P9-CQK-412

A23
35.00

DICTIONARY OF CANADIAN BIOGRAPHY

DICTIONARY OF CANADIAN BIOGRAPHY

DICTIONNAIRE BIOGRAPHIQUE DU CANADA

GENERAL EDITORS

GEORGE W. BROWN
1959–1963

DAVID M. HAYNE
1965–1969

FRANCESS G. HALPENNY
1969–

DIRECTEURS GÉNÉRAUX ADJOINTS

MARCEL TRUDEL
1961–1965

ANDRÉ VACHON
1965–1971

JEAN HAMELIN
1973–

UNIVERSITY OF TORONTO PRESS

LES PRESSES DE L'UNIVERSITÉ LAVAL

11624
920.071 DCB V.4

DICTIONARY OF CANADIAN BIOGRAPHY

VOLUME IV

1771 TO 1800

UNIVERSITY OF TORONTO PRESS
Toronto Buffalo London

STAFF OF THE DICTIONARY

TORONTO

MARY P. BENTLEY supervisory editor JANE E. GRAHAM associate editor

DAVID A. CHARTERS, ROBERT L. FRASER, GUS RICHARDSON, STUART R. J. SUTHERLAND
manuscript editors

PHYLLIS CREIGHTON translations editor

JOAN E. MITCHELL bibliographer

QUEBEC

HUGUETTE FILTEAU, MICHEL PAQUIN directeurs des recherches

GÉRARD GOYER assistant principal

MARIE-CÉLINE BLAIS, PIERRE DUFOUR, FRANCE GALARNEAU, GÉRALD KAMP
JAMES LAMBERT, THÉRÈSE P. LEMAY, JACQUELINE ROY assistants

JEAN-PIERRE ASSELIN assistant à l'édition

TRANSLATOR J. F. FLINN

© University of Toronto Press and
Les Presses de l'université Laval, 1979
Printed in Canada

Canadian Cataloguing in Publication Data
Main entry under title:

Dictionary of Canadian biography. – Laurentian ed.

Added t.p. in English and French.
Issued also in French.
Limited ed. of 500 copies.
Includes bibliographies and indexes.
Contents: v. 1. 1000–1700. – v. 2. 1701–1740. – v. 3. 1741–1770. – v. 9. 1861–1870. – v. 10. 1871–1880.
ISBN 0-8020-3139-0 (v. 1) ISBN 0-8020-3249-4 (v. 2)
ISBN 0-8020-3315-6 (v. 3) ISBN 0-8020-3320-2 (v. 9)
ISBN 0-8020-3288-5 (v. 10)

1. Canada – Biography – Dictionaries.

FC25.D52 920'.071 C75-4451-9
F1005.D49

CONTENTS

INTRODUCTION

VOLUME IV is the sixth volume of the *Dictionary of Canadian biography/Dictionnaire biographique du Canada* to be published. Volume I, presenting persons who died between the years 1000 and 1700, appeared in 1966; volume II (death dates 1701–40) in 1969; volume III (death dates 1741–70) in 1974. This numerical and chronological sequence was broken in 1972 with the publication of volume X (death dates 1871–80) as a consequence of a special grant from the Centennial Commission. Our staff and contributors have continued to work in the 19th as well as in the 18th century. Publication of volume IX (death dates 1861–70) followed in 1976; volume XI (death dates 1881–90) is now in press. The DCB/DBC is therefore at present concentrating its efforts, first on filling out, by volumes V, VI, VII, and VIII, the story for the years 1801–60, and then on completing its programme for the 19th century with volume XII. Readers are referred to the Introduction to volume IX for further comment on this programme.

The Introduction to volume I contains an account of the founding of the DCB by means of the generous bequest of James Nicholson (1861–1952), and of the establishment of the DBC with the support of Université Laval. The DCB/DBC, while continuing to develop the collaboration on which its immense bicultural and bilingual project depends, has maintained the principles and standards of operation and selection set out in the preliminary pages of its first volumes. Acknowledgements of volume IV record the gratitude of the DCB/DBC for the increased assistance of the Canada Council in 1973. Support then given has been maintained and amplified since by the Social Sciences and Humanities Research Council of Canada. This assistance has supported the effort to carry the project forward in the spirit and manner of its founders but with the great benefit for contributors and editors of working simultaneously in related time periods.

The 255 contributors to volume IV, writing in either English or French, have provided 504 biographies ranging in length from 600 to 10,000 words. They were invited to contribute because of their special knowledge of the period of the volume and the persons who figured in it, and all have been asked to write in accordance with the DCB/DBC's *Directives to contributors*. It sets out a general aim for articles:

> Each biography should be an informative and stimulating treatment of its subject, presented in readable form. All factual information should be precise and accurate, and be based upon reliable (preferably primary) sources. Biographies should not, however, be mere catalogues of dates and events, or compilations of previous studies of the same subject. The biographer should try to give the reader an orderly account of the personality and achievements of the subject, *against the background of the period in which the person lived and the events in which he or she participated.*

After editorial preparation in the offices of the DCB/DBC and final approval by the author, each biography was translated into the other language, and then the printer's manuscript for the two parallel volumes in English and French was assembled.

The time span of the death dates for volume IV is 30 years, and it has brought together a cast of characters who witnessed immense change and great tumult in affairs. People living beyond 1771 were to see the aftermath of the campaigns of the War of the Austrian Succession and the Seven Years' War, in which many of them had served and by which many more were affected; a different governing authority and new relationships to the old world after 1763 altered life for the inhabitants of the settlements along the St Lawrence. As a result of those campaigns the entire Maritime region came under the same authority. After a brief interlude the American War of Independence erupted into the northern British colonies and further changed the administrative arrangement of North America. Those who died before 1800 had already seen effects of the coming of the loyalists to the Maritime colonies and to the province of Quebec (in 1791 divided into Lower and Upper Canada), of the adoption of new governmental patterns in all the colonies, and of the changes consequent upon the dislocation of the well-established trading patterns linking New France with France and the building of other connections with merchants in Great Britain. After these years of turmoil, the colonies of British North America, expanding in population, would be greatly concerned with the ordering of government, society, and trade within the boundaries established by the conflicts of the last half of the 18th century. The effects of these years of change are reflected in our pages even in terminology, and particularly in the use of "Canadian," discussed in the Editorial Notes.

The biographies of related individuals, to which the generous number of cross-references is a guide, provide the means of following these themes through the volume. The French régime is here represented by such major figures as Governor Vaudreuil, intendants Hocquart and Bigot, Bishop Dosquet, the purveyor general Cadet, the merchant Ignace Gamelin, and the founder of the Grey Nuns, Mme d'Youville. Among the important artists and artisans are Delezenne and François-Noël Levasseur; an introduction to the professional life of the time is provided through such figures as Feltz, a doctor, and Boisseau, a notary. Glimpses of the social life of the period are contained in the biography of Mme Péan.

The conflicts of the Seven Years' War may be followed through the careers of an array of military officers, both French and British, such as Lévis, Ramezay, Amherst, and Saunders as well as those of lesser importance. The new society developing in the province of Quebec after the conquest is amply represented in a variety of people, among them Governor Murray, Chief Justice William Hey, Bishop Hubert, the Reverend David Chabrand Delisle, the merchant Jacobs, the seigneur Cuthbert, and such professional people as the journalist Brown, the doctor Lajus, and the notary Sanguinet. The biographies of Adhémar, Bishop Briand, Michel Chartier de Lotbinière, Chaussegros de Léry, Cugnet, Fleury Deschambault, and Glapion reflect experiences of the people of New France in adjusting to the new régime. The disruption of the American invasion in 1775–76 is sketched out in the biography of Richard Montgomery, who makes an appearance in volume IV under his own name primarily as a means of bringing together, with cross-references, the key events of the invasion for our readers. The effects of the liberal ideas associated with the American and the French revolutions may be seen through Jautard, Mesplet, Du Calvet, and others. The arrival of the loyalists, among them Chief Justice William Smith, produced an increase in population and introduced new cultural elements which led to the appearance of Upper Canada as a governmental entity; Christopher Robinson, founder of a prominent Upper Canadian family, appears in volume IV, as does Louis Roy, the colony's first king's printer.

Parts of the Maritimes had experienced a shift in rule some 50 years before the treaty of Paris (1763) confirmed a broader realignment. The biographies in volume IV bring before us once again the effects of wars in this region: in the struggles for Annapolis Royal (Du Pont Duvivier), Louisbourg (Du Pont Duchambon), and Fort Beauséjour (Monckton) and in the questions of allegiance for Acadians and Indians (Le Loutre). Volume IV also presents the groups involved in the administration and settlement of Nova Scotia, Prince Edward Island, and Newfoundland. Their stories may be followed through the careers of administrators such as Cornwallis, Patterson, and Palliser; officials such as Callbeck, Bulkeley, and Mathews; merchants and traders such as Mauger, Higgins, and Slade; and religious figures such as Bourg, Alline, MacDonald, and Coughlan. The effects of the increasingly strained relations between Britain and the American colonies in the 1760s and 1770s are reflected in the biographies of Danks, Fillis, Henry, and Salter. Towards the end of the century the loyalists are here too pushing out the frontiers of settlement in Nova Scotia and into what became New Brunswick; they are represented by such figures as Thomas Peters, Marston, Hardy, and Sower. The development of trade along the Labrador coast may be seen in the biographies of Darby, Coghlan, and others.

The story of the west is one of the fur trade and exploration. The Hudson's Bay Company's activities are represented by Hearne and Isbister, among others. The trade through Montreal continues to involve Canadian merchants such as Augé, but Scots families such as the Frobishers and Grants become increasingly important as time passes. With the interest in trading for the fur of the sea otter we come to Captain Cook and make a connection with the great age of exploration that in the 18th century was adding to the knowledge of the globe. Cook himself is in volume IV, as are Vancouver and the Spaniards Bodega and Martínez.

Inevitably the native peoples are affected by the activities in war and peace of the advancing whites, and biographies such as those of Akomápis and Kaieñˀkwaahtoñ make clear that their allegiance continues to be important. In volume IV we catch glimpses of Indian cultures at various stages of contact with the Europeans: when changes are relatively superficial (Muquinna); when a relationship of interdependence has developed (Matonabbee); and when the whites have become so powerful that the structure of Indian society is disintegrating (Teyohaqueande and Glikhikan). The Inuit of the Labrador coast make an appearance in volume IV both through individual biographies (Mikak) and the biographies of missionaries who encountered them (Drachart).

As in other volumes the DCB/DBC has endeavoured in volume IV to provide a broad spectrum of people through the many biographies of shorter length. Among them we find figures of questionable reputation: Pichon, Vergor, Ledru, and Roubaud; women of independence: Marie-Anne Barbel, Elizabeth Osborn, and Louise de Ramezay; modest artisans and tradesmen in a variety of occupations: Barsalou, Huppé, and Jacquet; men of scientific interests, both professional and amateur: Kalm, Wales, Lagarde, and Mounier; lesser-known artists: Beaucourt, Peachey, and Webber; colonizers: Clark, La Boularderie, and Owen; observers of Indian cultures: Long and Mackay. In our pages readers will also discover a black preacher of the Countess of Huntingdon's Connexion (Marrant), a student of French and Indian languages (Potier), an attorney general who was killed in a duel (White), a jealous husband (Pélissier), Lord Byron's grandfather (John Byron), the keeper of an orphan house (Wenman), a printer who combined journalism and the theatre (William Moore), and a shipbuilder who grew flowers in his spare time (Beatson).

Volume IV includes two essays as background for readers of the DCB/DBC. The first, by Professor Naomi Griffiths, provides an account of the Acadians from their first settlements to the end of the 18th century, and will thus be of interest to readers of volumes I–V. Professor Pierre Tousignant in his essay describes and analyses the various plans for the political organization of British North America after 1763, plans which can be seen in execution in the biographies of volumes IV and V. Other components of the volume are a glossary of native peoples, a general bibliography, and a full nominal index with cross-references to other volumes. Several biographies appear in an appendix and supplement for special reasons. In volume IV we are giving readers for the first time another short index which arranges the subjects of biographies by their occupations or other groupings; we should be glad to have comments from our readers on the usefulness of such an index.

The effort of preparation for contributors, consultants, and editorial staff represented in volume IV merits a special word. Each volume of the DCB/DBC means a concerted advance upon the history of the period under review in the course of which an impressive amount of original research occurs. A volume is thus much more than a reflection of research already done; it is also a significant contribution in its own right to research and, too, an indication of what gaps are still unfilled. Volume IV has had to face with particular force the challenge of not yet explored, or insufficiently known, subject areas and this fact has made the time of preparation longer than we would have liked. It has also made it necessary to make use of a supplement at the end of volume IV and hold for volume V the full text of the biography of Haldimand as well as the second section of the introductory essay on British North America with its annotated bibliography. All who have been associated with this volume hope that the research it has necessitated will constitute further suggestions for the future and that these will be pursued. A new edition of volume IV in later years would gladly reflect further inquiries. Volume V, now in advanced editorial preparation, has faced the same challenge of a period in which an enormous amount of original research remains to be done. The years covered by volumes IV and V are full of the interest that great social change brings, and we trust that they will be favoured by more and more students, in the widest sense of that term.

As a result of changes in the staff of the DCB/DBC during the preparation of the volume, a goodly number of persons were involved. Our lists on p.iv show those members of the DCB/DBC staff who had responsibility for the editing of texts and who worked in close association with the contributors. It is fitting that their care and concern in fulfilling their responsibilities for overseeing the contents of the volume and in leading the complex text through all stages of editorial preparation be acknowledged. Members of the staff who contributed to the volume in other ways are listed in the Acknowledgements. The DCB/DBC wishes to pay special tribute here to the contributions of two former staff members. Mary McDougall Maude, who resigned as Executive Editor on 1 Aug. 1978, made a noteworthy contribution to our work from her first appointment as a manuscript editor in October 1965; her historical sense, editorial skill, and insistence on high standards marked the final form of all the volumes with which she was associated. Gaston Tisdel joined the DBC in March 1966, became officially *directeur des recherches* on 1 June 1971, and resigned on 30 Oct. 1977. His concern for the project's well-being and its general acceptance as an historical authority, for ensuring the widest possible use for its volumes, and for obtaining a broad range of characters and of contributors to write about them was constant and lively. Together Mary Maude and Gaston Tisdel helped greatly to create the traditions of consultation, accommodation, and comradeship that have marked the relations of our two offices and made this project truly a *Dictionary of Canadian biography/Dictionnaire biographique du Canada*.

FRANCESS G. HALPENNY

JEAN HAMELIN

ACKNOWLEDGEMENTS

THE *Dictionary of Canadian biography/Dictionnaire biographique du Canada* receives assistance, advice, and encouragement from many institutions and individuals. They cannot all be named nor can their kindness and support be adequately acknowledged.

The DCB/DBC, which owes its founding to the generosity of the late James Nicholson, has been sustained over the years by its parent institutions, the University of Toronto and the University of Toronto Press and the Université Laval and Les Presses de l'université Laval. Beginning in 1973 the Canada Council provided generous grants to the two university presses which made possible the continuation and acceleration of the DCB/DBC's publication programme, and this assistance has been generously maintained and amplified by the Social Sciences and Humanities Research Council of Canada created in 1978. We should like to give special thanks to the SSHRCC not only for its financial support but also for the encouragement it has given us as we strive to complete our volumes. We also acknowledge with gratitude the assistance provided by the Ministry of Culture and Recreation of the Province of Ontario through its Wintario programme and also the assistance of the ministries of Education and Intergovernmental Affairs of the Province of Quebec in 1977–78.

Of the numerous individuals who assisted in the preparation of volume IV, we owe particular thanks to our contributors who made this work truly a community effort. We also have had the benefit of special consultation with a number of persons, some of them also contributors. We should like to thank: Phyllis R. Blakeley, Terence A. Crowley, André Desrosiers, Armand Gagné, Agathe Garon, Robert Garon, T. J. A. Le Goff, Monique Mailloux, André Martineau, Marianne Mithun, and Shirlee Anne Smith.

Throughout the preparation of volume IV we have enjoyed willing cooperation from libraries and archives in Canada and elsewhere. We are particularly grateful to the administrators and staffs of those institutions to which we have most frequently appealed: in Ontario, the Public Archives of Canada, the University of Toronto Library, and the Metropolitan Toronto Library; in Quebec, the Archives nationales du Québec and its regional branches, the *archives civiles* and *judiciaires*, the Archives de l'archidiocèse de Québec, the Bibliothèque générale de l'université Laval, the Bibliothèque and Archives du séminaire de Québec, and the Bibliothèque de l'Assemblée nationale. In addition, essential help was given by the Public Archives of Nova Scotia and the Hudson's Bay Company Archives in Winnipeg. We should also like to thank the staff of the *archives départementales* and *municipales* of France, who answered our numerous requests for information so kindly.

ACKNOWLEDGEMENTS

The editors of volume IV were assisted in the preparation of the volume by colleagues in both offices. In Toronto, editorial and research assistance has been given by Carol M. Judd, Marjorie E. Zavitz Robinson, Teresa Thompson, and James A. Ogilvy. Paula Brine Reynolds headed the secretariat during most of the work on volume IV, and with it concluded her long, enthusiastic, and trustworthy services to the DCB/DBC. Deborah Marshall, now in charge of secretarial services in Toronto, has also taken special responsibilities for the reading and handling of proof in volume IV. Secretarial assistance has been provided by Reni Grinfelds, Marcia Clunie, Lynne Hostein, and Anita Murnaghan. In Quebec, Marie-Aimée Cliche, Céline Cyr, Christiane Demers, Marcelle Duquet, Michel de Lorimier, Claudette Jones, Michèle Brassard, Pierrette Desnoyers, and Diane Verret aided the editors at one stage or another of volume IV; Pierrette Desrosiers was in charge of the secretariat, assisted by Hélène Lizotte, Suzanne East, Monique Baron, and Fabienne Lizotte. We have also benefited from the advice of Jacques Chouinard and Roch-André Rompré of the editorial department of Les Presses de l'université Laval.

We should like to recognize the guidance and encouragement we have received from the two presses with which the DCB/DBC is associated, and in particular Harald Bohne, H. C. Van Ierssel, and John Ecclestone at the University of Toronto Press, and Claude Frémont, J.-Arthur Bédard, Jacques Beaulieu, and Jacques Boivin at Les Presses de l'université Laval.

DICTIONNAIRE BIOGRAPHIQUE DU CANADA   DICTIONARY OF CANADIAN BIOGRAPHY

Editorial Notes

PROPER NAMES

Persons have been entered under family name rather than title, pseudonym, popular name, nickname, or name in religion, an arrangement which has the advantage of bringing together prominent members of the same family: DU PONT, RIGAUD. Where possible the form of the surname is based on the signature, although contemporary usage is taken into account. Common variant spellings are included in parentheses. Occasionally, research for a volume has suggested a change in spelling in a family name from that used in volumes published previously: for example, Mallepart (volume III) has been corrected in volume IV to Malepart.

In the case of French names, "La," "Le," "Du," and "Des" (but not "de") are considered part of the name and are capitalized; when both parts of the name are capitalized in the signature, French style treats the family name as two words: LE LOUTRE. Compound names abound: Charles-François BAILLY de Messein, Pierre de RIGAUD de Vaudreuil de Cavagnial; cross-references are made in the text from the compounds to the main entry under the family name: from Messein to Bailly and from Vaudreuil and Cavagnial to Rigaud. First names generally appear in the modern form: Jean rather than Jehan, Noël rather than Noel.

In the case of Spanish names, "la," like "de," is not considered part of the family name: Juan Francisco de la BODEGA y Quadra. Compound names have been given appropriate cross-references.

Married women and *religieuses* have been entered under their maiden names, with cross-references to the entry from their husbands' names or their names in religion: Frances MOORE (Brooke), Marie-Anne MIGEON de Branssat, *dite* de la Nativité.

Indian names have presented a particular problem, since an Indian might be known by his own name (written in a variety of ways by French and English unfamiliar with Indian languages) and by a French or English nickname or baptismal name; moreover, by the late 18th century some Indian families, such as the Brants, were beginning to use family surnames in the European style. Indian names have been used when they could be found, and, because it is impossible to establish an original spelling for an Indian name, the form chosen is the one found in standard sources or the one linguists now regard as correct. An effort has been made to include major variants of the original name, as well as European names, with appropriate cross-references: KOÑWATSIˀTSIAIÉÑNI (Gonwatsijayenni, Mary Brant).

For reference works useful in establishing the names of persons not receiving biographies in the DCB/DBC, the reader is referred to section III of the General Bibliography.

CROSS-REFERENCES WITHIN VOLUME IV

The first time the name of a person who has a biography in volume IV appears in another biography his family name is printed in capitals and level small capitals: François de LÉVIS, George VANCOUVER.

CROSS-REFERENCES TO OTHER VOLUMES

An asterisk following a name indicates either that the person has a biography in a volume already published – James Wolfe*, Louis-Joseph Papineau* – or that he will receive a biography in a volume to be published – François Baby*, Guy Carleton*. Birth and death (or floruit) dates for such persons are given in the index as an indication of the volume in which the biography will be found.

PLACE-NAMES

Place-names are generally given in the form used at the time of reference with the modern name included in parenthesis. Complete consistency, however, has not been possible nor has it been thought desirable. In biographies which have both French and English protagonists, for example, the alternate place-names may be either the contemporary French or the contemporary English form: e.g. Oswego (Chouaguen), Lac Saint-Sacrement (Lake George). The English edition cites well-known place-names in their present-day English form: St Lawrence River, Montreal, Quebec, Marseilles, Rome. The *Encyclopædia Britannica* has been followed in determining whether place-names outside Canada have accepted English forms.

Many sources have been used as guides to establish 18th-century place-names: *Atlas de la N.-F.* (M. Trudel); Clark, *Acadia*; Albert Dauzat et Charles Rostaing, *Dictionnaire étymologique des noms de lieux en France* (Paris, [1963]); *Encyclopædia Britannica*; Ganong, "Historic sites in N.B.," RSC *Trans.*, 2nd ser., V (1899), sect.II, 213–357; HBRS, XIV (Rich and Johnson), XV (Rich and Johnson), XXVII (Williams); "Historic forts and trading posts of the French regime and of the English fur trading companies," comp. Ernest Voorhis (mimeograph, Ottawa, 1930); Hunter, *Forts on Pa. frontier*; *Johnson papers* (Sullivan *et al.*); *Place-names of N.S.*; Rayburn, *Geographical names of P.E.I.*; P.-G. Roy, *Inv. concessions*; G. R. Stewart, *American place-names . . .* (New York, 1970); Walbran, *B.C. coast names*. For complete information about titles given in shortened form the reader is referred to the General Bibliography.

EDITORIAL NOTES

Modern Canadian names are based whenever possible on the Gazetteer of Canada series issued by the Canadian Permanent Committee on Geographical Names, Ottawa, and on the *Répertoire géographique du Québec* ([Québec], 1969), published by the Ministère des terres et forêts du Québec. For places outside Canada, the *National geographic atlas of the world*, ed. M. B. Grosvenor *et al.* (4th ed., Washington, 1975) has been a major source of reference. Place-names outside Canada are identified by administrative division if they are not to be found in *The Canadian Oxford desk atlas of the world*, ed. E. G. Pleva and Spencer Inch (3rd ed., Toronto, 1972) or the *Atlas Larousse canadien*, Benoît Brouillette et Maurice Saint-Yves, édit. (Québec et Montréal, 1971).

CONTEMPORARY USAGE

To avoid the anachronism of applying the terms "French Canadian" and "English Canadian" to the 18th century, volume IV follows the contemporary practice of referring to the French speaking inhabitants of the province of Quebec simply as "Canadians." Readers should be aware, however, that in the context of the fur trade the term "Canadian" is used, as it was in the 18th century, to refer to Montreal-based traders, whether French or English speaking.

QUOTATIONS

Quotations have been translated when the language of the original passage is different from that of the text of the biography. All passages quoted from works published in both languages are given in the accepted translations of these works. The wording, spelling, punctuation, and capitalization of original quotations are not altered unless necessary for meaning, in which case the changes are made within square brackets. A name appearing within square brackets has been added or substituted for the original in order to provide a cross-reference to a biography within the volume or in another volume.

DATES

The discrepancy between Old Style (Julian calendar, used in Britain until 1752 and Sweden until 1753) and New Style (Gregorian calendar, used in Italy, Spain, Portugal, and France from 1582) affects a number of biographies in volume IV. Most biographies, of course, present no problems: dates in those based entirely on British documents can be assumed to be Old Style; and in those based exclusively on French sources, New Style. But when an article draws on both British and continental or Quebec sources, authors have been asked to make the dates in the article uniformly Old or New Style and to indicate after the first date given (O.S.) or (N.S.). It should be noted that: (a) Old Style dates were 11 days behind New Style in the 18th century; (b) the Old Style new year began on 25 March and the New Style new year on 1 January (for Old Style dates between January and 25 March, the year is indicated as 1742/43).

BIBLIOGRAPHIES

Each biography is followed by a bibliography. Sources frequently used by authors and editors are cited in shortened form in individual bibliographies; the General Bibliography (pp. 797–833) gives these sources in full. Many abbreviations are used in the individual bibliographies, especially for archival sources; a list of these can be found on pp. 2, 796.

The individual bibliographies are generally arranged alphabetically according to the five sections of the General Bibliography: manuscript sources, printed primary sources (including a section on contemporary newspapers), reference works, studies and theses, and journals. Wherever possible, references to manuscript material give the location of the original documents, rather than of copies. In general the items in individual bibliographies are the sources listed by the contributors, but these items have often been supplemented by bibliographic investigation in the DCB/DBC offices. Any special bibliographical comments by contributors appear within square brackets.

TRANSLATION INTO ENGLISH (a note by the translator of French biographies)

Translation from French into English in volume IV has presented a continuity with the previous volume that might seem somewhat surprising but that presumably demonstrates the gradualness of the transition after the conquest from the French to the British régime. There is no sudden influx of new administrative terms based upon British usage. Indeed, for a time at least, the British administration apparently continued using certain French terms, *grand voyer* for example, rather than their English equivalents, and the continued existence of the seigneurial system meant the persistence of such terms as *lods et ventes* and *droit de quint*. (*A dictionary of Canadianisms on historical principles*, ed. W. S. Avis *et al.* (Toronto, 1967) has been helpful in decisions relating to translation.) The process of selecting English equivalents for new terms has, nevertheless, known no slackening in this volume, not only in new areas but also in old and now familiar ones: throughout the period covered by volume IV new activities such as printing and publishing and the considerable development of commercial and trading activities resulted in the increasing use of technical terms; the military struggle for North America led in its final stages to a more complex military organization and the appointment in New France of senior officers bearing titles and exercising new commands, such as *lieutenant général des forces navales* and *brigadier des forces navales*, for which exact equivalents did not exist in the British forces. Quotations from 18th-century documents, particularly from correspondence during the French régime, have continued to cause considerable difficulties. For the later period recourse has been had whenever possible to corresponding English versions, translations or even originals, of the French passages.

The Acadians

N. E. S. GRIFFITHS

ACADIAN HISTORY has been a lengthy story of cultural distinctiveness and political compromises. The territory called "Acadie" was the site of the first real attempt made by the French to settle in North America. Its centre was the south shore of the Bay of Fundy and its exact boundaries were never precisely defined. If one traces the placing of the word "Acadie" on maps made of North America during the 16th century, the name is to be found consistently south of the St Lawrence River but by no means equally consistently in one location. Many maps place "Acadie" across the region which is today divided into northern Maine, northern New Brunswick, and southeastern Quebec, including much of the Gaspé peninsula. On a map made in 1587 the name is specifically attached to what is today Nova Scotia. In 1601 Guillaume Levasseur, one of the most influential European mapmakers of the late 16th century, lettered the words "coste de Cadie" over what is now New Brunswick and Nova Scotia. Other maps of the same era, made during the last years of the 16th century or the first years of the 17th, have the word "La Cadie," "Lacadye," or "Acadie" placed over all the above regions combined as well as Prince Edward Island. There would be little agreement, at any period, among all the parties concerned with Acadian history – France, Great Britain, New France, New England, not to mention the people of Acadia themselves – as to where the frontiers should truly run.

Continual argument over the actual borders of Acadia became more important as the European settlement of North America progressed. The lands settled by the Acadians became a border country between New England and New France, a "continental cornice," as John Bartlet Brebner* terms it, in dispute between great empires. Acadian political traditions were decisively moulded by this fact. Claimed by France in the patents issued by Henri IV to Pierre Du Gua* de Monts in 1603, it was claimed with as much conviction and equal imprecision by the Scottish crown in 1621, when James VI granted Sir William Alexander* the authority to colonize what the charter in question called Nova Scotia, land whose boundaries were located somewhere between the Gaspé and the St Croix River. From that time until 1763 international treaties would refer to the area as "Acadie or Nova Scotia," underlining by dual title the experience of the Acadians, as much a people of the frontier as the inhabitants of Monmouthshire, Cumberland, Alsace-Lorraine, or the Basque country.

Whether or not England controlled the colony, as was the case between 1654 and 1670, the people of Massachusetts became and remained a most important influence for the Acadians. Although the treaty of Saint-Germain-en-Laye in 1632 acknowledged France as the rightful European authority for the development of "Acadie or Nova Scotia," the colony of Massachusetts Bay was a constant and never completely hostile force in their lives. It was almost always more important as a trading partner than anywhere else; and its influence was further strengthened during the years 1656 to 1670 when Thomas Temple* governed the Acadians for both Oliver Cromwell and Charles II, using Boston as his major source of supplies. Even when the treaty of Breda, signed in 1667 but not implemented for Acadia until 1670, restored the colony to France, the links remained. It was the opinion of the priests who were in the colony during the 1640s and 1650s, as well as the judgement of Governor Frontenac [Buade*], writing in the 1680s, that the Acadians had acquired a deplorable "parliamentary" turn of mind by associating too much with the colony of Massachusetts Bay. A report by the intendant of New France, Jacques de Meulles*, who visited Acadia in 1685–86, noted that Boston merchants had established the most considerable shops in the largest community in the colony, that of Port-Royal (Annapolis Royal, N.S.). By the end of the century, the English had become, in an Acadian phrase, "our friends the enemy," and contacts with them were more frequent, closer, and friendlier than is generally recognized.

In fact Acadian contacts with other people were considerably wider than has usually been accounted. Within their own lands their relations with the Indians were, for 150 years, most amicable, leading not only to the unmarried liaisons first deplored by missionaries in 1616, but to a significant number of church-registered unions. François-Edme Rameau* de Saint-Père, the French historian who published his first work on the Acadians in 1859, remarked that given the smallness of the Acadian population, the number of such registered partnerships was a significant formative factor for that community during the 17th century. From the time of Charles de Saint-Étienne* de La Tour the elder's first marriage to a Micmac in 1626, through Jean-Vincent d'Abbadie* de Saint-Castin's union with a Penobscot in the 1670s, until after the deportation of 1755, there was always at least one Acadian family in most settlements where one partner, usually the woman, was an Indian. The census returns of 1671 and 1686 indicate five families where the woman is described as a "sauvagesse," out of a total of some 75 and 135 families respectively. More important, perhaps, than this sprinkling of marriages is the general tenor of relationships with the Indians, relations which meant that the Acadians, as one of their governors, François-Marie Perrot*, remarked in the 1680s, quickly adopted Indian-styled small boats for coastal voyaging and accompanied the Indian bands as they travelled through the forests. The Indians, in Acadian eyes, were permanent neighbours, neither the middlemen in commercial enterprise nor a hostile force. It was particularly fortunate for both sides that the Micmacs, the Indians with whom the Acadians had the greatest contact, were people with a migratory way of life, whose demands on the land were not in immediate conflict with those placed upon it by the newcomers from Europe.

The excellent relations between Acadian and Indian were helped by the way the Acadian community struggled into existence and painfully developed. During the first 30 or so years of the 17th century, every effort to organize European development around the Bay of Fundy resulted only in the maintenance of a European presence, never in the establishment of a settlement. Even after 1632 when the French authorities actively encouraged migration, rather than exploration and the conversion of the Indian, the colonists who set sail from France were few [*see* Isaac de Razilly*; Charles de Menou* d'Aulnay]. By 1671, when an official census was made, the population of European descent was recorded as less than 75 families, 68 of them within the confines of Port-Royal, and the others at Pobomcoup (Pubnico, N.S.), Cap Nègre (Cape Negro, N.S.), Pentagouet (on Penobscot Bay, Maine), Mouscoudabouet (Musquodoboit Harbour, N.S.), and Saint-Pierre (St Peters, N.S.), making barely 500 souls in all. Even the developments of the last decades of the 17th century brought the population to no overwhelming number. When the British acquired "Acadie or Nova Scotia" by the treaty of Utrecht in 1713, the population of New France was more than 19,000, that of New England 92,000, but the official computation of the Acadians was under 2,000. So gradual had been the growth of settlement through migration, and so non-exploitative the Acadians' way of life, that unlike other European societies transferred to America they posed no serious threat to the indigenous population. New England settlement meant eventual extirpation of Indian groups, while the logic of the expansion of New France meant the relatively benign exploitation of dependent Indian populations. Only with the Acadians did something akin to a symbiotic relationship with the Micmacs and other tribal groupings emerge. From this relationship the Acadians reaped positive benefits, not only in their early adoption of Indian canoes, but also in their use of such articles of clothing as the moccasin and their consumption of herbs and vegetables unknown in Europe.

It was possibly the diversity of their origins, as well as their small numbers, that made the Acadians more open to learning from the Indians. The work of the French linguist, Geneviève Massignon, has established how lacking in communal "set" the Acadians were. She undertook to trace the roots of Acadian speech patterns and found that although certain centres in France, such as Loudun and its region, contributed significantly to the Acadian stock, in fact more than half the population came from other parts of the country. Indeed, she was able to show that by 1707 about five per cent of the Acadian population came from one part or another of the British Isles.

Massignon's main purpose had been to decide whether the Acadian speech patterns were primarily a matter of European heritage or if the North American environment had added a crucial ingredient to the vocabulary. Her conclusion was that the lack of any single, overwhelming influence from any particular locality in Europe made Acadian speech very much a matter of colonial development. It had evolved as an amalgam of a variety of dialects, mostly French, a few English, one or two Indian, compounded into a whole by the distinctive life of the Acadian community and its need for a special vocabulary to render the precise quality of Acadian experience.

Massignon restricted her work to linguistics. But her research was one of the first steps towards an understanding of Acadia's European heritage. Migrants such as the Leblancs, who sailed via La Rochelle, and the Bastaraches, Basques from the Pyrenees who sailed from Bayonne, not only spoke different dialects but had lived in villages ruled by differing legal customs and differing religious traditions. It must be remembered that the France that helped establish Acadia was the France of a multitude of local variations, each region linked to the central government in its own peculiar way and each region undeniably different from its neighbours. The time of arrival of each contingent of migrants to Acadia, the sorts of power the newcomers attained, and the ways in which one heritage rather than another would be chosen to solve a problem of community relations, to contribute the folk songs for weddings, or to be used as the basic source of recipes for the provision of food, are crucial factors in the development of Acadian life. Since at no time did a group of migrants arrive imbued with either a religious or a secular ideology that would dominate all others, the gradual melding of old and new migrants was of particular importance for the colony. It is in this context that the chains which link the first expedition of de Monts in 1604, with its ideals of settlement and its belief in the value of co-operation with the Indians, to all later migrations are so important.

To outline one of the most important of many such chains: Jean de Biencourt* de Poutrincourt et de Saint-Just was one of the most stalwart supporters of de Monts, sailed with him in 1604, and helped found Port-Royal in 1605. When he returned to Acadia in 1606 he brought his son, Charles de Biencourt* de Saint-Just, with him. As the father is linked to the founder of the colony, so is the son linked to its developer, Charles de Saint-Étienne de La Tour, who arrived in Acadie in 1610, barely a teenager. During the next decade, when the colony suffered attacks by the English and was claimed as Nova Scotia by James VI of Scotland, the two young men worked together for its survival; when Biencourt died in 1623 or 1624 he left La Tour all his rights in the colony. These two families illustrate a general process in the creation of an Acadian people.

For the next 40 or so years La Tour was one of the most important men in Acadia, working for the growth of the colony mostly as a landholder and official whose authority and rights stemmed from France, but occasionally as an official deriving title and authority from the king of Scotland. (His father, Claude*, obtained a Scottish baronetcy for the family from Charles I during the winter of 1629–30, while he himself was commissioned lieutenant-general of the French king in Acadia by Louis XIII in 1631.) The ability of the La Tours to accord their governance of Acadia with either of the most interested European countries meant the existence in the colony of a powerful and enduring family whose first loyalty was to the reality of life in North America. Charles de La Tour married three times and had five surviving children. Some of his descendants would intermarry with the children of settlers such as Charles Melanson* and his brothers, people who came to the colony as migrants in search of a new life rather than as administrators organizing a new endeavour. The daughter of La Tour's son Jacques and Anne Melanson (her descent was Scottish) was named Agathe*. She would marry in succession two English subalterns who came to the colony as a result of the settlement arrived at in Utrecht; her son John BRADSTREET was to become a major-general in the British army. It was family friendships and connections such as these which cemented a relationship between the visions of the earliest arrivals and the contributions made to the Acadian identity by those who came later.

A further strengthening of such relations was made possible by the longevity of the population. This was particularly significant for a community which knew a succession of differing authorities claiming its governance during a space of some 50 or 60 years. Politically, the colony became a reality under French authority during the years 1632–54. Between 1654 and 1670 a basically but not completely French population was ruled in the name of England. For the next 40 years, 1670–1710, it was once more officially French; however, during the last 20 years, 1690–1710, the colony suffered a succession of English forays, at least one of which, the expedition of Sir William Phips* in 1690, resulted in some Acadians' swearing an oath of loyalty to the English crown. The presence in the Acadian population throughout the hundred years preceding the deportation of a significant body of middle-aged people, capable, for the most part, of remembering two, if not three, changes of national allegiance, gave the Acadians a certain mistrust of the claims of either France or England as to permanent possession of the colony. It also gave the Acadians a most cheerful attitude to smuggling, since what was illegal in the eyes of one government was the sole permitted trade in the eyes of the other. But above all, given the slow accretion of population by migration, Acadian marriage patterns, coupled with the general health of the population, allowed the colony to absorb all newcomers into a slowly developing family net, a net that brought together old and new generations and old and new village settlements. During the crucial period between 1671 and the close of the century, the last years of any significant French immigration to the mainland of the colony, Acadia received something less than 100 people to add to the stock already there. As Rameau de Saint-Père has noted, some four-fifths of those considered Acadian in 1755 could claim an ancestor recorded in the nominal census of the colony taken in 1671. It is remarkable that the nucleus of the Acadian population developed from such a base.

The Acadians were a people of unusually large and flourishing families and their food supply was adequate and varied enough not only for the expansion of the population but for the maintenance of a high level of fertility. Further, diseases such as typhoid, smallpox, and cholera never reached epidemic proportions in the colony. Visiting in 1699, the French surgeon Dièreville* was astounded at the size of Acadian families, some of which numbered 18 or more children. The norm in his own country was an infant mortality rate that gave the newborn no more than one chance in three of survival into adulthood. In Acadia, however, families such as those of Pierre Commeau and Daniel Leblanc were common enough. Pierre Commeau had arrived in the colony in 1636 and was married at its major settlement, Port-Royal, in 1641. He had 9 children: his grandchildren by 4 of his sons numbered 46. From their sons came some 68 children. Daniel Leblanc, who was also married in Port-Royal, probably in 1645, had 7 children, 6 of them boys. There were 52 grandchildren from the male line alone. The great-grandchildren numbered over 200, including the offspring of René Leblanc. He was the notary immortalized by Henry Wadsworth Longfellow in *Evangeline*, and himself had 3 children with his first wife, and 17 with his second, including triplets born in 1721.

Such families did not merely provide cohesion for a particular village, they also linked each new settlement to all others in the colony. In particular, and during the greater part of the 17th century, kinship ties helped carry the influence of the first major Acadian settlement, Port-Royal, into almost every other part of the colony. Beaubassin (near Amherst, N.S.) was the first major village settled after the establishment of Port-Royal. It was begun in 1672 to a large extent as a result of the work of Jacques Bourgeois*, who had come to Acadia in 1642 and had spent some 30 years in and around Port-Royal before moving on. Companions in his endeavour included second-generation members of families such as the Bernards and the Commeaus, whose relatives were soon to be found in other new villages, such as Pisiquid (Windsor, N.S.) and Grand Pré. Newcomers to the colony, such as Pierre Arsenault who landed in 1671, often married in Port-Royal before setting out to join another village. Arsenault himself married the daughter of Abraham Dugas, and Dugas had come out to Acadia early in the 1640s to live throughout his life in Port-Royal. In sum, the increase in the Acadian population meant much more than just the growth and development of a number of separate families: it also meant an intricate net of kinship lines criss-crossing the entire colony.

As the 17th century drew to a close, Acadian history could be summarized as a tale of official neglect and a barely successful struggle towards settlement. Nevertheless when the treaty of Utrecht was concluded in 1713, bringing to an end yet one more phase of Anglo-French warfare and making the colony once more a British possession, "Acadie or Nova Scotia" had both an international identity and a colonial population. Both the British and the French governments had become aware of the strategic worth of the "continental cornice"; the French negotiators had in fact made a strenuous effort during the treaty negotiations to retain Acadia. "We have directed all our energies towards regaining Acadia," they wrote to Louis XIV on 18 April 1712, "but it has been absolutely impossible for us to achieve that end."

Acadia had been lost to France by the treaty, but not permanently, at least in French eyes. The continuation of strong French interest in the territory was of crucial significance to the Acadian position. The French not only had ambitions for the repossession of Acadia; under the terms of the treaty they had a case for recovery of part of it. The treaty stated that Great Britain was given "all Nova Scotia or Acadie with its ancient boundaries as also the city of Port Royal, now called Annapolis Royal, and all other things in those parts which depend on the said lands and islands." No map was appended, nor were the northern and western limits of "all Nova Scotia or Acadie" specified. By the treaty, the French kept Île Saint-Jean (Prince Edward Island) and Île Royale (Cape Breton Island). At the same time they maintained that the limits of the territory ceded to Britain were not those granted to de Monts in 1603 but the much smaller concession made to Poutrincourt in 1608. In other words, the expression "ancien" in the treaty did not mean "ancient" or "original" but "former," in reference to the 1608 grant or to other interpretations favourable to the French case. For the French, therefore, there were two parts of Acadia:

"Acadie française" comprising Île Royale, Île St Jean, and as much of the mainland between present-day New Brunswick and the St Lawrence as they were disposed to claim, and "Acadie or Nova Scotia," which they had ceded to the British and being as little of that peninsula as possible. A map submitted by the French government in an attempt to settle the boundaries of the territory after the treaty of Aix-la-Chapelle in 1748 even made a case for British rights extending only along a thin slice of the eastern coast of Nova Scotia. On the other hand, of course, the British were convinced that what was signed on 8 May 1713 had given them at the very least the whole of the peninsula of Nova Scotia, quite probably all present-day New Brunswick, and, if the French were but honest, some rights to the land between New Brunswick and the St Lawrence, including the Gaspé peninsula.

Border warfare between the two great powers was made almost inevitable by these arrangements. But the plight of the Acadians was further complicated by other provisions of the treaty. One of the articles negotiated gave them the liberty to "remove themselves, within a year to any other place, as they shall think fit, together with all their movable effects." If any decided to remain, however, they were "to be subject to the Kingdom of Great Britain" and "to enjoy the free exercise of their religion according to the usage of the Church of Rome as far as the laws of Great Britain do allow the same." These last stipulations were amplified in a letter dated 23 June 1713 from Queen Anne to Francis Nicholson*, governor of Nova Scotia and commander of the expedition that had captured Port-Royal in 1710. He was bidden to allow those Acadians who "are Willing to continue our Subjects to retain and Enjoy their said Lands and Tenements without any Lett or Molestation as fully and freely as other our Subjects do or may possess their Lands and Estates or to sell the same if they shall rather Chuse to remove elsewhere." As time passed, the Acadians were to be less and less certain whether the article of the treaty itself, or the instructions in the letter to Nicholson, defined the limits of their rights: once the year (from a time not specified – the moment the treaty was signed? the moment Acadians were told of the provisions?) had elapsed, did they still have the right to move? with only their "movable effects," as the treaty stipulated? or having sold their "Lands and Estates," as the letter said they might?

In many ways these problems were of more moment to the British and French than to the Acadians themselves. Between 1714 and 1719 both powers considered the advantages and disadvantages of moving the Acadians from their original lands. The authorities of Île Royale, in particular the governor, Philippe Pastour* de Costebelle, wished to see the Acadians people that colony. But the authorities of Quebec and the French minister of Marine, Pontchartrain, were of two minds whether it would be more useful to persuade the Acadians to remain under British rule in the hope of a French reconquest of the colony, in which the Acadians ought to prove of immense help, or to encourage their emigration. The British were equally uncertain. The lieutenant governor of the colony, Thomas Caulfeild*, wrote to the Lords of Trade in 1715 that it was necessary for the Acadians to remain, not only for their cattle and hogs, which they would take if they left, but also "in case ye french quit us we shall never be able to maintaine or protect our English family's from ye insults of ye Indians, ye worst of enemies."

The Acadian reaction to this situation has been the cause of quite as much debate among historians as has any other aspect of their history. In the minds of many, such as Francis Parkman and James Hannay*, Acadian policy was dictated by the priests. To others, such as Émile Lauvrière, it was the sole practical reaction to intolerable pressure from the British. It is possible, however, to consider the Acadian attitude at this time as an intelligent solution to an obvious dilemma: the need to evolve a policy that would permit them to live comfortably under British authority, for as long as that might continue, while losing neither their religious practices nor the confidence of the French. There is no doubt that the Acadians considered the provision of priests a matter of importance; there is also no doubt that they considered the priests part, not the leaders, of their community. As the Acadians tried to respond to the varying demands made upon them by French and British, the recorded advice of the priests among them, in the years immediately following the treaty of Utrecht, was diverse. Father Dominique de La Marche*, superior of the Recollets on Île Royale, tried with considerable eloquence to persuade the inhabitants of Minas (Wolfville) to migrate, but without success. Father Félix Pain*, on the other hand, seems to have ignored direct instructions from Pontchartrain to encourage Acadian migration, thinking Île Royale too harsh a land for his flock.

The Acadians' policy was of their own making. Asked to take the oath to King George I by the authorities at Annapolis Royal at the same time as the authorities of Île Royale were asking them to emigrate, the Acadians evolved their own strategy. They sent a temporizing reply to the

British and a delegation to the French. They told the British that they knew their reply had been slow in coming, but that not all could read, and those who did must travel through the settlements to translate the oath demanded to explain its terms. There is no suggestion here that the priests could be relied upon to speed the work. It was the villagers themselves who would consider how the demand should be answered, the answer being presented to the authorities signed, often with a full signature, sometimes with an X, by the men of the area and brought to Annapolis Royal by the village delegates. It took three years for the replies to be organized in many cases, the demand for the oath not having been formally made until 1715. In sum, the Acadians refused to comply because as those of Beaubassin remarked "while our ancestors were under English rule such an oath was never required of them." However, as the inhabitants of Minas noted, they would guarantee not to cause any trouble while the British remained in power and they remained in the colony. Further, as those of the Annapolis River suggested, they might consider some oath that bound them not to take up arms against either Britain or France.

If such replies exasperated the authorities at Annapolis Royal, they pleased the authorities at Île Royale no better. The Acadians temporized as skilfully with French demands for migration as with British demands for oaths of loyalty, remarking that it was too late in the season to think of even considering the problem of migration, or that, even if they wished to remove themselves, they had insufficient boats, or that, though they were considering the matter, lack of roads to Île Royale made the project very difficult. Some historians consider that the Acadians were prevented from leaving Nova Scotia by the British; however, as the Acadian historian Joseph-Henri Blanchard has pointed out, had the Acadians wished to quit their lands, the British could not have prevented them. A report written in 1720 by Paul Mascarene*, the French speaking Huguenot who was to become the lieutenant governor of the colony in the 1740s, remarked that the Acadians were able to muster a thousand men capable of bearing arms, noting that those along the Annapolis River alone were able to "arm and assemble four hundred men in twenty-four hours time," a force quite capable of overwhelming the small British force in the province.

In fact, as Governor Richard Philipps* accurately summed the matter up in 1719, the Acadians "will neither sweare allegiance, nor leave the Country." During the 1720s, however, as the Acadians realized that the British appeared firmly ensconced at Annapolis Royal, there was a clarification of their policy. In 1726 the lieutenant governor, Lawrence Armstrong*, persuaded the settlers around Annapolis Royal to take an oath of loyalty with an exemption from bearing arms, "the same," it being noted in the Council records but not reported to the Lords of Trade, "to be writt upon y[e] Margent of the french Translation in order to gett them over by Degrees." By the end of the decade the majority of Acadian communities had sworn an oath similar to that taken by the inhabitants of the Annapolis River area and with similar provisions for their neutrality [*see* Robert Wroth*]. In making the final report on this matter to the Lords of Trade on 2 Sept. 1730, Philipps stated that the Acadians, now numbering some 4,000, had sworn an oath reading: "I sincerely promise and swear on my faith as a Christian that I will be utterly loyal, and will truly obey His Majesty King George the second, whom I recognize as the sovereign lord of Acadia or Nova Scotia. May God so help me." He said nothing of the provisions of neutrality to which he had agreed verbally, merely mentioning that the Acadians were a "formidable Body and like Noah's progeny spreading themselves over the face of the Province."

By 1730 the situation of the Acadians in Nova Scotia had within it everything necessary for a first class débâcle. As far as they themselves were concerned they had managed to bring the British to agree to their own terms for remaining in Nova Scotia. From this year forward most Englishmen, as Brebner points out, "spoke of them as 'the Neutrals' or 'the neutral French.'" The policy of neutrality was, in Acadian eyes, not a passive position but a positive strategy adjusted to border life. It was an adaptation to the reality of their existence on lands ruled by one power while another, which had earlier controlled the area, established in their neighbourhood a massive fortress, Louisbourg. The British had little military strength within the colony, but more than enough to make their presence uncomfortable for any Acadian village they visited, and there was always the possibility of reinforcements from Massachusetts. The French were careful not to provoke open warfare but their presence was equally obvious. In the forests surrounding the Acadian villages were the Indians, whose clashes with the British were an ever present reminder of their strength and their partiality to the French, and of the weakness of the British. Although in their own eyes the Acadians were as native to the valleys and marshlands, the seashore and the forests as the Indians, to the French and British the matter was by no means so clear. To these struggling imperial powers the most important characteristics of the Acadians were their language and their religion, and these same characteristics made them natural allies of French interests, natural enemies of British rights.

The next 18 years, however, were for the Acadians a time of growth and prosperity. This period was the golden age, 1730 to 1748, that would be a significant memory for every Acadian over the age of ten at the time of the deportation. The expansion of the population, the growth of the flocks and herds, the ever expanding cultivation of the land have been admirably chronicled by Andrew Hill Clark* in *Acadia: the geography of early Nova Scotia to 1760* (1968). The statistical record reveals the base of what was to become the legend embodied by Longfellow in the poem *Evangeline*, the story of Acadia, a land flowing with milk and honey. The population of Annapolis Royal alone grew from about 900 people in 1730 to some 2,000 by 1748. From this community, during these same years, young people moved out towards Minas and Cobequid (near Truro, N.S.) to establish their own families. The livestock holdings for the total population in 1714 were likely 4,000 cattle, the same number of sheep, and some 3,000 swine. By 1748 Minas alone had 5,000 cattle and Clark's estimates for all the settlements in the years 1748–50 are 17,750 cattle, 26,650 sheep, 12,750 swine, and 1,600 horses. These bare details of economic growth indicate the Acadians enjoyed a life without famine and without epidemics. Their food was plentiful and varied, and Acadian apple cider added to the gaiety of their festivities.

Founded upon the reality of plenty, Acadian society in the pre-deportation period, as the Acadian writer Antonine Maillet has shown, owed much to the traditions that formed Rabelais and little to asceticism, whether of the Reformation or of the Counter-Reformation. The Acadians developed with enthusiasm the arts of singing, violin-playing, dancing, story-telling, feasting, and drinking. All of these activities are mentioned with disapproval by those who worked as missionaries in Acadia, starting with the Recollet reports of 1616 and 1617 and continuing with Capuchin and Sulpician complaints. Massignon's study of vocabulary traces phrases such as "jouer à monter l'échelette" (in reference to a child's game played with the hands) straight back to 16th-century France, and Maillet's study of Acadian folklore links Acadian songs and hymns to the same century. The tradition of Acadian violin-making, and of Acadian step-dancing, has been compared as it now exists in the Canadian Maritimes and in Louisiana: the similarity of music and dance has led authorities to conclude a pre-deportation origin for the themes exploited. Coming from such a variety of villages in Europe, Acadians were able to assemble a wide collection of folk-tale and legend, of customs for Christmas or customs for weddings, which would relieve any last vestige of monotony in the colony.

Acadian society was remarkably unconstrained by external governance, either of the Catholic Church or of the state. The tradition of clerical authority as a hallmark of Acadian society is a tradition that developed from the circumstances of Acadian life after the deportation. The Acadians' concern for religion up to, and during, the years of exile was very much a concern that a particular institution and activity should be observed, and they practised their faith with a secular utility, registering their baptisms, marriages, and deaths. Theirs was not a concern that produced vocations to the priesthood, the monastic or the conventual life; it was not something that gave the church saints for her altars. It was, instead, a concern that would be expressed in argument, such as that recorded disapprovingly by the Capuchins who encountered Charles de La Tour's second wife, Françoise-Marie Jacquelin*, in 1640. It was a concern that would make the village of Beaubassin complain bitterly in 1693 of the Sulpician Father Jean Baudoin*, who, they alleged, neglected to say mass for them, being more interested in missionary activity among the Indians than in Acadian souls; or similar concern voiced in 1695 by the inhabitants of Minas Basin against their priest, Father Cosme, for trying to interfere too rigidly in a domestic quarrel between husband, wife, and sister-in-law. The clergy were, for the Acadians, a necessity but not an unquestioned authority.

Part of their attitude towards Catholicism was rooted in the manner in which they were provided with priests. Secular priests were as important in their communities as the regular clergy and were by definition linked more directly with ordinary daily life. Moreover, no one religious order dominated Acadian development. Through their relations with the Indians the Acadians had been brought into contact from the earliest times with Jesuit missionaries, while in the settlements two branches of the Franciscans, the Capuchins and the Recollets, were influential. The presence of Jesuit and Franciscan meant the existence among the Acadians of more than one framework for Catholic belief. As the 17th century drew to a close priests were sent from the Séminaire de Saint-Sulpice in Montreal as well as from France. This diversity of experience in an important aspect of community life was yet another encouragement to the growth of a particular Acadian quality.

Acadian Catholicism, it is clear, was a religion far less authoritarian than the Catholicism of New France. Similarly, during the golden age the political demands of the British, at least in the Acadian consciousness, were mere shadows. Even during the War of the Austrian Succession the essential independence of Acadian community life remained. This was partly because the transformation of Port-Royal into Annapolis Royal in 1714 had helped to shift the centre of Acadian society both psychologically and in terms of population density to the settlements of Beaubassin, Minas, and Grand Pré, and away from the officials and the governor. As the years passed, the growth of the Acadian community meant a movement of settlement even further away and the Acadian population spread into settlements along the present-day New Brunswick shoreline as well as across to Île Saint-Jean. The Acadians might be subjects of the British crown, but their contact with its representatives, military or civil, was haphazard, erratic, and rarely such as to impress upon them its might. The garrison of the colony was always undersupplied during the first half of the 18th century and frequently harassed by the Indians. Although Acadian disputes over land ownership were brought often enough to the authorities at Annapolis Royal, many of the villagers preferred to have such matters settled during the visits of the priests. British government in the colony was as much a "phantom rule" as ever the rule of France had been over their ancestors.

That this golden age was coming to an end during the War of the Austrian Succession does not markedly alter the essentially peaceful aspect of the period for the Acadians. The hostilities of the 1740s [*see* François DU PONT Duvivier; Jean-Baptiste-Nicolas-Roch de RAMEZAY] merely served to make them believe that they had achieved recognition, at no very great cost, from both French and British for their policy of neutrality. It is ironic that the conclusion of warfare between France and Britain in 1748 is truly the conclusion of peace for the Acadians. The treaty signed that year signals a new interest in the Acadian lands on the part of both powers. The next seven years succeed one another with the beat of inevitable tragedy running through the events. The policy followed by the Acadians with such success until 1748 became, after that year, a major contribution to the tragedy of deportation.

Acadian strategy had been built up over nearly a century, had proven successful, and hence was confirmed after 1748 on the assumption that no major change in it was required to meet the circumstances of the day. During the 1660s, the time of Thomas Temple and William Crowne*, the Acadians had been made aware of plans for their deportation – which came to naught. Visitation by the English after 1671 resulted in oaths sworn to whoever held the English crown, as for example that to William and Mary, reported by Joseph Robinau* de Villebon to the Marquis de Chevry in 1690. From 1710 on, the Acadians were repeatedly threatened with deportation and were repeatedly requested to swear oaths they found unnecessarily restrictive. The oaths they did proffer were apparently accepted by British officials and they themselves were left unmolested on their lands. The arrival of Edward CORNWALLIS in 1749 as governor of the colony led, in Acadian eyes, to the customary conversation about an oath, the expected threat of deportation for non-compliance, their response of loyalty qualified by neutrality, and the expected result of acceptance by default – of being left in tranquillity. It is true that Halifax had been founded but to the Acadians it was a most unprepossessing town, where, in the words of a contemporary, one half of the population lived by selling rum to the rest. Certainly it was as nothing when compared to Louisbourg. The new immigrants gathered together at Lunenburg could be ignored with equal ease, since they tended to desert and join the French and those remaining in Nova Scotia showed little evidence of strength. Even though violence became more and more prominent in Acadian lives with the activities of Jean-Louis LE LOUTRE and his Indians, it was sporadic in nature and did not appear to dictate a major change of Acadian policy.

It is appropriate to emphasize that the Acadians, as a collectivity, did not waver during the 1740s from the policy they had evolved a generation earlier. A letter signed on 13 Oct. 1744 by the leaders of Minas, Rivière-aux-Canards (near Canard), Pisiquid, and the "neighbouring rivers" refused grain and meat to the French troops under François Du Pont Duvivier and then continued: "We are under a mild and peaceful government with which we have every reason to be content, we hope that you will not divide us from it and that you will do us the kindness of not plunging us into dire want." One might argue the sincerity of this letter and whether or not it was more than a safeguard for villagers left to British mercies after Duvivier's failure to capture Annapolis Royal. However, it was used by the defence during the investigations into the conduct of those officers charged with waging war incompetently against the British [*see* Michel de Gannes* de Falaise]. Such officers protested that the expedition could not have succeeded without Acadian aid and that not only was such aid not forthcoming but some of the priests, Jean-Baptiste de Gay* Desenclaves at Annapolis Royal and Claude-Jean-Baptiste Chauvreulx* at Pisiquid, openly discouraged the Acadians from contemplating any activity that would assist the French.

In the light of this evidence and of Mascarene's reports to London, both during the hostilities of 1744 and in succeeding years, concerning the Acadians' support for the British, the actions of men such as Joseph-Nicolas Gautier*, *dit* Bellair, and Joseph LEBLANC, *dit* Le Maigre, become the actions of, at best, an unsuccessful minority. Even with French troops actually in Grand Pré, the villagers would not unequivocally join their cause. Whatever following Joseph Brossard*, *dit* Beausoleil, and the others had, it did not include the majority of the farmers and their families. The loyalties of the Acadians were akin to those of the people of Alsace-Lorraine, mixed and centred above all in a wish for life without war.

What the Acadians did not grasp until too late was the new importance placed upon their lands after 1748. At the discussions which followed the signing of the treaty of Aix-la-Chapelle that year the British stated that the limits of Acadia or Nova Scotia were "the most important point to be Determin'd for settling the same Tranquillity in America as had been so happily established in Europe." The colony had now become not merely a junction of two jurisdictions but a place for rival empires to confront one another. The inability of the Acadians to perceive the new importance of their territory was matched by their inability to recognize the difference in force and character of the men who became responsible for the government of the colony. Cornwallis, Peregrine Thomas Hopson*, and Charles Lawrence* were people of much different political capacities than Philipps, Armstrong, and Mascarene. Above all, the Acadians seem to have been unable to comprehend what government by Colonel Lawrence, who was experienced only as a soldier in the field, would demand in terms of diplomacy. For so long, part of Acadian experience had been the political ability of Mascarene, who believed in the art of the possible and could write of Acadian difficulties in 1744 with the following sense of sympathy: "The French Inhabitants as soon as the Indians withdrew from us brought us Provisions and continue to testifie their resolution to keep to their fidelity as long as we keep this Fort. Two Deputies arriv'd yesterday from Mainis, who have brot me a Paper containing an association sign'd by most of the Inhabitants of that place to prevent Cattle being transported to Louisbourg according to the Prohibition sent them from hence. The french Inhabitants are certainly in a very perillous Situation, those who pretend to be their Friends and old Masters having let loose a parcell of Banditti to plunder them, whilst on the other hand they see themselves threatened with ruin & Destruction, if they fail in their allegiance to the British Government." Lawrence, on the other hand, looked upon the Acadian tradition of petition and remonstrance as "Presumption" and considered Acadian attempts to inform him of their attitude utterly unacceptable. Mascarene could regard the Acadians as a people of ordinary human complexity; Lawrence was unable to distinguish in them any distinctive features save a treasonable unwillingness to declare unequivocal loyalty, underlined by their French speech and Catholic beliefs, both traits naturally linking them with the enemy.

Guy Frégault*, in *La guerre de la Conquete* (1955), summarizes the deportation of the Acadians in 1755 as an act of war, essential for the proper colonization of Nova Scotia to render it a part of the British empire as that polity entered the final stages of the Anglo-French struggle for the domination of North America. It is tempting to set about the elaboration and refinement of this theory, but it is sufficient here to say that the deportation took place during a period of war and that it was defended by those who carried it out as a military operation, a necessity for the defence of the colony.

For the Acadians the events of the year 1755 itself provided undeniable evidence of a new firmness of purpose and commitment of resource on the part of the officials in Halifax. First to feel the impact of the policy were the inhabitants of the Minas area, requested in the spring of that year to surrender boats and guns to a force sent out by Captain Alexander Murray* at Fort Edward (Windsor). While complying with this request the inhabitants sent a petition on 10 June to Halifax arguing against it. Within the next seven days Fort Beauséjour (near Sackville, N.B.) was successfully attacked and captured by Robert MONCKTON, the French garrison under Louis DU PONT Duchambon de Vergor leaving on 17 June. Shortly thereafter the Acadians of the Chignecto Isthmus were required to bring in their arms, a demand with which the communities in question complied by the 25th of the month. Lieutenant Governor Lawrence and the members of the ruling Council of the colony were now sufficiently heartened by success to attempt to bring the Acadians, once and for all, to a declaration of unequivocal allegiance to British interests. War in America having begun, this decision seems reasonable enough.

The Council meeting of 3 July 1755 had as its business the discussion of the petition presented by the inhabitants of Minas. It provided the necessary opportunity for a demonstration to a significant part of the Acadian population of the rigour now intended. The minutes of this meeting were published first by Thomas Beamish Akins* in *Acadia and Nova Scotia* (1869). In the more than 200 works published since the middle of the 19th century about the deportation this meeting has been seen not merely as a decisive confrontation between the Acadians and the officials of the province but also as one revealing the essential nature of the conflict. Colonel Lawrence and the Council are presented as men secure in the knowledge of their own right, skilled in oratory, organized in policy, and speaking from a position of undoubted strength. The Acadians, on the other hand, are a "simple peasantry," of a different order of sophistication if not of intelligence than their interlocutors, and, in Brebner's words, "harshly questioned and inexcusably bullied" during the discussion.

There is no doubt that the meeting was crucial in the development of the events leading up to the deportation. What is in doubt is the interpretation of the meeting as a clash between the strong and organized and the weak and unprepared. The position of the lieutenant governor and Council was based upon fear, not strength and certitude. They knew just how weak the general British situation was, and they believed that the colony in which they lived was peopled primarily by inhabitants whose loyalty to British interests was still an open question. The Acadians pointed out that they had remained neutral in past hostilities and that no oath could bind unless the will to keep it was present. In other words, they argued confidently from a sense of their own undoubted, unquestionable ownership of the lands on which they lived, their sense of being in "their own, their native land," and from a total disbelief in the reality of any deportation threat.

As the months went by, the Acadians became less confident, the colonial officials more so. The arrival in Halifax on 9 July 1755 of a naval squadron under the command of Vice-Admiral Edward Boscawen* gave Nova Scotian officials a reinforcement of undoubted strength. Boscawen and his second-in-command, Rear-Admiral Savage Mostyn, attended Council meetings, and by 18 July the lieutenant governor could write to his superiors in England that he was determined to obtain an unqualified oath of allegiance from the Acadians. The last days of the month saw the opposing sides reach the position most often attributed to them in its opening days: Lawrence and the Council arriving, with the support of the fleet, at a decisive policy to which they had become fully committed and which they had confidence they could implement; the Acadians, on the other hand, losing their sense of security and for the first time confused about the prospect of deportation. The final, written petitions of the Acadians, which reached the lieutenant governor and Council on 25 July, contained repetitions of their belief in their rectitude, that from Annapolis River expostulating: "We have unanimously consented to deliver up our fire arms to Mr [John Handfield*], our very worthy commander, although we have never had any desire to make use of them against his majesty's government. We have therefore nothing to reproach ourselves with, either on that subject, or on the subject of the fidelity that we owe to His Majesty's government." Such an argument, however, was insufficient to convince their opponents of their reliability. The final meeting between Acadian and official on Monday morning, 28 July 1755, resulted in the unanimous decision by lieutenant governor and Council to distribute the Acadians "amongst the several Colonies on the Continent" and to hire "a sufficient Number of Vessels . . . with all possible Expedition for that purpose."

The organization of the deportation over the next months was based on explicit instructions drawn up by the lieutenant governor. The meticulous specification by Colonel Lawrence of the amount of food to be provided on board ship for each Acadian has been seen by the French historian Émile Lauvrière, writing his history of the Acadians in the early 1920s, as the mark of total callousness: "Only a criminal soul," he wrote, "could devise such a plot in all its details." Brebner, however, writing in North America at much the same time, concluded from reading the same document that "Lawrence had attempted in the beginning to be very painstaking in preparation and, by contemporary standards, careful to provide adequate ship room for his victims, allotting two persons to a shipping ton, and allowing methodically for their provisioning from captured food-stuffs with necessary supplement from Halifax." For the Acadians, however, whatever the motive the result was the same: the destruction of their society, the elimination of their communities, their exile to foreign lands.

The actual dimension of this catastrophe has been a matter of considerable debate but the work of A. H. Clark has helped to set the probable limits. He has shown that the Acadian population in 1755 could not have been less than 10,000 and was probably closer to 12,000. The majority of those exiled, numbering about 7,000, were sent away in 1755 and another 2,000–3,000 people were deported before the policy was officially abandoned. For once the lieutenant governor and Council of Nova Scotia had finally decided upon the deportation of the Acadians in 1755, it became a matter of policy, a decision to be carried to its logical conclusion. The rounding up of Acadians continued until 1762. The fall of Louisbourg in 1758 saw particularly vigorous measures. Some 700 Acadians from Île Saint-Jean were put on board the *Duke William* and the *Violet*, their destination England. Both ships sank in the English Channel, and there were but few survivors [*see* Jacques GIRARD].

In 1761 there was some chance that the policy might be brought to an end. Responding that year to a request from Jonathan BELCHER, Lawrence's successor as lieutenant governor, Major-General Jeffery AMHERST denied the Nova Scotia government permission to send a number of Acadians into exile in Massachusetts without authority from London. However, news of Charles-Henri-Louis d'ARSAC de Ternay's capture of St John's, Newfoundland, in June 1762 so aroused fears in Nova Scotia that Belcher was moved to ignore these instructions. On 18 August he sent transports with some hundred Acadians to Boston, from which port they were returned to Nova Scotia at the end of September. This abortive shipment marked the end of the official policy of deportation.

The actual terms of the peace concluded in 1763 were not seen in Nova Scotia as granting Acadians the legal right to settle there. This right was, however, granted the following year. Lieutenant Governor Montagu Wilmot* arrived to take charge of the colony in September 1763 to discover that a French Protestant, Jacques Robin, had plans to gather the remnants of the Acadians together. He had written to the leading persons among them, according to the report that Wilmot sent to London, "inviting them in the strongest terms from all quarters, wherever dispersed, to collect themselves at Mirimichi." Wilmot pointed out to the authorities in London that such a plan would probably have dangerous consequences for the security of the province. On 16 July 1764 the Lords of Trade informed Wilmot that he should allow the Acadians to settle in Nova Scotia, provided they took the oath of allegiance.

Nine years after the transports had left with the first Acadians to be sent into exile there were yet Acadians in the colony, a nucleus for the development of a reconstituted Acadian society. Representatives of some 165 families came forward to take the oath, a community apparently of less than 1,000 spread throughout the colony. Uncounted were the Acadians who did not come forward, including those settled at Saint-Basile on the upper Saint John River, those in the woods around the Miramichi, and scattered families in Cape Breton and St John's Island (formerly Île Saint-Jean). Some 30 families were still in Halifax, and each of the following places reported in the neighbourhood of ten families: St Margaret's Bay, Chester, Lunenburg, Dublin, Liverpool, Yarmouth, Barrington, Annapolis Royal, Montagu, Cornwallis, Horton (Wolfville region), Falmouth, and Newport. The oath exacted of the Acadians was in stern contrast to earlier oaths, with their implication of the right of neutrality. The new oath was explicit, lengthy, and altogether a message to the Acadians of how decisively their lives had changed. It read: "I do swear that I will bear faithfull and true Allegiance to His most Sacred Brittannick Majesty King George the Third and him will defend to the utmost of my power against all traitorous Conspiracies and all Attempts whatsoever against his person, Crown and Dignity. And I will do my utmost Endeavours to disclose or make known to His Majesty and his Successors, all Treason and traitorous Conspiracies, or any attempts whatever which I shall know to be against him or any of them. And these things I do plainly and sincerely promise and Swear, according to the express Words by me Spoken and according to the plain and Common Sense understanding of these same words, without any Equivocation, mental Evasion or secret Reservation whatsoever; And I do make this Acknowledgement and promise heartily, willingly and truly upon the true Faith of a Christian, So help me God."

The ensuing years were to demonstrate how fundamentally the position of the Acadians had been altered. France no longer was a presence in the region, and at the same time the demography of what had been Acadia changed radically. The Acadians, once the predominant European inhabitants, were overwhelmed by other groups to whom were assigned the most favoured localities, including the ancient Acadian lands. Prior to 1764 New Englanders in large numbers had occupied the Annapolis valley and the Nova Scotian south shore. Before the American revolution, these newcomers were supplemented by settlement from Yorkshire in the Chignecto Isthmus and by the beginnings of the massive movement of Scots to Nova Scotia and Cape

Breton. The revolution and its aftermath brought a major influx of loyalists to Nova Scotia and to what became the loyalist province of New Brunswick. In the new political configuration of the second British empire, the Acadians were a minority in every colony, a minority moreover with no cultural and little religious affinity with the many groups of new settlers.

In these circumstances the political leverage the Acadians once possessed vanished utterly. Their difficulties were compounded by the grant of representative government to the several colonies of the region. In former times the Acadians had been able to bargain with the governor or with his appointed councillors; the emergence of legislative assemblies, beginning with Nova Scotia in 1758, meant the total exclusion of the Acadians from the ordinary political processes of all the colonies. Their Catholicism, their demographic weakness, and their unfamiliarity with the forms and procedures of British colonial rule barred them from office and from influence upon office-holders. Moreover, to assemblymen and councillors dedicated to the building of commercial, expansive, new societies the Acadians were a negligible quantity, ranking somewhere between Europeans and Indians. Their fate was symbolized by the summary ejection of Acadian families from fertile intervale land in New Brunswick; as Edward Winslow* put it in 1785, "a number of Frenchmen ... have been most unjustly ousted from their land." These families, and others like them, retreated or were shoved to the peripheral lands of the colonies, and to an existence isolated from the mainstream of colonial life.

But in spite of all that had happened and was happening to them, in the last decades of the 18th century the Acadians succeeded in reconstituting themselves as a distinct people. The nucleus of the new Acadian community was the minority that had evaded deportation. Some, the Acadian families in Annapolis Royal and Halifax, for example, had survived because they were useful, or simply because of the humane feelings of people in the vicinity. Neither the hewers of wood in Annapolis nor the inmates of charity hospitals in Halifax posed a threat; they were suffered to stay. Then there were the escapees, such as those who had been imprisoned in Fort Lawrence (near Amherst, N.S.) in late September 1755. Monckton recounted the story to John WINSLOW in October of that year: "Eighty-six men," he wrote, "got away ... by making a Hole under Ground from the Barrack through the South curtain, about thirty feet. It is worse," he noted, "because they are all People whose Wives were not come in and of Chipoudi [Shepody], Pitcoudiack [Petitcodiac], and Memramcook." This particular group moved north and later established themselves at Caraquet, spending the years between 1755 and the late 1760s as much hiding in the forests as attempting settlement. The third general category of Acadians who escaped exile were those who were actually embarked but who either captured the ship they were on and returned immediately or, once landed in the colony of exile, immediately obtained a vessel and sailed back. Still others, such as Alexis LANDRY, had managed to avoid capture altogether and had taken refuge in remote areas.

To these groups were added the returning Acadians, coming back from Quebec, from Massachusetts and other colonies as far south as Georgia, from Saint-Pierre and Miquelon, as well as from across the Atlantic, from the Channel Islands and France. The final numbers of such Acadians were pitifully small, compared with the numbers who had sailed into exile. Exposure to diseases that had been practically unknown to them before 1755, smallpox, typhoid, yellow-fever, accounted for at least a third of those deported. Perhaps another third made their way to Louisiana (either via South Carolina and Saint-Domingue (Hispaniola) or via Virginia, England, and France) and remained there permanently. The ordinary hazards of life, plus the harsh conditions of exile, also took their toll. Nevertheless, a significant number not only survived what the Acadians christened the great upheaval, "le grand dérangement," but made their way back to Nova Scotia. Once arrived they found their old lands resettled and government restrictions placed upon where they might live. They could move north to where those who had remained were most firmly ensconced, to lands much less fertile and subject to harsher climates than their old properties. They could join the tiny enclaves of Acadians that remained on Cape Breton and St John's islands. They could attach themselves to those communities within the peninsula of Nova Scotia that were in places newly set aside for them.

The most important of the last named was brought into being by government warrant in 1767: St Mary's Bay, the township of Clare, now in Digby County. Its inhabitants had been collected together from all parts of the province, but particularly from the environs of Halifax. In 1768 the first of several groups from Massachusetts joined the growing settlement, although many of those who had been exiled to that colony went to Quebec rather than return to Nova Scotia [*see*

Louis ROBICHAUX]. During the next decade there was a steady stream of returning wanderers, among them Guillaume JEANSON, Pierre LE BLANC, and Pierre DOUCET. In general, those who had gone to other British North American colonies joined settlements in Nova Scotia, those who had crossed the Atlantic settled along the coastline of what became New Brunswick in 1784 or joined villages in what would be Prince Edward Island after 1798, and those who had been in Quebec and some parts of northern Maine added themselves to the community of Saint-Basile. By 1771 the number of Acadian families reported within the peninsula, along the north shore of the Bay of Fundy, and on the Atlantic coast of New Brunswick was 193. By 1800 the Acadians of Nova Scotia alone numbered an astonishing 8,000. At this point the further increase of the Acadians within the Maritimes was due to the preponderance of births over deaths rather than to the return of exiles.

The re-establishment of the Acadians between 1764 and 1800 meant the organization of the Acadian people in a new context, their adaptation to a new environment, politically, socially, and economically. This necessity, together with the impact upon them of the experiences of the deportation, resulted in changes not only in their style of life but also in several of the characteristics which had distinguished them before the deportation. The most outstanding of such traits was their sense of themselves as a family. Kinship lines, the demands of relatives, were as important as ever to the Acadian people. But whereas before 1755 these had encouraged the expansion and development of the Acadian communities, after 1764 the Acadian family was the encircling, protective unit. Before and during the deportation the Acadians had shown a capacity to assimilate people of varying backgrounds, building into their society contributions from the English and the Indian as well as from many parts of France. After the deportation those who associated with them noted their desire to remain, as Moses Delesdernier* commented, in "almost an inviolate Separation from all other classes of People."

In the same way, their attitude towards religion altered. Before 1755 their Catholic belief had been one feature of many in their mental landscape. After 1764 the reliance upon the institutions of Catholicism became more and more marked. This was partly because most of the Acadian villages were left without any civil authority, no magistrates being appointed for their governance, nor any form of municipal authority established. During the 17th century the governance of the Acadian settlements had evolved in an interplay between the authorities, English or French, and the inhabitants, the latter establishing internal controls through kinship ties. From 1710 until 1763 the system of sending delegates to the authorities in Annapolis Royal and in Halifax was part of the structure of Acadian life. But after 1763 those who ruled could afford to ignore the Acadians. The lack of validation of the Acadian community through endorsement from without was matched by a lack of cohesiveness within. The vast majority of settlements were but collections of survivors, brought together by chance rather than the intention to establish a new community, saddened by the absence of the loved and lost rather than invigorated by building new lives with chosen partners. To found Memramcook in the 17th century had been to set out as a group of young families, knowing that grandparents left behind were well established and confident that hard work would soon build a respectable community. To re-establish Memramcook after 1763 was to return with the bewildering experience of the deportation a constant memory, with little surety of entitlement to hold lands cleared, and with sorrows for relatives and friends lost. In this situation the priests came to exercise a much more central role in Acadian society, providing spiritual comfort to shattered families and organizing communities to settle internal disputes.

Abbé Jean-Mandé Sigogne*, for example, laid down rules of behaviour for his own community of St Mary's Bay. A native of France, he had left his country as a result of the revolution and in 1799 came to Nova Scotia, a priest of 36 years of age. For the next 45 years Sigogne strove to improve the lives of his parishioners. Within a year of his arrival he had drawn up his "Articles for the regulation of life," dealing not only with the conduct expected at mass but also with the best method of settling family disputes; by 1809 his precepts were followed throughout the Acadian settlements in Nova Scotia. In 1810 Sigogne was named a justice of the peace for Clare, a position which helped him both in his long struggle to provide his parishioners with schools and in his encouragement of Acadian commercial enterprises. His work was not an isolated matter. As the 19th century progressed, the work of the priests became central to the life of the Acadian communities, and Acadian culture was centred far more thoroughly in the tenets of Catholic institutions than it had been in the past.

Again, if one considers the economic life of the Acadians it is both linked to their past experience and greatly changed. Hunting, fishing, farming, trade, a little smuggling had been the pillars of an economy which had allowed the Acadians to sustain an extraordinary population growth and to believe themselves wealthy. Now their lives were bound up with much the same pursuits but to a very different result. The development of the lumbering industry in the Maritimes, the growth of an industrial and urban society, meant that the concentration of the Acadians upon their traditional occupations resulted in their poverty. Instead of being successful villagers, their lives most comfortable in comparison with the migratory Indians, the Acadians had become visibly less wealthy than most of their neighbours.

As the 18th century drew to a close, however, the most outstanding fact in the lives of the Acadians was the deportation itself, what they knew and believed it had destroyed, what experiences it had brought to them, what it implied for their future existence. As the years passed, the pre-1755 era seemed, especially in contrast to existing circumstances, to have been not Acadia but Arcadia, the closest thing possible to paradise on earth. All squabbles overlooked, all hardships forgotten, the time always summer, the light the late afternoon, the community never split by property disagreements or disturbed by accusations of witchcraft, pre-deportation had been the best of times. Further, partly because of the Acadians' engulfment by a majority of English speaking peoples, partly because of the truth – that the majority of the Acadian population had indeed gone into exile without violent protest – it was now believed this paradise had been unjustly lost. The policy of neutrality which the Acadians had preserved until 1755 led them to create the myth of themselves as sinless victims, the British as somewhat stupid criminals. The Acadians came quickly to the conviction that they had done nothing to warrant their expulsion. During the 19th century the tradition of their Catholic belief emphasized the necessity of forgiving one's enemies as well as the glories attendant upon suffering nobly the slings and arrows of the world. As a result, the Acadian myth of the deportation demanded some form of forgiveness of those who had so cruelly, so unjustly brought suffering upon them.

If paradise unjustly lost was one aspect of the Acadian reaction to the deportation, another, quite as important, was their shared experience of it. Dr Andrew Brown*, the Edinburgh preacher and physician who visited Nova Scotia at the close of the century and who brought together a considerable record of Acadian life in the 18th century, noted their habit of gathering in the evening to re-tell their experiences. He also recorded their talent for dramatic flair and mimicry, for comparing the attitudes and gestures of Protestant divines attempting their conversion in Massachusetts with like gestures of the Quaker citizens of Pennsylvania, also interested in converting them. Such practices would both unite the Acadians and place a considerable barrier between them and other groups. But what above all was produced by this exercise was a knowledge within the Acadians themselves of their capacity to endure.

Those who came back from South Carolina had been sent into exile on board ships, such as the *Cornwallis*, where more than half of those embarked died before they even reached their destination. Those who returned from Philadelphia had watched smallpox kill more than a third of the Acadians sent there. Those who came back from Massachusetts had known attempts to cope with the exiles that had involved separation of parent and child, the adults sent to farms and the young indentured as servants. Those who returned from across the Atlantic would relate the experiences of dealing with one set of officials after another and of finding it quite possible to correspond with one another across frontiers, even with the nations in question at war. Whatever else the deportation had brought to the Acadians it had also instilled into them a conviction of their own capacity for survival. It is a conviction that has not yet been proven false.

The Centre d'études acadiennes at the Université de Moncton is the logical place to begin a study of the Acadians, either through work at the centre itself or with the aid of the bibliographies of Acadian material which it has published. Developed during the late 1960s out of the Archives acadiennes, whose documents the university had inherited from the Collège Saint-Joseph, the CÉA set about gathering all available documentation concerning the Acadian people, in the original where possible and by the appropriate means of copying where necessary. In 1975 it published the first volume of a proposed three-volume study entitled *Inventaire général des sources documentaires sur les Acadiens* (Moncton, N.-B.). Subtitled *Les sources premières, les archives*, this volume not only describes those documents which the CÉA now possesses but also attempts to note material held elsewhere. Its organization is idiosyncratic but it serves to introduce the scholar to the richness of primary sources for Acadian history. In 1977 the second volume appeared, subtitled *Bibliographie acadienne, liste des volumes, brochures et thèses concernant l'Acadie et les Acadiens des débuts à 1975*. Once more, the organization needs a certain amount of study before its plan becomes apparent, but the volume is an invaluable introduction to the wealth of secondary source material on Acadian matters.

Among thematic studies, Brebner's *New England's outpost* is the clearest account in English of the political and diplomatic history of the Acadians until 1755. In French, the first volume of Robert Rumilly's *Histoire des Acadiens* (2v., Montréal, 1955) recounts events lucidly. In 1968 Clark published his *Acadia*, an excellent work which presents with great detail the economic development of the Acadians during the years leading up to the deportation. N. [E. S.] Griffiths, *The Acadians: creation of a people* (Toronto, 1973), outlines the evolution of the Acadian identity. The study by the French scholar Geneviève Massignon, *Les parlers français d'Acadie* . . . (2v., Paris, [1962]), is an exhaustive examination of Acadian speech patterns and their roots. Its volumes not only explore the relationship between the dialects of France, Quebec, and Acadia but also give a well-organized analysis of the historical influences that shaped Acadian speech patterns. Antonine Maillet's work, *Rabelais et les traditions populaires en Acadie* (Québec, 1971), examines the root of much Acadian folklore, and its introduction presents a powerful overview of the course of Acadian history through three centuries.

The religious history of the Acadians has yet to be written, although there are a number of works concerned with particular aspects of it. Nineteenth-century historians in particular produced works such as H.-R. Casgrain's *Les sulpiciens et les prêtres des Missions-Étrangères en Acadie (1676–1762)* (Québec, 1897), but there has as yet been no exhaustive work on the complex matter of religion. Acadian literature has been well documented, if not yet studied and analysed, in the work edited by Marguerite Maillet *et al.*, entitled *Anthologie de textes littéraires acadiens* (Moncton, 1979).

What might be called the external relations of the Acadians, the society's connections with New England and with Quebec, has been the focus of a number of doctoral dissertations now in the process of publication. That of Jean Daigle, "Nos amis les ennemis: relations commerciales de l'Acadie avec le Massachusetts, 1670–1711" (University of Maine, Orono, 1975), is centred upon the relations between Acadia and New England at the close of the 17th century; that of J. G. Reid, "Acadia, Maine and New Scotland: marginal colonies in the seventeenth century" (University of New Brunswick, Fredericton, 1976), is concerned with the earlier years of that century. G. A. Rawlyk's *Nova Scotia's Massachusetts; a study of Massachusetts-Nova Scotia relations, 1630–1784* (Montreal and London, 1973) is a clear account of the major events in the period. There has not yet been a full examination of Quebec-Acadian relations, although [F.-]E. Rameau de Saint-Père's works, *La France aux colonies: . . . Acadiens et canadiens* (Paris, 1859) and *Une colonie féodale en Amérique: l'Acadie (1604–1881)* (2v., Paris et Montréal, 1889), are worth consulting on this subject.

It might be said that in many ways the deportation is the most important theme in Acadian history. By 1900 nearly 200 works had already been published about it. The intensity of the drama has been rendered best by Émile Lauvrière in *La tragédie d'un peuple: histoire du peuple acadien, de ses origines à nos jours* (3e éd., 2v., Paris, 1922). This account, written in florid language, makes the most thorough condemnation of the British. The work of Acadian historian Antoine Bernard, especially in his *Le drame acadien depuis 1604* (Montréal, 1936), presents a less partisan view. In English the best short treatment is by A. G. Doughty, *The Acadian exiles: a chronicle of the land of Evangeline* (Toronto and Glasgow, 1920). The historiography of the deportation has been examined most recently by J.-P. Hautecœur in *L'Acadie du discours: pour une sociologie de la culture acadienne* (Québec, 1975).

The integration of the province of Quebec into the British empire, 1763–91

PART I: FROM THE ROYAL PROCLAMATION TO THE QUEBEC ACT

PIERRE TOUSIGNANT

THE CHOICE of this historical period – the first 30 years of the British régime in Quebec – is not arbitrary. It is a period that has its own peculiarities and is in many respects distinct, especially in that the history of Quebec is then identical with that of Canada from all perspectives, whether geographic or demographic, economic or political, social or cultural. It is important to remember at the outset that this former French possession, referred to as Canada and then called the province of Quebec by virtue of the Royal Proclamation of October 1763, was to remain a uniform colonial entity until 1791.

The year 1791 marked in fact both a fracture and an amputation, the territory of Quebec being divided into Upper and Lower Canada and the way left open to two destinies, two orientations, two evolutions, two distinct developments: English Canada and French Canada. That separation assumed even more importance in that the two newly created provincial governments were each at the same time endowed with institutional bases permitting them to exercise authority within a constitutional framework modelled on that of the government in London. And in the historical perspective adopted here this political linking with the British empire must be considered a culmination rather than a turning-point – the final outcome of a solution envisaged 30 years earlier, just after the signing of the treaty of Paris in 1763.

These considerations, which themselves suffice to explain and justify the chronological division chosen for this essay, lead to others bearing on its orientation. As the title indicates, emphasis will be given to the fundamental characteristic of the early years of the British régime: the implementation of various trial solutions to the major problem of incorporating into the British empire the most important colony in New France, first at a time of revolutionary crisis that made any imperial reorganization in North America risky until the end of the American War of Independence, and after 1783 within the framework of a restructuring made necessary by the loss of the Thirteen Colonies.

It seems essential to place this colonial history in its North American context and to examine it in relation to imperial policy in order to grasp fully the significance of the decisions taken in London and to understand their consequences and their effects on the evolution of Quebec. Such an approach necessarily involves a choice in the aspects to be considered in the essay. The reader will not find here a narrative account designed to reconstitute the fabric of the past. Rather the essay seeks to set forth the network of relations between facts that are more or less well known so as to obtain a better understanding of the process of Quebec's integration into the British empire.

It is important to recall the general capitulation signed at Montreal on 8 Sept. 1760. This document is fundamental because the commitments then consented to on a provisional basis were officially sanctioned by the British parliament in 1774. The decisive importance this capitulation agreement was to acquire after Canada had been finally ceded stemmed from two main factors: on the one hand, the rights the conquered people were acknowledged to have; on the other, the interest in retaining the inhabitants of New France for the good of the British empire and in making of them faithful and loyal subjects of the crown.

Since Canada had been conquered before the Seven Years' War ended, its surrender implied a more or less prolonged period of military occupation. The fate of the conquered people had therefore to be considered, after that of the troops, the senior officers, and the senior personnel of the French colonial administration had been settled. A willingness was shown to concede to the former subjects of the king of France certain rights that went well beyond the well-known guarantee of the "free exercise of the Catholic, Apostolic, and Roman religion," which was to be officially confirmed by the treaty of Paris in 1763. The secular clergy was maintained both in its organization and in its ecclesiastical functions, and all the religious communities kept "their moveables, the property and revenues of the

Seignories" with "their privileges, rights, honours, and exemptions." The preservation of the quarter of the seigneurial domain that had been granted the religious orders was thereby assured. As for the lands belonging to the non-clerical seigneurs and the fate of their *censitaires*, article 37 was explicit: "The Lords of Manors, the Military and Civil officers, the Canadians as well in the Towns as in the country, the French settled, or trading, in the whole extent of the colony of Canada, and all other persons whatsoever, shall preserve the entire peaceable property and possession of the goods, noble and ignoble, moveable and immoveable, merchandizes, furs and other effects." Those who decided to go to France would be free to sell their belongings and take the proceeds with them; those who remained in Canada could enjoy "all the privileges of trade . . . in the countries above [*pays d'en haut*] . . . [and in] the interior of the colony."

Such, in the main, were the conditions that the last governor of New France, Vaudreuil [RIGAUD], considered "very advantageous" from the viewpoint of the "interests of the colony and the settlers." Among the requests that AMHERST refused, two were utterly inadmissible: the continuation of the king of France's power to name the bishop of Quebec, and the right of the inhabitants to remain strictly neutral in the case of conflict with France. Another request exceeded the authority of the victorious general: he could not permit retention of the laws, usages, and customs established before the conquest.

This last question, however, would soon regain attention after civil government had been set up. Leaving the new subjects "entire peaceable property and possession of the goods, noble and ignoble," involved not only retaining the seigneurial system but also preserving the social organization that depended upon it. How then was the necessity of recognizing everything in French law pertaining to the ownership, transmission, and sale of landed property to be avoided? This conclusion was precisely that reached early on by the law officers of the crown, Charles Yorke and William de Grey (respectively attorney general and solicitor general), who advised in their noted report of April 1766 that the former property laws be retained. Eight years later the British parliament gave official sanction to this recommendation.

The capitulation of September 1760 would probably not have had the same significance had it not been for the self-interest which worked in favour of the conquered population once Great Britain's imperial designs in North America had been realized. If the supreme ambition of the conquest's chief architect, William Pitt, had been to eliminate from the North American continent Britain's rival, France, his successor as secretary for the Southern Department, Lord Egremont, was particularly anxious to keep the inhabitants of New France for the benefit of the British empire: "Nothing is more essential to His Majesty's Service," he declared, "than to retain as many French subjects as possible and to prevent them from leaving their homes to go off to the colonies that may remain in France's possession." General Amherst had reason to congratulate himself for having acted appropriately in taking the necessary measures for reconciling conquerors and conquered.

In this spirit and with this concern for reconciliation began the military occupation, which lasted until civil government was set up in August 1764. The directives from Amherst in his famous Placard of 22 Sept. 1760 were the basis for the organization of this temporary régime. Wishing the forces of occupation to "live with the habitants in harmony and good fellowship," he had provided for arrangements and compromises likely to facilitate governance by the conquerors. As far as possible he endeavoured to respect the administrative structures in existence before the conquest. The previous division of the colony into three governments (Montreal, Quebec, and Trois-Rivières) remained unchanged, but these jurisdictions were so constituted that they could function separately and independently of one another. Each was entrusted to a military governor directly under the commander-in-chief of the British troops in North America, who had headquarters in New York.

The administration of justice was not changed as drastically as has been claimed by historian François-Xavier Garneau*, for whom the institution of courts martial symbolized a state of siege. Naturally military courts replaced the various judicial authorities of the French régime that had been abolished. The suppression of these bodies did not, however, signify the rejection of established traditions in the functioning of the judicial system. In keeping with the spirit of Amherst's directives, governors Ralph Burton*, Thomas GAGE, and James MURRAY concerned themselves in their respective jurisdictions with seeing that justice was dispensed promptly and cheaply by employing the captains and officers of the Canadian militia, who constituted courts of first instance and judged legal disputes according to the customary law of Paris. Cases under appeal were referred to councils of military officers and as a last resort to the governors themselves. Far from appearing oppressive, this judicial organization left such a deep impression that on the eve of the promulgation of the Quebec Act both seigneurial and bourgeois spokesmen for the Canadians evoked memory of it in a petition to the king: "Our gratitude obliges us to acknowledge, that the frightful appearances of conquest . . . did not long continue to excite our lamentations and tears. . . . And even in the very moment of the conquest, we were far from feeling the melancholy effects of restraint and captivity. For the wise and virtuous general [Amherst] . . . left us in possession of our laws and customs . . . and our own former countrymen were appointed judges of our disputes concerning civil matters." Thus the policy of reconciliation that inspired the conduct of the military authorities had prepared the conquered population to accept the change of imperial authority when Canada was definitively ceded. Fewer than 300 individuals out of a population of 60,000 – only one in 200 – chose to take advantage of article 4 of the treaty of Paris, which allowed them 18 months to emigrate from the colony "with all safety and freedom."

That every possible means had been used to make the military régime acceptable to them did not, however, prepare the new British subjects for the constraints and vexations imposed by the establishment of civil government. They had to learn the risks of politics that subjected them to the ordeals of a struggle for rights which had seemed to them almost secured. In taking definitive possession of Canada the London authorities had not seriously contemplated the problems that would be created by the integration into the British empire of these former subjects of the king of France, who already formed a separate people with an inclination to remain so. In the period just after the treaty of Paris too many questions simultaneously required the imperial government's attention for it to be able to give proper consideration to the situation of the Canadians.

In accordance with the treaty of Paris, signed on 10 Feb. 1763, Great Britain assumed control of the former territory of New France, including Canada "with all its dependencies" (the Great Lakes basin or *pays d'en haut* with Detroit as its main centre and the vast *domaine de l'Ouest* extending from Lake Superior to the Rocky Mountains); the eastern portion of Louisiana bounded by the Mississippi River (the western part having been ceded to Spain by a secret pact); and everything on the Atlantic coast and the Gulf of St Lawrence that had been left to France by the treaty of Utrecht in 1713 (in particular Île Royale or Cape Breton Island and Île Saint-Jean or Prince Edward Island). For her part Spain surrendered Florida and all her territory as far as the Mississippi. Thus, with the Thirteen Colonies included, Great Britain found herself in possession of almost half of the North American continent, from the Gulf of Mexico to Hudson Bay. Suddenly her American colonial domain had more than doubled by comparison with what it had been before 1760.

The acquisition of such a vast geographical area, diversely peopled by whites and Indians, posed problems of territorial development, colonial administration, and military defence, and with these the British government had to contend in the months following the signing of the peace treaty. Their solution was considered within the framework of a programme of imperial reorganization designed to strengthen the home authority by tightening the lines of central control over commerce, taxation, and politics. Indeed, the Royal Proclamation of October 1763 was the first of a series of executive and legislative measures by George Grenville's ministry (April 1763–July 1765) for this purpose. It was not long, however, before the implementation of this programme roused the opposition and then the active resistance of the Thirteen Colonies, bringing down the ministry less than three months after parliament had passed the famous Stamp Act.

The Royal Proclamation was to constitute not only the first step in the imperial plan, but also the very foundation, so that the trials and reverses experienced in putting the programme into effect had direct repercussions upon it. Thus, by a series of revisions the proclamation was gradually abandoned, to be replaced finally by the Quebec Act, which marked a reorientation of imperial policy. The experience of this setback helped significantly to increase the importance of Quebec and its inhabitants in the view of the British government, and this change of emphasis took place progressively as the initial programme was abandoned. Just as the attention of the authorities in London was focused on the Indian question in 1763, so it would be absorbed by the case of the Canadians in 1774.

The most striking aspect of the territorial reorganization decreed in the Royal Proclamation was undoubtedly the transformation into Indian reserves of the whole interior of the continent, from the Mississippi River to the watershed of the Appalachian mountains, and from West Florida to the domain of the Hudson's Bay Company beyond the Great Lakes basin. The area of the three new "royal" colonies was comparatively well defined: south of the 31st parallel, the two Floridas (East and West), and north of the 45th parallel, the province of Quebec, which formed a sort of trapezoid taking in the valley of the St

Lawrence and was bounded on the east by the Rivière Saint-Jean (on the north shore across from the western tip of Anticosti Island) and on the west by Lake Nipissing. On Quebec's Atlantic side, to the already established province of Nova Scotia were added Cape Breton Island and Saint John's Island. Finally, Anticosti Island, the Îles de la Madeleine, and the vast territory of Labrador (from the Rivière Saint-Jean to Hudson Strait) were annexed to Newfoundland in order to take greater advantage of the monopoly to exploit the fisheries in the gulf and along the coasts, recognized as "the most obvious advantage" deriving from the peace treaty.

Although one need only read the Royal Proclamation to discern the pre-eminence of the Indian question in it, the reasons that Quebec was overlooked are not so evident. The uprising of the western Indians early in the summer of 1763 had made it imperative to seek their pacification. For the central role played by the Ottawa war chief Pontiac the reader should consult the biography in volume III of the *DCB*. The circumstances and events of this dramatic story are well recounted there, but the author does not emphasize one aspect that is absolutely fundamental to understanding the extent of the uprising, which in less than a month spread from the point of eruption, Detroit, to all the forts and trading posts in the Great Lakes region. Mention is made of the frustrations that had built up as a result of the policy of strict economy ordered by the commander-in-chief, Amherst, who refused to continue the system of exchanging presents as practised under the French régime. Certainly, given the habits formed and the meaning attached to presents, the Indians reacted badly to the privations and restrictions inflicted upon them (especially in rum, powder, and lead). Just as essential, however, was the shock of the British occupation, which made them fear their hunting grounds would be taken from them. In their eyes the Anglo-American conqueror personified the land-grabber. They could hardly have seen him otherwise, in view of their experience of the intrusive and devastating thrust of white settlement in North America spreading rapidly towards the west.

When Pontiac's uprising broke out, the Southern Department was at the point of formulating the imperial programme that would take shape in the Royal Proclamation. The Board of Trade, then under the presidency of the young Lord Shelburne, had already sketched out the main lines in its report of 8 June 1763. At this stage the particular case of Canada and its conquered people was still attracting attention. Likely having been impressed by the reports from Murray, Burton, and Gage, Shelburne had taken into account their population forecasts, which showed that in all probability Canadians would remain preponderant "for a very long time." Consequently he hesitated about the form of government to be set up, being unprepared to recommend the creation of a house of assembly, which, however, the royal edict of October 1763 was to proclaim with the aim of encouraging British settlement. Though he did not overlook the fate of future Protestant settlers, Shelburne did not give them preferential attention. Not only did he appear to want to honour the commitments already made to the "new French Subjects," but he also seemed concerned about the rights that might eventually be granted them. Such noble preoccupations could not, however, withstand the onrush of events, which brought about his resignation as well.

The news of the uprising of the western Indians reached London shortly before the secretary of state for the Southern Department, Lord Egremont, died in August 1763. To succeed him the king called upon Lord Halifax, who as president of the Board of Trade from 1748 to 1761 had acquired extended experience in the affairs of the North American colonies. Halifax hastened to put the final touches to the drafting of the Royal Proclamation. Taking advantage of the deteriorating situation in the American mid west, and with the full support of the new president of the Board of Trade, Lord Hillsborough, he implemented a strategy of imperial control that he had long since entered upon. This was a serious political error, for although the urgency of pacifying the Indians demanded an official declaration from the crown, there was no need to put through on the same occasion an imperial programme for the whole of British North America. To want all at once to create Indian reserves for the interior of the continent, regulate the expansion of white settlement, and set up new provincial governments was too ambitious not to be risky.

Anxious, under the pressure of events, to take quick action, Lord Halifax did not trouble himself with Shelburne's observations on the Canadian sense of identity, observations that suggested taking into account the problems created by the various socio-ethnic and cultural components in the population of Quebec and East and West Florida. For this minister, who had earlier had to deal with the fate of the Acadians, such considerations did not weigh heavily. He decided quite simply to treat Canada like the two Floridas and to retain from the Board of Trade report of June

1763 only what fitted in with the strategy of imperial control that he had been evolving since the founding in 1749 of Halifax, named in his honour. He did not deviate from the policy of "settlement for Trade and Defence" that he had adopted at that time. Just as he had favoured British colonization of Nova Scotia, so he wanted to encourage the early establishment of Protestant settlers in the St Lawrence valley by means of various enticements, including land grants to the officers and soldiers demobilized after serving in North America, the promise of constitutional rights and privileges, and the protection of British law. In order to direct and channel the wave of settlement that it was hoped would surge into Quebec from the southern colonies, the expansion of their population towards the west had to be checked. The containing line, which was set at the watershed of the Appalachian mountains, was supposed to serve two ends: to retain the white colonists along the Atlantic coast (the better to observe and control their activities) and to maintain peace and security in the interior of the continent.

The means envisaged to attain the second objective stemmed directly from the initiatives taken and the experience acquired during the Seven Years' War. The conflict of colonization that had set the Anglo-American expansionist forces against the Franco-Canadian military presence had broken out in the heart of the Ohio valley. Faced on one hand with the ascendancy of French influence over the Indian tribes and on the other with the inability of the British colonies to organize their own system of defence, London had had to intervene to assure the imperial defence of this vast region. In 1755 the decision had therefore been taken to put Indian affairs under the control and protection of British government and to this end to create two posts of superintendents answerable to the commander-in-chief, one for the tribes south of the Ohio, the other, entrusted to Sir William JOHNSON, for the Iroquois nations and their allies in the northern district. Observations and recommendations by the two superintendents were to be of great service in drawing up the programme of 1763.

Despite the conquest of Canada and the military occupation of the western posts, the situation in the west had remained unstable because of the serious deterioration of relations between the Anglo-American settlers and the Indians. Having been launched on the war path by imperial rivalries, the Indians continued to be subjected to increasingly strong pressure from traders eager to deceive them and from speculators greedy for lands, who were acting in collusion with the provincial governments. This invasion and cornering of land prompted the Southern Department, two years before the edict of October 1763, to point out to the various governors of the royal colonies the crown's desire to prevent land grants and settlement in Indian territories without permission from London. The Royal Proclamation not only prohibited this land-grabbing by formal decree, but set a limit to white settlement by the creation of Indian reserves. Lord Halifax went even further, attempting to subject trading relations with the Indians to strict control by London.

Although the fur trade was declared "free and open" to all British subjects, an official licence had to be obtained from either the commander-in-chief or a colonial governor. The regulations instituted were supposed to limit trade to the garrisoned posts and make traders pass inspections aimed at preventing fraudulent transactions. The management of Indian affairs was to come under the authority of the Indian department, which had undergone an administrative reorganization in the two districts already in existence south and north of the Ohio. But the fine plan for organization put forward by the Board of Trade in July 1764 was destined, after a few years' trial, to suffer the repercussions of the general failure of Lord Halifax's ambitious programme of imperial control.

Realizing the programme involved enormous operating expenses, largely for the maintenance and upkeep of a military presence over a vast area. In the period right after the signing of the treaty of Paris the British government had decided to bring the forces necessary for the defence of the new colonial empire in North America up to about 7,500 men (regrouped in some 15 battalions). Close to half of these troops were spread out from Halifax to Detroit; four battalions were kept in the Floridas, and four in the frontier outposts of New York and Pennsylvania, including Fort Niagara (near Youngstown) and Fort Pitt (Pittsburgh). Except for a few hundred soldiers (a good many of whom were in New York where the commander-in-chief had his headquarters), no regiment was stationed in the urban centres on the Atlantic coast. Parliament had voted the sums required – estimated at more than £250,000 annually (but which would amount to much more) – on condition that the Thirteen Colonies be required to pay taxes, as the Grenville ministry was going to try to ensure with the Revenue Act in 1764 (commonly called the Sugar Act) and the Stamp Act in 1765.

The presence of the army, considered essential to establishing the planned system of imperial control, was maintained at the various western posts even after Pontiac's uprising had been suppressed. To the central government the army appeared to be an indispensable strategic support in the management of political and trade relations with the Indians. Ultimately, the success or failure, the pursuit or abandonment, of this important part of the Royal Proclamation would depend upon the military forces. And its renunciation was in fact largely dictated by the necessity, given the turn of events in the Thirteen Colonies, of withdrawing a large number of the garrisons posted in the interior to bring them closer to the centres of ferment on the Atlantic coast.

The problem created by the dispersal of troops on a continental scale began to be felt acutely during the first serious colonial crisis, precipitated by the Stamp Act. The violent reaction to this fiscal legislation and the resistance movement organized against it prompted certain governors to call upon the services of the commander-in-chief, General Gage, who then drew to the attention of the home authorities his inability to regroup his forces swiftly in an emergency. Obliged to reduce military expenses as a result of the colonies' refusal to contribute to them, the secretary at war, Lord Barrington, reconsidered the existing system of defence and proposed as an alternative in the new circumstances that some of the western posts be evacuated and the forces concentrated at Quebec and Halifax in the north, and St Augustine in East Florida. Unlike Gage, he preferred to keep the troops off the scene in areas of trouble in order to prevent them from being needlessly provoked. But it took a new colonial crisis resulting from the Townshend acts for Lord Barrington's plan to materialize.

In January 1768, under the pressure of the incipient revolutionary movement, the British ministry created a third office of secretary of state, exclusively devoted to the affairs of the American colonies. Its first incumbent, Lord Hillsborough, who favoured a policy of firmness and wanted to discipline the rebellious colonies, ordered Gage to keep garrisons only in the main forts – in particular at Detroit, Niagara, and Michilimackinac (Mackinaw City, Mich.) – so as to concentrate the troops at strategic points such as New York and Philadelphia. This decision dealt the final blow to imperial control of trade with the Indians, as the various colonial governors were advised in the spring of 1768. Experience, the minister explained, had shown that "the value of the object" did not justify such great expense and that "for want of a due Authority in the Superintendents" of Indian affairs, the policy was too difficult to apply.

The effect of this first revision of the Royal Proclamation was to leave control of the fur trade entirely to the colonial governments. The provinces most directly concerned were Quebec, New York, and Pennsylvania. The British and Canadian merchants in Quebec were greatly relieved by London's decision, which lifted the constraints that had been imposed on them. They had unceasingly demanded the freedom of trade that had been practised during the French period, and particularly the possibility of wintering among the Indians. Their confinement to designated posts, they argued, not only hamstrung their individual trading operations but substantially harmed the economic development of the province; indeed, the fact that they were prevented from supplying merchandise to the Indians at their hunting grounds encouraged strong and dangerous competition from the French and Spanish using the Mississippi River as a route. Not only the trade network but the whole system of relations with the Indians risked being irretrievably compromised, to the great detriment of both colony and mother country.

Governor Guy Carleton* himself endorsed and defended this position – and was thus able to establish better relations with the English speaking bourgeoisie in Quebec than his predecessor Murray had had. But in Carleton's view it was above all important to win the affection of the Indians "by wise regulations, honest dealing, and by kind treatment to attach them to us," in order to divert them from the enticements of the French and Spanish in New Orleans, "who must always be our Rivals in Trade." To Sir William Johnson, who continually suspected the Canadians of complicity in this competition, Carleton replied that there was no point in accusing a particular group when, in the face of the common enemy, "all the King's Subjects should be considered as Brothers, or one Family," and should not let themselves be dragged into rivalries between provinces.

This reply went to the heart of the problem, which was to recur with renewed force once the programme of imperial control for the west had been abandoned. How indeed could one reconcile the competing interests of colonial bourgeoisies vying to exploit the same resource – furs – in a territory that had been given over to the rapacity of virtually insatiable greed? To centre attention too much on the century-old competition between the Dutch traders in Albany and the Montreal merchants entailed the risk of forgetting the many other rivalries distributed geographically from the Atlantic coast to the frontiers of New York, Pennsylvania, and Virginia, where the drive for land was as unbridled as the race for pelts. The region south of the Ohio especially excited the voracity of speculators, and they succeeded in having the frontier established in 1763 pushed back to the boundaries of the present state of West Virginia. Johnson initiated this scramble for spoils in Indian territory by the treaty he negotiated with the Iroquois in the autumn of 1768 at Fort Stanwix (Rome, N.Y.); the superintendent of southern Indians, John Stuart, followed suit with the Cherokees. A fine free-for-all ensued between Pennsylvanians and Virginians who fought so fiercely over this land taken from the Indian reserves through bribery that Lord Dunmore, the governor of Virginia, created a *casus belli* in 1773 by taking over Fort Pitt, from which the British garrison had withdrawn the year before. The situation reached such a critical point that early in 1774 the authorities in London decided to save the region north of the Ohio by annexing it to the province of Quebec.

But what were the grounds for this annexation? Although the Indian reserves north of the Ohio had not yet fallen prey to white settlers, they had not escaped the rapacity of the traffickers in furs. Since the greediest of these traders had caused the programme of imperial control to fail, it seemed vain to think that they would quietly submit to any system of regulations coming from the colonial governments interested in exploiting this vast domain. Fully aware of the prospect of anarchy and worried by it, the Montreal fur-traders alerted Governor Carleton's administration, which entrusted the study of this important question to a committee of council. Its report of April 1769 dealt at length not only with the seriousness of the situation but also with the impossibility of remedying it unless the civil jurisdiction of the government of Quebec were extended to the region, as London five years later agreed to do. This was the only valid solution to the impasse for two reasons. On the one hand, the committee members admitted: "We are at a loss to conceive how any Province can form a system . . . to give it its binding effect upon persons casually residing for the purpose of trade in a country not liable to receive a Law from them, or enforce obedience to it." On the other hand, they pointed out: "We do not comprehend how one General solid well formed system for the Regulation of the Trade, which must arise from an union of the different Provinces so at variance with one another, in either manners, constitution, forms and modes of government and so unconnected upon any one general principle, can possibly be established."

The committee was right in thinking that without the establishment of a general system for the regulation of trade agreed upon by the three provinces concerned (Quebec, New York, and Pennsylvania), the fur trade would fall into "confusion . . . and Licentiousness and terminate perhaps in consequences fatal to the Dominion of Great Britain over those Countries." The few initiatives that were taken in 1770 and 1771 brought no positive results. The project for an intercolonial congress advanced by the province of New York failed lamentably for want of response from the colonies to which it was directed, and particularly from Quebec. According to the lieutenant governor, Hector Theophilus Cramahé, who was responsible for administration in Carleton's absence, "The interests of the two Provinces [New York and Quebec] in regard to the Indian Trade differ too widely to expect they will ever perfectly agree upon general Regulations for carrying it on." No agreement was in fact possible when the fur trade was the object of so much competition and rivalry. In reality, a great deal more protection for the economic interests of Quebec could be expected from London than from New York, and it was in just that direction that the political efforts of the province's administrators were focused.

The task of dealing the final blow to the Royal Proclamation fell to Lord Dartmouth, Hillsborough's successor as secretary of state for the American Colonies. Appointed in August 1772, after he had gained some experience in colonial affairs as president of the Board of Trade, he spent more than a year making inquiries before concluding that nothing further could be hoped for from Lord Halifax's programme for the west. This he admitted to Cramahé in December 1773, giving him to understand that the ministry was on the verge of a fundamental revision of policy concerning Quebec and that various considerations argued for an extension of the province's "narrow Limits." Given that this acknowledgement came only a few months before the drafting of the 1774 legislation, it is easy to suppose that despite his deliberate discretion Dartmouth was contemplating restoring the former boundaries of Canada so as to extend the civil jurisdiction of the government of Quebec to the Ohio, where the situation had become "more critical than ever," according to Johnson's latest reports. The state of affairs there was probably what Lord Egremont had feared ten years earlier when he recommended that civil jurisdiction over the whole continental mid west be included in the governor of Quebec's commission specifically to avoid allowing this vast region to become a refuge for outlaws. Lord Halifax had attached little importance to the danger, which nevertheless was real, worrying instead that the former French colony might acquire too much influence over the Indians and become too dominant in the fur trade, to the detriment of the other colonies. After ten years of uncontrolled and uncontrollable pillage in the Indian reserves, it was time to overcome old fears and face reality.

Cramahé endeavoured to explain this reality to Dartmouth, insisting on Quebec's unfavourable situation in relation to the Thirteen Colonies, which drew great profit from their trade with the West Indies. The fur trade constituted the only important economic activity of which Quebec could take advantage, since for six months of the year it was cut off from sea communication with the rest of the empire. Leaving it to share the trade in pelts with New York by maintaining the 1763 boundaries meant not only giving too many advantages to "New Yorkers [who] have already obtained a very considerable Share," but also running the risk that they might take it over completely, thanks to "their Superior Wealth." The geographical situation of Quebec dictated as a natural solution that it be united with the interior of the continent in order that the various groups of people living there be brought under the same government and be bound by the same laws.

The inquiry Lord Dartmouth conducted with the governors of New York and Pennsylvania revealed to him how little importance they attached to the fur trade in comparison with other economic activities. In contrast to Quebec, where until the end of the 18th century furs remained the principal source of wealth (varying from three-fifths to three-quarters of the total value of the province's exports), the contribution of pelts to the economy of New York declined steadily in the period 1760–75, from about fifteen per cent to less than three per cent of the total exports to England alone. Among the export commodities of the North American colonies (including Canada) in 1770, furs and deerskins ranked sixth in value; they represented only £150,000 out of a total of £3,500,000, less than five per cent. Clearly, in handing control of the western fur trade over to Quebec London was not running the risk of upsetting the balance of economic forces in North America.

Reconstituting New France's former trading empire naturally met the wishes of all those, both British and Canadian, who were linked with the commerce in pelts. In the autumn of 1773 François Baby*, a Quebec merchant, even went to London to plead this cause with Dartmouth on behalf of his compatriots, the leading bourgeois and seigneurs of Montreal, who had prepared an address and a memoir for the king. "We desire," they said, "that as under the French government our colony was permitted to extend over all the upper countries known under the names of Michilimackinac, Detroit, and other adjacent places, as far as the river Mississippi, so it may now be enlarged to the same extent." Such a request meant, geographically, the integration into Quebec not only of the Great Lakes basin but also of the Illinois country, which extended southwest to the confluence of the Ohio and the Mississippi and under the French régime had been part of Upper Louisiana. The main settlements in it were Vincennes (Ind.) on the Wabash River, and Kaskaskia (Ill.) and Cahokia (East St Louis, Ill.) on the east bank of the Mississippi; these French outposts had been the last to come under British control with the military occupation of Fort de Chartres (near Prairie du Rocher, Ill.) in October 1765, five years after the capitulation of Montreal.

The Illinois country caused the secretary of state much concern. It proved virtually uncontrollable from the point of view of trade because of its proximity to Western Louisiana (formed after 1763), where French and Spanish took maximum advantage of their favourable situation to draw furs off to New Orleans. Competition was impossible to sustain because of the difficulties and cost of supplying trade goods from the main distribution centre, Fort Pitt, which was situated more than 600 miles from Fort de Chartres. Maintaining these two posts entailed such expense (consuming more than half the budget of the department of northern Indians), that the commander-in-chief, Gage, to his great relief, finally received permission to evacuate them. In September 1772 Fort de Chartres was razed and Fort Pitt abandoned. But the minister's decision did not settle the fate of the hundreds of Canadian settlers already ensconced on the rich agricultural lands of the upper Mississippi. General Gage had threatened to oblige the inhabitants of Vincennes, isolated in the midst of the Indian reserves, to move, and the Canadians took advantage of this threat to demand a civil government, founded on British principles, for the Illinois country. Lord Dartmouth gave so much attention to this problem that London finally decided to put the whole region under Quebec's jurisdiction through the 1774 legislation.

Although the various considerations outlined above strongly suggested restoring Canada's former boundaries in order to solve the numerous problems created by the acquisition of the vast domain that had belonged to France, it appears equally indisputable that the British ministry took advantage of the critical state of relations between the mother country and her Thirteen Colonies (more obvious than ever since the Boston Tea Party) to make a final decision on the subject in the spring of 1774. The old historiographical debate about the influence of the American revolution on that decision will not be resumed here, but it is impossible to disregard the moment chosen to submit the Quebec Bill to the imperial parliament. It was certainly not a matter of coincidence. Between two extreme interpretations, one identifying the Quebec Act with the series of so-called coercive acts which the British government successively passed in less than three months for the specific purpose of subduing the rebellious province of Massachusetts, and the other entirely separating the Quebec Act from the others, there is room for a more discriminating assessment.

The fundamental fact to keep in mind when considering the impressive area which came under Quebec's jurisdiction is that the issue was to find an alternative solution to Lord Halifax's system. What was being given up, in reality, was not the idea of exercising control, and still less the will to exercise it, but rather the type of strategy that had been tried out since the Royal Proclamation. The objective remained, but the means of achieving it was changing. At the beginning of 1774 it appeared more necessary than ever to hold on to the possessions acquired in 1763. While on the Atlantic coast preparations were being made to punish the disobedient children, it had become urgent "to give force and effect to the Power and Authority of the Crown within the Interior Country," in the view of William Knox, under-secretary of state for the American Colonies, who was closely associated with the drafting of the legislation for Quebec. Since the Sons of Liberty were largely responsible for the failure of imperial control in the west, what alternative remained but to leave it to the new Canadian subjects – even at the risk of conjuring up the spectre of the former French empire? The good relations they were known to entertain with the Indians would contribute to improving rapport with the latter and reassure them about the fate of their reserves since, unlike the Americans, the Canadians did not covet their lands. It would also be the best means to establish a uniform system of regulations for the fur trade, the British no doubt reasoned.

When King George III gave royal approval to the Quebec Act on 22 June 1774, he declared that it was founded "on the clearest principles of justice and humanity" and would undoubtedly have "the best effects in quieting the minds and promoting the happiness of my Canadian subjects." Such solicitude for the conquered population was in sharp contrast with the scant attention paid it at the time of the Royal Proclamation. So marked a change of attitude deserves an explanation at this point.

The Royal Proclamation assimilated Quebec to the case of the two Floridas. In anticipation of swift Protestant settlement from the supposed population overflow of several American colonies, it was intended to provide the new provinces with the constitutional model in use in the royal colonies on the Atlantic coast, such as New York or Virginia. The edict proclaimed that the governors would have power and authority, "as soon as the state and circumstances . . . will admit, . . . with the Advice and Consent of the Members of our Council, [to] summon and call General Assemblies within the said Governments respectively." These representatives of the people would be required to legislate and pass decrees "for the Public Peace, Welfare and good Government . . . as near as may be agreeable to the Laws of England." While waiting for such representative assemblies to be convoked, the existing inhabitants and new settlers would have the benefit of the protection and enjoyment of the laws of the realm, through the setting up of law-courts "for hearing and determining all Causes, as well Criminal as Civil, according to Law and Equity, and as near as may be agreeable to the Laws of England."

Conceived solely in the expectation of a great influx of Protestant settlers whose assimilating wave would obliterate the historical past of New France, the Royal Proclamation took no account of the hopes and expectations that the surrender in 1760 and the military régime had raised and kept alive. In his haste to settle everything at once Lord Halifax had not followed through on the recommendations of Lord Shelburne (made in the Board of Trade's report of 8 June 1763), who had foreseen "particular Regulations and Provisions to be adapted to the different Circumstances and Situation" of each of the new acquisitions. Gradually becoming aware of the size of the problems and perceiving the damaging results of so improvised a policy, London began to contemplate a more realistic solution – as it had done with the programme for imperial control of the west.

But pending a reappraisal of the 1763 policy, Governor Murray had to suffer its initial troublesome consequences. He might have been able to avoid many tribulations had it not been for this unfortunate royal edict, which helped sow great confusion and dissatisfaction, but worse still stirred up much dissension among various groups. To attribute the main responsibility for these difficulties to the governor himself would be to ignore the constraints of imperial policy and the directives from London, and thus to give the false impression that he could have changed the course of Canadian history on his own authority. Murray was more the victim than the author of the unbearable situation in which he found himself and which forced him to return to London.

The unrealistic assumption that a wave of settlement from an overcrowded Atlantic coast would surge into the country stemmed largely from ignorance of North American geography and of the difficult living conditions in the St Lawrence valley. Americans were attracted by the luxuriance of the west, not the cold of Quebec. Two years after the Royal Proclamation, Murray's census showed that only a couple of hundred British settlers had answered the call of the north, choosing to live for the most part in the towns of Quebec and Montreal. Of the 136 Protestant subjects in the District of Montreal, about a hundred had come from England, Scotland, and Ireland; some fifteen were from Germany, only a dozen from New England and New York, the rest from elsewhere. Some sixty were declared as merchants, about thirty as innkeepers, and fifteen or so as clerks. Faced with the considerable disproportion between "old and new subjects," Murray's successor, Carleton, concluded in November 1767 that barring some unpredictable cataclysm the numerical superiority of the Canadians, far from diminishing, would only increase: "While this severe Climate, and the Poverty of the Country discourages all but the Natives, it's Healthfulness is such . . . [that] this Country must, to the end of Time, be peopled by the Canadian Race, who already have taken such firm Root . . . that any new Stock transplanted will be totally hid . . . except in the Towns of Quebec and Montreal."

The limited numbers of British settlers, as opposed to the astonishing population growth of the Canadians, made the assimilation hoped for by Lord Halifax highly problematical. With the institution of civil government in August 1764 it became necessary to find a *modus vivendi* with the conquered people, and this requirement forced Murray to deviate from his instructions. The English speaking bourgeoisie soon reacted, demanding such strict application of the Royal Proclamation that the representatives of the Roman Catholic majority appealed to the "goodness and justice" of the king against the intolerance shown by the Protestant minority: "What would become of the general prosperity of the Colony, if those who form the principal section thereof, become incapable members of it through the difference of Religion?"

The fundamental question was thus posed. It would force London to revise its policy completely, and to have recourse ultimately to the Quebec Act. At the end of 1764 Lord Chief Justice Mansfield, indignant at learning that Canadians were subjected to the same discrimination as English penal law applied to "papists" at home, pressed the government to investigate the fate reserved for the new Roman Catholic subjects. This question brought up the whole problem of the Canadians' legal status. The Board of Trade sought the opinion of Attorney General Sir Fletcher Norton and Solicitor General William de Grey; in their report of 10 June 1765 they expressed the opinion that the conquered population was not subject to the "Incapacities, Disabilities and Penalties" imposed upon Roman Catholics in England. In so doing they were tracing the way to the eventual abolition of the oath under the Test Act. For the moment the Board of Trade proposed judicial reforms to allow Canadian lawyers and attorneys access to the courts, at the level not only of the Court of Common Pleas but also of the Superior Court.

These judicial reforms drew comment from the new attorney general, Charles Yorke, who in collaboration with de Grey prepared a report that became famous because it brought into question the advisability and validity of applying English civil law in a "big and old colony" like Quebec, which had had its own code of customary law for a long time. The report recommended particularly that, within the framework of the seigneurial system, the inhabitants be allowed to retain their laws concerning the possession, transmission, and sale of landed property. British settlers would be required when purchasing land to conform to the usages and customs of the country, as was the practice in certain parts of the realm or in other royal colonies. As for English criminal law, it seemed to suit local needs and could be adapted to them as far as possible.

This report of April 1766 was a decisive step in the revision of the Royal Proclamation, even though the implementation of Yorke's recommendations had to be postponed until they could be embodied in a draft bill. To attribute solely to Lord Chancellor Northington's stubbornness the delay in regularizing the confused situation created by the royal edict of 1763 would be a simplistic explanation. On the one hand there were too many possible consequences to give effect to the report without an assessment of their full significance, and on the eve of its fall Lord Rockingham's ministry was certainly in no position to proceed with such an evaluation. On the other hand Yorke's recommendations could be only a partial remedy for the numerous thorny problems involved. A solution of far greater scope was imperative, and it was necessary not only to map out its bases with a better knowledge of the complex colonial realities but also to have the assistance of a stable administration enjoying the king's confidence, as would be the case with Lord North's cabinet, which in 1770 put an end to ten years of chronic ministerial instability.

Although it did not have time to develop a valid solution, Rockingham's ministry (July 1765–July 1766) paid sufficient attention to the Quebec question to become aware of past errors and to initiate a change in the orientation of the policy of October 1763. It was under this Whig ministry, incidentally, that Canon Jean-Olivier BRIAND received permission to be consecrated bishop. But no less important were the appointments in 1766 of Guy Carleton as lieutenant governor and William HEY and Francis Maseres* as chief justice and attorney general of the province respectively. Through this trio the government in London was able to obtain all the information needed for preparing an initial plan for a wide-ranging solution to the various problems created by the integration of Quebec into the British empire.

The idea of using parliamentary legislation to clarify the confused situation created by the Royal Proclamation began to be given careful attention in London during 1767. In June Lord Shelburne, then secretary of state for the Southern Department, advised Carleton that the Privy Council was giving serious consideration to providing the province with a civil constitution to be established by the authority of parliament. And as it seemed to him to be extremely important to form such "a System as shall at once be Equitable & convenient, both for His Majesty's Old and New Subjects," Shelburne asked the lieutenant governor to supply any information that might enlighten the ministry.

Carleton, who had been administering the colony for nearly a year when he received this request, had already made up his mind about the most suitable type of social and political organization. In the late autumn and early winter of 1767–68 he expounded his ideas to Shelburne in three long dispatches, tracing the main lines of a plan inspired more by a conceptual model borrowed from Europe's feudal period than founded upon the seigneurial system as it actually existed in New France. Two fundamental concerns – corresponding to his dual role as commander-in-chief and civil administrator – determined his choice of this plan: the "security" of the colony and its "dependence" with regard to the British crown. "Securing the Kings Dominions over this Province" was of the utmost importance and any schemes that did not take this basic factor into account would "be little better than meer Castles in the Air."

Maintenance of the seigneurial system and restoration of former usages and customs would not only guarantee the retention of the colony through the Canadians' "firm attachment" to the crown but would assure peace and tranquillity in the province through the "Subordination" of all subjects, "from the first to the lowest," and their "Obedience to the Supreme Seat of Government." The security of the colony would likewise be assured by the ease with which a fair-sized Canadian militia could be recruited through the services of the seigneurs, who enjoyed prestige and influence and would willingly be a party to enlisting their *censitaires*. Their participation required that they be reinstated as militia officers and given honours and privileges, including membership in the Legislative Council and some offices in the administration of the province.

As to the form of government, Carleton made no secret of his prejudices against representative institutions. In the troubled circumstances prevailing in the Thirteen Colonies it seemed dangerous to him to set up an elective house: "The British Form of Government, transplanted in this Continent, never will produce the same Fruits as at Home, chiefly, because it is impossible for the Dignity of the Throne, or Peerage to be represented in the American Forests. . . . [Here] All Men appear nearly upon a Level. . . ." The main deficiencies were the governor's want of authority to "retain all in proper Subordination" and the absence of a legislative body of the nobility to enhance the prestige of the council and counterbalance the spirit of democratic independence and the republican tendencies of the colonial assemblies. "The better Sort of Canadians," he claimed, "fear nothing more than popular Assemblies, which, they conceive, tend to render the People refractory and insolent." Again, Carleton did not take seriously the demands of the English speaking bourgeoisie, which he considered excessive. The Protestant minority constituted too tiny a group to be representative of the whole population.

Carleton's long dispatches reached London when the first secretary of state for the American Colonies, Lord Hillsborough, had just entered upon his duties. He was so strongly impressed that he led the governor to hope for immediate measures that would "not only releive His Majesty's new Subjects from the uncertain, and consequently unhappy Situation, they are now in; but give them entire Satisfaction for the future." And with unbelievable inconsequence the minister went on to condemn Murray's administration for having put the Royal Proclamation into effect "in the most absurd Manner, oppressive and cruel to the last Degree . . . and entirely contrary to the Royal Intention." Even though he had collaborated in drafting this unfortunate edict as president of the Board of Trade, he dared claim that it had never entered the authors' minds "to overturn the Laws and Customs of Canada, with regard to Property." At the very least this attack must be considered a mean and unfair way of defending himself, given Lord Halifax's designs for assimilation and the justifications that Murray was obliged to furnish for the few concessions he had made to the Canadians, contrary to his instructions as governor. It must be said in the minister's defence, however, that Carleton had deliberately painted a black picture of the Canadians' situation, with the obvious aim of more readily obtaining endorsement of his feudal plan.

Once he had been promoted governor early in the autumn of 1768, Carleton showed himself more confident and more determined than ever to have his political views accepted. In March 1769 he presented Hillsborough with a list of 12 Canadian seigneurs, selected from the largest landowners in the colony, who in his view deserved to be members of his council. Ten of them were former militia officers, and nine had been awarded the cross of Saint-Louis. Heading the list were six men who would later become members of the Legislative Council under the Quebec Act: Gaspard-Joseph CHAUSSEGROS de Léry, Pierre-Roch de Saint-Ours Deschaillons, Charles-François TARIEU de La Naudière, Luc de LA CORNE, Claude-Pierre PÉCAUDY de Contrecœur, and François-Marie PICOTÉ de Belestre. Only Jean-Baptiste-Marie Blaise Des Bergères de Rigauville, who would occupy the remaining seat to which the Canadians were entitled, was not on the list. Carleton's choice was well calculated. In case of danger, as, for instance, during the American invasion of Canada in 1775–76, these knights of Saint-Louis would indeed set the example and respond to the governor's orders despite their advanced age and the risk to their lives. Through family connections created generation after generation within the seigneurial class, the administration of the colony was expected to hold in subordination all those who cherished the hope of obtaining through family influence royal favours for offices or positions, however minor these might be. What better guarantee of permanent support for the crown's authority!

In London, Lord Hillsborough, who wanted to reach a satisfactory arrangement as quickly as possible, had the Board of Trade prepare a draft constitution that he passed on to Carleton, recommending to him the "greatest Confidence." Some historians have discerned in the draft bill of July 1769 "an instrument of political freedom" contrasting with the governor's feudal plan. Closer examination of the two reveals more similarity than difference. To end the prevailing confusion in Quebec it was proposed to institute a legislature enjoying "a complete legislative power" through the establishment of a legislative council and a house of assembly. The council would be composed of 15 members appointed by the crown, five of whom, in keeping with Carleton's wishes, would be chosen from among the Canadian seigneurs. The assembly would consist of 27 members: the 14 Protestants who were to be the sole representatives of the towns of Quebec, Montreal, and Trois-Rivières would constitute the majority; the remaining 13 seats would be filled by representatives of the seigneurial class, who alone would be entitled to stand in the rural counties. Thus the more than 80 per cent of Canadians who lived in the country would be restricted to choosing from a group of landowners who constituted less than one three-hundredths of the rural population. Like Carleton's feudal plan, Hillsborough's aimed precisely at restricting to the Canadian nobility participation in the power to legislate.

The many pressures exerted by the British merchants to obtain a legislative assembly failed to counterbalance the attraction for the authorities in London of Carleton's feudal plan. Even though, ten years after the conquest, this dynamic minority could claim to be the principal agent of economic development in the colony (by 1770 controlling three-quarters of the trade there, it has been said), the Canadians constituted more than 95 per cent of the population and included the great majority of landholders. This basic fact alone, quite apart from any crisis in the North American colonies, made the setting up of representative institutions virtually impossible, since the British government was obviously not ready to hand legislative authority over to the conquered people. The problem was how to limit the representation of those possessing land in Quebec without going against the creed dearest to the hearts of the governing élite in England, who came from the landed classes and believed all political power had to rest upon ownership of land. The British constitution was seen as a bulwark for landed property, which formed the foundation of the social, political, and economic organization of English society in the 18th century. This dilemma explains why the prime minister, Lord North, declared at the time of the parliamentary debates on the Quebec Bill that it would be "oppressive" to institute a legislative assembly while restricting the participation in it of those who owned nearly all the land in Canada and who should naturally constitute the great majority of its membership. It was preferable to put off its creation.

However commendable Hillsborough's intention to reconcile the interests of the Protestant minority with those of the Catholic majority, his constitutional draft contained too many major drawbacks for the government in London to risk trying it out. It had, moreover, been prepared in haste: important documents in the Quebec file were still missing, in particular the results of an inquiry into the administration of justice, which were not known in London until the autumn of 1769. This inquiry, initiated by the Privy Council, would not only supply full information on the organization of justice but would also specify its deficiencies and suggest reforms. It was conducted by Carleton in concert with his two chief assistants in the administration of the colony, Hey and Maseres.

In a report submitted in September 1769 and signed jointly with Hey the governor described in detail how the administration of justice functioned under the French régime, emphasizing the advantages of the social order established through the seigneurial system. He did not blunt his criticisms of the judicial organization that had followed the setting up of civil government. The ordinance of September 1764, he wrote, "had in it's Operation a Manifest tendency to disjoint and break in pieces, if not totally annihilate, the whole Frame and System of the ancient Laws." Not only had the Canadians suffered "plentifull streams of disquiet and vexation" because of it; worse still, "feeling themselves loosened from those restraints, which formerly held them, [they] are every day wearing off those Habits of modesty and obedience, by which they were formerly distinguished." Their principal complaints came from "the uncertainty of the Law," "the dilatoriness [and] the severity of the proceedings," and "the expence of the Suit."

The rest of the governor's report was virtually an indictment of the introduction of English civil law, which he had already denounced as "ill adapted to the Genius of the Canadians, to the Situation of the Province, and to the Interests of Great Britain." To try to impose "the whole body of the English Law" would be unworthy of a civilized nation and reminiscent of the period of the barbarian invasions rather than that of William the Conqueror. Not only would it be going against every principle "either of sound Policy or Humanity," but it might carry the risk of provoking an uprising and would surely alienate the population of the province forever. It was therefore important to restore to the whole province all French laws and customs in everything pertaining to civil law. On the other hand, he observed, since the Canadians seemed to be "very well satisfied" with English criminal law, he saw no objection to continuing with its introduction. He also favoured instituting the rights of habeas corpus and trial by jury, in both criminal cases and legal actions for damages. As for the methods of administering justice, he recommended the adoption of a procedure similar to that used in the French régime. Finally he recommended reestablishing the division into three judicial districts, reinstating militia captains in their former duties and making them agents of the government's orders at the parish level, and also limiting the powers given to justices of the peace; on this final point he adopted the views of Pierre DU CALVET, who in a memoir to Hillsborough had denounced the abuses to which justices of the peace were prone in the performance of their duties.

Hey did not endorse all of the governor's proposals and made his disagreement known in a separate document. He objected principally to the all but complete restoration of French laws and customs desired by Carleton. Seeing it as a backward step detrimental to Great Britain's real interests on the North American continent, he asserted that it "would operate not only as an exclusive Bar to any Union or Resemblance with the other Colonies, but tend to preserve in the Minds of the Canadians Principles inconsistent with the Idea of British Subjects in General." Consequently he favoured measures likely to facilitate the progressive assimilation of the Canadians and to give Quebec "the Form and Figure of a British Colony." Hey nonetheless recognized the necessity of making generous concessions to the Canadians, because of their numbers, wealth in land, and influence and for reasons of "Justice, Humanity, or Policy." While favouring the predominance of the English legal system, he recommended retaining for the new subjects the parts of customary law to which they were most attached, such as those involving "the Descent, Alienation, and Incumbrance of their real Property, their Mode of Devising Assigning and conveying their Personal, their Marriage Contracts and all those Dispositions which tend to regulate their domestic Aeconomy"; these should be "Administered with Integrity, Expedition and Moderation in Point of Expence."

Hey was to play a decisive role when the

Quebec Bill was being prepared. His presence in London from 1773 to the spring of 1775 enabled him to follow its development closely, and through his advice to counterbalance Governor Carleton's influence. His intervention was particularly obvious at the moment when the bill began to take shape after passing through the first stage in the drafting process. One has only to compare the second and third drafts to appreciate the effect not only of his judicious advice but especially of the ideas he defended. Specifically, the text of what archivists Adam Shortt* and Arthur George Doughty* classify as the second draft reads: "That His Majesty's Subjects . . . in the . . . Province of Quebec . . . [and those] of all the Territories [which may be annexed] . . . may . . . hold and enjoy their Property, Laws, Customs, and Usages, in as large, ample and beneficial manner, as if the [Royal] Proclamation, Commissions [and] Ordonnances . . . had not been made. . . ." Its author, Solicitor General Alexander Wedderburn, consulted Hey, who raised a fundamental objection: "What is to be the condition of the English Canadian? Is he or is he not included in the description of His Majesty's Subjects . . . ?" The chief justice went on to observe that it would be far better to define clearly what rights were to be restored to the Canadians and to specify their limits. Wedderburn considered these observations "so weighty" that after submitting them to the secretary of state, Lord Dartmouth, he prepared a third draft stating this time that Canadians might "hold, and enjoy their Property & Possessions together with all Customs & Usages relative thereto," and all their other civil rights. But in addition any person, whether Canadian or British, would be free to dispose of his property or possessions by testament or during his lifetime "in such manner as he or she shall think fit, any Law, Usage or Custom; heretofore; or now prevailing in the Province, to the contrary hereof in any wise notwithstanding." Furthermore, as the draft finally approved by parliament would stipulate, any land granted in free and common soccage according to the English system of holding would not be subject to the legal dispositions provided for seigneurial tenure. This provision kept the way open to developing British settlement in the St Lawrence valley. Hey would have the same concern when the time came for the secretary of state for the American Colonies to prepare the text of the royal instructions to the colony's governor for implementing the Quebec Act: the specific result would be article 12, which provided for the introduction of English laws through Legislative Council ordinances, "in all Cases of personal Actions grounded upon Debts, Promises, Contracts, and Agreements, whether of a Mercantile or other Nature; and also of Wrongs proper to be compensated in damages."

Hey was better at pleading the cause of the English speaking bourgeoisie than was Maseres, notwithstanding the goodwill and ready availability of the former attorney general. After giving up his office to return to London in the autumn of 1769, Maseres continued to take an interest in Canadian affairs. Unfortunately he had inherited from his Huguenot ancestors religious prejudices against Catholics so strong that he constantly carried them over to the political arena, to the point of becoming out of phase with the London authorities' changed viewpoint on the Quebec question. Thus when the 1774 bill was being prepared, he persisted in bringing forward the British merchants' demands for a house of assembly composed exclusively of Protestants or, failing that, a legislative council from which Canadians would be excluded. In reality he did more harm than good to the cause of those who had relied on him to convince the minister of the legitimacy of their requests. Their hopes dashed, they lost their illusions about the jurist advocate who had attracted them with his Whig training and his zeal for furthering "English liberties." A theoretician with a versatile mind, he enjoyed thinking up "plans and systems" (as François-Joseph Cugnet aptly remarked) more than formulating realistic solutions. Even before coming to Quebec in the autumn of 1766 he had advanced the hypothesis that the Canadians would be assimilated "in one or two generations" if proper measures were taken. When the moment came to produce a report on the laws and the administration of justice, he proposed four solutions, and rather than taking a stand he outlined the advantages and disadvantages of each, leaving the choice to "the wisdom of your Majesty's counsels." Upon going through this report a member of the commission of inquiry, Maurice Morgann*, found it so "improper" that he had been unable to extract "a single idea." Maseres had, however, a preferred solution that he revealed in his criticism of the Carleton-Hey report: a legal code for the province. The governor did not leave him time to commence it, considering it better for his majesty's service to find him a post other than that of attorney general of a former French and Catholic colony.

Determined to push his feudal plan, Carleton had informed Hillsborough in the spring of 1769 of his desire to go to London. The governor had to wait for more than a year before receiving permission to depart in August 1770, leaving the administration in the hands of the faithful Cramahé. Less than a year after his arrival in London Carleton had the satisfaction of seeing the grant of crown lands "in Fief and Seigneurie" authorized by the Privy Council, through the additional royal instructions of June 1771. For all practical purposes the authorities in London were endorsing the central element of the governor's plan. The decision to retain the seigneurial system, confirmed by parliament three years later, constituted a fundamental revision of the policy laid down in the Royal Proclamation and had important consequences for the Canadians' future. Although the Privy Council committee maintained that such a measure would contribute to the welfare and prosperity of the province, the real intention, according to the undersecretary of state William Knox, was to give the crown "great power over the Seigneurs." Henceforth they would recognize in King George III their "Sovereign Seigneur."

In January 1771 the impatient Hillsborough, still seeking at least a temporary solution, had informed Cramahé that the ministry was preparing to submit to parliament a bill aimed at granting the governor and council, for a limited period, legislative powers that would afford the possibility of dealing with the unsettled situation in the colony. Another hope dashed. Five months later at the end of the parliamentary session the secretary of state had to confess to Cramahé that "Every proposition that hath been yet suggested, has been attended with so many difficulties as to prevent any final decision." Despite everything he did not despair of reaching before long an "arrangement" that would give the Canadians satisfaction yet keep the colony under the crown's authority. At the end of the year he returned to the subject, to deplore the "great delay" in finding a solution but to justify it on grounds of the "Delicacy and Importance" of the decisions to be taken, bearing in mind the necessity of consulting almost every department of the government.

It was Lord Dartmouth, his successor, who with the assent of the king and the prime minister, North, would sponsor the solution so ardently desired by Hillsborough. In contrast to his nervous and impetuous predecessor, the calm and thoughtful Dartmouth was not one to make sudden decisions. Before taking action – which he put off until the autumn of 1773 – he waited for reports by the law officers of the crown, the attorney general Edward Thurlow and the solicitor general Alexander Wedderburn. These two "pillars of the law and state," as historian Edward Gibbon called them, had been asked to examine the Quebec file and make recommendations. Wedderburn produced his report in December 1772, and Thurlow submitted his in January 1773.

A great protector of law and order as well as the uncompromising defender of the crown's sovereignty over the colonies, Thurlow is said to have once declared on the subject of the Quebec Act that what was at issue was "the only sort of Constitution fit for a Colony." His report was inspired by his profound respect for traditional values and his faith in the heritage of the past. Like Carleton he unhesitatingly gave highest praise to the system of laws and government that had existed in New France, asserting that the experience of the French régime had demonstrated their merits. Consequently it was on this basis that a "flourishing colony" had to be built, as the principles of humanity and reasons of state in any case suggested. Great Britain's true interests dictated as few transformations as possible. No change in the form of government should be made until it was deemed "essentially necessary" to the maintenance of the conqueror's sovereign authority and the preservation of a spirit of obedience in his subjects. The best means to attain these two objectives was precisely to leave the conquered people "in the utmost degree of private tranquillity and personal security" where their former laws and customs were concerned.

Distrusting the dangerous innovations of novelty-seeking theoreticians, Thurlow seized the opportunity to denounce the report of Advocate General James Marriott, which was later published in London, in 1774, as *Plan for a code of laws for the province of Quebec*. Marriott had to resort to this means of gaining public attention because, not being a member of cabinet or parliament, he was unable to influence the crown as Thurlow and Wedderburn could. Thurlow attacked the "speculations" of Marriott, whose proposals were diametrically opposed to his own. Far from praising the French régime, Marriott saw in it a system of military government instituted primarily to make war against the British colonies in America. As this system had been harmful to the spirit of commercial enterprise, effort should be made not only to abolish it but also to erase even its memory from the minds of the Canadians by gradually assimilating them. The best way of making Canada useful to Great Britain would be to encourage British settlement, which would promote economic development.

On the eve of the Quebec Act, when the future of such settlement in Canada seemed sufficiently hypothetical to be the object of "speculations," the actuality of 80,000 new subjects was of more importance to the authorities in London. Thus Solicitor General Wedderburn reported that more attention should be paid to the Canadians than to the English speaking settlers, not only because of their substantial numerical superiority but also because depopulation for the benefit of her colonies was not in Britain's interest. In his view the strength and greatness of a nation lay in the size of its population, as public opinion held. This preoccupation on the part of the empire's rulers was even more legitimate in that the population of England was about three and a half times less than that of her rival, France, which at roughly 25 million was the most populous country in Europe. It is understandable, therefore, that in 1774 Lord Dartmouth found the departure of several hundred British settlers for Nova Scotia "a circumstance of very alarming consequence."

To give stronger legal warrant to the concessions to the Canadian people that the situation necessitated, Wedderburn based his reasoning upon the principle that a civilized conqueror could not conduct himself barbarously and deprive the conquered of "the enjoyment of their property, and of all the privileges not inconsistent with the security of the conquest." He also took up the argument advanced in the Yorke and de Grey report of April 1766: since Quebec had been settled for a long time, its inhabitants had to be left the customary law to which they were so strongly attached. As to the form of government, Wedderburn objected to the setting up of an assembly, which to him implied a double risk: on the one hand it was a "dangerous experiment" with new subjects in whom principles of submission and obedience had to be inculcated, and on the other it constituted "an inexhaustible source of dissension" between British and Canadian inhabitants. He considered such a creation "totally inexpedient." But in contrast to Carleton, whose views in the end prevailed, Wedderburn believed it necessary to effect a separation of powers between the governor and his future legislative council, to prevent the members of council from being completely subordinate to the king's representative. To keep the council from abusing its legislative powers, he envisaged the imposition of certain restrictions, particularly in all matters related to the subjects' lives and possessions as well as in taxation. In these instances no ordinance could have the force of law without prior authorization from London. Finally, he recommended that this government be set up for only a limited period.

His ideas were to take form in the first draft of a bill he was asked to prepare in anticipation of a temporary settlement. It dealt simply with the organization of a civil government, placed under the direction of a legislative council that was destined to play the central role. The arrangement was to last for 14 years, unless the decision was taken to create a legislative assembly at an earlier date. This initial bill, probably devised in the autumn of 1773, did not touch upon any of three other fundamental aspects which the final bill would include: religion, the administration of justice, and the extension of the frontiers. It must therefore be assumed that no decision had yet been taken on these essential points. In fact, nothing was really settled before the beginning of the spring of 1774.

On 1 Dec. 1773 Dartmouth informed Lieutenant Governor Cramahé that "the Affairs of Canada" were receiving the ministry's attention and that there was reason to hope they would be settled shortly. The tone of this letter indicated, however, that nothing had yet been decided and that important questions were still not settled. Dartmouth had obviously not foreseen the events that took place a fortnight later in Boston and that made the carrying out of London's good intentions impracticable. Everything was then left in abeyance, in order to deal with the case of the province of Massachusetts, which was considered much more urgent and serious.

The crisis brought about by the Boston Tea Party marked a turning point in relations between London and her colonies in America: it ended the imperial government's policy of hesitation and compromise. Thus, when the Bostonians' insult became known in London – their not only having destroyed a large shipment of tea but especially having opposed the sale of the product on the colonial market by a crown company – Lord North's ministry, with the king's backing, demonstrated its determination to act with speed and resolution. Late in January 1774 the cabinet resolved unanimously to take the necessary measures "to secure the Dependance of the Colonies on the Mother Country." There ensued, from March to June, the series of so-called coercive acts which parliament endorsed by a large majority. The Massachusetts Government Act (20 May) received royal assent a month before the Quebec Act (22 June). For the first time in the history of the American colonies the British parliament was intervening to alter a colony's charter. The changes made in it were partly intended to render the governor's executive action more effective by giving him extended discretionary powers. This increase in the governor's power was an important precedent that influenced the choice of civil government to be set up in Quebec and favoured the creation there, under Guy Carleton and Frederick HALDIMAND, of "the system of the generals."

After numerous changes and transformations the Quebec Bill was introduced in the House of Commons late in May. The determination shown by the ministry in having it voted by parliament before the end of the session leaves no doubt as to the manifest desire to end a long gestation period. The moment chosen, as already noted, was no simple coincidence. The pressure of events was real. "The inducement to adopt that plan of lenity and indulgence was greatly heightened by a consideration of the avowed purpose of the old colonies to oppose the execution of the laws of England, and to deny the authority of the supreme legislature," William Knox asserted a few months after the Quebec Act received royal assent. In this he was recognizing the influence of the revolutionary crisis, which in large measure determined the act's exceptional and temporary nature. It is important to remember that this famous charter of Canadian civil and religious rights had been conceived as "essentially a temporary bill," in the words of Solicitor General Wedderburn to the House of Commons.

There are highly divergent interpretations of the Quebec Act in historical works. Under the influence of contemporary denunciations certain historians have detected in it the instrument of dark, Machiavellian designs to raise an army of Catholic militia for a crusade against the Boston rebels; in contrast, others have never ceased praising it, viewing it, with William Kingsford*, as "a legal monument of British justice and generosity." There is as much danger of falsifying reality in blackening it as in glorifying it. It is not necessary to regard this legislation as the "great charter of French liberties" to recognize in it a degree of liberality in the context of its period. What must above all be kept in mind, in the light of the variety of arguments used by those who most favoured generous concessions to the conquered people, was their shared objective of maintaining the authority of the British crown over the colony. Any liberality towards the new subjects was intended to reinforce, not weaken, control by London. From this perspective it does not seem paradoxical that the minds reputedly the most conservative were the most liberal towards the Canadians.

The attached bibliography is deliberately selective, containing only the archival and secondary works, studies, and articles most frequently used in the preparation of Part I of this essay; Part II: "From the Quebec Act to the constitution of 1791" will appear in volume V and will list additional material.

Printed primary sources to be consulted include *Docs. relating to constitutional history, 1759–91* (Shortt and Doughty; 1918), its essential counterpart *Reports on the laws of Quebec, 1767–1770*, ed. W. P. M. Kennedy and Gustave Lanctot (Ottawa, 1931), and *NYCD* (O'Callaghan and Fernow), particularly volumes VII and VIII which contain a great deal of documentary material on the imperial policy from 1754 to 1774. Volumes IV and V of G. B., Privy Council, *Acts of the P.C., col.*, which cover the years 1745–83, and *The parliamentary history of England from the earliest period to the year 1803*, ed. William Cobbett and John Wright (36 v., London, 1806–20) also proved essential. In the latter series, volumes XV, XVI, and XVII contain the parliamentary debates on imperial legislation relating to the North American colonies from 1763 to 1774. For the Quebec Bill itself, a useful source is the documentary material, based on Sir Henry Cavendish's notes in the house, published by Wright: G. B., Parl., *Debates of the House of Commons in the year 1774, on the bill for making more effectual provision for the government of the province of Quebec . . .* (London, 1839; repr. [East Ardsley, Eng., and New York], 1966).

Because of the importance of King George III's political role during the critical revolutionary period, the reader should consult his correspondence with his ministers in *The correspondence of King George the Third from 1760 to December 1783 . . .*, ed. J. [W.] Fortescue (6v., London, 1928). For the problems resulting from putting the Royal Proclamation into effect, see *Correspondence of General Thomas Gage* (Carter), and for the Department of Northern Indians, see *Johnson papers* (Sullivan *et al.*).

The ordinances of the civil government of Quebec from 1764 to 1791 were published in PAC *Report*, 1913, app.E, and 1917, app.C. For the ordinances and proclamations of the military régime, see PAC *Report*, 1918, app.B.

Of the numerous contemporary works, Thomas Pownall, *The administration of the colonies* (London, 1764) and Sir Francis Bernard, *Select letters on the trade and the government of America; and the principles of law and polity applied to the American colonies* (London, 1774), proved useful for the views of colonial officials. The pamphlets of William Knox, the under-secretary of state for the American Colonies, should also be mentioned: *The controversy between Great Britain and her colonies reviewed &c* (London, 1769), *The justice and policy of the late act of parliament for making more effectual provision for the government of the province of Quebec . . .* (London, 1774), and *Thoughts on the act for making more effectual provision for the government of the province of Quebec* (London, 1774). Two works by Francis Maseres, the attorney general, are also invaluable, both for personal observations and as an excellent documentary source: *An account of the proceedings of the British, and other Protestant inhabitants, of the province of Quebeck, in North-America, in order to obtain an house of assembly in that province* (London, 1775); *Additional papers concerning the province of Quebeck: being an appendix to the book entitled, "An account of the proceedings of the British and other Protestant inhabitants of the province of Quebeck in North America, [in] order to obtain a house of assembly in that province*" (London, 1776).

Of the general histories of Canada covering the period, the following are essential because of their divergent treatments of political, social, and economic aspects: Brunet, *Les Canadiens après la Conquête*; Burt, *Old prov. of Que.*; D. G. Creighton, *The commercial empire of the St. Lawrence, 1760–1850* (Toronto, 1937); Neatby, *Quebec*; and Ouellet, *Hist. économique*.

For the military régime and the establishment of civil government, Lionel Groulx, *Lendemains de Conquête* (Québec, [1920]) remains valuable. M. Trudel's thoroughly documented study, *Le Régime militaire*, sheds light on the organization and operation of the military régime in the Government of Trois-Rivières; unfortunately there is no comparable source for Montreal and Quebec. S. M. Scott, "Civil and military authority in Canada, 1764–1766," *CHR*, IX (1928), 117–36, is essential for understanding the sensitive problem of jurisdictional conflicts between the civil and the military authorities during Murray's term of office.

V. T. Harlow's impressive work, *The founding of the second British empire, 1763–1793* (2v., London and New York, 1964) is of fundamental importance for placing in global perspective the evolution and transformation of the British empire during the second half of the 18th century. However, as Ronald Hyam has noted in his excellent critical review in *Hist. Journal* (London), X (1967), 113–24, one cannot subscribe to all of the author's views.

C. W. Alvord, *The Mississippi valley in British politics: a study of the trade, land speculation, and experiments in imperialism culminating in the American revolution* (2v., Cleveland, Ohio, 1917; repr. New York, 1959) cleared the way for fruitful exploration of the diverse aspects of the problem of the west, from the Royal Proclamation to the Quebec Act. J. M. Sosin developed a new synthesis of this enormous subject in *Whitehall and the wilderness: the middle west in British colonial policy, 1760–1775* (Lincoln, Nebr., 1961). The reader should also consult Harlow's analysis (I, chap. V) since in the light of his insights one can more sensitively interpret R. A. Humphrey's article "Lord Shelburne and the Proclamation of 1763," *English Hist. Rev.* (London and New York), XLIX (1934), 241–64.

Peckham's *Pontiac* is the principal study on Pontiac's uprising and the Indian question, but for a thorough understanding of the deteriorating relations between the whites and the Indians under the impact of the western expansion of American settlement W. E. Washburn, *The Indian in America* (New York, 1975) and W. R. Jacobs, *Dispossessing the American Indian* (n.p., [1971]) should be consulted. The circumstances surrounding the first partition of Indian reserves for the benefit of Americans are carefully analysed by Peter Marshall in "Sir William Johnson and the treaty of Fort Stanwix, 1768," *Journal of American Studies*, I (1967), 149–79.

For the fur trade and commercial activity in the west, Innis' classic, *Fur trade in Canada*, is still valuable. P. C. Phillips, *The fur trade* (2v., Norman, Okla., 1961) gives a general North American survey (I, chaps. 26–30). M. G. Lawson, *Fur: a study in English mercantilism, 1700–1775* (Toronto, 1943) clarifies the role and importance of the fur trade in the colonial economy of North America. W. S. Dunn, "Western commerce, 1760–1774" (unpublished PHD thesis, University of Wisconsin, Madison, 1971) sheds light on the interests and rivalries at stake as a result of the Royal Proclamation.

For the British régime in the northwest, see N. V. Russell, *The British régime in Michigan and the old northwest, 1760–1796* (Northfield, Minn., 1939), a study which is still useful although somewhat outdated. J. M. Sosin, "The French settlements in British policy for the North American interior, 1760–1774," *CHR*, XXXIX (1958), 185–208, deals with the French posts at Vincennes and in Upper Louisiana.

I. R. Christie, *Crisis of empire: Great Britain and the American colonies, 1754–1783* (London, 1966), gives a brief introduction to imperial policy and the American revolution. By contrast, Merrill Jensen, *The founding of a nation; a history of the American revolution, 1763–1776* (New York and Toronto, 1968) presents a solid synthesis. For a deeper understanding of the policies of the imperial government and the thinking of British leaders with regard to the empire, *see*: Richard Kœbner, *Empire* (Cambridge, Eng., 1961); Bernhard Knollenberg, *Origin of the American revolution, 1759–1766* (New York, 1960); Bernard Donoughue, *British politics and the American revolution: the path to war, 1773–75* (London and New York, 1964); and R. W. Van Alstyne, *Empire and independence, the international history of the American revolution* (New York, 1965).

E. N. Williams, *The eighteenth-century constitution, 1688–1815; documents and commentary* (Cambridge, 1960) contains well-chosen texts illustrating the workings of the various constitutional elements – king, government, and parliament – in Great Britain. For a more thorough analysis, *see* L. [B.] Namier, *The structure of politics at the accession of George III* (2nd ed., London, 1957) and Richard Pares, *King George III and the politicians* (Oxford, 1953).

G. E. Mingay, *English landed society in the eighteenth century* (London and Toronto, 1963) is essential for understanding the social and economic bases of the political organization and hierarchical nature of British society. Dorothy Marshall, *English people in the eighteenth century* (London, 1956) is a good general survey of diverse social and economic aspects of 18th-century England. An excellent introduction to this subject is André Parreaux, *La société anglaise de 1760 à 1810* (Paris, 1966).

Since colonial policy was under the secretaries of state for the Southern Department and for the American Colonies, it is important to understand organization and operation of their offices. *See* M. A. Thomson, *The secretaries of state, 1681–1782* (Oxford, 1932); M. M. Spector, *The American department of the British government, 1768–1782* (New York, 1940); and F. B. Wickwire, *British subministers and colonial America, 1763–1783* (Princeton, N.J., 1966).

Glossary of Native Peoples

THIS GLOSSARY INCLUDES the names of native groups that appear most frequently in the biographies of volume IV. It is designed to assist the reader in identifying and locating geographically those groups of native people caught up in the development of the European colonies or encountered by traders, explorers, and missionaries. In their contacts with the indigenous population, Europeans often designated as tribes groups that would not be considered such by a modern ethnologist. These names appear in the documents of the 18th century, and they have therefore been used in volume IV. Although it is the usual practice among ethnologists to refer to a tribe by the collective singular form of its name, for example Cree, we have used the ordinary plural, Crees, as the 18th century generally did.

Full names of authors of the articles in this glossary will be found in the list of contributors, pp. 835–43. Unsigned entries have been compiled by the staff of the *Dictionary*. The following published sources have been useful in the preparation of the glossary; shortened titles are listed in full in the general bibliography.

GENERAL WORKS

T. S. Abler and S. M. Weaver, *A Canadian Indian bibliography, 1960–1970* (Toronto, 1974). *Canada, Indian treaties and surrenders . . .* [1680–1906] (3v., Ottawa, 1891–1912; repr. Toronto, 1971). E. S. Curtis, *The North American Indian . . .* (20v. and 4v. illus., Seattle, Wash., and Cambridge, Mass., 1907–30; repr. New York and London, 1970). *Handbook of American Indians* (Hodge). Diamond Jenness, *The Indians of Canada* (Ottawa, 1960). *JR* (Thwaites). G. P. Murdock and T. J. O'Leary, *Ethnographic bibliography of North America* (5v., New Haven, Conn., 1975). *North American Indians in historical perspective*, ed. E. B. Leacock and N. O. Lurie (New York, 1971).

EAST COAST

T.-M. Charland, *Hist. des Abénakis*. D. E. Dumond, "On Eskaleutian linguistics, archaeology, and prehistory," *American Anthropologist* (Menasha, Wis.), new ser., 67 (1965), 1231–57. C. [-I.] Gill, *Notes sur de vieux manuscrits abénakis* (Montréal, 1886). M. R. P. Herisson, *An evaluative ethno-historical bibliography of the Malecite Indians* (Ottawa, 1974). E. A. Hutton [Chard], "Indian affairs in Nova Scotia, 1760–1834," N.S. Hist. Soc., *Coll.*, 34 (1963), 33–54; "The Micmac Indians of Nova Scotia to 1834" (unpublished MA thesis, Dalhousie University, Halifax, 1961). E. [A.] [Hutton] Chard, "Truckhouse trading: a forgotten aspect of Anglo-Micmac affairs in Nova Scotia," *Journal of Education* (Halifax), 5th ser., XV (1965–66), no. 3, 20–24. J.[-P.]-A. Maurault, *Histoire des Abénakis, depuis 1605 jusqu'à nos jours* ([Sorel, Qué.], 1866). N.S., House of Assembly, *Journal*, 1848, app.24. "Selections from the papers and correspondence of James White, esquire, A.D. 1762–1783," ed. W. O. Raymond, N.B. Hist. Soc., *Coll.*, I (1894–97), no.3, 306–40. *Source materials relating to the New Brunswick Indian*, ed. W. D. Hamilton and W. A. Spray (Fredericton, [1977]). J. G. Taylor, *Labrador Eskimo settlements of the early contact period* (Ottawa, 1974). W. E. Taylor, "An archaeological perspective on Eskimo economy," *Antiquity* (Cambridge, Eng.), XL (1966), 114–20. L. F. S. Upton, "Indian affairs in colonial New Brunswick," *Acadiensis*, III, no.2, 3–26.

GREAT LAKES AND OHIO VALLEY

Archives of Maryland, ed. W. H. Browne *et al.* (70v. to date, Baltimore, Md., 1883–19). [Henry Bouquet], *The papers of Col. Henry Bouquet*, ed. S. K. Stevens *et al.* (19v., Harrisburg, Pa., 1940–43). "Cadillac papers," *Michigan Pioneer Coll.*, XXXIII (1903), XXXIV (1904). W. L. Chafe, *Seneca morphology and dictionary* (Washington, 1967). William Chazanof, *Joseph Ellicott and the Holland Land Company . . .* (Syracuse, N.Y., 1970). B. A. Chernow, "Robert Morris: Genessee land speculator," *New York History* (Cooperstown, N.Y.), LXXV (1977), 195–220. *Colonial records of Pa.* (Hazard), III–IX. *Documentary history of Dunmore's War*, ed. R. G. Thwaites and L. P. Kellogg (Madison, Wis., 1905). *Documentary history of the Fox project, 1948–1959*, ed. F. O. Gearing *et al.* (Chicago, 1960). R. C. Downes, *Council fires on the upper Ohio: a narrative of Indian affairs in the upper Ohio valley until 1795* (Pittsburgh, Pa., 1940). R. D. Edmunds, "Pickawillany: French military power versus British economics," *Western Pennsylvania Hist. Magazine* (Pittsburgh, Pa.), 58 (1975), 169–84. "The French regime in Wisconsin – II," ed. R. G. Thwaites, Wis., State Hist. Soc., *Coll.*, XVII (1906). *Frontier advance on the upper Ohio, 1778–1779*, ed. L. P. Kellogg (Madison, Wis., 1916). *Frontier defense on the upper Ohio, 1777–1778 . . .*, ed. R. G. Thwaites and L. P. Kellogg (Madison, Wis., 1912; repr. Millwood, N.Y., 1973). *Frontier retreat on the upper Ohio, 1779–1781*, ed. L. P. Kellogg (Madison, Wis., 1917). [Christopher Gist], *Christopher Gist's journals . . .*, ed. W. M. Darlington (Pittsburgh, Pa., 1893). Barbara Graymont, *Iroquois*; "New York state Indian policy after the revolution," *New York History* (Cooperstown, N.Y.), LXXIV (1976), 438–74. M. W. Hamilton, *Sir William Johnson, colonial American, 1715–1763* (Port Washington, N.Y., and London,

1976). C. A. Hanna, *The wilderness trail; or, the ventures and adventures of the Pennsylvania traders on the Allegheny path . . .* (2v., New York and London, 1911; repr. Ann Arbor, Mich., 1967). Henry, *Travels and adventures* (Bain). *The Iroquois Book of Rites*, ed. H. [E.] Hale, intro. W. N. Fenton (Toronto, 1963). *Johnson papers* (Sullivan *et al.*). W. V. Kinietz, *The Indians of the western Great Lakes, 1615–1760* (Ann Arbor, Mich., 1965). *NYCD* (O'Callaghan and Fernow). *The official records of Robert Dinwiddie, lieutenant-governor of the colony of Virginia, 1751–1758 . . .*, ed. R. A. Brock (2v., Richmond, Va., 1883–84). *Papiers Contrecœur* (Grenier). Peckham, *Pontiac*. *Pa. archives* (Hazard *et al.*), 1st ser., I–IV. *The revolution on the upper Ohio, 1775–1777 . . .*, ed. R. G. Thwaites and L. P. Kellogg (Madison, Wis., 1908; repr. Port Washington, N.Y., and London, 1970). A. A. Shimony, *Conservatism among the Iroquois at the Six Nations Reserve* (New Haven, Conn., 1961). *The valley of the Six Nations . . .*, ed. and intro. C. M. Johnston (Toronto, 1964). *The Vaudreuil papers: a calendar and index of the personal and private records of Pierre de Rigaud de Vaudreuil, royal governor of the French province of Louisiana, 1743–1753*, comp. Bill Barron (New Orleans, 1975). Va., *Calendar of Virginia state papers . . .*, ed. W. P. Palmer *et al.* (11v., Richmond, Va., 1875–93), I; *Executive journals of the Council of colonial Virginia*, ed. H. R. McIlwaine *et al.* (6v., Richmond, 1925–66). N. B. Wainwright, *George Croghan, wilderness diplomat* (Chapel Hill, N.C., 1959). A. F. C. Wallace, *The death and rebirth of the Seneca* (New York, 1970). P. A. W. Wallace, *The white roots of peace* (Philadelphia, Pa., 1946). C. A. Weslager, *The Delaware Indians, a history* (New Brunswick, N.J., 1972). S. F. Wise, "The American revolution and Indian history," *Character and circumstance: essays in honour of Donald Grant Creighton*, ed. J. S. Moir (Toronto, 1970), 182–200.

WEST AND NORTH

[William Beresford], *A voyage round the world: but more particularly to the north-west coast of America . . .*, ed. and intro. George Dixon (London, 1789; repr. Amsterdam and New York, 1968). C. A. Bishop, *The Northern Ojibwa and the fur trade . . .* (Toronto and Montreal, 1974). Cook, *Flood tide of empire*. G. M. Dawson, *Report on the Queen Charlotte Islands, 1878* (Montreal, 1880). Philip Drucker, *The northern and central Nootkan tribes* (Washington, 1951). Wilson Duff and Michael Kew, "Anthony Island, a home of the Haidas," B.C., Provincial Museum, *Report* (Victoria), 1957, 37–64. R. [A.] Fisher, *Contact and conflict: Indian-European relations in British Columbia, 1774–1890* (Vancouver, 1977). HBRS, XXVII (Williams). [J. R. Jewitt], *Narrative of the adventures and sufferings of John R. Jewitt . . .* (New York, [1815]; 2nd ed., Middletown, Conn., 1815). *Journals of Captain James Cook* (Beaglehole). J. M. Moziño Suárez de Figueroa, *Noticias de Nutka: an account of Nootka Sound in 1792*, trans. and ed. I. H. Wilson (Seattle, Wash., 1970). G. P. Murdock, "Kinship and social behavior among the Haida," *American Anthropologist* (Menasha, Wis.), new ser., 36 (1934), 355–85. A. J. Ray, *Indians in the fur trade: their role as trappers, hunters, and middlemen in the lands southwest of Hudson Bay, 1660–1870* (Toronto, 1974). Edward Sapir, "The life of a Nootka Indian," *Queen's Quarterly* (Kingston, Ont.), XXVIII (1920–21), 232–43, 351–67. Morris Swadesh, "Motivations in Nootka warfare," *Southwestern Journal of Anthropology* (Albuquerque, N. Mex.), 4 (1948), 76–93. J. R. Swanton, *Contributions to the ethnology of the Haida* (New York, 1905). Joyce Wike, "Social stratification among the Nootka," *Ethnohistory* (Bloomington, Ind.), 5 (1958), 219–41.

Abenakis of Saint-François. The inhabitants of a mission village on the Saint-François River near its confluence with the St Lawrence, probably settled between 1660 and 1670. The first occupants were apparently Sokokis. There appear to have been Abenakis and "Loups" in the village before 1700. In 1705 or 1706, the mission of Saint-François-de-Sales moved from the lower falls of the Chaudière River to the Saint-François, bringing some Abenakis from Maine and many additional Sokokis and "Loups," so that in 1711 the village was estimated to contain 260 warriors, perhaps 1,300 persons. This population was reduced by epidemics and the colonial wars in which the inhabitants of Saint-François were always allies of the French. In 1759 the village was burned and many of its people killed in an attack by a force of rangers under Robert ROGERS. It was rebuilt, however, and between the outbreak of the American revolution and 1800 received numerous new inhabitants from the upper Connecticut River and from Missisquoi, at the mouth of the Missisquoi River on Lake Champlain. Until at least 1880, the band was known officially as the Abenakis and Sokokis of Saint-François. G.M.D.

Agniers. *See* MOHAWKS

Chaouanons. *See* SHAWNEES

Chickasaws; in French Chicachas. A leading Muskogean tribe, in the 18th century the Chickasaws lived in the area which is now Pontotoc and Union counties in northern Mississippi. They claimed a much larger area, including the present state of Tennessee and northern Alabama. Warlike and independent, they dominated the region, and Chickasaw was the lingua franca of all the tribes on the lower Mississippi. The Chickasaws, always enemies of the French, especially resented French trade relations with their enemies the Choctaws. In the early 18th century the British, friendly with the Chickasaws, were attempting to enter the Mississippi valley, and this fact, together with Chickasaw raids on Mississippi convoys, made the French determined to subdue the tribe. In 1736 a force under Pierre d'Artaguiette d'Itouralde attacked them in their home territory but was severely defeated [*see* François-Marie Bissot* de Vinsenne]. The Chickasaws resisted successfully again when an expedition under Jean-Baptiste Le Moyne* de Bienville invaded their lands in 1739. Unable to defeat the Chickasaws by military means and incapable of providing the trade goods that would have enabled them to supplant the British among the tribe, the French attempted to contain British expansion by keeping the Chickasaws and Choctaws at war with each other.

Chippewas. *See* OJIBWAS

Crees; in French Cris, a shortened form of Kristinaux. (In English Cree is sometimes used to include the Maskegons (Swampy Crees), Naskapis, Montagnais-Naskapis, and Montagnais, but the French Cris is a more restrictive term.) An Algonkian speaking people closely related to the Montagnais-Naskapis, the Crees comprised a great number of related, but autonomous, villages and bands. At the height of their expansion in the late 18th century they occupied a region comprising most of the southern half of the Hudson Bay coast, extending westward to include large portions of what is now northern Ontario, Manitoba, Saskatchewan, and eastern Alberta. This expansion resulted in diversification into four main divisions: Swampy, Rocky, Woods, and Plains. From the mid 17th century Crees were active in the French and British fur trade as trappers and as middlemen to far inland tribes [*see* WAPINESIW; WINNINNEWAYCAPPO]. They traded at the HBC posts on James Bay, and the term Home Indians used by the HBC traders usually referred to them. Close allies of the Siouan Assiniboins, they were at various periods bitter foes of the Dakota Sioux, Blackfeet, and Chipewyans [*see* MATONABBEE]. H.H.

Delawares. English name for Algonkian speaking Indians of the middle and lower Delaware River and east to the seacoast; often applied also to the related Munsees on the upper Delaware. The French name Loups generally also included the Mahicans and smaller coastal groups. The Delawares styled themselves Lenape, men. Abandoning their homeland because of involvement in the fur trade, depletion of game, and pressure of white colonization, they resettled as Iroquois dependants on the Susquehanna and Allegheny rivers. In 1680 René-Robert Cavelier* de La Salle met a hunting party of 40 Loups near the southern end of Lake Michigan, and 12 years later a similar group escorted refugee Shawnees from the Ohio to the upper Delaware. Delaware settlement on the Ohio began about 1725. Despite grievances, Delaware relations with the British were close and generally friendly, though disrupted by French occupation of the upper Ohio, 1753–59, and strained by Pontiac*'s War, 1763–64 [*see* ANANDAMOAKIN]. Their westward movement accelerated by these hostilities, they established settlements on the Muskingum River by agreement with the Hurons; and a nativist revival in the 1750s gave impetus to a renewal of the "Delaware nation" under Netwatwees, "King Newcomer" (d. 1776). Neutrality in the American revolution was only partially successful; the Delawares suffered at the hands of both British and Americans [*see* GLIKHIKAN]. The steady influx of white settlers after the war completed the process of disruption and removal. Part of the Delawares (mostly Munsees) took refuge in southern Ontario and the rest moved beyond the Mississippi. W.A.H.

Eskimos. *See* INUIT

Foxes; in French Renards (also known as Mesquakies from their own designation for themselves, meaning red-earth people, or as Outagamis from their name among their Algonkian neighbours, meaning people of the other shore). Originally located in the lower peninsula of Michigan, they migrated, probably under pressure from the Iroquois, to the vicinity of Baie des Puants (Green Bay, Lake Michigan) where they were first met by French traders and missionaries in the 1660s. The Foxes spoke a central Algonkian language closely related to Sauk, Kickapoo, and Mascouten, the languages of the peoples with whom they were often allied and who had migrated with them. All these tribes lived in villages where they raised maize, beans, and squash; they held annual communal hunts for deer and bison. Drawn into the fur trade at an early date, they had a shortage of beaver in their own country but, occupying strategic positions on the important Fox-Wisconsin River trade route to the Mississippi, they demanded a share in the trade as middlemen or in the form of tolls. At the beginning of the 18th century the Foxes were on friendly terms with New France and her Indian allies [*see* Noro*], but after an Ojibwa massacre of a Fox village near Detroit in 1712 [*see* Pemoussa*] the Foxes became a major source of disruption. The nature of their raids was aggravated, in French eyes, by their attempts to ally themselves with the British. Temporarily subdued in 1716 [*see* Ouachala*], the Foxes finally suffered defeat in 1730 and 1731–32, when the French took prisoner their greatest war chief, Kiala*. In 1733 many joined the Sauks and with them began a westward migration. It appears that by the 1760s the Foxes had recovered from their losses in the French attacks. During the American revolution the Sauks and Foxes adopted a policy of playing one European group off against the other. Even after the close of the revolution, competition among Europeans for control of the fur trade south of the Upper Lakes gave the two tribes a measure of economic power. With the advance of settlement following the War of 1812, however, they were driven across the Mississippi into Iowa, where some of them live today. H.H.

Haidas; in French Haïdas. With the exception of one group which in the 1790s established a permanent winter village at Kaigani (on the southern tip of Prince of Wales Island, Alaska) the Haida speakers inhabited the Queen Charlotte Islands (B.C.). Villages were usually located on the sheltered harbours and bays, particularly of the leeward eastern coast. The people lived close to the sea and were well known for the skill with which they built and operated their canoes. Their large, plank houses were fronted by the great totem poles which displayed their family crests as well as their wood-carving and artistic skills. Today, Haida art is frequently used as the standard by which all Indian art of the northwest coast is judged. In the Haida social system, rank was clearly defined and of great importance [*see* KOYAH]. Villages were divided into two exogamous clans, eagle and raven, membership in which, as well as inheritance generally, was determined matrilineally. The potlatch (a ceremony in which rights and prestige were established by the giving away of property) was, with its attendant ritual, an important aspect of the Haida way of life. Like the Nootkas, the Haidas proved to be capable traders when Europeans came to their villages in search of sea otter pelts in the late 1780s, and in the following decade they were at the forefront of the maritime fur trade. Their wealth and power increased and, unlike the Nootkas, they developed new skills, such as argillite carving, and marketed new products, such as potatoes, when the maritime fur trade declined in the early 19th century. R.A.F.

Hurons (from the Old French hure, a bristly head). They were divided into four separate tribes: the Bear (Attignawantan), and the so-called Cord (Attingueenongnahac), Rock (Ahrendarrhonon), and Deer (Tahontaenrat). When Iroquois attacks led to the dispersal of the Huron confederacy early in 1649, many Hurons took refuge among the neighbouring Tionontatis (Petuns), who were closely allied to them in language and culture. After December 1649, however, the Tionontatis and their Huron guests were driven out of southern Ontario by the Iroquois, who did not wish to see the Huron trade fall into the hands of yet another tribe. About 800 Tionontatis and Hurons made an orderly retreat northward towards Lake Michigan. Although mostly Tionontatis, these people came to be known as the Wyandots, a corruption of Wendat, the old name the Hurons had applied to themselves. Between 1653 and 1670, the Wyandots wandered in the region of the upper Great Lakes, participating in the fur trade and living with and being influenced by the Ottawas and Potawatomis. In 1670 the Hurons founded a settlement at Mackinac. In 1701 the chief Kondiaronk* attended the peace conference convened at Montreal by Louis-Hector de Callière*, and the Hurons, among them Michipichy*, were persuaded to move to the vicinity of Fort Pontchartrain, which the French had just constructed at Detroit. About 1738 there was a division among the Wyandots. Some remained in the Detroit area, their descendants residing near present-day Sandwich, Ont.; the others, under war chief Orontony*, moved to Sandoské (Sandusky, Ohio). After many wanderings the latter group finally settled on the Wyandotte Reservation in Oklahoma. The Wyandot language died out in the first half of this century.

Another portion of the Huron people fled to Quebec after the overthrow of the confederacy in 1649 and finally settled at Lorette, where they still reside. During the Anglo-French wars of the 18th century their warriors frequently assisted the French [*see* Vincent*]. Although they have retained their sense of ethnic identity, the Hurons of Lorette have intermarried extensively with French Canadians and ceased to speak their own language early in the 19th century. B.G.T.

Inuit (singular **Inuk**); in English commonly called Eskimos and in French, Esquimaux. The Inuit are widespread circumpolar people inhabiting parts of the Canadian Arctic, northern Alaska, and Greenland. Canadian Inuit have occupied most of the northern coastline and adjacent tundra from the Mackenzie delta to the Strait of Belle Isle, as well as most of the large Arctic islands as far north as Parry Channel. All speak variants of a single dialect group known as Inupik, and for descriptive purposes they are customarily divided into the following regional subdivisions: Mackenzie, Copper, Netsilik, Iglulik, Caribou, Baffinland, and Labrador Inuit. Of these, all but the Caribou Inuit have had a relatively balanced dual economy, based on both land and sea resources. It was once thought that the latter, who have developed the land side of their economy to an unusual degree, were the survivors of ancient inland "proto-Eskimo." However, recent historical research suggests that their marked inland adaptation has developed in response to contact with Europeans during the last two centuries. The Inuit of the eastern Arctic met with European explorers as early as Martin Frobisher*'s 1576 voyage to Baffin Island, but for the next few centuries encounters with European explorers, fishermen, whalers, and traders remained sporadic and often hostile. The first continuous contact occurred on the coast of Labrador, where Moravian missionaries such as Jens HAVEN and Christian Larsen DRACHART established permanent posts at Nain, Okak, and Hoffenthal (Hopedale) in 1771, 1776, and 1782 respectively. These missions eventually succeeded in converting the Inuit of the coast to Christianity [*see* KINGMINGUSE; MIKAK; TUGLAVINA]; they also formed the nucleus of communities which, except for Okak, are still in existence. J.G.T.

Iroquois. *See* SIX NATIONS CONFEDERACY

Loups. *See* DELAWARES

Malecites; in French Malécites. In 1750 they numbered about 1,000 and occupied their aboriginal territory, which extended from the drainage basin of the Saint John River westward into Maine and northward to the St Lawrence River. They trapped for the fur trade and, in the Saint John valley, practised maize horticulture. Like their neighbours the Micmacs, the Malecites were friendly toward the French and hostile toward the British. During the American revolution they harassed British settlements in the Saint John valley [*see* Pierre TOMAH; Ambroise SAINT-AUBIN] and finally declared war in August 1778. Along with the Micmacs, they participated in a series of peace treaties with the British, beginning soon after the founding of Halifax in 1749 and culminating in the Menagouèche treaty of September 1778 which ended open hostilities [*see* Nicholas AKOMÁPIS]. After 1783 there was a rapid influx of loyalists and other settlers into Malecite hunting lands and the ensuing decline in the fur trade brought suffering among the Indians [*see* Pierre BENOÎT]. Although the Nova Scotia government set aside a small reserve for the Malecites as early as 1765, and again in 1779, the New Brunswick government created in 1784 did little for the Indians until after 1800, when it began to grant reserves because it feared the native people might side with the Americans in a war. In 1800 the Malecites numbered probably just under a thousand. V.P.M.

Miamis. An Algonkian people closely related to the Illinois. The name derives from Omamey, applied by neighbouring tribes. English records usually called them Twightwees (one of their own names) or Naked Indians, though the latter term may have included other groups. The name Miamis was used in the 18th century both for a group of tribes, including the Weas and Piankeshaws, and for one tribe of this group, the Atchatchakangouens (Cranes). Miamis were first met in Wisconsin before 1670, but some were living south of Lake Michigan in 1680 and probably had been there earlier. By 1721 the Miamis occupied the three-river area of the present St Joseph (southeast of Lake Michigan), Maumee (west of Lake Erie), and upper Wabash. Following Orontony*'s lead in 1747, at least part of the Weas and the Piankeshaws formed an alliance with the British and moved to the Rivière à la Roche (Great Miami River), in present southwest Ohio. In June 1752, when many of its warriors were absent, the Miami village of Pickawillany (Piqua, Ohio) was captured by a French and Indian force under Charles-Michel MOUET de Langlade. Its chief, Memeskia (La Demoiselle, Old Britain), was killed and the British trade offensive in the region halted. The Miamis were not conspicuous in the Seven Years' War. They joined Pontiac* in 1763 but accepted reasserted British authority in 1765. In the latter half of the century Shawnees replaced them on the Great Miami River and Potawatomis and Kickapoos occupied some of their Wabash lands. W.A.H.

Micmacs. In 1750 they numbered approximately 10,000 and occupied their aboriginal territory comprising present-day Nova Scotia, Prince Edward Island, eastern New Brunswick, and the Gaspé peninsula. They were a strong, bold tribe, friends of the French and persistent harassers of the British. For nearly 30 years following the founding of Halifax in 1749 the British tried vainly to win the Micmacs' friendship through a series of treaties. A truck-house trading system was established in 1760 [*see* Benjamin GERRISH], but it proved unsuccessful; after 1764 individual traders were licensed for the Indian trade. During the revolution the Americans were able to elicit some support from the Micmacs, but it was of a limited nature and ended when the tribe made peace with the British in 1778 [*see* Jean-Baptiste ARIMPH]. White encroachment on Micmac lands had been felt as early as 1762 and became critical after 1783 when loyalist settlers and others took over the Indians' hunting lands [*see* Philip BERNARD; Joseph CLAUDE]. The fur trade declined sharply and the Indians suffered. The Nova Scotia government granted some relief in the form of food and clothing and began to set aside parcels of land for the Indians' exclusive use, hoping to induce them to take up agriculture. By 1800 the Micmacs' traditional way of life had been destroyed. Their population was reduced through illness and disease to about 4,000, and they were thoroughly subservient to the British. V.P.M.

Mississaugas; in French Mississagués. The so-called Mississaugas are Ojibwas. In the Ojibwa language Mississaugas may signify either people who inhabit the country where there are many mouths of rivers, or people of a large lake. Their name probably is derived from the Mississagué (Mississagi) River on the north shore of Lake Huron. The French first encountered this group of Ojibwas in 1634 near the mouth of the Mississagué River and at Manitoulin Island. Nearly a century later the Mississaugas, together with other Ojibwas, advanced east and south into former Huron territory. In the mid 18th century the French referred to the Ojibwas newly established between lakes Huron, Erie, and Ontario as Mississagués; the English speaking settlers continued to call Mississaugas those Ojibwas residing between Lake Simcoe, Rice Lake, and Kingston. The Mississaugas, however, considered themselves Ojibwas. The Mississauga alliance with the French during the wars of mid century was less than firm. In 1756 they threatened to attack the French post at Toronto [*see* Pierre Pouchot*], and a certain division of sympathies apparently continued during Pontiac*'s uprising of 1763. In 1764 they ceded to the British a narrow strip of land on the west bank of the Niagara River. With the arrival of the loyalists in the 1780s, they were obliged to surrender most of their lands on the north shore of Lake Ontario [*see* WABAKININE]. D.B.S. and B.J.

Mohawks; in French Agniers. Their own name for themselves is Ganiengahaga, people of the place of the flint. They were one of the three Elder Brothers (Mohawks, Onondagas, Senecas) of the Six Nations Confederacy and were Keepers of the Eastern Door of the Confederacy. Anglican missionaries such as John OGILVIE laboured successfully among them during the 18th century, ministering at their two villages of Fort Hunter and Canajoharie (near Little Falls, N.Y.) [*see* SAHONWAGY]. The Mohawks remained allies of the British throughout the 18th century and sided with the king during the American revolution. The loyalist Mohawks were forced to flee during the war [*see* KOÑWATSIˀTSIAIÉÑNI] – the Canajoharies settling in the vicinity of Fort Niagara (near Youngstown), N.Y., and the Fort Hunter families, with the exception of a few neutralists who stayed behind [*see* TEIORHÉÑHSEREˀ], settling at Carleton Island, N.Y. After the war, Governor Frederick HALDIMAND rewarded the faithful service of the Six Nations with two land grants in western Quebec (present-day Ontario), at the Grand River and the Bay of Quinte. Most of the Mohawks, with other loyalist Iroquois, went to the Grand River under the leadership of Joseph Brant [Thayendanegea*]; but a group of Fort Hunter Mohawks under Deserontyon* settled at the Bay of Quinte. In 1797 Brant and Deserontyon negotiated a treaty with New York state officials at Albany, N.Y., whereby they obtained for their people a small compensation for the surrender of all their lands in the environs of the Mohawk River. *See* SIX NATIONS CONFEDERACY. B.G.

Nootkas. The Nootkas inhabited the west coast of Vancouver Island from Cape Cook in the north to Nitinat River in the south, and one group lived on Cape Flattery (Wash.). Linguistically they are closely related to the Kwakiutls to the north. Living on the heavily indented, storm-lashed coastline, their aspect was to the sea, and it was from the sea that they largely drew their livelihood. They were particularly famous for their whaling. The Nootkas lived in a seasonally abundant environment and by the time of European contact had evolved a culture of great richness and complexity. Their social structure involved a finely tuned system of ranking, of both individuals and groups, which was in turn founded on a strict and comprehensive concept of the ownership of property. Also important in Nootka culture was an elaborate ceremonial life. In 1774 the Spanish navigator Juan Josef PÉREZ Hernández became the first European to make contact with the Nootkas, but Captain James COOK's was the first extended contact. His expedition spent a month at Nootka Sound in 1778 and later revealed the possibility of a profitable trade with the coastal Indians in sea otter pelts. From 1785 the Nootkas, particularly those of Clayoquot and Nootka sounds, were heavily involved in the lucrative maritime fur trade, which they manipulated to their advantage. Under leaders such as MUQUINNA and WIKINANISH the fur trade increased the wealth and power of the Nootkas. Following the turn of the century, however, the maritime fur trade passed them by, their importance declined, and once more they became isolated from outside contact. R.A.F.

Ojibwas (Chippewas); in French now known as Ojibwé but referred to in the 18th century as Sauteux. The meaning of Ojibwa has not been satisfactorily determined. The most popular explanation translates the word as to roast until puckered up. Canadian usage favours the spelling Ojibwa or Ojibway. Chippewa, adopted by the Bureau of American Ethnology, is a corruption of the word. According to tribal tradition, the three Algonkian groups, the Ojibwas, Potawatomis, and Ottawas, were once united but separated about the time of European contact. Linguistically and culturally they are closely related. A loose confederacy, entitled the Council of the Three Fires, still existed early in the 20th century. The Jesuits met the Ojibwas near Sault Ste Marie in 1640. They translated their name Baouichitigouin (people of the rapids) literally to the French Saulteur (sometimes written Sauteur, Saulteux, or Sauteux). The Ojibwas who later occupied sections of northwestern Ontario, Manitoba, and Saskatchewan carried this name with them, and are known today as Saulteaux. The Ojibwas' successful struggle with the Foxes expelled that group from the northern part of present Wisconsin at the beginning of the 18th century. In subsequent skirmishes with the Sioux, the Ojibwas gained most of what is now Minnesota and a part of North Dakota. In the southeast, approximately a century after European contact, some Ojibwas advanced into former Huron territory between lakes Huron, Erie, and Ontario. These people were called Mississaugas by the French and British. By the end of the 18th century the Ojibwas occupied a region stretching a thousand miles from the Saskatchewan River to the St Lawrence. They were active in the uprising against the British in the west in 1763–64. Minweweh* led an attack on the garrison at Michilimackinac (Mackinaw City, Mich.), and WASSON brought a force of Ojibwa warriors to fight by Pontiac*'s side in the siege of Detroit. During the 1780s and 1790s they ceded to the crown portions of present-day southwestern Ontario, the harbours at Matchedash Bay and Penetanguishene (Ont.), and St Joseph Island (Ont.). *See* MISSISSAUGAS.

D.B.S. and B.J.

Oneidas; in French Onneiouts. Their own name is derived from Tiionenioteˀ or standing stone, from a geographical feature near one of their villages. With the Cayugas, and later the Tuscaroras, they were the Younger Brothers of the Six Nations Confederacy. After the Tuscarora Wars of the early 18th century, they adopted the refugee Tuscaroras from North Carolina and gave them land in their territory. They also invited the Stockbridge, or Moheconnuck, Indians of Massachusetts and the scattered southern New England and Long Island tribes to live in their territory; and these established New Stockbridge (Stockbridge) and Brothertown (Deansboro) respectively. In the mid 18th century, the Oneidas were settled principally at Kanõˀalohaleˀ (Sherrill), Old Oneida (Oneida Valley), Oriska (Oriskany), and Oquaga (near Binghamton). During the American revolution the Oneida nation divided, most of the Oneidas, along with their protégé tribes, siding with the Americans. As a result, their settlements near Lake Oneida were totally destroyed by the loyalist Iroquois under Joseph Brant [Thayendanegea*] in 1780 and they became refugees at Schenectady, N.Y., for the remainder of the revolution. After the war a loyalist faction followed Brant to the Grand River (Ont.). Despite their faithful service with the Americans, the Oneidas remaining in their old territory were the first to feel the importunities of New York officials, who coerced them in a series of separate treaties to sell most of their land to the state. *See* SIX NATIONS CONFEDERACY. B.G.

Onondagas; in French Onontagués. Their own name is Onontaˀge, on top of the hill. They were the most centrally located nation of the Six Nations Confederacy, and, along with the Mohawks and Senecas, one of the Elder Brothers of the Confederacy Council. Their village, Onondaga (near Syracuse, N.Y.), was the capital of the Confederacy, and they thus served as both the fire keepers and the wampum keepers of the league. In federal councils of the Confederacy, they held a mediating role between the Elder Brothers (Mohawks and Senecas) and the Younger Brothers (Oneidas, Cayugas, and Tuscaroras). They maintained a continuing friendship with the British during the 18th century [*see* HOTSINOÑHYAHTAˀ; TEYOHAQUEANDE], but with the outbreak of the American revolution they split into pro-British, pro-American, and neutral factions. Colonel Goose Van Schaick's expedition against their village in April 1779 solidified the nation in support of the British, and those who escaped fled to the Senecas. After the war, some of the Onondagas returned to live in their old territory and another portion went to the Grand River (Ont.) with the loyalist Iroquois. For a time the fire-place of the Confederacy was moved to Buffalo Creek, N.Y., which was the most central location between the Iroquois in Canada and New York state. Eventually, the fire-place was moved to the Onondaga settlement at the Grand River. As the two Iroquois factions on either side of the border grew apart, the New York Iroquois re-established the Confederacy capital at the traditional location on the Onondaga Reservation (near Syracuse), and there were then two confederacies and two fire-places. The New York Onondagas, like the other Iroquois nations, were continually pressed by the state to sell large tracts of their land until only their village and a few surrounding acres remained of their former vast holdings. *See* SIX NATIONS CONFEDERACY. B.G.

Ottawas; in French Outaouais, probably derived from the Ojibwa verb to buy and sell, to trade. The French first applied the name Ottawa to all the upper Great Lakes Algonkian groups because, as Father Claude Dablon* explained in 1670, the Ottawas had been the first to reach the French settlements and the others also were assumed to be Ottawas. Towards the start of the 18th century most commentators began to restrict the use of the term Ottawa to four Algonkian groups: the Kiskakons, Sinagos, Sable, and Nassawaketons. By the 1740s there were Ottawas living in the vicinity of Detroit and at L'Arbre Croche (Cross Village, Mich.) [*see* NISSOWAQUET]. In the early 1760s the Ottawa chief Pontiac* organized a coalition of Ottawas, Potawatomis, Ojibwas, and Hurons which besieged the British garrison at Detroit throughout the summer of 1763. During the American revolution the Ottawas sided with the British, and EGUSHWA, a war chief, was one of the leaders of the subsequent Indian resistance to American expansion in the Ohio country. In May 1790 the Ottawas living on the Detroit River surrendered to the crown their claims to lands in present-day southwestern Ontario. By the end of the century they were living along the southwest shore of Lake Erie in villages mingled with those of their old allies the Hurons. The Ottawas from L'Arbre Croche had spread out along the east shore of Lake Michigan as far south as the St Joseph River. In the north, Manitoulin Island was shared with the Ojibwas. D.B.S. and B.J.

Potawatomis; in French Potéouatamis; meaning in Ojibwa, keepers of the fire. The French first contacted this Algonkian group, closely related to the Ojibwas and Ottawas, around the Baie des Puants (Green Bay, Lake Michigan). By the end of the 17th century, many Potawatomis had migrated southward into former Miami country on the St Joseph River. A few journeyed to Detroit after it was founded by Lamothe Cadillac [Laumet*] in 1701. By 1760 at least a hundred warriors resided there. The other principal bands remained in the St Joseph area. Steadfast in their French alliance, the Potawatomis fought with Pontiac* against the British in 1763. On the outbreak of the American revolution, however, they sided with the British and continued hostilities against the Americans until the treaty of Greenville in 1795. In 1790 the Potawatomis residing on the Detroit River surrendered to the crown their claims to lands in present-day southwestern Ontario. At the end of the 18th century they controlled the country around the head of Lake Michigan. They practised agriculture in the summer and hunted in the winter. D.B.S. and B.J.

Renards. *See* FOXES

Sauteux. *See* OJIBWAS

Senecas; in French Tsonnontouans. They call themselves Onõtawaˀka, great hill people. The Senecas were the most westerly of the Six Nations Confederacy and were known as the Keepers of the Western Door of the Confederacy. Along with the Mohawks and Onondagas, they were the Elder Brothers of the Confederacy Council. Influenced by France through its control of Fort Niagara (near Youngstown, N.Y.), a portion of the Senecas took the French part during the Seven Years' War. A segment of the nation also supported Pontiac* in 1763 [*see* KAYAHSOTAˀ]. In 1777, when the Six Nations were drawn into the American revolution, almost the entire Seneca nation sided with the British, and its warriors participated in the siege of Fort Stanwix (Rome, N.Y.) and the battle of Oriskany nearby. The two war chiefs of the Confederacy at that time, KAIEÑˀKWAAHTOÑ and Kaiũtwahˀkũ (Cornplanter), were chosen from their nation. After the war a small number of Senecas followed Joseph Brant [Thayendanegea*] to the Grand River (Ont.), but the great majority remained in their homeland. Beginning in 1797 with the treaty of Big Tree, the Senecas gradually and systematically sold most of their territory in western New York to the various land companies that had the right of pre-emption. In June 1799, while living on the Cornplanter Grant (near Corydon, Pa), the Seneca chief Ganiodaio (Handsome Lake) had the vision that subsequently led to a great revival of the native religion among the Six Nations Indians. *See* SIX NATIONS CONFEDERACY. B.G.

Shawnees; in French Chaouanons, from an Algonkian word meaning southerners. They were an Algonkian people originally resident south of the Ohio on the Cumberland River (Rivière des Anciens Chouanons on a French map of 1744). Dispersed by Iroquois attack, some moved toward Carolina; others, who took refuge at René-Robert Cavelier* de La Salle's Fort Saint-Louis (near La Salle, Ill.), provided a basis for a later French claim to the Ohio country. In 1692, a few years after their encounter with La Salle, some of these Shawnees moved to the head of Chesapeake Bay and the upper Delaware River, where they established a long-lasting association with the Delawares. The Iroquois, lukewarm to their presence there, assigned a chief, Swatana*, to oversee them and, after a minor disturbance in 1727, ordered them to return to the Ohio, where they were supervised by another Iroquois chief, Scarroyady. Here, about 1730, French agents renewed contact with them and, to frustrate the British traders, undertook to resettle the Shawnees on the upper Ouabache (Wabash). The new arrangement was short-lived; part of the tribe returned to the mouth of the Scioto River and the rest went to present-day Alabama. The Shawnees accommodated themselves to the French military occupation of the upper Ohio begun by Paul Marin* de La Malgue in 1753; but when Fort Duquesne (Pittsburgh, Pa) was abandoned in 1758 they withdrew from that area to settle on the Scioto River and Rivière à la Roche (Miami River) and exploit the Kentucky hunting grounds to which they had a traditional claim. After the 1768 treaty of Fort Stanwix the Shawnees, whose hunting lands had been surrendered to the whites by the Iroquois, faced conflict with Virginia, whose charter lands extended limitlessly west and northwest. Following a series of incidents provoked by impatient settlers and unruly frontiersmen, the governor of Virginia took military action in 1774 (Lord Dunmore's War) to compel the Shawnees to yield the contested lands. In the American revolution, as in Pontiac*'s uprising, the Shawnees joined their neighbours in resisting the advance of white settlement. Subsequent attempts by the United States, by treaty and by force, to obtain a cession of land north of the Ohio were unsuccessful until the 1794 battle of Fallen Timbers (near Waterville, Ohio). By the ensuing treaty of Greenville, 3 Aug. 1795, the western tribes were forced to surrender most of the present state of Ohio, including the principal Shawnee settlements. W.A.H.

Six Nations Confederacy. Prior to their adoption of the Tuscaroras in the early 18th century, these people were known to the British as the Five Nations Confederacy and to the French as the Cinq-Nations. Their own name for themselves is Oñgwanonsioñni or Kanonsionni, we are of the extended lodge. Tradition ascribes the founding of the Confederacy to Dekanahwideh* and Hiawatha (Hayenwatha), who persuaded five Iroquois tribes, the Mohawks, Oneidas, Onondagas, Cayugas, and Senecas, to cease their internecine warfare and unite in a League of Peace. Estimates of the date of the founding vary from 1450 A.D. to 1570 A.D. The capital of the Confederacy was located in the land of the Onondaga nation. Their unity made the Iroquois a potent force in Indian diplomacy, and later in European colonial diplomacy. The chiefs of the original Confederacy Council were probably the existing village chiefs who consented to the league's formation. Notably, the Seneca deer clan does not have Council chiefs. Authorities differ as to whether the chiefly titles number 50 or 49. They have been preserved and are passed down to each successor in the office of Confederacy, or sachem, chief in his clan and nation. The chiefs are chosen by the mothers of the respective clans and the choice is confirmed by the nation. They are raised to office by means of the Condolence Council, at which time a new sachem chief receives the title of the departed one whose office he will fill. The clan mothers may also remove an unsatisfactory chief from office. Descent is matrilineal and the matrons are accorded great respect. The agricultural economy of the Six Nations, which was the domain of the women, was dependent upon maize, bean, and squash cultivation. Hunting and fishing, the domain of the men, provided an important supply of food, as well as skins for clothing.

The Mohawks were the Iroquois nation most firmly under British influence during the 18th century, and they provided a steady supply of warriors to fight as British allies in the War of the Austrian Succession, the Seven Years' War, and the American revolution. Their noted chief Theyanoguin* was killed in 1755 during the British and Indian attempt to relieve Fort Edward (also known as Fort Lydius; now Fort Edward, N.Y.). The appointment of William JOHNSON as Indian agent for New York and later as superintendent of northern Indian affairs deepened the friendship between the Six Nations and Great Britain. Johnson's conquest of Fort Niagara (near Youngstown, N.Y.) in 1759 further undermined the influence the French had had over the Senecas. During the American revolution, the Six Nations Confederacy split apart, with the overwhelming number of Mohawks, Onondagas, Cayugas, and Senecas supporting the British, and the majority of the Oneidas and Tuscaroras supporting the Americans. After the end of the war, and largely as a result of Great Britain's abandonment of its faithful Iroquois allies in the peace treaty, Governor Frederick HALDIMAND secured two land grants in western Quebec (present-day Ontario) for the Six Nations loyalists. Most of these loyalist Iroquois settled on the Grand River tract, with a smaller number of Mohawks from Fort Hunter, N.Y., going to the Bay of Quinte. At Grand River, a dispute of many years' standing developed between Joseph Brant [Thayendanegea*], the principal leader, though he never bore the title of sachem, and the Quebec governmental officials over the nature of the Haldimand grant and over Brant's contention that the Six Nations had the right to sell or lease large tracts to white settlers. For several years after the American revolution, the Six Nations attempted to maintain the unity of their confederacy; but the groups in Upper Canada and in New York ultimately divided and established two separate capitals, at the Onondaga village at Grand River and on the Onondaga Reservation (near Syracuse), N.Y., with two sets of sachem chiefs on each side of the border. *See* MOHAWKS, ONEIDAS, ONONDAGAS, SENECAS.

B.G.

Tsonnontouans. *See* SENECAS

Wyandots. *See* HURONS

BIOGRAPHIES

List of Abbreviations

AAQ	Archives de l'archidiocèse de Québec
ACAM	Archives de la chancellerie de l'archevêché de Montréal
ACND	Archives de la Congrégation de Notre-Dame
AD	Archives départementales
AHGQ	Archives de l'Hôpital Général de Québec
AMA	Archives du ministère des Armées
AMHDQ	Archives du monastère de l'Hôtel-Dieu de Québec
AN	Archives nationales
ANQ	Archives nationales du Québec
ANQ-M	Archives nationales du Québec, dépôt de Montréal
ANQ-MBF	Archives nationales du Québec, dépôt de la Mauricie et des Bois-Francs
ANQ-Q	Archives nationales du Québec, dépôt de Québec
ASGM	Archives des sœurs Grises, Montréal
ASJCF	Archives de la Compagnie de Jésus, province du Canada français
ASN	Archives du séminaire de Nicolet
ASQ	Archives du séminaire de Québec
ASSM	Archives du séminaire de Saint-Sulpice
AUM	Archives de l'université de Montréal
AUQ	Archives du monastère des ursulines, Québec
BL	British Library
BN	Bibliothèque nationale
BRH	*Le Bulletin des recherches historiques*
CCHA	Canadian Catholic Historical Association
CÉA	Centre d'études acadiennes
CHA	Canadian Historical Association
CHR	*Canadian Historical Review*
DAB	*Dictionary of American biography*
DBF	*Dictionnaire de biographie française*
DCB	*Dictionary of Canadian biography*
DNB	*Dictionary of national biography*
DOLQ	*Dictionnaire des œuvres littéraires du Québec*
DPL	Detroit Public Library
HBC	Hudson's Bay Company
HBRS	Hudson's Bay Record Society
IBC	Inventaire des biens culturels
JR	*Jesuit relations and allied documents*
NYCD	*Documents relative to the colonial history of the state of New-York*
OH	*Ontario History*
PAC	Public Archives of Canada
PANB	Provincial Archives of New Brunswick
PANL	Provincial Archives of Newfoundland and Labrador
PANS	Public Archives of Nova Scotia
PAO	Archives of Ontario
PRO	Public Record Office
QDA	Quebec Diocesan Archives
RHAF	*Revue d'histoire de l'Amérique française*
RSC	Royal Society of Canada
SCHÉC	Société canadienne d'histoire de l'Église catholique
SGCF	Société généalogique canadienne-française
USPG	United Society for the Propagation of the Gospel

BIOGRAPHIES

A

ABERCROMBIE (Abercromby), JAMES, army officer; b. 1732, probably in Scotland; d. 23 June 1775 at Boston, Mass.

James Abercrombie's family origins are uncertain but he may have been a relative of James ABERCROMBY. On 11 June 1744 he was made lieutenant in the 1st Foot, which served in Flanders during the War of the Austrian Succession and in Scotland during the 1745 rebellion; this may have been his first commission. He was promoted captain in the 42nd Foot on 16 Feb. 1756, and in April of that year his regiment reached North America. By May 1757 Abercrombie was aide-de-camp to the Earl of Loudoun, commander-in-chief in America, and that summer he took part in Loudoun's abortive campaign against Louisbourg, Île Royale (Cape Breton Island) [*see* Charles Hay*].

After the army returned to New York Abercrombie went on reconnaissance and raiding missions with Robert ROGERS' rangers; his knowledge of French was used in interrogating enemy deserters. In his reports to Loudoun he consistently urged aggressive tactics. By March 1758 he was aide-de-camp to Major-General Abercromby, who had succeeded Loudoun, and he reconnoitred Fort Carillon (Ticonderoga, N.Y.) before the unsuccessful attack that July. By December, with Jeffery AMHERST the new commander-in-chief, young Abercrombie was in New York awaiting a new assignment; Amherst appointed him his aide-de-camp on 5 May 1759. His duties included examining and reporting on preparations for the coming campaign against Canada. Abercrombie was exasperated by the lack of aggressiveness of Amherst and Brigadier-General Thomas GAGE, and he complained to Loudoun that by not taking Montreal they were missing a fine opportunity to relieve the pressure on Wolfe*'s army at Quebec. He was clearly a man of strong opinions and considerable self-confidence. His craving for action was partially satisfied by his participation in Joshua LORING's successful naval foray on Lake Champlain following the capture of forts Carillon and Saint-Frédéric (near Crown Point, N.Y.).

In the winter Abercrombie was summoned to London to testify at the court martial Lord Charles Hay had demanded to clear his name after the Loudoun expedition. While in London he secured the recommendation of General Sir John Ligonier, principal military adviser to William Pitt, that Amherst promote him major. Loudoun was likely influential in obtaining Ligonier's support. Abercrombie rejoined the army at Oswego, New York, in July 1760 and was soon commissioned major; on 7–8 September he was Amherst's emissary to Vaudreuil [RIGAUD] in negotiating the capitulation of Montreal. His new commission was in the 78th Foot and he apparently joined the regiment after the surrender. It may have served in the Quebec area until disbanded in 1763. Major Abercrombie was placed on half pay.

On 27 March 1770 James Abercrombie returned to duty as lieutenant-colonel of the 22nd Foot, which was stationed in Britain. He took his unit to Ireland in late October 1773 and became acting commandant of the Dublin garrison. His letters to his friend and former patron, Loudoun, reveal Abercrombie as a man of refreshing candour and wry wit. Much as he disliked Dublin, he hoped that he would not be ordered to America where he believed Gage, the commander-in-chief, faced a most difficult situation. Nevertheless he was directed there on 3 March 1775.

Abercrombie reached Boston on 23 April and was immediately appointed adjutant general. He was as critical as ever of Gage's lack of initiative and of the low morale and lack of supplies in the besieged British force. By the end of May major-generals William Howe, John BURGOYNE, and Henry Clinton had arrived to replace Frederick HALDIMAND on Gage's staff, and Abercrombie was shortly afterwards appointed to head a battalion of grenadiers. On 17 June he was wounded leading his men against the American positions near Bunker Hill; he died on 23 June and was buried at King's Chapel, Boston. Abercrombie was later commended by Gage for his performance at Bunker Hill.

PETER E. RUSSELL

[Secondary sources contain numerous unsupported references to the existence and nature of a family relationship between the subject of this biography and Major-General James Abercromby, commander-in-chief in America in 1758. He is described as the general's son in: *The national cyclopaedia of American biography* (57 v. to date, New York, 1892–), I; Wallace, *Macmillan dictionary*; Le Jeune, *Dictionnaire*, I; Amherst, *Journal* (Webster), 85. Two modern works refer to him as a nephew of his commander: Shy, *Toward Lexington*; J. R. Cuneo, *Robert Rogers of the rangers* (New York, 1959).

The general did have a son, James Abercromby, in the 42nd Foot during the Seven Years' War, but this young man was an ensign at the time that the subject was a captain; see the "List of commissions," *Military affairs in North America, 1748–65* (Pargellis), 332, and *Officers of the Black Watch, 1725–1952*, comp. Neil McMicking (rev. ed., Perth, Scot., 1953), 16. The subject's correspondence never refers to the general as his father and he consistently spells their names differently (he was a good speller for his time). Contemporary sources do not refer to him as the general's son or as James Abercromby Jr, and the ensign is explicitly designated as a son in the list cited above (Pargellis). It is therefore unlikely that the subject was the son of his famous near-namesake.

He may have been a relative. Two capable historians believe him to be a nephew, although his own correspondence makes no mention of such a relationship, nor does that of any contemporary. If he were a younger relative of the general, he may have been the "Jemmy Abercromby" of the 1st Foot who did an errand for and wrote to the famous Scottish philosopher David Hume in London in 1747: [David Hume], *The letters of David Hume*, ed. J. Y. T. Greig (2v., Oxford, 1932; repr. 1969). Hume was a friend of the general, then a colonel (*ibid.*, I, 102–8, 146–48, 190, 204; *DAB*, I, 28–29).

A third possibility has been advanced in T. N. Dupuy and G. M. Hammerman, *People and events of the American revolution* (New York, 1974), 279, and Boatner, *Encyclopedia of American revolution*, 1. These sources allege that the subject was not the son of Major-General James Abercromby but the brother of the future General Sir Ralph Abercromby; the latter was also a young officer in the Seven Years' War (European theatre) and became famous for successful campaigns in the West Indies in 1796 and Egypt in 1801. His biography is in the *DNB*, I, especially pp.43–44. He did have a brother James, but this officer was killed in action at Brooklyn in 1776 (*ibid.*). Their family, Abercrombie of Birkenbog, was related to that of the 1758 general, Abercromby of Glassaugh (*DAB*, I, 28–29; *DNB*, I, 43–44). P.E.R.]

Huntington Library, Loudoun papers. *Correspondence of General Thomas Gage* (Carter). *General Sir William Howe's orderly book at Charlestown, Boston and Halifax, June 17, 1775, to 1776, 26 May . . .*, ed. B. F. Stevens, intro. E. E. Hale (London, 1890; repr. Port Washington, N.Y., and London, 1970). Knox, *Hist. journal* (Doughty). Mass. Hist. Soc., *Proc.*, 2nd ser., XI (1896–97), 304–6 (James Abercrombie to Cadwallader Colden, 2 May 1775). G. B., WO, *Army list*, 1775. Pargellis, *Lord Loudoun*.

ABERCROMBY, JAMES, army officer; b. 1706 in Banffshire (now part of Grampian), Scotland, son of Alexander Abercromby and Helen Meldrum; m. Mary Duff, and they had one daughter; d. 23 April 1781 at Glassaugh, Banffshire.

James Abercromby started his military career at the age of 11 by entering the 25th Foot as an ensign. Promotion during the peaceful Walpole era was not promising, and by 1736 he was only a captain, albeit in the 1st Foot. Like many officers, Abercromby entered politics to seek advancement, and in 1734 he was elected member of parliament for Banffshire on the interest of his brother-in-law William Duff, later Lord Braco. The government partially rewarded Abercromby for his support by appointing him lieutenant governor of Stirling Castle in 1739. The outbreak of war with Spain and later France brought better times for the military profession, and Abercromby was promoted rapidly, becoming colonel in 1746. That year he served as quartermaster general in the unsuccessful expedition against Lorient, France. He continued on active service until wounded at Hulst (Netherlands) the following year.

After the treaty of Aix-la-Chapelle in 1748 Abercromby retired, and he remained in comparative obscurity until the outbreak of the Seven Years' War. Sent to North America early in 1756 as deputy to the Earl of Loudoun, the British commander-in-chief, he was promoted major-general and made colonel of the 44th Foot. Under Loudoun Abercromby showed himself a loyal, tireless, and entirely uninspired subordinate, commanding a brigade in the force that Loudoun assembled at Halifax, Nova Scotia, in 1757 for an expedition against Louisbourg, Île Royale (Cape Breton Island). Following Loudoun's recall to England later that year, Abercromby was promoted commander-in-chief in North America. For the 1758 campaign, the British army was divided into three corps: one under Jeffery AMHERST to renew the assault on Louisbourg, a second under John Forbes* to take the strategic post of Fort Duquesne (Pittsburgh, Pa), and the third under Abercromby to invade Canada by way of Lake George (Lac Saint-Sacrement) and Fort Carillon (Ticonderoga, N.Y.).

This operation gave Abercromby an opportunity to distinguish himself, but he was unhappy with his command. Amherst had been allocated the cream of the army and most of the supplies, leaving Abercromby with a large number of ill-disciplined provincial troops and insufficient artillery. But, aided by his energetic quartermaster general, John BRADSTREET, and his charismatic second in command, Viscount Howe (George Augustus Howe), Abercromby opened the campaign early in July 1758 with an army of 6,000 regulars and 9,000 provincials. Crossing Lake George he landed with his army three miles south of Carillon on 6 July. The army's initial advance ended in confusion as the troops lost their way in the dense forest. Lord Howe, the moving spirit of the expedition, was killed during a brief skirmish. Despite this setback, Abercromby regrouped his army. Early on the morning of the 8th he discovered that the French commander, Montcalm*, was hastily entrenching his force of some 3,500 men behind a rough breastwork of fallen trees. Led to believe that the French expected substantial reinforcement shortly, and advised by his engineers that the French works were as yet not formidable, Abercromby ordered an immediate assault without waiting for his artillery or attempting a formal siege. The attack was a disaster, for despite the heroic endeavours of the troops the enemy defences could not be breached. After four hours it was abandoned, leaving 1,944 British casualties.

His army shattered, Abercromby retreated up Lake George and waited for reinforcements. The retreat was his second serious error, for his forces were still superior to Montcalm's and by bringing up his artillery he might yet have compelled the French to retire. But disheartened by his heavy losses, especially in officers, and lacking confidence in his provincial troops, he decided to do nothing further until he heard from Amherst. Abercromby's responsibility for this disappointing end and his general incompetence for high command were now fully recognized by the government, and he was recalled in September.

Abercromby did not see active service again, though by the normal process of seniority he had risen to the rank of full general by 1772. He died at Glassaugh in 1781, having spent the last 20 years of his life there in retirement.

RICHARD MIDDLETON

BL, Add. MSS 32884. Huntington Library, Abercromby papers, AB 216. PRO, PRO 30/8/98. *Correspondence of William Pitt* (Kimball). [John Forbes], *Writings of General John Forbes*, ed. A. P. James (Menasha, Wis., 1938). *Gentleman's Magazine*, 1781, 242. *DAB*. Joseph Foster, *Members of parliament, Scotland* . . . (2nd ed., London and Aylesbury, Eng., 1882), 3. Sedgwick, *House of Commons*, I, 406. Pargellis, *Lord Loudoun*, 74.

ACKMOBISH. *See* AKOMÁPIS

ADHÉMAR, JEAN-BAPTISTE-AMABLE, merchant, militia captain, and justice of the peace; b. 29 Jan. 1736 in Montreal (Que.), son of Jean-Baptiste Adhémar* and Catherine Moreau; d. there 26 July 1800.

Nothing is known of Jean-Baptiste-Amable Adhémar's childhood or education. As royal notary in Montreal, the centre of the fur trade, his father was called upon to draw up numerous hiring contracts for the west, and it may have been through his influence that Adhémar turned to the trade at an early age. Thus on 14 April 1758 he signed a year's contract with the purveyor general, Joseph-Michel CADET, to serve as chief clerk at Fort Niagara (near Youngstown, N.Y.).

On 31 March 1761, in Montreal, Adhémar married Marguerite, the daughter of merchant René-Alexandre Lemoine, *dit* Despins. His marriage, which made him brother-in-law to Jacques-Joseph LEMOINE Despins, one of the most important merchants in the colony prior to the conquest, probably furthered his career in the fur trade. During the next 15 years his business seems to have prospered normally in the regions around Michilimackinac (Mackinaw City, Mich.), Detroit, and Lake Superior. In 1769 he invested £300 in the trade, and in 1770 £800. Four years later, he sent four canoes, 29 men, and goods worth about £1,300 to Lake Superior. In 1777, with James McGill* as surety, Adhémar alone sent ten canoes, 94 men, and goods worth £5,100 to the west.

In 1777–78, for reasons that are unknown, he made his first trip to France and England. On 9 April 1778 he was in London when a petition signed by 23 British merchants in Canada was presented to the secretary of state for the American Colonies, Lord Germain. Adhémar was the only Canadian to sign this document, which sought the repeal of the Quebec Act or its amendment so that trial by jury in civil cases and English commercial law would be reinstituted and Canadian law eliminated. This petition also asked for the freeing of trade with the Indians, which since 1777 had been regulated by an ordinance requiring a licence for each trader. For some years after 1778 trader Adhémar disappears from view, but his success in the business world, however modest it may have been, and his family connections seem to have given him some reputation in Montreal society.

Adhémar was also interested in church affairs. In 1769 he had been elected a churchwarden in the parish of Notre-Dame, at that time the only parish in Montreal. In June 1783 he and lawyer Pierre-François Mézière were delegated to present to Governor HALDIMAND a petition signed by 300 Notre-Dame parishioners asking him to suspend the order for the expulsion of François Ciquard* and Antoine Capel, two French Sulpicians who had entered Canada clandestinely. The scarcity of priests had been felt with increasing severity within the Catholic Church since the conquest. The problem became more acute from 1778 on, when France allied herself with the rebellious American colonies and the British authorities closed the door to the immigration of French priests. Haldimand refused to rescind his decision, but he declared his readiness to let other priests from Europe enter Canada. Relying on these encouragements, the people in Montreal decided to petition London. A memoir prepared with the aid of Étienne MONTGOLFIER, the superior of the Sulpician seminary, although probably not with the support of BRIAND, the bishop of Quebec, asked for permission not only to bring French speaking priests from Europe to Canada but also to establish an episcopal see in Montreal. A second memoir, however, dealing with the Canadians' "civil rights" failed to gain the unanimous support of Montrealers and had to be dropped. The petition to the king dealt with this subject in vague terms, asking only that Canadians be permitted to participate fully in political life "under whatever form of government it . . . will please the king to set up in this Province." It attracted a mere 130 signatures, and this small number, in addition to the fact that time constraints prevented Quebec citizens from being associated with it, considerably diminished its significance. To meet the expenses of sending a delegation to London, Adhémar wrote to the militia captains, calling upon them to take up collections in the parishes, but this plan failed because of pressure from Haldimand.

On 18 Aug. 1783 Adhémar and Jean De Lisle* de La Cailleterie informed the governor that they had been "lawfully elected" as delegates to London and requested his support in their dealings with the British authorities. Haldimand refused, basing his decision on a report by the judge Adam MABANE, who at his request had investigated the projected mission. The governor, who was obsessed by the fear of revolutionary plots, made a harshly critical report to Lord North, the Home secretary, comparing Adhémar's conduct – and in particular his letter to the militia captains – with the activities of the American rebels before the revolution. Adhémar and De Lisle nevertheless left Quebec on 25 Oct. 1783 as representatives of the Canadians. They were accompanied by William Dummer Powell*, who went armed with a petition from the British merchants reviving the campaign, suspended during the American revolution, to obtain for Canada a form of government and a legal system more closely resembling those in England.

Early in December the Canadian delegates, accompanied by Thomas Hussey, Bishop Briand's representative, handed Lord North their memoir of support for a bishopric in Montreal and the immigration to Canada of foreign priests. The moment was badly chosen, for a new government was on the eve of being formed. While waiting, Adhémar and De Lisle went to Paris at the beginning of 1784 with a view to recruiting priests for the Canadian clergy. In order to concentrate their efforts on the recruiting question, the two delegates had already decided to drop the idea of creating a bishopric in Montreal. In any event Briand doubted the wisdom of that particular proposal. Having returned from Paris and having secured Sir Guy Carleton*'s cautious support, they met North's successor, Lord Sydney, in March. They asked him for permission to take three young schoolteachers and three young Sulpicians, all of them French, to Canada. Sydney's negative reply led Adhémar and De Lisle, in a memoir to the government on 24 March, to assert the need and the right of the Canadians to make their own choice of priests in Europe. The next day they learned that the king would not receive their petition and that it was to be transmitted to Lord Sydney, who had little sympathy for their cause. Their failure was complete, as Sydney himself assured Haldimand on 8 April: "These gentlemen have met with very little encouragement here." Sydney emphasized to Haldimand that the government would allow the Catholic Church to recruit all the priests and teachers needed, provided they hailed from countries independent of the House of Bourbon, such as Savoy-Piedmont. Briand had been disappointed by the mercenary attitude of several Savoyard priests whom he had tried to bring to Canada in 1781 and 1782, and he was opposed to this solution which was dear to Haldimand's heart.

Adhémar and De Lisle remained optimistic, however, when they learned that Haldimand, whom they held responsible for their failure, was going to be replaced by Carleton. Adhémar decided to remain in London for another year, whilst De Lisle returned to Canada to report. Both of them asked Briand to support Adhémar publicly, in order to give his mission a more official character. Briand was anxious to remain discreet, but he wrote to Carleton on 30 June 1784 that although he could not publicly approve a mission he considered "hasty and somewhat ill-humoured," he was in agreement with the idea of bringing French priests to Canada, and he asked Carleton to use his influence in support of Adhémar. On 5 November Briand sent Adhémar a letter of encouragement and even permission to write an address in the clergy's name, provided that he did not implicate the church in any political mission.

Because of political instability in England, Adhémar and De Lisle had not succeeded in advancing the civil aspect of their mission. Consequently they, together with Powell, had spoken to Francis Maseres*, the political agent in London of the British merchants in Canada. On 13 March 1784 the four, along with Pierre DU CALVET, had declared themselves in favour of the demands of these merchants, including their request for an elective assembly. On 20 April Adhémar wrote to Henri-François Gravé* de La Rive, of the Séminaire de Québec, that the failure of the mission on immigration of foreign priests had led him to believe "that our rights of every sort will not be unquestionably assured for us until we become less dependent upon the ministry's will, through the creation of a house of assembly."

After his return to Canada in the summer of 1784, De Lisle sought more ample powers of representation and more precise instructions as to the nature of the reforms desired. In London the ex-Jesuit Pierre-Joseph-Antoine ROUBAUD, who may be suspected of having wanted to replace Adhémar as a delegate, reported that Adhémar "was residing quietly and out of sight in his inn, little known, visited by no one." There is nothing surprising in this seclusion given that Adhémar was living with uncertain expectations and could count on only a small income to meet his expenses. Briand, who was one of those who sent him money, described his contribution as "a small testimony of the satisfaction brought [him] by Adhémar's wise and prudent conduct" in his mission.

On 5 Jan. 1785 Adhémar wrote a letter, later signed by De Lisle, in which he harshly criticized the Canadian bourgeoisie's timidity in both their requests and their way of presenting petitions to the king alone, when these could really be dealt with and debated only in the House of Lords and the Commons. He also condemned them for having thought only of their class interests. "Since the farmer, the craftsman, and the workman form the most useful and most necessary class of men, their interests must not be neglected," he wrote, adding that inequality would soon lead to "complaints, discouragement, hatreds, and a dangerous separation among all the estates." But the Canadian bourgeoisie itself had become divided over the reform movement: business and professional people supported it, while the seigneurs and the Canadian officials fell back upon the Quebec Act. The Canadian merchants seemed increasingly to prefer acting through London merchants, who probably had more influence than Adhémar. Moreover, in February 1785 their committee in Montreal regretted the publication of a letter by Adhémar containing "a reflection which seems rash and very much out of place."

Towards the end of the winter of 1785 Adhémar realized that his mission had failed. However, he was on the scene when the news arrived of Briand's resignation as bishop, and he was able to thwart the efforts of Haldimand, now back in London, on behalf of two English monks, both totally unsuited to the circumstances, as potential successors to Briand. Adhémar took advantage of Haldimand's return to accuse the erstwhile governor on 8 March of being responsible for his misfortune and to ask him to show him the kindness of obtaining for him a commission as judge of the Court of Common Pleas. Receiving no reply, Adhémar changed his tactics, admitting on 17 September that he had been wrong in agreeing to be a delegate of the Canadians against Haldimand's wish. "I no longer feel sufficiently vigorous," he wrote, "to undertake again the labours of the Indian trade; a modest salary, the position of judge at Detroit or any other that is within my feeble powers will suffice for me." Haldimand refused to help him but assured him that he would not say or do anything that might harm him.

For unknown reasons, Adhémar does not seem to have left England until the beginning of 1786, to go to New York. When the ship was wrecked, Adhémar was detained in Lisbon and he did not reach Quebec until early June. He brought the papal brief authorizing HUBERT's consecration as coadjutor bishop of Quebec. Back in Montreal, Adhémar found himself once more in financial difficulties. In 1785 he had written to Haldimand that he had already lost "through a commercial set-back the modest fortune amassed through a long period of work." He probably attempted to engage in trade again, but his business does not seem to have prospered. In April 1789, even though the merchant Jean-Baptiste Lemoine Despins owed him 9,520 *livres*, Adhémar's debts amounted to 16,858 *livres* including 7,577 owing to the Sulpicians and 3,521 to the merchant Charles Lusignan* (Carolo Lucciniani); nevertheless he had 300 masses sung on credit for his wife, who had just died. The belongings in his stone house and his stable on Place d'Armes were worth 3,212 *livres*; he also owned a frame-house on Rue Saint-Joseph and an orchard at Coteau-Saint-Louis. Despite his difficulties Adhémar remained a figure of note in Montreal. Thus in February 1788 he was appointed captain of the town's militia, a post he retained until around

1797. In 1790 he turns up as a justice of the peace for the District of Montreal, and three years later as a commissioner in Montreal for administering oaths of office, both posts he held until his death on 26 July 1800. As a result of a legal action brought by Lusignan, the Court of King's Bench of the District of Montreal ordered the sale of his property in December 1800.

Adhémar, who died in poverty, deserved a happier end. Although his mission to England was destined to failure from the beginning because of Haldimand's opposition, it enabled him, as well as many other Canadian bourgeois, to discern the need for constitutional revision and above all for an elective house of assembly. Adhémar had devoted himself unselfishly to the interests of his compatriots, but they do not seem to have remembered him with any great gratitude.

JEAN-GUY PELLETIER

AAQ, 12 A, D, 12; 20 A, I, 183; II, 3, 17; 1 CB, VI, 42; 90 CM, I, 10, 11; 60 CN, I, 34, 37, 38, 39, 40, 43; V, 40, 44, 46; 26 CP, C, 61. ANQ-M, État civil, Catholiques, Notre-Dame de Montréal, 29 janv. 1736, 4 août 1763, 17 oct. 1768, 27 oct. 1793, 28 juill. 1800; Greffe de J.-G. Delisle, 6 avril 1789; Greffe de Pierre Panet, 14 avril 1758, 29 mars 1761. ANQ-Q, AP-P-11. ASQ, Doc. Faribault, no.268; Fonds Viger-Verreau, Carton 12, no.61; 17, nos.39–53; 18, no.67; 19, no.14; 47/16; Sér.O, 037, p.17; Lettres, T, 55, 61. AUM, P 58, Corr. générale, J.-B.-A. Adhémar à François Baby, 23 juill., 1er oct., 5 nov. 1770, 25 août 1771, 21 nov. 1776, 10 sept., 6 oct. 1777; J.-B.-A. Adhémar aux citoyens de Québec, 5 mars 1785; J.-F. Perrault à J.-N. Perrault, 30 oct. 1783. BL, Add. MSS 21724, p.457; 21736, p.105; 21866, pp.69–72, 74, 77, 82–86, 132–33, 136, 179–80, 184–85. PRO, CO 42/16, pp.203–4 (PAC transcripts); 42/44, ff.178–80; 42/46, ff.46–60. Ste Ann's Parish (Mackinac Island, Mich.), Registre des baptêmes, mariages et sépultures de Sainte-Anne-de-Michillimakinak (mfm. at Dept. of State, Lansing, Mich., and at PAC).

Doc. relatifs à l'hist. constitutionnelle, 1759–91 (Shortt et Doughty; 1921), II, 749–51, 779. Pierre Du Calvet, *Appel à la justice de l'État* . . . (Londres, 1784), 253. [Francis Maseres], *Questions sur lesquelles on souhaite de sçavoir les réponses de monsieur Adhémar et de monsieur De Lisle et d'autres habitants de la province de Québec* (Londres, 1784). "MM. Adhémar et Delisle," *BRH*, XII (1906), 325–41, 353–71. "La mission de MM. Adhémar et Delisle en Angleterre en 1783–84," *BRH*, XXXII (1926), 617–31. Wis., State Hist. Soc., *Coll.*, XIX (1910), 65. *Quebec Gazette*, 24 Nov., 1 Dec. 1766, 30 Oct. 1783, 16 June, 19 Aug. 1791, 11 Dec. 1800. Ivanhoë Caron, "Inv. de la corr. de Mgr Briand," ANQ *Rapport*, 1929–30, 127–28, 131–33; "Inv. de la corr. de Mgr Hubert et de Mgr Bailly de Messein," ANQ *Rapport*, 1930–31, 223; "Inventaire de la correspondance de Mgr Joseph-Octave Plessis, archevêque de Québec," ANQ *Rapport*, 1928–29, 174, 181; "Inv. de la corr. de Mgr Mariaucheau D'Esgly," ANQ *Rapport*, 1930–31, 186, 191. Le Jeune, *Dictionnaire*, I, 25–26. Massicotte, "Répertoire des engagements pour l'Ouest," ANQ *Rapport*, 1931–32, 247. PAC *Rapport*, 1890, 144, 146, 150.

Georges Bellerive, *Délégués canadiens-français en Angleterre, de 1763 à 1867* . . . (Québec, [1913]), 70–87. Michel Bibaud, *Histoire du Canada, et des Canadiens, sous la domination anglaise* (Montréal, 1844; repr. East Ardsley, Wakefield, Eng., and New York, 1968), 85–86. Thomas Chapais, *Cours d'histoire du Canada* (8v., Québec et Montréal, 1919–34), I, 235–37. A.-H. Gosselin, *L'Église du Canada après la Conquête*, II, 195–99, 201, 203–5, 263, 281. Lemieux, *L'établissement de la première prov. eccl.*, 15, 17–19, 22–23, 281, 283. Neatby, *Quebec*, 196–99. W. R. Riddell, *The life of William Dummer Powell, first judge at Detroit and fifth chief justice of Upper Canada* (Lansing, Mich., 1924), 43–44, 177–81. J.-E. Roy, *Hist. du notariat*, I, 152. Sulte, *Mélanges historiques* (Malchelosse), I, 114–15. Tousignant, "La genèse et l'avènement de la constitution de 1791," 272–95. Michel Brunet, "La Conquête anglaise et la déchéance de la bourgeoisie canadienne (1760–1793)," *Amérique française* (Montréal), XIII (1955), no.2, 75–79. Fernand Ouellet, "Mgr Plessis et la naissance d'une bourgeoisie canadienne (1797–1810)," SCHÉC *Rapport*, 23 (1955–56), 96. Benjamin Sulte, "La délégation envoyée en Angleterre en 1783," *BRH*, VII (1901), 213–16.

ADRAWANAH. *See* OTTROWANA

AGASHAWA. *See* EGUSHWA

AGMABESH. *See* AKOMÁPIS

AIDE-CRÉQUY, JEAN-ANTOINE, parish priest and artist; b. 5 April 1749 at Quebec, son of Louis Aide-Créquy, a mason, and Marie-Hélène Lefebvre; d. 6 Dec. 1780 at Quebec.

Jean-Antoine Aide-Créquy was educated, at least in part, at the Séminaire de Québec: the seminary records note under the date 18 Nov. 1768, "it has been decided that . . . Créquy should enter [his year of] philosophy next Easter if [he is] ready." He received the tonsure in the chapel of the seminary on 7 Dec. 1771 and minor orders two weeks later. Made subdeacon in 1772 and deacon the following year, he was ordained priest on 24 Oct. 1773 and given responsibility for the parish of Baie-Saint-Paul, to which he went at the beginning of November. Bishop BRIAND approved of Aide-Créquy's appointment to this parish, which since the death of its priest in 1771 had been ministered to by Jean-Jacques Berthiaume, parish priest of Les Éboulements and Île aux Coudres. On 8 Nov. 1773 Briand wrote to Father Berthiaume: "I was very glad that Providence sent you M. Créquy as your neighbour; he is a reliable man and, I hope, will be a good priest and a dedicated missionary; [also] because I knew you liked him and had ties with his family; now I can rest content about this corner of my diocese which has always caused me a good deal of anxiety.'' In addition to the parish of Baie-Saint-Paul, Abbé Aide-Créquy was to look after the mission of Saint-François-Xavier-de-la-Petite-Rivière. As early as 22 Dec. 1773 he informed the bishop that he intended to build a new church for his parish which would incorporate the reredos of the existing church. This project in fact was completed five years later.

Aide-Créquy's correspondence with Bishop Briand reveals that he had little concern for his own comfort, being content with the bare necessities of life; he took a genuine interest in parish affairs and had great sympathy for his parishioners. He was the first parish priest to keep regular accounts for Baie-Saint-Paul. He provided a bell for his church and bought a small boat so that he could go to Petite-Rivière. His sacristan and factotum, Élie Mailloux, appears to have been an educated, intelligent man. In 1777 Aide-Créquy acted as middleman between the priests of the Séminaire de Québec and the labourers who were repairing its mill at Baie-Saint-Paul. The seminary granted some land to his parish council in exchange. In ill health, the young priest left his parish in June 1780; on 6 December, in retirement at Quebec, he died prematurely.

Always in precarious health, Aide-Créquy had perhaps overestimated his own strength in dedicating himself not only to his ministry but also to painting. As an artist he tried to meet the needs of parishes and communities now unable to import religious works from France. In particular, he executed a number of large paintings for neighbouring parishes. Their needs were no doubt an important stimulus to the development of both his art and his career. All his paintings have religious subjects, inspiration having come from engravings or paintings to which he had access in the colony. In his brief career he produced a respectable number of artistic works of which a dozen are known today. The earliest, *Vierge à l'enfant*, which is in the Hôtel-Dieu of Quebec, was painted in 1774. His large paintings include *Vision de sainte Angèle* (1775) in the Ursuline convent of Quebec, an *Annonciation* (1776) in the church at L'Islet, *Vision de saint Roch* (1777) in the church of Saint-Roch-des-Aulnaies, *Saint Louis tenant la couronne d'épines*, done in 1777 for the church of Saint-Louis on Île aux Coudres and now kept in the bishop's palace in Chicoutimi, and *Saint Joachim offrant la Vierge au Très-Haut* (1779) in the church at Saint-Joachim. For the latter parish he may have painted two other works which are supposed to have been replaced in 1869 by works of Antoine Plamondon*. Two others were destroyed by fires: *Sainte Famille* at Notre-Dame cathedral in Quebec in 1866, and *Saint Pierre et saint Paul* in the Baie-Saint-Paul church in 1962. Two paintings in the Hôtel-Dieu of Quebec, *Saint Pierre* and *Saint Paul*, are also attributed to him.

Aide-Créquy was skilful at presenting persons in paintings in effective relief, his scenes had good perspective, and he could catch the play of light and shade. His sense of colour was usually sure, his brush strokes deft, and his handling of impasto well judged. The paintings drawn from engravings were often more expressive than the engravings themselves. These technical and pictorial characteristics make it impossible to accept the hypothesis that Aide-Créquy was self-taught. It is quite likely he received his training before he became a priest. He was not always successful, however, in blending elements taken from different paintings into a happy composition, and in devising backgrounds himself he showed a taste for heavy architectural settings. It must be emphasized that he was not a slavish imitator. Abbé Charles Trudelle's comment is a valid assessment: ''He was not a Raphaël, yet one can see that he had taste and aptitude for his art.''

JOHN R. PORTER

AAQ, 12 A, C, 124–25, 137, 139; 61 CD, Les Éboulements, I, 13; Baie-Saint-Paul, I, 7–8. ANQ-Q, État civil, Catholiques, Notre-Dame de Québec, 6 avril 1749, 8 déc. 1780. Archives paroissiales, Saints Pierre et Paul (Baie-Saint-Paul, Qué.), Charles Trudelle *et al.*, ''Recueil de lettres et de notes concernant la paroisse de la Baie St Paul, 1859 . . . ,'' 18–20, 330–31, 334–35 (manuscrit). ASQ, MSS, 13, 11 oct., 18 nov. 1778; Séminaire, 152, nos.368, 379a. IBC, Centre de documentation, Fonds Morisset, Dossier J.-A. Aide-Créquy. Allaire, *Dictionnaire*, I, 8. *Canada, an encyclopædia of the country: the Canadian dominion considered in its historic relations, its natural resources, its material progress, and its national development*, ed. J. C. Hopkins (6v., Toronto, 1898–1900), IV, 354. P.-V. Charland, ''Notre-Dame de Québec: le nécrologe de la crypte,'' *BRH*, XX, 244. J. R. Harper, *Early painters and engravers in Canada* (Toronto, [1971]). Musée du Québec, *Peinture traditionnelle du Québec* (Québec, 1967), 10–11. Thomas O'Leary, *Catalogue of the Chateau Ramezay museum and portrait gallery* (Montreal, 1901), 35. P.-G. Roy, *Fils de Québec*, II, 86–87. Tanguay, *Dictionnaire*. Claude Thibault, *Trésors des communautés religieuses de la ville de Québec* (Québec, 1973), 37–38, 88. *Treasures from Quebec* (Ottawa and Quebec, 1965), no.56.

Léon Bélanger, *L'église de L'Islet, 1768–1968*

(L'Islet, Qué., 1968), 49–50. [Georges Bellerive], *Les Éboulements et l'Île-aux-Coudres; souvenirs et impressions d'écrivains sur ces deux beaux endroits historiques* (s.l., s.d.), 11. Léonce Boivin, *Dans nos montagnes (Charlevoix)* (Les Éboulements, Qué., 1941), 115. Jean Des Gagniers, *L'Île-aux-Coudres* ([Montréal], 1969), 76–79. J. R. Harper, *La peinture au Canada des origines à nos jours* (Québec, 1966), 37–39. Alexis Mailloux, *Histoire de l'Île-aux-Coudres depuis son établissement jusqu'à nos jours, avec ses traditions, ses légendes, ses coutumes* (Montréal, 1879), 61; *Promenade autour de l'Île-aux-Coudres* (Sainte-Anne-de-la-Pocatière [La Pocatière], Qué., 1880), 52. Gérard Morisset, *Coup d'œil sur les arts*, 54; *Peintres et tableaux* (Québec, 1936), I, 67–69; *La peinture traditionnelle au Canada français* (Ottawa, 1960), 52–54; *La vie et l'œuvre du frère Luc* (Québec, 1944), 37. Luc Noppen, *Notre-Dame-des-Victoires à la Place royale de Québec* (Québec, 1974), 24. P.-G. Roy, *Les cimetières de Québec* (Lévis, Qué., 1941), 34. Nérée Tremblay *St-Pierre et St-Paul de la Baie St-Paul* (Québec, 1956), 97–98. Charles Trudelle, *Trois souvenirs* (Québec, 1878), 115–16. P.-V. Charland, "Les ruines de Notre-Dame; l'ancien intérieur," *Le Terroir* (Québec), V (1924–25), 153–57, 162. Hormidas Magnan, "Peintres et sculpteurs du terroir," *Le Terroir*, III (1922–23), 342–54. Gérard Morisset, "Un curé-peintre, l'abbé Aide-Créqui," *L'Événement* (Québec), 20 déc. 1934; "La peinture en Nouvelle-France; Sainte-Anne-de-Beaupré," *Le Canada français* (Québec), 2e sér., XXI (1933–34), 209–26. P.-G. Roy, "Jean-Antoine Aide-Créquy," *BRH*, XX (1914), 297; "La peinture au Canada sous le Régime français," *BRH*, VI (1900), 150–53.

AILLEBOUST DE CERRY (Cery, Cerry d'Argenteuil), PHILIPPE-MARIE D', mariner and merchant; b. 21 Oct. 1702 at Montreal (Que.), son of Pierre d'Ailleboust* d'Argenteuil and Marie-Louise Denys de La Ronde; m. 27 June 1735 Marie-Madeleine Chéron at Charlesbourg (Que.); four of their 14 children survived infancy; d. 14 April 1787 at Loches, France.

Although he held letters of nobility and his father had been a senior officer in the colonial regulars, Philippe-Marie d'Ailleboust de Cerry became a sea captain and merchant. His older brothers Louis, Sieur d'Argenteuil, and Hector-Pierre, Sieur de Saint-Vilmé, had been introduced to the sea by their redoubtable uncle, Simon-Pierre Denys* de Bonaventure, and during the early 1720s it was they who initiated Philippe-Marie. By 1728 he had command of his own ship, the 60-ton *Aimable*, on voyages from Quebec to Île Royale (Cape Breton Island) and he soon began to sail between Louisbourg, Île Royale, and Martinique. During the 1730s he sailed continuously between Quebec and France, and from Quebec to Île Royale and the West Indies. Whether he was a good businessman is questionable; an associate in Martinique complained that Cerry and Argenteuil were unfamiliar with commercial practices and failed to keep their books in order. Nevertheless his ventures represented colonial attempts to gain some freedom from metropolitan domination of Canadian trade. In 1739, for example, Cerry commanded a ship owned by Pierre Trottier* Desauniers, his wife's brother-in-law, on a voyage to Bordeaux and returned to Quebec via Martinique with a cargo from Provence. By that time he had become one of the more experienced masters and pilots on the St Lawrence, and in 1741 he was recommended for the position of port captain at Quebec. He did not receive the appointment and continued as a sea captain, frequently commanding ships owned by Trottier Desauniers.

During the War of the Austrian Succession Cerry served courageously. In 1744 he built and organized a system of fire beacons along the St Lawrence between Île Saint-Barnabé, off Rimouski, and Pointe-Lévy (Lauzon and Lévis) to warn of any British attack. Early the next year he carried dispatches to France and returned to Quebec in time to sail again in December with news of the deteriorating situation in the colony. In June 1746 he took part in carrying the Canadian expedition under Jean-Baptiste-Nicolas-Roch de Ramezay to Acadia. Later in the summer, while making a second voyage with supplies, he was trapped off Cap Des Rosiers, near Gaspé, by American privateers; he ran his ship aground and burnt it to prevent it from falling into enemy hands. He made his way to France late the same year and was still there at the beginning of 1748 when he was appointed port captain of Quebec in acknowledgment of his recent services to the crown. On his way to take up his duties he was captured by the British and reached Canada only in the summer of 1749.

His post offered many challenges. Nothing had been done to improve navigation of the St Lawrence since the death of port captain Richard Testu* de La Richardière eight years before. Of Cerry's immediate predecessors in office, the first had died at sea shortly after being appointed and the second, Charles Latouche* MacCarthy, had never taken up the post. But although Cerry remained in office until the end of the régime he viewed it as a sinecure. His attempt in 1749 to increase his income by charging anchorage fees was rejected and this setback may have dissuaded him from working. A second port officer, Gabriel Pellegrin, was named in 1751 and Cerry turned to his own interests. He clearly had the continuing support of the governor and intendant, who objected on his behalf when his assistant was elevated to fire-ship captain, a rank that Cerry did not enjoy. Although Cerry was a member of the council of war which recommended the capitulation of Quebec in 1759 [*see* Jean-Baptiste-Nicolas-Roch de Ramezay], he appears to have played no role in the Seven Years' War.

Evidence of Cerry's various commercial interests is limited. In 1738 he is known to have become associated with Abbé Louis Lepage* de Sainte-Claire in an abortive attempt to establish an ironworks. He may also have tried his hand at the timber trade. He acquired an arriere-fief from the seigneurs of Île-Jésus in 1739 but three years later the land was reunited to the seigneury owing to Cerry's failure to encourage settlement. His wife, the youngest daughter of a member of the Conseil Supérieur, was also the half-sister of Charles Chéron, a Quebec ship's captain who often sailed to Île Royale and Labrador, and in 1753 Cerry obtained a nine-year grant of a large concession at Saint-Augustin, on the Labrador coast, together with the trading, sealing, and fishing rights that had formerly belonged to Chéron.

The conquest apparently destroyed Cerry's fortunes. His wife had died in 1758 and in 1761 he departed Canada with his two sons. He joined the colony of expatriate Canadians in Touraine and the next year acquired a pension of 600 *livres* that became his sole support for the next quarter century. He returned to Canada in 1763 to collect his two daughters and a niece, who had been boarding with the Ursulines, and placed them in a convent near Paris. For his sons he obtained commissions in the Légion de Saint-Domingue but they died on the island (now Hispaniola) a few years later. Towards the end of his life, as the number of expatriates dwindled, Cerry moved to Loches where the largest group lived, and there he ended his days a leading member of the tiny community.

JAMES S. PRITCHARD

AN, Col., C[11A], 36, f.165; 46, f.300; 63, f.218; 75, f.92; 81, f.300; 91; 121, f.102; C[11E], 11; E, 2 (dossier Ailleboust de Cerry); 67 (dossier Cerry); F[2B], 11; Section Outre-mer, G[1], 466, no.3. PAC, MG 24, L3, pp.1270, 1314. *Inv. de pièces du Labrador* (P.-G. Roy), I. *NYCD* (O'Callaghan and Fernow), X, 55ff. Godbout, "Nos ancêtres," ANQ *Rapport*, 1951–53, 470. P.-G. Roy, *Inv. concessions*, I; *Inv. jug. et délib., 1717–60*, IV. Ægidius Fauteux, *La famille d'Aillebout: étude généalogique et historique* (Montréal, 1917).

AILLEBOUST DE LA MADELEINE, FRANÇOIS-JEAN-DANIEL D', merchant-voyageur; b. 7 Oct. 1702 in Montreal (Que.), son of Jean-Baptiste d'Ailleboust* Des Muceaux and Anne Le Picard; m. 24 Nov. 1732 Marie-Charlotte Godefroy de Linctot in Montreal; d. 23 July 1793 at Pointe-aux-Trembles, Montreal Island.

François-Jean-Daniel d'Ailleboust de La Madeleine belonged to a section of the Canadian nobility that in the 18th century, without relinquishing its class privileges and sometimes even because of them, gained a living from the fur trade. He did not own property from which he could draw a substantial income, and his chances of becoming an officer, the most prestigious of careers, were slim because of the limited number of commissions available. Thus he became a voyageur and then a merchant-voyageur. From 1731 to about 1754, by himself or in partnership, he directed some ten trading trips to Michilimackinac (Mackinaw City, Mich.) and Michipicoton (Michipicoten River, Ont.), almost all financed by important Montreal merchant-outfitters such as François Foucher*, Alexis Lemoine*, *dit* Monière, and Ignace GAMELIN.

La Madeleine was thus one of the agents who obtained trade goods on credit, hired a crew for one or more canoes, and left each summer for the western posts. In these enterprises he was first in partnership, from 1731 to 1736, with two of his brothers, Nicolas-Marie d'Ailleboust Des Muceaux and Jean-Baptiste-Alphonse d'Ailleboust de La Boulasserie. Then from 1737 at least until 1742 he was associated with two other brothers, Pierre-Joseph d'Ailleboust de Manthet and Ignace-René d'Ailleboust de Périgny, and after that with Louis Gastineau de Sainte-Marie, to whom Governor Charles de Beauharnois* had granted the trading rights at the post at Michipicoton in 1747. Finally, in 1750 he and Manthet formed a new company with an initial capital of 12,500 *livres*; this company was dissolved four years later. In 1757 he signed more fur-trade contracts, but he seems to have retired from the business shortly afterwards.

His activities as a merchant-voyageur had not led him to give up hope of becoming an officer in the colonial regular troops. He was nearly 40, however, when he first had the chance to take up this career; in 1742 he was a cadet with the Michilimackinac garrison. At that time he already had three children, so that, according to his superior officers, he was "forced to follow the fur trade to support them." Perhaps family obligations became too heavy for this would-be officer, or perhaps he was afraid of being transferred to a garrison less convenient for his trading activities than Michilimackinac. In any case he never rose in the military hierarchy.

La Madeleine spent his later years at Pointe-aux-Trembles. In February 1759 he and his brother Manthet had bought a piece of property there on which was built a modest house of squared timbers (*pièces sur pièces*). Twelve years later he bought his brother's share and became sole owner.

HÉLÈNE PARÉ

AN, Col., D^{2C}, 43. ANQ-M, Greffe de J.-B. Adhémar, 4 juin 1732; 12 juin 1733; 9, 27, 28 juin 1747; 9, 10 juill. 1747; 1er mai 1750; Greffe d'Henri Bouron, 11 juin 1750, nos.53, 54; Greffe de L.-C. Danré de Blanzy, 23 juin 1741, 13 juin 1745, 1er févr. 1759; Greffe d'Antoine Foucher, 28 juill. 1767; Greffe de N.-A. Guillet de Chaumont, 28 juin 1737. Archives paroissiales, Notre-Dame (Montréal), Registre des baptêmes, mariages et sépultures, 1702; Saint-Enfant-Jésus (Pointe-aux-Trembles, Qué.), Registre des baptêmes, mariages et sépultures, 1793, f.18. ASSM, 24, Dossier 6. Ste Ann's Parish (Mackinac Island, Mich.), Registre des baptêmes, mariages et sépultures de Sainte-Anne-de-Michillimakinak (mfm. at PAC, MG 8, G17). [G.-]J. Brassier, *Montréal en 1781, déclaration du fief et seigneurie de l'isle de Montréal au papier terrier du domaine de sa majesté en la province de Québec . . .*, Claude Perrault, édit. (Montréal, 1969), 136. Massicotte, "Répertoire des engagements pour l'Ouest," ANQ *Rapport*, 1929–30, 1930–31. Ægidius Fauteux, *La famille d'Aillebout: étude généalogique et historique* (Montréal, 1917).

AITKEN (Aitkin), ALEXANDER, surveyor; probably b. at Berwick-upon-Tweed, England, son of David Aitken and his wife, who may have been named Catherine; d. 1799 at Kingston, Upper Canada.

Raised in northern England and in Scotland, Alexander Aitken was trained as a surveyor, probably by his father. The date of his arrival in Canada is not known. Late in 1784 he was made a deputy surveyor at Cataraqui (Kingston, Ont.); his territory comprised the north shore of Lake Ontario. When what is now southern Ontario was divided into four districts in 1788, Aitken stayed on as deputy surveyor at Kingston, the district town of the new Mecklenburg (after 1792 Midland) District, but he continued to work in that part of the Nassau (Home) District which had been his responsibility before 1788. In 1792 he was transferred to the surveyor general's office, created that year for the new province of Upper Canada, but the nature of his duties did not change. He worked with the land board of the Mecklenburg District from its creation in 1788 until its abolition in 1794.

As deputy surveyor Aitken's duties included continuing the actual surveys of his area, usually a concession or two at a time, establishing township boundaries, drawing plans for the government, and assigning lots, principally to loyalists in the early years. The territory Aitken surveyed began at the western end of what is now Leeds County and included the present Frontenac, Lennox and Addington, and Hastings counties, basically in the first two rows of townships from the waterfront. John COLLINS had already surveyed the Kingston town plot but Aitken resurveyed parts of it, laid out the town extensions, and in 1790 made the surveys of Point Frederick. He also surveyed much of Prince Edward County and the islands east of it.

In the Home District to the west Aitken surveyed the first concessions of Murray Township in Northumberland County, the Presqu'ile peninsula, and the town plot for Newcastle. His most important work to the west, however, concerned the plans for York (Toronto). In 1788 he had prepared the first plan for Lord Dorchester [Carleton*], and when John Graves Simcoe* was appointed lieutenant governor of the new province, Aitken accompanied him on his expedition north to what is now Lake Simcoe, the shores of which he then surveyed. In 1793 he prepared a new town plan of York and surveyed the shores of Burlington Bay (Hamilton harbour) and the start of Dundas Street to the west. The following year saw him doing further work along Yonge Street, north of York, and at Penetanguishene harbour.

Much of his surveying was extremely frustrating. Basic equipment was frequently unavailable, pay for the crew was slow in coming, and settlers were dissatisfied with their locations. Poor farmland was a problem. Hungerford Township, for example, was all rock and swamp and he was afraid to offer it to anyone. Inaccuracy, or claims of inaccuracy, in surveys also caused problems. Aitken had to investigate claims that his predecessors had erred in the survey of Fredericksburgh (North and South Fredericksburgh) Township, and in 1797 he had to recommend the resurvey of Richmond Township. Peter Russell* claimed that Aitken and Augustus Jones* had made errors in the town plan of York. When Aitken was dying, however, Chief Justice John Elmsley* attested to his general competence, commenting that his death would be "a severe misfortune" for the public service.

Little is known of Aitken's personal life. Though not highly paid, like all surveyors he received a number of land grants; he obtained 1,500 rural acres and a town plot in Kingston. When in that city he attended St George's Church, to which he made various donations. The constant movement necessary to his work seems to have left little time for other interests. The conditions of his work were hardly conducive to good health, and he complained of "intermitting fever," possibly malaria; he hurt his chest in a fall from a carriole and by 1797 was suffering from tuberculosis. His burial in St George's cemetery (now St Paul's churchyard) took place on 1 Jan. 1800. He had never married and his land holdings passed to his father in Scotland.

FREDERICK H. ARMSTRONG

PAO, U.C., Lieutenant Governor's Office, letterbook, 1799–1800, John Elmsley to Peter Hunter, 12 Nov. 1799; RG 1, A-I-1, 1–3; A-I-6, 1–2, 30; A-II-1, 1; C-I-4, 40; CB-1, 9–11. Queen's University Archives (Kingston, Ont.), Hon. Richard Cartwright papers, account book, 1791–98; [E. E. Horsey], "Cataraqui, Fort Frontenac, Kingstown, Kingston" (typescript, 1937).

Correspondence of Lieut. Governor Simcoe (Cruikshank), II, 30, 71, 99, 111; III, 178, 263; V, 13, 14, 121, 163, 202, 237ff. *The correspondence of the Honourable Peter Russell, with allied documents relating to his administration of the government of Upper Canada . . .*, ed. E. A. Cruikshank and A. F. Hunter (3v., Toronto, 1932–36), I, 53, 65, 169–70, 226. *Kingston before War of 1812* (Preston), 107, 125, 130, 296. PAO *Report*, 1905, 310, 385, 389, 426, 458, 461–62, 466–68, 472, 495, 507. *Quebec Gazette*, 10 July 1788. *The town of York, 1793–1815; a collection of documents of early Toronto*, ed. E. G. Firth (Toronto, 1962), xxxii, xxxvi, 11, 14, 23, 37. F. M. L. Thompson, *Chartered surveyors, the growth of a profession* (London, 1968). D. W. Thomson, *Men and meridians: the history of surveying and mapping in Canada* (3v., Ottawa, 1966–69), I, 225–26, 231. "Alexander Aitken," Assoc. of Ont. Land Surveyors, *Annual report* (Toronto), 47 (1932), 100. Willis Chipman, "The life and times of Major Samuel Holland, surveyor-general, 1764–1801," *OH*, XXI (1924), 55–57.

AKOMÁPIS (also **Ackmobish** and **Agmabesh**), **NICHOLAS**, a Malecite captain; the name probably means the young snowshoer, although snowshoe strap is a possibility; fl. 1778–80 in the Saint John valley (N.B.).

During their war of independence the Americans persistently worked for an alliance with the Indians of the Saint John River and, encouraged by Chief Ambroise SAINT-AUBIN, Malecites participated in Jonathan Eddy*'s attack on Fort Cumberland (near Sackville, N.B.) in 1776 and John Allan*'s expedition to the Saint John valley in 1777. The concerned British established Fort Howe at the mouth of the river in the fall of 1777 [*see* Gilfred STUDHOLME] and in July 1778 appointed a deputy superintendent of Indian affairs for the area. Their concern was justified, for in August the Indians declared war on the British and ordered them from the area. Attempting conciliation, Nova Scotia's superintendent of Indian affairs, Michael FRANCKLIN, called a conference at Menagouèche (Saint John, N.B.). Nicholas Akomápis was one of four captains who attended, along with the Malecite chiefs Pierre TOMAH and François Xavier and eight principal Malecites. Also present were 12 Micmacs and the missionary Joseph-Mathurin BOURG.

The main meeting occurred on 24 Sept. 1778. The Indians took an oath of allegiance to the king and signed a treaty agreeing to compensate the British for property stolen or destroyed, to remain neutral in the war, and to notify the British of American activities in the area. They solemnized these promises with a wampum belt. In return the British presented the Indians with gifts, introduced Bourg as the missionary who had been promised them, and agreed to build a trading post on the Saint John River. The following day the Indians visited a British ship in the harbour, where they drank the king's health. On 26 September they departed after a period of final speech-making, singing, and dancing.

Akomápis was somewhat prominent in events surrounding the treaty. Along with two other Indians he served as a courier for the British. His sincerity in signing the treaty is suggested by his subsequent pursuit of two British deserters and by his attempt with another Indian to capture the crew of an American whale-boat operating in the area. It may have been the latter incident which caused the British to have "a gold laced Hatt" made for him in September 1779. Other mention of Akomápis reveals him to have been involved, like many other Indians of the time, in the fur trade; he was compensated by the British in 1778 for three beaver traps stolen by soldiers. After 1779 little further mention of Akomápis appears in written records. Along with the other Malecites of the Saint John River he undoubtedly accepted gifts from the British once again in May 1780 in exchange for a promise to protect men cutting masts in the area.

Despite Akomápis' apparent loyalty to the British, he may have found it expedient to deal with the Americans as well. One "Nichola Agmabesh" and two of his sons appear on a 1780 list of "Indians . . . that are and have Been in the Service of the United States."

VIRGINIA P. MILLER

PANS, RG 1, 45, docs.65–66; 212, 6 Nov. 1778, p.355. *Military operations in eastern Maine and N.S.* (Kidder), 284. "Selections from the papers and correspondence of James White, esquire, A.D. 1762–1783," ed. W. O. Raymond, N.B. Hist. Soc., *Coll.*, I (1894–97), no.3, 306–40.

ALEYRAC, JEAN-BAPTISTE D', officer in the French regular army; b. 2 April 1737 in Saint-Pierreville (dept of Ardèche), France, son of Noé d'Aleyrac and Jeanne-Marie Vernhes; d. 1796 in France.

Jean-Baptiste d'Aleyrac was a provincial nobleman from a military family. In 1754 he enlisted as a volunteer in the Régiment de Languedoc and in May of the following year sailed to Canada as a lieutenant. In September he served in the battle of Lac Saint-Sacrement (Lake George, N.Y.). His leadership of a detachment there was later praised by LÉVIS because, unlike some of his fellow officers, he did not sound a false alarm when harassed by the British. He then saw action at Fort William Henry (also called Fort George; now Lake George, N.Y.) in August 1757 and at Fort Carillon (Ticonderoga, N.Y.) in July 1758. During the winter of 1758–59 he was in command at Bécancour (Que.), where one of his duties was to maintain good relations between the regulars and the local Canadians and Abenakis. He succeeded so well that the Abenakis adopted him and gave him the name Soleil.

By July 1759 d'Aleyrac had come to join the defence of Quebec, and in that month he fought in the battle of Montmorency. Wounded in August while on guard duty at Quebec, he was still able to participate in the battle on the Plains of Abraham on 13 September. In April 1760 he was at the battle of Sainte-Foy. He is credited with saving Lévis's life in a skirmish before the battle by holding off a party of 100 British with his command of 28 grenadiers. He was present at the capitulation of Montreal on 8 September and shortly afterwards returned to France.

D'Aleyrac, who was later described as "young and hare-brained," was thought to be somewhat hasty by his superior officers. Montcalm* called him "hot-headed" but thought he had winning ways and the potential to be a good officer. He appears to have served with some distinction during the campaigns of 1759, for he received both a promotion to grenadier lieutenant and a gratuity from Montcalm of 200 *livres*.

D'Aleyrac is of particular interest for the memoirs of his experiences in Canada written in the last years of his life. He had a more positive attitude towards the Canadians and Indians than many of his fellow officers [*see* Pierre-André GOHIN]. The Canadians he found to be healthy and tall, expert hunters and builders, and possessed of an excellent French and cuisine. Appreciative of the Indians' courage and honesty, he found their independence remarkable. He admitted that they tortured some of their prisoners but pointed out that they adopted most. Judging from d'Aleyrac's memoirs, he appears to have been good natured and to have adapted easily to the new world. His few criticisms were charitable, and his one complaint echoes that of many subsequent historians: the court nobility got all the honours and high commands, although the provincial noblemen did all the work and were the more meritorious.

One of the incidents d'Aleyrac relates in his memoirs concerns the night of 12–13 Sept. 1759 and Wolfe*'s approach on Quebec. He writes that he heard boats rowing back and forth and reported the fact to his superior, Captain Charles-François Auger de Marillac, who did not, however, consider the news important enough to transmit to higher authority. D'Aleyrac thought that in the ensuing battle on the Plains of Abraham Marillac let himself be killed out of shame. D'Aleyrac is the sole source for this incident, and one can only note in connection with it that he seems generally to have been fair minded and not given to bragging.

After his return to France d'Aleyrac served between 1765 and 1768 in the campaign in Corsica. He was promoted captain in 1768 and grenadier captain in 1781. The following year he received the cross of Saint-Louis. He apparently accepted the French revolution and was approved of by the government, for he was made lieutenant-colonel in 1792. Ill health forced him to retire the next year and he died in 1796 without issue.

SUSAN W. HENDERSON

[J.-B. d'Aleyrac], *Aventures militaires au XVIIIe siècle d'après les mémoires de Jean-Baptiste d'Aleyrac*, Charles Coste, édit. (Paris, 1935).

AD, Ardèche (Privas), État civil, Saint-Pierreville, 3 avril 1737. AMA, SHA, Y^b, 121–22 (copies at PAC). La Chesnaye-Desbois et Badier, *Dict. de la noblesse*. Claude de Bonnault, "Les aventures de M. d'Aleyrac," *BRH*, XLIV (1938), 52–58. Armand Yon, "La 'dolce vita' en Nouvelle-France à la veille de la guerre (1740–1758)," *Cahiers des Dix*, 37 (1972), 168–70.

ALLARD (Alard, Dalard) DE SAINTE-MARIE, PHILIPPE-JOSEPH D', officer in the colonial regular troops; b. between 1704 and 1708 at Plaisance (Placentia, Nfld), son of Jean-Joseph d'Allard* de Sainte-Marie and Marie-Anne de Tour de Sourdeval; m. 9 March 1739 Jeanne Jacau, sister of Louis-Thomas JACAU de Fiedmont, at Louisbourg, Île Royale (Cape Breton Island), and they had two daughters; m. secondly, 31 Jan. 1751, Angélique, daughter of Philippe Carrerot* and Marie-Thérèse Gaultier (Gauthier), at Louisbourg, and they had eight children; d. 1778 in Tonnay-Boutonne (dept of Charente-Maritime), France.

Philippe-Joseph d'Allard de Sainte-Marie's career was typical of the sons of Louisbourg officers: he entered the colonial regular troops at a young age, in 1720, and left Louisbourg only when forced to by the defeats of 1745 and 1758. Promoted first ensign in 1730, he served routinely in Michel de Gannes* de Falaise's company until 1733 when he was assigned "engineering duties" under Étienne Verrier*. In 1734 at Verrier's request he was posted to Île Saint-Jean (Prince Edward Island) to serve in an engineering capacity. He returned to Louisbourg that same year and in late 1736 was again sent to Île Saint-Jean with Robert Tarride* Duhaget, who was to relieve the ailing Jacques d'Espiet* de Pensens. Back at Louisbourg in 1738, Sainte-Marie began, rather unspectacularly, his long connection with the artillery when the acting governor François Le Coutre* de Bourville ordered him to assume command because the officer usually in charge was on leave. In 1739 Sainte-Marie was promoted lieutenant, and because he had improved the state of the batteries he continued to serve with the artillery.

Sainte-Marie had a younger brother, known as the Chevalier de Sainte-Marie, and the similarity of their early careers has caused some confusion. The Chevalier followed Philippe-Joseph into the service as a cadet in 1725, received an *expectative* of second ensign in 1728, and in 1730 filled the vacancy caused by his brother's promotion to first ensign. Although he had been sent to Quebec in 1736 for treatment of insanity, several remedies at Louisbourg having proved unsuccessful, he was promoted ensign in 1737. That year Governor Saint-Ovide [Monbeton*] asked that the Chevalier be placed in a hospital "with rooms for lunatics" in France. Because of his poverty the crown provided a pension of 300 *livres* for his support.

Philippe-Joseph's association with the artillery coincided with a concern for artillery reform in France and with Isaac-Louis de Forant*'s efforts to organize an artillery company at Louisbourg. Previously members of the colonial regular troops had cooperated with a few trained cannoneers recruited in Rochefort to man the fortress's batteries. Forant sent his proposal for a company to Versailles in October 1739 and ordered the immediate selection of trainees. Although the proposal was not approved until 1742 and did not take effect until 1 Jan. 1743, Sainte-Marie was chosen to command the company in November 1739. By October 1741 both the new unit and a gunnery school had been established. The artillerists were an élite corps. Not only did they have special quarters, but they were better paid (receiving special payments for exceptional marksmanship) and were exempt from many garrison duties. Worthy of particular notice is their unwillingness to participate in the 1744 mutiny of the garrison. Sainte-Marie's duties with the company and the school occupied much of his time. Because he was unable to supplement his salary by operating an officer's canteen, the crown approved a gratuity of 300 *livres* to offset the loss. In May 1743 he was promoted captain.

Sainte-Marie served in the first siege of Louisbourg but neither he nor his company was prominent in action. The ineffectiveness of their counter-battery fire, however, had little to do with the French defeat [*see* Louis Du Pont Duchambon]. Nor did it reflect upon Sainte-Marie's abilities. The Louisbourg fortifications had been designed to withstand a naval assault and were low lying. Elevation was of paramount importance in artillery exchange and once William Pepperrell*'s force had established its siege batteries on commanding ground, the best of gunners could not have overcome the disadvantage. Sainte-Marie's report of 26 June 1745 on the state of munitions in the fortress combined with Verrier's report on the fortifications was crucial to the resolve of Louis Du Pont Duchambon and the council of war, of which Sainte-Marie was a member, to capitulate. Sainte-Marie had held out little hope for further resistance. Most of the cannon were inoperative, only 47 barrels of powder were left, and the supply of fuses for the cannon was exhausted.

After the capitulation Sainte-Marie and his company were stationed at Rochefort. In 1747 Sainte-Marie commanded a battery on Governor Taffanel* de La Jonquière's flagship, the 64-gun *Sérieux*. In a furious encounter lasting eight hours with ships of Vice-Admiral George Anson's squadron on 14 May 1747, Sainte-Marie was wounded and taken prisoner. In February 1749 he was back at Rochefort maintaining his company in readiness for its return to Louisbourg. That March he was awarded the cross of Saint-Louis; it was noted that "he has always served with great zeal especially since the formation of the artillery company." He returned to Louisbourg in 1749 as the captain of the first of two artillery companies sent there. Sainte-Marie was wounded during the second siege of 1758, but again the artillery companies were not conspicuous in action. His whereabouts immediately after the siege are uncertain. In 1762 he was posted to Saint-Domingue (Hispaniola) with 120 men to augment the two artillery companies there. The following year illness necessitated his return to France and in 1765 he was in the garrison at Rochefort. That year he was commissioned lieutenant-colonel and retired with a large family, without fortune, on a pension of 1,800 *livres*. At least two of his sons became artillery officers.

Sainte-Marie was not a brilliant officer, but he was dedicated and hard-working. Unlike his father and many of his contemporaries in the Louisbourg officer corps, he avoided involvement in trade, which indicates a pride in his profession as artillerist in a fortress that always had more guns than men to man them.

TERRENCE MACLEAN

AN, Col., B, 57, ff.643, 763; 65, f.482v; 68, f.10; 72, f.15v; 76, f.24v; 90, f.49; 114, f.1; 152, f.267; 174, f.246v; C^{11B}, 18, ff.20, 57; 19, f.28; 21, ff.9–12, 38, 44, 51, 59, 63–64, 68; 22, ff.43, 114–15; 24, f.33; 27, ff.73, 87; D^{2C}, 1, f.21; 2, ff.71, 79, 117; 3, ff.113–17, 121, 131; 4, ff.6–7, 21, 42, 106–58; 47/4, pp.238, 260, 340, 376, 379; 48/1, pp.9–10, 28, 43; 48/3, p.582; 60, pp.17–18 (page references are to PAC transcripts); E, 3 (dossier Allard de Sainte-Marie); F^3, 50, f.319v; Section Outre-mer, G^1, 407, pièce 16; 408/1, ff.31, 97; 408/2, ff.16v–17; 409/2, ff.4v, 26v; 466, f.76.

Æ. Fauteux, *Les chevaliers de Saint-Louis*, 122. Frégault, *François Bigot*, I, 224–26. Francis Parkman, *A half-century of conflict* (5th ed., 2v., Boston, 1893), II, 317. Rawlyk, *Yankees at Louisbourg*, 145. R. J. Morgan and T. D. MacLean, "Social structure and life in Louisbourg," *Canada, an Hist. Magazine* (Toronto), 1 (June 1974), 67–69.

ALLINE, HENRY, evangelist, hymnist, and theologian; b. 14 June 1748 in Newport, Rhode Island, second son of William Alline and Rebecca Clark; d. 2 Feb. 1784 in North Hampton, New Hampshire.

Henry Alline was born into an old New England family which could trace its roots back to the arrivals on the *Mayflower*. His father, who was probably a miller, had resided in Boston – where Henry's mother became his second wife in 1738 – before moving to Newport, a seaport centre of 6,000 people and the second largest city of New England. In Newport young Henry attended the local "publick school," being, as he later wrote, "something forward in learning." Although his father had never farmed to any extent, the need to provide for a large family made particularly attractive Governor Charles Lawrence*'s announcements in 1758 and 1759 of free fertile land in Nova Scotia.

William Alline was in a group of 113 inhabitants of Rhode Island and Connecticut granted land for a settlement on the north bank of the Pisiquid (Avon) River, and in 1760, "after a long consultation," the family immigrated to what would become the township of Falmouth [*see* John HICKS]. There the Allines participated in the allocation of land in accordance with traditional New England custom and faced the rigours of pioneering settlements in North America. Young Henry was at first more concerned with the dangers from Indians than with the more prosaic difficulties of erecting buildings, clearing lands, and growing food.

Within a few years the settlement at Falmouth had overcome its birth-pangs and developed into a typical frontier agrarian community based upon subsistence agriculture. Three factors in this environment were of fundamental importance to Alline as he grew from adolescence to manhood. Together they produced constraints and an absence of secular opportunity for a bright and energetic lad who was a natural leader, thus encouraging a search for other outlets. In the first place, government policy in Nova Scotia sought successfully to eliminate as much local political initiative as possible by centralizing decision making in Halifax. Since there were no well-developed institutions of local government in Falmouth, young Henry could not look forward to any meaningful political career in his community. Secondly, the isolation and poverty characteristic of rural Nova Scotia meant that there were no local religious, cultural, or educational institutions which might have offered the young man some opportunities for cultivating his natural intellectual gifts. Finally, as the eldest son still living at home, Alline was expected by his aging parents to defer his own expectations and remain with them as manager of the family farm. A loving and dutiful son, not only was Henry unable to consider striking out on his own, but because of the size and relative poverty of the Alline household he could not begin to think about marrying and raising a family at home. Trapped thus by circumstances, Alline carried on his external life as a typical member of his community, sharing in both its work and its occasional pleasures. Internally, however, he became increasingly concerned about the state of his soul.

Even before the family had moved to Nova Scotia, Alline had been "moved upon by the spirit of God" and had passed several stages along the traditional New England road to conversion. He had attained Christian knowledge and recognized his own helplessness in the face of his Creator. In Falmouth, where he had little access to formal religious institutions, he continued to study on his own, reading "many experiences and accounts of a work of grace in the souls of others" in the popular devotional literature then available even to a pioneer population. As he grew older and became more involved with his peers in innocent recreation (which he would later label "frolicking and carnal mirth"), his parents discussed with him the "controverted points" of religion and spoke of the dangers of "carnal passions." Henry and his parents appear to have had the same concerns. Henry was experiencing the normal sexual urgings of the young male, and his parents worried not only about possible sin but about potential loss of the family mainstay. As one of the visions Alline recorded in his journal makes quite clear, he was forced to reject not only the possibility of marriage but female company as well.

For many years Alline wrestled constantly with his soul, "groaning under a load of guilt and darkness, praying and crying continually for mercy." Final assurance of conversion came on 26 March 1775, a Sunday with, as usual, "no preaching" in Falmouth. Henry wandered in the fields, returned to his house, picked up a Bible, and turned to the 38th Psalm. Shortly afterwards, he recorded, "redeeming love broke into my soul with repeated scriptures with such power, that my whole soul seemed to be melted down with love." Later he felt a call to "labour in the ministry and . . . preach the gospel." A decision to respond to this call would involve more than a year of intense agonizing.

In his journal Alline recorded the travails of this period of indecision in some detail. His initial response to the call had been "amen, Lord I'll go, I'll go, send me, send me," but a number of obstacles stood in his way. A critical one, of course, was the uncertainty resulting from the outbreak of the American rebellion against Britain. Henry had reached the point of conversion virtually on the eve of the battles of Lexington and Concord, and the period of his deliberation more or less coincided chronologically with the efforts of New England to expel Lieutenant-General Thomas GAGE's forces from Boston. Another difficulty was the long-engrained New England tradition of a learned ministry, which Alline and his parents respected. As Henry realized, though "it was true I had read and studied more than was common for one in my station," the attainment "was but small" and largely "acquired of myself without schooling." Finally, there was the problem of the family. As he commented, "my father's estate was not very large, and my parents being almost past labour, I had the whole care of these temporal concerns."

In October 1775 Henry tried to proceed to New England, which held a virtual monopoly in North America on the higher education he lacked, but the war intervened. The vessel he intended to sail on was seized by privateers, and while waiting for another ship he received word that his family had caught smallpox and desired his return to Falmouth. When the government decided the following month to call up part of the provincial militia under Henry Denny DENSON, an action which forced Nova Scotians to a conscious decision on their position *vis-à-vis* the war, Alline was "solicited by some of the officers to put in for a commission." Finding a religious justification for the neutrality in which many Nova Scotians took refuge, he rejected the offer on the grounds that his only commission should be one "from heaven to go forth, and enlist my fellow-mortals to fight under the banners of King Jesus." Alline had thus broken free of primary political allegiances to Britain, but the force of New England Puritan tradition remained. Symbolically, he broke with it on the first anniversary of the battles of Lexington and Concord. On 19 April 1776, the day he made his final decision to preach, he became an emancipated man, free to offer to others what he himself had found: a spiritual assurance which rejected and transcended the tribulations of the secular world, whether British or American. It was a message unmistakably Nova Scotian in its emphasis. For the next three years Alline confined his preaching to the area around Minas Basin, partly because of the uncertainties of war, but also because he still felt tied by family loyalties. Not until 6 April 1779 was he ordained an evangelist by three Annapolis valley churches, two of which he had played a part in organizing, and not until after the ordination did he preach beyond his immediate region.

No artist in pioneer Nova Scotia painted Henry Alline's portrait, and only one contemporary left a description of the evangelist, a man of "medium size, straight, thin of body, [with] light complexion, light curly hair, and dreamy blue eyes." In his later years Alline was increasingly affected by the consumption which ultimately killed him, and he undoubtedly showed the usual signs of it: a sickly pale physical appearance contrasting with a hyperactive, occasionally feverish, mental state. A consumptive mien would likely have added to his impact upon others, making him seem a Nova Scotian John the Baptist. The basis of Alline's success as an evangelist was not his physical appearance, however, but his command of the standard techniques of 18th-century revivalism. Alline's doctrine was more than a bit unusual. But his use of itinerant preaching, extemporaneous sermons directed at sudden conversions, lay involvement in religious services, emotional extravagance, and open confrontation with "opposers" marked him as heir to the transatlantic evangelical tradition of his day.

Like all great evangelists Alline eschewed settlement for himself and emphasized constant movement (or "itinerancy," as it was called at the time). From his base in Falmouth – for he never entirely freed himself from his family – he travelled for six to nine months of the year by horseback, boat, snowshoe, or on foot. During the course of his career he covered most of Nova Scotia and the settled parts of what is now New Brunswick, including many off-shore islands. In 1782 he visited St John's (Prince Edward) Island. Few of his meetings were held in church buildings, for even those that existed were usually closed to him. In any case, Alline did not regard church edifices, organizations, or finances as matters of much priority. In pioneer Nova Scotia he met the people on their own terms.

Alline's sermons were extemporaneous, but like most evangelists he had a standard series of points to make and a firm grasp of the biblical idiom in which to make them. Although his sermons undoubtedly became repetitive over time, he was seldom in one place long enough to bore his listeners. His emphasis, typical of contemporary revivalist preaching, was upon the need for the "new birth," an experience of emotional catharsis during which the individual came to accept Christ as his saviour. Alline was not solely a preacher, however. He understood the value both of prayer and of song. He encouraged the singing of hymns during and away from his meetings, and in the absence of hymnals wrote many hymns himself. A posthumous collection was reprinted at least four times in the United States, and several were included in the standard hymnals of the 19th century.

Singing was only one of the ways by which Alline encouraged his audience to participate in his religious services. A woman at Windsor, in a typical response, became "so overjoyed, that she could not contain, but cried out in divine raptures, with shouts of praise to God, and exhorting souls to come and share with her." Since Alline insisted that the "new birth" was the sole qualification for the ministry, he encouraged converted listeners to speak out and even to preach. Such lay participation was considered "levelling" by the clerical leaders of the organized churches and formed a large part of their criticism of his evangelical movement. But Alline thrived on opposition. He knew what he believed, was totally assured of the righteousness of his position, and was virtually unassailable within his own assumptions. One of his principal clerical opponents, the Congregationalist Jonathan Scott* of Yarmouth, insisted that Alline publicly overstated the vehemence of the opposition, which "gained him Pity, to all Appearance, and served to enflame the People, and promote the End, no Doubt, which he aimed at." Alline may not have been quite so consciously calculating, but whenever he met opposition he turned it to his advantage.

Alline seems almost instinctively to have concentrated his evangelical efforts on those segments of the Nova Scotia population most likely to be psychologically and emotionally receptive to his message. Rural and frontier Nova Scotia, particularly in those areas settled by Yankees, was experiencing both economic hardship and the psychological anxiety of rootlessness, heightened after the rebellion forced the breaking of close ties with New England. Many of the former New Englanders were familiar with the golden days of the Great Awakening of the 1740s and were favourably disposed to their reappearance. But more important, as one scholar has recently observed, in isolated and economically unstable communities, where status based on landownership and official position might be insecure, "religious status could become almost autonomously important, thus encouraging large numbers to seek piety and conversion." The revival in Nova Scotia did not distract the people from sympathy with the American rebellion, but it served as an emotional outlet for those unable to act politically. It perhaps also helped produce a primitive form of local patriotism based upon the uniqueness of Nova Scotia's "mission" in North America.

Alline's career as an evangelist was virtually coterminous with the American rebellion, and his ecclesiological principles fitted well into the uncertainties of those years of crisis and chaos. Not particularly interested in institutions, he organized a number of ephemeral churches: two in the Minas region, one in Annapolis County, and others in Liverpool and Maugerville, all areas in which traditional churches were weak or absent. The revival in Nova Scotia did not so much compete with existing religion as move into a void of spiritual leadership at a critical period, poverty and the confusion of the war years having driven most of the settled clergy away. Alline's New Light churches were organized around his insistence upon the crisis conversion, and partially reflected his beliefs. Only those who had enjoyed "a Work of Grace in their Hart" were admitted to membership. With the exception of the church at Horton (Wolfville region), which was firmly set against infant baptism, the New Light churches accepted Alline's view that modes and standards of baptism were matters of indifference to the true Christian. Similarly, financial support for the pastor, in accordance with Alline's wishes, was a voluntary matter reserved to the individual's own conscience. Alline had no interest in material things, and at his death his personal effects consisted of "a horse and sleigh, his apparel, and about twelve dollars in money." Nor did he have much interest in matters of routine organization. Although the New Light churches were well adapted to a period of crisis, they found it difficult, lacking a formal structure, to adjust to less chaotic conditions. Alline both created and unified the movement in Nova Scotia, but it was an inherently unstable and singularly personal affair, unlikely to survive him. Except for John Payzant* and Thomas Handley Chipman, he had few personal followers who undertook a public ministry.

Perhaps the most controversial aspect of Alline's work, then and since, has been his theology. Given his lack of and ultimate hostility to formal education, the primitive nature of the environment in which he lived, and the evangelical pietism which was his basic emphasis, one might have anticipated that Alline would have been a typical anti-intellectual revivalist, the sort against whom the opponents of revival always inveighed. Instead, he made a serious effort to provide an intellectual framework for his insights into the nature of God, man, and their relationship. For his efforts he has received little commendation. John Wesley, sent Alline's writings by the Nova Scotia Methodist leader William Black*, pronounced them "miserable jargon," and most subsequent commentators have agreed. The fundamental problem was Alline's lack of intellectual sophistication, a naïvety that led him, in ignorance of the difficulties, to attempt far more than was wise. The obscure, self-educated young Nova Scotian sought single-handed not only to overthrow the hoary theology of Calvinism, but to replace it with a spirit of existential mysticism far easier to experience than to expound. Alline lacked the tools of imagery which men like William Blake and the 16th-century German cobbler Jacob Boehme enjoyed, but his vision of God and the world was remarkably similar to theirs.

Alline's theological formulations, expounded principally in the first 200 pages of his major work, *Two mites on some of the most important and much disputed points of divinity . . .* (published in Halifax in 1781 by Anthony HENRY), began with his own experiences. Isolated and self-educated as he was, Alline was unable to reconcile the doctrines of Calvinism, even as modified by New England Puritanism, with what had happened to him. For Alline, the central point is that God is Love. If God was loving, then the harsh and just deity of New England, who chose only some to be saved, was not credible. Alline found an intellectual system which rejected Calvinism in the writings of the 18th-century Jacobite Anglican, William Law. Although Law's earlier work influenced all evangelicals, only Alline seems to have followed him in adopting the mysticism of Jacob Boehme.

In *Two mites*, Alline insisted that God is good and that since man was himself responsible for the fall from grace, he was also capable of achieving his own redemption. Alline's position came close to an enunciation of universal salvation, though he did not insist that all would be saved, but only that all could be saved. However controversial, such thinking was far more comprehensible than the mysticism of some of Alline's other writings, especially in the concluding pages of *Two mites* and in the pamphlet *The anti-traditionist* (Halifax, [1783?]). Here Alline wrote about the "everlasting Outbirth" which transcended the created universe, and attempted to verbalize his feelings about God. In his published critique of Alline, Jonathan Scott accused the evangelist of appealing to the "Passions of the Reader, especially the young, ignorant and inconsistent, who are influenced more by the Sound and Gingle of the words." The charge echoed those made against Boehme and Blake.

Not surprisingly, given his own experience and the environment in which he functioned, Alline's doctrine was not only mystical, but ascetic, egalitarian, and other-worldly. Because the material world was fallen nature, the human body was naturally sinful and required mortification; Alline inveighed against "frolicking," drinking, horse-racing, and other forms of worldly pleasure. Although his asceticism may have been too difficult for most Nova Scotians to emulate, many found his attitudes appealing. His belief that all mankind was capable of salvation suggested that all men were equal in the sight of God, and both this conviction and his emphasis on salvation in another world had a powerful attraction for a frontier population in time of secular crisis.

Nevertheless, Alline's efforts at articulating his intellectual position, beginning with the publication of *Two mites*, marked a turning point in his ministry. Most of the churches he founded concurred with his beliefs about church practice, but they drew up statements of doctrine which in their traditional Puritanism virtually denied Alline's emerging position. In April 1781 one of the churches which had ordained him in 1779 admonished Alline for "Publishing Erronious principles in print," and many among his followers found his theological position difficult to accept. Other opposition to Alline grew as his evangelical territory widened and became more stable following the conclusion of peace between Britain and the United States. Always concerned to expand his mission, Alline started for New England late in 1783. He died early in 1784 at North Hampton, New Hampshire. The location of his death symbolized the future direction of his immediate influence, for it was not far from the home of Benjamin Randall, founder of the Freewill Baptist movement in the United States based largely upon Alline's ideas. Most of the churches Alline had founded in Nova Scotia and New Brunswick either collapsed or went over to Baptists who rejected his anti-Calvinistic theology.

Henry Alline has never been completely neglected by Maritime historians, particularly those writing within the traditions of denominational history, but his career and activities have taken on a new importance in recent years, as evidenced in the many studies of them which have appeared since 1945. The new interest reflects a changing emphasis in historical scholarship, away from the study of formalized and centralized élites and their institutions and toward the understanding of the lives, thoughts, and aspirations of ordinary people. The Great Awakening in Nova Scotia is no longer seen either as a curious aberration from the progressive development of the Maritimes or as merely providing the origins of later religious institutions in the region. It is now recognized as a popular movement, indeed the major popular movement of its time. Henry Alline, as its early leader, has begun to take on the character of a folk hero, articulating the concerns of a perplexed people attempting to come to terms with the harshness of everyday life and the rapidly changing developments of the outside world over which they had little control. In his anti-materialism, anti-institutionalism, and even in his mysticism, Alline was rebelling against his society and searching for a new meaning to life. Such responses seem far more comprehensible in our confused modern society than they did to our more optimistic ancestors.

J. M. BUMSTED

For a complete list of Henry Alline's published works and of the primary and secondary sources relating to his career *see*: J. M. Bumsted, *Henry Alline, 1748–1784* (Toronto, 1971). To the secondary materials listed there the following should be added: J. M. Bumsted and J. E. Van de Wetering, *What must I do to be saved? The Great Awakening in colonial America* (Hinsdale, Ill., 1976); Gordon Stewart and G. [A.] Rawlyk, *A people highly favoured of God: the Nova Scotia Yankees and the American revolution* (Toronto, 1972); Gordon Stewart, "Socio-economic factors in the Great Awakening: the case of Yarmouth, Nova Scotia," *Acadiensis*, III (1973–74), no. 1, 18–34; and T. B. Vincent, "Alline and Bailey," *Canadian Literature* (Vancouver), no. 68–69 (spring–summer 1976), 124–33.

ALYMPH. *See* ARIMPH

AMBROISE. *See* SAINT-AUBIN

AMHERST, JEFFERY, 1st Baron AMHERST, army officer; b. 29 Jan. 1717 (N.S.?) at Riverhead, Sevenoaks, England; d. 3 Aug. 1797 at his house Montreal near Sevenoaks.

Jeffery Amherst was the son of another Jeffery Amherst, a prosperous barrister whose family had lived in Kent for centuries, and Elizabeth Kerrill. At the age of 12 young Jeffery became a page in the household of Lionel Cranfield Sackville, 1st Duke of Dorset, at Knole, his great house adjacent to Sevenoaks. The circumstances of his early military career are somewhat obscure. It has been asserted that Amherst entered the 1st Foot Guards as an ensign in 1731 (when he was in fact only 14), and a list of officers in that regiment's history shows him as becoming an ensign in November 1735. But the earliest printed *Army list*, that for 1740, makes no mention of him in connection with the Guards and shows him as a cornet, appointed 19 July 1735, in Major-General Ligonier's Regiment of Horse, then in Ireland (Dorset was lord lieutenant of Ireland 1730–37 and 1750–55). It seems well established that in July 1740 Ligonier recommended Cornet Amherst to be a lieutenant in his regiment. There is little doubt that Amherst's formative years as an officer were spent, not as a guardsman in London, as has been assumed, but in Ireland in a highly efficient cavalry regiment under the eye of one of the best British soldiers of the age. Dorset and Sir John (afterwards Lord) Ligonier were the patrons who set Amherst's feet on the road to eminence. Ligonier called him his "dear pupil."

Amherst saw his first active service as aide-de-camp to Ligonier in Germany during the War of the Austrian Succession. He was present at the battles of Dettingen (Federal Republic of Germany) in 1743 and Fontenoy (Belgium) in 1745. The 1st Foot Guards' records show that in December 1745 he was appointed captain in that regiment, a commission carrying with it the rank of lieutenant-colonel in the army at large. In 1747 the Duke of Cumberland was appointed commander-in-chief of the allied forces in Europe and made Amherst one of his aides-de-camp. In this capacity he served in the battle of Laffeldt (Belgium) that year. The period of peace following the treaty of Aix-la-Chapelle (1748) he spent in England, presumably with his regiment.

Amherst's first responsibility in the Seven Years' War was acting as "commissary" in charge of the administration of 8,000 Hessian troops taken into British pay at the beginning of 1756. He went to Germany in February to undertake this task, in which his functions seem to have been largely financial, but returned to England in May with part of the Hessian force as insurance against a possible French invasion. Soon after his return he was appointed colonel of the 15th Foot. This commission did not involve taking active command of the regiment, and he went back to Germany with the Hessian detachment in March 1757. Still responsible for the Hessians, he was present at the battle of Hastenbeck on 26 July 1757 when the Duke of Cumberland was defeated by the French.

In October Ligonier succeeded Cumberland as commander-in-chief, an office which gave him, under the crown, command of the forces in Britain and a degree of direction over those in America, extending to the nomination of commanders. Lord Loudoun, in command in America, having failed to attack Louisbourg, Île Royale (Cape Breton Island), in 1757, Ligonier was determined to have the fortress taken in 1758, and it is clear that he saw Colonel Amherst, his former aide-de-camp, as the man for the task. The appointment to command the Louisbourg expedition was remarkable, not merely because Amherst was very junior in the army, but because so far as one can see all his operational experience had been on the staff; he had never commanded troops in action. Obtaining George II's sanction for the grant to Amherst of the local rank of "Major General in America" was a delicate operation, in which William Pitt, secretary of state for the Northern Department, and the Duke of Newcastle, the prime minister, seem to have sought the aid of the king's mistress, Lady Yarmouth. The king finally agreed at the end of 1757; the rank of "Brigadier in America" for James Wolfe*, one of Amherst's designated subordinates, was authorized at the same time.

Amherst sailed for America on 16 March 1758. It was a slow voyage. Pitt and Ligonier having issued detailed orders, including instructions that the expedition against Louisbourg sail before the end of May, Amherst's force was under way before he joined it. It left Halifax on 28 May, 157 sail of naval and transport vessels, and met Amherst just outside the harbour. The naval commander was Admiral Edward Boscawen*. The fleet anchored in Gabarus Bay, to the west of Louisbourg, on 2 June. The same day Amherst reconnoitred the shoreline with two of his brigadiers, Wolfe and Charles Lawrence*, the third, Edward Whitmore*, not having yet arrived. Before Amherst's arrival the plan had been to land to the east of Louisbourg. He decided to attack instead to the west of it. His first intention to land at three different places was changed in favour of a single landing at Anse de la Cormorandière (Kennington Cove) with feints elsewhere. Since La Cormorandière was the place the French had entrenched most heavily, it was a questionable decision. Amherst seems to have been led to it by the observation that the surf was less severe there than elsewhere. Bad weather postponed the landing until the morning of 8 June. The dash and resolution of the advanced troops, and the leadership in particular of Wolfe and Major George Scott*, turned into success what might have been a disaster. Wolfe wrote afterwards, "Our landing was next to miraculous . . . I wouldn't recommend the Bay of Gabarouse for a descent, especially as we manag'd it."

His army established ashore, Amherst undertook systematic European-style siege operations against Louisbourg. These were hampered in the beginning by continuing bad weather which interfered with landing guns. He used Wolfe as commander of a detached mobile force which was the most active element in the siege. On 12 June, hearing that the French had destroyed the Royal battery on the north side of the harbour and were calling in their outposts generally, he ordered Wolfe to move round the harbour and occupy Pointe à la Croix (Lighthouse Point), from which the Island battery and the French naval squadron in the harbour could be bombarded. Fire was opened from Pointe à la Croix on the 20th. (It appears that the surf had permitted the landing of guns east of the harbour, though on the main beach to the west none were landed until 18 June.) On the 26th, the Island battery having been silenced at least for the moment, Amherst asked Boscawen to provide guns to replace those at Pointe à la Croix so that Wolfe's force could come back around the harbour, bringing their artillery, and both continue operations against the ships and "advance towards the West gate." From this time Wolfe directed the attack against the inner flank of the main fortifications of the town.

Amherst prepared his batteries with deliberate care, laboriously building an approach road to carry his guns across boggy ground and an epaulement to cover it from French fire. Wolfe's guns on the British left were firing early in July, but it appears that Amherst's main bombardment did not begin until the 22nd. Much damage was immediately done to the fortifications and the town. Amherst records that he ordered his artillery commander, Lieutenant-Colonel George WILLIAMSON, to direct his fire as much as possible at the defences, "that we might not destroy the Houses."

Relations between Amherst and Boscawen were excellent and the cooperation of army and navy left nothing to be desired. Wolfe wrote: "Mr. Boscawen has given all and even more than we cou'd ask of him . . ." (the contrast with his comments on the navy at Quebec the following year is marked). The French ships in the harbour were gradually worn down. The frigate *Aréthuse*, boldly handled by Jean VAUQUELIN, harassed Wolfe's force with her fire and interfered with the building of Amherst's epaulement, but on 9 July Wolfe's guns damaged her severely. On the night of the 14th–15th she got out of the harbour and away to France. On the 21st three naval vessels were burned. Two remained, *Prudent* and *Bienfaisant*. On the night of the 25th they were (to quote Wolfe again) "boarded by the boats of the [British] fleet with incredible audace and conduct, and taken under the guns and within the reach of the musquetry of the ramparts." The end was now at hand. The Dauphin demi-bastion on Wolfe's flank had been breached and an assault was practicable. On 26 July the governor, Drucour [Boschenry*], asked for terms. Amherst and Boscawen replied that the garrison must become prisoners of war, and demanded an answer within an hour, failing which the town would be attacked by land and sea. After some painful discussion among the French officers, Drucour accepted, and the British occupied Louisbourg on 27 July. The French battalions, denied the honours of war, handed over their arms and colours. Drucour agreed that the French forces in Île Saint-Jean (Prince Edward Island) should be included in the capitulation.

Amherst's conduct of the siege was marked by the thoroughness and deliberation that became his trademarks. Wolfe, who in general respected Amherst, wrote, "our measures have been cautious and slow from the beginning to the end, except in landing where there was an appearance of temerity." Amherst wrote to Pitt on the day his troops entered Louisbourg, "If I can go to Quebeck I will," but there had never been much likelihood of attacking both Louisbourg and Quebec in one summer. Boscawen decided it was too late in the season, and the news of the reverse suffered by James ABERCROMBY, the commander-in-chief in America, before Fort Carillon (Ticonderoga, N.Y.) on 8 July led Amherst to resolve to move to his assistance with five battalions. At the same time he sent detachments under Wolfe to destroy French settlements in the Gulf of St Lawrence and under Lord Rollo* to take over Île Saint-Jean; Colonel Robert MONCKTON was ordered to lay waste the communities in the Saint John valley (N.B.). Leaving a garrison at Louisbourg under Whitmore, Amherst sailed for Boston. There the grateful citizens attempted to make his whole force drunk, and in great part succeeded. Amherst extricated his five battalions, marched them across country to Albany, New York, and himself reported to Abercromby at Lake George (Lac Saint-Sacrement). It was agreed that there could be no further action in that sector that year. Amherst made his way back to his own area of command at Halifax. There on 9 November he heard that Abercromby's defeat had led to that general's recall, while his own success at Louisbourg had made him commander-in-chief in America. He now went to New York, where he spent the winter making plans and logistic arrangements for the campaign of 1759.

It was clear to Amherst that there should be a double attack on Canada. It was necessary, he wrote to Lord George Sackville in January, "to lay the axe to the root, and there are but two roads to get to it, one up the River St Lawrence to Quebec, and the other to Ticonderoga and Montreal, we must go both to be sure of prospering in one, and whichever of the two succeeds, the business is done." In London Pitt and Ligonier had already reached the same conclusion, and Wolfe, who had returned to England, was appointed to command the expedition up the St Lawrence. Although formally subordinated to Amherst, his command would in practice be independent, for communication with Amherst would be virtually impossible. On 29 Dec. 1758 Pitt sent detailed orders to Amherst. Much attention was given to Wolfe's enterprise and the measures to be taken in preparation for it. Amherst was also directed to invade Canada from the south with an army of regular and provincial troops: "by the Way of Crown Point [Fort Saint-Frédéric] or La Galette [at the head of the St Lawrence rapids], or both, according as you shall judge practicable, and proceed, if practicable, and attack Montreal or Quebec, or both of the said places successively," by a unified operation or with separate forces as he might see fit. His attention was directed to the importance of re-establishing the port of Oswego (Chouaguen) on Lake Ontario, and capturing Fort Niagara (near Youngstown, N.Y.). Before these orders reached him, Amherst was already "getting everything ready for a successful campaign." "I can't stay any longer for orders from England," he wrote Sackville, "if I do I shan't have time for preparing the necessary things, they will cost, but I hope I shall buy the country by it. . . ." He busied himself with obtaining from the various colonies the provincial troops that Pitt had asked them for, and with this purpose in mind made a quick visit in April 1759 to Philadelphia in an unsuccessful attempt to gain the cooperation of the Pennsylvania assembly. On 3 May he was at Albany preparing to open the campaign.

Amherst had succeeded in mobilizing a force of some 16,000 regular and provincial troops. Of these 5,000 were allotted to Brigadier-General John Prideaux for the Oswego and Fort Niagara tasks; the rest, under Amherst himself, were to be employed in invading Canada by the Lake Champlain line. On 21 June he arrived at the head of Lake George with a large part of his army. Further advance would depend on water transport, and on sufficient naval power to overcome the French armed vessels on Lake Champlain. Large numbers of boats had been prepared, and these were dragged overland from the upper Hudson to Lake George, "batteaus on waggons and whaleboats on mens shoulders, 15 to a boat." On 21 July the army moved down the lake in boats formed in columns, and the following day landed close to Fort Carillon. The French commander, François-Charles de Bourlamaque*, withdrew his main force from the fort, leaving a small garrison; no attempt was made to defend the advanced lines which had defeated Abercromby. Amherst began a siege in form, but on 26 July the French retreated by water, blowing up the fort. The British boats were dragged around the falls above Carillon and launched on Lake Champlain. On 4 August the army moved up the narrow south arm of the lake to Fort Saint-Frédéric, where they found that Bourlamaque had blown up the post and withdrawn to Fort Île aux Noix in the Rivière Richelieu. Amherst, who seems to have been hypnotized by the Crown Point position, began to build an elaborate fortress here (its ditches, cut out of the solid rock, are still to be seen). "This is a great Post gained," he wrote, "secures entirely all the country behind it [i.e. to the south], and the situation and country about it is better than anything I have seen." Yet the fortress had little relevance in existing circumstances; the French had lost the initiative in North America. Information that Bourlamaque had four armed vessels at the north end of Lake Champlain led Amherst in September to enlarge his plans for a flotilla of his own. His naval assistant, Captain Joshua LORING, was already building a brig; now a large *radeau* or raft, capable of mounting heavy guns, was undertaken. An attempt to burn a new French vessel at Île aux Noix was unsuccessful, and it was decided to build a 16-gun sloop as soon as the brig was completed. Progress with this building program was slowed by repeated breakdowns of the one available sawmill. Finally, on 11 October, the imposing formation of craft carrying Amherst's army started down the lake, with the *radeau*, *Ligonier*, leading. Loring with the brig, *Duke of Cumberland*, and the sloop, *Boscawen*, went in search of the enemy's ships; on the 13th the French commander, Joannis-Galand d'OLABARATZ, sank two of these to avoid capture and ran a third ashore. But on the 18th Amherst heard of the fall of Quebec a month before. He wrote in his journal, "This will of course bring Mons de Vaudreuil [RIGAUD] & the whole Army to Montreal so that I shall decline my intended operations & get back to Crown Point." On this somewhat inglorious note his year's campaign ended.

The vital importance of naval control of Lake Champlain is of course beyond doubt, and the long process of building vessels was clearly the reason for the failure to obtain better results. Nevertheless, it is difficult not to feel that during the long summer of 1759 Amherst did not keep sufficiently before him what should have been his main object, assisting Wolfe's operations at Quebec. The capture of Fort Niagara – effected on 25 July, after Prideaux had been killed, by Sir William JOHNSON – immediately led Montcalm* to weaken his army at Quebec by sending troops west. Amherst's own cautious and ponderous operations had no such effect. More energy and more effective improvisation on his part might well have ended the war in Canada in 1759. As it was, another year's campaign was necessary.

Pitt's orders for 1760 indicated the capture of Montreal as "the great and essential object," and Amherst was instructed to invade Canada "according as you shall, from your knowledge of the Countries, thro' which the War is to be carried, and from emergent circumstances not to be known here, judge the same to be most expedient." He decided on a three-pronged attack: James MURRAY with the Quebec garrison moving up the St Lawrence, Brigadier-General William HAVILAND proceeding from Crown Point up Lake Champlain, and Amherst himself moving down the St Lawrence from Lake Ontario. The

French would thus be obliged to divide their limited forces, and would be denied any possibility of retreat into the interior such as they had made after the battle of the Plains of Abraham. Again large forces were requisitioned from the colonies. Amherst's own army, over 10,000 strong, was by far the largest. As in 1759, the winter and spring were devoted to logistic planning and preparation. Large numbers of bateaux and whale boats were built. The late arrival of the provincial troops, who provided the labour to move the boats and supplies, delayed the opening of the campaign, but from mid May great quantities of provisions were moving up the waterways and over the portages to Lake Champlain and Amherst's advanced base at Oswego.

On 9 July Amherst himself arrived at Oswego, and on the 14th two armed snows built by Loring at Niagara during the winter were sent east in the hope of capturing two French vessels similarly constructed. On 10 August Amherst embarked his army in boats and began the movement against Montreal. After the French vessel the *Outaouaise* was captured on the 17th by "row-galleys" manned by the Royal Artillery under Colonel Williamson, the one man-made obstacle impeding the advance was Fort Lévis (east of Prescott, Ont.), on an island at the head of the rapids. Amherst besieged it formally, landing his artillery to bombard it. Captain Pierre Pouchot*, the French commander, made a determined defence, but the fort was battered into surrender on 25 August. The advance on Montreal now continued. Amherst lost 84 men drowned in the rapids on 4 September, but effective human resistance was at an end. On the 6th his army landed at Lachine on the island of Montreal and encamped before the city. Haviland had occupied Île aux Noix on 28 August and was now on the south shore of the St Lawrence opposite Montreal; Murray, having moved up the river without meeting serious opposition, was in position just below the city. Amherst wrote, "I believe never three Armys, setting out from different & very distant Parts from each other joyned in the Center, as was intended, better than we did." Striking it was; but it must be said that the precision of the junction owed something to luck.

The French defenders of Montreal were in an impossible situation. The Canadian militia had virtually all deserted, and the army at Vaudreuil's and LÉVIS's disposal had shrunk to little more than 2,000 men. The British forces amounted to 17,000. Vaudreuil asked for a suspension of operations, pending news from Europe. Amherst "said I was come to take Canada and I did not intend to take anything less." As at Louisbourg, he refused the French the honours of war, on the ground of the atrocities committed by their Indian allies. The French battalions burned their colours rather than give them up. Montreal, and with it Canada, was surrendered to Amherst on 8 Sept. 1760. The conquering general visited Quebec, with its already famous battlefields, before returning to his headquarters at New York.

Though the fighting with France in North America was virtually over, the war was not. Amherst as commander-in-chief was concerned with organizing expeditions against Dominica and Martinique in 1761 and in 1762 he sent a contingent to take part in the attack on Havana, Cuba. In August 1762 he dispatched his younger brother William with a hastily collected force to recover St John's, Newfoundland, from the French under Charles-Henri-Louis d'ARSAC de Ternay. News of peace in Europe came early in 1763. Almost immediately, however, Amherst began to receive from the west reports of Indian attacks which were the opening shots of Pontiac*'s uprising.

Amherst's dislike and contempt for the Indians are amply reflected in his journals and correspondence, though it may perhaps be doubted whether he was more bigoted than the average official of his time. As soon as active hostilities with France were over, he had begun to economize on presents to the tribes, though people closer to the problem (notably Sir William Johnson) believed that continued generosity would be better policy. Amherst wrote Johnson that he did not believe in "purchasing the good behavior, either of Indians, or any others"; "When Men of What race soever, behave ill they must be punished but not bribed." As commander-in-chief Amherst was responsible for Indian policy, and his attitude doubtless contributed to producing the outbreak of 1763. He was slow to believe that the trouble could be really serious; he underestimated the Indians' capacity for military action. Nevertheless, there is no evidence that these views in any way delayed measures to deal with the rising. The moment he heard reports of "bad designs" among the tribes he put the inadequate force of regulars available in the east on the road to the threatened areas; when on 21 June he heard of Pontiac's blockade of Detroit [*see* Henry GLADWIN] he wrote, "As I have made all preparations I am able to do, I had nothing remaining to be done on the receipt of this news." He did however make to Colonel Henry Bouquet the "detestable suggestion" (Francis Parkman's phrase) that smallpox might be introduced among the dissident Indians. Bouquet cheerfully offered to try to infect them with blankets, and perhaps as a result of Bouquet's orders an attempt was indeed made to do so with infected blankets and handkerchiefs. Early in August Bouquet's column marching to relieve Fort Pitt (Pittsburgh, Pa) inflicted a serious reverse on the Indians at Bushy Run. Amherst had thought of taking the field himself in 1764, but in fact he embarked for England, after over five years in North America, in November 1763. He wrote to a friend in the following February, "I may tell you for your own information only, that I have no thought of returning to America." And indeed, though he was to have many opportunities, he never again visited the continent where his name was made.

His successes in America had won Amherst honours, though these honours were not extravagant by the standards of those days. In September 1759 he had been made governor of Virginia. He never functioned actively in this office, and it was well understood that the position was a mere sinecure, worth some £1,500 a year. The appointment of commander-in-chief in America brought him the office of colonel-in-chief of the Royal Americans (60th Foot), in addition to the colonelcy of the 15th Foot which he retained. He was made a substantive major-general in 1759 and a lieutenant-general in 1761. In the latter year he was made a knight of the Bath. After the death of his elder brother Sackville in 1763 he built a new country house, which he named Montreal, on the family estate near Sevenoaks. He does not seem to have been actively employed in the army at this period, but he declined successively the office of master general of the Ordnance in Ireland and the command of the forces there. In 1768 growing colonial discontent led King George III to the conclusion that there should be an active governor in Virginia, and Amherst was given the choice of going there or resigning the governorship and accepting an annuity instead. He took offence, rather unnecessarily it seems, and resigned his colonelcies. He was shortly reappointed to them, being given the 3rd Foot, a more lucrative appointment, instead of the 15th, but the rift with the king was fully closed only when he was made governor of Guernsey (1770) and lieutenant-general of the Ordnance (1772). In the absence of a commander-in-chief, this latter office seems to have made him in effect the king's chief military adviser.

In 1769 it was suggested to Amherst that he try to obtain a grant of the Jesuits' estates in Canada. The Jesuit order had been suppressed in France in 1762–64, and was in a state of suspended animation in Canada until 1775 when it was finally suppressed there too and its estates vested in the crown. Amherst had applied for a grant in 1769, and in 1770 an order in council directed the preparation of a legal instrument for it. No action was taken, however, supposedly for want of a precise description of the estates. Amherst raised the question again from time to time, and in 1787 the governor of Canada, Lord Dorchester [Guy Carleton*], was instructed to make a full inquiry into the status of the lands. Some agitation followed, both English and French speaking inhabitants of the colony arguing that the estates should be devoted to the support of education. The matter remained in abeyance. Since, however, it appeared that an undertaking had been given to Amherst, the British parliament in 1803, after his death, authorized an annuity of £3,000 to be paid to his heirs in lieu of the lands he had never received.

In January 1775 the king pressed Amherst to take the command in America, where war with the colonists was threatening. He declined, for reasons that remain uncertain. The following year he was raised to the peerage as Baron Amherst of Holmesdale. In 1778, on the urging of his ministers, the king again asked Amherst to take the American command, and again he refused. Later that year he was appointed in effect commander-in-chief, although it appears his actual title was general-on-the-staff; the *Army list* shows his rank of general as dating from 19 March 1778. In June 1780 he had the task of restoring order when London was devastated by the Gordon riots. He was dismissed from his command when Lord North's ministry went out of office in 1782. At the beginning of 1793, when war with France was approaching, Amherst, though now 76 years of age, was recalled and appointed commander-in-chief with a seat in the cabinet. He retired again two years later, being succeeded by the Duke of York. Promoted field marshal as of 30 July 1796, he died on 3 Aug. 1797, and was buried in the parish church of Sevenoaks.

In May 1753 Amherst had married his second cousin, Jane Dalison. The marriage was childless. Jane appears to have had neurotic tendencies and Amherst probably was not an ideal husband. The fact that he had an illegitimate son, apparently born shortly before his marriage, of a mother whose identity is uncertain, may have contributed to estrange them. This son, also called Jeffery Amherst, rose to the rank of major-general and seems to have died in 1815. In 1760 Amherst told Pitt that while passing through England en route to Louisbourg in 1758, he had "made a promise" that no inducement would keep him in America willingly once the war was over; this promise was clearly made to his wife.

When he returned in 1763, however, her depression had deepened into derangement, and she died in 1765. In 1767 Amherst married again, his second wife being Elizabeth, daughter of General George Cary. This marriage too was childless. Amherst's heir was his nephew, William Pitt Amherst, the son of his brother William. In 1788, after William's death, Amherst obtained from the crown the title of Baron Amherst of Montreal, Kent, with remainder to his nephew. William Pitt Amherst accordingly inherited the title. After a mission to China and a period as governor general of India he was created Earl Amherst of Arracan in 1826. In 1835 he was appointed governor of Canada, but as a result of the fall of the Peel ministry in England he never took up the appointment.

Jeffery Amherst sat for his portrait several times. Sir Joshua Reynolds' picture of him with the St Lawrence rapids in the background, the more conventional Reynolds portrait now in the National Gallery of Canada, and the Thomas Gainsborough portrait in the National Portrait Gallery of Great Britain have often been reproduced. His appearance accords with Sir Nathaniel William Wraxall's description of him: "His manners were grave, formal and cold."

Amherst had an unbroken record of success as a commander, but he was a solid rather than a brilliant soldier. He never conducted a battle; the successful siege of Louisbourg is the nearest thing to it. His style was slow and heavy, as the campaign of 1759 amply showed. But he was an organizer of victory, who left nothing to chance in the fields of supply and transport, and this thoroughness was what the war in America mainly required. Sir John Fortescue said of him, "He was the greatest military administrator produced by England since the death of Marlborough, and remained the greatest until the rise of Wellington." That judgement may well be accepted.

C. P. Stacey

[There are two biographies of Amherst, neither completely satisfactory: L. S. Mayo, *Jeffery Amherst; a biography* (New York, 1916), and J. C. Long, *Lord Jeffery Amherst: a soldier of the king* (New York, 1933). Mayo's is in some ways the better book, though written without benefit of the Amherst papers, which did not come to light until 1925. Louis Des Cognets, *Amherst and Canada* (Princeton, N.J., 1962), is of limited value, but publishes letters not available elsewhere. Rex Whitworth, *Field Marshal Lord Ligonier: a story of the British army, 1702–1770* (Oxford, 1958), is very useful. Other printed sources of value are: *Correspondence of William Pitt* (Kimball); *Gentleman's Magazine*, 1765, 46; 1815, 91; G.B., Hist. mss Commission, *Report on the manuscripts of Mrs. Stopford-Sackville . . .* (2v., London, 1904–10); House of Commons, *Journals* (London), 58 (1802–3); *Burke's peerage* (1963); *DAB*; *DNB*; G.B., WO, *Army list*; Burt, *Old prov. of Que.*; R. C. Dalton, *The Jesuits' estates question, 1760–1888: a study of the background for the agitation of 1889* (Toronto, 1968); J. P. De Castro, *The Gordon riots* (London, 1926); J. W. Fortescue, *A history of the British army* (13v. in 14, London, 1899–1930), II; F. W. Hamilton, *The origin and history of the First or Grenadier Guards . . .* (3v., London, 1874); Francis Parkman, *The conspiracy of Pontiac and the Indian war after the conquest of Canada* (2v., Boston, 1910), and *Montcalm and Wolfe* (2v., Boston, 1884; repr. New York, 1962); Shy, *Toward Lexington*; Stacey, *Quebec, 1759*; [H.] B. Willson, *The life and letters of James Wolfe* (London, 1909); J. M. Hitsman and C. C. J. Bond, "The assault landing at Louisbourg, 1758," *CHR*, XXXV (1954), 314–30; Bernhard Knollenberg, "General Amherst and germ warfare," *Mississippi Valley Hist. Rev.* (Cedar Rapids, Iowa), XLI (1954–55), 489–94 (*see also* 762–63); Rex Whitworth, "Field-Marshal Lord Amherst, a military enigma," *History Today* (London), IX (1959), 132–37.

The voluminous Amherst papers are in great part available at the PAC. Amherst's military papers are in the PRO as WO 34; the PAC has microfilms. Large portions of Amherst's more private papers are in the PAC in the form of transcripts, gathered in MG 18, L4. Among these private papers are Amherst's invaluable journals for the years 1756–63. The journals from 14 Jan. 1758 to the end are published in Amherst, *Journal* (Webster). A more limited version intended for contemporary publication forms app.1 to vol. III of Knox, *Hist. journal* (Doughty); the originals are in PRO, CO 5/54–63. *See also* [William Amherst], *Journal of William Amherst in America, 1758–1760*, intro. J. C. Webster (London and Frome, Eng., 1927). The Bouquet papers, containing a good deal of correspondence with Amherst, are in BL, Add. mss 21631–60 (transcripts in PAC, MG 21, G1); the notorious reference to infecting the Indians with smallpox is in Add. mss 21634 (vol. 4 of the PAC transcripts). c.p.s.]

ANANDAMOAKIN (Anondounoakum, Onondamokin; Long Coat, from his Iroquois name **Atiaʔtawìʔtsheraʔ**, a coat), a Munsee Delaware chief, probably a member of the turkey clan, possibly a son of the blind chief Allemewi (baptized Salomon); fl. 1756–72.

Having lost much of their former land to settlers and land speculators, the Munsees, also known as Minisinks, were living on the upper Susquehanna River at Tioga (near Athens, Pa) by the mid 1750s. The beginning of the Seven Years' War heightened competition between the British and the French for the friendship of the native people; in an attempt to curb Indian support of the French, Sir William Johnson, superintendent of northern Indians, met on 9–11 July 1756 with Shawnee and Delaware leaders at Fort

Johnson (near Amsterdam, N.Y.). Although unnamed in Johnson's reports, the heads of these two delegations are commonly identified as Paxinosa and Nutimus respectively; however, Paxinosa's son reported on 6 July that his father was accompanied by a "Chief of the Mennisink Nation whose name is Onondamokin."

The Delaware leader returned to Johnson's house late that month with some of his tribe, but on 18 April 1757 Governor Vaudreuil [RIGAUD] reported that he had attracted the Delawares of Tioga to Fort Niagara (near Youngstown, N.Y.). Although in July the British heard of dissension between the French commandant at Niagara and "some Munsey Indians with the King of that tribe who went there this spring," the commandant himself, Pierre Pouchot*, reported that "the principal Delaware chief of Théoga" had returned to Niagara on 12 June with 27 warriors. Four days later this chief, presumably Anandamoakin, and four others accepted an invitation to go to Montreal, where Vaudreuil received them in council in July. These Indians, the governor observed, "can extend their parties as far as New-York and in many other places where our Indians cannot conveniently go to strike."

The effects of French attention were visible a year later when Moses (Tunda) Tatamy, a Delaware sent by the governor of New Jersey to invite the Munsees to a conference, arrived on 5 July 1758 at Aghsinsing (near Corning, N.Y.). There, in "the King's House," as Moses reported, "live Alamewhehum [Allemewi] an old Man and Anandamoakin a fat Man well dressed in French Cloaths as are almost all the Warriors. The Old Man is a friend of the English . . . but the fat man is for the French and . . . is going soon to pay them a Visit." When the English invitation was delivered, "all the rest seemed much pleased . . . but the fat man hung his Head and made no answer or very little." In the outcome, a third chief, Eghohund, headed the Munsee delegation to the treaty.

Anandamoakin headed the small Munsee delegation that in 1760 accompanied the Delaware chief Teedyuscung on a western journey which included attendance at a treaty with British authorities at Pittsburgh on 12–17 August. When Teedyuscung reported at Philadelphia on 15 September, his company included "Anondounoakom the Son of the Chief of the Minisinks."

In 1763 discontent among the Senecas and western Indians resulted in an uprising against the British [*see* Pontiac*], and the Munsees were participants to such effect that in February 1764 Sir William Johnson offered a reward of $50 each for their chief warriors, Anandamoakin and Yaghkaposin (Squash Cutter). When Johnson's raiders destroyed the Munsee towns, their residents took refuge with the Senecas, at whose insistence the two proscribed leaders came to Johnson Hall (Johnstown, N.Y.) in 1765 as reluctant delegates; on 8 May they accepted peace terms that required them to remain as hostages for their people's compliance. On the following day the Munsees attempted to exculpate themselves by deposing Anandamoakin on the grounds that he had been the instigator of their hostile actions, but the Iroquois blocked this move. Squash Cutter died a month later of smallpox, but Anandamoakin was released in due time and apparently joined his people, who had resettled on the upper Allegheny River at Goshgoshing (midway between Warren and Franklin, Pa).

The chief at this place, Allemewi, became a Moravian convert in 1769, vacated his office, and moved with the mission Indians to the Beaver River near present Moravia, in western Pennsylvania. The mission diary at that place records a visit by Anandamoakin on 9–11 Oct. 1771 on his way to an Indian council on the Muskingum River (Ohio); on 10 Aug. 1772 the same diary reports the departure of Salomon's (Allemewi's) son, probably Anandamoakin, who was returning to the upper Allegheny after a long visit. No further references to him are known.

WILLIAM A. HUNTER

Moravian Church Archives (Bethlehem, Pa.), Indian missions, box 135, Goschgoschünk and Lawunakhannek; box 137, Langundo Utenünk. Pa. Hist. Soc. (Philadelphia), Christian Frederick Post journal, 1760. *Coll. des manuscrits de Lévis* (Casgrain), XI, 95–96. *Colonial records of Pa.* (Hazard), VII, 6 July 1756; VIII, 8 Oct. 1758, 15 Sept. 1760. [John Hays], "John Hays' diary and journal of 1760," ed. W. A. Hunter, *Pennsylvania Archaeologist* (Honesdale), XXIV (1954), 81. *Johnson papers* (Sullivan *et al.*), III, 695–97; IV, 336–37; VI, 652; XIII, 334. *NYCD* (O'Callaghan and Fernow), VII, 152–59, 173–75, 285, 720–25, 736; X, 588, 590. *Pa. archives* (Hazard *et al.*), 1st ser., III, 505–6.

ANGEAC (Dangeac, Danjaique, Don Jacque), FRANÇOIS-GABRIEL D', officer in the colonial regular troops and colonial administrator; b. 1708 at Plaisance (Placentia, Nfld), son of Gabriel d'Angeac and Marguerite Bertrand; d. 9 March 1782 at Soubise (dept of Charente-Maritime), France.

François-Gabriel d'Angeac entered the military at an early age, as had his father. He mounted his first guard at Port-Dauphin (Englishtown, N.S.) when he was only eight years old, but he had to wait until 1723 for a second ensigncy in his father's company at Louisbourg, Île Royale (Cape Breton Island). His promotions followed the usual slow pattern of the colonial regulars, but from 1738 to 1741 and 1743 to 1745 he was stationed at Port-Dauphin as lieutenant and he sometimes served as commandant there.

Recalled to Louisbourg to help defend the fortress in 1745, d'Angeac went to France after the defeat. In 1746 he recruited troops in France for colonial companies. Promoted captain in 1747, he went with part of Île Royale's garrison to Quebec and then returned to Louisbourg when it was reoccupied by France in 1749. As commandant of Port-Dauphin from 1751 to 1758, he supervised the reconstruction of that outpost and headed the detail that cleared Governor Jean-Louis de RAYMOND's road from Port-Toulouse (St Peters, N.S.) to Louisbourg. D'Angeac was awarded the cross of Saint-Louis while on leave in France in 1754. In 1758 he was wounded in the chest during the second siege of Louisbourg.

Back in France in 1760, d'Angeac was chosen to command the troops sent to Canada as reinforcements because of his bravery, experience, and familiarity with the region. To avoid the British, the commander of the French fleet, François Chenard de La Giraudais, sought refuge in the mouth of the Restigouche River (N.B.) with three armed vessels. With only 200 men, d'Angeac constructed a battery and picquet at Pointe-à-la-Garde (Que.), as well as two batteries upstream, and on 8 July they inflicted some damage on British ships commanded by John BYRON. D'Angeac remained with the frigate *Machault* until it was abandoned, and then led the French retreat into the woods.

During the succeeding months d'Angeac and his officers organized some 2,000 Acadians and Indians, bolstered French defences, and built ovens for the relief of the near-starving local populace. In August some of the sailors among his men took to privateering. After the capitulation of Montreal Major Robert Elliot* was sent to Restigouche to present Governor RIGAUD de Vaudreuil's order to surrender. D'Angeac defiantly detained the officer for two days before agreeing to terms. On 30 Oct. 1760 the troops surrendered. Upon his return to France later in the year he was awarded a gratuity of 900 *livres* for his valour.

In further recognition of his military service and familiarity with the North Atlantic region, in 1763 d'Angeac was appointed governor of the new French colony of Saint-Pierre and Miquelon at a salary of 8,000 *livres*. These tiny, barren islands off the southern coast of Newfoundland had finally been secured by France in the treaty of Paris to replace Louisbourg as a base for the French sedentary fishery and as a refuge for the deep-sea fishing fleet. By the treaty France was permitted to construct buildings on the islands for the fishery only and to station no more than 50 soldiers there as a police force.

D'Angeac raised the men for his garrison at Rochefort and arrived at Saint-Pierre on 15 June 1763; however, Captain Charles DOUGLAS delayed the transfer of territory until 4 July when James COOK had completed his survey of the islands. A few Canadians migrated to the new colony, but most prominent in its early commercial and administrative life were former residents of Île Royale, such as Antoine Morin, Alexandre-René Beaudéduit, Michel de COUAGNE, Philippe Leneuf de Beaubassin, Jean-Baptiste DUPLEIX Silvain, and Antoine RODRIGUE. Some were key figures in establishing the sedentary fishery, and d'Angeac favoured them by granting fishing space although he thus incurred criticism from French ship captains. The number of French ships visiting Saint-Pierre and Miquelon to engage in the deep-sea fishery grew steadily, as did the catch exported to France and the West Indies.

The Acadians who had flocked to the new colony caused d'Angeac great anxiety. Settled primarily on Miquelon, in 1767 they formed over two-thirds of the resident population of approximately 1,250 on the two islands. D'Angeac was empowered to distribute rations to new settlers, but the Acadians strained the limited resources of the colony. Wishing to restrict settlement to that associated with the fishery, in 1767 France ordered colonial officials to evacuate the Acadians. Although he thought the policy unjust, d'Angeac complied, and he deported 763 Acadians to France in that year. For reasons that remain obscure, in 1768 they mistakenly accused d'Angeac of being the source of their misfortune. Some remained in France supported by the government; others migrated back to Acadia, Cape Breton, Îles de la Madeleine, and even Saint-Pierre and Miquelon.

D'Angeac was also required to deal with the British authorities in Newfoundland. Saint-Pierre and Miquelon lacked wood for heating and construction, and the French sought it in the British colony. In 1765 Governor Hugh PALLISER, reflecting Britain's narrow interpretation of the treaty of Paris, formally protested this incursion into British territory, as well as the presence of French warships in the area, even for the purpose of provisioning the islands and protecting French fishermen. He further objected to the French fishing in the channel that separated the islands from Newfoundland. Referred to home authorities, these matters were disputed by the two governments for years. Palliser also increased naval patrols to try to reduce the trade in contraband, especially fish and spirits, with the islands. D'Angeac, however, closed his eyes to the smuggling, and the trade continued.

Discouraged by his relations with Palliser, d'Angeac requested permission to retire in 1765 but was denied it. His health was deteriorating in the damp, foggy climate and he again requested a recall in 1769. Promoted brigadier of the line infantry in 1770, he left Saint-Pierre for France in 1772 and was succeeded on his own recommendation by his nephew, Charles-Gabriel-Sébastien de L'Espérance. D'Angeac was granted a pension of 6,000 *livres* and retired to Soubise.

D'Angeac was a good officer in battle and a capable governor. Although he insisted at the time of his retirement that he had not profited from his years in service, he had owned a commercial vessel called the *Dauphine* at Île Royale in the 1750s. Moreover, his long posting at Port-Dauphin, the centre of much of the family trading activity of Louis Du Pont Duchambon, Louis Du Pont Duchambon de Vergor, and François Du Pont Duvivier, permits the conclusion that he engaged in trade. He had married Geneviève, sister of François Lefebvre de Bellefeuille, at Louisbourg on 31 Dec. 1735, and they had seven children. Two sons entered the military and one of them served under him at Saint-Pierre. Two of his daughters received a pension of 500 *livres* each after his death.

T. A. Crowley

AN, Col., B, 76, f.488; C[11A], 105, ff.179–84, 356–60, 567–75; C[11B], 31, f.19; 32, f.125; E, 5 (dossier d'Angeac). ASQ, Polygraphie, LVIII, 39. Knox, *Hist. journal* (Doughty), III, 368, 370, 386, 394–95, 418. Æ. Fauteux, *Les chevaliers de Saint-Louis*, 120, 156.

La Morandière, *Hist. de la pêche française de la morue*, II, 755–80, 796, 800, 808. Z. E. Rashed, *The peace of Paris, 1763* (Liverpool, Eng., 1951). J.-Y. Ribault, *Les îles Saint-Pierre et Miquelon des origines à 1814* (Saint-Pierre, 1962), 12–18, 41–42. Stanley, *New France*, 260. Henri Bourde de La Rogerie, "Saint-Pierre et Miquelon: des origines à 1778," *Le Pays de Granville; bull. trimestriel de la Soc. d'études historiques et économiques* (Mortain, France), 2e sér., nos.38–40 (1937). Ægidius Fauteux, "Les Du Pont de l'Acadie," *BRH*, XLVI (1940), 258. J.-Y. Ribault, "La population des îles Saint-Pierre et Miquelon de 1763 à 1793," *Revue française d'hist. d'outre-mer* (Paris), LIII (1966), 50–58.

AONGOTE. *See* Williams, Eunice

ARBUTHNOT (Arbuthnott), MARIOT (Marriot, Marriott), naval officer and colonial administrator; b. 1711 in Weymouth, England; married, with at least two sons; d. 31 Jan. 1794 in London, England.

Mariot Arbuthnot entered the Royal Navy about 1727 and rose slowly through the ranks, becoming a lieutenant in 1739, a commander in 1746, and a post-captain in 1747. He commanded the *Portland* at the battle of Quiberon Bay, France, during the Seven Years' War; after a period of command at Portsmouth he was appointed commander of the navy yard at Halifax, Nova Scotia, arriving there on 1 Nov. 1775. Less than a week after his arrival he retained the *Somerset* for the protection of Halifax, after learning that "a body of rebels" was marching "up the country" to an unknown destination. On 20 April 1776 Arbuthnot received his commission as lieutenant governor of Nova Scotia, replacing Michael Francklin. The governor, Francis Legge, sailed for England in May, and Arbuthnot became administrator of the province.

Legge had been a controversial figure who had created rifts in the community, and although Arbuthnot's chief concern was the defence of Nova Scotia, he was determined to have harmony at Halifax. He pledged himself to "conciliate the minds of the people in and about this neighbourhood of the Town." Accordingly, when the House of Assembly prorogued in June, he attended a public dinner at the Great Pontack Inn with members of the assembly and several prominent citizens, including Francklin. Legge's friends, however, saw the assembly's reception of Arbuthnot as an insult to Legge, and one of them, Henry Denny Denson, described a sermon preached by John Breynton as "the most fulsome praise to the L[t] G[r] that was parhaps ever heard, which would have made any other Man blush, but he swallowed all."

That summer Arbuthnot visited the Windsor, Cornwallis, and Truro areas. The inhabitants of the Truro region he described as "a strong, robust, industrious people, bigoted dissenters and of course great levelers," but they apparently assured him of their loyalty and subsequently sent him "a very handsome address." When they later sheltered American privateers Arbuthnot expressed surprise: "having no duplicity in my own Conduct [I] was not prepar'd to meet it in theirs." In November he had to dispatch troops to Fort Cumberland (near Sackville, N.B.), which was being besieged by forces under Jonathan Eddy* [*see* Joseph Goreham]. He also had troops sent to Liverpool and Yarmouth and armed vessels outfitted in an attempt to counter the raids of privateers. Arbuthnot was not, however, concerned solely with military affairs. At Halifax he dealt with dissent by ordering the prominent merchant Malachy Salter arrested and tried on suspicion of conducting a dangerous correspondence with Boston. To alleviate the plight of soldiers' families Arbuthnot gave the women work at the dockyard picking oakum.

On 23 Jan. 1778 Arbuthnot was promoted rear-admiral and recalled; he left Halifax on 17 August when Richard Hughes* was sworn in as lieutenant governor. In the spring of 1779 Arbuthnot received his most important and most contentious posting when he was appointed commander of the North American station. In this position he distinguished himself mainly through bitter quarrels with his fellow officers. He saw no further service after relinquishing the command in 1781 but was promoted admiral of the blue on 1 Feb. 1793 by virtue of seniority.

Some biographers have treated Arbuthnot harshly. According to one he was ignorant of his profession, was destitute of even a rudimentary knowledge of naval tactics, and appeared in contemporary stories as a coarse, blustering, foul-mouthed bully. Such assessments seem to be based mainly on the 1779–81 period, when his health declined precipitously as a result of what may have been minor strokes. In Nova Scotia he appears to have been, in John Bartlet Brebner*'s words, "well-meaning, but optimistic and gullible."

DONALD F. CHARD

A mezzotint by Charles Howard Hodges of the portrait by John Rising is in the National Maritime Museum, London.

PANS, RG 1, 45, docs. 12, 13, 17, 24, 28; 136, pp.230, 241; 168; 212, 6 Nov. 1775; 13 May, 9, 16 Oct. 1776; 10 Nov. 1777; 17 Aug. 1778; 342, p.275. PRO, CO 217/27. *Gentleman's Magazine*, 1794, 184. PAC *Report*, 1894, 354, 375. Perkins, *Diary, 1766–80* (Innis), 124. *The private papers of John, Earl of Sandwich, first lord of the Admiralty, 1771–1782*, ed. G. R. Barnes and J. H. Owen (4v., London, 1932–38), III, 265, 267; IV. *Nova-Scotia Gazette and the Weekly Chronicle* (Halifax), 7 Nov. 1775. *Times* (London), 4, 5 Feb. 1794. *DNB*. Brebner, *Neutral Yankees* (1969), 252. Murdoch, *History of N.S.*, II, 593–94. David Spinney, *Rodney* (London, 1969).

ARGENTEUIL. *See* AILLEBOUST

ARIMPH (Alymph), JEAN-BAPTISTE, a second chief of the Micmacs of Richibucto (N.B.); fl. 1776–78.

In the years immediately preceding the American War of Independence, both the Americans and the British attempted to win the Malecites and Micmacs as allies. In May 1775 the Massachusetts government petitioned these tribes for aid against the British, and in September the Indians agreed. Perhaps the Micmacs were so inclined because the British had virtually cut off gunpowder supplies to them during the summer. Realizing that their move had cost them the Indians' good will, the British hastily summoned the chiefs to a conference at Halifax, where they gave them gunpowder and clothing. This gesture swayed many of the Micmacs since they not only appreciated the gifts but also realized the power of the British and the potential threat they posed. The Malecites, encouraged by chiefs such as Ambroise SAINT-AUBIN and Pierre TOMAH, and at least some of the Micmacs continued nonetheless to affirm their friendship with the Americans, their leaders signing a treaty to that effect in the spring of 1776. In July the Malecites of the Saint John River, led by Saint-Aubin, and some unauthorized Micmac men signed a treaty with the government of Massachusetts committing the Indians to furnish 600 men to fight on the American side. When the Micmac chiefs heard of it two months later, they sent a letter in which they reaffirmed their friendship but declined to supply the men. Arimph, designated "Chief of Rechibouctou," signed this letter along with seven other leaders. It seems the older chiefs refused to provide so many fighting men because they realized that the British would learn of such aid and would destroy the Indians' undefended villages.

The Americans, using agents such as John Allan*, continued to incite the Indians, and their efforts culminated in the Indians' declaration of war against the British in August 1778. The British then called leading Malecites and Micmacs to a peace treaty session at Menagouèche (Saint John, N.B.) [*see* Nicholas AKOMÁPIS]. Arimph, still a leader among his people, attended and on 24 Sept. 1778 signed the treaty as "second chief of the Micmacs of Richibucto." On behalf of all the Micmacs he subsequently joined two Malecite chiefs in signing a letter to the Americans at Machias (Maine) warning them to leave the two tribes alone and to return items stolen from the Saint John River trading post by an American privateer in 1777. Arimph disappears from written history after these events.

VIRGINIA P. MILLER

PANS, RG 1, 45, doc.66. *Documentary history of Maine* (Willis *et al.*), XXIV, 165–95. *Military operations in eastern Maine and N.S.* (Kidder). "Selections from the papers and correspondence of James White, esquire, A.D. 1762–1783," ed. W. O. Raymond, N.B. Hist. Soc., *Coll.*, I (1894–97), no.3, 306–40.

ARMITINGER. *See* ERMATINGER

ARSAC DE TERNAY, CHARLES-HENRI-LOUIS D', naval officer; b. 27 Jan. 1723, probably at Angers, France, son of Charles-François d'Arsac, Marquis de Ternay, and Louise Lefebvre de Laubrière; d. 15 Dec. 1780 on board the *Duc de Bourgogne* in the roads of Newport, R.I.

Charles-Henri-Louis d'Arsac de Ternay was admitted to the Knights of Malta as a page to the grand master on 12 Dec. 1737, when he was not yet 15 years old. In October 1738 he joined the midshipmen's corps at Toulon, France; on 10 Oct. 1743 he was appointed sub-corporal, and on 1 Jan. 1746 sub-lieutenant. He lived in Malta from 1749 to 1752 before becoming a lieutenant-commander at Toulon in February 1756. On 10 Jan. 1761 he attained the rank of captain and took command of the *Robuste* at Brest.

The surrender of Montreal in September 1760 had virtually ended the French presence in North America. The war continued in Europe, however, and the Duc de Choiseul, the minister of War, Marine, and Colonies, attempted to harass the British on the oceans as well as overseas. At the end of 1761 he worked out a wide-ranging plan of action aimed at intercepting the British fishing vessels on the Grand Banks the following year, and even at attacking Canada in 1763. Ternay was chosen to head the initial expedition, whose immediate objectives were to seize St John's, Newfoundland, "to cause as much harm as possible to the English . . . [and to advance] if possible as far as Île Royale [Cape Breton Island] to assault the English there."

The expedition, which was organized in complete secrecy (only Ternay knew its true destination), assembled 750 soldiers – including 161 Irishmen as the nucleus of a battalion to be recruited from the Irish fishermen in Newfoundland. Transport consisted of two ships of the line, a frigate, and two flutes. They set sail from Brest on 8 May 1762. On 23 June, hoisting the British flag in order to avoid giving alarm, the five ships anchored at Bay Bulls, 20 miles south of St John's. The next day the infantry, under Colonel Joseph-Louis-Bernard de Cléron d'Haussonville, landed without opposition and immediately set off for St John's. The garrison there was weak, and on 27 June the French fleur-de-lis was raised over Fort William. Ternay and his sailors undertook a systematic destruction of the British establishments: all the fisheries were destroyed, and 460 ships of all sizes were captured or sunk. It is estimated that the British suffered more than £1,000,000 in damages.

The French established themselves in Newfoundland, certain that they would be remaining there until at least the next year; for they believed that the British would make no attempt before spring. But having learned on 15 July of the French attack, Jeffery AMHERST, the British commander-in-chief in North America, decided to expel them immediately. He appointed his brother, Lieutenant-Colonel William Amherst, to command seven ships, on which 1,500 British and American soldiers from the garrisons of New York, Halifax, and Louisbourg, Cape Breton Island, were embarked. These ships left Louisbourg on 7 September and joined the fleet commanded by Commodore Lord Colvill*.

Already worried at the presence of Colvill, who had been patrolling in the area since 25 August, Ternay had proposed to d'Haussonville that they embark the grenadiers and leave only the fusiliers at Fort William, either to obtain an honourable surrender in the event of a large-scale British attack, or to remain there all winter if the danger proved imaginary. However, when Amherst's squadron was sighted on 12 September, Ternay disembarked the grenadiers "to resist the enemy." On 13 September the British troops landed in force at Torbay, ten miles north of St John's, without any interference from the French fleet. Two days later, despite bitter resistance, the French were driven back into the fort. Ternay assembled the naval officers and grenadier captains in d'Haussonville's quarters for a last council of war. Against his advice – he apparently advocated the immediate abandonment of the fort – it was decided to leave the grenadiers in the fort until the very last moment, when they would regain the ships in longboats. The fusiliers of the Régiment de la Marine were to protect the operation by preventing the British from cutting the road giving access to the port. Ternay thereupon had the boom closing the entrance to the port destroyed; he also had the guns of the batteries covering the roadstead spiked to prevent the British from using them against the French as they sailed through the Narrows.

Taking advantage of a favourable wind, Ternay however moved forward the departure of his fleet to the night of 15 September. He was not even disturbed by the British, for, as he noted, "a thick fog and fresh easterly winds had forced the enemy squadron out to sea." While he succeeded in saving his entire squadron, Ternay nevertheless left the fusiliers of La Marine and all the grenadiers under d'Haussonville at St John's in a desperate situation. D'Haussonville had to surrender to Amherst on 18 September. The British, who had not been able to intercept the French ships, took their revenge a few days later. On 22 September they captured the *François-Louis*, en route for St John's with reinforcements of 93 men, and a short time later the *Zéphir*, under Captain François-Louis Poulin* de Courval.

Ternay did not reach Brest until 28 Jan. 1763, after he had been chased by two British ships off the French coast, had seized a British privateer, and had taken refuge in the Spanish port of Corunna. When, in accordance with the terms of capitulation, d'Haussonville returned to France, probably in October 1762, he apparently complained about Ternay's precipitous departure. The latter was not, however, censured, since it was appreciated that he had saved his little fleet. Moreover, negotiations about preliminary peace terms were under way between France, Spain, and Great Britain at Fontainebleau, and the terms were in fact signed on 3 Nov. 1762.

From 1764 to 1769 Ternay received command of various ships, and on 16 Aug. 1771 he was named commandant general of Île de France (Mauritius) and Île Bourbon (Réunion). On 22 December of the same year he attained the rank of brigadier of the naval forces. Appointed rear-admiral as of November 1776, Ternay took part in the War of American Independence as the senior naval officer in Lieutenant-General Rochambeau's expedition of 1780. Blockaded by a British fleet in the roads of Newport for six months, he died of typhus in December after eight days' illness. Since he had taken the three monastic vows of the Knights of Malta, he had never married.

GEORGES CERBELAUD SALAGNAC

AN, Col., B, 114; Marine, B[2], 370, 371; B[4], 104; C[1]. BN, MSS, NAF 9410 (Margry). [William Amherst], *The recapture of St. John's, Newfoundland, in 1762 as described in the journal of Lieut.-Colonel William Amherst, commander of the British expeditionary force*, ed. J. C. Webster ([Shediac, N.B.], 1928). *Liste de messieurs les chevaliers, chapelains conventuels et servants d'armes des trois vénérables langues de Provence, Auvergne et France* ([Valetta?], Malta, 1778). Lacour-Gayet, *La marine militaire sous Louis XV*; *La marine militaire sous Louis XVI*. Maurice Linyer de La Barbée, *Le chevalier de Ternay: vie de Charles Henry Louis d'Arsac de Ternay, chef d'escadre des armées navales* (2v., Grenoble, France, 1972). Warrington Dawson, "Les 2112 français morts aux États-Unis de 1777 à 1783 en combattant pour l'indépendance américaine," Soc. des américanistes, *Journal* (Paris), nouv. sér., XXVIII (1936), 1-154. E. W. H. Fyers, "The loss and recapture of St. John's, Newfoundland, in 1762," Soc. for Army Hist. Research, *Journal* (London), XI (1932), 179–215. "Une expédition française à Terre-Neuve en 1762," *BRH*, XIII (1907), 316–19.

ASSOMPTION, MARIE-JOSÈPHE MAUGUE-GARREAU, *dite* **DE L'.** *See* MAUGUE-GARREAU

ATIAˀTAWÌˀTSHERAˀ. *See* ANANDAMOAKIN

ATKINSON, GEORGE, HBC chief factor; d. 2 Oct. 1792 at Eastmain Factory (at the mouth of Rivière Eastmain, Que.).

Nothing is known of the life of George Atkinson before his engagement with the Hudson's Bay Company, other than that he was probably born in Stockton-on-Tees, England. His first years of service with the company evidently occurred during 1751–54, when crew lists for the company ship *Sea Horse*, engaged in the supply of posts on Hudson Bay, regularly included his name. An unexplained 14-year gap followed, but in 1768 he was once more engaged by the company, this time to serve as a sailor at Fort Albany (Ont.) for three years at £15 per annum.

In 1769 Atkinson was appointed mate of the Eastmain sloop at £25 annually after George Isbister was removed for bad behaviour. Thomas Moore, master at Eastmain, found Atkinson "a Very Worthy Man" and had him hunt, fish, and carry letters to Moose Factory (Ont.) and Albany, as well as care for the sloop. When Moore went to England in late 1772, Atkinson took charge of Eastmain as well as of its sloop. His 1772–73 journal suggests that he was on cordial terms with the Indians.

In the fall of 1773 Moore resumed the Eastmain command, and until 1777 Atkinson continued his service on company vessels. His assiduity and "knowledge of the Natives" led to his being proposed as leader of inland expeditions in the fall of 1773 and again in late 1776. On both occasions circumstances prevented his going. In late 1777, however, Atkinson did go inland. Eusebius Bacchus Kitchin, chief at Moose, had hoped Atkinson's party would travel up the Abitibi River (Ont.), but "the Ship arriving [at Moose] so late & the water being so shoal" defeated that plan. Instead, Atkinson wintered at Mesakamy Lake (Kesagami Lake, Ont.), only "half way to . . . [Lake] Abbitiby," after a "Longe fatiguen Journey." His letters to Kitchin document his problems there and the onset of the ill health he was to suffer thereafter. Disputing Kitchin's charge of misuse of provisions, he wrote "what could I dou the Indians That you was pleased to Send with us had nothing to mentain thar Selve with."

Kitchin ordered Atkinson to take the command of the Moose sloop in June 1778. In September Atkinson, being "very much beloved by the Natives there," was appointed master of Eastmain, a command he would hold almost continuously until his death. The post grew in size and importance under Atkinson's direction, and he was credited by Edward JARVIS, chief at Moose, with opening "new Channels of Trade, from the Northward to Richmond [on Lac Guillaume-Delisle] and Mistasin Lake [Lac Mistassini, Que.]." By September 1786 Eastmain had become independent of Moose and a "Factory distinct by itself." It was as well a base for resistance to Canadian competition. In 1790 Atkinson sent John Clarke* to Lac Mistassini to gather intelligence about rival Canadian traders, who were encroaching upon Eastmain's territory, and to recruit "any independent Men who wish to enter into this Service." Atkinson's salary suggests that his efforts were valued by the company: by 1791 he was receiving £130 per annum. His last years were beset by illness, however, and he returned to England in 1785–86 and in 1791–92. He was to survive his return to Eastmain in 1792 by only a few weeks, dying there in October.

Atkinson, like numerous other company officers of his time, had acquired a native family; to him and the Indian woman Necushin were born two sons and a daughter. The London committee, in an attempt to keep its posts free of traders' families, had forbidden passage of European women to the bay and had long ordered its servants not to consort with Indian women. But by the 1770s the latter rule had been defied by company men such as Joseph ISBISTER, Humphrey MARTEN, Moses NORTON, and Robert Pilgrim*. Long isolated from England, traders might accept Indian offers of female companionship for personal as well as commercial motives. By the time of Atkinson's death the company was coming to accept the presence of native-born women and children at its posts. The Indians commonly considered these women to be married, and by the 1830s they were earning legal and company recognition as wives "according to the custom of the country." The sons of these unions, if given paternal and company encouragement, could offer useful service to the HBC. Atkinson sent his son Sneppy to England in 1790, where he acquired his baptismal name George, in the hope that he would "shake of a little of the Indian & in so doing make him exert himself like a Man" on his return to Eastmain. Both of Atkinson's sons served the company, as did other Hudson Bay youths like Charles Thomas Isham* and William Richards*. George Jr had a fur-trade career of some note and left a large family to carry on the Atkinson name in the James Bay area.

JENNIFER S. H. BROWN

Durham County Record Office (Durham, Eng.), EP/Sto 2 (Holy Trinity Church, Stockton-on-Tees, register of baptisms, marriages, and burials, 1707–80). HBC Arch. A.1/39, pp.14, 127, 240, 388; A.1/43, ff.58, 105; A.1/46, f.74; A.5/2, ff.145–47; A.6/13, ff.124, 153; A.11/57, ff.122–22d; A.30/1, ff.2, 17, 30; A.30/3, f.33; A.30/4, f.11; A.32/3, f.12; A.36/1B, ff.14–16; B.59/a/40, ff.15, 29, 40, 44, 45; B.59/a/44, ff.6–8, 19, 21, 24; B.59/b/1; B.59/b/6, ff.6, 14–15; B.59/b/9, ff.14–15, 16; B.59/b/10, f.22; B.59/b/12; B.135/b/5, ff.3, 5–6, 10; B.135/b/6, ff.6, 8–9, 16–17, 40. PRO, Prob. 11/1238, will of George Atkinson, proved 28 Nov. 1793. *Moose fort journals, 1783–85*, ed. E. E. Rich and A. M. Johnson, intro. G. P. de T. Glazebrook (London, 1954). *Northern Quebec and Labrador journals and correspondence, 1819–35*, ed. K. G. Davies and A. M. Johnson (London, 1963).

ATQUANDADEGHTE. *See* OHQUANDAGEGHTE

ATTERWANA. *See* OTTROWANA

AUBERT DE GASPÉ, IGNACE-PHILIPPE, officer in the colonial regular troops and seigneur; b. 4 April 1714 at Saint-Antoine-de-Tilly (Que.), son of Pierre Aubert de Gaspé and Madeleine-Angélique Legardeur de Tilly; d. 26 Jan. 1787 at Saint-Jean-Port-Joli (Que.).

Ignace-Philippe Aubert de Gaspé gained a name for himself as much through his military career as through being a member of the Aubert family, who were related to the most notable families in Canada. He was the grandson of Charles Aubert* de La Chesnaye, a businessman, and of Charles Legardeur* de Tilly, governor of Trois-Rivières. Through his marriage in Quebec on 30 June 1745 to Marie-Anne Coulon de Villiers, daughter of Nicolas-Antoine*, he became the brother-in-law of Louis* and of Joseph Coulon* de Villiers de Jumonville.

In the course of a distinguished military career, Ignace-Philippe Aubert de Gaspé spent 33 years in the forces and was prominent himself in numerous combats and expeditions which marked the end of the French régime. A cadet at 13 he was successively promoted second ensign (1739), ensign (1745), lieutenant (1749), and captain (1756); he served all over New France from 1734 to 1760. He first participated in the 1734–35 expedition to subdue the Foxes, west of Lake Michigan [*see* Nicolas-Joseph de Noyelles* de Fleurimont], and in the 1739 campaign against the Chickasaws and Natchez in Louisiana [*see* Jean-Baptiste Le Moyne* de Bienville; Charles Le Moyne* de Longueuil]. After three years' garrison duty at Michilimackinac (Mackinaw City, Mich.), he left the west in 1746 to join Jean-Baptiste-Nicolas-Roch de RAMEZAY's expedition organized to help the fleet of the Duc d'Anville [La Rochefoucauld*] chase the British from Acadia. Four years later, when France was trying to consolidate the boundaries of its territories in that part of the country, he was called upon to build Fort Saint-Jean, on the Saint John River. He became commandant and remained there until he left for the west in 1753. Following a brief stay on the Ohio River, he participated in the attack on Fort Necessity (near Farmington,

Pa.), which was intended to avenge the death of Jumonville who had been killed by a detachment of Virginian militia led by George Washington [*see* Louis Coulon de Villiers]. In 1756, after a few months' stay at Fort Niagara (near Youngstown, N.Y.), he was sent to the Lake Champlain region, and he served at Fort Saint-Frédéric (near Crown Point, N.Y.) and Fort Carillon (Ticonderoga, N.Y.). He consequently took part in the capture of Fort George (also called Fort William Henry; now Lake George, N.Y.) in 1757 and in Montcalm*'s well-known victory over ABERCROMBY at Carillon in 1758. After the fall of Quebec he took part in the French army's siege of the city and fought at Sainte-Foy under LÉVIS.

Montcalm seldom praised the colonial regular troops; nevertheless Captain Aubert de Gaspé was among the small number he mentioned after the British were routed at Carillon. Aubert de Gaspé's merit was also recognized by Ramezay and Noyelles de Fleurimont, and by the king, who on 24 March 1761 named him a knight of the order of Saint-Louis. Whether he ever had the opportunity to go to France and be received officially as a member of that order is not clear.

In the autumn of 1760, after the surrender of Montreal, Aubert de Gaspé took refuge with his *censitaires* at Port-Joli. As his manor house had been burnt by the invader the previous autumn, he was forced to live for a time in what remained of the seigneurial mill at Rivière Trois-Saumons. Except for 1775 and 1776, which were marked by the American invasion, the 26 years that Aubert de Gaspé spent on his seigneury after the conquest were on the whole peaceful. Between 1764 and 1766 the manor house and all the houses burnt by Wolfe*'s army were rebuilt. The seigneur's personal presence so encouraged settlement that the population of the seigneury nearly tripled during his years there. In 1779 it was possible to build a church, develop the second line of homesteads, and begin on the third.

Captain Aubert de Gaspé, the fourth seigneur of Port-Joli, died in his manor house at the age of 72 and was buried on 28 Jan. 1787 in the parish church which he had helped build. He and Marie-Anne Coulon de Villiers had ten children. The sixth, Pierre-Ignace*, became a member of the Legislative Council and a militia colonel; he married Catherine Tarieu de Lanaudière and their son Philippe-Joseph* was the author of *Les anciens Canadiens*.

JACQUES CASTONGUAY

[Æ. Fauteux* states in *Les chevaliers de Saint-Louis*, 25ff., 182ff., that Ignace-Philippe Aubert de Gaspé never visited France and consequently was not admitted as a knight of the order. On the other hand, textual analysis of Philippe-Joseph Aubert de Gaspé's *Mémoires* (Ottawa, 1866) indicates that Ignace-Philippe was believed to have spent some time in France after the conquest. He might have been admitted as a knight at this time. This theory would explain why in 1786 he could write after his name "admitted to the royal and military order of Saint-Louis," an addition his grandson also made on two occasions. Further research is needed. J. C.]

ANQ-Q, Greffe de J.-N. Pinguet de Vaucour, 26 juin 1745. Archives paroissiales, Notre-Dame de Québec, Registre des baptêmes, mariages et sépultures, 30 juin 1745; Saint-Antoine-de-Tilly (Qué.), Registre des baptêmes, mariages et sépultures, 5 avril 1714; Saint-Jean-Port-Joli (Qué.), Registre des baptêmes, mariages et sépultures, 26 janv. 1787, 19 mars 1789. ASQ, MSS, 424, ff.8–10. Æ. Fauteux, *Les chevaliers de Saint-Louis*. P.-G. Roy, *Inv. concessions*, III, 170. P.[-J.] Aubert de Gaspé, *Les anciens Canadiens* (16e éd., Québec, 1970); *The Canadians of old*, trans. G. M. Pennée (Quebec, 1864); *Mémoires* (Ottawa, 1866). H.-R. Casgrain, *Philippe Aubert de Gaspé* (Québec, 1871). Jacques Castonguay, *La seigneurie de Philippe Aubert de Gaspé, Saint-Jean-Port-Joli* (Montréal, 1976). [François Daniel], *Histoire des grandes familles françaises du Canada, ou aperçu sur le chevalier Benoist, et quelques familles contemporaines* (Montréal, 1867). P.-G. Roy, *La famille Aubert de Gaspé* (Lévis, Qué., 1907).

AUGÉ, ÉTIENNE, merchant-trader; b. at Saint-Louis-de-Lotbinière (Lotbinière, Que.), son of Louis Augé and Antoinette Barabé; d. 18 Jan. 1780 in Montreal.

The date of Étienne Augé's arrival in Montreal is not known, but by 1751, when he married Louise-Françoise Dalgueuil, *dit* Labrèche, he was already a merchant-trader there. According to the marriage contract signed on 11 September before notary Jean-Baptiste Adhémar*, Augé owned a piece of land with a stone house on Rue Saint-Paul, Montreal's business street. His wife's aunt Jeanne Dalgueuil gave them a house built of squared timbers (*pièces sur pièces*) and a bakehouse with its fixtures, on condition that they lodge and feed her. Louise-Françoise Dalgueuil was then 41 and Augé was about the same age. Their late marriage probably accounts for their lack of children; in fact childless marriages were not uncommon among Montreal merchants. Augé and his wife associated with the town's most important merchant families – the Charly Saint-Anges, Giassons, Hervieux, Quesnels, Couagnes, and Guys. Over the years Augé was especially close to the Guys and in 1777 named "his friend" Pierre Guy* as his executor.

Augé was primarily involved in the import-export trade. He did not engage seriously in the fur trade, limiting his interest to outfitting several expeditions in the period 1751–55. He did, however, ship to the French market the pelts he received from outfitters in payment for trading goods. Augé also had a retail business in which he sold to local people, for cash or on credit, textiles, sewing and dressmaking supplies, manufactured goods, and even foodstuffs such as sugar, spices, coffee, and rum. If the volume of his purchases between 1755 and 1758 can be taken as a guide, his yearly turnover amounted to about 30,000 *livres*. This business was more profitable and entailed fewer risks than did trading in furs with the Indians.

For some time after the conquest Augé maintained contacts with his suppliers in La Rochelle, Denis GOGUET and the merchant-traders Paillet et Meynardie. But trade with France had in fact become impossible, and he had to enter into relations with the London merchant-traders Daniel and Antoine Vialars and Isidore Lynch, who had been recommended by his correspondents in La Rochelle. Besides selling the pelts he shipped, these suppliers also attended to clearing the 200,000 *livres* in bills of exchange held by Augé. Although he had reason to complain frequently of the greed of his new suppliers, and though the clearing of his bills was to drag on, Augé succeeded in significantly expanding his business from 1770 to 1775. His business correspondence deals primarily with the cost and quality of the merchandise he received, remittances in bills of exchange or in pelts, freight and insurance rates, frequency of shipments, and the economic situation in Britain. His accounting methods, like those of the town's other merchants, were rather rudimentary, but they sufficed for the needs of business in Montreal. There is no better proof of this than the fortune he accumulated. At his death he left 80,000 *livres* to his relatives and friends, including Pierre Guy, to various charities, and to his Indian slave Marguerite. His extensive assets included 10,000 *livres* in personal property, nearly 24,000 *livres* in accounts receivable, two pieces of land in the suburbs of Montreal, and 28,000 *livres* in merchandise in stock.

Étienne Augé, like other Montreal merchants, engaged in political activity. Between 1764 and 1766 he signed three petitions to the British authorities about the regulation of the fur business. He also signed the Montreal merchants' protest against the claims of the seigneurs in 1766 and the Canadian merchants' petition of December 1773 asking the king for the restoration of French laws and opposing the creation of a house of assembly.

The tempo of Augé's activities began to moderate around 1775. He may already have been stricken by the illness which would lead to his death in 1780. His nephew, Michel Augé, whom he apparently treated like a son and who helped him in his business, probably took over from him. Augé was one of the Montreal merchants who succeeded in living through the political and economic changes of the era of the conquest without being too seriously affected. He was probably the largest Canadian merchant-trader in Montreal near the end of the French régime and he seems to have done even better after 1760. Examination of various accounting documents, his business correspondence, and numerous contracts shows clearly the importance of his commerce.

JOSÉ E. IGARTUA

AN, Col., C^{11A}, 108, ff.1–90. ANQ-M, Greffe de J.-B. Adhémar, 11 sept. 1751, 14 sept. 1754; Greffe de Simon Sanguinet, 7 janv., 4, 16 mars 1780; Greffe de François Simonnet, 13 juin 1758, 8 juin 1766. BL, Add. MSS 35915, ff.228–33 (copies at PAC). PAC, MG 23, GIII, 25, ser.A (Étienne Augé); ser.B (Étienne Augé); GIII, 29; MG 24, L3, pp.1469–75, 1522–30, 1532–33, 2097–99, 2203–6, 2274–76, 2395–96, 2494–95, 2659–60, 2672–73, 3407–10. PRO, CO 42/1, pp.181–83; 42/2, pp.277–80; 42/5, pp.298–99 (PAC transcripts). *Doc. relatifs à l'hist. constitutionnelle, 1759–91* (Shortt et Doughty; 1921), 1, 490–94. "État général des billets d'ordonnances . . . ," ANQ *Rapport*, 1924–25, 231–342. "Protêt des marchands de Montréal contre une assemblée des seigneurs, tenue en cette ville le 21 février, 1766," É.-Z. Massicotte, édit., *Canadian Antiquarian and Numismatic Journal* (Montreal), 3rd ser., XI (1914), 1–20. *Quebec Gazette*, 20 Oct. 1766. Massicotte, "Répertoire des engagements pour l'Ouest," ANQ *Rapport*, 1930–31, 414, 433, 436, 438, 446; 1931–32, 304–5, 312. Tanguay, *Dictionnaire*. J. E. Igartua, "The merchants and *négociants* of Montreal, 1750–1775: a study in socio-economic history" (unpublished PHD thesis, Michigan State University, East Lansing, 1974). É.-Z. Massicotte, "La bourse de Montréal sous le Régime français," *Canadian Antiquarian and Numismatic Journal*, 3rd ser., XII (1915), 26–32.

AUGOOSHAWAY. *See* EGUSHWA

AUMASSON DE COURVILLE, LOUIS-LÉONARD, known as **Sieur de Courville**, notary, lawyer, and memorialist; b. at the end of 1722 or the beginning of 1723 at Sainte-Menehould, France, son of Claude Aumasson de Courville, an officer, and Judith de Chevreau; m. 6 June 1752 Marie-Anne, daughter of Étienne Amiot, *dit* Villeneuve, at Quebec; d. some time after 1782, perhaps in the Montreal region.

Louis-Léonard Aumasson de Courville, a secretary to the Marquis de La Jonquière [Taffanel*], governor of New France, may have arrived in Quebec with him in August 1749. On 28 May 1754 he was appointed royal notary for French Acadia and by July had taken up residence at Fort Beauséjour (near Sackville, N.B.). There he soon became the secretary of the commandant, Louis Du Pont Duchambon de Vergor, and he became acquainted with Abbé Jean-Louis Le Loutre and Louis-Thomas Jacau de Fiedmont, both of whom later figured prominently in his "Mémoires." After a siege by Robert Monckton Fort Beauséjour capitulated on 16 June 1755. As Vergor's secretary Aumasson de Courville drafted the terms of surrender.

Back in Quebec after his year in Acadia, Aumasson de Courville was appointed clerk of the Jesuits' seigneurial court at Notre-Dame-des-Anges on 26 March 1756. On 3 April Intendant Bigot granted him a commission as royal notary in the jurisdictions near Quebec of Notre-Dame-des-Anges, Saint-Gabriel, Sillery, Saint-Joseph, and Saint-Ignace. Courville apparently did not receive any deeds after 11 June 1758, when he was living at Ancienne-Lorette. He continued as clerk of the Jesuit court until 1759.

On 1 Oct. 1760 Aumasson de Courville received a new commission from the military governor of Montreal, Thomas Gage, to serve as "royal notary" in the parishes of Saint-Ours, Contrecœur, and Saint-Denis on the Richelieu River. Over the next five years he lived in the parishes of L'Assomption, Repentigny, Varennes, and Saint-Ours successively before settling in Saint-Denis, which had been supposed to be his place of residence. The profession of notary had been recognized by the military régime, but there was uncertainty about its continued existence after the treaty of Paris; this uncertainty, and the relatively low fees, probably explain why the Sieur de Courville felt a need for change. He settled in the *faubourg* Saint-Marie in Montreal in 1765 and seems at that point to have forsaken notarial practice for a new career; on 26 Nov. 1768 he was admitted to the bar. But he evidently earned no more as a lawyer than he had as a notary, since on 12 April 1770 the sheriff held a sale of his property. He was still in Montreal at the beginning of June 1773, when his oldest son, Charles-Léonard, died at 18 years of age. Aumasson de Courville gave up pleading, returned to notarial practice and by 1779 had settled in L'Assomption where he practised at least until 1781 or more likely 1782. After that date no further trace of him has been found.

After more than 20 years of research, Ægidius Fauteux* established in 1940 that the author of the "Mémoires du S . . . de C . . . contenant l'histoire du Canada durant la guerre, et sous le gouvernement anglais" was Louis-Léonard Aumasson de Courville, whose biography he wrote. The "Mémoires" recount events in New France between 1749 and the beginning of the British régime, and they were published in 1838. It may be that they were begun by Courville before the capture of Quebec, since some of them were transmitted to the anonymous author of the "Mémoire du Canada," who is known to have left New France for France by the spring of 1760. Fauteux's searching analysis of the "Mémoires" reveals Courville to have been a difficult man whose tenacious personal animosities sometimes obscured his view of events. Courville describes the activities of the administrators and embezzlers at the end of the French régime bluntly, and he also attacks the clergy, particularly Abbé Le Loutre, François Picquet, and the Jesuit Jean-Baptiste Tournois*. In this outspokenness Fauteux saw the explanation for the anonymity Courville maintained; the "Mémoires" contain so much "invective, a great deal of it flagrantly unfair," that "fear of reprisal made him keep silent."

Whether as secretary or as notary Courville was in subordinate positions; it is significant that he was not called as a witness at the trial of Vergor, who was accused of negligence after the loss of Fort Beauséjour. The change of régime did not favour his career. In 1779, when he was arguing with Valentin Jautard in the *Gazette littéraire pour la ville et district de Montréal*, he describes himself as an "old-fashioned jurist, living in a cottage, exposed to the full fury of disgrace and misfortune."

François Rousseau

[The "Mémoires du S . . . de C . . . contenant l'histoire du Canada durant la guerre, et sous le gouvernement anglais" were published in 1838 and reprinted in 1873 in "Mémoires sur le Canada, depuis 1749 jusqu'à 1760 . . . ," Literary and Hist. Soc. of Quebec, *Hist. Docs.*, 1st ser., I. Courville's memoirs, comprising 211 pages, constitute the most important section of the book. In an article entitled "Le S . . . de C . . . enfin démasqué," *Cahiers des Dix*, 5 (1940), 231–92, Ægidius Fauteux solved the problems posed by the memoirs and identified their author. The present biography takes this article as its point of departure. F.R.]

ANQ-M, Greffe de L.-L. Aumasson de Courville, 1754–81; the ANQ-Q holds the minutes for 1756–58. "Mémoire du Canada," ANQ *Rapport*, 1924–25, 96–198. "Les notaires au Canada sous le Régime français," ANQ *Rapport*, 1921–22, 56. P.-G. Roy, *Inv. jug. et délib., 1717–60*, VI, 78, 80, 88; *Inv. ord. int.*, III, 185, 196. Tanguay, *Dictionnaire*, II, 32. Vachon, "Inv. critique des notaires royaux," *RHAF*, IX, 560–61.

AUTERIVE. *See* Cuny

AVÈNE DES MÉLOIZES, ANGÉLIQUE RENAUD D'. *See* RENAUD

AYLWIN (Aylwyn), THOMAS, merchant and justice of the peace; b. *c.* 1729 in Romsey, Hampshire, England; m. 11 Sept. 1771 in Boston Lucy Cushing, and they had at least three sons; d. 11 April 1791 at Quebec.

Thomas Aylwin was probably one of the merchants who established themselves at Quebec immediately after its capture by Major-General Wolfe*'s troops. He was doubtless among that set of merchants of whom Governor MURRAY said in 1764: they "have resorted to a Country where there is No Money, and . . . think themselves superior in rank and fortune to the Soldier and the Canadian." In partnership for a few years with Charles Kerr, Aylwin specialized in the retail sale of imported products including dry goods, foodstuffs, wine, hardware, stationery, and other merchandise. After Kerr died in 1765 Aylwin pursued his commercial activities at Quebec until 1769, when he seems to have removed to Massachusetts for about six years.

Returning to Quebec at the beginning of the American revolution, Aylwin set up his business on Rue Saint-Jean and later rented a house on Rue Saint-Joseph. On 23 Oct. 1777 he bought two houses on Rue Notre-Dame, in the business district, from merchant and legislative councillor Thomas Dunn* for £948 (Halifax currency), paying £508 in cash. The range of products he advertised in the *Quebec Gazette* steadily broadened. As well, he was the supplier to certain merchants, including Jacob Bettez of Baie-Saint-Paul and also Abraham Morhouse who in June 1786 owed £1,100 to "Tho. Aylwin & Co." In the same period Aylwin undertook to sell Samuel JACOBS' wheat and went into the wholesale trade in biscuit. He seems to have enjoyed moderate prosperity; in fact, the inventory made after his death reveals that he lived comfortably, though not in luxury. For example, although he owned a gold-trimmed porcelain tea service, mahogany furniture, and plate worth £17, two of the 12 pieces of ornamental china on the mantel were broken and the carpet in his parlour was "much wore." His library of some 50 volumes included works of history, law, religion, and poetry, as well as books on business.

At the end of 1790, a few months before his death, Aylwin, who was probably ill or in financial straits, put up his house and his store with its adjoining dwelling for sale or rent. The inventory of his estate revealed a net deficit of £293, not counting a considerable debt to the Quebec firm of Fraser and Young which was discovered later. However, his London supplier, Breckwood Pattle and Company, likely remained his most important creditor. At the request of Montreal merchant John Gray* and of Ann, the widow of Alexander Gray of Quebec, Aylwin's immovables were seized and were put up for auction in 1792 to pay off the debts of his estate.

Along with his activities as a businessman Thomas Aylwin had also held office as justice of the peace from 1765 until his departure for Massachusetts; reappointed in 1785, he retained the post until his death. Aylwin collaborated in the endeavours of a group of merchants who sought recognition of their commercial interests from the political authorities. By 1764 he was a member of the Quebec grand jury chaired by merchant James JOHNSTON which opposed Murray's administration. On 10 and 17 Dec. 1767 the opinion of Attorney General Francis Maseres* favouring the application of British law to bankruptcy cases was published in the *Quebec Gazette*; Maseres himself asserted that Aylwin, with George SUCKLING, framed the anonymous response which appeared on the 24th and 31st. In this response they set out the position of the majority of merchants who, though generally favourable to the introduction of British commercial law, were opposed in this particular instance. They alleged that, because of the economic conditions prevailing in Canada, the law would, if put into effect, entail the bankruptcy of many businessmen who with more time might pay off their debts. Later, on the occasion of Lieutenant Governor Henry HAMILTON's departure in 1785, Aylwin was among the supporters who expressed satisfaction with the interest he had taken in commerce, and especially with his inauguration of trial by jury in commercial cases. A member of the Quebec grand jury again in 1787, Aylwin opposed any tax to finance construction of public buildings, including a new prison, until the colony was in a better position to assume this financial burden and had a constitution closer to the British model. However, in 1789, under his chairmanship, this body expressed its regret to Chief Justice William SMITH that there was no tax system to ensure the maintenance of Quebec streets, which were in poor condition. That same year the grand jury demanded that the government create a public fund to assist the poor, who were particularly hard hit by famine; it also suggested the organization of supervised programs of work to lessen the risk that ex-criminals left at loose ends after their release would return to crime. In 1789 also, he and other Quebec merchants signed a petition to Lord Dorchester [Guy Carleton*] requesting that importation free of excise duties be permitted temporarily for West Indian rum, a commodity Aylwin had been selling since at least 1776. They asked as well that the province of Quebec be favoured over any other country in trade with these islands. The following year Aylwin signed a petition in favour of a non-sectarian university [*see* Jean-François HUBERT; Charles-François BAILLY de Messein].

Like many other merchants Aylwin also took part in activities of the colony's Masonic organization. In 1769 he was treasurer of the Provincial Grand Lodge and a member of the committee set up to obtain a grand lodge seal. At the time of the American revolution when war led to the decline of military lodges and, by the same token, freemasonry in Canada was at its lowest ebb since the conquest, Aylwin sat on a committee established to remedy the situation by encouraging the revitalization of the civilian lodges. In October 1775 he undertook to be secretary to St Andrew's Lodge, No. 2, Quebec, at Quebec, and the following year became its master, again for a one-year period. Deputy provincial grand master by the end of 1776, he retained this post until at least 1781; as such he signed the commissions authorizing the creation of St Peter's Lodge, No. 4, Quebec, at Montreal, and Unity Lodge, No. 13, of Quebec, at Sorel.

Thomas Aylwin died in April 1791 leaving his wife, who survived him by only a month, and three sons who were still minors. One of his grandsons, Thomas Cushing Aylwin*, was a member of the Legislative Assembly under the Union, and later a judge of the Court of Queen's Bench.

JEAN LAFLEUR

ANQ-Q, AP-G-313/2, George Allsopp to A.M. Allsopp, 12 March 1785; État civil, Anglicans, Cathedral of the Holy Trinity (Québec), 14 April 1791; Greffe de M.-A. Berthelot d'Artigny, 13 nov. 1779; Greffe de J.-A. Panet, 23 oct. 1777; Greffe de Charles Stewart, 28 juill., 10 août 1786, 20 avril, 29 août 1789. PAC, MG 19, A2, ser.3, 2, p.53; 3, pp.91, 145–46; 4, pp.14, 95–96, 98–100; MG 23, GII, 1, ser.1, 2, p.55. "Charles Robin on the Gaspe coast, 1766," ed. A.-G. LeGros, *Revue d'hist. de la Gaspésie* (Gaspé, Qué.), IV (1966), 196. *Doc. relatifs à l'hist. constitutionnelle, 1759–91* (Shortt et Doughty; 1921), I, 189, 191. "A list of Protestant house keepers in the District of Quebec (Octr. 26th, 1764)," *BRH*, XXXVIII (1932), 754. Maseres, *Maseres letters* (Wallace), 19, 74, 79, 125–28. *Quebec Gazette*, 25 July 1765–17 Nov. 1768, 28 Nov. 1776–1 Nov. 1792 (there are over 140 references to Thomas Aylwin in the index of the *Quebec Gazette*). *Almanach de Québec*, 1780, 60; 1788, 18; 1791, 34, 82. "Juges de paix de la province de Québec (1767)," *BRH*, XLII (1936), 13. J. H. Graham, *Outlines of the history of freemasonry in the province of Quebec* (Montreal, 1892), 47–49, 56. Charles Langelier, *L'hon[ble] Thomas Cushing Aylwin, juge de la Cour du banc de la reine . . .* (Québec, 1903), 11. J. R. Robertson, *The history of freemasonry in Canada from its introduction in 1749 . . .* (2v., Toronto, 1900), I, 478. Pemberton Smith, *A research into early Canadian masonry, 1759–1869* (Montreal, 1939), 6–47. "La famille Aylwin," *BRH*, LI (1945), 241.

B

BABY, *dit* **Dupéront (Dupéron, Duperron), JACQUES**, fur-trader and Indian department employee; baptized 4 Jan. 1731 at Montreal (Que.); m. *c*. 23 Nov. 1760 at Detroit (Mich.) to Susanne Réaume (Rhéaume), *dit* La Croix; 11 of their 22 children survived to adulthood; d. *c*. 2 Aug. 1789 at Detroit.

Jacques Baby de Ranville, grandfather of Jacques Baby, *dit* Dupéront, was a scion of the decayed nobility of southern France and a sergeant in the Régiment de Carignan-Salières who married in Canada and settled as a rural merchant and farmer. Ranville's son Raymond first went west with the fur brigades at age 15. In 1721 Raymond married Thérèse Le Comte Dupré, daughter of a Montreal family deeply involved in the fur trade although of seigneurial rank. Their son Dupéront therefore shared that heritage so significant in early Canadian history of vague pretensions to nobility coupled with dynamic participation in the fur trade and residency in Montreal.

When Dupéront first went west is unknown, but by 1753 he was a trader and Indian agent at Chiningué (Logstown, now Ambridge, Pa). In the Seven Years' War he, his elder brother Louis, and his youngest brother Antoine were all trading in the west and saw military service in the Ohio valley alongside France's Indian allies. A fourth brother, François*, handled the Montreal end of Antoine's and Dupéront's business on a partnership basis that would last until the death of Antoine in 1765. After the fall of Canada in 1760 Dupéront refused to swear allegiance to George III; and being, in Colonel Henry Bouquet's words, "of a family noted for their influence among the Indians," he was prevented from touring the western posts to collect his debts before returning to Montreal. His posture as a French patriot led to his arrest and temporary incarceration at Detroit on a groundless charge of plotting with Indians against the British occupying forces.

Dupéront's intention was to leave Canada for France, there to join François, who had been sent to England as a prisoner of war. But upon arrival at Montreal in the autumn of 1761 Dupéront learned that François was moving their commercial relations from La Rochelle and Bordeaux to London, their French correspondents transferring cash balances and providing necessary letters of introduction. Dupéront also found that he was able to sell his furs advantageously at Montreal and that market prospects were good. He and his wife therefore returned to Detroit, the base of his operations, probably in the autumn of 1762.

Since he was permitted to return west, Dupéront had presumably taken the oath of allegiance at Montreal. He made his new position clear in Pontiac*'s uprising by first supplying the besieged British garrison at Detroit and then openly joining it. In 1777 he was appointed a captain and interpreter in the department of Indian affairs and was acting commissary in 1779. Although the latter office might seem to have entailed business advantages, Governor HALDIMAND's aide-de-camp, Dietrich Brehm, stated in a letter from Detroit to his superior that "Mr. Baby now is not able to mind his own bisnis of trade being interely taken up by the maniging of Indiens" and that he should therefore receive higher pay than the "common and lowlified interpreters."

Dupéront lost considerably by the discredit of Canada's paper money after the conquest. The difficult business climate of the decades that followed is mirrored in his letters to François. He notes the swelling of the ranks of traders after 1765 (rightly predicting "the confusion will be dispelled by the ruin of the greatest number"), a change in market demand from beaver to luxury furs, the increasing competition of traders from Albany and New York who, he wrote, "sell here at almost as low a price as we buy at Quebec," and the deterioration of the trade, especially after the American revolution. The year 1772 was the first in which he received fewer furs than he had anticipated.

But Dupéront survived and prospered. Indeed, his 1785 outfit was the largest of his career, £5,000. He was undoubtedly a vigorous trader, admired by the Indians, demanding with regard to the quality of his merchandise, insistent on the early arrival of outfits each year, and having the competitive advantage of residency. From an early date he diversified his economic base by the development of lands. He had received several grants of land from Indian tribes in addition to his purchases. By 1789 he had 1,440 acres of developed land with two water-driven mills on the American side of the Detroit River and 720 acres on the British side. He also had an immense timber reserve northwest of Lake St Clair, given him by the Ojibwas. The value of his estate at his death cannot be determined with certainty; his will forbade his children to bother their mother with demands for an inventory. When she did authorize an inventory in 1800, the estate totalled about £24,570, most of it invested with Alexander Ellice* of London. That this money had formerly been invested in New York, either by Dupéront or his heirs, suggests the possibility that he may have developed trade relations with that city in his later years. It was his son James* (Jacques) who withdrew these American investments in 1793 and transferred the proceeds to London.

At his death Dupéront was 58, one-eyed, worn down by the rigours of frontier life, but not an old man. He did not live long enough to enjoy the dignified appointments he had received: a commission of the peace in 1784, the lieutenant-colonelcy of the Detroit militia in 1787, and a seat on the land board for the District of Hesse in 1788. His correspondence and actions suggest that he was straightforward, impulsive, and marked by the stubborn tenacity of the self-made man. His letters contain many thundering denunciations of his competitors, yet they also bear witness to the warmth and humour of a generous personality. Certainly his contemporaries admired him. "Poor Baby died at Detroit about the first of August, universally regretted," wrote the fur-trader John Richardson*. "He has not left such a Frenchman behind him."

DALE MIQUELON

ANQ-M, État civil, Catholiques, Notre-Dame de Montréal, 4 janv. 1731. ANQ-Q, Greffe de J.-B. Planté, 8, 12 nov. 1800; 20 déc. 1800 (nos.2536–41). ASQ, Fonds H.-R. Casgrain, Sér. O, 0423, 0475, 0476. AUM, P 58. BL, Add. MSS 21638, pp.250, 253, 260, 268, 312; 21653, p.73; 21759, p.93 (transcripts at PAC). PAC, MG 18, I5, 1, pp.274, 887, 1052; 2, pp.8, 44, 362; 5/1, p.7; 5/2, pp.8, 350, 352; 6, p.124; MG 23, GIII, 7, John Richardson letters, Richardson to Porteous, 23 Sept. 1789; RG 4, B28, 115. PAO, Baby papers, commissions, 1777, 1784, 1787; livre de comptes, 1788–91; Potawatomie land grant. PRO, CO 42/37, p.46 (transcript at PAC).

Quebec Gazette, 2 April, 29 Aug., 10 Sept. 1789. Lefebvre, "Engagements pour l'Ouest," ANQ *Rapport*, 1946–47. Massicotte, "Répertoire des engagements pour l'Ouest," ANQ *Rapport*, 1931–32,

1932–33. [P.-]P.-B. Casgrain, *Mémorial des familles Casgrain, Baby et Perrault du Canada* (Québec, 1898–99). [François Daniel], *Nos gloires nationales; ou, histoire des principales familles du Canada* . . . (2v., Montréal, 1867). D. B. Miquelon, "The Baby family in the trade of Canada, 1750–1820" (unpublished MA thesis, Carleton University, Ottawa, [1966]). Peckham, *Pontiac*. P. J. Robinson, *Toronto during the French régime* . . . (Toronto and Chicago, 1933). P.-G. Roy, *La famille Le Compte Dupré* (Lévis, Qué., 1941).

BADEAUX, JEAN-BAPTISTE, notary, justice of the peace, and diarist; b. 29 April 1741 at Quebec, son of Charles Badeaux, a tailor, and Catherine Loisy; d. 12 Nov. 1796 at Trois-Rivières (Que.).

Jean-Baptiste Badeaux came from a family that had been established in Canada since 1647. In that year Jacques Badeaux and his wife, Jeanne Ardouin, both natives of La Rochelle, arrived in Canada with their three children and settled at Beauport. When he was 13, their great-grandson Jean-Baptiste, the ninth in a family of ten children, was living with an aunt at Trois-Rivières, where he was a cantor in the church of L'Immaculée Conception. Later he became the master cantor, a post that he held with pride all his life but for which he was never remunerated.

On 20 March 1767 Badeaux obtained a commission as a notary, and he remained in practice for the rest of his life. His deeds, which reflect a whole period in the history of Trois-Rivières, are drawn up so meticulously that he could legitimately be called the perfect notary. Badeaux won the confidence of the governmental authorities, who on several occasions entrusted him with tasks that fell within the area of his expertise. In December 1778 he wrote to Governor HALDIMAND for permission to assume custody of the deeds of notary Paul Dielle, who was seriously ill. The governor assented. Badeaux came to have in his keeping all the notarial records of the former notaries of the District of Trois-Rivières. In 1795 he was given the responsibility of preparing the land roll for the properties being claimed by the Abenakis of Saint-François. As notary and attorney for the Ursulines of Trois-Rivières, he went to Quebec several times to render fealty and homage to the governor on their behalf for their seigneuries of Rivière-du-Loup-en-Haut and Saint-Jean. A contract dated October 1772 indicates that his services as attorney for these seigneuries entitled Badeaux to "two *sous* per *livre* of the sums [in seigneurial dues] that he shall receive at the aforementioned seigneuries, in money as well as in poultry and grain."

At the time of the American invasion in 1775 Badeaux kept a diary in which he noted the events that took place in Trois-Rivières and the surrounding region. A convinced royalist, he commented, "I admit that although I find some virtues in several of the republicans, I find great defects in a republic in general; I see in it much more error and ostentation than true greatness of soul." He distinguished himself during this period by encouraging his compatriots to enrol in the militia and by attempting to moderate the enthusiasm of those in sympathy with the American cause. Early in November 1775, foreseeing that their town would soon be captured by the Americans, the inhabitants of Trois-Rivières sent Badeaux and an English speaking citizen, William Morris, to present a petition to Richard MONTGOMERY asking him to see that the lives and possessions of the citizens were respected. The general responded favourably to their request.

In 1781 Haldimand accorded Badeaux a commission as notary for the entire province of Quebec, probably as a reward for his loyalty and devotion during the American invasion. In July 1790 he was appointed justice of the peace for the District of Trois-Rivières. That same year merchant Aaron HART, who wanted to obtain payment for the goods supplied the Americans during 1775–76, asked Badeaux to serve as his attorney in dealings with Congress. The Ursulines did the same in order to obtain reimbursement for the expenses incurring in nursing the American soldiers. Badeaux's efforts met with no success, however.

On 29 Oct. 1764 Badeaux was married to Marguerite, daughter of wood-carver Gilles Bolvin*; on 10 Jan 1791 he took Marguerite Pratte as his second wife. He died "after a long and severe illness." The *Quebec Gazette* rendered him the following homage: "His active and able conduct in the execution of his duty as a magistrate and a notary, always received the merited approbation of all those who knew him . . . the public have cause to lament the loss of a useful and respectable citizen." His sons Antoine-Isidore and Joseph* took up the notarial profession; Joseph became a member of the assembly for the town of Trois-Rivières and the counties of Buckingham and Yamaska.

IN COLLABORATION WITH RAYMOND DOUVILLE

The manuscript journal of Jean-Baptiste Badeaux is held at PAC, MG 23, B35. The *Revue canadienne* (Montréal) published this manuscript in volume VII (1870) under the title "Journal des opérations de l'armée américaine, lors de l'invasion du Canada en 1775–76, par M. J. B. Badeaux, notaire de la ville des Trois-Rivières." It was reprinted the following year by the Literary and Hist. Soc. of Quebec in its *Hist. Docs*, 3rd ser., no.2, and in 1873 by Abbé Hospice-Anthelme-Jean-Baptiste Verreau* in *Invasion du Canada*. The register of Jean-Baptiste Badeaux (1767–96) is held at ANQ-MBF.

ANQ-MBF, Greffe de Paul Dielle, 27 oct. 1772. ANQ-Q, État civil, Catholiques, Notre-Dame de Québec, 29 avril 1741. PAC, MG 23, B3, CC 35, pp.117–19. *Quebec Gazette*, 8 July 1790, 17 March 1796. F.-J. Audet, *Les députés des Trois-Rivières (1808–1838)* (Trois-Rivières, 1934), 5–6. Gabriel Debien, "Liste des engagés pour le Canada au XVIIe siècle (1634–1715)," *RHAF*, VI (1952–53), 378. Le Jeune, *Dictionnaire*, I, 111. P.-G. Roy, *Fils de Québec*, II, 70–71. Jouve, *Les franciscains et le Canada: aux Trois-Rivières*. J.-E. Roy, *Hist. du notariat*, II, 42, 47, 59, 66–67, 131. Sulte, *Mélanges historiques* (Malchelosse), III, 99; X, 51; XIX, 75. *Les ursulines des Trois-Rivières depuis leur établissement jusqu'à nos jours* (4v., Trois-Rivières, 1888–1911), I, 361. Raymond Douville, "La dette des États-Unis envers les ursulines de Trois-Rivières," *Cahiers des Dix*, 22 (1957), 137–62.

BAILLY DE MESSEIN, CHARLES-FRANÇOIS, coadjutor bishop of Quebec; b. 4 Nov. 1740 at Varennes, near Montreal (Que.), eldest son of François-Augustin Bailly de Messein and Marie-Anne de Goutin; d. 20 May 1794 at Quebec.

The Bailly de Messein family is believed to have been ennobled in the 16th century, and the first of the family to leave France and settle in Canada was Nicolas, son of Michel and Anne Marsain, who came as an ensign in the colonial regular troops around 1700. In 1706 he was married in Quebec to Anne Bonhomme; in 1732 he was promoted lieutenant, and on 27 Sept. 1744 he died in Quebec at the age of 80. One of their two surviving children was François-Augustin, who had been born on 20 Aug. 1709. Like most French and Canadian noblemen, he chose a wife from the upper class, marrying Marie-Anne, the daughter of François-Marie de Goutin* and Marie-Angélique Aubert de La Chesnaye, of Île Royale (Cape Breton Island). The marriage contract was signed by such prominent men as Intendant Michel Bégon* de La Picardière, Charles Le Moyne* de Longueuil, Baron de Longueuil, and Louis-Joseph Rocbert de La Morandière, the king's storekeeper. François-Augustin went into business, first in Montreal and then at Varennes. He died in 1771; his widow lived until 1804.

Of François-Augustin's 16 children the best known was unquestionably his eldest son, Charles-François, whose godparents were Josué Dubois* Berthelot de Beaucours, governor of Montreal, and Marie-Charlotte Denys de La Ronde, widow of former governor Claude de Ramezay*. François-Augustin had prospered sufficiently to send his two oldest sons to do their classical studies at the Collège Louis-le-Grand in Paris around 1755. It is certain, however, that Charles-François did his year of rhetoric, the senior class, after he returned to Quebec in 1762. He is said to have come back from France with rather haughty manners and with needs that even his father's means could not support. The young man is supposed to have made approaches at this time to one of the daughters of Luc de LA CORNE, but when she responded with no more than friendship Charles-François decided to enter the Grand Séminaire de Québec.

On 10 March 1767 he was ordained priest and he left immediately for Nova Scotia to replace Pierre Maillard*, who had been missionary to the Micmacs and Acadians there until his death in 1762. Lieutenant-Governor Guy Carleton*, who had already noticed young Bailly, is supposed to have asked Bishop BRIAND to appoint him to this sensitive mission. The governor of Nova Scotia, Lord William CAMPBELL, was well pleased with the missionary, since he succeeded in pacifying the Indians and reassuring the Acadians who had just taken the oath of loyalty to George III. The young priest, however, felt isolated from Quebec and asked the bishop to recall him. He was back in 1772 and was appointed to teach the rhetoric and *belles-lettres* classes at the Petit Séminaire; in 1774 he was also elected one of its directors for two years.

In 1776, probably because of his peacemaking mission in Nova Scotia, Bailly became chaplain to Louis Liénard* de Beaujeu de Villemomble's volunteers, with the purpose of preaching loyalty to England and thwarting the intrigues of the American invaders, who were causing havoc in the parishes on the south shore of the St Lawrence from Saint-Thomas-de-Montmagny (Montmagny) to Notre-Dame-de-Liesse-de-la-Rivière-Ouelle (Rivière-Ouelle). That spring Bailly was shot in the abdomen and taken prisoner by the Americans [*see* Michel BLAIS]. Soon released, he returned to convalesce at the seminary and teach theology in 1777, before being named parish priest for Saint-François-de-Sales at Pointe-aux-Trembles (Neuville) in September.

In the ten years since his ordination Charles-François Bailly had progressed through the phases of an ecclesiastical career similar to that of many Canadian priests in the second half of the 18th century. Tall and handsome, he had acquired polish and ease in his manners and speech at the Collège Louis-le-Grand, where there were many sons of noblemen. It was this refinement that had doubtless brought him to Carleton's attention. The success of his mission in Acadia and the praise it had won him from the governor of Nova Scotia promised Bailly a brilliant future, if he were ambitious.

In 1774 Carleton had returned to Quebec with a young wife who had grown up at Versailles, and three children to provide with an education worthy of their parents. The governor therefore had sent for Bailly de Messein, whose loyalty was unquestioned and who had experience in teaching. Tradition has it that the tutor, wearing a silk cassock, used to travel to and fro between the seminary and the Château Saint-Louis in the governor's coach. When Carleton had to leave for England in July 1778, he was understandably anxious to take his children's tutor with him. Thus Bailly went to England and there was introduced to London society. Probably in order to maintain a tangible link with his parishioners at Pointe-aux-Trembles, he had one of them, young François-Xavier Larue, later a notary in the village, accompany him.

In 1782 Bailly returned to Canada and to his parish, which he had entrusted to Joseph-Étienne Demeule during his absence in England – an absence Bishop Briand had disapproved of but was unable to prevent. Bailly attended to his parish until 1786; he directed it according to the rules of ecclesiastical discipline, was always obliging to neighbouring parish priests, and was exemplary in conduct and character. When Carleton, now Lord Dorchester, returned to Quebec as governor in 1786, the parish priest of Pointe-aux-Trembles came back to the Château Saint-Louis, where his conversation and society were much sought after; but this association in turn brought him the label, in certain circles, of "the parish priest of the English."

As it happened, Louis-Philippe MARIAUCHAU d'Esgly, bishop of Quebec for the previous two years, had had to wait until the governor's arrival to consecrate his coadjutor, Bishop HUBERT, for whom bulls had reached Quebec early in June 1786. On 29 November Bishop Hubert received episcopal unction at the hands of retired Bishop Briand, who was attended by Henri-François Gravé* de La Rive, a priest from the seminary, and Bailly de Messein. When Bishop Mariauchau d'Esgly died in June 1788, Bishop Hubert had to choose a coadjutor. Dorchester designated his friend Bailly de Messein. Even though the candidate was not to the bishop's liking, it was necessary to avoid offending the governor, who had given many generous privileges to the Catholic Church and to the Canadians, especially since Bailly was in fact an educated and zealous priest. In September 1788 Bailly was named bishop *in partibus infidelium* of Capsa and on 12 July 1789 he was consecrated by Hubert, who was attended by Gravé and Pierre-Laurent Bédard. For the ceremony the priests and pupils of the seminary provided music that was beautiful and very moving. There were few priests present; "Monseigneur l'Ancien," as Bishop Briand was called, seemed inconsolable, and Bishop Hubert overwhelmed. Afterwards, at a meeting in Bishop Briand's residence with Joseph-Octave Plessis* and Gravé present in addition to Hubert and Bailly, Hubert is supposed to have notified his coadjutor that he was to return to Pointe-aux-Trembles, since he had made him bishop only to retain the bishopric for the province. In August Bailly asked Bishop Hubert to advise him, in writing, of his powers and whether Quebec or Montreal was to be his place of residence. Hubert replied that his grant to him of letters as vicar general on 20 June 1788 had been to honour Bailly's dignity as coadjutor and not to relieve himself of his episcopal duties, that the coadjutor was free to live wherever he pleased, but that the bishop could not give him two parish charges to provide for his newly added expenses. Hubert did however grant him half the income from the tithe of the parish of Saint-Ours in addition to his parish at Pointe-aux-Trembles. "The Château's bishop" had a way of life to keep up, and he aspired to high office, knowing perhaps that Hubert had received permission from Rome to install a bishop in Montreal.

Hubert thought of sending his coadjutor to visit the Acadian missions in the summer of 1790. But relations between them were soon to deteriorate over a plan for a university and the abolition of certain public holidays. On 13 Aug. 1789 Chief Justice William SMITH, who had been charged with inquiring into education in the province of Quebec, had written the two bishops to ask their opinion on the founding of a non-sectarian university. Bishop Hubert acknowledged the letter the day he received it but did not reply until 18 November, after reflecting, consulting people, and sending his report to his coadjutor. On 26 November Smith, as chairman of what was the first fact-finding commission on education in the province of Quebec, submitted his report to Dorchester, who published it in February 1790. On 5 April Bishop Bailly sent Smith a letter in favour of the mixed-university plan; presenting arguments opposite to those of Bishop Hubert, he called him a rhapsodist, even held out against him the threat of the revolution, and made a show of believing that the bishop of Quebec's reply had been dictated to him by someone else. The coadjutor sent a copy of his letter to Bishop Hubert. Embittered at having no role in the administration of the diocese, Bishop Bailly later took advantage of circumstances to attack his bishop again, this time publicly, in the *Quebec Gazette*. On 29 April he published a letter he had sent to the bishop about Hubert's slowness in abolishing certain public holidays. That was going too far. Some of the clergy and lay people in Quebec, Montreal, and rural areas publicly expressed disapproval of the bishop of Capsa; the *Montreal Gazette* commented ironically on the situation [*see* Fleury MESPLET]. In October, after a few months' lull, Bishop Bailly's statement on the project for a university was published. It is now known, through Samuel NEILSON's records, that Charles-Louis Tarieu* de Lanaudière paid for the printing. A month later the *Quebec Gazette* carried a petition addressed to the governor requesting the creation in the province of Quebec of a university to be endowed with a royal charter and to be open to all religious denominations. The petition was signed by 175 persons, of whom 56 were French speaking. Bishop Bailly, Father Félix Berey Des Essarts, the Recollet superior, and Edmund Burke*, who had just left the Séminaire de Québec, were among those signing. The *Montreal Gazette* published articles denouncing the bishop of Quebec as ignorant and requesting at thc same time the creation of the university.

Bishop Hubert, who made no comment in the newspapers, was so affected by these public debates that he felt obliged to write about them to Lieutenant Governor Alured Clarke* and to Cardinal Leonardo Antonèlli in Rome. The cardinal sided entirely with Bishop Hubert, sending him a letter for the coadjutor in which he threatened to remove Bailly from office if he did not mend his ways. Bishop Bailly seems to have adopted a more reasonable attitude even before the letter arrived from Rome, since the bishop of Quebec did not deliver it to him. After April 1790 all relations between the two bishops were broken off, and Bailly no longer went to the seminary. Priests no longer came to see him. Even the Château Saint-Louis seemed to treat him coldly. He attended to the affairs of his parish and often visited the sisters of the Congregation of Notre-Dame, who had a convent at Neuville and whom he personally aided by paying for the education of several young girls. His friend, Father Berey, would come to see him and entertain him. The presence of Bishop Bailly was noted at least once in Quebec society when he baptized Édouard-Alphonse*, son of Ignace-Michel-Louis-Antoine d'Irumberry* de Salaberry, and godson of Prince Edward Augustus*. In 1793 his health began to fail, and Father Berey came to live with him.

In April 1794, Bailly, much feebler, put his affairs in order and made his will in the presence of notary François-Xavier Larue. He gave £1,000 to his former mission in Acadia, £500 to his sister Félicité-Élisabeth, the wife of Jacques Le Moyne de Martigny, £700 to his "butler," Donald MacDonald, and the rest of his personal and real estate to the poor of Neuville and of Saint-Jean-Baptiste-des-Écureuils, a neighbouring parish. He was then taken by rowboat, via the St Lawrence and the Saint-Charles, to the Hôpital Général in Quebec. He made his peace with Bishop Briand and Bishop Hubert before breathing his last on 20 May. His body was on public view at the Hôpital Général for two days, and then was taken to Neuville, where he had wanted to be buried. The funeral service, held on 22 May, was attended by a large gathering of fellow priests and friends, and the vicar general, Gravé de La Rive, gave the absolution. The coffin was placed under the high altar on the north side. On 5 June the parish priest of Saint-Joseph-de-la-Pointe-Lévy, Jean-Jacques Berthiaume, published a short notice of the bishop of Capsa's death in the *Quebec Gazette*, mentioning that before he died Bishop Bailly had asked his bishop's pardon in the presence of witnesses. John Neilson* was obliged to apologize to Bishop Bailly's family and friends in the next issue of the *Gazette*, saying that the announcement had appeared without his authorization and that he had not wanted to tarnish the reputation of the deceased.

In French Canadian historiography Bailly de Messein has been judged harshly, and only in the writings of the sisters of the Congregation of Notre-Dame and of the Hôpital Général in Quebec is there any praise. In 1954 Émile Castonguay made a timid attempt to do him justice, but he continues to be ignored in textbooks. He could not even serve as a foil in French Canada's ecclesiastical golden legend, as did the renegade Charles Chiniquy*. He was not a bad priest – quite the contrary. He carried out with zeal all the missions and duties his bishop assigned him, and he administered his parish in an exemplary manner before and after his voyage to England. His noble rank, imposing appearance, talents as orator and conversationalist, and classical studies at the most distinguished college in France, had all brought him to the attention of the civil authorities. His loyalty to the crown had been the final factor in making him feel destined for the highest ecclesiastical offices, which he thought he had attained as coadjutor. Then he made the error of contradicting his bishop in public, thus humiliating him in front of the Catholics and, above all, in front of the English Protestants. The tone of some of his remarks was that of the enlightened man denouncing his bishop's despotism and obscurantism.

The catalogue of books in his library might have confirmed that he had an affinity for the *philosophes*. But in fact it does not. First and foremost it contains books on theology and religion, then literary works and books on history, geography, the arts, and science. There are only two works by Voltaire, Jean-Jacques Rousseau's *Lettres écrites de la montagne* and his *Œuvres*, and three books about Rousseau, one on the *Contrat social*. In short, this was the library of a good priest; the dozen books of Latin poets are witness to his classical studies under the Jesuits.

A collection of more than 1,200 volumes was certainly rare for a Canadian priest before 1800. It indicates that the owner, if not wealthy, at least was reasonably well off. The inventory after death reveals that Bailly had as much personal property as parish priests of that period were allowed, a well-filled stable and barn, a loft filled with wheat and oats, and a fully furnished presbytery. Table silver and flat candlesticks and candelabras stamped with his monogram attest to his rank as nobleman and bishop, as does the fact that he had a butler and two maids. Although some money was owing him, he apparently owed more to his creditors, the largest sum to his friend Louis Langlois, *dit* Germain, a merchant and bookseller.

Perhaps sensing that after his death he would be forgotten, during his lifetime he had given the name of his episcopal title, Capsa, to a back concession at Neuville. In June 1969 the archbishop of Quebec had Bishop Bailly's remains transferred to the crypt of the basilica of Notre-Dame in Quebec.

CLAUDE GALARNEAU

[C.-F. Bailly de Messein], *Copie de la lettre de l'évêque de Capsa, coadjuteur de Québec, &c, au président du comité sur l'éducation . . .* ([Québec, 1790]).

AAQ, 12 A, D, 109; 20 A, II, 49, 51; 22 A, V, 275. ACND, 312.640/1–2. AHGQ, Communauté, Journal, II, 239. ANQ-Q, AP-P-84; AP-P-86; Greffe de F.-X. Larue, 11 avril 1794. ASN, AP-G, L-É. Bois, Succession, XVII, 1, 3. ASQ, C 35, pp.268–69, 311; Lettres, M, 136, 138; P, 145; S, 6bis, C, I; MSS, 12, ff.41, 43, 45; 13, 12 août 1774, 10 août 1800; 433; MSS-M, 228; Polygraphie, VII, 134; XVIII, 65; XIX, 64b; Séminaire, 16, no.23. AUM, P 58, Corr. générale, C.-F. Bailly à Panet, 14 sept. 1782, 27 mars 1786. Bibliothèque du séminaire de Québec, A.-G. Dudevant, "Catalogue des livres de la bibliothèque du séminaire des Missions étrangères de Québec fait dans le mois de may 1782" (copy at ASQ). *Mandements des évêques de Québec* (Têtu et Gagnon), II, 385–426. PAC *Rapport*, 1890, 219, 261, 287. *Montreal Gazette*, 6, 13, 27 May, 3, 10 June, 4, 18, 25 Nov. 1790. *Quebec Gazette*, 6 July 1789; 29 April, 13, 27 May, 4 Nov. 1790; 2, 12 June 1794. [F.-]M. Bibaud, *Le panthéon canadien; choix de biographies*, Adèle et Victoria Bibaud, édit. (2e éd., Montréal, 1891), 193–94. Caron, "Inv. de la corr. de Mgr Hubert et de Mgr Bailly de Messein," ANQ *Rapport*, 1930–31, 199–299. Henri Têtu, *Notices biographiques: les évêques de Québec* (Québec, 1889), 392–429. Tremaine, *Bibliography of Canadian imprints*. Audet, *Le système scolaire*, II, 191–208. Ghislain Bouchard, "Les fêtes d'obligation en Nouvelle-France, du début de la colonie à 1791" (mémoire de licence, université Laval, Québec, 1955). O'Reilly, *Mgr de Saint-Vallier et l'Hôpital Général*, 466–67. P.-G. Roy, *La famille Bailly de Messein* (Lévis, Qué., 1917). E. C. Bailly, "The French-Canadian background of a Minnesota pioneer: Alexis Bailly," *BRH*, LV (1949), 137–75. M.-A. Bernard, "Mgr Charles-François Bailly de Messein," *BRH*, IV (1898), 348–50. Bernard Dufebvre [Émile Castonguay], "Mgr Bailly de Messein et un projet d'université en 1790," *L'Action catholique; supplément* (Québec), XVIII (1954), nos.10, 11. Placide Gaudet, "Un ancien missionnaire de l'Acadie," *BRH*, XIII (1907), 244–49. Ignotus [Thomas Chapais], "Notes et souvenirs," *La Presse* (Montréal), 6 avril 1901, 8; 20 avril 1901, 9; 4 mai 1901, 8.

BARBEL, MARIE-ANNE (Fornel), merchant and entrepreneur; b. 26 Aug. 1704 at Quebec, daughter of Jacques Barbel* and Marie-Anne Le Picard; m. 31 Dec. 1723 Louis Fornel*; seven of their 14 children survived infancy; d. 16 Nov. 1793 at Quebec.

Marie-Anne Barbel's father had risen swiftly from garrison sergeant of Quebec to office-holder, but he ended his life overwhelmed by debts. Barbel was an upstart, something not rare in the colony, and at the time of Marie-Anne's marriage his career was in the ascendant. The Fornel family, into which she married, was more stable; in the marriage contract signed by the governor and the intendant, both her prospective husband and his father are designated merchants and bourgeois of Quebec. Her future brother-in-law, Joachim Fornel*, was soon to be named a canon of the Quebec cathedral chapter.

The life of Marie-Anne Barbel is of historical interest in part because of what it reveals of the role of women in the merchant class. Her business knowledge and her continuation in trade after her husband's death were typical. Although the business role of a wife under the custom of Paris is difficult to trace, Louis Fornel's delegation to Marie-Anne on 15 May 1743 of full power of attorney over his affairs during his absence on the Labrador coast demonstrates that she was informed of his activities and considered capable of business decisions. Nevertheless, in the period of her marriage, the bearing and raising of children and the managing of her household would have been the focus of her life. This emphasis changed in 1745 when her husband died.

The couple's "community of property" was not dissolved after Louis Fornel's death, his rights devolving instead upon his heirs. Mme Fornel administered this property, carrying on the family business and extending it in size and in new directions. She continued to enjoy friendship and close business relations with François Havy* and Jean Lefebvre*, two Huguenot merchants who had been her husband's partners in several enterprises, including the Labrador sealing industry. She was unable to continue exploitation of their sealing station at Chateau Bay, which after the War of the Austrian Succession was granted to Jean-François Gaultier*, but she had more success with Baie des Esquimaux (Hamilton Inlet), a site Fornel had discovered in 1743 and renamed Baie Saint-Louis. At the time of his death he had been petitioning for a monopoly of its trade. Intendant HOCQUART planned instead to unite it with the Tadoussac trading posts (sometimes called the king's posts), so that it would not adversely affect their business; however, his successor, BIGOT, granted the Baie Saint-Louis monopoly to Mme Fornel on 20 Sept. 1749. He noted that she would be developing it in company with Havy and Lefebvre, her share being only one-third. Bigot may have made the grant as part of a general strategy of thwarting his predecessor's clients, in this case the farmer of the Tadoussac trading posts, François-Étienne Cugnet*, for Cugnet's lease on them was not renewed. Instead they too were leased to Mme Fornel in 1749. "Widow Fornel has a company," Bigot explained to the minister of Marine, "and nothing whatever will be lacking at the post of Tadoussac and . . . the king will be well paid each year." Circumstantial evidence suggests that Havy and Lefebvre were her active partners in this venture as well, although they remained in the background, perhaps because of Governor Jacques-Pierre de Taffanel* de La Jonquière's abhorrence of Protestants.

As her husband had done before her, Mme Fornel invested part of her profits in the relative security of real estate. The most original venture of her career was the establishment of a pottery to meet the demand arising from wartime shortages. As Havy and Lefebvre explained in a letter of 1746, "no earthenware is coming from France and it appears that as long as the war lasts it will be the same, but the country has a resource in Mademoiselle Fornel who has established its manufacture. She has a very good craftsman and her earth proves good." The pottery, finished with lead and copper glazes, was immediately successful and was even taken for the French product. The shop remained in operation until at least 1752. In that year François JACQUET signed a three-year contract with her which is revealing of the conditions of labour at the time: he was to be paid on a piece-work basis, she would provide stove wood and lighting, and, curiously, each was to hire a man and provide his food and wages. Jacquet worked in the "Briqueterie," a dilapidated building in the Lower Town.

The war of the conquest hastened Marie-Anne Fornel's withdrawal from trade. Her north shore and Labrador posts were liabilities in wartime. She made no effort to renew the lease on the Tadoussac trading posts which expired in 1755, and it is doubtful whether she was still operating at Baie Saint-Louis when her monopoly expired in 1761. Her numerous buildings in Quebec's Lower Town were destroyed in the bombardment of the city in 1759, and nothing more is heard of the pottery. In 1764 she and the Fornel heirs agreed to settle accounts with the Havy and Lefebvre heirs by paying them the sum of 12,000 *livres*, the last payment being made in 1769. An inventory of the Fornels' community property made the following year indicates a history of solid bourgeois comfort, but also considerable indebtedness resulting from wartime reversals. Between 1765 and 1771 Mme Fornel laboured to pay her debts, rebuild many of her houses, and consolidate her assets. In 1777 the Fornel property was divided among the heirs, and Mme Fornel entered into the last phase of her life, that of retirement, which lasted until her death in 1793.

DALE MIQUELON

AN, Col., B, 91, f.276; C11A, 85, ff.21, 375; 92, ff.229, 358–59; 93, ff.229, 241, 257; 96, f.101; 100, f.337; 101, f.398. ANQ-Q, AP-P-753; Greffe de Claude Barolet, 20 déc. 1752; Greffe de P.-L. Descheneaux, 1er mars 1794; Greffe de C.-H. Du Laurent, 15 mai 1743, 15 oct. 1750, 31 mai 1752; Greffe de Claude Louet, 10 mai 1765; Greffe de J.-C. Louet, 31 déc. 1723; Greffe de J.-C. Panet, 10 oct. 1764. PAC, MG 24, L3, pp.872–76, 886–90, 1144–45. *Inv. de pièces du Labrador* (P.-G. Roy), I, 90–91, 99; II, 88, 255–60. P.-G. Roy, *Inv. jug. et délib., 1717–60*. Tanguay, *Dictionnaire*, I, 24; IV, 84. Lilianne Plamondon, "Une femme d'affaires en Nouvelle-France, Marie-Anne Barbel" (thèse de MA, université Laval, Québec, 1976).

BARSALOU (Barçalo, Barsolou, Barsoloy, Bersalou, Borsalou), JEAN-BAPTISTE (baptized **Jean**), voyageur and merchant-tanner; b. 9 Sept.

1706 at Montreal (Que.), son of Gérard Barsalou and Marie-Catherine Legras; d. there 18 March 1776.

Jean-Baptiste Barsalou's father was related through his mother to the prominent Montreal merchant Charles Nolan* Lamarque. By marrying the daughter of merchant Jean Legras on 6 May 1700, Gérard Barsalou found himself strengthening his ties with the business world. On 19 April that year he had made a notarized contract to establish a tannery with Charles Delaunay*, who was married to another daughter of Legras. Delaunay supplied the capital while Barsalou contributed his experience as a master tanner. Their partnership lasted six years, after which Barsalou set up on his own account in the *faubourg* Sainte-Catherine. The location, being well supplied with streams, allowed him to establish the reservoirs indispensable in his trade. Nevertheless, the scarcity of manpower and the difficulty in procuring skins seem to have caused him some problems. Gérard Barsalou died prematurely in 1721, leaving 11 children, most of them young, and a widow, who the same year married the notary Nicolas-Auguste Guillet* de Chaumont.

After his marriage in August 1723 the eldest Barsalou son, Joseph, took possession for the duration of his minority of the tannery, a sawmill which had recently been built in collaboration with his uncle Jean-Baptiste Neveu*, and other buildings, on condition that he assume care of six of his brothers and sisters, including Jean-Baptiste; his mother and stepfather would keep the four remaining children with them. Later, in 1735, Jean-Baptiste was to quarrel with his stepfather, who would accuse the young man in court at Montreal of having attempted to kill him.

Jean-Baptiste Barsalou entered the working world by making a few trips to the fur country on behalf of his uncle Neveu and of another merchant, Ignace GAMELIN the younger. Meanwhile, at the beginning of the 1730s he assumed management of the tannery, making agreements with Montreal butchers to reserve the hides of oxen, cows, and calves for him, and with shoemakers to settle the price of leather prepared in his shop. In partnership with his brother Jean-François, who was also a merchant-tanner, Jean-Baptiste competed with two other families of Montreal tanners, by name Lenoir, *dit* Rolland, and Plessy, *dit* Bélair [*see* Jean-Louis Plessy*, *dit* Bélair]. From 1747 to 1765 Barsalou varied his activities by buying and selling land in the *faubourg* Saint-Laurent. Anxious to defend his own interests, he forbad the purchaser of one of his properties to carry on any tanning business on it, even going so far as to put flagstones in the stream running through the property.

In May 1733 Barsalou had married Marie-Jeanne Becquet, with whom he had had a daughter the previous January. Although at the time of her baptism the infant was declared to be of unknown parentage, Barsalou acknowledged his paternity when he signed his marriage contract on 10 May. Marie-Jeanne Becquet died in 1743, at the birth of their ninth child, and the following year Barsalou married Geneviève Bouchard, *dit* Dorval, the widow of Pierre Forestier. He was to be married again in 1763, this time to Élisabeth Urtebise.

The inflation to which Canadian business was subject during the final years of the French régime and the losses experienced when paper currency was regulated after the conquest strongly affected Barsalou's trade. Having worked hard to consolidate his father's business and to hand it down to his sons, he saw it gradually deteriorate and his efforts meet with failure. The inventory taken after his death shows the wretched state of his business: he owned no more than his house, his tannery, and some tools; he left no cash. His sons had become voyageurs, and the Barsalou name disappeared from the tannery business. A century later, however, a grand-nephew, Joseph Barsalou, would make his mark in an allied field, by founding the first, and very important, French Canadian soap industry in Quebec province.

YVES-JEAN TREMBLAY

ANQ-M, État civil, Catholiques, Notre-Dame de Montréal, 6 mai 1700, 10 sept. 1706, 6 nov. 1721, 4 mai 1744, 8 janv. 1763; Greffe de J.-B. Adhémar, 30 nov. 1718, 21 déc. 1731, 7 sept. 1749; Greffe de Pierre Raimbault, 10 mai 1733. Godbout, "Nos ancêtres," ANQ *Rapport*, 1953–55, 492. P.-G. Roy, *Inv. jug. et délib., 1717–60*, III, 260, 309; IV, 41; V, 273–74, 276, 294, 296, 298; VI, 2. Tanguay, *Dictionnaire*, II, 132. J.-N. Fauteux, *Essai sur l'industrie*, II. É.-Z. Massicotte, "Un notaire dans une ménagerie," *BRH*, XLII (1936), 132–35.

BATT, ISAAC, fur-trader; b. *c.* 1725, probably in Stanstead Abbots, Hertfordshire, England; m. there on 18 April 1761 Sarah Fowler; d. summer 1791 in the vicinity of Manchester House (near Pike's Peak, Sask.).

Isaac Batt first contracted with the Hudson's Bay Company in 1754 to serve as a labourer at York Factory (Man.) for five years at £10 per annum. In the fall of 1758 James Isham*, chief at York, sent Batt and George Potts inland with a group of Indians who had arrived at York with the traders Joseph Smith* and Joseph Waggoner. The trip was evidently a success, for on 29 Aug. 1759 Isham informed the London committee that "Isaac Batt who arrived att the head of 64 Canues Last June, is again Returned inLand." He added that Batt, who was by now experienced at inland travel and trade, would "Return home" unless he were offered a new contract of £20 annually. The committee's refusal of his request led Batt to return to England in September 1760. In September 1762, however, he was again at York, still a labourer at £10 per annum but with the promise of a £10 gratuity. By this time Batt was a married man, and during the years 1763–66 £4 or £5 was deducted annually from his wages at his request for the support of his wife Sarah, of whom, however, no later mention is found.

Inland service continued to dominate Batt's career, and his responsibilities expanded with the growth of the problems associated with the company's inland trade. In the autumn of 1763 he and Joseph Smith were sent inland with the hope that "they will bring down Strange Indians to trade." The next year they were instructed to "Prevent Warr among the Natives, and get what Inteligence they could of the Approaches of the Interlopers [rival Canadian traders]." Batt and Smith travelled inland under the personal guidance of leading Indians known at the bayside posts. The loyalty to the company of such Indians, WAPINESIW and MATONABBEE being among them, was strengthened by such arrangements, and as Ferdinand JACOBS, chief factor at York, explained to the London committee when urged to stop the custom, "the Individuals they [the traders] go with (who are Leading Indians of the first rank) may take offence and not come down to the Factory, and prevent other Indians from coming down to Trade . . . for they receive a considerable benifit by having these Men in their Families, which if suddenly taken from them, may irritate them to trade their Furrs with the Pedlers." By 1768 Batt, who travelled inland yearly, had established himself as one of the company's more influential servants among the Indians in the vicinity of present day The Pas, Man., and was considered "a very honest good Servant." In 1772, after continued useful service, he received permission to return home for a year and did so that fall.

Batt's advancement from his return to York in 1773 until his death was slowed by his shortcomings at a time when the conditions and requirements of inland trade were changing. Like numerous other company servants of the mid 1700s, he was illiterate and therefore had to be excused from keeping journals while inland. Younger inland traders such as Matthew COCKING and William Tomison* were not so handicapped. While Batt remained a labourer, canoeman, and steersman at wages never surpassing £20 a year, junior men better equipped to keep records rose to dominate the company's inland activities. Discouraged by the company's failure to promote him, he became receptive to the recruiting offers of its competitors. During the 1771–72 season he had been approached by Canadian traders, Thomas Corry among them, who hoped to attract him and Louis PRIMEAU to their side "because they draw the natives." In 1774, when he was involved with Samuel HEARNE, Charles Thomas Isham*, and others in the frustrations of trying to settle "Basqueawe" (The Pas) and Cumberland House (Sask.), he received a new offer. Hearne informed the London committee on 30 June 1775 of its results: "The advantage your honours expected from Isaac Batt's knowlage of those Part are entirely frustirated by his leaving your Service and entering with the Pedlors."

Despite his shortcomings Batt was still a useful servant, and his desertion to serve with Joseph Frobisher* and others concerned company officers. Humphrey MARTEN, chief at York, quickly sent a personal note urging him to return. By the time the letter reached him in October 1776, Batt was receptive, "being tired of the Pedlers." In the spring of 1777 Frobisher released him from his employ.

Although welcomed back into the company, Batt had diminished his standing by his defection. Marten noted that he was useful in transporting goods and at hunting moose but considered him "too light to have the command at any place." Cocking described him as "Open as a Scieve." Despite his detailed report to company superiors on the pedlars' posts and trade, Batt's loyalty was no longer taken for granted. His usefulness inland as canoeman, trader, and hunter continued, however, well into the 1780s and was appreciated, as the Cumberland and other inland journals of the time attest. But by 1791 he was "An old Servant – almost worn out." When Tomison left him at Manchester House on the North Saskatchewan River in May 1791, he described him as "not fitt for any duty, further than one of the Number [of men there]."

In October Tomison returned to Manchester to learn of "the unfortunate end of Isaac Batt, in which he himself [Batt] was highly culpable." That summer he and some others had gone hunting with two Indian "villians," taking six horses, two guns, and some supplies. The Indians, "having nothing of their own," were seeking booty, and while Batt was "handing the Calimet to one, the other shot him through the head," whereupon they "went off with the whole." He was the first HBC servant to be killed by Indians in the Saskatchewan area.

Batt was known to have had a native family as early as 1777, and at his death he left descendants in the fur trade country. An associate, James Spence Sr, left legacies to his "Indian Wife Nestichio daughter of the deceased Isaac Batt" and their four children.

JENNIFER S. H. BROWN

HBC Arch. Isaac Batt file; A.1/39, p.306; A.1/42, ff.34, 97–98, 126, 156, 187; A.11/115, ff.16, 22, 24–25, 50, 63, 74, 80, 85, 111, 120, 122, 137, 144, 153, 158, 171, 182; A.11/116, ff.22–23; A.11/117, f.135; A.30/1, ff.62, 79; A.30/2, f.12; A.30/3, ff.15, 38, 62; A.30/4, f.74; A.30/5, f.39; A.32/3, f.229; A.36/12, f.224; B.121/a/6, f.35; B.121/a/7, ff.13–14; B.239/a/72, f.43d. Hertfordshire Record Office (Hertford, Eng.), D/P102 1/3 (Stanstead Abbots register of marriages, 18 April 1761). HBRS, XIV (Rich and Johnson); XV (Rich and Johnson). *Saskatchewan journals and correspondence: Edmonton House, 1795–1800; Chesterfield House, 1800–1802*, ed. A. M. Johnson (London, 1967).

BEAR. *See* SAINT-AUBIN

BEATSON, PATRICK, ship's captain, shipbuilder, and ship owner; b. 21 March 1758, son of John Beatson and Elizabeth Bruce; d. unmarried on 4 Dec. 1800 at Quebec, Lower Canada.

Patrick Beatson issued from a Scottish middle-class background and, after receiving an adequate education, became a mariner. By age 23 he had become a ship's captain, and from 1781 to 1783 he sailed under wartime conditions in the annual Atlantic convoys from London to Quebec, but he was not among the ships' captains calling at Quebec from 1784 to 1791. His brothers, William and John, who were also ships' captains, continued to be part of the convoy until 1793. The Beatsons carried to Quebec industrial goods and bulk cargoes, such as salt for the fisheries, and returned to Britain with furs, and increasingly with timber and wheat. They also transported troops, families of officials, and merchants such as Simon McTavish,* John McGill, and George Auldjo*.

It is possible that between 1784 and 1791 Patrick Beatson was learning the art of draughting and acquiring practical experience in shipbuilding at a Scottish yard. In 1792 and 1793 he was back on the Quebec run, but he left the sea in the fall of 1793 to settle at Anse des Mères (at the foot of Cap Diamant) in the city of Quebec. There he leased from Louis Dunière a shipyard from which three or four large ships had been launched between 1787 and 1791; the yard comprised a dwelling house, stable, forge, "steam-house," sheds, quays, and building slips. Beatson threw himself wholeheartedly into the role of shipbuilder, and his soon became the first important commercial shipyard in Quebec.

The enterprise had not been hastily conceived. His visits to Quebec had acquainted him with the town and its waterfront facilities. Moreover, he and his brothers had experience and connections in the shipping business, and their contacts with the Montreal and Quebec merchants who had taken passage with them were also undoubtedly valuable to Patrick. Between 1794 and 1800 he built at least 15 vessels totalling over 4,000 tons. The largest, the 645-ton *Monarch*, launched in 1800, was almost twice the size of any locally constructed vessel to that time and was not to be equalled in size until 1811. Besides employing local labour, Beatson had 10 or 12 trained shipwrights and blacksmiths sent from Scotland each year, and he used annually an average of 60,000 feet of oak timber in the yard. The ships he built were registered in his own name, but he also served as the Quebec agent for his brothers, now in partnership as shipbuilders in London.

In 1794 Beatson's growing prosperity permitted him to buy a small beach-front property east of his yard from the bankrupt estate of shipbuilder William King. Two years later he bought Powell Place (Bois de Coulonge) from Henry Watson Powell*, legislative councillor and receiver-general, for £500 cash and the promise of £1,500 more. The 124-acre estate, a mile and a half west of his yard, had a large house and dependencies on a plain above nearly 2,000 feet of shoreline, where Beatson's hopes of building his own ships were frustrated by the shallow water. Beatson claimed to suffer from inadequate launching facilities, especially for large vessels, at the yard that he leased from Dunière. Dunière's refusal to improve the facilities, and the stranding of the *Caledonia* at her launching in 1798, prompted Beatson's unsuccessful attempt to buy from the government a beach lot 360 feet to the west of his yard. He nonetheless continued to launch large vessels and in February 1800, ten months before his death, tentatively agreed to buy from Dunière not only the leased shipyard but also the lease on an adjoining property to the west.

By the late 1790s Beatson was comfortably established in his long, low, galleried house at the shipyard. He was able to entertain graciously, having fine china, cut glass, and silverware. His study served as a drawing office, for Beatson was one of the rare Quebec shipbuilders able to draw up the plans for a ship. His walls were lined with paintings and engravings of sea scenes, ships, and naval heroes such as Horatio Nelson, whom he may have met at Quebec in 1782 since that year Nelson escorted the convoy from London with Beatson's ship in it. He grew flowers in a heated greenhouse through the winter and filled flowerpots in his home with them in summer. He was a man of many interests, who kept a collection of 39 small brass cannon in his drawing-room and amused himself with such devices as a camera obscura and a magic lantern. He had several conveyances, two of which were decorated by François Baillairgé*, who also carved the figure-heads for Beatson's ships.

Patrick Beatson died at age 42 in December 1800, but work continued at the yard, which was inherited by John and William Beatson. In 1801 the brothers sold Powell Place and in March 1802 bought from Dunière the shipyard and lease on the adjoining property which Patrick had intended to buy. In October, however, they leased the property back to Dunière, and in 1806 it was sold from the Beatsons' bankrupt estate to shipbuilder Alexander Munn*.

Patrick Beatson's obituary in the *Quebec Gazette* noted that those who dealt with him "experienced extreme punctuality in [his] commercial concerns," and this business sense, as well as his single-minded commitment to his Quebec enterprise, contributed in large measure to his success.

EILEEN MARCIL

ANQ-Q, AP-G-208; AP-G-398; État civil, Presbytériens, St Andrews (Québec), 6 Dec. 1800; Greffe d'Archibald Campbell, 22 déc. 1825; Greffe de P.-L. Descheneaux, 24 mars 1794; Greffe d'Alexandre Dumas, 7 nov. 1801; Greffe de Charles Stewart, 16 nov. 1795, 31 oct. 1796, 30 juin, 4 oct. 1798, 17 juin 1799; Greffe de Félix Têtu, 15 mars 1802; Greffe de Charles Voyer, 21 oct. 1791, 15 déc. 1800; Greffe de Jacques Voyer, 11 mai 1799. AUM, P 58, Corr. générale Joseph Frobisher à Patrick Beatson, 9 juin 1794. PAC, MG 24, F3, correspondence, 12 juill., 21 déc. 1800; RG 1, L3[L], 39, pp.19505–7; RG 4, B32; RG 68, General index, 1651–1841. "Les dénombrements de Québec faits en 1792, 1795, 1798 et 1805 par le curé Joseph-Octave Plessis," ANQ *Rapport*, 1948–49, 140. *Quebec Gazette*, 30 Aug. 1781, 31 May, 2 Aug., 27 Sept. 1792, 11 July 1793, 11 Dec. 1800, 13 Aug. 1801, 9 Sept. 1802. A. J. Beatson, *Genealogical account of the Beatson families* (Edinburgh, 1860). Geoffrey Bennett, *Nelson the commander* (London, 1972), 15.

BEAUCOURT, FRANÇOIS MALEPART DE. *See* MALEPART

BEAUSÉJOUR, JOSEPH GODIN, *dit* **Bellefontaine**, *dit*. *See* GODIN

BÉDARD, THOMAS-LAURENT, priest, professor, bursar, and superior of the Séminaire de Québec; b. 3 Feb. 1747 at Charlesbourg (Que.), son of Thomas Bédard and Marie-Angélique Fiset; d. 27 May 1795 at Quebec.

Thomas-Laurent Bédard studied at the Séminaire de Québec and was ordained priest by Bishop BRIAND on 23 Sept. 1775. His career was to be spent in the seminary. He had become a professor of philosophy and science in 1773, on 17 Oct. 1775 was received as a member of the community, and on 24 May 1776 joined the council. For a year he had the double task of director of the Petit Séminaire and prefect of studies; then on 17 Aug. 1778 he was elected first assistant to the superior, Henri-François Gravé* de La Rive, and was put in charge of the bursar's office. As bursar Bédard had in particular to supervise the building of two rest houses which the seminary had decided in 1777 to put at the disposal of its students: one called Bellevue at Saint-Joachim "on the Fortin hill [Petit-Cap]," and the other called La Canardière (now named Maizerets). He also helped to prepare the document for recognition of suzerainty and census for the fiefs and seigneuries of Côte-de-Beaupré, Île-aux-Coudres, Sault-au-Matelot, Coulonges, Saint-Michel, and Île-Jésus, which was presented by Gravé to Governor HALDIMAND on 11 July 1782.

Bédard's colleagues showed their confidence in him by choosing him as their superior on 13 Aug. 1781. It was the second time a Canadian had been appointed to this office [*see* Jean-François HUBERT]. Bédard held the office for two terms, resuming his duties as bursar in 1786. He served as treasurer in a subscription organized to aid the Hôtel-Dieu after the departure of the British soldiers who had been quartered in it from 1759 to 1784 [*see* Marie-Louise CUROT, *dite* de Saint-Martin]. "The purpose of this subscription," as a heading for his book of receipts and expenses indicated, was "to create a fund to obtain medicines, restore in the Hôtel-Dieu the rooms for the poor occupied up till now by the king's troops, and help it to begin again the charitable works which are the object of its rule." This collection among the clergy and citizens of Quebec, inaugurated in March 1784 under the honorary presidency of Lieutenant Governor Henry HAMILTON, continued until 15 June 1787 and brought in about £618.

From 1790 to 1793, while retaining his office as bursar, Abbé Bédard taught dogmatic theology at the Grand Séminaire. Just prior to the passing of the Constitutional Act, he again had occasion to attract public attention. The loyalists who had come to the province were at that time stepping up their campaign against the seigneurial system of land tenure. On 10 Oct. 1790 a special committee established within the Legislative Council to study the question came out in favour of free and common socage, the method of land granting practised in British colonies, and it supported its conclusions with a petition submitted to Lord Dorchester [Guy Carleton*] in 1788 by Charles-Louis Tarieu* de Lanaudière, seigneur of Sainte-Anne-de-la-Pérade. Abbé Bédard felt he ought to intervene, and on 11 Feb. 1791 he sent the governor a heavily documented memoir entitled "Observations sur le projet du changement de tenure." After pointing out numerous errors and inaccuracies in Lanaudière's text, Bédard concluded that the disappearance of the seigneurial régime would in the short run ruin the seigneurs by depriving them of their banal rights and *lods et ventes* and in the long run ruin the habitants by removing any possibility of their obtaining land for themselves and their children at little cost. On 10 March a petition signed by Abbé Gravé de La Rive, superior of the Séminaire de Québec, and 59 other Canadian seigneurs similarly affirmed that a change in tenure could only be detrimental to the working class. These interventions were probably not unrelated to the imperial government's decision to maintain the seigneurial régime in Lower Canada.

On 14 Aug. 1793 Thomas-Laurent Bédard was elected superior for a third term but he did not live to complete it. On 5 May 1795 he was admitted to the Hôpital Général, and he died there on the 27th at the age of only 48 years. He was buried the next day in the chapel of the Séminaire de Québec.

NOËL BAILLARGEON

AHGQ, Hôpital, Registre des prêtres malades, no.50. Archives paroissiales, Saint-Charles-Borromée (Charlesbourg, Qué.), Registre des baptêmes, mariages et sépultures, 3 févr. 1747. ASQ, MSS, 12, ff.44, 46–53; MSS, 437, f.35; MSS-M, 122, 251, 726; Polygraphie, XXVIII, 7b; S, Carton 11, nos.1, 1A, 13; S-184A; Séminaire, 33, no.43. PAC, MG 11, [CO 42], Q, 48/1, pp.5ff.; 51/2, pp.4ff., 506–35. *Quebec Gazette*, 24, 31 March, 7, 28 April 1791. Tanguay, *Dictionnaire*, II, 184; *Répertoire*, 141. Ivanhoë Caron, *La colonisation de la province de Québec* (2v., Québec, 1923–27), I, 141–42. Casgrain, *Hist. de l'Hôtel-Dieu de Québec*, 470. A.-H. Gosselin, *L'Église du Canada après la Conquête*, II. Maurice Séguin, "Le régime seigneurial au pays de Québec, 1760–1854," *RHAF*, I (1947–48), 382–402.

BELCHER, JONATHAN, lawyer, chief justice, and lieutenant governor of Nova Scotia; b. 23 July 1710 in Boston, Massachusetts, second son of Jonathan Belcher and his first wife, Mary Partridge; m. there on 8 April 1756 Abigail Allen, and they had five sons and two daughters; d. 30 March 1776 in Halifax, Nova Scotia.

Jonathan Belcher was born into a well-established New England family. His maternal grandfather was a lieutenant governor of New Hampshire, his paternal grandfather an important Boston merchant and member of the Massachusetts Council. Jonathan's father was successively a leading Boston merchant and councillor, governor of Massachusetts and New Hampshire (1730–41), and governor of New Jersey (1747–57). A serious student, Jonathan graduated from his father's alma mater, Harvard College, with an AB in 1728 and an AM in 1731. He pursued divinity studies in Boston from 1728 to 1730 and later studied mathematics at Cambridge University, where he obtained a second master's degree in 1733. He subsequently received a third AM from the College of New Jersey (Princeton University), founded by his father.

In March 1730 Belcher had been entered in the Middle Temple, London, and he arrived to study law a year later; in May 1734 he was called to the English bar. He appeared in a number of colonial causes but was unable to establish himself at Westminster Hall, the chief law court, because of "the Number of Gentlemen of Superior Merit and Interest" there. After his father's removal from office in 1741 ended his financial support, Belcher surrendered his rank at the English bar to try his fortunes in Dublin, where it was hoped family connections might aid him. After five years of unremunerative labour he was appointed deputy secretary to the lord chancellor of Ireland through the recommendation of Lord Hardwicke, chief justice of Great Britain. In 1754 Belcher, with Edward Bullingbrooke, published a new abridgement of the Irish statutes. Later the same year, and again through Hardwicke's intervention, he was appointed to a position which promised status, financial independence, and political significance: the first chief justiceship of Nova Scotia, at £500 per year. After he visited New Jersey in 1755–56, efforts were made to obtain for him the lieutenant governorship of that province and the succession to his father as governor. These attempts failed, however, and Belcher resided in Nova Scotia until his death.

Prior to Belcher's arrival Nova Scotia had no formally trained law officers. In 1752 and 1753 charges of libel and partiality against officers of the courts [*see* James Monk*] had led Governor Peregrine Thomas Hopson* to appeal to the Lords of Trade to appoint a chief justice and an attorney general for the province. Although the latter official was never sent, in October 1754 Belcher was installed at Halifax with much pomp as both chief justice and member of the Executive Council. His first duty was to establish the courts on an orderly and constitutional basis. The Supreme Court, which replaced the General Court of governor and Council, commenced sittings immediately, with Belcher presiding; its functions were the trial of criminal cases and of debt cases above a minimum sum, the review of cases appealed from the Inferior Court of Common Pleas, and the proclamation of acts passed by the Council.

The chief justice appears to have given weight to his position as senior legal officer largely through his learning and his capacity for legal argument, but he also unhesitatingly invoked the powers of his office, as in 1755 when he refused to allow the use of government funds to pay for the transport of witnesses from Lunenburg to Halifax in a case he considered unnecessary. Both his English training and his Irish experience equipped him to oppose the Massachusetts precedents which had dominated the Nova Scotia courts prior to his arrival. In accordance with the instructions to the governor that the laws of the province should be "as near as may be Agreeable" to the laws of Britain, Belcher promoted English precedents and laws. As a result of his work they became more widely applied in Nova Scotia. In the awkward and recurring question of the extension of English laws to the colonies, Belcher supplemented his own views in favour of extension with the opinions of Chief Justice Stephen Sewall of Massachusetts and the Lords of Trade. The English law officers to whom the lords referred Belcher's opinions for advice did not, however, agree that the colonists had taken English statute law to America as part of their cultural heritage.

Belcher was involved not only in the application and interpretation of the law in Nova Scotia but also in its creation. As the sole fully trained jurist in office for many years, he is credited with having drafted the laws passed by Nova Scotia's first and subsequent legislatures. The very small number of laws rejected on technical grounds by the English law officers testifies to his skill and attentiveness. Belcher's substantial legal library as well as his notebooks and long experience are evident in his revision and annotation of the first volume of Nova Scotian laws, published in 1767 by Robert FLETCHER, and in his supervision the following year of an index of English laws acknowledged to extend to the colonies.

Belcher's legal opinions also frequently formed the basis of his political duties. Upon his arrival in Nova Scotia he was instructed to determine whether the governor and Council alone possessed legal authority to constitute laws for the colony. He has long been credited with having precipitated the calling of the first elected house of assembly within Canada by rendering the judgement that the governor and Council did not possess the necessary authority. More recent studies have clearly shown, however, that he did no such thing. In a turgid report of January 1755 he argued instead that the primitive circumstances of Nova Scotian society justified the application of the 17th-century Virginian precedent of legislating for a colony in the absence of an elected assembly. The English law officers rejected his opinion and the Lords of Trade ordered Lieutenant Governor Charles Lawrence* to seek Belcher's assistance in drawing up a plan for the calling of an assembly. Unlike Lawrence, Belcher accepted the board's decision, and late in 1755 he presented a proposal for an assembly of town and country constituencies based on a system of minimum population and non-resident representation. Moreover, he actively opposed Lawrence's delay in calling an assembly; early in 1757 he organized the transmission of complaints to the Lords of Trade from a majority of the Council and a committee of Halifax freeholders who objected to the governor's procrastination. When an assembly was finally elected in 1758 the chief justice, as a member of the Executive Council, automatically became a member of the Legislative Council.

Having established supremacy in the Council through a struggle with Treasurer Benjamin GREEN and by representations to the Lords of Trade, Belcher became administrator of the province when Lawrence died in October 1760. In November 1761 he was commissioned lieutenant governor, while Henry Ellis, governor of Georgia, received the governorship for which Belcher had hoped. Since Ellis never came to Nova Scotia, Belcher functioned as governor until 26 Sept. 1763, when he was replaced as lieutenant governor by Montagu Wilmot*.

Although Belcher had supported the summoning of a representative assembly, his subsequent relations with it were marred by controversy. His background should have fitted him admirably for senior colonial office, but his aristocratic nature made him unsympathetic to the ambitions of the Halifax merchants who were Nova Scotia's popular leaders. His attitude was evident in his administration.

Since CORNWALLIS' day a piece of legislation known as the debtors' act had protected Nova Scotian residents against prosecution by their creditors for debts incurred before they came to the province. The resolutions and acts affording protection had always been temporary, and by 1761 Belcher and the Lords of Trade agreed that the measure had outlived its usefulness. Both regarded it as a "manifest injustice . . . that [had] so long prevailed to the Injury of honest Creditors." Belcher was determined that when the act expired at the close of the next session of the house it would not be renewed. In November 1761, only two and a half months after prorogation and despite advice to the contrary by councillor Joseph GERRISH, Belcher summoned the assembly. Although the prospect of the early expiration of the debtors' act cannot have displeased the lieutenant governor, his principal reason for calling the house together was to proclaim royal disallowance of an act that had established, under the Indian commissary Benjamin GERRISH, a government-supervised monopoly in the Indian trade. He also published the Lords of Trade's instructions to pass legislation which would create a licensing system to open the trade to all residents. Belcher believed that Gerrish's opposition to the summoning of the legislature was the result of investments in his brother's monopoly, but Joseph, Benjamin, and several assembly members were concerned with preventing the expiry of the debtors' act. When seven members of the house including Benjamin Gerrish, Philip Augustus KNAUT, and Malachy SALTER appeared in Halifax but refused to attend the session, Belcher was forced not only to prorogue throughout November for want of a quorum but finally to delay the sitting until March 1762, when a quorum was assembled. The Lords of Trade ordered the dismissal from office of the offenders and of Joseph Gerrish, and Belcher's gloating communication of this news nearly created a second stalemate.

Belcher experienced further conflicts with the legislature in the sessions of 1762 and 1763. In addition to refusing assent to a new debtors' act, he rejected a new impost and excise bill favouring local distilling interests on the grounds that it could not supersede legislation already before the Lords of Trade and that it contained provisions contrary to British mercantilist law and practice. To ensure representation of its point of view before the Lords of Trade, in April 1762 the assembly had appointed as its agent in London Joshua MAUGER, the influential associate of the Halifax merchants. Although Belcher's actions in 1762 and 1763 had been consistent with his instructions from the Lords of Trade, Mauger succeeded in persuading them to reverse their position on the debtors' act. In addition, they criticized Belcher for his faulty interpretation of British practice in his objections to the impost and excise bills. To these embarrassments Mauger added complaints that the lieutenant governor was "unacquainted with and unskilled in the Art of Government." Belcher's subsequent denial in Halifax of the Board's change in position, on top of his insensitivity and inability to reconcile the duties of his office with the demands of the assembly, quite undermined his credibility.

Belcher was not an innovative man, and in several respects he continued the policies of his predecessor. In January 1762 he completed his awkward assignment of investigating charges of favouritism and conflict of interest during Lawrence's governorship. With the experience of a year in office facing the same obstacles, Belcher exonerated Lawrence and his associates. Although he was thus sensitive to the dangers as well as the responsibility of patronage, he nevertheless proliferated minor appointments throughout the province.

In pursuing the late governor's policies towards Indians and settlers, Belcher encountered new difficulties. In April 1761 he had separated the supply of goods to the Indian trade from the operation of the truckhouses, giving the supply contract to Alexander Grant and retaining Benjamin Gerrish as commissary in charge of the truckhouses. This measure did not, however, reduce the costs of the service as he had hoped. As well, his order of May 1762 reserving northeastern Nova Scotia from the Musquodoboit River to Baie des Chaleurs for the Micmacs was strongly criticized by the Lords of Trade. On the advantages of settling New Englanders in Nova Scotia, Belcher shared the views of Lawrence and his contemporary, Governor William Shirley of Massachusetts. Belcher's greatest political success perhaps lay in his encouragement of the new settlements to which Lawrence had given impetus. The Lords of Trade refused, however, to authorize the continuance of the government assistance which Lawrence had offered and which Belcher, eager to further the settlements, had initially continued.

With the security of British North America assured by the capture of Montreal in 1760 Belcher, unlike his predecessors, faced a substantially reduced parliamentary grant and strict orders to economize. Yet despite continuous assurances of reductions and savings, he exceeded the annual estimates in 1761 and 1762, in the latter year by over 40 per cent. His actions inadvertently reduced the immediate economic impact of British retrenchment upon the province, but his broken promises and his irregular accounts eventually led Mauger, the province's principal creditor, to threaten that Belcher would be held personally responsible for the provincial bills issued by him.

Although a civilian without military experience Belcher was, by virtue of his office as lieutenant governor, commander-in-chief of the colony. An insecurity in military affairs is evident in his over-cautious embargo on shipping and his establishment of martial law in July 1762, when news of Charles-Henri-Louis d'ARSAC de Ternay's raid on Newfoundland renewed fears of a French attack upon the province. But the principal military act of his administration was a small-scale repetition of Lawrence's deportation of the Acadians. Belcher's experience with the Acadians centred on his participation in the Council decisions of July 1755 to deport all those Acadians who refused to take the unrestricted oath of allegiance. His memorandum of 28 July 1755 justifying the decisions has usually been regarded as either expedient or irrelevant. In the years after the dispersal Belcher, like most Nova Scotians, continued to regard the Acadians as a threat to the province, despite assurances to the contrary from Major-General Sir Jeffery AMHERST, commander-in-chief in North America. When, therefore, news of the French attack on Newfoundland reached Halifax, Belcher, urged on by the legislature and his own fears, accepted the advice of his council of war and on 30 July ordered all those Acadian "prisoners of war" who had earlier been concentrated at Halifax deported to Boston. The Massachusetts government refused, however, to receive further Acadians, and Belcher was faced with their return to Halifax. The pragmatic Lords of Trade rebuffed Nova Scotian fears as unwarranted and the expulsion as inexpedient.

Belcher's demonstrated lack of political judgement, the financial chaos of his administration, and his inability to offset Mauger's influence in London ensured that he received no further political opportunities from the Board of Trade after his replacement as lieutenant governor in 1763. As a result of complaints about the concentration of too much authority in one man, the board decided that no future chief justice should govern Nova Scotia. Although it also considered removing Belcher from the Council in 1764, he remained its president and the chief justice until his death. These positions involved him in the continuing conflicts of Nova Scotian politics. In 1764 the assembly succeeded in having John Collier* and Charles MORRIS appointed assistant judges of the Supreme Court. This attempt to curtail Belcher's powers was frustrated when he drafted the assistants' commissions so narrowly as to ensure his own pre-eminence. It was nearly a decade before the assistant judges were allowed to constitute the court by themselves or were called upon to provide opinions on legal matters in conjunction with Belcher. The assembly's pressure about the fees and services of the courts continued throughout Belcher's life, and, although criticism centred more upon the Inferior Court of Common Pleas than the Supreme Court, Belcher resisted such reforms as the requirement that the court go on circuit and the formation of a court of exchequer.

Despite Belcher's opposition to Mauger's associates during his lieutenant governorship, later events brought him within their network. In the 1760s his business affairs outside Nova Scotia were handled by a nephew in Boston, but by the 1770s his agent was Brook Watson* in London and his largest creditor John BUTLER. Such an alliance led to Belcher's participation in the Council's opposition to Governor Francis LEGGE. In turn Legge attributed "many errors and evils" in the administration of justice to what he considered to be Belcher's lack of independence. In January 1776 Belcher ceased to attend the Council and petitioned the king for permission to resign his office on account of age and infirmity; he died before action was taken.

The aloofness, pomposity, and learning which marked Belcher's role as Nova Scotia's leading jurist were incompatible with the political aspirations instilled by his father. His real interests were academic, and like many gentlemen of his age he dabbled in verse and was knowledgeable about scientific developments. As a stalwart of St Paul's Church and a member of the corresponding committee of the Society for the Propagation of the Gospel in Nova Scotia, Belcher was an ardent supporter of the Church of England, to which he had been converted in 1740. From 1760 until his death he served as Masonic grand master of Nova Scotia. During his brief lieutenant governorship he was continuously eager to serve the province's best interests and to please his masters the Lords of Trade. His strong conservatism was, however, out of touch with the predominant philosophy of the age, and his genuinely good intentions foundered on the political realities of a struggling colony. His contribution to Nova Scotian development, while limited, lay in the law, where his expertise was recognized and generally respected.

S. BUGGEY

BL, Add. MSS 32696, f.430; 35588, ff.33, 224; 35909, ff.92, 172, 206. Halifax County Court of Probate (Halifax), B37 (original estate papers of Jonathan Belcher). Halifax County Registry of Deeds (Halifax),

Deeds, 1749–1836 (mfm. at PANS). Mass. Hist. Soc., Jeffries family papers, XIII. PAC, MG 11, [CO 217], Nova Scotia A, 64–71; [CO 220], Nova Scotia B, 8, 10, 12; Nova Scotia C, 1–5; MG 23, A1, ser.1, 13. PANS, MG 1, 107–11 (Belcher papers); RG 1, 136; 163–65; 206; 286; RG 39, C, 1755–57, box 2. Princeton University Library (Princeton, N.J.), Jonathan Belcher papers, AM 1984, 9256, 9258. PRO, CO 217/15–21, 217/34, 217/43, 217/52; CO 218/5–6. USPG, B, 25; C/CAN/NS, 2.

"The Belcher papers," Mass. Hist. Soc., *Coll.*, 6th ser., VI (1893), VII (1894). G.B., Board of Trade, *JTP, 1759–63*. *The perpetual acts of the General Assemblies of his majesty's province of Nova Scotia* [1757–82] (Halifax, 1767–[82]). Shipton, *Sibley's Harvard graduates*, VIII, 343–64. Brebner, *Neutral Yankees*; *New England's outpost*, 200–61. A. G. Doughty, *The Acadian exiles; a chronicle of the land of Evangeline* (4th ed., Toronto, 1922), 115ff. *Essays in colonial history presented to Charles McLean Andrews by his students* (New Haven, Conn., and London, 1931; repr. Freeport, N.Y., 1966), 169–97. Placide Gaudet, *Le grand dérangement: sur qui retombe la responsabilité de l'expulsion des Acadiens* (Ottawa, 1922). Émile Lauvrière, *La tragédie d'un peuple: histoire du peuple acadien, de ses origines à nos jours* (3e éd., 2v., Paris, 1922), I, 408, 445–49; II, 315–28. C. J. Townshend, "Jonathan Belcher, first chief justice of Nova Scotia," N.S. Hist. Soc., *Coll.*, XVIII (1914), 25–57.

BELESTRE, FRANÇOIS-MARIE PICOTÉ DE. *See* PICOTÉ

BELLEFEUILLE, FRANÇOIS LEFEBVRE DE. *See* LEFEBVRE

BELLEFONTAINE, *dit* **Beauséjour, JOSEPH GODIN,** *dit*. *See* GODIN

BELLERIVE, LOUIS GROSTON DE SAINT-ANGE ET DE. *See* GROSTON

BENOIST, ANTOINE-GABRIEL-FRANÇOIS, officer; b. 6 Oct. 1715 in Paris, France, son of Gabriel Benoist and Françoise de Trevet; m. 11 Nov. 1743 in Montreal (Que.) Marie-Louise, daughter of Captain Jacques Le Ber de Senneville; d. 23 Jan. 1776 at Bourges, France.

Antoine-Gabriel-François Benoist entered the army as a cadet in 1734 and left France the following year to serve in Canada. In 1739 he took part in the campaign led by Jean-Baptiste Le Moyne* de Bienville, governor of Louisiana, against the Chickasaws. Made a second ensign on 1 April 1741, he was promoted ensign in 1745. He served as adjutant under François-Pierre de RIGAUD de Vaudreuil in northern New York during the summer of 1747. Benoist then spent some time at Fort Saint-Frédéric (near Crown Point, N.Y.) and in 1748 was named adjutant in Montreal. Promoted lieutenant on 1 May 1749, he was sent to France in October to raise recruits. On his return he resumed his duties as adjutant. In 1752 he was appointed commandant of Fort du Lac-des-Deux-Montagnes (Oka, Que.), and the following year he was sent to participate in Paul Marin* de La Malgue's expedition to the Ohio valley. In 1754 he was posted to command Fort de La Présentation (Oswegatchie, now Ogdensburg, N.Y.); he replaced Alexandre DAGNEAU Douville at Fort de la Presqu'île (Erie, Pa) in 1755. In the spring of 1757 he was recalled to Montreal, promoted captain, and sent to Fort Saint-Jean (Que.). He was with the army under Montcalm* at the siege of Fort William Henry (also called Fort George, now Lake George, N.Y.) in August.

The fall of Fort Frontenac (Kingston, Ont.) in August 1758 endangered several French posts in the region, particularly Niagara (near Youngstown, N.Y.), and the fort had to be reoccupied as soon as possible. Benoist was appointed its commandant in the autumn of 1758 and tried to make the site more secure. But the fort was too badly damaged for a garrison to be stationed in it for the winter, and Benoist was ordered to fall back to Fort de La Présentation; there he was to replace Claude-Nicolas de Lorimier* de La Rivière as commander. At that moment La Présentation was also strategic in the defence of the colony; his assignment to the post was certainly a mark of confidence, fully warranted by the reputation he had gained during his years of service. Montcalm considered him an "officer of real merit" and an "honest man." Louis-Antoine de Bougainville* even said that he was "the most upright man in the colony and that to honesty, [he added] knowledge, vision, and zeal." In November 1758 Benoist assumed his new duties, taking charge at the same time of the post at Pointe-au-Baril (Maitland, Ont.), where construction of ships for transport and defence on Lake Ontario was under way [*see* Louis-Pierre Poulin* de Courval Cressé]. Because Benoist feared a British attack the following spring, Governor Pierre de RIGAUD de Vaudreuil sent out the military engineer Pierre Pouchot*. To speed the ship-building, Pouchot assumed temporary command of the two posts and then sailed for Fort Niagara at the end of April. During the summer of 1759 Benoist took part in the attack led by Louis de La Corne*, known as the Chevalier de La Corne, against Chouaguen (Oswego) and was wounded in the thigh by a gunshot. His wound took more than a year to heal, and it ended his participation in the Seven Years' War.

Benoist returned to France after the conquest

and in March 1761 was made a knight of the order of Saint-Louis and given a pension of 900 *livres*. He came back to the colony in 1763 to get his family and then returned to France to live in Bourges. The abilities he had displayed in his years of service in Canada, and above all his integrity, had made him deeply appreciated by his superiors. At the time of the *affaire du Canada*, in the early 1760s, Benoist appeared before the court at the Châtelet and submitted a long report to the commission of enquiry giving his reflections on Canada. The author of his military dossier noted: "His sense of honour obliged him to reveal information that was troublesome and that perhaps formed the basis for judgement in a notorious trial, but in giving evidence he showed, with his customary gentleness and decency, the consideration due to those who are to be pitied as they enter upon misfortune." At his death the intendant of the province of Berry, Nicolas Dupré de Saint-Maur, reminded the minister of "the exemplary conduct the Sieur de Benoist maintained in the various posts he held." The intendant and the archbishop of Bourges, Georges-Louis Phélipeaux d'Herbault, recommended Benoist's widow, who was without means, to the benevolence of the king; she was granted a pension of 600 *livres*.

ÉTIENNE TAILLEMITE

AD, Cher (Bourges), État civil, Saint-Outrille-du-Château, 24 janv. 1776. AN, Col., E, 26 (dossier Benoist). PAC, MG 18, K4. Bougainville, "Journal" (A.-E. Gosselin), ANQ *Rapport*, 1923–24, 254, 373. *Coll. des manuscrits de Lévis* (Casgrain), I, 167–68, 171; IV, 156; V, 143, 281, 292, 295, 303, 305, 308; VII, 134, 481, 484, 491, 500–1, 509, 548, 568; XI, 218. "Mémoire du Canada," ANQ *Rapport*, 1924–25, 143–45. *NYCD* (O'Callaghan and Fernow), X, 302, 953. *Papiers Contrecœur* (Grenier). *Royal Fort Frontenac* (Preston and Lamontagne), 80, 468. Æ. Fauteux, *Les chevaliers de Saint-Louis*, 188. Le Jeune, *Dictionnaire*. [François Daniel], *Histoire des grandes familles françaises du Canada, ou aperçu sur le chevalier Benoist, et quelques familles contemporaines* (Montréal, 1867).

BENOÎT (Boneval, Bonwah), PIERRE, Malecite Indian; d. 20 May 1786 in Queensbury parish, York County, New Brunswick.

Pierre Benoît's importance to the early history of New Brunswick lies with the trial following his murder. Early in the morning of 20 May 1786 two settlers, William Harboard and David Nelson, veterans of the Queen's Rangers, were out fishing when they heard dogs barking in the distance. Returning home, they found two dogs mauling one of Nelson's hogs and the other hogs missing. They shot one of the dogs and, assuming that the missing animals had been carried off in a boat, went down to the Saint John River. As the incident was later reported, they called on two Indians in a canoe to stop: "You have got my hogs." "No, no," came the reply, "you have killed my dog." The whites then fired over the heads of the Indians. Nelson fired a second time and Pierre Benoît fell dead. The other occupant of the canoe was his wife.

Four days later Nelson and Harboard were examined by the justices of the peace for York County and bound over for trial. "The Indians . . . are clamorous for an instant decision," wrote Edward Winslow*, one of the justices who had taken the depositions. The band was camped around the home of the other justice, Isaac Allen, behaving with a "rudeness" that distressed the entire family. The settlers, Winslow commented, "cannot reconcile themselves to the idea that two men of fair character should be sacrificed to satisfy the barbarous claim of a set of savages."

The trial was held at St Ann's (Fredericton) on 13 June with Chief Justice George Duncan Ludlow presiding. The solicitor general, Ward Chipman*, prosecuted for the crown; the accused had no counsel and pleaded not guilty to a charge of murder. Only three witnesses were called, none of them Indians. The trial was attended by many of the inhabitants, who showed the "deepest concern and sympathy" for the accused. Nevertheless, the jury found Harboard and Nelson guilty as charged. Harboard was pardoned, apparently because he had not fired the fatal shot; Nelson was hanged on the 23rd.

The execution of David Nelson was credited with averting serious trouble from the Indians at the time. And, although the kind of "trifling provocation" that had led to the murder of Benoît was often to be repeated in the years to come, this early and visible demonstration of justice set restraints on whites and Indians alike.

L. F. S. UPTON

Military operations in eastern Maine and N.S. (Kidder), 284. *Royal Gazette and the New Brunswick Advertiser* (Saint John), 27 June 1786. *Winslow papers, A.D. 1776–1826*, ed. W. O. Raymond (Saint John, N.B., 1901), 332–33, 357n. W. O. Raymond, "The first trial for murder on the River St. John," *Dispatch* (Woodstock, N.B.), 13 Nov. 1895, 6; repr. without acknowledgement by "Observer" [E. S. Carter], "First criminal trial in Fredericton," *Telegraph-Journal* (Saint John, N.B.), 25 Oct. 1929, 4.

BERBUDEAU, JEAN-GABRIEL, surgeon and subdelegate of the financial commissary of Île

Royale; b. 17 Oct. 1709 at Saint-Georges d'Oléron (dept of Charente-Maritime), France, son of Jean Berbudeau, master surgeon, and Marie-Anne Duvivier; d. 4 Jan. 1792 at the hamlet of Saint-Antoine in the parish of Archigny (dept of Vienne), France.

The date of Jean-Gabriel Berbudeau's arrival at Île Royale (Cape Breton Island) is not known. He was apparently not the first of the name to set foot there, for in a letter dated 24 June 1727 to Beauharnois*, the governor of New France, the minister of Marine, Maurepas, mentioned a "Sieur Berbudeau, surgeon at Île Royale." The subject of this biography was certainly in Louisbourg in 1743, for on 19 September of that year he married Marie-Gervaise Paris there. In his marriage contract he described himself as "surgeon maintained [by the king] at Port-Toulouse [St Peters, N.S.]." Following a request made on 17 Oct. 1743 by Jean-Baptiste-Louis Le Prévost* Duquesnel, the commandant of Île Royale, and François Bigot, the financial commissary, Berbudeau was appointed to Île Saint-Jean (Prince Edward Island) to replace Martin Descouts*, "surgeon maintained by the king with a salary of 600 *livres*."

There is no record of Berbudeau and his wife during the British occupation of Île Royale and Île Saint-Jean from 1745 to 1749. After these and other territories were restored to France by the treaty of Aix-la-Chapelle, Berbudeau was commissioned to accompany Claude-Élisabeth Denys* de Bonnaventure to Île Saint-Jean in 1749. Bonnaventure had been instructed to take possession of the island, rebuild its fortifications, and promote settlement, which had languished. Berbudeau and his family, then including two children, settled at Port-La-Joie (Fort Amherst). In 1751 he replaced François-Marie de Goutin* as the subdelegate on Île Saint-Jean of the financial commissary of Île Royale. Three years later, with the support of the financial commissary Jacques Prevost de La Croix, he also received his brevet as military surgeon.

Berbudeau's whereabouts during the second siege of Louisbourg in 1758 are not known, but on 28 April 1759 he landed at La Rochelle with his family and a large number of refugees. He settled there and carried on a private practice among the Acadians; only the surgeon-major Louis Bertin had been kept on active service. There is some evidence that in 1763 Berbudeau went to Guiana with the Acadians whom the minister of Marine, Choiseul, hoped to settle there; if he did, however, his stay was short. In 1766 his name was put forward for service on the Île de Ré, but his candidature was not accepted. Some years later he devoted himself to the Acadian refugees whom the Marquis de Pérusse Des Cars was taking on his lands in Poitou, at Archigny, Monthoiron, La Puye, and Saint-Pierre-de-Maillé (dept of Vienne). At Des Cars's request, on 11 Nov. 1771 the king granted Berbudeau an annual pension of 354 *livres*.

Berbudeau passed away peacefully in 1792. Four of his seven children died in infancy. It seems that only his daughter Marie-Reine married; in 1783 her husband, Pierre-Alexis Texier de La Touche, became the syndic of the Acadians in Poitou.

Georges Cerbelaud Salagnac

AD, Vienne (Poitiers), E, 4, 16–17, 62. AN, Col., C[11B], 25, 33, 38; D[2C], 1 ter; E, 27 (dossier Berbudeau); Section Outre-mer, G[3], 2047/1, 18 sept. 1743, 19 août 1751. Archives communales, Archigny (dép. de la Vienne), Registres paroissiaux. Archives maritimes, Port de Rochefort (France), 1E, 133–39. Ernest Martin, *Les exilés acadiens en France au XVIIIe siècle et leur établissement en Poitou* (Paris, 1936), 777. Pierre Massé, "Descendances acadiennes: les quatre filles de Marie-Reine Berbudeau," *RHAF*, V (1951–52), 531–41; VI (1952–53), 252–62; VII (1953–54), 426–34; VIII (1954–55), 415–25; "Le syndic de la colonie acadienne en Poitou," *RHAF*, V (1951–52), 45–68, 252–64, 373–400.

BERNARD, PHILIP, chief of a group of Micmacs at St Margaret's Bay, Nova Scotia; fl. 1786.

After the founding of Halifax in 1749 and the take-over of all of present-day Nova Scotia by the British in 1758, the Micmacs felt increasing pressure on their land holdings from settlers. As early as 1754 the Indians had requested that some land be set aside for their own exclusive use. In 1762 Lieutenant Governor Jonathan Belcher issued a proclamation forbidding settlers to trespass on certain lands claimed by the Indians along the Nova Scotia coast from the Musquodoboit River to Canso and northwest to the Baie des Chaleurs. The influx of loyalist settlers following the American revolution intensified competition for land, while at the same time the wild game required by the Micmacs to support their traditional way of life diminished. The Indians consequently suffered and became increasingly dependent upon the British. The Nova Scotia government had already made some attempt to induce the Indians to settle in one place and live by agriculture, and it now intensified its efforts. In 1783 a policy was begun of issuing licences or tickets of occupation to groups of Indians for land on which they agreed to settle. Between September and December 1783 nine such licences were issued. During 1784 several more were granted in response to petitions from the Indians, who undoubtedly were increasingly alarmed at the amount of land claimed by settlers.

These licences merely granted the Indians permission to use the land. In 1786 the government made its first recorded grant of land title to Micmacs. The group living at St Margaret's Bay, led by Philip Bernard, were told that pending completion of a formal grant they could occupy a 500-acre tract on the bay. Before the grant could be accomplished, however, the land was found to be the property of Brook Watson*, who sold it and dispossessed the Indians. Chief Bernard, along with Solomon and Tawmaugh, two men of the group, then memorialized the government on 1 Feb. 1786, requesting a 500-acre grant at the head of the bay. In response, Governor John Parr commissioned a survey of the tract so that the Indians could be given title. This survey was reported accomplished on 3 March 1786.

Following the grant of land to the three petitioners, outright grants were also made to other Micmac groups around the colony. Some horticulture was undertaken by the Indians, but on the whole no great strides toward sedentary life were made as a result of the policy. The significance of the grant to Bernard was that the principle of giving Indians legal title to land was established, and the practice culminated in the creation of a reserve system in 1820. After 1786 there is no further mention of Philip Bernard in written records.

Virginia P. Miller

PANS, RG 1, 165, pp.224–25; 430, nos.23½, 26½, 27½, 28. *N.S. Archives, I*, 215. E. A. Hutton, "The Micmac Indians of Nova Scotia to 1834" (unpublished MA thesis, Dalhousie University, Halifax, 1961).

BERNIER, BENOÎT-FRANÇOIS (also called **Joseph-Pierre**), army officer and financial commissary of wars in New France; b. 24 April 1720 in Vienne, France, son of François Bernier, cloth merchant, and Marie Malen (Mallen); d. 1799, unmarried, probably in Vienne.

The military career of Benoît-François Bernier seems to have begun relatively late; the earliest record lists him as sub-lieutenant in the Régiment Royal-Suédois in 1746. After serving as a lieutenant in the siege of Maastricht (Netherlands) in 1748, he was put on half pay and from 1749 to 1755 was employed by the regiment at Paris and Versailles. He must have attracted favourable attention, for he was made aide-de-camp to Dieskau* when the latter was sent to Canada in 1755 as commander of the French regular troops despatched to the colony. For administrative purposes Bernier was attached to the Régiment d'Artois as a lieutenant, but the connection was purely nominal.

His first sojourn in Canada was destined to be short. He arrived with Dieskau in June 1755 and was captured at Lac Saint-Sacrement (Lake George, N.Y.) in September. Dieskau, seriously wounded, was abandoned on the battlefield by all save Bernier, who was himself slightly wounded. They were made prisoner by William Johnson's colonials.

It was thought for some time that both Bernier and Dieskau were dead; their personal effects were in fact auctioned off in Quebec before word of their survival and impending transfer to England was received. In England Bernier was parted from his general and sent to London where, according to a French memoir, he was held for two months and pressed by Lord Holland, the Duke of Newcastle, and the Earl of Loudoun to "join the British service." He was then sent "as if in punishment" to Edinburgh Castle.

Bernier was repatriated to France in 1757, promoted captain, and the following year appointed assistant to André Doreil*, the financial commissary of wars at Quebec. He arrived in Canada at the end of June 1758, gravely ill with a fever contracted in passage, and was not out of danger until late July. Bernier, although lacking in experience because of his illness, replaced Doreil as commissary of wars when the latter returned to France in the autumn of 1758. Doreil spoke of Bernier's "talent and intelligence" and arranged to have him assisted by his secretary, Alexandre-Robert Hillaire de La Rochette, "who is conversant with all the details of the Commissariat." Bernier had charge of the physical well-being of the regular troops, their rations, equipment, billeting, and hospitalization. By all accounts he served his troops well.

After the fall of Quebec in September 1759, Bernier remained for four months at Quebec and was particularly concerned with looking after the wounded. He acted as liaison officer with the British, and he was given full authority by Governor Pierre de Rigaud de Vaudreuil, then in Montreal, to deal with all difficulties involved in executing the capitulation of Quebec. This responsibility was delegated to Bernier because he spoke English, an uncommon accomplishment among 18th-century French officers. He had probably acquired it during his stay in England.

At the time of the capitulation of the colony in September 1760 Bernier was in Montreal, and he organized the passing of the troops in review. He then returned to Quebec to make provision with the British commissaries for the subsistence and lodging of the French troops. He was put in sole charge of the embarkation of all the French regulars as well as those families wishing immediate repatriation. It was a major task and one which he discharged to his superiors' satisfaction, judging by the fact that upon his return to France with LÉVIS late in November 1760 he was awarded the cross of Saint-Louis, given a pension of 1,200 *livres*, and appointed financial commissary at Dunkerque.

Bernier retired from government service on 2 Sept. 1776 and survived the French revolution. As "citizen Bernier" he received an annual pension from the Republic of France until his death in 1799.

J. R. TURNBULL

AMA, SHA, Y[4]. AN, Col., C[11A], 103, ff.419–22v, 423–26v. ANQ-Q, Greffe de J.-A. Saillant, 19 juill. 1758. Bibliothèque municipale de Vienne (dép. de l'Isère, France), État civil, Saint-André-le-Bas, 25 avril 1720. *Doc. relatifs à la monnaie sous le Régime français* (Shortt), II. Doreil, "Lettres" (A. Roy), ANQ *Rapport*, 1944–45, 16, 24, 31–32, 41, 45, 48, 71, 73–74, 77, 88, 93, 100, 106, 111–12, 143–44, 161–62. *NYCD* (O'Callaghan and Fernow), VI, 1004; X, 318, 340, 354, 356–57, 360, 384, 387, 422, 564, 692, 746, 765, 829, 861, 959, 965, 968, 1009, 1054, 1120, 1123–24. Le Jeune, *Dictionnaire*. J.-E. Roy, *Rapport sur les archives de France*, 371–72, 377, 415.

BERSALOU. *See* BARSALOU

BERTRAND DE LATOUR, LOUIS. *See* LATOUR, BERTRAND DE

BESNARD, *dit* **Carignant, JEAN-LOUIS** (he signed L. Carignant), merchant-trader; b. 22 Nov. 1734 in Montreal, son of Jean-Baptiste Besnard, *dit* Carignant, and Marie-Joseph Gervaise; m. 13 Aug. 1764 Charlotte Brebion in Montreal; m. there secondly on 20 Jan. 1770 Félicité, daughter of Montreal merchant Pascal Pillet; d. 3 Dec. 1791 at Michilimackinac (Mackinac Island, Mich.).

Jean-Louis Besnard, *dit* Carignant, followed in the footsteps of his father, a Montreal merchant and outfitter. Around 1770 he was engaged in the fur trade, outfitting voyageurs for amounts sometimes exceeding 20,000 *livres*; in addition he ran a flour mill at Lachine, near Montreal. Although he rapidly acquired many debtors, Carignant was not afraid to go into debt himself to his suppliers. Like every merchant in the colony, he had to speculate on credit and choose his debtors carefully. However, he had less luck in this game than others [*see* Jean ORILLAT], and on 30 Sept. 1776 he had to declare a bankruptcy that would have repercussions on the political life of the province.

On 9 Oct. 1776 Carignant submitted a balance-sheet to his creditors which showed 222,306 *livres* in debts and 140,640 *livres* in assets, 65,000 *livres* of the latter in accounts outstanding; his creditors were London merchants Brook Watson* and Robert Rashleigh, the firms of Pierre Foretier* and Jean Orillat and of John Porteous in Montreal, and also Montreal merchants Jean-Marie Ducharme*, Jacob JORDAN, Toussaint Lecavelier, Louis-Joseph and Charles-Jean-Baptiste Chaboillez*, Charles Larche, and Ignace Pillet (Carignant's brother-in-law). Carignant had contracted his largest debt – the sum of 88,000 *livres* – with the firm of Watson and Rashleigh. The balance-sheet also revealed the losses he had incurred in trading in furs and wheat, but these could not by themselves account for the bankruptcy, which Carignant attributed to "unfortunate events . . . bad promises and swindles of which he has been the victim."

Yet a few hours before declaring bankruptcy, Carignant had completed a series of deals with Montreal merchant Richard Dobie* through which Dobie had bought furs worth 130,000 *livres* from him and he, after deducting his debts to Dobie and Dobie's partner Adam Lymburner*, had made 63,000 *livres* not shown in the books. Carignant's creditors, to whom he had assigned his property, accused Dobie of fraud and took legal proceedings against him because, according to them, he had entered into secret agreements with Carignant to pay for the furs. When the Court of Common Pleas in Montreal decided in favour of the creditors, Dobie appealed to the Legislative Council, and as a result of Chief Justice Peter LIVIUS' summation it reversed the judgement on 30 April 1778. The next day Governor Sir Guy Carleton* dismissed Livius from his post without explanation. During the subsequent inquiry, Livius insinuated to the British authorities that Carleton had been influenced by Brook Watson, who was Carignant's principal creditor and who, according to Livius, "was in great habits with Sir Guy Carleton & was very much trusted by him in his private concerns, & in some matters of a public nature, particularly in Indian Affairs." Livius was reinstated but never returned to Canada. As for Carignant, his combined assets could in no way cover his debts at the time of his bankruptcy; his creditors allowed him to remain in business, hoping to be repaid gradually, but whether this hope was fulfilled is not known.

Carignant's business papers and the documents produced at the time of his bankruptcy provide some useful indications of his commercial practices and style of life. Of the 128 debts recorded in his accounts receivable ledger in 1776, only eight exceeded 1,000 *livres* but they amounted to nearly 50,000 *livres*, three-quarters of the total. His assets also included 12,500 *livres* in furs, ginseng, and merchandise, a house on the construction of which he had spent 26,000 *livres* (and which his creditors sold for 36,000 *livres* in 1777), furnishings valued at 12,000 *livres*, a library of some 40 titles appraised at 1,200 *livres*, and two black slaves, a man worth 1,600 and a woman worth 1,200 *livres*. Judging from the inventory of the house, Carignant lived comfortably, and he owned several expensive articles – a mahogany table, a faience fountain, some silverware, and some crystal.

Carignant's subsequent career seems to have been rather varied. He was trading in wheat again in 1777 and apparently received a contract for supplying flour to the army, perhaps in concert with his old creditor, Jacob Jordan. In 1780 he went into partnership with his brother-in-law, Antoine Pillet, to run a bakery. In the winter of 1781–82 he was in trouble with the authorities. Rebel sympathizers who had been taken prisoner accused Carignant of having established relations with the Americans; he was arrested and taken to Quebec. In his defence he submitted a certificate of loyalty signed by such residents of Montreal as Luc de LA CORNE, Pierre Guy*, Jacob Jordan, Christian Daniel CLAUS, James McGill*, and Edward William Gray*. He was released for lack of evidence at the beginning of 1782. But his bakery business fell off, and he had difficulty again with his creditors. In May 1785 he received a commission as notary at Michilimackinac, and he was living there in 1786 and 1787. In 1788 he was appointed superintendent of inland navigation at Michilimackinac. He drowned in Lake Michigan on 3 Dec. 1791.

Hilda Neatby*, after reviewing the Dobie case, decided that Carignant was simply dishonest. But if so, it is hard to see why he would of his own free will have made over all his belongings to his creditors in 1776, or why they would have agreed to let him continue in business once the supposed fraud had been discovered. Besides, why would he have been granted the official posts at Michilimackinac if his honesty or loyalty had been in doubt? As for his inability to succeed in business, Carignant like many others was probably a victim of the development in the fur trade which concentrated control increasingly in the hands of a small group of merchants and led to the creation of the North West Company in 1783.

JOSÉ E. IGARTUA and MARIE GÉRIN-LAJOIE

ANQ-M, État civil, Catholiques, Notre-Dame de Montréal, 22 nov. 1737, 13 août 1764, 18 sept. 1769, 20 janv. 1770; Greffe de Pierre Panet, 25 mai 1767, 22 déc. 1774, 9 oct. 1776, 29 avril, 12 mai, 1er juill. 1777; Greffe de Simon Sanguinet, 2, 10, 23 oct. 1769, 22 mars, 23 juill. 1770, 14, 25 juill. 1774, 17 févr. 1775; Greffe de François Simonnet, 11 mai 1750, 8 déc. 1770. AUM, P 58, Doc. divers, C2, 27 juill. 1787. BL, Add. MSS 21721, ff.182–83v, 192; 21734, ff.310–11, 320; 21791, ff.142, 146 (copies at PAC). PAC, MG 23, GIII, 25, ser. A (Louis Carignant); MG 24, L3, pp.27531–35, 30494; RG 4, A1, 38, p.12548; B8, 28, p.22; B28, 115. PRO, CO 42/2, pp.261–64; 42/42, pp.129–34 (PAC transcripts). Ste Ann's Parish (Mackinac Island, Mich.), Registre des baptêmes, mariages et sépultures de Sainte-Anne-de-Michillimakinak, 16 juill. 1786, 20 août 1787 (mfm. at PAC, MG 8, G17). *Quebec Gazette*, 17 Nov. 1766, 7 Sept. 1769, 16 Jan. 1777, 2 Dec. 1779. *Almanach de Québec*, 1791, 39. Massicotte, "Répertoire des engagements pour l'Ouest," ANQ *Rapport*, 1929–30, 327, 345, 347, 369, 406, 426–27; 1930–31, 353–54, 357, 372–74, 376, 400–2, 420. Tanguay, *Dictionnaire*. Burt, *Old prov. of Que.* (1968), I, 248–50. Neatby, *Administration of justice under Quebec Act*, 74–77.

BIGOT, FRANÇOIS, financial commissary of Île Royale and intendant of New France; baptized 30 Jan. 1703 in the parish of Saint-André, Bordeaux, France, son of Louis-Amable Bigot and Marguerite Lombard; d. 12 Jan. 1778 at Neuchâtel, Switzerland.

The Bigot family began to rise in the world at least three generations before that of François. At the end of the 16th century Bonaventure was a "merchant and citizen of Tours." His son Étienne left this city for Paris around 1619. Since his marriage to Marie Renard in 1617 had brought him into the circles of the Bonneaus and the Fleuriaus, Étienne's descendants could count on protection in the rank and fashion of French society. One of the Parisian cousins, Marie-Louise Bigot, married a Brulart de Sillery at the end of the 17th century.

It was with Louis, the son of Étienne, and in the south west of France, that the critical turning point in the family's history occurred. From then on its course followed a classic pattern: finance, the magistracy, the achieving of nobility. At the time of his marriage in 1657 Louis Bigot was attached to one of the most important tax farms in western France, financed in large measure by the Bonneaus, that of the import and export duties at Bordeaux (*le convoi et la comptablie*). He served in succession as clerk, controller, collector, and finally receiver general. This position apparently enabled him to participate actively in the major occupation of the inhabitants of Bordeaux, the fitting out of ships, and with bottomry loans he helped to finance several voyages to Quebec and Newfoundland. It was probably this important contribution to the commercial life of the city that gained him his letters as a citizen (*lettres de bourgeoisie*) on 26 March 1698. He had further ambitions nevertheless. In 1682 he had become seigneur of Monaday, a fief in the suburbs of Bordeaux. In 1700 he purchased the post of head clerk in the *parlement* of Bordeaux for 50,000 *livres* and six years later that of secretary to the king, an office conferring nobility. This extraordinary ascent was confirmed by the marriages of his daughters into old families of the local aristocracy.

Louis's son, Louis-Amable, father of François, the future intendant, maintained the level gained. His career was made in the *parlement*: after serving as lawyer and then councillor, he inherited the post of head clerk. In 1698 he married Marguerite Lombard, with a dowry of 40,000 *livres*. Newly arrived from Manosque, the Lombards had quickly settled into the local bourgeoisie and had specialized in maritime administration. One of François's brothers, Louis-Joseph, had a career as a naval officer. The eldest, Joseph-Amable, first tried the army but soon went into the magistracy, initially in the presidial court in Bordeaux and then in the *parlement* there. He sold the latter office in 1741, probably following financial difficulties. It was he who, so to speak, liquidated the patrimony; he abandoned the seigneury of Monaday in 1748, sold the house in Bordeaux in 1766, and died in 1780 at Saint-Dizant-du-Gua (dept of Charente-Maritime), apparently living as a noble, but in poverty, on his seigneury of Beaulon.

Nothing is known with certainty of François's education, though he probably took the courses offered by the Faculté de Droit in Bordeaux. In any case, at the age of 20, when legal studies were normally completed, he chose to enter the Marine administration. Two reasons are possible for his choice: first, a personal liking to which he later attested and which perhaps had come from his maternal ancestors; second, the appointment in March 1723 of his cousin, Charles-Jean-Baptiste de Fleuriau, Comte de Morville, as minister of Marine. His apprenticeship was lengthy and unremarkable; Morville was with the Marine for only a short period and was not able to secure rapid promotion for him. Taking the usual route, François first served as a scrivener and thus, in the port to which he was sent, was in charge of a limited sector under the authority of a commissary. He became a commissary himself in 1728, chief scrivener in 1729, and "resident commissary of the Marine" at Rochefort in 1732. This was his last post before his North American career.

His superiors at Rochefort took Bigot to task for his love of gambling. Though it was a passion common in his milieu, he probably gambled more often than was usual. His enemies also accused him of playing the gallant, and there is nothing improbable in this. Nevertheless, his administration must have been methodical and efficient. Moreover, his appointment to Louisbourg, Île Royale (Cape Breton Island), on 1 May 1739 as financial commissary replacing Sébastien-François-Ange LE NORMANT de Mézy definitely represented a promotion. Although the position did not correspond to his wishes, Bigot was prepared to accept it because the minister of Marine, Maurepas, had explained to him that "an intendancy in the ports of France cannot be expected if one has not served in the colonies." On 30 July Bigot sailed for Louisbourg with the newly appointed governor, Isaac-Louis de Forant*; they arrived on 9 September.

Anxious to impress his superiors in France, Bigot attended zealously to every aspect of the financial commissary's duties [*see* Jacques-Ange Le Normant* de Mézy]. He reorganized the bookkeeping and personally supervised operations in detail. He worked well with the agent of the treasurers general of the Marine, Jacques-Philippe-Urbain Rondeau*, and the controller and attorney general of the Conseil Supérieur, Antoine Sabatier*. Though he justly criticized the king's storekeeper, Philippe Carrerot*, he allowed him to retain his position. His only change in personnel was to advance the career of his protégé, Jacques PREVOST de La Croix, who himself became financial commissary on 1 Jan. 1749.

Bigot avoided the conflicts with the governor that had marked the administrations of his predecessors. Forant held his position only briefly for he died in May 1740, and Bigot had amicable relations with his successors, Commandant Jean-Baptiste-Louis Le Prévost* Duquesnel and interim commandant Louis DU PONT Duchambon. The Du Ponts, the pre-eminent military family in the colony, became personal favourites, particularly François DU PONT Duvivier and Louis DU PONT Duchambon de Vergor. The accounts for 1742 to 1744 indicate some of the ways in which this patronage worked. During these years Vergor received 714 *livres* in direct payments from the crown for the rental of a boat to carry Bigot about the island even though the financial commissary had already been granted 1,200 *livres* annually to defray his transportation costs. Similarly, in 1744 the crown was charged 33,000 *livres* to fit out Duvivier's schooner *Succès*, which he had rented to the administration for 6,300 *livres*.

Bigot's patronage of the Du Ponts raises the

question of his involvement in commercial activity at Louisbourg. To Guy Frégault* his participation seemed likely. With the outbreak of war between France and Britain in 1744 Bigot invested heavily in privateering. He had a two-fifths share in the *Cantabre*, which he purchased and fitted out at a total cost of more than 17,500 *livres* with his partners Joannis-Galand d'OLABARATZ, Duvivier, and Duquesnel. Again in partnership with Duvivier and Duquesnel and with Duvivier's brother Michel Du Pont de Gourville he held a quarter interest in the *Saint-Charles*, the total cost of which was 8,850 *livres*, and he obtained another quarter interest in a larger vessel, the *Brador*, acquired and fitted out for 34,590 *livres*.

A Louisbourg financial commissary's first concern was probably to assure adequate supplies for the troops and the civilian population. Throughout his administration Bigot thought, or wanted to give the impression, that the situation was dire. "If a scarcity of supplies were to occur in a year when we were attacked," he wrote, "what assistance could be obtained from people dying of starvation?" The problem of supply had been a recurrent one for his predecessor, Le Normant, who in 1737 had dispatched Prevost to Versailles to report on it. Bigot had no more success in solving the problem than Le Normant and like him had no reluctance in turning to New England for supply if he thought it warranted. In 1743, in response to Intendant Gilles HOCQUART's pleas for assistance, Bigot contracted with Duvivier to secure from his New England contacts fish and foodstuffs potentially worth 135,000 *livres*. Because the crisis at Quebec then dissipated, the supplies fortunately remained in Bigot's stores and made him certain of relative plenty for the winter. On the other hand, the following autumn nearly ended in disaster, hostilities having begun, but a few French ships sailing out of Quebec managed to reach Île Royale before winter and provided supplies for several months.

Bigot considered a variety of measures to remedy this ever precarious situation. Though in 1739 he had opposed Hocquart's plan to set up at Louisbourg "a granary of plenty," a type of permanent warehouse which was to serve the two colonies, he brought the subject up again three years later, proposing the establishment of a storehouse for flour from New England. The minister turned a deaf ear. The financial commissary also hoped to develop farming in the areas of Île Royale that were potentially suitable, or on Île Saint-Jean (Prince Edward Island), where the land appeared to him to be good. During his administration the court continued the practice of sending out salt smugglers released from prison to help work the land, but they were more of a nuisance than an aid to the colonists and the practice ceased in 1741. Rationing was another measure to protect supplies. Even though Bigot did not succeed in finding any long-term solution to the problem, he accomplished so much so well that the inhabitants never suffered from hunger, even during the siege of May–June 1745.

The management of Île Royale's economy entailed many other duties and Bigot had mixed success in these. His attempts to encourage the extraction of coal failed because no interested buyers could be found in France. In shipbuilding there was a different sequence of events: early successes – 15 ships were launched in 1741 – were not repeated; in 1743 the carpenters produced only four ships, while 17 were purchased from the Americans. When the minister expressed his astonishment, Bigot replied that the practice had a number of advantages: "I make every effort to enlist the inhabitants in building, but I am unable to succeed because of the benefits they see in purchasing English ships, these purchases procuring for them the disposal of their rum and molasses, so if that harms construction, it on the other hand is good for the sale of the cargoes coming from the islands [the West Indies]."

Among Bigot's other concerns, the two principal were fishing and trade. The French authorities had, after all, not assigned to Louisbourg a solely military function; they wanted it to replace Newfoundland as a base for fishing and to serve as a depot for French merchants plying the North Atlantic [*see* Philippe Pastour* de Costebelle]. In 1739 the fisheries might have seemed to be excellent; in reality they were far from good. The scarcity of labourers was beginning to diminish profits in alarming fashion. For many fishermen, and their financial backers, this decline meant ruin, in more or less short order. Bigot thought the government should intervene and on its own authority reduce the sailors' wages, thus sustaining the profits of the entrepreneurs; but then it would be absolutely essential to find markets. He was to suggest a few to his superiors; however, various factors, privateering being one, in the end brought his plans to nothing. A graph of the annual value of fishery production – the fish themselves or the oil – indicates a drop of more than 55 per cent between 1739 and 1744; the value of production fell from 3,161,465 to 1,481,480 *livres*.

The statistics on the balance of trade were more hopeful, at least in appearance. The information available suggests that trade underwent a notable expansion – nearly 50 per cent – in the period 1739–44 and that it almost always presented a favourable balance. A comparison of a graph for trade with the graph for the fisheries, the island's sole resource, makes it evident that Louisbourg's functions as a depot and an entrepôt had become more marked in these years. Trade, carried on in a fourfold direction, had decreased with Canada because of poor harvests, had stagnated with France, but had increased with the West Indies and the British American colonies [*see* Sébastien-François-Ange Le Normant de Mézy]. The minister was upset at the growth in foreign trade, but Bigot strongly denied the evidence. It is necessary to consider only the number of ships from British Acadia and New England that berthed at Louisbourg – 49 in 1739, 78 in 1743 – when in the same years French ships numbered respectively 56 and 58. Did the financial commissary want to conceal his own hand, his personal participation in business at Île Royale?

Bigot had also to take a close interest in military affairs. Fate indeed dictated that the 20 odd years of his North American adventure would be marked by constant war and that his name would be connected with two stunning defeats. By 1739 in fact, the year of his arrival at Louisbourg, tense situations had arisen between Paris and London; the following year Duquesnel and Duvivier even proposed an attack on Annapolis Royal (N.S.) and Placentia (Nfld). But no action occurred. The financial commissary busied himself with things that seemed much more mundane, the importance of which, apparently, eluded the officials at Versailles: securing decent living conditions for the soldiers (although he was reprimanded by the minister in 1739 for not suppressing the officers' canteens) and patching the stonework walls and bastions of a fortress that had never been completed and that had been badly maintained. If the colony, when war came in the spring of 1744, was relatively ill prepared and suffered mishap after mishap, it was not because of negligence on Bigot's part. He made an increasing number of appeals to Versailles and Quebec, and he organized privateering, though its effects were neutralized by the activity of American sailors. But there were some things he was powerless to control. In May 1744 Duquesnel appointed Duvivier to lead an expedition against Canso, whose commander, Patrick Heron*, surrendered on 24 May. Flushed by the easy success of the mission Duquesnel devised a plan for a joint assault on Annapolis Royal by Nova Scotia Micmacs led by the missionary Jean-Louis Le Loutre, a small naval squadron, and a detachment commanded by Duvivier. This time the enterprise was a failure. Bigot could organize the means for such an operation but not change military incompetency.

In December Bigot faced a more severe test. Depressed by the threat of a British attack [*see* Joannis-Galand d'Olabaratz] and by the flagrant abuses of which it had long been the victim, the Louisbourg garrison erupted into mutiny. Was it Bigot who by his boldness, as he boasted, succeeded in keeping the soldiers in check? His role is not clear. The general amnesty which Duchambon, interim commander since the death of Duquesnel in October, promised the mutineers had its desired effect, but since Bigot held the purse-strings and controlled the disposition of stores, his role in dealing with the mutiny must have been important.

To Maurepas Bigot pointed out the great danger Louisbourg was in from possible British attack. The long-expected fear was realized in April 1745 when warships under Commodore Peter Warren* began to blockade Louisbourg. On 11 May American provincial troops commanded by William Pepperrell* landed unopposed at Pointe Platte (Simon Point), one mile west of Louisbourg. Although outnumbered, the garrison held out for 47 days, but by the end of June it was necessary to accept the evidence in the reports of the artillery officer, Philippe-Joseph d'Allard de Sainte-Marie, and the chief engineer, Étienne Verrier*: from a military point of view, further resistance was futile. On 26 June, at a council of war which included Bigot, the unanimous decision was made to capitulate. Throughout the siege Bigot had ensured an adequate and fair distribution of provisions. The officers obtained an honourable capitulation, and Bigot at the same time effected an advantageous commercial transaction. Merchandise in the storehouse was sold to the British and "converted into bills of exchange on London"; for this transaction he received a substantial bonus from the minister, but he probably also benefited personally from it.

Bigot returned to France on the *Launceston*, arriving at Belle-Île on 15 July 1745. The period of rest he wanted was cut short by the minister's orders; he was sent to Rochefort to look after the soldiers of the garrison, and then to assist in equipping the ships leaving for Quebec. If he had hoped for a post in France, he must have been disappointed. His Canadian mission was beginning to take shape; the Acadian adventure was not yet concluded.

By the end of 1745 Maurepas had in fact decided that Île Royale was to be recaptured. The Duc d'Anville [La Rochefoucauld*] received command of the expedition and by January 1746 preparations were under way. The operation was no small affair; to ensure the supplies alone, 1,100,000 rations had to be prepared. Bigot, who was appointed commissary general only at the end of February, managed the task with diligence. On 10 April everything was ready, but it was already late if the meeting of all the French forces at Chebucto Bay (Halifax harbour) planned for 20 May was to be achieved. The gathering of the various parts of the expedition in western ports of France took place only on 17 May, it was not possible to sail until 22 June, and the Acadian shores were not reached until 10 September. Then came the misfortunes of severe storm, abrupt changes of command, and illness in the crews. In these circumstances it was not possible to undertake any action. Powerless, Bigot watched the ruin of the expedition he had prepared with such effort. Even the necessary return to France was made with difficulty, and the ship on which Bigot sailed was wrecked on a shoal off Port-Louis. He escaped with his life but lost a good part of his personal belongings.

By contrast, the next year, 1747, was one of the most tranquil of his busy life. He spent it completing reports about the previous year's expedition, closing the Louisbourg accounts, and resting at Bordeaux and Bagnères (probably Bagnères-de-Bigorre). He had only one cause for worry: Maurepas gave him to understand that he was to replace Hocquart as intendant at Quebec. At the time of his trial in 1763 Bigot had it recorded that he had "made the utmost attempt to get out of it." However he resigned himself. On 17 June he wrote to Maurepas: "If you have need, my lord, of my services in this colony, I would go there, I assure you, with great pleasure on the ships you will be sending, and I would leave the waters as soon as your order is received, the service of the king being dearer to me than my health." Bigot sailed on the *Zéphyr* and arrived at Quebec on 26 Aug. 1748. He was not going to return to France, except briefly, until 21 Sept. 1760 when he went aboard a British ship, the *Fanny*, put at his disposal at Montreal by article 15 of the capitulation Governor Vaudreuil [RIGAUD] had signed on 8 September.

Bigot's duties in Canada are usually described as those of the chief civil officer, but this designation is a misleading anachronism. Frenchmen knew no civil order in the British sense of the term until the revolution of 1789, and their paternal or absolute monarchs did not divide duties among officials according to whether they were civil or military. Besides, Bigot was not one of the usual intendants of police, justice, and finance chosen from among the *maîtres des requêtes* and commissioned to administer provinces; he was one of the *officiers de plume*, to use the 18th-century expression, commissioned to administer ports and colonies. He was thus a career officer in the Marine from that part of the ministry concerned with administering funds, supplies, equipment, timber, shipbuilding, housing, hospitals, the populace in general, and everything, indeed, except fighting. Neither his experience at Louisbourg and at French ports nor his new duties in Canada could fairly be described as "civil" administration except in the limited sense that he shared authority with a governor who was the military commander-in-chief. Bigot's task was to direct trade, finance, industry, food supplies, prices, policing, and other such matters in one of the march-lands of the French empire colonized and maintained for the purposes of imperial expansion. When Bigot arrived, five years of war had just been concluded by a peace treaty which intelligent observers, including Bigot, knew to be no more than a truce. His fundamental duty was to assist the governor in the tasks of imperial expansion.

A grand strategy for Canada as a bastion of a growing French American empire was already being worked out in 1748 by the commandant general, La Galissonière [Barrin*], but the part Bigot as intendant had to play in it he did not, it appears, play very well. He did not do well partly because the funds granted each year were not commensurate with the task and partly because the military and naval situations, which he thoroughly understood, made him pessimistic and ultimately cynical, as well they might. He pointed out after the Seven Years' War that an aggressive strategy had made Canada a theatre of struggles it could not cope with. Still, in 1750 he worked with Governor La Jonquière [Taffanel*] to stir up and arm the Indians in Acadia against Halifax and to promote emigration of French Acadians and also the resistance among them that was to lead to their expulsion [*see* Jean-Louis Le Loutre]. Bigot did not oppose the futile Ohio expedition in 1753 led by Paul Marin* de La Malgue but secretly joined in the profit-making preparations which made it so expensive. He expressed pessimistic fears at a meeting of the war council called by Vaudreuil just after the defeat of Montcalm* on the Plains of Abraham in 1759 and so did not help to prevent the fateful decision by Jean-Baptiste-Nicolas-Roch de RAMEZAY to surrender Quebec. Montcalm blamed him for the economies and shortages that hampered the forces, linking them with the tyranny and corruption he saw in Bigot's intendancy, but this accusation may be going too far. An intendant and *officier de plume* such as Bigot, by the very nature of his responsibilities, was likely to quarrel with an *officier d'épée* such as Montcalm or a governor such as Vaudreuil. Montcalm was hardly a reliable judge; his copious criticism betrays his own unstable, tempestuous character. His harsh opinions should be tempered by the knowledge that, on the whole, the calm and capable General LÉVIS maintained close and friendly relations with Bigot.

Bigot showed much greater ability at one of the intendant's traditional tasks of maintaining food supplies. Although his record was marred by a greedy attention to personal profit, he could fairly claim to have fed the forces and the populace better than might have been expected in the hungry winters of 1751–52, 1756–57, and 1757–58. War brought more French (and Irish) soldiers to feed and interrupted agriculture by taking men off the land to fight and to join in the swollen wartime supply trades. More vessels plied the St Lawrence than ever before to and from Europe, the West Indies, and Île Royale. Never the peasant people of the familiar legend, Canadians were excited by new opportunities for buying, selling, hoarding, profiteering, smuggling, and counterfeiting in the turbulent war and inter-war years. Bigot tried to keep tenants on the land by enforcing the edicts of Marly (6 July 1711), which provided that uncultivated land would escheat to the landlords, but he had little success. The growing need for a rational, controlled food supply is reflected in Bigot's many regulations for the distribution and pricing of grain, flour, and bread, a creditable administrative effort hard to appreciate except in the larger context of efforts to feed hungry peoples in, say, Bourbon France, British India, and some Third World countries today. History shows that authorities managing food supplies, however vigorously and successfully, are usually seen as corrupt, arrogant, and ineffectual. No one knows yet whether Bigot systematically starved the Canadian people in a rapacious *pacte de famine*, as Louis Franquet* and others then thought, or whether their accusations should now be viewed as one of those legends so common in 18th-century France. We do know that he appointed the purveyor general of the French forces in Canada, Joseph-Michel CADET, and supported his remarkable efforts to bring supplies from France in 1757–60.

The production of other commodities besides food was also declining during Bigot's term of office and the effects of Bigot's intendancy are not clear in this field. He quickly planned to improve the fur trade so as to rival the British trade but it is hard to know what he accomplished. The fur trade no doubt languished, like the ginseng trade, because of falling demands on overseas markets, but how did Bigot affect prices and sales by his secret monopoly of the annual fur auction? The Saint-Maurice ironworks failed before Bigot's time with the financial collapse of its director, François-Étienne Cugnet*, but Bigot did little or nothing to revive it. Nor did he revive the infant shipbuilding industry which his predecessor Hocquart had attempted to nurture but which still suffered from rising prices, shortages of materials and skilled labour, and the competition of captured prize ships from New England yards [*see* René-Nicolas LEVASSEUR]. He seems, on the other hand, to have done something to stimulate the growing of hemp and the making of rope which had been declining since 1744, soon after war broke out, and yet French merchants exported much rope to Quebec before and during his intendancy in response to rising prices which Bigot apparently could not control. In short, the wars depressed the colonial manufacturing of most commodities and encouraged importing from France in spite of higher customs duties imposed on imports and exports from 1753.

Bigot, like Bourbon officials generally, was more successful at public works, public order, and policing than at economic management. His record in such matters great or small shows no lack of intelligence or hard work, whatever his other deficiencies, and is comparable with the record of many an intendant in France. "Tyranny" is the word that springs to mind when reading the list of Bigot's ordinances directing people's movements and behaviour in detail, prescribing severe punishments for offenders, and relying in criminal cases on the stocks, the gibbet, the execution block, and the tortures of the boot, built by an official carpenter, Jean Turgeon. Yet tyranny of this type was standard French practice, and most of the 29 cases of torture of criminal suspects in Canada were before Bigot's time. He showed a rare tolerance of the Huguenot merchants in the colony and in dispatches of 1749 defended them against the bigotry of Bishop Pontbriand [Dubreil*] on the grounds that they were harmless in religion and indispensable in trade with France. Furthermore, many of Bigot's ordinances reflect a paternal effort to save the people of a turbulent frontier society from their own folly and lack of civic sense. Even more than previous intendants he tried to prevent people from firing guns in towns, fighting in church doorways, dumping rubbish in streets and harbours, and letting their livestock wander about untethered in the streets. He paved and maintained the streets of Quebec with the proceeds of a tax of 30 or 40 *livres* a year on tavern-keepers, and tried to regulate traffic. His authoritarian zeal went so far, in fact, that Rouillé and other ministers advised him to leave more of the policing work to the courts. But it was not in Bigot's nature to leave things to courts for he was, after all, an 18th-century Marine officer endeavouring to run the colony as he might have run the naval installations at Brest or Rochefort, where he would have preferred to be.

François Bigot did not want to live in Canada as, indeed, few Frenchmen did. Again and again he applied for a posting in France. A posting to Quebec was a kind of exile like a posting to any other remote bastion of the empire and he had to endure it for 12 years, except for an eight-month visit home between October 1754 and May 1755. He seems to have been demoralized by this exile, by his forebodings of imperial disaster, and by an 18th-century officer's natural propensity for graft, and it is perhaps surprising that he worked as well as he did. But his work as intendant has not yet been fairly judged or even clearly portrayed and will not be until the evidence for it has been distinguished from the testimony gathered in the *affaire du Canada*.

One version of Bigot's 12 years as the last French intendant in Canada was told by a tribunal of the Paris Châtelet criminal court, when it published a long judgement of him and other Canadian officials on 10 Dec. 1763, the same year that the treaty of Paris was signed. Bigot had then been imprisoned in the Bastille for two years and was now sentenced to banishment from France forever. This disgraceful end and the court's version of his career have made it even more difficult to form a just opinion of Bigot as intendant, not because he was innocent of the charges brought against him but because the Bourbon administration was in general founded upon venality, patronage, and corruption of the kind he was accused of, because Bourbon judicial procedures were notoriously unfair to the accused, and because the government needed scapegoats for the loss of Canada and excuses for defaulting on debts to ease its own perilous financial situation. We find that during and after the war, the minister of Marine was writing to other intendants, too, as though they were corrupt: Vincent de Rochemore in Louisiana and Pierre-Paul Le Mercier de La Rivière de Saint-Médard in Martinique, for example. "Either you are working for your own advantage or for that of the king. Which do you prefer us to think?" he wrote to Le Mercier on 13 Oct. 1761. Accused of gross profiteering by forming a trading company with English merchants, this intendant was recalled in disgrace on 30 March 1764. A few years later during the American War of Independence, French colonial affairs were being conducted with similar confusion and corruption. A knowledge of this background helps to put Bigot's career in proper perspective.

The fraud of which Bigot was accused was not based upon mere forgery or a surreptitious misuse of funds; it was a system of private enterprise on a grand scale with the collaboration of most of the other colonial officials and many army officers and merchants working under the terms of personal understandings or even formal companies. This sort of corruption was a part of the political culture in Bourbon France, a way of life inevitably promoted by authoritarian governments and not changed until after the revolution, when new standards of honesty and new methods of control to enforce them were gradually imposed upon officials by a series of elected legislatures. Until then, the French government had had a double standard: it blamed its poorly paid officials for what one naval officer called "the insatiable dragon of avarice," which could not in general be suppressed in a system based on venality and patronage. Furthermore, Bigot's system of corruption was merely part of a vice-regal court which he set up at Quebec and which was essentially modelled on the royal court at Versailles: the magnificent social life with gay parties and balls and sumptuous dinners in the midst of a wretchedly poor populace; the mistresses, usually the wives of ambitious officers and others – Michel-Jean-Hugues PÉAN, major at Quebec, for instance – glad of the endless favours they obtained in exchange and flattered by such distinguished company; the preferments, employments, contracts, and business opportunities shared out among these gay circles; the complicated pattern of loyalty and jealousy among the favoured few and the bitterness among the excluded or the neglected. Unlike Louis XV, however, an official such as Bigot might himself fall victim to sudden shifts of fortune and favour.

The principal difference between Bigot and the previous Canadian intendants was that his opportunities for enrichment were much greater at a time when more money was being spent in Canada than ever before; his career as an officer in the Marine had prepared him to seize every opportunity that might be safely exploited, just as other Marine and military officers did in that age, especially out in the colonies; and he had the misfortune to administer a colony lost to the enemy during a conflict that had been costly and inflationary. No doubt Bigot deserved his fate, but more research is needed before we shall know whether he was a particularly corrupt intendant or merely a typical intendant in a corrupt system.

Even before leaving France Bigot had made arrangements with a Jewish shipping firm of Bordeaux, David Gradis et Fils, to form a company for trading to Quebec. They signed an agreement dated 10 July 1748 by which Gradis was to put up whatever capital was required to dispatch a ship of about 300 tons loaded with wine, brandy, and other goods, and to take half of the profits or losses of the firm. Bigot held a 50 per cent interest in the firm but soon ceded a 20 per cent interest to the controller of the Marine at Quebec, Jacques-Michel BRÉARD, and so himself retained 30 per cent. This agreement was to stand for six years from the date of the first ship's departure from Bordeaux, but it was renewed in 1755 and not cancelled until 16 Feb. 1756. The first ship, the *Renommée*, sailed early in 1749 under Captain Jean Harismendy with a cargo valued at 106,000 *livres* and it also carried the personal belongings of Bigot, Bréard, and the new governor, La Jonquière. Each year thereafter Gradis sent off at least one ship, and usually more, loaded with the firm's goods, but not all of Gradis's ships were sent for this firm. He also shipped cargoes of food, equipment, and men for the crown and, during the war years, for the official purveyor general, Cadet. Bigot and Bréard disposed of the firm's shipments at Quebec, usually by purchasing them for the crown at prices set by Bréard, the controller, and then either sent the ship on to the West Indian colonies or found a return cargo to France. Furthermore, Bigot saw to it that the 3 per cent duty imposed from 1748 on goods entering or leaving Canada was not collected on the firm's shipments.

The seventh clause in the agreement with Gradis had provided that the partners in Canada could fit out ships for trade with the West Indies or elsewhere in the Americas provided they sent Gradis proper accounts of such business. Whether Gradis was kept informed is not clear, but Bigot and Bréard soon acquired shares in a considerable fleet of perhaps 15 schooners, snows, and other small vessels which plied between Quebec, Louisbourg, and the West Indies. These included the *Angélique*, named no doubt for Bigot's mistress, Mme Péan [Angélique RENAUD d'Avène Des Méloizes]; the *Saint Victor*, named after Jean-Victor VARIN de La Marre, the commissary in charge at Montreal; the *Saint-Maudet*, named for the fishing post of Saint-Modet on the Labrador coast belonging to Bréard; and the *Étoile du Nord*, *Jaloux*, *Aimable Rose*, *Finette*, *Trompeuse*, *Commode*, *Deux Sœurs*, and *Saint François*. Some of these were built at Quebec under Bréard's general supervision, and held up the building of other ships, even ships for the crown. War losses tended to discourage transatlantic shipping, but the profits rose along with the risks. In 1759 Gradis bought the *Colibry* (140 tons) through Verduc, Vincent et Cie of Cádiz and loaded it with Spanish wines and liqueurs at a total cost of 114,524 *livres*, of which Gradis's interest was 50 per cent; he induced Péan to take two-thirds of this 50 per cent interest. Péan sold half of his interest (i.e. one-third of Gradis's 50 per cent) to Bigot. The *Colibry* reached Quebec with a captured prize worth 140,000 *livres* and the partners made handsome profits.

In 1755 and 1756 Bigot had a business agreement of some kind with the receiver general of finance for La Rochelle, Gratien Drouilhet, whose attorney at his death on 30 Jan. 1756 acknowledged a debt of 554,546 *livres* "in cash and promissory notes" to Bigot. This money may have been simply a loan but was more probably the investment and profits from a trading partnership concealed in the trading company Drouilhet had formed with Péan, Louis PENNISSEAUT, and Pierre Claverie*, one of whom was probably Bigot's front man.

Within the colony, Bigot as intendant leased the fur-trading post of Tadoussac in 1749 to Marie-Anne BARBEL, widow of Louis Fornel*, instead of to François-Étienne Cugnet, who had had it formerly and expected it to be renewed, and Bigot thus held back a personal share in the profits. He also kept the two important concessions of La Baie and La Mer de l'Ouest, which included many forts, in the hands of such friends as Péan and Jacques Legardeur* de Saint-Pierre. In 1752 and the years following, Bigot formed a secret company to buy the furs from forts Niagara (near Youngstown, N.Y.), Frontenac (Kingston, Ont.), and Rouillé (Toronto) that were supposed to be auctioned to the highest bidders at Quebec. He held a 50 per cent interest in this company, Bréard a 25 per cent interest, and Guillaume ESTÈBE and another partner 12.5 per cent each. They sent the furs to Denis GOGUET, a prominent merchant of La Rochelle, who sold them in France.

Before Bigot's arrival in the colony, the contract to supply the government with flour had been awarded to Marie-Anne Guérin, the widow of the former contractor, Nicolas Jacquin*, *dit* Philibert. In 1750 Bigot granted this contract to Louise Pécaudy de Contrecœur, the wife of François Daine*, one of Bigot's subdelegates, who called in her nephew, Péan, adjutant at Quebec since 1745. For the next few years the army and the government posts were supplied with flour by a group including Garaud, Jean-Pierre La Barthe, Claverie, Jean Corpron*, and Bigot himself who either imported their supplies or bought them from the Canadian habitants. It was in connection with this trade that in 1752

Bigot asked Rouillé, the minister of Marine, to send out 70 bushels of flour on the *Saint-Maudet* and 45 bushels on the *Étoile du Nord*, two ships which he owned jointly with Bréard and Péan.

Varin later accused Bigot of holding a 25 per cent interest in a company with himself and a Montreal merchant, Jacques-Joseph LEMOINE Despins, for importing supplies; these were purchased for the crown at inflated retail prices in Montreal, whereas they ought to have been purchased at wholesale prices in Quebec. He further alleged that during the Seven Years' War the transporting of food and munitions to outlying posts was managed by another company in which Bigot had a share, along with Péan, Bréard, Varin himself, and two clerks. In 1756 Bigot, Péan, and Varin formed a company to buy a shop in Quebec from the importing merchants Jean-André LAMALETIE and Estèbe. The treasurers general's agent, Jacques Imbert*, was engaged to alter the records in order to make their large profits look smaller. Bigot almost certainly had a share, too, in the company formed under Cadet's name known as the Grande Société, which supplied food to the army, the garrisons, and the government in general from 1 Jan. 1757; and this company, a profit-making concern without check or hindrance, appears to have made great sums in various ways.

While Bigot and dozens of officials and officers in Canada were making private fortunes, the Canadian populace was suffering from inflated prices, food shortages, and occasional severe famines. A serious economic crisis developed in which prices rose by 1759 to perhaps eight times their pre-war level, and in the same year goods in Canada were estimated to cost about seven times more than in France. Bigot's rapacity certainly contributed to this deplorable situation, but several other factors must each have weighed as much or even more. First, it is clear to the 20th-century eye – and was to some 18th-century observers, including Bigot himself – that costs in Canada rose because of inflation caused in part by the purchases for the troops sent out in 1755 under Jean-Armand Dieskau*. There had been signs of inflation at the end of the previous war in 1748, and the crown spent even more money in the Seven Years' War. Secondly, inflation was promoted by wartime shipping costs and losses which made commodities scarce and expensive in Canada. The British fleet and privateers patrolled the seas even to the mouths of the French ports and, although many French ships still managed to reach Quebec, marine insurance, freight rates, and wages were very high [*see* Joseph-Michel Cadet]. Those costs were inevitably reflected in the prices of the imported goods. Thirdly, the various paper currencies on which the Canadian economy depended – the playing-card money, the payment orders, the treasury bills, and the bills of exchange drawn annually on the treasurers general in France by their Quebec agent, Imbert – all these depreciated in value during the 1750s.

The French government itself did much to cause this depreciation by taking steps which tended to shake confidence in the credit of the treasurers general and of the crown itself. As early as 15 June 1752, Rouillé wrote to Bigot that three-quarters of the bills of exchange drawn in Canada each autumn would have to be deferred for two or three years "in order that . . . the treasury of the colonies may gradually recover from its depleted state." These bills were consequently marked to be cashed in three terms, and in business circles the ones to be cashed in two years were soon at a discount of 12 per cent or more; those to be cashed in three years at a discount of 18 per cent or more. Even with these planned deferments, the two treasurers general for the Colonies had great difficulty in cashing the Canadian bills of exchange because of a large debt they were carrying and because of the crown's general financial difficulties.

Ultimately, the Canadian paper currencies depended for their value upon the soundness of the French government, but the government was in serious financial straits during the Seven Years' War. More and more pressed for cash to pay for the continental war against Frederick II of Prussia as well as the maritime war against Great Britain, the government resorted to desperate financial projects. The controllers general of finance appealed to every possible source of support and also deferred payments. For instance, an indemnity of 20,000 *livres* due to a Quebec merchant, Jean Taché*, with whom Bigot signed an agreement on 20 April 1751 for the use of a brigantine, the *Trinité*, wrecked entering Louisbourg harbour soon afterwards, was not authorized in Paris until late in 1757. Again, Abraham Gradis, Bigot's former partner, spent the spring and summer of 1759 in Paris trying to induce the government to pay him a few hundred thousand *livres* and talked of impending disaster unless he were paid. Some people at the ministry of Marine and Colonies, such as Sébastien-François-Ange Le Normant de Mézy in 1758 and Emilion Petit in 1761, could see how unpaid merchants, sailors, and port workers were discrediting the royal government. "Those who in good faith make contracts with the king," wrote Petit, "are cheated by the small degree of good faith and promptitude in both payments and receipts." A memorandum of 1758 had already ascribed the high prices in Canada partly to "the slowness in the payment of bills of exchange [drawn] on France." Merchants and others who were naturally, and as it turned out rightly, uneasy about the paper credit system on which trade to Canada was based, charged more and more for goods and services.

The inflation dramatically increased government expenses in Canada, and this expansion in turn increased the financial strain. In 1750 the colony cost the crown a little more than two million *livres*, in 1754 the cost more than doubled, and in a letter of 15 April 1759 the intendant reckoned that the bills of exchange for that year would amount to over 30 millions. Considering that the ministry had chided Bigot as early as 1750 for the relatively small sums he was then spending in excess of the king's accounts, we may imagine why the enormous demands of the later war years goaded the ministry to investigate and then to prosecute the intendant they held responsible. It was big bills rather than tales of corruption which brought the official wrath down on Bigot's head, for the government was nearing bankruptcy.

For historians unaware of the financial crisis of the crown, unaware of the normal corruption of Bourbon government, it has been easy to see Bigot's arrest in November 1761 as a natural result of denunciations sent in to the government. Anyone who makes this assumption, however, must be overlooking the timing and circumstances of the arrest and also the long delay of at least a decade between the first denunciations and the arrest. Various reports of Bigot's commerce and corruption began to reach Versailles soon after his arrival in Canada in 1748, and these were taken seriously as the minister's letters show throughout the 1750s. Bigot was denounced by the engineer Louis Franquet in 1753, the commissary of wars André Doreil* in the middle 1750s, Montcalm soon after his arrival in 1756, the commissary for Montreal, Varin de La Marre, in 1757, Louis-Antoine de Bougainville* in 1758, the commissary Charles-François PICHOT de Querdisien Trémais in 1759, and many merchants and others throughout his term in Canada. A buzz of more or less slanderous gossip surrounds anyone in authority in nearly any society, and experienced ministers of state know it for what it is. In Bourbon France, as Guy Frégault so rightly remarked, "the court, faithful to a system almost as old as the colony, encouraged spying." Gossip, rumour, and the secret denunciations of unknown accusers were regularly admitted as evidence in courts of law and this practice was in accord with the prevailing morality taught, for instance, at Jesuit schools. Had the minister of Marine wanted to commit Bigot to trial for corruption there would have been plenty of testimony against him at any time during his career in Louisbourg and Canada, but if allegations of corruption had been enough to bring an official to trial most officials would have been on trial most of the time. The truth seems to be that personal honesty or dishonesty weighed less in a man's career than personal loyalty, patronage, family reputation, the accidents of circumstances, and the ups and downs of the struggling factions which ramified throughout the social and political hierarchies.

Bigot's fate, like any official's fate, depended upon the esteem of patrons and superiors caught up in the struggles of factions. When the Seven Years' War began to go badly for France in 1757, the ruling faction of the Duc de Choiseul began to make changes and to look for scapegoats. "Too impotent to attack corrupt practices at their roots and to punish the chief offenders," Moufle d'Angerville wrote soon afterwards in his *Journal historique*, "it sought victims who did not have unduly powerful friends and yet [were] likely by their position, number, and the nature of their crimes, to create a sensation. Monsieur Berryer [minister of Marine and Colonies in a government Choiseul dominated] . . . found all the necessary conditions in the leaders and administrators of Canada. . . ." It was fatally easy for the government to link Bigot's evident corruption with the inflation in Canada, and by treating them as simple cause and effect to trump up a plausible excuse for suspending payments on the Canadian bills of exchange. It would have been an unwise betrayal and politically damaging, however, to suspend payments while the colony was engaged in a struggle for survival against an enemy siege, and the defeat on the Plains of Abraham was therefore a financial boon for the royal government. On 15 Oct. 1759, just after the first news of the defeat of 13 September had reached France, the government felt politically strong enough to suspend payment of the colonial bills of exchange and so ordered in an official ruling. In view of the defeat it seemed, indeed, necessary to suspend payments which might now profit the enemy as well as the corrupt officials. The crown was thus able to disguise its own inevitable bankruptcy as a politically and morally necessary suspension of payments. By association Bigot and the other officials from Canada were soon made to serve as scapegoats for the military and naval disasters as well as the financial ones.

The *affaire du Canada*, one of the most notorious of the century, was thus a many-sided affair. It began, so far as the general public was concerned, with the arrest and imprisonment of the Canadian officials, including Bigot, who was imprisoned on 17 Nov. 1761, and many of his former business associates, Cadet and Péan among them. It proceeded with their trial by a commission of the Châtelet numbering no fewer than 27 magistrates under the chairmanship of the lieutenant general of police, Antoine de Sartine. It ended with the judgement of 10 Dec. 1763, a lively 78-page essay in scandal, printed and circulated in hundreds of copies, announcing Bigot's banishment forever, the confiscation of all his property, and the heavy fines imposed on all the condemned men. For perfidious officials who seemed to have plundered a colony and lost it to the enemy, the observing public would in general have been pleased with the torture and death recommended by the prosecutor on 22 Aug. 1763. A clerk in one of the bureaux of the treasurers general of the Marine wrote to a friend on 22 Oct. 1763, "The gentlemen from Canada have not yet had judgement rendered, this is [due], it is said, at the end of the month; it is true that they were sentenced by the public a fortnight ago, Monsieur Bigot [to have] his head cut off, and Pean and Cadet [to be] hanged. . . ." Meanwhile, behind the scenes the case for the crown was being prepared under the supervision of a magistrate at the Châtelet criminal court, Étienne-Claude Dupont, acting in close consultation with Berryer and Choiseul. They sought evidence and testimony high and low throughout the kingdom, whereas Bigot's only recourse was a lawyer who drew up a factum, *Mémoire pour Messire François Bigot, ci-devant intendant . . .* , from the prisoner's unaided memory. Particular care was lavished by an impoverished government on the financial side of the trial, so that all possible funds could be recovered and government debts cancelled.

Like all the Canadian officials who made big profits in private business, Bigot had dispatched his savings to France so that he could enjoy them on his return. He had planned to live like a gentleman on a country property in an agreeable French province surrounded by family, friends, and servants. With the instincts of an 18th-century businessman, he had divided his fortune among several friends and agents and diversified his investments. A full list of his fortune, such as the government agencies compiled, would be tediously long, but the crown ordered him to pay a total of some one and one-half million *livres* as "restitution." Through a friend, Bernis, and by a notarial contract in Paris dated 24 Aug. 1758, Bigot had bought an estate near Versailles, the castle and fief of Vaugien, from a receiver general of finance, Jacques-David Ollivier, for 760,000 *livres*. Abraham Gradis in Bordeaux was found to hold 323,286 *livres* for Bigot and Denis Goguet of La Rochelle, who had earlier made his own fortune in Canada and continued to deal in Canadian furs, was ordered on 31 July 1764 to pay 279,400 *livres* in funds he was holding for Bigot. A large sum, probably several hundred thousands, was variously invested in royal and provincial tax farms and private annuities and mortgages by a Paris notary, Charlier, not under Bigot's own name but that of a front man, Nicolas-Félix Vaudive, a lawyer in the *parlement* and a clerk of the sessions in the Grand Conseil du Roi, son of a Paris merchant jeweller. This sum included 50,000 *livres* lent to a Bordeaux shipping merchant, Jean-Patrice Dupuy, who had been trading to Canada. Another large sum had been used to buy 60 shares in a firm of Paris bankers, Banquet et Mallet. He had also purchased an office of king's secretary in 1754, and considerable personal belongings, especially a magnificent and unusual set of silverware. When the crown eventually opened some crates held for Bigot by Denis Goguet at La Rochelle, they found large quantities of wine, preserves, and jam, by then quite spoiled.

Several agencies were entrusted with the recovery of Bigot's property and all other assets due to the crown as a result of the affair. From 4 May 1761 to 1774 the lapsed post of controller for the recovery of crown assets was revived for Pierre-François Boucher, whose business was to account for all property due to the crown. Then, as soon as the court had pronounced the final judgement on the prisoners, the crown was careful to issue a ruling on 31 Dec. 1763 turning over private claims on the confiscated property to the Commission Fontanieu, which had been busy with the settlement of naval and colonial debts since its appointment on 15 Oct. 1758 and had proved its ability and willingness to reduce the crown's obligations as far as possible [*see* Alexandre-Robert HILLAIRE de La Rochette]. Among hundreds of claims, it awarded Gradis 354,602 *livres* out of Bigot's estate by a judgement of 1 March 1768 and it settled the claims of Bigot's servants: his secretary, Joseph BRASSARD Deschenaux, his major-domo, Nicolas Martin, and his valet, Jean Hiriart, who had served him from March 1752 until 1 Oct. 1760 at 300 *livres* a year and then (while living with Bigot in the Bastille) at 400 *livres* a year plus 30 *sous* a day for food until the end of 1763. The commission's final report was not submitted until 7 May 1772. Meanwhile, various notaries and royal treasurers were employed as trustees for the funds collected, and Bigot's own notaries were approached for information about his affairs by the Châtelet, which thus violated the sacred confidentiality of the notarial profession. By such methods and agencies Bigot lost virtually all his property, and the crown's debt to him in uncashed bills of exchange was cancelled.

At the same time, the public scandal of Bigot's corruption made it easy for the crown to treat most of the paper credit instruments from Canada as tainted and so to justify reducing them in value. Even the suspension of these instruments, the delays, and the necessity for the holders of such paper to apply to the government saved over 18 millions in paper never officially reported. By 1764, there appeared to be paper to a total face value of over 83 million *livres* consisting of more than 49 million in bills of exchange, 25 million in currency notes, and nearly 9 million in notes receivable issued in Canada and never converted into bills of exchange. Ultimately, the total reached nearly 90 million *livres* of which the crown recognized only 37,607,000 *livres*, but it could not pay even this sum and so converted it into bonds bearing interest at 4 per cent per annum, a rate of interest at which the French government could not borrow on the money market. Bigot may have cost the government something during the Seven Years' War, but the cost was largely in paper credit notes that were subsequently reduced by more than half and merely added to the long-term debt, the debt that was to bring the crown to the brink of revolution.

As for the former intendant, he had left for Switzerland shortly after judgement was delivered on 10 Dec. 1763. He chose to call himself François Bar (de Barre, Desbarres), which was the name of his brother-in-law, the Sieur de Barre (Bar). He stayed for some time at Fribourg and then went to Neuchâtel. On 18 March 1765 he obtained permission to take up residence there. By the next day he had purchased a house in the *faubourg* Vieux Châtel, in the parish of Saint-Ulrich, for the sum of 10,000 *livres tournois*. He had a comfortable life, according to the Comte de Diesbach who, visiting him in 1768, noted, "I found him very well accommodated in a residence he had bought and repaired." He seems to have successfully fitted himself into local circles in Neuchâtel: Diesbach recounted that he had met Bigot "at the assembly," probably an official municipal reception, and he did, incidentally, bequeath 150 *livres* "to the senior pastors of the churches of Neuchâtel, to be distributed to the poorest people in town."

He was not, then, destitute. To be sure, his cousins gave him some assistance, but probably it was to his close relationship with the Gradis that he owed his relatively pleasant life in exile. Nevertheless, he felt the burden of dishonour that the 1763 conviction had attached to his name. He never became reconciled to it. In 1771 he obtained permission to spend a few weeks in his own country by claiming he had problems with his health that only the waters at Bagnères could clear up. These troubles were only too real, if Péan is to be believed, for he noted when he went to meet Bigot at Dijon: "I found him in a state of such great weakness that he would not have been able to endure public coaches; I took him in my own, where he several times made me afraid of continuing on the way . . . this respectable man is greatly to be pitied." For a few days Bigot visited the estate of the Péan family, whose loyalty does not seem to have faltered despite the years. He probably took advantage of his stay to interest the bishop of Blois in his cause, and the next year the bishop took steps with the minister of Marine, Bourgeois de Boynes. Bigot himself dispatched a "Mémoire justificatif" in 1773, and a proposal for *lettres de réhabilitation* in 1775. But too many influential people who had been party to his trial recalled both the man and his dossier in great detail. Matters remained at a standstill in Paris.

François Bigot died on 12 Jan. 1778 at Neuchâtel; he was buried in the little Catholic church of Saint-Martin-L'Évêque in Cressier, a village nearby, as he had requested in his will: "I desire that my body be buried in the cemetery at Cressier without any pomp, just as the poorest person in the parish would be."

J. F. Bosher and J.-C. Dubé

[The following sources provided essential information about the Bigot family: the records of notaries in Tours (AD, Indre-et-Loire); the parish registers of that city (Archives municipales); the minute-books of Paris notaries (AN, Minutier central); the genealogical series at the BN; and the records of notaries and parish registers of Bordeaux (AD, Gironde). (We should like to note here that we are much indebted to a Bordeaux researcher, Pierre Julien-Laferrière, who has done a great deal of work in tracing the Bigot family.) Nothing has been found on François Bigot's early life except his birth certificate; on the first phase of his career the Bigot file in AN, Col., E, should be consulted.

For the period commencing in 1739, the date at which his North American career began, the sources are extensive and scattered. The principal ones are in the AN (Col., B, C^{11A}, C^{11B}). The researcher will certainly find Bigot's name in the impressive collection of official papers generated by the *affaire du Canada*: among others, the incomplete but well-indexed Archives de la Bastille, held at the Bibliothèque de l'Arsenal; papers at the AN, V[7], cartons 362–65 (*commissions extraordinaires*); and numerous factums and printed materials, a comprehensive list of which appears in the bibliography of Frégault, *François Bigot*, a work that is still the best starting point for a study of the man. A great many documents of major interest are readily accessible and well edited in *Docs. relating to Canadian currency during the French period* (Shortt).

Certain series at the AN which have as yet been little studied – E (Conseil du roi) and Y (Châtelet), for example – probably contain documents concerning Bigot. A number of notarial archive groups furnish information of varying importance but unequalled detail; for example, AN, Minutier central, XVIII, LVII; AD, Gironde (Bordeaux), Minutes Baron, Minutes Dubos, Minutes Faugas (all notaries of Bordeaux); ANQ-Q, Greffe de Claude Barolet, Greffe de J.-C. Panet.

Few figures in the history of Canada have been the focus of a study as detailed and scholarly as the one Guy Frégault devoted to the last intendant of New France. This perceptive and well-documented work increased our knowledge of this figure who had so intrigued (or scandalized) authors and historians of the 19th and early 20th centuries. Frégault was particularly interested in Bigot as the last administrator of the French régime. Even while recognizing the high calibre of this work, one might criticize its author for not having put the case of Bigot in the general context of the institutions of Bourbon France and for having too literally reproduced the version of his intendancy circulated by the Châtelet at the time of his trial. Since the publication of Frégault's work, Denis Vaugeois has written a useful article on the end of Bigot's life, "François Bigot, son exil et sa mort," *RHAF*, XXI (1967–68), 731–48. J.F.B. and J.-C.D.]

BIRCH. *See* BURCH

BLAIS (Blay), MICHEL (Michel-Toussaint), militia captain and co-seigneur; b. *c.* 1711, probably at Berthier-en-Bas (Que.), son of Pierre Blais and Françoise Baudoin; d. 5 Sept. 1783 at Saint-Pierre-de-la-Rivière-du-Sud (Saint-Pierre-Montmagny, Que.).

Michel Blais came from a family of farmers. His grandfather Pierre Blais, a native of Angoulême, France, had arrived in the colony in 1664 and settled on the Île d'Orléans. His father lived in various places on the south shore, across from Île d'Orléans, and Michel, like his brothers and sisters, remained in the region. On 25 June 1741, at Sainte-Anne-de-la-Pocatière (La Pocatière, Que.), he married Marie-Françoise, the daughter of Joseph Lizot, major of militia at Saint-Roch-des-Aulnaies. In the marriage contract signed that day before notary Étienne Jeanneau*, Blais is said to be a "habitant on the seigneury of Bertier." Two years later he bought from Charles Couillard de Beaumont land with a frontage of eight *arpents* five *perches* and a depth of four leagues in the seigneury of Rivière-du-Sud; in 1775 he added eight and a half *arpents* to his holding.

Through the years Blais acquired a position of considerable importance in Saint-Pierre-de-la-Rivière-du-Sud. In 1762 he owned more livestock than most of the habitants in his parish and four servants were in his employ. His brother Joseph, who had settled in Saint-Pierre some years earlier, was no less well-to-do. But Michel was certainly more influential since his many properties had made him a co-seigneur; in 1763 he had to render homage and fealty for a quarter of the seigneury of Rivière-du-Sud and half of Lespinay. Four years later he joined the seigneurs in the region of Quebec in signing an address to the king protesting Governor MURRAY's recall. At the time of the conquest he had been militia captain at Saint-Pierre, a mark of the esteem and confidence in which he was held. Although the abolition of the militia by the British authorities in 1764 deprived him of his office for more than ten years, he acted as bailiff in his parish during this period, thus gaining an entry to the lower levels of the province's judicial system. In an exchange of land transacted in 1770 before notary François-Dominique Rousseau by Blais and William Ross, a merchant, Blais was called "first bailiff of the parish of St-Pierre."

Although a prominent landowner in his area, Blais nevertheless claimed privileges to which he was not entitled. In 1770 Marie-Geneviève Alliés, widow of Jean-Baptiste Couillard, the seigneur of Rivière-du-Sud, took legal action against him and a number of local habitants for having disregarded the banal rights. The Court of Common Pleas on 14 Aug. 1770 condemned them to pay milling dues to the banal mill of the seigneury. Blais would not give in so easily; on 6 Sept. 1774 another judgement ordered him to demolish the windmill he had "improperly put up" in this seigneury which belonged to the under-age son of Jean-Baptiste Couillard. This time, it seems, the authorities prevailed over his obstinacy.

At the time of the American invasion Blais remained loyal to the British government, but he does not appear initially to have adopted a firm position. Although he had resumed his office in the militia, in January 1776 he agreed to announce at the church door that a certain Pierre Ayotte was recruiting men for the American cause. Later he explained that he had done so "to prevent greater harm" and that his tone had been "so ironical that no one showed up." Nevertheless several habitants of the village, like many others in the region, joined the ranks of the rebels; the divisions thus caused among the population became evident on 25 March 1776 at Saint-Pierre, in Captain Michel Blais's home. At this time the Americans were still occupying a post at Pointe-Lévy, across from Quebec, and were preparing to make forays into the region of Côte-du-Sud. About mid March the British authorities had commissioned a former officer of the French colonial regulars, Louis Liénard* de Beaujeu de Villemomble, then living in retirement on Île aux Grues (downstream from Île d'Orléans), to assemble the royalist forces in the region for an attack on the American post. In a few days a force was raised, and its advance guard of some 50 men quickly reached the village of Saint-Pierre, where Michel Blais's house became their headquarters. The Americans, alerted by their supporters, sent a detachment of 80 men who were joined by some 150 Canadians, and on 25 March they attacked Blais's house, from which the British flag was flying. "In this action," wrote Simon SANGUINET, "fathers were to be found fighting against their sons, and sons against their fathers – which will no doubt seem quite extraordinary." Three of the royalists were killed and several were wounded, including Abbé Charles-François BAILLY de Messein, who was chaplain to the volunteers. All those unable to escape were captured by the Americans.

After the Congressional forces had withdrawn, Governor Guy Carleton* ordered an investigation in the parishes of the District of Quebec with the object of reinstating the militia there and of making a list of the habitants who had collaborated with the Americans. At Saint-Pierre Captain Blais and his son Michel, a lieutenant, were recognized as "the only persons in that parish who have been plundered by both Bostonians and rebel Canadians." In the face of such proof "of the Sieur Michel Blay's zeal and affection for his King," the investigators, François Baby*, Gabriel-Elzéar Taschereau*, and Jenkin Williams*, allowed father and son to retain their positions in the militia.

At the time of his death in 1783 Blais was serving as syndic in charge of building the new parish church at Saint-Pierre, and hence his name is on the cornerstone of the building. Eleven years later Bishop HUBERT gave permission for Blais's body to be transferred to the new church. Blais had had at least five children. Two daughters, Marguerite and Marie-Joseph, became Ursulines. His son Louis was a member of the assembly for Hertford County from 1800 to 1804.

MARIE-CÉLINE BLAIS and JACQUES MORIN

ANQ-Q, Greffe d'Étienne Jeanneau, 25 juin 1741. Archives paroissiales, Saint-Pierre-du-Sud (Qué.), Registre des baptêmes, mariages et sépultures, 8 sept. 1783, 22 oct. 1794. AUM, P 58, Doc. divers, B1, 14 août 1770, 6 sept. 1774. IBC, Centre de documentation, Fonds Morisset, Dossier Michel Blais. *Invasion du Canada* (Verreau), 105–6. "Journal par messrs Fran[s] Baby, Gab. Taschereau et Jenkin Williams . . . ," Ægidius Fauteux, édit., ANQ *Rapport*, 1927–28, 480, 485, 487. PAC *Rapport*, 1888, note B, 18–20. "Recensement du gouvernement de Québec, 1762," 31. Claude de Bonnault, "Le Canada militaire: état provisoire des officiers de milice de 1641 à 1760," ANQ *Rapport*, 1949–51, 336. Caron, "Inv. de la corr. de Mgr Hubert et de Mgr Bailly de Messein," ANQ *Rapport*, 1930–31, 308. Godbout, "Nos ancêtres," ANQ *Rapport*, 1957–59, 389–91. P.-G. Roy, *Inv. concessions*, I, 204–6. Tanguay, *Dictionnaire*. Burke, *Les ursulines de Québec* (1863–66), III, 367–68. Lanctot, *Le Canada et la Révolution américaine*, 148–50. G. F. G. Stanley, *L'invasion du Canada, 1775–1776, "Canada invaded,"* Marguerite MacDonald, trad. (Québec, 1975), 125, 133. F.-J. Audet, "La seigneurie de la Rivière du Sud," *BRH*, VII (1901), 118. "Le capitaine Michel Blais," *BRH*, VI (1900), 375–76. Ivanhoë Caron, "Les Canadiens français et l'invasion américaine de 1774–1775," RSC *Trans.*, 3rd ser., XXIII (1929), sect.I, 21–34. M.-M. Dumouchel-Butler, "William (Guillaume) Ross," SGCF *Mémoires*, XXV (1974), 170–82. Archange Godbout, "Les émigrants de 1664," SGCF *Mémoires*, IV (1950–51), 219–20.

BLAIS DE SURLAVILLE, MICHEL LE COURTOIS DE. *See* LE COURTOIS

BLEURY, CLÉMENT DE SABREVOIS DE. *See* SABREVOIS

BODEGA Y QUADRA (Cuadra), JUAN FRANCISCO DE LA, naval officer, explorer, and diplomat; baptized 3 June 1743 in Lima, Peru, son of Tomás de la Bodega y de las Llanas, a Spanish-born deputy of the Spanish consulate in Cuzco, and Francisca de Mollinedo y Losada, descendant of a prominent Peruvian family; d. 26 March 1794 in Mexico City.

Juan Francisco de la Bodega y Quadra entered the marine guard at the age of 19. He was promoted frigate ensign in 1767, ship's ensign in 1773, and ship's lieutenant in 1774. In that year he was assigned to the department of San Blas (state of Nayarit, Mexico), the administrative headquarters of Spain's west coast posts north of San Blas. Bodega's first visit to the northwest coast of North America came in 1775, when he served as captain of the schooner *Sonora*, sailing, along with Juan Josef PÉREZ Hernández, in the expedition commanded by Bruno de Hezeta. Intrepid and resolute, Bodega continued north when the companion vessel, *Santiago*, turned back; he reached 58°30′N and discovered and named Bucareli Sound (Alas.).

Bodega was sent to Peru in 1776 to secure a vessel for use on the northwest coast. He returned to San Blas the next year with the Callao-built frigate *Favorita*, which he captained to Alaskan waters in 1779 as second in command of Ignacio de Arteaga's expedition. The commanders had been instructed to explore the area, to determine the extent of Russian expansion east from the Aleutians, and to execute orders from Madrid calling for the interception of Captain James COOK's vessels. Bodega and Arteaga had no way of knowing that the famous navigator had already been slain in the Sandwich (Hawaiian) Islands, and they did not sail far enough west to meet Cook's ships, which Charles CLERKE had brought to Alaskan waters for a second season of exploration.

Bodega's superiors recognized him to be a valorous and competent officer. He had been awarded the military title of knight of the order of Santiago in 1776, and in 1780 he was made frigate captain. Before his transfer to Havana, Cuba, in 1783, Bodega served as commandant of the department of San Blas for a year. Promoted ship's captain in 1784, he was transferred to Cadiz, Spain, the following year. After Bodega left the department, command of Spanish activities on the northwest coast had, for want of more capable officers, been entrusted to hot-tempered Esteban José MARTÍNEZ. At this time maritime fur-traders of other nations were showing an increased interest in the region, and in 1789 Martínez, in an attempt to enforce Spanish claims there, seized a number of British vessels at Nootka Sound (B.C.). The British prime minister, William Pitt, took advantage of the incident to press Spain for drastic concessions in its claims to the northwest coast. Charles IV of Spain was reluctant to yield, however, and the Nootka Sound crisis of 1790 for a time threatened to involve all Europe and the United States in war. The crisis ended in the Nootka Convention of 1790, which appeared to commit Spain to returning all land in the sound taken from British subjects in 1789 [*see* John Meares*].

Bodega had again been appointed commandant of the department of San Blas in 1789, and in 1792 he sailed to Nootka to take command of the small Spanish naval base there. The base, with its barracks, hospital, and flourishing gardens, had been the sole European outpost between California and Russian Alaska for the preceding three years. The genial commandant from Lima, with his even-tempered governance of the base, earned the respect and admiration of the British and American fur-traders, and of the Nootkas. Captain Robert Gray*, an American trader, placed such high regard upon his friendship that he named his son Robert Don Quadra Gray. Bodega's many-course banquets, served on silver plate and accompanied by fine wines and brandies, to which captains and officers of all nationalities calling at Nootka were invited, were famous. The tolerance and interest Bodega displayed for the Nootkas' customs gained their lasting affection and strengthened Spain's hold over the area. MUQUINNA was often an overnight guest at Bodega's residence.

During his single summer in command at Nootka Bodega provided for construction of a second, short-lived base at Núñez Gaona (Neah Bay, Wash.), and for a more extensive exploration of Juan de Fuca Strait and the fjords of what are now British Columbia and Alaska in a search for the fabled northwest passage [*see* Dionisio Alcalá-Galiano*]. The explorations resulted in the most complete maps that had yet been made of the coastline and Captain George VANCOUVER's use of them is mirrored today in the many Spanish place names along the coast.

Bodega had taken command at Nootka in order to negotiate with Vancouver the terms of the 1790 Nootka Convention. He was convinced, however, by the testimony he gathered from fur-traders and Indians, and by the vaguely worded terms of the convention, that he was justified in withholding from Vancouver all but a small portion of Friendly Cove in the sound. Bodega's diplomacy effectively thwarted the British attempt to gain possession of the base. Two subsequent Anglo-Spanish conventions led to a mutual agreement to leave the sound uncolonized; British plans for settlements on the northwest coast were checked until the 19th century.

Spanish activities on the northwest coast had reached their apogee under the vigorous impetus provided by Bodega, but his conviction and firmness were not matched in Mexico City or Madrid, where greater importance was attached to placating London than to sustaining a costly dominion over the region. Bodega spent the winter of 1792–93 in Monterey (Calif.) providing for the strengthening of the posts in Alta California and hosting a visit to Monterey from the Vancouver expedition. He returned to San Blas in the spring of 1793. Broken in health, he applied for transfer to Callao. Despite a period of recuperation in Guadalajara (Mexico), a sudden seizure while he was in Mexico City on 26 March 1794 cut short his career.

WARREN L. COOK

[Some of the diaries and journals of Juan Francisco de la Bodega y Quadra have been printed as the following:

"Navegación hecha por Don Juan Francisco de la Bodega y Quadra . . . a los descubrimientos de los mares y costa septentrional de California," Spain, Consejo Superior de Investigaciones Científicas, Instituto Histórico de Marina, *Colección de diarios y relaciones para la historia de los viajes y descubrimientos*, ed. L. C. Blanco *et al.* (6v. to date, Madrid, 1943–), II, 102–33; "Primer viaje hasta la altura de 58° . . . 1775" and "Segunda salida hasta los 61 grados en la fragata Nuestra Senora de los Remedios (a) la Favorita . . . 1779," Spain, Dirección de Hidrografía, *Anuario* (Madrid), III (1865), 279–93, and 294–331. W. L. C.]

Huntington Library, HM 141, Juan Francisco de la Bodega y Quadra, "Viaje a la costa n. o. de la America Septentrional . . . en las fragatas . . . Sta. Gertrudis, Aranzazu, Princesa y goleta Activa." Museo Naval (Madrid), MS no.126, "Extracto del diario" (1775); MS no.618, Juan Francisco de la Bodega y Quadra, "Comento . . ." (1775); MS no. 622, Juan Francisco de la Bodega y Quadra, "Diario" (1775). [F. A. Mourelle], "Journal of a voyage in 1775, to explore the coast of America, northward of California, by the second pilot of the fleet . . . ," *Miscellanies*, ed. and trans. Daines Barrington (London, 1781), 469–534. J. M. Moziño Suárez de Figueroa, *Noticias de Nutka; an account of Nootka Sound in 1792*, trans. and ed. I. H. Wilson (Seattle, Wash., 1970). [George Vancouver], "Captain Vancouver's report to the Admiralty on the negotiations with Don Juan Francisco de Bodega y Quadra at Nootka Sound in 1792," B.C., Provincial Archives Dept., *Report* (Victoria), 1913, 11–30; *Voyage of discovery* (J. Vancouver). Cook, *Flood tide of empire*. M. E. Thurman, "Juan Bodega y Quadra and the Spanish retreat from Nootka, 1790–1794," *Reflections of western historians*, ed. J. A. Carroll and J. R. Kluger ([Tucson, Ariz.], 1969), 49–63; *The naval department of San Blas; New Spain's bastion for Alta California and Nootka, 1767 to 1798* (Glendale, Calif., 1967). Javier de Ybarra y Bergé, *De California á Alaska: historia de un descubrimiento* (Madrid, 1945). F. E. Smith, "The Nootka Sound diplomatic discussion, August 28 to September 26, 1792," *Americana* (New York), XIX (1925), 133–45.

BOIRET, URBAIN, priest and superior of the Séminaire de Québec; b. 6 Sept. 1731 in the parish of Saint-Thomas, La Flèche, France, son of René Boiret, master gardener; d. 5 Nov. 1774 in Quebec.

Urbain Boiret arrived in Canada on 26 July 1755. He had probably been ordained priest in Rouen, France, on 15 March of that year, at the same time as his travelling companion, Henri-François Gravé* de La Rive. He wanted to devote himself to the mission to the Tamaroas (Cahokia, now East St Louis, Ill.), but he never reached the banks of the Mississippi; he was kept at the Séminaire de Québec where he held various offices, including those of bursar and professor of theology. He also became a director of the seminary on 16 Feb. 1759.

At the beginning of the siege of Quebec in the summer of 1759, all the priests left the seminary, including the superior, Colomban-Sébastien PRESSART; only Boiret and Joseph-André-Mathurin JACRAU remained. When the latter fell ill in September and had to be hospitalized, Boiret was left alone to watch over the seminary. The building, situated just within Upper Town, was an easy target for the British guns and was seriously damaged; only two or three rooms remained fit for occupation. After the capitulation Boiret, who was still the bursar of the seminary, went to spend the winter at Saint-Joachim to take stock of the damage to its properties there and to replace the parish priest, Philippe-René Robinau* de Portneuf, who had been killed by the British. Everything had been destroyed, and the accounts of the bursar's office emphasize that during this winter Boiret "was housed in a hut in the middle of the fields and during the coldest periods . . . he had no ink nor any of the comforts of life." In the autumn of 1761 he was back in Quebec.

In 1762 the Séminaire des Missions Étrangères in Paris appointed a new superior for the Séminaire de Québec, Pierre Maillard*, vicar general of Acadia; Gravé de La Rive was nominated for the post in the event that Maillard could not go to Quebec. Governor MURRAY rejected this appointment, which had been made in France, and insisted on a local election, omitting the two names put forward by Paris. On 4 July Boiret was elected unanimously, and his three-year term of office was extended for a second term in 1765. It was during his six years as superior that the seminary painfully rebuilt on the ruins in Quebec and on its domains, particularly in the seigneury of Beaupré, where Boiret had spent the winter of 1759–60. The sale of some suburban lots to Murray and the merchant Thomas Ainslie*, among others, brought in the funds needed for reconstruction.

From 1764 to 1768 Boiret was also chaplain to the nuns of the Hôtel-Dieu, and in the autumn of 1765 he had to take on the delicate task of reopening the Petit Séminaire. The role of the Petit Séminaire had changed considerably: under the French régime it had accepted only pupils intending to enter the priesthood; now it was replacing the Jesuit college, which had been forced to close, and it had to provide means of instruction for all those with the ability to undertake classical studies. Boiret became its director at the end of his second term as superior of the seminary, in 1768. He ran it successfully until the summer of 1773, when the seminary council promoted him to head the Grand Séminaire. On 28 Sept. 1774 he was again elected superior, but he did not retain the office for long: he was already ill. He went to the Hôpital Général on 26 June and died there on 5 November. He was buried in the crypt of the seminary chapel. On 10 November the *Quebec Gazette* published an anonymous obituary notice in the form of a rather inflated poem in both Latin and French, to which another anonymous reader replied humorously in the issue of 17 November.

In the 19th century Bishop Edmond Langevin*, finding a parchment text in the attic of a Quebec printing house, made the surprising discovery that Boiret had received the dignity of apostolic protonotary from the Holy See. Abbé Boiret likely kept his appointment secret for fear of offending his fellow priests by having himself called "Monseigneur," since he was the first person to receive this dignity under the British régime. Rome had probably decided to accord him the honour at the prompting of his younger brother, Denis Boiret, a priest with the Missions Étrangères in Paris, who lived in the Holy City from 1771 to 1773 to promote the interests of the mission in Cochin China (Vietnam). It was to him that Abbé Boiret left some family property in France; his personal effects and library of 180 volumes went to the seminary.

HONORIUS PROVOST

AD, Sarthe (Le Mans), État civil, Saint-Thomas de La Flèche, 6 sept. 1731. ASQ, C 9; C 11; C 22; Lettres, M, 116, 117; P, 124; R, 20; MSS, 12, ff.30, 31, 32, 36, 41; Séminaire, 8, nos.43, 44. *Le séminaire de Québec* (Provost), 450–51. *Quebec Gazette*, 10, 17 Nov., 1774. Allaire, *Dictionnaire*, I, 61. Casgrain, *Hist. de l'Hôtel-Dieu de Québec*, 574. A.-H. Gosselin, *L'Église du Canada après la Conquête*, I. Adrien Launay, *Mémorial de la Société des Missions étrangères* (2v., Paris, 1912–16), II, 61–63. M. Trudel, *L'Église canadienne*, II, 27–96. J.-E. Roy, "L'abbé Urbain Boiret," *BRH*, II (1896), 93–94. P.-G. Roy, "Mgr Urbain Boiret," *BRH*, II (1896), 139.

BOISSEAU, NICOLAS, king's scrivener, notary, and court clerk; b. 1700 in Paris, France, son of Pierre Boisseau and Marguerite Gérin (Guérin); d. 9 Feb. 1771 at Quebec.

On 20 May 1722, following the death of his father, who had been an attorney in the *parlement* of Paris, Nicolas Boisseau obtained passage to Canada from the minister of Marine. Upon his arrival Boisseau, who had frequented "the Palais [de justice in Paris] for three years," was employed at Quebec as king's scrivener in the office of the Marine. He held this post until 1726. During the ocean crossing he had struck up a friendship with François Daine*, who was returning to Canada with the appointment of chief clerk of the Conseil Supérieur of Quebec. This relationship led to his being called upon to replace Daine in his duties on various occasions between 1723 and 1726. Their friendship was not limited to professional matters. Boisseau made the acquaintance of Daine's sister-in-law, Marie-Anne Pagé, *dit* Carcy, whom he married in Quebec on 9 Sept. 1725, in the presence of his friend, who acted as a witness.

Thanks to his experience in the legal field and the influence of his uncle, Abbé Gérin, dean of the parish priests of Paris, Boisseau was able to acquire on 23 April 1726 the office of chief clerk of the provost court of Quebec. In this capacity he kept a register of all deeds issued by the court and all documents brought to him for deposit in his office; in addition he was the depositary of the minutes of deceased notaries who had practised in the Government of Quebec. Since Intendant HOCQUART considered it necessary that there be a notary present when minutes were deposited (to give out receipts and ratify certain deeds) he appointed Boisseau a notary on 15 April 1731. On 22 April 1732 the king granted him a new commission, similar in every respect to his previous one; he was one of only four notaries under the French régime who were commissioned by the king.

For 13 years Boisseau held the posts of clerk of court and royal notary. In the latter capacity he drew up 392 deeds. However, following his appointment on 25 March 1744 to the post of chief clerk of the Conseil Supérieur, he relinquished his notarial duties. A son of his first marriage, Nicolas-Gaspard*, took over as clerk of the provost court, and Jean-Claude PANET succeeded him as royal notary. Boisseau was following in the steps of his friend Daine, whom he was once again replacing.

Some years earlier, after his first wife's death on 7 May 1739, Boisseau had made a second marriage, an advantageous one both financially and socially. On 4 June 1741, in the presence of the principal legal officers of the colony, he married Marie-Louise, the daughter of Jean-Baptiste Bissot* de Vinsenne (Vincenne), an officer in the colonial regular troops. She brought him a dowry of 1,000 *livres* and a fief of ten *arpents* by six leagues in the seigneury of Lauson. The attendance at this marriage of the most prestigious legal figures in the colony, and the size of his wife's dowry, indicate clearly the social standing that Boisseau enjoyed as early as 1741.

Nicolas Boisseau was installed in his duties as chief clerk of the Conseil Supérieur on 12 Oct. 1744 and fulfilled them without interruption until the council moved to Montreal in the autumn of 1759; Boisseau preferred to remain in Quebec. From then until his death in Quebec on 9 Feb. 1771 he undertook no official duties. The conquest seems to have placed him in an awkward financial position: not only did he lose his post as clerk of court, but during the siege of Quebec his house on Rue Saint-Pierre in Lower Town was burned and his possessions destroyed.

A prudent man and a good legal practitioner in the opinion of Beauharnois*, Hocquart, Vaudreuil [Rigaud], and Bigot, Nicolas Boisseau was always regarded as an efficient and competent official. Until the end of his life he was held in high esteem by his fellow citizens, who attended his funeral in large numbers on 11 Feb. 1771.

André Lachance

Nicolas Boisseau's register covering the period 1731–44 is held by the ANQ-Q.

AN, Col., B, 45, f.89; 49, f.670; 57, ff.694, 728; 65, f.439; 85, f.208; 87, f.2; 97, f.15; 117, f.73; C[11A], 120, ff.347, 350v; E, 37 (dossier Boisseau); F[3], 9, f.186. ANQ-Q, État civil, Catholiques, Notre-Dame de Québec, 9 sept. 1725, 8 mai 1739, 4 juin 1741, 11 févr. 1771; Greffe de Florent de La Cetière, 7 sept. 1725; Greffe de J.-N. Pinguet de Vaucour, 2 juin 1741; NF 2, 19, ff.82, 83; NF 25, 55, no.2011. "Recensement de Québec, 1744," 128. F.-J. Audet et Édouard Fabre Surveyer, *Les députés au premier parlement du Bas-Canada (1792–1796)* . . . (Montréal, 1946), 51–53. J.-B. Gareau, "La Prévôté de Québec, ses officiers, ses registres," ANQ *Rapport*, 1943–44, 122–23. Le Jeune, *Dictionnaire*, I, 199. P.-G. Roy, *Inv. jug. et délib., 1717–60*, I, 301; II, 48, 290; III, 199; IV, 210; VII, 26–27; "Les notaires au Canada sous le Régime français," ANQ *Rapport*, 1921–22, 42. Tanguay, *Dictionnaire*, II, 330. Vachon, "Inv. critique des notaires royaux," *RHAF*, IX, 425, 546–47.

BONEVAL. *See* Benoît

BONNEAU, LOUIS DE PREISSAC DE. *See* Preissac

BONNÉCAMPS, JOSEPH-PIERRE DE, Jesuit; baptized 3 Sept. 1707 at Vannes (dept of Morbihan), France, son of Nicolas de Bonnécamps and Anne Muerel; d. 28 May 1790 at the château of Tronjoly in the parish of Gourin (Morbihan).

Joseph-Pierre de Bonnécamps was admitted to the Jesuit noviciate of the province of Paris on 3 Nov. 1727. He studied philosophy at the Jesuit college in La Flèche (1729–32), taught grammar classes at Caen (1732–36) and the senior grades (*belles-lettres* and rhetoric) at Vannes (1736–39), and studied theology at the Collège Louis-le-Grand (1739–43). He then left for Quebec, where he was appointed á teacher of hydrography at the Jesuit college in 1744 and where he pronounced his solemn vows on 8 Dec. 1746.

From the beginning Bonnécamps was determined to give serious instruction using the most advanced instruments for his observations. On 29 Oct. 1744 Intendant Hocquart wrote to the minister of Marine, Maurepas, that Father Bonnécamps requested a second-pendulum and a telescope mounted on a quadrant, and that he was planning to build an observatory on the college roof. In 1747 the *Mémoires pour servir à l'histoire des sciences et des beaux-arts* (also called *Journal de Trévoux*) published a meteorological observation that Bonnécamps had made at Quebec on 12 June 1746.

On 9 Oct. 1748 Intendant Bigot asked the minister of Marine to send the instruments Hocquart had already asked for in 1744; obviously Bonnécamps had not yet received them, or at least not all of them. Bigot wrote: "Father Bonnécan, a Jesuit, a teacher of mathematics, has pointed out to me that for instructing young men who are going in for navigation he needed a second-pendulum, an observation telescope, a quadrant with a three-foot radius equipped with a telescope rather than sights, and a lodestone since the one he has is very weak."

Although he had still not received all the instruments, in 1749 Bonnécamps accompanied Pierre-Joseph Céloron* de Blainville on his expedition to the Ohio River. A man was needed who could map the regions traversed, and there was no one more capable than the teacher of hydrography at the Quebec college. The expedition left Lachine on 15 June and was back in Quebec on 18 November. On his return, Bonnécamps prepared a report for Commandant General La Galissonière [Barrin*], who had just gone to France; the report, accompanied by a map, was sent to him the following year. In it Bonnécamps described everything that might appeal to a man of scientific interests such as La Galissonière: fauna, trees, natural curiosities, climate, location of forts and villages, and Indians. The priest wrote: "The longitude is estimated throughout. If I had had a good watch, I could have fixed some points by observation, but could I count on a watch of mediocre quality?" The expedition was of major importance in Bonnécamps's life and scientific career, but it was not an isolated experience. On 25 June 1752 he was at Fort Frontenac (Kingston, Ont.) to make astronomical observations.

Meanwhile Bonnécamps had become known in the scientific community through the account of his trip to the Ohio and especially through the map he had drawn. In 1754–55 he was corresponding with Joseph-Nicolas Delisle, an astronomer and geographer in the French navy. Bonnécamps spent the winter of 1757–58 in France; in a letter of 8 Nov. 1757 to his friend and protector, Madame Hérault, Bougainville* had recommended the erudite Jesuit to her attention. On 25 March 1758 Bonnécamps again wrote to Delisle, this time to describe the desperate situation in Canada. After the capture of Quebec in 1759, he returned to France.

In 1761 Bonnécamps was again in Caen teaching mathematics at the Jesuit college, but he had to leave this post in 1762 when the colleges of the Society of Jesus in France were closed. Some years later, around 1765, he was serving on the islands of Saint-Pierre and Miquelon with Father François-Paul Ardilliers; it is not known exactly when he returned to France. In 1770, however, he was chaplain at the convict prison in Brest, in accordance with the royal wish that former Jesuits of France come under the jurisdiction of the diocesan bishop of their birthplaces. Bonnécamps had earlier made the acquaintance of François-Jean-Baptiste L'Ollivier de Tronjoly, a compatriot, when he was ministering in Saint-Pierre and Miquelon. He became tutor to Tronjoly's children, and in his château, near Gourin, he died on 28 May 1790, aged 82 years.

JOSEPH COSSETTE

Joseph-Pierre de Bonnécamps's writings include: "Observation météorologique faite à Québec en Canada, le 12 de juin 1746," *Mémoires pour servir à l'histoire des sciences et des beaux-arts* (Paris), mars 1747, 572–74; "Relation du voyage de la Belle Rivière faite en 1749, sous les ordres de M. de Céloron," *JR* (Thwaites), LXIX, 150–98. The map he drew when travelling through the Ohio valley is now held by the Service historique de la Marine (Château de Vincennes, Paris), Recueil de cartes anciennes, no.67, carte no.21.

ASJCF, 595; 596; 597; 4028, f.26c. Mélançon, *Liste des missionnaires jésuites*. Rochemonteix, *Les jésuites et la N.-F. au XVIIIe siècle*, II, 74–76, 156. L.-P. Audet, "Hydrographes du roi et cours d'hydrographie au collège de Québec, 1671–1759," *Cahiers des Dix*, 35 (1970), 13–35. A.[-H.] Gosselin, "Le château de Tronjoly, dernière résidence du P. de Bonnécamps," RSC *Trans.*, 2nd ser., IV (1898), sect.I, 33–34; "Encore le P. de Bonnécamps (1707–1790)," RSC *Trans.*, 2nd ser., III (1897), sect.I, 93–117; "Les jésuites au Canada; le P. de Bonnécamps, dernier professeur d'hydrographie au collège de Québec, avant la Conquête (1741–1759)," RSC *Trans.*, 2nd ser., I (1895), sect.I, 25–61. O. H. Marshall, "De Céloron's expedition to the Ohio in 1749," *Magazine of American History* (New York and Chicago), II (1878), 129–50.

BONWAH. *See* BENOÎT

BORSALOU. *See* BARSALOU

BOURASSA (Bouracas, Bourasseau), *dit* **La Ronde, RENÉ**, fur-trader; baptized 21 Dec. 1688 at Prairie-de-la-Madeleine (Laprairie, Que.), son of François Bourassa, *dit* La Ronde, and Marie Le Ber; m. there 23 Oct. 1710 Agnès Gagné, and they had three children; m. there secondly, on 28 Sept. 1721, Marie-Catherine Leriger de La Plante, and they had five children; buried 7 Sept. 1778 at Montreal.

In the early decades of the 18th century the merchants in the English colonies were paying on the average twice the French price for beaver pelts. Tempted by these profits, René Bourassa, *dit* La Ronde, ventured into the extensive illicit trade between Montreal and Albany, New York. He was caught, however, and in July 1722 fined 500 *livres*.

By 1726 he had entered the western trade, which his father had followed over 30 years earlier. In partnership with Nicolas Sarrazin and François Lefebvre* Duplessis Faber, Bourassa dispatched canoes to the *pays d'en haut* in 1726. The following year he traded to Baie-des-Puants (Green Bay, Wis.), where Duplessis was commandant. Although his main focus was the western trade, in March 1729 Bourassa carried letters to New England, a trip which was often cover for illegal trade. By 1735 he was connected with business associates of Pierre Gaultier* de Varennes et de La Vérendrye. In that year Bourassa hired *engagés* to go to La Vérendrye's posts at Fort Saint-Charles (on Lake of the Woods) and Fort Maurepas (a few miles above the mouth of the Red River). He himself was at Saint-Joseph (Niles, Mich.) in July but wintered with the explorer at Saint-Charles. Early in June 1736 Bourassa and four others set out for Michilimackinac (Mackinaw City, Mich.). Suddenly they were captured by some 100 Prairie Sioux warriors, who claimed the French were arming their enemies. The war party was preparing to burn Bourassa at the stake when his Sioux slave girl dramatically pleaded for his life and he was released. He and his men subsequently escaped empty-handed to Michilimackinac, but the Sioux ambushed Jean-Baptiste Gaultier* de La Vérendrye's party, which was following some miles behind, and killed its 21 members.

Bourassa returned to the west in the late fall. Ignoring the elder La Vérendrye's directive to join him at Fort Saint-Charles, Bourassa and Laurent-Eustache Gamelin, *dit* Châteauvieux, constructed a post at Vermillon (near the mouth of the Vermilion River, Minn.) and wintered there with a number of Ojibwas. In the spring of 1737 Bourassa went east to Michilimackinac.

After 1737 his trade appears to have centred around that post. He sold 45 pots of wine to Pierre-Joseph Céloron* de Blainville for the French and Indians going south to fight the Chickasaws in 1739 and in subsequent years he sold goods used in negotiations with various tribes. Despite unsettled conditions throughout the west, Bourassa moved his family to Michilimackinac during the 1740s. He became a prominent member of the small trading community, owning one of its 40 houses, another lot in the fort, and a meadow outside. A number of slaves helped manage his properties. By the late 1740s Bourassa was apparently semi-retired, and his business was handled primarily by his sons René and Ignace. He had an active social life, attending numerous baptisms and weddings. Marriage ties linked him to other prominent families in the fort. In 1744 his son René had married the daughter of Jean-Baptiste Chevalier* and in 1754 his daughter Charlotte-Ambroisine married Charles-Michel MOUET de Langlade.

When Ojibwas organized by Minweweh* captured Michilimackinac from the British garrison in 1763 Bourassa must have been apprehensive. The Indians disliked him and they killed all his horses and cows before the British returned in September 1764. Perhaps this disaster prompted his return to Montreal, for even though he apparently got along well with the new commandant, William Howard (who called him a man of "good character"), he soon left Michilimackinac. His son Ignace, however, continued trading there until 1775. René Bourassa's remaining years were spent in Montreal, where he died in 1778.

DAVID A. ARMOUR

AN, Col., C[11A], 73, ff.226, 263; 76, ff.183, 196, 250; 117, f.363; 118, f.31; 119, ff.116, 198, 284, 285. Clements Library, Thomas Gage papers, Supplementary accounts, A state of houses and lands at Michilimackinac. Pa. Hist. Soc. (Philadelphia), Simon Gratz autograph coll., Howard to Bradstreet, 15 Oct. 1764. PAC, MG 18, K3, map of Michilimackinac in 1749. *The Aulneau collection, 1734–1745*, ed. A. E. Jones (Montreal, 1893), 93–94. "État général des billets d'ordonnances . . . ," ANQ *Rapport*, 1924–25, 231–342. "État général des états et certificats tant de la ville de Montréal que des forts et postes . . . ," ANQ *Rapport*, 1924–25, 356–59. *Journals and letters of La Vérendrye* (Burpee). "Langlade papers – 1737–1800," Wis., State Hist. Soc., *Coll.*, VIII (1879), 209–23. "The Mackinac register," ed. R. G. Thwaites, Wis., State Hist. Soc., *Coll.*, XVIII (1908), 469–513; XIX (1910), 1–162. *NYCD* (O'Callaghan and Fernow), V, 726–33. "Procès-verbaux sur la commodité et incommodité dressés dans chacune des paroisses de la Nouvelle-France par Mathieu-Benoît Collet, procureur général du roi au Conseil supérieur de Québec," Ivanhoë Caron, édit., ANQ *Rapport*, 1921–22, 305–6. "The St. Joseph baptismal register," ed. George Paré and M. M. Quaife, *Mississippi Valley Hist. Rev.* (Cedar Rapids, Iowa, and Lincoln, Neb.), XIII (1926–27), 215.

"Congés de traite conservés aux Archives de la province de Québec," ANQ *Rapport*, 1922–23, 192–265. *Dictionnaire national des Canadiens français (1608–1760)* (2v., Montréal, 1958), I, 163. Godbout, "Nos ancêtres," ANQ *Rapport*, 1959–60, 334–35. Labrèque, "Inv. de pièces détachées," ANQ *Rapport*, 1971, 1–50. *Mariages de Laprairie (N.-D.-de-la-Prairie-de-la-Madeleine), 1670–1968*, Irenée Jetté et Benoît Pontbriand, compil. (Québec, 1970). É.-Z. Massicotte, "Congés et permis déposés ou enregistrés à Montréal sous le Régime français," ANQ *Rapport*, 1921–22, 189–223; "Répertoire des engagements pour l'Ouest," ANQ *Rapport*, 1929–30, 191–466. Tanguay, *Dictionnaire*. Antoine Champagne, *Les La Vérendrye et le poste de l'Ouest* (Québec, 1968). Martin Kavanagh, *La Vérendrye, his life and times . . .* (Brandon, Man., 1967).

BOURDAGES, RAYMOND, surgeon and merchant; b. 1730 or 1731 in France, son of Pierre Bourdages, a carpenter, and Marie-Anne Chevalier; d. 10 Aug. 1787 at Bonaventure (Que.).

Raymond Bourdages was a master surgeon in 1755, according to a deed of gift between him and his wife signed in Quebec on 17 Oct. 1760. He was probably in attendance on the garrison of Fort La Tour, at the mouth of the Saint John River (N.B.), which was under the command of Charles DESCHAMPS de Boishébert shortly before the deportation of the Acadians. It was in that vicinity early in 1756 that he married Esther, the daughter of René Leblanc, royal notary at Minas (near Wolfville, N.S.).

Bourdages left Acadia during the winter of 1756–57 and moved his family to Ancienne-Lorette (near Quebec), where several of his children were baptized. In 1760 he travelled to France, probably to settle an inheritance. Upon his return in 1762 he established two trading posts on the Baie des Chaleurs, one at Bonaventure and the other at Caraquet (N.B.). He employed his near relatives in his business, in particular his young brothers-in-law Benjamin and Jean-Baptiste Leblanc, who set up at Tracadièche (Carleton, Que.) at this time. Alexis LANDRY, a cousin by marriage, was already in the region having been a pioneer settler at Caraquet.

It is not known when Bourdages moved his family to his property at Bonaventure; the 1765, 1774, and 1777 censuses do not indicate their presence there. Although he lived at Bonaventure only in the summer months, he took an interest in developing the region; in addition to his trading posts and the 300 acres of land he had purchased around 1762, he owned two mills there which he had built at the request of local residents.

On several occasions Bourdages's properties

were threatened. He was obliged to defend himself first against William Van Felson, a Dutchman who had arrived in 1763 and asserted his right to all the land on the Baie des Chaleurs. Three years later, supported by a survey, Samuel Jan Holland* claimed a grant which took in Bourdages's land, and it was not until 1825 that Bourdages's heirs were able to obtain title. The American War of Independence brought further troubles – American privateers set fire to his property and his trading posts, along with those belonging to Charles Robin*. He was taken prisoner in June 1778. The influence of the American agent John Allan* stirred up coastal Micmacs the following year and, on 22 March 1779, 16 of them pillaged Bourdages's post at Caraquet alleging that a state of war existed. The date of Bourdages's release by the Americans is unknown, but he was apparently not present at the raid.

Bourdages and Esther Leblanc had 11 children. Their son Louis* repeatedly had to present memoirs on behalf of the heirs to obtain recognition of his ownership of the lands bequeathed by his father's will.

MARIO MIMEAULT

ANQ-Q, État civil, Catholiques, Notre-Dame de L'Annonciation (L'Ancienne-Lorette), 1750–85; Greffe de Simon Sanguinet, 17 oct. 1760. Archives paroissiales, Saint-Joseph (Carleton, Qué.), Registre des baptêmes, mariages et sépultures, 1787. PAC, MG 30, C20, 3. Patrice Gallant, *Les registres de la Gaspésie (1752–1850)* (6v., [Sayabec, Qué., 1968]). Le Jeune, *Dictionnaire*, I, 224–25. [Bona Arsenault], *Bicentenaire de Bonaventure, 1760–1960* ([Bonaventure, Qué., 1960]); *Hist. et généalogie des Acadiens*, I, 238–39; II, 897. Geneviève Massignon, *Les parlers français d'Acadie* (2v., Paris, s.d.), II, 65. F.-J. Audet, "Louis Bourdages," RSC *Trans.*, 3rd ser., XVIII (1924), sect.I, 73–101.

BOURDON DE DOMBOURG, JEAN-FRANÇOIS, officer in the colonial regular troops; b. 29 Dec. 1720 in the parish of Saint-Barthélemy, La Rochelle, France, son of Jean-François Bourdon de Dombourg et de La Pinaudière and Madeleine Poirel; m. 6 July 1752 at Port-La-Joie (Fort Amherst, P.E.I.) to Marguerite, daughter of the Acadian merchant Joseph-Nicolas Gautier*, *dit* Bellair, and they had eight children; d. in or after 1789, probably at La Rochelle.

Jean-François Bourdon de Dombourg was brought to Île Royale (Cape Breton Island) in 1733 by his uncle Claude-Élisabeth Denys* de Bonnaventure. He probably began his military career immediately, but he was made a gentleman cadet only in 1736. Evidently he had some skill with languages: by 1739 he was acting as an "interpreter for the Micmac Indians" and in 1741 he was formally posted to Abbé Pierre Maillard*'s mission on Île Royale in order to extend his knowledge of Indian tongues. The same year he blew off his left hand when proofing some guns which were to be given to the Indians as gifts from the king. This loss did not apparently lessen his fighting ability, however, for in May 1744 he was ordered to assemble the Indians in Acadia to "make war on the English." With 250 Indians, he participated in at least one unsuccessful attack on Annapolis Royal (N.S.) that summer [*see* Paul Mascarene*]. Returning to Louisbourg in November, he was taken prisoner at the siege the following year and sent to France. He served in the unsuccessful expeditions of the Duc d'Anville [La Rochefoucauld*] to Acadia in 1746 and Governor La Jonquière [Taffanel*] to Canada in 1747.

When Île Royale and its dependencies were reoccupied by France in 1749 following the treaty of Aix-la-Chapelle, Bourdon was immediately seconded to Île Saint-Jean (Prince Edward Island) as an interpreter. Promoted several times during the 1740s, he was finally made lieutenant in 1750. Like many of his fellow officers, he served at outposts such as Île Saint-Jean and Port-Toulouse (near St Peters, N.S.) before his final posting to Louisbourg.

One week before Louisbourg's capitulation to AMHERST on 27 July 1758, Bourdon was ordered to join Charles DESCHAMPS de Boishébert's "flying camp" of colonial regulars, Acadian partisans, and Indians. By 1759 he was at Restigouche (Que.) in charge of a handful of troops and more than a thousand Acadian refugees. The winter of 1759–60 was hard: he was reduced to eating "cowhides, beaver skins, and dogs." Hunger was not his only problem, for the missionaries Maillard, Jean Manach*, and Charles GERMAIN were treating for peace with the British. Although Manach attempted to explain his actions as being in the Acadians' best interests, Bourdon sent the Acadians at Miramichi (N.B.) a letter appealing to their pride. "Where on earth," he asked, "is [your] patriotism, [your] devotion to religion. . . ." Manach intercepted the letter, but its contents became generally known and Bourdon succeeded in attracting a group of Acadians to Restigouche. He also prepared a dossier for Governor Vaudreuil [RIGAUD] which virtually accused the priests of treason.

In late May 1760 Bourdon received unexpected aid. A French convoy destined for Canada had had to take refuge in the Baie des Chaleurs not far from Bourdon's post. François-Gabriel d'ANGEAC, captain of the troops aboard the vessels, took command of the post and with François Chenard de La Giraudais, commander of the convoy, improvised defences. On 27 June a British squadron under Captain John BYRON began an assault. The French forces held until 8 July, when the frigate *Machault* and most of the remaining supply ships were fired, and the troops retreated into the woods. Byron returned to Louisbourg and it was not until late October that Major Robert Elliot* arrived to take the surrender of the French forces. By the terms of the capitulation Bourdon was sent to France. His wife and children were taken to Halifax, Nova Scotia, and did not join Bourdon in La Rochelle until November 1764.

The later part of Bourdon's life is only sketchily known. In May 1764 he was retired from the colonial regulars with a pension of 400 *livres*. He seems to have been poor, for as late as 1773, when requesting a captain's commission in a new regiment, he referred to his "poverty-stricken state." In 1775 he was made a knight of the order of Saint-Louis, an honour that included a pension. Perhaps, however, his poverty was relative to his estate; our last record of him, in 1789, shows him sitting in the nobles' assembly of the seneschal jurisdiction of La Rochelle.

ANDREW RODGER

AN, Col., B, 59, f.547; 74, f.554v; 84, p.316; 86, p.312; 91, p.348; 120, f.577v; 181, f.225v; C[11A], 105/1, pp.82–162, 179–84; C[11B], 22, f.127v; 27, f.283; 28, ff.26, 68; 29, ff.26–28; 31, f.77v; D[2C], 4, p.132; 5, f.330; 48; E, 47 (dossier Bourdon de Dombourg); Section Outre-mer, G[1], 411/2; 458, f.20v; 459, f.12v (paginated references are to PAC transcripts). Knox, *Hist. journal* (Doughty), III, 353–421. Æ. Fauteux, *Les chevaliers de Saint-Louis*, 203. Archange Godbout, "Familles venues de La Rochelle en Canada," R.-J. Auger, édit., ANQ *Rapport*, 1970, 114–367. Régis Roy, "Bourdon de Dombourg," *BRH*, XXVIII (1922), 243.

BOURG, JOSEPH-MATHURIN, priest, Spiritan, missionary, and vicar general; b. 9 June 1744 at Rivière-aux-Canards (near Canard, N.S.), eldest son of Michel Bourg and Anne Hébert and grandson of Alexandre Bourg*, *dit* Belle-Humeur; d. 20 Aug. 1797 at Saint-Laurent, near Montreal (Que.).

Like many other Acadians, Joseph-Mathurin Bourg, along with his family, was deported from Nova Scotia in 1755 [*see* Charles Lawrence*]. He probably was sent to Virginia first, but by 1756 he was in England. Seven years later he crossed to France, where he lived at Saint-Suliac (dept of Ille-et-Vilaine) before moving to Saint-Servan in 1766. The following year he went to study philosophy at the Séminaire du Saint-Esprit in Paris, under the patronage of the Abbé de L'Isle-Dieu, the bishop of Quebec's vicar general in France. He received the tonsure on 27 May 1769 and minor orders on 9 June 1770, as did his half-brother and companion in exile, Jean-Baptiste Bro*.

Immediately after completing his third year of theology in 1772, Bourg was sent to Quebec, and on 19 September he was ordained priest by Bishop Jean-Olivier BRIAND in the chapel of the Hôtel-Dieu in Montreal. The following year he was sent to serve the scattered Acadian population in Nova Scotia, which then included New Brunswick, and Gaspé. He took up residence at Tracadièche (Carleton, Que.) and recorded his first act on 3 Sept. 1773 in the parish registers of Bonaventure. Shortly afterwards he travelled throughout his Baie des Chaleurs mission and even visited Memramcook and Minudie. In July 1774 he went to Quebec, where his family had been living since their return from France, and it was probably during the course of this trip that Bishop Briand appointed him vicar general in Acadia. That autumn he made his first visit to the Acadians of the Saint John River and southwestern Nova Scotia. Although these areas had been served in the past by Charles-François BAILLY de Messein, some Acadian communities had not seen a priest for many years.

In 1778 Bourg became of great service to the Nova Scotian authorities by agreeing to go and restore calm among the Indians of the Saint John River, who it was feared might join the rebel American forces. That they had no missionary was, in fact, one of the causes of the Indians' discontent, agents of the Nova Scotia government having promised the previous year to obtain one for them. In December 1777 Lieutenant Governor Mariot ARBUTHNOT had written to Governor Carleton* with a request that Bishop Briand be asked to send Bourg to Halifax. Briand agreed, and Bourg went to Halifax in August 1778 to receive instructions. On 24 September, accompanied by Michael FRANCKLIN, the superintendent of Indian affairs, and Gilfred STUDHOLME, the commandant of Fort Howe (Saint John, N.B.), he met with the Malecites and Micmacs at Menagouèche, near the fort, and showed them a letter from the bishop which threatened with excommunication all those who aided the rebels. A treaty was then signed in which the Indians promised to remain neutral [*see* Nicholas AKOMÁPIS].

Abbé Bourg played a similar role throughout the War of American Independence. He went to the Saint John River again in 1779, and in 1780 and 1781 he participated in various meetings with the Indians. The correspondence of John Allan*, the American superintendent of eastern Indians, indicates clearly Bourg's value to the British in their attempt to retain the Indians' support. For his services Bourg had received in August 1778 a sum of £50, as well as a £100 pension of unknown duration and two grants of land: Heron Island, off the south coast of the Baie des Chaleurs, and a property on the site of present-day Charlo. Since he never received the title-deeds, his heirs later encountered many difficulties; in 1806 surveyor George Sproule* contested their right to the land on the grounds that it had never been cultivated.

Abbé Bourg lived at Tracadièche until 1784, making annual visits to southwestern Nova Scotia from 1780 to 1783. In 1784 Bishop Briand asked him to go to Halifax; the number of Catholics there had increased and they had been demanding a priest since 1782. Believing that Halifax would become one of the most important postings in his diocese, the bishop considered it an appropriate place of residence for his vicar general, who could, moreover, speak English. Unable to move there until 1 Aug. 1785, Bourg was well received on his arrival by the civil authorities. However, when Father James Jones*, an Irish priest, arrived 27 days later, Abbé Bourg, realizing that the population could not support two priests, decided that Jones should have charge of the parish. He left Halifax in February 1786 and, after making a final visit to the Acadians of Nova Scotia, returned to the Baie des Chaleurs. Since there were not enough French speaking priests in the diocese of Quebec, after his departure the Acadians of Nova Scotia were served by English speaking priests until the arrival of Jean-Mandé Sigogne* in 1799.

In 1784 Bishop Briand had thought of sending Abbé Thomas-François LE ROUX to replace Abbé Bourg at Tracadièche, but Le Roux was too old to leave his post at Memramcook. On his return to the Baie des Chaleurs, Bourg found the mission under the direction of Antoine Girouard*, a young priest whom Bishop Louis-Philippe MARIAUCHAU d'Esgly had sent there in 1785. The bishop then gave charge of the north shore of the bay to Abbé Bourg and the south shore to Abbé Girouard. But Bourg continued to minister to the Indians of the entire mission. Soon after his return, the New England Company, a Protestant society, offered him the post of teacher to the Baie des Chaleurs Indians, but it is not known whether he accepted.

During the winter of 1789–90 Girouard, who was ill, stayed with Abbé Bourg and was able to observe the vicar general's manner of life. He then wrote a letter in Latin to the new bishop of Quebec, Jean-François HUBERT, describing Abbé Bourg's imprudent conduct with his servant Marie Savoye, a woman in her forties to whom the vicar general claimed to be related. Although Girouard acknowledged that she was a good servant and cook, he maintained that she ruled over the affairs of the presbytery and the parish and was the cause of quarrels between Bourg and his parishioners. The bishop admonished Bourg to be more prudent, and he promised to be so.

At the bishop's request Abbé Bourg again took charge of the south shore of the Baie des Chaleurs after Abbé Girouard left in 1790. In the winter of 1794–95 he contracted a violent fever and was supposed, in delirium, to have "talked too much" and expressed anti-religious sentiments. His parishioners therefore demanded another missionary and took advantage of Bourg's inactivity to remove his servant from the presbytery. In March 1795, when he had recovered, Abbé Bourg asked to be recalled, at the same time making clear his dissatisfaction and explaining his conduct to the bishop. He was given charge of the parish of Saint-Laurent, near Montreal, and in the summer of 1795 abbés Jean-Baptiste-Marie CASTANET and Louis-Joseph Desjardins*, *dit* Desplantes, succeeded him at the Baie des Chaleurs. Bourg remained parish priest of Saint-Laurent until his death on 20 Aug. 1797.

At a time when there were few missionaries, Abbé Bourg had not stinted himself in serving the Acadians, particularly those of the Baie des Chaleurs region. Parish registers show that he frequently travelled about his mission and that he visited southwestern Nova Scotia at least five times. Not only did he bring spiritual comfort to the Acadians, but his presence undoubtedly helped to renew their confidence. An Acadian himself, he had survived the great upheaval of 1755 and had, in spite of it, maintained good relations with the British authorities. He was not the first priest who had been born in Acadia, Bernardin de Gannes de Falaise having that honour, but he was the first Acadian missionary to return after the deportation.

ÉLOI DEGRÂCE

AAQ, 12 A, C, 125–26, 135; D, 106; 20 A, II, 6; 210 A, I, 131–32, 173–74; 22 A, V, 307–8; 1 CB, I, 8; II, 2, 6, 10, 15–16, 22; CD, Diocèse de Québec, I, 72a; 311 CN, VI, 1. Archives de l'évêché de Gaspé (Gaspé, Qué.), Casiers des paroisses, Restigouche, Indiens de Restigouche à l'évêque, 4 janv. 1787. ASQ, MSS, 12, f.40. N.B. Museum (Saint John), Simonds, Hazen, and White papers, folder 20, item 40, William Franklin to the Indians, 14 Sept. 1778. PANS, RG 1, 212, 21 Aug.

1778. *Documentary history of Maine* (Willis *et al.*), XVI, XVIII. "Selections from the papers and correspondence of James White, esquire, A.D. 1762–1783," ed. W. O. Raymond, N.B. Hist. Soc., *Coll.*, I (1894–97), no.3, 306–40. Patrice Gallant, *Les registres de la Gaspésie (1752–1850)* (6v., [Sayabec, Qué., 1968]), [VI], xxii–xxiv. Le Jeune, *Dictionnaire*, I, 228–29.

Antoine Bernard, *Histoire de la survivance acadienne, 1755–1935* (Montréal, 1935), 37–54. É.-P. Chouinard, *Histoire de la paroisse de Saint-Joseph de Carleton (baie des Chaleurs), 1755–1906* (Rimouski, Qué., 1906). A. A. Johnston, *A history of the Catholic Church in eastern Nova Scotia* (2v., Antigonish, N.S., 1960–71), I. H. J. Koren, *Knaves or knights? A history of the Spiritan missionaries in Acadia and North America, 1732–1839* (Pittsburgh, Pa., 1962), 108–21. Arthur Melanson, *Vie de l'abbé Bourg, premier prêtre acadien, missionnaire et grand-vicaire pour l'Acadie et la Baie-des-Chaleurs, 1744–1797* (Rimouski, Qué., 1921). Antoine Bernard, "Les Acadiens en Gaspésie," *L'Évangéline* (Moncton, N.-B.), 31 juin–11 juill. 1932. É.-P. Chouinard, "A travers les régistres de Saint-Joseph de Carleton," *Le Moniteur acadien* (Shédiac, N.-B.), 10, 20, 27 janv., 10, 24 févr., 3, 7, 10, 31 mars 1899; "L'abbé Joseph Mathurin Bourg," *Le Moniteur acadien*, 17, 24, 31 août 1899; "Le premier prêtre acadien – l'abbé Joseph-Mathurin Bourg," *La Nouvelle-France* (Québec), II (1903), 310–17, 403–11. Éva Comeau, "L'abbé Joseph-Mathurin Bourg, curé de Carleton en 1773," *Revue d'hist. de la Gaspésie* (Gaspé, Qué.), IX (1971), 239–42. Placide Gaudet, "Les premiers missionnaires de la baie Ste-Marie . . . ," *L'Évangéline* (Weymouth Bridge, N.-É.), 9 juill. 1891, [2]. J.-M. Léger, "L'abbé Bourg, pacificateur des Indiens," Soc. historique acadienne, *Cahier* (Moncton, N.-B.), II (1966–68), 243–45.

BOWMAN, JAMES, doctor and surgeon-major; b. probably in Ireland, son of Whitney Bowman; d. 1787 at Quebec.

James Bowman is thought to have come to Quebec as surgeon-major to the British forces, apparently shortly after the conquest. On his discharge from the army, he decided to set up an office in that town. In the spring of 1784 he began to work as a doctor at the Hôtel-Dieu, where he and another Quebec doctor, Joseph Détailleur, had been accepted in recognition of their selfless and unremitting care of smallpox victims during the epidemic of the previous winter. Since the conquest the wards of the Hôtel-Dieu had been reserved for military patients, but the epidemic had produced so many more sick persons than hospital facilities in Quebec could accommodate that early in 1784 the government had decided to return the wards to the hospital nuns [*see* Marie-Louise CUROT, *dite* de Saint-Martin]. Not only had Bowman and Détailleur provided constant care for all smallpox victims in the town, but they now volunteered to treat free of charge all those infected with the disease who were brought to the nuns' hospital.

On 18 April 1785 Lieutenant Governor Henry HAMILTON, faced with another widespread infectious disease, appointed Bowman official investigator of the Baie Saint-Paul malady. As far back as 1773 this strange disease, which was spreading through the villages along the St Lawrence, had come to the attention of Governor Guy Carleton*. The government had launched an enquiry but had abandoned it in 1775 because of the American invasion. In September 1782 a group of highly respected physicians in Quebec and Montreal, including Philippe-Louis-François Badelart*, James Davidson, Charles Blake*, Robert Sym, George Selby*, and Jean-Baptiste Jobert, had issued a warning to the authorities in a petition to the grand jury in Montreal. During 1785 and 1786 Bowman was given the responsibility of visiting all the regions to which the infection had spread. He examined 5,801 sick persons in 1785 and 4,606 the next year.

In contemporary medical circles there was prolonged discussion about the source of this disease. Its symptoms and developmental cycle, and the success of treatment with mercury-based medicine, convinced Blake, Davidson, Sym, Selby, and Bowman that it was syphilis. Two Montreal doctors, Robert Jones* and Jobert, were certain, however, that syphilis was not involved. Nevertheless all the physicians treated their patients with medicine containing mercury and expressed satisfaction with the results.

Bowman presented a documented report to the government and a claim for £2,500 for two years of study and travel. The claim was not honoured, and instead he was offered 100 guineas for expenses and 200 guineas as his fee. By the time of his death in 1787, however, the government had decided to accord him £825. Since Bowman had already received £500, the remainder was paid to his estate.

ÉDOUARD DESJARDINS

PAC, RG 4, B43. [P.-L.-F. Badelard], *Direction pour la guérison du mal de la baie St-Paul* (Québec, 1785); "Observations sur la maladie de la Baye . . . données au public par ordre de son excellence le gouverneur," *Quebec Gazette*, 29 July 1784. Robert Jones, *Remarks on the distemper generally known by the name of Molbay disease, including a description of its symptoms and method of cure chiefly intended for the use of the clerical and other gentlemen residing in the country* (Montreal, 1786). "Une correspondance médicale: Blake à Davidson," P.-A. Fiset, édit., *Laval médical* (Québec), 23 (1957), 419–48. Abbott, *History of medicine*. M.-J. et G. Ahern, *Notes pour l'hist. de la médecine*, 73–83. Heagerty, *Four centuries of medical history in Canada*, I, 131–60. A. W. Cochrane, "Notes on the measures adopted by government, between 1775 and 1786, to check the St. Paul's Bay disease," Literary and Hist. Soc. of Quebec, *Trans.*, IV (1854), 139–52. Émile Gaumond, "La syphilis au Canada français, hier et aujourd'hui," *Laval médical*, 7 (1942), 25–65. J.-E. Roy, "Maladie de la baie," *BRH*, I (1895), 138–41. Benjamin Sulte, "Le mal de la baie Saint-Paul," *BRH*, XXII (1916), 36–39.

BRADSTREET, JOHN (baptized **Jean-Baptiste**), army officer and office-holder; b. 21 Dec. 1714 at Annapolis Royal, Nova Scotia, second son of Edward Bradstreet and Agathe de Saint-Étienne* de La Tour; m. Mary Aldridge, and they had two daughters; d. 25 Sept. 1774 in New York City.

John Bradstreet and his brother Simon served in Nova Scotia as volunteers in Richard Philipps*' regiment (40th Foot) until 1735, when their mother, working through the regimental agent King Gould, secured commissions for them. John received an ensign's rank and thus began a military career which would be capped when he became a major-general in 1772.

Confusion surrounds the early years and family of John Bradstreet as the result of the presence in Nova Scotia of a cousin of the same name. After the latter's death John compounded the confusion by marrying his widow, and two of the four children believed to be his were actually his cousin's. In later years Bradstreet was reticent to discuss his family background and the Nova Scotian phase of his career. No doubt uneasiness about the effect his Acadian ancestry would have on his career in the British army, as well as his involvement in questionable trading activities, explain his silence. The result has been a historical picture of Bradstreet as an enigmatic figure who first emerged during the campaign against Louisbourg, Île Royale (Cape Breton Island) in 1745. As a young officer stationed at Canso in the 1730s, however, Bradstreet had been very active. In addition to carrying out his military duties, he had developed a lucrative trade in provisions and lumber with the French fortress. Despite advice from Gould to "Knock off" such activities lest they damage his military career, Bradstreet continued his mercantile connections with Louisbourg well into 1743. Not surprisingly, when Canso and its garrison were captured by the French in May 1744 [*see* François Du Pont Duvivier], Bradstreet was given preferred treatment. During the next few months he became the message bearer between the commandant of Louisbourg, Jean-Baptiste-Louis Le Prévost* Duquesnel, and Governor William Shirley of Massachusetts as prisoner exchanges were discussed. Bradstreet also worked at turning his knowledge of Louisbourg to good advantage in New England and improving his chances of promotion in Britain. The very day in September 1744 that the released Canso garrison reached Boston, Bradstreet and George Ryall, a fellow officer in the garrison, submitted a report on Louisbourg to Shirley which stressed the fortress's importance to the French empire and hinted at its vulnerability. Three months later, Bradstreet presented Shirley with a plan for an assault on the French stronghold. Whether it was used as the basis for the 1745 attack is uncertain since no copy is now available. William Vaughan* claimed to have been the author of the definitive plan; however, Bradstreet was described by William Pepperrell* as "the first projector of the expedition," and Shirley claimed that it was because of Bradstreet's "Intelligence and advice . . . that I set the Expedition on ffoot."

Although disappointed that he was not given command of the expedition, Bradstreet accepted a provincial commission as lieutenant-colonel of the 1st Massachusetts Regiment and contributed to the victory at Louisbourg. Pepperrell, Commodore Peter Warren*, and Shirley all applauded his performance. The day after the surrender Bradstreet was commissioned "Town Major of ye City and Fortress," but the more substantial rewards he clearly expected were not forthcoming. Moreover, after Charles Knowles became governor of Cape Breton in June 1746, even his position as town major was lost. Personal animosity developed between the two men, and rewarding sidelines for Bradstreet, such as providing rum and fuel to the garrison, were curtailed by Knowles, who claimed that he no longer permitted Bradstreet "to Plunder the Government." Although Bradstreet had been appointed captain in Pepperrell's newly established regular regiment garrisoning the fortress and on 16 Sept. 1746 was appointed lieutenant governor of St John's, Newfoundland, he remained bitter. Further attempts to improve his situation failing and continued frustration at Louisbourg being unacceptable, he journeyed to St John's in August 1747 to begin active service as lieutenant governor.

Newfoundland turned out to be only a temporary resting place, however, since in the fall of 1751 he went to England. Armed with his journal of the siege, reciting his contributions, and bemoaning his treatment, he soon regained the support of King Gould and Gould's son Charles which he had lost because of his trading activities, and he aroused the interest of powerful persons such as Sir Richard Lyttleton, an intimate of William Pitt, Charles Townshend, later chancellor of the exchequer under Pitt, and Lord Baltimore. Although both Townshend and Baltimore were ultimately unsuccessful in their attempts to obtain preferment for him, Lyttleton and Charles Gould were to prove more useful. Having gained badly needed "Easie Access" to patrons in England, Bradstreet returned to America in 1755 with Major-General Edward Braddock's expedition.

Now a captain in Pepperrell's newly raised 51st Foot, he was initially assigned to Shirley's campaign against Fort Niagara (near Youngstown, N.Y.) the same year. Lacking experienced personnel, the Massachusetts governor relied heavily on his old Louisbourg adviser. In the spring of 1755 he ordered Bradstreet to Oswego (Chouaguen) to improve its defences and prepare it as a base for the assault on Niagara. Bradstreet carried out his orders energetically and in August he was promoted brevet-major and adjutant-general. During the summer, however, Shirley had encountered difficulty in organizing and transporting his army to Oswego, and as the opportunity for a Niagara strike slipped away Bradstreet sought permission for an immediate attack on the French fort. Shirley had rejected this plan, and in September he abandoned the campaign altogether. He decided that an attack on Fort Frontenac (Kingston, Ont.), which he described as "the Key" to Lake Ontario, must be the first campaign of 1756, and he assigned the task to Bradstreet.

One of Bradstreet's first duties in the spring was to lead a convoy of bateaux to reinforce the garrison at Oswego. Once there he was to select the necessary men and supplies and attack Fort Frontenac. He had difficulty in reaching Oswego, however, and its weakened garrison and incomplete fortifications made it obvious that an offensive against Frontenac was impossible. Since French pressure on Oswego was now growing, Bradstreet directed his efforts to keeping the supply line between Oswego and Albany open. He returned to Oswego once more on 1 July 1756 and then waited impatiently in Albany to set out again. In mid August, however, Montcalm* captured Oswego.

By then Lord Loudoun had replaced Shirley as commander of the British forces in America. Shirley's enemies, such as Sir Charles HARDY and Sir William JOHNSON, identified Bradstreet as one of his cohorts, but Bradstreet was quick to dissociate himself from his former commander. Forewarned in March 1756 by Charles Gould that Shirley "is no longer in great esteem here," Bradstreet became somewhat uncooperative when Shirley attempted to collect information for his own vindication. He moved instead to endear himself to Loudoun and his staff, and his strategy worked perfectly. Of all the measures that Shirley had authorized, only Bradstreet's performance "won the unqualified praise of Shirley's successors." With Loudoun's approval the bills for his bateau service were honoured, he received a captaincy in the Royal Americans (60th Foot) when the 51st was disbanded early in 1757, and he became virtual quartermaster and aide-de-camp to Loudoun. During the spring of 1757 he assembled supplies and transports at Boston for Loudoun's expedition against Louisbourg, and at Halifax in August he was among those who felt that the attack should not be postponed.

Although disappointed by the cancellation of the expedition, Bradstreet was encouraged to learn that William Pitt had become the British prime minister, and he wrote to Lyttleton seeking "a favourable mention." He was quite willing to specify appointments to which he considered himself entitled, such as the governorship of New Jersey, the colonelcy of a regiment of rangers, or the post of quartermaster general. Moreover, once again offering schemes to his superiors, early in September 1757 he sent Lyttleton his thoughts on how Canada could be conquered. For complete victory in North America a three-pronged assault should be launched against the French possessions. One army should reduce Louisbourg and then proceed against Quebec while another should move from Albany to capture forts Carillon (Ticonderoga, N.Y.) and Saint-Frédéric (near Crown Point, N.Y.) and then link up with the third army, which was to attack across Lake Ontario from Oswego. The combined forces should then proceed "in a short time [with] the reduction of the Town of Montreal." Bradstreet thus offered a strategy which bears a striking resemblance to the basic plan that Pitt used to achieve the conquest of Canada in the campaigns of 1758 to 1760.

"Charmed with the Spirit and Enterprizing Genius" of Bradstreet, Lyttleton passed his ideas along to Pitt and Lord Ligonier, commander-in-chief of the British army. The latter was definitely influenced by them in drawing up his plans for the 1758 campaign. Quick action followed Bradstreet's request for promotion; on 1 Jan. 1758 Lyttleton reported to Charles Gould with obvious satisfaction that "I have Obtained for our Friend Bradstreet the rank of *Lt. Col in the Kings Service*, as Deputy Quarter Master General for America."

While he was winning promotion in England, Bradstreet was being assigned increasingly important tasks in America. Loudoun ordered him to oversee the construction of bateaux in the Albany region for service on Lake Ontario and the Hudson and St Lawrence rivers in the coming campaign, and he also approved Bradstreet's proposal for an attack on Fort Frontenac in the early spring. These plans were abruptly altered early in March, however, when Loudoun was replaced by James ABERCROMBY. In Pitt's orders to Abercromby, Bradstreet was assigned to quartermaster's duties in the southern colonies. Abercromby was aware of Bradstreet's talents, however, and in "an inspired piece of disobedience" decided to use him in his campaign against Fort Carillon. Accordingly, Bradstreet supervised the construction of bateaux and the movement of men and provisions up the Hudson River in preparation for the attack. When Viscount Howe (George Augustus Howe), Abercromby's second in command, was killed, Bradstreet "took up the slack" since Thomas GAGE, now second in command, failed to emerge as a key adviser to Abercromby. With Abercromby's permission he took a force of several thousand regulars and provincials on a more direct route to Carillon than the army had been following. Once before the fort with this advance guard, Bradstreet requested permission to launch an immediate attack. Abercromby did not take "the least Notice" of this request but instead came up with the rest of the army and ordered the attack for the next day. The delay proved costly: on 8 July the strengthened French forces and entrenchments hurled back successive waves of British attackers. Following Abercromby's decision to withdraw, Bradstreet took command at the landing place and converted a near disastrous rush for the boats into an orderly embarkation.

While others licked their wounds in the aftermath of the British defeat, Bradstreet resurrected his proposal for an attack on Fort Frontenac and secured Abercromby's approval. His largely colonial force of approximately 3,000 reached Lake Ontario on 21 August and four days later was within sight of the French fort. Frontenac was in no condition to resist a siege and the fort's commander, Pierre-Jacques PAYEN de Noyan et de Chavoy, surrendered on the 27th. After plundering, burning, and demolishing the fort, Bradstreet's force retreated to British territory. With this one brilliant stroke the lifeline of the French Great Lakes empire had been severed. More directly, the capture of French provisions at the post, the destruction of the French naval flotilla on Lake Ontario, and the resultant blow to French prestige among the Indians all contributed to the final defeat of New France.

Bradstreet's triumph was applauded in Great Britain, and he was promptly promoted colonel in America, the promotion being backdated to 20 August. But ironically, although his military career had risen to its apex during Britain's years of defeat, his feelings of frustration and neglect intensified as the victorious years of the British war effort began. Under his new commander, Jeffery AMHERST, Bradstreet served as deputy quartermaster general at Albany, winning Amherst's consistent respect for the conscientious performance of his duties. During the preparations for the 1760 campaign Bradstreet's ceaseless diligence caused his health to collapse and brought him to death's door. As Amherst's army embarked upon the final reduction of Canada, Bradstreet remained behind at Oswego, confined to his bed. Although his quartermaster's duties were financially rewarding and indeed increased his political and economic importance in the Albany region, as the war drew to a close he became increasingly concerned at what he considered the British government's failure to reward adequately his contributions to the victory. His cause was not helped by Lyttleton's departure from England in 1760 nor by Pitt's fall from power in 1761, but the faithful Charles Gould continued to solicit on his behalf and in October 1763 secured his appointment as lieutenant governor of either Montreal or Trois-Rivières once Ralph Burton*'s choice was known. By this time Pontiac*'s uprising had broken out, and Amherst offered Bradstreet command of an expedition to the Great Lakes against the Indians. Reasoning that the successful completion of this task would carry more weight with the British government than his service in Canada, he accepted.

The operations planned for 1764 were directed primarily against the Delawares and the Shawnees; Bradstreet was to command a northern force moving from Niagara to Detroit, while Henry Bouquet was to command a southern force moving from Fort Pitt (Pittsburgh, Pa) towards the Muskingum River (Ohio). Unable for various reasons to leave Niagara until early August, and bitterly disappointed at the limited size of his force, Bradstreet convinced himself that his mission was also one of peacemaking. Thus he offered tentative peace terms to an Indian delegation which met him near Fort Presque Isle (Erie, Pa) on 12 August and conducted further negotiations after his arrival at Detroit on 27 August.

By mid September Bradstreet had reached Sandusky (Ohio) on his return journey. Gage, who had succeeded Amherst as commander-in-chief, had by now been informed of Bradstreet's peacemaking activities and disavowed them, ordering Bradstreet to launch an overland attack against the Delawares and Shawnees. Bradstreet felt his weakened force was incapable of such a mission and remained at Sandusky until mid October, offering only a potential threat to the Indians and an indirect aid to Bouquet. The journey from Sandusky disintegrated into a nightmarish rout because of storms and lack of supplies, and it was not until 4 November that the remnants of the expedition began to arrive at Niagara. To his credit, Bradstreet had relieved Detroit, helped reopen the various posts on the Upper Lakes, and proved at least an indirect help to Bouquet's more successful campaign. But to Gage and Sir William Johnson, Bradstreet had mismanaged the campaign and exceeded his instructions, and he emerged from the Detroit campaign with his military record and reputation badly tarnished.

After the Detroit disappointment Bradstreet continued to serve as acting deputy quartermaster general at Albany, a virtual sinecure since his departmental expenditures and responsibilities were cut to the bone by Gage. The unsympathetic Gage remained as commander-in-chief for the remainder of Bradstreet's life, often thwarting his efforts at advancement. Bradstreet prospered financially through land speculation and other dealings, but his military career stagnated. Pet projects such as the establishment of a full-fledged colony at Detroit with himself as governor were still offered to the home authorities, but although the projects were at times carried to the brink of achievement they were ultimately unsuccessful. Equally futile were his requests for the governorships of Massachusetts, New York, or even Canada when he heard that Guy Carleton* contemplated "never returning" in 1770. In 1773 the possibility of his succeeding Gage was still being pursued, and his proposal for a Detroit colony was resubmitted the following year, only to be precluded by the Quebec Act. The old warrior was spared the news of this final rejection, as well as the spectacle of the open revolution he had long expected, since he died at New York City on 25 Sept. 1774. The next day, accompanied by an elaborate funeral *cortège*, Bradstreet's body was borne to its final resting place in Trinity Church.

For an Anglo-American-Acadian a successful career in the mid-18th-century British army was not an easy undertaking. Nevertheless, Bradstreet was able to combine a prominent role in military triumphs with proper timing, well-placed patrons, the support of his commanding officer, and a widespread recognition of his special talents, and he thus did remarkably well. The obscurity surrounding his background and the questionable side of many of his schemes and actions kept him beyond the pale, however. Although valued in a wartime emergency, he remained a somewhat irregular regular.

W. G. Godfrey

[Material concerning John Bradstreet is fairly extensive but widely scattered. The Tredegar Park coll. at the National Library of Wales (Aberystwyth) contains the immensely rewarding Bradstreet-Gould correspondence. At the PAC numerous collections (in microfilm and transcript) touch upon Bradstreet's activities. Among the more important are the Amherst family papers (MG 18, L4), AN, Col., C11B (MG 1), Nova Scotia A (MG 11, [CO 217]), PRO, Adm.1 (MG 12), CO 5, CO 194, CO 217 (MG 11), PRO 30/8 (MG 23, A2), and WO 1 (MG 13). At the PANS, RG 1, 5–26, 29–30, 34–35, and 38 were helpful. The Clements Library houses the extensive Thomas Gage papers; the American series contains substantial correspondence between Gage and Bradstreet. The American Antiquarian Soc. (Worcester, Mass.) has the John Bradstreet papers, 1755–77, and the New York Public Library, Manuscripts and Archives Division, has the somewhat disappointing Philip Schuyler papers. Both the New York Hist. Soc. (New York) and the New York State Library (Albany) have miscellaneous items dealing with Bradstreet. The Huntington Library has the Abercromby and Loudoun papers, which are worthwhile, particularly the latter, and the Mass. Hist. Soc. has the equally useful Belknap papers.

Among the more important printed primary sources are [John Bradstreet], *An impartial account of Lieut. Col. Bradstreet's expedition to Fort Frontenac . . .* (London, 1759; repr. Toronto, 1940); *The Colden letter books* (2v., N.Y. Hist. Soc., *Coll.*, [ser.3], IX, X, New York, 1876–77); *Correspondence of General Thomas Gage* (Carter); *Correspondence of William Pitt* (Kimball); *Correspondence of William Shirley* (Lincoln); *Diary of the siege of Detroit . . .* , ed. F. B. Hough (Albany, N.Y., 1860); *The documentary history of the state of New-York . . .* , ed. E. B. O'Callaghan (4v., Albany, 1849–51), I, IV; G.B., PRO, *CSP, col., 1710–11* to *1738*; *Johnson papers* (Sullivan *et al.*); *The Lee papers* (2v., N.Y. Hist. Soc., *Coll.*, [ser.3], IV, V, New York, 1871–72), I; *Louisbourg journals, 1745*, ed. L. E. De Forest (New York, 1932); Mass. Hist. Soc., *Coll.*, 1st ser., I (1792), VII (1800); 4th ser., V (1861), IX (1871), X (1871); 6th ser., VI (1893), X (1899); *Military affairs in North America, 1748–65* (Pargellis); *NYCD* (O'Callaghan and Fernow), VII, VIII, X; *Royal Fort Frontenac* (Preston and Lamontagne).

Bradstreet has never been examined in a full-length biography. S. McC. Pargellis contributed the brief biographical sketch in *DAB*. Arthur Pound attempted a more detailed look in *Native stock: the rise of the American spirit seen in six lives* (New York, 1931), but his account is exaggerated and inaccurate. Harvey Chalmers' historical novel *Drums against Frontenac* (New York, 1949) paints a fascinating, albeit largely imaginary, picture. Because of Bradstreet's participation in so many of the mid 18th-century American military campaigns, he is frequently mentioned but is only rarely subject to detailed examination. Examples are

Frégault, *François Bigot*; L. H. Gipson, *The British empire before the American revolution* (15v., Caldwell, Idaho, and New York, 1936–70), VII; McLennan, *Louisbourg*; Pargellis, *Lord Loudoun*; Usher Parsons, *The life of Sir William Pepperrell, bart. . . .* (2nd ed., Boston and London, 1856); Rawlyk, *Yankees at Louisbourg*; Shy, *Toward Lexington*; Stanley, *New France*; and Rex Whitworth, *Field Marshal Lord Ligonier: a story of the British army, 1702–1770* (Oxford, 1958).

The only recent detailed studies of particular phases of Bradstreet's career are W. G. Godfrey, "John Bradstreet at Louisbourg: emergence or re-emergence?" *Acadiensis*, IV (1974), no.1, 100–20, and Peter Marshall, "Imperial policy and the government of Detroit: projects and problems, 1760–1774," *Journal of Imperial and Commonwealth History* (London), II (1974), 153–89. A full-length study of Bradstreet's career in dissertation form is W. G. Godfrey, "John Bradstreet: an irregular regular, 1714–1774" (unpublished PHD thesis, Queen's University, Kingston, Ont., 1974). W.G.G.]

BRANSSAT (Bransac), *dite* **de la Nativité, MARIE-ANNE MIGEON DE.** *See* MIGEON

BRANT, MARY. *See* KOÑWATSIˀTSIAIÉÑNI

BRASSARD, LOUIS-MARIE, priest; b. 17 Dec. 1726 at Quebec, son of Jean-Baptiste Brassard, a beadle, and Marie-Françoise Huppé, *dit* Lagroix; d. 27 Dec. 1800 in Nicolet (Que.).

Louis-Marie Brassard was enrolled in the Séminaire de Québec on 4 Dec. 1742 and on 15 Dec. 1746 received the tonsure. He continued to live in the seminary until he was ordained priest by Bishop Pontbriand [Dubreil*] on 20 Dec. 1749. He was immediately given parish responsibilities as a curate. Historian Jean-Baptiste-Arthur Allaire* claims that his first assignment was to Île Royale (Cape Breton Island) as a missionary. If so, Brassard stayed there only briefly since by March 1750 he was curate at Charlesbourg. The following autumn he was appointed parish priest of Nicolet. Brassard also had to serve an area including the present-day parishes of Saint-Grégoire-le-Grand and Saint-Antoine-de-la-Baie-du-Febvre. He ceased ministering to the mission of Saint-Grégoire at an unknown date and to Saint-Antoine in 1786.

Brassard ran into difficulties with the faithful of Saint-Antoine over the building of a church and presbytery there. They argued strongly against his plan to construct these buildings on land he owned on the shore. It is significant that Brassard did not win this conflict. We do not know, however, how far he should be held responsible for the dispute. Brassard was devoted to his bishop and his flock at Nicolet, but he gave the impression of not being as interested in the people of Saint-Antoine as he should have been. Relations between them became so strained that in 1785 the latter complained to Bishop Louis-Philippe MARIAUCHAU d'Esgly that they had been ignored by their pastor.

On the other hand, Brassard had a tranquil and pleasant life with his Nicolet parishioners. Since he was near them and they had the chance to get to know him, they were in a position to recognize and value his talents. He reciprocated. In 1784 he built the stone church they wanted on land he had bought in Nicolet in 1770. A house and various other buildings were subsequently erected on the same site. He bequeathed his goods, as well as his rents and his lands, to the parish council of Nicolet, in order to provide his parish with a primary school. The need for such an institution was great, there being none in the vicinity. The school was opened in 1801, a few months after his death. It remained in existence until the Brothers of the Christian Schools came to Nicolet in 1887. The building which it had occupied became in 1803 the Séminaire de Nicolet, a classical college, but the school continued within the college building.

In his history of the Séminaire de Nicolet, Bishop Joseph-Antoine-Irénée Douville comments on Brassard's zeal and his affection for his parishioners. The few relevant documents which have been preserved seem to refute the assertion so far as the people of Saint-Antoine-de-la-Baie-du-Febvre are concerned, but Brassard apparently served the inhabitants of Nicolet to their complete satisfaction and he continued to minister to them until his death on 27 Dec. 1800, although after 1791 he was no longer the parish priest.

CLAUDE LESSARD

AAQ, 515 CD, I, 3; IV, 198; IX, 2a. ANQ-Q, État civil, Catholiques, Notre-Dame de Québec, 19 déc. 1726. Archives de l'évêché de Nicolet (Nicolet, Qué.), Cartable Saint-Jean-Baptiste-de-Nicolet, I, 5–8, 17. ASN, AO, Polygraphie, I, 4–42; Séminaire, IX, 53; Titres divers et contrats de l'abbé Louis-Marie Brassard; AP-G, L.-É. Bois, Garde-notes, 9, p.147; 11, p.84; 14, p.62. ASQ, MSS, 2, f.53. Allaire, *Dictionnaire*. J.-E. Bellemare, *Histoire de la Baie-Saint-Antoine, dite Baie-du-Febvre, 1683–1911* (Montréal, 1911), 59–160; *Histoire de Nicolet, 1669–1924* (Arthabaska, Qué., 1924), 104–62. J.-A.-I. Douville, *Histoire du collège-séminaire de Nicolet, 1803–1903, avec les listes complètes des directeurs, professeurs et élèves de l'institution* (2v., Montréal, 1903), I, 1–20.

BRASSARD DESCHENAUX, JOSEPH, secretary to the intendant, scrivener in the Marine, seigneur, and justice of the peace; b. 1 Aug. 1722

at Quebec, son of Charles Brassard Deschenaux, a shoemaker, and Marie-Joseph Hébert; d. there 16 Sept. 1793.

Born into a family of modest means, Joseph Brassard Deschenaux owed his education to a notary who lived with his parents on Rue Saint-Jean. (This notary may have been Christophe-Hilarion Du Laurent*, who at the time of the 1744 census was in practice and was a lodger in the Brassard Deschenaux home.) Joseph was thus able to join the Marine bureau, where he attracted attention because of his lively intelligence, his capacity for work, and his ambition. He became secretary to Gilles HOCQUART, who in February 1745 made him responsible for the census of the parishes and seigneuries on the south shore of the St Lawrence. Although the intendant put restrictions on the young man, with whom "it was necessary," he said, "always to keep the reins well in hand; . . . if one were to let them slacken on him, one might well experience dire results," he recommended him to his successor, François BIGOT. In 1750 Bigot entrusted Brassard Deschenaux with the collection of the tax levied for the maintenance of the Quebec barracks, and four years later he appointed him acting treasurers' agent in the absence of Jacques Imbert*, the agent of the treasurers general of the Marine in Canada, who was visiting France. By 1752 Brassard Deschenaux was in a position to buy at public auction the house of Nicolas Lanoullier* de Boisclerc, on Rue des Remparts, for the sum of 14,500 *livres*. He was to rent it to Montcalm* during the general's stay at Quebec. It was a good investment for Brassard Deschenaux, since the rent of high-ranking French officers was paid by the king and a high price could be obtained rather easily. He did not fail to take advantage of the situation judging by the remarks in Montcalm's journal: "An excuse for enriching the secretary . . . high rents, inflated or imaginary repairs."

Bigot's secretary succeeded in making himself indispensable both to his employer and to those who, seeking to enrich themselves through public funds, gathered around the intendant. Thus, in 1755, he helped Joseph-Michel CADET prepare a memoir in which the former butcher offered his services to the minister of Marine, Machault, for the supply of all necessary provisions to the king's stores and posts. Cadet had made a similar offer the preceding year, but the minister had ignored it. This time, as a result of Bigot's intervention, Machault responded positively and Brassard Deschenaux participated in the drawing up of the contract for the general supply of provisions in Canada which was to make Cadet a rich purveyor general and from which the secretary would also profit. In 1763, when trials were being conducted at the Châtelet in Paris regarding the *affaire du Canada*, Brassard Deschenaux was accused of having falsified five years earlier the figures in the accounts relating to the supplies he had undertaken to furnish, in partnership with Cadet, to the post at Miramichi (N.B.). The prices had been inflated excessively, and Bigot had refused to sign the accounts; the secretary had then reduced prices by half but doubled the quantity of supplies, so that "the king has suffered the same loss as if the first conditions had still applied." He was also accused of having distributed to the Acadians who had taken refuge at Quebec far fewer supplies than the quantity officially claimed, with the result that Cadet, the supplier, had been able once again to profit "at the expense of the king." Cadet testified to the court that he had given Brassard Deschenaux a pension of 40,000 *livres* for services rendered and had provided him with all the food he had needed. On 10 Dec. 1763 Brassard Deschenaux was sentenced to five years' banishment from Paris, given a fine of 50 *livres*, and ordered to make restitution of 300,000 *livres*. Because he had remained in Canada after the conquest, having been appointed king's scrivener by Governor Vaudreuil [RIGAUD] and Bigot "to take care of the hospitals, and whatever may relate to the service of his most Christian Majesty," this sentence had little effect on him. However, he seems to have gone to France in 1766 in order to have his name cleared there. An article in the *Quebec Gazette* on 14 May 1767 announced that "the several Persons concerned in the Canada Affair, who appealed from their Sentence, have obtained a Decision partly in their Favour. . . . M. des Chesneaux, who was . . . condemned to Banishment, and the Restitution of 300,000 Livres, is now ordered to restore only 100,000, till the Court has received further Information."

According to the anonymous author of the "Mémoire du Canada," Brassard Deschenaux was a member of the Grande Société, forming with Michel-Jean-Hugues PÉAN and Cadet "a kind of triumvirate," and amassed a fortune of 2,000,000 *livres* during the French régime, a claim that should be taken with caution. However it may be, Brassard Deschenaux was in a position to take advantage of the final departure for France of some of his former friends after the conquest to buy their seigneuries. From Péan he acquired the seigneuries of La Livaudière and Saint-Michel and from Nicolas Renaud* d'Avène Des Méloizes that of Neuville, known also as Pointe-aux-Trembles. In 1769 and 1770 he bought some parts, with seigneurial rights, of Beaumont and on 18 March 1770 he purchased a quarter of the seigneury of Bélair, adjoining that of Neuville. The numerous leases made between Brassard Deschenaux and new *censitaires* prove that he attended closely to the management of his properties. In Quebec he owned and lived in a magnificent house on Rue des Pauvres with a stone courtyard and buildings. Brassard Deschenaux seems to have made his fellow citizens forget his malpractices since they entrusted him with offices requiring honesty and disinterestedness; he was, in fact, churchwarden of Notre-Dame parish and cashier of the parish council at the time of the rebuilding of the cathedral (1768–71). He was among those persons of standing approached in 1773 by the English merchants of Quebec who, desiring a house of assembly, sought to enlist support from the leading Canadians of the city. He was also appointed a justice of the peace.

Brassard Deschenaux had married at Quebec on 21 Aug. 1747 Suzanne-Élisabeth Filion, who died the following year; he then married, on 21 May 1750, Madeleine Vallée. Four children survived him, including two sons: Charles-Joseph*, who was to become vicar general of the bishop of Quebec in 1809, and Pierre-Louis*, a notary and lawyer, who was to be appointed judge of the Court of King's Bench for Trois-Rivières in 1794. Brassard Deschenaux's funeral service was held on 18 Sept. 1793 in the cathedral of Quebec in the presence of the coadjutor bishop, Charles-François BAILLY de Messein. The honourable Gaspard-Joseph CHAUSSEGROS de Léry, Jean-Antoine Panet*, Nathaniel Taylor, Michel-Amable Berthelot* d'Artigny, and Thomas Scott* signed the burial certificate.

THÉRÈSE P. LEMAY

ANQ-Q, État civil, Catholiques, Notre-Dame de Québec, 2 août 1722, 21 août 1747, 21 mai 1750, 18 sept. 1793; Greffe de J.-B. Planté, 5 juin 1793. *Coll. des manuscrits de Lévis* (Casgrain), VII, 514. *Doc. relatifs à l'hist. constitutionnelle, 1759–91* (Shortt et Doughty; 1921), I, 11, 474. "Mémoire du Canada," ANQ *Rapport*, 1924–25, 116–18, 131, 197. "Recensement de Québec, 1744," 33. *Quebec Gazette*, 14 May 1767. P.-V. Charland, "Notre-Dame de Québec: le nécrologe de la crypte," *BRH*, XX, 249–50. J.-E. Roy, *Rapport sur les archives de France*, 875, 884. P.-G. Roy, *Inv. concessions*, II, 27–28, 259–61; III, 51–53; IV, 286; V, 60; *Inv. jug. et délib., 1717–60*, V, 136; VI, 129; *Inv. ord. int.*, III, 67, 145, 148, 188. Frégault, *François Bigot*, II. P.-G. Roy, *Bigot et sa bande*, 152–58. [P.-]P.-B. Casgrain, "La maison Montcalm sur les Remparts, à Québec," *BRH*, VIII (1902), 230–35. Leland, "François-Joseph Cugnet," *Revue de l'université Laval*, XIX, 145. P.-G. Roy, "La maison Montcalm sur les Remparts, à Québec," *BRH*, XXXII (1926), 380–81; "Les secrétaires des gouverneurs et des intendants de la Nouvelle-France," *BRH*, XLI (1935), 104–5.

BRASSIER, GABRIEL-JEAN, priest, superior of the Sulpicians of Montreal, and vicar general; b. 26 Aug. 1729 at La Tour (dept of Puy-de-Dôme), France; d. 20 Oct. 1798 in Montreal (Que.).

Gabriel-Jean Brassier entered the Grand Séminaire in Clermont-Ferrand, France, on 31 Oct. 1750 and was ordained priest in 1754, probably on the eve of Trinity Sunday. At the request of his superior, Jean Couturier, he at once chose Canada as the country in which to serve, and he remained there the rest of his life. He spent the years 1754–56 at the mission of Lac-des-Deux-Montagnes (Oka), among the Algonkins, where there were already some Sulpicians. He was made responsible for the parish of Saints-Anges at Lachine during the Seven Years' War (1756–63). For the last 35 years of his life he was in the parish of Notre-Dame in Montreal.

At the beginning of the 1780s Brassier became the right-hand man of his superior, Étienne MONTGOLFIER, whom he effectively replaced in 1789, and permanently succeeded in 1791. He assumed a fourfold responsibility as superior of the Sulpicians, administrator of their seigneuries, *ex officio* parish priest of Notre-Dame in Montreal, and vicar general of the bishop of Quebec. Unlike his predecessor, Brassier showed great interest in the Collège Saint-Raphaël, where teaching had begun in 1773 [*see* Jean Baptiste CURATTEAU]. He considered it important to remedy certain deficiencies pointed out by the churchwarden in charge, Louis Cavilhe, at a meeting of the churchwardens on 6 Sept. 1789. For some 15 years the college had been preparing for the clerical state those who had a vocation, and this policy had not fulfilled the expectations raised by a publicly owned college. Many former pupils had returned to their families disdainful of their fathers' trades and unsuited for any work whatever; they became useless and often a source of scandal. Cavilhe, speaking for the churchwardens and townspeople of Montreal, therefore proposed that the college, subject to the inspection of the Sulpician superior and the incumbent churchwardens, should be staffed with teachers not only of Latin but also of writing, geography, mathematics, and English. The superior and two representatives of the parish council were also to monitor the quality of the teaching and routine matters; in the case of large expenses they would have to refer to the body of churchwardens. These proposals were warranted, since the parishioners had assumed in

1773 the responsibility of paying for the land and the construction of the college.

On the day after the September meeting Brassier took up the improvement of the school situation in Montreal with Bishop HUBERT. Soon after, Jean-Baptiste Curatteau resigned because of his health and was replaced by fellow Sulpician Jean-Baptiste Marchand*. The bishop urged the churchwardens to extend a warm welcome to the new director and assured them that their deliberations, which he considered sensible, would bear fruit. The principal designate, he added, had "wit, virtue, skill in handling details, and . . . will merit, I hope, the confidence of the public"; he would moreover be released from his parish work. Hubert appointed two new assistant priests to the parish of Montreal, and chose a deacon, Ignace Leclerc, to teach rhetoric at the college. He advised Brassier to find a layman, a good, honest Catholic of upright moral character, to give daily lessons in writing and English. Leclerc could add two or three geography lessons per week to his load, and perhaps direct an hour of history every evening. Hubert also urged Marchand to protect the young pupils from the corruption of the world and to make them conscious of the honour of being Canadians, of belonging to the Catholic faith, and of being citizens of Montreal. He also insisted upon collaboration between the Sulpicians and the churchwardens, since the latter after all represented the owners of the college. At the end of October 1789 "Marchand's little school was growing every day," and three years later the philosophy year already had 20 pupils. In October 1794 the college was expecting to admit more than 184 students.

Brassier's reputation rests on his contribution to the coming of French Sulpicians to Canada, which had been his predecessor's dream. The persecutions suffered by the clergy during the French revolution had scattered them widely, in particular to England where 8,000 French priests took refuge. The conservative writer Edmund Burke and the refugee Philippe-Jean-Louis Desjardins*, vicar general of Orléans, obtained permission from the British government to send an investigating committee to Canada to examine the prospects for settling French ecclesiastics there. The British authorities had thus far opposed letting any Frenchmen into Canada, but now, still concerned to win the Canadians' trust, they had changed their minds, having become convinced that any such new immigrants would not seek to alienate former citizens of France from "a just and peaceful" government by inviting them to adopt a "barbarous and destructive" one. While spreading aversion for atheistic and Jacobin France, the exiled priests would at the same time counteract republican propaganda from the United States among the Canadians, and in so doing draw them closer to Britain.

Bishop Hubert looked favourably upon the immigration and immediately thought of it as a way of supplying the Collège Saint-Raphaël with teachers. Brassier promptly thanked him but expressed the opinion that few European vessels would venture forth in view of the imminent possibility of war between France and England. He hoped all the same that his superior general, Jacques-André Émery, would profit by circumstances to send him a dozen or so Sulpicians. His desire was fulfilled. Candide Le Saulniers* arrived in the autumn of 1793 and 13 more Sulpicians joined him in Montreal the following year. Four others, who had taken refuge in Spain, succeeded in crossing the Atlantic in 1796. Of the 35 priests or future priests who arrived from Europe in Canada over four years, more than half belonged to the Society of Saint-Sulpice. The survival of the Sulpician order in Canada was assured.

An active man, Brassier ended his days paralysed. He had served as a link between the difficult and delicate term of his predecessor, Étienne Montgolfier, and that, no less long and tense, of Jean-Henri-Auguste Roux*. A transitional figure, humble and discreet, Brassier worked to assure adequate pastoral services for Montreal as well as a renowned educational establishment.

LUCIEN LEMIEUX

AAQ, 210 A, I, 57–58, 61, 63–65, 71–72, 125; II, 144, 240–41; 22 A, I, 107–9. ACAM, 901.005, 773–7; 901.012, 784-3, 789-1, 789-5, 793-4, 793-7, 793-8, 794-3; 901.137, 792-3. ASQ, Lettres, I, 56; Polygraphie, XVIII, 20. *Mandements des évêques de Québec* (Têtu et Gagnon), II, 453–56. Gauthier, *Sulpitiana*. N.-E. Dionne, *Les ecclésiastiques et les royalistes français réfugiés au Canada à l'époque de la révolution, 1791–1802* (Québec, 1905). Galarneau, *La France devant l'opinion canadienne*. Lemieux, *L'établissement de la première prov. eccl.* Olivier Maurault, *Le collège de Montréal, 1767–1967*, Antonio Dansereau, édit. (2e éd., Montréal, 1967). J.-B.-A. Ferland, "L'abbé Philippe-Jean-Louis Desjardins," *BRH*, V (1899), 344–46. M. G. Hutt, "Abbé P. J. L. Desjardins and the scheme for the settlement of French priests in Canada, 1792–1802," *CHR*, XXXIX (1958), 121. É.-Z. Massicotte, "Une page de l'histoire du collège de Montréal," *BRH*, XXIII (1917), 207–9. Thomas Matheson, "La Mennais et l'éducation au Bas-Canada," *RHAF*, XIII (1959–60), 477.

BRÉARD, JACQUES-MICHEL, controller of the Marine, merchant, and member of the Conseil Supérieur of Quebec; baptized 7 Dec. 1711 at

Rochefort, France, son of Jacques Bréard, a notary and cashier in the Marine, and Marie-Anne Marcellin; d. 22 March 1775 and buried in the parish church of Saint-Mandé-sur-Brédoire (dept of Charente-Maritime), France.

Jacques-Michel Bréard joined the Marine as a cadet in March 1730 and became a writer in December. It is known that he made a voyage in 1731–32 to Martinique and Saint-Domingue (Hispaniola); otherwise he had various port duties at Rochefort. On 1 Jan. 1748 he was named controller of the Marine at Quebec with supervision over finances, stores, construction, and recruiting, and he arrived at Quebec on 26 August with the new intendant, BIGOT, on the *Zéphyr*. His main duty was to keep a watch on all Marine property and funds by verifying every transaction of the intendant, of the agents of the treasurers general of the Marine and Colonies (such as Jacques Imbert* and Alexandre-Robert HILLAIRE de La Rochette), and of others in a set of duplicate records which he was to keep for this purpose. The controller was all the more necessary because the agents at Quebec were not royal officials but salaried employees of the treasurers general for the Marine and Colonies, who managed naval and colonial funds in what amounted to a private banking system.

Bréard, like most Bourbon officials, did not consider himself morally bound to work only for the crown in return for his salary, which even in 1756 was a meagre 1,800 *livres*, and he evidently spent much of his time in more profitable ways. From the very beginning of his tour of duty in Canada, he held a one-fifth interest in a transatlantic trading company formed with Bigot and a Jewish firm of Bordeaux, David Gradis et Fils, in a contract of 10 July 1748 renewed in 1755. The partners shared in the profits of at least one annual shipment of about 300 tons of goods from Bordeaux to Quebec; and Bréard and Bigot fitted out some smaller vessels for trade with the West Indies, as the contract suggested they might. Bréard in fact had several schooners built at Quebec for the Martinique trade. According to Jean-Victor VARIN de La Marre, between 1755 and 1757 Bréard was also in partnership with Michel-Jean-Hugues PÉAN, Bigot, and Varin himself. Meanwhile, on 1 May 1749 he became a member of the Conseil Supérieur with a stipend of 450 *livres* annually, and in the same year he acquired a one-fifth interest in a seal and porpoise fishery on the Labrador coast at Chateau Bay through a partnership with Jean-François Gaultier*, the proprietor of the concession, and Charles-François TARIEU de La Naudière. On 5 Nov. 1748 Bréard and Guillaume ESTÈBE had been granted a nine-year fishing and trading concession on the Rivière Thekaapoin, between the concessions formerly granted to Jean-Baptiste Pommereau* and François Margane* de Lavaltrie. When this property proved useless for fishing because of the way the tides rose and fell among the islands there, Bréard was able to win the concession of Saint-Modet, previously exploited by Pierre Constantin*, on 6 April 1751. In Canada, Bréard went into the business of selling trading licences for western posts under the patronage of the governor, La Jonquière [Taffanel*], notably the posts at Detroit, which proved so profitable that he made a total of 1,100,000 *livres*. The capital funds needed he obtained from acquaintances in France and the management of the business he entrusted to Estèbe.

Bréard's brother, Marcellin-Nicolas (1714–1785), had become a writer in the Marine, then a minor supplier of wood to the Marine, and in April 1758 the agent at Rochefort for the treasurers general of the Colonies, a post he was to hold until 1768. We do not know whether this brother was directly involved in Bréard's business at Quebec but he was well placed to be. He had to settle all official accounts for the colonies at Rochefort, paying out, for instance, 144,969 *livres* for shipments to Canada in 1760 on three Bordeaux ships, the *Machault*, the *Fidélité*, and the *Marquis de Malauze*. In this post, Marcellin-Nicolas increased his fortune from about 40,000 *livres* to about half a million and as his appointment was founded on a bond of guarantee for 60,000 *livres* posted by Jacques-Michel in 1758, we may reasonably surmise that the two brothers were in business together. These suspicions are in no way reduced by the discovery that the Marine intendant at Rochefort, Charles-Claude de Ruis-Embito de La Chesnardière, was Marcellin-Nicolas's patron, instrumental in securing the post of treasurers' agent.

Having made a fortune at Quebec, Jacques-Michel Bréard became homesick for the gentle climate and civilized order of western France where, by notarial contract of 7 Feb. 1753, he had bought a manor house called Les Portes in the parish of Saint-Mandé-sur-Brédoire on the borders of Poitou and Saintonge. Besides he felt uncomfortable at Quebec since complaints about his business dealings had been sent to the minister at Versailles. Since 1752 he had, it was said, been suffering from a "maladie de langueur et d'Elizie" and with the permission of his superiors at Quebec he sailed away on 29 Oct. 1755. He arrived at La Rochelle on 19 December. There he learned that the day before he left Quebec the

Aimable Rose of Honfleur carrying all his belongings back to France in seven large packing cases had been seized and taken to Portsmouth as a prize. He may have recovered his papers for at his death he possessed a set of accounts for every year he had been in Canada. On 9 Feb. 1756 a ministerial order to return to Quebec prompted Bréard to arrange with Abraham Gradis for a shipment of goods to sell in Canada; but on doctor's orders he was allowed to remain in France at last and was posted to Marennes on 15 Aug. 1757 as commissary for naval conscription. Already on 18 May 1756 he had bought a royal magistrate's office with the title of treasurer of France and made other investments, especially in private loans.

Bréard and his family were now able to indulge their social ambitions. He had married Marie Chasseriau, daughter of a minor nobleman of Saintonge, in October 1741, and they had two sons who became minor noblemen themselves. The elder, Jean-Jacques Bréard*, born at Quebec on 11 Oct. 1751, became a councillor in the fiscal subdivision of Marennes, then mayor of the town, and went on to play a part in the French revolution as a member of the Convention and the Committee of Public Safety with a special interest in naval business. There were two daughters, also born at Quebec, who married poor noblemen and for the first of these marriages Jacques-Michel Bréard put up a dowry of no less than 80,000 *livres*. Without the disasters of the *affaire du Canada* the Bréard family might have blossomed like so many other French families with similar beginnings.

Suddenly, on 24 April 1762, orders were issued for Bréard's arrest and he was imprisoned in the Bastille with the other officials from Canada. He and they had often been denounced for their rapacious business dealings in Canada since 1748 and might well have been arrested earlier. But present-day high standards of conduct for public servants date from the 19th century; the 18th century saw nothing wrong with a royal official carrying on a private business on the side so long as it did not interfere with the royal service or harm the interests of the crown or the legal rights of others. Bréard, like Bigot and Joseph-Michel CADET, was a scapegoat for the crown's loss of Canada and its repudiation of colonial and naval debts. The trials were nicely timed to draw public anger onto the heads of these officials. In the general judgment of 10 Dec. 1763 Bréard was banished from Paris for nine years and ordered to pay a fine of 500 *livres* and a restitution to the crown of 300,000 *livres*. Bréard had indeed cheated the crown and the public, but no more so than was usual in Bourbon France. The political motives underlying his trial would be hard to deny in view of the royal *lettres de réhabilitation* which cleared his name on 27 Dec. 1771.

Long before then Bréard had retired to the life of a modest country gentleman living on his rents and annuities at his seigneury of Les Portes, with a few servants and tenants, horses and livestock of every kind, vineyards, and the acquaintanceship of a local circle of small office-holders, army officers, and minor noblemen. He had a library with books on many subjects, especially history, and also the works of Rousseau, Voltaire, Pascal, Bossuet, and the French classical dramatists. His little manor house, much altered, was still in the hands of his descendants in 1971 when their *métayer* was pleased to show its thick walls and two decorated fireplaces. The cottagers were still talking of the family's ancient connection with Canada.

J. F. BOSHER

AD, Charente-Maritime (La Rochelle), État civil, Saint-Mandé-sur-Brédoire, 24 mars 1775; Minutes Audouin (Aulnay), 17 juin 1775 (Bréard's inventory after death) [I wish to thank M. and Mme Lemercier, notaries at Aulnay, for generously helping me and for responding to my suggestion that they deposit their old minutes at the Archives départementales at La Rochelle. J.F.B.]; Minutes Bietry (Saint-Just), 6 oct. 1741 (Bréard's marriage contract); Gironde (Bordeaux), Minutes Dufaut (Bordeaux), 28 juill. 1784. AN, T, 590$^{1-4}$ (papers of Bréard's brother and descendants); V^{1}, 391 (concerning Bréard's office as treasurer of France); Col., C^{11A}, 98 (especially Bréard to the minister, 28 Oct. 1752); Marine, C^{7}, 44 (dossier Bréard). PRO, HCA 32/162, *Aimable Rose* (including a bill of lading for Bréard's property and other information). *Docs. relating to Canadian currency during the French period* (Shortt), II, 783–86.

BREWSE (Bruce), JOHN, military engineer; m. Mary —; d. 15 Sept. 1785 at Ipswich, England.

John Brewse first appears in the records of the Board of Ordnance for 1745 as a second engineer on the Newfoundland establishment. He is listed as occupying the same position three years later, but there is some doubt whether he resided on the island for the whole period. Back in England by 1749, Brewse accompanied CORNWALLIS' expedition to Nova Scotia as its engineer. He assisted Charles MORRIS in laying out the town of Halifax and was one of the first justices of the peace appointed by the governor. Brewse's main task, however, was to build defences for the new settlement. As protection was needed immediately he commenced a series of temporary fortifications. By winter a picketed fort had been built on Citadel Hill and two smaller forts in the town. A crude battery on George Island and two more forts were finished by late 1750, and the straggling barricade made of felled trees and brushwood that Brewse had been forced to use in 1749 after the settlers refused to work on the defences was replaced by a proper palisade erected by the troops.

These duties were interrupted in August 1750 when Brewse was assigned as engineer to the detachment sent by Cornwallis to establish a British presence in the Chignecto region. Brewse was wounded in the leg during a skirmish between Lieutenant-Colonel Charles Lawrence*'s men and a force under Jean-Louis LE LOUTRE, but he was able to proceed with the construction of Fort Lawrence (near Amherst, N.S.). The new post was largely completed by 25 September, when Brewse returned to Halifax.

Brewse may have accompanied Cornwallis to England in October 1752, since in December he and the ex-governor appeared before the Board of Trade to discuss the Nova Scotia estimates for 1753. He returned to Halifax in August 1754 with plans and equipment for a battery that the Board of Ordnance had directed him to build on the Dartmouth side of the harbour. Lawrence, now lieutenant governor, warned the board that he would "greatly fear" the battery, anticipating the verdict of later observers who pointed out that such an isolated and easily captured work was a positive danger to the town. He gave Brewse his full support for this project, however, as well as for the construction of three other batteries on the Halifax shore in 1755.

Brewse was assigned in 1755 as engineer to MONCKTON's expedition against Fort Beauséjour (near Sackville, N.B.). He directed the trenching operations during the siege with the help of Winckworth TONGE, who had been appointed his assistant. Monckton gave most of his praise to the artillery and merely noted that Brewse and his men "were likewise verry Active," but Lawrence, who seems to have had a high opinion of the engineer, reportedly believed that the ease with which the fort was captured was due to "the good conduct of Mr. Brewse." Brewse's own account of the siege is brief, sparse, and uninformative, but the plans he made of the Chignecto Isthmus form a valuable record of the operation.

Brewse attained the rank of captain-lieutenant when the engineers were given military status in 1757 and, along with several colleagues, was assigned to the expedition against Louisbourg, Île Royale (Cape Breton Island), in 1758. There he probably received his share of the low opinion which Wolfe* and AMHERST had of the engineers. According to Ordnance records, he was in Portugal in 1762 with the British force assisting in the defence of the country against Spanish invasion. He then appears to have spent some years at the Ordnance office in London, and in 1778, now a lieutenant-colonel, he was appointed chief engineer at Minorca following the death of Patrick MACKELLAR. It was his fate to hold this position when Minorca was successfully besieged by the French and Spaniards in 1782, just as it had been John Henry Bastide*'s fate to be present at an earlier loss of the island in 1756. Brewse was promoted colonel in 1780, and in 1782 he was appointed to the newly formed Tower Committee, a group of senior engineers whose task it was to review proposed engineering and fortification works. It is not known whether he continued to hold this appointment until his death three years later.

Brewse had a daughter Mary, who was the wife of Lieutenant William Kesterman of the engineers. They were the beneficiaries of his will along with John Boddington and Cuthbert Fisher of the Ordnance office.

MAXWELL SUTHERLAND

PAC, MG 11, [CO 220], Nova Scotia B, 4, p.21; MG 18, N15, pp.2–3, 6, 16; N25, p.2; National Map coll. PRO, CO 217/9, ff.70–74; 217/15; Prob. 11/1134, ff.184–86. *Annual Register* (London), 1762 (8th ed., 1810), 28–32. *The building of Fort Lawrence in Chignecto, 1750*, ed. and intro. J. C. Webster (Saint John, N.B., 1941), 7, 11. G.B., Board of Trade, *JTP 1749/50–53*, 376. [Joshua Winslow], *The journal of Joshua Winslow . . .*, ed. and intro. J. C. Webster (Saint John, N.B., 1936), 35–39. *Roll of officers of the corps of Royal Engineers from 1660 to 1898 . . .*, ed. R. F. Edwards (Chatham, Eng., 1898), 4, 6. Porter, *History of Royal Engineers*, I, 158, 171, 180, 188, 203, 209–13; II, 202–3.

BREYNTON, JOHN, Church of England clergyman; baptized 13 April 1719 at Trefeglwys (Powys), Wales, son of John Breynton; d. 20 July 1799 in London, England.

After receiving his early education at Shrewsbury School, John Breynton was admitted to Magdalene College, Cambridge, on 5 March 1738/39. He graduated with a BA in 1742. That same year he was ordained and entered the chaplaincy service of the Royal Navy, serving in the *Suffolk* in 1742, the *Deptford* in 1743, the *Prince Frederick* in 1744, and the *Norwich* in 1745–46. On 22 May 1746 he arrived at Louisbourg, Cape Breton Island, in Charles Knowles' small squadron and remained there as deputy chaplain to the garrison until the evacuation of the fortress in 1749. He returned to England and the following year received his MA from Cambridge.

Leaving the navy, Breynton entered the service of the Society for the Propagation of the Gospel on 17 April 1752 and was sent to Halifax, Nova Scotia, to replace William Tutty*. When he arrived early in October he found Thomas WOOD already there, and the presence of two missionaries in the same parish caused some difficulty. The situation between them was not finally regularized until 24 Sept. 1759, when Governor Charles Lawrence* appointed Breynton rector, and Wood vicar, of St Paul's Church.

In Halifax Breynton found a settlement of about 2,700 people, most of whom were listed as members of the Church of England but among whom were many dissenters from New England. Breynton's relations with the dissenters were cordial throughout his ministry. He learned German sufficiently well to be able to preach to the members of the little Dutch church in Halifax, and when they had no minister he served them as diligently as he did his own congregation at St Paul's. Both he and Wood extended their ministries beyond Halifax as far as Annapolis Royal. The expulsion of the Acadians in 1755 and the subsequent arrival of the New England planters opened up a further field for their missionary endeavours.

By 1769 Breynton was beginning to feel his work heavy on his shoulders. On 16 Jan. 1769 he wrote to the SPG requesting permission to visit England the following year, but it was not until 1771 that he was able to go. On 16 April of that year he was granted the degree of DD by Cambridge on the recommendation of influential friends in Nova Scotia. He returned to Halifax in 1772.

Writing to the SPG on 2 Jan. 1776, Breynton advised of "the breaking out of the Small Pox amongst us last Summer." "When that Distemper . . . began to Spread," he wrote, "I applied every Effort to promote Inocculation, preached a Sermon upon the Occasion and raised a Subscription towards Inocculating the Poor & I flatter myself I have been Instrumental in Saving Many Lives in this Province." The colony's difficulties were increased in 1776 by the unexpected influx of refugees who had accompanied Lieutenant-General Sir William Howe's troops from Boston. Their arrival placed a severe strain on the limited resources of the citizens of Halifax, and friction developed between the old and the new inhabitants. Breynton did all he could to reconcile the two factions, and he was especially helpful to the loyalist clergy. Jacob Bailey* was one of those who bore testimony to his kindness in letters to the SPG.

Physically worn out by his efforts, on 13 Jan. 1777 Breynton applied to the SPG for leave to go to England when peace was restored, but he was refused permission. After several subsequent requests he eventually left in the summer of 1785 and remained on leave of absence until 1789. It is stated that he had hopes of being nominated bishop of Nova Scotia, for which ambition he had many influential backers in the province. Disappointed in his hopes, since Charles Inglis* was named bishop in 1787, Breynton resigned his mission in 1789, and through the efforts of the SPG he applied for and received a pension from the Archbishop Tenison Fund. He was eventually replaced as rector of St Paul's by Robert Stanser*. During his years in Nova Scotia Breynton had held a number of offices and chaplaincies. As a result he has acquired a reputation for greed, but his various perquisites were not considered unusual at the time. It is not certain, moreover, that he had received any salary during the early years of his ministry.

Before his arrival in Halifax Breynton had married Elizabeth —, and they had seven or eight children. On 6 Sept. 1779, a year after his first wife's death, he married in Halifax Mary Cradock, the widow of Joseph GERRISH, and she accompanied him to England in 1785. At his death in London at age 80 Breynton was buried in the churchyard of St Mary's Church, Paddington Green.

C. E. THOMAS

National Library of Wales (Aberystwyth), Trefeglwys parish registers, 1695–1723, III, f.14. National Maritime Museum, RUSI/NM/137 a & b, List of chaplains of the Royal Navy, 1626–1916, by A. G. Kealy. PANS, RG 1, 19, no.16, Knowles to Newcastle, 8 July 1746. PRO, Adm. 6/6. University of Cambridge, Magdalene College (Cambridge, Eng.), admissions registers, no.3 (1716–1894), p.31. USPG, B, 20, pp.7, 25; 25, nos.135, 202, 212, 239; Journal of SPG, 12, p.136; 28, p.246 (mfm. at PANS).

Alumni Cantabrigienses . . . , comp. John and J. A. Venn (2 pts. in 10v., Cambridge, Eng., 1922–54), pt.I, I. R.V. Harris, *The Church of Saint Paul in Halifax, Nova Scotia: 1749–1949* (Toronto, 1949). C. F. Pascoe, *Two hundred years of the S.P.G.* . . . (2v., London, 1901). A. W. H. Eaton, "Old Boston families, number two: the family of Capt. John Gerrish," *New England Hist. and Geneal. Register*, LXVII (1913), 105–15.

BRIAND, JEAN-OLIVIER, Bishop of Quebec; b. 23 Jan. 1715 in the parish of Plérin (dept of Côtes-du-Nord), France; d. 25 June 1794 at Quebec.

Jean-Olivier Briand came from a humble peasant family of Saint-Éloi, a village in the parish of Plérin in Brittany. Early in this century Mgr

Henri Têtu* was able to see the little house, complete with thatched roof, in which he was born. He was the eldest of the five or six children of François Briand and Jeanne Burel; his godfather was an uncle on his father's side, Olivier Desbois, and his godmother an aunt on his mother's side, Jacquette Quémar. His father, who was born on 4 May 1688 and baptized the next day at Plérin, died around 1745; his mother, who apparently was born on 18 Jan. 1689, passed away at Plérin on 16 Sept. 1768 "at 80 years of age, less three or four months."

According to the "family record book" of Bishop Briand's sister, Catherine-Anne-Marie, who had been born on 20 May 1722 and who from 1779 to 1804 served as superior general of the Filles du Saint-Esprit in Plérin, a secular community she had joined on 27 Oct. 1742, François Briand and Jeanne Burel had "inspired" in their children "good manners . . . and above all the fear of God and the shunning of worldly things." The future bishop of Quebec was said to have had a kind, gentle, amiable, and patient father, "one of the most honourable men in Plérin"; this father loved and cherished his children, laboured and struggled for them, yet at the same time showed, as his wife did, great charity toward the poor, "especially widows and orphans, whose interests in the parish he had . . . at heart, never refusing [them] any pleasure within his means." Jean-Olivier never knew his maternal grandparents, Mathurin Burel and Jacquette Quémar, who had died young, but he did witness the devotion of his paternal grandfather, Yves Briand, and his grandmother, Jeanne Desbois, "both of whom virtually wore themselves out working to procure a comfortable situation and an honourable upbringing for their children."

Two priests from the diocese of Saint-Brieuc (to which Plérin belonged) were to influence Jean-Olivier's career. The first was his uncle, Jean-Joseph Briand, who was known as "a man of outstanding merit," and who was to be for many years the parish priest of Plérin, dying there on 20 April 1767 at the age of 80 years and two months. He imparted "the first principles of the sciences" to the young boy and guided him "in the path of virtue and knowledge of the saints." As he intended to enter the priesthood, young Briand, whose sister said that "he always did well at school," studied at the Séminaire de Saint-Brieuc; he was ordained priest in March 1739. Returning to his native parish, he became friendly with another priest, Abbé René-Jean Allenou* de Lavillangevin, who had been and perhaps still was the parish priest of Plérin, and with whom the Briand family seems to have had close ties. Abbé Lavillangevin was regarded – though inaccurately – as the founder of the Filles du Saint-Esprit; in fact the community had been established by his uncle, Abbé Jean Leuduger. In the late 1730s Catherine-Anne-Marie Briand was preparing to enter this community, where she would join Marie Allenou de Grandchamp and eventually succeed her as superior general; a Mlle Briand, a relative of the future bishop of Quebec, was to marry Mathurin Gaubert, who was related through his mother to Abbé Leuduger. It was Lavillangevin who "by his good advice and zeal" (notes Catherine-Anne-Marie Briand) "stole" Jean-Olivier Briand from his parents in 1741 "to make a good missionary of him" in Canada.

According to another version, which is not incompatible with the first, it was the appointed bishop of Quebec himself, Henri-Marie Dubreil* de Pontbriand, who made the appeal to Lavillangevin and Briand. In any event the two left Plérin on 11 May 1741 to embark at La Rochelle. Catherine-Anne-Marie Briand's account relates that Bishop Pontbriand had already appointed Lavillangevin vicar general and Briand a canon. Because, in her words, Briand was willing to go to Canada "only as a missionary priest," he relinquished his canonry when at La Rochelle, though he had to accept it once he was in Quebec. On 28 May Briand was still in France waiting to sail; he probably left on 8 June, since the *Rubis*, on which he travelled with the new bishop and the former parish priest of Plérin, cast anchor at Quebec on 30 August, after an 84-day crossing. Because Intendant HOCQUART had sent a boat to meet the ship, the bishop landed at Quebec on 29 August. Briand, from whom the bishop was never separated until his death, presumably accompanied him at that time.

On 31 August Briand took possession of his canonry. Thus began a long career in the service of the Canadian church, of which, following his severe test during the aftermath of the Seven Years' War, he would be proclaimed "the second founder." In the mean time, while serving as canon, treasurer of the chapter, and confessor of the nuns of the Hôtel-Dieu and the Hôpital Général, and as the person "responsible for the guidance of a host of young seminarists," Jean-Olivier Briand was also the secretary and confidant of his overburdened bishop. He accompanied Pontbriand on pastoral visits and virtually countersigned all of his pastoral letters, being in fact "his only resource." "For 17 years," Abbé de L'Isle-Dieu noted in 1757, Monsieur Briand has "never left" his bishop's side, and "without being absent from any canonical office, finds the way to be his worthy prelate's shadow." In 1752, for example, he went with

Bishop Pontbriand as far as the Iroquois mission of La Présentation (Oswegatchie; now Ogdensburg, N.Y.), more than 40 leagues from Montreal; and from May to November 1753 he stayed with him at Trois-Rivières while the Ursuline convent, which the bishop was personally raising from the ashes, was being rebuilt [*see* Marie-Françoise GUILLIMIN, *dite* de Saint-Antoine]. On these occasions the chapter was advised that the duties Briand was performing at the bishop's side excused him from his canonical offices, though he was to be considered present "so that he will not lose any of the benefits of his prebend."

Canon Briand was so adept at remaining in his bishop's shadow that for nearly 20 years he went virtually unnoticed; his timidity was such that he could not even preach; uninterested in intrigue and without personal ambition, he was a hard worker, a pious and devoted priest who was better acquainted with the situation of the Canadian church than anyone else and who had the most detailed knowledge of its administration. First his bishop, and then the diocesan chapter, turned to him when the Canadian church suddenly had to take up the greatest challenge in its history. Once he had entered the lists, this man who was the soul of humility and discretion was to become, in the words of a Quebec nun, "God's right-hand man."

On 1 July 1759, at the beginning of the siege of Quebec, Bishop Pontbriand, who was already ill, withdrew to Charlesbourg. On 13 and 14 July the Ursulines and the nuns of the Hôtel-Dieu took refuge at the Hôpital Général, where Briand, with the help of his colleague Charles-Régis Blaise Des Bergères de Rigauville, was bringing the rites of the church to the wounded, whose number and sufferings increased daily. The day of Montcalm*'s defeat on the Plains of Abraham, 13 September, Pontbriand appointed Briand vicar general of Quebec and then withdrew to Montreal with the French army. He also put him in charge of the three women's communities in the town, with the title of superior, and urged him to take up permanent residence in the Hôpital Général, where he had already been living for several months. It was from this institution on the banks of the Saint-Charles that throughout the winter Briand administered the section of the diocese fallen into enemy hands; at the same time he lavished attention night and day on the wounded, both French and British, who filled the hospital. In the spring of 1760 he watched with sorrow the first exchanges in the battle of Sainte-Foy, which took place "on a height opposite our house," as one of the nuns of the Hôpital Général recorded; "at the height of the action," she added, unable to restrain himself any longer, Briand betook himself to the battlefield, at the risk of his own life: "What made him take this decision, . . . he said, was that there were not enough chaplains to succour the dying. . . ."

While at the Hôpital Général Vicar General Briand also learned in close succession of Bishop Pontbriand's death in Montreal on 8 June 1760 and of the signing of the surrender of that town and all Canada on 8 September. The Canadian church found itself without a bishop at a moment when the political situation did not allow it to have any communication with France or to have a bishop sent out to Canada. Moreover, beside article 30 of the act of surrender of Montreal, which states that "If, by the treaty of peace, Canada should remain in the power of his British Majesty, his most Christian Majesty shall continue to name the Bishop of the colony, who shall always be of the Roman communion, and under whose authority the people shall exercise the Roman Religion," AMHERST had written: "Refused." Consequently, in September 1760 a long period of anxious, harrowing waiting began. Would Canada be restored to the king of France? If not, would it be possible to obtain from the British, who were so opposed to "popery," permission to bring in a bishop or to have one consecrated? Would the Catholic church not soon die in Canada for lack of priests?

According to the dispositions of the Council of Trent, during a vacancy in the episcopal see the administration of the diocese of Quebec fell by right to the chapter. But for some time the canons were prevented from meeting because of the restrictions placed on movements by the British. Since his letters of appointment as vicar general provided him with the necessary administrative powers, it was Briand who exercised ecclesiastical authority in the colony until the chapter was able to meet on 2 July 1760. Appointments were then made of three vicars general for Canada, and three for the distant parts of the colony. In the course of two other assemblies, Abbé de L'Isle-Dieu, who was living in Paris, was appointed vicar general for Louisiana and the Mississippi region (23 Sept. 1760) and Canon Joseph-Marie de LA CORNE de Chaptes vicar general for the diocese in France (30 Sept. 1760). Canon Briand, to whom was allocated the part of the diocese under the jurisdiction of the Government of Quebec, was also designated, according to Abbé de L'Isle-Dieu, to be "at the head and the first of the vicars general, the see being vacant." He was clearly going to play the leading role in this church without a bishop and acquire undoubted ascendancy over his colleagues, who consulted him eagerly.

For nearly a year, in administering his part of the diocese Briand as vicar general had had to take into account the presence of a political authority professing a religion still strongly opposed to that of the Canadians. The situation was delicate, as Briand was quite aware. From the beginning he adopted a moderate attitude, conciliatory in secondary matters, firm on what was essential, always respectful towards the new masters. It was an approach that would lead them little by little to serve the church, rather than to harm or simply ignore it. This timid man, in whom a historian of our times has seen only "a dullard," was on the contrary lively and sociable, and above all knew how to chase away "that fatal melancholy," as Abbé Joseph-Octave Plessis*, his secretary for ten years, said. In fact this Breton had a Norman's shrewdness, and towards the end of his life, when informing a correspondent of the consecration of the third coadjutor since the conquest, he would in a way admit it, laughing up his sleeve: ". . . for here I am with four bishops in Canada, where it was not possible, they said, to have any, and a little Daniel from Plérin in Saint-Brieuc overcame all the difficulties." (It was Daniel, prophet of the race of David, who through his talent for reading and interpreting dreams won the favour of the king of Babylon, without yielding to him in anything. . . .)

Briand's conduct with regard to the British authorities while he was vicar general and later bishop has been so little understood in our time that it must receive some attention. Right after the surrender of Quebec, Bishop Pontbriand had set forth the theological principles on which the Canadian church should order its conduct: "The Christian religion requires for victorious princes who have conquered a country all the obedience, the respect, that is owed to the others . . ."; "The king of England now being, through conquest, the sovereign of Quebec, all the feelings of which the apostle St Paul speaks are due him [Rom. 13: 1-7]." "One must beware of falling out with the governor, to avoid greater difficulties . . . ," he wrote to Briand. Pontbriand recommended his vicar general to James MURRAY, assuring him that he "will share my views." Moreover, Abbé de L'Isle-Dieu in Paris, and Rome itself, in turn urged upon the Canadians not only respect and submission, but also circumspection and tact: ". . . it will be necessary," wrote Cardinal Castelli in 1766, "that the ecclesiastics and the bishop of Canada conduct themselves with all possible prudence and discretion, in order not to cause the government any jealousy in state matters"; and, he added, "that they sincerely forget in this respect that they are French." All of these statements conformed with Catholic theology; from them, Briand was to derive for the Canadian church the greatest – and the most unpredictable – benefits.

Since the king of England was the new sovereign of Canadian Catholics, the church had to recognize and treat him as such. This duty Briand did not hesitate to call to mind, in both his pastoral letters and his correspondence. After some indecision he even decided to have King George's name mentioned in the prayers in the mass, despite the protestations of certain members of the clergy: "I have not allowed anyone to give me as a reason that it is very hard to pray for one's enemies. . . . They are our masters, and we owe them what we owed the French when they were our masters. Does the church now forbid his subjects to pray for their prince?" The theological basis was sound, and the reasoning flawless. Briand, who did not lack psychological insight (to the point of maintaining excellent relations with all the governors in his time), understood that to gain the new masters' goodwill it was necessary to interest them in the life of the church; to this end some unimportant interference had to be tolerated at the beginning, the better to oppose any more serious attempt to bring the church into tutelage. Consequently he let Murray intervene on a few occasions with certain parish priests and gave in for the time being to his demands regarding appointments to parishes; he even consulted him on occasion, and once he went so far as to appeal to the British secular arm. A close consideration of the situation reveals that his conduct could not have been more skilful: soon Murray would make no decisions concerning parish priests and religious matters without first speaking to the vicar general, and would, moreover, interest himself only in questions of discipline, interfering in no way with worship or religious teaching. In 1765 a nun at the Hôpital Général could record that Briand had "been able to maintain his rights and those of his parish priests, without ever encountering obstacles" from the British. Things were on the right track.

Briand was trying to get the British authorities in Canada – and also his clergy and people – to recognize the existence of two distinct jurisdictions: the religious, which came under the ecclesiastical authority, and the civil, which came under the political authority. According to the accepted concepts of his time, the ecclesiastical and the political powers had obligations towards one another, but Briand wanted them exercised on each side without interference. It is in this light that one must read the following extract from a letter he wrote, probably in 1762, to James ABERCROMBIE: "I beg you, Sir, to continue your protection to the church; I would almost dare to tell you that you are obliged to do so, just as the church is obliged to hold you in high esteem. *Non enim sine causa gladium portat* ["for he beareth not the sword in vain"], St Paul tells us in speaking of the secular power, which must lend itself to the support of religion, as the ecclesiastical power [must lend itself] to making peoples render the respect and obedience that they owe princes and superiors." In order to counter any attempted encroachment and maintain good relations with the civil authority, Briand applied two "principles," which are known to us because they were noted down by Bishop Plessis, his former secretary; these were on the one hand "to handle all his affairs with the governor himself, without having any of the subaltern officers intervene in them," and on the other hand "on every occasion to take the government's interests very much to heart, to declare very great loyalty towards the king, and to inspire the same loyalty in his clergy." Consequently it was a bitter experience for him to see priests and some of the faithful occasionally take their religious quarrels to the civil authorities, when the latter, as he observed in 1769, "refer all ecclesiastical matters to me."

In all these proceedings Briand showed no dull-wittedness, and even less weakness of character. Writing to Guy Carleton* himself in 1784, he noted that some had thought he had acted as he did in certain recent circumstances "through fear of the governor. Oh no! Never in my life have I feared any man." His meaning was plain: I fear no one, not even you. He immediately added humorously (he was capable of it): "I even blame myself, now when I am at death's door, for not having feared God and my dread Judge enough." The man who wrote this was neither easily taken in nor weak. At the time when Murray was venturing to intervene in parish charges, Briand wrote: "I had the honour to say to him that neither I nor the Pope himself could do anything about refusing, delaying, or granting absolution, because penitence was a secret and inner court whose judge had to render accounts to God alone." In every circumstance he was able to assert the fundamental rights of the church and make them respected, without ever reaching the stage of confrontation. The secret of his strength – and of his success – he revealed in a letter to his sister in 1782: the British "continue to show me marks of real esteem," he wrote, because they "are aware of my frankness and my sincerity" and know "that my conscience and duty are well above any other consideration."

It is futile, then, to look for complications and to suggest that Briand's poverty and timidity explain why he became "the candidate of Murray" – who liked his candour, moderation, and delicacy – when steps were being taken following the colony's permanent cession to Britain to give the Canadian church a bishop again. Vicar General Étienne MONTGOLFIER, the candidate chosen by the chapter on 15 Sept. 1763, was checkmated by Murray and withdrew on 9 Sept. 1764 in favour of Briand, who observed that he himself had "the approval of the clergy and people and the most obvious protection of the political government." The canons gathered at the Hôpital Général of Quebec on 11 September and unanimously agreed to elect Briand and put his name forward for the bishopric of Quebec. Although he felt "extreme repugnance" for the "burden" being thrust on him, fearing it "more than death," Briand understood nevertheless that he must not think of himself, but of the future of the church in Canada. He sailed for England almost immediately in order to "press for his high office" there. He had the recommendations of Murray, who had even exerted himself to get support for him, but the circumstances prevailing in London were scarcely favourable. The apostate Jesuit Pierre-Joseph-Antoine ROUBAUD had prejudiced people against the Canadian clergy; then the fall of the ministry in 1765 further complicated the situation; finally, even though there was general willingness to give Canada a bishop, no one knew how to do it without violating the laws of Great Britain. Briand was given to understand in ministerial circles that he had only to go to France and have himself consecrated there, and people would shut their eyes provided he contented himself with the title of "superintendent of the Catholic church in Canada." In December 1765, after a 13-month stay in London, Briand left for France on the official pretext of going to visit his mother in Brittany.

If it is true that in 1741, fearing his courage would fail, Abbé Briand had left Plérin secretly without saying goodbye to his parents and with only his breviary as luggage, the joy of reunion in Saint-Éloi on 19 Dec. 1765 can easily be imagined. Later recalling the scene to her mother, Catherine-Anne-Marie portrayed her brother's feelings during the few weeks he spent with his family: "I shall never forget the joy, the pleasure, the affection with which you embraced each other and all of us, brothers and sisters. We found him just the same as ever, a good son, a good brother, gentle, meek, . . . humbling himself and recognizing his unworthiness, scorning honours and dignities, without any ambition for wealth; and had he not feared opposing God's designs, he would have preferred . . . [to] remain hidden and unknown in his little family." He was, however, obliged to leave: farewells were said at Saint-Brieuc on 23 Jan. 1766, on Abbé Briand's 51st birthday. Before leaving his mother for ever – she "was ill because of it" – he ordered a large stone house to be built for her at his expense, near the cottage where he had been born; over its door was engraved the inscription: "Jean-Olivier Briand, bishop of Quebec, 1766."

Meanwhile, on 21 January, "after receiving from various sources . . . firm testimonials to his excellent qualities," Pope Clement XIII had signed the bull appointing Briand bishop of Quebec. It was on 16 March 1766, the anniversary of his first mass (a fact he drew to the attention of his mother), that he was quietly consecrated. The ceremony was performed, with the permission of the archbishop of Paris, in the private oratory of Mme Meny (born Marie-Madeleine Péan) at Suresnes (dept of Hauts-de-Seine) by the bishop of Blois, Charles-Gilbert Demay de Termont, assisted by the bishops of Rodez and Saintes. Leaving Paris on 21 March, Bishop Briand returned to London, received permission to return to Canada, took the oath of loyalty to the king, and sailed soon after, on 1 May, the day he thanked the bishop of Orléans for a gratuity of 3,000 *livres* granted him. On his arrival at Quebec on 28 June the new bishop was welcomed with a great display of joy from both Canadians and British. And on 19 July the seventh bishop of Quebec took possession of his see, in the chapel of the Séminaire de Québec.

Although the survival of the priesthood seemed assured in Canada for the time being, the church's situation nonetheless remained a constant source of worry for the bishop of Quebec. Besides the ever present danger that the civil authority's attitude to the clergy would harden, Briand had reason to fear that whatever he did the church might continue to grow weaker "imperceptibly . . . day by day," as he remarked in 1769. The war had left much ruin and distress: the parish church of Quebec, the bishop's palace, and numerous country churches had been destroyed; the habitants were impoverished, certain women's religious communities were in desperate straits because of their debts, and the diocese itself was deprived both of the revenues which had previously served mainly for the canons' upkeep and of the gratuities which the king of France used to pay annually "to the poor parishes." The number of priests had greatly decreased (180 in 1758, 138 in July 1766); Britain refused to permit the Jesuits and Recollets to recruit new members and would not allow French priests to come to Canada [*see* Jean-Baptiste-Amable ADHÉMAR]; hence in 1774 the bishop would note that "since I have been back, I have created 25 priests; 32 have died, and two are no longer serving," and that despite 90 ordinations under his episcopate, 75 parishes, it was said, would find themselves without a priest by 1783.

In addition, since the conquest the populace was no longer quite the same: "People's hearts have been disturbed during the troubles of the war," Briand remarked, observing that there was much "to improve" in the Canadians. There had been deplorable scandals throughout the country. Even more frequently, quarrels that sometimes verged on open rebellion against the parish priest or the bishop had erupted over the ministry or the site of a church, the building of a presbytery, or the payment of tithes; some churchwardens carried the spirit of independence to the point of wanting to run everything and were insolent with the bishop: "This is a terrible time where churchwardens are concerned," groaned Briand. And he complained that "the good Canadians want to organize the church's affairs themselves; they know more about religion and God's affairs than do the priests and the bishop." On the strength of his episcopal authority he warned, begged, threatened, and if pushed to the limit, excommunicated, while being ready to pardon at the slightest sign of repentance. In letters to his priests he occasionally judged too harshly the flock whom, he said, "I thought I knew," and no longer recognized; "the Catholics reject me"; "a very great number . . . declare their Christianity with their words but . . . contradict it with their behaviour, and have abjured it in mind and heart"; "if they do not change, religion will be lost in the colony." There was certainly some exaggeration in all of this; but it shows, more than anything, exasperation – which admittedly was not entirely unjustified. "Ah, my goodness! What a terrible pace: I should prefer being parish priest at Baie Saint-Paul or Kamouraska," he wrote to Vicar General Étienne MARCHAND in 1767. Seven or eight years later, after two pastoral visits of his diocese (1767–68 and 1771–73), and less harassed by the problems that had tormented his early years, the bishop would take a more serene view of his beloved Canadians: "Doubtless there are some bad Christians, there is licence, there is dissoluteness, but I do not think that there is as much as there was 15 or 20 years ago; and I am not without consolation on that score."

His priests had also felt the effects of the uncertainties born of war and conquest; particularly before he became bishop, during the military occupation, some of them had caused him many annoyances. This was not true of all of them, but to all he wrote letters that were often admirable and always frank and straightforward. He congratulated some, blamed others, exhorted them all, recalling to mind the "great perfection which . . . is so strongly recommended" to "a true priest," condemning the "passion for the easy life and all that ensues from it," and criticizing severely the various sorts of conduct apt "to give the English ideas . . . of an unfavourable nature about the clergy." He spoke of the need for gentleness, wanting his priests to live in harmony with their parishioners and act with moderation so as not to irritate them. It was necessary, of course, to "thunder" against licence, but "gently"; in sermons it was necessary to avoid "invectives" and to talk more "of virtue than of the ugliness of vice"; sinners were not to be rebuffed, but received with kindness. In many respects Briand seems to have been ahead of his time. "It is not always best to attack vices and abuses head-on," he wrote to one parish priest, "but it is good to take a roundabout way. It is better for sinners to say to themselves that they are sinners than for us to tell them ourselves or give them occasion to think that we belive they are." In 1766, discussing the departure of two nuns from their convent, he asserted to his vicar general that "at present we must not be too rigid on certain occasions: formerly that could work. Today things have changed, you know." And again it was he who decided in 1770 that no one must be forced to contribute to the building of a church, enunciating the lofty principle that "the building of a church is not a corvée; it is a religious act. . . ."

When he had had to reproach his priests, Vicar General Briand liked to call a spade a spade: "If I speak frankly and as I think, I shall tell you some truths that will grieve you. If I dissemble, I shall distress my own sincere and honest nature. Would it be more suitable to say nothing and to reply, as people say, like a Norman [equivocally]? A Breton, and perhaps a Christian, much less still a priest and fellow religious, even less a vicar general . . . must not conceal the truth." Nevertheless the Breton was sometimes a little harsh. Observing that he had not been aware of the faults of which a parish priest was accused, he told him, "I knew only that you were lazy or a sluggard." He bluntly called the parish priest of Quebec, Jean-Félix Récher*, an ignoramus. To another whom he removed from the ministry he said: "I love good priests, but those who are disobedient to their superiors, who recognize no chief, . . . who respect no rules, no canons of the church, and who act as they please, will never find favour with me." The storm past, he concluded his letters in a general manner by saying that, if he was severe, it was the better to bring his correspondent back to his duty, and that in this case he would forget all he had to reproach him for; or again, that he was acting only for the priest's good and retained every friendly feeling for him. In 1774 Briand told parish priest Pierre-Antoine PORLIER, with whom he had a dispute, of his intention to see him become parish priest of Quebec, and even a canon: "Despite all that you have done, written, and said against me, my heart has not changed, and feels the same way towards you as it did 25 years ago." All of which goes to show that Plessis, who had known him so well, was right in calling Briand "an intelligent man with character."

Briand perhaps never encountered a greater challenge in his own entourage than at the beginning of his episcopate. The strongest and most sustained opposition, as well as the longest, came from Jean-Félix Récher and his churchwardens and concerned the status of the church of Notre-Dame in Quebec, which had been destroyed during bombardments in 1759. Briand wanted it to be his cathedral, as it had been for his predecessors; the priest and churchwardens were willing to rebuild it, but on condition that it would serve solely for parish worship. Both sides, in seeking to impose their views, based themselves on long-standing rights. Reconstruction began slowly in 1767. Father Récher died in 1768, and the Séminaire de Québec relinquished the parish rights to which it could lay claim. The churchwardens did not relent, however, supported as they were from then on by two members of the seminary, Henri-François Gravé* de La Rive and Joseph-André-Mathurin JACRAU, who even became their lawyer in the matter. The church, which was nearing completion, was opened for worship in 1771. Bishop Briand, having vainly attempted to reach an agreement with the churchwardens, announced that he would not play his opponents' game by going to court; he would continue to celebrate mass in the chapel of the seminary, choosing it as his cathedral church, and he would abstain from celebrating mass or even from making an appearance in the parish while his rights were unrecognized. Carried on by their momentum, and despite Jacrau's death, the churchwardens wrote to Rome against their bishop. But resolution of the affair came from Quebec, in 1774, through the mediation of Lieutenant Governor Hector Theophilus CRAMAHÉ.

Cathedral church or parish church? "Cathedral church *and* parish church," it was decided. The compromise was a diplomatic one, and for the bishop's entry into his cathedral, on the eighth anniversary of his consecration, a "great ceremony" was held.

The pressure he was under in 1767 and 1768 was so great, and his love of peace was so confounded by it, that Bishop Briand thought of resigning as soon as he had chosen a coadjutor, especially since he felt he had little talent for either preaching or administering the diocese. Vicar General Marchand, to whom he had unburdened himself, tried to dissuade him; he commented further that "before being bishop you could not preach, today you easily surmount the timidity that until then you had not overcome, [and] you speak to your people with grace, with vigour, with ardour, and with persuasive eloquence." In any event, the bishop had to appoint a coadjutor to assist him. At his request Rome had authorized him in 1766 to choose the coadjutor himself, *cum futura successione* (with right of succession), and to present him to the sovereign pontiff. He asked Carleton's permission to go ahead; the lieutenant-governor hesitated to take a decision, did not give his consent until 1770, and then proposed Abbé Louis-Philippe Mariauchau d'Esgly, who was five years older than Briand. Briand did not think he should object to this choice since the candidate was "a good priest." The essential thing was that there should be a second bishop, and a worthy one; it was also important to set a precedent: "It meant a great deal to set the pattern," Briand himself remarked. The bishop has been accused rather casually of weakness on this occasion. To enter into discussions would have delayed a matter that Carleton had already let drag on for four years and would perhaps have compromised it, since the governor was on the point of sailing for London. Carleton's fear "that another governor may not be as kind to us," as Briand noted, and the very imminence of his departure led him to ask the bishop to consecrate Abbé d'Esgly "as soon as he [Carleton] had given his consent," without waiting for the required bulls. "I had to put up with a bit of a storm," wrote Briand (relatives of the coadjutor had got involved), "but I held firm, and gave such evident proof of the rightness of my refusal, that now all is quiet." Having once more saved the essential, the bishop wrote to the apostolic nuncio in Paris to present Abbé d'Esgly to him. The bulls were slow in arriving: it was on 12 July 1772, in the chapel of the seminary, that Bishop Briand consecrated the man who was to be his successor; to make the proclamation and confer the powers of office, he waited for the day of his solemn entry into his cathedral, 16 March 1774.

The year 1774 had been a particularly successful one for Briand. He had ceremonially taken possession of his cathedral and proclaimed his coadjutor; peace had returned to Quebec, and the bishop was not displeased with his flock; vicars general represented him in all parts of his immense diocese; more than 25 new parishes had been created since 1766, and an almost equal number of priests had been ordained. Had it not been for the cathedral chapter, whose authorities were never willing to agree to let him fill vacancies and which was itself to be doomed to extinction, Briand could have considered his work finished and carried out his plans to resign. Because of his coadjutor's age the bishop was kept from "laying down his charge" and "living in the retirement" to which he had always aspired.

But the American revolution broke out. Soon there was talk of an imminent invasion of Canada, and already rebel agents were urging the Canadians to revolt. Briand, who according to Plessis "had as a maxim that the only true Christians and sincere Catholics are subjects obedient to their lawful sovereign," urged his faithful to repulse the invaders and issued a pastoral letter supporting Carleton's proclamation concerning the re-establishment of the militia; he reminded his priests of their duty, founded on the teaching of the Gospel and of St Paul, and against those habitants collaborating with the enemy he had recourse to the punishments of the church, which could no longer recognize them as its children. Constantly and in all things he was faithful to authority and to the oath he had sworn to the king. The Canadians, who still retained painful memories of the war of the conquest, had not all resisted the desire to take vengeance on England; many did not understand the position taken by their bishop and the great majority of the priests. Exhorting, begging, threatening, and acting with severity, Briand suffered greatly from the obstinacy of this part of his flock – a tiny minority, in fact. Calm was slow in returning, and in certain parishes there was no rush to make peace with the church. The bishop was scarred by this. It has even been claimed that he was never afterwards able to bring himself to undertake a new pastoral visit of his diocese. But perhaps the state of his health no longer allowed him to do so.

Before becoming bishop, Briand had twice been sick, in 1750 and again in 1757, the second time rather seriously it seems. In 1770 he wrote his sister that during his pastoral visit he had not realized his strength had diminished; moreover, sciatica was making him suffer, "particularly in the morning." This malady grew worse as the years went by. In the descriptions of it, gout was also mentioned. When he had an attack, he had trouble with his chest and arms and was completely prevented from engaging in any activity. In 1784 he himself would tell Carleton that for more than eight months he had been unable to do more than write his name. "Three lines without a pause bring me pain that I can hardly bear," he added. The previous year the doctors had considered his illness "rather serious." It was also said that he was suffering from "a violent illness that the doctors call spasms"; in addition he had "a stubborn catarrh with all the symptoms of tympanitis," according to Bishop d'Esgly. Probably these illnesses, from which he was already suffering at the period of the American invasion, rather than bitterness, explain why he did not begin a third visit of his diocese. However that may be, judging himself to be on the verge of death, and seeing that his coadjutor was very old, he resigned on 29 Nov. 1784, to allow d'Esgly to consecrate a younger bishop. In retirement, being "no longer fit for anything but prayer," he took no part in the administration of the diocese except to give explanations and advice when asked, even though Bishop d'Esgly had appointed him vicar general on 2 Dec. 1784 and continued to accord him episcopal powers. He intervened only once, writing a fatherly rebuke to the impetuous coadjutor, Bishop Jean-François HUBERT. Having made his will on 22 March 1791, Briand died at the Séminaire de Québec on 25 June 1794, at the age of 79. Two days later, on 27 June, Plessis pronounced his funeral oration during the ceremonies in the cathedral of Quebec.

Of this truly humble priest, who was bishop against his own wishes and whose portrait has slowly emerged in this biography, we should remember two characteristic traits: his spirit of poverty and his faith in Providence. To his mother, his brothers and sisters, his sister Catherine-Anne-Marie, and his priests, he expressed the scorn that one must have for wealth – and that he himself had in the highest degree. By his own admission "born without wealth and given an honourable office without income," he lived, as Carleton noted, "in a poor little apartment in the seminary" and ate "at the common table"; he had just one secretary, sometimes employed only part-time, and a footman. Again, he had "neither coach, nor sleigh, nor horse"; he "wore many a cassock turned inside out" and had "not a morsel of bread or a glass of wine to offer a friend." "I am very fortunate," he observed, "that I am given my keep at the seminary." He refused, however, to request the help of the people in his diocese for the "restoration" of the bishop's palace, which was in ruins, and forbad a collection to be taken for the bishop. In his will he asked that after his death the crozier he had always used be returned to the Séminaire de Montréal, to which it belonged. At the time of his death the *Quebec Gazette* praised his moral virtues, both Christian and social, recalling "the abundant alms that he distributed among the poor."

He had told his sister that he feared "neither life, nor death, nor poverty," and that he had never been afraid of "lacking" anything whatsoever: in everything he put himself in the hands of Providence, "whose conduct is very often all the more merciful in that it agrees less with our desires and flatters our hopes less." This profound faith probably explains many of his attitudes: "I have always thought," he once wrote, "that obstacles came from God, and that He would put an end to them Himself." And in 1768 he told his vicar general, "It is up to the Lord who has put me [at the head of the diocese], unworthy though I am, to settle everything. I want only what He wants, and I hope that He will settle everything. People whisper to me, people push me, but I shall act only as favourable circumstances are presented to me by Providence."

Bishop Briand, who had a thorough knowledge of the last 20 years of the French régime, indirectly passed judgement on his own career and work when he told his secretary, Plessis, that "under the British government the Catholic clergy and the rural populace enjoyed more liberty than they had been accorded before the conquest." He would not have been contradicted by the Anglican bishop of Quebec, Jacob Mountain*; having arrived a year before Briand's death, Mountain complained a few years later that his Catholic counterpart "disposes as he sees fit of all the curacies in the diocese, sets up parishes, grants special permission for marriages as he wishes, and carries out freely all those duties that the king's instructions refuse him and that the Protestant bishop has never performed."

ANDRÉ VACHON

The AAQ holds most of the documents concerning Bishop Briand. Two of his letters have been published in *BRH*, XXI (1915), 122, 128.

PAC, MG 11, [CO 42], Q, 1–47; MG 23, GII, 1. [C.-A.-M. Briand], "Livre de raison de Mlle Briand, sœur de Mgr Briand, premier évêque de Québec sous la puissance anglaise," ANQ *Rapport*, 1946–47, 57–79. *Doc. relatifs à l'hist. constitutionnelle, 1759–91*, (Shortt et Doughty; 1921). La Rue, "Lettres et mémoires," ANQ *Rapport*, 1935–36; 1936–37;

1937–38. [M.-J. Legardeur de Repentigny, dite de la Visitation], "Relation de ce qui s'est passé au siège de Québec, et de la prise du Canada . . . ," *Le siège de Québec en 1759 par trois témoins*, J.-C. Hébert, édit., (Québec, 1972), 11–31. *Mandements des évêques de Québec* (Têtu et Gagnon), II, 160–63, 166, 168–71, 174–79, 185–309. J.-O. Plessis, "L'oraison funèbre de Mgr Briand," *BRH*, XI (1905), 321–38, 353–58. J.-F. Récher, *Journal du siège de Québec en 1759* (Québec, 1959). Desrosiers, "Corr. de cinq vicaires généraux," ANQ *Rapport*, 1947–48. Henri Têtu, *Notices biographiques: les évêques de Québec* (Québec, 1889), 259–355.

Brunet, *Les Canadiens après la Conquête*. Burke, *Les ursulines de Québec* (1863–66). [J.-B.-A.] Ferland, *Mgr Joseph-Octave Plessis, évêque de Québec* (Québec, 1878). A.-H. Gosselin, *L'Église du Canada après la Conquête; L'Église du Canada jusqu'à la Conquête*, III. Laval Laurent, *Québec et l'Église aux États-Unis sous Mgr Briand et Mgr Plessis* (Montréal, 1945). O'Reilly, *Mgr de Saint-Vallier et l'Hôpital Général*. Hermann Plante, *L'Église catholique au Canada (1604–1886)* (Trois-Rivières, 1970). Marcel Trudel, *L'Église canadienne; Louis XVI, le Congrès américain et le Canada, 1774–1789* (Québec, [1949]). Ivanhoë Caron, "La nomination des évêques catholiques de Québec sous le Régime anglais," RSC *Trans.*, 3rd ser., XXVI (1932), sect.I, 1–44. Fernand Combaluzier, "Le sacre de Mgr Briand à Suresnes," *BRH*, XLVI (1940), 3–9. Lionel Groulx, "Le conflit religieux au lendemain de 1760," SCHÉC *Rapport*, 7 (1939–40), 11–26. Arthur Maheux, "Difficultés religieuses après la cession," SCHÉC *Rapport*, 14 (1946–47), 11–24; "Notes sur Roubaud et sur sa responsabilité dans la nomination de M. Briand comme évêque de Québec," SCHÉC *Rapport*, 6 (1938–39), 45–60. "Mgr Briand et les rebelles de 1775," *BRH*, XLV (1939), 286. Fernand Ouellet, "Mgr Plessis et la naissance d'une bourgeoisie canadienne (1797–1810)," SCHÉC *Rapport*, 23 (1955–56), 83–99. Henri Têtu, "Souvenirs d'un voyage en Bretagne," *BRH*, XVII (1911), 130–40, 161–69, 197–202. Marcel Trudel, "Pourquoi Briand fut-il le candidat de Murray?" *RHAF*, VIII (1954–55), 463–95; "La servitude de l'Église catholique du Canada français sous le Régime anglais," SCHÉC *Rapport*, 30 (1963), 11–33.

BROOKE, FRANCES. *See* MOORE

BROOKE, JOHN, Church of England clergyman; b. *c.* 1709 probably in Norfolk, England; d. 21 Jan. 1789 at Colney, Norfolk.

Nothing is known with certainty of John Brooke's early life and education. He was ordained priest on 17 June 1733 and between 1733 and 1746 became rector or perpetual curate of five parishes in and around Norwich, England, all but one of which he held until his death. In 1756 he married Frances MOORE, already a prominent literary figure; they were to have a son and probably a daughter. Brooke was appointed acting chaplain in the British army in February 1757 and arrived in North America later that year. He was deputy chaplain in the 22nd Foot for one year and garrison chaplain at Louisbourg, Cape Breton Island, from August 1758 to July 1760, when he came to Quebec. In December Governor MURRAY, who was a personal friend of 20 years, unofficially appointed him minister of the town, served until then by Jean-Michel Houdin*, and chaplain to the garrison. He was formally commissioned garrison chaplain on 28 Oct. 1761, by which time he was also chaplain to the Royal Americans (60th Foot). In August 1761 about 100 civil officers and merchants in Quebec had petitioned the Society for the Propagation of the Gospel to appoint Brooke its missionary at Quebec with a French-language assistant.

After Brooke became unofficial minister for the town, Church of England services, which had been celebrated in the Ursuline chapel from September 1759 until the summer of 1760, were held in the Recollet church following the Roman Catholic service. Neither Brooke nor the Roman Catholic Church appreciated the arrangement; Brooke, in fact, considered it a humiliation for the state religion. Brooke's social role as minister prompted him to promote the establishment of Protestant education and the introduction of smallpox vaccination. In January 1764 he was chosen by the absentee auditor general, Robert Cholmondeley, as his deputy at Quebec. Murray reported to London in October the presence of 144 Protestant householders, Church of England and dissenters, in the town; the following month about 80 people repeated the petition of 1761 to the SPG. Murray officially supported the petition, but unofficially he began to criticize Brooke. To the SPG he regretted that Brooke did not understand French. To Cholmondeley he complained that Brooke "cannot govern his tongue and will perpetually interfere with things that do not concern him . . . ; Brookes certainly is an honest man and a man of parts, he is very well informed too and when passion does not interfere is a most agreeable companion [but] his sprightly imagination makes him . . . frequently forget that he wears Black. . . ."

Although Brooke, as garrison chaplain and unofficial minister of the town, was expected by Murray to be a peacemaker in the agitated relations between civilians and the military in the colony [*see* Thomas WALKER; Pierre DU CALVET], his meddlesome and prickly nature and his good relations with the merchants, the military's most persistent critics, so provoked the garrison as to limit his value as a chaplain. Particularly galling was his appearance on behalf of the merchant George Allsopp*, who, charged with failure to carry a light after dark as required by law, had brought a suit for brutality against the two soldiers responsible for his arrest. Murray himself was probably angered most by Brooke's friendship with Allsopp, the governor's obstreperous political opponent. Indeed in July 1765 Murray identified Brooke to the Earl of Hillsborough, secretary of state for the American Colonies, as a member of a cabal seeking to have him replaced; it was composed mainly of merchants who, unlike the more patient governor, sought the colony's rapid anglicization and protestantization in order to facilitate integration into Britain's political and economic empire.

Murray was succeeded in July 1766 by Guy Carleton*, who tended at first to sympathize with the merchants. Brooke became friendly with the new lieutenant governor and with his Huguenot attorney general, Francis Maseres*. Maseres to begin with found Brooke "a very sensible and agreeable companion," but shortly after wrote that, although Brooke was a fine minister, he was also "rather too warm in his Temper which hurries him now and then into indiscreet Expressions." Adam MABANE of the French party, which opposed the merchants' aspirations, was considerably more critical than Maseres of Brooke's conduct as minister: "The Church is . . . made instrumental in the good Cause," he complained, "Brookes in his sermons declaims in the praise of ye Lt. Governor & C. Justice [William HEY], (who by ye by are always present) . . . ." Carleton and Maseres soon parted ways as the former came to realize the necessity of Murray's policy of conciliation with the Roman Catholic Church while Maseres, strongly anti-Catholic, allied himself with the merchants. Brooke was caught in the middle when in the summer of 1767 Leger-Jean-Baptiste-Noël VEYSSIÈRE, a Recollet and parish priest converted to Protestantism, presented himself to the garrison chaplain to take the oath of abjuration, his first step towards the ministry. Maseres supported Veyssière, but Carleton was unwilling to see the convert become a minister in the colony. Maseres broke off all relations with Brooke when he learned that "in a low and foolish piece of flattery to General Carleton" the chaplain had refused to administer the oath to Veyssière, although before he became aware of Carleton's fears "he used to wish and intend that this convert should officiate. . . ."

But if Veyssière had been temporarily hindered by Brooke, it was the latter whose future was cloudier. The two petitions in favour of Brooke's appointment as an SPG missionary at Quebec were never granted, the SPG alleging insufficient funds. Brooke continued his unofficial ministry until 1768, even travelling back and forth between Montreal and Quebec for six months in 1766 until the arrival of David CHABRAND Delisle as Protestant chaplain in Montreal. In July 1768 he auctioned off the household belongings. Some of these indicate that he and his wife Frances, who had come to Quebec in 1763, lived comfortably; their home, a former Jesuit mission house at Mount Pleasant in Sillery, had been sublet to them by George Allsopp's father-in-law, the merchant John Taylor Bondfield. In August 1768 the Brookes left for England, a couple of months after the arrival of David-François De Montmollin* as the French-language assistant requested by Quebec's Protestants since 1761.

Carleton took advantage of Brooke's departure to send with him a letter explaining the lieutenant governor's ecclesiastical policy to Richard Terrick, bishop of London, who was responsible for the church in the colonies. Brooke was personally to give the bishop "very ample Information on the State of Religion in this Country." Carleton recommended the chaplain to Terrick, and regretted that, after serving eight years as minister at Quebec without any allowance, Brooke should find himself "dispossessed." Brooke, however, despite his absence from Quebec, drew full pay as garrison chaplain until his death.

Little is known of Brooke after his return to England, although he seems to have resumed his Norfolk posts. When George Allsopp was in London on business in 1785 he met the Brookes there. In 1769, a year after their return, Frances published in London *The history of Emily Montague . . .*, an epistolary novel, much of which was set in Canada. Émile Castonguay has speculated that John Brooke actually wrote the letters of one of the novel's characters, Sir William Fermor. Frances' dedication of the novel to Carleton, her husband's patron, as well as John's vocation and longer experience in the colony, would make it reasonable to speculate that, at the very least, John contributed substantially to the comments on religion, politics, and the character of the Canadians which predominated in Fermor's letters.

John Brooke died at Colney on 21 Jan. 1789. His eight years in Quebec left no lasting impression, and he is now all but forgotten. He represents, however, that group of clergy, all chaplains, who served as a stopgap while the Church of England pondered the best pastoral approach to a colonial population almost entirely French speaking and Roman Catholic, but onto which had been grafted a minuscule, religiously diverse, and fractious band of British and French Protestant merchants, office-holders, and soliders. Although his own unclerically febrile temperament and Murray's well-placed censures no doubt hurt Brooke's chances of remaining in Canada, it was the church's decision that a French-language clergy would best serve its cause which ultimately displaced Brooke and other British chaplains.

JAMES H. LAMBERT

AUQ, Journal, 2, avril–mai, août–sept. 1767; Livre des entrées et sorties des pensionnaires, 1766. Lambeth Palace Library (London), Fulham papers, 1, ff.108–12, 165–67. Norfolk and Norwich Record Office (Norwich, Eng.), VSC/8 Bk.20; VSC/9. PAC, MG 23, A4, 14, p.26; 16, pp.106, 117–18; GIII, 1, 2, pp.45–46, 182, 184–85, 226–27; 3, p.243; RG 1, L3[L], pp.24733–37; RG 68, 93, pp.8–9, 12–24; 190, p.57. PRO, CO 42/25, ff.195–96. QDA, 82 (D-1), 1 Sept. 1761, [1 Nov. 1764]. USPG, C/CAN/Que, I, 29 Aug., 1 Sept. 1761, 1 Nov. 1764; Journal of SPG, 15, pp.164–65; 16, pp.280–82 (copies at PAC).

Gentleman's Magazine, 1789, 90. Maseres, *Maseres letters* (Wallace), 25, 46, 57, 80. [Frances Moore (Brooke)], *The history of Emily Montague, by the author of Lady Julia Mandeville*, intro. L. J. Burpee (Ottawa, 1931). *Quebec Gazette*, 9 April 1765, 22 Sept. 1766, 7, 14 July 1768. *Alumni Cantabrigienses* . . . , comp. John and J. A. Venn (2 pts. in 10v., Cambridge, Eng., 1922–54), pt.I, I, 226. Kelley, "Church and state papers," ANQ *Rapport*, 1948–49, 301–16. André Bernier, *Le Vieux-Sillery* ([Québec], 1977), 21–22. Bernard Dufebvre [Émile Castonguay], *Cinq femmes et nous* (Québec, 1950), 30. H. C. Stuart, *The Church of England in Canada, 1759–1793; from the conquest to the establishment of the see of Quebec* (Montreal, 1893), 8–9, 12, 16–20, 25. C. S. Blue, "Canada's first novelist," *Canadian Magazine* (Toronto), LVIII (1921–22), 3–12. A. H. Young, "Lord Dorchester and the Church of England," CHA *Report*, 1926, 60–65.

BROWN, WILLIAM, journalist and printer; b. *c.* 1737 at Nunton (Dumfries and Galloway), Scotland, son of John Brown and Mary Clark; d. unmarried 22 March 1789 at Quebec.

When he was about 15 years of age William Brown was sent to live with relatives of his mother in America, and from 1751 to 1753 he studied mathematics and classics at William and Mary College in Williamsburg, Virginia. In 1754 he went into an office as clerk, and then began to learn his future trade in a printer's shop in Philadelphia. There in 1758 he went to work for William Dunlop, who two years later entrusted him with the management of two bookshops. Dunlop, who was related to Benjamin Franklin, may have been Brown's uncle. At the end of 1760 Brown is supposed to have entered into partnership for a short time with James Rivington in New York and to have opened a bookshop with him. But he soon went back to working for Dunlop, who decided to send him to Bridgetown, the capital of Barbados, to set up a printing shop. Brown found the climate there trying; after something over two years he returned to Philadelphia. He became interested in the city of Quebec, and is said to have obtained information through William Laing, a Quebec tailor and merchant. He then wrote Governor MURRAY for the necessary authorizations for the founding of a newspaper and for promises of moral and financial support. What Murray replied is not known; in any case, Brown got in touch with a former co-worker in Philadelphia, Thomas GILMORE, and the two decided to go to Quebec to start a newspaper. They prepared for their business venture with the help of Dunlop, who advanced them money.

On 5 Aug. 1763 Brown and Gilmore signed a partnership agreement, each putting up capital of £72. Travelling by way of Springfield (Mass.), Albany, Lake Champlain, and Montreal, Brown reached Quebec on 30 September after many adventures. Meanwhile Gilmore was off to England to purchase various materials, in particular from the London firm of William Caslon Sr, the supplier that Brown would continue to prefer.

Brown collected 143 subscriptions in response to a brochure, probably printed in Philadelphia, which announced the forthcoming publication of a weekly gazette. There were as many Canadian subscribers as there were British, most of the former being members of the clergy. On 21 June 1764 the first number of the *Quebec Gazette/La Gazette de Québec* came out. In addition to printing jobs, the two partners in 1765 extended their activities to publishing [*see* Thomas Gilmore], and they also received an annual allocation of £50 from the colonial authorities for official announcements. The enterprise met with fair success: on 29 April 1768 Brown and Gilmore wrote to William Dunlop to obtain the services of an apprentice and a translator; their former employer was repaid that year, and Brown purchased a new press for which he paid £26.

After his partner's death in 1773 Brown, who became sole owner of the business at the beginning of 1774, continued to issue many publications. The text of the Quebec Act came out in 1774, and the following year four legal works by François-Joseph CUGNET appeared. Brown later published the *Ordinances made and passed by the governor and Legislative Council of the Province of Quebec* (1777), *The order for morning and evening prayer* . . . , a collection in Iroquois edited by Christian Daniel CLAUS (1780), a

Pseautier de David . . . (1785), and a new collection of ordinances (1786). The Quebec almanacs, now an extremely rare and valuable source of information, had begun to appear in 1780. Then in 1789 the *Gazette* announced the opening of subscriptions at 2*s*. for the publishing of *Abram's Plains* . . . , a collection of poems by Thomas Cary*, who later founded the *Quebec Mercury*. This work was of interest both for its method of publication by subscription and for its contents, poetry seldom being a source of profit. The collection was published in March 1789 and sold quite well at the price of 2*s*. 6*d*. In all, Brown published about 250 or 260 works, mainly pamphlets, catechisms, and a variety of printed materials; only eight of them ran to more than 100 pages. Among these may be noted two pieces that had an interesting fate: a *Kalendrier perpétuel à l'usage des Sauvages* . . . , announced in the *Gazette* on 20 Oct. 1766, the whole edition of a thousand copies being bought by Father Jean-Baptiste de LA BROSSE for distribution in his missions; and *Direction pour la guérison du mal de la baie St-Paul* (1785), the first medical treatise, written by Philippe-Louis-François Badelard*, surgeon-major of the garrison of Quebec, paid for by the government, and distributed free of charge to fight a suspected outbreak of venereal disease [*see* James BOWMAN].

However the *Quebec Gazette* obviously remains William Brown's major work. This first periodical in the province of Quebec was published on the American model: Brown's printing shop relied for basic income on the publication of a newspaper in which advertisements, forming the content of the last two pages, and the numerous official government announcements were the essential matter. Brown's *Gazette*, bilingual from the first issues, consisted of four two-column pages, with English on the left and the French translation on the right. The translation was bad throughout the 25 years of Brown's administration. At the time of the founding of the *Quebec Gazette*, Brown had thought of making it a vehicle for information, entertainment, and service to the public. He explained his goals in the prospectus announcing that he and his associate Gilmore were establishing a printing-office in Quebec and launching a bilingual weekly: "we consider it as the most effectual Means of bringing about a thorough Knowledge of the *English* and *French* Language to those of the two Nations now happily united in one in this Part of the World . . . ; by which Means they will be enabled to . . . communicate their Sentiments to each other as Brethren. . . . Or, as the Means only of bringing to their Knowledge the Transactions of the different and most distant Nations of the World. . . ." Obviously eager to provide his readers with as much foreign news as possible, Brown indicated in the first issue in June 1764 the three main guidelines he would follow: the *Quebec Gazette* would offer "a view of foreign affairs, and political transactions," would take "particular care" in giving "the transactions, and occurrences of our mother-country," and would with "impartiality" lay out the real facts with regard to the Thirteen Colonies and the Caribbean islands. In the absence of foreign news during the harsh winter, the paper would publish "such *Originals*, both in *Prose* and *Verse*, as will please the FANCY and instruct the Judgment." Brown noted that in any case "we shall have nothing so much at heart, as the support of VIRTUE and MORALITY, and the noble cause of LIBERTY." But this fine, principled stand would prove difficult to sustain in face of the turn of events that plunged America into a situation of revolutionary crisis.

For a few years the publishers enjoyed a degree of freedom to inform the *Gazette*'s readers about British policy and the reactions of the colonial assemblies, especially in connection with the crucial question of taxation. Having themselves been directly affected by the notorious Stamp Act, which forced them to suspend the paper's publication for nearly seven months (from 31 Oct. 1765 to 29 May 1766), when publication resumed they immediately reprinted the speech William Pitt had made in the House of Commons against this legislative measure, now at last repealed. At the same time they asserted that there had been false rumours that their paper was being placed "under the Inspection" of the colonial government, and they took the opportunity to reaffirm their determination to defend freedom of the press. But with the increasing gravity of the revolutionary crisis the two publishers could not long maintain their British press "free from the Inspection or Restrictions." They were forced, whether they liked it or not, to submit to the restrictions of a colonial régime that put narrow constitutional limits on the exercise of Anglo-Saxon liberties. Now officially governor, Guy Carleton* made a show of much stricter and more severe vigilance than his predecessor James Murray had been able to carry out, especially after the harsh warning that George III had deemed necessary to give the Sons of Liberty in his speech from the throne on 8 Sept. 1768. In order to remove from Canadian sight the bad example of subjects rebelling against the authority of the British parliament it was better to silence the echoes of American newspapers in the *Quebec Gazette*. Thus from 1770 on, the province of Quebec was almost totally ignorant of what was happening in the colonies to the south. Carleton's guidelines and orders were so closely followed that in his absence from August 1770 to September 1774 Lieutenant-Governor Hector-Théophilus CRAMAHÉ, through the use of censorship, compelled the publishers to confine themselves to true foreign news, to such European affairs as the Russo-Turkish war and the first partition of Poland, and, for want of other news, to fill the paper's pages with assorted elementary facts, more or less amusing anecdotes, innocuous short tales, and edifying epistles.

The American invasion of Canada [*see* Richard MONTGOMERY] forced William Brown, now sole editor, to suspend the publication of his newspaper again, from 30 Nov. 1775 to 14 March 1776 and from 21 March to 8 Aug. 1776. He had to wait for the complete expulsion of the rebel forces to pick up his subscribers again and to operate without too much financial difficulty. The *Gazette* reappeared a month after the Declaration of Independence, and Brown thought it wise to reassure his subscribers by notifying them clearly of his intentions: "It has so far justly merited the Title of THE MOST INNOCENT GAZETTE IN THE BRITISH DOMINIONS; and . . . there is little likelihood of its loosing Claim to so laudible an Attribute." And Brown was to retain this reputation for it until his death on 22 March 1789.

Circumstances had thus prevented Brown from proceeding with his initial plan. Of the three elements (information, entertainment, and usefulness) which the founder had hoped to give his newspaper and of the role he had wanted it to play, there remained only the function of official gazette. It was left to his nephew, Samuel NEILSON, who had joined him some years earlier, to give the newspaper new life by reopening it to the outside world, where attention was focused on the unfolding of the revolution in France. The new awareness of local public opinion would find its outlet in the columns of the *Quebec Gazette* through controversial letters to the editor and writings by its readers, and from 1789 to 1793 the paper went through a joyous and glorious period of ideological effervescence unique in its history.

A group of Brown's friends had chosen Peter Stuart, Malcolm Fraser*, and James Fisher* as trustees of his estate. The absence of certain pieces of evidence makes it hard to draw conclusions about the data given in surviving estate records. Far from indicating a financial surplus as substantial as the £10,000 to £12,000 Ægidius Fauteux* claims, these records suggest instead a deficit. It is difficult therefore to give a final judgement on the estate.

Brown remains one of the outstanding figures in our history, as much for his enterprising spirit and pioneering qualities as for his success and his output. He was to be the source of inspiration for Fleury MESPLET in Montreal and then for the great names in printing and journalism, the Neilsons, Pierre-Édouard Desbarats*, Thomas Cary, William MOORE; he holds a place of primary importance, as his monument, the *Gazette*, illustrates.

IN COLLABORATION WITH
JEAN-FRANCIS GERVAIS

ANQ-Q, Greffe de Charles Stewart, 14 janv. 1791. ASQ, Polygraphie, XXX, 6[d], 6[e], 6[f]; Séminaire, 120, nos.259, 268; 152, no.227. PAC, MG 24, B1, 47–156. *Quebec Gazette*, 1764–89. Beaulieu et Hamelin, *La presse québécoise*, I, 1–12. Wallace, *Macmillan dictionary*. Æ. Fauteux, *Introduction of printing into Canada*. Galarneau, *La France devant l'opinion canadienne*. Elzéar Gérin, *La Gazette de Québec* (Québec, 1864). Gundy, *Early printers*. Eugène Rouillard, *Les premiers almanachs canadiens* (Lévis, Qué., 1898). F.-J. Audet, "William Brown (1737–1789), premier imprimeur, journaliste et libraire de Québec; sa vie et ses œuvres," RSC *Trans.*, 3rd ser., XXVI (1932), sect.I, 97–112.

BRUCE. *See* BREWSE

BRUCE, ROBERT GEORGE, military engineer; b. probably in Scotland, son of — Bruce and Margaret Hay; d. 8 April 1779 in London, England.

Robert George Bruce joined the Board of Ordnance in Great Britain as a practitioner engineer in December 1755; when the engineers were accorded military status in 1757 he received an ensign's rank. Later that year he took part in the abortive expedition against the French naval arsenal of Rochefort. He was promoted lieutenant in 1758 and captain-lieutenant in 1759, and in the summer of 1761 he received a posting to Annapolis Royal, Nova Scotia.

When Annapolis Royal became the British capital of Nova Scotia in 1710, the Board of Ordnance had assumed responsibility for its fortifications. During the 1730s and 1740s it authorized repairs to meet various emergencies, but the financial base to rebuild the crumbling earthworks in a more permanent fashion was lacking. After the martial situation eased in the late 1750s, however, the board was able to examine the state of Nova Scotia's defences, and in the process it gave Annapolis Royal a degree of attention it had never enjoyed during the period of conflict. Bruce was dispatched from England with orders to report on the condition of the old fort and recommend necessary improvements.

Bruce's North American experiences began

inauspiciously with the capture of his ship by a French privateer and the consequent loss of his instruments and personal effects. He reached Annapolis Royal in July and shortly thereafter reported to the board that the fort was in a "most ruinous condition." He recommended an ambitious proposal to rebuild the earthen walls and bastions in stone. No action was taken on this proposal for nearly two years while the board considered it; in the interim Bruce occupied his time inspecting forts Frederick (Saint John, N.B.) and Cumberland (near Sackville, N.B.), surveying on the Saint John River, and assisting his engineer colleagues Samuel Beardsley, John Marr, and William Spry at Halifax.

Approval to begin work at Annapolis Royal was received early in 1763, and by the summer Bruce had commenced extensive masonry foundations for a new fort. He negotiated contracts for construction materials with the Boston firm of Apthorp and Hancock and with local suppliers so that the Annapolis area experienced a period of brisk trade. The local labour shortage was solved by employing Acadians who had escaped deportation in 1755 and who had been allowed to remain as nominal prisoners. This activity brought a measure of prosperity to the former capital; wages rose, sub-contractors flourished, and lumber prices exceeded those at Halifax. Bruce, apparently an affable employer with a "kind disposition," virtually ruled at Annapolis, the engineers, overseers, and labourers outnumbering the regular garrison. By 1766 £15,000 worth of ordnance supplies, nearly half the estimated cost of the ambitious project, were stockpiled at the fort. In that year, however, continuing peace and tightened financial controls caught up with the Board of Ordnance; all work on Nova Scotian fortifications was halted and Bruce returned home. By 1770 almost no sign of his labours remained, the supplies having been dispersed, the new buildings dismantled and shipped to St John's, Newfoundland, and the costly masonry walls removed.

Bruce's career with the Board of Ordnance after his return to England is largely unknown. He was promoted captain in 1774. By 1778 he was in Dominica, where a small group of British engineers, including Gother Mann*, was building extensive fortifications. He had probably been there for several years, for he had acquired "estates and Plantations" by the time he made his will in February 1778. In it he bequeathed what appears to have been a good-sized fortune to a score of relatives and female acquaintances in both Britain and Dominica. He had been married, but his wife had apparently died in Dominica.

The defences of Dominica, although costly, were woefully undermanned, and the island fell quickly to a French invasion in September 1778. By the following April Bruce was back in London, where he died under pitiable circumstances. The *Gentleman's Magazine* reported that his death was a result of his fourth attempt at suicide in one day. His servant and attending physician had dressed his wounds from the previous attempts but had trustingly left him alone in his house "in a seeming composure." "Nothing but phrenzy," reported the *Magazine*, "could occasion this melancholy catastrophe," since Bruce had "just married an amiable young lady, and had himself a plentiful fortune."

While his efforts in Nova Scotia apparently came to nothing, Bruce had some significance beyond his role as a casualty of the military parsimony that followed the Seven Years' War. He was representative of a new brand of professional engineer which was beginning to appear in the British army: formally trained in comparison with his predecessors, well versed in financial procedures, concerned with the proper planning of fortifications, and insistent on sound surveys. He and his colleagues such as Beardsley, Marr, and Spry reveal in their correspondence a growing, almost ebullient *esprit de corps* arising from their identical training at the Royal Military Academy in Woolwich, shared experiences, and common disdain for the regular army. Six plans prepared by Bruce or under his direction survive to attest to the high standard of draftsmanship that was becoming the rule among the younger royal engineers of that day.

MAXWELL SUTHERLAND

Clements Library, Thomas Gage papers, American series, 11, R. G. Bruce to Gage, 26 Dec. 1763; 50, William Fenwick to Colonel Cunningham, 24 March 1766. PRO, Prob. 11/1054, ff.357–59; WO 34/12, William Forster to Jeffrey Amherst, 21 Aug. 1763; 47/58, f.21; 47/59, f.118; 47/62, f.113; 55/1558, pt.3, ff.55–56; 55/1820, pt.3, f.11; pt.5, f.7 (mfm. at PAC). *Gentleman's Magazine*, 1779, 211. *Roll of officers of the corps of Royal Engineers from 1660 to 1898* . . . , ed. R. F. Edwards (Chatham, Eng., 1898), 5, 7. Porter, *History of Royal Engineers*, I, 182–83.

BRUYÈRES (Bruyere), JOHN (Jean, Joseph), officer, secretary to Governor Ralph Burton*, and seigneur; d. some time before 1787.

Little is known about John Bruyères's origins. It has often been said that he was Swiss – as all French speaking Protestants were designated – but this is untrue. He came from a family of French Huguenots, the de Bruyères, who were probably of noble birth and who had emigrated to England at the time of the revocation of the edict of Nantes. Arriving in Canada in 1759 with Wolfe*'s army, as an ensign in the 35th Foot, he took part in the siege of Quebec and at the close of the battle of the Plains of Abraham was put in charge of guarding prisoners and captured belongings and papers. In 1760 he wrote an account of the battle of Sainte-Foy for Brigadier George Townshend*; he then followed the troops to Montreal. On 16 September, after the surrender, the commander-in-chief, Jeffery AMHERST, appointed Burton governor of the District of Trois-Rivières, and Burton chose Bruyères as his secretary. This choice, which was probably due to Bruyères's knowledge of French, may also be explained by the fact that his sister Marguerite was Burton's mistress. Burton created a scandal in Trois-Rivières by taking her there to live with him; he was, however, to marry her around 1763.

The first important document bearing the signature of Bruyères is the proclamation of 22 Sept. 1760 ordering the people of Trois-Rivières to lay down their arms and take the oath of allegiance to King George II. Subsequent edicts concerned in particular the census, *corvées*, and the supplying of food and animals to the troops. Some of the new government's demands may have seemed severe, but Bruyères managed to use tact and diplomacy in drawing up the edicts, and thus made relations between the authorities and the citizens of Trois-Rivières easier. He pursued this line of conduct throughout his two years there as Burton's secretary and during the short time he assisted HALDIMAND who temporarily took over during Burton's absence from May 1762 to March 1763.

More readily than they had in Burton's case the people of Trois-Rivières forgave Bruyères for his cohabitation with their compatriot Catherine-Élisabeth, daughter of the late Jean-Baptiste Pommereau* and Claire-Françoise Boucher de Boucherville (remarried since 1745 to Joseph-Michel LEGARDEUR de Croisille et de Montesson). Bruyères married Catherine-Élisabeth in 1764, thus allying himself with a much esteemed family and becoming co-seigneur of Bécancour. This mixed marriage, which was solemnized before a Protestant minister, caused a great stir. The church had, however, decided to pardon Catholics who had married Protestants, on condition that they did penance. On 8 July 1764 Louis Jollivet, the parish priest of Notre-Dame in Montreal, wrote to Vicar General BRIAND that Catherine-Élisabeth had done her penance and would soon be able to receive communion.

When Burton became governor of Montreal on 29 Oct. 1763, Bruyères followed him there. The last proclamation he signed was dated 1 Aug. 1764, at the end of the military régime in Montreal. He remained in the city, where on 11 August he bought a house that was destroyed by fire in April 1768. Along with other officials, in September 1764 Bruyères protested in writing against an address sent to MURRAY by the English merchants of Montreal expressing the hope that arbitrary imprisonments and the exactions committed by government employees would cease. On 21 June 1771, at Trois-Rivières, Bruyères signed a deed of transfer of the income from his fief of Bécancour in favour of his mother-in-law "for as long as she lived." The following month he asked Hector Theophilus CRAMAHÉ for the grant of a seigneury adjoining the rear of the seigneury of Bécancour; Cramahé does not seem to have assented to this request. In 1772 Bruyères was in Europe; he was also there in 1774. Jean-Baptiste BADEAUX, notary at Trois-Rivières, acted as his attorney during his absences as he did again during Bruyères's stay in England in 1784. Bruyères returned to Canada the following year.

Neither the place nor the exact date of Bruyères's death is known, but a petition by his son Ralph Henry*, dated 18 Jan. 1787, proves he had died some time before then. Ralph Henry and his wife Janet Dunbar had at least four children. Their daughter Anne-Françoise married wealthy fur dealer Jean-Baptiste-Toussaint Pothier* in January 1820; Jeanne-Marie-Catherine married doctor David Thomas Kennelly, and subsequently lawyer Michael O'Sullivan*.

IN COLLABORATION WITH RAYMOND DOUVILLE

ANQ-M, État civil, Catholiques, Notre-Dame de Montréal, 17 mai 1831. ANQ-MBF, Greffe de J.-B. Badeaux, 21 juin 1771; Insinuations, 1760–64. *Doc. relatifs à l'hist. constitutionnelle, 1759–91* (Shortt et Doughty; 1921), I, 75–77. *Quebec Gazette*, 20 Sept. 1764, 26 May 1785. P.-G. Roy, *Inv. concessions*, I, 255; V, 172. E.-H. Bovay, *Le Canada et les Suisses, 1604–1974* (Fribourg, Suisse, 1976), 10. Jouve, *Les franciscains et le Canada: aux Trois-Rivières*. M. Trudel, *Le Régime militaire*. F.-J. Audet, "John Bruyères," *BRH*, XXXI (1925), 342–43. Pierre Daviault, "Traducteurs et traduction au Canada," RSC *Trans*., 3rd ser., XXXVIII (1944), sect.I, 67–87. Gérard Malchelosse, "La famille Pommereau et ses alliances," *Cahiers des Dix*, 29 (1964), 193–222.

BUCK. *See* BURCH

BULKELEY, RICHARD, office-holder; b. 26 Dec. 1717 in Dublin (Republic of Ireland), second son of Sir Lawrence Bulkeley and Elizabeth Freke; m. 18 July 1750 Mary, daughter of John

Rous*, at Halifax, Nova Scotia, and they had four sons; m. secondly 26 July 1776 Mary Burgess at Halifax; d. there 7 Dec. 1800.

Richard Bulkeley's early life is somewhat obscure. It has been asserted that he attended school in Dublin and that he served as an officer in a British cavalry regiment during the War of the Austrian Succession, but neither of these claims has been substantiated by contemporary records. In 1749 Bulkeley was persuaded by Edward CORNWALLIS, newly appointed governor of Nova Scotia and a personal friend, to accompany him to the province as an aide-de-camp. Bulkeley was soon actively engaged in carrying out Cornwallis' orders for the establishment of Halifax, the new capital of Nova Scotia. Commissioned by the governor as an ensign in the 45th Foot in October 1749, he acted as paymaster of works, director of "sundry Publick Works," and, with Horatio Gates, "Commissary of Wet Stores for soldiers." His command of French and German was useful in dealing with the "Foreign Protestants" who were gathered at Halifax prior to the founding of Lunenburg in 1753. When Cornwallis left in October 1752, Bulkeley was retained as aide-de-camp and director of public works by Governor Peregrine Thomas Hopson*.

Charles Lawrence*, Hopson's successor, also employed Bulkeley as director of public works, and the two men became closely associated. Bulkeley was not actively engaged in the expulsion of the Acadians in 1755, but the "Vindication by Secretary Bulkeley and Judge [Isaac Deschamps*] of the Acadian Removal" published later showed that he supported it as necessary military strategy. In 1757 difficulties arose from his position as director of public works. When several Halifax inhabitants, including Jonathan Binney*, Malachy SALTER, and Otto William SCHWARTZ, petitioned for an assembly that year, one of their complaints was that a small clique of officials around Lawrence had control of too much public money. Bulkeley was calculated to control over £1,700, consisting of his own salary as overseer of the king's works (£182 10*s*.), the pay of five clerks as overseers (£273 15*s*.) and of three servants as labourers (£72), an allowance for 75 cords of wood (£45), his salary as commissary of rum and molasses (£300), his pay as an officer (£80), and "advantages on Contracts for the public Works, at the lowest Calculation £750.0.0." It was also asserted that since no government contracts were publicly advertised Bulkeley, together with a small staff, drew up the estimates for any public work, employed all the workmen, and valued the final result.

On 10 Oct. 1758 Lawrence appointed Bulkeley to succeed William Cotterell as provincial secretary, recommending to the Lords of Trade Bulkeley's "abilities, Integrity and attention to his Duty." At that period the duties and responsibilities of the secretary were not clearly defined, but they included keeping the Great Seal, conducting and having charge of government correspondence, and issuing letters patent, land grants, commissions, and other documents. An examination of the various commission-, order-, and letter-books reveals that the provincial secretary recorded orders he had been given by the governor and Council for pardons, licences to keep school, leaves of absence, writs, proclamations, and warrants. The beautiful copperplate handwriting and well-kept indexes bear witness to the efficiency of the clerks hired by Bulkeley. The secretary usually assumed the duties of clerk of the Council and was a Council member himself. Bulkeley was appointed to Cotterell's vacant Council seat on 16 Aug. 1759 but did not become clerk of the Council until 4 Nov. 1763.

When Lawrence died in October 1760, the administration of the province was assumed by Chief Justice Jonathan BELCHER, who was thankful to retain Bulkeley as secretary because of his experience and knowledge "of the respective views of our late Governor." In the difficulties between Belcher and the legislature Bulkeley was loyal to the chief justice. He and Charles MORRIS disagreed with Belcher in 1763, however, when their report on local government favoured the New England township system over the British and Virginian county grand jury system strongly supported by Belcher. Bulkeley and Morris seem to have won the Council to their view, but long negotiations between Council and assembly left the grand jury system intact. Bulkeley's support for the township system appears to have been a result of his wish to keep Lawrence's promise to the New England settlers that their former system of local government would be retained. His own predilection, however, as revealed in other ways, was for strong central control.

The two succeeding governors, Montagu Wilmot* and Lord William CAMPBELL, also retained Bulkeley as provincial secretary. In an attempt to enforce collection of customs duties and thereby reduce the provincial debt, Campbell instructed Bulkeley to impress upon the magistrates of the outports their responsibility to stop smuggling. In 1770 he appointed Bulkeley inspector of public works and buildings, inspector of workmanship and repair, and commissioner of escheats. Both Bulkeley and Campbell were interested in horses and Bulkeley imported thoroughbreds from Ireland. Horse-racing took place at Halifax and Windsor, where Bulkeley had acquired land in 1764 through a large grant made to him and several other councillors, including Michael FRANCKLIN and Joseph GOREHAM. He owned other property as well, but his holdings never became substantial.

When Governor Francis LEGGE arrived in Nova Scotia in October 1773, Bulkeley was still a councillor and provincial secretary. Since he held a multiplicity of other offices it would appear that he stood to lose from the governor's attacks on the spoils system, but he initially supported Legge because of his strong sense of loyalty. Legge considered Bulkeley's office so inefficient, however, that in November 1774 he replaced Bulkeley's son John as first clerk to the secretary, and Bulkeley became the governor's enemy. As a Council member he participated in the measures that body took to oppose Legge. By May 1775 the governor was sufficiently convinced that Bulkeley and other Council members such as Jonathan Binney and John BUTLER were actively hampering his efforts to investigate the provincial debt that he asked the British government for their dismissal. Although Bulkeley did not sign the Council petition to the king on 1 Jan. 1776 requesting Legge's removal (Butler noted that "Mr. Bulkeley is under Some fears"), he appears to have overcome his misgivings. In June 1776 he was a member of the Council committee that drew up an address thanking the king for Legge's recall the previous month.

Bulkeley was retained as secretary by lieutenant governors Mariot ARBUTHNOT, Richard Hughes*, and Sir Andrew Snape Hamond, naval officers with little knowledge of Nova Scotia who left most of the governing of the province to Bulkeley and other officials. Hughes appointed Bulkeley brigadier-general of the provincial militia in June 1780. The inflation of wartime caused Bulkeley to submit a memorandum to Hamond in May 1782 asking the British government for an increase in his salary as secretary. Although Bulkeley acknowledged that he might obtain some addition to his income from the assembly, "it could be only voted annually and the continuation of it would depend entirely on their consideration, how far his conduct pleas'd them to do which might, in many instances, be to sacrifice the interests of Government." Like most members of the executive, he preferred to remain independent of the assembly's control.

Governor John PARR found in Bulkeley a fellow Irishman only eight years his senior, and soon Bulkeley, Alexander Brymer, and Matthew Richardson formed an inner circle of advisers to the governor. In dealing with the problem of accommodating the thousands of loyalist refugees and disbanded soldiers who arrived in Nova Scotia at the end of the American revolution, Parr and Bulkeley sometimes worked 20 hours a day. The secretary's letter-book contains correspondence about rations and tools for the loyalists, surveying, and land grants, as well as material about the separation from Nova Scotia of the new provinces of New Brunswick, St John's (Prince Edward) Island, and Cape Breton, and the question of American vessels fishing in Nova Scotian waters.

In November 1785 some inhabitants of Halifax petitioned the Council for incorporation as a city, but the request was refused as neither "expedient or necessary." Bulkeley was blamed by the petitioners for having influenced this decision, and the stand would have been consistent with his desire for strong executive control since an independent city administration might have opposed the wishes of the Council. Two years later the assembly complained to Parr about the improper and irregular administration of justice by Isaac Deschamps and James Brenton*, the two puisne judges. The Council, after having investigated behind closed doors, unanimously exonerated the judges in February 1788, declaring the charges to be "Groundless and Scandalous." Bulkeley and the other Council members undoubtedly believed that it was in the interests of established authority that the judges be defended from attack.

Parr died suddenly on 25 Nov. 1791 and Bulkeley, as senior councillor, assumed the administration of the government until John Wentworth* took office as lieutenant governor on 14 May 1792. As administrator Bulkeley carried on Parr's arrangements for the emigration of black loyalists to Sierra Leone [*see* Thomas PETERS] and won Lieutenant John Clarkson's praise for the efficient way in which he assisted preparations for the embarkation.

Wentworth was an experienced ex-governor of New Hampshire who had lived in Nova Scotia as surveyor general of the king's woods. He did not need to depend on the opinion of Bulkeley, whom he described as "from his great age and infirmities, intirely incapable of attending the Duty [of secretary]." Wentworth may have hinted to Bulkeley that he resign; in any event Bulkeley did so as secretary and clerk of Council on 22 Dec. 1792 and was succeeded by his son James Michael Freke. A bachelor, Freke continued to live at home and paid a large share of the salary to his father by a family agreement. After

Freke's death in November 1796, Wentworth appointed his own brother-in-law Benning Wentworth to the vacant positions. This move apparently affected Bulkeley's financial position adversely, for Chief Justice Thomas Andrew Lumisden Strange* and the lord mayor of London, Sir Brook Watson*, both asked the British government to make some financial arrangement for Bulkeley and his wife. Wentworth accordingly paid Bulkeley £200 a year. Since Bulkeley retained his positions as judge of the Vice-Admiralty Court (to which he had been appointed on 18 May 1769) and commissioner of escheats, he had, according to Wentworth, "a decent and comfortable support." In view of the fact that a private income of over £1,000 a year has been claimed for Bulkeley, the attempt by his friends to secure financial support for him is curious; it may be that the deterioration in his "private circumstances" he was said to have suffered during the American revolution resulted in his need for government assistance.

Bulkeley was not to enjoy his judgeship long after this incident. In June 1798 Admiral George Vandeput forwarded to Wentworth a complaint from nine captains in Halifax against some of the Vice-Admiralty Court's decisions and the fact that trials were held in Carleton House, Bulkeley's residence. In a well-reasoned letter Bulkeley replied that any of his decisions could be appealed and that the court was held in a spacious room with "the doors always open for access to all persons." While the matter was being considered by the British government, however, Bulkeley resigned in favour of Brenton, evidently wishing to avoid a long dispute. He remained a councillor until his death on 7 Dec. 1800, when he was buried in St Paul's Church.

In his capacity as secretary, Bulkeley supervised the publication of Anthony HENRY's *Nova-Scotia Gazette* and for a time had edited the *Halifax Gazette*. He is believed to have been the author of an *Address to the public on the present state of the province of Nova Scotia*, published in 1785, which described how the province might be improved by attracting capital and settlers and by developing the export trade and agriculture. Bulkeley was deeply involved in organizations of various kinds. One of the members of the first masonic lodge at Halifax in 1750, he succeeded Parr as provincial grand master of the masonic lodges in December 1791 and held the office until his death. In January 1786 he helped found the Charitable Irish Society of Halifax and twice served as its president. He was also chosen president of a society for the promotion of agriculture founded in 1789 and was president of a chess, pencil, and brush club in Halifax from about 1787. Bulkeley was appointed churchwarden when St Paul's parish was formally organized in 1759 and was vestryman until his death; he also served as organist in 1759–60. Noted for his lavish hospitality, Bulkeley had entertained James Wolfe* and many other military men during the Seven Years' War and the American revolution. The dining-room of his mansion opposite St Paul's, which he built of stone brought from the ruins of Louisbourg, could seat 50. As administrator, he entertained in his own residence (still standing as the Carleton Hotel) and held large levees there on New Year's Day and the queen's birthday, as well as dinners on St Patrick's and St George's days.

One of the few officials in Cornwallis' expedition who remained in Nova Scotia, Richard Bulkeley, a healthy, vigorous, and hard-working civil servant, assisted 13 governors and lieutenant governors from Cornwallis to Wentworth. In half a century of service he took part in the founding of Halifax, the immigration of New Englanders and loyalists, and the prosperity of the French revolutionary wars. A man of "Inflexible integrity," in his obituary he was called "the Father of the Province."

PHYLLIS R. BLAKELEY

A small chalk self-portrait of Richard Bulkeley as an old man is in the PANS. Halifax County Court of Probate (Halifax), B175 (estate of J. M. F. Bulkeley), B176 (will and inventory of estate of Richard Bulkeley) (mfm. at PANS). PANS, MG 1, 258 (Isaac Deschamps docs.), nos.143, 156, 191, 195, 198, 200, 202, 206–21; RG 1, 48, nos.63–75; 134; 136, pp.157, 163ff.; 137, p.105; 164–72; 186–91; 215–18; 286–87; 348, no.43; F.-J. Audet, "Governors, lieutenant-governors, and administrators of Nova Scotia, 1604–1932" (typescript, n.d.). PRO, CO 217/16, ff.204–18, 221–22, 231–32, 307; 217/18, ff.48–49, 73–79, 135–36, 204–44, 280; 217/51, ff.190–93; 217/52, ff.116–18; 217/59, f.7; 217/63, f.163; 217/68, ff.3–5, 8; 217/75, f.33. St Paul's Anglican Church (Halifax), Registers of baptisms, burials, and marriages, 1752–56; registers of burials, 1776, 1796, 1800; registers of marriage licenses, 1753–90.

[Richard Bulkeley and Charles Morris], "State and condition of the province of Nova Scotia together with some observations &c, 29th October 1763," PANS *Report* (Halifax), 1933, app.B, 21–27. [John Clarkson], *Clarkson's mission to America, 1791–1792*, ed. and intro. C. B. Fergusson (Halifax, 1971), 77, 89, 92, 96–99, 109–11, 142. "Report on the present state and condition of his majesty's province of Nova Scotia," PANS *Report*, 1933, app.B, 28–34. "Vindication by Secretary Bulkeley and Judge Deschamps of the Acadian removal," N.S. Hist. Soc., *Coll.*, II (1881), 149–53. *Nova-Scotia Gazette and the Weekly Chronicle* (Halifax), 13 June 1775; 1785. *Nova-Scotia Magazine* (Halifax), 1789–92. *Royal Gazette and the Nova-Scotia Advertiser* (Halifax), 15 Nov. 1796, 9 Dec.

1800. Tremaine, *Bibliography of Canadian imprints*, 206–7, 599–601.

Brebner, *Neutral Yankees* (1969), 66, 76–77, 213–16, 236, 240–41, 243–46, 254–55, 262–63, 273, 287; *New England's outpost*, 256, 259–60. R. V. Harris, *The beginnings of freemasonry in Canada* (Halifax, 1938), 100, 106–9. Murdoch, *History of N.S.*, II, 356, 537–38, 571, 577, 585, 645; III, 4, 94, 97, 99, 152. A. S. Barnstead, "Development of the office of provincial secretary, Nova Scotia," N.S. Hist. Soc., *Coll.*, XXIV (1938), 1–31. Margaret Ells, "Nova Scotian 'Sparks of liberty,'" *Dal. Rev.*, XVI (1936–37), 475–92. J. S. Macdonald, "Hon. Edward Cornwallis, founder of Halifax," "Life and administration of Governor Charles Lawrence, 1749–1760," and "Richard Bulkeley, 1717–1800," N.S. Hist. Soc., *Coll.*, XII (1905), 1–17, 19–58, 59–87; "Memoir of Governor John Parr," N.S. Hist. Soc., *Coll.*, XIV (1909), 41–78; "Memoir, Lieut.-Governor Michael Francklin, 1752–1782," N.S. Hist. Soc., *Coll.*, XVI (1912), 7–40.

BUNT. *See* HOTSINOÑHYAHTA?

BURCH (Birch, Buck), JOHN, craftsman and local official; b. 1741 in England; m. *c.* 1779 Martha Ramsey, a widow, and they had one son; d. 7 March 1797 at Chippawa (Niagara Falls), Upper Canada.

In 1772 John Burch emigrated from London to New York City, where he advertised himself as a "Tin-Plate Worker and Japanner" with a large stock of tinware for sale. He was a successful tradesman and purchased an estate at Papacunk (N.Y.) on the east branch of the Delaware River. When the American revolution broke out Burch "was prest to sign an Association which he refused & retired to Albany to avoid it," leaving New York in 1775. He set up shop in Albany and undertook construction of a grist- and sawmill at Woodstock, but he was forced to remain on his farm as the disturbances increased. In 1778 Burch gave supplies to John BUTLER's rangers, as did his neighbours with his encouragement. In retaliation the rebels sacked his estate three times before razing it entirely and confiscating all his known property. His losses exceeded £4,500.

Burch was forced to flee to Fort Niagara (near Youngstown, N.Y.), where, unfit for active service, he was appointed keeper of the Indian stores and sutler to Butler's Rangers. In 1783, at the end of the war, he and his wife settled on land on the west bank of the Niagara River. Burch received several lots in what became Stamford Township and established his home at the mouth of Chippawa Creek (Welland River). A few miles to the north, beside the Niagara rapids, he constructed a grist- and sawmill in 1785–86. Its workmanship and the ingenious log flume were admired by travellers of the period. After his death, Burch's mill was sold to Samuel Street*, his former partner in a company for carrying goods over the Niagara Falls portage.

As a reward for his loyalty and enterprise Burch was appointed to several positions of local importance. In June 1786 he was made justice of the peace for the Niagara region and in 1791 he was named to the Nassau District land board. The following year Burch was appointed to the board for Lincoln County. He was further rewarded with land grants, including 500 acres for his services to the rangers. He later petitioned as a magistrate for an additional 700 acres but received less. By the time he died Burch had risen from craftsman to gentleman and squire. In 1785 one traveller described him as "a very sensible, well-informed character, his conversation pleasing and instructive and his communications very novel."

PETER N. MOOGK

PAC, MG 24, D4; E1; RG 1, L3. "The arts and crafts in New York, 1726–1776: advertisements and news items from New York City newspapers," N.Y. Hist. Soc., *Coll.*, [ser.3], LXIX (1936), 204. PAO *Report*, 1904, 992–94, 996, 999–1000, 1281; 1905, xcvii, 132, 211, 302–6, 313, 316, 334, 339, 344; 1928, 50, 160; 1930, 42, 79, 107, 137. "Records of Niagara . . . ," ed. E. A. Cruikshank, Niagara Hist. Soc., [*Pub.*] (Niagara-on-the-Lake, Ont.), 38 (1927), 69; 39 (n.d.), 21, 41, 115, 119; 40 (n.d.), 62; 41 (1930), 96, 111, 112, 117–34, 138. R. C. Bond, *Peninsula village: the story of Chippawa* ([Chippawa, Ont.], 1964), 12–13, 18, 21–22. H. C. Mathews, *The mark of honour* (Toronto, 1965), 53–54, 63, 128, 130, 134, 137. Janet Carnochan, "Inscriptions and graves in the Niagara peninsula," Niagara Hist. Soc., [*Pub.*], 19 ([2nd ed.], n.d.), 67; "Names only but much more," *ibid.*, 27 (n.d.), 2.

BURGOYNE, JOHN, known as Gentleman Johnny, army officer, politician, and dramatist; b. 1722, only son of Captain John Burgoyne of Bedfordshire and Anna Maria Burnestone of London; d. 3 Aug. 1792 and was buried in Westminster Abbey, London, England.

John Burgoyne was educated at Westminster School, where he developed an exaggerated classical style and a life-long friendship with Lord Strange, son of the wealthy and powerful 11th Earl of Derby. Commissioned a cornet in the 13th Dragoons in 1740, he purchased a lieutenancy the next year. In 1743 he eloped with Lady Charlotte Stanley, sister of his friend Lord Strange, and her father, after providing a modest dowry, cut her off. Burgoyne bought a captaincy with the money, but by 1747, deeply in debt, he sold his commission and retired with his wife to France. Burgoyne travelled extensively during his stay on the continent and was at this time first exposed to the European concept of "light dragoons" or "light horse," a type of mounted troops then unknown in England. He later submitted a plan to create such a force and in 1759 raised the 16th Light Dragoons, a light horse regiment.

In 1756, after a reconciliation with his father-in-law, Burgoyne returned to the army with a captaincy in the 11th Dragoons, which he exchanged in 1757 for a captaincy in the Coldstream Foot Guards, which gave him the army rank of lieutenant-colonel. In the Seven Years' War Burgoyne took part in raids on the French coast and from 1759 served as colonel of the 16th Light Dragoons. He took a radical approach to organization and discipline in his regiment, his views being well in advance of contemporary thought. He made his military name in the Portuguese campaign of 1762, capturing the towns of Valencia de Alcántara (province of Cácerio, Spain) and Vila Velha de Ródão (district of Castelo Branco, Portugal).

The next decade was the height of Burgoyne's success. Elected to parliament for Midhurst in 1761 through the Derby patronage, he was active in the house on foreign policy and military matters. He received military sinecures worth £3,500 annually, and a promotion to major-general in 1772. He was in the forefront of the great debate on India and the attack on Robert Clive. He also began a literary career and made a considerable success with a play, *Maid of the oaks*, presented in London by David Garrick in 1775.

At the outbreak of the American revolution Burgoyne was sent to Boston, and there he witnessed the battle of Bunker Hill. Without a field command, he spent much of his time writing letters home which were critical of his commander, Lieutenant-General Thomas GAGE. He also wrote a proclamation addressed to the rebels, which was ridiculed both in the colonies and at home for its high-flown language; Horace Walpole later characterized him as "Pomposo" and "Hurlothrumbo." Burgoyne returned to England in November 1775 and attempted, without success, to get an independent command. He sailed for Quebec in March 1776 with reinforcements for Guy Carleton*, who was besieged by American forces under the command of Benedict Arnold*.

The first of the troops arrived in May, Burgoyne himself late in June. Carleton then followed the Americans in their retreat up Lake Champlain, with Burgoyne as his second in command. In November, at the close of the campaign, Burgoyne returned to England. On 28 Feb. 1777 he submitted to the government his "Thoughts for Conducting the War from the side of Canada." It was a clear presentation of the campaign attempted in 1776, separation of the New England colonies from the rest by a British advance along the Lake Champlain-Hudson River line of communications. Burgoyne's plan was adopted almost verbatim and in 1777 the government ordered him to go to Albany, N.Y., there to effect a junction with the forces of Lieutenant-General Sir William Howe; he would thus come into the area of Howe's responsibility and place himself under Howe's command. The two men would later have conflicting interpretations of Howe's intended role at that stage of the campaign. At the same time Lieutenant-Colonel Barrimore Matthew ST LEGER was to advance towards Albany by the Mohawk valley and capture Fort Stanwix (Rome, N.Y.).

Burgoyne was back in Quebec by 6 May 1777 as the field commander; Carleton's powers were confined to Canada. Carleton resigned his governorship over this slight, but he nonetheless provided the necessary administrative support to the extent that Burgoyne was able to advance only six weeks after arriving at Quebec. His only real problem was inadequate assistance from the local inhabitants and the subsequent weakness of his transport.

Burgoyne's army, which gathered at Saint-Jean in June, was composed of about 7,500 regulars, 400 Indians, 100 loyalists, and over 2,000 non-combatants. During the advance up Lake Champlain, Burgoyne made speeches to his Indians and issued proclamations to the Americans, all of which were later ridiculed for their pretension. The British reached Fort Ticonderoga on 30 June and easily forced the Americans to evacuate it. Most of the garrison, however, got away. Burgoyne then moved to Skenesborough (Whitehall, N.Y.) and there made the mistake of advancing to the Hudson River cross-country instead of going via Lake George. It took four weeks to cover 22 miles of difficult terrain, under constant harassment by the enemy.

His need for supplies prompted Burgoyne to undertake a disastrous diversion to Bennington (Vt), which cost almost 1,000 men. Nearly stranded in the wilderness, he gathered supplies from the immediate countryside and then crossed the Hudson River on 13–15 September at Saratoga (Schuylerville, N.Y.). The American forces under Major-General Horatio Gates were gathering in strength to the south, and there was an encounter battle nearby in the vicinity of Freeman's Farm on the 19th. The British suffered heavy losses but held the field, and some commentators say that, had they attacked the next day, they might have won through. Instead, Burgoyne dug in. It appears that at this point he decided that a northern move by Howe was essential. But Howe was operating in Pennsylvania and was unable to come to Burgoyne's assistance. A second battle was fought nearby at Bemis Heights on 7 October. The British were defeated and fell back on Saratoga. The Americans surrounded them on the 12th, and on the 17th Burgoyne and his army surrendered.

After a winter in Boston with his men, Burgoyne was paroled and returned to Britain. Dropped by the government, he joined the Whigs and in 1780 published his *State of the expedition from Canada*, an ably argued defence of his campaign and conduct. He regained some of his offices when the Whigs returned to power in 1782, but he lost them again when they fell in 1783. He opposed the younger Pitt and made almost his last political appearance as manager of Warren Hastings' impeachment in 1787.

Most of his last decade was spent in literary efforts. He wrote the librettos for two comic operas and in 1786 produced his best comedy, *The heiress*, popular both in Britain and on the continent. Following his wife's death in 1776, Burgoyne had four illegitimate children by his mistress Susan Caulfield.

Burgoyne was almost an archetypal example of the 18th-century Englishman of public affairs. As a soldier, writer, and politician, he had some ability but not genius. In a society where connections were everything, his were effective but carried him beyond his depth. Scholars still dispute his merits, or lack of them, but because Saratoga is generally accepted as the turning point of the American revolution, Burgoyne remains best known as the general who lost that campaign.

JAMES STOKESBURY

[John Burgoyne], *The dramatic and poetical works of the late Lieut. Gen. J. Burgoyne; to which is prefixed, memoirs of the author* . . . (2v., London, 1808); *Orderly book of Lieut. Gen. John Burgoyne from his entry into the state of New York until his surrender at Saratoga, 16th Oct., 1777* . . . , ed. E. B. O'Callaghan (Albany, N.Y., 1860); *A state of the expedition from Canada* . . . (London, 1780; repr. New York, 1969). [Roger Lamb], *An original and authentic journal of occurrences during the late American war, from its commencement to the year 1783* (Dublin, 1809).

Boatner, *Encyclopedia of American revolution*. *DNB*. *The Oxford companion to English literature*, comp. and ed. Paul Harvey (4th ed., rev. Dorothy Eagle, Oxford, 1967). E. B. De Fonblanque, *Political and military episodes . . . derived from the life and correspondence of the Right Hon. John Burgoyne* . . . (London, 1876). F. J. Hudleston, *Gentleman Johnny Burgoyne: misadventures of an English general in the revolution* (New York, 1927). Hoffman Nickerson, *The turning point of the revolution, or Burgoyne in America* (2v., Boston and New York, 1928; repr. Port Washington, N.Y., 1967). W. M. Wallace, *Appeal to arms – a military history of the American revolution* (New York, 1951). C. [L.] Ward, *The war of the revolution*, ed. J. R. Alden (2v., New York, 1952).

BUSBY, THOMAS, soldier and innkeeper; b. 1735, apparently in Ireland; m. before 1768; d. 22 Oct. 1798 at Montreal (Que.).

Thomas Busby enlisted in the 27th Foot in 1756 at Cork, Ireland, and came out with the regiment the next year to Halifax, Nova Scotia, to take part in Lord Loudoun's planned expedition against Louisbourg, Île Royale (Cape Breton Island). Although the expedition was cancelled, Busby soon saw considerable action. In 1758 he participated in James ABERCROMBY's frontal attack on Fort Carillon (Ticonderoga, N.Y.), where, he claimed, his grenadier company left more than half its number dead and he had "seven Bullets through his Hat and seven thro' his Clothes." In 1759 he was present at the capture of Carillon and Fort Saint-Frédéric (near Crown Point, N.Y.). He took part that year in building the great stone fort with which AMHERST replaced the latter French stronghold, and he returned the following year as a "Miner" (probably a quarryman). After serving at Île aux Noix in 1760, he saw action in the West Indies in 1761 at Grenada and Fort-Royal (Fort-de-France), Martinique, and in 1762 at Havana, Cuba.

Most of Busby's remaining time with the 27th Foot was spent in Canada, where he was "on duty at nearly every Post in the Province" of Quebec. He took his discharge at Quebec on 26 July 1767, just before the regiment returned to Cork. He had not attained commissioned rank and was left with only a disabled arm as souvenir of his campaigns. In 1775 he was again in action, this time in the militia at Longue-Pointe, Montreal.

On 7 Dec. 1768 Busby was appointed assistant barrack-master at Montreal, a position he held until 1796 when his employment was abruptly terminated, effective 24 December. His dismissal was coupled with the appointment of William Stanton to relieve Barrack-Master James Hughes* of several functions, as Hughes had requested; the appropriations apparently did not cover the salaries of both Stanton and Busby. Hughes later protested that he had not anticipated Busby's removal and had unsuccessfully requested his reinstatement, praising him as "an Honest Man, and a faithful Servant."

Busby was not left destitute; like several other

Irish soldiers in Canada he had been operating an inn. Between 1769 and 1780 he repeatedly secured inn and liquor licences, and his inn may have been strategically located near the Quebec-gate barracks. In 1772 he bought a two-storey stone dwelling there, and by 1781 he had absorbed the neighbouring house and lot. At the time of his death Busby also owned three buildings in the *faubourg* Sainte-Marie nearby, one of them a bark mill, two town lots in William Henry (Sorel), and 300 acres in Upper Canada. There is some indication that he may have been in trade, but it was his son Thomas*, not he, who was the business agent of the barons of Longueuil.

A. J. H. RICHARDSON

ANQ-M, État civil, Anglicans, Christ Church (Montréal), 24 Oct. 1798. PAC, RG 8, I (C series), 187, pp.9–10; 505, p.89; 546, p.64. *John Askin papers* (Quaife), II, 593. *Montréal en 1781 . . .* , Claude Perrault, édit. (Montréal, 1969), 32. PAC *Rapport*, 1885, lxxvii–lxxviii. *Quebec Gazette*, 24 Aug. 1769, 23 July, 13 Aug. 1772, 27 May 1779, 24 May 1781, 28 Feb. 1799. Cameron Nish, *Inventaire sommaire des documents historiques de la Société historique de Montréal* (Montréal, 1968). *Service of British regiments* (Stewart), 157. W. H. Atherton, *Montreal, 1535–1914* (3v., Montreal and Vancouver, 1914), III, 566. Campbell, *History of Scotch Presbyterian Church*, 120.

BUTLER, JOHN, businessman and office-holder; probably b. in England; m. 29 Oct. 1753 Rachel Wall, a widow, in Halifax, Nova Scotia; d. 25 Oct. 1791 at Martock, Somersetshire, England.

John Butler came to Halifax via Long Island, New York. He received property in the first allotment of land in Halifax in 1749, acquired further large holdings in what later became Hants County, and some time before 1754 erected the Great Pontack Inn, the centre of social activities in Halifax. By 1758 he was referred to as a distiller, probably because of his connection with Joshua MAUGER. Butler acted as business agent for the English firm of Watson and Rashleigh [*see* Sir Brook Watson*], and when Mauger left Nova Scotia in 1760, Butler became his attorney-agent there. With Michael FRANCKLIN and Isaac Deschamps* he protected Mauger's economic and political interests in the province.

In 1762 Butler was elected to the House of Assembly as one of the members for Halifax County. Ten years later he was appointed to the Council on the recommendation of Francklin, then lieutenant governor, and became agent victualler and paymaster of the troops in Nova Scotia and Newfoundland on the death of Benjamin GERRISH. He was made lieutenant-colonel in the Halifax militia on 1 Jan. 1774, appointed a justice of the Inferior Court of Common Pleas three months later, and commissioned a full colonel in the militia on 1 Nov. 1776. During the American revolution he joined the Halifax merchants in outfitting an armed vessel, the *Revenge*.

Butler's chief concern, however, was the advancement of Mauger's interests in Nova Scotia. In 1761 he successfully petitioned the assembly against two bills which would have lowered the tariff protecting Mauger's distilleries. By 1767 Butler and John FILLIS controlled five-sixths of the provincial rum trade. In that year the Halifax-London mercantile alliance became alarmed when the governor, Lord William CAMPBELL, supported a bill to lower the protective tariff. Although Butler appeared before the Council to oppose the bill, the measure passed. Butler and Fillis promptly petitioned the Board of Trade against the act, however, and the London merchants Butler represented were able to use their control of the provincial debt to persuade the board to restore the old duty.

Political opponents, temporarily insolvent friends, and interfering governors received equal treatment from Butler: he pursued them relentlessly. John DAY, a political rival with a reputation for honesty, had his credit badly shaken by an anonymous letter which Butler forwarded to Watson and Rashleigh; Malachy SALTER would have lost his vessel the *Rising Sun* to Butler, had the latter been able to persuade Simeon Perkins* to seize the ship for debts owed; and Michael Francklin, heavily in debt to Mauger, was repeatedly embarrassed by Butler's contemptuous treatment. Butler's animus toward Governor Campbell took the form of incessant bullying, and in 1773 Butler and Mauger mounted a campaign to seek Campbell's removal.

Butler's fiercest confrontation was with Campbell's successor, Francis LEGGE. Legge's desire to bring financial order to the colony led to a complete review of the public accounts in 1774–75. For the first year Legge, with the assistance of the assembly, was successful and even managed to sue individuals for moneys owed the treasury; however, when Jonathan Binney* went to jail rather than accept the court verdict, Legge's enemies seized the opportunity to undermine the governor's position with the home authorities. Their methods were unprincipled, even by the standards of 18th-century politics. Legge fought back, labelling many of the assemblymen "Public Debtors," unsuccessfully seeking the dismissal of most of the Council, and investigating a charge, which proved false, that Butler was corresponding with American rebels. Legge was forced to leave Halifax on 12 May 1776 to try to defend himself in London. The following year Butler was fittingly described by a contemporary as the one "who calls himself lord, king, governor of Halifax." He is believed to have left Nova Scotia about 1781, but nothing is known of his subsequent career.

Allan C. Dunlop

Conn. Hist. Soc. (Hartford), Jonathan Trumbull papers, Mauger to Trumbull, 24 Nov. 1752. Halifax County Court House (Halifax), City of Halifax allotment book (mfm. at PANS). Halifax County Court of Probate (Halifax), Book 4, p.27, no.87 (mfm. at PANS). PAC, MG 23, A1, ser.1, 13, no.2474, Mauger to Pownall, 9 Dec. 1773. PANS, MG 1, 447 (D. C. Harvey docs.), folder 198; RG 1, 44, doc.67; 45, doc.7; 47, p.91; 136, p.255; 168, pp.349–50, 355–56, 480, 517–19; 211, 3 May 1762; 212, 3 March 1776. PRO, CO 217/26, pp.239, 271 (mfm. at PANS). St Paul's Anglican Church (Halifax), Registers of baptisms, burials, and marriages, 29 Oct. 1753 (mfm. at PANS). Somerset Record Office (Taunton, Eng.), Martock, Register of burials, 2 Nov. 1791. Brebner, *Neutral Yankees*.

BUTLER, JOHN, army officer, office-holder, and Indian agent; baptized 28 April 1728 at New London, Connecticut, son of Walter Butler and Deborah Ely, *née* Dennison; m. Catalyntje Bradt (Catharine Bratt) about 1752, and they had four sons and one daughter who survived infancy; d. 13 May 1796 at Newark (Niagara-on-the-Lake, Ont.).

Virtually nothing is known of John Butler's youth. It seems clear, though, that he began his association with the frontier and the Six Nations at an early age. His father, a captain in the British army, brought his family to the Mohawk valley of New York about 1742, and three years later John was at Oswego (Chouaguen) with him. Walter Butler was apparently on close terms with William Johnson and it is quite possible that John received some of his early training in dealing with the Indians from him. Certainly Johnson became impressed with Butler's abilities in Indian languages and diplomacy. In May 1755 he brought him as an interpreter to the great council at Mount Johnson (near Amsterdam, N.Y.); the same year, when Johnson was given command of the colonial expedition against Fort Saint-Frédéric (near Crown Point, N.Y.), he appointed Butler a lieutenant over the Indians, a loosely defined position which involved some nominal leadership. Butler continued to serve in this capacity throughout the Seven Years' War, reaching the rank of captain. He was with James Abercromby at the attack on Fort Carillon (Ticonderoga, N.Y.) and with John Bradstreet at the capture of Fort Frontenac (Kingston, Ont.) in 1758. The next year he was second in command of the Indians when Johnson took Fort Niagara (near Youngstown, N.Y.), and in 1760 he held the same post in Amherst's force advancing on Montreal.

After the war Butler continued to work under Johnson in the Indian department, appearing as an interpreter at councils with the Indians during the 1760s. He settled his family at Butlersbury (near Johnstown, N.Y.), the estate his father had left him, and was appointed a justice of the peace. In the early 1770s he apparently retired from the Indian department to devote himself to his growing properties. When Tryon County was established in 1772 he was appointed a justice of the Court of Quarter Sessions and lieutenant-colonel of the militia regiment commanded by Guy Johnson. Sir William died in 1774 and Guy became Indian superintendent; Butler was again appointed an interpreter.

At the outbreak of the Revolutionary War in 1775 Butler, together with other Mohawk valley loyalists including his sons Thomas and Walter, and Guy Johnson, left to join the British forces in Canada. Butler's wife and other children were interned by the rebels the following year and he did not see them again until an exchange was arranged in 1780. In Montreal, Johnson proposed to Governor Guy Carleton* that the Six Nations and the Indians of Canada be used to put down the rebellion in the "back settlements" of western New York and Pennsylvania. Carleton, however, refused to use them other than as scouts and in defence. Faced with this refusal, and aware of the arrival of Major John Campbell with a commission as agent for Indian affairs in Quebec, Johnson and Christian Daniel Claus decided to carry their case to Britain and left in November 1775. Butler remained as acting superintendent of the Six Nations and, with American forces threatening Canada, was sent to Fort Niagara. His instructions were to do all he could to keep the Six Nations out of the fighting but loyal to Britain, since the British considered the Iroquois to be allies. Although the inclination of the Indians, particularly those who were under the influence of Samuel Kirkland, a New Light missionary from Connecticut, was to sign pacts of neutrality with the rebels, Butler had considerable success in maintaining their alliance with Britain. During the following year and a half he established a network of agents among the tribes from the Mohawk River to the Mississippi, which became a valuable source of intelligence for the British and an aid to loyalists fleeing to

Canada. In the early summer of 1776 Butler also raised and dispatched a party of loyalists and Indians to aid in the expulsion of the American forces from Canada.

In 1777 the British government decided that its Indian allies should be used offensively against the rebels, and in May Butler was ordered to collect as large a force as possible from among the Six Nations and to join Lieutenant-Colonel Barrimore Matthew ST LEGER's expedition at Oswego for an attack against Fort Stanwix (Rome, N.Y.). Although Butler had only a month to accomplish this task, he succeeded in persuading 350 Indians, mostly Senecas, to accompany the expedition. By this time he had received a regular appointment as deputy superintendent of the Six Nations from Guy Johnson, who had arrived in New York in 1776. Nevertheless, at the beginning of the expedition Claus arrived with a commission as superintendent of all Indians employed on it. Butler was intensely disappointed at this supersession, but there is no indication that it affected his conduct towards Claus. Butler was present at the victory of Oriskany, near Fort Stanwix, on 6 Aug. 1777, where the Indians and some unorganized loyalist rangers bore the brunt of the fighting and casualties [*see* KAIEÑ?KWAAHTOÑ].

At the end of the St Leger expedition Butler travelled to Quebec. In September Carleton commissioned him to raise a corps of provincial rangers from among frontier loyalists who had fled to Fort Niagara. Promoted major commandant, Butler was assigned Niagara as his permanent base. His first orders called for him to join BURGOYNE's expedition, but it ended in disaster before he had even begun to recruit.

The following year, with recruiting now well under way, Butler's Rangers and a force of Indians led by Kaieñ?kwaahtoñ and Kaiũtwah?kũ (Cornplanter) undertook their first expedition against the American frontier settlements, the extraordinarily successful raid of 3–4 July on the Wyoming valley, Pennsylvania. Ill health forced Butler to spend the rest of 1778 at Niagara but in November his son Walter led the well-known raid against Cherry Valley (N.Y.). The enormous effect of these and other raids that year and early the next may be gauged by the fact that Congress was forced by public pressure in 1779 to divert to the frontier an army of several thousand men, many of them regulars, under Major-General John Sullivan. Its objectives were to destroy the settlements and lands of the Six Nations allied to the British and to capture as many prisoners as possible. The American campaign did indeed throw the British and Indians on the defensive and Butler, with a force of several hundred men, was defeated at Newtown (near Elmira, N.Y.) on 29 August. The Americans then devastated the Indian villages of the Finger Lakes region. Thousands of Indians were forced to turn to the British for subsistence, but the base at Niagara remained and in 1780 the rangers and Indians were back at their work. In the following years Butler's Rangers extended their operations. A company was assigned to the posts at Oswegatchie (Ogdensburg, N.Y.) and Detroit, and from all bases rangers and Indians carried out almost continuous harassing operations against the whole frontier from the Hudson River to Kentucky.

The Butlers and the war they waged have been condemned by generations of American historians as "treacherous," "barbarous," and "diabolically wicked and cruel." But there is little basis in fact for these charges. Frontier warfare was always cruel, and there is no evidence that the Butlers made it more so and some to support the contention of a few historians that they acted with all the humanity the situation would allow. Condemnations have usually been based on the assumption that the Butlers' raids were motivated by hate and by a desire for revenge. The operations of the rangers, however, had the important objectives of denying supplies to the Continental Army and of drawing off as many American troops as possible from seaboard operations. That these aims were achieved is indicated in part by the Sullivan campaign and also by the fact that Tryon County's prewar population of approximately 10,000 had been reduced, by an exodus away from the threatened area, to 3,500 by 1783.

Butler's interests during the revolution were not exclusively military. As early as 1776, by using his influence as deputy superintendent over the Indian trade, he managed to monopolize the trade with the loyalists at Fort Niagara as well as the lucrative Indian department trade for himself and Richard Pollard*, a merchant at the fort, and later for Thomas Robinson, Pollard's successor. This monopoly was, however, broken in 1779 when Guy Johnson assumed control of Six Nations affairs and was replaced by one operating in Johnson's interest.

Butler was closely involved in the first settlement on the Canadian side of the Niagara River. Early in the war he sited the ranger barracks opposite the fort. In 1779, when Governor HALDIMAND decided to encourage agriculture in the neighbourhood of the fort as a means of reducing the garrison's dependence on supplies from Montreal, he assigned Butler the task of finding appropriate people from among the loyalist refugees. Butler found in this responsibility an opportunity both to impress Haldimand with his competence and to establish himself as leader and source of patronage for the Niagara loyalists. By the end of the war he had settled a number of families opposite the fort, and some of his favourites on the best lots. Indeed, the first name of the new settlement was Butlersbury. When Butler's Rangers was disbanded in June 1784, Butler and his family and a large part of his corps settled there. From this settlement grew the town of Newark, and Butler remained one of the town's most prominent citizens until his death.

The end of the revolution had also brought Butler ill fortune. His property in New York had been confiscated in 1779, and, although he received half pay as a lieutenant-colonel and a 500-acre land grant, the loyalist claims commission refused to recognize many of his claims to Indian lands. In addition, the money he made during the war was lost, apparently in a speculation in Indian goods. In an attempt to reverse this trend, he travelled to Quebec and England in 1784 and 1785 but was unsuccessful in obtaining for his sons the concession giving exclusive use of the Niagara portage route and for himself the higher salary he desired.

Butler also played a prominent part in the local affairs of the Niagara region. He was appointed a justice of the Court of Common Pleas and a member of the district land board when the District of Nassau was established in 1788, and he also became lieutenant-colonel of the Nassau militia, and, at a later date, colonel of the Lincoln County militia. Sir John Johnson* was, however, able to use his influence to prevent Butler or any of his rangers from receiving important offices when the province of Upper Canada was formed in 1792. Similarly, Butler did not rise further in the Indian department. He tried to recoup his family's fortunes through an illegal attempt to supply trade goods to the Indian department involving his son Andrew, his nephew Walter Butler Sheehan, and Samuel Street*, a Niagara merchant. Butler also used his prestige as an Indian superintendent to cooperate with some Americans in a speculation involving Iroquois lands in New York state. When both these ventures failed, Butler turned to farming, milling, and land speculation, but he had only mediocre success.

As deputy superintendent of the Six Nations, Butler played a large part in the purchase of much of southwestern Ontario, including the Grand River lands, from the Mississaugas [*see* WABAKININE]. He had a significant role in the diplomatic and military manœuvring with the Americans and Indians in the years before the evacuation of the border posts in 1796. In 1792 the American government sought to arrange a treaty with the Indians of the old northwest. Butler attended the unsuccessful conference at Lower Sandusky (Ohio) the following year, and with Joseph Brant [Thayendanegea*] and the Six Nations opposed the intransigent position taken by the western Indians and Alexander MCKEE that the boundary between American and Indian territory be no farther west than the Ohio River. It was to be Butler's last significant public service. During the conference his health failed and he never fully regained it. Although he remained a valuable adviser to the government of Upper Canada, by late 1795 Lieutenant Governor Simcoe* regretfully considered removing him from his Indian department position because of his growing infirmities.

John Butler was one of the great figures in European-Indian relations in North America. His influence with the Indians was clearly based upon their trust of him. The success he had in keeping most of the Six Nations out of the fighting but attached to the British cause during the first two years of the revolution speaks to his influence, as does the fact that to him fell most of the burden of explaining to the Indians the British concession of the western lands in 1783. The greatest tribute probably came from Joseph Brant, who said at an Indian funeral ceremony for Butler that he "was the last that remained of those that acted with that great man the late Sir William Johnson, whose steps he followed and our Loss is the greater, as there are none remaining who understand our manners and customs as well as he did."

Butler's relations with the Johnson clan have been the subject of some speculation. He was part of the group closest to Sir William in the 1760s, and the suggestion has been made that when he apparently left his position in the Indian department about 1771 it was because of a falling out with Sir William. The more probable reason for his departure was Sir William's decision to give the limited number of deputy appointments in the department to relatives, such as Claus and Guy Johnson, his sons-in-law, and John Dease, his nephew. Butler, seeing little opportunity for his own advancement, probably chose to devote himself to the development of his estate. There is no evidence, however, of animosity in the break. When Johnson drew up his will in early 1774 he named Butler as one of his executors and a guardian of his children by Mary Brant [KOÑWATSIˀTSIAIÉÑNI]. Nor would Butler have received his various civil and military appointments in Tryon County without Johnson's approval. Indeed Butler, who later selected two of his own sons to be officers in the first company of his rangers, probably understood Johnson's motives completely.

The difficulties with the Johnson group appear to have been instead with Guy and Claus in Canada. Their departure for Britain in late 1775 in the face of the American invasion was considered by Carleton to be akin to desertion. This action, and Butler's obvious competence in dealing with the Indians, put him in great favour with both Carleton and Haldimand. Once Johnson and Claus returned to Canada they saw Butler as a threat to their positions and sought to undermine his reputation, but they were ultimately unsuccessful. Carleton retained him as agent at Niagara and commissioned him to raise the rangers despite Claus' derogatory letters, and Haldimand, not by chance, promoted him lieutenant-colonel in 1779, just when Guy Johnson arrived back in Canada. A short time later Haldimand intervened to prevent Johnson from removing Butler as agent at Niagara. Carleton's and Haldimand's support of Butler, however, was not merely a function of their dislike of Claus and Johnson. Both governors were clearly convinced that Butler was the most competent man for the job and probably appreciated his loyalty and deep sense of duty; Carleton later described him as "very modest and shy."

R. ARTHUR BOWLER and BRUCE G. WILSON

The only known picture of John Butler is a small profile print held by the PAC; Charles William Jefferys* based a portrait on this print. There is a memorial to Butler in St Mark's Church, Niagara-on-the-Lake, Ont.

BL, Add. MSS 21670, 21699, 21756, 21765–70, 21775, 21873. Metropolitan Toronto Library, U.C., Court of Common Pleas, Nassau District, minutes, 12 Jan. 1792. PAC, MG 11, [CO 42], Q, 13; 14, pp.157–58; 15, pp.225–27; 16–1, pp.91–98; 17–1; 26; 50; MG 24, D4; MG 29, E74; MG 30, E66, 22; RG 1, L3, 1, no.87; 2, nos.40, 99. PAO, Canniff (William) papers, package 13, Goring family; Reive (W.G.) coll.; Street (Samuel) papers, cancellation of articles of agreement between Andrew Butler and Samuel Street, 4 Jan. 1797; RG 1, A-I-1, 2. PRO, AO 12, bundle 117; 13/21; 13/89; 13/90; 13/109; CO 42/26, p.66; 42/36–40; 42/42, pp.144–47; 42/43, pp.786–89; 42/46, pp.395ff., 411–18, 431, 458ff., 479ff., 491ff.; 42/49; 42/50, pp.121–22; 42/55, pp.105–8; 42/69, p.245; 42/73 (PAC transcripts); 323/14; 323/15; 323/23; 323/30; WO 28/4; 28/10. *Correspondence of Lieut. Governor Simcoe* (Cruikshank), I, 246, 256, 324, 365–66, 373–74; II, 113, 155, 267; III, 278–79, 323; IV, 101, 125, 217, 264–65. *Johnson papers* (Sullivan *et al.*), I, 13, 27–29, 108, 380, 516, 625. *NYCD* (O'Callaghan and Fernow), VII; VIII, 304, 362–64, 497–500, 688–89, 718–23, 725–27. PAC *Report*, 1884–89. "The probated wills of men prominent in the public affairs of early Upper Canada," ed. A. F. Hunter, *OH*, XXIII (1926), 328–59. "Records of Niagara, 1784–9," ed. E. A. Cruikshank, Niagara Hist. Soc., [*Pub.*] (Niagara-on-the-Lake), 40 (n.d.), 24–27. *DAB*.

R. W. Bingham, *The cradle of the Queen City: a history of Buffalo to the incorporation of the city* (Buffalo, N.Y., 1931), 72–73. E. [A.] Cruikshank, *The story of Butler's Rangers and the settlement of Niagara* (Welland, Ont., 1893), 11–12, 23–25, 27–28, 33–37, 39–51, 59, 63–75, 79–88, 91–98. Howard Swiggett, *War out of Niagara: Walter Butler and the Tory rangers* (New York, 1933; repr. Port Washington, N.Y., 1963), 5, 7–13, 126–32, 169–201, 225–70, 286. P. H. Bryce, "Sir John Johnson, baronet: superintendent-general of Indian affairs, 1743–1830," N.Y. State Hist. Assoc., *Proc.* (New York), XXVI (1928), 233–71. E. [A.] Cruikshank, "The King's Royal Regiment of New York," *OH*, XXVII (1931), 193–323; "Ten years of the colony of Niagara, 1780–1790," Niagara Hist. Soc., [*Pub.*], 17 (1908), 2–10, 16–17, 24–31, apps.A, B. Reginald Horsman, "The British Indian department and the abortive treaty of Lower Sandusky, 1793," *Ohio Hist. Quarterly* (Columbus), 70 (1961), 189–213. W. H. Siebert, "The loyalists and the Six Nation Indians in the Niagara peninsula," RSC *Trans.*, 3rd ser., IX (1915), sect.II, 79–128.

BUTLER, WALTER, army officer; b. 1752 at Butlersbury (near Johnstown, N.Y.), eldest son of John BUTLER (1728–96) and Catalyntje Bradt (Catharine Bratt); d. unmarried, 30 Oct. 1781, at West Canada Creek, N.Y.

Having taken an early interest in military affairs, Walter Butler was recommended in 1768 to be an ensign in the militia. He studied law in Albany and was admitted to the bar in 1775. Father and son fled to Montreal in August that year, following the outbreak of the Revolutionary War; the rest of the family was interned at Albany. On 25 Sept. 1775 Walter helped capture Ethan Allen during the skirmish at Longue-Pointe (Montreal), and the following May he fought at Les Cèdres (Que.) as an ensign in the 8th Foot. The Butlers accompanied the Indians under Christian Daniel CLAUS on Barrimore Matthew ST LEGER's expedition against Fort Stanwix (Rome, N.Y.) and on 6 Aug. 1777 participated in the battle of Oriskany nearby.

After Oriskany, Walter led a party of soldiers and Indians down the Mohawk valley, under a flag of truce but recruiting for the crown as they went. Captured on 12 or 13 August, he was tried by court martial and sentenced by Major-General Benedict Arnold* to be hanged as a spy. Several American officers who had known him as a law student interceded, and he was merely interned in Albany. There he was eventually transferred to the home of Richard Cartwright, a loyalist sympathizer. On 21 April 1778 Walter got his sentry drunk and escaped to join his father at Fort Niagara (near Youngstown, N.Y.).

Conventional campaigns against the colonies by way of Canada ended with BURGOYNE's surrender at Saratoga (Schuylerville, N.Y.) in 1777, and a vicious guerrilla war of a type only too familiar to the North American frontier began. When Walter rejoined him, John Butler was recruiting a ranger battalion to serve with the Indians in raids against American settlements. Composed entirely of volunteers – highly mobile expert marksmen, familiar with the tactics of forest warfare – Butler's Rangers were considered by a contemporary writer to be among the "smartest, liveliest, and most useful troops in the British service . . . rarely known to be worsted in any skirmish or action."

In June 1778 John Butler sent Walter to Quebec where Governor HALDIMAND approved their plan "to break up the back settlements of New York, Pennsylvania, and [New] Jersey," largely to stem the flow of farm produce to the Continental Army. Walter was still in Quebec when John Butler led an expedition against the Wyoming valley of Pennsylvania, the first of several operations which earned Butler's Rangers a bloody reputation. Walter took command in September when his father was ill and on 11 Nov. 1778 led a force of 520 rangers, regulars, and Indians in a disastrous attack on Cherry Valley, N.Y. Lacking heavy cannon, the rangers and regulars were unable to capture the fort, and during the siege the Indians sacked the town. Despite the efforts of Butler and Joseph Brant [Thayendanegea*] to restrain them, they killed over 30 inhabitants.

Walter Butler's role in the incident has been distorted by myth and legend. James Clinton, the American commander in northern New York, never accused him of having ordered or conducted the massacre, and it seems unlikely that Walter would have taken such actions when members of his own family were vulnerable to reprisals. The evidence seems to point to Sequidonquee (Little Beard), a Seneca warrior. But local histories and novels of the 19th century, written largely on the basis of legend and hearsay, describe Walter as cruel and vindictive. The writers, according to Howard Swiggett, "fixed upon young Butler as the Devil, and made him part of every midnight murder of the long years." There is, however, no evidence to show that he instigated or took part in the Cherry Valley atrocities.

On the other hand, the incident may be attributed in part to Walter's poor relations with the Indians. He did not get along with Brant, who was senior in rank and may have resented serving under him. Butler later stated that he was unable to control the Indians; their actions at Cherry Valley appear to have shocked him, and he resolved never to conduct another operation where Indians were in the majority.

Though his family was released in 1780, Butler never achieved his other aims: promotion to major in the rangers and the purchase of a company in an established regiment. He was killed during Major John Ross's raid on the Mohawk valley in 1781. "So feared was the Butler name," George Francis Gilman Stanley has said, "that the rebels of the Mohawk valley rejoiced more over the news of his death than they did at the surrender of [Charles] Cornwallis at Yorktown."

DAVID A. CHARTERS

In March 1779 Walter Butler travelled the north shore of Lake Ontario from Niagara to Cataraqui (Kingston, Ont.). In his journal of the eight-day voyage – published as "Walter Butler's journal of an expedition along the north shore of Lake Ontario, 1779," ed. J. F. Kenney, *CHR*, I (1920), 381–91 – he carefully recorded time and distance and described sites for farming, naval stores, and hunting. BL, Add. MSS 21756/1, 21756/2, 21764, 21765. *NYCD* (O'Callaghan and Fernow), VIII, 499, 721. PAC *Report*, 1886, 640. *DAB*. G.B., WO, *Army list*, 1777. Sabine, *Biographical sketches of loyalists*, I, 280.

North Callahan, *Royal raiders, the Tories of the American revolution* (New York, 1963), 171. E. [A.] Cruikshank, *The story of Butler's Rangers and the settlement of Niagara* (Welland, Ont., 1893), 12, 25, 26, 33, 37, 54–56. Graymont, *Iroquois*, 79, 81, 118, 120, 143, 156, 164–65, 187–89, 191. P. M. Hamlin, *Legal education in colonial New York* (New York, 1939; repr. 1970), 152–53, 155. William Kirby, *Annals of Niagara* (Niagara Falls, Ont., 1896), 57. Lanctot, *Canada and American revolution*, 77, 141. H. C. Mathews, *The mark of honour* (Toronto, 1965), 27, 36, 45, 48–49, 57–59, 60–62. J. C. Miller, *Triumph of freedom* (Boston, 1948), 397, 399. Stanley, *Canada's soldiers* (1960), 125. W. L. Stone, *The campaign of Lieut. Gen. John Burgoyne and the expedition of Lieut. Col. Barry St. Leger* (Albany, N.Y., 1877; repr. New York, 1970), 208–9. Howard Swiggett, *War out of Niagara: Walter Butler and the Tory rangers* (New York, 1933; repr. Port Washington, N.Y., 1963). E. A. Cruikshank, "The King's Royal Regiment of New York," *OH*, XXVII (1931), 193–323. H. U. Swinnerton, "The story of Cherry Valley," N.Y. State Hist. Assoc., *Proc.* (n.p.), VII (1907), 74–93.

BYRON, JOHN, naval officer and governor of Newfoundland; sometimes called Foul-weather Jack for the storms his ships so often endured; b. 8 Nov. 1723, second son of William Byron, 4th Baron Byron, and his third wife Frances Berkeley; m. 8 Sept. 1748 Sophia Trevannion, and they had two sons and seven daughters; d. 10 April 1786 in London, England.

According to contemporary accounts, John Byron entered the Royal Navy in 1731. Nine years later he sailed as a midshipman in the *Wager* (24 guns), one of Commodore George Anson's squadron going to the Pacific. The *Wager* was wrecked on the southern coast of Chile, and after surviving this and other hardships Byron eventually found his way back to England in February 1745/46. By December he had been promoted post-captain and appointed to the *Siren* (24 guns), which he commanded until the end of the War of the Austrian Succession.

Byron commanded several ships during the Seven Years' War; in 1760, in the *Fame* (74 guns), he was sent in command of a small squadron consisting of the *Fame*, *Dorsetshire* (70 guns), *Achilles* (60 guns), and *Scarborough* (22 guns) to Louisbourg, Cape Breton Island, to assist the garrison in demolishing the fortifications. He arrived on 24 May but on 19 June interrupted the work to go in search of a French convoy which was reported to be in the Restigouche River (N.B.) supplying an armed force on the Gaspé coast. Byron was separated from the rest of his squadron, which had been joined by the *Repulse* (32 guns), so that between 22 and 26 June the *Fame* sounded her way alone up an extremely narrow unmarked channel in the Baie des Chaleurs in search of the French vessels. Joined the following day by the rest of his ships, Byron then painstakingly worked his way into the mouth of the Restigouche, accompanied by the *Repulse* and the *Scarborough*. On the 28th the *Fame* destroyed a battery on the north shore which had been impeding the progress of the British ships, and on 8 July the two frigates came within range of the French force, which included the frigate *Machault* (32 guns) and two flutes. The *Machault* struck and later blew up, while the storeships were burnt. Byron's men also burnt all the houses they could find ashore. This episode, sometimes called the battle of the Restigouche, was the last naval engagement of the Seven Years' War in North America [*see also* François-Gabriel d'ANGEAC].

Byron returned to England in November, and in 1764 he hoisted a commodore's broad pendant in the frigate *Dolphin* (24 guns) for a voyage to the Pacific in company with the sloop *Tamar* (16 guns). The expedition discovered several clusters of islands and returned to England in 1766 after having circumnavigated the world.

Three years later Byron was appointed governor of Newfoundland, going out in command of the *Antelope* (54 guns) in 1769 and the *Panther* (60 guns) in 1770 and 1771. He was governor at an interesting period in the island's history, but his achievements have been overshadowed by those of his predecessor, Hugh PALLISER. Byron did his best to satisfy both the Board of Trade and the inhabitants and cannot be said to have made any significant innovations of his own. Like Palliser, he received frequent complaints from both French and English about interference with each other's fishery. Byron was, however, less severe on French vessels found fishing outside treaty limits, and his relations with d'Angeac, the governor of Saint-Pierre and Miquelon, were smoother than those between Palliser and d'Angeac. Byron also turned his attention to the questions of customs and naval officers' fees, the salmon fishery, and the seal fishery of the Îles de la Madeleine. His effectiveness as governor in 1771 was limited by his inability to visit the outports, since he had been instructed by the Admiralty to make his seamen available for the building of fortifications at St John's. Byron was succeeded as governor in 1772 by Commodore Molyneux SHULDHAM.

In March 1775 Byron was promoted rear-admiral of the blue and by January 1778 had risen to the rank of vice-admiral of the blue. Four months later he was placed in command of a squadron fitting out for North America, and on 9 June he sailed, flying his flag in the *Princess Royal* (90 guns), in order to intercept a French fleet under the Comte d'Estaing. Byron reached New York alone on 18 August, his ships having been dispersed by storms, and then sailed to Halifax, Nova Scotia, where the squadron was reunited on 26 September. Bad weather frustrated further attempts to find the enemy, and it was not until 6 July 1779 that Byron caught up with d'Estaing off Grenada in the West Indies, where his 21 ships fought a bold but indecisive action against 25 French vessels. He returned to England in October. In September 1780 he was promoted vice-admiral of the white, but he had no further employment before his death. His eldest son John, "a handsome profligate," was the father of George Gordon, Lord Byron, the poet, and the sufferings of Don Juan in Byron's poem were, according to the author, based on "those related in my grand-dad's 'Narrative.'"

W. A. B. DOUGLAS

A portrait of John Byron by Sir Joshua Reynolds hangs in the Painted Hall at Greenwich Naval College, London. Byron was author of: *Byron's journal of his circumnavigation, 1764–1766*, ed. R. E. Gallagher (Cambridge, Eng., 1964); *The narrative of the Honourable John Byron (commodore in a late expedition around the world), containing an account of the great distresses suffered by himself and his companions on the coasts of Patagonia from the year 1740 till their arrival in England, 1746* . . . (London and Dublin, 1768).

PRO, Adm. 1/482; 1/486, ff.165, 231–40; 1/1442; 1/1491; 51/3830; CO 194/28; 194/29, ff.28, 47–50; 194/30, ff.3, 9–12, 15, 31, 57–65; 195/9; 195/10, ff.1–105; 195/15; 195/18; 195/21; Prob. 11/1140, f.202. Knox, *Hist. journal* (Doughty), II, III. Charnock, *Biographia navalis*, V, 423ff. Colledge, *Ships of Royal Navy*, I. *DNB*. [A list of the ships Byron served in is available in the entry. W.A.B.D.] G.B., Adm., *Commissioned sea officers*.

W. L. Clowes, *The Royal Navy; a history from the earliest times to the present* (7v., London, 1897–1903), III. John Creswell, *British admirals of the eighteenth century; tactics in battle* (London, 1972). [Creswell rehabilitates Byron's reputation as a tactician in his analysis of the battle off Grenada, bringing in considerations which had been overlooked by Byron's chief critics, A. T. Mahan and J. K. Laughton. W.A.B.D.] C. H. Little, *The battle of the Restigouche: the last naval engagement between France and Britain for the possession of Canada* (Halifax, 1962). A. T. Mahan, *The influence of sea power upon history, 1660–1783* (Boston, 1890). G. J. Marcus, *A naval history of England* (2v., London, 1961–71), I, 439. Bernard Pothier and Judith Beattie, *The battle of the Restigouche, 22 June–8 July, 1760* (Can., National Historic Sites Service, *Manuscript report*, no.19, [Ottawa], n.d.). [Consists of two reports, one by Beattie (1968) and the other by Pothier (1971).] Prowse, *History of Nfld*. W. H. Whiteley, "Governor Hugh Palliser and the Newfoundland and Labrador fishery, 1764–1768," *CHR*, L (1969), 141–63; "James Cook and British policy in the Newfoundland fisheries, 1763–7," *CHR*, LIV (1973), 245–72.

C

CADET, JOSEPH-MICHEL, merchant butcher, businessman, and purveyor general to the French forces in Canada; b. 24 Dec. 1719 at Quebec, son of François-Joseph Cadet (Caddé), a merchant butcher, and Marie-Joseph Daveine (Davesne, Davenne); his paternal grandfather was a merchant butcher of Quebec and his great-grandfather was also one in Niort, France; d. 31 Jan. 1781 in Paris, France.

When Joseph-Michel Cadet was only four years old his widowed mother on 29 Nov. 1724 married Pierre-Joseph Bernard, a son of one of Maurepas's secretaries and himself a scrivener in the Marine department, and a few years later she followed her husband to Rochefort leaving Cadet, aged 12, to fend for himself, or so he later declared. At first he stayed with his maternal grandfather, Gabriel Daveine, with whom he afterwards recalled studying mathematics. He evidently had little formal education, for his letters are composed of more colloquial expressions and phonetic spelling than were usual for merchants and their clerks at the time, and in September 1732, before he was 13, he joined the crew of a merchant ship for a voyage to Île Saint-Jean (Prince Edward Island) and then went to work buying cattle for Augustin Cadet, his father's half-brother, a Quebec butcher.

Cadet's family relationships are worth recording to show the milieu in which he got his start as a Quebec businessman. His uncle, Michel-François Cadet, Augustin's brother, kept a shop at Quebec dealing in imported French fabrics at one time, but he was also a butcher like the rest of the family. Cadet's father's sister, Marie-Anne Cadet, married a master locksmith, Pierre Amiot, in 1714 and their son, Cadet's first cousin, Jean-Baptiste Amiot*, became a successful importing merchant acting as the colonial agent of several French shipping merchants during the 1740s and 1750s. Another first cousin, Louise Cadet, Augustin's daughter, in 1755 married a Huguenot merchant, Joseph Rouffio*, member of a business family of Montauban. The two uncles, Pierre Amiot and Augustin Cadet, were among the seven witnesses at Cadet's marriage on 10 Sept. 1742 to Angélique Fortier, daughter of Michel, a Montreal businessman. Another witness was a certain "Monsieur Duburon," probably Jean-Joseph Feré Duburon, an officer in the colonial regulars, whose daughter, Louise-Élisabeth, in 1738 married Denis GOGUET, a La Rochelle merchant living at Quebec. After Goguet returned to La Rochelle, Cadet was one of the many Canadians who did business with him and in 1763 Goguet held over 323,000 *livres* in bills belonging to Cadet. Whether Cadet benefited by his mother's marriage to a scrivener in the Marine who died at Rochefort about 1737 as provost marshal, or by his sister Marie-Joseph's marriage (8 Sept. 1749) to a surgeon, Jean-Raymond Vignau, is not clear. His other relationships are enough to explain how he became a successful merchant butcher.

These relationships do not, however, account for Cadet's astonishing career as the last purveyor general to the French forces in Canada and a rich and powerful businessman. That career can only be explained by his ability to seize opportunities afforded by the two mid-century wars which brought more and more French troops to Canada. Throughout the history of France, and indeed of most countries, vast fortunes have been made supplying the armed forces in wartime. The Bourbon governments contracted out the supplying business to syndicates of businessmen whose histories have not yet been written, and the general context of Cadet's career is not well understood. It is helpful to remember, however, that while he was making a business of army victualling in Canada many other men of a similar type were victualling other forces in the French empire. For example, under the name of Nicolas Perny, a front man, 13 French businessmen formed a company of purveyors general to the ministry of Marine and Colonies for six years beginning on 1 Jan. 1757. Among them were figures such as Pierre Escourre of Bordeaux, son of a mayor of Tournon, who also invested in slaving ventures to Angola, in the company supplying French army hospitals and other similar enterprises, and who married the daughter of a purveyor general to the navy at Martinique, Laurens-Alexandre Dahon. Other such men contracted to supply the navy with timber, cannon, anchors, and clothing. All had their fingers in many pies. This is the context in which Cadet's career must be studied for it makes little sense in the national history of Canada. In France there were hundreds of similar businessmen who failed in some cases, grew rich in others, or had ups and downs but managed, like Cadet, to marry their daughters into families of the minor nobility. Françoise Cadet married François Esprit de Vantelon, son of a king's councillor in the fiscal subdivision of Châtellerault, mayor and captain general of Châtellerault; Angélique Cadet married Jérôme Rossay, seigneur of Les Pallus, officer of the Duc d'Orléans, municipal magistrate and militia captain of Châtellerault; one of Cadet's sons called himself by the sonorous name of Joseph Cadet Deschamps, seigneur of Mondon. How did their father, a mere colonial butcher, make all this possible?

According to what Cadet declared in 1761 during his interrogations in the Bastille, he had worked during the late 1730s for the official purveyor of meat to the crown at Quebec, Romain Dolbec, and had soon become an equal partner. In 1745, during the War of the Austrian Succession, he was asked by the intendant, Gilles HOCQUART, to provide all the meat required by the crown and continued to do so until 1756. This activity was very profitable. Meanwhile he carried on with his own butchering business for a few years, but also ventured into other commodities, milling flour and selling it to ships' captains, buying ships' cargoes and re-selling them, and dealing in fish, fur, and general shipping. During the early 1750s he contracted with Michel Mahiet, Antoine Morin, Louis Michaud, and others to go out and gather the fish and fur at posts on the fief of Les Monts-Louis to which he had acquired the rights. He began to buy boats and even ships. In 1752, for instance, he and a partner, Nicolas Massot, sent a ship of about 140 tons, the *Joseph de Québec*, under Captain Maurice Simonin, to Martinique with a cargo of fish, timber, and oil to be sold and exchanged for a cargo of sugar for the port of Bordeaux. At Bordeaux the ship was fitted out for the journey to Louisbourg, Île Royale (Cape Breton Island), and Quebec in summer 1753 by Pierre Desclaux using a bottomry loan of 11,000 *livres* from David Gradis et Fils at 12 per cent interest. As Cadet acknowledged and as the busy files of his principal notary, Jean-Claude PANET, show, the War of the Austrian Succession gave Cadet profits and opportunities enough to become a general entrepreneur in the expansive post-war period. He imported large quantities of wine, brandy, and general merchandise from France, particularly in association with Barthélemy* and Jean-Baptiste-Tropez Martin and, in 1759, with Pierre Delannes and Jean-Jacques Gautier and a controller of the Marine, Jean de Villers.

The most successful businessmen in the French empire, then as always, were those who could do business with the government and obtain such official influence, offices, titles, privileges, honours, and mates for their children as money could buy. As early as 1754 Cadet wrote to the minister of Marine and Colonies offering to sign a contract as purveyor general to the crown in Canada; that is, to provision the royal stores at Quebec, Trois-Rivières, Montreal, and the outposts. He got no reply. Then, some time during the summer in 1755, he mentioned the proposal to an army officer with many business interests, Michel-Jean-Hugues PÉAN, adjutant at Quebec, who aroused the interest and support of the intendant, François BIGOT. In October Bigot wrote to Versailles about Cadet's proposal and in July 1756 received the minister's permission to sign a contract for nine years beginning on 1 Jan. 1757. Cadet thus assumed responsibility for Canadian supplies that had hitherto been provided partly by smaller colonial contractors and partly by the French company of purveyors general working under the name of Claude Fort, whose contract expired on 31 Dec. 1756. Forty-two articles were drawn up in an official contract which Cadet and the intendant signed on 26 Oct. 1756.

Under the terms of this contract, Cadet was to give each soldier in the field a daily ration of two pounds of bread, a quarter of a pound of dried peas, and either a pound of beef or half a pound of bacon; and failing these rations he was to give cash instead. Soldiers in the town garrisons were to have one and one-half pounds of bread and a quarter of a pound each of dried peas and bacon. In winter, when fighting was usually suspended, Cadet normally paid the equivalent of these rations to the householders on whom the soldiers were quartered, and the rates were to be fixed by the intendant. This official contract concealed some secret contracts by which various officials and others were associated with the supply business. In the same month, October 1756, Cadet signed an agreement *sous seing privé* (binding but not recorded in notarial minutes) giving Péan a three-fifths share in the business, including one-fifth each for Intendant Bigot, Governor Vaudreuil [RIGAUD], and himself, or so Péan said, and he urged Cadet to keep this arrangement secret. About the same time, Cadet conceded another fifth share to be divided equally among three assistants: Jean Corpron*, who kept the books at Quebec, and François Maurin* and Louis PENNISSEAUT, who together managed a store at Montreal for supplying foodstuffs there and at the forts and posts beyond. This left Cadet with only one-fifth of the profits, but he recovered another fifth in spring 1759 when the aforementioned assistants withdrew from the association. Besides, he did not now lack opportunities for profitable contracts on the side. During 1757 and 1758 he was invited to supply Acadia and did so in association with Bigot's secretary, Joseph BRASSARD Deschenaux, and an army captain, Charles DESCHAMPS de Boishébert.

Joseph-Michel Cadet was now enmeshed in one of those dubious mixtures of private and public enterprise so characteristic of Bourbon France, and how it ramified may be seen in glimpses of the lives of his associates. From 1 July 1755 to 11 June 1756, Pennisseaut and Péan were in a joint-stock trading company with the receiver general of finances for La Rochelle, Gratien Drouilhet, and the government storekeeper at Quebec, Pierre Claverie*. Claverie, through his mother, Jeanne La Barthe, was first cousin to the government storekeeper at Montreal, Jean-Pierre La Barthe, who on 30 Oct. 1759 formed a business company with Pennisseaut and Pennisseaut's relatives, JACQUES-JOSEPH and Jean-Baptiste Lemoine Despins of Montreal. François Maurin had meanwhile been in business with his brother-in-law, Pierre Landriève Lamouline, a chief scrivener for the Marine at Montreal, and we know, too, that Maurin was a cousin of several Huguenot merchants at Quebec, including Pierre Glemet and JEAN-MATHIEU and François* Mounier, most of whom came from his own birth-place, Jarnac, on the Charente. Some of these, like Cadet himself, made large sums of money in the supply business during the Seven Years' War.

Cadet distinguished himself from the rest, however, by his heroic efforts to supply the colony with his own fleet of merchant ships not only in 1757 and 1758 but also in 1759 when most French shipping on the Atlantic had been stopped by the British navy and privateers. A full list of Cadet's ships would be difficult to establish because his shipping agents, especially Pierre Desclaux at Bordeaux and François Gazan and Joseph Aliés at La Rochelle, dispatched many consignments of goods to him in other men's ships. At one time or another during the three critical years, however, he bought more than two dozen ships in France and Canada, most of them late in 1758 when it was clear that no cargo space was to be had at any price for sending goods to Quebec the next spring. Many of the ships' officers and seamen were Canadian, a forgotten group in Quebec history: men such as Captain Jean Carbonnel of the *Venus* (200 tons), Captain Michel Voyer of the *Amitié* (130 tons), and Captain Joseph Massot, Second Officer André de Lange, and most of the 17-man crew of the *Magdeleine* (92 tons), a schooner which Cadet bought for 4,000 *livres* in May 1756 and lost to the enemy in April 1757. Perhaps half of Cadet's ships were wrecked or captured, but many others arrived safely at Quebec, notably a fleet of almost 20 ships under Jacques Kanon* in May 1759. As Governor Vaudreuil wrote to Versailles on 7 Nov. 1759, "It is because of the help he [Cadet] had brought from France that the colony was saved for the king." We need not pretend that Cadet was entirely disinterested in order to appreciate the vigour, scale, daring, and success of his campaign to feed the starving colony.

The French government never acknowledged Cadet's achievements for at least three reasons, none of them worthy of a great nation. First, Cadet was more successful than the French navy in maintaining the transatlantic links on which so much depended. The French fleet was defeated again and again and soon abandoned normal patrolling of the imperial sea routes and even the French coasts in favour of the perennial project for invading England with a fleet of troop ships which, in this case, was destroyed at the Baie de

Quiberon by Admiral Edward Hawke on 20 Nov. 1759. The ships would have been better employed in convoying merchant and troop ships, but the French authorities seemed incapable of organizing a convoy as efficient as Cadet's. Even the repatriation of the French officials and refugees after 1759 was largely done by British vessels. Mortified by its own failures, the French government was not in a frame of mind to recognize Cadet's successes. Secondly, once Quebec had been lost in September 1759 it was easy to ignore or to disparage Cadet's efforts to supply the colony and politically necessary to find scapegoats who could be blamed for the losses and failures. Cadet and other officials were natural scapegoats for the loss of Canada just as Jean LABORDE was for the loss of Louisbourg and the Comte de Lally and Joseph-François Dupleix were for the loss of French India, because they had made handsome profits in the ill-fated colonies. Here is a third reason why Cadet's achievements were not properly appreciated: he had garnered a fortune reckoned at several millions. The money was in property and bills of exchange and treasury notes deposited with Denis Goguet at La Rochelle; Barthélemy and Jean-Baptiste-Tropez Martin at Marseilles; Lanogenu and the firm of Veuve Courrejolles at Bayonne; and Pierre Desclaux, Jean-André LAMALETIE, and Jean Dupuy Fils et Cie at Bordeaux; and when Cadet could do nothing more in Canada he went to France to settle his many debts and make the most of his fortune. Taken off at Quebec on a British ship, the *Adventure*, on 18 Oct. 1760, he landed at Brest on 26 November, reached Bordeaux 12 days later, where his family had been living since 1759, and arrived in Paris on 21 Jan. 1761; he was arrested four days later and imprisoned in the Bastille with most of his official colleagues from Canada.

Historians who take the ensuing trial at its face value have no difficulty in pronouncing Joseph-Michel Cadet, as the Châtelet criminal court did on 10 Dec. 1763, a monstrous criminal fortunate to get off with banishment from Paris for nine years and what amounted to a fine of six million *livres*. To make a national hero of Cadet would be uphill work as there are signs that in 1759 he was in close contact with the enemy for some dark purpose. He was never tried for that, however, and various facts and circumstances show that his case was not so simple as the Châtelet made it seem. Not all observers in Canada thought him a criminal. "I believe him to be the least guilty of all," wrote a prominent merchant, François Havy*, on hearing of Cadet's arrest, "for he was only a tool that others made use of and he will perhaps be the only victim." The crown itself seemed to betray doubts when on 5 March 1764 it lifted Cadet's banishment and decided to release him from the Bastille and to reduce his fine by half. Whatever the significance of those decisions, French criminal justice was notoriously unfair to the accused and otherwise deficient, as many enlightened observers pointed out in that age, and it was not for nothing that the revolutionary governments abolished the Châtelet and made the taking of the Bastille on 14 July 1789 a symbol of victory over a tyrannical and backward régime. More to the point, the prosecuting ministers and magistrates made Cadet's crimes seem worse than they were by blaming him not only for selling food to the crown at high prices but also for the high prices themselves.

Cadet was faced with a typical 18th-century misunderstanding of the market mechanism which he in his commonsense way seemed to grasp clearly. He said that he "could not conceal that expenditures for the king in Canada were immense, [but] that the cause for this could only be attributed to the scarcity of goods," and goods were scarce because too few ships reached Quebec. This in turn was because "the dangers that ships and vessels faced in their freighting from France to Canada were not imaginary." In this matter the evidence seems to be on Cadet's side. Shipping insurance premiums rose from less than five per cent of the value insured in 1755 to 50 per cent or more in 1758; in 1759 insurance was often unobtainable. Freight rates to Quebec paid in France rose from 190 *livres* a ton in 1756 to from 240 to 280 *livres* in 1757; but for guaranteed delivery at Quebec in 1758 and 1759 freight rates were anything from 400 to 1,000 *livres* a ton when cargo space could be rented at all. The crown, in its infinite wisdom, took the view, on the advice of the Commission Fontanieu set up in 1758 to reduce naval debts [*see* Alexandre-Robert HILLAIRE de La Rochette], that anything charged above the 1756 rate of 190 *livres* was inadmissible profiteering and summarily reduced the claims of shipping merchants to that figure. The crown adopted the same principle when it explained the high wartime prices in Canada as the result of a conspiracy for which Cadet was partly to blame, and yet it now seems plain that whatever Cadet may have done, wartime conditions alone were enough to explain why food prices rose. The trial of Cadet and his associates led the general public to believe that they were particularly self-seeking, corrupt, and unscrupulous, whereas a little investigation shows that they were only doing what many other Bourbon officials did, especially in the colonies, but they had the misfortune to find unusually profitable circumstances in a colony that was subsequently lost to an enemy in wartime. The Bourbon monarchy was accustomed to reducing its short-term debts periodically by means of a *chambre de justice* which tried anyone suspected of profiteering at government expense, and the infamous *affaire du Canada* was carried out in that tradition.

Cadet's case went on for many years while various crown agencies set up to recover the money those involved in the *affaire du Canada* were condemned to pay slowly discovered that six million *livres* was too much to ask for. A commission established by a ruling of the Conseil d'État, 31 Dec. 1763, decided a year later that Cadet's debts amounted to the staggering figure of about seventeen million *livres*, of which about nine million was owing to the crown, but by 27 Nov. 1767 they had reduced the latter to 3,898,036 *livres*, which he duly paid by 20 Aug. 1768, although this was a higher figure than the royal controller for the recovery of crown assets, Pierre-François Boucher, arrived at. In the course of the investigation Cadet was imprisoned and interrogated once more from 17 February to 25 March 1766. At his death he was still compiling accounts which he hoped to render to the crown to justify himself. He had no intention, however, of paying out any more than he had to and at his death had still not satisfied his private creditors, who had formed a union in the manner of the age and elected directors who included Tourton et Baur, the well-known Paris bankers, Jean-Baptiste-Tropez Martin, a merchant formerly of Quebec but originally from Marseilles, and Arnoult, a former Paris notary. Cadet had, however, settled some of his debts, having paid 61,583 *livres* to his main Bordeaux agent, Pierre Desclaux, on 11 Jan. 1768; 52,856 *livres* to his old personal assistant, Étienne Cebet, on 23 April 1767; and so on as recorded in the files of his principal Paris notary, Maître Delage.

During the 1760s Cadet also sold off the property he owned in Canada, including a lot on the Rue Saint-Pierre, Quebec, measuring 120 feet by 90 feet (whereon had once stood a house built by a Mme Cugnet), which he sold for 22,500 *livres* to William Grant*, who visited him in Paris for this purpose; three other houses in Quebec, one ruined and one that was still standing on the old Rue Saint-Paul until the early 1970s; two pieces of land on the Rivière Saint-Charles about a league from Quebec; and his seigneury, Les Monts-Louis, on the St Lawrence River about 90 leagues below Quebec. Most of this property was sold for him either by his Quebec notary, Panet, or by his old friend and assistant, Antoine-Pierre Houdin, then at Quebec.

During the last 15 years of his life, Cadet used his remaining assets and his credit to build up what we might now call a trust and real-estate business in France. He bought, sold, and managed large properties. For example, in January 1767 he bought the seigneury of Barbelinière in the parish of Thuré (dept of Vienne) through an intermediary who hid Cadet's identity, and several other estates "consisting of ancient castles partly demolished, share-croppers' houses, farms, water-mills, forests, arable lands, meadows, vineyards, thatched cottages, feudal dues . . . in Poitou, Maine and Touraine." Like many other dealers and speculators in France, he lived partly in Paris or its suburbs where his business was done – and where he eventually died in the Hôtel Sainte-Avoye, in the parish of Saint-Nicolas-des-Champs – and partly on one of his estates near Blois in the valley of the Loire.

No lovelier part of the world is to be found than this, the land of French princely châteaux and of the *Très riches heures du duc de Berry*, but Cadet and his wife, two middle-aged Canadians in exile, missed the remembered things of home. On 5 May 1766, Cadet wrote to Houdin in Quebec to send him two birch-bark canoes, a Canadian carriage and harness, some ploughs and some axes, and "an honest habitant youth from the Côte de Beaupré or the Île d'Orléans; a good farmer and enterprising at this work." Cadet offered a nine-year contract at 200 *livres* a year. "This man is to work my land," he wrote. "I will have great satisfaction in seeing people from my native land there. But remember I want a bachelor and a first-rate farmer." So Cadet lived on comfortably, though never very wealthy, until he died on 31 Jan. 1781; his wife died on 1 Oct. 1791. His partners in the supply business at Quebec had dispersed soon after being released from the Bastille in the early 1760s, Corpron to Nantes where he established himself as a shipping merchant, Maurin to Bordeaux where in 1770 he was described as a resident of the city living in the Place Saint-Domingue. Pennisseaut we have not been able to trace.

Joseph-Michel Cadet's career was spectacular, but he was by no means alone in rising from humble origins to the splendours of a country estate. Jacques Imbert*, the Marine treasurers' agent at Quebec, whom Cadet must have known well, was born on 15 Nov. 1710 to a Montargis merchant tanner, later turned corporal in the mounted constabulary, who had married a surgeon's daughter, and after many years in Canada, where he married a Canadian girl, Imbert died a country gentleman at his château near Auxerre, having married off his only daughter, Catherine-Agathe (born at Quebec) to a royal magistrate there. The lives of Jacques-Michel BRÉARD, controller of the Marine at Quebec, and various merchants such as Denis Goguet, Michel Rodrigue, and Jean-Mathieu Mounier were marked by similar success. "It is a popular conviction," wrote another biographer of Cadet, Adam Shortt*, half a century ago, "that private profit and public benefit cannot possibly coincide." Shortt, reflecting on Cadet's career, did not share that conviction and why should we? After all, if France had not lost Canada, Joseph-Michel Cadet might have been acclaimed as a hero and a public benefactor!

J. F. BOSHER

AD, Charente-Maritime (La Rochelle), B, 259; 5746, no.5; Gironde (Bordeaux), Minutes Guy (Bordeaux), 3 mars 1759. AN, Col., E, 58 (dossier Cadet); 276 (dossier Lemoine-Despins); Minutier central, XIV, XXXIII. ANQ-M, Greffe de Pierre Panet [With many thanks to José Igartua, who sent me the references to the Montreal sources. J.F.B.]. ANQ-Q, État civil, Catholiques, Notre-Dame de Québec; Greffe de Claude Barolet, 8 nov. 1733 (marriage contract of Augustin Cadet); Greffe de C.-H. Du Laurent, 11 juin 1756; Greffe de J.-C. Panet. Bibliothèque de l'Arsenal, Archives de la Bastille, 12142, ff.267–70 (Cadet's statement to Sartine, 18 Nov. 1761); 12143–48. PRO, HCA, 32/175, *Chesine*; 32/200, *Hardy*; 32/233/1, *Magdeleine*.

Docs. relating to Canadian currency during the French period (Shortt), II. "Autographes de personnages ayant marqué dans l'histoire de Bordeaux et de la Guyenne," Soc. des archives historiques de la Gironde, [*Publication*] (Bordeaux), XXX (1895), 253–61. François Bluche, *L'origine des magistrats du parlement de Paris au XVIII*e *siècle (1715–1771): dictionnaire généalogique* (Paris, 1956). Tanguay, *Dictionnaire*. J. F. Bosher, " 'Chambres de justice' in the French monarchy," *French government and society, 1500–1850: essays in memory of Alfred Cobban*, ed. J. F. Bosher (London, 1973), 19–40; *French finances, 1770–1795: from business to bureaucracy* (Cambridge, Eng., 1970). Paul Butel, *La croissance commerciale bordelaise dans la seconde moitié du XVIII*e *siècle* (2v., Lille, France, 1973). Jean Egret, *The French prerevolution, 1787–1788*, trans. W. D. Camp, intro. J. F. Bosher (Chicago and London, 1977). P.-G. Roy, *Bigot et sa bande*. [L.-F.-G.] Baby, "Une lettre de Cadet, le munitionnaire de la Nouvelle-France," *Canadian Antiquarian and Numismatic Journal* (Montreal), 3rd ser., I (1898), 173–87. Alfred Barbier, "La baronnie de la Touche-d'Avrigny et le duché de Châtellerault sous François 1er," Soc. des Antiquaires de l'Ouest, *Mémoires* (Poitiers, France), 2e sér., IX (1886), 349–60; "Un munitionnaire du roi à la Nouvelle France: Joseph Cadet, 1756–1781," Soc. des antiquaires de l'Ouest, *Bull.* (Poitiers), 2e sér., VIII (1898–1900), 399–412 [This article is useful in spite of some serious inaccuracies, such as, for instance, Cadet's date of birth. J.F.B.]. J. F. Bosher, "The French government's motives in the affaire du Canada" (*English Hist. Rev.* (Harlow, Eng.), forthcoming); "French Protestant families in Canadian trade, 1740–1760," *Social History*, VII (1974), 179–201; "Government and private interests in New France," *Canadian Public Administration* (Toronto), X (1967), 244–57. Jean de Maupassant, "Les armateurs bordelais au XVIIIe siècle: les deux expéditions de Pierre Desclaux au Canada (1759 et 1760)," *Revue historique de Bordeaux et du dép. de la Gironde* (Bordeaux), VIII (1915), 225–40, 313–30. Honorius Provost, "La maison Cadet," *Cahiers d'hist.* (Québec), I (1947), 27–32 (with a sketch of the house in question).

CALLBECK, PHILLIPS, office-holder and administrator of St John's (Prince Edward) Island; b. *c.* 1744; m. in 1772 Ann Coffin; d. 21 Feb. 1790 at Charlottetown, St John's Island.

Little is known of the early life of Phillips Callbeck, although family tradition suggests that he was born and educated in Ireland. He came to St John's Island from England about 1770 and in September of that year was appointed to Governor Walter PATTERSON's first council. In the same year he became attorney general and surrogate general and judge of probate. He had a law practice as well, and Patterson, writing after the death of Chief Justice John Duport in May 1774, noted that Callbeck's appointment to the position could not be allowed since it would leave the island without a single lawyer. Callbeck also ran a mill and a store.

As senior councillor, Callbeck became administrator in 1775 when Patterson left for England to fight for a commitment to funding the island government. He had occupied this post for only four months when the colony was attacked in November by New England privateers. Charlottetown was looted and Callbeck, together with Surveyor General Thomas Wright*, was taken prisoner. Released in Salem, Massachusetts, Callbeck was in Halifax by January 1776.

After his return to the island in May, Callbeck attempted to improve the defensive state of the colony. He raised an independent company of militia and, as engineer, attended to the fortifications of the island. But he overstepped his authority in the construction of defence works (his bill for £14,000 was later rejected by the British military officials) and was never able to raise the full complement of 100 men for the company. According to Chief Justice Peter Stewart* all this activity made for him "an independent fortune": in addition to his salaries as administrator and attorney general and profits made as the colony's principal merchant and shopkeeper, Callbeck collected perquisites as acting engineer and militia colonel.

Patterson returned to the colony in 1780 and the next year seized several townships for arrears in quitrents. Callbeck was among those who supported the action and who purchased land at the auction which followed in November 1781. The reaction of such proprietors as Robert CLARK and Captain John MacDonald* was strong, and they pressured the British officials to reverse the move. Probably in the fall of 1783 Patterson received a draft bill from Lord North, secretary of state for the Home Department, providing for the land's return to the original proprietors. Patterson put off introducing this legislation until he could secure an assembly more sympathetic to his own views. In the election of March 1784 he was opposed by the Country party, led by John Stewart*, son of the chief justice. Callbeck ran unsuccessfully for an assembly seat in the election, which resulted in a victory for the Country party. A new election in March 1785 resulted in a more compliant assembly, and Callbeck assisted Patterson in forcing defeat of the draft bill in November 1786. Patterson then introduced a private bill which returned all land to its original proprietors save that bought by Callbeck, Thomas Desbrisay*, and Peter Stewart, provided that the 1781 purchasers were compensated. In the same month, however, Lieutenant Governor Edmund Fanning* arrived to serve as acting governor in the place of Patterson, who was summoned by the Home secretary to explain his actions. Patterson clung to office until June 1787, when he returned to England. Fanning, now governor, set about establishing his own faction.

Callbeck had no real place in the new government. He attended meetings of council infrequently and, when present, obstructed the passage of its motions and the conduct of its business. Dropped from the council by Fanning as a result, Callbeck was reinstated the same year, but he did not attend any more meetings. The summer of 1787 saw the election of an anti-Fanning assembly led by Captain Alexander Fletcher. Callbeck, who had been elected as a member of Fletcher's party, was voted speaker in January 1788. In London, the last of the series of events begun in 1781 was being played out before the Privy Council. Criminal charges against Patterson and the members of his administration were maintained, and in July 1789 Callbeck was removed from his seat on council and dismissed as attorney general. His death followed within a year.

Callbeck's career had been ruined by the land question, which would destroy many more before it was settled. He, like Patterson, has been judged harshly by historians, but he appears to have had a dedication to the struggling colony's interests as well as to his own. After his death the assembly voted to place a monument on his grave as a "grateful Tribute to the General Benefactor of this Island."

H. T. HOLMAN

PRO, CO 226/1, pp.15, 29; 226/6, pp.18, 76–83; 226/7, pp.34–35, 60–66, 71–73; 226/12, pp.53–54, 185; 227/1, pp.4, 71–73; 227/2, pp.61, 63–73, 81; 227/4, p.3. Public Archives of P.E.I. (Charlottetown), accession 2541/35, diary; MacDonald papers, Captain John MacDonald to Nelly MacDonald, 12 Sept. 1789; Smith-Alley coll., M. J. Young to George Alley, 4 Dec. 1894; RG 5, Executive Council, Minutes, 19 Sept. 1770, 18 April, 23 May, 29 Sept. 1787. Island of St John's (P.E.I.), House of Assembly, *Journal*, 3 April 1790. [John MacDonald?], *Remarks on the conduct of the governor and Council of the Island of St. John's, in passing an act of assembly in April 1786 to confirm the sales of the lands in 1781 . . .* (n.p., [1789?]).

CAMPBELL, JOHN, army officer and Indian agent; b. *c.* 1731 in Glendaruel (Strathclyde), Scotland; d. 23 June 1795 at Montreal (Que.).

John Campbell early embarked on a military career, joining the 43rd (later the 42nd) Foot in 1744. Promoted lieutenant on 16 May 1748, he accompanied his regiment to North America in 1756, and two years later he was wounded in ABERCROMBY's assault on Fort Carillon (Ticonderoga, N.Y.). In March 1762 Campbell, now a captain, exchanged into the 27th Foot, with which he served at the siege of Havana, Cuba. From the autumn of 1763 the regiment was stationed at Trois-Rivières (Que.), and in that year Campbell married Marie-Anne, daughter of Luc de LA CORNE, who had played an important role in French-Indian relations during the Seven Years' War. The continuing influence of his father-in-law may have been one of the factors in Campbell's later appointments in the Indian department.

In March 1765 Governor James MURRAY of Quebec, whose instructions had ordered him to appoint "a proper Person or Persons" to treat with the Indians, named Campbell "Inspector of Indian Affairs." A jurisdictional dispute developed, however, when Sir William JOHNSON, superintendent of northern Indians, pointed out that Christian Daniel CLAUS was already serving as deputy agent to the Canadian Indians. The matter was referred to the British government and Johnson's claim was apparently upheld, since Campbell was later to petition for the position to which he had been appointed. In late 1766 Campbell was caught up in the Thomas WALKER affair when he was accused of being one of the magistrate's assailants. Imprisoned, he was subsequently freed when charges against most of the accused were dropped.

The 27th Foot left Quebec for Ireland in August 1767 and four years later, seeing no chance for advancement, Campbell exchanged to half pay. He maintained his interest in obtaining a post in the Indian department, and in September 1772 the Duke of Argyll supported his petition for the superintendency of the Indians in Quebec. Through the influence of Governor Guy Carleton*, Campbell was named superintendent of Indian affairs in Quebec on 3 July 1773. His appointment was part of Carleton's campaign to reduce the Johnson family's influence in the department, and Campbell's arrival at Montreal in September 1775 to claim the superintendency meant the displacement of Claus, who bitterly resented his supersession. In November Claus joined Guy JOHNSON, Joseph Brant [Thayendanegea*], and others on a voyage to England, where he hoped to obtain redress from the home government. Campbell, who had remained in Montreal, was active in resisting the American invasion, leading a sortie in September which resulted in the capture of Ethan Allen and a part of his force. He was later taken prisoner himself, however, and only in late 1776 was he released and allowed to go to New York.

The next year Campbell was given charge of the western Indians on the BURGOYNE expedition, although no military duties were attached to the post. According to Burgoyne, neither Campbell nor his deputy Alexander Fraser spoke any Indian language, and this deficiency was partially responsible for their being "of no weight" in Indian councils. The majority of the Indians left the army in August, and either Campbell accompanied them or he was soon exchanged after the army's surrender in October 1777 since he was back in Montreal by July 1778. That year, the pressure of the Johnson group combined with Carleton's replacement by HALDIMAND, who was more favourable to the Johnsons, led to a resurgence of their interests. Perhaps because of Campbell's failure to keep the Indians with the Burgoyne expedition and Claus's fluency in several Iroquoian languages, Claus was appointed deputy agent to the Six Nations in Canada in October, and Campbell's responsibilities were thereby reduced to some extent. But since Haldimand seems to have been friendly to him and Guy Johnson was preoccupied with difficulties of his own at the time, Campbell was not dismissed as Claus had been.

Campbell's title of "Commandant of the Indians and Superintendent and Inspector of Indian Affairs" made him responsible for all Indians in Canada other than the Six Nations, and because of the largely military character of his work during the revolution he reported directly to Haldimand, although he was expected to inform the Johnson group of his activities. He was ordered to send Indians on scouts and raids into rebel territory, to transmit trade goods and presents to the upper posts, and to supply and provision Indians on government service. In addition, he took part in government councils with the Indians, especially during the later phase of the revolution when some of the Six Nations were preparing to enter Canada. Campbell seems to have worked well with Haldimand, although like other officials of the department he incurred the governor's criticism for its large expenses. In late 1782 Sir John Johnson* was appointed superintendent general of Indian affairs, whereupon Campbell became responsible to him.

Problems about an exact definition of Campbell's position led to difficulties on occasion. As early as spring 1774 he petitioned for the rank of lieutenant-colonel in the army, and he repeated this request on several occasions. Twice in 1779 he also claimed the command of the Montreal garrison in the absence of the senior military officer. Haldimand adamantly refused all the requests made during his governorship, and he was supported by the British government. From the correspondence over the matter, it appears that Campbell's titles of major (which he had received in 1773) and lieutenant-colonel (1777) were courtesies only since his position was a civil one. Thus although the *Army list* mentioned him as having local rank in America, he was allowed neither the rank nor the pay of an officer. With the end of the war Campbell's courtesy rank of colonel, awarded him in 1782, was taken away, and he reverted to lieutenant-colonel. He petitioned the British government for reinstatement as colonel, but it was not until 1790 that this advancement occurred. In 1792 he again attempted to assert his authority when he claimed the command of the department in Sir John Johnson's absence. Lieutenant Governor Alured Clarke* was no more helpful than Haldimand: he replied that Campbell's appointment was confined to Lower Canada and gave him no claim to command the entire department. Campbell's frustration at not having his Indian department service recognized in a suitable military fashion was at the centre of the department's ambiguous position in government; not until 1830 was its status finally determined.

Campbell seems to have dealt with departmental business in a responsible way but on at least one occasion his normal routine was interrupted by the displeasure of Lord Dorchester [Carleton]. During the early 1790s a sensitive situation developed as the British government became involved in the dispute between the Americans and Indians over the Ohio country. When one of Dorchester's speeches to an Indian council appeared in the American press early in 1794, he ordered Campbell to discover how the speech had been obtained and accused the Indian department of Lower Canada of being in a "deranged state." Campbell reported that he did not know how the speech had been acquired and evaded the second issue by attempting to explain instead the "deranged state" of Lower Canada's Indians. One year later his career was ended by his death.

It is difficult to assess Campbell's career. Some authorities have seen him as a grasping incompetent, an 18th-century version of the later American carpetbagger. But this assessment is probably unjust; his difficulties were as much the product of Indian department upheavals during the revolution as they were of his own shortcomings.

DOUGLAS LEIGHTON

BL, Add. MSS 21771–73; 21873, ff.146–47v; 21882, f.10. PAC, MG 19, F1, 23; MG 23, A1, ser.1, 8, ff.2285, 2287. *Johnson papers* (Sullivan *et al.*), VIII, 1103, 1109; XII, 114, 691, 698. PAC *Report*, 1888, note A. "State papers," PAC *Report*, 1891, 27, 65–66, 105. "State papers – Lower Canada," PAC *Report*, 1890, 76, 89, 111, 112. *Quebec Gazette*, 2 July 1795, 18 March 1813. G.B., WO, *Army list*, 1758–95. PAC, *Preliminary inventory, Record Group 10: Indian affairs* (Ottawa, 1951), iii. Graymont, *Iroquois*, 81, 148, 150–55, 175. R. S. Allen, "The British Indian department and the frontier in North America, 1755–1830," *Canadian Historic Sites: Occasional Papers in Archaeology and History* (Ottawa), no.14 (1975), 5–125.

CAMPBELL, Lord WILLIAM, naval officer and colonial administrator; b. *c.* 1730, fourth son of John Campbell, 4th Duke of Argyll, and Mary Bellenden; d. 4 Sept. 1778 in Southampton, England.

As a younger son of a peer William Campbell possessed no inherited income, and he therefore entered the Royal Navy in search of a career. From 1752 to 1760 he served in the Indian theatre, taking part in two actions against the Comte d'Aché's fleet and participating in the battle of Plassey. By August 1762 he had risen to the rank of captain. Campbell then spent several years in American waters, and while in command of the *Nightingale* he visited South Carolina. There, on 7 April 1763, he married Sarah Izard, daughter of one of the principal planters of the province. Two daughters and a son were born to the couple.

In 1764 Campbell was elected to parliament from the family constituency of Argyllshire, but he resigned two years later after being named governor of Nova Scotia, an appointment that owed much to his family's influence at court. The death of the previous governor, Montagu Wilmot*, in May 1766 necessitated Campbell's speedy assumption of his duties. He arrived at Halifax on 26 November and the following day took over the administration from Lieutenant Governor Michael FRANCKLIN.

In a report to the British government submitted soon after his arrival Campbell stated that Nova Scotia was £23,000 in debt and was contributing little towards its annual expenditure. Since complaints had been received about Francklin, Campbell also, as instructed, commented upon the lieutenant governor's suitability to hold office. He criticized Francklin's "overbearing Influence" and his ability to "sit Judge, and Arbitrator in cases, where his own Interest is most immediatly concerned," but Francklin's influence in London protected him.

Late in 1767 the assembly passed a bill raising the excise on locally produced rum and lowering the impost on imported spirits. Campbell had supported the measure in order to make cheaper rum available to the population and to break the monopoly of John BUTLER and John FILLIS, who controlled the wholesale rum trade in the province. Butler and Fillis appealed to Joshua MAUGER in London for assistance, and Mauger, supported by several other merchants, petitioned the Board of Trade to repeal the legislation, which they claimed would injure Nova Scotia's allegedly large trade with the West Indies. In spite of an "able, convincing statement" by Campbell in defence of his actions, the board accepted the merchants' arguments and ordered the legislation annulled.

Campbell was able to appear personally before the board to present his case since he had been granted leave in 1767 to return to England to bring out his wife. He was absent from Nova Scotia from October 1767 to September 1768, and upon his return he travelled to Boston for a month. Although in total his absences eventually amounted to nearly two of his seven years of governorship, Campbell was genuinely interested in the welfare of the province. He visited much of it to see conditions for himself and as a result urged that the British government finance road building to connect the various settlements and townships; he also pointed out the desirability of encouraging settlement in the "Infant Colony."

But although Campbell believed that the province could, with proper support, become "equal to any of his Maj.s Colony's upon the Continent," he was prevented from exercising efficient government in many instances by economic constraints which the home authorities imposed. In 1767 he was refused permission to use the Cape Breton coal mines or the revenue from quitrents to finance road building, and in 1768 he was forced to spend £100 of his own money to rent a schooner to observe the French islands of Saint-Pierre and Miquelon. Campbell utilized his visit to London to convince the Board of Trade not to reduce the parliamentary grant further. He was also able to obtain a £500 grant to pay for road building but upon his return discovered that Francklin had already incurred £423 worth of debts for the construction of roads on his own initiative. Although the governor's request for reconstruction of the decayed Halifax fortifications was refused, the threat of war with Spain in 1770 secured approval for repairs. The removal of the garrison of Halifax to Boston in 1768 caused Campbell concern, and he pointed out that the "thinly settled nature of the colony" meant that Nova Scotia was now more exposed to enemy attack.

Campbell had suffered from ill health and problems with his eyes for some time, and in 1771 these difficulties became increasingly troublesome. Leave was granted him to go south for treatment and he spent from October 1771 to July 1772 in Boston. The treatment appears to have been effective, since he returned to work with vigour, urging the British government to establish naval patrols in the Strait of Canso and in the Baie des Chaleurs to protect the fisheries and prevent smuggling. The patrols were refused, but during the winter of 1772–73 Campbell organized his own investigation into smuggling at Halifax and on the Saint John River (N.B.).

Despite his avowed intention of remaining in Nova Scotia, Campbell had twice petitioned for the vacant governorship of South Carolina, and in June 1773 his wish was fulfilled. He left Halifax in October and after spending over a year in England arrived at Charleston in June 1775. The governor met a hostile reception since the revolution was already well advanced, and his attempts to secure cooperation from the assembly were fruitless. He spent the last four months of his term of office, from September 1775 to January 1776, on a British warship in Charleston harbour. In June 1776 he participated in the British attack on Charleston as commander of a gun-deck on the *Bristol*. Wounded in the battle, he went to England to recover but died two years later of his injury.

Campbell's governorship of Nova Scotia has been described as uneventful by historians, and there is little doubt his term of office lacked the controversy associated with that of his successor, Francis LEGGE. His relations with assembly and Council were generally good and he was popular with the community at large. He was one of the more energetic governors in trying to improve communications and defence and to increase settlement; it was his misfortune that the economic climate was unfavourable to his plans.

FRANCIS A. COGHLAN

PANS, F.-J. Audet, "Governors, lieutenant-governors, and administrators of Nova Scotia, 1604–1932" (typescript, n.d.). PRO, CO 217/44, ff.11–19, 157–59, 167–68; 217/45, f.245; 217/46; 217/47, ff.23–24; 217/48, ff.41–43, 45, 140. *Burke's peerage* (1927). *DAB*. Murdoch, *History of N.S.*, II, 463, 468–72, 474, 478, 480, 488–94. J. S. Macdonald, "Memoir, Lieut.-Governor Michael Francklin, 1752–1782," N.S. Hist. Soc., *Coll.*, XVI (1912), 7–40.

CAMPION, ÉTIENNE-CHARLES, fur-trader and merchant; baptized 15 Jan. 1737 at Montreal (Que.), son of Étienne Campion, *dit* Labonté, an innkeeper, and Charlotte Pepin; m. there 23 Nov. 1773 Madeleine Gautier; m. secondly 17 Feb. 1794 Marie-Josephte Maillet at Trois-Rivières (Que.); buried 23 Dec. 1795 at Montreal.

Étienne-Charles Campion first went into the *pays d'en haut* in 1753. By 1761 he was well acquainted with the region and was recommended as a guide and assistant to Alexander Henry* the elder, who planned a trading voyage to Michilimackinac (Mackinaw City, Mich.). Campion's knowledge and support proved invaluable when Henry arrived at the post before the British force of occupation and was in some danger from the local Indians [*see* Minweweh*]. Campion continued as his assistant until 1763 and behaved, according to Henry, "with honesty and fidelity."

Although Campion's residence was in Montreal, he was active in religious and community affairs at Michilimackinac from 1765 to 1794. He traded to the south and to the northwest as well as at Michilimackinac, and he sold merchandise to the Indian department there. During the American revolution he occasionally went on missions for the department. In 1779 a group of Michilimackinac traders including Campion pooled their goods in a partnership known as the General Store. Disorder connected with the revolution complicated their business, however. They had merchandise and furs at Fort St Joseph (Niles, Mich.) when in the fall of 1780 it was pillaged by raiders from Illinois. With a force of local Potawatomis, Campion overtook the party at a place called Rivière-du-Chemin (Michigan City, Ind.) and recovered most of the plunder, but in 1781 an attack in his absence destroyed the St Joseph post.

Once peace had been restored, Campion resumed his southwestern trade on an extensive scale. There was a marked increase in trading generally in the region during the years after the revolution, and competition was destructive of profits. In 1785 Campion joined with a number of merchants at Michilimackinac (Mackinac Island, Mich.) in a partnership known as the General Company of Lake Superior and the South, or as the General Society, which concentrated on the trade south to the Illinois country and west to the headwaters of the Missouri. In that year also, Campion became one of the 19 founding members of the Beaver Club in Montreal. The General Society apparently dissolved in 1787. Campion, along with William Grant* of Montreal and some others, formed Grant, Campion and Company, which moved into the trade west of Lake Superior as far as the Saskatchewan country. It became an important rival of the North West Company. Campion's group was party to a 1792 arrangement by which Joseph Frobisher* of the North West Company secured agreement among a number of the opposing concerns to diminish the competition at the western posts. Grant, Campion and Company continued to outfit wintering traders and to sell wholesale to small merchants at Michilimackinac; it also became associated with James GRANT in the Timiskaming trade.

Campion was involved in a murder at Michilimackinac in 1792. According to the commandant, Edward Charlton, an Ojibwa named Wawenesse attempted to stab a trader and two others. Overpowered, his hands tied behind him, he was being led to the authorities when he was attacked and killed by seven men including Campion. The incident was considered by a grand jury at Detroit, but the resolution is not known.

Campion went on with his normal business activities. The tendency to new alliances in the fur trade continued to exert itself, and in 1795 Grant, Campion and Company acquired one of the 46 shares in the North West Company. Campion was in poor health, however, and he died in December.

IN COLLABORATION

ANQ-M, État civil, Catholiques, Notre-Dame de Montréal, 15 janv. 1737, 23 nov. 1773, 23 déc. 1795; Greffe de J.-B. Adhémar, 30 avril 1754; Greffe de J.-G. Delisle, 19 déc. 1795; Greffe de Pierre Panet, 22 nov. 1773; Testaments, Testaments olographes, Étienne Campion, 19 déc. 1795. PAC, MG 19, B3, p.4. Ste Ann's Parish (Mackinac Island, Mich.), Registre des baptêmes, mariages et sépultures de Sainte-Anne-de-Michillimakinak.

Correspondence of Lieut. Governor Simcoe (Cruikshank), I. *Docs. relating to NWC* (Wallace). Henry, *Travels and adventures* (Bain). *Michigan Pioneer Coll.*, IX (1886), X (1886), XI (1887), XIII (1888), XIX (1891), XXIII (1893), XXIV (1894). Lebœuf, *Complément*, 1re sér., 24. Lefebvre, "Engagements pour l'Ouest," ANQ *Rapport*, 1946–47. C. W. Alvord, *The Illinois country, 1673–1818* (Chicago, 1922; repr. 1965). Rich, *History of HBC*, II. W. S. Wallace, *The pedlars from Quebec and other papers on the Nor'Westers* (Toronto, 1954). W. E. Stevens, "Fur trading companies in the northwest, 1760–1816," Mississippi Valley Hist. Assoc., *Proc.* (Cedar Rapids, Iowa), IX, pt.2 (1918), 283–91.

CANNARD, PIERRE RENAUD, *dit*. *See* RENAUD

CAPTAIN JECOB. *See* WINNINNEWAYCAPPO

CARIGNANT, JEAN-LOUIS BESNARD, *dit*. *See* BESNARD

CARPENTIER, BONAVENTURE (baptized **Étienne**), priest and Recollet; b. and baptized 18 Sept. 1716 at Beaumont (Que.), probably the son of Étienne Carpentier and Marie-Charlotte Blanchon; d. 6 Jan. 1778 at Saint-Nicolas (Que.).

Étienne Carpentier took his vows on 29 April 1737 and on 23 Sept. 1741 was ordained priest with the name Father Bonaventure. After a few months' ministry at Lotbinière and a two-year stay at the Recollet monastery in Trois-Rivières, he became chaplain at Fort Saint-Frédéric (near Crown Point, N.Y.) at the beginning of 1747. From 1750 to 1753 he ministered to the parishes of Sainte-Marie-de-la-Nouvelle-Beauce (Sainte-Marie, Que.) and Saint-Joseph-de-la-Nouvelle-Beauce (Saint-Joseph, Que.); then from 1753 to 1754 he acted as chaplain at Fort Frontenac (Kingston, Ont.). For some years afterward there is no trace of him.

In 1758 Father Bonaventure was a missionary to the Acadians and the Indians along the Miramichi River (N.B.). In September of that year MURRAY, under Wolfe*'s orders, destroyed their settlement (since that time called Burnt Church), forcing Father Bonaventure and his flock to flee into the woods in the direction of Baie des Chaleurs. In 1764 Father Bonaventure became the first resident priest at Bonaventure (Que.). Two years later he wrote Bishop BRIAND that his age and health no longer allowed him to minister to his immense territory, where he had to cover seven or eight leagues to visit the sick, and furthermore that the mission at Bonaventure could no longer support a missionary unless that person "is willing to follow the trade of a Recollet" and beg.

In 1767 accusations of scandalous conduct were made against Father Bonaventure – he and an Indian woman were said to have had a child – and Bishop Briand called him to Quebec to give an account of himself. Ignoring this order, he was suspended from all his functions as parish priest including that of saying mass in the diocese. Faced with such sanctions he entrusted his mission to Father Ambroise, the priest at Restigouche, and retired to Paspébiac, promising Bishop Briand in January 1768 that he would go to Quebec in the spring. This repentance did not, however, last long, for he seems to have resumed his ministry on the pretext "that having been appointed by the king and the governor no one had the right to remove him." The Indian chiefs of the Miramichi region had protested the loss of their missionary to the bishop, who replied rather sternly in a pastoral letter dated 9 Oct. 1768 and addressed to the inhabitants of Baie des Chaleurs: he ordered them "to have no further dealings or association with Brother Bonaventure Carpentier, Recollet, for purposes of religion, . . . to expel him from the presbytery, where he has no longer any right to be, to take away from him the key to the church and sacristy and all the vestments and sacred vessels. . . ."

Father Bonaventure finally went to Quebec, where Bishop Briand, out of consideration for François Bonaventure, the parish priest of Trois-Rivières and the Recollet's cousin, appointed him parish priest of Saint-Nicolas in 1769. After only a few months there, he quarrelled with the churchwardens and sought shelter in his cousin's house where he remained three years, helping out in that parish. The bishop, who had again removed his authority to exercise the ministry, returned it except for confession in 1772. Two years later Father Bonaventure resumed his parish charge at Saint-Nicolas, where he died on 6 Jan. 1778.

FIDÈLE THÉRIAULT

AAQ, 22 A, III, 391, 617; 311 CN, I, 141; 33 CR, A, 37, 49. Archives de l'archevêché de Rimouski (Rimouski, Qué.), Correspondance. Archives de l'évêché de Gaspé (Gaspé, Qué.), casier des paroisses, Bonaventure, lettre de Louis-Joseph Desjardins à Mgr Hubert, 30 sept. 1795. N.B. Hist. Soc., *Coll.*, III (1907–14), no.9, 303 (James Abercrombie to James Wolfe, 24 Sept. 1758). Allaire, *Dictionnaire*, I, 100. Jouve, *Les franciscains et le Canada: aux Trois-Rivières*, 180–81, 236, 243–44. Archange Godbout, "Les aumôniers de la vallée du Richelieu," SCHÉC *Rapport*, 12 (1945–46), 74–75. Henri Têtu, "M. Jean-Félix Récher, curé de Québec, et son journal, 1757–1760," *BRH*, IX (1903), 305.

CASOT, JEAN-JOSEPH, priest and Jesuit; b. 4 Oct. 1728 at Paliseul, in the bishopric of Liège (Belgium), son of Jacques Casot and Jeanne Dauvin; d. 16 March 1800 in Quebec.

Jean-Joseph Casot entered the Jesuit noviciate in Paris on 16 Dec. 1753 and arrived in Canada in 1757 as a lay brother. He became cook at the Jesuit college in Quebec. He experienced the war of the conquest, the rationing, the capture of Quebec by the British, the occupation of the college by troops, and the upheavals that ensued for the Society of Jesus in Canada, including the prohibition after the treaty of Paris (1763) from recruiting or receiving new members.

In the autumn of 1759 Brother Casot had taken refuge in the outskirts of Quebec. He returned to the college as cook in June 1761 and was put in charge of the primary school, along with Brother Alexis Maquet; Father Augustin-Louis de GLAPION was the sole teacher for secondary studies. (The English garrison was still occupying two-thirds of the college.) Father Glapion, who became superior in 1763, noticed Brother Casot's ability and soon appointed him bursar of the college. Because of the steadily diminishing number of Jesuit priests, Bishop BRIAND ordained him priest on 20 Dec. 1766, with Brother Jean-Baptiste Noël; Brother Alexis Maquet was ordained in September 1767. Father Casot spent the rest of his life as bursar of the college in Quebec; he was also confessor to the hospital nuns of the Hôtel-Dieu from 1783 to 1796.

In 1768 Father Glapion, who had given up expecting any early replacements, had dropped instruction at the level of classical studies, maintaining only the primary school, which would be shut down in 1776. On 21 July 1773 the papal brief *Dominus ac Redemptor* suppressed the Society of Jesus throughout the world. Bishop Briand in 1774 called together the Jesuits residing in Quebec and told them he had the brief and the order to notify them. But, with Governor Carleton*'s agreement, he did not put the order into effect; the Jesuits kept their name and religious habit, and possession of their property. Indeed, since notice of the brief had not been properly given, they remained Jesuits, as did those in Prussia and White Russia. At the time there were only 12 members of the order in Canada, four in Quebec; nine died between 1775 and 1785.

Upon Father Glapion's death in 1790 Jean-Joseph Casot became administrator of the Jesuit estates and acted as if he were the owner. When Father Bernard Well, the last Jesuit in Montreal, died in March 1791, Father Casot immediately went there and gave all the movables used by his colleague to the Hôpital Général and the poor, claiming these belonged to his order.

On 14 Nov. 1796 Father Casot drew up a testament in which he left the furnishings of his church in Quebec to Coadjutor Bishop Pierre Denaut*, the other churches in the city, the Ursulines, and the diocesan missions. However, he had previously deposited part of the college archives at the Hôtel-Dieu of Quebec and had given the books from the library to the seminary and the table service and pharmaceuticals to the Hôpital Général.

The lieutenant governor, Sir Robert Shore Milnes*, refused to recognize the legality of the will but made sure that most of its provisions were respected. The Ursulines' annalist, recording Casot's death on 16 March 1800, noted: "In this month of March passed away at the age of 71 years and 6 months Reverend Father J. Joseph Casot, the last of the sons of Ignatius in this country, who has left as many orphans as there are poor and needy. . . . He used all his income, which we know was large, to aid them, whilst denying himself the necessities of life. His death has been mourned by all men of good will." With his death began the controversy over the Jesuit estates that was to plague the 19th century.

JOSEPH COSSETTE

ASJCF, 740; 741; BO 80, C. Nelisse à A. Mélançon, 6 août 1924; Cahier des vœux, f.42. Bas-Canada, chambre d'Assemblée, *Rapport du comité spécial . . . nommé pour s'enquérir de l'état actuel de l'éducation dans la province du Bas-Canada* (s.l., [1824]). Isaac Weld, *Voyages au Canada dans les années 1795, 1796 et 1797* . . . (3v., Paris, An XI [1803]), II, 80. Allaire, *Dictionnaire*, I, 164–65. Caron, "Inv. de la corr. de Mgr Briand," ANQ *Rapport*, 1929–30, 68; "Inv. de la corr. de Mgr. Denaut," ANQ *Rapport*, 1931–32, 166. Mélançon, *Liste des missionnaires jésuites*. Burke, *Les ursulines de Québec* (1863–66), III. Rochemonteix, *Les jésuites et la N.-F. au XVIIIe siècle*, II, 182, 201, 214, 235. J.-E. Roy, "La liste du mobilier qui fut saisi en 1800 par le shérif de Québec, à la mort du père jésuite Cazot," *Revue canadienne* (Montréal), XXV (1889), 271–82.

CASTAING, PIERRE-ANTOINE (he was usually known as **Antoine**), merchant and colonial official; b. at Bordeaux, France, son of Antoine Castaing, a merchant, and Isabau (Élisabeth) Sareillier (Sarcelié, Lecarulier); d. 1779 in France.

Pierre-Antoine Castaing immigrated to Louisbourg, Île Royale (Cape Breton Island), about 1740. His age and previous experience are unknown and he had no close relatives in Île Royale, but it appears he intended to enter business. Initially his commercial dealings were small, and he supported himself by his appointment on 5 Nov. 1740 as translator to the Louisbourg admiralty. The arrival of trading ships from New England created a need for translation and surviving documents attest to Castaing's ability.

Shortly before the capitulation of Louisbourg in 1745 and the deportation of the inhabitants, Castaing married Charlotte-Isabelle Chevalier, the daughter of a shipping and trading family established at Louisbourg since the colony's foundation. Castaing and his wife returned in 1749 with a daughter, two servants, and his brother Jean and sister Rose. He had probably improved his commercial connections in Bordeaux between 1745 and 1749, for he developed a substantial and diversified business on his return to the colony. He rented a fishing property near Louisbourg and bought the catches of independent fishermen. He also bought ships, contracted with some of the fishermen he employed to have them build schooners for him during the winter, and chartered other vessels to carry his cargoes to Bordeaux, where he was represented by his brother-in-law, Joseph-Guillaume Lapeire. To extend his business Castaing imported for sale in his storehouse such varied goods as coffee, sugar, wine, rum, and rope, and he exported shingles, bricks, planks, and staves, in addition to cod. Castaing had only one close business associate, his brother Jean, who died in 1755, but he frequently formed short-term partnerships with fishermen, ship captains, and merchants.

Despite his expanding business, Castaing did not give up translation. In 1752 he was nominated as translator and interpreter to the admiralty. In 1755 he was ordered not only to translate documents for English captains, but also to perform a surveillance role for the admiralty by ensuring that restrictions on foreign trade were obeyed by visiting captains, crews, and passengers.

Though most of Castaing's commercial links were with Bordeaux, he did some business with the French Caribbean colonies and had a rather unusual New England connection through his second wife. His first wife had died in 1749 and in 1752 he married Willobe King, known as Olive Le Roy, of Rhode Island. Despite the trading links between Île Royale and the British colonies, relatively few New Englanders actually settled in the French colony. Castaing's wife and her sister, who also married a Louisbourg merchant, Jean-Jacques Brunet (Brunnet), were two of the small number of New England residents. Castaing's sister Rose married another Louisbourg merchant, Pierre Rodrigue.

Castaing's business dealings were typical of the more active Louisbourg merchant, as were his ties to France and his local family connections. His Louisbourg career ended with the capture of the fortress in 1758. With his wife and children, he returned to Bordeaux where he pursued new business interests, apparently without success. In 1779 he disappeared while "in the mountains on a logging operation," and his family was left dependent upon charity.

CHRISTOPHER MOORE

AD, Charente-Maritime (La Rochelle), B, 271, ff.16v–17, 22v–24; 276, 9 sept., 21 nov. 1740. AN, Col., C[11B], 30, 33; E, 65 (dossier Élizabeth Castaing); Section Outre-mer, G[1], 407/2, f.54v; 408/2, ff.39, 40, 49v; 409/1, f.74v; 410; 466, pièce 76; G[2], 209, dossier 499; 210, dossier 517; G[3], 2041/1, 16 nov. 1749; 31 juill. 1750; 9 juill., 1er déc. 1751; 20 nov. 1752; 2047/1, 20 sept., 28 nov. 1743; 2047/2, 23 juill., 29 nov. 1752. McLennan, *Louisbourg*. Christopher Moore, "Merchant trade in Louisbourg, Île Royale" (unpublished MA thesis, University of Ottawa, 1977). H.-P. Thibault, *L'îlot 17 de Louisbourg (1713–1768)* (Can., Service des lieux historiques nationaux, *Travail inédit*, no. 99, [Ottawa], 1972), 87–91.

CASTANET, JEAN-BAPTISTE-MARIE, priest and Recollet; b. 1766 in the diocese of Rodez, France; d. 26 Aug. 1798 in Quebec City.

Little is known about the early years of Jean-Baptiste-Marie Castanet. He was ordained a priest by the Recollets around 1790 and over the next two years served his order in France. Like many of his religious brothers, he was forced into exile by the progress of the revolution, and he left his homeland for England in late 1792 or early 1793. Some time after his arrival there the bishop of Quebec, Jean-François HUBERT, through the agency of Jean-François de La Marche, the bishop of Saint-Pol-de-Léon then residing in London, issued an open invitation to the French refugee clergy to settle in Canada. Castanet was among those who accepted. Approximately 45 French priests in exile left England for Canada between 1791 and 1802. Castanet arrived at Quebec in June 1794, in the company of abbés Louis-Joseph Desjardins*, *dit* Desplantes, Jean-Denis Daulé*, and François-Gabriel Le Courtois*.

Castanet had a reputation as a scholar and teacher and, since the staff at the seminary of Quebec was limited, he was gratefully accepted there as a professor of philosophy. Not in good health, he found the pressures of regular teaching too demanding and requested a transfer to one of the missions in the Atlantic region. In the summer of 1795 Castanet, Desplantes, and Philippe-Jean-Louis Desjardins* accompanied Hubert on his first pastoral visit to Acadia. On the bishop's return to Quebec Castanet took up residence at Caraquet, while Desplantes went to Bonaventure on the Gaspé coast. As successor to Joseph-Mathurin BOURG, Castanet had charge of the Acadian communities on the Baie des Chaleurs, from Caraquet to Nepisiguit (Bathurst) and along the Nepisiguit River. His first mass was celebrated at Caraquet on 28 Aug. 1795. The following year his mission was extended to include the Miramichi region and settlements as far south as Richibucto. In 1798 he informed Governor Thomas Carleton* of New Brunswick that his mission numbered 349 families.

It was a poor region whose chief source of income was fishing. Castanet appears to have been the only missionary who served the area without receiving at least a nominal pension from the government. Nonetheless, he persevered. He commenced construction of a small chapel at Caraquet and attempted to provide some kind of basic instruction, sacred and secular, for the Acadians, most of whom had received little or no education of a formal kind. He also spent a large part of his time among the Micmacs and did much to calm the mounting tensions between Indians and whites. He is said to have negotiated an agreement with the colonial government whereby the Indians were granted lands and exclusive fishing rights on various streams within the area of his mission.

It had presumably been Castanet's hope that a change in climate and responsibilities might restore his health, but it continued to decline. His last sacerdotal act in the Miramichi region was performed on 29 Oct. 1797 and at Caraquet on 6

March 1798. Two months later he entered the Hôpital Général of Quebec, leaving his mission in the hands of Desplantes and Abbé Jacques de La Vaivre, who had been sent out in 1796 to assist both missionaries. On 26 August 1798 Castanet succumbed to tuberculosis at the age of 32, the first of the French clergy in exile to die in Canada. He was buried under the church of the Hôpital Général.

Upon Castanet's death the parish priest of Notre-Dame de Québec, Joseph-Octave Plessis*, wrote, "This young priest was endowed with a remarkable spirit of order and regularity." Castanet was eventually succeeded at Caraquet by Abbé René-Pierre Joyer.

DELLA M. M. STANLEY

CÉA, Fonds Placide Gaudet, 1.52–2, "Notes sur les missionnaires de la baie des Chaleurs." PAC, MG 9, A5, 3. Allaire, *Dictionnaire*, I. Caron, "Inv. de la corr. de Mgr Denaut," ANQ *Rapport*, 1931–32, 129–242; "Inv. de la corr. de Mgr Hubert et de Mgr Bailly de Messein," ANQ *Rapport*, 1930–31, 199–351. L.-C. Daigle, *Les anciens missionnaires de l'Acadie* ([Saint-Louis de Kent, N.-B., 1956]). Tanguay, *Répertoire*.

Antoine Bernard, *Le drame acadien depuis 1604* (Montréal, 1936). *Caraquet: quelques bribes de son histoire, 1967, année du centenaire*, Corinne Albert-Blanchard, compil. ([Caraquet, N.-B.], [1967?]). N.-E. Dionne, *Les ecclésiastiques et les royalistes français réfugiés au Canada à l'époque de la révolution, 1791–1802* (Québec, 1905). Robert Rumilly, *Histoire des Acadiens* (2v., Montréal, 1955), II. M. Trudel, *L'Église canadienne*, I.

CAVAGNIAL, Marquis de VAUDREUIL, PIERRE DE RIGAUD DE VAUDREUIL DE. *See* RIGAUD

CERRY (Cerry d'Argenteuil), PHILIPPE-MARIE D'AILLEBOUST DE. *See* AILLEBOUST

CHABERT DE JONCAIRE DE CLAUSONNE, DANIEL-MARIE (he signed **Joncaire Chaber**), Indian agent, interpreter, and military officer; baptized 6 Jan. 1714 at Repentigny (Que.), son of Louis-Thomas Chabert* de Joncaire and Marie-Madeleine Le Gay de Beaulieu; m. 19 Jan. 1751 at Montreal Marguerite-Élisabeth-Ursule Rocbert de La Morandière; buried 5 July 1771 at Detroit.

Daniel-Marie Chabert de Joncaire has frequently been confused with his father and with his brother Philippe-Thomas*, both of whom were also agents of France among the Iroquois. By his own account Chabert went to live among the Iroquois as a young boy, and in the following years he resided for some time among the Ottawas, Ojibwas, and Shawnees also. As a young man, when not employed on military expeditions, he was travelling among the Indians "to cultivate friendship, check imprudence, dispel plots, or break off the treaties of these people with the enemy." His influence was enhanced by his status as an adopted son of the Iroquois and the fact that he had a Seneca wife and children.

In 1739 and 1740 Chabert served with the force that travelled from Canada to the lower Mississippi valley to aid Jean-Baptiste Le Moyne* de Bienville in an attack on the Chickasaws, and he acted as interpreter in the subsequent negotiation of a peace treaty. He held the rank of cadet at this time but in 1748 was promoted ensign in the colonial regular troops.

Since 1701 the Iroquois had been officially neutral in the struggle between France and Britain, but pressure on them to take sides intensified during the 1740s and 1750s. Although the personal influence of Chabert and his brother was great, especially among the Senecas, William JOHNSON gained similar power among the Mohawks, and the Six Nations Confederacy was slowly torn apart. In 1748, when Philippe-Thomas resigned his position as principal agent among the Iroquois, he was replaced by Daniel-Marie. Despite Iroquois objections, Daniel-Marie began constructing a new fort, which became known as the little Niagara fort or Fort du Portage, about a mile and a half above the falls. It was intended to intercept furs that might otherwise have been taken to the British at Oswego (Chouaguen) once the difficult portage had been made. He commanded at the new post and was subsequently given a monopoly on the portage traffic. In 1757 he was promoted lieutenant.

During the 1750s, as Franco-British competition for influence among the Indians grew, Chabert made numerous visits to the various nations. On a 1758 mission to negotiate with the Iroquois and the Delawares he carried 80,000 *livres* in trade goods and 30,000 in presents. Demonstrations of British strength finally prevailed, however, and in 1759 the Iroquois allowed Johnson's forces to besiege Fort Niagara (near Youngstown, N.Y.). Chabert was among the officers who signed the capitulation on 25 July. An exchange of prisoners in December brought him from New York to Montreal, and he served with the army under LÉVIS, who besieged MURRAY at Quebec in the spring of 1760. Chabert retreated with the rest of the troops to Montreal when the siege was lifted, and Governor Vaudreuil [RIGAUD] sent him to gather Indians for the defence of that city.

Along with other French officers he left Canada in 1761, much to the relief of the British who feared his influence with the Indians. After stopping in England he crossed to France where he was imprisoned in the Bastille in connection with the *affaire du Canada* [*see* BIGOT]. He maintained that because he had relied on Vaudreuil's promise that losses would be charged to the king's account, he used his own money and credit to provide goods to the Indians. His records had been destroyed at Fort du Portage when he burned it before moving his garrison to reinforce Fort Niagara in 1759, but he estimated that the king owed him 1,661,281 *livres*. At his trial he explained the considerable wealth he had had by claiming to have engaged in a profitable trade in ginseng; but it was the fur trade, in which he like other officers engaged despite orders, that was the source of his wealth. In 1763 the court found him guilty of carelessness in examining the inventories of provisions in the forts he commanded and warned him against repeating the offence – a virtual acquittal.

Chabert went to London after his trial and on 18 Oct. 1764 he unsuccessfully petitioned the king for land on the east bank of the Niagara River from the site of his former fort to and including the present Buffalo River, land that he asserted had been given to his father by the Iroquois. That same month Governor Murray was warned by British authorities that Chabert planned to return to Canada and should be hindered from going among the Indians. When he arrived with a large stock of trade goods bought in Britain, he was prevented by Murray from taking them to Niagara. Murray was soon succeeded by Guy Carleton*, and Chabert applied to the new governor for permission to trade with the Indians. Carleton took his side, arguing that there were no legal barriers to his going. After visiting Johnson personally in 1767 and assuring him of his future good conduct, Chabert was at last allowed to go to Detroit. A rumour soon reached Johnson that at Niagara Chabert had privately assured Gaustrax, a Seneca chief, that the French would return, an accusation Chabert denied.

All the delay had placed him in financial difficulties, and his situation was worsened by the rejection of his land claim at Niagara and the failure of his attempt to get compensation from France for his losses during the siege of Niagara. As well, the minister of Marine asserted that the bills of exchange Chabert sent for redemption bore false signatures and that if he were in France he would be arrested. He was reduced to begging permission from Johnson to write to the commander-in-chief, Major-General GAGE, "that he may put my wife and children in the way to have a bit of bread, and that it would be shameful at my age to see me dragging out my life along the lakeside, to be the laughing stock to the entire rabble." His fortunes seem to have improved in the year or two before his death in 1771 at Detroit.

IN COLLABORATION WITH WALTER S. DUNN JR

AN, Col., D^{2C}, 58, f.19; Marine, C^7, 58 (dossier Joncaire-Chabert). Buffalo and Erie County Hist. Soc., Daniel Joncaire MS coll. Bougainville, "Journal" (A.-E. Gosselin), ANQ *Rapport*, 1923–24, 202–393. *Coll. des manuscrits de Lévis* (Casgrain), VII, 344, 483. *Johnson papers* (Sullivan *et al.*). *NYCD* (O'Callaghan and Fernow), X, 39, 146, 234, 377, 392, 698. PAC *Report*, 1899, supp., 188–89; 1905, I, pt.VI, 104, 330, 390. "State papers," PAC *Report*, 1890, 10, 14. Tanguay, *Dictionnaire*, I, 325. F. H. Severance, *An old frontier of France: the Niagara region and adjacent lakes under French control* (2v., New York, 1917).

CHABRAND DELISLE, DAVID, Church of England clergyman; b. 31 Dec. 1730 at Anduze (dept of Gard), France, son of David Chabrand, baker, and Marguerite Roussel; m. 1 Oct. 1768 Margaret Henry, and they had eight children, at least five of whom survived childhood; d. 28 June 1794 at Montreal, Lower Canada.

David Chabrand, known in France as Chabrand, *dit* Veyrac, *dit* La Chapelle, was in 1745 among the postulants of the synod of Basses-Cévennes, which four years later accepted him as a divinity student. From 1750 to 1753 at least, he studied at the clandestine French Protestant seminary at Lausanne, Switzerland, but in the latter year the synod of Basses-Cévennes refused to extend his period of studies. Renouncing a career as a pastor in France, he eventually went to England, where he was ordained priest of the Church of England on 23 Dec. 1764 and appointed to a London parish. On 14 April 1766 he was appointed garrison chaplain of Montreal with an annual salary of £115. With this move the name Delisle, which he was already using in England, began to replace Chabrand as his family name.

Delisle's appointment reflected the decision of the British government and the Church of England, encouraged by Governor MURRAY of Quebec and the Protestant merchants there, to appoint bilingual ministers to Canada, not only to serve the British and the few French Protestants but also to proselytize the Canadians. It was a rare point of unanimous agreement between Murray and the colony's predominantly mercantile

Protestant population. Murray felt that British rule could be secured only by winning over the Canadians and he sought to reassure them by protecting their laws and institutions and by cooperating with the Roman Catholic Church, all the while hoping that time and subtle measures would bring about a conversion of the heart to England from France and to Protestantism from Roman Catholicism. The quiet conversion of the Canadians by a respectable French-language Protestant clergy was such a measure. The Protestant merchants, disadvantaged in competition with the merchants of the Thirteen Colonies by the language and institutions of Quebec, sought to have the colony immediately anglicized in all ways, a policy Murray feared would provoke a revolt. For the merchants the proselytism of the Roman Catholics by a clergy capable of speaking both languages would facilitate the overall programme.

Soon after his arrival in Canada in late summer 1766, Delisle made the acquaintance of the Huguenot attorney general, Francis Maseres*, who found him "a very good man." Delisle also ministered unofficially to the "Protestant Congregation of Montreal," which had been served since the conquest by the chaplains John OGILVIE and Samuel Bennett. In 1764 the city counted 56 Protestant families of which a few were French, many English and Church of England, but most Scots Presbyterians, who had no minister of their own. Unable to use the run-down Jesuit chapel, granted to it by Lieutenant Governor Guy Carleton* some time before September 1767, the congregation was obliged to share places of worship with the Roman Catholics, and on the latter's terms. Delisle objected that this arrangement made the Catholic clergy arrogant towards the Protestants, but his efforts to obtain from government an exclusively Protestant church were in vain. He complained as well that the Canadians were "the most ignorant and bigotted People in the world, and the most devoted to the Priests, especially to the Jesuits."

Delisle's services to the Protestant congregation were normalized in 1768 when he was appointed its minister with an additional salary of £200. He became a freemason and chaplain of St Peter's Lodge, No. 4, Quebec at Montreal; he was also appointed chaplain to the Montreal prison. Although his requests to become a missionary of the Society for the Propagation of the Gospel were denied, he performed the functions of one, visiting the Chambly garrison and Protestants dispersed outside Montreal. By 1771 his proselytism had produced only two Canadian converts. On the other hand, he and the congregation did succeed in bringing a Protestant schoolmaster to Montreal in 1773. The American revolution substantially increased Delisle's activities; not only did the number of Protestant soldiers greatly expand, but the German troops preferred French services. As well, his civilian congregation was swelled by the arrival of the loyalists.

Delisle and his two French-language colleagues, Leger-Jean-Baptiste-Noël VEYSSIÈRE at Trois-Rivières and David-François De Montmollin* at Quebec, seem to have got on well with the bilingual British merchants who had been partially responsible for their appointment. Delisle, for example, had close relations with the Frobisher family, particularly Joseph*. The loyalists, however, were unilingual and not inclined to accustom themselves to the peculiar English idiom of the French ministers. In 1788 their complaints, including those by Christian Daniel CLAUS, but particularly by the Reverend John Doty*, pointed to the few French Protestant families (about 20) in comparison with the English (5,000) and to the sparseness of attendance, of the giving of the sacraments, and of catechizing. The complaints reached the ears of the newly appointed bishop of Nova Scotia, Charles Inglis*, a loyalist himself, who determined to replace all three men with English-language ministers.

In the summer of 1789 Inglis conducted a pastoral visit of the province of Quebec. He found Delisle to be "a sensible, well-bred man," and often dined at his house. He also found that he could scarcely understand his English, and that the congregation was eager to get an English-speaking assistant for him. Under pressure from Inglis, Delisle agreed to limit himself to preaching in French and to continuing his proselytism among the Canadians. Though by early August he had changed his mind, he could elicit from Inglis only the concessions that he would remain titular minister and be allowed to preach occasionally in English. The English assistant, James Marmaduke Tunstall*, was to assume the bulk of the minister's responsibilities.

Inglis had persuaded Governor Lord Dorchester [Guy Carleton] to have the Jesuits' chapel repaired for the exclusive use of the Montreal congregation, and, in a gesture of goodwill, Delisle was invited by the congregation to preach the dedicatory sermon at the inaugural service in Christ Church on 20 Dec. 1789. He accepted, and from this point on continued, in spite of Inglis' instructions, to take a principal share of the minister's duties. Through Joseph Frobisher he even persuaded the congregation to ask Inglis in

1792 to remove the restriction on his preaching in English.

Delisle, hampered by illness at least since 1791, died on 28 June 1794. His total salary of over £300 per annum had enabled him to become a man of property; he owned three houses and a small farm in Montreal. Although he had obtained a land grant of 5,000 acres in 1766 when appointed chaplain, his persistent petitions to have it designated and transferred were ignored. In August 1795 a group of associates including the merchants Joseph Perinault*, Pierre Foretier*, and John Welles, of which Delisle had been leader, was granted 1,000 acres in Godmanchester Township, and in October 1816 Delisle's heirs finally received his 5,000-acre grant in Hinchinbrook Township. As a French-language Protestant minister, Delisle appears to have fared better than Veyssière and De Montmollin, but he too found the fruits of his appointment bitter, since he tasted the aversion for him of the Canadians, the insulting indifference towards him of most of his own congregation, and, finally, near abandonment by the Church of England.

JAMES H. LAMBERT

David Chabrand Delisle is the author of *Sermon funèbre prononcé à l'occasion de la mort de Mr. Benjamin Frobisher* (Montréal, 1787; repr. York, Eng., 1796).

AD, Gard (Nîmes), Etat civil, Anduze, 31 déc. 1730. BL, Add. MSS 1699, ff.41–42; 21661, p.2342 (PAC copies). Christ Church Cathedral (Montreal), Minute book register, July 1789 to May 1802, 7 July, 23 Aug., 20 Sept. 1789, 3 May, 19 June, 2 July 1791, 2, 9 April 1792; "Register of the Parish of Montreal commenced 20th June 1784 by Mr. D[d] Ch[d] Delisle Rector of the Parish and Chaplain of the Garrison [1784–95]," 30 June 1794; "The register of the Protestants of Montreal, made by one D[d] Ch[d] Delisle Rector of the Parish & Chaplain to the Garrison, the 31st Dec[r] 1792 [1766–1793]," 17 Aug. 1769, 10 Oct. 1770, 15 March, 27 Sept. 1772, 16 May 1774, 7 Jan. 1776, 8 April 1777, 3 Jan. 1780, 6 March, 23 July 1786. Lambeth Palace Library (London), Fulham papers, 1, ff.163–65; 33, f.1; 38, ff.6v, 58. McGill University Libraries, Dept. of Rare Books and Special Coll., MS coll., CH132.S2, Joseph Frobisher to Thomas Dunn, 10 April 1788. Montreal Diocesan Archives, C-11, 28 Dec. 1793, Request from Delisle *et al.* to Jacob Mountain. PAC, MG 23, A1, 2, pp.1432–53; A4, 13, pp.33–34; 14, pp.26, 42; 16, p.106; GIII, 1, 2, p.182; RG 1, E15, A, 1780; L3[L], 1, pp.11–26, 45–57; 3, p.1129; 4, p.1583; 5, pp.1629–30, 1634; 7, pp.2165, 2345–51; 10, pp.2737, 2747, 2913–40, 3229–50; 47, pp.24264–65; 72, pp.36037–45; 127, pp.62481–95; 173, pp.84176–261; RG 4, A1, pp.6214–15, 17820–21; RG 8, I (C series), 933, p.8. PRO, CO 42/25, f.197; 42/27, f.149; 42/28, ff.387v–88, 390; 42/49, ff.46, 47; 42/51, f.189; 42/72, ff.231–33. QDA, 84 (D-3), 27 Aug. 1789, 27 Oct. 1792. Trinity Cathedral Archives (Quebec), Register of marriages, 1768–95, p.1. USPG, C/CAN/Que., I, 14 April 1766, 30 Sept. 1767, 14 July 1771, 15 Dec. 1773, 9, 20 Oct. 1782, 13 Oct. 1788; Journal of SPG, 16, pp.264–65; 17, pp.465–67; 21, pp.497–98 (copies at PAC).

Coll. of several commissions (Maseres). *Doc. relatifs à l'hist. constitutionnelle, 1759–91* (Shortt et Doughty; 1921), I, 56, 72, 516. Fabre, dit Laterrière, *Mémoires* (A. Garneau), 44–46. Charles Inglis, *A charge delivered to the clergy of the province of Quebec, at the primary visitation holden in the city of Quebec, in the month of August 1789* (Halifax, 1790). *Montreal Gazette*, 1 Feb. 1787, 9 July, 12 Nov. 1789. *Quebec Gazette*, 29 Sept. 1766, 28 April 1768, 3 May 1787, 16 July, 13 Aug. 1789. Kelley, "Church and state papers," ANQ *Rapport*, 1948–49, 305–8, 312–17; 1953–55, 94–96, 102–5, 113, 119. F. D. Adams, *A history of Christ Church Cathedral, Montreal* (Montreal, 1941), 11–49. Campbell, *History of Scotch Presbyterian Church*, 201–2. J. I. Cooper, *The blessed communion; the origins and history of the diocese of Montreal, 1760–1960* ([Montréal], 1960), 7–19. R.-P. Duclos, *Histoire du protestantisme français au Canada et aux États-Unis* (2v., Montréal, [1913]), I, 35–36. J. S. Moir, *The church in the British era, from the conquest to confederation* (Toronto, 1972), 43, 45, 59, 66. H. C. Stuart, *The Church of England in Canada, 1759–1793; from the conquest to the establishment of the see of Quebec* (Montreal, 1893), 24–25, 31, 78–86, 88, 107. F.-J. Audet, "David Lynd, 1745–1802," *BRH*, XLVII (1941), 89. Philéas Gagnon, "Le ministre Delisle," *BRH*, XVIII (1912), 63–64. Leland, "François-Joseph Cugnet," *Revue de l'université Laval*, XVII, 834–35. É.-Z. Massicotte, "La famille du pasteur Delisle," *BRH*, XLVI (1940), 105–7; "Les mariages mixtes, à Montréal, dans les temples protestants, au 18e siècle," *BRH*, XXI (1915), 84–86; "Le ministre Delisle," *BRH*, XVIII (1912), 123–25. T. R. Millman, "David Chabrand Delisle, 1730–1794," *Montreal Churchman* (Granby, Que.), XXIX (1941), no.2, 14–16; no.3, 14–16. J.-E. Roy, "Les premiers pasteurs protestants au Canada," *BRH*, III (1897), 2. A. H. Young, "Lord Dorchester and the Church of England," CHA *Report*, 1926, 60–65.

CHAMPAGNE, LOUIS FOUREUR, *dit*. *See* FOUREUR

CHAPTES, JOSEPH-MARIE DE LA CORNE DE. *See* LA CORNE

CHAPTES (Chap, Chapt) DE LA CORNE, LUC DE LA CORNE, known as. *See* LA CORNE

CHAREST, ÉTIENNE, seigneur, merchant, and militia captain; b. 4 Feb. 1718 at Pointe-Lévy (Lauzon, Que.), son of Étienne Charest and Anne-Thérèse Duroy; d. 6 Aug. 1783 at Loches, France.

Étienne Charest's father, who had built his fortune upon lucrative business houses, industries, and real estate, was one of the richest landowners in the colony. When he died in 1735,

Étienne and his younger brother Joseph Dufy Charest were not old enough to inherit and take over the administration of the seigneury of Lauson, and Jacques Charly Saint-Ange, their brother-in-law, assumed control. Fearing that Charly Saint-Ange would misuse his authority, their guardian and trustee Pierre Trottier* Desauniers obtained letters of emancipation and benefit of age for them in 1737.

In 1738 the two young seigneurs named Jean de Latour, a royal notary at Quebec, as a judge of bailiff's court for Lauson, which had been without seigneurial justice since 1712. That year Étienne issued an ordinance appointing surveyor Ignace Lafleur, *dit* Plamondon, to establish the boundaries between the seigneuries of Beaurivage, Lauson, and Tilly. A census in 1739 enumerated 1,237 persons in Lauson, an increase of 806 in 33 years.

Since their father's death the two brothers had continued to run his business and industries in partnership, concentrating in Labrador on the cod- and seal-fisheries. Joseph, who had chosen a sailor's career, and Étienne, who lived on Rue Sault-au-Matelot in the lower town of Quebec in their father's shop (one of the most flourishing and best stocked in the city), overlooked nothing, however, that might encourage more settlement in the seigneury. In the spring of 1745 they had their *censitaires* provide new title-deeds to their property in the seigneury. The following year Étienne built a flour mill on the Rivière Etchemin for the habitants' convenience, and this step led to the founding of the parish of Saint-Henri, for whose church and presbytery he gave a piece of land. Between 1750 and 1754 he made 20 land grants in an area which covers the present parishes of Saint-Joseph-de-la-Pointe-de-Lévy, Saint-Romuald-d'Etchemin, and Saint-Nicolas.

In 1759 MONCKTON landed at Pointe-Lévy and established a camp from which the city of Quebec could be bombarded. As militia captain, Charest led some 40 of his *censitaires* and about 300 Indians against the invaders, putting up a strong and resolute resistance and slowing their advance by some hours. Seventeen years later, in 1776, he was rewarded with the cross of Saint-Louis for his services, the only militia soldier from the colony ever to receive this decoration.

Following the treaty of Paris in 1763, Étienne Charest signed the address from the citizens of Quebec to Governor MURRAY proclaiming their loyalty to their new sovereign. In October that year he went to England, with a commission from his compatriots to ask for the maintenance of their religious institutions in Canada, the re-establishment of French laws, a reform of justice, and a more favourable financial settlement. Disappointed with his lack of success – London did not permit the appointment of BRIAND as Catholic bishop of Canada until three years later – and despairing of every finding tranquillity, Charest left Canada with all of his family in August 1765, shortly after his return from England, and went to live at Loches, in Touraine. Before departing he sold his houses in Quebec and his seigneury; Governor Murray purchased the latter, which at that time had 1,540 *censitaires* holding 33,706 acres, for the sum of 80,000 *livres*.

Étienne Charest was the last seigneur of Lauson under the French régime. On 22 Oct. 1742 he had married Marie-Catherine, daughter of Pierre Trottier Desauniers, at Saint-Joseph-de-la-Pointe-Lévy; on the same day his brother Joseph married Marguerite, her sister. Étienne Charest and his wife had 13 children; his sons settled in Saint-Domingue (Hispaniola).

ROLAND-J. AUGER

ANQ-Q, NF 25, 38, no.1381; 39, no.1397; 41, no.1496. Archives paroissiales, Notre-Dame de Québec, Registres des délibérations du conseil de la fabrique, IV, 164. Æ. Fauteux, *Les chevaliers de Saint-Louis*, 204–5. P.-G. Roy, *Inv. ord. int.*, II, 242; III, 3, 193. Georges Bellerive, *Les délégués canadiens-français en Angleterre, de 1763 à 1867* . . . (Québec, [1913]), 8–22. Burt, *Old prov. of Que.* (1968), I, 86, 100. J.-E. Roy, *Histoire de la seigneurie de Lauzon* (5v., Lévis, Qué., 1897–1904), II, 138–43, 157–59, 175–77, 186, 211–13, 282–86, 360–64, 370–79, 385, 416. "Comment fut reçut le traité de Paris," *BRH*, LI (1945), 310–11. O.-M.-H. Lapalice, "Étienne Charest," *BRH*, XXXIV (1928), 500–1.

CHARTIER DE LOTBINIÈRE, EUSTACHE (baptized **François-Louis**), Recollet, cordelier, and member of the Knights of Malta; b. 13 Dec. 1716 in Quebec, son of Eustache Chartier* de Lotbinière and Marie-Françoise Renaud d'Avène de Desmeloizes; d. some time after 1785 in the United States of America.

The young François-Louis Chartier de Lotbinière must have studied either at the Jesuit college or the Petit Séminaire at Quebec, as did his brothers. In 1736 his father put him on a ship bound for France, where he was to prepare for a career. But in the first of the scandals of his career the young man, not yet 20, broke his journey on the Labrador coast and, returning to Quebec, immediately joined the Recollets, in spite of the opposition of his father who was aware that he was neither serious nor pious. Chartier de Lotbinière took his vows on 17 Oct. 1738 under the name of Brother Eustache. But he had to wait until a new bishop, Pontbriand [Dubreil*], arrived to receive the minor and major orders, including the priesthood; these he was given in a four-day interval from 20 to 23 Sept. 1741. He then travelled to France where, according to Odoric-Marie Jouve, "he obtained admission as a member of the Friars Minor of the Observance [cordeliers]; but he subsequently went back to the Recollets, and in 1749 returned to Canada." This stay in France is confirmed by a letter dated 24 March 1748 from Canon Pierre HAZEUR de L'Orme to his brother Joseph-Thierry Hazeur* in Quebec, in which he casually mentions Canon Eustache Chartier de Lotbinière's sons: "There's one of them parish priest at Pointe-aux-Trembles [Neuville]; another one a Recollet after being a cordelier, who is now in Rouen where he is busy preaching badly. . . ."

Upon his return to Canada, Chartier de Lotbinière exercised his ministry, mainly at Trois-Rivières, until the end of 1756, but also served as chaplain to various forts. François-Clément Boucher de La Perrière, the commandant of Fort Niagara (near Youngstown, N.Y.), was in fact speaking of Father Eustache when he wrote on 11 June 1755 "that he can be considered a deserter from his post." This evidence is of some significance. According to letters written much later by Bishop BRIAND the famous Father Eustache had already ruined his career publicly through the twin vices of drunkenness and dissoluteness. Although the document cannot be found, around 1756 Bishop Pontbriand issued a declaration of interdict and suspension from all the orders. The interdict theoretically excluded him from all churches and even from the colony. It seems likely that his elder brother Eustache, the parish priest of Pointe-aux-Trembles, and his younger brother MICHEL, a respectable army engineer, allied to make him return to France. According to Bishop Briand, Chartier de Lotbinière suffered a serious illness there; he remained a Recollet, "after that [was] apostate . . . for two years; then, becoming a member of the Order of Malta without mending his ways, [and] expelled from Martinique by the Capuchins and the governor because of his disorderly conduct, he was not ashamed to return to Canada."

He arrived in Quebec in August 1768. According to François-Xavier Noiseux*, "he had obtained a situation as a lay brother in the Order of Malta and wore a cassock with the cross of Malta." He went to his brother Eustache at Pointe-aux-Trembles, where Bishop Briand allowed him to administer the sacraments. On 2 Oct. 1770 Briand took the risk of naming him parish priest at Saint-Laurent, on Île d'Orléans, under the supervision of Chartier's first cousin, Louis-Philippe MARIAUCHAU d'Esgly, the new coadjutor bishop of Quebec and priest of the neighbouring parish of Saint-Pierre. But Chartier de Lotbinière's loose living forced the coadjutor in May 1772 to suspend him from all public functions. He then retired to a private home at Beaumont and drew up lists of charges against Bishop Briand which he sent to London and Rome. The bishop had no difficulty in clearing himself of the charges; always gracious, he accepted the culprit's apologies and had restored to him a suitable pension which the governor had granted but then withdrawn. The bishop did, however, administer a stinging rebuke to Abbé Antoine Huppé, *dit* Lagroix, the parish priest at Saint-Michel (Saint-Michel-de-Bellechasse), who was responsible for the mission church at Beaumont, for having let Chartier de Lotbinière administer the sacraments to his flock.

The American invasion in the autumn of 1775 was perfectly timed to relieve the Quebec church of this chronic scandal. With Bishop Briand preaching loyalty to the Catholic Canadians, the ex-Recollet took the rebels' side, setting himself up as chaplain to the handful of Canadians who had become militiamen in the pay of the Bostonnais under James Livingston* and taking part in the siege of Quebec that winter. The odds were excellent for him; the Americans had given him £1,500 and promised him a bishop's mitre. "M. de Lotbinière then came out of retirement to minister and give the sacraments to the rebels, without any authority. He took over the church at Ste-Foy and performed the duties of ministry there." He was designated chaplain for the Canadian militiamen by Benedict Arnold* on 26 Jan. 1776. After the siege of Quebec was lifted, he followed his regiment in retreat across the border with the Americans. On 12 Aug. 1776 Congress ratified his appointment as military chaplain, and he was paid a monthly salary until February 1781. After that Chartier de Lotbinière is believed to have retired to the home of his brother Michel, who was also living in the United States, having taken up the Americans' cause, although under different circumstances. At the end of 1785 and again on 2 Jan. 1786, "in danger of dying of cold and hunger," Eustache Chartier de Lotbinière, who was then at Bristol, Pennsylvania, demanded from Congress what he believed was his due for his commitment and services to the cause of American independence. No further trace of him has been found.

HONORIUS PROVOST

ANQ-Q, AP-P-378. ASQ, MSS, 425; Fonds Viger-Verreau, Carton 2, no.132; Sér. O, MSS 097. [Thomas Ainslie], "Journal of the most remarkable occurences in the province of Quebec from the appearance of the rebels in September 1775 until their retreat on the sixth of May 1776," ed. F. C. Würtele, Literary and Hist. Soc. of Quebec, *Hist. Docs.*, 7th ser. (1905), [9]–89. U.S., Continental Congress, *Journals of the Continental Congress, 1774–1789*, ed. W. C. Ford *et al.* (34v., Washington, 1904–37), P.-G. Roy, *Fils de Québec*, I, 189–90. Jouve, *Les franciscains et le Canada: aux Trois-Rivières*, 181, 202. Laval Laurent, *Québec et l'Église aux États-Unis sous Mgr Briand et Mgr Plessis* (Montréal, 1945). Têtu, "Le chapitre de la cathédrale," *BRH*, XVI, 362.

CHARTIER DE LOTBINIÈRE, MICHEL, Marquis de LOTBINIÈRE, officer in the colonial regular troops, military engineer, and seigneur; b. 23 April 1723 at Quebec, son of Eustache Chartier* de Lotbinière and Marie-Françoise Renaud d'Avène de Desmeloizes; m. 20 Nov. 1747 at Quebec Louise-Madeleine, daughter of Gaspard-Joseph Chaussegros* de Léry, the king's engineer; they had eight children, of whom a son and daughter reached adulthood; d. 14 Oct. 1798 in New York.

Michel Chartier de Lotbinière's mother died at his birth, and he was also deprived of the presence of his father, who entered a religious order three years after his wife's death. As a boy Michel attended the Jesuit college in Quebec, and then in adolescence joined the colonial regulars as a cadet, thus breaking with the family tradition of winning fame on the bench. Commissioned second ensign in 1744, he served in the Acadian campaign of 1746–47 under Jean-Baptiste-Nicolas-Roch de RAMEZAY, and during this baptism of fire earned a reputation as a capable and courageous officer. In 1749 the commandant general of New France, Roland-Michel Barrin* de La Galissonière, appointed him ensign and entrusted him with a reconnaissance mission in the west to gather information of strategic and scientific interest in the region between Montreal and Michilimackinac (Mackinaw City, Mich.).

After his return to France, La Galissonière sent for his protégé in 1750 so that he could take training there as an engineer and artillery officer in the colonial regulars. Three years later Chartier de Lotbinière returned to Canada with the title of king's engineer and the rank of lieutenant. He worked under his father-in-law on the rebuilding of Quebec's ramparts. In 1755 Governor Vaudreuil [RIGAUD], his cousin, put him in charge of building Fort Carillon (Ticonderoga, N.Y.). Although promoted captain in 1757, he was refused the post of chief engineer in New France which he had asked for after his father-in-law's death in March 1756; the court chose instead to appoint Nicolas Sarrebource* Maladre de Pontleroy, an engineer in the French regulars. Pontleroy's arrival marked the beginning of a series of disappointments for Chartier de Lotbinière: the chief engineer and his friends not only hindered his work at Carillon, but also sent reports to Paris accusing him of incompetence and malversations. From then on, for more than 20 years, Chartier de Lotbinière had no credibility with the ministry of Marine, and the court of France accorded him no further reward or honour. On the other hand, in 1758 Vaudreuil granted him the seigneury of Alainville, southwest of Lake Champlain.

From Montcalm*'s successful defence of Carillon in 1758 until the British capture of Quebec in 1759, Chartier de Lotbinière stayed in the region of the capital, where the governor employed him to build defence works. He took part in the campaign of September 1759 as Vaudreuil's aide-de-camp. In the spring of 1760 he was put in charge of fortifying Île aux Noix to stop the enemy's advance from the south, but he had to abandon this post to Brigadier-General William HAVILAND's troops and fall back on Montreal. After the capitulation he went to France with his son, Michel-Eustache-Gaspard-Alain*, leaving his wife and his daughter, Marie-Charlotte, in Canada.

The conquest, which had altered the circumstances of life for Canadians, had particularly affected the group of seigneurs whose career was the army. Each member of this minor nobility of the sword had to adapt to prevailing conditions: Chartier de Lotbinière stood out through the originality, if not the success, of his attempts to adjust to the new situation. Having met with nothing but disappointment in France, where he had tried to resume his military career, he turned his hopes to his native land again. He decided to become a large landowner, and he purchased seigneuries: Vaudreuil, Rigaud, and Saint-François-de-la-Nouvelle-Beauce, which had belonged to Vaudreuil; Villechauve, which had been held by Charles de Beauharnois*; and, on the southeast shore of Lake Champlain, Hocquart, which had been granted to the former intendant and bore his name. These transactions completed, he went to London on his way to Canada and there learned that his two seigneuries on Lake Champlain, Alainville and Hocquart, which since the Royal Proclamation of 7 Oct. 1763 had been within the boundaries of New York, were in danger of being occupied by neighbouring settlers. He therefore prolonged his stay in the British capital to get his ownership of them recognized by the Board of Trade, but a year of representations resulted in only a vague promise, which Chartier de Lotbinière took to be a guarantee.

From 1764 to 1770 the new owner applied himself to developing his seigneury of Vaudreuil and had his family home, a mill, and the church of Saint-Michel (which is still standing) built there. Since his income was insufficient to meet his obligations, particularly those he had contracted with the Vaudreuils, he was forced in 1770 to sell his son the seigneury of Lotbinière, which he had inherited from his father, and then in 1771 to make over to him the seigneuries of Rigaud, Vaudreuil, and Saint-François-de-la-Nouvelle-Beauce; he kept only Villechauve, which was also mortgaged. In addition, despite numerous representations made to the governor of New York on the basis of London's promise, he was unable to recover his two seigneuries on Lake Champlain. In December 1771 he decided to return to London to plead his cause a second time. In its decision of February 1776 the Board of Trade rejected his claims to the Alainville lands and offered him as compensation for the seigneury of Hocquart a grant of equal size in the province of Quebec. Chartier de Lotbinière refused this compromise, left Great Britain, and decided to be a British subject no longer. He was all the more embittered since he had already suffered a severe setback in 1774, when he opposed Governor Guy Carleton*'s plans and put himself forward as the spokesman for the Canadian seigneurs, despite the fact that the latter gave him little support. When invited to express his views before the House of Commons committee responsible for studying the Quebec Bill, he had suggested the creation of a house of assembly made up of all the large landowners, whether new or old subjects, Catholic or Protestant, in order to re-establish the predominance of the seigneurial class, which the governor had reduced to subordinate rank. He had also pleaded for the maintenance of French civil and criminal laws and the use of French in public matters. The adoption of the bill put an end to his political ambitions in Canada and convinced him of the despotic nature of the régime.

Chartier de Lotbinière then turned to France; there, on the advice of his former superior officer the Chevalier de LÉVIS, he offered his services to the Comte de Vergennes, minister of Foreign Affairs, who entrusted him with an unofficial mission as an observer. Chartier de Lotbinière left France in June 1776 and arrived in Massachusetts in November. He immediately wrote to the president of the Continental Congress, John Hancock, introducing himself as Vergennes's unofficial envoy, even though the minister had expressly forbidden him to use the French government as a reference. He spent some six months in Boston, where his agitating incurred him the animosity of many citizens. In reality, though he wished France to intervene in America, it was out of personal interest rather than sympathy for the rebels' cause, which left him lukewarm despite what he said in his letters to his son, a prisoner of the Americans since November 1775. He thought France should take advantage of the conflict to regain possession of her former colony, in which case he would be able to re-establish himself in his properties and enjoy the good graces of the state. He returned to France in August 1777 to make his report, but the minister did not deem it advisable to entrust other missions to him. Nevertheless, Chartier de Lotbinière still clung to his hopes of reconquest as late as 1782, when he sent Vergennes a memoir advocating it. The treaty of Versailles in 1783 deprived him, however, of any hope of returning to Canada.

Chartier de Lotbinière remained for about ten years in France, trying to improve his situation. With Lévis's support he re-established his reputation, which had been tarnished by Pontleroy's accusations, and then obtained the cross of the order of Saint-Louis, a pension of 600 *livres* which was increased to 1,200 in 1781, and finally a marquisate in 1784 for the sacrifices he had made by allying himself with the French cause in 1776.

In 1787 the indefatigable Chartier de Lotbinière again crossed the Atlantic to try once more to recover his seigneuries of Alainville and Hocquart from the American states, but two years of effort proved futile. Furthermore, when upon his arrival in New York he had tried to obtain permission to go to his own country, Lord Dorchester categorically refused. In October 1790, however, he crossed the border quite straightforwardly and unhindered, in the company of his son, who was Lord Dorchester's confidential agent. After 19 years' absence he revisited his family and his seigneury of Villechauve. But the euphoria of the reunion was short-lived, and he took the road to exile again after selling Villechauve to Alexander Ellice* on 30 July 1795. To receive her share from the sale, Mme Chartier de Lotbinière asked for and obtained a property separation in June 1796.

Embittered and at odds with his family, Chartier de Lotbinière, who had set himself apart from the other seigneurs by the bold stance he had adopted against Governor Carleton, ended his days alone in New York. He died of yellow fever in October 1798, at the age of 75.

F. J. THORPE and
SYLVETTE NICOLINI-MASCHINO

[The sources for a biography of Michel Chartier de Lotbinière are extensive: a rough estimate of the manuscript material is some 2,000 folios. Serious biographers will be frustrated by gaps in the diaries and personal correspondence, because enough of these sources exist to provide a tantalizing, beclouded image of the private man without revealing more about his relations with the wife, son, and daughter from whom he was separated for more than 25 years. The Lotbinière papers are scattered among repositories in Quebec, New York, and elsewhere, but fortunately have been copied and consolidated at the PAC and to some extent at the ANQ-Q. S.N.-M. and F.J.T.]

Some of Lotbinière's letters have been published in the *BRH*: "Lettre du marquis de Lotbinière à John Hancock, président du Congrès," XLIX (1943), 114–15; "Lettre du marquis de Lotbinière à son fils," 190–92; "Lettre du marquis de Lotbinière au président du Congrès," LIV (1948), 115–18.

AMA, SHA, A[1], 3498, no.175; 3499, nos.31, 83, 156. AN, Col., B, 96, ff.96, 179; 105, f.181; C[11A], 91, f.214; 101, ff.333, 335; D[1], 10, f.59; D[2C], 48, f.268; E, 75 (dossier Chartier de Lotbinière). ANQ-Q, AP-G-229, E.-G.-M.-A. de Lotbinière à Nicolas Renaud d'Avène Des Méloizes, 24 oct. 1803; Greffe de C.-H. Du Laurent, 15 nov. 1747. Archives du ministère des Affaires étrangères (Paris), Corr. politique, Angleterre, 508, ff.49–54v; 516, ff.247–48v; 519, ff.440–46; États-Unis, 1, ff.96–98, 107–8, 255–56; Mémoires et doc., Angleterre, 47, ff.283–308v, 327, 339–40. ASQ, Polygraphie, XXX, 30; Séminaire, 14/7, nos.18a, 18d. N.Y. Hist. Soc. (New York), Canada-Lotbinière, MSS, Correspondence, 1746–90; Journals, reports, miscellaneous papers. PAC, MG 18, K3. Private archives, Henry de Lotbinière-Harwood (Vaudreuil, Qué.), Acte de cession des seigneuries de Vaudreuil et de Rigaud, 14 sept. 1771. PRO, CO 42/1, f.139. *American archives* (Clarke and Force), 5th ser., III, 642–46, 1079–80, 1412–15, 1564. "Au sujet de la famille de Lotbinière," *BRH*, XXXIII (1927), 392, 395–96. *Coll. des manuscrits de Lévis* (Casgrain), II, 66–72; VI, 38–41; VII, 409; IX, 7–8, 19–21. *Docs. relating to constitutional history, 1759–91* (Shortt and Doughty; 1918), I, 532. *Inv. des papiers de Léry* (P.-G. Roy), II, 117–32. *NYCD* (O'Callaghan and Fernow), VII, 320–21, 642–43; VIII, 577–79, 669–70; X, 746, 769. Brunet, *Les Canadiens après la Conquête*, 240–42. Sylvette Nicolini-Maschino, "Michel Chartier de Lotbinière: l'action et la pensée d'un Canadien du 18e siècle" (thèse de PHD, université de Montréal, 1978). L.-L. Paradis, *Les annales de Lotbinière, 1672–1933* (Québec, 1933). Marcel Trudel, *Louis XVI, le Congrès américain et le Canada, 1774–1789* (Québec, [1949]), 15, 118. E. [M.] Arthur, "French Canadian participation in the government of Canada, 1775–1785," *CHR*, XXXII (1951), 304, 306. C.-A. de Lotbinière-Harwood, "L'honorable M. E.-G.-A. Chartier de Lotbinière," *BRH*, XL (1934), 73. R.-L. Séguin, "La persévérance d'un Canadien en quête d'une croix de Saint-Louis," *RHAF*, IX (1955–56), 361–75.

CHAUSSEGROS DE LÉRY, GASPARD-JOSEPH (Joseph-Gaspard), military engineer, seigneur, chief road commissioner (*grand voyer*), and legislative councillor; b. 20 July 1721 at Quebec, son of Gaspard-Joseph Chaussegros* de Léry and Marie-Renée Legardeur de Beauvais; m. 24 Sept. 1753 at Quebec Louise, daughter of François Martel* de Brouague, and they had 18 children, of whom seven survived to adulthood; d. 11 Dec. 1797 at Quebec.

The son and grandson of military engineers, Gaspard-Joseph Chaussegros de Léry was prepared from childhood for the same profession in Canada. As a cadet in the colonial regular troops from the age of 12, he learned surveying, mapping, and construction; in 1739 he was named an assistant engineer at a time when his father was chief engineer in the colony. In 1739–40 he took part in Pierre-Joseph Céloron* de Blainville's expedition against the Chickasaws. Commissioned second ensign in 1742, he carried out engineering duties until 1748 at Fort Saint-Frédéric (near Crown Point, N.Y.), where the defences, left in his charge by his father, were subsequently condemned as badly laid out and constructed; he had similar duties at Montreal, Chambly, and Quebec. In August 1746 Léry accompanied François-Pierre de RIGAUD de Vaudreuil in the raid that captured Fort Massachusetts (Williamstown, Mass.), and in October 1747 he led 50 Indians and French soldiers into New England to strike at the British, Mohawks, and Delawares. Promoted ensign in 1748, he directed the construction of Fort Saint-Jean on the Richelieu. His work earned him the praise of the commandant general in New France, Roland-Michel Barrin* de La Galissonière, and his financial management the sharp criticism of François BIGOT. In 1749 La Galissonière sent him from Montreal to Detroit on a reconnaissance mission that provided useful strategic data, as well as geographical and astronomical information.

Following his return from Detroit Léry resigned as assistant engineer while remaining ensign in the army; he probably believed his future would be brighter under the supervision of military officers, several of whom had a high regard for his work, than under that of Bigot, who was attempting a tighter civilian control over fortifications and for whom Léry's resignation was "no great loss." Nevertheless, in order to relieve the pressure on the small engineering establishment in New France, Governor La Jonquière [Taffanel*] continued to make wide use of Léry's engineering knowledge in the field, away from the intendant's scrutiny, and expressed considerable satisfaction with his work. In 1750 and 1751 Léry worked in the Chignecto Isthmus, mapping, writing papers on the geography of the region, and building stockade forts. In the latter year he was sent by La Jonquière to France and delivered the reports and plans made in Acadia to the minister of Marine, Rouillé. He arrived back at Quebec in November 1752. Between 1753 and 1756 he was on the frontier from Fort Niagara (near Youngstown, N.Y.) and Detroit to Fort Duquesne (Pittsburgh, Pa), building fortifications and bringing supplies and trade goods from Montreal.

In March 1756 Léry led a party of 360 Indians, Canadians, and French regulars through nearly impracticable woods and under bad weather conditions to destroy the supply depot of Fort Bull (east of Oneida Lake, N.Y.). His success disrupted British plans for a spring offensive in the lower Great Lakes region and earned Léry a promotion to captain in 1757 (he had been lieutenant since 1751) and the cross of Saint-Louis in January 1759. The victory at Fort Bull had also given the French time to prepare Montcalm*'s important capture of Fort Oswego (Chouaguen) in August 1756 when Léry commanded the left flank of François-Pierre de Rigaud de Vaudreuil's advance party of Canadians and Indians. Montcalm, generally unimpressed with Canadian officers, found Léry an agreeable exception. In June 1757 Governor Vaudreuil [RIGAUD] assigned Léry, whom he too had come to regard highly, to improve the fortifications of Quebec until the arrival of Nicolas Sarrebource* Maladre de Pontleroy in September. In July 1758 Léry accompanied Paul-Joseph LE MOYNE de Longueuil on a diplomatic mission to secure the support of the Six Nations Confederacy, and in May and June 1759, as the British advanced up the St Lawrence, he organized the evacuation of the region from the seigneury of L'Islet-du-Portage to Rimouski. He took part in the battle of the Plains of Abraham and was confined by the British as a wounded prisoner in the Hôpital Général. Late in 1761 he and his family were sent to France.

Léry's career after the conquest is a case study in those divided loyalties occasioned by a transfer of territorial sovereignty. He tried to obtain employment in the French service but received only vague promises of future military appointments or offers of uncleared land in tropical colonies. His liquid assets in French colonial paper currency were worth little, despite a face value of 94,000 *livres*. Mindful of his property in Canada – especially as seigneur of Léry – he arranged in 1763 with British officials in Paris and London to return home by way of England. Although he assiduously courted Canada's new masters, and had the distinction of being the first Canadian seigneur to be presented to King George III, he received a cool reception from Governor MURRAY upon arriving at Quebec in September 1764, chiefly because he had left two sons in France to be educated for military careers. Discouraged, Léry proposed late in 1765 to sell his Canadian holdings at a loss and commit himself irrevocably to France. The French authorities, however, had been watching his movements since his first *démarches* toward the British; and now, far from being welcome in France and able to obtain a position there, he was in danger of being arrested if he returned. When he found in 1766 that the British government had no objection to his sons' remaining in France (since as Roman Catholics they might never obtain British commissions), he decided to stay in Canada.

In Governor Guy Carleton* he found a friend and advocate, and under Carleton's administration he prospered. In 1768 Carleton named him successor to François-Joseph CUGNET as chief road commissioner for the District of Quebec. The governor supported Léry's claim to a British pension (promised in 1763), arguing that leading Canadians preferring to live under British rule rather than in France or a French colony deserved encouragement. In 1775 he procured Léry an appointment to the Legislative Council of the enlarged province of Quebec, and in 1792 appointed him a member of the new Legislative Council for Lower Canada, a position Léry held until his death.

Léry prospered financially as well as politically under the British régime. He had inherited from his father the fief of Beauvais and the family seigneury of Léry, and, although he sold the latter to Gabriel CHRISTIE in 1766, between 1768 and 1783 he acquired the seigneuries of Perthuis, Rigaud-Vaudreuil, Gentilly, Le Gardeur, and Sainte-Barbe. By 1797 these properties, with a total population of 356 habitants, produced a revenue of 2,813 *livres* per annum. He had, as well, two grist-mills, two saw mills, and two houses in Quebec providing an annual net revenue of 2,892 *livres*.

Some British contemporaries and at least one eminent historian have tended to dismiss Léry as a mediocrity. In 1764 the Earl of Hertford described him as "a person of . . . very shallow . . . capacity"; in 1775 Colonel Henry Caldwell*, who was often in conflict with Carleton, characterized Léry's devotion to the governor as "servile adulation"; and in 1789 Alexander Fraser described all the Canadians on the Legislative Council, including Léry, as "illiterate." Elizabeth Arthur has assessed his voting record in council as uninformed and inconsistent, adding that after François Baby*'s appointment, Léry had no other motive for voting than to oppose Baby.

It is difficult to agree with these judgments. Léry's military reports under the French régime gave evidence of analytical ability. In the Legislative Council after 1775 he advocated the preservation of public records, improved measures for fire prevention, the founding of a law school and a school of surveying with salaried teachers and free tuition, a sufficient number of notaries to meet the demand for their services, and effective disease-control measures. He voted against martial law in 1778, preferred voluntary restraint to compulsory price control in 1780, and sponsored legislation concerning highways and land surveys in 1785. Two years later he supported the abolition of slavery in principle, though he opposed making Quebec a refuge for escaped slaves from abroad, and he was the only councillor to vote against the postponement of the bill to the next session. That Léry was not a lawyer and probably had difficulty grasping the principles of English and French law may explain some inconsistency in his voting on juridical questions. As for his attitude toward Baby, the record clearly shows him voting sometimes with, and sometimes against, that merchant on a wide range of issues. He was nonetheless, in his general political outlook, associated with the French party or faction in the council, favouring retention of the Quebec Act and opposing the introduction of such reforms as English commercial law and a legislative assembly.

Léry had survived the disruption of the conquest by fastening his loyalties tightly to self-interest. He had been able before 1760 to cultivate influential men such as La Galissonière and Vaudreuil, and after the conquest he continued to use this ability to good effect with Carleton, Charles and George* Townshend, Governor HALDIMAND, and Prince Edward Augustus*. Recognizing in 1775 that he was beholden to the British, he described as "credulous" and "simple" those habitants who had espoused the American cause. He was also guided by his devotion to his sons and spared no effort to assure their future. He sent his second son back to France in 1783 only after unsuccessful attempts to obtain for him a commission in the British army; and again in 1796 and 1797 he sought military careers in the British service for two of his sons. While the French monarchy lasted, however, he received, in recognition of his previous service, a pension of 590 *livres*, which, as long as his sons studied in France, was used for their benefit. Three years before his death Léry reaffirmed his allegiance to the British crown, from whom he received a pension of £200 per annum, by signing a petition denouncing American and republican French conspiracies in the Canadas.

Léry's funeral on 14 Dec. 1797 is testimony to the relative prosperity and social prominence he had achieved. He was buried in the cathedral of Notre-Dame with Joseph-Octave Plessis*, the coadjutor bishop of Quebec, officiating at the service and several of his former colleagues on the council in attendance.

F. J. THORPE

AN, Col., C^{11A}, 72, f.239; 93, ff.55, 285; 99, f.498; 100, f.253; C^{11E}, 10, ff.200–3; D^{2C}, 48, ff.278v, 298, 316; E, 77 (dossier Chaussegros de Léry); Marine, 3JJ, 271, no.2, Mémoire de Chaussegros de Léry sur le lac Ontario; Section Outre-mer, Dépôt des fortifications des colonies, Am. sept., nos.317, 503, 522, 533–35, 546–49. Archives du ministère des Affaires étrangères (Paris), Mémoires et doc., Amérique, 10, ff.256–57. PAC, MG 11, [CO 42], Q, 69, pp.329, 349; MG 23, A4, 16, pp.36, 39; GII, 1, ser. 3, Lord Elibank to Murray, 22 May 1764; RG 1, El, 6–7; RG 4, B6, 10–18; RG 14, A1, 1–2. PRO, CO 42/29, f.9; 42/66, f.400. [G.-J. Chaussegros de Léry], "Journal de la campagne que le Sr de Léry . . . a faite au Détroit en l'année 1749 . . . ," A.[-E.] Gosselin, édit., ANQ *Rapport*, 1926–27, 334–48, 372–94; "Journal de Joseph-Gaspard Chaussegros de Léry, lieutenant des troupes, 1754–1755," ANQ *Rapport*, 1927–28, 355–429. *Coll. des manuscrits de Lévis* (Casgrain), X, 22–25. *Inv. des papiers de Léry* (P.-G. Roy), II, III. *NYCD* (O'Callaghan and Fernow), X, 307, 528–34. PAC *Report*, 1904, app.D, 118; 1929, app.A, 41–42. *Papiers Contrecœur* (Grenier), 46–47, 51, 182, 210, 224, 248, 307. *DBF*, VIII, 882–83. Æ. Fauteux, *Les chevaliers de Saint-Louis*, 170. [François Daniel], *Nos gloires nationales; ou, histoire des principales familles du Canada* . . . (2v., Montréal, 1867), II, 141. Stanley, *New France*, 138–40. E. [M.] Arthur, "French Canadian participation in the government of Canada, 1775–1785," *CHR*, XXXII (1951), 303–14. P.-G. Roy, "La famille Chaussegros de Léry," *BRH*, XL (1934), 589–92.

CHAVOY, PIERRE-JACQUES PAYEN DE NOYAN ET DE. *See* PAYEN

CHENUGHIYATA (Chinoniata). *See* HOTSINOÑHYAHTA?

CHERRIER, FRANÇOIS-PIERRE (François, Pierre-François), merchant and notary; baptized 3 Sept. 1717 at Savigné-l'Évêque (dept of Sarthe), France, son of François Cherrier, a merchant, and Périnne Isambart; d. 21 July 1793 at Saint-Denis, on the Richelieu River (Que.).

François-Pierre Cherrier came to Canada in 1736 on the advice of his maternal uncle, Sulpician Joseph Isambart, who had been parish priest of Saint-Antoine-de-Longueuil since 1721. Isambart persuaded him to take up residence in this village, and thanks to him Cherrier acquired a certain importance, signing as a witness when deeds were drawn up, acting as a godfather by the year after his arrival, and establishing relations with the principal local families. He opened a store next door to the presbytery, and he seems to have been fairly successful in business. On 9 Nov. 1738, in the presence of notary François SIMONNET, Cherrier bought a piece of land, paying three-quarters of the price in cash and the remainder "in goods from his store." Appointed seigneurial notary in 1738 – probably through his uncle's support – he continued to attend to his business.

On 14 Jan. 1743 Abbé Isambart blessed Cherrier's marriage to Marie, daughter of the former churchwarden Michel Dubuc. Charles Le Moyne* de Longueuil was among the witnesses signing their marriage contract, which had been drawn up the previous day in the presence of notary Antoine Loiseau. The couple had 12 children. Cherrier's business connections enabled him to ask Jean-Marie LANDRIÈVE Des Bordes, the supervisory clerk of the king's stores in Montreal, to be godfather to his son Joseph-Marie-Simon in 1747; Marie Gauvreau, the wife of Jean-Baptiste-Grégoire Martel de Saint-Antoine, king's storekeeper in Montreal, became the godmother.

In order to diversify his commercial interests, Cherrier in 1748 bought all the wood on a piece of land belonging to the fief of Du Tremblay, adjoining Longueuil; he paid 480 *livres* in payment orders and 120 *livres* in Canadian "playing card" money. In addition he leased out his land at Longueuil. On 18 Nov. 1750 Intendant BIGOT appointed him royal notary for the parish of Longueuil. A notary's income was certainly not enough by itself to meet the needs of Cherrier, who had a large family, and he continued to be active in trade, like many other notaries at the time.

After the conquest, Thomas GAGE, the governor of Montreal, renewed Cherrier's commission as a notary on 1 Oct. 1760. As a merchant, however, Cherrier suffered heavy loss as a result of the settlement of the paper money. Since his protector, Isambart, had died in December 1763, Cherrier went to try his luck in Montreal in August 1765. Here his eldest daughter, Marie-Charlotte, married surgeon Jean-Jacques Lartigue in September 1766. Because his financial difficulties did nothing but increase, Cherrier and his family returned to Longueuil in August 1767. The notary was not clear of trouble yet; at the beginning of 1770 he owed Jacques PERRAULT, known as Perrault *l'aîné*, a Quebec merchant, the sum of £380 18*s*. 6*d*. His stone house and the land surrounding it on the main street were put up for sale at auction, along with a piece of land, 12 by 30 or 40 *arpents*, in the barony of Longueuil. In the absence of buyers Perrault acquired the latter property in partial payment of Cherrier's debts. Finally, in May 1770 the notary lost his house and its outbuildings in a fire.

Broken, but not desperate, Cherrier left Longueuil on 16 May 1770, to seek shelter with his wife and children in the presbytery of the parish of Saint-Denis, on the Richelieu, where his eldest son, François*, had become parish priest the previous year. Cherrier owed fairly large sums to a certain M. Dupré, a Quebec merchant, to Jacques-Joseph LEMOINE Despins in Montreal, and to MM. Mercure and Perrault, also in Montreal. He took up residence at Saint-Denis, in a house opposite the church and presbytery, where he continued to practise as a notary until 1789.

Though Cherrier was not successful in making a fortune, he had the consolation of seeing his children succeed in establishing themselves securely. François became vicar general of the bishop of Quebec; Joseph-Marie, a surveyor and later a merchant, was the father of lawyer Côme-Séraphin*. Benjamin-Hyacinthe-Martin was a surveyor and member of the legislative assembly for Richelieu, while Séraphin, also a member for Richelieu, practised medicine and engaged in trade. Cherrier's daughter Marie-Charlotte was the mother of Jean-Jacques Lartigue*, the first bishop of Montreal; Périne-Charles, who married Denis Viger*, was the mother of Denis-Benjamin*. Finally, Rosalie, who married notary Joseph Papineau*, became the mother of the great tribune Louis-Joseph Papineau*.

YVES-JEAN TREMBLAY

François-Pierre Cherrier's register (1750–89) is held at ANQ-M.

AD, Sarthe (Le Mans), État civil, Savigné-l'Évêque, 3 sept. 1717. ANQ-M, État civil, Catholiques, Saint-Antoine (Longueuil), 14 janv. 1743; Greffe d'Antoine Foucher, 30 déc. 1748; Greffe d'Antoine Loiseau, 13 janv. 1743. PAC *Rapport*, 1918, app.B, 29. Allaire, *Dictionnaire*, I, 119, 277. F.-J. Audet, *Les députés de Montréal (ville et comtés), 1792–1867* (Montréal, 1943), 411–12. F.-J. Audet et Édouard Fabre Surveyer, *Les députés au premier parlement du Bas-Canada (1792–1796)* . . . (Montréal, 1946), 65. É.-Z. Massicotte, "Les tribunaux et les officiers de justice de Montréal sous le Régime français," *BRH*, XXXVII (1931), 307. "Les notaires au Canada sous le Régime français," ANQ *Rapport*, 1921–22, 47. P.-G. Roy, *Inv. ord. int.*, III, 152. Tanguay, *Dictionnaire*, III, 52–53. Vachon,

"Inv. critique des notaires royaux," *RHAF*, XI, 105. J.-J. Lefebvre, "La famille Cherrier, 1743–1945," SGCF *Mémoires*, II (1947), 148–64; "La vie sociale du grand Papineau," *RHAF*, XI (1957–58), 472–73. É.-Z. Massicotte, "L'essaimage des Français et des Canadiens-français dans l'Amérique du Nord," *BRH*, XXXIV (1928), 45. Henri Morrisseau, "La famille Cherrier de Saint-Denis-sur-Richelieu; un salon aristocratique à la fin du dix-huitième siècle," *Revue de l'université d'Ottawa*, XVI (1946), 301–38.

CHEW, JOSEPH, Indian department official; probably b. in Virginia (U.S.A.) in the 1720s; d. 24 Sept. 1798 at Montreal (Que.).

Joseph Chew apparently began his military career as an officer in the Virginia troops. In 1747 he was a captain in the New York forces and was captured near Saratoga (Schuylerville, N.Y.) by Luc de LA CORNE. He was taken prisoner to New France, but his release was obtained in or before the summer of 1748. The war having been concluded, Chew set out for Maryland in January 1748/49 since he had the offer of "disposing of a Cargoe of goods" there. By 1752 he was living in New London, Connecticut, where he was marshal of the Vice-Admiralty Court. He was probably also still engaged in trade. In 1762, perhaps because he knew Sir William JOHNSON, a group of Connecticut speculators involved in a controversial land purchase along the Susquehanna River [*see* John Hendricks LŸDIUS] sent him to discuss the settlement of the tract with the Indian superintendent.

During the late 1760s Chew encountered financial difficulties and was, he wrote, "Support'd almost wholy by . . . [Johnson's] Bounty." He moved to the vicinity of Johnson Hall (Johnstown, N.Y.) and became a justice of the peace, undoubtedly through Johnson's influence. On 6 July 1774 he was appointed secretary to the Indian department. In effect he was secretary to Guy JOHNSON, Sir William's successor, and in this capacity attended various conferences with the Six Nations.

In November 1775 Chew accompanied Guy Johnson, Christian Daniel CLAUS, Joseph Brant [Thayendanegea*], and others to England in connection with Governor Guy Carleton*'s reorganization of the Indian department. When the party returned to North America several months later, he seems to have undertaken active military service in the New York City area against the American rebels. During a campaign in eastern Long Island in 1777 he was captured by Americans. Evidently paroled, he subsequently served in the Connecticut region. These activities separated Chew from his wife and children, whom he had left at Johnstown in 1775, and their welfare was a constant anxiety to him. At the war's end he sought compensation for his family's losses, going to England as late as 1789 for that purpose. Apparently he was successful, for he received various benefits including a grant of land in Carleton County, New Brunswick.

During the war the Indian department had fallen into disorganization. Particularly acrimonious was a dispute between Daniel Claus and John CAMPBELL over responsibility for the Canadian Indians. Sir John Johnson*'s appointment as superintendent general in 1782 alleviated some of the tension but Chew must have encountered difficulties when in the 1780s he again took up his duties as secretary. Sir John was somewhat ineffective as an administrator, and it was Chew who kept the department functioning. Working mostly in Montreal, he was responsible for the day-to-day correspondence with agents in the field and with other government departments. While the British retained the western posts and dreamed of creating a sphere of influence among the Indians of the Ohio-Mississippi country, Chew's role was vital. In 1794 the signing of Jay's Treaty, which relinquished the posts, reduced the department's importance. Chew remained active as secretary until his never robust health deteriorated in the autumn of 1798. He died on 24 September apparently of a bronchial disorder.

Chew's last years had been marked by renewed concern for his family's welfare. He asked that his son John succeed him as secretary and sought a departmental appointment for his younger son William Johnson Chew. It is an indication of the high regard in which Joseph Chew was held that both requests were granted. John Chew served as secretary from 1798 to 1806 and William Johnson Chew was departmental storekeeper at Fort Niagara (near Youngstown, N.Y.) and Fort George (Niagara-on-the-Lake, Ont.) from 1794 to 1809.

DOUGLAS LEIGHTON

PAC, MG 19, F1, F2, F6; MG 23, HI, 1, ser.3–4; RG 4, D1, 13, no.1242; RG 8, I (C series), 1203½, p.11; RG 10, A1, 486; A2, 11, pp.22, 37. PRO, PRO 30/55, 1, no.133. Conn. Hist. Soc., *Coll.* (Hartford), XVI (1916), 200, 322, 383; XVII (1918), 291. *Johnson papers* (Sullivan *et al.*). *Quebec Gazette*, 29 Feb. 1816. Graymont, *Iroquois*, 81. E. C. Wright, *The loyalists of New Brunswick* (Fredericton, 1955), 269. R. S. Allen, "The British Indian department and the frontier in North America, 1755–1830," *Canadian Historic Sites: Occasional Papers in Archaeology and History* (Ottawa), no.14 (1975), 5–125.

CHRISTIE, GABRIEL, army officer and seigneur; b. 16 Sept. 1722 at Stirling, Scotland, son of James Christie, a merchant, and Catherine Napier; d. 26 Jan. 1799 in Montreal (Que.).

Unlike his two brothers, a solicitor and a banker in Stirling, Gabriel Christie chose a military career, and his rise was like that of many sons of middle class families who were drawn towards the aristocracy. On 13 Nov. 1754 he became a captain in the 48th Foot. He took part in the siege of Quebec as a major, a rank he obtained on 7 April 1759. Christie was still in the colony when he was promoted lieutenant-colonel in 1762. In 1764–65 at the time of Pontiac*'s uprising, Christie as deputy quartermaster general used the public *corvée* to transport military supplies from Montreal to Lachine, the loading point for Detroit and Michilimackinac (Mackinaw City, Mich.). This action brought him into conflict with the governor, MURRAY, who objected to using the *corvée* now that civil government had been established; the incident was only one example in a series of quarrels that developed between Murray and the military [*see* Ralph Burton*] and reveals Christie as having personal ends in view in the use of his official position.

In 1776 the post of quartermaster general was assigned to Thomas Carleton*, brother of Governor Guy Carleton*. Christie protested but received the reply that he would have a better chance for advancement if he were in England. Christie did, indeed, go back there at this time. The following year he was promoted colonel. His battalion was stationed in the West Indies during most of the American revolution, but in the 1780s, when his active role in the army was over, he had settled upon Canada as his place of residence though he continued to make trips back to England. On 19 Oct. 1781, before the end of the revolution, he became major-general, and on 10 May 1786 was made colonel commandant of the 1st battalion of the 60th Foot. Nor was this his last promotion, for on 12 Oct. 1793 he became lieutenant-general and on 1 Jan. 1798 general. In other words, Christie's military career was notable although not one of brilliant feats of arms. His portrait would be incomplete, however, if his activities as a large landowner were not taken into consideration.

Unlike Henry Caldwell*, who also had an interest in becoming a landowner and who consequently partook of the same upper-class mentality, Christie does not seem to have been attracted to the fur trade. He had a substantial fortune when his plans began to centre upon life in Canada, and he preferred to use it for landed property. The economic situation favoured his plans. After 1760 many seigneurs, both noble and bourgeois, were prepared to sell their fiefs because they were returning to France or were in financial difficulties. Christie's conduct, which was socially significant, was also motivated by economic considerations: rapid population growth, large forest reserves in the seigneuries, and the beginnings of commercial prospects in the agricultural sector. In September 1764 he bought the seigneury of L'Islet du Portage from Paul-Joseph LE MOYNE de Longueuil, a good long-term investment. Christie, however, was more interested in having land in the District of Montreal and thus he sold this seigneury to Malcolm Fraser* in 1777. In 1764 he and Moses Hazen* had acquired the seigneuries of Bleury and Sabrevois from the Sabrevois de Bleury family for £7,300. After a dispute with his partner, Christie temporarily lost part of the seigneury of Bleury to Hazen, but court battles between the two were far from over. In 1764 Christie bought the seigneury of Noyan from the Payen de Noyan family, sharing ownership with John CAMPBELL. In 1765 the seigneury of Lacolle, owned by the Liénard de Beaujeu family, fell into his hands, and the following year he acquired the seigneury of Léry from Gaspard-Joseph CHAUSSEGROS de Léry. Around 1777 he added the seigneuries of Lachenaie and Repentigny to his lands. These acquisitions were not enough to satisfy his ambition, even though he also owned land in England. In April and October 1792 he made two requests for land grants in the Eastern Townships, but evidently without success. Then on 23 Nov. 1796 Jean-Baptiste Boucher de Niverville sold him the seigneury of Chambly.

Christie lived partly on his seigneurial dues, which he said brought him £700 in 1790. Since he resided in Montreal and since his military career sometimes took him out of the country, he visited his seigneuries only occasionally and administered them through agents, but he had some concern for his rural property, valued at £20,000 in 1775. A dispute with the *censitaires* of Lachenaie over the right of banality revealed a man who was both alive to his interests and open to compromise. His attitude was paternalistic but also stemmed from a sense of his own importance. He remained interested for a long time in the exploitation of the forest resources of his seigneuries. As early as 1766 he travelled to Lake Champlain and afterwards began trading in forest products. Indeed the "seigneur" was, for a time, also a businessman.

Christie believed above all in the need to safeguard the integrity of patrimonies. Consequently he supported Francis Maseres*' projected reform to secure greater freedom in making wills. He personally favoured his male offspring when he wrote his will. When he died in 1799 his lands went to his son Napier, who on his death in 1835 left them to his half-brother William Plenderleath*, on condition that Plenderleath take the name of Christie. Gabriel Christie was typical of a number of immigrant British officers who in their way of thinking closely resembled the nobility of New France.

Christie and his wife Sarah Stevenson had a son Napier and two daughters: Catherine, born 15 Jan. 1772, and Sarah, born 20 Nov. 1774, who married the Reverend James Marmaduke Tunstall*, rector of Christ Church in Montreal. He also had a natural son, James, and with his mistress Rachel Plenderleath, three other sons, Gabriel, George, and William: all of these he recognized on 13 May 1789 when he made his will in Leicester, England.

FERNAND OUELLET

PAC *Rapport*, 1890, 17–18, 76–79, 260; 1891, 15, 19–20. *Quebec Gazette*, 26 May 1785. P.-G. Roy, *Inv. concessions*, I, 261, 267; II, 200; IV, 242–43, 245, 253, 261, 265. Ivanhoë Caron, *La colonisation de la province de Québec* (2v., Québec, 1923–27), II. A. S. Everest, *Moses Hazen and the Canadian refugees in the American revolution* (Syracuse, N.Y., 1976). Neatby, *Quebec*, 40–41, 60–61. J.-B.-A. Allaire, "Gabriel Christie," *BRH*, XXIX (1923), 313–14. F.-J. Audet, "Gabriel Christie," *BRH*, XXX (1924), 30–32. P.-G. Roy, "Un amateur de seigneurie, Gabriel Christie," *BRH*, LI (1945), 171–73.

CIRIER, ANTOINE (although **Cirié, Cirrié, Cyrier, Sirier**, and **Syrier** are found, he signed Cirier), cabinet-maker and wood-carver; b. 10 Aug. 1718 in Montreal, son of Martin Cirier, cabinet-maker and wood-carver, and of Marie-Anne Beaune (Bône); m. 10 Oct. 1740 at Longue-Pointe (Montreal) to Marie-Joseph Lenoir, granddaughter of cabinet-maker Vincent Lenoir; m. secondly 19 May 1774 Marguerite Desroches at Pointe-aux-Trembles, Montreal Island; d. 2 Sept. 1798 at Pointe-aux-Trembles.

Antoine Cirier probably apprenticed with his father. In 1738 the latter withdrew from his contract with the churchwardens of the parish of Saint-François-d'Assise, Longue-Pointe, in favour of his son, who completed the decoration of the church retable around 1743. He was to work there again from 1767 to 1770. Between 1737 and 1758 Antoine did much of the interior decoration of the church of La Purification at Repentigny; after 1756, however, he had to deal with lawsuits for having failed to complete the contracts within the periods stipulated. The woodwork and carving for the church of L'Enfant-Jésus at Pointe-aux-Trembles kept him busy for several years from 1743 on, and here perhaps his principal work was accomplished. Nevertheless the central retable and cornice of the church of Saint-Laurent on Montreal Island, begun in late 1756, are also among his more important creations. He had some commissions from the sisters of the Congregation of Notre-Dame of Montreal, and in 1756 he undertook to prepare wainscoting for the Château de Ramezay in Montreal, which belonged to the Compagnie des Indes. Since his craft required him to travel, he stayed in several places near Montreal: Lachenaie, L'Assomption, Longueuil, Saint-Joseph-de-la-Rivière-des-Prairies, Saint-Denis on the Richelieu, Saint-François-de-Sales (Laval), Saint-Sulpice, Varennes, and Verchères.

Cirier lived in Montreal until 1740 and then spent three or four years at Longue-Pointe before finally settling at Pointe-aux-Trembles. In all three towns he made a large number of property deals. These transactions and the fact that he was a militia captain clearly indicate that he had been successful professionally and socially. Cirier had at least seven apprentices, including a nephew, Joseph Bachand, *dit* Vertefeuille. He had contacts with the leading wood-carvers of the Montreal region, and in 1761 he became the cousin by marriage of Philippe Liébert*, whom he had known for at least ten years. In 1771 he and wood-carver Jean-Louis Foureur*, *dit* Champagne, were given the task of examining three retables made by Liébert in the church of Saint-Louis, Terrebonne. It is also possible that Cirier, Liébert, and wood-carver François Guernon*, *dit* Belleville, collaborated on the church of Pointe-aux-Trembles in 1773–74 and that Cirier and Guernon continued to work together the following year for the mission of Lac-des-Deux-Montagnes.

Demolition and fire having relentlessly taken their toll, little remains of Cirier's abundant and varied work as a wood-carver and cabinet-maker. The loss is all the more regrettable since Cirier had obviously played a leading role in the Montreal region in his time and had created works of great value. Writing in 1742 of Cirier's work for the church of Longue-Pointe, Bishop Pontbriand [DUBREIL] urged upon the parishioners all the precautions needed "to secure the retable which lends such grace to your altars and sanctuary [so as not] to render useless so many works made with so much courage and success for the house of the Lord."

JOHN R. PORTER

ANQ-M, Doc. jud., Registres des audiences pour la juridiction de Montréal, 22, f.447; 25, f.82v; 26, ff.58v, 163, 171, 268; 28A, ff.36, 40v, 44, 94, 357; 28B, ff.15v, 19v, 34, 148v; État civil, Catholiques, Notre-Dame de Montréal, 10 août 1718; Saint-Enfant-Jésus (Pointe-aux-Trembles), 5 janv. 1765, 19 mai 1774, 4 sept. 1798; Greffe de J.-B. Adhémar, 14 juin 1744, 2 janv. 1749; Greffe de Louis Chaboillez, 14 sept. 1797; Greffe de François Comparet, 4 oct. 1740, 8, 11 mars 1744, 3 oct. 1745, 18 juill. 1749, 30 juin, 7 sept. 1751, 21 mai, 28 déc. 1754, 8 janv., 4 avril, 6 sept. 1755; Greffe de C.-F. Coron, 12 nov. 1747, 11 oct. 1756, 13 mars 1764; Greffe de L.-C. Danré de Blanzy, 1er mars 1741, 4 août 1744, 1er août 1746, 14 févr. 1749, 19 janv. 1755, 24 avril, 27 sept. 1756; Greffe de J.-C. Duvernay, 30 juin, 28 août 1751; Greffe d'Antoine Foucher, 16 nov. 1771; Greffe d'Antoine Loiseau, 26 févr. 1746, 13 mars 1748; Greffe de P.-F. Mézière, 17 janv. 1766; Greffe de Pierre Panet, 13 nov. 1773, 27 juin 1774; Greffe de François Racicot, 17 nov. 1779, 10, 26 janv. 1780; Greffe de François Simonnet, 15 oct. 1745, 30 mars, 11 juin 1751. Archives paroissiales, Saint-Enfant-Jésus (Pointe-aux-Trembles, Qué.), Livre de comptes, 1726–1865. IBC, Centre de documentation, Fonds Morisset, Dossier Antoine Cirier.

Quebec Gazette, 28 Oct. 1779. Tanguay, *Dictionnaire*. Émile Falardeau, *Artistes et artisans du Canada* (5 sér., Montréal, 1940–46), 4e sér., 49–81. Gowans, *Church architecture in New France*, 85, 132, 143–44. Gérard Morisset, *Coup d'œil sur les arts*, 18, 32–33; *Les églises et le trésor de Varennes* (Québec, 1943), 12. Jean Palardy, *Les meubles anciens du Canada français* (Paris, 1963), 390. J. R. Porter et Jean Trudel, *Le calvaire d'Oka* (Ottawa, 1974), 93, 101. Ramsay Traquair, *The old architecture of Quebec* (Toronto, 1947), 249, 292. A. Bellay, "L'église de Saint-François d'Assise de la Longue-Pointe," *Revue canadienne* (Montréal), XXIX (1893), 420–28. É.-Z. Massicotte, "Maçons, entrepreneurs, architectes," *BRH*, XXXV (1929), 132–42. Gérard Morisset, "Martin et Antoine Cirier," *La Patrie* (Montréal), 12 nov. 1950, 26–27, 50.

CLARK, ROBERT, merchant and colonizer; b. in London, England, son of Wotherton and Mary Clark; m. *c.* 1750 Elizabeth — ; m. secondly 6 July 1775 Ann Berry in London; d. July or August 1794, probably in St John's (Prince Edward) Island.

Details of Robert Clark's early life are unknown. He became a Quaker some time before 1753 and was active in the Society of Friends; in 1767 he was stated to have been a minister, or leader, for some years. He and his wife lived in Reading from 1753 to 1758 and in Faringdon from 1761 to 1764, when they moved to London. After 1773 legal documents list his occupation as salesman or merchant. He purchased Lot 21 on St John's Island in March 1773 and later added other lots, or townships, to his holdings. The next year he brought over 100 settlers, many of them indentured servants, to the north shore of the island and founded the settlement of New London. There is some indication that he was motivated by religious enthusiasm. Governor Walter PATTERSON stated that Clark "really thought himself a second Penn" and added that he "hoped to make New London a place for the recovering of sinners." Few of Clark's settlers shared his religious affiliation, however, and New London was to provide instead the roots of Methodism on the Island.

Clark returned to England in 1774, leaving his colonists without proper shelter or provisions. He had painted an attractive picture of the new world for prospective emigrants, but the diary of one settler, Benjamin Chappell*, details the near starvation which prevailed the first winter. By 1775 there were 16 houses and a sawmill at New London, but the settlement did not meet the expectations of the London investors, who had hoped for quick returns of timber, and colonization efforts do not appear to have been repeated. In 1779 Clark offered land at £100 for 500 acres, but there were no land sales before 1787 and few after. Many people left New London to settle nearby. Patterson wrote in 1784 that the settlers had been supplemented by "all the Vagabonds of the Island." He also felt that Clark was ruining himself by allowing his settlers "Wages, Victuals and Drink at Will" and by letting them do "as they pleased."

Patterson's account of New London may have been coloured by his conflict with Clark over land sales. In 1781 Patterson had seized several lots, including some of Clark's, for non-payment of quitrents and had resold them to himself and his friends. Clark, one of the loudest in protesting this action, petitioned the Privy Council in 1785. His efforts, together with those of Captain John MacDonald*, another proprietor, led to the successful prosecution of Patterson and several members of his council in 1789.

Clark returned to St John's Island in 1786, possibly only for a visit. By 1792 he was identified as a resident of the colony. The last years of his life were difficult. The lack of any financial return from the New London settlement, along with a heavy debt, involved him in several law suits. One of these, with his New London agent John Cambridge*, whom he had appointed in 1784, had to be appealed to the governor in council and eventually to the king in council. The suits did not end with his death in 1794 and his widow remained in the colony for several years attempting to regain his property. By 1800 the estate had been sold and the houses of New London torn down or moved; the dream of a Quaker colony on St John's Island was at an end.

H. T. HOLMAN

P.E.I., Supreme Court, Estates Division, will of Robert Clark (unregistered) (mfm. at Public Archives of P.E.I.). PRO, CO 226/8, pp.165–67; 226/10, pp.94–126, 135–43, 234–41, 253–94; CO 388/62, p.1207. Public

Archives of P.E.I. (Charlottetown), Benjamin Chappell, diary; RG 3, House of Assembly, Journals, 1775–89; RG 6, Courts, Supreme Court case papers, 1784–1800; RG 16, Registry Office, Land registry records, conveyance registers, liber 1234, ff.4, 5, 6, 8, 9. Thomas Curtis, "Voyage of Thos. Curtis," *Journeys to the Island of St. John or Prince Edward Island, 1775–1832*, ed. D. C. Harvey (Toronto, 1955), 9–69. [John MacDonald?], *Remarks on the conduct of the governor and Council of the Island of St. John's, in passing an act of assembly in April 1786 to confirm the sales of the lands in 1781 . . .* (n.p., [1789?]). *A short description of the Island of St. John, in the Gulph of St. Lawrence, North America* (n.p., 1779). "Dictionary of Quaker biography" (typescript), available only at Haverford College Library (Haverford, Pa.) and Library of Religious Soc. of Friends (London). D. C. Harvey, "Early settlement and social conditions in Prince Edward Island," *Dal. Rev.*, XI (1931–32), 448–61. [R. W. Kelsey], "Quakerism on Prince Edward Island in 1774," Friends' Hist. Soc. of Philadelphia, *Bull.*, XII (1923), 75–77.

CLARKE. *See* CLERKE

CLAUDE (Glaude), JOSEPH, principal chief of the Restigouche Micmacs; d. 1796 in their village at Restigouche (Pointe de la Mission, Que.). His successor, Jacques (Joseph) Gagnon, took office 18 May 1796.

The Restigouche Indians, whose territory included the coast from the Baie de Cascapédia (Que.) to the Miramichi River (N.B.) and all the land drained by the rivers between, were the survivors of the Gaspesian branch of the Micmac people. It is not clear whether it was Joseph Claude or his father who was appointed chief of Restigouche village by Governor Beauharnois* on 8 April 1730. By 1760 Joseph was certainly chief. At that time a British estimate placed the village's population at 100, although a contemporary French census put its number at 350. The former number is probably more accurate, for a 1765 census shows 87 members of the band at Restigouche.

At the time of the capitulation of Montreal in 1760 Claude's village was a refuge for over 1,000 Acadians from various parts of Nova Scotia and the base for about 200 French troops under François-Gabriel d'ANGEAC. The French and Indians made peace with the British separately in October, and Claude received a few blankets and supplies for his tribe. The influx of Acadians posed a threat to the small band. Writing in January 1761 to Roderick MacKenzie, the British commander at Restigouche, Claude complained that the Acadians treated his people like dogs, prevented them from fishing, and were preparing to sail off with the king's stores as soon as the ice broke.

The Acadians were deported [*see* Joseph DUGAS], but white fishermen and settlers again began moving into the Baie des Chaleurs region by the 1770s. Campbellton (N.B.) was founded in 1773, and in the next ten years some Acadians returned to the area. In 1778, when the French vice-admiral Comte d'Estaing, in the name of the king of France, invited Canadians to take up arms with the American rebels against the British, the missionary Joseph-Mathurin BOURG was able to intervene with Claude's people and maintain peace. After the American revolution the influx of whites continued. Justus Sherwood*, looking for new sites for incoming loyalists in June 1783, noted that the land at the mouth of the Restigouche River was of good quality and would yield many hundred thousand tons of hay; it was, however, "claimed by the Restigouch Indians." Although the Indians had granted settlers the right to cut hay for a fee of a dollar a year, it was inevitable that disputes should arise between them and the settlers as more Acadians and loyalists arrived from New Brunswick.

In 1786 the Quebec government, anxious to placate the Indians in order that white settlement might continue uninterrupted, appointed a commission to investigate their claims and grievances. The commissioners – Nicholas Cox, lieutenant governor of Gaspé, John COLLINS, deputy surveyor general of Quebec, and Abbé Bourg – were at Restigouche village from 29 June to 1 July. On 30 June they interviewed Claude, who claimed for his band the hunting grounds on the north side of the Restigouche River and an exclusive right to the salmon fishery. As his authority he produced Beauharnois's appointment of 1730.

Claude's people took particular exception to the land claims of Edward Isaac Mann, a Massachusetts loyalist, and to the indiscriminate use of seines by Robert Adams, another settler. Cox argued, however, that the lands occupied by the Restigouche Indians did not belong to them and were in fact French seigneuries which, through the exercise of the *droit de retrait*, now belonged to the British crown. Consequently, the king expected his Indians to make room for "others of his Children the English & Acadians, who are to be regarded by you as brothers." The commissioners promised the Indians a gratuity in return for the relinquishment of their "pretensions" to the land and for a "trifling concession" between the Rivière Nouvelle (Que.) and Point Macquache (probably Pointe à la Croix) up to a boundary line that would be drawn to mark off Indian and white holdings. As for the salmon fishery, "your pretensions as Natives of the Country" would be favourably reported to the governor,

Lord Dorchester [Guy Carleton*]. The band's three chiefs, Claude, Gagnon, and François Est*, *dit* Coundo, signed the agreement.

The problems of the Restigouche Indians did not end with the signing of the agreement. Although Claude apparently felt secure enough to rent out, in 1787, six *arpents* of land at Point Bourdon (probably Pointe à Bourdeau), which he claimed as his personal property, he was never able to retrieve them. Two separate surveys were made of the Indians' grant to the government in the 1786 agreement. The first, conducted by William Vondenvelden* in October 1787, cut deeply into the territory the Indians had retained. It was modified by John Collins in the following year. Unfortunately, both surveys were approved by the Legislative Council of Quebec in 1790 and the resulting confusion remained long after Claude's death. A number of protests were made in the first half of the 19th century, resulting in a detailed review of the situation in 1840 by Duncan Campbell Napier*, who as military secretary for Lower Canada was responsible for Indian affairs. He recommended a grant of crown lands adjoining the village as indemnification for past losses, but nothing was done. In 1865 the issue was reopened, and at that time William Prosperous Spragge, the deputy superintendent general for Indian affairs, admitted that the procedures followed by the 1786 commission in its negotiations with Claude had violated the principle "universally recognized that the Crown assumes no Indian Territory until a Deed of Cession & Surrender has been executed by the Indians & compensation agreed upon."

L. F. S. Upton

PANB, RG 2, RS8, Indians (William Spragge to commissioner of crown lands, 12 April 1865). Can., Prov. of, Legislative Assembly, *Appendix to the journals*, 1847, I, app.T, app.96. "Papiers Amherst (1760–1763) concernant les Acadiens," R.-S. Brun, édit., Soc. historique acadienne, *Cahier* (Moncton, N.-B.), III (1968–71), 273, 284, 288. "Recensement des gouvernements de Montréal et de Trois-Rivières, 1765," 116. Justus Sherwood, "Extracts from my journal of my voyage from Quebec to Gaspy, Bay Chaleurs, and Merimishi," PAC *Report*, 1891, 21–23. P. K. Bock, *The Micmac Indians of Restigouche: history and contemporary description* (Ottawa, 1966), 14–21. Père Pacifique [de Valigny] [H.-J.-L. Buisson], "Ristigouche: métropole des Micmacs, théâtre du 'dernier effort de la France au Canada,'" Soc. de géographie de Québec, *Bull.* (Québec), 19 (1925), 129–62; 20 (1926), 95–110, 171–85. L. F. S. Upton, "Indian affairs in colonial New Brunswick," *Acadiensis*, III (1973–74), no.2, 3–26.

CLAUS, CHRISTIAN DANIEL, Indian department official; b. 13 Sept. 1727 at Boennigheim (near Heilbronn, Federal Republic of Germany), son of Adam Frederic Claus, the town prefect, and his wife Anna Dorothea; d. 9 Nov. 1787 near Cardiff, Wales.

Christian Daniel Claus was born into a prominent family of southwestern Germany. In 1748 or 1749 a German emigrant visiting from America involved him in a plan to export raw silk and tobacco from America for processing in Germany. When Claus arrived in Philadelphia in the autumn of 1749, he discovered that the scheme was more imaginary than real. With few contacts and apparently unable to afford the voyage home, he resolved to find employment during the winter and return to Germany in the spring. He made the acquaintance of Johann Conrad Weiser, Pennsylvania's Indian agent, and was probably hired at that time as a tutor for Weiser's son. In 1750 Claus accompanied Weiser on a journey to the Hudson-Mohawk valley of New York, and during their stay with the Onondagas he began to compile a vocabulary of Indian words. On his return to Philadelphia he met the governor who, recognizing his interest in languages, arranged for him and Weiser's son to be sent to live among the Mohawks. He stayed for a while with King Hendrick [Theyanoguin*], who instructed him in the language, history, and customs of the Six Nations.

In 1755, when the management of Indian affairs in the northern colonies was centralized under the direction of William Johnson, Claus was made a lieutenant in the Indian department and a deputy secretary of Indian affairs. With the outbreak of the Seven Years' War at this time, the department was strained to its utmost for some years. Johnson's connection with the Six Nations became a vital part of the British effort to wrest control of eastern North America from France. Claus played an important role as an interpreter and diplomat in the frequent conferences and negotiations with the Indians. The collapse of New France added new pressures to the department; Johnson found that his traditional role with the Six Nations and his new concerns with the Indians of the Ohio country left him no time to look after Canada. Claus was accordingly made the deputy agent to the Canadian Indians on 20 Sept. 1760. He was based at Montreal and reported both to Johnson and to the local military government.

The world of the Indian department was a quasi-military one. In 1756 Claus had been made a lieutenant in the Royal Americans (62nd, later 60th Foot). With Johnson's financial assistance he purchased a captaincy in 1761, but he sold it the following year. He became colonel of the Albany County militia on 18 Feb. 1768 and acquired the colonelcy of another militia regiment on 7 July 1772.

These middle years of Claus's career were busy but pleasant. He married Ann (Nancy), the daughter of Johnson and Catherine Weissenberg (Wisenberg), on 13 April 1762. He occupied an important government post, and he owned considerable land in the vicinity of Albany. His success was deserved: he was charming, honest, and hardworking. The American revolution and administrative change in the Indian department, however, ended this comfort.

Sir William Johnson died suddenly on 11 July 1774 and was succeeded in the department by another son-in-law, Guy JOHNSON. Governor Guy Carleton*, resenting the Johnson influence over Indian administration in Quebec and wishing to place the Montreal agency more nearly under his own control because of the approaching conflict with the Americans, used this opportunity to institute a change in personnel. Daniel Claus, who according to his own statement had for 15 years borne "the whole weight and management of . . . the Indian Department" in Canada, was summarily dismissed from office in 1775 and replaced by John CAMPBELL, the son-in-law of Luc de LA CORNE. On 11 Nov. 1775 Claus took passage to England in company with Guy Johnson, Joseph Brant [Thayendanegea*], and others seeking the cancellation of Carleton's arrangements.

Claus returned in June 1777 with an appointment as superintendent of the Six Nations Indians who were to accompany Barrimore Matthew ST LEGER on an expedition into the Mohawk valley by way of Oswego, and he was present at St Leger's unsuccessful siege of Fort Stanwix (Rome, N.Y.) in August. With John BURGOYNE's defeat at Saratoga (Schuylerville) in October, the loyalist cause in the upper Hudson valley was lost, and Claus's family fled to Canada, abandoning lands and possessions.

The final period of his career opened with his appointment in August 1778 as a deputy agent for the Six Nations in Canada, subordinate to Guy Johnson. Several factors were involved. Frederick HALDIMAND had replaced Carleton as governor in June. He knew Claus and was sympathetic to the needs of the Indian department. Burgoyne's surrender had left the future of the Six Nations, especially the Mohawks, in doubt, and someone was needed to act as an official liaison with Indian leaders. Claus, who was familiar with the Iroquois and spoke some of their dialects, was the obvious choice; Campbell did not speak any Indian tongue and was fully occupied with the affairs of the Canadian Indians.

In his last years Claus supervised, along with John BUTLER, the establishment of various groups of Six Nations Indians on British soil, particularly at the Bay of Quinte and the Grand River (Ont.). His time was spent chiefly in Montreal and Quebec, but he made regular journeys to the western country. He was also greatly concerned to obtain compensation for his losses in the American revolution, and he died in Britain in 1787 while pursuing this interest. His son William* later became deputy superintendent of Indian affairs.

Claus's career demonstrates the intricacies of office-holding and the complexity of Indian-white relations in the late 18th century. He was a consummate politician, who strongly defended the Johnson interests in the Indian department, and an ambitious official who took his responsibilities seriously and carried them out with great competence.

DOUGLAS LEIGHTON

The PAC has two portraits said to be of Daniel Claus, but according to M. W. Hamilton, "The Johnson portraits," *Johnson papers* (Sullivan *et al.*), XIII, the one in civilian dress may be of his son William. Claus was author of *Daniel Claus' narrative of his relations with Sir William Johnson and experiences in the Lake George fight*, [ed. A. S. Walcott] ([New York], 1904).

PAC, MG 11, [CO 42], Q, 61/2, pp.353–56; 73/2, p.340; MG 19, F1, 20, 23, 25. *Johnson papers* (Sullivan *et al.*). *NYCD* (O'Callaghan and Fernow). *Orderly book of Sir John Johnson during the Oriskany campaign, 1776–1777 . . .*, ed. W. L. Stone (Albany, N.Y., 1882). *The valley of the Six Nations. . .*, ed. and intro. C. M. Johnston (Toronto, 1964). Graymont, *Iroquois*. P. A. W. Wallace, *Conrad Weiser, 1696–1760, friend of colonist and Mohawk* (Philadelphia and London, 1945).

CLAUSONNE, DANIEL-MARIE CHABERT DE JONCAIRE DE. *See* CHABERT

CLERKE (Clarke, Clerk), CHARLES, naval officer and explorer; b. 1741 at Weathersfield Hall (near Braintree), England; d. 22 Aug. 1779 on board the *Discovery*, near Avacha (Tar'ya) Bay, Kamchatka peninsula (U.S.S.R.).

Charles Clerke, the son of a justice of the peace, entered the Royal Navy in 1755. After serving throughout the Seven Years' War, he became a midshipman on John BYRON's expedition around the world in 1764–66. On his return Clerke wrote a sensationalized account of the notorious "Patagonian giants," which, despite its publication in the *Philosophical Transactions* of the Royal Society of London in 1768, was probably a hoax, for its author already had a reputation as a high-spirited young man. The turning point of Clerke's professional life came in 1768 when he joined the *Endeavour*, under James COOK, as master's mate on the first of the great explorer's Pacific voyages. Clerke's service began an association which lasted until Cook's death. After promotion to lieutenant in May 1771 during the first voyage, Clerke sailed on the second voyage as second lieutenant in the *Resolution*; in 1776, now a captain, he was given command of the *Discovery* and sailed with Cook to the north Pacific in search of a northwest passage.

For Clerke the seeds of personal tragedy had been sown before he left England in 1776, for a spell in the Fleet prison in London as the guarantor of another's debts had left him with tuberculosis. As Cook's vessels made their slow way towards the northwest coast of America Clerke seems to have considered resigning his command, in the hope of recovering in warmer climes, but was presumably held back by his strong sense of duty. The journal he kept in 1778, as the expedition worked its way northward along the coasts of what are now British Columbia and Alaska in a vain search for the northwest passage, contains more complete and precise natural history observations than those of most of his colleagues, as well as good descriptions of the Nootkas. But Clerke's strength was failing rapidly. In April 1778 he was able to accompany Cook on a visit to a Nootka village at Nootka Sound (B.C.), but when he assumed command of the expedition after the awful shock of Cook's death in February 1779 he referred to "my own unhappy state of Health which sometimes is so bad as hardly to suffer me to keep the Deck." Despite his poor health, he ordered the vessels back into the icy and fogbound waters of the north in another attempt to find a route through Bering Strait and east along the Arctic coastline of the American continent. The strait was reached on 5 July (ship time), but on the 7th the great ice-barrier which had blocked Cook's progress the previous year was sighted. After repeated attempts to penetrate the ice the expedition was forced back in latitude 70°33′N, five leagues short of their farthest point north in 1778. Clerke's last journal entry, dated 21 July 1779, concluded: "this Sea is now so Choak'd with Ice that a passage I fear is totally out of the question." The battered vessels put back to Avacha Bay, Kamchatka, for repairs, but before they reached port Clerke, long since "reduced to almost an absolute skeleton," as one of his officers wrote later, died at the age of 38. Of his last months Lieutenant James KING wrote, "nor did he swerve in any instance from persevering on account of his health, preferring his duty to his Country, to even his own life."

GLYNDWR WILLIAMS

[Charles Clerke's report on the "Patagonian giants" is printed as "An account of the very tall men, seen near the *Streights* of *Magellan*, in the year 1764, by the equipage of the *Dolphin* man of war, under the command of the Hon. Commodore *Byron* . . . ," Royal Soc. of London, *Philosophical Trans.*, LVII (1768), pt.1, 75–79. His journals for 1776–79 are in the PRO, Adm. 51/4561/217 and Adm. 55/22, 55/23, 55/124, and extracts are printed in *Journals of Captain James Cook* (Beaglehole), III, 531–49, 569–82, 591–603, 632–50, 655–59, 678–97, 1301–40. The section relating most directly to Canada, which concerns the expedition's stay at Nootka Sound from March to April 1778, is printed on pp.1323–33. A collection of Clerke's letters to Sir Joseph Banks* is in the State Library of New South Wales, Mitchell Library (Sydney, Australia), Banks papers (Brabourne coll.), II. Those written on the last voyage are printed in *Journals of Captain James Cook*, III, 1508, 1509, 1518–19, 1542–44; Clerke's final report to the Admiralty, in PRO, Adm. 1/1612, pt.35, is found on pp.1535–40. For additional information, *see*: BL, Egerton MSS 2591, f.275A; James Burney, *A chronological history of north-eastern voyages of discovery; and of the early eastern navigations of the Russians* (London, 1819), 233–34, 268; [John Byron], *Byron's journal of his circumnavigation, 1764–1766*, ed. R. E. Gallagher (Cambridge, Eng., 1964), 207n; *The Banks letters; a calendar of the manuscript correspondence of Sir Joseph Banks . . .*, ed. W. R. Dawson (London, 1958), 220–21; and *DNB*. G.W.]

COCKING (Cochin, Cockan, Cockings), MATTHEW, HBC chief factor and explorer; b. 1743, apparently in York, England, probably the son of Richard Cochin, tailor, and Jane Carlton; d. 17 March 1799 in York.

Little is known of Matthew Cocking before 1765, when the Hudson's Bay Company "entertained" him as a writer at an annual rate of pay of £20 for five years at York Fort (York Factory, Man.). There he transcribed post journals and correspondence in his elegant hand, kept accounts, and checked shipments of goods and furs inward and outward against indents and inventories. His intelligence and diligence were recognized in 1770, when he was made second at York with a salary of £50 per annum.

In 1772 Cocking volunteered to go inland when Andrew Graham*, acting chief at York, complained that the accounts of the trade situation given by the company's servants who had been sent on trips inland were "incoherent and unintelligible." On 27 June 1772, under the guidance of a reluctant "Indian Leader," Cocking began an arduous journey in an Indian canoe which he did not know how to steer. The Indians were "sickly" and a canoe mate died. They travelled slowly by the usual route up the Hayes, Fox, and Minehage (Minago) rivers (Man.) and so to the Saskatchewan River. At the site of an old French post, where friends awaited them, they "threw away" their canoes and then proceeded overland from Peonan Creek (Sask.), across the South Saskatchewan, to the Eagle Hills (south of Battleford). Cocking wandered with the Indians, hunting out on the open plains southwest of modern Biggar and in the parklands until it was time again to build canoes for the journey down to the bay. He arrived back at York on 18 June 1773. In his detailed journal, log, and concluding "Thoughts on making a settlement inland," Cocking gave, as Graham had expected, a "rational account" of the buffalo country and of the life and customs of its people, among them the "stranger Indians" of the plains, notably the Siksikas (Blackfeet). He described the prairies and parklands, their wildlife and vegetation, and the route that connected them with the bay. He discussed the posts, procedures, and trade standards of the Canadian pedlars who were intercepting the York trade. He made clear how urgent it was that the company push trading operations inland and identified the many problems to be overcome, among them the company's lack of canoes and experienced men.

Cocking's next trip inland in 1774–75 gave him bitter experience with one of these difficulties: total dependence on the Indians for "carriage." He left on 4 July 1774 to help Samuel HEARNE establish Cumberland House, the company's first permanent western inland settlement, at Pine Island Lake (Cumberland Lake, Sask.). Cocking took a route via Lake Winnipeg (Man.) which he hoped would be feasible for large canoes. On the way he "came up with" Isaac BATT, an experienced inland traveller, and Charles Thomas Isham*, who had been abandoned by their Indian guides. Cocking stayed with them, not wishing to leave them to starve. His own Indians could not be persuaded to go on up the Saskatchewan where many of the natives were ill; eventually other Indians came to take him on, not to Basquia (The Pas, Man.), where Hearne awaited him, but to their own country up the Red Deer River, west of Lake Winnipegosis. He wintered at Witch Lake (perhaps Good Spirit Lake, Sask.). Undaunted, Cocking described this new territory in his journal and sought to attach to the company the stranger Indians he met. He set off down the Red Deer River on his return journey on 20 May 1775 and arrived at York on 27 June.

Although Cocking had in 1774 been appointed master of Severn House (Fort Severn, Ont.), Ferdinand JACOBS, chief at York, and the York council reported that he had been sent inland once more, despite his great reluctance and "an ugly rupture." Travelling by way of the Nelson River (Man.), he took command of Cumberland House from Hearne on 6 Oct. 1775. From that post he led the opposition to the Canadian pedlars, sending out Robert Longmoor*, Malchom Ross, and William WALKER, among others, to compete with them. Cocking was sent inland to Cumberland once more in 1776 on direct orders from the London committee.

In August 1777 Cocking at last received permission to take up his appointment at Severn. Severn, like York, was suffering from the pedlars' competition, but there, besides dealing with the Indians, Cocking was concerned mainly with the routine provisioning and daily management of the post. Although ill-health was "growing on him," he took command of York in 1781 when illness forced its chief, Humphrey MARTEN, to return to England. At York, Cocking's last recorded official act was to try to check the spread of the devastating smallpox epidemic of 1781–82 by sending urgent warnings to Severn, Albany (Fort Albany, Ont.), and Moose Factory (Ont.) in August 1782. Marten returned to relieve Cocking just before the Comte de Lapérouse [GALAUP] captured York. Cocking sailed for England on 24 August on the *King George*, which, with a cargo of furs, eluded the French force. His "long services and good Behaviour" had earned the "Approbation" of the company. The records he left are today an invaluable source of information about the early west.

Settled in the suburbs of York, where a sister and a half-brother lived, Cocking did not forget his transatlantic family ties; he secured permission from the company to send an annual remittance for "the use of his children and their parents in Hudson's Bay." When he died his major legatees were English relatives, but his will provided for goods worth £6 a year to be supplied to each of his three mixed-blood daughters, the eldest to receive the full amount, the others to share their portion with their mothers. The council at York requested that part of this legacy might be "laid out in Ginger Bread, Nuts &tc. as they have no other means of obtaining these little luxuries, with which the paternal fondness of a Father formally provided them."

IRENE M. SPRY

[Matthew Cocking], "An adventurer from Hudson Bay: journal of Matthew Cocking, from York Factory to the Blackfeet country, 1772–73," ed. and intro. L. J. Burpee, RSC *Trans.*, 3rd ser., II (1908), sect.II, 89–121.

HBC Arch. A.1/42–45; A.5/1–3; A.6/10–19; A.11/115–18; A.16/32–33, A.16/37; A.30/1–2; B.49/a/1–5, B.49/a/7; B.135/b/4–13; B.198/a/20–27; B.198/d/26–33; B.239/a/53–54, B.239/a/66, B.239/a/68–76, B.239/a/78–80; B.239/b/36–42, B.239/b/78–79; B.239/d/56–57, B.239/d/59–62, B.239/d/65 66, B.239/d/68, B.239/d/70, B.239/d/84–85, B.239/d/87, B.239/d/93, B.239/d/95–96, B.239/d/98–99, B.239/d/101–2; C.1/386; E.2/6, f.51; E.2/11, ff.41–73d. PAC, MG 18, D5. University of York, Borthwick Institute of Hist. Research (York, Eng.), general MS indexes of wills and administrations (Prob. Index plus date); PR. Y/ASP.19, 7 Sept. 1743, 17, 20 March 1799; Prerogative Court of York probate records, April 1799 (will of Matthew Cocking). *Docs. relating to NWC* (Wallace). HBRS, XIV (Rich and Johnson); XV (Rich and Johnson); XXVII (Williams). Henry, *Travels and adventures* (Bain). *Journals of Hearne and Turnor* (Tyrrell). *Letters from Hudson Bay, 1703–40*, ed. K. G. Davies and A. M. Johnson, intro. R. [G.] Glover (London, 1965). *The registers of All Saints' Church, Pavement, in the city of York*, ed. T. M. Fisher (2v., Yorkshire Parish Register Soc., *Pubs.*, C, CII, Leeds, 1935–36). *The registers of St. Michael le Belfrey, York*, ed. Francis Collins (2v., Yorkshire Parish Register Soc., *Pubs.*, I, XI, Leeds, 1899–1901). J. N. L. Baker, *A history of geographical discovery and exploration* (London, 1931). Morton, *History of Canadian west*. Rich, *History of HBC*. [Much kind help from HBC archivists is gratefully acknowledged. I.M.S.]

COGHLAN, JEREMIAH, merchant and ship-owner; m. Joanna —, and they had four sons and one daughter; fl. 1756–88.

Jeremiah Coghlan captained several Bristol merchant ships on voyages to the Mediterranean, the West Indies, and North America in the 1750s. He visited Newfoundland in 1756 as the master of a trading vessel and in 1762–63 made a voyage there on his own account in the *Lovely Joanna*, a 25-ton vessel with a crew of five. By the summer of 1764 Coghlan was established in the fishery on the island of Fogo, off the northeastern coast of Newfoundland, both as an independent entrepreneur and as an agent for Bristol merchants.

The following year, under the protection of Governor Hugh PALLISER, who favoured the development of a Labrador fishery, Coghlan established a sealing post at Chateau Bay near the Strait of Belle Isle and fitted out an armed sloop to survey the northern coast for likely places for cod and salmon fisheries. He rapidly became one of the pillars of the Fogo community and in 1769 Governor John BYRON appointed him naval officer for the port. Coghlan usually returned each fall to Bristol, where he resided in a spacious house on Trinity Street.

In 1769 Coghlan formed a partnership with Thomas Perkins of Bristol, and to this association were later added two men familiar with Labrador: George Cartwright*, a former army officer, and Francis Lucas*, who had served in the naval garrison at Chateau Bay. A settlement presided over by Cartwright was made at Cape Charles, north of Chateau Bay, and Lucas was sent north to trade with the Inuit. Unfortunately, Lucas was lost on the return voyage to Europe in 1770 and Coghlan found it prudent to end his connection with Cartwright, "having been subject to a heavy loss." (The partnership with Perkins was dissolved in 1773.) Coghlan and Cartwright then essentially divided the Labrador coast north of Chateau Bay between them, Cartwright retaining Cape Charles and, far to the north, Sandwich Bay while Coghlan took the intervening coast.

Coghlan steadily prospered, prosecuting the cod fishery in the summer and leaving crews for sealing and furring in the winter and salmon fishing in the spring. By 1777 he could boast that he employed four times the men Cartwright did, "being bred in this business," and he regularly sent two ships a year to the Labrador coast. At the peak of his career Coghlan annually employed between eight and ten ships to carry supplies out to Newfoundland and Labrador and cargoes of cod, salmon, furs, sealskins, and oil back to England. The miscellaneous outgoing cargoes included virtually all the basic needs of people living in isolated communities: for the household, casks of bread, biscuits, pork, and beef, firkins of butter, pipes of olive oil and vinegar, cartons of soap and candles, and bales of clothing, hats, and gloves; for the fishery, hogsheads of twine, salt, and other supplies.

By 1776 Coghlan had become the governor's right-hand man in northeastern Newfoundland. He enforced payment of customs duties, dispatched law-breakers to St John's for trial, and recruited men for the defence of Quebec against the Americans. During the American revolutionary war he cooperated closely with the governors in the defence of Newfoundland, and his settlements survived largely unscathed. During the summer of 1778, however, the American privateer John Grimes appeared off the coast of Labrador. He sacked the establishment at Chateau Bay, attacked Coghlan's posts on the Alexis River, and took one of his ships. Fearing an attack upon Fogo itself, Coghlan summoned a meeting of local merchants, "but it was with great difficulty he could get even the voice of one Englishman, who would engage to stand by him, although there were 250 able men capable of bearing arms." He decided to depend upon his own people, and he put his largest ship, the *Resolution*, in a state of defence. Governor John Montagu dispatched two warships to intercept Grimes, but he escaped after plundering Cartwright at Sandwich Bay. A grateful Coghlan forwarded to Montagu an address of thanks signed by 67 merchants and fishermen of Fogo who had assembled under arms as volunteers and who were headed by Coghlan as their "colonel-commandant." In the spring of 1779 Coghlan asked Governor Richard EDWARDS for arms with which to defend Fogo, and that August a warship delivered 200 muskets to him. In the summer of 1780 Edwards supplied him with four six-pounders for Fogo and three six-pounders for his post at Spear Harbour, at the mouth of the Alexis River. In addition, for the remainder of the conflict ships of the Newfoundland squadron regularly patrolled the southern Labrador coast and escorted the ships of the Labrador merchants to St John's in the fall. For his part, Coghlan kept up the drilling of his fishermen-soldiers, mounted his cannon in hastily built forts, and was so vigilant that no privateer dared attack him.

Towards the end of the war rumours began to circulate about Coghlan's solvency, with such effect that he had to take court action. In September 1781 his eldest son presented his petition for redress before Edwards in St John's. Coghlan's evidence included letters written by his erstwhile partner Cartwright and by John Codner, a St John's merchant, which threw doubt on the worth of his credit notes. Edwards had no difficulty in declaring the reports to be "malicious, ill-founded, and industriously spread for the purpose of injuring the said Jeremiah Coghlan's trade and credit."

Ironically, the reports were all too true, or else they had the desired effect, for Coghlan was forced into bankruptcy in July 1782. The news threw Fogo into confusion and Governor John Campbell sent one of his captains to help sort matters out. Coghlan's fish, oil, and other effects were seized to pay his fishermen's wages and his debts. He apparently remained active in the Newfoundland trade to some extent thereafter, for in 1788 he protested to Palliser on behalf of English merchants about the newly established Bermudian fishery on the Grand Banks. Little further is known of his career. He is thought to have been the father of Pamela Simms, who would later marry the Irish patriot Lord Edward Fitzgerald, but there is no documentary evidence to support this Newfoundland legend.

In the 1770s Jeremiah Coghlan may well have been the most prominent merchant in northern Newfoundland and on the Labrador coast. His fishing, sealing, and furring crews were to be found on the coasts of Newfoundland from the Exploits River to St Barbe, while on the Labrador coast they ranged far north from Chateau Bay, perhaps even to Hamilton Inlet. Coghlan was an example of a West Country merchant who was successful, at least for a time, in carrying on a migratory fishery and exploiting new areas on the Labrador coast. When the collapse of his empire came, however, it was swift and complete.

WILLIAM H. WHITELEY

[Jeremiah Coghlan's residence in Bristol can be traced in the records in the Bristol Record Office of St Augustine parish – the poor rate books, 1761–83; the lighting and cleansing rate books, 1761–64, 1770–86; and the land tax books, 1763–64, 1766–69, 1770, 1780–87 – and in the register book of christenings, burials, and weddings, 1738–91, held by St George's Church (Bristol). Information on the cargoes his ships carried out to Newfoundland can be found in the Bristol Presentments, exports, 1773–80, at the Bristol Reference Library. Although Coghlan was not a member of the Society of Merchant Venturers, the Seamen's Hospital order book, 1747–69, the Hospital for Decayed Seamen, book no.1, 1748–87, and the ships' muster rolls, 1751–94, in the society's archives at Merchants' Hall (Bristol) contain several references to his ships.

Much information about Coghlan's career in Newfoundland is to be found in the correspondence of the Colonial Secretary's Department (GN2/1) in PANL, in particular vols. 3–9. Scattered references may be found in PRO, CO 194/21 and 194/34. The journal of Governor John Montagu for 1778 in PRO, Adm. 50/17, has a good account of the privateer raids on the Labrador coast and Coghlan's spirited action. The unpublished diaries of Trinity merchants Isaac and Benjamin* Lester in the Dorset Record Office, Dorchester (D.365), contain several references to Coghlan's activities from 1765 to 1782. Typewritten extracts from the diaries are located in the archives of the Maritime History Group at Memorial University of Newfoundland in St John's (MHG-B-2A, MHG-B-2B). Coghlan also appears in George Cartwright's *A journal of transactions and events, during a residence of nearly sixteen years on the coast of Labrador* . . . (3v., Newark, Eng., 1792).

Printed material on Coghlan is generally scarce, except for his alleged connection with Pamela Simms. There are scattered references in W. G. Gosling, *Labrador: its discovery, exploration, and development* (2nd ed., London, 1910), and Prowse, *History of Nfld.*, and references to his ships in *Lloyd's list* (London), 1763–81. With regard to Pamela Simms *see* S. P. Whiteway, "The romantic Pamela Simms, wife of Lord Edward Fitzgerald, the Irish rebel" (paper presented to the Nfld. Hist. Soc., St John's, 31 March 1942), which tends to discount the supposed Newfoundland connection. For a contrary view *see* William Pilot, "This Newfoundland girl might have become queen of France," *The book of Newfoundland*, ed. J. R. Smallwood (6v., St John's, 1937–67), V, 137–42. The biography of Pamela Fitzgerald in the *DNB* inclines to the belief that she was indeed born in Fogo, but makes no mention of Coghlan. W.H.W.]

COIGNE. *See* COUAGNE

COLE, JOHN, Canadian fur-trader; b. in New England; killed 22 April 1779 in the Eagle Hills (south of Battleford, Sask.).

Little is known of John Cole's life prior to 1771. In that year he engaged with the Canadian Thomas Corry and helped in the establishment of his post at Cedar Lake (Man.). Cole deserted the next year and, seeking employment with the Hudson's Bay Company, arrived at York Factory (Man.) on 11 July in company with three canoes of Indians. Corry complained to Andrew Graham*, acting chief at York, that Cole and another of his servants, a Canadian named Bove, had absconded with "a Consetrable Sum in goods," and he condemned the two as "notras vellons." Graham, however, was impressed by Cole and described him as "a strong, tall, able Man, [who] speaks the English, French, & Indian Languages, was formerly one of the Battoe Men, & has travelled over a large extent of Ground from Bristol in New-Jersey, but never was at Quebeck or Montreal, talks very sensible, & can write a little, & very much belov^{d}. by the Natives."

Graham had always opposed the establishment of inland posts by the Hudson's Bay Company, but Corry's post at Cedar Lake had cut deeply into York's fur returns. In one instance Corry had side-tracked 125 of the 160 canoes that Louis PRIMEAU and Isaac BATT were bringing down to York. Describing the pattern of Canadian trade, Cole easily persuaded Graham that "nothing will do but the establishment of a Settlement Inland." He declared that he would engage to conduct large loaded canoes up the Saskatchewan River in 40 days, and he got from Graham a contract for £12 per annum, twice the usual starting rate. He was then sent inland to recruit Bove and to bring down to York two large birch-bark canoes; he had insisted such canoes were essential for inland settlement, but materials for them did not exist as far north as Hudson Bay.

Cole spent the winter of 1772–73 inland and reappeared at York Factory in the early summer of 1773, with neither Bove nor the canoes. Sent inland once more to the Saskatchewan, Cole deserted back to the Canadians. The details of his further career are uncertain. In July 1776 he was reported to be serving as an interpreter for some pedlars who were building a post upstream from the HBC's Cumberland House (Sask.) on the Saskatchewan River. Farther upstream, on the North Saskatchewan River three miles above its junction with the South Saskatchewan, he constructed for Booty Graves a post that was never used. Cole subsequently remained in the upper Saskatchewan area.

By 1779 Cole was apparently in the employ of Peter Pangman*. At this time the Indians were suffering from ill treatment at the hands of some Canadian traders in the upper Saskatchewan. In the autumn of 1778 the traders at the upper settlement in the Eagle Hills had killed an Indian by administering a dose of laudanum in his grog. Cole himself certainly had lost the respect of the Indians which Graham had claimed for him, for Peter Fidler* was later to describe him as being possessed at that time of "a very irriscarable Temper, & frequently ill using the Natives without any just cause." The Indians returned the next spring and, in an argument on 22 April with the Canadians over a horse, one of them shot and killed Cole and another trader.

E. E. RICH

Docs. relating to NWC (Wallace). HBRS, XIV (Rich and Johnson); XXVII (Williams). *Journals of Hearne and Turnor* (Tyrrell). Morton, *History of Canadian west*. Rich, *History of HBC*, II.

COLLÉGIEN, JEAN-ANTOINE SAILLANT DE. *See* SAILLANT

COLLIER, Sir GEORGE, naval officer; b. 11 May 1738 in London, England, eldest son of George Collier; m. 3 Sept. 1763 Christiana Gwyn, and they had one son; m. secondly on 19 July 1781 at Exeter, England, Elizabeth Fryer, and they had two sons and four daughters; d. 6 April 1795 in London.

A man of obvious leadership qualities, George Collier made a successful career in the Royal Navy. He entered in 1751 and three years later was promoted lieutenant. In July 1762 he was made captain and in 1775 was knighted. The next year, following the outbreak of the American revolution, he was part of Commodore William Hotham's squadron convoying Hessian troops to New York City. There he participated in Lieutenant-General Sir William Howe's operations against the rebel army. It was with "inexpressible astonishment and concern" that he witnessed Howe's failure to destroy the retreating American forces after the battle of Long Island on 27 Aug. 1776.

The next month Collier was sent to organize the naval defence of Nova Scotia, and he discharged this command with great success until his departure in 1778. His squadron was particularly successful in taking American vessels. By the end of 1777 some 76 enemy ships had been captured or burnt, perhaps a third of them British vessels that had previously been seized by the Americans; in July 1777 the squadron took the "flag ship" of the New England privateering fleet, the *Hancock* (32 guns). As senior naval officer at Halifax Collier was also responsible for collecting the transports necessary for the evacuation to France of the population of Saint-Pierre and Miquelon, who were forced to leave their homes by a British squadron under Commodore John Evans in 1778 [*see* Charles-Gabriel-Sébastien de L'ESPÉRANCE].

Collier was no less active in dealing with invasion threats to Nova Scotia. Soon after his arrival at Halifax he dispatched a squadron to relieve Fort Cumberland (near Sackville, N.B.), where the garrison under Joseph GOREHAM was being besieged by "an inconsiderable number of New England banditti" led by Jonathan Eddy*. The ships arrived after Eddy's attacks had been beaten off, but they landed troops who cooperated with the garrison to rout the rebels on 29 Nov. 1776. In June 1777 Collier heard that a group of rebels had concentrated at Machias (Maine) to secure an Indian alliance and to attack Nova Scotia. He promptly dispatched a force of six ships which landed troops under Brigade-Major Gilfred STUDHOLME; following a skirmish, the American threat was nullified.

After the recall of Rear-Admiral James Gambier in the spring of 1779 Collier assumed command of the North American squadron. In May he convoyed an expeditionary force to Virginia and captured or burnt 137 enemy vessels there. On his return to New York he assisted in the capture of Fort Lafayette (near Verplanck, N.Y.). In August Collier went to the relief of Fort Majebigwaduce (Castine, Maine), whose garrison under Brigadier Francis McLEAN was being besieged by a large American force. His powerful squadron routed the Americans and destroyed their fleet of 19 armed and 24 provision and transport vessels. When George III was informed of his successes, he commented that "It is remarkable that Sir G. Collier, with so scanty a force, should have been during the five months able to effect more objects against the rebels than the admirals that commanded such large fleets."

Collier's remarkable achievements were curiously unrewarded. Upon his return to New York from Maine he was relieved of his command, which had in any case been only a temporary one, by Rear-Admiral Mariot ARBUTHNOT. He later served in the Channel fleet and was present at the relief of Gibraltar in 1781, but he never again held an independent command. His failure to be promoted to flag rank or to secure any other public acknowledgement of his services – he twice applied unsuccessfully for a baronetcy – led Collier to resign his command in the Channel fleet later in 1781. In 1784 he was elected to parliament from Honiton. He was finally promoted rear-admiral in 1793 and vice-admiral the following year; in 1795 he was appointed commander-in-chief at the Nore. Forced to resign because of ill health, Collier died in April of that year. He had made a small fortune from prize money, and the principal asset mentioned in his will was £16,667 in three per cent Consols.

JULIAN GWYN

[George Collier], "'To my inexpressible astonishment': Admiral Sir George Collier's observations on the battle of Long Island," ed. L. L. Tucker, N.Y. Hist. Soc., *Quarterly* (New York), XLVIII (1964), 292–305.

Clements Library, Sir Henry Clinton papers. National Maritime Museum, HIS/7 "A detail of some particular services performed in America during the years 1776, 1777, 1778 and 1779, by Commodore Sir George Collier . . . ," comp. G. J. Rainier; JOD/9 "A journal of the war in America by Sir George Collier." PRO, Adm. 1/1611–12; 6/19–21; PRO 30/8/124, ff.166–68; Prob. 11/1259, ff.115–17. Sheffield City Libraries (Sheffield, Eng.), Wentworth Woodhouse Muniments, R.111/32–40. *Naval Chronicle* (London), XXXII (1814), 265–96, 353–400. *The private papers of John, Earl of Sandwich, first lord of the Admiralty, 1771–1782*, ed. G. R. Barnes and J. H. Owen (4v., London, 1932–38), III, 135. *DNB*. Namier and Brooke, *House of Commons*, II, 239.

COLLINS, JOHN, surveyor and office-holder; d. 15 April 1795 at Quebec.

The creation of the office of surveyor general of lands of the province of Quebec arose from the recognition by the British that they needed more and better geographical information about the country ceded to them in 1763. Samuel Jan Holland* was appointed to head the office in March 1764 and in the same month was commissioned surveyor general of the Northern District of North America. His authority extended as far south as Virginia and required his prolonged absence from Quebec. On 8 Sept. 1764 John Collins was therefore named deputy surveyor general of Quebec, and until 1779, when Holland took up his duties relating to the province on a full-time basis, he was responsible for the operation of the surveyor general's office.

Few details are known of Collins' previous life, although some evidence suggests that he was a Quebec merchant at the time of his appointment. According to Holland he had been "imployed for many years as a deputy Surveyor in the Southern Colonys" and had been recommended by Governor MURRAY and others. Within months of receiving his commission Collins was busy fixing the boundary between Quebec and New York eastward from the St Lawrence River to Lake Champlain along the 45th parallel. In 1765 he also surveyed and set out lands for settlement on the harbours of the Gaspé and Baie des Chaleurs. In addition to his general survey work he prepared maps for the governor, made plans relating to property disputes, and drew up reports such as that on the use of the king's wharf in Quebec. Between 1771 and 1773 Collins and Thomas Valentine, New York's representative, continued the delimitation of the boundary between the two provinces.

During the American revolution Collins remained at Quebec performing his surveying duties. With the end of hostilities, the government faced the enormous problem of the refugee loyalists. Land had to be surveyed and laid out in advance of settlement. On 11 Sept. 1783 Governor HALDIMAND directed Collins to go to Cataraqui (Kingston, Ont.) and proceed with this task. During 1783 Collins outlined the townships of Kingston, Ernestown, Fredericksburgh, and Adolphustown, one of the earliest surveys in present-day Ontario. He continued to work in the upper St Lawrence area and in 1785 led a survey party charged with establishing a communication route between Cataraqui and Lake Huron. In May 1787, because of discord resulting from such matters as the distribution of land and the issue of rations, stores, and clothing, a board of inquiry was appointed to hear and examine the complaints of the loyalists and others in the western regions of the then province of Quebec. The board, consisting of Collins, Holland, William Dummer Powell*, and others, first dealt with grievances in the seigneury of Sorel. Collins and Powell subsequently conducted hearings in the Kingston area.

Collins had also become involved in the political life of the colony. In January 1773 he was sworn in as a member of the Council. In 1775 he became a legislative councillor, a position he held for the duration of the Quebec Act and, under the Constitutional Act of 1791, until his death. He was also one of the legislative councillors whom Sir Guy Carleton* chose in August 1776 to be his "board of privy council." This group of trusted advisers to the governor continued its existence under Haldimand until 1782, although it was condemned as unconstitutional in 1779 by the British government. Collins served on such bodies of the Legislative Council as the committee on commerce and police and the land committee. He held general commissions of the peace for various places and received commissions of oyer and terminer for Quebec in 1788 and for Quebec and Montreal in 1791.

After completing surveys in large unsettled areas Collins often petitioned for land; he thus acquired property on the harbour of Bonaventure, on the Baie des Chaleurs, on Bay Tonegeyon (Collins Bay, Ont.), and in Hereford Township, Quebec. A dispute arose over the size and location of the Hereford grant; the matter occupied Collins during the last years of his life and was still unresolved when he died in 1795 at his house on Rue Saint-Louis in Quebec.

Little is known of Collins' personal life. An active Freemason, he was Quebec provincial grand master from 1767 to 1785. His wife Margaret died at Quebec on 24 Jan. 1770. They had at least one child, Mary, who married James Rankin, a surveyor.

ROBERT J. HAYWARD

ANQ-Q, État civil, Anglicans, Cathedral of the Holy Trinity (Québec), 25 Jan. 1770. BL, Add. MSS 21721, 21732, 21784, 21786, 21791, 21798, 21884. PAC, National Map coll., VI/300-1795; VI/325-Grand Rivière-1765; VI/325-Sorel-1790; VI/340-Gaspé-1765; VI/340-Paspébiac-1765; VI/340-Port Daniel-1765; F/350-Québec-1766; VI/409-Nassau-1790; H3/410-Ontario-1785; VI/1001-1774; H1/1100-1790; R/1100-1790; RG 1, E15, A, 1, 2, 11–13, 29; L3L, 1, p.144; 10, p.3201; 63, pp.31519–20, 31523–24; 163, p.79510; RG 4, A1, 32, pp.10656–75; 33, pp.10697–868; RG 68, 89, ff.1, 53, 81, 84; 91, ff.247, 250, 253, 260, 264, 267, 427, 446; 97, ff.100, 105, 110, 115. PRO, CO 42/32–33.

Quebec Gazette, 16 April 1795. Joseph Desjardins, *Guide parlementaire historique de la province de Québec, 1792 à 1902* (Québec, 1902). PAC, *Catalogue of the National Map collection . . .* (16v., Boston, Mass., 1976). Burt, *Old prov. of Que.* L. F. Gates, *Land policies of Upper Canada* (Toronto, 1968). D. W. Thomson, *Men and meridians: the history of surveying and mapping in Canada* (3v., Ottawa, 1966–69). I. F.-J. Audet, "Trois géographes canadiens," Soc. de géographie de Québec, *Bull.* (Québec), XVIII (1924), 85–98. Willis Chipman, "The life and times of Major Samuel Holland, surveyor-general, 1764–1801," *OH*, XXI (1924), 11–90. A. R. Davis, "Samuel Holland and John Collins, pioneer Canadian surveyors," Assoc. of Ont. Land Surveyors, *Annual report* (Toronto), 45 (1930), 185–90. "Hon. John Collins, deputy surveyor general," Assoc. of Ont. Land Surveyors, *Annual report*, 47 (1932), 105–10.

CONTRECŒUR, CLAUDE-PIERRE PÉCAUDY DE. *See* PÉCAUDY

COOK, JAMES, naval officer, surveyor, and explorer; b. 27 Oct. 1728 in Marton-in-Cleveland

(Marton, North Yorkshire), England, the son of James Cook, a Scottish agricultural labourer, and Grace Pace, a local woman; d. 14 Feb. 1779 at Kealakekua Bay, Sandwich (Hawaiian) Islands.

James Cook spent most of his childhood at Great Ayton, a town not far from his birthplace, where his father moved to take a job as a farm foreman. At the age of 17 he found his first regular employment in a shop at the little fishing port of Staithes (Cleveland). In 1746 he signed a three-year apprenticeship agreement with John Walker, a Whitby shipowner, and combined an arduous but invaluable period of training in that hard school of seamanship along the east coast of England – a shoreline of treacherous, shifting shoals, uncharted banks and shallows, and difficult harbours – with voyages at times to the Baltic. On 17 June 1755 Cook turned down the offer of command of one of Walker's vessels to enlist in the Royal Navy as an able seaman. Volunteers of Cook's calibre were rare; within a matter of weeks he was master's mate on the *Eagle* (where he was to become acquainted with Captain Hugh PALLISER). In June 1757 he passed his master's examinations and became qualified for that most responsible of naval posts, the navigation and handling of a royal ship.

Cook spent most of the Seven Years' War in North American waters and saw his first campaigning off Louisbourg, Île Royale (Cape Breton Island), where, as master of the 60-gun *Pembroke*, he was present at the surrender of the fortress to AMHERST's forces in July 1758. His posting to this vital arena of the Anglo-French struggle was to have substantial and unforeseen results for Cook. An incipient interest in surveying probably already existed – it would be a strange master who was not professionally interested in charts – but the sight of unknown shores, crudely represented on existing maps and yet playing vital parts in the strategy and diplomacy of the war, seems to have stimulated Cook in a way which service in home waters might not have. As early as the summer of 1758 Cook made his first chart, of Gaspé bay and harbour (Que.), good and useful enough to be published in London the next year. The winter of 1758–59 was an important one for Cook, who was by now under the general command of Philip Durell*. Encouraged by both the *Pembroke*'s captain, John Simcoe, and a new acquaintance, military engineer Samuel Jan Holland*, he pursued his studies in navigation and surveying, subjects in which considerable technical advances – particularly in instrument design – had recently been made. Knowing of the forthcoming assault on Quebec, Cook and Holland apparently spent much time that winter constructing as good a preliminary chart of the St Lawrence gulf and river as the indifferent existing maps of the region would allow. The dramatic arrival of Wolfe* and Charles SAUNDERS off Quebec the next summer was made possible only by the care with which the masters of the British vessels, including Cook, sounded out a channel through the tortuous St Lawrence navigation so that the great armada of warships and transports could pass in safety. Cook was one among a group of skilled and dedicated men, but there is evidence which points to his having a large share in the construction of the "New Chart of the River St. Lawrence," which was published in London in 1760. This was an elaborate affair with many insets and coastal profiles, and it immediately became the standard chart of this difficult waterway. Holland's later recollections and a comparison of the published chart with manuscript drafts both suggest that Cook's role was a dominant one, though the internal evidence is by no means conclusive because of the difficulty in dating the variant versions. A further sign that Cook was beginning to attract attention came with the award to him in January 1761 of £50 (two-thirds of his normal annual salary) "in consideration of his indefatigable Industry in making himself Master of the pilotage of the River Saint Lawrence, &c." By now Cook was becoming a compulsive surveyor, and his presence in Lord Colvill*'s squadron off Newfoundland after Charles-Henri-Louis d'ARSAC de Ternay's attack in 1762 gave him the opportunity to chart part of the island's eastern coastline, including St John's harbour, Placentia road, Bay Bulls, Harbour Grace, and Carbonear Bay.

With the end of the war in sight, Cook returned to England and was discharged in November 1762 from the *Northumberland*, on which he had served as master since September 1759. On 21 Dec. 1762 he married Elizabeth Batts of Barking (London), though his spell of domesticity was short-lived, for in April 1763 the Admiralty, finding him "a Person well skilled in making Surveys," instructed him to chart the coasts of Newfoundland. Despite the island's importance to the North Atlantic cod fishery, and indirectly to Britain's maritime strength, no detailed and reliable maps of its coastline existed; this deficiency Cook was now to remedy in five seasons of painstaking and conscientious survey work. Cook owed his appointment at least in part to the favourable impression his surveying methods had made the previous year on Captain Thomas Graves*, governor of Newfoundland, and in May 1763 Cook sailed with Graves for Newfoundland.

In his first season's work Cook surveyed Saint-Pierre and Miquelon before they were restored to the French under the terms of the treaty of Paris of February 1763, and he then went on to chart stretches of coastline around the northern tip of the island, including the harbours of Croque, Noddy Bay, and Quirpon, parts of the "French shore" along which France retained fishing rights by the peace. Both sets of surveys were clearly related to the treaty terms and serve as a reminder of the political and commercial implications of Cook's work in Newfoundland.

The pattern of Cook's life for the next four years was set when he returned to spend the winter of 1763–64 in London. During that winter he bought the house in East London where his six children were to be born. When Cook sailed again for North America in the spring of 1764 he did so as commander of his own craft, the little 68-ton schooner *Grenville*. Using her as a base, he worked his way steadily along the intricate and rugged coasts of Newfoundland, surveying the northwest stretch in 1764, the south coast between the Burin peninsula and Cape Ray in 1765 and 1766, and the west coast as far north as the southernmost point of his old 1763 survey in 1767. For all his modesty, Cook already possessed a firm sense of the value of his work, and perhaps of its commercial possibilities, for, with the blessing of the Admiralty, he published his surveys in quick succession: two charts in 1766, another in 1767, and a final one in 1768. These charts, which marked a new standard in British hydrographic surveys, combined land-based trigonometrical surveys with small-boat work on the seaward side, and they were set out with a scrupulous attention to detail and a multitude of soundings, coastal profiles, and sailing notes. Reprinted many times, and incorporated in the famous *North American pilot . . .* of 1775, they were the firm basis for sailors' knowledge of the dangerous coasts of Newfoundland for the best part of a hundred years. Cook did not forget the political direction behind his work. The charts contained a mass of information about existing fisheries, as well as hints for establishing new ones, since he carefully marked promising sites for harbours and drying stages. He even located a fishing bank off the south coast which was unknown to the fishing fleets. In general, his surveys helped not only to turn the legal position of sovereignty over North America gained by Britain at the peace negotiations into practical reality, but to encourage the expansion of the fishery into previously unknown waters. Throughout these years Cook showed a steadily developing self-reliance and sense of authority. His requests for extra men and equipment, his improvements in the routine and often strenuous techniques of surveying work, and his conversion of the *Grenville* from a schooner to a brig, all point to a man intent on perfection. And always there was the zest for self-improvement, for new intellectual experiences, best shown by his successful management of the tricky (and not strictly relevant) business of carrying out observations of the sun's eclipse in July 1766, apparently from Eclipse Island off the south coast. His figures, printed in the *Philosophical Transactions* of the Royal Society of London in 1768, were introduced as by "Mr. Cook, a good mathematician, and very expert in his Business." Cook's five seasons in Newfoundland produced the first large-scale and accurate maps of the island's coasts; they also gave Cook his mastery of practical surveying, achieved under often adverse conditions, and brought him to the attention of the Admiralty at a crucial moment both in his personal career and in the direction of British overseas discovery.

When Cook returned to England for the winter of 1767–68 his work in Newfoundland was far from complete, but he was never to return to North America's Atlantic coastline. Instead, in April 1768 he was given command of a former Whitby collier, renamed the *Endeavour*, and, as a newly commissioned first lieutenant, left for the South Seas in August. This voyage, completed in 1771, and his second circumnavigation during the period 1772–75, revolutionized Europe's knowledge of the South Pacific, making precise and certain information which before 1775 had been fragmentary and confused. During the first voyage New Zealand, the east coast of Australia, and Torres Strait emerged from the mists of rumour and myth; during the second Cook sailed farther south than previous explorers had ever been, destroying the speculative geographers' concept of a great and fertile southern continent. These accomplishments occurred without the loss of a single man from scurvy, an achievement so remarkable that it would have overshadowed the geographical results of the voyages had they been less momentous. On his return Cook was given post rank in the navy, but his fame had spread far beyond naval circles – he was, as the Earl of Sandwich, first lord of the Admiralty, described him to the House of Lords in November 1775, "the first navigator in Europe." In March 1776 he was admitted as a Fellow of the Royal Society and at the same time awarded the society's Copley gold medal for his paper on scurvy.

For Cook there was to be little respite from exploration. His appointment in August 1775 to a post of retirement as captain at Greenwich Hospital lasted only until April 1776, when he decided to accept a challenge which had defeated Europe's finest seamen for almost three centuries, the quest for a northwest passage. Cook was tempted to undertake such a voyage because of recent discoveries, which had renewed optimism that a navigable passage might be found and the £20,000 award offered by an act of parliament in 1775 claimed. Samuel HEARNE's epic overland journey to the mouth of the Coppermine River (N.W.T.) in 1771 had, for the moment, discredited the apocryphal narratives of Juan de Fuca*, Bartholomew de Fonte*, and others who were supposed to have passed eastward along straits from the Pacific coast to Hudson Bay, for Hearne had crossed neither strait nor navigable river. Hearne's sighting of the Arctic coastline, however, indicated that a seaway might be found around rather than through the North American continent. Moreover, in 1774, at the same time that the Admiralty received news of Hearne's explorations, a Russian map, showing a more easterly and open route from the Pacific to the polar sea than Vitus Jonassen Bering's dimly known straits, was published in London. The map, allegedly based on the accounts of Russian fur-traders who were moving along the Aleutian Islands towards the American mainland, showed Alaska to be an island, with a wide strait between it and America through which ships could sail north. The search for a northwest passage was accordingly shifted northwards, and while Cook was looking for the Pacific entrance, expeditions under Richard Pickersgill in 1776 and Walter Young in 1777 were sent to Baffin Bay in search of the Atlantic entrance. Cook's instructions recommended him to sail to latitude 65°N before beginning the search for a passage, "taking care not to lose any time in exploring Rivers or Inlets, or upon any other account, until you get into the beforementioned latitude." These orders explain the uncharacteristic haste with which Cook sailed along the coast of what is now British Columbia in the summer of 1778.

Cook left England in the *Resolution* and *Discovery* in July 1776, sailed around the Cape of Good Hope, crossed the Pacific by way of New Zealand, Tahiti, and the Sandwich Islands, and so on to the northwest coast of America. On 7 March 1778 the coast of what is now Oregon was sighted in latitude 44°33′N, but the weather was misty and stormy and only tantalizing glimpses of the shore were caught through the rain. Cook's main concern was to find a harbour where he could take on wood and water and repair his vessels. He had hopes of finding such a spot inside an opening which appeared on the far side of a headland in latitude 48°15′N, but as the ships drew nearer he decided that the opening was too small to afford shelter and renamed the point Cape Flattery (Wash.), adding in his journal, "It is in the very latitude we were now in where geographers have placed the pretended *Strait of Juan de Fuca*, but we saw nothing like it, nor is there the least probability that iver any such thing exhisted." Although it was unusual for Cook to be dogmatic without good reason, he had not seen enough of the coast at close quarters to justify this pronouncement, for Cape Flattery forms the southern tip of the entrance to the strait now named after Juan de Fuca. During the night Cook headed away from the strait, intending to close again with the land at daybreak, but severe gales prevented the expedition from approaching the coast for nearly a week. When the vessels sighted land again on 29 March they were off the densely wooded oceanic shores of Vancouver Island (B.C.), supposed by Cook to be part of the mainland. Here the vessels anchored in Ship Cove, King George's Sound (now Resolution Cove, Nootka Sound), where they were to remain almost a month. The crews saw a good deal of the local Indians (Nootkas), physically unalluring to them with their faces and bodies heavily decorated and smeared with grease and filth, but a people skilled in handling their heavy dugout canoes and in constructing long wooden buildings with intricate totemic carvings. Considerable quantities of furs, mostly the thick, lustrous pelts of the sea otter, were obtained from them. The Nootkas' dexterity in trade and their possession of two silver spoons and some iron tools led Cook and his officers, Charles CLERKE among them, to guess that they had already been in direct or indirect contact with Europeans: perhaps Spaniards from the south, Russians from the north, or even Canadians or Hudson's Bay Company men from the east. The first of these possibilities was the most likely, for Spaniards had sailed along this coast on reconnaissance in 1774 and 1775, and one probe, under the command of Juan Josef PÉREZ Hernández, had anchored off Nootka Sound. News of these ventures had reached England two months before Cook sailed, but in abbreviated and misleading form. Just as misleading were some of the rumours about Cook's expedition which reached Madrid in 1776. Spanish authorities were alarmed by these reports because they feared the establishment of a British presence along the Pacific coast of America, which had been claimed by Spain as early as 1493. Instructions were issued by Madrid to the viceroy of New Spain (Mexico), Antonio María Bucareli y Ursúa, to hinder Cook if he reached California; the viceroy protested in vain that these instructions could not be carried out, and he managed to delay the sending of Spanish ships in search of Cook until 1779.

On 26 April 1778 Cook's vessels left Nootka and headed north. Bad weather forced them out to sea, and they did not sight land again until they were well beyond the boundary of modern Canada and into Alaskan waters. Cook sailed steadily along a coastline which became harsher and bleaker and then began to bend inexorably westward, away from the area where Hearne, more than a thousand miles to the northeast, had sighted the shores of the polar sea. At last the long tongue of the Alaskan peninsula was rounded, and the ships passed through the strait reached by Bering in 1728, turning northeast in a hopeless attempt to sail along the northern shoreline of the American continent. The grim reality of polar navigation soon emerged as the expedition encountered a massive wall of ice which blocked the way eastward, imperilling the ships as it drove down upon the shore. The ships retreated through Bering Strait and away to winter in the Sandwich Islands, where Cook met his death at Kealakekua Bay on 14 Feb. 1779 in an incident where he showed perhaps less than his usual judgement.

Cook had been set an impossible task in the Arctic by speculative geographers who drew absurd maps and by pseudo-scientists who insisted that ice would not present a serious obstacle to summer navigation in the polar sea; he understandably did not always show his normal certainty of touch and professional detachment. Yet, judged by any standard, the results of his single season of exploration were extraordinary. He had charted the coastline from Mount St Elias (at the northern end of the Alaska panhandle) to Bering Strait and beyond, and south of Mount St Elias he had touched, as had the Spanish explorers of 1774 and 1775, along a coast previously unvisited by Europeans. The maps brought home by his officers and published with the official account of the voyage in 1784 showed the immensity of his achievement. As the title-page of the 1784 account put it, the voyage had been one "for making discoveries in the Northern Hemisphere, to determine the position and extent of the west side of North America; its distance from Asia; and the practicability of a northern passage to Europe." In outline at least, the shape and position of the northwest coast of America were known at last. This advance in knowledge could not be matched by either the Russians or the Spaniards; they had no seamen on the coast who approached Cook in experience and determination, and their surveys tended to be issued in garbled form, or not at all. Admittedly Cook was not the first explorer to touch at many places along the northwest coast. He and his officers were the first, however, to reveal to the world, through narratives, maps, and drawings, where they had been and what they had seen [*see* James KING; John WEBBER]. Moreover, Cook's explorations were not the conclusive exercises they had been in the South Pacific, for neither he nor his Spanish and Russian predecessors had determined whether the stretches of coastline they had sailed along were islands or mainland. The interior, sometimes even a few yards from the water's edge, was still unknown, and so were its peoples. The coastal explorations of this period provided little information that would solve the question of how far north the Rocky Mountains extended, a major preoccupation of geographers. But for the first time public and mercantile interests in Europe and the United States were attracted to the northwest coast, whose dramatic scenery and inhabitants became familiar images to readers of the accounts of Cook's last voyage. More important, these narratives, with their tales of Nootkas trading for a handful of beads sea otter pelts worth a hundred dollars apiece on the Chinese market, drew attention to the commercial potentialities of this remote region. The quest for beaver had drawn men from the Atlantic seaboard of the continent almost to within sight of the Rockies; now there was a rush to fit out seaborne expeditions for the northwest coast [*see* James HANNA; John KENDRICK]. Prominent among the commanders of these trading expeditions were several of Cook's men, among them George DIXON and Nathaniel Portlock*, whose voyages demonstrated that Cook had underestimated the tenacity of his own countrymen when he reflected in June 1778 that "a very benificial fur trade might be carried on with the Inhabitants of this vast coast, but unless a northern passage is found it seems rather too remote for Great Britain to receive any emolument from it." The commercial ventures of the 1780s were to reveal that Cook's surmise in 1778 that he was coasting the mainland at all times between Cape Flattery and Alaska was wrong. It was singularly appropriate, however, that the Englishman who provided the definitive 18th-century survey of the coastline of western Canada was George VANCOUVER, who had sailed with Cook on his second and third voyages and who saw his detailed work as complementary to the broad outlines sketched in by his old commander. Once more trade had followed exploration, and international competition had accompanied both. Cook's last voyage was the prelude and in a very real sense the stimulus to a long period of intense international rivalry on the northwest coast, through which in 1790 Britain and Spain came to face each other in a conflict which almost led to war (*see* Esteban José MARTÍNEZ]; their respective positions, however, were gradually submerged by the rising tide of American activity. The developments of this rivalry – the Nootka crisis, the arrival on the coast of explorers, traders, and settlers from the east, and finally the Oregon question and the treaty of June 1846 – all played their part in the shaping of modern Canada.

GLYNDWR WILLIAMS

[Biographies of James Cook abound, but all are now overshadowed by the definitive work by J. C. Beaglehole, *The life of Captain James Cook* (London, 1974). An essential accompaniment to this monumental work of scholarship is the Hakluyt Society's edition of Cook's Pacific journals, *The journals of Captain James Cook on his voyages of discovery*, ed. J. C. Beaglehole (4v. in 5 and portfolio, Cambridge, Eng., 1955–74); most relevant to this biographical sketch is volume III, *The voyage of the 'Resolution' and 'Discovery,' 1776–1780*. This volume contains not only the full text of Cook's manuscript journals (BL, Egerton MSS 2177A, 2177B), but also long extracts from the journals of various members of Cook's crews. For Cook's views this modern edition should always be consulted in preference to the official contemporary account, James Cook and James King, *A voyage to the Pacific Ocean . . .* (3v. and atlas, London, 1784), for although the first two volumes were Cook's in name, they were Dr John Douglas' in style. As Douglas wrote at the time, "The Public never knew, how much they owe to me in this work" (BL, Egerton MSS 2181, f.48); and until Professor Beaglehole's labours scholars could only guess at how much of the published account was Cook's and how much his meddlesome editor's. Cook's logs, letters, and charts relating to his earlier surveys in northeast America are scattered among the great libraries of the world: the British Library, the Public Record Office, the archives of the Hydrographer of the Navy, Ministry of Defence (Taunton, Eng.), the National Maritime Museum, the Public Archives of Canada, and Harvard University (Cambridge, Mass.). Cook's work is listed and analysed in the following: R. A. Skelton, "Captain James Cook as a hydrographer," *Mariner's Mirror* (Cambridge, Eng.), 40 (1954), 92–119; *James Cook, surveyor of Newfoundland . . .*, intro. R. A. Skelton (San Francisco, 1965); and R. A. Skelton and R. V. Tooley, *The marine surveys of James Cook in North America, 1758–1768 . . . a bibliography . . .* (London, 1967). The political and commercial implications of Cook's Newfoundland surveys are discussed in W. H. Whiteley, "James Cook and British policy in the Newfoundland fisheries, 1763–7," *CHR*, LIV (1973), 245–72. For additional material, see: *DNB*; *Captain Cook, navigator and scientist: papers*, ed. G. M. Badger (Canberra, 1970); and Glyndwr Williams, *The British search for the northwest passage in the eighteenth century* (London and Toronto, 1962). G.W.]

CORBIN, ANDRÉ, blacksmith and maker of edge-tools; baptized 2 May 1709 in Quebec, son of André Corbin, also a blacksmith and maker of edge-tools, and Charlotte Rainville; d. 26 March 1777 in Trois-Rivières.

André Corbin's father had an ironworking shop in Quebec, and as an apprentice there André Jr learned the various techniques of working in iron. On 16 July 1731 at the age of 22, he married Louise, daughter of Pierre Petit*, in Trois-Rivières. He does not seem to have settled in this region at that time but instead returned to Quebec, where his first child was born in April 1732. That spring Corbin probably helped his father to test the quality of the iron extracted from the mines along the Rivière Saint-Maurice which François Poulin* de Francheville was beginning to work.

In 1734 Corbin returned to Trois-Rivières, where he had a house built of squared timbers (*pièces sur pièces*) and an ironworking shop in which he made tools and articles for everyday use. He also took on bigger jobs at the Saint-Maurice ironworks, where Pierre-François OLIVIER de Vézin hired him. But the quality of his work was not satisfactory, if a report written in 1741 by François-Étienne Cugnet* is to be believed: "As early as 1738 . . . we had discovered examples of money badly spent, for instance a double forge built by the aforementioned Corbin, an edge-tool maker, which the Sieur Olivier had set up at Saint-Maurice, and which he tore down two years later because he acknowledged that Corbin was more of a hindrance than a help." This opinion must be treated with caution, however, because Cugnet's chief purpose was to place responsibility for bad management of the ironworks upon Olivier de Vézin and thus clear himself with Intendant HOCQUART and the minister of Marine, Maurepas.

In 1744 Corbin was working in Quebec as a blacksmith and edge-tool maker in the king's shipyards. His ninth child was baptized at Pointe-Lévy (Lauzon and Lévis) in July 1744. He was back at Trois-Rivières in 1746, and his mother-in-law, Marguerite Véron de Grandmesnil, granted him "a piece of timbered land" in the seigneury of Yamaska. He continued to work as a "master ironsmith," filling orders from private customers and doing jobs for the ironworks, to which he owed the sum of 110 *livres* in 1747.

On 8 Jan. 1748 André Corbin was married again at Trois-Rivières, to Véronique Baby, a cousin of

René-Ovide HERTEL de Rouville who later became director of the Saint-Maurice ironworks. Corbin probably carried out some contracts for the ironworks during this period. Although his name does not appear in its general statement of accounts, we know he was a master ironsmith there in 1751. During the same period he made "the cross for the tower and other pieces of ironwork" for the second church at Saint-Antoine-de-la-Baie-du-Febvre (Baieville) and received the sum of 74 *livres*.

Corbin remained an active ironsmith and took part in community life in Trois-Rivières until his death on 26 March 1777. His fellow citizens seem to have appreciated his sense of responsibility since, according to Benjamin Sulte*, Corbin was elected syndic of the town of Trois-Rivières in 1757. Although a decree of the Conseil Supérieur dated 4 Dec. 1758 refused him "the position of syndic of the citizens and bourgeois of the aforesaid town" so long as he had not proven his right to "assume the aforesaid position," notarial acts show that Corbin for several years after the conquest bore that title.

RENÉ BOUCHARD

ANQ-MBF, État civil, Catholiques, Immaculée-Conception de Trois-Rivières, 16 juill. 1731, 8 janv. 1748, 27 mars 1777; Greffe de J.-B. Badeaux, 18 juill. 1768, 28 nov., 11 déc. 1770, 23 mars, 29 mai 1773, 7 févr., 10, 11 avril 1777; Greffe de Jean Leproust, 6 mars 1752, 20 juill. 1756, 21 déc. 1757; Greffe de Louis Pillard, 25 juill. 1746, 30 janv. 1747, 7 janv., 25, 28 juin 1748, 18 janv., 27 juin 1758, 27 juill. 1762, 15, 17, 21 avril 1763, 8, 9 juill., 10 août, 24 sept. 1764, 17 mai 1765, 5 déc. 1766, 22 déc. 1767; Greffe de H.-O. Pressé, 7 juill. 1742. Archives paroissiales, Saint-Antoine-de-Padoue (Baieville, Qué.), Livres de comptes. IBC, Centre de documentation, Fonds Morisset, Dossier André Corbin. *Recensement de Québec, 1716* (Beaudet), 36. P.-G. Roy, *Inv. jug. et délib., 1717–60*, VI, 127. Tanguay, *Dictionnaire*. J.-E. Bellemare, *Histoire de la Baie-Saint-Antoine, dite Baie-du-Febvre, 1683–1911* (Montréal, 1911), 63–64. J.-C. Dupont, "Les traditions de l'artisan du fer dans la civilisation traditionnelle au Québec" (thèse de PHD, université Laval, Québec, 1975). J.-N. Fauteux, *Essai sur l'industrie*, I, 58. Mathieu, *La construction navale*, 96. Morisset, *Coup d'œil sur les arts*, 126. Sulte, *Mélanges historiques* (Malchelosse), VI, 112–13.

CORNWALLIS, EDWARD, army officer and colonial administrator; founder of Halifax, Nova Scotia; b. 22 Feb. 1712/13 in London, England, sixth son of Charles Cornwallis, 4th Baron Cornwallis, and Lady Charlotte Butler, daughter of Richard Butler, 1st Earl of Arran; m. 17 March 1753 in London, Mary, daughter of Charles Townshend, 2nd Viscount Townshend; d. 14 Jan. 1776 at Gibraltar.

Born into a family with influential connections, Edward Cornwallis and his twin brother Frederick became royal pages at the age of 12. A captain in the 8th Foot by 1734, Cornwallis acted as a courier for the diplomatic service between 1738 and 1743 and became major of the 20th Foot in 1742. In December 1743 he was appointed by his father to represent the family borough of Eye in parliament. The following year he joined his regiment in Flanders and assumed command when the lieutenant-colonel was killed at Fontenoy (Belgium) in 1745. Promoted lieutenant-colonel of the 20th the same year, Cornwallis participated in the "pacification" of Scotland, including the near-massacre at Culloden, before ill health compelled him to relinquish his command to Major James Wolfe* in 1748. The previous year he had been appointed a groom of the royal bedchamber, and in March 1749 he was promoted colonel.

Cornwallis' career in Nova Scotia began on 21 June 1749, when he arrived off Chebucto Bay in the sloop *Sphinx* as the newly appointed governor of the province. His appointment inaugurated a new policy on the part of the British government. For years after Nova Scotia had become a British possession in 1713, it had been neglected by the home authorities. The War of the Austrian Succession, however, demonstrated the province's strategic importance. In order to ensure the safety of the New England colonies, an Anglo-American force under William Pepperrell* and Peter Warren* attacked and captured the French fortress of Louisbourg, Île Royale (Cape Breton Island), in 1745. Although Louisbourg was restored to France in exchange for Madras, India, by the treaty of Aix-la-Chapelle in 1748, the British government well understood that "it was essential to provide in that area a British military station of comparable strength as a counterweight and as a protection for New England and her trade."

The scheme to establish a British settlement in the province proceeded with startling rapidity. In March 1749 Lord Halifax, president of the Board of Trade, submitted a report to the Duke of Bedford, secretary of state for the Southern Department, which proposed that a town be started on Chebucto Bay, "the great long harbour" on the south shore of the peninsula whose potential was already well known. Halifax had received suggestions for the settlement plan from various sources in contact with the Nova Scotia situation, among which New England influence was the most noticeable. Indeed, he considered the redressing of New England's grievances over the peace the most important reason for the establishment of the new settlement. But it was from Great Britain that the original settlers were recruited. That spring alluring newspaper advertisements appeared inviting persons to volunteer for the settlement in Nova Scotia. Prospective settlers were promised both free transportation and free victualling for one year; military protection was to be provided by two regiments from the Louisbourg garrison under Colonel Peregrine Thomas Hopson*. In May Cornwallis and 2,576 settlers departed for the province.

The initial problem facing Cornwallis after his arrival was the selection of the precise spot for the settlement, and this decision caused him no little difficulty. Commodore Charles Knowles, a former governor of Louisbourg, and Captain Thomas Durell, who had charted parts of Nova Scotia, had recommended the high bluff overlooking Bedford Basin (the inner part of the bay, renamed for the Duke of Bedford), but it was too far inland to suit Cornwallis. Some persons in England had suggested what is now Point Pleasant, at the mouth of the harbour, but Cornwallis rejected it because of the stony soil and the likelihood of high seas in winter; he likewise turned down the suggestion of the Dartmouth side of the harbour because it could be commanded from the higher ground opposite. In the end he himself chose the side of a hill on the west side of the bay which commanded the whole peninsula for the new settlement, named Halifax for the president of the Board of Trade. In favour of the site was the gentle slope of the hill (later named Citadel Hill), its good soil, the convenient landing place for small boats, and the excellent anchorage for larger vessels close to the shore. In the words of Archibald McKellar MacMechan*, "Time has approved the wisdom of [Cornwallis'] choice."

With the arrival of acting governor Paul Mascarene* and some of his councillors from Annapolis Royal, Cornwallis was able to organize his government. On 14 July 1749 his first council, which included Mascarene, John Gorham*, Benjamin GREEN, and others, was sworn in. Cornwallis' commission and instructions stipulated that he was to enact laws only with the consent of a council and a house of assembly, but the Board of Trade recognized that under the existing circumstances the calling of an assembly was impossible. For various reasons, no assembly was formed until 1758 under Governor Charles Lawrence*. The first laws of the new government tended to follow the Virginian models that had influenced previous Nova Scotian administrations. Similarly, in establishing a system of courts Cornwallis turned to Virginian examples and erected a general court to deal with major offences and a county court to deal with minor offences.

The governor's main concern, however, was to make the settlement habitable before winter. In spite of difficulties, he was able to report steady progress. On 24 July he forwarded to the Board of Trade detailed plans of the town, and on 20 August he announced that lots had been drawn and every settler knew where he was to build. Already many persons had arrived from Louisbourg, and a migration from New England was beginning. In mid September the soldiers were raising a line of palisades and in October two of the forts were finished. By September Cornwallis expressed his satisfaction that "every thing goes on very well indeed much better than coud have been expected." While he lamented the "irregularity and indolent disposition" of many of the settlers, mostly disbanded soldiers and sailors, he applauded the few Swiss among them as "honest industrious Men [who are] easily governed and work heartily." The Board of Trade subsequently decided to send out a "mixture of Foreign Protestants" who "by their industrious and examplary dispositions [would] greatly promote and forward the settlement in its infancy," but Cornwallis found that the first group sent out in 1750 were "in general old miserable wretches." More Swiss and Germans arrived during Cornwallis' governorship, and in 1753 they began a settlement of their own at Lunenburg [*see* Jean Pettrequin*; Sebastian ZOUBERBUHLER].

Beyond Halifax, however, Cornwallis' difficulties were many times greater. In October 1749 the acting governor of Canada, the Marquis de La Galissonière [Barrin*], sent forces under Charles DESCHAMPS de Boishébert and Louis de La Corne* to the Saint John River (N.B.) and the Chignecto Isthmus, hoping thereby to limit British settlement. The following year, Cornwallis sent Lawrence with a force to the isthmus to reinforce British claims to the region, and after a confrontation with La Corne in April, in September Lawrence erected Fort Lawrence (near Amherst, N.S.) across the Missaguash River from the French positions. In 1749 Jean-Louis LE LOUTRE, the French missionary to the Indians, had arrived back in the province, and on him, "a good for nothing Scoundrel as ever lived," Cornwallis put the blame for his troubles with the Indians. The governor had initially established friendly relations with the Micmacs around Halifax, but he soon heard that the Indians throughout the province had "colleagued" with Le Loutre. In August 1749 they began their depredations, seizing a vessel at Canso, attacking another at Chignecto, and ambushing four men near Halifax. Cornwallis proposed "to root [the Micmacs] out entirely," but the board warned him that such a course might imperil neighbouring British colonies by producing "a dangerous spirit of resentment" among other tribes. Indian attacks continued until well into the Seven Years' War.

Shortly after Cornwallis' arrival, several Acadians had appeared before him and had requested to know their position under his government. On his instructions, they returned later with all their deputies, who petitioned to be allowed to take the qualified oath of allegiance administered by former governor Richard Philipps*. Cornwallis, who had a low opinion of Philipps, wanted to show the Acadians that "tis in our power to master them or to protect them" and demanded an unequivocal oath of allegiance which obliged them to bear arms for the British crown. In September 1,000 Acadians answered that they would rather leave the province than take the unqualified oath. Unable to force their acceptance of this demand, Cornwallis decided to leave the Acadians alone until he had received instructions from the Board of Trade. In the mean time, he attempted to cut off their communication with the French on the Saint John and the isthmus, and he improved his own ability to supervise them by establishing small posts in the Minas region (near Wolfville) and by building a road there. On the board's instructions, he did nothing for the remainder of his governorship to cause the Acadians to leave.

The troubles outside Halifax had convinced Cornwallis that more military force would be needed, and in October 1749 he asked the board for two additional regiments, assuring them that with this reinforcement he would make Nova Scotia "more Flourishing than any part of North America." When he was sternly lectured on the necessity of frugality in public spending in February 1750, he did not take it kindly: "My Lords without money You could have had no Town no Settlement & indeed no Settlers." So began a long battle over expenditure in which, MacMechan wrote, Cornwallis was "outspoken, frankly abrupt." Although the board was sympathetic to Cornwallis' difficulties and obtained the additional regiment for Lawrence's expedition in the autumn of 1750, it generally had to follow the dictates of a government which was becoming increasingly alarmed at the cost of Nova Scotia. Thus in June 1750 the board listed numerous complaints against Hugh Davidson, Cornwallis' secretary, especially for his "negligence" in not transmitting accounts of the great sums being expended at Halifax, enquiring, among other things, why enough "pound weight of Bread" to victual 3,000 persons for a year had been sent out, when only between 1,500 and 2,450 persons had actually been fed. Perturbed that "any person under me should have given even suspicion of male Practice," Cornwallis sent Davidson home to answer the charges. He pointed out, however, that there was little reason for the board to be surprised at over-expenditure, since £44,000 had been spent in Britain alone that year, £4,000 more than the entire parliamentary grant. In November Cornwallis changed his tactics somewhat, hoping that by showing the immensity of his difficulties in establishing the settlement he would win the board's approval and justify his excess expenditures. Alarmed most by the expense of maintaining a garrison at Chignecto, he hoped it would be accepted because of "the great Step It is towards making this Peninsula, what it was intended to be, a Florishing Colony."

The dispute came to a climax in 1751. In March of that year the board informed Cornwallis that he would not retain the good opinion of parliament unless he refrained from "exceedings" in the future. Cornwallis' reply was even blunter than usual: to "flatter Your Lordships with hopes of savings" would be "dissimulation of the worst kind." This reply crossed a further letter from the board, dated June, which in effect accused him of negligence for not keeping it informed of events since the previous November, and when Cornwallis replied in September he indicated that he had reached the end of his patience. With apparent relish, he listed numerous specific difficulties he had previously presented to the board, implying he might as well have spared himself the trouble for all the help he had received, and ended with a wish that his successor be appointed. His appointment had been only for two or three years, and his health had been indifferent, but his inability to develop the colony as he wished may well have hastened his desire to return home. He left Halifax in October 1752 and was succeeded by Hopson.

Cornwallis subsequently returned to his political and military career. In 1752 he exchanged the colonelcy of the 40th Foot (to which he had been appointed in March 1750) for that of the 24th Foot. The following year he was elected to parliament from Westminster, a seat he held until

1762. At the outbreak of the Seven Years' War Cornwallis embarked part of his regiment on Admiral John Byng*'s fleet bound for the relief of Minorca. The fleet returned without accomplishing its task, and Cornwallis and two other colonels were tried by court martial for participating in the decision to leave Minorca to its fate. A favourable board exonerated them on technical grounds, but all three men were harshly lampooned in the press. Cornwallis' powerful friends were influential enough, however, to allow him not only to remain in the army but also to be promoted major-general in 1757. In October of that year Cornwallis took part in a second Minorca-like incident when he served as a brigade commander in General Sir John Mordaunt's expedition against the French naval arsenal of Rochefort. After a week of indecisive councils in which Cornwallis participated, it was decided to return to England. Cornwallis was not tried this time, but he was again attacked in the press. Following a tour of duty in Ireland, he was promoted lieutenant-general in 1760 and became governor of Gibraltar in 1762. The post was not to his liking, but although he requested a transfer several times, Minorca and Rochefort perhaps told against him and he remained at Gibraltar until his death.

From the letters of Edward Cornwallis there emerges a picture of a stern man with a strong sense of duty, one who became convinced of the importance of his mission to develop a British presence in Nova Scotia and who was not averse to lecturing the authorities for failing to provide the means he felt necessary to carry out this task. He was sometimes too outspoken, and probably took advantage of friends at court to offer criticisms of a kind and in a manner that no ordinary governor would have done. None could question his intention to do what he thought best for Nova Scotia, however; almost no one has questioned the basic decisions he made relating to Halifax. Because bad luck or personal weakness dogged his European ventures, the three years Cornwallis spent in Nova Scotia may well have been the most successful of his career.

J. Murray Beck

A portrait supposedly representing Cornwallis was placed in Government House in Halifax in 1923. An authentic portrait was acquired in 1929 by the government of Nova Scotia; it hangs in the PANS. A large statue of Cornwallis was unveiled in the plaza of the Hotel Nova Scotian in 1931.

PANS, RG 1, 29; 35, pp.29, 33, 42; 209. G.B., Board of Trade, *JTP, 1741/42–49; 1749/50–53*. *N.S. Archives, I*, 559–66, 583–86, 588, 590–93, 601–2, 608, 614, 627, 629, 631, 633, 638. Akins, *History of Halifax City*. Brebner, *New England's outpost*, 133, 237. Murdoch, *History of N.S.*, II. T. B. Akins, "The first Council," N.S. Hist. Soc., *Coll.*, II (1881), 17–30. J. S. Macdonald, "Hon. Edward Cornwallis, founder of Halifax" and "Life and administration of Governor Charles Lawrence, 1749–1760," N.S. Hist. Soc., *Coll.*, XII (1905), 1–17 and 19–58. A. McK. MacMechan, "Ab urbe condita," *Dal. Rev.*, VII (1927–28), 198–210. W. S. MacNutt, "Why Halifax was founded," *Dal. Rev.*, XII (1932–33), 524–32. C. P. Stacey, "Halifax as an international strategic factor, 1749–1949," CHA *Report*, 1949, 46–56.

COTTÉ (Côté), GABRIEL, merchant and fur-trader; baptized 12 June 1742 at Saint-Louis-de-Kamouraska (Kamouraska, Que.), son of Nicolas Cotté and Marie-Claude Levasseur; d. 5 Feb. 1795 at Montreal.

Gabriel Cotté first went to the *pays d'en haut* in 1760 and for the next 35 years, in varied capacities, he was to remain there. On 17 Aug. 1765 at Michilimackinac (Mackinaw City, Mich.), he married Agathe Roy-Desjardins by mutual consent before a number of witnesses, as was the custom in the absence of a priest. Their first child, Marianne, was born in 1767 and baptized on 25 July 1768 by Vicar-General Pierre Gibault*, who on this same date blessed the parents' marriage.

By 1772 Cotté had begun his activities as a merchant-trader, engaging voyageurs to transport merchandise from Montreal to Michilimackinac. A few years later he was granted a licence "for Michilimackinac and beyond to Neppigon [Nipigon, near the mouth of the Nipigon River] . . . for trading between 13 April and 4 June 1778." On 23 July 1778 Cotté signed a petition of ten Michilimackinac merchants to Governor Sir Guy Carleton* requesting a resident missionary, and two days later he subscribed to the fund for the maintenance of such a person. In 1779 he became associated with two merchant-traders, Maurice-Régis Blondeau*, whose sister Angélique* he was to marry on 29 Dec. 1783, and John Grant. This partnership, established to trade in the Lake Superior region, continued until 1785. In 1783 Cotté led an expedition into that country, where he found the Indians dying of hunger and where he lost four of his own men. Cotté was a founding member of the Beaver Club of Montreal in 1785.

During the years 1786 and 1787 he signed documents at Michilimackinac (which had been relocated on Mackinac Island) relating to protection for the Indian trade and the maintenance of the church of which he was a warden. Letters from Pierre Grignon, a business connection in La Baye (Green Bay, Wis.), reveal that Cotté intended to leave the west permanently in the fall of 1792 and return to Montreal for reasons of health. His signature as justice of the peace at Michilimackinac, a position he had held since about 1780, demonstrates his presence at the post again on 24 Aug. 1794. Several years earlier Cotté had apparently become a captain of militia in Montreal. His name with that title appears on several documents, but it could have been that of another Gabriel Cotté.

Cotté's son Pierre-Gabriel, who had been born in 1775, probably at Michilimackinac, continued in business there after his father's retirement and death and held office as justice of the peace. He moved to St Joseph's Island (Ont.) in 1800 when the status of Michilimackinac was in doubt, but there is no further record of him. Cotté's second wife bore three daughters, Lucie-Angélique, who became the mother of Judge Maurice Laframboise*, Marie-Josephte, who married Jules-Maurice Quesnel*, and Marie-Catherine-Émilie, who married François-Antoine Larocque*. After Cotté's death his widow founded the Orphelinat Catholique de Montréal and thus carried on the religious and public service which had long been a part of her husband's life.

RUTH R. JARVIS

ANQ-M, État civil, Catholiques, Notre-Dame de Montréal, 10 nov. 1777; Greffe de P.-F. Mézière, 29 déc. 1783. PAC, MG 19, B3, p.4. Ste Ann's Parish (Mackinac Island, Mich.), Registre des baptêmes, mariages et sépultures de Sainte-Anne-de-Michillimakinak, 25 juill. 1768, 22, 23 juill. 1787, 24 août 1794, 20 avril 1800, 16 juin 1804 (mfm. at Dept. of State, Lansing, Mich.). [This document, which covers the years 1695–1821, was published with notes as "The Mackinac register" in Wis., State Hist. Soc., *Coll.*, XVIII (1908), 469–513; XIX (1910), 1–162; certain errors are found in this version. R.R.J.] *Docs. relating to NWC* (Wallace), 451, 460. "Fur-trade on the Upper Lakes, 1778–1815," ed. R. G. Thwaites, Wis., State Hist. Soc., *Coll.*, XIX (1910), 270–71. *Michigan Pioneer Coll.*, IX (1886), 650; X (1886), 286–87, 290; XI (1887), 485, 488; XX (1892), 671–72. *Quebec Gazette*, 16 June, 3 Nov. 1785, 11 Oct. 1787, 22 Jan. 1789. Massicotte, "Répertoire des engagements pour l'Ouest," ANQ *Rapport*, 1932–33, 299–300; 1942–43, 265–392. Morice, *Dict. historique des Canadiens et Métis*, 71. Tanguay, *Dictionnaire*, III, 145, 149. Benoît Brouillette, *La pénétration du continent américain par les Canadiens français, 1763–1846; traitants, explorateurs, missionnaires* (Montréal, 1939), 85, 161. M.-C. Daveluy, *L'Orphelinat catholique de Montréal (1832–1932)* (Montréal, 1933), 294ff. Morton, *History of Canadian west*, 260. É.-Z. Massicotte, "Quelques rues et faubourgs du vieux Montréal," *Cahiers des Dix*, 1 (1936), 127–28.

COTTON (Couton), BARTHÉLEMY, hatter and receiver and inspector of furs for the Compagnie des Indes; b. 2 July 1692 at Quebec, son of Barthélemy Couton and Jeanne Le Rouge; d. 27 May 1780 at Quebec.

Barthélemy Cotton's father was a soldier from Dauphiné who, after being discharged from the colonial regular troops, worked as a hatter and lived at Saint-Jérôme-de-L'Auvergne, in Charlesbourg parish. As the oldest son, young Barthélemy seems to have learned hat-making and also farming from his father. He was a dutiful child. In July 1712 his parents sold him a farm in Notre-Dame-des-Anges seigneury and, after he had paid off the debts encumbering the concession, they wanted to repossess it. In 1714 he formally declared that he would acquiesce "to retain their love, give them peace of mind, and preserve his inheritance" while protesting the loss to himself. He later took care of his aged parents and lent them money. Barthélemy possessed a farm at Saint-Jérôme-de-L'Auvergne from the 1720s until his death, but his interests were elsewhere.

From 1718 he worked at various times as a butcher, a hatter, and an employee of the Compagnie des Indes at Quebec, where he was receiver and inspector of pelts at the company's principal office. He possibly owed this position to his knowledge of beaver fur acquired in hat-making since 1719 or even before, and to a trip to France from which he returned with his brother in 1724. His instructions were contained in a dispatch from France dated 9 May 1725; Cotton was to receive, grade, and pack the beaver skins in 120-pound bales with suitable identifying marks. Traders were obliged to deliver the pelts to him by virtue of the company's export monopoly of beaver. He and a comptroller, who kept the accounts, worked under the supervision of the company's agent.

Perhaps in part because of his new position, even though it was probably a seasonal occupation that ended with the yearly departure of the ships to France, Cotton had little time for manufacturing hats in the shop that occupied the lower floor of his house on Rue Saint-Jean, close to the Jesuit college. In 1730 and 1731 he shared the shop and the dye works behind the house with his apprentice Joseph HUPPÉ, *dit* Lagroix. In the latter year another hatter, Jean Létourneau, assumed Cotton's functions. Both Huppé and Létourneau were to pay rent to Cotton, but there was apparently a disagreement between Cotton and Huppé. Huppé defaulted and later moved to Montreal. A second blow fell in September 1736 when the Conseil de Marine forbade hat-making in Canada because in producing, selling, and exporting beaver hats the colonial craftsmen infringed the monopoly of the Compagnie des Indes. When Cotton's shop was closed that month by royal order, the hat-making equipment confiscated was valued at 590 *livres*. Officials estimated that his yearly revenue from the business was only 400 *livres*.

Still an employee of the Compagnie des Indes, Cotton continued to make a comfortable living despite this setback. On 13 Nov. 1741 he married Marie Willis, a widow 12 years his senior who had been kidnapped by the Abenakis in New England as a child and brought to Canada. Possibly with his wife's dowry, he acquired in the same year a tile-works from Nicolas-Marie Renaud* d'Avène Des Méloizes. The kilns were inactive beginning in 1743, a year of bad harvests. The kiln venture, the hat shop, and the fact that the couple had a man-servant in 1744 indicate that Cotton had money, but he exhibited little enthusiasm for business.

Without any children of his own, Barthélemy Cotton made five different wills to bequeath his property to his nearest blood relations. At first he favoured his sister Marguerite, who was a dressmaker, and his brothers Jean-François and Michel* who were, among other things, silversmiths. Of the three only Michel was married and his children were the principal beneficiaries of Barthélemy's later wills. In the first testament, drawn up in 1752, Cotton showed the charitable inclinations of a devout man. Bequests were made to the poor, to the parishes of Quebec and Charlesbourg, and to various religious houses. Particularly favoured was the Hôpital Général of Quebec, for which Cotton had acted as secular agent in the 1720s and where three of his nieces were nuns. In 1771 Cotton made a special bequest to another nun of the Hôpital Général. His last will was made on 10 Dec. 1773. The frequent revisions were necessitated by the death of relatives or their departure for France after the conquest as well as by the reduction of his fortune; he seems to have found no replacement for his lost post with the Compagnie des Indes after the conquest. Cotton's wife died in 1776 and four years later he passed away at the age of 87.

PETER N. MOOGK

AN, Col., B, 43, ff.507–9; 62, ff.110–11; 78, ff.25–33 (mfm. at PAC); C[11A], 51, pp.10–16 (PAC transcripts). ANQ-Q, État civil, Catholiques, Notre-Dame de Québec, 2 juill. 1692, 13 nov. 1741, 28 mai 1780; Greffe de Louis Chambalon, 30 oct. 1709, 27 avril 1713; Greffe de C.-H. Du Laurent, 15 juin 1752; Greffe de François Genaple de Bellefonds, 27 févr. 1686, 23 sept. 1691; Greffe de J.-C. Panet, 31 août 1761, 3 mars 1767, 25 oct. 1771, 10 déc. 1773; Greffe de J.-N. Pinguet de Vaucour, 18 févr. 1728; Greffe de Pierre Rivet Cavelier, 31 déc. 1715; NF 25, 23, no.879; 57, nos.2299, 2318. Archives maritimes, Port de Rochefort (France), 1E, 105, f.323. "Recensement de Québec, 1744," 33. *Quebec Gazette*, 3 Feb., 27 May 1785. P.-V. Charland, "Notre-Dame de Québec: le nécrologe de la crypte," *BRH*, XX, 242–44. *Dictionnaire national des Canadiens français (1608–1760)* (2v., Montréal, 1958), I, 310. P.-G. Roy, *Inv. ins. Cons. souv.*, 166–67; *Inv. jug. et délib., 1717–60*, I, 57, 59, 61, 186; II, 71, 75, 107, 276, 320; III, 150; V, 177–78; VI, 3. Tanguay, *Dictionnaire*, I, 142; III, 159. J.-N. Fauteux, *Essai sur l'industrie*, I, 169; II, 488. Lionel Groulx, "Note sur la chapellerie au Canada sous le Régime français," *RHAF*, III (1949–50), 383–401. É.-Z. Massicotte, "L'anéantissement d'une industrie canadienne sous le Régime français," *BRH*, XXVII (1921), 193–200.

COUAGNE (Du Coigne), JEAN-BAPTISTE DE, fur-trader and interpreter; baptized 3 March 1720 at Montreal (Que.), son of René de Couagne* and Louise Pothier; father of at least two mixed-blood sons; d. after 1795.

Member of a prominent family of Montreal merchants, Jean-Baptiste de Couagne entered the fur trade at a young age. He went to the Illinois country as an *engagé*, an indentured employee, in the late 1730s and spent a number of years in the region, where he acquired a good knowledge of Indian customs and languages. At one point he was captured by the Cherokees, who subsequently adopted him. At Montreal in 1747 he contracted to go to Detroit as an *engagé*; in 1749 he was hired to go to Lake of the Woods.

Like Peter Bisaillon*, Jacques de Noyon*, and others, de Couagne eventually decided to try his fortunes with the English. He spent the winter of 1750–51 at Fort Edward (known to the French as Fort Lydius), New York, with John Hendricks LYDIUS, a relation by marriage. In the spring William JOHNSON wrote to Governor George Clinton* of New York asking permission for de Couagne "to follow Business" in the colony. Minimizing his connections with Montreal, de Couagne had told Johnson that he had spent the previous 14 years in the Illinois country. For a considerable time during the early 1750s de Couagne lived among the Six Nations. The authorities of New France were far from pleased with his activities, and in 1751 Governor La Jonquière [Taffanel*] ordered his arrest.

Having an independent view of his own interests, de Couagne stayed in communication with New France. When war broke out between

Britain and France in the mid 1750s his ties became particularly suspect to the British. He and a partner were imprisoned at Albany in the autumn of 1757 but soon escaped. The consequences of the incident appear to have been light, however. The next May they arrived at Fort Johnson (near Amsterdam) after spending some time among the Six Nations, and Johnson dispatched them to James ABERCROMBY, the commander-in-chief, for questioning. Abercromby sent them back to Six Nations country to spy.

When Fort Niagara (near Youngstown, N.Y.) fell to the British in the summer of 1759, de Couagne was hired by Johnson to serve there as an interpreter and was employed in that capacity for the rest of his career. His work took him on various missions. Late in the summer of 1759 he went to Oswego, where British forces were gathered for an attack down the St Lawrence. The next year Johnson ordered him to go with the Indians accompanying Robert ROGERS to Detroit to "prevent any difference which might arise between our people and them for want of understanding each other." He travelled there again in 1765 with Wabbicommicot*, who was carrying a message for the nations that had been involved in Pontiac*'s war. When in 1769 rumours of an uprising of Ojibwas, Potawatomis, and Ohio valley Indians began to circulate, de Couagne was sent to investigate.

By 1773 he was rapidly losing his sight. He retired to Montreal and in 1780 was described as "old blind DeCouagne who is here in the Gray Sisters Hospital." He had so recovered his strength and vision the next spring that he thought of returning to work at Niagara, but there is no evidence that he went. His name was on the Indian department pension list for 1796; "Invalid Interpreter," he was to receive a dollar a day.

JANE E. GRAHAM

AN, Col., C[11A], 97, f.165. PAC, MG 18, O6, p.24; MG 19, F1, 2, pp.161–62; 25, pp.208–9. *Coll. des manuscrits de Lévis* (Casgrain), VII, 168. *Johnson papers* (Sullivan *et al.*). *Michigan Pioneer Coll.*, XXV (1894), 108. *Handbook of American Indians* (Hodge), I, 405. Massicotte, "Répertoire des engagements pour l'Ouest," ANQ *Rapport*, 1929–30, 378; 1930–31, 367, 383.

COUAGNE (Coigne), MICHEL DE, officer in the colonial regular troops; b. 5 Oct. 1727 at Louisbourg, Île Royale (Cape Breton Island), eldest son of Jean-Baptiste de Couagne* and his first wife Marguerite-Madeleine de Gannes de Falaise; m. 19 Feb. 1758 at Louisbourg Jeanne Loppinot, and they had six children; d. 28 Oct. 1789 at Saint-Marc (Haiti).

It was a frequent practice of the French crown to recognize the services of deceased officers by appointing their sons to posts in the armed forces. Michel de Couagne was created a gentleman cadet in the colonial regulars in 1740, soon after the death of his father, who had served on Île Royale as an engineer for 23 years. Michel served as a voluntary assistant engineer in 1742 and 1743, and participated in the taking of Canso in 1744 and the defence of Louisbourg in 1745 [*see* François DU PONT Duvivier ; Louis DU PONT Duchambon]. Transported to France by the terms of the surrender of the fortress, he was commissioned lieutenant and assistant engineer on 6 Jan. 1747, and that year he took part in the ill-fated expedition to Canada of Jacques-Pierre de Taffanel* de La Jonquière. Having finally reached Canada in 1748, he assisted Gaspard-Joseph Chaussegros* de Léry for the next six years on the fortifications of Quebec, Montreal, and other places. In 1754, at the request of Louis Franquet*, director of fortifications for New France, he returned to Louisbourg with the full grade of engineer and was employed there until the capitulation of 1758 [*see* Augustin de Boschenry* de Drucour]. Franquet, who considered him one of his best engineers, procured him a promotion to captain on half pay in 1756, an advancement probably designed to give him the authority an engineer at Louisbourg required. During the siege of 1758 de Couagne demonstrated courage, diligence, and skill in siegecraft. In particular, he supervised repairs to the Island battery.

De Couagne spent the years 1759 to 1763 at La Rochelle, completing the detailed fortifications accounts not only for Île Royale but also for Canada, writing appreciations of different kinds concerning the two colonies, and longing to return to his native island. It was the quality of his work on the Louisbourg accounts, with which he was intimately acquainted, that led the court to have him verify the Canadian records, of which he had no firsthand knowledge but with which he apparently also dealt competently. His letter of 4 Nov. 1760 on Île Royale (an excellent geographical source) strongly recommended the construction of a new fortified capital on Spanish Bay (Sydney harbour) if France repossessed the colony. Agricultural settlement, he urged, should be encouraged by the establishment of the seigneurial system in several fertile areas that had been largely neglected during more than 40 years of French occupation of the island. De Couagne further noted that the proper role of Louisbourg and the south coast had always been as a base for the fishery; this they should remain. His letter of 26 Aug. 1761 on Canada was concerned with the management of fortifications, the need for more trained engineers and fewer amateurs, and the improvement of procedures. He also recommended an end to the disastrous practice whereby officers in charge of construction at isolated posts sold wine and spirits to soldier-workers.

Promoted captain in January 1763, de Couagne was made a knight of Saint-Louis the following month. The same year he was transferred to Saint-Pierre and Miquelon, where he directed the construction of government buildings and harbour facilities, drew accurate maps and plans, and collected natural history specimens. He was unsuccessful in his bid to be designated second in command to his former colleague, François-Gabriel d'ANGEAC, now governor of the diminutive colony. Following his return to France at the end of 1766, de Couagne was posted to the colonial military depot on the Île de Ré, where he eventually became second in command and briefly served as commander of the company of cadets. Reduced to half pay in 1781, he complained to his relative the Comte d'Argenson of financial hardship – he and his wife had lost all their possessions at Louisbourg in 1758 – and in 1783 he was appointed king's lieutenant of Saint-Marc on the island of Saint-Domingue (Hispaniola). A distaste for tropical climates, his continuing financial distress, and adverse decisions on promotion all made his years in the Caribbean colony difficult. So too did the severe fine he incurred in 1786 for failing to prevent a violation of the foreign-trade regulations in his district. His death in 1789 left his widow in desperate economic circumstances.

F. J. THORPE

AMA, Inspection du Génie, Bibliothèque, MSS *in-4°*, 66, f.65. AN, Col., B, 78, f.393; 85, f.199; 87, f.208v; 91, f.261; 99, ff.244, 252v; 103, f.188; 121, f.649; 133, ff.139, 144; 136, f.104; C11A, 98, f.78; 105, f.296; C11B, 25, f.27; 34, f.12; 35, ff.282–83; 36, ff.268–70; 38, ff.169–70; C11C, 8, ff.82–91; C12, 1, f.100; 14, f.6; D1, 11, ff.59, 60v, 102, 118v, 241v; D2C, 2, ff.115v–16; 4, f.114; E, 94 (dossier Michel de Couagne); Section Outre-mer, Dépôt des fortifications des colonies, Am. sept., no.488; Saint-Pierre et Miquelon, carton 1, nos.7, 9–14; G1, 409/2, p.210; G3, 2045. PAC, MG 18, O6. *Inv. des papiers de Léry* (P.-G. Roy), II, 95, 110. Æ. Fauteux, *Les chevaliers de Saint-Louis*, 192–93.

COUGHLAN, LAURENCE, Methodist preacher, Church of England clergyman, and local official; founder of Methodism in Newfoundland; probably b. at Drummersnave (Drumsna, Republic of Ireland); d. probably in 1784 in London, England.

Laurence Coughlan was reared a Roman Catholic, but converted to Methodism at Drummersnave in 1753. Although he had, according to John Wesley, "no learning at all," in 1755 he was recruited as an itinerant preacher and became known for his zeal and persistence. Two years later he was transferred to England, serving first at Whitehaven and later at Colchester, where he had conspicuous success. In 1760 he returned to Ireland for a period and worked in Waterford, a port through which great numbers of Irish travelled to Newfoundland. By 1763 Coughlan had become one of Wesley's most valued helpers, but in 1764, when Coughlan had himself ordained by Erasmus, a Greek Orthodox bishop now thought to have been an impostor, Wesley was angered because he did not think the uneducated Coughlan worthy of the honour. Wesley claimed in 1768 that Coughlan had brought another "blot" upon himself when he "married and ruined" an unnamed woman. The ruin alluded to was evidently financial. There may also have been theological differences between the two men. In any event, by 1765 Coughlan's usefulness to Wesley as a preacher was at an end.

Since there is confusion in many sources about the date of Coughlan's first arrival in Newfoundland and the circumstances of his formal ordination as a Church of England priest, it is important that the facts be clearly stated. On 22 Nov. 1765 the people of Harbour Grace, Mosquito, and Carbonear authorized George Davis, a London merchant who was probably about to leave Newfoundland for the winter, "to procure and agree with a Protestant Minister of the Gospel, to come and reside among them." The following April Davis informed the Earl of Dartmouth, president of the Board of Trade, that Coughlan seemed "a proper Person" to serve as minister "if he could obtain Holy Orders," and urged Dartmouth to "use your endeavours to get him ordained." Coughlan was made deacon on 25 April, "licensed to perform the ministerial office in the province of Newfoundland" the following day, and then ordained priest on the 27th. Since Dartmouth's letter of recommendation had indicated that a ship was waiting for Coughlan at Poole "& will sail as soon as he gets thither," the date of Coughlan's arrival in Newfoundland was therefore 1766, probably in June. On 19 December of the same year Coughlan himself appeared before the Society for the Propagation of the Gospel and presented a petition from the people of Harbour Grace and vicinity asking that he be appointed the society's missionary and given an annual stipend. By that date he had already resided "some Time" among the people as "their Minister." The petition was granted, and Coughlan returned to Harbour Grace in September 1767. He was the first Church of England priest to serve in Conception Bay and the third then resident in Newfoundland [*see* James Balfour* and Edward LANGMAN]. Accompanying Coughlan during most of his stay on the island were his wife, who was also an ardent Methodist, and his daughter Betsey.

The record of Coughlan's ministry shows that he led a kind of double religious life. As a Church of England priest he administered the sacraments to a growing number of communicants, held regular services in Harbour Grace and, after 1768, in Carbonear, and on occasion preached in Irish to Irish fishermen to make them see "the Errors of Popery." In February 1768 he opened a school and despite difficulties kept it functioning during his ministry. By 1772 Coughlan could justly claim that he had served the SPG well. This appearance of success as Church of England clergyman, however, cloaked his real Methodist ambition, which was to be an instrument of evangelical conversion among the people. In this effort he met with no success for nearly three years, though he laboured "Night and Day," preaching "from house to house" in the manner favoured by Wesley. At length he grew discouraged and determined not to stay "in such a poor desolate Land," but his dogged efforts eventually bore fruit and a Methodist "awakening" began and spread "like fire."

As the revival grew, Coughlan began to encounter opposition from his more orthodox parishioners. His Methodist theology now, it seems, began to appear more openly in sermons to his regular congregation, and he urged its members to attend the private meetings he was organizing throughout his parish. In 1770 Coughlan's promised stipend from his parishioners was not forthcoming, and in July Governor John BYRON felt it necessary to order them to live up to their pledge; at the same time he appointed Coughlan a justice of the peace for Conception Bay. In November the stipend was still unpaid.

The following year certain incidents took place which brought Coughlan and some leading residents of Harbour Grace into open conflict. In February, Coughlan publicly denounced the merchant Hugh Roberts for adultery and advised his parishioners to avoid dealing with Roberts in future; five months later, he tried physically to prevent some of Roberts' labourers from working on a Sunday. As a result of these two episodes, Roberts and 12 other Harbour Grace merchants petitioned Byron that Coughlan be "silenc'd or remov'd" as a "very unfitt Person for a Justice of the Peace as well as a Missionary, being Ignorant of the Laws of his Country & a Person of no Education"; they also alleged that as a magistrate Coughlan was guilty of accepting bribes. Although, according to Coughlan's account of the subsequent inquiry, all his enemies "were found Liars," his commission as justice was revoked by Byron on 25 October because of his "many unwarrantable proceedings to the great obstruction & discouragement of the trade & fishery."

The antagonism which Coughlan aroused in the merchants contrasts strikingly with the affection and loyalty he inspired in the ordinary people who joined his movement. That movement continued to grow during his stay in Newfoundland, spreading northward from Carbonear to Blackhead, where a new church capable of holding 400 people had been built in the winter of 1768–69. The establishing of Methodist societies beyond Harbour Grace indicated Coughlan's desire to "travel up and down in this land" to spread his message. If he could have carried on in this fashion, he told Wesley in 1772, he would have stayed in Newfoundland, "but as I cannot, except by water, in small boats, I am not able to stand it." It was not only his "dreadful Apprehensions" of the sea, however, which drove him from the island. The enmity of the merchants had continued unabated, and in May 1772 a quarrel broke out between Coughlan and Nicholas Fiott, one of the 13 petitioners of the previous year. Coughlan flatly refused to allow Fiott to stand as godfather of two children, accusing the merchant of leading "an immoral life." A heated confrontation ensued during a Sunday church service, but Coughlan stood his ground and the children were not baptized. In October Fiott formally complained to Governor Molyneux SHULDHAM, who in turn asked the SPG to remove their missionary from Harbour Grace. The same month Coughlan himself asked the society for permission to return to England, and he left in October 1773. Two months later he appeared before the SPG in London and resigned his mission.

Coughlan's career from 1773 to his death is obscure. A letter to Wesley in 1772 seems to hint that he wished to return to the Methodist itinerancy in Britain, but these tentative overtures were not encouraged. In 1776 he was minister of Cumberland Street Chapel, London. On 25 Feb. 1785, Wesley wrote to John Stretton, one of Coughlan's followers in Newfoundland, that Coughlan had died some time previously, "utterly broken in pieces."

Laurence Coughlan had begun a movement that was to transform religious and social life in Conception Bay. To judge from reports by later missionaries, his own accounts of his success as a preacher cannot be doubted. After he left Newfoundland, devoted followers like Stretton, Thomas Pottle, and Arthur Thomey carried on his work, and the Methodist denomination which he established in the populous district of Conception Bay has flourished to this day. Though a fiery, fastidious, and perhaps irascible man, it is evident that Coughlan had great sympathy for the people he served and a good understanding of their character. His work, *An account of the work of God in Newfoundland . . .*, published in London in 1776, displays his charismatic and sympathetic personality.

PATRICK O'FLAHERTY

Laurence Coughlan, *An account of the work of God in Newfoundland, in series of letters* (London, 1776), 8–11, 18–19, 50ff.

Lambeth Palace Library (London), Fulham papers. PANL, GN2/1, 4, 5; N. C. Crewe coll., dossier on Methodism in Newfoundland. USPG, A; B, 6, pp. 168–69; C/CAN/Nfl., 1, pp. 58–62; Journal of SPG, 17–21. *Arminian Magazine* (London), VIII (1785), 490–92. SPG [*Annual report*] (London), 1767–76. [John Wesley], *The letters of the Rev. John Wesley*, ed. John Telford (8v., London, 1931; repr. [1960]), IV, 56, 204, 289–90; V, 101–3, 109; VII, 260. C. H. Crookshank, *History of Methodism in Ireland* (3v., Belfast and London, 1885–88), I, 100–1, 107, 149. Jacob Parsons, "The origin and growth of Newfoundland Methodism, 1765–1855" (unpublished MA thesis, Memorial University of Nfld., St John's 1964), 17, 148–49. Warwick Smith, "Rev. Laurence Coughlan" (paper presented to the Nfld. Hist. Soc., St John's, 20 March 1942).

COULON DE VILLIERS, FRANÇOIS, captain in the colonial regular troops; b. 1712 at either Montreal or Verchères (Que.), son of Nicolas-Antoine Coulon* de Villiers and Angélique Jarret de Verchères; d. 22 May 1794 at New Orleans, Spanish Louisiana.

François Coulon de Villiers was a member of a distinguished military family of the Canadian nobility. In 1733, while holding the non-commissioned rank of brevet cadet, which would indicate his having already had several years of military service, he was severely wounded in an encounter with a Fox war party near Baie-des-Puants (Green Bay, Wis.). His father, the district commandant, and a brother were killed in this skirmish. To compensate the family for their loss, his brothers Louis* and Nicolas-Antoine* were promoted second ensign and lieutenant respectively, and François was commissioned ensign on 15 Aug. 1736. In his report to the minister of Marine in 1739 Governor General Beauharnois* remarked that Coulon de Villiers was "a good officer, zealous for the service, [and] of a good conduct." He was subsequently transferred to the Louisiana establishment and promoted lieutenant in 1746. While serving in the Illinois territory he was married twice: first to Élisabeth Groston de Saint-Ange, of Illinois, and secondly to Marie-Madeleine Marin of Fort de Chartres (near Prairie du Rocher, Ill.). He had one daughter by his first wife in 1740 and one son by his second in 1757.

On 1 Feb. 1754 Coulon de Villiers was commissioned captain. The same year, while England and France were still at peace, a detachment of Virginia militia led by George Washington ambushed a French emissary party commanded by François's brother, Joseph Coulon* de Villiers de Jumonville, who was killed in the affray. During the ensuing hostilities François lost no opportunity to avenge his brother's death. In 1756 he led a force of 23 colonial regulars and 32 Indians in an assault on Fort Granville (near Lewiston, Pa), some 60 miles from Philadelphia, captured it, took about 30 prisoners, burned the fort with its six months of supplies, and safely retired. The following year he was acting adjutant of Fort de Chartres and continued to lead war parties that ravaged the frontiers of Virginia. In September 1758 he was with the force that inflicted a defeat on Brigadier-General John Forbes*'s advance guard near Fort Duquesne (Pittsburgh, Pa). The tables were turned in 1759 when the Anglo-Americans laid siege to Fort Niagara (near Youngstown, N.Y.). A relief force from the Ohio garrison rushed to its aid and was cut to ribbons in an ambush. Among those taken prisoner was Coulon de Villiers. After being exchanged at New York for an English officer held by the French he made his way to New Orleans where he was awarded the cross of Saint-Louis on 1 Aug. 1759.

When Louisiana was ceded to Spain Coulon de Villiers resigned his commission in the French regulars, entered the Spanish service, and was appointed to the command at Natchitoches. On 28 June 1762 he married Marie-Geneviève Énault de Livaudais at New Orleans and acquired a plantation, most likely from her, at Pointe Coupée (near New Roads, La). In 1768, while he was serving at Natchitoches, the prominent Canadians of New Orleans rose in revolt against their Spanish rulers. The following year the revolt was sternly suppressed by 3,000 Spanish troops sent from Cuba. Probably in recognition of his not having participated in the uprising, Coulon de Villiers was appointed an alcalde of New Orleans, an important administrative and judicial post in the local government. He now took up residence in his wife's commodious New Orleans house, tended by eight domestic slaves.

When he made his will on 18 Feb. 1794 Coulon de Villiers could look back on a distinguished career under two crowns. He had been fortunate to survive the wars and was fortunate also to die when he did. To have lived another decade and thereby come under American rule would have been bitter indeed for a nobleman who had named his youngest son Jumonville, in memory of the brother slain by George Washington.

W. J. ECCLES

AN, Col., D[2C], 47, ff.688–89; 48, ff.38, 41; 49, ff.320, 326; 61, f.89. La. State Museum (New Orleans), Cathédrale Saint-Louis de la Nouvelle-Orléans, Registre des mariages, 28 juin 1762. Natchitoches Court Record Office (Natchitoches, La.), Conveyances, 5, f.826; 6, f.865; 10, f.1220; 11, f.1257; Spanish translations, 45, no.1198. New Orleans Court Record Office, Greffe de François Broutin, 18 févr. 1794. New Orleans Public Library, Department of Archives, Census of New Orleans, 6 Nov. 1791. St Martin Parish Court House (St Martin, La.), Original acts, 1–15, 1760–94. G. R. Conrad, *First families of Louisiana* (2v., Baton Rouge, La., 1970), I, 170. Stanley, *New France*. A.[-E.] Gosselin, "Notes sur la famille Coulon de Villiers," *BRH*, XII (1906), 174, 257–75.

COURREAUD (Courraud) DE LA COSTE (La Côte), PIERRE, merchant; baptized 7 May 1696 in the parish of Saint-André, Angoulême, France, son of Élie Courreaud de La Coste, a merchant, and Catherine Coulaud; d. 26 March 1779 in Montreal (Que.).

Pierre Courreaud de La Coste was in Quebec in May 1717, when he signed a contract to serve for two years as apprentice to barber-surgeon Simon Soupiran* Sr. But Courreaud, a merchant's son, soon gave up the apprenticeship to go into business in Montreal, where he had relatives. There, on 26 Sept. 1718, he married Marie-Anne Massé (Macé), the widow of a blacksmith and edge-tool maker, Guillaume Malhiot. Courreaud was then only 22 but pretended to be 26, while his wife, who was 34 and had four dependent children, claimed to be only 30. These white lies allowed the husband to pass as being of age and his wife to avoid scandal. She died in September 1721 following childbirth, and six months later Courreaud married a girl of 20, Marguerite Aubuchon, *dit* L'Espérance, whose father was a merchant at Longue-Pointe, near Montreal. They had seven children but apparently none survived their father.

Neither of his wives brought Courreaud much wealth, but he was probably able to make use of family connections in his business affairs. At the time of his first marriage he established himself on Rue Saint-Paul, the business street of Montreal, and sold goods to fur-traders. With Julien Trottier Desrivières as his partner, he supplied trade goods to his second cousin, Marin Hurtebise, who from 1733 to 1735 was involved in the ventures of explorer Pierre Gaultier* de Varennes et de La Vérendrye. After Trottier's death in 1737, Courraud evidently maintained business relations with his cousin; when in July 1741 the Compagnie des Indes, which held a monopoly on the fur trade, conducted general searches in Montreal for undeclared beaver pelts, he was found to have merchandise belonging to Hurtebise on his premises. Courreaud was also associated with Jean-Baptiste Latour in the sale of goods to Île Royale (Cape Breton Island), and with Pierre Latour, a merchant who, like him, had interests in the trade with the *pays d'en haut*. As a result of these various endeavours Courreaud acquired a degree of wealth. He owned a two-storey stone house, which he renovated in 1733 and to which he added a storage vault the following year. By 1729 he had a maidservant, and in 1737 he was even able to purchase a young black slave of 12 or 13 years of age.

Towards the end of the 1730s Courreaud added speculation in land to his business activities. Some of this land probably came from insolvent or recalcitrant debtors, such as Gabriel Descary, whose indebtedness occasioned legal proceedings from 1743 till 1759. In 1739 Descary, Marin Hurtebise' partner, had received trade goods from Courreaud but contested their value, and succeeded in having what he owed reduced from 5,264 *livres* 14 *sols* 4 *deniers* to 4,251 *livres* 1 *sou* 4 *deniers*. Courreaud appealed to the provost court of Quebec against this reduction but lost his case. Finally in 1759 a decision by the Conseil Supérieur enabled him to seize Descary's property and sell it at auction. To avoid similar situations Courreaud had made those to whom he extended credit mortgage property to him with a fixed term as soon as their debts became significant.

Courreaud retired from business shortly after the conquest. In August 1764 he bought from Marie-Thérèse Migeon de La Gauchetière a piece of land called "presville," near the *fau-*

bourg Saint-Laurent, as well as the arriere-fief of La Gauchetière. Four years later he renounced his feudal rights, thus escaping the *droit de quint*, which he should have paid when he bought the fief in 1764. Like most influential Montrealers, Courreaud had signed the petition to George III in 1763 asking him to let merchandise that had remained in France during the war come into Canada and to use his influence with the court of France to speed settlement of all Canada paper. The "La Coste fils" who signed with him was probably his son Marin.

JOSÉ E. IGARTUA

ANQ-M, État civil, Catholiques, Notre-Dame de Montréal, 26 sept. 1718, 22, 24 sept. 1721, 27 mars 1779, 20 avril 1784; Greffe de J.-B. Adhémar, 6 août, 29 sept., 24 nov., 6 déc. 1752, 2, 3 févr., 10 mai, 12 oct., 16, 24 nov. 1753, 9, 15 janv., 8 juill. 1754; Greffe de L.-L. Aumasson de Courville, 10 oct. 1770; Greffe de Gervais Hodiesne, 12 déc. 1754, 20 févr., 20, 21 mars, 28 juin, 11 oct. 1755, 25 juin 1756, 9 janv. 1761, 27 oct. 1763; Greffe de M.-L. Lepallieur de Laferté, 25 sept. 1718; Greffe de Pierre Panet, 14 mars 1757, 18 sept. 1760, 22 août 1764, 17 juill., 30 oct. 1767, 8 juin 1768; Greffe de Simon Sanguinet, 2 mai 1778; Greffe de Nicolas Senet, 20 mars 1722; Greffe de François Simonnet, 25 sept. 1750, 9 nov. 1754, 21 mars 1755, 14 févr. 1756, 16 juin 1758, 14 mai 1768, 18 févr. 1769, 6 oct. 1773. ANQ-Q, NF 11, 59, ff.74–77; 61, ff.19v–26; 69, ff.19, 31v–32, 39v–41. Archives municipales, Angoulême (dép. de la Charente, France), État civil, Saint-André d'Angoulême, 7 mai 1696. PRO, CO 42/24, ff.72–74v (mfm. at PAC). "Aveu et dénombrement de messire Louis Normand, prêtre du séminaire de Saint-Sulpice de Montréal, au nom et comme fondé de procuration de messire Charles-Maurice Le Pelletier, supérieur du séminaire de Saint-Sulpice de Paris, pour la seigneurie de l'île de Montréal (1731)," ANQ *Rapport*, 1941–42, 27. *Doc. relatifs à la monnaie sous le Régime français* (Shortt), II, 968, 970. *Montréal en 1781* . . . , Claude Perrault, édit. (Montréal, 1969), 23–24, 121–24. "Recensement de Montréal, 1741" (Massicotte), 26. "Marguilliers de la paroisse de Notre-Dame de Ville-Marie de 1657 à 1913," *BRH*, XIX (1913), 279. P.-G. Roy, *Inv. jug. et délib., 1717–60*, IV, 110, 149, 188; VI, 133, 140, 143–44, 148–49. Tanguay, *Dictionnaire*. P.-G. Roy, "La famille Courault de La Coste," *BRH*, XLV (1939), 366–68.

COURVILLE, LOUIS-LÉONARD AUMASSON DE COURVILLE, *dit* **Sieur de.** *See* AUMASSON

COUTON. *See* COTTON

COX, NICHOLAS, army officer and colonial administrator; b. *c.* 1724 in England; m. Deborah —; d. 8 Jan. 1794 at Quebec.

Nicholas Cox joined the 58th Foot as an ensign in 1741 and served during the rebellion in Scotland four years later. In 1750 his regiment (now the 47th Foot) was sent to Nova Scotia, where Cox participated in the capture of Fort Beauséjour (near Sackville, N.B.) and the expulsion of the Acadians in 1755 [*see* Robert MONCKTON; John WINSLOW]. He also saw action at the siege of Louisbourg, Île Royale (Cape Breton Island) in 1758 and at Quebec the following year. He had risen to the rank of captain by 1764.

In 1775 Governor Guy Carleton* chose Cox, now a major, to fill the newly created position of lieutenant governor of the District of Gaspé; the post probably had its origin in the French practice of appointing a subdelegate of the intendant to represent the government on the remote and rugged Gaspé coasts [*see* François LEFEBVRE de Bellefeuille]. When Cox arrived at Quebec with his family in August, Canada was threatened with attack by American forces and he was immediately put to work training recruits. It was not until the summer of 1777 that he was able to travel to the Gaspé.

Following closely Carleton's instructions, Cox took a census on his first trip and reported 631 Europeans permanently settled on the coastline between Gaspé Bay and the Restigouche River, in addition to 572 men brought out to labour on the fisheries for the summer only. He found that the Acadians of the Baie des Chaleurs were successfully combining fishing and agriculture to gain their living. North of Paspébiac, however, the population depended almost entirely on the fisheries. Cox discovered little sympathy for the American revolutionary cause but organized militia forces in any case. He again visited the district for brief periods in 1778 and 1780 but spent the remainder of the war in England and Quebec. Since Gaspé was constantly harassed by American privateers during the war, Cox urged HALDIMAND, who had succeeded Carleton in 1778, to provide naval protection as well as economic assistance to the region. His entreaties had little effect, however, and the Gaspé experienced both depopulation and starvation in the period of the American revolution.

In 1784 Cox journeyed to Gaspé again, this time to supervise the settlement of over 500 loyalists. He found this task unpleasant because of the loyalists' quarrelsome dispositions and their desire to obtain large land grants, often at the expense of the established Indian and Acadian inhabitants. The loyalists were not granted land, but were instead given "location tickets," documents which assigned plots of land. Although Cox succeeded in obtaining the same documents for the Acadians, he recognized the necessity of acquiring regular title deeds for everyone in the region. He failed to impress this need upon the government, however, and the result was nearly a century of uncertain land holding in the Gaspé.

Much of the land at the head of the Baie des Chaleurs, where both loyalists and Acadians were expanding, was claimed by the Micmacs of the Restigouche River, and in 1786 Cox, as a member of a commission responsible for investigating the Indians' grievances, averted a violent clash between the Indians and the settlers. He persuaded the Micmac chiefs, Joseph CLAUDE among them, to relinquish their land claims and offered them in exchange his mere opinion that the government would consider granting them an equivalent amount of land nearby and would protect their rights to the Restigouche salmon fisheries and give them a "gratuity." Although these compensations were not granted the Indians' fears were assuaged, and it was not until the 1820s that they again became militant over the land question.

Cox was eager to establish a strong agricultural economy in the district to provide an alternative to the traditional fishing industry, but he could offer only moral encouragement to the farmers of the Baie des Chaleurs region. At the same time he supported the fishing industry, and in particular the interests of Charles Robin*, the leading fish merchant in the area. In 1787 Cox successfully urged the government to grant Robin extensive tracts of land and fishing privileges; it is perhaps significant that Cox was deeply in debt to Robin at the time.

The office of lieutenant governor of Gaspé was not high in the government hierarchy, and Cox often reported to the lieutenant governor of Quebec. Certain supplementary functions were attached to the office; for example, Cox was superintendent of trade and fisheries on the Labrador coast. The government did not, however, supply a vessel with which to patrol the Labrador and Gaspé coasts, and there is no evidence that Cox ever went to Labrador. He did live permanently in the Gaspé for a few years after 1784. He received a salary of £400 per year and a house at New Carlisle; in 1787 he was granted Île Bonaventure. Cox was also colonel of the Gaspé militia and a member of the district land board. He died in office and was succeeded by Francis Le Maistre*. Cox's successors were, however, much less attentive to their duties. The office eventually became redundant in 1826.

DAVID LEE

AN, Col., C[11B], 35, f.136. BL, Add. MSS 21723, pp.355–60; 21743, p.5; 21862 (PAC transcripts). PAC, MG 11, [CO 42], Q, 25, pp.178–79; 27, pp.240, 460–64; 28, p.193; 63, pp.124–25, 135–36; 67, pp.57–59; MG 28, III, 18; RG 1, L3[L], 67, pp.33313–32; 168, p.81836; RG 4, A1, 21, p.7310; 29, pp.9488–90; 31, pp.10084–99. [Thomas Ainslie], *Canada preserved: the journal of Captain Thomas Ainslie*, ed. S. S. Cohen ([Toronto, 1968]), 94. *Quebec Gazette*, 24 Aug. 1775, 27 Nov. 1788, 14 May 1789, 16 Jan. 1794. *Almanach de Québec*, 1792, 120. Langelier, *List of lands granted*, 4, 13–14. W. H. Siebert, "The loyalist settlements on the Gaspé peninsula," RSC *Trans.*, 3rd ser., VIII (1914), sect.II, 399–405.

COYA (Coyour). *See* KOYAH

CRAMAHÉ, HECTOR THEOPHILUS. *See* Supplement

CRÉQUY. *See* AIDE-CRÉQUY

CRESPEL, EMMANUEL (baptized **Jacques-Philippe**), priest, Recollet, provincial commissioner of the Recollets, and author; b. 13 March 1703 at Douai, France, son of Sébastien Crespel and Louise-Thérèse Devienne; d. 29 April 1775 at Quebec.

At the age of 16 Emmanuel Crespel joined the Recollets in Avesnes, France, where he made his profession on 20 Aug. 1720. Four years later he left for Quebec, arriving 8 October on the *Chameau*. While familiarizing himself with life in the colony, he pursued his ecclesiastical training and was ordained priest by Bishop Saint-Vallier [La Croix*] on 16 March 1726. His ministry was to be divided into two periods: one as military chaplain, the other as the administrator of his religious order.

From 6 Oct. 1726 until 2 June 1728 Crespel served as priest at Fort Richelieu (Sorel, Que.), where he left a reputation for devotion and saintliness. On 5 June 1728 he went as chaplain with a force being sent under Constant Le Marchand* de Lignery to fight the Foxes in the Great Lakes region. In face of an enemy who kept slipping away, the contingent had to be satisfied with burning villages and destroying crops. After this exploit, which Father Crespel considered "absolutely useless," the expedition returned to Montreal at the end of September. The following summer he went back to the Great Lakes region to serve as chaplain, first at Fort Niagara (near Youngstown, N.Y.) from 27 July 1729 until 1732, then at Fort Frontenac (Kingston, Ont.) until 1735, and finally at Fort Saint-Frédéric (near Crown Point, N.Y.) from 17 Nov. 1735 until 21 Sept. 1736.

His superiors having recalled him to France, Crespel sailed on the *Renommée*, a new ship under the command of Joseph Damours de Freneuse, who had 46 years of experience at sea. The ship left Quebec on 3 Nov. 1736 with 54 passengers but 11 days later ran aground on the southern tip of Anticosti Island. Seeing that there was no possibility of help before spring, the group decided to break up: 24 men remained at the scene of the shipwreck, the others attempted to get to the Mingan Islands where some Frenchmen were spending the winter. On 27 November, 13 men climbed into the dinghy while 17 others, including Father Crespel and Captain Damours, crowded into the longboat. The latter soon lost sight of the dinghy, which evidently was dashed to pieces, since debris from it was found the following spring. Father Crespel and his companions succeeded in rounding the western tip of Anticosti Island. The weather, however, was steadily becoming colder, and on 7 December, unable to go farther because of ice, they had to take shelter in a bay on the north shore of the island. Bad weather, famine, fever, and other illnesses killed nearly all the Recollet's companions. At the end of April, the three survivors obtained help from some Indians. On 1 May Crespel succeeded in reaching the post of Mingan, which at that time was under the command of Jean-Louis Volant d'Haudebourg. With d'Haudebourg accompanying him, Crespel returned to the scene of the shipwreck, and found four men still alive; one of them died soon after. Crespel has left us an account of this shipwreck written in the form of letters to his brother. Although his narrative cannot be described as a masterpiece, it has a quality of sincerity that is moving. As a simple adventure story, and for this very reason, the book met with astonishing success from the moment of its publication in 1742 and went through many subsequent reprintings as well as translation into German and English.

Father Crespel returned to Quebec on 13 June 1737. One can imagine the amazement that greeted him, since he was believed to be in France. After a few weeks spent regaining his strength, he was appointed to be parish priest at Soulanges (Que.), a post he held for a year. Having been recalled to France again, he sailed on 21 Oct. 1738 on the king's vessel *Rubis*, which reached Port-Louis in Brittany on 2 December; he arrived in Paris at the year's end. Early in 1740 he was named vicar of the monastery in Avesnes. The quiet weighed upon him, however; returning to Paris, he resumed his duties as a military chaplain and for eight years served in the force under the Maréchal de Maillebois which took part in the campaign against Austria. Incidentally, it was at Maillebois's residence at Paderborn (Federal Republic of Germany) that he wrote the account of his voyage.

Having returned to Canada – in 1750, it seems – he became the provincial commissioner of the Recollets, an office he retained for the rest of his life except for the period 1753–56, when he served as superior of the monastery in Quebec. He was in charge of his order at a difficult time, when the British authorities prevented the recruitment of new members. In 1762 Colonel Frederick HALDIMAND was indignant that Father Crespel changed the superiors in Montreal and Trois-Rivières without having asked his permission. Although Crespel remained inflexible on this matter, he nevertheless finally won the respect of the new rulers.

Emmanuel Crespel died on 29 April 1775 and was buried in the Recollet church on 1 May. When the church was destroyed by a fire, his remains were transferred to the cathedral of Notre-Dame in Quebec. It was his book that in the end made him famous. In addition to the story of his shipwreck, Father Crespel included one letter recounting the expedition against the Fox tribe, and another describing his years at Niagara, Detroit, and Saint-Frédéric, the country he had traversed, and the Indians' customs. Crespel had a real gift as a storyteller that won him the public's favour.

JEAN-GUY PELLETIER

Father Emmanuel Crespel is the author of *Voiages du R. P. Emmanuel Crespel, dans le Canada et son naufrage en revenant en France*, Louis Crespel, édit. (Francfort-sur-le-Main, 1742). The work was well received and was first republished at Amsterdam in 1757 with the title *Voyage au Nouveau-Monde et histoire intéressante du naufrage du R. P. Crespel, avec des notes historiques et géographiques*. Subsequent reprints include those issued in 1808 and 1884 at Quebec and in 1968 at Montreal. The work was translated into German as *Des Ehrwürdigen Pater Emanuel Crespels merkwürdige Reisen nach Canada . . . aus dem Französischen übersezt* (Frankfurt am Main and Leipzig, 1751) and into English as *Travels in North America, by M. Crespel . . .* (London, 1797). The account was also published in serial form in various magazines, including the *Magazin du Bas-Canada* (Montréal), I (janv.–juin 1832), 122–28, 162–70, 204–13, under the title "Relation du naufrage du navire *la Renommée*, sur les côtes de l'isle d'Anticosti; extraite d'une série de lettres du P. Emmanuel Crespel, récollet, à son frère"; and *Mélanges religieux* (Montréal), 14, 16, 21, 28 mars, 1er, 4, 8 avril 1851, under the title "Voyages au Canada et naufrage du R. P. Emmanuel Crespel, récollet, sur l'isle d'Anticosti, en 1736." The English version may also be found as "Voyages of Rev. Father Emmanuel Crespel, in Canada, and his shipwreck, while returning to France" in *Perils of the ocean and wilderness . . .*, ed.

J. [D.] G. Shea (Boston, Mass., [1856]), 131–206. An analysis of Crespel's work, signed "Actidès," has been published in *L'Abeille* (Québec), 27 mars 1850, 1–2; 4 avril 1850, 1–2. A portrait of Crespel, believed to have been executed around 1758 by another Recollet, Brother François, is held by the Musée du Québec.

AAQ, 12 A, C, 32, 34; 66 CD, I, 25, 29. ACAM, 901.001, 761-1. Archives municipales, Douai (dép. du Nord, France), État civil, Saint-Pierre, 13 mars 1703. ASQ, Fonds Viger-Verreau, Sér.O, 081, p.10; Lettres, M, 142, 143; S, 4, 4[Bis]; MSS, 146, 191b; Polygraphie, XXV, 4e; XXXI, 40. PAC, MG 18, E15. PAC *Rapport*, 1886, 520. *Quebec Gazette*, 4, 25 May 1775. Allaire, *Dictionnaire*, I, 138–39. *Biographie universelle* (Michaud et Desplaces), IX, 481. *DOLQ*, I, 183, 214, 788–89. Jouve, *Les franciscains et le Canada: aux Trois-Rivières*, 190, 203. J. H. Kennedy, *Jesuit and savage in New France* (New Haven, Conn., and London, 1950), 178. M. Trudel, *Le Régime militaire*, 138–39. Archange Godbout, "Les aumôniers de la vallée du Richelieu," SCHÉC *Rapport*, 13 (1945–46), 69–71. O.-M. Jouve, "Les anciens récollets, le R. P. Emmanuel Crespel," *Revue du Tiers-Ordre et de la Terre-Sainte* (Montréal), 1905, 1906, 1907. Hugolin Lemay, "Le P. Emmanuel Crespel, commissaire des récollets au Canada," *BRH*, XLIV (1938), 169–71. P.-G. Roy, "Le capitaine de Freneuse et le naufrage de la *Renommée*," *BRH*, XXII (1916), 60–61.

CROISILLE (Croizille) ET DE MONTESSON, JOSEPH-MICHEL LEGARDEUR DE. *See* LEGARDEUR

CUADRA. *See* BODEGA

CUGNET, FRANÇOIS-JOSEPH, seigneur, judge, attorney general, chief road commissioner (*grand voyer*), French translator and French secretary to the governor and Council of Quebec, clerk of the land rolls, and lawyer; b. 26 June 1720 at Quebec, eldest son of François-Étienne Cugnet* and Louise-Madeleine Dusautoy (Dusaultoir); d. there 16 Nov. 1789.

Little information can be gleaned about François-Joseph Cugnet's childhood and adolescence. He does not appear to have attended the Jesuit college in Quebec. He was a descendant of a family of Parisian lawyers – his paternal grandfather, Jean (Jean-Baptiste), and his uncle, Jean-Baptiste Cugnet, had taught law at the Université de Paris, and his father, François-Étienne, had been a lawyer in the *parlement* of Paris before being appointed director general of the Domaine d'Occident in New France – and he was naturally drawn to the study of law. This choice is even less surprising since, according to an inventory of property, his father had a library that was astonishingly rich for the period in treatises on all types of law, civil, criminal, and canonical. As a youth François-Joseph, like his three brothers and sister, was able to familiarize himself with the profession. Three of the family in fact would engage in legal activities: François-Joseph, Thomas-Marie, who became a member of the Conseil Supérieur, and Gilles-Louis, who, although he was a canon, pursued law studies up to the doctoral level in France, where he sought refuge after the capitulation of Quebec.

From October 1739, it seems, until September 1741, François-Joseph took the courses given by Attorney General Louis-Guillaume Verrier*. Then, from 1741 to 1747, a period during which his father was in the greatest financial difficulty due to the bankruptcy of the Saint-Maurice ironworks and when, as well, the elder Cugnet was using all possible means to retain the trading lease to the Tadoussac post, François-Joseph completely disappears from sight. He reappears in Saint-Domingue (Hispaniola), where from 1747 to 1750 he stayed as a scrivener in the Marine. From 30 Sept. to 31 Dec. 1751 he was incarcerated in the La Rochelle prison on a charge of having attacked Denis GOGUET, the former agent at Quebec of a La Rochelle merchant. In the summer of 1752, after managing to borrow 2,400 *livres* to pay his passage, François-Joseph returned to Quebec for good. The debt obliged him not only to give up his share in his late father's house, but also to relinquish all rights to the estate, as accounts rendered by his mother on 5 May 1753 indicate.

In this period, after an investigation into his conduct, Cugnet on 21 May 1755 was refused a commission as assessor to the Conseil Supérieur, an office his brother Thomas-Marie had obtained on 4 Oct. 1754. François-Joseph was able to find the means, however, to put his knowledge of law into practice as a scrivener in the head office of the Domaine d'Occident from 1755 to 1758. On 14 Feb. 1757, at the age of 36, Cugnet married Marie-Josephte de Lafontaine de Belcour at Notre-Dame in Quebec. She was 20 years younger than he. They were to have five children, of whom only two reached adulthood. The elder, Jacques-François, became a lawyer and served with his father as joint French secretary and French translator; the younger, Antoine, never attracted much attention and died unmarried.

Marie-Josephte de Lafontaine de Belcour was the great-granddaughter of François Byssot* de La Rivière and Cugnet was drawn into defending her share in the seigneuries of Île aux Œufs, Anticosti Island, the Mingan Islands, and especially the mainland seigneury of Mingan, which was the object of protracted litigation. The latter case had begun in 1763 with a quarrel between Governor MURRAY and Cugnet's father-in-law, Jacques de Lafontaine* de Belcour; after Belcour's death in 1765 Cugnet took the case in hand, at a time when many in Quebec, with Murray first and foremost, were hoping that an impending decision by London would restore to the province the north shore of the St Lawrence and Labrador, which had been joined to Newfoundland, and so allow it to continue exploiting the lucrative winter fishing grounds. However, in 1768 London refused to recognize the claims of the heirs to the mainland seigneury of Mingan. At the time of his marriage, François-Joseph had acquired three-quarters of the seigneury of Saint-Étienne, which his mother and his two brothers turned over to him. This action was tantamount to recognition at the opportune moment of the title seigneur of Saint-Étienne that Cugnet had assumed in 1751.

At the end of the French régime, at the time of the final French attempt to retake Quebec after the victory of Sainte-Foy, Montcalm*'s successor, François de LÉVIS, kept Cugnet under guard on board one of his frigates. Because accusations of treason were being spread about Cugnet, Governor Vaudreuil [RIGAUD] even proposed an investigation into his conduct at the time of the capture of Quebec in September 1759. This rather obscure episode in Cugnet's life has yet to be cleared up.

With the advent of the British régime Cugnet found the way to a brillant career as a bureaucrat, an achievement probably beyond his reach under French rule, since he had been held in little esteem. In December 1759 Murray appointed him judge for the parishes of Charlesbourg, Beauport, and Petite-Rivière; on 2 Nov. 1760 he became attorney general for the north shore in the District of Quebec, an office he may have held until his appointment on 20 Nov. 1765 as chief road commissioner for the District of Quebec. He retained that office until 1768.

Cugnet would lose no time, furthermore, in winning the confidence and esteem of Murray's successor as head of the colonial government, Lieutenant Governor Guy Carleton*. His legal knowledge also impressed the new attorney general, Francis Maseres*, who considered him "a very ingenious and able Canadian gentleman . . . well acquainted with the Custom of Paris." Maseres found in Cugnet an associate competent to initiate him into the usages and customs of the Canadians and able to interpret the regulations of the former French administration. Cugnet succeeded in making himself so valued that on 24 Feb. 1768 he was awarded the post of French translator and French secretary to the governor and the Council of Quebec.

Carleton had been ordered by the British government to carry out an inquiry into the state of the laws and the administration of justice in the colony, and he immediately pressed his French secretary into service. At his request Cugnet drew up a brief summary of the "Coutumes et usages anciens De La Province de Quebec," which the governor hastened to send to the secretary of state for the Southern Department, Lord Shelburne, in the spring of 1768. The following year Cugnet prepared an "Extrait des Edits, Déclarations, Règlemens, ordonnances, Provisions et Commisions des Gouverneurs Généraux & Intendants, tirés des Registres du Conseil Supérieur faisant partie de la Legislature En force dans la Colonie du Canada, aujourd'huy Province de Quebec."

But in the mean time a controversy had arisen over Cugnet's summary, which drew criticism from both Attorney General Maseres and Chief Justice William HEY. They considered its form too "concise" and its terminology too "technical" for it to be clearly understood by the law officers of the crown. Governor Carleton therefore decided to call upon other competent people including Abbé Joseph-André-Mathurin JACRAU and Abbé Colomban-Sébastien PRESSART, of the Séminaire de Québec, who undertook a new codification. Their collective work finally resulted in the publication in London in 1772–73 of what was known as the "Extrait des Messieurs," a text in five parts, of which one was none other than the "Extrait des Edits . . ." prepared by Cugnet in 1769. Although he had collaborated in the joint work, Cugnet was nevertheless jealous because the exclusive right to perform the task had been taken away from him. In addition to suffering from hurt pride, he was apprehensive in view of the prevailing uncertainty about the fate Great Britain was holding in store for the long-standing usages and customs of the conquered people. And indeed, until the introduction of the Quebec Act, which was to reassure and calm him, Cugnet worked up a great deal of anxiety and aggressiveness in defence of the old property laws, to which, as a small seigneur, he especially clung.

It was just after the publication of the "Extrait des Messieurs" that the celebrated quarrel occurred between Cugnet and Maseres which, for historian Thomas Chapais*, had the appearance of a struggle in which Cugnet – "this Canadian by heart as well as by birth" – figured as the "national champion" for the defence and preservation of his compatriots' rights. Maseres, the former attorney general, had returned to England after three years in Canada but continued to take an interest in Canadian affairs. Hence in August 1772 he had published in London at his own expense a *Draught of an act of parliament for settling the laws of the province of Quebec*. This draft recommended the adoption of the "Extrait des Messieurs" as the civil code of the province, while making provision for the possible introduction of certain parts of British law. Maseres proposed in particular that the succession laws be modified in a way that he considered "a softening" of the law of primogeniture.

When Cugnet learned of this plan, he was unable to restrain his anger and criticized it in terms Maseres considered "venomous." He protested against adopting the "Extrait des Messieurs" as the only civil code for the province without recourse to various treatises and commentaries of French jurists, and he violently opposed the changes proposed in the succession laws, invoking principles of natural justice to support the method of land partition under the seigneurial system. He declared peremptorily that "if the British government imposed these new [succession] laws on its new subjects without their consent, it would be harsher than the Turkish government." And Cugnet unhesitatingly attempted to prejudice the famous jurist William Blackstone against Maseres, daring to assert that the Canadians had always considered the former attorney general "as their sworn enemy." Intellectually and emotionally a Whig, Maseres was a great admirer and defender of the British constitution and laws quite as much as he was a fierce upholder and zealous adherent of the Protestant faith, and he was deeply offended. In August 1773 he published in London a *Mémoire à la défense d'un plan d'acte de parlement pour l'établissement des loix de la province de Québec* . . . in which he refuted point by point the objections raised by Cugnet. This memoir, largely devoted to the proposed change in the law of primogeniture, sheds some light on Cugnet's fixed views. Having agreed to become a British subject in the hope of keeping "the entire peaceable property and possession" of all his belongings (according to the terms of the articles of capitulation of 1760), Cugnet showed himself determined to resist as best he could the "attempts" to deprive him of them. Judging that the seigneurial system offered him the best guarantee of protection and seeing in every effort at change a danger of encroachment, he worked furiously to defend the cause of the old property laws so as to establish a better claim to the preservation of his rights to his own seigneury of Saint-Étienne. All this controversy between the former attorney general and the governor's French secretary did not prevent Maseres, when called to testify before the House of Commons committee at the time of the debates on the Quebec Bill, from several times naming Cugnet in support of his affirmations.

In the climate of uncertainty prevailing in the colony, only the fear of seeing "the king alter and change at will the former laws of every conquered country" prompted Cugnet to contemplate the creation of a house of assembly composed of the representatives of the seigneurial class, in order to guarantee that the old property laws would not be changed without the consent of those having the greatest interest in their preservation. Feverishly active in the period of unrest that marked the introduction of the Quebec Act, Cugnet busied himself at the end of 1774 with the preparation of a circular letter under the pseudonym "Le Canadien Patriote": his intention was to put his compatriots on guard against the activities and intrigues of British merchants such as Thomas WALKER and Isaac Todd* who "were working" at antagonizing them and making them dissatisfied. "Those people must surely take us to be wonderfully stupid, and totally blind to our own interest, that they venture to request us to join with them in complaining of an act of parliament which . . . grants us every thing we had desired, – the free exercise of our religion, – the use of our ancient laws, – and the extension of the boundaries of our province. . . ." Once the Quebec Act relieved him of his worries, Cugnet showed himself so completely satisfied with it that he opposed any change in the form of government. Like his son Jacques-François, he considered as "madmen" the Canadian "reformers" who after 1783 headed a movement for an appeal to the people with a view to forming a representative government in which laws would be subject "to the whim of an ignorant majority."

While preparing the French translation of the Quebec Act which appeared in the *Quebec Gazette* on 8 Dec. 1774, Cugnet was actively compiling four treatises on French civil law, which were to be the first published in Canada. Governor Carleton himself subsidized their publication, as the accounts of printer William BROWN prove. It was largely through these treatises that Cugnet acquired a degree of fame, and we must be grateful to him for having shown how the customary law of Paris was applied in the colony.

The seigneur of Saint-Étienne could not put aside the convictions, preoccupations, and claims which had led him to regard property law and seigneurial tenure as highly important. He readily assimilated His Britannic Majesty to a sovereign lord to whom his Canadian vassals had to render fealty and homage at his Château Saint-Louis at Quebec. With such a feudal concept of the organization of society in the colony, Cugnet had no difficulty in getting his views endorsed by Governor Carleton. Carleton used many arguments to plead with the authorities in London for the preservation of the seigneurial system, because he saw in it the surest means not only of winning for the British crown the "firm attachment" of the Canadian seigneurs and their *censitaires*, but also of ensuring that order and submission to authority reigned in the colony "from the first to the lowest."

The governor could not haggle over favours of the new régime with so close a collaborator who in his writings supported the British crown's domination over the colony and also favoured consolidation of the power of the colonial authorities. Consequently, after re-establishing the office of clerk of the land rolls in 1777, Sir Guy Carleton appointed none other than his French secretary to it, without much concern for the conflict of interest that might arise in the exercise of the two offices. In effect, as clerk of the land rolls Cugnet had to certify the value of the documents presented by the seigneurs, while as secretary he had to make an inquiry to establish their authenticity. Consequently there is no reason to be surprised that Cugnet endeavoured to take advantage of this situation to assert or to make the most of his own seigneurial rights and those of members of his family, particularly in the case of the mainland seigneury of Mingan. But he had to endure a stinging defeat when he made a vain attempt in 1781 to get his claims and those of five co-seigneurs of Anticosti, the Mingan Islands, and the mainland Mingan seigneury recognized by Governor HALDIMAND and Attorney General James Monk*, since both refused to sign their act of fealty and homage.

One of the last favours Cugnet had been able to obtain from Carleton before he was replaced by Haldimand was a commission as a lawyer; he received it on 1 May 1777, at the same time as his son Jacques-François, who was less than 20 years of age. It constituted official recognition of the title of "lawyer in the *parlement*" that Cugnet had assumed in 1771. In truth, his reputation was so great and his legal opinions so widely sought, that he had acted as a consulting lawyer long before receiving his commission. Governor Haldimand himself, during his noted lawsuit against John Cochrane, made use of an argument put forward by this expert in French law – and in 1783 won his case. Cugnet naturally acquired personal renown as a result.

During the final period of his life Cugnet no longer showed the fighting spirit that had but lately led him to engage so fiercely in the defence of his own and his compatriots' seigneurial rights. Since by virtue of the Quebec Act his title as seigneur of Saint-Étienne was secure, he no longer felt the need to be vindictive. This assurance explains why he did not take a really active part in the struggle of 1784–89 between the partisans of constitutional change and the defenders of the régime set up in 1775. He was content to espouse the cause of the defenders, whose principal spokesmen were drawn from among the seigneurs.

After an exciting and busy public life, Cugnet saw the end of his career darkened by lawsuits and legal proceedings. On 27 Sept. 1783 he initiated an action against his sister's heirs and his mother's executor, Michel-Amable Berthelot* d'Artigny; he contested his mother's will in the hope of obtaining more money from the estate than she had left him. Knowing her eldest son's financial difficulties, she had wanted to protect the share of the capital she intended for her grandsons and to give him only a life interest in it. Dissatisfied, Cugnet even went so far as to lay claim to his father's estate, which circumstances had obliged him to renounce in 1753; he also tried to arrogate to himself the share belonging to his brothers Gilles-Louis and Thomas-Marie, who by that time had died. He came off badly and had to give up all his claims in 1784. In 1786 judge Pierre-Méru Panet* had to settle the litigation over the claims to the seigneury of Saint-Étienne that Cugnet had advanced at the expense of his sister's heirs. In all these actions François-Joseph showed himself a self-seeking haggler, capable of taking advantage of his posts to make the old records say what he wanted.

Financial worries embittered the last years of his life. Up to his ears in debt, Cugnet was unsuccessful in pacifying his most recent creditor, Michel-Eustache-Gaspard-Alain Chartier* de Lotbinière, who sued him on behalf of the estate of Louis-Joseph GODEFROY de Tonnancour. From 1786 to 1789 Cugnet carried on an interesting correspondence with his creditor. He was a lively and prolific writer, and his personal writings are of great value for an understanding of him. This personal correspondence, and, as well, his "Observations succintes" of 1786 concerning the seigneury of Saint-Étienne and all the documents related to his numerous lawsuits, must be examined: in these he shows himself sometimes arrogant, sometimes despairing, but always possessed by the delusions of grandeur that caused his misfortunes and disappointments.

On 29 May 1788 Cugnet had the joy of seeing his son Jacques-François named by Lord Dorchester to the office of joint secretary and joint translator to the governor and Council of Quebec. The first French secretary's succession was assured.

Cugnet passed away at Quebec on 16 Nov. 1789. His funeral was held in the church of Notre-Dame in Quebec, where he had been baptized and where he had been married. The seigneur of Saint-Étienne received the honour of being buried under his pew, in keeping with custom, on 18 November. The Cugnet name was soon to disappear in Canada, since François-Joseph's two sons had no descendants.

PIERRE TOUSIGNANT and MADELEINE DIONNE-TOUSIGNANT

[The four treatises on French civil law prepared by François-Joseph Cugnet were published by William Brown at Quebec in the period from February to May 1775 and bore the following titles: *Traité abrégé des ancienes loix, coutumes et usages de la colonie du Canada . . .* ; *Traité de la loi des fiefs . . .* ; *Traité de la police . . .* ;*Extraits des édits, déclarations, ordonnances et règlemens, de Sa Majesté Très Chrétienne . . . .* These treatises demonstrate that as a pupil Cugnet followed the example of his teacher, Attorney General Louis-Guillaume Verrier, who paid particular attention to the practical aspects of law rather than to its theoretical side. They are the work of an intelligent and opportunistic bureaucrat who knew how to put to use his legal knowledge and the experience acquired in various posts; but we can only regret that Cugnet did not take the trouble to prepare carefully certain of them that seem rather slapdash and superficial. On the other hand, the two manuscripts dealing with municipal law merit close study, including comparison of the 1775 copy with that sent to Blackstone in 1773. It would be interesting to know what importance Cugnet's contemporaries attributed to his writings, but unfortunately the documents of the period say nothing about this. P.T. and M. D.-T.]

AN, Col., B, 72, f.48; C11A, 72, f.228; 75, f.166; E, 101 (dossier Cugnet). ANQ-M, Doc. jud., Cour des plaidoyers communs, Registres, 8 août 1781–11 mai 1785, 1786. ANQ-Q, État civil, Catholiques, Notre-Dame de Québec, 27 juin 1720, 14 févr. 1757, 18 nov. 1789; Greffe de Nicolas Boisseau, 28 août 1742; Greffe de P.-L. Descheneaux, 2–4 sept. 1783, 1er–22 déc. 1785; Greffe de J.-C. Panet, 5 mai 1753; NF 2, 40, f.108; NF 11, 67, ff.67v, 154v, 159; 68, ff.7, 12, 41, 128v; QBC 16, 1, ff.355–61. ASQ, Polygraphie, V; 52a. AUM, P 58, Corr. générale, J.-F. Cugnet à P.-P. Margane de Lavaltrie, 1er févr. 1787. BL, Add. MSS 21719, f.47v; 21873, f.293v; 21883, ff.75–75v. McGill University Libraries, Dept. of Rare Books and Special Coll., MS coll., CH9.S44, CH191.S169, CH243.S221b. PAC, MG 11, [CO 42], Q, 1, pp.186–89; 2, pp.1–2, 104, 111–25; 5, pp.316–22, 432, 477–81, 482–559; 56, pp.352–87; RG 68, 89, ff.113, 175; 90, ff.64, 78; 91, f.207. PRO, CO 42/1, pp.224–360; 42/5, pp.13, 15–17; 42/6, pp.93–94 (copies at PAC). Bégon, "Correspondance" (Bonnault), ANQ *Rapport*, 1934–35, 160. *Coll. des manuscrits de Lévis* (Casgrain), VIII, 169, 180; IX, 94. *Docs. relating to constitutional history, 1759–91* (Shortt and Doughty; 1918), I, 288–91, 299–301. G. B., Parl., *Debates of the House of Commons in the year 1774, on the bill for making more effectual provision for the government of the province of Quebec, drawn up from the notes of Sir Henry Cavendish . . .* (London, 1839; repr. [East Ardsley, Eng.] and [New York], 1966). [Francis Maseres], *An account of the proceedings of the British, and other Protestant inhabitants, of the province of Quebeck in North-America, in order to obtain an house of assembly in that province* (London, 1775); *Additional papers concerning the province of Quebeck: being an appendix to the book entitled, "An account of the proceedings of the British and other Protestant inhabitants of the province of Quebeck in North America, [in] order to obtain a house of assembly in that province"* (London, 1776); *Maseres letters* (Wallace), 99–100, 103; *Things necessary to be settled in the province of Quebec, either by the king's proclamation, or order in council, or by act of parliament* ([London, c.1772]). *Rapports sur les lois de Québec, 1767–1770*, W. P. M. Kennedy et Gustave Lanctot, édit. (Ottawa, 1931), 11.

F.-J. Audet, "Commissions d'avocats de la province de Québec, 1765 à 1849," *BRH*, XXXIX (1933), 578. P.-V. Charland, "Notre-Dame de Québec: le nécrologe de la crypte," *BRH*, XX, 249. P.-G. Roy, *Inv. concessions*, III, 198–99; *Inv. ins. Prév. Québec*, I, 185; III, 127, 130; *Inv. jug. et délib., 1717–60*, V, 279; VI, 32; *Inv. ord. int.*, III, 188; *Inv. procès-verbaux des grands voyers*, I, 176–92; V, 96–141, 158. Brunet, *Les Canadiens après la Conquête* [In this historian's work Cugnet appears as "a precursor of parliamentary democracy in Quebec." Such a portrayal of him can only be understood by making a scenario from historical reality based on fragmentary and abbreviated documentation, and disregarding the profound motivations that led Cugnet to take certain initiatives in the name of the "True Canadian Patriots" before the Quebec Act calmed this seigneur's lively apprehensions. P.T. and M.D.-T.]. Burt, *Old prov. of Que.* Thomas Chapais, *Cours d'histoire du Canada* (8v., Québec et Montréal, 1919–34), I, 126–27. Gonzalve Doutre et Edmond Lareau, *Le droit civil canadien suivant l'ordre établi par les codes . . .* (Montréal, 1872). Adélard Gascon, "L'œuvre de François-Joseph Cugnet; étude historique" (thèse de MA, université d'Ottawa, 1941). Roger Huberdeau, "François-Joseph Cugnet, jurisconsulte canadien; essai historique" (thèse de bio-bibliographie, université de Montréal, 1947). Edmond Lareau, *Histoire du droit canadien depuis les origines de la colonie jusqu'à nos jours* (2v., Montréal, 1888–89). Neatby, *Administration of justice under Quebec Act*. Marine Leland, "François-Joseph Cugnet," *Revue de l'université Laval*, XVI–XXI; "Jean-Baptiste Cugnet, traîte?" *Revue de l'université d'Ottawa*, XXXI (1961), 452–63; "Histoire d'une tradition: 'Jean-Baptiste Cugnet, traître à son roi et à son pays,'" *Revue de l'université d'Ottawa*, XXXI (1961), 479–94 [This series of articles, which deserve to be assembled in one volume, is the fruit of prolonged, patient, and meticulous research. They constitute the only thoroughly researched study so far undertaken of this man, whom the author tracks through an extensive documentation of primary sources drawn from the great collections of historical archives. We can only be grateful to this specialist in French literature for having provided such full documentation, while making no claim to be undertaking a historian's work. P.T. and M.D.T.] André Morel, "La réaction des Canadiens devant l'administration de la justice de 1764 à 1774," *La Revue du Barreau de la prov. de Québec* (Montréal), XX (1960), 53–63. Benoît Robitaille, "Les limites de la terre ferme de Mingan," *BRH*, LXI (1955), 3–15. P.-G. Roy, "Les grands voyers de la Nouvelle-France et leurs successeurs," *Cahiers des Dix*, 8 (1943), 215–17.

CUNY DAUTERIVE (Auterive), PHILIPPE-ANTOINE DE, writer in the Marine and cashier at Montreal for the treasurers general of the Marine and Colonies; b. 9 May 1709 at Langres, France, son of Philippe-Antoine Cuny, *directeur des étapes* in charge of army provisioning in Langres, and Élisabeth Dupont; m. 25 Aug. 1749 at Quebec Madeleine-Thérèse, daughter of Louis-Thomas Chabert* de Joncaire; d. 1 July 1779 in the parish of Saint-Diez, Loches, France.

Philippe-Antoine de Cuny Dauterive arrived in Canada as a secretary with Commandant General La Galissonière [Barrin*] and remained in the Marine bureaux after La Galissonière's departure in 1749. In 1753 he was appointed cashier in Montreal for the treasurers general of the Marine and Colonies under Jacques Imbert*, their agent; Mme de Cuny in 1770 claimed in letters to the French government that her husband had been sent to Montreal even earlier "to keep a closer watch over the administration of the crown's finances in which some embezzlement had already been suspected by Monsieur le comte de la Galissonière. After this general's departure, Sieur Dauterive was obliged to accept the post of [Montreal cashier to the] treasurers on the pretext [that he merited] greater confidence and usefulness, and orders were given for the treasury to remain at the house of the financial commissary [Jean-Victor VARIN de La Marre]." That house was destroyed by fire in 1754 along with the Cunys' own and they lost all their belongings worth, she claimed in 1770, some 300,000 *livres*, including 200,000 *livres*' worth of goods recently imported from France. Various officers in Montreal certified in 1769 that Cuny had sacrificed his own property in order to save property belonging to the crown and he applied for a pension on the strength of this sacrifice.

The loss of imported merchandise in the fire suggests, as was the case, that Cuny had an importing business on the side. We know from the records of a legal case that in 1759 Cuny and an army officer, Laurent-François Lenoir de Rouvray, brother of a Paris notary, received 16 barrels of wine and as many half-barrels of brandy from Bordeaux through the agency of the Quebec firm of François Mounier* and Thomas Lee. These goods had been shipped to Quebec that spring by the Bordeaux firm of Lamaletie, Latuilière et Cie [*see* Jean-André LAMALETIE], which eventually had to go to law to make Cuny and Lenoir pay their bills. By a ruling of 10 July 1760 the *parlement* of Paris ordered them to pay principal and interest totalling 6,000 *livres*.

Some time late in 1758 Cuny suddenly quit his post to return to France and was replaced by Jean-Simon Imbert, nephew of Jacques Imbert. The minister, Berryer, regarded Cuny's hasty departure as a proof of dishonesty, as he remarked in January 1759 in one of his angry letters to the intendant, BIGOT. Whether Cuny made profits in trade or by fraud, he was wealthy enough once back in France to invest in an office of lawyer in the Paris *parlement*, in various annuities on the Hôtel de Ville and the royal tax farms, and in some "inventions and enterprises of Monsieur Darles de Lignières." During the *affaire du Canada* he was arrested along with other officials from Canada, possibly early in 1762 at the same time as his brother-in-law, Daniel-Marie CHABERT de Joncaire de Clausonne, but he was discharged after only a brief imprisonment in the Bastille, perhaps because of some powerful friends, and granted a pension of 300 *livres* on 1 July 1765. Cuny and his wife complained to their friends about the difficulty of living on that pension; it was soon raised to 600 *livres* "and let us hear no more about it," the minister scribbled with the royal "Bon" on a memorandum of 30 June 1768. The Cunys nevertheless did not give up their financial appeals. Meanwhile, to reduce expenses and to be near friends and relations, they went to live at Henrichemont near Bourges, and then in Tours; finally they settled near Loches.

J. F. BOSHER

AN, Col., E, 111 (dossier Dauterive); Minutier central, Minutes Semillard, 21 avril 1763, 11 févr. 1765; Minutes Le Noir, le jeune, 25 oct. 1759; Minutes Prignot de Beauregard, 15 sept. 1761 (all notaries of Paris). *NYCD* (O'Callaghan and Fernow), X, 937–39 (Berryer to Bigot, January 1759).

CURATTEAU, JEAN-BAPTISTE, Sulpician priest; b. 12 June 1729 in Nantes, France, son of Pierre Curatteau, a merchant, and Jeanne Fonteneau; d. 11 Feb. 1790 in Montreal (Que.).

Jean-Baptiste Curatteau came from a lower

middle class background. His oldest brother, Pierre, was captain of a slaver and died in Jamaica, a prisoner of the British, during the Seven Years' War. The second son, Claude, a priest and brilliant teacher, was parish priest of Saint-Pierre in Bouguenais, near Nantes, at the time of his death in 1765. Jean-Baptiste also had two Curatteau half-brothers; René, the elder, went into business, then became a priest, and died a victim of the French revolution. An orphan in 1744, at 15 years of age, Jean-Baptiste made two trips to Guinea. Probably educated at the Collège de l'Oratoire, he was tonsured on 19 Dec. 1750 at the Grand Séminaire des Enfants Nantais, and early in January 1754 he left Nantes to enter the Séminaire de Saint-Sulpice in Paris. Although the family property was heavily mortgaged, he made arrangements for an annuity of 60 *livres* to provide for his entry into the priesthood. He became a member of the community of Saint-Sulpice on 22 March 1754, received minor orders in Paris on 30 March, and left La Rochelle for Canada on 13 May.

After his arrival in Montreal Curatteau assisted in the parish ministry. He completed his theological studies and was ordained priest on 2 Oct. 1757. From that month to March 1764 he continued to serve in Montreal and also taught in the small schools maintained by the Séminaire de Saint-Sulpice.

In March 1764 Curatteau became parish priest of Sainte-Trinité-de-Contrecœur, not an easy post since the building of a much needed presbytery had been prevented for 15 years by a dispute between the parishioners of the seigneury of Contrecœur and those of Saint-Ours. In 1762 Curatteau's predecessor, Amable-Simon Raizenne, had asked Thomas GAGE, the governor of Montreal, for permission to tax the Contrecœur residents for this purpose. On 23 May 1764 Gage's successor, Ralph Burton*, granted this power and Curatteau was able to get the presbytery built. Dissatisfied with the mood pervading the parish, he left it at his own request in September 1765. On 6 November he was appointed missionary priest in Saint-François-d'Assise-de-la-Longue-Pointe, near Montreal, where he laboured for seven years.

By 1766 he had enlarged his presbytery and on 1 June 1767 he opened a secondary school, which later became the Collège de Montréal. At the end of two years the school had two masters and 31 boarders, 16 of whom had begun to study Latin. The school grew and Curatteau added to its property. Governor Guy Carleton* visited the school in 1770 and encouraged him in his work. Curatteau had founded the school without the support of his superior, Étienne MONTGOLFIER, but the institution met a real need. On 26 July 1773 the parish council of Notre-Dame in Montreal purchased the Château de Vaudreuil; on 7 October Curatteau moved his school there, changing its name to the Collège Saint-Raphaël. After repairing and equipping the building at great personal expense, he began courses on 21 October. There were 130 students, including 55 boarders, divided among five classes, as well as five masters and eight domestic servants. British officials had raised objections to moving the school but Bishop BRIAND managed to straighten out the difficulties. The Collège Saint-Raphaël provided a course in Latin and French authors. Curatteau's handwritten rules indicate that the college régime was typical of a *petit séminaire*, educating devout Christians and prospective priests.

In 1764 the Sulpicians constituted the largest religious community for men in Canada and the youngest (in terms of the average age of its members). In time, as a result of death, lack of recruits, and legal difficulties, the surviving Sulpicians entered an era of insecurity. Montgolfier's administration also brought financial problems since he drew heavily on Sulpician funds with what seems excessive generosity. Around 1785 Curatteau and two others urged that the Sulpician property be sold and the proceeds divided amongst the members of the community, but in the end this step was not taken.

Curatteau often alluded to the possibility of returning to France, but the need for priests kept him in Canada. In spite of his commitments at the school, he served as chaplain to the nuns at the Hôtel-Dieu in Montreal from 1783 until his death. His health appears to have deteriorated in 1789, and he announced his resignation as principal of the school in the *Montreal Gazette* on 11 June. On 28 September he left an inventory of his assets with notary Louis Chaboillez*, bequeathing a life interest in them to Jean-Baptiste Marchand*, his successor. Curatteau estimated that they were worth between 35,000 and 40,000 *livres*. When he left the school on 25 Sept. 1789, the churchwardens of the parish council of Notre-Dame in Montreal expressed their appreciation for his work. Curratteau retired to the Séminaire de Saint-Sulpice in Montreal, where he died suddenly on 11 Feb. 1790. He was buried two days later under Notre-Dame church. In his will, drawn up on 29 Jan. 1774, the Collège Saint-Raphaël was named his beneficiary.

Curatteau distinguished himself by his dedication as a priest. He apparently had a rather difficult disposition, which explains why his superiors wanted him to serve outside the confines of the seminary. His work as an educator earned him the admiration of his contemporaries. In 1770 Jean De Lisle* de La Cailleterie had noted, "This kindly man is considered a father to the young, a pillar of education, the epitome of patience, a model of virtue, and a very worthy priest."

J.-BRUNO HAREL

AD, Loire-Atlantique (Nantes), E, 774, 775 (copies at PAC); État civil, Nantes, 12 juin 1729. ANQ-M, État civil, Catholiques, Notre-Dame de Montréal, 13 févr. 1790; Saint-François d'Assise (Longue-Pointe). ASSM, 11; 14; 21; 24. [L.-A. Huguet-Latour], *Annuaire de Ville-Marie; origine, utilité et progrès des institutions catholiques de Montréal* (Montréal, 1863–77). F.-J. Audet, *Contrecœur, famille, seigneurie, paroisse, village* (Montréal, 1940). Olivier Maurault, *Le collège de Montréal, 1767–1967*, Antonio Dansereau, édit. (2e éd., Montréal, 1967); *Saint-François-d'Assise-de-la-Longue-Pointe, abrégé historique* (Montréal, 1924).

CUROT (Curaux), MARIE-LOUISE, *dite* **de Saint-Martin**, hospital nun of the Hôtel-Dieu in Quebec and superior; b. 27 Jan. 1716 in Montreal (Que.), daughter of Martin Curot, a storekeeper at Fort Frontenac (Kingston, Ont.), and Madeleine Cauchois; d. 18 Jan. 1788 at Quebec.

We do not know the circumstances which preceded Marie-Louise Curot's entry into the convent of the Hôtel-Dieu in Quebec. Received into the noviciate on 3 Oct. 1736, she took the veil on 3 April 1737 and made her profession on 9 April of the following year. There is every indication that the Curot family, which included four daughters and three sons, was well educated and quite prosperous. Marie-Louise entered the convent with "her full trousseau" and her father provided 3,225 *livres* "in silver" for her upkeep and dowry.

Marie-Louise de Saint-Martin had the advantage, as a chapter member, of being introduced to the community's affairs under the skilled guidance of Marie-Andrée Regnard* Duplessis, *dite* de Sainte-Hélène, before she assumed the chief administrative responsibilities. Her signature appears first in the "Actes capitulaires" on 2 Sept. 1748, in connection with a grant of land near the fortifications of the intendant's palace. On 12 March 1759 she was elected senior hospital nun. The next year Vicar General Jean-Olivier BRIAND named her depositary for the poor and renewed her appointment in 1761 and 1762. The community's business adviser in Paris, François SORBIER de Villars, mentioned the neatness of her written work and the accuracy of her accounts. The community, taking notice of these skills, on 9 Nov. 1762 elected her superior to succeed Marie-Ursule Chéron, *dite* des Anges, who had died in office. Forty-six years old, Marie-Louise de Saint-Martin became the youngest superior in the country. She was re-elected in 1765 for a second term and later served from 1771 to 1777 and from 1780 to 1786.

During her first 12 years as superior she worked hard to pay off the debt resulting from the rebuilding in 1757 of the convent-hospital, which had burned down in 1755. In 1760 there was still 100,000 *livres* owing. Marie-Louise de Saint-Martin's exceptional ability and her unflagging efforts to restore her community to a sound financial position are clearly revealed in the annals, the deliberations of the chapter, the relations maintained with civil and religious leaders both in the colony and abroad, and above all in her regular correspondence with Sorbier de Villars. The required funds were secured through close attention to collecting rents, the sale of building sites in the town, the development of the seigneuries, the acceptance of boarders, and also through humble labour, such as the laundering of sacramental linen for the parish of Notre-Dame and the making of artificial flowers. In a letter dated March 1778 Sorbier de Villars expressed his pleasure at "the successful discharge" of the debts of the Hôtel-Dieu and praised the "sound administration" of Marie-Louise de Saint-Martin.

From 1759 to 1784 British forces occupied the wards of the Hôtel-Dieu, which became in effect a British military hospital. The sisters rarely served there since the occupation forces took care of their own sick. The alien presence did not, however, disrupt the monastic rule, and the superior's correspondence with Governor MURRAY and with Hector Theophilus CRAMAHÉ suggests that cordiality and mutual respect were maintained between the community and its guests. In the spring of 1784 the troops were installed in barracks and the sisters were able to reopen their hospital, with the help of a public subscription [*see* Thomas-Laurent BÉDARD].

When Marie-Louise de Saint-Martin died on 18 Jan. 1788, the community paid her the following tribute: "a virtuous and very able nun . . . , she was sober, steadfast and gentle, impartial in her treatment of subordinates, discreet, of sound and enlightened judgement, indeed perfectly suited to rule; she has left a void deeply felt by the community which relied on her counsel."

CLAIRE GAGNON

AMHDQ, Actes capitulaires, I; Annales, II; Bienfaiteurs, Papiers Curot; Chroniques, III, 1736; Corr., Évêques, J.-F. Hubert; Corr., Procureurs, B.-L. Villars; Élections triennales et annuelles, I, pp.145–93; Notices biographiques, M.-L. Curot; Registre des comptes du monastère, V, 15–17; Registre des dots, III, 1736. ANQ-M, État civil, Catholiques, Note-Dame de Montréal, 28 janv. 1716; Greffe d'Antoine Adhémar, 21 août 1713. ANQ-Q, NF 11, 62, f.168v; NF 25, 64, no.3904. Tanguay, *Dictionnaire*, III, 209. Casgrain, *Hist. de l'Hôtel-Dieu de Québec*, 437ff. M. Trudel, *L'Église canadienne*, II, 255–87. [On p.263 the author confuses Marie Louise Curot de Saint-Martin with Angélique Viger, who took Saint-Martin as her name in religion. C.G.]

CUTHBERT, JAMES, army officer, merchant, justice of the peace, and legislative councillor; b. *c*. 1719, probably at Farness (Highlands), Scotland, son of Alexander and Beatrix Cuthbert; m. 1749 Margaret Mackenzie; m. secondly 1766 Catherine Cairns, and they had three sons and seven daughters; m. thirdly 23 March 1786 Rebecca Stockton; d. 17 Sept. 1798 at Berthier-en-haut (Berthierville, Que.).

The descendant of an old noble family, James Cuthbert began his career in the Royal Navy. Captain and commanding officer of an independent infantry company by October 1760, he was also a captain in the 101st Foot until December 1762, when he transferred to the 15th Foot. Cuthbert was a member of MURRAY's staff at Quebec; in 1765 he left the army.

The following year, before departing for England, Murray appointed Cuthbert to the Council of Quebec (14 June) and made him a justice of the peace. The new councillor quickly found himself in conflict with Lieutenant Governor Guy Carleton*, Murray's successor. The circumstances of Murray's departure – he had been recalled to England as a result of pressure applied by the colony's merchants – led his supporters to give Carleton a chilly reception. Carleton responded by immediately classing them as an opposition party. Like the other hostile councillors, Cuthbert was severely critical of Carleton when in 1766 the new lieutenant governor, having consulted only part of the council, made a temporary ruling on a dispute over access to the king's posts; the decision was contrary to Murray's policy and favoured his enemy George Allsopp*. In addition, Cuthbert and Murray's other appointees fiercely opposed Carleton when he gave precedence in council to members appointed by the king.

Cuthbert carved out a place for himself in society by becoming a seigneur; on 7 March 1765 he bought the seigneury of Berthier, where he had a manor-house built, and between 1770 and 1781 he acquired Du Sablé, known as Nouvelle-York, and part of Lanoraie, Dautré, and Maskinongé. However, he was severely affected by the American invasion of 1775–76. He alienated his *censitaires* by the authoritarian methods he used to have them perform their military service. In June 1776 the Americans burned his manor-house and did more than £3,000 damage to his property at Berthier, in revenge, according to Cuthbert, for his having saved Lieutenant-Colonel Simon Fraser, 700 to 800 soldiers, and seven British ships at Trois-Rivières. He was, moreover, sent as a prisoner to Albany, New York. After his release, he spent some time in England in 1777 before returning to Canada, probably the following year, to resume his seigneurial activities. He immediately rebuilt the manor-house at Berthier on an imposing scale. In January 1781 he made a 14-year contract to sell all the wheat from his seigneuries to Allsopp.

On his return to Canada, Cuthbert also took his place in the Legislative Council set up by the Quebec Act, to which he had been appointed in 1775. He clashed with Governor HALDIMAND on two issues in particular. First, perhaps because he was himself a justice of the peace, he opposed any decrease in the salaries of government officials, which Haldimand considered too heavy a burden for the people. Then in 1779 and 1780, when prices were sky-rocketing, and according to Haldimand Cuthbert was preparing to plunge into the wheat market, he opposed a freeze on the prices of wheat and flour and the issuance of an edict against the monopoly of certain foodstuffs. When Cuthbert spent the years 1781 to 1784 in England on business, the governor complained of his prolonged absence; in 1786 he was barred from the council and dismissed from his post as justice of the peace, without being given a reason.

Proud of his aristocratic Scottish origins, Cuthbert clung to his seigneurial status. Although often haughty and difficult, he could be generous and affable, and his manor-house at Berthier was known for its hospitality; at the end of the century Prince Edward Augustus* visited weekly. Between 1786 and 1787 Cuthbert, a Presbyterian, built St Andrew's Church at Berthier, probably the first Protestant church erected in the colony. Since his *censitaires* were nearly all Catholic, however, he endeavoured to display a degree of religious tolerance. In 1766 he had participated in the creation of the parish of Saint-Cuthbert by donating 60 *arpents* of land as the site for a church. In 1779 he supplied the stone for building the church and, later, a painting of his patron saint as well as two bells. He also gave land and materials for the construction of the church of Sainte-Geneviève on his seigneury between 1782 and 1787. Nevertheless in 1789 he publicly protested the action of Bishop HUBERT in authorizing the parish priest of Berthier, Abbé Jean-Baptiste-Noël Pouget*, to receive the renunciation of the Presbyterian faith by two of his sons, Alexander and James*. He had sent them, along with their brother Ross*, to study French civil law and language at the English Catholic college of Douai in France, and they had returned determined to convert. Since he was not a Catholic, Cuthbert was unable to take advantage of his seigneurial pew or the precedence due him at religious ceremonies, and so he seized the few occasions that came along to make a public display of his station – for example, the annual May planting and the seigneur's reception of his *censitaires* at the manor-house when they came to pay homage.

Prosperous and distinguished, Cuthbert nevertheless made many enemies and had little political influence, especially from the 1780s on. Since 1763 he had been demanding 3,000 acres of land to the rear of Berthier, on the strength of his captain's rank in the British army at the time of the conquest; it was wasted effort. Moreover, from 1786 he made sustained but unsuccessful protests to the authorities against his exclusion from the Legislative Council and his dismissal as justice of the peace, and for several years vainly sought compensation for the damage his seigneuries had suffered during the American revolution. In 1788 he went to England where he made a fruitless attempt to have himself reinstated in his former positions, and especially to obtain compensation for damage that he claimed had been done to his seigneuries in 1779 by soldiers who had accidentally set fire to 54 acres of valuable white pine while cutting wood for the Quebec citadel. In 1792 he ran as a candidate for the House of Assembly and was defeated by Pierre-Paul Margane* de Lavaltrie in the county of Warwick, where the vast majority of voters were his own *censitaires*. He disputed the election results with the authorities in the colony and in London, but without success. In 1795 he returned to England in a final effort to make good his political claims, to get monetary compensation, and to obtain both a colonelcy in the militia for his seigneuries and a baronetcy in recognition of his activity and his losses during the American revolution. He was repeatedly rebuffed.

Despite these failures Cuthbert remained one of the most prosperous of seigneurs: in 1790 his land yielded £1,700. With the acquisition of Dorvilliers after 1790, his seigneuries stretched about 50 miles along the St Lawrence. He also owned a summer house at Beauport and, in December 1797, he bought properties in Montreal, including a large lot with a stone house at Côteau Saint-Louis. After his sudden death at Berthier in September 1798, his sons divided his landed property among themselves, James, the eldest, inheriting Berthier, Alexander receiving Dorvilliers and the Montreal properties, and Ross inheriting the remainder.

JEAN POIRIER

ANQ-M, Greffe de J.-J. Jorand, 1er mai 1793; Greffe de P.-F. Mézière, 13 oct. 1770; Greffe de Pierre Panet, 7 mars 1765. ANQ-MBF, État civil, Anglicans, Église protestante (Trois-Rivières), 23 mars 1786. Archives civiles, Richelieu (Sorel, Qué.), État civil, Christ Church (Berthierville), 18 Sept. 1798; Greffe de Barthélemy Faribault, 10 Sept. 1771, 13 Sept. 1774, 26 June 1777, 19 Sept., 12 Oct. 1778, 21 March 1786. Archives de la Soc. historique de Joliette (Joliette, Qué.), Cartable famille Cuthbert. Archives de l'évêché de Joliette, Registre des lettres, Cartable Saint-Cuthbert, 1766–94; Cartable Sainte-Geneviève-de-Berthier, 1766–94. McCord Museum (Montreal), Cuthbert-Bostwick papers, 1765–1957. *Doc. relatifs à l'hist. constitutionnelle, 1759–91* (Shortt et Doughty; 1921), I, 167. P.-G. Roy, *Inv. concessions*, I, 165; II, 186; III, 56–57, 87, 92–93; V, 55.

S.-A. Moreau, *Précis de l'histoire de la seigneurie, de la paroisse et du comté de Berthier, P.Q. (Canada)* (Berthierville, 1889). F.-J. Audet, "James Cuthbert de Berthier et sa famille; notes généalogiques et biographiques," RSC *Trans.*, 3rd ser., XXIX (1935), sect.I, 127–51. Du Vern [Richard Lessard], "Le fief Dorvilliers," *L'Écho de Saint-Justin* (Louiseville, Qué.), 24 mars 1938, 1. Édouard Fabre Surveyer, "James Cuthbert, père, et ses biographes," *RHAF*, IV (1950–51), 74–89. D. R. McCord, "An historic Canadian family, the Cuthberts of Berthier," *Dominion Illustrated* (Montreal), VII (1891), 110–12, 123–25. S.-A. Moreau, "L'honorable James Cuthbert, père, seigneur de Berthier," *BRH*, VII (1901), 341–48. Jacques Rainville, "Vers notre tricentenaire," *Le Courrier de Berthier* (Berthierville), 19 janv. 1967, 24 oct. 1968, 12, 26 juin, 3, 14 juill., 4, 18 sept., 2, 16, 30 oct., 13, 27 nov. 1969.

CYRIER. *See* CIRIER

D

DAGNEAU DOUVILLE, ALEXANDRE, officer in the colonial regular troops, interpreter, and fur-trader; b. in April or May 1698 at Sorel (Que.), son of Michel Dagneau Douville and Marie Lamy; d. 1774 at Verchères (Que.).

At the age of 18 Alexandre Dagneau Douville

entered the fur trade, and for the next 15 years, while serving as a cadet in the colonial regulars, he traded heavily among the Miamis, with some side trips to Fort des Sables (Irondequoit, N.Y.), to Baie-des-Puants (Green Bay, Wis.), and to Michilimackinac (Mackinaw City, Mich.). At Montreal on 7 Aug. 1730 he allied himself with an important trading family when he married Marie, daughter of Nicolas-Antoine Coulon* de Villiers Sr. Three years later he was in a confrontation with the Sauks and Foxes near Baie-des-Puants and witnessed the death of his father-in-law and other relatives [*see* Nicolas-Antoine Coulon* de Villiers Jr].

It was intended that Dagneau be promoted second ensign in 1734, but the ministry of Marine confused him with his brother Philippe Dagneau Douville de La Saussaye, and a correct commission was not issued until 1736. In that year Dagneau served as an officer and interpreter at Fort Frontenac (Kingston, Ont.), and in 1739 he was in charge of taking presents to Detroit for the Ottawas. Two years later he was promoted first ensign. After serving again at Fort Frontenac in 1743, Dagneau was sent to Fort des Miamis (probably at or near Fort Wayne, Ind.) in the spring of 1746 to escort Miami representatives to Montreal. The threat of a general Indian uprising in the west [*see* Orontony*] and word of a Mohawk war party at the Niagara portage kept him from bringing the delegation farther than Detroit, and in his absence Miamis pillaged Fort des Miamis. Intendant BIGOT later obtained for him 300 *livres* for the goods he lost.

At a major conference in Quebec in November 1748 Dagneau served as an interpreter between French authorities and some Iroquois chiefs. He became a lieutenant in 1750 and commanded at Sault-Saint-Louis (Caughnawaga, Que.). In June 1754 he replaced Jacques-François Legardeur de Courtemanche in charge of Fort de la Presqu'île (Erie, Pa). This was a key post, the first in a line of forts being built into the Ohio valley by which the French hoped to block British expansion, and Dagneau commanded about 100 regulars and militia. The following year he was replaced by Antoine-Gabriel-François BENOIST. Then on 17 March 1756 he retired as a captain on half pay and thereafter lived on family lands at Verchères. Dagneau's military career had been solid, if undistinguished. He was engaged in no major battles but made his contribution through his familiarity with Indian customs and languages, especially those of the Iroquois and Miamis.

In 1763 Dagneau was one of the 55 accused of misconduct in connection with the *affaire du Canada*. Although summoned to Paris to appear before the Châtelet, he did not go. The court decided to await fuller information about him and the outcome of the case is not certain. Any misconduct was no doubt little different from that of other officers serving on the frontier; their military positions gave them an opportunity to engage in trade, much of it illicit. The Dagneau Douville trade network was one of the most important in New France. Louis-Césaire Dagneau* Douville de Quindre, Guillaume Dagneau Douville de Lamothe, and Philippe Dagneau Douville de La Saussaye were also prominent traders in the west and, like their brother, married into families with similar pursuits.

Alexandre had at least five children, two of whom were killed in the Seven Years' War. A third son, Alexandre-René, spent his career as an officer in the West Indies and at his death in 1789 was a retired lieutenant-colonel of infantry and a knight of the order of Saint-Louis.

DONALD CHAPUT

AN, Col., D^{2C}, 57, p.167; 59, p.63; 61, p.26; E, 103 (dossier Dagneau Douville) (copies at PAC). ANQ-M, État civil, Catholiques, Notre-Dame de Montréal, 16 févr. 1734, 13 sept. 1740, 12 nov. 1744, 15 août 1748. [G.-J. Chaussegros de Léry], "Journal de Joseph-Gaspard Chaussegros de Léry, lieutenant des troupes, 1754–1755," ANQ *Rapport*, 1927–28, 366, 376. "The French regime in Wisconsin – II," ed. R. G. Thwaites, Wis., State Hist. Soc., *Coll.*, XVII (1906), 188–89, 278–87, 432. *NYCD* (O'Callaghan and Fernow), X. PAC *Rapport*, 1904, app.K, 215, 228. *Papiers Contrecœur* (Grenier). Godbout, "Nos ancêtres," ANQ *Rapport*, 1951–53, 466. Massicotte, "Répertoire des engagements pour l'Ouest," ANQ *Rapport*, 1929–30, 218, 245, 257, 298. P.-G. Roy *et al.*, *Inv. greffes not.*, XVI, 99. Tanguay, *Dictionnaire*. [The author is wrong in indicating that Alexandre Dagneau Douville married a second time, to Marie Legardeur de Courtemanche; all of Dagneau's children were from his marriage to Marie Coulon de Villiers in 1730. D.C.] Hunter, *Forts on Pa. frontier*, 70–89, 122–23. Cameron Nish, *Les bourgeois-gentilshommes de la Nouvelle-France, 1729–1748* (Montréal et Paris, 1968), 87, 161–62. P. J. Robinson, *Toronto during the French régime . . .* (2nd ed., Toronto, 1965). P.-G. Roy, *Bigot et sa bande*, 225–26. R. de Hertel, "Michel d'Agneau d'Ouville et sa famille," *Nova Francia* (Paris), IV (1929), 218–19. "Une conférence de M. de la Galissonnière avec les chefs iroquois," *BRH*, XII (1916), 347–49.

DALARD. *See* ALLARD

DANGEAC (Danjaique). *See* ANGEAC

DANKS, BENONI, army officer and office-holder; b. *c.* 1716 in Northampton, Massachusetts, son of Robert Danks and Rebecca

Rust; m. first, 28 Nov. 1745, Mary Morris, and they had three surviving children; m. secondly, before May 1768, Lucy — ; d. 1776 at Windsor, Nova Scotia.

Nothing is known about the career of Benoni Danks before he came to Nova Scotia. He may have participated in the siege of Fort Beauséjour (near Sackville, N.B.) in 1755 and been recruited into the ranger companies by George Scott* in the spring of 1756. The "Company of Rangers commanded by Benoni Danks Esq." was serving in the Chignecto area in 1756, 1757, and 1758 and was active in guerrilla warfare against the French and their Indian allies. An officer skilled in forest fighting, in June 1758 Danks commanded a force of rangers and regulars in a successful action against an enemy raiding party near the present city of Moncton; he returned to Fort Cumberland (formerly Beauséjour) "with all his party, prisoners, and plunder; and had not a man of his whole detachment killed or wounded." Tradition relates that "Capt Danks, who ever rode to the Extreme of his Commission in every barbarous Proceeding," allowed his men to bring in scalps of Acadians, pretending that they were Indian to claim the bounty of £50.

After the capture of Louisbourg, Île Royale (Cape Breton Island), in 1758, Lieutenant-Colonel Robert MONCKTON sent Captain Silvanus Cobb* to Fort Cumberland to bring Danks's rangers to the Saint John River for an expedition against the French settlements. In November Danks's company formed part of George Scott's detachment which raided and burned French villages on the Petitcodiac, and in 1759 it was with James Wolfe*'s forces at the siege of Quebec, providing valuable services in reconnoitering the countryside. Sent with Scott on a mission of destruction along the St Lawrence, the rangers were not present at the battle on the Plains of Abraham.

Danks decided to return to Nova Scotia to settle on former Acadian lands. In 1761 he was granted 25 acres near Fort Cumberland, and five years later he received an additional six shares in Cumberland Township. In September 1761 he was established on his land with seven in his household and 51 head of livestock. He was a member of the committee to admit settlers to the township, and he may have been operating a small store or acting as a sutler to the troops at the fort. Over the years he received large grants of land "for service formerly done by him in a military capacity," including 10,000 acres in the vicinity of Quaco Bay (N.B.).

Danks was present at the siege of Havana in 1762, serving under Joseph GOREHAM; while there he sold his commission in the rangers. On 17 July 1764 Governor Montagu Wilmot* appointed him justice of the peace and major commandant of the militia for Cumberland County. The following year he was appointed lieutenant-colonel commandant and also granted a licence "to Traffick with the Tribe of Argimaux and other Indians inhabiting on the Coast of the Bay of Vert." On 28 May 1765 Danks was listed on the rolls of the Nova Scotia House of Assembly. He represented Cumberland County until 2 April 1770 but was not an active member. His appointment on 30 July 1767 as collector in Cumberland County for duties on wine, beer, rum, tea, coffee, and playing cards appears to have brought him trouble, for on 13 July 1775 the committee of the assembly investigating accounts found that he owed over £87. The difficulties of collection had been increased by the scarcity of cash in the province. In 1770 he had written to the provincial treasurer, Benjamin Green Jr, suggesting that the government accept grindstones, an important item in Nova Scotia's trade with the American colonies, in lieu of money. "I never have taken five Pound in money for the hole year Past," he stated. "I am Bringing Down some fat oxen and horses to Pay the Ballance as their is no money to be had here."

In the early years of the American revolution, Danks was one of the justices of the peace appointed by the governor and Council to administer the oath of allegiance to all persons coming into the province, and he was still in command of the militia in November 1775. He apparently sympathized with the revolution, however, and seems to have participated in the rebellion led by Jonathan Eddy*. He was taken prisoner by Goreham late in 1776 and sent to Halifax. He died on the way at Windsor from the effects of "a spent Ball in his thigh, which he conceal'd until a Mortification ensued."

PHYLLIS R. BLAKELEY

BL, Add. MSS 19071, f.243 (transcript in PANS, RG 1, 363, f.31, p.12). Cumberland County Registry of Deeds (Amherst, N.S.), Book B, pp.37–40. Forbes Library (Northampton, Mass.), J. R. Trumbull, "History of Northampton: Northampton genealogies, v.3, pt.1" (typescript), pp.158, 160. Halifax County Court of Probate (Halifax), D32 (will of Benoni Danks, proved 12 Sept. 1777). PANS, RG 1, 136, pp. 176, 230–31, 246, 257; 164/2, pp.60, 284, 314; 165, p.367; 167, pp.49–50; 204, 3 Aug. 1761; 210, 14 May 1756; 211, 25 July 1764, 8 Aug. 1766; 222, f.4; 286, f.63; RG 37, Halifax County, 21A; MS file, Nova Scotia militia, Danks' Rangers, "Capt. Scott's bill for the rangers of Capt. Danks's company [7 July 1756–4 Aug. 1757]."

Cinco diarios del sitio de La Habana, ed. A. A.

Rodríguez (Havana, 1963), 200. Knox, *Hist. journal* (Doughty). N.S., House of Assembly, *Journal*, 1765–75, especially 28 May 1765; 17 June 1766; 18, 21, 23, 29 July 1767; 24 Oct. 1769; 13 July 1775. PAC, *The Northcliffe collection* . . . (Ottawa, 1926). *Directory of N.S. MLAs*. W. B. Kerr, *The maritime provinces of British North America and the American revolution* (Sackville, N.B., [1941?]; repr. New York, [1970]), 36–39, 69. Murdoch, *History of N.S.* J. C. Webster, *The forts of Chignecto: a study of the eighteenth century conflict between France and Great Britain in Acadia* ([Shediac, N.B.], 1930), 72–78. W. C. Milner, "Records of Chignecto," N.S. Hist. Soc., *Coll.*, XV (1911).

DARBY, NICHOLAS, ship captain and merchant; b. *c.* 1720; m. 4 July 1749 Hatty Vanacott of Bridgwater, England, and they had one son and one daughter; d. 5 Dec. 1785 in Russia.

From an early age Nicholas Darby was engaged in the Newfoundland fishing trade as a ship captain, particularly along the northern coasts of the island. He may have been born in St John's and was certainly living there in 1758, when he joined with other merchants in subscribing for the building of a new church for Edward LANGMAN, the Church of England missionary in St John's. Darby had strong connections with the West Country and probably resided in Bristol during the winter.

Towards the end of the Seven Years' War the British government asked merchants trading to Newfoundland for advice about the future defence of the island. Darby was sent by the Society of Merchant Venturers of Bristol to present its views to the Board of Trade, and he gave a detailed account of French fishing operations on the French Shore north of Cape Bonavista and their trade with the Labrador Inuit. In 1763 Darby himself took part in the fishery north of Cape Bonavista as part-owner of a vessel fitted out from Bristol.

In 1765 Darby embarked on a scheme that, as his daughter later wrote, was "as wild and romantic as it was perilous to hazard": the establishment of seal, salmon, and cod fishing posts on the southern coast of Labrador around the Strait of Belle Isle, territory that had been British only since 1763. With 150 men from England, he made his initial headquarters at Chateau Bay, with which he was familiar.

Darby benefited initially from the policies of Governor Hugh PALLISER. Determined to allow only English-based ship fishers on the Labrador coast, in August 1765 Palliser evicted the agent of the Quebec merchants Daniel Bayne* and William Brymer from their post at Cape Charles. The fishing station was then given to Darby, who made it his headquarters and constructed lodgings, a workshop, and a fishing stage. He also established fishing crews at other likely places in the region, such as Forteau and Île aux Bois (Que.).

Although Darby found the Labrador fisheries extremely productive, he soon encountered difficulties. His men refused to winter on the coast, and pillaging Inuit burnt houses and boats and destroyed his salt. Undaunted, he formed a partnership with Michael Miller, a Bristol merchant, and sailed to Labrador in the summer of 1766 with 180 men and ships and equipment worth over £8,000. Palliser built and garrisoned a blockhouse known as York Fort at Chateau Bay for his protection, and some of Darby's men agreed to stay the winter. But he and his crews lacked the experience and technical knowledge necessary for successful sealing and found, as the Quebec merchants had before them, that experienced Canadians and permanent possession of the sealing places were required. In spite of financial losses, Darby was able to bring out 160 men in 1767, but he had difficulty controlling unruly crews and began to run foul of the authorities. In August, for instance, Palliser ordered the arrest of ten of his men on murder charges arising from fights at the posts.

The Cape Charles fishery ended abruptly in November 1767 when a band of Inuit, apparently seeking revenge for depredations by New England whalers, attacked a crew preparing for winter sealing. They killed three men, drove the rest off, stole some boats, and burnt vessels and equipment worth more than £4,000 [*see* Francis Lucas*]. Darby's losses resulted in the dissolution of his partnership with Miller and in the scattering of his family. The house in Bristol had to be sold and the family moved to London. The children were placed in boarding schools, and without his knowledge Darby's wife started a small school to earn money, which hurt and offended the proud man. He repeatedly petitioned the Privy Council for compensation, but without result.

By 1769, however, Darby was zealously promoting yet another scheme for exploiting the Labrador fisheries, and with the help of friends he was able to fit out a vessel from London. This time he hired four experienced Canadians for help in the winter fishery. It was a great success, and by the summer of 1770 Darby had seal oil and skins worth almost £1,000 ready for market. On 11 August, however, Lieutenant Samuel Davys of York Fort arrived at Darby's post at Forteau and seized all his goods and equipment on the grounds that he was illegally employing Frenchmen and using French-built equipment. George Cartwright*, who had taken over Darby's old post at Cape Charles, supplied Davys with a vessel to convey the confiscated goods and the four Canadians to St John's.

In late October the Canadians appeared before Governor John BYRON. Darby, marooned on the Labrador coast, was unable to defend himself, and the oil and sealskins were confiscated. Just as Bayne and Brymer had been evicted in 1765 in his favour, so Darby was in turn displaced, the fruits of his labour falling to officials such as Davys and traders now in official favour such as Cartwright. Eventually arriving back in England, Darby asked the Board of Trade for compensation; he claimed he did not know that his Canadians were French subjects "as has been pretended." The board decided, however, that it had no jurisdiction in the case. The Court of King's Bench awarded him £650 damages against Davys, an inadequate sum and in any case uncollectable.

Darby may have visited the Labrador coast after 1770; little is known of his later years. His daughter Mary, as the famous Perdita, swept the London stage and was briefly the mistress of the Prince of Wales. Contracting rheumatic fever at 24, she became an invalid and supported herself by writing poems and stories. According to her *Memoirs*, Darby commanded a small armed ship during the American revolution and later, at the age of 62, entered the Russian navy, dying three years later.

An able and courageous seaman, Darby was a pioneer in the attempt to establish a year-round fishery on the Labrador coast. However, his poor relations with the Inuit and his lack of technical knowledge of the winter fishery inevitably brought conflict and ruin. Later entrepreneurs were able to avoid these pitfalls at least in part: Cartwright, for example, gained the trust of the Inuit. It is only fair to add that in the 1770s British officialdom relaxed its tight hold over the Labrador fisheries, allowing traders to operate more freely and permitting them greater proprietary rights in their posts.

WILLIAM H. WHITELEY

BL, Add. MSS 35915, ff.92–93. PANL, GN2/2, 20 Sept. 1763, 9, 15 Aug. 1767, 2 Oct. 1770. PRO, CO 194/15, ff.45–46; 194/16; 194/18, ff.82–84; 391/69, ff.310–11; 391/71; 391/78; 391/79; PC 2/113, ff.467, 576. Soc. of Merchant Venturers (Bristol, Eng.), Letterbooks and books of proceedings, 1762–63. George Cartwright, *A journal of transactions and events, during a residence of nearly sixteen years on the coast of Labrador . . .* (3v., Newark, Eng., 1792). Mary [Darby] Robinson, *Memoirs of the late Mrs. Robinson, written by herself*, ed. M. E. Robinson (4v., London, 1801), I, 18; II, 22. W. G. Gosling, *Labrador: its discovery, exploration, and development* (2nd ed., London, 1910). A. M. Lysaght, *Joseph Banks in Newfoundland and Labrador, 1766: his diary, manuscripts and collections* (London and Berkeley, Calif., 1971).

DAUTERIVE, PHILIPPE-ANTOINE DE CUNY. *See* CUNY

DAVIDSON, WILLIAM (John Godsman), lumber merchant, shipbuilder, and office-holder; b. John Godsman *c.* 1740, at Cowford, parish of Bellie (Grampian), Scotland, son of William Godsman and a daughter of William Davidson; m. Sarah, daughter of Phineas Nevers, probably at Maugerville (N.B.) some time between 1777 and 1779, and they had five children; d. 17 June 1790 at Miramichi, New Brunswick.

As a young man, John Godsman was engaged in the salmon fishery in Scotland. In 1765 he immigrated to Nova Scotia with the idea of establishing a fishery on some river in that colony. He arrived in Halifax, assumed the name of William Davidson, and formed a partnership with John Cort, a native of Aberdeenshire, about whom little else is known. Davidson became the dominant member of the partnership. The two men visited the Miramichi in the summer of 1765 and on their return to Halifax applied for and received a grant of 100,000 acres (two-thirds to Davidson and one-third to Cort). The concession, which included land originally part of the seigneury of Richard Denys* de Fronsac, extended 13 miles on either side of the Miramichi River and conveyed rights to the fishery and the timber, including white pine. Davidson and Cort were required to clear and improve the land and to establish one Protestant settler for every two acres. Since they were primarily interested in the fishery, these stipulations were to cause trouble later.

Davidson was a capable man and he made considerable progress in the next ten years in spite of a number of setbacks. After receiving the grant he travelled to New England to secure men and supplies and in the spring of 1766 arrived at Miramichi with about 25 men. In the following years more settlers and labourers were brought from New England and Britain. Davidson was soon shipping fish and furs to the West Indies and Europe. Most of the work in the fishery ceased in the winter, however, and the men were usually idle for several months. In order to provide year-round employment, Davidson, who had quickly realized the potential of the fine stands of pine on the river, had the men employed cutting timber. In 1773 he brought out a master-builder, shipwrights, and other craftsmen from Britain and began the construction of the first ship ever built on the river, the schooner *Miramichi*. She was lost off the coast of Spain on her maiden voyage, and a second vessel, launched in 1775, was wrecked off the northern tip of St John's (Prince Edward) Island. Other cargoes reached Europe safely, but the American revolution was to curtail Davidson's shipping activities.

At the outbreak of the war Davidson entered into a contract with a British firm, which guaranteed markets for his fish and timber for seven years. However, all shipping activities in North American waters became risky because of American privateers. Moreover, rebel sympathizers such as John Allan* stirred up the Indians, and the settlers at Miramichi were raided on several occasions. When the firm buying his timber and fish closed its business in North America, Davidson was left with tons of wood and no market for it. By 1777 he had become discouraged and in November moved inland to Maugerville. He took most of his workers with him, leaving John Cort behind to look after their interests at Miramichi. Some time during the war Cort died.

In 1779 Davidson visited Lieutenant Governor Richard Hughes* in Halifax and proposed a scheme whereby he would deliver masts and yards, trimmed and ready for shipping, to the mouth of the Saint John River. Davidson's proposal was encouraged but he received no financial support because rebel activities in the area made the venture risky. However, that November Michael FRANCKLIN, the superintendent of Indian affairs, wrote to Pierre TOMAH, an influential Malecite chief, requesting that the Indians protect Davidson from rebel attack. As well, he gave Davidson letters for the magistrates and settlers on the river asking them to assist and protect the project. With this support Davidson decided to take the risk and thereby began the timber industry of the Saint John. He was so successful that he soon attracted competitors, chief among them William Hazen* and James White, who had been established in a trading partnership at the mouth of the river since 1765. Davidson soon had a large section of the population in the Maugerville area employed in the woods. With their support he was elected in 1783 a member for Sunbury County in the Nova Scotia House of Assembly.

As the war drew to a close, Davidson, apparently because of the competition on the Saint John River, decided to return to the Miramichi. He must have known that large numbers of refugee loyalists would soon be arriving to demand grants on the Saint John, and he certainly hoped to exploit the valuable timber that covered much of his own grant on the Miramichi. Most of the men who had come to Maugerville with him agreed to go back, and in May 1783 he purchased two vessels in Halifax, loaded them with provisions, and set out to re-establish his business. When he arrived at Miramichi, he discovered that all his buildings and fishing craft had been destroyed by the Indians. Re-establishing proved to be an expensive undertaking. He furnished provisions and supplies to the settlers on credit and expended some £5,000 in building stores, a shipyard, and a sawmill. He was soon shipping fish, furs, and lumber, and between the years 1783 and 1785 he built three vessels. He also pursued his masting operations on the Saint John through agents there. Bad luck continued to plague Davidson, who lost several vessels and cargoes during the period 1783–85. As before, he encouraged settlement but brought out only craftsmen who could be employed in the fishery or the shipyard and mill until they established themselves on the land. He also tried to expand his business by sending vessels out of the river to fish for cod.

In 1785 Davidson faced a new problem. The British government, looking for homes for the thousands of loyalists who had come to Nova Scotia and the new colony of New Brunswick, was no longer eager to make large grants like that given to Davidson and Cort in 1765. It also began to escheat those holdings which had not been improved. Davidson asked for two years to fulfil the conditions of his grant, but his request was turned down. An investigation found that only 30 settlers had actually been established on the land. Davidson's workers, who numbered about 50, were not counted since they owned no property. His grant was therefore escheated, and he was given a smaller one of 14,540 acres which included his improvements, stores, shipyard, and mill site.

By 1785 the organization of the new colony of New Brunswick had begun and Davidson became one of the first justices of the peace for Northumberland County. That year, in New Brunswick's first election, Davidson and Elias HARDY, a Saint John lawyer, were elected as the county's representatives in the provincial assembly. Davidson, the only local candidate, had supported Hardy against two government candidates. He had no love for the loyalist hierarchy, responsible for the escheat of his old grant, or for the government it dominated. Hardy was its leading opponent in Saint John, and it was to be expected that Davidson, opposed to its attempts to extend its influence into Northumberland

County, would assist him. Benjamin MARSTON, the county sheriff, had tried to secure the election of the government candidates, and he referred to Davidson as "an ignorant, cunning fellow . . . who has great influence over the people here, many of them holding land under him, & many others being tradesmen & laborers in his employ."

Even after losing much of his land, Davidson continued to bring out settlers; 11 lots were sold between 1785 and 1787. He borrowed large sums of money in Halifax and mortgaged his property to expand his business. He also made several contracts with William Forsyth* and Company of Greenock, Scotland, and Halifax, including one in 1789 to supply the company with masts and yards for the British navy. He had markets for his fish in Europe and the West Indies and, by 1789, three sawmills in operation with contracts for all the lumber he could produce. But bad luck continued to haunt him. In February 1790, while travelling up the river on snowshoes, he was caught in a severe storm and had to seek shelter in a haystack. He nearly froze to death and never recovered from the cold he caught. He died four months later at the age of 50.

Davidson was a man of vision and great energy. He founded the first English speaking settlement in northern New Brunswick, developed the fishing industry far beyond that begun earlier by the Acadians, and was the principal founder of the lumber industry on the Miramichi and Saint John rivers.

W. A. SPRAY

N.B. Museum (Saint John), Davidson family, papers, 1765–1955. Northumberland County Registry Office (Newcastle, N.B.), Registry books, 1, 2. PANB, "New Brunswick political biography," comp. J. C. and H. B. Graves (11v., typescript), XI, 28–29; RG 4, RS24, S1-P9, petition of William Davidson, 28 Feb. 1786; RG 10, RS108, Land petitions, series I, Northumberland County, nos.57, 70, 75; RG 18, RS153, Minutes of the Court of Quarter Sessions, 1789–1807. University of N.B. Library, Archives and Special Coll. Dept. (Fredericton), Winslow papers, 20, 21, 22; Benjamin Marston, Diary, 1776–87. [Patrick Campbell], *Travels in the interior inhabited parts of North America in the years 1791 and 1792*, ed. H. H. Langton and W. F. Ganong (Toronto, 1937), 63. "Historical-geographical documents relating to New Brunswick," ed. W. F. Ganong, N.B. Hist. Soc., *Coll.*, III (1907–14), no.9, 308–41. "The James White papers," ed. W. O. Raymond, N.B. Hist. Soc., *Coll.*, II (1899–1905), no.4, 30–72. PAC *Report*, 1894, 265, 313. *Winslow papers, A.D. 1776–1826*, ed. W. O. Raymond (Saint John, N.B., 1901), 298–310. *Royal Gazette and the New Brunswick Advertiser* (Saint John), 22 Aug. 1786.

W. H. Davidson, *An account of the life of William Davidson, otherwise John Godsman, of Banffshire and Aberdeenshire in Scotland and Miramichi in British North America* (Saint John, N.B., 1947). James Hannay, *History of New Brunswick* (2v., Saint John, N.B., 1909), I, 70. MacNutt, *New Brunswick*, 9, 62–63. Louise Manny, *Ships of Miramichi; a history of shipbuilding on the Miramichi River, New Brunswick, Canada, 1773–1919* (Saint John, N.B., 1960). Raymond, *River St. John* (1910), 304–12. E. C. Wright, *The Miramichi* . . . (Sackville, N.B., 1944). W. O. Raymond, "The north shore; incidents in the early history of eastern and northern New Brunswick," N.B. Hist. Soc., *Coll.*, II (1899–1905), no.4, 93–125.

DAVISON (Davidson), GEORGE, entrepreneur, officer-holder, and agriculturist; son of Alexander Davison, a prosperous farmer, and Dorothy Neal, of Kirknewton parish, Northumberland, England; d. 21 Feb. 1799 in London.

George Davison first came to Canada about 1773, and by the early 1780s he had accumulated an extensive tract of land in the seigneury of Rivière-du-Loup, near Trois-Rivières, largely as a result of the business dealings of his older brother, Alexander*. A justice of the peace in 1780, Davison was appointed to the Legislative Council in 1783 as a protégé of Governor HALDIMAND, who was, along with the Duke of Northumberland and Evan Nepean, under-secretary of state for the Home Department, his most important political friend. He was frequently absent from council meetings and made few important contributions to those he attended, but he generally voted with the French party through loyalty to his patron and in line with his own deeply conservative outlook. He opposed the introduction of jury trial, favoured by Lieutenant Governor Henry HAMILTON and his supporters, on the grounds that "in all small communities as well as in this there must necessarily be a degree of connection or dependance thro' Interest, alliance or friendship, which argues strongly against the Impartiality of the Trial by Jury."

During his stay in Canada Davison accumulated a sizeable fortune, largely through government patronage and by deals in which his brother Alexander took the initiative and the risk. In 1786 the two brothers, in partnership with François Baby*, obtained a lease of the king's posts for 16 years. They thereby acquired a monopoly on the fur trade and fisheries on the north shore of the lower St Lawrence, one of the choicest morsels of government patronage available since it demanded almost no risk or managerial skill on the part of the lessees and produced at least £2,500 per annum. This lease had been held by William Grant* and Thomas Dunn*, political allies in the

English party of Lieutenant Governor Hamilton, who had in 1785 caused a scandal by renewing it for them although it was widely known that he would shortly receive orders from London to award the lease to the Davisons. The brothers had their triumph in 1786, despite the replacement of their friend Haldimand by the unsympathetic Lord Dorchester [Carleton*].

George was in London in 1787 when Sir Thomas MILLS, the receiver general, appointed him his deputy for a term of five years. The position promised to be lucrative and he rushed back to Quebec in August. He was disappointed, however, for a financially embarrassed Sir Thomas dismissed him within two months. Sir Thomas was himself soon ousted, but the support of Lord Lovaine, a relative of the Duke of Northumberland, did not secure the position of receiver general for Davison. In partnership with David Monro* and Mathew Bell*, Davison obtained the lease of the Saint-Maurice ironworks from his brother in 1793. These crown-owned ironworks proved highly profitable under the management of Bell, who took care of most of Davison's Canadian affairs.

In 1791 Davison returned to England and remained in London until his death except for one short visit to Lower Canada. However, he continued to derive revenue from Canada and to interest himself in Canadian affairs. His brother was supply agent to the British forces in North America and George assisted him, partly by carrying on a correspondence with Governor Simcoe* of Upper Canada. While Alexander's attentions were totally occupied by the Continental wars and the enormous fortunes to be made by military suppliers, the younger brother took full charge of the Canadian market, obtaining in 1794 a contract to supply 855,012 pounds of flour and 6,000 bushels of peas to His Majesty's forces. These purchases were actually made by his agents in Canada and earned for Davison a five per cent commission.

Throughout the last 20 years of his life George Davison was chronically ill; he had had to excuse his frequent trips to England from Canada on the grounds of poor health. However, he was always ready to return when a profitable situation presented itself. Between 1788 and 1793 he crossed the Atlantic no fewer than eight times, and he quit the province for good only when a realignment of political forces lessened the influence of his protectors. Davison's career, then, was not that of a man firmly attached to Canada.

Although business and politics occupied a great deal of Davison's time, especially in the later years of his life, he was always much more interested in agriculture. His favourite residence in the 1780s was the 400-acre Lanton Farm, near Saint-Antoine-de-Padoue, Rivière-du-Loup (Louiseville), where he maintained a large household. He considered himself an agricultural innovator and a model for his Canadian neighbours. His farms were run by English managers who made use of some of the latest British and Continental improvements. Lanton had a threshing machine (then still a novelty in parts of England) and apparently produced an exceptionally high yield of good quality wheat. Davison also owned or leased at least three mills, one of them quite substantial, in Saint-Antoine-de-Padoue and Sainte-Anne-d'Yamachiche (Yamachiche) as well as a great many *censives* scattered throughout the area.

Davison's interest in agriculture was not limited to that practised on his own estates. He was chairman of a committee of the Legislative Council concerned with the cultivation of hemp. Furthermore, when the Quebec Agricultural Society was formed in 1789, he was elected to the board of directors and was by far the most active member during the first few months of the society's existence. He arranged for seed grain to be sent from abroad and agreed to have certain experiments with wheat performed on his lands. Within a year, however, his interest waned and the society later declined in importance. Still, it is in the realm of agriculture more than in other areas that George Davison appears as an independent and public-spirited citizen.

ALLAN GREER

[Two short biographical articles on George Davison have been published. Both are confused and riddled with errors: Turcotte, *Le Cons. législatif*, 43–44; Charles Drisard, "L'honorable Georges Davidson," *L'Écho de Saint-Justin* (Louiseville, Qué.), 7 juin 1934, 1. A.G.]

Information on George Davison's life was found scattered throughout a number of primary sources, most of them manuscripts: ANQ-MBF, Greffe de Joseph Badeaux, 8 janv. 1800; Greffe de Benoit Le Roy, 17 sept. 1791, 12 oct. 1793. ANQ-Q, AP-G-323. BL, Add. MSS 21715, 17 July 1782; 21717, 12 June 1783; 21718, 25 Oct. 1784; 21723, 4 March 1783; 21727, 16 July 1782; 21735/2, 1 March 1784 (copies at PAC). PAC, MG 11, [CO 42], Q, 25, pp.246–94; 49, pp.36–41; 74/2, pp.291–305; MG 23, HI, 1, ser.3, 2, p.63; 3, pp.206–7, 220–21, 234, 275–76, 284–86; 4, pp.105–6, 281–83; 5, pp.3–5, 139–40; RG 14, A1, 2–8. [Joseph Hadfield], *An Englishman in America, 1785, being the diary of Joseph Hadfield*, ed. D. S. Robertson (Toronto, 1933), 163–64. [Robert Hunter], *Quebec to Carolina in 1785–1786; being the travel diary and observations of Robert Hunter, Jr., a young merchant of London*, ed. L. B. Wright and Marion Tinling (San Marino, Calif., 1943),

27–28. PAC *Rapport*, 1889. *Quebec Gazette*, 5 June, 18 Dec. 1783, 27 Oct. 1785, 30 Aug., 6 Sept. 1787, 11 Dec. 1788, 23 April 1789, 25 March 1790, 5 May, 20 Oct. 1791, 11 July 1793, 11 June 1795, 2 Aug. 1798, 21 Aug., 4 Dec. 1800, 25 Aug. 1803.

DAY, JOHN, naval surgeon, merchant, and office-holder; son of Dr George Day and his first wife; d. November 1775 at sea.

John Day must have been in Nova Scotia as early as 1755, since on 2 October a marriage licence was issued to the bachelor Day and Sarah Mercer, a widow. She died in 1763 and that same year Day married Henrietta Maria Cottnam. At least four children were born of the second marriage. Between 1757 and 1765 Day was involved in several careers; in the late 1750s his name appears in land transactions in Halifax County as a naval surgeon and a merchant, and from approximately 1762 to 1765 he was a merchant at Halifax in partnership with Edward Vause. In 1764 he was appointed a justice of the peace in Kings County, where he leased lands, and the following year he moved from Halifax to the Mantua Estate, a property near Newport which he had purchased. In 1765 also he was elected to the House of Assembly as the first representative for Newport Township. Although Day, like so many non-Halifax members, was irregular in his attendance, he was a dominant figure when present, becoming the most active and influential of the members who supported the township and reform interests. This group demanded a greater share for the townships in local and central government, the reform of the provincial treasury, and more efficient methods of collecting revenue. In 1765 and 1766 Day, by his strength of personality and involvement in committee work, played a leading part in the assembly's temporary achievement of the right to approve the provincial estimates. In the summer of 1766 he was one of a committee appointed to examine the accounts of Benjamin GREEN, the provincial treasurer; their report explicitly connected the growing provincial debt with Green's neglect of correct procedure.

In March 1769 Day left the province and took up residence in Philadelphia as a druggist. Returning four years later, he resumed his mercantile activities. In 1775 he was in partnership with Joseph SCOTT, an association that may have been formed before his departure. In August 1774 he announced his candidacy for the assembly for the town of Halifax and was elected by "a great majority." As before, the most contentious issues in the assembly were the control of the estimates and past unauthorized expenditures. In Day's view, the Council, "a Junta of cunning and wicked Men," had consistently thwarted the assembly's attempts to improve Nova Scotia's financial status, since their views "extend no further than their own private Emolument, and [they] further the Distresses of the Community in order to produce a slavish Dependance on themselves." Appointed to a committee which was to audit and report on the provincial accounts, he assisted in its main work, which resulted in the condemnation of such defaulters as Jonathan Binney*, George Cottnam, and John Newton. He resigned in April 1775 for unknown reasons.

Day was also prominent in the stormy legislative session of 1775. Adept in political debate, he initiated the assembly's famous loyal address to the crown, which delicately enumerated that body's grievances but took pains not to prejudice the parliamentary grant on which the province depended. In addition, he succeeded in having passed several bills which were largely his own work: among these were measures for reform in the statement and examination of public accounts and the proper regulation of elections.

In November 1775 Day, who was also an agent victualler to the British army, left for Boston on board a vessel loaded with supplies for the garrison there. While engaged in this endeavour, he was lost at sea. Unlike many of his colleagues, Day was apparently both a loyalist and a critic of the oligarchical system prevailing in Nova Scotia. At times his independence from faction mystified both his allies and his opponents; John BUTLER declared in 1775 that he had "Perplext the House." Day's importance is perhaps best described by John Bartlet Brebner*, who wrote that his "distinguished public career made him the leading, perhaps the only, independent, public-spirited statesman in Nova Scotia."

WENDY L. THORPE

John Day is thought to be the author of *An essay on the present state of the province of Nova-Scotia . . .* ([Halifax, 1774?]).

Halifax County Court of Probate (Halifax), D26 (original estate papers of John Day). Halifax County Registry of Deeds (Halifax), 3, pp.55–56; 4, pp.21, 103; 5, pp.84–85; 10, pp.25, 201. Hants County Registry of Deeds (Windsor, N.S.), Deeds, 1765–68 (mfm. at PANS). Kings County Registry of Deeds (Kentville, N.S.), 7, p.126 (mfm. at PANS). PANS, RG 1, 163, p.64; 164, pp.177, 184, 196, 242, 274, 324; 168, p.102; RG 20, A, 3A; 33. *Halifax Gazette*, 9 Dec. 1758. *Nova-Scotia Gazette and the Weekly Chronicle* (Halifax), 16, 30 Aug., 6 Sept. 1774; 28 May, 17 Sept. 1776. J. B. Brebner, *Neutral Yankees* (1969), 182–83, 199, 215, 264; "Nova Scotia's remedy for the American revolution," *CHR*, XV (1934), 171–81.

DÉCHAMBAULT (D'echambault). *See* FLEURY

DECOSTE, JEAN-BAPTISTE (sometimes called **Sieur de Letancour**), court officer; b. in 1703 in Paris, France, son of Louis Decoste and Catherine Coré; d. 26 Feb. 1778 at Pointe-Claire (Que.).

Nothing is known about Jean-Baptiste Decoste's arrival in New France. On 18 Aug. 1725, in Montreal, he married Marie-Renée, the under-age daughter of Nicolas Marchand, a tailor. Although he was only 22, he seems to have been sufficiently wealthy for the notary to set the jointure at 6,000 *livres*. Apparently his principal sources of income were not in the colony, however, since in the marriage contract Nicolas Marchand agreed to lodge the couple in his house once they were wed and to "heat and keep" them for two years. Marchand also gave his daughter a piece of land on Rue Saint-Paul, next to the family home.

Around 1730 Decoste served as captain of the guards of the Domaine d'Occident. In this capacity he worked to prevent fraud in import and export duties on a certain number of products. He also helped his father-in-law, who since September 1727 had been a court officer in the royal jurisdiction of Montreal, acting either as a witness for him or as an appraiser. Because Decoste was also a legal practitioner and attorney, he knew the ways and customs of the lawcourts and judicial procedure. Hence on 22 Nov. 1731 Intendant HOCQUART granted him a commission as court officer for the entire royal jurisdiction of Montreal. After passing the investigation into his character, on 3 Jan. 1732 he entered upon his duties. Six months later, on 23 July, he was appointed court crier for the royal jurisdiction of Montreal, with the duty of attending court sittings and seeing that the silence and respect befitting the court room were maintained. He held this office until 1757, when he was replaced by court officer Nicolas-François Robert. In the mean time, on 8 July 1743, Decoste had succeeded Jean-Baptiste Adhémar* as court officer of the Conseil Supérieur for Montreal; in this capacity he had to carry out in the Government of Montreal all the "decrees, judgements, and other acts" emanating from the council. In 1746 François Dumergue came from Quebec to replace him in this post.

Jean-Baptiste Decoste's eldest son, Jean-Christophe, was to follow him in court service. Born in Montreal on 14 Aug. 1726, he had received early the rudiments of religion and reading from a lay school-teacher, Louis Fourier. His father then introduced him to the work of a court officer, and on 9 Feb. 1751, when he was 24, he was appointed a royal notary in the jurisdiction of Montreal. Since his commission does not seem to have been registered in Montreal and there is no trace of a Decoste notarial registry, it may be assumed that he never practised as a notary. Two years later, on 3 March 1753, he became a "process server," and continued in this occupation until the conquest. But although his honesty and his assiduity in taking the sacrament had been extolled by witnesses at the investigation into his character, it seems that Jean-Christophe began to lead a dissolute life, despite the indignation and constant remonstrances of his parents. He paid no heed and married a widow of no means and little repute, Marie-Joseph Dumouchel. The marriage further displeased his parents, and by an act drawn up before notary Gervais Hodiesne* on 22 Nov. 1757 they disinherited their son, thus banishing him from the family. Jean-Christophe died on 18 Nov. 1767; a few days earlier he wrote that "he has no reason to be content with the way he has been treated by his brothers and sisters, who on different occasions have insulted him in public."

ANDRÉ LACHANCE

ANQ-M, Doc. jud., Pièces détachées, 7 mars, 25, 27 avril, 3, 4 mai, 6 juin, 19, 27, 30 juill., 17 sept., 30 déc. 1731, 2, 3, 5 janv. 1732, 10, 13, 15 mars 1753, 5 janv., 27 mars 1759; État civil, Catholiques, Notre-Dame de Montréal, 18 août 1725, 15 août 1726, 18 févr., 2 mars 1728, 15 mars, 29 juill. 1729, 21 nov. 1757, 19 nov. 1767; Saint-Joachim (Pointe-Claire), 28 févr. 1778; Greffe de L.-L. Aumasson de Courville, 5 nov. 1767; Greffe de Gervais Hodiesne, 22 nov. 1757; Greffe de F.-L. Lepallieur de Laferté, 23 nov. 1738; Greffe de M.-L. Lepallieur de Laferté, 16 août 1725; Greffe de Pierre Panet, 18, 19 nov. 1757; Greffe d'André Souste, 17 sept. 1754. C.-J. Ferrière, *Dictionnaire de droit et de pratique, contenant l'explication des termes de droit, d'ordonnances, de coutumes et de pratique* (3e éd., 2v., Paris, 1749). É.-Z. Massicotte, "Les tribunaux et les officiers de justice, à Montréal, sous le Régime français, 1648–1760," RSC *Trans.*, 3rd ser., X (1916), sect.I, 291, 293. P.-G. Roy, *Inv. ord. int.*, II, 108, 126–27, 272; III, 43, 154–55, 205. Tanguay, *Dictionnaire*, III, 269. Vachon, "Inv. critique des notaires royaux," *RHAF*, XI, 105.

DEGEAY, JACQUES, Sulpician and parish priest; b. 31 March 1717 in the parish of Saint-Nizier, Lyons, France, son of Henri Degeay and Marie Bournicat; d. 6 Aug. 1774 in Montreal (Que.).

In February 1740 Jacques Degeay, who had already received the tonsure, entered the Séminaire de Saint-Irénée in Lyons, which was directed by the Sulpicians. His teachers considered him both innocent and somewhat stubborn. These traits, which were demonstrated throughout his life, probably explain why in January 1742 the council of the Society of Saint-Sulpice in Paris asked for more information before they accepted him as a member. He was apparently ordained priest in the spring of that year.

Degeay arrived in Montreal on 21 July and served in Notre-Dame parish until October. In November he succeeded Pierre Le Sueur* as parish priest of Saint-Pierre-du-Portage (L'Assomption, Que.). For 32 years he laboured there not just as a missionary but also as a builder, businessman, and Christian shepherd to the humblest of his flock. Degeay found Le Sueur's unpretentious parish buildings in a state of decay. He reorganized parish finances, bought land with his own funds, and, after discussion with his parishioners, a few of whom remained stubbornly opposed, began the construction of a stone church and presbytery in 1750. The same year he opened a new cemetery. These projects had all been approved by Bishop Pontbriand [Dubreil*] during his pastoral visit in June 1749, and Louis Normant* Du Faradon blessed the corner-stone on 23 June 1750. Degeay embellished the church by adding a bell-tower with three bells (one of them his personal property) and by acquiring suitable decoration. Until his death he employed at different times three wood-carvers: Gilles Bolvin*, Philippe Liébert*, and François Guernon*, *dit* Belleville. In years of rapid expansion – the parish grew from about 500 persons in 1742 to more than 3,000 in 1774 – he exercised his ministry faithfully and showed outstanding organizational ability. He fostered the village's development, encouraged school education, assisted parishioners from his own funds, and transferred land he owned to them.

Degeay became the guardian angel of the Acadians who came to settle in the Saint-Sulpice seigneury. After consultation with the government, the Sulpicians had offered land to these exiles who had spent ten years wandering in New England. In September 1766 some 80 of them arrived at Saint-Pierre-du-Portage and 37 families followed a year later. They settled about 12 miles north of Saint-Pierre, thus establishing the nucleus of the future parish of Saint-Jacques-de-l'Achigan. Degeay provided them with the necessities of life and also undertook to validate marriages and hold baptismal services.

Degeay's stubbornness led to difficulties with the civil authorities in Quebec. He incurred the wrath of Lieutenant Governor Guy Carleton* after having performed a marriage unaware that the man involved was a deserter from the British army. After an exchange of acrimonious letters between the two, the priest finally had to ask Carleton's pardon in 1766 for the tone of his remarks. On this occasion Étienne MONTGOLFIER noted in a letter to Bishop BRIAND that he distrusted the "rather impetuous nature of this priest."

In 1771, Degeay, feeling the symptoms of the illness that would prove fatal, was hospitalized for the first time in the Hôtel-Dieu in Montreal. He returned there at the beginning of July 1774 and at that time made his will. Its provisions included leaving his bell to the church of Saint-Jacques-de-l'Achigan, a bequest that led to a quarrel between the parishioners of this parish and those of Saint-Pierre-du-Portage. Degeay died on 6 August and was buried on 8 August under Notre-Dame. As the historian Christian Roy notes, his legacy was "personal accomplishments of great fruitfulness, a seigneury almost fully settled, and a parish which was probably the only one of its kind."

J.-BRUNO HAREL

ACAM, 355.114. Archives du séminaire Saint-Irénée (Lyon, France), Registre des ordinations, 1740–41. Archives municipales, Lyon (dép. du Rhône, France), État civil, Saint-Nizier, 31 mars 1717. Archives paroissiales, L'Assomption-de-la-Sainte-Vierge (L'Assomption, Qué.), Registre des baptêmes, mariages et sépultures, 1742–74. ASSM, 15, testament de Jacques Degeay; 24, Dossier 6. "Sur deux retables de l'église de L'Assomption," Raymond Douville, édit., *RHAF*, XII (1958–59), 30–34. Guy Courteau et François Lanoue, *Une nouvelle Acadie, Saint-Jacques de L'Achigan, 1772–1947* ([Montréal, 1947]). Christian Roy, *Histoire de l'Assomption* ([L'Assomption, 1967]).

DEGUIRE, *dit* **Desrosiers, JOSEPH** (he also signed **J. Desrosiers** or **Joseph Derosiers**), militia captain and seigneur; b. 1 Oct. 1704 at Lavaltrie (Que.) and baptized 1 Nov. 1704 at Contrecœur (Que.), son of Pierre Deguire, *dit* Desrosiers, and Jeanne Blet (Belet, Blette); m. 16 March 1731 Angélique Pepin at Saint-Michel-d'Yamaska (Yamaska, Que.) and they had at least 13 children; d. 12 Feb. 1789 in the same parish.

Nothing is known about the early years of Joseph Deguire, *dit* Desrosiers. In 1731 he purchased some land at Petit-Chenal-d'Yamaska, where his father had settled as early as 1707. He made his first fur-trading trip to the *pays d'en haut* in 1733, returning there in 1738. Around 1737 he was chosen militia captain by the parishioners of Saint-Michel-d'Yamaska and received his commission from Pierre de RIGAUD de

Vaudreuil, then governor of Trois-Rivières. He was to serve as captain for 25 or 26 years and thus became influential in the parish. "Empowered to receive official acts" such as marriage contracts, wills, and bills of sale, he had judicial as well as military duties. He seems to have been reasonably well off judging by the way in which he set up his children and the fact that he increased his land holdings at Yamaska in 1744 and 1745.

On 4 Sept. 1751 Governor La Jonquière [Taffanel*] and Intendant BIGOT granted Joseph Deguire, *dit* Desrosiers, the seigneury of Rivière-David, which was also called Saint-Joseph or Deguire. At the time it was granted, most of the seigneury was wooded and rich in fur-bearing animals. This fact in addition to the Seven Years' War would explain why settlement did not begin until January 1767. After that date the number of land grants was large enough for Deguire to build a banal mill. There is no proof, however, that he ever resided on the seigneury. On the contrary, he seems to have lived always at Petit-Chenal-d'Yamaska.

The new régime which began in 1760 was to bring numerous difficulties for seigneur Joseph Deguire, including the elimination of his post as militia captain. Although the census of 1765 shows that he was the second-largest landowner at Yamaska, with 451 acres of land and 28 animals, he was not secure from financial worries. In 1768 he had to borrow money from Joseph Depin, promising to repay it the following year. On 3 July 1769 Deguire sent a letter to Governor Guy Carleton* protesting against legal proceedings that were being instituted "for nothing at all" and that were causing a "multitude of expenses." Although he was speaking on behalf of "poor people," Deguire was also pleading his own cause, because the deal made with Depin had led to legal difficulties. The governor nevertheless considered his protest important enough to mention in a report on his travels across the country dated 28 March 1770 and sent to Lord Hillsborough, secretary of state for the American Colonies, from Quebec, and he endeavoured to rectify abuses of which the justices of the peace were guilty.

After owning the seigneury of Rivière-David for 21 years, Joseph Deguire sold it on 29 Dec. 1772 to Christophe L'Huissier of Varennes, for £8,000. His decision undoubtedly arose from the economic situation in the colony since the advent of the British régime and the decline in profitability of his seigneury. After the sale Joseph Deguire substantially reduced his activities; he continued to live at Petit-Chenal-d'Yamaska, in the home of his son-in-law, Pierre Leverrier. On 31 Oct. 1788 he made his will, and on 12 Feb. 1789 died. His widow, Angélique Pepin, asked the executor to request that the will be revoked, because Joseph Deguire had made his daughter Marie and Pierre Leverrier his sole heirs.

RENÉ DESROSIERS

ANQ-M, Doc. jud., Cour des plaidoyers communs, Registres, 21 mars, 14, 18, 29 sept. 1789, 22, 23, 26 mars, 1er juill., 15 nov. 1790; État civil, Catholiques, Sainte-Trinité (Contrecœur), 1er nov. 1704; Greffe de F.-M. Lepallieur de Laferté, 1er juin 1733, 30 mai 1738; Greffe de J.-C. Raimbault, 28 juin 1731, 5 sept. 1734; Greffe de François Simonnet, 29 déc. 1772. ANQ-MBF, Greffe de Louis Pillard, 30 déc. 1751, 17 févr., 29 avril, 4 nov. 1753, 13 janv. 1761, 4 mai 1763, 23 juin 1766; Greffe de H.-O. Pressé, 19 févr. 1744, 14, 24 juin 1745; Greffe d'É.-F. Rigaud, 26 janv. 1767, 14, 22 mars, 2 avril 1774; Procès-verbaux des arpenteurs, J.-B. Leclerc, 16 mars 1740; Antoine Lepellé, dit Desmarets, 12 déc. 1732. Archives civiles, Richelieu (Sorel, Qué.), Greffe de Barthélemy Faribault, 28 mars 1789; Greffe de Puyperoux de La Fosse, 15 mars 1731; Greffe d'Antoine Robin, 18 oct. 1768, 16 août 1769, 16 janv., 11 oct. 1771, 2 avril 1774, 14 mars, 8 août 1775, 17 oct. 1778. Archives paroissiales, Saint-Michel (Yamaska, Qué.), Registre des baptêmes, mariages et sépultures, 16 mars 1731, 13 févr. 1789. PAC, MG 11, [CO 42], Q, 7, pp.55–58; MG 17, A7–2–6, 20.

PAC *Rapport*, 1890, xvii–xxi, 1–6. "Recensement des gouvernements de Montréal et de Trois-Rivières, 1765," 104; "Recensement du gouvernement de Trois-Rivières, 1760," 47–50, 52–53. Claude de Bonnault, "Le Canada militaire: état provisoire des officiers de milice de 1641 à 1760," ANQ *Rapport*, 1949–51, 514. P.-G. Roy, *Inv. concessions*, V, 78–79. Tanguay, *Dictionnaire*, I, 165; III, 277–78. Azarie Couillard-Després, *Histoire de Sorel de ses origines à nos jours* (Montréal, 1926), 110. O.-M.-H. Lapalice, *Histoire de la seigneurie Massue et de la paroisse de Saint-Aimé* (s.l., 1930), 5–85. Sulte, *Hist. des Canadiens français*, VII, 45.

DEGUISE, *dit* **Flamand (Flamant), JACQUES,** master mason, stone-cutter, and contractor; b. 5 March 1697 and baptized the next day in Notre-Dame at Quebec, son of Guillaume Deguise, *dit* Flamand, a mason, and Marie-Anne Morin; d. 18 Nov. 1780 at Quebec.

Jacques Deguise, *dit* Flamand, belonged to the second generation of masons working in New France, as did Pierre RENAUD, *dit* Cannard. One of the earliest Canadian master masons, Jean-Baptiste Maillou*, *dit* Desmoulins, had trained Jacques's brother, Girard-Guillaume*, and in the absence of any apprenticeship contract bearing Jacques Deguise's name, it is reasonable to assume that he too was one of Maillou's group.

Jacques Deguise was active over a period of about 36 years. His name first appears in a notary's minute-book in 1721, when he was building the foundations for a square-timbered house on Rue Saint-Flavien in Quebec. He was then still a minor and had to have his contracts ratified by his mother. Deguise completed his training in the period from 1722 on, when he worked on the big building site for the prison and court-house in Trois-Rivières. At this time he was working with his brother and with Jean-Baptiste Boucher, *dit* Belleville, a stone-cutter and masonry contractor whose name often recurs on contracts for fortifications at Quebec and Montreal.

As for domestic architecture Deguise was in charge of preliminary work on several residences in Quebec, including one constructed on Rue des Remparts in June 1725 according to plans by Gaspard-Joseph Chaussegros* de Léry and known today as the Maison Montcalm, one built in 1728 on Place Royale for Joseph Duburon, an officer, and another built in 1729 on Rue Saint-Roch for navigator Abel Olivier*.

From 1730 on Deguise found himself in a difficult situation. Thérèse Rinfret, *dit* Malouin, whom he had married in Quebec on 10 Sept. 1725, died on 21 Nov. 1730. At that moment Deguise was being harassed in his professional activity because he was unable to meet certain due dates for payment which had been laid down when contracts were signed. In an attempt to restore his fortunes he engaged in various property transactions, for example with Jean-Eustache Lanoullier* de Boisclerc.

Deguise resumed his building activities in 1734, constructing a house for surgeon Michel Bertier* on Rue des Pauvres, and one for Charles Normand at the corner of Rue Saint-Jean and present-day Rue Sainte-Angèle, and then, in the period up to 1745, a number of other buildings designed as dwellings in the neighbourhood of Rue des Pauvres near the site originally granted to the Hôtel-Dieu. Deguise's technique for assuring his profit consisted in buying a piece of land in this quarter, building a stone house on it, and selling the two together.

The master mason's career took a new direction when in 1747 he became involved in the undertaking to improve the fortifications of Quebec. Five years later, his brother having died, he took over his role as contractor of the king's works for the fortifications and barracks. The pace of his financial transactions from that moment indicates a significant degree of prosperity: obviously these works were profitable for him. With funds that must have been increasing rapidly, he was able to make numerous property deals in the present-day quadrilateral bounded by Rues Saint-Jean, Saint-Stanislas, Elgin, and Sainte-Angèle, which was being developed at that time. Moreover, it was Deguise who in 1755 loaned chief engineer Chaussegros de Léry the money required for the dowry of his daughter Josephte-Antoinette, who wished to enter the Hôpital Général – a transaction that has the odour of clientage.

Deguise also worked for the religious communities. In 1754 he supervised the building of a wing for the parlours of the Ursulines' convent and the measuring for a masonry wall around their property. He was also entrusted with the rebuilding of the convent of the hospital nuns of the Hôtel-Dieu in Quebec which had been destroyed by fire in 1755; the contract amounted to 24,000 *livres*. In the field of religious architecture the only building that can be attributed to Deguise with certainty is the church of Saint-François-Xavier-de-la-Petite-Rivière (Petite-Rivière). This small, half-timbered, field-stone church is proof that masons in the 18th century were still using the techniques imported from France by their predecessors. Like most of the master masons working in the colony, Deguise had trained apprentices and hired journeymen. Among the names associated with his are those of Thomas Allard, Jean-Baptiste Rouillard, and Joseph Morin. But none of them carried on the master's work; none even acquired much of a reputation.

Jacques Deguise and Thérèse Rinfret, *dit* Malouin, had had three children, but only one, François, outlived them. François carried on his father's occupation, and in 1749 he married into a mason's family, wedding Marie-Françoise, daughter of Pierre Jourdain, *dit* Bellerose. After his wife's untimely death, Jacques Deguise married Marie-Élisabeth Laisné, *dit* Laliberté, on 5 Feb. 1742 at Saint-Augustin; they had 11 children.

At the time of his death on 18 Nov. 1780, at the age of 83, Jacques Deguise was living in the home of his daughter Élisabeth and his son-in-law Joseph Falardeau on Rue Saint-Stanislas. He was buried the next day in the Cimetière des Picotés.

RAYMONDE GAUTHIER and MARTHE LACOMBE

AMHDQ, Registre des comptes du monastère, IV, 331–32. ANQ-Q, État civil, Catholiques, Notre-Dame de Québec, 6 mars 1697, 4 juill. 1729, 8 févr. 1774, 19 nov. 1780; Saint-Augustin, 5 févr. 1742; Greffe de Gilbert Boucault de Godefus, 10 juill. 1747; Greffe de Louis Chambalon, 26 déc. 1711; Greffe de J.-É. Dubreuil, 23 janv., 20 nov. 1721, 8, 18 mars, 21 avril 1722, 18 janv. 1723, 3 mars 1724, 5 août, 10 sept., 29 déc. 1725, 11 janv. 1727, 5 oct, 1729, 20 oct. 1731, 4 avril 1734; Greffe de C.-H. Du Laurent, 24 mai 1735, 1er mars 1755; Greffe d'Henri Hiché, 1er févr. 1734; Greffe de N.-C. Pinguet de Bellevue, 27 avril 1749; Greffe de J.-N. Pinguet de

Vaucour, 16, 26 févr. 1728 (nos.112, 113, 115), 8 mars 1731, 26 févr. 1737, 17 avril 1738, 31 déc. 1740, 27 mars 1741, 28 janv. 1742; NF 19, 68, ff.174v–90. AUQ, Fonds construction, 20 août 1735, 14 oct. 1754.

P.-G. Roy, *Inv. coll. pièces jud. et not.*; *Inv. ord. int.*, II, 48, 59–60, 82. Tanguay, *Dictionnaire*, I, 165; III, 44, 279–80. Marthe Bergeron-Hogue, *Un trésor dans la montagne* (Québec, 1954), 225–39. D'Allaire, *L'Hôpital Général de Québec*, 108. Marthe Lacombe, "Les réalisations du maçon Jacques Deguise, dit Flamand, au quartier du palais," *Le parc de l'Artillerie et les fortifications de Québec; études historiques présentées à l'occasion de la conférence des Sociétés savantes* (Québec, 1976), 27–36. O'Reilly, *Mgr de Saint-Vallier et l'Hôpital Général*, 720.

DEIAQUANDE. *See* TEYOHAQUEANDE

DELAGARDE. *See* LAGARDE

DELEZENNE, IGNACE-FRANÇOIS, silversmith, merchant, and seigneur; baptized 30 April 1718 in the parish of Sainte-Catherine in Lille, France, son of Martin Delezenne and Marie-Christine Jacquemart; buried 1 May 1790 at Baie-du-Febvre (Baieville, Que.).

Ignace-François Delezenne probably learned his craft in his home town. He sailed for New France around 1740 with his partner Charles Barthe. The two silversmiths first set up in business in Quebec but could not meet the competition from the numerous local artisans. Barthe appears some ten years later at Detroit. Delezenne went to Montreal, where the only silversmiths were Jacques Gadois*, *dit* Mauger, and Roland Paradis*. He was living there on Rue Saint-François by the summer of 1743, and he started in business under the aegis of the influential Gadois, who introduced him to Montreal society. Delezenne made many utensils, even working in copper, and he probably also made silver articles for the fur trade. But his career only really got under way when he received his first orders for church silver.

Prosperity came soon after his marriage on 8 Jan. 1748 to Marie-Catherine Janson, *dit* Lapalme, niece of architect Dominique Janson*, *dit* Lapalme. The following summer Delezenne bought a large piece of silver, weighing 27 marks 2 ounces and valued at 1,553 *livres 5 sols*, from the estate of merchant Pierre Guy*. This purchase, for which Gadois and Dominique Janson went surety, freed Delezenne from one of the major constraints hampering silversmiths of the period, the scarcity of material; it enabled him to make, among other things, a monstrance and some ampullae for holy oil – which have since disappeared – for the church of Saint-Charles-de-Lachenaie.

Delezenne's shop on Rue Saint-Jacques received enough orders for him to engage one Dominique-François Mentor, a black emancipated slave, as an apprentice in 1749. About the same time he changed his first stamp, a rather simple one (an open crown, I, a period, F,D), for a more elaborate one (a closed crown, IF, D). Between 1748 and 1752 he created a piece that is one of the masterpieces of Quebec silverwork, the superb chalice with highly original decorative motifs that belongs to the Religious Hospitallers of St Joseph in Montreal.

A property on Rue Notre-Dame, across from the Recollets, became the cause of a quarrel between Delezenne and Dominique Janson after the death in June 1748 of its owner, Michel-Étienne Couturier, *dit* Le Bourguignon, an uncle of Marie-Catherine Janson on her mother's side. Delezenne finally bought it from Janson for 5,000 *livres*. Having decided to set up business in Quebec, he sold it on 9 July 1752 to surgeon Claude Benoist for 9,000 *livres*. Just before his departure a dispute with his apprentice Mentor brought him before the royal jurisdiction of Montreal. Mentor followed him to Quebec, however, and in 1756 signed a contract to work as a journeyman for two years, with the option of a third year. Mentor had probably sued because his master was devoting more time to real estate than to his craft. A skilful administrator, Delezenne through these transactions acquired money for ambitious works in silver which he could not otherwise have undertaken. At this time also, the market for silversmiths' products in Quebec was favourable: only two of the ten silversmiths in business in 1740 were still there. It was in these circumstances that Delezenne set himself up as a merchant on Rue de la Montagne in Quebec, in November 1752; he quickly acquired a degree of renown.

In January 1755, for 4,923 *livres*, he obtained at auction a property on Rue Saint-Joseph (Rue Garneau) from the estate of Marie-Madeleine Sasseville. The terms of the award of this fief included the right to levy *cens et rentes* on various persons, and Delezenne became a seigneur. In 1755 and 1756 a succession of lawsuits brought the new owner into conflict with his neighbours and showed him to be grasping, vindictive, and stubborn. Only two of his neighbours stood up to him, notary Simon Sanguinet Sr, and Dominique Janson, *dit* Lapalme, who had been living in Quebec since 1751. Three others sold their properties, one to Delezenne, because they could not assume the expenses occasioned by the court actions and by the construction of dividing walls.

With the aid of his connections and his commercial dealings, Delezenne soon set up an enterprise that was new for the colony: the manufacture on a large scale of trade silver. Through his friendship with Christophe PÉLISSIER, a king's scrivener, and with Jacques Imbert*, the agent of the treasurers general of the Marine, he was able to obtain Intendant BIGOT's favour and became his appointed silversmith. Bigot had Delezenne melt down treasury *écus*, including the 15,000 *livres* found at Chouaguen (Oswego). From 1756 to 1759 Delezenne ran a veritable small industry manufacturing trade silver and hence neglected the production of church and table silver. A single agreement, signed in 1758, stipulated that Jean Robaille and four workmen were to utilize 1,000 marks of silver for manufacturing ornaments and trinkets for the fur trade; this silver would have been worth at least 57,000 *livres*, over five times the value of Delezenne's house and workshop on Rue de la Montagne. Several silversmiths – Dominique-François Mentor, Étienne Marchand, and Jean Robaille and his apprentice Claude-Marie-François Morin – worked with Delezenne. In much the same way as Gadois had assisted him some years earlier, Delezenne assisted Louis-Alexandre PICARD, who supervised the work of Amable Maillou, Jean-François Risbé, and Charles Diverny, *dit* Saint-Germain. But the siege of Quebec in the summer of 1759 put an abrupt stop to their work. Not only was his house on Rue de la Montagne demolished, but Delezenne saw part of his profits, 15,756 *livres* in paper money, destroyed. However the Delezenne family had moved to Rue Saint-Joseph the previous summer, and so was unharmed.

With the change in allegiance Delezenne adopted a new stamp (a crown, DZ) that was more in keeping with the British tradition. Whether or not this adaptation was a clever commercial device to win the conqueror's sympathies, more than half of his extant work bears this stamp. Most of these pieces were made between 1764 and 1775 and mark the peak of his production, which was divided equally between silver articles for the fur trade and church and table silver. It seems that during this period Delezenne worked with a conscientious apprentice with a splendid future, François Ranvoyzé*. Ranvoyzé's early works closely followed forms and decorative motifs inherited from Delezenne. Indeed, at the time of Ranvoyzé's marriage in 1771 Delezenne was described as "his friend who is a father to him." It would, however, be risky to claim, as some writers have, that François Ranvoyzé trained Delezenne's son as a silversmith, even though their names followed one another in the "Rôle général de la milice canadienne de Québec . . . ," drawn up in the autumn of 1775. A plausible explanation is that Joseph-Christophe Delezenne* worked with his father, who lived near Ranvoyzé, and hence their names appear together on the roll. Joseph-Christophe Delezenne's career as a silversmith was, moreover, limited to his apprenticeship. Joining the American ranks early in 1776, he accompanied the invading army when it withdrew from the province of Quebec and he settled in the United States. In 1788 he served as engineer and captain at West Point, New York. When he returned to Lower Canada in 1807 he was accused of treason.

Ignace-François Delezenne's life changed after his daughter Marie-Catherine*'s marriage on 8 March 1775 to Christophe Pélissier, the director of the Saint-Maurice ironworks. It was a financial transaction as much as a marriage: for an exorbitant price, the silversmith "sold" his daughter, who had promised her hand to Pierre Fabre*, *dit* Laterrière, to his longtime friend. Delezenne went to live at the ironworks at the end of 1775, and there he and Pélissier collaborated with the Americans. Circumstances led Pélissier to go into exile in France. Various documents confirm that between the time of Pélissier's departure and return to Canada for a visit in the summer of 1778, Delezenne directed the Saint-Maurice ironworks, while Laterrière ran the operation. Indeed, when the lease for the ironworks was made over to Alexandre Dumas* in February 1778, it was Delezenne who carried out the transaction. Shortly afterwards he moved to Trois-Rivières, acquiring several pieces of property there in April; Laterrière went to live at Bécancour with Marie-Catherine. Before returning to France in the autumn of 1778 Pélissier, who could not resign himself to losing his wife to Laterrière, hatched an intricate plot against him which Delezenne organized. At the instance of Bishop BRIAND, who had already excommunicated the notorious lovers, and of HALDIMAND, Laterrière was imprisoned after a hasty trial on the basis of false witness by Delezenne's son Michel, who accused him of having collaborated with the Americans. Haldimand refused him any form of recourse; he thus satisfied his friend Pélissier's demands by separating the lovers, and he made Laterrière an example of official repression, even though Laterrière claimed to be a staunch royalist. After many vicissitudes Laterrière and Marie-Catherine finally took up residence at Gentilly in October 1783.

At this period Delezenne was still active as a silversmith, working particularly for the fur trade and training John Oakes*. The Saint-Cuthbert chalice and case for holy oils (Birks collection) can be attributed to the period 1783–84. They greatly influenced Oakes, who passed the models on to Michael Arnoldi*, Robert Cruickshank*, and Charles Duval* soon after his master's death. In the autumn of 1784 Delezenne disposed of his properties in Trois-Rivières at a profit and bought a farm at Baie-du-Febvre. From these deals he acquired 2,000 *livres* in cash. Land speculation had always been profitable for him, as is illustrated by the sale of his property in Montreal in 1752; similar transactions at Quebec in 1779 involved the sum of 25,000 *livres*.

After his wife's death in November 1787, Delezenne was reconciled with his daughter and Laterrière, who came to live with him until his death in 1790. As there was no inventory after his death it is impossible to appraise his financial and professional situation, but he had probably lived comfortably during the last six years of his life. He had enjoyed good health and seems to have been active until his death producing trade silver, which explains why he set up business near the fur-trading post among the Abenakis at Saint-François. Later a number of silversmiths in the region from Trois-Rivières to Lake Champlain adopted this plan of setting themselves up in business near the Indian trading posts: the list included John Oakes, Michael Arnoldi and his brother Johann Peter, Michel Roy, Dominique Rousseau*, Henry Polonceau, Charles Duval, Jean-Baptiste Decaraffe, and Jean-Baptiste-François-Xavier Dupéré, *dit* Champlain.

In addition to being the first silversmith in Trois-Rivières and the master of the famous François Ranvoyzé, Ignace-François Delezenne may be considered the father of the manufacture of trade silver in Canada, which was indeed his major professional concern. He was successful in developing a market for such goods, a market which, because of the prominent role of furs in the economy, became important itself. He made the creation of trade silver an activity of the colony and gave the product a significance it had not had when its manufacture was the prerogative of the mother country. To tokens and medals were added more elaborate ornaments; silversmith Picard perfected new tools; production on a nearly industrial scale, by numerous apprentices or journeymen, replaced small-scale or part-time operations by artisans; and trade silver became more important than church silver in the economy.

Only a few religious articles by Delezenne remain, but the quality of their execution, and the vigour and finesse of their style show that he was an absolute master of his art. These works are almost all masterpieces of their kind, as numerous imitations have subsequently attested. If only a score of Ranvoyzé's or Laurent Amiot*'s religious works had survived the wear and tear of time, it is not certain that they would have reflected glory upon their creators to the same degree. As for table silver, Delezenne left a few specimens in Quebec of a kind not made by any other silversmith – for example, the flat candlestick and the chafing dish at the Séminaire de Québec and the wedding cup in the Musée du Québec.

Delezenne was unusual in that he began a career as a silversmith at the height of the French régime and he was able to continue it after the conquest with merit and honour, exerting a great influence on others. He was the leader in his field for more than 20 years, and his activity illustrates the evolution of the silversmith's art in a transitional period. His role as Bigot's appointed silversmith and his share in the transfer of the lease of the Saint-Maurice ironworks and in the conspiracy against Laterrière give to his career an interest beyond his profession.

ROBERT DEROME

[Ignace-François Delezenne's works can be seen in Quebec in the Musée du Québec, the museum of the Séminaire de Québec, the archbishop's palace, the Hôpital Général, the Hôtel-Dieu, and the private collection of Gérard Morisset*. Other works are held in Montreal in the Musée des Beaux-Arts, the Hôtel-Dieu, the church of Notre-Dame, and the convent of the sisters of the Congregation of Notre-Dame; in Toronto in the Henry Birks collection and the J. E. Langdon collection; and at the Musée d'Odanak (Que.) and the churches of Notre-Dame-de-Foy at Sainte-Foy, Sainte-Marguerite-de-Blairfindie at L'Acadie, Saint-François-Xavier at Caughnawaga, and Saint-Michel at Vaudreuil.

It is impossible to list here all the exhibition catalogues, books, and articles in which Ignace-François Delezenne's name appears; Robert Derome's work *Les orfèvres de N.-F.* and his article "Delezenne, le maître de Ranvoyzé" in *Vie des Arts* (Montréal), XXI (1975–76), no.83, 56–58, can be consulted. There is a descriptive catalogue of Delezenne's work and a more detailed biography of the silversmith in Robert Derome, "Delezenne, les orfèvres, l'orfèvrerie, 1740–1790" (thèse de MA, université de Montréal, 1974). There are illustrations of some of Delezenne's works in J. Trudel, *L'orfèvrerie en N.-F.* R.D.]

AAQ, 20 A, I, 181. AD, Nord (Lille), État civil, Sainte-Catherine, 30 avril 1718. ANQ-M, Doc. jud., Registres des audiences pour la juridiction de Montréal, 24, 25, 26, 27; État civil, Catholiques, Notre-Dame de Montréal, 8 janv. 1748, 9 mars 1749, 16 févr., 13 sept. 1750, 26 déc. 1751; Saint-Laurent, 31 janv. 1751; Greffe de J.-B. Adhémar, 10 août 1743, 6 janv., 12 sept. 1748, 8 déc. 1749, 9 juill. 1752; Greffe de L.-C. Danré de Blanzy, 22 avril 1749, 2 sept. 1750, 14 janv., 13 sept. 1751; Greffe de Gervais Hodiesne, 11 mars 1751; Greffe de Simon Sanguinet, 21 sept. 1772. ANQ-MBF, Greffe de J.-B. Badeaux, 16, 17 avril, 24 sept. 1778, 10 févr. 1779, 5 sept., 16 oct., 4, 8 nov. 1780, 23 août 1781, 8 janv. 1782, 15 oct., 6 déc. 1783, 31 août, 15, 28 sept. 1784; Greffe de C.-L. Maillet, 12 févr., 22 juin, 6, 23 oct., 1er nov. 1778, 15 sept. 1779 (the items cited for 1778 have disappeared; the information was taken from the calendar). ANQ-Q, AP-P-526; AP-P-2213; État civil, Catholiques, La Nativité de Notre-Dame (Beauport), 23 févr. 1763; Notre-Dame de Québec, 24 déc. 1752, 26 mars, 23 juill. 1754, 26 mars 1755, 12, 13 sept. 1756, 23 sept. 1757, 16, 25 oct. 1758, 7 mai 1759, 7 nov. 1761, 25 janv. 1762, 26 janv., 2 déc. 1763, 24 févr. 1764, 14 oct. 1765, 19 janv., 18 avril 1770, 7 sept. 1772; Saint-Charles-Borromée (Charlesbourg), 5 sept. 1759; Greffe de Claude Barolet, 5 mars 1755, 25 juin, 13 déc. 1756, 4 mai 1757, 31 mai 1758, 6 mai 1759; Greffe de M.-A. Berthelot d'Artigny, 8 mai 1775, 2 oct. 1777; Greffe de J.-B. Decharnay, 23 juill. 1756; Greffe de C.-H. Du Laurent, 20 août 1748, 25 juill. 1757, 3 mai 1758; Greffe de P.-A.-F. Lanoullier Des Granges, 15 déc. 1750, 20 oct., 12 nov. 1754; Greffe de François Lemaître Lamorille, 25 juin, 12 sept. 1761; Greffe de Claude Louet, 20 oct. 1766; Greffe de F.-E. Moreau, 22 juill. 1763; Greffe de J.-A. Panet, 12, 13 févr. 1779, 17 févr. 1781; Greffe de J.-C. Panet, 24 août, 27 nov. 1752, 22 juin, 31 août 1765; Greffe de J.-N. Pinguet, 26 oct. 1780; Greffe de J.-A. Saillant, 10 avril 1764, 24 nov. 1771; Greffe de Simon Sanguinet, 26 oct. 1751, 21, 22, 25, 26 juin 1754, 10 mai, 20 juin 1755, 24 oct. 1760, 15 nov. 1766, 22 févr. 1768; NF 6, 4, p.428 (copy at PAC); NF 11, 67, f.177; NF 19, 103, 104, 107; NF 20, 30 mars, 5 avril 1742, 14, 24 janv. 1755, 24 août 1756; QBC 26, 1, 1re partie, p.25; 2e partie, pp.17, 41. ASQ, C 11, 10 nov. 1764; Fonds Viger-Verreau, Sér. O, 040A, pp.34–35, 76, 84–85; Polygraphie, XXVII, 21. BL, Add. MSS 21845/1, pp.162–251; 21845/2, pp.353, 356 (copies at PAC). IBC, Centre de documentation, Fonds Morisset, Dossier I.-F. Delezenne. PAC, RG 4, A1, 4, 3 avril 1764; 16, 3 févr. 1767; 28, 3 août 1785 (original not located); 95, 13 sept. 1807.

Pierre Du Calvet, *Appel à la justice de l'État . . .* (Londres, 1784), 151–52. Fabre, dit Laterrière, *Mémoires* (A. Garneau). *Invasion du Canada* (Verreau). *Inv. des papiers de Léry* (P.-G. Roy), III, 257–66. *Mémoire pour messire François Bigot, ci-devant intendant de justice, police, finance & marine en Canada, accusé: contre monsieur le procureur-général du roi en la commission, accusateur* (Paris, 1763), 666–68. "Témoignages de liberté au mariage (15 avril 1757–27 août 1763)," ANQ *Rapport*, 1951–53, 49–50, 83–84. *Quebec Gazette*, 29 Sept. 1766, 5 July 1770, 25 June, 17 Dec. 1772, 30 Jan. 1777, 6 Aug., 3 Sept. 1778, 5 Jan. 1792. P.-G. Roy, *Inv. concessions*, I, 8. Tanguay, *Dictionnaire*. Raymond Douville, *Visages du vieux Trois-Rivières* (Trois-Rivières, 1955). Arthur Maheux, *Ton histoire est une épopée . . . nos débuts sous le Régime anglais* (Québec, 1941), 71–72. P.-G. Roy, *Bigot et sa bande*, 247–48. Sulte, *Mélanges historiques* (Malchelosse), VI. Tessier, *Les forges Saint-Maurice*.

DELISLE, DAVID CHABRAND. *See* CHABRAND

DELOR, JEAN-BAPTISTE-ANTOINE LEVASSEUR, ***dit***. *See* LEVASSEUR

DEMINIAC. *See* MINIAC

DENIS (Denys) DE SAINT-SIMON, ANTOINE-CHARLES, officer in the colonial regulars; b. 3 Nov. 1734 in Quebec, son of Charles-Paul Denys* de Saint-Simon and Marie-Joseph Prat; d. 8 June 1785 at Port-au-Prince, Saint-Domingue (Hispaniola).

Antoine-Charles Denis de Saint-Simon entered the colonial regulars as a cadet in January 1746 and from the outbreak of the Seven Years' War served in the military campaigns in the Ohio River region. On 9 July 1755 he fought in the battle between the troops of Daniel-Hyacinthe-Marie Liénard* de Beaujeu and Edward Braddock near Fort Duquesne (Pittsburgh, Pa); the following year Governor RIGAUD de Vaudreuil wrote to the minister of Marine: "He has been on all the reconnaissance missions and was involved in the General Braddock affair. He is still at the Belle Rivière [Ohio River], where he is constantly out skirmishing with the enemy." Named second ensign in the colonial regulars on 1 May 1757, Saint-Simon was promoted ensign on the active list on 1 Jan. 1759. That year he campaigned in the Acadian borderlands, and in June 1760 made his way through the woods from Baie des Chaleurs to Montreal carrying the royal dispatches as soon as they arrived from Bordeaux.

His exploit had attracted the attention of Bougainville*, who in 1763 asked Choiseul that "this courageous and robust young man" be posted to his service for an expedition he was organizing to the Îles Malouines (Falkland Islands). Moreover, because Saint-Simon was used to dealing with native people and could command their respect, Bougainville wanted to appoint him to the general staff of the new colony. At this time Saint-Simon was in Tours with a group of Canadian officers who had been brought back to France after the conquest and he was finding life tedious. He raised some objections to Bougainville's offers, because he wanted to return to Canada to settle family affairs, but the promise of a commission as an infantry captain to act as adjutant in the Îles Malouines finally persuaded him.

The expedition, which included some 40 Canadian or Acadian settlers, left Saint-Malo on 6 Sept. 1763. Saint-Simon sailed on board the corvette *Sphinx*, commanded by François Chenard de La Giraudais, and reached the Îles Malouines on 3 Feb. 1764. He was immediately sent on reconnaissance in the north and west of the archipelago. He helped to found the first settlements but in April returned to France with Bougainville, coming back to the new colony in January 1765 with 40 men of the colonial regular troops formerly stationed in Canada, a captain's commission, and a brevet as adjutant.

In 1766, at the time of an expedition in the Straits of Magellan, Saint-Simon was instructed to conclude an alliance with the Patagonians. He sailed on the flute *Étoile*, commanded by La Giraudais, which left the Îles Malouines with the *Aigle* on 24 April. The first contacts with the Patagonians were made on 5 May. Saint-Simon handed over to them the traditional gifts of harpoons, blankets, red woollen caps, knives, cloth, pipes, and tobacco. The alliance was formally concluded on 1 June with a presentation of the king's colours. When Bougainville sailed through the straits with the *Boudeuse* and the *Étoile* 18 months later he found this flag still in their possession. On this voyage Saint-Simon had proven himself a skilled diplomat, able to avoid incidents between the French and Patagonians, and the description he left of the people reveals he was also a good observer.

When the Îles Malouines were evacuated by the French in April 1767 after their cession to Spain, Saint-Simon boarded the Spanish frigate *Liebre*, which sailed for Montevideo, Uruguay, on 27 April. He did not reach El Ferrol (El Ferrol del Caudillo) in Spain until 12 Jan. 1768, and arrived in Lorient, France, in February. A new request to return to Canada does not seem to have met with success, and he went back to Tours, which was still serving as a reception centre for former Canadian officers. On 16 April 1769 he was appointed a captain in the Légion de Saint-Domingue; when this corps was disbanded, he transferred on 18 Aug. 1772 to the Régiment du Port-au-Prince and ended his career in the garrison there. On 24 Dec. 1773 he became a knight of the order of Saint-Louis.

Denis de Saint-Simon was always well regarded by his superiors. The governor of Saint-Domingue, the Marquis de Vallière, noted that he had "served at all times with the distinction of an excellent and brave officer." His last commander, the Marquis de Laval, colonel of the Régiment du Port-au-Prince, wrote: "One can only speak highly of the zeal and the manner in which M. de Saint-Simon carried out his duties and did his service. . . . This officer is all the more worthy of the king's favours because he sacrificed his fortune in Canada to continue to serve in France."

ÉTIENNE TAILLEMITE

AN, Col., C[11A], 101, f.160v; D[2C], 4, f.176; 59, f.44; 96, f.29; E, 363 bis (dossier Saint-Simon); F[2A], 14; Marine, C[7], 296 (dossier Denis de Saint-Simon); Section Outre-mer, G[1], Port-au-Prince (Haïti), 8 juin 1785. ANQ-Q, État civil, Catholiques, Notre-Dame de Québec, 4 nov. 1734. *Coll. des manuscrits de Lévis* (Casgrain), I, 166; VII, 176; X, 141; XI, 82. [A.-J.-H. de Maurès de Malartic, comte de Malartic], *Journal des campagnes au Canada de 1755 à 1760 . . .*, Gabriel de Maurès de Malartic et Paul Gaffarel, édit. (Dijon, France, 1890), 335. [F.-]M. Bibaud, *Le panthéon canadien; choix de biographies*, Adèle et Victoria Bibaud, édit. (2e éd., Montréal, 1891). [Bibaud confuses the career of Antoine-Charles Denis de Saint-Simon with that of Claude-Anne de Saint-Simon, Marquis (then Duke) of Saint-Simon (1743–1819), a major-general who took part in the War of American Independence and immigrated to Spain during the French revolution. É. T.] Tanguay, *Dictionnaire*. J.-É Martin-Allanic, *Bougainville navigateur et les découvertes de son temps* (2v., Paris, 1964). C.-F. Bouthillier, "La bataille du 9 juillet 1755," *BRH*, XIV (1908), 222–23.

DENSON, HENRY DENNY, army officer, landowner, and office-holder; b. *c.* 1715 in County Mayo (Republic of Ireland); d. 3 June 1780 at Falmouth, Nova Scotia.

Little is known of Henry Denny Denson's background. He was married in 1735 but soon afterwards joined the British army as a lieutenant and left Ireland. His wife, Edith, lived in Dublin throughout her life. The couple had one daughter, Elizabeth, who married George Cartland, a Dublin lawyer.

In 1743 Denson went on half pay and then disappears from view until 1760, when he was at Pisiquid (Windsor, N.S.) as an agent for the Nova Scotia government during the New England migration. He apparently decided to settle in Nova Scotia and was one of the first proprietors of the township of Falmouth on the Pisiquid (Avon) River. Since Denson was in Falmouth before the arrival of its New England settlers, he had his pick of choice lands and buildings abandoned by the Acadians. He was one of the first to build in the township and clearly intended to become a country squire. Undoubtedly he had recognized the difficulty of an Irish adventurer's achieving such an ambition in Britain and had therefore chosen to establish himself in the new colony.

One basis of a squire's position was his country estate, and Mount Denson, as Henry's was called, gradually became prosperous and comfortable, although the number of its tenants did not approach that of neighbouring Castle Frederick, the home of Joseph Frederick Wallet DesBarres*. By 1764 Denson had installed Mrs Martha Whitefield as "housekeeper"; through an ingenious legal arrangement, she managed to realize most of his estate after his death, although only after a legal battle with Mrs Denson and the Cartlands. The census of 1770 shows Mount Denson's household at 22 persons, mainly tenants and blacks, and livestock to a total of eight horses, 18 oxen, 34 cows, 34 young cattle, 150 sheep, and 12 swine. On hand were 250 bushels of wheat, 10 bushels of flax seed, and 40 bushels of oats. Such prosperity deserved a mansion house, and Denson built his around 1772.

Denson realized a substantial income through stock-raising. At his death, his inventoried estate included five black slaves, lavish household furnishings, and one of the larger private libraries in the province, including an extensive shelf of legal reference books. The inventory might well have been that of a comfortable Virginia planter or Sussex squire.

The successful squire not only held land but was also the political leader of his community. Denson dutifully accumulated a variety of elective and appointive responsibilities. From 1761 he was a justice of the Inferior Court of Common Pleas and, except for the years 1765 to 1769, a member of the House of Assembly for various constituencies until his death. He was a militia officer from the founding of Falmouth and road commissioner and collector of impost and customs for Kings County. In 1773 he served as acting speaker of the assembly during William NESBITT's illness.

Denson's local leadership did not always go unchallenged in the county. In 1762 a substantial body of his neighbours complained to the Board of Trade of his "most arbitrary and illegal conduct," including his "prophane Cursing, swearing, Sabbath-breaking, and other Immoralities." They were also upset that Denson, under martial law, had collected farmers at hay harvest time and marched them 50 miles "to do Duty as Soldiers," and they protested that because he held so many commissions from Halifax he informed, judged, and received in excise cases. Similarly, when Denson was appointed lieutenant-colonel of the Loyal Nova Scotia Volunteers in 1775 by Governor Francis LEGGE he encountered much opposition from his Yankee neighbours on attempting to recruit for the regiment.

Throughout most of his political career in Halifax, Denson trimmed. He was neither one of the "Halifax Gang" nor one of its articulate critics. This neutrality changed in 1775 and 1776, when he supported Legge in his struggles with the assembly and Council. The classic squire to the end, Denson suffered from gout in his later years, which forced him to resign his military commission shortly before his death in 1780.

J. M. BUMSTED

BL, Add. MSS 19069, f.54. Halifax County Court of Probate (Halifax), D46 (original estate papers of Henry Denny Denson). PAC, MG 23, A1. PANS, RG 1, 443, nos.2–17. *Directory of N.S. MLAs*, 89. Brebner, *Neutral Yankees* (1969), 185. J. V. Duncanson, *Falmouth – a New England township in Nova Scotia, 1760–1965* (Windsor, Ont., 1965), 30.

DENYS DE VITRÉ, THÉODOSE-MATTHIEU, ship's captain and pilot; baptized 8 Nov. 1724 at Quebec, son of Guillaume-Emmanuel-Théodose Denys de Vitré and Marie-Joseph Blaise Des Bergères de Rigauville, grandson of Paul Denys* de Saint-Simon; d. 1775 in England.

The son of a ship's captain, Théodose-Matthieu Denys de Vitré probably went to sea early. In 1746, a year before being granted legal status as an adult with benefit of age, he commanded a bateau with a crew of 12 sent to Acadia with supplies for troops. In the 1750s he sailed regularly between Bordeaux and Quebec, commanding in 1752 the *Angélique* owned by Guillaume ESTÈBE and in 1756 the 350-ton *Renommée* belonging to Abraham Gradis, a Bordeaux businessman. Returning to New France with the latter ship in 1757, he was intercepted by an English cruiser and taken prisoner.

Vitré himself is the only source for the events which occurred between his capture and his appearance before Quebec in 1759 with the vanguard of the British fleet. Some years after his imprisonment, he prepared a memoir designed to return him to favour in France. Portions of his account, in which he styled himself the Marquis de Vitré and claimed service in the French navy, are so filled with falsehoods that his remarks must be used with caution. According to Vitré, after his capture in 1757 he was lodged with other French prisoners at Alresford, Hampshire, where the British proposed that he pilot the invasion fleet to Quebec. He was dissuaded by a senior French naval officer from trying to escape, but got word to Gilles HOCQUART, then intendant at Brest, and other French officials, who arranged an exchange. The French sent two British officers to England in February 1758, but the British refused to return Vitré, who was thereafter under constant surveillance. This tale appears dubious because Vitré was not a senior ship's master. He may have been under tremendous pressure to aid the enemy, as he later claimed; more than likely, he decided to make the best of a bad situation and cooperate.

Whatever Vitré's particular case may have been, it is certain that in preparation for the coming campaign the British were actively gathering pilots who knew the route to Quebec. During the autumn of 1758 Rear-Admiral Philip Durell*, who had been left with a fleet at Halifax, collected from Louisbourg, Cape Breton Island, and different settlements of the Gaspésie – Gaspé, Mont-Louis, and Grande-Rivière – at least 17 French pilots familiar with the St Lawrence river and its gulf. In March 1759 Vice-Admiral Charles SAUNDERS requested the governors of New York and Massachusetts to send him any pilots acquainted with the St Lawrence. A number were taken from prisons in England. Vitré was sent on the *Neptune*, flagship of the British fleet, to Halifax. There, because of his specialized knowledge of the south shore of the St Lawrence, he was transferred to the advance squadron under Durell, and during May and June the ships made their way to Quebec.

Vitré later stated that almost immediately afterward he was returned to England still a prisoner and brought back to Canada the next year on the pretext that he would be allowed to settle his losses. But in 1763, when he petitioned the Privy Council for assistance, Vitré claimed to have piloted warships and transports on the St Lawrence during the summer of 1759 and served the following year in the squadron of Commodore Robert Swanton*, sent to relieve Brigadier-General James MURRAY at Quebec. Vitré acknowledged then that "his Services on those Occasions are too Notorious ever to admit of his returning to France"; and Admiral Saunders stated on his behalf that "the said Pilot exerted a most uncommon Zeal and Assiduity in the Services on which he was employed, many of which were of very great Importance and Utility to the Success of that expedition."

Vitré does not appear to have wished to settle in Canada. In 1763 the British Privy Council, acting on Saunders' recommendation, granted him permission to bring his family from France to England (he had married a woman from a Bordeaux family in 1755) and endowed him with an annual pension of £200, increased by £50 a year later. Considering that other Canadian pilots were paid only £15, and that Augustin RABY, one of the principal pilots of the invasion fleet, received a life pension of 5*s*. a day, there can be little doubt that Vitré was a collaborator who had done more than pilot a single British ship.

Vitré's son John became a lieutenant in the Royal Navy and saw service in the West Indies and India. Some time after Vitré's death in 1775 he tried to obtain redress from the British government for his father's losses, which he estimated at £10,000. This figure appears to have been based on Vitré's own dubious claims that his Canadian and French losses amounted to 235,000 *livres*. Whether any compensation was granted is not known.

J. S. PRITCHARD

[Both F.-X. Garneau, *Hist. du Canada* (H. Garneau; 1913–20), II, 230, and Francis Parkman, *Montcalm and Wolfe* (2v., London, [1908]), II, 130, confuse Théodose-Matthieu Denys de Vitré with his son John. This error, the result of a misreading of the "Mémorial du lieutenant John Denis de Vitré au Très Honorable William Pitt" published in *Siège de Québec en 1759 . . .* (Québec, 1836) (and in *Le siège de Québec en 1759 par trois témoins*, J.-C. Hébert, édit. (Québec, 1972), 51–123, 130), has caused lasting confusion. Stanley, *New France*, 203, compounds the error, stating that "the last ship Gradis sent to Canada in 1759 was captured by the British on her return voyage, and her captain, Jean Denis de Vitré, was forced, by threat of hanging, to pilot the vessels bearing Wolfe's army to the walls of Quebec." The distinction between father and son was established by Philéas Gagnon, "Le sieur de Vitré," *BRH*, III (1897), 178–186, but Æ. Fauteux, the editor of "Journal du siège de Québec," ANQ *Rapport*, 1920–21, 146, n.85, is one of the few historians to have made use of the information. J.S.P.]

AD, Gironde (Bordeaux), 6B, 100, f.56v; 102, ff.5v, 73; 272; 402; 409; 412. AN, Col., C[11A], 51, ff.103–4; 118, ff.77–78; F[2b], 2. ANQ-Q, État civil, Catholiques, Notre-Dame de Québec, 22 sept. 1722, 8 nov. 1724. "Commission de pilote côtier à Louis Roberge, de l'île d'Orléans," *BRH*, XXIII (1917), 56. *Despatches of Rear-Admiral Philip Durell, 1758–1759, and Rear-Admiral Lord Colville, 1759–1761*, ed. C. H. Little (Halifax, 1958). G.B., Privy Council, *Acts of P.C., col., 1745–66*, 565. [Charles Saunders], *Despatches of Vice-Admiral Charles Saunders, 1759–1760: the naval side of the capture of Quebec*, ed. C. H. Little (Halifax, 1958). P.-G. Roy, *Inv. jug. et délib., 1717–60*, I, 148; V, 41. Tanguay, *Dictionnaire*, I, 181; III, 343. Jean de Maupassant, *Un grand armateur de Bordeaux, Abraham Gradis (1699?–1780)* (Bordeaux, 1917). W. R. Riddell, "The pilots of Wolfe's expedition, 1759," RSC *Trans.*, 3rd ser., XXI (1927), sect.II, 81–82.

DE PEYSTER, ABRAHAM, army officer and office-holder; b. 1753 in New York City, son of James (Jacobus) De Peyster and Sarah Reade; m. 1783 in New York City Catherine Livingston, and they had six children; d. 19 Feb. 1798 at Saint John, New Brunswick.

Abraham De Peyster is the loyalist's loyalist. He fits exactly the popular stereotype, although that image is actually true only of a small minority. He was a member of a wealthy, landed, New York family which had a tradition of office-holding and military service under successive administrations, and which was joined by common interest and marriage to similar families, forming the aristocracy of colonial New York.

Abraham and his two younger brothers joined the loyalist side soon after the outbreak of the American revolution. Abraham was commissioned captain in the King's American Regiment in December 1776, served throughout the war, and saw a good deal of fighting in several states. As second in command of the British force at the battle of King's Mountain (S.C.) on 17 Oct. 1780, he had the unpleasant duty of surrendering after the death of Major Patrick Ferguson. By late 1783 he had been exchanged and had returned to New York. When the city was evacuated by British troops in November, he sailed to Nova Scotia, where he was placed on half pay and granted land in Parrtown (Saint John). Two years later, when the new province of New Brunswick was divided into counties, De Peyster became the first sheriff of Sunbury County. He moved to Maugerville to take up his duties and was granted land across the Saint John River in Burton.

In February 1792 Lieutenant Governor Thomas Carleton* appointed De Peyster treasurer of the province. The treasurer gathered the provincial revenues, chiefly derived from customs duties levied on incoming goods, and disbursed the resulting funds. In addition the position included the responsibilities of the present-day auditor general. It did not, however, carry with it an appointment to the Executive Council. De Peyster returned to Saint John after his appointment not only to be convenient to the customs offices but also to maintain a degree of independence from the legislature in Fredericton, which was probably believed necessary for the successful functioning of the office.

Although he was evidently considered a competent treasurer, De Peyster did not occupy the post long; he died in 1798 from "a short and painful disease." A son seems to have died about the same time, since the cost of their coffins is listed on the same bill. De Peyster appears to have lived with some style in Saint John (there is, for example, a statement of purchase for two slaves in 1797, and among the contents of his estate is a piano valued at £10), but he was found to have died insolvent. Since he left no will, his estate was settled by a series of decrees by the Executive Council. His wife and remaining children returned to New York City after his death.

JO-ANN FELLOWS

Portraits of Abraham De Peyster are to be found in the works by Draper and Lawrence cited below. N.B. Museum (Saint John), Hazen coll., Ward Chipman papers, bill, 2 March 1798. PANB, RG 2, RS6; RS 8, Appointments and commissions, register of commissions, 1785–1840; RG 10, RS108, Sunbury County. Saint John Regional Library (Saint John, N.B.), Primary source material, nos.32, 71–73, 93–94, 97–100, 102, 112.

Royal Gazette and the New Brunswick Advertiser (Saint John), 20 Feb. 1798. Sabine, *Biographical sketches of loyalists*, I, 372–73. [A. S. De Peyster], *Miscellanies, by an officer*, ed. J. W. De Peyster ([2nd ed.], 2v. in 1, New York, 1888). L. C. Draper, *King's Mountain and its heroes . . .* (Cincinnati, Ohio, 1881). J. W. Lawrence, *Foot-prints; or incidents in the early history of New Brunswick* (Saint John, N.B., 1883), 54, 55, app.

DESANDROUINS, JEAN-NICOLAS, army officer and military engineer; b. 7 Jan. 1729 at Verdun, France, eldest child of Benoît-Nicolas Desandrouins and Marie-Scholastique Hallot; d. unmarried 11 Dec. 1792 in Paris, France.

After a classical education at the local Jesuit college, Jean-Nicolas Desandrouins was commissioned lieutenant in the Régiment de Beauce in 1746. Five years later, following active combat service in the War of the Austrian Succession, he entered the military engineering school at Mézières (Charleville-Mézières). He graduated with distinction, and was admitted to the engineer corps in 1752.

Following three years' service at Dunkerque, Desandrouins was promoted second captain and sent to Canada as assistant to Jean-Claude-Henri de Lombard* de Combles. Arriving at Quebec on 18 May 1756 and at Fort Frontenac (Kingston, Ont.) a month later, he drew up plans for improving the latter's defences and on 8 July reconnoitred Oswego (Chouaguen) with François-Marc-Antoine LE MERCIER in preparation for Montcalm*'s attack. After Lombard's death on 11 August, Desandrouins, the sole remaining regular engineer, played a key role in the siege and capture of Oswego. He constructed an approach road for Le Mercier's artillery through wooded and partly swampy country in one day, and his advice on the siting of trenches was accepted by Colonel François-Charles de Bourlamaque* after the trenches dug by Captain Pierre Pouchot* were found to be vulnerable to British artillery fire.

Desandrouins's contribution to Montcalm's victories of 1757 and 1758 was similarly important. In 1757 he carried out a reconnaissance of Fort William Henry (also called Fort George; now Lake George, N.Y.), and during the siege directed the digging of approach trenches by 300 men who worked night and day in relays under fire. After wintering at Quebec, Desandrouins went to Fort Carillon (Ticonderoga, N.Y.) to help Nicolas Sarrebource* Maladre de Pontleroy reconnoitre, prepare defensive positions, and advise infantry commanders on field fortifications. The speed at which Desandrouins worked under fire during ABERCROMBY's attack of 8 July 1758 earned him the cross of Saint-Louis.

During the winter of 1758–59 Desandrouins prepared appreciations of Carillon and of Canada in general. In 1759, as Bourlamaque's senior engineer, he constructed new defensive positions in the Richelieu River-Lake Champlain sector against Jeffery AMHERST's cautiously advancing force. From mid August until March 1760 he was responsible for the construction and command of Fort Lévis (east of Prescott, Ont.). As engineer and aide-de-camp to LÉVIS, he supervised the digging of trenches during the siege of Quebec, and when Lévis's army was retreating upstream to Montreal, he assisted in delaying actions at Sorel.

Later that year, after the surrender of the colony, Desandrouins returned to France and continued a distinguished career in the engineer corps for another 31 years. Between 1761 and 1780 he served first in Malta and then in various places in France, at Strasbourg, Neuf-Brisach, Thionville, Saint-Omer, Bapaume, Nancy, and Sarrelouis (now in the Federal Republic of Germany), constructing all kinds of works including a canal, a hospital, and a bridge. Promoted lieutenant-colonel in 1774 and colonel in 1779, he became in 1780 commander of engineers in the Comte de Rochambeau's expeditionary force to America. Although illness prevented him from taking part in the siege of Yorktown, Virginia, his services won him not only a special French pension but also membership in the Society of the Cincinnati, an American military and patriotic organization. After a devastating shipwreck off Curaçao in February 1783 which resulted in the loss of many of his possessions, including a large part of his private papers, Desandrouins returned to France. Appointed director of fortifications at Brest in 1785, he was promoted major-general in 1788. Three years later, however, along with other senior officers of the engineer corps, he was forced to retire by the revolutionary government. His income sharply reduced by a new pensions policy, Desandrouins was considered for appointment to a committee on the fortifications of Paris but died before he could be assigned to the post.

Desandrouins's extant writings, maps, and plans are useful source material for the Seven Years' War in North America. Though his comments on Canada reflect the prevalent bias of the French regular army against Canadians and Indians, within those limits he reveals himself as an astute observer of the events and conditions of his time. Like other engineer officers, who tended to have a superior education, he played an important staff role as adviser to commanders in matters not directly related to his technical duties.

F. J. THORPE

AMA, Inspection du Génie, Archives, art. 3; art. 8; art. 14; SHA, A[1], 3417, 3457, 3498, 3499, 3540, 3574, 3733; Mémoires historiques et reconnaissances militaires, art. 247; Y^b, 685; Y^{3d}, 3251. AN, Col., B, 103, 104, 107; C^{11A}, 103, 105; D^{2C}, 59, f.14; Section Outre-mer, Dépôt des fortifications des colonies, Am. sept., no.538. PAC, MG 18, K9; K13. Bougainville, "Journal" (A.-E. Gosselin), ANQ *Rapport*, 1923–24, 205, 216, 221, 226–28, 255, 290, 320, 323, 331, 333. [F.-J. Chaussegros de Léry], "Lettres du vicomte François-Joseph Chaussegros de Léry à sa famille," ANQ *Rapport*, 1933–34, 55. *Coll. des manuscrits de Lévis* (Casgrain), I–VIII, X. Doreil, "Lettres" (A. Roy), ANQ *Rapport*, 1944–45, 137, 142. "Mémoire du Canada," ANQ *Rapport*, 1924–25, 148, 177. *NYCD* (O'Callaghan and Fernow), X. PAC *Rapport*, 1929, 88–104. [J.-G.-C. de Plantavit de Margon, chevalier de La Pause], "Mémoire et observations sur mon voyage en Canada," ANQ *Rapport*, 1931–32, 24. *DBF*, X, 1182.

A.-M. Augoyat, *Aperçu historique sur les fortifications, les ingénieurs et sur le corps du génie en France* ... (3v., Paris, 1860–64), II, 639. Henri Doniol, *Histoire de la participation de la France à l'établissement des États-Unis d'Amérique, correspondance diplomatique et documents* (6v., Paris, 1886–99), V, 311–590. L.-É. Dussieux, *Le Canada sous la domination française d'après les archives de la Marine et de la Guerre* (3e éd., Paris, 1883), 291–310, 331–42, 409–29. Frégault, *La guerre de la Conquête*, 57, 96, 183, 188, 193, 307, 379. [C.-N.] Gabriel, *Le maréchal de camp Desandrouins, 1729–1792; guerre du Canada, 1756–1760; guerre de l'Indépendance américaine, 1780–1782* (Verdun, France, 1887). Marcel Trudel, *Louis XVI, le Congrès américain et le Canada, 1774–1789* (Québec, [1949]), 181. "Le maréchal de camp Desandrouins," *BRH*, XXXVI (1930), 607–8.

DESAUNIERS, THOMAS-IGNACE TROTTIER DUFY. *See* TROTTIER

DES BORDES, JEAN-MARIE LANDRIÈVE. *See* LANDRIÈVE

DESCHAMBAULT, JOSEPH FLEURY. *See* FLEURY

DESCHAMPS DE BOISHÉBERT ET DE RAFFETOT, CHARLES, officer in the colonial regular troops; b. 7 Feb. 1727 at Quebec, son of Henri-Louis Deschamps* de Boishébert and Louise-Geneviève de Ramezay; m. 7 Sept. 1760 his cousin Charlotte-Élisabeth-Antoinette Deschamps de Boishébert et de Raffetot at Cliponville (dept of Seine-Maritime), France, and they had one son; d. 9 Jan 1797 at Raffetot (near Rouen), France.

Charles Deschamps de Boishébert entered upon a military career early in life. His name appears on a list of gentlemen cadets dated 1 Oct. 1739, with the comment "a promising young man, very steady." In 1742 he joined the Quebec garrison as assistant adjutant. During the years

1744 and 1745 he participated in several expeditions along the New York frontier.

To counterbalance the British presence in Acadia, which had increased since the capture of Louisbourg, Île Royale (Cape Breton Island), by William Pepperrell*'s troops in 1745, a force of some 700 soldiers, with Indian support, left Quebec for Acadia in June 1746 under the command of Jean-Baptiste-Nicolas-Roch de RAMEZAY. On his arrival Ramezay learned of the presence of British troops at Port-La-Joie (Fort Amherst, P.E.I.) and he sent Boishébert there on reconnaissance. Boishébert reported two British warships and 200 soldiers, and he apparently accompanied the party of Micmacs and a few young officers under Joseph-Michel LEGARDEUR de Croisille et de Montesson which returned to attack the enemy at Port-La-Joie. In October, and until 3 November, he took part in the unsuccessful siege of Annapolis Royal (N.S.), the British administrative and military headquarters in Acadia. During the winter Ramezay prepared an expedition against the force under Arthur Noble* which was stationed at Grand Pré. Boishébert was wounded in the battle fought there on 11 Feb. 1747 (N.S.). Following this French victory he returned to Quebec with the rest of the troops. In August he was placed in command of a cartelship leaving for Gaspé, where he was to effect an exchange of prisoners with the British. The mission accomplished, he returned again to Quebec.

On 28 Feb. 1748 Boishébert was promoted lieutenant, and he soon was engaged in operations in yet another part of New France. The previous year had seen the threat of a general Indian uprising in the west [*see* Orontony*], and in the spring of 1748 Boishébert was among the reinforcements sent under Pierre-Joseph Céloron* de Blainville to Detroit, which was particularly endangered. He took part in an expedition that took revenge on the Indians for attacks that had been made on the French in the vicinity.

From 1749 Boishébert was again in Acadia. At this time the boundary question, unresolved since 1713, was taking a new turn: France had decided to set the limits of Acadia at the Missaguash River [*see* Jean-Louis LE LOUTRE]. Boishébert was sent to the mouth of the Saint John River to oppose any attempt by the British to establish themselves there. A lively discussion took place immediately after his arrival when John Rous*, the senior British naval officer on the Nova Scotia station, arrived to claim the mouth of the Saint John for the British. Boishébert nonetheless remained firm. He rebuilt Fort Menagouèche (Saint John, N.B.) and, disguised as a fisherman, went up and down the coasts of Acadia in order to assess the Acadians' loyalty to France.

In 1751 Governor La Jonquière [Taffanel*] gave Boishébert the honour of carrying the official dispatches to France; at court he received a gratuity of 2,000 *livres*. The next year he was back in Canada, and he soon became involved in the west once more. To counter the threat of British expansion into the Ohio valley, Governor DUQUESNE had decided to link Lake Erie to the Ohio by a series of forts. Boishébert, whom the governor described as "a very zealous and deserving officer," led an advance detachment which left Montreal in February 1753 to prepare for the arrival of the main force. He landed at Presqu'île (Erie, Pa) early in May 1753 and apparently spent the summer in the region, under the orders of Paul Marin* de La Malgue, who was in command of the expedition. On 28 August he was put in charge of Fort de la Rivière au Bœuf (Waterford, Pa), but he held this posting only briefly.

By late autumn Boishébert was back in Quebec. In 1754 he again left for Acadia, with the title of commandant of Fort La Tour, at the mouth of the Saint John, and there he worked to counter persistent British efforts to establish themselves. He also made a study of the harbours between Acadia and Boston. The capture of Fort Beauséjour (near Sackville, N.B.) on 16 June 1755 by MONCKTON's forces marked a turning-point in Boishébert's career. Immediately after the fort fell, the British commander dispatched a large detachment against the handful of militiamen at Fort La Tour. As there was no hope of a successful outcome, Boishébert burned his fort before the enemy arrived and sought refuge among the local populace, continuing meanwhile to fight the enemy. The rest of his career in Acadia was spent working to secure the Acadians' loyalty to France, bringing to French territory as many of those in British-occupied regions as possible, and with the Indians' help constantly skirmishing against the enemy.

Shortly after the capture of Fort Beauséjour Boishébert learned that the British intended to attack the villages of Chipoudy (Shepody), Petitcodiac (near Hillsborough), and Memramcook; he immediately left for Chipoudy but arrived too late to prevent the village from being destroyed. On 3 Sept. 1755, however, he confronted a British detachment at Petitcodiac. After three hours of desperate struggle, during which they suffered heavy losses, the British fled. Boishébert, who had lost only one man, returned to the Saint John River with 30 of the most destitute families.

In order to forestall any British notion of taking revenge on the Acadians, Boishébert sent his lieutenant, François Boucher de Niverville (Nebourvele) Grandpré, to the Petitcodiac region. This officer was also to prevent supplies and munitions from being transported between the Fort Beauséjour region and Baie-Verte. In the mean time Boishébert himself went to Memramcook to keep the British from landing there. He spent part of the winter of 1755–56 at Cocagne (near Shediac). On 24 January he was caught in a British ambush nearby but succeeded in escaping without loss. On 17 March 1756 he was promoted captain.

Boishébert's constant vigilance over these settlements shows clearly that he wanted at all cost to prevent further systematic deportations of the Acadians by the British. The settlers had already been deported from the region of Tintemarre (Tantramar), despite Boishébert's attempts to evacuate the most destitute families. His efforts were limited by a scarcity of supplies, which coincided from 1756 to 1758 with a period of extreme poverty for most Acadians. Boishébert's position was further complicated by the enemy's constant advance. According to prisoners who had been taken to Quebec, there was a permanent detachment of 1,000 British at Fort Cumberland (the former Fort Beauséjour), 150 in the Baie-Verte region, and 150 at Fort Lawrence (near Amherst, N.S.). Boishébert nevertheless held his ground on the Saint John River under difficult conditions. On 12 Oct. 1756 he even undertook an expedition against Fort Monckton (formerly Fort Gaspereaux, near Port Elgin, N.B.), but the enemy evacuated the fort and set fire to it before he arrived. In January 1757 he went to the Miramichi River and there set up his headquarters and a refuge for the Acadians. With Father Charles GERMAIN's help he tried to sustain the Acadians' resistance to the British.

Boishébert's orders were to go to the aid of Louisbourg, if necessary. In 1757 rumours of a planned British attack on the fortress led Augustin de Boschenry* de Drucour, governor of Île Royale, to send for him. The anticipated attack did not take place, and Boishébert withdrew to Quebec where he spent the winter. He was to leave for Louisbourg early in the spring of 1758, but he delayed his departure until the beginning of May. Bougainville* predicted that "having left too late, Boishébert will probably amuse himself trading in furs at Miramichi." No evidence has been found that Boishébert was involved in trade, but he did indeed arrive too late. By the time he had collected a small force of Acadians and Indians and reached Louisbourg it was the beginning of July, and the British had landed a month earlier. He took up position at Miré (Mira), north of the fortress, and was expected to conduct guerrilla operations against the British siege lines. His efforts were of limited effectiveness, mainly because of the lack of munitions and supplies, the small number of soldiers under his command, and their poor physical condition. Some of the Indians and Acadians deserted so that he had but 140 able-bodied soldiers. In this precarious situation Boishébert succeeded in killing only one British soldier, taking one prisoner, and burning a guardhouse. Drucour and Abbé Pierre Maillard*, who was with the expedition, reproached him for his inactivity; Maillard later wrote that Boishébert had "from his earliest youth received more protection and favours than anyone else and so had been able to go to command at posts where there was more opportunity to become rich through trade than to win fame through military deeds." Boishébert, who had been made a knight of the order of Saint-Louis earlier that year, was aware that a greater effort had been expected of him on the expedition.

After Louisbourg fell on 26 July 1758, Boishébert withdrew, with the enemy in pursuit. He brought back a large number of Acadians from the region around Port-Toulouse (St Peters, N.S.) to the security of his post on the Miramichi. On 13 August he left Miramichi with 400 soldiers for Fort St George (Thomaston, Maine). His detachment reached there on 9 September but was caught in an ambush and had to withdraw. This was Boishébert's last Acadian expedition. In the autumn he left for Quebec. Montcalm*, who did not like Boishébert, wrote to LÉVIS: "He has made a hundred thousand *écus* in the last campaign," and, indulging his inclination to gossip, added: "I think he is lavishing his youth and his money on you-know-who."

With a corps of Acadian volunteers Boishébert took part in the defence of Quebec in the summer of 1759, and also in the decisive battle on the Plains of Abraham. In the winter he returned for the last time to Acadia, to gather reinforcements for the defence of Canada and to restore the morale of the discouraged Acadians. Learning upon his arrival that certain missionaries, among them abbés Jean Manach* and Pierre Maillard, had encouraged the Acadians to submit to the British, Boishébert spoke out against this attitude and vigorously reproached the missionaries for their baseness towards the mother country.

After the fall of Canada in 1760 Boishébert returned to France. He was accused of having participated in Intendant BIGOT's schemes and shortly after was imprisoned in the Bastille. It was claimed that he had profited personally from the purchase in Quebec of supplies for the starving Acadians. After 15 months in prison he was acquitted.

In 1763 Boishébert was involved in plans for settling Acadians at Cayenne (French Guiana) and vainly tried to obtain a military appointment there. In 1774 his request for an appointment as inspector of colonial troops was turned down. His Canadian seigneury of La Bouteillerie, also known as Rivière-Ouelle, was sold that year. Until his death, on 9 Jan. 1797, he lived in France at Raffetot, a property he had acquired through his marriage.

PHYLLIS E. LEBLANC

AN, Col., C[11A], 87, ff.314–64; 105, ff.47–50; C[11B], 35, f.130; C[11D], 8, ff.153–57; E, 36 (dossier Charles Deschamps de Boishébert). Bougainville, "Journal" (A.-E. Gosselin), ANQ *Rapport*, 1923–24. Clos, *Memorial on behalf of the Sieur de Boishébert . . .*, trans. Louise Manny, ed. J. C. Webster (Saint John, N.B., 1942). *Coll. de manuscrits relatifs à la N.-F.*, III, IV. *Coll. des manuscrits de Lévis* (Casgrain), VI, VII. *Les derniers jours de l'Acadie* (Du Boscq de Beaumont). Placide Gaudet, "Généalogie des familles acadiennes avec documents," PAC *Rapport*, 1905, II, IIIe partie, 236–43, 353–54, 365, 402–6, 409. "Journal du siège de Québec" (Æ. Fauteux), ANQ *Rapport*, 1920–21, 184, 235. [D.-H.-M. Liénard de] Beaujeu, "Journal de la campagne du détachement de Canada à l'Acadie et aux Mines, en 1746–47," *Coll. doc. inédits Canada et Amérique*, II, 25–27. *NYCD* (O'Callaghan and Fernow), X, 79–80. *Papiers Contrecœur* (Grenier). [John Witherspoon], "Journal of John Witherspoon, 1757–1759," N.S. Hist. Soc., *Coll.*, II (1881), 31–62.

P.-G. Roy, *Inv. concessions*, II, 250. H.-R. Casgrain, *Une seconde Acadie: l'île Saint-Jean – île du Prince-Édouard sous le Régime français* (Québec, 1894). Hunter, *Forts on Pa. frontier*. Corinne LaPlante, "Le traité d'Utrecht et l'Acadie, une étude de la correspondance secrète et officielle qui a entouré la signature du traité d'Utrecht" (thèse de MA, université de Moncton, Moncton, N.-B., 1974). P.-G. Roy, *Bigot et sa bande*; *La famille Des Champs de Boishébert* (Lévis, Qué., 1906). Stanley, *New France*. J. C. Webster, *Charles Des Champs de Boishébert, a Canadian soldier in Acadia* (n.p., 1931). Marquis de Grosourdy de Saint-Pierre, "Un cousin canadien en Normandie au XVIIIe siècle," *Nova Francia* (Paris), II (1926–27), 25–27. P.-G. Roy, "Charles Des Champs de Boishébert et de Raffetot," *BRH*, XII (1906), 105–11.

DESCHENAUX, JOSEPH BRASSARD. *See* BRASSARD

DESDEVENS DE GLANDONS, MAURICE, surveyor; b. 1742 in France, son of Joseph Desdevens de Glandons and Gabrielle Avet Forel; m. 19 Jan. 1767 Marie-Thérèse Mathon at Sainte-Geneviève-de-Batiscan (Batiscan, Que.); d. some time after 6 May 1799.

The date of Maurice Desdevens de Glandons' arrival in Canada is not known, nor is the date of his first commission. He did, however, work as a surveyor from 1767 until 1799 except for a ten-year period of exile in the United States. He had to take refuge there because he had helped the American invaders of Canada in 1775–76.

Desdevens de Glandons officially enlisted as a militia captain in 1775 with the approval of the American commander, Richard MONTGOMERY. During the siege of Quebec he transported munitions and foiled attempts at desertion. On 1 Jan. 1776 Benedict Arnold* ordered him to recruit as many men as possible to help form a company, and on 12 March named him a notary and surveyor under the senior engineering officer, Edward Antill.

On 7 Aug. 1776 Desdevens de Glandons was at Albany, New York; here, until September 1781, he worked with Canadian refugees who were not attached to any specific regiment. On 18 Oct. 1781 the pension and food rations he had been receiving since 10 Aug. 1776 were cut off. To supplement his now inadequate income, he worked illegally as a pedlar and innkeeper, having been refused a licence. His right to rations was reinstated on 6 May 1782, but these were quite inadequate for his family, which at that time included only two children, two daughters having starved to death at Albany in 1776. Each year until 1786 he vainly petitioned to have his pension restored. Finally, tired of it all, Desdevens de Glandons returned to Canada, probably that year; his surveying reports indicate he was working at Lake Champlain in 1786 and at Nicolet the following year.

On 8 May 1787 the governor general, Lord Dorchester [Carleton*], pardoned him, but a new commission as a surveyor was not issued to him. In March 1788 Desdevens de Glandons again requested a commission, apparently with success, and he continued in practice until at least 1799. The burial certificate for his wife, who died 6 May 1799, is the last document mentioning surveyor Desdevens de Glandons; he was then living at Verchères.

RUTH GARIÉPY SMALE

ANQ-M, État civil, Catholiques, Saint-François-Xavier (Verchères), 6 mai 1799; Procès-verbaux des arpenteurs, Maurice Desdevens de Glandons, 1767–99 (there is a gap from 6 Nov. 1775 to September 1786). Archives paroissiales, Sainte-Geneviève-de-Batiscan (Qué.), Registre des baptêmes, mariages et sépultures, 19 janv. 1767. PAC, MG 23, B3, CC35, pp.74–118;

B45; MG 30, D1, 10, pp.571–87. Corinne Rocheleau-Rouleau, "Maurice Desdevens de Glandon et l'invasion américaine, 1775–1776," *BRH*, XLI (1945), 372.

DESGLIS (Desgly). *See* MARIAUCHAU

DES MÉLOIZES, ANGÉLIQUE RENAUD D'AVÈNE. *See* RENAUD

DESPINS, JACQUES-JOSEPH LEMOINE. *See* LEMOINE

DESPINS, MARGUERITE-THÉRÈSE LEMOINE. *See* LEMOINE

DESROSIERS, JOSEPH DEGUIRE, *dit*. *See* DEGUIRE

DEVAU, *dit* **Retor, CLAUDE** (also spelled **Devaux, de Veaux, de Vox**), salt smuggler and blacksmith; b. *c.* 1704 in France, son of Benoît Devau and Marie Potier; d. 14 April 1784 at Sainte-Anne-de-la-Pérade (La Pérade, Que.).

Claude Devau, *dit* Retor, was banished from France for his involvement in the contraband salt trade and arrived in Canada in the 1730s with one of the numerous groups of salt smugglers deported to the colony between 1730 and 1742 [*see* Pierre Révol*]. The colonial authorities, who deplored the scattering of population and the marked decrease in immigration to Canada since the end of the 17th century, looked favourably upon the arrival of these men who swelled the ranks of the colonists, and they urged the king to send more of them to Canada. They feared the influence of the salt smugglers on the population much less than that of convicts or ne'er-do-well young men of good family; however, the quality of these recruits apparently deteriorated, since after 1735 correspondents from the colony praised them less.

On their arrival most of the salt smugglers were put to work on settlers' farms or enrolled in the troops. What became of Devau is not fully known, but he apparently set himself up as a blacksmith at Saint-Charles-de-Lachenaie. In January 1742 he underwent a premarital examination before Jacques-Joseph Lacombe, by means of which the parish priest was assured that he knew his prayers. To take a wife in Canada he also had to prove he had "come as a single man from France to Canada," and to do this he obtained a certificate from the commissary of Marine in Quebec, Jean-Victor VARIN de La Marre. On 1 Feb. 1742, at Sainte-Anne-de-la-Pérade, Devau married Marie-Madeleine Gendron, the daughter of a settler of that parish. The marriage settlement of six *livres* suggests that his means were slender. After his marriage he settled at Sainte-Anne-de-la-Pérade. There he first practised his blacksmith's trade and then began to farm. On 24 July 1747 the local seigneur, Pierre-Thomas Tarieu de La Pérade, granted him a piece of land with a frontage of four *arpents* and a depth of 20. On this land Claude Devau and his wife raised their large family. Nine children survived him when he died at Sainte-Anne-de-la-Pérade on 14 April 1784 "at about 80 years of age," according to the burial certificate. He was interred the next day in the parish cemetery.

One of a special class of immigrant, Claude Devau, *dit* Retor, is a good illustration of the salt smuggler turned settler who proved well suited to help colonize New France.

ANDRÉ LACHANCE

ANQ-MBF, État civil, Catholiques, Sainte-Anne-de-la-Pérade (La Pérade), 1er févr. 1742, 15 avril 1784; Greffe d'A.-B. Pollet, 11, 12, 13 mai 1743, 20 oct. 1746, 24 févr., 24 juill. 1747, 22 mai 1748; Greffe de Joseph Rouillard, 31 janv. 1742. Tanguay, *Dictionnaire*. Hamelin, *Économie et société en N.-F.*, 87–88. Gérard Malchelosse, "Faux sauniers, prisonniers et fils de famille en Nouvelle-France au XVIIIe siècle," *Cahiers des Dix*, 9 (1944), 161–97.

DIAQUANDE. *See* TEYOHAQUEANDE

DIMOCK, SHUBAEL, Baptist preacher; b. 27 May 1707 at Mansfield, Connecticut, son of Timothy Dimock (Dimmick) and Abigail Doane; d. 10 May 1781 at Newport, Nova Scotia.

Shubael Dimock originally belonged to the Congregational Church, the established church in Connecticut. He was, however, influenced by the religious revival known as the Great Awakening and became a leader in a group which separated from the church in Mansfield. Considered a threat to legitimate authority, the separates were persecuted by local officials in Windham County, and those who preached without being licensed ministers, including Dimock, were sentenced to jail. Dimock continued to preach, however, and told the magistrate he would persevere "unless you cut out my tongue." He stubbornly refused to pay rates for the support of the established church, although his wife sometimes paid them to avoid confiscation of valuables by the constable.

To escape further persecution the Dimocks immigrated to Nova Scotia, attracted by the promise in Governor Charles Lawrence*'s proclamation of 1759 of free grants of land, "full liberty of Conscience," and freedom from tithes. Family tradition relates that while Shubael was in jail, his son Daniel had visited Nova Scotia and later persuaded his father to immigrate there and that the Dimocks were in the Falmouth area six months before the other New England planters arrived in the spring of 1760 [*see* John HICKS]. Certainly Dimock was one of the holders of the first Falmouth grant of 1759, only 18 of whom actually settled in Falmouth. When a second grant was made in 1761, he received one share of 500 acres. At the same time Daniel obtained half a share in the township of Newport across the Pisiquid (Avon) River.

Shubael gave temporal as well as spiritual guidance in the new settlement. He was elected moderator of the first meeting of the Falmouth proprietors on 10 June 1760, when a standing committee of three was appointed to settle the grantees on their lands and to make regulations for local government. For several years he was chosen moderator of the town meetings. He presided when lots were drawn in the summer of 1760 for former Acadian homes and buildings and for all boards and timber in the township, when the formal Falmouth grant was received from Henry Denny DENSON on 23 March 1762, and when the arrangements were made in September 1762 for the repair of the dykes of the Great Marsh. He had brought with him from New England a stubborn belief in the right of the individual to participate in the decisions of local government; he was one of the inhabitants of what was then Kings County who in 1762 joined Robert Denison* in protesting to the Lords of Trade that the promises made by Lawrence for "the Protection of the Government in all our civil and Religious Rights and Liberties" had not been kept, in demanding their own township government, and in condemning the conduct of Denson, who was "a Reproach to Authority, and a great Discouragement to Religion and Piety among Us."

In his new home Shubael Dimock gathered a few pious persons "round him to hear him preach." Although Daniel had become converted to baptism by immersion and was baptized in 1763, Shubael was not convinced. After prolonged study of the Scriptures, however, he was baptized in the Kennetcook River by his son. Both worked to promote the cause of religion in Newport and Falmouth, the one preaching in the morning and the other in the afternoon. In 1771 Shubael was regarded as having the pastoral care of "a Considerable Number" of Baptists in Newport, where he then lived, and in 1776 the Dimocks shared in the fellowship of Baptists and Congregationalists which the New Light preacher Henry ALLINE established there. According to his grandson Joseph*, Dimock did not agree with all the peculiarities of Alline's creed but nevertheless regarded him as "an eminent instrument in the hands of the Almighty to call sinners to repentance." Although Dimock's own preaching talents may have been small, Alline praised his eloquent gifts in prayer and exhortation, saying "I never heard any person pray who looks so directly into heaven and leads others with him as he does."

Shubael Dimock was married three times: to Percilla Hovey on 11 Dec. 1731 at Mansfield; to Eunice Marsh on 10 Nov. 1747, also at Mansfield; and to Sarah Knowlton, widow of Abraham Masters (Marsters), on 22 Oct. 1768 at Newport. Altogether he had 13 children, two of whom died young. A pioneer among the Baptists of Nova Scotia, he was a firm believer in the right of the individual to make his own decisions about his religion. Three generations of his family carried on missionary work for the expansion of the Baptist denomination.

PHYLLIS R. BLAKELEY

Hants County Court of Probate (Windsor, N.S.), loose petitions and wills, 1761–98 (will of Shubael Dimock, proved 9 Aug. 1781). PAC, MG 9, B9, Newport, 1 (mfm. at PANS). PANS, MG 4, no.31 (Falmouth Township records). *Births, baptisms, marriages and deaths, from the records of the town and churches in Mansfield, Connecticut, 1703–1850*, comp. S. W. Dimock (New York, 1898). *A genealogy of the Dimock family from the year 1637*, comp. J. D. Marsters (Windsor, N.S., 1899), 5–20.

M. W. Armstrong, *The Great Awakening in Nova Scotia, 1776–1809* (Hartford, Conn., 1948). I. E. Bill, *Fifty years with the Baptist ministers and churches of the Maritime provinces of Canada* (Saint John, N.B., 1880), 28–29. J. M. Bumsted, *Henry Alline, 1748–1784* (Toronto, 1971). J. V. Duncanson, *Falmouth – a New England township in Nova Scotia, 1760–1965* (Windsor, Ont., 1965). H. Y. Hind, *Sketch of the old parish burying ground of Windsor, Nova Scotia . . .* (Windsor, 1889), 48–50, 52. *Baptist Missionary Magazine of Nova-Scotia and New-Brunswick* (Saint John and Halifax), new ser., III (1836), 171–77. J. M. Bumsted, "Origins of the Maritime Baptists: a new document," *Dal. Rev.*, XLIX (1969–70), 88–93.

DIXON, GEORGE, naval officer and maritime fur-trader; fl. 1776–91.

George Dixon, an armourer in the Royal Navy per a warrant dated 16 April 1776, joined the *Discovery* on the same day. In July he sailed for the Pacific on Captain James COOK's third voyage of exploration. As an armourer Dixon was a skilled mechanic, with the rating of petty officer first-class, whose duty it was to assist the gunner in keeping the ship's arms in order. The *Discovery* was at King George's Sound (Nootka Sound,

B.C.) in March and April 1778 and touched at other places along the northwest coast before returning to England in 1780. The voyage must have fired in Dixon an interest in discovery, for in August 1784 he wrote to Sir Joseph Banks*, the influential president of the Royal Society of London, to suggest the mounting of an overland expedition, with himself as "astronomer," to cross North America via Quebec and the Great Lakes. Nothing came of this venture, perhaps, as he himself observed, because of the "troubled state" of America.

Cook's voyage had initiated the maritime fur trade in sea otter pelts with China. In 1785 Dixon and Nathaniel Portlock*, a shipmate in the *Discovery*, became partners in Richard Cadman Etches and Company, commonly called the King George's Sound Company, one of several commercial associations formed to prosecute the trade. Two vessels were fitted out that year by the company, the *King George* and the *Queen Charlotte*, and a licence to trade on the northwest coast was purchased from the South Sea Company, which held the monopoly for the Pacific coast. Portlock was given command of the *King George* and of the expedition, Dixon command of the *Queen Charlotte*. William Beresford, the trader assigned to the expedition, wrote that Dixon and Portlock had been chosen for their ability as navigators, their knowledge of the Indians and of the best trading spots, and because they were "men of feeling and humanity, and pay the most strict attention to the health of their ships companies, a circumstance of the utmost consequence in a voyage of such length."

The vessels left London on 29 Aug. 1785 and arrived at Cook Inlet (Alas.) the next July. There they traded with the Indians before sailing to winter in the Sandwich (Hawaiian) Islands. In the spring of 1787 they sailed to Prince William Sound (Alas.), where they met another British trader, John Meares*, whose ship had been iced in. Meares's crew was in great disorder, either from scurvy, as he claimed, or from "uncontrolled application to spirituous liquors," as Beresford later charged. Dixon and Portlock lent aid but exacted from Meares, who was trading illegally within the bounds of the South Sea Company's monopoly, a bond not to trade on the coast.

From Prince William Sound, Dixon, having separated as planned from Portlock, sailed south to trade. He came across a large archipelago, which he named the Queen Charlotte Islands (B.C.). Although Captain Robert Gray*, of the American sloop *Lady Washington*, was to call these islands after his own ship in 1789, British possession of the coast allowed for the continuance of Dixon's appellation. Dixon sailed along the western shores of the islands, named Cape St James, and then went up their eastern coasts as far as Skidegate. Along the way he purchased a large number of sea otter pelts from the Haidas, trading at one time with the village of the chief KOYAH. Dixon reached Nootka Sound in mid August, only to find that he had been preceded by captains James Colnett* and Charles DUNCAN, who had obtained most of the furs. Since Portlock failed to appear at Nootka, Dixon steered for the Sandwich Islands and China. He sold his furs there and then returned to England in September 1788.

Although there is no record that Dixon was ever again at sea, he retained an interest in the exploration of the northwest coast of America and the search for a northwest passage. In 1789 he met with both the hydrographer Alexander Dalrymple and Evan Nepean, an influential government official, and in July he urged on the latter Dalrymple's plan for a settlement on the northwest coast in order to prevent the Russians, Americans, or Spaniards from establishing themselves there. Dixon was afraid that if the government did nothing the coast and its trade would be lost to Britain, "and in consequence of that Loss the Traders both from Hudson's Bay and Canada will find themselves in a bad neighbourhood." In October he wrote Banks regarding the expedition being outfitted under the command of Captain Henry Roberts and George VANCOUVER, offering suggestions about the type of vessels that should be used and the best place to establish a settlement on the northwest coast. The opinions of Christopher Middleton* and Cook to the contrary, Dalrymple still believed in the existence of a northwest passage, and he persuaded the Hudson's Bay Company to explore once more the west coast of Hudson Bay. In May 1790 the company entrusted the expedition to Charles Duncan. Dixon, who was to accompany him, was instructed to take the expedition inland from the Dubawnt and Yathkyed lakes (N.W.T.) to the Pacific by way of Great Slave Lake. For some reason Dixon's part of the journey was subsequently cancelled, and he did not accompany Duncan.

Dixon had published *A voyage round the world; but more particularly to the north-west coast of America . . .* , in London in 1789. He wrote the introduction and the appendix, but the body of the text consists of a series of letters written by Beresford. When Meares published an account of his voyages of 1788 and 1789, Dixon wrote a pamphlet criticizing its many inaccuracies; there followed a minor pamphlet war between the two men, from which Dixon emerged the victor.

It has been suggested that Dixon taught navigation at Gosport and wrote *The navigator's assistant* . . . , published in 1791. There are no references to him after that date. A skilled navigator and successful trader, Dixon rose from obscurity to become an important figure in the history of the northwest coast.

BARRY M. GOUGH

[George Dixon's pamphlets, *Remarks on the voyages of John Meares, esq., in a letter to that gentleman* (London, 1790) and *Further remarks on the voyages of John Meares, esq.* . . . (London, 1791), have been reprinted in *The Dixon-Meares controversy* . . . , ed. F. W. Howay (Toronto and New York, 1929; repr. Amsterdam and New York, 1969). Dixon may also have authored *The navigator's assistant; or, a new and methodised system of naval mathematics* . . . (London, 1791). Certain of his letters have been published: "Letters of Captain George Dixon in the Banks collection," ed. R. H. Dillon, *British Columbia Hist. Quarterly* (Victoria), XIV (1950), 167–71. B.M.G.]

The Banks letters; a calendar of the manuscript correspondence of Sir Joseph Banks . . . , ed. W. R. Dawson (London, 1958). [William Beresford], *A voyage round the world; but more particularly to the north-west coast of America* . . . , ed. and intro. George Dixon (London, 1789; repr. Amsterdam and New York, 1968). Nathaniel Portlock, *A voyage round the world; but more particularly to the north-west coast of America* . . . (London, 1789; repr. Amsterdam and New York, 1968). PAC *Report*, 1889, 29. *DNB*. Walbran, *B.C. coast names*. Cook, *Flood tide of empire*. H. T. Fry, *Alexander Dalrymple (1737–1808) and the expansion of British trade* (Buffalo, N.Y., and Toronto, 1970). Glyndwr Williams, *The British search for the northwest passage in the eighteenth century* (London and Toronto, 1962).

DOANE, ELIZABETH. *See* OSBORN

DOGGETT, JOHN, mariner, merchant, office-holder, and militia officer; b. 6 Feb. 1723/24 at Plymouth, Massachusetts, son of Ebenezer Doggett and Elizabeth Rickard; m. 3 Nov. 1748 Abigail House, at Scituate, Massachusetts, and they had eight children; d. 20 March 1772 at Port Mouton Island (Mouton Island), Nova Scotia.

John Doggett had moved to Scituate by 1748, and he worked as a sea-captain and then as keeper of a ferry. His attention was turned towards Nova Scotia as early as 1757, for when Governor Charles Lawrence* went to Boston that year he urged Doggett to accept a grant of a Nova Scotia township for himself and others. Lawrence was eager to promote settlement of the lands formerly held by the Acadians and of the other vacant lands in the colony, but security and representative government had to be provided before New Englanders in substantial numbers would migrate to Nova Scotia. Shortly afterwards circumstances began to change. In 1758 Louisbourg, Île Royale (Cape Breton Island), was captured, and the first elected legislature was convened in Nova Scotia.

By 1759 Doggett and other New Englanders were showing a keen interest in the colony, and the government developed a settlement scheme which projected 14 townships along the south shore, through the Annapolis valley, along Minas Basin, and across the Chignecto Isthmus. Doggett endeavoured to procure settlers by journeying throughout New England, and on behalf of themselves and others he, his brother Samuel, Elisha Freeman, and Thomas Foster applied for a tract of land. A grant of Liverpool Township was issued to them on 1 Sept. 1759. There were to be 41 grantees for the first settlement by the "last [of] September next" and a total of 164 families by the end of September 1762. In the spring of 1760 the first 50 families arrived in the township. Some came in their own fishing schooners; others were brought in provincial vessels such as the *York and Halifax* (Capt. Silvanus Cobb*). The local responsibility for the promotion of the settlement was largely Doggett's. He hired ships to transport the immigrants and distributed relief to the needy. For his services he was afterwards paid £90 by the Nova Scotia government.

Although Liverpool had difficulties in its early days it made progress, and the energetic, able Doggett was a leading resident. The second town meeting was held at his house on Doggett's Point on 8 July 1760. He had a store and in 1762 he purchased a half interest in a sawmill on Mill Brook. In 1761 he had received a licence to occupy and improve Port Mouton Island, and on 31 Dec. 1763 the Nova Scotia Council advised that it be granted to him.

Doggett held numerous offices in the township. On 26 May 1760 he was appointed one of its first two justices of the peace, and in July he became a member of the proprietors' committee and of a committee to lay out a common for fish flakes. On 22 July 1761 he was made truckmaster for the management of trade with the Indians, a position he seems to have held until Simeon Perkins* was commissioned in 1766. Doggett's appointment to a committee for dividing forfeited lands in the township and for admitting other settlers was authorized by the Nova Scotia Council on 15 Aug. 1761. He became collector of impost and excise for the township on 23 Nov. 1761 and major in the militia on 20 July 1762. On 6 Jan. 1764 he was appointed judge of the Inferior Court of Common Pleas for Queens County and in the same year he became the county's first registrar of deeds.

When news of the repeal of the Stamp Act was received on 3 June 1766 there was a day of rejoicing in Liverpool. During the proceedings some of the militia marched to Major Doggett's home, where they were entertained. In 1770 Doggett was elected to the House of Assembly and on 9 June of the following year he was commissioned lieutenant-colonel in the county militia. He died on 20 March 1772 "after a tedious and lingering illness" at Port Mouton Island, to which he may have been isolated on account of a contagious disease.

CHARLES BRUCE FERGUSSON

PANS, MG 1, 828 (T. B. Smith genealogy); MG 4, no.77 (Liverpool Township docs.); RG 1, 164, 165, 211, 359. Private archives, Seth Bartling (Liverpool, N.S.), R. J. Long, "The annals of Liverpool and Queen's County, 1760–1867" (1926) (typescript at Dalhousie University Library, Halifax; mfm. at PANS). N.S., House of Assembly, *Journal*, 1770–71. Perkins, *Diary, 1766–80* (Innis). "Vital records of Liverpool, N.S.," *New England Hist. and Geneal. Register*, CXXVI (1972), 94–102. *Directory of N.S. MLAs*. S. B. Doggett, *A history of the Doggett-Daggett family* (Boston, 1894). C. B. Fergusson, *Early Liverpool and its diarist* (Halifax, 1961). J. F. More, *The history of Queens County, N.S.* (Halifax, 1873; repr. Belleville, Ont., 1972). F. E. Crowell, "New Englanders in Nova Scotia: no.39 – Doggett, Daggett," *Yarmouth Herald* (Yarmouth, N.S.), 6 Nov. 1928.

DOLOBARATS. *See* OLABARATZ

DOMBOURG, JEAN-FRANÇOIS BOURDON DE. *See* BOURDON

DON JACQUE. *See* ANGEAC

DOSQUET, PIERRE-HERMAN, Sulpician, priest of the Missions Étrangères, and fourth bishop of Quebec; b. 4 March 1691 at Liège (Belgium), son of Laurent Dosquet, a merchant and bourgeois, and Anne-Jeanne Goffar; d. 4 March 1777 in Paris, France.

Nothing is known of Pierre-Herman Dosquet's youth other than that in 1715 he entered the Sulpician seminary in Paris, where he was ordained priest the following year. Admitted to the Society of Saint-Sulpice in 1721, he then volunteered for the mission in Canada, arriving there in July that year. For two years he served as chaplain of the Congregation of Notre-Dame in Montreal, to the nuns' satisfaction. Poor health and the climate led him to return to France in 1723.

Dosquet then became the superior of the Séminaire de Lisieux, retaining this office until 1725. At this period the Society of Saint-Sulpice supplied the Séminaire des Missions Étrangères with some of its members, and Abbé Dosquet was one. He became a director of the Paris seminary and was sent to Rome as its procurator. On 25 Dec. 1725 he was named bishop of Samos *in partibus*, with the honorary title of assistant to the papal throne. He also held the position of procurator general for the apostolic vicars of the East Indies.

In December 1727 Bishop Saint-Vallier [La Croix*] died in Quebec. For nearly two years Quebec had no resident bishop, since the coadjutor, Bishop Louis-François Duplessis de Mornay, never set foot in Canada. On 25 May 1729 Dosquet was appointed administrator of the diocese by Mornay, now titular bishop, and Pope Clement XII signed the bull naming him coadjutor on 24 July 1730.

In mid June 1729 Dosquet sailed from Rochefort on the *Éléphant*, accompanied by an imposing retinue. His arrival was not, however, as impressive as had been anticipated, because on 2 September the ship struck a reef near Île aux Grues. In a letter of 15 May 1735 to his brother, Canon Pierre HAZEUR de L'Orme noted: "The bells, the cannon, the dais . . . demonstrated perfectly the joy everyone felt at his coming, [a joy] which, according to what you wrote to me, he did not fully reciprocate."

The new coadjutor was to find himself confronted with several problems. He stayed at the Séminaire de Québec initially, since the bishop's palace was in disrepair and in addition he was unsure whether the bishop was its owner. In his will Bishop Saint-Vallier had made the nuns of the Hôpital Général his sole legatees, but he had bequeathed the bishop's palace to his successor, on condition that he maintain it. This ambiguity concerning the ownership engendered a quarrel that would only be settled later under Bishop Pontbriand [Dubreil*]. However, after costly repairs Dosquet was able to move into the bishop's palace; he never felt at home there because the palace had a rampart walk on which the public used to gather.

At the time of Dosquet's arrival in Quebec certain religious communities of women, particularly the hospital nuns and the Ursulines, were living under difficult conditions resulting from the discord that had arisen upon Bishop Saint-Vallier's death [*see* Claude-Thomas Dupuy*; Étienne Boullard*]. Dosquet criticized the religious life of these communities harshly, and this action scarcely made him popular, especially since Governor Charles de Beauharnois* and Intendant HOCQUART did not share his opinion. The bishop even required the Ursulines to destroy about 25 pages of their annals which described their dispute with the chapter of Quebec over their confessor.

Dosquet enjoyed no better relations with the chapter; there was nothing but mutual recrimination. The bishop almost systematically took the opposite view to the chapter's decisions. However, neither meanness nor personal rivalries were the reason for the bishop's attitude. In the opinion of Beauharnois and his contemporaries "the coadjutor is a saintly man . . . who applies himself to putting everything in order." He simply lacked a modicum of tact and diplomacy, as for instance when he set the governor and the intendant against him by getting the minister of Marine to forbid them free access to the convents.

Dosquet shared his predecessors' opinion about the liquor trade. He differed from them, however, in visiting his diocese only once, in the summer of 1731, and he availed himself of the occasion to have his priests sign a condemnation of Jansenist ideas. During this visit he became aware of the straitened circumstances of his parish priests, and as a result asked that the tithe be increased to a thirteenth from a twenty-sixth – a request refused by the king, to the great relief of the Canadian settlers. The coadjutor himself was in a difficult position financially, since he had not received the revenues of the benefices attached to the bishopric of Quebec. Dosquet therefore decided to return to France to secure either Bishop Mornay's resignation or his move to Canada. Dosquet sailed on the *Rubis* on 15 Oct. 1732, after selling some of his possessions, for in the event that he should meet with a refusal he did not wish to return to Canada as coadjutor.

In France Dosquet made efforts to clarify the situation of the episcopal see of Quebec. In the autumn of 1733 Mornay resigned, and Dosquet succeeded him, receiving various gratuities granted by the king. The new titular bishop left La Rochelle on 31 May 1734, with an entourage of 11. On 8 August Canon Eustache Chartier* de Lotbinière, archdeacon of the chapter, took possession of the bishop's palace in the name of Dosquet, who reached Quebec on 16 August. No description of his arrival has been found; Beauharnois and Hocquart simply mention in a dispatch that "he has been received with all the honours due his position." Dosquet took up virtually permanent residence at Samos, a house in Sillery that he had bought in 1730. His remoteness from the centre of the city assuredly did nothing to foster good relations between the bishop and his people, who saw little of him during his term of office, especially since he made no episcopal visits. Indeed, certain of his decisions displeased the Canadians: in February 1735 he issued a pastoral letter revoking all the powers accorded the priests in his diocese by his predecessor, and on the pretext of correcting certain abuses he forbade priests to be served by women in their presbyteries unless they were close relatives. In addition he prohibited ecclesiastics from wearing wigs and barred schoolmasters from teaching classes with pupils of both sexes. Only one directive seemed likely to win him praise from posterity: in February 1735 he urged parish priests to teach Latin to the children who seemed to have a priestly vocation.

As Beauharnois and Hocquart noted, Dosquet felt that he was "held in little esteem by the people," and relations between him and his clergy had become strained. Alleging that the air of his native land would do his health good, and that financial matters particularly required his presence in France, he sailed on the *Héros* on 19 Oct. 1735. As he was far from sure he would return, he took all his staff with him; in addition he ordered the doorkeeper of the bishop's palace to sell his furniture, and to offset his debts he assigned Samos to the seminary, as well as half of his seigneury of Bourgchemin, bought from Vaudreuil [Pierre de RIGAUD] in 1731.

Dosquet spent his last years as bishop of Quebec travelling in France. Correspondence between him and the court on the subject of his resignation began in 1736. As he did not wish to return to Canada, he finally agreed to resign, provided the king would guarantee him attractive benefices. Having at last obtained the revenues from the abbey of Breine, near Soissons, and settled the question of the repairs to the bishop's palace in Quebec, he signed his resignation early in 1739. Bishop François-Louis de Pourroy* de Lauberivière succeeded him. Dosquet then lived alternately in Rome and Paris. As vicar general of the archbishop of Paris he had the opportunity to render certain services to his successors until his death on 4 March 1777.

It is difficult to make a judgement about Bishop Dosquet's service in Canada. Everyone praised his piety and intelligence. However, Beauharnois stressed that "his administration [was] too autocratic, which alienated people from the trust they might have had in him," and that to make matters worse he was a Walloon and therefore a foreigner. Moreover, unlike his predecessors, Dosquet was not ready to make sacrifices, money matters having preoccupied him far too much. Yet, it must be emphasized that he arrived in Quebec at a time of great difficulty for the Canadian church, which was still troubled by the dissensions that followed Bishop Saint-Vallier's death.

JEAN-GUY PELLETIER

AAQ, 20 A, I, 19; 22 A, II, 273, 285, 287, 298, 299, 301–4, 393, 425, 428, 431, 434, 445, 446, 460, 477, 486, 487, 492, 494, 507, 508; 10 B, 72, 77, 84; 11 B, IV, 45; VI, 27, 28, 63, 65, 70, 76, 81; VII, 47; CD, Diocèse de Québec, I, 39; 10 CM, I, 62; 91 CM, I, 8; 60 CN, III, 83; 167 CN, I, 88; Dosquet, P.-H., note personnelle de l'archiviste sur son lieu de sépulture. AN, Col., C[11A], 51–72. ASQ, Chapitre, 146; Doc. Faribault, no.230; Évêques, no.179a, b; Fonds Viger-Verreau, Sér. O, 035, p.7; Lettres, M, 48, 67, 79, 80, 88, 90, 93, 95, 99; R, 8; S, 105; Y, 75; Paroisse de Québec, 19; Polygraphie, V, 22, 40; IX, 33; XI, 3; Séminaire, 3, no.51; 5, nos.73, 74; 12, nos.2a, 2f; 14/5, nos.16, 27, 28, 33, 35; 34, no.137; 40, no.71b; 79, no.4. AUQ, "Annales," I.

"Liste des passagers sur la flutte du roy l'Éléphant destinée pour Québec," *BRH*, XXXVII (1931), 61–62. *Mandements des évêques de Québec* (Têtu et Gagnon), I, 529–52. "Mgr Dosquet et le naufrage de l'Éléphant," *BRH*, XIII (1907), 315–16. *DBF*, XI, 631. Le Jeune, *Dictionnaire*. PAC *Rapport*, 1886, xcvi–cxl; 1904, app. K, 108–269. P.-G. Roy, *Inv. concessions*, IV, 108–11, 114–15, 237–38; V, 276–77; *Inv. jug. et délib., 1717–60*, II, 77. Tanguay, *Répertoire*. Louis Bertrand, *Bibliothèque sulpicienne, ou histoire littéraire de la Compagnie de Saint-Sulpice* (3v., Paris, 1900), III, 168–84. P.-J.-O. Chauveau, *Bertrand de La Tour* (Lévis, Que., 1898). A.-H. Gosselin, *L'Église du Canada jusqu'à la Conquête*, II, 48–363. O'Reilly, *Mgr de Saint-Vallier et l'Hôpital Général*, 280–304. Rochemonteix, *Les jésuites et la N.-F. au XVIIIe siècle*, I, 157–68. P.-G. Roy, *La ville de Québec sous le Régime français* (2v., Québec, 1930), II, 129–32. *The storied province of Quebec; past and present*, ed. William Wood *et al.* (5v., Toronto, 1931–32), I, 490–96. L.-É. Bois, "Mgr Duplessis-Mornay," *BRH*, XVIII (1912), 311–19. [P.-]P.-B. Casgrain, "L'habitation de Samos," RSC *Trans.*, 2nd ser., XII (1906), sect.I, 3–35. Micheline D'Allaire, "Les prétentions des religieuses de l'Hôpital Général de Québec sur le palais épiscopal de Québec," *RHAF*, XXIII (1969–70), 53–67. N.-E. Dionne, "Le naufrage de l'Éléphant," *BRH*, XI (1905), 119–21. A.-H. Gosselin, "Mgr Dosquet et M. Voyer," *BRH*, VII (1901), 366–67; "Québec en 1730 . . . ," RSC *Trans.*, 2nd ser., V (1899), sect.I, 3–62. Têtu, "Le chapitre de la cathédrale," *BRH*, XIII, 225–43, 257–83, 289–307, 321–27, 353–61; XIV, 3–21, 33–39, 65–79, 97–109.

DOUCET (Dowset), PIERRE (Pitre), ship's captain and merchant; b. 16 May 1750 at Annapolis Royal (N.S.), son of François Doucet and Marguerite Petitot, *dit* Saint-Sceine (Sincennes); m. 1773 Marie-Marguerite Le Blanc at Salem, Massachusetts; d. after September 1799.

In 1755 François Doucet and his family were deported to Boston and settled in Salem. Like most Acadian families exiled in Massachusetts, the Doucets were in dire poverty, and the children were soon placed in foster homes. Pierre Doucet was adopted by a sea captain who instructed him in navigation and saw to it that he received an education. In 1773 Doucet married and settled with his wife in Casquebaye (Portland, Maine), where his first child, Olivier, was born on 20 Dec. 1774.

Two years earlier Doucet's father had left Massachusetts and, along with Pierre LE BLANC and some others, settled along St Mary's Bay in the district of Clare (N.S.). In the spring of 1775 Pierre Doucet bought from Joseph Gravois, one of these settlers, a tract of 360 acres near Sissiboo (Weymouth). Gravois had already built a house there, and Doucet and his wife moved in. Their second child was born there in 1776.

It is not known when Doucet received captain's papers, but by the time of his arrival in St Mary's Bay he was commanding vessels. In December 1775 he sailed from Halifax in his schooner *Eunice*, bound for Grenada. In the years that followed he established a triangular trade between Nova Scotia, the West Indies, and Boston. He usually carried lumber, potatoes, apples, and dried cod to the West Indies, whence he sailed for Boston with a mixed cargo of sugar, rum, and molasses. From there he returned to St Mary's Bay with some of the West Indian cargo together with cloth, utensils, building materials, and flour. These articles he sold in his warehouse at Belliveau Cove. Raw materials and manufactures were not his only cargo; in August 1791 he cleared Kingston (Jamaica) in his schooner *Peggy*, bound for Havana with ten slaves. By 1795 the French revolution and the consequent activities of French privateers had disrupted the pattern of his trade, and he turned his interest to local freighting operations. In that year he planned, according to James Moody*, to carry coal between Cape Breton and Halifax "for the use of the government, on freight."

In spite of his travels as a sea captain, Doucet still found time for the affairs of the Acadian community at St Mary's Bay. He was a major in the Acadian militia of Annapolis County in 1794, and in March 1797 he and some other Clare inhabitants petitioned the government for aid in making and repairing roads.

Although it has been written that Doucet was drowned near the Grand Passage in 1798, it is quite possible that the report was erroneous. In September 1799 Simeon Perkins* noted in his diary that "Capt. Dowset of Sissiboo, puts on here [Liverpool, N.S.] in his way to Halifax."

Credit is due Doucet for having shown the people of Clare the opportunities offered by the type of commerce in which he engaged. Many followed his example, and the district of Clare prospered for a century from this triangular trade.

J.-ALPHONSE DEVEAU

Archives du Centre acadien, Collège Sainte-Anne (Church Point, N.-É.), Pierre Doucet, généalogie. PAC, MG 30, C20, 6, pp.1435–1, 1435–2, 1438–1. Private archives, Adolphe Doucet (Belliveau Cove, N.S.), Pierre Doucet papers (copies at Archives du Centre acadien). Perkins, *Diary, 1797–1803* (Fergusson), 76, 169, 191. Antoine Bernard, *Histoire de la survivance acadienne, 1755–1935* (Montréal, 1935), 238. P.-M. Dagnaud, *Les Français du sud-ouest de la Nouvelle Écosse* . . . (Besançon, France, 1905). I. W. Wilson, *A geography and history of the county of Digby, Nova Scotia* (Halifax, 1900). Placide Gaudet, "Unknown yet prominent," *Halifax Herald*, 10 Nov. 1897, 1, 5.

DOUGLAS, Sir CHARLES, naval officer; m. Lydia Schimmelpinck, and they had two sons and one daughter; m. secondly Sarah Wood, and they had one son and one daughter; m. thirdly Jane Baillie; d. 16 March 1789 at Edinburgh, Scotland.

Little is known of Charles Douglas' early life except that he served as a midshipman at the siege of Louisbourg, Île Royale (Cape Breton Island), in 1745. After some delay he was promoted lieutenant in 1753. During the Seven Years' War he came to the attention of the Admiralty and was promoted commander in February 1759; that year, in command of the armed ship *Boscawen*, he performed useful service for Vice-Admiral Charles SAUNDERS' fleet during the Quebec campaign. Having been promoted post-captain in March 1761, the following year he commanded the sixth-rate *Siren* (24 guns) on the Newfoundland station. When a French force under Charles-Henri-Louis d'ARSAC de Ternay attacked the island that summer, Douglas helped to contain the invasion with his marines and was the first to inform Commodore Lord Colvill* of the situation. He also commanded the naval force covering Lieutenant-Colonel William Amherst's landing at Torbay on 13 September, and in recognition of his services he was given the honour of carrying Colvill's dispatches to London in October. He remained on the same station the following year in command of the frigate *Tweed* (32 guns) and ensured, by ingenious delays, that James COOK could finish the survey of Saint-Pierre and Miquelon before the islands were turned over to their new French governor François-Gabriel d'ANGEAC.

In 1764 and 1765, apparently through influence at the British court, Douglas served as a flag officer in the Russian navy. He commanded various ships during the next ten years. In 1776, in the *Isis* (50 guns), he again played a vital role when on 6 May he brought relief to Quebec, then under siege by Benedict Arnold*. The early arrival had been achieved by forcing the *Isis* through thick pack ice in the Gulf of St Lawrence, a remarkable feat of seamanship which Douglas described in extravagant terms to the Admiralty. Douglas remained in Canada during the campaigning season of 1776, and by clever improvisations involving difficult transport from the St Lawrence as well as innovations in methods of naval construction he and his subordinates created a fleet of small ships on Lake Champlain which defeated Arnold's flotilla in the battle of Valcour Island (11–13 October). This feat required no embroidery, and it bespoke great personal expertise, whether or not the measure was entirely necessary.

In recognition of his services in helping to repulse the American invader, Douglas was created a baronet in January 1777. He subsequently commanded the *Stirling Castle* (70 guns) from 1777 to 1778 and the *Duke* (90 guns) from 1778 to 1781, and he served as captain of the fleet to admirals Sir George Brydges Rodney and Hugh Pigot in the West Indies from 1781 to 1783. Douglas is chiefly remembered for his innovations in naval gunnery, especially when he commanded the *Duke* and was captain of the fleet to Rodney. It is also generally accepted that he persuaded Rodney to steer through the French line at the battle of the Saintes on 12 April 1782.

Appointed "to the Naval Command in Nova Scotia and Seas adjacent" following the American revolution, Douglas arrived at Halifax on 30 May 1784. He played a large part in adjusting the region to the postwar situation by interpreting and applying treaty obligations with the United States and making transports available to Governor John PARR for provisioning loyalist settlements. In November he demanded his recall, however, when the Admiralty refused to stand behind the measures he thought were necessary to reform the Halifax dockyard, whose commissioner, Henry Duncan*, was responsible not to him but to the Navy Board. Douglas was promoted rear-admiralof the blue in September 1787. Two years later he was again appointed to the command at Halifax, but he died before taking it up. His youngest son Howard* became a governor of New Brunswick.

W. A. B. DOUGLAS

An engraving of Henry Singleton's portrait of Sir Charles Douglas hangs in the National Maritime Museum in London.

National Maritime Museum, SAN/1–5, SAN/T/1–8. PAC, MG 18, L4, pkt.20. PRO, Adm. 1/482, ff.413, 429–35, 441; 1/487; 1/491; 1/1704; 1/1706; 1/1709; Prob.

11/1176, ff.143–44. *Burke's peerage* (1953). Charnock, *Biographia navalis*, VI, 427ff. *DNB*. G.B., Adm., *Commissioned sea officers*. William Playfair, *British family antiquity; illustrative of the origin and progress of the rank, honours and personal merit of the nobility of the United Kingdom* . . . (9v., London, 1809–11), VII, pt.1, app., lxxxix. W. L. Clowes, *The Royal Navy; a history from the earliest times to the present* (7v., London, 1897–1903), III. John Creswell, *British admirals of the eighteenth century; tactics in battle* (London, 1972). Howard Douglas, *Naval evolutions* . . . (London, 1832). S. W. Fullom, *The life of General Sir Howard Douglas* . . . (London, 1863). A. T. Mahan, *The influence of sea power upon history, 1660–1783* (Boston, 1890). [W. C.] B. Tunstall, *Flights of naval genius* (London, 1930).

[S. W. Fullom referred to private Douglas papers that can no longer be located. It seems likely that Playfair relied on such papers. Unfortunately, the elevation of Douglas to a baronetcy seems to have caused a discreet curtain to be drawn upon the period of his early life, and more attention than necessary has been paid to his lineal descent from James, 4th Earl of Morton. This concealment is a pity, because knowledge of his early years might shed light on his innovative abilities. W.A.B.D.]

DOUGLAS, FRANÇOIS-PROSPER, Chevalier de DOUGLAS, officer in the French regular troops; b. 21 Feb. 1725 at Montréal, in Bugey (dept of Ain), France, son of Charles Douglas, Comte de Douglas, syndic of the nobility of Bugey and officer, and Marie-Anne de Lilia; d. 26 April 1781 at Nantua, France.

In keeping with family tradition, François-Prosper Douglas took up a military career. In 1743 he was a second lieutenant in the Régiment du Languedoc, the next year he was promoted lieutenant, and he subsequently took part in several European campaigns. In 1746 he was made captain of a company in the second battalion of his regiment, and he still held this command when he arrived in Canada in 1755 with the French troops under Dieskau*.

Douglas's military record seems undistinguished, although he participated in several actions during the Seven Years' War. He was at Lac Saint-Sacrement (Lake George) in 1755, at the capture of Oswego (Chouaguen) in 1756, and at Fort Carillon (Ticonderoga, N.Y.) in 1758. According to the casualty list he was wounded "very lightly" in the last battle. In his letters to his family he did not mention the injury, complaining only of the hardships he had endured since coming to Canada, where soldiers had to be ready for action whenever the weather permitted. The wound may nevertheless have been the reason for his being made a knight of the order of Saint-Louis on 20 Oct. 1758.

During the siege of Quebec the next year, Douglas was second in command of a party led by Jean-Daniel DUMAS which attempted to dislodge the British from Pointe-Lévy (Lauzon) on the night of 12–13 July. The force consisted of Indians, regulars, militia, townspeople, and some seminarians whom a wag christened "the Royal Syntax." It became separated in the dark; its members mistook one another for the British, fired, and retreated precipitately without having attacked the enemy. It is not known whether Douglas was at all at fault in this fiasco. He appears to have been in charge of the Samos battery, which fired on the British fleet during the landing at Anse au Foulon on 13 September but which was abandoned after being attacked by Wolfe*'s men. A ministerial note in the muster-roll of captains says that he "served well. A good captain, without other talent." His record in Canada would seem to bear out that judgement.

Douglas was more remarkable for having been one of the fewer than 20 regular officers to marry Canadian women. Montcalm*, who generally disapproved on the grounds that the officers were marrying below their social class and thereby jeopardizing their careers, approved of Douglas's match. Charlotte de La Corne, whom Douglas married on 13 April 1757, was of noble descent through her father Louis, known as La Corne *l'aîné*, and her mother Élisabeth de Ramezay. Montcalm described her as "a woman of quality, with very good family connections in the colony and a suitable fortune." As a nobleman Douglas would in turn have been considered a highly desirable match in Canada.

He returned to France after the conquest, taking his wife and family with him. Two sons had been born in Canada, Louis-Archambaud, later made a knight of the order of Saint-Louis and imprisoned in 1794 during the Terror, and Charles-Luc. Another child was born in Touraine, where Douglas stayed some time after his arrival in France. In 1763 he embarked for Corsica; he remained there for six years, during which he took part in several military operations. He then retired and returned to France in 1769. Subsequently he wished to come back to Canada to settle on the seigneury of Terrebonne, which he had inherited from his father-in-law, but he was unable to carry out the scheme and he died in 1781 at Nantua, near his birthplace.

SUSAN W. HENDERSON

AMA, SHA, A[1], 3457, no. 60; X[b], carton 77 (copies at PAC). AN, Col., C[11A], 120; F[3], 15, pp.172, 275 (copies at PAC). ANQ-M, État civil, Catholiques, Notre-Dame de Montréal, 13 avril 1757. *Coll. des manuscrits de*

Lévis (Casgrain), III, 131. Doreil, "Lettres" (A. Roy), ANQ *Rapport*, 1944–45, 3–32. "Journal du siège de Québec" (Æ. Fauteux), ANQ *Rapport*, 1920–21, 170, 229. Æ. Fauteux, *Les chevaliers de Saint-Louis*, 229. La Chesnaye-Desbois et Badier, *Dict. de la noblesse* (1863–76), VI, 989. Tanguay, *Dictionnaire*. Stanley, *New France*, 224. Pierre Gauthier, "De Montréal (en Bugey) à Montréal (au Canada)," *RHAF*, III (1949–50), 30–44. "Officiers du régiment de Languedoc," *BRH*, LI (1945), 285. P.-G. Roy, "Les officiers de Montcalm mariés au Canada," *BRH*, L (1944), 260, 280–81.

DOUVILLE, ALEXANDRE DAGNEAU. *See* DAGNEAU

DOWSET. *See* DOUCET

DRACHART, CHRISTIAN LARSEN (Lorenz, Lauritsen), Moravian missionary in Labrador; b. 23 June 1711 at Skaelskør, Zealand, Denmark; d. 8 Sept. 1778 at Nain, Labrador.

Christian Larsen Drachart, the son of a merchant, was brought up after his father's death by his uncle, a Lutheran clergyman. He took a theological degree at Copenhagen and then entered the Seminarium Groenlandicum, a Lutheran institution founded in 1737 to train prospective missionaries for Greenland. In 1739 he was ordained and sent to the mission at Godthaab.

Drachart had shown an interest in pietism while a student and he soon made contact with the Moravian Brethren who were settled at New Herrnhut, in the immediate vicinity of Godthaab. Their influence on Drachart was profound, and he began to adopt some of their practices. As a result he came into conflict with his superiors in the Lutheran mission; they had never approved of the Moravians' missionary tactics, which in their view played too much on the emotions. In 1745 he married a Moravian and was accepted into the New Herrnhut congregation. He retired from Greenland after his wife's death in 1751 and lived at the Moravian settlement of Herrnhut, in Saxony. He worked as a porcelain painter there until 1765 when he volunteered to help found a mission for the Inuit of Labrador.

That summer Drachart joined Jens HAVEN and two other Moravian Brethren on a voyage to Labrador to find a place for a settlement and "try the tempers of the Eskimaux." Haven sailed north along the coast but Drachart was detained at Chateau Bay, in southern Labrador, by Hugh PALLISER, the governor of Newfoundland. Palliser needed an interpreter to persuade the Inuit to cease trading with the French and harassing the British whom he was encouraging to establish a fishery on the south Labrador coast [*see* Nicholas DARBY]. For three weeks in August Drachart combined the roles of government agent and missionary, a situation he found distasteful. His position was made more difficult by the fact that he did not speak English and had to rely on the assistance of an English Moravian, John Hill. Drachart nonetheless succeeded in winning the confidence of the Inuit in the area, some of whom had met Haven the year before, and persuaded them to meet with Palliser. On 21 August a form of treaty was made; the Inuit agreed to regard the British flag as a sign of friendship and to stay away from the British fishermen. Once Palliser had left Labrador in early September Drachart, rejoined by Haven, resumed the more congenial role of evangelist.

Following the 1765 voyage, the Moravians refused to return to Labrador unless they were given a land grant, a request which Palliser and the Board of Trade rejected. Drachart went to live at the Moravian settlement of Fulneck (near Pudsey, West Yorkshire), England. Here, from June until October 1769 he cared for Karpik, an Inuit boy captured by a detachment from Fort York (Labrador) in November 1767 [*see* Francis Lucas*]. Under Drachart's influence Karpik accepted Christianity, and his death from smallpox was a bitter disappointment. This incident reversed Drachart's decision not to return to Labrador.

In 1770, the land grant conceded, he joined Haven on another exploratory voyage. Accounts of this journey indicate that Drachart preached with the utmost persistence at every opportunity and conducted the negotiations by which the Inuit "sold" a tract of land to the Moravians. The following year he sailed to Labrador for the last time as one of the missionary party that was to establish a settlement at Nain. Too old for travelling, Drachart nevertheless took an active part in the spiritual work of the mission. He died at Nain in 1778, and his body was laid out for the Inuit to visit, so that they could see his "friendly and smiling look" and learn not to fear death. It was an appropriate end for a life dedicated to the conversion of the Inuit.

J. K. HILLER

PAC, MG 17, D1. PRO, CO 194/16. L. T. A. Bobé, *Hans Egede, colonizer and missionary of Greenland* (Copenhagen, 1952), 187–88. J. W. Davey, *The fall of Torngak, or the Moravian mission on the coast of Labrador* (London, 1905), 104–6. Finn Gad, *The history of Greenland* (2v., London and Montreal, 1970–73), II, 254–60. Hiller, "Foundation of Moravian mission," 47–54. "Grønlandsmissionæren Christian Drachart," *Atuagagdlitit/Groenlandsposten* (Godthaab, Greenland), 1963, no.13, 17.

DRAKE, FRANCIS WILLIAM, naval officer and governor of Newfoundland; d. 1788 or 1789.

Francis William Drake was a younger brother of Sir Francis Henry Drake, the last baronet in succession from Sir Francis Drake*. The date and place of his birth are not known, and in accounts of his life some details have been interchanged with others concerning his younger brother, also a naval officer, who died about the same time. Before 1750 Drake commanded several ships. One of these, the *Fowey*, was wrecked in the Gulf of Mexico in 1748, but Drake was exonerated by a court martial. He was appointed governor of Newfoundland in 1750, serving as *de facto* governor under Commodore George Brydges Rodney, the senior naval officer on the station, in 1750 and 1751, and succeeding to the full office in 1752.

The significance of Drake's governorship lies in the establishment of criminal courts in Newfoundland; previously, persons accused of criminal offences had been transported to England for trial. Although the draft instructions of Governor Philip Vanbrugh in 1738 had contained provisions for establishing such courts, the provisions were later removed because of the parliamentary opposition of the West Country merchants, who feared any increase in the power of the naval governors would limit the authority of their own ships' captains. The British government obtained legal advice which indicated that the creation of the courts would not contradict previous laws, however, and established courts of oyer and terminer in 1750. Drake was authorized to appoint commissioners, who would preside over regular trials by jury. He was also given the power to pardon all offenders except wilful murderers, to whom he could grant reprieves if the circumstances warranted. In the case of sentences involving "loss of life or limb" Drake had to report fully to the home government, submitting complete transcripts of court records in order that capital sentences might be allowed or disallowed by the crown. He was subsequently given authority to permit executions without recourse to the crown, except in cases involving officers and men of the navy or merchant marine.

Despite the fact that the courts sat only during the short period of the governor's annual presence on the island, they were effective in curtailing the lawlessness prevalent in Newfoundland, particularly in St John's. Drake was reluctant to pass sentences of death, however, and referred most if not all capital cases to England for review. It is not known whether this reluctance stemmed from his unfamiliarity with criminal law, or from a belief that the knowledge, rather than the example, of his power to execute was sufficient to deter potential criminals.

Drake was succeeded as governor in 1753 by Captain Hugh Bonfoy* and during the Seven Years' War served on the American station and in the West Indies. In the American revolutionary war he held posts at the Downs and at Portsmouth, and in September 1780 he was promoted vice-admiral of the blue and appointed to command a squadron of the Channel fleet under Vice-Admiral George Darby. Severe attacks of gout limited his ability to command, however, and terminated his active career abruptly that year; he was nevertheless promoted vice-admiral of the red in September 1787. On 23 Jan. 1788 in Ripley he was married by special licence, because she was a minor, to the only daughter of George Onslow, for many years the member of parliament for Guildford. Drake died towards the end of that year or early in 1789.

FREDERIC F. THOMPSON

Robert Beatson, *Naval and military memoirs of Great Britain from 1727 to 1783* (2nd ed., 6v., London, 1804). Charnock, *Biographia navalis*, VI, 61. *DNB* (biography of Sir Francis Samuel Drake). R. G. Lounsbury, *The British fishery at Newfoundland, 1634–1763* (New Haven, Conn., 1934; repr. New York, 1969), 275–76, 298, 300. A. H. McLintock, *The establishment of constitutional government in Newfoundland, 1783–1832: a study of retarded colonisation* (London and New York, [1941]).

DRUILLON DE MACÉ, PIERRE-JACQUES, officer in the colonial regular troops; baptized 9 Sept. 1727 in the parish of Saint-Solenne at Blois, France, son of Pierre-Jacques Druillon, lieutenant-general for the bailiwick of Blois, and Marie Bachaddelebat; m. 1769 Marie-Anne Petit de Thoizy at Blois; d. there 26 June 1780.

Members of the Druillon family had held high judicial office in Blois for 200 years. Pierre-Jacques Druillon de Macé broke with tradition in 1749 by abandoning advanced legal studies for a military career. Through the influence of his relative Roland-Michel Barrin* de La Galissonière, commandant general of New France, he obtained an appointment in the colonial regulars at Louisbourg, Île Royale (Cape Breton Island), as second ensign. He was subsequently transferred to Canada, where there was still some opportunity for officers of the colonial troops to learn by direct experience the arts of gunnery and fortification. Posted in 1752 to Fort Niagara (near Youngstown, N.Y.), he was sent the following year to undertake the construction of Fort de la Presqu'île (Erie, Pa) and Fort de la Rivière au

Bœuf (Waterford, Pa) under the general supervision of François-Marc-Antoine LE MERCIER. In 1754 he participated in the building of Fort Duquesne (Pittsburgh, Pa).

Druillon is remembered chiefly for his part in the Jumonville affair. One of the party under Joseph Coulon* de Villiers de Jumonville which was attacked on 28 May 1754 near present-day Jumonville, Pa, by George Washington's force, he was wounded and made prisoner. Druillon and the 20 other survivors of the French detachment were taken first to Winchester, then to Williamsburg, Virginia. Governor Robert Dinwiddie rejected repeated bids for their release, though he agreed to make their lot easier by allowing them to purchase clothing from local merchants. Druillon later claimed that he had been repeatedly interrogated and accused of espionage. Under the terms of Washington's surrender of Fort Necessity (near Farmington, Pa) to the French on 3 July 1754, Druillon and his men were supposed to be exchanged for two British captains, Robert Stobo* and Jacob Van Braam [*see* Louis Coulon* de Villiers]. Sharp disagreements precluded the exchange, however, and the British hostages were sent to Quebec, while Druillon and his party were moved to Alexandria, Virginia. After having been detained in Virginia almost a year, Druillon and three others were put aboard merchant vessels at Hampton. Druillon landed at Bristol, England, on 10 June 1755 and made his way to the French embassy in London. Soon his complaints to the French ambassador of maltreatment during his detention in Virginia and his voyage to England became part of the accelerated Anglo-French diplomatic war of 1755–56. Druillon himself crossed to France to report to the minister of Marine.

Following his return to Canada in 1756, Druillon served mainly in the Lake Champlain sector. As a full ensign, he participated in RIGAUD de Vaudreuil's campaign around Lac Saint-Sacrement (Lake George) during the winter of 1756–57 and saw action at the siege and capture of Fort William Henry (also called Fort George; now Lake George, N.Y.). He spent the winter of 1757–58 on leave in France and the summer and fall of 1758 at a forward post between Fort Carillon (Ticonderoga, N.Y.) and Fort Lydius (also called Fort Edward; now Fort Edward, N.Y.). On 1 Jan. 1759 he was promoted lieutenant and assigned to the construction of works at Île aux Noix (in the Richelieu River), Laprairie, and Châteauguay. Subsequently, and until November 1759, he commanded 200 men in a camp between La Présentation (Oswegatchie; now Ogdensburg, N.Y.) and Fort Lévis (east of Prescott, Ont.). After taking part in the battle of Sainte-Foy in April 1760, he was transferred to Île Saint-Hélène, where he was serving when Montreal was surrendered in September.

Upon his return to France in 1760, Druillon retired to Blois and remained there until his death. He received a yearly pension of 300 *livres* for his services but, despite good references and repeated requests from 1761 to 1775, he was unable to obtain the cross of Saint-Louis and the additional pension he desired.

F. J. THORPE

AD, Loir-et-Cher (Blois), État civil, Saint-Honoré, 27 juin 1780; Saint-Solenne, 9 sept. 1727, 18 sept. 1769. AN, Col., B, 96, f.298v; 102, ff.91–92v; 105, f.211; 108, f.537; D[1], 3, f.90v; D[2C], 4, f.158; 48/1, f.161; 48/2, ff.236v, 312v; E, 139 (dossier Druillon). Archives du ministère des Affaires étrangères (Paris), Corr. politique, Angleterre, 439, ff.194, 197, 214–16, 221–23, 232–33. *Coll. des manuscrits de Lévis* (Casgrain), I–VIII, X. [Robert Dinwiddie], *The official records of Robert Dinwiddie* . . . (2v., Richmond, Va., 1883). *NYCD* (O'Callaghan and Fernow), X, 264–65. *Papiers Contrecœur* (Grenier), 11, 19, 42, 46, 157, 188, 257, 260, 262, 271, 305. [George Washington], *The writings of George Washington*, ed. W. C. Ford (14v., New York and London, 1889–[93]), I, 76–89. L.-C. Bergevin et Alexandre Dupré, *Histoire de Blois* (2v., Blois, France, 1846–47), II, 44, 60, 62–64, 67, 189–90, 198–99, 309, 633–34. É.-Z. Massicotte, "Pierre-Jacques Druillon, seigneur de Macé," *BRH*, XXVI (1920), 125–26.

DU CALVET, PIERRE, storekeeper, merchant, justice of the peace, and seigneur; b. 1735 at Caussade (dept of Tarn-et-Garonne), France, son of Pierre Calvet and Anne Boudet; d. March 1786 at sea.

Pierre Du Calvet was the eldest in a family of at least five children. In 1758 he sailed for Quebec, eager to try his luck in the new world. The son of a "bourgeois" father, but claiming to be of a "noble family," he left his country for "reasons of religion." He knew what it cost to adhere to the Protestant faith, which his father had been obliged to renounce when he had had his children baptized in the Catholic church.

He left Bordeaux intending to become a merchant, but a shipwreck on his arrival at Quebec in June 1758 cost him the merchandise he had brought. Unable to set up business on his own, he accepted a post as storekeeper at Miramichi and Restigouche (N.B.). He remained in Acadia from July 1758 till the autumn of 1759, having been made responsible by Louis XV for providing for "three or four thousand" destitute Acadians, victims of the policy of deportation initiated in 1755 [*see* Charles Lawrence*]. Back in Canada in the autumn of 1759, he was entrusted with the mission of returning to Acadia to make a count of the Acadian refugees and report on the state of this war-torn region. He spent the four months from January until April 1760 on the task.

At the time of the capitulation of Montreal, Lieutenant Cæsar McCormick brought Du Calvet to AMHERST's attention. Held prisoner in Acadia when Du Calvet was living there as storekeeper, McCormick had been freed in 1759 and sent to Fort Cumberland (near Sackville, N.B.) with some 30 companions. Du Calvet had been a member of the escort of Acadians accompanying them from Restigouche to Caraquet.

In 1761 MURRAY had no hesitation in turning to Du Calvet for help in settling the thorny problem of the Acadians, who, far from accepting capitulation, were threatening to intercept British merchant ships in the Gulf of St Lawrence. He was given the task of enumerating the last of the Acadians, in preparation for their removal to Quebec. His assignment lasted three and a half months.

In the period immediately after the conquest Du Calvet devoted his energies to setting up an export business, which within a few years became very prosperous. He dispatched entire cargoes of wheat to England and Spain, on ships chartered by the London firm of Watson and Rashleigh. From 1772 to 1776 he supplied them with nearly 35,000 bushels of wheat and 800 of pease, as well as "beavers and peltries." The wheat exported was in itself worth more than 150,000 *livres* at the average price of 4*s*. 6*d*. per bushel. In exchange he procured various kinds of goods in Europe including, on occasion, lead shot and "German steel," as well as spirits.

While attending to his commercial activities, Du Calvet did not neglect family matters. In 1763, within the space of a few months, he lost his uncle, who had immigrated to South Carolina, and his father. To obtain possession of his uncle's property he thought it wise to protect himself with two notarial deeds: an affirmation of his rights of inheritance, and a power of attorney given to Joseph Myer, a London merchant, to oppose the "distribution . . . of the aforementioned estate" before he himself arrived in London. He quickly organized his departure for England. Since his business could not suffer any interruption, he left it in the hands of two men whom he trusted, Jean DUMAS Saint-Martin and Pierre Jussaume, *dit* Saint-Pierre. He was absent from Canada for nearly two years. The settlement of his father's estate also required his presence in Europe. As he was already established in America, he wanted to get rid of the property in France left him by his father. Using diplomatic channels, and the good offices of both the secretary of state for the Southern Department, Lord Halifax, and the British ambassador in Paris, he obtained the permit necessary for release of the properties. However, according to Du Calvet himself, he had "to sacrifice most [of his] inheritance" as a result of his allegiance to his new king and to the Protestant faith.

Du Calvet returned to Canada in June 1766, and that month obtained a commission as justice of the peace. Leaving again five months later, he was absent until April 1767, when his business and his commission as justice of the peace brought him back to Montreal. The appointment, a final proof of Murray's esteem, allowed him to play a role that suited him in the administration of justice in the colony. He was, in fact, a born dispenser of justice, attentive to abuses and ever ready to denounce them. A man of passionate temperament and inexhaustible enthusiasm, he used his pen like a stiletto, not hesitating to censure both the vices of the judicial system and the dishonesty of certain of his colleagues. He proved equally apt at conceiving constructive reforms. In 1769 he submitted to Governor Guy Carleton* a plan to standardize the administration of justice throughout the province. On 28 Oct. 1770 he sent Lord Hillsborough, secretary of state for the American Colonies, a "Mémoire sur la forme judiciaire actuelle de la Province de Québec." Examining the establishment of civil government, he enumerated for Hillsborough the dangers of giving too many powers to justices of the peace. Since September 1764 they had been authorized to judge without appeal "all Causes or Matters of Property, not exceeding the Sum of *Five Pounds*, current Money of *Quebec*," and were taking advantage of this power to get rich without even "inquiring into the heart of the matter" under dispute. They were helped by the bailiffs who, armed with blank warrants, were drumming up an extensive clientele for them. By contrast Du Calvet praised the rigorous but honest way in which justice had been dispensed under the military régime.

Convinced of the need to eliminate the most flagrant abuses, Carleton on 1 Feb. 1770 issued an ordinance to take away from justices of the peace "all Jurisdiction, Power, and Authority in Matters of private Property." It is probable that Du Calvet's representations were not unconnected with this reform, since some of his ideas were embodied in it. He was not, however, completely satisfied. The preamble to the ordinance made no exception for the justices of the peace "whose conduct has been prudent and correct," and he considered it "insulting" to be associated with those whom he had just denounced.

Du Calvet's zeal and vigilance were praised by Governor Carleton, Chief Justice William HEY, and Francis Maseres*, the former attorney general; Maseres even deemed him worthy of appointment to the Legislative Council. But not everyone had such sentiments about this reformer. Through his virulent denunciations Du Calvet had made implacable enemies among his colleagues on the bench. His quarrels, including those with judge John Fraser of the Court of Common Pleas for the District of Montreal, became so notorious that he had to appeal to the speaker and members of the Legislative Council. He also had a dispute with the military forces. Like his bourgeois fellow citizens who in the name of English liberty were asserting the rights of private property, he chafed at being obliged to billet troops in his residence. The soldiers' presence caused mutual resentment, and on several occasions he complained of having been harassed by them and other assailants who attacked his property in Montreal and the animals on his seigneury of Rivière-David, near Sorel.

A tenacious, punctilious, and captious habitué of the courts, Du Calvet knew how to use, even misuse, them. His *causes célèbres* with two London firms, Watson and Rashleigh and François Ribot, kept the court reports filled for many years. He even alerted public opinion by having his own arguments published.

Du Calvet had no place on the bench after the Quebec Act came into effect in 1775. However, the administration of justice did not hold any the less interest for him. His quarrels in the courts gave him the opportunity to renew his censure of the judges' conduct and their decisions. The *Gazette littéraire pour la ville et district de Montréal*, founded by Fleury MESPLET, proved a suitable medium for his attacks on the judicial system. Its editor, the lawyer Valentin JAUTARD, entered the fray and exchanged open letters with Du Calvet. From April till June 1779 denunciations of the administration of justice filled the columns of the weekly. On 26 May Du Calvet triggered a sequence of events when he called to account two judges of the Court of Common Pleas, Edward Southouse and René-Ovide HERTEL de Rouville, in an indictment aimed particularly at the latter. The next day Hertel de Rouville lodged a complaint with Governor HALDIMAND on behalf of himself and his colleague. The *Gazette littéraire* was suspended; its editor and printer were imprisoned.

The attorney general, James Monk*, brought libel proceedings against Du Calvet. The gravity of the accusation and the importance of the persons involved made association with this case compromising. No member of the bar felt ready to defend the accused. William Dummer Powell*, a young lawyer newly arrived in Montreal, agreed to plead the case, against Monk's advice. Du Calvet was acquitted by a jury composed of English merchants from Montreal.

Sixteen months later, on 27 Sept. 1780, Du Calvet was arrested, not on account of his recent quarrels with the law but because of suspicions of treason which had hung over him since the American invasion. His arrest had been ordered by the commandant of Montreal, Brigadier Allan MACLEAN, on the basis of allegations by Major Thomas Carleton*, who was head of a counter-espionage service at Saint-Jean. Three letters dated 7 and 8 Sept. 1780 and addressed to General George Washington, the Marquis de La Fayette, and the members of the Philadelphia Congress had been intercepted, and they provided the evidence brought against him. In a deposition on 20 October Boyer Pillon, a doctor, acknowledged that he was their author; one, however, the letter addressed to the Congress, implicated Du Calvet since Pillon admitted that he had signed both their names to it – weak evidence, all things considered. Without taking time to consult the governor and obtain a written order Maclean had Du Calvet arrested. When confronted with the *fait accompli* of the arrest, Haldimand did not question his subordinate's action. His letters to Maclean, however, show that he considered the evidence of the correspondence unconvincing. The assertions of certain others facing charges of complicity with the rebels seemed to the governor to warrant more credence, and it was on their testimony that Haldimand upheld Du Calvet's and Pillon's arrests. Some of the witnesses for the prosecution reported that Du Calvet had incited them to join the rebels and had offered to furnish them with supplies. When an investigation was made, there was almost no clear proof. Haldimand admitted, moreover, that he had only presumptive evidence against Du Calvet. Somewhat embarrassed, he gave Major Carleton the task of seeing if there were grounds for a trial.

On 6 Dec. 1780 Haldimand agreed to the request of a member of the Legislative Council, François LÉVESQUE, that Du Calvet be freed. It was only a matter of being patient for another 24 hours, the time required for Hector Theophilus CRAMAHÉ, the lieutenant governor, to prepare the certificate for his release. But a badly timed letter from the prisoner, written in a vindictive style, offended Haldimand so deeply that he would make no further concessions to Du Calvet. His imprisonment stretched out to two years and seven months, with no right to any trial whatever. The precarious situation of the colony, which was threatened with a second invasion by the Americans, in fact enabled the governor to suspend habeas corpus.

What were the charges against Du Calvet? The matter had dragged on for five years. On 7 and 9 Oct. 1775 he had already appeared before a jury of nine commissioners on the accusation of siding with the rebels. For want of sufficient evidence he had been set free. The following month he had been among those to whom Richard MONTGOMERY sent his message urging the inhabitants of Montreal to surrender without resistance, in order to avoid useless bloodshed. In April 1776 he received a member of the delegation sent by the American Congress to persuade the Canadians to join the Thirteen Colonies. Even more disturbing, a certain Pierre Du Calvet was said to have been in the Canadian regiment recruited by Colonel Moses Hazen* to assist the Americans. A compromising document attested that this Pierre Du Calvet had received an advance on his ensign's pay. In August 1776, after the invaders had retreated, the American Congress authorized his appointment as lieutenant and the payment of eight months' service as an ensign. How could our Du Calvet have abandoned his business interests in this manner? An alternative hypothesis seems reasonable. Du Calvet was accommodating in his home a nephew who bore his name, and for whom he had sought a lieutenancy in 1770. By the time of the American invasion this second Pierre Du Calvet would have had the training required by a soldier. It was probably he who joined the Canadian volunteers under Hazen.

The most serious charge, but one for which there was "little . . . legal evidence" according to judge William Renwick Riddell*, would seem to be Du Calvet's more or less forced collaboration with the invading American army which occupied Montreal for six months. There is nothing surprising in the fact that this rich merchant had been requisitioned to provide the invaders with essential supplies. Subsequently Du Calvet was to seek reimbursement for the promissory notes made out to him in exchange for his merchandise, claiming the sum of 56,394 *livres*. On a couple of occasions he asked the Marquis de La Fayette for his support. Twice, in October 1783 and June 1785, he had meetings in Paris with Benjamin Franklin, who was then the ambassador of the United States to France. More important still, he went to New York to present both a detailed account of costs and petitions to the Continental Congress on 3, 15, and 26 Sept. 1785. His vouchers enabled him to obtain an amount equivalent to 5,352.50 Spanish dollars, about half the sum he had requested.

Believing that he was the victim of the worst persecutions, Du Calvet had found his years in prison a nightmare. Discovering an outlet in writing, he never stopped proclaiming his innocence and demanding his release. He had to wait until 2 May 1783 to obtain freedom and to seek justice in England, that "empire of liberty." Anxious to bring an action against Haldimand, for a year he vainly petitioned the king and the ministers in London. Tired of these futile endeavours, Du Calvet turned to the printed word to set out his grievances. In March 1784 appeared in London *The case of Peter Du Calvet . . .*, which was described as a factum intended for the lawyers who were attempting to clear his name. In it the facts are presented in chronological order with occasional explanations for readers unfamiliar with the colonial context, and they are supported by the plaintiff's extensive correspondence. Properly speaking, Du Calvet was not the author of this text, which was written in English in a balanced manner that contrasts with his other writings. It is in fact said to be the work of the former attorney general, Francis Maseres, and the chief justice, Peter LIVIUS. Livius had already taken a stand against the legality of incarcerating political prisoners without trial, and hence was all the more in sympathy with Du Calvet's case.

In June – July 1784 Du Calvet once more stirred up public opinion by publishing, again in London, *Appel à la justice de l'État*; this was a veritable indictment of the system of justice, with vehement remonstrances and sharp recriminations, written in an inflammatory style. In it he appealed to the king, the Prince of Wales, and the Home secretary, Lord Sydney. He adroitly linked his fate with that of his fellow citizens harassed by Governor Haldimand's despotism. He drew on John Locke and on legal authorities Samuel von Pufendorf and Grotius for material to support and defend their national rights. Earlier, in November 1783, when denouncing the abuses of power in the colonial administration, he had bluntly told Lord North: "You will not allow our oppression to justify in the eyes of all Europe the detaching of the thirteen provinces." Only immediate changes and return to a constitutional régime could make it possible for hope to be held of retaining "the province for his majesty."

Du Calvet devoted most of his "Lettre à messieurs les Canadiens," a key piece in his indictment which took up more than half the book, to the exposition of a "detailed plan of government" designed to bring about a "salutary revolution." He attacked the Quebec Act fiercely, seeing in it "the real, though unpremeditated, establishment of the enslavement of the province." He denounced the régime of guardianship imposed upon the Canadians since the conquest and emphasized the vices and gaps in the parliamentary legislation of 1774. Being anxious to reinstate the Canadians in their rights and privileges as British subjects, he proposed a series of constitutional and judicial reforms. The maintenance of French civil law being assured, he demanded "the restoration of the law of habeas corpus [and] trial by jury." Determined to limit the governor's powers, he suggested making him subject to the laws of the province and depriving him of the right to throw a subject into prison or to dismiss from office, on his own authority, members of the Legislative Council or the legal profession. Despite the prejudices and preconceptions of his fellow citizens, who were afraid of seeing the province overwhelmed with taxes, Du Calvet sought to convince them of the value of a legislative assembly, which would give them not only "the pleasure and glory of being [their] own taxing officials," but also the means of complete control of public expenditures. He was thus anticipating what was to be the great subject of debate in the House of Assembly of Lower Canada 30 years later: the control of funds granted. He also suggested a reform of the Legislative Council by doubling the number of members and making it in part elective, so that it would cease to be simply a "reserve body," submissive to the governor's will. No bigot, this Protestant recommended "the free entry of Roman priests into Canada." The six other articles of his plan bore particularly on the appointment of six representatives of the colony to the "British senate," naturalization of Canadians, the restoration of the Conseil Supérieur as a judicial court, the formation of a regiment of native-born Canadians, freedom of the press, and "the founding of colleges for educating the young." In this connection Du Calvet recommended that the Jesuit estates be appropriated to support "public schools, suited to all types of education." The *Appel à la justice de l'État* had a great impact on his contemporaries. He was one of the men who contributed the most to making them aware of the necessity and urgency of constitutional reforms and to prompting them to ally themselves with the British residents in the colony to win their case. He polarized public opinion so effectively and to such an extent that the Canadian reformers found him an inspiration, as is clear from the tributes accorded him by the committees of reform leaders in Quebec and Montreal. Unfortunately Du Calvet too often gave free rein in his writings to his resentment, and according to Captain John Schank* and Father Félix Berey Des Essarts, he had imagined rather than experienced the bad treatment he complained he had undergone on board the *Canceaux* and at the Capuchin monastery in Quebec, where political prisoners had been held. Objective testimony should not, then, be sought in Du Calvet's two works. They should be considered rather as the cry of a man driven to despair because he was unable to obtain "prompt justice from the state."

In working out his plan for reform Du Calvet had the assistance of his friend Maseres who gave him the benefit of his legal knowledge. The collaboration of Pierre-Joseph-Antoine ROUBAUD was a much less happy experience; Du Calvet probably regretted bitterly having been caught in the designs of so perfidious a man as his secretary. Roubaud did not hesitate to betray Du Calvet's trust and played the role of spy and informer on behalf of Evan Nepean, the under-secretary of state for the Home Department, and Haldimand himself.

On 3 Oct. 1771, in Christ Church, Montreal, Du Calvet had married Marie-Louise, the daughter of Pierre Jussaume, *dit* Saint-Pierre; she was 15 years younger than he. Their married life was brief. Three years later the young woman passed away, having borne three sons; only one of them, John, soon called Jean-Pierre and finally, like his father, Pierre, survived. The last of Du Calvet's sons, born in October 1774, two months before his mother's death, had been named Guy, after his godfather Guy Carleton.

Du Calvet thought of himself as belonging to "the class of the leading citizens of Montreal." He possessed not only the land that the Jussaumes had owned on Rue Saint-Jean and Rue Saint-Paul but other properties, orchards, and gardens on Rue Saint-Paul and the Place du Marché, as well as the seigneury of Rivière-David and two other arriere-fiefs. However he had had to put his landed property up for sale or permit others to do so in order to pay for his lawsuits and numerous trips to France, England, and the United States. The impressive inventory drawn up after his death shows that his liabilities (94,000 *livres*) exceeded his assets. The estate was by no means negligible. Unfortunately it was encumbered with too many unpaid accounts (he was owed 82,000 *livres*) and unsold goods.

Death prevented Du Calvet from bringing his

lawsuit against Haldimand to a conclusion and seeing his *Appel à la justice de l'État* bear fruit. After a brief stay in Canada, where he again gave full power of attorney to Jean Dumas Saint-Martin, Du Calvet hastened to return to England in March 1786. Leaving New York on 3 March in a Spanish ship, Du Calvet and the other passengers were driven into port by unfavourable winds a few days later. The ship set sail again on 15 March but was lost with all hands during a violent gale. Thus Du Calvet perished.

Apparently it was Maseres who after Du Calvet's sudden disappearance took responsibility for his friend's only son, a lad barely 12 years of age who had been living in England since August 1783.

PIERRE TOUSIGNANT and
MADELEINE DIONNE-TOUSIGNANT

Pierre Du Calvet, *Appel à la justice de l'État; ou recueil de lettres au roi, au prince de Galles, et aux ministres; avec une lettre à messieurs les Canadiens, . . . une lettre au général Haldimand lui-même; enfin une dernière lettre à milord Sidney* . . . (Londres, 1784); *The case of Peter Du Calvet, esq., of Montreal in the province of Quebeck, containing, amongst other things worth notice, an account of the long and severe imprisonment he suffered in the said province* . . . (London, 1784) [This work was drawn up not by Du Calvet but by two of his friends, Francis Maseres and Peter Livius.]; *Mémoire en réponse à l'écrit public, de Me Panet, fondé de procuration de Watson & Rasleigh de Londres, demandeurs, contre Pierre Ducalvet de Montréal, écuyer, défendeur* . . . (Montréal, 1779).

[The analysis and inventory of the Haldimand collection for the PAC *Report*, 1888, led archivist Douglas Brymner* to judge Du Calvet harshly. Some members of the Royal Society of Canada, such as Benjamin Sulte* (*Mélanges historiques* (Malchelosse), VII, 76–98), Francis-Joseph Audet* ("Sir Frédéric Haldimand," RSC *Trans.*, 3rd ser., XVII (1923), sect.I, 127–49), and Gustave Lanctot* (*Le Canada et la Révolution américaine*), followed his lead and attempted to exonerate Haldimand by refuting the accusations brought against him. They even claimed he was "one of the best governors that Downing Street sent out." Unable to understand the direction and significance of Du Calvet's political action, they saw in this liberal and reforming spirit only a "cynical traitor," whose reputation they took pleasure in sullying. Disregarding as too categorical the judgements of Du Calvet's detractors, the historian Lionel Groulx* (*Hist. du Canada français* (1950–52), III, 94–95), like François-Xavier Garneau* (*Hist. du Canada* (1859), III, 51–54), recognized the originality of the contribution made by Du Calvet, who showed "a boldness of thought well in advance of his time." P.T. and M.D.-T.]

AD, Gironde (Bordeaux), Registre d'embarquement de passagers: certificat de catholicité, 1758; Tarn-et-Garonne (Montauban), État civil, Caussade, 1735. ANQ-M, État civil, Anglicans, Christ Church (Montréal), 3 Oct. 1771, 7 July, 3 Aug. 1772, 8 Nov. 1773, 16 Oct. 1774, 11 May 1775; Greffe de P.-F. Mézière, 29 mars, 29 mai 1764, 11 févr. 1786. ASQ, Fonds Viger-Verreau, Carton 13, nos.33, 34; 17, nos.44, 49, 51; 20, no.43; 42/3, no.2; Sér.O, 040A, p.17. BL, Add. MSS 21791, p.80; 21795, pp.156, 163; 21807, p.278; 21843, pp.202–3; 21845, p.353; 21865, pp.1, 5, 45–46, 97, 148–49, 166–75, 242, 260, 268–86; 21886, pp.40–41, 65–68, 109–12, 141–42, 198, 200, 211 (copies at PAC). PAC, MG 11, [CO 42], Q, 7, pp.7–8; 19, pp.171–73, 253; 20, p.184; MG 23, B3, CC41, pp.15–19. PRO, CO 42/5, ff.270–70v; 42/20, ff.8–9, 28; 42/30, ff.105, 168v, 170, 175–80, 184, 188–88v, 193v, 194, 197, 198; 42/34, f.261; 42/43, ff.24–25, 30. *American archives* (Clarke and Force), 5th ser., I, 1604. [Félix Berey Des Essarts], "Réplique par le P. de Berey aux calomnies de Pierre Du Calvet contre les récolets de Québec," PAC *Rapport*, 1888, 40–43. Fabre, dit Laterrière, *Mémoires* (A. Garneau). [Benjamin Franklin], *The works of Benjamin Franklin; containing several political and historical tracts not included in any former edition and many letters, official and private, not hitherto published; with notes and a life of the author*, ed. Jared Sparks (10v., Boston, Mass., 1840), X, 330. *Journals of the Continental Congress, 1774–1789; edited from the original records in the Library of Congress*, ed. W. C. Ford *et al.* (34v., Washington, 1904–37), XXVI, 260–61; XXX, 90. [Francis Maseres], *An account of the proceedings of the British, and other Protestant inhabitants, of the province of Quebeck, in North-America, in order to obtain an house of assembly in that province* (London, 1775); *Additional papers concerning the province of Quebeck: being an appendix to the book entitled, "An account of the proceedings of the British and other Protestant inhabitants of the province of Quebeck in North America, [in] order to obtain a house of assembly in that province"* (London, 1776). "Pierre Du Calvet," J. J. Lefebvre, édit., ANQ *Rapport*, 1945–46, 341–411. "Pierre Du Calvet," J.-M. Le Moine, édit., *BRH*, I (1895), 14–15. *La Gazette littéraire pour la ville et district de Montréal*, 7, 14, 21, 28 avril, 26 mai, 2 juin 1779. *Quebec Gazette*, 22 March, 9 Aug. 1770; 31 May–27 Dec. 1781; 1782; 1785; 1786.

[F.-M.] Bibaud, *Le panthéon canadien: choix de biographie dans lequel on a introduit les hommes les plus célèbres des autres colonies britanniques* (Montréal, 1858). *DOLQ*, I, 35–37. L.[-H.] Frechette, *La légende d'un peuple* (Paris, 1887), 211–15. Adélard Gascon, "Pierre Du Calvet: monographie" (thèse de PHD, université d'Ottawa, 1947). Émile Lauvrière, *La tragédie d'un peuple: histoire du peuple acadien, de ses origines à nos jours* (3e éd., 2v., Paris, 1922), II. Tousignant, "La genèse et l'avènement de la constitution de 1791." Auguste Vachon, "Pierre Roubaud, ses activités à Londres concernant les affaires canadiennes, 1764–1788" (thèse de MA, université d'Ottawa, 1973). E. C. Wright, *The Miramichi, a study of the New Brunswick river and of the people who settled along it* (Sackville, N.B., 1944). É.-Z. Massicotte, "Pierre Ducalvet inculpé en 1775," *BRH*, XXIX (1923), 303–4. W. R. Riddell, "Pierre Du Calvet: a Huguenot refugee in early Montreal; his treason and fate," *OH*, XXII (1925), 239–54.

DUCHAMBON, LOUIS DU PONT. *See* Du Pont

DUCHAMBON DE VERGOR, LOUIS DU PONT. *See* Du Pont

DUCHARME, LAURENT, fur-trader; baptized 10 Aug. 1723 at Montreal (Que.), son of Louis Ducharme and Marie Picard; m. 26 Nov. 1753 Marguerite Métivier in Montreal, and they had at least three children; d. after 1787.

Laurent Ducharme was born into a Montreal family that had extensive experience in the western fur trade, and in 1754 he embarked on a modest fur-trading career around the western lakes. By 1758 Ducharme had moved his wife to the small, fortified, fur-trading village of Michilimackinac (Mackinaw City, Mich.). His family lived in a house on Rue du Diable where a slave girl, Madeleine, assisted with the housekeeping.

In 1761 British soldiers came to garrison Michilimackinac, but they never gained the friendship of the local Ojibwas. In the spring of 1763 Ducharme learned of Indian intentions to attack the garrison at Michilimackinac, but when he warned Captain George Etherington of their plans, the commandant berated him and also threatened to send prisoner to Detroit the next person to tell such a tale. On 2 June 1763 Ducharme watched in horror as the Ojibwas, organized by Minweweh*, surprised the garrison and killed or captured all the soldiers. Ducharme and the other French inhabitants were not harmed.

As a result of the uprising, trade in the Upper Lakes region was severely disrupted, but when peace returned Ducharme once again became an active participant. During the late 1760s and early 1770s he was licensed to take trade goods from Montreal to the interior. Most of his business centred at Michilimackinac, but in 1769 he traded at Milouaqui (Milwaukee, Wis.) and in 1772 at both La Baye (Green Bay) and Milouaqui.

When the American revolution began to trouble the Upper Lakes in 1777, Ducharme served as an informer at Milouaqui for Captain Arent Schuyler De Peyster, commanding officer at Michilimackinac. On 15 May he sent the alarming message that the Spanish were attempting to get the Potawatomi chief, Siginakee (called Letourneau or Blackbird), to incite the Indians in the upper Mississippi valley against the British. This is Ducharme's only recorded involvement in the war.

Concerned about the "profaneness and impiety" at Michilimackinac during these unsettled times, Ducharme joined with a number of other merchants in 1778 in petitioning Sir Guy Carleton* to send a missionary to Michilimackinac. No regular missionary had resided there for nearly ten years. Many merchants pledged their financial support. Ducharme promised £18 per year, a modest sum indicating that he was not one of the wealthier traders.

Economic conditions were also unstable. To combat the uncertainty a number of merchants, including Étienne-Charles Campion and Ducharme, pooled their resources and in 1779 set up a general store at Michilimackinac for one year. Ducharme invested half a canoe load, worth £7,500, again a comparatively modest sum. At this time he is listed as a resident of Montreal. Apparently he lived there only part of the year and, like many other small traders, wintered among the Indians to obtain furs at better prices. One of his posts was on the Fond du Lac River in Wisconsin where he traded with the Winnebagos.

In 1787 Ducharme witnessed an election of church wardens to serve the church of Sainte-Anne which had been moved, along with the fort and town, to Mackinac Island in 1780. Here the record of Laurent Ducharme ends. The date and place of his death are not known.

David A. Armour

BL, Add. mss 21758, ff.33–35, 37–38. Clements Library, Thomas Gage papers, supplementary accounts, A state of houses and lands at Michilimackinac. Wis., State Hist. Soc. (Madison), Canadian archives, Abstracts of Indian trade licences in Canadian archives, 1767–76, 27 July 1769, 17 May, 12 July 1770, 13 May 1773, 17 July 1774. Augustin Grignon, "Seventy-two years' recollections of Wisconsin," Wis., State Hist. Soc., *Coll.*, III (1857), 233, 250–51. Henry, *Travels and adventures* (Bain). "Langlade papers – 1737–1800," Wis., State Hist. Soc., *Coll.*, VIII (1879), 217–19. "Langlade's movements in 1777," Wis., State Hist. Soc., *Coll.*, VII (1876), 406. *Michigan Pioneer Coll.*, IX (1886), 658; X (1886), 275–76, 286–90, 305, 307; XIII (1888), 69 70. Godbout, "Nos ancêtres," ANQ *Rapport*, 1951–53, 471. Massicotte, "Répertoire des engagements pour l'Ouest," ANQ *Rapport*, 1931–32, 277, 281–83, 351, 356–58; 1932–33, 285, 287–89, 291, 294–99, 301–2. Tanguay, *Dictionnaire*, III, 491–92. L. P. Kellogg, *The British regime in Wisconsin and the northwest* (Madison, Wis., 1935), 47, 95, 146; *The French regime in Wisconsin and the northwest* (Madison, 1925; repr. New York, 1968), 295. R. G. Carroon, "Milwaukee and the American revolution," Milwaukee County Hist. Soc., *Hist. Messenger* (Milwaukee, Wis.), XXIX (1973), no.4, 118–44. Charles Lart, "Fur trade returns, 1767," *CHR*, III (1922), 351–58.

DU COIGNE. *See* Couagne

DUDEVANT, ARNAULD-GERMAIN (baptized **Arnaud**), priest; b. 30 May 1751 in the parish of

Sainte-Croix, Bordeaux, France, son of Jacques Dudevant, a merchant, and Jeanne Barbequière; d. *c.* 1798.

Arnauld-Germain Dudevant presumably received a classical education at Bordeaux, and he must have begun theological studies there, since he brought to Canada some handwritten notebooks on grace and the church dated 1774. He and his compatriot Jean-Baptiste Lahaille* arrived in Quebec in 1775, with Governor Guy Carleton*'s permission. Admitted a member of the Séminaire de Québec on 5 April 1777, Dudevant was ordained priest two weeks later. From 1775 to 1777 he is reported to have taught the third form in the Petit Séminaire; he was named director of the Grand Séminaire in August 1777, second assistant to the superior the following year, and first assistant in 1780. For reasons unknown Dudevant resigned in the winter of 1782 and began an inventory of the seminary's library while waiting for a ship to take him back to France.

He returned to Bordeaux in 1783 and became a canon of the metropolitan church of Saint-André in succession to his uncle, Louis-Hyacinthe Barbequière, who had resigned the canonry in his favour. Again dissatisfied, Dudevant thought of joining the priests of the Missions Étrangères in Paris; the procurator of the Séminaire de Québec, François SORBIER de Villars, would have liked Dudevant as his successor there. But the authorities of the Séminaire de Québec were opposed, and Dudevant remained at Bordeaux. During the revolution he emigrated to Madrid and wrote to Bishop HUBERT from there in 1794, asking him to accept him again in Quebec. The bishop replied that he would be happy to receive him but could not pay his passage, having already promised this help to 12 *émigré* priests. Poor Dudevant is believed to have sailed from Spain in 1798 on an American vessel bound for America, but nothing further was ever heard of him and it is assumed that he perished at sea.

Thanks to Dudevant, however, we know what the library of the Séminaire de Québec was like at the end of the 18th century. The catalogue he made shows that it was by far the most important library in Canada at that period; it contained 4,883 volumes comprising 2,121 titles. The plan of the library was, for the most part, that of 18th-century French libraries: first, seven sections for books on theology and religion; then works on civil and canon law, history, and *belles-lettres*; and a final section for textbooks. The *belles-lettres* section included both sciences and arts. The functions of the Grand and Petit Séminaires accounted for the number of books in each category. Religious works were most numerous with 1,306 titles and 2,866 volumes, *belles-lettres* included 298 titles, history 147, and law 135. The textbooks comprised 701 volumes under 235 titles. Only a third of the works were in Latin, and these were mainly textbooks. In the library were found not only the great authors of the 17th and 18th centuries, but also historical works, scientific treatises, and dictionaries. Even Voltaire appears in the catalogue with the *Dictionnaire philosophique portatif*. . . and *Le siècle de Louis XIV*. It was a library perfectly adapted to the dual function of the institution: the provision of a classical and a religious education.

CLAUDE GALARNEAU

AD, Gironde (Bordeaux), État civil, Sainte-Croix, 30 mai 1751; G, 779, f.195. ASQ, Lettres, M, 165; P, 26[a], 29, 32, 34, 82; S, 85; MSS, 12, ff.45–48; 13, 4 avril 1777, 18 oct. 1779, 5 déc. 1794; 433; 437; MSS-M, 199–202; Polygraphie, XVII, 29, 30, 30a; Bibliothèque du séminaire de Québec, A.-G. Dudevant, "Catalogue des livres de la bibliothèque du séminaire des Missions étrangères de Québec fait dans le mois de may 1782" (copy at ASQ). Caron, "Inv. de la corr. de Mgr Hubert et de Mgr Bailly de Messein," ANQ *Rapport*, 1930–31, 310. Antonio Drolet, *Les bibliothèques canadiennes (1604–1960)* (Ottawa, 1965). Monique Laurent, "Le catalogue de la bibliothèque du séminaire de Québec, 1782" (thèse de DES, université Laval, Québec, 1973). "L'abbé Germain Dudevant," *BRH*, XLVII (1941), 207. Antonio Drolet, "La bibliothèque du collège des jésuites," *RHAF*, XIV (1960–61), 487–544; "La bibliothèque du séminaire de Québec et son catalogue de 1782," *Le Canada français* (Québec), 2e sér., XXVIII (1940), 261–66.

DUFROST, CHARLES. *See* YOUVILLE, CHARLES-MARIE-MADELEINE D'

DUFROST DE LAJEMMERAIS, MARIE-MARGUERITE (Youville), founder of the Congregation of the Sisters of Charity of the Hôpital Général of Montreal (Grey Nuns); b. 15 Oct. 1701 at Varennes (Que.); d. 23 Dec. 1771 in Montreal.

Marie-Marguerite Dufrost de Lajemmerais belonged to one of the great families of New France. Her mother, Marie-Renée Gaultier de Varennes, was the daughter of René Gaultier* de Varennes, governor of Trois-Rivières, and Marie Boucher, the daughter of Pierre Boucher*. Her father, François-Christophe Dufrost de La Gemerais, who descended from an old noble family in France, had come to Canada in 1687. Marguerite, the eldest child, had three brothers: Charles and Joseph, who became priests, and Christophe*, who accompanied his uncle, Pierre Gaultier* de Varennes et de La Vérendrye, on his expeditions in western Canada. Her sisters, Marie-Clémence and Marie-Louise, married respectively Pierre Gamelin* Maugras and Ignace GAMELIN, two prominent Montreal merchants.

Marguerite was not yet seven when her father died, leaving his family financially insecure. With the aid of relatives she was nevertheless admitted in August 1712 to the Ursulines' boarding-school at Quebec, where she spent two years. Returning to Varennes, she shared the heavy family responsibilities with her mother until 1720, when Mme Dufrost married Timothy Sullivan*, a doctor who although a commoner was well off. The marriage, a *mésalliance* at that period, stood in the way of a projected marriage between Marguerite and a young nobleman.

Towards the end of 1721 the family moved to Montreal, where Marguerite became acquainted with François-Madeleine d'Youville, the son of Pierre You* de La Découverte. On 12 Aug. 1722 they were married in the church of Notre-Dame. Their marriage contract, which had been signed the day before, is interesting because its signatures show that nearly all those eminent in the colony were present, among them Governor Philippe de Rigaud* de Vaudreuil, Claude de Ramezay*, governor of Montreal, and Charles Le Moyne* de Longueuil, first Baron de Longueuil and the governor of Trois-Rivières. The contract guaranteed Marguerite a jointure of 6,000 *livres* and an additional legacy with first claim on the estate for 1,000 *livres* as well as rings and jewels. It was a great deal for a period when people in average circumstances usually had a jointure of 300 to 500 *livres* and an additional legacy of 200 to 300 *livres*.

The young couple went to live on the Place du Marché, in the home of Mme You de La Découverte, who perhaps was miserly, as some have claimed, but who nonetheless lived in quite a comfortable house, as the inventory made after d'Youville's death in 1730 reveals. Little is known of the couple's eight years together, but there seem to have been two distinct periods. At the beginning, from 1722 to 1726, two boys and two girls were born in close succession; all died in infancy except François, who would later be parish priest of Saint-Ours. These early years were marked by repeated complaints from Indians and merchants against d'Youville's trading practices at Île aux Tourtres [*see* Pierre You de La Découverte], and by Mme You de La Découverte's almost constant presence in the house. Apparently, however, the couple sometimes resided at the farmhouse in Sainte-Anne-du-Bout-de-l'Île (now Sainte-Anne de Bellevue) which belonged to the You de La Découverte family, since one of their infant daughters was buried not far from there, at Saint-Joachim-de-la-Pointe-Claire. The second period in their married life, from 1727 to 1730, was strongly marked by Marguerite's concentration upon the practice of religion. The year 1727 seems particularly important; her son writes that she was then seen "to renounce vain adornments and to embrace the way of piety"; in a letter written to Abbé de L'Isle-Dieu in 1766 she herself traced her devotion and her "confidence in the Eternal Father" back to this time. Moreover, it was in 1727 that she began to join different religious sisterhoods. During this period d'Youville's mother died, leaving him the means to live comfortably, and a fifth child, CHARLES-MARIE-MADELEINE, was born in July 1729.

When d'Youville himself died on 4 July 1730, Marguerite was 28. She had to take care of two infants and was expecting a sixth child, who was born on 26 Feb. 1731 and died less than five months later. She inherited an estate burdened with debts – since d'Youville had wasted no time in squandering his inheritance – and had no better course open to her than to renounce it. By a court lease she was, however, awarded the house she was living in, and from its premises she carried on a trading business for several years.

A new stage in her life was beginning which would lead Mme d'Youville, again in two phases, to assume responsibility for the Hôpital Général of Montreal. She devoted the first period, from 1730 to 1737, to prayer, good works, and the education of her two sons; François entered the Séminaire de Québec in 1737 and Charles followed him in 1742. Under the direction of Sulpician Jean-Gabriel-Marie Le Pape* Du Lescöat, who had been her adviser since 1727, she worked actively within sisterhoods and applied herself to easing the lives of the poor. Her lively awareness of the surrounding poverty prompted her to increasingly concrete acts, in which she had the encouragement of Sulpician Louis Normant* Du Faradon, her spiritual director since Le Pape Du Lescöat's death in 1733. Thus, on 21 Nov. 1737, she took Françoise Auzon, a blind woman in her sixties, into her home. On 31 December Marie-Louise Thaumur de La Source, Catherine Cusson, and Marie-Catherine Demers Dessermont pledged with Mme d'Youville to devote themselves to the service of the poor. Although theirs was still only a lay association, they apparently took vows of poverty, chastity, and obedience, and this moment is considered the date of the founding of the order.

In October 1738 they moved into a house large enough to lodge them all and to allow them to receive other unfortunates, whom they looked after with the proceeds from various endeavours. Marguerite d'Youville's work was started, but the next ten years had harsh labour and painful suffering in store for her. She had to face her family's lack of understanding; indeed in November 1738 her two brothers-in law, along with others, signed a petition against the Sulpicians' alleged intention to put Mme d'Youville and her companions in charge of the Hôpital Général in place of the Brothers Hospitallers of the Cross and of St Joseph. She had to put up with the hostility of the populace, which looked on the little community with disfavour. Some people called them "les grises," meaning tipsy women; they were accused of getting drunk and continuing the illicit sale of liquor to the Indians which Mme d'Youville's father-in-law and her husband had carried on. The slander spread quickly, and a Recollet even went so far as to refuse them communion. From 1738 to 1744 Mme d'Youville, who suffered from a bad knee, had to stay in her room. When she was better again and everything seemed to be more in order, a raging fire destroyed the house on 31 Jan. 1745. She experienced many difficulties in finding lodgings for her inmates and the community, which by now had five members, until 1747, when she assumed charge of the Hôpital Général. Two days after the fire Mme d'Youville and her companions signed a deed drawn up by Normant Du Faradon, called "Engagements primitifs," in which they promised formally to live and die together in submission and obedience to the one person who would be entrusted with the administration of the house, to divest themselves of all belongings except landed property and put them into a common fund, and to devote themselves unreservedly to the welfare of the poor. This deed formed the basis of the community founded by Mme d'Youville, and a copy was included in the earliest collection of its rules, published in 1781 by Étienne MONTGOLFIER.

The ten years of difficulty had not, however, been unprofitable: with Mme d'Youville's strength of character, practical turn of mind, and tireless devotion to duty, the community had been consolidated and had managed to continue its chosen work. Consequently the Sulpicians persuaded Governor Charles de Beauharnois*, Bishop Pontbriand [Dubreil*], and Intendant HOCQUART, who were all trustees of the Hôpital Général, to charge her with its management. An ordinance promulgated on 27 Aug. 1747 appointed her director of the hospital "temporarily and at His Majesty's pleasure and until he has given other instructions for it."

Mme d'Youville was taking in hand a bankrupt institution [*see* Jean Jeantot*; Louis Turc* de Castelveyre, named Brother Chrétien]. Founded in 1692 by François Charon* de La Barre, the Hôpital Général was burdened with a debt of nearly 40,000 *livres*, and its building was in a lamentable state. The last period of Mme d'Youville's life was devoted to getting the hospital running again, administering it with limited financial means, and establishing on a permanent basis the community she had formed. After completing an inventory of the hospital's possessions, which gives some idea of its dilapidated condition, Mme d'Youville had it cleaned up and had the most urgent repairs done. On 7 Oct. 1747 she moved into it with six associates, two of whom had not yet been admitted into the community [*see* Agathe Véronneau*], and eight inmates. She found two old Brothers Hospitallers and four sick old men in the hospital. Soon large rooms were ready for the sick and poor of both sexes, a change in the policy of the Hôpital Général which until then had been reserved exclusively for men. At the request of Sulpician Antoine Déat*, Mme d'Youville had 12 rooms made ready to receive those then called "fallen women."

Things were going well and Mme d'Youville had every reason to think that she would succeed in re-establishing the Hôpital Général. But the court opposed the creation of new religious communities in the colony; the king considered them a source of expense since when they received official recognition they became entitled to an income to provide for their continuing existence. Intendant BIGOT, Bishop Pontbriand, and the new governor, La Jonquière [Taffanel*], were afraid that, without this assured income, the community would disintegrate when the founder died and the Hôpital Général would fail for a second time. Therefore in October 1750 Bigot issued an ordinance terminating the provisional contract of 1747 and uniting the Hôpital Général of Montreal with the one in Quebec. The hospital nuns of Quebec were authorized to sell the institution's buildings and dependencies and the furniture they did not want to keep, "in return for assuming the responsibility for feeding and keeping the infirm, elderly, disabled, and orphans of the Government of Montreal," who would be taken to Quebec. Because of the lateness of the season, however, Mme d'Youville could remain in the hospital and continue her work until the following July. This ordinance dismayed Montrealers, who had come to appreciate the work done by Mme d'Youville and her sisters. Normant Du Faradon sent the minister of Marine a petition signed by 80 citizens, among them the governor of Montreal, Charles Le Moyne* de Longueuil, second Baron de Longueuil, which recalled that at the founding of the Hôpital Général in 1692, the "letters patent contained the clause and express reserve that the aforesaid establishment should serve in perpetuity without the possibility of being changed either as to place or into any other pious work." Marguerite d'Youville and her sisters also drew up a petition in which they described the improvements made to the Hôpital Général since they had taken over and indicated the irreparable harm that would be done the poor of Montreal in depriving them of a place "where they are assured of finding certain help in their old age." Finally they offered to repay Brother Chrétien's debts if they were themselves confirmed in "the rights, favours, and privileges" granted to the Brothers Hospitallers at the time the hospital was founded. Mme d'Youville went in person to Quebec to carry this petition to Bishop Pontbriand and Bigot, who both received her coldly. They had no confidence in the community's permanence, and like many of their contemporaries they saw its founder as an instrument of the Sulpicians, whom they suspected of wanting to gain control of the Hôpital Général. Consequently they refused to support her petition. Only Governor La Jonquière was sympathetic towards her and promised her his help.

Athough Mme d'Youville found little support in Quebec, Jean Couturier, the superior of the Sulpicians in Paris, took up her defence at the court and stressed her offer to repay the hospital's debts on condition that the king recognize her community by letters patent and put her definitely in charge of the Hôpital Général. He also brought up a clause in the contract between the Sulpicians and François Charon which stipulated that if the hospital ceased to exist, and if the Brothers did not buy the land, the land would revert to the seminary, along with all the buildings on it. As the Brothers had never bought it, Bigot could not dispose of a property that belonged to the Sulpicians. On 14 Dec. 1751 the intendant was obliged by royal order to issue an ordinance revoking the union of the Hôpital Général of Montreal with that in Quebec and leaving Mme d'Youville in charge of the institution. On 12 May 1752 the king in council ordered the trustees of the hospital to sign a contract with Mme d'Youville determining how it would be administered. This contract, which was made public by an ordinance of 28 Sept. 1752, was prompted by a memoir that Mme d'Youville had delivered to the trustees on 19 June in which she set out the methods she intended to adopt to discharge the hospital's debts – methods that reveal an administrative ability the government and merchants of the time might have envied. As a prudent woman who had almost lost everything, she also set out her conditions: she and her sisters would be dispensed from teaching and would close the school that the Brothers Hospitallers conducted in the hospital; they would have all the rights and privileges granted the Brothers; if the king one day decided to take the administration of the institution away from them, the 18,000 *livres* they were sacrificing to pay off the debts would have to be repaid them. The letters patent, dated 3 June 1753, in which the king recognized the community as a legal entity and placed Mme d'Youville and her companions officially in charge of the administration of the Hôpital Général, reached Quebec in the autumn and were registered in the Conseil Supérieur on 1 October. In June 1755 Bishop Pontbriand made his pastoral visit to the community and officially approved the rules drawn up by Normant Du Faradon at the beginning of their life in common. On 25 August, 11 of those who had already made their profession received the habit from the hands of the Sulpician. They took the name Sisters of Charity of the Hôpital Général, or Grey Nuns (Sœurs Grises), in memory of the sobriquet given them by the people of Montreal. In France in the mean time, thanks to Abbé de L'Isle-Dieu's successful handling, the creditors of the Hôpital Général were paid off and the institution's debts finally settled in 1756.

The Hôpital Général, which took in poor men and women, fallen women, and abandoned children, was in fact a hospice; but in 1755 a smallpox epidemic transformed it into a real hospital. The following year Bigot called on Mme d'Youville to attend to the sick soldiers and prisoners, at government expense. The intendant was stingy with payments and cut them down, and the hospital had to assume the major share of the costs. Marguerite d'Youville proved remarkably ingenious at lodging and feeding all these people. She knew how to turn everything to profit: needlework, the making of sails and tents, production of consecrated wafers and candles, curing of tobacco, burning and sale of lime, renting of plots of land, and sale of produce from the sisters' farms. She also received ladies of quality who paid board and lodging. Able to make herself both feared and loved, she succeeded in turning everyone's skills to profit. Even among those hospitalized were found persons with strength enough to work as occasional tailors, shoemakers, and bakers. She hired British prisoners who had been treated at the hospital, either for labour on her farms or as hospital attendants to help the nuns who had little knowledge of English. The community continued its tasks despite epidemics, poor harvests, the war, and then the new régime.

For the founder the trials multiplied. In 1757 illness almost carried her off and she drew up her first will, leaving everything she owned to the hospital. Later she had the grief of separation from the friends and members of her family who returned to France after the conquest. There was the devaluation of the currency, at a time when France owed the hospital 120,799 *livres*. The year 1765 brought the heaviest trial, for on 18 May, in the space of a few hours, fire destroyed the Hôpital Général, which then was sheltering 18 sisters, 17 ladies paying board and lodging, 63 poor persons, and 16 illegitimate children. She wrote to Abbé de L'Isle-Dieu: "My dear Father, pray that God will give me the strength to bear all these crosses and to make saintly use of them. So much at one time: to lose one's king, one's country, one's possessions."

She had no choice but to rebuild, and the last years of her life were as active as the early ones. With the help of the Sulpician seminary – Étienne Montgolfier advanced her 15,000 *livres* – she began the rebuilding, and seven months after the fire the poor were able to return to their lodgings. She sold a piece of property at Chambly which was producing little income, and from one of her boarders, Marie-Anne Robutel de La Noue, bought the seigneury of Châteauguay, which was still largely uncultivated but whose possibilities she foresaw. She had a large water-mill and a bakehouse built there, had several acres of land cleared and sown, and an orchard planted, supervising everything herself despite the fatigue of the trips by cart and canoe between Montreal and Châteauguay. Marguerite d'Youville saw to everything, with the result that on the eve of her death she left a house that was firmly established, both spiritually and materially. In a second will she bequeathed half of her possessions to her two sons and the remainder to the Hôpital Général on condition that if the occasion arose her sons could retire to live there for nothing. She died on 23 Dec. 1771 after a paralytic stroke, remembered by all as an exceptional woman. To Sister Marguerite-Thérèse LEMOINE Despins fell the task of continuing her work.

If Mme d'Youville possessed remarkable administrative talent, her unselfishness was equally evident. And the indomitable courage which enabled her to stand up to her many trials, to defend herself against the unfair accusations of those in power in Canada, and to put up with the insults and calumnies of the populace, should not obscure the sensitivity of this woman, who was moved by the misfortunes as well as by the moments of happiness of her relatives and friends and whom every form of human affliction touched deeply. Her correspondence reveals the intensity of her spiritual life, and tradition attributes miracles and certain prophetic utterances to her.

CLAUDETTE LACELLE

[A great deal has been written on Marguerite d'Youville and her work. Three bibliographies cover the period before her beatification in 1959 and they list 808 titles: Catherine Barry, "La vénérable Mère d'Youville et les Sœurs de la Charité de Montréal (sœurs grises)" (thèse de bibliothéconomie, université de Montréal, 1938); Sœur Sainte-Fernande [Albina Côté], "Bibliographie, 1950–1958, de la bienheureuse Marguerite d'Youville" (thèse de bibliothéconomie, université Laval, Québec, 1963); Sœur Saint-Hyacinthe [Gertrude Pelletier], "Bienheureuse Marguerite d'Youville; bibliographie canadienne, 1938–1949" (thèse de bibliothéconomie, université Laval, 1963). Much has been written since 1959. In the majority of the studies, however, the years before she took charge of the Hôpital Général are treated only briefly, since it was not until 1747 that she began a sustained correspondence. At that time she was 46 and had been a widow for 18 years; two-thirds of her life, then, remains obscure. Nevertheless, recent studies based on notarial acts illuminate these years to some degree. Only the most useful primary and secondary sources are listed here. C.L.]

AN, Col., C11A, 90–96; F3, 13, 14 (copies at PAC). ANQ-M, Chambre des milices, 1–5; Greffe de J.-C. Raimbault, 24 avril 1731; Greffe de Pierre Raimbault, 11 août 1722. ASGM, Dossier: Maison mère, Historique, Doc., 146–253; Mère d'Youville, Corr.; Famille; Antoine Sattin, "Vie de madame Youville, fondatrice et première supérieure des Sœurs de la Charité de l'Hôpital Général de Montréal, communément nommées sœurs grises, dédiée à cette même communauté, 1828"; C.-M.-M. d'Youville, "Mémoires pour servir à la vie de Mde Youville et tirés pour la plupart des dépositions des sœurs Despins, Lasource, Rinville et de Mde Gamelin, et d'une autre sœur"; "La vie de madame Youville, fondatrice des Sœurs de la Charité à Montréal." PAC, MG 8, E6, 1–5; MG 17, A7-2-1, 3, pp.877–82, 971–75; A7-2-3, 8, pp.88–91; A15, 1, pp.15–124. Bégon, "Correspondance" (Bonnault), ANQ *Rapport*, 1934–35. *Édits ord.* (1854–56), II, 404. La Rue, "Lettres et mémoires," ANQ *Rapport*, 1935–36, 1936–37, 1937–38.

[M.-R. Côté], *Une disciple de la croix, la vénérable Marguerite d'Youville, Marie-Marguerite Dufrost de La Jemmerais, veuve d'Youville, 1701–1771, fondatrice à Montréal en 1737 du premier institut canadien, les Sœurs de la Charité (sœurs grises)* ([Québec], 1932). [É.-M. Faillon], *Vie de Mme d'Youville, fondatrice des Sœurs de la Charité de Villemarie dans l'île de Montréal, en Canada* (Villemarie [Montréal], 1852). A. Fauteux et Drouin, *L'Hôpital Général de Montréal*, I. Albertine Ferland-Angers, *Mère d'Youville, vénérable Marie-Marguerite Du Frost de Lajemmerais, veuve d'Youville, 1701–1771; fondatrice des Sœurs de la Charité de l'Hôpital-général de Montréal, dites sœurs grises* (Montréal, 1945); *Pierre You et son fils François d'Youville* ([Montréal, 1941]). A.-H. Gosselin, *L'Église du Canada après la Conquête*, I; *L'Église du Canada jusqu'à la Conquête*, II, III. Estelle Mitchell, *Le vrai visage de Marguerite d'Youville (1701–1771)* (Montréal, 1973). M. Trudel, *L'Église canadienne*. Albertine Ferland-Angers, "Varennes, berceau d'une sainte," *RHAF*, XIII (1959–60), 3–17. É.-Z. Massicotte, "La famille Dufrost de la Gemmeraye," *BRH*, XXII (1916), 71–76.

DUFY DESAUNIERS, THOMAS-IGNACE TROTTIER. *See* TROTTIER

DUGAS (Dugast), JOSEPH, merchant, privateer, and militia officer; b. 1714 at Grand Pré, Nova Scotia, second son of Joseph Dugas and Marguerite Richard; m. first Marguerite Leblanc, daughter of Joseph LEBLANC, *dit* Le Maigre, and they had seven children; m. secondly Louise Arseneau at Chedabouctou (Guysborough, N.S.) in 1762; d. 11 Jan. 1779 at Saint-Servan, France.

Joseph Dugas was brought by his family to the new colony of Île Royale (Cape Breton Island) as an infant. In 1729 at the age of 15 he was commanding the *Nouveau Commerçant* in the coasting trade between Louisbourg and Île Saint-Jean (Prince Edward Island). Working with his father until the latter's death in 1733 and then on his own, he supplied firewood to the Louisbourg garrison. Between 1730 and 1737 the annual income from this business averaged 5,567 *livres*, phenomenal earnings compared with a garrison captain's pay of 1,080 *livres*.

In 1737 Dugas, in partnership with Jean Milly, *dit* La Croix, and François Poinsu, was granted a three-year charter to provide both the garrison and the civilian population of Louisbourg with fresh beef, an important contract because virtually all Île Royale's foodstuffs were imported. The enterprise began well in July 1738, but difficulties arose when the minister of Marine, Maurepas, pursuing French trade policies, stipulated that cattle were to be imported from Canada rather than from British Nova Scotia. Moreover, in the same year local merchants objected that the Dugas enterprise was a front for François DU PONT Duvivier's monopoly. In 1740 the charter was modified slightly to stipulate that Dugas draw at least 30 head of cattle from Canada each year. The conditions of the charter were, however, never stringently enforced, probably as a result of the protection of the Louisbourg administration [*see* Du Pont Duvivier]; in 1744 Acadian deputies reported to Paul Mascarene* that Dugas had driven both cattle and sheep overland from Minas to Baie-Verte (N.B.) and then taken them by sea to Louisbourg. Dugas continued to supply the needs of the garrison until 1745.

Because of these drives Dugas was able to provide the French with military intelligence. In October 1744 he informed Claude-Élisabeth Denys* de Bonnaventure, commander of the naval detachment which was supposed to combine with Duvivier's land force for an attack on Annapolis Royal, Nova Scotia, that the latter had already withdrawn. On 17 May 1745 Louis DU PONT Duchambon, the commandant at Louisbourg, dispatched Dugas to locate Paul Marin* de La Malgue in Acadia and communicate the necessity of immediate relief for the besieged fortress. After Louisbourg's fall, William Pepperrell* and Peter Warren* sent Dugas to Nova Scotia to encourage the Acadians to provision the occupying force. Dugas's association with Pepperrell and Warren was short-lived. When Indians from Île Royale plundered his ship at Tatamagouche and threatened him, Dugas retired to Minas until Île Royale was returned to France in 1749; he then settled at Port-Toulouse (near St Peters, N.S.). The census of 1752 described him as a "habitant-caboteur" (coaster); his holdings were meagre: three cattle, two pigs, a dozen fowl, and two acres under turnips which, he complained, "have never grown well there." The purchase of a vessel undoubtedly improved his situation. The historian François-Edme Rameau* de Saint-Père reports that up to 1756 Dugas and several others were paid 60,000 *livres* for making more than 300 voyages transporting refugee Acadians and their provisions to Île Saint-Jean.

Following the second capitulation of Louisbourg on 26 July 1758 Dugas escaped to Quebec where he was issued a commission as a privateer. In January 1759 he passed information to the commander of the Miramichi region (N.B.) about British preparations at Halifax and Louisbourg and noted the plight of the Acadians, who had suffered "all the hardships imaginable." He also indicated that the villagers of Port-Toulouse intended to join the growing force of Acadian partisans and refugees to the north of the Chignecto area who continued to elude the British dragnet.

In February 1760 Dugas was at Richibucto (N.B.), where he strongly protested missionary Jean Manach*'s encouragement of Acadian submission. By the winter of 1760 Dugas was a major in the partisan militia around the Baie des Chaleurs. The resistance of this last French stronghold had slowly crumbled after the capitulation of François-Gabriel d'ANGEAC on 30 Oct. 1760. The continued presence of the Acadian partisans and privateers and of a small detachment of 12 colonial regulars commanded by François Boucher de Niverville (Nebourvele) Grandpré alarmed Jonathan BELCHER, the administrator of Nova Scotia, and in October 1761 Captain Roderick MacKenzie with 56 soldiers was sent to pacify the region. Owing to the number of Acadians and the lack of ships, MacKenzie was able to transport only the Acadian leaders, including Dugas (Di Gaw in some British records), to Fort Cumberland (near Sackville, N.B.), and then to Halifax where they were imprisoned. Among those left behind was Alexis LANDRY. When Dugas was captured, he seems to have owned two 20-ton shallops (one in partnership with Joseph Leblanc, *dit* Le Maigre) which may have been used as privateers.

A year later Dugas had escaped and was hiding at Chedabouctou, where on 2 Oct. 1762 he married Louise Arseneau, without a priest, "because they were unable to present themselves at a church." By 1764 Dugas had emigrated to Miquelon; his marriage was regularized there in May 1766. The fate of those Acadians who, to remain loyal to French authority, moved to Saint-Pierre and Miquelon was not a pleasant one. In 1767, as a result of French policy, many were deported or left the islands [*see* d'Angeac], and Dugas was among them. He arrived at Saint-Malo in November 1767, only to be forced along with other Acadians to return the following spring.

Joseph Dugas lived out his last years in penury. In 1776, after a half-century of enterprise on the Acadian frontier, he had only a share of a beach lot, a house, a stable, and two head of cattle. Two years later, aged 64, Dugas suffered his final hardship: the British, in retaliation for the French sheltering of Yankee privateers during the American revolution, captured Saint-Pierre and Miquelon and deported its nearly 1,300 inhabitants to France. Dugas and his wife disembarked once again at Saint-Malo, on 6 Nov. 1778. He died at nearby Saint-Servan on 11 Jan. 1779; his wife died five months later on 10 June.

BERNARD POTHIER

AD, Ille-et-Vilaine (Rennes), État civil, Saint-Servan, 11 janv. 1779. AMA, SHA, A[1], 3498, no.6. AN, Col., B, 65, ff.447v-48v; 66, ff.297–98; 70; C[11A], 105, ff.49–49v, 60–60v; C[11B], 19, f.133; 20, ff.52, 304–6v; 22, ff.202, 288–89; 25, f.43; C[11C], 11; 12, f.155; Section Outre-mer, Dépôt des fortifications des colonies, Am. sept., no.216; G[1], 413A, ff.26, 65; 467, f.28; G[2], 180, ff.350–53; 182, ff.629–39; 191, ff.58–58v; G[3], 2037, f.66; 2038/1, f.18; 2045, f.29. CÉA, Fonds Patrice Gallant, les Acadiens à Miquelon, dossier VII, 191–91b. PRO, CO 217/1, ff.222–22v; WO 34/1, pp.47–52, 63–70, 117–26, 139–44, 313–28 (PAC transcripts).

Placide Gaudet, "Acadian genealogy and notes," PAC *Report*, 1905, II, pt.III, 175, 191–96, 260–64, 271–72. *N.S. Archives, IV*, 52, 76–77. PAC *Report*, 1894, 226–27, 229–30; 1905, II, pt.I, 17. "Papiers Amherst (1760–1763) concernant les Acadiens," R.-S. Brun, édit., Soc. historique acadienne, *Cahier* (Moncton, N.-B.), III (1968–71), 257–320. [F.-E.] Rameau de Saint-Père, *Une colonie féodale en Amérique: l'Acadie (1604–1881)* (2v., Paris et Montréal, 1889), II, 386–87. Bernard Pothier, "Acadian emigration to Île Royale after the conquest of Acadia," *Social History*, no.6 (November 1970), 116–31.

DU JAUNAY, PIERRE (Pierre-Luc), priest, Jesuit, and missionary; said to have been b. 11 Aug. 1704 (or 10 Aug. 1705) at Vannes, France; d. 16 July 1780 at Quebec.

Pierre Du Jaunay entered the Jesuit order in Paris on 2 Sept. 1723 and studied theology at La Flèche from 1731 to 1734. Following his ordination he sailed for Canada in 1734, and the next year he accompanied Jean-Baptiste de Saint-Pé* to Michilimackinac (Mackinaw City, Mich.) where he first met the Ottawa Indians, to whom he would minister for nearly 30 years.

The risk involved in missionary work among the western tribes was made tragically clear to Du Jaunay when his friend Jean-Pierre Aulneau* was killed at Lake of the Woods in 1736. Undaunted, he made several requests to be sent to the Mandans and other tribes of the far west. These wishes were not honoured by his superior. Instead his career centred at the trading town of Michilimackinac, and with this settlement as a base he served several other small communities in the Upper Lakes region. His first documented baptism took place on 21 June 1738 at Saint-Joseph (Niles, Mich.), but he was apparently at this mission only briefly before returning to Michilimackinac. He visited it again for short times in 1742, 1745, and 1752. He also journeyed to Sault Ste Marie (Mich.), where he said mass in 1741. Extensive travel was not necessary for him because the voyageurs and traders of the Upper Lakes made frequent trips to Michilimackinac. The parish register there records the presence of people from Saint-Joseph, La Baye (Green Bay, Wis.), Sault Ste Marie, and Chagouamigon (near Ashland, Wis.). Though he attended to the French, his primary love was for the Indians, and he was deeply distressed by the reprehensible conduct of nominally Christian whites, which was a stumbling block to potential Indian converts.

The focus of Du Jaunay's ministry was the log church of Sainte-Anne, situated within the palisaded town. Behind the church a door in the palisade opened into a court enclosing a bake oven and an ice-house. Close by the rectory was a blacksmith shop where Pascal Soulard and Jean-Baptiste Amiot* worked under contract to the priest. In 1739 Du Jaunay supplied corn and ironwork for Pierre-Joseph Céloron* de Blainville's expedition against the Chickasaws.

When the Ottawas who lived close to Michilimackinac decided to relocate their village in 1741, Du Jaunay helped persuade them to move only as far as L'Arbre Croche (Cross Village, Mich.). From then on he divided his efforts between the parish ministry at Sainte-Anne's and the mission of Saint-Ignace at L'Arbre Croche, where he had a farm. In the 1740s he compiled a 396-page manuscript dictionary of the Ottawa language.

In 1743 a new church was constructed at Michilimackinac to accommodate the growing community. During his ministry in the parish from 1742 until 1765 Du Jaunay conducted 25 weddings and 120 baptisms. Thus he directly touched the lives of most families who lived in the Upper Lakes region. Working with him at various times were fellow priests Claude-Godefroy Coquart*, Jean-Baptiste de Lamorinie*, and Marin-Louis (Marie-Louis) Le Franc; several Indian slaves and an occasional lay worker also assisted.

In 1754, after nearly 20 years in the interior, Du Jaunay visited Montreal. He apparently missed the tragic smallpox epidemic in the Michilimackinac region in 1757 [*see* NISSOWAQUET]. On his return shortly after he found an impoverished and desolate community.

In 1760, following the British capture of Canada, Du Jaunay spoke out for a peaceful acceptance of the new régime. His influence assisted the smooth transition when British troops finally arrived at Michilimackinac in 1761. Although Du Jaunay had persuaded the French and the Ottawas to accept the British, he had little success with the nearby Ojibwas. On 2 June 1763, encouraged by Pontiac*'s attack on Detroit, the local Ojibwas led by Minweweh* and Madjeckewiss* surprised and overpowered the British garrison. Appalled by the slaughter, Du Jaunay risked his life in sheltering some of the soldiers and traders in his house. A short time later the Ottawas from L'Arbre Croche arrived and took the survivors under their protection. In a letter to Henry GLADWIN, George Etherington, the commandant, remarked that the priest was "a very good man, and had a great deal to say with the savages hereabout, who will believe everything he tells them." Du Jaunay himself carried the letter to Detroit, arriving there on 18 June. Two days later Gladwin sent him back with verbal instructions and a wampum belt for the Ottawas. The pious priest, who "never told a lie in his life," had refused to carry a letter that he could not reveal if stopped by hostile Indians. Before leaving Detroit he held a council with Pontiac in an unsuccessful effort to free the English prisoners.

Affairs at the straits of Mackinac remained chaotic until the post was regarrisoned. Du Jaunay tried to restore order and wrote to Sir William JOHNSON to give assurances of the goodwill of the French and Ottawas. On 22 Sept. 1764, when British troops returned, the priest was at the water side to welcome them. He was the first to sign the oath of allegiance, and he demonstrated his good faith by supplying food for them and delivering up a captive soldier whom his servant had ransomed from the Indians.

Du Jaunay's long career at Michilimackinac was nearly over. In 1765 he was recalled and the mission closed. After celebrating his last baptism at the straits on 3 July 1765, he packed up the sacred vessels of the mission and took them to Detroit. At Quebec he was appointed spiritual director of the Ursulines there on 2 Aug. 1767. He maintained his interest in western affairs, however. In 1769 he briefly became embroiled in the events stirred up by the court martial of Robert ROGERS. When Joseph-Louis Ainsse* of Michilimackinac, a prosecution witness, was himself charged with theft, Du Jaunay travelled to Montreal to testify to Ainsse's good character.

Despite the turmoil of the American revolution the old priest continued his work at Quebec until his death in 1780. At Michilimackinac and at L'Arbre Croche his memory lingered. As late as 1824 the Ottawas were still pointing out the spot "where Du Jaunay used to walk up and down, saying his office."

DAVID A. ARMOUR

AN, Col., C11A, 72, f.125; 73, ff.212, 258, 273; 76, ff.183, 192, 213; 86, f.244; 119, f.328. Clements Library, Thomas Gage papers, American ser., 84, Roberts to Gage, 30 March 1769; 85, memorial of Louis Joseph Ainse in Carleton to Gage, 30 May 1769. Newberry Library (Chicago), MSS coll., Gage to Langlade, 17 July 1763. Pa. Hist. Soc. (Philadelphia), Simon Gratz coll., case 4, box 7, Howard to Bradstreet, 15 Oct. 1764. PRO, WO 34/49, Etherington to Gladwin, 12 June 1763. Ste Ann's Parish (Mackinac Island, Mich.), Registre des baptêmes, mariages et sépultures de Sainte-Anne-de-Michillimakinak.

The Aulneau collection, 1734–1745, ed. A. E. Jones (Montreal, 1893), 66, 104, 110–12, 122–25, 136–38.

[Michel Chartier de Lotbinière], "Fort Michilimackinac in 1749: Lotbinière's plan and description," trans. and ed. Marie Gérin-Lajoie, *Mackinac History* (Mackinac Island), II, no.5 (1976). [G.-J. Chaussegros de Léry], "Journal de Joseph-Gaspard Chaussegros de Léry, lieutenant des troupes, 1754–1755," ANQ *Rapport*, 1927–28, 400. *Diary of the siege of Detroit* . . . , ed. F. B. Hough (Albany, N.Y., 1860), 29–32. Henry, *Travels and adventures*. *Johnson papers* (Sullivan *et al.*), III, 412–16; XI, 273, 336. *Journals and letters of La Vérendrye* (Burpee), 365. *JR* (Thwaites), LXX, 87, 250–53; LXXI, 171. *Michigan Pioneer Coll.*, I (1874–76), 485; VIII (1885), 367–68; XXVI (1894–95), 535; XXVII (1896), 669. "The St. Joseph baptismal register," ed. George Paré and M. M. Quaife, *Mississippi Valley Hist. Rev*. (Cedar Rapids, Iowa, and Lincoln, Neb.), XIII (1926–27), 216–17, 223. *The siege of Detroit in 1763: the journal of Pontiac's conspiracy, and John Rutherfurd's narrative of a captivity*, ed. M. M. Quaife (Chicago, 1958), 140–41, 147. Wis., State Hist. Soc., *Coll.*, VII (1876), 162–64; VIII (1879), 219–20; XVII (1906), 370–74, 413; XVIII (1908), 471–80, 482–83, 486; XIX (1910), 6–30, 33–37, 42–44, 47–48, 52–53, 56, 58, 63–71. Caron, "Inv. de la corr. de Mgr Briand," ANQ *Rapport*, 1929–30, 70, 84, 85. Martin Kavanagh, *La Vérendrye, his life and times* . . . (Brandon, Man., 1967). Laval Laurent, *Québec et l'Église aux États-Unis sous Mgr Briand et Mgr Plessis* (Montréal, 1945). George Paré, *The Catholic Church in Detroit, 1701–1888* (Detroit, 1951).

DUMAS, JEAN-DANIEL, officer in the colonial regular troops; b. 24 Feb. 1721 at Montauban, France, son of Samuel Dumas and Anne Martin; d. unmarried on 2 Aug. 1794 at Albias (dept of Tarn-et-Garonne), France.

Having joined the Régiment d'Agenois as a volunteer, in 1742 Jean-Daniel Dumas was named second lieutenant in the grenadier company and the following year, lieutenant. During the War of the Austrian Succession, he served in Bavaria, Italy, and Provence, and in 1747 he was promoted captain. With that rank, but in the colonial regulars, he arrived in Canada three years later. He was sent to Acadia, where an uneasy situation existed because of the failure of the treaty of Utrecht to define the frontiers conclusively [*see* Jean-Louis LE LOUTRE]. He rapidly acquired a reputation as a skilful negotiator with the Indians. This was probably why he was posted to Fort Duquesne (Pittsburgh, Pa), in the Ohio valley, in 1754. The battle of the Monongahela on 9 July 1755 gave Dumas an opportunity to distinguish himself. When the French commander, Daniel-Hyacinthe-Marie Liénard* de Beaujeu, was killed early in the combat, it was Dumas who took command of the fewer than 900 men, including about 600 Indians, and routed the much larger British force. For this feat he was made a knight of the order of Saint-Louis on 17 March 1756, at 35 years of age. He would have liked, however, to see the decoration accompanied by a promotion; as he wrote to the minister Machault on 24 July 1756, he believed that his victory had been "the salvation of a whole colony" and had enabled France to make allies of Indians friendly to the British. Dumas had created a strong impression on the Indians; entrusted with the command of Fort Duquesne after the victory, he made use of his new position to negotiate alliances with several Indian groups and to organize numerous expeditions against British settlements.

By his services Dumas attracted the esteem and protection of Governor RIGAUD de Vaudreuil. In May 1757 he was named town major of Quebec. That year he served under François-Pierre de RIGAUD de Vaudreuil and later Montcalm* in the August campaign which would bring the capitulation of Fort William Henry (also called Fort George, now Lake George, N.Y.). He acted as adjutant, administering the affairs of all the militia units, to the great satisfaction of Vaudreuil who claimed that "because of his diligence, our troops, and even our Canadians, yielded nothing to the *troupes de terre* [French regulars] in the most precise execution of [their] military duties." On 1 Jan. 1759 Dumas was appointed adjutant general and inspector of the colonial regular troops in Canada. This important promotion permitted him to play an active role in the 1759 and 1760 campaigns.

During the siege of Quebec in 1759 the Lower Town was threatened with destruction by batteries which the British set up at Pointe-Lévy (Lauzon) in July. Under pressure from a number of citizens, Governor Vaudreuil agreed to the recruitment of volunteers to surprise the British by night. Dumas led this raid, and François-Prosper DOUGLAS was second in command. In all, about 1,500 men – militiamen, regulars, townsmen, and even some students – crossed the St Lawrence on the night of 12–13 July. They had scarcely reached the south shore when, believing themselves surrounded by the enemy, they opened fire upon one another. Despite Dumas's efforts to regroup them, the whole force was seized with panic, and the raid was a complete failure. Shortly after, on the night of 18–19 July, five or six British ships (including a 50-gun ship of the line) under John Rous* sailed past Quebec to cast anchor at Anse des Mères (between Place Royale and Anse au Foulon). Dumas was ordered to follow their movements with 600 men, but he was unable to prevent them from destroying the last fireship, which was being fitted out at Anse des Mères. Nor could he prevent British grenadiers from landing at Pointe-aux-Trembles (Neuville) on 21 July and carrying off more than 200 women and children, who were, however, released the following day. In the battle of the Plains of Abraham on 13 September, Dumas commanded a brigade; after the capture of Quebec he took up position on the Rivière Jacques-Cartier intending with the aid of field works to bar the British advance to Montreal. He spent the winter in this position.

In command of a brigade at the battle of Sainte-Foy on 28 April 1760, Dumas took an active part in the combat, which could have resulted in the recapture of Quebec if help had arrived from France and if the French artillery under Fiacre-François POTOT de Montbeillard had not proven much inferior in number and quality to the British. Dumas directed the retreat and with 1,500 men endeavoured to delay Brigadier-General James MURRAY's advance on Montreal. In September 1760, after the capitulation, he went to France. His services in Canada had been thought so valuable that Jean de Rigaud de Vaudreuil, Vicomte de Vaudreuil and brother of the governor, observed on 13 Jan. 1761: "If my brother had been aided by everyone as he was by [Dumas], I can assure you that that country would still belong to the king."

In March 1761 Dumas was promoted to the rank of colonel. In 1765 he was named second in command at Saint-Domingue (Hispaniola), but he did not take up his post, and the following year he received command of Île de France (Mauritius) and Île Bourbon (Réunion). In 1768 he was made a brigadier-general of the armies, and that same year he was recalled to France. His stay on Île de France had been marked by a sharp conflict with the intendant, Pierre Poivre, and the Conseil Supérieur of the colony, but he vindicated himself fully of the accusations against him and in 1772 received an annual gratuity of 3,000 *livres*. Two years later he obtained a pension of 7,200 *livres* for his services, and on 1 March 1780 he was promoted major-general. On several occasions he asked to be allowed to go on active service, but without success.

Possessed of a sense of humour, Dumas was a brave, talented, and experienced officer and was also scrupulously honest. Antoine de Sartine, who at the time of the *affaire du Canada* headed the commission on the malpractices committed in the colony, acknowledged that "everywhere the Sieur Dumas was in command, expenses diminished by half on the day of his arrival, and upon his departure rose again to their normal level."

ÉTIENNE TAILLEMITE

AMA, SHA, Y^{3d}, 2672. AN, Col., C^{11A}, 102, f.153; 104, ff.177, 180, 275f., 440; 105, ff.16, 20; D^{2C}, 4, f.126; 48, f.309; 59, ff.7, 10; 94, f.10; 181, f.3; E, 153 (dossier Dumas); Marine, B^4, 98, f.11v. Bougainville, "Journal" (A.-E. Gosselin), ANQ *Rapport*, 1923–24, 219, 234, 251, 271, 275. *Coll. des manuscrits de Lévis* (Casgrain). "Journal du siège de Québec" (Æ. Fauteux), ANQ *Rapport*, 1920–21, 151, 218. Knox, *Hist. journal* (Doughty), I, 418–19. "Mémoire du Canada," ANQ *Rapport*, 1924–25, 113, 121, 130, 133, 176–77, 189. *NYCD* (O'Callaghan and Fernow), X. *Papiers Contrecœur* (Grenier), 221. *Siège de Québec en 1759 . . .* (Québec, 1836; republished in *Le siège de Québec en 1759 par trois témoins*, J.-C. Hébert, édit. (Québec, 1972), 79, 82–84, 88). *Dictionary of Maurician biography*, ed. Auguste Toussaint (2v. to date, [Port Louis, Mauritius], 1941–). Æ. Fauteux, *Les chevaliers de Saint-Louis*, 161. J.-E. Roy, *Rapport sur les archives de France*, 1025–27. P.-G. Roy, *Les officiers d'état-major des gouvernements de Québec, Montréal et Trois-Rivières sous le Régime français* (Lévis, Qué., 1919), 88–94. F.-J. Audet, *Jean-Daniel Dumas, le héros de la Monongahéla; esquisse biographique* (Montréal, 1920). Henri Bourde de La Rogerie, *Les Bretons aux îles de France et de Bourbon (Maurice et la Réunion) au XVIIe et au XVIIIe siècle* (Rennes, France, 1934), 212, 236, 277. J.-É. Martin-Allanic, *Bougainville navigateur et les découvertes de son temps* (2v., Paris, 1964).

DUMAS SAINT-MARTIN, JEAN, merchant-trader and justice of the peace; b. February 1725 at Montauban, France, son of Pierre Dumas and Marie Calquieres; d. 18 June 1794 in Montreal (Que.).

Jean Dumas Saint-Martin probably arrived in Quebec a few years before the conquest with Alexandre Dumas*, a merchant-trader to whom he was related. On 30 Oct. 1756, in the presence of notary Jean-Claude PANET, the two signed a document which saved the merchant-trader Pierre Révol* from ruin: with Jean Dumas Saint-Martin going surety for him, Alexandre Dumas agreed to pay Révol's numerous creditors a part of their claims. Subsequently Dumas Saint-Martin settled in Montreal as a merchant-trader, the occupation given on his marriage contract with Madeleine Gimbal, *née* Morisseau, signed on 7 Jan. 1764 in Montreal.

Of Huguenot origin, Dumas Saint-Martin was chosen by Governor MURRAY in January 1765 to be a justice of the peace for the District of Montreal. In 1767 he was a partner of Christophe PÉLISSIER and others, who in June that year obtained a lease of the Saint-Maurice ironworks for 16 years. Dumas was to sell its products in Montreal; around 1770 he was replaced in this function by Jacob JORDAN. Among those with whom the partnership involved Dumas were Alexandre Dumas, Thomas Dunn* and Benjamin Price*, both members of the Council of Quebec, and Brook Watson*, an important British merchant. Dumas thus gained entry to an influential circle, but how much use he made of it in his business is unknown. His commercial affairs are not mentioned in available documents, not even in his will, which was drawn up in 1791. There Dumas stated that he did not know "what condition [his] estate will be in."

Like other merchants in the colony, Dumas Saint-Martin took an interest in its political life, calling for the creation of a house of assembly and the preservation of French laws except in commercial dealings. In 1789 he signed the address of the Montreal Protestants welcoming the Church of England bishop Charles Inglis*. Close to the English speaking community through his religion and his business interests, Dumas Saint-Martin was linked by language and culture to the Canadians. In his will "poor Canadians" and "poor Protestants" were treated with equal generosity.

No children were born of Dumas's marriage to Madeleine Morisseau; however, the couple became fond of their nephew Michel, the son of Antoine-Libéral Dumas*, whom they had "as it were brought up" and whom they designated as their sole legatee. Dumas Saint-Martin died on 18 June 1794 and was buried the next day in the Church of England cemetery in Montreal; his wife received a Catholic burial upon her death six years later.

José E. Igartua

ANQ-M, État civil, Anglicans, Christ Church (Montréal), 19 June 1794; Greffe de Louis Chaboillez, 21 déc. 1791, 28 janv. 1794, 24 nov. 1804; Greffe de P.-F. Mézière, 7 janv. 1764. ANQ-Q, État civil, Catholiques, Notre-Dame de Québec, 7 oct. 1766; Greffe de J.-C. Panet, 30 oct. 1756. *Doc. relatifs à l'hist. constitutionnelle, 1759–91* (Shortt et Doughty; 1921), II, 786–88. *Quebec Gazette*, 4 Oct. 1764, 15 Oct. 1767, 18 May, 16, 23 June, 3 Nov. 1785, 18 Dec. 1788, 16 July 1789, 19 July 1792. Tanguay, *Dictionnaire*. Sulte, *Mélanges historiques* (Malchelosse), VI, 144. Tousignant, "La genèse et l'avènement de la constitution de 1791," 309. É.-Z. Massicotte, "Jean Dumas Saint-Martin, négociant et magistrat," *BRH*, XXVIII (1922), 86–89; "Les tribunaux de police de Montréal," *BRH*, XXVI (1920), 181–82. P.-G. Roy, "La famille Dumas," *BRH*, XLV (1939), 161–64; "Le faux-saunier Pierre Revol," *BRH*, L (1944), 227, 234.

DUNCAN, CHARLES, naval officer, explorer, and maritime fur-trader; fl. 1786–92.

It may be assumed that Charles Duncan had spent many years in the naval service before taking part in voyages between 1786 and 1788 as a member of the merchant marine. The evidence is his own "Sketch of the entrance of the Strait of Juan de Fuca," published in 1788 by Alexander Dalrymple, the hydrographer, which notes that he then held the rank of master in the Royal Navy.

In 1786 Richard Cadman Etches and Company, commonly known as the King George's Sound Company, fitted out the *Prince of Wales* and its tender, the *Princess Royal*. James Colnett* was given command of the former; Duncan of the latter. The company, one of several commercial associations formed to pursue the trade in sea otter furs with China, had sent vessels under Nathaniel Portlock* and George Dixon to the northwest coast the year before. Duncan and Colnett left England in September 1786 and, after establishing a sealskin and oil factory on Staten Island (Isla de los Estados, Argentina), arrived at King George's Sound (Nootka Sound, B.C.) the next July. There they traded with the Nootka Indians and, in mid August, met Dixon, who had spent the season trading to the north. Duncan and Colnett then sailed to winter in the Sandwich (Hawaiian) Islands. They returned to the coast in March 1788 and parted, Duncan putting in to Nootka Sound for repairs. In May he headed to the Queen Charlotte Islands, on Dixon's recommendation that trade there would be good. He was the first to prove that they were islands by sailing through Hecate Strait and Dixon Entrance, thus confirming the speculations of Dixon and the Comte de Lapérouse [Galaup].

Duncan spent June and July shuttling between these islands and those lying off the mainland between the mouth of the Skeena River and Calvert Island. He named this chain Princess Royal's Isles, but only one island has retained this appellation. His chart of the area was subsequently used by George Vancouver. On 5 August he continued south to Nootka Sound, where he met another trader, John Meares*. Farther south, in Clayoquot Sound, Duncan anchored off the Nootka village of Ahousat, then located on Vargas Island, and traded with the tribe of Wikinanish. Duncan then sailed by the mouth of Juan de Fuca Strait. His map and sketch of the entrance, dated 15 August, contains some comments on the Indians of Cape Claaset (Cape Flattery, Wash.). It also includes a drawing of Pinnacle Rock (Fuca's Pillar, Wash.), off the cape. The resemblance of the rock to the one described in Juan de Fuca*'s account of the Strait of Anian, and the Indians' comment that a "Great Sea" lay to the east, stimulated belief in England that the strait led to the polar sea.

On 17 August Duncan sailed for the Sandwich

Islands, where he joined Colnett, and together they sailed for China. Duncan's season on the coast had been profitable; almost 2,000 furs had been obtained. He did not return to the northwest coast but exchanged ships with Colnett and sailed to England from Canton in the *Prince of Wales*.

Duncan's discoveries on the northwest coast made him a firm, even fanatical, believer in the existence of a northwest passage. His return to England coincided with a growing interest in the fabled passage aroused by the Nootka crisis [*see* Esteban José MARTÍNEZ], the explorations of Peter Pond* and Samuel HEARNE, the promotions of Dalrymple, and a planned government expedition to establish a settlement on the northwest coast. In May 1790 Duncan received instructions from the Hudson's Bay Company to sail for the west coast of Hudson Bay, find the passage, sail through it to the entrance of Juan de Fuca Strait, and either return or proceed to China. If he did not find such a passage, he was to push inland from Chesterfield Inlet (N.W.T.) as far as the Yathkyed and Dubawnt lakes. Dixon was to accompany Duncan and from the lakes was to travel overland to the Pacific; this plan was subsequently cancelled, and Duncan went alone. He made a voyage in 1790 and another in 1791. On the second occasion he wintered at Churchill (Man.); he examined the shores of the bay and Chesterfield Inlet in July 1792 but found no indications of a passage. Duncan, who "prior to his Sailing, entertained the most positive Assurances that he should discover the often sought for North West Passage . . . felt the disappointment so severely, that whilst on his Voyage home he was attack'd by a Brain Fever." He made several attempts to commit suicide and had to be tied to his bunk, but he still held to the existence of a passage, believing that a rising of land on the west coast of Hudson Bay had made it impassable. There are no further known references to Duncan.

BARRY M. GOUGH

[William Beresford], *A voyage round the world; but more particularly to the north-west coast of America . . .*, ed. and intro. George Dixon (London, 1789; repr. Amsterdam and New York, 1968). *The Dixon-Meares controversy . . .*, ed. F. W. Howay (Toronto and New York, 1929; repr. Amsterdam and New York, 1969). Meares, *Voyages*. Walbran, *B.C. coast names*. H. H. Bancroft [and H. L. Oak], *History of the northwest coast* (2v., San Francisco, 1884). Cook, *Flood tide of empire*. H. T. Fry, *Alexander Dalrymple (1737–1808) and the expansion of British trade* (Buffalo, N.Y., and Toronto, 1970). Glyndwr Williams, *The British search for the northwest passage in the eighteenth century* (London and Toronto, 1962).

DUPÉRONT (Dupéron, Duperron), JACQUES BABY, *dit*. *See* BABY

DUPLEIX SILVAIN (also **Sylvain**), **JEAN-BAPTISTE**, merchant and colonial official; b. 1721 at La Baleine (Baleine Cove, N.S.), fifth son of Claude Duplaix (Duplex Silvain) and Catherine de Gonillon; m. 24 Feb. 1753 Geneviève Benoist at Louisbourg, Île Royale (Cape Breton Island), and they had 14 children; d. in or after 1796 in France.

Claude Duplaix, a merchant and ship captain, left his native Quebec for Plaisance (Placentia, Nfld) in 1710. When Newfoundland and Acadia were awarded to Great Britain in 1713, he went to Île Royale, where he died about 1721. Jean-Baptiste Dupleix Silvain was raised by his stepfather (and uncle), Michel Daccarrette*, and worked in Daccarrette's business from 1737 until the latter's death in action during the siege of Louisbourg in 1745.

Throughout the siege Dupleix Silvain served bravely in the town militia (as he was to do again in 1758) and after the fall of the fortress was deported to La Rochelle. There, in 1747, he formed a business association, ratified at Louisbourg in October 1749, with Philippe Leneuf de Beaubassin and Blaise Lagoanere. All three were among the heirs of Michel Daccarrette and the aim of the association was in part to acquire his property and manage his concerns. By a definitive arrangement of 1754 the partners took over his merchandise, effects, and ships; the buildings and land were left to the other heirs, except for the fishing habitation at La Baleine, which the partners retained for one more year. At the end of three years the real property was to be put back into a common fund. The partners had made a previous arrangement with Jeanne de Picot, Léon Brethous's widow, the principal creditor of the Daccarrette estate, which would have allowed them to press further claims against the estate, but they seem never to have exercised this right.

While securing their interest in the Daccarrette estate the partners set up a fishing and shipping concern and traded supplies to France, Saint-Domingue (Hispaniola), and Quebec. In the early 1750s with Antoine RODRIGUE, they managed, badly it seems, the contract to supply meat for the Louisbourg fortress, eventually falling out with Rodrigue over the sharing of expenses. In 1753 they bid unsuccessfully to work on the Louisbourg fortifications. By the mid 1750s the business appears to have been directed by Dupleix Silvain and Leneuf de Beaubassin; Lagoanere had died before 1754 and had been replaced by his children, none of whom were prominent in the firm.

Despite its initial difficulties, the company prospered, judging from what the partners claimed to have abandoned when Louisbourg fell in 1758: a share in the Daccarrette property in and near the town and three other fishing habitations they had acquired at Rochefort Point and La Baleine. In 1753, when he married Geneviève Benoist, Antoine Rodrigue's niece, Dupleix Silvain had estimated his share in the company to be worth over 20,000 *livres*; in 1758 he valued it at 71,000 of a total of 215,000 *livres*. The company was said to have earned 150,000 *livres* during its existence and in January 1757 Leneuf de Beaubassin claimed that its fishing operations were the basis of the colony's commerce.

The partners had, however, experienced difficulties before 1758. They had extended credit to fishing expeditions which had become insolvent and they had had trouble with their French creditors. Between 1755 and 1758 they had lost at least seven ships as well as money invested in a share of a privateer, cargoes shipped in other vessels, and eight fishing shallops at La Petite Brador (Little Bras d'Or, N.S.). On their return to France after the capitulation in 1758, the partners (Dupleix Silvain, Leneuf de Beaubassin, and the Lagoanere heirs) assumed equal responsibility for their debts and agreed to pay the creditors 50 per cent, or 43,000 *livres*. To discharge his share, Dupleix Silvain in 1763 left for Saint-Pierre and Miquelon, where he set up a fishing enterprise. By 1778 he had recouped some of his fortune; he had three fishing habitations, five schooners, and two shallops, and he employed 80 to 100 men each year. In 1769 he had returned briefly to France to try to make a new arrangement with his creditors because his partners had not discharged their share of the debts and had died insolvent.

Deported from Saint-Pierre in 1778, in 1783 Dupleix Silvain returned to the islands from France with a pension of 150 *livres* and a position as judge of the jurisdiction and lieutenant (by commission) of the admiralty court. His affairs seem to have been in good order, despite further claims advanced by creditors from his Louisbourg days. He earned 6,000 *livres* a year from his position and may for a time have been doing business under his children's names. By 1787 he had paid 10,500 *livres* of the former company's debts.

Between 1789 and the British capture of Saint-Pierre and Miquelon in 1793, Dupleix Silvain was reluctantly entangled in the factionalism and the challenges to the military authorities by some of the merchants which passed for revolutionary activity on the islands. He was taken prisoner by the British for the fourth time in 1793 and held captive for 28 months. He surfaced again in Saint-Malo in February 1796 and was awarded a small pension. His eldest son is known to have been in business at Bayonne in 1802.

T. J. A. Le Goff

AN, Col., B, 110, f.3; 117, f.192v; 174, f.271v; 181, ff.360v, 403; 183, f.156; C[12], 2, f.147; 3, f.81; 8, ff.9, 42; 14, f.49; 16, ff.16, 40; 17, ff.18–18v, 20, 30; E, 159 (dossier Dupleix Silvain); 356 (dossier Rodrigue); Section Outre-mer, G[1], 414; 415; 467, pièces 21, 24, 28–30; G[3], 479 (extrait du registre des baptêmes, mariages et sépultures de l'église de la Balleine); 2042, 19 déc. 1753; 2044, 16 déc. 1755; 2047/1, 16 oct. 1749; 2047/2, 16 déc. 1752, 24 févr. 1753. J.-Y. Ribault, *Les îles Saint-Pierre et Miquelon des origines à 1814* (Saint-Pierre, 1962), 95, 98–109; "La pêche et le commerce de la morue aux îles Saint-Pierre et Miquelon de 1763 à 1793," Congrès national des soc. savantes, Section d'hist. moderne et contemporaine, *Actes du quatre-vingt-onzième congrès, Rennes, 1966* (3v., Paris, 1969), I, 251–92; "La population des îles Saint-Pierre et Miquelon de 1763 à 1793," *Revue française d'hist. d'outre-mer* (Paris), LIII (1966), 45.

DU PONT DUCHAMBON, LOUIS, officer in the colonial regular troops, king's lieutenant, and merchant; baptized 1 Jan. 1680 at Sérignac (dept of Charente), France, sixth son of Hugues Du Pont Duvivier and Marie Hérauld de Gourville; m. 11 Feb. 1709 at Port-Royal (Annapolis Royal, N.S.) to Jeanne Mius d'Entremont de Pobomcoup, granddaughter of Philippe Mius* d'Entremont, Baron de Pobomcoup; d. 22 Aug. 1775 in the parish of Curat (dept of Charente).

Louis Du Pont Duchambon arrived in Acadia in 1702 as an ensign in a new company in which his brothers, François Du Pont* Duvivier and Michel Du Pont* de Renon, served as captain and lieutenant. He was promoted lieutenant in 1704. The two older brothers and Duchambon moved to Louisbourg, Île Royale (Cape Breton Island), after its establishment in 1713. Even with the early death of the eldest brother, Duvivier, in 1714, the Du Pont family remained entrenched in the officer corps of the garrison. That year Renon became adjutant and by 1717 Duvivier's sons had become officers. With Renon's death in 1719 family leadership devolved upon Duchambon, and under his tutelage the foundations were laid by which the Du Ponts became the most important military family in the colony.

Duchambon spent much of his early career on Île Royale at the outpost of Port-Dauphin (Englishtown, N.S.). Posted as a lieutenant there in

Renon's company, he was promoted captain in 1720 and made commandant in 1723. His wife was employed as Indian interpreter until French authorities recognized in the early 1720s that "the Indians do not like to inform women about their treaties and concerns." The command was small and Duchambon asked to be recalled to Louisbourg in 1731, yet Port-Dauphin remained almost the personal fief of the Du Ponts until the 1740s. His sons François Du Pont Duchambon (known as Duchambon *l'aîné*) and Louis Du Pont Duchambon de Vergor and his nephews François Du Pont Duvivier and Philippe-Michel Du Pont de Renon either served or commanded there at various times in these years. Outposts of Louisbourg such as Port-Dauphin and those on Île Saint-Jean (Prince Edward Island) allowed officers to pursue commercial interests away from the eye of the Louisbourg administration, and it is not surprising that Vergor and Duvivier were among the colony's military officers most active in trade.

After taking leave in France in 1728, Duchambon returned to Île Royale and became major of Louisbourg in 1733, the year after his nephew Duvivier had been promoted adjutant. As the third and fourth ranking officers of the general staff, both men were responsible for routine military discipline, garrison life, and constabulary functions in the town, but not for military provisioning, which was handled by the civil administration. Duchambon and his nephew were also in a position to start their relatives on the ladder of the military hierarchy. Duchambon himself had at least seven sons by his marriage and most were launched on military careers early in their lives at Île Royale. In 1734 four of the first 16 boys chosen as cadets belonged to the Du Pont family.

Although an unexceptional officer, Duchambon gained promotions through seniority and his friendship with Governor Saint-Ovide [Monbeton*]. In 1730 he became a knight of Saint-Louis and in 1737 he was appointed to replace Jacques d'Espiet* de Pensens as king's lieutenant of Île Saint-Jean. During his uneventful command on that island Duchambon was joined by Vergor, several other sons, and later by Joseph Du Pont Duvivier, a nephew. Here and at Louisbourg Duchambon's own commercial activities appear to have been circumscribed. With François Du Pont Duvivier and André Carrerot*, he sold the schooner *Union* in 1732 to the French merchants Girard de La Saudrais of Saint-Malo and Charles Maccarty of La Rochelle. On Île Saint-Jean he maintained a farm where he raised livestock and in 1741 he purchased a bateau for 3,000 *livres*. It was probably this vessel that Duchambon dispatched with François Du Pont Duvivier's expedition against Canso in 1744.

Duchambon's appointment in April 1744 to replace François Le Coutre* de Bourville as king's lieutenant of Île Royale – the highest rank an officer could attain at Louisbourg and one which carried with it a seat on the Conseil Supérieur – came as a symbolic tribute to a family with extended roots in Acadia. In October fate thrust Duchambon to the helm of the colony when Commandant Jean-Baptiste-Louis Le Prévost* Duquesnel died suddenly. Although he wished to be governor, Duchambon was ill suited by age and temperament to assume even interim command at a time when France and Britain were at war. He remained in command, however, because Duquesnel's replacement, Antoine-Alexis Perier de Salvert, was unable to reach Louisbourg.

As soon as he assumed command Duchambon made preparations to defend the fortress from the Anglo-American attack that Joannis-Galand d'Olabaratz had led him to expect would come the following spring. Believing New England to be stronger than in the last war, Duchambon was even more pessimistic than his predecessors in warning French authorities that Louisbourg could not be held with so few men, guns, and munitions. With François Bigot, the financial commissary, he also dispatched a plan to capture Annapolis Royal and Placentia (Nfld) in 1745 with the aid of a French squadron and reinforcements from France.

In December 1744, however, nearly the entire Louisbourg garrison, sparked by the soldiers of the Régiment de Karrer, mutinied and held its officers for ransom. The colonial regulars harboured genuine grievances: exploitation by officers, rotten vegetables and poor rations, and Duquesnel's failure to distribute the booty from the capture of Canso earlier in the year. Clearly shaken and fearing further upheaval, Duchambon could do little but accede to the soldiers' demands and release the supplies they had requested. Once the soldiers had been pacified, Louisbourg returned to its winter hibernation.

Despite his alarmist warnings intended to shock the French authorities, Duchambon appears to have been little disturbed by the prospect of an attack. Accepting the traditional wisdom that the defences of the fortress were adequate in the face of a naval assault, he ignored the possibility of an enemy landing west of Louisbourg and laying siege to the fortress from its vulnerable landward side. This sequence of events is what in fact was to occur. During April 1745 British warships under Commodore Peter Warren* arrived to blockade Louisbourg, while transport vessels assembled in Gabarus Bay. On the morning of 11 May American provincial troops commanded by William Pepperrell* began landing unopposed at Pointe Platte (Simon Point), one mile west of Louisbourg.

Inside the fortress, a shaken Duchambon undertook his first military command seconded by a thoroughly demoralized officer corps. Indecisive in the extreme, he watched from the ramparts as the American landing proceeded and finally dispatched a small detachment led by the famed privateer Pierre Morpain* to oppose the New Englanders. Duchambon's tactical indecisiveness was crucial: having forfeited the initiative by not providing enough troops to oppose successfully the New Englanders' landing at an early stage, he was now forced to contend with the constricting circumstances of a long, formal siege. Louisbourg's weakness, particularly on its landward side, became painfully apparent. The ground, though swampy, proved to be no serious obstacle to the progress of the enemy, who moved onto the high ground dominating the fortress on three sides. As the New Englanders began their siege works, Duchambon ordered the abandonment of the highly rated but vulnerable Royal battery [*see* François-Nicolas de Chassin* de Thierry], the destruction of buildings outside the fortress walls, and the scuttling of vessels to block the harbour entrance. On 14 May the besiegers opened fire against the French fortress, and, after rendering the abandoned French artillery serviceable, they turned even the guns of the Royal battery against the town.

Despite Duchambon's weakness and the early advantages of the attackers, the siege lasted nearly seven weeks. The American irregulars' lack of discipline and their distaste for the harsher realities of warfare prevented commitment to a frontal assault on the fortress. In the end it was the damage wrought by the enemy artillery which forced the French to surrender. Though the French guns had replied vigorously until their ammunition ran out, the town had suffered much damage. Ultimately, the combination of military necessity – formalized by the reports of both Philippe-Joseph d'ALLARD de Sainte-Marie, the commander of the artillery, and Étienne Verrier*, the chief engineer – and the substantial pressure of the Louisbourg merchants moved Duchambon to capitulate on 28 June. He was thus exempted from surrendering the fortress on military grounds alone, and from sole responsibility for the French defeat. Although Duchambon contributed to the French defeat through his irresolution, the outcome of the siege was critically influenced by forces outside his control. Faults in fortification design, poor garrison morale, limited artillery and munitions, the ministry of Marine's failure to realize the full danger of an Anglo-American attack until April 1745, the limited resources of the French navy, misfortunes that prevented more adequate naval support for the French defence, and the failure of Paul Marin* de La Malgue with his Canadians and Indians to relieve Louisbourg in time: all these factors contributed to the Anglo-American victory.

Duchambon secured favourable terms for the capitulation of Louisbourg, including the honours of war, and stoutly protested subsequent breaches of the terms by the victors. He wanted to be the last to leave but was forced to depart on 15 July 1745. He arrived in France four weeks later. The trial of the mutineers began shortly after at Rochefort with revelations of officers' misconduct and a claim by the soldiers that Duchambon had promised them a general amnesty on 1 Jan. 1745. Ordered by the minister to remain with Bigot at Rochefort and to write a detailed account of the siege, apparently never done, he was granted leave late in September to go to Versailles. As events surrounding the mutiny were exposed, Bigot shielded Duchambon by accusing others, and in March 1746 Duchambon retired with a pension of 1,000 *livres* and a gratuity of 1,200.

Duchambon spent his later years at Chalais in his native Saintonge, where he lived off his pension and a small income from property. His family, however, continued to advance in the colonies. By 1758 one-tenth of the Louisbourg regular officer corps present during the siege, including five company captains, were Du Ponts. Duchambon's sixth son, Mathieu Du Pont Duchambon Dumaine, became adjutant in 1758. Although launched early on military careers, his sons gained social and economic prominence through commercial activity and advantageous marriages. Vergor found instant wealth through his association with François Bigot; Duchambon *l'aîné* owned a bateau and schooner enlisted for royal service in 1745 and also contracted in 1750 to supply wood for the Louisbourg guardhouses; about 1750 Dumaine outfitted two fishing shallops in concert with another military officer and Jean-Pierre-Michel Roma. Duchambon's daughters married military officers, but his sons married into the bourgeoisie: Anne Du Pont Duchambon de Mézillac, for instance, was married to Louis de Coux, a lieutenant and later captain; Vergor to Marie-Joseph, daughter of Joseph Riverin*; Jean-Baptiste-Ange Du Pont

Duchambon to Marie-Anne, daughter of Jean-Pierre Roma*; Dumaine to Barbe-Blanche, daughter of André Carrerot; and Charles-François-Ferdinand Du Pont Duchambon to Marguerite-Josephte, daughter of Michel Rodrigue. Although an uninspired officer, Duchambon was the patriarch of an enterprising family which had carved a distinguished position in colonial society.

T. A. CROWLEY and BERNARD POTHIER

AD, Charente (Angoulême), État civil, Curat, 23 août 1775. AN, Col., B, 23, f.106v; 36, f.433; 54, f.503v; 65, f.482½; 81, f.338; 82, ff.11, 145; 189, f.142; C[11A], 88, ff.150–52; C[11B], 5, f.398; 11, f.220; 26, f.77; 27, ff.34, 55–58v, 177v; D[2C], 47, 48; E, 143 (dossier Du Pont Duchambon); Section Outre-mer, Dépôt des fortifications des colonies, Am. sept., nos.137, 216–18; G[2], 188, f.367; 194, f.79; G[3], 2038/2, 9 déc. 1733; 2046/1, 22 août 1737; 2046/2, 5 oct. 1741; 2047/1, 15 juin 1751. ANQ-Q, AP-P-659. PANS, RG 1, 26 (mfm. at PAC). *Louisbourg in 1745: the anonymous "Lettre d'un habitant de Louisbourg" (Cape Breton), containing a narrative by an eye-witness of the siege in 1745*, ed. and trans. G. M. Wrong (Toronto, 1897; repr. 1901). Frégault, *François Bigot*. McLennan, *Louisbourg*. Rawlyk, *Yankees at Louisbourg*. Ægidius Fauteux, "Les Du Pont de l'Acadie," *BRH*, XLVI (1940), 225–37, 257–71.

DU PONT DUCHAMBON DE VERGOR, LOUIS, officer in the colonial regular troops; b. 20 Sept. 1713 at Sérignac (dept of Charente), France, second son of Louis DU PONT Duchambon and Jeanne Mius d'Entremont de Pobomcoup; m. 8 July 1752 at Quebec Marie-Joseph, daughter of Joseph Riverin*; d. after 1775 in France.

Louis Du Pont Duchambon de Vergor began his military career in 1730 as a gentleman cadet; he saw routine service at Île Royale (Cape Breton Island) and in 1737 was detached to his father's command on Île Saint-Jean (Prince Edward Island). In the early 1740s he commanded at Port-Dauphin (Englishtown, N.S.), and in 1744 he participated in the Canso and Annapolis Royal raids led by his cousin, François DU PONT Duvivier. In 1745 Vergor was injured by flying masonry during the Anglo-American bombardment of Louisbourg. After its capitulation, he returned to France. Thanks to his family connections, Vergor had been initiated into trade at Île Royale: in 1744 he had received a share of the cod that the Canso raid had yielded as booty, had invested in privateering, and had earned 1,550 *livres* from renting to the crown buildings at Port-Dauphin and Port-La-Joie (Fort Amherst, P.E.I.) and from transporting troops and materials in his vessels.

In 1747 Vergor was posted to Canada; he was promoted lieutenant in 1749 and captain in 1750. In mid September 1750 he was dispatched aboard the brigantine *Saint-François* to convoy the schooner *Aimable Jeanne*, which was carrying munitions and supplies from Quebec to the small French post on the Saint John River (N.B.). Early on 16 October, about ten leagues west of Cape Sable (N.S.), the French vessels were overtaken by a British sloop commanded by Captain John Rous*. Despite inferior armament, Vergor engaged the sloop, allowing the *Aimable Jeanne* to reach the Saint John. The action lasted the better part of the day, after which, with only seven men fit out of 50 and the *Saint-François* unmasted and sinking, Vergor was obliged to yield. The incident soon assumed full-fledged diplomatic proportions, because the French protested both the attack, which had occurred in peacetime, and Vergor's treatment by Governor Edward CORNWALLIS in Halifax. According to Vergor, Cornwallis "lost his temper to the extent of saying that Captain Roux ought to have sunk him and had he been in the place of this captain he would have done it." His rage notwithstanding, Cornwallis thought it prudent to release Vergor, who, soon back in France, enjoyed the distinction, for one of his rank, of personally reporting the incident to the minister of Marine, Rouillé.

Though in 1750 he had been posted to Louisbourg, Vergor, earnestly supported by Intendant BIGOT, sought a company in Quebec, which was granted in 1751. The following year he became a knight of the order of Saint-Louis. In August 1754 he was appointed to command at Fort Beauséjour (near Sackville, N.B.), which with Fort Gaspereau (near Port Elgin, N.B.) had been built on the Chignecto Isthmus in the early 1750s to establish a *nouvelle Acadie* in the face of the British presence in Nova Scotia. According to the traitor Thomas PICHON, Vergor owed the Beauséjour posting to Bigot.

The key to understanding Vergor's career seems to be his intimacy with Bigot; based on an affinity of character, it dated from the 1740s when they served together at Louisbourg. The strongly biased and gossipy Louis-Léonard AUMASSON de Courville, who became Vergor's secretary at Beauséjour, wrote that the basis for this intimacy "honoured neither the one nor the other": "the intendant being a womanizer, he owed gratitude to this officer." Pichon was more explicit; Vergor, he claimed, "served more than once as [Bigot's] pimp." Although his courage cannot be doubted, events at Beauséjour in 1755 and Quebec in 1759 show that Vergor was unfit for military command. Moreover, according to Courville and Pichon, Vergor's mental and physical characteristics were no more commendable than his morals. Courville observed: "this officer lacked sense and education; even his face was displeasing; . . . [he was] in all respects incapable." Pichon claimed that "the stupid commandant" stuttered, could not so much as read, and scarcely knew how to sign his name. We have only one letter in Vergor's hand, written "a bocegour" in May 1755. It reveals he could only reproduce his native tongue phonetically: ". . . je neux vous sanpeche pas . . . da gette toute la cargeson au si bien que le vingt et audevis . . ." (je ne vous empêche pas . . . d'acheter toute la cargaison aussi bien que le vin et eau-de-vie . . .). Mme Bégon [Rocbert*], who had no reason to prejudge him, had written after a brief meeting in Montreal in 1749: "He is the most dull-witted fellow I have ever met but he knows all the angles." An official marginal note of 1761 is a summary of many of these reactions: he was "mediocre in every respect."

The weight of testimony points to greed as the vice which dominated Vergor and which, coupled with a general moral laxity, probably made him especially attractive to the Bigot set. Courville claimed that Vergor was "avaricious in the extreme," and it is in his memoirs that we find the famous quotation attributed to Bigot: "Profit, my dear Vergor, by your opportunity [at Beauséjour]; trim, – cut – you have the power – in order that you may soon join me in France and purchase an estate near me." Pichon claimed that Vergor's only interest at Beauséjour was "skimming the cream off this colony" by monopolizing control of firewood and beverage supplies, which he estimated brought Vergor 60,000 *livres* a year.

Forts Beauséjour and Gaspereau, which the authorities in Massachusetts and Nova Scotia viewed as a threat, became the objects of an expedition in the spring of 1755. The British, under Lieutenant-Colonel Robert MONCKTON, landed unopposed in June under the cover of Fort Lawrence (near Amherst, N.S.) across the Missaguash River from Beauséjour. Vergor's situation, though by no means hopeless, was disadvantageous. He had at his disposal a regular fortification, sufficient artillery, and 160 colonial regular troops, but upon his arrival he claimed Beauséjour was "in a very sad state . . . and capable because of its poor fortifications of disgracing even the bravest officer." Louis-Thomas JACAU de Fiedmont, who commanded the artillery, agreed. As for the 1,200 to 1,500 recalcitrant Acadians in the area, severe deprivations precluded their usefulness as an effective militia force. Many invoked the oath of neutrality, which made them vulnerable to reprisals if found in arms by the British, hundreds deserted, and Vergor, in order to placate the fears of the remainder, agreed to state in writing that he had forced them to bear arms under pain of death. It was an inauspicious beginning to a frontier incident which within days would precipitate the definitive solution to the onerous problem of the neutrality of the French population of Nova Scotia.

On 13 June, after seizing a ridge within range of the fort, Monckton began mortar fire with telling effect upon the French position. Though the French artillery responded in kind, inside the crowded fort demoralization rapidly gave way to quaking terror, and on 16 June, with the Acadians in service now mutinous, the helpless Vergor capitulated. The next day Benjamin Rouer* de Villeray surrendered Fort Gaspereau without being attacked. The fall of these forts marked the collapse of the *nouvelle Acadie* and settled the Acadian boundary dispute finally in favour of the British. In the following weeks the Acadians of this region who did not make good their escape into the wilderness north of Chignecto were rounded up and deported to the American seaboard colonies.

The minister of Marine, Machault, had good reason to believe, from private advice and published British accounts, that the Chignecto forts had been "very ill defended," official reports from Vaudreuil [RIGAUD] and Drucour [Boschenry*] notwithstanding. Machault ordered an inquiry to be conducted "without regard for anyone." Vergor and Villeray were summoned before a court martial at Quebec in September 1757. Under the protection of Bigot and the military, both were acquitted, despite Vergor, who, according to Courville, "not having a shred of sense often made remarks that could work against him." Certain secondary accounts and popular lore of the surrender of Beauséjour have featured with disapproval the "banquet" which Vergor had prepared for Monckton's officers, but the gesture was consistent with the military courtesies of the day and was not invoked at Vergor's trial as contrary to proper military conduct.

Vergor continued his service, at Lake Champlain, in 1757 and 1758. In 1759 he was back at Quebec, besieged from June by James Wolfe* and Charles SAUNDERS. Early in September he was detached to command a sentry post on the high cliff above the Anse au Foulon, at the head of a narrow trail which linked the river bank to the Plains of Abraham. It was, as Vergor's fortune would have it, at this very point that the indecisive Wolfe finally had chosen to attempt a landing on the night of 12–13 September. A first party of redcoats landed undetected after responding to the challenges of the sentries in passable French, followed within minutes by several light infantry companies who rapidly scaled the cliff and fell upon Vergor's detachment with complete surprise. The men, certainly not as alert as warranted by the circumstances, offered only negligible resistance before dispersing. Vergor was shot in the right leg and in the hand and was captured with several of his men. The rest fled to the safety of Quebec and gave the alarm. By this time it was daybreak, and the British, after months of siege, had dramatically established a bridgehead whence, in a matter of hours, the fortunes of New France would be sealed.

It is significant that, once repatriated to France, Vergor suffered no official reprimand for his part in the British landing. Yet another of Courville's disparaging allegations has graced most subsequent French-language accounts of the events: "This captain had with him many inhabitants of Lorette . . .; they asked him for permission to go home to work for the night; he granted it to them; (it is claimed that this was on condition they also work for him on an estate he had in this parish . . .)." There is no evidence that supports this allegation.

Back in France in 1760, Vergor sought to continue in the service, but it appears that his wounds prevented him. In April of that year he was awarded an invalid's pension, and he journeyed regularly to the baths. The shattering of his leg at the Foulon left him crippled and in constant pain. One of his numerous solicitations was dictated "from my bed, suffering."

In 1762 Vergor was living in Paris. He later retired first to La Flèche, where his wife died in April 1770, then to the parish of Saint-Clerc-de-Cosnac (dept of Charente) in Saintonge, his family's province of origin. His circumstances are unclear: an entry on a 1761 official list describes him as "rich"; yet his annual journeys to the baths were subsidized, and he solicited the patronage of the bishop of Orleans. In 1763 the minister of Marine assured this prelate that "I will remember with pleasure the interest you are taking in this officer when arrangements are made for all the officers who served in Canada." In 1768 he was awarded 2,510 *livres*' indemnity for his Canadian losses. He died in poverty after 1775 "without lands or revenue." Of his eight children, a son, Joseph Du Pont Duchambon de Vergor, returned to Lower Canada during the French terror of 1794.

BERNARD POTHIER

AD, Charente-Maritime (La Rochelle), B, 275, ff.69–92v. AN, Col., B, 94, ff.45–45v; 117, f.462; 122, f.159v; 131, f.203½; C[11B], 23, f.64; 26, f.176v; 27, f.264; 34, ff.46–47v; C[11C], 12, ff.99, 115, 146; D[2C], 43, p.22; 47/4, p.345; 48/1, p.29; 48/3, p.647 (PAC transcripts); E, 143 (dossier Du Pont Duchambon de Vergor); F[3], 50, f.465. Archives du ministère des Affaires étrangères (Paris), Mémoires et doc., Amérique, 9, ff.309–9v, 314–15v, 334–39, 346–47v (mfm. at PAC). PAC, MG 18, F37. PANS, RG 1, 341–41½ (Thomas Pichon papers). Bégon, "Correspondance" (Bonnault), ANQ *Rapport*, 1934–35. "Extrait d'un journal tenue à l'armée que commandait feu M. le marquis de Montcalm, lieutenant général," Literary and Hist. Soc. of Quebec, *Hist. Docs.*, 7th ser. (1905), 29–78. [L.-T. Jacau de Fiedmont], *The siege of Beauséjour in 1755; a journal of the attack on Beauséjour . . .*, ed. J. C. Webster, trans. Alice Webster (Saint John, N.B., 1936). Knox, *Hist. journal* (Doughty), II. *Mémoires sur le Canada, depuis 1749 jusqu'à 1760*. PAC, *The Northcliffe collection . . .* (Ottawa, 1926), 35. PAC *Report*, 1904, app.G, 303, 313–21. Æ. Fauteux, *Les chevaliers de Saint-Louis*, 152–53. Le Jeune, *Dictionnaire*.

H.-R. Casgrain, *Guerre du Canada, 1756–1760; Montcalm et Lévis* (2v., Québec, 1891; réimpr. Tours, France, 1899). A. [G.] Doughty and G. W. Parmelee, *The siege of Quebec and the battle of the Plains of Abraham* (6v., Quebec, 1901). Frégault, *François Bigot*; *La guerre de la Conquête*. Francis Parkman, *Montcalm and Wolfe* (2v., Boston, 1884; repr. New York, 1962). Édouard Richard, *Acadie: reconstitution d'un chapitre perdu de l'histoire d'Amérique*, Henri D'Arles [M.-J.-H.-A. Beaudé], édit. (3v., Québec et Boston, Mass., 1916–21). P.-G. Roy, *Bigot et sa bande*, 239. Stacey, *Quebec, 1759*. J. C. Webster, *The forts of Chignecto: a study of the eighteenth century conflict between France and Great Britain in Acadia* ([Shediac, N.B.], 1930); *Thomas Pichon, "the spy of Beausejour," an account of his career in Europe and America . . .* ([Sackville, N.B.], 1937). Ægidius Fauteux, "Les Du Pont de l'Acadie," *BRH*, XLVI (1940), 260–62.

DU PONT DUVIVIER, FRANÇOIS (usually referred to in documents as Sieur Duvivier), officer in the colonial regular troops and merchant; b. 25 April 1705 at Port-Royal (Annapolis Royal, N.S.), son of François Du Pont* Duvivier and Marie Mius d'Entremont de Pobomcoup; d. 28 May 1776.

Following a brief interlude in France after the surrender of Port-Royal to Francis Nicholson* in 1710, the elder François Du Pont Duvivier was sent to the new colony of Île Royale (Cape Breton Island) with the first colonizing expedition in 1713. His premature death the following year and the presence in the colonial officer corps of two of his brothers, Louis DU PONT Duchambon and Michel Du Pont* de Renon, hastened the military advancement of his surviving sons. François Du Pont Duvivier, the eldest, became a cadet in 1716, a midshipman at Rochefort, France, in 1718, and returned to Louisbourg as an ensign in 1719. The two others, Joseph DU PONT

Duvivier and Michel Du Pont de Gourville, soon joined their brother in the colonial regulars. Despite the death of their father, the family seems to have fared reasonably well; the 1720 census of Louisbourg shows that they employed two servants.

Little is known of Duvivier's early military career, but he enjoyed the favour of Governor Saint-Ovide [Monbeton*]. In 1730 he was promoted lieutenant and in 1732, the year before his uncle Duchambon became major at Louisbourg, Duvivier was appointed adjutant there. Following Louisbourg practice he was accorded the rank of captain to lend authority to his position on the general staff, but he did not receive his captain's commission through seniority until 1737.

A member of Île Royale's most prestigious military family in the early 1730s, Duvivier launched himself in a variety of business pursuits. Although the source of his earliest capital remains obscure, by 1745 he was probably the colony's wealthiest officer, having a fortune crudely estimated by one contemporary at 200,000 *livres*. In 1732 Duvivier and his uncle Duchambon, together with André Carrerot*, the king's storekeeper at Louisbourg, sold a schooner to French merchants. In the same year he began wholesaling when he supplied 40 large barrels (*barriques*) of imported rum to the fishing company at Port d'Orléans (North Bay Ingonish, Cape Breton Island) in the concession of Louis-Simon Le Poupet* de La Boularderie. He also ventured into the sedentary fishery in 1732 through the lease of fishing space on the Louisbourg harbour belonging to the wealthy merchant-fisherman Nicolas Bottier, *dit* Berrichon. The fishing industry preoccupied him for some time; in 1736 he exported 73 large barrels of fish oil aboard the king's ship *Rubis* to the La Rochelle merchant Joseph-Simon Desherbert de Lapointe.

To diversify his operations and enter the lucrative trade with the West Indies, Duvivier formed a partnership with the experienced West Indian merchant-captain, Louis Jouet. Between 1735 and 1751 Jouet regularly sent his 60-ton *Aigle*, often alternating command with Jacques Le Roy, to trade at Martinique once or twice a year. In a formal contract signed in 1736 Jouet and Duvivier agreed to purchase a property belonging to Duvivier's mother near the Louisbourg quay, where they intended to build a frame house and stone storehouse. The cooperation between the two captains extended further. When Duvivier acquired the 120-ton brigantine *Reyne du Nord*, Jouet commanded it on a voyage to Martinique in 1741, although he reported to port officials there that he himself was the vessel's owner. The following year Duvivier sold the brig to Jean and Louis Medoux, Bordeaux merchants, for 13,000 *livres*.

Duvivier worked closely with his brother Michel and entrusted his business affairs to him during his frequent trips to France. Both were shrewd businessmen who knew how to manipulate credit and use the law to protect their investments. Duvivier had charged five per cent interest on credit to La Boularderie's company at Port d'Orléans, and in 1736 when he was away in France and it appeared the company would go bankrupt, Michel moved to ensure payment of the debt. In response to his initiative, the financial commissary, Sébastien-François-Ange LE NORMANT de Mézy, dispatched the bailiff of the Conseil Supérieur to seize the company's moveables. When Duvivier returned he argued that according to the customary law of Paris he should be paid before the other creditors. Le Normant would not issue an order to that effect but required all creditors to appear before him to seek a solution.

In the 1740s Duvivier and Michel enlarged their enterprises. Michel had benefited from the 10,000-*livre* dowry that Marie-Josephe Gautier, a daughter of Joseph-Nicolas Gautier*, *dit* Bellair, brought to their marriage in 1737. In 1742 Michel purchased the 75-ton *Saint-Charles* from another officer, Michel Leneuf de La Vallière, for 4,600 *livres*. Duvivier bought a larger ship of the same name about that time. Both vessels were sent to Martinique in 1743 loaded with the usual cargoes of wood products and fish. Duvivier also dispatched the 90-ton *Succès* that he had purchased from drydock in 1743 for 10,000 *livres*. The *Succès* reached Martinique early in 1744, followed shortly by another vessel Duvivier had acquired, the 90-ton *Magdeleine*.

Duvivier clearly displayed business acumen, but just as his military career was furthered by his uncle and by Saint-Ovide, so too his commercial empire was nurtured by official favouritism, especially on the part of two Louisbourg financial commissaries, Le Normant and François BIGOT. In 1737 Le Normant, who was said to have lent money to Duvivier, secured approval from France to establish a monopoly of the fresh meat supply for the fortress which Duvivier allegedly controlled through Joseph DUGAS. Duvivier then set about buying land and acquired four properties along the Rivière de Miré (Mira River) in 1739. On two of these lots which he had begun to purchase from Saint-Ovide he attempted to raise livestock but a severe winter in 1740–41 wiped out 50 head. Bigot later continued Le Normant's preferential treatment and, despite a protest from the engineer Étienne Verrier*, permitted Duvivier to charge the crown a rent of 750 *livres* annually for buildings at Port-Dauphin (Englishtown) that Duvivier's soldiers had constructed. Bigot also gave Duvivier government contracts. In 1743, when it was feared that the Canadian harvest would be consumed by grasshoppers and the Intendant Gilles HOCQUART pleaded with Louisbourg administrators to secure supplies for Quebec from New England, Bigot contracted with Duvivier to bring fish and foodstuffs potentially worth 135,000 *livres* from Boston, where Duvivier had contacts, notably Peter Faneuil, a leading merchant.

Tough, ambitious, and privileged, Duvivier could afford to be heedless of others and to engage in unscrupulous business practices in order to gain advantage in the local market-place. In the early 1730s he infringed on the property of his neighbours, Blaise Cassaignolles and Bernard Decheverry. They took the dispute to court, but Duvivier was able to enlist the support of Le Normant, who issued a direct order that led the Conseil Supérieur to defer judgement. Cassaignolles and Decheverry were forced to carry the case to the king's council in France to receive satisfaction.

Other local merchants and fishermen were frustrated by Duvivier's conduct but rendered impotent by his military rank and the protection afforded by Le Normant. In 1738 Cassaignolles and 20 others, including François Milly*, Pierre Martissans, and Michel Daccarrette* (d. 1745), sought recourse through petition to the minister of Marine. Citing specific instances of underhanded manœuvring and unfair advantage, they indicted Duvivier for seeking profit at the expense of the local community in a manner unbecoming to a Christian. Also criticizing Michel and mentioning Jean-Baptiste Lascoret, Duvivier's clerk, they evoked a picture of their own enterprises ruined by illicit competition with the result that "one sees on the beaches only [these] two officers who, with sword at side, buy up the cod and deliver it to the captains with whom they do business and make them take the cod in payment at whatever price they judge appropriate." The minister's reaction to this rare instance of collective protest is unknown, but in 1739 Le Normant was transferred amid a series of revelations and Saint-Ovide resigned the governorship. The new governor, Isaac-Louis de Forant*, received official instructions to reform the military of Île Royale.

Duvivier's commercial activity and Acadian family connections gave him a familiarity with the Atlantic region which heightened his military usefulness to France. In 1740 Île Royale's new commandant, Jean-Baptiste-Louis Le Prévost* Duquesnel, worked with Duvivier to revise plans for the recovery of Acadia should a rupture with Great Britain occur. In May 1744, when Duquesnel received word that France had declared war on Britain, he appointed Duvivier to lead an expedition of some 350 men against the British fishing station at Canso. There was no resistance from the defenders and at dawn on 24 May their commander, Patrick Heron*, surrendered. This attack had been the first formal venture into warfare for Duvivier and the Louisbourg garrison and it brought booty to the French victors.

The war brought other profits. While Duvivier was at Canso, Jean-Baptiste Lannelongue* acted on his behalf. On 7 June 1744 Lannelongue rented one of Duvivier's houses to Bigot for the housing of British prisoners. Two weeks previously Lannelongue had supplied the administration with peas and flour amounting to nearly 56,000 *livres*, most probably for Duvivier's account. Duvivier's schooner *Succès*, his flagship at Canso, was leased to the administration by Lannelongue for 6,300 *livres* and then outfitted at a cost of 33,000 *livres* before it was placed in the command of privateer Pierre Morpain*. In June 1744 Duvivier also invested substantially in two privateers with Michel, Duquesnel, Bigot, and Joannis-Galand d'OLABARATZ. Three years later he was paid over 5,000 *livres* by Bigot in compensation for livestock from his Miré habitation consumed during the war.

Formal business was put aside temporarily when the easy victory at Canso persuaded Duquesnel to attempt the capture of Annapolis Royal. The missionary Jean-Louis LE LOUTRE agreed to lead 300 Nova Scotia Micmacs against the British fort in mid July on the understanding that they would be joined shortly by a detachment of colonial regular troops under Duvivier and a small naval squadron. When the warships failed to arrive the Micmacs withdrew in disgust. Nothing daunted, on 29 July Duquesnel dispatched Duvivier to Nova Scotia with 50 colonial regulars, an undetermined number of Île Royale Micmacs, and the expectation that the warships would soon appear.

Having landed at Baie-Verte (N.B.) on 8 August, Duvivier cast himself as the Acadian liberator back among his own, but despite strong emotional appeals along the route to Annapolis Royal, he succeeded in detaching no more than a dozen Acadians from the strict neutrality which by this time had become the practical expedient of government and governed in Nova Scotia.

Keenly disappointed, he retaliated with threats which served only to alienate the Acadian community. He fared little better with the Indians; after the miserable fiasco of July, only 230 Micmacs and Malecites rallied to his side on 7 September, the day he invested the British fort.

The siege lasted a full four weeks. Despite decided tactical and psychological advantages, the French effort was compromised from the start by Duvivier's singular lack of offensive spirit. Aided not a little by the ailing Duquesnel's ambiguous, even contradictory, communications from Louisbourg (instructing him to attack if a favourable occasion presented itself, but not to take unnecessary risks), Duvivier adamantly refused to seize the opportunity afforded by the decrepit state of the British fort and the low morale of its garrison. Jean-Baptiste de Gay* Desenclaves, a priest to the Acadians, observed Duvivier and pronounced contemptuously that the only glory he gained from this venture "was being more skilful in trade than in the art of war," noting further that "in his camp he spoke only of hogsheads of molasses and brandy."

The garrison at Annapolis Royal, which consisted of no more than 75 able-bodied soldiers, was commanded by Lieutenant Governor Paul Mascarene*. Shrewd, practical, and courageous, Mascarene inspired an effective and confident defence. His efforts were considerably assisted by the arrival on 26 September of two vessels bringing reinforcements and supplies from Boston. Although the morale of his detachment was shaken, Duvivier refused to withdraw. The fate of the French effort, however, was sealed abruptly on 2 October with the arrival from Louisbourg of Michel de Gannes* de Falaise bearing the news that the naval squadron had not sailed and the order to withdraw to winter quarters at Minas. Duvivier feigned disgust at the prospect of retreat, "prodded in the arse," at a time when an assault on the British fort would have been warranted, but Duquesnel's order was in reality fortunate for him because it enabled him to divert attention from his own indecisiveness.

With the Acadians refusing even to supply foodstuffs for the detachment, the French declined to winter at Minas and withdrew precipitately from Nova Scotia on 5 October: "It is flight," Duvivier wrote, "not retreat." When he arrived back in Louisbourg on 23 October, Duvivier found in command not Duquesnel, who had died on 9 October, but his own uncle Duchambon. Thinking that he might be blamed for not having upheld "the honour of the king's arms" before Annapolis, Duvivier immediately requested a council of war to hear his version of events. When de Gannes arrived the next day he found the entire town and garrison against him, for Duvivier had led them to believe that Annapolis could have been taken had the siege been continued.

Duvivier carried the colony's dispatches to Versailles in late November. There is no doubt he welcomed the opportunity to relate the story of the Acadian expedition to the minister of Marine himself. The exercise proved to be a fruitful one, for in consideration "above all of the Canso expedition and that in Acadia" he was received into the order of Saint-Louis on 17 May 1745 at Brest, where he was preparing to join Antoine-Alexis Perier de Salvert's Louisbourg relief squadron. Having learned at sea of the fall of the fortress to William Pepperrell*'s troops, the expedition returned to port. His plans to return to his post thwarted, Duvivier spent the next few years pressing claims for compensation for supplies he claimed were furnished for use at Île Saint-Jean (Prince Edward Island) and others which were consumed at his Miré properties during the siege.

Duvivier retired from the service rather abruptly in 1747 but rejoined as half-pay captain in 1749 when Île Royale was reoccupied by the French. He attempted to give status to his wealth by vigorously soliciting the governorship of the colony. Although his career continued to be promoted by Bigot and Le Normant, who were now intendants at Quebec and Rochefort, Duvivier's notoriety had spread and there was opposition to his bid for power. At Quebec the governor general, La Jonquière [Taffanel*], reacted with righteous scorn to Duvivier's rash pretension to a governorship: "They will never convince me that M. Duvivier should be governor of Île Royale . . . to speak frankly, Duvivier would do much better to enjoy in France his profits from trade than to aspire to positions which he does not merit, especially to the prejudice of a number of deserving officers in your government who have served the king well, [while] M. Duvivier was busy enriching himself." The position, as it turned out, was already promised to Charles Des Herbiers* de La Ralière, but through Le Normant's solicitation Duvivier was appointed king's lieutenant and commandant of Île Saint-Jean in 1750.

Duvivier had been too successful, too accustomed to having his own way, to accept this consolation prize. He remained in Paris, and on several occasions he was received by the minister of Marine, Rouillé, at Versailles. But he was also observed making clandestine visits to the English commissioners who were in France negotiating the settlement of the Acadian boundary. Rouillé's suspicions were aroused, and he ordered an investigation by the Paris lieutenant-general of police late in 1750. Subsequently he issued a stern rebuke to Duvivier and advised his erstwhile patron, Le Normant, that the captain had fallen short of his high opinion of him. Duvivier's commission as commandant was revoked in May of the following year, and, pleading ill health, he retired from the service in 1753 with a pension of 1,200 *livres*.

In 1752 Duvivier was living on his estate at Le Vivier, near Chalais in the commune of Sérignac (dept of Charente), and owned the seigneury of Médillac nearby. After the investigation of his conduct and his subsequent resignation, he disappears mysteriously from public view. Although he had acquired great wealth in North America, at his death his estate was valued at only 25,000 *livres*; it was inherited by his sister-in-law, the widow of Michel.

T. A. Crowley and Bernard Pothier

[What became of François Du Pont Duvivier in the last 20 years of his life is not known. His personal dossier (AN, Col., E, 169) ends with his retirement from the service in 1753, and his absence from official records after that date is seemingly complete. Although his dossier indicates that he received a pension from the Invalides in 1753, no record of it is to be found in AN, Col., D^{2D}, 13 (Pensions et gratifications, 1763–87); D^{2D}, 14 (Pensions et gratifications, états des colonies, 1752–88); D^{2D}, 15 (Pensions et gratifications, états des ports, 1770–85). It is worth noting, however, that his brother Michel and several cousins appear in these records. Duvivier is known to have been residing at his château in 1752 (AN, Section Outre-mer, G^3, 2041/1, 4 nov. 1752), but in 1763, when his niece's child was baptized at Sérignac, he was not among those who signed the baptismal act (AD, Charente (Angoulême), État civil, Sérignac, 10 déc. 1763). Nor does he appear in the lists of persons exempt from the *taille* in the 1760s and 1770s (AD, Charente, 7C, 282), though as a noble he would have been entitled to such exemption. It is unlikely, then, that he was living on his estate after the 1750s. Moreover, there is no record of his death in the parish registers of Sérignac or the nearby communes of Chalais, Yvier, or Monboyer; the only mention of it found is in a list of collateral inheritances paid (AD, Charente, 11C, 1115, "Table alphabétique des successions collatéralles payées"). One possibility that the silence surrounding him suggests is that he ended his days in prison; if he did, however, it was not in the Bastille since he is not in the lists published by Frantz Funck-Brentano: *Les lettres de cachet à Paris, étude suivie d'une liste des prisonniers de la Bastille (1659–1789)* (Paris, 1903). We are indebted to Raymonde Litalien of the PAC for her research in the Archives nationales and to T. J. A. Le Goff for examining local records and in particular for establishing Duvivier's date of death. We are also grateful to Christopher Moore for making available evidence concerning Duvivier's commercial connections with New England.

It should be noted that secondary sources, published archival documents, and printed calendars to archival material frequently fail to distinguish between, and in some instances confuse, the careers of François Du Pont Duvivier and his brother Joseph. T.A.C. and B.P.]

AD, Charente (Angoulême), État civil, Sérignac, 1761, 1763; Charente-Maritime (La Rochelle), B, 275, ff.69, 72, 78v; B, 6113. AN, Col., A, 2, ff.89–94; B, 41, ff.592–96v; 86, f.369; 92, ff.219v, 253, 461; C^{8A}, 17, 20, 21; C^{11A}, 95, f.51; 121, f.192; C^{11B}, 20, f.304; 25, f.83v; 26, f.134; 29, ff.58v–59, 106–9v; C^{11C}, 12, f.138; E, 169 (dossier Duvivier); F^{1A}, 35, f.54; 95, f.51; Section Outre-mer, G^2, 183, f.195; 186, f.14, p.135; 187, ff.126–27, p.43; 188, ff.337–40; G^3, 2041/1, 18 nov. 1739, 27 sept. 1751, 4 nov. 1752; 2041/2, 8 nov. 1739; 2046/1, 26 juill. 1737; 2046/2, 18 juill. 1742. Archives maritimes, Port de Rochefort (France), 1E, 124, f.296. PANS, RG 1, 26 (mfm. at PAC).

Knox, *Hist. journal* (Doughty), III, 346. *NYCD* (O'Callaghan and Fernow), X, 9, 18, 40. Æ. Fauteux, *Les chevaliers de Saint-Louis*, 141–42, 174–75, 195. Crowley, "Government and interests," 126–34, 136–37, 223–24. Frégault, *François Bigot*. McLennan, *Louisbourg*. Rawlyk, *Yankees at Louisbourg*. Ægidius Fauteux, "Les Du Pont de l'Acadie," *BRH*, XLVI (1940), 225–37, 257–71. H. A. Innis, "Cape Breton and thc French régime," RSC *Trans.*, 3rd ser., XXIX (1935), sect.II, 80–81. R. J. Morgan and T. D. MacLean, "Social structure and life in Louisbourg," *Canada, an Hist. Magazine* (Toronto), 1 (June 1974), 60–77.

DU PONT DUVIVIER, JOSEPH. *See* Appendix

DUPRÉ, known as **Saint-Georges Dupré, GEORGES-HIPPOLYTE LE COMTE.** *See* Le Comte

DUQUESNE (Du Quesne, Duqaine, Duquêne) DE MENNEVILLE, ANGE, Marquis DUQUESNE, naval officer and governor general of New France; b. *c.* 1700 at Toulon, France, third son of Abraham Duquesne and Ursule-Thérèse Possel; d. 17 Sept. 1778 at Antony (dept of Hauts-de-Seine), France.

From the beginning of the 17th century the Duquesnes were sailors, privateers, merchants, and soldiers. The family, which belonged to the Norman gentry, was Huguenot, but following the revocation of the edict of Nantes in 1685 Abraham Duquesne accepted conversion to Catholicism and remained in the royal navy. He became a rear-admiral and for several years held the post of commandant of the port of Toulon, the principal French naval base at that period. Following his example, four of his sons became sailors.

Ange Duquesne de Menneville joined the navy at a young age; by 1713 he was serving as a midshipman at Toulon. In 1726 he became a second ensign and three years later had his first contact with Canada while serving on the flute *Éléphant* under Louis-Philippe de Rigaud* de Vaudreuil. The ship, which was carrying the captain's brothers, Pierre de RIGAUD de Vaudreuil de Cavagnial and François-Pierre de RIGAUD de Vaudreuil, ran aground near Île aux Grues in the St Lawrence. The circumstances surrounding the loss of the ship and the pillaging of the wreck by salvagers aided neither the commandant's career nor Duquesne's, which was delayed as a result. Duquesne was not rich enough to buy commissions. In 1735, when he received the certificate attesting to his Catholicity, he was promoted lieutenant-commander and then received command of his first ship, the *Inconnu*. He was made a knight of the order of Saint-Louis in 1738 and until 1744 served on the high seas.

The War of the Austrian Succession gave Duquesne the opportunity to demonstrate his abilities. He was stationed at Toulon, where he associated with figures who would become influential: La Galissonière [Barrin*], La Jonquière [Taffanel*], and Louis-Philippe de Rigaud de Vaudreuil, who belonged, as he did, to the fleet of Claude-Élisée de Court de La Bruyère. Duquesne distinguished himself in actions against the British and the African pirates. His drive was recognized, and in 1746 he received the rank of major and became port commandant of Toulon. Three years later he relinquished this post to go to sea again.

Seeking a successor to La Jonquière, the governor general of New France, in the autumn of 1751 the court selected Duquesne, whose name had been put forward by La Galissonière. By making this choice the court ensured continuity in its colonial policy, which was aimed particularly at protecting the fur trade and at French settlement of the Ohio valley. Duquesne received the title of marquis, a gratuity of 15,000 *livres*, and advances amounting to 27,000 *livres*. After several meetings with La Galissonière, he obtained his written instructions on 15 April 1752. The king asked him to devote special attention to ensuring the territorial integrity of the French empire in America. In particular he was to drive the British merchants out of the Ohio valley and establish peace with the Indian tribes that had been hostile since the uprising in 1747 [*see* Orontony*]. The minister of Marine, Rouillé, gave him a strict injunction to rely on Abbé LE LOUTRE in matters concerning Acadia. He indicated Oswego (Chouaguen) as a place to be taken if the British gave France reason for reprisals. Finally he asked him to help Intendant BIGOT limit the expenses to which Canada was giving rise. These instructions – which were heavily influenced by La Galissonière – did not, however, set down any precise lines of conduct to be followed.

Marquis Duquesne landed at Quebec on 1 July 1752, to everyone's surprise. Charles Le Moyne* de Longueuil had been serving as acting governor since La Jonquière's death on 17 March 1752; it was not known that La Jonquière's successor had already been provided for, and it was thought that the appointment of a new governor would be a long time in coming. Duquesne quickly attracted hostility in the colony. First he undertook to instil discipline in the troops and militia through reviews, inspections, and training for the numerous Canadians who had enrolled. Then, in October 1752 the Canadians learned that despite the officers' protests Duquesne was going to launch a military expedition under Paul Marin* de La Malgue to occupy the Ohio valley.

Marin was to command a detachment of about 2,000 men, almost all of them whites in accordance with the orders of the court, which wanted France rather than its Indian allies to oppose the British merchants. During the winter of 1752–53 Duquesne devoted his attention to raising and equipping his army; with Bigot he regulated the sale of foodstuffs from Louisbourg, Île Royale (Cape Breton Island), and New England. His original plan was simple: Marin was to take the route followed by Pierre-Joseph Céloron* de Blainville in 1749 and to establish a series of forts. The expedition of 1753–54 would, however, encounter enormous difficulties and in the end was a partial failure, thus doing Duquesne serious harm. The minister of Marine blamed him for having lacked prudence and particularly for having chosen Marin, who was not the most senior officer in Canada. For his part Bigot denounced the means that Duquesne had utilized, considering it too costly for settling a small problem. In the summer of 1753 Bishop Pontbriand [Dubreil*] of Quebec had even asked that the expedition be abandoned. Duquesne succeeded, however, in convincing Rouillé that he had been unable to act otherwise under the circumstances, and he not only remained in charge in New France despite his critics, but also organized a new expedition.

Duquesne was aware that he had to take action early in the spring of 1754; George Washington, representing the governor of Virginia, had ordered Marin's successor, Jacques Legardeur* de Saint-Pierre, to leave Fort de la Rivière au Bœuf

(Waterford, Pa). Duquesne put Claude-Pierre Pécaudy de Contrecœur in charge of this new expedition; Pécaudy dislodged the small party of British from the forks of the Ohio and immediately undertook the construction of Fort Duquesne (Pittsburgh, Pa).

After Louis Coulon* de Villiers's victory on 3 July 1754 at Fort Necessity (near Farmington, Pa) and Washington's ensuing capitulation, Duquesne was able to proclaim his success. He was conscious, however, of the grave errors made in the Ohio valley: he expressed serious reservations about the clause in the capitulation that barred the Americans from the valley for only one year. Having transmitted to the minister his version of the affair and Washington's journal and being satisfied with the way things had gone during his term of office, Duquesne asked in October 1754 for his recall.

During the winter of 1754–55 Duquesne learned that the British were preparing to retaliate; while assuring him they would do nothing of the sort, the minister of Marine, Machault, had advised him of Edward Braddock's departure for America as commander of the armed forces. Consequently Duquesne took steps early in the spring to reinforce Fort Duquesne and the outlying posts. He again concentrated his forces to defend New France's southwest frontier, even though he was aware of the British moves in the direction of Acadia and New York. In so doing he was complying with the instructions he had received to do nothing in Acadia and around Lake Champlain. Moreover, he knew that his successor would arrive with reinforcements for Canada and Louisbourg. He therefore entrusted the defence of the centre to the militia, moved his available forces to the west, and left the defence of the east to Louisbourg. These were ideal tactics for a man who underestimated the Americans' military talents and who as well was about to be relieved of his post.

Indeed Pierre de Rigaud de Vaudreuil de Cavagnial landed at Quebec on 24 June 1755 during his absence; Duquesne, however, quickly returned from Montreal. The new governor general did not hesitate to criticize Duquesne's actions: he presented a sombre picture of the colony, exhausted by the harsh Ohio campaign, and blamed him for having put all his efforts into that region, neglecting the other sectors where forts and posts were in poor shape just when the British were organizing a general offensive. All these criticisms were justified, but the responsibility did not lie with Duquesne alone, since in its desire for economy the court had rejected all his plans for repairing the defences. Vaudreuil and Duquesne did not cooperate and for a time were in open conflict. Duquesne sailed for France outraged by Vaudreuil's attitude.

In France he explained his actions to the minister of Marine, who was satisfied, the more so since Braddock's force in America had been cut to pieces. Only Fort Beauséjour (near Sackville, N.B.) had fallen [*see* Robert Monckton], but Duquesne laid that responsibility on Le Loutre. Duquesne was generously rewarded for his services in Canada, being forgiven the 27,000 *livres* advanced to him in 1752; he was consulted on Canadian matters, and seems to have met Montcalm* before the latter left for Canada.

Duquesne resumed his naval career. In April 1756 he was named inspector general of the coasts of France; on 23 June 1757 he assumed acting command of the fleet at Toulon and took part in minor actions until 1758. Defeated in an engagement with a British squadron commanded by Henry Osborn, Duquesne lost his vessel the *Foudroyant* and was captured and taken to England. The minister of Marine, Choiseul, treated him severely, but the king absolved him of blame and granted him a pension of 3,000 *livres*. This defeat did, however, raise questions about his future active career. Little is known of his subsequent endeavours, other than the fact that the king made him a commander of the order of Saint-Louis in 1763.

Duquesne's retirement became final on 8 April 1776. Although as a result of the loss of the *Foudroyant* he was not appointed lieutenant-general of the Marine, in consideration of his 20 campaigns he was awarded continuation of his rear-admiral's pay and the honorary title of lieutenant-general of the naval forces. On 4 Dec. 1776 Duquesne informed the court that in view of his age he no longer intended to visit the ports. He spent his last days in one or other of his residences in Paris and at Antony. As he had no offspring when he died in September 1778, he left his fortune, estimated at 200,000 *livres*, to his nephews and nieces, and his servants.

Duquesne had had an active career, serving and fighting energetically. During his stay in New France this overbearing, proud, but obedient man was unpopular. It was said that Bigot himself feared him. Putting his "special" mission ahead of all else, he carried out his task resolutely, intransigently, and unhesitatingly. Warned in advance that many would disapprove of the military occupation of the Ohio valley because the economy of the colony could not stand such a drain on its manpower and resources, he was mistrustful of the colonials, and they did not appreciate him. Only the recommendations from Rouillé and Machault for clemency and prudence softened his behaviour towards dirty soldiers, undisciplined militiamen, insolent officers, and merchants without strong ties to the mother country.

PIERRE-L. CÔTÉ

AN, Col., B, 95–97, 99; C[11A], 99, 100. Bégon, "Correspondance" (Bonnault), ANQ *Rapport*, 1934–35, 271. *Coll. des manuscrits de Lévis* (Casgrain), VII. Doreil, "Lettres" (A. Roy), ANQ *Rapport*, 1944–45. *Papiers Contrecœur* (Grenier), 15, 96–98, 117–19, 223–24. W. L. Clowes, *The Royal Navy; a history from the earliest times to the present* (7v., London, 1897–1903), III, 189–90. C. W. Dahlinger, *The Marquis Duquesne, Sieur de Menneville, founder of the city of Pittsburgh* (Pittsburgh, Pa., 1932). Frégault, *François Bigot*, II. Régis Roy, "Le gouverneur Du Quesne," *BRH*, XII (1906), 53.

DUSOURDY, LOUIS-NICOLAS LANDRIAUX, *dit*. *See* LANDRIAUX

DU TREMBLAY, FRANÇOIS GAULTIER. *See* GAULTIER

DUVIVIER, FRANÇOIS DU PONT. *See* DU PONT

DUVIVIER, JOSEPH DU PONT. *See* DU PONT [Appendix]

DYADEROWANE. *See* OTTROWANA

E

EAGLESON, JOHN, clergyman; b. in Ulster; m. 16 Aug. 1781 Sophia Augusta Pernette, and they had at least two daughters; fl. 1765–90.

John Eagleson came to Cumberland Township, Nova Scotia, about 1765 to serve as a Presbyterian missionary. His abilities soon brought him to the attention of influential men in the province, and in 1767 Lieutenant Governor Michael FRANCKLIN, Chief Justice Jonathan BELCHER, Provincial Secretary Richard BULKELEY, and Reverend John BREYNTON, the rector of St Paul's in Halifax, recommended him to the authorities in London for reordination within the Church of England. Eagleson's motives in seeking the change may only be surmised. His later life shows him capable of acting from conviction, but there were definite financial, political, and social advantages in belonging to the established church, and it probably appealed in any case to a man of Eagleson's personality and convivial tastes. Whatever his reasons he was ordained in England by the bishop of London in 1768 and returned to Nova Scotia under the auspices of the Society for the Propagation of the Gospel late in June of that year.

Instead of proceeding directly to Cumberland as he had expected, Eagleson was sent first to St John's (Prince Edward) Island and then to Cornwallis Township, Nova Scotia. He was back in Cumberland in 1770, the first permanent Church of England clergyman in the area and the first chaplain at Fort Cumberland (near Sackville, N.B.) since the conquest. He seems to have taken over the glebe lands previously held by a dissenting clergyman, Caleb Gannett, although not without a lawsuit; as garrison chaplain he probably had access to quarters within the fort as well. For two decades he served the area near the fort, procuring the services of a schoolmaster there and establishing congregations in several outlying districts. He also made a few excursions up the Petitcodiac River and travelled occasionally to the Annapolis valley and Halifax. In 1773 he led a mission to St John's Island, the first Protestant clergyman to visit the colony since it had become a separate jurisdiction in 1769. He discouraged the work of dissenting missionaries in Cumberland and on one occasion instigated a military raid on a meeting led by William Black*. He seems to have been popular with both his parishioners and the garrison, but apparently he began to drink to excess.

In 1776, during the local rebellion led by Jonathan Eddy*, Eagleson was captured and carried prisoner to Boston. After 16 months he escaped and returned to Cumberland, where he found his property almost destroyed. Throughout the period of the American revolution he considered himself a target for rebels in the Cumberland area and, fearing recapture, he fled to Halifax in 1781. He married that year in the Windsor area, and in 1782, after his return to Cumberland, he purchased a farm near the fort and seems to have settled down to a more routine way of life. By 1788, however, complaints about his drinking and its effect on his ministerial activities had reached Bishop Charles Inglis*. After an inquiry lasting several months, Inglis dismissed Eagleson from his priestly functions in June 1790 on the grounds of drunkenness and incompetence.

Eagleson, mentally disturbed for at least part of the time, seems to have spent his last years estranged from his family. He made his home with a Siddall family near present-day Oxford, N.S. In July 1811 his widow married Hallet Collins of Liverpool.

GERTRUDE TRATT

Cumberland County Registry of Deeds (Amherst, N.S.), Book D, p.49 (mfm. at PANS). PANS, MG 4, no.100, folder 12 (Canon E. A. Harris' notes on Pernette family). Private archives, Seth Bartling (Liverpool, N.S.), R. J. Long, "The annals of Liverpool and Queen's County, 1760–1867" (1926) (typescript at Dalhousie University Library, Halifax; mfm. at PANS). St Paul's Anglican Church (Halifax), Registers for Windsor-Falmouth-Newport, 1774–95, 16 Aug. 1781 (mfm. at PANS). University of King's College Library (Halifax), P. S. Hamilton, "History of the county of Cumberland" (typescript, 1880) (copy at PANS). USPG, B, 25, nos.118, 119, 121, 123, 126, 127, 135, 146, 147, 152, 158, 182, 186, 231; C/CAN/NS, 2, nos.110, 111 (mfm. at PANS).

PAC *Report*, 1913, app.I. M. W. Armstrong, *The Great Awakening in Nova Scotia, 1776–1809* (Hartford, Conn., 1948). A. W. [H.] Eaton, *The Church of England in Nova Scotia and the Tory clergy of the revolution* (New York, 1891). I. F. Mackinnon, *Settlements and churches in Nova Scotia, 1749–1776* ([Montreal, 1930]). C. F. Pascoe, *Two hundred years of the S.P.G. . . .* (2v., London, 1901). C. W. Vernon, *Bicentenary sketches and early days of the church in Nova Scotia* (Halifax, 1910). W. B. Kerr, "The American invasion of Nova Scotia, 1776–7," *Canadian Defence Quarterly* (Ottawa), XIII (1935–36), 433–55. *Saint John Globe* (Saint John, N.B.), 17 Nov. 1923. E. M. Saunders, "The life and times of the Rev. John Wiswall, M.A., a loyalist clergyman in New England and Nova Scotia, 1731–1821," N.S. Hist. Soc., *Coll.*, XIII (1908), 1–73.

EDWARDS, RICHARD, naval officer and governor of Newfoundland; b. *c.* 1715; d. 3 Feb. 1795 at Fordwich, Kent, England.

Richard Edwards has often been confused with his namesake, who was also a naval officer and governor of Newfoundland. Promoted lieutenant in the Royal Navy by 1740, by 1753 Edwards had risen to the rank of captain, in command of the *Assistance*. Four years later, during the Seven Years' War, he was appointed governor of Newfoundland, succeeding Richard Dorrill*. During Edwards' term of office the ships under his command were active in capturing French vessels, and these prizes provided an important source of revenue to both naval personnel and local officials. Militia units were also formed – or more probably resurrected – for defence against a possible French attack. The protection of the island also required Edwards to keep a careful watch on the increasing number of poor Irish, whose loyalty was thought to be doubtful. Although Edwards shared Dorrill's adverse opinion of these unfortunate people, he did not carry out Dorrill's order to have all transients returned to England at the end of each fishing season.

Edwards was succeeded as governor in 1760 by James Webb*. In 1778, commanding the *Sandwich*, he was present at the battle of Ushant as part of Admiral Augustus Keppel's fleet. The following year he was made rear-admiral of the blue and was again appointed governor of Newfoundland, replacing Vice-Admiral John Montagu. Edwards' major problem during his second term was once more the defence of the island. American privateers were numerous off the coasts [*see* Jeremiah COGHLAN], although many were captured by Edwards' squadron. To provide for the island's protection, by May 1780 Edwards had recruited through the efforts of the chief engineer, Robert PRINGLE, about 400 men to form the Newfoundland Volunteers. This corps disbanded because the home government declined to support all the terms of its engagement, and in September Edwards authorized the raising of the Newfoundland Regiment, a provincial infantry unit. He also had batteries built or repaired in several places adjacent to St John's that were vulnerable to attack from the sea. Because of the disruption of trade with New England and the West Indies, his activities concerning defence were complemented by earnest attempts to provision the island to meet the needs of the permanent population and the large yearly influx of transients.

In civil matters Edwards experienced difficulty with the problem of legal jurisdiction. Although empowered to hear only appeals in civil cases, by 1780 Edwards and his deputies were in practice presiding over both civil and criminal cases. The exigencies of Newfoundland's unusual status, without clear assignment of legal jurisdiction, were largely responsible for this situation, which continued as long as all concerned accepted the judgements. The inevitable happened in 1780 when a group of Exeter merchants refused to agree to a decision and sued the governor. The case was eventually settled by arbitration, but it exposed the inadequacies of the island's civil administration. The system nevertheless persisted long after Edwards had left Newfoundland.

In April 1782, as a consequence of Lord North's resignation, Edwards relinquished his governorship and was succeeded by John Campbell. He was promoted vice-admiral of the white in February 1787 and the following year was appointed commander-in-chief at the Medway and at the Nore. The remaining item of note in his career was his promotion to admiral of the blue in 1794.

FREDERIC F. THOMPSON

Metropolitan Toronto Library, Richard Edwards letterbooks, 1779–81. Charnock, *Biographia navalis*, VI, 105. A. H. McLintock, *The establishment of constitutional government in Newfoundland, 1783–1832: a study of retarded colonisation* (London and New York, [1941]), 59–62. G. W. L. Nicholson, *The fighting Newfoundlander; a history of the Royal Newfoundland Regiment* (St John's, [1964?]). Paul O'Neill, *The story of St. John's, Newfoundland* (2v., Erin, Ont., 1975–76), I: *The oldest city*, 95–96, 137–38. Charles Pedley, *The history of Newfoundland from the earliest times to the year 1860* (London, 1863), 130, 136. Prowse, *History of Nfld*. (1895), 349–51.

EGUSHWA (Agashawa, Augooshaway, Negushwa), Ottawa war chief; b. *c*. 1730, probably in the Detroit River region; d. *c*. 1800 in southeastern Michigan.

Egushwa, who reputedly had fought as a young man for the French against the British, came into prominence among the Indians in the Detroit River region in the 1770s as a successor to Pontiac*, to whom he was apparently related. Although at first he achieved note as a war chief and was listed as such at a Detroit council in June 1778, he was to become a major spokesman on all issues for the Ottawas, Ojibwas, Potawatomis, and at times the Wyandots, of the vicinity. In 1778 he was the main Indian leader on Henry HAMILTON's expedition against Vincennes (Ind.), whose inhabitants had declared for the rebels. He advised Hamilton, acted as liaison between him and the other chiefs, and led scouting parties into the surrounding country. Later in the revolution, in 1780, he probably accompanied Captain Henry Bird on an expedition into Kentucky.

By the late 1780s Egushwa's power and influence extended through the Detroit River region, southern Michigan, and the area south of Lake Erie. He was in contact with the Indians in Ohio who had been converted by the Moravian Brethren. During the revolution these Indians had first been forcibly removed from their villages by the British and had subsequently been fallen upon by the Americans [*see* GLIKHIKAN]. He assured them that they were safe in their new town of New Salem (about 12 miles south of Sandusky, Ohio). Missionary David Zeisberger* emphasized that Egushwa held authority in the region and that most important questions were referred to him. At Detroit in 1790 the chief was one of the signatories to a treaty by which the Ottawas, Ojibwas, Potawatomis, and Wyandots ceded land in present southwestern Ontario to the British.

Although Britain had agreed at the end of the American revolution to withdraw from the country south of the Great Lakes, she had not done so, hoping that with her encouragement the Indians of the Ohio country would be able to resist the advance of American settlement. The Americans, however, were determined to assert their authority over the region. Egushwa helped organize the Indian resistance to American advances across the Ohio River. He was particularly active at the time of Major-General Anthony Wayne's expedition in 1793 and 1794, sending messages among the Ojibwas, Potawatomis, and Ottawas encouraging them to assemble on the Miamis (Maumee) River and resist the American forces. Speaking and acting on behalf of these tribes, he was one of the most important chiefs among the Indians who gathered to meet Wayne's advance. He fought against the Americans at the battle of Fallen Timbers (near Waterville, Ohio) in August 1794, when the Indians, unassisted by the nearby British, were defeated. Lieutenant Governor Simcoe* of Upper Canada referred to him as "that Great Chief and firm Friend of the British."

Egushwa recovered from a serious wound in the head which he received during the battle, and in the mid 1790s he was living in the Raisin River (Mich.) area. In the late spring of 1795 he journeyed to Greenville (Ohio) to negotiate with Wayne. He spoke at the council and signed the treaty of Greenville, which surrendered most of present Ohio to the Americans. On his return to Raisin River he sent the copy of the treaty and the large peace medal given to him by Wayne to the British Indian agent Alexander MCKEE.

Egushwa died in southeastern Michigan about 1800. According to the trader Pierre Navarre, his brother Nodowance was also a war chief and another brother, Flat Button, was a warrior.

REGINALD HORSMAN

Correspondence of Lieut. Governor Simcoe (Cruikshank), II, 8, 126–29, 189, 195, 224, 233, 345, 396; III, 19, 274, 292, 325; IV, 26, 71, 92–93, 304; V, 130. [L. C. Draper], "Biographical field notes of Dr. Lyman C. Draper: Toledo and vicinity, 1863–1866," Hist. Soc. of

Northwestern Ohio, *Quarterly Bull.* (Toledo), 5 (1933), no.4, items 82, 142, 151. *Frontier defense on the upper Ohio, 1777–1778 . . .* , ed. R. G. Thwaites and L. P. Kellogg (Madison, Wis., 1912; repr. Millwood, N.Y., 1973). *Henry Hamilton and George Rogers Clark in the American revolution, with the unpublished journal of Lieut. Gov. Henry Hamilton*, ed. J. D. Barnhart (Crawfordsville, Ind., 1951). *Indian affairs: laws and treaties*, comp. C. J. Kappler (5v., Washington, 1904–41; repr. New York, 1971), II, 44. *Michigan Pioneer Coll.*, IX (1886), 442, 483; X (1886), 394; XX (1892), 350. U.S., Congress, *American state papers: documents, legislative and executive, of the Congress of the United States . . .* (38v., Washington, 1832–61), class II, v.[1], 566. [David Zeisberger], *Diary of David Zeisberger, a Moravian missionary among the Indians of Ohio*, ed. and trans. E. F. Bliss (2v., Cincinnati, Ohio, 1885), I, 437–38; II, 26–27, 39–40, 83–84, 154. R. F. Bauman, "Pontiac's successor: the Ottawa Au-goosh-away (E Gouch-e-ouay)," *Northwest Ohio Quarterly* (Toledo), XXVI (1954), 8–38.

ELLICE, ROBERT, merchant and fur-trader; b. 1747, probably in Auchterless (Kirktown of Auchterless, Grampian), Scotland, third son of William Ellice of Knockleith and Mary Simpson of Gartly; d. 1790, probably in Montreal (Que.).

Robert Ellice was the son of a prosperous miller, who prior to his death in 1756 had provided his children with some education and who may have left them a modest estate. In 1765 the five Ellice brothers emigrated from the Aberdeenshire family homestead to America, their mother and two sisters remaining behind. The brothers made their way to Schenectady, New York, a small farming and commercial centre on the frontier. Alexander*, the eldest, formed a partnership with John Duncan and James Phyn, two local merchants, in 1766. Duncan had been active in the fur trade around the Mohawk valley, Niagara (near Youngstown, N.Y.), and Detroit; his new partners aggressively expanded the business into grain and general merchandise. Following Duncan's retirement in 1767 the firm, now known as Phyn, Ellice and Company, moved into larger quarters. Their affairs prospered, and in the autumn of 1768 Robert Ellice was brought into the firm. Additional business arrangements, including a co-partnership with John Porteous, a Montreal-based merchant, were established in Detroit, Albany, New York, Montreal, London, and Bristol. These reflected the growing volume of business but were also a deliberate response to the mounting friction between the American colonies and Great Britain. The firm was aware that Montreal merchants had been unaffected by the non-importation agreements in force in the American colonies in the late 1760s, and as early as 1770 they made arrangements to import their trade goods for the interior and market their furs through Quebec.

As an adjunct to the fur trade, during the late 1760s the firm sought and obtained government contracts to supply goods and provisions to military posts on the Great Lakes, principally Detroit and Michilimackinac (Mackinaw City, Mich.). It also secured contracts with the Indian department to supply presents for the Indians. In addition to proving quite profitable, these government contracts helped to secure access to regions beyond the posts, and Phyn, Ellice and Company often transported non-government goods along with the official supplies. The contracts continued throughout the American revolution and quite likely up to the British evacuation of the frontier posts in 1796.

In 1774, anticipating further strife between Britain and her American colonies, James Phyn established a London office while Alexander Ellice established one in Montreal. Most of the firm's assets were converted to cash and bills of exchange and were safely removed to England. Late in 1775 the remaining assets in the colony of New York were transferred to James Ellice, also a partner in the firm, who protected the firm's interests at Schenectady during and after the American revolution. Robert Ellice also appears to have remained in New York, for in 1776, despite taking the oath of allegiance to the state, he was turned back at Fort Stanwix (Rome, N.Y.), on his way from Schenectady to the interior to collect some of the firm's debts. He sailed from New York City on 11 Sept. 1778 and joined Alexander in Montreal, where the outbreak of hostilities had afforded merchants new opportunities in the shape of supply contracts with the British military for foodstuffs and other goods.

In 1779 the Montreal concern became Robert Ellice and Company, managed jointly by Ellice and John Forsyth*. By purchasing outright the assets of the Detroit firm of Graverat and Visgar instead of utilizing the system of transactions specified by contractual agreements, Ellice was able to take a leading personal role in expanding the trade to the areas south and west of the Great Lakes and subsequently in the region beyond Lake Superior. John Richardson* had joined the Ellices as an apprentice in 1774, and upon Robert's death in 1790 the firm was reorganized as Forsyth, Richardson and Company; this partnership, tied to the Ellice house in London, subsequently became part of the XY Company. In 1787 Robert Ellice became a partner in the London firm, from that year known as Phyn, Ellices, and Inglis. Through these interlocking partnerships, reinforced by kinship ties, the Ellices supplied a substantial portion of the trade goods for the interior (dealing with such early North West Company traders as Peter Pond*, Simon McTavish*, and Benjamin FROBISHER), acted as middlemen at the fur depots, and marketed furs in Europe. They owned vessels on both the Great Lakes and the Atlantic and acquired extensive landholdings in North America. The keys to their success were bold planning, fortunate timing, careful accounting, and financial acumen. Although Robert Ellice's early death prevented him from sharing in it, the family amassed a considerable fortune which played a significant role in early Canadian commerce.

JAMES M. COLTHART

BL, Landsdowne MSS LXXII, ff.455–58. National Library of Scotland (Edinburgh), Dept. of Manuscripts, MSS 15113; 15115, f.1; 15118, ff.1–12; 15125, ff.82–99; 15130, ff.1–76; 15131, ff.1–177; 15135; 15138; 15176, ff.75f.; 15193, f.33. PRO, BT 6/190; CO 47/80–82. J. M. Colthart, "Edward Ellice and North America" (unpublished PHD thesis, Princeton University, Princeton, N.J., 1971). R. H. Fleming, "Phyn, Ellice and Company of Schenectady," *Contributions to Canadian Economics* (Toronto), IV (1932), 7–41. H. A. Innis, "The North West Company," *CHR*, VIII (1927), 308–21. W. S. Wallace, "Forsyth, Richardson and Company in the fur trade," RSC *Trans.*, 3rd ser., XXXIV (1940), sect. II, 187–94.

ERMATINGER (also **Ermintinger, Armitinger**), **LAWRENCE**, merchant; baptized 29 Oct. 1736 at Schaffhausen, Switzerland, son of Laurenz Ermatinger, gunsmith, and Anna Maria Buhl; d. 6 Oct. 1789 in Montreal (Que.).

Lawrence Ermatinger, a partner in the firm Trye and Ermatinger, merchants of London, England, arrived in Montreal soon after the British conquest and quickly became involved in trade. His first recorded business transaction in Montreal was on 16 Feb. 1762. On 15 Oct. 1763 he signed an article of agreement with Forrest OAKES for a term of three years. After the expiration of this agreement, Ermatinger continued to furnish trade goods to Oakes and also to other partnerships for their fur trade ventures. He sent these goods to Michilimackinac (Mackinaw City, Mich.) and Grand Portage (near Grand Portage, Minn.). He also acted as an agent for the transport of goods and passengers to England.

In 1767 Ermatinger's partner, James Trye, died in England, and Ermatinger attempted unsuccessfully to settle the affairs of the firm. He was obliged to return to England in November 1769 and declare bankruptcy, but he was able to salvage some of his business and with the aid of friends and creditors returned to Montreal in June 1770. He rented a house, got his store ready for retail trade, and had his goods landed. On 10 July 1770 a fire destroyed the house and his offices, but with the goods he rescued and others not yet arrived he returned to business. His premises were burned again on 19 Nov. 1772. On 7 Nov. 1774 Ermatinger purchased a house on Rue Saint-Paul, which he insured for £400 in London and intended to make fireproof with iron plates imported from England. During the occupation of Montreal (1775–76), the American administrator of the town ordered the arrest of Ermatinger and nine other prominent supporters of the crown when he heard of Brigadier-General Richard MONTGOMERY's defeat at Quebec. His arbitrary action drew a strong protest from Montrealers and the prisoners were released. Ermatinger was obliged to store his goods and go to the country to avoid the Americans. He suffered some financial loss but was soon involved in the trade in military supplies for the British army.

Despite adversity Ermatinger managed to continue his fur trading activities. His name appears regularly among the recipients of fur trade licences from 1769 to 1778. He was also involved in the financing of partnerships such as that of Forrest Oakes and Charles Boyer. In 1779 a short-lived North West Company consisting of 16 shares held by nine different partnerships was organized; one share was held by Oakes and Company, a partnership between Ermatinger and Forrest Oakes.

Ermatinger acted also as an agent for several London merchants throughout most of his business career in Montreal. He kept his principals informed of the state of the Canadian market and with this advice goods were shipped to him on consignment. He sold these and purchased cargoes to be shipped back to England or sent direct to some foreign market. He was sometimes sent instructions about the disposal of goods but his principals relied largely on his judgement in both buying and selling. While acting as an agent Ermatinger sometimes also worked on a commission basis for London merchants; he was engaged in commerce on his own account as well. Prior to 1773 he imported goods for his own business directly from the English manufacturers but because of their many irregularities he found it more profitable to pay a commission and have all his stock shipped from one firm.

Ermatinger's prosperity did not endure. He amassed large debts and in August 1783 was forced to mortgage all his real property and personal estate to a London merchant firm. He felt obliged to sell his property and his house on Rue Saint-Paul. From 1783 until his death Ermatinger was no longer active in the business community of Montreal. He died intestate on 6 Oct. 1789.

During his active years Ermatinger had been a member of the community of English merchants who sought to benefit from the trade of Canada after the conquest, and who formed committees, wrote petitions, passed resolutions, and generally sought to influence political and economic events in Canada. He was also one of the first members of a Masonic organization in Montreal, along with his wife's brother-in-law Edward William Gray*.

Within a few years of his arrival in Canada Ermatinger had married Jemima Oakes, the sister of Forrest. They had eight children, including Frederick William*, sheriff of Montreal and one of the first directors of the Bank of Montreal, Charles Oakes*, fur-trader, and Lawrence Edward, assistant commissary-general in the British army.

M. Momryk

ANQ-M, État civil, Anglicans, Christ Church (Montréal), 8 Oct. 1789; Greffe d'E. W. Gray, 18 août 1783; Greffe de J. A. Gray, 25 août 1809. PAC, MG 19, A2, ser.1, 1, 3; ser.3, 31, 63, 192, 193, 199, 201, 203; ser.4, 1; MG 30, D1, 12; RG 4, B28, 24–25. PRO, B 4/20, f.11; B 6/4, f.66. *Docs. relating to NWC* (Wallace). *Quebec Gazette*, 20 June, 25 July 1765, 16 March 1767, 23 July, 3 Dec. 1772, 9 Sept. 1779, 25 Sept. 1783. E. H. Capp, *The story of Baw-a-ting, being the annals of Sault Sainte Marie* (Sault Sainte Marie, Ont., 1904; repr. 1907). Isabel Craig, "Economic conditions in Canada, 1763–1783" (unpublished MA thesis, McGill University, Montreal, 1937). D. B. Miquelon, "The Baby family in the trade of Canada, 1750–1820" (unpublished MA thesis, Carleton University, Ottawa, [1966]). A. S. Morton, "Forrest Oakes, Charles Boyer, Joseph Fulton, and Peter Pangman in the north-west, 1765–1793," RSC *Trans.*, 3rd ser., XXXI (1937), sect.II, 87–100.

ESGLY (Esglis), LOUIS-PHILIPPE MARIAUCHAU D'. *See* Mariauchau

ESTÈBE, GUILLAUME, merchant-trader, entrepreneur, storekeeper, member of the Conseil Supérieur, and seigneur; b. 1701 in the parish of Sainte-Trinité, Gourbit (dept of Ariège), France, son of Arnaud (Armand) Estèbe and Élisabeth Garde; probably d. in France some time after 1779.

Guillaume Estèbe, the son of a merchant, already had contacts with a number of French merchants before he sailed for New France. He was in Quebec in 1729 as an itinerant trader bearing a proxy from a La Rochelle merchant, Joseph-Simon Desherbert de Lapointe. He may have returned soon after to France but, having decided to settle in Canada, he married Élisabeth-Cécile, daughter of merchant Étienne Thibierge, at Beaumont, near Quebec, on 8 Nov. 1733. The 5,000 *livres* of property he declared when his marriage contract was signed, the 3,000-*livre* marriage settlement he provided for his wife, and the social rank of the witnesses present in the office of notary Jacques Barbel* suggest that Guillaume Estèbe already enjoyed a degree of wealth and had rapidly established new connections. Among the witnesses at the marriage itself were Jean Crespin, a member of the Conseil Supérieur and militia colonel for whom Estèbe was to serve two years later as executor; Louis-Jean Poulin* de Courval, king's attorney; and Nicolas Boisseau, notary and clerk of the provost court of Quebec.

During the years that followed, Estèbe carried on various activities simultaneously. In 1737 he bought a house on Rue Saint-Pierre which he sold in 1750 to Jean-Baptiste Amiot* (1717–69) for 30,000 *livres*. In 1752 he had another house built on that street by Nicolas Dasilva*, *dit* Portugais, and sold it in 1757 to the king's purveyor, Joseph-Michel Cadet, for 50,000 *livres*. In 1743 he received his first land grant, the seigneury of Sabrevois on the Richelieu, but he had the grant annulled the following year after he learned the land was "worthless." In 1744 he obtained a grant of the seigneury of La Gauchetière on the shores of Lake Champlain and in 1753 became the holder of Mistanguienne, an arriere-fief belonging to the seigneury of Notre-Dame-des-Anges, which he sold four years later to storekeeper François-Joseph de Vienne.

In 1739 Estèbe acquired interests in the seal fisheries off the Labrador coast by entering into partnership with Jean-Baptiste Pommereau*, who had obtained a concession at Gros Mécatina (Que.) the previous year. He kept these interests after Pommereau's death in 1742 [*see* Joseph-Michel Legardeur de Croisille et de Montesson]. In 1740 Estèbe and Henri-Albert de Saint-Vincent set up a company to exploit the concession at Petit Mécatina, next to Gros Mécatina, and in 1748, with Jacques-Michel Bréard, he obtained another concession in that region. This concession was by no means the only undertaking in which Bréard and Estèbe were partners: Estèbe acted as business agent for Bréard and the two men were also important members of Intendant Bigot's famous clique.

Before Bigot's arrival in the colony, Estèbe had already made a place for himself within the colonial administration. In 1736 he was appointed a councillor of the Conseil Supérieur, and on 1 Feb. 1758, after he resigned the office prior to his departure for France, the king appointed him an honorary councillor, an honour given to only one other person in New France, François Daine*. In 1740, moreover, he had obtained the office of king's storekeeper in Quebec. Intendant HOCQUART also recognized his competence in a number of fields. In 1741, after the collapse of the company formed by François-Étienne Cugnet* to operate the Saint-Maurice ironworks, Hocquart appointed Estèbe his subdelegate to manage the establishment. In the autumn Estèbe went to the ironworks and drew up a complete inventory. He was chosen by the intendant to replace the commissary of Marine when the decision was taken early in 1744 to make an appraisal of the ironworks. That year Hocquart twice commissioned him to go to the Côte de Beaupré and the Île d'Orléans to buy or borrow from the habitants the wheat and flour needed for the troops and residents of Quebec and the troops on Île Royale (Cape Breton Island).

Guillaume Estèbe amassed most of his fortune in his last ten years in New France, during Bigot's term as intendant. After the conquest, at the time of the *affaire du Canada*, he admitted he had left the colony with nearly 250,000 *livres*, and this was probably an understatement. The anonymous author of the "Mémoire du Canada" estimated Estèbe's fortune at 1,800,000 *livres*. Estèbe's connections with Bigot and some of his entourage, particularly Bréard and Pierre Claverie*, enabled him to participate in highly profitable commercial undertakings. For example, in the early 1750s, he and Claverie were involved in a store which the other Quebec merchants called, not without reason, "La Friponne" ("The Rogue"). Moreover, as king's storekeeper until 1754, Estèbe was in a favourable position to carry out certain fraudulent operations at Bigot's request. When the ships of David Gradis et Fils, a Bordeaux firm with which Bigot was associated, arrived at Quebec, Estèbe would declare to the bureau of the Domaine d'Occident that their cargoes were for the king's account. Thus the company evaded payment of import duties, which had been in effect since 1749.

Estèbe had gone to France shortly before the *affaire du Canada* broke in 1761. He was imprisoned in the Bastille, as were other colonial administrators accused of corruption. During his trial at the Châtelet he was charged, among other things, with having profited illegally through the sale of goods to the king's store at exorbitant prices by companies in which he had an interest, with selling to the king at an inflated price the provisions for Île Royale, and with having had interests in the coasters chartered in the king's name which traded on the St Lawrence or transported goods to Acadia. The decision rendered on 10 Dec. 1763 sentenced him to be reprimanded before the council chamber at the Châtelet, to donate six *livres* to charity, and to repay 30,000 *livres*.

This conviction does not seem to have affected Estèbe's administrative career. For more than 20 years after his return to France, he apparently held the office of king's secretary at the chancery in Bordeaux. In 1779 Estèbe asked that his *lettres d'honneur* to the post at Bordeaux be registered with the Conseil Supérieur of Saint-Domingue (Hispaniola), where he wanted to join members of his family; the transfer was refused on the pretext that he did not live there himself. No further trace of him has been found.

FRANCINE BARRY

AN, Col., E, 172 (dossier Estèbe). ANQ-M, Greffe de F.-M. Lepallieur de Laferté, 9 mars 1737. ANQ-Q, AP-G-322, 61ff.; Greffe de Jacques Barbel, 6 nov. 1733; NF 12, 16, cahier 8, pp.6–7; cahier 10, pp.57–58. *Inv. de pièces du Labrador* (P.-G. Roy), I, 83–84, 88–89; II, 11–16, 20–45, 50–57, 61, 66. "Mémoire du Canada," ANQ *Rapport*, 1924–25, 134, 197–98. PAC *Rapport*, 1887, cciii.

Marion, *Dict. des instit.* J.-E. Roy, *Rapport sur les archives de France*, 870, 874, 881. P.-G. Roy, *Inv. concessions*, I, 23–24; IV, 252, 271–72; *Inv. jug. et délib., 1717–60*; *Inv. ord. int.*, II, 304; III, 16–17, 57, 59–60, 62. Tanguay, *Dictionnaire*. Frégault, *François Bigot*. P.-G. Roy, *Bigot et sa bande*, 59–65. Tessier, *Les forges Saint-Maurice*, 74–85. J.-E. Roy, "Les conseillers au Conseil souverain de la Nouvelle-France," *BRH*, I (1895), 180, 183. P.-G. Roy, "Le sieur Guillaume Estèbe," *BRH*, LII (1946), 195–207.

F

FELTZ (Felx, Fels, Felts), CHARLES-ELEMY-JOSEPH-ALEXANDRE-FERDINAND, surgeon-major; b. *c.* 1710 in Germany, son of Elemy-Victor Feltz, a doctor, and Marie-Ursule Mouthe; d. 9 March 1776 at or near Blois, France.

Charles-Elemy-Joseph-Alexandre-Ferdinand

Feltz landed in New France in 1738 as a recruit. He probably already had some experience as a surgeon, since the nuns of the Hôtel-Dieu of Montreal selected him "to take care of the ailing inhabitants in their hospital." In September 1740 he was called to Quebec and succeeded Michel Bertier* as surgeon to the Hôtel-Dieu and surgeon-major of the town. Governor Charles de Beauharnois* hoped to get him the latter position permanently, but the home authorities appointed Antoine Briault. Fortune nevertheless favoured him. The surgeon-major of Montreal, Joseph Benoist, who was old and crippled, retired from professional practice, and with Intendant HOCQUART's support Feltz obtained the post. He returned to Montreal with his commission as surgeon-major at the beginning of August 1742.

The surgeon's prospects quickly improved. He soon moved into his own house on Rue Notre-Dame and shortly after acquired a second property, with a garden and orchard, in the *faubourg* d'Ailleboust. He bought a piece of land in the *faubourg* Saint-Laurent, subdivided it into lots, and sold about 20 of them between 1754 and 1759. All these investments brought good returns, and Feltz profited from similar transactions in the fief of La Gauchetière, near Montreal. With the income he was able to buy two-thirds of the fief of Île Saint-Paul (Île des Sœurs) from Jean Le Ber de Senneville on 11 Aug. 1758.

His professional practice made him even wealthier. Every year he was paid 1,008 *livres tournois* as surgeon-major of Montreal and 300 "for his calls and trips to treat the Indians." As surgeon of the Hôtel-Dieu of Montreal until 1760, and the Hôpital Général from 1747 to 1766, Feltz regularly received fees from these institutions. He also had an income from selling medicaments. In his consulting room he kept more than 1,000 *livres*' worth of remedies including *poudre divine*, vitriol, and the famous theriac, a current panacea. The Seven Years' War gave new impetus to this lucrative business.

Ferdinand Feltz had a way of life that matched his fortune. He not only had a maidservant but also owned slaves, and although his wealthiest colleagues were content with two, or even one, he had to have ten. He associated with the socially prominent. Madame Bégon [Rocbert*] used to meet him at receptions where the "gentlefolk" of the town congregated. On Twelfth Night he entertained Charles Le Moyne* de Longueuil and Jean-Victor VARIN de La Marre at his home, and François-Pierre de RIGAUD de Vaudreuil found refuge under his roof after a quarrel with his brother, Governor RIGAUD de Vaudreuil. Mother d'Youville [DUFROST] took him into her confidence and made a friend of him.

On 4 Nov. 1741 Feltz had married Marie-Ursule, daughter of François Aubert* de La Chesnaye, in Quebec. This marriage had probably facilitated his entry into the inner circle of Montreal society. When he married Cécile Gosselin, widow of merchant Charles-Dominique Douaire de Bondy, on 16 Feb. 1757 in Lachine, he gained new and equally useful connections.

Feltz's competence as a surgeon and physician was valued by the people about him. He treated several prominent members of the colony's "high society." Madame Bégon, who was at times sceptical of his diagnoses and admitted that she did not believe all his "charades," nevertheless turned to him for treatment. Like the majority of his profession, Feltz made frequent use of blood-lettings and enemas. Sometimes his treatment was less conventional – for example he used toads to try to relieve a sore on Mother d'Youville's knee. But what largely established his reputation was his prescription for curing ulcers, a secret which surgeons Louis-Nicolas LANDRIAUX and Pierre-Joseph Compain* inherited when he left. Finally, his well-informed opinion was sought when nurses had to be chosen for foundlings, and he was called on to adjudicate disputed bills of certain of his colleagues.

Feltz, who had received his naturalization papers on 3 Feb. 1758, thought of leaving for France after the conquest, but the authorities in Britain ordered him to remain to take care of the sick and wounded soldiers hospitalized in Montreal. In June 1766 James MURRAY gave him a certificate acknowledging his services, and at the end of August he left Canada for good. In France he continued to practise in the region of Blois until his death ten years later.

Ferdinand Feltz, a jovial character who at times liked to make fun of the failings of his fellow citizens, attained a prosperity which came to few in his profession, thanks to good marriages and his skill as a practitioner and businessman. He remains one of the most interesting figures in the medical annals of the French régime.

GILLES JANSON

AMHDQ, Corr., Anciennes mères, Brouillon de lettre de sœur Geneviève Duplessis de l'Enfant-Jésus à M. de Laporte, 20 oct. 1751; Brouillon de lettre s.d. et sans destinaire (vers 1751); Registre des malades, V, 37, 61, 71. AN, Col., B, 74, pp.160–61, 243–44, 253–55; 76, pp. 172–73; 107, pp.89–91 (PAC transcripts); 113, f.194v; C11A, 73, ff.54–55; 75, ff.101, 317–18; 77, f.14; 79, f.355; E, 26 (dossier Benoist), 181 (dossier Feltz). ANQ-M, Doc. jud., Registres des audiences pour la juridiction de Montréal, 15 mars, 13 sept. 1748, 7 mars 1750, 23 mars

1751, 18 avril 1755; État civil, Catholiques, Notre-Dame de Montréal, 3 oct. 1756, 16 févr. 1757, 13 mai 1758; Greffe d'Henri Bouron, 21 mars 1750, 5 juin 1751; Greffe de L.-C. Danré de Blanzy, 16 nov. 1742, 13 août 1743, 14, 20 sept., 24 nov., 19 déc. 1754, 21, 25 févr., 10 mars 1755, 19, 29 juin, 3 sept., 9, 20, 30 oct., 17 nov. 1756, 15, 16 févr., 29 avril, 11, 14, 15 mai 1757, 28 avril, 3, 17 juin, 11, 16, 19, 21, 23 août 1758, 29 avril, 10 mai, 16 août, 29 sept. 1759, 1er avril, 17 sept. 1760; Greffe de P.-F. Mézière, 15 oct. 1764; Greffe de C.-C.-J. Porlier, 3 avril 1743; Greffe de François Simonnet, 7 mai 1748. ANQ-Q, Greffe de J.-N. Pinguet de Vaucour, 2 nov. 1741. Archives générales des Religieuses hospitalières de Saint-Joseph (Montréal), Registre des recettes et dépenses de l'Hôtel-Dieu de Montréal, 1743–83. ASGM, Ancien journal; Corr. générale, no.6; Maison mère, Historique, Médecins; Maison mère, MY/D; Mémoire de mère Élisabeth McMullen; Registre des recettes et dépenses, II. ASSM, 1M1.62, 940. AUM, P 58, Doc. divers, G2, 2 juill. 1748.

Bégon, "Correspondance" (Bonnault), ANQ *Rapport*, 1934–35, 193–94, 197, 207, 209, 215, 250. *Coll. des manuscrits de Lévis* (Casgrain), VII, 515; IX, 17–18, 62; X, 91–92. *Édits ord.*, II, 395–96. *Monseigneur de Lauberivière, cinquième évêque de Québec, 1739–1740*, Cyprien Tanguay, édit. (Montréal, 1885), 133–37, 143–46. [M.-A. Regnard Duplessis, dite de Sainte-Hélène], "Lettres de mère Marie-Andrée Duplessis de Sainte-Hélène, supérieure des hospitalières de l'Hôtel-Dieu de Québec," A.-L. Leymarie, édit., *Nova Francia* (Paris), V (1930), 249–50, 359–61, 368–70. [C.-M.-M. d'Youville], "La vie de madame Youville, fondatrice des Sœurs de la Charité à Montréal," ANQ *Rapport*, 1924–25, 367. *Quebec Gazette*, 23 July 1767. M.-J. et G. Ahern, *Notes pour l'hist. de la médecine*. Albertine Ferland-Angers, *Mère d'Youville, vénérable Marie-Marguerite Du Frost de Lajemmerais, veuve d'Youville, 1701–1771; fondatrice des Sœurs de la Charité de l'Hôpital-général de Montréal, dites sœurs grises* (Montréal, 1945), 180, 190, 218, 235–39, 241, 244–47, 255–56, 259. M. Trudel, *L'esclavage au Canada français*. Henri Têtu, "M. Jean-Félix Récher, curé de Québec, et son journal, 1757–1760," *BRH*, IX (1903), 300.

FERNÁNDEZ Y MARTÍNEZ DE LA SIERRA, ESTEBAN JOSÉ MARTÍNEZ. *See* MARTÍNEZ

FIEDMONT, LOUIS-THOMAS JACAU DE. *See* JACAU

FILLIS, JOHN, businessman and office-holder; b. *c.* 1724 in Boston, Massachusetts, son of John Fillis; d. 16 July 1792 in Halifax, Nova Scotia.

The son of a prosperous carter in Boston, John Fillis came to Nova Scotia around 1751. Apparently possessed of considerable capital, he founded a thriving shipping business in Halifax, and at the outbreak of the American revolution he had a branch in Boston. Payment of a guinea a month for the support of the poor had enabled Fillis to obtain a licence to sell liquor in Halifax, and in 1752 he established a distillery. He and Joshua MAUGER enjoyed a monopoly of the wholesale rum trade in the province and frequently acted together to protect their common interest. In 1767, for example, when Governor Lord William CAMPBELL supported a bill to lower the impost and raise the excise duty on spirits, Fillis and Mauger's agent, John BUTLER, protested to the Board of Trade and were supported in London by Mauger and other British merchants interested in Nova Scotia. Campbell was soon ordered to restore the old rate of duty. The demand for rum resulting from the large-scale immigration to the province from Europe, Great Britain, and New England in the three decades after the founding of Halifax meant wealth for both Fillis and Mauger. Like many Nova Scotians Fillis invested heavily in land, and he came to own properties in Halifax, Grand Pré, Cornwallis, Horton (Wolfville region), Granville, and what is now Bridgetown. At the time of his death his estate was valued at nearly £30,000.

Fillis' high standing in the community won him a seat in the first House of Assembly in 1758. Ten years later he succeeded Benjamin GERRISH as a member for Halifax County, a seat he held until 1770. In the fifth assembly (1770–85) he replaced Richard GIBBONS as the representative for Barrington Township, and in 1784 he was offered the position of speaker, an honour he refused. From 1785 until his death he represented Halifax Township. He seems to have played an active role in the Halifax community. He was appointed a justice of the peace in 1771 and was a prominent member of Mather's (St Matthew's) Church.

The increasingly strained relations between Britain and the American colonies in the 1760s and 1770s created a dilemma for Fillis as for many other New Englanders in Nova Scotia. In the summer of 1774 the Council recommended that Fillis and William Smith, a fellow merchant and JP, be stripped of their offices for having protested the landing of East India Company tea in Halifax. The two men were also linked to another rebellious act, the burning of some hay intended for the British forces at Boston. Stories of their revolutionary tendencies were circulated by rebels in New England and eventually reached the ears of Lieutenant-General Thomas GAGE. Alarmed, Fillis and Smith appealed to the assembly in June 1775 to clear their names, and a resolution attesting to their loyalty was passed by the house that month. Partly to regain his position in the province Fillis became a leader in the assembly's successful campaign in 1775–76 to have Governor Francis LEGGE removed. The fact that

Fillis had been named a defaulter by the committee appointed by Legge to examine the provincial accounts may also explain his activities against the governor.

A dissenter, landowner, merchant, and politician, Fillis was one of the most vigorous of the New England transplants that rooted themselves so firmly in Nova Scotian soil. He was twice married: first to Elizabeth Stoddard on 24 Dec. 1747 in Boston, and secondly to Sarah Cleveland, *née* Rudduck, on 19 Oct. 1756 in Halifax. He seems to have had ten children, four of whom probably died young. His son John became a substantial merchant in Halifax.

A. A. MacKenzie

PANS, MS file, Fillis family docs.; MG 9, nos.1, 4, 109. PRO, CO 217/22. St Paul's Anglican Church (Halifax), Registers of baptisms, burials, and marriages. *Royal Gazette and the Nova-Scotia Advertiser* (Halifax), 17 July 1792. *Directory of N.S. MLAs*. Brebner, *Neutral Yankees*. *Acadian Recorder* (Halifax), 29 May 1926. "A merchant of the early days of Halifax . . . ," *Maritime Merchant* (Halifax), XLIV (1935–36), no. 19, 49, 86. J. F. Smith, "John Fillis, MLA," *Nova Scotia Hist. Quarterly* (Halifax), 1 (1971), 307–23. *Yarmouth Herald* (Yarmouth, N.S.), 8 May 1928.

FLAMAND (Flamant), JACQUES DEGUISE, *dit*. *See* Deguise

FLETCHER, ROBERT, printer and merchant; fl. 1766–85.

Robert Fletcher's early life is obscure. He was likely born in London, where he presumably followed the printing trade before coming to Halifax, Nova Scotia, in the early summer of 1766. He brought with him a new printing press, as well as an extensive stock of books and stationery with which he immediately set up shop. Until this time Anthony Henry had enjoyed the monopoly of government printing, but he had incurred official displeasure by criticizing the Stamp Act of 1765. Fletcher may well have been invited and encouraged by some local officials to immigrate to Nova Scotia with the incentive of government patronage. On 15 Aug. 1766 he published the first issue of his newspaper, the *Nova-Scotia Gazette*, a semi-official weekly of four pages consisting of a single sheet in folio, the immediate successor to Henry's *Halifax Gazette*.

Late in 1766 Fletcher printed his first edition of the *Journal and votes of the House of Assembly for the province of Nova Scotia*, for which he charged the government £18 16*s*. 4*d*. In the mean time he had secured the contract for printing the first revision of the laws of the province, the agreement being that he would furnish 200 copies for the sum of £180. *The perpetual acts of the General Assemblies of his majesty's province of Nova Scotia*, known today as the Belcher edition because of the notes supplied by Chief Justice Jonathan Belcher, was compiled by John Duport and published by Fletcher on 13 May 1767.

Fletcher showed a definite aptitude for printing, but unfortunately his work appears to have been wholly restricted to government commitments, though he advertised printing of every kind "done in the most expeditious, neat and correct manner." His orderly composition and layout stand in marked contrast with the crude and rather flamboyant style of Anthony Henry. Yet by 1770, because of financial reasons or loss of interest, he appears to have been willing to abandon the printing field to Henry, who had established a rival paper in 1769. The last issue of the *Nova-Scotia Gazette* having been published on 30 Aug. 1770, Fletcher sold his press to John Boyle of Boston and from then on devoted his interest exclusively to his bookstore, one of the first in Canada. He apparently felt no rancour towards Henry, however, for his merchandise was extensively advertised in the columns of the latter's *Nova-Scotia Gazette and the Weekly Chronicle* during the next few years. Fletcher expanded his business to include general merchandise in 1772 and, from all indications, experienced frequent financial crises. In 1780 he planned to leave the province but did not do so; in January 1782 he went into bankruptcy and his stock and household effects were sold at public auction. For the next three years, however, he continued to maintain a store, but no record of him remains after the autumn of 1785.

Though little is known of Fletcher's personal life he apparently had some standing in the community, for he served as churchwarden at St Paul's Anglican Church in 1775 and also acted as agent for absentee landowners. As a printer he had unquestionable ability; it is unfortunate that he abandoned his craft in favour of a less creative trade. His first revised edition of Nova Scotia statutes, a volume of some 200 pages, today may be regarded as the first official publication of any stature produced in Canada.

Shirley B. Elliott

[As far as can be ascertained there are no original copies of Fletcher's *Nova-Scotia Gazette* in Canada today. The Mass. Hist. Soc., Boston, and the New York Public Library have small collections of broken runs, but the major portion of the newspaper has disappeared. S.B.E.]

PANS, RG 1, 212, p.213. N.S., House of Assembly, *Journal*, October-November 1766, 47, 77. *Nova-Scotia Gazette* (Halifax), 26 Nov. 1767. *Nova-Scotia Gazette and the Weekly Chronicle* (Halifax), 7 May 1771; 1 Sept., 10 Nov. 1772; 26 Jan., 22 June, 28 Dec. 1773; 24 Oct. 1775; 23 May, 21 Nov. 1780; 8 May 1781; 22 Jan., 19 Feb., 9 July 1782; 24 Feb., 27 May 1783; 25 May 1784; 25 Jan., 4 Oct. 1785. Tremaine, *Bibliography of Canadian imprints*. R. V. Harris, *The Church of Saint Paul in Halifax, Nova Scotia: 1749–1949* (Toronto, 1949). Isaiah Thomas, *The history of printing in America, with a biography of printers, and an account of newspapers* . . . (2nd ed., 2v., Albany, N.Y., 1874; repr. New York, 1972). J. J. Stewart, "Early journalism in Nova Scotia," N.S. Hist. Soc., *Coll.*, VI (1888), 91–122.

FLEURY DESCHAMBAULT, JOSEPH (he signed **Déchambault** or **D'echambault**), office-holder and merchant; b. 1 May 1709 at Quebec, the second son of Joseph de Fleury* de La Gorgendière and Claire Jolliet; m. 19 Jan. 1738 Catherine, daughter of Étienne Véron* de Grandmesnil, merchant and receiver of the admiral of France at Quebec; six of their nine children survived to adulthood; d. 13 July 1784 at Montreal (Que.).

Nothing is known of Joseph Fleury Deschambault's early life or career, but by 1736 he was employed at Montreal as general agent for the Compagnie des Indes. His father was the company's agent-general in Canada, which position Deschambault himself attained by 1754. Prior to 1751, Deschambault's official capacities with the company seem to have included the financing of or granting of credit to numerous traders and merchants, among them Paul Marin* de La Malgue, Louis Ducharme, Louis-François Hervieux*, and François-Marie de Couagne, and he was thus indirectly a significant contributor to the Canadian side of the colonial economy. His position was such that when Mme Bégon [Rocbert*] mentioned his presence in France in 1751 she referred to him as the "representative for Canadian business."

Deschambault was also involved from at least the early 1740s in private fur-trading ventures as a partner, an outfitter, or a financier. In the 1750s he expanded his operations, holding trade licences for Lac des Deux-Montagnes, Lake Huron, Rivière Saint-Joseph (St Joseph River), and Michilimackinac (Mackinaw City, Mich.). At the latter place he owned a "house and lot" which he let for 1,300 *livres* annually. Most of his undertakings appear to have been joint ventures begun with such partners as Jacques Giasson, Nicolas Dufresne, and Jacques Hervieux, all important fur-trade outfitters in Montreal. However, Deschambault seems to have undertaken his most costly venture alone. Prevailed upon by his uncle by marriage, Governor General Vaudreuil [Rigaud], in 1758 he acquired six-year leases for the trade at Chagouamigon (near Ashland, Wis.), Michipicoton (Michipicoten River, Ont.), and Kaministiquia (Thunder Bay, Ont.). As these posts were bases for Vaudreuil's attempts to buy off the western Indians in order to prevent them from joining the British, they were let to Deschambault on favourable terms, there being no *droit de ferme* to pay. There was as well an assured market for him in the goods to be given by the posts' military commanders as gifts to the Indians. In the event, these apparently lucrative posts were only sources of loss: war-generated inflation increased Deschambault's costs far beyond his expectations, the conquest brought his leases to an early end, and the French government and some individuals defaulted on payment for the goods they had received, leaving an unpaid balance of over 170,000 *livres*.

Deschambault's business affairs contributed to his social position in New France, but status was measured not simply by wealth. He had good family connections, particularly with the official and mercantile groups. His grandfathers had been the explorer Louis Jolliet* and the judge Jacques-Alexis Fleury* Deschambault; his sisters married into the Taschereau, Trottier Dufy Desauniers, Marin de La Malgue, and Rigaud de Vaudreuil families. In 1754 he obtained increased access to the military and landed nobility through the marriage of his 13-year-old daugher Marie-Anne-Catherine to Charles-Jacques, son of Charles Le Moyne* de Longueuil. Although in character Deschambault appears to have been self-important, he was possibly no more so than others of the minor nobility. It is, therefore, not surprising that he sought marks of recognition "befitting his station." As early as 1751 he had supplied plans for reorganization of the militia and had petitioned to be made colonel of militia – a position then held at Quebec by his father. Although successive governors general consistently supported his many applications, the minister of Marine rejected the dissemination of such ranks in Canada, for fear that "a colonist who became colonel could easily acquire too much influence," and suggested that Deschambault be made a major instead. There is no evidence that he was ever offered the lesser rank. Only under the British did he receive this form of recognition, when he was made inspector of militia in 1775. Deschambault may nonetheless have had some informal "influence" with the habitants: in 1759 and 1760 he was charged with finding grain and cattle in the Montreal area and was successful. This success, however, may have been due more to his ability to disburse personally over 200,000 *livres* in cold cash than to his other attributes.

The conquest considerably changed the nature and direction of Deschambault's business activities. The Compagnie des Indes was no longer of any consequence in Canadian affairs; and the fact that Deschambault himself no longer participated in the fur trade may perhaps indicate the extent to which he had commingled his own and the company's activities. Moreover, an unknown proportion of his liquid capital was first frozen, then lost, in the 325,000 *livres* of payment orders that he personally held at the end of the war, and for which he was only partially reimbursed. After 1760 what remained of Deschambault's capital, or what he was able to borrow, became primarily concentrated in life annuities in France and in revenue-producing real property, mainly in the Montreal area, rather than in more speculative commerce. This type of investment may have been a natural development, for in the late 1750s, following the death of his son-in-law Charles-Jacques Le Moyne de Longueuil, Deschambault was named trustee for his daughter, thus becoming responsible for managing the barony of Longueuil and the seigneury of Belœil. He nevertheless appears to have considered seriously the possibility of leaving Canada in the 1760s. As early as 1763 he attempted to have the Longueuil and Belœil seigneuries sold, and it was probably also about this time that he purchased the life annuities in France. In 1765 and in 1768–69 he travelled to France, not only to see to his troubled financial affairs but also to visit his three sons, who had gone there after the conquest.

Deschambault's interest in France, however, undoubtedly waned as his economic and social prospects in Canada improved. The relatively short distance of the seigneuries of Longueuil and Belœil from Montreal, the amount of fresh and unconceded land they contained, and the increasing importance of grain in the Canadian economy under the British régime enhanced their value, making them attractive investments. As early as 1764 such newcomers as Moses Hazen* and Gabriel Christie had received grants from Deschambault. During the two decades under his management the seigneuries seem to have made good economic progress – he granted several hundred concessions in Longueuil alone – but not apparently enough to satisfy David Alexander Grant, husband of Deschambault's granddaughter Marie-Charles-Joseph Le Moyne* de Longueuil, heiress of the seigneuries. By a judicial award he was replaced as trustee by Grant in 1781. From then until his death Deschambault appears to have done little.

The change in Deschambault's business activities can be directly attributed to the conquest; he did not change his attempts to assert and improve his social status – all his daughters married into the new British hierarchy. Indeed in 1768 he was accused in France of being "more English than French" and in 1774 Governor Guy Carleton* wrote that "He and His family have ever been remarkably civil to the English." However, any assessment as to whether he or other members of his class had quickly or easily accommodated themselves to British rule must take into account the variety of social, political, and financial pressures which had acted upon them.

Deschambault died on 13 July 1784 and was buried on the 15th in Notre-Dame church in Montreal. His estate, valued at more than 100,000 *livres*, was, however, encumbered with a claim for 69,040 *livres* by his son-in-law the judge John Fraser, and possibly by other claims concerning the unpaid 10,000 *livres*' dowry of his daughter Thérèse-Josèphe, wife of Major William Dunbar. Nonetheless, the inventory of his possessions, compiled over two years after his death, shows that Deschambault had maintained an ostentatious style of life. Among his many possessions were several dozen armchairs and a sofa, a number of large and small mirrors, an extensive amount of silver plate, a gold and crystal chandelier, a Chinese table, and six Persian curtains. Curiously, no books were listed. These articles were in his 15-room stone house on Rue Saint-Paul in Montreal; he also left a stone house at Longueuil, half of a warehouse in Quebec, and land in at least six seigneuries.

Historians are at total variance about Deschambault's significance: Édouard-Zotique Massicotte* suggests he was probably "the most important Canadian financier of the time," while Robert La Roque* de Roquebrune speaks of him as being "among the small shopkeepers of Quebec." He seems to have had little in common with the bourgeoisie which was developing in Britain and France, for he apparently saw power as a function of inherited social position rather than of acquired wealth. However, until further study can clarify the social milieu in which Deschambault lived, he may be looked on either as an important mercantile figure and member of the bourgeoisie or as a minor member of the Canadian nobility, commercially minded but striving to improve his social standing.

ANDREW RODGER

[The registers of Jean-Baptiste Adhémar*, Henri Bouron, François-Pierre CHERRIER, Louis-Claude Danré* de Blanzy, Antoine GRISÉ, Pierre Lalanne, Pierre-François Mézière, Claude-Cyprien-Jacques Porlier, and François SIMONNET, held by the ANQ-M, contain almost 500 deeds that concern Deschambault; the registers of Danré de Blanzy, Grisé, Lalanne, and Porlier are particularly interesting. A.R.]

AN, Col., B, 93, f.29; 105, f.13; C[11A], 95, ff.341–51; 100, f.90; 102, f.182; E, 185 (dossier Deschambault). ANQ-M, État civil, Catholiques, Notre-Dame de Montréal, 15 juill. 1784; Greffe d'Antoine Foucher, 27 juill. 1786; Recensement, Compagnie des Indes, 1741. ANQ-Q, AP-P-545; Greffe de Claude Barolet, 12 avril 1750; 24 mai 1752; 1er mai 1758; Greffe de J.-N. Pinguet de Vaucour, 17 janv. 1738; NF 2, 24, 16 oct. 1736; 35, 27 mars 1778; NF 11, 51, ff.32v-33; 52, ff.131v-132v; 64, f.137v. BL, Add. MSS 21699, p.602; 21715, pp.49–50; 21716, p.154; 21731, p.262; 21732, p.82; 21734, pp.407–8; 21735/1, pp.197–98, 226; 21831, pp.6–8, 16 (copies at PAC). McGill University Libraries, Dept. of Rare Books and Special Coll., MS coll., CH218.S196. PAC, MG 8, F51; MG 11, [CO 42], Q, 8, pp.99–110; 12, pp.241–46; 17, p.117; MG 24, L3, pp.3030–31, 3917–18, 17367–68, 17481–83, 20048–52, 20426–27, 21801–7, 21825–29, 22960–64, 24010–11, 24088–95, 26098–110, 28234–40. PRO, CO 5/115, pp.260–262; 5/176, pp.32–58 (copies at PAC). "Congés de traite conservés aux Archives de la province de Québec," ANQ *Rapport*, 1922–23, 192–265. "Pierre Du Calvet," J.-J. Lefebvre, édit., ANQ *Rapport*, 1945–46, 341–411. *Quebec Gazette*, 12 July, 8 Nov. 1764, 7 July 1768, 28 Dec. 1769, 21 Feb. 1771, 26 Sept. 1772, 31 July 1783, 23 Dec. 1784. Claude de Bonnault, "Le Canada militaire: état provisoire des officiers de milice de 1641 à 1760," ANQ *Rapport*, 1949–51, 269–71. Louise Dechêne, "Les dossiers canadiens du notaire Pointard," ANQ *Rapport*, 1966, 115–27. Alexandre Jodoin et J.-L. Vincent, *Histoire de Longueuil et de la famille de Longueuil* . . . (Montréal, 1889). O.-M.-H. Lapalice, "Bancs à perpétuité dans l'église de N.-D.-de-Montréal," *BRH*, XXXV (1929), 354–55. Odette Lebrun, "Épouses des Le Moyne: les baronnes de Longueuil," Soc. d'hist. de Longueuil, *Cahier* (Longueuil, Qué.), 2 (1973), 7–10. J.-J. Lefebvre, "Études généalogiques: la famille Fleury d'Eschambault, de La Gorgendière," SGCF *Mémoires*, III (1948–49), 152–74. É.-Z. Massicotte, "Maçons, entrepreneurs, architectes," *BRH*, XXXV (1929), 139; "Où est né le bienheureux André Grasset de Saint-Sauveur," *BRH*, XXXIII (1927), 95; "Quelques rues et faubourgs du vieux Montréal," *Cahiers des Dix*, 1 (1936), 130.

FLOQUET, PIERRE-RENÉ, Jesuit; b. 12 Sept. 1716 in Paris; d. 18 Oct. 1782 in Quebec.

Pierre-René Floquet entered the noviciate in Paris on 6 Aug. 1734 after two years of philosophy. He taught the grammar and classics classes at Quimper (1736–40), studied theology at the Jesuit Collège de La Flèche (1740–44), and arrived in Canada on 17 Aug. 1744. After teaching for five years at the Jesuit college in Quebec, he tried missionary life at Sault-Saint-Louis (Caughnawaga) in 1749–50 and then returned to Quebec as bursar of the college (1750–56). In 1757 he replaced Father Nicolas Degonnor as superior of the Jesuits in Montreal, holding this office until his retirement in 1780. At the same time he was involved with the Congrégation des Hommes de Ville-Marie and served as a priest at the Jesuit chapel.

Until 1775, when he had the bad luck to become involved in political matters, he never attracted public attention. But during the Americans' occupation of Montreal in 1775–76 [*see* Richard MONTGOMERY] his frequent relations with them compromised him in the eyes of the British authorities and of Bishop BRIAND, who had appealed to the clergy and the Canadian people to remain loyal.

On 15 Feb. 1776 the second Continental Congress in Philadelphia appointed Benjamin Franklin, Samuel Chase, and Charles Carroll to go to Canada to win Canadians to its cause; Charles Carroll brought along his cousin John Carroll, a Jesuit and the future archbishop of Baltimore, Maryland, who was to make contact with Canadian clergy. Arriving in Montreal on 29 March 1776, the delegation was received by Brigadier-General Benedict Arnold* and stayed in the home of Thomas WALKER, a merchant sympathetic to the American cause. John Carroll visited Floquet, who was still living in the Jesuit residence. As he was bearing a letter of introduction from Father Ferdinand Farmer, his superior in Philadelphia, Carroll obtained permission from Étienne MONTGOLFIER, the vicar general in Montreal, to say mass in Father Floquet's church, but he dined only once in the Jesuit residence. Unfortunately Floquet compromised himself further.

In a letter of 15 June 1776 to Bishop Briand, who was threatening to place him under an interdict, Floquet gave an explanation for the actions thought rash: he did not like the Quebec Act and had said so too bluntly; by dealing tactfully with the Bostonnais he thought he could protect his *confrères* in Maryland and Pennsylvania from persecution; misled by the attitude of neutrality adopted by the representatives sent to meet with the invaders in Montreal, he had been tolerant in the confessional towards militiamen who had joined the American forces; he had thought fit to give communion secretly to three such men who had been refused it at the parish church; he had gone to dine with Colonel Moses Hazen*, along with Father John McKenna, a friend of the colonel who had been driven from New York by the anti-Catholic Whig party and had retired to live in the Jesuit residence in Montreal in the spring of 1776. Floquet did not consider that he had acted badly; nevertheless, he admitted that in the best interests of religion he ought to have followed his bishop's directives in political matters.

The interdict opened his eyes. On Bishop Briand's orders he went to Quebec. There, on 29 Nov. 1776, he wrote the bishop to ask that his punishment be lifted. The interdict was removed, and Floquet continued his ministry in Montreal. But on 27 April 1777 in a letter to Sébastien-Louis Meurin, a Jesuit missionary to the Illinois, Bishop Briand wrote: "Father Floquet has behaved very badly; for six months he has been under interdict because of his obstinacy. . . . He does not believe that he was wrong and says so when he is not afraid of his listeners." Floquet, who died in Quebec on 18 Oct. 1782, stood out as an exception among his fellow Jesuits who "had behaved themselves, and were much distressed" by his conduct.

JOSEPH COSSETTE

ASJCF, 583; 856.16. *Bannissement des jésuites de la Louisiane, relation et lettres inédites*, Auguste Carayon, édit. (Paris, 1865). Rochemonteix, *Les jésuites et la N.-F. au XVIIIe siècle*, II, 217–18. T.-M. Charland, "La mission de John Carroll au Canada en 1776 et l'interdit du P. Floquet," SCHÉC *Rapport*, 1 (1933–34), 45–56. Têtu, "Le chapitre de la cathédrale," *BRH*, XVI, 37.

FONFAY, JEAN-BAPTISTE MORIN DE. *See* MORIN

FORK. *See* NISSOWAQUET

FORNEL, MARIE-ANNE. *See* BARBEL

FORTIER, MICHEL, navigator and merchant; b. 31 Aug. 1709 at Saint-Laurent, Île d'Orléans (Que.), eldest son of Michel Fortier and Angélique Manseau; m. 30 Sept. 1748 Marie-Anne Cureux, *dit* Saint-Germain, at Quebec; of their six children, one, Pierre-Michel, also became a merchant-trader; d. 29 March 1776 in Quebec.

The earliest known documents concerning Michel Fortier date back to 1743, when he signed an engagement with Guillaume ESTÈBE and his partners in the presence of notary Gilbert Boucault* de Godefus. His job at that time was to go to the post of Gros Mécatina on the Labrador coast as master of a ship, to hunt seals there and trade with the Indians. During each of the three years of this contract Fortier brought back 3,000 to 4,000 sealskins and 450 barrels of oil.

On 13 Oct. 1751 Governor La Jonquière [Taffanel*] and Intendant BIGOT granted him land with about two leagues' frontage on the Labrador coast, bounded by Pointe de Blanc-Sablon on the southwest and Pointe de la Forté or Grincedents on the northeast. He was authorized to engage in cod-fishing, seal-hunting, and trading with the Indians there for six years. In return he had to pay two beaver pelts or four *livres* annually. Fortier was not, however, able to enjoy free use of this grant, for François Martel* de Brouague, owner of Baie de Phélypeaux (Baie de Brador), disputed its territorial limits. The Canadian authorities then had to intervene to settle the dispute. Through an ordinance dated 15 May 1752, Bigot initially allowed Fortier to continue exploiting his grant in Baie de Sainte-Claire, but only for a year. Meanwhile Gabriel PELLEGRIN was to determine the exact boundaries of the two grants. While waiting for Pellegrin's geographical specifications, Fortier got the authorities to renew his fishing permit for 1753. But in the summer of 1754 Fortier, who had in fact established a post on the territory allocated to Martel de Brouague, had his grant revoked. He consequently lost all his hunting and fishing gear, except some 200 barrels of oil and about a hundred shallops, to the profit of Pierre Glemet and François-Joseph de VIENNE, the lessees of the concession of Baie de Phélypeaux.

For 20 years after this brief venture Michel Fortier's career is obscure, although he is known to have remained a merchant. In 1775, after Governor Guy Carleton* had proclaimed martial law in the province of Quebec, he was commissioned a militia captain, at 66 years of age. On 31 Dec. 1775, leading the 77 men of the 9th company of the *faubourg* Saint-Roch, he played his part in repulsing Brigadier-General Richard MONTGOMERY's attack on Quebec. Shortly afterwards, on 29 March 1776, Michel Fortier died; his burial in the crypt of Notre-Dame in Quebec suggests that he enjoyed a certain prestige in Quebec society.

MICHEL ROBERGE

ANQ-Q, Greffe de Claude Barolet, 29 sept. 1748; Greffe de Gilbert Boucault de Godefus, 18 sept. 1743; Greffe de J.-C. Panet, 15 mars 1753; NF 2, 40, ff.31, 44, 91, 103. *Inv. de pièces du Labrador* (P.-G. Roy). "La milice canadienne-française à Québec en 1775," *BRH*, XI (1905), 227, 261. P.-V. Charland, "Notre-Dame de

Québec: le nécrologe de la crypte," *BRH*, XX, 241. P.-G. Roy, *Inv. coll. pièces jud. et not.*; *Inv. contrats de mariage*; *Inv. ord. int.* Tanguay, *Dictionnaire*. "La chasse des loups-marins autrefois," *BRH*, XXIV (1928), 734.

FOUREUR (or **Le Fourreur**), *dit* **Champagne, LOUIS**, cabinet-maker, wood-carver, and clock-maker; b. 2 June 1720 in Montreal (Que.), son of Pierre Foureur, a blacksmith and locksmith, and Anne-Céleste Desforges; m. 9 Nov. 1744 Catherine Guertin in Montreal; d. there 16 April 1789.

Louis Foureur may have learned the trade of cabinet-maker and wood-carver under the guidance of François Filiau, *dit* Dubois, since the two men knew each other well. Filiau was at Foureur's wedding and the following year was godfather to his eldest son. Little is known about Foureur's career as a wood-carver. He took on at least six apprentices, the first in 1744 for a period of four years, the last in 1775 for six years. In 1757 he made six wooden candlesticks for the church of Sainte-Geneviève (Pierrefonds), and in 1760 he received money for the retable and tabernacle of the Chapelle du Père Éternel in the Hôpital Général of Montreal. Two years earlier he had signed a contract with mason and stone-cutter François Périnneau, *dit* Lamarche, for the stonework of a chapel in the Recollet church in Montreal. Work was to begin in April 1759, and it is probable that Louis Foureur had made the plans for the chapel since the contract refers to him as "architect."

Even less is known about Louis Foureur's career after the conquest, and care must be taken not to confuse it with that of his son Jean-Louis*, who was also a cabinet-maker and wood-carver and who used the signature and name of Louis Foureur. From 1760 on the senior Foureur may have been responsible for the maintenance of the organ in Notre-Dame, Montreal, a task subsequently carried out by his son. His work as a clockmaker is known thanks to an article published in 1813 in the Montreal weekly *Le Spectateur* and devoted to Foureur and another Montreal clockmaker, Jean-Baptiste Filiau, *dit* Dubois, the brother of François. Described as "an amiable man" known for "his wit and the liveliness of his conversation," whose entire education consisted of "having learned to read and write in his youth," Foureur is said to have been a friend of the Sulpician Gabriel-Jean BRASSIER, who supposedly often extolled to him the superiority of Europeans over Canadians in the fine arts. Using a clock imported from Europe as an example, Brassier is said to have asked Foureur "if a Canadian workman would be capable of contemplating the execution of such a work." The story goes that Foureur, having taken up the challenge by studying clockmaking in secret and by making an excellent clock, continued to make clocks until his death.

Louis Foureur spent his entire life in Montreal. At first a tenant in a merchant's house on Rue Notre-Dame, in 1747 he had a single-storey stone house built on that street and lived in it until his death. Being rather well-off, he owned two other houses with the land they stood on, one on Rue Notre-Dame and the other on Rue Saint-Jacques, as well as a large piece of land on the Côte Saint-Louis. After 1776 Foureur and his wife began to sell their property, the last transaction being in 1784, the year in which they drew up their will. Their seven children included, besides Jean-Louis, Pierre, a silversmith, and Charlotte, who married Dominique Rousseau*, a silversmith and fur-trader.

JOHN R. PORTER

ANQ-M, Doc. jud., Registres des audiences pour la juridiction de Montréal, 28B, f.83v; État civil, Catholiques, Notre-Dame de Montréal, 2 juin 1720, 9 nov. 1744, 23 août 1745, 23 août 1756, 18 avril 1789; Greffe de L.-C. Danré de Blanzy, 24, 25 mai 1745, 12 mai 1752, 24 avril 1759; Greffe de Jean Delisle, 4 avril 1771, 17 oct. 1774, 10 mars, 17 juin 1779, 20 janv., 12 juin 1780; Greffe de J.-B. Desève, 12 mars 1791; Greffe d'Antoine Foucher, 15 janv. 1755, 15 janv. 1775, 28 janv. 1776; Greffe de P.-F. Mézière, 15 août, 4 nov. 1767, 29 janv. 1776, 24 avril 1781, 31 juill., 6 nov. 1784; Greffe de François Simonnet, 14 sept., 8 nov. 1744, 20 févr. 1746, 10 avril 1747, 29 juin 1750, 22 févr. 1753, 2 nov. 1758, 15 avril 1763. IBC, Centre de documentation, Fonds Morisset, Dossier Louis Foureur, dit Champagne. [F.-M.] Bibaud, *Dictionnaire historique des hommes illustres du Canada et de l'Amérique* (Montréal, 1857). Tanguay, *Dictionnaire*. Émile Falardeau, *Artistes et artisans du Canada* (5 sér., Montréal, 1940–46), 5e sér., 59–60, 67–71. Morisset, *Coup d'œil sur les arts*, 18, 34. "Arts libéraux et mécaniques," *La Bibliothèque canadienne, ou miscellanées historiques, scientifiques, et littéraires* (Montréal), I (1825), 174–78. "Communication," *Le Spectateur* (Montréal), 16 sept. 1813, 65–66. O.[-M.-H.] Lapalice, "Les organistes et maîtres de musique à Notre-Dame de Montréal," *BRH*, XXV (1919), 245.

FRANCKLIN (Franklin), MICHAEL, merchant, office-holder, colonial administrator, and Indian agent; b. 6 Dec. 1733 at Poole, England, second son of Michael Francklin and Edith Nicholson; m. 7 Feb. 1762 Susannah Boutineau in Boston, Massachusetts, and they had at least four children; d. 8 Nov. 1782 at Halifax, Nova Scotia.

In the years prior to the American revolution

Halifax was dominated by a merchant élite. Michael Francklin was a member of this group of merchant-politicians; involved in the major events of the period, he provides an excellent case study of how private and public goals were melded by these men.

Any influential figure, particularly one with a strong personality, is bound to be controversial, and Francklin was no exception. In his own time he attracted ardent supporters and no less committed enemies. A similar phenomenon has occurred among historians. He has been labelled "pompous and arrogant" and "incompetent" by those who have not approved of his role in provincial affairs, while one of his defenders has described him as "a man of great personal magnetism combined with courage, integrity, energy, and independence." Perhaps the most common view comes from the most respected chronicler of 18th-century Nova Scotia, John Bartlet Brebner*, who saw him as a "puppet" almost completely under the control of Joshua MAUGER. Such a characterization is misleading, however, for although Francklin acted in concert with Mauger when his interests so compelled him, on other occasions he exasperated and infuriated Mauger and his followers.

As the fourth child and second son, Francklin had little prospect of advancement in early life through parental aid. His father was able to provide contacts with relatives in London, however, and Francklin made a brief but abortive attempt to establish himself in the business world there. Before reaching age 18, he had made two trips to the new world, visiting Jamaica and assessing its mercantile prospects. Evidently he did not find them bright, for in the summer of 1752 he booked passage for Halifax on the *Norfolk*.

At the time of Francklin's arrival the leading merchant in Halifax was probably Joshua Mauger. Early in his career Mauger had been associated with Francklin's relatives, perhaps even with his father. It is possible that Francklin emigrated at Mauger's suggestion, and it is certain that the older man sponsored Francklin's first Halifax enterprise, a dram-shop on George Street. Business was obviously successful, for Francklin soon opened a second establishment in partnership with Thomas Gray.

Although many merchants failed during the highly unstable times of the mid 1750s, Francklin's business concerns, now diversified to include trading and retailing in general merchandise, boomed. In 1755 he returned to England briefly to recruit promising young men for future mercantile ventures. The Seven Years' War proved to be a financial windfall for Francklin. He secured several lucrative contracts to provision the British forces at Halifax and later at Quebec. Problems of wartime supply led to scarcities which increased both prices and profits, particularly in rum and fish. Investments in privateering brought him additional income. It is difficult to estimate precisely how much money he made during the war, but he certainly became an exceedingly wealthy man. His connections with Mauger, who had moved to London in 1760, gave him excellent access to the British market, while his marriage to the granddaughter of Peter Faneuil, one of the most important Boston merchants, cemented his business relations with New England. As a result, in 1766 a resident of Halifax described him as "the first Merchant in the Place."

Francklin, Jonathan Binney*, John BUTLER, Richard Codman, and John Anderson became the nucleus of a group which formed around Mauger in the 1750s. Building on their close personal and mercantile connections and financed chiefly by Mauger and Brook Watson* in London, they came to dominate Halifax trade almost totally by the mid 1760s. This mercantile élite recognized the potential of government connections to assist private enterprise. The advantages of a close relationship between men of business and the government were well known; politics in Britain was largely based on the principle that influential men should be attached to the government to increase its stability. There were, however, obvious disadvantages to this system. The interconnection of business and government meant that a potential source of political criticism was muted. Moreover, the merchant-politicians in Halifax tended to pass laws which benefited business but did little for other groups.

Francklin's involvement in politics began in 1759, when he was elected to the House of Assembly to fill one of the first two seats for Lunenburg Township; in 1761–62 he served as a member for Halifax County. A promising young man, he was appointed to important committees. Few were surprised, therefore, when in May 1762 he was appointed to the Council, becoming its youngest member. He soon became identified with a faction opposing Lieutenant Governor Jonathan BELCHER whose members included Joseph GERRISH and Charles MORRIS in the Council and Benjamin GERRISH and Malachy SALTER in the assembly.

On the surface, Francklin's motives for joining this faction seem clear. The mercantile leaders of Halifax opposed Belcher partly because of his efforts to control illegal trade, a profitable enterprise for many, including Francklin. In addition, the lieutenant governor showed no inclination to grant Francklin's almost constant petitions for land. Francklin was also peeved over Belcher's refusal to grant him the monopoly of the Indian trade. The Council had approved his application in 1761, but Belcher denied it after evidence was produced that the application was fraudulent in several respects. In London, meanwhile, Mauger had conceived a special dislike for Belcher and was actively lobbying with the Board of Trade for his removal. By linking Mauger's interests with his own, Francklin was consolidating his association with the Mauger group, an association which continued until the American revolution.

Through the influence of Mauger, Francklin secured the post of lieutenant governor in March 1766. Since his mandamus did not reach Nova Scotia until 22 August, however, the treasurer, Benjamin GREEN, became administrator on the death of Governor Montagu Wilmot* in May. Francklin served as acting governor for three months until the arrival of Lord William CAMPBELL. Because of Campbell's frequent absences, he held the reins of government on three other occasions, from 1 Oct. 1767 to 10 Sept. 1768, from 4 Nov. to 4 Dec. 1768, and from 2 June to 10 July 1772.

During his periods in power Francklin aroused considerable controversy. In 1766 he revived a project to mine coal for export in Cape Breton, banned eight years earlier by the Board of Trade, by simply assuming that the ban no longer existed. When it was discovered that he had not only exceeded his authority but given the licence to mine and export coal to Benjamin Gerrish and other business associates, protests arose from unhappy competitors, forcing the board in February 1768 to order that the "highly irregular" contract not be renewed. Similarly, in 1768, on the basis of ambiguous instructions from London, Francklin expended the entire Nova Scotia contingency fund on the establishment of townships and of government offices on St John's (Prince Edward) Island and attempted to grant property to his land-hungry friends. Although his actions were probably not deliberate attempts to circumvent the will of the British government, they demonstrate again the tendency to equate private and public goals. Francklin found his proceedings "highly disapproved" by the king and was forced to travel to England to clear his name.

The uproar needs to be put in its proper perspective. Colonial governors frequently exceeded their authority; in fact, every governor of Nova Scotia before Francklin had at some point been chastised by the Board of Trade for so doing. The practice of combining politics with profit was also common, particularly in colonies as poor as Nova Scotia, where governmental largesse assumed great importance. More virtuous citizens, or those with insufficient connections to take advantage of the spoils of office, might decry such occurrences, but generally only minor note was taken of them in Britain and Nova Scotia.

The merchant community generally retained its confidence in Francklin, but by the early 1770s his political opponents were becoming increasingly shrill. In 1774 Richard GIBBONS revived charges that Francklin "and others connected with him" had provided "an unreasonable credit" to the settlers at Lunenburg during the 1750s. When these debt-ridden settlers could not repay their loans, Francklin "consented to take their [bounty] certificates [awarded for local improvements] in Discharge of their Debts . . . at Sixty per Cent discount." Gibbons also charged that Francklin was "immediately dependant and other wise closely connected with" Mauger and that he had used his "Influence and that of his Party" to impoverish Nova Scotia. Although Francklin may have been guilty of usury, Gibbons missed the mark in intimating that he was Mauger's puppet. In the 1750s, eager to rise and greatly dependent on Mauger's patronage, Francklin seldom deviated from the lead set by the more powerful merchant. But after his appointment as lieutenant governor he pursued his own interests without Mauger's sanction. The attempts to exploit St John's Island, for example, were disapproved of by Mauger and embarrassed him when he was called upon to defend them before the Board of Trade. Also, in the early 1770s Francklin became involved in colonization schemes in which Mauger did not figure. By the time of Governor Francis LEGGE's administration Francklin and Mauger once again seemed to be pursuing similar goals. Their motives, however, were not identical. Francklin opposed Legge not only because of instructions from Mauger but also because the governor, by showing a preference for other advisers, notably James Monk*, was challenging the source of his power.

Despite charges that he was reaping fantastic monetary rewards, on the eve of the American revolution Francklin suffered acute shortages of cash. Part of the problem was the usual shortage of specie in America, but Francklin's difficulties also stemmed from his penchant for investing virtually every shilling in land. Although he had accumulated thousands of acres and was widely regarded as one of the richest men in the province, by 1774 he owed the crown "above five hundred pounds Sterling" in quitrents. In order to make his idle land productive, he seized upon a scheme to import settlers from overseas. Yorkshire quickly became his favourite source, and before the revolution impeded the flow, over 1,000 people had emigrated to become tenants on his lands. The cessation of immigration placed him in a precarious financial situation, and John Butler advised Mauger to write off Francklin's debts, observing "He owes a very considerable Sum here." According to Legge, Francklin was reduced "from being an opulant Merchant to distress."

Still, Francklin remained an influential man, and his position as a leader of the anti-Legge forces during the protracted controversy surrounding the governor's administration may have coloured Legge's view of his financial difficulties. Relations between the two men reached such an impasse that Legge recommended to Lord Dartmouth, secretary of state for the American Colonies, that Francklin be stripped of his office or transferred from the colony. Although the claim that Francklin was the first to plan the governor's demise is sheer speculation, his role in Legge's recall was undeniably crucial. He had both the political resources and the motive to challenge Legge, and in his exploitation of the incidents surrounding his old business partner Binney he effectively capitalized on Legge's ineptness. In the spring of 1776, however, after Legge's recall to England, Francklin was replaced as lieutenant governor by Mariot ARBUTHNOT. His removal, combined with the governor's recall, seems to have been an attempt by the Board of Trade to lessen controversy in Nova Scotia politics at a time of crisis.

During the American revolution Francklin remained loyal to the crown. Unlike most merchants, however, he was not passive in his loyalty. In 1777 he was appointed superintendent of Indian affairs for the province, a position for which he was uniquely qualified. In 1754 he had been captured by a band of Micmacs and taken to the Gaspé. During his three months of captivity he learned their language and developed a respect for the Indian culture. Although he had varying luck throughout the war ensuring the adherence of the Micmacs and Malecites to the British cause, he was ultimately successful. Through a series of meetings, the judicious distribution of gifts, and the provision of the services of a missionary [*see* Joseph-Mathurin BOURG], he countered the efforts of John Allan* and other supporters of the Americans [*see* Pierre TOMAH; Gilfred STUDHOLME]. Characteristically, Francklin had refused to serve as superintendent until he was granted a fixed salary and provisions were made for his expenses.

Francklin, who spoke French, was also influential among the Acadians. As lieutenant governor he had allowed those who had returned following the expulsion to settle around Minas Basin on terms far more generous than the Council had recommended. In addition, he permitted the unrestricted practice of the Roman Catholic religion and gave guarantees that there would not be a second deportation. Francklin was not specifically empowered to give these guarantees, but he managed to convince the Board of Trade that his policies were wise, and they were eventually ratified by that body. It is impossible to ascertain how many Acadians returned, but a 1771 census counted 1,249 persons in 274 families throughout the province.

Francklin survived the hostilities of the American revolution, but he did not live to see the peace. On 8 Nov. 1782 he died at his town home in Halifax. An age was drawing to a close. The old Nova Scotia, dominated by a Halifax-based mercantile élite, was being transformed by the influx of thousands of loyalists; the distinctive community that Francklin had done so much to shape was being dramatically altered.

If historians have been unable to reach a consensus about Michael Francklin, it is perhaps because they have failed to grasp the role that he played. He was in many ways a typical colonial merchant-politician, meshing private and public concerns in an age when such intermingling was widely accepted. It is therefore in terms of the success that he had in helping to build the foundations for Nova Scotia that he must be evaluated, not in terms of 20th-century morality superimposed on an earlier age. In these terms, Francklin must be considered one of the truly important founders of the province.

L. R. FISCHER

PAC, MG 11, [CO 217], Nova Scotia A, 72; 77, p.59; 78, p.41; 81, pp.125, 129; 83, p.127; 88–93; [CO 220], Nova Scotia B, 14; MG 23, A1, ser.1, 2, no.1119; 13, nos.2494, 2496. PANS, RG 1, 136, p.114; 187, 16 March, 11 April 1754; 188, 26 March, 10 April, 15 May 1761, 3 May 1762, 25 July, 13 Nov. 1764; 189, 23 Aug. 1766. PRO, CO 217/19, f.130; 217/20, f.65; 217/45, f.7. *Nova Scotia Chronicle and Weekly Advertiser* (Halifax), 14 Nov. 1769. *Nova-Scotia Gazette and the Weekly Chronicle* (Halifax), 16 Nov. 1782. *Directory of N.S. MLAs*, 126–27. Brebner, *Neutral Yankees*. G. A. Rawlyk, *Nova Scotia's Massachusetts: a study of Massachusetts–Nova Scotia relations, 1630 to 1784* (Montreal and London, 1973), 234. W. B. Kerr, "The rise of Michael Francklin," *Dal. Rev.*, XIII (1933–34), 489–95. J. S. Macdonald, "Memoir, Lieut.-Governor

Michael Francklin, 1752–1782," N.S. Hist. Soc., *Coll.*, XVI (1912), 7–40.

FRASER, ALEXANDER, army officer and seigneur; b. *c.* 1729 in Scotland; m. *c.* 1765 Jane McCord; d. 19 April 1799 at Saint-Charles, near Quebec.

Untangling the several Alexander Frasers who served with the 78th Foot in the campaigns of the Seven Years' War has been a perennial problem. The subject of this biography, who appears to have come from a good Highland family, entered the 78th as an ensign and was promoted lieutenant on 12 Feb. 1757. He participated in the captures of Louisbourg, Île Royale (Cape Breton Island), and Quebec, and he was wounded in 1760, possibly at the battle of Sainte-Foy [*see* LÉVIS]. Fraser remained in Canada after his regiment was disbanded and in August 1763 he purchased from Governor James MURRAY the seigneury of La Martinière, near Quebec. He added the adjoining seigneury of Vitré in 1775 and that of Saint-Gilles, approximately 20 miles above Quebec, in 1782.

With the outbreak of the American revolution Fraser returned to military service; he was commissioned captain in the Royal Highland Emigrants on 14 June 1775 [*see* Allan MACLEAN]. Along with other officers of this regiment he was commended by Governor Sir Guy Carleton* in 1777 for his "indefatigable zeal and good conduct" during the American siege of Quebec in the winter of 1775 [*see* Richard MONTGOMERY]. There was more behind this commendation than good service, however. Fraser and his fellow officers had assumed that their regiment would be placed on the regular establishment so that when it was reduced they would enjoy their rank and half pay. Their assumption proved wrong, and they had "the Mortification to find themselves now obliged to serve in a provincial Regiment and to do duty in a manner very disagreeable to them as their Rank is not ascertained in the Army." Carleton sympathized with their plight, praised their contribution, and urged that their regiment be established or the officers placed in regular regiments. In Alexander Fraser's case, nothing came of this recommendation. Instead, he was assigned as a captain to the militia stationed at Saint-Jean on the Richelieu and "Constantly did duty" from some time in 1777 until April 1778. Service with the militia was not common practice for regular officers, but because Fraser belonged to a provincial regiment, which did not have the rights and privileges of regular regiments, his transfer to the militia would not have been regarded by the authorities as unusual or demeaning.

In August 1778, claming that he had "No other friens to apply to," he begged Governor HALDIMAND for "some small Provision" and hinted at a pension, while maintaining that he remained ready to serve in "any Garrison of foot." In May 1779 Major John Nairne*, his friend and superior officer, urged that Fraser be allowed to retire since the state of his health rendered him "totally unfit for further service." Nairne emphasized that only his shattered health had caused Fraser to make such a request. No doubt the frustration caused by the indifference shown to his various complaints had also helped. Fraser probably left the regiment the same year; ironically, in April 1779 the British government had approved the inclusion of the Royal Highland Emigrants into the regular army, as the 84th Foot.

Fraser's private life was as disappointing as his Revolutionary War service. His wife died in 1767, and he was left to raise their two infant daughters, Jane and Margaret. Jane died a few years after her own marriage and her son Walter Davidson*, born in 1790, became the only male heir to the Fraser seigneurial holdings. In June 1791, when his grandson was ten months old, Fraser gave him title to the Saint-Gilles seigneury, where he had granted land to 15 German veterans in 1783. Fraser successfully sought further grants in the 1790s, at times using his former military service as justification. He died at Saint-Charles on 19 April 1799 and was buried at Quebec on the 22nd.

W.G. GODFREY

ANQ-Q, Greffe de J.-A. Panet, 18 sept. 1782; Greffe de J.-C. Panet, 2 août 1763; Greffe de J.-A. Saillant, 28 mars 1775. PAC, MG 11, [CO42], Q, 61/2, pp.265, 270; MG 23, GIII, 11; MG 24, B1, 25, pp.13–53; RG 1, L3, 1, pp.207, 212; 12, pp.3694, 3702; 87, pp.42899, 42905. Wallace, *Macmillan dictionary*, 244. Arthur Caux, "Notes sur les seigneurs de Beaurivage," *BRH*, LV (1949), 155–61. W. S. Wallace, "Alexander Fraser of Beauchamp," *BRH*, XLIII (1937), 176–79; "Some notes on Fraser's Highlanders," *CHR*, XVIII (1937), 131–40.

FROBISHER, BENJAMIN, fur-trader; b. *c.* 1742, probably in Halifax, England, son of Joseph Frobisher and Rachel Hargrave; d. 14 April 1787 in Montreal (Que.).

Benjamin Frobisher apparently immigrated to Canada with his brother Joseph* around 1763, and their brother Thomas joined them about 1769. The lives of all three became linked with the fur trade and its expansion into the northwest. They developed this orientation at a time when most fur-traders were based at Niagara, Detroit, or Michilimackinac (Mackinaw City, Mich.) and traded actively in the Illinois country. The brothers' initial investments, between 1764 and 1768, took them into the Lake Superior region. They were traders who would in time reach top rank and who acted both in concert and apart, and like many others they sought partnerships to share the risks of their ventures. They joined forces financially from time to time with such men as James McGill*, Isaac Todd*, Richard Dobie*, Charles Paterson, and Thomas Corry, and they did not hesitate to go security for other fur-traders, whether French or English speaking. The same complexity of relationships existed in the expeditions themselves: thus in 1765 Benjamin Frobisher was John Welles's partner; then in 1769, when the Frobisher brothers decided to extend their trade beyond Lake Superior, they took part with Richard Dobie in a small venture of one canoe, eight crew, and goods worth £500. Although on this occasion the expedition was stopped by the Indians at Rainy Lake, the brothers made a fresh attempt the following year, still in partnership with Dobie, and the expedition went well beyond Fort Bourbon, at the mouth of the Saskatchewan River, with three canoes, 18 men, and goods worth £1,200.

A division of labour was soon established among the Frobisher brothers; any business that was to expand could not depend on one man both to organize and to lead trading ventures. Within the enterprise, which was largely a family one, Benjamin was the organizer and administrator. He managed the business in general, dealt with importers and suppliers in England, and saw to financing and to the hiring of personnel, who, he noted one year, live "in the parish of Laprairie and are farmers by occupation." From 1771 on he seems to have been in partnership solely with his brothers, who undertook to work in the field. In 1772, with six canoes and 45 men, they apparently reached the Red River and the following year they got to the Saskatchewan. Two years later Benjamin organized an expedition of four canoes and 30 men.

There was intense competition among traders in the 1770s, whether they were on their own or in small partnerships. This rivalry caused numerous problems: it increased costs and stimulated territorial expansion which in turn caused fresh expenses and resulted in decreasing profits. The American revolution occasioned a scarcity of trade goods and set off an inflation that threatened the existence of small enterprises. In 1775 the Frobishers had joined with James McGill and Maurice-Régis Blondeau* in outfitting 12 canoes and a crew of about 103. They reached Grand Portage (near Grand Portage, Minn.) and afterwards formed a coalition with others to exploit the resources of the northwest. Benjamin and Joseph later explained: "Taught . . . by experience that separate Interests were the Bane of that Trade, we lost no time to form . . . a Company." In connection with the event Matthew COCKING, the Hudson's Bay Company's master at Cumberland House (Sask.), noted in his journal after a visit by Joseph Frobisher and Alexander Henry* the elder: "French Laws having been established in Canada last April [1775] they suspect the Pedling Business will be confined to few hands as in the French time and consequently that the present Quantities of Furrs Yearly carried down will be much deminished tho' the Profitts accruing will be much greater in proportion." Whether this forerunner of the North West Company survived more than one season is not known. The tendency towards combination was nevertheless established, and the war helped to reinforce it.

In 1779 the Frobishers set up a company with Charles Paterson and outfitted a large expedition. This company owned two of the 16 shares in the North West Company established that year, whose total investment comprised a flotilla of 43 canoes, 367 men, and merchandise worth £20,920. In 1781 Isaac Todd and James McGill replaced Paterson as partners in the Frobishers' enterprise. The years 1781–84 seem to have been difficult for the brothers because competition remained keen in the northwest. New agreements made by the partners of the NWC in 1783 suggest both a change in personnel and a reinforcement of the Frobishers' position, as well as that of Simon McTavish*. The partners were conscious of the dangers posed by Britain's surrender of the posts in the Great Lakes region to the Americans by the treaty of Versailles (1783). Worried that Americans might seize possession of their trade and harvest the fruits of their labours, they sent Edward UMFREVILLE and Venance Lemaire, *dit* Saint-Germain, to search out a new route between Lake Superior and Lake Winnipeg through British territory. The Frobishers even went so far as to ask Governor HALDIMAND on 4 Oct. 1784 to grant the NWC a monopoly of the fur trade in the northwest. They met with a refusal.

From 1783 on, the Frobishers significantly increased their investments. In 1785–86 they fitted out 55 canoes and six bateaux, hired crews totalling 585 men, and invested £46,000. Through the securities they made available, they seem at that time to have put money indirectly into the fur trade over the whole northwest; for example, with James McGill they put up security in 1785 for 31 canoes, 64 bateaux, and 568 men, covering investments of about £41,300.

Benjamin Frobisher died on 14 April 1787, just when the northwest was beginning to gain ascendancy in the fur trade and when the NWC was on the point of acquiring a virtual monopoly in that region. He had sensed that the future of the fur trade would be in the northwest and had concentrated his efforts there. He took an understandable pride in his accomplishments; in a letter of 1784 to Adam MABANE he placed himself among those "animated with that spirit natural to men who can Boast of having brought . . . [the fur trade] to its present Value & Extent." He nevertheless left an estate in some confusion, with greater debts than assets. After it had been wound up, his brother Joseph, who carried on the enterprise, assumed responsibility for his debts.

FERNAND OUELLET

PAC, RG 4, B28, 110–15. *Docs. relating to NWC* (Wallace). F.-J. Audet, *Les députés de Montréal (ville et comtés), 1792–1867* (Montréal, 1943). Davidson, *NWC*, 1–50. W. S. Dunn, "Western commerce, 1760–1774" (unpublished PHD thesis, University of Wisconsin, Madison, 1971). Innis, *Fur trade in Canada* (1962), 166–233. W. S. Wallace, *The pedlars from Quebec and other papers on the Nor-Westers* (Toronto, 1954).

G

GAGE, THOMAS, army officer and colonial administrator; b. 1719 or 1720, the second son of Thomas Gage, 1st Viscount Gage in the Irish peerage, and his first wife, Benedicta Maria Theresa Hall; d. 2 April 1787 in London, England.

The Gages of Firle in Sussex were an old Catholic family. Thomas Gage's parents found it expedient to convert to the Church of England in 1715, but though they resumed the old faith before their deaths, their son was raised and remained an Anglican. He attended Westminster School in London and subsequently entered military service; by 1743 he was a captain in the 62nd Foot. In 1745 he was aide-de-camp to the Earl of Albemarle at Fontenoy (Belgium), fought at Culloden the next year, and in 1747–48 was again aide-de-camp to Albemarle in Flanders. He was stationed in Ireland from 1748 to 1755 with the 44th Foot, becoming its lieutenant-colonel by purchase on 2 March 1750/51.

Gage's career to this point had been of no particular distinction. When Major-General Edward Braddock was sent to America in 1755 with the 44th and 48th Foot to halt French advances in the Ohio country, James Wolfe* observed a little condescendingly that "My honest friend Gage is to be of the Ohio party." Gage's part in the disaster that overtook Braddock's force near the forks of the Ohio on 9 July aroused some controversy, it being claimed that as commander of the advance party he should have stopped the rout of the head of the column, which caused the disorganization of the main force. Gage displayed personal bravery in the encounter; one witness (possibly Gabriel CHRISTIE) stated that he "distinguish'd himself by Encouraging the men as much as he Could and after they were broke, in rallying them." It is equally clear that he failed to take possession of the high ground from which the French and Indians launched their attack, perhaps because, as he later claimed, he lacked irregular forces.

In his subsequent career in America, Gage earned a reputation as a sound officer and an effective administrator. In 1757 Lord Loudoun, then commander-in-chief, thought the 44th one of his two best regiments because Gage "keeps up Discipline Strictly; the Regt is in Rags but look like Soldiers." Gage saw little active service under Loudoun, although he did accompany him to Halifax, Nova Scotia, on the "cabbage planting expedition" of 1757, when plans to attack Louisbourg, Île Royale (Cape Breton Island), went awry. Gage was convinced that Braddock would not have been defeated had he possessed regular troops trained for forest war and in December 1757, taking advantage of Loudoun's displeasure with the conduct of Robert ROGERS' ranger companies, he proposed to raise a regular regiment of light troops, provided the government met the costs and appointed him its colonel. The regiment so raised was the 80th, the first in the British army to be trained in both regular and irregular tactics. In 1758 it served in ABERCROMBY's assault upon Fort Carillon (Ticonderoga, N.Y.), where Gage, second in command after the death of Viscount Howe (George Augustus Howe), was slightly wounded. He had recruited the regiment in New Jersey, and found a wife there as well. On 8 Dec. 1758 he married Margaret, the daughter of Peter Kemble, a wealthy New Jersey merchant and politician, and Gertrude Bayard, who was connected with the important Schuyler, De Lancey, and Van Cortlandt families of New York. Five daughters and six sons were to be born to the couple. By the time of his marriage Gage had become a brigadier-general in America.

In July 1759 Gage got his first independent command. AMHERST ordered him to take the French post at La Galette (near Ogdensburg, N.Y.) to help Wolfe's siege of Quebec and to "make a frontier" along with Crown Point (N.Y.), Oswego, and Niagara (near Youngstown) in case Wolfe was defeated. Before he reached Oswego to take over from Sir William JOHNSON, Amherst further directed him to advance toward Montreal after capturing La Galette. Gage's subsequent conduct disclosed his shortcomings as a commander. Doubts assailed him even as he reached Oswego; he told Johnson that he did not believe in "running his head against a wall, or attempting impossibilities." Rather than viewing his command as a chance to achieve strategic results by applying pressure from the west, he saw only problems. The Oswego defences needed strengthening, supplies were short, French vessels controlled the St Lawrence, and La Galette, if taken, would prove vulnerable to counter-attack during the winter. In a "long discourse" with Johnson on 6 September, he argued that Amherst had left his assistance to Wolfe too late, and that unless a concerted movement was made upon Montreal, "an expedition this way would be of no service." Four days later he wrote to Amherst informing him of his decision not to attack the French post or move on Montreal. But Johnson's scouts inconveniently reported La Galette to be lightly held, and Gage thereupon consulted his senior officers. Finding them divided, he decided to stick to his original decision. A furious Amherst upbraided Gage for missing a great opportunity, charging that he and his officers had "found out difficulties where there are none." This criticism was not altogether fair, but certainly Gage's chief virtues as a soldier were caution and a diligent attention to details, not boldness and the urge to battle. Where another man might have seen a golden opportunity to end the war in 1759, he saw only obstacles. It is noteworthy that when Amherst took Montreal in 1760, Gage commanded the rear-guard.

Despite their differences, Amherst respected Gage's administrative capacities and in September 1760 appointed him military governor of Montreal, along with Ralph Burton* at Trois-Rivières; James MURRAY was already military governor at Quebec. Gage was the senior officer of the three, and in 1761 was promoted major-general, but he never claimed authority over the others, and indeed referred to the military governors collectively as "the Three Kings." Characteristically, he thought of himself "in no other light, than as a Military Governor," appointed by Amherst, responsible only to him, and under his orders and direction. Thus in May 1763, when the Board of Trade sent him a series of questions about Canada, he told Amherst that since "I know of no general Governor thereof (but yourself as Commander in Chief)," he had sent duplicates of the questionnaire to Murray and Burton.

There is no full account of Gage as military governor of Montreal, although his biographer John Alden has a short chapter on the subject and brief references are to be found in Alfred Leroy Burt*, *The old province of Quebec* (2v., Toronto and Minneapolis, Minn., 1933; repr. Toronto, 1968), and in Hilda Neatby*, *Quebec: the revolutionary age, 1760–1791* (Toronto, 1966). That the three governments were separate jurisdictions and their governors responsible to Amherst seems either to have been missed or to have been treated perfunctorily by most historians. Burt was certainly aware of the situation, and indeed draws attention to Gage's distinctive policy with respect to the administration of justice, while Neatby mentions specific actions taken by Gage within his jurisdiction. But quite naturally their attention, and that of other historians, focussed on Murray, since he was governor of Quebec, the capital of the colony and its traditional centre. Gage's work at Montreal merits more attention than it can be given here, in part because of his special responsibility for the fur trade and the interior.

Since Amherst chose never to intervene significantly in the administration of Canada, the three governors were virtually supreme within their territories, and since they consulted one another infrequently, their administrations in some respects took different paths. It is true that Murray and Burton came to Montreal in early 1762 to discuss, among other things, the danger of famine in the District of Quebec, and also that during the period when Frederick HALDIMAND replaced Burton at Trois-Rivières, Gage had some influence on him, as their correspondence shows. Since there was so little interchange among the governors it was scarcely surprising that Gage should note, "I don't find, in many Particulars, that we have all acted alike." Nevertheless, there were no radical divergences;

for the most part Gage, like his colleagues, was content to discover and apply the laws and customs of New France. Thus he enforced the king's right to feudal dues upon the sale or transfer of seigneuries and obliged all new seigneurs "to do Homage for their Manors, according to Custom." On the whole he seems to have favoured the seigneurs in their disputes with tenants; he supported them in deciding against those to whom land had been conceded but who had failed to take occupancy, and in ruling that tenants must pay their dues in "current money" rather than in the discredited paper of the former régime. In his ordinances regulating such varied matters as snow removal, garbage disposal, and the maintenance of roads, bridges, and ferries he conformed to the traditional procedures of the intendancy. In the same vein were his ordinances against forestalling and coin-clipping, and his regulation of the prices of such necessities as bread and firewood, in the latter case because high prices were "to the great prejudice of the poor, and caused solely by the avidity of the owners."

In important respects Gage departed from previous practice. He made innovative use, for example, of the captains of militia in their judicial capacity. Instead of retaining the courts of individual captains, as Murray did, one of his first acts in Montreal was to constitute all the captains of the town as a single court, to meet weekly to "settle all disputes of private individuals." He found that this system worked well, telling Amherst that the captains had "acted with so much uprightness and Justice in their Decisions, as to gain great Reputation to themselves, & to ease me of a great deal of Trouble." As a result, in 1761 he extended the arrangement to the rest of his territory, in order to make justice "more prompt and easy and less expensive to those who are obliged to have recourse to it." Haldimand copied the system in Trois-Rivières, and in both governances it remained unchanged until the commencement of civil rule.

Gage was also innovative in his attitude toward trade. The French policy of granting monopolies for the interior fur trade was not "Worthy our Imitations," he thought, and in an ordinance of 1 April 1761 he declared that "the trade is free for everybody" though subject to a passport system. He believed that the interior trade should be controlled by restricting the number of posts and placing them under the surveillance of military detachments in order to prevent trouble with the Indians, a policy he was later to promote as commander in chief, in collaboration with Sir William Johnson. He was nevertheless generally sympathetic towards merchants, whether French or English, and feared what he termed the "heavy hand" of the Board of Trade. Unless the Board cramped Canada's trade, he thought the province would become a rich and flourishing one, attractive to people of property, and a place where "many branches of Trade will be struck out, which the French never thought of, or were prevented from pursuing." He was encouraged in 1762 when some of the Canadian merchants began to trade their furs on the London market.

While in Montreal Gage was regarded as an honest, fair, and conscientious administrator, a reputation he was to enjoy in the southern colonies as well. There is no reason to doubt his assertion that he had endeavoured to treat the Canadians with kindness and humanity, and had made it his business to protect them in their laws, religion, and property, despite the fact that his private feelings for some elements of the population were unfriendly. He cared little for the seigneurs, especially the officers among them; "the sooner these Croix de S^{t}. Louis, with the rest of the idle Noblesse, leave the Country, the better it will be for it." As for the priests, "those black Gentry," he distrusted them all as the hidden promoters of French influence.

By 1763 Gage was ready to give up his command and return to England; as he told Amherst, it was not that he was tired of America, but "very much of this cursed Climate, and I must be bribed very high to stay here any longer." He was. In October he left Montreal for New York, where he became acting commander-in-chief on Amherst's departure the next month. Confirmed in this appointment in 1764, he remained in it until his recall in 1775. His work in this post touched the northern colonies in many ways, not only with respect to their military establishments but also in such matters as Indian affairs. But his chief concerns were with the thirteen southern colonies, especially as politics there grew more turbulent.

Gage's advice to the home government on the situation in America was invariably cautious. Yet while on leave in England in 1774 he encouraged George III to believe that strong measures would curb the Americans, a point of view he had expressed in private letters for some years. Summarizing Gage's views, the king told Lord North, the prime minister, that Gage "says they will be Lyons, whilst we are Lambs but if we take the resolute part they will undoubtedly prove very meek." He returned to America in May 1774 with the additional post of governor of Massachusetts, and his early dispatches led the home government to believe that the crisis was passing. Subsequently, however, the situation worsened; Gage transferred the bulk of his forces to Boston, where they were to be effectually locked up; and during September and October gave such bleak accounts to Lord Dartmouth, secretary of state for the American Colonies, that he lost all credit at home. On receipt of Dartmouth's instructions "to take a more active & determined part," he ordered the seizure of rebel stores at Concord on 19 April 1775 that inaugurated hostilities in the revolutionary war.

Gage has been held responsible by a number of American historians for encouraging the use of Indians against the rebels. As early as 4 Sept. 1774, when withdrawing two regiments from Quebec to reinforce the Boston garrison, he asked Governor Guy Carleton* whether it would be possible to raise "a Body of Canadians and Indians" for service outside the province "should matters come to Extremities." He waited, however, until some Stockbridge Indians had been identified among the American forces investing Boston before telling Dartmouth, on 12 June 1775, that "we need not be tender of calling upon the Savages, as the Rebels have shewn us the Example." As his critics have suggested, this was something of a pretext; Gage himself admitted to Carleton that the Stockbridges were scarcely the formidable Indians of the frontiers but rather "what the French would call Domiciliés, and not of great worth." But Gage cannot be saddled with major responsibility for the Indian participation in the revolution. Indian peoples such as the Six Nations had good reason to enter the war, and it was inevitable that most Indian tribes would side with the British.

By mid 1775 Gage's days in America were numbered. In June Lord George Germain, the new secretary of state for the American Colonies, anticipated his removal when he observed that despite his good qualities, Gage was "in a situation of too great importance for his talents." Though a capable administrator, Gage had never shown high military abilities and indeed had lost the confidence of his troops and senior officers [*see* John BURGOYNE]. He was recalled in August, ostensibly for consultations, and sailed from Boston on 10 October. His only further military appointment was to command the defence forces of Kent in 1781. In 1782 he was made a full general.

Thomas Gage was a representative product of the 18th-century British army. His family and political connections, the system of purchase, and his own solid administrative abilities had helped him rise to positions of responsibility. His personal reputation as a fair-minded commander, a devoted family man, and an amiable and charming host remained unblemished. In Montreal all these qualities won him a reputation as a just and competent governor. As a soldier, however, his record in actual operations was not distinguished. Neither in the La Galette affair nor during the far more complex crisis in Boston in 1774–75 did he display the political and strategic grasp which those situations demanded.

S. F. WISE

[The volume of documents relating to Thomas Gage is immense. The largest collections are in the Clements Library, University of Michigan, and in the PRO, CO 5 series. Selections from these collections are printed in *Correspondence of General Thomas Gage* (Carter). Gage's correspondence with Amherst from 1758 to 1760 can be found in PAC, MG 11, which contains transcripts of CO 5/56–59, and his correspondence with Amherst during his governorship of Montreal in PAC, MG 13, which contains transcripts of PRO, WO 34/5. His correspondence with Frederick Haldimand from 1758 to 1763 is in PAC, MG 21, which contains transcripts of BL, Add. MSS 21661.

J. R. Alden, *General Gage in America; being principally a history of his role in the American revolution* (Baton Rouge, La., 1948), is a scholarly and sympathetic biography. Much less favourable are two studies by John Shy, *Toward Lexington*, and "Thomas Gage, weak link of empire," in *George Washington's opponents: British generals and admirals in the American revolution*, ed. G. A. Billias (New York, 1969). Short biographies are included in the *DAB* and the *DNB*.

Sources for particular episodes in Gage's career are as follows: for the Braddock expedition, *Military affairs in North America, 1748–65* (Pargellis) and *Correspondence of William Shirley* (Lincoln), II. Captain Robert Orme of Braddock's staff attributed the disaster to the collapse of Gage's advance party, and to "a manner of fighting" to which the troops were unused (*Correspondence of William Shirley*, II, 208). In response to an inquiry instituted by Shirley, the new commander-in-chief, Gage and Thomas Dunbar, the two regimental commanders, claimed that the morale of the troops was low, partly because of the influence of "the Provincial Troops and Country People," who had told them that "if they engaged the Indians in their European manner of fighting, they would be beat." They also drew attention to the shortage of light troops – only "three or four" scouts were in front of the column – and to "the Novelty of an invisible Enemy and the Nature of the Country, which was entirely a Forest" (*Correspondence of William Shirley*, II, 313). Shirley did not accept this response. He blamed Gage for failing to occupy the high ground and for losing control of the vanguard, but agreed that the French should be imitated in their use of screens of irregulars to protect regular forces. Alden (pp.24–27) argues that Gage lacked the requisite authority to occupy the high ground, while Shy (*Toward Lexington*) and L. H. Gipson (*The British empire before the American revolution* (15v., Caldwell, Idaho, and New York, 1936–70), VI, chap.4) take the view that he should have displayed more initiative. Contemporary descriptions of the action are found in *Military affairs*, 96–117. For Loudoun, *see* Pargellis, *Lord Loudoun*, 234, 299–305. Sir William Johnson's revealing account of Gage's hesitations in 1759 is in Knox, *Hist. journal* (Doughty), III, 187–232; *see also* Amherst, *Journal* (Webster).

There is no full account of Gage as military governor of Montreal, though brief references are in Burt, *Old prov. of Que.*, and Neatby, *Quebec*. Gage's ordinances as governor are printed in PAC *Report*, 1918, app.B, 21–77, and his "Report of the state of the Government of Montreal" of 20 March 1762 in *Docs. relating to constitutional history, 1759–91* (Shortt and Doughty; 1918), I, 91–95. Excerpts from his correspondence with Carleton in 1774–75 are in *ibid.*, II, 583–84, and 661–62.

Indictments of Gage for encouraging the use of the Indians can be found, in descending order of vehemence, in Allen French, *The first year of the American revolution* (Boston, 1934; repr. New York, 1968), 403–10; J. M. Sosin, "The use of Indians in the war of the American revolution: a re-assessment of responsibility," *CHR*, XLVI (1965), 101–21; and D. [R.] Higginbotham, *The war of American independence: military attitudes, policies, and practice, 1763–1789* (New York, 1971), 319–22. The inevitability of Indian participation is argued in S. F. Wise, "The American revolution and Indian history," *Character and circumstance: essays in honour of Donald Grant Creighton*, ed. J. S. Moir (Toronto, 1970), 182–200. S.F.W.]

GAIACHOTON. *See* KAYAHSOTA?

GALAUP, JEAN-FRANÇOIS DE, Comte de LAPÉROUSE, naval officer; b. 23 Aug. 1741 in the parish of Saint-Julien in Albi, France, son of Victor-Joseph de Galaup and Marguerite de Rességuier; m. 18 June 1783 Louise-Éléonore Broudou in Paris; they had no children; d. in June 1788, at Vanikoro, Santa Cruz Islands.

Jean-François de Galaup joined the navy as a midshipman at Brest on 19 Dec. 1756, and the following March sailed with the *Célèbre* in the squadron under Comte Dubois de La Motte [Cahideuc*] being sent to relieve Louisbourg, Île Royale (Cape Breton Island). He returned to Brest on 12 Nov. 1757, escaping the terrible epidemic that ravaged both the ships and the town. On 22 Feb. 1758 he joined the frigate *Zéphyr* in the squadron sent to Louisbourg under Comte Du Chaffault de Besné. On 15 August he was posted to the *Cerf*, and the following 16 May to the *Formidable*, a ship of the line in the squadron that the Comte de Conflans was with difficulty fitting out at Brest to protect a prospective landing in England. On 20 November, at the entrance to the Baie de Quiberon, this fleet of 21 ships encountered 23 vessels commanded by Edward Hawke. The *Formidable*, which was in the rear squadron, had to bear the brunt of the attack and put up admirable resistance. Twice wounded, Lapérouse was taken prisoner but was almost immediately exchanged.

In May 1762 Lapérouse sailed on the *Robuste*, in the division under Charles-Henri-Louis d'ARSAC de Ternay which set out to destroy the British fisheries in Newfoundland. Lapérouse was promoted sub-lieutenant on 1 Oct. 1764, and from 1765 to 1769 he was assigned duties relating to coastal transport in France. In 1771 he saw active service at Saint-Domingue (Hispaniola) aboard the frigate *Belle-Poule*. Early the following year he left for Île de France (Mauritius) with his patron Arsac de Ternay, who had just been named its commandant general. He left there in April 1773 for a long expedition in the Indian Ocean. Back at Île de France in March 1774, he returned to France in May 1777. On 4 April 1777 he had been promoted lieutenant-commander, and the following month was made a knight of the order of Saint-Louis.

In 1779 Lapérouse received command of the *Amazone* which, as part of La Motte-Picquet's division, left on 1 May for the West Indies, escorting a convoy bound for Martinique. Joining the fleet under Vice-Admiral the Comte d'Estaing, Lapérouse took part in the capture of Grenada and in the battle against John BYRON's squadron on 4, 5, and 6 July. Then, on board the *Amazone*, he was put on the lookout outside Charleston, South Carolina.

On 4 April 1780 Lapérouse was promoted captain, and the following 18 December received command of the frigate *Astrée*. By this time an expedition had been planned against the British establishments in Hudson Bay, but various difficulties forced a postponement. On 21 July 1781, while patrolling in the waters off Cape Breton Island with the *Astrée* and the *Hermione*, Lapérouse fought a brilliant battle with a British convoy and captured two ships. Then he escorted a convoy bound for the West Indies (December 1781) and took part in an attack on Saint Christopher (February 1782) and in battles off the Îles des Saintes against the squadron under Admiral George Brydges Rodney (9 and 12 April 1782). The French fleet was defeated but Lapérouse managed to reach Cap-Français (Cap-Haïtien, Haiti) without mishap. There on 14 May he took command of the ship of the line *Sceptre*, and on 31 May he set sail for Hudson Bay with the frigates *Astrée* and *Engageante*. He took with him 250 soldiers, 40 gunners, four artillery pieces, and two mortars. Despite extreme difficulty in navigating he arrived in Hudson Strait in mid-July, and on 8 August was in sight of the entrance to the Churchill River (Man.). The next day he landed his troops and called upon Chief Factor Samuel HEARNE to surrender; Hearne immediately complied. Fort Prince of Wales was partially destroyed, and the stocks of supplies and furs were taken. On 24 August Lapérouse successfully attacked York Factory (Man.). Hard pressed by bad weather, he left immediately, having faithfully carried out his mission without losing a single man; at the same time he had treated his prisoners with the greatest kindness. This campaign earned him a pension of 800 *livres*.

After peace returned, Lapérouse was chosen by the king because of his extensive experience and his humanity to take charge of an expedition to the Pacific, where numerous regions, including the west coast of North America, were still unexplored. In July 1785, shortly before his departure, Lapérouse was promoted brigadier of the naval forces, and during his voyage was to receive a commission as rear-admiral.

The *Astrolabe* and the *Boussole*, the two frigates in the expedition that had been organized with the help of the Académie des Sciences, left Brest on 1 Aug. 1785, easily rounded Cape Horn, and arrived in Concepción Bay (Chile) on 23 Feb. 1786. On 9 April Lapérouse called at Easter Island, and in May at the Sandwich Islands (Hawaii), where he discovered Maui Island, missed by James COOK. On 23 June the frigates came in sight of Mount St Elias (on the Alaska-Canada border). Lapérouse then sailed down the west coast of America, undertaking many hydrographic surveys. On 14 September he reached Monterey (Calif.), where Esteban José MARTÍNEZ came to his aid to pilot the two frigates into port. Crossing the Pacific from east to west, he went into Macao, China, on 3 Jan. 1787, and entered Manila Bay on 26 February before heading north. The first European navigator to sail into the waters between China and Japan, Lapérouse found the strait between Yezo (Hokkaido, Japan) and Sakhalin (U.S.S.R.) which bears his name, before putting into Avacha (Tar'ya) Bay on the coast of Kamchatka Peninsula (U.S.S.R.) on 7 September. The interpreter Jean-Baptiste-Barthélemy de Lesseps went ashore to return to France via Siberia, taking with him the reports and maps prepared by his chief.

Lapérouse then sailed in the direction of the central Pacific and cast anchor on 9 December at Maouna (Tutuila, Samoa). He continued towards the Friendly Islands (Tonga) and on 26 Jan. 1788 reached Botany Bay in Australia. He left about 15 March, sailing to the north-east. Caught up in a cyclone, his two frigates were wrecked in the vicinity of the Santa Cruz Islands in mid-June 1788. Lapérouse's disappearance remained a mystery until Peter Dillon, in 1826, and Jules-Sébastien-César Dumont d'Urville, in 1828, discovered the wreck of the *Astrolabe*. Finally, Reece Discombe identified the remains of the *Boussole* in 1964.

Lapérouse is representative of the most accomplished of the 18th-century sailors. An excellent navigator, a brilliant combatant, a humane leader with a mind open to all the sciences of his time, he was always able to combine to advantage prudence and audacity, experience and theory. As resourceful as he was indefatigable, as amiable as he was firm, he had a talent for making everyone like him.

ÉTIENNE TAILLEMITE

AN, Marine, B[4], 125, 138, 142, 145–47, 150, 163–68, 183–85, 191–95, 206, 266, 318–20; C[1], 173, p.1439; 179, p.211; 180, p.299; 182, p.454v; 184, p.704; C[7], 165 (dossier Lapérouse). H. H. Bancroft [and H. L. Oak], *History of the northwest coast* (2v., San Francisco, 1884). Georges Bordonove, *Grands mystères et drames de la mer* (Paris, 1975). M.[-R.] de Brossard, *Lapérouse, des combats à la découverte* (Paris, 1978); *Rendez-vous avec Lapérouse à Vanikoro* (Paris, 1964). John Dunmore, *French explorers in the Pacific* (2v., Oxford, 1965–1969), I. Paul Fleuriot de Langle, *La tragique expédition de Lapérouse et Langle* (Paris, 1954). Édouard Goepp et Henri de Mannoury d'Ectot, *Les marins* (2v., Paris, 1877). Lacour-Gayet, *La marine militaire sous Louis XV*; *La marine militaire sous Louis XVI*. O.[-J.] Troude, *Batailles navales de la France* (4v., Paris, 1867–68), I, II.

GAMELIN, IGNACE, merchant, receiver for the king's domain, militia captain, and judge; b. 10 Dec. 1698 in the parish of Saint-François-Xavier (Batiscan, Que.), son of Ignace Gamelin* and Marguerite Le Moyne; m. 31 Jan. 1731 in Montreal Marie-Louise Dufrost de La Gemerais, sister of MARIE-MARGUERITE, and they had 15 children; d. 9 March 1771 in Montreal.

Ignace was a member of the important Gamelin family who were prominent as merchants in New France. He was introduced to trade at a young age and started his career as a businessman early in the 1720s, when he seems to have taken over from his father, a Montreal merchant. He soon enlarged his field of action by entering into partnership with Charles Nolan* Lamarque, and in 1721 he invested 24,000 *livres tournois* in fitting out voyageurs for the *pays d'en haut*. From then on he exhibited the enterprising spirit that would enable him to become one of the outstanding figures in the 18th-century fur trade.

Gamelin's interest in that trade led him to participate in the venture of Pierre Gaultier* de Varennes et de La Vérendrye, his wife's uncle.

Although La Vérendrye was commandant of the *poste de l'Ouest* and theoretically had a monopoly of the fur trade in the region of Lake Ouinipigon (Winnipeg), he lacked funds to realize the old dream of discovering the western sea. He succeeded in interesting Gamelin, who agreed to participate in the undertaking. In 1731 La Vérendrye formed a nine-man partnership made up of four separate sub-partnerships; one of the members was Gamelin. For the first expedition Gamelin and Nolan Lamarque supplied trade goods worth 33,000 *livres tournois*, payable in beaver pelts at the price offered by the Montreal merchants on the return of the canoes in August the following year. In the spring of 1734 a new company replaced the one created in 1731; Gamelin and Nolan Lamarque again participated, supplying goods worth 26,405 *livres tournois*. As exploration was not proceeding at the desired pace, it was agreed on 18 May 1735 that a new company would be formed for three years. The contract stipulated that La Vérendrye would confine himself to exploration, leaving the running of the business and trading to his partners. In a sense La Vérendrye was farming out his posts to the merchant-outfitters in return for an annual salary of 3,000 *livres*; in addition the partners were to pay Governor Charles de Beauharnois* for the trading lease of Kaministiquia (Thunder Bay, Ont.). The company undertook to obtain all its trade goods from the warehouses of Gamelin and Nolan Lamarque, who in that one year invested more than 50,000 *livres tournois*. On 21 April 1738, when another company replaced the one set up in 1735, the terms of the agreement remained approximately the same.

In 1740, disappointed by La Vérendrye's never-ending delays in paying his debts, Nolan Lamarque and Gamelin instituted proceedings against him. The explorer, who had been short of money since the beginning of his enterprises, promised to pay off his debts in the next two years. When this agreement was reached, La Vérendrye appointed Gamelin his agent on 1 June 1747 and for a period of three years leased Fort Maurepas on the Red River and Fort La Reine (Portage-la-Prairie, Man.), as well as their dependent posts, to his son Pierre Gaultier* de La Vérendrye de Boumois and Pierre-Julien Trottier-Desrivières. Gamelin became the sole supplier of goods and the sole receiver of furs from these posts. It may well be asked why merchants played such an important role in the attempts to discover the western sea. La Vérendrye had tried in vain to obtain funds from the minister of Marine, Maurepas, who distrusted him. Thus he constantly had to have recourse to the merchants, who as financial backers were scarcely disinterested collaborators; they had, however, the merit of making his expeditions possible.

Gamelin's considerable activity in the fur-trading field was not limited to his partnership with the explorer. A summary inventory of hiring contracts shows that between 1727 and 1752 he signed on his own behalf and that of his partners with more than 370 voyageurs going to the *pays d'en haut*, principally to Michilimackinac (Mackinaw City, Mich.) and the numerous western posts.

Gamelin also took part in another large-scale venture. In 1729 François Poulin* de Francheville undertook to organize the Saint-Maurice ironworks. In order to make such an enterprise successful he had to ally himself with experts, financial backers, and officials. Consequently on 16 Jan. 1733 Francheville signed a contract with his brother Pierre Poulin*, Gamelin, François-Étienne Cugnet*, director of the Domaine d'Occident, and Louis-Frédéric Bricault* de Valmur, Intendant HOCQUART's secretary. Nevertheless the enterprise encountered great difficulties; in November 1733 Francheville's death led to a temporary shut-down of the ironworks. In the autumn of 1735 Gamelin and Cugnet, who still had faith in the project, formed an alliance with Pierre-François OLIVIER de Vézin to reorganize the ironworks, on condition that they received financial aid from the king. A new company was formed on 16 Oct. 1736 by Gamelin, Cugnet, Thomas-Jacques Taschereau*, agent of the treasurers general of the Marine in New France, and two ironmasters, Vézin and Jacques Simonet* d'Abergemont. On 20 Aug. 1738 the fires were lit. Gamelin, the only partner who was a native of Canada, maintained rigorous control of operations, but to no avail. Since they were unable to make the undertaking profitable, Cugnet and Gamelin resigned in October 1741, as did the other partners soon after. Gamelin was the only one to pay a share of the enterprise's debts.

In addition to his activities in the *pays d'en haut* and the ironworks, Gamelin operated a wholesale and retail business in the Montreal region and was one of the main suppliers to the government for various products. He obtained his supplies in La Rochelle, from the Pascaud brothers in particular. To transport their goods between France, the West Indies, and New France, Gamelin and his partners Francheville, Nolan Lamarque, and Jean-François Malhiot* could depend on their ship the *Montréal* (1731–35) and a schooner, the *Magnonne*, which belonged to Gamelin. The brigantine *Dauphin* also sailed on their account between Montreal and Louisbourg, Île Royale (Cape Breton Island). It is not known whether Gamelin had these ships built in New France, but in 1743 he paid part of the cost when the *Caribou* was built at Quebec. For voyages to the *pays d'en haut* he employed the usual birch-bark canoes built for six to ten men, which were made in Trois-Rivières.

As a prominent businessman Gamelin was solicited for services which increased his prestige in Montreal society. In 1734 he was named a churchwarden for the parish of Notre-Dame. He often acted as arbitrator, guardian, appraiser, and legal representative. In 1739 he was commissioned receiver for the king's domain within the Government of Montreal, a post he had held on a temporary basis since 1735, and in 1754 he was assistant director of a Montreal merchants' guild. From 1750 to 1760 he held the office of militia captain in Montreal and the amount of time he devoted to it may explain the decrease in his commercial activity, which ceased towards the middle of the Seven Years' War.

Under the British régime Gamelin was appointed a lower court judge of the Montreal Chamber of Militia. During his term, which lasted from 1760 to 1764, he played a rather ambiguous role: sitting with his fellow judges on this military court, he signed 23 decisions in cases in which he was plaintiff or party.

At the end of the military government in 1764 Gamelin was penniless and still had seven children at home to feed. The final years of his life were sad: from 1768 until his death he was paralysed, deaf, dumb, and almost blind. He left his heirs debts of 49,719 *livres* and receivables amounting to 79,543 *livres*, including numerous bonds of which some dated from 1721. One of the principal merchants in Montreal, Ignace was probably the most important member of the Gamelin family.

RAYMOND DUMAIS

The Château de Ramezay has an unsigned portrait of Ignace Gamelin.

ACND, Doc. du dépôt général, 13 (livres de comptes d'Ignace Gamelin, 1720–57). AN, Col., B, 65, pp.681, 688; 81, pp.304–5; C[11A], 65, pp.17, 24, 30; 67, pp.63, 83–84; 73, pp.120, 122; 74, pp.132, 147; 95, f.346v; 110; 111; 112; F[3], 13, pp.96, 114 (copies at PAC). ANQ-M, Chambre des milices, 1760–64; Doc. jud., Cour des plaidoyers communs, Registres, 1765–71; Juridiction de Montréal, 11; 14, 12 avril, 12 août 1724, 22 avril, 24 mai 1725, 4 avril 1727, 20 mai, 19 juin 1739, 2 juin 1740, 9 juin 1745, 10 juin 1748, 24 mai 1749, 7 juin 1751; Registres des audiences pour la juridiction de Montréal, 1720–60; État civil, Catholiques, Notre-Dame de Montréal, 31 janv. 1731, 10 mars 1771; Greffe de J.-B. Adhémar, 29 janv., 4 juin 1731, 17 mai 1735; Greffe de L.-C. Danré de Blanzy, 29 mai 1744, 12 juill. 1747, 15 juin 1754, 13 déc. 1758; Greffe de F.-M. Lepallieur de Laferté, 10 juin, 14 nov. 1734, 14 juin 1735; Greffe de P.-F. Mézière, 18 juin 1764; Greffe de Pierre Panet, 26 avril 1757, 12 sept. 1765, 8 mai 1771; Greffe de C.-C.-J. Porlier, 25 sept. 1740; Greffe de J.-C. Raimbault, 25 août, 29 sept. 1732 (some thousand acts were checked in researching this biography; only the most important are cited here); Livres de comptes, Charles Nolan Lamarque, 1727–34; Recensement, Compagnie des Indes, 1741. ANQ-MBF, État civil, Catholiques, Saint-François-Xavier (Batiscan), 10 déc. 1698. ANQ-Q, Greffe de J.-N. Pinguet de Vaucour, 16 janv. 1733, 23 oct. 1735, 18 oct. 1736, 30 oct. 1737. ASQ, Fonds Viger-Verreau, Carton 1, no.48; 2, no.157; 3, no.180; 8, no.28; 20, no.40. Private archives, J.-B. Porlier (Boucherville, Qué.), Lettres de la famille Gamelin, 1764–77. Bégon, "Correspondance" (Bonnault), ANQ *Rapport*, 1934–35, 56. "Documents sur Pierre Gaultier de La Vérendrye," J.-J. Lefebvre, édit., ANQ *Rapport*, 1949–51, 51–67. [Louis] Franquet, "Voyages et mémoires sur le Canada," Institut canadien de Québec, *Annuaire*, 13 (1889), 29–240. [Nicolas Renaud d'Avène Des Méloizes], "Journal militaire tenu par Nicolas Renaud d'Avène Des Méloizes, ch[er], seigneur de Neuville, au Canada, du 8 mai 1759 au 21 novembre de la même année . . . ," ANQ *Rapport*, 1928–29, 15. *Quebec Gazette*, 27 April 1769. Claude de Bonnault, "Le Canada militaire: état provisoire des officiers de milice de 1641 à 1760," ANQ *Rapport*, 1949–51, 443. Labrèque, "Inv. de pièces détachées," ANQ *Rapport*, 1971, 45, 258. P.-G. Roy, *Inv. coll. pièces jud. et not.*, I, 120; *Inv. concessions*, II, 226, 229, 234; IV, 224; *Inv. ins. Cons. souv.*, 218–19; *Inv. jug. et délib., 1717–60*, IV, 34, 60, 211; V, 84–85, 281; *Inv. ord. int.*, I, 184; II, 186, 266; III, 15–16, 26, 54–55.

Antoine Champagne, *Les La Vérendrye et le poste de l'Ouest* (Québec, 1968). Albertine Ferland-Angers, *Mère d'Youville, vénérable Marie-Marguerite Du Frost de Lajemmerais, veuve d'Youville, 1701–1771; fondatrice des Sœurs de la Charité de l'Hôpital-général de Montréal, dites sœurs grises* (Montréal, 1945). Cameron Nish, *Les bourgeois-gentilshommes de la Nouvelle-France, 1729–1748* (Montréal et Paris, 1968); *François-Étienne Cugnet, 1719–1751: entrepreneur et entreprises en Nouvelle-France* (Montréal, 1975). Sulte, *Mélanges historiques* (Malchelosse), VI. Tessier, *Les forges Saint-Maurice*. M. Trudel, *L'esclavage au Canada français*. Philéas Gagnon, "Nos anciennes cours d'appel," *BRH*, XXVI (1920), 346–47. É.-Z. Massicotte, "Une chambre de commerce à Montréal sous le Régime français," *BRH*, XXXII (1926), 121–24.

GAMELIN, PIERRE-JOSEPH (he signed **Pierre**), storekeeper, trader, militia captain, and justice of the peace; b. 16 April 1736 at Saint-François-du-Lac (Que.), son of Joseph Gamelin, a merchant, and Angélique Giasson; m. 29 Jan. 1759 at Lachine Marie-Louise de Lorimier and they had six daughters; m. secondly on 15 Sept. 1785 at Saint-Vincent-de-Paul (Laval) Marie-

Anne Lemaître-Lamorille and they had one son; d. 19 Oct. 1796 in Montreal.

Baptized provisionally the day he was born, Pierre-Joseph Gamelin received the full ceremonies of baptism from Canon Joseph-Thierry Hazeur* on 5 June 1736; his godmother was Jeanne-Charlotte de Fleury Deschambault, who later was to marry his godfather, Pierre de RIGAUD de Vaudreuil de Cavagnial, in 1736 governor of Trois-Rivières. Gamelin, who was a descendant of a famous Montreal merchant family, was initiated into the business world at an early age. At 22 he was the king's storekeeper at Fort Frontenac (Kingston, Ont.), and he then served at Fort La Présentation (or Oswegatchie; now Ogdensburg, N.Y.).

Since he had performed these duties during BIGOT's administration, Gamelin was accused of complicity in the *affaire du Canada*. On 29 March 1762 the Paris Châtelet ordered his arrest, and he was tried *in absentia*. The judgement rendered on 10 Dec. 1763 found Bigot and his accomplices guilty but deferred Gamelin's case "for further inquiry before pronouncing [him] contumacious." As he was anxious to protect his reputation and dispel doubts about his activities, Gamelin went to Paris to defend himself and in the end was acquitted. On 4 April 1767 he asked the Council of Marine for reimbursement of 69,000 *livres* in Canada paper, alleging that he was entitled to this favour because of the heavy expenses he had incurred in coming to clear himself in France.

Gamelin had been in business as a wholesale and retail merchant since at least 1762. His account books, kept from 1766 to 1778, show that Canadians constituted 70 per cent of his clientele; among his suppliers were the London merchants Davis and Sharp; John and Robert Barclay, who were to launch lawsuits against him in 1786; Aymare Mavit and Daniel Vialars; and Ogier Renaud and Company. He was an agent for the latter firm, which often served as his middleman with European suppliers, the firms of Paillet et Meynardie and Tourons et Frères in La Rochelle. Gamelin also went into partnership with Antoine Vitally and Jérôme Jugier, tobacco manufacturers in Canada, but the company went into bankruptcy in 1786. In addition he continued to have an interest in the *pays d'en haut*: in the spring of 1789 and 1794 he hired 22 voyageurs, most of them for Michilimackinac (Mackinac Island, Mich.). On 18 May 1795 he carried out his last commercial transaction, transferring merchandise to Grant, Campion and Company, including some cases of Jamaica rum that had been sent to Michilimackinac the previous year.

In 1762 some of the British in Montreal took the initiative in bringing together about 30 citizens, of whom ten were Canadians, with a view to founding a Masonic lodge. Wishing to form a connection with the upper-class British, Gamelin joined the group. On the other hand, on 27 Dec. 1770 he was named the third churchwarden of the parish of Notre-Dame in Montreal. A week later, on 3 Jan. 1771, having become master of the lodge, he appeared in public at a Masonic ceremony. The clergy, who pretended to be unaware of the freemasons' activities, were dumbfounded, and they envisaged the possibility of dismissing him as churchwarden, but Gamelin's importance and his family's considerable role within the church and Montreal society since the end of the 17th century persuaded them to be prudent. Not wishing, moreover, to aggravate an affair that was already causing too much stir, the clergy decided to settle the disagreement amicably. After taking counsel together, the parish priest, Louis Jolivet, the vicar general Étienne MONTGOLFIER, and Bishop BRIAND brought pressure to bear on Gamelin to give up one or other of his posts, which were considered incompatible. Gamelin probably gave in to the ecclesiastics' wishes; in fact on 30 June 1771, when reconstruction of the church of Notre-Dame-de-Bonsecours began, in his capacity as churchwarden he laid one of the cornerstones. In addition, when four of his daughters married Britons, three of whom were Protestants, he did not attend the Protestant weddings because of "certain religious reasons."

As a member of the business élite in the 18th century, the owner of property at Saint-Vincent-de-Paul, Prairie-de-la-Madeleine (La Prairie), Île Bouchard, and particularly at Verchères, where he farmed out 190 acres of land, Gamelin was entrusted with some important duties. A militia captain at the time of the American invasion, he was taken prisoner when the garrison of Saint-Jean was captured in November 1775. In 1784–85 he went to London with some of his compatriots [*see* Jean-Baptiste-Amable ADHÉMAR] to defend the interests of the Canadians, and in particular to ask for priests, who were urgently needed in Canada. In 1792 Gamelin stood for the county of Effingham in the elections to the first House of Assembly but was defeated by Jacob JORDAN, the seigneur of Terrebonne. That year he became a justice of the peace. In 1769 Gamelin had bought a two-storey stone house, built on the present site of the Bonsecours market. After his second marriage he lived at Saint-Vincent-de-Paul. In 1795 he was back in Montreal, where on 14 Sept. 1796, being ill, he made his will.

As an important trader under the British régime

Pierre-Joseph Gamelin had to come to terms with the conquerors. At his death his assets were valued at £4,172 and his debts at £4,455, while his accounts receivable amounted to £88,104. Pierre-Joseph was, it seems, the last of the merchants of the Gamelin dynasty, of whom there had been no fewer than ten in the 18th century, including Ignace* the elder, IGNACE the younger, and Pierre Gamelin* Maugras.

RAYMOND DUMAIS

ANQ-M, Chambre des milices, 13 juill. 1762, 14 janv., 7 sept. 1763, 24 juill. 1764; Doc. jud., Cour des plaidoyers communs, Registres, 1765–96; État civil, Anglicans, Christ Church (Montréal), 30 Jan. 1784, 17 Sept. 1793; Catholiques, Notre-Dame de Montréal, 20 oct. 1766, 7 janv. 1783; Saint-François-du-Lac, 5 juin 1736; Saints-Anges (Lachine), 29 janv. 1759, 20 févr. 1784; Saint-Vincent-de-Paul (Laval), 15 sept. 1785, 31 mai 1789; Greffe de J. G. Beek, 30 janv. 1784, 17 sept. 1793; Greffe de Louis Chaboillez, 8, 11, 15, 22, 29 mai 1789, 5, 10, 13, 14 juin 1794, 7 déc. 1796, 5 juill. 1797, 27 mars 1798; Greffe de Jean Delisle, 29 mars 1780; Greffe de J.-G. Delisle, 13 nov. 1791; Greffe de J.-C. Duvernay, 8 août 1762, 13 juin 1766, 9 oct. 1767, 21 sept. 1771, 9 oct. 1772, 28 juill., 5 août, 5 oct. 1773; Greffe d'Antoine Foucher, 9 avril 1782, 10 juill. 1786, 23 mars, 1er mai 1787; Greffe de François Leguay, 4 janv. 1783, 16 juin 1785; Greffe de P.-F. Mézière, 18 janv. 1779; Greffe de Pierre Panet, 27 janv., 27 févr. 1759, 12 août 1766, 3 déc. 1767, 30 juin 1769, 13 juill. 1770, 12 déc. 1772, 4 janv., 21 févr., 29 mars 1774, 23 févr. 1775; Greffe de Joseph Papineau, 20 févr. 1784, 14 nov. 1792, 18 mai 1795, 6 févr., 4 sept. 1796; Greffe de François Simonnet, 22 juill. 1768, 2 juin, 30 août 1769; Greffe de L.-J. Soupras, 20 juin 1783; Greffe d'André Souste, 2 juill. 1764; Tutelles et curatelles, 15 juin 1785, 19 mars 1795, 1er déc. 1796. Archives paroissiales, Notre-Dame (Montréal), Registre des délibérations d'assemblées générales des marguilliers, I, ff.342, 346–47, 354–55, 359; II, ff.18, 93, 94, 95, 96. ASQ, Fonds Viger-Verreau, Carton 9, no.1; 17, no.51. AUM, P 58, Corr. générale, Pierre Gamelin à Mlle Despinassy, 21 oct. 1772. PAC, MG 24, D3, 1. *Jugement rendu souverainement et en dernier ressort, dans l'Affaire du Canada, par messieurs les lieutenant général de police, lieutenant particulier et conseillers au Châtelet, et siège présidial de Paris, commissaires du roi en cette partie, du 10 décembre 1763* (Paris, 1763), 6, 45–47, 77. "MM. Adhémar et Delisle," *BRH*, XII (1906), 325, 353. "Première réunion de la grande loge de Montréal," PAC *Rapport*, 1944, xxxii. *Quebec Gazette*, 12 Oct. 1780, 17 Nov. 1785, 7 Aug., 13 Nov. 1788, 15 July 1790. F.-J. Audet et Édouard Fabre Surveyer, *Les députés au premier parlement du Bas-Canada (1792–1796)* . . . (Montréal, 1946), 282. Thomas Chapais, *Cours d'histoire du Canada* (8v., Québec et Montréal, 1919–34), I, 235–37. A.-H. Gosselin, *L'Église du Canada après la Conquête*, I, 380–84. Lemire-Marsolais et Lambert, *Hist. de la CND de Montréal*, IV, 192–94, 432; V, 232–33. P.-G. Roy, *Bigot et sa bande*, 191–93. Ægidius Fauteux, "Marguillier et franc-maçon," *BRH*, XXVI (1920), 240. "La première loge maçonnique," *BRH*, LI (1945), 179. Louis Richard, "La famille Lœdel," *BRH*, LVI (1950), 78–89.

GANNENSTENHAWI. *See* WILLIAMS, EUNICE

GARREAU. *See* MAUGUE-GARREAU

GARREAU (Garo, Garrau, Garaut), *dit* **Saint-Onge, PIERRE,** priest, canon of the chapter of Quebec, and vicar general; b. 20 Dec. 1722 in Montreal (Que.), son of Pierre Garreau, *dit* Saint-Onge, and Marie-Anne Maugue; d. 20 Sept. 1795 at Trois-Rivières (Que.).

Ordained by Bishop Pontbriand [Dubreil*] on 18 Dec. 1745, Pierre Garreau, *dit* Saint-Onge, served as a priest at Saint-Étienne-de-Beaumont (Beaumont) from 1745 to 1748. From 1748 to 1749 he was parish priest of Saint-Louis on Île aux Coudres, and from 1749 to 1755 of Sainte-Anne-du-Petit-Cap (Sainte-Anne-de-Beaupré). Having been appointed a canon of the chapter of Quebec on 6 Nov. 1755, he was elected secretary on 27 Sept. 1756 and lived in Quebec until 1760. From 1760 to 1764 he was parish priest of Saint-François-Xavier-de-Batiscan (Batiscan) and also served the mission church of Sainte-Geneviève-de-Batiscan. In 1764 BRIAND appointed him vicar general at Trois-Rivières to replace Joseph-François PERRAULT; he held this office until 1788, ministering at the same time to both La Visitation-de-la-Pointe-du-Lac and Sainte-Marie-Madeleine-du-Cap-de-la-Madeleine.

Garreau was a close friend of Briand, whose political views concerning the representatives of the new régime he shared, and he was entrusted with numerous responsibilities, such as restoring peace and agreement between certain parish priests and their flocks and smoothing out conflicts of jurisdiction between priests of neighbouring parishes. The latter task was a delicate one which required tact, persuasion, and also an authoritative manner. He seems to have had recourse in particular to authority, at least in the opinion of the population of Trois-Rivières, and their view was sometimes shared by the Recollets, who were responsible for ministering to this parish. On several occasions his superior thought it necessary to remind him to be more charitable. On 24 March 1777, when Bishop Briand wrote outlining the dissensions in his area, he asked him to examine his conduct and be careful not to give grounds for slander. A few months later Briand took him to task for his attitude towards parish priest Benjamin-Nicolas

Mailloux* and the Recollets. As vicar general Garreau often had disputes with the civil authorities and the churchwardens, and particularly with the directors of the Saint-Maurice ironworks, Christophe PÉLISSIER and Pierre Fabre*, *dit* Laterrière, who lodged bitter complaints with the bishop about his intransigence.

The inhabitants of Trois-Rivières became more distrustful of him when they perceived that he was much more conciliatory with the British authorities than with those to whom he had to give spiritual direction. An event that stirred further resentments and susceptibilities was the occupation of Trois-Rivières by the Americans during 1775–76 [*see* François GUILLOT, *dit* Larose]. The great majority of the inhabitants of Trois-Rivières were sympathetic to the Bostonnais. The vicar general was openly hostile and, obeying the bishop of Quebec, he ordered public prayers, processions, benedictions, and novenas for the British cause. The parishioners obeyed, but not without grumbling, as one may well imagine. The situation would probably have been different if the vicar general had resorted to persuasion rather than to his authority. But such was his character.

Father Garreau finally sought peace and quiet in his position as chaplain to the Ursulines. Old and infirm, in 1788 he humbly sought Bishop HUBERT's permission to finish his days in their convent. He was poor, close to destitution even, as he wrote to the bishop on 29 Nov. 1788: "All I have to eat is what my garden produces . . . I find myself in the dire necessity of coming forth, not like the wolf out of the woods, but out of my present situation, to knock on some charitable doors." He died in the Ursuline convent on 20 Sept. 1795.

RAYMOND DOUVILLE

AAQ, 20 A, I, 136, 138, 139, 141, 143, 144, 149, 175; 22 A, IV, 547; V, 7, 215; 10 B, 219v, 220, 221v, 245v, 253v, 254; 1 CB, IX, 84, 86, 87, 90, 92, 93; 81 CD, II, 22, 56; 33 CR, A, 3, 5, 6, 7, 17, 18, 20, 31, 39, 97, 98, 117, 123, 141, 142, 145. ASQ, Lettres, S, 48; T, 52; Polygraphie, VII, 6; Séminaire, 8, no.42. Caron, "Inv. de la corr. de Mgr Briand," ANQ *Rapport*, 1929–30, 45–136. Hervé Biron, *Grandeurs et misères de l'Église trifluvienne (1615–1947)* (Trois-Rivières, 1947). A.-H. Gosselin, *L'Église du Canada après la Conquête*. Jouve, *Les franciscains et le Canada: aux Trois-Rivières*. Sulte, *Mélanges historiques* (Malchelosse), VI. Albert Tessier, *Les Trois-Rivières: quatre siècles d'histoire, 1535–1935* (2e éd., s.l., 1935). M. Trudel, *Le Régime militaire*. *Les ursulines des Trois-Rivières depuis leur établissement jusqu'à nos jours* (4v., Trois-Rivières, 1888–1911), I. Raymond Douville, "La dette des États-Unis envers les ursulines de Trois-Rivières," *Cahiers des Dix*, 22 (1957), 137–62; "La maison de Gannes," *Cahiers des Dix*, 21 (1956), 105–35.

GASPÉ, IGNACE-PHILIPPE AUBERT DE. *See* AUBERT

GATROWANI. *See* OTTROWANA

GAULTIER DU TREMBLAY, FRANÇOIS (also called **Gaultier de La Vérendrye**), explorer and soldier; b. 29 Oct. 1715 and baptized on 22 December at Sorel (Que.), third son of Pierre Gaultier* de Varennes et de La Vérendrye and Marie-Anne Dandonneau Du Sablé; d. 30 July 1794 in Montreal (Que.).

François Gaultier Du Tremblay was not yet 16 when he left for the west with his father and his brothers Jean-Baptiste* and Pierre* in 1731. After wintering at Kaministiquia (Thunder Bay, Ont.), he spent the summer of 1732 helping build Fort Saint-Charles on Lake of the Woods. In 1737 he went with his father to Fort Maurepas on the Red River and in the autumn of 1738 to the Mandan country, a region corresponding roughly to present-day North Dakota. When the explorers entered the main Mandan village on 3 Dec. 1738, François was at their head, carrying a flag with the arms of France.

A few years later François returned to this area in the course of a long expedition to the southwest organized by his brother Louis-Joseph*, the Chevalier de La Vérendrye. They set out in the spring of 1742, with two Frenchmen and some Indian guides, and went first to the Mandan country. After passing through many Indian villages, they arrived among the Gens de l'Arc – probably a Pawnee tribe – from whom they hoped to obtain information about the western sea. The Chevalier was obliged to take part in a war these Indians were waging, but François remained with the non-combatants to guard the expedition's belongings. In March 1743 the explorers encountered some Gens de la Petite-Cerise, a Pawnee-Arikara clan, and stayed with them for some time. Near their fort, situated at the juncture of the Bad and Missouri rivers, opposite present-day Pierre in South Dakota, the Chevalier buried a plaque to mark their passage. It bears François's name, shortened to "tblt" (for Tremblet, a spelling frequently found), as well as those of the Chevalier and the two Frenchmen accompanying them.

After his father's resignation in 1744 François remained in the west and served under Nicolas-Joseph de Noyelles* de Fleurimont, who replaced La Vérendrye as commandant of the *poste de l'Ouest*. In 1746 La Vérendrye again became commandant and Pierre went to join François at the post, arriving during the winter of 1747–48. François was still in this region when his father died in December 1749 in Montreal. On 1 Oct. 1750 he was appointed a gentleman cadet in the colonial regular troops by Governor La Jonquière [Taffanel*], and in 1750 or 1751, after more than 19 years' absence, he returned to the St Lawrence valley.

François was not to remain long in the east. In February 1752 his brother Louis-Joseph entered into partnership with Luc de LA CORNE to run the trading post at Chagouamigon (Ashland, Wis.), and François signed on to work for them as an interpreter at a salary of 500 *livres* a year. In 1755 François was back in Montreal with his brother, and on 13 June 1756 he made over to Louis-Joseph all his rights to the family property, including his share in the fief of Du Tremblay, in return for a life annuity of 400 *livres* per annum. In a laborious and awkward handwriting, he signed this deed "tranblei," his only extant signature. On Louis-Joseph's death in 1761 François found himself, against his own wishes, once more in possession of the family heritage; on 29 Nov. 1769 he again surrendered his rights, this time to his brother's widow, Louise-Antoinette de Mézières de Lépervanche, on condition that she maintain and support him or pay him an annual allowance of 450 *livres*. In a petition addressed to Governor HALDIMAND in 1781 she spoke of the burden presented by her brother-in-law, "an old man incapable of providing for his needs."

François Gaultier Du Tremblay, who was almost completely illiterate, does not seem to have possessed his brothers' abilities or initiative. He lived modestly and unobtrusively and would probably have remained unnoticed had he not belonged to a great family of discoverers. With his death in 1794 the La Vérendrye family came to an end.

ANTOINE CHAMPAGNE

AN, Col., C[11A], 100, ff.28, 30, 32; C[11E], 16, ff.308–13; D[2C], 61, f.125. ANQ-M, Greffe de L.-C. Danré de Blanzy, 13 juin 1756; Greffe d'Antoine Foucher, 18 févr. 1752; Greffe de Pierre Panet, 5 juill. 1764, 29 nov. 1769; Greffe de François Simonnet, 15 juill. 1750. BL, Add. MSS 21734, 3 Feb. 1781 (PAC transcript). [Besides the two works of Antoine Champagne, *Les La Vérendrye et le poste de l'Ouest* (Québec, 1968) and *Nouvelles études sur les La Vérendrye et le poste de l'Ouest* (Québec, 1971), there are a great many studies and printed source materials that concern the La Vérendrye family. Readers should consult the bibliographies to the articles on Pierre Gaultier* de Varennes et de La Vérendrye and his sons Jean-Baptiste*, Louis-Joseph*, and Pierre* in volumes II and III of the *DCB*. A.C.]

GAYAHGWAAHDOH. *See* KAIEÑ?KWAAHTOÑ

GERMAIN, CHARLES, Jesuit, priest, and missionary; b. 1 May 1707 in Luxembourg; d. 5 Aug. 1779 at Saint-François-du-Lac (Que.).

Charles Germain entered the Jesuit order at Tournai (Belgium) on 14 Sept. 1728. Until 1739 he divided his time between study and teaching, going from Tournai to Lille and then to Douai. After his ordination he decided to serve in the missions of New France. He arrived there in the autumn of 1739 and the following year succeeded Jean-Pierre Daniélou* as missionary to the Malecites of the Saint John River (N.B.), remaining with them until just before the treaty of Paris was signed.

Germain's name is, in fact, still associated with this mission. He distinguished himself there mainly by the central role he played as liaison between the government of New France and the Indians under his guidance. This role was complex: not only was he the correspondent of the authorities of New France (HOCQUART, Beauharnois*, La Galissonière [Barrin*], and Vaudreuil [RIGAUD] all praised his zeal), but he also acted as chaplain to the garrison at Fort Menagouèche (Saint John, N.B.), advised upon the strength of the Indian forces in his region, and served as military chaplain in the field, go-between, and informer. In these various capacities he was involved in the many events that marked the War of the Austrian Succession and the Seven Years' War in Acadia.

The ecclesiastical authorities clearly thought Germain an exceptional person: in 1752 they recommended to Rome that he be made superior general of the Jesuits in New France. But Abbé de L'Isle-Dieu, the bishop of Quebec's vicar general in France, succeeded in getting Father Charles-Michel Mésaiger*, the Jesuits' procurator in Paris, to keep Germain at Aukpaque, his principal place of residence (about seven miles from Fredericton, N.B.), because his presence there was deemed indispensable for the success of French policy. Abbé de L'Isle-Dieu was evidently aware of Germain's role in Acadian affairs, for he judged him to be "a statesman." Describing the missionary's activities to Bishop Pontbriand [Dubreil*], he acknowledged that "the good of the cause is even more at stake than the advancement of religion."

Not unnaturally, Germain's name is almost always associated with that of Abbé Jean-Louis LE LOUTRE for the period 1744–55. Later, however, their paths differed. After the capture of Fort Beauséjour (near Sackville, N.B.) by Robert MONCKTON in 1755 and the deportation of the

Acadians, Le Loutre, attempting to reach France, was captured by the British. Germain remained in Acadia where he worked with Charles DESCHAMPS de Boishébert in an attempt to consolidate the remnants of Acadian resistance. But his situation became increasingly difficult as the French position worsened. It is known that he went to Quebec with his Indians to participate in the 1759 campaign. In 1760 he was the only missionary in Acadia who still had faith in a French victory, but the following year, resigned to defeat, he offered the Nova Scotian government his help in pacifying the Indians. On 21 Sept. 1761 the British authorities granted him a pension, as they had Abbé Pierre Maillard*: he received £50 for his services.

In the autumn of 1762, while he was visiting Quebec, Germain seems to have been detained by James MURRAY, probably because of continuing fears about his influence among the Indians. Although his flock was promised a successor, none was sent and they burned his church in protest. Germain pursued his career in the new British colony, serving in the region of Trois-Rivières (specifically at Cap-de-la-Madeleine and Batiscan) from January 1763 to 1767. He left the area temporarily in 1763 when Ralph Burton* ordered the expulsion of the Jesuits in the Government of Trois-Rivières, but he returned in December, shortly after Burton had been replaced by HALDIMAND.

His long experience with the Indians probably explains Germain's appointment in 1767 to Saint-François-du-Lac, where he served both the parish and the mission. In 1779 he was indirectly connected with incidents of espionage in the south of his parish which marked the threat of American invasion and had involved the treason of Joseph-Louis GILL, but he managed to exonerate himself in Haldimand's eyes. At his death on 5 Aug. 1779 Germain was one of the last Jesuits in North America.

MICHELINE D. JOHNSON

AN, Col., B, 91, f.352; 98, f.42 (copies at PAC). Archives de l'évêché de Nicolet (Nicolet, Qué.), Cartable Odanak; Cartable Saint-François-du-Lac. ASJCF, 573, 675, 708, 779, 808–3; 4018, ff.372, 379, 393, 405, 417, 421, 485, 489, 492, 506, 509, 511, 517, 529, 532, 533, 534, 553, 559; 4021, f.18. BL, Add. MSS 21777 (transcripts at PAC). *Coll. de manuscrits relatifs à la N.-F.*, III, 210, 273, 277, 281, 287, 304, 326, 345, 359, 369, 403, 409, 516; IV, 27, 104. *Les derniers jours de l'Acadie* (Du Boscq de Beaumont), 86n, 91, 95, 96, 98, 131, 132, 167, 185, 282. Placide Gaudet, "Généalogie des familles acadiennes avec documents," PAC *Rapport*, 1905, II, IIIe partie, 236–58, 318–27, 369–71. *JR* (Thwaites), LXIX, 76, 290; LXX, 84; LXXI, 26, 172–73, 398. La Rue, "Lettres et mémoires," ANQ *Rapport*, 1935–36, 317, 377, 389; 1936–37, 346–47, 357, 402, 406, 436; 1937–38, 187. *N.S. Archives, I*, 83, 309, 319–21, 362–76.

H.-R. Casgrain, *Une seconde Acadie: l'île Saint-Jean – île du Prince-Édouard sous le Régime français* (Québec, 1894), 159, 223, 264. T.-M. Charland, *Hist. des Abénakis*, chaps.IX–X; *Histoire de Saint-François-du-Lac* (Ottawa, 1942), 152, 155–56, 203–5, 214. R. C. Dalton, *The Jesuits' estates question, 1760–1888: a study of the background for the agitation of 1889* (Toronto, 1968), 3–20. Antonio Dragon, *L'Acadie et ses 40 robes noires* (Montréal, 1973), 235–41. M. D. Johnson, *Apôtres ou agitateurs: la France missionnaire en Acadie* (Trois-Rivières, 1970), 11, 13, 112, 131, 138. Raymond, *River St. John* (1910), 175, 185, 189, 202, 210, 221, 235, 260–61. Rochemonteix, *Les jésuites et la N.-F. au XVIIIe siècle*, II, 99–103. M. Trudel, *L'Église canadienne*, I, 47, 93, 352, 353; II, 131, 136, 139, 155, 157–58, 166, 172, 211; *Le Régime militaire*, 7, 141–42, 153, 173.

GERRISH, BENJAMIN, merchant and office-holder; b. 19 Oct. 1717 in Boston, Massachusetts, youngest son of John Gerrish and Sarah Hobbes (Hobbs); m. 1744 Rebecca Dudley in Boston; d. 6 May 1772 in Southampton, England.

Benjamin Gerrish was reared in Boston, where his father was a prosperous merchant, and he was probably involved in business there with his older brother JOSEPH after their father's death in 1737. Following his brother, Gerrish moved to Halifax, Nova Scotia, apparently in 1751. Like other New England merchants who established themselves in Halifax at this time, he was attracted by the prospects of the profits to be gained from supplying both the military and the civilian sectors of the population and from exploiting the area's resources. He entered into partnership with Joseph Gray, and their firm became one of the most successful in Halifax, partly because of profits realized during the Seven Years' War.

The Gerrishes were among those New England merchants who applied pressure on Governor Charles Lawrence* and the Board of Trade in the mid 1750s to establish a house of assembly in Nova Scotia. They achieved their goal in 1758. When Joseph, who was elected to the first assembly, was appointed to the Council the following year, Benjamin successfully contested his seat. His appointment to three positions of importance in 1760 indicated his standing as a member of Halifax's political élite; he was named a captain of militia, a justice of the peace for Halifax County, and finally, the most lucrative of all, Indian commissary. The latter post made him in effect the director of a government monopoly, in which the government assumed all the risks, paid his subordinates, and guaranteed him a percentage of proceeds from all sales to the Indians and purchases of furs from them. In addition, he was permitted to retain his private business and provide goods for the trade from his own store. Gerrish appears to have profited considerably from the appointment.

When Lawrence died in 1760, his successor, Jonathan BELCHER, sought to cut the enormous losses being incurred in the Indian trade by turning the monopoly over to a private contractor. In the spring of 1761 the Council recommended Michael FRANCKLIN, but Belcher insisted that Francklin was a cover for Gerrish and awarded the contract to Alexander Grant. Gerrish was permitted to retain the nominal title of Indian commissary, but he protested to the Board of Trade, claiming that the provincial government owed him some £2,500. To press his case in London, he enlisted the support of Joshua MAUGER; he eventually received about one-quarter of his claim.

The Indian trade affair proved to be one of several factors which led to an anti-Belcher movement among the Halifax merchants, supported by Mauger. In 1761, when the Lords of Trade instructed Belcher to allow the lapse of the debtors' act, a measure which stopped foreign creditors from prosecuting their Nova Scotian debtors in Nova Scotia courts, the Gerrishes led the resistance. They organized a boycott of the assembly by such members as Jonathan Binney*, Philip Augustus KNAUT, and Malachy SALTER, which prevented Belcher from obtaining a quorum during the winter of 1761–62. The debtors' act, which had been renewed in 1760 until the end of the first session after 1 Oct. 1761, was thus extended into 1762. The Gerrishes' task was made easier because the Halifax group had successfully contested elections in a number of communities outside the capital and thus virtually controlled the assembly. The merchants, supported in person by Mauger, also denounced Belcher to the Board of Trade. The eventual outcome was Belcher's replacement by Montagu Wilmot* in 1763. Although Benjamin and his brother had been removed from nearly all their offices for their role in the boycott, they were immediately reinstated upon Belcher's removal. Benjamin was elected to the assembly from Halifax in 1765 and three years later was appointed to the Council.

A leading Congregationalist layman and member of Mather's (St Matthew's) Church, Gerrish undertook with Salter in 1770 to appeal for financial aid from large churches in Boston on behalf of the Congregational churches and clergy in Nova Scotia. The generous response, much of which came in the form of scarce commodities, may well have strengthened Nova Scotian sympathies for the American revolution, at least during its early stages.

Gerrish, however, seems not to have become directly involved in the growing revolutionary controversy. He appears to have been something of a commercial opportunist who supported or disobeyed British regulations according to his own interest. While doing business with the British military he also participated, under Francklin's authority, in defying British restrictions on the export of coal from Cape Breton Island in 1767–68.

Gerrish made his will at Boston in 1772 before leaving for England, where he died. He left considerable property in Nova Scotia, including a large farm and mansion named Gerrish Hall in Windsor; most of the estate went to his wife and his nephew, Benjamin Gerrish Gray*.

STEPHEN E. PATTERSON

Mass. Hist. Soc., Andrews-Eliot papers, Benjamin Gerrish and Malachy Salter to Andrew Eliot and Samuel Cooper, Halifax, 18 Jan. 1770; Benjamin Gerrish to Andrew Eliot and Samuel Cooper, Halifax, 10 May 1770; Nehemiah Porter to Andrew Eliot, Yarmouth, 16 Nov. 1770. Akins, *History of Halifax City*, 52, 61, 237, 253. J. G. Bourinot, *Builders of Nova Scotia* . . . (Toronto, 1900), 133, 146. Brebner, *Neutral Yankees* (1937), 18–22, 71–73, 78–79, 81–82, 84–89, 136–37, 191, 216n, 218n. MacNutt, *Atlantic provinces*, 68–69. A. W. H. Eaton, "Old Boston families, number two: the family of Capt. John Gerrish," *New England Hist. and Geneal. Register*, LXVII (1913), 105–15. W. S. MacNutt, "The beginnings of Nova Scotian politics, 1758–1766," *CHR*, XVI (1935), 41–53.

GERRISH, JOSEPH, merchant, army officer, and office-holder; b. 29 Sept. 1709 in Boston, Massachusetts, third son of John Gerrish and Sarah Hobbes (Hobbs); d. 3 June 1774 in Halifax, Nova Scotia.

Joseph Gerrish was tutored in the counting-house of his father, a substantial Boston merchant. He eventually became a business partner, and upon his father's death in 1737, a beneficiary of his estate. Gerrish first came to Nova Scotia when he was commissioned an ensign in the 3rd Massachusetts Regiment and participated in the campaign against Louisbourg, Île Royale (Cape Breton Island), in 1745. The following year he was part of the force under Arthur Noble* which was sent to reinforce the garrison of Annapolis Royal, and he was wounded in the defeat of the New England forces at Grand Pré on 31 Jan. 1746/47. Back in Boston by July 1747, Gerrish then entered into partnership with John Barrell and supplied goods to the Annapolis Royal garrison. He does not seem to have prospered in Boston and moved to Halifax soon after its founding in 1749, investing in a number of houses and a fishing business. The fishing enterprise failed, and by 1755 he had been forced to turn to farming "for the support of my unfortunate Family." Some time before 1759 he was appointed to the lifetime position of naval storekeeper for the royal dockyard.

Gerrish entered public service in 1753 with his appointment as a justice of the peace for Halifax County and a judge of the Inferior Court of Common Pleas. Elected a member of the first Nova Scotia House of Assembly in October 1758, he served on its committee to answer Governor Charles Lawrence*'s address; the following year he was appointed to the Council.

When in 1761 Lieutenant Governor Jonathan BELCHER was instructed to prevent the renewal of the debtors' act, which kept foreign creditors from prosecuting their Nova Scotian debtors in Nova Scotia courts, Gerrish and his brother BENJAMIN helped organize a boycott of the assembly during the winter of 1761–62. Gerrish's indebtedness to Barrell seems to have contributed to his fervent resistance. Although the Board of Trade ordered him removed from civil office because of his role in organizing the boycott, he was reinstated after Belcher's replacement by Montagu Wilmot* in 1763.

Gerrish appears to have been fairly conservative in political affairs thereafter, devoting himself to his mercantile interests and official duties. In 1764 he unsuccessfully applied for permission to mine and export coal from Cape Breton. Two years later he was appointed a surrogate judge of the Vice-Admiralty Court in Halifax. When the court system was reorganized in 1769, Jonathan Sewell was appointed judge instead, but with the recommendation of Governor Francis Bernard of Massachusetts Sewell deputed Gerrish to serve in his office; Gerrish held the position until his death.

In 1740 Gerrish had married Mary Brenton and they had one son and two daughters. She died in Halifax some time after 1754, and in 1768 he married Mary Cradock of Boston. There were no children by this second marriage. Gerrish died in Halifax in 1774 and was buried in St Paul's churchyard. His widow later married John BREYNTON, the rector of St Paul's.

STEPHEN E. PATTERSON

A portrait by John Singleton Copley presumed to be of Gerrish is in the Chicago Art Institute.

Harvard College Library, Harvard University (Cambridge, Mass.), MS Sparks 4, Governor Bernard's official papers, V (letterbooks, 1765–68), 68, 141; VII (letterbooks, 1768–69), 153–55. Akins, *History of Halifax City*, 52, 61, 218–19, 246–61. J. G. Bourinot, *Builders of Nova Scotia . . .* (Toronto, 1900), 139–49. Brebner, *Neutral Yankees* (1937), 75, 79–81, 216n, 218n, 223n. Carl Ubbelohde, *The vice-admiralty courts and the American revolution* (Chapel Hill, N.C., 1960), 105, 128–29, 148–49, 179. A. W. H. Eaton, "Old Boston families, number two: the family of Capt. John Gerrish," *New England Hist. and Geneal. Register*, LXVII (1913), 105–15.

GEYESUTHA. *See* KAYAHSOTA?

GIBBONS, RICHARD, lawyer, office-holder, and chief justice; b. *c.* 1734 in London, England, son of Richard and Susannah Gibbons; m. 10 May 1783 Susanna Sheperd in Halifax, Nova Scotia, and they had one son and one daughter; d. 3 Aug. 1794 at Nantes, France.

Richard Gibbons' father was one of the earliest settlers of Halifax, arriving from Virginia by May 1750. Gibbons received legal training in England and in May 1765 became a solicitor at the Court of Chancery in Halifax; the following October he became clerk of the Inferior Court of Common Pleas. In June 1771 he took his seat in the House of Assembly as member for Barrington Township, but the election was annulled when an investigation conducted at his own request revealed irregularities in the campaign. A supporter of Governor Francis LEGGE's attempt to reform the provincial administration, Gibbons prepared memoranda on the judicial system and the provincial debt which were critical of Michael FRANCKLIN and other established officials opposed to Legge. Gibbons was not interested solely in reform, however. An ambitious man, he hoped that his connection with Legge would lead to a government appointment if any officials were dismissed by the governor.

Despite Legge's recall in 1776, Gibbons did achieve higher office; in January 1777 he was appointed solicitor general, and four years later he became attorney general. He was, however, unpopular with Governor John PARR and other members of Parr's administration. In 1784 a dispute arose between Gibbons and Parr over the issuing of land grants to loyalists. Gibbons' signature was required on each grant, and he claimed to be entitled to a fee for each name on the grant, even when hundreds of names were involved. After loyalists complained, Parr allowed grants without Gibbons' signature.

Because of his poor relations with Parr, Gibbons was probably glad to accept the offer of Joseph Frederick Wallet DesBarres*, the new lieutenant governor of Cape Breton and a personal friend, to appoint him chief justice of the infant colony. Gibbons was named to the chief justiceship, which carried with it the ex officio presidency of the Executive Council, on 25 July 1785, and shortly afterwards he began to organize Cape Breton's judicial system.

DesBarres was a controversial administrator during whose term of office frequent disagreements divided the Council, and in these clashes Gibbons supported the lieutenant governor against his principal opponents, Attorney General David MATHEWS, Registrar Abraham Cuyler*, and Colonel John Yorke, the garrison commander. In the winter of 1785 DesBarres quarrelled with Yorke over the right to distribute military supplies to some inhabitants, and Gibbons used legal processes in an attempt to force Yorke to allow this distribution by DesBarres. DesBarres' opponents succeeded in having him recalled by the British government in November 1786, and before leaving Cape Breton he sent Gibbons to London to plead for his reinstatement. When Parr, who had also quarrelled with DesBarres, heard of this measure, he wrote to Lord Sydney, secretary of state for the Home Department, attacking Gibbons as the "worst of characters." Gibbons was unsuccessful in having DesBarres restored.

William Macarmick* became lieutenant governor in 1787, and in a conciliatory gesture retained Gibbons in his positions. The chief justice, however, resented the apparent increase in influence of Mathews and Cuyler, and he determined to regain the power he had enjoyed before DesBarres' removal. Using as a basis a volunteer militia formed from DesBarres' supporters, he organized the Friendly Society, a quasi-military association which he conceived as a protection against any possible tyranny of Macarmick, Mathews, or Cuyler. When the society attempted to form a select militia company, Macarmick countered by trying to organize a regular militia composed of all groups because he feared any increase in Gibbons' importance and the danger of violence between the society and Mathews' and Cuyler's supporters. Gibbons, in his capacity as chief justice, rejected the plan, and Macarmick outlawed the society as a possible "Seed of Rebellion."

Despite this setback, Gibbons was undaunted. Early in 1788 he placed himself at the head of a movement which was seeking a house of assembly for Cape Breton, and in February he addressed the grand jury as "the only representative body of the People," proposing that it act as a legislative assembly. Macarmick refused to recognize the jurors as "a check on the Governor and Council" and, influenced by Mathews' views that the incident represented another challenge to his power, dismissed Gibbons from his positions in March. The dismissal brought a storm of protest from Gibbons' supporters, and the chief justice travelled to Quebec, Halifax, and finally London in an effort to justify his actions, although he was forced to sell his farm and belongings in Sydney to pay his expenses. After arguing his case for three years he was reinstated in March 1791 because of his generally good character. He did not attempt, however, to return to Cape Breton for another three years, and on the voyage Gibbons, his wife, and their son were captured and imprisoned in France. Gibbons' family was released after 22 months of confinement, but he had already died on 3 Aug. 1794.

His son Richard Collier Bernard DesBarres Marshall served as attorney general of Cape Breton for a time and was active in the agitation before 1820 to have a house of assembly granted to the colony. After Cape Breton was reannexed to Nova Scotia that year, he became a leader of the Cape Breton separatist movement which was active until 1846. Gibbons Jr died in 1863.

R. J. MORGAN

PAC, MG 11, [CO 217], Cape Breton A, 2, pp.39–41, 141–44; 3, pp.1–9, 84–93; 5, pp.68–70, 83, 86, 93; 7, pp.125–26; 8, pp.85, 125–26, 152–53, 158–59, 163, 167; Nova Scotia A, 90, p.218; 91, p.208; 98, p.4; 99, pp.156–59; MG 23, F1, ser.5. PANS, MG 1, 262B (Dodd family docs., 1788); RG 1, 53, pp.440–41. PRO, CO 217/112, ff.138–39. John Doull, *Sketches of attorney generals of Nova Scotia* (Halifax, 1964), 9–18. G. N. D. Evans, *Uncommon obdurate: the several public careers of J. F. W. DesBarres* (Toronto and Salem, Mass., 1969). R. J. Morgan, "Orphan outpost: Cape Breton colony, 1784–1820" (unpublished PHD thesis, University of Ottawa, 1972); "Joseph Frederick Wallet DesBarres and the founding of Cape Breton colony," *Revue de l'université d'Ottawa*, XXXIX (1969), 212–27.

GIENGWAHTOH. *See* KAIEÑˀKWAAHTOÑ

GILL, JOSEPH-LOUIS, known also as **Magouaouidombaouit**, meaning friend of the Iroquois, a principal chief of the Abenakis of Saint-François; b. 1719 at the Saint-François-de-Sales mission (Odanak, Que.); d. there 5 May 1798.

Joseph-Louis Gill was the most notable of the children of Samuel Gill and his wife Rosalie (*née* James?), who had both been captured by Abenakis on the New England coast. Around 1740 he married Marie-Jeanne Nanamaghemet, daughter of a principal chief of the Abenakis of Saint-François. Some time before 1749 Gill was elected a principal chief; in that year he and the four other principal chiefs signed the letter to the canons of the cathedral of Chartres, France, renewing the Abenakis' vow to Our Lady of Chartres [*see* Atecouando* (Jérôme)].

Although Gill spent his life among the Indians as had his parents, he did not totally adopt the Abenaki way of life, preferring farming and business, which brought him a comfortable living, to hunting. Mrs Susanna Johnson, a captive whom he had bought and who was living in his home in 1754, wrote: "He kept a store of goods and lived in a style far above the majority of his tribe." The Gills had two sons, Xavier and Antoine; the latter has been identified by Abbé Joseph-Pierre-Anselme Maurault* as the Sabatis mentioned by Mrs Johnson. Gill escaped the massacre perpetrated by Major Robert ROGERS, who destroyed the Abenakis' village in October 1759, but his wife and two children were taken captive and only Antoine survived.

On several occasions after the conquest Gill was the tribe's spokesman to the British authorities. Thus on 24 Nov. 1763 he went to meet the new military governor of Trois-Rivières, Frederick HALDIMAND, to assure him that the Indians of Saint-François had no dealings with those in the *pays d'en haut* who had been incited to revolt by Pontiac* and to request that the Jesuit Jean-Baptiste de LA BROSSE replace Father Pierre-Joseph-Antoine ROUBAUD as missionary. In February 1764 he met Haldimand again, to complain of encroachments by the whites on Abenaki hunting grounds.

Gill's loyalty to the British crown was questioned during the American revolution. In the summer of 1778 five Americans who had escaped from prison in Quebec were recaptured by Abenaki scouts ten leagues from the village of Saint-François-de-Sales. They had in their possession a map of the Rivière Saint-François which Gill had drawn to guide them to New England. Upon learning of their capture, Gill fled and was not seen again for two years. In 1780, to win over his supporters in the tribe, the superintendent of Indian affairs in Montreal, Lieutenant-Colonel John CAMPBELL, proposed sending to Cohoes (Newbury, Vt) for him, since he was known to be living there, and promising him a pardon. At the end of August Gill gave himself up to Captain Luke Schmid, whom he met at the blockhouse at Saint-Hyacinthe on the Yamaska River. Haldimand, now governor of the province, granted him a pardon and administered the oath of allegiance. To prove his loyalty to the government and to dispel the other Abenakis' prejudices against him, Gill went off towards Cohoes in May 1781 to take a prisoner. Through a trick he succeeded in capturing Major Benjamin Whitcomb, but his prisoner escaped when they were a few leagues from Saint-François-de-Sales. Some Abenakis accused Gill of having let him escape because Whitcomb was supposed to have promised him that he would spare the village if the Bostonnais succeeded in taking Canada. This charge was probably unjustified, for it was learned the following year that Whitcomb was planning to come to capture Gill and burn his house as well as the rest of the village.

Towards the end of his life Gill was made prayer leader. In this capacity he was the most important person in the church after the missionary, and in the latter's absence he led the daily communal prayers. This role also made him a sort of prefect responsible for religious discipline. He died on 5 May 1798 and was buried in the Abenaki church.

On 2 Nov. 1763, at Baie-du-Febvre (Baieville, Que.), he had remarried; he and his wife Suzanne, daughter of the militia captain Antoine Gamelin, *dit* Châteauvieux, had six sons and two daughters, from whom are descended the best known representatives of the Gill family, including Ignace*, member of the assembly for Yamaska during the Union.

THOMAS-M. CHARLAND

BL, Add. MSS 21662, ff.23, 24, 27, 33; 21669, ff.23, 24; 21722, f.322; 21771, ff.54, 55, 57; 21772, ff.3–7, 9; 21773, ff.6–9, 31, 36, 42, 58, 110, 120, 121; 21777; 21794, ff.11, 12, 54; 21795, f.186; 21796, f.64; 21841, ff.186, 187; 21844, f.47; 21865, f.186 (copies at PAC). PAC, RG 10, A6, 1833, pp.339–41. *Johnson papers* (Sullivan *et al.*), XIII, 430, 619, 717. [Susannah Willard], *A narrative of the captivity of Mrs. Johnson, containing an account of her sufferings, during four years, with the Indians and French* (Walpole, N.H., 1796; [new ed.], New York, 1841). T.-M. Charland, *Hist. des Abénakis*. C.[-I.] Gill, *Notes historiques sur l'origine de la famille Gill et histoire de ma propre famille* (Montréal, 1887), 35, 49. J.[-P.]-A. Maurault, *Histoire des Abénakis, depuis 1605 jusqu'à nos jours* ([Sorel, Qué.], 1886), 349–50, 422–23, 501, 507. J. C. Huden, "The white chief of the St. Francis Abnakis – some aspects of border warfare: 1690–1790," *Vermont History* (Montpelier), new ser., XXIV (1956), 199–210, 337–55.

GILMORE (Gilmour), THOMAS, journalist and printer; buried on 3 Feb. 1773 in Quebec.

Thomas Gilmore is believed to have been born in 1741 either in Philadelphia or Stone, a village now in the suburbs of Dublin (Republic of Ireland). At 17 years of age he was hired by printer William Dunlop in Philadelphia, and he worked there for a time alongside William BROWN. In 1763 Brown, who had returned from Barbados, met Gilmore again, and on 5 August the two signed a partnership contract to set up a printing-press in the province of Quebec. With difficulty Brown made his way to Quebec on horseback and there distributed a handbill announcing the publication of a weekly gazette. Gilmore sailed to London, where he bought type from founder William Caslon Sr, a press and ink, and paper from the shop of Kendrick Peck; he also subscribed to various newspapers. On 7 June 1764 he rejoined his partner Brown in Quebec. They had 143 subscribers, and on 21 June the first number of the *Quebec Gazette/La Gazette de Québec* was published. The subscriptions and the £50 paid annually by the colonial authorities for official announcements were insufficient to meet the sundry expenses and the monthly rent of 14*s*. 6*d*. for their shop on Rue Saint-Louis, which belonged to a J. Thomson. The press therefore turned out announcements of sales, blank certificates, calendars, and the first books printed in the province. For example, in 1765 they published for James JOHNSTON, foreman of the Grand Jury of Quebec, 300 copies of a bilingual brochure known under the title of *Presentments to the Grand Jury*. In November 1765 *Le catéchisme du diocèse de Sens*, a 180-page work in octavo by Mgr Jean-Joseph Languet de Gergy, was printed in 2,000 copies (eight or nine are extant) and delivered to Louis Langlois, *dit* Germain, at a price of £91 16*s*. A French translation of the Stamp Act was published in 1766, followed in 1767 by a work in Montagnais by Jean-Baptiste de LA BROSSE, *Nehiro-Iriniui; Aiamihe Massinahigan . . .* (96 pages), as well as by *Ordinances, made for the Province of Quebec . . .* (81 pages in folio) and *The Trial of Daniel Disney . . .*, a work on the Thomas WALKER affair, probably by Francis Maseres*.

Because the *Gazette* was published in two languages Gilmore and Brown had difficulty finding suitable staff, and they regularly advertised positions. On 29 April 1768 they wrote their former employer, Dunlop, to ask him to send them a young black who knew English, French, and printing techniques, who was honest, and who had had smallpox. JOE, the young black, evidently did not meet all these criteria; the firm's account book records amounts paid on 19 Aug. 1771 to get Joe out of prison and on 21 Jan. 1777 to Dr James Davidson for treatment of Joe's smallpox.

Growing disagreement between the two partners was perhaps not unconnected with Gilmore's marriage to Mary Lillicoe on 6 Nov. 1768 in Quebec. On 4 Oct. 1770 Gilmore signed a promissory note for £250 in favour of Brown, who through his lawyer, Arthur Davidson*, demanded payment of the debt before the Court of Common Pleas on 4 Feb. 1771 and on 6 July 1772. Gilmore died an alcoholic early in 1773 at 32 years of age. During that summer there was more wrangling between his widow and Brown, who accused each other of dishonesty in the *Quebec Gazette* on 12 and 19 August and 2 September. The issue of 27 Jan. 1774 announced the dissolution of the partnership between Gilmore (in the person of his widow) and Brown, who remained sole owner of the newspaper.

Although Brown was certainly the dominant figure, Gilmore was also a pioneer in the development of printing in Quebec.

JEAN-FRANCIS GERVAIS

ASQ, Polygraphie, XXXV, 6e; Séminaire, 152, no.182. Cathedral of the Holy Trinity (Anglican) (Quebec), Registers of baptisms, burials, and marriages, 6 Nov. 1768, 3 Feb. 1773. PAC, MG 24, B1, 49. Beaulieu et Hamelin, *La presse québécoise*, I, 2. Tremaine, *Bibliography of Canadian imprints*. Æ. Fauteux, *Introduction of printing into Canada*. H. P. Gundy, *Canada* (Amsterdam, 1972), 29–31. F.-J. Audet, "William Brown (1737–1789), premier imprimeur, journaliste et libraire de Québec; sa vie et ses œuvres," RSC *Trans*., 3rd ser., XXVI (1932), sect.I, 97–112. Raoul Renault, "Les débuts de l'imprimerie au Canada," *BRH*, XII (1906), 86–88.

GIRARD (Giran, Gyrard), JACQUES (his Christian name is not certain), missionary; b. *c*. 1712 in the province of Auvergne, France; d. January 1782 at Jouarre (dept of Seine-et-Marne), France.

When Abbé Jacques Girard was sent to Quebec in the spring of 1740, he was described by the directors of the Séminaire des Missions Étrangères in Paris as "a little priest from Auvergne, of a candid nature and great zeal." Sick upon arrival, he did not recover until the following year. In 1742 Bishop Pontbriand [Dubreil*] sent him, along with Jean-Pierre de MINIAC, to Acadia, where he became parish priest at Cobequid (near Truro, N.S.). The British authorities did not accept the bishop's right to send missionaries to Acadia, and Paul Mascarene*, president of the Nova Scotia Council, raised difficulties before agreeing to the appointment of the two priests.

At the outbreak of the War of the Austrian Succession in North America Girard considered leaving his mission, but he changed his mind and agreed to work with the French army. He became closely involved in Jean-Baptiste-Nicolas-Roch de RAMEZAY's Acadian campaigns in the winter of 1746–47, transmitting information on British troop movements to Ramezay, undertaking with Abbé Pierre Maillard* to obtain provisions for the forces, acting as liaison between the various detachments, and sheltering wounded French soldiers in his presbytery. Early in 1750 Governor Edward CORNWALLIS had him arrested, along with four Acadian deputies, for having advised his parishioners not to take an unconditional oath of allegiance to the British king. After three months in prison Girard was allowed to settle in the region of Minas Basin, the inhabitants there having petitioned Cornwallis for a priest to assist Claude-Jean-Baptiste Chauvreulx*. He had, however, to take the oath himself and to promise explicitly not to counsel against it again or to return to his former parish. For having kept his word Girard was criticized in 1752 by the Baron de Longueuil [Le Moyne*], administrator of New France, who believed that the missionary "could with a perfectly clear conscience have used his authority over the habitants at Cobequid to alienate them from the English."

According to the Abbé de L'Isle-Dieu, the bishop of Quebec's vicar general in France and the only one to mention the incident, Girard was captured by Micmacs in 1751 and taken into the woods for a time. In the spring of 1752, on the bishop's order, he crossed to Île Saint-Jean (Prince Edward Island). The bishop's decision to send him there reflected the French government's policy of attracting to the island the Acadians living under British rule [*see* Claude-Élisabeth Denys* de Bonnaventure]. He became parish priest at Saint-Paul-de-la-Pointe-Prime (Prim Point), where many Acadians from Cobequid had settled. Distressed by the abject poverty of his parishioners, he asked for help from Louisbourg, Île Royale (Cape Breton Island), describing to the authorities there the refugees' utter destitution.

After the fall of Louisbourg in 1758 Girard and more than 300 of his parishioners were put on board the *Duke William* on 20 October. On 13 December the ship sank off the coast of England. Girard explained that "the crew saved themselves and rescued me and four of my habitants and parishioners"; however, a 19th-century account implies that he had been urged by the captain to abandon his flock after having exhorted them to submit to their unhappy fate. After a month of misery, difficulty, and privation, Girard arrived in France at the end of January 1759. He was badly received at the Séminaire des Missions Étrangères, where he was accused of having left his parish without permission and where he was required to pay for his keep. He was able to support himself only through the gratuities which the Abbé de L'Isle-Dieu obtained for him from the king. His difficulties led him in 1761 to launch a law suit, with Abbé Jean Manach*, against the directors and superior of the seminary. After losing the case on 6 Sept. 1764, Girard was struck from the society's list of members.

In June 1765 the Abbé de L'Isle-Dieu obtained for Girard the post of prefect apostolic of Saint-Pierre and Miquelon, but the ship taking him and his colleague Manach there was wrecked and ran aground on Martinique. Girard was unable to return to France until 1766 and was then in poor health. The following year the new bishop of Quebec, Jean-Olivier BRIAND, tried to get permission to send him to Île Saint-Jean, but the plan failed. Girard stayed in France and was made perpetual chaplain of the abbey of Jouarre, near Meaux. In 1774 he turned down an offer to become parish priest of the Acadian colony in Poitou [*see* Jean-Gabriel BERBUDEAU]. He remained at Jouarre, where he died in January 1782 "in the odour of sanctity."

MICHELINE D. JOHNSON

AAQ, 12 A, C, 222; 20 A, I, 106; 22 A, II, 519; 11 B, III, 277; 1W, VII, 101–8, 133–36, 209–26, 229–49, 273–83. AN, Col., B, 110, ff.60, 119, 243; 115, ff.54, 187; 117, f.522; 120, f.361; 122, ff.55, 190; 125, f.104; C[11A], 78, ff.407, 423; 82, f.326; 98, f.338; C[11B], 29, f.73; 33, f.288; F[3], 50, ff.639–41 (mfm. at PAC). ASQ, Lettres, M, 98, 99, 115, 117, 118, 121, 122, 122[a]; P, 26; R, 8, 90; S, 7[a]; Polygraphie, V, 40; VII, 5, 109, 114; IX, 29; XI, 2, 3, 4; Séminaire, 14/6, no.3.

Coll. doc. inédits Canada et Amérique, I, 12–16, 41–46; II, 10–75; III, 60–80, 181–91. *Les derniers jours de l'Acadie* (Du Boscq de Beaumont), 237. Placide Gaudet, "Généalogie des familles acadiennes avec documents," PAC *Rapport*, 1905, II, IIIe partie, 375–76. La Rue, "Lettres et mémoires," ANQ *Rapport*, 1935–36, 301, 317, 346, 382, 390, 408; 1936–37, 401, 423; 1937–38, 184, 203, 214, 219. *N.S. Archives, I*, 121–26, 170, 180–85, 188. H.-R. Casgrain, *Les sulpiciens et les prêtres des Missions-Étrangères en Acadie (1676–1762)* (Québec, 1897), 365, 374, 404, 406, 408; *Une seconde Acadie: l'île Saint-Jean – île du Prince-Édouard sous le Régime français* (Québec, 1894), 160, 275–78, 302, 307, 360, 362; *Un pèlerinage au pays d'Évangéline* (2e éd., Québec, 1888), 308–11. Harvey, *French régime in P.E.I.*, 110–200. J.-W. Pineau, *Le clergé français dans l'île du Prince-Édouard, 1721–1821* ([Québec, 1967]), 27–33. Édouard Richard, *Acadie: reconstitution d'un chapitre perdu de l'histoire d'Amérique*, Henri D'Arles [M.-J.-H.-A. Beaudé], édit. (3v., Québec et Boston, Mass., 1916–21), III, 307–11. Albert David, "Les missionnaires du séminaire du Saint-Esprit à Québec et en Acadie au

XVIIIe siècle," *Nova Francia* (Paris), I (1925–26), 9–14, 52–56, 99–105, 152–59, 200–7.

GLADWIN (Gladwyn), HENRY, army officer; b. 1729 or 1730, probably in Derbyshire, England, elder son of Henry Gladwin and Mary Dakeyne; m. Frances Beridge, and they had ten children; d. 22 June 1791 at Stubbing Court, Derbyshire.

Henry Gladwin became a lieutenant in the 48th Foot on 28 Aug. 1753 and in 1755 was wounded at the battle of the Monongahela (near Pittsburgh, Pa). His regiment spent the rest of 1755 and 1756 refurbishing near Albany, New York, and in 1757 it accompanied Lord Loudoun to Halifax, Nova Scotia, as part of the abortive expedition against Louisbourg, Île Royale (Cape Breton Island). On 26 Dec. 1757 Gladwin was commissioned captain in the 80th Foot, a new light infantry regiment being raised by Thomas GAGE. He was wounded in James ABERCROMBY's attack on Fort Carillon (Ticonderoga, N.Y.) in 1758, and in 1759 AMHERST promoted him acting major. He served as *de facto* commander of his regiment in the successful British campaign against forts Carillon and Saint-Frédéric (near Crown Point, N.Y.) in 1759. He held the same command in 1760 but was detached early in the summer to assist Colonel Henry Bouquet in building Fort Presque Isle (Erie, Pa). By late October he was in command of Fort William Augustus (formerly Fort Lévis; east of Prescott, Ont.). He secured his permanent commission as major on 13 Dec. 1760.

In 1761 Gladwin accompanied Sir William JOHNSON on a diplomatic mission to the Upper Lakes tribes but became ill at Detroit and returned east. He took command at Detroit in the summer of 1762, and the episode for which he is best known occurred there in 1763. That spring the able Ottawa chief Pontiac* raised the Upper Lakes tribes against the British and by June they had captured most of the western posts. Pontiac attempted to gain entry at Detroit for himself and a war party by means of feigned peace parleys but Gladwin was not deceived, having been informed beforehand of Pontiac's intentions. About a thousand warriors then laid siege to the fort. Their attempts to starve and harry it into submission failed because of the commandant's sound defensive strategy and the timely arrival of several relief expeditions. Throughout the siege the garrison never numbered more than 450 men. One expedition, which reached Detroit on 29 July, consisted of 280 men (including Robert ROGERS and 20 rangers) under Amherst's aide Captain James Dalyell (or Dalzell). He proposed to abandon Gladwin's successful strategy of relying on the Indians' unwillingness to assault strong defences in favour of a night attack on the Indian villages. Gladwin reluctantly allowed the sortie but word reached Pontiac, who successfully ambushed the force of about 250 men on 31 July. The British sustained 60 casualties including the death of Dalyell. The garrison returned to the defensive and by the end of October many Indians had sued for peace and gone home. Detroit had been the only upper post not captured, and both Amherst and Bouquet, the senior officer in the west, approved of Gladwin's measures; Amherst demonstrated his favour by appointing him nominal deputy adjutant general in America and recommending his promotion to lieutenant-colonel, effective 17 Sept. 1763.

In late 1763 and early 1764 Gladwin wrote to his superiors of his dislike for further service in America and of his desire to return to England to settle his deceased father's affairs. After John BRADSTREET's force relieved Detroit in August 1764, Gladwin returned to England by way of New York. He settled on his estate and saw no further active service. Seniority brought him the rank of colonel on 29 Aug. 1777 and major-general on 20 Nov. 1782. He died in 1791.

PETER E. RUSSELL

Clements Library, Thomas Gage papers, letterbooks, 1759–63; American series, Gladwin to Gage, 26 Oct. 1760; 4, 24, 25 Feb., 5, 8, 24 March, 5, 7 April 1762. PRO, WO 34/2, ff.1–11, 14, 16–18, 29; 34/6, f.12; 34/7, ff.2–3, 31, 50, 96, 100–1, 112–14; 34/49. Amherst, *Journal* (Webster). [Henry Bouquet], *The papers of Col. Henry Bouquet*, ed. S. K. Stevens *et al.* (19v., Harrisburg, Pa., 1940–43). *Diary of the siege of Detroit . . .*, ed. F. B. Hough (Albany, N.Y., 1860). *Johnson papers* (Sullivan *et al.*), III, 421, 468–500, 512, 521, 524, 670, 730, 747, 751, 820. Knox, *Hist. journal* (Doughty), I, 40–41. Thomas Mante, *The history of the late war in North-America and the islands of the West Indies, including the campaigns of MDCCLXIII and MDCCLXIV against his majesty's Indian enemies* (London, 1772). *Michigan Pioneer Coll.*, XIX (1891), 27–295; XXVII (1896), 605–80. *Military affairs in North America, 1748–65* (Pargellis), 223, 232, 235, 239–40, 265. *The siege of Detroit in 1763: the journal of Pontiac's conspiracy, and John Rutherfurd's narrative of a captivity*, ed. M. M. Quaife (Chicago, 1958). Peckham, *Pontiac*. M. M. Platt, "Detroit under siege, 1763," *Michigan History* (Lansing), XL (1956), 465–97.

GLANDONS, MAURICE DESDEVENS DE. *See* DESDEVENS

GLAPION, AUGUSTIN-LOUIS DE, Jesuit and superior general; b. 8 July 1719 at Mortagnesur-Huisne (Mortagne-au-Perche), France; d. 24 Feb. 1790 at Quebec.

Augustin-Louis de Glapion entered the Jesuit novitiate in Paris on 10 Oct. 1735 and had spent two years studying philosophy at the Collège de La Flèche before going to Quebec in 1739. There he taught liberal arts and the third- and fourth-year classes at the Jesuit college. On his return to France in 1746 he studied philosophy and theology at the Collège Louis-le-Grand in Paris until 1751. His tertianship completed, he took his major vows in 1753 at the Collège de Nevers, where he was a professor of philosophy in 1752 and 1753. The next five years he spent as prefect of studies at the Collège d'Arras, which he left in 1758 intending to return to Quebec.

Glapion left Paris on 25 March 1758 and made the crossing with Joseph-Pierre de BONNÉCAMPS, a former colleague in Quebec. In May the two Jesuits rejoined Jean-Baptiste de Saint-Pé*, who was still serving as superior general of the Jesuits and rector of their college in Quebec, the spiritual and intellectual centre of the Society of Jesus in North America. Saint-Pé may indeed have been responsible for Glapion's return to Canada. The ageing superior, then 72, was undoubtedly glad to see Glapion, whom he knew and esteemed and whom he thought of as his successor. The appointment of the newly arrived Jesuit as minister and procurator of the college, and hence as Saint-Pé's principal assistant, would seem to corroborate this suggestion.

In order to maintain essential contacts with the civil and religious authorities after the capitulation of Quebec in September 1759, Saint-Pé had to seek refuge outside the occupied region as they had done. In Montreal he would be in a better position to communicate with most of the members of his order, who were scattered across America. He left Glapion as vice-rector at the college in Quebec and hence as his deputy to the Jesuits there. In October 1759 James MURRAY asked the Jesuits to vacate the college so that it could be converted into a military storehouse. Glapion found refuge at the mission of Lorette until 1761, when part of the college was restored to the order. He returned to Quebec in June and was joined there by Saint-Pé, who from then on seems to have transferred the duties of superior general to Glapion, although his official appointment came only in 1763.

Glapion's historical importance as superior general results primarily from the specific circumstances that kept him in office as the last incumbent for almost 30 years. Many factors – the British conquest and the treaty of Paris, the diverse constitutional régimes and the policies of the various governors, and later the suppression of the Jesuits by Rome – moved his order inexorably toward extinction, which the deaths of its members ultimately made inevitable. As superior general Glapion lived through the whole painful progression of events and was necessarily involved in the major issues – the order's struggle for existence, the disposition of the Jesuit estates, and the closely linked incidents involving Pierre-Joseph-Antoine ROUBAUD.

In the act of capitulation of Montreal in 1760, AMHERST recognized the property rights of the religious orders but made their continuation in the colony subject to the king's pleasure. By 1762 Murray had decided to demand total suppression of the Jesuit order, which he disliked, and seizure of its estates. In 1764 when Roubaud, who was collaborating with the governor though still a Jesuit, was authorized by him to go to England as his agent to inform the British authorities about the new colony, Glapion behaved with firmness, wisdom, and dignity towards both men.

The Jesuits in Canada were shielded by the treaty of Paris from the termination of the society's civil existence that their *confrères* were suffering in France. Murray, however, received instructions dated 13 Aug. 1763 to limit the order to its existing members and to forbid recruitment in Canada. Glapion made use of Étienne CHAREST's visit to London to ask that this restriction be removed and that the college be restored to its original purpose, education. Murray's replacement by Guy Carleton* in 1766 coincided with the return of Jean-Olivier BRIAND as bishop and the filling of a see that had been unoccupied for six years. Glapion had already planned for three of his colleagues who were lay brothers to be ordained. Jean-Baptiste Noël and Jean-Joseph CASOT became priests on 20 Dec. 1766 and Alexis Maquet in September 1767. After securing Carleton's support, Glapion wrote to the secretary of state, Shelburne, on 12 Nov. 1766; he raised the question of recruitment from among those of Canadian origin or from Europe, he asked that the order be allowed to reoccupy fully all the buildings belonging to it, and he requested compensation for the army's occupation of the college. Glapion's demands went unanswered. The Americans in 1776, however, gave to the Jesuits their Montreal residence, which had been converted into a prison by colonial officials.

The *Quebec Gazette* had for years been publishing reports of the treatment the Jesuits were suffering in various Catholic countries in Europe. Even a rumour that Rome would totally suppress them gained ground. Some time in 1774 the papal brief *Dominus ac Redemptor* reached Quebec;

this decree, suppressing the Society of Jesus, had finally been signed at the end of August 1773. Bishop Briand, who was personally well disposed towards the Jesuits, was apparently dumbfounded. A letter he wrote on 6 Nov. 1774 to the prefect of the Sacred Congregation of the Propaganda shows that he had not grasped the consequences of the incredible news or the importance of the role which Rome was entrusting to him as bishop. With Carleton's agreement, he did not proclaim the suppression of the order, and its survival as a religious body resulted in its civil survival. Canonical regulations made the bishop the hierarchical superior of the Jesuits in Canada; civil arrangements made the bishop subordinate to the governor. Carleton never raised the issue of the Jesuits' continuation although he always advocated that the government take over their estates. In this he – and Glapion – took a position opposite to that of Amherst, who from 1769 on, in collusion with Roubaud, was claiming the estates for himself. The stance taken by Carleton's successor, HALDIMAND, towards the Jesuits was closer to that of Murray. When Carleton took up office again in Quebec along with Chief Justice William SMITH in 1786, he displayed greater determination to take over title to the Jesuits' property in order to use the proceeds for education. In 1788 when Glapion was required to produce copies of the Jesuits' property deeds for a commission established to investigate their estates, he specified that he would do so only in the presence of a notary. Again, in 1789 he maintained that the right to private property was sacred. And in a final gesture, two months before he died, he legally transferred "to the Canadian people" all the property belonging to his order. A hundred years of discussion would fail to breach the untransferrable character of the estates.

In spite of all these disputes Glapion fulfilled his calling as a priest. He was confessor at the Hôpital Général in Quebec and to Bishop Louis-Philippe MARIAUCHAU d'Esgly, and it was as confessor that he apparently saved the father of La Corriveau from being hanged [*see* Marie-Josephte Corriveau*]. Glapion died at Quebec on 24 Feb. 1790; there were then only two surviving Jesuits, Bernard Well and Jean-Joseph Casot.

G.-É. GIGUÈRE

AAQ, 20 A, I, 173, 176. Archivum Romanum Societatis Iesu (Rome), Canada I, fasc.1, Varia de pristina missione canadensi, XVII, XVIII, XIX. ASJCF, 727; 4021; IC, 4244.43. ASQ, Polygraphie, XXVII, 54. *JR* (Thwaites), LXXI, 15–16. Laval Laurent, *Québec et l'Église aux États-Unis sous Mgr Briand et Mgr Plessis* (Montréal, 1945). Rochemonteix, *Les jésuites et la N.-F. au XVIIIe siècle*, II. M. Trudel, *L'Église canadienne*. T.-M. Charland, "La mission de John Carroll au Canada en 1776 et l'interdit du P. Floquet," SCHÉC *Rapport*, 1 (1933–34), 45–56. Luc Lacourcière, "Le destin posthume de la Corriveau," *Cahiers des Dix*, 34 (1969), 239–72; "Le triple destin de Marie-Josephte Corriveau (1733–1763)," *Cahiers des Dix*, 33 (1968), 213–42. "La mort de Mgr d'Esgly," *BRH*, XI (1905), 111. J.-E. Roy, "Biographies canadiennes," *BRH*, XIX (1913), 305. Têtu, "Le chapitre de la cathédrale," *BRH*, XVI, 37.

GLASIER (Glasior, Glazier), BEAMSLEY (Bemsley, Bensley) PERKINS, army officer, land agent, and office-holder; baptized 4 July 1714 at Ipswich, Massachusetts, the son of Stephen Glasier and Sarah Eveleth; m. 17 April 1739 Mrs Ann Stevens at Newbury, Massachusetts, and they had one son and one daughter; d. August 1784 aboard the *Nancy* en route from Halifax, Nova Scotia, to England.

Beamsley Perkins Glasier's first recorded military service was in 1745, when he served as an ensign in the 5th Massachusetts Regiment on William Pepperrell*'s expedition against Louisbourg, Île Royale (Cape Breton Island). During the siege 40 men signed an agreement "Voluntarily to go on ye attack of the Island Battery . . . Provided Beamsley Glaizer is our Capt, on sd attack." After Louisbourg's surrender, Glasier was commissioned a captain in August. Ten years later he again served with the Massachusetts forces, this time as a major in Jonathan Bagly's regiment. William JOHNSON made Glasier adjutant general of the provincial forces at Lake George (Lac Saint-Sacrement), New York, that September, remarking that "He is a Very Active and Serviceable man." Johnson's opinion was not shared by everyone, for a month later about 45 Massachusetts officers demanded that Glasier and William Eyre* be relieved of their commands, called Glasier a "Murd[erer?]," and threatened that if the two were not removed "ye Camp Should be too hott for them." The commanding officers refused to entertain their complaints. Shortly afterwards Glasier became a lieutenant-colonel in the New York regiment. In July 1756 Glasier, now a colonel, participated in a meeting of colonial field officers at Ford Edward (N.Y.) that pointed out the difficulties preventing cooperation between colonial and regular forces [*see* John WINSLOW].

In March 1757 Glasier, while continuing to serve as a colonel in the New York regiment, was commissioned lieutenant in the Royal Americans (60th Foot), a unit especially formed for service in North America; many of its officers were Americans, Germans, and Swiss. In April he was placed in charge of Fort Herkimer (Herkimer, N.Y.). He probably served in the west throughout the campaigns of 1758, 1759, and 1760, although it is related that he visited Quebec to make an exchange of prisoners. There he is supposed to have met his close relative Captain Benjamin Glasier, who had been captured by Indians at Fort William Henry (also called Fort George; now Lake George, N.Y.). In 1760 Glasier was promoted captain.

Glasier was one of the principal founders of the Massachusetts outpost on the lower Saint John River that was to develop into the core area of the later colony of New Brunswick. He was a member of a group of army officers, mostly from the 44th and 60th regiments, who decided at Montreal in 1764 to enter into a venture to settle Nova Scotian lands. An association, later known as the Saint John River Society or occasionally as the Canada Company, was formed under the leadership of Captain Thomas Falconer. The association later added members from Halifax, Boston, New York, Philadelphia, and Ireland, and it came to include such officers as Thomas GAGE and Ralph Burton*, after whom townships were named, and prominent colonial leaders such as Governor Thomas Hutchinson of Massachusetts and Philip John Livingston of New York.

Glasier, the association's appointed agent, left Quebec in August 1764 to choose suitable lands in Nova Scotia. He arrived at Halifax in late October and, crossing over to Fort Frederick (Saint John, N.B.), conducted a preliminary survey of the lower Saint John. Impressed by the area, he reported back to his associates that "it looks like a Park as far as ever your eye can carry you." He returned to Halifax and in December received the Council's promise that the land would be reserved until the following June. In the spring of 1765 Glasier returned to the Saint John, this time with Charles Morris* Jr, to conduct a more rigorous survey. In April, while he was still there, the region, partly through his advocacy, was erected into Sunbury County. He and Falconer were elected shortly afterwards as its first representatives, but Glasier was never in Halifax when the assembly was sitting. In fact, neither of them took his seat.

There was great competition for lands in Nova Scotia, and to get support in the Council Glasier had listed two councillors, Michael FRANCKLIN and Surveyor General Charles MORRIS, as members of the association the previous December. In July 1765 Francklin wrote Glasier confidentially, urging him to complete his selection of land soon because the government was embarrassed at the number of land applicants who were "put off on your acct." The society had begun work on the establishment of a settlement, having engaged the services of Richard Barlow, a former sergeant in the 44th, to act as its storekeeper; by the summer, tools, six oxen, and supplies had arrived at Fort Frederick for the future settlers. In October the society received from the Nova Scotia government a grant of five townships on the Saint John River, comprising about 400,000 acres.

Glasier spent the early months of 1766 in New York organizing a meeting of the society, at which it was decided to establish a township, to be called Gagetown, on the site of an old French settlement and to build mills at Nashwaak Falls (Marysville). In July Glasier sailed from Newburyport, Massachusetts, to Fort Frederick, stopping at Portsmouth to pick up five millwrights. In the following months he was engaged in "building the mills, surveying . . . clearing up the land, bilding Houses, making Roades, hiring oxen . . . and in fine so much I shall never pretend to write it." In the spring of 1767, however, he left the Saint John for New York and rejoined his regiment in August. The mills were uncompleted, and, although a number of settlers were brought out by the proprietors in the following years, the terms of the grants to the society were not met and most of the lands were escheated with the arrival of the loyalists in 1783. Glasier's letters show that he had some skill as a promoter but that he failed to persuade the proprietors to subscribe enough money to finance his activities; their parsimony was almost certainly the main reason for his abandoning the enterprise. The Indians of the Saint John River, who raided the settlements a few years later and drove the settlers from his own estate at the mouth of the Nerepis River, do not appear to have objected seriously to Glasier's attempt to build mills a few miles from their main settlement at Aukpaque (near Fredericton). Indeed, on his first visit to the river Glasier had described them as "well pleased at our coming here."

Between 26 July 1768 and 24 May 1770 Glasier served as commandant of the garrison at Michilimackinac (Mackinaw City, Mich.). There, in August 1768, he met the Ottawa chiefs, NISSOWAQUET among them. He was impressed by their demeanour but refused their request for food, pointing out that "they m[ust not] expect he cou'd maintain them in time of profound peace." He reported that copper deposits in the Lake Superior area were plentiful and of high quality. In June 1769 he recommended to Gage that the fort be moved to nearby Mackinac Island. He was living in Albany County, New York, in 1772 and was promoted major in 1775; during the American revolution he served in the West Indies and the southern colonies as commandant of the fourth battalion of his regiment. In 1778 he was the commandant at St Augustine (Fla) and the next year served at the siege of Savannah (Ga). From February 1780 to October 1782 he was again commandant at St Augustine. Glasier's battalion then went by way of New York to Halifax, where it was disbanded in October 1783.

Although most of the Saint John River Society's grants were escheated in 1783, Glasier, because he had lost property in Florida and because of his efforts to promote settlement, was permitted to keep his estate and was also given an adjoining grant of 1,000 acres. Just before his death he sold his estate to Major John Coffin*.

D. MURRAY YOUNG

[Benjamin Glasier], "French and Indian war diary of Benjamin Glasier of Ipswich, 1758–1760 . . . ," Essex Institute, *Hist. Coll.* (Salem, Mass.), LXXXVI (1950), 65–92.

BL, Add. MSS 21661, pp.28–30. Clements Library, Sir Henry Clinton papers; Thomas Gage papers. Huntington Library, Loudoun papers, LO 1575, LO 1680, LO 2699, LO 4219, LO 4258, LO 4397, LO 5215. Mass. Hist. Soc., Parkman coll.; St John's Soc. coll. PRO, PRO 30/55; WO 34/191. "The James White papers," ed. W. O. Raymond, N.B. Hist. Soc., *Coll.*, II (1899–1905), no.4, 30–72. *Johnson papers* (Sullivan *et al.*). [Charles Morris], "The St. John River: description of the harbour and river of St. John's in Nova Scotia, and of the townships of Sunbury, Burton, Gage, and Conway, lying on said river . . . dated 25th Jan. 1768," *Acadiensis* (Saint John, N.B.), III (1903), 120–28. *Muskets, cannon balls & bombs; nine narratives of the siege of Savannah in 1779*, ed. and trans. Benjamin Kennedy (Savannah, Ga., 1974), 101, 106n. *Old Fort Michilimackinac: reproductions of two maps from the papers of General Thomas Gage in the William L. Clements Library . . .* (Ann Arbor, Mich., 1938), 10–11. "Old townships on the River St. John; papers relating to the St. John's River Society," ed. W. O. Raymond, N.B. Hist. Soc., *Coll.*, II (1899–1905), no.6, 302–57. W. H. Siebert, *Loyalists in east Florida, 1774 to 1785; the most important documents pertaining thereto* (2v., De Land, Fla., 1929; repr., intro. G. A. Billias, Boston, Mass., 1972), II, 63.

J. B. Butcher, "Eveleth genealogy" (typescript; copy at office of *New England Hist. and Geneal. Register*, Boston). G.B., WO, *Army list. Massachusetts officers in the French and Indian wars, 1748–1763*, ed. N. S. Voye (Boston, 1975). *Vital records of Ipswich, Massachusetts, to the end of the year 1849* (3v., Salem, Mass., 1910–19), I, 159–60; II, 186, 567–68. *Vital records of Newbury, Massachusetts, to the end of the year 1849* (2v., Salem, 1911), I, 182; II, 193–94, 598. L. M. B. Maxwell, *An outline history of central New Brunswick to the time of confederation* (Sackville, N.B., 1937). C. L. Mowat, *East Florida as a British province, 1763–1784* (Berkeley, Calif., and Los Angeles, 1943; repr. Gainsville, Fla., 1964), 123. W. O. Raymond, *Glimpses of the past: history of the River St. John, A.D. 1604–1784* (Saint John, N.B., 1905); *River St. John*. N. W. Wallace, *A regimental chronicle and list of officers of the 60th, or the King's Royal Rifle Corps, formerly the 62nd, or the Royal American Regiment of Foot* (London, 1879). L. M. [B.] Maxwell, "Benjamin Glasier, early settler of central New Brunswick," *Maritime Advocate and Busy East* (Sackville, N.B.), 45 (1954–55), no.8, 11–13.

GLAUDE. *See* CLAUDE

GLIKHIKAN (**Glickhican**, usually translated as gun sight or sight on a gun barrel; baptized **Isaac**), Munsee Delaware warrior and orator, Moravian convert and "native elder"; probably b. *c.* 1730 in Pennsylvania; d. 8 March 1782 at Gnadenhutten (Ohio).

An eminent Delaware war captain, Glikhikan journeyed to Canada in support of the French during the Seven Years' War. In 1763 he participated in the siege of Fort Pitt (Pittsburgh, Pa) during Pontiac*'s uprising. He was the most influential counsellor to Packnake, head chief of the Munsee Delawares at Kuskuski (near New Castle, Pa). An early opponent of Christianity, Glikhikan had contested the efforts of the Jesuits among the tribes bordering on lakes Erie and Ontario. In 1769 he journeyed to the new Moravian mission at Lawunakhannek (near Franklin, Pa), intending to force David Zeisberger* and other missionaries from the region. While at Lawunakhannek, he listened to Zeisberger preach and soon was converted to Christianity. During the following year he was instrumental in extending the Delaware invitation to the Moravians to establish a new mission, Languntoutenünk (probably near Darlington), on the Beaver River in western Pennsylvania. On Christmas eve 1770 he was baptized into the Moravian congregation there.

Glikhikan remained a dedicated Christian and assisted Zeisberger and John Gottlieb Ernestus Hackenwelder (Heckewelder) in their attempts to spread the Moravian faith among the tribes of the Ohio valley. Glikhikan's former stature as an orator and warrior enabled him to exert considerable influence, and he soon became a "national helper" or "native elder." In 1772 he and the Moravian Indians moved to the present Tuscarawas River in eastern Ohio, where they founded two new settlements: Schoenbrunn (near New Philadelphia) and Gnadenhutten.

During Lord Dunmore's War (between Virginia and the Shawnees in 1774), Glikhikan assisted the Delaware chief White Eyes in keeping his tribe out of the conflict, and when the American revolution erupted, he used his influence to prevent large numbers of Delawares from joining the British. Although the Moravian villages proclaimed neutrality, the missionaries and the converts favoured the Americans and occasionally supplied American leaders at Pittsburgh with intelligence of British raiding parties. Between 1777 and 1781 Glikhikan successfully persuaded several groups of pro-British Indians who were passing through the Moravian towns to return to their villages without striking the Americans. He also protected Zeisberger and other missionaries from hostile warriors.

In September 1781 a large British war party led by Matthew Elliott*, the Wyandot chief Pomoacan (Half-King), and the Delaware chief Konieschguanokee (Captain Pipe) forced Glikhikan, the missionaries, and the Moravian Indians to abandon their settlements in the Tuscarawas valley and resettle at Captives' Town on the upper Sandusky River. During late October Glikhikan, Zeisberger, Hackenwelder, and several of the Moravian Indians journeyed to Detroit, where they were interrogated by the British commander, Major Arent Schuyler De Peyster. De Peyster found them innocent of the charges that they had actively aided the Americans, and in November 1781 Glikhikan and the missionaries returned to Captives' Town.

During the winter of 1781–82 the refugees on the Sandusky suffered from a severe shortage of food. In February 1782 Glikhikan led about 100 of the Indians back to the Tuscarawas towns, hoping to harvest the corn they had been forced to abandon the previous September. At Gnadenhutten, Glikhikan and his followers were surprised by a force of Pennsylvania militia commanded by Lieutenant-Colonel David Williamson. The Pennsylvanians accused the Moravian Indians of supporting the British, and on 8 March 1782 Glikhikan, his wife Anna, and 88 others died under the hatchets and mallets of the Americans.

R. DAVID EDMUNDS

Documentary history of Dunmore's War, ed. R. G. Thwaites and L. P. Kellogg (Madison, Wis., 1905), 28. *Frontier advance on the upper Ohio, 1778–1779*, ed. L. P. Kellogg (Madison, 1916), 240–61. *Frontier retreat on the upper Ohio, 1779–1781*, ed. L. P. Kellogg (Madison, 1917), 120–346. [J. G. E. Hackenwelder], *Narrative of the mission of the United Brethren among the Delaware and Mohegan Indians . . .* (Philadelphia, 1820; repr. New York, 1971), 100–226; *Thirty thousand miles with John Heckewelder*, ed. P. A. W. Wallace (Pittsburgh, Pa., 1958), 85–200. "John Ettwein and the Moravian Church during the revolutionary period," ed. K. G. Hamilton, Moravian Hist. Soc., *Trans.* (Bethlehem, Pa.), XII (1940), 342–62. *Michigan Pioneer Coll.*, X (1886), 523, 538–41. *Pa. archives* (Hazard *et al.*), 1st ser., VII, 541–42; IX, 524–42. [David Zeisberger], *Diary of David Zeisberger, a Moravian missionary among the Indians of Ohio*, ed. and trans. E. F. Bliss (2v., Cincinnati, Ohio, 1885), I, 1–65. *Handbook of American Indians* (Hodge).

C. W. Butterfield, *History of the Girtys . . .* (Cincinnati, Ohio, 1890), 98–102. Edmund De Schweinitz, *The life and times of David Zeisberger . . .* (Philadelphia, 1871), 350–550. Gnadenhuetten Monument Soc., *A true history of the massacre of ninety-six Christian Indians, at Gnadenhuetten, Ohio, March 8th, 1782* (New Philadelphia, Ohio, 1844), 1–12. E. [E. L.] and L. R. Gray, *Wilderness Christians, the Moravian mission to the Delaware Indians* (Toronto and Ithaca, N.Y., 1956), 40–75. Reginald Horsman, *Matthew Elliott, British Indian agent* (Detroit, 1964), 25–40. W. H. Rice, *David Zeisberger and his brown brethren* (Bethlehem, Pa., 1897). P. A. W. Wallace, *Indians in Pennsylvania* (Harrisburg, Pa., 1961), 173. C. A. Weslager, *The Delaware Indians, a history* (New Brunswick, N.J., 1972), 221–317.

GODEFROY DE LINCTOT, DANIEL-MAURICE, officer in the colonial regular troops, merchant, and Indian agent; baptized 5 May 1739 at Montreal, son of Louis-René Godefroy de Linctot and Catherine-Apolline Blondeau; d. before 30 April 1783 in the Illinois country.

Daniel-Maurice Godefroy de Linctot belonged to the fifth generation of Godefroys to serve in the military forces in New France. His brothers Hyacinthe and Maurice-Régis were also officers in the colonial regulars and there is some confusion about the three careers prior to 1760. By the early 1750s Daniel-Maurice was a cadet, and he and a brother participated in Jean-Daniel DUMAS's defeat of Edward Braddock near Fort Duquesne (Pittsburgh, Pa) in July 1755. He became an ensign in 1759. After the fall of New France he and most of his family went to France, arriving on 1 Jan. 1762. In 1764 several members of the family were given permission and funds to return to Canada to settle their affairs, and it may have been at this time that Daniel-Maurice left France. Two Linctot brothers, probably Hyacinthe and Daniel-Maurice, were reported to be living at Verchères in 1767, but by 1770 they had apparently moved west. Daniel-Maurice became a successful trader at Prairie du Chien (Wis.) and Cahokia (East St Louis, Ill.) and was considered a leader among the French of the Illinois country.

With the coming of the American revolution Linctot faced the problem of allegiance once again. As late as June 1778, Charles Gautier de Verville, a leading British advocate in the Upper Lakes region, spoke favourably of the Linctot brothers, and on 4 June Daniel-Maurice was reported to be visiting with Charles-Michel MOUET de Langlade, the most effective British partisan on the frontier. When the revolution reached the Illinois country with George Rogers Clark's forces in July, Linctot changed his stance. Perhaps influenced by community leaders such as Linctot, Jacques-Timothée Boucher de Montbrun, Father Pierre Gibault*, and the merchant Jean-Gabriel Cerré*, the French inhabitants of the Illinois country generally welcomed the rebels. Linctot was elected militia captain by the residents of Cahokia, and during the next few months he made expeditions with a troop of horse soldiers against La Pée (also called Peouarea; now Peoria, Ill.), Vincennes (Ind.), and Ouiatanon (near Lafayette, Ind.). Pleased with his work, Clark named him Indian agent for most of the Illinois country in the spring of 1779. The appointment, carrying the rank of major in the Virginia troops, was later confirmed by Thomas Jefferson, governor of the state.

Linctot spent most of the winter of 1779–80 in Virginia, and while there conferred with the French admiral, Louis-Philippe de Rigaud de Vaudreuil, Marquis de Vaudreuil, who encouraged him to attract more frontier French to the rebel cause. By mid 1780 Linctot was at Fort Pitt (Pittsburgh) with the assignment of engaging the Shawnees, Delawares, and other Ohio valley tribes to fight the British. That Linctot, who knew several Indian lanugages, was an effective irritant can be seen in a letter to the Ohio valley Indians from Arent Schuyler De Peyster, the British commandant at Detroit: "Send me that little babbling Frenchman named Monsieur Linctot, he who poisons your ears." Clark later referred to Linctot's "singular service" as an Indian agent.

Travelling was common for Linctot in these years. He was in St Louis (Mo.) from July to September 1781 and conferred there with Francisco Cruzat, the Spanish lieutenant governor of Upper Louisiana. Late in September he was back in Cahokia, involved in a minor land case. After this date nothing is known of him. He had died by 30 April 1783, as a letter from Clark to Jefferson makes clear.

DONALD CHAPUT

AN, Col., D^{2C}, 48, 58, 59; F^3, 12. ANQ-M, État civil, Catholiques, Notre-Dame de Montréal, 5 mai 1739. *Cahokia records, 1778–1790*, ed. C. W. Alvord (Springfield, Ill., 1907). *Frontier retreat on the upper Ohio, 1779–1781*, ed. L. P. Kellogg (Madison, Wis., 1917). *George Rogers Clark papers . . .* [1771–84], ed. J. A. James (2v., Springfield, Ill., 1912–26). *Kaskaskia records, 1778*–1790, ed. C. W. Alvord (Springfield, Ill., 1909). *The papers of Thomas Jefferson*, ed. J. P. Boyd *et al.* (19v. to date, Princeton, N.J., 1950–). Wis., State Hist. Soc., *Coll.*, XI (1888), 100–11. *Dictionnaire national des Canadiens français (1608–1760)* (2v., Montréal, 1958). Tanguay, *Dictionnaire*. Va., *Calendar of Virginia state papers . . .* (11v., Richmond, Va., 1875–93), III. F. L. Billon, *Annals of St Louis in its early days under the French and Spanish dominations* (St Louis, Mo., 1886; repr. [New York], 1971). G. A. Brennan, "De Linctot, guardian of the frontier," Ill. State Hist. Soc., *Journal* (Springfield), X (1917–18), 323–66.

GODEFROY DE TONNANCOUR, CHARLES-ANTOINE (also called the **Chevalier de Tonnancour**), soldier and seigneur; b. 4 Nov. 1755 at Trois-Rivières (Que.), son of Louis-Joseph GODEFROY de Tonnancour and Louise Carrerot; m. 21 Nov. 1785 in Quebec, Reine, daughter of Jean-Louis Frémont, a merchant-trader, and they had ten children; d. 6 Nov. 1798 in Trois-Rivières.

Like his father and two brothers, Charles-Antoine Godefroy de Tonnancour took part in the defence of the province of Quebec during the American invasion in 1775. He seems subsequently to have undergone a period of inactivity, and on 13 May 1781 he begged Governor HALDIMAND to keep him in mind if an opportunity arose to employ a young officer who for a long time had "been languishing in a kind of idleness . . . quite contrary to his nature."

For some years before his marriage in 1785 the Chevalier de Tonnancour probably divided his time between Trois-Rivières and Quebec; he may even have acted as an agent in Quebec for his father who had various business interests including the fur trade. When his father died in 1784 Tonnancour acquired the family estate which he had to share with his eight brothers and sisters. This inheritance consisted mainly of landed property located between Trois-Rivières and the seigneury of Maskinongé, primarily the fiefs of Vieuxpont, Labadie, Pointe-du-Lac, and Yamaska.

Tonnancour finally took up residence in Trois-Rivières in 1785 and began to sell off his lands little by little. He was by no means the only one thus to dissipate his paternal inheritance; his co-heirs often joined him in disposing of the properties. The proceeds of the sales were never sufficient, however, to maintain his luxurious way of life; he had to resort to loans that he could not always repay on the due date. Thus in 1788 Pierre-Édouard Desbarats*, a Trois-Rivières merchant with whom he had a current account, demanded payment of a bill for 200 *livres*; later a merchant-trader in Quebec, Jacques Curchot, brought a protest against him for his delay in paying £100, for which Curchot demanded interest.

When a new district of Trois-Rivières was created in July 1790, Tonnancour was one of 17 people chosen by Lord Dorchester [Carleton*] to oversee "keeping the peace in the aforementioned new District." Four years later he and George Dame were jointly appointed commissioners for granting lands in this district. In March 1797 he was appointed head of the grand juries for the Court of King's Bench. The following year he died at Trois-Rivières.

Although the inventory compiled after Tonnancour's death shows that he owned a handsome and well-furnished house, personal belongings worth 2,902 *livres*, and five pieces of land in Trois-Rivières and its suburbs, it also reveals that his financial situation was desperate. His debts amounted to 48,949 *livres*, whereas there were only 9,597 *livres* in outstanding accounts to be recovered by his estate. Nearly all the landed property went to pay debts owed to William Grant*, a Trois-Rivières merchant, and his partner James McKenzie. In view of this situation the Chevalier's widow, who was to live until 1858, had no choice but to exercise her right to renounce the community of property with her husband, "without being held responsible for its debts."

Charles-Antoine Godefroy de Tonnancour's life illustrates well the precarious financial position in which many Canadian seigneurs found themselves at the end of the 18th century, a plight which became inevitable with the rise of the lower middle class.

NORMAND PAQUETTE

ANQ-MBF, Greffe d'A.-I. Badeaux, 13 sept. 1797, 21 déc. 1798; Greffe de J.-B. Badeaux, 29 oct. 1784, 13 sept. 1785, 15 mars, 4 déc. 1787, 15 mars, 18 juin, 18 août 1788, 5 mars 1789. BL, Add. MSS 21830, pp. 213–14. *Quebec Gazette*, 24 Nov. 1785, 8 July 1790, 16 Oct. 1794, 16 Oct. 1797, 3 Jan., 30 Oct. 1800. P.-G. Roy, *La famille Godefroy de Tonnancour* (Lévis, Qué., 1904), 57, 61; "Les ancêtres du général Frémont," *BRH*, IV (1898), 277–78.

GODEFROY DE TONNANCOUR, LOUIS-JOSEPH, keeper of stores, king's attorney, seigneur, and merchant; baptized 27 March 1712 at Trois-Rivières (Que.), son of René Godefroy* de Tonnancour and Marguerite Ameau; d. 15 May 1784 at Trois-Rivières.

Louis-Joseph Godefroy de Tonnancour began to make his mark in the Trois-Rivières region in 1730, when the chief road commissioner (*grand voyer*), Jean-Eustache Lanoullier* de Boisclerc, chose him as his clerk. The following year he was entrusted with the duties of king's storekeeper, a post he retained along with that of king's attorney for the jurisdiction of Trois-Rivières which he received on 1 April 1740. He had also succeeded his father as apostolic syndic for the Recollets of Trois-Rivières in 1738.

Godefroy de Tonnancour inherited from his father the seigneury of Pointe-du-Lac, on which he tried to build a village for nomadic Indians. Visiting Canada in 1752, the military engineer Louis Franquet* took note of this undertaking, indicating that it involved "houses all built alike and laid out in straight lines; there were already nine of them." Five more fiefs were added to Godefroy de Tonnancour's properties in the Trois-Rivières region – Labadie, Yamaska, Roquetaillade, Godefroy, and Île-Marie.

In addition, Godefroy de Tonnancour achieved recognition as a merchant. Having been a supplier to the state in the 1740s, for shipbuilding among other things, he was one of three people granted a licence in 1760 for "sedentary trade" in Trois-Rivières and the surrounding area. About 1760 the Hotel-Dieu of Quebec borrowed 9,600 *livres* from him, and Bishop Pontbriand [Dubreil*] 9,000 *livres*. Godefroy de Tonnancour remained in Canada after the Seven Years' War, and he continued to be active under the new régime. Thus, from 16 March to 30 April 1764 he sat as commissioner for the registration of Canada paper, along with Jean-Baptiste Perrault and René-Ovide HERTEL de Rouville. He declared that he had over 150,000 *livres* of it in his own possession, more than any of his fellow merchants claimed; he lost a great deal of it at the time of the settlement of paper money by the king of France [*see* Alexandre-Robert HILLAIRE de La Rochette; Bernard Cardeneau*]. In March 1769 Governor Guy Carleton* recommended him as a member of the Legislative Council, but he was not appointed.

During the American invasion in 1775–76 [*see* Richard MONTGOMERY] Godefroy de Tonnancour showed his loyalty to George III. Having been appointed a colonel of militia on 7 Sept. 1775, he tried to overcome the desire of the inhabitants of Trois-Rivières to remain neutral; in this effort he was aided by the notary Jean-Baptiste BADEAUX. When the Americans occupied the town in February 1776, Godefroy de Tonnancour was the only militia officer who refused to hand over his commission, alleging that it was "something that belonged to him and formed part of his property." In the face of the enemy's intransigence, however, he had to give in.

On 11 Feb. 1740 at Trois-Rivières Godefroy de

Tonnancour had married a former captive of the Indians, Mary Scamen (Scammon), and they had four children. On 2 Nov. 1749 in Quebec he took as his second wife Louise Carrerot, daughter of André Carrerot*; the couple had 12 children. All his life Godefroy de Tonnancour maintained ties with the leading citizens of Trois-Rivières. An important local figure, he was able to adapt to the change of régime and to win the good will of both Governor HALDIMAND and Bishop BRIAND.

FRANCES CAISSIE

AN, Col., C11A, 57, pp.40–41 (PAC transcripts). ANQ-MBF, État civil, Catholiques, Immaculée-Conception (Trois-Rivières), 27 mars 1712, 11 févr. 1740, 17 mai 1784; Greffe de Paul Dielle, 26 mars 1766; Greffe de Jean Leproust, 15 mars, 3, 17 mai 1756; Greffe de Louis Pillard, 9 sept. 1749, 7 mars 1755, 15 mai 1764; Greffe de H.-O. Pressé, 11 févr. 1740. ANQ-Q, État civil, Catholiques, Notre-Dame de Québec, 2 nov. 1749; Greffe de Claude Barolet, 26 oct. 1749. [J.-B. Badeaux], "Journal des opérations de l'armée américaine, lors de l'invasion du Canada en 1775–76, par M. J. B. Badeaux, notaire de la ville des Trois-Rivières," *Revue canadienne* (Montréal), VII (1870), 186–202, 267–76, 329–45. Le Jeune, *Dictionnaire*, II, 721. P.-G. Roy, *Inv. concessions*, I, 154, 289; II, 48, 126, 254, 268; III, 147, 263–64; IV, 117; *Inv. procès-verbaux des grands voyers*, V, 155–56. Tanguay, *Dictionnaire*, IV, 314.

Coleman, *New England captives*, II, 147–48. Alexandre Dugré, *La Pointe-du-Lac* (Trois-Rivières, 1934). Jouve, *Les franciscains et le Canada: aux Trois-Rivières*. Cameron Nish, *Les bourgeois-gentilshommes de la Nouvelle-France, 1729–1748* (Montréal et Paris, 1968), 58, 65–67, 113, 141, 147, 152, 178. P.-G. Roy, *La famille Godefroy de Tonnancour* (Lévis, Qué., 1904), 50–51, 82. Sulte, *Mélanges historiques* (Malchelosse), II, 79; XI, 29; XVIII, 39, 58. M. Trudel, *L'Église canadienne*, II, 98, 270, 406; *Le Régime militaire*, 11–15, 18, 22, 25–27, 75, 120, 146.

GODIN, *dit* **Bellefontaine**, *dit* **Beauséjour, JOSEPH**, militia officer, merchant, and interpreter; b. 1697 in the parish of Sainte-Anne-du-Pays-Bas (Fredericton, N.B.), son of Gabriel Godin, *dit* Chatillon, *dit* Bellefontaine, and Marie-Angélique Robert Jasne (Robertjeanne); m. 1725 Marie-Anne Bergeron d'Amboise; d. after 1774, probably in Cherbourg, France.

When Joseph Robinau* de Villebon, governor of Acadia, built Fort Saint-Joseph (known as Fort Nashwaak, now Fredericton) in 1692, he brought to the area a number of Acadian and Canadian settlers, including Gabriel Godin, *dit* Chatillon, a naval officer, and his wife. Robinau made Godin second lieutenant at the fort and granted him land with a frontage of three leagues on the Saint John River. This land was the origin of the name Bellefontaine. Godin developed the property and used it as a base for a substantial trade with other French colonies and with the Indians – Abenakis, Malecites, and Micmacs. He became so adept in the Indians' languages that Robinau appointed him king's interpreter. Joseph Godin worked closely with his father and inherited both his goods and his prestige. He too was a leading settler of the parish, and it was later claimed that "the Indians, like the French, did [nothing] without consulting him and submitted docilely to all his [decisions?]." Governor Beauharnois* commissioned him king's interpreter, and in 1736 Godin and his brother-in-law, Michel Bergeron d'Amboise, went as deputies from the Saint John Acadians to the Annapolis Royal Council. They were imprisoned there by Governor Lawrence Armstrong* for failing to report to the Council immediately, but they were soon released and sent home with instructions to invite the Saint John Indians to the British post.

In 1749 Charles DESCHAMPS de Boishébert organized the Saint John Acadians into a militia, and on 10 April Godin was appointed to its command. During the Seven Years' War he supported and encouraged the Indians in their opposition to the British and even led some of their war parties. When a party of rangers, under the command of Moses Hazen*, sacked Sainte-Anne in February 1759, they killed Godin's daughter and three of his grandchildren because he had refused to swear allegiance to the British king and "by his speech and largess . . . had instigated and maintained the Indians in their hatred and war against the English." Godin was taken prisoner by the rangers and brought, after having been joined by his family, to Annapolis Royal. From there he was taken to Boston, Halifax, and England; later he was sent to Cherbourg. In 1767 he was living there and was one of a group of Acadians who asked for life annuities. He obtained a pension of 300 *livres* for his losses and services. In 1774 a proposal was made to place him and his wife in a religious house where they could be cared for. Recalling his services to the king, which he claimed had cost him 60,000 *livres*, Godin asked that instead they be allowed to remain at Cherbourg with a pension.

GEORGE MACBEATH

AD, Calvados (Caen), C 1020, mémoire de Joseph Bellefontaine, dit Beauséjour, 15 janv. 1774. Placide Gaudet, "Acadian genealogy and notes," PAC *Report*, 1905, II, pt.III, 140, 241. *N.S. Archives, III*. [Joseph Robinau de Villebon], *Acadia at the end of the seventeenth century; letters, journals and memoirs of Joseph Robineau de Villebon . . .*, ed. J. C. Webster (Saint

John, N.B., 1934), 99, 149, 154. L. M. B. Maxwell, *An outline of the history of central New Brunswick to the time of confederation* (Sackville, N.B., 1937).

GODSMAN, JOHN. *See* DAVIDSON, WILLIAM

GOGUET, DENIS, merchant-trader, receiver of the admiralty court of Quebec, and treasurer of France; b. 1704 at La Flotte, Île de Ré, France, son of Denis Goguet, merchant, and Marguerite-Thérèse-Sibylle — ; m. 24 Nov. 1738 at Quebec Louise-Élisabeth, daughter of Jean-Joseph Feré Duburon, lieutenant in the colonial regular troops, and Jeanne Durand; d. 30 Jan. 1778 at La Rochelle, France.

Denis Goguet first came to Canada in 1731 and 1732 as the agent of Simon-Pierre Thiollière, a La Rochelle trader, and probably remained in the colony only during the summer months. He may not have returned to Canada on Thiollière's behalf the next year, for in October 1733 the latter's procurator at Quebec was Jean Taché*, another young Rochelais. Whatever Goguet's activities may have been that year, in the spring of 1734 he was at Quebec as supercargo aboard the *Comte de Toulouse*, bearing bills of lading, instructions, and the power of attorney for Pascaud Frères, the most important La Rochelle firm trading to Canada [*see* Antoine Pascaud*]. Goguet had forged a link that would support a brilliant career.

Goguet was, as a document of 1734 described him, a *marchand forain*, a metropolitan trader spending each summer in the colony, sometimes a winter as well, lodging with one settled trader one year and another the next. But as the Pascauds' trade with Canada was large and regular, Goguet spent more winters at Quebec than many *forains* and stayed for so many years as the Pascauds' factor that he became at least a semi-permanent resident of Quebec's Lower Town business community. A document of 1737 describes him as a "trader of Quebec," but another of the following year calls him a "trader ordinarily resident in the town of La Rochelle presently in this town of Quebec." Goguet's link with Canada was strengthened by his marriage to a Canadian in 1738. The decade that followed saw many signs of growing ties with the community: the renting of a pew in the cathedral church, the purchase of a house (the title later proved invalid), and the birth of eight children in Canada, three of them surviving infancy.

In 1741 the Pascauds received a monopoly of the cod fishery and the seal and walrus hunt in the Îles de la Madeleine. It became one of Goguet's responsibilities to administer the seal and walrus "fishery," as it was called. A contract dated 1742 outlines the method of exploitation. A small ship was sent out from Quebec from September to September with captain, master of the hunt, ship's carpenter, barrel maker, five sailors, and a "boy." All except the boy, who was given a salary of 120 *livres*, were paid by granting them one-third of the product of the hunt, Goguet having the right of first refusal for the purchase of their part. In 1744 the Pascauds, who had always been prominent in Canadian trade, received the contract to supply the king's warehouse at Quebec and kept it for several years. The prestige of the factor was invariably a consequence of his metropolitan connections, and the Pascauds' success contributed to making the 1740s the high point of Goguet's Canadian career. Commerce remained the *raison d'être* of his residence in Canada, but he did not refuse the prestige of office, being appointed receiver of the admiralty court in Canada on 23 April 1743.

Goguet's return to France in 1747 either ended his residence in Canada or was the preparation for a definitive departure. Certainly in 1750 he was once again a "trader of La Rochelle," with his own Quebec agent, apparently Jacques PERRAULT. Goguet is reputed to have become the leading recipient of Canadian furs, numbering the Intendant BIGOT among his clients. In 1750 also, Goguet became a treasurer of France, something that seems astonishing for a colonial factor so recently returned to the metropolis. On 16 June 1756 he was elected syndic of the La Rochelle merchants and in 1769 purchased the office of king's secretary, a sinecure which bestowed many privileges and conferred hereditary nobility. He also provided himself with the landed estate necessary to his high station, becoming the seigneur of La Sauzaie.

In Denis Goguet we are confronted with a great ambition. His early career closely parallels that of Antoine Pascaud, the father of Goguet's own associates, who had similarly made his fortune in Canada, married a Canadian, and transferred his business to La Rochelle. However, the Pascauds' climb to distinguished office and nobility required two generations. The difference is perhaps not so much a measure of Goguet's greater ability or different inclinations as an indication that by the 1750s the line of demarcation between the nobility and the upper bourgeoisie was beginning to wear thin.

DALE MIQUELON

AD, Charente-Maritime (La Rochelle), État civil, Saint-Jean de La Rochelle, 21 janv. 1778. ANQ-Q, Greffe de Claude Barolet, 22 oct. 1731, 15 oct. 1734, 18 août 1738, 2 sept. 1742, 18 août 1751; Greffe de Nicolas

Boisseau, 15 avril, 30 oct. 1741, 30 oct. 1743; Greffe de Jean de Latour, 18 nov. 1738, 6 oct. 1740; Greffe de Claude Louet, 21 mars, 1er oct. 1765; Greffe de J.-C. Panet, 26 juin 1746, 11 oct. 1747, 4 oct. 1753, 8 nov. 1758, 7 oct. 1761, 1er sept. 1762; NF 25, 27, no.1008. PAC, MG 24, L3; *Rapport*, 1904; 1905, I. P.-G. Roy, *Inv.jug. et délib., 1717–60*, III, 61, 233; IV, 226; V, 144, 161, 195; *Inv. ord. int.*, II, 262; III, 18, 39, 46, 52, 66, 85. Tanguay, *Dictionnaire*, IV, 317. Frégault, *François Bigot*, II, 84, 360. Émile Garnault, *Le commerce rochelais au XVIIIe siècle, d'après les documents composant les anciennes archives de la chambre de Commerce de La Rochelle* (5v., La Rochelle et Paris, 1887–1900), I, 87. Robert Henri, "Les trafics coloniaux du port de La Rochelle au XVIIIe siècle," Soc. des antiquaires de l'Ouest, *Mémoires* (Angoulême, France), 4e sér., 4 (1960), 23, 29, 35, 186, 190–91.

GOHIN, PIERRE-ANDRÉ, Comte de MONTREUIL, officer in the French regular troops; b. 16 Nov. 1722 at Angers, France, son of Nicolas Gohin de Montreuil and Monique-Françoise Petit; d. after 1793.

Pierre-André Gohin joined the Régiment de Piémont at the age of 20 as a second lieutenant. Promoted captain in 1746, he served during the War of the Austrian Succession and in 1755 was made a knight of the order of Saint-Louis. That same year he was raised to the rank of lieutenant-colonel and appointed assistant chief of staff of the French regular troops in Canada, then under the command of Jean-Armand Dieskau*. Montreuil arrived at Quebec on 26 June and by August was preparing to join his commander at Fort Saint-Frédéric (near Crown Point, N.Y.). On 8 September he served as second in command to Dieskau in the encounter with British forces under William JOHNSON near the site of the future Fort William Henry (also called Fort George, now Lake George, N.Y.). After the battle Montreuil conducted the French retreat towards Fort Saint-Frédéric. He had attempted to rescue Dieskau, wounded during the engagement, but the commander had ordered him to concentrate his energies on the fighting.

Montreuil's failure to remove Dieskau from the field and prevent his capture by the British drew considerable criticism. Governor Vaudreuil [RIGAUD], on 25 September, declared to Machault, the minister of Marine, that he could not forgive Montreuil for abandoning Dieskau, pointing out that the British would cite his capture "as a proof of their triumph . . . though in truth, [they] have lost three times more men than we." The anonymous diarist of the "Mémoire du Canada" stated that Montreuil had retreated against Dieskau's orders and had deserted his commander in a cowardly manner. Dieskau, however, in letters written from England in 1758, completely exculpated his second in command of any wrongdoing, and the Duc de Belle-Isle, the minister of War, assured him the same year that he considered him blameless. Indeed, the criticism of his action does not seem to have affected his career, for in March 1756 Montreuil was appointed assistant chief of staff under Montcalm*.

Because of the competition for place and honour, relations between French and colonial regular officers in Canada were at best strained. Montreuil shared the low opinion of the Canadians held by Montcalm and his general staff. He attributed Dieskau's failure on 8 Sept. 1755 not only to his having advanced too near the British positions but to his unwarranted faith in the Canadians and the Indians. "The Canadian," he wrote in a report dated 12 June 1756, "is independent, wicked, lying, braggart, well adapted for skirmishing, very brave behind a tree and very timid when not covered." Montreuil also accused Vaudreuil and the colonial officers of prejudice against the French and criticized what he considered to be wasteful and extravagant expenditures on the part of the colonial government.

Montreuil served at the siege of Fort William Henry in 1757 and in the battle at Fort Carillon (Ticonderoga, N.Y.) in 1758, where both Montcalm and LÉVIS reported that he had distinguished himself. Active during the Quebec campaign of 1759, he claimed that he had counselled Montcalm against combat on the Plains of Abraham because he thought the French had not enough men to ensure success. He served as second in command at Sainte-Foy in 1760, returning to France after the fall of Montreal that year. Promoted brigadier in 1761, the next year he was made major-general and served as second in command at Saint-Domingue (Haiti). When the governor, Vicomte Armand de Belzunce, died on 4 Aug. 1763, he assumed full command as governor general of Saint-Domingue until the arrival of the new appointee on 23 April 1764. He probably left the island shortly after and returned to France, where he was promoted lieutenant-general in 1781. On 1 Nivôse, Year II (21 Dec. 1793) of the French Republic the provisional executive committee offered him the nation's thanks and awarded him an annual pension of 837 *livres* 10 *sols* for life in recognition of his service, during which he had participated in ten military campaigns.

Montreuil's character and abilities are difficult to assess. In 1755 André Doreil*, the commissary of wars, described him as an honest man, but weak and astonishingly naïve. Although Montreuil claimed that he was "never happier than when I have a great deal to do," it was Doreil and the Chevalier de La Pause [Plantavit*] who performed much of the assistant chief of staff's work while Montcalm was in command. Montcalm seems to have best summed up Montreuil's abilities when he described him, as he did several times, as a brave, honest, and honourable man, who had little talent for the position he held.

SUSAN W. HENDERSON

AD, Maine-et-Loire (Angers), E, 26; 263. AMA, SHA, A[1], 3498, no.4; 3499, no.90; 3540, no.98; Y[2d] (copies at PAC). *Coll. de manuscrits relatifs à la N.-F.*, III, 547. *Coll. des manuscrits de Lévis* (Casgrain), I–XII. Doreil, "Lettres" (A. Roy), ANQ *Rapport*, 1944–45, 62. "Mémoire du Canada," ANQ *Rapport*, 1924–25, 114, 132, 171, 189. [M.-L.-É.] Moreau de Saint-Méry, *Description topographique, physique, civile, politique et historique de la partie française de l'isle de Saint-Domingue*, Blanche Maurel et Étienne Taillemite, édit. (3v., Paris, 1958). *NYCD* (O'Callaghan and Fernow), X, 324, 419, 862. P.-G. Roy, "Le chevalier de Montreuil," *BRH*, XI (1905), 121–24.

GON?AONGOTE. *See* WILLIAMS, EUNICE

GONWATSIJAYENNI. *See* KOÑWATSI?TSIAIÉÑNI

GOREHAM (Gorham), JOSEPH, army officer and officer-holder; b. 29 May 1725 in Barnstable, Massachusetts, sixth son of Shobal (Shubael) Gorham and Mary Thacter and brother of John Gorham*; m. 29 Dec. 1764 Anne Spry at Halifax, Nova Scotia, and they had six children; m. secondly in 1787 Elizabeth Hunter; d. 20 July 1790 at Calais, France.

Unlike his brother, Joseph Goreham entered military service at an early age. In 1744, just after he left school, he was appointed lieutenant in his brother's company of rangers, which was sent to reinforce the garrison of Annapolis Royal (N.S.) against French attacks. When his brother left for Boston later that year, Joseph assumed temporary command of the company. By 1752 he had been promoted captain and commanded his own company, the only one on the Nova Scotia establishment.

The rangers were used to protect the nascent British settlements such as Lunenburg against Indian raids until the outbreak of the Seven Years' War, when they became increasingly involved in major military operations because of their skill in irregular warfare. In July 1757, for example, Goreham and some of his men were dispatched to reconnoitre Louisbourg for Lord Loudoun's expedition, and a year later they served under AMHERST at the successful siege of the fortress. In 1759 the company formed part of the expedition against Quebec commanded by Wolfe*, and like the other rangers they were used by the general in his campaign of terror against the Canadian settlements. On 9 August Goreham and his men levelled the village of Baie-Saint-Paul in retaliation for attacks on British shipping by the inhabitants, and followed up by burning the hamlets of La Malbaie and Sainte-Anne-de-la-Pocatière (La Pocatière). In September the company was included in Major George Scott*'s force which destroyed the settlements from Kamouraska to Quebec.

In August 1760 Goreham was promoted major in the British army, and the next September he succeeded in having his company taken on the regular establishment, probably because of his good relations with former commanders such as Amherst and George Townshend*. No other ranger unit was so honoured. In 1762, after garrison duty at several places, Goreham's Rangers sailed to Havana, Cuba, and participated in the siege of that city. Like the rest of the British force, the unit was decimated by sickness; Goreham records that he himself was twice "given over" by the surgeons. The following year some rangers accompanied Captain James Dalyell's relief column to Detroit [*see* Henry GLADWIN].

With the disbanding of his unit after the peace in 1763 Goreham returned to Nova Scotia, probably that year. During the next few years he was granted a considerable amount of land in the province, including over 20,000 acres on the Petitcodiac River (N.B.). During his regular trips to England he actively used his connections to seek official positions, and in 1764 he was recommended to Governor Montagu Wilmot* for appointment as lieutenant governor. When he eventually arrived back in Halifax, however, he found to his chagrin that Wilmot had already chosen Michael FRANCKLIN. Goreham then again went to England and petitioned for "appointments . . . adequate to the Salary of the Lieutenant Governor" as compensation for his disappointment. He was rewarded with an appointment to the Council, the position of deputy agent for Indian affairs in the province, and the award of the fuel contract for the troops in Nova Scotia, but he did not return to Halifax until late in 1766. Goreham attended Council meetings infrequently but was genuinely interested in the welfare of the Indians; his overspending, however, was criticized by Guy JOHNSON and other officials of the Indian department.

Despite these appointments, Goreham's financial position grew steadily worse. His numerous journeys in search of preferment had caused him to amass large debts, and even after selling most of his property except his land grants, which he mortgaged, he remained considerably in arrears. In September 1768 he suffered "a very considerable loss of revenue" from the fuel contract when the Halifax garrison was withdrawn to Boston, and the following year a change in Indian department organization caused his dismissal as deputy agent. He regained the post on the personal appeal of Lord Hillsborough, secretary of state for the American Colonies, to Sir William JOHNSON, and in the course of another English visit in 1770 was given the position of lieutenant governor of Placentia, Newfoundland, as well. The salary of the latter appointment proved to be less than he had expected, however, and although he was promoted lieutenant-colonel in 1772 he was not given rank in a regiment as he had hoped. Moreover, that year he was finally dismissed as deputy agent, and he incurred more debts by continuing to draw the salary after his dismissal. Worse followed. By 1774 the time limit for the settlement conditions on his grants had nearly expired with only a few settlers located; in order to stave off the ruin the escheat of these lands would have caused, he appealed to Lord Dartmouth, secretary of state for the American Colonies, and secured a ten-year extension on the settlement grants. The drinking problem which was attributed to him at this time may have contributed to his financial woes.

Under such circumstances, Goreham was probably thankful to be able to enter active military service again. In 1774, with rebellion impending in the southern colonies, he submitted a plan for raising a corps of "His Majesty's Loyal North American subjects"; it was quickly approved. By June 1775 officers were recruiting in Boston, Nova Scotia, and Newfoundland for the Royal Fencible Americans, as the unit was named. Although Goreham hoped to recruit mainly from New England, he gathered only a few rebel deserters, and in Nova Scotia his officers competed with those of Lieutenant-Colonel Allan MACLEAN and Governor Francis LEGGE, who were also raising provincial regiments. Forced to turn to Newfoundland, he still had only 190 men at Halifax in December.

The following May most of the regiment was ordered to garrison Fort Cumberland (near Sackville, N.B.) on the Chignecto Isthmus. In early November a motley rebel force under Jonathan Eddy* appeared in the region and, after capturing an outpost, laid siege to the fort itself. Fortunately for Goreham, Eddy's attacks were poorly handled, and the garrison easily repulsed them with minimal casualties to both sides. Goreham was cautious in defence, preferring to await reinforcements rather than have his half-trained and ill-equipped men attack an enemy believed to be much superior in numbers. British troops arrived from Windsor on the 27th and cooperated with the garrison to rout the rebels two days later, thus ending the only concrete military threat to Nova Scotia of the American revolution. In the aftermath, Goreham tried to ease tension by pardoning the local inhabitants who he felt had been forced to join Eddy. Several of his own officers and the loyal settlers sharply disagreed with his decision, and Major Thomas Batt even attempted, unsuccessfully, to have Goreham dismissed for neglect of duty, but Goreham's policy was probably correct.

In 1780 the Fort Cumberland garrison was transferred to Halifax, remaining there until the regiment was disbanded in October 1783. Goreham was promoted colonel in 1782 and was absent much of 1783 in England, presumably soliciting appointments to ease his financial difficulties. He appears to have lived a good deal in France thereafter, possibly to evade his creditors. Three months before his death Goreham was promoted major-general, one of the few native Americans and the only ranger officer to attain that rank. Goreham's career bears some resemblance to that of Robert ROGERS, another ranger officer. Like Rogers, Goreham had a successful military career in the Seven Years' War, and like Rogers, he was "a veteran of many years in eighteenth-century patronage technique." But despite the financial problems both he and Rogers were prey to, Goreham ended his career on a more favourable note, and if he never really surmounted his financial difficulties, at least the outward trappings of success must have provided some consolation.

DAVID A. CHARTERS and
STUART R. J. SUTHERLAND

PAC, MG 9, B1, 1; B3; MG 23, A1, ser.1, 3, nos.1182, 1184, 1199, 1202; 5, nos.1064–65; ser.2, 5, nos.67–74; MG 25, 47. PRO, CO 217/13, f.309; 217/20, ff.315–16; 217/21, ff.373–75; 217/25, ff.12–14; 217/26, ff.93–94, 120–21, 221–22; 217/28, ff.21, 138, 146; WO 17/1497; 17/1498, ff.1, 7, 8, 15; 24/750, f.5; 25/3096, bundle 2, no.3. *Cinco diarios del sitio de La Habana*, ed. A. A. Rodríguez (Havana, 1963), 197–200. *Gentleman's Magazine*, 1784, 556; 1787, 546; 1790, 763; 1791, 279; 1805, 474; 1807, 687; 1808, 565. *Johnson papers* (Sullivan *et al.*), V, 534–36, 771–72, 789; VII, 75–76, 90–91, 105–6; XII, 195–98, 378–80, 556–67, 641–42, 731–33, 805–6. Knox, *Hist. journal* (Doughty), I, 32; II, 17, 23, 26, 37, 38, 136. [Alexander McDonald], "Letter-book of Captain Alexander McDonald, of the Royal Highland Emigrants, 1775–1779,'' N.Y. Hist. Soc., *Coll.*, XV (1882), 205–498. *Military operations in eastern Maine and N.S.* (Kidder), 67–74, 153, 157, 169, 196–97, 228–31, 261–62. PAC *Report*, 1894, 311, 324, 328, 332, 339, 340, 346, 353–63, 368. G.B., WO, *Army list*, 1756–90. E. A. Jones, *The loyalists of Massachusetts: their memorials, petitions and claims* (London, 1930), 150–51.

Brebner, *Neutral Yankees* (1969), 80n, 190n, 194n, 197, 215n. P. H. Smith, *Loyalists and redcoats: a study in British revolutionary policy* (Williamsburg, Va., 1964), 14, 67–69. G. T. Bates, ''John Gorham, 1709–1751: an outline of his activities in Nova Scotia, 1744–1751 . . . ,'' N.S. Hist. Soc., *Coll.*, XXX (1954), 27–77. ''Colonel John Gorham's 'Wast Book' and the Gorham family,'' *New-York Geneal. and Biographical Record* (New York), XXVIII (1897), 197–202. Harry Piers, ''The fortieth regiment, raised at Annapolis Royal in 1717; and five regiments subsequently raised in Nova Scotia,'' N.S. Hist. Soc., *Coll.*, XXI (1927), 115–83.

GRANT, CUTHBERT, fur-trader; son of David Grant of Letheredie (Highlands), Scotland, and Margaret Grant; d. 1799 at Kaministiquia (Thunder Bay, Ont.).

Cuthbert Grant belonged to the Clan Grant of Strathspey, members of which were active in the Canadian fur trade during the 1770s, and Grant became one of the first Nor'Westers to enter the trade in the Athabasca country. The exact date of his arrival in Canada and his early activities are unknown. He may have accompanied Peter Pond* to the Athabasca River in 1778, but he is not mentioned by name in the documents until Pond sent him in 1785 or 1786 to establish a North West Company post at the mouth of the Slave River. In opposition was Laurent Leroux* of Gregory, MacLeod and Company, who built nearby at about the same time. Grant was in the Athabasca region in 1788, and the continued existence of both posts was noted by Alexander Mackenzie* in 1789 and by Peter Fidler* and Philip TURNOR in 1791.

In 1793 Grant travelled with his clerk John Macdonell* from Grand Portage (near Grand Portage, Minn.) to the confluence of the Souris and Assiniboine rivers (Man.) where he established Fort La Souris (also known as Fort Assiniboine), the first North West Company post in the area. It was to counter one already built by former Nor'Westers who had become free traders. The same year Donald ''Mad'' MacKay built Brandon House nearby for the Hudson's Bay Company. By 1795 there were about 21 posts in the upper Assiniboine district competing to control the supply of furs and pemmican. Grant was in charge of the seven belonging to the North West Company. His headquarters appear to have been a post (southwest of Togo, Sask.) variously called Cuthbert Grant's House, the Upper House, Fort de la Rivière Tremblante, and Aspen House. In 1795 Alexander Mackenzie's efforts resulted in a reorganization of the North West Company, and Grant became a partner.

Grant spent the winter of 1797–98 in the Fort Augustus (Edmonton) area, replacing Duncan McGillivray*. According to John McDonald* of Garth, he was then middle-aged and not active enough for the district. He became ill in the spring of 1799 and was being taken out of the fur-trading country, presumably to Montreal, when he died. He had sent his eldest son James there the year before and the boy had been baptized at St Gabriel Street (Presbyterian) Church, to whose building fund Cuthbert Grant had contributed.

Grant had married a woman of the Qu'Appelle district, the daugher of a white trader and a Cree or Assiniboin woman. This trader may have been French, for some of Grant's children were associated with the Métis community at Red River. Cuthbert* was a leader at the battle of Seven Oaks (now part of Winnipeg) in 1816; Mary married Pierre Falcon*, the Métis balladeer.

HARTWELL BOWSFIELD

[The existence of at least two other Cuthbert Grants – one a merchant at Quebec, the other at Trois-Rivières – has led to some confusion among historians. For example, Wallace, in *Docs. relating to NWC*, identifies the subject of this biography with Cuthbert Grants still living in the period 1801–7. H.B.]

Les bourgeois de la Compagnie du Nord-Ouest (Masson). *Five fur traders of the northwest; being the narrative of Peter Pond and the diaries of John Macdonnell, Archibald N. McLeod, Hugh Faries, and Thomas Connor*, ed. C. M. Gates ([2nd ed.], St Paul, Minn., 1965). *Journals of Hearne and Turnor* (Tyrrell). Alexander Mackenzie, *Voyages from Montreal on the River St. Laurence through the continent of North America to the Frozen and Pacific oceans in the years 1789 and 1793* . . . (London, 1801; new ed., intro. Roy Daniells, Edmonton, 1971). *New light on the early history of the greater northwest: the manuscript journals of Alexander Henry . . . and of David Thompson . . .*, ed. Elliott Coues (3v., New York, 1897; repr., 2v., Minneapolis, Minn., 1965). [David Thompson], *David Thompson's narrative, 1784–1812*, ed. R. [G.] Glover (new ed., Toronto, 1962). L. J. Burpee, *The search for the western sea* (2nd ed., 2v., Toronto, 1935). Davidson, *NWC*. Innis, *Fur trade in Canada*; *Peter Pond, fur trader and adventurer* (Toronto, 1930). M. A. MacLeod and W. L. Morton, *Cuthbert Grant of Grantown, warden of the plains of Red River* (Toronto, 1963). Morton, *History of Canadian west*. Rich, *History of HBC*. H. R. Wagner, *Peter Pond, fur trader & explorer* ([New Haven, Conn.], 1955).

GRANT, JAMES, fur-trader; b. in the parish of Kirkmichael, Strathavon (Grampian), Scotland; fl. 1777–99.

James Grant was one of the numerous Grants in the Canadian fur trade after 1763; their relationships are obscure and there were even several James Grants. The subject of this biography may have been related to William Grant* of Montreal, who came from the same parish, although their letters do not suggest any family connection.

James Grant's name first appears among the fur-trading licences for 1777. He was then trading at the Timiskaming posts, which he seems to have taken over from Richard Dobie* that year. He apparently maintained his interests in the Timiskaming and Rivière Dumoine (Que.) areas for the next 18 years, in partnership with John Porteous until 1783, Daniel Sutherland* until 1786, Richard Dobie until 1791, and Grant, Campion and Company (of which William Grant was senior partner) until 1795. Before 1787 he was also concerned in the Michilimackinac and Illinois trade, sending canoes to Michilimackinac with George McBeath* in 1783 and Daniel Sutherland in 1785 and 1786. McBeath seems to have had an interest in the Timiskaming posts as well.

In all these ventures James Grant was apparently the wintering partner, although just how he divided his time is not clear. In 1783 he may have been at Cahokia (East St Louis, Ill.), but from 1787 until 1793 he wintered at Fort Timiskaming (near Ville-Marie, Que.). By 1793 he was suffering from leg trouble (the symptoms suggest ulcers) and he did not return to the fort that autumn, although he visited the district in the summers of 1794 and 1795. In December 1795, however, McTavish, Frobisher and Company bought the Timiskaming posts for the North West Company and Grant retired.

As early as 1787 Grant was in financial straits. Although he seems to have been an excellent trader, at home in the woods and with the Indians, affable and kindly in disposition, he apparently lacked the managerial qualities necessary for an increasingly complex and competitive trade. It was presumably this defect, combined with advancing age and physical disabilities, that prompted Simon McTavish* to retire him.

The last years of Grant's life are as elusive as the early ones. According to Dobie, McTavish ("a liberal hearted man as ever existed") offered him an annuity of £100 on his retirement. In May 1797 Samuel Gerrard*, formerly of Grant, Campion and Company, thought him "as great a Bear as ever," who "certainly deserves well of the fair Sex whose Service he faithfully adheres to." A year later Grant was living in Montreal, although Gerrard did not know "whether a NoWest or Tg [Timiskaming] Partner, I imagine neither, but the humble Servant of both." In March 1799 Grant refused to sign the annuity papers, declaring that the sum was to be paid in sterling, not Halifax currency, but McTavish, Frobisher and Company declined to alter it. No record of Grant's death has been found.

ELAINE ALLAN MITCHELL

ANQ-M, Greffe de J. G. Beek, 28, 30 mars 1787. HBC Arch. F.3/1, f.314. Private archives, E. A. Mitchell (Toronto), Cameron family papers, letters of James Grant to Æneas Cameron (mfm. at PAO). *Docs. relating to NWC* (Wallace), 450. W. S. Wallace, *The pedlars from Quebec and other papers on the Nor'Westers* (Toronto, 1954).

GRASSET DE SAINT-SAUVEUR, ANDRÉ, merchant and secretary to the governor; b. 1724 in Montpellier, France, son of Jean Grasset de Saint-Sauveur and Louise Roussel; d. 1794 in Paris, France.

On 10 May 1747 André Grasset de Saint-Sauveur sailed for Canada on the warship *Sérieux* as secretary to the new governor general of New France, La Jonquière [Taffanel*]. Four days later, the convoy of 39 vessels in which the *Sérieux* was travelling was attacked by a British squadron off Cape Ortegal, Spain. Grasset was taken prisoner with La Jonquière and they were brought to England. Freed in 1748 by the treaty of Aix-la-Chapelle, they were finally able to take up their posts and they landed at Quebec on 14 Aug. 1749.

On 1 May 1750 Grasset obtained letters of appointment as councillor of the Conseil Supérieur of Quebec, but since he had settled in Montreal, he never presented his letters to the council. However, he retained his official title of secretary until 1752. At the request of Charles Nolan* Lamarque, a Montreal merchant whose daughter Marie-Anne he married on 2 October of that year, he then gave up office to devote himself to Lamarque's business. Grasset was not unfamiliar with colonial trading: since his arrival he had succeeded in accumulating 20,000 *livres* by importing French goods which as merchant-outfitter he then used to trade with the Indians.

In 1755, following the appointment of Vaudreuil [RIGAUD] as governor general, Grasset agreed to resume his former post as secretary. Vaudreuil had nothing but praise for him: "He carries out his role as first secretary with zeal, diligence, and dispatch," he wrote to the minister of Marine, Nicolas-René Berryer. After the death of Grasset's wife in childbirth on 18 Oct. 1755, the governor personally found a match for him with a rich Canadian, Marie-Joseph, daughter of Jacques Quesnel Fonblanche, an important merchant in Montreal. She was already an experienced businesswoman, having engaged in business with her father from the age of 14. Grasset continued to serve as secretary to the governor, but from 1756 on the Grassets turned their attention primarily to their trade with the Indians. At that time they owned two retail stores on the Montreal market square.

When Vaudreuil returned to France in 1760, Grasset remained in Canada. Given powers of attorney by the former governor, he attended to the administration and disposal of the marquis's possessions in the colony. Meanwhile, in Paris in 1761 he was accused at the Châtelet of breach of trust, along with François BIGOT and others involved in the *affaire du Canada*. On 10 Dec. 1763 the court issued an order against him deferring the case "for further inquiry before condemning him for failure to appear in court." When Grasset was informed of this decision, he resolved to return to France. He sailed on 1 Nov. 1764, taking his wife and five small children, and his father-in-law, who was 83. He was in Paris on 23 Dec. 1764. On 21 Jan. 1765 he appeared before the court of the Châtelet to give himself up and obtain a ruling on the order of deferral issued against him. Numerous accusations had been made by his contemporaries. Montcalm* called him "ignorant and greedy." The author of the "Mémoire du Canada" thought him "devoid of honour and feelings" and "a traitor to his master" and saw in him nothing but "roguery and illicit trade." Even Joseph-Michel CADET, who had also been accused, testified to his illicit activities. In April 1765 the court nevertheless dismissed his case, because it had received no information enabling it to find him guilty.

According to the author of the "Mémoire du Canada," Grasset had amassed 1,900,000 *livres* during his stay in Canada. Yet, seven years after the conquest, in August 1767 Grasset claimed that his entire fortune consisted of 317,292 *livres* in bills of exchange that he had acquired honestly through his two advantageous marriages and his trading activities. In 1772, when he was appointed French consul in Trieste (Italy), his financial situation had become so bad that he had to put his family in the care of a religious community because he lacked the means to support them. In May 1778 his wife wrote to the minister of Foreign Affairs, the Comte de Vergennes, that as all her resources were exhausted she was "reduced to the most dire want." In 1794, André Grasset de Saint-Sauveur died in Paris at the Hôpital des Incurables, a completely ruined man.

Two sons of his second marriage made names for themselves in France. Jacques, the elder, was one of the fashionable novelists of the early 19th century; André, a priest and canon of the metropolitan church of Sens, was one of the martyrs of the Commune in September 1792 and was beatified at the beginning of the 20th century.

ANDRÉ LACHANCE

AN, Col., B, 91, f.30; 95, f.51; 109, f.29; 127, f.362; C11A, 104, f.113; E, 211 (dossier Grasset de Saint-Sauveur). ANQ-M, État civil, Catholiques, Notre-Dame de Montréal, 2 oct. 1752, 3 juill. 1756; Greffe de L.-C. Danré de Blanzy, 29 sept. 1752, 7 avril, 2 juill. 1756. "Mémoire du Canada," ANQ *Rapport*, 1924–25, 102, 144, 188, 197. PAC *Rapport*, 1899, suppl., 182–83. Tanguay, *Dictionnaire*, V, 350. P.-G. Roy, *Bigot et sa bande*, 159–63; *Les petites choses de notre histoire* (7 sér., Lévis, Qué., 1919–44), 3e sér., 257–73; "Les secrétaires des gouverneurs et des intendants de la Nouvelle-France," *BRH*, XLI (1935), 91.

GREEN, BENJAMIN, merchant and office-holder; b. 1 July 1713 at Salem Village (Danvers, Mass.), the son of Reverend Joseph Green and Elizabeth Gerrish; m. November 1737 Margaret Pierce, and they had at least three sons and two daughters; d. 14 Oct. 1772 at Halifax, Nova Scotia.

Benjamin Green reputedly began his career as a merchant with his brothers Joseph and John at Boston, where he was twice elected constable. On 1 March 1745 he was appointed secretary to William Pepperrell*, commander of the expedition against Louisbourg, Île Royale (Cape Breton Island). He was joint treasurer to the New England forces after the surrender of the fortress, and he also served as secretary to the Council at Louisbourg until at least May 1746. The same year he succeeded Thomas Kilby* as commissary. In July 1749 Green sailed to Chebucto Bay and met Edward CORNWALLIS' expedition; he soon became a member of Cornwallis' first Council as well as naval officer for the new town of Halifax and judge of the Vice-Admiralty Court. The following year he was appointed secretary to the Council and provincial treasurer. Green resigned as secretary in 1752, declaring that it was a full-time position and that his other offices required considerable attention. The following year he resigned as judge of the Vice-Admiralty Court because of an apparent conflict with his position as naval officer; he chose to retain the latter office because of his need for its "Certain Income." In 1758 Green, as senior councillor, unsuccessfully contested with Chief Justice Jonathan BELCHER the right to administer the government of the province in the absence of the governor and lieutenant governor. In March 1760 he was appointed a justice of the peace at Halifax.

Late that year Green departed for England, apparently to assist in the review of unaudited accounts of former governor Peregrine Thomas Hopson* as the latter had requested. Still in England in 1762, Green was experiencing financial problems because the authorities refused to reimburse him for his expenses until the Treasury had approved the auditors' report of Hopson's accounts. In 1761, possibly because of these problems, Green had mortgaged much of his property in Nova Scotia, including four large warehouses in Halifax, to two London merchants for £6,000. He satisfied the claims on his property by November 1765, but the exact nature of the settlement is unclear. At least some of Green's land was surrendered and later became the property of Brook Watson*.

While in England Green had faced problems other than financial; the Board of Trade asked him to explain charges of misconduct made by Robert Sanderson, first speaker of the Nova Scotia House of Assembly. Sanderson accused Green of having given the Halifax merchant Malachy SALTER two government contracts in return for a share in the profits. Green admitted his partnership with Salter but denied ever having made undue use of his influence as a Council member. The board found Green "highly blameable," but because of his good record it only reprimanded him and he continued in his offices on his return to Halifax in 1763. The following year a reduction in his salary as provincial treasurer led him to express doubts that the income from his remaining appointments would be sufficient to support his family. Green remained on the Council, and on the death of Governor Montagu Wilmot* in 1766 he became the administrator of Nova Scotia until Michael FRANCKLIN received his commission as lieutenant governor. During his three-month tenure the assembly, anxious to assert its authority in fiscal matters, attacked him for neglecting to follow correct procedure in handling the province's finances.

In December 1767 Green made his will, admitting himself "Something Infirm." Two months later he resigned as provincial treasurer, but in October 1771 he assumed the administration of the province again on the departure of Governor Lord William CAMPBELL. Continued sickness made his duties onerous, and in March 1772 he asked to resign his post as naval officer because his health was "very much impair'd." In June Francklin reported that Green was too unwell to transact business and might never again attend Council meetings. He died four months later.

In 1775 the Council initiated an audit of Green's accounts, conducted by James Monk*, Charles MORRIS, and others. Green's son Benjamin, who had succeeded his father as provincial treasurer, placed many obstacles in the way of the auditors. At first he denied ever having seen any of the records for the period previous to his appointment, but eventually he admitted having "worked hard for two days on his father's records with Francklin's 'Assistance & Direction.'" The auditors finally reconstructed the missing records from various official sources, and although they claimed to have given Green Sr the benefit of doubt wherever they could, they still found him deficient by almost £7,000. Their report contrasts sharply with the tablet erected in St Paul's cemetery, which declared that Green "was of a public spirit and a great encourager of the good of the Town and Province from the settlement of which to his death he was employed in the principal affairs of the Government with honour to himself and the approbation of all."

DONALD F. CHARD

Halifax County Court of Probate (Halifax), Book 2, pp.84–85 (will of Benjamin Green, 4 Dec. 1767). Halifax County Registry of Deeds (Halifax), 6, nos.129, 130. Mass. Hist. Soc., Louisbourg papers, 1745–58; Thomas Hancock, letterbook, April 19, 1745 – June 16, 1750. PANS, RG 1, 163; 164, p.20; 209, 10, 23 Oct. 1752; 211, 20 May 1758, 11 March 1760, 23 May 1766; 212, 2 Feb. 1768, 8 March 1776; 491, p.5; 492; 493. PRO, CO 217/16, f.264; 217/17, f.48; 217/18, ff.58, 73–78, 113–17; 217/19, f.20; 217/20; 217/21, f.222; 217/23–25; 217/26, ff.103, 114; 221/28, f.4. *Correspondence of William Shirley* (Lincoln), I. *Louisbourg journals, 1745*, ed. L. E. De Forest (New York, 1932), 235. Massachusetts (Colony), General Court, House of Representatives, *Journal* (Boston, 1755; repr. 1957), 316. Mass. Hist. Soc., *Coll.*, 6th ser., X (1899), 3n, 32, 90. *Nova-Scotia Gazette and the Weekly Chronicle* (Halifax), 20 Oct. 1772. Shipton, *Sibley's Harvard graduates*, IV, 133, 230; VI, 314. Brebner, *Neutral Yankees* (1969), 84, 198ff., 201, 224–27. A. S. Burrage, *Maine at Louisburg in 1745* (Augusta, Maine, 1910), 117n. R. F. Seybolt, *The town officials of colonial Boston, 1634–1775* (Cambridge, Mass., 1939), 220, 229. A. S. Barnstead, "Development of the office of provincial secretary, Nova Scotia," N.S. Hist. Soc., *Coll.*, XXIV (1938), 1–31.

GRIDLEY, RICHARD, army officer, military engineer, and entrepreneur; b. 3 Jan. 1710/11 in Boston, Massachusetts, son of Richard and Rebecca Gridley; m. 25 Feb. 1730/31 Hannah Dem-ing in Boston, and they had nine children; m. secondly 21 Oct. 1751 Sarah Blake in Boston; d. 21 June 1796 in Stoughton, Mass.

Richard Gridley became an apprentice to a Boston merchant at an early age, but by the 1740s he apparently was a "scholar" of John Henry Bastide*, a British engineer engaged in improving colonial defences. His study of military engineering may have led to his being chosen lieutenant-colonel in command of the artillery in William Pepperrell*'s expedition against Louisbourg, Île Royale (Cape Breton Island) in 1745. During the siege Gridley had "direction of the Batteries," in particular the one at Pointe à la Croix (Lighthouse Point), and he also undertook some minor engineering tasks. Praised by Governor William Shirley of Massachusetts for his work, Gridley was rewarded with a captain's commission in Shirley's American Provincials (67th Foot), which garrisoned Louisbourg from 1746 to 1749.

Placed on half pay at the disbanding of his regiment in 1749, Gridley saw no military service until 1755, when he was appointed colonel of a Massachusetts regiment in William JOHNSON's expedition against Fort Saint-Frédéric (near Crown Point, N.Y.). Gridley commanded the garrison at Fort Edward and built fortifications at various points around Lake George (Lac Saint-Sacrement), earning Johnson's praise that "if all the Officers of his Rank in the Army were equal to him I should have thought myself verry happy in my Station." The following year Gridley became colonel, artillery commander,.and chief engineer in John WINSLOW's force of provincials. During the acrimonious debate between Winslow and Lord Loudoun, the commander-in-chief, over a proposed amalgamation of the regular and provincial forces, Gridley supported his commander to such an extent that Loudoun believed him to be the real leader of the provincial officers opposed to amalgamation.

In 1758, as a volunteer under AMHERST, Gridley again served at Louisbourg. He was consulted by the British general and also took command of some American carpenters after the death of their commander. The following year he raised a similar unit for James Wolfe*'s expedition and was allegedly present at the battle of the Plains of Abraham.

With the end of the war in North America, Gridley returned to civilian pursuits, and in 1760 he petitioned Amherst for a grant of the Îles de la Madeleine in the Gulf of St Lawrence in order to carry on a seal and walrus fishery. Although Amherst could only give a temporary permit pending British governmental approval of the grant, Gridley went to the islands and, after hiring some Canadians and Acadians, began to prosecute the fishery. By 1763 he had 12 families there, with five houses, six vessels, and all necessary equipment for converting the catch into oil. But the "considerable expence" Gridley had incurred went for nought; in late 1763 the Board of Trade refused his petition, apparently because a general policy for the Gulf fisheries had not then been decided upon. Undaunted, Gridley continued to frequent the islands; in 1765 he, four sons, and 22 Canadians and Acadians fished there during the summer. His son Samuel, a Bristol merchant, continued unsuccessfully to petition for a grant of the islands on behalf of his father, and in 1777, after Gridley had joined the American rebels, for himself alone. Gridley was not, however, involved only in the fishery; in 1772 he was operating an iron smelter at Stoughtonham (Sharon) in Massachusetts.

With the outbreak of the American revolution in 1775 Gridley offered his services to the rebels, and the Massachusetts Congress commissioned him major-general, colonel of an artillery regiment, and chief engineer of the state's forces. He supervised the construction of earthworks on Breed's Hill near Boston and was wounded in the subsequent battle of Bunker Hill on 17 June. The following March he was responsible for the erection of batteries on Dorchester Heights overlooking Boston, the step which is generally considered to have forced the British evacuation of the city on the 17th. In November 1775 Gridley's "advanced age" had led to his replacement as colonel of artillery, but he remained chief engineer until August 1776 and served as an engineer until January 1781. After his retirement that month he apparently lived at Stoughton until his death. The present-day United States Army Corps of Engineers considers Gridley to be its founding father.

STUART R. J. SUTHERLAND

PRO, CO 194/16, ff.254–57; 217/19, f.174; 217/20, ff.5–17. Boston, Mass., Registry Dept., *Records relating to the early history of Boston*, ed. W. H. Whitmore *et al.* (39v., Boston, 1876–1909), [24]: *Boston births, 1700–1800*, 68; [28]: *Boston marriages, 1700–1751*, 154, 247. *Correspondence of William Shirley* (Lincoln), I, 288; II, 168n, 479, 501–10. G. B., Board of Trade, *JTP, 1759 63*, 407; *1764–67*, 6, 134; *1768–75*, 288; *1776–82*, 86. *Johnson papers* (Sullivan *et al.*), II, 223–24, 236ff., 281. *DAB*. F. B. Heitman, *Historical register of officers of the Continental army during the war of the revolution . . .* (Washington, 1893), 201. Rawlyk, *Yankees at Louisbourg*, 102.

GRISÉ, ANTOINE (also called **Grisé**, *dit* **Villefranche**), royal notary; b. 19 Oct. 1728 at Chambly (Que.), son of Antoine Grisé and Françoise Poyer; m. 24 June 1754 Françoise Marcoux at Chambly; d. there 12 July 1785.

Antoine Grisé's father, a corporal in Jacques-Hugues Péan* de Livaudière's company, came originally from one of the places in France called Villefranche, hence the nickname sometimes given father and son. On 24 July 1756 the younger Grisé received a commission as royal notary for the seigneuries of Chambly and Rouville. That year either his father (who lived until 1781) or more probably he himself became storekeeper at Fort Chambly. In any event "Villefranche, formerly storekeeper of Fort Chambly," in 1763 was sentenced in the *affaire du Canada* to five years' banishment from Paris and a fine of 30 *livres* for accepting bribes and falsifying accounts. The sentence was pronounced *in absentia*, since the two Grisés had remained in Canada.

On 1 Oct. 1760 Antoine Grisé Jr was commissioned notary for the seigneuries of Chambly, Belœil, and Rouville, with the requirement that he live in Chambly. After that date his minute-book (there is no inventory) shows that his practice became busier, especially in the recording of land grants. Antoine Grisé was relied on by all the local seigneurs, for whom he drew up deeds of land grants. Some are done on printed forms which are perfectly preserved and are fine specimens of early Canadian printing.

Grisé became embroiled with the famous jurist, François-Joseph CUGNET, who was trying to obtain the title-deeds of the heirs of François-Joseph Bissot* [*see* Jacques de Lafontaine* de Belcour]. On 4 Dec. 1769 Grisé had acquired from Antoine de Lafontaine de Belcour, a brother of Marie-Josephte, Cugnet's wife, all the rights to the Mingan islands which Lafontaine de Belcour had inherited from his mother, Charlotte Bissot. On 10 April 1775 Grisé in turn sold these rights to William Grant* of Saint-Roch. At least in Cugnet's eyes the 1769 deed was illegal, and on 13 April 1775 (and again during the following weeks) he inserted a notice in the *Quebec Gazette* in which he denounced the 1775 transaction and warned the public about Grisé: "The public can be assured that this deed of transfer is defective (*if not fraudulent*)." We do not know the result of the affair.

On 23 Aug. 1781 Antoine Grisé's commission was extended to include the city and district of Montreal. In June 1785 he signed his 2,775th deed and laid down his pen. He passed away at Chambly the following month. His son Jean-Baptiste, who was also a surveyor, had been granted a commission as notary the preceding February and succeeded him immediately. His career was short. He died early in 1796, asphyxiated by fumes from a stove in a Montreal inn.

JEAN-JACQUES LEFEBVRE

ANQ-M, État civil, Catholiques, Saint-Joseph (Chambly), 12 janv., 19 oct. 1728, 24 juin 1754, 14 juill. 1785; Greffe d'Antoine Grisé, 1756–85; Greffe de J.-B. Grisé, 1785–96. Private archives, J.-J. Lefebvre (Montréal), Lettre de Raoul Raymond, 29 août 1974 (notes sur la famille Grisé). PAC *Rapport*, app.B, 1918, 28. J.-E. Roy, *Rapport sur les archives de France*, 871, 875. P.-G. Roy, *Inv. concessions*, III, 194, 196; *Inv. ord. int.*, III, 198. Tanguay, *Dictionnaire*. Vachon, "Inv. critique des notaires royaux," *RHAF*, XI, 272. P.-G. Roy, *Bigot et sa bande*, 186–88. Leland, "François-Joseph Cugnet," *Revue de l'université Laval*, XVII, 151–52; XX, 149–50.

GROSTON (Grotton) DE SAINT-ANGE ET DE BELLERIVE, LOUIS, officer in the colonial regular troops; baptized *c.* 1700 at Montreal, son of Robert Groston* de Saint-Ange and Marguerite Crevier; d. 27 Dec. 1774, unmarried, at St Louis (Mo.).

Robert Groston de Saint-Ange took his family to the west around 1720, when he was stationed at Fort Saint-Joseph (Niles, Mich.). In 1723 he and Louis accompanied Étienne de Véniard* de Bourgmond to Fort d'Orléans, some 280 miles up the Missouri River. On several missions Louis, a cadet and then an ensign, led detachments of troops. He remained on the Missouri until 1736.

In that year his father persuaded the governor of Louisiana, Jean-Baptiste Le Moyne* de Bienville, to promote Louis lieutenant on half pay and give him command of the Ouabache post (Vincennes, Ind.), succeeding François-Marie Bissot* de Vinsenne. Saint-Ange de Bellerive, as Louis was usually known, remained in charge there until 1764. Trade at the settlement was only moderately successful and the farming produced few surplus crops. An account from the mid 1750s referred to the post as "a pretty village" of about 80 inhabitants. Over the years Saint-Ange de Bellerive made many grants of farm lands and village lots which were notarized but for which no register was kept, and this casualness led to many problems of title after the area became American territory.

In 1748 Saint-Ange de Bellerive was promoted captain on half pay. There was little military activity around the Ouabache post, and during the frontier wars some of its soldiers were sent elsewhere to participate. Louisiana authorities frequently said that the establishment cost more than it was worth. The alignment of some Miamis with the British early in the 1750s did threaten the post and led to some minor skirmishes, but Saint-Ange kept most of the nearby Piankeshaws, a Miami group, from the troubles.

Commandant of an obscure outpost, Saint-Ange de Bellerive achieved a place in history because of the vacuums he filled. During the French withdrawal from the west, he was given interim command at Fort de Chartres (near Prairie du Rocher, Ill.) in June 1764 and, despite pressure from Pontiac* and other Indian leaders, turned the post over peacefully to Captain Thomas Sterling (Stirling) on 10 Oct. 1765. He then led his small garrison and some local inhabitants across the Mississippi to St Louis. Although the west bank of the river had been ceded to the Spaniards, they had some difficulty arranging its government, and Saint-Ange de Bellerive remained in command at St Louis even after the arrival of Spanish troops in 1767. He turned over his authority to Pedro Josef Piernas in 1770 but continued as an adviser, particularly with regard to "the management and government of the Indians." Until his death in 1774 he was captain of infantry in the Spanish service.

DONALD CHAPUT

[According to Tanguay, *Dictionnaire*, IV, 382, a Louis Groston de Saint-Ange was baptized on 16 Oct. 1698 and a Louis-Daniel was baptized 20 Feb. 1702. Although the subject of this biography was always known as Louis, his stated age in various reports seems to correspond more closely to Louis-Daniel's baptismal date. D.C.]

AN, Col., D^{2C}, 59, 222. Huntington Library, Loudoun papers, LO 336, LO 362. PAC, MG 8, G14, 1. *NYCD* (O'Callaghan and Fernow), VII, 882; X, 247, 1157–62. *Ouiatanon documents*, ed. and trans. Frances Krauskopf (Indianapolis, Ind., 1955). "The St. Joseph baptismal register," ed. George Paré and M. M. Quaife, *Mississippi Valley Hist. Rev.* (Cedar Rapids, Iowa, and Lincoln, Neb.), XIII (1926–27), 201–39. "Spain in the Mississippi valley, 1765–1794: I, the revolutionary period, 1765–1781," ed. Lawrence Kinnaird, American Hist. Assoc., *Annual report* (Washington), 1945, II. *The Spanish régime in Missouri . . .* , ed. Louis Houck (2v., Chicago, 1909; repr. 2v. in 1, [New York], 1971). "Will of St. Ange de Bellerive," ed. O. W. Collet, *Magazine of Western History* (Cleveland, Ohio), II (1885), 60–65.

DAB. Tanguay, *Dictionnaire*, I, 285. J. D. Barnhart and D. L. Riker, *Indiana to 1816, the colonial period* (Indianapolis, Ind., 1971). H. P. Beers, *The French & British in the old northwest . . .* (Detroit, 1964). Louis Houck, *A history of Missouri . . .* (3v., Chicago, 1908; repr. 3v. in 1, [New York], 1971). W. B. Douglas, "The sieurs de St. Ange," Ill. State Hist. Soc., *Trans.* (Springfield), XIV (1909), 135–46. G. J. Garraghan, "Fort Orleans of the Missoury," *Missouri Hist. Rev.* (Columbia), XXXV (1940–41), 373–84.

GUERNE, *See* LE GUERNE

GUGY, CONRAD, secretary to HALDIMAND, justice of the peace, seigneur, and director of the Saint-Maurice ironworks; b. *c.* 1734 in The Hague, Netherlands, son of Hans George Gugi, a French speaking Swiss officer serving in the Dutch army, and Thérèse Reis; d. unmarried 10 April 1786 and was buried in Montreal on 12 April.

Conrad Gugy seems to have served in the Dutch army before joining a newly formed British regiment, the Royal Americans (62nd, later 60th, Foot), as a lieutenant in 1756. This regiment, which included Haldimand and a great many other foreign Protestants, saw action at Quebec under Wolfe* in 1759. Appointed governor of the District of Trois-Rivières in October 1763, Haldimand chose Gugy, who spoke French and English with equal ease, as his secretary. Gugy succeeded John BRUYÈRES, who had held the post when Ralph Burton* was governor of the district. In addition to his regular work of translating and drafting numerous proclamations, in March 1764 Gugy had to record statements and administer oaths to those holding "bills of exchange of Canada, payment orders, card-money and certificates," who were to be reimbursed by France. Three commissioners, Louis-Joseph GODEFROY de Tonnancour, René-Ovide HERTEL de Rouville, and Jean-Baptiste Perrault, were named to assist him in this task.

Later in 1764 Gugy resigned his post as secretary and bought at auction the seigneury of Grandpré, also called Petit-Yamachiche, and part of the seigneury of Grosbois-Ouest, or Petite-Rivière-Yamachiche, where he built a manor-house. In 1771 he purchased Dumontier which adjoined Grosbois-Ouest. He likewise acquired Frédérick, located behind Pointe-du-Lac, and some lands forming part of Rivière-du-Loup-en-haut, which was owned by the Ursulines of Trois-Rivières.

Gugy, who remained loyal to the British crown during the American revolution, had to deal with various troublesome situations occasioned by local sympathizers. In 1775 François GUILLOT, *dit* Larose, a merchant of Rivière-du-Loup (Louiseville), accused him of threatening to whip Canadians who supported the American cause. Cleared of this charge following a trial at Trois-

Rivières that year, Gugy continued to be the victim of all kinds of petty annoyances. Moreover, when the Americans were retreating in 1776, they burned some buildings on his seigneuries.

In 1778 a great many loyalists took refuge in the area along Lake Champlain and northwards to Yamachiche. In mid September Gugy wrote to Haldimand, now governor of Canada, of his intention to establish these people, who were mainly women and children, on his seigneury of Grosbois, "to the end of having an eye upon them." The idea appealed to Haldimand, who was not eager to have the refugees mingling with the local populace. On 6 October the governor gave his official consent to the plan, issued orders for buildings to be erected, and gave Gugy the authority required to maintain order among the new arrivals. Six days later work was begun on a dozen houses with space for 240 persons, and construction was finished by the end of a month, thanks to *corvées* from five neighbouring parishes. Gugy had nine other houses and a school erected. For six years, from the autumn of 1778 until late 1784, the seigneury served as a refugee camp for large numbers of loyalists – 440 were listed as present in October 1779; they remained for long intervals, or for short periods prior to moving away to establish themselves elsewhere. Gugy's settlement cost the government £1,350, a sum which included the services of the seigneur, who acted as supervisor, and judging from the correspondence exchanged between Gugy and Haldimand, it was not always an easy role.

Gugy had been appointed a justice of the peace in 1765. Named to the first legislative council at its inception in August 1775, he retained the post until his death. In 1780 he served on a committee of legislative councillors charged with finding ways to reduce the price of wheat and flour. On 3 Feb. 1783 Gugy took a 16-year lease of the Saint-Maurice ironworks, for an annual rent of £18 15*s*., but he died three years later, and Alexander Davison* and John Lees* took back the lease. There seems to have been a link between Gugy's sudden death and his loss of a court case brought against him by François Le Maître Duaime, the owner of a neighbouring fief who claimed that Gugy was responsible for wilful damage to his property during the construction of buildings for the loyalists. In 1787 Gugy's seigneuries were put up for auction to pay the damages for which the jury had held him liable. Shortly after, however, the judgement was reversed. By an *inter vivos* deed of gift for services rendered, which was drawn up on 13 Jan. 1786, Gugy had left a life interest in his seigneuries, movables, and immovables to Elizabeth Wilkinson*, who lived in his manor-house, and all his properties passed to her. It was intended that after her death they should go to Gugy's brother Barthélemy, whose son Louis* in fact inherited them, Barthélemy having predeceased her.

IN COLLABORATION WITH
RAYMOND DOUVILLE

Doc. relatifs à l'hist. constitutionnelle, 1759–91 (Shortt et Doughty; 1921), II, 685, 703. PAC *Rapport*, 1892, 275. *Quebec Gazette*, 25 Jan., 22 Feb., 1, 8, 15 March, 10, 17 May 1787. P.-G. Roy, *Inv. concessions*, II, 269–70, 272; IV, 117–19, 205–6; V, 198. Raphaël Bellemare, *Les bases de l'histoire d'Yamachiche, 1703–1903* (Montréal, [1903]). É.-H. Bovay, *Le Canada et les Suisses, 1604–1974* (Fribourg, Suisse, 1976). Ivanhoë Caron, *La colonisation de la province de Québec* (2v., Québec, 1923–27), II, 43, 120–21, 125, 286. Sulte, *Mélanges historiques* (Malchelosse), VI. Tessier, *Les forges Saint-Maurice*. M. Trudel, *Le Régime militaire*. Napoléon Caron, "Les Gugy au Canada," *BRH*, VI (1900), 89–92. Pierre Daviault, "Traducteurs et traduction au Canada," RSC *Trans.*, 3rd ser., XXXVIII (1944), sect.I, 67–87. É.-Z. Massicotte, "Famille Gugy," *BRH*, XXIII (1917), 312–14; "Les tribunaux de police de Montréal," *BRH*, XXVI (1920), 181. P.-G. Roy, "Le fief Dumontier," *BRH*, XXXIV (1928), 3–5. W. H. Siebert, "The temporary settlement of loyalists at Machiche, P.Q.," RSC *Trans.*, 3rd ser., VIII (1914), sect.II, 407–14.

GUICHART, VINCENT-FLEURI (also called **Guichart de Kersident**), Sulpician priest and missionary; b. 13 April 1729 at Bannalec, France, son of Sylvestre Guichart and Françoise-Marie Cozer; d. 16 Oct. 1793 in Montreal (Que.).

On 17 Oct. 1749 Vincent-Fleuri Guichart joined the Robertins in Paris, a religious community which provided training for the priesthood under the guidance of the Sulpicians. He joined the Séminaire de Saint-Sulpice on 22 March 1754, was ordained priest eight days later, and left for Canada on 13 May, reaching Montreal on 5 September. Guichart was to serve in the mission of Lac-des-Deux-Montagnes (Oka) for the rest of his life, except when he was curate of Notre-Dame in Montreal from 1767 to 1777.

On his arrival at Lac-des-Deux-Montagnes on 9 Nov. 1754, he was given the responsibility of ministering to the Algonkins, whose language he quickly learned. Manuscripts that he wrote in this language, including a dictionary, sermons, prayers, songs, and examinations of conscience, are still extant. He also began to learn Iroquois, and sermons written in it have been found dating from 1761.

In 1777, at the end of his service as curate at

Notre-Dame in Montreal, Guichart was reappointed to Lac-des-Deux-Montagnes. The following year he became the mission's bursar and in 1784 its superior, succeeding Pierre-Paul-François de LAGARDE. As a missionary he administered the sacraments, preached, taught both Canadians and Indians, and managed the Sulpicians' seigneury.

The registers indicate that from 1777 to 1793 there was an average of 65 baptisms, 12 marriages, and 30 burials annually. Bishop Jean-François HUBERT made pastoral visits in 1786 and 1791, confirming 143 persons on the first occasion. Since there were not many Sulpicians in Canada, Guichart was assisted during his first three years as superior by Antoine-Théodore Braun, a priest of German extraction who served as bursar and missionary to the Iroquois. Braun was able to exercise a good influence despite the mission's poverty and lack of food but he left suddenly in September 1787. The stir caused by his departure subsided only slowly after the arrival of Michel-Félicien Leclerc*, the first Canadian Sulpician missionary.

Guichart had to resolve numerous difficulties in the practical management of the mission. From 1763 the community had been disturbed by Iroquois claims to a part of the seigneury [*see* François-Auguste MAGON de Terlaye]. It is possible that he mentioned quitting his post; on 25 Sept. 1787 a group of Mississaugas and Algonkins presented him with a necklace "six feet long and half a foot wide" to keep him from going away and abandoning them and also four dollars, in return for which Guichart said a high mass for them. The presence of whites posed other problems for the missionaries, since merchants brought spirits into the mission. Étienne MONTGOLFIER, superior of the Sulpicians, had urged Guichart in 1784 to avoid violence in fighting the traders. The whites also wanted to settle on lands belonging to the Sulpicians, and from 1784 to 1793 Guichart had to resist the claims of Eustache-Ignace Trottier Desrivières-Beaubien, who even took his case to the Court of Appeal but without success.

During the final months of his life Guichart lost the use of his legs. While Michel Leclerc carried on the ministry, Guichart kept the parish registers. He was recalled to the Séminaire de Saint-Sulpice in Montreal because of his health and died there on 16 Oct. 1793. He was buried the next day beneath Notre-Dame. Montgolfier noted in 1784 that Guichart was intelligent but could be employed in virtually no work other than that of the mission. Contemporary accounts often mention the beauty of his voice, which was said to have been "sweeter than the swan's song."

J.-BRUNO HAREL

AD, Finistère (Quimper), État civil, Bannalec, 13 avril 1729. Archives civiles, Terrebonne (Saint-Jérôme, Qué.), État civil, L'Annonciation (Oka) (copy at PAC). ASSM, 8, A; 24, Dossier 2, Dossier 6. Gauthier, *Sulpitiana* (1926), 221. Louis Bertrand, *Bibliothèque sulpicienne, ou histoire littéraire de la Compagnie de Saint-Sulpice* (3v., Paris, 1900). Olivier Maurault, *"Nos Messieurs"* (Montréal, 1936). Pierre Rousseau, *Saint-Sulpice et les missions catholiques* (Montréal, 1930). J.-A. Cuoq, "Anotc kekon," RSC *Trans.*, 1st ser., XI (1893), sect.I, 137–79.

GUILLIMIN (Guillimen), GUILLAUME, office-holder, merchant, judge, and lawyer; b. 13 July 1713 at Quebec, son of Charles Guillimin* and Françoise Lemaître-Lamorille; d. 30 July 1771 at Quebec.

Guillaume Guillimin's father Charles was a prominent merchant in New France, whose fluctuating business career ended in reduced circumstances and a stream of petitions to the court seeking financial relief for himself and his family. One petition, dated 1735, which requested that Guillaume be made a scrivener in the civil bureaucracy of New France, was rejected by Maurepas, the minister of the Marine. But when Charles Guillimin died in 1739, Maurepas relented somewhat. Recognizing, as did Intendant HOCQUART, that the elder Guillimin's sad fortunes were due in part to the government's financial instability, he offered to do something for the family. Hocquart, who had yearned since his arrival in Canada to improve the legal capacities of those serving on the Conseil Supérieur, pointed out that Guillaume had been studying law under the attorney general, Louis-Guillaume Verrier*, since 1736 and, though still too young to be named a councillor, could be made an assistant councillor for a probationary period, with the expectation of one day filling a vacant seat on the council. After some hesitation on the part of Governor General Charles de Beauharnois*, who was wrangling with Hocquart at that time over a number of appointments in their respective spheres of patronage, Guillimin was named assistant councillor, without pay, on 20 Sept. 1741. He was the first person to serve in that capacity in New France and, on 25 March 1744, he became a councillor. Since Marie-Geneviève Foucault, whom he married in May 1744, was the daughter of another councillor, François Foucault*, Guillimin was obliged to obtain from the king letters of dispensation from this family connection before he could be sure of his position. These were accorded him on 28 April 1745.

Guillimin served capably on the council for the next eight years, and during that time he was employed by Beauharnois and Hocquart in other capacities. He was, for example, a member of Hocquart's informal advisory council, which assisted the intendant in times of crisis. In 1746, during the War of the Austrian Succession, he was chosen to serve as commissary for an expeditionary force of 700 men, under Jean-Baptiste-Nicolas-Roch de RAMEZAY, that campaigned in Acadia. He raised supplies for the expedition and sailed with it to Acadia in June. After returning to Quebec later that year, he continued to supply the military with agricultural produce as a private entrepreneur. This was the most profitable activity for Canadian merchants in wartime.

In 1752 Guillimin resigned his seat on the council in order to become judge of the admiralty court at Quebec, a more lucrative post. Five years later, on 24 April 1757, he succeeded Nicolas-Gaspard Boucault* as local lieutenant (judge) of the provost court of Quebec. It was not unusual for one man to hold both positions, and he continued to do so until the conquest. That epic event left him in a precarious position. As a Canadian official he had little hope of obtaining a suitable post in France and no other alternative than to try to make his way in the new, alien régime. He made the transition successfully and, on 14 March 1765, he received a licence from Governor MURRAY to serve as attorney and lawyer in the Court of Common Pleas. Thus, on 9 July 1766, the date when his commission was signed, he became French Canada's first lawyer. He was also given a commission as notary, but he seems to have done little in that field, his registry consisting of only a few entries. By the time of his death in 1771 he had paved the way for the three of his ten children who had reached maturity to live comfortably in the British colony. His second daughter married James McGill*, a prominent Scottish resident of Montreal and founder of the university which took his name. Guillimin's success in the professional ranks following the conquest was perhaps a harbinger of the ambitious French-Canadian's role in the decades to come.

DONALD J. HORTON

AN, Col., B, 70, f.78; 72, ff.2–2v, 275; 73, ff.33, 69–69v; 78, f.140; C[11A], 73, f.8; 75, f.260; 81/1, f.14; F[3], 14, f.38. *DCB*, III, 74–77, 646–48. P.-G. Roy, "La famille Guillimin," *BRH*, XXIII (1917), 129–39.

GUILLIMIN, MARIE-FRANÇOISE, *dite* **de Saint-Antoine**, Ursuline and superior of the convent of Trois-Rivières (Que.); b. 10 Jan. 1720 in Quebec, daughter of Charles Guillimin* and Françoise Lemaître-Lamorille; d. March 1789 at Trois-Rivières.

Marie-Françoise Guillimin entered the Ursuline noviciate in Trois-Rivières on 8 April 1735 and pronounced her perpetual vows two years later. She then performed almost all the tasks required of the nuns, who devoted themselves to teaching children and caring for the sick.

In May 1752 a disastrous fire destroyed the convent and 45 houses in Trois-Rivières. The Ursulines had to spend the next 18 months in the house of the Recollets, who in turn accepted the hospitality of a brother-in-law of Marguerite-Renée de la Croix, the superior of the Ursulines and a daughter of René Godefroy* de Tonnancour. In the spring of 1753, Bishop Pontbriand [Dubreil*] arrived to direct in person the rebuilding of the convent-hospital. According to a letter written at this time to his brother, the Comte de Nevet, the bishop had, over a period of six months, "to foresee what has continually to be done on the building site to make my people work." He added: "From being a bishop I have become a joiner, a carpenter, a labourer." In the absence of documents it is not easy to picture the financial situation of the nuns during the years after the fire, but the loans they had to raise suggest that they must have been in considerable difficulty. Marie-Françoise de Saint-Antoine, entrusted in 1754 with the office of bursar, displayed great organizing abilities in putting the convent and hospital back on solid foundations; she had the encouragement of Bishop Pontbriand, who continued to take an interest in the fate of the Ursulines of Trois-Rivières.

In 1765 Marie-Françoise de Saint-Antoine was appointed superior of the community for a three-year term. In January 1769 she was recalled to this office to replace Marie-Geneviève Godefroy de Tonnancour, *dite* de Sainte-Hélène, who had had to resign because of ill health. During the American invasion in 1775–76 Marie-Françoise de Saint-Antoine was in charge of the hospital, assisted by another nun born in Quebec, Marie-Josephte Paquet, *dite* de la Nativité. The Ursulines' annalist wrote that "all the Boston soldiers were suffering from want of the most necessary articles; . . . they were reduced to wretched poverty; they lived largely on alms in our town, and many were in our hospital for several months." Promissory notes signed by American military commanders to pay for care given to the wounded were not honoured; "they have never been worth more than the paper they are printed on." Some historians have suggested that at the beginning the nuns used pressure to obtain reimbursement. In fact they had entrusted this commission to notary Jean-Baptiste BADEAUX, and the list of sums due, signed by the bursar, Marie-Josephte de la Nativité, and certified by the commander of the American forces, Colonel William Goforth, on 12 March 1776, is in his registry. The American debt to the Ursulines, according to this document, amounted to "£26 36*s*. (in Halifax currency)."

Marie-Françoise de Saint-Antoine was again called to direct her community from 1778 to 1784 and from 1787 until her death in March 1789. She was buried in the Ursuline cemetery.

RAYMOND DOUVILLE

ANQ-MBF, Greffe de J.-B. Badeaux, 10 sept. 1792. ANQ-Q, État civil, Catholiques, Notre-Dame de Québec, 10 janv. 1720. Archives des ursulines de Trois-Rivières, Annales. J.-B. Badeaux, "Journal des opérations de l'armée américaine lors de l'invasion du Canada en 1775–76...," *Revue canadienne* (Montréal), VII (1870), 186–202, 267–76, 329–45. Hervé Biron, *Grandeurs et misères de l'Église trifluvienne (1615–1947)* (Trois-Rivières, 1947). A.-H. Gosselin, *L'Eglise du Canada jusqu'à la Conquête*, III, 183–84, 188–93. Jouve, *Les franciscains et le Canada: aux Trois-Rivières*. *Les ursulines des Trois-Rivières depuis leur établissement jusqu'à nos jours* (4v., Trois-Rivières, 1888–1911), I. Raymond Douville, "La dette des États-Unis envers les ursulines de Trois-Rivières," *Cahiers des Dix*, 22 (1957), 137–62.

GUILLOT, *dit* **Larose, FRANÇOIS**, soldier, merchant, and militia captain; b. 25 Dec. 1727 at Asnelles (dept of Calvados), France, son of Jacques Guillot and Marguerite Loiseleur; m. 25 July 1763 Marie Létourneau, *née* Rateau, at Quebec; d. some time before 1785, probably in the United States.

It seems likely that François Guillot, *dit* Larose, arrived in Canada as a soldier in 1740 and, after the conquest, set himself up in Quebec as a merchant. In 1767 he settled in Rivière-du-Loup (Louiseville), where he became bailiff and later also militia captain. In 1770 he leased a mill from the Ursulines of Trois-Rivières, which he gave up four years later.

Primarily a businessman, Guillot also gambled on the possibilities that developed during the American invasion in 1775, particularly when the majority of his fellow citizens were won over to the American cause. As soon as the Americans arrived at Trois-Rivières, he let his sympathies be known. He accused Conrad GUGY, who owned several seigneuries in the region, of threatening to have Canadians who were in sympathy with the rebels whipped, a charge from which Gugy was cleared on 4 Dec. 1775.

At the beginning of May 1776 François Guillot and a companion, Pierre Dupaul, joined the American troops that had just raised the siege of Quebec and those evacuating Trois-Rivières. He went with them to Sorel, where reinforcements from New England soon reached them. Early in June both men took part in preparations for an attack on Trois-Rivières designed to retake the town and check the advance of British troops. A regiment under Brigadier-General William Thompson crossed the St Lawrence and landed at Pointe-du-Lac during the night of 7 June. François Guillot served as guide and led Thompson to the home of a local inhabitant, Antoine Gautier, who was asked to guide the force to the gates of Trois-Rivières. Gautier, who seemed to fall in readily with this order, advised Thompson not to venture on the king's road, which was swarming with scouts, and suggested going through the woods of Sainte-Marguerite and the region of the Saint-Maurice ironworks. But at the same time he sent his wife with a message to Landron, the militia captain; the latter went to Trois-Rivières to alert the local garrison and give it time to prepare for the attack. Meanwhile Guy Carleton*'s army reached Trois-Rivières.

After a battle in which the Americans had more than 500 officers and men killed or wounded, Thompson was taken prisoner. François Guillot returned to Sorel with what was left of the little army and then went on to Chambly, Saint-Jean, and Île aux Noix. According to François-Xavier Garneau*, he was given command of a company of "brave French Canadians" under the orders of Colonel Moses Hazen* and fought in the Hudson River region.

After that no more is heard of him. It appears that he died in the United States, but we do not know where or when. He may have been dead when the administrators of his estate, Alexander Davison* and John Lees*, published an announcement on 13 Aug. 1778 in the *Quebec Gazette* that his properties were to be sold in pursuance of an order of the Court of Common Pleas. In any case he was dead in 1785, for on 20 January of that year his widow married Augustin Sicard of Rivière-du-Loup, her third husband.

RAYMOND DOUVILLE

AD, Calvados (Caen), État civil, Asnelles, 25 déc. 1727. ANQ-MBF, Greffe de J.-B. Badeaux; Greffe de Benoît LeRoy. *Invasion du Canada* (Verreau). *Quebec Gazette*, 8 Sept. 1768, 7 Sept. 1769, 4 Oct. 1770.

J.-E. Bellemare, *Histoire de Nicolet, 1669–1924* (Arthabaska, Qué., 1924). Lanctot, *Le Canada et la Révolution américaine*, 162–63. Germain Lesage, *Histoire de Louiseville, 1665–1960* (Louiseville, Qué., 1961). J.[-P.]-A. Maurault, *Histoire des Abénakis, depuis 1605 jusqu'à nos jours* ([Sorel, Qué.], 1866). Raymond Douville, "La dette des États-Unis envers les ursulines de Trois-Rivières," *Cahiers des Dix*, 22 (1957), 137–62. J.-J. Lefebvre, "Les Canadiens-français et la Révolution américaine," Soc. historique franco-américaine, *Bull.* (Boston, Mass.), 1946–47, 50–71. Riclès [Richard Lessard], "François Guillot, dit Larose," *L'Écho de Saint-Justin* (Louiseville), 11 juin 1936, 1.

GUIYAHGWAAHDOH. *See* KAIEÑ?KWAAHTOÑ

GUYASUTA. *See* KAYAHSOTA?

GYRARD. *See* GIRARD

H

HALDIMAND, Sir FREDERICK. *See* Supplement

HAMILTON, HENRY, army officer and colonial administrator; b. *c.* 1734, probably in Dublin (Republic of Ireland), younger of two sons of Henry Hamilton, member of the Irish parliament for Donegal and collector of the port of Cork, and Mary Dawson; m. 19 March 1795 Elizabeth Lee, and they had at least one daughter; d. 29 Sept. 1796 on Antigua.

Commissioned ensign in the 15th Foot in 1755 and promoted lieutenant in September of the following year, Henry Hamilton saw service in the Seven Years' War at Louisbourg, Île Royale (Cape Breton Island), Quebec, and in the Caribbean; he received his captaincy at Havana, Cuba, in 1762. In early 1766 Hamilton was in garrison at Trois-Rivières, and was placed in command later that year at Crown Point (N.Y.). In 1767 he became a brigade major with Lieutenant Governor Guy Carleton*, who recommended him highly. Hamilton left North America with his regiment in 1768, but by 1775 was back and stationed in Montreal. In that year he was sent by Carleton to quell an uprising by the habitants of Terrebonne against their seigneur, and managed to accomplish the task through diplomacy. Later in 1775 he sold his commission. According to his reminiscences, a military career was not traditional in his family; moreover, his education had been classical and his interests were political. Indeed, his later career, especially in Quebec, seems to bear out Alfred Leroy Burt*'s judgement that he "had a thoroughly civilian mind, a thoroughly civilian conception of government."

When the boundaries of Quebec were extended by the Quebec Act of 1774 to include the triangle of land between the Ohio and Mississippi rivers, it became necessary to invest some officials with the symbols of British power to govern the area. In retrospect, it was easy to argue that these officials should have held high military rank, but in 1775 it was decided to create civil governorships, and Hamilton, Edward Abbott, and Mathew Johnson were appointed to the posts at Detroit, Vincennes (Ind.), and Kaskaskia (Ill.) respectively. Hamilton's appointment, made by Carleton, was probably suggested by Lord Dartmouth, secretary of state for the American Colonies, to whom Hamilton had been recommended by the chief justice of Quebec, William HEY.

Understandably, Hamilton was much concerned about the nature of his office and the extent of his powers, but most of his questions were never answered by officials in Quebec and London. Part of the problem lay in the fact that American armies were already in Canada by the time Hamilton undertook his journey westward in the autumn of 1775, and communication between Detroit and the St Lawrence region remained more than ordinarily difficult. His first problem was the administration of justice. New judicial arrangements were postponed because of the war, and Hamilton resorted to a most unsatisfactory and irregular method of settling property disputes, while Philippe Dejean*, whose authority as a temporary judge had ended with the Quebec Act, continued to hand down judgements in criminal cases. In 1778 the grand jurors of the District of Montreal indicted Hamilton for tolerating illegal actions by Dejean. Predictably, Governor HALDIMAND excused any high-handed actions on the grounds that the paramount need was security in the midst of war, and the British government, unsure how to deal with Hamilton given the novelty of his office and the wartime conditions, took the same view.

Hamilton's position at Detroit in the early

years of the American revolution was far from enviable. The British had not yet established any suitable government or firm policy for the upper Great Lakes-Illinois region, so that neither the Indians nor the Canadian settlers had much confidence in the new rulers. Moreover, since Hamilton's commission was a civil one, the limits of his authority in a wartime situation were not clear. As early as 1776 his dispatches urged military action, but at first his superiors were reluctant to agree to such a move. Early in 1778, however, the situation changed with the arrival of George Rogers Clark and his Virginia militia in the Illinois country. Philippe-François Rastel* de Rocheblave surrendered Kaskaskia to them in July, and the inhabitants of Vincennes declared for Virginia the same month, Abbott having left for Detroit in February. Hamilton asked for instructions but the possibility of recapturing Vincennes was still under discussion in Quebec when he decided to act. With about 60 Indians [*see* EGUSHWA] and 175 white troops, mostly Canadian militia with about 30 British regulars from Detroit, he set out on 8 Oct. 1778 to cut off American trade at Vincennes, and, it has been suggested, to escape from the intolerable position in which he had been placed at Detroit for the past three years.

Vincennes was taken in December, and Hamilton decided to wait for spring before making any further moves, relying on leniency to keep the 500 residents of the town on the British side. He believed that the arrival of Clark with the news of the Franco-American alliance of February 1778 had eroded whatever support the British had among Indians and Canadians. In any case, when Clark attacked without warning, the entire garrison was forced to surrender unconditionally on 25 Feb. 1779. Hamilton and a number of his associates, including Jehu HAY, were sent off to Virginia, and British power in the old northwest received a serious setback. Hamilton blamed the disaster on the defection of Canadian volunteers and the continuing correspondence of the residents of Vincennes with the Americans. "The conduct of the canadians in general has shown that no ties that have force upon enlightened and generous minds, can bind them, and that they prefer any subjection, to the freedom of Englishmen," he lamented to Haldimand in an account written in 1781 of the Vincennes expedition. Once news of the defeat reached him, Haldimand was prompt to explain that the expedition had been undertaken without his specific authorization, although in obedience to his general instructions to Hamilton. The farthest that he went in criticizing the lieutenant governor personally was to suggest, in strict confidence to a fellow general, that the mission might have been successful if Hamilton had had the prudence to retire from Vincennes in time.

If there was any thought of censure, it seems to have been obliterated by news of the treatment Hamilton received in Virginia. Held in Williamsburg and Chesterfield for 18 months, during many of them in irons, he was denied any consideration as a prisoner of war and was treated as the common criminal his captors believed him to be. Efforts to secure his parole and eventual exchange succeeded at last through the intervention of George Washington, but only after the Virginia authorities, Governor Thomas Jefferson in particular, had resisted all appeals for many months.

The explanation for the Americans' treatment of Hamilton lies in their fear of Indian attacks on their western settlements and the conviction that he typified a brutal and relentless British policy in using Indians; the "hair-buyer general," Clark dubbed him. So intense was the hatred of Hamilton that a century and a half passed before American historians conceded that there was no positive proof that he had ever offered rewards for scalps. The judgment of Milo Milton Quaife that Hamilton was "a brave and high-minded soldier" exemplifying an old tradition that was beginning to be seen as inhumane betrays more of Quaife's belief in the progress of moral perceptions and of American leadership in that progress than it does knowledge of events in the old northwest in the 1770s. Any effort to exonerate Hamilton from responsibility for Indian raids on the grounds that he was simply carrying out orders from his superiors is unconvincing. As early as 1776 he had apparently proposed employing Indians against the Americans, and in March 1777 he was authorized to assemble as many Indians as possible and to use them in "making a Diversion and exciting an alarm upon the frontiers of Virginia and Pennsylvania." He was, however, to restrain them from any acts of violence against "well-affected and inoffensive inhabitants." Hamilton undoubtedly realized the contradiction in these orders – if Indians were used, settlers, whatever their political stance, would become victims – but he saw alliance with the Indians as the only means of retaining British power in the old northwest. There is no indication that revulsion against the policy caused the Americans to refrain from using similar tactics throughout the war.

Early in 1781 Hamilton was at last free to go to England, and there he received word that on Haldimand's recommendation he had been appointed lieutenant governor of Quebec, succeeding Hector Theophilus CRAMAHÉ. When Haldimand had first been appointed governor in 1777, Hamilton had told the Indians at Detroit: "I shall rise up, or sit down, as he orders me." Almost from the moment of his arrival in Quebec in June 1782, however, relations with his superior were strained. Haldimand and his supporters in the French party had created a set of policies that they justified as long as the war continued, and at the same time they had come to regard any opposition as fundamentally disloyal. Yet as early as December Hamilton supported the opposition group in the Legislative Council, led by George Allsopp*, in a motion critical of past decisions. It would appear that from this point on Haldimand lost confidence in the man he had recommended and could not immediately have dismissed.

With the signing of the treaty of Paris in September 1783, pressure for change in Quebec, particularly from the British merchants, mounted; at the very least, there would have to be some steps toward the implementation of instructions to the governor left in abeyance through nearly a decade of war. Much of the debate that raged in council was over the introduction of habeas corpus and the extension of English law to commercial cases. The French party urged the least possible change and defended its charter theory in which the Quebec Act (isolated from the instructions accompanying it) was seen as a sacred document enshrining the inalienable rights of the Canadians. Hamilton from the beginning challenged this worshipful attitude, desiring free discussion of individual clauses of the act. The territorial provisions had been made obsolete by the peace treaty and, he argued, Quebec society had altered sufficiently within the past decade that other clauses also deserved re-examination. Whenever this charter theory formed part of a motion before council, Hamilton felt impelled to record his dissent, although it might have been wiser to refrain from doing so on the motion congratulating George III on the conclusion of peace! Prominent among Hamilton's supporters during the 1784 session was Hugh Finlay*, the deputy postmaster general. Although the council passed an ordinance granting habeas corpus, the two other ordinances approved were renewals of previous ones, and both men claimed that the measures passed fell short of what they believed to be "His Majesty's gracious intention toward his Canadian subjects" to introduce a greater measure of English institutions into the province.

The French party, with the governor's support, was able to win most of the battles at that session, but during the summer its members were alarmed when it became known that Haldimand was about to depart for England, reluctantly leaving the administration of the colony in the hands of the lieutenant governor. Repeatedly Hamilton begged for orders, instructions, copies of dispatches, and other documents in time to examine them carefully and discuss problem areas with his superior. But Haldimand chose to have documents delivered to Hamilton on the day of his departure and even then did not include copies of his own dispatches to London. Again, Hamilton was entrusted only with civil powers, and Haldimand made an effort to confine that authority as much as possible. Military command was assumed by Barrimore Matthew ST LEGER, the ranking army officer after Haldimand, and to him and others the governor entrusted much of the business dealing with the loyalists and Indians. The governor's rather meagre instructions did include a statement of his own support for the Quebec Act as a charter and his conviction that all petitions against it were the work of designing men. It has been suggested that he hoped to force Hamilton into consultation with Adam MABANE and the French party. But Hamilton had already had occasion to quarrel with the favouritism Haldimand had shown towards Mabane. "He gave the helm into another person's hand, but would not entrust me with the management of an Oar," Hamilton complained in November 1784. No mayor of the palace would be tolerated during the Hamilton administration. Instead, he resolved to open up the council to free discussion, and his attitude encouraged various groups of citizens to present petitions in favour of an elected assembly and against certain ordinances currently in force. When these petitions appeared, Hamilton, whether or not he was in agreement with their contents, resolved that they must be transmitted to the king. It soon became evident that, whatever the reasons for his actions, Haldimand had set the stage for a stormy legislative session in 1785.

During that session Hugh Finlay presided over a council that was almost equally divided on each issue brought before it. Hamilton's supporters were able to push through an ordinance introducing jury trials in some civil cases, but the strength of the French party was sufficient to postpone for one more year any amendments to the militia ordinance which had re-established the corvée. Its victory came about in the midst of furious debate throughout the colony. There had been a petition against this ordinance (which Hamilton duly transmitted to London) and certain of its statements were regarded by military men in the colony as unfair attacks on their past conduct. Colonel Henry HOPE published a denial of these statements in the *Quebec Gazette*, and another petition was then circulated protesting Hope's remarks. Hamilton's desire that public opinion should have free expression was fulfilled with a vengeance.

With Haldimand in London representing the French party's view on each issue, Hamilton was finding it difficult to retain the confidence of His Majesty's government. Just after the legislative session ended in May he took the decision that made his recall certain. He had asked Haldimand about the matter of a new lease for the king's posts, a question that would likely have to be decided during his administration of the colony. He had been told that the matter had been laid before the British government and that nothing was to be done until His Majesty's pleasure was known. The first mail packet in 1785 contained a number of letters to citizens of Quebec announcing that Alexander* and George DAVISON and François Baby*, friends of the French party, had been chosen as the new lessees, but the official letter informing Hamilton of the decision did not arrive for several days. During this period, although the decision was common knowledge in Quebec, Hamilton chose to reconfirm the lease of a different group, Thomas Dunn* and his associates William Grant* and Peter Stuart. Hamilton seems to have been convinced that an injustice was being planned to the Dunn group which it was in his power to remedy, and the purity of his motives does not seem to have been seriously questioned, even though Dunn and Grant had been his supporters in crucial debates in the council over the past two years. It was his political wisdom, not his probity, that came under attack. If he hoped for a last minute change of heart in Britain, he had miscalculated. In August a curt letter of dismissal ordered him to hand over authority to Hope, who also assumed the military command on St Leger's departure, and to return to England at once.

Hamilton sailed for England on 2 Nov. 1785, the same day on which he handed the seals of office to his successor. For more than two years humiliated and financially embarrassed, he awaited vindication. But during those two years, events in Quebec made it possible to see Hamilton's actions in perspective. He left behind at least two measures that his enemies sought to set aside as illegal. In both cases they failed. The lease he had granted to the Dunn group for the king's posts was to be reviewed on 1 Oct. 1786, and the government clearly recognized its legality by granting the posts to the Davisons and Baby only from that date. The conclusion would seem to be inescapable: Hamilton's actions had cost him his position, but he had acted within his power. The second illustration revealed even more about the animosity of his opponents and aroused new sympathy for him. In the council session of 1786 Mabane led an attempt to refuse payment of accounts authorized by Hamilton in the previous year, a move which would have made Hamilton liable for the charges. Even Hope, Mabane's friend, refused to accept his argument; in his report accompanying the minutes of council, Hope left no doubt of his support for Hamilton's conduct. With the arrival of Governor General Lord Dorchester [Carleton] and the new chief justice, William SMITH, in October 1786 the balance of power within Quebec altered. Their views of the situation in the colony, which seemed to echo some of Hamilton's judgements, had placed the British government by 1788 in a position to evaluate some of the problems which Hamilton had faced, and a new appointment for him followed. For six years he served as governor of Bermuda and the new capital, founded during his term of office, was named for him. These were years of political calm in the colony. In 1794 he became governor of Dominica, and he died in office two years later.

Twice in his lifetime, opponents in their fury made Hamilton a symbol of what they hated and feared. The French party in Quebec saw him as an innovator who pandered to the wishes of the lower classes, and as an enemy of the kind of social order set up by MURRAY, Carleton, and Haldimand. Its denunciations of Hamilton's conduct at Quebec were, in their way, as extreme as Clark's description of "the hair-buyer" of the war years. Yet when this group of detractors charged that Hamilton's actions were preparing the way for an American expansion into Canada, they had, perhaps wilfully, forgotten what he had suffered at American hands. In Quebec he represented change at a time when fears for the future dominated the ruling party, and even those such as Hope, who admired his qualities, or Finlay and Evan Nepean, under-secretary of state for the Home Department, who also sympathized with his aspirations, sometimes questioned his political judgement. It was his misfortune that the American revolution and its aftermath created circumstances that doomed his missions not only at Detroit but also at Quebec.

ELIZABETH ARTHUR

BL, Add. MSS 21702, pp.32, 36; 21717, p.489; 21726, p.137; 21733; 21734; 21736, p.198; 21739, p.255; 21755, pp.122, 200, 267; 21781, pp.8, 25, 37, 40; 21782, pp.54, 156, 235, 506; 21783, pp.53–102; 21807 (copies at PAC). PAC, MG 11, [CO 42], Q, 12, p.212; 15, pp.9, 102, 105,

215; 18, pp.216–17; 23, pp.389, 393–400, 438–39; 24, p.235; 25, p.6; 26, pp.214, 419; MG 23, A4, 29, p.207; GII, 11. PRO, CO 42/16, pp.42, 55; 42/17, pp.56, 97; 42/18, p.13; 42/19, pp.119, 121, 212, 226 (copies at PAC). *The capture of old Vincennes: the original narratives of George Rogers Clark and his opponent, Gov. Henry Hamilton*, ed. M. M. Quaife (Indianapolis, Ind., 1927). *Docs. relating to constitutional history, 1759–91* (Shortt and Doughty; 1907), 735–805. *Henry Hamilton and George Rogers Clark in the American revolution, with the unpublished journal of Lieut. Gov. Henry Hamilton*, ed. J. D. Barnhart (Crawfordsville, Ind., 1951). *Michigan Pioneer Coll.*, III (1880), 16; IX (1886). *The Windsor border region, Canada's southernmost frontier . . .*, ed. E. J. Lajeunesse (Toronto, 1960). *Appleton's cyclopædia of American biography*, ed. J. G. Wilson *et al.* (10v., New York, 1887–1924). H. J. Morgan, *Sketches of celebrated Canadians, and persons connected with Canada, from the earliest period in the history of the province down to the present time* (Quebec and London, 1862). Wallace, *Macmillan dictionary*. Burt, *Old prov. of Que.* (1968), II, 125, 129–32. O. J. Jæbker, "Henry Hamilton, British soldier and colonial governor" (unpublished PHD thesis, Indiana University, Bloomington, 1954). J. A. James, *The life of George Rogers Clark* (Chicago, 1929), 51–53, 132. Neatby, *Quebec*, 183, 194–203. Frederick Palmer, *Clark on the Ohio* (New York, 1929). F.-J. Audet, "L'honorable Henry Hamilton," *BRH*, XXXI (1925), 487–88. J. D. Barnhart, "A new evaluation of Henry Hamilton and George Rogers Clark," *Mississippi Valley Hist. Rev.* (Cedar Rapids, Iowa, and Lincoln, Neb.), XXXVII (1950–51), 643–52. Reginald Horsman, "Great Britain and the Illinois country in the era of the American revolution," Ill. State Hist. Soc., *Journal* (Springfield), LXIX (1976), 100–9. N. V. Russell, "The Indian policy of Henry Hamilton: a re-valuation," *CHR*, XI (1930), 20–37. D. C. Skaggs, "Between the lakes and the bluegrass," *Northwest Ohio Quarterly* (Toledo), XLVIII (1976), 89–101.

HANNA, JAMES, pioneer in the maritime fur trade on the northwest coast of North America; d. 1787.

Nothing is known about James Hanna prior to his departure from Macao, China, on 15 April 1785 in the brig *Harmon* (60 tons) with a crew of 20 men. It is not clear whether the vessel sailed under Portuguese colours or under the British flag with a licence from the East India Company. Hanna, who had the financial backing of John Henry Cox, a merchant residing in China, headed for Nootka Sound (B.C.), which had been described by Captain James COOK as a likely place to acquire a profitable cargo of sea otter pelts.

Arriving there in August, Hanna and his men were attacked by the Nootka Indians, and in the ensuing struggle 20 Indians, including several chiefs, were killed. Hanna claimed that the attack occurred after he fired on the Indians in retaliation for their theft of a chisel. The Nootka chief MUQUINNA told Esteban José MARTÍNEZ in 1789, however, that it had been in response to a humiliating and painful practical joke played on him by Hanna and his men, which involved setting off a charge of gunpowder under his chair as he sat on the deck. Whatever the cause, peaceful relations were established after the battle, and in the resulting trade Hanna acquired 560 sea otter pelts. As a token of friendship he exchanged names with Cleaskina, chief of Ahousat, a Nootka village then located on Vargas Island, who was known to later voyagers as "Captain Hanna." Hanna returned to Macao in December, selling his furs for up to $60 apiece and realizing $20,600.

Encouraged by the profit made from such a short cruise, Hanna's backers fitted him for a second trip. He left Macao in May 1786 in the snow *Sea Otter* (120 tons) with a crew of 30. When he arrived at Nootka in August, he found the situation greatly altered. James Charles Stuart Strange* of Bombay had already been there in July with two ships and had bought all the furs. Hanna remained at anchor in Nootka for a fortnight, purchasing only about 50 good pelts. He then sailed northward, discovering and naming several sounds, islands, and harbours on his way. He appears to have thought that the north end of Vancouver Island was a separate island, naming it after Cox, and he is said to have sighted the Queen Charlotte Islands, to which, with the land north of them, he gave the name Nova Hibernia. By the end of September Hanna had managed to collect about 100 prime pelts, and on 1 October he sailed for China, reaching Macao on 8 Feb. 1787. The cargo brought $8,000, despite its small size. Plans were made for a third trip, but Hanna died before they were completed.

Hanna's visits to the northwest coast were brief, and the information he kept concerning them was scanty, but his observations were useful to others. George DIXON, John Meares*, and George VANCOUVER all consulted his charts. In 1790 Alexander Dalrymple, the British geographer, cited Hanna's explorations when he advanced British claims to the northwest coast and its fur trade.

RICHARD A. PIERCE

Provincial Archives of B.C. (Victoria), *Sea-Otter* (ship), Journal of a voyage from Macoa towards King Georges Sound in the Sea Otter, Captain Hanna, commander; Brig Sea Otter from Macao towards America through the northern Pacific ocean (1785). [William Beresford], *A voyage round the world; but more particularly to the north-west coast of America . . .*, ed. and intro. George Dixon (London, 1789; repr. Amsterdam and New York, 1968). [Alexander] Dalrymple, *The Spanish pretensions fairly discussed* (London, 1790). *The Dixon-Meares controversy . . .* , ed. F. W. Howay (Toronto and New York, 1929; repr. Amsterdam and New York, 1969). *Geschichte der Reisen, die seit Cook an der Nordwest- und Nordost-Küste von Amerika und dem nördlichsten Amerika selbst von Meares, Dixon, Portlock, Coxe, Long u.a.m. unternommen worden sind . . .* , ed. and trans. Georg Forster (3v., Berlin, 1791). Meares, *Voyages*. G. Vancouver, *Voyage of discovery* (J. Vancouver). *Voyages of 'Columbia'* (Howay). Howay, *List of trading vessels in maritime fur trade*. Walbran, *B.C. coast names*. H. H. Bancroft [*et al.*], *History of Alaska, 1730–1885* (San Francisco, 1886); [and H. L. Oak], *History of the northwest coast* (2v., San Francisco, 1886). Cook, *Flood tide of empire*.

HANTRAYE, CLAUDE (often incorrectly written **Hautraye**, but he signed Hantraye), notary; b. probably 10 Dec. 1723 at Saint-Hilaire-du-Harcouët, France, son of Noël Hantraye and Marie Hamond; m. 9 Jan. 1753 Marie-Marguerite Debuire in Quebec; m. secondly 26 Nov. 1759 Marie-Françoise Viger in Montreal; d. 15 Jan. 1777 at Saint-Jean-François-Régis (now Saint-Philippe-de-Laprairie, Que.).

In 1754 Claude Hantraye was sent to be storekeeper at Fort Saint-Frédéric (near Crown Point, N.Y.), where he apparently remained for only a year. He stayed long enough, however, to be one of the minor figures accused in the *affaire du Canada* and he was sentenced *in absentia* on 10 Dec. 1763 to banishment from Paris for five years and a fine of 50 *livres*.

Hantraye lived at Prairie-de-la-Madeleine (La Prairie, Que.) after the surrender of Montreal, and he was still there in 1765; in that year he began drawing up deeds as a notary, although his commission has not been found. Most of the deeds he prepared during this period are land grants for René Cartier, seigneur of La Salle. In November 1767 Hantraye moved to Saint-Antoine-de-Padoue (Saint-Antoine-sur-Richelieu), where he became the first resident notary.

In May 1772 he settled in Saint-Jean-François-Régis. He drew up deeds there for nearly five more years, continuing to devote his time in part to René Cartier's land grants and many commercial transactions. Hantraye apparently continued his professional activities uninterrupted by the American occupation in 1775–76 and he signed his last deed on 30 Dec. 1776. He died on 15 Jan. 1777 and was buried in the crypt of the parish church of Saint-Jean-François-Régis.

JEAN-JACQUES LEFEBVRE

ANQ-M, État civil, Catholiques, Saint-Philippe; Greffe de Claude Hantraye, 1765–76. Tanguay, *Dictionnaire*, IV, 459, 469. P.-G. Roy, *Bigot et sa bande*, 188–89.

HARDY, Sir CHARLES, naval officer, colonial administrator, and office-holder; b. *c.* 1714, son of Vice-Admiral Sir Charles Hardy and Elizabeth Burchett; m. July 1749 Mary Tate; m. secondly 4 Jan. 1759 Catherine Stanyan, and they had three sons and two daughters; d. 18 May 1780 at Portsmouth, England.

Charles Hardy entered the Royal Navy in 1731 under his father's patronage; he was promoted lieutenant six years later and captain in 1741. His early years at sea were spent in American waters; from 1741 to 1743 he served off the coast of South Carolina and Georgia. Appointed governor of Newfoundland on the outbreak of war with France in 1744, Hardy failed to take up his post and was tried by court martial for neglect of duty. He was exonerated, however, after it was shown that he had unsuccessfully battled contrary winds for 63 days before returning to port. The following year, in command of the *Torrington*, he helped convoy reinforcements from Gibraltar to the newly captured fortress of Louisbourg on Cape Breton Island. He served off the coasts of Spain and Portugal from 1746 until the peace in 1748, when he was placed on half-pay.

In 1755 Hardy was knighted and appointed governor of New York. The post became one of considerable importance since, in preparation for war with France, London decided that year to make New York City the arsenal of British arms in North America. A rather self-effacing man, Hardy proved to be an effective governor. He was especially useful to Lord Loudoun, commander-in-chief in North America, who expressed his gratitude for "the assistance and friendship I have met with from him on every occasion." In the spring of 1757 Hardy suggested that a trade embargo be laid on the British colonies in order to ensure an adequate supply of transports for Loudoun's planned attack upon Louisbourg and to prevent the French learning of the British plan from captured ships. The embargo affected shipping from Nova Scotia to Virginia and was the cause of many complaints from the business community, probably because it was enforced more effectively than any other embargo in colonial America.

In June Hardy convoyed the transports intended for the siege of Louisbourg to Halifax, Nova Scotia. He had been promoted rear-admiral in 1756, and at Halifax he became second in command to Vice-Admiral Francis Holburne.

The presence in Louisbourg harbour of a large French naval force under Comte Dubois de La Motte [Cahideuc*], intelligence about which came in part from Hardy's observations, led to the cancellation of the expedition. Hardy had advised against it in any case, arguing that the season was too advanced for British ships to keep their stations off Île Royale. His opinion was well founded since in September a hurricane wreaked havoc in Holburne's fleet cruising off Louisbourg.

In July 1758, as second in command to Vice-Admiral Edward Boscawen*, Hardy took part in the successful siege of Louisbourg and the following month convoyed three regiments under Wolfe* to the Baie de Gaspé and the lower St Lawrence River. The force did considerable damage, burning about 200 fishing boats and numerous stages, storehouses, lines, and nets; the hamlet of Mont-Louis, taken by surprise, was razed. Hardy, however, did not agree with Wolfe's proposal to sail farther up the river, and he turned back off Île du Bic. He was probably fearful of the dangerous navigation and anxious to return to Louisbourg in case he had received orders to sail to England.

From 1759 to 1762 Hardy served in home waters as second in command to Vice-Admiral Sir Edward Hawke and to Boscawen; in November 1759 he participated in Hawke's celebrated success off Quiberon Bay, France. He was promoted vice-admiral in 1762 and two years later was elected to parliament from Rochester, a seat he held until 1768. In 1771 he was returned for Plymouth and was appointed governor of Greenwich Hospital at £1,000 per annum. Seven years later he became, through seniority, admiral of the fleet.

When Admiral Augustus Keppel resigned the command of the Channel fleet in 1779, no active officer would agree to succeed him, and Hardy was drawn out of his long retirement. His ships were greatly outnumbered by a Franco-Spanish fleet which appeared in the Channel in August and he was forced to retreat, but the enemy neither attacked nor attempted to capture a bridgehead for the 40,000 troops waiting in France to invade England. The following May, on the very day Hardy resumed the command, he was seized "with an inflamation of the bowels (a disorder to which he was much subject) and expired on Thursday (18 May) morning at three o'clock." In his will he left an annuity of £1,000 to his wife, and his seat at Rawlins, Oxfordshire, to his eldest son.

JULIAN GWYN

Huntington Library, Abercromby papers, AB 705; Loudoun papers, LO 3545, LO 4035, LO 4298, LO 5361. N.Y. Hist. Soc. (New York), Sir Charles Hardy papers. PRO, Adm. 1/480, 1/1882–86, 1/5284, 6/15–16; PRO 30/8/95, ff.290–92, 294; Prob. 11/1066, ff.241–46. *Horace Walpole's correspondence* . . . , ed. W. S. Lewis *et al.* (39v. to date, New Haven, Conn., and London, 1937–), XXV, 48. *Johnson papers* (Sullivan et al.). *The letters and papers of Cadwallader Colden* [1711–75] (9v., New York, 1918–37). *NYCD* (O'Callaghan and Fernow), VI, VII. *The private papers of John, Earl of Sandwich, first lord of the Admiralty, 1771–1782*, ed. G. R. Barnes and J. H. Owen (4v., London, 1932–38), III, 3–115. *DNB*. Namier and Brooke, *House of Commons*, II, 583–84. Pargellis, *Lord Loudoun*, 265.

HARDY, ELIAS, lawyer and office-holder; b. *c.* 1744 at Farnham, England; m. Martha Huggeford of New York; d. 25 Dec. 1798 at Saint John, New Brunswick.

Elias Hardy, the son of a nonconformist minister, read law and in 1770 was admitted as a solicitor in the courts of Chancery and King's Bench. In 1775 he decided to seek his fortune in the new world and went to Virginia where, finding the courts closed because of the colonists' dispute with the British government, he worked briefly as a tutor. Hardy publicly criticized Thomas Paine's inflammatory pamphlet *Common sense* . . . (1776), which led to his seizure by a mob of Virginia partisans. He escaped and fled first to Maryland, and then to New York City, where he remained for the duration of the American revolution. In 1778 he was commissioned to act as a notary public. Hardy took no part in the war although he tried to obtain a military commission, but he was clearly identified as a loyalist. In 1782 he was one of the nine petitioners, including such loyalist notables as Charles Inglis*, Samuel Seabury, and Christopher Billopp*, who begged Sir Guy Carleton* to see that loyalist interests were safeguarded during the peace negotiations.

Hardy originally intended to return to England at the end of the war, when an outburst of dissension within the loyalist ranks permanently altered the course of his life. A group of 55 New York professional men and Church of England ministers petitioned the British government in July 1783 for extraordinary grants of 5,000 acres of land in Nova Scotia, in recognition of their special merits and wartime sacrifices. Many common loyalist refugees were enraged by this Petition of Fifty-five and asked a committee consisting of Hardy, Samuel Hake, Tertullus Dickinson (Hardy's brother-in-law), and Captain Henry

Law to express their opposition formally. Hardy himself drafted the angry, eloquent counter-petition, which, signed by 600 loyalists, accused the 55 of trying to secure all the best lands in Nova Scotia for themselves and force other refugees "to be tenants to those whom they consider as their superiors in nothing but deeper art and keener policy." For the refugees, the counter-petition elicited an assurance from Carleton that all loyalist exiles would receive equitable grants of good land in Nova Scotia. For Hardy, it set the mould for his subsequent career in British North America.

Henceforth Hardy's public activities were marked by an active, though always legally correct, opposition to the attempts of loyalists favoured by wealth, official position, or other special privilege to use their influence to take advantage of the less fortunate. He was not a radical, but his political and legal career from 1783 until his terminal illness in 1795 displays a consistent determination to protect the rights of the common citizen against more powerful, aggrandizing interests.

In 1783 Hardy decided to accompany the loyalist exiles who were resettling around the Saint John harbour area of Nova Scotia. There he encountered widespread discontent over the prejudicial manner in which the loyalist agents in charge of the settlements along the Saint John River were distributing the best commercial lots to themselves and their friends. At the request of a loyalist militia company, Hardy drafted a petition of grievances which accused the agents of favouritism in the distribution of land and supplies and threatened to take the case to London if a fairer system were not introduced. This petition thoroughly alarmed both the agents and Governor John PARR of Nova Scotia. It not only impugned the agents' management of the settlement process, but potentially endangered their effort to get the British government to partition Nova Scotia and create a separate loyalist province north of the Bay of Fundy. The governor saw in the petition a challenge to the conduct of his administration.

At first, Parr was inclined to blame Hardy for the troubles along the Saint John. Hardy, however, went to Halifax during the winter of 1783–84 and convinced the governor that his real enemies were the loyalist agents, both because of their partiality in allocating lands and, more important, because of their desire to use the discontent within the settlements to discredit the Parr administration so as to achieve the partition of Nova Scotia. Parr and Hardy thereupon allied themselves to undermine the power of the agents and oppose the partition movement. In the spring of 1784, Hardy returned to the Saint John with Parr's chief justice, Bryan Finucane, who promptly redistributed the contested commercial lots and began to organize a political opposition to partition. In addition, the Nova Scotia Council set up a committee of inquiry to investigate the conduct of the agents, with Hardy as its chief investigator. The agents reacted predictably to Hardy's activities. In Lieutenant-Colonel Edward Winslow*'s opinion, Hardy was not only "a pettifogging notary public" but "a viper"; Major John Coffin* condemned him as a "vagabound," and George Leonard* as the leader of "Malcontents" and "undeserving people." Hardy was undeterred, but his efforts came too late. The British government had already decided to partition Nova Scotia, and in June 1784 New Brunswick was created with the loyalist agents and their colleagues firmly entrenched in the most important positions of power.

In spite of this setback, Hardy chose to stay on in New Brunswick and settled in Saint John. His role in the hotly contested election of 1785 is ambiguous. Although Hardy declined to be a candidate in the city, Governor Thomas Carleton* was probably correct when he identified him as the mastermind behind the slate of candidates who opposed the government nominees. The lower cove party, as it was called, was headed by Dickinson, and five of the party's six candidates were members of the first Masonic lodge in Saint John, formed in September 1784, to which Hardy also belonged. Hardy was the recognized spokesman for the opposition slate during the election itself, but he personally worked to damp down the threat of violence which eventually led to a riot. He later defended the rioters against government prosecution. Hardy himself was elected to the assembly from the remote county of Northumberland, thanks to the sponsorship of his client, the fishing magnate William DAVIDSON. His voting record in the assembly was decidedly liberal but not intransigently anti-government, demonstrating the delicate balance which Hardy tried to maintain between the need for a well-established system of law and order within the province and the equally important need for its inhabitants to be able to enjoy their rights and express their grievances. Thus while Hardy supported the administration's bill to discourage "tumults and disorders," he opposed its effort to limit political meetings to 20 persons. Likewise, although he voted to establish the Church of England in the province, he at the same time sought to extend the right to perform the marriage ceremony to Presbyterian and

Methodist ministers. Hardy was unequivocal in his support of bills to pay assembly members for their expenses while attending legislative sessions and in opposing a residence requirement for assembly candidates, in both instances wishing to see a broadening of the choice open to the electorate. Yet Hardy's professional respect for the law caused him to oppose popular efforts to reduce the jurisdiction of the Supreme Court. By 1790 Hardy's politics had become sufficiently acceptable to the Carleton government that he was appointed, with the Executive Council's assent, common clerk of the City of Saint John.

It has been stated that, as a lawyer, Hardy was "well nigh without a peer," and inevitably he attracted clients among the well-to-do as well as the indigent, although even the most prosperous were not accepted members of New Brunswick's governing élite. In October 1783 he and John Le Chevalier Roome had formed a partnership in New York to collect loyalist claims and forward them to London, and during the 1780s he drafted and presented the claims of many New Brunswickers for compensation from the loyalist claims commission. His most famous trial cases were his defence of Munson Hoyt against charges of slander by Benedict Arnold* in 1790, his representation, which began in 1793, of James Simonds* against his former partners in the Simonds, Hazen and White Company, and his opposition to the attempts of the landowners along the Saint John River to reduce the fishing rights of the citizens of Saint John. In all these cases, opposing counsel was New Brunswick's other great trial lawyer, Ward Chipman*.

In 1793 Hardy relinquished his seat in Northumberland County and was elected to the assembly from Saint John. Henceforth, he became a much more conspicuous advocate of that city's populace. Thus, he supported bills to establish local grammar schools in preference to a college at Fredericton, he joined the effort to move the provincial capital back to Saint John from Fredericton, and, most notably, he used his political and legal skills to protect the rights of the Saint John fishermen. Throughout these disputes, Hardy did not attack the Carleton government head-on but in 1795, when the Legislative Council chose to question the assembly's power to initiate revenue measures, Hardy drafted a sophisticated, terse reply for the assembly, emphatically asserting its exclusive right to originate money bills. This impassioned defence of the people's representatives proved to be Hardy's last significant political act, for ill health forced him out of public life later in the same year. It seems a most fitting climax to his career.

Neither Hardy's person nor his politics ever won him entry into New Brunswick's elegant social circles, but, as Ward Chipman ruefully admitted, he maintained his popular base of support throughout his life. Even after Chipman and Mayor Gabriel George Ludlow* engineered Hardy's dismissal from the Saint John clerkship in 1795 as part of a fisheries dispute, the Common Council voted Hardy a sum of £80 in 1797 for his "past services." Like so many of his clients and supporters, Hardy was buried in an unmarked grave in Saint John upon his death in 1798. His estate was valued at £61. Soon thereafter Hardy's wife Martha and their four children moved to the New York home of her father, Dr Peter Huggeford, a New York loyalist who had lived briefly in Saint John after the revolution and then resettled permanently in the United States.

In the 20th century Hardy's contribution to the provincial legal tradition has been acknowledged, but his contributions as a political reformer still remain largely unrecognized. In part this neglect is because he has been overshadowed in Canadian historiography by the more flamboyant and politically aggressive assembly champion, James Glenie*. Yet Glenie's opposition to the Carleton government was sporadic and limited to select issues, and it sometimes seemed motivated more by a desire to advance his political position in England than to improve the lot of the people of New Brunswick. The bulk of the evidence suggests that Hardy's milder, but broader and more constant, defence of the impoverished refugee, the subsistence farmer, the city mechanic, and the common fisherman made him the most effective advocate of individual liberties and popular participation in government during New Brunswick's earliest years.

ANN GORMAN CONDON

PANB, RG 4, RS24; RG 5, RS32C/1; RG 7, RS71B/1, pp.177–79 (estate of Elias Hardy). PAO *Report*, 1904. *Winslow papers, A.D. 1776–1826*, ed. W. O. Raymond (Saint John, N.B., 1901). MacNutt, *New Brunswick*. W. O. Raymond, "Elias Hardy, councillor-at-law," N.B. Hist. Soc., *Coll.*, IV (1919–28), no.10, 57–66.

HARRISON, EDWARD, merchant, shipowner, office-holder, and seigneur; b. *c.* 1729 (according to a census of Quebec's English population about 1773) or *c.* 1734 (according to his burial certificate); buried 17 Oct. 1794 at Quebec. He was married and had at least two daughters and possibly one son.

Edward Harrison first appeared in Canada in 1763, when he came to Quebec and Montreal to collect debts for the London merchant Charles

Crokatt. He also performed this work for Crokatt's associate James Strachan and several other London merchants grouped with Crokatt and primarily interested in trading to the Carolinas. He retained connections with them for his own trade, which he carried on from 1763 at Quebec, with an interval at Montreal in 1769–70. In the 1760s and 1770s Harrison was associated with a group of Montreal merchants including Richard Dobie* and Lawrence ERMATINGER who drew funds and outfits for the fur trade from Strachan; he sometimes helped support their ventures or bought from their returns of peltries. He seemed more committed to the grain business, however, and in 1770 was described as its "greatest Shipper." By 1772 he was "running Madd" in the trade, as James Morrison, his agent at Montreal, distributed Harrison's cash "round the country." Some time after 1774 he built a granary at Quebec on land he had acquired. The quantity of his purchases from the Richelieu region in 1787, and his request in 1788 that John Antrobus* not be granted a certain plot of land because access to Harrison's granary would be obstructed, suggest that he retained a lively interest in wheat into the late 1780s. By that time, however, he was imprudently failing to take the time to examine the quality of the grain he purchased. Harrison was also involved in other business: in the 1770s several consignments of his jewellery, wine, and cloth were sold by auction in Montreal. A shipowner from the beginning of his Canadian career, in 1774 he had a "fine" vessel built in the Rivière Saint-Charles for the Atlantic run. He may well also have had an interest in one of the most popular transatlantic sailers of the period, the *Peters*, since he was usually the Quebec agent who allotted passenger and freight accommodation on it.

Harrison was also active politically. He served on the Council of Quebec from January 1773, and from August 1775 on its successor under the Quebec Act, the Legislative Council. He was in addition a member of the unofficial executive councils of governors Guy Carleton* and Frederick HALDIMAND and, from 1792, belonged to the Legislative Council of Lower Canada. A faithful workhorse on important committees such as those dealing with public accounts and land grants, he voted with the English party and occasionally took a leading part. For example, in 1777 he moved an amendment in the Legislative Council to the ordinance on civil courts to introduce "substantially, English law and English practice" in those institutions. His sympathies for the English party had already appeared in the 1760s and did not spring from an attachment to Sir John Johnson*, as one observer suggested.

In 1785 Harrison was still "among . . . the first characters" of Quebec, but late in 1788 he failed to make payment on a debt owed to the estate of Samuel JACOBS, and by 1791 his fortunes had collapsed completely. The cause of his problems is not known, but they may have been connected with the uncertainty of the grain market between 1783 and 1793. By 1791 his only income was his allowance of £100 a year as a member of the Legislative Council, and that too ceased on 26 December with the division of Quebec into Upper and Lower Canada; members of the new legislative councils were not paid. Nevertheless, in 1792 Harrison still retained his house on an important business street in Quebec, his servant, and his fief of Grosse-Île, acquired in February 1784.

In addition to his council positions, Harrison had served as an officer of the Quebec militia at least since 1775, attaining the rank of major by the time of his death. As well, in 1791 he was appointed a commissioner of oyer and terminer for Trois-Rivières. In 1786, on orders from Lieutenant Governor Henry HOPE, Harrison made an inventory of crown property at the "king's posts" on the lower St Lawrence, so careful that it is an important document for Canadian architectural history.

A. J. H. RICHARDSON

ANQ-M, Doc. jud., Cour des plaidoyers communs, Sentences, 15 sept. 1765, 26 févr. 1766 (copies at PAC). ASQ, Polygraphie, XXXVII, 1. BL, Add. MSS 21668, f.3 (mfm. at PAC). PAC, MG 19, A2, ser.1, 1, pp.4, 27, 43; ser.3, 55, 31 May, 12 July 1787; 56; 65, ff.439, 492; 71, ff.1455f., 1459, 1468, 1485, 1524, 1526; 82, 16 Aug., 9 Nov. 1764, 14 Jan., 6 May 1765, 25 Aug., 17 Oct. 1769; 86, 24 Oct. 1770; 87, 3 Nov. 1770; 88, 15 Oct. 1770; 223, 14 May 1766, 29 Sept. 1770, 19 Aug., 7 Sept. 1772, 28 June, 30 Sept. 1774; MG 23, GII, 3, 5, 27 June, 18 July, 2 Nov. 1791, 11 June, 19 July 1792; GIII, 5, ff.102, 288, 291; RG 1, E1, 29, pp.111–13, 126, 128, 130, 136, 146, 148–50; 108, pp.50–56; 111, pp.74, 134; E15, A, 4, 8, 10, 11, 32; L3[L], 102, pp.50380–85; RG 4, B28, 28, 20 May, 8 Aug. 1765; 110, 6 April 1769; RG 68, 202, f.55. PRO, CO 42/24, ff.133, 135–38; 42/25, ff.23–24, 195–96; 42/32, f.13; 42/34, f.84; 42/40, f.178; 42/59, f.204; 42/66, f.399; 42/98, f.18 (mfm. at PAC).

Doc. relatifs à l'hist. constitutionnelle, 1791–1818 (Doughty et McArthur; 1915), 17. [Joseph Hadfield], *An Englishman in America, 1785, being the diary of Joseph Hadfield*, ed. D. S. Robertson (Toronto, 1933), 125–26. *John Askin papers* (Quaife), II, 181. *Johnson papers* (Sullivan *et al.*), VII, 162, 220. [Henry Laurens], *The papers of Henry Laurens*, ed. P. M. Hamer *et al.* (4v. to date, Columbia, S.C., 1968–), I, 2n; IV, 287n.

"Orderly book begun by Captain Anthony Vialar of the British militia . . . ," ed. F. C. Würtele, Literary and Hist. Soc. of Quebec, *Hist. Docs.*, 7th ser. (1905), 226. *Select documents in Canadian economic history*, ed. H. A. Innis and A. R. M. Lower (2v., Toronto, 1929–33), I, 524. [William Smith], *The diary and selected papers of Chief Justice William Smith, 1784–1793*, ed. L. F. S. Upton (2v., Toronto, 1963–65), II, 167, 169. "Visite générale de la paroisse de Québec, commencée le 30 juillet 1792," ANQ *Rapport*, 1948–49, 36. *Quebec Gazette*, 19 July 1764; 3 Jan., 13 June, 25 July, 29 Aug., 31 Oct. 1765; 16 June, 3 July 1766; 4 June, 8 Oct. 1767; 18 May 1769; 28 July 1774; 18, 25 May 1775; 17 July 1777; 5 July 1787; 2 Sept. 1790; 8 Dec. 1791; 7 March 1793; 3 July, 2, 23 Oct. 1794; 16 Oct. 1806. *Almanach de Québec*, 1792, 98; 1794, 65. P.-G. Roy, *Inv. concessions*, I, 221–22. Turcotte, *Le Cons. législatif*, 33. Neatby, *Administration of justice under Quebec Act*, 47–48, 204. C. E. Peterson, "The houses of French St. Louis," *The French in the Mississippi valley*, ed. J. F. McDermott (Urbana, Ill., 1965), 35. G. C. Rogers, *Charleston in the age of the Pinckneys* (Norman, Okla., 1969), 13–14.

HART, AARON, businessman; b. *c.* 1724, perhaps in Bavaria (Federal Republic of Germany), but more likely in England; d. 28 Dec. 1800 at Trois-Rivières (Que.).

Nothing is known of Aaron Hart's origins. Family tradition long kept up the legend of a regiment named the Hart New York Rangers which was supposed to have joined AMHERST's troops at the time of the conquest of Canada. Some Jewish historians have made of Aaron Hart an officer serving with the British forces and on Amherst's general staff. More realistically, the scholarly J. R. Marcus alleges that he was a purveyor, a sutler who is believed to have followed the troops. At that time the commissariats of European armies did in fact welcome many Jews. A masonic certificate dated 10 June 1760 at New York is the earliest document known to refer to Aaron Hart; having made up his mind to follow Amherst and HALDIMAND's troops northwards, Hart had probably considered it wise to provide himself with a sort of letter of introduction. Military documents, however, never mention his presence, and the next known reference to him is a receipt dated 28 March 1761 which indicates that he and Eleazar Levy had supplied merchandise to Samuel JACOBS. On 21 Oct. 1761 Jacobs wrote to Hart, and thereafter a regular correspondence confirms Aaron Hart's presence in Trois-Rivières.

In May 1762 Haldimand took over the administration of Trois-Rivières while the governor, Ralph Burton*, was absent. He became patron to Hart, who was already purveyor to the troops quartered there. On 4 July 1762 a fire broke out in the town; according to Haldimand, "the merchant Hart, an English Jew who has suffered the most, may have lost [£]400 or 500." Three days later notary Paul Dielle drew up a lease between Théodore Panneton the younger and Aaron Hart. On 23 Aug. 1763 the authorities opened a post office at Trois-Rivières "in the house of Mr. Hart, merchant" that was to remain there for seven years. In the summer of 1764 Haldimand, now officially governor, wrote to GAGE that "the group of British merchants in Trois-Rivières" was "composed of a Jew and of a sergeant and an Irish soldier on half pay." Hart soon became interested in the fur trade. He engaged the best-known voyageurs in the region, among them Joseph Chevalier, Louis Pillard the younger, and Joseph Blondin. His initiatives paid off and he continued to expand this lucrative undertaking.

On 7 Feb. 1764 Aaron Hart acquired his first land, buying 48 acres from the Fafard de La Framboise estate for the attractive price of £350 in cash. Seven months later he purchased a large section of the seigneury of Bécancour. In May 1765 part of the Bruyères fief came into his possession; within six months he had paid off the £500 Simon Darouet demanded for it. His enthusiasm for acquiring new properties never diminished. Hart foresaw the extraordinary possibilities present in this country, newly conquered by the British. Believing in its progress, its development, he thought of establishing a solid dynasty in Canada and he methodically laid the foundations. In 1767, convinced of the promise of his new country, he went to London to take a wife. On 2 Feb. 1768 he married Dorothy Judah and through his marriage found himself at the centre of a large family connection. One of Aaron's brothers, Moses, had already joined him in his ventures; another, Henry, had settled at Albany, New York, and a third, Lemon, was launching the London Red Heart Rum distillery in London. At least two of Dorothy Judah's brothers, Uriah and Samuel, had gone to Canada ahead of her. Their correspondence indicates that "Mama Judah" lived in New York around 1795. The same letters give information about the close links which joined the couple to the large interrelated circle of Jews in New York, principal members being the Gomezes, Meyers, Levys, Cohens, and Manuels.

Upon his return from London in the spring of 1768 Aaron rejoined his brother Moses, who had kept a successful watch over his business affairs. Aaron dreamt of a large family and never missed a piece of land for sale or a landowner short of funds. He made loans easily and was willing to bide his time, letting the debt increase; then he would ask for security, suggest a mortgage. The old seigneurs, defeated in 1760, became his steadiest clients, and he showed some sympathy for them. He became, as it were, the accomplice of Joseph-Claude Boucher* de Niverville, Charles-Antoine GODEFROY de Tonnancour, Jean-Baptiste Poulin de Courval Cressé, and Jean Drouet de Richerville. Through generous and discreet loans he made the post-conquest period almost attractive for them. Time enough later to brandish his claims in front of the heirs, who, caught unawares, would scarcely know where to turn. The future belonged to the new settlers, English, Scottish, or Jewish. Aaron Hart grasped the true meaning of the events that had opened the valley of the St Lawrence to him and his people. The fact that only a small number of English speaking persons had settled in the province prompted the British to rely on Jewish merchants. The latter regarded themselves as British and attached their names to the numerous petitions drawn up by His Majesty's old subjects. They established themselves throughout the new British colony: Eleazar Levy, Elias Salomon, Levy Simons, Hyam Myers, Abraham Franks, and some others at Quebec; Moses Hart, Aaron's brother, in Sorel; Uriah Judah in Verchères; Pines Heineman in Saint-Antoine-de-Padoue, Rivière-du-Loup (Louiseville); Emmanuel Manuel in Sainte-Anne-d'Yamachiche (Yamachiche); Joseph Judah and Barnett Lyons in Berthier-en-Haut (Berthierville); Samuel Jacobs in Saint-Denis, on the Richelieu; Chapman Abraham, Gershom, Simon, and Isaac Levy, Benjamin Lyons, Ezekiel and Levy SOLOMONS, David Lazarus, John and David Salisbury Franks, Samuel and Isaac Judah, Andrew Hays, and many others in Montreal. This list, compiled mainly from the business papers of Aaron Hart and Samuel Jacobs, is in no way complete. Most of these Jews had arrived in the province of Quebec at the time of the conquest or shortly thereafter. Some had first engaged in fur-trading in the Great Lakes region, and then had come to Quebec and Montreal around 1763; others had come directly with the troops. For instance, Samuel Jacobs was at Fort Cumberland (near Sackville, N.B.) in 1758 and then followed in the wake of the 43rd Foot and Wolfe*'s troops, reaching Quebec in the autumn of 1759.

Samuel Jacobs could in fact easily rival Aaron Hart for recognition as the first Canadian Jew. Both engaged in business on a large scale and left evidence of their activity that could supply valuable material for a whole generation of historians. For his Jewish compatriots, however, Aaron Hart's good fortune lay in having made a Jewish marriage and having been able to bring up his children, or at least his sons, in Jewish traditions. Since he lived to a respectable age, he also had the opportunity of initiating them into business himself. From 1792 he associated them closely with his enterprises. While the eldest, Moses*, went off to try his luck at Nicolet, and then at Sorel, Aaron gave his shop on Rue du Platon over to the firm of Aaron Hart and Son and entrusted specific responsibilities to Ezekiel*. When Moses returned he converted the company and also took advantage of the occasion to bring young Benjamin in. Carrying out a plan conceived earlier, Aaron and his sons opened a brewery across from the Ursuline convent, near the St Lawrence. By assigning large landed properties to his sons, especially the two eldest, he quite simply forced them to establish themselves at Trois-Rivières, the chosen birthplace for the Hart dynasty.

In the spring of 1800 Aaron fell ill. He fought against his illness until mid December, and then he resolved to dictate his will, "bearing in mind that there is nothing so certain as death and so uncertain as the moment of its coming." His eldest son, Moses, was to inherit the seigneury of Sainte-Marguerite and the marquisate of Le Sablé, Ezekiel the seigneury of Bécancour, Benjamin the main store, and Alexander two plots in town. To his four daughters, Catherine, Charlotte, Elizabeth, and Sarah, he left the sum of £1,000 each, but he attached all sorts of conditions linked in particular to their marriages and their prospective offspring. Clauses of the will invariably restore assets to those who bear the Hart name. The inventory of his property carefully drawn up by notaries Joseph Badeaux* and Étienne Ranvoyzé* reveals not only the merchant's fortune, but also his practices and dodges. He had several bags containing large reserve funds in Spanish piastres. As for moneys owing, their entry covered 11 pages in the notaries' ledger. Not a single parish within a radius of 50 miles could boast of not having at least one inhabitant who was in debt to Hart. Of these innumerable debts, only one left unpleasant memories. In 1775, at the time of the American invasion, the Trois-Rivières merchant had supplied both sides; the Americans had paid him in paper money that had still not been honoured a quarter of a century later. For the rest, the heirs had excellent prospects. At the time of the abolition of the seigneurial system, the lists prepared by a descendant of the Judahs around 1857 revealed that the Hart clan owned entirely or in part four fiefs (Boucher, Vieux Pont, Hertel, and Dutort) and seven seigneuries (Godefroy, Roquetaillade, Sainte-Marguerite, Bruyères, Bécancour, Bélair, and Courval). The total of the *cens et rentes* and the *lods et ventes* amounted at that time to $86,293.05.

Although in large measure supplanted, the people of Trois-Rivières had not had their final word: in 1807 they elected Ezekiel Hart to the assembly. Without quite realizing it, Ezekiel to some extent was becoming one of them. Three or four generations later the Harts would experience more fully the true meaning of the deep-rooted and tenacious resistance of the "long-time Canadians." Gradually Aaron Hart's descendants would blend into the French speaking and Catholic population of Trois-Rivières which had somehow managed to live through the drama of 1760. Some joined the ranks of the Anglo-Protestants for a time; yet hundreds of Aaron Hart's descendants, who were firmly attached to their properties, refused to lose everything by leaving a region which resolutely remained French and Catholic. They chose to remain there, though threatened with slow but inexorable assimilation by the local majority. Today some of them jealously guard the secret of their origins and of their relative prosperity; many others are completely ignorant of them. Aaron Hart could not foresee this curious historical reversion in which those defeated in 1760 would gradually become vehicles of assimilation. The Harts of the Trois-Rivières region would have the same experience as the Burnses, Johnsons, and Ryans: mingling with the "long-time Canadians" they too would become the progenitors of the Québécois of today.

Denis Vaugeois

[The papers of the Hart family are held at the Archives du séminaire de Trois-Rivières in the Fonds Hart, estimated by Marcel Trudel to contain about 100,000 items in 3,000 folders. Hervé Biron, who classified the material, has drawn up a 98-page inventory entitled "Index du fonds Hart." The papers constitute the richest collection of documents tracing the history of the Jews in Canada from 1760 to 1850. During this period in which Sephardic Jews were dominant, the Hart family allied itself to most of the Jewish families in Canada and the United States. The Jacobs papers at PAC (MG 19, A2, ser.3), which form part of the Ermatinger family collection and comprise more than 300 volumes, cover a much shorter period, from 1758 to 1786. To the present, only one Jewish historian, J. R. Marcus, director of the American Jewish Archives in Cincinnati, Ohio, and author of *Early American Jewry* (2v., Philadelphia, 1951–53), has studied these two important collections in depth. Under the auspices of the Canadian Jewish Congress, a Canadian Jewish historian, B. G. Sack, published *History of the Jews in Canada*, trans. Ralph Novek, [ed. Maynard Gertler] ([2nd. ed.], Montreal, 1965); it is a general survey of uneven historical value. Using the Hart papers, Raymond Douville brought out an interesting biography of Aaron Hart entitled *Aaron Hart; récit historique* (Trois-Rivières, 1938). In *Les Juifs et la Nouvelle-France* (Trois-Rivières, 1968), Denis Vaugeois details the story of the first Canadian Jews. It is interesting to note that L.-P. Desrosiers drew inspiration from the lives of Aaron Hart and Nicolas Montour for his novel *Les engagés du Grand-Portage* (Paris, 1938). A number of documents relating to Aaron Hart may be found in AUM, P 58, and in the McCord Museum, Montreal. D.V.]

Chronological list of important events in Canadian Jewish history, comp. Louis Rosenburg ([Montreal], 1959). *Printed Jewish Canadiana, 1685–1900. . .* , comp. R. A. Davies (Montreal, 1955). *A selected bibliography of Jewish Canadiana*, comp. David Rome (Montreal, 1959). A. D. Hart, *The Jew in Canada* (Toronto, 1926).

HAUTRAYE. *See* Hantraye

HAVEN, JENS, founder of the Moravian mission in Labrador; b. 23 June 1724 in Wust, Jutland, Denmark; m. 12 April 1771 Mary Butterworth of the Moravian settlement of Fulneck (near Pudsey, West Yorkshire), England, and they had two sons; d. 16 April 1796 at Herrnhut, Saxony (German Democratic Republic).

Born into a Lutheran farming family, Jens Haven was in his youth apprenticed to a joiner in Copenhagen who belonged to the Moravian Church. In June 1748, his apprenticeship completed, Haven was admitted to the Moravian settlement at Herrnhut. He remained there for ten years until, having volunteered for foreign mission work, he was sent to the Greenland Inuit mission in 1758. He spent four years at the new station at Lichtenfels (near Fiskenæsset) before returning to Herrnhut on leave early in 1763.

Even before going to Greenland, Haven had become convinced that it was his destiny to establish a mission for the Labrador Inuit; the Moravians' first attempt to do so had failed in 1752 [*see* John Christian Erhardt*]. Early in 1764 Haven asked and obtained permission from the Moravian authorities to go to Labrador, which had been placed under the jurisdiction of the governor of Newfoundland in 1763. In February, knowing no English, he set out on foot for London, and through the good offices of the Moravian congregation there obtained an interview with the newly appointed governor, Hugh Palliser, who arranged passage for him to St John's. Palliser hoped that Haven could help end the endemic Inuit-white conflicts which plagued the

Strait of Belle Isle and southern Labrador, seriously impeding the development of a fishery there.

Haven spent the summer of 1764 at the strait. As a result of long conversations with the Inuit, he was able to provide Palliser with a detailed report on the situation there and an accurate analysis of the factors underlying the outbreaks of violence. Both the governor and the Moravians welcomed the results of Haven's expedition: Palliser reported that "good use may be made of this Man next Year"; the Moravians decided that a Labrador mission could, and should, be established. In 1765, under Palliser's auspices, Haven returned to the strait on a ship commanded by Francis Lucas*. He was accompanied by three other Moravians, one of whom, Christian Larsen DRACHART, could also speak the Inuit language. The Moravians wanted primarily to find a site for a mission house, but because Palliser had decided to use them as interpreters to assist in making a form of treaty with the Inuit, their freedom of movement was restricted. Angered by Palliser's attitude, the Moravian authorities decided that there would be no further expeditions to Labrador until they were given the land grants there for which they had applied in February 1765. Both Palliser and the Board of Trade were unwilling to make the grants, and it seemed that an impasse had been reached. Haven spent 1766 and 1767 in Moravian settlements at Fulneck and Zeist (Netherlands).

Early in 1768 Haven received permission to renew pressure on the Board of Trade for a land grant, and he returned to London. After protracted negotiations, an order in council of May 1769 granted the Moravian Church 100,000 acres in Labrador [*see* MIKAK]. In 1770 Haven, accompanied by Drachart and Stephen Jensen, sailed once again to Labrador. In August they chose land in the Nuneingoak region, and purchased it from the local Inuit. Haven was greeted enthusiastically by the natives, to whom he was known as Jens Ingoak, the Inuit friend.

Haven returned to London in 1770 and spent the winter and early spring preparing the frame of a mission house and joining in the final arrangements for the establishment of the mission in 1771 – arrangements that included his marriage. Fourteen persons composed the missionary party which was led, not by Haven, but by Christoph Brasen, a Danish surgeon. Haven was passed over, probably because of "the natural impetuosity and roughness of [his] disposition," and his tendency to be "warm and overbearing." On 12 Aug. 1771 the missionaries began to erect a house on their land in Labrador, and they called it Nain.

Haven spent the next 13 years in Labrador with the exception of a furlough in 1777–78. He took a leading part in the spiritual activities of the mission and made important exploratory voyages along the northern coast of Labrador. In 1776 he built a station at Okak and remained in charge there until 1781, when he was recalled to Nain to oversee preparations for the establishment of Hoffenthal (Hopedale), which he built in 1782 and where he stayed two years. In 1784, old and weak, and with failing sight, he retired to Herrnhut and lived there until his death in 1796. He was blind for the last six years of his life.

It was due to Haven's persistence that a Moravian mission was established in Labrador. As a contemporary remarked, he was "a *Mauerbrecher* . . . a bold adventurer in different emergencies." But at the same time he had a hot temper and a blunt single-mindedness which made him a difficult colleague. He was aware of these defects and fought against them, but without them the mission would never have become a reality.

J. K. HILLER

[Manuscripts relating to the Moravian missions in Labrador are held by the Moravian Church Archives in Bethlehem, Pa., and London, England, and include diaries, letters, minutes, plans, maps, church books, etcetera. This material is on microfilm either at Memorial University of Newfoundland (St John's) or the PAC (MG 17, D1). The following memoir is largely by Haven himself: "Memoir of the life of Br. Jens Haven, the first missionary of the Brethren's Church to the Esquimaux, on the coast of Labrador," *Periodical accounts relating to the missions of the Church of the United Brethren, established among the heathen* (London), II (1798), 99–110. J.K.H.] PRO, CO 194/16. Daniel Benham, *Memoirs of James Hutton; comprising the annals of his life, and connection with the United Brethren* (London, 1856). Hiller, "Foundation of Moravian mission." W. H. Whiteley, "The establishment of the Moravian mission in Labrador and British policy, 1763–83," *CHR*, XLV (1964), 29–50.

HAVILAND, WILLIAM, army officer; b. 1718 in Ireland, son of Captain Peter Haviland; m. 5 July 1748 Caroline Lee; m. secondly in 1751 Salusbury Aston, and they had one son and one daughter; d. 16 Sept. 1784 at Penn, Buckinghamshire, England.

William Haviland was commissioned ensign in the 43rd Foot (Gooch's American Regiment) in December 1739, and he took part in the siege of Cartagena (Colombia) in 1741. The following year he obtained a company in the 27th Foot and during the Jacobite rebellion in Scotland served as an aide-de-camp to the regimental commander

Major-General William Blakeney. Haviland was promoted major in 1750 and lieutenant-colonel in 1752.

In July 1757 Haviland brought the 27th to Halifax, Nova Scotia, by way of New York to serve in Lord Loudoun's proposed expedition against Louisbourg, Île Royale (Cape Breton Island). He probably returned with the regiment to New York the following month, and during the winter of 1757–58 he was in command of Fort Edward on the Hudson River. Here he discovered the difficulties inherent in leading colonial troops. Attempting to punish some mutinous rangers, Haviland clashed with Captain Robert ROGERS and incurred the wrath of the ill-tempered provincials, who wanted no part of British discipline. Loudoun and Major-General James ABERCROMBY, Haviland's commanding officers, were dissatisfied with the rangers' behaviour but allowed Haviland's request for a court martial to drop. Although they failed to support Haviland completely, his superiors' confidence in his ability was reflected in the fact that the rangers continued as part of his command until the surrender of Montreal in 1760.

In the summer of 1758 Haviland took part in Abercromby's unsuccessful attack on Fort Carillon (Ticonderoga, N.Y.), and the following year he commanded the advance force of Jeffery AMHERST's expedition up lakes George (Lac Saint-Sacrement) and Champlain. Because of the qualities of leadership Haviland had demonstrated at Fort Edward and during the 1759 campaign, he was selected by Amherst to lead one of the three independent commands intended to converge on Montreal in 1760; the others were to be commanded by Amherst, advancing from Oswego, and James MURRAY, advancing from Quebec. In command of 3,400 troops, Haviland, now appointed brigadier-general, left Crown Point in August. Moving up Lake Champlain, his force encountered the French under Colonel Louis-Antoine de Bougainville* at Fort Île aux Noix on the Richelieu River. Bougainville hoped to delay Haviland's advance long enough to prevent his rendezvous with the other British forces. With the capture of the French flotilla on the river, however, Bougainville considered the fort indefensible and withdrew to Saint-Jean under cover of night on 27 August. François BIGOT, in assessing the significance of the capture of Île aux Noix, wrote that had Bougainville been able to hold out for as long as had been hoped, "Canada might have perhaps been saved for this year." With the rangers in the vanguard, Haviland advanced on Saint-Jean, which the French quickly abandoned. He established communications with Murray and captured Chambly soon afterwards. With the arrival of Amherst's force Montreal was surrounded, and on 8 September the city surrendered. Haviland had played a significant role in completing the conquest of Canada and had taken part in what was probably the most brilliant British military manœuvre of the Seven Years' War.

In December 1760 Haviland was made a colonel commandant in the Royal Americans (60th Foot). In 1761 he accompanied Major-General Robert MONCKTON's expedition to the West Indies, where the following year he commanded a brigade at the reduction of Martinique and at the siege of Havana, Cuba. Promoted major-general in 1762 and lieutenant-general in 1772, he was appointed colonel of the 45th Foot in 1767. During the American War of Independence he served in England on Amherst's staff and in 1779 was appointed to command the Western District with headquarters at Plymouth. There he won praise for skilfully maintaining cordial relations between the regulars and the militia. In 1783 he was promoted general. After his death his widow and children were looked after by Edmund Burke, a former friend and neighbour; the two families were later linked by marriage.

JOHN D. KRUGLER

A half-tone portrait of William Haviland (artist and date unknown) is in L. W. G. Butler and S. W. Hare, *The annals of the King's Royal Rifle Corps . . .* (5v., London, 1913–32), I.

Clements Library, Thomas Gage papers, American series; Sir John Vaughan papers. Huntington Library, Abercromby papers; Loudoun papers. PRO, WO 34/10, 34/51–52, 34/116–23, 34/125–29, 34/132–43, 34/147, 34/161–65, 34/188, 34/231–39, 34/241. Amherst, *Journal* (Webster), 15, 115, 127, 145, 148, 204, 207, 210, 218, 220, 222, 239, 245–46, 254, 260–61, 275. *Annual Register* (London), 1760, 57–60. *Coll. des manuscrits de Lévis* (Casgrain), IV, 256–57, 290–91, 297, 300; X, 137–49; XI, 224–25, 248–49. *The correspondence of Edmund Burke*, ed. T. W. Copeland *et al.* (10v., Cambridge, Eng., and Chicago, 1958–78), IV, 126; V, 86, 102, 238, 278, 374, 405; VI, 66, 262, 391; VII, 4, 85, 190–91, 493; VIII, 274, 290, 294, 296, 317, 320, 353; IX, 5, 453–54. *Correspondence of William Pitt* (Kimball), II, 280, 308, 322, 338, 342, 345. *Gentleman's Magazine*, 1784, 718–19. *Johnson papers* (Sullivan *et al.*), III, 260; X, 208. Knox, *Hist. journal* (Doughty), I, 157, 473, 478, 486, 497, 508; II, 488, 504, 515, 527, 529, 565, 600; III, 82, 94, 330–31, 333. *NYCD* (O'Callaghan and Fernow), X, 713–14, 1103–5, 1121. Robert Rogers, *Journals of Major Robert Rogers . . .* (London, 1765; repr. Ann Arbor, Mich., [1966]), 70–71, 80–88, 90–102, 187–97.

British manuscripts project: a checklist of the microfilms prepared in England and Wales for the American Council of Learned Societies, 1941–1945, comp.

L. K. Born (Washington, 1955). [J.] B. Burke, *A genealogical and heraldic history of the landed gentry of Great Britain & Ireland* (5th ed., 2v., London, 1871), 600. *DNB*. J. S. Corbett, *England in the Seven Years' War: a study in combined strategy* (2nd ed., 2v., London, 1918), II, 106–17, 220–21, 250. J. R. Cuneo, *Robert Rogers of the rangers* (New York, 1959), 64–74, 88–89, 118–28. J. W. Fortescue, *A history of the British army* (13v. in 14, London, 1899–1930), II, 395–99, 540. Frégault, *Canada: war of the conquest*, 282–87. L. H. Gipson, *The British empire before the American revolution* (15v., Caldwell, Idaho, and New York, 1936–70), VII, 155, 238, 448–62; VIII, 191–93. D. E. Leach, *Arms for empire: a military history of the British colonies in North America, 1607–1763* (New York, 1973), 471–75. J. C. Long, *Lord Jeffery Amherst: a soldier of the king* (New York, 1933), 99, 126–36, 153, 261, 266–67, 306, 309. Francis Parkman, *Montcalm and Wolfe* (2v., Boston, 1884; repr. New York, 1962), 361, 590, 594. *The Seven Years' War in Canada, 1756–1763 . . .* , comp. Sigmund Samuel (Toronto, 1934), 59–64, 180–82. G. M. Wrong, *The fall of Canada . . .* (Oxford, 1914), 194, 203, 206, 218–22.

HAY, CHARLES, merchant; fl. 1770–83.

Charles Hay, a Scottish merchant, seems to have settled in Quebec some years after the treaty of Paris, since his name is not on the list of heads of Protestant households in the District of Quebec drawn up on 26 Oct. 1764. The first document referring to Hay's activities that we have found is a bond dated 9 Feb. 1770 and signed by Pierre Dextreme, *dit* Comtois, an innkeeper, in favour of Hay for deliveries of rum, brandy, wine, and other hard liquor. In it Hay is described as a master cooper. He also had a flourishing trade, importing rum and wine and exporting wood, especially barrel staves. Alfred Leroy Burt*, the historian, presents him as a prominent Scot in Quebec, but there is little trace of his commercial activities except for the 1770 document. It seems surprising that if Hay were an important merchant his name was not on the petitions of the British merchants for the abrogation of the Quebec Act and for the creation of a house of assembly.

At the time of the American revolution the numerous commercial contacts that he seems to have had with the American colonies made the authorities suspect his loyalty. The evidence for suspicion increased, especially when Charles and his brother Udney stayed outside the city during the American siege of Quebec. Following Richard MONTGOMERY's defeat, Charles returned to Quebec, but Udney joined the American army as a colonel and served as quartermaster at Albany, New York.

After the American troops withdrew in 1776, the colonial authorities adopted severe measures against supporters of the American cause who were thought to have been *agents provocateurs* or traitors. These measures reached a climax some years later, when Governor HALDIMAND in 1780 intercepted letters revealing a new invasion scheme. The principal suspects, including Pierre DU CALVET, Fleury MESPLET, and Charles Hay, were taken into custody, Hay being one of the few English speaking persons arrested as a traitor. In a letter of 21 March 1780 Brigadier-General Allan MACLEAN stated that Hay was an out-and-out rebel and that he maintained close contact with the enemy.

The prisoners, confined without trial, were well treated. Pierre Fabre*, *dit* Laterrière, Valentin JAUTARD, Hay, and Mesplet had a room 30 feet square, were well fed, and were allowed visitors. These imprisonments without trial engendered a wave of protest, especially in Charles Hay's case. His wife Mary went to England to defend his interests. In February 1782 she presented a statement to Welbore Ellis, the secretary of state for the American Colonies, which led Lord Shelburne, the new secretary of state for the Home Department, to ask Governor Haldimand for an explanation some months later. Despite these steps, Charles Hay had to wait more than a year to regain his freedom. He was released in May 1783, and no further trace of him has been found.

GUY DINEL

[The catalogue of minute books at the ANQ-Q was checked for all those notaries who practised at Quebec between 1760 and 1785 and the minute books of the following were consulted: Antoine Crespin, Sr, 1750–82, Antoine Crespin, Jr, 1782–98, J.-C. Panet, 1744–75, and J.-A. Saillant, 1749–76. G.D.] *Doc. relatifs à l'hist. constitutionnelle, 1759–91* (Shortt et Doughty; 1921). "A list of Protestant house keepers in the District of Quebec (Octr. 26th, 1764)," *BRH*, XXXVIII (1932), 753–54. PAC *Rapport*, 1890, 135. Burt, *Old prov. of Que.* (1968), II, 17–18. J. N. McIlwraith, *Sir Frederick Haldimand* (London and Toronto, 1926), 279.

HAY (Hayes, Hays), JEHU (John), army officer, Indian department official, and lieutenant governor of Detroit; probably b. at Chester, Pennsylvania; m. 1764 Julie-Marie Réaume at Detroit, and they had a large family; d. 2 Aug. 1785 at Detroit.

Jehu Hay purchased an ensigncy in the Royal Americans (60th Foot) and was formally commissioned on 2 April 1758. He was assistant engineer at Fort Niagara (near Youngstown, N.Y.) in 1760 and from about the beginning of August 1761 was adjutant there. On 27 April 1762 he was promoted lieutenant and shortly after was sent to Detroit with Henry GLADWIN. Hay played an active role in the defence of the fort against Pontiac*'s siege in 1763 and his diary is a major source for the history of this episode. The disbanding of much of his regiment in 1763 caused Hay anxiety over his prospects, especially when his improvident father died that year and left him responsible for a brother and sister. On Gladwin's recommendation he was made fort major in August 1764. Later that fall, however, he was placed on half pay.

In February 1765 Hay sought employment in the Indian department from Sir William JOHNSON and in mid 1766 was appointed commissary for Indian affairs at Detroit with a salary of £200 a year. In this capacity he supervised trade with the Indians, attended conferences, and procured intelligence on Indian affairs. He experienced his first problems with the Detroit mercantile community at this time because he had to enforce unpopular restrictions on the Indian trade [*see* Sir William Johnson]. It has been alleged that his handling of crown funds would not have stood close scrutiny; Hay, however, felt that his superiors' auditing was already too rigorous.

As a result of the British government's decision in 1768 to turn over responsibility for Indian affairs to the colonies, the department's funds decreased and the commissaries were discharged as of 25 March 1769. Hay did not secure another appointment in the department until early 1774, when he was made the Indian agent at Detroit. At this time Thomas GAGE commissioned him to tour the Ohio valley and report on the increasingly chaotic situation there. Hay left in July but had to turn back because of the hostility of the Shawnees, who were at war with Virginia.

In 1775 Detroit received a lieutenant governor in Henry HAMILTON. He and Hay became close, and by 1778 Hay was Indian agent, acting engineer, barrack master, and major, commanding six companies of the local militia. He played an important role in Hamilton's expedition against Vincennes (Ind.) in the fall of 1778, supervising preparations, obtaining intelligence, conferring with the Indians, and leading the advance party in the final successful approach to the fort. Over the winter he assisted in rebuilding and supplying it. When George Rogers Clark attacked Vincennes in February 1779 Hay took part in the negotiations for its surrender. Clark believed that Hamilton and Hay were responsible for Indian raids on frontier settlements in Kentucky and the Ohio valley and spoke of executing them as murderers. Governor Thomas Jefferson of Virginia shared Clark's hostility and delayed releasing them as long as he could. They gave their paroles on 10 Oct. 1780, proceeded to New York, and sailed for England on 27 May 1781.

On 23 April 1782 Hay was appointed lieutenant governor of Detroit as a reward for his service, and he reached Quebec late in June. He soon came into conflict with Governor HALDIMAND, who was unwilling to change the command at Detroit at what he felt to be a critical juncture in the western campaigns. Haldimand did not want to remove the commandant, Major Arent Schuyler De Peyster, or to insult him by requiring him to serve under an ex-lieutenant. By the end of October 1783 he had decided to transfer De Peyster to Niagara and send Hay to Detroit, but he angered Hay by leaving responsibility for Indian affairs in the hands of Alexander MCKEE.

Hay reached his post on 12 July 1784. He was soon in trouble with both Haldimand and the inhabitants about the enforcement of strict and unpopular British controls over shipping on the Great Lakes, and about expenses at Detroit, the eviction of non-residents, and the removal of local records to Quebec. Once again he was the man in the middle and could satisfy neither party. He repaired Detroit's fortifications and barracks and worked well with McKee, an old associate, in gathering intelligence and conducting diplomacy among the tribes. His health was poor, however, and he died on 2 Aug. 1785.

PETER E. RUSSELL

Clements Library, Jehu Hay, diary. [Henry Bouquet], *The papers of Col. Henry Bouquet*, ed. S. K. Stevens *et al.* (19v., Harrisburg, Pa., 1940–43). *The capture of old Vincennes: the original narratives of George Rogers Clark and of his opponent, Gov. Henry Hamilton*, ed. M. M. Quaife (Indianapolis, Ind., 1927). G.B., Hist. MSS Commission, *Report on the manuscripts of Mrs. Stopford-Sackville . . .* (2v., London, 1904–10), II, 225–48. *Johnson papers* (Sullivan *et al.*). *Michigan Pioneer Coll.*, IX (1886), X (1886), XI (1887), XIX (1891), XX (1892). *The siege of Detroit in 1763: the journal of Pontiac's conspiracy, and John Rutherfurd's narrative of a captivity*, ed. M. M. Quaife (Chicago, 1958). M. M. Quaife, *Detroit biographies: Jehu Hay* (Burton hist. coll. leaflets, VIII, [Detroit], 1929), 1–16. N. V. Russell, *The British régime in Michigan and the old northwest, 1760–1796* (Northfield, Minn., 1939).

HAZEUR DE L'ORME, PIERRE, parish priest and delegate in France of the chapter of the cathedral of Quebec; b. 22 Dec. 1682 at Quebec, son of François Hazeur*, a merchant, and Anne Soumande; d. 1771 in Paris, France.

Pierre Hazeur de L'Orme followed in the steps of his older brother, Joseph-Thierry*; after studies at the Petit Séminaire de Québec, which he began in May 1692, he prepared to enter the priesthood. He received the tonsure on 24 July 1701, the minor orders on 24 Aug. 1703, the subdiaconate on 19 Dec. 1705, and the diaconate on 2 Feb. 1706; on 25 April 1706, at the same time as Joseph-Thierry, he was ordained priest by Bishop Laval*, in the absence of Bishop Saint-Vallier [La Croix*]. From 1707 to 1722 Hazeur de L'Orme was parish priest at Champlain, from which he was absent only for a voyage to France, from October 1711 to November 1712. Few traces of this first ministry remain.

In 1722 Hazeur de L'Orme sought and obtained the position of delegate of the chapter of the cathedral of Quebec, which had been vacant since Pierre Le Picart's death in 1718. On 14 Oct. 1722 he received his canonry and a procuration as agent general in France, with the mission of overseeing in particular the administration of the abbey of Saint-Pierre de Maubec (Méobecq, dept of Indre), which belonged to the chapter. Leaving Quebec four days later, he landed at La Rochelle on 27 November. As soon as he arrived the delegate was confronted with the problems that were to be his lot for the duration of his mission: the need for costly repairs to the abbey, the necessity of putting its finances in order, the defence of the chapter's jurisdiction against neighbours and the bishop of Bourges, and endless lawsuits with servants guilty of embezzlement. Although Hazeur de L'Orme promised quick redress, the canons thought that he was taking far too long, that Maubec was bringing in too little, that his accounts were not sufficiently detailed, and above all that his personal expenditures were too heavy. Every year the delegate had to give a long account of himself, and he was on the point of convincing his colleagues when the dissensions following Bishop Saint-Vallier's death [*see* Claude-Thomas Dupuy*] prompted certain of the canons to examine his accounts even more closely. Three of them were appointed to go through them with a fine-tooth comb; furthermore, in 1731 the dean of the chapter, Bertrand de LATOUR, went to France himself "to manage all the business affairs of the chapter in France, that is to say, to examine and agree to the accounts, those of M. Delorme as well as of all the other accountants . . . all M. Delorme's powers will remain wholly suspended without his being able to deal with any matter." He was in disgrace. But not for long, for Hazeur de L'Orme had little difficulty in proving that Latour's management of the property was worse than his own; he succeeded in persuading the canons to recall the dean in October 1732. He himself recovered his rights in 1734, and for five years he had to keep dunning Latour to recover the 691 *livres* the latter owed the chapter.

Then a calmer period began for him, during which he brought most of the lawsuits to an end and had less difficulty in getting his accounts accepted by the chapter. He even succeeded in sending it an additional 2,000 *livres* each year. Unfortunately, in 1746 illness cast a shadow over this tranquil period; he got over a bout of pneumonia, but three weeks later had a relapse and for six months struggled against "mortal maladies"; he even received the sacrament of extreme unction. He recovered but was handicapped by listlessness and weakness in his legs; he had to hand over some of his administrative duties to subordinates, and his accounts felt the effects. The chapter again began to question him about certain items in his budget. In 1750 his colleagues renewed his procuration for five years, but at the same time they sent Canon Joseph-Marie de LA CORNE de Chaptes to France as their delegate with instructions "to work efficiently" with Hazeur and particularly to take charge of an important lawsuit against the Séminaire de Québec over the parish ministry of Quebec [*see* René-Jean Allenou* de Lavillangevin; Jean-Félix Récher*]. Although the two colleagues got along reasonably well, Hazeur de L'Orme was gradually ousted, and on 1 Oct. 1756, "in view of the aforesaid Sieur De Lorme's infirmities and his great age," the chapter decided to cancel his procuration on 1 May 1757 and to entrust it to Canon La Corne.

Hazeur de L'Orme was no longer able to return to Canada, but his request to the civil authorities and the chapter of Quebec for a pension was unsuccessful. The chapter did, however, pay him his prebend, at least until 1763; a little later La Corne paid him a life annuity of 400 francs on behalf of the chapter. The former delegate was nevertheless not in distress since he lived in the home of his nephew Claude-Michel Sarrazin, a son of the surgeon and naturalist Michel Sarrazin*. It was there that he died at the end of 1771.

Hazeur de L'Orme had been a good servant of the chapter: La Corne called him "a very upright man, who always strove for [its] greatest good," a judgement in which even the aged delegate's critics concurred. But the canons had not always openly displayed such confidence and their agent had had cause to complain regularly of being treated with a certain suspicion. He had tried to defend himself against it with closely reasoned arguments, and perhaps he was not wrong to accuse the canons of ingratitude when they decided to remove him from office after 34 years of loyal service.

Hazeur de L'Orme's correspondence with his brother Joseph-Thierry is particularly interesting because of the valuable information it gives about his compatriots who had returned to France and other people in Paris who had some connection with Canada; it shows the canon to have been a devoted uncle attentive to his nephews François Hazeur and Joseph-Michel and Claude-Michel Sarrazin, who had come to France to complete their education. It also reveals a delegate eager for social advancement. The first of the Hazeurs to add to his name "de L'Orme," which he had borrowed from his mother's family, the Soumandes, Hazeur had obtained royal nomination as precentor of the chapter of the cathedral of Quebec in 1723. In his letters he prided himself on the friendship of the Comte de Maurepas and of several court officials, and to keep the friendship up he would have liked to go and live in Versailles, if his constituents had not required him to stay in exile at Maubec; as often as possible, however, he took time off and his winters at least were spent in Paris. There he could not live as he would have liked, for he was often short of money, and, as his only asset was some silverware of little value, he could hardly borrow. On his death he even owed the chapter 1,300 francs.

NIVE VOISINE

AAQ, 12 A; 10 B; 11 B, Corr. de Hazeur de L'Orme. A.-H. Gosselin, *L'Église du Canada jusqu'à la Conquête*, II. P.-G. Roy, *La famille Hazeur* (Lévis, Qué., 1935); "La famille Hazeur, émule de Aubert de La Chesnaye," *BRH*, XLI (1935), 321–49. Têtu, "Le chapitre de la cathédrale," *BRH*, XIII–XVI.

HEARNE, SAMUEL, explorer, fur-trader, author, and naturalist; b. 1745 in London, England, son of Samuel and Diana Hearne; d. November 1792 in London.

Samuel Hearne's father, who had shown energy and imagination as managing engineer of the London Bridge Water Works, died in 1748. Mrs Hearne then took her son and daughter to Beaminster, in Dorset. After some elementary education, Hearne joined the Royal Navy in 1756 as a servant to Captain Samuel Hood. He saw considerable action during the Seven Years' War, including the bombardment of Le Havre, France. He left the navy in 1763, and his activities during the next three years are unknown. In February 1766 he joined the Hudson's Bay Company as a mate on the sloop *Churchill*, which was then engaged in the Inuit trade out of Prince of Wales's Fort (Churchill, Man.). Two years later he became mate on the brigantine *Charlotte* and participated in the company's short-lived black whale fishery.

In the mid 18th century the HBC was heavily criticized for not fulfilling its charter responsibilities to explore. The company's enthusiasm for exploration had waned after the tragic ending in 1719 of James Knight*'s expedition, remains of which were discovered by Hearne on Marble Island (N.W.T.) in 1767. Probes by sea for a northwest passage out of Hudson Bay, such as that conducted by Christopher Middleton* in 1742, had run into dead ends. Nonetheless, an incentive for further exploration remained in the long reputed presence of pure copper in the remote northwestern interior. In 1762 Moses NORTON sent two Indians, Idotliazee and another (probably MATONABBEE), to explore to the northward of Churchill. On their return in 1767 they reported the existence of "a River wh[ch] Runs up between 3 Cooper mines . . . and is a very Plentifull Country of ye Best of furrs," and they brought a sample of the ore. Norton went to England in 1768 and persuaded the company's London committee to authorize the sending of a European to pin down the mines' location and to report on the navigability of the adjacent river (Coppermine River, N.W.T.). The company hoped that the mines would prove large enough to provide "handy lumps" of copper to ballast its supply ships returning from the bay; at the very least, the overland journey would be a kind of propaganda tour to encourage distant tribes to trade at Churchill. Somewhat to his surprise, Hearne was "pitched on" as the proper person to head the expedition. He was young and fit and had a reputation for snowshoeing. He had improved his navigational skills by watching the astronomer William WALES, who had spent the 1768–69 season at Prince of Wales's Fort.

Norton insisted on planning Hearne's first two attempts to reach the Coppermine. Unfortunately, his choice of Indian guides was less than astute. The first, Chawchinahaw, was told to conduct Hearne to Matonabbee somewhere in the "Athapuscow Indians country" but abandoned him shortly after they started out on 6 Nov. 1769. The second attempt began on 23 Feb. 1770 with Conneequese, who claimed to have been near the Coppermine River. He got lost after months of arduous travel northwards into the bleak Dubawnt River country (N.W.T.), and he could not even prevent passing Indians from robbing Hearne and his two Home Guard Crees.

The accidental breaking of Hearne's quadrant simply confirmed the futility of proceeding.

Upon returning to Prince of Wales's Fort on 25 Nov. 1770, Hearne greatly provoked Norton by refusing to use any of his guides again. Norton did not, however, allow this animosity to "interfere with public business," and he provided Hearne with all necessary supplies and accepted his choice of Matonabbee as guide. Matonabbee's appointment was most auspicious. He had been to the Coppermine, had recently met and developed a liking for Hearne, and was devoted to the mission. More important, as a leading Indian he had great prestige among the Chipewyans and the Athabascan Crees and had developed as well a relatively organized pattern of movement between the trade posts on the coast and the interior. Hearne simply attached himself to Matonabbee's "gang," which included his six wives and from time to time picked up other Indians.

The third expedition left Prince of Wales's Fort on 7 Dec. 1770. The hardships Hearne faced on this as well as the two previous expeditions can scarcely be exaggerated. Since the tiny canoes used by the Indians were suitable only for crossing rivers, Hearne and his companions had to make their way by foot across trackless wastes. Hearne himself was burdened by a 60-pound pack made awkward by a quadrant and its stand. Snowstorms hit viciously even in July and he frequently had no tent or dry clothes. On the barren lands it was "either all feasting, or all famine." Although he became accustomed to eating caribou stomachs and raw musk-ox, he drew the line at lice and warbles; after long fasts eating caused him "the most oppressive pain." Eventually he learned what the Indians already knew from experience – that travel was possible only by patiently following the seasonal movements of buffalo and caribou, their only source of food. Hearne's success as an explorer was largely the result of his adaptation to their way of life and movement.

After travelling westward to Lake Theleweyaza-yeth (probably Alcantara Lake, N.W.T.), Hearne and his companions headed north and reached the Coppermine River on 14 July 1771. He quickly saw that shoals and falls made the river useless for navigation. Hearne had been ordered "to smoke your Calimut of Peace," but when Matonabbee's men came across a band of Inuit he was forced to take part in the preparations for their massacre. His protests were derided, and to avoid his companions' contempt he had to arm himself. During the massacre he "stood neuter in the rear," but an Inuit girl was speared so close to him "that it was with difficulty that I could disengage myself from her dying grasps." He named the place Bloody Falls and could never "reflect on the transactions of that horrid day without shedding tears." Continuing his survey of the river another eight miles, he came to the partially frozen Arctic Ocean on 17 July – the first European to reach it overland in North America. The Indians then took him 30 miles south to one of the copper mines. Hearne was totally disillusioned when an intensive search of the area yielded only one four-pound lump of copper. The Indians, anxious to get to Cogead (Contwoyto) and Point lakes, where their wives awaited them, doubled the pace of their return journey, causing Hearne to lose his toenails and suffer excruciating pain. In midwinter he became the first European to see and cross Great Slave Lake. The expedition arrived back at Prince of Wales's Fort on 30 June 1772, in time to meet the supply ship from England.

The results of his 32 months of travel were, Hearne recognized, "not likely to prove of any material advantage to the Nation at large, or indeed to the Hudson's Bay Company." Nevertheless, his failure to find an east-west waterway crossing his northern route was important in casting doubt on its existence. Despite his careful attempt at calculation of the latitude at Congecathawhachaga (near Kathawachaga Lake, N.W.T.) on 1 July 1771, he placed the mouth of the Coppermine River 200 miles too far to the north, but the error reinforced his important conclusion that there was no northwest passage via Hudson Bay. It was on the basis of this judgement that Captain James Cook was told not to begin a serious search for a passage from the Pacific side until reaching 65°N latitude. The geographer Alexander Dalrymple nevertheless still believed in the existence of a northwest passage, and in pointing out some of Hearne's exaggerations he discredited his standing as an explorer for years to come.

Following his travels Hearne served briefly as mate on the *Charlotte* but, despairing of the coastal trade, he requested "some Principal station in the land service." Undoubtedly on the strength of his impressive journals, which reached the London committee at about the same time as Andrew Graham*'s persuasive memorandum urging the establishment of inland posts to meet Canadian competition, Hearne was chosen in 1773 to found the company's first western inland post. Having learned to live off the land, he took minimal provisions for the eight Europeans and two Home Guard Crees who accompanied him. They went inland on 23 June 1774 as passengers in the canoes of the Indians who had come to trade at York Factory (Man.). Matthew COCKING and reinforcements failed to connect with Hearne's party at Basquia (The Pas, Man.). After consulting some local chiefs, Hearne chose a strategic site on Pine Island Lake (Cumberland Lake, Sask.), 60 miles above Basquia. The site was linked to both the Saskatchewan River trade route and the Churchill system. There he directed the construction of Cumberland House, the oldest permanent settlement in the present province of Saskatchewan. Although instructed to keep "a distant civility" with the surrounding pedlars from Montreal, he appreciated their rescue of an HBC servant and returned the favour. He inspired his men to endure the first hard winter by restricting himself "to the very same allowance in every artical." On 30 May 1775 he took out the first furs with the Indian canoes going down to York. On the return journey to Cumberland, he complained that the "villins of Indians that accomp[d] me embezzeld at least 100 gal[ns] of the Brandy besides a Bag containing 43 lb[s] of Brazil Tobaco, & 56 lb[s] of Ball." Hearne advised the London committee that the company's ability to extend its trade inland was hampered by its lack of canoes, and he suggested the development of a prototype of the later York boat. Eager to found more posts, he was instead appointed chief at Prince of Wales's Fort, which he reached on 17 Jan. 1776.

Through circumstances largely beyond his control, Hearne's years at Churchill were less productive than those he had spent inland. As the competition of the Canadian pedlars in the interior cut into the company's profits, the London committee began to place an unrealistic emphasis on the white whale fishery of Hudson Bay as a source of supplies and on the northern coastal trade conducted by the ships of the bay posts. The whale fishery was not, however, productive and demanded as well the expense of highly paid whalers, which offset its usefulness. Hearne felt that the northern trade only intercepted the established trade at Churchill and allowed Indians to avoid paying their debts there, but his reluctance to press the trade earned for him the displeasure of the committee. The distant American revolution had an impact on his career as well. His fort, despite its 40-foot-thick stone walls, was scarcely defensible. It lacked drinking water, a ditch, and a military garrison, and its fortifications suffered from poor masonry, defective embrasures, and low elevation [*see* Ferdinand JACOBS]. On 8 Aug. 1782 Hearne and his complement of 38 civilians were confronted by a French force under the Comte de Lapérouse [GALAUP] composed of three ships, including one of 74 guns, and 290 soldiers. As a veteran Hearne recognized hopeless odds and wisely surrendered without a shot. Most authorities who comment on his generally complacent attitude excuse it in this instance, as did the HBC at the time. Hearne and some of the other prisoners were allowed to sail back to England from Hudson Strait in a small sloop.

In September 1783 Hearne returned to build a modest wooden house (named Fort Churchill) five miles from the partially destroyed stone fort and on the exact site of the original post at Churchill. He found that the trade situation had deteriorated markedly. The Indian population had been decimated by smallpox and starvation due to the lack of normal hunting supplies of powder and shot. Matonabbee had committed suicide on learning of the fort's capture, and the rest of Churchill's leading Indians had moved to other posts. The competition of the Canadians, who by now had penetrated the homeland of the Chipewyans, was more intense than ever. Hearne grew sensitive about criticism of his handling of the northern coastal trade, the whale fisheries, and the smuggling activities of the company's Orkney servants. He bitterly asserted to the London committee that he had "served you too *Scrupulous* and too Faithfully to become a Respectable character in your Service." His health began to fail and he delivered up command at Churchill on 16 Aug. 1787.

During his retirement in London Hearne was mollified by the attentions of scientists and HBC directors. In the last decade of his life he used his experiences on the barrens, on the northern coast, and in the interior to help naturalists like Thomas Pennant in their researches. He also worked on the manuscript of what was to become *A journey from Prince of Wales's Fort, in Hudson's Bay, to the northern ocean . . . in the years 1769, 1770, 1771, & 1772*, the book which would establish his claim to fame. His original travel journals and maps of 1769–72 had not been intended for the public, but interest in the geography and life of the largely unexplored interior had led to their being lent by the company to the Admiralty and to scientists. In the years after his journey he had continued to compile material, and the Comte de Lapérouse, when he read the manuscript following his capture of Hearne, had urged its publication. In this opinion he was joined in England by Dr John Douglas, the editor of Cook's journals, and William Wales.

Hearne's *Journey* was published in London three years after he died. Before his death he had added to the manuscript two chapters on the Chipewyans and the animals of the northern regions and had inserted into his narrative, at appropriate places, descriptions of hunting methods, the treatment of women, Inuit artifacts, and the habits of beaver, musk-ox, and wood bison. His anthropological generalizations are backed by vivid accounts of actual individuals and events, and his portrait of the Chipewyans is one of the best of any tribe in the early contact phase. At pains to refute critics of the HBC's inactivity in exploration, Hearne is still sufficiently philosophic to wonder if the Indians of the interior really benefited from the fur trade. The book, directed at the general public rather than at specialists, is written in a plain, unadorned style. It went through two English editions and by 1799 had been translated into German, Dutch, and French.

Hearne the fur-trader served his company well by land and by sea in a variety of responsibilities. The skill in observation and desire for realism revealed in his book mark him as a significant early naturalist. As an explorer and writer, he represents an interesting combination of physical endurance and intellectual curiosity.

C. S. MACKINNON

[Samuel Hearne's *A journey from Prince of Wales's Fort, in Hudson's Bay, to the northern ocean . . . in the years 1769, 1770, 1771 & 1772* (London, 1795) was reprinted in Ireland (Dublin, 1796) and the United States (Philadelphia, 1802) and was translated into German (Berlin, 1797), Dutch (2v., The Hague, 1798), Swedish (Stockholm, 1798), French (2v., Paris, 1799), and Danish (Copenhagen, 1802). Two modern editions have been published, one edited by Joseph Burr Tyrrell* (Toronto, 1911; repr. New York, 1968) and the other by R. G. Glover (Toronto, 1958). Thanks to the work of these two men, in particular that of Glover, Hearne's reputation is now secure. C.S.M.]

HBC Arch. A.11/14, ff.78, 81, 174; 11/15, ff.47, 80, 112; B.42/a/103, 14 Sept. 1783, 16 Aug. 1787; B.42/b/22, letter from Hearne, 21 Jan. 1776. *Journals of Hearne and Turnor* (Tyrrell). "Some account of the late Mr. Samuel Hearne," *European Magazine and London Rev.* (London), XXXI (1797), 371–72. [David Thompson], *David Thompson's narrative, 1784–1812*, ed. R. [G.] Glover (new ed., Toronto, 1962). George Back, *Narrative of the Arctic land expedition to the mouth of the Great Fish River, and along the shores of the Arctic Ocean, in the years 1833, 1834, and 1835* (London, 1836), 144–55. J. C. Beaglehole, *The life of Captain James Cook* (Stanford, Calif., 1974). Morton, *History of Canadian west*. Rich, *History of HBC*, II. Gordon Speck, *Samuel Hearne and the northwest passage* (Caldwell, Idaho, 1963).

G. H. Blanchet, "Thelewey-aza-yeth," *Beaver*, outfit 280 (Sept. 1949), 8–11. R. [G.] Glover, "Cumberland House," *Beaver*, outfit 282 (Dec. 1951), 4–7; "The difficulties of the Hudson's Bay Company's penetration of the west," *CHR*, XXIX (1948), 240–54; "Hudson Bay to the Orient," *Beaver*, outfit 281 (Dec. 1950), 47–51; "La Pérouse on Hudson Bay," *Beaver*, outfit 281 (March 1951), 42–46; "A note on John Richardson's 'Digression concerning Hearne's route,'" *CHR*, XXXII (1951), 252–63; "Sidelights on St Hearne," *Beaver*, outfit 277 (March 1947), 10–14; "The witness of David Thompson," *CHR*, XXXI (1950), 25–38. Glyndwr Williams, "The Hudson's Bay Company and its critics in the eighteenth century," Royal Hist. Soc., *Trans.* (London), 5th ser., XX (1970), 149–71. J. T. Wilson, "New light on Hearne," *Beaver*, outfit 280 (June 1949), 14–18.

HENRY, ANTHONY (also **Anton Heinrich** or **Henrich**), printer and publisher; b. 1734 near Montbéliard (France) of German parents; d. 1 Dec. 1800 in Halifax, Nova Scotia.

Little is known of Anthony Henry's early life, but he probably served a regular apprenticeship in the printing trade in Europe. He was proficient in English, German, and French. In 1758 he served with the British forces as a regimental fifer at the capture of Louisbourg, Île Royale (Cape Breton Island). It is believed that after his discharge Henry worked in a New Jersey printing office for two years. He then joined John Bushell*'s shop in Halifax. He was made a partner in the business on 23 Sept. 1760 and assumed control of it after Bushell's death in 1761.

Henry continued the publication of the *Halifax Gazette*, but his business was mainly government printing and stationery. He worked closely with the provincial secretary, Richard BULKELEY, who had been responsible for the editing of the *Gazette* since 1758, and with the administration's financial support he gradually succeeded in improving his equipment and expanding his business. In the autumn of 1765 Henry hired a young apprentice by the name of Isaiah Thomas, and on 21 November, presumably with his employer's knowledge, Thomas published in the *Gazette* a paragraph indicating that the people of Nova Scotia were opposed to the Stamp Act. Government officials were incensed, and when the *Gazette* continued to comment on the act Bulkeley withdrew the administration's patronage. The newspaper ceased to appear some time between March and August 1766.

Henry was succeeded as government printer by Robert FLETCHER, who began the semi-official *Nova-Scotia Gazette*. Three years later Henry founded the *Nova Scotia Chronicle and Weekly Advertiser*, the first Canadian newspaper to run independent of government patronage. The *Chronicle* presented a variety of the "freshest Advices both Foreign and Domestic," as well as essays excerpted from European and American publications. Henry somehow managed to obtain the proceedings of the House of Assembly, which he printed seriatim, and this feature must have appealed to a politically conscious community. The *Chronicle* contained few advertisements, and its survival was perhaps partly the result of its consistent support for the Whig position. Henry may well have had financial support from Whig sympathizers.

In 1770 Fletcher's publication was absorbed by Henry's more popular newspaper to form the *Nova-Scotia Gazette and the Weekly Chronicle*. In the same year, probably because he was the one skilled printer with presses in Halifax, Henry resumed publication of government documents. His newspaper, renamed the *Royal Gazette and the Nova-Scotia Advertiser* in 1789, lasted for 30 years and became more an outlet for official information as his political preference for the Whigs diminished. In 1788 Henry was officially commissioned king's printer, an appointment which removed much of the uncertainty in his contract with the government. His commission is one of the earliest and most important documents in the history of Canadian publishing. After receiving it Henry became noticeably cautious and avoided controversies that might jeopardize his official position.

Besides many government documents and the Nova Scotia statutes, Henry published some of the religious works of the celebrated evangelist Henry ALLINE, and almanacs such as *The Nova-Scotia calender . . .* and *Der Neuschottländische calender. . . .* The *Nova-Scotia calender* for 1776, with its wood-cut engraving of Halifax harbour, was the first Canadian book to contain an illustration. A total of some 200 items, not including newspapers, which bear Henry's name or are attributed to him, are listed in Marie Tremaine's *Bibliography of Canadian imprints*. By the time of his death the position of king's printer had gained considerable stability and authority as a result of his consistent work. His technical skills improved over the years, but his productions never reached a standard of uniformly good printing and design to match that of Fletcher or of John Howe*, his successor as king's printer.

Mainly on evidence provided by Isaiah Thomas – whose account of his sojourn in Halifax is, however, generally looked upon as unreliable – it is said that around 1761 Henry married a black pastry cook who owned some property and with whose financial help he was able to purchase Bushell's press and also to build a home where they lived until she died two or three years later. On 23 Feb. 1773 Henry was married to Barbara Spring, a widow 15 years his senior. In 1780 Margaret Greese, whose maiden name may have been Miller, became his third wife, and she survived him by 26 years. One daughter is known to have been born of this marriage. Socially Henry mixed with the German element in Halifax and at one time was a warden of the little Dutch church (St George's). He was the godfather of Anthony Henry Holland*, who became an important publisher in Halifax.

DOUGLAS G. LOCHHEAD

There is a portrait in crayon of Anthony Henry in PANS.

N.S. Legislative Library (Halifax), N.S., Lieutenant Governor (Parr), commission appointing Anthony Henry king's printer of the province of Nova Scotia dated at Halifax, 8 April 1788. Tremaine, *Bibliography of Canadian imprints*. Bell, *Foreign Protestants*. Brebner, *Neutral Yankees*. Æ. Fauteux, *Introduction of printing into Canada*. H. P. Gundy, *Canada* (Amsterdam, 1972). Isaiah Thomas, *The history of printing in America, with a biography of printers, and an account of newspapers . . .* (2nd ed., 2v., Albany, N.Y., 1874; repr. New York, 1972). J. J. Stewart, "Early journalism in Nova Scotia," N.S. Hist. Soc., *Coll.*, VI (1888), 91–122.

HERNÁNDEZ, JUAN JOSEF PÉREZ. *See* PÉREZ

HERTEL DE ROUVILLE, RENÉ-OVIDE, lieutenant general for civil and criminal affairs, director of the Saint-Maurice ironworks, chief road commissioner (*grand voyer*), and judge of the Court of Common Pleas; b. 6 Sept. 1720 at Port-Toulouse (near St Peters, N.S.), son of Jean-Baptiste Hertel* de Rouville and Marie-Anne Baudouin; d. 12 Aug. 1792 in Montreal (Que.).

Unlike his father, his brother Jean-Baptiste-François, his numerous uncles, and his paternal grandfather Joseph-François Hertel* de La Fresnière, René-Ovide Hertel de Rouville did not win renown through the noble feats of arms that glorified the Hertel name. Quite early in life he turned to the study of law, taking the courses given at Quebec by the attorney general, Louis-Guillaume Verrier*, who listed him as one of his new pupils in October 1743. Two years earlier Hertel de Rouville's marriage had been the talk of the town. Against the wishes of his mother and guardian – his father had died in 1722 – he had married Louise-Catherine André* de Leigne, a woman 11 years his senior, in Quebec on 20 May 1741. His mother took the matter to court and won. On 12 June the Conseil Supérieur annulled the marriage and forbad the two parties concerned to live as man and wife. But their plight was brief, since on 22 October they again entered into wedlock, this time, it seems, with the consent of the two families. The couple were to have three daughters and two sons. Jean-Baptiste-Melchior*, the best known of their children, became a member of the first assembly in 1792 and later a member of the Legislative Council.

On 1 April 1745, at the age of 24, Hertel de Rouville was named to the office of lieutenant general for civil and criminal affairs in the royal jurisdiction of Trois-Rivières, probably through the influence of his father-in-law, Pierre André* de Leigne, who had been lieutenant general for civil and criminal affairs of the provost court of Quebec; this appointment was confirmed on 17 Oct. 1746. While performing these duties he was given a number of other responsibilities, the most important being that of director of the Saint-Maurice ironworks.

When François-Étienne Cugnet* had gone into bankruptcy in 1741 the Saint-Maurice ironworks reverted to the Domaine d'Occident and were placed under the intendant's direct control. Numerous problems, including not insignificant difficulties related to the hiring of qualified workmen and to the workers' productivity, had arisen. Loose behaviour and insubordination often created disorder and dissension. In 1747, therefore, Intendant HOCQUART decided to delegate his lieutenant general of Trois-Rivières to investigate any dispute arising among the workers. In 1749 the new intendant, BIGOT, renewed Hertel de Rouville's commission, and in October of that year extended his responsibilities: the subdelegate was to conduct an inspection in order to "correct abuses . . . cut down expenses . . . and do everything that could contribute to the good and the advantage of this establishment." Having thus become familiar with the operation, Hertel de Rouville was named to succeed Jean-Urbain Martel* de Belleville as director of the ironworks, probably in 1750. He would retain this post until the end of the French régime. Despite the critical remarks made by engineer Louis Franquet* during his inspection of the ironworks in 1752, it is difficult to judge Hertel de Rouville's management of this enterprise, which was to be brought to a virtual standstill by the war of the conquest.

At the time of the conquest Hertel de Rouville went to France, anxious to find a position there. According to Abbé François Daniel he is supposed to have become steward of the Prince de Condé's household. But when peace returned in 1763, he decided to rejoin his family in Trois-Rivières. He soon succeeded in entering into the good graces of Governor MURRAY, who on 20 Nov. 1765 appointed him chief road commissioner for the District of Montreal. On 5 Feb. 1767, a year after the death of his first wife, Hertel de Rouville married Charlotte-Gabrielle Jarret de Verchères, widow of Pierre-Marie-Joseph Raimbault de Saint-Blaint, in Montreal.

Hertel de Rouville retained the post of chief road commissioner until 1775, when Governor Guy Carleton* granted him a commission as conservator of the peace and commissioner for the District of Montreal. A similar commission, for the District of Quebec, was issued at the same time to notary Jean-Claude PANET. These appointments of the first two French Canadian judges under the British régime took effect on the very day the Quebec Act came into force, 1 May 1775. Although Carleton counted on winning over the conquered Canadians in this way, he would have been more successful had he fixed his choice on anyone but Hertel de Rouville, whose appointment produced more displeasure than satisfaction among the Canadians. As soon as he received word of the appointment, even before its official confirmation, the seigneur of Beauport, Antoine Juchereau* Duchesnay, hastened to express the most profound indignation. Writing to François Baby*, a prominent Quebec merchant and later a member of the Legislative Council, he commented: "How could the government possibly have cast its eye upon the greatest scoundrel and the biggest rogue on earth, and have him dispense what he has never known? . . . whether the government is badly informed or whether it wishes us ill . . . the name of the judge [Hertel de Rouville] makes me shudder for all remaining arrangements." Baby, who shared this opinion and consequently considered the "promotion" dangerous for the public good, was equally pessimistic about the results to be expected from the Quebec Act: "I am very much afraid that the time is not far off when Canadians will be unable to console themselves for having asked for the new form of government."

These fears and apprehensions were not unfounded, given the way in which Hertel de Rouville acted in carrying out his new duties. After seeing him in action, and suffering the repercussions of a judicial system which left a good deal of room for arbitrary decisions, Pierre DU CALVET, a fellow Montrealer, commented: "M. de Rouville is . . . [a man] of such an overbearing nature, of such an arrogant character, of a temperament so nearly despotic that it betrays itself everywhere. . . . A man completely puffed up with the pretensions of vanity . . . , unyielding in his opinions . . . , intolerant . . . , very much a formalist, biased . . . , warm enough towards his friends, whom I should more aptly call his clients and his protégés, but all fire and flame against his enemies." This portrait quite accurately conveyed the salient traits of his personality, which, being well known to the public, earned him an unenviable reputation.

According to documents emanating from English speaking circles in the colony, the choice of Hertel de Rouville met with such general disapproval from his fellow citizens in Montreal that, had it not been for the events disturbing the province on the eve of the American invasion, they would have petitioned against his appointment. The British minority especially condemned the means Hertel de Rouville used to bring himself to the attention of the colonial authorities. It was common knowledge that the new judge had not hesitated to act as a "toady" as a way of courting the administration: "M. de Rouville is remarkable for taking every opportunity (as he speaks a little English) to throw himself in the way of the English inhabitants of Montreal in order to pick up what tales he can, to send them up to the Governour." Indeed, less than a month before his appointment he had told Governor Carleton of his altercation with Thomas WALKER in the market-place in Montreal. When Walker, expressing sympathy with the revolutionary cause, had declared publicly "that the peoples of the [American] colonies were honest folk who did not want to be slaves and who would defend their liberty and their rights as long as they had blood," Rouville had publicly retorted: "The people who are listening to you, myself included, have never been slaves, any more than you have; and our submission to the king and his government guarantees us that we will always be free."

By his own admission, through "his conduct and his zeal" as a loyal subject of his majesty Hertel de Rouville "drew the wrath of the rebels, who made him feel it as soon as they were in possession of the town of Montreal." In fact he was speedily subjected to the severity of the impetuous Brigadier-General David Wooster, who after Richard MONTGOMERY's death had assumed command of the American occupation. In January 1776, having decided to proceed by force with the expulsion of the most prominent loyalists in the town, Wooster "ordered M. Hertel de Rouville to get ready to leave for the colonies." Although the citizens of Montreal protested, the unfortunate magistrate got off with taking the road to Lake Champlain and being "kept a prisoner for 18 months."

Upon his return to the province Hertel de Rouville was reinstated in judicial office as judge of the Court of Common Pleas for the District of Montreal; an ordinance of 25 Feb. 1777 had set up such a court of justice in each of the two main districts of the province. During the greater part of the last 15 years of his life this faithful collaborator with the new régime sat on this court along with his colleagues, Edward Southouse and John Fraser. Hertel de Rouville found he was better able to adopt his preferred methods of working with Fraser, who already had long experience as a judge and who in addition belonged to the French party within the Legislative Council.

The system set up by the Quebec Act for administering justice mirrored the authoritarian régime established by the British parliament at a crucial moment in the relations between the mother country and her North American colonies. Since this régime did not provide for the separation of powers or control over them, and hence favoured their concentration in the hands of the governor and of a small oligarchy in the Legislative Council, the persons enjoying the patronage dispensed by those in power could expect almost unlimited immunity. Justice Hertel de Rouville was thus able to perform his duties as a magistrate with impunity, despite all the complaints and criticisms he brought upon himself through his obviously unfair judgements, his arbitrary decisions, and the incongruity of his sitting drunk on the Bench, as he frequently did in the afternoon sessions. An irascible man, prone to violent fits of anger, he could easily make improper use of annoying procedures in order to impose his will.

Judges were so strongly protected by the established system that the initiative taken by Chief Justice William SMITH, whose influence was predominant on Carleton (Dorchester), to conduct a "full investigation" into the administration of justice resulted in no change. This investigation, held during the summer and early autumn of 1787 and primarily aimed at the "conduct and partiality" of the Common Pleas judges, brought such a defensive reaction on their part that Smith was unable to obtain any positive results. Not only were the three principally involved – Adam MABANE, John Fraser, and Hertel de Rouville – not censured in any way by London, but their chief adversary, Attorney General James Monk*, was ordered to resign in the spring of 1789.

The chief justice's setback was to render quite futile the bold attack made upon Justice Hertel de Rouville's vexatious proceedings by Louis-Charles Foucher*, a young lawyer who later became solicitor general of Lower Canada. In a petition to Lord Dorchester dated 4 Oct. 1790,

Foucher demanded that justice be done him against his "oppressor," who he said had "persecuted, stigmatized, and demeaned" him, and caused him "irreparable damage and harm" through "deliberate and constant opposition to the practice and exercise of his profession as a lawyer" and through the threat of depriving him of his right to plead, which "would have. . . completely destroyed his clients' confidence [and] would have forced him to withdraw ignominiously from the bar." As there was ample matter for an investigation, the decision was taken to set up a committee of the Legislative Council to hear witnesses.

The committee's make-up left no room for doubt about the outcome of this unequal contest. Its chairman, François-Marie PICOTÉ de Belestre, seigneurs Joseph-Dominique-Emmanuel Le Moyne* de Longueuil and René-Amable Boucher* de Boucherville, and the judge John Fraser were all either friends of the accused or allies connected with him through marriage or otherwise. The conclusions of their report – written in English and then translated into French – are even more revealing of the vices of the judicial system itself than they are of the obvious partiality of the members of the investigating committee; it asserted that "the whole complaint . . . is futile, ignorant, ungrateful, rash and scandalous." Not content simply to reject Foucher's complaints they went further, recommending that "as amends to the judge and to the government's dignity" he be deprived of his "permit to pettifog . . . in order to set an example." Things had reached such a point that the publisher of the *Montreal Gazette*, Fleury MESPLET, printed some letters from readers who, having followed the affair closely, could not refrain from making derisive comments on this travesty of justice.

To conceal this lamentable denial of justice Lord Dorchester invited Foucher to argue his case before a plenary meeting of the Legislative Council on 7 April 1791. The members of the council were then called upon to submit a conclusive report to the governor after a thorough examination of the whole dossier. It was not until 23 July that three reports – a majority one, a minority one, and one by the chief justice – were laid on the council table. The majority of the councillors (who constituted the French party) backed the committee's conclusions, finding Foucher's grievances "baseless, vulgar, and malicious." Only a minority recognized that the plaintiff had indeed been prevented from practising his profession as a lawyer and had been treated "with unnecessary harshness." For his part, the chief justice criticized Hertel de Rouville's conduct but did not dare advocate that he be dealt with severely; such a recommendation would have risked the annulment of Hertel de Rouville's commission as judge for the District of Montreal, and also might have deprived him of his right to sit on the Court of Common Pleas in Trois-Rivières (recently set up through an ordinance of 29 April 1790), as well as on that in Quebec, the various judges in office having recently been authorized to take turns in each of the province's three districts.

Although Hertel de Rouville had succeeded in escaping severe sanctions, thanks to the established system, he had nevertheless been affected by the affair's repercussions, which made him feel that he had been a victim of persecution. In the hopes of being "justified in the eyes of his sovereign" and of receiving "a striking token to avenge him for the insult as a [final] consolation before going to his grave," he took the initiative of informing the Home secretary, Lord Grenville, of his unhappy lot as a poor 70-year-old who had been "slandered . . . and made a public spectacle." He died less than a year later, without any consolation, and judging by the way in which his death was reported in the *Montreal Gazette* and the *Quebec Gazette*, it may be supposed that his departure occasioned little regret: "His Honour Mr. Justice Hertel de Rouville, one of the judges of the Court of Common Pleas, died on Sunday the twelfth inst. [12 Aug. 1792] between 7 and 8 in the evening."

PIERRE TOUSIGNANT and
MADELEINE DIONNE-TOUSIGNANT

AN, Col., C^{11A}, 80, pp.113–14 (PAC transcripts). ANQ-M, Greffe de Pierre Panet, 5 févr. 1767. ANQ-Q, Greffe de Nicolas Boisseau, 11 oct. 1741; NF 2, 34, f.88; 36, ff.69, 124. ASGM, Laïcs, H. PAC, MG 8, C10, 2, pp.1–3, 4–7, 404–7; MG 11, [CO 42],Q, 11, pp.149–51; 53, pp.202–573; MG 24, L3, pp. 3896, 3904; RG 1, E1, 1, pp.155–65; RG 4, A1, 31, p.39; 32, pp.1–3; RG 68, 89, f.112. PRO, CO 42/88, f.137. *American archives* (Clarke and Force), 4th ser., III, 1185–86, 1417. Pierre Du Calvet, *Appel à la justice de l'État* . . . (Londres, 1784), 90–91. [Louis] Franquet, "Voyages et mémoires sur le Canada," Institut canadien de Québec, *Annuaire*, 13 (1889), 22, 113–14. *Invasion du Canada* (Verreau). [Francis Maseres], *Additional papers concerning the province of Quebeck: being an appendix to the book entitled, "An account of the proceedings of the British and other Protestant inhabitants of the province of Quebeck in North America,* [*in*] *order to obtain a house of assembly in that province*" (London, 1776). PAC *Rapport*, 1914–15, app.C, 48–51, 244–46; 1918, app.C, 17–18. *Montreal Gazette*, 5 May 1791, 16 Aug. 1792. *Quebec Gazette*, 16 Aug. 1792. P.-G. Roy, *Inv. ins. Prév. Québec*, II, 73; III, 37; *Inv. jug. et délib., 1717–60*, IV, 24–26; V, 11–12; *Inv. ord. int.*, III, 90,

126, 135–36; *Inv. procès-verbaux des grands voyers*, V, 170. Turcotte, *Le Cons. législatif*, 75.

Burt, *Old prov. of Que*. [François Daniel], *Histoire des grandes familles françaises du Canada, ou aperçu sur le chevalier Benoist, et quelques familles contemporaines* (Montréal, 1867). Neatby, *Administration of justice under Quebec Act*. Cameron Nish, *François-Étienne Cugnet, 1719–1751: entrepreneur et entreprises en Nouvelle-France* (Montréal, 1975), 83–118. P.-G. Roy, *La famille Jarret de Verchères* (Lévis, Qué., 1908), 28. Sulte, *Mélanges historiques* (Malchelosse), VI, 131. Tessier, *Les forges Saint-Maurice*. P.-G. Roy, "Les grands voyers de la Nouvelle-France et leurs successeurs," *Cahiers des Dix*, 8 (1943), 225–27; "L'hon. René-Ovide Hertel de Rouville," *BRH*, XII (1906), 129–41; "René-Ovide Hertel de Rouville," *BRH*, XXI (1915), 53–54.

HERTEL DE SAINT-FRANÇOIS, JOSEPH-HIPPOLYTE (called the **Chevalier Hertel**), army officer and interpreter; b. 23 July 1738 at Saint-François-du-Lac (Que.) and baptized two days later at Sorel, son of Joseph Hertel de Saint-François and Suzanne Blondeau; d. 10 Aug. 1781 in Montreal.

Like his five brothers, Joseph-Hippolyte Hertel de Saint-François took up a military career. He served as a cadet in the Ohio region and in 1755 took part in the battle of the Monongahela [*see* Daniel-Hyacinthe-Marie Liénard* de Beaujeu]. The following year he was commissioned second ensign. Thanks to his aunt, Catherine Jarret de Verchères, the wife of Pierre-Joseph Hertel de Beaubassin, he enjoyed Montcalm*'s favour. On 20 June 1757 Montcalm wrote to Bourlamaque*: "I commend the Hertels to you: they are nephews of a lady of whom you are fond and who is devoted to you." On 30 June Bourlamaque dispatched a detachment of Indians on an expedition under three officers; two were Hertel brothers and Joseph-Hippolyte may have been one of them. In 1759 he was promoted ensign on the active list. During the year Hertel, who had been serving at Fort Carillon (Ticonderoga, N.Y.) for two years, was sent out at the head of Indian war parties.

After the conquest Hertel de Saint-François went to France, arriving at Le Havre on 1 Jan. 1762 on the *Molinieux*. His stay in France was short, for in 1763 he returned to Canada and went to live in Montreal. Like some other Canadians at this period, Hertel joined the new English Protestant community and became a member of a Masonic lodge in Montreal. As early as 1764 his name appears on a list of the heads of Protestant families in Montreal signed by Governor MURRAY. Three years later, on 3 Aug. 1767, in Montreal's Christ Church he married Marie-Anne, daughter of Jean-Baptiste Le Comte* Dupré and Marie-Anne Hervieux. As the latter opposed the marriage before a Protestant minister, another ceremony was held on 24 August in the church of Notre-Dame in Montreal.

Hertel's experience with the Indians during the Seven Years' War was put to good use at the time of Pontiac*'s War. In 1764 he was placed at the head of an Iroquois contingent from Sault-Saint-Louis (Caughnawaga) which was sent to the Detroit region to help John BRADSTREET put down the uprising. Hertel was subsequently entrusted by Colonel Henry Bouquet with several missions that aided the peace negotiations with the Delawares, Shawnees, and Senecas. The colonel recommended him to the superintendent of northern Indians, Sir William JOHNSON. Hertel returned to Montreal in the spring of 1765. Because he was in straitened circumstances, his widowed mother approached Johnson twice on his behalf.

On 17 June 1769 Governor Guy Carleton* appointed Hertel interpreter for the Abenakis who had sought refuge among the Iroquois at St Regis after the destruction of their village of Saint-François-de-Sales (Odanak) on 4 Oct. 1759 [*see* Robert ROGERS]. The St Regis Iroquois asked the authorities to remove these refugees, who were provoking conflict by intruding on their hunting grounds and those of the Six Nations proper. They wanted to be rid also of the interpreter, whom they accused of encouraging the Abenakis "to remain so that he might continue to carry on the fur trade with them." After the Iroquois brought further pressure to bear in 1770, Hertel decided to give up. The Abenakis left St Regis at the end of the year.

Back in Montreal, Hertel in 1775 enrolled in the volunteer detachment that was commanded by François-Marie PICOTÉ de Belestre and Joseph-Dominique-Emmanuel Le Moyne* de Longueuil, raised to help repulse the American troops invading Canada. When Fort Saint-Jean capitulated on 2 Nov. 1775, he was taken prisoner. He was recognized as an officer by Brigadier-General Richard MONTGOMERY, who had met him during the campaign against Pontiac, and was sent by him into exile in the American colonies. Freed in an exchange of prisoners, Hertel returned in 1777 to Montreal, where he died four years later. His widow applied twice to Governor HALDIMAND for a life pension. On 29 Oct. 1781 she wrote to him: "M. Hertel left me as his entire fortune one son, who is only waiting to be old enough to offer his services to his king." The son, Louis-Hippolyte, who had been born in Montreal in 1771, became a lieutenant in the

Royal Canadian Volunteer Regiment. On 2 April 1792, two months before her death, Madame Hertel sold to the Presbyterian congregation of Montreal the site on which it built St Gabriel Street Church.

THOMAS-M. CHARLAND

AN, Col., C[11A], 101, f.15; D[2C], 3, p.127; 48 (copies at PAC). ANQ-M, Greffe de Joseph Papineau, 2 avril 1792. BL, Add. MSS 21651, pp.75–76, 88, 115; 21653, pp.463, 489–90; 21669, pp.72–73; 21687, p.29; 21772, p.73; 21773, p.149; 21831, p.130; 21879, pp.38, 48 (PAC transcripts). PAC, MG 11, [CO 42], Q, 2, p.335; 4, p.13; 13, p.164; MG 19, F1, 1, p.136. *Coll. des manuscrits de Lévis* (Casgrain), I, 170; V, 173; VI, 27. [Antoine Foucher], "Journal tenu pendant le siège du fort Saint-Jean, en 1775, par feu M. Foucher, ancien notaire de Montréal," *BRH*, XL (1934), 144, 212–13. "The French regime in Wisconsin – III," ed. R. G. Thwaites, Wis., State Hist. Soc., *Coll.*, XVIII (1908), 218. [Thwaites confuses the two Hertel brothers, Pierre-Antoine and Joseph-Hippolyte. This error was perpetuated by N. B. Wainwright, editor of "George Croghan's journal, 1759–1763 . . . ," *Pennsylvania Magazine of History and Biography* (Philadelphia), LXXI (1947), 399. T.-M.C.] *Invasion du Canada* (Verreau), 249. *Johnson papers* (Sullivan *et al.*). "Liste des membres; première réunion de la Grande Loge de Montréal," PAC *Rapport*, 1944, xxxii. "A list of Protestant house keepers in Montreal (1764)," *BRH*, XXXIX (1933), 158. "La mission de M. de Bougainville en France en 1758–1759," ANQ *Rapport*, 1923–24, 38. *Papiers Contrecœur* (Grenier), 104, 344, 407. [Nicolas Renaud d'Avène Des Méloizes], "Journal militaire tenu par Nicolas Renaud d'Avène Des Méloizes, ch[er], seigneur de Neuville, au Canada, du 8 mai 1759 au 21 novembre de la même année . . . ," ANQ *Rapport*, 1928–29, 32, 39, 46.

[François Daniel], *Nos gloires nationales; ou, histoire des principales familles du Canada . . .* (2v., Montréal, 1867), II, 369, 371. Francis Parkman, *The conspiracy of Pontiac and the Indian war after the conquest of Canada* (10th ed., 2v., Boston, 1886; repr. New York, 1962). C.-F. Bouthillier, "La bataille du 9 juillet 1755," *BRH*, XIV (1908), 222. T.[-M.] Charland, "Les neveux de madame de Beaubassin," *RHAF*, XXIII (1969–70), 84–90. J.-J. Lefebvre, "Louise Réaume-Fournerie-Robertson (1742–1773) et son petit-fils le colonel Daniel de Hertel (1797–1866)," *RHAF*, XII (1958–59), 330. "La loyauté des Canadiens en 1775," *BRH*, XXXI (1925), 373. É.-Z. Massicotte, "A propos de mariage," *BRH*, XXXII (1926), 536–37. "La reddition du fort Saint-Jean en 1775," *BRH*, XII (1906), 315.

HEY, WILLIAM, chief justice of Quebec; b. *c.* 1733 in England, son of Thomas and Elizabeth Hey; m. *c.* 1783 a Miss Paplay of Jamaica; d. 3 March 1797 in London, England.

William Hey was educated at Eton, at Corpus Christi College, Cambridge, and at the Middle Temple, from which he was called to the bar in 1756. His subsequent career stemmed from his Kentish connections. Recommendation to Lord Hardwicke secured his appointments in 1763 as deputy recorder of Dover and as recorder of Sandwich, Kent. When Hardwicke's son, Charles Yorke, became attorney general in Lord Rockingham's ministry, Hey's career was further advanced. With the support of Yorke and another Kentish Whig, Lord Sondes, Hey was chosen chief justice of Quebec. The royal mandate for his appointment was issued on 3 Feb. 1766.

Hey arrived at Quebec on 9 Sept. 1766, having travelled with the colony's new attorney general, Francis Maseres*. He was soon busied with pressing legal cases arising from the later stages of the Thomas WALKER affair and from the crown's attempt of November 1766 to collect customs duties [*see* Sir Thomas MILLS]. By refusing bail to Joseph HOWARD and others accused in the attack on Walker and by attempting to secure a special verdict from the jury in the customs case, Hey became embroiled in issues of great significance to the English speaking community in Quebec.

The attempt to establish a legal system generally acceptable to the entire population provided Hey with his largest task. Governor MURRAY had tried to create a structure that would introduce English law without doing injustice to the Canadians, but many difficulties arose in an immensely complicated situation. Before Hey's departure from England the law officers had recommended to the British government that Hey and Maseres "prepare a suitable *Plan* adapted to the Jurisdiction of the different Courts, and the convenience of the Suitors." Simplicity and speed of justice should be the essential considerations. No rapid response to the law officers' recommendation was forthcoming from the government, however. Only on 28 Aug. 1767 did the Privy Council resolve that investigations be undertaken into "Whether any and what defects are now subsisting in the present state of Judicature," and what grievances were expressed and changes required by Canadians. This task was to be carried out by a "fit & proper person" – Maurice Morgann* – who, however, did not arrive in Quebec until 22 Aug. 1768.

Hey and Maseres had already made an attempt at linking French and English law. The chief justice possessed no formal knowledge of the French system and in court required an interpreter, but Maseres thought that the advice of an assessor would prove sufficient since "Mr: Hey has already had occasion to determine two or three cases that turned upon points of the French law, and did it very ably and so as to give general satisfaction.'' No claim to authority on matters of detail could, however, be made and it seemed impossible for this deficiency to be remedied. François-Joseph CUGNET had recently drawn up a code of relevant law, but it was, though ably done, ''very difficult to Mr: Hey and me to understand from the great conciseness and the technicality or peculiarity of the French law-language,'' Maseres confessed.

On his return to England in September 1769 Morgann took with him three reports on the legal situation: two giving the contrasting views of Maseres and Governor Guy Carleton* and the third expressing Hey's dissents from the governor's report, which he himself had helped prepare. Carleton recommended the general retention of English criminal law and the use of French civil law except for mercantile disputes. Although the chief justice had no wish to impose a purely English legal procedure, he felt that a more limited restoration of French civil law was advisable. He considered that any policy should be shaped by the ''desire to establish such a System as shall tend to draw this Province into some Resemblance with the rest of Your Majesty's Dominions upon this Continent,'' but that the change should be made ''with the gentlest Hand.'' No Canadian could object to English law being the leading element in an English government, ''provided those Points which most sensibly affect them such as the Descent, Alienation and Incumbrance of their real Property, their Mode of Devising Assigning and conveying their Personal, their Marriage Contracts and all those Dispositions which tend to regulate their domestic Æconomy, and keep up Family Connection, are preserved entire, and the Laws concerning them well understood and Administered. . . .'' Hey differed from Maseres, who wanted a code to be drawn up; the chief justice believed there was not enough time to prepare one.

When the future of Quebec was being considered in England, Hey's views were taken into account: reports by the law officers contain respectful references to the chief justice's recommendations. Having been granted permission to return home on leave, Hey arrived in London early in 1774, in time to participate in the final stages of the preparation of the proposed legislation. Solicitor General Alexander Wedderburn later told Lord Dartmouth, secretary of state for the American Colonies, that he had ''had much conversation with Mr. Hey'' concerning the unsuitability of French criminal law and had found the chief justice's opinions ''weighty.'' In the first week of June 1774, when in the course of its consideration of the Quebec Bill the House of Commons examined witnesses, Hey appeared before it, following Carleton and Maseres. The leader of the government, Lord North, having denied the opposition copies of their reports on the laws of Quebec on the grounds that these submissions were too long to reproduce, had deprived his critics of useful sources of information. In response to opposition questions seeking to magnify the extent to which Canadians had been denied English constitutional and legal advantages Hey delivered measured and distant answers. He did not agree with assertions that trial by jury or an elected assembly were rights demanded by most Canadians. Although he believed he might in time master their system of law he could not be certain of this. He still thought it desirable that the English and Canadian systems of civil law be reconciled – the question on which he had originally differed with Carleton – but he admitted that the plan seemed less practicable than it had in 1769, since the Canadians had grown less submissive. However they still retained from the old régime much of their respect for authority, submitting naturally and perfectly to the crown rather than yearning for an assembly; that was their attractive aspect, to be ''in general a very attentive and obedient people.'' On the other hand he also found them ''a very ignorant people – a very prejudiced people.'' Perhaps because he held these mixed views Hey neither supported nor attacked the bill, which with regard to the legal system essentially followed Carleton's recommendations of 1769.

In the last week of September 1774 parliament was prematurely and unexpectedly dissolved. On 27 September Hey submitted to Dartmouth his resignation as chief justice. That these events were linked by more than coincidence was proved by Hey's nomination and unopposed return as member for Sandwich. His offer to resign as chief justice had been made in the knowledge of his approaching election and in the belief that he could not occupy both positions.

Nevertheless, in December 1774 Dartmouth wrote to Carleton to dispel any assumptions that Hey would not return to Quebec. The chief justice, he asserted, was resolved to resume his duties, even if he would have to relinquish his seat, ''which however we hope and think may be avoided.'' Whether Hey's resolution was entirely voluntary may be doubted; his presence in Quebec was urgently required if new courts of justice, a necessary consequence of the enforcement from 1 May 1775 of the Quebec Act, were to be organized.

By the end of 1774, still in England, Hey had

prepared the draft of an ordinance for establishing courts of justice in the province. He did not, however, return to Quebec sufficiently promptly to allow for the preparation of an ordinance by the appointed date. After his arrival on 15 June 1775 he found it difficult to carry out the task assigned him by the Legislative Council of conducting the committee that would prepare a new judicial structure. Hey continued to assert the superiority of English commercial law and of trial by jury in cases relating to personal wrongs. Carleton's instructions reveal that the British government intended these practices to be established by the governor and council, but Carleton, in alliance with the seigneurs on the council, offered an opposition sufficient to fend off proposals for their introduction. The controversy was in any case overtaken by the American invasion of the summer of 1775.

In the face of American attack, Canadian intransigence, and the governor's opposition, Hey was only too anxious to abandon his post. "Let me say in general," he wrote to Lord Apsley, the lord chancellor, in August 1775, "that this country affords as gloomy . . . [a prospect] in point of security & in the ill humours & evil dispositions of its inhabitants . . . as can be imagined." He consequently felt that his ten years' service deserved compensation by "the first office of distinction or Profit that the Crown has to bestow." He had no military ardour to encourage him to remain. When he finally closed his letter to Apsley in mid September it was with the prediction that Saint-Jean, Montreal, and Quebec would soon fall to the invaders. "In this situation I hold myself in readiness to embark for England where I possibly may be of some use your Lordship will I hope agree with me that I can be of none here. . . ."

Hey did not stay to see his fears of defeat fully confirmed. He sailed for England in November 1775 and later that winter made his only recorded contribution to parliamentary debate. Speaking in opposition to Charles James Fox's motion of 20 Feb. 1776 which proposed an inquiry into British military failure in North America, Hey defended the Quebec Act from charges that it had contributed to that failure and he praised Carleton who, he declared, had not received proper support. The *Public Advertiser* placed Hey's speech among the three "most general and important." Through his acquaintance with the state of Canada "it is said great information was given to the whole House. . . ."

In the course of the summer of 1776 it became clear that Hey would not return to Quebec. He held firmly to the understanding on which he had entered the Commons: that he would soon thereafter leave Quebec and acquire other office. In August he declined the request of Lord Germain, the new secretary of state for the American Colonies, that he resume his duties. He resigned office and "strenuously pressed" his claim for a commissionership of excise or customs. His appointment to the customs post on 31 Oct. 1776 vacated his parliamentary seat and closed his legal and political careers.

As chief justice of Quebec Hey had discharged his duties with reasonable diligence. Although he was altogether more competent than his predecessor, William Gregory, and not a centre of controversy like his successor, Peter LIVIUS, his efforts were for the most part confined to presiding over a legal system which he but partially understood and failed to amend. It has been concluded by Alfred Leroy Burt* that "with one possible exception [an aspect of the Walker case] no fault has been found with his administration of justice" and Hilda Neatby* has asserted that the council's blocking of his bill to reorganize the courts in the summer of 1775 "meant the loss of the first and best chance of building, on the settlement of the Quebec Act, a reasonable compromise between the English merchants and the French party." Unfortunately, Hey's general competence and ability to contribute to the revision of Quebec's court system proved of less significance to him than his desire to secure a safe office in England.

IN COLLABORATION WITH PETER MARSHALL

Docs. relating to constitutional history, 1759–91 (Shortt and Doughty; 1918). G.B., Hist. MSS Commission, *The manuscripts of the Earl of Dartmouth* (3v., London, 1887–96), I–II; Parl., *Debates of the House of Commons in the year 1774, on the bill for making more effectual provision for the government of the province of Quebec, drawn up from the notes of Sir Henry Cavendish* . . . (London, 1839; repr. [East Ardsley, Eng.] and [New York], 1966). Maseres, *Maseres letters* (Wallace). *Reports on the laws of Quebec, 1767–1770*, ed. W. P. M. Kennedy and Gustave Lanctot (Ottawa, 1931). Namier and Brooke, *House of Commons*. Burt, *Old prov. of Que*. (1968). Bernard Donoughue, *British politics and the American revolution: the path to war, 1773–75* (London and New York, 1964). Neatby, *Administration of justice under Quebec Act*.

HICKS, JOHN, land agent and office-holder; b. 23 April 1715 at Portsmouth, Rhode Island, son of Thomas Hicks and Ann Clarke; m. 8 May 1740 Elizabeth Russell at Tiverton, Rhode Island; d. 6 March 1790 at Hicks' Ferry (Bridgetown, N.S.).

John Hicks was born into an influential and

prosperous Quaker family in Rhode Island. His father, a descendant of one of the Pilgrim Fathers, had amassed a considerable estate in Portsmouth, and his maternal grandfather had held high government office in the colony. After his marriage in 1740 Hicks settled in King's County, where he farmed and was soon made a justice of the peace for Charlestown. It was therefore as a man of considerable influence that he travelled to Nova Scotia in April 1759 to represent the citizens of the Rhode Island and Providence Plantations who were interested in settling in the province. The previous October the governor of Nova Scotia, Charles Lawrence*, had published a proclamation in the *Boston-Gazette* informing the people of New England that the time was ripe for the settlement and cultivation not only of the lands made vacant by the expulsion of the Acadians but of other parts of "this valuable province" as well. His proclamation had created immediate interest, particularly in Rhode Island and Connecticut where a rapid increase in population was making agricultural land scarce.

Hicks sailed to Halifax with Robert Denison*, Jonathan Harris, Joseph Otis, and Amos Fuller, all agents from Connecticut. On 18 April they met with Lawrence and four of his councillors at the governor's home. Agreement was quickly achieved on settlement terms, and the agents were taken at government expense in the armed snow *Halifax* to view the proposed lands. The surveyor general, Charles MORRIS, accompanied them to aid in the choice of township sites. Rounding Yarmouth, they sailed into the Bay of Fundy, examined the lands along the Annapolis River, and proceeded to Minas Basin. The agents returned to Halifax so well pleased that Denison, Harris, and Otis immediately entered into an agreement with the Council for settlement of the townships of Horton and Cornwallis to the west of Minas Basin. They then returned to New England, but Hicks and Fuller stayed on to present their own plan of action. They chose the site of a former Acadian settlement on the north bank of the Pisiquid (Avon) River opposite Fort Edward (Windsor), where they proposed to bring 100 families, 50 in 1759 and 50 in 1760. On 21 July they were granted 50,000 acres to form the township of Falmouth. Before the grant was made, however, word had reached Halifax that a large party of French and Indians had appeared before Fort Edward. Although no engagement had taken place there, violence had been reported in other parts of the province. Hicks informed the Council on 16 July that in his opinion the settlers would prefer to come the following year.

The Rhode Island planters arrived at Falmouth in four ships in May 1760. Hicks and his family were among them. Township records show that Hicks played a prominent role in the new community. Not only was he given responsibility for providing housing "for the soldiers to live in while we need them in the village," but he was also appointed a justice of the peace for the township and served on its first grand jury.

In 1765 Hicks moved to lands he had purchased along the Annapolis River in Granville Township. On the resignation of Henry Munro he was elected in July 1768 to the House of Assembly for Granville. He took his seat on 31 October and served until the general election of 1770. In 1772 he moved across the river to Annapolis Township, where he purchased and improved extensive lands. He established a ferry linking the two townships and the community that grew up around it was called Hicks' Ferry until the name was changed to Bridgetown in 1824. Hicks died there in 1790 and was survived by six of his 11 children. Three of his sons appear in the Capitation Tax Act returns of 1794, and their rates show them to have been among the wealthiest residents of Annapolis Township.

John Hicks was representative of the planters who gave a distinctive New England character to the Annapolis valley. Although the Board of Trade eventually supported Lawrence's promotion of settlement from New England, they had originally wanted these lands reserved for disbanded soldiers. The enthusiasm of Hicks and his energy in arranging the Rhode Island immigration were essential contributions to the success of the governor's policy.

F. H. HICKS

PANS, MG 9, no. 109; RG 1, 211, 12 Oct. 1758, 18 April, 18–19 May, 16 July 1759. *Ancestry of Jeremy Clarke of Rhode Island and Dungan genealogy*, comp. A. R. Justice (Philadelphia, [1922]), 53. *Directory of N.S. MLAs*, 158. Calnek, *History of Annapolis* (Savary), 332, 526–27. W. E. Chute, *A genealogy and history of the Chute family in America* . . . (Salem, Mass., 1894), ci–cii. E. R. Coward, *Bridgetown, Nova Scotia: its history to 1900* ([Kentville, N.S., 1955]), 25–26. J. V. Duncanson, *Falmouth – a New England township in Nova Scotia, 1760–1965* (Windsor, Ont., 1965), 11–22, 267–68. A. W. H. Eaton, *The history of Kings County, Nova Scotia* . . . (Salem, Mass., 1910), 58–69. H. Y. Hind, *Sketch of the old parish burying ground of Windsor, Nova Scotia* . . . (Windsor, 1889), 7, 46–50. W. C. Milner, *Grand Pre; a chapter in colonial history* (Wolfville, N.S., n.d.), 11–14, 20. Murdoch, *History of N.S.*, II, 364–65, 476. R. S. Longley, "The coming of the New England planters to the Annapolis valley," N.S. Hist. Soc., *Coll.*, XXXIII (1961), 81–101.

HIGGINS, DAVID, ship captain, merchant, colonizer, and office-holder; m. 6 June 1773 Elizabeth Prince at Boston, Massachusetts; d. April 1783 at Charlottetown, St John's (Prince Edward) Island.

Nothing is known of David Higgins' background or early life. He first appears in the 1760s as a ship captain in the Gulf of St Lawrence fishery. In 1767, with merchants Hutcheson Mure and Robert Cathcart, he drew Lot 59 on St John's Island in the Board of Trade lottery. Two years later he went into partnership with James William Montgomery, lord advocate of Scotland. Their plan was to develop Lot 59, which fronted on Cardigan Bay, and Montgomery's adjacent Lot 51 as a fishing, lumbering, and mercantile centre. Probably as a result of his connections with Montgomery, Higgins was appointed naval officer of the Island as well as one of the first members of its Council. He was also authorized by the Earl of Hillsborough, secretary of state for the American Colonies, to take over custody of stores and provisions ordered to Charlottetown in 1768 by Lieutenant Governor Michael FRANCKLIN of Nova Scotia as part of his abortive attempt to favour his friends and business associates.

Higgins arrived on the Island in September 1769 and reported to Whitehall that Governor Walter PATTERSON would be disappointed if he expected "good houses provisions many utensils boats &c" from the Nova Scotia effort, since the buildings were unfinished and uninhabitable, the provisions spoiled, the boats in bad repair, and the stores and tools badly rusted and useless. Montgomery had supplied Higgins with a shipload of trade goods to sell to prospective settlers and an open letter of credit to the prominent Boston merchant Job Prince, Higgins' future father-in-law. Higgins had no trouble disposing of these goods and subsequent provisions obtained in New England, which helped keep many newcomers to the Island from starvation, but most of his dealings were solely on credit. Higgins kept a store at Georgetown, and on Lot 59 he built a sawmill and grist-mill, cleared 30 acres for St Andrew's Farm, and settled 32 small tenants, including a dozen Acadian families familiar with the fishery. He sent 22 shiploads of timber to Britain in the early 1770s, but because of depressed prices the expenses of preparation and shipment were barely cleared. Higgins served as foreman of the Island's first grand jury, and he was appointed a "Public Pass Officer" for Georgetown in 1771 to prevent unauthorized departures from the Island by indentured servants. He was himself dismissed from the Council in 1773 for being absent from its meetings without leave.

By 1774 Montgomery was appalled at the charges on him, which totalled nearly £4,000 without visible return, and that year he stopped payment on Higgins' bills of exchange and called him home for an accounting. On his way Higgins stopped at Boston to convey to Job Prince his interest in Lot 59 (and the buildings on it, which belonged to Montgomery) in repayment of some of his debts. In Scotland, Montgomery could make little sense of his partner's books, but he wrote off the debt in return for Higgins' third of Lot 59 (whose sale to Prince he did not discover until after Higgins' death), another third of Lot 59 and half of Lot 12, which Higgins had come to acquire, and a bond for £2,400. In return, Higgins became lessee from Montgomery of two-thirds of Lot 59, half of Lot 12, all of Lot 51, and Panmure Island for a yearly rental of £100, which was to rise ultimately to £300. Having already invested and lost his wife's "little fortune" and having resided on the Island for five years "in not much better a state than slavery," Higgins felt obliged to return there in the summer of 1775 with another load of trade goods and an elaborate outfit for distilling molasses. With these items, presumably obtained on credit, he hoped to use Three Rivers (the region around Georgetown) in a triangular trade with Britain and the West Indies in fish, timber, molasses, and trade goods. The American War of Independence ruined his plans. His vessel was taken by privateers on the voyage out and he was able to ransom himself and his cargo only at great expense. Although he saved the precious distilling equipment this time, it was carried off in American raids on Three Rivers later in the war.

In July 1779 Higgins was elected to the House of Assembly but he resigned in March 1780 after serving as speaker. He was still trying to stay in business in 1781, when he wrote HALDIMAND offering to serve as his agent in the Gulf, but in 1782 he gave up and moved his family to Charlottetown, returning to Three Rivers in a schooner upon which he loaded everything movable for sale at the capital. Most of the Island's officials helped Higgins in his distress by taking off his hands at bargain prices such items as doors, windows, and blacksmiths' equipment, although according to one observer, "Non will confess any part of it." As a final indignity, one "Mr Barry" (probably Captain Walter Berry) carried off Higgins' wife. Overwhelmed by his debts and his "Wife defiling his Bed," Higgins went on a four-month drinking-bout that culminated in a fatal fever in April 1783. Another of Montgomery's agents, David Lawson*, undertook administration of the Higgins estate and gained custody of the account books which Island rumour held showed large debts owed by leading government officials, especially Attorney General Phillips CALLBECK. Montgomery, the principal creditor, was never able to recover the books despite years of litigation.

David Higgins was one of the Island's most active and enterprising early adventurers, and he helped many settlers. Lieutenant Governor Thomas Desbrisay* wrote at Higgins' death that he was "a man that did more service to the Lower Class of People here, than all the officers of Government, put together." But service did not pay bills or satisfy creditors. Most of the money involved did not belong to Higgins, and he died a virtual bankrupt, testimony to the problems of the early merchants of St John's Island.

J. M. BUMSTED

BL, Add. MSS 21734, f.127. PRO, CO 226/1, f.55; 226/4, ff.1–2, 29–32, 119–21, 175–78. Scottish Record Office (Edinburgh), Montgomery estate papers in the muniments of Messrs. Blackwood and Smith, W.S., Peebles, Estate papers, GD293/2/78/23, 28, 30, 45, 47, 61; 293/2/79/1, 19, 46, 49, 51, 52. Brebner, *Neutral Yankees* (1969), 85–86. A. H. Clark, *Three centuries and the Island: a historical geography of settlement and agriculture in Prince Edward Island, Canada* (Toronto, 1959).

HILLAIRE (Hilaire) DE LA ROCHETTE, ALEXANDRE-ROBERT (D'), *écuyer* and agent in Quebec of the treasurers general of the Marine and Colonies; son of Charles-Robert Hillaire de Moissacq et de La Rochette and Élizabeth Martin of the parish of Notre-Dame in Versailles, France; m. 21 Nov. 1760 Marie-Anne Levasseur at Montreal; d. in or after 1772.

Alexandre-Robert Hillaire de La Rochette first appeared in Canada in 1755 as secretary to André Doreil*, who had been appointed chief commissary in Jean-Armand Dieskau*'s expedition. At Quebec, Montcalm* and BIGOT, as well as Doreil, took an interest in his career and a few months after Doreil's return to France late in 1758 La Rochette succeeded Jacques Imbert* as the Quebec agent of the treasurers general of the Marine and Colonies. He held that post from 16 Oct. 1759 until the formal cession of the colony to Great Britain in 1763. His principal employers were Claude Baudard de Sainte-James and Noël-Mathurin-Étienne Perichon, who had both purchased their offices for the enormous sum of 600,000 *livres* and assumed their duties on 31 Jan. 1758, just as the financial crisis of the Seven Years' War was beginning. La Rochette's main duties were to make payments for the crown in the various forms of paper currency used in Canada and to maintain public confidence in that currency by converting it annually into bills of exchange drawn on his employers in Paris. To carry out such duties in the war years, with inflation, profiteering, and the frequent loss of the mails at sea, was extremely difficult, as Imbert well knew when he quit the post. Furthermore, on 15 Oct. 1759, at the time La Rochette assumed his new duties, the French government made them impossible by suspending all payments on bills of exchange drawn in the colonies on the treasurers general. There was much talk of La Rochette's being incompetent or worse, but the best of men could only have failed in such a post at such a time.

The minister, at any rate, thought highly of La Rochette and after his return to France appointed him agent for the colonies on 16 Oct. 1763 to supervise the supplies purchased for the colonies and the colonial service. In addition he was put in charge of the liquidation of Canadian paper money; he was to receive, examine, and verify all outstanding private claims on the crown, especially bills of exchange and currency notes, and, when these claims had at last been officially approved (and reduced after years of delay), to make the necessary payments [*see* Bernard Cardeneau*]. He proceeded under the direction of the Commission Fontanieu (named after its chairman, Gaspard-Moïse-Augustin de Fontanieu, Marquis de Fiennes), first established on 18 Oct. 1758 as "La Commission de liquidation des dettes de la Marine et des Colonies" and ordered on 28 Nov. 1761 to turn from naval debts to Canadian debts. Their work on the Canadian debts was not finished until 1768 when, on 20 February, the crown published an *Arrêt* which disqualified all claims that had not been presented to the commission by the prescribed deadlines. In 1772 La Rochette, still agent for the colonies, made arrangements for his temporary replacement in order to spend a year or two in India. We lose track of him thereafter.

La Rochette's family connections cast a revealing light on his career and show in rare detail the patronage by which a Bourbon official might get ahead in life. On his mother's side of the family were two businessmen of Marseilles who set up as bankers and traders at Quebec in the late 1740s, Barthélemy Martin*, son of Vincent Martin, and Jean-Baptiste-Tropez Martin, son of Charles-Bruno Martin. The Martin and Hillaire families were, of course, useful to each other, but members of both married into the even more useful family of Levasseur, which was connected with rich and powerful farmers general. Barthélemy Martin in 1752 and La Rochette in 1760 married daughters of René-Nicolas LEVASSEUR, the chief royal shipwright posted at Quebec, whose brother Louis-Armand was a career naval officer serving as financial commissary at Rochefort when he died on 9 Aug. 1760. When much later, on 18 Jan. 1771, Jean-Baptiste-Tropez Martin, then in Paris, married La Rochette's sister, Barbe-Madeleine, among the guests at the wedding were Élizabeth-Françoise Ferrand, *née* Levasseur, first cousin of Mme de Pompadour's father, and her husband, Laurent-René Ferrand, a farmer general. Clearly, La Rochette was not without influence either in Paris or in Quebec. He had substantial business interests in France during the 1760s in association with his future brother-in-law, Jean-Baptiste-Tropez Martin, investing over 20,000 *livres* in the Société de Guadalcanal alone, but whether he profited by his brief career in Quebec is not clear, as he was not arrested in the *affaire du Canada*. His powerful family relations no doubt protected him.

J. F. BOSHER

AN, Col., E, 257 (dossier La Rochette); Marine, C[7], 167 (dossier La Rochette); Minutier central, IV, no.693 (marriage contract, 18 Jan. 1771). Yves Durand, *Les fermiers généraux au XVIIIe siècle* (Paris, 1971), 75–76. John Keyes, "Un commis des trésoriers généraux de la Marine à Québec: Nicolas Lanoullier de Boisclerc," *RHAF*, XXXII (1978–79), 181–202. Henri Legohérel, "Une commission extraordinaire du Conseil d'État du roi: la commission de liquidation des dettes de la marine et des colonies (1758–1768)," Université de Dakar, faculté de Droit et des Sciences économiques, *Publications*, 1968, 1–32.

HIYOUA. *See* WIKINANISH

HOCQUART, GILLES (sometimes **Hocart** in old family documents), financial commissary and intendant of New France; b. 1694 in the parish of Sainte-Croix, Mortagne-au-Perche, France, third of 14 children born to Jean-Hyacinthe Hocquart and Marie-Françoise Michelet Du Cosnier; m. 23 Aug. 1750 Anne-Catherine de La Lande in Brest, France; the marriage was childless; d. 1 April 1783 at Paris.

The Hocquarts originated in Champagne, where documents bearing their name date from 1189. They were local officials near the village of Sainte-Menehould whose claims to nobility were not officially recognized until 1536 and whose material circumstances were hardly better than the surrounding peasantry's. Gilles Hocquart's ancestors, the Hocquarts de Montfermeil, migrated during the 16th century from Champagne to Paris, where they entered the king's financial bureaucracy. Through the acquisition of tax offices and the fashioning of advantageous marriage ties, with the Colbert family for example, they climbed gradually into the upper echelons of the robe nobility. By the mid 1700s they were wealthy residents of the Place des Victoires district, with influence in the magistracy and government bureaucracy as well as in finance. Their offspring married into leading families of the sword nobility. It was, in fact, the revolution and the brutal stroke of Mme Guillotine that finally halted their social progress.

Jean-Hyacinthe Hocquart, Gilles's father, was one of the chief architects of the family's success. At age 21 he was a secretary and clerk under Jean-Baptiste Colbert in the finance ministry. His marriage, in 1681, to a relative of the prestigious Talon family of the judicial robe helped the Hocquarts to gain a foothold in that branch of the robe nobility – a foothold which his grandson Jean-Hyacinthe-Louis-Emmanuel converted into the presidency of the second chamber of the *parlement* of Paris. In 1686, however, Jean-Hyacinthe abandoned his promising financial career and, responding to an appeal for men of talent to staff the Marine commissariat, began a new life in the port cities. After many years of service he was named intendant of Toulon in 1716 and of Le Havre in 1720. His two eldest sons followed his first career and became successful administrators and financiers at Paris. Jean-Hyacinthe, for example, was a wealthy farmer general. His younger sons, including Gilles, entered the Marine service under his direction and pursued lengthy careers far from Paris and the lavish style of life of their siblings.

Gilles, who spent his entire working life in the Marine commissariat, began in 1702 as a scrivener at Rochefort. Since he was just eight, it is unlikely that he performed all of the duties of that post until much later. Moving with his father to Brest in 1706, he remained there until 1716 when, after briefly considering a vocation in the priesthood, he went to Toulon and was promoted junior commissary. In 1721 he was named commissary and a year later was transferred to Rochefort, where he served until his appointment to New France in 1729. Rochefort was a training school for Marine personnel and, during his tenure there, Hocquart performed a wide assortment of tasks, from supervising ship repairs to serving as the port's financial controller. It was this practical training and the knowledge of commercial, legal, and administrative details which it provided that contributed to his successes in Canada. Though his progress through the ranks had been slow, by 1728 he was second in command to the intendant, François de Beauharnois* de La Chaussaye, Baron de Beauville, and was highly regarded in the ministry of Marine. At age 34, he was ready for a more challenging appointment.

It is not certain, however, that Hocquart's appointment, on 8 March 1729, as financial commissary and acting intendant in New France, was based solely on his administrative record. His family may have intervened on his behalf with the minister of Marine, Maurepas. Several relatives were well placed for such action, including his brother Jean-Hyacinthe, who purchased the office of Marine treasurer in 1729 and who, as a farmer general, had financial dealings with Maurepas. Patronage based on family influence often determined whose career advanced and whose remained in limbo. On the other hand, Hocquart possessed specific abilities that were desperately required in Canada. As controller at Rochefort he had earned a reputation for honest and efficient financial administration, whereas in Canada the intendant, Claude-Thomas Dupuy*, had plunged the finances into a confused morass of large deficits, jumbled accounts, and doubtful dealings. Dupuy had not been trained in the Marine and he apparently regarded the details of financial administration as a proper field for unimaginative clerks. Moreover, his economic proposals, which he elaborated without first gaining knowledge of or experience in Canada, were seldom tempered by considerations of financial feasibility. Maurepas, it is clear, was anxious to replace him with a more realistic and experienced bureaucrat.

Then again, Hocquart's personality may have been his strongest recommendation. By 1729 relations between Dupuy and Governor Charles de Beauharnois* de La Boische had degenerated from mutual dislike into the sort of bellicosity that infected New France's upper social strata and brought effective government to a standstill. Beauharnois was undoubtedly correct when he wrote, "it is enough that I say white for him to say black." It was for this reason that Maurepas finally decided to recall Dupuy and to send a more congenial partner for Beauharnois. Hocquart fitted this role perfectly. Everything about him suggested a person of calm temperament and unassuming disposition. He was physically nondescript, with the sleepy eyes and heavy features of one who enjoys sedentary pleasures. Although intelligent, he was not brilliant or devastatingly perceptive. The historian Guy Frégault* has described him as a "hard-working clerk . . . without any daring initiatives or broad syntheses." Though unbending once he decided on a course of action, he was flexible in his methods and almost always sought the road of least resistance. Maurepas described him to Beauharnois as "judicious, industrious, and pleasant to deal with." But although he may have suited the administrative needs of New France in 1729, there was no evidence that he possessed the experience or economic vision to cope with the colony's long-term economic problems. The scope and magnitude of those problems were revealed to him in his memoirs of instructions.

Hocquart's instructions were rooted in classic mercantilist maxims. "Since the colony of Canada is of value only insofar as it is useful to the kingdom," they stated, "Sieur Hocquart must apply himself to finding ways of contributing to that end." But the thrust of French mercantilism had changed significantly since the days of Louis XIV and Colbert. Under Cardinal Fleury, Louis XV's first minister from 1726 to 1743, the maintenance of peace with Great Britain for the purposes of commercial expansion was seen as the key to France's eventual hegemony in Europe. To further this policy Fleury emphasized political stability and strict governmental economy; the impact in the colonial sphere was to tighten the grip of the commerce-oriented robe bureaucrats on policy and to restrict the funds available for state initiatives. Hence Maurepas laid great stress on the expansion of trade, but through private rather than state initiative. Hocquart was urged to promote Canada's trade within the French Atlantic empire, but without increasing government spending.

The instructions pointed out that while the potential for a larger trade between Canada and France in fish, furs, lumber, and other items was great, the potential for Canadian agriculture and industry to supply the growing slave population of the French West Indies was greater still. Like so many mercantilist thinkers before him, Maurepas envisaged an integrated commerce between France's Atlantic colonies which would have the added benefit of reducing the illegal trade between New England and the French West Indies. Louisbourg, Île Royale (Cape Breton Island), Hocquart was informed, was an ideal entrepôt and naval shield for this three-cornered trade, as well as a market for Canadian products, but since its construction few ships had arrived there each year from Quebec. In the minister's view responsibility for this development lay with Hocquart's predecessors, Michel Bégon* de La Picardière and Dupuy, for they had failed to develop the commercial possibilities of Canadian industry and agriculture. The instructions left no doubt that Hocquart's own administration would be judged in the light of his ability to do so. He was to succeed where every intendant since Jean Talon* had failed in shifting the axis of Canada's export economy from the fur trade to agriculture and industry. Only in this way would New France achieve long-term economic stability, while serving a more useful purpose for France.

Hocquart arrived at Quebec in September 1729, having escaped without injury when his ship, the *Éléphant*, ran aground near Île aux Grues. He stayed for some time with the governor general at the Château Saint-Louis and was pleased to discover that Beauharnois, chastened somewhat by the minister's severe criticism of his role in Dupuy's recall, was friendly and supportive. Indeed, over the next ten years both men found it mutually beneficial to cooperate and to respect each other's sphere of authority. They had a mutual enemy in Bishop Pierre-Herman DOSQUET and, apparently, a genuine liking for each other. It was Beauharnois who petitioned the minister in 1730 to have Hocquart promoted intendant and Hocquart warmly recommended Beauharnois for the *cordon rouge*. When differences did arise, they were careful not to allow the dispute to grow into a personal confrontation. Instead, they requested a decision from the minister. The administrative crisis that had led to Dupuy's recall was thus easily defused and Hocquart was free to concentrate on broader issues.

As intendant Hocquart had jurisdiction in a number of areas – the administration of the judicial system, the maintenance of public order, and the development of economic policy. In fact, however, his activities in relation to justice and police constituted but a minor aspect of his intendancy and were focused largely on improving the quality of the bureaucracy. His instructions had stressed his role in the economic sphere, and it was this field that claimed his attention. If he had had any doubts about the feasibility of those instructions, they must have been confirmed by his first impressions in Canada. In fact, his dispatches to the court from the date of his arrival until 1731 were cautiously pessimistic. His initial scepticism can be partly attributed to the culture shock experienced by upper-class Europeans who were venturing for the first time to the extremities of the known world. To them, Canada was an isolated and forlorn outpost surrounded by an infinity of rock and forest. But Hocquart was also a practical man who observed that Canada lacked the human resources and material conditions necessary for rapid economic progress. He was discouraged, for instance, by the quality of the civil bureaucracy in New France. In his view it was inefficient, understaffed, and poorly paid. Many of the financial officers who had served with Dupuy, including the agent of the treasurers general of the Marine, Nicolas Lanoullier* de Boisclerc, were suspected of wrongdoing, while death and retirements left him without a single experienced commissary. "I have borne almost entirely alone the brunt of all the operations I have undertaken," he complained in 1730; "having found no one here capable of unravelling the chaos of all the outstanding business, I have had to direct, give instructions for, and supervise all the work." He found many of the judicial officers, including the king's attorney at Montreal, François Foucher*, and several councillors of the Conseil Supérieur, to be incompetent, and he saw no possibility of finding suitable replacements in the colony. He asked for help from France and, in the mean time, relied heavily on those officials, such as Louis-Frédéric Bricault* de Valmur, his secretary, and Jean-Victor VARIN de La Marre, the controller, who had accompanied him to Quebec.

Hocquart was even more disappointed with the merchant community in Canada. He was aware from his long experience in the French port cities that the commercial bourgeois there were largely responsible for France's commercial resurgence since the treaty of Utrecht. He was predisposed therefore to look upon the merchants as the spearhead of economic growth. And the budgetary restrictions placed upon his administration left no doubt that his success in Canada would depend heavily upon his ability to persuade the merchants to develop agriculture and industry. But in 1729 this possibility seemed remote. The wealthiest merchants, men such as Pierre de Lestage* and Louis Charly* Saint-Ange, invested primarily in the fur trade, where profits were high and the demands for managerial skills, secondary facilities, and long-term commitments relatively modest. Hocquart learned from experience, moreover, that merchant capital was not easily attracted to other branches of the economy. There were a few entrepreneurs, he acknowledged, especially at Quebec, who were involved in the fisheries, lumbering, and the grain trade, but their operations made only a slight impact on external trade. Although he assisted those who were striving to develop export industries, such as Abbé Louis Lepage* de Sainte-Claire, who had established a sawmill on his seigneury of

Terrebonne, or Michel Sarrazin* and François Hazeur, who operated a slate quarry at Grand Étang in Gaspé, he noted that these ventures often suffered from poor management. After one failure in 1730 he stated, "in this country only the king can establish industries and keep them going in their early stages."

This view was partly based on Hocquart's recognition of the difficulties facing entrepreneurs in Canada. A thriving agricultural trade depended, for example, on the regular production of agricultural surpluses. But such surpluses could not be produced, he claimed, when seigneurs were lax in settling their fiefs and in fulfilling their seigneurial obligations. In taking note of these abuses, Hocquart also maintained that some seigneurs charged unfair and illegal rents and that others sold rather than rented wooded land. He considered the habitants, whose qualities he would later praise, lazy and insubordinate. He could not help comparing their subsistence level of farming with conditions in France, where the peasants, he believed, were more industrious. Between 1729 and 1731 he instigated the reunion of 400 undeveloped habitant concessions to their seigneuries under the second edict of Marly, more than double the number reunited under the two previous intendants. Hocquart also accepted the argument of Canada's merchants that the supply of currency was inadequate to stimulate exchanges between habitants who did have surplus crops and the merchants. He pointed out that the 400,000 *livres* in card money that he had been authorized to circulate in 1729 was not enough. He also commented on the high cost and inadequacy of transportation, noting that the small ships constructed in Canada could not service the trade with the West Indies. But merchants who wanted to build large ships were faced with high labour costs. "It is true that . . . the majority of resident merchants take naturally to the building [of ships]," he wrote, "but labour is so expensive here, and the inhabitants have so little money, that they cannot undertake large enterprises."

Although Hocquart acknowledged the material obstacles to economic diversification, he accepted the view of his French superiors that the unenterprising attitude of Canada's commercial élite, evidenced by its narrow preoccupation with the fur trade, was primarily responsible. His initial assessment, in other words, was that of an unsympathetic outsider. But in 1731 and 1732 his views changed. He began to distinguish sharply between Canadian and French merchant interests and to ascribe the inadequacies of the former to the suffocating preponderance of the latter. The Canadian merchants, only a few of whose fortunes, he later claimed, were as large as 50,000 to 60,000 *livres*, did not have enough capital to invest in industry and the agricultural economy because trade was for the most part controlled by French commercial houses such as Robert Dugard et Cie of Rouen, represented in Canada by a permanent factor, François Havy*, and Mme Pascaud et Fils of La Rochelle, whose directors, the widow and sons of Antoine Pascaud*, were associated in the Canadian trade with Pierre de Lestage. French merchants gained the lion's share of profits from the transactions of their agents in Canada and from the interest they collected on the debts the Canadian merchants owed them. In 1732 Hocquart estimated these debts at 250,000 *livres*. Since the French merchants were not generally interested in reinvesting their profits in other Canadian ventures, it was extremely difficult to promote economic diversification.

From a stern critic of the Canadian merchants, Hocquart had become their advocate. He was convinced that the crown would have to intervene to protect their interests and to help them gain a larger share of Canadian commerce, even if that meant interfering with the trade of French merchants. If the Canadians were ever to develop the non-fur economy, and Hocquart stated more than once that they were better suited to the task than were French merchants whose base of operations was far away, the crown would also have to provide them with financial aid. Hocquart summed up this line of thought in a seminal dispatch in 1732: "It is for you, my lord, to consider whether it would be more suitable in this case to assure the advantage for the resident merchants or for those from outside. It is true that freedom of trade benefits all the inhabitants because of the abundance and cheapness of goods that result. On the other hand, it would be desirable to have in this country some wealthy merchants, even if they were few in number, because they would be in a position to start and enlarge businesses that the slenderness of their means does not allow them even to attempt." Hocquart wanted to create a Canadian commercial bourgeoisie, like those in the French ports, that could, with the crown's initial support, diversify and expand the economy. Such was the policy that informed his actions, that brought him into conflict with his French superiors, and that characterized his intendancy.

There were three main factors which led Hocquart to adopt this policy. First, he was appointed intendant in 1731, a promotion that allowed him to shed some of the discretion that had been required during his probationary period as financial commissary. As intendant he was in a stronger position to express his views and to adopt his own goals. Second, after two years in Canada he had developed strong ties to elements of the commercial élite, particularly merchants and officials at Quebec involved in commerce. The views of men like François-Étienne Cugnet*, who spoke from the Canadian merchant perspective, had an impact on his thinking. Third, Hocquart was anxious to add to his prestige and wealth. Unlike many of his predecessors, however, he did not pursue this goal through proposals designed to increase the intendant's political power. Instead he sought to add to his sphere of patronage by favouring the economic enterprises of his clients. He borrowed from and lent funds to them and invested in some of their ventures. The Canadian merchants, like the civil and judicial officials under his authority, were his natural clients. Whereas French merchants trading in Canada could appeal to the minister, the Canadian merchants turned to the intendant. This patron-client relationship contributed greatly to Hocquart's protection and support of them.

Hocquart was anxious to gain the minister's support for his ideas, but Maurepas was far from convinced. He doubted, as he explained in a dispatch of 1733, whether the Canadians were as deeply in debt to French merchants as Hocquart claimed or whether this indebtedness accounted for the slow development of agriculture and industry. The Canadian merchants, he suggested, were simply trying to become masters of the entire trade so that they could set their own prices and gouge the habitants. He warned Hocquart not to interfere with trade except on those occasions, during a crop failure for example, when the welfare of the colony was clearly at stake. Although Maurepas was prepared to support Canadian enterprise, he was not prepared to do so at the expense of French merchants. Nor was he willing to invest more crown funds in Canadian development. "As to the funds with which you believe the country must be assisted," he wrote, "they have never been so considerable as during your administration . . . it is easy to judge that you have been more favourably treated . . . than your predecessors. . . ." Hocquart would do better, he contended, to find a profitable way to raise taxes so that the Canadians would finally pay their fair share of the 600,000 *livres* that the crown spent annually on Canada.

This refusal to provide the moral and material support Hocquart considered vital severely restricted the effectiveness of his initiatives between 1733 and 1736. Although he convinced Maurepas that the time was not yet ripe for collecting taxes in Canada, he was unable to gain approval for more than 25,000 *livres*, or 2.5 per cent of the total expenditures for the period, in loans and direct aid to Canadian enterprises. In these circumstances, his efforts on behalf of ventures such as François Poulin* de Francheville's ironworks at Saint-Maurice, Nicolas-Marie Renaud* d'Avène Des Méloizes' tile industry near Quebec, Louis Denys* de La Ronde's copper mine on Lake Superior, and Abbé Lepage's lumber business, produced meagre results. None of them gave any sign of developing into significant export industries. On the contrary, Francheville's forge shut down in 1735 [*see* Thérèse de Couagne*] and by 1736 Lepage was on the verge of bankruptcy. Hocquart was now convinced that small-scale enterprises could not succeed and that the Canadian merchants would never transform the economy without substantial support from the crown. "I know, my lord, that the expenditures the king makes in support of this colony are great, and that they are even a burden on the Marine," he explained in 1736, "but . . . the colony is about to become still more useful to France through the cultivation of tobacco, the construction of ships, the mining of iron and copper: but the efforts that will be made here can produce an effect only slowly, if His Majesty does not consent to help us." The previous year he and Beauharnois had sought approval for a 110,000 *livres*' loan to a new company, headed by Cugnet, which intended to develop the Saint-Maurice ironworks into a major industry. In 1736 Hocquart returned to France to appeal personally for more support.

By then, however, the outlook in the ministry had changed. For one thing, Fleury and Maurepas were fearful that a European war would soon erupt over the Austrian succession and that the French navy would be unable to protect France's growing Atlantic trade. This concern led to a new emphasis on the construction of war vessels and to renewed interest in Hocquart's glowing – and, as it proved, over-optimistic – accounts of Canada's timber resources and shipbuilding capability. Later, in 1738, Pierre-Arnaud de Laporte succeeded Pierre de Forcade as first clerk of the colonial bureau in the ministry of Marine. More ambitious and less experienced than Forcade, Arnaud de Laporte was also more dependent on the views of the colonial intendants. Hocquart, it seems clear, convinced him that big industries like the Saint-Maurice ironworks and state shipbuilding would flourish in Canada. In any event, the ministry's financial austerity was relaxed and, between 1736 and 1741, more than 500,000 *livres* in crown funds were invested in or lent to these industries. This largesse contributed significantly to rapid economic growth during the same period.

But if the ministry's financial policy was important, so too was Hocquart's administration of the Canadian finances. He believed that there was a close relationship between government spending and the growth of trade. "The expenditures the king makes in this country," he wrote in 1735, "are responsible for part of the returns. If . . . His Majesty increased those outlays not only would his service benefit from it, but it is clear that trade would expand commensurately." After his first two years at Quebec, when unravelling Dupuy's accounts and stabilizing the financial system were imperatives, he took advantage of every opportunity to increase expenditures. For example, he proposed numerous public works and fortifications from completing the Lachine canal to the construction of a stone wall around Quebec, the estimates for which totalled hundreds of thousands of *livres*. And the projects that were approved, such as the construction of Fort Saint-Frédéric (near Crown Point, N.Y.), always proved more costly than his estimates. Hocquart also made a number of inflated or unauthorized expenditures that were vaguely explained in his annual accounts. This laxity, which perhaps was deliberate, was a constant source of irritation for Maurepas, who reprimanded him repeatedly. Annual expenditures rose very gradually during the 1730s, but Hocquart did all in his power to increase them.

Although government spending benefited a wide cross-section of Canadian society, Hocquart favoured his clients above all others. He did this, first of all, by maintaining control of financial affairs in a closely knit group of civil officials who remained in place through most of his administration. Chief among them were Thomas-Jacques Taschereau*, the agent of the treasurers general of the Marine; Jean-Victor Varin de La Marre, the controller; Honoré Michel* de Villebois de La Rouvillière, the commissary at Montreal; François Foucault*, the king's storekeeper at Quebec and, later, financial officer of the state shipyards; and Cugnet, director of the Domaine d'Occident. These men also formed the corps of Hocquart's judicial clientele in the Conseil Supérieur. Although he continued to ask for administrative help from France, Hocquart had gradually abandoned his criticisms of the Canadian bureaucracy. Instead, he praised his staff of financial officers and civil officials as able men beleaguered by an excess of work. This assessment seems, on the whole, to have been accurate and several officials, Louis-Guillaume Verrier*, Michel de Villebois, and Jean-Eustache Lanoullier* de Boisclerc, were remarkably vigorous and effective. It is true, of course, that Hocquart tended to put too much confidence in his lieutenants, and near the end of his tenure several of them, including Cugnet and the king's storekeeper Louis-Joseph Rocbert de La Morandière, were guilty at times of abusing his trust. On balance, however, Hocquart had one of the most efficient administrative teams in New France's history.

Many of these officials were privately involved in the industrial and agricultural enterprises supported by the intendant. They were given crown loans, fur-trade leases, seigneurial grants, fishing-post leases, advances on their salaries, and extraordinary bonuses; several of them profited from state contracts. On occasion their contract arrangements went well beyond 18th-century standards of public morality. Foucault, for example, purchased bread for the king's store from himself under an assumed name. These bureaucrat-entrepreneurs were in a good position to second Hocquart's efforts to assist other entrepreneurs, such as Denys de La Ronde and Lepage. It is clear, in fact, that the intendant and his team of officials were the driving force behind the expansion of the non-fur economy during the late 1730s.

But Hocquart's energetic efforts extended far beyond government finance. He strove in numerous ways to increase the Canadian merchants', and especially his clients', share of New France's commerce. Despite Maurepas's admonitions, for instance, he made matters difficult for many French merchants trading in Canada. He was slow to assist their agents in collecting debts from Canadians and he used his influence in the Conseil Supérieur to frustrate their legal proceedings. He worked, moreover, to discourage those transient merchants (*marchands forains*) who came to Quebec on a seasonal basis and who took all their profits out of the colony. He did this by nurturing uncertainty whether or not the grain crop would be sufficient to permit exports; by introducing shipping and milling regulations that complicated their transactions; by favouring the spread of resident merchants' stores into the countryside to reduce the *forains*' on-the-scene trading advantages; and by increasing the supply of card money to offset the appeal the *forains* enjoyed when they paid in coin. By the late 1730s fewer and fewer transients were risking the trip to Canada.

In a more positive vein, Hocquart favoured the expansion of the fur trade, particularly the expeditions of Pierre Gaultier* de Varennes et de

La Vérendrye and his sons in the 1730s to open the far west to French influence. Fur-trade profits, he realized, were the major source of investment capital for Canadians interested in developing agriculture and industry. He encouraged prominent fur-traders, such as Lestage and Charly Saint-Ange, to diversify in this way. He also leased government trading posts at Tadoussac, Fort Frontenac (Kingston, Ont.), and Fort Niagara (near Youngstown, N.Y.) to private entrepreneurs such as Cugnet and François Chalet. In the 1740s he advocated leasing all posts then exploited by their military commandants to merchants. He recognized that his proposal was a direct assault on Beauharnois's sphere of patronage which could only result in a deterioration of their relationship, but by that time he was less concerned with Beauharnois's attitude than with pushing aggressively forward with his policy of commercial expansion. This concern helps account, too, for his reluctance to destroy the illegal fur trade, even though he admitted in 1737 that it represented as much as one-third of the traffic in beaver pelts. He explained to the Compagnie des Indes that "the country is so vast and the profits made there so great that it is not possible to destroy [the trade] entirely"; but it is also evident that he regarded those profits as indispensable for the Canadians. Similarly, when the sedentary fisheries along the Labrador and St Lawrence coasts became profitable during the 1730s Hocquart, in cooperation with Beauharnois, recommended grants to several of his clients, including Foucault and Nicolas-Gaspard Boucault*, and stoutly resisted the claims of older concession holders and French merchants, though not always with success [*see* Pierre Constantin*]. As always, he wanted to channel the existing commercial wealth to Canadian entrepreneurs.

Hocquart also strove to eliminate the obstacles to the commercial success of industrial and agricultural ventures. For instance, he was an effective spokesman for Canadian exports, forwarding samples and extolling the qualities of products from beeswax to buffalo hides. He argued vigorously when French inspectors differed with his assessment of these products and others such as lumber, hemp, tar, and tobacco. He took the lead in sending trial shipments of Canadian staples to Martinique and he endeavoured to expand the agricultural trade to Louisbourg. In the latter regard, he supported the claims of Quebec's merchants that the Louisbourg officials, particularly Governor Saint-Ovide [Monbeton*], were tolerant of the illegal trade in foodstuffs with New England which was so detrimental to their interests. He warned that "the merchants of Canada who send [goods] there can sell them only at a loss, and are consequently reluctant to send anything there . . . a disadvantage that leads to others, the price of wheat drops, and the habitants neglect the cultivation of their lands." Secure and substantial markets, Hocquart understood, were vital to the success of Canadian commerce.

Within Canada, Hocquart endorsed virtually every proposal, plausible or bizarre, which offered some hope of developing into a trading enterprise. He even approved a scheme, originating with Cugnet and Jean-Baptiste Gastineau* Duplessis, to transport live buffaloes from the Mississippi River to Quebec which, while it did not amuse the officials at Versailles, must have put the Mississippi Indians' stoicism to a severe test. The intendant also oversaw many improvements to Canada's internal trading system. They included annual expeditions by Quebec's port captain, Richard Testu* de La Richardière, to sound and chart the St Lawrence and its tributaries; the upgrading of Quebec's port facilities, including the construction of a breakwater in the Rivière Saint-Charles, which Hocquart described as "the most useful undertaking I could conceive for the advancement of trade"; ordinances governing the quality and transportation of exports such as flour; and regulations to raise standards in town markets. The ordinances reflecting that aspect of Hocquart's administration devoted to public order are filled with regulations designed to improve exchanges between the countryside and the towns and to promote a more stable and consistent economic atmosphere. It was under Hocquart's direction, furthermore, that the chief road commissioner (*grand voyer*), Jean-Eustache Lanoullier de Boisclerc, constructed two great roads, from Quebec to Montreal and from Montreal to Lake Champlain, which facilitated settlement and the movement of goods within the central colony. Hocquart, in short, was the most industrious intendant since Talon at fostering New France's commercial potential.

Nowhere was this more apparent than in his contribution to the two major colonial industries, the Saint-Maurice ironworks and shipbuilding. Hocquart not only persuaded the ministry in 1736 to lend the Saint-Maurice company the original 110,000 *livres* required to establish the ironworks, but he advanced additional sums on his own authority. When the end came in 1741, the company owed the crown 192,627 *livres*. He also defended Cugnet, the company's financial officer, when it was discovered that he had "borrowed" another 64,302 *livres* from the funds of the Domaine d'Occident. Hocquart intervened with Maurepas on three occasions to delay repayment of the loans and, when iron was finally produced, he permitted the company to sell it to obtain operating capital rather than use it as repayment. In 1740 he loaned the company 3,000 *livres* of his own money. He also helped the Saint-Maurice partners to acquire additional seigneurial grants in the vicinity of the ironworks and facilitated the transportation of iron to both Louisbourg and France. Despite his having recommended the project as a stimulus to other iron-mining ventures, he blocked Abbé Lepage's efforts to establish one at Terrebonne on the grounds that it would injure the Saint-Maurice enterprise. Finally, in 1740, when the company was unable to surmount a number of managerial difficulties, he stepped in to reorganize its operations. From then until the collapse of the Saint-Maurice venture the following year, Hocquart functioned as an unofficial government watchdog.

Besides supervising state shipbuilding, Hocquart's major contribution to that industry was in keeping both the state and the private shipyard supplied with carpenters. He had played down New France's chronic shortage of skilled labour when he confidently asserted that the two shipyards could flourish in harmony. But there were just 50 carpenters at Quebec in 1739, only 20 of whom could be rated first-class. The high wages they were able to command, up to three *livres* per day for a master carpenter, threatened to close down private shipbuilding. Between 1739 and 1743 Hocquart employed various expedients to keep both yards operating. He persuaded the king's shipbuilder, René-Nicolas LEVASSEUR, to employ men from related trades and even unreliable axemen. Carpenters were brought from France and he searched as far afield as Acadia and Louisbourg for more. He also attempted to speed up the training of those in the royal shipyard. On one or two occasions he suspended work on the king's vessels to supply the private shipyard and he allowed carpenters to work on certain religious feast-days. It was largely because of his efforts that private vessels were constructed during this period [*see* Pierre Trottier* Desauniers].

For a number of reasons Hocquart's promotion of agriculture was much less paternalistic. He was unfamiliar with agriculture himself and his close associates in Canada were also town dwellers. Industry, moreover, seemed to offer better prospects for immediate commercial returns. Lumber, ships, iron, copper, and fish were needed in France, whereas grain was not. He believed, too, that a vibrant shipbuilding industry was a necessary prerequisite for the expansion of the grain trade with the other French colonies. Hocquart may also have been discouraged by his initial insights into the unambitious attitudes of the seigneurs and habitants. If so, he became convinced in time that harsh measures, like the edicts of Marly, would be less effective in spurring them on than would a more positive approach. For example, he abandoned his earlier resolve to withhold new seigneurial grants until the existing ones were well established. Instead he and Beauharnois launched the most significant expansion of the seigneurial system since the 17th century. Between 1733 and 1743, 32 new fiefs were granted in previously unsettled areas of the St Lawrence and along key tributaries such as the Chaudière and Richelieu. When not given to military officers in Beauharnois's circle, such as Jean-Baptiste-Nicolas-Roch de RAMEZAY, they went to Hocquart's clients – Taschereau, Cugnet, Foucault, Guillaume ESTÈBE. He trusted that these hand-picked seigneurs would expand settlement. Similarly, he was convinced that promoting the trade of the town merchants, so that they could offer high prices for the habitants' produce, was a better way to encourage surplus productivity than was seizing the habitants' concessions. "Since the habitant has no tax to pay," he wrote in 1741, "[the prospect of] luxury is necessary to encourage him to work. . . ." He acted on this premise by offering unprofitably high prices in the king's stores for hemp and tobacco. Once the habitants saw the advantages of growing these crops, he argued, prices would come down and the merchants would take over. Thus, despite the fact that he issued many ordinances relating to life in the countryside, Hocquart depended mainly on the initiative of his merchant-clients and on the dynamics of the market-place to achieve his goals there.

By 1740 it seemed as though Hocquart was on his way to achieving the economic transformation called for in his instructions. Canada's volume of trade that year was 4,375,184 *livres* compared with 2,817,742 *livres* in 1730, a 39 per cent increase. Exports had increased during the same period by 712,780 *livres*, or 51 per cent, and, between 1739 and 1741, New France enjoyed a favourable balance of trade totalling 262,118 *livres*. Most important, over 50 per cent of the exports during that three-year span were in agricultural and industrial products. Between 20 and 30 ships left Quebec each year with agricultural goods for Louisbourg and the West Indies; in 1739, for instance, their cargoes were valued at 162,017 *livres*. Hocquart could fairly claim that "various kinds of meal and biscuits now constitute a considerable item in Canada's trade." The private ship-building industry had expanded during his tenure to the point where merchants from Bordeaux and Martinique were making plans to build ships at Quebec, and the Saint-Maurice ironworks, which was finally producing iron, promised to add significantly to Canada's exports. Hocquart was also hopeful that state shipbuilding would spur private initiatives in the lumber, tar, and rope-making industries [*see* Médard-Gabriel Vallette* de Chévigny]. Although the state had played a major role in the economic progress of the period, Hocquart saw this role as a kind of midwifery that would give birth to a vibrant Canadian bourgeoisie in the years ahead.

But none of this promise was realized. Between 1741 and 1748, when he left New France, Hocquart witnessed the collapse of his economic policy and, with it, the end of the mercantilist rationale for Canada's role within the French empire. There were many reasons for this collapse and several of them – human failings, natural calamities, and the perils of war – were beyond his control. Yet the shortcomings of his approach to economic development, some typical of the thinking in that era and others the result of his own short-sightedness, played a key part.

The initial shock came in 1741, when the Saint-Maurice ironworks went bankrupt. The ironworks was, in many ways, the linchpin of Hocquart's emphasis on industrial development and its failure revealed many of the drawbacks of that orientation. It was clear, first of all, that the five partners – Cugnet, Taschereau, Jacques Simonet* d'Abergemont, Ignace GAMELIN, and Pierre-François OLIVIER de Vézin – had never possessed enough capital to succeed. Not only did they borrow all of the money to establish the ironworks from the king, but they also borrowed large sums at high interest rates from private sources, Denis GOGUET, Jean Taché*, and Trottier Desauniers among them, to meet operating expenses. In the end, they had incurred total debts of more than 390,000 *livres*. Cugnet, the company's financial officer and the most favoured of all Hocquart's clients, was ruined. He was saved from the dismal consequences of bankruptcy only by Hocquart's intervention. The partners also committed a number of managerial blunders which, taken together, demonstrated that Hocquart had overvalued their entrepreneurial abilities. In financial resources and bourgeois qualities, then, Hocquart's clients were not at all like the successful merchants in the French ports who diversified into primitive industrial ventures.

But still more notable in the Saint-Maurice failure were the material and environmental difficulties that made such an enterprise unprofitable in a remote setting like Canada. Though he had always recognized these problems of markets, transportation, labour, technical expertise, and climate, Hocquart had consistently underestimated them. Now, however, they proved instrumental in transforming the Saint-Maurice project from an example of private initiative into an industrial albatross that the state was obliged to take over. These same problems, particularly high labour costs, led to the collapse of the private shipbuilding industry in 1743. They contributed, too, to the high cost of state shipbuilding, which made a mockery of Hocquart's prediction that the accessibility of lumber would make that industry more economical in Canada. Needless to say, no timber barons emerged to supply the shipyards or to export lumber to France. Pierre Lupien*, *dit* Baron, had some success, but his sons, like Clément de SABREVOIS de Bleury, retreated to the less risky task of supplying the lumber needs of the small domestic economy. As Hocquart dejectedly stated in 1744: "Today I find myself obliged to have the exploitations [of the forests] undertaken economically, that is embarrassing, and to abandon the means of private enterprise for lack of skilled and solvent people." Nor, in this atmosphere, were Canadian merchants interested in taking over any of the smaller export industries operated by the state, such as rope-making and the manufacture of turpentine and glue.

Although the emasculation of private industry that occurred during these years was primarily due to the long-term problems peculiar to that branch of the economy, the process was hastened by agricultural set-backs. Three consecutive crop failures between 1741 and 1743 led to a rise in prices for bread and other staples, the suspension of work on many industries, and ultimately to widespread unemployment among the town-workers. The devastating impact of these natural calamities was at least partly due to Hocquart's neglect of agriculture. This neglect first became apparent in 1741, when he was forced to reunite 21 undeveloped seigneuries to the king's domain, the majority of which were grants that he and Beauharnois had recommended during the previous decade. With the exception of Taschereau his clients had not extended the frontiers of settlement and his own lack of emphasis on immigration, combined with the fact that a high proportion of the rapidly growing population that came of age during the 1730s was attracted to the industrial towns, meant that there were few new tenants available. The intendant's industrial orientation had reinforced the centripetal pattern of settlement which saw most of New France's grain produced within a 30-mile radius of the two main towns. And his relative complacency in promoting the trade of the town merchants, without emphasizing reforms in the countryside, meant that while trade and wheat production increased, the amount of new land brought under cultivation and agricultural methods did not improve commensurately. All of this heightened the colony's vulnerability to crop failure. By 1742 all exports of grain were suspended and Hocquart was obliged to fix the price of wheat to discourage hoarding. When caterpillars destroyed the crops in 1743, he appealed to France for emergency shipments of flour. That winter, rations were distributed by armed guards to the hungry Quebec townsfolk, whose numbers were swelled by starving habitants who poured into the capital to find food. From the bright prospects of the late 1730s, Hocquart found himself struggling to save the colony.

War between France and Britain from 1744 to 1748 dealt a finishing blow to any hopes Hocquart may have had for reviving private initiative in the industrial-agricultural economy. The British naval blockade was so effective during the first two years of the war that trade to and from New France virtually ceased. Between August 1744 and November 1746 only five ships from France dropped anchor at Quebec. According to Hocquart, only 98,744 *livres* in dry goods reached Canada from France in 1745 and only 331,782 *livres* from all sources. Prices rose far above the level that would have permitted profitable industrial activity and trade goods of all types were scarce. "We are totally lacking in blankets, in dry goods, both for the needs of the inhabitants and for the Indians," Hocquart and Beauharnois reported in 1745 and, until a fresh supply of goods reached the western posts in 1747, the fur trade declined sharply. Meanwhile, British privateers ravaged the fishing industry, and agricultural exports, which were just beginning to rebound from the series of crop failures, were hit by military expropriations and by the fall of Louisbourg to Anglo-American forces under William Pepperrell* and Peter Warren*. After Louisbourg was lost Hocquart wrote that "the trade in food, and in other products of the country, has fallen off completely. . . ." From then on, Canadian merchants, who were already intimidated by high wartime insurance and freight rates, kept their ships in port. The most successful of them turned from external trade to supplying the state with war supplies. Instead of commercial bourgeois, they became state contractors.

The war was also disastrous for Hocquart's financial administration. During the early 1740s expenditures on Canada had increased dramatically owing to the high costs of operating state industries and because the economic hardships of the period necessitated extraordinary outlays. Whereas expenditures had averaged 519,180 *livres* from 1738 to 1741, they reached 859,052 *livres* in 1743. The deficit of revenues to expenditures in 1743 was 172,926 *livres*. Yet these statistics paled before the wartime expenditures. The high cost of equipping the numerous war parties led by such men as François-Pierre de RIGAUD de Vaudreuil and Jacques Legardeur* de Saint-Pierre, in Acadia and on the New York frontier, and the staggering sums spent on presents and equipment for Indian allies, not to mention the expense of maintaining as many as 4,000 of their dependants at any one time, raised the average annual expenditure between 1744 and 1748 to 2,056,869 *livres*. Although opinions vary, the deficit for the war years was about 2,500,000 *livres*.

When the treasurer Taschereau resorted to the desperate expedient of issuing millions of *livres* in letters of exchange, drawn on the treasurers general at Paris, as payment for the card money and other secondary currencies brought to him in 1746, Maurepas was beside himself with consternation. "The extraordinary efforts that have had to be made to honour these bills of exchange have so upset the Marine service," he explained to Hocquart in 1747, "that it has been necessary to suspend the most essential operations . . . if the other colonies had caused in proportion half of the expenditures that have been made in Canada since the war, there would not have been enough left to fit out a single ship. . . ." He warned the intendant that his reputation in the Marine service depended upon his ability to reduce expenditures substantially. But Hocquart, who was exhausted by the wartime demands upon his ingenuity and despondent about his own debts which had risen to 24,000 *livres* because of the failure of his personal supplies to reach Quebec, could offer no solution. "You recommend economy to me and reduction in expenditures," he had written as early as 1745, ". . . I have always made that my main concern and if things go otherwise, it must be attributed to the circumstances of the war." He contended then and repeated often thereafter that the governor was solely responsible for war expenditures and that "economy is by no means the commanding virtue of the military."

This comment pointed to yet another aspect of Hocquart's intendancy that had deteriorated since the 1730s. He and Beauharnois had enjoyed amicable relations throughout most of that decade, but as Hocquart's economic proposals found favour in the ministry, bringing him much additional financial patronage, Beauharnois became frustrated and jealous. The governor's patronage had not expanded during the long peace because the military establishment remained relatively static and because the minister was opposed to new western initiatives. Thus, in spite of the absence of any significant constitutional changes, Beauharnois's position had slipped relative to Hocquart's. In peace-time government finance was the main lever of power and as Beauharnois admitted in 1739, "I do not know where Mr. Hocquart is in terms of funds nor what use he makes of them." This state of affairs was aggravated by Hocquart's intrusions into Beauharnois's sphere of authority, especially with respect to the fur-trade role of the commandants at the western posts. By 1740 Beauharnois was criticizing Hocquart in a number of areas, including his favouritism for the Saint-Maurice company in spite of its wasteful expenditures and his direction of state shipbuilding. The governor may also have been the source of rumours about irregularities in Hocquart's financial administration that began in 1739 [*see* Jean de Laporte* de Lalanne] and surfaced regularly thereafter. Although they cooperated during the war, Hocquart suggested to Maurepas that Beauharnois and his senior officers were too old to pursue an aggressive military policy in the Canadian style. He may well have contributed thereby to the governor's recall to France in 1746.

Hocquart was recalled himself in 1748. Although he had been requesting a new post for over a year, it seems likely that Maurepas had decided to replace him with François BIGOT, the financial commissary at Louisbourg, soon after the war began. A number of factors had delayed Bigot's appointment, and he did not reach Quebec until 1748. Hocquart returned to Paris in September of that year and on 1 April 1749 he was appointed intendant at Brest. During his 15-year tenure there he had many contacts with persons passing to and from Quebec and he maintained a private interest in the fishing post of Saint-Modet on the Labrador coast (later traded for Gros Mécatina) and in a seigneury on Lake Champlain, purchased in the early 1760s by Michel CHARTIER de Lotbinière. During the Seven Years' War he fitted out several fleets bound for Canada and helped Acadian refugees resettle in France. After his retirement in 1764 to accept the sinecure of intendant of maritime conscription, he lived frugally in Paris on pensions and his 12,000 *livres*' salary. When he died, he was quite poor. He wanted to leave 13,500 *livres* – a portion to his domestics and the poor of various parishes where he had lived, the rest to be used by the minister of Marine as he saw fit – but he had only 10,554 *livres* in liquid assets.

It is clear from dispatches he wrote in later life that Hocquart regarded his Canadian intendancy as a failure. He had expressed the same view at the end of his tenure when he wrote, "I have gladly sacrificed in the king's service both my youth and the expectations I could have of an advantageous situation. . . . My administration has been more difficult than any of those that preceded it and perhaps several of them together . . . ." The judgement of history, however, is mixed. During Hocquart's 19-year administration, New France experienced its golden age of commercial prosperity. Economic development was more diversified under his direction than at any other time, and his policies served to stabilize the colony's internal social structure. Given the peace-time conditions of the 1730s, some progress in these areas was inevitable. But it was Hocquart who pursued a deliberate economic policy which stressed the private initiative of Canadian merchants in the non-fur economy. It was Hocquart who, through his control of state finance, made the majority of enterprises possible. And it was Hocquart who worked tirelessly to improve the material conditions upon which their success depended. In the process he brought order, if not strict economy, to the Canadian finances and, for more than a decade, harmony to Canadian politics. On the other hand, he placed unreasonable confidence in the good will and entrepreneurial skills of his Canadian clients and underestimated the serious drawbacks of Canada's frontier economy, especially with regard to the lack of trained manpower, the absence of a strong local market for industrial goods, and the costs of transportation that made Canadian products uncompetitive overseas; in consequence he misdirected economic development towards large industries instead of agriculture. By so doing, he increased the colony's vulnerability to the periodic agricultural crises that were a common feature of the *ancien régime*. If he was not responsible for the devastating set-backs of the war years, it was nonetheless true that his departure at the end of the war marked the permanent eclipse of those mercantilist goals that had been the *leitmotiv* of his original instructions. Perhaps Roland-Michel Barrin* de La Galissonière, interim governor of New France from 1748 to 1750, wrote the best epitaph to Hocquart's intendancy in his remarkable memoir on Canada in 1750: "In this memoir, I shall consider Canada strictly as an unproductive frontier. . . ."

DONALD J. HORTON

A portrait of Gilles Hocquart is reproduced in P.-G. Roy, *La ville de Québec sous le Régime français* (2v., Québec, 1930), II, facing 112, and in Régis Roy, "Les intendants de la Nouvelle-France," *infra*, 101. The dispatches that Hocquart wrote after his return from Canada are held at Archives maritimes, Port de Brest (France), 1E, 505–12.

AD, Paris, D[26], no.277; Yvelines (Versailles), F, Fonds Montfermeil. AN, E[1], 1084–89; F[7], 4744; F[12], 76–95; F[15], 3492; T, 77–78, 123, 1100; Col., B, 27–89, 92, 97–98, 102; C[11A], 49–92, 94, 110–21; C[11B], 11, 19–27; C[11E], 13, 16; C[11G], 9–11; D[2C], 2–4, 18, 47/2, 48, 58, 60–61, 222; D[2D], 1; E, 43 (dossier Boucault), 68 (dossier Chalet); F[1A], 25–36; F[2B], 4, 6–7; F[2C], 6; F[3], 11–15, 50; Marine, B[1], 63–98; B[2], 62–191, 279, 286, 337–79, 453; C[1], 153–54; C[7], 20 (dossier Beauharnois de la Boëche), 23 (dossier Bégon, Michel), 143 (dossier Hocquart), 246 (dossier Pichot de Kerdisien de Tremois); Section Outre-mer, G[1], 460–61; Minutier central, XC. ANQ-Q, Greffe de Claude Barolet, 1737–39; Greffe de Nicolas Boisseau, 1733–44; Greffe de Gilbert Boucault de Godefus, 1740–49; Greffe de J.-É. Dubreuil, 1714–39; Greffe d'Henri Hiché, 1728–35; Greffe de Jean de Latour, 1737–41; Greffe de J.-C. Louet, 1723–35; Greffe de J.-N. Pinguet de Vaucour, 1735–43; NF 2, 9–18; NF 4; NF 6, 3; NF 7, 3–9; NF 8. Archives du ministère des Affaires étrangères (Paris), Corr. politique, Angleterre, 498–99; États-Unis, 23; Mémoires et doc., Amérique, 2, 3, 5/3, 7/2, 10, 24 (PAC transcripts). Archives maritimes, Port de Rochefort (France), 1E, 101–13, 350–60; G, 261. ASQ, Fonds Viger-Verreau, Cartons 10, 17. BN, MSS, Coll. Clairambault, 866; Fr., Carrés d'Hozier, 341, no.30570; Coll. Chérin, 106, no.2203; Dossiers bleus, 358, no.9293; Nouveau d'Hozier, 188, no.4131; Pièces originales, 1525, nos.28009, 34774; NAF, Coll. Margry, 9218, 9275, 9281, 9331; Manuscrits isolés, 11332, 20534, 22313. PAC, MG 8, A1, 7–9; MG 18, B12, G9, H13, H40; MG 23, A1, ser. 1, 3–5. PRO, CO 5/133.

Mercure de France (Paris), juin 1739, avril 1750, déc. 1755, juin 1760, janv. 1761, juin 1772. Martin de Malros, *Généalogie de la famille Hocquart* (Auxerre, France, 1958). P.-G. Roy, *Inv. ord. int.* Claude Aboucaya, *Les intendants de la Marine sous l'Ancien Régime . . .* ([Aix, France], 1958). François Bluche, *Les magistrats du parlement de Paris au XVIIIe siècle, 1715–1771* (Paris, 1960). Albert Deschard, *Notice sur l'organisation du corps du commissariat de la Marine française depuis l'origine jusqu'à nos jours . . .* (Paris, 1879). J.-C. Dubé, *Claude-Thomas Dupuy, intendant de la Nouvelle-France, 1678–1738* (Montréal et Paris, [1969]). Maurice Filion, *La pensée et l'action coloniales de Maurepas vis-à-vis du Canada, 1723–1749: l'âge d'or de la colonie* ([Montréal], 1972). Guy Frégault, *La civilisation de la Nouvelle-France, 1713–1744* (2e éd., Ottawa, 1969); *Le XVIIIe siècle canadien: études* (Montréal, 1968; réimpr. 1970). D. J. Horton, "Gilles Hocquart: intendant of New France, 1729–1748" (unpublished PHD thesis, McGill University, Montreal, 1975). Cameron Nish, *François-Étienne Cugnet, 1719–1751: entrepreneur et entreprises en Nouvelle-France* (Montréal, 1975). A. McC. Wilson, *French foreign policy during the administration of Cardinal Fleury, 1726–1743 . . .* (Cambridge, Mass., and London, 1936). J.-C. Dubé, "Origine sociale des intendants de la Nouvelle-France," *Social History*, no.2 (1968), 18–33. P.-G. Roy, "Les commissaires ordinaires de la Marine en la Nouvelle-France," *BRH*, XXIV (1918), 51–54. Régis Roy, "Les intendants de la Nouvelle-France," RSC *Trans.*, 2nd ser., IX (1903), sect.I, 101–3.

HOLMES, WILLIAM, fur-trader; of Irish descent; d. 17 Aug. 1792 in Montreal (Que.).

William Holmes apparently came to Canada some time after 1763, and by 1774 he was actively engaged in the fur trade into the Saskatchewan country. In October 1774 Holmes, Charles Paterson, and François Jérôme, *dit* Latour (Franceway), were reported on their way up the Saskatchewan River with seven canoes to their post at Fort des Prairies (Fort-à-la-Corne, Sask.), where they spent the winter. Holmes was there the next season and on 5 Feb. 1776 set out on an expedition with Alexander Henry* the elder to visit the winter villages of the Assiniboins in the parklands of the Saskatchewan. In May 1777 he was reported going down to Montreal with 12 canoes of furs. About this time he must have formed a partnership with Robert Grant, another Canadian trader, for in April and May of 1778 Holmes, Grant and Company engaged at least four men in Montreal to go to Fort des Prairies. That October Holmes and Booty Graves, an Englishman who had been a partner of Peter Pond* in 1775, travelled up from Montreal with ten canoes to the Canadians' lower settlement, often known as Sturgeon River Fort, on the Saskatchewan River just below its confluence with the Sturgeon River.

During the 1770s competition among the Canadian traders, and between them and the Hudson's Bay Company, was intense; the rivals, pursuing furs and each other, pushed farther and farther into the Saskatchewan country. By March 1779 Holmes had moved up the Saskatchewan River to the Canadians' middle settlement (near Wandsworth, Sask.). There in a space of a few hundred yards were located the HBC's Upper Hudson House and, as the company servant Philip TURNOR wrote, four Canadian houses as well as "about ten small Houses inhabitet by their men, which in fact are trading Houses every one of their men being a trader." Such competition was destructive of profits, and on 1 April Holmes informed Turnor that "the Canadian traders in that River except Blondeaux [Joseph-Barthélemy Blondeau] had then entered into a General Partnership, and they expected he would likewise join them." Partnerships of this kind were common in the Canadian settlements along the Saskatchewan River, and Holmes had probably been party to them. For example, Henry reported that in 1776 the traders at Fort des Prairies had agreed to pool their resources and profits, and this arrangement appears to have been renewed the next year. These local and temporary agreements undoubtedly made Holmes receptive to the idea of one great partnership, for some time in 1779, probably after he returned to Montreal in the late spring, he and Grant were to become joint partners in the founding of the 16-share North West Company.

Despite the "General Partnership" at the middle settlement, Holmes still faced a major rival in the HBC, and he had to resort to tactics the company's servants found offensive. In April 1779 he and his men locked up some Indians who had come down to the settlement, forcing them to trade all their furs with them. When Magnus Twatt, one of the company's servants, protested this action, Holmes was reported to have beaten him "in a cruel manner." Holmes had other problems as well. On the 25th the traders learned of the killing of John COLE three days before by Indians at the Canadians' upper settlement in the Eagle Hills (southwest of Battleford, Sask.). A nervous Turnor wrote that the news had incensed the French Canadian *engagés*, who thought that the HBC had incited the Indians, and he reported that Holmes had had to arm himself against his own men who were "much sett against us and likewise against every Englishman." There being a ratio of 27 Englishmen to about 300 French Canadians, the traders had some cause for worry, but nothing came of the incident.

The fierce competition for furs ensured that Holmes's relations with the HBC would never be good. In October 1779, after William Tomison* had established the HBC's Hudson House about 14 miles downstream from the old post, Holmes arrived to build a post opposite. From there he and Peter Pangman* informed Tomison in December that Cumberland House (Sask.) had been destroyed by Indians. Tomison, however, dismissed the story as untrue, which it was, and the Canadians as "a parcle of villains." The next May Holmes and Pangman obtained from the Indians beaver coats that had been loaned them by the HBC. In retaliation Robert Longmoor*, at Cumberland, impounded the trade goods of Patrick Small, a Canadian trader, and released them only when Small gave him three beaver coats.

Holmes remained active in the Saskatchewan country in the 1780s. The smallpox epidemic that swept through the western Indians in the early years of the decade reduced the fur returns of Holmes and his partners severely; between 1781 and 1782 they dropped from 330 packs to 84. The destruction, by the French under the Comte de Lapérouse [GALAUP], of York and Churchill factories on Hudson Bay in the summer of 1782 cut the source of the HBC servants' supplies and put Holmes in an advantageous position. In October 1783 he was able to sell supplies to Tomison, at Cumberland House, for a price which the latter considered "rather too much." Holmes had a post at Battle River, near the upper settlement, in 1784, but two years later he moved down the Saskatchewan to build at Fort de l'Isle, opposite the HBC's newly established Manchester House (near Pike's Peak, Sask.).

Holmes, who had remained a partner in the NWC throughout the 1780s, retired from the fur trade in 1790. Some time after August 1791 he sold his share in the company to John Gregory*.

ARTHUR J. RAY

Docs. relating to NWC (Wallace). Henry, *Travels and adventures* (Bain). HBRS, XIV (Rich and Johnson); XV (Rich and Johnson). *Hudson's Bay miscellany, 1670–1870*, ed. and intro. Glyndwr Williams (Winnipeg, 1975). *Journals of Hearne and Turnor* (Tyrrell). [Alexander Mackenzie], *The journals and letters of Sir Alexander Mackenzie*, ed. and intro. W. K. Lamb (Toronto, 1970). PAC *Report*, 1888, 59–61. *Saskatchewan journals and correspondence: Edmonton House, 1795–1800; Chesterfield House, 1800–1802*, ed. A. M. Johnson (London, 1967). Massicotte, "Répertoire des engagements pour l'Ouest," ANQ *Rapport*, 1946–47, 306–7. Morton, *History of Canadian west*.

HOPE, HENRY, army officer and colonial administrator; probably b. after 1746, perhaps at Craigie Hall, in Linlithgowshire, Scotland, son of Charles Hope Weir and Lady Anne Vane, grandson of the 1st Earl of Hopetoun; m. Sarah Jones of Mullaghbrack (District of Armagh, Northern Ireland); d. 13 April 1789 at Quebec.

Henry Hope was commissioned captain in the 27th Foot in 1764 while it was in Canada. It is likely that he served with the regiment in Ireland from 1767 to 1775 and met his wife there. In 1775 he went with it to Boston but at once transferred to the 44th Foot, with which he was serving in

Halifax the following spring when he received promotion to major. He campaigned for at least three years in New York, New Jersey, and Pennsylvania, and in 1777 he received his lieutenant-colonelcy. He was absent in England in 1779 and again from 1780 to 1781. The next year he was in Canada once more; he was promoted colonel and visited Michilimackinac (Mackinac Island, Mich.) as a member of a board investigating excessive expenditures at that post. Hope was made quartermaster general in the colony in 1783, and by 1785 he was also commandant at Quebec since the commander-in-chief, Barrimore Matthew St Leger, based himself in Montreal. In October 1785 Hope succeeded St Leger as commander-in-chief.

Hope had secured the patronage of key ministers in the British government. Recommended by Thomas Townshend, Viscount Sydney, who was then in charge of the colonies, on 2 Nov. 1785 he was sworn in as lieutenant governor of Quebec, succeeding Henry Hamilton who had been administrator of the colony since Governor Haldimand's departure. Hope's instructions were to subdue party strife until a new governor should arrive. However, he was already committed to the French party, led by his close friend Dr Adam Mabane, which opposed the commercial interests of the English merchants. His view of colonial administration was profoundly influenced by the American revolution. Convinced that he was preventing a dangerous infringement of the royal prerogative, he was one of those who delayed the consecration of Jean-François Hubert as coadjutor bishop. Because of the "invincible obstacle of having to do with an *Assembly* composed of *Americans*," he refused the lieutenant governorship of New Brunswick. Although in the provision of mill sites he offended the loyalists in Quebec by insisting on the preservation of seigneurial limitations to the crown's benefit, his genuine concern for the refugees shows in his extension of the duration of their provisioning, his facilitation of their claims for war losses, and his support of the isolated Gaspé settlers. He had been delegated much responsibility by British ministers unwilling to be involved openly in the use of Indians to protect Quebec's western flank, and he revealed a shrewd appreciation of the dangers of the developing confrontation between the Indians and Americans in the Ohio country [*see* Egushwa].

Hope was apparently hot-tempered but "a very polite Man," and he kept table "in very genteel Fashion," in fact beyond his means. He was thought an efficient administrator, and after the arrival of Lord Dorchester [Carleton*] as governor general late in 1786, he retained "the management of all business, both civil and military." The new leader of the English party, Chief Justice William Smith, thoroughly disconcerted him, however. Cool and subtle, Smith repeatedly drew Hope into admitting ignorance of council business though he was chairman, changing his votes at meetings, and giving the impression that he lacked self-control and impartiality. In his weakness Hope foolishly tried to hide his association with the French party from the British government and his compromises at council and his gestures to Smith from his party. As opposition to the chief justice grew, however, Hope found it easier again to maintain himself as a champion of the Canadians.

Hope visited Britain in 1788 on private business – perhaps reunion with a wife he had not seen for years, for she accompanied him back to Quebec that autumn. A stormy voyage brought him down with what Mabane diagnosed as a consumption with complications, complications which soon proved to be venereal disease. In April he died from "his improper Gallantries . . . the most shocking object that can be imagined – his Features & the greatest part of his Face entirely destroy'd."

A. J. H. Richardson

BL, Add. mss 21734, ff.419–19v, 421–22; 21736, ff.183–84, 232–37, 276–80, 312–14; 21737, ff.87–88v, 111–11v, 112, 132–33, 204; 21758, ff.679–80. PAC, MG 23, GII, 12, 14 April 1779, 30 April 1789; 21, 30 June 1789; 22, 8 July 1785; HI, 8; MG 24, L3, p.5201. PRO, CO 42/16, p.240; 42/17, pp.94, 110, 119, 131, 146; 42/18, pp.88–93, 133; 42/22, p.29 (copy at PAC); CO 42/47, ff.298–302; 42/48, ff.23–24, 29–29v, 31–33, 34–34v, 168–68v, 174–74v, 176–76v, 194–99v, 209–10v, 215–16v; 42/49, ff.59–67, 77–79, 104–8, 208–10v, 242–44v, 338–41, 371–73 (mfm. at PAC).

[C. L. Baurmeister], *Revolution in America: confidential letters and journals, 1776–1784 . . .*, trans. and ed. B. A. Uhlendorf (New Brunswick, N.J., 1957), 395. *General Sir William Howe's orderly book at Charlestown, Boston and Halifax, June 17, 1775, to 1776, 26 May . . .*, ed. B. F. Stevens, intro. E. E. Hale (London, 1890; repr. Port Washington, N.Y., and London, 1970). *Gentleman's Magazine*, 1746, 164. Thomas Hughes, *A journal . . . 1778–1789*, intro. E. A. Benians (Cambridge, Eng., 1947), 137. *Michigan Pioneer Coll.*, X (1886), 656–59. PAC *Report*, 1889, 138–39, 226–27. PAO *Report*, 1904, 23, 1326, 1331, 1357–58, 1367. *Quebec Gazette*, 16 May 1765, 27 June 1782, 25 Sept. 1788, 9 July 1789. [William Smith], *The diary and selected papers of Chief Justice William Smith, 1784–1793*, ed. L. F. S. Upton (2v., Toronto, 1963–65), II, 157, 161–80, 197, 204, 270. *Burke's peerage* (1967), 1283, 1523, 1526. *DNB*. G.B., WO, *Army list*, 1763–84. A. L. Burt, *Old prov. of Que.* (1933), 352–53, 360,

386–87, 419–21; *The United States, Great Britain and British North America from the revolution to the establishment of peace after the War of 1812* (Toronto and New Haven, Conn., 1940), 142. Neatby, *Quebec*, 209–10. W. C. Trimble, *The historical record of the 27th Inniskilling regiment . . .* (London, 1876), 36–37. L. F. S. Upton, *The loyal whig: William Smith of New York & Quebec* (Toronto, 1969), 177, 180–82.

HOTSINOÑHYAHTA? (written **Chenughiyata, Chinoniata, Kotsinoghyâtà, Otsinughyada, Rozinoghyata**), Onondaga chief; fl. 1748–74. The name the **Bunt**, by which he was generally known to the British, may be a corruption of the German *band*, a cord or sinew, since that is the meaning of his Onondaga name.

Hotsinoñhyahta? was acquainted with the British as early as 1748. He may have been Racsenagate, one of the Onondagas who in March 1751 (o.s.) agreed to deed a large piece of land near their village to William JOHNSON rather than sell it to the French as some of their nation had proposed. In the summer of 1756, when Johnson (now superintendent of northern Indians) accompanied a delegation of Six Nations sachems to a condolence council at Onondaga (near Syracuse, N.Y.), Hotsinoñhyahta? received the mourners. Later that year he sent Johnson word that he was going to Canada and would report on his journey.

The meeting Hotsinoñhyahta? attended at Montreal in December was a large one composed of high French officials and representatives of the domiciliated Indians living near Montreal and of the Ottawas and Potawatomis from the *pays d'en haut*. Governor Vaudreuil [RIGAUD] had called the conference to solicit the neutrality or support of the native people in the war which had broken out between the French and British. Hotsinoñhyahta? stressed the neutrality of the Six Nations and promised to burn the British forts in their villages. When he returned home in the spring of 1757 he sent Johnson word that the French were planning an attack on German Flats, a part of the Mohawk valley near the mouth of West Canada Creek. At a meeting with Johnson in June the Onondagas, Cayugas, and Senecas emphasized their intention to remain neutral.

In the summer of 1758 Hotsinoñhyahta? went to meet Paul-Joseph LE MOYNE de Longueuil near Chouaguen (Oswego, N.Y.). He warned Longueuil, an adopted son of the Six Nations, that the British were assembling men and barges at Fort Bull (east of Oneida Lake) and that an attack on Fort Frontenac (Kingston, Ont.) was rumoured – an attack which occurred a few weeks later. Hotsinoñhyahta? went to Canada in the autumn of 1758. On his return he advised Johnson that a French expedition was preparing to go against Fort Stanwix (Rome, N.Y.).

Johnson's capture of Fort Niagara (near Youngstown, N.Y.) in July 1759 encouraged Iroquois participation on the British side in the war. Hotsinoñhyahta? and his sons joined the forces gathered at Oswego (being rebuilt by the British) for an attack down the St Lawrence. The expedition was postponed, but Hotsinoñhyahta? returned the next year and accompanied AMHERST and Johnson to Montreal.

In September 1762 Hotsinoñhyahta? informed Johnson that "being very old" he needed help in managing the affairs of the Six Nations Confederacy. He asked that his two assistants be given identification papers so that they would be known at the various posts. In following years he attended numerous conferences with the British and privately advised Johnson on various occasions. The missionary Samuel Kirkland described him in 1765 as "a venerable old chief . . . [who] spoke like a Demosthenes." In the autumn of 1768 Hotsinoñhyahta? took part in the negotiations at Fort Stanwix in the course of which the Six Nations and their dependent tribes gave up a large amount of their land to the whites and agreed to a boundary line that was supposed to protect their remaining territory. The treaty was witnessed by one chief for each Iroquois nation; Hotsinoñhyahta? signed for the Onondagas.

The old chief decided to retire in 1771, but Guy JOHNSON, Sir William's deputy, persuaded him to withdraw his resignation. Hotsinoñhyahta? now found walking difficult, and the Indian department accounts for 1771 and 1772 show the purchase of a bateau for him. In 1773 he accompanied Christian Daniel CLAUS, another deputy, to a conference at Canassadaga, the Iroquois village on Lac des Deux-Montagnes (Que.). The Six Nations at this time were concerned with reuniting to the Confederacy those who had separated themselves from it during the wars between Britain and France, and this objective may have prompted the old man to make the journey. In 1774 his resignation on account of his great age was announced, and his long career as a diplomat and politician came to a close.

IN COLLABORATION WITH ARTHUR EINHORN

Hamilton College Library (Clinton, N.Y.), Kirkland MSS, journal of 1764–1765. *Johnson papers* (Sullivan *et al.*). "Mémoire du Canada," ANQ *Rapport*, 1924–25, 142. *NYCD* (O'Callaghan and Fernow). Graymont, *Iroquois*.

HOWARD, JOSEPH, merchant and fur-trader; b. in England; m. *c.* 1763 Marguerite Réaume; d. 5 Dec. 1797 at Berthier-en-Haut (Berthierville, Que.).

Joseph Howard, who may have come from Bristol, arrived in Montreal in 1760 and became one of the first British merchants of that city to enter the western fur trade; he formed a trading partnership with John or Edward Chinn (or both of them) and with Henry Bostwick which sent canoes to Michilimackinac (Mackinaw City, Mich.) in 1761. Soon he was linked by marriage to a large family network of Canadian fur-traders, among whom were the Lemoines and the Couagnes. In December 1763 Howard and other Montreal merchants signed a petition to Thomas GAGE, the acting commander-in-chief, asking that any peace terms made with the then hostile western Indians include the payment of their debts to the traders. After peace was eventually declared, Howard experienced difficulty because of defaulting correspondents at Michilimackinac in 1765 and 1767. He ended his partnership with the Chinns and Bostwick about the latter year, perhaps as a result of an increasingly straitened financial situation: in 1768 his business failed, leaving him with debts that included £4,506 owed to the London firm of Brook Watson*.

Howard had also entered the eastern fur trade. By 1766 he, George Allsopp*, and Edward Chinn had established unlicensed posts in competition with those of the Tadoussac trade (sometimes called the king's posts). In August they were ordered by the Council to remove their posts, but political manœuvring delayed action until after their final appeal was rejected by the Privy Council in the autumn of 1768. Howard may have added lumbering to his business interests. In August 1765 he purchased the seigneury of Ramezay on the Rivière Yamaska, a property which had a good sawmill.

Howard was one of those merchants who became embroiled in a struggle with the British military authorities in the early 1760s. On one occasion he and Thomas WALKER objected, at a merchants' club, to making a courtesy call on the new military governor of Montreal, Ralph Burton*, on New Year's Day, 1764: "very indecent language was made use of, chiefly so by . . . Howard." "Upon clear & undoubted proofs of His disrespect," Howard was dismissed shortly after by Burton from his post as king's auctioneer. Howard does not appear to have carried his opposition to the authorities as far as Walker did, and indeed they were to fall foul of each other in 1766. Walker charged Howard and five military officers in November with responsibility for the beating he had received from masked assailants in 1764. They languished in jail until March 1767 when the charges were finally dropped.

Howard's relations with the authorities who controlled access to the western trade do not appear to have been particularly good. In 1779 HALDIMAND, for military reasons, delayed issuing the passes for the western traders, and Howard, afraid of missing the Indians who had come down to trade, set off for Michilimackinac without one. He was stopped at the post in June by the commandant, Arent Schuyler De Peyster, and sent back. In December he was accused of having aided the escape of Thomas Bentley, a Kaskaskia (Ill.) merchant arrested for corresponding with the Americans, and he was placed on bond. The next March Howard was fined £50 for his unlicensed trip to Michilimackinac, and in May his agent, John Sayer*, was allowed to "collect his effects" from the post but not to trade. In July 1781 Howard received a pass, too late for it to be of use. After missing three trading seasons he faced bankruptcy. He pleaded with the government in October 1781 for an early pass for the next season; he claimed that lack of one "will not only compleat my ruin but hurt some very worthy merchts in London." The next month his request was granted.

Little is known of Howard's later affairs, except that he continued his involvement in the western trade. He signed the 1786 petition of Montreal merchants concerning the disruption in the fur trade caused by an inter-tribal war among the western Indians. That winter he proposed to the government that the fur trade be organized into a monopoly of 100 shares, these to be sold by public auction; he was concerned in part to "restrain the Sale of Rum" to the Indians. His son John and William Oldham formed a short-lived partnership in 1791 to compete with the North West Company, and Howard may have supported the venture. In 1793 he was still sending traders to Michilimackinac (which had been moved to Mackinac Island), but in 1794 his business was bankrupt, probably from losses in the crumbling fur market. Two years later he retired to a quiet life as a rural merchant in Berthier-en-Haut.

A. J. H. RICHARDSON

ANQ-M, Greffe de Peter Lukin, 12 juill. 1794. BL, Add. MSS 21844, ff.465–68, 470, 473. PAC, MG 23, GIII, 5, ff.102–3; 8, pp.100–1; MG 29, A5, 26, James Hallowell to Simon McTavish, 24 Oct. 1791; 27, John Gregory to Simon McTavish, 24 Oct. 1791; RG 68, 238, pp.97–99 (entry listing debts of Joseph Howard, 1768). PRO, CO 42/1, ff.164–65, 180–90; 42/5, f.30; 42/26, pp.234, 242–44, 270–73; 42/53, p.162. *Docs. relating to NWC* (Wallace). *Johnson papers* (Sullivan *et al.*), V, 345, 755–57; X, 992–93. *Michigan Pioneer Coll.*, IX (1886), 357–58, 363, 383–84; X (1886), 504–5; XI (1887), 389–92, 483–86, 503–4, 524–25, 662–63, 669–70; XIX (1891), 491–92, 525. PAC *Report*, 1885, lxxxvii, xciii; 1888, note A, 1–2; 1918, app.B., 38–39, 66. Wis., State Hist. Soc., *Coll.*, XIX (1910), 237–38. Massicotte, "Répertoire des engagements pour l'Ouest," ANQ *Rapport*, 1932–33, 267, 301; 1942–43, 326, 328. P.-G. Roy, *Inv. concessions*, IV, 218–19. Burt, *Old prov. of Que.* (1968), I, 95n, 96–98, 118–19, 122; II, 160.

HUBERT, JEAN-FRANÇOIS, bishop of Quebec; b. 23 Feb. 1739 at Quebec, son of Jacques-François Hubert, a baker, and Marie-Louise Maranda; d. there 17 Oct. 1797.

Jean-François Hubert was educated at the Petit Séminaire de Québec and then in 1755 began theological studies at the Grand Séminaire. In the summer of 1759, when Quebec was under siege, he took refuge at the Sulpician seminary in Montreal where the most advanced students of the Séminaire de Québec had been brought together. There he continued to study under the direction of Abbé Colomban-Sébastien PRESSART. In October 1759 Bishop Pontbriand [Dubreil*] also came to the seminary in Montreal where he again encountered Hubert; Hubert had previously served as the bishop's secretary and he resumed these duties. In the spring of 1760 Pontbriand conferred minor orders on him. At his death in June the prelate bequeathed 300 *livres* to his young secretary. The following year Hubert was one of the first students to return to Quebec, and when the seminary reopened on 15 Oct. 1762 he resumed theological studies. Hubert, who had become secretary to Vicar General Jean-Olivier BRIAND in 1761, had to wait until Briand returned from London as bishop before he received major orders and then, on 20 July 1766, the priesthood. He was the first priest to be anointed by the new bishop.

Devoted to his former teachers and drawn to the missionary ideal of the Séminaire de Québec, Hubert had long sought acceptance into the seminary. He had held the office of bursar since September 1764, and on 7 Aug. 1765 was admitted to the community. During his years at the seminary Hubert would carry out numerous important tasks, while at the same time teaching philosophy and theology and also continuing as Briand's secretary for some 12 years. In the autumn of 1765 he was a director of the Petit Séminaire, at the time when that institution took over from the Jesuit college the responsibility for secondary education and began offering it to all young men who wanted it, not just to those intending to become priests. On 26 April 1768 he was admitted to the seminary's council and on 20 August was appointed a director of the Grand Séminaire. Bursar of the seminary from 1770 to 1777, in 1773 he was again a director of the Petit Séminaire. The next year, on 3 December, he became the first Canadian superior of the Quebec seminary. In choosing a Canadian its members had probably taken into account the desires expressed by MURRAY when he was governor, as well as by the British authorities, who clearly favoured the Canadianization of the clergy, hoping in this way to hasten the breaking of all existing ties between France and the Canadians.

On 12 Aug. 1778 – two years before his term of office as superior was to end – Hubert resigned, to everyone's surprise. The work now being undertaken by the seminary, which had had to give up its missions to devote itself solely to teaching, was no longer to his liking, nor did it suit his health. He joined the Illinois mission as Briand's envoy extraordinary, and was succeeded as head of the seminary by Henri-François Gravé* de La Rive. Returning to Quebec early the next spring, Hubert was appointed vicar general and accepted the office of parish priest of Sainte-Famille on Île d'Orléans. On 27 July 1779 he renounced his membership in the seminary. His stay among the Illinois and his brief stay at Sainte-Famille since 24 March had only confirmed him in his "decision to work at the holy ministry in the missions."

Hubert had probably conceived the idea of devoting himself to the missions through his association with his bishop, and Briand naturally rejoiced in his former secretary's decision. In September 1781 Hubert left his parish charge of Sainte-Famille to fill the gap that Pierre-Philippe POTIER's death had left in Notre-Dame-de-l'Assomption near Detroit; he had visited the parish when he travelled to the Illinois mission. Governor HALDIMAND had furnished Briand's vicar general with a letter of recommendation couched in flattering terms. Hubert served the parish until 1784, building a new church and presbytery and taking an active role in educating the young. In September 1784 he wrote to his bishop: "I should like to be able to reform morals as easily as one can rebuild a presbytery; but alas, how many obstacles there are!" Soon after, Hubert learned of his appointment as coadjutor to the bishop of Quebec.

Bishop Briand had long been thinking of resigning from office. His health left much to be desired, and his coadjutor, Louis-Philippe MARIAUCHAU d'Esgly, was very old; there was great danger that the two bishops would have no successor. On 29 Nov. 1784 Briand resigned in favour of d'Esgly. The delicate question of the choice of a coadjutor had to be faced, and it was important that a young, dynamic priest in good standing with the government be appointed quickly. On 30 November d'Esgly and Briand jointly recommended Jean-François Hubert to the Holy See and signed the act of nomination, on condition that Hubert meet with the approval of London and the authorities in Rome. The clergy, prominent figures in Quebec, and several members of the Legislative Council praised this judicious selection. London, however, was to wait two years before accepting the choice: Haldimand, displeased that Briand had waited for him to leave before resigning, thereby depriving him of a say in the choice of a coadjutor, had intervened, favouring two English monks, a Dominican and a Recollet, for the vacant office in the see of Quebec. On 30 April 1785 Lord Sydney, the Home secretary, informed Lieutenant Governor Henry HAMILTON that the office had to be offered first to the superior of the Sulpicians. In July 1785 Étienne MONTGOLFIER refused it for various reasons, one being his advanced age. Rome had sent the bulls naming Hubert bishop *in partibus* of Almyra and coadjutor of Quebec, and d'Esgly received them early in June 1786. Approval by London, which was slow in coming, followed shortly upon the arrival of the new governor, Lord Dorchester [Guy Carleton*], and on 29 Nov. 1786 Hubert was consecrated bishop by Briand in the cathedral of Quebec.

Scarcely had he been appointed coadjutor when Hubert undertook the first full visitation of the diocese to be made in 15 years. In 1787 he confirmed more than 9,000 people in the District of Montreal alone. The sick and aged d'Esgly, who remained in his parish of Saint-Pierre on Île d'Orléans, could in all tranquillity have left things to his coadjutor. However, his intransigence and his desire that nothing be done without his permission created a number of problems for Hubert and for Vicar General Gravé de La Rive, who were often obliged by circumstance to take decisions without consulting their bishop. In April 1788 d'Esgly threatened Gravé with severe penalties, even going so far as to withdraw his powers as vicar general. Hubert took Gravé's side, while Briand, who was distressed "to see the peace disturbed in this poor church of Canada," exhorted the coadjutor to be patient and advised him to treat his bishop with deference. On 4 June 1788, when Bishop Hubert was on a pastoral visit in the region of Saint-Hyacinthe, d'Esgly died. Hubert returned to Quebec immediately and took possession of his see on 12 June 1788.

The responsibilities the new bishop was assuming were not without their problems; the situation in the diocese worried him particularly. Although the population of the province of Quebec had grown in 30 years from 60,000 to 160,000, in 1790 the clergy numbered only 146 priests, as opposed to 163 in 1760. Furthermore many parishes had no resident priest, and most priests were often called upon to serve two or three parishes. Hubert foresaw no immediate solution. The British authorities opposed the immigration of French priests and denied the Recollets and Jesuits the right to take in novices; moreover, the Society of Jesus had been suppressed by the pope in 1773. There were, on the average, only four ordinations a year of young Canadians, and this scarcely sufficed to fill the vacancies left by deaths. Nevertheless, though conscious of the "small inclination" of Canadian students for the clerical state and of the growth of "the spirit of independence and libertinage" amongst them, the bishop counted heavily on recruiting Canadian subjects; in a memoir to Dorchester on 20 May 1790 he stressed that "in the present state of affairs foreign priests would be of virtually no assistance to the Canadian clergy." As for English priests, he was afraid that "being accustomed to arguing freely on all political matters, [they] might make some unfavourable impressions on the minds of a people to whom [the Canadian clergy] had always preached strict obedience to the orders of the sovereign or his representatives, and complete submission to any legitimate system of laws, without examination or discussion."

The freedom the Canadian church enjoyed was in fact highly relative. Despite certain compromises London had not given up the exercise of its right to keep a vigilant eye on the church, indeed to keep it under its thumb. This limitation was not unknown to Hubert, who later, when writing to the prefect of the Sacred Congregation of Propaganda to suggest that the diocese of Quebec be split, remarked that "on this subject, as on many others, we in Canada are forced to innumerable precautions." He envied the bishop of Baltimore, John Carroll, his liberty of action, since it was entirely within Carroll's discretion in 1791 to entrust the administration of his seminary to Sulpicians who had come from France. "In the United States of America, there is a church that is becoming established with brilliant success. The Congress is protecting it. Is this for [any] motive except those of politics? Not so, but by the consent of Providence who employs all things to accomplish His eternal purposes." The bishop had nevertheless adapted himself to this not too uneasy situation, to the point that in November 1792 he wished the superior of the Missions Étrangères in Paris "as happy a lot as ours in this country, where we enjoy, at least on the government's part, liberty for our holy religion, without worry and without dissension." However, his fears of witnessing both the subjugation of the Canadian church and the Protestantizing of the Canadians by London would be aroused again with the arrival in Quebec of the Anglican bishop, Jacob Mountain*, in 1793.

One of the new bishop's first tasks had been to fill the office of coadjutor. Just as he had designated d'Esgly in 1770, so Dorchester now imposed Charles-François BAILLY de Messein, the parish priest of Saint-François-de-Sales at Pointe-aux-Trembles (Neuville), who was nicknamed "the parish priest of the English." Known for his pro-British sentiments and held in esteem by the governor – he had been tutor to his three children at Quebec and then in England – "the Château's bishop," as Bailly was called, was consecrated on 12 July 1789. Hubert, who was well acquainted with the sensibilities and "the extreme touchiness of the British government," had thought it wise not to object. He had, however, taken care to warn Bailly that he did not intend to entrust him with any specific task or "to lay down in any way the burden that Providence alone" had laid upon him. Bailly did not take kindly to the rather unobtrusive role to which Hubert had condemned him. He publicly opposed his bishop in the *Quebec Gazette* on 29 April 1790: he complained in the name of the clergy about a pastoral letter of 10 Dec. 1788 that restricted the jurisdiction of the priests of the diocese and he blamed his bishop in the name of the citizenry for maintaining too many public holidays, to the detriment of the rural Canadian populace. The split between the bishop and his coadjutor was public, "something that had never been seen in the church of Canada," wrote Hubert to Cardinal Antonèlli. The *Montreal Gazette* supported Bailly on this occasion, but Briand and the Canadian clergy publicly disavowed the coadjutor bishop.

Believing in a church free from political pressure, Hubert always endeavoured to strengthen the Canadian church and to establish relations of friendship and absolute confidence with his clergy and the faithful. At the beginning of his episcopate he wanted to convoke a synod at Quebec but had to abandon the idea because of the governor's opposition. He also early considered splitting his diocese, which was inordinately large, by creating a bishopric in the District of Montreal. But apart from the possibility of government opposition, the conduct of his coadjutor, who was a likely candidate for this bishopric, postponed the execution of this project. Because of his concern for the religious education of the Canadians, who were being increasingly tainted with "impiety" and "the spirit of independence," he encouraged several movements, including the Congrégation des Hommes de Notre-Dame de Québec; indeed upon Augustin-Louis de GLAPION's death in 1790 he took charge of that organization. The well-being and material circumstances of the clergy also engaged Hubert's attention and in 1796 he took an interest in the creation of an ecclesiastical fund to provide for the needs of priests who were "worn out or ill." Believing in order and efficiency, Hubert asked that his letters be transcribed into a special notebook, contrary to the practice of his predecessors who had merely summarized their most important letters on loose sheets. In so doing he initiated the series of registers of correspondence which has continued until the present.

One of the most important of the many problems with which Hubert had to deal was the scheme to establish a university for Catholics and Protestants. This project was to bring the bishop into conflict with his coadjutor Bailly and cause a sensational incident, which was taken up in the newspapers. On 31 May 1787, in view of the lamentable state of education in the province, Dorchester set up a special committee to investigate all aspects of teaching. Chaired by Chief Justice William SMITH, this commission had nine members, of whom four were Canadians. On 13 Aug. 1789 Smith sought the advice of the bishop of Quebec and of Bailly about the establishment of a mixed university at Quebec. Hubert made known his response in a long memoir dated 18 November in which he expressed the opinion that such a project was premature; he emphasized in particular the limited number of students for the professors and the Canadians' general lack of interest in university studies. Hubert also posed several questions. On what level was the proposed new institution to be set up? Who was going to take charge of it? Who would appoint the director? What role would the bishop of Quebec be called upon to play in it? Who exactly would be the "men without prejudices" to be put in charge of the institution as protection for both Catholics and Protestants? Was it not better to support and promote the two existing colleges in Quebec and Montreal and, using the income from the Jesuit estates, to facilitate the reopening of the Jesuit college, which could later be raised to a university? The bishop, like Briand earlier, considered himself the natural guardian of the estates and thought he alone was capable of both utilizing them and making them bear fruit in accordance with the donors' intentions.

The coadjutor's reply to the commission's questionnaire was quite different. On 5 April 1790, four months after the investigating committee had completed its report and adopted a series of resolutions to present to the governor, Bailly sent Mr Justice Smith a long statement, in which he came out in favour of the project and refuted one by one his bishop's arguments. Some months later, in October 1790, Bailly made his letter public. The clergy of the diocese and most of the leading citizens took a stand in favour of Hubert on this occasion, just as they had supported him in May 1790 during the controversy between the two bishops over the reduction in the number of public holidays. The dispute with Bailly was referred to the authorities in Rome, who pronounced in favour of the bishop of Quebec. Bailly was to make his peace with his bishop at the time of his death on 20 May 1794.

The project for a non-sectarian university at Quebec, which was so dear to Dorchester's heart, was not followed up, despite a request presented to the governor on 31 Oct. 1790 by 175 prominent French and English speaking citizens of the province of Quebec and an important legacy from Simon SANGUINET for the founding of such a university. Hubert had not wanted to become involved in a project which, according to him, could have been disastrous to the Canadian people and which, in his view, on the whole presented no guarantee for his compatriots' language and faith. Not that the bishop distrusted the governor's intentions. He considered him "a man without prejudices against Catholics and full of kindnesses for the Canadians." Besides, Dorchester was thinking less of subjugating the church than of entrusting to the state a leadership role in the field of education. But for Hubert teaching was a responsibility of the church, not the state. For his part, Bailly had expressed the opposite view: the projected university was a responsibility of the state, which offered equal guarantees to Catholics and Protestants. Hubert was to claim that the frustrated ambitions of his coadjutor had led to this difference of opinion with him; he was probably not entirely mistaken. But the coadjutor bishop, who had been educated at the Collège Louis-le-Grand in Paris, who read the philosophers of his time and was accustomed to frequenting the English Protestant environment in London and Quebec, showed a rare open-mindedness by his stance. In short, the problem of the denominational school, which would not soon be resolved, had arisen for the first time. Bishop Hubert's attitude, which prevailed at that period in the Canadian clerical milieu, constituted a condemnation of the ideas of the French revolution. He was probably afraid that the projected institution would become the vehicle of ideas hostile to religion and authority. Hubert noted in October 1792 that Canada "is not entirely sheltered from the spiritual evils that afflict Europe. A prodigious number of bad books have come into this country, and with them a spirit of philosophy and a mood of independence which can only have dire consequences." The bishop must have had in mind the struggle against religion, the clergy, and the nobility in which the *Montreal Gazette* and its founder, the Frenchman Fleury MESPLET, were engaged.

This distrust of revolutionary ideas on the part of the religious leaders was all the greater since it coincided with the rise of a new lay élite directly opposed to the clergy and bent on contesting the traditional role of the church in Canadian society. The introduction of parliamentary rule in 1791 was hardly to the clergy's liking. Gravé de La Rive wrote: "Those who, in my opinion, reflect a little are very angry at this change, for there are several of our vain Canadians and many English, admirers of the [French] National Assembly, who are already talking of establishing the rights of man as principles in the laws." As the uncontested spokesman for the Canadians until then and the leading nationalist leader at the end of the 18th century, the bishop of Quebec from then on was engaged in a struggle for power with the new group of lay leaders whose viewpoints and objectives he did not share. The presence in Canada of French emissaries, whose aim was to incite the people to rebel against England, and the vague desires of the former mother country to reconquer Canada, only heightened the bishop's opposition to any return of ungodly France to the shores of the St Lawrence. In November 1793, when a French naval expedition was sailing towards Canada, Hubert called upon the parish priests in his diocese to remind the people of the loyalty, obedience, and fidelity owed to the government. The dangerous state of agitation into which the Canadians were being drawn made "harmony between the state and the priesthood more necessary." In 1796 Hubert issued another vigorous reminder that the Canadians "are under the strict obligation to adhere to the loyalty they have sworn to the king of Great Britain, in prompt obedience to the laws, and in antipathy to any way of thinking that might inspire in them those ideas of rebellion and independence which have for some years made such sad ravages, and from which it is so strongly to be desired that this part of the globe be preserved for ever."

The struggle against the revolutionary ideology was accentuated by the arrival of French royalists who had been driven from their country by the revolution. From 1791 on, 51 *émigré* priests came to Canada; 40 stayed here, including 18 Sulpicians. Although their numbers were small, they were nonetheless of great importance. Before 1790 Canada had received only a handful of French ecclesiastics and at that time had only 146 priests; this number increased by nearly a third in the space of ten years. The French clergy would win renown in the Acadian missions and in the church in Canada, where it would play an important spiritual and cultural role [*see* Jacques-Ladislas de Calonne*; Louis-Joseph Desjardins*, *dit* Desplantes]. At the very time when the Canadian church was approaching a period of austerity which would not come to an end until shortly after 1837, these priests gave the church its second wind. The bishop of Quebec would have liked to receive more *émigré* priests in his diocese. He had several times unburdened himself on this subject to the bishop of Saint-Pol-de-Léon (France), Jean-François de La Marche. "An 'unconstitutional' priest from France, who is hostile to the oath . . . [to the Civil Constitution of the Clergy] and the principles which engendered it, is always welcome in Canada." He had not been afraid to receive with open arms these "zealous and fervent workers," at the risk of displeasing the Canadian clergy, who did not always look favourably on the arrival of the foreign priests. But as long as the diocese could not meet its own needs, Hubert had to act as the protector of the *émigrés*. "Let us get rid of a certain national prejudice; let us adopt a broader and more liberal point of view; let us prefer the general good of the faith to personal views of [our own] interest, and there will not be so much opposition to strangers who are seeking a useful and honourable refuge," he wrote.

Bailly's death in May 1794 again raised the problem of the appointment of a coadjutor. On this occasion Dorchester presented a list of three names to Hubert, who chose Pierre Denaut*, parish priest of Longueuil and since 1790 vicar general. Denaut was consecrated bishop in Montreal on 29 June 1795. Soon after, in July, Hubert left on a pastoral visit to the Baie des Chaleurs region, despite the fears of those close to him. He came back worn out and seriously ill. The following year he was unable to proceed with his plans to go to Halifax. His health worsened. After several stays in hospital, he resigned his office on 1 Sept. 1797 in favour of his coadjutor. He was named parish priest of Château-Richer, but spent barely two weeks there before he was taken to the Hôpital Général in Quebec, where he died a short time later, on 17 October.

GILLES CHAUSSÉ

AAQ, 12 A, C, 111; D, 55v, 60v, 100v, 150v; 20 A, I, 188; II, 1, 16, 28, 36, 51; VI, 25, 30, 101, 104; 210 A, I, 44–46, 102, 221, 273; II, 4, 10, 63, 65–67, 130–31, 222; 22 A, III; 30 A, I, 106–23; 1 CB, V, 6; VI; 516 CD, I, 8a, 9; 61 CD, Sainte-Famille, île d'Orléans, I, 4; CD, Diocèse de Québec, I, 86; II, 47; 7 CM, V, 65–71; 60 CN, I, 31, 32. ACAM, 901.012. ANQ-Q, AP-P-997; État civil, Catholiques, Notre-Dame de Québec, 24 févr. 1739. ASN, AP-G, L.-É. Bois, Succession, XVII, 5–15. ASQ, Évêques, no.159; Fonds A.-H. Gosselin, Cartons 6, 7; Fonds Viger-Verreau, Sér.O, 081, p.21; Lettres, M, 125, 126, 136, 161; P, 158, 165; R, 20; S, 6[Bis], AA; MSS, 12, ff. 32, 34, 36, 38–47; 13; Polygraphie, XVIII, 1; Séminaire, 4, no.133; 73, nos.1, 1a, 1b, 1c, 1d, 7e; 14/3, nos.3, 4. ASSM, 19, tiroir 60; 21, cartons 42, 51; 27, tiroir 94. McGill University Libraries, Dept. of Rare Books and Special Coll., MS coll., CH193.S171.

"Échec de l'université d'État de 1789," Y.-A. Lacroix, édit., *Écrits du Canada français* (Montréal), 28 (1969), 215–56. *Mandements des évêques de Québec* (Têtu et Gagnon), II, 341–502. *Le séminaire de Québec* (Provost), 452. *Montreal Gazette*, 6, 13, 27 May, 3, 10 June, 4, 18, 25 Nov. 1790. *Quebec Gazette*, 29 April, 13, 27 May 1790. Allaire, *Dictionnaire*, I, 272–73. [F.-]M. Bibaud, *Le panthéon canadien; choix de biographies*, Adèle et Victoria Bibaud, édit. (2e éd., Montréal, 1891), 121. Gérard Brassard, *Armorial des évêques du Canada . . .* (Montréal, 1940), 92. Caron, "Inv. de la corr. de Mgr Hubert et de Mgr Bailly de Messein," ANQ *Rapport*, 1930–31, 199–351. Desrosiers, "Corr. de cinq vicaires généraux," ANQ *Rapport*, 1947–48, 76–78, 113–23. Le Jeune, *Dictionnaire*, I, 773–74. P.-G. Roy, *Fils de Québec*, II, 65–68. Tanguay, *Dictionnaire*, IV, 533; *Répertoire*, 7, 136. Henri Têtu, *Notices biographiques: les évêques de Québec* (Québec, 1889), 381–407. L.-P. Audet, *Histoire de l'enseignement au Québec* (2v., Montréal et Toronto, 1971), I: *1608–1840*. N.-E. Dionne, *Les ecclésiastiques et les royalistes français réfugiés au Canada à l'époque de la révolution, 1791–1802* (Québec, 1905). Galarneau, *La France devant l'opinion canadienne*. Lemieux, *L'établissement de la première prov. eccl.* George Paré, *The Catholic Church in Detroit, 1701–1888* (Detroit, 1951). M. Trudel, *L'Église canadienne*.

L.-É. Bois, "L'Angleterre et le clergé français réfugié pendant la Révolution," RSC *Trans.*, 1st ser., III (1885), sect.I, 77–87. D.-A. Gobeil, "Quelques curés de la première paroisse ontarienne, de M. Hubert au curé A. MacDonell, Sandwich, 1781–1831," SCHÉC *Rapport*, 23 (1955–56), 101–16. E. C. Lebel, "History of Assumption, the first parish in Upper Canada," CCHA *Report*, 21 (1953–54), 23–37. Léon Pouliot, "L'enseignement universitaire catholique au Canada français de 1760 à 1860,'' *RHAF*, XII (1958–59), 155–69.

HUGUET, JOSEPH (baptized **Jacques-Joseph**), Jesuit and missionary; b. 25 May 1725 at Saint-Omer, France, son of Jean Huguet and Scholastique-Geneviève Verhoune; d. 5 May 1783 at Sault-Saint-Louis (Caughnawaga, Que.).

Joseph Huguet joined the Society of Jesus at Tournai (Belgium) on 30 Sept. 1744. Between 1746 and 1752 he taught grammar classes at the Collège de Namur and classics and rhetoric at Cambrai; from 1752 to 1756 he studied theology at Douai. On 15 Oct. 1757 his name first appears in the register of the Sault-Saint-Louis mission to the Iroquois. A missionary at Saint-Régis from 1757 to 1759, he returned to Sault-Saint-Louis in 1759. On the death of Father Jean-Baptiste de Neuville in 1761 he became superior of the mission and served in that office for the rest of his life. From 1769 to 1777 Huguet also ministered to Châteauguay.

After the conquest Huguet was virtually the only priest among the Iroquois of Sault-Saint-Louis, and he had to deal with civil authorities who were generally unfriendly. By 1762 he found himself indirectly in conflict with his congregation over the boundaries between the seigneury of Prairie-de-la-Madeleine, which was owned by the Jesuits alone, and that of Sault-Saint-Louis, which belonged jointly to the Jesuits and the Iroquois. The governor of Montreal, Thomas GAGE, first decided in favour of the Iroquois, despite the fact that the Jesuits' claims to Prairie-de-la Madeleine were clear, established in 1647 and reaffirmed by the king of France in 1718. Six months later, however, Gage reversed his decision and ordered the boundary markers replaced in their original location. The matter came before the courts in 1766 and 1768; the Jesuits' rights were upheld, but the strong resentment of the Iroquois caused Huguet deep pain and his prestige was lowered among them. In 1770, however, Huguet had the consolation of seeing how loyal the Iroquois still were to their faith and their missionary when a certain ''Klingancourt'' (probably Mathieu-Benjamin Damours de Clignancour) attempted to stir up trouble in the village; he insulted and slandered Father Huguet. The Iroquois defended their priest saying that he was a peaceful, upright man who did his utmost to settle disturbances. They appealed to Sir William JOHNSON, the superintendent of northern Indians, who promised to settle the matter. Klingancourt had to decamp.

The American revolution was a trying period for Father Huguet. It was uncertain which side the Iroquois of Sault-Saint-Louis would choose. The change of flag in 1760 does not seem to have moved them deeply; they had early made a distinction between political allegiance and the faith brought by the French missionaries. Although loyal to their faith, they had learned through the unbroken relations they had maintained, despite French protests, with the merchants in Albany, New York, that their material interests were better served by the British. At the beginning of the revolution the Iroquois of Sault-Saint-Louis were undecided; British and Americans alike were but invaders. Early American successes had impressed them, however, and they were perhaps more sympathetic to the rebels. Father Huguet might remind the Iroquois of their obligations towards Britain, but in general they did not listen. Nevertheless, from the beginning some Iroquois from the village fought on the British side. On 8 Oct. 1775 Father Huguet buried Ignace and Pierre, ''killed by Bostonnais'' at Saint-Jean, and on 16 October he buried André. But the authorities in Quebec attributed the Iroquois warriors' lack of enthusiasm to Father Huguet; he was suspected, if not of preaching disloyalty, at least of encouraging a spirit of neutrality from which even Claude-Nicolas-Guillaume de Lorimier*, who had great influence in the village because of his long association with them, was unable to move them. Huguet was denounced and in 1776 was removed temporarily from the village.

In June 1777 Father Antoine Gordan, the missionary at Saint-Régis who was to serve as chaplain to the Iroquois warriors accompanying John BURGOYNE's army, asked Governor Sir Guy Carleton* to allow Father Huguet to return to Sault-Saint-Louis, so that the Iroquois would not be without spiritual succour. His request was granted. Father Huguet was the last of New France's Jesuit missionaries. He died at Sault-Saint-Louis on 5 May 1783 and was buried under the church in which he had ministered devotedly for more than 22 years.

JOSEPH COSSETTE

Archives municipales, Saint-Omer (dép. du Pas-de-Calais, France), État civil, Saint-Denis, 25 mai 1725. Archives paroissiales, Saint-François-Xavier (Caughnawaga, Qué.), Registres des baptêmes, mariages et sépultures, 1735–1808. *Invasion du Canada* (Verreau). Caron, ''Inv. de la corr. de Mgr Briand,'' ANQ *Rapport*, 1929-30, 71–78. Mélançon, *Liste des missionnaires jésuites*. E. J. Devine, *Historic Caughnawaga* (Montreal, 1922), 272–331. Lanctot, *Le Canada et la Révolution américaine*. Rochemonteix, *Les jésuites et la N.-F. au XVIIIe siècle*, II, 218. J. Gras, ''The return of the Jesuits to the Iroquois missions,''

Woodstock Letters (Woodstock, Md.), XXXV (1906), 91–100.

HUIQUINANICHI. *See* WIKINANISH

HUPPÉ (Hupé), *dit* **Lagroix (La Groy, Lagroye, Lagrouais), JOSEPH,** mason, joiner, and hatter; b. 6 Nov. 1696 at Beauport (near Quebec) to Jacques Huppé, *dit* Lagroix, and Suzanne Le Normand; d. after 16 Feb. 1776.

Joseph Huppé, *dit* Lagroix, had apparently been a joiner and mason for some time when in 1730 he decided to learn the hatter's trade. His grandfather Michel Huppé, *dit* Lagroix, a Norman who had come to Canada in the mid 17th century, had followed the trade, and Joseph may have had some knowledge of it from his father, who was evidently a farmer.

Huppé apprenticed with the hatter Barthélemy COTTON. On 29 Jan. 1730 the two men signed an agreement by which Cotton undertook to teach his trade to Joseph Huppé, "master mason and joiner." Their association was not long, however. There was apparently a disagreement between them and, in violation of his three-year contract, Huppé left Quebec in the winter of 1731–32. He set himself up in Montreal, where in March 1732 he leased a house on Rue Capitale for six months. Cotton took legal proceedings against him, but nonetheless Huppé stayed in Montreal and followed the hatter's trade until 1736.

The only other hat-maker in Montreal at the time was a Parisian, Jean-Baptiste Chaufour. Neither man enjoyed a considerable trade; they were, according to Governor Charles de Beauharnois* and Intendant Gilles HOCQUART in 1735, "common workers." By official estimate their output and that of Cotton amounted to 1,200 or 1,500 beaver hats a year. They each employed one or two journeymen at most. Since Huppé's wife, Charlotte Jérémie, *dit* Lamontagne, *dit* Douville, whom he had married at Quebec on 27 Nov. 1728, had died in February 1733, he had only one dependant, a daughter.

Insignificant though they were, the three hatters in New France were important to the French government. In 1735 the minister of Marine, Maurepas, claimed that by sending unfinished beaver hats to France they encroached on the Compagnie des Indes's monopoly of the export of beaver pelts. The governor and intendant rejected the claim and were reluctant to forbid hat-making in the colony as the minister wished. Instead, they limited the hatters to the Canadian market and forbad the export of unfinished or incomplete hats. Maurepas was not moved by their appeal on behalf of the Canadian hatmakers; he insisted in his dispatch of May 1736 that the establishments be destroyed.

On 12 September Barthélemy Cotton's shop in Quebec was closed and on the 24th the royal officials in Montreal took action. It was found that Jean-Baptiste Chaufour had not worked as a hat-maker for two years. He accompanied the officials as they proceeded to Huppé's shop, Au Chapeau Royal, in a suburb of Montreal. They inventoried the contents, smashed the basins and the dyeing and fulling vats, and carried off the rest of the hat-making equipment to the king's storehouse. Huppé's loss was put at 676 *livres*, and he later received some compensation from the Compagnie des Indes. His activities after the closing of his shop are unknown, but he seems to have drifted back and forth between Montreal and Quebec. On 16 Feb. 1776 he made his will before the Charlesbourg notary, André Genest. His death date remains unknown.

Historians have tried to make sense of the suppression of the Canadian hatters in 1736. Joseph-Noël Fauteux and Paul-Émile Renaud saw the event as the outcome of French mercantilism, a policy concisely stated in a royal memoir of 1704: "whatever might compete with the manufactures of the realm must never be produced in the colonies." French colonial policy in Canada was, however, not rigidly mercantilistic. Colonial industries duplicating those of the mother country were usually tolerated and often encouraged by France with the aim of fostering colonial self-sufficiency. Lionel Groulx* suggested that the minister's decision was shaped instead by the Compagnie des Indes, which was suffering from a reduced supply of beaver pelts and may have objected to the Canadian diversion of beaver from the export trade. The crown believed that if French hatters had first choice of pelts they would increase their share of the European hat market, and it had a fiscal interest through its connection with the Compagnie des Indes in maintaining the volume of beaver sent from Canada. Therefore the suppression of Canadian hat-making could have been considered to be in the national interest of France.

PETER N. MOOGK

AN, Col., B, 62, f.110; 64/3, ff.608–12; C11A, 63, pp.62–65; 64, pp.69–70; 65, pp.10–16 (copies at PAC). ANQ-Q, Greffe de Claude Barolet, 8 mars 1745, 8 févr. 1755; Greffe d'André Genest, 16 févr. 1776; Greffe de J.-C. Louet, 28 déc. 1731; Greffe de J.-N. Pinguet de Vaucour, 27 nov. 1728; NF 2, 24, f.104; NF 25, 23, nos.876, 879, 891. ASQ, Séminaire, 21, no.2, p.25. ASSM, 24, Dossier 6, cahier NN, 48. IBC, Centre de documentation, Fonds Morisset, Dossier Joseph Huppé, dit Lagroix. P.-G. Roy, *Inv. jug. et délib., 1717–60*, II, 262, 265, 276. Tanguay, *Dictionnaire*. J.-N. Fauteux, *Essai sur l'industrie*, II, 485–90. P.-É. Renaud, *Les origines économiques du Canada; l'œuvre de la France* (Mamers, France, 1928). Sulte, *Hist. des Canadiens français*, IV, 68; V, 83. Lionel Groulx, "Note sur la chapellerie au Canada sous le Régime français," *RHAF*, III (1949–50), 383–401. É.-Z. Massicotte, "L'anéantissement d'une industrie canadienne sous le Régime français," *BRH*, XXVII (1921), 193–200; "Les enseignes à Montréal, autrefois et aujourd'hui," *BRH*, XLVII (1941), 354.

HUTCHINS, THOMAS, HBC chief factor, surgeon, and naturalist; d. 7 July 1790 at Hudson's Bay House, London, England; survived by his wife Margaret.

Thomas Hutchins is an intriguing figure whose importance lies less in his official career with the Hudson's Bay Company than in the controversial subject of his contribution to North American natural history. Hutchins first entered the service of the company in February 1766, when he was appointed surgeon at York Fort (York Factory, Man.) for five years at £36 per annum. He sailed for Hudson Bay that summer in the company of Ferdinand Jacobs, who was returning to his command at York, and arrived in August. During the next few years he became friendly with another company officer, Andrew Graham*, master of the outpost at Severn (Fort Severn, Ont.). When Graham became acting chief at York for the 1771–72 season the two men collaborated in keeping detailed meteorological and natural history observations. The astronomer William Wales had already sent Hutchins directions for observing the eclipse of the sun expected on 6 Nov. 1771, and although Graham helped with the recording of meteorological observations, Hutchins was clearly the leading spirit. In the collecting and describing of natural history specimens for the Royal Society of London, however, Graham was the more experienced partner. In the covering letter to the descriptive notes he sent home in August 1772, Hutchins acknowledged that he had followed "Mr Graham's advice" and described his notes as "not wrote by one who is skilled in zoological affairs, but by a young person seeking after knowledge and improvement, who would think himself extremely happy to be of service to the learned. . . ." The two men sent back to England notes that were separate, but based on the same specimens and measurements, and in general the classification scheme of both the 1772 lists was Graham's. The dedication Graham and Hutchins displayed is the more creditable since the winter of 1771–72 was exceptionally severe, and Hutchins was kept busy tending the sick, sometimes "night as well as day."

In 1773 Hutchins returned to England for a year's leave and during this time agreed with the Royal Society to keep observations on the dipping-needle on his voyage back to the bay, and to carry out experiments at Fort Albany (Ont.), where he had been appointed chief, on congealing mercury by cold. His report on his findings was printed in the society's *Philosophical Transactions* for 1776, and in 1781 he carried out further tests on mercury at Albany. The results were printed in the *Philosophical Transactions* for 1783, were acclaimed by scientists, and gained for Hutchins the award of the Royal Society's Copley medal that year. He was the second HBC servant to be so honoured; Christopher Middleton* had received the medal in 1742.

Hutchins had retired from active service in the bay in 1782, but the next year he took up the post of corresponding secretary to the company at £150 per annum, a position he held despite failing health until his death in July 1790. During this last period of his life Hutchins came into contact with the prominent naturalists Thomas Pennant and John Latham and in his dual role as amateur naturalist and secretary of the HBC supplied them with information on Canadian wildlife. A letter from Hutchins to Pennant in February 1784 shows the two men corresponding on natural history topics, and in the second volume of his celebrated *Arctic zoology*, published in 1785, Pennant noted "I had the good fortune to meet with Mr. *Hutchins*, a gentleman many years resident in *Hudson's Bay*; who with the utmost liberality, communicated to me his MS. observations, in a large folio volume. . . ." In reality, the volume was one of those written by Graham. That its attribution to Hutchins was no accidental misunderstanding is shown not only by continuing references to Hutchins in Pennant's *Supplement* of 1787 but by a repetition of the same process in John Latham's *A general synopsis of birds*. In his third volume, published in 1785, Latham declared himself "indebted to the observations of Mr. *Hutchins*, of the *Hudson's Bay Company*, an intelligent and communicative Naturalist." The many extracts which follow, however, are taken from a manuscript volume of Graham's "Observations on Hudson's Bay" which can be precisely identified as that classified as E.2/10 in the archives of the HBC. The acknowledgements by Pennant and Latham were to be followed by many standard works until the publication in 1969 of parts of Graham's original manuscript, together with related Hutchins papers. These documents showed that while certain volumes of Graham's natural history notes contained some Hutchins material, Hutchins himself, though undoubtedly a genuine enthusiast – "Natural history is my delight" he told Pennant in 1784 – was in comparison with Graham a minor figure. Hutchins apparently appropriated as his own large portions of Graham's notes stored at Hudson's Bay House, thereby winning an undeserved reputation as the leading authority on the natural history of Hudson Bay.

GLYNDWR WILLIAMS

[Most of Thomas Hutchins' known manuscripts are in the archives of the Hudson's Bay Company: B.239/a/17, journal of meteorological observations kept at York Fort in 1771–72; Z.4/1, his letter of February 1784 to Pennant together with notes on "Fish in Hudson's Bay"; E.2/11, volumes of Graham's "Observations" which include notes of Hutchins' scientific experiments; E.2/10 (pp.199–213), another volume of Graham's "Observations" which contain natural history notes kept by Hutchins at Albany, probably between 1780 and 1782. Hutchins' natural history observations written at York in 1771–72 are in the archives of the Royal Society of London, MS.129. His reports to the Royal Society were published as: "An account of the success of some attempts to freeze quicksilver, at Albany Fort, in Hudson's Bay, in the year 1775: with observations on the dipping-needle," *Philosophical Trans.*, LXVI (1776), 174–81, and as "Experiments for ascertaining the point of mercurial congelation," *ibid.*, LXXIII (1783), [303–70]. Much of this material, together with a full discussion of Hutchins' standing as a naturalist, is in HBRS, XXVII (Williams); see in particular R. G. Glover's introduction, xiii–xx, xxxii–xxxvi, and appendices C and E. Some additional notices of Hutchins' activities are to be found in HBC Arch. A.1/42, p.370; A.1/142, p.135; in his obituary, *London Chronicle*, 8 July 1790; in Thomas Pennant, *Arctic zoology* (2v., London, 1784–85), and *Supplement* (London, 1787); and in John Latham, *A general synopsis of birds* (3v. in 6, London, 1781–85). Readers should also consult Glyndwr Williams, "Andrew Graham and Thomas Hutchins: collaboration and plagiarism in 18th-century natural history," *Beaver*, outfit 308.4 (spring 1978), 4–14. G.W.]

I

IMBERT (Imber), BERTRAND, merchant; b. 7 July 1714 at Bayonne, France, son of Pierre Imbert and Saubade Castera (de Cassera); m. 10 April 1752 at Louisbourg, Île Royale (Cape Breton Island), to Anne-Louise Lagrange, daughter of Jean-Baptiste-Martin Lagrange and Marie-Anne Maisonnat, *dit* Baptiste, and granddaughter of Pierre Maisonnat*, *dit* Baptiste; d. 26 Nov. 1775 at Bayonne.

Bertrand Imbert was the son of a master tailor of Agen who had married and settled in Bayonne in 1712. Imbert's godfather, Bertrand Duvergé, a Bayonne merchant with whom Imbert appears to have maintained business relations during his years in Louisbourg, may have provided him with access to the world of commerce. In 1735 Imbert was in Louisbourg and formed a partnership that year with Jean-Baptiste Lannelongue*. Little is known of their early activities, but by the mid 1750s they had become successful merchants and privateers. Imbert's marriage in 1752 may have supplied the partnership with the financial backing necessary to their commercial ventures.

On the eve of the Seven Years' War the fishing enterprise of Imbert and Lannelongue was one of the most considerable on Île Royale. In 1758 they reckoned their holdings at 124,000 *livres*, consisting of a fishing habitation, 40 shallops, and two half-shallops at Petit Lorembec (Little Lorraine), two schooners of 50 tons each, presumably for the metropolitan and intercolonial trade, and a third 50-ton schooner for the coasting trade. The capitulation of Louisbourg in that year entailed severe property losses for Imbert; subsequently his deteriorating financial position was exacerbated by his inability to claim the Louisbourg property he had inherited from his mother-in-law, who died en route to France in 1758, or to collect some 30,000 *livres* – confiscated by the British, according to Imbert's wife.

The partners' activities resumed in Bayonne but were plagued by setbacks. During the war they lost several ships, either wrecked or captured by the British: the snow *Comte de Guiche*, the frigate *Rencontre*, and a 66-ton schooner sent for delivery in 1759 to Joseph-Michel CADET in Quebec for which they had been unable to secure insurance. In 1761 they held 28,000 *livres* of suspended bills of exchange on the treasurers of the Marine and the Colonies and the Compagnie des Indes. In the same year a lawsuit resulting from the loss of a ship, the *Probité*, whose purchaser they had guaranteed at Louisbourg, paralysed their affairs. Nevertheless, with the help of business friends in France, the partners set up a fishery on the island of Saint-Pierre in 1764. Between 1763 and 1766 they sent supplies to the fishery but by 1766 poor catches and the loss of the *Saint-Michel*, wrecked in 1764, had left their affairs in a bad state.

Apparently Imbert weathered the setbacks better than Lannelongue. In 1759, after they had returned to Bayonne, both paid about the same head tax, but by 1766 Lannelongue's assessment had shrunk to four *livres* whereas Imbert was assessed at 11 *livres* plus three *livres* for his household. After Lannelongue's death in 1768, Imbert continued in business; as late as 1771 he shipped a cargo of cod from Bayonne to Bordeaux. He seems to have retired in 1772, for he no longer maintained a clerk at his residence. His wife survived him and was living in Bordeaux in 1789.

T. J. A. Le Goff

AN, Col., B, 95, f.280v; 99, f.34; C[11C], 12–14; E, 227 (dossier Imbert et Lannelongue); Section Outre-mer, G[1], 408/2, ff.231–32; 458, ff.237, 244; 459, f.283v; 466, pièce 76 (1749); 467, pièce 21 (1764); G[2], 202, dossier 289; 209, dossier 496; G[3], 2041/1, 23 sept. 1751; 2047/2, 4 mars 1752. Archives communales, Bayonne (dép. des Basses-Pyrénées), CC, 133–45; EE, 62–72; GG, 56–58, 62, 123, 129. L. M. Hoad, "Surgeons and surgery in Île Royale," *History and Archaeology* (Ottawa), 6 (1976), 259–335.

IRVING, PAULUS ÆMILIUS, army officer, councillor, and administrator of the province of Quebec; b. 23 Sept. 1714 in Dumfriesshire (now part of Dumfries and Galloway), Scotland, son of William Irving, laird of Bonshaw; m. Judith, daughter of Captain William Westfield of Dover; d. 22 April 1796 in England.

Except for a few months in 1766, the life of Paulus Æmilius Irving followed a familiar pattern for British officers serving in Canada in the 18th century. A captain in the 15th Foot in 1753 and a major by 1758, Irving sailed with his regiment early in 1759 to join James Wolfe*'s expedition against Quebec. Although he was slightly wounded in an engagement on 8 August, Irving was ready for action by the time of the battle on the Plains of Abraham in September. His role on that occasion was a minor one since his regiment was stationed at the extreme left of the line towards the rear and was very early detached to protect Côte Sainte-Geneviève where no action developed.

In October 1759 Brigadier-General James Murray appointed Irving quartermaster general to succeed Colonel Guy Carleton* who was recovering from wounds. Irving apparently carried out his responsibilities efficiently during the military régime at Quebec both as quartermaster general and as a member of the Military Council. Promoted lieutenant-colonel in January 1762, he was an obvious choice as one of the members of the council Murray was empowered to select when the civilian government was established in August 1764. He was commissioned lieutenant governor for the District of Montreal just two weeks after he took office as councillor, but the British government doubted that such officials were required in each of the three subdivisions of the colony, and Murray's impassioned defence of Irving's appointment failed to convince the authorities. The turbulent character of Montreal during the two years which followed has been blamed both on the absence of a lieutenant governor and on the quarrel between Brigadier Ralph Burton*, commanding the military forces of the colony, and Governor Murray, who was greatly disappointed to find himself limited to a civilian role.

Events in Montreal, the attack on the merchant Thomas Walker on 6 Dec. 1764 in particular, produced the chaos that resulted in the recall of both Burton and Murray to Britain. As the senior member of the council, Irving, on 30 June 1766, became president of the council and administrator of the colony, a role he was to fill until the arrival from New York of Lieutenant Governor Carleton in late September. Although most ordinances and proclamations passed that summer represented only the official action of the Quebec council on matters previously decided in Britain, one decision was made on 8 August based on the particular point of view of Irving and the majority of the council present. George Allsopp* and other merchants had persisted in regarding the king's posts, lands reserved to the crown, as open for trade in spite of a monopoly granted to certain merchants by Murray, and they had erected buildings on the land in dispute. On 8 August these buildings were ordered removed. Faced by protests against this ruling, Carleton summoned some but not all of the councillors to meet him on 9 October. Irving, who was included, seems to have seen nothing irregular in the meeting at the time; his concern appeared after the event, when four of his friends, James Cuthbert, Adam Mabane, François Mounier*, and Walter Murray, sought and received his support in a remonstrance to the lieutenant governor. Irving, by virtue of his senior position, discussed the matter privately with Carleton. Irving's report of what was said at that meeting differed materially from what Carleton remembered of his own statements. In correspondence with the home government, the lieutenant governor evaded the central legal questions: had the meeting of 9 October been a regular meeting of council or only a committee meeting and had the lieutenant governor the authority to select individual councillors to attend a regular meeting? Within the colony, however, the issue had become the dominance of the king's representative over both factions in the council, the supporters of British merchants on one hand and, on the other, James Murray's friends, known as the French party, of whom Irving and Adam Mabane were the most conspicuous and influential. Within six weeks, both men had been dismissed from the council, ostensibly because they had signed a petition asking for bail for several men accused of complicity in the attack on Thomas Walker two years earlier. Carleton chose to interpret the signatures of Irving and Mabane, but not of other councillors who had signed the petition, as an attempt "to disturb the peace and interrupt the free course of justice." He reasoned that the removal of two would serve as an example to all.

Irving and Mabane protested their dismissal and continued to do so even after Irving had returned to England with his regiment in July 1768. Both eventually regained official confidence; in 1771 Irving was appointed lieutenant governor of Guernsey, serving again with Jeffery AMHERST. His last appointment was the honorary one of lieutenant governor of Upnor Castle, Kent. But the military rewards he received from the British government paled in comparison with those conferred upon his son Paulus Æmilius, a baronet and a general by 1812. Irving seems to have been a worthy career officer caught in a political crisis that was not of his making and beyond his powers to resolve or even descry. It is perhaps significant that, at the height of the dispute when Carleton was ascribing the meanest of motives to his opponents, the worst he could say of Irving was that he had signed documents "because his Friends desired him."

ELIZABETH ARTHUR

PAC, MG 11, [CO 42], Q, 2, pp.32, 206; 26, pp.40, 193; MG 23, A4; GII, 1, ser.1, 3; RG 1, E1, 1–6. *Docs. relating to constitutional history, 1759–91* (Shortt and Doughty; 1918). Knox, *Hist. journal* (Doughty). *Quebec Gazette*, 21 July 1768. Burt, *Old prov. of Que.* Neatby, *Quebec*. A. L. Burt, "Sir Guy Carleton and his first council," *CHR*, IV (1923), 321–32.

ISAAC. *See* GLIKHIKAN

ISBISTER, JOSEPH, HBC chief factor; b. *c.* 1710, son of Adam Isbister and Helen MacKinlay; m. 1748 Judith, daughter of Christopher Middleton*; buried 20 Oct. 1771 at Quebec.

Little is known of Joseph Isbister's youth, but he probably grew up in Stromness, Orkney Islands (U.K.), where his father was a merchant. In 1726 he was apprenticed to Captain Christopher Middleton of the Hudson's Bay Company and served under him in Hudson Bay for the next four years. Isbister was then employed by the company as a sailor in James Bay until 1735, when he was appointed mate of the *Beaver*, an HBC sloop engaged in trade along the East Main (the eastern coasts of Hudson and James bays), and given command of Eastmain House (at the mouth of Rivière Eastmain, Que.), an outpost of Fort Albany (Ont.). Three years later he succeeded Robert Pilgrim* as master of the *Moose River* (II), and in August 1740, after the sudden death of his superior, Rowland Waggoner*, he was elected to the command of Albany.

The first Orkneyman to attain a governorship in the HBC, Isbister proved to be one of the company's most noteworthy officers in the mid 1700s. A man "of great strength and independence of mind," he was not afraid to challenge the authority of the company's London committee, as he did over the matter of inland trade. The company, lacking both the experienced personnel and the birch-bark to build the large canoes necessary for trade in the interior, and also afraid that inland posts would draw trade away from its more easily provisioned bayside posts, had long preferred that its servants persuade the Indians to travel down to Hudson Bay. But this policy placed the company at a disadvantage with its Canadian competitors. In 1743 Isbister reported that Albany's trade had fallen off because some Canadian pedlars had established a post about 120 miles up the Albany River at "the very part that all Cannoes must pass that Come Down to Albany Fort." Convinced that Albany's trade could be saved only by disregarding the company's official policy, in June 1743 he took a small party of men to a strategic spot upstream from the Canadian post, built Henley House (at the junction of the Albany and Kenogami rivers, Ont.), and appointed his brother William* master.

Although the committee approved Isbister's action, it insisted that the function of the small outpost was to be for "defense rather than trade." Isbister, however, displayed an astute and far-sighted appreciation of the needs of the company's trade: inland posts would eventually dominate the company's activities. He was also the first to grapple with the problem of inland transport, and his efforts to build a boat "to draw as little watter as a Canno & Carie more goods" presaged the introduction of the flat-bottomed York boat.

Ill health forced Isbister to relinquish the

command of Albany in 1747. During the following year in Britain he married, and he recovered his health sufficiently to return to Hudson Bay as chief of Prince of Wales's Fort (Churchill, Man.). He retained this post until 1752 when he was again appointed chief at Albany.

Isbister's career provides insight into the company's problems of management and discipline. Although the London committee had drawn up strict rules of conduct for its servants, it depended on the capability and inclination of its overseas officers for their enforcement. Life on the bleak shores of Hudson Bay was hard and monotonous, and it is not surprising that the men sought solace in liquor and Indian women. In 1740 the committee specifically commanded Isbister to stamp out drunkenness, private trade, and "the detestable Sin of Whoring." Following these instructions, he instituted a strict military regimen at Albany and, being a powerful, quick-tempered man, he frequently resorted to physical force to punish those who were refractory or careless. On Christmas day, 1743, he chastized a man for "Caballing" by knocking him down so hard he broke his leg. To another servant, who had neglected his duties while drunk, he applied six lashes with a cat-o'-nine-tails.

The London committee's standing regulation prohibiting the harbouring of Indian women in the posts was more difficult to enforce, in part because it was at variance with the realities of life on the bay. By the mid 18th century it had become customary for chief factors to keep an Indian wife, and Isbister, despite his marriage in 1748, was no exception. These alliances helped cement trade ties with the Indians, and the women, besides answering the men's physical needs, performed important domestic tasks around the post, such as making moccasins and netting snowshoes. As a result, many HBC chief factors allowed their officers and men varying degrees of licence with Indian women. Isbister, however, was particularly strict: everyone but himself was prohibited contact with Indian women. His double standard earned him the bitter resentment of the garrison at Churchill and ultimately culminated in tragedy after his return to Albany. His attempts to re-establish strict discipline there antagonized the men and alienated the Home Guard Indians (Crees), who had been given free access to the fort and its supplies by the previous factor. Wappisis*, one of the leading Indians at Albany, was so enraged when William Lamb, master at Henley, followed Isbister's example that in December 1754 he and some relatives plundered the post and killed the men.

Isbister, who refused to acknowledge that his own behaviour had been an indirect cause of Henley's destruction, blamed the whole affair on French intrigue. Fearful that the post would fall into French hands, he ordered a party of Indians to burn it, but his prime concern was to bring the responsible parties to justice. When his suspicions concerning the involvement of Wappisis, who had returned nonchalantly to Albany, were confirmed, he brought him and his two sons to trial, found them guilty, and sentenced them to hang. Although determined "to let the Indians Know that the English will not put up with Such Villainous Treatment," Isbister delayed carrying out the sentence until he had received the approbation of the Moose council. The London committee reprimanded him not for his execution of the Indians but rather for his failure to re-establish Henley. Isbister was prevented from doing so, however, by the refusal of most of his men to go inland again.

In 1756 Isbister's contract expired and, in compliance with his wishes and in fear for his safety should the Indians seek revenge, the London committee recalled him. A gratuity from the committee several years later indicates that he did not leave the company on bad terms.

In 1760 Isbister, along with his wife and six small children, immigrated to Quebec City. Governor James MURRAY was instrumental in securing for him the lease of the post of Mingan from Jacques de Lafontaine* de Belcour. Isbister got along well with the Indians because of his knowledge of their language, and Murray later observed that "prudence made it Necessary at that time of War to be careful who occupied the Posts in the Gulph and River of St Lawrence." In 1763 Isbister purchased a property on the Rue des Remparts in Quebec. He died in the city in October 1771 "of a Decay and wore out lungs." His wife and children returned to England.

SYLVIA VAN KIRK

ANQ-Q, État civil, Anglicans, Cathedral of the Holy Trinity (Québec), 20 Oct. 1771. HBC Arch. A.1/37, ff.253, 296; A.1/43, ff.150, 172; A.1/144, f.56; A.5/1, f.13d; A.6/6, f.96; A.6/7, ff.1, 157; A.6/8, f.112; A.6/9, f.9; A.11/2, ff.101–2, 164, 173–75d; A.11/3, ff.10–11; A.16/2, f.50; A.16/10, f.19; B.3/a/30, f.8; B.3/a/34, ff.8, 36–37; B.3/a/35, f.17; B.3/a/37, f.11; B.3/a/46, ff.5, 17; B.3/a/47, ff.41–42d; B.42/a/36, f.20; B.42/a/38, ff.25d, 27d. PAC, MG 8, G24, 10, f.19; RG 4, B28, 24, 9 Nov. 1771; RG 68, 331, f.551. PRO, CO 42/1, ff.155–56, 293–95. HBRS, XXVII (Williams). *Letters from Hudson's Bay, 1703–40*, ed. K. G. Davies and A. M. Johnson, intro. R. [G.] Glover (London, 1965). Rich, *History of HBC*. J. S. Clouston, "Orkney and the Hudson's Bay Company," *Beaver*, outfit 267 (March 1937), 38–43, 63.

J

JACAU (Jacault, Jacob) DE FIEDMONT, LOUIS-THOMAS, artillery officer; b. *c.* 1723, probably on Île Royale (Cape Breton Island), son of Thomas Jacau, a master gunner, and Anne Melanson, *dit* La Verdure; d. unmarried, 25 Aug. 1788 at Belleville (Paris), France.

Louis-Thomas Jacau de Fiedmont rose from the ranks to become an officer. He entered the army as a non-commissioned officer and in 1743 was admitted to the gunners of Île Royale as a cadet under his brother-in-law Philippe-Joseph d'ALLARD de Sainte-Marie. He was subsequently in France, but in May 1747 as part of Governor Taffanel* de La Jonquière's squadron he sailed on the *Sérieux* from the Île d'Aix, off Rochefort, for New France. On 14 May he was taken prisoner in a battle fought with a British squadron under Vice-Admiral George Anson off Cape Ortegal, Spain. The following year he was promoted ensign in the artillery company of Île Royale, a rank he retained when he went to Canada in 1750. Commended as "very reliable," on 1 April 1753 he was named lieutenant and given command of the artillery in Acadia. He apparently was serving as an engineer at Fort Beauséjour (near Sackville, N.B.) when it was captured by the British under Robert MONCKTON in 1755. The next year he served with distinction in Montcalm*'s attack on Oswego (Chouaguen), no doubt the reason for his promotion to captain in March 1757.

The year 1757 brought Jacau other satisfactions. In May he was instructed to take a detachment of workmen organized in Quebec by the artillery commander, François-Marc-Antoine LE MERCIER, to Fort Carillon (Ticonderoga, N.Y.). Upon reaching Lake Champlain he suggested to the officer commanding the sector, Bourlamaque*, that boats armed with one cannon each be constructed to serve as redoubts cruising lakes Champlain and Saint-Sacrement (Lake George) as veritable floating batteries. This project, which Montcalm had already approved, greatly interested Bourlamaque. On 1 August a boat built according to Jacau's plans headed the French fleet which sailed under Montcalm's orders towards the southern end of Lac Saint-Sacrement to lay siege to Fort William Henry (also called Fort George; now Lake George, N.Y.). Similar boats, called "jacobites" probably after their inventor, Jacau or Jacob, were used on many occasions throughout the Seven Years' War.

Jacau returned to Fort Carillon with workmen in May 1758 and was in the battle there on 8 July. In May 1759 he was employed building a bridge over the Rivière Saint-Charles near Quebec. During the siege of Quebec he served with the artillery under Le Mercier and later Fiacre-François POTOT de Montbeillard. In the council of war that Jean-Baptiste-Nicolas-Roch de RAMEZAY assembled on 15 Sept. 1759 to decide what policy should be adopted after the defeat on the Plains of Abraham, Jacau de Fiedmont alone declared himself in favour of a last-ditch stand, suggesting that "rations be reduced and the fortress be defended to the very end." Some days later Governor Vaudreuil [RIGAUD] noted that "he behaved admirably and deserves the highest praise and His Majesty's favours." On 8 Feb. 1760 Jacau was made a knight of the order of Saint-Louis.

Jacau sailed for France on the *Félicité* which was wrecked some 130 leagues from the Azores; he reached the islands in a small open boat in May 1760. Promoted lieutenant-colonel on 15 April 1762, he was sent to French Guiana that year to command the artillery. In September 1763 he was appointed second in command of the colony, and two years later became its governor. He remained in Guiana until 1783, reaching the rank of infantry brigadier in 1769 and major-general in 1780. He had found the colony in great disorder and governed it wisely, trying among other things to increase settlement, in particular by assisting Canadians who had taken refuge in France to establish themselves in Guiana. In 1771 the king had granted him a pension of 2,000 *livres* and praised his administration, "his good services and his impartiality."

By nature gentle and quick to make friends, Jacau de Fiedmont was known for his integrity and was always well respected. During his years of service in Canada he earned a great deal of praise from his superiors. In 1761 Bourlamaque testified that "nothing can be added to the esteem that the Sieur de Fiedmont has acquired through his courage and the particular talents he has demonstrated on a host of occasions when he was extremely useful. The success of most of his ideas was ensured by his zeal and was a complete fulfilment of objectives." Nevertheless he was reproached as governor of Guiana for being too stubborn and headstrong and showing "too much leniency to the officers who are almost all Canadians like himself."

ÉTIENNE TAILLEMITE

AMA, SHA, A[1], 2794. AN, Y, 15682; Col., C[11A], 105, ff.348, 349, 469v; 120, f.299; C[14], 25–28, 31bis, 32, 34, 36, 38, 43, 44, 50; D[2C], 4, ff.76, 133; 5, ff.214v, 224v, 252; 58, f.1v; 59, p.17; 127, f.3; 137, f.1; E, 183 (dossier Fiedmont); Section Outre-mer, G[2], 184, ff.368–75; Minutier central, LXXVIII, no.936. Bougainville, "Journal" (A.-E. Gosselin), ANQ *Rapport*, 1923–24, 294, 309, 331, 342, 345, 359. *Coll. des manuscrits de Lévis* (Casgrain), IV, 43, 86, 127; V, 147, 151, 155, 166, 173, 183, 221, 253, 275; VI, 49, 173, 183, 216; VII, 190, 202, 207, 274, 386, 405, 411, 477, 479, 529, 531, 561, 573; XI, 7. *Doc. relatifs à la monnaie sous le Régime français* (Shortt), II, 814, 816. "Journal du siège de Québec" (Æ. Fauteux), ANQ *Rapport*, 1920–21, 144, 210. "Mémoire du Canada," ANQ *Rapport*, 1924–25, 103, 109–10, 132–33, 151. "La mission de M. de Bougainville en France en 1758–1759," ANQ *Rapport*, 1923–24, 15–16, 34, 41. *NYCD* (O'Callaghan and Fernow), X. PAC *Rapport*, 1905, I, VIe partie, 233. Æ. Fauteux, *Les chevaliers de Saint-Louis*, 173–74.

JACOBS, FERDINAND, HBC chief factor; b. *c.* 1713, probably in England; buried 21 Nov. 1783 in the parish of St Sepulchre, West Ham (Greater London), England.

Ferdinand Jacobs was engaged as an apprentice by the Hudson's Bay Company in London on 20 April 1732. During his seven-year term the company was to supply him with clothes and "other necessaries" and at the end he was to receive £10. He sailed for Prince of Wales's Fort (Churchill, Man.) that spring. In 1739 the chief factor there, Richard Norton*, described him as a "very Sober Deserving Young Man," and he was granted an annual salary of £12. The following year he was appointed "accomptant" and assistant to the chief for three years, with a salary of £20 per annum.

Jacobs was a diligent and reliable officer who worked vigorously at the various jobs assigned to him. In addition to his duties as accountant he had charge of one of the main spring goose hunts, when in a month almost 3,000 geese would be shot and salted. In 1746 he took responsibility for obtaining the fort's supply of wood, involving 20 men in four months of work. Jacobs, who had been appointed second under Robert Pilgrim* in 1745, continued in that position until 1752 when he succeeded Joseph ISBISTER as chief and began receiving an annual salary of £70.

The servants at Prince of Wales's Fort, described by Isbister in 1748 as "a most intolerable Set of Sots," sorely tested Jacobs' patience during his first two years as chief. He sent the two worst offenders back to England and quickly brought order to the management of the fort. He sent the sloop north on exploring missions every year and also secured the services of MATONABBEE, who became a leading Indian at the post. The construction of the post's fortifications proceeded under his guidance, and at the end of three years the southwest curtain had been completed, part of the west bastion rebuilt, and new gun platforms laid. On 18 Aug. 1757 he informed the London committee with unconscious irony that "Better work Never was Done to the Building . . . which I am sure will stand for many Centurys." In August 1782 it fell to the Comte de Lapérouse [GALAUP], who blew holes in the walls Jacobs had so painstakingly built.

Private trade in furs among company officers and servants was a serious problem for the London committee. In 1755 they wrote to Jacobs saying that they were "apprehensive from the large quantity of Furrs & Skins sent home on your account . . . you include therein those given by the Leading Indians in return for Presents made them of our goods." The following year he received the strongest company censure of his long and active career: he was again reprimanded and told that the number of furs he had claimed exceeded that of all "our other Chiefs in the Bay put together." Although Jacobs attempted to defend himself by saying that the furs had been given him in a "bond of friendship," he was thoroughly familiar with the company's trade policies and must have known that a three-year total of private furs with a net value of over £200 would be questioned.

Jacobs sailed to England on a year's leave of absence in 1759 and returned to Churchill the following year with an increased salary of £100 per annum. On the death of James Isham* in 1761 he asked to be made chief at York Factory (Man.), "[my] State of Health being much Impair'd by my Constant application & Constant attention to the many works [at Churchill]." The request was granted and he arrived at York in 1762. By this time Jacobs had spent 30 years on Hudson Bay and had an unrivalled knowledge of the company's business and the preferences of his Indian customers.

Jacobs continued to implement the London committee's policy of trying to persuade the Indians to bring their furs down to the bay by sending a number of expeditions inland from York. The policy was not successful in the long run. The Indians dreaded the long, arduous journey to the bay, and when Canadian pedlars entered their territory they traded with them. In the years after the conclusion of the Seven Years' War and Pontiac*'s uprising, when trade through Montreal began to revive, fur returns at York dropped precipitously. In 1768 Jacobs wrote to the London committee urging that a post be built inland to compete with the Canadian traders. Consent was grudgingly given, but a shortage of qualified men and river craft delayed the project. It was not until 1774 that he was able to send Samuel HEARNE and Matthew COCKING up the Saskatchewan River to found Cumberland House (Sask.), the company's first western inland establishment. The next year, after 43 years of service at the bay, Jacobs retired from the company and returned to London. He died in November 1783.

Although it has been stated that Jacobs was "Canada's first Jew," no record of his religion has been traced in the HBC Archives. From the fort journals it is evident that he supported the Church of England. Like many company officers Jacobs formed an alliance with an Indian woman, and it is known that they had a son and a daughter. His son Samuel, who later served as an officer in the East India Company at Madras, India, was christened by the surgeon at Churchill on 22 Feb. 1756, and Jacobs himself was buried in a Church of England cemetery.

The HBC was well served by Ferdinand Jacobs. He realized the importance of initiating inland trade and advocated the building of inland posts to meet the competition of the Montreal traders. When the days were too short for the Indians to hunt, he fed them. He tried to curb the drunkenness of the company's servants and encouraged them as well to attend divine service on Sundays. He treated both master and servant with fairness and understanding.

SHIRLEE ANNE SMITH

Guildhall Library (London), parish of St Sepulchre [1774–92], register of the book of burials, 1774, no.34. HBC Arch. A.1/41, f.100; A.1/45, f.43d; A.1/140, f.76; A.1/144, f.10; A.5/1, ff.10d, 15d, 30; A.6/6, f.78; A.6/7, ff.75d, 183; A.6/10, f.31; A.6/12, ff.106, 164; A.6/13, f.135d; A.6/16, f.179d; A.11/13, ff.60, 122, 128–28d, 132d, 134, 138, 144, 150, 150d, 162, 174; A.11/15, f.22; A.11/115, ff.80, 116d, 168, 176d; A.11/155, ff.65, 77; B.42/a/25, f.32; B.42/a/28, ff.18d, 20d, 30; B.42/a/32, f.13d; B.42/a/40, f.26; B.42/a/46, f.22d; B.42/d/14–19; B.239/a/59, f.203; B.239/a/65, f.18; C.1/379, f.35. India Office Records (London), file FL2/PS/606 (letter from Mrs Judith Chibbett). PRO, Prob. 11/1110, f.569. Hearne, *Journey from Prince of Wales's Fort* (Glover). A. A. Chiel, "Manitoba Jewish history – early times," Hist. and Scientific Soc. of Man., *Trans.* (Winnipeg), 3rd ser., no.10 (1955), 14–29.

JACOBS, SAMUEL, merchant; date and place of birth unknown; d. on or about 10 Aug. 1786, probably at Saint-Denis, on the Rivière Richelieu (Que.).

According to American historian Jacob Rader Marcus, Samuel Jacobs was probably of Alsatian origin. He arrived in Canada with the British army during the Seven Years' War and did business as a purveyor to the troops, especially the officers. Some promissory notes and receipts confirm his presence in January 1758 at Fort Cumberland (near Sackville, N.B.), where he apparently engaged mainly in the liquor trade. From 1759 to 1761 he was in partnership on equal terms with William Buttar and Alexander Mackenzie in a brewery at Louisbourg, Cape Breton Island. Jacobs seems to have devoted little time to it, choosing instead to take his schooner *Betsey* and follow the British fleet when it sailed for Quebec in the summer of 1759. That autumn he was preparing to send his vessel to Oporto (Porto), Portugal, but General James MURRAY requisitioned the little ship to ply between Île d'Orléans and Quebec. He later requested compensation for the losses he had suffered in consequence.

The end of the war led Jacobs to try his luck in the new British colony. A few papers which seem to be in his handwriting, in particular a large invoice made out to Laurent Bertrand (Bertrend) dated 20 Oct. 1760, suggest that Jacobs spoke French. He seems to have been a wealthy merchant already, since by the transaction Bertrand consigned £2,525 worth of furs to him and Jacobs sold him wine, spirits, salt pork, coffee, sugar, and salt, for £1,444. By 3 November Jacobs had paid what he still owed Bertrand.

Jacobs evidently was at home among both old and new subjects of His Britannic Majesty; he did business with the Canadians as easily as with the British or his fellow Jews. Around 1760 he was trading with Aaron HART, who later set up business in Trois-Rivières, and with Eleazar Levy, who after settling for a time in Quebec finally moved to New York about 1771. Through his Jewish connections Jacobs established firm commercial relations with New York, where Hyam Myers was his principal agent. Myers also travelled frequently to Quebec and in 1772 lived in Levy's house before returning to New York, where he disappears from sight.

Jacobs early grasped the importance of the Richelieu route. He set up stores along it from Crown Point (N.Y.) to Sorel. In 1763 he thought it advisable to open a store at Saint-Denis, which he entrusted to Charles Curtius. Jacobs' account books show the extent of his trading activity. In the single month of November 1763 he received at least 18 different shipments, carefully noting the names of the ships and captains. These deliveries included coffee, salt, and sugar, and especially a large number of pipes of wine and spirits. He exported mainly wheat, apples, and furs.

While living in Quebec, where he owned some property, he concentrated his activity along the Richelieu. In a document dated 3 April 1770 he listed the plots of land he had bought at Saint-Denis from 31 Jan. 1769 on, valuing them at £2,700. On 1 July 1770 he made a list of his accounts at his store in Sorel: 183 debtors owed him £5,270 18*s*. 11*d*. He also did a good deal of business at Saint-Ours and Saint-Charles.

Jacobs finally settled at Saint-Denis. In addition to buying and running a general store, he operated a distillery and had an interest in pearl-ash, which he exported to England. One of his business associates at that time was George Allsopp*. As well as being Allsopp's partner in these various industries, Jacobs acted as his supplier of wheat in exchange for wholesale goods.

Innumerable letters bear witness to the attention that Samuel Jacobs paid to his children's education. Although English seems to have been the language used at home, he entrusted at least two of his daughters to the Ursulines of Quebec and wanted them to learn French thoroughly. Thus, in a letter of 16 March 1763 he exhorted his daughter Mary Geneviève, who was living in Charles Grant's home, to continue to be "a good girl, virtuous, obediant," adding "I charge you to write to me at least once a month in french." His oldest son, Samuel, boarded for a time in Elias Salomon's home and studied at John Reid's private school in Quebec. Writing to Samuel's father, on 2 Nov. 1780, Salomon emphasized that the son was, at 16, beginning to be almost a man and asked that the father increase his board and also his pocket money. The two failed to reach agreement, however, not least because Jacobs accused Salomon's two daughters of having been "very generous" under their mother's lenient eye: the three of them had spoiled his boy for him. Samuel moved to Reid's home, and Charles Grant was asked to keep an eye on him.

Unlike most Jews of the period, Samuel Jacobs married a French Canadian, not a Jewess. In 1784 he regularized his situation with Marie-Josette Audette, *dit* Lapointe, the marriage licence being issued by Governor HALDIMAND on 15 October. How old Jacobs was at that time is not known. He may not have been in good health. In any case, he made his will that day: "If I die at St. Denis aforesaid," he wrote, "my will is that I be Buried at Sorel, . . . near to some old soldier there." He bequeathed his furniture and household goods to his wife, as well as the usufruct of £1,500, with the obligation to bequeath the capital to at least three of his children. He left the rest of his estate to his "two eldest natural daughters, Mary Geneviève and Mary Marianne," and his son Samuel. He did not forget his other children: John Levy, John Baptist, Baptist Samuel, and his youngest daughter Angélique. On 3 Aug. 1785, after having threatened Mary Geneviève that he would cut her off with a shilling if she married Stanislas Vigneault without his consent, he did in fact cut off her inheritance, except for the shilling, and forbad his wife, on pain of being herself disinherited, to give her any assistance whatever.

Jacobs died on or about 10 Aug. 1786. He left his executor, Edward William Gray*, a heavy task, since the value of the property involved made it necessary for him to guard the rich merchant's papers carefully. Jacobs' widow took as her second husband Jean-Baptiste Rieutord*, a doctor from Trois-Rivières. She in turn died in 1806. An extremely complex notarial deed, now in the Baby collection, again left Edward William Gray the task of settling the delicate question of the inheritance, raised this time by the new will left by the widow, in which she is called "mother and step-mother" of Samuel Jacobs' children.

The Saint-Denis merchant was a colourful man and his correspondence shows an original mind. A musician in his leisure, he was fond of reading plays and was not unwilling to use a theatrical style himself. Even though he did not attend the synagogue in Montreal and had made a Protestant marriage, he gave proof of his Jewish conscience on many occasions. He knew a little Hebrew and enjoyed signing certain letters "Shemuel," shaping the final "l" in the Hebrew manner. He even left a long account of the American invasion in Hebrew characters which no one so far has succeeded in fully understanding. The learned Dr Marcus and his colleagues at Hebrew Union College and the American Jewish Archives in Cincinnati have not been able to decipher much of it.

Samuel Jacobs left numerous business papers which shed some light on the earliest Jews in Canada, with whom he had throughout his life maintained close relations. To those previously mentioned should be added his brother Thomas, Gershom and Isaac Levy, Simon Nathan, Lazarus David, Samuel Judah, and Abraham

Jacobs. He remains, however, an enigmatic personality. More knowledge of him could not fail to provide new insights into "the morrows of the conquest."

DENIS VAUGEOIS

[The Jacobs papers at the PAC (MG 19, A2, ser.3, 1–246) are the most important primary source. They form part of the Ermatinger family collection; one of the Ermatingers was the executor for Edward William Gray, who was himself responsible for Samuel Jacobs' estate. The papers permit a close examination of Jacobs' commercial activities but tell us little about his family situation. At the Archives du séminaire de Trois-Rivières, the Fonds Hart, 1760–1865, contain numerous references to Jacobs, and the parish archives of Saint-Denis (Saint-Denis-sur-Richelieu, Que.) includes documents (23 oct. 1772, 6 août 1776, 14 mai 1780, 27 juill. 1781) concerning Jacobs' children, who were raised as Catholics. Additional information is to be found in ANQ-Q, Greffe de P.-L. Descheneaux, 13 déc. 1787.

The most important printed sources and studies include: *American Jewry: documents; eighteenth century; primarily hitherto unpublished manuscripts*, ed. J. R. Marcus (Cincinnati, Ohio, 1959); J. R. Marcus, *Early American Jewry* (2v., Philadelphia, 1951–53), I, 240–51; II, 497; David Roberts, "George Allsopp, Quebec merchant, 1733–1805" (unpublished MA thesis, Queen's University, Kingston, Ont., 1974); Denis Vaugeois, *Les Juifs et la Nouvelle-France* (Trois-Rivières, 1968), 118–28; *Canadian Jewish Archives* (Montreal), I (1959), nos.4 and 5; P.-G. Roy, "La maison Montcalm sur les Remparts à Québec," *BRH*, VIII (1902), 265. D.V.]

JACQUERAULT (Jacquero). *See* JACRAU

JACQUET (Jacquiers), FRANÇOIS, potter; b. *c.* 1731, probably at Bourgoin-Jaillieu, France, son of Joseph Jacquet, a manufacturer of faience, and Louise Giroux; d. some time after 1777.

François Jacquet came to Canada as a soldier in the colonial regular troops and was discharged on 2 Dec. 1751. On 10 Jan. 1752 he married Élisabeth Bourget in Quebec. The marriage contract, concluded the previous day before notary Gilbert Boucault* de Godefus, indicates that he was living in the house of the widow Fornel [Marie-Anne BARBEL] "in his capacity as a potter," and this evidence suggests that he must have apprenticed in France with his father. On 31 May 1752 Jacquet engaged himself to work for Marie-Anne Barbel for three years, but by the end of the summer problems had developed. Jacquet wanted to leave the shop, located near the Rivière Saint-Charles, alleging that "the building which constitutes the pottery is uninhabitable . . . is in danger of collapsing" and "has holes all over, with water leaking in." At the beginning of the winter he complained that "the clay . . . in the aforementioned pottery is frozen so hard that it cannot be used for its intended purpose."

Whether she liked it or not, Marie-Anne Barbel had to do without the services of her potter, because on 18 Nov. 1752 he went into partnership with merchant Pierre Révol*. According to the contract, Révol advanced 2,913 *livres* 14 *sols* to buy clay and the "tools necessary to use it," while Jacquet undertook to work for him for five years, with profits and losses to be shared equally. Their association lasted less than two years since on 16 March 1755 Jacquet went into partnership with Jean Teissier to manufacture bricks and hired "as brick-maker, Pierre Fournier living at Cap-Rouge." This new partnership was dissolved on 2 July.

Between 1752 and 1766 François Jacquet acquired some lots on the right bank of the Rivière Saint-Charles. He apparently found usable clay on the spot and set up shop there. There is no indication that he trained apprentices, but in 1757 he hired Joseph François, *dit* Saint-François, "to be and in his capacity as journeyman potter," and in 1763 he hired a potter named Jacob Steinner. From 1762 on, probably because there were no longer imports from France, Jacquet signed numerous contracts to make earthenware articles for Quebec merchants, such as François Dambourgès. He received orders for cooking pots, plates, and dishes of all sorts. Many such items dating from this period have been found, but none can be attributed with certainty to Jacquet.

Jacquet seems to have been in financial difficulties in the spring of 1770. He disposed of part of his land in March, and a little later his remaining properties, together with their buildings – two houses, a barn, and a shop with a kiln – were seized. In April he took legal action against Guillot Poulin to obtain payment for earthenware. His situation does not seem to have improved subsequently, since in September he signed a bond for 1,739 *livres* 19 *sols* in favour of Gabriel Messayé, a Quebec baker. He probably left the city at that period to set up business in Montreal. On 18 Oct. 1777 he took inventory of his shop in the *faubourg* Saint-Joseph, after the sudden departure of his partner Joseph, who was identified as "Irish by birth." In the shop there were many earthenware soup bowls, chamber pots, cooking pots, butter crocks, soup tureens, and dishes, and some unused "powdered clay." This is the last record of François Jacquet; the date and place of his death remain unknown.

François Jacquet was one of the few potters working in New France, a situation no doubt explained by the massive importation of pottery from France. In 1747 earthenware goods worth 250,000 *livres* were exported from La Rochelle to the West Indies, Louisiana, and Canada, and in 1758 51,000 *livres*' worth. It was only after the conquest that this craft really began to develop, and more information about Jacquet's career might illustrate its growth.

IN COLLABORATION WITH MICHEL GAUMOND

AMHDQ, Papier terrier, Quartier Saint-Sauveur, Procès-verbal du terrain des pauvres . . . , 18 août 1762, no.4, ff.62, 63. ANQ-M, Doc. jud., Cour des plaidoyers communs, Registres, 1770–85; Greffe d'Antoine Foucher, 18 oct. 1777. ANQ-Q, État civil, Catholiques, Notre-Dame de Québec, 10 janv. 1752; Greffe de Claude Barolet, 20 déc. 1752; Greffe de Gilbert Boucault de Godefus, 9 janv., 26 juill. 1752, 21 août 1753, 16 mars 1755; Greffe de C.-H. Du Laurent, 31 mai 1752, 20 mai 1757; Greffe de Claude Louet, 13 déc. 1764; Greffe de F.-E. Moreau, 14 mai, 1er sept., 21 nov. 1764, 15 mai 1765; Greffe de J.-C. Panet, 18 nov. 1752; Greffe de J.-A. Saillant, 28 oct. 1762; Greffe de Simon Sanguinet, 2 sept. 1763, 7 mars, 12 sept. 1770; NF 19, 100, f.41v; QBC 28, Conseil militaire, 1er, 11 avril 1761; IBC, Centre de documentation, Fonds Morisset, Dossier François Jacquet. Private archives, J.-P. Cloutier (Prescott, Ont.), Lettre de Jean Chapelot. *Quebec Gazette*, 10 May 1770. P.-G. Roy, *Inv. jug. et délib., 1717–60*, V, 249–50; *Inv. procès-verbaux des grands voyers*, II, 247. Tanguay, *Dictionnaire*.

JACRAU (Jacquero, Jacquerault), JOSEPH-ANDRÉ-MATHURIN, parish priest, procurator of the seminary of Quebec, and promoter of justice in the diocesan tribunal; b. *c.* 1698 in the diocese of Angers, France; d. 23 July 1772 in Quebec.

Joseph-André-Mathurin Jacrau must have arrived in Canada by 1725; he received the tonsure and minor orders from Bishop Saint-Vallier [La Croix*] on 16 March 1726 in the chapel of the Hôpital Général in Quebec, where he was also ordained priest on 24 November. Since he had already attained the mature age of 28 years by the time of his ordination, the bishop put him in charge of the parish of Ancienne-Lorette at the beginning of 1727. He had some legal quarrels with his predecessor, Charles-Joseph Le Berre, and with habitants who were unwilling to comply with the public ordinance concerning the parish districts. In 1737 Jacrau asked to be admitted as a member of the community of the Séminaire de Québec; his request was granted on 15 October and approved the same day by the vicar general, Jean-Pierre de MINIAC. The new member, who was recognized for his business acumen, received the office of procurator, probably at the end of 1738. In order that he might hold the office, he was admitted without delay to the council of the community, a decision which the directors in Paris approved without hesitation. In addition, in 1739 the superior, François-Elzéar Vallier*, who was about to sail to France for reasons of health, delegated to him his powers as procurator for Bishop DOSQUET, who had been absent from the colony since 1735.

Jacrau was promoter of justice in the diocesan tribunal from 12 Dec. 1740 and, after the death of Charles Plante* in 1744, the seminary appointed him substitute priest for the parish of Quebec. He is known to have prepared the nominal census of Quebec and its suburbs which was begun on 15 Sept. 1740. In addition, Jacrau became acting superior of the seminary, succeeding Abbé Vallier, who died on 16 Jan. 1747. In this capacity he had a number of disagreements with Bishop Pontbriand [Dubreil*]. Jacrau claimed that the seminary of Quebec was neither an episcopal nor a diocesan seminary, and that it was subject solely to the authority of the Missions Étrangères in Paris. Bishop Pontbriand, who could not admit such claims, took over the direction of the seminary. When informed of this conflict the authorities in Paris sent Christophe de Lalane to Quebec and he replaced Jacrau as superior in the summer of 1748. On 20 Sept. 1749 the seminary relieved him of his parochial duties in the parish church of Notre-Dame in Quebec with the appointment of a new titular parish priest, Jean-Félix Récher*, so that Jacrau was able to devote himself entirely to the office of procurator, which he had resumed in November 1748; from the following year on he was assisted by a layman, David Mouisset. In 1752 he was replaced as procurator by Colomban-Sébastien PRESSART, whose assistant he became, but he resumed the office in 1756. When various lawsuits were subsequently brought against the seminary, particularly by the chapter of Quebec, the procurators of the seminary were provided with ample material to keep them busy as archivists [*see* René-Jean Allenou* de Lavillangevin].

Jacrau was one of the five priests of the seminary who went through the crucial period of the conquest. Having remained alone in Quebec with Urbain BOIRET to watch over the seminary's property during the siege in 1759, he was devoting himself to the spiritual care of the patients in the Hôpital Général when he fell seriously ill in September; he hovered between life and death until March of the following year. He recovered somewhat but remained an invalid, which did not prevent him when the war was over from helping in the restoration of the seminary, and also of the seigneury of Beaupré, which had been completely devastated by the British. Jacrau was also chaplain to the nuns of the Hôtel-Dieu from 1761 to 1764.

Jacrau, who had been Canon Jean-Olivier BRIAND's regular confessor since 1753, took advantage of Briand's voyage to England in the autumn of 1764 to accompany him as far as Dover, before returning to his native land for a while in the hope of recovering his health. They met again at the beginning of 1766 in Paris, where Jacrau was a witness at the inquiry into the character of the future bishop of Quebec, and on 28 June they returned to Canada together. Jacrau made some attempt to attend again to the business of the seminary but his health continued to deteriorate. He made known his last wishes, which he had written down before his departure for France, and died on 23 July 1772. He was buried the next day in the crypt of the chapel.

At the time of his voyage to France Jacrau had asked the king for a pension, which was granted in 1768, and thus he was able to acquire a personal library of about 200 volumes, which he left to the seminary. This library, whose inventory has been preserved, included at least 45 works on ecclesiastical, civil, and criminal law, since along with his business sense Jacrau had an acknowledged talent for legal matters; the attorney general Francis Maseres* described him as "a very learned French lawyer."

It was probably because of the competence in legal matters of Jacrau and of his colleague Pressart that in 1767 or at the beginning of 1768 Lieutenant Governor Guy Carleton* referred to the priests of the seminary the abridgment of the French civil laws in effect in Canada which had been prepared by François-Joseph CUGNET at the request of the Privy Council. The priests were not satisfied with the document, and Carleton asked them to write an abridgment of the customary law of Paris. Their text met with no more favour than had Cugnet's with a number of Canadian gentlemen who cannot be identified with certainty; according to Maseres they were three or four of the most prominent seigneurs in the country. Carleton therefore invited these critics to collaborate with Cugnet and the priests of the seminary in the preparation of a document that he could submit to the Privy Council. Their work, known in Canada as the "Extrait des Messieurs," was composed of five fascicules which were published in London under Maseres's instructions. The first three appeared in 1772 and the remaining two the following year. Although the texts were written in French, each bore a long English title. One of these fascicules had Cugnet as its author; the other four were the work of "a Select Committee of Canadian Gentlemen, well skilled in the Laws of France and of that Province," and Abbé Jacrau was certainly a member of this committee.

HONORIUS PROVOST

AAQ, 12 A, C, 34, 37 (Jacrau's certificates of ordination to the diaconate and priesthood are written in his own hand). ASQ, C 9; C 11; C 22; Chapitre, 150, 152; Évêques, no.206; Lettres, M, 91, 93, 112; R, 8, 132, 134, 135; S, 72, 74; MSS, 12, ff.3, 7, 13, 23; Polygraphie, III, 61; VII, 102, 102a, 115, 120; XV, 24b; XXIII, 1; Séminaire, 3, no.7; 4, nos.128–29d; 28, no.22. Philéas Gagnon, *Essai de bibliographie canadienne . . .* (2v., Québec et Montréal, 1895–1913), I, 2. P.-G. Roy, *Inv. jug. et délib., 1717–60*, II, 184, 199; III, 266. A.-H. Gosselin, *L'Église du Canada après la Conquête*, I. M. Trudel, *L'Église canadienne*. Leland, "François-Joseph Cugnet," *Revue de l'université Laval*, XVII, 448, 450–53, 455–56, 820, 822–23.

JADIS, CHARLES NEWLAND GODFREY, naval officer, army officer, and merchant; b. 6 Nov. 1730 at Portsmouth, England, only child of John Godfrey Maximilian Jadis and Elizabeth Newland; m. Margaret —, and they had at least seven children; d. some time after August 1788.

Most of what is known about Charles Newland Godfrey Jadis comes from the several petitions and claims he set out in later life. The son of an officer in the Royal Navy, Jadis joined the *Bedford* in 1741 as a midshipman and served in the Mediterranean during the War of the Austrian Succession. He left the navy after the peace of 1748 and seven years later was commissioned ensign in the 54th Foot (renumbered 52nd Foot in 1757), an unusual but not unique change of career. Promoted captain-lieutenant by January 1762, he accompanied his regiment from Ireland to Quebec in 1765 but was shipwrecked in the St Lawrence during the voyage. The accident undermined his health, and two years later he sold his commission and returned to Ireland.

With the conclusion of the Seven Years' War, what is now New Brunswick had been opened up to British settlement, and in 1764 a society of military officers was formed in Montreal for the purpose of obtaining a large land grant on the Saint John River [*see* Beamsley Perkins GLASIER]. Whether Jadis was connected with this society before his departure from Canada is not known, but in 1768 he purchased lands at Grimross (Gagetown, N.B.) from Synge Tottenham, one of the grantees. In August of the following year he and his family arrived at Halifax equipped with merchandise for trade with the Indians of the Saint John valley. On his arrival at Fort Frederick (Saint John) in May 1770, Jadis found that the Malecite Indians there were hostile to British settlement, and he was several times threatened "with Immediate distruction." When he moved to his lands soon thereafter he met with a similar reception from Pierre TOMAH and others. After several months of harassment his house, store, and trade goods were destroyed by fire in February 1771 and he and his family returned to Halifax. Jadis blamed the fire on the Indians, incited, he believed, by James Simonds*, a rival trader living at Portland Point (Saint John). An employee of Simonds stated in an affidavit that Simonds had declared an intention to have the Indians burn Jadis' house. The allegation is scarcely necessary to sustain the reputation of the firm of Simonds, William Hazen*, and James White as the monopolists of the Saint John trade prior to the American revolution. They regarded the valley as their own commercial preserve and the appearance of Jadis as an act of effrontery.

Temporarily set back, Jadis travelled to England, where he received some compensation for his losses from the British government. In the winter of 1772–73 he returned to Nova Scotia and with James Burrow conducted an investigation into smuggling on the Saint John and at Halifax. He returned to his lands in 1774, just as the turmoil of the American revolution was spreading to Maugerville, principal settlement of New Englanders on the Saint John. One of the few supporters of British and Nova Scotian authority in a region that was still largely wilderness, Jadis soon incurred the hostility of the Maugerville settlers, and their attempt to force his acceptance of the authority of Congress brought systematic persecution. In September 1775 he wrote to Governor Francis LEGGE, "I am daily in dread of my and family's lives. . . . They have broke my ribs and . . . carried me into the woods." The following year, as Maugerville's leaders prepared to assist a rebel invasion of Nova Scotia [*see* Jonathan Eddy*], pressure on Jadis mounted and he was threatened with imprisonment. After begging for permission to leave the province, in July he was given a pass by Jacob Barker, chairman of the Maugerville committee of safety, to go to New England. Instead, he made his way to Halifax, where he reported events to the magistrates and unsuccessfully offered to return to the Saint John with a party of soldiers to restore provincial authority.

Jadis' whereabouts until 1784 are unknown, but in October of that year he reappeared in Halifax and was granted lands by Governor John PARR to replace those he had been forced to leave. Parr refused, however, to restore his property on the Saint John or to grant Jadis the financial compensation he demanded. Jadis went to England to press his claim, and his last appearance in the records is in August 1788.

IN COLLABORATION WITH W. S. MACNUTT

PRO, AO 13, bundle 92; CO 217/26, ff.111–13; 217/35, ff.2, 10–11, 191–93; 217/48, ff.92–93. G.B., WO, *Army list*, 1756–68. Brebner, *Neutral Yankees* (1969), 109n. Murdoch, *History of N.S.*, II, 502. Raymond, *River St. John* (1910), 192; "Brigadier General Monckton's expedition to the River Saint John in September, 1758 . . . ," N.B. Hist. Soc., *Coll.*, III (1907–14), no.8, 113–65.

JARVIS, EDWARD, HBC chief factor; d. *c.* 1800.

Edward Jarvis was initially employed by the Hudson's Bay Company in 1771 to serve as surgeon to Fort Albany (Ont.) for three years at £40 per annum. Within two years he had mastered the Home Guard (Cree) language, and this achievement, along with his youthful energy, made him the logical and willing choice as leader of a proposed survey of the company's territories bounded by the Moose and Albany rivers, James Bay, and Lake Superior. The company considered the survey vital to its fortunes. In order to counter the increasing competition of the Canadian pedlars, whose trade was making serious inroads into company fur returns, it was necessary to map strategic points for the establishment of posts on the yet unknown rivers of the interior. Jarvis' work, along with that of Philip TURNOR, was intended to locate those points.

Jarvis' first expedition, which left Albany on 29 March 1775, ended abortively at Henley House (at the junction of the Albany and Kenogami rivers), when the Indians there refused to provide guides. He returned to Albany and on 3 October set out for the Chepysippy (Kabinekagami) River, in company with Questach, the captain of the Albany goose hunters. He crossed over to the Missinaibi River and on 19 Nov. 1775 reached Moose Factory (Ont.). Back at Henley in February 1776, he set out that May to survey the Canadian establishments on Lake Superior at Michipicoten (Michipicoten River, Ont.). He arrived there on 19 June and made detailed observations of the two groups of Canadians, one of them composed of servants of Alexander Henry* the elder. He then left on his return journey, reaching Albany on 5 July. Jarvis' explorations gave the company considerable insight into the geography of the Albany-Moose area and an idea of the strengths and weaknesses of the Canadian opposition.

Jarvis' journals indicate that he was particularly ill suited to face the problems that plagued most early explorers. He suffered from extreme temperatures, diarrhoea, black flies and mosquitoes, and starvation; at the end of his last trip he was so thin that he had to wear a "bandage" over his shoulder to keep his "trouzers" up. Unaccustomed to the Indians' habit of feast or famine, he balked when they expected him to eat 15 pounds of cooked beaver at one meal. Jarvis was also totally dependent on the Indians of the interior for guides; the HBC servants might desire a clearer knowledge of company territory, but the Indians were not always willing to grant it to them. According to Thomas HUTCHINS, chief at Albany, the Indians had refused to guide Jarvis on his first journey because they were opposed to company exploration, finding "it more beneficial to have two places of opposite Interests to resort to, where each by presents endeavours to gain them for the other."

The remainder of Jarvis' career was neither remarkable nor exciting. Having refused to go inland again after the 1776 expedition, he spent the years 1776–78 shuttling between Albany and Henley. In September 1778 he went to England; he re-enlisted with the company the next year as chief at Moose for five years at £130 per annum. In 1781 the command at Albany fell vacant and he requested and was granted a transfer to that post.

As chief Jarvis advocated a policy of inland expansion, supporting the establishment of posts in order to "distress the North West Company and cut their Communication with the Interior Country where their whole trade is Carried on." Like Hutchins and Humphrey MARTEN, his predecessors at Albany, he encouraged the hiring of Canadians to man these posts, although by 1791 both he and the London committee had cooled to the idea. In 1792 the precarious state of his health forced his retirement to England.

Jarvis was re-engaged by the company in 1796 and appointed chief inspector and supervisor of the posts on Hudson and James bays. The appointment was an effort on the part of the London committee to reconcile the sometimes conflicting aspirations of its chief factors in Rupert's Land. Jarvis, a noted advocate of Albany's interests, was given a cool reception at York Factory (Man.) on his arrival in August. His ill health prevented the completion of his overhaul of the company's posts, and in 1797 he retired on an annual pension of 50 guineas. He probably died some time after March 1800, the date of the last payment to him.

Little is known of Jarvis' personal life, except that he had a brother in desperate financial straits and an aged relative, both of whom he supported. The mixed-blood mother of his son was "the daughter of an Englishman" with "few or no Indian friends." Fearing for his son in case of his wife's death, Jarvis had thought it best to send the boy to England in 1784 to be educated.

F. PANNEKOEK

HBC Arch. A.1/43, f.116; A.1/47, ff.75, 108d; A.1/140, f.79; A.6/16, f.34; A.11/3, ff.197, 199; A.11/4, ff.23d, 162, 210; A.11/5, ff.102, 189d; A.11/55, p.123; A.19/2, f.87; B.3/a/71–74; B.86/a/29, ff.2–14, 29; B.86/a/30–32. *Moose Fort journals, 1783–85*, ed. E. E. Rich and A. M. Johnson, intro. G. P. de T. Glazebrook (London, 1954). Morton, *History of Canadian west*. Rich, *History of HBC*.

JAUTARD, VALENTIN, lawyer and journalist; b. *c.* 1738 in France; d. 8 June 1787 in Montreal (Que.).

Valentin Jautard, a much abused figure in Quebec history, arrived in America at an unknown date. On 4 June 1765 he bought from Jean-Baptiste Lagrange the property of the Sainte-Famille mission among the Tamaroas at Cahokia (East St Louis, Ill.) [*see* Jacques-François Forget* Duverger]. Some time later the bishop of Quebec's vicar general, Sébastien-Louis Meurin, was successful in preventing him from reselling it to an Englishman. Although he had left Cahokia, Jautard retained possession until November 1786, when the ownership of the mission's property was submitted to arbitration, which went against him.

Jautard arrived in the province of Quebec in 1767 and on 31 Dec. 1768 was appointed a lawyer. He must have had a good education and probably an attractive personality to obtain such a privilege so soon after settling in Canada. The American revolution fired him with such enthusiasm that in November 1775 he welcomed the invading army to Montreal with an address that he had had signed by several dozen "residents of three *faubourgs*": "our chains are broken, blissful liberty restores us to ourselves . . . , we accept union as we accepted it in our hearts from the moment we learned of the address of 26 Oct. 1774 [the letter of the Continental Congress to the people of Quebec]." Early in 1776, the commandant of Montreal, Brigadier-General David Wooster, the highest-ranking American officer after the death of Richard MONTGOMERY, appointed Jautard a notary, but it seems unlikely that Jautard went into practice since the Americans left the city in June.

At about this time Jautard met another Frenchman, printer Fleury MESPLET, who had arrived in Montreal in May. When Mesplet undertook in June 1778 to publish *La Gazette du commerce et littéraire, pour la ville et district de Montréal*, he enlisted the talented and educated Jautard as editor. In the spring of 1779 Jautard ventured to criticize in the *Gazette*, now renamed *La Gazette littéraire, pour la ville et district de Montréal*, some of Justice René-Ovide HERTEL de Rouville's judgements that he disagreed with as a lawyer. Judges Hertel de Rouville and Edward Southouse barred him from the court, but he and Mesplet appeared there on 27 May to defy the judges and perhaps to force them into a blunder. At least this is the suggestion Hertel de Rouville made when he wrote Governor HALDIMAND that day asking him to intervene. The pro-American attitude of the two friends had certainly not brought them into favour with the administration, and they were arrested on 2 June. The paper immediately ceased publication. Jautard and Mesplet were not released until September 1782.

On 23 Aug. 1783 Jautard signed a contract in Montreal for his marriage with Thérèse Bouat, widow of Louis-Jean Poulin* de Courval and of Jean-Baptiste de Gannes de Falaise; he thus joined an old Canadian family and at the same time gained access to some ready money. Jautard, who was only 45, may have thought that his wife, aged 72, would leave him well provided for. The contract stipulated that the wedding would take place "in a church ceremony as soon as possible." Some wag hastened to announce in the *Quebec Gazette* that the wedding had been celebrated in the Recollets' church "at 10 o'clock in the evening," and praised the bride for "the charms and attractions of youth, which seem always to be renewed in her . . . who has been won over by someone who is as good a rhetorician as he is a gallant."

In August 1785 Fleury Mesplet began publishing the *Montreal Gazette/La Gazette de Montréal*; Jautard was responsible for translation into English. On 13 October Jautard, "former courtroom lawyer," advised its readers that henceforth he would be living in the home of Fleury Mesplet and offered his services "for counselling, written statements, and translating from English into French." Less than two years later Valentin Jautard died. His widow lived until 1801, bequeathing her estate to the Hôpital Général to which she had retired.

Historians have treated Valentin Jautard severely, not so much because of his enthusiasm for the Americans, but because of the "Voltairianism" he displayed in *La Gazette littéraire*. "The quiet spectator" – his pseudonym – made no secret of his fondness for Voltaire. But in the earlier newspaper he gave as much space to anti-Voltairian writings as to Voltairian texts or pieces by Voltaire himself. Historians and scholars have not given Jautard, Quebec's "first literary critic," sufficient credit for having stimulated the Montreal intelligentsia; he was a man of the Enlightenment leading the *philosophes'* campaign from Fleury Mesplet's back room. It was in this context that the Académie de Montréal was founded; though it had sought incorporation from Governor Haldimand on 30 Dec. 1778, it did not obtain this status because of the opposition of the Sulpician superior, Étienne MONTGOLFIER. These intellectuals – enlightened citizens fighting against obscurantism and the somewhat oppressive presence of the Sulpicians, who claimed the right to direct intellectual life in Montreal – were a group like those found in small provincial towns in France. After the war with the Americans, which had deprived the group of its two best men, Jautard and Mesplet, the circle formed again around them, this time through the agency of the *Montreal Gazette/La Gazette de Montréal*.

As the historian Séraphin Marion notes, Valentin Jautard was an astute man, a skilful polemist who, far from being a sycophant or time-server, was an avant-garde fighter of undoubted courage and independence of mind. It is regrettable that many aspects of his life – his origins, education, and much of his activity in Montreal – remain unknown.

CLAUDE GALARNEAU

ANQ-M, Greffe de Louis Chaboillez, 18 mai 1799; Greffe de François Leguay, 23 août 1783; Greffe de P.-F. Mézière, 12 août 1783. *Cahokia records, 1778–1790*, ed. C. W. Alvord (Springfield, Ill., 1907). Fabre, dit Laterrière, *Mémoires* (A. Garneau), 117–18. *Old Cahokia: a narrative and documents illustrating the first century of its history*, ed. J. F. McDermott (St Louis, Mo., 1949), 24–25, 83–84. *La Gazette littéraire pour la ville et district de Montréal*, 3 juin 1778–2 juin 1779. *Montreal Gazette*, 25 Aug. 1785–Jan. 1794. *Quebec Gazette*, 25 Sept. 1783. Jules Léger, *Le Canada français et son expression littéraire* (Paris, 1938). Séraphin Marion, *Les lettres canadiennes d'autrefois* (9v., Hull, Qué., et Ottawa, 1939–58), II. Camille Roy, *Nos origines littéraires* (Québec, 1909), 65–69. J.-E. Roy, *Hist. du notariat*, II, 58–59. Robert Rumilly, *Histoire de Montréal* (5v., Montréal, 1970–74), II, 57, 70–72, 82. Marcel Trudel, *L'influence de Voltaire au Canada* (2v., Montréal, 1945), I, 94–110. Raymond Douville, "La maison de Gannes," *Cahiers des Dix*, 21 (1956), 119. R. W. McLachlan, "Fleury Mesplet, the first printer at Montreal," RSC *Trans.*, 2nd ser., XII (1906), sect.II, 197–309. É.-Z. Massicotte, "La famille

Bouat (deuxième génération)," *BRH*, XXX (1924), 39–45; "L'ultime aventure du journaliste Jautard," *BRH*, XLVII (1941), 328–30.

JEANSON (Jeançonne), GUILLAUME (also **William Johnson**; he signed **Gilliom Shanson**), soldier and settler; b. August 1721 at Annapolis Royal (N.S.), son of William Johnson, a Scottish soldier, and Isabelle Corporon, an Acadian; m. *c.* 1751 Marie-Josette Aucoin; d. after 1777, probably at Tracadièche (Carleton, Que.).

Guillaume Jeanson is reputed to have served with the garrison at Annapolis Royal until he was accused of stealing supplies and discharged. He then joined the Acadian community, probably at Rivière-aux-Canards (near Canard, N.S.), where his son Jean-Baptiste was born in 1752.

During the expulsion of 1755 Jeanson and his family escaped to Miramichi (N.B.). He appears to have been active among the refugees who gathered there, for in 1758 he was reported in command of the Acadian irregulars harassing the British in Nova Scotia. In the spring of that year he was at Annapolis Royal, encouraging disaffected Acadians to join the forces of Charles DESCHAMPS de Boishébert at Miramichi. In June 1762, however, he and his family were among Acadian prisoners being held at Fort Edward (Windsor, N.S.).

With the end of the Seven Years' War in 1763 the Jeansons were released and probably chose to settle in the Windsor area. In 1768 Jeanson was listed among those Acadians willing to take the oath of loyalty to the British king, and in that year he and 37 others at Windsor petitioned the government for provisions and a resident priest. From Windsor Jeanson appears to have moved to St Mary's Bay. The date of his move is not known but he may have been with a group of Acadians that arrived there in 1769. This group obtained land grants in 1775; the same year Jeanson received a lot of 360 acres in the present village of Grosses Coques. Tradition has it that he established a sawmill there and, because he spoke English, acted as a spokesman for the Acadians.

Some time after 1774 Jeanson left St Mary's Bay. The census of 1777 for Tracadièche lists him, his wife, and six of their children; the New Brunswick legislator Urbain Johnson* was a great-grandson.

J.-ALPHONSE DEVEAU

N.S., Dept. of Lands and Forests, Crown Lands Office, Old book 12, ff.5–17 (mfm. at PANS). PAC, MG 30, C20, 11, pp.2604, 2605; 12, p.2613. "Prisonniers acadiens du fort Edward, N.-É., 1763, et pétitions des Acadiens de cette région, avec les listes des signataires, 1764–1768 (papiers Deschamps)," R.-S. Brun, édit., Soc. historique acadienne, *Cahier* (Moncton, N.-B.), III (1968–71), 188–92. Arsenault, *Hist. et généalogie des Acadiens*. L.-C. Daigle, *Histoire de Saint-Louis-de-Kent: cent cinquante ans de vie paroissiale française en Acadie nouvelle* (Moncton, [1948]).

JOE, black slave and pressman; b. *c.* 1760 in Africa; fl. 1771–89.

Joe is first mentioned in Canadian records in August 1771 as a slave belonging to William BROWN and Thomas GILMORE, publishers of the *Quebec Gazette*; the partners were paying the sum required to get him out of prison. It is not known when Joe had become their property, but they seem to have owned black slaves since at least 1769. In a letter dated 29 April 1768 Brown had complained to his former employer in Philadelphia, William Dunlop, about the difficulties that the young Canadians hired for the printing shop were causing him: it was impossible to keep them long, for as soon as they acquired some experience, they demanded higher wages and became insolent. Consequently the two partners had decided to buy a black slave, 15 or 20 years of age, who was honest and had already had smallpox. They asked Dunlop to buy one for them – they were ready to pay a good price – and to send him by ship, taking care to have him insured. Dunlop may have sent several blacks in this way to his two former employees, and perhaps Joe came to Canada through his agency. After Gilmore's death in February 1773 and the dissolution of the partnership in January 1774, Brown remained owner of the black slaves then working in the printing shop.

Brown had Joe imprisoned in August 1774 for a theft of over £4. After his stay in prison, which cost his master nearly £3, the slave returned to the shop, and there practised the craft of printer's pressman. He must have liked this work quite well, for there is no mention of him until April 1777 when he ran away. Brown had to pay 17*s.* 9*d.* to get him back. In November Joe repeated his action, and this time Brown put him back in prison, again incurring some expense. On the following 25 January Joe ran away again, and Brown paid 10*s.* reward to the people who caught him. A few days before Christmas, another flight. This time Brown was not satisfied with putting Joe in prison; he had him flogged by the hangman, thus adding to his costs. In April 1779 Joe absconded after stealing a small sum from his master, who once more had to pay to get him back. When in September Joe ran off again, he was found on board a ship about to sail. Brown, who probably had had enough, made an unsuccessful attempt to sell his slave; however, Joe now had a reputation for his name had appeared regularly in the *Gazette* as a thief or runaway. At the end of 1785, there was another flight by Joe, and fresh expenses for Brown. On 18 February of the following year, the slave, who was then in prison, escaped along with John Peters, a criminal. The sheriff offered a reward of £5 for each of the fugitives; Brown promised three guineas to anyone who found his pressman, described by the *Quebec Gazette* of 4 May as "twenty-six years of age, about five feet seven inches high, a little pitted with the smallpox, has several scars on his legs, speaks English and French fluently." Joe returned to Brown's shop in June and seemed to settle down. In 1788, however, he stole some liquor for which his owner had to pay. To encourage him in the right path Brown gave him weekly pocket money.

Brown's persistency in retrieving Joe should occasion no surprise; "ebony wood" (as black slaves were called at the time) was costly, £40 to £50 each on the average, or twice the price of an Indian slave. Since no slave ships came to supply Canada, black slaves were rare. They had to be bought at second hand, either in the American states or through merchants trading with the West Indies or sometimes with Guinea. Blacks may also have been considered more useful, since several of them learned a trade, whereas the Indians were content to be servants or canoemen.

In the context of the times Joe was not so badly off in Brown's shop. The printer's disbursement books reveal that he was not stingy with food or clothing for his slave. Shoes in particular cost him a great deal – little wonder in view of Joe's numerous flights. In addition the slave always received money as a New Year's gift. During the American siege of Quebec in the winter of 1775–76 Brown, who was enrolled in the militia, sometimes had Joe replace him during his tour of guard duty and rewarded him with a shilling. But the slave's greatest luck was that his master took it upon himself to punish him for his crimes by making him have a taste of prison or the hangman's lash. Had he handed him over to the law, Joe could have been hanged for his first theft. Such a crime meant the gallows, for the free man as well as for the slave. Both were equal in the eyes of Canadian justice, and in fact appeared before the same judges, had the right to appeal to a superior court, and suffered the same punishments.

On Brown's death at the end of March 1789, Joe became by the terms of his will the property of Samuel NEILSON. In the month of August he ran away once more. Profiting from his uncle's experience, Neilson did not persist; although his masters treated him humanely, Joe evidently preferred freedom. No further trace of him has been discovered.

THÉRÈSE P. LEMAY

[Volumes 47, 57, 59, 101–3 of the Neilson collection at the PAC (MG 24, B1) contain several references to the expenditures made for the slave Joe by the printers Thomas Gilmore and, in particular, William Brown. From 1777 to 1789 the *Quebec Gazette*, then owned by Brown, printed many notices, often repeated in the *Montreal Gazette*, concerning the sale of Joe and his flights. T.P.L.]

M. Trudel, *L'esclavage au Canada français*. Hubert Neilson, "Slavery in old Canada before and after the conquest," Literary and Hist. Soc. of Quebec, *Trans.*, [new ser.], 26 (1905), 19–45.

JOHNSON, GUY, Indian department official; b. *c.* 1740 in Ireland; d. 5 March 1788 in London, England.

Guy Johnson may have been the midshipman of that name who served on HMS *Prince* in 1755. On arriving in North America Guy claimed that Sir William JOHNSON, the British superintendent of northern Indians, was his uncle but their relationship was probably more distant. Although young, he served through the Seven Years' War as an officer in the provincial forces, commanding a company of rangers under Jeffery AMHERST in 1759 and 1760. He acted as secretary in the northern Indian department until 1762 when Johnson appointed him a deputy agent. In 1763 he married Sir William's youngest daughter, Mary (Polly), and established his home at Guy Park near present Amsterdam, N.Y. While performing his duties in the Indian department, he was also active in military and political affairs, rising to colonel and adjutant-general of the New York militia and being elected to the New York assembly for 1773–75.

Upon Sir William's death in July 1774, Guy was directed by Lieutenant-General GAGE to assume the duties of superintendent pending confirmation by the crown. Faced with mounting revolutionary activity, Guy, his brother-in-law Sir John Johnson*, and Christian Daniel CLAUS attempted to organize resistance in the Mohawk valley to the usurpation of authority by the Tryon County committee of safety. With the beginning of armed rebellion in 1775, he devoted his full energies to retaining the allegiance to the crown of the powerful Six Nations Confederacy. He was unable to fulfil this task in the increasingly hostile environment of the Mohawk valley, and he and a few hundred loyal residents left in May

1775. At Oswego Johnson met with more than a thousand Iroquois and secured their pledge to protect the St Lawrence River–Lake Ontario supply route should the rebels threaten it. He failed, however, to obtain their active support for the crown's effort to suppress the spreading rebellion. At Oswego his young wife died on 11 July, leaving him with two small daughters.

Johnson proceeded to Montreal where he secured assurances of aid from the Canadian Indians, but finding his authority challenged by the newly arrived agent of Indian affairs for the province of Quebec, John CAMPBELL, he left for England in November to clarify the scope of his superintendency. He failed to have the Canadian Indians returned to his jurisdiction, but he accepted appointment as superintendent of the Six Nations and returned to America in the summer of 1776. He joined Sir William Howe's army at New York and, expecting the rebellion in the colony to be crushed by the campaign of 1777, remained in the city until BURGOYNE's defeat near Saratoga (Schuylerville) dashed such hopes. He then attempted to reach Canada by ship, but the scarcity of transport, the activity of the French fleet, and bad weather prevented him from reaching Montreal before the spring of 1779. Johnson was criticized for leaving the management of his department to two subordinates, John BUTLER at Niagara (near Youngstown, N.Y.) and Daniel Claus at Montreal, during the crucial years 1776–79. He maintained that he had kept in contact with his deputies and even claimed credit for planning the devastating raids against the Wyoming valley in 1778 and the Schoharie valley settlements in 1780 [*see* KAIEÑˀKWAAHTOÑ]. It is clear, however, from the correspondence of Claus, Butler, Sir John Johnson, General HALDIMAND, and others that he had little or no influence on the operation of the Indian department from 1776 to late 1779. Circumstances may have justified his long stay in New York City, but the regular communications that existed between there and Montreal provided him with the means by which he could have guided departmental policy. His neglect was inexcusable.

Johnson reached Niagara in the autumn of 1779. Despite Haldimand's protests about costs, he succeeded in providing for the thousands of Iroquois driven from their homes by the American campaign of 1779, and he directed large-scale Indian and loyalist raids against the frontier, destroying massive quantities of produce needed by the rebel army. In 1783 he turned over the Indian department to Sir John Johnson, who after 1778 had become Haldimand's chief adviser on Indian affairs, and returned to England to obtain restitution for property confiscated by the rebels. While still pressing his claim, he died in London on 5 March 1788.

JONATHAN G. ROSSIE

There is a portrait of Johnson by Benjamin West in the National Gallery of Art (Washington) and one by an unknown painter in the N.Y. State Hist. Assoc. Museum (Cooperstown). BL, Add. MSS 21766; 21769–70; 24323, ff.11, 14, 20, 22, 26. Huntington Library, Loudoun papers, LO 683, LO 2505. PAC, MG 19, F1; RG 10, A2. PRO, Adm. 36/6373, p.42. *Johnson papers* (Sullivan *et al.*), I, VIII, XIII. *The minute book of the committee of safety of Tryon County . . .* , ed. J. H. Hanson and S. L. Frey (New York, 1905). *NYCD* (O'Callaghan and Fernow), VIII. *DNB*. Graymont, *Iroquois*.

JOHNSON, WILLIAM. *See* JEANSON, GUILLAUME

JOHNSON, WILLIAM. *See* TEKAWIROÑTE

JOHNSON, Sir WILLIAM, superintendent of northern Indians; b. *c.* 1715, eldest son of Christopher Johnson of Smithstown (near Dunshaughlin, Republic of Ireland) and Anne Warren, sister of Vice-Admiral Sir Peter Warren*; d. 11 July 1774 at Johnson Hall (Johnstown, N.Y.).

In 1736 William Johnson began acting as agent for Peter Warren, receiving rent from Warren's Irish tenants. Early in 1738 Johnson came to America to oversee an estate that Warren had acquired near Fort Hunter, in the Mohawk valley of New York. He arrived at a propitious moment, since the struggle between France and Britain for hegemony in eastern North America came to a climax during his lifetime. To this conflict Johnson gave the remainder of his life, and through it he built his fortune, one of the largest in colonial America.

With much capital supplied by his naval uncle, Johnson became within a decade of his arrival the most substantial businessman on the Mohawk. Employing white indentured labourers and black slaves, he established a 200-acre farm on the south bank of the river; in 1739 he bought an 815-acre tract on the north side with access to the King's Road, which reached as far west as the Oneida Carrying Place (near Oneida Lake). Through an agent he began trading in imported English goods to the Indian settlement of Oquaga (near Binghamton). He also contracted with farmers for their surpluses of wheat and peas. By 1743 he had opened trade to Oswego (Chouaguen), the principal fur-trading post of British America. His shop on the King's Road served as the supply centre for all his dealings, and he thus cut into the long-established monopoly of the Dutch houses in Albany. He also shipped his own goods to New York City, where they were sold or transported either to the West Indies or to London.

Such business skill and success inevitably led to involvement in public affairs. In April 1745 he was made a justice of the peace for Albany County. Between 1745 and 1751 he was colonel of the Six Nations Indians, a responsibility formerly held in commission by several Albany fur-merchants. His influence with the Six Nations, especially his neighbours the Mohawks, soared, for he had ready access to provincial funds to pay the Indians regularly for their services. During the War of the Austrian Succession he attempted to organize Indian scouting and raiding parties on the frontier in support of a planned attack on Fort Saint-Frédéric (near Crown Point, N.Y.), but he was not particularly successful since the Six Nations generally remained committed to neutrality. In February 1748 he was made colonel of the 14 militia companies on the New York frontier, and in May colonel of the militia regiment for the city and county of Albany, positions which he held for the rest of his life and which opened great opportunities for patronage. He was appointed to the New York Council in April 1750, but he rarely attended its sittings.

Most of his time during the interval of relative peace from 1748 to 1754 he spent in pursuit of his private fortune. In April 1746 he had won the contract to supply the garrison at Oswego, and by 1751 he had provided goods and services amounting to £7,773, New York currency. Though he claimed a loss of about five per cent on the contract, he clearly profited from it by collecting duties at Oswego and by padding his accounts. With the approach of the Seven Years' War he once again became deeply involved in provincial affairs. A member of the New York delegation to the Albany Congress in June and July 1754, he advocated increased expenditure for garrisons among the Indians at strategic points and called for a regular policy of paying Indians for their services. He wanted young men to be sent among the native people as interpreters, schoolmasters, and catechists. The congress came to no agreement, but a month later the Board of Trade decided on its own initiative to create a regular Indian administration financed by parliament. In April 1755 Edward Braddock, commander-in-chief in North America, selected Johnson to manage relations with the Six Nations and their dependent tribes. As he explained to the Duke of Newcastle, Johnson was "a person particularly qualify'd for it by his great influence with those Indians." In February 1756 Johnson received a royal commission as "Colonel of . . . the Six united Nations of Indians, & their Confederates, in the Northern Parts of North America" and "Sole Agent and Superintendant of the said Indians."

In April 1755 Braddock had also made Johnson commander, with the provincial commission of major-general, of an expedition to take Fort Saint-Frédéric. The campaign, which called as well for a force under Braddock to seize Fort Duquesne (Pittsburgh, Pa) and one under William Shirley to take Fort Niagara (near Youngstown, N.Y.), was a dismal failure except for one engagement in which Johnson was involved early in September. At Lake George (Lac Saint-Sacrement) with part of his force of some 300 Indians headed by Theyanoguin* and 3,000 Americans, Johnson learned that a strong French column under Jean-Armand Dieskau* was moving towards Fort Edward, where the rest of his men were encamped. Johnson's relief detachment was ambushed and the survivors hotly pursued by some French regulars, who rashly attempted to take the hastily fortified position at Lake George by storm. They were cut to pieces by the Americans, and Dieskau was wounded and captured. Johnson, himself wounded early in the attack, played little part in the battle but was given credit for its outcome. When he visited New York City at the end of the year, he was greeted as a hero, and the king created him a baronet. In 1757 parliament made him a gift of £5,000. Never was such an insignificant encounter so generously rewarded.

Johnson had resigned his military commission late in 1755, and thereafter his duties largely concerned Indian affairs. With Indian raids disturbing the Pennsylvania frontier, he was given permission to appoint a deputy there, George Croghan. Their attempts to enlist Indians in the British cause were unrewarding during the early years of the war, which were marked by singular British setbacks. Fort Bull (east of Oneida Lake) was overrun by forces under Gaspard-Joseph CHAUSSEGROS de Léry in March 1756. Oswego fell to Montcalm* that August and was destroyed. Fort William Henry (also known as Fort George, now Lake George) surrendered in August 1757, and German Flats (near the mouth of West Canada Creek) was attacked in November. In 1758 a huge force under James ABERCROMBY failed to take Fort Carillon (Ticonderoga). The Indians largely remained neutral, and Johnson's prestige, despite his numerous conferences with them, waned.

This situation was altered by the string of victories beginning with AMHERST's capture of Louisbourg, Île Royale (Cape Breton Island), in 1758 and culminating in the fall of Fort Niagara and Quebec. The successful attack on Niagara was an important military encounter for Johnson. Undetected by Pierre Pouchot*'s garrison, the British under John Prideaux concentrated at Niagara a force of about 3,300 regular and provincial troops early in July 1759. Johnson, as second in command, was responsible for the contingent of some 940 Indians. After less than two weeks of siege Prideaux was killed and Johnson assumed command. Five days later a French force under François-Marie Le Marchand* de Lignery, coming from the Ohio valley, approached to relieve the garrison. Johnson sprang an ambush so successfully that the enemy not slain or taken prisoner fled in panic. The next day, 25 July, the fort surrendered. With it went control of the strategically important portage; the main artery of the French fur trade had been cut.

In the final campaign of the war Johnson accompanied Amherst to Montreal in 1760. Although he started out with almost 700 Indians, Johnson led only 185 into the city, the rest having departed following the surrender of Fort Lévis (east of Prescott, Ont.). After a few days in Montreal, he appointed Christian Daniel CLAUS his resident deputy there and returned to the Mohawk valley.

Indian affairs acquired a new dimension and a new importance with the fall of Canada. Problems that had necessarily been dealt with piecemeal during the war now demanded broader approaches. Johnson's policy, never spelled out in much detail despite various promptings from London, had four main points. The purchase of Indian lands should be controlled at a pace determined by the tribes' willingness to sell. Trade should be restricted to designated posts and be carried on at fixed prices by traders required to post bond and licensed annually. To oversee the administration the superintendent would have need not only of deputies but also of commissary-inspectors, interpreters, and gunsmiths. To finance its operation he suggested a tariff on rum.

What happened was rather different. Though much of the administration was established it was paid for by parliament. Prices were never fixed, and traders were never wholly restricted by bonds, licences, or designated trading posts. Moreover, the governors of Canada, through which most of the fur trade passed, issued their own licences and took measures to control the trade without reference to Johnson or his deputy there. Worse still for Johnson was the fact that since his regulations never had legal force he was powerless to punish those who ignored his sanctions. From 1768, when London abandoned its centralized control of Indian affairs, each colony was left to develop as best it could its relations with the Indians on its frontier. This decision coincided with another the home authorities made for economy, to withdraw garrisons from the western posts. Thereafter Johnson ought to have had close dealings with the New York government, yet he was never consulted about Indian affairs. Nor did he bother to build a party of support in the council or the assembly.

As superintendent he was under the orders of the commander-in-chief in North America, until 1763 Amherst, with whom Johnson greatly differed in opinion. Since the real instrument of British power in America was the army, Amherst's views carried the day. Whereas Johnson wished to encourage the supply of arms and ammunition to the Indians, Amherst, who put little value on their services, wished to restrict it. Whereas Johnson always worked diplomatically for an accommodation with the Indians, Amherst wished to deal forcefully with any tribe that opposed British arms. The 1763–64 Indian uprising would doubtless have resulted in a serious clash between Johnson and the commander-in-chief had not Amherst, at the height of the crisis, been given leave to return home to England. His successor, GAGE, reverted to the policy Lord Loudoun and Abercromby had followed; he issued no direct orders and left the superintendent free to work out details. In this way peace was made with Pontiac* and his allies, and little retribution was taken for the deaths of nearly 400 soldiers and perhaps 2,000 settlers.

After 1760 Johnson conferred frequently with the Indians, settling grievances and renewing covenants of friendship with them on behalf of the crown. In 1766 he met with Pontiac at Oswego, and in 1768 at Fort Stanwix (Rome, N.Y.) he settled the new boundary line for Indian lands with KAIEÑˀKWAAHTOÑ and other leaders. Thereafter he confined himself largely to meeting the Six Nations at his home. It was in the midst of one such conference in July 1774 that he fell ill "with a fainting and suffocation which . . . carried him off in two hours." Gage remarked: "The king has lost a faithful, intelligent servant, of consummate knowledge in Indian affairs, who could be very ill spared at this juncture, and his friends an upright, worthy and respectable man, who merited their esteem." This verdict has generally been endorsed by historians and biographers.

In fact Johnson served himself at least as well as he served his king. From April 1755 until his death some £146,546 came into his hands as superintendent, an annual average of £7,700. From it he received his salary, as well as salaries for his son John* and sons-in-law Guy JOHNSON and Daniel Claus. He arranged for the crown to rent his store and pay his storekeeper's wages and he charged the crown two and one-half per cent commission on all goods he supplied to the Indians as superintendent. He had the crown build a school for the Indians and pay a schoolmaster's salary, though he took credit for both. Perhaps the principal item in value furnished to the Indians was rum. The same accounts charged the crown with the cost of burying Indians killed while drunk. He never submitted vouchers, only the bald accounts, which, though unaudited, were always paid.

There was also considerable conflict of interest in Johnson's dealings in Indian lands. Publicly he represented a policy to prevent the despoliation of such lands, yet privately he arranged for their purchase by himself and by others. These tracts were without value to whites unless settled and cultivated, and by that process the Indian way of life, in which hunting played an important part, was destroyed. As superintendent, Johnson negotiated the land deal between the prospective purchaser and the Indians, and at least from 1771 he had the permission of the Six Nations to set the price of their land.

The territory he acquired for himself was not insignificant.He accepted a 130,000-acre grant from the Mohawks of Canajoharie (near Little Falls, N.Y.). For £300, New York currency, he bought about 100,000 acres on the Charlotte Creek, a tributary of the Susquehanna River though as a result of boundary limits set by the Fort Stanwix agreement of 1768 he was obliged to abandon his purchase. In 1765, less than three months after a treaty had been concluded with Pontiac, designed in part to allay Indian fears for their land, Johnson purchased some 40,000 acres from the Oneidas. In all this he acted no differently from dozens of other speculators in Indian lands. He was distinguished only by the great advantages he possessed through his office and through his long intimacy with the Indians. He was indeed one of their principal exploiters; his actions speak louder than any words of his. He was a typical imperial servant, in an area where he had few competitors able to match his intelligence and interest – an almost unbeatable combination in the 18th century.

Johnson was a man of some intellectual curiosity, and he amassed a substantial library of books and periodicals. On occasion he purchased scientific instruments. In January 1769 he was elected a member of the American Philosophical Society, but he never went to its meetings. He also belonged to the Society for the Promotion of Arts and Agriculture and to the board of trustees of Queen's College (Rutgers University, New Brunswick, N.J.), though he never attended its sessions.

There is no evidence that Johnson ever married. In his will he acknowledged as his wife Catherine Weissenberg (Wisenberg), an indentured servant who had escaped from her New York City owner. He took her in in 1739, and by the time of her death in April 1759 they had had three children. He is thought to have cohabited with many Indian women, but his most important liaison, for personal and political reasons, was with Mary Brant [KOÑWATSIˀTSIAIÉÑNI]. Eight of their children survived him.

JULIAN GWYN

The earliest portrait of Johnson, completed about 1751, is attributed to John Wollaston and is in the Albany Institute of History and Art (Albany, N.Y.). There is a miniature in the PAC. The N.Y. Hist. Soc. holds an 1837 copy by Edward L. Mooney of a portrait done in 1763 by Thomas McIlworth. A fourth was painted in 1772 or 1773 by Matthew Pratt and hangs in Johnson Hall, the site also of a celebrated bronze statue.

[Johnson has appeared in much fiction, and in the opinion of the noted Johnson scholar Milton W. Hamilton, it was the novels of Robert William Chambers that "gave many Americans their only conception of Sir William." Johnson has been the subject of several biographies, none adequate. Errors in the earliest, W. L. [and W. L.] Stone, *The life and times of Sir William Johnson, bart.* (2v., Albany, N.Y., 1865), have often been repeated. The most recent, M. W. Hamilton, *Sir William Johnson, colonial American, 1715–1763* (Port Washington, N.Y., and London, 1976), adds useful detail but misunderstands the central feature of Johnson's career, his relations with the Indians.

Johnson's role as an Indian agent has figured prominently in numerous monographs, the best of which are unpublished. Dissertations include D. A. Armour, "The merchants of Albany, New York, 1686–1760" (PHD thesis, Northwestern University, Evanston, Ill., 1965), especially chap.IX; C. R. Canedy, "An entrepreneurial history of the New York frontier, 1739–1776" (PHD thesis, Case Western Reserve University, Cleveland, Ohio, 1967), especially chaps. II–III; E. P. Dugan, "Sir William Johnson's land policy (1739–1770)" (MA thesis, Colgate University, Hamilton, N.Y., 1953); W. S. Dunn, "Western commerce, 1760–1774" (PHD thesis, University of Wisconsin, Madison, 1971), especially chap.V; E. R. Fingerhut, "Assimilation of immigrants on the frontier of New York, 1764–1776" (PHD thesis, Columbia University, New York, 1962); E. M. Fox, "William Johnson's early career as a frontier landlord and trader" (MA thesis,

Cornell University, Ithaca, N.Y., 1945); F. T. Inouye, "Sir William Johnson and the administration of the Northern Indian Department" (PHD thesis, University of Southern California, Los Angeles, 1951); D. S. McKeith, "The inadequacy of men and measures in English imperial history: Sir William Johnson and the New York politicians, a case study" (PHD thesis, Syracuse University, Syracuse, N.Y., 1971); Peter Marshall, "Imperial regulation of American Indian affairs, 1763–1774" (PHD thesis, Yale University, New Haven, Conn., 1959).

Most of Johnson's manuscripts have been published in *Johnson papers* (Sullivan *et al.*), the last editor of which was M. W. Hamilton, who has also written a number of short articles on aspects of Johnson's life and on Johnsoniana. Other collections with many Johnson letters are *The documentary history of the state of New-York* . . . , ed. E. B. O'Callaghan (4v., Albany, N.Y., 1849–51) and *NYCD* (O'Callaghan and Fernow), especially vols. VI–VIII. Still unpublished are a number of his accounts in the Clements Library, Thomas Gage papers, and in PRO, AO 1 and T 64.

Two further works dealing with aspects of Johnson's life are F. J. Klingberg, "Sir William Johnson and the Society for the Propagation of the Gospel (1749–1774)," which appears in his *Anglican humanitarianism in colonial New York* (Philadelphia, 1940), 87–120, and Julian Gwyn, *The enterprising admiral: the personal fortune of Admiral Sir Peter Warren* (Montreal, 1974), which treats Johnson's relations with his uncle. J.G.]

JOHNSTON, ALEXANDER, judge of the Court of Vice-Admiralty and legislative councillor; b. *c.* 1737; d. 26 Oct. 1778.

It is difficult to identify Alexander Johnston. The historian Francis-Joseph Audet* thought him "very likely" the Alexander Johnston who during the military régime of 1760 to 1764 was captain of a company in the 46th Foot stationed at Saint-François-du-Lac in the Government of Trois-Rivières. Audet seems to have been in error, however, since in 1770 this man was a lieutenant-colonel in the 70th Foot serving in the West Indies. We know that by November 1767 the future legislative councillor and judge was a barrister-at-law in the province of Quebec. He may therefore have been the "counsellor Johnston" who was in Quebec that very month with a young wife described by Francis Maseres* as "a very beautiful woman."

On 2 March 1769 Johnston was appointed judge of the Court of Vice-Admiralty for the province of Quebec. In criminal matters this court was empowered to judge, without a jury, all crimes and offences committed at sea. In non-criminal matters it had jurisdiction over commercial litigation, whether maritime or civil, between merchants and shipowners. Acting with a jury it could also investigate shipwrecks, unclaimed property, treasure-trove, and accidents at sea. Johnston's salary, when the first payments were finally approved nearly four years after his appointment, was a generous £200 per annum, and his duties were light. As his predecessor James Potts had admitted, "by the situation of this Port [Quebec], very little business is done in the Court of Admiralty, in comparison with what happens in Ports nearer the Sea, which are open all the year." Johnston secured the position of examiner in the Court of Chancery on 22 Dec. 1769, and about the beginning of 1770 he also became clerk of the crown. He first took over the clerkship in an acting capacity from Henry KNELLER, who had become attorney general, but was probably appointed to full rank the following summer. Although the position paid less than the judgeship, it likely occupied more of Johnston's time, since he was responsible for most of the detailed presentation and recording of King's Bench business, work which also took him more often to Montreal.

In November 1775 William Gordon and Peter LIVIUS arrived in Quebec bearing mandamuses for positions which included Johnston's clerkship and judgeship. Gordon took over the former position, but Johnston managed to hang on to the higher paid post, since Livius was made judge of the Court of Vice-Admiralty for Montreal only. Some time after 31 Oct. 1777, however, Johnston relinquished his judgeship as well. Meanwhile the loss of his salary as clerk had been compensated for by his appointment in August 1775 to the first Legislative Council set up under the terms of the Quebec Act. He was a faithful attendant at the few meetings convened before the emergency of the American invasion of 1775–76 caused a lapse in the use of the council. He was also present at the frequent sessions held in the first four months of 1777 and served on most of the important committees, including the one which drafted ordinances establishing courts of justice [*see* Adam MABANE]. It is surprising, then, that he disappears completely from the council minutes after attending a "privy" council meeting in July 1777. He continued to be a member, as Governor HALDIMAND's instructions of 1 April 1778 indicate. Since he died prematurely, it is not too fanciful to suspect broken health in the last year of his life; it was brought on perhaps by his very frequent guard, picket, and fatigue duty as a militia captain during the winter siege of 1775–76, a service that was said also to have injured William Gordon's constitution.

A. J. H. RICHARDSON

ASQ, Polygraphie, XXXVII, 1. BL, Add. MSS 9913, ff.186, 214 (copy at PAC). PAC, MG 23, A1, ser.1, 7, no.1767; GII, 3, 1; MG 24, B1, 46, p.3; RG 1, E1, 6, pp.1–49; 13, p.14; E15, A, 2; 8; 9; 10; 11; 13/3; 16; RG 4, A1, 14, p.6209; 20, pp.6846, 6947. PRO, CO 42/35, f.114; CO 217/19, p.171 (mfm. at PAC). *Doc. relatifs à l'hist. constitutionnelle, 1759–91* (Shortt et Doughty; 1921), I, 74; II, 685. *Gentleman's Magazine*, 1763, 314–15; 1765, 147. Maseres, *Maseres letters* (Wallace), 64. "Orderly book begun by Captain Anthony Vialar of the British militia . . . ," ed. F. C. Würtele, Literary and Hist. Soc. of Quebec, *Hist. Docs.*, 7th ser. (1905), 155–265. *Quebec Gazette*, 1 Sept. 1768, 18 Jan. 1770, 25 July 1771, 14 July 1774, 29 Oct. 1778. G. B., WO, *Army list*, 1758–60, 1763, 1766, 1768, 1770. Turcotte, *Le Cons. législatif*, 3–4, 21–43. Neatby, *Administration of justice under Quebec Act*. G. F. G. Stanley, *Canada invaded, 1775–1776* (Toronto, 1973), 160. A. L. Burt, "The quarrel between Germain and Carleton: an inverted story," *CHR*, XI (1930), 205–6.

JOHNSTON (Johnstone), JAMES, merchant; b. *c.* 1724, probably at Stromness, in the Orkneys, Scotland; d. 8 April 1800 at Quebec.

James Johnston, whose origins and career before he came to Canada are unknown, arrived at Quebec during or soon after the conquest, probably to establish himself there as a merchant. On 22 June 1761 he rented a house on Rue des Pauvres for 1,000 *livres* a year, with the assurance that if the colony remained a British possession, he could purchase it for 12,000 *livres*, 3,000 in cash and the remainder in bills of exchange drawn on London. Although a Presbyterian, two months later he signed the petition requesting that John BROOKE, the Anglican garrison chaplain, be named a missionary to Quebec. On 22 July 1762 Johnston went into partnership with another Scottish merchant, John Purss*, with whom he was to remain closely connected in both business and friendship until his death.

As a member of the British merchant community in the new colony Johnston joined in its political demands. In 1764 he was chosen foreman of the first grand jury by Williams Conyngham. An adversary of Governor MURRAY, Conyngham had succeeded in persuading the official responsible for appointments to the jury to entrust him with the task; according to the attorney general, George SUCKLING, the 14 British jurors he selected were "malcontents from not having been made magistrates and a few others whose want of understanding and whose situation in life rendered them [his] fit tools." Johnston himself had been thwarted by the governor in his attempt to obtain a share of public property. The jury, most of whom were British merchants, opposed the ordinance of 17 Sept. 1764 which, it was thought, might well make the legal system costly, complicated, oppressive, and even unconstitutional since it allowed Catholics to act as jurors and lawyers in civil cases. During the assizes on 16 Oct. 1764 the Grand Jury proceeded, moreover, to make virulent denunciations of Governor Murray's political, economic, and social policies. That year the Quebec merchants sent a petition demanding the governor's recall, and Johnston was one of its signatories. In 1768, although deeming that Johnston had been "entering into Party against Mr. Murray with too much Warmth," Guy Carleton* recommended him to Lord Shelburne, the secretary of state for the Southern Department, for a vacant seat on the Council at Quebec; he remarked that Johnston was "a Man of a very excellent Understanding, and likewise very fit." Although he reiterated this recommendation the following year, it was not acted upon.

In 1767 Johnston, probably acting in the name of the firm of Johnston and Purss, and eight other shareholders took a lease on the Saint-Maurice ironworks; the two Scotsmen, however, parted with their shares to Christophe PÉLISSIER some time before 1771. As early as 1770 at least, the firm of Johnston and Purss was conducting business from a rented site on the king's wharf, adjoining the Cul-de-Sac in Quebec's Lower Town. The two partners had good personal relations with various other Quebec merchants, including George Allsopp*, Jacob JORDAN, and Adam Lymburner*. In addition John Johnston, one of James's brothers, was their agent in London, and a young relative, David Geddes, represented them in the West Indies from 1772 on. At least during the 1780s Johnston and Purss engaged in the wheat trade, but a large share of their commerce with New York and the West Indies apparently consisted of a preparation called "essence of spruce for making beer," the discovery of which they attributed to Johnston's brother-in-law Henry Taylor, the owner of a Quebec distillery.

From 1784 Johnston, like most of the British merchants who had been silenced during the American revolution, began to attack the judicial system once more and again demanded a system of regulations more favourable to trade. Hence in November he signed a petition expressing these concerns and demanding a new constitution. He also supported Lieutenant Governor Henry HAMILTON, who was favourable to the merchants' demands, when he was recalled to England for having given the lease of the king's posts to a group of his sympathizers in 1785. Two years later Johnston backed Chief Justice William SMITH's stand in favour of bringing the judicial system into line with that of England. Moreover in 1789, after the merchants' spokesman in their protest against the administration of justice, Attorney General James Monk*, was dismissed for questioning the judges' competence, Johnston was one of the merchants who assured him of their support.

Towards the end of the 1780s Johnston received tangible proof of the respect he had earned in the community. In 1787, in an ordinance providing for the construction of prisons and other public buildings, Lord Dorchester [Guy Carleton] appointed him one of the commissioners to draw up the plans and estimate costs for them, grant the contracts for land sales, and provide for the collection of the necessary taxes. Johnston did not, however, undertake these duties, since the application of the ordinance had been linked by the governor to approval by the British authorities and it never came into force. That year, when he was 63, he became an artillery captain in the British militia for the city and suburbs of Quebec, a post he retained until 1794, when he was promoted lieutenant-colonel. The firm of Johnston and Purss seems to have been only relatively prosperous during this period. Although it had an operating deficit of £756 in 1800, it owned real estate valued at £5,252 consisting of Johnston's house and four others, ten warehouses, two wharfs, and a piece of land comprised of two building sites bought in 1782 in the parish of Beauport.

In the autumn of 1783 Johnston had married a young Scottish woman, Margaret Macnider, sister of the Quebec merchants Mathew and John* Macnider. The couple had two children, John Purss and Ann. Johnston, who had a strong feeling for family, maintained close ties with relatives in the Orkneys. Moreover, as guardian of his nephews John and Henry Taylor of Quebec, he sent the elder to England in 1779 "for the best school Education in England (at any Expence) preparative to his becoming in time a good man and a compleat Distiller." To that end the young man was to study French, English, arithmetic, bookkeeping, geometry, trigonometry, natural sciences, and chemistry, but with the proviso that "none of his time be murdered in Latin or any other dead business Language." In 1783 Henry followed his brother.

In November 1798 James Johnston made his will, and on 8 April 1800 he died at Quebec in his house on Rue Champlain. With his death the firm of Johnston and Purss was dissolved and its property holdings were divided by lot between his widow and children, who were still minors, on the one hand, and his former partner on the other.

ANDRÉ BÉRUBÉ

ANQ-Q, Greffe de M.-A. Berthelot d'Artigny, 17 août 1782; Greffe d'Alexandre Dumas, 2 août 1794, 9 sept. 1795; Greffe de J.-C. Panet, 22 juin 1761; Greffe de J.-A. Saillant, 4 avril 1771; Greffe de Charles Stewart, 17 juin 1793, 4 juin 1798; Greffe de Charles Voyer, 12, 16 mai, 8, 10 juin, 23 août 1800. Archives civiles, Québec, Testament olographe de James Johnston, 17 nov. 1798 [*see* P.-G. Roy, *Inv. testaments*, III, 64]. Orkney Archives, Orkney Library (Kirkwall, Scot.), D15/1/3; D15/3/1–3; D15/3/6; D15/3/10–11. PAC, MG 11, [CO 42], Q, 2, pp.233–49; 29, pp.534–39, 870–72; MG 23, GII, 19, 2, p.10; RG 4, A1, pp.6053–58. PRO, CO 42/28, ff.155–56; 42/29, f.31; 42/115, f.13. USPG, C/CAN/Que., I, 29 Aug. 1761.

"Les dénombrements de Québec faits en 1792, 1795, 1798 et 1805 par le curé Joseph-Octave Plessis," ANQ *Rapport*, 1948–49, 78, 80, 128, 131. *Doc. relatifs à l'hist. constitutionnelle, 1759–91* (Shortt et Doughty; 1921), I, 187–91, 202–5. PAC *Rapport*, 1914–15, app.C, 205–7. *Quebec Gazette*, 22 Nov., 27 Dec. 1764, 29 Sept. 1766, 17 Dec. 1767, 3 Nov. 1785, 5, 26 July 1787, 11 Dec. 1788, 12 Nov. 1789, 28 Oct. 1790, 28 April, 16 June, 18 Aug. 1791, 28 Nov. 1793, 13 Feb., 3, 10, 24 July, 23 Oct. 1794, 11 June 1795, 29 June 1797, 16 July 1799, 10 April 1800, 14 May 1801, 5, 26 May 1803. Burt, *Old prov. of Que.* (1968), I, 99–100. Neatby, *Administration of justice under Quebec Act*, 344; *Quebec*, 37–38.

JOHNSTONE, JAMES, known as the **Chevalier de Johnstone** (he occasionally signed **Johnstone de Moffatt**), army officer; b. 25 July 1719 in Edinburgh, Scotland, son of James Johnstone, a merchant; his mother belonged to a lesser branch of the Douglas family; d. after 1791, probably in Paris, France.

It is known that James Johnstone's relations with his father were stormy and that he was indulged by his mother, but his early education has not been recorded. He is described as short in stature and slight of build. His youth appears to have been spent wantonly. After a visit to two uncles in Russia in 1738, he resided in London but was forced by his father to return to Scotland in 1740. When news reached Edinburgh in 1745 that Prince Charles, the Young Pretender, had landed in Scotland, Johnstone sped to join his army. Through his relatives he was introduced to Lord George Murray, second in command of the rebels, who appointed him his aide-de-camp. Johnstone moved with the army during the Jacobite uprising and occasionally served as aide-de-camp to the prince. After the battle of Prestonpans (Lothian) in September 1745, Charles granted Johnstone a captain's commission. The young officer raised some men and joined the

Duke of Perth's Regiment. Following the rout at Culloden in 1746, he escaped north and was concealed by a protectress who seems to have been Lady Jane Douglas, wife of Colonel John Stewart. Johnstone made his way to London in the disguise of a pedlar and then to Rotterdam dressed as a servant in the company of his protectress. In Paris he was introduced to the Marquis de Puysieux, minister of foreign affairs, by influential friends and was granted a pension from funds accorded by Louis XV for Scottish rebels exiled in France.

Despite promises from Puysieux, Johnstone's captain's commission was not recognized in France, and he received only an ensigncy in the colonial regular troops of Île Royale (Cape Breton Island). Although his derogation vexed him, he went to Louisbourg in 1750. He described his life there as purgatory, but he lived comfortably; his servant attended to his material wants and he indulged in reading military history. In the quarrel between Governor Jean-Louis de RAYMOND and the financial commissary, Jacques PREVOST de La Croix, Johnstone sided with the former and was rewarded with an appointment as English interpreter in 1752 and a promotion to lieutenant in 1754.

In June 1758, when Louisbourg was attacked by Jeffery AMHERST, Johnstone was stationed on Île Saint-Jean (Prince Edward Island). He escaped to Acadia and was charged with conducting some English prisoners from Miramichi (N.B.) to Quebec. Arriving there in September, he later became aide-de-camp to LÉVIS. He also served as interpreter and as voluntary engineer for the entrenchments constructed by Lévis between the French camp and the Rivière Montmorency. But when Lévis left for Montreal, Johnstone remained in Quebec as aide-de-camp to Montcalm*. Following the siege of Quebec and the death of the general, he retreated with the army. At Île aux Noix from April to August 1760, he escaped to Montreal when the French were forced to abandon the Champlain-Richelieu front. After the capitulation of the city, he returned to Quebec and sailed for France on 16 Oct. 1760.

Johnstone's role in the momentous events in New France was minor. Although egocentric, he was timid by nature and had made his escape at Culloden by having a younger officer dislodge a servant from a horse. His principal legacy was his memoirs, composed, or at least completed, after his return to France, in which he recounted in ungrammatical French what he had witnessed and heard during his campaigns in Scotland and in New France. Although he sometimes erred in matters of detail and frequently bemoaned his unhappy fate, Johnstone often wrote with shrewd insight and philosophical reflection.

Johnstone's later life was less eventful. He was retired from the Marine service with a pension of 300 *livres* in 1761 and the following year was made a knight of the order of Saint-Louis. He lived in Paris but visited Scotland in 1779 to settle personal matters. By 1790 his pension had been increased to 1,485 *livres*, and in 1791 he successfully petitioned the assembly for 500 *livres* for losses incurred during the Jacobite rebellion. Johnstone's adventures were the inspiration for the character of Maxwell in the Canadian novel entitled *The span o' life: a tale of Louisbourg and Quebec*, written by William McLennan and Jean Newton McIlwraith and published in New York and Toronto in 1899.

T. A. CROWLEY

[The main source for James Johnstone's life is his memoirs; the PAC has a copy (MG 18, J10). Charles Winchester edited a poor translation of this manuscript as *Memoirs of the Chevalier de Johnstone* (3v., Aberdeen, Scot., 1870–71). The work has also been printed in parts: *Memoirs of the rebellion in 1745 and 1746 . . .* (London, 1820; repub., ed. Brian Rawson, 1958); "Mémoires de M. le Cher. de Johnstone," Literary and Hist. Soc. of Quebec, *Hist. Docs.*, 9th ser. (1915). Parts of the Canadian memoirs were first published in translation in Literary and Hist. Soc. of Quebec, *Hist. Docs.*, 2nd ser. (1868), and in *Coll. de manuscrits relatifs à la N.-F.*, III, 465–84; IV, 231–43, 245–65. T.A.C.]

AN, Col., C^{11C}, 13, p.162 (PAC transcript); E, 230 (dossier Johnstone). McLennan, *Louisbourg*. Stacey, *Quebec, 1759*. Édouard Fabre Surveyer, "Le chevalier Johnstone," *BRH*, LXI (1955), 85–92. William Howitt, "Le chevalier Johnstone," *BRH*, VII (1901), 56–58.

JONCAIRE DE CLAUSONNE, DANIEL-MARIE CHABERT DE. *See* CHABERT

JONES, JOHN, soldier and dissenting minister; b. 1737 in Wales of dissenting parents; d. 1 March 1800 at St John's, Newfoundland.

John Jones joined the Royal Artillery at the age of 20. According to his biographer, "The Ox never drank water more greedily than he drank iniquity," and his conduct grew worse after his company's transfer to St John's in 1765. Even allowing for some exaggeration, it is evident that Jones's behaviour was no example of Christian probity.

In 1770 he was converted, apparently as a result of hearing a soldier curse God before he died from injuries received in a brawl, and the conversion became permanent, partly because of the encouragement Jones obtained from Laurence

Coughlan, whom he met in 1771 and with whom he subsequently corresponded. After his company's return to England in 1773 he joined a congregation influenced by the ideas of the dissenting preacher George Whitefield. Two years later, by then sergeant-major, quartermaster, paymaster, and clerk of his company, he returned with his unit to St John's and became a regular attendant at the Church of England services conducted by Edward Langman, the only legal form of worship on the island. At the same time, however, he organized a dissenting society, which at first included a jailer, a sergeant and his wife, and three other soldiers. During the winter of 1775–76 he received permission from local officials to hold services in the court house, but he was almost immediately opposed by Langman. The following summer Langman succeeded in convincing Governor John Montagu to enforce the English law against dissenters and to forbid the rental of accommodation for dissenting services; Jones's society was forced to meet secretly on the "Barrens" outside St John's until Montagu's departure at the end of the fishing season. In the governor's absence two members of Jones's society erected a meeting house, which Montagu closed on his return the next year. He threatened to demolish the building and transfer Jones to Placentia, but did not, perhaps because Jones was a good soldier and received the support of his commanding officer.

Jones returned to England in the summer of 1778. Shortly afterwards his society requested him to leave the army and return to St John's as their minister. He was ordained by a dissenting clergyman and arrived in St John's in July 1779. One of his first acts was to petition Governor Richard Edwards for permission to preach, but his first petition and a further appeal were refused. Langman's influence on the governor was, however, counteracted by more favourable opinions from London and these, combined with a recommendation from the chief engineer Robert Pringle, made Edwards respond to a third petition in 1780 by allowing Jones to preach. The meeting house was reopened on 1 August; four years later Governor John Campbell issued a proclamation granting full liberty of conscience and freedom of worship in Newfoundland.

The society encountered financial difficulties from its foundation, but Jones managed to organize a school and contributed from his army pension to help pay for an assistant master and defray the fees of poorer children. In 1790 funds from London eased the situation and enabled him to establish a charity school for all denominations. A new meeting house was completed in 1789, and by 1794 Jones had a congregation of 400 persons. He maintained cordial relations with Methodists, Presbyterians, and Roman Catholics, and lived to see an end to the old feud with members of the Church of England, who used his meeting house in the winter of 1799 while their new church was being built. Jones suffered a stroke in that year and died, appropriately, on St David's day, 1800; the funeral oration was given by John Harries*, the Church of England minister. In his will Jones bequeathed everything to his charity school. He was never married.

Frederic F. Thompson

St David's Presbyterian Church (St John's, Nfld.), Journal of John Jones. "The life of the Rev. John Jones, late of St. John's, Newfoundland," *Evangelical Magazine* (London), VIII (1800), 441–49. J. S. Armour, "John Jones and the early dissenter movement in Newfoundland" (paper presented to the Nfld. Hist. Soc., St John's, 17 Nov. 1975). St David's Presbyterian Church, *The dissenting Church of Christ at St. John's, 1775–1975 . . .* (St John's, 1975). Prowse, *History of Nfld.* (1895), supp., 49–51. J. R. Thoms, "Twenty-six notable men," *The book of Newfoundland*, ed. J. R. Smallwood (6v., St John's, 1937–75), VI, 177–78.

JORDAN, JACOB, merchant, seigneur, and MHA; b. 19 Sept. 1741 in England; m. 21 Nov. 1767 Ann Livingston at Montreal and they had at least ten children; m. secondly 2 Nov. 1792 Marie-Anne Raby at Montreal and they had one son; d. 23 Feb. 1796 at Saint-Louis-de-Terrebonne (Terrebonne, Que.).

Jacob Jordan came to Canada, before August 1761, with weighty credentials. At Montreal that year he was distributor of stamps under the Stamp Act and agent for the highly influential London firm of Fludyer and Drummond, a company with political connections and capital of the first order. It held a large contract to victual troops in America and in 1767 acquired one to supply cash for army pay and expenses in the colonies. Jordan's part in this remitting contract gave him a command of cash not enjoyed by most of his fellow businessmen, and he was able enough to use the advantage to build up a personal empire. Already in 1765 he was the holder of a land grant in what is now New Brunswick as a member of the Saint John River Society [see Beamsley Perkins Glasier]. In 1770 he petitioned with Colin Drummond, a brother of one of the principals in the London firm and its Quebec agent, for a township on the Winooski River (Vt). In each of these ventures he was joined by John Livingston, a prominent Montreal fur-trader and possibly his father-in-law.

Perhaps to aid his army victualling Jordan entered the grain trade and in 1767 formed a partnership with Drummond and John Halstead to purchase wheat and bake biscuits. The partnership lasted two years, and both Jordan and Drummond subsequently continued in the grain trade. One of Jordan's suppliers was Jacques Cartier*, an important trader from the Richelieu valley and grandfather of George-Étienne*. By 1770 Jordan was creditor of Jean ORILLAT of Montreal and had replaced Jean DUMAS Saint-Martin as Montreal agent for the Saint-Maurice ironworks.

With the advent of war in 1775 Jordan was able to pick up further business on his own account. He was given a contract to provide firewood for the Montreal garrison and one to supply horses and wagons for John BURGOYNE's expedition; the government, however, was slow in arranging the latter contract and remiss in paying. On 5 July 1776 Jordan had been appointed a deputy paymaster general, and the same year Drummond's son John succeeded his father as a deputy paymaster general and deputy commissary general. Jordan and John Drummond were also at this time agents for Harley and Drummond of London, who now had the contract to remit currency for army pay and expenses. Forewarned in the spring of 1779 of an "amazing price of wheat and flour in other parts of America", Jordan and Drummond, joined by several other important merchants, hurried to purchase wheat before the expiry of the export embargo on 1 August. They cornered the Richelieu wheat crop and were largely responsible for the doubling of prices to the public. To buy the wheat, Jordan and Drummond had apparently used £15,000 of public money from the remitting contract. They were promptly dismissed as agents by Harley and Drummond, but they retained their official posts and probably the profits made in the speculation. Three years later Jordan was entrusted by the government with large-scale wheat purchases.

At the close of the war Jordan continued to expand his independent business ventures. He secured ownership of the Terrebonne mills in 1784 by buying the seigneury from Pierre-Paul Margane* de Lavaltrie. By 1788 the mills were apparently the second most productive in Canada, and the seigneury was "famous for its *Astonishing* production of wheat." In the 1790s Jordan established Samuel Birnie, his clerk at least since 1778, in a "very eligible" baking business at Montreal, and in 1792 he was Birnie's partner in a Montreal tobacco factory. As chief Canadian backer of the Montreal Distilling Company, Jordan had sent Birnie to the Caribbean in 1785 to purchase molasses. This combination of products – rum, tobacco, and biscuit – seems to have been aimed at the great fur-trade market. From 1791 to 1794 Jordan put his money for the first time directly behind a fur-trade firm, one which was attempting to enter the trade in the northwest as the southwest was closing to Canadians. The visible partners involved were Jordan's nephew William Oldham and John Howard, son of the veteran trader Joseph HOWARD. Jordan also bought furs elsewhere, notably from the Nipigon trader Gabriel COTTÉ. A London broker, John Brickwood, recently bypassed by the North West Company which had formerly dealt with him, backed Jordan and may have given him promises of strong support. A second partnership in 1792, Jordan, Forsyth and Company, perhaps represents an alliance with another bypassed fur-trade interest, Alexander Ellice* and his associates. An attempt was made to bring Peter Pond* and Alexander Henry* the elder into this opposition to the North West Company.

Nearly all Jordan's enterprises ran into trouble, however. In his later years he lacked the access to cash that his earlier banking functions had given him. The wheat market was generally hazardous from 1783 to 1793. In 1788 Jordan was forced to sue the distillery to recover his heavy advances. Six years later the bakery burned. The French revolution upset the European fur market, triggering many failures and giving the *coup de grâce* to Jordan, who lost £18,000 on his peltry shipments of 1793. His sufferings were increased by ill health and by reflections, apparently, on the falsity of Brickwood's promises, which he termed a "vile (not to say worse) snare." His obituary, however, suggests that he bore his troubles with dignity. From 1792 to 1796 he was a member of the House of Assembly for Effingham County, Lower Canada, and he was at one time considered for the office of speaker.

A. J. H. RICHARDSON

ANQ-M, Greffe de François Leguay, 25 oct. 1786; Greffe de Peter Lukin, 1er mai, 12 juill. 1794; Greffe de Pierre Panet, 2 juill. 1770; Greffe de Joseph Papineau, 31 mai 1794; Greffe de Simon Sanguinet, 10 mars 1784. AUM, P 58, Doc. divers, G2, 17 août 1776. BL, Add. MSS 21714, f.121; 21733, ff.80–81, 197; 21734, ff.381, 489–92; 21851, f.82; 21854, ff.77–79, 172–73; 21870, ff.117, 253; 21873, f.272 (mfm. at PAC). PAC, MG 11, [CO 42], Q, 38, p.231; MG 19, A2, ser.3, 18, 16 April 1779; 54, 28 Oct. 1778; 63, f.276; 76, pp.44, 46, 68–70, 72–76, 80–82, 84–87; 86, 22 Dec. 1770; 143, ff.91, 95; F1, 14, p.317; MG 23, GIII, 5, 11 Feb. 1790, 18 Oct. 1791; 8, ff.2–3, 11–14, 17–18, 100–1, 103–5, 107–8; 25, ser.D, Jordan family papers, 17 Feb. 1767, 3 Nov. 1770, 22 May 1777, 30 July, 24 Oct. 1784, 20 Oct. 1785, 15 Oct.

1786, 17 Oct. 1787, 10 Oct. 1788, 20 Oct. 1789, 5 March 1794, 16 Oct. 1795; MG 24, L3, pp.3804–5, 3810, 4497, 4506, 4578–82, 26295–305; RG 4, B17, 20 Jan., 21, 26 Feb. 1789.

Les bourgeois de la Compagnie du Nord-Ouest (Masson), I, 46. *The later correspondence of George III*, ed. Arthur Aspinall (5v., Cambridge, Eng., 1962–70), I, 42–43, 47, 49, 89, 97, 105–8, 144–45. PAC *Rapport*, 1888, 979; 1889, 96, 105, [John Watts], *Letter book of John Watts, merchant and councillor of New York, January 1, 1762–December 22, 1765* (New York, 1928), 344, 399. *Montreal Gazette*, 29 Feb. 1796. *Quebec Gazette*, 17 Oct. 1765, 16 June 1766, 15 Oct., 17 Dec. 1767, 29 June 1769, 22 Aug. 1771, 1 Oct. 1795, 19 Nov. 1807. F.-J. Audet et Édouard Fabre Surveyer, *Les députés au premier parlement du Bas-Canada (1792–1796)* . . . (Montréal, 1946), 275–78, 282–85, 288–90. *DNB*, VIII, 1278, 1283–87, 1290. G.B., Hist. MSS Commission, *Report on American* MSS, I, 33, 339. Massicotte, "Répertoire des engagements pour l'Ouest," ANQ *Rapport*, 1942–43, 317–44. Raymond Masson, *Généalogie des familles de Terrebonne* (4v., Montréal, 1930–31), 1841. N.Y., Secretary of state, *Calendar of N.Y. colonial manuscripts, indorsed land papers; in the office of the secretary of state of New York, 1643–1803* (Albany, 1864), 506, 608, P.-G. Roy, *Inv. concessions*, III, 220.

Hector Bolitho, *The Drummonds of Charing Cross* (London, 1967), 22–23, 36, 56–57, 110–11. Burt, *Old prov. of Que.* (1933), 308. I. R. Christie, *The end of North's ministry, 1780–1782* (London and New York, 1958), 182, 258–59. E. B. De Fonblanque, *Political and military episodes . . . derived from the life and correspondence of the Right Hon. John Burgoyne* . . . (London, 1876), 234–35. Namier and Brooke, *House of Commons*, II, 341–44, 442–44, 586–87; III, 194–95. Ouellet, *Hist. économique*, 115–16, 127–31, 151. Raymond, *River St. John* (1910), 356–80. Rich, *History of HBC*, II, 190–96, 200–1. "A brief account of the fur trade to the Northwest country, carried on from Lower Canada, and of the various agreements and arrangements under which it was conducted," *Canadian Rev. and Literary and Hist. Journal* (Montreal), 1 (July 1824), 155. Édouard Fabre Surveyer, "Notre Alexandre Dumas (1727–1802), député de Dorchester," RSC *Trans.*, 3rd ser., XLI (1947), sect.I, 4. "Panet vs Panet," *BRH*, XII (1906), 120–23.

K

KAIEÑ?KWAAHTOÑ, chief-warrior of the lower or eastern Senecas, member of the turtle clan (the name means disappearing smoke or mist; it appears most often as spoken in Mohawk, **Sayenqueraghta** or **Siongorochti**; attempts to write the Seneca pronunciation have included **Gayahgwaahdoh, Giengwahtoh, Guiyahgwaahdoh**, and **Kayenquaraghton**; he was also known as **Old Smoke, Old King**, the **Seneca King**, and the **King of Kanadesaga**); b. early 18th century; d. 1786 on Smoke Creek (in present-day Lackawanna, N.Y.).

Kaieñ?kwaahtoñ was the son of a prominent Seneca chief in what is now western New York and resided for most of his life in the Seneca town of Ganundasaga (Geneva). Early in life he established a military reputation in expeditions against the Cherokees and by 1751 had apparently achieved the rank of war chief. Soon after, he began to take an active role in diplomacy with the whites, being present at negotiations in Philadelphia in July 1754 and at Easton (Pa) four years later.

It seems probable that Kaieñ?kwaahtoñ, like most of the eastern Senecas, did not espouse the French cause in the Seven Years' War. In the summer of 1756 his brother proclaimed his own and Kaieñ?kwaahtoñ's loyalty to the British. In January 1757 the superintendent of northern Indians, Sir William JOHNSON, sent Kaieñ?kwaahtoñ presents to curry his favour. The Seneca chief and a number of warriors served at Johnson's side in the capture of Fort Niagara (near Youngstown, N.Y.) in 1759.

The fall of New France left the native population wholly dependent upon the British for manufactured goods. The Indians had grown accustomed to the generosity of white diplomats anxious for their allegiance, and they still expected such liberality. The British became parsimonious, however, and the result was the uprising of 1763 [*see* Pontiac* and KAYAHSOTA?]. The role of Kaieñ?kwaahtoñ in this confrontation is in doubt. The testimony of a Seneca, Governor Blacksnake [Thaonawyuthe*], who knew him well and who was a boy at the time, identifies him as the chief of the Seneca forces who inflicted a severe defeat on the British at the Niagara portage. Blacksnake's memory, though generally reliable, may have failed him here, for while the Senecas were fighting the British at the carrying place, Johnson was reporting that Kaieñ?kwaahtoñ "who had ever been our freind" had been sent by the Onondagas and other Iroquois to bring the warring Senecas to peace. Other testimony also asserts that Kaieñ?kwaahtoñ was a friend of the crown during this war.

In Indian diplomacy it was normal to return a captive or two as part of peace overtures. At the close of the uprising Kaieñ?kwaahtoñ approached the Seneca family that had adopted Mary Jemison and stated that he was going to return her to the authorities at Niagara. Her foster family hid her, however, and he went to Niagara empty handed. He later found another prisoner to deliver to the British, and on 21 March 1764 he arrived with the captive at Johnson Hall (Johnstown, N.Y.). Four days after, he addressed a conference there, using the usual metaphors to declare the coming of peace. The hatchet was buried and washed by a stream to the ocean where it would be lost forever, and the dead on both sides were buried so that both British and Indians could forget the conflict. Kaieñ?kwaahtoñ's name heads the list of Seneca chiefs on the preliminary articles of peace signed on 3 April. He also played a role in the conference at Fort Stanwix (Rome, N.Y.) which in 1768 attempted to draw a firm boundary between white settlement and Indian lands.

Between the treaty of Fort Stanwix and the outbreak of the American revolution, Kaieñ?kwaahtoñ remained in the background. He was seemingly of considerable influence among the eastern Senecas, but the focus of diplomatic activity in Indian affairs was farther west. He appeared at Johnson Hall at least twice in 1771 with news from the west, and when Guy JOHNSON succeeded to the post of superintendent of northern Indians he apparently cultivated the friendship of Kaieñ?kwaahtoñ in particular.

The outbreak of rebellion in the British colonies gave the ageing chief another chance to exhibit his military prowess. When the Senecas and most of the other Six Nations decided in the summer of 1777 to enter the war as allies of the British, he and Kaiũtwah?kũ (Cornplanter) were named to lead the Senecas in the war. Since they had as many warriors as the rest of the Six Nations combined, Kaieñ?kwaahtoñ was to play an important part in the conflict. Although his advanced years compelled him to ride a horse on military expeditions, he was active throughout. Indians under his command, and the British and loyalists with whom they cooperated, ran up an impressive series of victories on the northern frontier.

Full of energy, Kaieñ?kwaahtoñ immediately left the 1777 council to harass Fort Stanwix, now a rebel-held post, which guarded the western entrance to the Mohawk valley. It was more than a month before Barrimore Matthew ST LEGER's force arrived and the siege began in earnest. The Indians had been invited to smoke their pipes and watch their white allies take the fort, but on 5 August word arrived from Mary Brant [KOÑWATSI?TSIAIÉÑNI] that Brigadier-General Nicholas Herkimer and 800 Mohawk valley militia were advancing to raise the siege. The task of intercepting them was delegated to the Indians and a small body of loyalist troops. Kaieñ?kwaahtoñ, Cornplanter, and Joseph Brant [Thayendanegea*] were all present to lead the Six Nations warriors. The engagement at nearby Oriskany proved one of the bloodiest of the war, given the numbers involved. The rebels lost between 200 and 500 killed, and Indian losses were significant. Although Herkimer's force was practically exterminated, the lack of siege artillery doomed the British attempt to take the fort.

Kaieñ?kwaahtoñ was again on the war trail in the summer of 1778. He, Cornplanter, and John BUTLER led a force of about 450 Indians and 110 rangers to attack the Wyoming valley, Pa. The first two forts they approached surrendered but the third, Forty Fort, refused to capitulate. On 3 July over 400 of its garrison marched out to challenge the attackers. After firing three volleys the rebels were outflanked by the Indians and they panicked. Their retreat became a rout and more than 300 were killed. The Indian-loyalist force lost fewer than ten. The next day Forty Fort and the remaining stockades in the valley surrendered. The eight forts and a thousand houses were burned but no civilians were harmed.

Kaieñ?kwaahtoñ seems to have spent September chasing a small rebel force under Colonel Thomas Hartley from Delaware country in the Susquehanna valley. The rebels burned two Indian towns and the two sides subsequently fought at Wyalusing, Pa, with few casualties. The Seneca chief did not participate in the other major military action of that year, the raid on Cherry Valley, N.Y. [*see* Walter BUTLER].

Late in the summer of 1779 several thousand Continental soldiers under John Sullivan, supported by artillery, invaded the Iroquois homeland. Butler, Brant, Kaieñ?kwaahtoñ, and others marshalled a small force to oppose them. Butler and Brant advised harassing the invaders while retreating slowly. Other, less wise, heads prevailed, and an attempt was made to block the enemy's path. The rebel artillery and a strategic blunder by the Indians led to a rout, and Sullivan proceeded to burn his way through the Cayuga and Seneca country, devastating 40 villages including Ganundasaga. His army destroyed 160,000 bushels of corn, "a vast quantity" of other vegetables, and extensive orchards. The agricultural base of the Indian economy had been ravaged. With winter at hand the Iroquois, including Kaieñ?kwaahtoñ, fled to Niagara to subsist on British rations.

The devastation of their homeland did not break the spirit of the Senecas or their ancient chief. He was on the war trail again in July and August 1780 as a leader in the expedition that destroyed the Canajoharie and Normans Kill district, netting 50 or 60 prisoners. In October he was in the field again, joining Sir John Johnson* in a raid into the Schoharie valley. He may have shared command with Brant of the force which during this expedition captured 56 rebels who sallied forth from Fort Stanwix. The raiders also destroyed some 150,000 bushels of grain and burned 200 houses.

In this same year Kaieñ?kwaahtoñ, his family, and others moved their homes to Buffalo Creek. They frequently visited the British posts and on one of these occasions Kaieñ?kwaahtoñ paid his only documented visit to present-day Canada. It was reported that, after being handsomely entertained by the officers at Fort Erie (Ont.), the family was in some danger as he attempted to manœuvre his canoe back across the Niagara River.

During the war Kaieñ?kwaahtoñ and his warriors had succeeded in pushing the white frontier back almost as far as Albany but had in turn been driven from their homes to cluster about Niagara, the shores of Lake Erie, and the Allegheny River. Britain, in negotiating a peace with the Americans, chose to ignore the Iroquois who had fought at the side of her armies. A home on the Grand River (Ont.) for a portion of the Six Nations was obtained by Joseph Brant. The Senecas for the most part did not follow the Mohawk chief but remained in what is now New York state to make their own peace with the Americans. Abandoned by their British allies, they faced an aggressive and greedy American government in negotiations at Fort Stanwix in 1784. Kaieñ?kwaahtoñ was not there; he was hunting. Perhaps he chose not to attend.

He died in 1786 on Smoke Creek. Years later, Governor Blacksnake recalled him: "he was pretty tall – over 6 feet – & large in size – of a commanding figure. His eloquence was of a superior order – & in intellect he towered far above his fellows; He fully enjoyed the confidence of his people."

THOMAS S. ABLER

Wis., State Hist. Soc. (Madison), Draper MSS, ser.F, ser.S. *Colonial records of Pa.* (Hazard), V, 12 Aug. 1751, 6 Aug. 1754. *Johnson papers* (Sullivan *et al.*), IX, 588; X, 514, 519, 830; XI, 113, 139–40; XII, 626–28, 899, 912; XIII, 88. *Journals of the military expedition of Major General John Sullivan against the Six Nations of Indians in 1779 . . .* , ed. Frederick Cook (Auburn, N.Y., 1887). *NYCD* (O'Callaghan and Fernow), VII, 623; VIII, 282, 484, 506, 559, 721. *Pa. archives* (Hazard *et al.*), 1st ser., III, 558; VII, 508. J. E. Seaver, *A narrative of the life of Mrs. Mary Jemison . . .* , intro. A. W. Trelease (New York, 1961), 68–70, 76. *The Sullivan-Clinton campaign in 1779: chronology and selected documents . . .* (Albany, N.Y., 1929). [William Walton], *The captivity and sufferings of Benjamin Gilbert and his family, 1780–83*, ed. F. H. Severance (Cleveland, Ohio, 1904), 110. G. S. Conover, *Sayenqueraghta: king of the Senecas* (Waterloo, N.Y., 1885), 3. Graymont, *Iroquois*, 167–72.

KALM, PEHR (baptized **Petter**), natural historian; b. 6 March 1716 (N.S.) in Ångermanland province, Sweden, son of Gabriel Kalm, a Finnish clergyman, and Catherine Ross, of Scots ancestry; m. February 1750 Anna Magaretha Sandin, *née* Sjöman, in Philadelphia (Pa); d. 16 Nov. 1779 at Åbo (Turku), Finland.

Pehr Kalm was born in Sweden but was taken to Finland after 1721. Although brought up in poverty, he was able to attend school in Vaasa and matriculated to the University of Åbo in 1735. There he studied under the utilitarian mineralogist Herman Diedrich Spöring and two followers of the naturalist Carl Linnaeus (Linné), Johan Browallius and Carl Fredrik Mennander. He tutored in various parts of Finland in 1738 and 1739, noting the natural history of the country.

In 1740 Kalm came to the attention of Baron Sten Carl Bielke, an Åbo judge and member of the Royal Swedish Academy of Sciences. Becoming Bielke's ward, he went to the baron's estate in Sweden to manage his experimental plantations. In December he entered the University of Uppsala, where he heard the lectures of the noted scientist Anders Celsius. From 1741 he was a friend and student of Linnaeus. Under the influence of Bielke and Linnaeus, Pehr Kalm developed a strong interest in utilitarian botany, that is, botany as applied to problems of agriculture and industry. Linnaeus began to plan an expedition to North America in order to collect information on economically useful plants that might be viable in Scandinavia, and in 1747 Kalm was chosen to undertake the trip. Just before his departure he was appointed professor of *oeconomia* (economic natural history) at Åbo.

Kalm sailed for England in November 1747 and remained there for some months; he reached Philadelphia in September 1748. He met the leading American naturalists and set out to learn all he could about the natural history of the British colonies. His instructions from the Royal Swedish Academy of Sciences, however, were to spend as much time as possible in Canada since its climate was thought to be similar to that of Sweden and Finland, and so he proceeded north.

On 2 July 1749 Kalm entered New France at Fort Saint-Frédéric (near Crown Point, N.Y.). The commandant general of the colony, La Galissonière [Barrin*], had been instructed by the minister of Marine to defray Kalm's expenses and the fort's officers were expecting him. Kalm was surprised to learn that they collected rocks and botanical specimens on La Galissonière's orders. After three weeks of botanizing, Kalm moved to Montreal, where he was entertained by the Baron de Longueuil [Le Moyne*].

Having reached Quebec on 5 August, Kalm met La Galissonière, by whom he was greatly impressed. He had already praised American naturalists, but in the commandant general, he wrote, "I imagined I saw our great Linné under a new form." Accompanied by the physician and naturalist Jean-François Gaultier*, Kalm collected seeds of various economic plants in the area. He found Quebec's climate more extreme than Sweden's and felt that some Canadian plants would not thrive in his homeland. After his return to Montreal on 26 September he continued collecting. He wished to return to the British colonies via Fort Frontenac (Kingston, Ont.), where he had been told there were important dye plants and wild rice, and Fort Niagara (near Youngstown, N.Y.), but his request was refused by the new governor general, La Jonquière [Taffanel*], on account of frontier tensions. Instead he was obliged to go by way of Fort Saint-Frédéric.

On 29 October he reached Albany. During the winter he was able to obtain permission to visit Niagara, which he did in August 1750. Its officers received him well and aided in his seed collecting. His account of the falls was published by Benjamin Franklin and by John Bartram, but unfortunately his diary of his trip to Niagara is lost and a full account never appeared. His journeys in New France yielded considerable information and valuable seeds, among which were several such as sugar maple, walnuts, and fast-ripening maize which he had high hopes of domesticating in Scandinavia.

Kalm's diary of his travels formed the basis of a three-volume book, *En resa til Norra America* (Stockholm, 1753–61). He provides an important account of Canadian society, its religious and social institutions, economic and political structure, customs and traditions, fashions and food. The native peoples interested him greatly and he recorded various observations and reports of their ways, appearance, and origins. His diary shows that his impression of Canadians was much higher than his book suggests. In his published account he speaks glowingly of their personal qualities. He praises the politeness and cheerfulness he found at all levels of society and contrasts the industrious women with the colonial Englishwomen "who have indeed taken the liberty of throwing all the burden of housekeeping upon their husbands." In his manuscripts he is even more favourable, comparing Canada with the British colonies as heaven compares with earth, white with black. No doubt part of this feeling stemmed from the royal treatment he had received in New France, thanks to the intervention of the Swedish minister to Paris. Kalm recognized, however, that men such as La Galissonière were rare; what he did not realize was that he had arrived at the zenith of French scientific interest in New France.

Kalm sailed for Europe in February 1751, reaching Stockholm in May, and late that year he returned to Åbo to take up his post. There he remained for the rest of his life teaching, and publishing, in addition to his account of the North American voyage, numerous articles of which many dealt with North American natural history. Missing from Kalm's published account is a good deal of botanical information on Canadian plants. He hoped to produce a "*Flora canadensis*" on his return to Finland but the work never materialized. Nevertheless most of the information he had gleaned appeared in dissertations written under his direction.

Kalm was one of the outstanding utilitarian Linnaean botanists, one genus and 90 species of plants being named for him. His major legacy, his book, stimulated natural history in Sweden and provided Europeans with an accurate and wide-ranging account of North American conditions and customs. Kalm's descriptions of Canadian life and *mores* are among the best found in travel literature concerning the country.

RICHARD A. JARRELL

[The part of Pehr Kalm's account of his journey relating to North America appeared in English as *Travels into North America . . .* , trans. J. R. Forster (3v., Warrington, Eng., and London, 1770–71) and was republished with additional material as *The America of 1750: Peter Kalm's travels in North America*, ed. A. B. Benson (2v., New York, 1927; repr. 1966). It was also translated into French as *Voyage de Kalm en Amérique*, L.-W. Marchand, trad. (2v., Montréal, 1880) and into Dutch; the entire work appeared in German. Kalm's description of Niagara is included in [John Bartram], *Observations on the inhabitants . . . and other matters worthy of notice, made by Mr. John Bartram, in his travels from Pensilvania to Onondago, Oswego and the Lake Ontario . . .* (London, 1751), reprinted under the title *Travels in Pensilvania and Canada* (Ann Arbor, Mich., 1966). In addition to his book, Kalm wrote a number of articles on specific plants and animals of North America which appeared in the publications of the Royal Swedish Academy of Sciences. Eight of these were translated into English by Esther Louise Larsen and published in *Agricultural History* ([Baltimore, Md.?]) between 1935 and 1950.

Monographs and articles relating to Kalm include: Israel Acrelius, *A history of New Sweden; or, the settlements on the River Delaware*, trans. W. M. Reynolds (Philadelphia, 1874); *Dictionary of scientific biography*, ed. C. C. Gillispie *et al.* (14v., New York, 1970–76), VII, 210–11; Martti Kerkkonen, *Peter Kalm's North American journey; its ideological background and results* (Helsinki, 1959); P.-G. Roy, "Le voyageur Kalm et les cloîtres de Québec," *BRH*, XXXV (1929), 449–51; Carl Skottsberg, "Pehr Kalm: levnadsteckning," *Levnadsteckningar över Kungl. Svenska vetenskapsakademiens ledamöter* (Stockholm), 8 (1949–54), 219–505; Armand Yon, "Pour un IIe centenaire: du nouveau sur Kalm," *RHAF*, III (1949–50), 234–55. R.A.J.]

KAYAHSOTA? (written **Gaiachoton, Geyesutha, Guyasuta, Kayashoton, Kiashuta, Quiasutha**), Seneca chief and diplomat; b. *c.* 1725, probably on the Genesee River (N.Y.), but his family moved to the Ohio region when he was young; d. on the Cornplanter Grant (near Corydon, Pa), probably in 1794. His name, spelled Kayahsota? according to Wallace L. Chafe's phonemic orthography of modern Seneca, means it stands up (or sets up) the cross.

Although the Iroquois Confederacy had since 1701 been officially committed to neutrality in the wars between the French and the British, the Iroquois of the Ohio country and the Senecas whose homes were on the Genesee tended to pursue a pro-French policy. The French strengthened their position in the region in the early 1750s by building a string of forts from Lake Erie to the forks of the Ohio [*see* Paul Marin* de La Malgue]. The British responded in 1753 by sending the young George Washington to demand that the French withdraw from the area, which both powers claimed. Years later, Washington remembered Kayahsota? as being among the Indian escort on his fruitless journey. In 1755 Major-General Edward Braddock attempted to capture Fort Duquesne (Pittsburgh, Pa), and Kayahsota? was part of the force of French and Indians which met and, under Jean-Daniel DUMAS, routed him. In the autumn Kayahsota? led a delegation of 20 Senecas to confer with Governor Pierre de RIGAUD de Vaudreuil in Montreal.

The fortunes of war turned against the French and their native allies, and despite the assistance given by Kayahsota? and other western Senecas, in 1758 Fort Duquesne fell to the British under John Forbes*. The French effectively withdrew from the west in 1759, but hostilities were not at an end. The miserly attitude adopted by AMHERST with respect to Indian presents aggravated the difficulties between the native population and the British, and the result was the outbreak generally known as the Pontiac* rebellion, although it has been called the Kiyasuta and Pontiac war.

Political leaders in the egalitarian societies found in most of North America prior to its conquest by the white man lacked the authority to compel their constituents to action and relied instead upon suasion. As he had no power to dictate public policy, and only his personal diplomatic skills to shape public opinion, Kayahsota? would not seem to merit a major share of the blame, or praise, for the conflict which flared on the western frontier in 1763. The native population was nearly unanimous with respect to the desirability of attacking the red-coated troops who had so recently replaced the French in that region, but Kayahsota? was influential in focusing resentment and was among the first to urge the use of force. As early as 1761 he and his fellow Seneca Tahahaiadoris were circulating a large red wampum belt, known as the war hatchet, among the native population clustered about Detroit. According to Sir William JOHNSON's deputy, George Croghan, they privately admitted to him that the purpose was to bring on a general uprising from Detroit to the Mohawk valley. Sir William himself came to Detroit in September 1761 to counteract their efforts. At the conference Kayahsota? denied the charges made against him but found himself contradicted by a Wyandot, and the resulting uproar was calmed only by the efforts of Johnson. Later an Ottawa speaker, Mécatépilésis, publicly identified Kayahsota? as "the bad Bird lately Amongst us." Johnson met with Kayahsota? privately and tried to convince the Seneca leader of the error of his ways, but his diplomacy obtained only a brief respite. In June 1763 the frontier erupted in a general war. Most of the Six Nations, including the eastern Senecas, remained at peace, but the western Senecas were active against the British. Kayahsota? and a few other Senecas fought alongside the Delawares in the siege of Fort Pitt (formerly Fort Duquesne) and against the relief force under Colonel Henry Bouquet. Native testimony also suggests that he took part in the capture of the British post at Venango (Franklin, Pa).

After the fighting had run its course, Kayahsota? was among those who signed a preliminary peace agreement on 12 Aug. 1764, and he was given the task of carrying the conditions of peace to those groups still at war. At the end of October 1764 Kayahsota' came to Tuscarawas (near Bolivar, Ohio) with delegates of the Delawares, Shawnees, and Senecas to meet with Bouquet. Bouquet's major concern by this time was the release of white captives still in Indian hands. He reported the negotiations a success, despite the necessity of dispatching Kayahsota' to the Delawares to protest the murder of a British soldier. Over 200 white captives were released (although some proved so reluctant to rejoin white society that Bouquet had to post guards to prevent them from returning to their native captors). Following the conference, Bouquet sent Kayahsota' to fetch white captives held by the Wyandots.

In the spring of 1765 George Croghan met with the western Indians at Fort Pitt, and the return of prisoners was again a central issue. Kayahsota' was there and was appointed a delegate to yet another conference, this time with Sir William Johnson at Johnson Hall (Johnstown, N.Y.). Kayahsota' and other western Indians met there from 4 to 13 July to negotiate a final peace. On the last day Kayahsota' affixed the sign of a wolf, the eponym of his clan, to the treaty.

In the following decade Kayahsota' served continually as an intermediary between the British authorities and the native inhabitants of the Ohio region. Frequently journeying between Johnson Hall and the Ohio, he carried wampum belts and Johnson's words in attempts to preserve peace in the west or to isolate diplomatically such uncooperative groups as the Shawnees. The Indian superintendent considered him a "Chief of much Capacity and vast Influence" and found him "very useful on such Occasions." When a group of Shawnees appeared at Fort Pitt in the spring of 1773 with a complaint about Virginia surveyors, it was Kayahsota' who received them and presented them with a wampum belt. On the other hand the western Indians often conveyed their grievances to Johnson through him. For example, the participants in a major conference held at Fort Pitt in October 1773 sent Kayahsota' to Johnson Hall with their complaints about unregulated trade, particularly in liquor.

Kayahsota' was never able to carry out one of Johnson's major aims, the removal of the Mingos, Iroquois emigrants to the Ohio country, back to their old homes in what is now upstate New York. The superintendent feared that these warriors, far from the moderating influence of the Onondaga council and even farther from Johnson Hall, and carrying with them the well-earned reputation that the Iroquois enjoyed as fighting men, might join their Algonkian speaking neighbours against the British. Johnson had first asked Kayahsota' to persuade the Mingos to return in 1765, and the Seneca chief was still trying unsuccessfully to carry out the policy in 1773.

In addition to all his diplomatic activity, Kayahsota' found time to work for various whites in the Ohio valley. His knowledge of the geography and the inhabitants of the region enabled him to serve as guide and intermediary for travellers and traders. His duties took him several times to Fort de Chartres (near Prairie du Rocher) in the Illinois country.

When the American revolution broke out, Kayahsota' had already established a close working relationship with Guy JOHNSON, successor to Sir William as Indian superintendent. The rebels, however, were active in courting the chief's favour. Kayahsota' was among the Indian leaders meeting representatives of the Continental Congress at Fort Pitt in October 1775. He agreed that the Shawnees should surrender prisoners and booty captured in their war with Virginia, which had just concluded, and consented to go to their towns to make sure the surrender was carried out. In return, he asked for assurance that the boundary of white settlement established by the treaty of Fort Stanwix (1768) would be honoured. He also observed astutely that disputes among the rebel representatives might well inhibit the kindling of a bright council fire so necessary for effective Indian-white communication.

The Six Nations held a neutral stance during the early years of the American revolution. Kayahsota' moved freely between the rebel post at Fort Pitt and the loyalist stronghold at Niagara (near Youngstown, N.Y.). To the commandants at both forts he proclaimed the determination of the Six Nations to take no part in any war between Britain and the colonies. At Fort Pitt on 6 July 1776 he emphasized native opposition to the movement through Indian lands by armies of either side. Later, he went on an embassy to the Mingos to bring them into line with the neutral position assumed by the other western tribes. In recognition of his services, the Continental Congress awarded him a colonel's commission and a silver gorget.

It was inevitable, however, that the native population would eventually enter the contest on the side of the crown. There were too many grievances against the encroaching Americans and, although the war disrupted normal economic life, an active role in the conflict promised ample material rewards. With the decision of the Six Nations in the summer of 1777 to abandon neutrality, Kayahsotaʔ began to work actively for the royal, and Indian, cause. Later in the summer he was one of a large body of Indians who accompanied Barrimore Matthew ST LEGER against the rebels at Fort Stanwix (Rome, N.Y.). The siege of this fort at the western end of the Mohawk valley was in its initial phase when word came from Mary Brant [KOÑWATSIʔTSIAIÉÑNI] that 800 militiamen were marching to attack the besiegers. It was primarily the Indians who were dispatched to meet them, and the rebels were repulsed in the bloody battle of Oriskany nearby. Kayahsotaʔ was in the field again soon; in December 1777 Simon Girty* reported that the Seneca chief or members of his war party had killed four people near Ligonier, Pa. When in 1779 a rebel army commanded by Daniel Brodhead marched from Fort Pitt up the Allegheny river valley, burning Seneca villages, Kayahsotaʔ appeared at Niagara demanding 100 soldiers to aid against the invaders. The hard-pressed British commander refused, and Brodhead's destructive expedition went largely unopposed.

Kayahsotaʔ was sent from Niagara in 1780 on a familiar diplomatic task. Anxious to keep the alliance of the western Indians, Guy Johnson dispatched him on a tour of the Ohio country to call a conference at Detroit. Most of the chiefs of the region were absent carrying the war into Kentucky with Henry Bird's expedition; so the messages were left with the Wyandots for delivery later in the summer. There is some evidence that Kayahsotaʔ then commanded a party of 30 Wyandots who raided near Fort McIntosh (Rochester, Pa) in July. In the spring of 1781 Kayahsotaʔ was again on the diplomatic trail, but illness detained him for some time at Cattaraugus (near the mouth of Cattaraugus Creek, N.Y.). The ageing chief went to war once more, leading the party which on 13 July 1782 burned Hannastown, Pa, and then went on to attack Wheeling (W. Va).

For all intents and purposes, the American revolution was over, and the Senecas soon made their peace with the United States. There is one report that the new republic tried to use Kayahsotaʔ as a peacemaker in the Ohio region, but for the most part the role devolved on Kaiũtwahʔkũ (Cornplanter), probably a nephew of Kayahsotaʔ. The Ohio Indians, however, were bent on a major confrontation with the Americans which Seneca diplomacy was powerless to stop. As events moved towards a climax, Kayahsotaʔ carried personal and public messages to the American commander, Anthony Wayne, at Pittsburgh in 1792, and accompanied Cornplanter to a meeting with Wayne in 1793. Wayne was organizing and training his force so that he could invade the Ohio country and subdue its native inhabitants, and he was to achieve success at the battle of Fallen Timbers (near Waterville, Ohio) in August 1794.

Cornplanter's diplomatic efforts earned him a grant of land in Pennsylvania, and he and his Seneca followers gathered on it at the close of the century. There Kayahsotaʔ died and was buried, probably in 1794.

THOMAS S. ABLER

BL, Add. MSS 21767. Wis., State Hist. Soc. (Madison), Draper MSS, ser.F, ser.S. *Anthony Wayne . . . the Wayne-Knox-Pickering-McHenry correspondence*, ed. R. C. Knopf (Pittsburgh, Pa., 1960). *Colonial records of PA.* (Hazard), IX, 23 Aug., 5 Dec. 1764, 4 June 1765. [George Croghan], "George Croghan's journal, 1759–1763 . . . ," ed. N. B. Wainwright, *Pennsylvania Magazine of History and Biography* (Philadelphia), LXXI (1947), 303–444. *Frontier defense on the upper Ohio, 1777–1778 . . .* , ed. R. G. Thwaites and L. P. Kellogg (Madison, 1912; repr. Millwood, N.Y., 1973). *Frontier retreat on the upper Ohio, 1779–1781*, ed. L. P. Kellogg (Madison, 1917). "John Adlum on the Allegheny: memoirs for the year 1794," ed. D. H. Kent and M. H. Deardorff, *Pennsylvania Magazine of History and Biography*, LXXXIV (1960), 265–324, 435–80. *Johnson papers* (Sullivan *et al.*), III, 488; IV, 607; V, 681; VIII, 615–16, 641, 643, 679, 835, 1012; X, 347; XII, 994, 1016, 1034–35, 1044–61, 1090, 1095–1100, 1115; XIII, 233, 253–55, 666–67, 681–82, 686. *NYCD* (O'Callaghan and Fernow), VII, 750–57; VIII, 315, 363–64, 501, 503; X, 345–47. *The revolution on the upper Ohio, 1775–1777 . . .* , ed. R. G. Thwaites and L. P. Kellogg (Madison, 1908; repr. Port Washington, N.Y., and London, 1970). W. L. Chafe, *Handbook of the Seneca language* (Albany, N.Y., 1963). R. C. Downes, *Council fires on the upper Ohio: a narrative of Indian affairs in the upper Ohio valley until 1795* (Pittsburgh, 1940). H. R. Schoolcraft, *Information respecting the history, condition and prospects of the Indian tribes of the United States* (6v., Philadelphia, 1851–57), IV, 269–78. N. B. Wainwright, *George Croghan, wilderness diplomat* (Chapel Hill, N.C., 1959).

KENDRICK (Kenwick, Kenwrick), JOHN, fur-trader; b. *c.* 1740 in Harwich, Massachusetts, son of Solomon Kenwrick and Elizabeth Atkins; m. December 1767 Huldah Pease; d. 12 Dec. 1794 at Honolulu harbour, Oahu (Hawaii).

John Kendrick went to sea at an early age, and by the time he was 20 he was engaged in the whaling industry of the St Lawrence. He served in one campaign in the Seven Years' War but then returned to sea, entering the New England coastal trade. During the American revolution he commanded several privateers which preyed on British commerce.

The third Pacific voyage of James COOK revealed the high prices sea otter furs from the northwest coast would bring in China. As news of the trade possibilities filtered through the commercial world, merchants responded by sending expeditions to the northwest coast; James HANNA, sailing from Macao, China, in 1785, was the first to exploit the trade. In 1787 Kendrick was placed in command of a trading expedition organized by Joseph Barrell, a Boston merchant, and composed of two ships, the *Columbia Rediviva* and the *Lady Washington*, the latter under Captain Robert Gray*. The vessels bore cargoes of trade goods, chiefly items of copper and iron, special medals for the Indians, and passports and letters from the American government and the Commonwealth of Massachusetts.

The expedition left Boston in September 1787 but Kendrick, according to Gray, was not a "nimble leader." The ships dawdled in several ports along the way. One of these stops, at the island of Juan Fernández (Isla Robinson Crusoe), off the coast of Chile, alerted Spanish authorities to their destination and caused concern about possible American encroachments on Spanish claims to the Pacific coast. Kendrick and Gray finally arrived at Nootka Sound (B.C.) in September 1788, after taking three months longer than the normal sailing time, and decided to spend the winter there. Kendrick systematically courted MUQUINNA, one of the principal chiefs of the Nootka Indians. In March 1789, while his partner sailed south, trading along the coast as far as Juan de Fuca Strait, Kendrick moved his ship farther up the sound to Mawinna Cove (Marvinas Bay, B.C.) and erected a house and battery, which he named Fort Washington.

On 5 May the Spanish warship *Princesa*, under the command of Esteban José MARTÍNEZ, arrived at Nootka. Martínez had been instructed to establish a temporary post to ensure that Spanish claims to the Pacific coast would be recognized. Kendrick was able to persuade the Spaniard that his two vessels were in Nootka for repairs, not for trade. Several British vessels, however, including the *Argonaut*, under the command of James Colnett*, were seized by Martínez for infringing on Spanish sovereignty. The seizure of these vessels touched off the Nootka crisis, which was to bring England and Spain to the brink of war in 1790. Kendrick appears to have helped establish the Spanish presence at Nootka: he introduced Martínez to Muquinna, trained his guns on the *Argonaut* upon request, and ordered his armourer to make leg-irons for the British prisoners. During the stay at Nootka Kendrick's son John embraced Catholicism and changed his name to Juan; he later served on Spanish vessels.

With two good ships and with his competitors in irons, Kendrick had a chance to make a fortune for himself and his owners. The northwest coast was then a fur-traders' paradise; in one instance the expedition had received 200 sea otter pelts valued at $8,000 for an equal number of iron chisels worth about $100. In July 1789 Kendrick exchanged commands with Gray, and while the *Columbia* sailed for China, Kendrick traded in the *Lady Washington* along the coast from Nootka to the Queen Charlotte Islands (B.C.). There he anchored off what is now known as Anthony Island, and in the process of trading with the Haidas subjected their chief, KOYAH, to intense personal humiliation by locking him to a gun-carriage until some of Kendrick's laundry, which had been pilfered by the Indians, was returned.

On his voyage to China Kendrick visited the Sandwich (Hawaiian) Islands and became one of the first to see the possibility of trade with the Orient in pearls and sandalwood. He left three men to collect these commodities, but on such short notice they had no means of conducting their mission effectively. When George VANCOUVER saw them in March 1792 they were destitute and had failed in their task. Once in China, Kendrick spent a leisurely 14 months disposing of his cargo and rerigging the *Lady Washington* as a brig. In March 1791 he again sailed for the northwest coast, visiting Japan on the way.

On 13 June 1791 the *Lady Washington* arrived at Barrell Sound (Houston Stewart Channel, B.C.). Three days later, off Anthony Island, the Haidas, led by Koyah, attacked the vessel. Kendrick and his crew repulsed the Indians, killing many. As he had not been very successful in trade in the Queen Charlotte Islands, Kendrick turned south along the coast and on 12 July entered Nootka Sound. Uncertain of the intentions of the Spaniards, he went to his old anchorage of Mawinna, where he obtained about 800 sea otter pelts. He pleased the Indians by paying high prices for their furs; by supplying them with guns, he contributed to subsequent violence in the fur trade. Kendrick also purchased large tracts of land, obtaining deeds signed by the Nootkas and duly witnessed. John Howell, an American trader, later reported that Kendrick "one day told the Commandant at Notka Sound, that he bought his Territories, whilst other nations stole them; and that if they (the Spaniards) were impertinent he would raise the Indians and drive them from their settlements." Sailing south to Clayoquot Sound, Kendrick obtained more furs, met with Gray, took time to repair his ships, and then left for China on 29 September.

Kendrick spent 14 months in Macao, to Gray's exasperation, before sailing in the spring of 1793 for the northwest coast. He spent the summer trading along the coast and then wintered in the Sandwich Islands. Late in 1794, after having spent the summer in trade, he revisited the Sandwich Islands, where one faction of the natives had just won an inter-island war. While Kendrick was at anchor in Honolulu harbour witnessing a victory celebration, a fellow trader fired a broadside in salute. Unfortunately, one of his guns had not been unshotted, and its ball pierced the side of the *Lady Washington*, killing Kendrick and several of his crew.

Although Kendrick was noted for his enterprise and good spirits, he was also dilatory and often entertained fantastic schemes. Howell reported that two "of his favourite plans were to change the prevalence of the westerly winds in the Atlantic Ocean, and turn the Gulf Stream into the Pacific, by cutting A Canal through Mexico." Convinced of the feasibility of colonizing the land he had purchased at Nootka, Kendrick wrote to Thomas Jefferson suggesting that it be settled under the protection of the American government. In 1795 his owners advertised in London for immigrants to the region, but none were forthcoming. Petitions later made to the United States Congress on behalf of his family for title to the land failed in 1854 for lack of documentation.

RICHARD A. PIERCE

"Captains Gray and Kendrick; the Barrel letters," ed. F. W. Howay, *Washington Hist. Quarterly* (Seattle), XII (1921), 243–71. "Later affairs of Kendrick; Barrell letters," ed. N. B. Pipes, Oreg. Hist. Soc., *Quarterly* (Eugene), XXX (1929), 95–105. "Letters relating to the second voyage of the 'Columbia,' " ed. F. W. Howay, Oreg. Hist. Soc., *Quarterly*, XXIV (1923), 132–52. Meares, *Voyages*. G. Vancouver, *Voyage of discovery* (J. Vancouver). *Voyages of 'Columbia'* (Howay). *DAB*. Howay, *List of trading vessels in maritime fur trade*. Walbran, *B.C. coast names*. Cook, *Flood tide of empire*. F. W. Howay, "John Kendrick and his sons," Oreg. Hist. Soc., *Quarterly*, XXIII (1922), 277–302; "Voyages of Kendrick and Gray in 1787–90," Oreg. Hist. Soc., *Quarterly*, XXX (1929), 89–94.

KERDISIEN. *See* PICHOT

KERRIVAN, PETER. *See* Appendix

KERSIDENT, VINCENT-FLEURI GUICHART DE. *See* GUICHART

KIASHUTA. *See* KAYAHSOTA?

KING, JAMES, naval officer and explorer; b. 1750 at Clitheroe, Lancashire, England; d. late October or early November 1784 in Nice (France).

James King, the second son of the curate of Clitheroe, entered the Royal Navy in 1762. He served on the Newfoundland station under Captain Hugh PALLISER and in the Mediterranean, being promoted lieutenant in 1771. He then studied science, first in Paris in 1774 and then at Oxford. In 1776 he was appointed second lieutenant of the *Resolution* and sailed on the last of James COOK's Pacific voyages, with specific responsibility for astronomical observations. He succeeded to the command of the consort vessel, the *Discovery*, when Charles CLERKE died in August 1779, and he was given post rank after the expedition returned to England.

During the voyage King kept an admirably full and detailed journal, in which factual descriptions are accompanied by more reflective passages. Important for its careful listing of navigational, astronomical, meteorological, and other observations, the journal also forms one of the most reliable running accounts of the famous voyage, and in particular of the explorations of the 1778 and 1779 seasons when the expedition searched in vain for a northwest passage along the coasts of what are now British Columbia and Alaska and through Bering Strait. It shows King to have been better versed in the controversial geography of the northwest coast, and in the accounts of earlier Russian explorations, than any other officer on board except Cook himself. It was no surprise, then, that after the expedition's return King (who was elected a fellow of the Royal Society of London in 1782) was entrusted with the writing of the third volume of the official account of the voyage – though its style owes much to Dr John Douglas' busy editorial pen. The volume reflects King's uneasiness about the haste with which Cook had sailed along the west coast north of Nootka Sound (B.C.). He suggests another venture to "trace the coast with great accuracy from the latitude of 56° to 50°, the space from which we were driven out of sight of land by contrary winds," adding that the expense might be met by trading in sea otter pelts with the Indians. King's account of the sale of such furs by Cook's men in Canton (People's Republic of China) at more than 100 dollars apiece for the best, officially verified rumours about the money to be made in the fur trade with China and may well have helped to secure the capital needed for the private expeditions which were beginning to leave for the northwest coast of America [*see* James HANNA; John KENDRICK].

King did not long survive the publication, in June 1784, of *A voyage to the Pacific ocean*. After service in the West Indies and with the Channel fleet he went to what is now the south of France for health reasons in the late summer of 1784 and died in Nice of tuberculosis. An unusual man to find serving as a naval officer, King had been interested in science and politics, and was a friend of Edmund Burke's family and of the political reformer John Cartwright. In the tributes paid to him by friends and colleagues perhaps the most striking came from James Trevenen, one of Cook's officers, who, meeting William Wilberforce in 1785, "was much struck with the resemblance between him and Capt: King (I kiss the name) the same quickness in his manner, the same ease in his behavior, the same mildness gentleness and persuasion."

GLYNDWR WILLIAMS

[James King's journals for 1776–79 are in PRO, Adm. 55/116, 55/122; extracts are printed in *Journals of Captain James Cook* (Beaglehole), III, 549–69, 582–91, 603–32, 650–54, 659–78, 1361–455. King's journal for 1779–80, "Journal of the proceedings of his may sloop Discovery from Kamchakta to Cape of Good Hope . . . ," has recently (1973) been discovered in the archives of the Hydrographer of the Navy, Ministry of Defence (Taunton, Eng.), and is numbered OD279. Letters concerning King's authorship of the third volume of James Cook and James King, *A voyage to the Pacific Ocean* . . . (3v. and atlas, London, 1784), are in BL, Egerton MSS 2180. Additional information can be found in *The correspondence of Edmund Burke*, ed. T. W. Copeland *et al.* (10v., Cambridge, Eng., and Chicago, 1958–78), III, V; in *The Banks letters; a calendar of the manuscript correspondence of Sir Joseph Banks* . . . , ed. W. R. Dawson (London, 1958), 486–87; and in the *DNB*. G.W.]

KINGMINGUSE (baptized **Peter**), Labrador Inuk; fl. 1776–92.

Although the Moravian Brethren established a mission at Nain, Labrador, in 1771 [*see* Jens HAVEN], the missionaries did not formally accept a candidate for baptism until October 1775. On 19 Feb. 1776 Kingminguse, a young *angakok* (shaman) from a nearby band, renounced his traditional beliefs and was baptized. Appropriately, he was named Peter. The event caused a stir among the local Inuit and aroused considerable interest in the new religion, especially since Kingminguse proved at first a model convert. This general enthusiasm evaporated during the summer of 1776, and as a result Kingminguse found his ideological isolation difficult to endure. In August he went inland to hunt caribou and, when his wife (a candidate for baptism) fell sick, called in two *angakut* to cure her. He confessed his relapse to the missionaries, and his behaviour during the winter of 1776–77 seems to have satisfied them. But the long summer caribou hunt, far from mission influence, was again his undoing. In November 1777 the missionaries reported that Kingminguse had "during the hunting season . . . quite gone from his heart and had taken such courses that we were obliged to tell him that we could not acknowledge him as our brother or admit him to the meetings of the believers." It was not until August 1779 that he was thought to be sufficiently contrite and allowed to rejoin the congregation. However, the familiar pattern soon reappeared. During the summers of 1780 and 1781, he used traditional methods to cure sickness. He confessed and was pardoned on both occasions. In 1783 he became affected by a general restlessness generated among the Nain Inuit by the news that guns were available from a trader at Chateau Bay in southern Labrador. Telling the missionaries that he had lost his faith, he left for the south.

Kingminguse did not return to Nain until the summer of 1785, by which time he had apparently resumed his trade as an *angakok*. The missionaries did their best to persuade him to return to the congregation, but their pleas were in vain. The last reference to Kingminguse in mission records (1792) describes him as "sunk in heathenism" on Nukasusuktok, an island not far from Nain.

Kingminguse's position had been difficult. Although baptism initially gave him a special status, it deprived him of the respect he had gained as an *angakok* and a hunter. His frequent returns to the old ways – typical of the early converts – reflect an attempt not only to regain that respect, but also to eliminate the cultural isolation which conversion implied. While close to a mission, a convert could bear this isolation more easily; but when far away, or when under stress, there was a natural tendency to discard new, alien practices in favour of the old. If Kingminguse's vacillations were not unusual, his final abandonment of the mission was. Most converts, no matter how regular their lapses, remained within the mission orbit. Kingminguse, however, had told the missionaries that he could never return, because when he saw others baptized after him continuing in the faith he was ashamed.

J. K. HILLER

PAC, MG 17, D1, Nain mission diaries, 1771–1893. Hiller, "Foundation of Moravian mission," 201–6.

KING OF KANADESAGA. *See* KAIEÑ?KWAAHTOÑ

KNAUT, PHILIP AUGUSTUS (sometimes referred to as **George Philip** or **John Philip**), fur-trader, merchant, and local official; b. 1716 in the Electorate of Saxony (German Democratic Republic); m. 30 July 1750 Anna Grob at Halifax, Nova Scotia, and they had three surviving children; m. secondly on 15 July 1781 Jane Brimner at Lunenburg, Nova Scotia; d. 28 Dec. 1781 at Lunenburg.

Philip Augustus Knaut accompanied Edward CORNWALLIS' expedition to Nova Scotia in 1749, and he soon secured a pass to travel on business anywhere in the province; since the pass was in French it is likely he was trading in furs with the Acadians. Although not associated with the general migration of foreign Protestants, in 1753 he accompanied the Germans to Lunenburg, where he quickly won the confidence of the government at Halifax and received small official positions such as justice of the peace, militia officer, and coroner. One of the first storekeepers in the town, Knaut was also operating a sawmill near Lunenburg as early as 1754 and accumulating wood lots to supply it. In 1755 Lieutenant Governor Charles Lawrence* bought the entire output of the mill to encourage this kind of entrepreneurial activity.

A German who spoke English, Knaut had the trust of his fellow Lunenburgers, and in the elections to the first House of Assembly in 1758 he had the support, almost to a man, of the 44 freeholders with foreign names. Knaut was elected for the township of Lunenburg and remained a member for either the township or the county of Lunenburg until his death. As an assemblyman, he considered it almost his only function to act as a spokesman for his constituents. Thus in his first two sessions he sought an English speaking minister and schoolmaster for the German community and protection for its outsettlers against the Indians.

After the Halifax merchant Benjamin GERRISH had acquired a near monopoly of trade with the Indians in 1760, he made Knaut the Indian truckmaster at Lunenburg, one of six such salaried officers. Since the bargain with Gerrish proved disastrous for the government, Lieutenant Governor Jonathan BELCHER terminated it on instructions from London. The lieutenant governor was also ordered to take other action that would have been injurious to Gerrish and his brother JOSEPH. To forestall steps to implement these measures, the Gerrishes organized a strike by some members of the assembly and prevented it from meeting between October 1761 and March 1762. For taking part in the strike, Knaut was stripped of the offices he held under commission. Apparently indignant, he absented himself from the meetings of the commission for assigning lots in Lunenburg and finally resigned in "a churlish manner." Knaut later reinstated himself, however, and in November 1767 he again became a justice of the peace. Although by now a veteran member of the assembly, he played only a minor role in its proceedings and committee work. He continued to air his constituents' grievances, however, appearing twice before the Council in 1774 to press their land claims.

All the while his business operations had prospered, and the result at his death was an unseemly contest for the control of his estate between his second wife, who had remarried within six weeks of his death, and his daughters and sons-in-law. In the end John Newton, collector of impost and excise at Halifax, who had married Knaut's elder daughter Catherine, was granted letters of administration and the guardianship of Knaut's third child, Benjamin. The estate's net value of about £9,000, a small fortune in the 18th century, represents one of the first success stories in the Lunenburg region.

J. MURRAY BECK

Halifax County Court of Probate (Halifax), K58 (original estate papers of Philip Augustus Knaut). N.S., House of Assembly, *Journal*, 1758–81. Bell, *Foreign Protestants*, 346, 483, 485n, 539, 540, 575n. Brebner, *Neutral Yankees* (1937), 58–65. M. B. DesBrisay, *History of the county of Lunenburg* (2nd ed., Toronto, 1895), 110.

KNELLER, HENRY, lawyer and attorney general; d. March 1776 in England.

Henry Kneller came to Canada shortly after the conquest, in 1763 or the following year. On 2 Oct. 1764 he was appointed clerk of the crown, on 3 November he took his oath as deputy clerk of the Council, and on 13 November he was appointed register of the Court of Chancery. On 23 March 1765 Kneller obtained a commission as an attorney, which (with that given to Williams Conyngham) is the earliest known to have been issued in Quebec. He had apparently obtained permission to practise law before this date, however, since the *Quebec Gazette* announced on 28 Feb. 1765 that he had been admitted to practise in the Court of King's Bench at its first sitting (as were Conyngham, Jeremy Condy Russell, and John Burke) and had taken the required oaths. Kneller resigned as deputy clerk of the Council on 11 June 1765 because of his many activities.

Shortly thereafter he ceased being register of the Court of Chancery; after August 1765 his signature is not on any of its documents. On 22 July 1767 he was commissioned a barrister.

Kneller was held in high regard by governors James MURRAY and Guy Carleton*. When the latter gave Francis Maseres* a year's leave of absence to return to England in the autumn of 1769, he appointed Kneller acting attorney general, that is, acting king's attorney. This appointment was confirmed by the king early in 1770. Carleton also recommended that, should it prove impossible to find a qualified jurist who knew French, Kneller should be given the permanent post.

At the Council's request, Kneller drew up an ordinance, passed on 1 Feb. 1770, to make the administration of justice more efficient and to regulate the civil courts of the province. This decree resulted from the report of a committee which had been established to investigate the work of the justices of the peace, in response to numerous complaints about their incompetence and irregularities. The ordinance abolished the jurisdiction of the justices of the peace in matters of property, established a court of common pleas in the district of Montreal independent of the one in Quebec, decreed that in future these courts would sit throughout the year, and reduced the severity of rules governing execution of judgements. It was ill received by the English merchants. Many of them were justices of the peace and were disappointed at losing their powers in matters of private property. They also complained that the measure enabled their business creditors to hound them all year round and gave their debtors too much protection. Their protests, however, had no effect.

In October 1771 Kneller was appointed advocate general in the Court of Vice-Admiralty, succeeding George SUCKLING. According to the *Quebec Gazette* he was given official appointment as attorney general in 1772. Kneller returned to England in 1775 and died there in March the following year.

JACQUES L'HEUREUX

PAC, MG 11, [CO 42], Q, 7, p.1; 8, p.83; MG 23, GII, 1, ser.1, 2, p.190; RG 1, E1, 1, p.56; 2, pp.9–10; RG 4, B8, 28, p.86. PRO, CO 42/2, pp.98, 100; 42/3, p.136; 42/6, p.213 (PAC transcripts). *Doc. relatifs à l'hist. constitutionnelle, 1759–91* (Shortt et Doughty; 1921), I, 376–96; II, 703. *Rapports sur les lois de Québec, 1767–1770*, W. P. M. Kennedy et Gustave Lanctot, édit. (Ottawa, 1931). *Quebec Gazette*, 28 Feb., 20 June 1765, 1 Oct. 1772. P.-G. Roy, *Les avocats de la région de Québec*, 232. Wallace, *Macmillan dictionary*, 373. Brunet, *Les Canadiens après la Conquête*, 227–29. Burt, *Old prov. of Que.* (1968), I, 156–58. Neatby, *Quebec*, 97–99. L'Heureux, "L'organisation judiciaire," *Revue générale de droit*, 1, 288–90, 294–95, 314–16, 318, 322. W. R. Riddell, "The first court of chancery in Canada," *Boston University Law Rev.* (Boston, Mass.), II (1922), 241.

KNOX, JOHN, army officer and author; third son of John Knox, a merchant of Sligo (Republic of Ireland); d. 8 Feb. 1778 at Berwick-upon-Tweed, England.

John Knox is reported to have served as a volunteer in the British army during the War of the Austrian Succession. He distinguished himself in the action at Laffeldt (Belgium) on 2 July 1747 and in consequence was appointed to an ensigncy in the 43rd Foot in 1749. Five years later he purchased a lieutenancy in the 43rd. In 1757 Knox went with his regiment from Ireland to Halifax, Nova Scotia, to participate in Lord Loudoun's intended expedition against Louisbourg, Île Royale (Cape Breton Island). The attack was postponed, and the 43rd spent the winter in posts on the Bay of Fundy, Knox being stationed at Annapolis Royal. The regiment was not employed in Jeffery AMHERST's successful operation against Louisbourg in 1758 and suffered what Knox called "inglorious exile" in the Fundy region until the spring of 1759, when it was incorporated into James Wolfe*'s force for the expedition against Quebec. Knox was present with his regiment in the battle on the Plains of Abraham, served throughout the winter 1759–60 under James MURRAY at Quebec, and fought in the battle of Sainte-Foy on 28 April 1760. He was with Murray's force which advanced up the St Lawrence, and he was present at the capitulation of Montreal in 1760.

In the winter of 1760–61 Knox, now probably in England, was appointed captain of one of a number of newly formed independent companies, many of which were soon amalgamated to constitute new infantry regiments. Knox's company became part of the 99th Foot but this unit was short-lived, being disbanded in 1763 after the peace. Knox was placed on half pay. He evidently used this enforced leisure to write his two-volume work *An historical journal of the campaigns in North-America for the years 1757, 1758, 1759 and 1760 . . .* (London, 1769). Knox, then living in Gloucester, dedicated the book by permission to Amherst. Attempts to obtain military preferment failing, he remained on half pay until February 1775, when he was appointed to command one of three independent companies of invalids stationed at Berwick-upon-Tweed. He still held this position when he died.

Knox's *Historical journal*, as the name implies, is a combination of history and personal record. Parts of it are apparently portions of his own diary. Episodes in which he did not participate, although often written in diary form, are largely described by including contemporary documents. The operation orders and other papers which Knox reproduces are one of the valuable features of the work. Though notably uncritical, it is an important source for the history of the Seven Years' War in North America. A reviewer in the *Monthly Review; or, Literary Journal* remarked, sensibly enough, that Knox's method of compilation resulted in many trivia being recorded along with the important events. He added, however, "Mr. Knox appears to be a man of sense, with more literature than usually falls to the share of officers in the army." Knox's will mentioned that he had compiled an index containing many "additional anecdotes" to Tobias George Smollett's *The present state of all nations* . . . (8v., London, 1768–69) and had prepared a revised version of his own *Journal*, "very different in many respects" from the first edition. It appears that these works were never published. When the will was made in April 1777, part of the first edition of the *Journal* remained unsold, and it is evident Knox made little money by it.

In 1751 Knox had married Jane Carre, a lady of Cork whose considerable fortune appears to have been dissipated by a trustee. She survived her husband, poorly provided for. They had at least one child, a son who had died by the time Knox made his will.

C. P. Stacey

[The best account of Knox is that by Arthur George Doughty* in the editor's preface to his Champlain Society edition of the *Historical journal* (3v., Toronto, 1914–16; repr. New York, 1968). Some additional information has been gleaned from Knox's will in PRO, Prob. 11/1040, dated 12 April 1777, and also from the *Monthly Review: or, Literary Journal* (London), XLI (1769), pt.2, 395–96, various G.B., WO, *Army lists*, and J. W. Fortescue, *A history of the British army* (13v., London, 1899–1930), II. C.P.S.]

KOINTAGUETTEZ. *See* Ohquandageghte

KOÑWATSI?TSIAIÉÑNI (**Gonwatsijayenni**, meaning someone lends her a flower, **Mary Brant**), Mohawk, head of the Six Nations matrons; b. *c*. 1736; d. 16 April 1796 at Kingston (Ont.).

Details of Mary Brant's birth, parentage, and early years are obscure. She may have been born at the upper Mohawk castle of Canajoharie (near Little Falls, N.Y.), her family's home; or, like her younger brother Joseph [Thayendanegea*], she may have been born while her parents were living in the Ohio region. John Norton* in his *Journal* states that Joseph was born at Cayahoga (near Akron, Ohio) and was "descended from Wyandot prisoners adopted by the Mohawks on both the father and the mother's side." William Allen, who had interviewed Joseph Brant's son Joseph, stated, perhaps on the son's authority, that Brant's father was an Onondaga chief. This assertion would not negate Norton's claim that the Brants were of Wyandot ancestry and Mohawk nationality since, in the matrilineal Iroquois society, children took the nationality of their mother. Some authorities claim that the father of Mary and Joseph was a respected sachem. According to Norton, he was "a great Warrior" who died when the children were young. The mother then took Mary and Joseph with her to Canajoharie shortly before the outbreak of the Seven Years' War. Eleazar Wheelock, at whose mission school in Connecticut Joseph Brant once studied, said that the Brants were "a Family of Distinction" among the Mohawks.

There was a persistent tradition in the Mohawk valley among both whites and Indians that Mary and Joseph Brant were descended from King Hendrick [Theyanoguin*]. The 19th-century historian and archivist Lyman Copeland Draper, who did painstaking research on the Brant genealogy, found confirmation of such a relationship. A Mohawk woman named Katy Moses, aged 77 in 1879 and "distantly related to Brant's last wife," stated that "she learned many years ago from aged Mohawks, that Brant's mother was a daughter of Old King Hendrick." Joseph Brant's granddaughter Charlotte told Draper that Joseph's mother was a granddaughter of Hendrick.

Mary, or Molly as she was generally known, possibly attended one of the Church of England mission schools in the Mohawk valley. Her later letters, if authentically from her own hand, show that she was mistress of a fine penmanship and a proper English style. There is some evidence, however, that she was only semi-literate and that the letters were dictated to an amanuensis.

She evidently accompanied the delegation of 12 Mohawk principal men who, under the leadership of Hendrick, went to Philadelphia in the winter of 1754–55 to discuss with Pennsylvania officials the fraudulent sale of lands in the Wyoming valley to a group of Connecticut speculators [*see* John Hendricks Lÿdius]. Christian Daniel Claus, who had accompanied the delegation, stated that at Albany on the return trip an English captain "fell in Love wth. Ms. Mary Brant who was then pretty likely not havg. had the small pox."

According to a Mohawk valley tradition, Molly first attracted Sir William JOHNSON's attention at a militia muster, when she leaped upon the back of a horse behind an officer and hung on to him as the horse dashed about the field, much to the amusement of the spectators. Their first child, Peter Warren Johnson, was born in 1759, the same year that Johnson's wife Catherine Weissenberg died. Molly and Sir William had seven more children who survived infancy. Although Johnson referred to her in his will as his "prudent & faithfull Housekeeper" and to the children as his natural children, there is a persistent tradition that they were married according to Indian ceremony, which was not recognized as legal for members of the white community. Johnson treated her with every respect, furnished her and the children with every comfort and luxury befitting an upper class family, and provided generously for them in his will. He also permitted the children to bear his surname. The eldest, named in honour of Johnson's uncle, Sir Peter Warren*, probably received his early education in the Mohawk valley but in 1772 was sent to Montreal for further schooling. In 1773 Johnson sent him to Philadelphia, where he was apprenticed to a dry-goods merchant. Indicative of his genteel upbringing were his requests to his father for a watch so that he might be on time for dinner appointments and for work, some French and English books to read at leisure, a Mohawk book so that he would not forget his Indian tongue, and help in securing a violin. Of his mother, he requested some Indian curiosities to show his Philadelphia friends. His letters indicate a close and affectionate relationship between Johnson, his Mohawk consort, and their children.

Mary Brant presided over Johnson's household with intelligence, ability, grace, and charm, and she effectively managed the estate during Johnson's many and prolonged absences. A contemporary author described her as a "daughter to a sachem, who possessed an uncommonly agreeable person, and good understanding." Because of her important family connections among the Iroquois, she was also of inestimable value to Sir William during his negotiations with the Indians.

After Sir William's death in 1774, she and her children moved to Canajoharie, for the Johnson Hall estate had passed into the hands of John Johnson*, Sir William's white son. At Canajoharie she was highly respected both as the relict of Sir William and as a woman of quality in her own right. She maintained a comfortable existence in a well-furnished house and dressed in Indian style, but in the finest cloth. In his will Sir William had left her a lot in the Kingsland Patent (in present-day Herkimer County), a black female slave, and £200, New York currency. With her legacy she opened a store among the Indians, where she traded chiefly in rum.

Upon the outbreak of hostilities between Great Britain and the colonies, the Brants became staunch loyalists. Early in the conflict Mary Brant did all in her power to feed and assist those loyalists who had taken refuge in the woods, and she also sent ammunition to supporters of the king. In August 1777 she performed one of her most noteworthy achievements when she dispatched Indian runners to inform Barrimore Matthew ST LEGER's forces, then besieging Fort Stanwix (Rome, N.Y.), of the approach of a large body of American militia. This timely warning resulted in the successful ambush of the Americans by the Indians and loyalists at nearby Oriskany.

After the battle the Oriska Indians, a part of the Oneida nation who had supported the Americans in the campaign, revenged themselves upon the Mohawks, and particularly upon Mary Brant, by attacking and despoiling both Canajoharie and Fort Hunter, N.Y., the lower Mohawk castle. Mary Brant and her family, who had lost most of their possessions in the attack, took refuge at Onondaga (near Syracuse), the capital of the Six Nations Confederacy, where she submitted her grievances to the confederacy council and was promised satisfaction.

She then moved to Cayuga (south of present Cayuga, N.Y.), where she had distant relatives; and during the months of discouragement after the Stanwix campaign, when the Indians pondered their losses and wavered in their support of the king, she rendered invaluable service by encouraging and steadying them in their alliance. In one important council she even publicly rebuked the venerable KAIEÑʔKWAAHTOÑ, leading war chief of the confederacy, for counselling peace with the Americans. Her entreaties won over the whole council. Daniel Claus correctly assessed her influence with the Iroquois: "one word from her goes farther with them than a thousand from any white Man without Exception who in general must purchase their Interest at a high rate."

Soon afterwards Major John BUTLER prevailed upon Mary Brant to come to live at Niagara (near Youngstown, N.Y.), a major military base where she could be of much use to the British by advising and interceding with the Indians. As head of a society of Six Nations matrons, which was particularly influential among the young warriors, she was highly esteemed in the confederacy. She arrived at Fort Niagara in the late fall of 1777 and for the next several months was of inestimable assistance there as a diplomat and stateswoman. She was consulted by the Indians on all issues of importance and often cautioned them against making unwise proposals to the commander of the fort.

In July 1779, at the suggestion of the commander, who found his facilities at the fort strained, she reluctantly left her elderly mother behind and went with her family to Montreal, where she placed two of her daughters in a boarding school. In the autumn of 1779, when she heard of the destruction being wrought in Iroquois country by the forces of the Sullivan-Clinton expedition [*see* Kaieñ?kwaahtoñ], she hastened to return to Niagara to be of what assistance she could. But she never reached Niagara, for she agreed instead to remain at Carleton Island, N.Y., where there was a large Six Nations settlement and where she was able to assuage the disgruntled and resentful Indians during the discouraging winter of 1779–80. The commander, Alexander Fraser, highly praised her leadership during those months, affirming that the Indians' "uncommon good behaviour is in a great Measure to be ascribed to Miss Molly Brants Influence over them, which is far superior to that of all their Chiefs put together." A woman of spirit and sometimes of temper, she remained fiercely loyal to her family and to the memory of Sir William and bitter towards the American rebels, who had driven her and her people from their homeland.

In 1783, at the end of the war, she moved to Cataraqui (Kingston, Ont.), where HALDIMAND ordered a house to be built for her. She lived the remainder of her life at Kingston, highly respected by her neighbours. In 1783 also, Haldimand set her pension at £100 annually, the highest paid to an Indian. In addition she received compensation from the British government for her losses during the war. She made a trip back to the Mohawk valley in 1785 and visited Schenectady, where the Americans attempted to persuade her to return with her family. Several years later she was offered financial compensation by the Americans for her confiscated lands if she and her children would return and settle, which offer she "rejected with the utmost contempt."

Little is known of her later years, though reports of travellers afford the occasional glimpse. On 13 Sept. 1794 Mrs John Graves Simcoe [Elizabeth Posthuma Gwillim*] permitted Mary Brant, who was ill, to travel with her aboard the *Mississauga* from Niagara to Kingston. "She speaks English well," noted Mrs Simcoe in her *Diary*, "and is a civil and very sensible old woman." In April of the following year Mary Brant successfully prescribed a favourite Indian remedy, the root of sweet flag (*acorus calamus*), for Governor Simcoe*, who had been extremely ill with a persistent cough. The medicine relieved his malady "in a very short time."

Mary Brant remained a devout Anglican, regularly attending services at St George's in Kingston, where she "sat in an honourable place among the English." She died on 16 April 1796 and was buried in the cemetery (now St Paul's churchyard) in a ceremony conducted by the pastor John Stuart*, who had once been missionary to the Mohawks at Fort Hunter. All her daughters, save one who remained single, married white men of distinction in Upper Canada. Her son George Johnson, known among the Indians as Big George, farmed and taught a day school not far from Brantford for many years. Peter died in 1777 in Philadelphia while serving with the 26th Foot.

A woman of high intelligence and remarkable ability who was at ease in two cultures, Mary Brant personified the dignity and influence accorded to respected mothers among the Iroquois people. In a society in which the mothers chose the sachems and influenced the warriors, Mary Brant played a unique role. Her descent from a high ranking Indian family, her liaison with Sir William Johnson, and her own talents enabled her to wield great power at a critical moment. This power she exerted at much personal cost in a cause which she believed just. Her loyalty to her own family, to her people, and to the traditional Iroquois alliance with the crown was steadfast and enduring. The military officials who had most to do with Indian affairs during the American revolution recognized how essential her leadership was in maintaining the morale and loyalty of the Iroquois. History has subsequently been less than kind to her in often overlooking her achievements. Unquestionably she was one of the most devoted United Empire Loyalists.

BARBARA GRAYMONT

BL, Add. MSS 21661–892 (transcripts at PAC). Clements Library, Sydney papers, secret service payments, 1782–91, Nepean papers, compensation for Joseph and Mary Brant, 31 March 1786. N.Y. Hist. Soc. (New York), Misc. MSS Haldimand, Haldimand to John Johnson, 27 May 1783. New York Public Library, Manuscripts and Archives Division, American loyalist transcripts, XXI, p.331; XLIV, pp.107, 118; Schuyler papers, Indian boxes, box 14. PAC, MG 19, F1; RG 1, L3, 186. PRO, CO 42 (mfm. at PAC). Wis., State Hist. Soc. (Madison), Draper MSS, ser. F.

Can., Dept. of Militia and Defence, General Staff, *A*

history of the organization, development and services of the military and naval forces of Canada from the peace of Paris in 1763, to the present time . . . (3v., [Ottawa, 1919–20]), II. [C. D. Claus], *Daniel Claus' narrative of his relations with Sir William Johnson and experiences in the Lake George fight*, [ed. A. S. Walcott] ([New York], 1904). [A. MacV. Grant], *Memoirs of an American lady* . . . (2v., London, 1808). [E. P. Gwillim (Simcoe)], *The diary of Mrs. John Graves Simcoe* . . . , ed. J. R. Robertson (Toronto, 1911; repr. 1973). [S. A. Harrison], *Memoir of Lieut. Col. Tench Tilghman* . . . (Albany, N.Y., 1876; repr. New York, 1971). *Johnson papers* (Sullivan *et al.*). *Kingston before War of 1812* (Preston). [John Norton], *The journal of Major John Norton, 1816*, ed. C. F. Klinck and J. J. Talman (Toronto, 1970). *NYCD* (O'Callaghan and Fernow), VIII. *The Susquehannah Company papers*, ed. J. P. Boyd (4v., Ithaca, N.Y., 1962), I. Eleazar Wheelock, *A plain and faithful narrative of the original design, rise, progress, and present state of the Indian charity-school at Lebanon, in Connecticut* (Boston, Mass., 1763).

William Allen, *The American biographical dictionary* . . . (3rd ed., Boston, Mass., 1857), 131–32. *Notable American women, 1607–1950: a biographical dictionary*, ed. E. T. James *et al.* (3v., Cambridge, Mass., 1971), I, 229–30. Graymont, *Iroquois*. W. L. [and W. L.] Stone, *The life and times of Sir William Johnson, bart.* (2v., Albany, N.Y., 1865). H. P. Gundy, "Molly Brant – loyalist," *OH*, XLV (1953), 97–108. M. W. Hamilton, "Sir William Johnson's wives," *New York History* (Cooperstown), XXXVIII (1957), 18–28. Jean Johnston, "Ancestry and descendants of Molly Brant," *OH*, LXIII (1971), 86–92.

KOTSINOGHYÂTÀ. *See* HOTSINOÑHYAHTAʔ

KOUATEGETÉ. *See* OHQUANDAGEGHTE

KOYAH (Coya, Coyour, Kower, Kouyer; phonetically the name is xo'ya, and means raven), ranking chief of the Kunghit-Haidas, the southernmost division of the Queen Charlotte Islands Haidas; probably d. 21 June 1795.

What little is known of Koyah's life comes from the journals of a few New England seamen, which provide a fragmentary and biased account. Yet it is apparent that Koyah, a "little diminutive savage looking fellow," was embroiled in more clashes with trading vessels than any other northwest coast chief, and his life throws some light on the origins of the violence that often marred the Pacific fur trade.

As elsewhere on the northwest coast of Canada, the fur trade at Red-Cod-Island-Town (Ninstints, Anthony Island, B.C.), the principal village of Koyah's people, began on peaceful terms. The settlement, called Koyah's by the traders, who followed the practice of naming each village after its chief, had been visited in 1787 by George DIXON and in 1788 by Charles DUNCAN. In June 1789 the *Lady Washington*, commanded by Robert Gray*, arrived. As Robert Haswell* recorded in the ship's log, "A brisk trade was soon set on foot by Coya the Chief, who bartered for all his Subjects, and a number of Sea Otter skins were purchased before night." Business was conducted with "the strictest friendship."

In July Gray exchanged vessels with his partner, John KENDRICK, and sailed to China. Kendrick, who lacked Gray's experience in the trade, returned to Koyah's. He permitted too many Indians on board and became angered when some minor items, including his personal linens, were pilfered. Seizing Koyah and another chief, Skulkinanse, Kendrick bolted one leg of each chief to a gun-carriage and threatened them with death until all the stolen items were returned and all the furs in the village were traded to him. As the Indians later reported to Gray, Kendrick "took Coyah, tied a rope round his neck, whipt him, painted his face, cut off his hair, took away from him a great many skins, and turned him ashore."

Although Koyah could always count on the loyalty of his kin, his ability to command the other villagers depended on his prestige. The treatment he had received at the hands of Kendrick was in Haida terms a shocking violation of a noble person. For this reason Koyah was driven to seek revenge when Kendrick returned to the village on 16 June 1791. The episode is known in unusual detail, from several second-hand accounts in journals and one first-hand account which survived as a song, "The ballad of the bold northwestman." Trade was brisk and Kendrick, "in liquour" that day, again permitted too many Indians on board. They overran and seized his ship. Koyah is reported to have pointed to his leg and gloated, "Now put me into your gun carriage." After a brief scuffle with the captain, however, Koyah and his followers were driven overboard with a loss of about 40. Among the dead were his wife and two of his children; he himself was wounded. To Koyah's previous humiliation had been added defeat in battle, personal injury, and bereavement.

This second encounter with Kendrick must have had a disastrous effect on Koyah's standing. Gray visited the village on 8 July (he was told of Kendrick's first visit but not of his second) and reported that Koyah "appeared to be much frightened, being in a constant tremor the whole time." Moreover, as the Indians explained to him, "Coyah was now no longer a Chief, but an 'Ahliko,' or one of the lower class; they have now no head Chief, but many inferior Chiefs."

The next events show Koyah engaged in activities that would regain for him some of his prestige. On 27 August Captain Joseph Ingraham, at anchor in Cumshewa Inlet (Moresby Island, B.C.), saw Koyah and Skulkinanse leading 12 large canoes to war against a traditional enemy, Chief Skidegate. The outcome of that raid is not known. In the summer of 1794 Koyah, along with the chiefs Cumshewa and Scorch Eye, captured at Cumshewa an American brig manned by 11 men and put to death all but one, who was held in slavery for a year. During the winter of 1794–95 he captured a large British vessel which had anchored nearby to replace broken masts. The entire crew was killed.

On 21 June 1795 the Boston sloop *Union*, commanded by John Boit, dropped anchor off Koyah's village. Forty canoes containing 300 men surrounded the vessel, and eight of the chiefs, including Koyah, came aboard. In Boit's words, "Scorch Eye the head chief began the attack by seizing Mr. Hudson, the 2nd officer. At the same time the Indians along side attempted to board, with the most hideous yells. . . . I killed their first chief, Scorch Eye, in the 2nd mates arms, while they was struggling to gether. The rest of the Chiefs on board was knock'd down & wounded & we kill'd from the Nettings & in the Canoes along side above 40 more. . . . Suppose in this fracas we kill'd and wounded about 50 but the Indians said we killed 70." Next day the Indians ransomed back the captured chiefs, who had been held in irons. Boit's identification of Scorch Eye as the head chief, together with the report of this incident made by Captain Charles Bishop*, who wrote that "Koyer . . . attacked Captain Boyds vessel," has led historians to conclude that it was Koyah, rather than Scorch Eye, who was killed in the attack. At all events, this is the last time that Koyah is mentioned in contemporary accounts.

The Kunghit-Haidas survived for a time, but Koyah's dynasty did not; in the following decade the Eagle chief, Ninstints, took ascendancy. Reduced by the encounters with Kendrick and Boit and by the smallpox epidemic of 1862, the remnants of the tribe abandoned their village about 1885, moved to Skidegate (B.C.), and became Christians.

WILSON DUFF

Provincial Archives of B.C. (Victoria), *Hope* (ship), "Journal of the voyage from Boston to the north west coast of America, 1790–1792," by Joseph Ingraham, photocopy of original; *Ruby* (ship), "Commercial journal, copy's of letters and accts. of Ship Rubys voyage to N. Wt. coast of America and China, 1794.5.6," by Chas. Bishop. *The sea, the ship, and the sailor: tales of adventure from log books and original narratives*, ed. Elliot Snow (Salem, Mass., 1925). *Voyages of 'Columbia'* (Howay). K. E. Dalzell, *The Queen Charlotte Islands, 1774–1966* (Terrace, B.C., 1968); *The Queen Charlotte Islands, book 2, of places and names* (Prince Rupert, B.C., 1973). J. R. Swanton, *Contributions to the ethnology of the Haida* (New York, 1905). Wilson Duff and Michael Kew, "Anthony Island, a home of the Haidas," B.C., Provincial Museum, *Report* (Victoria), 1957, 37–64. F. W. Howay, "The ballad of the bold northwestman: an incident in the life of Captain John Kendrick," *Washington Hist. Quarterly* (Seattle), XX (1929), 114–23; "Indian attacks upon maritime traders of the north-west coast, 1785–1805," *CHR*, VI (1925), 287–309.

L

LABORDE (La Borde), JEAN, agent of the treasurers general of the Marine and Colonies, attorney general of the Conseil Supérieur of Île Royale (Cape Breton Island), royal notary, and merchant; b. 21 Nov. 1710 at Bidart, diocese of Bayonne, France, son of Martin Laborde (Borda) d'Aloperca and Catherine Dechart (Duhart); m. 2 Feb. 1734 at Louisbourg, Île Royale, Louise Milly, *née* Dupuy, a Canadian; they had eight children of whom only one son and two daughters are known to have been still alive in 1761; d. 3 Sept. 1781 at Eysines, near Bordeaux, France.

There is no evidence that Jean Laborde was related to the famous Bayonne families of court bankers and farmers general, and the patronage by which he got his start in life is not clear. He first went to Île Royale in June 1730 as clerk to the king's storekeeper, André Carrerot*, and late in 1733 he became secretary to the acting financial commissary, Sébastien-François-Ange LE NORMANT de Mézy. When Le Normant returned to France in 1737, Laborde continued working under the next financial commissary, François BIGOT, and the Marine controller, Antoine Sabatier*, at a salary of 900 *livres* a year. He also took the post of clerk of the Conseil Supérieur at Louisbourg on the death of the previous clerk, Claude-Joseph Le Roy* Desmarest. When Anglo-American forces under William Pepperrell* and Peter Warren* captured Louisbourg in

1745, the Labordes retired with Bigot to Rochefort where Laborde spent part of the next three years drawing up the treasurers' accounts for Île Royale, the treasurers' agent, Jacques-Philippe-Urbain Rondeau*, having died. He also spent some time at sea as treasurers' agent to the fleet of the Duc d'Anville [La Rochefoucauld*].

When the War of the Austrian Succession ended in 1748, Laborde went to Canada with Bigot and helped to clear up the affairs of the late agent of the treasurers general of the Marine, Thomas-Jacques Taschereau*. The next year Jacques PREVOST de La Croix, the financial commissary of Île Royale, had him appointed a royal notary and treasurers' agent for that colony. Laborde went to Louisbourg where he was to remain until the loss of the colony to Jeffery AMHERST in 1758. Although working under the direction of the financial commissary, Laborde was in fact the paid agent or clerk of the treasurers general of the Marine and Colonies. Beginning with the year 1750 and until 1771 the financing of the colonial service was separated from that of the naval service. Therefore, two new offices of treasurer general for the Colonies were created, one for even-numbered years and the other for odd-numbered years, and agents such as Laborde had to serve four treasurers general, although most of their business was for the colonial service. The four treasurers general were big financiers in Paris who had bought their offices at high prices and who held and disbursed all royal funds allotted to the navy and the colonies, like so many bankers, on orders from the crown's minister at Versailles or from a local representative of the crown such as the financial commissary at Louisbourg. Tables of authorized payments, drawn up in the ministry in Paris, were sent out to the colony each year and Laborde's job was to pay soldiers, sailors, officers, supply merchants, and others for the crown. He paid in cash when he had it and otherwise in promissory notes or bills of exchange drawn on the treasurers general in Paris. These were printed forms, duly filled out, as were the receipts he was supposed to keep and to send to the treasurers general with his accounts. Laborde's accounts, like nearly all accounts for the French government, were several years late because the accounting system required that all transactions pertaining to a certain year be completed before the accounts for that year could be drawn up and submitted to the Chambre des Comptes. Meanwhile, nothing prevented Laborde, or any other treasurers' agent, from using royal funds, or funds borrowed on the considerable credit of his post, in private business ventures.

Laborde had already established himself in a small way as a shipping merchant during the War of the Austrian Succession. No doubt he began to trade much earlier than that, but war offered new opportunities which he seized in partnership with a merchant of the colony, Jean Marguerie. In 1744 they invested, for example, 1,000 *livres* in a privateer, the *Brador*, and a larger sum in a 60-ton vessel, the *Trompes*, sent to Martinique. The loss of Louisbourg the next year interrupted Laborde's trade but he was ready to begin again as soon as France recovered the colony at the end of the war, blessed as he then was with the financial commissary's patronage and the prospect of abundant capital from his treasury funds and credit. His favoured position soon encouraged two prominent local merchants to link their fortunes with his by marrying his daughters: in 1749, Antoine Morin, who was brother of Jean-Baptiste MORIN de Fonfay, soon to become the king's storekeeper, and in 1753, Michel Daccarrette*, who was willing to bring 4,000 *livres* to a marriage to which Laborde gave only 1,500 *livres*. Laborde bought ships: the *Hazard* in 1750, as agent for the Martinique firm of Delatesserie et Guillemin, the *Grignette* in 1751 from Pierre Rodrigue, the *Charmante Polly* in 1752 from Bernard Decheverry, and others. These he worked as fishing schooners and in the West Indian trade. So successful was he that in 1753 a group of Saint-Malo merchants formally accused him of monopolizing the Louisbourg market, together with the Morin brothers and Nicolas LARCHER, by dealing in illegal British goods and so undercutting French merchants. But Laborde was now in an unassailable position and the next year, without ceasing to be treasurers' agent, he became attorney general of the Conseil Supérieur for Île Royale which brought him prestige and another 400 *livres* a year.

Laborde was ready to grasp the opportunities offered by the Seven Years' War. He began to supply French forces and in the years 1755–58 made 165,000 *livres* in molasses alone. No fewer than five privateers scoured the Atlantic on his behalf and the best of them, the *Vigilant*, with a crew of more than 50, netted him 150,000 *livres*, or so he claimed. Encouraged by Prevost's patronizing willingness to hire his vessels for official dispatches to France, Laborde went into transatlantic shipping through the agency of such prominent merchants as Dominique Cabarrus at Bordeaux, Jean Lanne at Bayonne, and Yves-Augustin Bersolles at Brest. In the spring of 1757, the *Dauphin* (60 tons) left Bayonne with a cargo for him, including wine, brandy, onions, shallots, stockings, pins, and powder, worth 17,568 *livres*, and early that summer he dispatched the *Victoire* (100 tons) to France with a cargo of dried cod, linseed, pepper, brown sugar, mahogany, and other American produce. The brokerage business, buying and selling British and French ships and their cargoes, was a natural addition to so large a business, for Laborde had become one of the colony's most successful merchants. A census of 1750 shows that even then the Labordes had seven domestic servants, and the family landed in France in 1758 with four black slaves. Laborde might soon have grown rich enough to settle in France like Denis GOGUET or Michel Rodrigue, but unfortunately for him the British captured the *Victoire*, the *Dauphin*, the *Charmant*, and then Île Royale itself. Laborde later claimed to have lost a privateer, the *Vigilant*, and its cargo, two houses in Louisbourg, "one of the finest fishing establishments in the harbour" including a warehouse measuring 80 feet by 30 feet and a lodge big enough to house 80 fishermen, shares in two other such fisheries, and property on the Rivière de Miré (Mira River), acquired in part by official grant as early as 1741, now stocked with 12 cows, a bull, and two horses, forming three *métairies* (share-cropper's properties) and a meadow.

That was only the beginning of Laborde's misfortunes. When the British shipped him back to France, he thought of settling in Bordeaux, where the Daccarrettes went to live, and he bought a large house there, but decided to stay in La Rochelle in order to settle his accounts with the treasurers general. While working on these accounts for the 1750s, Laborde discovered in 1760 – or pretended to discover – that he had left a lot of records together with money in a strong-box in Louisbourg and without them was unable to account for several hundred thousand *livres* of royal funds. This loss soon reached the ears of the minister, the suspicious and tough-minded Berryer, who on 28 Nov. 1760 wrote to ask the naval intendant at Rochefort to help in the search for the missing papers. Three weeks later, Laborde had a notary draw up a power of attorney for someone in Louisbourg to try to recover them from the British governor there. During the next few months, Laborde's son (probably Sébastien-Charles) spent his time in London working on this affair through the good offices of Lord Holderness and even proposed to go to Halifax, Nova Scotia. Laborde himself began to press the former financial commissary of Louisbourg, Prevost de La Croix, then at Rochefort, for the missing records. Nothing turned up and on 10 March 1763 the minister wrote to ask the Atlantic ports to hunt for Laborde, who was suspected of trying to flee to England or Canada. Laborde was soon arrested in Paris, where he had gone on 19 Feb. 1763, was imprisoned in the Bastille on 16 March, and stayed there for the next 17 months.

Was Laborde in earnest or was he merely putting up a determined show of innocence to cover a fraudulent misuse of royal funds? The government evidently doubted his sincerity, for they were quick to arrest him once he left La Rochelle. Under interrogation in March 1763 Laborde declared, probably to save himself, that Prevost had taken the strong-box from Louisbourg and in September 1758 brought it ashore with him at Santander, Spain, where he had turned it to private account through the agency of the French merchant firm of Darragory Frères et Cie. Laborde claimed that he had not wanted to report the loss until he could prove it and so had sent his stepson, Thomas Milly, to Santander to gather evidence from Darragory's clerks, and even thought of sending Daccarrette to Madrid. "I think as you do, Monsieur," one of the magistrates wrote to Antoine de Sartine, lieutenant-general of police, "that poor Laborde is losing his grip." The ministers took Laborde's story seriously enough, however, to arrest Prevost and an uncle and associate, Michel-Henri Fabus, a well-connected businessman and venal office-holder. They also imprisoned Daccarrette and Laborde's son, Sébastien-Charles, at Bordeaux, as they were determined to get to the bottom of the case and had the authority to arrest and hold people on the mere suspicion, or even in anticipation, of a crime.

Sartine was asked to inquire into the case. By February 1764 he had decided that Laborde was dishonestly trying to cover up debts to the crown incurred by excessive personal spending in Louisbourg, Bordeaux, La Rochelle, and Paris. Prevost was freed in June 1763 and declared innocent the next year; his uncle, Fabus, soon went bankrupt no doubt as a result of the scandal; Daccarrette was released in 1764 but only after his house in Bordeaux had burned down in December 1763 and the claims of his creditors had bankrupted him as well; and Laborde was presented with a bill for 455,474 *livres*, the price of his release. Laborde signed over all his assets to the crown in a detailed notarial document on 12 July 1764, and although they were worth only 336,104 *livres*, the crown released him on 25 August. He went to live at Eysines, a village near Bordeaux, with only a stipend of 400 *livres* a year as a former attorney to the Louisbourg Conseil Supérieur. The priest of Saint-Martin-d'Eysines certified for pension purposes on 16 Aug. 1779 that Laborde was still in good health, but he died two years later and was buried under the porch of the village church.

J. F. Bosher

AD, Charente-Maritime (La Rochelle), B, 230, 20 déc. 1758; 1790, 12 juin 1759; 1798, 18 avril 1763; Minutes Fredureaux-Dumas (La Rochelle), 20 déc. 1760; Minutes Laleu (La Rochelle), 11 avril 1749; Gironde (Bordeaux), État civil, Saint-Martin-d'Eysines, 4 sept. 1781. AN, Col., C[11A], 125; E, 238 (dossier Laborde); Section Outre-mer, G[1], 406–9, 467/3; G[3], 2041/1; Minutier central, XXXIII, no.553, 12 juill. 1764. Archives maritimes, Port de Rochefort (France), 1E, 172, Choiseul à Ruis-Embito, 10 et 26 mars 1763; 417, Ruis-Embito à Berryer, 25 nov. 1760. Bibliothèque de l'Arsenal, Archives de la Bastille, 12200, ff.57–58, 72, 306–7, 350ff., 454–55, 473ff.; 12145, f.256. PRO, HCA, 32/180/1, *Dauphin*; 32/254, *Victoire*. Crowley, "Government and interests."

LA BOULARDERIE, ANTOINE LE POUPET DE. *See* Le Poupet

LA BROSSE, JEAN-BAPTISTE DE, Jesuit, priest, missionary, and professor; b. 30 April 1724 at Magnac, a hamlet in the parish of Jauldes (dept of Charente), France, son of Jean de La Brosse, seigneur of La Chabrouillère and of Magnac, and Louise Dubois-Cuvier; d. 11 April 1782 at Tadoussac (Que.).

After studying at the Jesuit college in Angoulême, Jean-Baptiste de La Brosse began his noviciate with the Jesuits in Bordeaux on 9 Oct. 1740. He took his first vows on 10 Oct. 1742, studied philosophy for two years, and taught in various schools until 1749. He completed his training as a Jesuit by a third year of philosophy and four years of theology.

Ordained priest early in April 1753, La Brosse came to Canada with a number of other Jesuits the following year. He stayed at Quebec and then in the autumn of 1755 went to join Father Charles Germain in Acadia, where he ministered to the Abenakis, Malecites, and Acadians of the St John River region (N.B.). Since July 1755, when the deportation of their people had begun [*see* Charles Lawrence*], these Acadians had been pursued and had had to take refuge in the forests. As soon as he arrived Father La Brosse went along, helping them and encouraging them to flee. Early in March 1756 he narrowly escaped being taken by the British.

Returning to Quebec in the autumn, La Brosse lived in the Jesuit college until 1758, serving as procurator, adviser to the rector, confessor, and professor of philosophy. On 2 Feb. 1758 he pronounced his solemn vows in the presence of Father Claude-Godefroy Coquart* and then worked as chaplain in the Hôpital Général in Quebec until April. In the summer he went to assist Father Pierre-Joseph-Antoine Roubaud, who was with the Abenakis at Saint-François-de-Sales (Odanak), and at the same time he undertook regular duties in the parish of Saint-Michel-d'Yamaska. In July 1759 La Brosse went with a party of Abenakis to Quebec, which was under siege. He was taken prisoner at Pointe-aux-Trembles (Neuville) but the next day was liberated as a military chaplain. On 4 October he and Father Roubaud escaped Major Robert Rogers' raid on the Abenakis at Saint-François. The following year he still claimed the title of "missionary to the Abenakis" and was ministering occasionally in the parish of Saint-Louis-de-Terrebonne. During his years with these Indians he had improved his knowledge of their speech and in 1760 completed a basic dictionary of the Abenaki language.

From his earliest days in Canada, Father La Brosse had espoused the cause of the Acadians, Abenakis, and Malecites. In 1761, however, he was given the tranquil parish of Saint-Henri-de-Mascouche, and remained there until the middle of 1766 despite requests from the Indians of Saint-François for his return. He was then appointed missionary to the Montagnais, who inhabited an immense territory stretching from Île aux Coudres to Sept-Îles and from Tadoussac to Chicoutimi, and he began the most significant work of his life, through which he would make an outstanding contribution and attain both historical fame and legendary renown. In 1770 Bishop Briand also made him responsible for ministering to the area from Cacouna to Rimouski on the south side of the St Lawrence, as well as to Acadia, St John's (Prince Edward) Island, and Cape Breton Island. In 1773, however, Joseph-Mathurin Bourg took over his responsibilities for the Acadians and Micmacs.

Annals containing his annual summaries of his activities from 1766 to 1776, two Tadoussac registers recording his official acts – the "Miscellaneorum Liber" and the "Magnus Liber" – his letters, and various other statements reveal the nature of his work. His chief concern was to establish a Montagnais Christian community on firm human foundations. As early as 1767 he had William Brown and Thomas Gilmore print 3,000 spellers and 2,000 prayer books in Montagnais, designed, as he noted, for "those who know how to read and for those who will learn." He devoted winters to the education of the Montagnais, showing them how to read and write, teaching them the catechism, liturgical rites, singing, and the rudiments of music, and training catechists to carry on his work in his absence and after his death. He also served the French on both sides of the St Lawrence and the Acadians of Baie des Chaleurs, since registers of at least 15 parishes record his ministrations. But his creative work was primarily with the Montagnais, among whom he established a church which was respectful of their language and which could sustain itself.

Employees and clerks of the trading posts made his task difficult because of their general conduct and their trade in spirits with the Indians. In his concern to save his Montagnais Christian community Father La Brosse did not hesitate to write in 1780 to the vicar general of Quebec, Henri-François Gravé* de La Rive, to censure the diocesan authorities for their spinelessness and indulgence towards the French living at the posts. Despite these obstacles his forceful personality enabled him to accomplish his purpose in large measure. We can form some idea of his achievement by the number of prayer books and spellers he had printed, the large quantity of Indian religious calendars he bought from Brown and Gilmore, and above all from the records he entered in the registers of Tadoussac. The "Catalogus generalis totius Montanensium gentis" kept by his successor, Abbé Jean-Joseph Roy, is also a valuable source of detailed information. Written around 1785 and now housed in the Archives de l'archidiocèse de Québec, this "Catalogus" is clearly a continuation of one which Brown and Gilmore printed for Father La Brosse in 200 copies in 1767. Virtually a census of the Montagnais Christians, it gives for each person a number, names of parents, date of birth, assessment of literacy and of religious performance, date of first communion, and date of death where applicable.

In spite of extensive travel every year, Father La Brosse successfully engaged in work which reveals his ability as a scholar and professor. Wherever he went he made use of his Jesuit predecessors' studies. He did further research, made comments and corrections on their work, and developed it in his own writings. He used the dictionary of Father Joseph Aubery* as a basis for his etymological dictionary of the Abenaki language, and for his book of Montagnais prayers he drew inspiration from one by Father Pierre-Michel Laure* on which he wrote numerous comments. The catechetical instructions written by Father Antoine Silvy* are covered with comments and notes by La Brosse from which he drew the materials for a Montagnais grammar and speller. He laboured for eight years compiling a Montagnais dictionary. He also translated selections from the Bible into that language and, since there was no money to get the translations printed, he had students make manuscript copies.

La Brosse's efforts to teach reading and writing were certainly not wasted. When James McKenzie* passed through Tadoussac in 1808, 26 years after La Brosse's death, he noted that the Montagnais could read and write their own language well enough to be able to correspond with one another, that they excelled in singing hymns, and that those who sang in church read music well enough to sing accurately.

La Brosse was no ordinary man and legends soon sprang up about him. His medical knowledge, his gifts of healing, and the admiration, sympathy, and deep respect he attracted were all magnified to make him the hero of many tales, two of which are particularly well known. According to the "legend of the bells" La Brosse had predicted the exact moment of his own death and when he died, at midnight, the bells in all the chapels and churches that he served began to toll spontaneously. In another legend, the missionary kept back a forest fire by tracing a line on the ground with a stick. The sculptor Alfred Laliberté* did a bronze statue illustrating this story early in the 20th century.

LÉO-PAUL HÉBERT

[Information about Jean-Baptiste de La Brosse's work as a teacher at the Jesuit college can be found in the notes of one of his students, André Couillard, in ASQ, MSS-M, 67. For his ministry from 1766 to 1781, sources include the third register kept for Tadoussac, "Miscellaneorum Liber," and the fourth register, "Magnus Liber," which are in AAQ, U, Registre des postes du domaine du roy, A[1]; B. The "Miscellaneorum Liber" also contains the "Annales Missionis ab anno 1766," ff.87v–90, which in effect is La Brosse's "relation" in Latin of his annual comings and goings from 1766 to 1776. Part of the "Annales" appeared, with a French translation and notes by Biblo [Jean-Philéas Gagnon], in *L'Union libérale* (Québec), 24 août 1888, 3. Victor Tremblay included a translation of a large part of the text in his *Hist. du Saguenay*. The whole text, with translation and commentaries, was published in "Les annales du père Jean-Baptiste de La Brosse, s.j.," edited by L.-P. Hébert, *Saguenayensia* (Chicoutimi, Qué.), 16 (1974), 75–94. "Les lettres du père Jean-Baptiste de La Brosse," edited by L.-P. Hébert, was published in this journal in no.17 (1975), 73–83.

Father La Brosse frequently signed his work with the pseudonym Jan-Batist Nudenans. The Musée d'Odanak has a bound manuscript of an etymological dictionary of the Abenaki language which bears the title "Radicum Wabanakaerum Sylvae Collecta a J. B. Nudenaus Anno 1760." The Archives historiques oblates in Ottawa holds manuscripts of a Montagnais-Latin dictionary begun at Tadoussac in 1766 and completed at Île-Verte in 1774–75, a Montagnais grammar dated 1768, and a Latin-Montagnais dictionary dated 1772. Both this archives and AAQ hold a Montagnais alphabet entitled *ABEGHJIKMNOPRSTU* (Uabistiguiatsh [Québec], 1767), of which 3,000 copies were printed. The BNQ in Montreal holds an Abenaki alphabet, *Akitami Kakikemesudi-Arenarag' Auikhigan* . . . (Kebec-Dari [Quebec], 1770) signed Jan Batist Nudenans, of which 600 copies were printed. *Nehiro-Iriniui Aiamihe Massinahigan* . . . (Uabistiguiatsh [Quebec], 1767; 2nd ed., 1817; 3rd ed., 1844), containing a collection of prayers and a Montagnais catechism, had a run of 2,000 copies in its first edition; copies can be found at AAQ, the Archives historiques oblates, the Bibliothèque de l'Assemblée nationale, and the Bibliothèque de la ville de Montréal. L.-P.H.]

AAQ, 12 A, C, 250v, 308; 22A, IV, 83; 61 CD, Saint-Laurent, île d'Orléans, I, 6. Archives de l'archevêché de Rimouski (Rimouski, Qué.), 355.106, lettre du père J.-B. de La Brosse à Mgr Gravé, 21 avril 1780. Archives de l'évêché de Gaspé (Gaspé, Qué.), casier des paroisses, Bonaventure, lettre du père J.-B. de La Brosse à Mgr Briand, 28 déc. 1771. ASJCF, D-7, 1. PAC, MG 24, B1, 49–50, 52–53, 57, 59, 100–2. *Les bourgeois de la Compagnie du Nord-Ouest* (Masson), II, 405–54. *JR* (Thwaites). *L'Oiseau-mouche* (Chicoutimi, Qué.), I (1893), 15, 19, reproduces in Montagnais and in French Bishop Briand's pastoral letter to the Montagnais of 13 May 1769. This document does not appear in *Mandements des évêques de Québec* (Têtu et Gagnon). H.-R. Casgrain, *Œuvres complètes* (4v., Montréal, 1884–88), I. Alexandre Chambre, *Un grand apôtre du Canada, originaire de l'Angoumois: le R. P. J.-B. de La Brosse, né à Jauldes (Charente), mort à Tadoussac (Saguenay)* (Jauldes, France, [1904]). Antonio Dragon, *Trente robes noires au Saguenay*, Adrien Pouliot, édit. (Chicoutimi, 1971). Rochemonteix, *Les jésuites et la N.-F. au XVIIIe siècle*. A. E. Jones, "Quelques notes sur le P. Jean-Baptiste de La Brosse," *L'Union libérale* (Québec), 23 nov. 1888, 3; 26 avril 1889, 3. Yves Tremblay, "Le père de La Brosse, sa vie, son œuvre," SCHÉC *Rapport*, 35 (1968), 47–59.

LA CORNE, LUC DE, known as **Chaptes (Chap, Chapt) de La Corne** or as **La Corne Saint-Luc**, officer in the colonial regular troops, merchant, interpreter, and member of the Legislative Council; b. at Contrecœur (Que.), probably in the autumn of 1711, son of Jean-Louis de La Corne* de Chaptes and Marie Pécaudy de Contrecœur; d. 1 Oct. 1784 in Montreal.

Luc de La Corne came from a large and illustrious family. He and his brother Louis*, known as the Chevalier de La Corne, were destined to participate in military and commercial endeavours which took them to the same battlefields south of Lake Champlain and the same fur-trading territories in the west. Consequently their names were often confused in the last decade of the French régime but, unlike the Chevalier, La Corne Saint-Luc did not fight in Acadia.

Like many others [*see* Joseph MARIN de La Malgue], La Corne Saint-Luc was able to take advantage of his military career to carry on profitable commercial activity over a lengthy period. He benefited from the increased number of western posts and the expansion of the fur trade beyond Lake Superior at the time of the La Vérendryes' explorations [*see* Pierre Gaultier* de Varennes et de La Vérendrye]. For the period from 1738 to the end of the French régime more than 80 of his hiring contracts have been found for the fur trade at Detroit, Michilimackinac (Mackinaw City, Mich.), Sault Ste Marie (Mich.), Chagouamigon (near Ashland, Wis.), Kaministiquia (Thunder Bay, Ont.), and Nipigon (Ont.). In turn merchant-outfitter and fur-trader, La Corne Saint-Luc went into partnership at least twice to take charge of one of these posts. From 1742 to 1743 he exploited Kaministiquia with his brother François-Josué de La Corne* Dubreuil, its commandant. Then on 18 Feb. 1752 he signed articles of partnership for three years with Louis-Joseph Gaultier* de La Vérendrye to pursue the trade at Chagouamigon, south of Lake Superior. La Vérendrye took command of the post, while La Corne Saint-Luc acted as financial backer and outfitter. He assumed three-quarters of the expenses incurred and received three-quarters of the profits. In 1754–55 he was said to be in commercial partnership with Captain Robert Stobo*.

In all these transactions La Corne Saint-Luc seems to have shown himself a shrewd merchant. His three marriage contracts attest to his affluence, and at the conquest the Sieur de Courville [Louis-Léonard AUMASSON de Courville] included him among the richest Canadians, with a fortune of 1,200,000 *livres*. When he died, his debtors owed him more than 152,000 *livres*, and the moneys owed him with the merchant Lavallée in Paris amounted to 241,314 *livres*. The inventory of his property reveals his love of ostentation: his wardrobe was rich and impressive. His substantial income enabled him to surround himself with many slaves who performed domestic duties. The majority of slaves in 18th-century New France were Indians, mainly Pawnees from the Mississippi valley; blacks made their appearance principally under the British régime. The nearly 4,000 slaves who are known to have existed during the French régime belonged to some 1,500 individuals, about 30 of whom held more than 10. Among these large owners La Corne Saint-Luc was second only to Governor Beauharnois*.

La Corne Saint-Luc distinguished himself through an eventful life in which courage and endurance were a constant necessity. Having taken up a military career, he attracted the attention of Beauharnois, who in 1742 recommended him for an ensigncy because of his bravery the previous year at Fort Clinton (Easton, N.Y.). It was on 10 Dec. 1742 in Montreal that La Corne Saint-Luc married for the first time, his wife being Marie-Anne Hervieux. In the ten years of marriage before her death in January 1753, they had four sons and three daughters; only the daughters survived.

A long association with the Indians acquainted La Corne Saint-Luc with "four or five Indian languages," which he "spoke fluently." He was to be present as interpreter at two important conferences between Governor Vaudreuil [RIGAUD] and the Senecas in October 1755, and at one with a broader delegation of Indians in December 1756. As he had discovered how to win the Indians' confidence, his services had for a number of years been put to use in an extremely sensitive double task: recruiting warriors from the allied Indian tribes and leading them into battle. During the War of the Austrian Succession he commanded a detachment of 150 Canadians and Indians sent to assist Jacques Legardeur* de Saint-Pierre at Fort Saint-Frédéric (near Crown Point, N.Y.), which at that time was considered essential for the defence of Canada. For four months, from January to April 1746, this force harassed the enemy around Lac Saint-Sacrement (Lake George). It was not, however, until the end of June 1747 that another detachment of some 200 men, led by La Corne Saint-Luc and others, was successful in capturing part of the garrison of Fort Clinton.

La Corne Saint-Luc, who became a lieutenant in 1748, made various appearances at Montreal or Quebec to report on his expeditions, see to business matters, or escort Indian delegations sent from the *pays d'en haut*; he also busied himself leading a convoy to Michilimackinac, where the enterprising Legardeur de Saint-Pierre had just succeeded Louis de La Corne as commandant.

Luc de La Corne continued to distinguish himself in his military career. Two years in a row, in 1753 and 1754, Governor DUQUESNE recommended him for the command of a company, emphasizing that he was "a brave man and skilled in recruiting." His captain's commission was granted on 15 March 1755. That year he served under Baron de Dieskau*'s orders as one of the "officers attached to the Indians" in an important expedition which Governor Vaudreuil intended to ward off the threat of an Anglo-American advance by way of Lake Champlain – a threat that was manifested in the building of Fort Lydius (also called Fort Edward, now Fort Edward, N.Y.) and Fort George (also called Fort William Henry, now Lake George). It was against Fort George that in August 1757 Montcalm* won one of the most brilliant French victories, and La Corne Saint-Luc, commanding the Indians on the left flank, shared it. Unfortunately the exploit was tarnished after the surrender; on 10 August the Indian allies killed some members of the British garrison, which the French were allowing to go to Fort Lydius. The court of France was even held accountable for the Indians' behaviour. La Corne Saint-Luc, who along with other officers had been responsible for escorting Lieutenant-Colonel George Monro and his garrison, was not able to prevent the unprovoked assault.

La Corne Saint-Luc returned to Montreal and there, on 3 Sept. 1757, he took as his second wife Marie-Joseph Guillimin, the widow of Jacques Legardeur de Saint-Pierre, who had been killed two years earlier and under whose orders La Corne Saint-Luc had fought on several occasions. The marriage, which was childless, lasted 11 years.

In 1758 La Corne Saint-Luc distinguished himself in a type of military action that fitted in perfectly with the strategy of guerrilla warfare advocated by Vaudreuil. At the end of July he was able to take advantage of Montcalm's victory at Carillon (Ticonderoga, N.Y.) to launch an attack with a detachment of 400 Canadians and Indians on an enemy convoy en route to Fort Lydius. Acting quickly for fear of a surprise counter-attack by the enemy, they took 64 prisoners and 80 scalps, killed many oxen, and destroyed the supplies. This trophy-taking in the Indian manner made many of La Corne Saint-Luc's contemporaries, including the Americans, indignant. But in Governor Vaudreuil's eyes the exploit merited the cross of Saint-Louis. Hence on 6 Nov. 1758, he made a note of commendation in the margin of his roster: "This captain has rendered very fine service at all times. He has fought in all the campaigns in this war and has always distinguished himself, particularly in this last campaign at Carillon, having been at the head of a detachment that laid an ambush on the road to Fort Lydius in which he completely vanquished an enemy convoy." On 1 Jan. 1759 he was made a knight of Saint-Louis.

Shortly before the capture of Quebec in September 1759, La Corne Saint-Luc helped prepare plans for defensive action on Lake Champlain, and Vaudreuil approved the suggestions that he and Louis-Joseph Gaultier de La Vérendrye made. As commander of the Indians he was in the advance guard under François-Charles de Bourlamaque* at the battle of Sainte-Foy in April 1760, and he was wounded there.

After the final defeat La Corne Saint-Luc considered going to France. On 15 Oct. 1761 he sailed on the *Auguste* with quite a number of the Canadian nobility including Louis-Joseph Gaultier de La Vérendrye. He was accompanied by his brother Louis, two of his children, and two of his nephews, all of whom he was unfortunately to lose a month later when the ship was wrecked near Cape North, on Cape Breton Island. Only seven of the 121 passengers and crew escaped death. One of the lucky survivors, La Corne Saint-Luc published an account of this voyage. In it he relates how, after many adventures, despite the autumn chill and the lack of supplies and transportation, he succeeded in finding help for his unfortunate companions; he then travelled 550 leagues, going right across Cape Breton Island to Canso Strait, following the northwest coast of Nova Scotia to Baie Verte (N.B.), taking the Saint John River to the portage at Témiscouata, and then journeying from Kamouraska to Quebec. He arrived on 23 Feb. 1762 after a hundred days of impossible travel.

Fate having taken a hand, La Corne Saint-Luc made a new life for himself in Canada. Believing that the British occupation would be temporary, he endeavoured to use his influence with the Indians to foster their discontent with the conquerors. He even went so far as to spread the rumour that a French fleet would come to recover the territory. In a letter of 19 Dec. 1763, during Pontiac*'s uprising, Lieutenant Governor Cadwallader Colden of New York accused him of having been engaged for two years in inciting the western Indians to conspiracy and insurrection.

Nevertheless La Corne Saint-Luc's family had no difficulty integrating itself into the society that emerged under the British régime. It made links through marriage with the best matches in the colony. His eldest daughter, Marie-Anne, married John CAMPBELL, probably in 1763. His eighth child, Marie-Marguerite (whose mother, also Marie-Marguerite, a daughter of the seigneur Pierre Boucher* de Boucherville, had become La Corne's third wife in 1774), was to marry Major John Lennox. Among La Corne Saint-Luc's compatriots alliances were to be made with Jacques Viger*, Marie-Marguerite's second husband; Charles-Louis Tarieu* de Lanaudière, who would accompany La Corne Saint-Luc in 1777 at the time of John BURGOYNE's campaign; and Georges-Hippolyte LE COMTE Dupré, for whom he apparently had little liking since in December 1769 he opposed the marriage with his daughter Marie-Louise-Charlotte. The ceremony nevertheless took place early the following year.

During the American invasion La Corne Saint-Luc played a rather questionable role. In the autumn of 1775, fearing the capture of Montreal was imminent, he took the initiative, with the approval of certain other leading citizens of Montreal, in making an offer through his Iroquois friends at Sault-Saint-Louis (Caughnawaga, Que.) to surrender to Richard MONTGOMERY. Mistrustful of such scheming, the American general hesitated but agreed to negotiate under certain conditions. However at this juncture, Colonel Ethan Allen's detachment having been intercepted at Longue-Pointe (Montreal), La Corne Saint-Luc thought better of his plan. To avoid suspicion he handed Montgomery's reply to Governor Guy Carleton*, who chose to put an end to the incident by having the letter officially burned. Considering La Corne Saint-Luc to be "a great villain and as cunning as the devil," the American general forbad him to come to Montreal after its capitulation in November 1775 and relegated him to Boucherville. Soon after, La Corne Saint-Luc was taken to La Prairie on the orders of Montgomery's replacement, Brigadier-General David Wooster, who suspected him of intrigue. Wooster, after he had become the leading commander in the occupying army, sent him off to Philadelphia the following February, and he was kept for some time at Kingston (also called Esopus), N.Y.

This ordeal did not dampen the martial ardour of La Corne Saint-Luc, who by this time was 66. Immediately after his release he had conversations with the loyalist ex-governor of New York, William Tryon, and suggested that what was necessary was "to unleash the Indians against the wretched rebels" as a means of ending the revolutionary war and revenging his imprisonment. Convinced that at his call his friends would dig up the hatchet, he agreed to take part in the campaign under Major-General Burgoyne, who entrusted command of the Indians to him. This large military operation, which was to mark a turning point in the revolutionary war, came to a lamentable end on the battlefield at Saratoga (Schuylerville), N.Y., in October 1777 as a result of serious errors of strategy. Burgoyne had to surrender his army, which La Corne Saint-Luc considered "one of the finest . . . [the] country had yet seen."

Upon his return to London after the disaster, Burgoyne did his best to justify his stinging defeat before British opinion. A member of parliament, he accused La Corne Saint-Luc in the House of Commons itself of having been responsible for the Indians' desertion before the final outcome of the campaign and denounced him as "by nature, education, and practice, artful, ambitious, and a courtier." It was, however, the same Burgoyne who had earlier called him "a Canadian gentleman of honour and parts, and one of the best partizans the French had last war." In replying to him, Lord Germain, who as secretary of state for the American Colonies was responsible for the military operations, took the occasion to express his displeasure by repeating La Corne's own judgement of Burgoyne: "a very brave man, but as heavy as a German."

La Corne Saint-Luc had too great a sense of honour not to take up the gauntlet. He replied publicly to Burgoyne in a letter of 23 Oct. 1778 addressed to the London newspapers. In the courteous but proud tone of an officer who had many times proved his courage and military competence he made an apt retort to the defeated general. Having first expressed his astonishment at the way in which Burgoyne had acted, he then set out the facts once more to show that his former commander bore full responsibility for the flight of the Indians, who had been not only indignant but disgusted at his "indifference" and callousness towards their dead and wounded after the battle at Bennington (Vt.) two months before the disaster at Saratoga.

Burgoyne deserved this lesson in civility, since La Corne Saint-Luc merited treatment as a gentleman. Not only had he been rewarded with the cross of Saint-Louis at the end of the French régime, but following the Quebec Act he had become a member of the Legislative Council, created in May 1775. It had not taken long for Carleton to appreciate the importance of this prominent citizen and to recommend his appointment as a councillor on the highly selective list he had presented in March 1769 to the secretary of state for the American Colonies, Lord Hillsborough. He had fixed his choice on those whom he considered to be "men of First Property and Consequence." In his eyes La Corne Saint-Luc belonged to the seigneurial élite, which should enjoy the patronage of the British crown.

But for the conquered subjects such favours had definite limits. Although Carleton's successor, General HALDIMAND, agreed that La Corne Saint-Luc should serve as his aide-de-camp, he was not prepared to support his request for promotion in the militia to the rank that his commission as "colonel of the Indians" conferred upon him. Since the Franco-American alliance of 1778 the new governor had had an almost obsessive distrust of the ex-subjects of the king of France, and he advised against such a promotion for this former officer of the French colonial regulars.

Six months before his death La Corne Saint-Luc had occasion to assert his political creed when he took the initiative in the Legislative Council of proposing an address to Governor Haldimand calling upon him to make known to the king his councillors' "sincere desire" to see the Quebec Act "continued in all its force," in order "to be able to transmit it to posterity as a precious charter." This motion, presented on 21 April 1784 at the end of the legislative session, was favourably received by the French party, which included a majority of councillors, and by the governor himself; Haldimand adopted the language used by La Corne Saint-Luc and reiterated to the authorities in London his personal conviction that maintaining the 1774 legislation constituted "the most likely means to attach the People to the Mother Country, and make them happy in the Enjoyment of their Religion, Laws, and Liberties."

On 1 Oct. 1784 La Corne Saint-Luc passed away at his residence on Rue Saint-Paul in Montreal. He was buried on 4 October in the chapel of Sainte-Anne in the church of Notre-Dame. His third wife survived him by 35 years.

PIERRE TOUSIGNANT and
MADELEINE DIONNE-TOUSIGNANT

[Luc de La Corne], *Journal du voyage de M. Saint-Luc de La Corne, écuyer, dans le navire l'Auguste, en l'an 1761* (Montréal, 1778; 2e éd., Québec, 1863); "A letter from the Chev. St Luc de la Corne, colonel of the Indians, to Gen. Burgoyne," *Scots Magazine* (Edinburgh), XL (1778), 715–16.

AN, Col., C^{11A}, 85, pp.110–11, 115–16; 87, pp.166–67; 99, pp.94–101; 103, f.438; 120, pp.84–91; D^{2C}, 48, ff.56, 233, 236, 253, 315v, 316; F^{3}, 13, ff.268–70 (page references are to PAC transcripts). ANQ-M, État civil, Catholiques, Notre-Dame de Montréal, 10 déc. 1742, 3 sept. 1757, 9 avril 1774, 4 oct. 1784; Sainte-Trinité (Contrecœur), 1702–19 [La Corne Saint-Luc's birthdate remains uncertain because the parish registers for 1711 are missing. P.T. and M.D.-T.]; Greffe de J.-B. Adhémar, 8 déc. 1742; Greffe de L.-C. Danré de Blanzy, 1er sept. 1757, 29 sept. 1784; Greffe d'Antoine Foucher, 18 févr. 1752, 29 sept. 1784; Greffe de Pierre Panet, 25 avril 1772, 17 mars 1774; Greffe de Simon Sanguinet, 6 déc. 1784. ASQ, Fonds Viger-Verreau, Carton 9, no.6. BL, Add. MSS 21714, pp.123–26; 21770, pp.54–55 (copies at PAC). PAC, MG 8, A1, 9, pp.204–8; MG 11, [CO 42], Q, 6, pp.34–40; 23, pp.321–22; RG 1, E1, 7, pp.202–7.

American archives (Clarke and Force), 4th ser., III, 973, 1095–96, 1098–99; IV, 156–57, 1482; VI, 609, 769. John Burgoyne, *A state of the expedition from Canada*

. . . (London, 1780; repr. New York, 1969). *Docs. relating to constitutional history, 1759–91* (Shortt and Doughty; 1918), II, 594–95. [J. M. Hadden], *Hadden's journal and orderly books: a journal kept in Canada and upon Burgoyne's campaign in 1776 and 1777, by Lieut. James M. Hadden . . .*, ed. Horatio Rogers (Albany, N.Y., 1884; repr. Freeport, N.Y., [1970]), 134–35, 517–37. *Invasion du Canada* (Verreau). "Inventaire des biens de Luc Lacorne de Saint-Luc," J.-J. Lefebvre, édit., ANQ *Rapport*, 1947–48, 31–70. *Johnson papers* (Sullivan *et al.*). "Mémoire du Canada," ANQ *Rapport*, 1924–25, 196. *NYCD* (O'Callaghan and Fernow), VII, 590; VIII, 707–8; X, 32, 39–40, 79–80, 112, 183, 345, 500, 512, 607, 621, 629, 643, 750, 760, 801, 803, 817, 849, 913–14, 1080, 1086. *The parliamentary history of England from the earliest period to the year 1803*, ed. William Cobbett and John Wright (36v., London, 1806–20), XIX, 1181, 1195. "Procès de Robert Stobo et de Jacob Wambram pour crime de haute trahison," ANQ *Rapport*, 1922–23, 314, 321–22, 324. Caron, "Inv. de la corr. de Mgr Briand," ANQ *Rapport*, 1929–30, 83, 116. Æ. Fauteux, *Les chevaliers de Saint-Louis*. Massicotte, "Répertoire des engagements pour l'Ouest," ANQ *Rapport*, 1929–30, 354–59, 366, 374, 383–84, 417, 419, 433; 1930–31, 419, 424, 451; 1931–32, 243–49, 254, 275, 277, 279, 294–95, 308–14, 326, 333.

P.[-J.] Aubert de Gaspé, *Les anciens Canadiens* (Québec, 1863). Burke, *Les ursulines de Québec* (1863–66), III, 147. Antoine Champagne, *Les La Vérendrye et le poste de l'Ouest* (Québec, 1968). Frégault, *La guerre de la Conquête*, 218, 325. A.-H. Gosselin, *L'Église du Canada après la Conquête*, II, 107–8. W. D. Lighthall, *La Corne St-Luc, the "General of the Indians"* (Montreal, 1908). James Lunt, *John Burgoyne of Saratoga* (New York, 1975). Stanley, *New France*, 28, 88, 101–4. M. Trudel, *L'esclavage au Canada français*, 57–98, 156–57. Ægidius Fauteux, "Le chevalier de La Corne," *BRH*, XXVI (1920), 352. Henri Têtu, "M. Jean-Félix Récher, curé de Québec, et son journal, 1757–1760," *BRH*, IX (1903), 322–23.

LA CORNE DE CHAPTES, JOSEPH-MARIE (Jean-Marie) DE, parish priest, ecclesiastical councillor, dean of the chapter, and vicar general; b. apparently at Contrecœur (Que.), son of Jean-Louis de La Corne* de Chaptes and Marie Pécaudy de Contrecœur; he is believed to have been baptized at Verchères on 2 Nov. 1714; d. 7 Dec. 1779 at Maubec (Méobecq, dept of Indre), France.

Having entered the Séminaire de Québec on 1 May 1730 Joseph-Marie de La Corne de Chaptes received the tonsure from Bishop DOSQUET on 6 May 1735. Three years later, the bishop being absent from the colony, La Corne had to go to France to be ordained; he was received into the priesthood at Rennes in the autumn of 1738. On his return to the colony the following year, he was immediately named parish priest at Saint-Michel (Saint-Michel-de-Bellechasse), and there with the parishioners' agreement built a stone presbytery.

In July 1747 Bishop Pontbriand [Dubreil*] made La Corne a canon of the cathedral of Quebec and thought of him as a replacement for ecclesiastical councillor François-Elzéar Vallier* on the Conseil Supérieur. The bishop observed that "he has intelligence and talent and is a man of good family." On 25 Aug. 1749 the canon was appointed to the council. The experience he gained there in legal matters, combined with what he had learned as treasurer of the chapter, a position he had been holding for some time, was subsequently of great service to him. Indeed, in 1750 he was delegated by his colleagues in the chapter to go to France to defend their interests in the lawsuit about the conferring of the charge of the parish of Quebec which they had brought against the seminary and in which Canon René-Jean Allenou* de Lavillangevin played a leading role for the chapter [*see also* Jean-Félix Récher*]. This protracted suit, which went on until after the conquest, would summon up all La Corne's zeal and talent.

In Paris the chapter of Quebec had already had a representative for some years in Canon Pierre HAZEUR de L'Orme. La Corne thought his visit would be brief and hoped that, with the lawsuit under way, he would be able to return to Canada before the end of 1751 leaving Hazeur with power of attorney. On arrival he consulted lawyers who concluded that the chapter's requests were well grounded. He then harassed the offices of the administration at Versailles with representations but had little success. Believing, however, that his presence was no longer necessary in Paris, he decided to return to Canada in the spring of 1751. On his way he stopped at the abbey of Saint-Pierre in Maubec, a benefice of the chapter, to assess the state of its premises. When he reached La Rochelle, he learned that the Séminaire des Missions Étrangères in Paris had undertaken to delay the legal proceedings by refusing to recognize the validity of Canon de L'Orme's power of attorney. Reluctantly La Corne returned to the capital, where he again embarked, to no purpose, on a round of representations. In a letter to Canon Lavillangevin on 19 June 1751 he listed the connections and the line of action through which he intended to win the favours of those in high office; in the end these dealings were of no use. Incidentally La Corne seems to have exercised restraint in using the funds put at his disposal for his upkeep, but the lawsuit, now getting bogged down – in particular, in May 1753 the judge in charge of the inquiry died of smallpox – would prove expensive for the chapter of Quebec. Because of de

L'Orme's ill health, La Corne also attended to the administration of Maubec. He did not, however, lose hope of returning to Canada, although at the Paris seminary it was being said that he was prolonging the lawsuit to extend his stay in France.

La Corne informed his colleagues in a letter dated 26 Feb. 1755 that he had received royal appointment as dean of the chapter. The following year the chapter put him officially in charge of the administration of the Maubec abbey and in 1757 Hazeur's power of attorney was cancelled in favour of La Corne. De L'Orme expressed some regret about these decisions: "I do not think [he] is as skilled yet as I can be." La Corne kept up the struggle over the parish of Quebec, preparing memoir after memoir. In 1759 the king gave him the abbey of L'Étoile, in the diocese of Poitiers ten leagues from Maubec. Beginning that year, the year of the siege and capitulation of Quebec, La Corne attempted to help his colleagues in Quebec as much as he could; he lent them his income as dean and his canon's prebend and agreed to allow them to draw a bill of exchange on him for 5,000 *livres*.

The loss of Canada gave a new direction to the career of La Corne. Until his appointment as vicar general on 30 Sept. 1760, he had attended to the lawsuit in Paris during the winter and in the summer had travelled to and fro between his abbeys. In 1762 he wanted to be relieved of his duties as the chapter's agent; he felt that two canons from Quebec who had sought refuge in France in the autumn of 1759, Gilles-Louis Cugnet and Charles-Ange Collet*, would be capable of succeeding him. But his colleagues, who were satisfied with his services, increased his responsibilities; on 1 Oct. 1761 the chapter appointed him vicar general for Louisiana and the Mississippi region.

Bishop Pontbriand's death in June 1760, at a dramatic moment in the history of the Canadian church, raised the problem of the succession to the bishopric. When the treaty of Paris was signed in February 1763, Canon La Corne went to London to plead for the maintenance of the Catholic hierarchy. He first called upon Lord Shelburne, the president of the Board of Trade, and presented him with a memoir in which he concluded that election of a bishop by the chapter would be the solution most acceptable to the British government. This solution was adopted in August 1763; the chapter of Quebec then hastened to elect Canon Étienne MONTGOLFIER as bishop, and it appointed La Corne his "special procurator to report the above-mentioned election" to the authorities in London. In the spring of 1764 Britain indicated its willingness to turn a blind eye to Montgolfier's appointment, on condition that he bear the title of "Supérieur du Clergé." But Governor MURRAY categorically refused the appointment and put forward the name of Canon Jean-Olivier BRIAND. In March 1766 Briand was consecrated bishop in the château of Suresnes (dept of Hauts-de-Seine), France; La Corne's negotiating for appointment of a bishop was finally crowned with success. Briand had recognized the major role played by the canon in the affair; he had indeed claimed that "If there is a bishop, it is he to whom we shall owe it."

In a letter dated 29 March 1766 La Corne announced the good news to his colleagues in Quebec. He also informed them that the king of France was taking the Maubec abbey away from them to give it to him personally, on condition that he pay his colleagues who were in France – canons de L'Orme, Jean-Pierre de MINIAC, and Joseph-Ambroise Gaillard – an annual pension of 400 francs each.

La Corne continued, however, to represent the chapter in Paris, and in its name he attended to various financial matters. On 21 Sept. 1767 Briand appointed him vicar general, and in July 1770 gave him the task of carrying out with the papal nuncio in Paris all the steps needed to obtain bulls for Bishop Louis-Philippe MARIAUCHAU d'Esgly, the new coadjutor; La Corne complied, even though his health was not good that year. In a letter on 15 March 1770 he offered his resignation as dean, asking that he be allowed to retain the honorary title since he did not want to sever his links with the chapter. This request for permission to resign was refused. His final years, marked by illness and infirmity, were spent mainly in Berry. He died of pneumonia at the Maubec abbey on 7 Dec. 1779.

A man of great energy, who was not always easy to get along with, Canon La Corne was an effective agent for the Canadian church, both in London and in Paris, and one of our great diplomats.

JEAN-GUY PELLETIER

AAQ, 12 A, B, 312; C, 56; 20 A, I, 43, 44, 103, 153; 22 A, II, 688; 10 B, 167v, 168, 193, 193v, 194, 200, 218, 218v, 219, 220, 222, 227, 241, 241v, 244, 248v, 250, 261; 11 B, II, 453; V, 99, 101, 112; VI, 59; VII, 1–77, 87; VIII, 37, 48; X, 28, 49, 53; 1 CB, VI, 18, 19; CD, Diocèse de Québec, I, 58, 59; 91 CM, I, 102; 60 CN, V, 19; VI, 18, 22. AD, Indre (Châteauroux), Archives de l'abbaye de Méobecq, H281–H324; État civil, Méobecq, 7 déc. 1779. ASQ, Chapitre, 50, 85, 132, 258; Évêques, nos. 88, 138, 146, 147; Fonds Viger-Verreau, Sér. O, 035, p.18; Lettres, M, 121, 122, 122[a], 129; P, 24; S, 48, 92, 169; MSS, 13, 18 oct. 1779; Polygraphie, VII, 2, 3, 4, 9; XIII, 24; XVII, 4; Séminaire, 14/6, no.11; 14/7, nos.2, 3, 14; 75, no.58.

La Rue, "Lettres et mémoires," ANQ *Rapport*, 1935–36, 323, 331, 345, 388, 402; 1936–37, 398, 414, 459; 1937–38, 248–50. Allaire, *Dictionnaire*, I, 289. Caron, "Inv. de la corr. de Mgr Briand," ANQ *Rapport*, 1929–30, 47, 61, 63–64, 71, 104, 106. Le Jeune, *Dictionnaire*, II, 18–21. P.-G. Roy, *Inv. jug. et délib., 1717–60*, V, 125; *Inv. ord. int.*, II, 283. Henri Têtu, *Notices biographiques: les évêques de Québec* (Québec, 1889), 272, 359. A.-H. Gosselin, *L'Église du Canada après la Conquête*, I, 2, 64, 69, 72, 77, 79, 81, 83, 87, 95–96, 115, 120–21, 124, 127–32, 148, 151, 156, 158–59, 194–96, 204, 208–9, 403; II, 118, 246; *L'Église du Canada jusqu'à la Conquête*, II, 159, 330; III, 76, 106–7, 124–25, 168, 248, 253, 271–72, 280, 290–92, 297–304, 350, 462. Lemieux, *L'établissement de la première prov. eccl.*, 3–9. M. Trudel, *L'Église canadienne*. Lionel Groulx, "Le conflit religieux au lendemain de 1760," SCHÉC *Rapport*, 7 (1939–40), 13, 18, 23. Arthur Maheux, "Difficultés religieuses après la cession," SCHÉC *Rapport*, 14 (1946–47), 20. J.-E. Roy, "Les conseillers au Conseil souverain de la Nouvelle-France," *BRH*, I (1895), 182. P.-G. Roy, "Les conseillers clercs au Conseil souverain de la Nouvelle-France," *BRH*, XXII (1916), 352. Têtu, "Le chapitre de la cathédrale," *BRH*, XIII–XVII.

LA COSTE (La Côte), PIERRE COURREAUD DE. *See* COURREAUD

LA CROIX, JACQUES PREVOST DE. *See* PREVOST

LA FOURCHE. *See* NISSOWAQUET

LAGARDE (Delagarde), PIERRE-PAUL-FRANÇOIS DE, Sulpician, priest, and missionary; b. 19 July 1729 at Séguret (dept of Vaucluse), France; d. 3 April 1784 in Montreal (Que.).

Pierre-Paul-François de Lagarde entered the Séminaire Saint-Charles d'Avignon on 1 Nov. 1743 and by 21 Oct. 1746 was studying in Paris. He became a member of the Séminaire de Saint-Sulpice in Paris on 22 March 1754, was ordained deacon, and left for Canada on 25 May. He travelled on the frigate *Gloire* with the Sulpician François PICQUET and his delegation of Indians who were returning home. The voyage from Rochefort to Quebec took until 15 September.

Ordained priest in Quebec on 24 May 1755, Lagarde rejoined Picquet at the mission of La Présentation (Oswegatchie, now Ogdensburg, N.Y.). Here he concentrated on work with the Iroquois and his involvement enabled Picquet to carry out other than religious projects during the Seven Years' War. For five years Lagarde ministered to the Indians and the French, at one time with the help of François-Auguste MAGON de Terlaye and at another time with Jean-Claude MATHEVET, and frequently in the absence of Picquet. He also familiarized himself with the difficulties of the Indians' language. In his spare time he took up botany, and it was reported that he had transformed the parish register into a herbarium. He studied, among other plants, the wild ginger (*Asarum Canadense L.*), the matgrass (*Nardus Stricta L.*), the marguerite (*Chrysanthemum Leucanthemum L.*), the ox-eye daisy (*Anthemis Tinctoria L.*), and the daisy (*Bellis Perennis L.*).

When the British army invaded New France from the west in 1760, Lagarde remained at the mission to give spiritual solace to the defenders. On 23 July he signed the records at La Présentation for the last time, and a month later he was taken prisoner by AMHERST at Fort Lévis (east of Prescott, Ont.). Released on parole, he made his way to Montreal, where he served as a priest from November 1760 to May 1761. After a year and a half at the mission of Lac-des-Deux-Montagnes (Oka, Que.), he was appointed in January 1763 to the rural parish of Lachine. Each year until 1 June 1777 he performed about 50 baptisms, as many burials, and ten or so weddings. In 1769 his presbytery burnt down, and he quickly rebuilt it. After this disaster a new register traces the administration of the parish; the balance-sheets show surpluses increased six-fold from 1769 to 1776.

When Magon de Terlaye died in 1777 Lagarde was recalled to the Lac-des-Deux-Montagnes mission as bursar, and he became the superior after Mathevet left in 1778. In this position he had a double responsibility. As the representative of the Séminaire de Saint-Sulpice, seigneur and landowner, the superior granted sites to the Indians which they might use without charge but could not own; in addition he was often called upon to provide material assistance. From 1778 to 1783 Lagarde devised regulations which were approved by the elders of the tribes, tried to get the Indians to adopt an orderly way of life, and resisted Iroquois claims to ownership of the land. His other role as shepherd of his flock is revealed in the manuscripts he left: a catechism and sermons in French, but especially his work in Iroquois, a grammar and sermons (though his knowledge of that language shows no real sense of its spirit).

By 1782 Lagarde had fallen ill, but he remained

at his post until February 1784. He died at Montreal on 3 April 1784 and was buried beneath the chancel of Notre-Dame.

J.-BRUNO HAREL

ANQ-M, État civil, Catholiques, Notre-Dame de Montréal; Saints-Anges (Lachine). ASSM, 8, A; 24, Dossier 2, Dossier 6. Allaire, *Dictionnaire*. Gauthier, *Sulpitiana*. Louis Bertrand, *Bibliothèque sulpicienne, ou histoire littéraire de la Compagnie de Saint-Sulpice* (3v., Paris, 1900). André Chagny, *Un défenseur de la "Nouvelle-France," François Picquet, "le Canadien" (1708–1781)* (Montréal et Paris, 1913). J.-A. Cuoq, "Anotc kekon," RSC *Trans.*, 1st ser., XI (1893), sect.I, 137–79.

LAGROIX (La Groy, Lagroye, Lagrouais), JOSEPH HUPPÉ, *dit*. *See* HUPPÉ

LEJEMMERAIS, MARIE-MARGUERITE DUFROST DE. *See* DUFROST

LAJUS, FRANÇOIS (baptized **Louis-François**; also called **François-Xavier**), surgeon-major; b. 28 Aug. 1721 in Quebec, son of Jordain Lajus*, surgeon, and Louise-Élisabeth Moreau, *dit* Lataupine; d. 6 Oct. 1799 in Quebec.

François Lajus learned surgery from his father. He then became a military surgeon, and on 11 Jan. 1745 Intendant HOCQUART granted him a commission to go to Acadia as surgeon-major with a detachment under the command of Paul Marin* de La Malgue. Lajus evidently was back in Acadia some years later, for he was at Louisbourg, Île Royale (Cape Breton Island), when the British captured it in 1758 [*see* Augustin de Boschenry* de Drucour]. Accompanied by an Indian guide, he immediately returned to Quebec, bringing the news that the fortress had fallen.

During the siege of Quebec in the summer of 1759, Lajus treated the many wounded brought to the Hôpital Général. After the conquest he practised surgery in the town and, although he was not attached to any particular hospital, he was often called into consultation at the Hôtel-Dieu. Like his father, he was surgeon to the Recollets and a churchwarden of the parish of Notre-Dame in Quebec. He was a close friend of the seigneur of Lauson, Étienne CHAREST, and corresponded with him after Charest left for France in 1765.

A notice in the *Quebec Gazette* of 29 March 1770 shows that surgeons were not exempt from criticism or calumny. Its author, William Laing, cleared up rumours that Lajus had been guilty of "blameable conduct" during Mrs Laing's confinement. Not only were these reports untrue, he wrote, but his wife thought that Lajus "was the Means of saving her Life, by his great Skill and Care, and hereby desires to return him her public Thanks for the same, and would rather have him on such an Occasion than anyone that she knows."

It seems in fact that Dr Lajus had a good reputation and a large practice, which was not true of all doctors or surgeons. The profession was not organized at this time. In 1750, under the French régime, Intendant BIGOT had issued an ordinance requiring any newcomer to be examined by the king's physician before he could practise, but it had fallen into disuse and had not been replaced after the conquest. Consequently there were more charlatans of every sort passing themselves off as doctors and doing serious harm to the inhabitants' health than there were qualified doctors and surgeons. To end these abuses Lord Dorchester [Carleton*] issued an ordinance in 1788 which forbade anyone, under pain of a heavy fine, to practise medicine, surgery, and obstetrics without first appearing before the Board of Medical Examiners, in either Quebec or Montreal. Because of his knowledge and wide experience Lajus was chosen by the governor to be a member of the first board in Quebec.

On 14 Nov. 1747 Lajus had married Marguerite Audet de Piercotte de Bailleul in Quebec, and they had several children who died in infancy. On 11 Aug. 1776 he took as his second wife Angélique-Jeanne Hubert, whose brother, Jean-François HUBERT, was superior of the seminary and later bishop of Quebec. Their eldest child, François-Marie-Olivier-Hubert, died tragically from a shot in the head in 1795, when he was 17. The alleged murderer, Abel Willard, committed suicide in prison, and the inquiry concluded that this action was a case of "Insanity." Lajus's two other sons, Jean-Baptiste-Isidore-Hospice and René-Flavien, were ordained to the priesthood, and his daughter, Jeanne-Françoise-Louise-Luce, married Pierre-Stanislas Bédard* in 1796.

THÉRÈSE P. LEMAY

ANQ-Q, AP-P-1106; État civil, Catholiques, Notre-Dame de Québec, 28 août 1721, 14 nov. 1747, 11 août 1776, 8 oct. 1799. *Quebec Gazette*, 29 March 1770, 7 May 1795. P.-G. Roy, *Fils de Québec*, II, 16–18; *Inv. concessions*, V, 3; *Inv. contrats de mariage*, IV, 25; *Inv. jug. et délib., 1717–60*, V, 245; VI, 26; *Inv. ord. int.*, III, 66, 150. Tanguay, *Dictionnaire*, I, 339; V, 97. Abbott, *History of medicine*. M.-J. et G. Ahern, *Notes pour l'hist. de la médicine*, 325–31. Heagerty, *Four centuries of medical history in Canada*, I, 226. J.-E. Roy, *Histoire de la seigneurie de Lauzon* (5v., Lévis, Qué., 1897–1904), II. P.-G. Roy, *A travers l'histoire de l'Hôtel-Dieu de Québec* (Lévis, 1939), 181; "La famille Lajus," *BRH*, XL (1934), 243–47.

LALANCETTE, LOUIS-NICOLAS LANDRIO, *dit. See* LANDRIAUX

LA MADELEINE. FRANÇOIS-JEAN-DANIEL D'AILLEBOUST DE. *See* AILLEBOUST

LAMALETIE, JEAN-ANDRÉ, merchant and clerk of the marshalcy of Quebec; baptized 8 Jan. 1718 at Bordeaux, France, son of Louis Lamaletie, merchant and consul of the consular jurisdiction of Bordeaux, and Marie-Anne Benet; m. 14 Nov. 1747 at Quebec, Marie-Thérèse, daughter of François Foucault*, member of the Conseil Supérieur; of their nine children only two or three survived infancy; d. after 1774 in France.

Conflicting sources have placed Jean-André Lamaletie's first appearance in Canada in 1739 and 1741, but the articles of his partnership with the well-known La Rochelle outfitter, Joseph-Simon Desherbert de Lapointe, dated 14 June 1744, constitute the earliest document to provide significant information on his career. Lamaletie brought to the partnership only "his work, industry, and application." Lapointe agreed to contribute trade goods worth 60,000 *livres* to the firm over a three-year period, taking three-quarters of the profits and bearing alone the risk of losses. Lamaletie, in addition to his one-quarter share of profits, was to receive 200 *livres* per year for handling an additional 8,000 *livres* of merchandise from a Louisbourg merchant named Delort (possibly Guillaume Delort*) and 500 *livres* per year for handling additional cargo as Lapointe's agent. Lamaletie's contract exemplifies the dependence of Quebec's Lower Town traders, generally young men making their way in the world, upon metropolitan French capital and connections. Whether as salaried clerks, commission agents, or junior partners, they extended the reach of French traders into Canada by supplying manufactures to the community wholesale and retail and by outfitting the Montreal fur-traders. They then collected return cargoes, mostly furs and bills of exchange, remitting them to La Rochelle, Bordeaux, or Rouen, where they were received by the outfitters whose investment and patient extension of credit had made them the masters of the trade.

In 1746 Lamaletie's contract with Lapointe was extended to December 1752 and his share of the profits increased to one-half. It was thus a successful young man in the ascendant phase of his career who married into the prominent Foucault family in 1747, although the marriage contract reveals that he still had no assets beyond his business. The distinguished signatures on the contract, including those of the governor, bishop, and intendant, indicate the social significance of the marriage. So too, in all probability, does Lamaletie's appointment as clerk of the marshalcy, an office he held from July 1748 until 1758. A Catholic, Lamaletie did not suffer from the social and civil disabilities that circumscribed the lives of his many Huguenot *confrères* in the Lower Town.

In 1750, Lapointe died. Lamaletie spent the winter of 1751–52 in France, making new business connections. He returned to Quebec secure in a new partnership with another La Rochelle outfitter, Pierre-Gabriel Admyrauld. At Quebec he became linked with Guillaume ESTÈBE and another trader, Jean Latuilière, who moved to Bordeaux in 1757. In the same year Lamaletie withdrew from his partnership with Admyrauld and in 1758 he too went to Bordeaux. The new firm name of Lamaletie, Latuilière et Cie appeared shortly thereafter. As Estèbe also made the move to Bordeaux in 1758, it is possible that in some manner he too was connected with the firm. It was probably through Estèbe that Lamaletie first became acquainted with the Canadian purveyor general, Joseph-Michel CADET, a customer to whom Lamaletie, Latuilière et Cie sent many ships in the closing years of the Seven Years' War. The breaking of links with La Rochelle and the transfer of the seat of operations to Bordeaux were undoubtedly intended to facilitate the handling of state contracts.

Although his accounts were seized, Lamaletie was never himself arrested for wartime profiteering and escaped the fate of Estèbe and Cadet. His profits suffered heavily when the state suspended payments on its bills of exchange. The war and the loss of Canada, which Lamaletie regarded as an "irreparable loss to the state & for which I will never console myself," left him a much poorer man, but Lamaletie, Latuilière et Cie remained in business. In the 1760s Lamaletie acted on behalf of many Canadians who were winding up their affairs in France, particularly with regard to government drafts and other obligations. After 1774 no further references to his name can be found in Canadian sources.

DALE MIQUELON

AN, Col., B, 87, f.3; 110, f.76. ANQ-Q, Greffe de Claude Barolet, 16 sept., 11 nov. 1747, 11 juin 1748; Greffe de C.-H. Du Laurent, 26 oct. 1751; Greffe de Claude Louet, 24 oct. 1763, 9 août 1766; Greffe de J.-C. Panet, 28 avril 1749, 9, 14, 18, 21, 22, 23 oct., 4 nov. 1751, 19 oct. 1753, 23 sept. 1754, 28 févr., 16 déc. 1757, 1er avril, 22, 28 mai, 23 août, 18 sept. 1758, 30 août, 3 sept. 1762, 28 oct. 1763, 9 mars, 8 juill. 1768; Greffe de J.-A. Saillant, 13 oct. 1755, 4 nov. 1756; Greffe de Simon Sanguinet, 7 juill. 1766; NF 25, 56, no.2119.

PAC, MG 24, L3. *Archives de la Bastille, documents inédits*, François Ravaisson-Mollien, édit. (19v., Paris, 1866–1904), XVIII, 276, 362, 376. P.-G. Roy, *Inv. ins. Cons. souv.*, 248, 277; *Inv. jug. et délib., 1717–60*, V, 20, 75, 150, 165; VI, 76, 135, 137; *Inv. ord. int.*, III, 96. Tanguay, *Dictionnaire*, V, 105. Frégault, *François Bigot*, II, 138. Jean de Maupassant, *Un grand armateur de Bordeaux, Abraham Gradis (1699?–1780)* (Bordeaux, 1917), 53–54, 78. J. F. Bosher, "A Québec merchant's trading circles in France and Canada: Jean-André Lamaletie before 1763," *Social History*, IX (1977), 24–44.

LA MALGUE, JOSEPH MARIN DE. *See* MARIN

LA MARRE, JEAN-VICTOR VARIN DE. *See* VARIN

LA NAUDIÈRE, CHARLES-FRANÇOIS TARIEU DE. *See* TARIEU

LANDRIAUX (Landrio, *dit* Lalancette; Landriaux, *dit* Dusourdy), LOUIS-NICOLAS, surgeon; b. *c.* 1723 at Luçon, France, son of Louis Landriaux and Marie-Louise Bourond; d. 24 Aug. 1788 in Montreal (Que.).

Louis-Nicolas Landriaux's presence in Canada was first noted on 10 April 1748, when he appeared as a witness in a lawsuit in Montreal. He was then a soldier serving under Louis de La Corne* and was practising surgery at the Hôtel-Dieu of Montreal, probably as an assistant to Charles-Elemy-Joseph-Alexandre-Ferdinand FELTZ, who was also a surgeon at the Hôpital Général. On 7 May 1748, when Landriaux was about to leave Montreal to take up the position of surgeon at Fort Saint-Frédéric (near Crown Point, N.Y.), he named Feltz as his proxy and entrusted him with receiving the 480 *livres tournois* granted annually by the king for his new position. He returned to Montreal some months before July 1759 when the fort was abandoned.

Good surgeons were rare in Montreal in the mid 18th century, and Landriaux, who had acquired experience treating the sick and wounded in the Lake Champlain region, probably built up a practice quite quickly. In September 1766, after Feltz left for France, he became surgeon-in-chief at the Hôpital Général and served there until August 1782, when Dr George Selby* replaced him. He received 300 *livres tournois* per year for his services at first, and in 1780 the nuns raised this salary to 400 *livres*. Mother d'Youville [DUFROST], expressing her satisfaction with Landriaux, noted: "He is acquiring a large practice through his good sense and prudence."

Louis-Nicolas Landriaux was apparently an important resident of Montreal. In 1762 he was living in a house he owned on Rue Saint-Pierre, near the Recollets' house; 20 years later he was still there. The statement by several historians that Landriaux lived in Quebec is erroneous, to be explained by a misreading of a text in the *Quebec Gazette*, 7 and 21 March 1782. Landriaux had some servants, and even a slave; in addition he owned "many good houses in town." In 1773 he was one of a number of prominent people who signed a petition to King George III asking him to grant the "Canadians" their former laws.

Having been trained by Feltz, an excellent surgeon who had initiated him into the secrets of his art – for example he had passed on to him a method for curing ulcers – Landriaux knew how to win the confidence and liking of his patients. Between 1770 and 1773 three inmates of the Hôpital Général left him part of the properties they said they owned in France; however, it was up to the surgeon to undertake proceedings at his own expense to acquire possession of these hypothetical legacies. To further his education Landriaux acquired a medical library that was outstanding for the time; Ambroise Paré's works and the *Aphorisms* of Hippocrates stood alongside treatises on pregnancy, venereal diseases, anatomy, and medicaments.

Though Landriaux seems to have lived a comfortable and affluent life, he died heavily in debt. In 1788 he owed various creditors more than 30,000 *livres*. His wife renounced the inheritance, and his possessions were sold at auction.

His marriage with Marie-Anne Prud'homme had taken place on 8 June 1756 in the chapel of Fort Saint-Frédéric and they had had 22 children; the first, baptized at the fort, died a few months later, and all the others were born in Montreal. Descendants live today in Quebec and Ontario.

GILLES JANSON

ANQ-M, Doc. jud., Registres des audiences pour la juridiction de Montréal, 10 avril 1748; État civil, Catholiques, Notre-Dame de Montréal, 21 juill. 1758, 16 mars 1784, 26 août 1788; Greffe de L.-L. Aumasson de Courville, 3 août 1770, 25 janv. 1772, 4 août 1773; Greffe de Louis Chaboillez, 9 sept. 1788 (marriage contract of Louis-Nicolas Landriaux and Marie-Anne Prud'homme drawn up at Fort Saint-Frédéric on 7 June 1756), 15, 16 sept., 1er oct. 1788; Greffe de L.-C. Danré de Blanzy, 29 janv. 1760; Greffe de François Simonnet, 7 mai 1748. ASGM, Corr. générale, no.6; Maison mère; Historique, Médecins, 3; Registre des baptêmes et sépultures de l'Hôpital Général de Montréal, II, f.29; Registre des recettes et dépenses, II. PAC, MG 8, G10.

Docs. relating to constitutional history, 1759–91 (Shortt and Doughty; 1907), 354–55. *Quebec Gazette*, 23 July 1767, 7, 21 March 1782. M.-J. et G. Ahern, *Notes pour l'hist. de la médecine*. [É.-M. Faillon], *Vie de Mme d'Youville, fondatrice des Sœurs de la Charité de Villemarie dans l'île de Montréal, en Canada* (Villemarie [Montréal], 1852). Albertine Ferland-Angers, *Mère d'Youville, vénérable Marie-Marguerite Du Frost de Lajemmerais, veuve d'Youville, 1701–1771; fondatrice des Sœurs de la Charité de l'Hôpital-général de Montréal, dites sœurs grises* (Montréal, 1945), 245, 256. P. J. Robinson, *Toronto during the French régime* . . . (2nd ed., Toronto, 1965). P.-G. Roy, *Hommes et choses du fort Saint-Frédéric* (Montréal, 1946). M. Trudel, *L'esclavage au Canada français*. É.-Z. Massicotte, "Le chirurgien Landriaux," *BRH*, XLVI (1940), 148–49; "Les chirurgiens, médecins, etc., de Montréal, sous le Régime français," ANQ *Rapport*, 1922–23, 143; "Les médecins, chirurgiens et apothicaires de Montréal, de 1701 à 1760," *BRH*, XXVII (1921), 79. P.-G. Roy, "La famille du chirurgien Landriaux," *BRH*, XLIII (1937), 46–48.

LANDRIÈVE DES BORDES, JEAN-MARIE, chief king's scrivener and commissary of the Marine; b. 12 Aug. 1712 at Aubusson, France, son of Gabriel-Alexis Des Bordes Landriève, presiding judge of the province of Marche, and Marguerite Mercier; buried 21 May 1778 at Artanes (dept of Indre et Loire), France.

Jean-Marie Landriève Des Bordes arrived in Canada towards the end of the 1730s. In May 1740 he was in Montreal, where in addition to engaging in trade he was employed as an inspection clerk in the king's stores, a job for which he was commissioned on 21 Oct. 1741. As he was satisfied with Landriève's services, the minister of Marine, Maurepas, granted him letters patent as king's scrivener on 23 Jan. 1748. In 1751, following a visit to France on personal matters, Landriève returned to Canada at Intendant François BIGOT's request in order to serve as chief scrivener at Detroit. The next year he was commissioned subdelegate of the intendant for Detroit, to succeed Robert NAVARRE. The office was resumed by Navarre in 1754, when Landriève was recalled to Quebec; there he was put in charge of the quartermaster and pay services for troops in the governments of Quebec and Trois-Rivières, replacing Jacques-Michel BRÉARD. He became one of the confidential agents of the intendant, who entrusted him with the inspection and management of the forts in the *pays d'en haut* from La Présentation (Oswegatchie, now Ogdensburg, N.Y.) to Fort Duquesne (Pittsburgh, Pa); he carried out an inspection in 1755. In 1758 he served as commissary at Fort Carillon (Ticonderoga, N.Y.).

At the time of the conquest, in keeping with article 20 of the terms of surrender for Montreal, Landriève was chosen by Governor Vaudreuil [RIGAUD] for the office of commissary with responsibility for the king's affairs in the colony. He got along well with the British authorities, who showed high regard for him. Indeed Thomas GAGE, governor of Montreal, and his wife were present on 23 June 1761 at the signing of the contract for Landriève's marriage with Marie-Gilles, the youngest daughter of Gaspard-Joseph Chaussegros* de Léry, the king's engineer in New France. Also present were various French military officers and Jacques-Joseph LEMOINE Despins, with whom Landriève had done business during the final years of the French régime. Landriève declared that he was bringing 200,000 *livres* in cash to the joint estate, and his wife 12,000 *livres*. At that time, according to the author of the "Mémoire du Canada," Landriève's fortune was estimated at 900,000 *livres*.

In France, however, Landriève was accused at the Châtelet of having participated in the breaches of trust committed by Bigot and his circle, in particular as a member of an association of merchant-traders with François Maurin*, Joseph-Michel CADET, and Jean Corpron*. On 10 Dec. 1763, after due investigation, he was accused of failure to appear in court, and he was found guilty of having received gifts from Cadet, signed false statements, and forged or signed false bills for the purchase from Maurin, Corpron, and Cadet of supplies that were paid for but never delivered. The court of the Châtelet sentenced him to be banished from the city of Paris for nine years, to pay the king a fine of 500 *livres*, and to make 100,000 *livres*' restitution to the state. Landriève returned to France on the *Chevalier de Lévis* in January 1765. He immediately asked for and obtained a safe conduct for six months, on condition that he give himself up at the end of that time to face the sentence hanging over him. In June of that year he demanded a new trial and spent all his time justifying his conduct in Canada. On 24 Nov. 1766 the court of the Châtelet acquitted him of all charges and declared him blameless in the *affaire du Canada*. Once exonerated in France, Landriève insisted upon clearing his name completely in Canadian eyes by publishing letters and messages in the *Quebec Gazette*, the only one of the 55 accused officials who took such action. In 1769 he obtained from the king letters patent as a commissary of the Marine and a pension of 600 *livres*.

In the summer of 1770 Jean-Marie Landriève Des Bordes left Paris and retired to his property at Artanes, where he died in May 1778. According to his nephew, François-Joseph Chaussegros de Léry, he left his wife and three children "a respectable fortune." His two sons went into the king's service, Antoine-Gilles joining the king's bodyguards, and Pierre-Paul the colonial regular troops.

ANDRÉ LACHANCE

AD, Indre-et-Loire (Tours), État civil, Artanes, 21 mai 1778. AN, Col., B, 71, f.43; 74, f.18v; 84, f.17; 87, ff.11, 11v; 89, f.15; 91, ff.32, 32v; 113, f.273; 164, f.347; C[11A], 93, f.264; 96, ff.54, 54v; 105, ff.199, 382, 407, 409; E, 253 (dossier Landriève Des Bordes). ANQ-M, État civil, Catholiques, Notre-Dame de Montréal, 25 juin 1761; Greffe de Pierre Panet, 23 juin 1761. [F.-J. Chaussegros de Léry], "Lettres du vicomte François-Joseph Chaussegros de Léry à sa famille," ANQ *Rapport*, 1933–34, 55. *Inv. des papiers de Léry* (P.-G. Roy), II, 289; III, 54–56, 113, 135–41, 146–50, 157–60. "Mémoire du Canada," ANQ *Rapport*, 1924–25, 174, 187, 197. PAC *Rapport*, 1899, suppl., 182–83; 1905, I, VIe partie, 72, 108, 130, 319, 359, 361, 364, 383. *Quebec Gazette*, 14 May, 26 June 1767, 2 Feb. 1769. J.-E. Roy, *Rapport sur les archives de France*, 875, 884. P.-G. Roy, *Inv. ord. int.*, III, 16, 169, 185, 189, 191. Tanguay, *Dictionnaire*, V, 127. P.-G. Roy, *Bigot et sa bande*, 168–72. [P.-]P.-B. Casgrain, "Landrieffe," *BRH*, II (1896), 45–46. J.-E. Roy, "Landriève," *BRH*, II (1896), 89–90. Benjamin Sulte, "Jean-Marie Landrieff," *BRH*, II (1896), 50–53.

LANDRY, ALEXIS, merchant; b. at Grand-Pré, Nova Scotia, and baptized 25 Aug. 1721, son of Jean Landry and Claire Le Blanc; d. 6 March 1798 at Caraquet, New Brunswick.

Alexis Landry left Grand-Pré in 1743 and went to live on the seigneury of Beaubassin at Aulac (N.B.), where he married Marie Terriot, the widow of Jean Cormier; they were to have at least 11 children. In 1755 he took part in the defence of Fort Beauséjour (near Sackville, N.B.); forced to leave Aulac after the fort's surrender to Robert MONCKTON on 16 June, he and his compatriots took refuge at Cocagne on the Ruisseau des Malcontents, where they remained until the end of the winter. In the spring of 1756 Landry, along with many other Acadians, decided to go north to Miramichi, hoping to escape from British raids and to make a living by hunting and fishing. They went through a terrible winter of war, famine, and pestilence; more than 350 Acadians perished, including five of his own children. It is likely that in the spring of 1757 Landry made his way to Caraquet with three families. The date of their arrival is unknown, but the census taken by Pierre DU CALVET in July 1761 reports Landry's presence there. In October 1761 Captain Roderick MacKenzie conducted a raid against the settlements on the Baie des Chaleurs. His Acadian prisoners were to be taken to Fort Cumberland (formerly Beauséjour), but 157 of them, including Landry and his family, were left behind because of lack of space in the boats. Shortly afterwards, probably for security, Landry left Caraquet for Miscou and settled at what is now called Landrys River.

In the spring of 1768 Landry brought his family back to Caraquet; on 13 March 1769 George Walker, the magistrate at Nepisiguit (Bathurst, N.B.), gave him official permission to settle on the land he had occupied in 1761, provided that it had not been granted to someone else. In 1784 Landry received title to this land and three years later Governor Thomas Carleton* granted him "the meadows and tidal flats located along the Rivière du Nord." From 1766 on Landry had engaged in a lively trade in imported goods, which he obtained from traders in Nepisiguit and Bonaventure and Paspébiac (Que.) in exchange for cod. In 1775 he even became a shipbuilder; the following year he delivered to Walker's company in Nepisiguit a brigantine intended for a London company.

In 1791 Landry took steps to have a chapel erected at Caraquet. The missionary Joseph-Mathurin BOURG wanted it built near the cemetery, and on 10 July 1793 Landry officially made over land for the purpose, with the condition that he and his heirs have the use without payment of a four-seat closed pew and that the cost of his funeral service and burial in the chapel be paid by the parish council. Two years later he wrote to Pierre Denaut*, coadjutor of the bishop of Quebec, expressing the hope that Bishop HUBERT would remember the people of Caraquet and send them a resident priest; in the letter he mentioned that a fire had destroyed his barn and part of his grain. Landry was evidently much concerned about the spiritual welfare of his fellow citizens, for he took the place of a priest when necessary at baptisms, marriages, and burials. On 14 July 1794 he had been appointed tax assessor and road commissioner for the parish of Caraquet.

Alexis Landry died at Caraquet at 76 years of age and was buried in a small cemetery near the sanctuary of Sainte-Anne-du-Bocage. Since 1961 a monument has overlooked the grave of this Acadian, one of the few survivors of the deportation period whose exact place of burial is known.

ALBERT LANDRY

AN, Section Outre-mer, G[1], 466, no.30. Archives of the Archbishopric of Baton Rouge (Baton Rouge, La.), Registre des baptêmes, mariages et sépultures de Saint-Charles-des-Mines (Grand-Pré, N.-É.), 1707–42. Private archives, Laura Cormier (Caraquet, N.-B.), Coll. Livin Cormier (factures, états de compte, lettres, reçus, documents officiels sur Alexis Landry et sa famille). PRO, WO 34/239, ff.160–64. Soc. jersiaise (St Helier, Jersey), Journal de Charles Robin, 1767–84. [Transcripts or microfilm copies of archival materials are available at CÉA.]

"Papiers Amherst (1760–1763) concernant les Acadiens," R.-S. Brun, édit., Soc. historique acadienne, *Cahier* (Moncton, N.-B.), III (1968–71), 257–320. *Caraquet: quelques bribes de son histoire, 1967, année du centenaire*, Corinne Albert-Blanchard, compil. ([Caraquet, N.-B.], [1967?]). W. F. Ganong, *The history of Caraquet and Pokemouche*, ed. S. B. Ganong (Saint John, N.B., 1948). Placide Gaudet, "Alexis Landry," *L'Évangéline* (Moncton, N.-B.), 12, 19 mai, 9 juin, 19 juill. 1927 (p.11 in each issue).

LANGLADE, CHARLES-MICHEL MOUET DE. *See* MOUET

LANGLOISERIE, *dite* **Saint-Hippolyte, MARIE-MARGUERITE PIOT DE.** *See* PIOT

LANGMAN, EDWARD, Church of England clergyman and local official; b. 1716, son of John Langman of Totnes, England; married, with one daughter; d. 1784 in St John's, Newfoundland.

Edward Langman graduated BA from Balliol College, Oxford University, in 1739 and was then ordained to the curacy of St Ive, Cornwall. In 1750 he journeyed to St John's, presumably with the fishing fleet, and officiated as a clergyman for the summer. His conduct made a favourable impression on the inhabitants, and the following December they successfully petitioned the Society for the Propagation of the Gospel that he be appointed to succeed their last missionary, William Peaseley*. Langman was allotted a salary of £50 per annum by the SPG and the inhabitants of St John's implied that they would also give financial support.

In May 1752 Langman arrived in St John's and began to minister to the 40 Church of England families living there. He held divine service every Sunday, preaching in the morning and evening, administered the sacrament four times a year, and added prayers on Wednesdays and Fridays in Lent. In 1759 he made the first of a series of missionary journeys when he spent two weeks in Placentia. The following year he went to Renews, Fermeuse, and Ferryland, and in 1761 he travelled to Bay Bulls and Witless Bay. At the latter places he was upset to find that "the few Protestants there are in danger even of their lives" since the Roman Catholics were restrained from attacking them only by "fear of the civil power."

The French invasion of Newfoundland in 1762 [*see* Charles-Henri-Louis d'ARSAC de Ternay] resulted in a heavy loss to Langman, whose property was plundered of £130 during the occupation of the town. To add to his misfortune, his wife died in childbirth at the same time, and only his own serious illness prevented him from being exiled from the town with the other Protestants. His finances never recovered from the shock; since his parishioners had never provided a house he found it difficult to live "with any tolerable decency" on the little money they gave him. Twice in 1763 he asked the SPG to move him elsewhere, but he nevertheless extended his visits with a journey to Trinity in the summer of 1764. His virtue was unappreciated by some, however, for in 1765 several merchants, upset by his justified financial requests and his criticisms of their behaviour, organized a petition to the SPG which complained of his "immoral, drunken, disagreeable" conduct. Governor Hugh PALLISER and others rebutted the charges, but Langman's hopes for increased local financial support faded. In 1768 he suffered a further loss when all his belongings and the church plate were destroyed by fire. Langman managed to survive these troubles, aided by Palliser's grant of land for a house and by SPG funds.

Langman believed that Protestantism found its natural home in the Church of England, and he was opposed to anything which would undermine this unity. Nevertheless, he was friendly with dissenters, welcomed them to communion, and agreed to baptize their children. He balked at the creation of dissenting ministers or congregations, however, perhaps because he feared that they would compete with his church. Thus in 1772 he was indignant when a man named Garnett, claiming to be an SPG missionary, held Methodist meetings, and he was hostile when John JONES, "a common soldier," sought permission to function as a dissenting minister in 1779.

With his work as a clergyman, Langman combined an active participation in St John's fledgling judicial system. Appointed justice of the peace in 1754, he was the first clergyman to hold that position. He was also a commissioner of the court of oyer and terminer as early as 1762, and in 1773 his ability was recognized with his appointment to the important position of *custos rotulorum* for St John's. Two years later he was again involved in controversy when he accused his fellow justices of partiality and perjury. On their complaining to Governor John Montagu, Langman was dismissed, but he was reinstated by Governor Robert Duff the following year.

By 1781 the new Anglican church in St John's, whose construction Langman had initiated in 1758, possessed a large porch, a tower for five bells, and a handsome clock, the gift of Governor Richard EDWARDS. Langman, however, was in ill health: years of missionary work and cold weather had left him stricken with gout. Moreover, in 1784 several merchants again complained about his behaviour, and this, together with Langman's letters about his gout, led to his dismissal in January 1784. Some of the merchants' complaints seem to have been justified, since Walter Price, Langman's successor, reported finding the mission neglected, with the dead unburied and no plate for the sacrament. Langman died in St John's shortly after his dismissal.

During the 32 years that Edward Langman spent in Newfoundland as a missionary he built up the Church of England in St John's, and by his work as a justice of the peace he enhanced the church's semi-official position on the island. He thus generated the pan-Protestant, Erastian ethos which was dominant in Newfoundland Anglicanism until the appointment of Bishop Edward Feild* in 1844.

FREDERICK JONES

USPG, B, 6, nos.137, 141, 144, 147, 151, 152, 164, 171, 177, 188, 193, 201, 206, 214; Journal of SPG, 13, pp.88–90, 199–200; 14, pp.18–19, 120; 15, pp.319–20; 16, pp.258–60, 505–6; 17, pp.62–64; 20, pp.52–54; 22, pp.188–200; 23, pp.263–64. *Alumni Oxonienses; the members of the University of Oxford, 1715–1886 . . .*, comp. Joseph Foster (4v., Oxford and London, 1888). [C. F. Pascoe], *Classified digest of the records of the Society for the Propagation of the Gospel in Foreign Parts, 1701–1892* (5th ed., London, 1895). Prowse, *History of Nfld.*

LAPÉROUSE, JEAN-FRANÇOIS DE GALAUP, Comte de. *See* GALAUP

LA PISTOLE, JACQUES VARIN, *dit*. *See* VARIN

LARCHER, NICOLAS, merchant and colonial official; b. 18 June 1722 at Paris, France, son of Henri-Michel Larcher and Marie-Anne Marinier; d. 27 Dec. 1788 at Paris.

Nicolas Larcher arrived in Quebec in 1747 as his father's agent in the shipping trade, but by 1751 he had moved to Louisbourg, Île Royale (Cape Breton Island), which he had visited earlier. There his association with Jacques PREVOST de La Croix, the financial commissary, proved to be a useful business connection. Dissatisfied with the quality of materials sent from the royal stores at Rochefort, Prevost began to order directly from the Larchers. He also authorized Larcher to seek grain in New England when a shortage threatened Île Royale in 1752. By 1753 Larcher had built a house, storehouses, and a large wharf on a property he owned just outside the town walls. An interest in a fishing property at Petit Degrat (Petit-de-Grat Island, N.S.), which employed 39 Basque fishermen in 1752, provided Larcher with supplies of dried cod for export to Europe or the West Indies. He travelled to France most winters, leaving a clerk to superintend his affairs.

Prevost's support made Larcher unpopular with the financial commissary's many enemies, particularly the governor, Jean-Louis de RAYMOND. Larcher's quick financial success and New England mercantile connections also brought criticism. In 1753 Raymond charged that Larcher's wharf and storehouses might be used for foreign trade, a complaint echoed in 1754 by the minister of Marine, Antoine-Louis Rouillé. Later in 1753 some Saint-Malo merchants cited Larcher as an example of the Louisbourg merchants who were trying to drive metropolitan shippers from Île Royale by undercutting prices with cheaper New England goods.

Neither charge is entirely credible. Raymond in fact supported an increase in the foreign trade that Île Royale was authorized to conduct. In the 1750s this trade with the British American colonies, particularly Massachusetts, formed about 20 per cent of Île Royale's commerce and involved all important Louisbourg merchants. In attacking Larcher, Raymond may have been indulging Rouillé's suspicions of foreign links at the expense of an associate of his rival Prevost. The complaint of the Saint-Malo merchants may be related to the competition for West Indian markets between Île Royale cod and the French and Irish salt beef exported by the Malouins. The Saint-Malo traders never abandoned their trade with Île Royale, however, and they did not compete directly with the New Englanders there. Saint-Malo sent preserved foods, cloth, liquor, wine, manufactures, and salt to Louisbourg, while the British colonies sent ships, building supplies, and fresh foods. In any case, the specific complaints of the Saint-Malo merchants ring hollow. How could Larcher, a recent immigrant and a member of a Paris firm, be considered a colonial out to wreck the metropolitan trade? Despite their professed concern for the "poor inhabitants in a harsh slavery," the Saint-Malo merchants' prime purpose was to promote their own interests by casting suspicion on their competitors.

Despite his detractors and his brief residence at Île Royale, Larcher was one of four acting councillors appointed to the Conseil Supérieur in September 1754, probably by Prevost. The appointment, made permanent on 1 June 1755, may have been partly an attempt to strengthen the legal competence of the council. Larcher was frequently assigned to investigate complex civil and criminal cases and his detailed briefs suggest a knowledge of commercial law and a bent for analysis.

In the mid 1750s Larcher diversified his business interests by adding local industrial projects to his import-export trade. He opened a sawmill on a tributary of the Rivière de Miré (Mira River) and took over the contract for the annual supply of 12,000 large barrels (*barriques*) of coal to the Louisbourg garrison. Both these projects, as well as a small farm, were supervised by his associate Antoine RODRIGUE, who may have initiated their development before selling to Larcher. In 1756 and 1757 Larcher supplied the required amount of coal, chartering many coastal vessels to carry it from Glace Bay and Mordienne (Port Morien) to Louisbourg. In 1758 over 16,000 large barrels were reported mined, but war and blockade prevented shipments to Louisbourg. Industry had not replaced trade in Larcher's interests, however, and he continued shipping goods to Quebec and France, partly under government contracts.

When Louisbourg capitulated on 26 July 1758, Larcher's North American activities ended. He had been remarkably successful. In 1752 his Petit Degrat fishery was capable of producing cod worth perhaps 35,000 *livres* annually, and the coal sales were worth a minimum of 50,000 *livres* a year. His shipping, lumbering, farming, and other business interests resist evaluation, but his claim that the fall of Île Royale cost him a business worth 250,000 *livres* does not seem exaggerated, and the variety of his investments in Île Royale was unmatched. Larcher rejoined the family business in Paris, married, and appears to have been relatively prosperous, though he insisted on the continuation of his pension of 300 *livres* as a former councillor.

Larcher's success in Île Royale is attributable to his access to the investment capital of his family in France, which enabled him to undertake ambitious projects. Yet Larcher differed from most French merchants in his willingness to commit both his money and his energy to Île Royale. In 1758 he was essentially a local merchant because of his property and capital investment, his council appointment, and his local residence. Perhaps Louisbourg's fall vindicated the metropolitans' reluctance to invest in Île Royale, but Raymond had earlier pointed out how the colony might have been strengthened had more attempts been made to develop its land resources.

CHRISTOPHER MOORE

AMA, Inspection du Génie, Bibliothèque, MSS *in-f°*, 210[d], no.6. AN, Col., B, 99, p.260 (PAC transcript); 101, f.5; C^{11B}, 19, ff.283–84v; 32, ff.155, 180, 192; 33, f.79; 38, f.307; C^{11C}, 9, ff.202–5; E, 256 (dossier Nicolas Larcher), ff.11–13; F^{5B}, art.14, f.79; Section Outremer, Dépôt des fortifications des colonies, Am. sept., no.139; G^1, 466, no.84, f.21; G^2, 204, dossier 470, f.89; 212, dossiers 551, 576–82, 584; G^3, 2041/1, 25 oct. 1749, 18 oct. 1750, 16 déc. 1751; 2044, 16 déc. 1756. Archives de Paris, Reconstitution des actes de l'état civil de Paris, paroisse Saint-Jacques-de-la-Boucherie, 18 juin 1722; paroisse Merry, 27 déc. 1788. PAC *Report*, 1905, II, pt.I, 32. McLennan, *Louisbourg*. Christopher Moore, "Merchant trade in Louisbourg, Île Royale" (unpublished MA thesis, University of Ottawa, 1977).

LA ROCHETTE, ALEXANDRE-ROBERT HILLAIRE DE. *See* HILLAIRE

LA RONDE, RENÉ BOURASSA, *dit. See* BOURASSA

LAROSE, FRANÇOIS GUILLOT, *dit. See* GUILLOT

LA SALLE, JOSEPH PERTHUIS DE. *See* PERTHUIS

LA SIERRA, ESTEBAN JOSÉ MARTÍNEZ FERNANDEZ Y MARTÍNEZ DE. *See* MARTÍNEZ

LATOUR, BERTRAND DE (several sources wrongly give him the Christian name of Louis and the surname Bertrand de Latour), Sulpician, priest, vicar general, superior of the religious communities of women in the diocese of Quebec, and ecclesiastical councillor on the Conseil Supérieur; b. 6 July 1701 in Toulouse, France, son of Pierre de Latour, a lawyer in the *parlement*, and Catherine de Jonquières; d. 19 Jan. 1780 at Montauban, France.

Bertrand de Latour was descended from a family of lawyers raised to the nobility through their office as magistrates in Toulouse. Educated first in the town where he was born, he commenced the study of law but entered the Séminaire de Saint-Sulpice in Paris on 12 June 1724. There he "gave proof of as much talent as piety [and] completed his licentiate with honours." He must also have completed his legal education, since by 1729 he bore the title of doctor of laws.

On 2 May 1729 Latour, who had been transferred to the Séminaire des Missions Étrangères, was appointed dean of the chapter of Quebec by Louis XV. On 17 May he became the ecclesiastical councillor on the Conseil Supérieur of New France, replacing Jean-Baptiste Gaultier* de

Varennes. The minister of Marine, Maurepas, told Governor Charles de Beauharnois* that the king had appointed Latour to these offices in consideration of "the favourable testimony which has been given to him about the good moral character, ability, and sound beliefs of this ecclesiastic." The king's ship, the flute *Éléphant*, which brought him from France with the new coadjutor of Quebec, Bishop DOSQUET, was shipwrecked the night of 1-2 Sept. 1729 on the sandbank at Cap Brûlé, some ten leagues from Quebec. This mishap presented the chapter's young dean with a splendid opportunity for making his first appearance in Quebec. The canons were insistent that their dean rather than the archdeacon, Eustache Chartier* de Lotbinière, should receive the new coadjutor. Consequently they sent a canoe to fetch Latour, and he, reaching Quebec on 2 September, some hours earlier than Bishop Dosquet, was able to welcome him officially, thus depriving Chartier de Lotbinière of another chance to assert his authority.

Some days later the Conseil Supérieur admitted its new ecclesiastical councillor into its ranks. He astonished the whole assembly when he refused the president's invitation to take a seat at the end of the council table, the other councillors being senior to him. The young doctor of laws protested that this was not his place and that "in conformity with his letters of appointment he should be seated right after the senior councillor." The affair was brought to the king's attention, and Latour won out. This firmness and, equally, this legalistic attitude, marked his stay in Quebec and roused vigorous opposition. Made Bishop Dosquet's vicar general before the end of 1729, he was appointed superior of the religious communities of women on 7 March 1730 and carried out his duties in a dictatorial manner, which brought protests from the nuns [*see* Marie-Thérèse Langlois*, *dite* de Saint-Jean-Baptiste]. He provoked a quarrel within the chapter by demanding an increase in his prebend which most of his *confrères* refused him. This situation deteriorated to the point that in October 1730 the canons appealed to the Conseil Supérieur, which decided against Latour. On leaving the sitting he was booed by his *confrères* in the chapter.

On 29 Oct. 1731 Latour sailed for La Rochelle, with instructions from the Quebec chapter to audit the accounts of Pierre HAZEUR de L'Orme, whose administration of the Abbaye de Saint-Pierre de Maubec (Méobecq, dept of Indre), a benefice belonging to the chapter, satisfied neither the dean nor the canons. Latour was never to return to Canada, although on 3 Oct. 1733 the Séminaire des Missions Étrangères appointed him parish priest for the cathedral parish of Quebec. He resigned from this office on 8 May the following year, but kept his title of dean of the chapter until 1738, refusing however to accept the income from it.

In France Bertrand de Latour became a prolific preacher, with a pronounced taste for polemics. He took part in various theological and canonical quarrels which shook the church of France, including the one stirred up by the bull *Unigenitus* [*see* Dominique-Marie Varlet*], and he became the ardent defender of Roman orthodoxy against Gallicanism. In 1736 he was a canon of the cathedral of Tours, vicar general, and official, as well as superior of the religious communities of women in the city. In 1740 he was parish priest of Saint-Jacques in Montauban, and in December of that year he became a member of the town's Académie des Belles-Lettres.

From 1739 to 1779 Latour published an imposing number of sermons, panegyrics, treatises on dogma, and liturgical, canonical, and other papers. When he left Canada he had taken with him a manuscript copy of the annals of the Hôtel-Dieu of Quebec written by Jeanne-Françoise Juchereau* de La Ferté, *dite* de Saint-Ignace. He published this text in Montauban in 1752 under the title *Histoire de l'Hôtel-Dieu de Québec*. In 1761 he became the first historian to take Bishop Laval* for his subject, publishing in Cologne the *Mémoires sur la vie de M. de Laval, premier évêque de Québec*; he had written the text during his stay in Canada, where he had been able to consult documents at first hand and question people who had known the bishop. Vigorously opposed to the theatre, from 1763 to 1778 he published in Avignon 20 volumes of *Réflexions morales, politiques, historiques et littéraires sur le théâtre*.

Bertrand de Latour was a man out of the ordinary. Nature and education had endowed him with qualities that could have secured an equally brilliant career for him in a variety of fields. A priest by vocation, a jurist by family tradition, intelligent and hard-working, he was consumed with enthusiasm for the defence of what was right and just. Everywhere he went he aroused interest, sometimes admiration, and often opposition. He had not maintained much contact with Canada, but at his death he bequeathed an endowment of 225 *livres* on the diocese of Toulouse "in favour of the three [women's religious] communities in Quebec and the fund for [their] poor."

JULES BÉLANGER

[The *Œuvres complètes de La Tour, doyen du chapitre de la cathédrale de Montauban, réunies pour la première fois en une seule collection* . . . , J.-P. Migne, édit.

(7v., Paris, 1855) contains, among other items, sermons, addresses, memoirs, and devout works the author had published during his lifetime, as well as his *Mémoires sur la vie de M. de Laval, premier évêque de Québec* (Cologne, République fédérale d'Allemagne, 1761) and his *Réflexions morales, politiques, historiques et littéraires sur le théâtre* (20v., Avignon, France, 1763–78). J.B.]

AAQ, 10 B, ff.70v–71, 77v–79, 83, 84; 11 B, V, 55, 10–13; VI, 27. AD, Tarn-et-Garonne (Montauban), G, 238. AN, Col., B, 53, f.573v; C[11A], 51, f.186. ANQ-Q, NF 11, 39, f.188v; 40, ff.7v, 68v; NF 12, 6, f.130v. Archives de la Compagnie de Saint-Sulpice (Paris), Registre des entrées, 1713–40, p.14. Archives municipales de Toulouse (dép. de la Haute-Garonne, France), GG 278, f.74. ASQ, MSS, 12, f.2; 208; Paroisse de Québec, 5. Bibliothèque municipale de Montauban (dép. de Tarn-et-Garonne, France), MSS 5. [J.-F. Juchereau de La Ferté, dite de Saint-Ignace, et M.-A. Regnard Duplessis, dite de Sainte-Hélène], *Histoire de l'Hôtel-Dieu de Québec*, Bertrand de Latour, édit. (Montauban, [1752]). Jules Villain, *La France moderne; grand dictionnaire généalogique, historique et biographique* (4v., Montpellier, France, 1906–13), II, 1029–30. Jules Bélanger, "Bertrand De Latour et la querelle du théâtre au dix-huitième siècle" (thèse de D. ès L., université de Rennes, France, 1969). P.-J.-O. Chauveau, *Bertrand de La Tour* (Lévis, Qué., 1898). Émerand Forestié, *La Société littéraire et l'ancienne Académie de Montauban; histoire de ces sociétés et biographie de tous les académiciens* (2e éd., Montauban, 1888), 209–10. H.-A. Scott, "Louis Bertrand de la Tour & son œuvre," RSC *Trans.*, 3 rd ser., XXII (1928), sect.I, 113–40.

LAUBARA. *See* OLABARATZ

LA VÉRENDRYE, FRANÇOIS GAULTIER DE. *See* GAULTIER DU TREMBLAY

LAVIGNE, PAUL TESSIER, *dit. See* TESSIER

LE BLANC, PIERRE, co-founder of Pointe-de-l'Église (Church Point, N.S.); b. *c.* 1720 at Grand Pré, Nova Scotia, son of Jacques Le Blanc and Élisabeth Boudrot; m. 4 Oct. 1745 Marie-Madeleine Babin and they had at least ten children; d. 6 July 1799 at Pointe-de-l'Église.

Soon after his marriage Pierre Le Blanc settled on the Rivière aux Canards (Canard River, N.S.), and at the time of the Acadian deportation in 1755 he owned three horses, five oxen, seven cows, 13 head of young cattle, 18 pigs, and 55 ewes. With their four children Pierre and his wife were deported to Boston, Massachusetts, where on 25 Nov. 1755, soon after their arrival, a fourth daughter was born on the quay. The Le Blancs apparently lived at Lynn, near Boston, and they were still there in April 1767 when a tenth child was born. They must have been reasonably well off since, unlike most of the Acadians in Massachusetts, they did not leave the colony in 1766. Of those that did, a number returned to Nova Scotia, where, in the interests of opening up the colony, the British authorities had since 1764 allowed Acadians who took the oath of allegiance to settle.

It was not until 1771 that Le Blanc and François Doucet, a fellow exile, set out by boat to explore the coast of the district of Clare in Nova Scotia, where Acadians had been established since 1768. They returned to the region with their families in 1772 and settled at a place later called Pointe-de-l'Église. Tradition has it that on their arrival one of the Le Blanc daughters, Madeleine, *dite* La Couèche, revived the flagging courage of her weary and discouraged elders by seizing an axe and beginning to cut the trees and branches needed for a shelter. By 1775 22 families were settled in the region, including that of Pierre DOUCET, François's son.

That year Pierre Le Blanc obtained a grant of 200 acres of land, and in 1785 he bought or was granted 350 more. His descendants and those of François Doucet today constitute the majority of the population of Church Point and Little Brook. One of Le Blanc's sons, Joseph, was a pioneer of present-day Wedgeport, settling in that area in 1778; many of his descendants are still there.

J.-ALPHONSE DEVEAU

Archives paroissiales, Sainte-Marie (Church Point, N.-É.), Registre des baptêmes, mariages et sépultures, 1799–1801. N.S., Dept. of Lands and Forests, Crown Lands Office, Index sheet no.6. PAC, MG 30, C20, 13. Arsenault, *Hist. et généalogie des Acadiens*, 733. P.-M. Dagnaud, *Les Français du sud-ouest de la Nouvelle Écosse* . . . (Besançon, France, 1905), 24–25. C. J. d'Entremont, *Histoire de Wedgeport, Nouvelle-Écosse* (s.l., 1967). I. W. Wilson, *A geography and history of the county of Digby, Nova Scotia* (Halifax, 1900), 42.

LEBLANC, *dit* **Le Maigre, JOSEPH,** farmer, trader, and Acadian patriot; b. 12 March 1697 at Les Mines (near Wolfville, N.S.), son of Antoine Leblanc and Marie Bourgeois; m. 13 Feb. 1719 Anne, daughter of Alexandre Bourg*, *dit* Belle-Humeur, and Marguerite Melanson, *dit* La Verdure; d. 19 Oct. 1772 at Kervaux, in the parish of Le Palais, Belle-Île, France. [See *DCB*, III.]

AD, Morbihan (Vannes), État civil, Le Palais, 20 oct. 1772.

LE COMTE DUPRÉ, GEORGES-HIPPOLYTE, known as **Saint-Georges Dupré**, merchant, militia officer, military transport officer, deputy chief road commissioner (*grand voyer substitut*), and politician; b. 23 March 1738 at Montreal (Que.), son of Jean-Baptiste Le Comte* Dupré and Marie-Anne Hervieux; d. 26 Nov. 1797 at Montreal.

Son and grandson of successful merchants, Georges-Hippolyte Le Comte Dupré traded in his early years, till at least 1770. His inclination, however, like that of his older brother Jean-Baptiste*, was for a military and government career; both men felt strong loyalty to the crown. Georges-Hippolyte, a major in the Canadian militia in Montreal at the beginning of the American invasion in 1775, later became a colonel, as did his brother in Quebec. One of the six Canadians among the 12 notables who signed the capitulation of Montreal on 12 Nov. 1775, Le Comte Dupré was also one of the ten Montrealers "recognized as good Royalists" and disarmed by order of the American general, David Wooster. On 6 Feb. 1776 he and three other militia officers were imprisoned at Fort Chambly for refusing to surrender their commissions. On 25 June 1776, after the departure of the Americans, Le Comte Dupré was one of three officers, including Edward William Gray* with whom he had been imprisoned, appointed in the District of Montreal to collect arms and American commissions from disaffected militia and to seize and try spies and fifth columnists – experience no doubt helpful for his peacetime role as inspector of police in Montreal (1788–97).

From 1775 till his death Le Comte Dupré was a militia commissary for corvées and for transport of military provisions and stores in the District of Montreal; his son Pierre-Hippolyte succeeded him. During the war Le Comte Dupré had been largely responsible for transport to the western posts, which comprised a vast and difficult hinterland where logistics were the key to military control. This hinterland provided a vital shield for Canada and Le Comte Dupré's management of transport there was probably his most significant achievement. He served on the frontier, probably as transport commissary, in the campaign of 1777 under BURGOYNE and William Phillips. He should not be blamed for the "inactivity and desertion of the Canadian corvées" deplored by Burgoyne, for he was specifically held back from accompanying them as superintendent by Governor Sir Guy Carleton* who felt he could not "be spared from the duty of collecting and forwarding" them. Le Comte Dupré's competence was acknowledged at the end of the war by HALDIMAND, who in 1783 appointed him deputy chief road commissioner in the District of Montreal to act in the region for the chief road commissioner of the province, François-Marie PICOTÉ de Belestre, who treated his office as a sinecure.

Like most Canadian gentlemen in the 1780s, Le Comte Dupré was opposed to an elective legislature and the extension of English law, but like many others, when the change came, he secured election to the House of Assembly, representing Huntingdon, a county in Lower Canada which extended west from the Richelieu River on the southern shore of the St Lawrence, from 1792 to 1796. He doubtless won the voters' "affection" through a breadth of outlook that had been revealed in his just administration of the corvée and in his humane treatment of suspected American sympathizers during the war.

The two wives of Georges-Hippolyte Le Comte Dupré died young. On 9 Jan. 1764 he had married at Montreal Marie-Charlotte, daughter of Daniel-Hyacinthe-Marie Liénard* de Beaujeu; she died in 1769 after the birth of their second son. His second wife was Marie-Louise-Charlotte de La Corne, the daughter of Luc de LA CORNE. The young woman left home because of her father's objections to her marriage and only after "much noise" was his consent given. They were married on 22 March 1770 at Saint-Vincent-de-Paul (Laval) on Île Jésus. Marie-Louise-Charlotte died in January of the following year at the age of 20.

A. J. H. RICHARDSON

[An oil portrait in the Château de Ramezay, Montreal, painted by Louis-Chrétien de Heer* as late as 1799, is claimed to represent Le Comte Dupré: A.J.H.R.]

ANQ-M, État civil, Catholiques, Notre-Dame de Montréal, 24 mars 1738, 9 janv. 1764; Saint-Vincent-de-Paul (Laval), 22 mars 1770. BL, Add. MSS 21733, f.3; 21789, ff.203, 204 (copies at PAC). PAC, MG 24, L3, pp.116–22, 2684–92, 2952–54, 2980–81, 3150–51, 3166, 3180–81, 3200–1, 3215, 3379–81, 3790–91, 3832–33, 3871–72, 3898, 3968, 4139–40, 4187, 4223–26, 4233–34, 4245–47, 4300–1, 4357–59, 4432–34, 4468–70, 4533–34, 4571–74, 4585–94, 4648–49, 4656–58, 4750–53, 4762–64, 4802–4, 4841–42, 4878–80, 4924–25, 4975–77, 4994–95, 5008–10, 5017–18, 5025–26, 5042–43, 5065–67, 5083, 5332–34, 5371–72, 5381–83, 5391–92, 5403–5, 5440–48, 5467–68, 5474–75, 5480, 5484–86, 5490–91, 5533–35, 5566–68, 5577–82, 5585–91, 5595–97, 5675–76, 5737–38, 5760, 5779–82, 5795–96, 5903–4, 5923–24, 6477–78, 6537–38, 6746, 6863, 6893–94, 7100–1, 7141, 7178–80, 7191, 7210–11, 32753–54, 33247–52; RG 8, I (C series), 201, p.118.

American archives (Clarke and Force), 4th ser., IV, 991, 1004–5. *Invasion du Canada* (Verreau), 34, 37, 93, 96–98, 319. "Inventaire des biens de Luc Lacorne de Saint-Luc," J.-J. Lefebvre, édit., ANQ *Rapport*, 1947–48, 33, 35, 88–89. PAC *Rapport*, 1887, 332, 336. *Montreal Gazette*, 10 July 1792. *Quebec Gazette*, 22 Jan. 1789, 20 Dec. 1792, 7 Dec. 1797. *Almanach de Québec*, 1788, 1795. Caron, "Inv. de la corr. de Mgr Briand," ANQ *Rapport*, 1929–30, 83. Burt, *Old prov.*

of Que. (1933), 286–87, 412. E. B. De Fonblanque, *Political and military episodes . . . derived from the life and correspondence of the Righ Hon. John Burgoyne* . . . (London, 1876), 239, 248. Neatby, *Quebec*, 149, 164, 201–3, 251–52. P.-G. Roy, *La famille Le Compte Dupré* (Lévis, Qué., 1941).

LE COURTOIS DE SURLAVILLE (Le Courtois de Blais de Surlaville), MICHEL (he sometimes signed **Achille-Michel-Balthasar**), army officer; baptized 17 July 1714 at Bayeux, France, son of Thomas Le Courtois and Charlotte Le Blais; d. unmarried 8 Jan. 1796 in Paris.

Michel Le Courtois de Surlaville's service in North America was a brief interlude in a long and illustrious military career. The son of a lawyer, he entered the army in 1734 as a second lieutenant in the Régiment de Foix. After serving in Italy and Germany, he purchased the adjutancy of the Régiment de La Couronne for 2,000 *écus* in 1742. The following year he participated in several sieges in Bohemia and Bavaria, where he was wounded, and he again saw active service in Flanders in 1744. He obtained a captain's commission in 1745, and the same year he fought at the battle of Fontenoy (Belgium), where his valiant conduct in leading the La Couronne brigade after all the other officers had been killed or wounded won him the cross of Saint-Louis. At the siege of Tournai (Belgium) in 1746 he led a sortie from the fortress; at Brussels, shortly afterwards, he was wounded a second time. Named major of a militia brigade in 1747, he was placed in command of the town of Tubize (Belgium) by the Maréchal de Saxe. He joined the newly formed regiment the Grenadiers de France in 1749 as an adjutant.

At some point in his career, probably during his service in Bavaria, Surlaville had encountered Jean-Louis de RAYMOND, who in 1751 was appointed governor of Île Royale (Cape Breton Island). Raymond wanted to take Surlaville with him as his aide-de-camp, but the ministry of Marine, fearing that other colonial governors would also want such military aides, made him instead troop major of Louisbourg on 1 April 1751, simultaneously appointing him colonel of infantry, a rank Surlaville had asked for when he had accepted Raymond's proposal. The arrangement was unusual, since the duties of town and troop major were usually performed by one person, at this time Michel de Gannes* de Falaise. The minister of Marine, Rouillé, decided that an army officer could improve the state of the garrison, however, and with Surlaville's appointment de Gannes's duties were limited to the regulation of affairs in the town.

The Louisbourg garrison which Surlaville was to command was a rowdy crew of ill-disciplined exiles, culled from France and surrounding countries. Two factors served to lower the quality of the troops. Unlike men in the army, the colonial regulars and other Marine troops were recruited throughout France, and they lacked the tradition of service with any one regiment. Moreover, colonial troops were frequently selected from a pool, and Marine officials did not have the same concern for quality that an officer recruiting for his own regiment would. Since most enlistments were open-ended, the men felt condemned to exile for life. Desertion was a major problem. A royal amnesty of 1750 attempted to curb the high rate within the colony, but it had little effect. Worse still, there had been a revolt among the troops at Louisbourg in 1744 [*see* Louis DU PONT Duchambon], and a mutiny in 1750 among a detachment at Port-Toulouse (near St Peters, N.S.) had resulted in the execution of nine soldiers.

Surlaville set about vigorously to reform this state of affairs. Soldiers were ordered to have their hair cut, uniforms and equipment were required to pass inspection under penalty, the garrison was drilled regularly, and the movements of soldiers were circumscribed. Discipline was strict but justice fair. Surlaville's excellent records show that corporals and sergeants who abused their soldiers were sentenced in the same manner as the men. As a result of these reforms the desertion rate fell, and Louisbourg's garrison was better regulated than it had ever been before.

An officer who possessed a critical intelligence and a literary ability far beyond most of his contemporaries, Surlaville quickly gained an understanding of the colony's history, strategic value, commerce, and administration. He criticized numerous acts of the ministry of Marine, including the uniforms and supplies sent annually from France for the troops, and he investigated the illicit practices of Jacques PREVOST de La Croix, the financial commissary. Shortly after his arrival in the colony, Raymond dispatched Surlaville to Halifax as his official representative, and the major returned to Louisbourg with a report on the newly established British settlement. Together with Thomas PICHON, he assessed the strategic weakness of the French position in Acadia and made recommendations to improve it. Surlaville also kept a journal during his two years on Île Royale in which he recorded events and heaped scorn on Raymond, whom he had come to detest. In addition, he copied and annotated some of the governor's correspondence in a petulantly sarcastic manner to reveal how preposterous Raymond's conduct had been. Thus when

Raymond asked the minister of Marine to remember him to the king, Surlaville commented: "his imagination has actually convinced him that he is an important person who merits some of the king's attention. . . . What folly!"

Surlaville's posting to Louisbourg has been called the most important military appointment made there during its last decade. Yet most of his reforms were abandoned after he returned to France with Raymond in the fall of 1753, apparently because of poor health. The duties of town and troop major were reunited and once again given to a colonial officer, Robert Tarride* Duhaget. Surlaville was accorded a pension of 800 *livres* from the ministry of Marine for his efforts but found himself passed over for promotion in the Grenadiers de France because of his absence, and so in March 1754 he exchanged his adjutancy for a retired colonel's brevet in the Régiment de La Couronne. In March 1757 he was appointed assistant chief of staff of infantry in the Army of the Lower Rhine, and two years later assistant chief of the army staff. Until the fall of Louisbourg in 1758 he continued to correspond with fellow officers in Acadia. These letters, his journal, and other writings have been preserved, and together they provide an intimate portrait of French activity in the region during the 1750s.

Promoted brigadier in 1761, Surlaville again served as assistant chief of staff with the French army in Germany, and in 1762 he became major-general. During this period he appears to have been in considerable financial difficulty, the causes of which are unknown. In 1759 he stated that he was about 16,000 *livres* in debt. Several pensions and gratuities appear to have wiped out the debt by 1763, one pension being of 12,000 *livres*. Little is known of his later life apart from his service in Picardy and Boulonnais from 1763 to 1771 and his promotion to lieutenant-general in 1781.

T. A. Crowley

AD, Calvados (Cæn), État civil, Saint-Sauveur de Bayeux, 1714; F, 1894 (fonds Surlaville). AMA, SHA, Mémoires historiques et reconnaissances militaires, art.1105, pièce 1; Y[2d], 1170 (dossier Surlaville). AN, Marine, C[7], 314 (dossier Surlaville). ASQ, Polygraphie, LV, esp. 41; LVI-LVIII (Surlaville papers; copies in PAC, MG 18, F30). *Les derniers jours de l'Acadie* (Du Boscq de Beaumont). Crowley, "Government and interests," 103–89. McLennan, *Louisbourg*, 191, 193, 329. Stanley, *New France*. J. C. Webster, *Thomas Pichon, "the spy of Beausejour," an account of his career in Europe and America* . . . ([Sackville, N.B.], 1937).

LEDRU (Le Dru), JEAN-ANTOINE, priest; b. 1752 in France; d. in or after 1796.

It appears that Jean-Antoine Ledru made his religious profession with the Dominican order at Arras, France. In 1773 he moved to its convent in Paris, where he remained until the winter of 1774. The date of his ordination is unknown. It seems likely that he left the order for the secular priesthood, although it is possible that he remained with it and joined a contingent of Dominican missionaries in the West Indies. He was referred to as a Dominican while in North America.

Ledru arrived in Nova Scotia in the summer of 1786 and was sent by Vicar General Joseph-Mathurin Bourg to serve St Mary's Bay and Cape Sable. That fall he began an extensive missionary tour, without the permission of his superiors. At Shelburne he was asked to go to St John's (Prince Edward) Island, whose Catholic inhabitants had been without the services of a priest since the death of James MacDonald in 1785. Having first visited Arichat and Pictou, Ledru crossed to the island just before Christmas Day, 1786, and spent the winter at Fortune Bay. The following spring he travelled to the Îles de la Madeleine and Cape Breton. His long absence from St Mary's Bay does not seem to have worried him, for he visited Thomas-François Le Roux at Memramcook, New Brunswick, before returning to his mission.

After Ledru's arrival in Nova Scotia, correspondence had passed between Bourg and the bishop of Quebec concerning the validity of his qualifications. The fact that he had arrived in the area without any letters of authorization from the Dominicans had caused some suspicion, and when parishioners began to complain about his irresponsibility, the question arose whether or not he was an impostor. Although Abbé Bourg was able to confirm that Ledru had been regularly ordained, in 1787 Bishop Louis-Philippe Mariauchau d'Esgly ordered his immediate dismissal from Acadia. It was the bishop's opinion that Ledru was unreliable, in view of his inability to stay in one location, and dishonest since "in the guise of probity and zeal, [he] has taken, in the absence of missionaries, large sums of money from people too simple to mistrust the deceit." Given the British government's suspicion of French priests from abroad, it must have seemed even more unwise to harbour Ledru longer.

Ledru nevertheless remained in Nova Scotia until the late spring of 1788 and created dissension which was to last for some years. On his return to St Mary's Bay in 1787 he had discovered that the people there no longer regarded him as their priest. Perhaps in revenge he petitioned Lieutenant Governor John Parr that certain religious vessels which were in private hands be given to the church at Cape Sable. The people of St Mary's Bay, who also needed a communion service, were incensed, and the controversy over possession of the vessels was not finally settled until 1806, when Bishop Joseph-Octave Plessis* made an official decision in favour of the larger community at St Mary's Bay.

In 1789 Ledru accepted an appointment to settle at Kaskaskia in the Illinois country. Within a few months of his arrival in September, his bishop, John Carroll of Baltimore, became concerned about him. No letter had come from France attesting to Ledru's character and authorizing his stay in North America; moreover, the bishop had received unsettling news concerning his activities in Acadia. Meanwhile, Ledru, finding the tithes at Kaskaskia insufficient for his support, had been persuaded by a better offer to move to St Louis (Mo.), in Spanish Louisiana. He was forced to leave there, probably in the fall of 1793, after a quarrel with the commandant, who claimed that Ledru had "discontented these parishioners by an interest and a commerce which give him lawsuits with everybody, vexing them further by extravagant fees in all the ceremonies of his ministry." Ledru apparently wintered at Fort St Joseph (Niles, Mich.) before travelling to Michilimackinac (Mackinac Island, Mich.), where he exercised his ministry without authorization and where his name appears on the baptismal registers from May to July 1794. He then went to Detroit, intending to carry on to Fort Erie, but the governor general, Lord Dorchester [Carleton*], had received disquieting reports about his republican sympathies and in June 1794 advised Lieutenant Governor Simcoe* of Upper Canada to deny him entry. Ledru had to stay at Detroit, where he was forced to rely on rations from the commandant. In the delicate period before the signing of Jay's treaty in November 1794, the British were much concerned about republican agitation in the vicinity of the western posts, particularly those close to the Upper Canadian border. The authorities intended to return Ledru to Michilimackinac, but because no boat was available, he was sent to Fort Erie. "If he is ill disposed or his principles considered republican," wrote the commandant at Detroit, "this is by no means a proper place to suffer him to remain. . . ." In September Dorchester secured the transfer of the Reverend Edmund Burke* to Raisin River, south of Detroit, "expressly to counteract the Machinations of Jacobin Emissaries." Although it is not clear if Ledru had visited the Raisin River area, the governor general had perhaps been alarmed by a petition from the inhabitants to have Ledru as their priest.

In October 1794 Ledru received an official order of banishment from Simcoe for having behaved "so improperly." He was to leave Upper Canada by way of Oswego, N.Y., and never to return to any British province. His subsequent activities are unknown. Writing to Bishop Jean-François HUBERT of Quebec in March 1796, Bishop Carroll noted apropos of Edmund Burke that "ill-intentioned people, and especially an apostate Dominican named Le Dru, have found a way of inspiring certain officers of the American troops posted in the vicinity of Fort Detroit, with prejudices against that priest." This letter suggests that Ledru had found his way back to Detroit. No further record of him has been found. The image he projects is not that generally associated with French missionaries in British North America, for wherever he had gone he had come into conflict with the authorities.

DELLA M. M. STANLEY

AAQ, 7 CM, I, 12. Archivo General de Indias (Seville, Spain), Sección, Papeles de Cuba, legajo 208A. CÉA, Fonds Placide Gaudet, 1.54–15, 1.88–9, 1.88–12. *Before Lewis and Clark: documents illustrating the history of the Missouri, 1785–1804*, ed. and intro. A. P. Nasatir (2v., St Louis, Mo., 1952), I, 132, 203. *Correspondence of Lieut. Governor Simcoe* (Cruikshank), II–V. *Kaskaskia records, 1778–1790*, ed. C. W. Alvord (Springfield, Ill., 1909). "The Mackinac register," ed. R. G. Thwaites, Wis., State Hist. Soc., *Coll.*, XIX (1910), 97–102. Allaire, *Dictionnaire*, I, 330. Caron, "Inv. de la corr. de Mgr Hubert et de Mgr Bailly de Messein," ANQ *Rapport*, 1930–31, 199–351; "Inv. de la corr. de Mgr Mariaucheau D'Esgly," ANQ *Rapport*, 1930–31, 185–98.

Antoine Bernard, *Histoire de la survivance acadienne, 1755–1935* (Montréal, 1935), 241–42. P.-M. Dagnaud, *Les Français du sud-ouest de la Nouvelle Écosse . . .* (Besançon, France, 1905), 49–50. A.-H. Gosselin, *L'Église du Canada après la Conquête*, II, 164–65, 289. A. A. Johnston, *A history of the Catholic Church in eastern Nova Scotia* (2v., Antigonish, N.S., 1960–71), I, 120–32, 150, 170. Émile Lauvrière, *La tragédie d'un peuple: histoire du peuple acadien de ses origines à nos jours* (2v., Paris, 1922), II, 343. W. R. Riddell, *The life of John Graves Simcoe, first lieutenant-governor of the province of Upper Canada, 1792–96* (Toronto, [1926]), 264–65. Placide Gaudet, "Les premiers missionnaires de la baie Ste-Marie . . . ," *L'Évangéline* (Weymouth Bridge, N.-É.), 9 juill. 1891, p.[2]; 16 juill. 1891, p.[3].

LEFEBVRE DE BELLEFEUILLE, FRANÇOIS, seigneur; baptized 4 March 1708 at Plaisance (Placentia, Nfld), second son of Jean-François Lefebvre* de Bellefeuille and Anne Baudry; m. 17 March 1749 Marie-Josephte Hertel de Cournoyer, and they had 11 children; d. 11 April 1780 at Trois-Rivières (Que.).

François Lefebvre de Bellefeuille helped his father and his brothers Georges and Pierre develop the family seigneury of Grand-Pabos, which had been acquired in 1729. Theirs was the only seigneury on the Gaspé coast permanently settled during the French period. In June 1745 François hurried from Pabos to Quebec with the first news of the siege of Louisbourg, Île Royale (Cape Breton Island). The next year, Georges, who had been a subdelegate of the intendant of Quebec since 1737, went to France; his title was bestowed upon François in 1749. François's duties were to settle disputes among both the resident fishermen and the French who came every summer to fish along the Gaspé coast.

After the death of his father around 1744, François had continued to develop the fishing resources of the seigneury with the help of his younger brother Pierre. Its most important assets were excellent beaches for dry-curing the codfish which could be caught a short distance offshore. Besides the money gained from selling his fish at Quebec Lefebvre de Bellefeuille obtained income by leasing space on his beaches to the summer fishermen from France. He seems to have lived well, since his seigneurial manor house was reported in 1758 to have been large and well furnished. Of the many seigneuries on the Gaspé coast only Grand-Pabos had a resident seigneur; it was thus the only one successfully developed. Lefebvre de Bellefeuille prospered without any assistance from the government.

Although his concession was restricted to the area around the mouth of the Rivière Grand-Pabos, Lefebvre de Bellefeuille extended his seigneurial authority to include the good beaches at the mouth of the Grande Rivière, a few miles to the northeast. Indeed, it was at Grande-Rivière that he lived with his family. The Gaspé coast was remote from Quebec and the government cared little that Lefebvre de Bellefeuille exceeded his authority. By the 1750s he had been given the vaguely defined military title of "king's commandant for the entire Gaspé coast and the Baie des Chaleurs."

In September 1758 Brigadier-General James Wolfe* visited the Gaspé coast with a small fleet of warships. Lefebvre de Bellefeuille was in no position to resist, and the British devastated French fishing operations all along the coast. At Grande-Rivière and Pabos they destroyed one sloop, more than 100 shallops, about 100 houses, over 10,000 quintals of codfish, and all goods and provisions. Lefebvre de Bellefeuille left and never returned to the Gaspé coast, choosing instead to live at Trois-Rivières near his wife's family.

In 1765 Lefebvre de Bellefeuille sold the seigneury of Grand-Pabos to Colonel Frederick Haldimand. The proceeds of the sale helped him purchase part of the Cournoyer seigneury (near Trois-Rivières), and with his wife's inheritances he gained control of most of the rest. He died on 11 April 1780; his son Antoine inherited the seigneury.

David Lee

AN, Col., C[11A], 83, ff.94, 170, 175; F[3], 50, ff.361f.; Marine, C[7], 24 (dossier Lefebvre de Bellefeuille). ANQ-Q, NF 2, 36, ff.80v–81. BL, Add. mss 21726, pp.7–8 (PAC transcripts). PAC, MG 9, B8, 1, Pabos; MG 18, M, ser.3, 24, no.2. P.-G. Roy, *Inv. concessions*, IV, 98–101, 127–30. Tanguay, *Dictionnaire*. La Morandière, *Hist. de la pêche française de la morue*, II, 601–3. David Lee, "The French in Gaspé, 1534 to 1760," *Canadian Historic Sites: Occasional Papers in Archaeology and History* (Ottawa), no.3 (1970), 25–64. A. C. de L. Macdonald, "La famille Le Febvre de Bellefeuille," *Revue canadienne* (Montréal), XX (1884), 168–76, 235–47, 291–302.

LE FOURREUR. *See* Foureur

LEGARDEUR DE CROISILLE (Croizille) ET DE MONTESSON, JOSEPH-MICHEL, officer in the colonial regular troops and seigneur; baptized 30 Dec. 1716 at Bécancour (Que.), son of Charles Legardeur* de Croisille and Marie-Anne-Geneviève Robinau de Bécancour; d. *c.* 1776 in Pennsylvania.

Joseph-Michel Legardeur de Croisille et de Montesson grew up on the seigneury of Bécancour, where equal numbers of Canadians and Christian Abenakis lived side by side. This background probably explains how he gained the linguistic and social skills that enabled him to act as liaison between Canadians and Indians during his military career. In 1739, as a cadet, Montesson was part of the force of Canadians and Indians that travelled to the lower Mississippi valley to assist Louisiana in its wars against the Chickasaws [*see* Jean-Baptiste Le Moyne* de Bienville]. He was promoted second ensign in 1742. In 1746 he was with Jean-Baptiste-Nicolas-Roch de Ramezay's expedition against the British in Acadia. He led a raid on a British provisioning party at Port-La-Joie (Fort Amherst, P.E.I.) in July. The raiders, mainly Micmacs, killed or captured almost 40 of the enemy at slight cost to themselves, and Montesson was commended for having distinguished himself in his first independent command. In August, while conveying a cargo of provisions across the Bay of Fundy, his small vessel was run aground and wrecked when pursued by a British ship.

On 25 Oct. 1745 at Quebec he had married Claire-Françoise Boucher de Boucherville, widow of Jean-Baptiste Pommereau*. The marriage involved him in the seal fishery at Gros Mécatina, which Pommereau had carried on in association with Guillaume ESTÈBE and Daniel-Hyacinthe-Marie Liénard* de Beaujeu. Their concession expired in 1747 but was renewed for six years dating from 1748, with Montesson acting on behalf of his wife.

Made full ensign on 15 Feb. 1748, he was one of several interpreters at an important negotiation between the Iroquois and the Canadians at Montreal that autumn [*see* Kakouenthiony*]. When Governor DUQUESNE decided to send a fort-building expedition to back up the Canadian claim to the Ohio country, Montesson was made a member of the advance detachment under Charles DESCHAMPS de Boishébert which left Montreal in February 1753. Reports of Montesson's quarrels with Boishébert angered the governor, who considered recalling him. Unaware of Duquesne's displeasure, the minister of Marine promoted him lieutenant on 1 April 1753. He remained with the expedition, and during August and September his special responsibility was directing a small squad building dug-out canoes. The following year he coordinated assistance being given to the expedition by a party of Abenakis and made at least one trip to the site of Fort Duquesne (Pittsburgh, Pa) with supplies. In that year also he acquired an island which had originally been part of the seigneury of Bécancour, and in 1755 he purchased the seigneury itself from his mother.

During the Seven Years' War Montesson's tasks were varied: providing liaison with Abenaki allies in 1755, reconnoitring by night around Fort Carillon (Ticonderoga, N.Y.) and guarding the signal station at Kamouraska in 1758, retiring guns from the Île d'Orléans and commanding small squads being moved about Quebec City's outskirts in 1759, and recruiting residents of the south shore for the last big effort in 1760.

He had been promoted captain on 1 May 1757. In 1761 he went to France and received the cross of Saint-Louis. He may have been considering resettlement there, but by New Year's 1764 he was back in Canada exchanging greetings with Governor MURRAY of Quebec. One of his stepdaughters married John BRUYÈRES, secretary to the governor of Trois-Rivières, in a Protestant ceremony; the other married a British officer. Nevertheless Montesson was not employed by the new régime until 1775, when with other seigneurs he rallied to defend the government against the American invasion. (The Bécancour militia, however, refused to be called up.) Montesson was a civilian volunteer at Saint-Jean when the fort there was captured on 3 Nov. 1775. Prisoners were sent to Pennsylvania, and Montesson died before an agreement of 1777 permitted the men taken at Saint-Jean to return home.

Writing in 1753, Governor Duquesne castigated his "spirit of insubordination, proceeding from his having independent means" and called him "a busybody, a shameless liar, and very difficult to get along with." Montesson may not have been an attractive personality, and he may have tolerated members of the British occupation force within his family circle, but he showed himself ready to defend Canada against all comers, in the 1770s as in the 1750s.

MALCOLM MACLEOD

AN, Col., C[11A], 85; F[3], 14, 15. ANQ-Q, NF 6, 4, pp.300–5, 321–26 (PAC transcripts). Library of Congress (Washington), George Washington papers, 9, 19, 20, 21, 22, 34, 42. PAC, RG 4, D1, 7. [G.-J. Chaussegros de Léry], "Journal de Joseph-Gaspard Chaussegros de Léry, lieutenant des troupes, 1754–1755," ANQ *Rapport*, 1927–28, 365, 375. *Coll. des manuscrits de Lévis* (Casgrain), VII, VIII. *Inv. de pièces du Labrador* (P.-G. Roy), I, 88–89. [D.-H.-M. Liénard de] Beaujeu, "Journal de la campagne du détachement de Canada à l'Acadie et aux Mines, en 1746–47," *Coll. doc. inédits Canada et Amérique*, II, 16–75. "Mémoire du Canada," ANQ *Rapport*, 1924–25, 154. *NYCD* (O'Callaghan and Fernow), X, 186–88. *Papiers Contrecœur* (Grenier). "Recensement du gouvernement de Trois-Rivières, 1760," 52–53. "Une expedition canadienne à la Louisiane en 1739–1740," ANQ *Rapport*, 1922–23, 181–82. Æ. Fauteux, *Les chevaliers de Saint-Louis*. P.-G. Roy, *Inv. concessions*, I, 251–57. P. E. LeRoy, "Sir Guy Carleton as a military leader during the American invasion and repulse in Canada, 1775–1776" (unpublished PHD thesis, 2v., Ohio State University, Columbus, 1960). Marcel Trudel, "Les mariages mixtes sous le Régime militaire," *RHAF*, VII (1953–54), 7–31.

LEGARDEUR DE REPENTIGNY, LOUIS, officer in the colonial regular troops; b. 5 Aug. 1721 in Montreal (Que.), son of Jean-Baptiste-René Legardeur de Repentigny and Marie-Catherine Juchereau de Saint-Denis; d. 11 Oct. 1786 in Paris, France.

Louis Legardeur de Repentigny began military service at the age of 13 and in 1741 was breveted second ensign in the colonial regular troops. After this appointment he remained in the region of Fort Saint-Frédéric (near Crown Point, N.Y.) and was sent on various reconnaissance and scouting operations along the frontier. In 1745 he took part in an expedition against Saratoga (Schuylerville, N.Y.). Repentigny was promoted ensign in 1748, lieutenant in 1751, and captain in 1759, and during this period he participated in nearly all the campaigns fought in Canada. He served mainly in the region of Michilimackinac (Mackinaw City, Mich.), taking charge of Fort Saint-Joseph (Niles) in 1750, and then of a fort he built two years later on his seigneury of Sault-Sainte-Marie (in the vicinity of Sault Ste Marie, Mich.), whose command he retained until 1758 or 1759. As well, Repentigny received special commissions and served in Acadia in 1746 and 1747 as leader of a detachment of 30 Canadians [*see* Jean-Baptiste-Nicolas-Roch de RAMEZAY]. In 1757 he took part in the military operations against Fort George (also called Fort William Henry; now Lake George, N.Y.) and in the battle at Carillon (Ticonderoga, N.Y.) in 1758.

The next year, and throughout the Quebec campaign, he commanded the army reserve. On 31 July he repulsed Wolfe*'s landing at the ford across the Montmorency, and he fought in the battle of the Plains of Abraham, afterwards withdrawing to Pointe-aux-Trembles (Neuville), where he was in charge until November 1759. As officer commanding the colony's militia units, Repentigny distinguished himself at the battle of Sainte-Foy on 28 April 1760. With his force he played a decisive role in blocking the British centre and twice repulsing it. "This brigade was the only one that the enemy did not make yield an inch of ground," wrote Governor Vaudreuil [RIGAUD]. Repentigny joined the retreat to Montreal; then, refusing British domination, he went to France after the colony's surrender. He said that he was ruined, for he had left landed property in Canada worth 278,000 *livres*. In 1762, at the head of a 200-man detachment being sent to reinforce Charles-Henri-Louis d'ARSAC de Ternay's expedition, Repentigny set out for Newfoundland, but he was taken prisoner en route by the British vessel *Dragon*. He was also made a knight of the order of Saint-Louis that year.

Although Repentigny, like all former officers of the colonial regular troops, complained of being passed over in favour of officers from the regular army, he continued to serve in colonial forces. In 1769 he was in command of the depot for colonial recruits on the Île de Ré and the following year was promoted lieutenant-colonel. He took command, as colonel, of the Régiment d'Amérique in 1773 and of the Régiment de Guadeloupe four years later; in June 1780 he also received command, against his wishes, of the Régiment de Martinique. In 1783 Repentigny was named governor of Senegal and assigned responsibility for resuming possession of this colony, which had been restored to France by the treaty of Versailles; his main task was to protect the trade in gum arabic. Difficulties that developed with traders led to his recall in October 1785. He was ill when he left the island of Gorée on 24 April 1786 in the *Bayonnaise*, and he arrived back in France only to die.

Repentigny, who had to his credit 16 campaigns, 12 battles, and 2 sieges, was held in varying esteem by his superiors. In 1759 LÉVIS praised his talents and zeal, and in 1774 the Comte de Genlis noted that he "has served the king for 35 years and on every occasion has given proof of his zeal and conscientiousness"; on the other hand, at Guadeloupe he was blamed for lacking firmness, discernment, and impartiality. The king's order for his appointment to Senegal stated: "This officer, [although] ill-fitted to command a corps, is endowed with honesty and unselfishness."

Repentigny had married Marie-Madeleine, the daughter of Gaspard-Joseph Chaussegros* de Léry, at Quebec on 20 April 1750. They had at least one son, Louis-Gaspard, who was born at Quebec on 10 July 1753 and was lieutenant-commander and port captain at Point-à-Pitre, Guadeloupe, at the time of his death on 2 July 1808.

ÉTIENNE TAILLEMITE

AN, Col., C[11A], 105, f.12; D[2C], 7, f.152; 101, ff.153, 225; 204, f.2; 205, f.1; E, 72 (dossier Legardeur de Repentigny). *Coll. des manuscrits de Lévis* (Casgrain), II, 257. Æ. Fauteux, *Les chevaliers de Saint-Louis*, 191. Le Jeune, *Dictionnaire*, II, 520. Tanguay, *Dictionnaire*, V, 293. Léonce Jore, "Un Canadien gouverneur du Sénégal, Louis Le Gardeur de Repentigny (1721–1786)," *RHAF*, XV (1961–62), 64–89, 256–76, 396–418. P.-G. Roy, "La famille LeGardeur de Repentigny," *BRH*, LIII (1947), 238.

LEGARDEUR DE REPENTIGNY, PIERRE-JEAN-BAPTISTE-FRANÇOIS-XAVIER, officer in the colonial regular troops; b. 24 May 1719 in Montreal, son of Jean-Baptiste-René Legardeur de Repentigny and Marie-Catherine Juchereau de Saint-Denis; d. 26 May 1776 at Pondicherry, India.

The son of an officer, Pierre-Jean-Baptiste-François-Xavier Legardeur de Repentigny enlisted in the colonial regulars in 1733. He was promoted second ensign when he was 15, ensign in 1742, and lieutenant six years later. Posted to Île Royale (Cape Breton Island) in 1750, he received the rank of captain that year.

In 1757 Legardeur, who had returned to Canada, was decorated with the cross of the order of Saint-Louis. His brother LOUIS was also serving in the colonial regulars, and reports on the military campaigns of these years refer to both brothers, who were captains, by the name of M. de Repentigny. Louis, however, campaigned primarily along the Ohio River with Jean-Baptiste-Philippe TESTARD de Montigny and Joseph MARIN de La Malgue, while Pierre won renown in the Quebec region. LÉVIS and Vaudreuil [RIGAUD] considered Pierre a zealous, talented, and intelligent officer, and Montcalm* called him "a man of merit."

After the conquest Legardeur went to France and settled at Tours. In 1769 he entered the service of the Compagnie des Indes as adjutant general and commander of the troops. Promoted infantry colonel in 1771, in 1774 he was made commandant at Mahé, India, and in 1775 became colonel of the Régiment de Pondichéry. He died at Pondicherry the following year.

Legardeur is best known as the murderer of a Quebec merchant, Nicolas Jacquin*, *dit* Philibert. This homicide, committed in January 1748, is supposed to have stemmed from Philibert's desire to have the order billeting Legardeur in his house changed. The officer took offence and insulted the merchant, who replied in kind and struck him. Finally Legardeur fatally wounded the merchant with his sword. Upon being condemned by the provost court of Quebec to pay a fine of 8,000 *livres* and to be decapitated, he sought refuge at Fort Saint-Frédéric (near Crown Point, N.Y.). He asked the king for letters of remission, stressing his service and his military ability; Commandant General Roland-Michel Barrin* de La Galissonière and Intendant BIGOT lent him their support. He obtained his reprieve in 1749. Back in Quebec he ran up against public opinion, which never forgives as readily as a king. Governor La Jonquière [Taffanel*] decided to transfer him to Île Royale.

This murder was the origin of the famous legend of the Golden Dog [*see* Nicolas Jacquin, *dit* Philibert], which has been given several interpretations. According to one of them, Bigot – who was not even in Canada at the time – is supposed to have been the instigator of the murder; another brings into it Intendant Michel Bégon* de La Picardière and one of Philibert's brothers, who is supposed to have succeeded in avenging the merchant by killing Legardeur in India. Legardeur and Philibert became principal characters in William Kirby*'s novel *The Golden Dog*.

Legardeur had married Catherine-Angélique, the daughter of Pierre-Jacques PAYEN de Noyan et de Chavoy, in Montreal on 30 Jan. 1753. She had two stillborn infants and died at Lachenaie on 19 Dec. 1757. On 26 June 1766 at Saint-Vincent de Tours, France, Legardeur married Marguerite-Jeanne, the daughter of Philippe-Jean-Baptiste Mignon, and they had a son and a daughter.

CÉLINE CYR

AN, Col., E, 272 (dossier Legardeur de Repentigny). Archives paroissiales, Notre-Dame de Montréal, Registre des baptêmes, mariages et sépultures, 24 mai 1719. *Coll. des manuscrits de Lévis* (Casgrain), I, II, V, VII, VIII. "Journal du siège de Québec" (Æ. Fauteux), ANQ *Rapport*, 1920–21, 137–241. Claude de Bonnault, "Le Canada militaire: état provisoire des officiers de milice de 1641 à 1760," ANQ *Rapport*, 1949–51, 282–83. Æ. Fauteux. *Les chevaliers de Saint-Louis*, 163–64. Tanguay, *Dictionnaire*, V. Léonce Jore, "Pierre, Jean-Baptiste, François-Xavier Legardeur de Repentigny," *RHAF*, XV (1961–62), 556–71. P.-G. Roy, "La famille LeGardeur de Repentigny," *BRH*, LIII (1947), 234–36; "L'histoire vraie du Chien d'Or," *Cahiers des Dix*, 10 (1945), 103–68.

LEGGE, FRANCIS, army officer and colonial administrator; b. *c.* 1719; d. 15 May 1783 near Pinner (Greater London), England.

Little detailed evidence survives of Francis Legge's origins and private life, of his army career, or of his life after his recall from Nova Scotia in 1776. Only a distant kinship with a man who could make colonial appointments, and who recommended him somewhat surprisingly in 1773 to the governorship of Nova Scotia, prevented him from living and dying in anonymity. For a few brief and hectic years, however, Legge was in the spotlight. He was not a successful governor, in large measure because he was a product of 18th-century British ruling-class nepotism and patronage, unable to comprehend the rules of a society where men were forced to make their own careers by whatever means came to hand. The real conflict which developed between Legge and the Nova Scotian oligarchy from 1774 to 1776 was not between virtue and corruption, but between two incompatible views of how one managed to survive and prosper.

Legge's early military career was undistinguished. He became an ensign in the 35th Foot in May 1741 and on 16 Feb. 1756 obtained a captaincy in the 46th Foot, serving through the American campaigns of the Seven Years' War without distinction or promotion. He achieved his high point, the command of five companies at Trois-Rivières, in July 1761 and was considering retirement in 1765 because of the difficulties of advancement. His career prospects brightened, however, when his distant kinsman the Earl of Dartmouth (the exact relationship is not entirely clear) became president of the Board of Trade in

July 1765. Around 1766 Dartmouth received the detailed proposal for action requisite from every suitor for patronage – "Captain Legge's proposal of a Company of 100 Axmen, to make and preserve roads in the interior parts of North America" – and, soon afterwards, a letter requesting assistance in purchasing the majority of the 28th Foot. Although Legge did not gain the post in the 28th, he was mysteriously promoted major of his own regiment on 13 April 1767.

In 1772 Dartmouth was appointed secretary of state for the American Colonies and, like all 18th-century ministers, he remembered his clients, since "Great Men" measured their power largely in terms of their ability to attract and place supporters. Legge was offered two posts not yet actually available: the superintendency of southern Indians when the expected death of incumbent John Stuart occurred and the governorship of Pittsylvania, a proposed settlement on the Ohio River. He also found support for his efforts to obtain a lieutenant-colonelcy; he was able to purchase the rank in the 55th Foot in 1773. When in that year Dartmouth suggested that he succeed Lord William CAMPBELL as governor of Nova Scotia, Legge jumped at the chance. It was the first concrete offer made to him; the sorts of uncertain sinecures which had been bandied about demonstrate that the Earl did not have great plans for or much confidence in his kinsman. Nova Scotia was an opening, albeit not one of the preferred posts in the empire, and Legge was a client. The match was not entirely unreasonable. Legge was a soldier, and Nova Scotia a frontier colony of military importance. Having no influence of his own, he would be totally dependent on his superior and hence loyal. Unfortunately, as one of his more sympathetic later chroniclers, John Bartlet Brebner*, has observed, Legge was basically a stupid man. He completely failed to understand the dynamics of Nova Scotia politics and what was expected of him as governor.

Nova Scotia was run by a small but amorphous group of merchants based in Halifax under the London patronage of Joshua MAUGER, one of its former members, and the local direction of Lieutenant Governor Michael FRANCKLIN. Most of this group were swashbuckling entrepreneurs who had been initially attracted to Nova Scotia by its lack of rules and structure. They were not particularly polite or genteel, and they had to work hard to wrest success from the limited public and private resources of the province, on which demands were heavy. Prominent everywhere in public positions (John BUTLER and Jonathan Binney* sat on the Council; John Newton and others were assemblymen), the members of the clique engaged in much mutual patronage. They were the sorts of local figures who dominated nearly every society and government in colonial North America. Royal governors appointed from outside could either cooperate with such an oligarchy, a choice made by most successful governors, or do battle with it. In any conflict at any time the governor was at a substantial disadvantage, but he was particularly so in the early 1770s, when many of the American colonies seemed to be teetering on the verge of rebellion, and especially so in Nova Scotia, where there was no alternative political faction such as a "country" party of agrarian interests with which to cooperate. Whatever Dartmouth may have told Legge before his departure for America about being tough-minded and independent, the British government above all wanted political quiet, and that requirement demanded an alliance between the governor and the local merchant élite which ran the province. Legge failed to produce that alliance. Part of the reason was his assumption of social superiority to the élite. As a soldier, he had an "honourable" occupation for a ruling-class Englishman; in Britain, kinship and connections were far more important than ability or energy, and individuals in "trade" seldom achieved political power. Moreover, in his developing opposition to the oligarchy there was always more than a faint aroma of inconsistency and bullying, a point his opponents were quick to exploit.

Legge arrived in Halifax on 6 Oct. 1773 aboard the brigantine *Adamant*. Soon after, the House of Assembly voted on a case which would become central in Legge's downfall, declaring on the 21st that "the charge of £75 per Annum to Jonathan Binney Esquire for being first Magistrate at Canso, is and has been repeatedly disallow'd by this House." Funds to pay Binney had been allocated in 1764 for one year only, argued the assembly, and he had been illegally deducting his salary from his customs receipts. Legge was in no position to understand the intricacies of the Binney dispute, which was only part of a long argument between assembly and Council over the control of provincial funds, and he wrote to Dartmouth supporting Binney as a "serviceable and necessary" magistrate who seemed to be doing his job at Canso. He then proceeded to work fiercely to find out about his province and its governance. Unfortunately for himself, he was not content to identify the sources of local power in order to make peace with them; he also wanted to know who was abusing that power.

The first year of Legge's tenure was a busy

one. He tried to find a way for Nova Scotia to benefit from the boycott which the southern colonies were imposing on trade with Britain, but his hope that the province would replace New England in the triangular trade with the West Indies proved unjustified. Moreover, the British government refused his request for a grant for the construction of roads, which he was eager to advance in order to improve communications and trade. In the political field, Legge looked for friends in the group of assemblymen who should have been the "country" party, those gentlemen like Henry Denny DENSON and Winckworth TONGE who represented constituencies outside Halifax. He also sought legal advice and a legal adviser from home to replace Attorney General William NESBITT, citing the latter's inability and his laxity in collecting debts. In addition, he advocated changes in such provincial institutions as the lighthouse on Sambro Island and the orphan house in Halifax. In the latter case, an effort to secure money for repairs led to a new contract at reduced salaries for the supervisors, Richard WENMAN and his wife, and elimination of the fee for the visitor, the Reverend John BREYNTON. Alterations in such institutions were potentially troublesome for the Halifax oligarchy, and they increasingly pointed to the fact that the governor threatened the oligarchy's patronage system. Each step made enemies; Legge's papers were rifled as early as March 1774. He finished the job of alienating the élite by acquiescing in the Council's decision in November to appoint a committee to audit the provincial books and by attempting to influence the results.

Nova Scotia had suffered from a large debt for many years, a constant problem for every governor. Not surprisingly, the committee, which included John DAY, Charles MORRIS, and the new solicitor general James Monk*, found few records surviving, and it attempted to reconstruct them from other official sources, a process which uncovered substantial irregularities and shortages [*see* Benjamin GREEN]. There were some legitimate explanations for the bad practices, and Legge might have found considerable support for the institution of a better system for the future. Instead Monk, with Legge's backing, began looking for villains and attempted to recover the missing funds by suing defaulters, a difficult process in the absence of an equity court, which could sit without a jury; juries in colonial North America were notorious for backing local residents against the efforts of government to bring them to account. Binney and Newton were eventually tried before a jury which Legge found it necessary to pack – because of the influence "among the common people" of the two defendants, he informed Dartmouth, a "special jury" of the most reliable of the inhabitants had been assembled – and to supervise by ostentatiously sitting in the gallery of the courthouse throughout the trial. Judgements were obtained against both men, but Binney refused to put up surety for his release and remained with his family in jail, a martyr to persecution. Legge further compounded the obvious comparisons with "Stuart despotism" by creating on his own authority a court of exchequer with equity jurisdiction to try further default cases.

By the spring of 1775, when the Americans were erupting into rebellion, Legge had alienated the Halifax élite to the point where he had virtually lost control of the government, a fact symbolized by the problems he had with the 1775 legislature; his best efforts to be conciliatory were seen as signs of weakness. The assembly, which until then had cooperated reasonably well with the governor, decided to petition the Privy Council "on the subject of the Grievances the People of this Province labour under." One can only speculate on the reason for this reversal of opinion, but Legge's high-handed conduct of Binney's trial undoubtedly had much to do with it. The Council also turned against him. Although the majority of its members wanted to know the state of the provincial finances, they did not intend to collect outstanding debts or to bring those involved to court.

During the summer session the assembly cleared many of the defaulters and reduced the amounts owed by others, and both Council and assembly petitioned the British government to remove Legge because of the danger of rebellion if he continued as governor. Fortunately for Britain, those critical of Legge preferred to seek relief in Whitehall rather than in Philadelphia; firm economic ties to Britain ensured the loyalty of most Halifax merchants. Equally fortunately, the Americans decided that their lack of naval power made it impracticable to support the group headed by Jonathan Eddy* in Cumberland County or that in Maugerville (N.B.), both of which were petitioning for armed assistance in throwing off the British yoke. The rebel decision was especially happy for Legge since the widespread desire for neutrality outside Halifax had made it difficult for him to recruit the Loyal Nova Scotia Volunteers, a provincial regiment he had been commissioned to form, or to assemble the provincial militia. Nor could he offer much in the way of men or supplies to Lieutenant-General Thomas GAGE in Boston.

Soon after Legge prorogued the 1775 legislature, the contending parties turned to Whitehall to make their respective cases. Unfortunately for Legge, Mauger had the ear of one of the permanent under-secretaries at the Board of Trade, John Pownall, and Dartmouth had been succeeded by Lord George Germain, whose analysis of the situation – ". . . the Universal Cry is against Mr. Legge, & . . . the Province will be lost, utterly lost; and, if I take no notice, of these matters, should any mishap befall, tho' the Governor, is [ever] so good a man, . . . they'll on purpose counteract his measures, must I be answerable" – was awkwardly expressed but irrefutable at the time. Legge was ordered home in February 1776 to answer charges and left the province in May. The Board of Trade, after a long hearing, decided his fate in July, assessing the situation along the same lines as had Germain; it refused to countenance the specific accusations against him but found him "wanting in that Gracious and Conciliating Deportment which the delicacy of the times and the Tempers of Men under agitation & alarm more particularly demanded." The Board emphasized that there was no evidence of "serious and well grounded matters of misconduct" to prevent the royal confidence on future occasions; Legge had, indeed, been warmly received by George III and Germain the day he had arrived in London to defend himself. But he was not permitted to return to Nova Scotia, for his recall had given "such satisfaction" to the province that he could hardly be allowed to resume the helm. As a reward for its loyalty, the Halifax élite was permitted, under a series of naval lieutenant governors who took little interest in local matters, to govern itself until the crisis of rebellion was resolved. Not until 29 July 1782 did Legge lose his appointment to John PARR. He died ten months later.

The Nova Scotia career of Francis Legge well illustrates the difficulties which faced the first British empire and its appointed representatives in governing the North American colonies. Legge's problems were in no way unique, and the speed of his inevitable downfall (the only unusual feature) is attributable mainly to his own shortcomings.

J. M. BUMSTED

PAC, MG 11, [CO 217], Nova Scotia A, 95, p.151; 96, pp.113, 153; [CO 220], Nova Scotia B, 15, pp.185, 190, 191; MG 23, A1. PANS, RG 1, 44, docs.1, 6, 33, 38. *Gentleman's Magazine*, 1783, 453. *Nova-Scotia Gazette and the Weekly Chronicle* (Halifax), 12 Oct. 1773, 29 March 1774. F.-J. Audet, "Governors, lieutenant-governors, and administrators of Nova Scotia, 1604–1932" (typescript, n.d.; copy at PANS). B. D. Bargar, *Lord Dartmouth and the American revolution* (Columbia, S.C., 1965). Brebner, *Neutral Yankees* (1969), 180–212, 215–16, 222ff., 229–46, 270ff. W. B. Kerr, *The maritime provinces of British North America and the American revolution* (Sackville, N.B., [1941?]; repr. New York, [1970]), 62ff. L. W. Labaree, *Royal government in America: a study of the British colonial system before 1783* (New Haven, Conn., 1930). J. K. Martin, *Men in rebellion: higher governmental leaders and the coming of the American revolution* (New Brunswick, N.J., 1973). V. F. Barnes, "Francis Legge, governor of loyalist Nova Scotia, 1773–1776," *New England Quarterly* (Brunswick, Maine), IV (1931), 420–27.

LE GUERNE, FRANÇOIS (sometimes written **Guerne** or **De Guerne**), Spiritan, priest, and missionary; b. 5 Jan. 1725 at Kergrist-Moëlou (dept of Côtes-du-Nord), France, son of Yves Le Guerne; d. 6 Dec. 1789 at Saint-François-de-Sales, Île d'Orléans, Quebec.

On 1 July 1749, after a few years at the Séminaire du Saint-Esprit in Paris, François Le Guerne entered the Séminaire des Missions Étrangères, where Abbé de L'Isle-Dieu, the bishop of Quebec's vicar general in Paris, paid his board. Early in the summer of 1750 he left for Quebec, sailing on the frigate *Diane* from Rochefort; at that time he was only a tonsured cleric. He spent more than a year in Quebec, completed his theological studies, and was then ordained priest by Bishop Pontbriand [Dubreil*] on 18 Sept. 1751.

Le Guerne went to Acadia, probably in 1752, to minister to the settlers around Fort Beauséjour (near Sackville, N.B.). At first he served some 80 families at Tintemarre (Tantramar), but after the departure of Abbé Le Guet (Du Guay) early in 1754 he had at least 200 families scattered over nearly 40 leagues along the Shepody, Petitcodiac, and Memramcook rivers. Obliged to travel from one post to another for two months of every year, he asked the bishop of Quebec for another missionary to assist him with his heavy burden. He worked in cooperation with Jean-Louis LE LOUTRE, who ministered to the Indians in the region.

In June 1755 Fort Beauséjour was captured by British troops under Robert MONCKTON. Le Guerne refused to compel the Acadians to resist the British because Louis DU PONT Duchambon, the commandant of the fort, and Abbé Le Loutre "had said on leaving that it was in the habitants' interest to be quite submissive." So strongly were the Acadians attached to their lands that Le Guerne doubted many would heed a counsel of disobedience, and he was reluctant to be held responsible for the misfortunes of those who did.

On seeing the sad fate that befell them anyway – those who presented themselves at the fort were imprisoned with a view to deportation – Le Guerne changed his mind; accompanied by a large number of his parishioners he took to the woods north of the Shepody, Petitcodiac, and Memramcook rivers. With Charles DESCHAMPS de Boishébert he attempted to facilitate the escape of families still at liberty and to organize the resistance of those Acadians who wished to continue harassing the enemy. He had repeatedly to go into hiding because Monckton sought to have him arrested. Nearly 200 families shared his lot, living in extreme poverty, without flour, salt pork, cooking fat, molasses, or adequate rations of meat. By March 1756 Le Guerne had managed to get some 500 Acadians across to Île Saint-Jean (Prince Edward Island) [*see* Gabriel ROUSSEAU de Villejouin]. Many of his former flock, however, were too attached to their lands and paid no heed to his appeals, hoping that Acadia would again become French.

In order to escape the British Le Guerne left Acadia for good in August 1757. On his arrival in Quebec he immediately wrote to Governor Vaudreuil [RIGAUD] to request aid for the Acadians; however the situation was critical in the St Lawrence valley and the governor refused his request. Abbé de L'Isle-Dieu wanted to send Le Guerne to the mission to the Tamaroas (Cahokia, now East St Louis, Ill.), but Bishop Pontbriand kept him in Quebec hoping that he would be able to return to Acadia once peace had been restored. Since the war did not end, the bishop entrusted him in 1758 with the parish of Saint-François-de-Sales on Île d'Orléans.

Le Guerne spent the remainder of his career in that parish, absenting himself for a year (1768–69) to give a course in rhetoric at the Petit Séminaire in Quebec. In October 1789 about 50 of his parishioners, citing Le Guerne's "state of languor and infirmity," asked Bishop HUBERT to recall him, and the bishop advised him to retire. They complained that they had been harshly treated by their pastor and reproached him for denying his services to a large number of his flock and for seeking to enrich himself by every means. He died two months later. Among other legacies in his will Le Guerne left 360 *livres* to the Séminaire de Québec, 3,600 *livres* to the Séminaire du Saint-Esprit in Paris, and 3,600 *livres* to his relatives in Brittany.

GÉRARD FINN

AD, Côtes-du-Nord (Saint-Brieuc), État civil, Kergrist-Moëlou, 6 janv. 1725. AN, Col., B, 92, ff.54, 86, 137v; C[11A], 87, f.388; 96, ff.221, 245; 100, f.241. ASQ, C 35; Lettres, P, 83; R, 14; S, 6bis, C; MSS-M, 225, f.6; Polygraphie, XXV, 21; Séminaire, 14/6, no.14. La Rue, "Lettres et mémoires," ANQ *Rapport*, 1935–36, 294–306; 1936–37, 354–61, 395–408; 1937–38, 197–98, 202–3, 235–36, 246–48. Le Jeune, *Dictionnaire*. René Baudry, "Un témoin de la dispersion acadienne: l'abbé LeGuerne," *RHAF*, VII (1953–54), 32–44.

LE LOUTRE, JEAN-LOUIS (he signed LeLoutre), priest, Spiritan, and missionary; b. 26 Sept. 1709 in the parish of Saint-Matthieu in Morlaix, France, son of Jean-Maurice Le Loutre Després, a paper maker and member of the provincial bourgeoisie, and Catherine Huet, daughter of a paper maker; d. 30 Sept. 1772 in the parish of Saint-Léonard in Nantes, France.

In 1730 Jean-Louis Le Loutre entered the Séminaire du Saint-Esprit in Paris; by that time he had lost both his parents. When his training was completed, he transferred to the Séminaire des Missions Étrangères in March 1737, intending to serve the church in foreign parts. As soon as he had been ordained, he sailed for Acadia and in the autumn of that year appeared at Louisbourg, Île Royale (Cape Breton Island). Le Loutre was supposed to replace Abbé Claude de La Vernède de Saint-Poncy, the parish priest at Annapolis Royal (N.S.), whose relations with the British governor, Lawrence Armstrong*, had become strained [*see* Claude-Jean-Baptiste Chauvreulx*]. By the time he set foot on the American continent, however, the difficulties between Saint-Poncy and Armstrong had been ironed out and the governor had agreed that the parish priest should retain his post. Taking advantage of this situation, Pierre Maillard*, a missionary on Île Royale, wrote to the home authorities requesting that Le Loutre be allowed to replace Abbé de Saint-Vincent, a missionary to the Micmacs, and make his residence at Shubenacadie, on the river of the same name, 12 leagues from Cobequid (near Truro, N.S.). Before joining his flock Le Loutre spent some months at Maligouèche (Malagawatch) on Île Royale in order to learn the Micmac language. Maillard described him as a zealous missionary and diligent student, although Le Loutre had a difficult apprenticeship in this language without grammar or dictionary.

On 22 Sept. 1738 Le Loutre left Île Royale for the Shubenacadie mission, an immense territory stretching from Cape Sable to Chedabucto Bay in the north and present-day Cumberland Strait in the west. Le Loutre was to minister to the Indians as well as to the French posts at Cobequid and Tatamagouche, where Abbé Jacques GIRARD would replace him in 1742, and he concerned himself indirectly with the Acadians on the east coast of Nova Scotia. With the cooperation of the authorities at Louisbourg he immediately undertook to build chapels for the Indians. Although his relations with Armstrong were strained at first, the governor having protested because Le Loutre had not presented himself at Annapolis Royal, on the whole he remained on cordial terms with the British authorities until 1744.

With the declaration of war between France and Great Britain that year, the French authorities made a distinction in Acadia between the missionaries ministering to parishes with a French population and those serving among the Indians. The former were advised to remain neutral, at least in appearance, in order to avoid being expelled; the others were advised to support the intentions of the governor of Louisbourg and encourage the Indians to make as many forays into British areas as the military authorities considered necessary. The two major events of this period were the French siege of Annapolis Royal in 1744 under François Du Pont Duvivier, and the arrival in Acadia, two years later, of the French squadron commanded by the Duc d'Anville [La Rochefoucauld*]. Despite the assertions of several historians, it was Abbé Maillard who accompanied Duvivier's expedition. His presence, however, does not mean that Le Loutre was not also involved. From Canseau (Canso), Duvivier hastily dispatched a letter to Le Loutre asking him to keep watch on the route from Annapolis Royal to Minas, the place where they were to join forces, and Duvivier noted in his journal the value of Le Loutre's presence during the siege of Annapolis Royal in September.

The siege was unsuccessful and less than a year later, in June 1745, Louisbourg fell to Anglo-American forces. The new masters of Île Royale tried to seize Le Loutre. Peter Warren* and William Pepperrell* invited him to come to Louisbourg, warning that his life would otherwise be in danger, but Le Loutre chose to go to Canada for consultation with the authorities. He arrived at Quebec on 14 September, accompanied by five Micmacs, and left seven days later with specific instructions which in fact made him a military leader; henceforth it was through him that the French government was able to exercise control over the Indians in Acadia. He was also to keep watch on communications between the Acadians and the British garrison at Annapolis Royal, and he spent the winter with his Micmacs near Minas for this purpose.

With Louisbourg in enemy hands, Le Loutre became the liaison between the settlers and French expeditions by land or sea. The authorities had given him instructions to receive at Baie de Chibouctou (Halifax harbour) the squadron under the Duc d'Anville that France was sending in 1746 to recover Acadia. Le Loutre knew the signals which would identify the ships of the fleet, and was the only person who did except for Maurice de La Corne, a missionary at Miramichi (N.B.); the British having put a price on Le Loutre's head, La Corne had been seen as a possible replacement for him. Le Loutre was to coordinate the operations of the naval force with those of Jean-Baptiste-Nicolas-Roch de Ramezay's army, sent to Acadia early in June 1746 by the authorities in Quebec. Ramezay and his detachment arrived at Beaubassin (near Amherst, N.S.) in July, when only two frigates of the French squadron had reached Baie de Chibouctou. Without seeking the agreement of the two captains, Le Loutre wrote to Ramezay suggesting that an attack be made on Annapolis Royal with no delay for the remainder of the fleet; but his advice was not acted upon. In September the squadron finally arrived, but not in full strength since a number of ships had been sunk or damaged by gales and the crews had been reduced in numbers and weakened by sickness. As for the two ships that had come in June, in view of the delay of the fleet they had already set off on the return voyage. After d'Anville's death and Constantin-Louis d'Estourmel*'s attempted suicide, La Jonquière [Taffanel*] assumed command of the squadron. Ramezay and Le Loutre went to Annapolis Royal to rendezvous with it, but to no avail; the squadron had to return to France and Le Loutre took the opportunity to sail on the *Sirène*.

While in his native land Le Loutre was preoccupied with his brother's promotion and with the fate of the nuns from Louisbourg who had been deported to France after the fall of the fortress [*see* Marie-Marguerite-Daniel Arnaud*, *dite* Saint-Arsène]; he also managed to obtain gratuities for himself as well as a pension of 800 *livres* deducted from the diocese of Lavaur, thanks to the efforts of Abbé de L'Isle-Dieu, the bishop of Quebec's vicar general in Paris. He returned to Acadia in 1749 on the *Chabanne*, in company with Charles Des Herbiers* de La Ralière, the new governor of Île Royale, which had been restored to France by the treaty of Aix-la-Chapelle the previous year. He had already made two attempts to return but both times had ended up in British prisons, from which he had been released after successfully concealing his identity by using the names of Rosanvern and Huet.

The situation in Acadia had changed considerably since Le Loutre's departure: Louisbourg was again French, and the British had just founded Halifax. The missionary was ordered by the ministry of Marine to set up his headquarters at Pointe-à-Beauséjour (near Sackville, N.B.) rather than at Shubenacadie, too close to the authorities in Halifax who were clamouring for the missionary's head. The French claimed that Pointe-à-Beauséjour was outside the "old" Acadia, ceded to Great Britain in 1713 by the treaty of Utrecht, whereas the British maintained that Acadia extended as far as the Baie des Chaleurs. It was in this disputed territory, with ill-defined frontiers, where the two countries were demanding territorial concessions from each other, that Le Loutre's career was now to be played out. While the boundary commissioners were engaged in discussions in Paris, the French attempted to reinforce their claims to the region north of the Missaguash and to Île Saint-Jean (Prince Edward Island) by using the Indians to harass the British and restrict their settlements and by trying to persuade as many Acadians as possible to leave enemy territory and settle in the area under French control.

With regard to the use of the Indians Le Loutre revealed his thinking in a letter of 29 July 1749 to the minister of Marine: "As we cannot openly oppose the English ventures, I think that we cannot do better than to incite the Indians to continue warring on the English; my plan is to persuade the Indians to send word to the English that they will not permit new settlements to be made in Acadia . . . I shall do my best to make it look to the English as if this plan comes from the Indians and that I have no part in it." The attacks made by the Indians led Edward CORNWALLIS, the governor of Nova Scotia, to swear that he would have Le Loutre's head, and to describe him in October 1749 as "a good for nothing Scoundrel as ever lived." Cornwallis tried to capture him dead or alive by promising a reward of £50. Tension increased in Acadia in 1750 with the murder of Edward How*, a militia officer from Fort Lawrence shot on the banks of the Missaguash after negotiations under a flag of truce. A certain number of historians have accused Le Loutre of instigating this murder, but there is no conclusive evidence of it. Louis-Léonard AUMASSON de Courville, James JOHNSTONE, Jacques PREVOST de la Croix, the Marquis de La Jonquière, Pierre Maillard, and La Vallière (probably Louis Leneuf de La Vallière) have left descriptions of the episode. In some of these Le Loutre is said to have plotted the killing, but the versions contradict one another. Except for La Vallière, none of the authors was at the scene of the murder, and several of the accounts were written some years after the event. Yet it seems that Le Loutre must bear a certain responsibility for the murder as the admitted agent of French policy, which sought constantly to identify in the minds of the Indians the interests of Catholicism and those of the state. The killing was an open act of hostility on the part of the Micmacs against the Protestant authorities in Halifax, who understandably saw in it the complicity of both Le Loutre and Pierre-Roch de Saint-Ours Deschaillons, commander at Beauséjour. Even if the two had not directly plotted the crime, they were witnesses who remained passive.

As for the Acadians, the missionary thought that they were ready to abandon their land, and even to take up arms against the British, rather than sign an unconditional oath of allegiance to King George II. They were, however, perhaps not as determined to emigrate as Le Loutre maintained. Since 1713 the Acadians had always accommodated themselves to the British régime, and it was difficult for them to leave fertile lands that they had cleared and settle in French territory without being assured that sooner or later it would not become British. On behalf of the French government Le Loutre promised to establish and feed them for three years, and even to compensate them for their losses. They were not easily convinced, and the missionary apparently used questionable means to force them to emigrate – threatening them, among other things, with reprisals from the Indians. The Acadians who moved, whether of their own free will or not, found themselves in an unenviable situation. Both on Île Saint-Jean and in the Fort Beauséjour region it was difficult to produce sufficient food to meet the needs of the new arrivals. The correspondence of Le Loutre, Des Herbiers, and La Jonquière, who was then governor of New France, makes daily mention of the supply problems in Acadia. In the spring of 1751 the missionary described the situation: the supply ships had not reached Baie Verte, consumption was greater than had been anticipated, the settlers were on the point of running out of meat and had received no wine whatever. Le Loutre was forced to divert certain presents intended for the Micmacs to the Acadians and the garrison at Fort Beauséjour. The situation on Île Saint-Jean was also desperate, and in the face of these problems the Acadians indicated their wish to return to their former lands. The missionary accused François-Marie de Goutin*, the storekeeper and subdelegate of the financial commissary on Île Saint-Jean, of having left the settlers to starve when the warehouses were full of supplies. After asking the authorities in Louisbourg to put the bad administration on Île Saint-Jean to rights, Le Loutre complained of the commandant and the storekeeper at Baie-Verte (N.B.). In August 1752 he went to Quebec to meet Intendant BIGOT and Governor DUQUESNE, but being dissatisfied with the results of his representations, he came back to Acadia, entrusted his Micmacs to Abbé Jean Manach*, and crossed the Atlantic.

At the end of December 1752 Le Loutre arrived in France. As soon as he reached the mother country, he asked for an audience at court; Rouillé, the minister of Marine, received him on 15 January. Although Rouillé, and particularly Abbé de L'Isle-Dieu, would have preferred seeing the missionary in Acadia rather than in France – it had been suggested to him that he postpone his voyage – relations between the three men were soon cordial. In collaboration with the minister Le Loutre wrote a report, denouncing British claims, for Roland-Michel Barrin* de La Galissonière, who was in charge of the commission negotiating the frontiers in North America. With Abbé de L'Isle-Dieu he also drew up detailed reports on the Acadians and the territory they occupied or could occupy, with a plan of divisions showing areas to be kept and those to be given up. The two men submitted these reports with the declared aim of suggesting to the court how negotiations should be conducted. Le Loutre insisted to the royal officials that the Acadians could not continue to live in uncertainty, tossed about between two powers; he recommended negotiating firmly in order to define strictly the territories ceded in 1713 and to adhere to the articles of the treaty of Utrecht, which granted the British only a strip of land at the southwest tip of Acadia including the former Port-Royal and the surrounding area. If, as a last resort, a larger block of territory had to be given up, the missionary proposed that the line of demarcation between the French and British possessions in Acadia be drawn from Cobequid to Canso. The Baie des Chaleurs and Gaspé regions, which Le Loutre included in Acadia, should remain French, and the port of Canso should become neutral, with fishing rights reserved solely for the French. The aim of the plan was to keep the enemy posts at a distance, hem in Nova Scotia with a solid band of fortified posts, and ensure communications by land and sea between Louisbourg, the posts in French Acadia, and Quebec. This proposition meant the evacuation of Beaubassin by the British and the destruction of Fort Lawrence. The French would thus recover fertile lands, and the confrontations which the proximity of forts Beauséjour and Lawrence made inevitable would be eliminated. If the Acadians wanted to remain subjects of the king of France, they would have to abandon the region of Annapolis Royal and Minas Basin. According to Le Loutre, France had an obligation to resettle them in order to keep them from being dominated by a nation that wanted to wipe out Catholicism. He proposed that they be established in the region of Beaubassin and the Shepody, Memramcook, and Petitcodiac rivers. The French authorities would have to construct *aboiteaux* or dikes to protect the low-lying lands against the high tides. He maintained that at the end of four years the settlers would be able to produce more than they consumed, and hence could meet the needs of the garrison of Beauséjour and even have surpluses of wheat and cattle for export to Louisbourg. He estimated the cost of building the dikes at 50,000 *livres*, a sum that the court granted him. In fact, however, this sum was to be greatly exceeded; in March 1755 the missionary assessed the expenditures required for the dikes at 150,000 *livres* and asked the court for a supplement of 20,000 *livres*, the balance to be supplied by the Acadians' labour and materials. Le Loutre had perhaps concealed the high cost of construction in order to gain the court's assent for the project.

During his stay in France Le Loutre also discussed with his religious superiors "certain circumstances in which he [might] find himself in relation to his Indians' warring and even that of the French, especially those who are still under the domination of the English."[5] He pondered over his activity with the Acadians. What means could he use to persuade them to leave British territory? As for those Acadians who had taken the oath of allegiance to Great Britain, could he ask that they be deprived of the sacraments? Was he empowered to threaten them with excommunication in order to persuade them to take refuge in territory claimed by France, or again could he ask his Micmacs to force recalcitrants to abandon their lands? Le Loutre also wondered whether he could encourage the Indians to attack and scalp British settlers in peace-time. At the same time he was busy obtaining certain favours for his mission, his colleagues, and himself. Among other things he managed to have the annual pension of 1,200 *livres* that the court paid to the missionaries among the Acadians shared with the missionaries in charge of the Micmacs, as he was. The king also granted him a gratuity of 2,438 *livres* to buy flour at Louisbourg, 2,740 *livres* for various liturgical articles, and 600 *livres* for medicines. Le Loutre recruited new missionaries for Acadia, including Pierre Cassiet*, and obtained for each a special gratuity of 600 *livres*.

At the end of April 1753 Le Loutre sailed for Acadia on the *Bizarre*, and the following year he was made vicar general there by Bishop Pontbriand [Dubreil*]. Upon his return he made persistent efforts to persuade the Micmacs to break the peace that had been signed with the British during his absence [*see* Jean-Baptiste Cope*], and he made use of them to harass the British settlers. He bought the trophies they brought back from hunts and raids; for example, he paid 1,800 *livres* for 18 British scalps. According to Courville, who had arrived at Fort Beauséjour in 1754 – and whose testimony cannot be ignored as some authors suggest it should because of the anticlericalism of the French at the time – Le Loutre threatened to abandon the Acadians, withdraw their priests, have their wives and children taken from them, and if necessary have their property laid waste by the Indians. A parallel can be drawn between what Courville reported and the Acadians' petitions to Cornwallis, in which they declared that they could not sign an unconditional oath because the Micmacs would not forgive them for doing so. Nevertheless, all Le Loutre's efforts proved vain. In June 1755 the British forces obliged Louis Du Pont Duchambon de Vergor to surrender Fort Beauséjour, and the deportation of the Acadians in the region began shortly thereafter. Knowing that he was in danger, the missionary had slipped out of the fort in disguise and reached Quebec through the woods. Late in the summer he went to Louisbourg and from there sailed for France. On 15 September the ship on which he was sailing fell into the hands of the British. Le Loutre was taken prisoner, and despite the minister of Marine's efforts he was not released until eight years later, on 30 Aug. 1763, after the signing of the treaty of Paris.

When he arrived in France Le Loutre was refused free lodgings at the Séminaire des Missions Étrangères because of his income of 800 *livres* a year. Acting in concert with Jean Manach and Jacques Girard, who had been refused in the same way, he sued the seminary, challenging the rules of the institution and asking that its missionaries have a part in its operation. The *parlement* of Paris resolved the question, judging the request by Le Loutre and his colleagues inadmissible on all counts. This setback did not discourage Le Loutre; he turned to the Duc de Choiseul, the minister of Marine, in order to obtain a pension. Despite Choiseul's insistence, the bishop of Orléans was unable to secure one for him, and the coffers of the Marine had to provide it. In May 1768 the court granted Le Loutre an annual pension of 1,200 *livres*, retroactive to 1 Jan. 1767, a stipend that he could enjoy until he had "been provided with an equivalent benefice." These gratuities did not prevent him from carrying on his attempt to make the Séminaire des Missions Étrangères provide for his needs.

Besides these preoccupations with money matters, Le Loutre concerned himself actively with the deported Acadians who had taken refuge in France. The court had several plans for settling them; the most serious was the one put forward by the Estates of Brittany in October 1763 which advocated settling at Belle-Île 77 Acadian families who were in the regions of Morlaix and Saint-Malo. The three Acadian delegates who visited the island in July 1764 found it difficult, however, to convince their compatriots to go to settle there. In the face of their indecision the court appealed to Le Loutre, who had no trouble persuading them to move. After numerous negotiations and several trips by Le Loutre between Paris, Rennes, and Morlaix, the Acadians arrived at Belle-Île late in 1765, under his guidance. They were provided with lands, houses, farm buildings, livestock, and tools and were granted certain financial advantages. Nevertheless, in 1772, after six years of hard work, they were unable to support themselves and certain of them indicated their wish to return to Acadia, a desire which could only displease the former missionary who had so devoted himself to removing them from the authority of the British. In 1771 Le Loutre had already inquired into the possibility of settling the Acadians in Corsica, but the island presented few advantages. He continued looking for more fertile lands, and in 1772 he organized a tour of Poitou in order to visit the area around Châtellerault that the Marquis de Pérusse Des Cars wanted to grant the Acadians [*see* Jean-Gabriel Berbudeau]. Fate ordained that Le Loutre should not see these lands; during the trip, which he was making in company with four Acadians, he died at Nantes on 30 Sept. 1772.

Historians are unanimous in recognizing the importance of Le Loutre's activity in Acadia but differ in their assessment of the significance of his role as a missionary. Several, particularly those writing in English, have criticized him for having acted more as an agent of French policy than as a missionary, and they hold him largely responsible for the deportation of the Acadians from Nova Scotia in 1755, because in threatening them with reprisals if they signed the oath of loyalty, he condemned them to a forced exile. Before a judgement is made on Le Loutre's career in Acadia, however, three important points must be considered: in the 18th century France claimed to be the defender of the Catholic faith; Acadia was populated with French Catholics governed by the Protestant British; missionaries were the only representatives of the French government among the Acadians tolerated by Great Britain. According to Le Loutre almost any means could be used to remove the Acadians, who were in danger spiritually, from British domination. He used the means at his disposal: arguments of a religious nature and the Indians. His method was debatable, but it was in keeping with the logic of his age, when in France as in England religion was at the service of the state.

Le Loutre was a leader of men, and the situation in Acadia was favourable to his activity. He was a politically involved missionary, stubborn and prepared to make up for the lack of French civil government in Acadia. His activity was displeasing to the government in Halifax, and even to certain French officers. He was probably excessively zealous, and his conduct was often questionable, but his sincere devotion to the cause of French Acadia cannot be doubted. He cannot be held responsible for the deportation of the Acadians.

GÉRARD FINN

Le Loutre's autobiography, the original of which is held by the Archives du séminaire des Missions étrangères (Paris), 344, has been published by Albert David as "Une autobiographie de l'abbé Le Loutre," *Nova Francia* (Paris), 6 (1931), 1–34. This text was published in translation by John Clarence Webster* as an appendix to *The career of the Abbé Le Loutre in Nova Scotia . . .* (Shediac, N.B., 1933), 32–50. A number of Le Loutre's letters have been published in *Coll. de manuscrits relatifs à la N.-F.*, III, and *Coll. doc. inédits Canada et Amérique*, I. For a discussion of the way Le Loutre has been regarded by both English and French speaking historians *see*: Gérard Finn, "Jean-Louis LeLoutre vu par les historiens," Soc. historique acadienne, *Cahiers* (Moncton, N.-B.), 8 (1977), 108–47.

AD, Finistère (Quimper), État civil, Saint-Matthieu de Morlaix, 1687, 1703–5, 1707–11, 1716, 1720; Saint-Mélaine de Morlaix, 1706–10; G-150-51, rolle de capitation; Registres du contrôle des actes de notaires, 1720–21; Loire-Atlantique (Nantes), État civil, Saint-Léonard de Nantes, 1er oct. 1772; Morbihan (Vannes), E, 1.457–1.464; Vienne (Poitiers), Cahier 3, no.245. AN, Col., B, 65, 68, 70–72, 76, 78, 81, 83–84, 88–89, 93, 95, 97–98, 100, 104, 110, 117, 120, 122, 125, 131, 134, 139, 143; C11A, 82, 83, 85, 87, 89, 93–96, 98–100, 102, 125; C11B, 20–22, 26–27, 29–30, 33–34; C11C, 9, 16; C11D, 8; C11E, 4; E, 169 (dossier Duvivier [François Du Pont Duvivier]), 265 (dossier Joseph Le Blanc), 275 (dossier Le Loutre); F3, 16; F5A, 1; Section Outre-mer, Dépôt des fortifications des colonies, Am. sept., no.34. Archives du séminaire de la Congrégation du Saint-Esprit (Paris), Boîte 441, dossier A, chemise II. Archives du séminaire des Missions étrangères (Paris), 25, 26, 28, 344. ASQ, Lettres, M, P, R; Polygraphie, IX. PRO, CO 217/7–9, 217/11, 217/14–15, 218/3; SP 42/23. Brebner, *New England's outpost*. Gérard Finn, "La carrière de l'abbé Jean-Louis LeLoutre et les dernières années de l'affrontement anglo-français en Acadie" (thèse de doctorat, université de Paris I (Sorbonne), 1974). M. D. Johnson, *Apôtres ou agitateurs: la France missionnaire en Acadie* (Trois-Rivières, 1970). Ernest Martin, *Les exilés acadiens en France au XVIIIe siècle et leur établissement en Poitou* (Paris, 1936).

LE MERCIER (Mercier), FRANÇOIS-MARC-ANTOINE, artillery officer; b. 29 Dec. 1722 at Caudebec, France, son of Nicolas-François Le Mercier, lieutenant-colonel of infantry in the Régiment d'Agenois, and Charlotte Le Rebours; m. Françoise Boucher de La Bruère (La Bruyère) at Sainte-Foy, near Quebec, on 15 Nov. 1757, three days after he was baptized by Bishop Pontbriand [Dubreil*] in Notre-Dame in Quebec; d. *c.* 1798 in the region of Lisieux, France.

In 1734 François-Marc-Antoine Le Mercier was a militia lieutenant, and the following year he joined the Régiment d'Agenois at Philippsburg (Federal Republic of Germany) with the rank of second lieutenant. At the end of the War of the Polish Succession he was put on half pay and shortly after left the army to study mathematics at Strasbourg and La Fère in France. He arrived in Canada in 1740 as a cadet in the colonial regular troops. Serious and ambitious, Le Mercier began to study engineering and gunnery; in 1743 he was appointed second ensign and was attached to the service of the commissary of artillery, Jean-Baptiste Dupin de Belugard.

When the War of the Austrian Succession spread to America in 1744, Le Mercier found himself in sole charge of the artillery at Quebec. He supervised 500 workmen, having batteries built, setting up defence lines near the Rivière Saint-Charles, and repairing a barrack block. The following year he served as an engineer and artillery officer in the Acadian campaign under Paul Marin* de La Malgue. After the surrender of Louisbourg, Île Royale (Cape Breton Island) in June 1745, he proceeded to Beaubassin (near Amherst, N.S.), which was being used as a rallying point; on the way there he sank a privateering sloop. He then returned to Quebec. At the beginning of 1746 he was ordered by Governor Charles de Beauharnois* to go to Fort Saint-Frédéric (near Crown Point, N.Y.) to help in readying its defences and to take an inventory of its munitions and supplies. During his stay at the fort he discovered the Lac Saint-Sacrement (Lake George) portage and went as far as Fort Lydius (also called Fort Edward; now Fort Edward, N.Y.). He was recalled to Quebec after the spring thaw and left immediately for Acadia with the force that Jean-Baptiste-Nicolas-Roch de RAMEZAY was leading to meet the Duc d'Anville [La Rochefoucauld*]. At the beginning of the following winter he was at Beaubassin, and in February 1747 was one of 300 Canadians and Indians commanded by Nicolas-Antoine Coulon* de Villiers who, in extremely cold weather and after a forced march, successfully attacked a detachment of New Englanders led by Arthur Noble* at Grand Pré, Nova Scotia.

In 1748 Le Mercier was appointed artillery aide. When the war ended, he was sent to France specifically to study artillery drill, the manufacture and casting of artillery pieces, and the basic concepts of defence works, and he subsequently sat an examination. He stayed in several towns and to acquire experience visited some ironworks, including those at Rancogne (dept of Charente) where cannons were cast. At the beginning of 1750 he was promoted lieutenant and put in command of an artillery company, the first such unit to be sent to Canada. From Rochefort he went to the Île de Ré, where he trained his artillery recruits. When he was back in Canada with his company, he made a strong impression on Governor La Jonquière [Taffanel*] because of the discipline he maintained among his gunners and the care he took of the artillery. In 1751 Le Mercier supervised the casting of some 100 guns and a dozen mortars at the Saint-Maurice ironworks at Trois-Rivières, but apparently Intendant BIGOT put an end to the arms production at the ironworks after 1752, for a number of reasons including the lack of specialized master founders.

In 1753 the new governor of the colony, DUQUESNE, who was determined to ensure French supremacy in the Ohio region, organized a major campaign [*see* Paul Marin de La Malgue]. Le Mercier took part in it as an engineer; he was also made responsible for the transport of rations. In April he left Montreal with a small detachment and headed towards Fort Niagara (near Youngstown, N.Y.). During the summer he helped build Fort de la Presqu'île (Erie, Pa) and Fort de la Rivière au Bœuf (Waterford, Pa), which were erected to undercut British claims to the Ohio valley. That year he was promoted captain, but he was not given the cross of the order of Saint-Louis which Duquesne had sought for him. The governor did, however, entrust him with command of engineering and artillery forces in the colony.

The following spring Le Mercier returned to Fort de la Rivière au Bœuf with a force of 360 soldiers and militiamen. He was immediately ordered by Claude-Pierre PÉCAUDY de Contrecœur to dislodge the British who had begun building a fort on the Ohio River. He was successful, and he continued construction of the fort under the name of Fort Duquesne (Pittsburgh, Pa). In early summer an expedition was organized to avenge the death of Joseph Coulon* de Villiers de Jumonville, killed on 28 May 1754 in an ambush set by George Washington. Louis Coulon* de Villiers, Jumonville's brother, led the 500 men, and Le Mercier was made his second in command. They forced Washington and his detachment out of Fort Necessity (near Farmington, Pa), where they had taken refuge, and returned to Fort Duquesne. In the autumn Le Mercier was sent to France to give an account of the operations in which he had participated during the last two campaigns in America. On 15 October he sailed on board the *Parfaite Union*, in company with Bigot, Michel-Jean-Hugues PÉAN, and Péan's wife, Angélique RENAUD d'Avène Des Méloizes.

Le Mercier returned to Quebec in the spring of 1755. In September he took part in the battle at Lac Saint-Sacrement, in the course of which he probably served as adviser to Dieskau* – Montcalm*, who had not witnessed the event, later ventured to say that Le Mercier had "caused M. de Dieskau's defeat and capture." During the French army's retreat Le Mercier had the rear-guard, and with his ten men succeeded in getting out of an ambush laid by 250 British soldiers. The following summer Le Mercier commanded the artillery at the capture of Oswego (Chouaguen), Montcalm's first military operation in New France, and his intrepidity overcame the general's hesitations about the emplacement and laying of the guns. In six hours Montcalm succeeded in bringing about the fall of Oswego with a single battery of nine guns, firing over the parapet, but he never forgave Le Mercier, whom he characterized as "an ignorant and weak man," for having taught him a lesson.

In 1757 the artillery in the colony counted eight officers including Louis-Thomas JACAU de Fiedmont and 180 gunners; Le Mercier was still only a captain, but he received a brevet as artillery commander and a pension of 400 *livres*. That year the king bestowed upon him the cross of the order of Saint-Louis. During February and March 1757 Le Mercier participated in the expedition led by François-Pierre de RIGAUD de Vaudreuil against Fort William Henry (also called Fort George; now Lake George, N.Y.). The attack was called off, but after setting fire to the area around the fort, Rigaud sent Le Mercier to call upon the British commander to surrender. This demand was rejected, however, and the siege was lifted. In May Le Mercier was at

Quebec and was busy assembling men and supplies for Fort Carillon (Ticonderoga, N.Y.), where he went at the end of June. In August he took part in the siege of Fort William Henry. After spending the winter in the colony, he returned to Fort Carillon in the summer of 1758. On 8 July he commanded the artillery and also distributed ammunition and fresh provisions during James ABERCROMBY's attack, which turned into a signal victory for Montcalm. He spent the rest of the year in Montreal and Quebec. His long winter evenings were often passed in the company of Bigot and other members of the Grande Société, with whom he indulged in gambling.

In late March 1759 Le Mercier went to Les Cèdres, upstream from Montreal, to ensure the transport of supplies to Fort Niagara. In April he was in Quebec, where he apparently reported on the measures taken for the defence of the city. During the siege of Quebec he commanded the artillery and was also responsible for distributing supplies to the army which, like the population, was rationed. In addition he had to provide powder and ammunition for some 300 cannon and mortars of different calibres ranged in batteries over ten miles and to see to their security, which was threatened by bombardment and fire. Moreover, Le Mercier constantly had to cope with the confusion of authority, making the best of the orders and counter-orders of Montcalm and Governor Vaudreuil [RIGAUD], of their changes of mood, and above all of their jealousy. On a number of occasions he bore the flag of truce between the governor and Vice-Admiral Charles SAUNDERS. Using well-directed artillery fire on 23 July he prevented several British ships from forcing their way upstream of the city. This action delayed by five weeks the exploit that assured the British of victory. On 9 August, having heard of the fall of Fort Niagara, Vaudreuil sent Le Mercier, with LÉVIS and La Pause [Plantavit*], to complete construction of Fort Lévis (east of Prescott, Ont.). Fiacre-François POTOT de Montbeillard replaced Le Mercier as commander of the artillery.

After the fall of Quebec, Le Mercier went to Montreal, where he looked after provisioning the army. Fearing that Fort de l'Île aux Noix, on the Richelieu River, might be attacked, he went there in October, returning to Montreal after the danger had passed. When he sailed for France on 25 Nov. 1759 on the *Machault*, he was charged with informing the court of the situation and needs of the colony, a mission he performed competently. He found himself, however, among the accused when a commission was set up to deal with the embezzlement that had occurred in the colony before the conquest. Le Mercier was arrested and incarcerated in the Bastille but was cleared of all accusations and released when the decision in the *affaire du Canada* was finally rendered in December 1763. Subsequently he seems to have taken up residence at Lisieux, in Normandy, where he was still living in 1798, well off but completely forgotten.

François-Marc-Antoine Le Mercier did not play a leading role in the drama of the loss of New France. He never held the rank or the power that would have enabled him to effect major changes in either the civil or the military organization and administration of the colony. He certainly profited from the system to make his fortune – Montcalm said in 1759: "This officer, who came out twenty years ago as a simple soldier, will soon be worth about 6 or 700,000 *livres*, perhaps a million, if these things continue." The general did not conceal his dislike of Le Mercier, and he left many unfair statements about him, accusing him of being preoccupied with his finances and neglecting his military obligations. "M. Mercier, who is never anywhere because he is everywhere," he wrote, ". . . perhaps neglects only that which concerns his profession." In reality Le Mercier always tried to carry out to the best of his ability all the responsibilities entrusted to him, but those responsibilities, which were sometimes too numerous, prevented him from devoting himself entirely to his profession as an artillery officer.

JEAN PARISEAU

AN, Col., E, 276 (dossier Le Mercier). Bibliothèque de l'Arsenal, 5769 (papiers du comte d'Argenson), pp.298, 327, 330, 339 (PAC transcripts); Archives de la Bastille, 12128; 12142–48; 12501, ff.74, 78, 96, 115, 130, 138, 169, 174; 12502, ff.4, 18, 23, 29–30, 69, 72, 77, 88, 117bis, 198, 201, 212, 232; 12503, ff.224–25, 227, 231, 237, 242–43, 253, 262; 12504, ff.8, 9, 71, 124, 139, 164, 170, 180, 209, 227, 259; 12506, ff.23, 30, 31, 37, 42, 56, 81, 90. *Coll. des manuscrits de Lévis* (Casgrain). *Doc. relatifs à la monnaie sous le Régime français* (Shortt), II, 894, 896, 898. "Journal du siège de Québec" (Æ. Fauteux), ANQ *Rapport*, 1920–21. Knox, *Hist. journal* (Doughty). [A.-J.-H. de Maurès de Malartic, comte de Malartic], *Journal des campagnes au Canada de 1755 à 1760 . . .*, Gabriel de Maurès de Malartic et Paul Gaffarel, édit. (Dijon, France, 1890). *Mémoires sur le Canada, depuis 1749 jusqu'à 1760*. [Pierre] Pouchot, *Memoir upon the late war in North America, between the French and the English, 1755–60 . . .*, ed. and trans. F. B. Hough (2v., Roxbury, Mass., 1866), I, 23–25, 27–28, 31, 35–36, 46, 65–66, 69, 224.

Æ. Fauteux, *Les chevaliers de Saint-Louis*, 164–65. Le Jeune, *Dictionnaire*. J.-E. Roy, *Rapport sur les archives de France*, 870, 873, 875. Tanguay, *Dictionnaire*. Thomas Chapais, *Le marquis de Montcalm*

(1712–1759) (Québec, 1911), 113, 116, 120, 122–24, 139. Frégault, *François Bigot*, II; *La guerre de la Conquête*. P.-G. Roy, *Les petites choses de notre histoire* (7 sér., Lévis, Qué., 1919–44), 1re sér., 213–16; 3e sér., 273; 7e sér., 135, 193; *La ville de Québec sous le Régime français* (2v., Québec, 1930), II, 289, 385–86. Stanley, *New France*. Tessier, *Les forges Saint-Maurice*. Henri Têtu, "M. Jean-Félix Récher, curé de Québec, et son journal, 1757–1760," *BRH*, IX (1903), 141, 332, 344, 354.

LEMOINE DESPINS, JACQUES-JOSEPH, merchant; b. 15 July 1719 at Boucherville (Que.), son of René-Alexandre Lemoine, *dit* Despins, and Marie-Renée Le Boulanger; d. 16 April 1787 in Montreal.

Jacques-Joseph Lemoine Despins probably acquired his knowledge of business from his family; his father was a merchant, and one of his uncles, Alexis Lemoine*, *dit* Monière, had had great success in the fur trade. In 1743 or 1744 Lemoine Despins went into partnership with Jean-Baptiste-Grégoire Martel de Saint-Antoine, who had just been appointed king's storekeeper in Montreal. This partnership brought him into the king's service as Martel's clerk, and by this means into increasingly lucrative enterprises. On 22 April 1747, when his marriage contract with Marguerite, the daughter of merchant Jean-Baptiste Guillon (Guyon), was signed in Montreal, some ten Montreal merchants were present. The contract indicates that Lemoine Despins possessed 16,000 *livres*, "both in cash and in merchandise," and that he reserved about two-thirds of what he owned as property separate from the joint estate. This unusual clause allowed him to allocate most of his wealth to his business without legal obstacle.

Lemoine Despins quickly prospered in his business dealings. Indeed, in 1748 the commissary of the Marine in Montreal, Jean-Victor VARIN de La Marre, became associated with Despins and Martel. This "important business company" as Madame Bégon [Rocbert*] wrote in December that year, was the exclusive contractor for the king's supplies; it also sold goods retail and had commercial interests in the *pays d'en haut*. Louis PENNISSEAUT, who was a cousin by marriage of Lemoine Despins and a merchant-trader later linked with assistant purveyor François Maurin*, also entered the partnership in 1755. The company lasted until 1757. In 1763, during his trial at the Châtelet in the *affaire du Canada*, Martel declared that it was Lemoine Despins who had administered the partnership.

Lemoine Despins also was involved in the fur trade. In 1751 and 1752 he hired some voyageurs and in the autumn of 1752 went into partnership with Louis de La Corne* to operate the *poste de l'Ouest*. Subsequently he had a share in the fur trade at Detroit, and from 1755 at Fort Témiscamingue (near Ville-Marie, Que.).

His first wife having died in 1752, Lemoine Despins remarried in Quebec on 6 Nov. 1755; his second wife was Madame Bégon's niece, Marguerite-Charlotte, daughter of Louis-Joseph Rocbert de La Morandière, who had been storekeeper in Montreal. Lemoine Despins had had two sons by his first marriage, Jacques-Alexis and Jean-Baptiste, who on their mother's death were entitled to half their parents' estate. Thus Lemoine Despins had an inventory made of his property in September 1756 which reveals the extent of his commercial interests. The furnishings of his house seem modest, but the goods stocked in the vault, the warehouse, and the courtyard, belonging to the partnership that Lemoine Despins ran for Martel and Varin, were valued at more than 100,000 *livres*; the moneys owing to the partnership amounted to about 200,000 *livres* and the debts to only 30,000 *livres*. It is difficult to know what belonged to Lemoine Despins in his own right, but in addition to the partnership's business he certainly had personal business interests; he owned a bakery and shares in a schooner, and he had a correspondent in Quebec, the merchant Jacques PERRAULT, who owed him 50,000 *livres*.

At the end of 1756 Lemoine Despins signed a contract with purveyor Joseph-Michel CADET to enter "the service of the king." Martel later wrote that "for economy's sake the Sieur Lemoine had been charged with furnishing all the flour, salt pork, and peas to the armed forces and with the general victualling of the forts; these supplies were enormous," and Martel accused Lemoine Despins of having falsified invoices. In 1758 Lemoine Despins asked Jacques Perrault to "include in the expenditures those for whom this [would be] advantageous." These unsavoury practices and the resulting profits were resented in Montreal.

After the conquest Lemoine Despins's name was on the list of those charged in the *affaire du Canada*, but when the judgement was rendered it simply declared "that there will be a further inquiry into the facts mentioned in the trial." According to Pierre-Georges Roy*, Lemoine Despins went to England in 1765 and then to France where he obtained letters of rehabilitation before returning to Canada. Whether or not this is so, Lemoine Despins seems to have had little difficulty in starting up in business again under the British régime. He was put in contact with the merchants Daniel and Antoine Vialars in London, who often acted as suppliers to Canadian traders, and with whom he did business through Jacques Perrault in Quebec. He seems to have remained in business until his death. When his sons came of age, he gave them their share of their mother's estate, 60,000 *livres* to each. They received merchandise, real estate, and funds which enabled them to form a company for "trade in merchandise suitable to this country." Lemoine Despins had little to do with politics under the new régime. At the request of the citizens of Quebec in 1765, he did, however, secure the nomination of eight representatives from Montreal "to be present at Quebec when a general assembly for the common good is convoked." On the advice of his correspondent Perrault, he had acted unobtrusively. In 1775 he helped carry out defence preparations before the Americans reached Montreal.

In the course of his career Lemoine Despins, like several other merchants, had been a churchwarden and a militia captain. Using his family and business connections, he acquired substantial wealth, more through questionable privileges than by honest trade; this route to success set him apart from most of the Montreal merchants.

José E. Igartua

AN, Col., E, 276 (dossier Le Mercier). ANQ-M, État civil, Catholiques, Notre-Dame de Montréal, 16 juill. 1719, 24 avril 1747, 17 avril 1787; Greffe de J.-B. Adhémar, 9 mars 1752, 17 juin, 8 juill., 2 oct. 1753; Greffe de L.-C. Danré de Blanzy, 22 avril 1747, 28 sept. 1756, 22 mai 1759; Greffe de Pierre Panet, 24 sept. 1757, 13 juill. 1763, 25 mai, 7 juill., 14 nov. 1764, 7 juin, 20 sept. 1765, 27 avril 1767, 30 avril, 23 juill., 25 oct., 15 nov. 1768, 11 sept. 1769, 10 nov. 1770, 21 sept. 1771, 19 mai 1772; Greffe de François Simonnet, 6 déc. 1754. ANQ-Q, État civil, Catholiques, Notre-Dame de Québec, 6 nov. 1755; Greffe de Claude Barolet, 5 nov. 1755. PAC, MG 18, H50.

Bégon, "Correspondance" (Bonnault), ANQ *Rapport*, 1934–35, 17, 176. J.-B.-J. Élie de Beaumont, *Observations sur les profits prétendus indument faits par la société Lemoine des Pins, Martel & Varin* (Paris, 1763). "État général des billets d'ordonnances . . . ," ANQ *Rapport*, 1924–25, 246–342. [J.-B. Martel de Saint-Antoine], *Mémoire pour Jean-Baptiste Martel, écuyer, ci-devant garde des magasins du roi à Montréal* (Paris, 1763). *Mémoires sur le Canada, depuis 1749 jusqu'à 1760*. *Quebec Gazette*, 8, 29 Dec. 1766, 1 Sept. 1768, 19 Dec. 1771, 12 March 1772, 8 Jan., 28 Nov. 1778, 29 April 1779, 18 May, 15 June 1780, 17 May 1781, 20 June 1782, 31 March, 12 May 1785, 29 June, 19 Oct. 1786. "Marguilliers de la paroisse de Notre-Dame de Ville-Marie de 1657 à 1913," *BRH*, XIX (1913), 279. É.-Z. Massicotte, "Inventaire des actes de foi et hommage conservés aux Archives judiciaires de Montréal," ANQ *Rapport*, 1921–22, 105; "Répertoire des engagements pour l'Ouest," ANQ *Rapport*, 1930–31, 421, 426, 429, 443; 1931–32, 330, 337–40, 360. J.-E. Roy, *Rapport sur les archives de France*, 871, 875. Tanguay, *Dictionnaire*. Frégault, *François Bigot*, II, 86, 89–91. P.-G. Roy, *Bigot et sa bande*, 163–68. Jacques Mathieu, "Un négociant de Québec à l'époque de la Conquête: Jacques Perrault l'aîné," ANQ *Rapport*, 1970, 46, 56, 80.

LEMOINE DESPINS, MARGUERITE-THÉRÈSE, superior of the Sisters of Charity (Grey Nuns) of the Hôpital Général of Montreal; b. 23 March 1722 at Boucherville, near Montreal (Que.), daughter of René-Alexandre Lemoine, *dit* Despins, and Marie-Renée Le Boulanger; d. 6 June 1792 in Montreal.

Marguerite-Thérèse Lemoine Despins received a careful upbringing. After her mother's death, she was entrusted, at her own request, to the care of Madame d'Youville [Dufrost], who took her into the Grey Nuns' house as a boarder on 2 July 1739. She thus observed from within the growth of both the community and the charitable work with which she would become associated 12 years later.

On 2 July 1751 she was admitted as the first regular novice of the Grey Nuns and the same day was entrusted with the office of mistress of novices. For 20 years she worked closely with her companions, sparing neither health nor fortune to establish securely the work to which she was devoted. It was, in fact, her inherited wealth that enabled the community to purchase the seigneury of Châteauguay during Madame d'Youville's administration.

On 27 Dec. 1771, a few days after the founder's death, Sister Despins was chosen by the community as superior. The 30 years she had spent at Madame d'Youville's side had prepared her well for this task: while still young she had been initiated into the spiritual practices dear to the founder, and perhaps more than anyone else she was aware of the spirit of charity which Madame d'Youville wanted to instil into her community. In addition for 20 years she had taken an active part in the community's administration.

As soon as she had assumed office, Sister Despins entrusted responsibility for the temporal affairs of the house to Thérèse-Geneviève Coutlée* as bursar; she devoted her own attention to bringing the projects left unfinished by Madame d'Youville to a successful conclusion. She resolved the problems raised by the Indians at Sault-Saint-Louis (Caughnawaga), who were claiming part of the seigneury of Châteauguay, by coming to an arrangement with the government whereby the community ceded to the Indians 16 *arpents* of land in return for the government's cancellation of the *droit de quint*, which the nuns had not yet paid; she also had the manor house at Île Saint-Bernard rebuilt. In addition she took steps to ensure that the rules, constitutions, and dress of the community were laid down more precisely; in 1781 Étienne MONTGOLFIER completed a draft collection of rules and constitutions. Under her administration the sisters continued their charitable assistance to the poor and the underprivileged, and they diversified their sources of income to ensure provision for their pensioners.

Sister Despins was known as the soul of gentleness and kindness and these qualities marked her administration. The peace of her final years was disturbed by pain and suffering; at the beginning of 1792 her illness worsened, and she died some months later.

CLAUDETTE LACELLE

ASGM, Corr. générale, Supérieures, II; Maison mère, Historique; Mère Despins, Personnel. A. Fauteux et Drouin, *L'Hôpital Général de Montréal*, I.

LE MOYNE DE LONGUEUIL, PAUL-JOSEPH, known as the **Chevalier de Longueuil**, seigneur, officer in the colonial regular troops, and governor of Trois-Rivières; b. 17 Sept. 1701 at Longueuil (Que.), son of Charles Le Moyne* de Longueuil, first Baron de Longueuil, and Claude-Élisabeth Souart d'Adoucourt; d. 12 May 1778 at Port-Louis, France.

Paul-Joseph Le Moyne de Longueuil was a member of a family with a strong military tradition and close connections to the Indian nations. He apparently spent much of his early life amongst the Iroquois, was accepted by them as a blood-brother, and spoke their language. This association, coupled with his family's important social and political position within the colony's administrative and military élite, shaped the course of his life.

He began his military career in France in 1717, and by 1719 was a lieutenant in the Régiment de Normandie. He returned to Canada only in 1726 when, in quick succession, he was made a lieutenant in the colonial regular troops, commandant at Fort Frontenac (Kingston, Ont.), and in 1727 captain of his own company. These rapid promotions were doubtless aided as much by his father's position as governor of Montreal as by his own qualities. But his military capabilities were soon tested, for in 1728, after having been replaced as commandant at Fort Frontenac by the elderly René Legardeur* de Beauvais, he was ordered west under Constant Le Marchand* de Lignery in the unsuccessful campaign against the Foxes. He apparently led a party of Iroquois from Lac-des-Deux-Montagnes (Oka) against the Foxes in 1730; during this fighting he may have been wounded, for an ailing "M. de Longueuil" travelled to France in the autumn of that year, and on a document dated 1739 an anonymous hand notes that Longueuil "is able to serve usefully," as if he had not been so earlier.

Whatever the reasons, Longueuil seems to have attended more to his personal affairs than to his military career during the 1730s. On 19 Oct. 1728 he had married Marie-Geneviève Joybert de Soulanges, and they were to have 11 children, only four of whom survived infancy. Through this marriage he acquired an interest in the seigneuries of L'Islet-du-Portage, Pointe-à-l'Orignal on the Ottawa River, and Soulanges, to the latter of which he added in 1733 lands originally conceded to Gabriel and Pierre Hénault. The following year he was granted the seigneury of Nouvelle-Longueuil, the westernmost seigneury conceded on the St Lawrence before the conquest.

Longueuil was recalled to military activity in 1739 and was posted commandant at Fort Saint-Frédéric (near Crown Point, N.Y.), but by September 1740 he was replaced there. In 1743 he succeeded Pierre-Joseph Céloron* de Blainville as commandant at Detroit, a post which Governor Beauharnois* and Intendant Gilles HOCQUART considered a reward for officers having distinguished themselves in the service, and he remained there for the following six eventful years. Detroit played a major part in Canada's system of western Indian alliances because it serviced the fur trade to the west and south. Both the British and the French employed the trade to use the Indian tribes for their own ends: the French to drive out encroaching British traders and settlers, and the British to break the French hegemony in the interior. During Longueuil's service at Detroit the War of the Austrian Succession was exacerbating French difficulties in the west, for British naval successes on the Atlantic and local war requirements led to scarcities of merchandise and munitions among Canadian traders, at once creating discontent among the Indians and depriving the French of the means of defence.

In 1744 Longueuil frustrated a developing Indian conspiracy against the French [*see* NISSOWAQUET], and the following year he noted that the Indians around Detroit were quietly leaving the region. During 1746 British traders, intent on fomenting an uprising, increased their intrigues and the crisis came in the spring of 1747 with a plan by several tribes to kill the Detroit garrison and settlers. When their intention was revealed to

Longueuil by a Huron woman, he called all settlers to the fort, and then revealed his knowledge of the affair to the Indians. For the entire summer the settlers ventured no great distance from the fort and no crops were planted; buildings in the vicinity were burned and cattle slaughtered as the Hurons under Orontony*, with the encouragement of Mikinak*, revolted against the French. Elsewhere the situation was equally grave: in the spring five Frenchmen had been killed at Sandusky (Ohio) and there had been a rising at Michilimackinac (Mackinaw City, Mich.). Longueuil's position was strengthened in September by the arrival of a convoy with troops, but the food, military supplies, and trade goods it brought were barely sufficient for the winter. He immediately reinforced the detachments at Fort Saint-Joseph (Niles, Mich.), Ouiatanon (near Lafayette, Ind.), and in the Illinois country. One tribe after another sent delegations to negotiate a pardon and a peace. Longueuil, preferring a policy of conciliation to that of exemplary punishment advocated from Quebec, released a number of Indian prisoners. He was subsequently censured by the government for this action, but his policy was undoubtedly wise. Although isolated incidents occurred to the west throughout the winter, at a general conference held at Detroit in April 1748 the Ottawas, Potawatomis, Hurons, and Ojibwas returned to French allegiance. The arrival in the summer of another convoy with abundant supplies sealed the issue.

During Longueuil's tenure as commandant at Detroit it seems probable that he was involved privately in the fur trade, even though Beauharnois and Hocquart wrote circumspectly in 1744 that they had not been informed whether this was so. About 1725 the king seems to have granted to the commanders at forts Frontenac and Niagara (near Youngstown, N.Y.), as well as at Detroit and Michilimackinac, the exclusive right to buy and sell furs in the *pays d'en haut* in hopes that the ties thus established between the officers and the Indians would facilitate the control of the tribes. This privilege would have been very lucrative, but it is not known if it was still valid when Longueuil was in command at Detroit. Longueuil's seigneuries of Nouvelle-Longueuil, Pointe-à-l'Orignal, and Soulanges were all located on the fur trade routes to the west, and in 1750, after his return to Quebec from Detroit, he was granted land, which was probably used as a trading counter, near the Ottawa village opposite Detroit. He was said to have a number of *engagés* working for him in various posts.

Longueuil's tenure at Detroit had been extended beyond that expected by the imperial authorities; he had been appointed town major of Quebec in 1748, and in 1749, before his return in the summer from the *pays d'en haut*, he was named king's lieutenant. After Detroit, his term as king's lieutenant in Quebec appears relatively uneventful. In 1754, however, he commanded the Iroquois on Claude-Pierre PÉCAUDY de Contrecœur's Ohio valley expedition, and three years later he was second in command to François-Pierre de RIGAUD de Vaudreuil and at the head of the Indians who covered the flanks in the attack on Fort George (also called Fort William Henry; now Lake George, N.Y.). He was also given more administrative duties: on 1 May 1757 he became governor of Trois-Rivières, although he does not appear to have taken up his position until later. In 1758 Governor Vaudreuil [RIGAUD] planned to send a small army in the direction of Corlaer (Schenectady, N.Y.) to contain the Six Nations Confederacy, or if possible gain their support, but when he discovered the extent of British preparations to attack Fort Carillon (Ticonderoga, N.Y.), most of the troops were diverted there. However, Longueuil was sent in July at the head of a small force which included Gaspard-Joseph CHAUSSEGROS de Léry and 300 soldiers on a diplomatic mission to Cataraqui (Kingston, Ont.) and Chouaguen (Oswego; today Oswego, N.Y.) to induce the Iroquois to support the French. This expedition was his last major operation for in 1759 and 1760 he devoted his energies to preparing for the defence of Trois-Rivières. However, when Brigadier-General James MURRAY finally led the British expedition upriver from Quebec in July 1760, he bypassed Trois-Rivières and proceeded directly to Montreal, the capture of which brought the end of hostilities.

In conformity with article 16 of the capitulation at Montreal, in which he was specifically mentioned, Longueuil was transported to France. He was placed in charge of the Canadian officers in the province of Touraine, and in 1764 he received permission to return to Canada to settle his affairs and persuade his family to go to France. Although in September he sold to Gabriel CHRISTIE the seigneury of L'Islet-du-Portage, he left Canada for the last time in September 1766 without having completely settled his affairs, and without his family. Longueuil spent the remainder of his life at Tours, France, but died at Port-Louis aged and infirm on 12 May 1778. The seigneuries of Soulanges, Pointe-à-l'Orignal, and Nouvelle-Longueuil passed to his son Joseph-Dominique-Emmanuel*.

Longueuil's superiors often praised him as an intelligent, energetic, and capable officer. On 24 April 1744, while at Detroit, he had been awarded the cross of Saint-Louis, and then was given the exceptional privilege of wearing the decoration before being officially received into the order. He was sufficiently fit to undertake an arduous mid-winter campaign even in his late fifties, and his abilities in Indian diplomacy were tested on several occasions. At the height of western Indian risings in 1747 Beauharnois and Hocquart wrote that "we have great confidence in the adroitness of this officer to place the [Indian] nations again in our interest." A decade later Governor Vaudreuil wrote that he "is generally liked, especially by the Indian nations." He had probably had fur trade and other mercantile interests and had acquired in Canada four seigneuries and urban land holdings as well as investments, possibly in life annuities, in France. Longueuil's military and administrative career was almost foreordained by his family's position in Canada, and through his personal talents and interests he was able to continue its tradition of public service coupled with private gain.

ANDREW RODGER

AN, Col., B, 50, f.492v; 51, f.522; 115, f.137; C[11A], 53, p.107; 81, f.12; 89, p.219; 93, pp.121–23, 161; 103, p.159; 104, pp.128, 163; 116, f.157v; D[2C], 2, pp.36–37, 48–50; 4, p.30; 47, ff.7, 529; 48, f.36v; 49, f.350; 57, ff.100v, 117; 61, ff.87v, 102v; 222 (page references are to PAC transcripts); E, 203 (dossier Germaine); 290 (dossier Le Moyne de Longueuil). ANQ-M, État civil, Catholiques, Saint-Antoine (Longueuil), 19 sept. 1701. ANQ-Q, État civil, Catholiques, Notre-Dame de Québec, 19 oct. 1728. PAC, MG 8, F113. *Coll. des manuscrits de Lévis* (Casgrain), VII, 172; XI, 74, 77, 79. "The French regime in Wisconsin – III," ed. R. G. Thwaites, Wis., State Hist. Soc., *Coll.*, XVIII (1908), 38. *JR* (Thwaites), LXIX, 258. *NYCD* (O'Callaghan and Fernow), IX, 1099–100; X, 83–86, 115–16, 118–19, 128, 138–41, 145, 148–51, 156, 161–63, 169, 450–51. *The Windsor border region, Canada's southernmost frontier . . .*, ed. E. J. Lajeunesse (Toronto, 1960), lxix, 40.

[F.-M.] Bibaud, *Dictionnaire historique des hommes illustres du Canada et de l'Amérique* (Montréal, 1857), 159–60. Æ. Fauteux, *Les chevaliers de Saint-Louis*, 139–40. Le Jeune, *Dictionnaire*. P.-G. Roy, *Inv. concessions*, II, 143; IV, 176, 273. Tanguay, *Dictionnaire*. N. W. Caldwell, *The French in the Mississippi valley, 1740–1750* (Urbana, Ill., 1941; repr. Philadelphia, 1974), 86–100. Alexandre Jodoin et J.-L. Vincent, *Histoire de Longueuil et de la famille de Longueuil . . .* (Montréal, 1889), 250–53. C. M. Burton, "Detroit rulers: French commandants in this region from 1701 to 1760," *Michigan Pioneer Coll.*, XXXIV (1905), 334. P.-G. Roy, "Les commandants du fort Saint-Frédéric," *BRH*, LI (1945), 324.

LE NORMANT DE MÉZY, SÉBASTIEN-FRANÇOIS-ANGE (he signed **Lenormant Demesi**), colonial official; b. 20 Nov. 1702 in Dunkerque, France, eldest son of Jacques-Ange Le Normant* de Mézy and Anne-Marie Debrier; d. 3 Feb. 1791 at Paris.

Sébastien-François-Ange Le Normant de Mézy belonged to a family of lesser royal servants that had begun to achieve recognition during the reign of Louis XIV, and his career was to reflect its traditional loyalties and associations. When his father came to Louisbourg, Île Royale (Cape Breton Island), in 1719 as financial commissary, Le Normant accompanied him and served unofficially in Mézy's office, mastering the rudiments of colonial administration. Late in 1721 Le Normant carried official dispatches to France and acted as his father's emissary to the council of Marine. He returned in 1722 as a scrivener in the Marine, responsible for maintaining lists of Louisbourg land grants, keeping the rolls for naval conscription, and preparing detailed fishing and trade reports.

In 1724 Mézy appointed Le Normant to settle judicial disputes in outlying areas; at the same time he charged him with preparing a census of the fishing settlements and inspecting soldiers on detached duty. Mézy's lax administration having been criticized by Maurepas, the secretary of state for the Marine, Le Normant sailed later that year to France to present his father's defence. He returned to Louisbourg in 1725 as a member of the Conseil Supérieur, a mark of favour from Maurepas who regarded the son with approval in spite of his displeasure with the father. In 1728 Le Normant became chief scrivener, the second ranking civil administrative officer in the colony. To his previous responsibilities were added the maintenance of the garrison muster rolls and supervision of the general stores. By this time his father, whose career was in serious jeopardy, was chiefly occupied in reviewing and completing his financial records, and Le Normant gradually assumed control of the daily operation of colonial government. When Mézy was recalled to France in 1729 to explain his administration, Le Normant was empowered to authorize royal expenditure (*ordonnancement*). Mézy returned to Île Royale only briefly, and during the early 1730s Le Normant's authority was challenged by rumours impugning his father's rectitude, by his own youth, and by the fact that, though he exercised the powers of financial commissary, he did not have the position. His father was not retired until 1733, and even then there seems to have been some reluctance to appoint a young man who had never served in France. With no one willing to accept a post in unpopular Louisbourg, Le Normant remained in his ambiguous position until 1734 when he sailed to France. The following year he returned with his commissions as financial commissary and first councillor of the Conseil Supérieur.

Le Normant's years at Louisbourg, like his father's, were marked by quarrels with Governor Saint-Ovide [Monbeton*], who had never learned to share authority with civil officials. As early as 1728 the two had come into conflict over Le Normant's newly assumed duty to keep the muster rolls. While Saint-Ovide was in France from 1729 to 1731, Le Normant also clashed with the interim governor, François Le Coutre* de Bourville, who exploited the ambiguity of Le Normant's position to oblige the younger man to defer to him. After 1731 Saint-Ovide once again led the attacks on Le Normant's authority and initiated attempts to have him replaced. It has been suggested that Le Normant's difficulties were the inheritance of his father's conflicts with the governor, but Le Normant made these conflicts his own, defending his jurisdiction with granite-like resistance, and the quarrels usually ended in his favour. Both Saint-Ovide and Bourville received ministerial rebukes for their pretensions as did Le Normant on one occasion in 1737.

The frustrations of Le Normant's position were undoubtedly exacerbated by the difficult economic climate of the 1730s, when the weakness of Louisbourg's economic base – fishing, trade, and the artificial support of government expenditures on fortress construction – was underscored by progressively more serious food shortages. Fishing, the mainstay of the economy, had worked against the development of agriculture because the seasonal demands of both on available labour were coincidental. Though its population was small, the colony was unable to feed itself. After 1731, moreover, the expenditures on fortress construction, which provided temporary cash circulation and facilitated local commerce before profits drained back to France, were reduced by about ten per cent from the average outlay of the previous seven years. More significant was the decline in the cod fishery. The outport fisheries had peaked between 1729 and 1733, but the total value of the Île Royale fishery declined rapidly after the latter date. At the same time. local food shortages, high wages for fishermen at Île Royale, and poor European market conditions led French outfitters to reduce the number of ships sent to the colony. Île Royale came increasingly under the sway of New England merchants, who revolutionized earlier transatlantic trading patterns based on metropolitan supply. Le Normant pointed out to the minister of Marine that economic conditions made the application of French mercantilist trade restrictions unrealistic, and during his term of office Louisbourg became more of a free port than before.

The contraction of the fishery was Le Normant's most serious economic problem and, although there was little he could do about it, his concern was expressed in several perceptive analyses of the situation. Confronted in 1738 with the petition of the Louisbourg merchants accusing him of supporting the monopolistic commercial practices of François Du Pont Duvivier and his brother Michel Du Pont de Gourville, Le Normant (on leave in France) replied in a blistering report which revealed both his understanding of the fishery and his contempt for the colonists, whom he described as "ignorant, without order in their business, susceptible to an ardent desire for gain but unable to take suitable measures, and without industry but capable of artifice." He argued that the colony's under-capitalization and the fishery's low profit margin could be remedied by resorting to the oligopolistic structures of the Canadian fur trade. But local merchants, he claimed, resisted attempts to supervise or regulate their customary commercial practices, which included debauching their fishermen and domestics with drink on credit and avoiding their metropolitan creditors under special protection against seizure for debt.

The merchants' charges of favouritism combined with revelations of other irregularities led the minister to make major changes in the Louisbourg administration in the late 1730s. The case against Saint-Ovide had been building up over a number of years and it was decided to retire him. While in France in 1738 Le Normant learned that he himself would be posted elsewhere. From a personal point of view, his years at Louisbourg had been difficult, darkened by persistent rumours of his father's malfeasance, embittered by defamatory attacks from the authoritarian and hot-tempered Recollet Zacharie Caradec, and complicated by the quarrels instigated by Saint-Ovide. Professionally, however, they provided a good foundation for a career that was just beginning. Within the limitations imposed by economic conditions beyond his control, Le Normant had served the colony well, as his successor François Bigot testified. Learning from his father's mistakes, he had transformed the colony's fiscal records into models of exactness, and his acute analyses of the changes in its trade and fishery later became the basis of government policy. The clarity of his reports and the accuracy of his accounts attracted the favourable attention of Maurepas. Perhaps more important, however, his years at Louisbourg had given him a familiarity with all aspects of colonial administration and constituted a unique apprenticeship for Marine service elsewhere. Le Normant had learned from his conflicts to check his own unruly temper, to maintain a glacial calm before provocation, and to moderate his own grievances when corresponding with the secretary of state for the Marine.

In April 1739 Le Normant was appointed financial commissary at Cap-Français (Cap-Haïtien) on the island of Saint-Domingue (Hispaniola), and he left for the colony that autumn. He had been chosen because Maurepas needed an administrator of sufficient ability, experience, and ruthlessness to force several of the colony's former financial officials to disgorge over two million *livres* in unpaid accounts. His four years at Cap-Français were notable for the harmony between him and the district governor and for his smooth relations with the island's intendant.

In 1744, his difficult task at Saint-Domingue near completion, Le Normant was promoted commissary general and appointed *ordonnateur* of Louisiana. He arrived at New Orleans in October 1744 with harsh royal instructions for the even more difficult task of liquidating the inflated paper currency that was destroying confidence in Louisiana's economy. By now an experienced ministerial hatchet man, Le Normant ruthlessly implemented the Draconian measures with no special consideration for the difficulties Governor Vaudreuil [RIGAUD] was having as a result of an inflammable Indian situation in the lower Mississippi valley and the renewal of Anglo-French hostilities. In fact, an angry Vaudreuil learned of the measures only after they had been promulgated in the Conseil Supérieur on 2 Jan. 1745. His attitude toward military governors having been shaped at Louisbourg, Le Normant probably enjoyed Vaudreuil's discomfort and certainly ignored his ire. By March he had confiscated 850,000 *livres*, and six months later he reported only 5,000 *livres* outstanding. In spite of promises that he would succeed to the intendancy of Saint-Domingue, the minister was unable to secure a replacement for him in Louisiana during the war and he was forced to remain there until the spring of 1748. He then returned to Cap-Français for little more than a year before being appointed intendant of Rochefort. He took up his new position in May 1750.

Le Normant's major effort at Rochefort was the reorganization of the arsenal. During his four years there, he increased its personnel, rebuilt long neglected facilities, and vastly expanded its shipbuilding and armament capability. In Paris between August and December 1751, and for most of 1753, he acted as a confidential adviser to Rouillé, the minister of Marine, who recognized his administrative talents. Promoted intendant of naval forces in 1754, he took up the post in October under the new minister, Machault. For years this position had been honorary, but the coming of war and changes within the ministry probably led to the appointment of someone with Le Normant's administrative abilities. His new post, which he continued to hold under Machault's successor, Peirenc, was largely advisory and few records of his duties or activities exist.

His own ability was probably as important a consideration as the influence of Mme de Pompadour, to whom he was distantly related by marriage, when in June 1758 he was made intendant general of the Marine (the equivalent of deputy minister). The office was designed for Le Normant because the new secretary of state and titular head of the Marine, Massiac, was the first member of the nobility of the sword to hold the charge and was unwilling to act as an administrator. During the next five months Le Normant attended to the daily administration of the ministry. He had little to do with the conduct of military and naval operations, but the fall of Louisbourg, the loss of the island of Gorée (off the coast of Senegal), British attacks along the Brittany coast, and France's deteriorating performance in the naval war, as well as internecine struggles within the Marine, all demanded a scapegoat. At the end of October both Le Normant and Massiac were removed from their posts. Le Normant departed with the honorary office of state councillor, the crowning achievement of an intendant's career. He was allowed to keep his rank for life and was granted an annual pension of 20,000 *livres*.

Le Normant was married twice. His first marriage, in January 1744 to Élisabeth Letellier, *née* Lescoffier, a wealthy widow at Cap-Français, provided the basis for his wealth. She owned, in whole or in part, two plantations. In 1745 the intendant of Saint-Domingue remarked to Maurepas that the marriage of Le Normant's cousin was "one of the most advantageous marriages there has [ever] been in this colony and which matched that of M. Le Normant." Le Normant may have acquired another plantation during his stay in Saint-Domingue in 1748–49.

Élisabeth Le Normant died in 1754 and on 5 May 1760 Le Normant married Marie-Louise-Augustine de Salignac de La Mothe-Fénelon, great-niece of the famous archbishop of Cambrai, François de Salignac de La Mothe-Fénelon. This marriage was the reverse of his first; he used his wealth to buy his way into an old, eminent, but poor, noble family. In 1760 Le Normant owned property and assets worth half a million *livres* in France and three plantations, with 500 slaves, worth an estimated two million *livres* in Saint-Domingue. He built his subsequent fortune in the usual way of an absentee planter by milking his plantations and putting the income into French lands and other investments. In retirement he lived the life of a wealthy Parisian *rentier*, accumulating nearly one million *livres*' worth of land in the Soissonnais and placing at least another million in perpetual annuities with the royal house of Orléans. At his death in the midst of the French revolution he still owned his plantations, and his French assets had grown to more than three million *livres*.

Zealous, ambitious, and intelligent, Sébastien-François-Ange Le Normant de Mézy was a ruthless defender of his class, his service, and his conception of his role under the monarch. Though a Marine rather than a royal provincial intendant, he was thoroughly imbued with the attributes and prejudices of his counterparts, who saw themselves as the king's most loyal servants. His scrupulous implementation of royal instructions and his vigorous defence of the prerogatives of his office illustrate his own dictum that the "intendant . . . is the king's man and reliable agent."

JAMES S. PRITCHARD

[Ministerial correspondence sent to Le Normant is found chiefly in AN, Col., B, and AN, Marine, B[2]. His personal dossier is contained in AN, Marine, C[7], 180. His official correspondence is in three colonial series: AN, Col., C[11B] (Louisbourg), 4–21 (his response to the 1738 petition is in vol.21, ff.297–304v); C[9A] (Saint-Domingue), 49–65; and C[13A] (Louisiana), 28–32. Notice of his marriages is given in AN, Minutier central, LXVIII, no.474, and CXIX, no.509. The originals of some of his dispatches are in AN, Marine, B[3], but the most complete collection is in Archives maritimes, Port de Rochefort (France), 1E, 379–82. Among several important documents in the BN, two deserve mention: MSS, Coll. Joly de Fleury, 1726, and MSS, NAF 126. For his later life, evidence is widely scattered through several registers in AN, Minutier central. J.S.P.]

LE POUPET DE LA BOULARDERIE, ANTOINE, officer in the French regular and colonial regular troops, colonizer, and colonial official; b. 23 Aug. 1705 at Port-Royal (Annapolis Royal, N.S.), son of Louis-Simon Le Poupet* de La Boularderie and Madeleine Melançon; m. Éléonore-Jeanne de Beaugny (Beaunier), and they had six sons; d. at Paris on or about 16 Sept. 1771, the day on which his pension was stopped.

Good family connections are implied by Antoine Le Poupet de La Boularderie's early position as a page to the Duc d'Orléans and his entry on 1 Jan. 1724 into the Régiment de Richelieu, in which he attained the rank of captain. La Boularderie appears to have sold his company for financial reasons prior to his father's death in 1738. At that time he inherited a non-seigneurial but noble concession (*en franc alleu noble*) at Île de Verderonne (Boularderie Island, N.S.) and a fishery at Niganiche (Ingonish); by royal brevets of 1 March 1739 he also succeeded to his father's local military command of Port d'Orléans (North Bay Ingonish), Île de Verderonne, and the east shore of La Petite Brador (Little Bras d'Or) passage. It was characteristic of the *ancien régime* that a costly function such as the commandant's would be undertaken by a private party in return for an economic advantage such as the concession. The command involved maintaining law and order, and his authority, although not extending to colonial officers, caused concern at Louisbourg.

La Boularderie went to Île Royale (Cape Breton Island), a young man with both military and courtier experience and highly placed protectors, notably the Duc de Richelieu. According to La Boularderie's own account, he "conveyed farmers from Normandy, workers, and all the necessary tools for farming. I had twenty-five people in my service for eight years. . . ." He was improving his father's estate when the War of the Austrian Succession diverted his attention from private affairs. In 1744 he served in the capture of Canso [*see* François DU PONT Duvivier] and in 1745 in the defence of Louisbourg [*see* Pierre Morpain* and Louis DU PONT Duchambon]. Taken prisoner, he was sent to Boston for three months. For the remainder of the war, he served as a half-pay captain in Canada. In 1749, holding the same rank, La Boularderie was a member of the force that repossessed Louisbourg, where he served until the end of August 1750. His estate had been completely destroyed by "French freebooters and Indians" while Île Royale was in English hands and he now proceeded to rebuild it on a modest scale.

Official correspondence of this period includes many references to the poverty of the La Boularderies. They were the recipients of some gratuities from the ministry of Marine, and local officials apparently built them a house, either at Louisbourg or La Petite Brador. The capture of Île Royale by British forces in 1758 completed La Boularderie's ruin. A visit to England in 1758 failed to secure indemnification for his lost estates, and in 1759 he returned to France for good.

Testimonials in La Boularderie's Marine department dossier from every stage of his intermittent military career indicate he was a capable and courageous officer, and his conduct at the time of his capture in 1745 even earned him the esteem of the enemy. When he left Boston the authorities gave him a certificate stating that he "conducted himself very well and as a gentleman with the approval of the government and was also of great service to the French prisoners." Yet in spite of Richelieu's intervention and a good service record, La Boularderie did not receive a promotion. On 12 Aug. 1760 Louis XV conferred upon him the cross of Saint-Louis, although he seems to have been motivated as much by La Boularderie's sufferings as by his military record.

The *ancien régime* saw La Boularderie as a gentleman. That he could not handle his money and in 1764 became hopelessly indebted to the inns of Versailles was regarded as – indeed was – a natural consequence of his class. A paternal government simply paid his bills and exiled him to the provinces, where he could live on his pension. But La Boularderie got no farther than Paris, where he was fortunate in finding a protector, the Princesse de Courtenay, Marquise de Bauffremont (Beauffremont), who fed and housed him. After her death in 1768, he lived from hand to mouth, dying like a pauper in the Paris hospital of the Frères de Saint-Jean-de-Dieu. From his many supplications to the minister of Marine, couched in the whimpering style then regarded proper in addressing a superior with favours to grant, there emerges a pathetic picture of him in his last years: "covered with wounds, deeply attacked by the stone which torments me cruelly, an ulcer on my leg resulting a long time ago from a cannonball explosion . . . my eyesight is suffering, my linen was stolen during my illness, for three years I have had the same black suit on my body."

Antoine's wife, who also found her Marine pension inadequate, lived all the while in a convent at Niort. There is evidence of their estrangement as early as 1751, when he turned over to her the fishery at Niganiche, she promising to demand nothing more from him "for any reason." After his death, she moved to Tours, complaining of her poverty in a series of letters to Marine officials, the last of which is dated 1784.

DALE MIQUELON

AN, Col., B, 68, f.27; 70, ff.7, 32; 71, f.7; 72, ff.20–21; 78, f.15; 80, f.44; 89, ff.30, 63; 90, f.66; 94, f.4; 110, ff.208, 279½; 112, f.93½; 118, f.197; 130, f.88; 149, f.432; C[11B], 20, ff.60, 118, 137; 21, f.307; 22, ff.31, 49, 274; 23, ff.21, 37, 225; 28, ff.38, 73; 33, f.97; E, 240 (dossier Antoine Le Poupet de La Boularderie [three documents pertaining to Antoine's son, "Le chevalier," have inadvertently been included in the dossier: pièces 22, 36, and 37]); Section Outre-mer, G[3], 2047/1, 8 oct. 1751. PAC, MG 9, B8, 24 (registres de Saint-Jean-Baptiste du Port-Royal), pp.50–51 (originals for 1702–28 are at the PANS, RG 1, 26). *Les derniers jours de l'Acadie* (Du Boscq de Beaumont), 287–92. Le Jeune, *Dictionnaire*, II, 7–8. Clark, *Acadia*, 283–84. La Morandière, *Hist. de la pêche française de la morue*, II, 671–72. Régis Roy, "Mr. Le Poupet de La Boularderie," *Le Pays laurentien* (Montréal), II (1917), 91–94.

LE ROUX (Leroux), THOMAS-FRANÇOIS, priest and missionary; b. 15 Jan. 1730, probably in the diocese of Tours, France; d. 5 Feb. 1794 at Memramcook, New Brunswick.

The generally accepted date of Thomas-François Le Roux's ordination is 1756. There is some evidence to suggest that he may have been a member of the Congrégation du Saint-Esprit. Other than that, there is no information available concerning his upbringing or religious vocation in France. He arrived in Canada in late 1773 or the summer of 1774 in response to a call from Charles-François BAILLY de Messein, who with the support of Bishop Jean-Olivier BRIAND of Quebec had written to the Séminaire des Missions Étrangères in Paris requesting the aid of French clergy with the Acadian missions.

Upon his arrival Le Roux was sent to minister to about 15 Acadian families at Havre-Aubert on the Îles de la Madeleine. His services were divided between this outpost and the Acadian settlements on Cape Breton and St John's (Prince Edward) Island. After several years Bishop Briand decided to move him to a mainland mission at Memramcook. He arrived there in the fall of 1781 or the spring of 1782. Although he had been preceded in the region by Abbé Joseph-Mathurin BOURG, Le Roux is regarded as the first resident priest of Memramcook. The parish established there was given the name of his patron saint, Saint Thomas.

The climate may have been less rigorous than at Havre-Aubert, but the Memramcook mission was no less demanding. It comprised an area approximately 40 miles square, much of which Le Roux reached by canoe, and included the poor Acadian farming and fishing communities of Barachois, Cocagne, Grande-Digue, Shediac, Le Coude (Moncton), Saint-Anselme, Petitcodiac, and Minudie. His flock in 1785 numbered about 160 families or 960 persons. Despite a suggestion that he should replace Abbé Bourg at Tracadièche (Carleton, Que.) that year, Le Roux remained at Memramcook, largely because of his age but also because his parishioners were anxious to retain his services. He seems, however, to have been strict with his flock. In 1789 he informed Bishop Jean-François HUBERT that he had abolished "all assemblies, dances, balls, social evenings, [and] catechized two and three times a day, during the winter, until Easter." For some time after his arrival at Memramcook Le

Roux continued to serve the village of Malpeque on St John's Island, and in 1788 he came into conflict with Dr William Phelan, missionary at Arichat, Cape Breton, who claimed that the island fell within his jurisdiction. Le Roux may have continued to serve the island after 1788, but by 1791 his visits there had ceased.

As the years progressed Le Roux found it more and more difficult to travel to the communities within his extensive mission. In 1791 he was invited by Bishop Hubert to retire to the Hôpital Général of Quebec if his age and infirmities made it impossible for him to continue his work. Later his eyesight began to fail, and in 1793 he asked Hubert to send him new spectacles to enable him to read the mass. His last letter to his bishop, written in Abbé Bourg's hand, was dated 16 July 1793, and in it he reiterated his request to be replaced. He was again invited to retire to Quebec, but his death intervened.

Le Roux was twice buried and disinterred before his body came to rest under the sanctuary of the church at Saint-Joseph on the west side of the Memramcook River. According to the Acadian historian Placide Gaudet*, he "had the reputation of a saint and it was said that he had performed several miracles." He was succeeded at Memramcook by the bilingual Irish priest Thomas Power.

DELLA M. M. STANLEY

AAQ, 311 CN, III, 1–14 (copies at CÉA). CÉA, Fonds Philias Bourgeois, 13.1–1; Fonds Placide Gaudet, 1.28–13, 1.51–14, 1.54–15, 1.66–5, 1.69–7, 1.72–5, 1.74–18, 1.75–5. Allaire, *Dictionnaire*, I. Caron, "Inv. de la corr. de Mgr Hubert et de Mgr Bailly de Messein," ANQ *Rapport*, 1930–31, 199–351; "Inv. de la corr. de Mgr Mariaucheau D'Esgly," ANQ *Rapport*, 1930–31, 185–98. L.-C. Daigle, *Les anciens missionnaires de l'Acadie* ([Saint-Louis de Kent, N.-B., 1956]). Tanguay, *Répertoire*.

Arsenault, *History of Acadians*. [H.-R. Casgrain], *Mémoire sur les missions de la Nouvelle-Écosse, du Cap Breton et de l'île du Prince-Édouard de 1760 à 1820 . . . réponse aux "Memoirs of Bishop Burke" par Mgr O'Brien* . . . (Québec, 1895). Albert David, *Les missionnaires du séminaire du Saint-Esprit à Québec et en Acadie au XVIIIe siècle* (Mamers, France, 1926). Père Pacifique de Valigny [H.-J.-L. Buisson], *Chroniques des plus anciennes églises de l'Acadie: Bathurst, Pabos et Ristigouche, Rivière Saint-Jean, Memramcook* (Montréal, 1944).

LÉRY, GASPARD-JOSEPH CHAUSSEGROS DE. *See* CHAUSSEGROS

L'ESPÉRANCE (also **Sivert de L'Espérance**), **CHARLES-GABRIEL-SÉBASTIEN DE, Baron de L'ESPÉRANCE**, baron of the Holy Roman Empire, officer in the French regular and colonial regular troops, and colonial administrator; b. 1 Dec. 1725 at Louisbourg, Île Royale (Cape Breton Island), son of Charles-Léopold-Ébérard de L'Espérance* and Marguerite Dangeac; d. 5 Jan. 1791, probably at Versailles, France.

Like his father, Charles-Gabriel-Sébastien de L'Espérance chose a military career. When he was ten years old, he enrolled as a cadet in a detachment of the Swiss Régiment de Karrer at Louisbourg and in 1742 he was promoted second ensign. He was present at the siege of the fortress in 1745 and returned to France with the rest of the defeated garrison. Although he embarked with troops bound for Canada in the fleet commanded by La Jonquière [Taffanel*] in 1747, L'Espérance was charged with escorting two troop detachments to the Antilles. Promoted lieutenant in the colonial regulars at Île Royale in 1754, he served under his uncle, Captain François-Gabriel d'ANGEAC. In 1755 L'Espérance married Anne-Claire Du Pont de Renon, granddaughter of Michel Du Pont* de Renon. Following the fall of Louisbourg in 1758, L'Espérance returned to France.

Although his early career was not exceptional, L'Espérance advanced, aided by his family connections and persuasive powers. Promoted captain in 1763, he accompanied d'Angeac to the newly acquired fishing station of Saint-Pierre and was dispatched to take possession of Miquelon. He was stationed there with some 20 soldiers for nine years and in 1770 was awarded the cross of Saint-Louis.

Placed in command at Saint-Pierre when d'Angeac returned to France in 1772, L'Espérance succeeded to the governorship of the two islands on his uncle's recommendation in 1773. Two years later he allied himself with Saint-Pierre's closely knit merchant community by his marriage to Jeanne-Françoise, the 21-year-old daughter of Antoine RODRIGUE. The census of 1776 put the islands' population at 1,984; in a summer of good fishing that increased by as much as 1,000 men. The sedentary fishery was concentrated on Saint-Pierre, and its residents owned two brigantines, 67 schooners, and 225 shallops. Acadian settlers, less involved in the fishery, preferred to live on Miquelon.

As Great Britain and her American colonies moved towards war, relations between the French colony and Newfoundland became critical. In 1776 an agreement with John Montagu, governor of Newfoundland, settled two long-standing disputes between the two colonies. Thereafter the French were allowed to cut wood in Newfoundland and fish in the channel separating the two territories. Trade between Saint-Pierre and New England stopped in that year, but the position of the island became even more precarious when France allied with the Americans in 1778. With only 31 soldiers and six cannon, L'Espérance could do little when in September 1778 an English squadron under Commodore John Evans appeared off Saint-Pierre and demanded that the French surrender. Always vainglorious, the governor capitulated with great pomp after having secured the honours of war. When he and his officers had left for France, the British pillaged and burned the settlement.

Promoted brigadier in the colonial infantry in 1778, L'Espérance was awarded a pension of 4,000 *livres*. He had planned to settle in Alsace, where he had relatives, but in 1783 he was recalled to the governorship of Saint-Pierre and Miquelon when the islands were returned to France by the treaty of Paris. Sometimes in debt, and frequently requesting advances and gratuities from the government, he was doubtless pleased that his salary was raised from 10,000 to 15,000 *livres*. The number of troops in his command was also increased threefold, and in 1784 he was promoted brigadier of the line infantry.

French attachment to the North Atlantic fishery was such that the government had provided subsistence for refugees from Saint-Pierre and Miquelon while they were in France from 1778 to 1783. In order to begin the colony anew, the monarchy induced fishermen to return by offering rations for up to a year and a half, fishing hardware, and advances for the reconstruction of buildings. The British also permitted the colonists to cut wood on Newfoundland and mine coal on Cape Breton Island. Within a year the population reached 1,204; about one-half were fishermen. L'Espérance urged that the colony receive more troops and be fortified.

In 1784 a three-man commission was sent to Saint-Pierre to determine whether the islands could be more securely defended. After considering the report, the minister of Marine, Castries, decided against any fortified installation on Saint-Pierre as both impractical and too costly. The islands were relegated to the position of a simple fishing station and the civil and military establishments were reduced. The governorship was abolished and replaced by the command of an infantry captain, reporting to the French naval captain sent annually to protect the fisheries.

L'Espérance crossed the Atlantic for the last time in 1785. Although awarded a pension of 6,000 *livres* in 1786, both he and his wife plagued the government with petitions for more. Promoted major-general in 1788, he officially retired in April 1789.

T. A. CROWLEY

AN, Col., E, 281 (dossier L'Espérance); Section Outre-mer, G^3, 2044, 23 août 1755. Æ. Fauteux, *Les chevaliers de Saint-Louis*, 215. La Morandière, *Hist. de la pêche française de la morue*, II, 810–16, 823–26. J.-Y. Ribault, *Les îles Saint-Pierre et Miquelon des origines à 1814* (Saint-Pierre, 1962), 65–67, 80–86. Henri Bourde de La Rogerie, "Saint-Pierre et Miquelon: des origines à 1778," *Le Pays de Granville; bull. trimestriel de la Soc. d'études historiques et économiques* (Mortain, France), 2e sér., nos.38–40 (1937). J.-Y. Ribault, "La population des îles Saint-Pierre et Miquelon de 1763 à 1793," *Revue française d'hist. d'outre-mer* (Paris), LIII (1966), 43.

LETANCOUR. *See* DECOSTE

LEVASSEUR (Le Vasseur), FRANÇOIS-NOËL (generally referred to as **Vasseur**), master woodcarver and sculptor; baptized 26 Dec. 1703 in the church of Notre-Dame, Quebec, son of Noël Levasseur* and Marie-Madeleine Turpin; m. 18 Aug. 1748, in Quebec, Marie-Geneviève Côté, widow of Gilles Gabriel; no children; d. 29 Oct. 1794 at the Hôpital Général in Quebec.

François-Noël Levasseur came from a famous family of craftsmen in wood. From the time of their arrival in New France in the mid 17th century, his great-grandfather, Jean Levasseur*, *dit* Lavigne, and the latter's brother Pierre Levasseur*, *dit* L'Espérance, had virtually monopolized fine woodwork and carving. François-Noël, and his younger brother Jean-Baptiste-Antoine LEVASSEUR, *dit* Delor, whose works indeed cannot be distinguished from his, kept traditional wood-carving alive in New France throughout the 18th century.

François-Noël Levasseur completed his first orders in 1740 after the death of his father and teacher, who had been the regular craftsman supplying many of the parishes and religious communities at the beginning of the 18th century. When François-Noël took over the workshop on Rue Saint-Louis he faced strong competition. His uncle, Pierre-Noël Levasseur*, then at the peak of his fame, was turning out important pieces of religious furniture and fine statues in which the baroque influence was still evident. Apparently, however, newly established parishes such as those founded at the end of the 17th century were not always able to acquire his works. Pierre-Noël may have been unable to keep up with the demand, or he may have set his price too high. Thus there was a need for simpler carving, virtually mass-produced, that would be within easier reach of rural parishes. François-Noël turned to this task.

Almost all the parishes that had been established within the Government of Quebec before 1775 ordered furnishings or statues from the Levasseurs' workshop. Their business also spread into the Government of Trois-Rivières, but the Government of Montreal, except for the parish of Saint-Sulpice, remained less open to the Levasseurs' influence. There were fewer parish councils there, and other craftsmen such as Paul-Raymond Jourdain*, *dit* Labrosse, were also offering their services. Parishes erected during the 18th century had to attend to their most urgent needs first, and so they would initially order a tabernacle, crucifixes, and candlesticks. Then, when permanent places of worship were built, the interior decoration of the church could be completed, according to need or financial means, by the addition of various furnishings which would stop the parishioners from envying neighbouring parishes. The account books of the parish councils list numerous payments for processional crosses, statues, small pedestals, reliquaries, pulpits and communion tables, churchwardens' pews, frameworks for altars and pots. Apparently contracts had to be made almost a year before the anticipated delivery date, and the wood-carvers never made anything not expressly ordered or of a design not approved in advance. Payments were made over long periods after delivery and might sometimes be settled in kind, according to the wood-carvers' requirements, by wheat, tobacco, or garden produce.

After their father's death François-Noël and Jean-Baptiste-Antoine continued for a time to turn out works much like those he produced. To furniture of simple workmanship but carefully designed proportions they would apply piece by piece a classical decoration mainly of acanthus leaves in scroll pattern or as fleurons. When they had acquired dexterity, they were able to chisel motifs of roses or other flowers in which one was conscious of the relief. With the late discovery of the rococo style, production underwent an important change. Curiously, the rocaille motif so characteristic of the final period of the rococo style was used in a spirit completely contrary to the one in which it had been created in France under Louis XV. Relying on technical skill and imbued with a tradition now almost routine, François-Noël Levasseur failed to understand that asymmetry was one of the major characteristics of this new decorative art; he produced motifs in the rococo style but applied them to his furniture according to classical criteria, as if fidelity to his predecessors' models took precedence over any need for change. This turning-point in the history of the workshop occurred around 1749 and was first illustrated in the tabernacle of the church of Sainte-Famille on Île d'Orléans.

One might be tempted to think that the conquest would mean a drop in production for the wood-carving shop but such was not the case. Numerous furnishings had been moved and hidden during the war, some had been damaged, and with the return of peace everything had to be repaired. The Levasseur workshop was busier than ever, and production continued until 1782, even after Jean-Baptiste-Antoine's death in 1775. There was no important change in its methods at that time and the large pieces of furniture such as tabernacles were still decorated with the rococo motif, which was by then completely out of fashion in France.

After Pierre-Noël Levasseur's death in 1770, François-Noël seems to have concentrated on producing works carved in the round. It had originally been intended that the shop's statues would be placed in niches on the tabernacles. Marked by a hieratic character that contrasted with the feeling of movement in Pierre-Noël Levasseur's work, they retained with their polychromatic treatment a coarser, almost peasant workmanship. But following the conquest statues of all sizes came out of the workshop on Rue Saint-Louis, in particular because the parish councils had to replace those that had disappeared from the portals of their churches during the war or had been seriously damaged by the passage of time.

Despite the size of the Levasseurs' workshop there is no information extant about the hiring of the workmen or apprentices needed for a successful operation. We know, however, that they called upon experienced men labouring elsewhere in the city (for instance, a turner) to finish commissioned works. The pieces made in the workshop were gilded at first by the Ursulines, and later, at the end of the French régime and after the conquest, by the Augustinian nuns at the Hôpital Général.

François-Noël Levasseur, who after 28 Sept. 1782 lived in rooms usually occupied by the chaplain of the Hôpital Général, spent the last 12 years of his life with his niece, Sister Marie-Joseph de Saint-François-d'Assise; probably with the help of the old craftsman, she herself did some pieces of wood-carving for her community at that time. The last important wood-carver of the Levasseur dynasty passed away at the age of 90. Other craftsmen in wood were, however, ready to carry on, in particular the Baillairgés [*see* Jean Baillairgé*].

Art historians have on the whole treated

François-Noël Levasseur's work with deference. To be sure, his atelier was productive and a large number of its works have been preserved; this very availability helps to make judgements favourable. But if the work is put into context, one notices that the articles turned out on Rue Saint-Louis show that development of woodcarving traditions had halted. The excessive simplification of line and tendency to repeat decorative motifs seem to indicate an absence of the spirit of inquiry. The craftsmen were cut off from creative centres such as Paris, and they lacked easy access to the great models. Thus although their dexterity remained unchanged, their creative power deteriorated.

RAYMONDE GAUTHIER

AHGQ, Hôpital, Registre des décès, 30 oct. 1794. ANQ-Q, État civil, Catholiques, Notre-Dame de Québec, 26 déc. 1703, 9 janv. 1775; Greffe de C.-H. Du Laurent, 18 août 1748. ASQ, Polygraphie, XXVI, 17. IBC, Centre de documentation, Fonds Morisset, Dossier F.-N. Levasseur. "Recensement de Québec, 1744," 10. Labrèque, "Inv. de pièces détachées," ANQ *Rapport*, 1971, 188. Tanguay, *Dictionnaire*, V, 391. Raymonde [Landry] Gauthier, *Les tabernacles anciens du Québec des XVIIe, XVIIIe et XIXe siècles* (Québec, 1974), 25–26. Morisset, *Coup d'œil sur les arts*, 27–28. Jean Palardy, *Les meubles anciens du Canada français* (Paris, 1963). J. R. Porter, *L'art de la dorure au Québec, du XVIIe siècle à nos jours* (Québec, 1975), 105, 110, 116, 181. Jean Trudel, *Un chef-d'œuvre de l'art ancien au Québec, la chapelle des ursulines* (Québec, 1972), 49–50, 100–1. Marius Barbeau, "Les Le Vasseur, maîtres menuisiers et statuaires (Québec, *circa* 1648–1818)," *Les Archives de folklore* (Québec), 3 (1948), 35–49. Raymonde [Landry] Gauthier, "Un art de vivre et de créer: la dynastie des Levasseur," *Critère* (Montréal), 12 (1975), 127–39.

LEVASSEUR, RENÉ-NICOLAS, head of royal shipbuilding and inspector of woods and forests in Canada; probably born at Rochefort, France, in 1705 or 1707; d. 2 Aug. 1784 at Aubagne, France.

René-Nicolas Levasseur belonged to a family that had been associated with the Marine for nearly a century. Members of it had held the offices of intendant and financial commissary, and his father had been engaged in naval construction. First a shipbuilder in Rochefort, in 1717 the elder Levasseur had become chief supervisor of naval construction at Toulon. René-Nicolas was to follow faithfully in his father's steps, serving as an apprentice under his orders; one of his brothers became an engineer and the other, Louis-Armand, became financial commissary of Rochefort. René-Nicolas entered the king's service in 1727 as assistant shipbuilder at Toulon. In 1733 he supervised the building there of a 40-gun ship, the *Aquilon*. He was by now experienced and reliable, priding himself on his honesty, zeal, and usefulness, and he was ready for all the tasks he would assume in the colony.

In the spring of 1738 the minister of Marine, Maurepas, finally responded favourably to the request that colonial authorities had been making for more than 20 years for a royal shipyard at Quebec. At the same time he announced that René-Nicolas Levasseur was being sent to manage the operation. Levasseur sailed for Canada immediately and took up residence in Quebec with his wife, Angélique Juste, and their children in a house on Rue Champlain, near the future shipyard.

That autumn Intendant HOCQUART sent him into the forests to verify information gathered in previous explorations [*see* David Corbin*; Médard-Gabriel Vallette* de Chévigny], to specify the quantity and quality of wood needed for the yards, and to choose the regions to be exploited. Subsequently Levasseur returned to the forest nearly every year, looking for wood suitable for ships of 500 to 700 tons burden. The shipbuilding enterprise was the result of the minister's decision to increase the number of warships in the royal fleet in case of armed conflict with Britain. Previous estimates, except those of the expert Vallette de Chévigny, proved to be too optimistic however: the wood required for building large ships was becoming scarce and expensive and was of mediocre quality. The forest resources of Canada would have been more suitable for constructing merchant ships of 250 to 300 tons. The decision taken in France caused misgivings and created all kinds of difficulties. The trees had to be felled in the distant region of Lake Champlain, the operation cost more than had been foreseen, and to obtain lumber of the required dimensions wood of poor quality had to be used. Hence the enterprise in the colony fell into disrepute which increased when big ships, such as the *Caribou*, a flute of 700 tons launched in 1744, rotted in less than five years.

Organizing the work left Levasseur practically no free time. Once the cutting areas had been marked out, he would return to Quebec to prepare for the summer season, draw plans for future ships, and procure the supplies needed for their construction. But he often had to return to the forest before the end of winter to supervise woodcutting, make sure he would have all the logs necessary, and arrange for them to be floated from Lake Champlain to Quebec. From April to

November or December he had to coordinate and supervise all the workmen in the shipyards.

In 1746 the yards, which had first been located on the Rivière Saint-Charles at the spot where private individuals were accustomed to build ships, were moved to Cul-de-Sac, not far from the Place Royale. Because of its depth the St Lawrence was better suited for launching big ships than the Saint-Charles. In summer some 200 men supervised by a dozen foremen from France worked on the site from early morning until nightfall. The tempo of work made it possible to build a ship in two years. From 1738 until the conquest Levasseur launched about ten warships, plus some small service craft. He undertook to train his son Pierre and Louis-Pierre Poulin* de Courval Cressé as assistant shipbuilders and they built light warships to cruise the lakes at the time of the Seven Years' War.

These successes were not achieved without difficulty. The home authorities considered the cost of the vessels excessive. The search for large logs was costly. It took all Levasseur's imagination and tenacity to deal with almost catastrophic situations. Setting up and then moving the shipyards entailed a considerable outlay of money. He even had to complain of the exactions of colonial administrators. Some of them – for example Jacques-Michel BRÉARD – made personal use of the services of foremen paid by the king and wood intended for building the king's ships. The scarcity of manpower at all times made it necessary to pay high salaries. At first craft masters qualified to take charge of the various workshops had to be brought from France. Later the intendant was obliged to ask the minister year after year for ordinary journeymen in order to ensure the survival of the enterprise, since Canadian labour was becoming scarce.

Despite the good will of the builder and the colonial authorities, the difficulties resulting from the system and from the economic situation meant that the shipbuilding programme could not attain its objectives. It served only briefly as the catalyst for private enterprise that Hocquart had wished for. After remarkable progress from 1739 to 1742, the secondary industries – rosin and pitch for caulking, linen and hemp for cordage and sails, iron for nails and tackle – rapidly declined. A slump in agriculture in 1742 and 1743 caused such a large rise in prices that the small contractors, who could sell only at prices fixed by the intendant, went out of business. From 1744 on, Levasseur had to order from French arsenals essential parts for completing the ships. When the British navy undertook to blockade the St Lawrence, particularly after 1756, the operation was seriously threatened. Moreover, the royal enterprise monopolized material and human resources to the exclusion of private enterprise. Satisfaction of France's needs had been achieved to the detriment of the colony's development. Of Hocquart's plan there remained only a metropolitan industry which had been implanted in a colonial setting to derive greater profit from its resources.

In contrast to the Saint-Maurice ironworks, where administrators, foremen, and workmen were not always qualified, the shipyard had in Levasseur a competent and conscientious man. His work was unanimously and constantly praised, despite failures such as the loss of the *Orignal*, which broke her back on the day of her launching in 1750. He was sought out whenever there were serious difficulties. He was the expert who had to solve the problems presented by the supply of wood. His methods of floating wood allowed rapids to be passed without danger. He had to blast dangerous rocks in watercourses. It was he, rather than the king's engineer, Gaspard-Joseph Chaussegros* de Léry, who was charged with building the quays when the shipyards were moved to Cul-de-Sac. He had come to New France as an assistant shipbuilder with an annual salary of 1,800 *livres*; the following year he received letters patent as a shipbuilder, and in 1743 his salary was increased to 2,400 *livres*. In 1749 he became chief shipbuilder and in 1752 was appointed inspector of woods and forests. Every ship-launching also meant important gratuities for him. During the siege of 1759 he was called upon to direct the squads of workmen responsible for fighting the fires which resulted from the bombardment of the city. The colonial administrators never lost their confidence in Levasseur's talents and effectiveness.

The French authorities were also to recognize his aptitudes and put them to use. He lost almost everything in the war. During his voyage back to France in 1760 the ship put into port on the coast of Spain, and he had to leave his family at Bayonne, near the Spanish frontier, for lack of money. The minister of Marine granted him 1,200 *livres* a year for his upkeep. In addition the minister quickly found a way to make use of his competence, putting him in charge of exploitation of wood in the Pyrenees to supply Bayonne with masts. For this challenge, with which the administration had been struggling for nearly 30 years, Levasseur once more received a salary of 2,400 *livres*. He succeeded so well – with the court's congratulations, as his personal file records – that he was appointed commissary of the Marine on 21 May 1764.

When he asked to be retired in March 1766, he received a pension of 1,800 *livres*. However, the memory of his exceptional services gradually faded. His son Pierre, who had become a writer in the Marine after the family returned to France, was refused his letters patent as deputy commissary. At Levasseur's death in 1784 his wife had great difficulty in obtaining the minimum pension of 600 *livres* awarded the widows of commissaries of the Marine. The able and effective man of action had been forgotten.

JACQUES MATHIEU

[The sources for a study of René-Nicolas Levasseur are cited in my book, *La construction navale*. Readers may also consult Levasseur's personal dossier in AN, Marine, C[7], 184 (copy at PAC). J.M.]

LEVASSEUR (Le Vasseur), *dit* **Delor, JEAN-BAPTISTE-ANTOINE** (generally referred to as **Vasseur**), master wood-carver and sculptor; baptized 20 June 1717 in the church of Notre-Dame in Quebec (Que.), son of Noël Levasseur* and Marie-Madeleine Turpin; d. 8 Jan. 1775 at Quebec.

The son of an important wood-carver in New France, Jean-Baptiste-Antoine Levasseur was always to be overshadowed by his older brother FRANÇOIS-NOËL. Together they ran a busy workshop which mainly produced religious furnishings. It is not known exactly what Jean-Baptiste-Antoine's tasks were within the small company, nor how the brothers divided their profits, because they seem to have constituted a unit referred to as "Les Vasseurs." His signature is only rarely found on notarized contracts, but Jean-Baptiste-Antoine Levasseur seems to have enjoyed a certain authority. In his brother's absence, it was he who signed the receipts concluding business with parishes and religious communities.

On 10 April 1747 Jean-Baptiste-Antoine married Marie-Régis Cartier in Notre-Dame in Quebec, and the couple set up housekeeping with François-Noël on Rue Saint-Louis. The two brothers had shared the house since the outset of their career. René-Nicolas LEVASSEUR, "naval engineer maintained for the king's service in this country," who was not related to Jean-Baptiste-Antoine, was at the signing of the marriage contract, and his presence suggests that the wood-carver was one of those ornamenting ships built in the Quebec shipyards. The bride's father, René Cartier, was a navigator, who is known to have ordered at least one ship, the *Saint-Joachim*, from the Quebec shipyards. A list of suppliers and workmen at the king's shipyards includes several Levasseurs, although Jean-Baptiste-Antoine is not mentioned. Woodcarvers always stayed within easy reach of the busiest shipyards and since the Levasseurs' competence was well known, the services of their workshop were undoubtedly called upon. Undated sketches held by the Séminaire de Québec testify to the contribution that Jean-Baptiste-Antoine and his brother made to ship decoration. The drawings are of carving for the stern of a ship which was intended for the seminary's use. Probably meant to bear the name *Sainte-Famille*, this barque was to be decorated with classical motifs derived from the acanthus leaf; on it would appear in bas-relief the traditional figures: an infant Jesus in swaddling clothes, and a St Joseph and Virgin Mary with rather primitive features.

In the 18th century craftsmen in wood worked in anonymity. Because orders seem to have been placed on the basis of good faith, supported by the craftsman's reputation, transactions were rarely notarized. The atmosphere of anonymity was increased by the presence within extended families of individuals with the same name. In the Levasseur family the name Noël was regularly in use among the wood-carvers. Art historians consequently have difficulty in identifying the works by Jean-Baptiste-Antoine Levasseur and others of the family.

As we learn more of 18th-century wood-carvers and their creations, it becomes evident that the production of each workshop as a whole should be analysed and placed in perspective. Indeed, Jean-Baptiste-Antoine Levasseur and other wood-carvers of his period would probably have considered it improper to give a personal character to a work; in their opinion, whatever is a beautiful creation makes itself known and its origins clear by its very existence.

Jean-Baptiste-Antoine Levasseur was buried in Quebec on 9 Jan. 1775. He and Marie-Régis Cartier had seven children, of whom only one lived. This sole descendant of wood-carver Noël Levasseur does not seem to have engaged in the family's traditional occupation.

RAYMONDE GAUTHIER

ANQ-Q, État civil, Catholiques, Notre-Dame de Québec, 20 juin 1717, 10 avril 1747, 9 janv. 1775; Greffe de J.-N. Pinguet de Vaucour, 9 avril 1747. ASQ, Polygraphie, VI, 37; XXVI, 17. IBC, Centre de documentation, Fonds Morisset, Dossier J.-B.-A. Levasseur, dit Delor. "Recensement de Québec, 1744," 10. Tanguay, *Dictionnaire*, II, 569; V, 390–91. Mathieu, *La construction navale*, 95–105. Morisset, *Coup d'œil sur les arts*, 27–28, 35, 162. Jean Palardy, *Les meubles anciens du*

Canada français (Paris, 1963). Marius Barbeau, "Les Le Vasseur, maîtres menuisiers et statuaires (Québec, *circa* 1648–1818)," *Les Archives de folklore* (Québec), 3 (1948), 35–49.

LE VERRIER DE ROUSSON, LOUIS, officer in the colonial regular troops; b. 11 April 1705 in Montreal, son of François Le Verrier* de Rousson and Jeanne-Charlotte de Fleury Deschambault; d. in or after 1789 in France.

Like his father, Louis Le Verrier de Rousson joined the colonial regulars, initially serving as a half-pay ensign until that rank was abolished in New France in 1722. He then became a second ensign, was promoted ensign in 1731, and lieutenant in 1739. In the latter year he accompanied Charles Le Moyne* de Longueuil to the Mississippi valley on his campaign against the Chickasaws.

Le Verrier's fortunes began to rise after Pierre de RIGAUD de Vaudreuil started to court his widowed mother (he married her in 1746). When Vaudreuil was appointed governor of Louisiana in 1742, he obtained permission to take Le Verrier along as an officer. Le Verrier became a captain in Louisiana in 1744 and for most of the next ten years served with the New Orleans garrison.

Although in the early 1750s Le Verrier was one of the senior captains in Louisiana, he followed Vaudreuil to France in 1753. On 1 Feb. 1754 he was created a knight of the order of Saint-Louis; Vaudreuil presented the order to him. When Vaudreuil was appointed governor general of New France in 1755, Le Verrier obtained a transfer into the Canadian colonial regulars. In the early campaigns of the Seven Years' War he served with LÉVIS at Lake Champlain. He had rheumatism in the summer of 1756, and Vaudreuil solicitously suggested to Lévis that Le Verrier might recover better in the comfort of Montreal.

From 1757 to the summer of 1759 Le Verrier was commandant at Fort Saint-Joseph (Niles, Mich.), with a gratuity of 2,000 *livres* and control of the local fur trade. He managed to send several contingents of Indian warriors to Montreal, but a smallpox epidemic and British agitation among the tribes interfered with the smooth operation of the post. In early 1758 Vaudreuil tried to have Le Verrier appointed town major of Quebec, succeeding Jean-Daniel DUMAS, but he was hindered by his own arrangements, having already recommended Pierre-Paul Margane de Lavaltrie. He then suggested that Lavaltrie be pensioned instead. The commission came through in January 1759, and Le Verrier returned from the west that summer. He must have been present during Wolfe*'s siege of the capital, but his role in its defence and in the subsequent operations leading to the fall of Canada is unknown.

After the conquest, Le Verrier went to France, where he continued to try to obtain preferment through his stepfather. Since Vaudreuil was preoccupied with his own troubles at this time, it is unlikely that Le Verrier achieved much. In 1767 he was living in Paris and he was still alive in 1789. He does not appear to have married. Although he had served in many regions and had rank and position, he seems to have been of mediocre talent. What he became was due to the good graces of the Marquis de Vaudreuil.

DONALD CHAPUT

AN, Col., D^{2C}, 48; 58, f.23; 59; 222. Huntington Library, Loudon papers, LO 16, LO 36, LO 259, LO 261. *Coll. des manuscrits de Lévis* (Casgrain), VIII, 31–33. "The French regime in Wisconsin – III," ed. R. G. Thwaites, Wis., State Hist. Soc., *Coll.*, XVIII (1908), 184, 205, 210. "Notes sur MM. Leverrier, père et fils," *BRH*, XXXV (1929), 288–91. PAC *Report*, 1905, I, pt.VI, 283. Æ. Fauteux, *Les chevaliers de Saint-Louis*, 156. Le Jeune, *Dictionnaire*, II, 544. Tanguay, *Dictionnaire*, V, 395. P.-G. Roy, "Les deux Leverrier," *BRH*, XXIII (1917), 3–13.

LÉVESQUE, FRANÇOIS, merchant, justice of the peace, legislative and executive councillor; probably b. 29 June 1732 at Rouen, France, to François Lévesque and Marie Pouchet; m. 16 Aug. 1769 Catherine Trottier Desauniers Beaubien in an Anglican service at Quebec, and they had nine children; d. 15 Jan. 1787 at Quebec.

Nothing is known of François Lévesque's early years, except that he came from a Huguenot family, prosperous weavers originally of Bolbec, France. His reasons for leaving that country are also unknown, as is the precise date of his arrival at Quebec. Nevertheless, it seems that before 1756 he joined forces with his two cousins François Havy* and Jean Lefebvre*, who were already established at Quebec as merchants. The Seven Years' War then caused separation of the associates: Havy went to La Rochelle and Lefebvre left Quebec for France in 1760. After Lefebvre's departure Lévesque was given responsibility for recovering the debts owing to his partners.

Lévesque quickly gained the confidence of the existing authorities, and was able to take advantage of favourable business opportunities. Thus in 1764 Governor HALDIMAND made him the sole trustee of 87 stoves and 310,000 pounds of iron from the Saint-Maurice ironworks, which was later liquidated. The administrators of the

Séminaire de Québec entered into numerous transactions with him: for example, he lent them 3,000 *livres* in 1761 and supplied 6,000 paving stones in 1774. In another connection, on 11 Aug. 1781 the bursar of the seminary, Thomas-Laurent BÉDARD, granted Lévesque a lot with a frontage of 60 feet in Quebec's Lower Town.

Lévesque embarked on a large wheat business which greatly enhanced his wealth and status. About 1773 he is even said to have owned a fleet of vessels for his trade with Europe. While engaged in commercial activities, he also pursued a career in public office. In 1769, in his marriage contract, he was termed a justice of the peace; then in 1772 he became a member of the Council and in 1775, under the Quebec Act, of the Legislative Council. As councillor he opposed the fixing of wheat and flour prices, which was proposed in 1780.

On 6 Nov. 1786 Lord Dorchester [Carleton*] announced the creation of a committee of council on commerce and police, which was to study "External and Internal Commerce and regulation of the Police, having an Eye to the ancient Laws and usages of the Province," and to report to Lord Dorchester. The committee's appointed members, Edward HARRISON, John COLLINS, William Grant*, George Pownall*, and François Lévesque, were authorized to summon witnesses and undertake interrogations, and to examine records and pertinent documents. The committee met for the first time on 13 November, and its report was submitted shortly before Lévesque's death on 15 Jan. 1787.

There is a well-established tradition that Lévesque was converted to Catholicism through his wife's influence. Nevertheless, his burial certificate is to be found in the Anglican register at Quebec. The obituary in the *Quebec Gazette* of 18 January bears witness to the respect in which his compatriots held him: "His social and patriotic virtues have long since acquired him the esteem, love and gratitude of this province, to whose interests he always shew'd his attachement, which renders his loss the more regretted by the public in general, and his friends in particular." The important political offices he assumed, as well as his social success, make him typical of the bourgeoisie of his time.

Lévesque's wife died in 1807 at Saint-Denis on the Richelieu, where she had retired to be near her daughter Catherine and her nephew Pierre-Guillaume Guérout.

JEAN-FRANCIS GERVAIS

ANQ-Q, État civil, Anglicans, Cathedral of the Holy Trinity (Québec), 16 Aug. 1769, 17 Jan. 1787; Greffe de Claude Barolet, 14 sept. 1748; Greffe d'André Genest, 11 juin 1775; Greffe de J.-C. Panet, 16 août, 10 oct. 1769. ASQ, C 22, sept.–oct. 1761; S, Carton 10, no.38; Séminaire, 82, no.50; 121, no.112; 152, nos.28, 215, 236. *Doc. relatifs à l'hist. constitutionnelle, 1759–91* (Shortt et Doughty; 1921), II, 685, 703, 780, 802, 859, 885–87, 897, 900, 908. PAC *Rapport*, 1890, 43, 51–53, 214. *Quebec Gazette*, 18 Jan. 1787.

F.-J. Audet et Édouard Fabre Surveyer, *Les députés au premier parlement du Bas-Canada (1792–1796)* . . . (Montréal, 1946), 258–59. Tanguay, *Dictionnaire*, VII, 358. Turcotte, *Le Cons. législatif*, 28. Liliane Plamondon, "Une femme d'affaires en Nouvelle-France, Marie-Anne Barbel" (thèse de MA, université Laval, Québec, 1976), 79. M. Trudel, *L'Église canadienne*, I, 189–90; *Le Régime militaire*, 115–16. M.-F. Beauregard, "L'honorable François Lévesque, son neveu Pierre Guérout, et leurs descendants," SGCF *Mémoires*, VIII (1957), 13–16. A.[-E.] Gosselin, "François-Joseph de Vienne et le journal du siège de Québec en 1759," ANQ *Rapport*, 1922–23, 413. J.-J. Lefebvre, "François Levêque (1732–1787), membre des Conseils législatif et exécutif," *BRH*, LIX (1953), 143–45.

LÉVIS, FRANÇOIS (François-Gaston) DE, Duc de LÉVIS, army officer; b. 20 Aug. 1719 at the Château d'Ajac, near Limoux, France, son of Jean de Lévis, Baron d'Ajac, and Jeanne-Marie de Maguelonne; d. 26 Nov. 1787 at Arras, France.

François de Lévis was born into an impoverished branch of one of the more ancient noble families of France. He entered the army in his teens, merely another poor Gascon cadet, but one with excellent family connections; his cousin was the Duc de Lévis-Mirepoix, who became a marshal of France in 1751. On 25 March 1735 he was commissioned a second lieutenant in the Régiment de la Marine, and was promoted lieutenant on 3 June. He served in the campaign on the Rhine during the War of the Polish Succession and on 1 June 1737, aged 17, was raised to captain. In 1741 he served in the French "auxiliary" force in the Bavarian army which invaded Bohemia during the War of the Austrian Succession, and took part in the capture and defence of Prague and in the disastrous retreat of 1742. On 19 Feb. 1743 he crossed the Rhine into France with 73 men, exchanged prisoners from four shattered regiments. He fought at Dettingen (Federal Republic of Germany) later that year, then served with his regiment in upper Alsace under the Maréchal de Coigny, and distinguished himself in several battles and sieges in south-western Germany. Two years later he served with the army of the lower Rhine under the Prince de Conti. In 1746 his regiment joined the army of Italy, in which he served as assistant chief of staff in the force commanded by his cousin. In August 1747, while his regiment was aiding in the defence of Provence, he relinquished his company in exchange for a supernumerary colonel's brevet and continued to serve until the end of the war as assistant chief of staff.

Lévis had established a reputation as a brave and competent officer noted for his sang-froid, but he lacked the money required to support a regiment of his own. When, therefore, it was decided in 1756 to send reinforcements and a new general staff under the Marquis de Montcalm* to the army in Canada, Lévis accepted the post of second in command of the French regulars with the rank of brigadier. The position carried with it a salary of 18,000 *livres*, a supplement of 18,000 *livres* per year, and a kit and departure allowance of 9,000 *livres*. He also received secret sealed orders to be opened in the event of Montcalm's death or incapacitation which named him to the command of the French regulars. In the event of Governor Vaudreuil [RIGAUD]'s demise, Montcalm would automatically succeed him, and were Montcalm subsequently to die or be incapacitated, Lévis was then empowered to assume the office. Accompanied by five servants, he sailed from Brest, France, on 6 April and arrived at Quebec on 31 May.

After seeing to the disembarkation of the troops, Lévis proceeded to Montreal where Vaudreuil and Montcalm were making preparations for the Oswego (N.Y.) campaign. Vaudreuil received him courteously, then dispatched him to take command at the Lac Saint-Sacrement (Lake George) frontier. While Montcalm hesitantly proceeded to lay siege to Oswego, Lévis made his dispositions to repel an attack on Fort Carillon (Ticonderoga, N.Y.). He decided that the best place to engage an approaching force would be at the northern end of Lac Saint-Sacrement, where the enemy would have to disembark and then be most vulnerable. The Anglo-American forces under Lord Loudoun gathered around Fort Edward (also known as Fort Lydius; now Fort Edward, N.Y.) declined to oblige him, however, and he spent the summer in sending out Indian and Canadian war parties to ravage the American frontier settlements in order to tie down their forces and to take prisoners who might provide intelligence of the enemy's dispositions and intentions.

Upon learning of the success of the Oswego expedition, Lévis was very concerned for fear his own efforts would be overlooked. He wrote to the Comte d'Argenson, minister of War, declaring that it would be most disagreeable were Montcalm to receive recognition and favours, and he to be forgotten. He added, however, that were Montcalm to receive nothing then he desired nothing for himself. In the event, Lévis was rewarded with a 1,000-*livre* pension drawn on the order of Saint-Louis.

Lévis was eager to advance his own career; hence he had to make sure that no opportunity was missed to bring himself to the favourable attention of those in power. At the same time he did not begrudge his colleagues any credit that they earned. After François-Pierre de RIGAUD de Vaudreuil's 1757 winter raid on Fort William Henry (also called Fort George; now Lake George, N.Y.), he informed the minister that had Vaudreuil offered him the command he would gladly have accepted, "but," he went on, "I could not have done better than he did. That enterprise had all the success that could have been expected of it." This generous comment contrasts markedly with Montcalm's sneering attempt to belittle the results of the raid and to denigrate Rigaud.

By this time relations between Vaudreuil and Montcalm were more than strained. When the minister of War cautioned Lévis to maintain good relations with the governor general, he replied that he got on very well with Vaudreuil and would have a closer relationship with him but for the fact that Montcalm would take umbrage. Lévis declared that he detested intrigue, had avoided it all his life, and would continue to do so. There is abundant evidence that he meant what he said.

In the summer of 1757 Lévis organized the artillery siege train and the transport boats for the assault on Fort William Henry, then took command of the advance guard. When Montcalm arrived at the head of Lac Saint-Sacrement with the siege guns Lévis and his 3,000 men had the fort invested. After a nine-day siege, the garrison surrendered. Relations between Vaudreuil and Montcalm neared the breaking point after Vaudreuil severely criticized Montcalm for refusing to follow up the victory by capturing Fort Edward as he had ordered. For Lévis, however, Vaudreuil had nothing but praise. In a dispatch to the minister he pleaded that Lévis be promoted major-general, expressing the fear that were his career not advanced he would request his recall to France, which, Vaudreuil asserted, would prove a grave loss to the colony.

The following year marked the turning point in the war. The Anglo-American army received heavy reinforcements of regulars from Britain, and assaults were planned on Louisbourg, Île Royale (Cape Breton Island) to be followed by an attack on Quebec, on the French forts on lakes Champlain and Ontario, and on Fort Duquesne (Pittsburgh, Pa) on the Ohio River. In an attempt to disrupt this strategy Vaudreuil gave Lévis command of 3,000 men – 400 of the fittest of the French regulars, 400 colonial regulars, the rest Canadian militia and Indian allies. He was ordered to march into the Mohawk canton and try to force them to join him in an attack on the British settlements on the Mohawk and Hudson rivers. To have forced the Mohawks, the most pro-British of the Iroquois nations, to enter the war on the French side would have been a devastating blow to the Anglo-Americans. A further objective was to prevent Oswego and its supply line forts being rebuilt and manned. In addition, a thrust towards Schenectady and Albany (N.Y.) would have disrupted the enemy's plans for an assault on the French position on Lake Champlain and allowed Montcalm to manœuvre the main French force against the Anglo-Americans on Lac Saint-Sacrement.

The strategy was bold but sound, provided the enemy cooperated by awaiting events. This they declined to do. Lévis's force had not gone far when it was hastily recalled; word had been received that the British and Americans were preparing to attack Carillon with an army rumoured to be 25,000 strong. Lévis with 400 of his élite troops headed for Carillon with all speed. They arrived late on 7 July to find the 3,000-odd French troops labouring to finish a log entrenchment and abatis on the crest of the slope before the fort. When the British under James ABERCROMBY launched their assault the next day Lévis was in command of the exposed right flank. Fortunately for the French the British made no attempt to turn it. The battle raged until sunset. The British columns suffered shattering casualties but kept reforming and attacking again and again. Lévis displayed his habitual sang-froid. When Bougainville*, who commanded on the left, was momentarily stunned by a spent musket ball, an officer called to Lévis that Bougainville had just been killed. Lévis, who had a low opinion of Bougainville, is said to have replied, "Ah well, he will be buried tomorrow along with a great many more."

Immediately after the French victory the smouldering resentment Montcalm felt towards Vaudreuil erupted into open conflict. Vaudreuil wrote to the minister of Marine pleading that Montcalm's request for his recall be granted and that Lévis be named commander of the French regulars in his place. Unfortunately for all concerned this request was turned down, but Lévis was promoted major-general. At the end of October he retired to his winter quarters at Montreal, well out of the parlour intrigue and savage squabbling that occupied the time of the senior officers and officials at Quebec.

In mid May 1759, when a renewed British assault was expected, Lévis still expressed confidence in the outcome, provided that they waged a war of manœuvre and did not lock themselves up in the fortified places. Montcalm privately expressed some resentment that Lévis's views on how the defence should be conducted prevailed over his own with Vaudreuil and the regimental officers. It was, however, fortunate on occasion that Lévis's plans were adopted. When Wolfe*'s army arrived before Quebec in June it was at Lévis's insistence that the Beauport shore from the Saint-Charles to the Montmorency rivers was fortified and the line extended up the latter river when it was discovered that the Montmorency could be forded above the falls and the French position taken in the rear. Lévis was given command of this left flank and when, on 31 July, Wolfe launched a major assault at Montmorency it was beaten back with heavy losses.

Following on the loss of Fort Niagara (near Youngstown, N.Y.) at the end of July [*see* Pierre Pouchot*], when it appeared likely that the British would make a thrust at Montreal from Lake Ontario, Montcalm felt compelled to detach Lévis with 800 men to counter the threat. Lévis left Quebec on 9 August; thus he was not present at the disastrous defeat of 13 September on the Plains of Abraham. Vaudreuil later declared that had Lévis been there the outcome would have been very different, since he surely would have restrained Montcalm from launching his precipitate attack in column on the British lines.

As soon as Lévis received word of what had transpired he opened his secret sealed orders and instantly departed for Quebec, joining the demoralized French army at Jacques-Cartier on 17 September. He was livid when he learned what had happened, declaring that he had never seen anything to equal the disorder he found among the troops. He declared bluntly that the defeat and shameful rout, just when they believed they would end the campaign with glory, had resulted from Montcalm's decision to attack before he had assembled his entire force. That said, he added that Montcalm had done what he thought was for the best. To Bourlamaque* he wrote that they must try to show things in as good a light as possible. When Vaudreuil asked that he and Lévis should go through Montcalm's papers since they would contain much that concerned the colony, Lévis bluntly refused, stating that he alone was empowered to look at them since they concerned only the French regulars, and he was responsible for them to the minister of War and Montcalm's family. He then set to work to restore order in the ranks, reinforce Quebec before it had to capitulate, and prepared to launch an attack on the British camp. It was, however, too late; on the 18th Jean-Baptiste-Nicolas-Roch de

RAMEZAY surrendered the city. All that could be done was to maintain a defensive position at Jacques-Cartier and send the rest of the army into winter quarters. Once the British fleet had departed in October the remaining French ships slipped down the river bearing pleas for strong reinforcements and supplies to be dispatched at the opening of navigation in order to arrive before the British. Were this not done, or peace not made by spring, Lévis warned, it would be unlikely the colony could be saved.

Those ships also carried dispatches from Lévis to the minister of War relating what had happened. He was particularly concerned lest responsibility for the disaster should rub off on him and damage his career. He informed the minister that in no way could he be held accountable for the mistakes committed during the past campaign and therefore requested that he be given assurance of promotion to lieutenant-general should he be able to impress on the British that the final conquest of Canada would not be as easy as they now appeared to think. This promotion, however, was not accorded him.

During the winter Lévis and Vaudreuil made their plans for a desperate attempt to beat back the assaults that were sure to come with the spring. Fortunately, their relations remained excellent. They were in accord that the only hope was to retake Quebec as early as possible, then shift the entire force to the Lake Champlain or the upper St Lawrence defensive positions, whichever was threatened first. It was hoped to use the speed afforded by river communication routes to defeat the invading armies one at a time. Everything depended on the initial success at Quebec and the receipt of reinforcements from France.

Orders were issued by Lévis in late November to the battalion commanders. Discipline had to be tightened and uniforms and equipment distributed fairly. The only shortages were in camp kettles, hooded winter coats, and underwear; beef was in short supply but there was enough bread. Vaudreuil ordered the militia captains to see to it that the habitants with soldiers billeted on them had eight days' rations always available so that a detachment could be called out, or the entire army, ready to march on the instant. The militia likewise had to be ready to march on first receipt of the order. Lévis also instructed the regular officers that they were to cooperate with the militia captains, establish good relations with them and treat the habitants gently, there having been too many complaints in the past on that score. To make this last point more firmly, he repeated the order five days later, on 29 March.

Lévis also carried on a polite correspondence with James MURRAY concerning the French casualties left behind in the Quebec hospital and an exchange of prisoners. Although they could not reach agreement on these issues, they clearly held each other in high regard as professional soldiers. When Lévis sent Murray a small supply of scurvy antidote, the latter reciprocated with a Cheshire cheese. They also exchanged newspapers brought by released prisoners sent from New York on cartel and Lévis commented on the disturbing fact that there was no mention of their particular theatre, that they appeared to have been forgotten in Europe, and then added tartly that he hoped to bring Murray more interesting news in the near future.

Throughout the winter Canadian detachments kept Murray's garrison closely invested, denied them any provisions from the countryside, and launched savage attacks on their outposts. But the worst enemies for the British were the bitter cold and scurvy. By spring Murray's garrison of 7,500 men had shrunk to some 4,000 fit for action.

On 20 April, before the river was free of ice, Lévis set out from Montreal with his 7,000-man army, 3,000 of them militia. Eight days later, after a terrible march through slush and mud, they stood before Quebec. Murray had received warning of their approach and was able to withdraw his advance forces, numbering 1,500 men, from Sainte-Foy and Lorette before Lévis could cut them off. Instead of shutting himself up in Quebec Murray decided to give battle, hoping to defeat the French forces piecemeal. He marshalled his army, 3,900 strong with 20 cannon, on the heights of the Plains of Abraham, the same ground that Montcalm had held in September. Lévis avoided Montcalm's mistake of attacking in column. He mustered his battalions, by now reduced to 5,000 men, in line more swiftly than Murray expected. Owing to a misinterpreted order the La Reine brigade and a body of militia, over 1,400 men, moved to the wrong flank and were left out of the action. The actual opposing forces engaged were therefore about equal in number.

Murray's plan was to hold the heights and pound the advancing French with his cannon. When Lévis's army moved up to attack, the units on the right got some distance ahead of the main body. Murray attempted to seize the opportunity and abandoned the heights, advancing down to marshy ground to attack. Lévis withdrew his right into the shelter of the nearby woods and also ordered the retreat of his left, which had meanwhile become embroiled in a fight for some houses. Jean d'Alquier* de Servian countermanded the latter order and led his men in a bayonet attack which stopped the British short. At the same time Lévis led an advance on the right that turned the British left flank, threatening to cut it off. The units there swiftly drew back, followed by the centre and then the right. Retreat became a rout. Had the La Reine brigade been in position Murray's army would have been crushed against Quebec's walls and destroyed. As it was, the survivors gained the safety of the town and Lévis was obliged to lay siege, with a totally inadequate siege train. He had won a resounding victory. His casualties were considerably less than Murray's, but the British still held Quebec. Everything now depended on which ships arrived first.

On 9 May the British frigate *Lowestoft* [*see* Robert Swanton*] sailed into the basin. The fleet under Lord Colvill* was close behind. Nothing remained for Lévis but to raise the siege and retire to Montreal for a last stand. Three British armies now converged on the town, Murray from Quebec, Jeffery AMHERST down the St Lawrence from Lake Ontario, and Brigadier-General William HAVILAND down the Richelieu. Murray ordered all the farms from Jacques-Cartier to Cap-Rouge burned, the people driven south to be a burden on the foe. All the way up the river the habitants were ordered to lay down their arms and return to their homes. Deserted farms were put to the torch. The militia now began to desert en masse, heading to their homes to save them from destruction by laying down their arms. The French regulars also, even the élite grenadiers, deserted in batches. The French army was rapidly melting away; its officers were in despair.

Further resistance was clearly hopeless, and Lévis admitted as much, but he insisted on fighting on to preserve the honour of French arms. In May 1759 he had declared that the army would defend the colony tenaciously and that it would be more honourable to perish, arms in hand, than to submit to a capitulation as shameful as that of Louisbourg. He may well have been strengthened in this resolve by the minister of War's directive dated 19 Feb. 1759 to Montcalm, ordering him to hold out to the last extremity rather than accept terms as shameful as those accepted at Louisbourg, and thereby erase that memory.

On 6 September Amherst's army was at Lachine. Vaudreuil called a council of war and it was agreed that nothing remained but to draw up terms for the surrender of the colony. Amherst concurred with most of them, but demanded that the regular troops not serve again during the war. What was worse in the eyes of the French officers was that he churlishly refused to grant them the customary honours of war. Lévis thereupon demanded that negotiations be broken off and a last stand made to preserve the honour of the army. It would, he declared, be unthinkable to submit to such humiliating terms before the enemy had been obliged to launch an assault on the town. When Vaudreuil refused to agree to the destruction of Montreal merely for the sake of punctilio, Lévis requested permission to withdraw the French regiments in defiance to Île Sainte-Hélène, where they could only have succumbed to starvation. Again Vaudreuil refused. He commanded Lévis to conform to the terms of the capitulation and order his troops to lay down their arms. All that was left to Lévis was to have the regimental colours burned to deny them to the foe, and to refuse to meet with Amherst and extend him the courtesies customary between generals.

Lévis sailed from Quebec on 18 October, leaving his junior officers to fend for themselves, and arrived at La Rochelle, France, after a rough crossing on 27 November. That same day he wrote to the minister of War informing him, among other things, that Vaudreuil had, to the end, done everything that prudence and human experience were capable of. Under the circumstances, that was generous of him. Five days later he was on his way to Paris. There he petitioned for promotion to lieutenant-general, for a supplement to his Canadian pay and allowances to bring his emoluments up to the 48,000 *livres* that Montcalm had enjoyed, and for release from the term of the capitulation that barred his serving further in the war. He was accorded all three. On 6 Feb. 1761 the treasurer general was instructed to pay Lévis 23,598 *livres*; on the 18th he was granted the rank of lieutenant-general and on 24 March William Pitt wrote from Whitehall to inform Lévis that His Britannic Majesty had been pleased to free him to serve anywhere in Europe. Two weeks later the Duc de Choiseul, minister of War, informed him that he was to serve with the army of the lower Rhine under the Prince de Soubise. Lévis did not, however, exhibit great impatience to return to the field; it was early December before he reported to the marshal. On Christmas eve he received permission to return to Paris and left Düsseldorf (Federal Republic of Germany) in the morning. This swift departure may have been occasioned by his forthcoming marriage, in March, to Gabrielle-Augustine, daughter of Gabriel Michel de Danton, the treasurer general of the artillery and a director of the Compagnie des Indes. He subsequently commanded the advance guard of the Prince de Condé at the battle of Nauheim/Johannisberg (Hesse, Federal Republic of Germany) and distinguished himself by capturing the enemy's guns.

When the war ended in 1763 Lévis left active service and in 1765 was appointed governor of Artois. In 1771 he received the highly honorific commission of commander of one of the four companies of the newly formed guards of the Dauphin's next eldest brother's military household (Gardes du Corps de Monsieur). He subsequently appears to have divided his time between Paris, Versailles, and Arras, seat of the Estates of Artois. He was quite assiduous in his duties and concerned himself with the improvement of communications in his province, in particular the construction of a canal from Béthune to the river Lys, and of a road from Boulogne-sur-Mer to Saint-Omer. During the War of American Independence he corresponded amicably with his old adversary James Murray, now governor of Minorca. They clearly still held each other in high regard. When officers of the Minorca garrison had to return to England during these years Murray wrote to Lévis asking him to use his good offices to procure passports allowing them to return overland through France rather than by sea or the long way round through Italy, Austria, Germany, and the Low Countries. Lévis was always pleased to oblige, even after Murray's nephew Captain Richard Johnston abused Lévis's kindness by drawing on his purse to the amount of 4,800 *livres* with a letter of exchange that both the London bank it was drawn on and Captain Johnston's father refused to honour. Murray hastened to make it good. Lévis declared that nothing gave him greater pleasure than to be of service to Murray. He went on to say that he hoped the war would soon end and that Murray would then return to England by way of Paris so that they could renew their old friendship.

During these years Lévis's career continued to advance. He received the baton of a marshal of France on 13 June 1783, and the following year he was created a duke. Four years later, in his 67th year, although in poor health, he insisted on travelling to Arras to preside at the opening of the provincial Estates. It proved too much for him. He died shortly after his arrival. A monument in his memory was erected by the Estates in the cathedral of Arras. He left a son, Pierre-Marc-Gaston de Lévis, who inherited the title of duke and command of the company of the Gardes du Corps de Monsieur, then went on to a notable career as a member of the Constituent Assembly, and as an *émigré*, economist, Anglophile, author, and member of the Academy. His widow and two of his three daughters were less fortunate; they went to the guillotine in 1794.

The life of François de Lévis was a remarkable old régime success story. Starting out as an impoverished Gascon cadet he ended his career as a marshal and a duke; beyond that no one could go. During his early career he had the powerful support in the army and at court of his kinsman the Maréchal de Mirepoix, whom Lévis regarded as his foster father. He lived in an age when patronage was all important, ability counted for little, and intrigue was endemic. He carefully avoided making enemies, but refused to play the sycophant. He remained aloof from factionalism, particularly in his relations with Montcalm and Vaudreuil, and earned the respect of both, which in itself was no small achievement. His competence as a military commander is beyond question; his victories at Montmorency and Sainte-Foy are proof of that. Finally, the esteem in which he was clearly held by his old antagonist Murray speaks volumes.

W. J. ECCLES

[The bulk of the manuscript material dealing with Lévis's service in Canada is contained in the *Coll. des manuscrits de Lévis* (Casgrain), in AN, Col., C^{11A}, and in AMA, SHA, A^1 and Y^{1d}. There is reference to his service in Europe in the last two series. Transcripts of his post-war correspondence with Murray are in PAC, MG 23, GII, 1, ser. 1, 5.

There are no complete biographies of Lévis except Gustave de Hauteclocque, *Le maréchal de Lévis, gouverneur général de l'Artois (1765–1787)* (Arras, France, 1901); however, brief entries have been devoted to him in several reference works, such as *Almanach royal* (Paris), 1700–92, L.-C. Waroquier de Méricourt de La Mothe de Combles, *Tableau historique de la noblesse militaire* . . . (Paris, 1784), and Le Jeune, *Dictionnaire*, and in the memoirs of his son, [P.-M.-G. de Lévis, duc] de Lévis, *Souvenirs et portraits, 1780–1789* (Paris et Londres, 1813). For the Canadian campaigns in which Lévis took part *see*: Frégault, *La guerre de la Conquête*, Stacey, *Quebec, 1759*, and Stanley, *New France*. A more detailed bibliography for the military history of the period may be found in *DCB*, III, xxii–xxiii. W.J.E.]

LEWIS, WILLIAM, printer and journalist; b. in Kent, England; m. Elizabeth —, who died June 1782; fl. 1777–87.

Except that he had emigrated to New York province by 1777, little definite is known of William Lewis' early life. Possibly he served his apprenticeship in the colony under James Robertson, a prominent royalist newspaperman. Lewis fell afoul of the Americans for his pro-British printing activities at Albany, where Robertson owned the *Albany Gazette*, and in 1777 he was arrested by the New York committee of public safety. He was released in Kingston,

N.Y., that October to "remain in the Service of Mr [John] Holt Printer." Some time after that he must have eluded his overseers and made his way to New York City, for on Friday, 3 Sept. 1779, he and Samuel Horner began publication of the *New-York Mercury; or, General Advertiser*, thereby filling the only gap in the week when a British paper was not printed. In 1783 John Ryan* joined Lewis as a partner and together they continued publishing the *Mercury* until 15 August, by which time the American revolution was over and the evacuation of New York all but complete.

Arriving in Nova Scotia as a captain in a loyalist company, Lewis was granted a lot on Prince William Street in Parrtown (Saint John, N.B.). Since he began publishing almost immediately, Lewis unquestionably had taken the *Mercury* press with him. On 12 Dec. 1783, with Ryan still a partner, he issued a four-page journal, the *Royal St. John's Gazette, and Nova-Scotia Intelligencer*, the first paper to be published in what is now New Brunswick. Lewis and Ryan advertised themselves as "Printers to His Majesty's Loyal Settlement of St. John's River, Nova Scotia, at the Printing and Post Office . . . King St., where all manner of Printing Work is performed with Accuracy and Despatch." Official printing was the essential source of income for the *Gazette*, but they published non-government matter as well, including almanacs and books.

The *Gazette*'s news section contained international, regional, and local items, and there were attempts at literature and humour. The doggerel of Charles Loosley either amused or annoyed readers in Saint John by unmasking "The clamorous faction and the party wars,/The noisy tavern, and the scenes of riot." Conditions there were chaotic during the first few years, and Lewis, who thrived on the inflammatory rhetoric of the American revolution, lost no opportunity to expose the misfortunes and sufferings of the loyalists between 1783 and 1785. He lashed out at the incompetence and unfairness of the officials and demanded a "second Spanish Inquisition" for the land agents who "The choicest tracts for some reserv'd,/Whilst their betters must be starv'd." The creation of the separate colony of New Brunswick in 1784 solved few problems and in July the *Gazette* offered by subscription "An accurate history of the settlement of His Majesty's exiled loyalists," a book, no doubt to be written by Lewis, which promised to reveal the "unparalled neglect, or willful fraud" perpetrated on "distressed soldiers and poor refugees." "Rank or station" would provide no shield from the attack. The book never did appear.

Even though the government was displeased with Lewis and Ryan, it was compelled to use their services because they were the only printers in the province. The contract for printing the charter of the city of Saint John in 1785, for example, went to the *Gazette*, but by then the authorities had had enough. Christopher SOWER, a former competitor of Lewis in New York, was appointed king's printer on 8 April 1785, and he arrived from London with his press in time for New Brunswick's first elections that November. Lewis and Ryan, forced to change the name of their paper to the *Saint John Gazette and Weekly Advertiser* when Sower claimed the title the *Royal Gazette and the New Brunswick Advertiser* for himself, flayed the officials who had given preferential treatment to one who had not suffered through the colony's first two years. The elections provided the opportunity for attacks on the establishment, and Lewis and Ryan, now freemen of the new city, were especially active in securing the defeat of the government candidates. Governor Thomas Carleton*, who would not tolerate such opposition, used the excuse of an election riot to arrest a number of the government's leading critics, including Lewis and Ryan. He also had the elections of unacceptable candidates overturned.

Bound over to the Supreme Court in May 1786, and charged with "criminal libel," Lewis and Ryan pleaded guilty, throwing themselves at the mercy of the court. Each was fined £20 and required to deposit £50 security as a guarantee of good behaviour for six months. Authoritarianism, not freedom of the press, held sway then and for another half century.

On 21 March 1786 Lewis had dissolved his partnership with Ryan, who retained the business and eventually replaced Sower as king's printer. Lewis had been unable to accept the conventions of a non-revolutionary society. He apparently departed from Saint John in 1786 or 1787, leaving no record of his destination.

C. M. WALLACE

N.B. Museum (Saint John), W. F. Ganong coll., papers relating to the Saint John election, 1785–86. N.Y. Hist. Soc., *Minutes of the committee and of the first commission for detecting and defeating conspiracies in the state of New York, December 11, 1776–September 23, 1778* . . . (2v., New York, 1924–25). *Rivington's New York newspaper; excerpts from a loyalist press, 1773–1783*, comp. Kenneth Scott (New York, 1973). *Royal Gazette and the New Brunswick Advertiser* (Saint John, N.B.), 21 March 1786, 2 May 1787. *Royal St. John's Gazette, and Nova-Scotia Intelligencer* (Saint John, N.B.), 29 Jan., 9 Sept. 1784. J. R. Harper, *Historical directory of New Brunswick newspapers*

(Fredericton, 1961). W. H. Kesterton, *A history of journalism in Canada* (Toronto, 1967). Sidney Kobre, *The development of the colonial newspaper* (Pittsburgh, Pa., 1944; repr. Gloucester, Mass., 1960). J. W. Lawrence, *The judges of New Brunswick and their times*, ed. A. A. Stockton [and W. O. Raymond] ([Saint John, N.B., 1907]). MacNutt, *New Brunswick*. E. C. Wright, *The loyalists of New Brunswick* (Fredericton, 1955). J. R. Harper, "Christopher Sower, king's printer and loyalist," N.B. Hist. Soc., *Coll.*, no.14 (1955), 67–109. D. R. Jack, "Early journalism in New Brunswick," *Acadiensis* (Saint John, N.B.), VIII (1908), 250–65. W. O. Raymond, "Elias Hardy, councillor-at-law," N.B. Hist. Soc., *Coll.*, IV (1919–28), no.10, 57–66.

LIDIUS. *See* LŸDIUS

LINCTOT, DANIEL-MAURICE GODEFROY DE. *See* GODEFROY

LITTLE ABRAHAM. *See* TEIORHÉÑHSERE?

LIVIUS, PETER, chief justice of Quebec; b. 12 July 1739 at Lisbon, Portugal, son of Peter Livius; d. 23 July 1795 on his way to Brighton, England.

Peter Livius was the sixth child of a Hamburg German employed in the English factory at Lisbon. His English mother sent him to school in England where, about 1758, he married Anna Elizabeth, daughter of Colonel John Tufton Mason. This marriage was the foundation of his personal fortune.

In 1763 Livius moved to New Hampshire, where his wife's family had large land claims. He established himself in lavish style near Portsmouth and from the first showed a marked ability to generate personal animosities; his Portuguese birth and ostentatious living were not to be forgiven. He gained his credentials in colonial society by a gift of books to Harvard College in 1764 and received an honorary MA three years later. In September 1765 his English connections obtained for him an appointment to the council of New Hampshire, and in 1768 he became justice of the Inferior Court of Common Pleas. He was accused of partiality as a judge, even of counselling litigants who were to appear before him. Governor Benning Wentworth, with whom he quarrelled over land grants, considered his political conduct to be factious and self-serving, alleging that he had been "a principal Abettor in the Disturbances at the Time of the Stamp Act" and had ever since been ready to court popularity in a manner unbefitting a judge. In 1772 Wentworth removed Livius from the bench.

Livius went to London to fight his dismissal, representing himself as the victim of the Wentworth family compact. The affair was widely reported in the colonial press. The Board of Trade accepted his charges, but the Privy Council upheld Wentworth's decision. He went to work to improve his credentials in England by a gift of elk horns to the Royal Society, which made him a fellow in 1773 for being "well versed in various branches of Science." He studied law at the Middle Temple and was called to the bar in 1775; an honorary DCL from Oxford University followed immediately.

Livius still planned to return to New Hampshire with honour vindicated, and he persuaded the secretary of state for the American Colonies, Lord Dartmouth, that he should be appointed chief justice with a salary paid directly by the crown. Wentworth protested vehemently and successfully; Livius had to settle for the posts of judge of the Court of Common Pleas and judge of the Court of Vice-Admiralty, in Montreal. Dartmouth wrote Governor Guy Carleton* that a man of Livius' abilities deserved a place on the Council and a seigneury. Livius arrived at Quebec on 4 Nov. 1775, just in time to experience the siege by the Americans [*see* Richard MONTGOMERY]. He later wrote of serving "day and night . . . with a musquet on my shoulder as a private soldier." He was rewarded with the office of chief justice in August 1776 and, *ex officio*, a senior place in the Council. He tried his hand at secret correspondence with the rebel general John Sullivan, urging him to turn over New Hampshire to the royal forces. The letter was intercepted and widely published; the new state responded by confiscating his estates and banishing him forever.

Within the beleaguered province of Quebec, history began to repeat itself as once again Livius generated strong animosities. Carleton had had his own nominee for the post of chief justice and complained bitterly that Livius had been sent "to administer justice to a people, when he understands neither their laws, manners, customs nor their language." Late in the summer of 1777 Livius clashed in the Council with Lieutenant Governor Hector Theophilus CRAMAHÉ who was replacing Carleton during the latter's visit to the west of the province. Later, when Cramahé arrested the Quebec tanner Louis Giroux and his wife for seditious utterances and lodged them in a military jail, Livius protested bitterly at this invasion of his civil authority. Governor Carleton supported the chief justice in this case, but early in 1778 they too came to a parting of the ways. Carleton, anxious to maintain the uneasy calm of wartime Quebec, had never revealed his instructions to the Council, instructions which would have made concessions to the English minority and introduced *habeas corpus* with its guarantee against arbitrary imprisonment. Sensing this omission, Livius at first tried privately to persuade Carleton to reveal his instructions; unsuccessful, he publicly moved in Council in April 1778 that the instructions be produced. The motion was lost, and Livius proceeded to move a remonstrance against Carleton's practice of routinely consulting a small number of councillors of his choice rather than the full board. At the end of that same month Livius made a powerful summation in a civil suit involving Jean-Louis BESNARD, *dit* Carignant, and Richard Dobie* which persuaded the Council, sitting as an appeals court, to find for Dobie. Carleton had earlier and quite improperly expressed his opinion to Livius that Dobie was at fault. The day following Dobie's vindication, 1 May 1778, Carleton dismissed Livius as chief justice without giving him any reasons for his removal.

On 31 July Livius left to plead his case in London, in the same convoy as Carleton but on a different ship. When asked by the Board of Trade to give grounds for his action, Carleton replied that he considered Livius "turbulent and factious," and a danger to the peace of the colony. A committee of the Privy Council restored Livius to office in March 1779, but he showed a marked reluctance to return to Quebec. He feared another collision, this time with the new governor, Frederick HALDIMAND, who was reputedly far less concerned with civil liberties than Carleton had been. Livius never saw Quebec again, for when he finally set sail in the autumn of 1780 his ship was beaten back from Newfoundland.

In the spring of 1782 Livius brought suit against Carleton for damages. He refused to go to Quebec unless the British government pledged that he would not be dismissed without a warrant from home. He claimed payment of arrears of salary, plus the expenses incurred in defending himself, and he wanted the seigneury and ironworks of Saint-Maurice as additional compensation. The secretary of state for the Home Department, Lord Sydney, who had to fend off these demands, found Livius pompous and unpleasant: he "asks a Silk Gown [KC] & Money, the Lord knows what. . . . He is a talking Man of Parade, with a strange Cast of Eye."

In December 1784 Livius first heard rumours that he was to be replaced in office by the former chief justice of New York, William SMITH. He tried negotiating with Smith through Dr Thomas Bradbury Chandler, stating that he would rather have £600 a year in England than £1,500 in Quebec; he forgot to say that he was only on half pay since the remainder went to the three provincial judges who held the chief justice's place in commission. The prolonged absence of a chief justice seriously weakened the judicial system of Quebec at a difficult time. Carleton chose Smith for the office, and in 1786 Livius lost a position that for eight years had been nothing but a hollow title.

From then until his death Livius existed in obscurity, yet another disappointed place-seeker. He presented William Pitt with a list of 50 offices he would accept, but he several times declined a pension. He claimed no compensation for his losses as a loyalist and, when no new office was forthcoming, agreed to accept a pension in June 1789.

Livius is a difficult man to evaluate. In the great crises of his life, such as the controversies over Wentworth's land holdings and Carleton's instructions, he was technically in the right but reckless to a fault. He could also be devious in political manœuvring as was shown quite explicitly in New Hampshire and insinuated in Quebec. Above all, he was a foreigner who tried to gain acceptance by following the norms of the English establishment: marriage into a family on the fringes of the aristocracy, honorary degrees from Oxford and Harvard, and membership in the Royal Society and Middle Temple. But he was never accepted as an Englishman, and this fact put a sharper edge on every controversy in which he engaged. Ironically, it was another foreigner in English service, Frederick Haldimand, who, grasping for the ultimate disparagement, raised the question whether a Portuguese of German parentage could hold any office under the crown without being prosecuted at the whim of a common informer.

L. F. S. UPTON

The memorial of Peter Livius . . . to the lords commissioners for trade and plantations; with the governor's answer, and the memorialist's reply . . . also their lordships report thereon . . . ([London], 1773). *Proceedings between Sir Guy Carleton, K.B., late governor of the Province of Quebec, and Peter Livius, esquire, chief justice of the said province . . .* ([London], 1779). *Proceedings in the case of Peter Livius* ([London, 1790]). [William Smith], *The diary and selected papers of Chief Justice William Smith, 1784–1793*, ed. L. F. S. Upton (2v., Toronto, 1963–65), I, 166–68, 174–75; II, 21, 115. Shipton, *Sibley's Harvard graduates*, XIII, 261–70. Burt, *Old prov. of Que.* (1933), 267–75. Neatby, *Administration of justice under Quebec Act*, 66–86. A. L. Burt, "The tragedy of Chief Justice Livius," *CHR*, V (1924), 196–212. R. P. Stearns, "Colonial fellows of the Royal Society of London, 1661–1788," *William and Mary Quarterly* (Williamsburg, Va.), 3rd ser., III (1946), 208–68.

LONG, JOHN, fur-trader; b. London, England; fl. 1768–91.

All that is known of John Long is contained in his *Voyages and travels of an Indian interpreter and trader*. According to this account he arrived in Montreal in 1768 as an articled clerk and spent the next seven years in the vicinity learning the Indian trade under the direction of a merchant. He grew particularly familiar with the Mohawks of Caughnawaga, in whose language he became fluent. During the early years of the American revolution he accompanied Indian parties on scouting expeditions and in several actions against the invaders in the Montreal area.

Having learned Ojibwa, the lingua franca of the fur trade, Long was employed in 1777 by an unnamed merchant to lead a trading party into the region north of Lake Superior. At Pays Plat (near the mouth of the Nipigon River, Ont.) he was adopted by the Ojibwa chief Madjeckewiss*. Although the ceremony was painful, adoption was believed by traders to be worthwhile for the business advantages it brought. Long and his men then went inland to Dead Lake (east of Lake Nipigon) and wintered there, doing a considerable trade. In the summer they returned to Pays Plat where their employer's agents picked up their furs and gave them a fresh supply of goods and provisions. The traders returned inland to Weed Lake (possibly Nighthawk Lake) for the winter of 1778–79. In the spring Long left the severe hardships of the interior for the more comfortable life of Michilimackinac (Mackinaw City, Mich.).

Disturbances connected with the American revolution were affecting the fur trade in the southern hinterland of Michilimackinac. In June 1780 word reached the post that the traders in that region had left their winter's furs at Prairie du Chien (Wis.) under the care of the interpreter Charles-Michel MOUET de Langlade rather than risk bringing them in. Long, with 36 Foxes and Sioux under Wahpasha* and 20 Canadians, went to the Mississippi to fetch the furs.

Long's next trading venture took him up the Saguenay River (Que.) in the autumn of 1780. He wintered at Chicoutimi and in the spring went west to Lake Shaboomoochoine (possibly Matagami Lake, Que.). In August 1781 he returned to Quebec. Seeing no further prospects for himself in Canada, he left for England in 1783. He contracted with a relative there to supply him with goods and by 1784 was in Canada again. His fortunes declined, however, and he was almost continually out of work and in debt for the next three years. He spent time in New York and in the new loyalist settlements on the Bay of Quinte (Ont.) but was unable to manage a trip to the fur-trading country. When he received money in 1787 from a friend, he decided to go back to England while he could, and he left Canada in October.

His book was published in London in 1791. It was, he claimed, "not the pages of a professed *Tourist*, but such observations as a commercial man flatters himself may be found acceptable to the merchant and the philosopher." It is significant for its detailed and relatively unbiased descriptions of Indian life. He deplored the behaviour of the Indians when they were intoxicated, but he recognized that many of the problems they were experiencing were directly attributable to the influence and example of whites. (He himself had pushed the priest of Tadoussac (Que.) into the St Lawrence during a drunken quarrel.) Of considerable importance also are his lengthy vocabularies of Inuit, Mohawk, Algonkin, Mohegan, Shawnee, and Ojibwa terms.

CHARLES A. BISHOP

John Long's *Voyages and travels of an Indian interpreter and trader, describing the manners and customs of the North American Indians; with an account of the posts situated on the River Saint Laurence, Lake Ontario, &c. to which is added a vocabulary of the Chippeway language, names of furs and skins in English and French, a list of words in the Iroquois, Mohegan, Shawanee, and Esquimeaux tongues, and a table shewing the analogy between the Algonkin and Chippeway languages* (London, 1791) was translated into German in 1791 and into French in 1794. An edition by R. G. Thwaites appeared as volume II of *Early western travels, 1748–1846* . . . (32v., Cleveland, Ohio, 1904–7); one by M. M. Quaife was published in Chicago in 1922. The original edition was reprinted in New York, 1968, and Toronto, 1971.

LONG COAT. *See* ANANDAMOAKIN

LONGUEUIL, PAUL-JOSEPH LE MOYNE DE LONGUEUIL, known as the **Chevalier de.** *See* LE MOYNE

LORING, JOSHUA, privateer and naval officer; b. 3 Aug. 1716 in Roxbury (Boston), Massachusetts, son of Joshua Loring and Hannah Jackson, and descended from Thomas L. Loring who settled in Massachusetts in 1634; m. 1740 Mary Curtis of Roxbury, and they had four sons and a daughter; d. 5 Oct. 1781 at Highgate (London), England.

As a boy Joshua Loring, a tanner's apprentice, decided to go to sea. During the War of the Austrian Succession he became master of a privateer and in 1744 was captured by the French and imprisoned briefly at Louisbourg, Île Royale (Cape Breton Island). Through the influence of Governor William Shirley of Massachusetts, Loring was made lieutenant in the Royal Navy on 23 May 1745. He continued to serve until 1749 and then went on half pay. In 1752 he acquired an impressive estate in Roxbury, presumably with prize money won during the war.

Following the outbreak of the Seven Years' War, Loring went to England where, on 13 March 1756, he was promoted commander, given command of a brigantine, and appointed agent for transports leaving English dockyard ports. He arrived at New York with some of the transports on 21 June. His energetic preparations for operations on the Great Lakes planned by Lord Loudoun came to nothing when Montcalm*'s capture of Oswego (Chouaguen) drove British seamen off Lake Ontario. All that Loring could manage was a reconnaissance on Lake George (Lac Saint-Sacrement) in September. He then asked for a sea command, but it was not until 19 Dec. 1757 that he was given the *Squirrel* (20 guns). It seems to have been nothing more than a paper transaction to give him the rank of post captain in charge of all naval construction and operations on the "Lakes of America" for the ensuing campaign.

In 1759 Loring played an important part in acquiring vessels of all kinds, both in Boston for the attack on Quebec and at Ticonderoga (N.Y.) for AMHERST's planned thrust down the Richelieu valley. In October, with a brig and a sloop he had constructed, he put to flight the old French privateer Joannis-Galand d'OLABARATZ on Lake Champlain. Loring had taken so long to prepare vessels, however, that Amherst decided it was too late in the season to pursue his advantage against the now exposed fort on Île aux Noix in the Richelieu River. In August of the following year Loring accompanied Amherst's army in the advance down the St Lawrence River from Oswego towards Montreal. Amherst pushed ahead with shallow draft gunboats while Loring's two larger vessels, the *Onondaga* (22 guns) and the *Mohawk* (18 guns), picked their way slowly through difficult channels in the river and fell behind the main body. Loring did not appear fully to appreciate his tactical role. At Fort Lévis, the strong French outpost on Île Royale (Galop Island, east of Prescott, Ont.) commanded by Pierre Pouchot*, the gunboats had captured the French vessel *Outaouaise* before Loring arrived. When he did come up he failed to coordinate naval bombardment with that of the batteries set up on adjacent islands. All his vessels drifted out of range save the *Onondaga*, which received heavy French fire. Eventually its crew struck the colours, under circumstances which Loring himself was unable to explain, and he prevented the wholesale desertion of his men only by threatening to shoot the first to try. One of Amherst's staff officers sent out a party of grenadiers to hoist the colours again. At this moment Loring "had the misfortune to loose the Calf of my right leg to a Cannon Ball," and he took no further active part in the campaign. In the following years he provided vessels for operations on Lake Erie during Pontiac*'s uprising of 1763 and its aftermath.

Loring never received an active sea command. After six months' leave in England in 1766 he returned in 1767 to his Roxbury estate. There he remained until "On the morning of the Lexington Battle [19 April 1775] . . . he mounted his horse, left his home and everything belonging to it, never to return again, and, pistol in hand, rode at full speed to Boston. . . ." He presumably left Boston for England during the evacuation in March 1776. In 1778 the state of Massachusetts proscribed and banished him, and Loring was driven back upon his personal resources. He died in England three years later; his widow survived him by eight years. The children of his eldest son included Robert Roberts Loring*, military secretary to Lieutenant-General Gordon Drummond*, governor of the Canadas during the War of 1812.

Joshua Loring placed great importance upon his quality as a naval officer, and his career served him well. Both in this capacity and as an agent of Amherst's decisions he played a dramatic minor role in the defeat of France in North America. But it was as a resourceful New England opportunist that he made the momentous decisions of his life, including the last. "I have always eaten the King's bread," he had remarked on going into exile, "and always intend to." Like other important choices, this was thrust upon him by main chance – and like the others it served him well in the end.

W. A. B. DOUGLAS

[Some of the primary sources have conflicting accounts of the events concerning the *Onondaga* on 22 Aug. 1760. John KNOX and Pouchot, like Amherst, assumed Loring ordered the colours struck. Loring himself said the colours were struck against his wishes. That Amherst chose to believe him is clear from Loring's subsequent employment. *Onondaga*'s second in command, Captain Joshua Thornton, a provincial officer who had taken a boat ashore on Île Royale, was dismissed from the service, even though Loring claimed to have sent him ashore as a stratagem. There must always be an element of doubt concerning this episode. W.A.B.D.]

An indifferent portrait was sold at Christie's in 1969. There is a black and white photographic reproduction at the National Maritime Museum, London. AMA, SHA, A[1], 3574, no.102. PAC, MG 18, L4, pkt.19. PRO, Adm. 1/2045–52, 3/64, 6/17–18; AO 13, bundle 47; Prob. 11/1084, f.539; WO 34/64, ff.133–225; 34/65. *Correspondence of William Shirley* (Lincoln). Knox, *Hist. journal* (Doughty). [Pierre] Pouchot, *Memoir upon the late war in North America, between the French and the English, 1755–60* . . . , ed. and trans. F. B. Hough (2v., Roxbury, Mass., 1866). Charnock, *Biographia navalis*, VI, 259. G.B., Adm., *Commissioned sea officers*. John Marshall, *Royal Navy biography* . . . (4v. in 6, and 2v. supp., London, 1823–35), II, pt.2, 544–49. Frégault, *La guerre de la Conquête*. Stanley, *New France*. J. H. Stark, *The loyalists of Massachusetts and the other side of the American revolution* (Boston, 1910).

L'ORME, PIERRE HAZEUR DE. *See* HAZEUR

LOTBINIÈRE, EUSTACHE CHARTIER DE. *See* CHARTIER

LOTBINIÈRE, MICHEL CHARTIER DE LOTBINIÈRE, Marquis de. *See* CHARTIER

LŸDIUS (Lidius, Lydieus), JOHN HENDRICKS (baptized **Johannes Hendricus**, also called **John Henry** and **Jean-Henri**), trader and interpreter; baptized 9 July 1704 in Albany, New York, son of Johannes and Isabella Lÿdius; m. 13 Feb. 1727 Geneviève Massé at Montreal (Que), and they had nine children; d. March 1791 at Kensington (London), England.

John Hendricks Lÿdius' father served as a pastor to fellow Calvinists in Antwerp (Belgium). On 20 July 1700 he arrived in Albany, where he was to be the minister of the Albany Dutch Reformed Church for the next ten years. He also ministered to the Iroquois. Young John Lÿdius seems to have lived an unsettled life in upper New York province before his appearance in Montreal in 1725. The French authorities believed he had fled to Canada to escape his creditors. He converted to Roman Catholicism and in 1727 married a Canadian, said by some to have been part Indian. He made his living from trade with, among others, the Iroquois.

In 1727 Intendant Claude-Thomas Dupuy* became alarmed at the number of English speaking artisans and merchants in Montreal, and two years later the minister of Marine ordered the proclamation in New France of the royal edict of October 1727 which prohibited foreigners from participating in the commerce of the colonies. Governor Beauharnois* and the financial commissary, HOCQUART, asked the minister to grant Lÿdius exemption since he was well regarded by the Iroquois, whose language he spoke, and since he might prove troublesome if forced to return to the British colonies. They suggested in addition an appointment as interpreter at 300 *livres* a year. The minister, in March 1730, merely granted the exemption "as long as he conducts himself well and faithfully." But Lÿdius was soon deprived of his special immunity and prosecuted for violating the edict. However, illegal trade with the British colonies and not the right of an alien to engage in commerce was the major issue at the trial. It seems unlikely that Lÿdius' actions were newly discovered. Since he traded with the Indians it must have been known that he was involved in the lively illicit trade between Albany and Montreal. During the hearing Lÿdius named other Montrealers and even Pierre de Lauzon*, the Jesuit missionary at Sault-Saint-Louis (Caughnawaga), as parties to the smuggling. Apparently the missionaries there and at Lac-des-Deux-Montagnes had complained to the authorities that Lÿdius bribed their Indians, encouraged their warlike spirit, and ridiculed the Roman Catholic faith. He had refused baptism for his son and had presided at the burial of an English Protestant. The court concluded that he was a relapsed heretic and a smuggler, and he was imprisoned in August 1730.

The mission Indians wanted him released, but on 28 September the Conseil Supérieur fined him 3,000 *livres* and banished him. He was put on board the *Héros* bound for Rochefort, and although his wife was allowed to accompany him, their newborn son was kept behind as a ward of the crown. Beauharnois and Hocquart stated that the banishment would make a strong impression "on those who are in the habit of carrying on, or favoring foreign trade." Although he had not paid his fine, Lÿdius did not stay long in the jail at Rochefort. By convincing the council of Marine that he was Dutch and that he had left an estate worth 12,000 *livres* in Montreal, he obtained permission to go to the Netherlands on the proviso that he never return to New France. It was the unhappy duty of Beauharnois and Hocquart in 1731 to tell their superiors in France that they had been hoodwinked. Lÿdius had left no property in Montreal.

Lÿdius made his way to New York province, and in 1732 the Iroquois gave him land on Otter Creek, Vermont, out of gratitude for his father's missionary work. However, Lÿdius settled on the Hudson River at the great portage between the Hudson valley and Lake Champlain. His establishment, called Fort Lydius (Fort Edward), was astride the trade route between New France and New York, and it annoyed many. In 1735 a council of the Dutch speaking merchants of Albany told the French mission Indians that the post would not be tolerated. It was the French, however, who took action. After war between Britain and France was declared in 1744, the small settlement near the fort was spied out, and in November 1745 an expedition led by Paul Marin* de La Malgue burned it. Lÿdius escaped and made several trips to Boston that winter to plead for the destruction of Fort Saint-Frédéric (near Crown Point, N.Y.), the French stronghold closest to his establishment. Failing, he then attempted to organize his own raiding expedition against Canada. As a trader and as a crown agent he supplied goods to friendly Indians gratis and encouraged them to form war parties against the French.

Lÿdius was next attacked by the Indian commissioners of New York, who blamed him for the Iroquois' lack of zeal for the British cause. In 1747 in the council of the province of New York he was accused of "abjuring his Protestant religion in Canada; of marrying a woman there of the Romish faith; and of alienating the friendship of the Indians from the English." Although Lÿdius may have been considered an opportunist and unreliable, he was highly regarded by some as an expert on the Iroquois. He served as a counsellor to William JOHNSON, colonel of the Six Nations, and in 1749 Johnson seems to have recommended him for the post of secretary of Indian affairs for New York. But although he could tolerate Lÿdius as a subordinate, he could not as a rival. In 1755 Johnson complained of Governor William Shirley's use of the trader as his military agent to the Six Nations. Lÿdius was, he wrote, "a Man extreamly obnoxious to the public in general and to me in particular . . . the very Man whom the Indians had at their public meeting so warmly complained of. To this Man he gave a Col[one]l's Commission over the Indians and set him up to oppose my interest and management with them."

The "public meeting" had been held at Mount Johnson (near Amsterdam, N.Y.) and when Lÿdius intruded, in search of recruits for an expedition against Niagara (near Youngstown, N.Y.), an Oneida denounced him as "a Devil . . . [who] stole our lands." The lands were on the Susquehanna River in Pennsylvania's Wyoming valley and had been purchased in 1754 by Lÿdius for the Connecticut Susquehannah Company. He had already acquired considerable territory from the Indians for himself and in this case he had dealt with six Iroquois sachems separately rather than, as was customary, in conference [*see* Karaghtadie*]. Lÿdius travelled to England via Quebec in 1764 to present his version of the Susquehanna affair. His land transactions, past association with the French, and the departure of Shirley made Lÿdius an isolated and distrusted figure.

In 1776 he returned to England to seek compensation from the government for past expenditures and services and to visit the Netherlands. In Holland he caught a crippling chill and was bedridden three years before establishing himself at Kensington, England, in 1788. There he gave an embellished account of his career, land holdings, linguistic accomplishments, and ancestry. He posed as the Baron de Quade and wore a military hat and cockade and a black suit sometimes adorned with the Prussian order of the Red Eagle. He was described as "a tall, well-made man, . . . a staunch Whig" and Calvinist. He retained a lively interest in current affairs until his death at 91 or 92. His heirs were a daughter and granddaughter.

PETER N. MOOGK

AN, Col., B, 54, ff.330v, 331, 393v; 55, ff.109, 482v; 81, f.283; C[11A], 51, pp.8–9; 52, pp.20–24; 53, p.41; 54, pp.148–54; 55, p.181; 56, pp.6–12; 75, ff.113–46 (paginated references are to PAC transcripts). ANQ-M, État civil, Catholiques, Notre-Dame de Montréal, 13 févr. 1727; Greffe de M.-L. Lepallieur de Laferté, 12 févr. 1727. ANQ-Q, Greffe d'Henri Hiché, 20 sept. 1735; NF 13, Matières criminelles, 3, ff.389–93. *Abstracts of wills on file in the surrogate's office, city of New York* (17v., N.Y. Hist. Soc., *Coll.*, [ser.3], XXV–XLI, New York, 1892–1908), II: *1708–1728*; III: *1730–1744*; V: *1754–1760*; VII: *June 6, 1766–November 29, 1771*; XI: *Abstracts of unrecorded wills prior to 1790*; XII: *June 17, 1782–September 11, 1784*; XVI: *Corrections: abstracts of wills, volumes I–V*. *The Colden letter books* (2v., N.Y. Hist. Soc., *Coll.*, [ser.3], IX, X, New York, 1876–77), I, 65, 238, 244. *Coll. de manuscrits relatifs à la N.-F.*, III, 153, 176–77, 276, 366, 488–89. James Duane, "State of the evidence and argument in support of the territorial rights and jurisdiction of New York against the government of New Hampshire . . . ," N.Y. Hist. Soc., *Coll.*, [ser.3], III (1870), 8. *Édits ord.*, I, 519. *Gentleman's Magazine*, 1791, 383–85. *The letters and papers of Cadwallader Colden* [1711–75] (9v., New York, 1918–37), II, 52–54; III, 115, 192, 366; IV, 127, 151, 186–87, 203, 247; V, 286, 292; IX, 10, 46. *NYCD* (O'Callaghan and Fernow), VI, 372, 385, 561, 569, 577, 603, 662, 664, 982, 984, 986, 994–95; VII, 29, 174, 456; VIII, 624; IX, 1019–21, 1101–2; X, 42, 144, 146, 210, 215. [John Sharpe], "Rev. John Sharpe's proposals, etc., March 1713," N.Y. Hist. Soc., *Coll.*, [ser.3], XIII (1880), 348. "The Susquehannah title stated and examined," Wyoming Hist. and Geological Soc., *Proc. and Coll.* (Wilkes-Barre, Pa.), XX (1925–26), 143, 148, 150–52. *Appleton's cyclopædia of American biography*, ed. J. G. Wilson *et al.* (10v., New

York, 1887–1924), IV, 58. *Calendar of wills on file and recorded in the offices of the clerk of the Court of Appeals, of the county clerk at Albany, and of the secretary of state, 1626–1836*, comp. Berthold Fernow (New York, 1896). N.Y. State, *Ecclesiastical records* ..., [ed. E. T. Corwin] (7v., Albany, 1901–16). Jonathan Pearson, *Contributions for the genealogies of the first settlers of the ancient county of Albany, from 1630 to 1800* (Albany, N.Y., 1872), 76. P.-G. Roy, *Inv. jug. et délib., 1717–60*, II, 119, 141. W. H. Hill, *Old Fort Edward before 1800; an account of the historic ground now occupied by the village of Fort Edward, New York* (Fort Edward, 1929).

LYON, JAMES, Presbyterian minister and composer; b. 1 July 1735 in Newark, New Jersey, son of Zopher and Mary Lyon; m. first, on 18 Feb. 1768, Martha Holden of Cape May, New Jersey, and they had nine children; m. secondly, on 24 Nov. 1793, Sarah Skillen in Boston; d. 12 Oct. 1794 in Machias (Maine).

James Lyon was educated at the College of New Jersey (Princeton), where he received his BA in 1759 and his MA three years later. Ordained a minister by the presbytery of New Brunswick, New Jersey, on 5 Dec. 1764, he accepted a call to Nova Scotia and arrived there the following year, his first pulpit being as minister to the Protestant dissenting congregation in Halifax until 1766. He then went to Onslow Township, where a number of families from Massachusetts had settled, and in 1768 moved to the Pictou area. This last move was the result of his connection with the Philadelphia Company, a land speculation group which, using Alexander McNutt* as agent, had obtained in 1765 a grant of 200,000 acres at Pictou known as the Philadelphia Grant. Lyon was a grantee there, as a member of the company, and between 1765 and 1775 he received a number of large grants in other parts of the province. In fact, in 1768 the presbytery of New Brunswick found it necessary to warn him of his reputation as a "land jobber," which it was feared would destroy his influence as a minister.

Of the many families from Pennsylvania expected to settle in Pictou only a few arrived, and Lyon soon returned to the Onslow area hoping to find enough families to support a minister. The fact that his name appears in the censuses for both Pictou and Onslow in 1770 suggests that he moved that year. In 1770 he also participated at Halifax in the ordination of Bruin Romkes Comingo* as minister of the Dutch Calvinistic church in Lunenburg. All four of the dissenting ministers in Nova Scotia officiated at the ordination: John SECCOMBE, James Murdoch, Benajah Phelps, and Lyon. Lyon's duties included delivering the charge to the candidate.

In August 1771 Stephen Jones of Machias met Lyon in Boston and offered him the pulpit of the Machias Congregational church. Lyon accepted and remained in Machias, with two intermissions, until his death. During the American revolution he supported the rebels, was chaplain in the militia, and in June 1775 led the group which captured some British ships off Machias. On 25 December of that year he wrote to George Washington suggesting a plan for the capture of Nova Scotia and offering his services as leader.

James Lyon was the first American composer to appear in print. In 1761 he had edited a psalm-tune collection, *Urania*, which included at least six of his own tunes. In addition he wrote the music for a composition entitled "Ode" for his graduation ceremony in 1759, and he is thought to have composed *The military glory of Great-Britain* for his 1762 commencement. Although *Urania* was the only collection he published, he continued to compose after 1762 and his tunes appear in other compilations. Surprisingly, however, the inventory of his possessions at his death lists no music, no musical instruments, and no copy of *Urania*. The memorial window in the present Congregational Church in Machias is silent also but bears witness of another kind: "In memory of Rev. James Lyon, A Noble Patriot, A Faithful Minister, A Good Man, and Full of the Holy Ghost."

TIMOTHY J. MCGEE

No copy of the composition entitled "Ode" has been found. [James Lyon and Samuel Davies], *The military glory of Great-Britain* . . . (Philadelphia, 1762; repr. Tarrytown, N.Y., 1925). *Urania, or a choice collection of psalm-tunes, anthems and hymns* . . . , ed. James Lyon (Philadelphia, 1761).

PANS, MG 1, no.742 (Rev. George Patterson docs.); MG 9, no.31, p.5; RG 1, 37. Presbyterian Hist. Soc. (Philadelphia), Presbyterian Church in the U.S.A., New Brunswick presbytery, minutes, v.2 (1756–71). Private archives, William Riddiough (Machias, Maine), papers. Washington County Probate Court (Machias, Maine), Probate records, v.2 (1790–1801), p.205, petition for administration of estate of James Lyon. G. W. Drisko, *Narrative of the town of Machias, the old and the new, the early and the late* (Machias, Maine, 1904). G. T. Edwards, *Music and musicians of Maine . . . 1604–1928* (Portland, Maine, 1928). I. F. Mackinnon, *Settlements and churches in Nova Scotia, 1749–1776* ([Montreal, 1930]). O. G. [T.] Sonneck, *Francis Hopkinson, the first American poet-composer (1737–1791), and James Lyon, patriot, preacher, psalmodist (1735–1794): two studies in early American music* (Washington, 1905; repub. 1967). A. W. H. Eaton, "The settling of Colchester County, Nova Scotia, by New England Puritans and Ulster Scotsmen," RSC *Trans.*, 3rd ser., VI (1912), sect.II, 221–65.

M

MABANE, ADAM, physician, judge, and councillor in the province of Quebec; b. *c.* 1734, probably in Edinburgh, Scotland; d. unmarried, 3 Jan. 1792 at Sillery, Lower Canada.

The first 26 years of Adam Mabane's life remain obscure; one source gives his mother's name as Wedel, asserts that his father, although a Protestant, had refused to swear allegiance to the Hanoverians, and claims for him relationship to James Thomson, author of *The seasons*. Mabane seems to have attended the University of Edinburgh but did not graduate; the amount of medical training he received remains in doubt. As a surgeon's mate in AMHERST's army he entered Quebec from New York in the summer of 1760.

There is little evidence that Mabane arrived with any of the advantages of birth or connection that would mark him out for preferment; only his appointment as assistant to the surgeon at the Quebec military hospital elevated him to commissioned rank in the army. At the same time he began a private medical practice which was to continue throughout his life and which became the source of much of his popularity. How skilful he was as a physician was always a matter of dispute among his political friends and enemies; the latter described him as antiquated in his methods by the time he had reached his thirties, but, surprisingly, they seldom stressed the inadequacy of his early training. His willingness to sacrifice his own comfort, his casualness about payment, and his sympathy for his patients, many of whom were Canadians, gave him a reputation for unselfishness, devotion, and honesty that constituted a genuine appeal to the emotions of many in the colony, including a number who held important offices in Quebec in the three decades after the conquest. These powerful friends, and less demonstrably this popular affection, made possible a political and judicial career for which Mabane had no training whatever.

That career began in August 1764 when Governor MURRAY appointed him to the Council of Quebec; in the following month he became a judge of the Court of Common Pleas for the district of Quebec. At first there was no payment for the judicial duties, and the new judge pointed out the financial loss he suffered in curtailing a lucrative medical practice to undertake other responsibilities. During the two years of Murray's administration Mabane became identified as the governor's constant supporter in the triangular feud that developed between Murray, the English merchants, and the Montreal military authorities. Mabane may have exacerbated the feud by his own partisanship and tactlessness in denying the right of the brigadier of the Northern Department, Ralph Burton*, to inquire into his expenses as surgeon of the Quebec garrison; Murray, however, regarded Mabane as the victim of the conflicting interests of the civil and military authorities. After Murray's departure for England on 28 June 1766 Mabane, because of the support he had shown the governor, came to symbolize the political position of his administration. Murray, however, was no longer present to offer protection.

Lieutenant Governor Guy Carleton* arrived in the colony on 22 Sept. 1766, determined to dissociate himself from the disputes of the previous régime. He chose to exclude Mabane, among others, from the first meeting of councillors held on 9 Oct. 1766. Mabane's participation in the ensuing remonstrance, and his unwise visibility in the protest against the refusal of bail in a celebrated court case, marked him out for dismissal. Compared to Paulus Æmilius IRVING, who was dismissed at the same time and for the same reasons, Mabane was extremely vulnerable, although Carleton, in spite of threats, did not go so far as to secure his dismissal from the bench. Mabane thus continued in the Court of Common Pleas, continued to protest his removal from council, and became a major property owner in Sillery, near Quebec, with the purchase of Woodfield, an estate once owned by Pierre-Herman DOSQUET. By the early 1770s, with Murray's return no longer a threat, there seems to have been some easing of the tension between Governor Carleton and Mabane; Carleton was able to see Mabane's position in the colony as a potential support for his own. Mabane's agreement with the political principles of the Quebec Act, horror at the increasing turbulence in the American colonies, and commitment to the British cause were all consistently evident, and his convictions were rewarded with an appointment to the new Legislative Council in 1775. Several Canadians were appointed to the council at the same time, and although few of them assumed positions of leadership, Mabane's influence was enhanced by their support. These councillors reinforced the strength of the French party, a group headed by Mabane which had emerged during Murray's administration and which claimed to speak for and protect the rights of a Canadian majority against English merchants who wished to destroy both French traditions and British imperial power.

Mabane's influence in judicial matters also increased during the 1770s. On 26 April 1775, four days before the implementation of the Quebec Act, which would establish a new judicial organization, Carleton reappointed the judges of the former courts and added two new names, Jean-Claude PANET and René-Ovide HERTEL de Rouville. It was popularly believed that these two looked to Mabane for guidance. With his fellow judge and councillor, John Fraser, Mabane was a member of the committee of council that drafted new ordinances for the establishment and regulation of civil and criminal courts in the province. For criminal cases, a court of king's bench, presided over by three commissioners in the absence of a chief justice, was established, and for civil cases the province was divided into two districts, Quebec and Montreal, with a court of common pleas in each. A court of appeals, composed of the governor, lieutenant governor, or chief justice, and five members of the council, served both districts. These ordinances became law in early 1777, and although they were to be in effect for a two-year period only, the system was continued until 1786. When Peter LIVIUS assumed office as chief justice he protested in vain against the arbitrary proceedings in the Court of Appeals and the unchallenged power of the governor and council in judicial affairs. His countervailing influence was removed in 1778 when Carleton, with Mabane's enthusiastic support on this occasion, chose to dismiss him. Livius was able to win his case for reinstatement, but he never returned to Canada. For the next eight years Mabane performed many of the duties of chief justice and came to believe that he would secure the appointment.

The continuance of the American war, the legacy of Carleton's policies, and the character of Frederick HALDIMAND, who became governor in 1778, all combined to make Adam Mabane a virtual mayor of the palace during these years. Haldimand relied upon Mabane as the most experienced man in the colony; he found his company congenial, his eccentricities lovable, and his financial position worthy of sympathy and such assistance as a governor could bestow. The most passionate critic of the Haldimand-Mabane association was Pierre DU CALVET, charged with treason in 1780 and imprisoned for almost three years. That Du Calvet, whose guilt was beyond doubt, considered himself a victim of the governor and his council does not invalidate all his criticisms of the government. His character sketch of Mabane, with his "habitually grimacing expression," bears the stamp of truth, and no better description of the laws of the period has been found than Du Calvet's "masquerade of alleged French jurisprudence."

The dangers inherent in placing the rights of all citizens within the discretionary powers of the governor and the judges were forcibly illustrated by the case of *Haldimand* v. *Cochrane*, where the plaintiff was the governor of the colony and the judge, Mabane, his closest adviser. In the years of Mabane's greatest power, Quebec was operating outside any principle of the rule of law, outside any legal system known to England or France, guided only by Mabane's personal concept of justice in specific cases. His prejudices were well known. The poor received more sympathy than the rich, and the one crime that was never forgotten, no matter how irrelevant it might have seemed to the case before the courts, was any failure in loyalty to the crown, especially during the American invasion of 1775–76. Such a bias was even more significant in view of Mabane's close association with other judges, most of them lacking his experience, and with some of the lawyers, such as Alexander Gray, who were pleading cases before him by the 1780s. Only the personal integrity of governor and judges prevented this lack of system from degenerating into intolerable tyranny.

Within the Legislative Council any attempt to break the stranglehold of the French party had little chance of success before 1784. Governor Haldimand used the American war as a reason for consulting only part of his council on occasion, even though the practice had been condemned by the home government. Any question of revising legal ordinances or considering the plight of prisoners detained without trial was easily postponed by the votes of Mabane and his supporters in council, and their advice also determined which petitions and remonstrances reached council for consideration.

As soon as peace with the United States was signed it became evident that, in some matters at least, the French party had been sincere in its claim that postponement was merely a war measure. In April 1784 one of the party members introduced a motion, unanimously supported by the council, to introduce the English law of habeas corpus. But when William Grant* moved that "the common and statute law of England insofar as it concerns the liberty of the subject" be instituted – a resolution which would have extended habeas corpus to civil cases as well as criminal ones – Mabane's group opposed the motion, since it went against the principles of the Quebec Act, and united to defeat it by a vote of nine to seven. Supporting the substantial minority was Lieutenant Governor Henry HAMILTON, who became responsible for the administration of the province on the departure of Haldimand a few months later. Hamilton was critical of the position adopted by the French party, while Mabane believed that the implementation of Hamilton's policies would involve the destruction of the Quebec Act, which he regarded as a charter, and introduce dangerous American ideas of government. Hamilton proceeded to admit for debate, and perhaps even to encourage, petitions which Mabane would have been able to suppress in earlier years. For the first time ordinances were passed with Mabane registering his dissent from the majority; in his private correspondence he denounced his opponents as "wasps and vipers," in a style reminiscent of Governor Murray's dispatches of two decades before.

Late in 1786 Carleton, raised to the peerage as Lord Dorchester, began his second term as governor of Quebec, and with him came a new chief justice, William SMITH. It soon became apparent that the tribulations of the French party under Hamilton had been no temporary discomfiture. The year 1787 marked the climax of debate in the council, and the fierce battles of that year were far more important in their cumulative effect than any single piece of legislation passed or committee report accepted. In isolated engagements the French party could still muster the larger force, and on at least one occasion the law officers of the crown found Mabane's legal argument more convincing than that of the chief justice. Nevertheless, the political power of the French party was crumbling. Dorchester divided the council into committees to consider such questions as agriculture, colonization, trade, and education. Since several of Mabane's opponents were senior to him on the council, he rarely served as chairman on any of these committees or cast the deciding vote that was so often required. More important, the French party had not developed new policy in any of these areas during the previous decade; they chose to defend the Quebec Act as the charter of all freedoms, whatever the specific subject of debate.

By far the most important of the committees from Mabane's point of view was the one investigating the administration of justice after 1775. In the midst of debate over conflicting motions before the council such a lengthy and public attack on the conduct of the judges had been made that on 18 May 1787 Dorchester had ordered a somewhat reluctant chief justice to undertake the investigation. There was no lack of evidence concerning the inadequacies and complexities of the judicial system, but the personal attack on Mabane and the ridicule and humiliation to which he was subjected aroused much popular sympathy. Neither side in the political dispute emerged from the affair with much credit, but Mabane remained as firmly entrenched as ever in the common pleas and in popular esteem. When the time came for appointments to the new Executive and Legislative councils established under the Constitutional Act of 1791, his name could not be ignored. His death occurred, however, before he had been sworn into office. It was only then that his opponents could effect real change, as Smith's comment on the news of his death made clear: "Mr. Mabane having made a vacancy in the two councils and in the Common Pleas Bench, on the 3rd instant, I beg leave to suggest that his death, and the resignation, hourly expected, of Mr. de Rouville, will open a door for the amendment of the jurisprudence of the province without detriment to individuals."

In contrast to the coldness of the Smith letter there was the warmth of friendship many felt for Mabane and his sister Isabell. John Craigie*, Henry Caldwell*, and Dr James Fisher* acted on her behalf to settle her brother's estate. His creditors were mollified to some extent by the sale of his books and furniture, and the immediate renting and eventual sale of Woodfield. It was found, however, that the doctor's possessions were insufficient to meet his debts.

Such a career as Mabane's inevitably evokes powerful responses. Smith's frustration and Du Calvet's exaggerated attacks had their echoes in later critical evaluations of Mabane. Nearly a century after his death, however, Abbé Louis-Édouard Bois* attempted to revive the memory and vindicate the reputation, portraying Mabane as the victim of persecution among his own people because of his sympathy for the Canadians. Now it would appear that Mabane's 30-year defence of what he conceived to be the Canadian interest is significant in that it helped to establish the framework within which early French Canadian nationalists were to operate. His career, moreover, offers an insight into the nature of 18th-century society in Canada, both through the record of his personal acquisition of power and through the social and political concepts he defended.

ELIZABETH ARTHUR

BL, Add. MSS 21661–92. PAC, MG 23, GI, 5; GII, 1, 15, 23. *Docs. relating to constitutional history, 1759–91*

(Shortt and Doughty; 1918). Pierre Du Calvet, *Appel à la justice de l'État* . . . (Londres, 1784). E. [M.] Arthur, "Adam Mabane and the French party in Canada, 1760–1791" (unpublished MA thesis, McGill University, Montreal, 1947). [L.-É. Bois], *Le juge A. Mabane, étude historique* (Québec, 1881). Neatby, *Administration of justice under Quebec Act; Quebec.*

MACAULAY (McAulay, McCauley), ROBERT, merchant; b. 1744 near Omagh (Northern Ireland), son of William Macaulay and Susan Gilliland; m. 13 Feb. 1791 Ann Kirby* at Crown Point, N.Y., and they had three sons, including John* and William*; d. 1 Sept. 1800 at Kingston, Upper Canada.

According to family tradition the Macaulays, originally from Scotland, had been living in Ireland for almost 100 years when their lease was not renewed, and in 1763 Robert's family moved to London. The next year Robert Macaulay and his brothers went to New York to live with their uncle William Gilliland. Together they developed land holdings at Willsboro (south of Plattsburgh, N.Y.) and Robert started a farm and a lumber business. At the beginning of the revolution his farm and business were confiscated or destroyed by the rebels. In 1776 he was taken prisoner during Benedict Arnold*'s retreat from Canada and held for some time at Crown Point. Later released, he was arrested again in 1778 for giving information to the British about the garrison at Ticonderoga. He was jailed at Albany for six months. After being freed on bail he escaped to Canada.

By April 1780 Macaulay was established as a merchant at Carleton Island (near Kingston, Ont.). He handled a variety of goods, including rum, wine, blankets, cloth, tea, guns, and gunpowder, and apparently conducted some trade with the Indians. According to a claim in 1797 he was also a captain of the Associated Loyalists on the island and as such he was granted 1,200 acres of land.

In 1784, when the local garrison moved to Cataraqui (Kingston), the merchants followed. Along with his partner Thomas Markland*, Robert Macaulay was one of the merchant forwarders, including Peter Smith*, Richard Cartwright*, Robert Hamilton*, and Joseph Forsyth*, who controlled much of the trade on Lake Ontario. In April 1788 Macaulay and Markland contracted with Archibald Thomson to build a log house for Sir John Johnson*, their firm to supply all the materials. They also acted as collecting agents for subscriptions to fund the construction of the first St George's Church (Church of England) in Kingston and were themselves benefactors of the church.

Family tradition states that Robert Macaulay had visited New York state in 1786 to see what property he could recover and that he met Ann Kirby there. He returned in 1791 to marry her. At the end of that year Macaulay dissolved his partnership with Markland and expanded the business, building a wharf and store on the water lot opposite his house. In 1796 John Kirby*, Ann's brother, became Robert's partner and carried on the business with Ann after Robert's death. Macaulay's will mentions, among other assets, six town lots, two dwellings, a blacksmith shop, and hundreds of acres of farm lots. The merchant family he established eventually became related to other prominent Upper Canadian families such as the Hamiltons, Marklands, and Kirkpatricks.

MARGARET ANGUS

BL, Add. MSS 21787, p.338; 21818. Metropolitan Toronto Library, John Ross Robertson coll., "Account of the losses of Robert Macaulay . . ." (1776). PAC, MG 23, HI, 1, ser.3, book 1, p.385; RG 1, L3 (index); RG 8, I (C series), 930, pp. 64–67. PAO, Macaulay family papers; RG 1, A-I-1, 1–2. Queen's University Archives (Kingston, Ont.), Hon. Richard Cartwright papers, letterbook, 14 Jan. 1798; Kirby Macaulay papers, William Macaulay to John Macaulay, 10 May 1843. St George's Anglican Cathedral (Kingston, Ont.), Vestry minute book, 1791–1800. *Kingston before War of 1812* (Preston). PAO *Report*, 1904, 436. S. W. Eager, *An outline history of Orange County . . . together with local traditions and short biographical sketches of the early settlers, etc.* (Newburgh, N.Y., 1846–47). W. C. Watson, *Pioneer history of the Champlain valley* . . . (Albany, N.Y., 1863), 178–84. Margaret Angus, "The Macaulay family of Kingston," *Historic Kingston* (Kingston, Ont.), 5 (1955–56), 3–12.

McCARTY (McCarthy), CHARLES JUSTIN (James), itinerant preacher; b. in Ireland, date of birth unknown; m. Catherine Lent, and they had four children; d. *c.* 1790.

Charles Justin McCarty was living in the province of New York when he became an ardent follower of the evangelist George Whitefield. He came to Canada in 1788 and preached effectively in the homes of loyalists in the Bay of Quinte area. His attempt to settle there was frustrated by the Mecklenburg land board, which turned down his petition for land "for want of due Proofs," despite McCarty's claims of persecution and imprisonment in the Hudson valley area for his loyalty to the crown. His preaching and personality had a polarizing effect in the townships west of

Kingston. The Reverend John Stuart*, who sat on the land board with Neil McLEAN and Richard Cartwright*, considered McCarty "an illiterate Irishman . . . a Man of an infamous private Character," and noted, "I think we shall be able to banish him for Crimes of a henious Nature." On the other hand, 41 residents of the area signed a petition that he "continue with us," recommending his sobriety, honesty, piety, and religion.

In April 1790 McCarty was arrested and tried on charges of being a vagabond, impostor, and disturber of the peace. The Court of Quarter Sessions, held on 13 and 14 April at Kingston and presided over by Cartwright, McLean, and Archibald McDonell*, ordered McCarty to leave the district. He apparently left but came back, for on 13 July he was again tried and ordered deported to Oswego, N.Y. He was never seen alive again, and accounts of his death have varied from starvation on an island, which seems probable, to murder, based on the discovery of a stabbed body.

Though McCarty had no official connection with the Methodists, his loyalist followers were largely of that faith and he had the Methodist style and emphasis. He has thus been claimed by Methodist historians as a martyr. Formally organized in 1785 in the United States, the Methodists were a new and unknown denomination, generally scorned by members of older churches as being enthusiasts and dissenters. Nathanael Burwash* later described this derisive attitude as "a spirit of arrogant enmity towards the Methodist body" and claimed that "the extreme instance" of it was McCarty's death "through the action of the civil authorities at Kingston." At least two other dissident preachers were in the Kingston area at the time and did not meet such hostility. A teacher in Adolphustown by the name of Lyons had preached the Methodist message without opposition, and William Losee*, a deacon of the Methodist Episcopal Church in the United States who had arrived just before McCarty's trial, was able to form lasting Methodist societies which included many of McCarty's supporters.

Other writers have defended the integrity of the court's decision, pointing out that even a grand jury had been consulted on the final verdict and that at least one of the judges at his second trial, Robert Clark*, was or soon became a Methodist. Yet with his loyalty questioned and his request for land refused, McCarty was indeed a rootless wanderer in a post-war era suspicious of opportunists and unproven newcomers.

Four years after McCarty's death, his widow married John McDougall of Ernestown. Some of McCarty's children settled in the Cobourg area, and his youngest son John became one of the original trustees of Upper Canada Academy, the forerunner of Victoria University.

J. WILLIAM LAMB

PAC, RG 1, L3, 281, 3232 A; L4, 7, p.30; RG 31, A1, 1851 census, Hamilton Township (mfm. at PAO). PAO, RG 1, C-IV, Hamilton Township papers, concession 5, lot 15; RG 21, A, Assessment rolls: Northumberland and Durham counties, Hamilton Township, 1808–15. United Counties of Northumberland and Durham Surrogate Court (Cobourg, Ont.), no.1251, will of John McCarty, 4 Dec. 1877 (mfm. at PAO). *Kingston before War of 1812* (Preston), 156–63. "Marriage register of St John's Church, Ernest Town, no.2," *OH*, I (1899), 20. PAO *Report*, 1904. *Encyclopedia Canadiana*, VI, 236. *Illustrated historical atlas of the counties of Northumberland and Durham* (Toronto, 1878). H. C. Burleigh, "The fate of McCarthy the martyr" (mimeograph, 1974) (copy at United Loyalists' Assoc. of Canada, Toronto). G. F. Playter, *The history of Methodism in Canada . . .* (Toronto, 1862), 18. Thomas Webster, *History of the Methodist Episcopal Church in Canada* (Hamilton, Ont., 1870), 36–39. W. S. Herrington, "The trial of Charles Justin McCarty," RSC *Trans.*, 3rd ser., XXI (1927), sect.II, 63–70. C. B. Sissons, "The martyrdom of McCarty – fact or myth?" *Canadian Journal of Religious Thought* (Toronto), IV (1927), 12–18.

McCARTY (McCarthy), RICHARD, military officer, lawyer, and fur-trader; b. in Hartford County, Connecticut; m. January 1765 Ursule Benoît, probably at Trois-Rivières (Que.); d. May or June 1781 in the Ohio valley.

Richard McCarty was probably the man of that name who served as a private in the Connecticut militia in August 1757 when Fort William Henry (also called Fort George; now Lake George, N.Y.) was lost to Montcalm*. McCarty may have been a commissary with the Connecticut militia in William HAVILAND's advance against Montreal in 1760. On 7 Nov. 1765 he was recorded on a list of Protestants in the Montreal district as a former commissary (whether with the army or the fur trade is not indicated) who had become a freeholder and notary at Chambly. He was commissioned a barrister and attorney-at-law in 1768. Two years later, on 11 April, he was issued a trading licence to depart from Montreal for Michilimackinac (Mackinaw City, Mich.) with goods worth £100, for which he assumed the bond himself. He may have been acting in conjunction with François Baby*, his uncle by marriage. During the next few years McCarty apparently traded between Michilimackinac and the Illinois country, and he may have developed connections at Cahokia (East St Louis, Ill.) quite soon. In 1775 he began to lay off land on the east bank of the Mississippi near Cahokia at a place he named St Ursule's, where he later built a water-mill. He apparently continued to trade from Michilimackinac. A map in his hand of the country around present Lake Winnipeg, the Saskatchewan River, and the upper Churchill was probably copied when Alexander Henry* the elder passed through Michilimackinac during the summer of 1776, returning from his only visit to that part of the interior. There is no evidence that McCarty participated in the expedition.

On 7 June 1778 McCarty wrote from St Ursule's with intelligence for the military commander at Michilimackinac concerning Indian and rebel activities in Illinois. The information was apparently both valid and important, but later that year McCarty supplied goods and services to the Illinois-Virginia forces. This acceptance of a commercial opportunity, for which his earlier experience as a commissary made him well qualified, may merely have reflected a neutral position. Early in the following year, however, he captained a small group of mainly French speaking volunteers from Cahokia which participated in the rebel attack on Fort Sackville (Vincennes, Ind.) in which Henry HAMILTON was taken prisoner. Thereafter McCarty was appointed captain in the regular forces of the state of Virginia (within which Illinois had been incorporated as a county). To his wife in Montreal he explained his change of allegiance as an attempt to establish a fortune for their children and a pension for herself in the event of his death.

As military commander at Cahokia from August 1779 McCarty soon mellowed his initially autocratic attitude towards the civilians and by October he was criticizing the Virginians' treatment of them. For this or some other reason he was arrested for treason, but whether he was tried is not known. In May 1781 he departed from Kaskaskia to present a petition from the civilians of that place to the Virginia legislature, complaining of their mistreatment by Virginian officials. A few days later he is believed to have been killed by Indians. Joseph-François Perrault*, who married McCarty's daughter Ursule in Montreal, eventually succeeded in obtaining on behalf of McCarty's heirs 400 acres of the land to which they laid claim in the United States.

Richard McCarty would seem to have been an opportunist whose aspirations exceeded his abilities. He probably married above his social status and may have abandoned the legal profession for the fur trade in the hope of building a fortune. The commander at Michilimackinac after 1774, Arent Schuyler De Peyster, must have known him reasonably well. On learning that McCarty had deserted to the Virginians he wrote "so poor a creature never entered into any service before – yet he was a very principal actor at Fort Sackville."

G. MALCOLM LEWIS

BL, Add. MSS 21757, ff.7, 47, 106–7v; 21842, ff.24–25. Clements Library, Harmar papers, 12, f.122a. Conn. State Library (Hartford), Connecticut archives, Colonial War, ser.1, no.21a. Ill. State Archives (Springfield), J. Nick Perrin coll., Cahokia records, notarized statement, 11 Jan. 1774. Ind. Hist. Soc. Library (Indianapolis), Armstrong papers. PAC, MG 24, L3, pp.2888–90, 3177–79. PRO, CO 42/5, ff.30–31. Wis., State Hist. Soc. (Madison), Canadian archives, abstracts of Indian trade licences in Canadian archives, 1767–76.

Cahokia records, 1778–1790, ed. C. W. Alvord (Springfield, Ill., 1907). *George Rogers Clark papers . . .* [1771–84], ed. J. A. James (2v., Springfield, 1912–26). *Kaskaskia records, 1778–1790*, ed. C. W. Alvord (Springfield, 1909). PAC *Report*, 1910, 17, 23. *The papers of Thomas Jefferson*, ed. J. P. Boyd *et al.* (19v. to date, Princeton, N.J., 1950–), IV, 207–8, 442; V, 494, 574. *The St. Clair papers . . .*, ed. W. H. Smith (2v., Cincinnati, Ohio, 1882). *Guide to the manuscript maps in the William L. Clements Library*, comp. Christian Brun (Ann Arbor, Mich., 1959). [P.-]P.-B. Casgrain, *La vie de Joseph-François Perrault, surnommé le père de l'éducation du peuple canadien* (Québec, 1898).

MACDONALD, JAMES (Seumas MacDhomhaill), priest and missionary; b. 1736 in the West Highlands, Scotland, probably in Moidart; d. 1785 on St John's (Prince Edward) Island.

James MacDonald was one of those bright lads the Scottish Catholic Church liked to send abroad for education. He entered the Jesuits' Scots College at Rome in 1754 and was ordained to the secular priesthood there in 1765 after completing his studies in philosophy, theology, and dogmatics. Returning to Scotland, he served until 1772 as a missionary priest based mainly at Drummond, near Crieff (Tayside). In May of that year he left Glasgow on the *Alexander* with more than 200 Highland Catholics for St John's Island, part of the first major emigration of Catholics from Scotland to America since the 1745–46 rebellion.

The group was led by laymen John MacDonald* of Glenaladale, known as Fear-a-Ghlinne, and his brother Donald (cousins of Father James), but the scheme had been conceived and the financing arranged by two bishops of the Scottish Catholic Church, John MacDonald and George Hay. Bishop MacDonald, fearful that the persecution initiated by Colin MacDonald of Boysdale on South Uist would spread, and unable to protest it legally, argued that emigration would relieve the sufferers on Uist by threatening the Highland lairds with depopulation of their estates. The church was aware of St John's Island through contact with the lord advocate of Scotland, James William Montgomery, who had extensive holdings there [*see* William MONTGOMERY], and it chose this site because of the Catholic Acadian population, and because the Scots "being all together on an Island, . . . would be the easier kept together & Religion the more flourish among them." The Scottish Church hoped to be given jurisdiction over the Island, but Rome decided to keep it under the bishop of Quebec, Jean-Olivier BRIAND. Father James, who had always been eager to go with his people, was selected to accompany the emigrants. He was in many ways an ideal choice for the venture, particularly since he was fluent in Gaelic, English, Latin, and French.

In spite of the bishops' hopes only 11 of 36 families on the Boysdale estate were willing to leave and the bulk of the emigrants came from the mainland MacDonald of Clanranald lands of Arisaig and Moidart. After a five-week voyage, the *Alexander* made its way up the Hillsborough River to Glenaladale's Lot 36, where Father James celebrated the Island's first mass under British rule. The only alternative leader to the Glenaladale MacDonalds, the priest found himself acting as spokesman for dissidents among the immigrants, many of whom were old friends and relations. He had other trials to contend with as well. The Acadians refused to mix with the Scots in a single settlement, and MacDonald was ordered by Briand to minister to the Acadians at Malpeque, where he settled for the first winter. There being no other priest on the Island, MacDonald could not himself receive the sacraments and felt extremely isolated.

In June 1773 Father James travelled to Quebec to explore the possibility of removing his "poor People" from the Island; though they had come out a year before with tools and food for a year, there was now, as he wrote home, "no money, no Cloathes, no meat to be met with there without paying four times the price of it, and it gives me a heart break that my poor friends who were in a tolerable good condition before they left Scotland are now upon the brink of the greatest misery and poverty." In Quebec he met Father Bernard-Sylvestre Dosque, the former priest at Malpeque, and was offered lands in Quebec for his parishioners. From the standpoint of the Scottish Church, Father James's activities were extremely dangerous, for dispersion of the settlement would imply its failure, and success was essential to frighten the Hebrides lairds and prevent further persecution. Fortunately conditions on the Island improved just in time. The arrival of Glenaladale later in 1773 with supplies combined with a better harvest to prevent the priest, in Bishop MacDonald's words, "from near destroying the whole affair," for those few who followed his advice were "irrecoverably" ruined and heartily repented of their removal to Quebec. There is no evidence that Father James's role in this episode damaged his relations with either the Glenaladales or his parishioners.

The immediate crisis of adjustment to the new land behind him and his people, Father James settled down to a routine of parochial activities among both Highlanders and Acadians. A church was built at Scotchfort, and the priest also often performed his duties in private houses as he had done in Scotland. Overcoming his fears of isolation, he refused an invitation from mainland Acadians to become their priest, insisting on the need to remain with his Island flocks. By 1776 he was fully reconciled to his situation and was even hearing confessions by Indians through interpreters as Dosque had done. There is unfortunately little record of his activities because of wartime interruptions in correspondence. Years of itinerant pastoral work, including occasional visits to Nova Scotia, in a land with only rudimentary communication and transportation took their toll and in 1785 Father James's worst fear was realized when for want of another priest he died of fever without receiving the last rites. He lies buried in an unmarked grave in Scotchfort. The Island was left without a resident priest until the arrival of Angus Bernard MacEachern* in 1790.

J. M. BUMSTED

Scottish Catholic Archives (Edinburgh), Blairs Letters, 11 Nov. 1770, Bishop George Hay to John Geddes; 25 Nov. 1771, Hay to Peter Grant; 14 Feb. 1772, Bishop John MacDonald to Hay; 23 April 1772, Bishop John MacDonald to Charles Cruickshank; 19 Jan. 1773, John MacDonald of Glenaladale to Hay; 9 June 1773, Father James MacDonald to John Grant; 25 Oct. 1773, Bishop John MacDonald to Hay; 4 Nov. 1776, Father James MacDonald to Hay. J. C. MacMillan, *The early history of the Catholic Church in Prince Edward Island* (Quebec, 1905), 41–50. J. M. Bumsted, "Highland emigration to the Island of St. John and the Scottish Catholic Church, 1769–1774," *Dal. Rev.*, LVIII (1978–79), 511–27. Ada MacLeod, "The Glenaladale pioneers," *Dal. Rev.*, XI (1931–32), 311–24.

MACÉ, PIERRE-JACQUES DRUILLON DE. *See* DRUILLON

MACKAY, JOHN, assistant ship's surgeon; fl. 1785–87.

Little is known of John Mackay's life until late in 1785. At that date he embarked with an expedition which was sailing from Bombay (India) under the leadership of Madras merchant James Charles Stuart Strange* to trade with the coastal Indians of present-day British Columbia. According to Alexander Walker*, who took part in the venture and who later interviewed him, Mackay was a native of Ireland who had received some medical training but had enlisted in the service of the East India Company as a private soldier. He had been selected for the voyage because he had sufficient medical background to act as surgeon's assistant on board the snow the *Experiment*, accompanying the *Captain Cook*, which carried a fully qualified surgeon. Strange had originally planned to leave a garrison of soldiers at Nootka Sound but decided on the spot against such an establishment because of its potential cost. Instead he left one man, John Mackay.

Later accounts of Mackay, based on scanty information, have tended to inflate his medical background. There is no doubt that in his journal Strange exaggerated Mackay's credentials; it was hardly in his interest to admit that the one individual left behind on his departure from the sound in July 1786 was not particularly well qualified. According to Strange, Mackay was a bright young man who had already won the affection of Nootka chief MUQUINNA by curing the chief's child of scabby hands and legs, and "as his [medical] Practice encreased, his Consequence in the Eyes of these people could not fail daily to gain ground." Nevertheless, Strange demonstrated a distinct lack of confidence in Mackay, emphasizing that he was supplied only with drugs which would not prove poisonous. Mackay was also left with full provisions, large quantities of seed, a pair of goats, as well as books, ink, and paper so that he might record "every Occurrence, however trivial, which might serve to throw any Light on our hitherto confined knowledge of the Manners, Customs, Religion & Government of these people." It was a golden chance for ethnography.

Unfortunately Mackay did not prove to be an ideal choice. He agreed to remain at Nootka Sound largely to avoid returning to the ranks in India, and in Alexander Walker's opinion, he was a man with "neither much Education nor much understanding." Captain George DIXON, who met Mackay in 1787, concurred, describing him as a "very ignorant young fellow . . . possessed of but an ordinary capacity." The difficulties were nevertheless not entirely of Mackay's making. The first problem was that Muquinna had insisted that Strange leave Mackay a musket and ammunition, since the natives viewed their guest principally as a smiter of the enemy. They also demanded that Mackay be left a red coat because such a garment would in itself awe their opponents. Strange tried to impress upon them that the gun was powerful only in the hands of a white man, but Mackay failed to capitalize on this advantage. A month after the departure of the Bombay vessels, the *Sea Otter* (Capt. James HANNA) called at Nootka Sound. Mackay was reported "healthy and contented, dressed and living like the natives"; indeed Mackay later recalled that by the time of Hanna's visit he had begun "to relish dried fish and whale oil," and was extremely "satisfied with his way of life." The Nootkas proudly displayed the gun to the *Sea Otter*'s crew, an understandable gesture to the Europeans who had first used firearms against them a year earlier. The Indians soon persuaded Mackay to let them examine the gun. He even dismantled the lock. Pieces were handed around, admired, and promptly vanished.

Despite the loss of his weapon, Mackay continued to be well treated until one day he inadvertently broke a taboo by stepping over the cradle of Muquinna's child when it was situated in front of the door. The chief chased him out of his house and assaulted him. For some weeks Mackay was forced to remain outdoors, his banishment prolonged by the child's death soon afterwards. Eventually he was given a hut and fed, but he never regained Muquinna's patronage. The writing instruments were destroyed shortly after by another chief; the goats died through neglect. When the village moved inland for the winter, Mackay was not fed on the journey and kept himself alive by eating all his garden and grain seed. Whatever skill in medicine he may have had, the women would not let him practise; they had their own remedies. Without his gun he was of no value in hunting, and he was left behind with the women and children whenever the men went food gathering. Naturally he came down with the bloody flux and spent a miserable winter.

In June 1787 the *Imperial Eagle* (Capt. Charles William Barkley*) moored in Friendly Cove and, according to the lost diary of Mrs Barkley (Frances Hornby Trevor), Mackay soon appeared on board, dressed only in a sea-otter skin and filthy beyond belief. Although Captain Dixon, who arrived in August, reported that Mackay had little command of the Nootkas' language – hardly surprising since he had spent most of his residence in disgrace – Mackay was able to help Barkley gain a cargo of 700 skins from the village. He was obviously eager to leave and apparently did so with Dixon aboard the *King George*. Upon his arrival in Canton (People's Republic of China), Mackay claimed that he had been forcibly removed and that given "a free choice he would not have quitted his station. . . ." By the time he returned to India he was drinking so heavily as to be nearly incomprehensible. Shortly after his interviews with Walker in Bombay (apparently some time in 1788), Mackay vanished. He probably soon died, his American experience a curiosity rather than a significant source of knowledge for others.

J. M. BUMSTED

National Library of Scotland (Edinburgh), Dept. of Manuscripts, MSS 13778, p.4; 13780, pp.262–78, 313. Provincial Archives of B.C., G.B., India Office, East India Company, Madras records, 1785–95, James Strange to Archibald Campbell, 22 Feb. 1788 (transcript); John Walbran, "The cruise of the Imperial Eagle" (typescript). [William Beresford], *A voyage round the world: but more particularly to the north-west coast of America* . . . , ed. and intro. George Dixon (London, 1789; repr. Amsterdam and New York, 1968), 232–33. [James Strange], *James Strange's journal and narrative of the commercial expedition from Bombay to the north-west coast of America* . . . (Madras, India, 1928; repr. 1929), 21, 23. Cook, *Flood tide of empire*, 102. F. W. Howay, "The voyage of the 'Captain Cook' and the 'Experiment,' 1785–86," *British Columbia Hist. Quarterly* (Victoria), V (1941), 285–96. W. K. Lamb, "The mystery of Mrs. Barkley's diary: notes on the voyage of the 'Imperial Eagle,' 1786–87," *British Columbia Hist. Quarterly*, VI (1942), 31–47.

MCKEE, ALEXANDER, Indian agent, fur-trader, and local official; b. *c.* 1735 in western Pennsylvania, son of Irish trader Thomas McKee and a Shawnee woman (or possibly a white captive of the Indians); d. 15 Jan. 1799 on the Thames River, Upper Canada.

As a young man Alexander McKee was a lieutenant in the Pennsylvania forces during the early part of the Seven Years' War. He entered the Indian department in 1760 as an assistant to George Croghan and until the outbreak of the American revolution he served the department and traded, achieving considerable importance among the tribes north of the Ohio River. He was married to a Shawnee woman and in the early 1770s had a home in one of the Shawnee villages on the Scioto River (Ohio).

As McKee was sympathetic to the British cause at the beginning of the revolution, he was kept under surveillance. In March 1778, with Matthew Elliott*, Simon Girty*, and others, he fled from the Fort Pitt (Pittsburgh, Pa) region into the Ohio country. Later in the year he joined the British at Detroit. The Americans considered his departure a major blow because McKee had extensive influence among the Indians. At Detroit he became a captain and interpreter in the Indian department and for the rest of the revolution helped direct operations among the Indians in the Ohio valley against the Americans. He participated in many of the main actions in that region, including Henry HAMILTON's capture of Vincennes (Ind.) in 1778, Henry Bird's expedition against Kentucky in 1780, and the attack on Bryant's Station (near Lexington, Ky) in August 1782.

After the revolution McKee obtained land on the Canadian side of the Detroit River, but he served at Detroit as deputy agent in the Indian department, which used his influence among the tribes in present Ohio and Indiana to encourage Indian resistance to American settlement beyond the Ohio River. He also traded along the Miamis (Maumee) River and was a prominent leader in the Detroit River region. He became lieutenant-colonel of the local militia in the late 1780s, justice of the Court of Common Pleas for the District of Hesse in 1788, member of the district land board in 1789, and lieutenant for the county of Essex in 1792.

When in the early 1790s full-scale hostilities broke out between the Americans and the Indian tribes, McKee and his assistants helped to gather and supply the Indians who resisted American expeditions [*see* EGUSHWA]. With John Graves Simcoe*, lieutenant governor of Upper Canada, he tried to devise a workable plan for an Indian buffer state between American and British possessions. McKee played a major role in organizing the Indians to meet Major-General Anthony Wayne's advances in 1793 and 1794 and was present at the battle of Fallen Timbers (near Waterville, Ohio) in August 1794, but only as an observer. Wayne's victory and the failure of the British regulars to support the Indians diminished British influence among the tribes. McKee was given formal command of Indian affairs in Upper Canada at the end of 1794 when he was appointed deputy superintendent and deputy inspector general of Indian affairs.

After the British withdrew from Detroit in 1796, McKee made his home on the Canadian side of the river. At his death three years later he was living on the Thames River. In the tumultuous years of the 1790s he had been the most important official organizing Indian resistance to the American advance across the Ohio River. To him, the British policy was not merely official, it was the culmination of a lifetime spent with the Indians of the Ohio valley. His son Thomas* also served in the Indian department, becoming agent at Amherstburg in 1801.

REGINALD HORSMAN

BL, Add. MSS 21661–892 (transcripts at PAC). PAC, MG 19, F1; RG 8, I (C series); RG 10, A1, 1–4; A2, 8–12. *Correspondence of Lieut. Governor Simcoe* (Cruikshank). *Frontier defense on the upper Ohio, 1777–1778 . . .*, ed. R. G. Thwaites and L. P. Kellogg (Madison, Wis., 1912; repr. Millwood, N.Y., 1973). *Johnson papers* (Sullivan *et al.*), III, VIII, X, XII. *Michigan Pioneer Coll.*, IX (1886), X (1886), XIII (1888), XIX (1891), XX (1892). PAO *Report*, 1905, 1928–29, 1931. *The Windsor border region, Canada's southernmost frontier . . .*, ed. E. J. Lajeunesse (Toronto, 1960).

R. C. Downes, *Council fires on the upper Ohio: a narrative of Indian affairs in the upper Ohio valley until 1795* (Pittsburgh, Pa., 1940). Reginald Horsman, *Matthew Elliott, British Indian agent* (Detroit, 1964). N. B. Wainwright, *George Croghan, wilderness diplomat* (Chapel Hill, N.C., 1959). Frederick Wulff, "Colonel Alexander McKee and British Indian policy, 1735–1799" (unpublished MA thesis, University of Wisconsin–Milwaukee, Milwaukee, Wis., 1969). W. R. Hoberg, "Early history of Colonel Alexander McKee," *Pennsylvania Magazine of History and Biography* (Philadelphia), LVIII (1934), 26–36; "A Tory in the northwest," *Pennsylvania Magazine of History and Biography* (Philadelphia), LIX (1935), 32–41.

MACKELLAR, PATRICK, military engineer; b. 1717; m. Elizabeth Basaline, probably on Minorca, and they had two sons; d. 22 Oct. 1778 on Minorca.

Patrick Mackellar entered the Ordnance service as a clerk at Woolwich (London) in 1735 and four years later was promoted clerk of the works and posted to Minorca. He soon displayed an aptitude for military architecture and engineering, which was officially recognized on 7 Dec. 1742 when he was granted a warrant as practitioner engineer. Thereafter he was employed in improving the defences of Port Mahón (Mahón, Minorca). He had risen to the rank of engineer in ordinary by July 1751.

Recalled to England in 1754, Mackellar was promptly dispatched to North America and was first employed on active service when he took part in Major-General Edward Braddock's expedition against Fort Duquesne (Pittsburgh, Pa) in 1755 [*see* Jean-Daniel DUMAS]. He was severely wounded in the battle of the Monongahela on 9 July, but by the following spring he was at Oswego (Chouaguen) as chief engineer of the frontier forts. Mackellar was ordered to replace obsolete fortifications at Oswego but his task was far from complete when the post was captured on 13–14 Aug. 1756 by a force under Montcalm*.

After some months as a prisoner of war at Quebec and Montreal, Mackellar was exchanged. He returned to Britain early in 1757 and on 14 May was commissioned captain in his corps. On 4 January of the following year he was promoted sub-director of engineers and major and was appointed deputy to Colonel John Henry Bastide*, chief engineer in Jeffery AMHERST's expedition against Louisbourg, Île Royale (Cape Breton Island). The British forces disembarked near the fortress on 8 June, and one month later Mackellar succeeded Bastide, who had been wounded. Although James Wolfe* was impatient with the slow progress of the siege, it appears that not a little of the credit for the capitulation of Louisbourg on 27 July was due to Mackellar's professional skill.

A few months later Mackellar was selected to serve as chief engineer in the expedition Wolfe was to command against Quebec. Mackellar was uniquely qualified for his new post. Not only was he highly respected in his profession but, following his release from imprisonment, he had submitted to the Ordnance Office a detailed report of the topography and defences of Quebec, together with a map of the area. Although much of his information was inaccurate or out of date – the original of his map had been included by Pierre-François-Xavier de Charlevoix* in his *Histoire et description générale de la Nouvelle France . . .* (3v., Paris, 1744) – it nonetheless provided Wolfe with the only substantial body of intelligence about his objective, and Mackellar became one of his few trusted advisers. He sited the British batteries and conducted all preliminary siege operations, despite a serious wound suffered during the attack on the Beauport shore on 31 July, and he devised and tested methods of landing infantry from floating stages. He also advised Wolfe against a frontal attack upon the city and accompanied the general on his final reconnaissance.

Immediately after the victory on the Plains of Abraham on 13 September, Mackellar engaged in preparations to besiege Quebec, but its capitulation five days later made these efforts redundant. During the autumn of 1759 and the spring of 1760 he strengthened the defences of the city against an anticipated French counter-attack, and had the direction of the artillery in the force under Brigadier-General James MURRAY at the battle of Sainte-Foy on 28 April. Although critically wounded in the British defeat, Mackellar supervised the defence of Quebec during his convalescence until the arrival of a British squadron in May forced the French to raise the siege. He also participated in the subsequent operations which completed the conquest of Canada.

In November 1760 Mackellar was appointed chief engineer at Halifax, where he initiated important works to improve the defences and devoted much time and energy to training troops for siege operations. He served with distinction as chief engineer in Major-General Robert MONCKTON's expedition against Martinique the following year and in the Earl of Albemarle's expedition against Cuba in 1762. He was dangerously wounded during the siege of Morro Castle, Havana, and never completely recovered. After the peace Mackellar was posted back to Minorca, where he again worked on improving the defences. He was promoted brevet lieutenant-colonel on 3 Jan. 1762, lieutenant-colonel on 2 Feb. 1775, and director of engineers and colonel on 29 Aug. 1777. His elder son John, who rose to the rank of admiral of the blue, served in Halifax from 1804 to 1810 as agent for prisoners of war and transports and governor of the naval hospital.

It is curious that Mackellar, despite a most respectable and distinguished career, was never the recipient of honours. His promotions, however, prove that he was one of the most esteemed military engineers of his generation, and certainly he deserves recognition for his contribution to the British successes in Canada during the final campaigns of the Seven Years' War.

JOHN W. SPURR

[Mackellar left interesting and valuable accounts of the principal operations in which he had been involved, including a priceless journal of the expedition to Quebec. This journal, when originally published in *Papers on subjects connected with the duties of the corps of Royal Engineers* (London), IX (1847), was incorrectly attributed to Major James Moncrieff. The originals of Mackellar's papers plus many pertinent maps are preserved in the BL, the Cumberland papers in the Royal Library at Windsor Castle, and the PRO, and many are conveniently available in *Military affairs in North America, 1748–65* (Pargellis). Copies of those papers relating directly to Canada are also available in the PAC. J.W.S.]

Knox, *Hist. journal* (Doughty). Frederic Boase, *Modern English biography* . . . (3v. and 3 supps., privately printed in England, 1892–1921; repr. London, 1965), II, 621–22. *DAB*. *DNB*. G.B., WO, *Army list*, 1758–1836. W. R. O'Byrne, *A naval biographical dictionary* . . . (London, 1849), 699–700. *Roll of officers of the corps of Royal Engineers from 1660 to 1898* . . . , ed. R. F. Edwards (Chatham, Eng., 1898), 4. L. H. Gipson, *The British empire before the American revolution* (15v., Caldwell, Idaho, and New York, 1936–70), VI, VII. Christopher Hibbert, *Wolfe at Quebec* (London and Toronto, 1959). Porter, *History of Royal Engineers*, II, 386–87. Stacey, *Quebec, 1759*, 44–46, 107–8, 129–30.

McLANE (McLean, M'Lane), DAVID, merchant; b. possibly in Ayrshire, Scotland; hanged at Quebec on 21 July 1797, at about 30 years of age.

From the summer of 1789 until April 1793 articles appeared in Quebec and Montreal newspapers praising the French revolution; these were written by both Canadians and Englishmen, the former being converts to the Enlightenment and the latter welcoming the establishment at last by the French of a parliamentary régime. Although Canadian priests opposed the revolution, they remained silent in public. When the revolutionaries declared war on Great Britain, however, the situation changed radically, and at this point colonial officials launched what was essentially a psychological campaign. Each week Montreal and Quebec newspapers published proclamations against sedition, denunciations, addresses, and speeches by the governor and other officials. Collections of these texts were published as pamphlets and distributed at public expense to magistrates, militia captains, justices of the peace, and other leading persons, all of whom were urged to expose anyone making seditious remarks. At the same time, the House of Assembly, on 2 May 1797, suspended the right of habeas corpus and ordered foreigners – especially Frenchmen – to leave the colony. Clerical denunciation of the "horrors" of a parricidal and diabolical revolution came in pastoral letters from the bishop, circular letters, homilies, and sermons.

In the autumn of 1793, and each autumn until 1797, the colonial authorities feared an attack by the French fleet from Saint-Domingue (Hispaniola). And throughout this period, French spies, who proved elusive, were hunted. Indeed the British became increasingly persuaded that the Canadians were being manipulated by spies. They were led to this conviction by the refusal of Canadians to enrol in the militia under the terms of the new law of 1794 in the fear that they would have to serve far away from their homes, and by hostile incidents in 1796 when another new law required the habitants to give their time, tools, and teams to work on road construction. It was necessary to discover these dangerous emissaries, and the search led to David McLane, a merchant from Providence, R.I.

On 1 Dec. 1796 in Montreal, William Barnard declared under oath that he had met McLane the preceding July in Vermont and later in Montreal, and that McLane had admitted he wanted to promote revolution in Canada. On 10 May 1797 in Quebec, John Black*, a ship carpenter and member of the House of Assembly, declared to an executive councillor that he had that very day met one Charles Frichet who had told him in confidence that "a French general" hiding in the forest wanted to see him; Black said he had then met David McLane, who revealed his subversive plans to him. He proposed to overthrow the government by enlisting seven or eight influential people including Black, and as many Canadians as possible. Assisted by recruits from the United States and armed with eight-foot pikes, the force would make a surprise attack on the Quebec garrison. That evening McLane was arrested in the home of Black, who had denounced him to the authorities. On 14 June, the court named as his lawyers George Germaine Sackville Francklin, son of Michael FRANCKLIN, and George Pyke*, both of whom had practised for only a few months. The trial began on 7 July, before 12 English jurors. The crown was represented by Attorney General Jonathan Sewell* and Alexis Caron*. Six witnesses were called for the prosecution, among them Charles Frichet and John Black, and all gave evidence incriminating the accused. In his own statement McLane declared that he had come to Canada for the sole purpose of selling wood. No witnesses were called for the defendant, but Pyke brought out the absurdity of the scheme attributed to McLane and the lack of supporting evidence. Francklin, moreover, contended that neither Frichet nor Black should be trusted as witnesses because they were accomplices. After a half hour's deliberation the jury pronounced McLane guilty. The defence demanded that the judgement be quashed on the ground that McLane, as a foreigner, could not be charged with treason. Their request was refused and the chief justice of the province, William Osgoode*, sentenced McLane to be hanged, to be disembowelled while still alive, and to have his head and limbs severed from his body. On 21 July, attended by two Protestant ministers, he was executed outside the city walls in the presence of a large crowd. He was already dead when the hangman cut off his head and disembowelled him; his body was not dismembered. The witnesses for the prosecution, Black in particular, had received land for their collaboration. Charles Frichet, an illiterate of no ability, was condemned to life imprisonment for having failed to denounce the American spy, but he was pardoned and immediately released.

The McLane affair horrified the population and caused much comment. The government had 2,000 copies of the trial transcript printed by William Vondenvelden*, and gave a subsidy to John Neilson* for two editions of a summary of the trial after he had written long articles in the *Quebec Gazette* about it. By autumn a pamphlet described to Americans McLane's trial and barbarous punishment. Although informed about the affair, the American government chose to ignore it in order not to endanger its relations with Great Britain. The following year Abbé Augustin de Barruel, a counter-revolutionary French intellectual, proceeded to use the McLane affair to demonstrate "the universal successes of the faction, accounted for by its universal conspiracies." The proceedings and the transcript of the trial were even included in a collection of important trials compiled by Thomas Bayley Howell in 1819, and the case continued to engender debate among British and American jurists in the 19th century.

The scheme attributed to McLane involved many improbabilities. Both French and English Canadian historians, with the exception of Douglas Brymner* and William Kingsford*, have in general agreed that McLane was an unlucky fool rather than a conspirator. The affair is a good example of what happens in wartime when the effects of fear and psychological propaganda lead to exaggeration so that some lose their heads and others become informers for profit.

CLAUDE GALARNEAU

[The proceedings of the trial were published by William Vondenvelden in a 127-page work entitled *The trial of David McLane for high treason, at the city of Quebec, in the province of Lower-Canada; on Friday, the seventh day of July, A.D. 1797: taken in short-hand, at the trial* (Quebec, 1797). John Neilson published a summary of the trial both in English and in French. The English pamphlet has 21 pages and bears the title *The trial of David M'Lane for high treason, before a special court of oyer and terminer at Quebec, on the 7th July 1797* (Quebec, 1797). The pamphlet published in the United States is entitled *The trial, condemnation and horrid execution of David M'Lane, formerly of Pennsylvania, for high treason . . .* (Windham, Ohio, 1797). *See also*: [Augustin de] Barruel, *Abrégé des mémoires pour servir à l'histoire du jacobinisme* (Londres, 1798), and *A complete collection of state trials and proceedings for high treason and other crimes and misdemeanors from the earliest period to the year 1783*, comp. T. B. Howell (33v., London, 1809–26), XXVI, no.622. C.G.]

ANQ-Q, AP-P-1061, 68–69. Archives du ministère des Affaires étrangères (Paris), Corr. politique, États-Unis, 49, ff.146, 155–65. PAC, MG 11, [CO 42], Q, 78, pp.135–44. PAC *Rapport*, 1891, xxxii–xli; note D, 57–85. T.-P. Bédard, *Histoire de cinquante ans (1791–1841), annales parlementaires et politiques du Bas-Canada, depuis la constitution jusqu'a l'Union* (Québec, 1869). Thomas Chapais, *Cours d'histoire du Canada* (8v., Québec et Montréal, 1919–34), II. Robert

Christie, *A history of the late province of Lower Canada, parliamentary and political, from the commencement to the close of its existence as a separate province* . . . (6v., Quebec and Montreal, 1848–55), I. Galarneau, *La France devant l'opinion canadienne*. F.-X. Garneau, *Hist. du Canada* (1845–48), III. William Kingsford, *The history of Canada* (10v., Toronto and London, 1887–98), VII. J.-F. Perrault, *Abrégé de l'histoire du Canada* . . . (5 parties en 4v., Québec, 1832–36), II.

MACLEAN, ALLAN, army officer; b. 1725 at Torloisk on the island of Mull, Scotland, third son of Major Donald Maclean, fifth laird of Torloisk, and Mary Campbell; m. 4 Feb. 1771 in London, England, to Janet Maclean; d. 18 Feb. 1798 in London, without issue.

Like many of his Highland contemporaries, Allan Maclean joined the Jacobite army in 1745. He served as a lieutenant in the Clan Maclean battalion and was present at Culloden. After the defeat of Charles, the Young Pretender, Maclean fled to the Netherlands and enlisted in the Scots brigade of the Dutch army in May 1746. In 1747 he and his kinsman Francis McLEAN were captured by the French at the siege of Bergen op Zoom (Netherlands). Allan Maclean returned to Great Britain in 1750 following the amnesty granted by George II to all Jacobite officers willing to swear allegiance to the house of Hanover.

On 8 Jan. 1756 Maclean was commissioned lieutenant in the Royal Americans (62nd, later 60th Foot) and served in North America until 1761. He was wounded in James ABERCROMBY's futile assault against Montcalm*'s forces at Fort Carillon (Ticonderoga, N.Y.) in 1758, and again while commanding an independent company of New York provincial troops at the siege of Fort Niagara (near Youngstown, N.Y.) in 1759. Later that year he joined James Wolfe*'s force before Quebec. Returning to Britain in 1761, Maclean raised his own unit, and on 18 Oct. 1761 he was gazetted major commandant of the 114th Foot (Maclean's Highlanders). He proceeded to North America with his men, but in 1763 the regiment was disbanded and Maclean went on half pay. A number of his men settled on St John's (Prince Edward) Island. Maclean himself later received a land grant there along with several other Maclean gentry, but he does not appear to have settled on the island.

Maclean was restored to full pay in 1772 and the next year offered to raise a battalion of Highlanders for service in Bengal, but the East India Company rejected the offer. As the political situation in the American colonies deteriorated, Maclean proposed to raise a regiment from disbanded Highland soldiers living in North America. This proposal was accepted and on 12 June 1775 Maclean was empowered by Lieutenant-General GAGE to raise "a Corps of two Battalions . . . to be cloathed, Armed and Accoutred in like manner with His Majesty's Royal Highland Regiment [42nd Foot] and to be called the Royal Highland Emigrants." The first battalion was recruited in Canada and New York and the second in Nova Scotia and St John's Island. Maclean, who was designated lieutenant-colonel commandant of the whole regiment, took personal command of the first battalion.

During the revolutionary war the second battalion never served as a unit, although some detachments were sent to the Carolinas. The first battalion, however, played a notable part in the defence of Canada during the American invasion of 1775. When Governor Guy Carleton*'s attempts to relieve Fort Saint-Jean (on the Richelieu River) collapsed, Maclean, who had assembled a force of regulars and Royal Highland Emigrants on the river and was endeavouring to enlist Canadian support, withdrew to Quebec. He arrived in time to discourage pro-American elements from surrendering the city to Benedict Arnold*. Maclean's energy and firm direction, combined with the efforts of Lieutenant Governor Hector Theophilus CRAMAHÉ, strengthened the morale of the defenders. Although Carleton took over the supreme command upon his arrival after the fall of Montreal, Maclean was responsible for the military arrangements which led to the defeat of the Americans on 31 Dec. 1775 and the death of their commander, Richard MONTGOMERY. The Americans continued the siege, however, until May 1776, when British reinforcements arrived.

On 11 May 1776 Allan Maclean was appointed adjutant general of the army in North America, a position he held until 6 June 1777 when he was promoted brigadier-general and made military governor of Montreal. Following BURGOYNE's surrender at Saratoga (Schuylerville, N.Y.), Maclean, as the officer responsible for the defence of Montreal, was forced to abandon Fort Ticonderoga (formerly Fort Carillon) and concentrate his troops along the Richelieu River for a more effective defence against any renewed American invasion. After strong appeals from Maclean, the Royal Highland Emigrants were finally regimented in 1779 as the 84th, and the authorized strength was raised from 700 to 1,000 for each battalion.

Maclean returned to Great Britain after the

peace settlement of 1783. He retired from the army in 1784 and lived quietly in London until his death.

G. F. G. STANLEY

BL, Add. MSS 21661–892. Private archives, J.N.M. Maclean of Glensanda, the younger (Edinburgh), Torloisk MSS and transcripts. G.B., Board of Trade, *JTP, 1764–67*, 404–14. Boatner, *Encyclopedia of American revolution. DNB. Gentleman's Magazine*, 1798, 354–55. G.B., WO, *Army list*, 1756–84. J. N. M. Maclean, *Reward is secondary; the life of a political adventurer and an inquiry into the mystery of 'Junius'* (London, 1963). J. P. MacLean, *An historical account of the settlements of Scotch Highlanders in America prior to the peace of 1783* . . . (Cleveland, Ohio, and Glasgow, 1900; repr. Baltimore, Md., 1968); *Renaissance of the clan Maclean* . . . (Columbus, Ohio, 1913). G. F. G. Stanley, *Canada invaded, 1775–1776* (Toronto, 1973).

McLEAN, FRANCIS, army officer; b. *c.* 1717, one of two sons of Captain William Maclean and Anne Kinloch; d. 4 May 1781 at Halifax, Nova Scotia. Apparently he never married.

Francis McLean served with his more famous kinsman Allan MACLEAN in the Scots brigade in the Dutch service and was captured at Bergen op Zoom (Netherlands) in 1747, where Maréchal Lowendahl, the French commander, praised him for his bravery. In October 1758 McLean joined the British army as a captain in the 2nd battalion, 42nd Foot, and was wounded in the capture of Guadeloupe in 1759. He exchanged into the 97th Foot in 1761, became lieutenant-colonel in 1762, and went on half pay in 1763. From 1762 to 1778 he was in the Portuguese service, attaining the rank of major-general and appointment to the government of Lisbon. At the same time he dabbled in land in North America. He acquired a lot on St John's (Prince Edward) Island and in 1773 was among several petitioners for 250,000 acres in upper New York.

In 1777 the 82nd Foot was raised for service in North America and Francis McLean appointed its lieutenant-colonel. He sailed with the regiment for Nova Scotia in the spring of 1778, arriving in September. There he replaced Major-General Eyre Massey as military commander at Halifax and was appointed to the local rank of brigadier in Nova Scotia by Sir Henry Clinton, the commander-in-chief in North America. In addition to his military duties, McLean was responsible to Clinton for overseeing Indian affairs and looking after arriving loyalists.

On 16 June 1779, under Clinton's orders, McLean took an expedition of about 650 men to Fort Majebigwaduce (Castine, Maine) to find a refuge for loyalists and to forestall an anticipated attack on Nova Scotia by troops from New England. From 25 July an American force of between 2,000 and 3,000 soldiers and sailors in some 40 vessels under the command of Dudley Saltonstall besieged him there. McLean faced desperate odds. Although he had not had nearly enough time to complete his fortifications, he resolved to stand his ground while sending for help. A gale drove back one relief force from Halifax, but Sir George COLLIER sailed from Sandy Hook (N.J.) on 3 August and engaged the Americans on the 14th, routing them completely. McLean's casualties amounted to only 23 killed, 35 wounded, and 11 missing. He returned to Halifax in the late fall.

McLean was certainly a brave and resolute soldier. John Moore, later a famous general, served as a subaltern under him at Majebigwaduce and formed a fondness for his superior. He enjoyed McLean's military library, which he considered one of the finest of its sort, and later extolled the soundness of his military knowledge.

As an administrator, McLean proved controversial. Superintendent of Indian affairs Michael FRANCKLIN stated that in 1781 McLean refused to release trade goods to him without explicit instructions from Clinton. Francklin, however, had a personal grievance; until the fall of 1779 the government had allowed him to draw all provisions from military stores, but in 1780 he was required to obtain the permission of the commander-in-chief. Another contemporary, the Reverend Jacob Bailey*, found McLean "opinionated and headstrong," and "insensible to every softer feeling." Bailey asserted that McLean arbitrarily took rations away from 200 or 300 loyalist refugees, allowing them to only about 20 people. But Clinton checked McLean's expenditures on loyalists closely and at the same time approved heartily some of McLean's administrative arrangements, such as the establishment of regimental hospitals.

McLean grew visibly ill during the winter of 1780–81, and died on 4 May 1781 at Halifax, where he was buried two days later.

FRANKLIN B. WICKWIRE

[Henry Clinton], *The American rebellion: Sir Henry Clinton's narrative of his campaigns, 1775–1782* . . . , ed. W. B. Willcox (New Haven, Conn., 1954), 135, 419–20. *The correspondence of King George the Third from 1760 to December 1783* . . . , ed. John Fortescue (6v., London, 1928), III, 531. G.B., Board of Trade, *JTP, 1764–67*, 402, 413; Hist. MSS Commission, *Report on American MSS*, I, 250–51, 301; II, 14–17, 172, 371, 416, 460, 466; *Report on manuscripts in various collections* . . . (8v., London, 1901–14), VI, 151; Privy Council, *Acts of P.C., col., 1766–83*, 63, 597; PRO, *CHOP, 1773–75. NYCD* (O'Callaghan and Fernow), VIII, 757, 791. H. M. Chichester and George Burges-Short, *The records and badges of every regiment and corps in the British army* (London, 1895). *DNB* (biography of Allan Maclean). J. B. M. Frederick, *Lineage book of the British army, mounted corps and infantry, 1660–1968* (Cornwallville, N.Y., 1969).

G. W. Allen, *A naval history of the American revolution* (2v., New York, 1913; repr. 1962), I, 420–21. W. S. Bartlet, *The frontier missionary: a memoir of the life of the Rev. Jacob Bailey . . .* (Boston, 1853), 165. Brebner, *Neutral Yankees* (1937), 328–29. James Browne, *A history of the Highlands and of the Highland clans* (4v., Glasgow, 1843). *A history of the Scottish Highlands, Highland clans, and Highland regiments . . .*, ed. J. S. Keltie (2v., Edinburgh and London, 1875), II, 452. J. C. Moore, *The life of Lieutenant-General Sir John Moore . . .* (2v., London, 1834). Murdoch, *History of N.S.*, II, 600–1. Carola Oman, *Sir John Moore* (London, 1953), 50, 94. G. G. Patterson, *Studies in Nova Scotian history* (Halifax, 1940), 17–33.

McLEAN, NEIL (Neal), commissary, businessman, and local official; m. secondly Mary Herkimer, and they had one daughter; buried 1 Sept. 1795 at Kingston, Upper Canada.

Details of Neil McLean's early life are not known. He has been wrongly identified with other people of the same name, and it should be noted that he was not an officer in the 84th Foot or the father of Archibald McLean*. He probably joined the commissariat department of the British army in 1759. At that time, except for a few on colonial establishments, commissaries were recruited from civilian life for particular campaigns and were usually men with commercial or financial experience. They ranked as officers but had no power of command, and were frequently suspected of enriching themselves at the expense of the government and the troops.

Since McLean later claimed that he had had continuous service in the department, he must have been kept on the establishment after the peace in 1763, perhaps in America. In 1776 he was ordered to Canada. There, according to his own statement, he was constantly employed on dangerous and disagreeable service and was the "drudge" of the department. Appointed assistant commissary general on 2 Jan. 1777, he served from 1778 in the "transport business" at Carleton Island (N.Y.). He forwarded supplies and reinforcements to the Upper Lakes posts and performed some duties connected with the distribution of gifts to the Indians. At times he had difficulty collecting his pay and allowances from the government.

In 1783, when the loyalist regiments were disbanded, McLean's pay was reduced, but he was kept on as assistant commissary and storekeeper for the loyalist settlement at Cataraqui (Kingston, Ont.). As one of the first "Habitants," he became a leader of the community, and in July 1784, along with John Ross, he was appointed justice of the peace. McLean became a deputy inspector of land surveys and of loyalists on 14 Jan. 1786, and on 10 Sept. 1788 was made inspector for loyalist land claims and a member of the land board for the District of Mecklenburg. On 14 June 1788 he had been appointed judge of the Court of Common Pleas along with James Clark*.

McLean prospered in Kingston. By 1788 he and his wife had received 700 acres from the government. His property included choice waterfront and other lots on both sides of the Cataraqui River. He maintained a house and farm staffed by two black servants. In 1789, along with other "principal inhabitants" of Kingston, he petitioned unsuccessfully for possession of the Kingston mills. By July 1793 he had received another 2,000 acres from the government, and he may have purchased land from other grantees.

In 1790 McLean was made a justice of the Court of Quarter Sessions and a trustee for the Kingston hospital. He was a benefactor of St George's Church, and on his death in 1795 he was buried in its cemetery (now St Paul's churchyard). His widow, who later married Robert Hamilton*, described as McLean's "close friend and business partner," inherited most of McLean's property. The remainder of his estate went to his daughter by his first marriage, Harriet, who later married Allan MacLean*, Kingston's first practising lawyer. She obtained more land in recognition of her father's services, but in 1798 the Executive Council of Upper Canada struck Neil McLean's name from the list of loyalists on the grounds that it had been inserted improperly.

RICHARD A. PRESTON

BL, Add. MSS 21661–892. PAC *Report*, 1884–89. PAO *Report*, 1905, 1917, 1928–29, 1931. *The parish register of Kingston, Upper Canada, 1785–1811*, ed. A. H. Young (Kingston, Ont., 1921), 25, 32, 37–38, 49, 54, 155. "The probated wills of men prominent in the public affairs of early Upper Canada," ed. A. F. Hunter, *OH*, XXIII (1926), 328–59.

MACLEOD, NORMAND, army officer, Indian department official, and fur-trader; b. on Skye, Scotland; m. Cécile Robert, probably the daughter of Antoine Robert of Detroit (Mich.); d. 1796 at Montreal (Que.).

Normand MacLeod first saw military service

in 1747 in the Netherlands. He came to America in 1756 as an ensign in the 42nd Foot, and during the Seven Years' War he transferred to Thomas GAGE's 80th Foot. He attained the rank of captain-lieutenant and in the early 1760s was stationed at Fort Niagara (near Youngstown, N.Y.). At that time he also became acquainted with the Detroit region. After the war he was placed on half pay, and in the mid 1760s he lived in New York City. He was a friend of Sir William JOHNSON and others of his circle and Johnson became his patron. MacLeod visited Johnson Hall (Johnstown), performed personal commissions for Johnson in New York, and was a brother Mason.

In the summer of 1766 MacLeod was appointed commissary for Indian affairs at Fort Ontario (Oswego, N.Y.). That year he entertained Pontiac* and his party when they came to the post for a meeting with Johnson. MacLeod became commissary at Niagara in 1767 but lost the position in the spring of 1769 during a general retrenchment by the British government. He went to New York City in an unsuccessful attempt to obtain patronage from General Gage. By the summer of 1770, however, he was established on a farm at Caughnawaga (Fonda, N.Y.) in the Mohawk valley under Johnson's patronage.

Named commandant at Fort Ontario in the fall of 1773, MacLeod requested permission to delay taking up his post until the following summer. Johnson died in July 1774, and it was likely then that MacLeod moved west to establish himself as a trader at Detroit in partnership with Gregor McGregor and William Forsyth. In October 1774 he bought property there in partnership with McGregor. In the fall of 1778, as a captain in the Detroit militia, MacLeod went on Henry HAMILTON's expedition against Vincennes (Ind.), whose inhabitants had declared for the rebels. He returned to Detroit early in 1779 before Hamilton's garrison was captured. Hamilton had attempted to make MacLeod town major at Detroit, but the appointment was not confirmed since no such position had been provided for the upper posts.

By 1779 MacLeod had a new partner – John Macnamara, who was a prominent merchant at Michilimackinac (Mackinaw City, Mich.) – but at the end of the revolution he became associated with John Gregory* of Montreal in the firm of Gregory, MacLeod and Company. This firm provided the main opposition to the North West Company; one of its wintering partners was Alexander Mackenzie*. MacLeod moved to Montreal at this time, and when in 1787 the North West Company absorbed his firm he received one of the 20 shares in the reorganized company. In 1790 he sold his share and retired. He died six years later.

Throughout his life MacLeod was well thought of by those who knew him and employed him. Sir William Johnson commented that he had "great Esteem for Capt MacLeod who is a Worthy Man and one I am always disposed to Serve." Frederick HALDIMAND referred to him as "a Gentleman for whom I have a particular regard."

REGINALD HORSMAN

Les bourgeois de la Compagnie du Nord-Ouest (Masson), I, 10–11. *Docs. relating to NWC* (Wallace), 11, 13, 82–84, 453, 474, 481–82. *Henry Hamilton and George Rogers Clark in the American revolution, with the unpublished journal of Lieut. Gov. Henry Hamilton*, ed. J. D. Barnhart (Crawfordsville, Ind., 1951), 104–5, 150, 171, 222. *Johnson papers* (Sullivan *et al.*), V–VIII. [Alexander Mackenzie], *The journals and letters of Sir Alexander Mackenzie*, ed. and intro. W. K. Lamb (Cambridge, Eng., 1970), 3, 6, 11, 447; *Voyages from Montreal on the River St. Laurence through the continent of North America to the Frozen and Pacific oceans in the years 1789 and 1793 . . .* (London, 1801; new ed., intro. Roy Daniells, Edmonton, 1971), xix, xxii. *Michigan Pioneer Coll.*, IX (1886), 484, 633, 658; X (1886), 283–84, 316–17, 374–75, 456, 608; XI (1887), 625; XIX (1891), 31, 110, 320–21, 588, 654–55, 665–66; XX (1892), 206, 249. *The new régime, 1765–67*, ed. C. W. Alvord and C. E. Carter (Springfield, Ill., 1916), 513–14. *NYCD* (O'Callaghan and Fernow), VII, 854; VIII, 228. PAO *Report*, 1904, 370–71. *Trade and politics, 1767–1769*, ed. C. W. Alvord and C. E. Carter (Springfield, Ill., 1921), 83. *The Windsor border region, Canada's southernmost frontier . . .* , ed. E. J. Lajeunesse (Toronto, 1960), 316–17. Wis., State Hist. Soc., *Coll.*, XII (1892), 28; XVIII (1908), 234, 239–40. James Browne, *A history of the Highlands and of the Highland clans* ([new ed.], 4v., London, 1848–52), IV, 155. Davidson, *NWC*, 62. Innis, *Fur trade in Canada* (1956), 199–200.

MACUINA. *See* MUQUINNA

MAGON DE TERLAYE, FRANÇOIS-AUGUSTE, Sulpician, priest, and missionary; b. 10 July 1724 at Saint-Malo, France, son of Luc Magon de La Balluë and Pélagie Porrée; d. 17 May 1777 at the mission of Lac-des-Deux-Montagnes (Oka, Que.).

François-Auguste Magon de Terlaye entered the Maison des Philosophes in Paris in October 1748. Ordained deacon in 1754, he became a member of the Séminaire de Saint-Sulpice in Paris on 22 March that year and on 25 May joined a group under Sulpician François PICQUET which travelled to Canada on the frigate *Gloire*. Ordained priest on 24 May 1755, Magon de Terlaye rejoined Picquet at La Présentation (Oswegatchie, now Ogdensburg, N.Y.) to assist him in both his priestly ministrations and his political activity. During the Seven Years' War Picquet took an active part in the defence of New France, with substantial help from Magon de Terlaye, the "Chevalier de Terlaye" as he is termed in the diary of Louis-Antoine de Bougainville*. Magon de Terlaye served both the Iroquois and the garrison as a priest. On 6 March 1756 he gave the mission church three paintings depicting the Last Supper, the Descent from the Cross, and the Virgin and Child with John the Baptist.

In May 1758 he was appointed to the Lac-des-Deux-Montagnes mission as an assistant to the superior, Hamon Guen*. Under Guen's successor, Jean-Claude MATHEVET, Magon de Terlaye became bursar as well as missionary to the Iroquois. In the former capacity he had small rough shelters built which he let the Indians use. The land itself was lent to the Indians and by 1763 the most settled Iroquois were beginning to claim ownership of it. Their claims would give rise to proceedings at law, to renunciations of religious faith, and in 1877 to arson at the mission; they were only settled by a Supreme Court judgement in March 1910 [*see* Nicolas Dufresne*; Joseph Onasakenrat*].

Around 1775–76 Magon de Terlaye commissioned a number of wooden sculptures in relief carved by François Guernon*, *dit* Belleville, remarkable works of art which symbolize Terlaye's fine taste and generosity. They were commissioned to reproduce and replace the oil paintings bought in France that had decorated the seven chapels of the Way of the Cross at Oka.

Magon de Terlaye left numerous manuscripts in Iroquois: a grammar, an Onondaga- and Cayuga-French dictionary, sermons, and a history of God's chosen people. He was also known for his charity to the nuns of the Congregation of Notre-Dame. Over a number of years his gifts amounted to 12,000 *livres* in dowries for sisters from humble families. Stricken with an infectious disease, Terlaye died suddenly at the Lac-des-Deux-Montagnes mission on 17 May 1777.

J.-BRUNO HAREL

ASSM, 24, Dossier 2; Dossier 6; 8, A. Louis Bertrand, *Bibliothèque sulpicienne, ou histoire littéraire de la Compagnie de Saint-Sulpice* (3v., Paris, 1900). André Chagny, *Un défenseur de la "Nouvelle-France," François Picquet, "le Canadien" (1708–1781)* (Montréal et Paris, 1913). Lemire-Marsolais et Lambert, *Hist. de la CND de Montréal*, V, 42, 140, 291–94. J. R. Porter et Jean Trudel, *Le calvaire d'Oka* (Ottawa, 1974). M. Trudel, *L'Église canadienne*. J.-A. Cuoq, "Anotc kekon," RSC *Trans.*, 1st ser., XI (1893), sect. I, 137–79. Olivier Maurault, "Quand Saint-Sulpice allait en guerre . . . ," *Cahiers des Dix*, 5 (1940), 11–30.

MAGOUAOUIDOMBAOUIT. *See* GILL, JOSEPH-LOUIS

MALARTIC, ANNE-JOSEPH-HIPPOLYTE DE MAURÈS DE MALARTIC, Comte de. *See* MAURÈS

MALEPART DE BEAUCOURT, FRANÇOIS (he generally signed F. Beaucourt and sometimes F.·. Beaucourt.·., the three dots in a triangle constituting a Masonic symbol), painter; b. 25 Feb. 1740 at La Prairie (Que.), son of painter Paul Malepart* (Mallepart) de Grand Maison, *dit* Beaucour, and Marguerite Haguenier; d. 24 June 1794 in Montreal (Que.).

François Malepart de Beaucourt is remembered primarily as the first Canadian painter to have developed his technique in Europe, but little is known of certain periods in his life. It was probably his father who first instructed him in painting. In 1757, less than a year after his father's death, his mother married Romain Lasselin, a corporal in the Régiment de Guyenne. According to the contract signed for her second marriage, François, the only living child of her previous marriage, was to be "fed and kept at the expense of the aforesaid joint estate . . . until the age of 25 years." After the conquest Corporal Lasselin may have decided to return to France with his family. In any event François Beaucourt was at Bordeaux in 1773, where on 12 July he married Benoîte, the daughter of Joseph-Gaëtan Camagne, a theatre artist and decorator.

Beaucourt probably had acquired some proficiency in his art, since in 1775 he tried to become a member of the Académie de Peinture, Sculpture, et Architecture Civile et Navale de Bordeaux. His candidature was supported by two members of the academy, Richard-François Bonfin, the city architect, and one of the Lavau brothers, well-known engravers, but it was none the less rejected.

Four years later Beaucourt received a commission to paint the curtains of the boxes and stage of the Grand-Théâtre of Bordeaux for 2,000 *livres*. At the same period he did several paintings in the chapel of the Benedictine monastery of La Réole, a town not far from Bordeaux: six pictures dealing with the life of St Peter for panels in the chancel, and six medallions representing different saints for the arches of the nave.

In 1783 Beaucourt again became a candidate for the Bordeaux academy, and he was named an academician on 14 Feb. 1784. That year, at the request of the city of Bordeaux, he executed two allegorical transparencies for the festivities marking the announcement of the treaty of Paris. He also did the *Martyre de saint Barthélemy* for the church of Saint-Genès-de-Fronsac (Fronsac, dept of Gironde) in 1784. Theoretically the members of the academy displayed their pictures every two years, but there was no showing in 1785. Hence five of Beaucourt's paintings, including the one done for his admission to the academy, *Le retour du marché*, were not exhibited until the *salon* of 1787. Beaucourt himself was not present and was probably no longer in France, for the minutes of the academy for 18 Dec. 1784 record that "Mr. Beaucour being on the point of departing for America, has taken leave of the academy." All the works Beaucourt painted while living in Bordeaux have disappeared today, except the *Martyre de saint Barthélemy*, which is so damaged that its quality cannot be judged.

There is no further trace of the artist until 1792. He may have sailed for the West Indies around the end of 1784. His best-known picture, *Esclave à la nature morte* (1786), is West Indian in inspiration, as is shown by the madras the young woman wears on her head, her beaded necklace, and the basket of exotic fruit in her hand. Moreover, certain French authors have asserted that Beaucourt died at Guadeloupe. Although this claim is quite wrong, it does suggest that the artist stayed there. Another canvas executed during this period, *Portrait de jeune fille* (1787), gives no indication of where the painter was living.

During January and February 1792 Beaucourt was in the United States, at Philadelphia, where he published an advertisement in the *General Advertiser*. In it he described his particular skills as an artist, offered his services, and suggested that he would take on a few pupils. The same advertisement, except that the artist no longer called himself a French painter, but rather a Canadian one, appeared on 14 June 1792 in the *Montreal Gazette*. According to this newspaper, the artist had practised his profession and "had met with considerable encouragement in several cities in Europe; namely, Paris, St. Petersburg, Nantes, Bordeaux." According to another advertisement in the same newspaper on 28 June 1792, Beaucourt had "just arrived in Canada."

There are many works of Beaucourt's, done in the Montreal region, from this time on. He painted numerous portraits, including those of Mother d'Youville [DUFROST] (dated 1792, a replica of an earlier unsigned portrait), Mother Marguerite-Thérèse LEMOINE Despins (1792), Abbé Claude Poncin* (1792), Eustache-Ignace Trottier Desrivières-Beaubien (1792 or 1793) and his wife, Marguerite-Alexis Malhiot (1792 or 1793). François Beaucourt produced a substantial body of religious paintings. In 1792 and 1793 he executed several for the church of Sainte-Anne-de-Varennes (Varennes), depicting St Augustine, St Jerome, St Ambrose, and St Gregory. Two pictures painted at the beginning of 1794 for the church of Saint-Joseph-de-Lanoraie (Lanoraie), *La nativité de la vierge* and *Saint Jean-Baptiste au désert*, were destroyed by fire in 1917. Two oil paintings, *Marie, secours des chrétiens* (1793) and *Miracle de saint Antoine* (1794), decorated the church of Saint-Martin, Île Jésus, which was burned in 1942. These paintings were saved, but the first now exists only in fragments in various collections. Numerous works which bear no signature have been attributed to Beaucourt. These attributions would seem to be erroneous since the artist generally signed his works.

Although he is important historically, Beaucourt was not a great painter. His heavy touch and his often ill-defined relief remove any claim to such a title. As a painter of religious scenes he was essentially only a mediocre imitator of European works. As a portrait artist, however, he showed a certain talent and was able to give life to his subjects through his warm colours. He seems to have excelled particularly in decorating private dwellings and theatres, although since his work in this field has disappeared we cannot evaluate it.

François Malepart de Beaucourt died in Montreal in 1794. In 1810 his widow married Gabriel Franchère, the father of Gabriel*, the well-known traveller; she died in Montreal in 1844.

MADELEINE MAJOR-FRÉGEAU

AD, Gironde (Bordeaux), C, 1208; 3E, 20338, 3 juin 1773; G, 3108, f.40, 5 juin 1784. ANQ-M, État civil, Catholiques, La Nativité-de-la-Très-Sainte-Vierge (Laprairie), 25 févr. 1740; Notre-Dame de Montréal, 25 juin 1794, 16 janv. 1844. ANQ-Q, État civil, Catholiques, Notre-Dame de Québec, 16 juill. 1756, 7 févr. 1757; Greffe de Simon Sanguinet, 5 févr. 1757. Archives municipales, Bordeaux, CC 311–12, 28 sept. 1779; DD 36 e, 1er, 4 mars 1780; GG 105, 8 avril 1754; 806, 12 juill. 1773; MSS 331, ff.371, 379, 380; 332, ff.71, 187, 190, 191; 333, f.29; 334, ff.34, 35; 338, f.18. ASGM, MS., Mémoire particulier, 1705–1857, ff.296, 297, no.I. Bibliothèque municipale de Bordeaux (dép. de la Gironde, France), MSS 712, f.136; 1539, ff.96, 97, 217, 218, 226, 350. IBC, Centre de documentation, Fonds Morisset,

Dossier François Malepart de Beaucourt. *General Advertiser* (Philadelphia), 3 Jan.–20 Feb. 1792. *Montreal Gazette*, 7, 14, 28 June 1792. *Album d'objets d'art existant dans les églises de la Gironde*, J.-A. Brutails, compil. (Bordeaux, 1907).

J. R. Harper, *La peinture au Canada des origines à nos jours* (Québec, 1966), 29, 53–58, 70, 78, 115, 419. C.-C. Marionneau, *Les salons bordelais, ou expositions des beaux-arts à Bordeaux au XVIIIe siècle (1771–1787), avec des notes biographiques sur les artistes qui figurèrent à ces expositions* (Bordeaux, 1883), xi, 71, 99, 117–18. Gérard Morisset, *Coup d'œil sur les arts*, 57–58; *Les églises et le trésor de Varennes* (Québec, 1943), 18, 21, 34–35; *La peinture traditionnelle au Canada français* (Ottawa, 1960), 55–58. É.-Z. Massicotte, "Le peintre Malepart de Beaucour," *BRH*, XLV (1939), 42–44; "Le peintre Malepart de Beaucours," *BRH*, XXVII (1921), 187–88. Maurice [Meaudre de] Lapouyade, "Essai de statistique archéologique: La Réole," Académie royale des sciences, belles-lettres et arts de Bordeaux, *Actes* (Bordeaux et Paris), 8 (1846), 324–25. Robert Mesuret, "Les premiers décorateurs du Grand-Théâtre de Bordeaux," Soc. de l'hist. de l'art français, *Bull.* (Paris), 1940, 119–26. Gérard Morisset, "Généalogie et petite histoire, le peintre François Beaucourt," SGCF *Mémoires*, XVI (1965), 195–99; "Saint-Martin (île Jésus) après le sinistre 19 du mai," *Technique* (Montréal), XVII (1942), 597–605.

MAQUINNA (Maquilla). *See* MUQUINNA

MARCHAND, ÉTIENNE, priest and vicar general; b. 26 Nov. 1707 at Quebec, son of Étienne Marchand, a carpenter, and Marie-Anne Durand; d. 11 Jan. 1774 in the Hôpital Général of Quebec.

Étienne Marchand was the eldest of seven children. His parents were ardent Christians who had joined the brotherhood of Sainte-Anne in 1715. According to Jacques Viger*, Marchand attended the Collège de Québec and then went to France to do his studies in theology. He remained there for three years. Returning to Quebec in 1731, he was ordained priest on 21 October by Bishop DOSQUET in the chapel of the episcopal palace. The following year he succeeded Joseph Dufrost de La Gemerais as parish priest of Champlain. In October 1735 he became priest of the parish of Sainte-Famille-de-Boucherville. On 30 Sept. 1740, shortly after the death of Bishop François-Louis de Pourroy* de Lauberivière, the chapter of Quebec appointed him vicar general for the administrative district of Montreal after the Sulpician Maurice Courtois had refused the post. At the request of the seigneur and habitants of Boucherville, the chapter at the same time acknowledged him as the incumbent of the parish and sent him papers indicating this appointment was permanent. He remained vicar general until the death of Bishop Pontbriand [Dubreil*] in 1760.

After 1764 Abbé Marchand played a more prominent role in the church in Canada. On 9 September of that year, Étienne MONTGOLFIER, superior of the Séminaire de Montréal, faced with MURRAY's prejudices against him, resigned as vicar general of the District of Montreal and invited the chapter to replace him with someone "who is not even from the Saint-Sulpice community." Two days later, the chapter chose Marchand. Murray prided himself on having instigated the appointment. He considered "This Marchand . . . a good honest hearty fellow . . . & w[t] proper Address may be brought to speak out and answer every purpose." When BRIAND returned to Canada as bishop in the summer of 1766, Marchand was confirmed in his responsibilities. On 25 July the new bishop sent him his letters of appointment and at the same time announced that Montgolfier was being appointed as a second vicar general of Montreal, in order to ease Marchand's burden. In addition to his other duties Montgolfier was given special responsibility for the *pays d'en haut* and was made ecclesiastical superior of the female religious orders; Marchand had only to guide the parishes on the south side of the St Lawrence.

Marchand enjoyed both the confidence and the respect of his bishop. Briand entrusted him with many tasks requiring sensitive handling and at one point even considered proposing him as coadjutor. In July 1766 when Joseph-François Perrault, vicar general of the District of Quebec, suggested that the parish priests and communities should be called upon to provide for the bishop's maintenance through an annual contribution, Marchand supported the proposal. The plan fell through only because Bishop Briand had reservations about it, being convinced "that nothing should be taken from the people or the parish priests for the bishop."

In May 1773, weakened by illness, Marchand entered the Hôpital Général in Quebec; he died there on 11 Jan. 1774. According to Pierre-Georges Roy*, it was during his stay in hospital that the vicar general wrote a mock-heroic poem in two cantos entitled "Les troubles de l'Église en Canada en 1728." The poem recounts the dispute between ecclesiastical and civil officials at the time of the burial of Bishop Saint-Vallier [La Croix*] at the Hôpital Général [*see* Claude-Thomas Dupuy*]. This poetic endeavour, Roy states, "is not a masterpiece but contains poetry of unusual satirical vigour."

Devoted and retiring, Marchand served the

Canadian church with zeal and love. His sense of balance and prudence stood Bishop Briand in good stead when the church, with little freedom of action, was going through difficult times.

GILLES CHAUSSÉ

[Jacques Viger was probably the first to transcribe, from an unknown source, the poetic exercise attributed to Étienne Marchand. His manuscript is in ASQ, Fonds Viger-Verreau, Sér.O, 0181. François-Maximilien Bibaud* cited the poem as "La querelle de l'Église" in his *Dictionnaire historique des hommes illustres du Canada et de l'Amérique* (Montréal, 1857), but in his *Bibliothèque canadienne, ou annales bibliographiques* (Montréal, [1858]), he entitled it "Les troubles de l'Église du Canada en 1728." Pierre-Georges Roy published it in *BRH*, III (1897), 114–21, 132–38. G.C.]

AAQ, 10 B, 119v, 123v, 124, 253v, 254v; 1 CB, V, 16f., 20, 22f., 25–28. ACAM, 901.004. ANQ-Q, État civil, Catholiques, Notre-Dame de Québec, 27 nov. 1707. ASQ, Fonds Viger-Verreau, Sér.O, 0181; 0227, pp.22–24; Polygraphie, XXIX, 16, p.460. PAC, MG 23, GII, 1, ser.1, 2, 206; GIV, 8. *Mandements des évêques de Québec* (Têtu et Gagnon), II, 180–82. Allaire, *Dictionnaire*, I, 362. Desrosiers, "Corr. de cinq vicaires généraux," ANQ *Rapport*, 1947–48, 76, 101–9. P.-G. Roy, *Fils de Québec*, I, 171–73. Tanguay, *Dictionnaire*, I, 409; V, 492; *Répertoire*, 108. P.-G. Roy, "Les troubles de l'Église du Canada," *BRH*, II (1896), 141–42, 173.

MARGUERITE (Margarett, Maria, Marie). *See* WILLIAMS, EUNICE

MARIAUCHAU D'ESGLY (d'Esglis, Desglis; he signed **Desgly), LOUIS-PHILIPPE**, bishop of Quebec; b. 24 April 1710 at Quebec, son of François Mariauchau* d'Esgly and Louise-Philippe Chartier de Lotbinière; d. 4 June 1788 at Saint-Pierre, Île d'Orléans (Que.).

Louis-Philippe Mariauchau d'Esgly descended from prominent families on both his father's and his mother's side and at baptism had Governor Philippe de Rigaud* de Vaudreuil as godfather. Nothing is known of his childhood and education except that he entered the Séminaire de Québec on 15 Oct. 1721. After ordaining him to the priesthood on 18 Sept. 1734, Bishop DOSQUET immediately named him to the parish of Saint-Pierre, Île d'Orléans. Because of the scarcity of priests after the conquest, d'Esgly also had to minister to the neighbouring parish of Saint-Laurent virtually without a break from 1764 to 1774.

After the conquest the episcopal succession became an issue of importance. Anxious to avoid the difficulties that had surrounded his own appointment, Bishop BRIAND of Quebec wanted a coadjutor named as quickly as possible. Although Étienne MONTGOLFIER appeared to be the ideal candidate, Governor Guy Carleton*, who wanted to have a Canadian in the post and was under pressure from the Lotbinière family, insisted on Abbé d'Esgly, who had, "among other merits, that of not offending anyone." Briand was somewhat disappointed with this candidate, who was older than he and deaf as well, but he resigned himself to ratifying the choice, which had the advantage of implying that the government recognized the principle of there being a succession in the bishopric of Quebec. On 28 July 1770 Briand hastened to ask the Holy See for the necessary bulls. As he had to go to England, Governor Carleton wanted the question settled as soon as possible, and he pressed Briand to consecrate d'Esgly without waiting for Rome's authorization. The nephews of the parish priest of Saint-Pierre also became involved; d'Esgly, amused at their eagerness, observed that they wanted "to have the pleasure of saying 'Monseigneur, my uncle.' " Despite the pressures, Briand waited until the bulls, signed by Pope Clement XIV on 22 Jan 1772, were received in Quebec. On 12 July he consecrated his coadjutor bishop *in partibus* of Dorylaeum. D'Esgly thus became the first Canadian-born bishop. Because of the dispute, dating back to 1766, between the bishop of Quebec and the churchwardens of Notre-Dame over the use of the parish church as a cathedral [*see* Jean-Félix Récher*], the ceremony was held "secretly, although everyone knew of it," in the chapel of the Séminaire de Québec. The public and official proclamation of the choice of d'Esgly was, however, delayed until March 1774. Although now coadjutor, d'Esgly insisted upon remaining in Saint-Pierre, where he continued to carry out his duties as parish priest with the help of curates. He published his only pastoral letter as coadjutor on 6 June 1778, prior to an official visit of the parishes on Île d'Orléans. In it he reproached the habitants for their sins and called upon them to make his visit the occasion for a return to virtuous living.

When d'Esgly's health deteriorated, Briand feared that the principle of succession would again be called into question; this fear led him to resign on 29 Nov. 1784. On 2 December d'Esgly signed the act of accession to his see. On the same day he named his vicars general, confirming in office Abbé Henri-François Gravé* de La Rive at Quebec, Pierre GARREAU, *dit* Saint-Onge, at Trois-Rivières, and Montgolfier at Montreal. In Paris Abbé François SORBIER de Villars was also reappointed as vicar general. The only innovation was the appointment of a vicar general in

London, where Father Thomas Hussey, an Irish priest, was to be the bishop's representative to the British government.

On 4 December the new bishop published his first pastoral letter. He had no illusions: in view of his age and infirmities he knew he would hold the post only briefly. He informed the faithful that they should continue to take their concerns to Briand, adding, "If his infirmities do not permit him to attend to [them], our vicar general in Quebec will settle them or send them on to us." D'Esgly returned to his parish in Saint-Pierre on 6 Jan. 1785, even though Briand had hastened to give up to him the apartments reserved for the titular bishop at the Séminaire de Québec.

One of the new bishop's first concerns was to find himself a coadjutor; on 22 Dec. 1784 he sent a letter to Abbé Jean-François HUBERT, who was the missionary at Detroit, announcing that he had been chosen. As Rome and London were slow in approving this nomination, Hubert was not consecrated bishop until November 1786. The next year Hubert undertook a pastoral visit in the bishop's name; there had been none following one Bishop Briand had been unable to complete in 1775, except for d'Esgly's visit to Île d'Orléans.

As a transitional bishop, d'Esgly contented himself, in the main, with administering the diocese, rather than seeking to govern through the adoption of long-term policies. Thus he settled local disputes over the choice of new church sites at Saint-Gervais, Baie-du-Febvre (Baieville), and particularly Yamachiche. He had to resolve a few problems of ecclesiastical discipline, such as the case of the Sulpician Pierre Huet* de La Valinière. He also had to deal with the famous Baie-Saint-Paul malady, and he signed a circular letter to announce Dr James BOWMAN's visit to the parishes. But the main question that concerned him, as it did his predecessor and immediate successors, was the lack of priests. The bishop wanted to bring priests from Europe to serve in the missions and teach in the colleges and seminaries, thus freeing the Canadian priests for parish ministry. Although he himself was not worried about whether the foreign priests were French, Savoyards, or Irishmen who knew French, the British government's opposition to the French and Briand's to the Savoyards forced him to appeal to the Irish priests, and he gave Father Hussey the task of recruiting them.

D'Esgly paid particular attention to the Maritimes, a region somewhat neglected since the conquest, where the scarcity of priests was being felt acutely. In January 1785 he confirmed Joseph-Mathurin BOURG there as vicar general. Later that year he posted James Jones*, who had arrived from Ireland, to Halifax, giving him jurisdiction over the priests whom John Butler, bishop of Cork, was sending. On 17 Oct. 1787 he sent the Catholics in the Maritimes a pastoral letter in which he congratulated them on having kept the faith, even when "mingled with foreign Protestants" and enjoying less spiritual support than the Canadians. He exhorted them to receive generously and obediently the European missionaries who had come to bring them succour.

During his final months as bishop of Quebec d'Esgly perceived that his authority, which he exercised from Île d'Orléans, was not being accorded sufficient respect and he sought to strengthen it. He reproached certain priests of the Séminaire de Québec, among them Thomas-Laurent BÉDARD and Gravé, for insubordination and even deprived Gravé of his authority as vicar general. He criticized Hubert, who had rather a low opinion of his superior's abilities, for not having given him an account of his pastoral visit. Only Briand's intervention with Hubert, recommending obedience, averted a crisis.

D'Esgly became unable to say mass in March 1788, and died on 4 June. The funeral, at which Gravé officiated, was held two days later in the church of Saint-Pierre; as d'Esgly had requested in his will, he was buried there. Nearly two centuries later, on 8 May 1969, his remains were transferred to the crypt of the basilica of Notre-Dame in Quebec. D'Esgly had not sought the office of bishop, but in accepting his elevation he made it possible for the problem of the episcopal succession to be resolved. Nevertheless, as historian Marcel Trudel has suggested, he may be criticized for having seriously complicated ecclesiastical administration by his insistence on living on his island until his death.

JEAN-GUY PELLETIER

AAQ, 12 A, D, 54v; 22 A, IV, 545; 30 A, III, 2; 10 B, 115v, 118, 123v; 1 CB, VI, 26, 39–41, 53, 55; 61 CD, Saint-Laurent, île d'Orléans, I, 1–6. ANQ-Q, AP-P-1385; AP-P-1386; État civil, Catholiques, Notre-Dame de Québec, 25 avril 1710; Saint-Pierre, île d'Orléans, 1734–88; QBC 28, Conseil militaire, 7, 4 mars 1761. ASQ, C 35, pp.240–47; Évêques, no.125; Fonds Viger-Verreau, Sér.O, 081, p.11; Lettres, M, 136; P, 15; MSS, 13, 29 nov. 1787, 10 nov. 1791; Polygraphie, XVII, 42; Séminaire, 10, no.56; 14/3, no.2; 15, nos.68a, 68b; 34, no.138. PAC, MG 23, GV, 1. "Lettres de noblesse de la famille Juchereau Duchesnay," *BRH*, XXVIII (1922), 137. *Mandements des évêques de Québec* (Têtu et Gagnon), II, 252–56, 297–99, 311–39, 349–51. PAC *Rapport*, 1905, II, IIe partie, 346–49.

Caron, "Inv. de la corr. de Mgr Briand," ANQ *Rapport*, 1929–30, 85, 107; "Inv. de la corr. de Mgr

Mariaucheau D'Esgly," ANQ *Rapport*, 1930–31, 185–98. Hugolin Lemay, "Bibliographie des ouvrages concernant la tempérance . . . depuis l'établissement de l'imprimerie [1764] jusqu'à 1910," *BRH*, XVI (1910), 212; XVII (1911), 251. "Papiers d'État," PAC *Rapport*, 1890, 153–54, 157, 164. Henri Têtu, *Notices biographiques: les évêques de Québec* (Québec, 1889), 297–304, 357–79, 386–91. Burke, *Les ursulines de Québec* (1863–66), II, 351; III, 174–78. A.-H. Gosselin, *L'Église du Canada après la Conquête*, I; II. P.-G. Roy, *La famille Mariauchau d'Esgly* (Lévis, Qué., 1908), 9–10. M. Trudel, *L'Église canadienne*, I, 94, 158, 349; "La servitude de l'Église catholique du Canada français sous le Régime anglais," SCHÉC *Rapport*, 30 (1963), 14, 22.

MARIE-ANNE DE LA NATIVITÉ. *See* MIGEON

MARIE-FRANÇOISE DE SAINT-ANTOINE. *See* GUILLIMIN

MARIE-JOSEPH DE L'ENFANT-JÉSUS. *See* WHEELWRIGHT

MARIE-LOUISE DE SAINT-MARTIN. *See* CUROT

MARIN DE LA MALGUE, JOSEPH (usually referred to as Marin *fils*), officer in the colonial regular troops and explorer; baptized 5 Feb. 1719 at Montreal (Que.), son of Paul Marin* de La Malgue and Marie-Joseph Guyon Desprez; d. 1774 at the Baie d'Antongil, Madagascar.

Born of a military family whose members distinguished themselves in the wars against the British, in Indian affairs, and in the fur trade, Joseph Marin de La Malgue entered the king's service at an early age. In 1732, when barely 13, Marin was sent to explore the *pays d'en haut* under the orders of his father, and he was to spend most of the next 13 years in that region. He explored the area around Michilimackinac (Mackinaw City, Mich.) in 1737. Although ill, he performed well under Pierre-Joseph Céloron* de Blainville in the Chickasaw campaign of 1739–40. In 1740 he made peace and trade agreements with the Sioux west of Baie-des-Puants (Green Bay, Wis.). Marin spent most of his time during this period at the Baie-des-Puants post, and became thoroughly familiar with the complexities of the fur trade and fluent in Sioux and several Algonkian dialects.

In 1745 Marin and his father, like many other French in the *pays d'en haut*, were recalled to fight the British in Acadia and at Louisbourg, Île Royale (Cape Breton Island). The first news of the fall of Louisbourg was brought to Montreal by Marin on 1 August. He then went to Quebec where on 20 September he married Charlotte, daughter of Joseph de Fleury* de La Gorgendière, thereby becoming related to François-Pierre de RIGAUD de Vaudreuil and to the future governor of New France, Pierre de RIGAUD de Vaudreuil. Late in the year, under his father's command, he took part in the expedition which destroyed Saratoga (Schuylerville, N.Y.).

Marin was in Acadia again in 1746. He later claimed to have led a raid against a British provisioning party on Île Saint-Jean (Prince Edward Island), although a contemporary journal records that Joseph-Michel LEGARDEUR de Croisille et de Montesson was in command. In 1747 Marin was at Grand-Pré, Nova Scotia, with Nicolas-Antoine Coulon* de Villiers and on the New York frontier with François-Pierre de Rigaud de Vaudreuil. In the summer of 1748 he returned to Acadia and in September went on to Île Royale. Not knowing that hostilities had ended, he probed the area near Louisbourg with a small force, taking some prisoners. Marin was only partially convinced of the peace by the captives. He released some of them, who reported the incident to the British governor of Louisbourg, Peregrine Thomas Hopson*. When the matter had been clarified, Marin freed all but one who was accused of treason by the French. It was in that year that he received the rank of second ensign.

In 1749, at the request of Governor La Jonquière [Taffanel*], Marin was given command at Chagouamigon (near Ashland, Wis.) on western Lake Superior. This post placed him in the trade network of his father, the commander at Baie-des-Puants, and La Jonquière. The elder Marin, largely because of the understandings he had with the governor and Intendant BIGOT, was more than a colonial officer serving at a frontier post: he was virtually in charge of the west. Joseph Marin was given the assignment of making peace with the Sioux and Ojibwas, who were fighting each other as well as the French, and he claimed to have succeeded. In 1750 he was promoted full ensign. His father and La Jonquière tried to have him appointed second in command of the Baie-des-Puants post, but gave up, apparently when the farmers of Chagouamigon requested that he be retained there. He spent most of 1751 in garrison at Quebec.

Marin returned to Baie-des-Puants in 1752 with an important commission: to relieve his father of command, to search for a route to the western sea via the Missouri, and to arrange treaties with the various Indian tribes. Jacques Legardeur* de Saint-Pierre, who in 1752 negotiated a truce between the Crees and the Sioux, reported that "M. Marin junior was not less occupied than I in arranging this peace." A journal begun at Michilimackinac by Marin on 17 Aug. 1753 provides information on his activities in that year and the next. On 14 October he was at the mouth of the Wisconsin River, where he began construction of Fort Vaudreuil and where he stopped a potential quarrel between local Ojibwas and Sioux. During the winter of 1753–54 Marin and Louis-Joseph Gaultier* de La Vérendrye, who had succeeded him at Chagouamigon, disputed over trading territories near the present border of Minnesota and Wisconsin. Marin accused La Vérendrye of interfering with his traders and with showing a partiality towards the Ojibwas that was certain to embitter the Sioux. The Marin mission was a failure in that no route to the Pacific was found; yet his diary is the most significant record of exploration in Minnesota during this era. He commented not only on military matters, trade, and Indian affairs, but also on La Vérendrye, Luc de La Corne, and other prominent personalities.

In 1754 Marin returned to Quebec but was sent west again the next year by Governor Duquesne. On 11 July 1756, having been recalled to participate in the campaigns against the British, he arrived in Montreal with a large contingent of Menominee warriors from Baie-des-Puants. During the next two years Marin, now a lieutenant, took part in a number of engagements on the New York frontier. He saw action in 1756 near Oswego (Chouaguen), where he and his Menominees were successful against larger British detachments. That August, near Fort George (also called Fort William Henry, now Lake George, N.Y.), he and a party of 100 defeated a force of some 65 men, killing or capturing all but their leader, whom he believed to have been Robert Rogers. In December he led a force of 500 French and Indians to attack the settlements along the Connecticut River. When his Huron and Iroquois guides objected, Marin shifted towards Albany. Again the Indians protested, and the force proceeded against Saratoga instead.

In July 1757 Marin undertook a reconnaissance mission in the vicinity of Fort Lydius (also called Fort Edward, now Fort Edward, N.Y.). Despite some desertions Marin made his way close to the British fort, where he wiped out first a ten-man patrol and then a 50-man guard. His little detachment next had to face a substantial force which it held off for more than an hour before retiring in good order. Marin had lost only three men. The financial commissary of wars André Doreil* called it a "most daring expedition." At the beginning of August 1758 Marin encountered a detachment commanded by Robert Rogers in the woods near Lake Champlain. Marin gradually withdrew from the combat, blaming the lack of a complete victory on the Canadian militia, most of whom deserted. In the report of the battle, Doreil referred to Marin as "a Colonial officer of great reputation."

Joseph Marin was made captain in January 1759. He spent the first part of the year in the vicinity of Fort Machault (Franklin, Pa) and the British Fort Cumberland (Cumberland, Md), where he harassed the frontier settlements. In the summer he joined the relief force that François-Marie Le Marchand* de Lignery led to Fort Niagara (near Youngstown, N.Y.) to raise the British siege. The force was ambushed by the British as it neared the fort, and Marin was taken prisoner. This was the end of glory for him. He later wrote that "they announced my capture as a great triumph in their newspaper." The imprisonment was a "horror." In the final battle for New France, the Marin home in Quebec was plundered and burned by the British. He estimated his loss at more than 60,000 *livres* and reported that all the family's personal and business papers had been destroyed.

Marin, with other important prisoners, was sent to England and eventually released to France, the mother country he had never seen. In 1762 he was among the reinforcements who embarked for St John's, Newfoundland, following its capture by Charles-Henri-Louis d'Arsac de Ternay, but he became a prisoner once again on 22 September, when the *François-Louis* was taken by the British. He was again repatriated to France.

His years in France were not happy: his fortune lost, he lived on a meagre pension from the crown. He tried to have the court acknowledge his status as a noble, claiming to be descended from the Marini family of Toulon, Toulouse, and Marseilles. There is some possibility that the Marins may have been of the minor nobility of southern France. Paul and Joseph had considered themselves nobles and were certainly considered as such in the colony. In 1767 Lieutenant Governor Guy Carleton* included Joseph Marin's name in a report on the Canadian nobility. Although the French court acknowledged Marin as "a man of war, courageous by nature, thirsting for glory and eager for the dangers through which it is gained," it did not deem these qualities sufficient to grant him his request. He did receive the cross of Saint-Louis in 1761, when the king tried to compensate the officers from New France for their service in a lost cause.

Probably in 1773, Marin was appointed lieutenant-colonel in the troops which were to take part in the Count de Benyovszky's attempt to establish a French settlement at the Baie d'Antongil, Madagascar. Shortly after their arrival on the island in 1774, both Marin and the son who had accompanied him died of fever.

The Marins were among the several families who dominated exploration, trade, and military affairs in the *pays d'en haut* prior to 1760. The continuing control of the best trading posts by the same families was often criticized, and the Marins did not escape censure. The wealth of the trade is difficult to assess, but it is certain that the Marins' association with La Jonquière, Bigot, and Legardeur was profitable. Joseph Marin was no doubt aided in his activities in the west by his relationship to the Vaudreuil family. One might conclude, as Louise Phelps Kellogg does, that La Jonquière and the Marins began the trading system which "by favoritism, corruption, and undue profits hastened the downfall of New France." But such a generalization ignores the effective frontier work of the Marins. They maintained peace in the west, explored new territory, and by their diplomatic skills tied the tribes so closely to the French that great numbers of Indians from the *pays d'en haut* fought in campaigns against the British. Marin claimed that he brought at least 20 tribes to the side of the French.

Marin was one of the ablest French military leaders, at various times successfully commanding regular, militia, and Indian detachments. He was, of course, a colonial officer, a type despised by regulars. Yet Montcalm*, who consistently preferred his regulars and who detested Marin's relative, Governor Vaudreuil, was nevertheless forced to give Marin credit for some victories, although he described him as "brave but stupid." André Doreil, who shared Montcalm's contempt for colonials, always praised Marin as an aggressive, effective officer.

DONALD CHAPUT

[Joseph Marin de La Malgue], "Journal de Marin, fils, 1753–1754," Antoine Champagne, édit., ANQ *Rapport*, 1960–61, 235–308. BN, MSS, NAF, 9286 (Margry), ff.273–79. Bougainville, "Journal" (A.-E. Gosselin), ANQ *Rapport*, 1923–24, 207–10, 288. *Coll. de manuscrits relatifs à la N.-F.*, III, 217–19, 410–12, 418; IV, 110–11, 188–89. *Coll. des manuscrits de Lévis* (Casgrain), VI, 35. *Découvertes et établissements des Français dans l'ouest et dans le sud de l'Amérique septentrionale . . . mémoires et documents inédits* [1614–1754], Pierre Margry, édit. (6v., Paris, 1879–88), VI, 648–49, 653–54. "The French regime in Wisconsin – II" and ". . . III," ed. R. G. Thwaites, Wis., State Hist. Soc., *Coll.*, XVII (1906), 315, 430, 439–40, and XVIII (1908), 63–64, 133–36, 158, 192–93, 196. [D.-H.-M. Liénard de] Beaujeu, "Journal de la campagne du détachement de Canada à l'Acadie et aux Mines, en 1746–47," *Coll. doc. inédits Canada et Amérique*, II, 16–75. "La mission de M. de Bougainville en France en 1758–1759," ANQ *Rapport*, 1923–24, 37, 54. *NYCD* (O'Callaghan and Fernow). PAC *Rapport*, 1886, clvii–clxiii; 1888, note C, 35; 1905, I, VIe partie, 334–35. Robert Rogers, *Journals of Major Robert Rogers . . .* (London, 1765; repr. Ann Arbor, Mich., [1966]). *Pennsylvania Gazette* (Philadelphia), 9, 23 Aug. 1759.

Æ. Fauteux, *Les chevaliers de Saint-Louis*, 56–57, 183–84. L.-P. et A.-M. d'Hozier, *Armorial*. Le Jeune, *Dictionnaire*. Massicotte, "Répertoire des engagements pour l'Ouest," ANQ *Rapport*, 1929–30, 426, 444; 1931–32, 303. Tanguay, *Dictionnaire*. L. P. Kellogg, *The French régime in Wisconsin and the northwest* (Madison, Wis., 1925; repr. New York, 1968). P. L. Scanlan, *Prairie Du Chien: French, British, American* (n.p., 1937), 29–46. Claude Bonnault de Méry, "Les Canadiens en France et aux colonies après la cession (1760–1815)," *Revue de l'hist. des colonies françaises* (Paris), XVII (1924), 529. E. W. H. Fyers, "The loss and recapture of St. John's, Newfoundland, in 1762," Soc. for Army Hist. Research, *Journal* (London), XI (1932), 179–215. G. L. Nute, "Marin versus La Vérendrye," *Minnesota History* (St Paul), 32 (1951), 226–38. Régis Roy, "Les capitaines de Marin, sieurs de la Malgue, chevaliers de Saint-Louis, officiers canadiens, etc., en la Nouvelle-France, de 1680 à 1762," RSC *Trans.*, 2nd ser., X (1904), sect.I, 25–34.

MARRANT, JOHN, freeborn black American, author, and minister of the Countess of Huntingdon's Connexion; b. 15 June 1755 in New York; d. 15 April 1791 in Islington (London), England.

John Marrant's early life was exceptional in that he was able to obtain an education despite the severe restrictions placed on blacks in colonial America. He attended school until the age of 10 or 11, first in St Augustine, Florida, where his mother had moved on the death of her husband in 1759, and then in Georgia. When the family later settled in Charleston, South Carolina, it was intended that Marrant should learn a trade. Instead, at his own wish, he studied music for two years before being apprenticed for over a year in an unknown trade. At the age of 13 he experienced Christian conversion at a George Whitefield meeting and, finding his family unsympathetic, he abandoned his home for the wilderness beyond Charleston. There he was found by an Indian hunter and taken among the Cherokees, with whom he lived for two years before returning to South Carolina.

At the outbreak of the American revolution Marrant was impressed into the Royal Navy as a musician and saw action in 1780 at the siege of Charleston and in 1781 off the Dogger Bank, where he was wounded. After his discharge he worked for three years with a London cotton merchant and joined an evangelical group known as the Countess of Huntingdon's Connexion. When he received from his brother, one of the 3,500 black loyalists transported to Nova Scotia after the revolution, a letter describing their yearning for Christian knowledge, Marrant determined to go there as a missionary. He was ordained a minister in the Connexion on 15 May 1785 at Bath.

Marrant's education and conversion combined to produce the two achievements for which he is remembered: the publication in London in 1785 of his account of the first 30 years of his life and his Christian ministry among the black loyalists of Nova Scotia. Between 1785 and 1835 *A narrative of the Lord's wonderful dealings with John Marrant, a black . . .* appeared in at least 21 different printings, including one in Welsh. Its amazing success can be attributed to the fact that it made important contributions to three literary genres: the American slave narrative, the Indian captivity tale, and the evangelical Christian conversion record. Although Marrant was never a slave, his *Narrative* is numbered among the most influential of early black writings because the pattern of his life paralleled the classic slave pattern of suffering and oppression, eventual escape, and journey to the promised land. After his death publishers, perhaps wishing to avoid the abolition controversy and stress the story of a Christian's progress, omitted the reference to his colour in the title and even lightened his frontispiece portrait to obliterate his racial characteristics. These amended versions depended for their appeal on Marrant's account of his residence among the Cherokees; his is considered to be one of the three most popular Indian captivity stories ever published.

Marrant himself seems to have regarded his *Narrative* as significant chiefly for its Christian message. It is tantalizingly silent on the details of his secular life, portraying instead a series of spiritual tests and victories often embodied in symbolic incidents that are hardly credible to modern readers. His conversion and subsequent adventures are all marked by miraculous escapes and prayers answered spontaneously. Marrant clearly saw himself as a living sermon. His struggle as a black Christian in an irreligious, white, slave-owning world that made little distinction between slaves and freeborn blacks was intended to inspire not just people of his own colour but his white readers as well.

In Nova Scotia Marrant's preaching contributed to a movement that had its parallel in the impact of his published *Narrative*. Although the black loyalists lived in poverty and oppression, they were able to create a vibrant culture centred on their Christian chapels and thus to endure as a distinct community. Marrant organized his first congregation at Birchtown, near Shelburne, and then embarked on a tour that took him to most of the black loyalist settlements. Occasionally he preached to white congregations and visited Micmac villages. His effectiveness as a preacher is acknowledged in his condemnation by several white ministers whose black parishioners deserted them for Marrant's message and for the all-black chapels he introduced. One important legacy of his ministry, therefore – and of the ministries of the Baptist preacher David George* and the Methodists Moses Wilkinson, John Ball, and Boston King – was the creation of exclusive black religious groups dedicated to the preservation of a unique Christian experience.

In 1787 Marrant travelled to Boston, where he joined the first black Masonic lodge, founded in 1784 by Prince Hall. He became chaplain to the lodge, and several of his Boston sermons were published in both England and America. He did not, however, lose contact with his Nova Scotian flock, for he returned to the province to marry black loyalist Elizabeth Herries at Birchtown on 15 Aug. 1788. In 1789, apparently believing his mission had been accomplished, he left for England. He continued his ministry at the main Huntingdonian chapel in Islington and on his death was buried in the adjoining churchyard.

John Marrant's brief career is less important for its accomplishments than for its influence upon historical and literary trends among black people in North America and in Africa. His was a message of perseverance, a testimony to the success a black man and a Christian could achieve through faith in God and in himself, and his *Narrative* served as a model for generations of black American writers. Marrant's followers became preachers and teachers in the Nova Scotian black community, and with the migration of some 1,200 black loyalists to Sierra Leone in 1792 [*see* Thomas PETERS], his message was spread to thousands of Africans. His work survives in the descendants of his black congregations.

JAMES W. ST G. WALKER

The following works by John Marrant have been published: *A journal of the Rev. John Marrant, from August the 18th, 1785, to the 16th of March, 1790 . . .* (London, 1790); *A narrative of the Lord's wonderful dealings with John Marrant, a black . . .*, ed. Rev. Mr Aldridge (London, 1785); and *A sermon preached the 24th day of June, 1789 . . .* (Boston, n.d.).

BL, Add. MSS 41262A, 41262B, 41263, 41264. PANS, MG 1, 479 (Charles Inglis docs.), no.1 (transcripts).

[John Clarkson], *Clarkson's mission to America, 1791–1792*, ed. and intro. C. B. Fergusson (Halifax, 1971). [David George], "An account of the life of Mr. David George . . . ," *Baptist Annual Register* (London), I (1790–93), 473–84. *Great slave narratives*, comp. A. [W.] Bontemps (Boston, 1969). *Held captive by Indians: selected narratives, 1642–1836*, comp. Richard VanDerBeets (Knoxville, Tenn., 1973). [Boston King], "Memoirs of the life of Boston King, a black preacher . . . ," *Methodist Magazine* (London), XXI (1798), 105–10, 157–161, 209–13, 261–65. C. [H.] Fyfe, *A history of Sierra Leone* (London, 1962). J. W. St G. Walker, *The black loyalists: the search for a promised land in Nova Scotia and Sierra Leone, 1783–1870* (London, 1976); "The establishment of a free black community in Nova Scotia, 1783–1840," *The African Diaspora: interpretive essays*, ed. M. L. Kilson and R. I. Rotberg (Cambridge, Mass., and London, 1976). R. W. Winks, *The blacks in Canada: a history* (Montreal, 1971). C. [H.] Fyfe, "The Countess of Huntingdon's Connexion in nineteenth century Sierra Leone," *Sierra Leone Bull. of Religion* (Freetown, Sierra Leone), 4 (1962), 53–61. D. B. Porter, "Early American Negro writings: a bibliographical study," Bibliographical Soc. of America, *Papers* (New York), 39 (1945), 192–268. A. F. Walls, "The Nova Scotian settlers and their religion," *Sierre Leone Bull. of Religion*, 1 (1959), 19–31.

MARSTON, BENJAMIN, merchant, surveyor, and office-holder; b. 22 Sept. 1730 at Salem, Massachusetts, eldest son of Benjamin Marston and Elizabeth Winslow; m. 13 Nov. 1755 at Marblehead, Massachusetts, Sarah Swett; d. 10 Aug. 1792 at Bolama, Portuguese Guinea (Guinea-Bissau).

Benjamin Marston obtained his AB from Harvard College in 1749 and later went into business with two of his brothers-in-law at Marblehead, where he achieved prosperity and respectability. With the onset of the American revolution Marston emerged as a marked, outspoken loyalist. In November 1775 he fled to Boston after his house was attacked by a patriot mob; his wife, left behind to watch his property, died soon afterwards. In March 1776 Marston accompanied the British garrison of Boston to Halifax, Nova Scotia, where he was to have a chequered career as a merchant and supercargo, mainly in the West Indian trade. He was captured three times by American privateers but was exchanged each time. In December 1781, on a voyage from Annapolis Royal to Halifax, his ship was blown off course and trapped in ice near Cape Canso. It was almost three months before Marston reached Halifax. There he lived in poverty until April 1783, when he was appointed surveyor of the new loyalist settlement of Port Roseway (Shelburne).

For the next 15 months Marston carried out a difficult task, exacerbated by what he called "This curs'd Republican Town meeting Spirit" of the disputatious refugees. In the summer of 1784 he was forced to flee to Halifax when disbanded troops rioted against free blacks [*see* David George*]. He was accused, probably unjustly, of partiality in the surveying and distribution of land and was dismissed by Governor John PARR.

Soon afterwards, on the recommendation of his cousin Edward Winslow*, Marston was appointed by the surveyor general of the king's woods in North America, John Wentworth*, to be his deputy in the newly created province of New Brunswick. In December 1784 he took up residence in Parrtown (Saint John), where he shared a house with Ward Chipman*. Appointed sheriff of Northumberland County, Marston travelled to the Miramichi River in June 1785. There he surveyed the woods, worked as deputy surveyor of crown lands, operated a mill, and, in partnership with John Mark Crank Delesderniers, traded with Indians and settlers. He found the sheriff's pay inadequate and his economic prospects poor, however, and in March 1786 he resigned as sheriff, returning to Saint John in November.

In March 1787 Marston went to Boston and obtained documentation to aid the Winslow family's claim as loyalists for compensation from the British government. Late that summer he left to press his own claim in London, where, sometimes close to starvation, he eked out a living for four years. To his great disappointment he was awarded only £105, less than one-quarter of his claim and sufficient only to pay his debts. In 1792 he accepted a position as surveyor for a private company intending to settle Bolama, a West African island. Most of the colonists, including Marston, died of fever shortly after arrival.

Benjamin Marston kept a diary from 1776 to 1787 which is an important source for the history of Nova Scotia and New Brunswick. A versatile person, with an attractive, blunt, optimistic personality, and liberal political views, he was a loyal friend and something of a poet and an artist. Like many loyalists he remained an American patriot and had high hopes for New Brunswick.

WALLACE BROWN

PANB, RG 10, RS107, Letterbook of George Sproule, surveyor-general, 1785–89. University of N.B. Library, Archives and Special Coll. Dept. (Fredericton), Winslow papers, 20, 21, 22; Benjamin Marston, Diary, 1776–87. W. O. Raymond, "Benjamin Marston of Marblehead, loyalist: his trials and tribulations during the American revolution," N.B. Hist. Soc., *Coll.*, III

(1907–14), no.7, 79–112; "The founding of Shelburne: Benjamin Marston at Halifax, Shelburne and Miramichi," *ibid*, no.8, 204–77. M. M. Vesey, "Benjamin Marston, loyalist," *New England Quarterly* (Orono, Maine), XV (1942), 622–51. J. L. Watson, "The Marston family of Salem, Mass.," *New England Hist. and Geneal. Register*, XXVII (1873), 390–403.

MARTEL, PIERRE-MICHEL (Philippe or **Philippe-Michel** can be found, but ordinarily he signed Pierre-Michel), commissary of the Marine; b. 2 May 1719 in Quebec, son of Jean Martel* de Magos, and Marie-Anne Robinau; m. 1751 Marie-Agathe Baudoin; d. 29 Sept. 1789 in Tours, France.

The Martel family seems to have reached a rather high rank in society, which perhaps explains why Pierre-Michel was able at an early age to enjoy the protection of the most prominent people in the colony. His godfather was François-Pierre de RIGAUD de Vaudreuil and his godmother Jeanne-Élisabeth Bégon, the intendant's daughter. His brother Jean-Urbain Martel* de Belleville was the director of the Saint-Maurice ironworks from 1742 to 1750. By 1738 Martel was evidently in HOCQUART's service, since that year the president of the council of Marine asked the intendant about the capabilities of his subordinate, who was seeking a position as king's writer. Hocquart praised the young man and was assured that Martel would receive the appointment at the first opportunity. It did not come until 12 April 1742. At that time, and until 1749, Martel was living with his mother on Rue Saint-Nicolas in Quebec, near the intendant's palace.

When François BIGOT succeeded Hocquart, he took Martel under his protection and recommended him on several occasions to the minister and council of Marine. Martel was principal writer in the Marine by 1754 and was "in charge of administration for the building of His Majesty's ships." In 1755 he received a commission from the intendant to act as comptroller of the Marine during the absence of Jacques-Michel BRÉARD; on 10 Aug. 1757 Bigot named him commissary of the Marine in Montreal to replace Jean-Victor VARIN de La Marre, who had received permission in April to return to France. Martel finally had the office he coveted, but he apparently wanted the commission to come direct from the king. In spite of appeals by the Chevalier de LÉVIS, Governor Pierre de RIGAUD de Vaudreuil, Bigot, and his Jesuit brother Joseph-Nicolas Martel, who was at that time at Moulins, France, he had to be content with a simple commission and the minister's promise to grant him the position he requested as soon as possible. The conquest was to put an end to his ambitions.

About 1757 Martel had entered into partnership with Michel-Jean-Hugues PÉAN, Bigot, Pierre-Arnaud de Laporte, Jean Corpron*, François Maurin*, and Louis PENNISSEAUT in the Grande Société [*see* Péan]. Thus when he was nominated on 30 Jan. 1761 to assist Charles-François PICHOT de Querdisien Trémais in France in settling Canada's accounts, he had little interest in investigating his partners and protectors. He managed to remain in the colony and so elude the task. Nevertheless he was one of those charged, as was his brother Jean-Baptiste-Grégoire Martel de Saint-Antoine, who had been storekeeper in Montreal.

Believing that he could get off lightly, he decided in 1764 to go to France, where he gave himself up. He was imprisoned in the Bastille, and in April 1765, after what Pierre-Georges Roy* calls "a semblance of a trial" at the Châtelet, he was acquitted of all charges. He then joined his family in the parish of Saint-Vincent, Tours, where he resided until his death.

MICHEL ROBERGE

AN, Col., C[11A], 100, f.128; 103, ff.23, 256. ANQ-Q, AP-P-1395; Greffe de P.-A.-F. Lanoullier Des Granges, 15 mars 1755; NF 2, 40, 20 sept. 1752; 42, 23 oct. 1755, 10 août 1757. "Les malignités du sieur de Courville," *BRH*, L (1944), 114. "Recensement de Québec, 1744," 48. Gustave Lanctot, "L'Affaire du Canada; bibliographie du procès Bigot," *BRH*, XXXVIII (1932), 8–17. Le Jeune, *Dictionnaire*. P.-G. Roy, *Inv. coll. pièces jud. et not.*, I, 123, 163; II, 362; *Inv. concessions*, II, 157, 160; IV, 131; *Inv. jug. et délib., 1717–60*, VI, 92, 110; *Inv. ord. int.* Tanguay, *Dictionnaire*, V, 533. Frégault, *François Bigot*. P.-G. Roy, *Bigot et sa bande*; *La famille Martel de Magesse* (Lévis, Qué., 1934). Guy Frégault, "La guerre de Sept Ans et la civilisation canadienne," *RHAF*, VII (1953–54), 198. Antoine Roy, "Jean Martel," *BRH*, VI (1900), 21–24. P.-G. Roy, "Les commissaires ordinaires de la Marine en la Nouvelle-France," *BRH*, XXIV (1918), 54.

MARTEN (Martin), HUMPHREY, HBC chief factor; b. *c*. 1729 in England; d. between 1790 and 1792, probably in England.

Humphrey Marten was first engaged by the Hudson's Bay Company in 1750 as a writer at York Factory (Man.) on a five-year indenture at £15 per annum. He must have been satisfactory to his superiors at York, for in 1755 he was suggested as a possible master of Flamborough House, an outpost of York, and he was later delegated to act as chief of York during James Isham*'s absence in England in 1758–59. He nevertheless felt that his services were not receiving due recognition, and in 1759 he pressed for an increase in pay to £50 per annum. He was almost dismissed for his temerity; however, the company appointed him second at York and master of a post planned for the mouth of the Severn River (Ont.) to counter possible French penetration there.

Following the death of Isham in April 1761, Marten was appointed acting chief of York by the factory's council. Much to his chagrin the London committee did not make the appointment permanent, and in September 1762 Ferdinand JACOBS was placed in command of the post. Recalled to London, Marten was appointed second at Fort Albany (Ont.); he arrived there in August 1763 and became chief the next year.

Throughout Marten's career the HBC was under increasing pressure from competition in the interior by Montreal-based traders. After his appointment to Albany, the primary object of Marten and the London committee became the re-establishment of Henley House (at the junction of the Albany and Kenogami rivers), which had been sacked by Wappisis* in 1755. Without company servants on the Albany River encouraging Indians to go down to the coast, Albany's trade system would be controlled by the Canadians. Despite stalling by Marten's men, who feared for their scalps, the new post was finally completed in 1768.

In September 1775 Marten was promoted chief of York. The London committee urged him to push trading operations into the Saskatchewan country to compete directly with the Canadians. He strongly supported the activities of William Tomison* and Robert Longmoor* at Cumberland House (Sask.). Their endeavours were plagued, however, by a shortage of canoes, men, and trade goods, and the Canadians remained dominant. Nevertheless, by 1780 the proceeds of the Saskatchewan trade were helping to ensure that York remained the principal company post in North America, in spite of the fact that Samuel HEARNE at Prince of Wales's Fort (Churchill, Man.) continually enticed York's Indians to trade at his post. The company's push inland was stopped by the decimation of the beaver hunters in the smallpox epidemic of 1781–82, and by Marten's surrender of York to the French under the Comte de Lapérouse [GALAUP] in August 1782. Taken prisoner to France, Marten was unable to return to the bay until September 1783. His surrender of York, although considered the cowardly act of a drunken man by Edward UMFREVILLE, was a realistic move in light of the fact that his men were greatly outnumbered by the French.

Marten's interests had not been centred solely on the fur trade. In an effort to curry favour with the influential members of the Royal Society of London, the company had ordered him to collect specimens of the bay's flora and fauna. He became interested in the project by 1771, but although his efforts were prodigious, they were amateurish and lacked the importance of those of Isham or Andrew Graham*.

Marten's private life is difficult to unravel. It is known that he had at least two relatives in England. His domestic relations in Rupert's Land involved numerous liaisons with the daughters of leading Home Guard (Cree) Indians. At Albany he shared his bed with Pawpitch, the daughter of Questach, or Cockeye, the captain of the Albany goose hunters and a powerful and respected figure at the bay. Pawpitch died on 24 Jan. 1771, leaving a son, John America, who was sent to England by his father for schooling. In 1781, when Marten was thinking of permanent retirement, an old Indian came to York from Albany to claim his daughter and her two children, who were living with him. By 1786 Marten had made new domestic arrangements; he kept two or three young women with him at York that year. Such multiplicity was not unusual at the bay, in part because liaisons were necessary to cement relationships with the Indians upon whom the company relied for food and furs. There is no record of any provision made by Marten for his women or children when he retired from Rupert's Land in 1786.

Some debate exists as to Marten's character, but it is certain that he grew increasingly difficult as his various afflictions – gout, stomach disorders, kidney problems, growing blindness, and the pains of numerous accidents – accumulated. His pain-racked frame seems to have soured an already mercurial disposition, and by the 1780s he had few friends. He threw food in his surgeon's face, tried to shove him down the stairs, and dismissed him from his mess, all out of "peevishness." Tomison and Hearne were barely on writing terms with Marten, and the York carpenter was on the point of open rebellion. In spite of his illness and the tremendous pressure from his subordinates, the frugal but impecunious Marten would not leave Rupert's Land. He was prepared to suffer much for a salary of £130 per annum. In 1786, unable to tolerate longer his pain and the insults of his subordinates, he resigned. No trace of his subsequent career is to be found. He was probably still living in 1790 when Umfreville, in *The present state of Hudson's Bay . . .*, damned him as a drunkard, a bully, and a coward, but fearing a lawsuit did not mention his name. However, some time before his own death in 1792 Hearne, revising his journals for publication, referred to the late Humphrey Marten.

F. PANNEKOEK

HBC Arch. A.5/1, f.36; A.11/3, ff.57, 69, 105, 114, 145, 166, 202d; A.11/114, f.141; A.11/115, ff.24, 27, 63, 65, 106; A.11/116, ff.85, 180–81; A.14/12, f.70; A.16/13, f.62; B.3/a/60, f.10; B.3/a/63, f.19; B.198/a/1; B.239/a/37, f.7; B.239/a/78; B.239/a/79, f.45; B.239/a/81; B.239/a/87, f.2; B.239/b/37, f.9; B.239/b/39, ff.9d, 27d. Hearne, *Journey from Prince of Wales's Fort* (Tyrrell). HBRS, XIV (Rich and Johnson). *Journals of Hearne and Turnor* (Tyrrell). Edward Umfreville, *The present state of Hudson's Bay . . .* (London, 1790). Rich, *History of HBC*.

MARTÍNEZ FERNÁNDEZ Y MARTÍNEZ DE LA SIERRA, ESTEBAN JOSÉ, naval officer and explorer; b. 9 Dec. 1742 in Seville, Spain; m. there 10 Sept. 1770 to Gertrudis González; d. 28 Oct. 1798 in Loreto (Baja California, Mexico).

Esteban José Martínez entered Seville's famous marine Seminario de San Telmo when he was 13 and went to sea within three years. By 1773 he was serving as a second pilot in the small naval department of San Blas (state of Nayarit, Mexico), the supply port for Spain's missions and posts in the Californias. He was subsequently to play a major role in the events that led Spain and Britain to the brink of war in 1790.

After the division of the new world between Spain and Portugal by the papal bull of 1493 and the treaty of Tordesillas (1494), Spain had considered the Pacific coast of the Americas to be part of her empire. Her claims had not prevented encroachments on the part of other countries and independent traders. By the 1770s rumours of Russian expansion south from Alaska were reaching Madrid. To forestall further erosion of Spanish sovereignty an expedition was dispatched in 1774, under the command of Juan Josef PÉREZ Hernández, with instructions to sail north from San Blas as far as possible. Martínez served as second officer on this voyage. Pérez reached what are now the northern Queen Charlotte Islands (B.C.) on 16 July. Prevented from going beyond 55° 30′N by unfavourable conditions, the expedition turned south and on 8 August anchored off what Pérez named Surgidero de San Lorenzo (Nootka Sound, B.C.). After making contact with the Nootka Indians, the expedition returned to San Blas.

Although several Spanish expeditions visited the northwest coast after 1774, little attempt was made to establish posts or to exploit the region's natural resources. However, James COOK's survey of the coast publicized its potential for a rich commerce in furs with China, and during the 1780s British vessels, often sailing under the Portuguese flag to avoid the monopolistic restrictions of the East India and South Sea companies, began to open up the trade in sea otter pelts [*see* James HANNA].

From 1775 until 1788 Martínez had been engaged in supplying Spanish posts in the province of Sonora (Mexico), and those at Loreto, Monterey (Calif.), San Diego, and San Francisco. In 1786, while on a routine mission to Monterey, he piloted the French expedition of the Comte de Lapérouse [GALAUP] into the harbour. Questioning the French on their discoveries, Martínez was left with the erroneous impression, duly reported to the viceroy of New Spain, that the Russians had established a post at Nootka. This report, together with those concerning Russian expansion being made by Spain's ambassadors to Russia, moved Madrid to order Martínez in 1788 to sail north to at least 61° latitude and make a full reconnaissance of Russian activities. Leaving San Blas on 8 March, the expedition of two vessels visited Russian trading posts on Kodiak Island and Unalaska in the Aleutians (Alas.). While he found no present threat to Spanish territory, Martínez learned that frigates were expected from Siberia in 1789 to establish the Russians at Nootka. On his return to San Blas on 5 December he recommended that Spain set up a post at Nootka no later than May 1789, and volunteered for the assignment. His report, and the arrival at the islands of Juan Fernández, off the coast of Chile, of two American ships under Robert Gray* and John KENDRICK, bound for the north Pacific coast, finally convinced Viceroy Manuel Antonio Flórez that Spain could no longer afford to ignore infringements of her sovereignty there.

Martínez was the only officer available to Flórez and he was accordingly placed in command of the new expedition, despite his low rank and his record of conflicts with subordinates during the 1788 voyage. Afraid of being beaten to Nootka by the Russians and lacking time to consult Madrid, Flórez instructed Martínez to set up a temporary post sufficient to guarantee Spanish sovereignty. The expedition arrived at Nootka on 5 May 1789 to discover several vessels, that of Kendrick among them, already in the sound. Martínez decided that the Americans did not pose any great threat to Spanish claims; indeed, he received no little assistance from Captain Kendrick, who introduced him to the Nootka chief MUQUINNA. However, another ship, the *Efigenia Nubiana*, was easy to identify as a

British vessel under a Portuguese flag of convenience. Claiming that the ship carried instructions in Portuguese to capture weaker foreign vessels, Martínez seized, but later released, the *Efigenia*.

Although Martínez had been instructed to create a temporary post at Nootka, he believed that Spain should take a more active interest in the northwest coast. On the 1774 voyage he had seen that it was not a cold and mountainous desert as had been thought, and he envisaged the creation of a Spanish society which would prosper from shipbuilding and other industries. When a schooner he had dispatched from Nootka on 21 June 1789 returned on 5 July with reports of the entrance to Juan de Fuca Strait, Martínez became convinced that the strait had its terminus near New Orleans on the Mississippi River. Although few were to accept his theory, Spain could not afford to relinquish control over the area until a full investigation had been completed. While at Nootka Martínez was tireless in his efforts to convince his government that the base should be made permanent. He ordered a large bell and complete ornaments for a proposed church there, as well as copper sheets for the Indian trade. He formulated a plan, based on the conquest and settlement of the Sandwich (Hawaiian) Islands, for a triangular transpacific trade system in which Mexican products would be exchanged on the northwest coast for sea otter pelts and lumber, which would in turn be sold in China for oriental luxury goods and the mercury needed in the Mexican mining industry.

By the time a British ship, the *Argonaut*, under the command of James Colnett*, arrived from Macao, China, on 2 July, Martínez's men had constructed a small battery and some buildings and had planted gardens on the site of the Indian village at Friendly Cove (B.C.). Colnett, no more suited for diplomacy than Martínez, claimed to have orders from England to create a permanent settlement. Polite relations between the two irascible commanders soon degenerated into disputes. In the final confrontation Colnett, according to Martínez, placed his hand on his sword and shouted "the evil-sounding and denigrating words 'Gardem España [God damn Spain].'" Martínez ordered the arrest of Colnett and the capture of his ship. When another British ship, the *Princess Royal*, arrived on 12 July, it too was detained, and both were sent to San Blas.

The events at Nootka were to create a major incident between Britain and Spain in 1790. That year John Meares*, a British trader who had visited Nootka in May 1788 and who had money invested in the captured vessels, published in London a biased account of the affair which served to whip up British feeling against Spain. Meares claimed to have purchased land from the Indians which had been taken by the Spaniards, and he condemned Martínez for killing an Indian chief and for having forced Colnett's Chinese artisans to work in mines. All these claims lacked substance: Muquinna subsequently denied having sold the land, the murder was the rash act of a Spanish soldier, and there were no mines. The Spanish policy of keeping all documents secret, however, led contemporary writers, including some Spaniards, to accept Meares's version of the events.

After waiting in vain until the end of October 1789 for orders to make the base at Nootka permanent, Martínez sailed for San Blas. Flórez, who was about to leave Mexico, wanted to avoid any responsibility for the events at Nootka and turned the affair over to his successor, the Count de Revilla Gigedo. Revilla Gigedo considered Martínez's handling of the situation "imprudent, inopportune, and ill-founded." Despite his criticism, however, he was dismayed to learn that Nootka had been abandoned, and in 1790 he sent Francisco de Eliza* y Reventa, with Martínez as second in command, to re-establish the base. While at Nootka Martínez received instructions from Madrid, issued at the request of his wife, to return to Spain. At San Blas by February 1791, he obtained an extension to allow him to dispose of the cattle ranch he had acquired in Tepic (Mexico). In September he set sail for Spain. After a few years' service out of Cadiz, his petitions for return to San Blas were granted, on condition that his wife consent to follow him, "otherwise not, because of the long time in which he had been separated from her, since he went to those realms." Promoted frigate ensign, he was transferred to San Blas in February 1795. In 1796 he was in Mexico City with renewed schemes for the settlement of the northwest coast. The last years of his life were probably spent commanding supply vessels between San Blas and Alta (present day) California, for he died at Loreto on one such voyage.

Under other circumstances, Martínez could have won a reputation as a Spanish hero rather than as a precipitous hot-head. He had prevented the British from establishing a post in territories claimed by Spain and had drafted plans that would have assured Spanish domination of the northwest coast. In his own mind he was defending the interests of his nation, and his letters from Nootka Sound had some impact on Spanish policy. But in the clash of imperial designs at Nootka he won only the condemnation of fur-traders and criticism from many of his own superiors.

CHRISTON I. ARCHER

Esteban José Martínez's diary for 1789 has been published in: Spain, Consejo Superior de Investigaciones Científicas, Instituto Histórico de Marina, *Colección de diarios y relaciones para la historia de los viajes y descubrimientos*, ed. L. C. Blanco *et al.* (6v. to date, Madrid, 1943–), VI.

Archivo General de Indias (Seville, Spain), Audiencia de México, legajo 1529, nos.702, 1182; legajo 1530, no.244; Sección de Estado, legajo 43, no.12. Archivo General de la Nación (Mexico City), Sección de Historia, vol.61, exp.14, Diario de la navegación y exploración del piloto segundo don Esteban José Martínez – 17 Dec. 1774; vol.65, exp.2, Martínez to Flórez, 13 July 1789. Archivo Histórico Nacional (Madrid), legajo 4289, Martínez to Valdés, San Blas, 5 Dec. 1788; legajo 4290, Robert Gray and Joseph Ingraham to Juan Francisco de la Bodega y Quadra, Nootka Sound, 5 Aug. 1792.

[James Colnett], *The journal of Captain James Colnett aboard the Argonaut from April 26, 1789, to Nov. 3, 1791*, ed. F. W. Howay (Toronto, 1940). Meares, *Voyages*. J.M. Moziño Suárez de Figueroa, *Noticias de Nutka; an account of Nootka Sound in 1792*, trans. and ed. I. H. Wilson (Seattle, Wash., 1970). *Voyages of 'Columbia'* (Howay). Cook, *Flood tide of empire*. W. R. Manning, *The Nootka Sound crisis* (Washington, 1905). M. E. Thurman, *The naval department of San Blas: New Spain's bastion for Alta California and Nootka, 1767 to 1798* (Glendale, Calif., 1967). Javier de Ybarra y Bergé, *De California á Alaska: historia de un descubrimiento* (Madrid, 1945). C. I. Archer, "The transient presence: a re-appraisal of Spanish attitudes toward the northwest coast in the eighteenth century," *BC Studies* (Vancouver), no.18 (summer 1973), 3–32.

MATHEVET, JEAN-CLAUDE, Sulpician, priest, missionary, and superior; b. 20 March 1717 at Saint-Martin-de-Valamas (dept of Ardèche), France, son of Claude Mathevet and Blanche Ranc; d. 2 Aug. 1781 in Montreal (Que.).

Jean-Claude Mathevet entered the Grand Séminaire de Viviers on 31 Oct. 1736. Having received the tonsure on 15 June 1737 and minor orders the following 21 December, he was ordained deacon on 23 May 1739. He left for Canada on the *Rubis* on 10 June 1740, accompanied by two other Sulpicians, Antoine Faucon and Jacques-Joseph Masson de Montbrac. The new bishop of Quebec, François-Louis de Pourroy* de Lauberivière, sailed on the same ship. The crossing proved calamitous, a quarter of the passengers succumbing to an unknown illness. The youthful Masson de Montbrac was among the victims, as was Bishop Lauberivière, who died a few days after reaching Quebec.

Mathevet taught Latin at the school conducted by the Séminaire de Saint-Sulpice in its Montreal house, and he assisted in the parish church of Notre-Dame. On 5 March 1747 he was ordained priest by Bishop Pontbriand [Dubreil*] in the Ursuline chapel at Quebec. He had begun ministering to the Indians of the Lac-des-Deux-Montagnes mission (Oka) on 12 Sept. 1746, when he was still a deacon. He was to devote the rest of his life to serving the Algonkins and later the Iroquois.

In July 1757, during the Seven Years' War, Mathevet and François PICQUET served as military chaplains to the Indians who accompanied Montcalm*'s expedition against Fort George (also called Fort William Henry, now Lake George, N.Y.). After a year as parish priest of Sainte-Anne-du-Bout-de-l'Île (Sainte-Anne-de-Bellevue), he transferred to the mission of La Présentation (Oswegatchie, now Ogdensburg, N.Y.) in 1758 and for two years he and Pierre-Paul-François de LAGARDE supported or replaced Picquet in ministering to the Indians at this defence outpost of New France.

After his return to the Lac-des-Deux-Montagnes mission, Mathevet became its fourth superior and from 1761 to 1778 carried on a rewarding ministry there. With the assistance of François-Auguste MAGON de Terlaye he energetically combatted the drunkenness that was causing havoc among the Indians to whom whites were illegally providing liquor. But Mathevet was above all a great specialist in the Algonkin language, in which he wrote a grammar (dated 1761), sermons, a sacred history, and a life of Christ. The last two works were printed in two editions in the 19th century. He had a good knowledge of Iroquois and 11 note-books of his sermons in Iroquois are extant. He also compiled a glossary of "Loup" words. Although the manuscript survives (it is in the archives of the Séminaire de Saint-Sulpice in Montreal), the identity of the language has not been positively established. It may be that of the Pocumtucks, an Algonkian speaking group originally from southern New England.

Mathevet was stricken with paralysis in March 1778 and had to retire to the seminary, where he died on 2 Aug. 1781. He was buried beneath the chancel of Notre-Dame. Called Ouakoui – the sky – by the Algonkins, Mathevet was held in the highest esteem by the Indians.

J.-BRUNO HAREL

[Two manuscripts in Algonquin by Jean-Claude Mathevet were published in the 19th century: a life of

Jesus and an Old Testament history. They appeared in a single volume entitled *Ka titc tebeniminang Jezos, ondaje aking. Oom masinaigan ki ojitogoban ka ojitogobanen Aiamie tipadjimo8in masinaigan 8ak8i ena8indibanen* (Montreal, 1861). The manuscripts were republished separately in Montreal, the Old Testament history appearing in 1890 under the title *Aiamie-tipadjimowin masinaigan ka ojitogobanen kaiat nainawisi mekatewikonaiewigobanen/L'histoire sainte en algonquin* and the life of Jesus in 1892 as *Ka titc Jezos tebeniminang ondaje aking enansinaikatek masinaigan ki ojitogoban kaiat pejik kanactageng daje mekatewikonaietc/Vie de Notre-Seigneur Jésus-Christ*. In 1975 G. M. Day published *The "Mots loups" of Father Mathevet* (Ottawa). J.B.H.]

Archives de l'évêché de Viviers (dép. de l'Ardèche, France), Registre des ordinations. ASSM, 8, A; 24, Dossier 2, Dossier 5. Allaire, *Dictionnaire*. Gauthier, *Sulpitiana*. Louis Bertrand, *Bibliothèque sulpicienne, ou histoire littéraire de la Compagnie de Saint-Sulpice* (3v., Paris, 1900). André Chagny, *Un défenseur de la "Nouvelle-France," François Picquet, "le Canadien" (1708–1781)* (Montréal et Paris, 1913). Pierre Rousseau, *Saint-Sulpice et les missions catholiques* (Montréal, 1930). M. Trudel, *L'Église canadienne*. J.-A. Cuoq, "Anotc kekon," RSC *Trans.*, 1st ser., XI (1893), sect.I, 137–79. Olivier Maurault, "Quand Saint-Sulpice allait en guerre . . . ," *Cahiers des Dix*, 5 (1940), 11–30.

MATHEWS, DAVID, office-holder; b. in New York City, son of Vincent Mathews and his second wife Catalina Abeel; m. Sarah Seymour, and they had at least two sons and two daughters; d. July 1800 at Amelia Point, Cape Breton Island.

David Mathews received his AM from the College of New Jersey (Princeton University) in 1754. After holding some minor offices in the administration of New York City, he was appointed mayor in February 1776. Soon afterwards, he was accused of "treasonable practices against the States of America" in connection with his alleged involvement in the "Hickey Plot" to assassinate George Washington and was jailed in Litchfield, Connecticut. He escaped, however, and returned to New York; in 1779 his property, which included 26,000 acres and two houses, was confiscated by the New York Congress. Mathews continued as mayor of New York until shortly before the evacuation of the city by British troops in November 1783.

Following his departure from New York, Mathews travelled, like many other loyalists, to Nova Scotia, where he applied unsuccessfully for the position of attorney general; it is not known whether he had ever received any formal legal training. In 1785 he was persuaded by Abraham Cuyler*, a former mayor of Albany and now registrar of the new colony of Cape Breton, to move to Sydney, its capital. In July he was appointed attorney general and a member of the Executive Council by Lieutenant Governor Joseph Frederick Wallet DesBarres*.

Although a provision had been made for a house of assembly in Cape Breton, none was established. As a result, the Council became the scene for debate over local issues; such debates frequently divided the Council into factions, thereby impairing effective government. The first such split occurred in December 1785 when DesBarres failed to consult the Council about the distribution of supplies to the inhabitants. The self-important Mathews, who had already begun to chafe under DesBarres's strict control of the Council, promptly resigned in protest. When DesBarres then attempted to seize military supplies in order to feed the settlers, Colonel John Yorke of the 33rd Foot objected and soon afterwards joined a faction, led by Mathews and supported by Cuyler and other Council members, which worked for DesBarres's removal. The group sent a petition protesting DesBarres's conduct to Governor John PARR of Nova Scotia, DesBarres's immediate superior. Parr forwarded the petition to the British government, and DesBarres was recalled in November 1786 as a result of this and other complaints.

On the arrival of Lieutenant Governor William Macarmick* in 1787 Mathews rejoined the Council. He soon managed to have his main opponent, Richard GIBBONS, the chief justice, removed from office, and later became Macarmick's principal confidant in the colony. After some time, however, the lieutenant governor objected to what he considered were Mathews' efforts to dominate him. The controversy reached a head in 1794 when Mathews formed an organization for the ostensible purpose of resisting "the rise and progress of sentiment and opinions subversive to our happy Establishment in Church and State" and preventing an influx of refugees from Saint-Pierre and Miquelon, who were fleeing an outbreak of revolutionary activity there. Macarmick claimed, however, that the association included "all the principle people, [so] that I might be obliged to fill vacancies out of this society." By persuading the Council's anti-Mathews faction, led by the Reverend Ranna Cossit*, to submit a petition which claimed that the organization would "subvert the good order of Society," Macarmick was able to ban Mathews' association in July. Mathews' followers threatened to riot, and only a stern reprimand to all concerned from the Duke of Portland, secretary of state for the Home Department, prevented the calamity.

Macarmick left Cape Breton in 1795 and Mathews, as senior councillor, became administrator of the colony. He soon used the office for personal aggrandizement, appointing his sons David and William Tryon acting attorney general and provost-marshal respectively, and naming to the Council Richard Stout*, Sydney's principal merchant, to whom he was deeply in debt. Mathews was also able to attack his opponents on the Council. He denied Cossit's right to appoint a schoolteacher and imprisoned the minister on debt charges, removed William McKinnon* from his position as secretary and registrar of the colony, and dismissed Chief Justice Ingram Ball*, replacing him with his crony Archibald Charles Dodd*. Both Ball and McKinnon were also eventually jailed on charges of debt. At the end of June 1798 Major-General James Ogilvie* arrived in Sydney to replace Mathews as administrator. In the year he served Ogilvie conducted an investigation into Mathews' conduct, but he left without being able to prove Mathews guilty of any wrongdoing.

The next administrator, General John Murray*, who arrived in June 1799 attempted to repair the divisions in the Council, but Mathews refused to be reconciled with his opponents. Moreover, he and Murray clashed over the appointment of a schoolteacher. After this and other quarrels Murray dismissed Mathews as attorney general in January 1800. Mathews promptly made an alliance with Edward Augustus*, Duke of Kent, who harboured a personal grudge against Murray, and Murray was replaced by Major-General John Despard* in June. Mathews did not live to enjoy his victory long, however, for he died at his home near Sydney the following month. Although he was doubtless an ambitious and quarrelsome man, David Mathews' career illustrates the loyalists' difficulties in adjusting to the political restrictions of the postwar British empire, particularly in a colony without a house of assembly.

R. J. MORGAN

Halifax County Court of Probate (Halifax), M60 (original will of David Mathews). PAC, MG 11, [CO 217], Cape Breton A, 3, pp.105–10; 12, pp.52–53, 55, 89, 276–77; Nova Scotia A, 108, pp.240–42; [CO 220], Cape Breton B, 1, pp.118–21. PRO, CO 217/112, ff.2–4, 143–44, 176, 284–85; 217/113, ff.152–53, 275; 217/115, ff.1–2, 51, 106–8, 120–21, 148; 217/117, ff.21, 76, 143–48, 157, 195–96, 198–99, 291–92; 217/118, ff.19–20, 23. Sabine, *Biographical sketches of loyalists*, II, 51–52. G. N. D. Evans, *Uncommon obdurate: the several public careers of J. F. W. DesBarres* (Toronto and Salem, Mass., 1969). A. C. Flick, *Loyalism in New York during the American revolution* (New York, 1901), 146–47. Lena Johnston, *Memories* (Sydney Mines, N.S., 1931). R. J. Morgan, "Orphan outpost: Cape Breton colony, 1784–1820" (unpublished PHD thesis, University of Ottawa, 1972), 42–50, 102–15; "Joseph Frederick Wallet DesBarres and the founding of Cape Breton colony," *Revue de l'université d'Ottawa*, XXXIX (1969), 212–27.

MATONABBEE, leading Indian; b. *c*. 1737 of Chipewyan parents at Prince of Wales's Fort (Churchill, Man.); d. after the destruction of the fort in August 1782.

Unlike most Chipewyans, who seldom visited Hudson's Bay Company posts and then only for a few days, Matonabbee was familiar with Europeans and the fur trade from his youth; his mother, formerly the captive of a Cree band, had married one of Churchill's hunters after company traders bought her freedom. Matonabbee was still a young boy when his father died, and Richard Norton*, chief factor at Churchill, accepted responsibility for him. Some time after 1741 relatives of Matonabbee's father took him away from the post because the new factor, James Isham*, showed little interest in the boy; but when Ferdinand JACOBS became factor in 1752 Matonabbee was again given special attention. His time at Churchill provided him with an opportunity to learn the Cree language as well as some English, and the years among his own people gave him a knowledge of the land and how to live on it. These skills, combined with his knowledge of the fur trade, made him a valuable asset to the company.

Continuing conflict between the "Athapuscow Indians," Crees living near Lake Athabasca (Alta), and Chipewyan groups disrupted trade in that area. It was probably in the late 1750s that Matonabbee was chosen by the company to serve as an ambassador living among the Crees in order to mediate between the two groups. The assignment was dangerous, since the Athabascan Crees were still raiding and sometimes killing small parties of Chipewyans near or within Cree territory. Matonabbee's success in terminating the hostilities was undoubtedly based on his personal qualities and his highly respected association with the HBC.

Matonabbee had made at least one trip to the Coppermine River (N.W.T.) by the late 1760s, and his report, together with the suasion of Moses NORTON, chief at Churchill, encouraged the company to order Samuel HEARNE to survey the area. Hearne's first two attempts to reach the Coppermine, in 1769 and 1770, ended abortively, and Matonabbee blamed their failure on the absence of women. He agreed to guide Hearne on his third trip, which was to last from 1770 to 1772, but insisted that women, including his many wives, accompany the travellers. Women were necessary to cook and sew and were, he claimed, "made for labour; one of them can carry, or haul, as much as two men can do." Hearne developed a high esteem for him and his capacity to organize the long, arduous journey. Matonabbee's ability to adapt the expedition to the Indian manner of transportation and to the exigencies of living off the land ensured its success.

In addition to being an ambassador and a guide, Matonabbee was a "leading Indian" of Churchill throughout his adult life. As such, he collected furs from Indians who were reluctant to make the difficult trip down to the distant bay to trade; he organized "gangs" of Indians who, for a share of the proceeds, agreed to carry the furs to the bay and bring back trade goods; and he distributed the trade goods among the inland Indians. He also served as a middleman to the Copper or Yellowknife Indians, the farthest inland Chipewyan group, as well as to some Dogribs. Matonabbee brought more furs to Churchill than any other Indian, but, even when his prestige was highest with the traders, his occupation was not all glory. Except for the brief times at the fort, where he was treated royally and provided with fancy goods, he had to travel extensively, often under great hardships and always under the threat of starvation.

In 1772 he was proclaimed head of the Chipewyan people by the company traders. HBC men had the illusion that "leading Indians" were important at all times, but in fact they often had little influence when away from the post. They did not replace or resemble traditional leaders but were considered by their people a necessary feature of their society's relationship with the traders. Matonabbee's occasional bullying behaviour, described by Hearne, was tolerated because of his successful dealings with the company. His role as a leading Indian bound Matonabbee inextricably to the fortunes of the fur trade; Andrew Graham* wrote that he committed suicide, a rare form of death among Indians, "for grief that the French had destroyed Churchill Factory, Anno Domini 1782."

BERYL C. GILLESPIE

[Matonabbee is known primarily for his guidance and leadership of Samuel Hearne's expedition to the mouth of the Coppermine River in 1770–72. Hearne's account of this expedition, *Journey from Prince of Wales's Fort* (Glover), includes many references to Matonabbee as well as a biographical sketch (pp.222–28). Brief mention of Matonabbee is made in HBRS, XXVII (Williams), 201–2, and in *Letters from Hudson Bay, 1703–40*, ed. K. G. Davies and A. M. Johnson, intro. R. [G.] Glover (London, 1965), xxvii–lii. The latter work also contains some discussion of the role of the leading Indian (pp.xxii–xxxvi). B.C.G.]

MAUGENEST (Maugenest, *dit* **Saint-Auron, Saint-Horan, Saint-Jorand**, or **Saint-Terone), GERMAIN**, independent fur-trader and HBC master; b. in France, son of François Maugenest and Marie-Anne Saint-Horan (Saint-Jorand); m. 5 March 1764 Rosalie Barrère in Montreal; m. there secondly on 12 Jan. 1767 Louise Descary; d. 10 Nov. 1792 in London, England.

Germain Maugenest arrived in Montreal some time before 1763. He traded to the Mississippi valley until about 1770, when he began to operate in the country between Lake Nipigon (Ont.) and Lake of the Woods. He fell heavily in debt to Ezekiel Solomons, the Montreal fur trade entrepreneur, and decided to escape by joining the Hudson's Bay Company. On 22 July 1779 he, his assistant John Coates, and seven Canadians, guided by three Indians, arrived at Albany Fort (Ont.) from Sturgeon Lake (east of Sioux Lookout, Ont.), where they had been trading. The event placed Chief Factor Thomas HUTCHINS in a quandary; his standing orders required him to order such pedlars to leave immediately, but he realized that Maugenest's expertise might be invaluable to the company, which only recently had decided to push into the interior instead of waiting by the bayside for trade [*see* Ferdinand JACOBS]. He therefore suggested that Maugenest go to England and deal with the company's London committee. Meanwhile Coates and the voyageurs, accompanied by George SUTHERLAND, an HBC employee, would return to winter at Sturgeon Lake, rendezvous with Maugenest at Gloucester House (Washi Lake, Ont.) in the autumn of 1780, and proceed inland once again.

Strongly recommended by Hutchins, Maugenest sailed for England and on 24 Nov. 1779 he appeared before the London committee. It approved his proposal to expand the company's inland trade and gave him a contract of £100 per annum as well as the promise of a commission on the furs he delivered to the bayside posts. He returned to Albany in September 1780 but did not proceed to Gloucester because Sutherland and Coates had nearly starved during the winter.

In May 1781, however, Maugenest set off up the Albany with a commission to act as HBC factor "Inland beyond the distance of 200 miles above Gloucester." The bateau carrying most of the gunpowder was lost in a rapid, however, and the expedition did not proceed beyond that post. The next spring Maugenest refused to go inland because the water was too low and the HBC men not skilful enough at handling canoes. His reluctance may in fact have been due to reports that Ezekiel Solomons was in the vicinity. When his request to be given charge of Gloucester was refused, Maugenest threatened to return to Canada. Probably as a result, he was transferred in 1783 to Moose Factory (Ont.), away from the Indians with whom he had influence. The London committee instructed him to accompany Philip TURNOR on an inland expedition and noted "Your Salary was Established in Consideration of your Inland Exertions, in Execution of which the Company have been wholly Disappointed." Turnor wrote "I promise my self very little assistance from Mr. Maugenest." The remark epitomizes the hostility towards Maugenest in the company, particularly among the employees, who did not relish taking orders from a Frenchman who, according to John Thomas, chief factor at Moose, "can scarcely talk English enough to be understood."

Maugenest spent the rest of his career working at Moose or one of its subordinate posts. He had command at Brunswick House (near the junction of the Opasatika and Missinaibi rivers, Ont.) from 1785 to 1789 and was subsequently at New Brunswick House (on Brunswick Lake). For a long time the London committee expected great things of him, although by 1789 it was threatening to dismiss him because his work was not producing a significant increase in trade. He did not get on well with Thomas, who felt that he gave too many presents to the Indians and permitted employees to spend too much of their wages on luxuries. In 1792, having complained of ill health for several years, Maugenest received permission to go to England; he died there on 10 November, shortly after his arrival. He left no will, and the HBC secretary in London, Alexander Lean, wrote to Todd, McGill and Company in Montreal for assistance in tracing Maugenest's heirs there. A male heir was discovered and the estate turned over to him in 1793.

Maugenest's chief contribution to the HBC was in the improvement of the logistics of the fur trade, especially at Albany where the chiefs had great difficulty in supplying their outposts at Henley (at the junction of the Albany and Kenogami rivers, Ont.) and Gloucester. He convinced Hutchins that goods should be packed in casks, chests, and bales to make bundles of roughly 90 pounds each, and covered with light, waterproofed canvas. Meat should be packed without bone in small casks, rather than in hogsheads which were impossible to portage. Although boats were already being used on the Albany, Hutchins was pleased with Maugenest's design of a bateau for inland transport, and it may have been a prototype of the future York boat. Maugenest also suggested the use of light, lidded, copper kettles as trade goods, and it was apparently on his advice that point blankets were introduced (points were short parallel lines on one edge of a blanket denoting its value in beaver). Both items became staples of the HBC trade.

GEORGE E. THORMAN

ANQ-M, État civil, Catholiques, Notre-Dame de Montréal, 5 mars 1764; Saints-Anges (Lachine), 12 janv. 1767. HBC Arch. A.1/47, ff.2, 22, 24; A.5/2, ff.94f., 114, 158, 195, 226, 259, 302; A.5/3, ff.105d, 106; A.6/12, ff.305–11; A.6/13, ff.2–126; A.6/14, ff.9–127; A.6/15, ff.19, 56; A.11/44, ff.158–87; A.11/45, ff.21–170; B.3/a/75–80; B.3/b/16–19; B.23/a/8–14; B.135/a/68–78; B.135/b/16–22. *Moose Fort journals, 1783–85*, ed. E. E. Rich and A. M. Johnson, intro. G. P. de T. Glazebrook (London, 1954), 354–65. A. M. Johnson, "Mons. Maugenest suggests . . . ," *Beaver*, outfit 287 (summer 1956), 49–53.

MAUGER, JOSHUA (baptized **Josué** but he signed Joshua), sea-captain, businessman, and politician; baptized 25 April 1725 in the parish of St John, Jersey, eldest son of Josué Mauger and Sarah Le Couteur; believed married to Elizabeth Mauger, his cousin; only known child, Sarah, baptized 8 April 1754 in Halifax, Nova Scotia; d. 18 Oct. 1788 at Warborne, near Lymington, Hampshire, England.

Joshua Mauger's career before he went to Halifax in 1749 is obscure. In 1743, at the age of 18, he was master of the *Grand Duke*, quarantined at an unknown British port in December after a voyage from Naples and Leghorn. He later served for some time as master of the *Duke of Cumberland* transport until its discharge at London in March 1747. Mauger then established a base of operations at Louisbourg, Cape Breton Island. By the time the British evacuated the fortress in 1749 he had become victualler to the Royal Navy there, an appointment which suggests that he already had influential friends in London. He moved to Halifax that year and, aside from a trip to England in 1749–50, seems to have remained there until 1760.

Mauger soon came into conflict with the Nova Scotian authorities over certain of his dealings with Louisbourg. The evidence which is available suggests that Halifax citizens who had been resident in Louisbourg were permitted to remove their possessions or the proceeds from their sale for a year or so after Louisbourg officially reverted to French control. In the autumn of 1749 Mauger received "Sundry Merchandise &

Stores" which he had left there. It appears, however, that Mauger used recovery of his Louisbourg possessions as a means of avoiding the trade restrictions imposed by Governor Edward CORNWALLIS, who was anxious to discourage contact with the French. In 1750 Mauger obtained permission to land ten hogsheads of wine from Louisbourg, but he must have imported a much larger quantity since in July and August Cornwallis ordered him to send back over 22 hogsheads. The governor claimed that efforts were being made to make Halifax "a repository for goods from Louisbourg and this chiefly supported and carried on by Mr. Mauger." In November 1751 he ordered the seizure of a sloop believed to have landed contraband from Louisbourg and, suspecting Mauger of having received some of the goods, authorized a search of his warehouse. Mauger argued that the Vice-Admiralty Court had no jurisdiction on land and refused to permit the search, but on the governor's orders James Monk* Sr broke open the warehouse and seized a quantity of rum. In Mauger's defence Isaac Deschamps* testified that the rum was part of 100 casks imported with the governor's permission in November 1750. Mauger explained that at the evacuation of Louisbourg he had had to dispose of large quantities of goods and had provided some of them to French residents there on credit. Sebastian ZOUBERBUHLER, acting on Mauger's behalf, had been unable to obtain acceptable bills of exchange or cash for the goods and had therefore accepted rum and molasses, which he had sent to Halifax. The Vice-Admiralty Court accepted the explanation and ordered Mauger's rum returned.

Cornwallis, obviously dissatisfied, suggested to the Board of Trade that Mauger be dismissed as victualler to the navy. He was convinced that unless the authorities were firm Nova Scotia would become "a rendezvous for smugglers and people who keep a constant correspondence to Louisbourgh." Admitting that the trade was "so very detrimental," the board noted, however, that it was not forbidden by any valid treaty or law and was therefore not illegal. The lords of the Admiralty were willing to terminate Mauger's contract if Cornwallis thought it necessary, but others apparently requested its continuation. Mauger seems to have retained his position until his departure for England, and he continued to receive goods from Louisbourg at least until 1754.

Perhaps the most serious challenge to government authorities in which Mauger was involved began in December 1752 as a result of the dissatisfaction of a number of Halifax residents with their justices of the peace. When Ephraim Cook, a prominent merchant and shipowner from England, lost his commissions as JP and judge of the Inferior Court of Common Pleas and was subsequently indicted for issuing a warrant without authority, his lawyer, David Lloyd, charged the justices with partiality in the performance of their duties. Mauger, quick to support a fellow merchant, joined with 13 other Halifax citizens calling themselves "the principal Inhabitants of this Town" to support Lloyd's protest. Early in March 1753 the Council cleared the justices of the charge, but by the end of the month Governor Peregrine Thomas Hopson* had appointed four new justices "to prevent any suspicion of Partiality in the Bench for the future."

During his 11 years in Nova Scotia Mauger developed wide economic interests, some of which, like his trade with Louisbourg, led to conflicts with local authorities. In the summer of 1751 he applied to Cornwallis for permission to establish a distillery in a "great store" behind his home. Refused permission on the grounds that the establishment would constitute a fire hazard, Mauger built outside the town, "with much hard labour and at great Expence having been obliged to remove almost a Mountain." Erection of the works was apparently underway by August 1751. In July the government had placed a 3*d*. a gallon duty on rum and other spirits, except for the products of Britain and the British West Indies, specifically to encourage the establishment of a distillery and undoubtedly with Mauger's interests in mind. By the autumn of 1752 Mauger was shipping large quantities of rum to outposts such as Fort Lawrence (near Amherst) and Fort Edward (Windsor); in 1766 the annual output of his distillery was 50,000 gallons. When William Steele applied in 1754 for permission to erect a distillery inside the town, Mauger warned that if it were situated near any of his properties he would be obliged to protest "in a public manner" because of the hazard, and the Council unanimously rejected Steele's proposal. It is not known, however, if Mauger objected when John FILLIS established his distillery in 1752, or if Fillis built within the town. The two men came to enjoy a virtual monopoly of the provincial rum trade, and Fillis and Mauger's agent, John BUTLER, acted in concert in the early 1760s to persuade the House of Assembly to increase the protective duty. Because Nova Scotia was seriously in debt and the duties on spirits were the one reliable means of replenishing the local treasury, their adjustment in the interests of maximum revenue became the prime object of those wishing to improve the credit of the province, and they were to involve Mauger and his friends in renewed conflicts with colonial governors in the 1760s and 1770s.

William Steele probably would have found it difficult to build on land in Halifax not near any of Mauger's. Between 1740 and 1760 Mauger took part in some 52 property transactions there. He received some land in the form of direct grants from the government and acquired other properties from bankrupt merchants or from tradesmen who were indebted to him. Outside the town he owned land in Lunenburg, Annapolis Royal, and Windsor, and more extensive properties in Cumberland County, along the Saint John River, and on St John's (Prince Edward) Island. These included a 20,000-acre tract in Cumberland County, which Mauger acquired from Alexander McNutt* in a legal action in 1769, and an estate of similar size on St John's Island, which he was granted in 1767 and which he disposed of in 1775. Mauger seems to have played a considerable role in the economic development of Lunenburg, where he was involved in shipbuilding and the lumber trade. In 1754 Lieutenant Governor Charles Lawrence* advised that the inhabitants of the town be discouraged from seeking work in Halifax because "Their lots at Lunenburg and the Employment Mr. Mauger finds them is as much full as they can accomplish."

Mauger's extensive property holdings were overshadowed in importance by his trading activities. The largest shipowner in Halifax in the years 1749–60, he owned, wholly or in part, 27 vessels, some bought in New England, others acquired by public auction after the Halifax Vice-Admiralty Court had condemned them for illegal trade, and still others purchased as prize vessels. Mauger shipped fish and lumber to the West Indies and obtained rum, molasses, and sugar in exchange. The timber in some cases undoubtedly came from his sawmills near Lunenburg, and the fish may have come from a fishing establishment he is said to have maintained at Halifax. His ships were used to carry rum from his distillery to a store he owned at Annapolis Royal and to Minas and Chignecto, where he may also have had stores. From England, Ireland, and New England he imported a wide assortment of items, ranging from beer and raisins to glass beads, lead shot, and grindstones. He seems also to have dealt in slaves. The Seven Years' War provided him with a new outlet for his energies; he invested in privateers, as well as in the purchase of prize vessels, and acted as agent for the officers and crews of British navy vessels which captured French ships off Cape Breton.

Not all of Mauger's shipping ventures were profitable. In 1750 the French destroyed one of his vessels in the inner reaches of the Bay of Fundy. Three years later he arranged a sham sale of a schooner to Matthew Vincent of Louisbourg in order to facilitate a trading venture to Martinique only to have the mate abscond with the vessel. Each of the privateers he owned jointly with John Hale, the *Wasp* and the *Musquetto*, made one recorded capture, but neither proved profitable. The vessel taken by the *Wasp* was worth only about £342 with its cargo. The second prize was ordered released by the Vice-Admiralty Court because it was Dutch; subsequently its crew accused their captors of having tortured them, and the court, presided over by John Collier*, ordered the captain and crew or their agents to pay damages to the injured parties as well as the costs of the month-long trial.

As victualler to the navy Mauger drew large amounts of provisions from both Britain and New England, especially during the war years. Mauger's British suppliers are not known, but his American source was a Connecticut partnership headed by Jonathan Trumbull, one of the colony's largest provisions dealers by the 1750s and later its governor. Mauger used his acquaintanceship with the clergyman Aaron Cleveland* to make contact with Trumbull and employed John Butler to arrange the first shipment of goods in the fall of 1752. For Trumbull and his partners the trade was invaluable because for some years it provided them with virtually the only bills of exchange they could obtain. For Mauger, however, it was less than satisfactory. The provisions he received did not always meet his demanding standards, and in 1754 he began to turn to Ireland as a source of beef, pork, and butter. He complained to Trumbull that he had lost more than £100 sterling on meat sent from Connecticut. At least one lot of beef had proven inedible in spite of his having had it repacked, newly salted, and pickled on arrival. When wartime inflation made Irish goods less expensive than Connecticut provisions, Mauger ceased buying from Trumbull.

Mauger departed for England in 1760, apparently in the summer, but he maintained a lively interest in Nova Scotia. The key to his continued involvement in provincial affairs lies, of course, in the immense fortune he had built up there, a fortune he was able to protect and advance even at a distance of 2,500 miles. Exactly why he was so successful in this endeavour is not entirely clear. Contemporaries believed that by the 1770s a Mauger "party" had developed in Halifax, but it is not always easy to identify the members of this group or to determine how they were attached to Mauger. Some, like Fillis, had similar economic interests; others, like Butler, were employed by him; and still others, like Michael FRANCKLIN, became indebted to him. Perhaps more important than particular links, however, was the fact that in defending his own interests Mauger was defending a colonial financial structure from which many members of the Halifax mercantile élite benefited. He had, therefore, a base of support in Halifax, which, combined with his knowledge of Nova Scotia and his substantial investment in the provincial debt, must have given him a certain authority in England. These factors alone, however, do not explain his considerable influence with successive governments. His election to parliament for Poole in 1768, a seat he held with only a brief interruption until 1780, undoubtedly added to his prestige, but he does not appear to have been a major political figure. Nevertheless, as Sir Lewis Bernstein Namier points out, "he seems to have been listened to, even when in Parliament he sided with the Opposition." In short, his relations with the home authorities remain something of a mystery.

In April 1762 the Nova Scotia House of Assembly chose Mauger as the colony's agent in London. In that capacity he conducted a bitter campaign against Jonathan BELCHER, the chief justice and lieutenant governor. On several occasions in 1762 and 1763 he appeared before the Board of Trade to demand Belcher's removal from administrative office for such offences as his refusal to permit continuation of the fur monopoly, of which Benjamin GERRISH was the principal beneficiary, and his unwillingness to extend the debtors' act, which protected settlers who had left debts behind them in other colonies and in which many members of the Halifax mercantile community had a vested interest. He complained to the board of Belcher's "Impudent Conduct" and charged that the lieutenant governor was "so unacquainted and unskilled in the Art of Government, and has behaved in such improper manner, as to have occasioned a General Dislike to him . . . and Disgust to his Measures." More important for Mauger's interest was the fact that in 1762 Belcher for some time refused assent to two bills which would have modified the duties on spirits in such a way as to favour local distillers. Perhaps another reason for his attack was his inability to secure payment of bills of exchange he had supplied the government of Nova Scotia during Belcher's administration. In March 1763 Belcher was replaced by Montagu Wilmot*. On Wilmot's death three years later, Michael Francklin was appointed lieutenant governor. Whether Mauger had anything to do with this appointment is not clear, but Francklin was one of his protégés and, along with Butler and Isaac Deschamps, had been entrusted with guarding Mauger's interests after his departure for England. He eventually fell heavily in debt to Mauger as well, and it would seem that his ten-year tenure of the lieutenant governorship could only have been advantageous for his patron.

Although by December 1763 Mauger had ceased to act as Nova Scotia's agent in London, he remained the colony's unofficial spokesman, with more apparent influence than a succession of governors. In that year he had been influential in securing to New Englanders along the Saint John River lands on which they had settled but to which British army officers had a prior claim; their settlement, Maugerville, was named in his honour. He also became involved in the appeals of individuals in Nova Scotia against government decisions which affected them adversely. The Nova Scotia issue which concerned him most, however, was distilling. In 1767 the House of Assembly, with a view to increasing the colony's revenue and with the support of Governor Lord William CAMPBELL, passed a law reducing the impost on imported spirits and raising the excise duty. Since Butler, Fillis, and Francklin had been unable to block the bill, they turned to Mauger for assistance. Along with Brook Watson* and other London merchants interested in Nova Scotia, Mauger petitioned the Board of Trade against the duties, which would, it was claimed, "tend to Distress the Trade and Fishery" of the province. Campbell argued that Mauger and Fillis had unjustly enjoyed a monopoly of Nova Scotia's rum trade "to the detriment of all the Merchants traders & Almost every other person in the province" and that the new duties would benefit the colony as a whole by permitting a reduction in the debt. The power of the merchants' lobby was such, however, that the board rejected Campbell's mercantilist arguments as "contrary to all true policy," and the old rates of duty were restored. The fact that Mauger and his friends held a substantial proportion of the provincial treasury notes – as they did not hesitate to point out to the board – no doubt weighed strongly in their favour. Since Campbell continued to make a nuisance of himself, Mauger and Butler began a campaign to have him removed. Although it was reasons of health that brought about the governor's transfer to South Carolina in 1773, Mauger's friends gave him credit for the removal.

The conflict over the duties on spirits clearly reveals what John Bartlet Brebner* has described as "the whole apparatus of influence and dependence" that ensured "Nova Scotian subservience to London." Campbell's successor,

Francis LEGGE, reported in 1775 that Mauger's influence was so extensive that the governor of Nova Scotia could not without complaint "introduce any measure for the public good" that was opposed to the interest of Mauger's supporters. By 1775 other voices had been raised against Mauger's "plan of Dominion" and against the "notorious" power of his agent, John Butler, but the opposition was not strong. Legge's desire to reform the customs and excise duties would have been enough in itself to attract Mauger's enmity, but his attack on the whole structure of privilege in Nova Scotia ensured his fate. Utilizing the protests sent to him by Legge's enemies in the colony, Mauger conducted a deft campaign against the governor in London. Legge was recalled in 1776, and Mauger's friends boasted that he was the third governor they had removed.

With his interests secure Mauger seems to have been content during the American revolution to reap the benefits of his investments. Indeed, those investments constituted one of the major ties linking Nova Scotia to Britain in the war years. Only in 1779 did he begin to disengage himself from Nova Scotian affairs. That year he gave his able lieutenant, John Butler, power of attorney to sell a considerable number of his holdings there. Three years later Butler's nephew, John Butler Dight* Butler, was authorized to sell all his remaining property, except for two 20,000-acre tracts on the Bay of Fundy, one of them apparently the property acquired from Alexander McNutt, and his distillery and related lands in Halifax. Finally, in 1784, Mauger sold his distillery as well. Although it is impossible to be certain, Mauger may have been experiencing financial problems in the late 1770s. The list of bankrupts in the *Gentleman's Magazine* for 1777 mentions a J. Mauger, broker, but it cannot be confirmed that this man was Joshua.

Little is known of Mauger's personal or business affairs in England. At his death he was a director of the French Hospital and an elder brother of Trinity House, both concerns that reflect his origins and background. He left most of his estate to the children of his nieces. His wife and daugher are not mentioned in his will and had presumably predeceased him.

DONALD F. CHARD

Conn. Hist. Soc. (Hartford), Jonathan Trumbull papers. Halifax County Court of Probate (Halifax), Book 3, pp.47–51 (will of Joshua Mauger) (mfm. at PANS). Halifax County Registry of Deeds (Halifax), 1, p.136; 2, pp.110, 411; 18, p.97; 20, pp.193–95 (mfm. at PANS). Hampshire Record Office (Winchester, Eng.), 84M70/PR2 (parish register of Boldre), 24 Oct. 1788. PANS, RG 1, 29, no.8; 35, no.15; 164/2, pp.54, 57; 209, 31 July 1751, 29 Dec. 1752, 1 March 1753; 210, 28 Feb. 1754; 491, pp.84–87, 90, 141; 492, pp.14, 31, 34; 493, pp.7, 8, 10, 13, 14, 28, 33, 46, 47–50, 182, 183, 191–93. PRO, Adm. 106/275; CO 217/13, ff.8, 66, 83; 217/19, f.167; 217/20, ff.202, 203; 217/21, f.52; 217/22, ff.113, 122, 127; 218/7; 221/28, ff.4, 9, 11, 77, 80, 103, 110, 139, 209. St John's Church (Jersey), Registre des baptêmes, 25 avril 1725. St Paul's Anglican Church (Halifax), Registers of baptisms, burials, and marriages, 8 April 1752 (mfm. at PANS).

G.B., PRO, *CHOP, 1773–75*, 431–32; *CTBP, 1742–45*, 387. *Boston Evening-Post* (Boston, Mass.), 12 Aug. 1751. *Boston Weekly News-Letter* (Boston, Mass.), 8 Nov. 1750. Namier and Brooke, *House of Commons*, III, 119–20. Brebner, *Neutral Yankees* (1969), 67; *New England's outpost*, 246. J. G. Lydon, *Pirates, privateers, and profits* (Upper Saddle River, N.J., 1970), 237. Glenn Weaver, *Jonathan Trumbull, Connecticut's merchant magistrate, 1710–1785* (Hartford, Conn., 1956), 50, 54, 70, 80.

MAUGUE-GARREAU, MARIE-JOSÈPHE, *dite* **de l'Assomption**, sister of the Congregation of Notre-Dame and superior of the community (superior general); baptized 30 Dec. 1720 in Montreal (Que.), daughter of Marie-Anne Maugue and Pierre Garreau, *dit* Saint-Onge; d. there 16 Aug. 1785.

Marie-Josèphe was the first Maugue-Garreau in Canada. Her name derived from the linking of the family names of her mother, the daughter of Claude Maugue*, clerk of court at Montreal, and of her father. She and other children of Marie-Anne and Pierre Garreau were called Maugue-Garreau to distinguish them from the children of Pierre and his first wife.

Marie-Josèphe entered the noviciate of the Congregation of Notre-Dame in Montreal in 1738 and made her profession two years later as Sister de l'Assomption, the name Marie Barbier* had borne. When the contract of her profession was signed on 22 Dec. 1740 some 20 days after her father's death, her mother promised to pay the community a dowry of 2,000 *livres*. In 1766, after 26 years of service, Sister de l'Assomption was elected to replace Marie-Marguerite PIOT de Langloiserie, *dite* Saint-Hippolyte, as superior general. Like her predecessor, she had to contend with the prevailing poverty and try to reorganize the community's temporal affairs. Sister de l'Assomption's correspondence with Abbé de L'Isle-Dieu, vicar general in France for the colonies, and with the new procurator general for the community in France, Jean-Louis Maury, reveals the financial losses it had suffered. In the 1763 liquidation of "Canada paper," bills of exchange had been reduced to half their face value, and orders for payment, card money, and certificates to a quarter. As a result the community had lost 7,700 *livres* on bills of exchange, more than 12,500 *livres* on orders for payment and card money certified in France, and nearly 20,000 *livres* on orders for payment and certificates declared in Canada. In 1770 a royal decree lowered the interest rate on all Canadian assets in France from four to two and a half per cent, putting them in the same category as securities held in France. The correspondence also lists the stocks and securities that the community then held in France, as well as its annual income from them. This income was steadily diminishing, a development that could only make more critical the situation created by war and the conquest.

Sister de l'Assomption's administrative problems were compounded by the fire that on 11 April 1768 destroyed part of Montreal, including the house and church the community had reconstructed after the fire of 1683. The sisters found refuge at the Hôtel-Dieu, where the "salle Royale" was divided "by using curtains and blankets, into various parts which became dormitories, classrooms, an infirmary, a common room." There they continued to teach their boarders and day pupils. On 8 September they returned to their house, which had been rebuilt and enlarged by a storey as a result of many gifts amounting to about 50,000 *livres*. To provide the additional sums needed for the reconstruction and for the organization of a school for day pupils, the sisters had to sell some land, as well as silver cutlery, cups, and goblets. They also gave up the services of a doctor, for which they were paying 200 *livres* a year, "until some serious malady should strike them unexpectedly." The community was soon confronted with a new worry. The increasing poverty of the population meant that there were fewer and fewer boarders. To ensure that "the order not slow down" the sisters had to resign themselves to taking day boarders, a solution they had been reluctant to accept. In 1769 the community's situation prevented their making a financial contribution to the rebuilding of the mission in Lower Town, which had been destroyed during the siege of Quebec [*see* Marie Raizenne*, *dite* Saint-Ignace].

It was probably these difficulties that prompted Sister de l'Assomption to concentrate the community's real estate in one area in order to put it to greater profit. She sold nearly all the lands acquired by the community as legacies of various sisters and decided to purchase the fief of Saint-Paul, which was being put up for auction. This fief, which covered two-thirds of Île Saint-Paul (Île des Soeurs), was close to the fief of La Noue at Pointe-Saint-Charles, which the nuns already owned through purchase and through a donation by Jeanne Le Ber*. They acted through an intermediary, Étienne AUGÉ, to whom the fief was sold for 832 *louis* on 16 Aug. 1769. A few people challenged the ensuing sale before Governor Guy Carleton*. But having given Sister de l'Assomption verbal permission to acquire the property, Carleton ratified his authorization with a document bearing his signature and seal. The immense farm on Île Saint-Paul and the sharecropping farm at Pointe-Saint-Charles together constituted a veritable agricultural complex.

During Sister de l'Assomption's term as superior the community maintained its spiritual life through the momentum built up during the first hundred years of its existence. Financial difficulties forced the nun to bring all her efforts to bear upon the community's temporal organization. She did so in an innovative spirit and with business acumen.

ANDRÉE DÉSILETS

ACND, Fichier général; Personnel, III; Registre général. ANQ-M, État civil, Catholiques, Notre-Dame de Montréal, 30 déc. 1720. Tanguay, *Dictionnaire*, IV, 170; V, 578. Galarneau, *La France devant l'opinion canadienne*. Lemire-Marsolais et Lambert, *Hist. de la CND de Montréal*, V. Claude Lessard, "L'aide financière donnée par l'Église de France à l'Église naissante du Canada," *RHAF*, XV (1961–62), 171–88.

MAURÈS DE MALARTIC, ANNE-JOSEPH-HIPPOLYTE DE, Comte de MALARTIC, officer in the French regular troops; b. 3 July 1730 at Montauban, France, son of Pierre-Hippolyte-Joseph de Maurès de Malartic, Comte de Montricoux, an officer in the Gardes Françaises, and Antoinette-Charlotte de Savignac; d. unmarried 28 July 1800 at Port-Louis, Île de France (Mauritius).

After studying at the Collège de Nanterre, near Paris, Anne-Joseph-Hippolyte de Maurès de Malartic entered the army in 1745 as a sub-lieutenant in the Régiment de la Sarre. On 8 Aug. 1746 he was named a second lieutenant in the Régiment de Béarn and on 1 November was promoted captain. He took part in campaigns in Flanders, Italy, and Provence and after the War of the Austrian Succession became assistant adjutant on 30 Oct. 1749. In 1755 he accompanied the Régiment de Béarn to Canada. Landing at Quebec on 19 June, he was sent to Fort Frontenac (Kingston, Ont.) and at that point began to keep a record of his regiment's movements and the events in which he participated. The following summer Malartic took part in Montcalm*'s expedition against Oswego (Chouaguen). Although defended by more than 1,700 men, the British stronghold capitulated on 14 August, yielding considerable booty. Three days later Montcalm wrote to LÉVIS: "I cannot praise too highly my aides-de-camp, Lapause [Plantavit*], Malartic; I would have collapsed under the task without them." Malartic subsequently went to the Lake Champlain region – to Fort Saint-Frédéric (near Crown Point, N.Y.), and to Fort Carillon (Ticonderoga), where in the summer of 1757 he joined the forces Montcalm was assembling to besiege Fort William Henry (also called Fort George, now Lake George, N.Y.). Malartic took part in the operation and was present on 9 August when the fort surrendered. Early in the autumn he went with the troops to Montreal. There he supervised distribution of food to the soldiers, who, like civilians, were subject to rationing. The task was not always easy because the soldiers were unwilling to eat the horsemeat served them.

In June 1758 Malartic left with the Régiment de Béarn for Fort Carillon and worked at preparing abatis to protect the fort against the assault that Major-General James ABERCROMBY's troops were preparing. The attack was launched on 8 July, but the French troops put up a vigorous defence and, despite numerical inferiority, forced the British to retreat with serious losses. Wounded in the knee, Malartic arrived back in Montreal on 17 August and spent the winter as major of his regiment, keeping an eye on its billets. He had meanwhile been made a knight of the order of Saint-Louis. The following summer he assisted in the hasty reinforcement of Quebec's fortifications, which offered poor protection. The British under James Wolfe* had landed in considerable force on the Île d'Orléans late in June and were beginning to besiege the city. Although their advance was checked on 31 July when they attacked the camp at Montmorency, below Quebec, their hold tightened inexorably, ending in their victory on the Plains of Abraham on 13 September. After the battle, in which he had a horse killed under him, Malartic withdrew to Montreal to organize winter quarters for the troops. He took an active role in the final campaign and suffered chest wounds in the battle of Sainte-Foy on 28 April 1760. He remained at Quebec until 5 June to take responsibility for the sick and wounded at the Hôpital Général, and to negotiate their evacuation with Brigadier-General MURRAY. Then he went to Montreal and with Jean-Daniel DUMAS tried to delay the British advance, but to no avail.

After the surrender of Montreal in September, Malartic left Canada with the Régiment de Béarn, landing at La Rochelle in November. The following year he was put on half pay. In April 1763 he was named major of the Régiment Royal-Comtois, and on 5 June colonel of the Régiment de Vermandois, a regiment he commanded for 17 years in Guadeloupe, Martinique, Saint-Domingue (Hispaniola), and Corsica. In 1770 he was promoted brigadier in the infantry and ten years later was named major-general.

In some measure won over to the ideas of the French revolution, Malartic became lieutenant-general of the armies on 25 Jan. 1792, commandant general of the French establishments beyond the Cape of Good Hope, and on 17 June governor general of Île de France. He found this colony in ferment with revolutionary ideas, and through prudent measures he restored calm. In June 1796 he sent back to France the agents of the Directory who had come to enforce the decree abolishing slavery; his action spared the colony the disorders that broke out in the West Indies. He died at Port-Louis in 1800 and an impressive mausoleum was built for him there in gratitude for his service.

Always held in high esteem by his chiefs, Malartic was regarded as a "well-trained, zealous, firm officer [who] has served well and has led his regiment to serve well." Honest and unselfish, and without personal means, he was described by a settler on Île de France in the following terms: "Austere in character, reserved and rather cold in manner, he had won the affection of the whole colony, which had long since seen him less as a governor than as a father . . . he probably offers the sole example of a general who survived the most unhappy periods of the revolution with honour, steadfast in the post in which the king had placed him."

ÉTIENNE TAILLEMITE

[A.-J.-H. de Maurès de Malartic, comte de Malartic], *Journal des campagnes au Canada de 1755 à 1760 . . .*, Gabriel de Maurès de Malartic et Paul Gaffarel, édit. (Dijon, France, 1890). AMA, SHA, A[1], 3498, 3574; LG, 1272/1. AN, Col., C[11A], 105. *Coll. des manuscrits de Lévis* (Casgrain). *Doc. relatifs à la monnaie sous le Régime français* (Shortt), II, 922, 924. *NYCD* (O'Callaghan and Fernow), X. *Dictionary of Maurician biography*, ed. Auguste Toussaint (2v. to date, [Port-Louis, Mauritius], 1941–). Le Jeune, *Dictionnaire*. "Officiers du régiment de Béarn," *BRH*, LI (1945), 354–55.

MENNEVILLE, Marquis DUQUESNE, ANGE DUQUESNE DE. *See* DUQUESNE

MERCIER. *See* LE MERCIER

MESPLET, FLEURY, printer, publisher, and bookseller; b. 10 Jan. 1734 in Marseilles, France, son of Jean-Baptiste Mesplet and Antoinette Capeau; d. 24 Jan. 1794 in Montreal (Que.).

It has always been assumed that Fleury Mesplet was born in Lyons rather than in Marseilles, and he did in fact spend his youth in Lyons, where his family had settled. His father, a native of Agen, was a printer, but it is not known whether he was a master printer or a journeyman; it is uncertain, therefore, whether Fleury apprenticed with his father, who died in 1760, or in a master printer's shop in Lyons. Nothing in Fleury's career up to this point explains his departure in 1773 for England, where he set up a printing business near Covent Garden in London, but the economic situation in France and the difficulties facing the printing trade in Lyons perhaps led him to seek his fortune elsewhere.

Mesplet may have met Benjamin Franklin in London; he was certainly well aware of the conflict between Great Britain and her colonies on the American continent. In any case, a wish to try his luck overseas is sufficient explanation for his departure for America. Taking his printing equipment with him, he settled in Philadelphia in 1774 with his wife, Marie Mirabeau, whom he had married around 1765 at Lyons, and went into partnership with another printer. Except for the *Lettre adressée aux habitans de la province de Québec, ci-devant le Canada*, which the first Continental Congress had him print, Mesplet received almost no orders. But he did meet Charles Berger, a compatriot in better circumstances, who was to become his financial backer. Mesplet was attracted by the province of Quebec, where, as he had no doubt learned, there was only one printing firm, and he set out for the capital early in 1775. In Philadelphia, meanwhile, Charles Berger had to redeem Mesplet's personal belongings and printing equipment, which had been seized by his partner; he also had to pay the rent and other debts. Mesplet's visit led to a decision to move to the province, and he returned to Philadelphia, visiting Montreal on the way. All he lacked was capital, but political events were going to work in his favour.

After Richard MONTGOMERY had captured Montreal in November 1775, Mesplet succeeded in convincing the second Continental Congress that a French printing firm was necessary for the success of the revolution in that city. The modest sum of $200 was granted him for moving his family and shop to Montreal. Having dissolved his partnership, Mesplet formed another with Berger, from whom he borrowed $2,666 to buy new type, paper, and other supplies. He hired Alexandre Pochard as editor for the newspaper he intended to found, Jacques-Clément Herse* and John Gray as journeymen printers, and a manservant. Bearing a printer's commission from the Congress, Mesplet left Philadelphia on 18 March 1776 and arrived in Montreal on 6 May. The American venture into the province was already at an end: the army left Montreal on 15 June, abandoning Mesplet and his company to the vengeance of those who had remained loyal to the crown. Mesplet was arrested and imprisoned along with his employees, but he was soon released and set up a shop on Rue Capitale; although Alexandre Pochard returned to France, Mesplet was able to publish five works in 1776.

Despite the war Mesplet soon felt it possible to publish a weekly paper, of which lawyer Valentin JAUTARD became editor. The first issue of *La Gazette du commerce et littéraire, pour la ville et district de Montréal* came out on 3 June 1778; from September on the paper was called *La Gazette littéraire, pour la ville et district de Montréal*. The first entirely French newspaper in Canada, it lasted only a year. Because of the war Mesplet had promised the government not to criticize the civil and religious authorities, and Jautard, although himself a fervent Voltairian, gave a great deal of space to anti-Voltairian writings. The superior of the Sulpicians, Étienne MONTGOLFIER, intensely disliked these men who were engaged in a contest with him for intellectual influence. When Jautard founded his Académie, and then asked Governor HALDIMAND to recognize it at the end of December 1778, Montgolfier hastened to write to the governor to denounce both the academy and the *Gazette littéraire*. In the spring of 1779 Jautard criticized some of Judge René-Ovide HERTEL de Rouville's judgements, which concerned him as a lawyer. In turn the judge complained to Haldimand, who gave way to the pressure and had Jautard and Mesplet arrested on 2 June. The two men remained in custody until September 1782; even then they were not officially set free but, with the connivance of the authorities, simply allowed to leave the prison.

Undaunted, Mesplet returned to his shop. But his situation was precarious. Heavily in debt, he was being dunned by his creditors, including Charles Berger; their partnership had been dissolved in September 1778 but Mesplet still owed him $4,800. Berger came to Montreal in September 1784 to collect his money. The matter was so complicated that four referees had to be appointed, and these sought the advice of Benjamin FROBISHER, one of the most important merchant-traders in Montreal. Berger agreed to settle for $1,200, but received only $460. For his part Mesplet, who had claimed an indemnity of $9,450 from the American Congress in June 1784, received only $426.50 from it. Another large creditor, tailor Joseph-Marie Desautels, to whom Mesplet owed $4,000, had Mesplet's property seized in November 1785, but the sale brought in only $600. Ironically, Edward William Gray*, who acquired the printing equipment, had to rent it to Mesplet, since he was the only person able to use it.

Having got rid of his creditors, and been freed from owning his shop, so to speak, Mesplet again turned to the idea of a paper, and on 25 Aug. 1785 the first edition of the *Montreal Gazette/La Gazette de Montréal* came out. His business seems to have been doing well, and two years later he set up a new shop on Rue Notre-Dame. On 1 Sept. 1789 his wife Marie, a faithful companion for almost 25 years, died at about 43 years of age. Six months later Mesplet took as his second wife a 23-year-old Montreal woman, Marie-Anne, daughter of his friend Jean-Baptiste Tison, a wig-maker. After he had founded his bilingual news-sheet, Mesplet had published a few books and pamphlets, but it is safe to assume that his paper accounted for the bulk of his income. The fact that in 1793 he ordered new type from France, with financial help from merchant Jean-Baptiste-Amable Durocher*, is a sure sign that the business was prospering. And yet at his death a year later Mesplet left his young widow in financial difficulties.

Printing had been initiated in the maritime provinces by British settlers from the south [*see* Bartholomew Green*; John Bushell*]. A similar pattern occurred in Quebec: printers William Brown and Thomas Gilmore had come from Philadelphia, and Fleury Mesplet, though a native of Lyons, had also set out for Montreal from that city. The first printer west of Quebec, Mesplet did not equal William Brown, who issued more than 250 titles, eight of them over 100 pages in length, and who was prosperous at his death. Mesplet encountered enormous difficulties in the course of 20 years' work in London, Philadelphia, and Montreal. About 80 titles are attributed to him, including the two periodicals. A quarter were religious works, as might be expected in a small town whose population, mainly Catholic, was guided by the Sulpicians. Besides being seigneurs of the territory, the Sulpicians had a classical college and provided Montreal's parish priest and vicar general. Orders for religious and educational works consequently bulked largest among those that came to Mesplet's shop, as was true for printers in French towns in the 18th century. Ten of his books ran to more than 100 pages; these included *Cantiques de l'âme dévote . . .* by Laurent Durand, known as *Cantiques de Marseille* (610 pages), *Formulaire de prières à l'usage des pensionnaires des religieuses ursulines* (467 pages), and a *Pseautier de David, avec les cantiques à l'usage des écoles* (304 pages), all works previously published in Europe and printed by Mesplet without authorization, a common practice at the time. The remainder of his output consisted of works concerning justice and pamphlets such as one on the Baie Saint-Paul malady [*see* James Bowman]. His shop printed in four languages – French, English, Latin, and Iroquois – and his varied output is proof of Mesplet's excellence as a printer.

If his output resembled that of French printers, it was also North American, particularly in its almanacs and calendars. Between 1777 and 1784 he published seven almanacs, from 48 to 62 pages each, with a variety of information such as a register of the priests and religious in Canada, a list of post offices, a table of weights and measures, nomenclature for contemporary currencies, and an index of known kingdoms and republics, the whole interspersed with stories and anecdotes. Mesplet fits the American model in having been primarily a printer and journalist, in contrast to his European counterpart, who was a printer and bookseller. The newspaper medium was well suited to the needs of North Americans, who lived in small centres far from their native lands and out of contact with the world beyond. The newspaper became the source of information from far and near, as well as the medium for the offering of services. The latter role guaranteed a basic income for a printing shop. Such a security Mesplet had wanted before coming to Montreal and had unsuccessfully sought once before. Yet his *Gazette littéraire* was an exclusively literary publication, with virtually no advertisements save those for the books he published and the paper he sold. His editor, Valentin Jautard, may have urged the publisher to this policy. In its year of existence the *Gazette* published philosophical, literary, and anecdotal articles, poems and letters, all material which lent itself to discussion but did not bring money to the printer. Mesplet seems to have respected this fact with his second weekly, begun in 1785. His *Montreal Gazette* (today the *Gazette*), adopting the model of the *Quebec Gazette/La Gazette de Québec* with French in the left-hand column and English in the right, had four pages half filled with advertisements and announcements of all sorts; these reveal the rapid development of Montreal's economic, social, and cultural life. The other half of the paper offered foreign and local news, often reprinted from the *Quebec Gazette* because of the *Montreal Gazette*'s limited means; it had articles on education, religion, literature, and after 1788, politics, for the paper was then resolutely demanding that a legislative assembly be established in Quebec. Mesplet's *Gazette* became Voltairian and anticlerical, condemning the ignorance of clerics engaged in teaching; it called Bishop HUBERT of Quebec a Christian despot in articles criticizing the excessive number of public holidays and denounced his obscurantism for opposing as premature a proposal for a mixed Catholic and Protestant university.

In contrast to William Brown's paper, Mesplet's second *Gazette* was first written in French and then translated into English by Valentin Jautard, who seems to have been the editor until his death in 1787. The back room of the *Montreal Gazette*, like that of the *Gazette littéraire*, served as a meeting place for the French speaking intelligentsia of Montreal, with Jautard at its head. It was there that young Henry-Antoine Mézière* found his calling on leaving college. The *Montreal Gazette* led the *philosophes*' combat against intolerance, the abuses of the clergy, and the feudal system. The paper burst forth in exultation when the French revolution dawned, still borrowing news from its rival in Quebec but also from French newspapers. It went even further in wanting to apply the principles of the revolution to the province of Quebec. France's declaration of war against Great Britain in 1793 obviously put a stop to this current. For the second time in 15 years war had prevented a group of young and middle-aged intellectuals from developing. Mesplet's two papers had been the centre of the Enlightenment in Montreal. Historians and scholars have referred particularly to the first, condemning its "Voltairianism," and have ignored the second, which for eight years constituted the point of convergence for Montreal's intelligentsia and was an important source of information for the public. Eight months after the paper was forced to change its tone, Mesplet was dead.

Following the practice in France, Fleury Mesplet had actually called himself a printer and bookseller, although he apparently did not sell many books other than those he printed. The inventories made when his property was seized in 1785 and after his death show few books other than those from his own press. The second inventory lists, however, a great quantity of high quality paper, ink, and pens. Thus, like his counterparts in the 18th century, Mesplet was printer-bookseller, publisher, and printer-journalist. But he was not the editor of his newspapers as was often the case in America, because he was not well enough educated. The few letters available show that he had difficulty expressing himself: hence his hiring of Alexandre Pochard in Philadelphia and Jautard in Montreal. Mesplet was, nevertheless, a first-class printer. His books may have been typeset rather quickly, but they show that he knew all the secrets of his trade and that he worked with a master's hand. We know only a few of his workers. He had brought John Gray and Jacques-Clément Herse from Philadelphia; the latter is supposed to have left him in 1785 to become a merchant. Mesplet took only one apprentice, Alexander, the young son of a Montreal schoolmaster, William Gunn, who joined his shop in December 1789. The available information suggests that until her death in September of that year his first wife, Marie Mirabeau, had almost certainly acted as a journeyman for her husband, as was the custom in France.

Impecunious always, a victim of seizures and imprisonment, a bad administrator but a good printer, Mesplet showed constancy and an extraordinary aptitude for convincing his friends and financial backers of his imminent success. Though his estate was in some confusion any claim that he died destitute is exaggerated: the inventory taken after his death proves that he owned furniture and a wardrobe that many Montrealers of quality might have envied. Prominent on the Rue Notre-Dame because of his backroom office and his newspaper, Mesplet had built up a circle of friends which included intellectuals such as Valentin Jautard, Pierre DU CALVET, and Henry-Antoine Mézière, small businessmen such as Jacques-Clément Herse, Jean-Baptiste-Amable Durocher, Joseph-Marie Desautels, and Charles Lusignan*, and men from the liberal professions such as notaries Antoine Foucher*, François Leguay Sr, Pierre-François MÉZIÈRE, Henry-Antoine's father, and Jean-Guillaume De Lisle*. Making him out to have been a "republican" and a "revolutionary" was exaggerated and anachronistic. Mesplet was a craftsman who was also an enlightened thinker in the 18th-century sense.

CLAUDE GALARNEAU

AD, Bouches-du-Rhône (Marseille), État civil, Marseille, 13 janv. 1734. ANQ-M, AP-199. Fabre, dit Laterrière, *Mémoires* (A. Garneau), 117–18. "Some unpublished documents relating to Fleury Mesplet," ed. R. W. McLachlan, RSC *Trans.*, 3rd ser., XIV (1920), sect.II, 85–95. *La Gazette littéraire pour la ville et district de Montréal*, 3 June 1778–2 June 1779. *Montreal Gazette*, 25 Aug. 1785–Jan. 1794. Tremaine,

Bibliography of Canadian imprints. Æ. Fauteux, *Introduction of printing into Canada*. Galarneau, *La France devant l'opinion canadienne*. H. P. Gundy, *Book publishing and publishers in Canada before 1900* (Toronto, 1965); *Early printers*. Séraphin Marion, *Les lettres canadiennes d'autrefois* (9v., Hull, Qué., et Ottawa, 1939–58), II. Camille Roy, *Nos origines littéraires* (Québec, 1909), 62–69. Marcel Trudel, *Louis XVI, le Congrès américain et le Canada, 1774–1789* (Québec, [1949]), xvi, 27, 70–71. Ægidius Fauteux, "Fleury Mesplet: une étude sur les commencements de l'imprimerie dans la ville de Montréal," Bibliographical Soc. of America, *Papers* (Chicago), 28 (1934), 164–93. R. W. McLachlan, "Fleury Mesplet, the first printer at Montreal," RSC *Trans.*, 2nd ser., XII (1906), sect.II, 197–309. Victor Morin, "Propos de bibliophile," *Cahiers des Dix*, 19 (1954), 11–46.

MESSEIN, CHARLES-FRANÇOIS BAILLY DE. *See* BAILLY

MÉZY, SÉBASTIEN-FRANÇOIS-ANGE LE NORMANT DE. *See* LE NORMANT

MIGEON DE BRANSSAT (Bransac), MARIE-ANNE, *dite* **de la Nativité**, Ursuline and superior; baptized 27 Jan. 1685 in Montreal (Que.), daughter of Jean-Baptiste Migeon* de Branssat and Catherine Gauchet de Belleville; d. 31 Aug. 1771 at Quebec.

Marie-Anne Migeon de Branssat joined the Ursulines in Quebec in 1702 with the required dowry of 3,000 *livres* as well as her board and furniture. She pronounced her vows two years later in the presence of the vicar general, Joseph de La Colombière*. In turn she was mistress of boarders, mistress of novices, assistant superior, and then for many years superior. Elected superior in 1735 and re-elected in 1738, she served again from 1744 to 1750 and from 1753 to 1760.

Her first election brought her authority in delicate and trying circumstances. The disputes which had been growing apace in the Canadian church since the death of Bishop Saint-Vallier [La Croix*] had exposed the Ursulines to difficulties, and they had had occasion to complain to the Conseil Supérieur about the highhanded way the chapter was treating them. Bishop DOSQUET himself had appointed the two preceding superiors, Anne Anceau, *dite* de Sainte-Thérèse, in 1732, and Marie-Louise Gaillard, *dite* de la Sainte-Vierge, in June 1735. The latter appointment does not appear to have been a successful one, since at the regular election four months later Marie-Anne de la Nativité was chosen.

She set to work immediately, and the records contain many illustrations of her intelligence and ability in all areas of responsibility. She completed work on the chapel, used for worship since 1723, by having the altar reredos which Noel Levasseur* had carved put in place in 1736. In 1739, at her suggestion, some of the infirmary's silver pieces, which had belonged in large part to Mme de La Peltrie [Marie-Madeleine de Chauvigny*], were given to make a sanctuary lamp with the hallmark of Paul Lambert*, *dit* Saint-Paul. That year, in honour of the hundredth anniversary of the Ursulines' arrival in Canada, she organized celebrations which, according to the annals, were of an unprecedented splendour.

Marie-Anne de la Nativité also energetically pursued the material interests of her community. She bought, sold, and leased property, built a storehouse and a small wing for boarders, and erected mills on the Sainte-Croix seigneury and the Portneuf barony. In 1739 she repaired the classroom used for day pupils in Mme de La Peltrie's house and in 1755 the bell-tower which had been knocked down by a hurricane and earthquake. On 7 June of the latter year, after a fire at the Hôtel-Dieu, she took in 49 hospital nuns for three weeks, reciprocating the kindness that community had shown the Ursulines in 1650 [*see* Marie Guyart*, *dite* de l'Incarnation] and in 1686 [*see* Jeanne-Françoise Juchereau* de La Ferté, *dite* de Saint-Ignace].

Marie-Anne de la Nativité was superior throughout the Seven Years' War. On 13 and 14 July 1759 the Ursulines, except for ten sisters, took refuge in the Hôpital-Général, as did the hospital nuns of the Hôtel-Dieu; the ten, along with the chaplain Pierre-Joseph Resche* and two other priests, remained to guard the convent. On 21 September, a few days after the capitulation, the Ursulines, reduced to the most abject poverty, returned to their cloister, which was unfit for use in winter. Brigadier-General MURRAY, wanting the nuns to care for some of his wounded soldiers, came to see their premises. He immediately furnished them with the necessities of life and, observing their inability to pay workers, decided to attend to the repairs to the convent personally. The work of restoration began with the chapel, the only building suitable for a parish church; in it Catholic and Protestant services of worship were held alternately. Only the most essential repairs were undertaken because by 4 October the wounded were being transferred to the convent; the sisters were thereafter provided for at the king's expense. They took their new task as hospital nuns seriously and by autumn they were even knitting long woollen stockings for the Scottish soldiers, whose uniforms were hardly suitable for Canadian winters.

The final year of Marie-Anne de la Nativité's

last term as superior was 1759 and custom dictated that she be replaced, but Bishop Pontbriand [Dubreil*], learning that she was highly regarded by the British, authorized the Ursulines to elect her for a seventh year if they wished. She received a majority of more than two-thirds. No one had cause to regret the breach of the rules, because on numerous occasions in the period up to 15 Dec. 1760 she succeeded in reconciling the interests of the community with those of the British. For instance, she obtained a pardon for a young British soldier who, wanting to see the nuns in procession, had slipped into the chancel of the cloister's chapel. When the British wounded left early in June 1760, it was again she who requested and succeeded in getting Murray's continued financial support for the community.

After three years' rest, Marie-Anne de la Nativité was elected in December 1763 to assist Esther WHEELWRIGHT, *dite* de l'Enfant-Jésus. In 1766, at the end of her term of office, she was released from all official responsibilities, but she continued to participate in the community's religious exercises. After being confined to the infirmary for two years, she died on 31 Aug. 1771.

Perhaps none save the founders was more deserving of her community's respect than Marie-Anne de la Nativité. In the words of the "Vieux Récit," "Our Lord endowed her with great intelligence and spirituality; she was learned, she spoke easily and wrote with a courteous and skilful pen, and her beautiful voice faithfully rose in support of the choir; she gave of all her talents for the benefit of her beloved house." Her life showed that this praise was well merited.

GABRIELLE LAPOINTE

ANQ-M, État civil, Catholiques, Notre-Dame de Montréal, 27 janv. 1685. AUQ, Actes d'élection des supérieures; Actes des assemblées capitulaires, 1, pp. 74, 215, 264f; Actes de professions et de sépultures, 1, p. 61; Annales, 1, pp. 190, 217, 220, 223, 273; Conclusions des assemblées des discrètes, 1, pp. 78, 82; Livres de comptes, 1; Registre des entrées, vêtures, professions et décès des religieuses, 1. Le Jeune, *Dictionnaire*. É.-Z. Massicotte, "Les actes de foi et hommage conservés à Montréal," *BRH*, XXVI (1920), 93–96. Tanguay, *Dictionnaire*. Burke, *Les ursulines de Québec* (1863–66), II, III. A.-H. Gosselin, *L'Église du Canada jusqu'à la Conquête*. [Joséphine Holmes, dite de Sainte-Croix], *Glimpses of the monastery, scenes from the history of the Ursulines of Quebec during two hundred years, 1639–1839* . . . (2nd ed., Quebec, 1897). Régis Roy, "Migeon de Bransat," *BRH*, XXVI (1920), 313–16.

MIGNAC (Mignaque). *See* MINIAC

MIKAK (Micoc, Mykok), Labrador Inuk; b. *c.* 1740, daughter of Inuk chief Nerkingoak; m. *c.* 1762 the son of an Inuk chief, m. *c.* 1770 TUGLAVINA, m. 1783 Serkoak; mother of at least one son and one daughter; d. 1 Oct. 1795 at Nain, Labrador.

Mikak is one of the first Inuit to emerge as a distinct individual in the history of the relations between the Europeans and the natives in Labrador. In 1765 the Moravian Brethren sent four missionaries on an exploratory expedition to contact the Labrador Inuit. From the British base of Chateau Bay on the Strait of Belle Isle the missionaries visited nearby encampments of Inuit who had come south for summer trade. A sudden September storm forced the missionaries Jens HAVEN and Christian Larsen DRACHART to stay overnight in the tent of a native religious leader or *angakok*. Mikak was present in the tent, learned the names of the missionaries, and memorized a prayer taught her by Drachart.

Mikak's next known contact with Europeans occurred under less happy circumstances. In November 1767 an Inuit band attacked Nicholas DARBY's fishing station at Cape Charles, northeast of Chateau Bay, killing some men and taking away boats. A detachment from Fort York at Chateau Bay pursued the Inuit, killing the men and capturing the women and children. Mikak was carried to Chateau Bay with the other prisoners and spent the winter at the blockhouse. Her evident intelligence attracted the attention of the second in command of the garrison, Francis Lucas*. With his help she picked up English quickly and in return taught him some Inuit words. In the autumn of 1768 Hugh PALLISER, then governor of Newfoundland, arranged for Mikak, her son Tootac, and an older boy, Karpik, to be taken to England. His intention was to impress them with the power and grandeur of England so that they would advocate cooperation and trade when they returned to their people. Upon arrival in London Mikak again met Jens Haven, and learned that the Moravians were eager to secure a land grant for a mission post on the Labrador coast.

In an age when "noble savages" were in fashion, Mikak was patronized by London society. Among other gifts, she received from Augusta, Dowager Princess of Wales, a costly dress trimmed with gold lace. At the instance of the naturalist Joseph Banks* Mikak sat to the society painter John Russell. The portrait was exhibited at the Royal Academy of Arts and now hangs in the Ethnological Institute at Göttingen University (Federal Republic of Germany). Clothed in the dress given her by the dowager princess,

Mikak looks out with a shrewd and observant eye. She repeatedly urged the cause of the Moravians before her well-connected patrons, and partly because of her efforts the Moravians received their grant in May 1769. The missionaries, however, disapproved of Inuit being taken to England, feeling that contact with European society spoiled them for the life to which they must return.

In the summer of 1769 Lieutenant Lucas landed Mikak on an island northwest of Byron Bay (north of Hamilton Inlet), and in the following year the Moravians dispatched a ship to look for a likely mission site. In July 1770 the missionaries Drachart and Haven met Mikak and her family near Byron Bay. She received them in her golden gown, with the king's medal on her breast, and her new husband Tuglavina at her side. As an *angakok* Tuglavina wielded great influence among his countrymen and came to be both respected and feared by the Moravians for his intelligence, courage, and "turbulent spirit." The missionaries told Mikak they had come to find a suitable place for a mission, if the Inuit approved, but warned sternly that stealing or murdering would be punished. According to their report, she replied with some spirit that she was "sorry to hear that we had such a bad opinion of their country people" and pointed out that the English also stole, but ended by saying that "they loved us very much and desired that we would come and live with them." Subsequently Mikak and Tuglavina guided the missionaries northwards and helped them pick a suitable site for Nain, the first mission post.

When the Moravians established Nain in August 1771, Mikak and her family visited but preferred not to live at the station. Mikak and Tuglavina entered a baptismal class but did not proceed further. Indeed from 1782 onward they joined other Inuit in frequent voyages, against the advice of the missionaries, to visit the European traders around Chateau Bay, trading whalebone and furs for guns, ammunition, and liquor. Mikak was attracted to the rough and ready European traders and returned to Nain only at the end of her life in 1795. Then she turned to the missionaries for comfort, saying that she had not forgotten what she had heard about the Saviour or what she had promised when she became a candidate for baptism.

In 1824, a Methodist missionary, Thomas Hickson, met in Hamilton Inlet two Inuit, father and son, each with two wives. The older Eskimo was none other than Tootac. One of his wives wore the golden gown presented to Mikak so many years before, and Tootac himself bore the name of Palliser, after the Newfoundland governor who had befriended them.

Mikak was highly intelligent, observant, and quick to learn. She could be generous and kind, as when she pleaded the cause of the Moravians in London and helped them to settle in Labrador. She seems to have remained her own woman, receptive to the Moravians' teachings but not without a degree of reserve, enjoying European society but conscious of her influence and place in the Inuit community.

WILLIAM H. WHITELEY

Methodist Missionary Soc. (London), Wesleyan Methodist Missionary Soc. correspondence, T. Hickson's journal on the Labrador C. (mfm. at United Church Archives (Toronto)). PAC, MG 17, D1, Voyage to Labrador, 1770. PRO, Adm. 51/629; CO 194/16; 194/27; 194/28. "Account of the Esquimaux Mikak," *Periodical accounts relating to the missions of the Church of the United Brethren, established among the heathen* (London), II (1798), 170–71. Daniel Benham, *Memoirs of James Hutton; comprising the annals of his life, and connection with the United Brethren* (London, 1856). Hiller, "Foundation of Moravian mission." *The Moravians in Labrador* (Edinburgh, 1833). H. W. Jannasch, "Reunion with Mikak," *Canadian Geographical Journal* (Ottawa), LVII (1958), 84–85.

MILLS, Sir THOMAS, army officer and office-holder; d. 28 Feb. 1793 in London, England.

Thomas Mills entered the army as an ensign in the 15th Foot on 26 April 1759 and was promoted lieutenant in the 47th Foot on 11 May 1760. The date of his arrival in North America has not been determined, but during the military régime in Quebec he served under MURRAY in Quebec City as adjutant and then as town major. Although his origins are unknown, he was evidently well connected; he enjoyed the friendship of Frederick HALDIMAND and the patronage of the influential Lord Mansfield. (William SMITH later alleged that Mills was Mansfield's illegitimate son.) After several years in England he returned to Quebec in June 1766 with appointments as receiver general, member of the Council, and brigade major.

The financing of colonies was a controversial matter in the 1760s. Murray's instructions as civil governor in 1763 forbade him to impose taxes without the consent of an assembly, and he seems consequently to have ceased collecting the customs duties which had been continued from the French régime. The law officers of the crown, however, gave the opinion that the duties could legally be collected "by proper authority," and Mills's royal appointment as receiver general on 10 July 1765 was the result.

When Mills took up his duties, he revealed a

vanity bordering on arrogance and an almost complete lack of integrity. The administrator of the colony, Paulus Æmilius IRVING, found him quite unfit for office. According to Irving he had little understanding of the question he had been appointed to solve and claimed totally unrealistic prerogatives. The receiver general was responsible to the Treasury Board for the collection and expenditure of public funds. In Mills's view he was therefore not obliged to submit accounts to the Council; nor was he required to have the governor's warrant in order to make payment. Indeed the governor and Council should merely decide what needed to be done; the receiver general would allot the contracts. These doctrines were quite impractical given the governor's personal responsibility for administering the colony in an economical manner. In the face of determined opposition by Irving, Mills quickly backed down.

Politically, Mills was one of the first councillors to abandon the vulnerable Governor Murray after the arrival of Guy Carleton* as lieutenant governor in September 1766. Murray was certain that the "Corrupt Boy Mills" had secretly worked with his enemies to bring about his recall. Mills aligned himself with Carleton, who at first had the favour of Murray's enemies. When in October Carleton decided to support George Allsopp* and other fur merchants seeking free access to the "king's posts," Mills went along despite the fact that he had publicly taken a diametrically opposed position favouring the claims to monopoly by his close friend Thomas Dunn*, one of the lessees.

Mills returned to London in August 1767 and for ten years his office was administered by acting appointees because he did not have the power to name a deputy. Carleton first appointed Hector Theophilus CRAMAHÉ and then in July 1770, Thomas Dunn. Mills's influence in London was sufficient to obtain a knighthood in 1772 and a new commission as receiver general in 1777, this time with the right to appoint a deputy. He named William Grant* of Saint-Roch. Grant was forced to retire in July 1784 when his malversation of funds was discovered, and Haldimand replaced him with Henry Caldwell* a year later. On 1 Sept. 1787 Mills chose George DAVISON as Caldwell's replacement but, financially embarrassed, returned himself to take up the post two months later.

Mills again cut a prominent social figure with his choice wines, fine fowling pieces, and the brown mare, Coquet, which he raced on the Plains of Abraham. When he was unable to meet certain payments in 1789 the Legislative Council investigated his accounts and found he had used more than £3,000 of public money to pay his debts. Despite his attempts to mystify Governor Dorchester [Carleton] with figures suggesting the crown owed him money, he was suspended by the governor on 25 August and returned to England later that year. He died insolvent in London in 1793, the same year a government audit revealed that he and his deputies owed the crown more than £18,500.

Mills had a remarkable capacity for self-deception. He even claimed credit for the passage of the Quebec Act. In a letter of June 1774 to Haldimand, he asserted that in face of Lord North's deplorable ignorance, his own lobbying of the House of Commons had saved the day for "King and Country" and had done "Justice to the Conquered." Indeed it was not too much to say that "The Limits – the Religion, the French Law, & the Council they owe to me."

F. MURRAY GREENWOOD

BL, Add. MSS 21687, 21728, 21858. Greater London Record Office (London, Eng.), P89/MRY1/314, 6 March 1793. PAC, MG 23, A4, 64; GII, 1, ser. 1, 2, pp.289–95; MG 55/14, 2. PRO, CO 42/26, 42/66, 42/86. [Frederick Haldimand], "Private diary of Gen. Haldimand," PAC *Report*, 1889, 123–299. Maseres, *Maseres letters* (Wallace), 43. [William Smith], *The diary and selected papers of Chief Justice William Smith, 1784–1793*, ed. L. F. S. Upton (2v., Toronto, 1963–65). *Quebec Gazette*, 21 Feb. 1765; 3 July, 11 Aug. 1766; 21 Sept., 1 Oct., 12 Nov. 1789; 13 June 1793. *Quebec Herald, Miscellany and Advertiser*, 21 Sept. 1789. Caron, "Inv. de la corr. de Mgr Briand," ANQ *Rapport*, 1929–30, 65. G.B., WO, *Army list*, 1760, 1763. Burt, *Old prov. of Que.* F.-J. Audet, "Les législateurs de la province de Québec," *BRH*, XXXI (1925), 484. H. R. Balls, "Quebec, 1763–1774: the financial administration," *CHR*, XLI (1960), 203–14. A. L. Burt, "Sir Guy Carleton and his first council," *CHR*, IV (1923), 321–32.

MINIAC (Mignac, Mignaque, Minire, Deminiac), JEAN-PIERRE DE, Sulpician, priest, missionary, vicar general, and archdeacon; b. *c.* 1691 in the diocese of Rennes, France; d. 8 May 1771 in Nantes, France.

Jean-Pierre de Miniac joined the Sulpicians on 23 Dec. 1717 and obtained a licence *in utroque jure* (civil and canon law). He arrived in Canada on 5 July 1722 and was put in charge of the parish of Saint-Laurent on Montreal Island, which belonged to the Séminaire de Saint-Sulpice. At the end of 1724 he was sent to the parish of Sainte-Trinité-de-Contrecœur, to which was attached the mission church at Saint-Ours. Miniac probably had a personal fortune, since he bought some land in the parish, including a lot of 17 acres. In September 1731 Bishop DOSQUET brought him to Quebec and entrusted him with the office of vicar general for the region of Quebec in succession to Bertrand de LATOUR, although he did not receive his letters of appointment until 4 Sept. 1732. The choice surprised the chapter; its archdeacon, Eustache Chartier* de Lotbinière, a Canadian, had been expected to get this important office, since the Canadian clergy felt it was time they were invited to take part in the administration of the church in Canada.

Miniac now lived at the Séminaire de Québec and assumed increasingly important roles in the ecclesiastical administration. From 1733 to 1736 he was confessor to the Ursulines. On 10 Sept. 1734 he received his benefice as a canon, and he was admitted to the chapter of the cathedral of Quebec on 26 Jan. 1735 as the official, succeeding Bernard-Joseph Boulanger who had resigned. During Bishop Dosquet's prolonged absences, from 15 Oct. 1732 to 16 Aug. 1734 and from 19 Oct. 1735 until his resignation in March 1739, Miniac really directed the Canadian church, and the civil authorities had nothing but praise for the "wisdom and prudence" of his administration. On 5 Feb. 1739 he became archdeacon of the chapter of Quebec in consequence of Chartier de Lotbinière's appointment as dean.

On the day of Bishop François-Louis de Pourroy* de Lauberivière's death, 20 Aug. 1740, the chapter, in accordance with ecclesiastical law, appointed Miniac vicar capitular for as long as the see was vacant. By October, however, he was involved in a dispute with the chapter over the appointment of a parish priest for Château-Richer. He planned to assign one of his friends, Abbé Roger-Chrétien Le Chasseur, to this parish; the chapter supported the incumbent, Louis-François Soupiran, a Canadian. The controversy again raised the question of the Canadianization of the clergy in New France. The case was brought before the provost court of Quebec, and just when Soupiran was intending to appeal to the Conseil Supérieur, Miniac took everyone by surprise by sailing unexpectedly for France. His departure, on 3 Nov. 1740, led the chapter to take away his powers both as vicar general and as vicar capitular. In Paris he met several prominent persons who were deeply concerned about the fate of the church in Canada, and one of them, Canon Pierre HAZEUR de L'Orme, contended that Miniac was hoping to succeed Bishop Lauberivière, which may well have been true. After the appointment of Bishop Pontbriand [Dubreil*], Miniac hesitated before returning to Canada.

He was back, however, in August 1742. The Canadian clergy seem to have been uneasy about the information Miniac might have given the new bishop about the situation of the church in Canada. Whatever the case may have been, that autumn Miniac was appointed vicar general for Acadia by Bishop Pontbriand, who counted on him to settle the problems disrupting that distant mission. An important witness to the difficulties that the church in Canada had just gone through was thus cleverly removed.

Miniac left Quebec on 12 Sept. 1742 and reached Rivière-aux-Canards (near Canard, N.S.) after a long and arduous trip. In the name of Governor Richard Philipps* of Nova Scotia, Paul Mascarene* raised difficulties in approving his appointment. Miniac would always be keenly aware of the difficult material conditions of his new position; nevertheless he behaved with great generosity during his exile and devoted himself to his task. At the time of the War of the Austrian Succession he did not conceal from his correspondents his fears about the military expeditions from Canada as a danger for the population. "I should consider it the final calamity for these settlers," he wrote on 23 Sept. 1745, "if another armed party arrived from Canada." Consequently it is not surprising that Intendant HOCQUART and the minister of Marine, Maurepas, criticized Miniac's conduct during that summer, as they did that of other missionaries, accusing them of being sympathetic towards the English. Bishop Pontbriand, however, vigorously defended the patriotic ardour of his Acadian priests, whose role in this period was ultimately ambiguous [*see* Claude-Jean-Baptiste Chauvreulx*]. In one and the same report, for example, Miniac sent information to the Canadian troops and obtained a pardon for an English prisoner named Newton.

Miniac left his post in September 1749 and returned to France, aged, ill, and almost blind. After a short stay in Provence to recover his health, he retired to the community of Saint-Clément in Nantes. There he spent the last 20 years or so of his life, not without remaining in contact with his correspondents in Quebec, who managed the few pieces of property he yet had in Canada. He was, moreover, still archdeacon of the chapter of Quebec. An attempt was apparently made on 23 Oct. 1751 to force him to resign by taking away his prebend, but it was returned to him on 30 April 1753.

Jean-Pierre de Miniac died on 8 May 1771. Considered by some to be "harsh in his conduct and in his manner of expressing himself," he had come close to playing a great role in the church in Canada. Circumstances allowed him to play only a small part on the troubled stage of the Acadian missions.

MICHELINE D. JOHNSON

AAQ, 12 A, A, 297v; B, 306v, 314, 315, 323, 325v; C, 170, 171; 22 A, II, 643; 10 B, 93v, 95v, 103v, 107, 110v, 126v, 127v, 144, 200v, 205v; 11 B, VI, 33; VII, 6; VIII, 58, 59, 60, 61; X, 13, 54; CD, Diocèse de Québec, II, 5, 172. AN, Col., B, 66, f.36; 68, f.53; 70, ff.16v, 24, 30, 31v, 42; 71, f.42v; 72, f.7; 74, f.24; 76, f.6; 81, f.64; C[11A], 59, ff.163–66; 61, ff.65–70; 65, ff.28–30; 67, ff.110–13; 73, ff.5–8; 78, ff.407, 423–29; 80, ff.340–53; 82, f.326; 86, f.140; 89, f.255. ANQ-Q, NF 19, 80. ASQ, C 8, pp.226–29, 518, 519; C 9, p.181; C 10, p.17; Lettres, M, 95; S, 7a–p; T, 57, 59; Polygraphie, III, 61, 115; V, 26; VII, 2, 102, 102a, 103, 105–11, 113–19, 121, 122; IX, 29; XVII, 2, 112, 117; XXVI, 39b, 39g; Séminaire, 3, no.51; 4, nos.129b, 130, 131; 12, nos.29, 29a, 29b; 14/6, nos.3, 7.

Coll. doc. inédits Canada et Amérique, I, 41–43; II, 10–75. *Édits ord.* (1854–56), II, 372. La Rue, "Lettres et mémoires" ANQ *Rapport*, 1935–36, 276–77, 301. *Mandements des évêques de Québec* (Têtu et Gagnon), I, 550–52. *N.S. Archives, I*, 319. Gauthier, *Sulpitiana* (1926), 234. Tanguay, *Répertoire*, 88 (copy annotated by the archivist of the Séminaire de Québec). H.-R. Casgrain, *Les sulpiciens et les prêtres des Missions-étrangères en Acadie (1676–1762)* (Québec, 1897), 343–417. A.-H. Gosselin, *L'Église du Canada jusqu'à la Conquête*, II, III. M.-A. Bernard, "Sainte-Trinité de Contrecœur," *BRH*, IV (1898), 193. J.-E. Roy, "Notes sur Mgr de Lauberivière," *BRH*, I (1895), 4–11. Têtu, "Le chapitre de la cathédrale," *BRH*, XIV, 35, 76, 98, 105, 131–32, 145; XV, 14, 293; XVI, 7, 98, 138.

MOFFATT, JAMES JOHNSTONE DE. *See* JOHNSTONE

MONCKTON, ROBERT, army officer and colonial administrator; b. 24 June 1726 in Yorkshire, England, second son of John Monckton, later 1st Viscount Galway, and Lady Elizabeth Manners; d. 21 May 1782 in London, England. Although apparently never lawfully married, he raised and was survived by three sons and a daughter.

In 1741, at age 15, Robert Monckton was commissioned in the 3rd Foot Guards, which sailed to Flanders the following spring to serve in the War of the Austrian Succession. Monckton saw action at Dettingen (Federal Republic of Germany) and at Fontenoy (Belgium), staying on in Flanders after the British army was recalled to suppress the Jacobite rebellion in 1745. Commissioned captain in the 34th Foot on 27 June 1744, he was promoted major on 15 Feb. 1747/48 and lieutenant-colonel of the 47th Foot on 28 Feb. 1751/52. On his father's death later that year Monckton became member of parliament for the family-controlled seat of Pontefract but was soon posted to Nova Scotia.

Monckton's introduction to Canada was as commander of Fort Lawrence (near Amherst, N.S.), which faced the French Fort Beauséjour across the Missaguash River near Chignecto Bay. This military frontier was calm between his appointment in August 1752 and the following June; Monckton and Jean-Baptiste Mutigny de Vassan, his counterpart at Beauséjour, exchanged notes, deserters, and runaway horses. Undoubtedly both sides were also gathering intelligence and reinforcing prejudices. Called to Halifax in June 1753 to preside over a court martial, Monckton stayed on to accept membership in the colony's Council.

German settlers at the new south shore community of Lunenburg were restive that autumn, and when news of an armed confrontation between the settlers and the local garrison reached the Council on 18 Dec. 1753, Monckton volunteered to lead a 200-man force to restore peace. Lieutenant Governor Charles Lawrence* and his Council advocated a reasonable approach so that "afterwards the consequences will lye on themselves should you be obliged to proceed to Extremitys." Monckton was courteously received at Lunenburg and negotiated a return to order by what Lawrence called "moderate and most judicious measures" [*see* Jean Pettrequin* and Sebastian ZOUBERBUHLER].

The aftermath, however, reveals the contrast between Monckton's humane perspective and the sterner views of his superior, Lawrence. Having disarmed the settlers peaceably and traced the source of the rumours that had caused the trouble, Monckton then advocated forgiveness. Lawrence would not accept this counsel and informed Monckton rather ominously: ". . . tho the merciful part is always the most agreable (particularly with Foreigners unacquainted with our laws and Customs) in disturbances of this nature, yet it is seldom the most effectual." Though one of the participants in the troubles was imprisoned for crimes and misdemeanors after Lawrence tried but failed to obtain a charge of high treason against him, most of the lieutenant governor's suggestions for legal retribution were ignored.

Robert Monckton's most memorable independent military command in North America was the successful campaign against the Chignecto forts, Beauséjour and Gaspereau (near Port Elgin, N.B.), in June 1755. Lawrence had joined Massachusetts Governor William Shirley in preparing the plan of operations during the preceding winter, based upon a general British order to counter French "encroachments." Monckton spent the winter in Boston using his knowledge of Fort Beauséjour in detailed preparation for the attack. Here he quarrelled with John WINSLOW, one of his subordinate commanders, and relations between the two men were poor throughout the campaign. A convoy of 31 transports and three warships left Boston on 19 May 1755, carrying nearly 2,000 New England provincial troops and 270 British regulars, and dropped anchor near the mouth of the Missaguash River on 2 June. Secrecy and careful planning resulted in an unopposed landing and relatively light resistance as Monckton's troops moved to invest Fort Beauséjour two days later. The garrison under Louis DU PONT Duchambon de Vergor, though outnumbered more than four to one, should have been able to resist longer than two weeks. Monckton's careful professional approach along a ridge northeast of the fort had hardly begun when the disheartened defenders proposed terms of capitulation on 16 June. Monckton granted the garrison passage to Louisbourg, Île Royale (Cape Breton Island), and pardoned Acadian irregulars who had taken up arms under threat of death. The next day Benjamin Rouer* de Villeray, the commander of Fort Gaspereau, accepted the same terms without a shot being fired. Monckton's success in the campaign was based upon surprise and good deployment of superior resources.

Precipitate collapse of the French defence of the Chignecto Isthmus left Monckton and Lawrence in command of an army of some 2,500 men, most of whom had volunteered for a whole year and all of whom were being paid and provisioned by the British government; in fact, unknown to the Treasury, the operation was being financed out of the annual parliamentary grant for the administration of Nova Scotia. Following supplementary orders, Monckton dispatched a small squadron to investigate the situation at the mouth of the Saint John River (N.B.), and by 2 July he had learned that the French garrison there had blown up its fort and retired. With his major responsibilities carried out so quickly, Monckton used his own men and hired Acadians to repair Fort Beauséjour (renamed Fort Cumberland) and to improve area roads. Many of the local inhabitants surrendered their arms, including the prominent partisan Joseph Brossard*, *dit* Beausoleil. But when the Acadian deputies negotiating with Lawrence refused the unqualified oath of allegiance, as they had done successfully for decades, Lawrence used his unprecedented military forces to respond with unprecedented severity: he ordered the expulsion of the Acadians. With characteristic efficiency but no apparent enthusiasm, Monckton carried out his orders to lure the inhabitants into custody, to burn their villages, and to supervise the deportation of the 1,100 people he collected in Chignecto.

Sole victor in a year of British defeats in North America, Monckton was made lieutenant governor of Nova Scotia in December 1755. During the next three years he acted as governor twice, both times handling preparations for the colony's first legislature. He was thus occupied in the summer of 1758 when AMHERST captured Louisbourg. That autumn he was given command of an expedition to scourge the Saint John River country (N.B.). A force of nearly 2,300 men, including the 2nd battalion Royal American Regiment (60th Foot) of which Monckton was now colonel, provided the base and advance troops for a cautious, deliberate expedition which destroyed houses, cattle, and crops for some 70 miles up the river. Few people were captured, but the expedition's purpose was to force any Acadians raiding British-held territory to retire to Quebec by spring. Begun on 11 September, the operation was completed on 21 November. Early in 1759 Amherst called Monckton south to New York, intending he should command the southern region. Monckton was still in New York when James Wolfe* chose him to be second in command in the campaign against Quebec that summer.

Monckton's role in the capture of Quebec was considerable. Shortly after the arrival of the British fleet at Quebec [*see* Sir Charles SAUNDERS], Monckton led the four regiments that established control of the south shore of the St Lawrence River at Pointe-Lévy (Lauzon and Lévis). Initially intended to protect the fleet, this position was soon used by Wolfe to establish powerful batteries facing the city. Monckton commanded the unsuccessful attempt to land on the Beauport shore on 31 July, though he had been sceptical of the plan. As the summer wore on, Wolfe's frustration prompted harsh measures against vulnerable settlements. There is evidence that Monckton delayed and moderated the execution of these orders in his command on the south shore. Tension between Monckton and Wolfe appeared briefly, though it was not as serious as Wolfe's differences with the other senior members of his staff. At the end of August, Wolfe asked his brigadiers for their written opinion on three alternative battle plans, all focusing on the Beauport shore. Monckton, MURRAY, and George Townshend* rejected all three plans, and proposed attacking above Quebec – a concept which proved successful. Monckton commanded the crucial landing at Anse au Foulon early on 13 September and the British right on the Plains of Abraham later that day, being wounded through the chest during the battle. He resented Townshend's excluding him from the negotiations for the capitulation of the city and recovered quickly enough to assume command of the city and its environs. In the month he served in this capacity Monckton displayed firmness in punishing soldiers who committed crimes and showed concern for the civilian population. One of his last orders, urging commanders not to allow their men to marry local girls, was a grudging admission that the army's relations with the Canadians were improving.

Monckton left Quebec for New York on 26 October. Honours were mixed with new responsibilities; he had been made colonel of the 17th Foot earlier that month and on 29 April 1760 became commander of the British troops in the southern provinces. In February 1761 he was promoted major-general and on 20 March became governor and commander-in-chief in the province of New York. Monckton crowned his successful military career the following winter as commander of the army that captured the West Indian island of Martinique. His overwhelming forces took the supposedly impregnable French position within three weeks of landing. The terms of capitulation, modelled on the surrender of Guadeloupe in 1759 with minor changes, suggest that Monckton was a careful and well-informed negotiator. By June 1762 he was back at his post in New York. Monckton left North America for England on 28 June 1763, though he retained the governorship of New York until 14 June 1765, and was subsequently regarded as a "friend of America." After exoneration by a court martial in 1764 on charges brought by a dismissed officer, Monckton became governor of Berwick-upon-Tweed on 14 June 1765 and was promoted lieutenant-general in 1770.

Luckless investment in the East India Company in this turbulent period of its history stimulated Monckton's interest in, and need for, a post in India. Though he first had royal support, and later had the company's nomination, he was not appointed commander-in-chief of the army there. He declined the government's alternative offer of the command of the army in America when that post became vacant but accepted a valuable land grant on the West Indian island of St Vincent. In 1774 he served briefly again as MP for Pontefract, but seems to have played no part in the Coercive Acts or the Quebec Act.

Governor of Portsmouth, England, from 1778, and MP for the town in the Admiralty interest, Monckton held these positions until his death in 1782. He was buried in St Mary Abbot's Church, Kensington (London).

I. K. STEELE

BL, Add. MSS 21638. Huntington Library, Loudoun papers. Library of Congress (Washington), Peter Force papers, VIII-D, Robert Monckton, correspondence, 1754–63. Newberry Library (Chicago), Edward E. Ayer coll., MS 341. Northamptonshire Record Office (Northampton, Eng.), Monckton of Fineshade records. PAC, MG 18, M. PRO, PRO 30/8, bundle 98. University of Nottingham Library (Nottingham, Eng.), Manuscripts Dept., Galway MSS, 11599, 11601–3, 11611. *Correspondence of William Pitt* (Kimball), II, 69, 163, 302. *N.S. Archives, I*, 269, 270, 376, 393–400, 443, 444, 448. *DAB*. *DNB*. D. H. Monckton, *A genealogical history of the family of Monckton . . .* (London, 1887). J. C. Webster, *The forts of Chignecto; a study of the eighteenth century conflict between France and Great Britain in Acadia* ([Shediac, N.B.], 1930), 49–50, 53–60, 110–16.

MONTBEILLARD, FIACRE-FRANÇOIS POTOT DE. *See* POTOT

MONTESSON, JOSEPH-MICHEL LEGARDEUR DE CROISILLE ET DE. *See* LEGARDEUR

MONTGOLFIER, ÉTIENNE, priest, superior of the Sulpicians in Montreal, and vicar general; b. 24 Dec. 1712 at Vidalon (dept of Ardèche), France, son of Raymond Montgolfier, and uncle of Joseph-Michel and Jacques-Étienne de Montgolfier, the famous inventors of the balloon; d. 27 Aug. 1791 in Montreal (Que.).

Having chosen the priesthood when he was 20, Étienne Montgolfier entered the diocesan seminary in Viviers, France, where he undertook classical studies and courses in philosophy and theology. Ordained priest on 23 Sept. 1741, he obtained his bishop's permission to join the Sulpicians. He went to Issy-les-Moulineaux to spend his year of seclusion (the equivalent of a noviciate). During the next nine years he taught theology in various Sulpician seminaries in France. In compliance with a request from his superior general, Jean Couturier, he left La Rochelle on 3 May 1751 to join the Sulpicians in Montreal, where he arrived in October.

Montgolfier soon gained a natural authority over the Sulpicians in Montreal. In January 1759 he was named superior, replacing Louis Normant* Du Faradon. This title automatically conferred on him the duties of administrator of the seigneuries belonging to the Sulpicians, titular priest of the parish of Montreal, and vicar general of the bishop of Quebec for the District of Montreal; he gave up this last office in 1764. No superior ever held office under such difficult circumstances. Quebec had just surrendered to the British, Bishop Pontbriand [Dubreil*] took refuge at the Sulpician seminary only to die there on 8 June 1760, and Montreal surrendered to the enemy on 8 September. Major-General AMHERST, however, left the Canadians free to practise the Catholic faith, and Montgolfier was able to remain in contact with the vicar general of Quebec, Jean-Olivier BRIAND, who following the bishop's death was considered to be the "first vicar general."

After the ratification of the transfer of Canada by France to Great Britain, Montgolfier decided to go to Europe, initially to see his superior general in France, and then to meet with the British government in London. His objective was to secure the Sulpicians' enjoyment of their property by getting the Sulpicians in France to relinquish it in their favour, and by keeping his group from being identified as a religious community like the Recollets or Jesuits. In this way the Sulpicians were to avoid being despoiled by the new colonial government.

On the occasion of the trip which he undertook in October 1763, Montgolfier had also been entrusted by the chapter of Quebec with the task of working for the appointment of a new bishop in North America. Putting forward the ancient right by which they were to elect a new bishop when the see was vacant, the canons had made the customary arrangements on the preceding 15 September: a mass of the Holy Spirit, a swearing-in of electors, and an election. They had confided to the Sulpician superior the name of the person whom they wanted for bishop – Montgolfier himself. The election was deemed null and void by the Sacred Congregation of Propaganda, because from the time the provisions of the Council of Trent (1545–63) had come into force the choice of bishops had rested with the pope, even though his choice might be made from among candidates put forward by other bishops or even, as in the present circumstances, by the canons. Pope Clement XIII indeed accepted the canons' choice of Montgolfier, and no one in Rome, Paris, or London was opposed to it. However, before the date set for his consecration, June 1764, Montgolfier learned that the governor general of Canada, MURRAY, preferred Canon Briand. The Sulpician did not insist; he returned to Canada and gave his resignation as bishop elect to the chapter of Quebec. After Briand had become bishop in 1766, he appointed Montgolfier second vicar general of Montreal, in order to ease the burden on Étienne MARCHAND.

Later Montgolfier took part in an attempt to set up a bishopric in Montreal. Briand and his coadjutor, Louis-Philippe MARIAUCHAU d'Esgly, seldom went to Montreal, mainly because of their advanced age and the primitive state of transportation at the period. The population of Montreal was growing rapidly, however, and the need for a bishop was being felt. Consequently two Canadian delegates were chosen to go to London bearing a memoir drawn up with Montgolfier's help which advocated the creation of an episcopal see in Montreal and the coming to Canada of French speaking priests from Europe. Jean-Baptiste-Amable ADHÉMAR and Jean De Lisle* de La Cailleterie went to London in 1783, but they found it difficult enough to pursue the second objective and confined themselves to it. When Briand resigned the following year and the question of appointing a coadjutor for d'Esgly arose, both of these men, along with Governor HALDIMAND, thought of Montgolfier, but in July 1785 the latter indicated his unwillingness. He felt that he was too old and he preferred to continue directing his efforts to having French Sulpicians come to Montreal.

Meanwhile Montgolfier had found himself obliged to take a stand on various political occasions in Canada. Opportunities to do so were not lacking. There was, for example, the incident on 7 Oct. 1773 on the occasion of the erection in Montreal's Place d'Armes of a monument of thanksgiving to George III. Montgolfier had not been invited to be present, and not being in the habit of taking part in military or civil ceremonies, he remained in the Sulpician house. Luc de LA CORNE suggested to the military commander that church bells should be rung to accompany the artillery salvoes. The officer did not object, but Montgolfier, the ecclesiastical superior, who was approached three times by La Corne, retorted: "You know we consider our bells as instruments of religion that have never been used in military or civil ceremonies." He finally added, when pressed by his importunate visitor: "If the commandant demands that the bells be rung, he is free to order the beadle, and I shall have nothing to say." The commandant, in fact, was less insistent than La Corne, and the bells did not peal.

The invasion of Quebec by Americans [*see* Richard MONTGOMERY] led to Montgolfier's taking more significant action. At Bishop Briand's request, the Sulpician prepared an outline of an appropriate sermon and distributed it to parish priests in the District of Montreal. In order to counteract American propaganda he elaborated in the sermon four points to prove the importance of supporting the British government: as a patriot, the Canadian must defend his country against the invaders; as a subject, a citizen who has taken an oath of loyalty to the king is violating the law if he refuses to obey orders; as a Catholic, the Canadian must show that his religion teaches him to obey his sovereign; finally, Canadians have a debt of gratitude towards the king, who has treated them well, and towards Governor

Guy Carleton*, who has defended their cause in London. Montgolfier concluded his model sermon with a reminder of what had happened to the Acadians some 20 years earlier [*see* Charles Lawrence*]; was it not wiser to choose the established power?

His correspondence with Bishop Briand reveals that Montgolfier was well informed of the comings and goings of the American rebel forces and the British soldiers. Carleton's presence in Montreal in 1775 prompted the Indians and certain French speaking whites to take a stand; having been neutral, they now came out in favour of the king. At the same time, moreover, Montgolfier wrote a circular letter to all the parishes in his district, supporting Carleton's decision to re-establish the militia units. During the period the Americans were in Montreal, from November 1775 to the spring of 1776, Montgolfier avoided relations with them; he considered them rebels and had difficulty understanding the neutrality of most Canadians. Once the town had been liberated, he expressed appreciation that tranquillity had been restored through "the protection of an equitable government; integrity is respected, and virtue protected." He assured Briand that parish priests were admitting to the holy sacraments only those of the pro-Americans who had recognized their error and had recanted in public through word or deed. A small number, however, refused to accept these conditions. For their part, the clergy seemed to be completely submissive to the legitimate authority, with the exception of Jesuits Joseph HUGUET, a missionary at Sault-Saint-Louis (Caughnawaga), and Pierre-René FLOQUET, the priest in charge at Montreal, and Sulpician Pierre Huet* de La Valinière, parish priest at L'Assomption.

The other stands taken by Montgolfier were in particular cases usually related to his office as vicar general: approval or refusal of marriages between Catholics and Anglicans, recruiting and training of candidates for the priesthood, restoration of the old chapel of Notre-Dame-de-Bon-Secours which had been destroyed by fire in 1775, a new printing of the shorter and longer catechisms, the appointment of priests, the possibility of holding Church of England services in certain Catholic churches. These subjects were dealt with in his correspondence with the bishop of Quebec, who had the final responsibility for the decisions taken by his vicar general.

Montgolfier was also concerned about the influence in Montreal of the French philosophers of the Enlightenment. The first poem published in French in a North American newspaper, *La Gazette de Québec/Quebec Gazette*, was an epistle from Voltaire to a cardinal; in it he criticized the church's intolerance and sectarianism. When the Académie de Montréal established its own official organ, *La Gazette littéraire pour la ville et le district de Montréal*, ten years later, in 1778, this paper praised Voltaire's writings, thinking, and wit [*see* Fleury MESPLET]. Montgolfier asked Bishop Briand to intervene with the authorities in order that the harm might be checked. "Scorning it as it deserves, I had always hoped that this gazette would disappear by itself; but since it looked to me as if the government's protection was being sought for it, I thought it opportune to anticipate events." In any case, the newspaper had to be given up the following year, 1779. The academicians' infatuation with the French encyclopaedists, and especially with Voltaire, had in truth done their cause harm, for the spirited replies of the readers ultimately had greater influence on the thinking of Canadians than had the academicians' ill-chosen remarks.

At the end of his life Montgolfier was extremely concerned about a drop in the number of priests. His numerous efforts to bring Sulpicians or other priests from France were never rewarded by the hoped-for results. In the autumn of 1784 he tried to make contact with his superior general, Jacques-André Émery, through former Governor Carleton who was in England at that time: "Could you not send me someone reliable, chosen by yourself, to succeed me in the position I hold in Montreal, and have him accompanied by one or two equally reliable persons?" But Governor Haldimand insisted upon respecting the king's instructions of 1764 which dictated that no Frenchman could come to Canada. Yet the Sulpicians were recruiting few Canadians, one among many reasons being to maintain a majority of Frenchmen within the group; the attitude was a hangover from colonialism. In any event, few Canadians had a calling to the priesthood at that period. Montgolfier, in short, reached the end of his life fearing that he would see the Sulpicians disappear from Canada. In 1787 he resigned from his double charge as ecclesiastical superior and chaplain to the Congregation of Notre-Dame, having just written *La vie de la vénérable sœur Marguerite Bourgeois . . .*, which was to be published in 1818. In 1789, his faculties failing and no longer able to read or write, he got his colleague Gabriel-Jean BRASSIER to assist him in his role as superior of the Sulpicians and vicar general to the bishop of Quebec. He died in Montreal on 27 Aug. 1791.

A dignified, affable, and well-mannered man, Montgolfier tried to collaborate as far as possible with the bishop of Quebec in the ecclesiastical organization of his adopted country. More a pragmatist than a thinker, more a jurist and canonist than a theologian, he wanted to ensure the survival of Catholicism in new and delicate circumstances. Had he been titular bishop, Montgolfier might have displayed his personality in more striking fashion, and he would in the process have become more Canadian. In fact, throughout his stay in Montreal he remained French, and he preserved a European turn of mind in the Sulpicians which made them feel closer to the new British masters than to the Canadian people.

LUCIEN LEMIEUX

[Étienne Montgolfier], *La vie de la vénérable sœur Marguerite Bourgeois, dite du Saint-Sacrement, institutrice, fondatrice, et première supérieure des filles séculières de la Congrégation Notre-Dame, établie à Ville-Marie, dans l'isle de Montréal, en Canada, tirée de mémoires certains et la plupart originaux* (Ville-Marie [Montréal], 1818).

ACAM, 901.005, 763-2, 766-4, 768-5, 768-6, 769-1, 769-5, 769-6, 771-2, 771-6, 773-2, 773-3, 773-6, 773-7, 775-11; 901.115, 776-3, 776-5, 777-2, 777-3, 777-6, 779-1, 779-2, 780-2, 780-7, 780-8, 780-9, 781-1, 781-4, 782-6, 782-7, 782-8, 782-9, 783-2, 783-4, 783-7. PRO, CO 42/16, ff.280–82. *Mandements des évêques de Québec* (Têtu et Gagnon), II, 265–66. Allaire, *Dictionnaire*. Louise Dechêne, "Inventaire des documents relatifs à l'histoire du Canada conservés dans les archives de la Compagnie de Saint-Sulpice à Paris," ANQ *Rapport*, 1969, 149–288. Desrosiers, "Corr. de cinq vicaires généraux," ANQ *Rapport*, 1947–48, 79–100. Gauthier, *Sulpitiana* (1926), 234–36. Lanctot, *Le Canada et la Révolution américaine*, 65. Lemieux, *L'établissement de la première prov. eccl.*, 1–8, 18–23. M. Trudel, *L'Église canadienne*, I, 260–96. T.-M. Charland, "La mission de John Carroll au Canada en 1776 et l'interdit du P. Floquet," SCHÉC *Rapport*, 1 (1933–34), 45–56. Séraphin Marion, "Le problème voltairien," SCHÉC *Rapport*, 7 (1939–40), 27–41. É.-Z. Massicotte, "Un buste de George III à Montréal," *BRH*, XXI (1915), 182–83. Henri Têtu, "L'abbé Pierre Huet de La Valinière, 1732–94," *BRH*, X (1904), 129–44, 161–75.

MONTGOMERY, RICHARD, army officer; b. 2 Dec. 1736 near Swords (Republic of Ireland), third son of Thomas Montgomery, member of the Irish parliament for Lifford, and Mary Franklyn (Franklin); m. 24 July 1773 Janet Livingston; d. 31 Dec. 1775 at Quebec.

Richard Montgomery was born into a respectable family of Irish gentry and after his initial schooling was sent to Trinity College, Dublin, in 1754. He did not take a degree, however, but instead on 21 Sept. 1756 entered the army as an ensign in the 17th Foot. His regiment saw much active service overseas during the Seven Years' War. In 1759 it was with AMHERST on Lake Champlain and in 1760 with William HAVILAND in the operations leading to the conquest of Canada, and in 1762 it participated in the attacks on Martinique and Havana, Cuba. Montgomery rose steadily in rank in these years. In July 1758 he became a lieutenant, in May 1760 the regimental adjutant, and in May 1762 a captain. But soldiering during the period of peace after 1763 proved frustrating because of his inability to advance, and in April 1772 he sold his commission and emigrated to America. There he purchased a farm near New York City where he indulged his newly acquired "violent passion" for farming. His marriage the following year to a member of the powerful and strongly pro-colonial Livingston family, was, in view of his background, unusual, but he was a friend of liberal politicians in England and had formed a sympathy for the American cause. The couple settled on the wife's estate near Rhinebeck (N.Y.).

The armed clashes between British troops and colonists at Lexington and Concord (Mass.) in April 1775 touched off hostilities elsewhere, and in May the frontier forts of Crown Point and Ticonderoga (N.Y.) were seized by Ethan Allen and Benedict Arnold*. Allen and Arnold followed up their successes by raiding into Canada as far as Saint-Jean (Que.), and their relatively good luck convinced them that an invasion of the province would be successful. The Continental Congress had been concerned for some months about the potential danger to the northern colonies posed by British troops, Canadians, and Indians operating from Canada, but apart from several addresses to the Canadian population urging solidarity with the other colonies it had hitherto given Canada little attention, and on 1 June had in fact forbidden any invasion of Canada. Now, however, with Allen's and Arnold's reports of weak British defences and their belief that the Canadians were inclined to remain neutral if the Americans invaded, and with much the same information coming from American sympathizers and emissaries in Canada, Congress reversed its policy. On 27 June it ordered Major-General Philip John Schuyler, commanding in New York, to assemble an army and capture Île aux Noix on the Rivière Richelieu, Saint-Jean, and Montreal and defeat the British forces in Canada "if practicable and . . . not . . . disagreeable to the Canadians." The Canadians and Indians in Canada were to be urged to remain neutral and even to join the colonial union, and emissaries were dispatched to attain these ends. During July and August some 2,000 men began to gather in upper New York. The second in command of the expedition was Montgomery. His support of the American cause had led to his election to the New York provincial congress earlier in 1775, and on 22 June he was appointed a brigadier-general in the newly formed Continental Army, doubtless because of his previous military experience. Montgomery was, however, at first reluctant to accept the rank. He was unwilling to leave his wife and the comforts of civilian life or to take arms against his countrymen, but he at length consented, in part because he believed that "the will of an oppressed people . . . must be respected."

Governor Guy Carleton* of Quebec was meanwhile experiencing considerable difficulty in raising a defensive force. When he had called up the militia in June as a response to the American raids, he was faced with considerable resistance to militia service and a widespread feeling for neutrality among the population. Although the militia had finally been embodied in August, Carleton was convinced that it would be "unadvisable to attempt assembling any Number of them, except it becomes absolutely necessary. . . ." With only about 800 British regulars available to garrison the entire province, the government position was weak.

There were several reasons for the population's reaction. Since late 1774 letters, addresses, pamphlets, and reports had been entering Canada from the southern colonies urging neutrality in any conflict, and they had had a considerable effect, especially since the terms of the Quebec Act of 1774 had been misrepresented in the province. Such propaganda had been spread mainly by British and American merchants such as Thomas Walker, who had been angered by the British government's refusal to give them English laws and a house of assembly in the Quebec Act and had subsequently become sympathetic to the American cause. These merchants were allowed to disseminate their views throughout the summer of 1775, and even after the beginning of hostilities. Moreover, while the seigneurs, clergy, and bourgeoisie were almost uniformly loyal to the British thanks to the religious and legal guarantees contained in the Quebec Act, the bulk of the population was still alienated enough by language, religion, and the memory of the conquest to be receptive to American requests for neutrality. During the raising of the militia, Carleton had erred in placing too much responsibility for its embodiment with the seigneurs. Not only had they lost influence after the conquest owing to economic factors and a rise of independence among their tenants, but they had displayed favouritism in selecting militia officers as well as a generally haughty attitude and had thus succeeded in alienating otherwise moderate habitants. Nor did the church's threat of ecclesiastical punishment for recalcitrant militiamen have much effect. One final factor was the weak British garrison; the population could reason that since the British seemed unable to defend them, they had little reason to antagonize the Americans. Carleton had small prospect of reinforcements from Gage in Boston, moreover; as the governor himself expressed it, "every Individual seemed to feel our present impotent situation." There were, it is true, undercurrents of support among the Canadians which might result in some help for the government, but that aid would be determined very much by developing circumstances.

Early in September Schuyler's troops established themselves on Canadian soil at Île aux Noix. Schuyler proclaimed that he would "receive in the most favourable manner every inhabitant of Canada and every friend to liberty," would protect their possessions, and would ensure religious freedom. From the beginning, numbers of Canadians came forward to offer their services. The Richelieu parishes were particularly forward, having been especially receptive to American propaganda, and James Livingston*, a former Sorel grain merchant and a relation of Montgomery, was appointed to command the volunteers. Many more took no active part but furnished provisions and transportation to the American troops. Payment for these services had to be in cash, however; Canadians had bitter memories of paper money from the French régime.

The first objective of the invaders was Fort Saint-Jean, where large amounts of military stores were kept. It was also the garrison for about 500 British regulars under Major Charles Preston, who were aided by a group of Canadian volunteers under François-Marie Picoté de Belestre. Because Schuyler had "not enjoyed a moment's health" for some time, he handed over command to Montgomery on 16 September and went home. The latter was hampered in the siege by bad weather, weak artillery, and insufficient supplies, and by the poor discipline of his disease-ridden men; he nearly resigned in frustration. Until the end of September only a blockade and an intermittent bombardment were possible, "which never annoyed the Enemy in the least." In Montreal, Carleton had still not been able to raise an effective militia force, but late in September the situation suddenly changed. On the 25th Ethan Allen and a mixed force of Canadians and Americans, attempting to capture Montreal by surprise, were defeated by a hastily assembled group of regulars, militia, and Indians under Major John CAMPBELL. The effect of the victory was so great that, according to the lawyer Simon SANGUINET, some 1,200 militiamen came into Montreal within a week to offer their services, including 300 from rebel-threatened Varennes, who arrived "with the best will in the world." Carleton was now able to muster a force of 2,000 men, mostly militia, and it was hoped that he would soon counter-attack.

But for three weeks the governor made no move, in part because he distrusted the militia for their earlier reluctance and their leaders for their loss of influence, and in part because he wished to avoid more fighting with the Americans in hopes of a reconciliation. Discouraged and bored, militiamen began to leave by permission or to desert to harvest their crops and protect their homes and families from possible reprisals. Then on 18 October, Fort Chambly surrendered to an American force largely made up of Canadians. Quantities of ammunition and stores were thus available for the besiegers of Saint-Jean. Elsewhere in the province Canadians remained unwilling to serve a cause they now saw in jeopardy. Adam MABANE was confronted by 250 men armed with sticks when he tried to raise the militia on the Île d'Orléans, and it was reported that only 15 men came to support the government from the parishes below Quebec. Farther west, Louis-Joseph GODEFROY de Tonnancour and Jean-Baptiste-Marie Blaise Des Bergères de Rigauville were forcibly prevented by other Canadians at Berthier-en-Haut (Berthierville) and Verchères from joining government forces with the militia they had collected. Upon receipt of this last news, 30 to 40 militiamen began to desert each night in Montreal. It was now obvious that Carleton had to mount a counter-offensive or watch his force disappear, but he did so only on 30 October. Some 1,000 militia, Indians, and regulars were to land at Longueuil and march to relieve Saint-Jean, but the Americans prevented their landing. The fort's defenders were growing short of provisions, Montgomery had new batteries which were destroying the buildings, and ammunition was low. After hearing of the relief force's failure, the garrison surrendered on 3 November. Some 2,000 Americans and several hundred Canadians were now opposed around Montreal to about 150 British regulars and a rapidly disappearing Canadian militia. Carleton had little choice but to evacuate Montreal on the 11th with his regulars and sail for Quebec. The fleet was halted at Sorel by the threat of American batteries, and though Carleton and his aide-de-camp Charles-Louis Tarieu* de Lanaudière managed to escape with the aid of Jean-Baptiste Bouchette*, the rest of the force had to surrender on 19 November, thus limiting effective government resistance to the city of Quebec.

Montgomery had landed troops on Île des Sœurs near Montreal on 11 November, and the next day he received a committee of Montreal citizens including James McGill*, Jean-Louis BESNARD, *dit* Carignant, and Pierre-Méru Panet*. Although rejecting their request for acceptance of a formal capitulation, the American general promised not to force loyalists to oppose the government actively, to guarantee the "peaceable enjoyment of property," and to allow the "free exercise . . . of religion." Montreal was occupied on the 13th, and Valentin JAUTARD presented an address of welcome from some pro-American inhabitants. Shortly thereafter Montgomery received a delegation from Trois-Rivières which included Jean-Baptiste BADEAUX and he promised good treatment for their town. But although British resistance in almost all the province had collapsed and the Canadians were generally observing a benevolent neutrality towards the Americans, Montgomery wished to secure their active support. Believing that he would not obtain it unless Quebec was taken, he started out on this objective with 300 men on 28 November, posting a garrison of 500 under Brigadier-General David Wooster in Montreal, Saint-Jean, and Chambly.

At Quebec meanwhile, Lieutenant Governor Hector Theophilus CRAMAHÉ was trying to defend the city, but he too was hampered by pro-American sympathies among the population. Early in November matters had worsened when it was learned that a second American army was close to Quebec. This force, commanded by Benedict Arnold, had left Cambridge (Mass.) in September with orders from George Washington himself to attempt to surprise Quebec or at least join Montgomery. The march, up the Kennebec River (Maine) and thence over the height of land to the Rivière Chaudière, had been a gruelling one through a trackless wilderness, and only some 600 of the original 1,100 reached Pointe-Lévy (Lauzon, Lévis) on 9 November. The Americans crossed to the Plains of Abraham on the night of the 13th, but six days later retreated upriver to Pointe-aux-Trembles (Neuville) to wait for Montgomery. Although local inhabitants had received the starving rebels with provisions and transportation, the Americans were nevertheless "almost naked," low in ammunition, and apprehensive of a British sortie. Montgomery arrived on 3 December and took command; two days later the siege of Quebec began. With reinforcements of local Canadians [*see* Maurice DESDEVENS de Glandon] and those from Livingston's unit (which had been made an American regiment), there were about 1,000 Americans and 200 Canadians, scattered in groups across the Plains down to the Rivière Saint-Charles. The local population supplied them with wood and provisions (although again for cash) and morale was high, although stores were low. Within Quebec, morale had improved with the arrival of Lieutenant-Colonel Allan MACLEAN and 100 of his newly raised Royal Highland Emigrants on 11 November and of Carleton himself on the 19th. The governor immediately expelled all those refusing to serve in the militia, and he made preparations for a vigorous defence; guns were mounted on the walls and barricades and blockhouses constructed. The garrison of 1,800 men, composed of British and Canadian militia, regulars, seamen, and some artificers, had provisions for themselves and the 3,200 inhabitants for eight months, and abundant military stores.

Montgomery soon discovered the British artillery was considerably superior to his own, but he had never intended to bombard Quebec into surrender. The urgings of his superiors in Boston and Philadelphia, who badly needed the military stores in Quebec, smallpox among his men, the imminent expiry of many enlistments, and the small likelihood of immediate reinforcement all combined to convince him he should attack rather than blockade the city until spring. It was finally decided to mount a concentric attack on Lower Town, relying on confusion and collaborators to force Carleton to abandon the strongly fortified Upper Town and give battle. The attack was ordered for the first dark night.

That condition was fulfilled on the night of 30–31 December. At about five o'clock in the morning, in a raging snowstorm, Montgomery and 200 men travelled along the river bank from Cap Diamant towards the district of Près-de-Ville. Simultaneously, Arnold's 600 men were advancing from the suburb of Saint-Roch towards Rue Sault-au-Matelot and an eventual junction with Montgomery in Lower Town. The defenders had been warned by deserters and, alerted by Captain Malcolm Fraser*, they turned out rapidly. At Près-de-Ville were British seamen under Captain Adam Barnsfare and Canadian militia under François Chabot and Louis-Alexandre PICARD, accompanied by John Coffin*. Themselves unseen in the blizzard, they watched until Montgomery and some others moved in front of the main body, then delivered a volley which cut them down. The other Americans retreated hastily. On the other front, Arnold was wounded and evacuated, but his men pressed on to overrun a barricade at Sault-au-Matelot and take some prisoners. They were then halted by stiff resistance from regulars and militia under Henry Caldwell*, in which John Nairne* and François Dambourgès were prominent. Informed of Montgomery's repulse, Carleton transferred troops and surrounded Arnold's men, who capitulated at about eight o'clock. The boast of a British officer that the garrison had won "as compleat a little victory as ever was gained" was justified. Between 60 and 100 rebels had been killed or wounded and another 400 or so captured for the loss of not quite 20 British and Canadians.

Although the remaining Americans, now commanded by Arnold, were apprehensive of a British counter-attack, Carleton was dubious of the morale of his garrison and cautiously remained in Quebec for the remainder of the winter. Rebel strength remained low despite reinforcements, thanks to continuing smallpox epidemics and expiring periods of enlistment. They could therefore only maintain a blockade with an intermittent artillery bombardment, which in four months only "killed a boy, a cow, wounded a sailor and a turkey, and frightened an old woman into fits." On 1 April 1776 a discouraged Arnold was replaced by Wooster and went to command at Montreal; one month later Wooster was himself superseded by Major-General John Thomas. The latter could muster 1,900 men, but only 1,000 were fit for duty, and of those 300 were clamouring for discharge since their periods of enlistment had ended.

In the mean time, Canadian attitudes had been changing. An undercurrent of loyalism had persisted in many areas, and in March a group of Canadians had even attempted to attack the American camp at Pointe-Lévy [*see* Charles-François BAILLY de Messein; Michel BLAIS]. If the majority did not choose such overt action, they nevertheless were becoming more anti-American, if not pro-British. The clergy, strongly loyal, had a noticeable influence, as did the upper classes. Moreover, the continued low strength of the American forces was leading the inhabitants to the same conclusions as they had previously drawn with the British. Nor were Canadians any more eager to fight for the rebels: Moses Hazen* complained that recruiting for the regiment he was raising for Congress went poorly and that the men were unsuitable, deserting at the first opportunity. The greatest single factor for change was the Americans' growing use of paper money and promissory notes in payment for goods and services, which seemed to indicate to the population the financial bankruptcy of the American cause. And considering that the Americans commandeered supplies frequently as well, the increasing alienation of the population is understandable. Montreal in particular had cause to regret the invasion. Wooster had embarked on a series of arbitrary and ill-judged actions over the winter of 1775–76 which broke most of Montgomery's promises. He closed the "Mass Houses" on Christmas eve, attempted to arrest loyalists such as Simon Sanguinet and Georges-Hippolyte LE COMTE Dupré, and announced that all who opposed congressional wishes would be arrested as traitors. Not content with these actions, he took Edward William Gray* and René-Ovide HERTEL de Rouville hostage to ensure the disarming of three suburbs thought hostile to the Americans, and he arrested Le Comte Dupré and Thomas-Ignace TROTTIER Dufy Desauniers when they refused to exchange their British militia commissions for American ones. By the spring of 1776 American fortunes had sunk to such a low ebb that Benjamin Franklin, Charles Carroll, and Samuel Chase, who arrived in Montreal in April as commissioners appointed by Congress to undertake the political conversion of the Canadians, soon became discouraged and even counselled abandonment of the country.

But any Canadian support for the British was still mainly covert, and only large British reinforcements could really make the Canadians active in opposition. On 6 May 1776 a small squadron under Charles DOUGLAS arrived off Quebec and landed troops. Carleton sortied the same day. The Americans, caught off guard as they prepared to raise the siege, retreated "in the utmost hurry and confusion," not stopping until they reached Sorel. Carleton declined to pursue and instead waited for the massive reinforcements of British and German regulars under John BURGOYNE approaching from Britain. In mid May 400 Americans were captured at Les Cèdres, west of Montreal, by an *ad hoc* force of regulars, Indians, and Canadians drawn from the Upper Lakes posts. American troops now controlled only the Montreal-Richelieu valley region, but substantial reinforcements released by the end of the siege of Boston enabled Brigadier-General John Sullivan, now commanding in Canada (Thomas was mortally ill with smallpox and Wooster had been recalled to explain his conduct at Montreal), to concentrate 5,000 men at Sorel by late May. As the first stage in a planned counter-offensive, Sullivan sent Brigadier-General William Thompson and 2,200 men against Trois-Rivières, which was believed to be lightly held. But Thompson's advance slowed down [*see* François GUILLOT, *dit* Larose], and when the Americans arrived before the town on 8 June they found it held by 7,000 British regulars from Burgoyne's force. The rebels were soundly defeated with the loss of 200 prisoners, one of whom was Thompson. Thereafter their position in Canada rapidly crumbled. Some 10,000 British and German regulars were pressing hard down the St Lawrence in pursuit, almost 3,000 Americans were ill, and Canadians were now beginning to turn openly against the invaders. By 18 June the forces of Arnold (who narrowly escaped from Montreal) and Sullivan had fallen back to Saint-Jean and two weeks later, closely pursued by the British, they had retreated over the frontier. No further attempt was made during the war to invade Canada, although rumours kept HALDIMAND worried.

As the Americans retreated, normal life returned to Quebec. Carleton was generally lenient with the inhabitants who had supported the rebels, perhaps because of his prediction before the invasion that Canadians would not aid the government in large numbers. All the same, some punishments were meted out. A commission consisting of Gabriel-Elzéar Taschereau*, François Baby*, and Jenkin Williams* was appointed by the governor to investigate the extent and nature of collaboration in the Quebec region, and between 22 May and 16 July it toured thc parishes. The commission found that many parishes had actively supported the encouraged the invaders, that others had been neutral, and that a small number had been sympathetic to the government. Nevertheless, the only reprisals generally taken were the replacement of many militia officers, who had been particularly pro-American, and the billeting of troops on especially stubborn parishes. Although the punishments were mild, complaints arose that they had not been equitably distributed, and after the invasion was over Carleton was much harsher with American sympathizers and imprisoned several. In his efforts to restore order he had the support of the church, which pursued a strict policy towards rebel supporters and backsliders. Bishop BRIAND decreed that the sacraments would be refused to those American sympathizers who did not atone for their transgression by public penance, but some time elapsed before this order was generally obeyed, and many remained unrepentant.

The invasion of Canada was a minor campaign in what soon became a much wider and more complicated conflict, and it was by and large unnecessary. The Americans had no clear idea of their objectives in invading the country, and when it became obvious that Canada had to be completely occupied and pacified, their rudimentary organization was incapable of sustaining such a full-scale effort. In any case, it was practically inevitable that the British would sooner or later mount a counter-offensive – the loss of Canada would have been a serious blow to their hopes of quickly crushing the rebellion – and that, given their unchallenged naval supremacy, they could concentrate enough troops to reconquer the province. But the invasion would not have succeeded or, if it had, the reconquest would have been more bloody and drawn out than it actually was, had the Canadians inclined strongly to one side or the other. That they chose to maintain a changeable neutrality is indicative of their lack of sympathy with either side and of their realization that a flexible policy of neutrality was the course which could best serve their interests in the fluid and uncertain circumstances of the invasion and spare them the misery which had accompanied the conquest 15 years previously.

On the morning after the American defeat before Quebec in December 1775 the frozen bodies of Montgomery and several companions were discovered beneath a snow-drift. Thomas Ainslie* recorded that those in Quebec who had known the dead American officer (he had been made major-general on 9 December but had never received the news) expressed sincere regrets at his death, and even Carleton apparently grieved for his "deluded friend." Cramahé had Montgomery's body "decently interred" at his personal expense; in 1818 it was returned to the United States. Montgomery was also mourned by his compatriots, who considered him a promising and popular officer. Captain Simeon Thayer of Arnold's force left this description: "a genteel appearing man, tall and slender of make, . . . of an agreeable temper, and a virtuous General."

STUART R. J. SUTHERLAND

[Since Montgomery had such a short career in the revolution, there has been comparatively little written about him. There is a biography by A. L. Todd, entitled *Richard Montgomery: rebel of 1775* (New York, 1966), but its superficial research and naive style of writing make it of little value. There are entries in the *DAB* and *DNB*. Sources used for biographical material include G.B., WO, *Army list*, 1756–72; F. B. Heitman, *Historical register of officers of the Continental Army during the war of the revolution* . . . (Washington, 1893); and T. H. Montgomery, "Ancestry of Gen. Richard Montgomery," *New-York Geneal. and Biographical Record* (New York), II (1871), 123–30. S.R.J.S.]

[Thomas Ainslie], "Journal of the most remarkable occurences in the province of Quebec from the appearance of the rebels in September 1775 until their retreat on the sixth of May 1776," ed. F. C. Würtele, Literary and Hist. Soc. of Quebec, *Hist. Docs.*, 7th ser. (1905), [9]–89. *American archives* (Clarke and Force), 4th ser., III–VI. [Henry Caldwell], "The invasion of Canada in 1775: letter attributed to Colonel Henry Caldwell," Literary and Hist. Soc. of Quebec, *Hist. Docs.*, 2nd ser. (1868), 1–19. Can., Dept. of Militia and Defence, General Staff, *A history of the organization, development and services of the military and naval forces of Canada, from the peace of Paris in 1763, to the present time* . . . (3v., [Ottawa, 1919–20]), I. [Jacob Danford], "Quebec under siege, 1775–1776: the 'Memorandums' of Jacob Danford," ed. J. F. Roche, *CHR*, L (1969), 68–85. *Docs. relating to constitutional history, 1759–91* (Shortt and Doughty; 1907), 450–59. *Invasion du Canada* (Verreau). "Journal of the most remarkable occurences in Quebec since Arnold appear'd before the town on the 14th November 1775," Literary and Hist. Soc. of Quebec, *Hist. Docs.*, 7th ser. (1905), 93–154. "Journal of the siege and blockade of Quebec by the American rebels, in autumn 1775 and winter 1776," Literary and Hist. Soc. of Quebec, *Hist. Docs.*, 4th ser. (1875), [3]–25. "Journal par Messrs Fran[s] Baby, Gab. Taschereau et Jenkin Williams . . . ," Ægidius Fauteux, édit., ANQ *Rapport*, 1927–28, 431–99. *March to Quebec: journals of the members of Arnold's expedition*, ed. K. L. Roberts (New York, 1938). "Orderly book begun by Captain Anthony Vialar of the British militia . . . ," ed. F. C. Würtele, Literary and Hist. Soc. of Quebec, *Hist. Docs.*, 7th ser. (1905), 155–265. PAC *Report*, 1914–15, app.B, 5–25. [Rudolphus Ritzema], "Journal of Col. Rudolphus Ritzema, of the First New York Regiment, August 8, 1775, to March 30, 1776," *Magazine of American History* (New York), I (1877), 98–107. "Rôle général de la milice canadienne du Québec . . . ," Literary and Hist. Soc. of Quebec, *Hist. Docs.*, 8th ser. (1906), 269–307. "State papers," PAC *Report*, 1890. Boatner, *Encyclopedia of American revolution*. *The toll of independence: engagements and battle casualties of the American revolution*, ed. H. H. Peckham (Chicago, 1974). Allen French, *The first year of the American revolution* (Cambridge, Mass., 1934). Lanctot, *Canada and American revolution*. J. H. Smith, *Our struggle for the fourteenth colony: Canada and the American revolution* (2v., New York, 1907). G. F. G. Stanley, *Canada invaded, 1775–1776* (Toronto, 1973).

MONTGOMERY, WILLIAM, army officer; b. 25 Jan. 1765 at Edinburgh, Scotland, son of James William Montgomery and Margaret Scott; d. 25 Oct. 1800 at Hounslow (Greater London), England.

As eldest son and prospective heir to the family estate, William Montgomery was carefully groomed by his father from an early age to assume direction of the Montgomery fortune. His father, lord advocate of Scotland from 1766 to 1775 and lord chief baron of the exchequer of Scotland from 1775 to 1801, had through marriage, astute business practice, and political influence acquired substantial lands in Peeblesshire and Stirlingshire in Scotland, and by 1775 he also owned nearly 100,000 acres on St John's (Prince Edward) Island.

Beginning in 1769, James Montgomery had set under way two major entrepreneurial ventures on St John's Island, one a fishing and trading operation in partnership with David HIGGINS on Lot 59, and the other a commercial flax farm on Lot 34. Financed by Montgomery for seven years on a profit-sharing basis, a flax farmer from Perthshire, David Lawson*, was sent to the Island in 1770 with nearly 50 indentured servants from the same region. The lord chief baron was unable to settle his accounts with Lawson in 1777 because of the disruption of communication brought about by the American revolution, and indeed was forced that year to appoint Lawson general agent of the Montgomery interests on the Island, with full power of attorney, in order to maintain any supervision of the investment during the war. With its conclusion, Montgomery sought a financial statement for Lawson's activities on the farm at Stanhope Cove (Covehead Bay) and as agent.

Realizing that Lawson was a working farmer and not an estate manager, Montgomery asked Chief Justice Peter Stewart* to assist in preparing the statement, which was further complicated by Lawson's assumption of administration of Higgins' estate in 1783. To his dismay, the lord chief baron learned that Lawson was a fervent political supporter of Governor Walter PATTERSON and outspoken opponent of the chief justice, the leader of the anti-Patterson forces on the Island. Mutual enmity between Stewart and Lawson made cooperation impossible. Moreover, it gradually became apparent from Stewart's letters and the absence of communications from Lawson that the latter had kept few records of his financial dealings and feared an accounting could not properly reward him for his many years of sacrifice on the Island. Ultimately, Montgomery came to suspect that Lawson had become unable to distinguish between his own property and that of his partner, who had put up the capital, about £1,500 in cash advances. The proprietor was unable to gain any satisfaction until 1788, when William Montgomery, a lieutenant in the 4th Foot posted to Halifax in 1787, received a four-month leave of absence to go to St John's Island to settle his father's affairs.

Upon his arrival in July 1788, William was offered a number of counter-proposals by Lawson, all falling far short of a full accounting. In a letter to William, Lawson later protested that nothing would satisfy but the impossible – and "to state Every day's labor for 18 year back with Everything purchased for the farm and Everything sold of the farm to this day and to whom sold" would produce "the longest Account Ever was on the Island." William, under close instructions from his father, undoubtedly saw Lawson's efforts to compromise as those of a desperate man finally confronted with someone on the spot to call him to account, and he suspected that Lawson's continued delays were the tactics of a man who knew the young officer would eventually have to return to duty. As the end of his leave drew near and with Lawson still procrastinating, William decided on drastic measures. He appeared unannounced at Stanhope Cove in late October 1788 with three assessors who inventoried the farm's improvements, stock, and crops. They found, not surprisingly, that the improved value of the farm did not begin to approach James Montgomery's substantial advances. Lawson was summarily evicted and was replaced with a loyalist family named Bovyer.

Out of the fiasco came one bright point, for William was well pleased with the work of one of the assessors, comptroller of customs James Douglas*, and recommended to his father that Douglas be appointed Montgomery agent for the Island. For his part, David Lawson remained convinced that William had treated him unfairly, although in 1793 an arbitration panel composed of Island residents did not agree. But Lawson was certainly correct in his assumption that William's actions would be fully supported by his father, whatever their merit. While he was on the Island, William's candidacy to parliament representing Peeblesshire was successfully canvassed and arranged by his father, and he was elected without opposition upon his return to Scotland in 1790. During his years in parliament, William increasingly took over protection of the Montgomery interests in Whitehall while his father withdrew from political life. The young man was active behind the scenes in the proceedings arising from the complaints against Lieutenant Governor Edmund Fanning* and other Island officers in 1791 and 1792, assisting Fanning's agent Robert Gray* on several occasions. He also regularly reported to his father on government discussions relating to the Island and especially to the proprietors.

Since he had obtained a safe seat in parliament and, in 1799, a lieutenant-colonelcy in the 43rd Foot, William's career was clearly on the rise when he unexpectedly died in 1800, much grieved by his aged father. The Montgomery estates and their management passed to a younger brother, James (later the brother-in-law of the Earl of Selkirk [Douglas*]), who lacked the benefit of William's general background and Island experience.

J. M. BUMSTED

BL, Add. MSS 35541, f.158. PAC, MG 23, E6, pp.30–32. Public Archives of P.E.I. (Charlottetown), Ira Brown papers, item 122. Scottish Record Office (Edinburgh), Montgomery estate papers in the muniments of Messrs. Blackwood and Smith, W.S., Peebles, Estate papers, GD293/2/21/93; 293/2/78/6, 17, 55–56; 293/2/79/10, 16, 26, 30, 31, 38; 293/2/81/2; RH4/56. University of B.C. Library (Vancouver), Special Coll. Division, Macmillan coll., James Montgomery to Edward Fanning, 30 April 1798. [William Drummond], "Diary of William Drummond," ed. David Weale, *Island Magazine* (Charlottetown), 2 (1977), 28–31.

MONTIGNY, JEAN-BAPTISTE-PHILIPPE TESTARD DE. *See* TESTARD

MONTRESOR (Montrésor), JOHN, military engineer; b. 22 April 1736 at Gibraltar, son of James Gabriel Montresor and Mary Haswell; m. 1 March 1764 Frances Tucker, in New York City, and they had six surviving children; d. 26 June 1799 in Maidstone prison, England.

John Montresor was raised in Gibraltar, where he probably learned the rudiments of military engineering from his father, the chief engineer there. In 1754 he went to North America when his father was designated chief engineer in Major-General Edward Braddock's force. John was commissioned an ensign in the 48th Foot in March 1755 and was appointed engineer in June; he was wounded in the battle on 9 July which ended Braddock's ill-fated expedition to Fort Duquesne (Pittsburgh, Pa) [*see* Jean-Daniel DUMAS]. Montresor spent most of 1756 on works at Fort Edward (sometimes called Fort Lydius), New York, and the following year joined Lord Loudoun's abortive expedition against Louisbourg, Île Royale (Cape Breton Island). Montresor was officially commissioned a practitioner engineer in May 1758 but subsequently lost his position in the 48th. In June he accompanied Jeffery AMHERST's expedition against Louisbourg and took an active part in the reduction of the fortress. He remained there after the capitulation and in March 1759 led a scouting party to the Bras d'Or lakes to search for Acadians.

Later that year Montresor was assigned to Wolfe*'s expedition against Quebec. During the siege he became quite friendly with Wolfe and made a profile drawing of the general which was published in 1783. After the fall of Quebec he remained there under James MURRAY's command and was employed in surveying the resources of the countryside, disarming the Canadian militia, and administering the oath of allegiance. In January 1760 he made a difficult overland journey to deliver dispatches to army headquarters in the American colonies and in the summer accompanied the vanguard of Murray's army to Montreal.

Montresor remained in Canada for some time after its surrender. In 1761 he explored the unknown region between Quebec and the Kennebec River (Maine). His account of this journey later fell into the hands of Benedict Arnold*, who used it as a guide for his expedition against Quebec in 1775. He was also employed by Murray, whom he disliked intensely and referred to as "A madman," in producing a monumental map of the St Lawrence, the so-called "Murray Map." Questions of responsibility and credit for the project led to quarrels between Montresor and two other engineers, Samuel Jan Holland* and William Spry.

By 1763 Montresor was stationed in New York, but Pontiac*'s uprising brought him back to Canada when he was sent by Amherst with dispatches for Major Henry GLADWIN, besieged at Detroit. The following year he was sent with Colonel John BRADSTREET's expedition to Detroit as chief engineer and commander of a detachment of Canadian volunteers, the first such force raised for the British service. The expedition assembled at Niagara (near Youngstown, N.Y.), where Montresor spent the summer constructing fortifications along the Niagara River, including the first Fort Erie (Ont.).

Following a trip to England in 1766, Montresor was promoted captain-lieutenant and appointed chief barrack-master of the Ordnance for America. He was in Boston when the War of American Independence broke out and in the following years served several times as chief engineer in America. He was promoted captain in January 1776. In October 1778 Montresor returned to England and retired from the army.

Although he lived to see several of his sons obtain preferment in the army, Montresor's last years were clouded. Throughout his later career he bore a grudge against the army and the Ordnance office for their failure to appoint him to the rank he felt his achievements and talents merited. But while his accomplishments were significant and his abilities undoubted, his journals reveal an arrogance which probably contributed to his lack of promotion. His bitterness, the huge amounts of money he could detail to purchase engineering supplies, and a lax auditing system probably led him to use his position as chief engineer to accumulate a small fortune for himself. Four years after he returned to England, however, his accounts were subjected to close scrutiny, and the auditors disallowed £50,000 out of claimed expenditures of about £250,000. Montresor contested this decision but the government eventually recovered £48,000 through the seizure and sale of his estate, which included a house in London and lands in Kent. He died in prison, a confinement apparently related to the money still owed to the authorities.

R. ARTHUR BOWLER

[There is a portrait of John Montresor by John Singleton Copley in the Detroit Institute of Arts. Four copies of the St Lawrence map on which Montresor worked are known to exist. The Clements Library and the PAC each have one, and the BL possesses two.

John Montresor left private papers which were used by G. D. Scull when he prepared "The Montresor journals" and by Montresor's descendant F. M. Montrésor in the preparation of his *CHR* article. The papers are not now listed in any manuscript inventory and I have been informed by D. W. Marshall of the Clements Library that the present owner does not permit access to them. Montresor's official correspondence is scattered in the Amherst papers (WO 34), the War Office papers (WO 1), the Ordnance Office papers (WO 44), the Audit Office papers (AO 12) in the PRO, the Haldimand papers (Add. MSS 21661-892) at the BL, and the Thomas Gage papers at the Clements Library. R.A.B.]

[John Montresor], "Journal of John Montresor's expedition to Detroit in 1763," ed. J. C. Webster, RSC *Trans.*, 3rd ser., XXII (1928), sect.II, 8–31; "Lt. John Montresor's journal of an expedition in 1760 across Maine from Quebec," *New England Hist. and Geneal. Register*, XXXVI (1882), 29–36. "The Montresor journals," ed. G. D. Scull, N.Y. Hist. Soc., *Coll.*, [ser.3], XIV (1881). *DAB*. *DNB*. R. A. Bowler, *Logistics and the failure of the British army in America, 1775–1783* (Princeton, N.J., 1975), 175–78. F. M. Montrésor, "Captain John Montrésor in Canada," *CHR*, V (1924), 336–40. F. H. Severance, "The achievements of Captain John Montresor on the Niagara and the first construction of Fort Erie," Buffalo Hist. Soc., *Pubs.* (Buffalo, N.Y.), V (1902), 1–19. J. C. Webster, "Life of John Montresor," RSC *Trans.*, 3rd ser., XXII (1928), sect.II, 1–8.

MONTREUIL, PIERRE-ANDRÉ GOHIN, Comte de. *See* GOHIN

MOORE, FRANCES (Brooke), author; baptized 24 Jan. 1724 in Claypole, Lincolnshire, England, daughter of the Reverend Thomas Moore, curate of Claypole, and Mary Knowles; m. *c.* 1756 the Reverend John BROOKE, and they had one son, and probably a daughter; d. 23 Jan. 1789 at Sleaford, Lincolnshire, England.

Frances Moore spent her childhood and adolescence in the various country rectories of clerical relatives. On her father's death in 1727 she moved with her mother and her younger sister Sarah to the rectory of her maternal grandparents at Peterborough. When their mother died the two sisters went to live with an aunt and uncle at the latter's rectory of Tydd St Mary (Lincolnshire).

By 1748 Frances had left this family home; in the 1750s she was writing poetry and plays and was reported to be moving in the literary circle of the novelist Samuel Richardson. She first attracted literary attention with her editorship, under the pseudonym, "Mary Singleton, Spinster," of a weekly periodical, *The old maid*, which appeared from 15 Nov. 1755 to 24 July 1756. In the vein of the *Spectator* of Addison and Steele, the journal included essays and letters written in a lively style commenting on theatre, politics, society, and religion. *The old maid* was to be reprinted in volume form in 1764. In 1756 Frances published a number of poems and a play, *Virginia*, which was never produced. By that summer she had married John Brooke, rector of Colney, Norfolk, and several parishes in Norwich, who left for North America in 1757 as a military chaplain.

Three years later Frances published *The letters of Lady Juliet Catesby, to her friend Lady Henrietta Campley*, a translation of Marie-Jeanne Riccoboni's epistolary novel first published in French in 1759; at least six editions of this popular work appeared during Mrs Brooke's lifetime. Her own first novel, *The history of Lady Julia Mandeville*, also epistolary, appeared in 1763 and it was reprinted eight times before her death. *Julia Mandeville* departs from the conventional novel of sensibility in its portrayal of a witty, intelligent feminist in the character of Julia's friend, Anne Wilmot. It shows the influence of Frances' husband, chaplain at Quebec since 1760, in its opposition to a proposal that the British leave Canada to France in exchange for Guadeloupe, and in its suggested guiding principles for governing the colony. "Canada, considered merely as the possession of it gives security to our colonies, is of more national consequence to us than all the Sugar-islands on the globe: but if the present inhabitants are encouraged to stay, by the mildness of our laws, and that full liberty of conscience to which every rational creature has a right; if they are taught, by every honest art, a love for that constitution which makes them free, and a personal attachment to the best of Princes; if they are allured to our religious worship, by seeing it in its genuine beauty, equally remote from their load of trifling ceremonies and the unornamented forms of the dissenters: if population is encouraged; the waste lands settled; and a whale fishery set on foot, we shall find it, considered in every light, an acquisition beyond our most sanguine hopes!"

By 1763 Mrs Brooke was a writer of some note, included in the literary circle surrounding Samuel

Johnson. In July of that year she sailed for Quebec to join her husband. Although she made at least one trip to England in 1764, returning late in 1765, she is thought to have lived in Quebec until her husband's return to England three years later. Frances and her sister Sarah, who had accompanied her to Canada, participated in the social life around Governor MURRAY and such men as Attorney General Francis Maseres*, who described her in 1766 as "a very sensible agreeable woman, of a very improved understanding and without any pedantry or affectation"; Henry Caldwell*, Murray's land agent and later receiver general of Lower Canada; Adam MABANE, a member of the Council of Quebec who is thought to have been related to James Thomson, author of *The seasons*; and George Allsopp*, a leader of the merchant group in its political opposition to Murray. The governor, who found John Brooke irascible, with a tendency to be politically and socially meddlesome, had hoped that the presence of Frances and her sister "would have wrought a change" in the chaplain, but found that "on the contrary they meddle more than he does."

While in Canada Frances Brooke wrote *The history of Emily Montague*, published in England in 1769. The novel employs the epistolary style of *Julia Mandeville*, and voices the author's experience of Quebec and her observations of its society, politics, religion, and natural surroundings. Most of the letters are written by Colonel Ed Rivers, Emily Montague's lover, and by Arabella Fermor, her friend and confidante. The character of Colonel Rivers is reputed to be modelled on Henry Caldwell and that of Arabella Fermor on Anna Marie Bondfield, the wife of George Allsopp. Arabella Fermor is also, it might be noted, the name of the young lady to whom Alexander Pope addressed *The rape of the lock*; Belinda, the central character of Pope's poem, is a beautiful and frivolous coquette; Mrs Brooke's Arabella is an intelligent and witty one. The plot of *Emily Montague*, sentimental and romantic, revolves around a courtship and its complications. A disparity between the two central viewpoints – that of the conventional, rather prosaic man of sensibility and that of the witty, lively, and perceptive woman – contributes to the tension of the novel. The setting of much of the action is Sillery, where at Mount Pleasant the Brookes lived in a former Jesuit mission house. Canada is first perceived by the English characters as a wilderness. One who tames it, however, will participate in creation, for he will "see order and beauty gradually rise from chaos." Detailed descriptions are given of Montmorency Falls in summer and winter, of the breakup of ice on the rivers in spring, of the immensity of the St Lawrence, and of Quebec and its surroundings viewed from the river. Winter is a season of cheerfulness and festivity in which the bitterness of the cold is offset by balls, sightseeing expeditions, and carriole races across the snow.

In general Mrs Brooke's English characters find the Canadian women beautiful, vivacious, and charming, but lacking in the important English virtue of sensibility – until a young widow from Kamouraska demonstrates that sensibility is not solely a British quality. Country girls, too, are charming, but the men are often described as "indolent," although hospitable and courteous. Indians are remarked as disdainful of rank or riches, and at one point Indian government and way of life are described at length. Indian women meet with more approval than men, and their role in selecting leaders is contrasted with the lack of power of European women.

The religion of the French inhabitants is of considerable interest to the British, and the comparative severity of the different religious orders and attractiveness of their costumes are noted. Individual members of religious orders are much admired. The superior of the Ursulines, a character resembling Sister Esther-Marie-Joseph de l'Enfant-Jésus [Esther WHEELWRIGHT], is described by Rivers as "one of the most amiable women I ever knew, with a benevolence in her countenance which inspires all who see her with affection; I am very fond of her conversation, tho' sixty and a nun."

A series of 13 letters in the novel, written by Sir William Fermor to a senior member of the British government, comment on the religion, politics, and character of the French inhabitants. Fermor foresees and endorses assimilation through the teaching of English, and through the provision of a liberal education, which would lessen the impact of a "superstitious" religion. He recommends that, although freedom of worship be allowed, "the inhabitants be gently led by reason to a religion which is not only preferable as being that of the country to which they are now annexed, but which is much more calculated to make them happy and prosperous as a people." The Brookes were themselves viewed as adherents of the English party, composed largely of British merchants operating from Quebec and Montreal, who in the interests of their commerce sought to have Quebec assimilated politically, socially, and economically into the British empire. Frances makes a point of indicating in her novel that politics is outside the realm of women; according to Adam Mabane, however, "particular Attention is paid to Mrs Brookes [by the English party] either from fear of her bad Tongue, or from Gratitude for the good offices'' she was able to render ''at the Tea Tables of London.'' It is likely, nonetheless, that John Brooke was the principal source of the reports and attitudes contained in William Fermor's letters.

Mrs Brooke's English characters leave Canada with regret. Arabella, who in November viewed Quebec as ''like a third or fourth rate country town in England,'' by June has decided, ''I had rather live at Quebec, take it for all in all, than in any town in England, except London: the manner of living here is uncommonly agreeable: the scenes about us are lovely, and the mode of amusements makes us taste those scenes in full perfection.'' Mrs Brooke herself returned to England with her husband late in 1768. Her younger contemporary Fanny Burney, another author in Johnson's literary circle, met her in February 1774, and in her diary recorded her first impression that ''Mrs. Brooke is very short and fat, and squints; but has the art of showing agreeable ugliness. She is very well bred, and expresses herself with much modesty upon all subjects; which in an *authoress*, a woman of *known* understanding, is extremely pleasing.''

In the 20 years following her return to England and publication of *Emily Montague*, Frances Brooke published two translations, wrote one tragedy, and wrote the libretti for two comic operas, of which *Rosina*, produced at Covent Garden in 1782, was an instant success both on stage and in printed form. About 1773 she had become, with her close friend, the great tragic actress Mary Ann Yates, joint manager of the Haymarket Opera House. This venture lasted for several years, but seems to have been, financially at any rate, not entirely a success. Frances published at least two more novels, *The excursion* in 1777, similar in theme to Fanny Burney's *Evelina*, published the following year, and *The history of Charles Mandeville*, published posthumously in 1790 and continuing the earlier *Julia Mandeville*. She may also have been the author of *All's right at last; or, the history of Miss West*, published in 1774, an epistolary novel set largely in Canada. Although hastily written, with several errors in fact, the novel has themes, attitudes, and elements of style that suggest Frances Brooke as possible author; it contains a number of lively letters by Canadian correspondents, absent from *Emily Montague*, and provides another record, this time including Montreal and Trois-Rivières, of British upper-class society in 18th-century Canada. By 1787 Mrs Brooke had moved to Sleaford with her son, John, then vicar of Helpringham and rector of Folkingham. Here on 23 Jan. 1789 she died, two days after her husband, apparently ''of a spasmodic complaint.''

Frances Brooke was a celebrated member of London's literary circle, respected for her skills as novelist, dramatist, translator, and essayist. In fiction, she contributed to the 18th-century novel of sensibility, to a renewed interest in the epistolary form, and to the newer movement toward realism in the novel. Her most successful opera, *Rosina*, continues to be of interest. Both *Julia Mandeville* and *Emily Montague* have been reprinted in this century. Mrs Brooke indicates her feminist stance through the wit, humour, and independent mind of the central women characters of these two novels. Her major contribution to Canadian literature remains the first novel written in North America, *Emily Montague*, which conveys with grace, wit, intelligence, and perception what it meant to experience Canada in the 18th century.

LORRAINE MCMULLEN

Frances Moore wrote several novels published in London; in Canada the best known of her works is *The history of Emily Montague, in four volumes, by the author of Lady Julia Mandeville* (1769). This novel was republished in London in 1777, 1784, and 1800; in Canada it first appeared in Ottawa (in 1931, with an introduction and notes by Lawrence Johnston Burpee* and an appendix by Frederick Philip Grove*) and then in Toronto (in 1961, with an introduction by Carl Frederick Klinck). It also appeared as *Histoire d'Émilie Montague, par l'auteur de ''Julie Mandeville''*, J.-B.-R. Robinet, trad. (4v. in 2, Amsterdam, 1770), and *Historie van Emelia Montague, door den schryver van ''Lady Julia Mandeville''* (2v., Amsterdam, 1783). In 1770 another French version appeared in Paris under the title *Histoire d'Émilie Montague, par M. Brooke, imitée de l'anglois par M. Frenais*; it was followed in 1809 by *Voyage dans le Canada, ou histoire de Miss Montaigu*, translated by ''T.G.M.'' *All's right at last; or, the history of Miss West* (2v., London, 1774), another novel which takes place largely in Canada, has been attributed to Frances Moore. It was translated as *Histoire de Miss West, ou l'heureux dénouement, par Mme ***, auteur de ''L'histoire d'Émilie Montagu''* (2v. in 1, Rotterdam, 1777).

ANQ-Q, AP-G-313/2, George Allsopp à A. M. Allsopp, 12 mars 1785. AUQ, Journal, 2, avril-mai, août-sept. 1767; Livre des entrées et sorties des pensionnaires, 1766. Lincolnshire Archives Office (Lincoln, Eng.), Claypole, Bishop's transcript of the register of christenings, marriages and burials, 24 Jan. 1724; Sleaford, Register of burials, 27 Jan. 1789; Stubton Deposit, 3E/5/D6, F6. QDA, 82 (D-1), memoir of 1764 concerning John Brooke. PAC, MG 23, GII, 1, ser. 1, 2, pp.21, 44–46, 184–85. ''Anecdotes of Mrs Frances Brooke,'' *European Magazine and London Rev.* (London), XV (1789), 99–101. *Critical Rev., or Annals of*

Literature (London), XVI (1763), 41–45. *The early diary of Frances Burney, 1768–1778; with a selection from her correspondence, and from the journal of her sisters Susan and Charlotte Burney*, ed. A. R. Ellis (2v., London, 1889), I, 273. *Gentleman's Magazine*, 1789, 90. [William Johnson], *Lincolnshire church notes made by William Johnson, FSA, 1828–1840 . . .* , ed. W. J. Manson, 9th Baron Manson ([Hereford, Eng.], 1936), 316–17. *Literary anecdotes of the eighteenth century; comprising biographical memoirs of William Bowyer and many of his learned friends . . .* , ed. John Nichols (9v., London, 1812–15), II, 346–47. Maseres, *Maseres letters* (Wallace), 46. "Stubton strong room – stray notes (2nd series); Moore and Knowles families – two sisters," ed. Edmund Royds, Associated Architectural Societies of Lincoln, *Reports and Papers* (Lincoln, Eng.), 38 (1926–27), 213–312. *Theatre, Haymarket* (3v., n.p., [1757–1829]), Haymarket Theatre, 1765. *Public Advertiser* (London), 23 May 1788. *Quebec Gazette*, 8 Nov. 1764, 14 July 1768.

DNB. André Bernier, *Le Vieux-Sillery* ([Québec], 1977), 21–22. Bernard Dufebvre [Émile Castonguay], *Cinq femmes et nous* (Québec, 1950), 30. John Genest, *Some account of the English stage from the restoration in 1660 to 1830* (10v., Bath, Eng., 1832), VI, 191–92. P.-A. Lamontagne et Robert Rumilly, *L'histoire de Sillery, 1630–1950* (Sillery, Qué., 1952), 27. J. M. LeMoine, *Maple leaves: history, biography, legend, literature, memoirs, etc.* (7 ser., Quebec, 1863–1906), VII, 83. G. S. Marr, *Periodical essayists of the eighteenth century, with illustrative extracts from the rarer periodicals* (New York, 1970), 162–63. C. S. Blue, "Canada's first novelist," *Canadian Magazine* (Toronto), LVIII (1921–22), 3–12. Desmond Pacey, "The first Canadian novel," *Dal. Rev.*, XXVI (1946–47), 143–50.

MOORE, WILLIAM, actor, printer, and journalist; m. 11 March 1790 at Quebec to Agnes McKay; fl. 1779–98.

William Moore began his career as an actor in England, playing at the Liverpool Theatre Royal in the years 1779–80. By 1781 he was in Jamaica with the American Company, a group of English actors managed by Lewis Hallam who had taken refuge from the American revolution. In July 1782 Moore printed at the *Royal Gazette* printing office a small work called *The elements of freemasonry delineated*, the first masonic book published in Jamaica. Following the war the members of the American Company gradually returned to the new republic. In 1785 Moore toured British North America with his one-man show, *Fashionable raillery*, a series of artistic impersonations. In May and June he performed in Nova Scotia, first in Shelburne, and then in Halifax, where his entertainment was so well received that he gave a command performance for Governor John PARR.

By July 1785 Moore had rejoined Hallam, who was then in Philadelphia with a small company, and in August they opened the John Street Theatre in New York. On 20 September, when Moore had his benefit, the company presented Arthur Murphy's comedy *The citizen*, the first regular drama to be performed in New York after the revolution. Moore completed the evening with his *Eulogy on freemasonry*. In November Moore and Edward Allen organized their own company and set off for Canada, travelling via Albany, where they remained until the middle of February. The Montreal theatre season opened in Mr Levy's assembly room on 16 March with a performance of *She stoops to conquer*. On 7 July the company left for Quebec, Allen and Moore having previously made arrangements to rent a room there in the inn owned by Miles Prentice, an important freemason. The room, which could seat around 300 people, was made into a theatre with boxes and two galleries. The first Quebec performance took place on 21 July 1786. The disappearance of the detailed advertisements from the *Quebec Gazette* after a few weeks was probably the result of their cost, and also of the influence of the Catholic Church and the puritanism of some of the New England Protestants who had recently settled in Quebec. The main part of the company returned to Montreal for a few months in early 1787, but Moore remained in Quebec where he became associated with a theatrical group from the United States. The Allen-Moore company had a second full summer season in Quebec in 1787 and gave a command performance of *She stoops to conquer* that August for Prince William Henry. By November they were back in Montreal for their last season together and, performing in Basile Proulx's room, they repeated their Quebec program. The opening night was held under the patronage of Lord Dorchester [Carleton*].

In Quebec, as in Jamaica, Moore combined his acting career with an interest in printing. In December 1786, at the end of his company's first season there, he had tried to find 40 subscribers for the publication of his *Elements of freemasonry*, but he apparently had no success. Two years later, in October, he announced the opening of his printing shop, and the first number of his *Quebec Herald and Universal Miscellany* appeared on 24 Nov. 1788. The newspaper, a weekly, was printed in quarto with new type purchased from William Caslon Jr of London; it was announced that "at the expiration of twelve months a title page and index will be added gratis to form an annual volume." The paper sold for one guinea annually, to be paid half yearly. The

French edition, *Le Courier de Québec ou Héraut françois*, ceased after only three issues, "there not being subscribers sufficient to pay for the paper." Moore continued to publish the *Herald* for over four years, a period of important constitutional change in Canada and of war and revolution elsewhere. For news content he relied on American and European papers, as well as on those from the West Indies and the Maritime provinces. Politically his paper represented the new ideals sweeping the western world: freedom of the press, democratic government, and opposition to all forms of arbitrary authority. For Moore, in Canada, these ideals took the form of opposition to the seigneurs, both French and English, to the clergy reserves, and to any attempt at censorship by either church or state. The *Montreal Gazette* [*see* Fleury MESPLET] and the *Herald* had much in common politically, and the two papers frequently exchanged articles. In November 1789 Moore decided to print the newspaper twice a week, on Monday and on Thursday, under the title *Quebec Herald, Miscellany and Advertiser*. Although the Thursday edition ran for only two volumes, the other continued until early 1793.

In addition to his newspaper Moore published a number of works of considerable interest. His father-in-law, Hugh McKay, marshal of the Court of Vice-Admiralty, acting overseer of chimneys, and high constable, had been commissioned by the government to enumerate the male inhabitants of Quebec, and in August 1790 he printed on Moore's press the first Canadian city directory. The second directory, for the year 1791, listed 1,347 householders, but the publishing venture ceased because of inadequate demand. In 1791 Moore printed Adam Lymburner*'s *The paper read at the bar of the House of Commons . . .*, which outlined the case of the Montreal and Quebec merchants for an elected assembly. Later that year he printed the text of the Constitutional Act.

Serious financial difficulties forced Moore to stop regular publication of the *Herald* after July 1792. He noted in it that he had been "disappointed in the receipt of sundry publications" and that a "vast number of subscriptions" to the newspaper had not been paid. In June 1793 his effects were seized for non-payment of debts. He left immediately for New York, where he returned to his music hall entertainments. Later he joined the Harper Rhode Island Company in Newport, and on 3 Oct. 1793, when he had his benefit, he again delivered his *Eulogy on freemasonry*, which was printed in the *Newport Mercury*.

Moore's activities over the next four years are uncertain. In 1798 John Durang, a member of Rickett's circus, noted in his diary that he had met Moore in Quebec. He may have returned to Quebec in July of that year because of the death of Hugh McKay, but nothing further is known of him.

William Moore was one of Canada's pioneer printers. From his press came several pamphlets which have lasting historical value, and, in contrast with William BROWN's *Quebec Gazette*, which contains little local news, Moore's *Quebec Herald* gives information on the political and social life of the province. The lively correspondence column in his newspaper is of special interest. Moore was the first Canadian actor-manager, and even if there is reason to believe that his troupe could be termed only second-rate, nevertheless for two years the company played alternate seasons in Montreal and Quebec. He was also a freemason, a member of the Quebec Fire Society, and a founding member of the Quebec Benevolent Society. During the short period of seven years that he was active in Quebec, Moore made a contribution to the political life of the city through his printing, and to its social life through his theatrical entertainments and his membership in various organizations.

DOROTHY E. RYDER

ANQ-Q, État civil, Presbytériens, St Andrews (Québec) (copy at PAC). PAC, MG 24, B1, 65, 71. [John Durang], *The memoir of John Durang, American actor, 1785–1816*, ed. A. S. Downer ([Pittsburgh, Pa., 1966]). *Montreal Gazette*, 1786–93. *Port-Roseway Gazetteer and the Shelburne Advertiser* (Shelburne, N.S.), 12 May 1785. *Quebec Gazette*, 1786–98. *Quebec Herald, Miscellany and Advertiser*, 1788–93. *Royal Gazette* (Kingston, Jamaica), 6–13 July 1782. Tremaine, *Bibliography of Canadian imprints*. Æ. Fauteux, *Introduction of printing into Canada*. J. N. Ireland, *Records of the New York stage from 1750 to 1860* (2v., New York, 1866–67; repr. 1966). G. C. D. Odell, *Annals of the New York stage* (15v., New York, 1927–49). H. P. Phelps, *Players of a century: a record of the Albany stage, including notices of prominent actors who have appeared in America* (2nd ed., Albany, N.Y., 1880; repr. New York, 1972). G. O. Seilhamer, *History of the American theatre* (3v., Philadelphia, 1888–91; repr. New York, 1968). Lionel Vibert, *Rare books of freemasonry* ([London], 1923). R. [L.] Wright, *Revels in Jamaica, 1682–1838 . . .* (New York, 1937; repr. [1969]). L.-P. Desrosiers, "Le Quebec Herald," *Cahiers des Dix*, 16 (1951), 83–94. É.-Z. Massicotte, "Recherches historiques sur les spectacles à Montréal de 1760 à 1860," RSC *Trans.*, 3rd ser., XXVI (1932), sect.I, 113–22. Victor Morin, "Syndicalisme et mutualité," *Cahiers des Dix*, 24 (1959), 51–84. R. [L.] Wright, "Freemasonry on the island of Jamaica,"

American Lodge of Research (Freemasons), *Trans.* (New York), III (1938–39), 126–58.

MORIN DE FONFAY, JEAN-BAPTISTE (usually known as Morin), colonial administrator; b. *c.* 1717 at Louisbourg, Île Royale (Cape Breton Island), eldest son of Claude Morin and Madeleine Lamouraux-Rochefort; still alive in 1793.

In 1696 Claude Morin emigrated from Chinon, France, to Plaisance (Placentia, Nfld) and in 1713 moved to Île Royale. Jean-Baptiste entered the service of the Louisbourg financial commissary in 1737, acting as a clerk under André Carrerot* until the fall of the fortress in 1745. Morin then was employed by the port administration at Rochefort, France, except for a seven-month interval when he set out for Canada in the disastrous expedition of the Duc d'Anville [La Rochefoucauld*]. During his exile in France Morin married Marie-Charlotte Boschet de Saint-Martin, the daughter of a Louisbourg merchant.

On his return to Louisbourg in 1749 Morin was appointed royal notary and clerk of the Conseil Supérieur, a post he held until 1753. He was also employed in the service of the financial commissary, Jacques Prevost de La Croix. In 1752, when Prevost dismissed the storekeeper, Pierre-Jérôme Lartigue, Morin was appointed to replace him, subject to ministerial approval. The following year, Séguin, the controller and Lartigue's ally, contested Morin's nomination claiming that Morin and his brother Antoine were conniving to sell their friends' merchandise to the government. The Morins provided a few supplies between 1737 and 1757, but it is hard to say whether they were more dishonest in their methods than anyone else. The minister ordered Morin dismissed; Prevost defended him, and Intendant Bigot wrote in his support. Morin apparently answered the charges successfully because he continued as storekeeper although he never obtained the post on a permanent basis.

Whether or not he profited from his positions, Morin was prosperous enough in the 1750s to invite jealousy and incur denunciations. In 1753 an anonymous petition accused Morin and his brother, along with Jean Laborde and Nicolas Larcher, of undercutting the prices of Saint-Malo suppliers by importing foodstuffs from the American colonies. The actual extent of Morin's wealth is difficult to determine but he claimed to have invested 10,500 *livres* from savings in privateering ventures in 1757.

After the siege of 1758, in which he was wounded, Morin returned to France and fell on hard times. It was not until 1762 that he was appointed to the post of colonial storekeeper at Rochefort; even then the supervision of packing material was removed from his purview for fear that his honesty might be put to the test. This post was eliminated by an administrative reform in 1771, but he continued to work on accounts until 1773. After a short term as commissary for maritime conscription at Rochefort, he was retired in 1776 on 2,000 *livres* a year.

Morin apparently decided to re-enter the naval administration after his elder son, an officer in the colonial regular troops, then serving in Guadeloupe, got heavily in debt, and with the support of the Prince de Conti he obtained in 1781 a position again as commissary for maritime conscription, serving first at Saintes and then at Angers. In April 1783 officials discovered that Morin had misappropriated 15,000 *livres* from the invalids' pension fund to meet bills of exchange which his son had drawn on him. He was imprisoned until October 1786. In spite of supplements to his wife's pension and the placement of his younger son in the naval administration, Morin was reduced to poverty. His pleas for a pension were rejected, although in 1792 his wife's pension was raised again.

In petitions to the ministry throughout his career, the last in 1793, Morin took care to emphasize his service to the crown. He claimed that during the mutiny of 1744 he had helped Carrerot gain the troops' confidence; had seen to the provisioning of troops and inhabitants during and after the siege of 1745; and in 1749 had managed the embarkation for Louisbourg. He stressed his efficiency in reorganizing the storehouse after Lartigue's dismissal; his altruism in keeping the archives of Île Royale at his own expense after the return to La Rochelle in 1758; the dispatch with which he had supervised the expedition of 150 supply ships to the colonies in 1763–64; and his honesty in refusing to take a share in freighting them. How true were his claims? All one can say is that the government disputed only his allegations about the archives.

Despite Séguin's accusations, which apparently clouded his career, Morin seems to have been a competent administrator. He profited, like many others in the royal administration, from the vagueness of the boundary between the public and the private sectors, from advancement by influence and patronage, and from slipshod accounting procedures which encouraged the king's servants both to use royal funds in their own interest and to engage their own money in the king's service in the hope of later recompense. Like some others, Morin later became a victim of this system.

T. J. A. LE GOFF

[AN, Col., C^{8B}, f.21, and F^{2C}, 4, ff.198, 227, detail voyages made from Louisbourg to Martinique twice in 1752 and to Saint-Domingue (Hispaniola) once in 1755 by a J.-Bte. Morin (Maurin). Fortress of Louisbourg parish records and occupants files suggest that these trips could not have been made by Morin de Fonfay. A document in AN, Section Outre-mer, G^3, 2047/2, 3 juill. 1753, confirms the existence of a Jean Maurin of Saint-Domingue who died in 1753 and whose estate was executed by Morin de Fonfay's brother, Antoine. T.J.A. LE G.]

AN, Col., B, 97, f.316; 168, f.232; C^{11B}, 29, f.171; 33, ff.328, 424–25, 475; 34, f.122; 36, ff.28, 36, 145; C^{11C}, 11; 12; D^{2C}, 7, p.111; 101, p.186; E, 317 (dossier Morin, Jean-Antoine-Charles); Marine, C^2, 42, pp.48–63; 43, p.120; 45, p.317; 48, p.155; 55, f.244; C^7, 220 (dossier Morin de Fonfay, Jean-Baptiste); CC^7, dossier Morin de Fonfay; dossier Pierre-Louis-Joseph Morin; Section Outre-mer, G^1, 408; 410; G^3, 2045, 21 oct. 1757; 2047/2, 21 juill. 1752; 2055, 15 janv. 1713.

MORRIS, CHARLES, army officer, officeholder, and judge; b. 8 June 1711 in Boston, Massachusetts, eldest son of Charles Morris, a prosperous sailmaker, and Esther Rainsthorpe; m. *c.* 1731 Mary, daughter of John Read, attorney general of Massachusetts, and they had 11 children; buried 4 Nov. 1781 at Windsor, Nova Scotia.

In 1734 Charles Morris was teaching at the grammar school at Hopkinton, Massachusetts, and living with his wife on his late father's farm, but his activities from then until 1746 are unknown. In that year he was commissioned captain by Governor William Shirley to raise a company of reinforcements for the defence of Annapolis Royal, Nova Scotia [*see* Paul Mascarene*]. On 5 Dec. 1746 Morris and 100 men were ordered to march from Annapolis Royal to the Minas region (near Wolfville) as the advance guard of Colonel Arthur Noble*'s detachment. Morris was present during the battle between Noble's force and the Canadians and Indians under Nicolas-Antoine Coulon* de Villiers at Grand Pré on 31 Jan. 1746/47.

The New England reinforcements for Annapolis were ordered home to be disbanded in October 1747, but Morris and the other officers remained in service and spent the winter in Massachusetts recruiting for the Annapolis garrison. In October he had presented a memorial to Shirley stressing the need for a strong fort among the Acadians at Minas, and the governor evidently took this interest as a reason to send Morris to make a survey of the region. In the spring of 1748 Morris arrived at Annapolis; in May Mascarene, acting on Shirley's orders, sent him to survey the Minas area and a month later ordered him to do the same in the Chignecto region. With 50 men, Morris traversed the Chignecto Isthmus, and he also surveyed the Bay of Fundy, at that time "Utterly unknown to the English." During the course of the survey Morris collected from every Acadian district the number of inhabitants and the state of their settlements. Poor weather prevented him from carrying the survey along the north shore of the bay to Passamaquoddy Bay (N.B.). In February 1749 Shirley forwarded Morris' "Draught of the Bay of Fundy" and his "observations taken upon the Spot" to the Duke of Bedford, secretary of state for the Southern Department, recommending that Morris be given further employment as a surveyor in Nova Scotia.

Morris' observations, contained in a 107-page manuscript entitled "A breif survey of Nova Scotia," led Andrew Hill Clark* to identify him as Nova Scotia's first practical field geographer. The "survey" contains a "General Discription of Nova Scotia, its Natural Produce, Soil, Air, Winds etca," identifies three climatic regions, and describes the Indians. It also includes an account of the trade, husbandry, settlements, and population of the Acadians and is an important source of information about them.

In "A breif survey" Morris had recommended that a strong fort be built on the Atlantic coast to offset Louisbourg, Île Royale (Cape Breton Island), and to protect British fisheries. When Halifax was founded by CORNWALLIS in 1749, Morris became one of its first settlers, and with the assistance of John BREWSE laid out the town. On the recommendation of the Earl of Halifax, president of the Board of Trade, the governor appointed Morris "Chief Surveyor of Lands within this Province" on 25 September. In 1750 Cornwallis ordered Morris to survey the peninsula of Halifax and report on its acreage exclusive of the town and suburbs. Morris performed this task, suggesting that 240 acres be laid out as a common for firewood and later pasturage.

Morris must have been upset at how slowly the new British settlements of Halifax and Dartmouth progressed. In a report submitted in 1753 which analysed their slow rate of growth he described the new towns as garrison communities only and pointed out that many settlers, lacking employment, abandoned the colony as soon as they had expended the provision bounty. In his view, the settlements could not prosper until farmers and fishermen had migrated into the region.

In 1751 and 1752 Morris surveyed the coast from Port Rossignol (Liverpool) to the Chezzetcook region to examine possible sites for a new township which would house the "Foreign Protestants" then gathered at Halifax. Governor Peregrine Thomas Hopson* selected Mirligueche as the site because of its good harbour and at the end of April 1753 accompanied the expedition of Swiss and Germans to the region. From the first landing Morris and his assistant James Monk* Sr, with ten settlers to cut the brush, were busy laying out the new town of Lunenburg, and by 18 June he was staking individual lots. He also prepared a plan setting out the town and blockhouses and indicating existing clear land. During the summer Morris and his team laid out "garden lots" and made a tentative "Plan of Thirty Acre Farm Lotts continuous to the Town of Lunenburg," which they presented to the Council on 15 September. The actual laying out of town lots went on until the summer of 1754. Since it was impossible to make complete surveys of hundreds of lots in the heavily wooded country around Lunenburg, the surveyors ran the baselines, established the corners, and blazed enough of the dividing lines to show their courses, leaving the settlers to continue them.

Morris was appointed to the Council on 30 Dec. 1755; he was therefore not a member when it was decided in July of that year to expel the Acadians. In 1751, however, he had already made the significant suggestion that the Acadians be rooted out of the Chignecto region in his "Representation of the relative state of French and English in Nova Scotia," which he transmitted to Shirley, then leaving for England as one of the British commissioners empowered to settle the Anglo-French dispute over the boundaries of Acadia. Morris believed that the presence of the Indians and French on the north shore of the Bay of Fundy and at Chignecto made effective British settlement of the province impossible, and he recommended that the Acadians be removed "by some stratagem . . . the most effectual way is to destroy all these settlements by burning down all the houses, cutting the dykes, and destroy[g] All the Grain now growing." As the official most knowledgeable about the Acadians Morris was consulted by the Council during its deliberations on their fate. His opinions had not changed, and the Reverend Andrew Brown* found his report "little honourable to his heart . . . cruel advice and barbarous Counsel."

Morris was among the councillors who complained to the Board of Trade in March 1757 about Governor Charles Lawrence*'s delay in calling a house of assembly; he favoured settlement of the province by New Englanders and knew that immigration would not occur unless prospective settlers were guaranteed an assembly. When the first legislature met on 2 Oct. 1758, Morris and Benjamin GREEN were the Council members who swore into office the first assembly representatives.

In the spring of 1759 the movement of New Englanders to the province was in its early stages, and on 18 April agents from Connecticut and Rhode Island appeared before the Council to discuss the lands being offered [*see* John HICKS]. It was agreed that Morris would accompany them on one of the province vessels and show them the "most convenient parts of the Country to settle Townships." The Council having decided to make arrangements for a number of families to be settled at Minas, Rivière-aux-Canards (near Canard), Pisiquid (Windsor), and Grand Pré, it is apparent that Morris' knowledge of the number of Acadian families which had been supported by each district must have been invaluable. Preliminary plans were made for townships at Chignecto and Cobequid (near Truro) as well, and on 17 August the Council, basing its decisions on a map of the province prepared by Morris, divided the province into five counties.

With the capture of Quebec, further arrangements were made in the spring of 1760 for the arrival of settlers from New England. On 8 May Morris was ordered to "proceed along the Coast Westward . . . to lay out and adjust the limitts of Townships." During his voyage he visited the new town of Liverpool, where he left the inhabitants "in high spirits extremely well pleased with their Situation"; at Annapolis Royal he found 40 settlers, who had already formed a committee to lay out lots for Granville Township. At Pisiquid he discovered that the six transports which had arrived for Minas Township had "been out 21 days and suffered much for want of sufficient provender and Hay for their Stock." He asked the Council for advice about whether to send the vessels back to New London (Conn.) for more settlers and about the location of settlements in the Pisiquid region, and he requested boards to construct shelter for troops and stores. The Council left all these problems to Morris' judgement and ordered that he was to "have credit on the Treasury here or on Mr. [Thomas] Hancock in Boston for procuring lumber or paying labour as may be necessary." Morris spent the summers of 1760 to 1762 looking after the new settlements, but he attended Council meetings in winter and proposed such practical measures as the procurement of various sorts of seeds, the appropriation of £25 to buy salt for the river fisheries at Horton, Cornwallis, and Falmouth, and a further allowance of pork and flour for the settlers of Liverpool.

The new townships were up to 100,000 acres in size, and "at [the time of] the first settlement" a "Town Plot was projected and laid out by the Chief Surveyor; and the boundaries of the Whole Tract fixt." To cut and clear the lines in wilderness lands, Morris had the assistance of as many as 30 or 40 men, paid at public expense. Each township was granted in shares to a number of settlers ranging up to several hundred, and once the township boundaries were laid down, the divisions into the lots of land belonging to each settler were carried out by Morris' appointed deputies, who were paid by the owners of the lots.

On 3 Nov. 1761 Administrator Jonathan BELCHER forwarded to the Board of Trade three accurate maps prepared by Morris of places settled on Minas Basin, Cobequid Bay, and Chignecto. The following January Belcher transmitted Morris' report of new settlements and his description of several towns. The 1761 report contains a good description of the natural resouces of each township and their present and future use, and Morris' shrewd observations and comments give a picture of Nova Scotia valuable to the government of the time and to historians, geographers, and environmentalists of today. Morris also described the New England migration and pointed out that during the summer the south coast had "a good Cod Fishery," predicting that in a few years fishing would "be transferred from New England to this Coast." He also claimed that a large trade in timber could be undertaken if the British government put a duty on Baltic timber equal to the cost of freight from Nova Scotia.

In the spring and summer of 1762 Morris was busy fixing settlers in the townships of Barrington, Yarmouth, and Liverpool and making a chart of the coast from Cape Sable to Cape Negro. The following year he and Henry Newton were sent to Annapolis County to investigate land disputes and to the Saint John River (N.B.) to inform the Acadians living near Sainte-Anne (Fredericton) that they were to move to another part of the province. They also told the New England settlers living at Maugerville that their lands were reserved for military settlement. Morris and Newton supported the New Englanders, however, by writing to Joshua MAUGER, the provincial agent in London, asking him to use his influence with the Board of Trade to allow them to remain. The settlers were in fact later confirmed in possession of their lands. In the summer and autumn of 1764 Morris was sent to survey Cape Breton and St John's (Prince Edward) islands and to inquire into the nature of the soil, rivers, and harbours, but poor weather confined his efforts to Cape Breton and Canso. The next year he surveyed Passamaquoddy Bay and the Saint John River, and in 1766 he surveyed the townships of Sunbury and Gage on the Saint John.

The large-scale speculation that was taking place at this period [*see* Alexander McNutt*] resulted in some extensive grants being made, and among these were concessions of 750,000 acres on the Saint John and grants covering all of St John's Island. In 1768 Morris prepared a plan and description of the harbour of Saint John and the townships of Burton, Sunbury, Gage, and Conway, enclosing them in a letter to William Spry, one of the grantees on the river. In it he described the reversing falls, the intervales, the navigability of the river for vessels of 100 tons as far as Sainte-Anne, the spring flooding, and the yield of the region. He later recommended that at least 25 miles on each side of the river be reserved to the crown in order to provide pine timber as masts for the Royal Navy.

St John's Island had been surveyed by Captain Samuel Jan Holland* in 1765–66, but no surveyor had laid out lots for prospective settlers. Accordingly, when Lieutenant Governor Michael FRANCKLIN drew up plans for the administration of the island in 1768, he ordered Morris to make further surveys. Morris was absent from May to October laying out "the ground on which the town of Charlotte Town" and other settlements were to be built. On his way home he was directed to inquire how "the lands in the Township of Truro, Onslow and Londonderry have been occupied." In June 1769 Morris was instructed by Governor Lord William CAMPBELL "to go from Hence to New York to settle the Limits and boundaries of the Governments of New York and the New Jerseys." He was away for about a year completing this task, which appears to have been his last major surveying job, since he was never absent long enough from Council meetings thereafter to have undertaken other such work.

By the 1770s, inflation and the expense caused by new methods of granting land had made the salary and fees of the surveyor general's office increasingly inadequate. By the new land instructions, a particular survey of each lot as well as the general survey of the whole tract had to be carried out at the expense of the surveyor general, "as no provision beforehand is made which was previously defrayed by govt or by grantees." Morris' son Charles* estimated in 1772 that from 1749 to 1771 his father had spent over £2,500 of his personal fortune on surveying expenses such as equipment and instruments which had not been paid by the government and, since the fees of the office averaged only £15 per annum, requested that a yearly increase be added from the parliamentary grant. The British government refused the request, but it agreed that Morris should be paid a certain sum for each 100 acres surveyed, the rate being left to the governor's discretion. Governor Francis LEGGE supported Morris' attempts to obtain more pay, and the Morris family remained loyal to Legge during his difficulties with the Council and merchants. Morris did not sign the Council's petition to the king against Legge.

Morris was appointed a justice of the peace for the town and county of Halifax in December 1750 and a justice of the Inferior Court of Common Pleas for that jurisdiction in March 1752. When a memorial submitted to the Council in January 1753 accused the justices of favouring Massachusetts law and practice over those of England, Morris asserted that his decisions were based upon "the constant Practices in the Court here and in England." Although the justices were renominated by Hopson, the dissatisfaction influenced the governor's decision to ask for a chief justice, and in 1754 a person with legal qualifications presided in the courts of Nova Scotia for the first time when Belcher became chief justice.

In 1763 the assembly presented an address to Lieutenant Governor Montagu Wilmot* urging, among other things, the appointment of two assistant judges to the chief justice. John Collier* and Morris were appointed the next year, receiving salaries of £100 a year. Belcher drafted his subordinates' commissions so narrowly, however, that Collier and Morris could try a case only in conjunction with the chief justice, and they could not even open or adjourn court without his presence and assent. The result was that Belcher could and did ignore them. Richard GIBBONS described a case in which Belcher invited his assistants to address the jury. The chief justice then recapitulated the evidence, gave his own altogether different opinion, and instructed the jury to find the verdict as he had advised. Morris was appointed master in the Court of Chancery on 12 May 1764. In that court "Suitors . . . have been so poor, that the Masters have given their Attendance & trouble for nothing."

After Belcher's death in March 1776, Legge appointed Morris, as senior assistant judge, to be chief justice until the British government decided upon a permanent appointment. Most of the civil cases tried before Morris were for debt and trespass, and it is evident he had learned considerable law by listening to Belcher. He also presided over criminal cases for larceny, counterfeit, and murder, the trial of Malachy SALTER for seditious conversation, and the treason trials of those persons involved in Jonathan Eddy*'s rebellion in Cumberland County. On 15 April 1778 Bryan Finucane took over as chief justice and Morris reverted to the position of first assistant judge of the Supreme Court, a position he held until his death. It was in this role as judge that Morris and his family took the most pride, regarding it as a position of prestige.

The Morris family had the reputation in Nova Scotia of being good administrators and surveyors. Charles Morris was surveyor general of lands for the province for 32 years, a period which saw the founding of Halifax and Lunenburg and the coming of the pre-loyalists, when the colony's foundations were laid. The Council had every confidence in his decisions and actions, and the chronicler of 18th-century Nova Scotia, John Bartlet Brebner*, praised him for his honest impartiality. Indeed, in spite of the difficulties of these early years of the colony, Charles Morris was "a faithfull Servant of the Crown."

PHYLLIS R. BLAKELEY

[The BL and the archives of the Ministry of Defence, Hydrographer of the Navy in Taunton, Eng., hold plans by Morris, but since he did not sign all his work, there are complications in identification. There are numerous map references in G.B., PRO, *Maps and plans in the Public Record Office* (2v. to date, London, 1967–), II. PRO, CO 221/38 "is composed of various survey plans, descriptions and notes prepared by Charles Morris" (mfm. at PAC). Some of the PAC holdings are listed in its *Report* of 1912.

A number of Morris' works have been published: "Judge Morris' remarks concerning the removal of the Acadians," N.S. Hist. Soc., *Coll.*, II (1881), 158–60; "Observations and remarks on the survey made by order of His Excellency according to the instructions of the 26th June last, on the eastern coasts of Nova Scotia and the western parts of the island of Cape Breton," PANS *Report* (Halifax), 1964, app.B, 20–28; "The St. John River: description of the harbour and river of St. John's in Nova Scotia, and of the townships of Sunbury, Burton, Gage, and Conway, lying on said river . . . dated 25th Jan. 1768," *Acadiensis* (Saint John, N.B.), III (1903), 120–28. His joint report with Richard Bulkeley, "State and condition of the province of Nova Scotia together with some observations &c, 29th October 1763," is in PANS *Report*, 1933, app.B, 21–27. P.R.B.]

Halifax County Court of Probate (Halifax), M154 (will of Charles Morris) (mfm. at PANS). PAC, MG 23, Fl, ser.5, 3, ff.421–61 (mfm. at PANS). PANS, RG 1, 29, no.4; 35; 36; 37, nos.18, 20; 39, nos.37–47, 62–63; 163/2, p.54; 164/1, pp.16–18, 33, 48–53, 73–75, 85; 164/2, pp.89–95, 260, 277, 302–4, 315; 165, pp.58–59, 229, 269; 166; 166A; 167; 168, pp.458–60; 169, p.6; 170, p.21; 209, 3 Jan., 29 Dec. 1752, 9 Jan., 5 March 1753; 210; 211, 18 April, 17 May, 17 Aug. 1759, 5 June 1760, 16 Feb., 14 April, 15, 22 May 1761; 212, 22 Oct. 1768, 16 June 1769, 19 Sept. 1770; 359; 361; 363, nos.34, 35, 38; 374; RG 39, J, Books 1, 6; 117. PRO, CO 217/19, ff.290–97; 217/20, ff.43–50; 217/29, f.49; 217/50, ff.85–87, 91–94; 217/51, ff.51–52, 59–61, 70–73, 190–93; 217/52, ff.116–17; 217/55, ff.196–99. Royal Artillery Institution, Old Royal Military Academy (Woolwich, Eng.), "A breif survey of Nova Scotia, with an account of the several attempts of the French this war to recover it out of the hands of the English." St Paul's Anglican Church (Halifax), Registers for Windsor–Falmouth–Newport, 1774–95, 4 Nov. 1781 (mfm. at PANS).

Boston, Mass., Registry Dept., *Records relating to the early history of Boston*, ed. W. H. Whitmore *et al.* (39v., Boston, 1876–1909), [24]: *Boston births, 1700–1800*, 76. PAC *Report*, 1904, app.F, 289–300; 1912, app.H. "Trials for treason in 1776–7," N.S. Hist. Soc., *Coll.*, I (1878), 110–18. PAC, *Catalogue of maps, plans and charts in the map room of the Dominion Archives* (Ottawa, 1912). Bell, *Foreign Protestants*, 104n, 237n, 331n, 408, 425–26, 428, 446, 468–74, 569–75. Brebner, *Neutral Yankees* (1937), 82–84, 90–91, 95–96; *New England's outpost*, 131, 234–50, 254. Clark, *Acadia*, 189n, 344n. Raymond, *River St. John* (1910), 277–78, 353, 375–76, 473–79. Ethel Crathorne, "The Morris family – surveyors-general," *Nova Scotia Hist. Quarterly* (Halifax), 6 (1976), 207–16. A. W. H. Eaton, "Eminent Nova Scotians of New England birth, number one: Capt. the Hon. Charles Morris, M.C.," *New England Hist. and Geneal. Register*, LXVII (1913), 287–90. Margaret Ells, "Clearing the decks for the loyalists," CHA *Report*, 1933, 43–58. W. F. Ganong, "A monograph of the cartography of the province of New Brunswick," RSC *Trans.*, 2nd ser., III (1897), sect.II, 313–425. R. J. Milgate, "Land development in Nova Scotia," *Canadian Surveyor, special edition; proceedings of the thirty-ninth annual meeting of the Canadian Institute of Surveying . . . 1946* ([Ottawa, 1946]), 40–52; "Surveys in Nova Scotia," *Canadian Surveyor* (Ottawa), VIII (1943–46), no.10, 11–14.

MOUET DE LANGLADE, CHARLES-MICHEL, fur-trader, officer in the colonial regular troops, and Indian department employee; baptized 9 May 1729 at Michilimackinac (Mackinaw City, Mich.), son of Augustin Mouet de Langlade, a prominent trader, and Domitilde, sister of NISSOWAQUET; m. 12 Aug. 1754 at Michilimackinac Charlotte-Ambroisine, daughter of René BOURASSA, *dit* La Ronde, and they had two daughters; he also had a son Charles by an earlier liaison with an Ottawa woman; d. during the winter of 1800–1 at La Baye (Green Bay, Wis.).

Throughout his long active career Charles-Michel Mouet de Langlade was known for his influence with the Indians. His authority derived from his relationship to Nissowaquet, an important chief, from his personal qualities, and from an incident during his childhood. As a ten-year-old boy he had accompanied Nissowaquet on a successful attack against the Chickasaws. The Ottawas, who had twice previously been defeated, decided that a special protecting spirit must dwell with him.

By 1750 Langlade was a cadet in the colonial regulars. His first recorded military exploit occurred in 1752 at Pickawillany (Piqua, Ohio). The British and the French were in bitter competition for control of the Ohio valley and its native population. When Pierre-Joseph Céloron* de Blainville was unable to persuade the Miamis under Memeskia (La Demoiselle) to move from Pickawillany, which was within the British sphere of influence, Langlade was sent there with a force of perhaps 300 Indians and French. Attacking on 21 June when most of the Miamis were away hunting, Langlade forced the remaining few and the British traders present to surrender. Memeskia was boiled and eaten. Governor DUQUESNE wrote of Langlade: "He is acknowledged here to be very brave, to have much influence on the minds of the Indians, and to be very zealous when ordered to do anything."

Promoted ensign on 15 March 1755, Langlade was active in the Seven Years' War. He claimed to have planned the ambush that led to Jean-Daniel DUMAS's defeat of Edward Braddock near Fort Duquesne (Pittsburgh, Pa) in 1755. In August 1756 he and his Indian followers returned to Fort Duquesne as scouts. They remained in the east during the winter and on 21 Jan. 1757 were part of a force which successfully ambushed Robert ROGERS and his rangers near Fort Carillon (Ticonderoga, N.Y.). Langlade was by this time an ensign on half pay. While serving under Montcalm* during the siege of Fort William Henry (also known as Fort George, now Lake George, N.Y.) that summer, he was instrumental in capturing a British flotilla. In September 1757 Governor Vaudreuil [RIGAUD] made him second in command at Michilimackinac. Langlade was present at the siege of Quebec two years later. If the reinforcements he had requested of LÉVIS had arrived in time, he and his Indians might have destroyed the detachment Wolfe* took to reconnoitre up the Montmorency River on 26 July. Instead, both sides withdrew after a brief skirmish. In 1760 Langlade came from Michilimackinac to Montreal, where he learned he had been promoted lieutenant on half pay. Ordered to leave the city just before its surrender, he returned to Michilimackinac where he held command until the British arrived in September 1761.

Langlade's time had not, however, been exclusively taken up by military service. In October 1755 he had been ordered by the commandant at Michilimackinac to establish a trading post at the mouth of the Grand River (Grand Haven, Mich.) and to use it to help maintain control of the Ottawas and Potawatomis along the western shore of Lake Michigan. Langlade continued to do his winter trading at this site through 1790, having as many as 15 men working for him.

Like many residents of Michilimackinac, Langlade appears to have adjusted to British rule with little difficulty. When in 1763 he heard rumours of an Ojibwa uprising he warned the commandant, George Etherington. Etherington did not listen, however, and the Ojibwas under Madjeckewiss* seized the fort. Langlade, at great risk to his life, rescued Etherington and William Leslye from the stake where they were to be sacrificed. He has been criticized for refusing refuge in his home to Alexander Henry* the elder. Langlade was unwilling to hazard the safety of his family but he did see to it that Henry was saved, and with his help and that of his Ottawa relatives the survivors of the attack were eventually taken to Montreal. Langlade took command of the fort until the British presence was reasserted the next year. He then moved his permanent home to La Baye, where his father was already living.

Early in the American revolution Governor Guy Carleton* referred to Langlade, by then a captain in the Indian department, as "a man I have had every reason to be very much satisfied with and who from his influence among the Indians of that district may be very much use." After bringing Indians to help defend Montreal in 1776 Langlade, with Luc de LA CORNE, joined BURGOYNE in the summer of 1777. Although many of Burgoyne's Indians left, Langlade and his Ottawa followers stayed until the attack on Bennington (Vt). When Langlade returned to the west from Montreal in the fall of 1778 he was called upon to gather an Indian force to assist Henry HAMILTON against rebel sympathizers at Vincennes (Ind.). Unsuccessful in the fall because the Indians had gone to their winter hunting grounds, Langlade collected a force in the spring. The Indians refused to move, however, when they heard that Hamilton had been captured by George Rogers Clark. Clark sent an agent, Daniel-Maurice GODEFROY de Linctot, to destroy Langlade's influence with the Indians but Langlade and his nephew, Charles Gautier de Verville, used generous gifts to maintain their support. In 1780 Langlade took an Indian force into the Illinois country to assist in the attack on Spanish St Louis (Mo.) but was chased back to Lake Michigan by Linctot's horsemen [*see* Wahpasha*].

After the war Langlade continued to serve in the Indian department. He received goods that Gautier had embezzled from the British storehouse on Mackinac Island, but although Gautier was discovered and dismissed from his post as storekeeper and interpreter in 1793 Langlade retained his position. He remained active until his death and enjoyed telling about 99 battles in which he had participated. A companion, recalling Langlade's actions, said he "never saw so perfectly cool and fearless a man on the field of battle."

PAUL TRAP

AN, Col., C[11A], 98, p.27 (transcript at PAC). Newberry Library (Chicago), Edward E. Ayer coll., MSS 490, 810. PAC, MG 25, 186; RG 10, A2, 1824, pp.107–14, 487–93; 1828, pp.8021–24. Wis., State Hist. Soc. (Madison), Benjamin Sulte, "Origines de Langlade."

Bougainville, *Adventure in wilderness* (Hamilton), 81–82. John Burgoyne, *A state of the expedition from Canada . . .* (London, 1780; repr. New York, 1969), app.VIII, xxxvi–xxxix. [A. S. De Peyster], *Miscellanies, by an officer*, ed. J. W. De Peyster ([2nd ed.], 2v. in 1, New York, 1888), 4–15. Henry, *Travels and adventures. John Askin papers* (Quaife), I, 136–37, 352–53. [James Johnstone, known as Chevalier de Johnstone], "A dialogue in Hades," Literary and Hist. Soc. of Quebec, *Manuscripts relating to the early history of Canada* (Quebec, 1868; repr. 1927), 12–18. John Long, *Voyages and travels of an Indian interpreter and trader . . .* (London, 1791; repr. New York, 1968, and Toronto, 1971), 148, 151. *Michigan Pioneer Coll.*, VIII (1885), 367–68, 466–67; IX (1886), 361–63, 371–73, 377–78, 380–81, 383–86, 392, 545–46, 558–60; X (1886), 270–71, 275–78, 372–73; XI (1887), 419; XII (1887), 42; XV (1889), 112–13; XIX (1891), 366, 411, 425–26, 448–49, 455–56; XX (1892), 668–69; XXVII (1896), 631–32, 665–70. *NYCD* (O'Callaghan and Fernow), X, 245–51, 303–4, 591–621. Wis., State Hist. Soc., *Coll.*, I (1855), 39; III (1857), 195–295; VIII (1879), 209–23, 227–30; XI (1888), 97–125; XII (1892), 39–41, 44–46, 97–99; XVIII (1908), 128–31, 135–40, 149, 163, 209–11, 253–58, 278–79, 355–56, 371–74, 391, 403–4, 406–8, 415, 417–19, 443–46, 462–68, 475, 481–82, 484, 486, 493–95; XIX (1910), 3, 5, 9, 29, 37, 44, 48, 51, 54–56, 62–63, 80, 82, 88–89, 299–300.

MOULTON, EBENEZER, Baptist minister; b. 25 Dec. 1709 in Windham, Connecticut, son of Robert Moulton and Hannah Grove; m. the widow of John Bound; d. in March 1783 at South Brimfield (Wales, Mass.).

A leader in the establishment of the first Baptist church at South Brimfield in 1736, Ebenezer Moulton was ordained its pastor on 4 Nov. 1741. Since he received little financial support from the congregation, he also engaged in "merchandizing." In 1761, apparently to escape his creditors, he sailed to Nova Scotia, where he became an itinerant preacher to the scattered fishing settlements along the southern shore of the colony. Most of his activity was concentrated in the Yarmouth area; he was the first minister to preach to the pre-loyalist settlers there. He received a land grant and established a residence at Cape Fourchu. A member in 1761 of the committee to divide lands in and admit settlers to Yarmouth Township, in the same year he was authorized to administer the oath of office to justices of the peace. Economic conditions were so difficult that Moulton could not expect regular remuneration for his clerical services; for ten years he remained an itinerant preacher, occasionally travelling as far as Horton (Wolfville region) and Cornwallis. In the early and middle 1760s he was the most important preacher in the Yarmouth area, and many who were not of the Baptist faith attended his sermons and sought his help for baptism and marriage.

In the late 1760s Moulton became embroiled, to his own disadvantage, in local religious controversies. His position was ambiguous. Nearly all those who were active in church affairs in Yarmouth were non-separating New Light Congregationalists, and Moulton attracted support through his evangelical style of preaching. Because he was a Baptist, however, his position was weak, for the New Lights had no wish to seem disloyal to their church. His ambivalent status brought him into conflict with the two other preachers in the community, John Frost and Jonathan Scott*, both of whom became Congregationalist ministers. In 1769, when the church at Chebogue ordained Frost as its minister, Moulton was not asked for advice or assistance, even though he was the only other prominent preacher in the region. In the following year, Scott, who had succeeded Frost as Congregationalist preacher, refused to use the same meeting house as Moulton. On one Sunday before public worship began, Scott openly criticized Moulton, led a large part of the congregation out of the meeting house, and left Moulton with only the rump to be edified by his preaching. That Scott had willingly listened to Moulton's preaching in the mid 1760s and had actually requested Moulton to perform his marriage ceremony in 1768 gives some indication of the bitter, personal nature of local religious disputes.

By the spring of 1771 Moulton had lost most of his support and he ceased preaching. After a decade of religious service to the Yarmouth area he was left without a following and without a role. He returned to South Brimfield, having apparently obtained letters of licence from his creditors, and died there 12 years later.

GORDON STEWART

PANS, MG 4, no.12 ("The records of the church of Jebogue in Yarmouth . . ."). Isaac Backus, *A history of New England with particular reference to the denomination of Christians called Baptists*, ed. David Weston (2nd ed., 2v., Newton, Mass., 1871; repr. 2v. in 1, New York, 1969). [Jonathan Scott], *The life of Jonathan Scott*, ed. C. B. Fergusson (Halifax, 1960). M. W. Armstrong, *The Great Awakening in Nova Scotia, 1776–1809* (Hartford, Conn., 1948). I. F. Mackinnon, *Settlements and churches in Nova Scotia, 1749–1776* ([Montreal, 1930]). Gordon Stewart and G. [A.] Rawlyk, *A people highly favoured of God: the Nova Scotia Yankees and the American revolution* (Toronto, 1972). M. W. Armstrong, "'Elder Moulton' and the Nova Scotia Baptists," *Dal. Rev.*, XXIV (1944–45), 320–23.

MOUNIER, JEAN-MATHIEU, merchant; baptized 2 Oct. 1715 at the parish church of Saint-Pierre in Jarnac, near Cognac, France, son of Adam Mounier and Suzanne Liard; d. in or after 1774.

Jean-Mathieu Mounier was born into a large scattered family of Huguenots with connections at Cognac, Saint-Maixent (Saint-Maixent-l'École), La Rochelle, Limoges, and elsewhere. He lived at Quebec from 1736 to 1758 as a wholesale importer in association with various Huguenot firms of La Rochelle and Bordeaux, especially the brothers Jean and Pierre Veyssière, originally from Limoges, with whom he was linked in a partnership. Bills of lading for shipments in the years 1744 to 1756 show that Mounier imported shoes and other leather goods, guns, mirrors, paper, cotton, draperies from Montauban, soap, oil, and, of course, wine and brandy. During those years he was joined in Quebec by several Huguenot relations who were also in business: three nephews, Henry, Jean, and François* Mounier; and two cousins, Pierre Glemet and François Maurin*, both of Jarnac. By the Seven Years' War, Jean-Mathieu Mounier had a considerable reputation and was the agent to whom Pierre-François Goossens, a Paris merchant banker and shipping agent, addressed three shiploads of food sent for the crown from Dunkerque in 1758.

In that year Jean-Mathieu Mounier returned to

France by way of Spain and soon bought various properties at La Rochelle, including a house on the Place d'Armes for 15,000 *livres* where he lived with an English maid and a black slave. With a fortune of 300,000 *livres* gathered in trade at Quebec, he intended to continue trading to Canada but these hopes were dashed by the British conquest and after various efforts to establish himself he went bankrupt in 1773. His bankruptcy was due in part to the French government's cunning manipulation of the Canadian bills after its own financial failure in autumn 1759, and in part to the bankruptcies of his cousin, Pierre Glemet, and two of his brothers, Michel Mounier in Cognac and Jean Mounier in Limoges.

It is only fair to add that Mounier did not share the single-minded devotion to business usual in French merchants of his time. He bought maps, microscopes, telescopes, and other scientific equipment and gathered a library of some 1,500 works on Newtonian science, astronomy, physics, mechanics, navigation, agriculture, history, and so on. At his bankruptcy, when these books were put up for sale, they were estimated to be worth 8,633 *livres*. Mounier also travelled a great deal in France during the 1760s and spent two years in Paris where he took an interest in the intellectual life of the time. He had business dealings meanwhile with the Paris banker Louis Jullien, and with various merchants of Quebec, Montreal, and the West Indies, but the character and extent of these affairs are difficult to assess, and the bankruptcy of 1773 shows what they all came to. He reported to his assembled creditors, in a balance sheet of 8 Nov. 1773 entitled "État à Peu Près de mes Malheureuses Affaires": "The habit of useless, frivolous spending, purely for pleasure, so easily adopted in comfortable circumstances such as I enjoyed before my reversal of fortune: this is, I believe, the only thing for which I need reproach myself. By useless spending I mean all which has dissipation as its object, and occasions for it are unfortunately only too frequent. Among them are the theatre, the ball, the country party, and the little games of polite society. With these I rank also the expenses occasioned by my experiments in physics and agriculture etc. These last are perhaps more excusable. I took them up because of the idleness forced upon me by my overwhelming losses of the last few years which took from me all means for trading enterprises, after the loss of Canada on which I had founded all my hopes."

Mounier was a prominent member of the Huguenot merchant group so important in Canadian trade during the 1750s; like others, he went bankrupt after the loss of the colony, either because he was unable to turn his hand to any other business once back in France or because all his funds were lost during the war or tied up in the ill-fated Canadian bills. But Mounier was not typical in his intellectual pursuits.

J. F. BOSHER

AD, Charente-Maritime (La Rochelle), B, 1754 (Mounier's seals dated from 21 Oct. 1773 to 15 Jan. 1774); 1757 (Mounier's bankruptcy balance sheet signed 8 Nov. 1773 and turned in to the authorities on 28 Jan. 1774); Minutes Fleury (La Rochelle), 14 janv. 1774 (Mounier's inventory including a catalogue of his books). Archives municipales, Jarnac (dép. de la Charente, France), État civil, Saint-Pierre, 2 oct. 1715. PRO, HCA 32/253, *Vainqueur* (including several letters by and to members of the Mounier family). J. F. Bosher, "French Protestant families in Canadian trade, 1740–1760," *Social History*, VII (1974), 179–201.

MUNRO, JOHN, soldier, merchant, and office-holder; b. 1728 at Fyrish, parish of Alness (Highlands), Scotland, son of Hugh Munro; m. 5 April 1760 Mary Brower, in Schenectady, New York, and they had eight children; d. 27 Oct. 1800 at Dickinson's Landing (probably Long Sault, Ont.).

John Munro, a soldier in the 48th Foot, came to America in 1756 and served in the Seven Years' War, after which he was granted land as a disbanded soldier and settled in the province of New York. He became a merchant-trader in Albany and quickly prospered. He acquired land holdings of over 11,000 acres and about 1765 he moved to an estate near Bennington (Vt), where he farmed and operated mills, a pot and pearl ashery, and a nail factory. Munro was an elder of the "English Presbyterian Church" in Albany, and as a magistrate of Albany County he was actively involved in the dispute between New York and New Hampshire over the ownership and jurisdiction of the "Hampshire grants" (now Vermont).

Since Munro was a prominent Tory, his family and property were harassed in the pre-revolutionary period, and he was twice imprisoned by the rebel forces. From 1776 to 1784 he served under Sir John Johnson* as a captain in the 1st battalion King's Royal Regiment of New York and among other services led a successful raid on Ballston (Ballston Spa, N.Y.) in October 1780 and commanded the garrison at Coteau-du-Lac (Que.) in 1781. In 1783, at HALDIMAND's request, he undertook a tour of exploration from Quebec to Halifax via the Témiscouata route on behalf of a group of loyalists who had obtained land in Nova Scotia. Munro reported on the route and on the suitability of lands in Nova Scotia and present-day New Brunswick.

John Munro was placed on half pay in 1784 and settled that year with his company in what became the Luneburg District of Upper Canada. From 1784 to 1787 he was in England, supporting himself and his family in Canada on borrowed money while trying to get adequate compensation for the loss of his New York property, whose worth he estimated at more than £10,000. He eventually received less than £300 and returned to Canada disillusioned and nearly penniless. He was, however, rewarded in other ways. In 1788 he was made sheriff and a member of the land board of the Luneburg District. He built and operated grist- and sawmills on the St Lawrence River as early as 1791. Munro was one of a number of loyalist leaders who were granted townships for settlement in 1792 and 1793. Although these grants were later rescinded, Munro and his family were given large amounts of land in Matilda Township and elsewhere in the Eastern District. He was an original member of the Legislative Council of Upper Canada, appointed 12 July 1792, and in December of that year he became a justice of the district Court of Common Pleas. Munro also held a number of minor or temporary posts. He was a magistrate of the Eastern District; in 1794 he served as one of the commissioners who conferred with representatives from Lower Canada on the division of customs duties in an attempt to secure for Upper Canada a share of the revenue from goods destined for that province. In 1797 he served on the Heir and Devisee Commission, which was established to hear claims to loyalist grants which had passed out of the hands of the original grantees. Munro was a conscientious legislator and judge but his public career was notable mainly for unswerving loyalty to authority. In 1794 he had voted, at Lieutenant Governor Simcoe*'s request, for the abolition of the Court of Common Pleas, as part of Simcoe's attempt to make the legal system of Upper Canada more like that of Great Britain.

Munro had acquired land and offices in Upper Canada, but he never regained the affluence he had enjoyed before the American revolution and he died in relatively modest circumstances.

J. K. JOHNSON

BL, Add. MSS 21779, 21826–29. DPL, Burton hist. coll., John Munro papers (copies at PAO). PAC, MG 24, A6; RG 1, L3, 150, 177, 327, 328, 331; RG 68, General index, 1651–1841. PRO, AO 12/21, 12/101, 13/56 (copies at PAC). [Patrick Campbell], *Travels in the interior inhabited parts of North America in the years 1791 and 1792*, ed. H. H. Langton and W. F. Ganong (Toronto, 1937). [François Daniel], *Nos gloires nationales; ou, histoire des principales familles du Canada . . .* (2v., Montréal, 1867), II, 48. [A.] E. Ryerson, *The loyalists of America and their times: from 1620 to 1816* (2nd ed., 2v., Toronto, 1880), II, 261–64. Grant Carr-Harris, "Ancestry of Captain, the Honourable, John Munro (1728–1800)," *Families* (Toronto), 16 (1977), 71–84. E. A. Cruikshank, "The King's Royal Regiment of New York," *OH*, XXVII (1931), 193–323.

MUQUINNA (Macuina, Maquilla, Maquinna), Nootka chief on the west coast of what is now Vancouver Island, B.C.; the name, written $muk^{w}ina$ in proper native orthography, means possessor of pebbles; he apparently was active as early as 1778 and probably died in 1795.

Muquinna was the name of a series of ranking chiefs of the Moachat group of Nootka Indians. This group had its most important summer village at Yuquot, at the mouth of Nootka Sound, and its winter village at Tahsis. Although it is not absolutely certain, there is evidence that the subject of this biography assumed leadership on the death of his father, Anapā, in 1778 and that he died in 1795, to be succeeded by another chief with the same name. Muquinna's leadership among the Nootka Indians coincided with the early years of contact with Europeans on the northwest coast and with the development of a maritime fur trade. This same period was one of rivalry between Britain and Spain on the coast in which the Indians became involved. In fact, most of what we know about Muquinna is related in or must be inferred from the journals of European explorers and fur-traders.

Although the Spanish navigator Juan Josef PÉREZ Hernández was in the Nootka Sound area in 1774, the first extended contact between Nootka Indians and Europeans came in 1778 when Captain James COOK spent nearly a month at Ship Cove (Resolution Cove) refitting his ships. It is quite possible that the Indian leader, not named by Cook, who held many discussions and arranged transactions with him was Muquinna. Friendly trading relations were established with the people of Yuquot, and a variety of items changed hands, including sea otter pelts, which Cook's crews later traded at great profit in Canton (People's Republic of China). The publication of the journals of Cook's third voyage revealed the profits to be made in a maritime fur trade with China. From its beginning Nootka Sound was a popular port of call for traders, and it soon became an important centre of the trade. Muquinna emerges as the dominant Indian leader at the sound.

Muquinna

The first expedition to the northwest coast after Cook's was that of James HANNA in 1785. In August Muquinna led an unsuccessful attack on his ship; a later Spanish account records him as saying it was provoked by a practical joke Hanna played on him. Initially most of the trading ships that called at Nootka Sound were British, but in the following years American vessels, mainly out of Boston, increasingly dominated. Muquinna traded with the British captain John Meares* in 1788 and allowed him to erect a small building on some land at Yuquot, an action that was later to embroil his people in international politics. Meares describes Muquinna as "of a middle size, but extremely well made, and possessing a countenance that was formed to interest all who saw him."

The developing intensity of the maritime fur trade placed Muquinna in a strategic position. Astute Indian leaders like him could exercise a great deal of control over the trade and mould it to serve their own ends. Those who had the good fortune to be in the right place at the right time, and were sagacious enough to use their situation, became extremely wealthy as a result.

On the one side, Muquinna was able to take advantage of the popularity of Nootka Sound to manipulate competition between traders which forced prices upwards. On the other side, he was able to regulate the activities of other Indians in the area. From the time of Cook's visit it was apparent the people of Yuquot were attempting to control contacts between Europeans and other Indian groups, a pattern consolidated under Muquinna's leadership as he endeavoured to ensure that all furs traded at Nootka passed through his hands, or, at least, through those of his people. By 1792 he controlled a trading network with the Kwakiutl group at the mouth of the Nimpkish River (on the east coast of Vancouver Island); his agents used the well-established trade routes to cross the island and purchase furs which were then sold to crews visiting Nootka. Like the European captains, Muquinna knew a good deal about price differentials, and the trader John Hoskins reports that his profits as a broker were considerable.

Meanwhile, however, international rivalries had begun to create problems for Muquinna and his people. Spain, dismayed by the number of British vessels now off the Pacific coast to which she had long laid claim, had sent a frigate north in 1789. Muquinna had seen it arrive in May at Nootka under the command of Esteban José MARTÍNEZ, who claimed the sound for Charles III. When Martínez arrested the trader James Colnett* for infringing on Spanish sovereignty, the threat to a profitable trade was felt by the Indians. On 13 July Muquinna's brother, Callicum, paddled out to berate the Spanish, only to be shot dead by a seaman. Muquinna thereupon moved to Opitsat, the village of WIKINANISH, Callicum's father-in-law, in Clayoquot Sound. Indian rivalries, however, required him to watch events at Yuquot closely, and when a rival visited Martínez on 1 August, Muquinna also came for a visit. He was at Yuquot again on 1 September and promised Martínez, then departing, to take care of the buildings in the small post he had established.

Much more was seen of the Spaniards in 1790. Madrid having decided to reoccupy Nootka Sound, a force under Francisco de Eliza* y Reventa arrived at Yuquot in April and began to build a small settlement. The Nootka Indians, suspicious of the Spaniards, tended to avoid the cove, and their fears were not allayed by Eliza's plunder of a local village for planks. In June Muquinna encountered an exploring mission under Manuel Quimper at Opitsat and was reassured enough that in October he helped search for survivors of a shipwreck. But Colnett arrived at Yuquot in January 1791 and before he departed on 2 March tried to win Muquinna to the British cause; Muquinna asked "to see a larger ship." He had to keep on good terms with the Spaniards, for Eliza, having heard about ritual cannibalism, had threatened to destroy his village if the act were repeated. Muquinna remained at Tahsis, and when Alexandro Malaspina* visited there in August, he ratified the cession to the Spanish of land at Yuquot made in 1790.

Spain and Britain were on the brink of war in 1790 following Martínez' seizure of Colnett in 1789 and Meares's claim to own by purchase the land now occupied by the Spanish at Yuquot. The quarrel was eventually settled by the diplomatic action of the Nootka Conventions. When in 1792 Juan Francisco de la BODEGA y Quadra arrived at Yuquot to arrange application of the terms, Muquinna struck up a close relationship with him and was his frequent dinner guest. Bodega became convinced, partly by Muquinna's testimony, that Meares's claim to all Yuquot was unfounded, and when George VANCOUVER arrived in August to repossess Meares's land, Muquinna found himself fêted by both sides during the negotiations. He proved adept in the art of diplomacy, entertaining the foreign emissaries at Tahsis. When Bodega left Nootka Sound in September, Yuquot was still in Spanish hands, and only in March 1795, after further negotiations between Spain and Britain, did the Europeans abandon the sound. Muquinna's people soon tore down the buildings and reasserted their dominance over the area they had earlier abandoned; in September a visitor, Charles Bishop*, reported an Indian village stood at Yuquot. Muquinna was said to be "very ill of an ague," and a few weeks later Bishop was told by Wikinanish at Clayoquot Sound that he had died.

Muquinna was a Nootka chief in the traditional sense but also a leader whose role was changing with the impact of the Europeans. He had almost certainly attained his position of leadership at the time of Cook's visit by traditional Indian usages and validated it by potlatching as had his predecessors. But since the measure of a leader's influence and prestige was largely the wealth that passed through his hands, his position was enhanced by the profits he acquired through the control of trade with foreign visitors and exploitation of existing trading relationships with other Indian groups. Thus he probably became more powerful through the fur trade than he might otherwise have done, and this new power of Muquinna and his people was expressed in their relations with other groups in the Nootka Sound area. Nevertheless it is possible that his position was exaggerated in the journals of European visitors simply because Nootka was so important to them at this time; perhaps Muquinna's neighbour and intermittent ally, Wikinanish, the Clayoquot leader, was more powerful. Neither, however, was the kind of ruler ship captains tended to suppose: they led by influence rather than by authority and by prestige rather than power [*see* KOYAH]. There is no doubt, however, that Muquinna was one of the most important Indian leaders in the area during the early contact period, and his role in this phase of northwest coast history is as significant as that of any of the Europeans who sailed into Nootka Sound.

ROBIN A. FISHER

The journal and letters of Captain Charles Bishop on the north-west coast of America, in the Pacific and in New South Wales, 1794–1799, ed. and intro. Michael Roe (Cambridge, Eng., 1967). *Journals of Captain James Cook* (Beaglehole), III. Meares, *Voyages*. J. M. Moziño Suárez de Figueroa, *Noticias de Nutka; an account of Nootka Sound in 1792*, trans. and ed. I. H. Wilson (Seattle; Wash., 1970). G. Vancouver, *Voyage of discovery* (J. Vancouver). *Voyages of 'Columbia'* (Howay). Cook, *Flood tide of empire*. Philip Drucker, *The northern and central Nootkan tribes* (Washington, 1951). Robin Fisher, *Contact and conflict: Indian-European relations in British Columbia, 1774–1890* (Vancouver, 1977).

MURRAY, JAMES, army officer and colonial administrator; b. 21 Jan. 1721/22 at Ballencrieff (Lothian), the family seat in Scotland, fifth son and 14th child of Alexander Murray, 4th Baron Elibank, and Elizabeth Stirling; m. 17 Dec. 1748 Cordelia Collier, d. 26 June 1779; m. secondly on 14 March 1780 on Minorca, Anne Witham (Whitham), d. 2 Aug. 1784, and they had six children, four of whom reached maturity; d. 18 June 1794 at Beauport House, near Battle, Sussex, England.

On 6 Dec. 1736, fresh from the schooling of William Dyce in Selkirk, James Murray enrolled as a cadet in Colyear's regiment, part of the Scots brigade of the Dutch army, then stationed at Ypres (Belgium). In February 1739/40 he joined the British army as a second lieutenant with the 4th Marines (Wynyard's) but in November 1741 transferred as a captain to the 15th Foot, with which he remained till 1759. In January 1749/50 he purchased the majority, and a year later the lieutenant-colonelcy, of his regiment. From October 1759 he was colonel commandant of the 2nd battalion of the Royal Americans (60th Foot), and in July 1762 he was promoted major-general. Appointed governor of the garrison of Quebec on 12 Oct. 1759, he became governor of the District of Quebec on 27 Oct. 1760 and governor of the province on 21 Nov. 1763.

During these years as a professional soldier, Murray saw a fair amount of active service. From November 1740 to December 1742 he was in the West Indies, where he took part in the attack on Cartagena (Colombia) and the Cuban operations; from July to October 1745 he fought in Flanders, being seriously wounded in the defence of Ostend (Belgium), and in September 1746 he participated in the Lorient expedition. During the Seven Years' War he was with the 15th for the attempt on Rochefort, France, in September 1757, and from 1758 to 1760 he was in North America. He served under James Wolfe* at the siege of Louisbourg, Île Royale (Cape Breton Island), in 1758, and the following year at the siege of Quebec, where he commanded the left wing of the battle line on the Plains of Abraham. Left in charge of Quebec during the winter of 1759–60, he was forced to retreat inside the walls after the battle of Sainte-Foy on 28 April 1760; however, he managed to hold the city until the arrival of a British squadron in May [*see* Robert Swanton*]. The next month he set off up the St Lawrence to rendezvous with William HAVILAND and Jeffery AMHERST and force the capitulation of Montreal in September.

As a military commander Murray has been criticized as "hot-headed and impetuous, inclined to underrate the offensive power of his opponents"; he has also been acclaimed as "a man of the most ardent and intrepid courage, passionately desirous of glory." Wolfe held him in high regard, commending his "infinite spirit" and "great services" during the Louisbourg campaign, and personally selecting him as the junior brigadier at the siege of Quebec. For Murray, however, the latter was not an unqualified success. Although he joined Robert MONCKTON and George Townshend*, the other brigadiers, in urging the establishment of a force above the city, he did not, as he later claimed, recommend "the very place" where Wolfe landed; and if he maintained that a "superior authority" checked his pursuit of the French right flank, no evidence has been found to support this disclaimer of a costly tactical error. In any event, Murray was dissatisfied with both the reporting of his conduct and the amount of credit he was given for the victory.

Still more controversy surrounds his defence of Quebec. Lacking sufficient funds, adequate supplies of fuel, and fresh provisions, and with a garrison of some 6,000 able-bodied men, whom illness reduced to fewer than 4,000 during the winter, when confronted in late April by a force almost twice his strength, he decided, characteristically, to attack. The resulting battle has generally been considered a British defeat, though again Murray defended not only his conduct but his decision to fight. At any rate, from a strategic viewpoint, judgements range from the opinion that his losses might have incited LÉVIS to assault the city if the British fleet had not arrived in time, through the conviction that Lévis would not have chanced an assault unless the French fleet had arrived first, to the view that Lévis suffered a mauling that left him incapable of preventing Murray's advance to Montreal and that the battle of Sainte-Foy thus played a crucial part in the conquest.

Following the capitulation of Montreal on 8 Sept. 1760, Canada was subjected to a military régime. The colony was divided into three independently administered districts – Quebec, Trois-Rivières, and Montreal – which were placed under Murray, Ralph Burton*, and Thomas GAGE respectively, each of them being in turn responsible to Amherst, the commander-in-chief, in New York. On the establishment of civil government, proclaimed in Britain on 7 Nov. 1763 and inaugurated in Canada on 10 Aug. 1764, the districts were united into the province of Quebec. Provision was made for Murray, as governor, to be assisted by two lieutenant governors, but these positions were discontinued after both Gage and Burton declined to fill them.

However, Murray did not enjoy unbridled authority. On his proclamation as governor the civil and military commands were separated, and later in 1764 command of all the troops in the province was given to Burton who, as brigadier of the Northern Department, was responsible only to the commander-in-chief, by now Gage. Whether it was caused by Burton's jealousy of Murray's nomination as governor, or by Murray's resentment of Burton's independence as brigadier, or simply by the practical inseparability of the two offices, friction soon developed between these former friends and contributed to the recall of both in 1766. Murray was surely right to maintain that in Quebec, which was not only a conquered colony but one where the governor had always been the military chief, authority could not be shared; and the home authorities admitted as much when they granted both commands to Murray's successor, Guy Carleton*, in 1766.

Another hindrance was the lack of qualified and dependable advisers. Fortunate in his civil secretary, Hector Theophilus CRAMAHÉ, whom he appointed to the Council in 1764 and then sent as his representative to London, Murray had to rely principally on serving officers – notably Paulus Æmilius IRVING and Samuel Jan Holland*, both of whom became councillors – and on former military men, such as Adam MABANE (likewise a councillor), John Fraser, and John Nairne*. He also came to trust a few merchants, particularly Thomas Ainslie*, Hugh Finlay*, Thomas Dunn*, James Goldfrap, and Benjamin Price*, the last three being Council members as well. However, the patronage system, under which many colonial offices were dispensed in England, saddled him with a number of difficult officials, headed by Chief Justice William Gregory and Attorney General George SUCKLING. Although he apparently changed his mind about the latter, Murray at first considered them both "needy lawyers," not only "entirely ignorant of the Language of the Natives" and "ignorant of the World" but "readier to puzzle and Create Difficultys than to remove them." Nor were they the exceptions: Murray had to contend with Coroner Williams Conyngham, whom he described as "the most thorough paced Villain who ever existed"; an assortment of British patentees, some of whom could not "read a word of French"; and so many inept justices of the peace that the office fell into disrepute and had to be rehabilitated by Carleton. In addition, he faced several unruly officers, such as Gabriel CHRISTIE, deputy quartermaster general for the Northern Department, and Arthur Brown, who commanded the 28th Foot, as well as a pack of disgruntled traders led by George Allsopp*, William

Grant*, Edward HARRISON, Eleazar Levy, James JOHNSTON, and the brothers Alexander and William Mackenzie.

As if that were not enough, the Southern Department, Board of Trade, War Office, and Treasury all meddled in colonial affairs, sometimes acting without consultation among themselves, sometimes avoiding issues altogether for want of clear-cut responsibility. Moreover, Murray enjoyed the confidence of only two of the four ministries that held office while he was in Quebec: those of the Duke of Newcastle and the Earl of Bute, which together lasted from June 1757 to April 1763. This support was lost with the advent of the Whigs, after which Murray seems to have encountered some discrimination because of his association with the "King's Friends." Under the ministries of George Grenville and Lord Rockingham, he had to account to such politicians as Lord Halifax, Lord Shelburne, and Lord Dartmouth, who were at best unsympathetic; and if he was faithfully backed by the Duke of Argyll, Lord Egremont, Lord Mansfield, Lord North, Lord George Sackville, Charles Jenkinson, William Pitt, and Charles Townshend, a list of his detractors, who included the Duke of Bedford, Lord Camden, Lord Northington, Isaac Barré, Welbore Ellis, Horace Walpole, and John Wilkes, indicates the odds against him.

Murray's primary concern throughout the military régime of 1760–63 was security, for neither the return of the French nor a revolt by the Canadians could be ruled out. Determined to "slip no Opportunity to keep up the dread of our Arms," he warned in November 1759 that reprisals would follow any aiding of the enemy; he also sanctioned the retributions exacted at Pointe-Lévy (Lauzon), Sorel, and Lorette in 1759 and 1760; and as late as July 1765 he advised the expulsion of the Acadians from Bonaventure and the stationing of troops at Gaspé and Baie des Chaleurs. On the other hand, he listened to complaints against his troops, punished any of them who exploited the inhabitants, urged Amherst to restrain the crews of ships putting in at Quebec, and encouraged both the merchants and the military to relieve the indigent. The strategic motive behind this policy of harshness and humanity was revealed even before the fall of Montreal: the Canadians, Murray reckoned, "hardly will hereafter be easi[ly] persuaded to take up Arms against a Nation they admire, and who will have it allways in their [power?] to burn or destroy." Indeed, he was soon hoping for more: "to cultivate close connections with such of them as hereafter may be of use to Us in case of another war."

It was obvious, however, that the new subjects could not be controlled, much less conciliated, if either their accustomed usages or their former officials were disregarded. Consequently, although the articles of capitulation had not guaranteed the preservation of French laws, customs, or institutions, Murray modelled the council for his district on the old Conseil Supérieur, permitted the use of French law in cases not referred to this council, gave the captains of militia new commissions, and appointed several Canadians (such as Jacques de Lafontaine* de Belcour, whom he named attorney general and commissary for the south shore) to administrative posts. But it must be admitted that these measures were neither unique nor entirely successful: Murray's arrangements were in accordance with Amherst's directives to all the governors, similar expedients were employed in Trois-Rivières and Montreal, and complaints of unjust imprisonments and ruined family affairs – often attributed to ignorance of French usages and the French language – did occur in the District of Quebec.

The church was another concern during the military régime. The articles of capitulation signed at Quebec guaranteed "the free exercise of the Roman religion," while specific safeguards, added at Montreal, covered the chapter, priests, curates, missionaries, and communities of nuns – though not the Jesuits, Recollets, or Sulpicians. Murray's wartime experience had not predisposed him towards the clergy: identifying them as "the source of all the mischiefs which have befallen the poor Canadians," he doubted whether much reliance could be placed on oaths when "the Conscience can be so easily quieted by the Absolution of a Priest." He accordingly intervened in the appointment of parish priests, whom he was determined to keep "in a state of necessary subjection," cautioned the home authorities against expatriate clerics such as Joseph-Marie LA CORNE de Chaptes, and revealed a deep distrust of the religious orders, particularly the Jesuits.

Gradually, however, his attitude changed. Beginning with a promise to protect all parish priests who did not prove troublesome, Murray came to rely on them to maintain order in the parishes. In return he doled out aid: to the "charitable Priest" Jean-Baptiste-Laurent Morisseaux, who was awarded the benefit of Saint-Augustin in Labrador; to the parish priests of Saint-Laurent, Île d'Orléans, and Sainte-Foy, who received restoration grants; and to Jean-Olivier BRIAND, vicar general of Quebec, who was presented with a gratuity of £480 for "his good behaviour." Similarly, Murray's gratitude to the nuns for their impartial nursing during the hostilities induced him to supply their communities with fuel and provisions, remunerate them for their services, support the claim of the Hôpital-Général to "a large sum" due from the king of France, and obtain the remission of debts owed to the French government by the Hôtel-Dieu and the Ursuline convent in Quebec [*see* Marie-Louise CUROT; Marie-Anne MIGEON de Branssat]. Even the Jesuits became entitled to some consideration: rejecting a request to lay an attachment on their effects, Murray went so far as to recommend their being paid pensions if dismissed.

He also helped to resolve the problem of the episcopal succession. The death of Bishop Pontbriand [Dubreil*] in June 1760 raised the question of how priests could be ordained without infringing British laws – which, as Lord Egremont, secretary of state for the Southern Department, enjoined, "prohibit absolutely all Popish Hierarchy in any of the Dominions belonging to the Crown." Although opposed to the presence of a bishop in Quebec, Murray would accept a "Superintendent of the Romish Religion," to be elected by the Quebec chapter and, following approval by the British government, consecrated by the pope. He balked, however, at the chapter's initial choice of Étienne MONTGOLFIER, vicar general of Montreal and superior of the Sulpicians, and it was largely through his influence that in 1764 Briand was elected instead. With the consecration of the latter in March 1766, the continuance of the priesthood, and so of the church in Quebec, was secured.

As he acknowledged as early as July 1763, Murray's change of attitude was fostered by Briand's ability to act "with a Candour, Moderation, and a Delicacy in such circumstances, as deserve the highest Commendation, such indeed as I little expected from one of his Gown." Well briefed on the need to conciliate the British authorities and acutely aware of the governor's prejudices, Briand took care to obtain his approval of ecclesiastical appointments, to issue the numerous *mandements* and circular letters he requested, and, in general, to accept the same kind of governmental intervention that had occurred during the last century of French rule. A working concordat was the result: in exchange for toleration, some support, and – of special significance for the shaping of Canadian society – permission to continue its educational role, the church counselled not merely submission but cooperation. This collaboration was rewarded in the Quebec Act of 1774, which recognized the claims of the clergy to their accustomed dues, and then in the Constitutional Act of 1791, which effectively established Roman Catholicism in Lower Canada.

The last major concern during the military régime was the economy. With both the means of production and the importing agencies disrupted to such an extent that sufficient supplies could not be obtained, Murray was moved to issue the population with military stores. More fundamentally, an imbalance between supply and demand during the last years of French rule had resulted in a chronic shortage of cash, and so induced the authorities to issue more than a million *livres* of paper money. The French government's decision in 1760 to suspend payment on this paper threatened not only to wipe out the savings and capital of many Canadians but to deprive Quebec of its principal means of exchange. And meanwhile, speculators were hoarding goods in order to force up prices. The immediate economic problems confronting Murray were thus how to solve the currency crisis and how to check an already rife inflation.

The first problem entailed two questions: what to do about the French paper money and how to obtain more specie. Finding that he could neither enforce the exclusive use of cash nor persuade the home government to substitute a British equivalent, Murray had to be content with registering the paper in circulation. He also tried to curb speculation on it by advising against its sale, at least until the rumours concerning its possible redemption were confirmed. But although he claimed that the result was a rise in market value – which benefited the Canadians at the cost of alienating the British merchants in Quebec – speculation continued well into the period of civil government. Moreover, when the French authorities decided in 1764 to discharge the debt with bonds rather than cash, and then repudiated it altogether in 1771, those who had taken Murray's advice were caught out. It has been argued that their losses, which contributed to a series of bankruptcies between 1764 and 1771, placed the Canadians at a disadvantage in the contest for commercial dominance.

To obtain specie, each of the governors resorted to the conventional palliative of overvaluing foreign currencies. Murray considered the Halifax standard of five shillings to the Spanish dollar the most suitable rate of exchange for Quebec; Gage and Burton, however, preferred the eight shilling rate applied in New York, with which their districts had close trading connections. Speculation naturally followed this difference, and once in charge of the whole province Murray decided to compromise on the New England standard of six shillings, which was convenient for the Canadians since it made the English shilling equivalent to the French *livre*. In practice, though, all three rates figured in business accounts till 1777, when Carleton reverted to Murray's original choice of the Halifax standard.

But the great hope was to increase exports, and although Pontiac*'s uprising hampered the restoration of the fur trade, the resources of the St Lawrence basin seemed propitious. Reporting in 1760 on its quantities of fish, seals, whales, hemp, flax, tar, pitch, and potash, and noting that the region contained "Iron enough to supply all Europe," Murray predicted that within a few years Canada would be exporting foodstuffs. In particular, he set out to popularize the potato, which was soon produced commercially on the Île d'Orléans, and encouraged the sowing of wheat, for which he expected to find a market in Britain. Most of his calculations were based only on potential development, however, and lack of capital, high freight rates, shortage of labour, and deficient techniques combined to delay economic expansion till the 1770s. Murray never saw the balance of trade that would have been the cure for Quebec's currency problem.

In contrast, the problem of inflation was handled rather successfully. Realizing that a principal cause was the hoarding practices and monopolistic arrangements derived from Joseph-Michel CADET's Grande Société, Murray imposed a system of price controls reinforced with sales regulations: the justices of the peace were ordered to fix prices according to supply, bakers and butchers had to obtain permission to sell their products, and importers were supervised. It is difficult to assess the effect of such measures on the middlemen, who were the chief culprits in hoarding, but deflation must have been at least expedited. In any event, prices did fall after 1760 – by as much as 50 to 80 per cent during the next six years – and Murray may well be entitled to a share of the credit for this achievement.

He also continued some of the measures employed by the French to raise revenue. These included fines on the alienation of fiefs; a tax on houses in the town of Quebec (for which he substituted, as more equitable, a tax on horses in the parishes); proceeds from the lease of the fur-trading stations known as the "king's posts"; and customs duties, which were by far the most lucrative, and contentious, source of income. Concluding that many of the French tariffs had been unfair and that the one on textiles would be unacceptable in a British colony, in 1761 Murray consolidated them all into a single duty on liquor, of which "The quantity the Canadians Consume is incredible." Although this duty netted £8,725.8*s*.1*d*. in a little over four years, objections from the British merchants in Quebec eventually forced its discontinuance, after which Murray had to manage with bills drawn on London. However, the home authorities not only tacitly admitted the legality of his imposition but approved Murray's general aim of making Quebec contribute to its administrative costs when they later reproached him for not having resumed some of the other French duties as well.

On 10 Feb. 1763, by the treaty of Paris, France formally ceded Canada to Great Britain. To judge by the subsequent proclamation of 7 October, the original intention was to anglicize the new colony: British settlement was to be promoted through the offering of lands on a quitrent basis, while British usages were to be imposed by implementing English criminal and civil law and making provision for a house of assembly. Both Murray's commission as governor and the accompanying instructions reflected this policy: "So soon as the Situation and circumstances" admitted, he was to summon an assembly, elected by "the Major Part of the Freeholders." He was also to appoint a council, consisting of four *ex officio* members and eight persons chosen by him "from amongst the most considerable of the Inhabitants of, or Persons of Property in Our said Province". Pending the making of laws "by & with the advice and Consent" of the assembly and council, rules and regulations were to be issued "by the Advice" of this council. And courts of justice were to be established with the council's consent and advice, although the judges and law officers were to be appointed by the governor alone.

There was some doubt, however, concerning the ecclesiastical implications. The fourth article of the treaty of Paris granted Roman Catholics in Quebec religious liberty "as far as the laws of Great Britain permit." But those laws included the Corporation Act of 1661 and the Test Acts of 1673 and 1678, by which Catholics were barred from all offices under the crown, disabled in the courts, deprived of the vote, and banned from both houses of parliament. Did this mean that Canadians would be prohibited from occupying civil offices, taking part in the administration of justice, and either electing to or sitting in the proposed assembly? If so, the government of Quebec would be not only a religious but a racial oligarchy, with a legislature in which the representatives of a handful of British Protestants – estimated by Murray in October 1764 as no more than 200 householders in the entire province – would make laws for some 70,000 Canadian Roman Catholics.

Once again, Murray tried to compromise. In his ordinance of 17 Sept. 1764, he established two districts, Quebec and Montreal, placing Trois-Rivières in the latter until it had enough Protestants to provide its own law officers. He then set up a three-tier system of civil courts. At the top was the Court of King's Bench, from which certain appeals lay to the governor in council and thence to the king in council; next was the Court of Common Pleas, from which certain appeals lay to the Court of King's Bench; at the bottom were the courts of the justices of the peace, from which certain appeals also lay to the Court of King's Bench. Only English law was applicable in the highest and lowest courts, only practitioners of that law were admitted to the Court of King's Bench, and only Protestants could become justices of the peace. However, in the Court of Common Pleas – which Murray designed "to please the Canadians & to prevent their being made a Prey to our upright Lawyers" – cases were determined "agreeable to Equity, having regard nevertheless to the laws of England"; French laws and customs were "allowed and admitted" (providing the cause of action was between Canadians and had arisen before 1 Oct. 1764); exponents of the civil law were permitted to practise; and either party might request a trial by jury, on which Canadians were eligible to serve. In addition, three men noted for their sympathy towards the Canadians – Adam Mabane, François Mounier*, and John Fraser – were chosen as judges for the Court of Common Pleas; a prerogative court was created to facilitate testamentary business; the grants and rights of inheritance in force before the treaty of Paris were recognized, thereby "quieting people in their possessions"; and an alternative to the English law of primogeniture was provided by sanctioning the French custom of coparcenary, which, as Murray also maintained, "contributes to the better cultivating and peopling of the country."

Although they might have helped to conciliate the Canadians, these concessions had the opposite effect on many of the British. As each bulwark of privilege was breached, their disquiet increased, and when it became apparent that Murray had no intention of summoning an assembly, their specific and sporadic complaints gave way to a personal and unremitting campaign against the governor. Acquiring a permanent agent, Fowler Walker, in London and enlisting the support of business associates there, the British merchants in Quebec embarked on a heady series of presentments, remonstrances, and petitions.

Oddly enough, in view of what was happening in the American colonies, the home authorities do not appear to have been alarmed by either Murray's refusal to summon an assembly or the pretensions of the grand jury of 1764 – who, "as the only body Representative of the Colony," claimed the right to be consulted before any ordinances became law and to have public accounts laid before them at least once a year. Murray was questioned about his recalcitrance after his return to England in 1766; but by allowing Carleton to continue a conciliar form of administration, the British government implicitly sanctioned what was perhaps the most significant departure from both the proclamation of 1763 and Murray's commission.

Another grievance of the British settlers concerned the social side of the anglicizing policy. With the dual object of promoting British immigration and converting the French, Murray was instructed to carry out a survey, advertise for settlers, make grants of land, and provide for a Protestant church and school in every district, township, and precinct. He accordingly carried out the surveying and advertising; recommended a reduction of the quitrents (to make crown lands more competitive with the seigneurial holdings offered for rent); and granted large tracts to two settlers, John Nairne and Malcolm Fraser*. He also engaged a renegade Jesuit, Pierre-Joseph-Antoine ROUBAUD, to act as a go-between in London, and solicited the Society for the Propagation of the Gospel for Bibles, prayer-books and French speaking "missionaries." He also hoped that his appointment of the Huguenot Mounier to both the Court of Common Pleas and the Council would "induce many to embrace our Religion, that they may be admitted to the like advantages."

As the British merchants complained, however, much of this activity seemed only dutiful, if not perfunctory. Evidently believing that it was even more important to reassure the Canadians, who were "uneasy on account of Apprehensions for the Future existance of their Religion," Murray continued to co-operate with their clergy, particularly Joseph-François Perrault, vicar general of Trois-Rivières, and Étienne MARCHAND, who replaced Montgolfier as vicar general of Montreal in late 1764. Similarly, his promotion of British settlement could scarcely be described as whole-hearted. Questioning the validity of grants acquired by British settlers during the military régime, he was reluctant to make new ones, and by the end of 1764 had limited these to the pair awarded Nairne and Fraser. Moreover, he allowed seigneurial grants to be surveyed privately, with the result, according to the deputy surveyor of Quebec, John COLLINS, that many of those buildings were "Extended to a very considerable distance beyond the Real Boundarys," and the amount of land available for British settlement was proportionately reduced.

If he was criticized for not following the political and social guidelines of the proclamation of 1763 closely enough, Murray was castigated for enforcing its economic injunctions too strictly. A boundary line that isolated the western hinterland, including the Great Lakes and Ohio valley, gave the Indians their promised reserve but left the fur-traders from Quebec in an impossible position. Now required to obtain licences and furnish recognizances before entering the territory and then to conduct their business from within the military posts, they had to compete with traders from the Mississippi who were able to enter and move about freely. Murray could appreciate their difficulties and did recommend against the restrictions, which were finally removed in 1768. He was nonetheless subjected to numerous aspersions, which direct attention to the discord that generally characterized his relations with the merchants.

The fact is that Murray found it difficult to get along with people in trade, who in turn considered him incapable of understanding, let alone furthering, their interests. Duties, shipping, fisheries, posts, and wharfs were recurring subjects of dispute, and it was not enough for him to reply that he had helped on several occasions: as when he proposed an embargo on French commodities, or promoted British participation in the seal fishery, or backed some of the Canadian claims to seal-oil posts. What the merchants felt he lacked was a business sense; and what they coveted was something he was determined to withhold – political power. For although some businessmen were given administrative positions, including membership on the Council, they were carefully selected, had usually acquired land, and always remained in the minority. Above all, the governor would not summon an assembly.

The common explanation of Murray's behaviour is that he was prejudiced against the British merchants and captivated by the Canadians. He certainly made no effort to dissemble his contempt for the former: "the most cruel, Ignorant, rapaćious Fanatics, who ever existed," these "birds of passage" were "chiefly adventurers of mean Education, either young beginners, or if old Traders, such as have failed in other Countrys, all have their Fortunes to make and little sollicitous about the means, provided the end is obtained." In contrast, the Canadians, "soldiers to a man," were "perhaps, the best and bravest Race on the Globe, a Race, that have already got the better of every National Antipathy to their Conquerors, and could they be indulged with a very few Privileges, which the Laws of England do not allow to Catholics at home, must in a very short Time become the most faithful & useful Set of Men in this American Empire."

In the mean time, however, they had to be protected. "You know, Cramahe," Murray wrote in late 1764, "I love the Canadians but you cannot conceive the uneasiness I feel on their Acc!, to see them made the prey of the most abandoned of Men while I am at their head is too much for me to endure much longer." This was not empty rhetoric. When Gage decided to raise a force of Canadians during Pontiac's uprising, Murray advocated the calling of volunteers rather than a draft, was able to fill his quota for the District of Quebec without resorting to induction, and insisted that service conditions for the Canadians should be the same as those for the militiamen from New York. His objection to billeting without due payment, refusal to issue general warrants as a means of obtaining forced labour, opposition to the impressment of boatmen, and preference for contracts instead of the corvée, likewise illustrate his "infinite tenderness" for the "brave, Valuable Race" he had grown to "admire and love."

But that is not the only way in which Murray's behaviour can be interpreted. Indeed, this essentially ethnic construction might be not only anachronistic but obscurantist. For, it is argued, the crucial distinction at the time was not between two races, but between two classes – "bourgeois" and "landed." Furthermore, from a modern perspective, it was the former that represented progress: whereas the British government was intent on fitting Quebec into the old colonial system and Atlantic triangle, the merchants were attempting to create a commercial empire inland; and North America was to be developed not by concentrating on the seaboard regions but by opening up the west. No matter how "Ignorant, factious, Licentious" they might have seemed, the merchants should have been supported because they alone possessed the initiative, energy, and skill required for that enterprise.

It is also argued that such support would not have been simply tantamount to siding with the British against the Canadians. Regardless of who they were and how effectively they managed, some Canadians did participate in business activities after the conquest. In fact, this event freed them from the mercantilist restrictions imposed by the French authorities; and not only was the British colonial system much more liberal, but the beginning of the industrial revolution and development of capitalism in England opened up limitless prospects. Integration into the British empire should have provided Canadian business interests with an unprecedented opportunity for both economic and social advancement. If only they too had been encouraged, or at least left unhampered, the disadvantages under which they laboured might have been reduced, and relations between Canada's two founding peoples might have begun, and continued, on more harmonious lines.

Murray, however, would have denied that such a partnership was either actually or potentially possible. To him those Canadians – "the few exceptions" – who occasionally, and often inadvertently, abetted the British merchants were only "the little Dealers in the Towns of Quebec and Montreal who are at the mercy of the British Traders their Creditors." At the same time, he would not have denied – if brought to think in such terms – that class was a potent, if not determining, factor in his behaviour. As he admitted, "It was a maxim of mine to shun Addresses from the Traders, they wanted to make themselves of Consequence by Addresses, presentm[ts]. and Remonstrances; I discouraged such things from them, and upon all Occasions consulted the Men of property in the Colony."

These consisted of two groups, who also crossed ethnic lines: the British governmental supporters and the Canadian seigneurs. The former, mostly military men but including a few merchants (such as Benjamin Price, who owned 20,000 acres), were supposed to shelter Quebec from that "turbulent, levelling spirit" which, according to Chief Justice William SMITH after the American revolution, had caused the Thirteen Colonies to be "abandoned to democracy." However, this "French party" came to uphold not only conciliar as opposed to representative government, but also those Canadian institutions, laws, and customs that seemed indispensable to the continuance of a hierarchical society. They accordingly found their natural allies not among members of their own race but in the other group that wished to "preserve" Quebec, the seigneurs [*see* Gaspard-Joseph CHAUSSEGROS de Léry; Charles-François TARIEU de La Naudière].

So long as security was his primary concern, Murray had been wary of the latter: "impecunious, haughty, tyrannical, contemptuous of trade and authority, attached to French rule," they were the one group of Canadians whose departure was "rather to be wished than regretted." Then he began to notice, or fancy, the "healthy" respect shown them by the peasantry, the forbearance with which they asserted their rights and privileges, and the order and stability that seemed to flow from the relationship. Before the end of 1763 he had decided that "I would not advise their expulsion, because I foresee they may become very usefull to us if properly managed." Soon afterwards, he recommended the employment of former officers of the colonial regulars in the campaign against Pontiac, and in March 1764 offered the command of the Canadian corps to Pierre-Jean-Baptiste-François-Xavier LEGARDEUR de Repentigny. By 1766 he was counselling the magistrates in Montreal not to billet soldiers on the seigneurs, since "This Distinction they had the right to Expect, decency and regard paid to People of Family in all Civilized Countries required it."

The incident that prompted Murray's recall occurred on 6 Dec. 1764 in Montreal. Relations between the military and the merchants had always been rancorous in that town, where billeting was particularly troublesome and where Burton had his headquarters. On the night in question a party of men from the 28th Foot, bent on teaching the tradesmen a lesson, broke into the house of one of the principal offenders, Thomas WALKER, thrashed him soundly, and cut off one of his ears. The ensuing wrangle over where and by whom a trial should be held enabled Murray's critics to marshal their grievances, and this time their protest to the British government proved effective. In October 1765 Murray was told that he would have to account in London for both the disorders in Montreal and, in general, his administration of Quebec. He was ordered home the following April and left Canada on 28 June 1766.

Murray was accused of not merely obstructing the course of justice in the Walker affair but, among other malpractices, of improperly remitting fines imposed by the chief justice; wrongfully seizing and detaining ships and merchandise; billeting troops unnecessarily and unfairly; imposing duties and taxes contrary to law; establishing a special court for the Canadians; favouring the seigneurs; bolstering Roman Catholicism; issuing ordinances that were "Unconstitutional, Vexatious, Oppressive, Calculated to serve private purposes, Absurd and Unjust"; and instead of conciliating the two races, managing only "to kindle Animositys, and to raise Jealousies among them, and to keep them Disunited." Not one of these charges could be made to stick, however, and on 13 April 1767 the Lords of Committee of

Council dismissed them all as "groundless, scandalous and Derogatory to the Honor of the said Governor, who stood before the Committee unimpeached."

Murray could now have returned to Quebec, where he had often spoken of settling permanently and had obtained extensive properties across the river from the town, as well as on lakes Champlain and Saint-Pierre. But although he retained the nominal governorship of the province till 12 April 1768, he never did get back. Various explanations have been suggested, including a reluctance to leave his wife, who was disinclined to accompany him overseas; pressure from his brother Lord Elibank, who looked to his support in the House of Commons, for which Murray considered standing; apprehension that friction would recur, especially since Carleton, who had been made lieutenant governor in September 1766, was opposed to some of Murray's policies and several of his appointees; and a general feeling of disenchantment, possibly indicated by his reluctance to participate in the framing of the Quebec Act in 1773.

Whatever the reasons, Murray resumed his military career soon after returning to England. Serving on the Irish staff in 1766 and subsequently as an inspecting general of the Southern District, in December 1767 he exchanged his colonelcy in the 60th Foot for that of the 13th, and in May 1772 was promoted lieutenant-general. Two years later he began his second colonial assignment, an eight-year stint in Minorca. Since the titular governor, General John Mostyn, was not resident, Murray, although designated as only the lieutenant governor, was effectively in charge from the start. In April 1779 he was finally gazetted governor and was given a lieutenant governor of his own, Sir William Draper, the next month.

Between August 1781 and February 1782, when Fort St Philip was besieged by a Franco-Spanish army, Murray relived his defence of Quebec. Resisting this time any impulse to launch his men, reduced by the end of the siege from 2,000 to 600 combatants, against a force of 16,000, he bore himself so gallantly – to the extent of spurning a bribe of £1,000,000 to surrender – as to earn the honorific title of "Old Minorca" before being obliged to capitulate. A court of inquiry was afterwards convened to look into various charges brought by Draper, whom Murray had dismissed for insubordination and who was now retaliating with accusations of misconduct ranging from embezzlement to cruelty. Murray was not only acquitted on all except two trifling charges but had the satisfaction of being complimented by both the court and the king on his "zeal, courage and firmness" in defending Fort St Philip. He thereupon retired to his Sussex estate where, becoming a full general in February 1783 and acquiring the honours of colonel of the 21st Foot and governor of Hull, he passed his remaining 12 years.

Weaknesses of character, or personality, cannot be overlooked and go a long way to explain, if not entirely to account for, the antagonisms Murray encountered throughout his life. He was arrogant, irascible, authoritarian, and snobbish, and he could be harsh, impetuous, inconsistent, and intemperate. It is equally impossible to ignore his valour, resolution, fortitude, compassion, generosity, altruism, and code of honour. He was, in short, very much a soldier and an aristocrat, and he reflected both the shortcomings and the qualities – perhaps not altogether inappropriate or unfortunate for Canada at that juncture – of the type. Admirers, especially among the Canadians, were not wanting and petitions begging for his return proclaimed that "he gained our hearts," affirmed that his "clear-sightedness, Equity and wisdom continually afford him efficacious means for maintaining the people in tranquillity and obedience," and lamented the loss of "Our protector, our father," without whom "what will become of us?" But the epitaph that Murray might well have chosen himself is contained in his report to Shelburne of 20 Aug. 1766: "I glory in having been accused of warmth and firmness in protecting the King's Canadian Subjects and of doing the utmost in my Power to gain to my Royal Master the affection of that brave hardy People; whose Emigration, if ever it shall happen, will be an irreparable Loss to this Empire, to prevent which I declare to your Lordship, I would chearfully submit to greater Calumnies & Indignities if greater can be devised, than hitherto I have undergone."

From a constitutional standpoint, Murray's governorship is notable mainly because of the modifications he made in the anglicizing policy of 1763. His refusal to summon an assembly, and reliance on a council instead, provided Carleton with a precedent that was ratified in the Quebec Act of 1774. The form of administration established by this act in turn served as a prototype for the development of crown colony government, which became an alternative to representative government in the reorganization of the British empire after the American revolution. Murray's incorporation of French principles and practices into the English legal system was another precedent on which Carleton could build, also received statutory recognition in 1774, and has persisted in

Quebec to the present day. As illustrated by the retention of French laws and institutions in Santo Domingo and Martinique and of Romano-Dutch laws and institutions in British Guiana and Cape Colony, this "policy of continuation" became an alternative to the "policy of anglicization" in the second British empire.

From an economic standpoint, Murray left his mark by restraining the mercantile interests. The restrictions he enforced in the western hinterland, the "clogs of commerce" with which he burdened merchants within the province, and, most important, his thwarting of their efforts to gain political power through the acquisition of an assembly, all helped to transform Quebec from a fur-trading region, which might have become the heart of an inland commercial empire, into an agricultural belt that was principally concerned with the exploitation of its own resources and oriented towards the Atlantic. Murray has therefore been held at least partly responsible for both the perpetuation of Quebec as a quasi-feudal enclave and the delay in its attaining a capitalist economy.

Finally, from a social standpoint, Murray made his greatest impact through his efforts to counter the policy of anglicization. Whether or not the Canadians could have been thoroughly anglicized without a substantial British immigration, the possible effects of completely subordinating the Roman Catholic church, extensively promoting British settlement, establishing exclusively English laws and institutions, and firmly entrenching the British merchants as the dominant political force should not be discounted. In any event, Murray's aversion to the bourgeoisie (British and Canadian alike), together with his partiality for their adversaries (the clergy, seigneurs, and French party), led him to champion the Canadian cause. And this is probably what lies behind much of the praise, and blame, that has been heaped upon him. During the years immediately following the conquest, a serious attempt might have been made to turn Quebec into an anglicized colony. Murray's ultimate achievement, or failure, was that he helped to impede this movement. His apology was that he thereby helped to prevent the total subjugation of the Canadians.

G. P. Browne

[Two portraits in oil of James Murray, by anonymous artists, are known to exist: one is in the National Portrait Gallery, London; the other is in the PAC. J. S. Neele published an engraving, ascribed to James Gillray, and S. A. Cumberlege another, by an anonymous artist; the BL holds copies of both and the PAC a copy of the latter. James Murray is the author of: "Journal of the siege of Quebec, 1759–60," Literary and Hist. Soc. of Quebec, *Hist. Docs.*, 3rd ser. (1871), no.5, 1–45, which also appeared as a separate publication under the title *Governor Murray's journal of Quebec, from 18th September, 1759, to 25th May, 1760: journal of the siege of Quebec, 1759–60* ([Quebec and Montreal, 1871]); *Report of the state of the government of Quebec in Canada, by General Murray, June 5, 1762 . . .* (Quebec, 1902); *The sentence of the court-martial . . . for the trial of the Hon. Lieut. Gen. James Murray . . .* (London, 1783). G.P.B.]

BL, Add. MSS, 15491, ff.1–14; 21628, f.302; 21668, ff.1–57; 21686, ff.61, 81. PAC, MG 23, GII, 1. PRO, CO 42/1–7; 42/24–25. Scottish Record Office (Edinburgh), GD 32/24. *Annual Register* (London), 1759, 1760, 1763, 1782. *Coll. of several commissions* (Maseres). *Correspondence of William Pitt* (Kimball), IV. *Docs. relating to Canadian currency during the French period* (Shortt), II. *Docs. relating to constitutional history, 1759–91* (Shortt and Doughty; 1918). William Draper, *Observations on the Honourable Lieutenant-General Murray's defence* (London, 1783). John Entick, *The general history of the late war: containing it's rise, progress, and event, in Europe, Asia, Africa, and America . . .* (4th ed., 5v., London, 1779). G. B., Hist. MSS Commission, *Fifth report* (2v., London, 1876); *The manuscripts of the Marquess Townshend* (London, 1887), 315–16; PRO, *CHOP, 1760–65*; *CHOP, 1766–69*. *Gentleman's Magazine*, 1759–60, 1763–66. [James Johnstone], "The campaign of 1760 in Canada," Literary and Hist. Soc. of Quebec, *Hist. Docs.*, 2nd ser. (1868). Knox, *Hist. journal* (Doughty), II. Maseres, *Maseres letters* (Wallace). PAC *Report*, 1918. [Horace Walpole], *The letters of Horace Walpole, fourth Earl of Orford . . .* , ed. [Helen] and Paget Toynbee (16v. and 3v. supp., Oxford, Eng., 1903–25), IV, 396. [John Wilkes], *The correspondence of the late John Wilkes with his friends, printed from the original manuscripts, in which are introduced memoirs of his life*, ed. John Almon (5v., London, 1805). *Lloyd's Evening Post and British Chronicle* (London), 7 Nov., 24–26 Dec. 1766, 2–5 Jan. 1767. *Quebec Gazette*, 1764–68.

DNB. G. L. Beer, *British colonial policy, 1754–1765* (New York, 1922). Brunet, *Les Canadiens après la Conquête*. Burt, *Old prov. of Que.* D. [G.] Creighton, *The empire of the St Lawrence* (Toronto, 1956). A. [G.] Doughty and G. W. Parmelee, *The siege of Quebec and the battle of the Plains of Abraham* (6v., Quebec, 1901), II, 8, 219, 222, 227, 266; III, 81, 161; IV, 288; V, 44–45; VI, 50–52, 141. Frégault, *La guerre de la Conquête*. R. H. Mahon, *Life of General the Hon. James Murray, a builder of Canada . . .* (London, 1921). A. C. Murray, *The five sons of "Bare Betty"* (London, 1936). Neatby, *Quebec*. Ouellet, *Hist. économique*. M. Trudel, *L'Église canadienne*. M. G. Reid, "The Quebec fur-traders and western policy, 1763–1774," *CHR*, VI (1925), 15–32. S. M. Scott, "Civil and military authority in Canada, 1764–1766," *CHR*, IX (1928), 117. Marcel Trudel, "La servitude de l'Église catholique du Canada français sous le Régime anglais," CHA *Report*, 1963, 42–64.

MURRAY, WALTER, member of the Council of Quebec, commissioner of the port of Quebec, and justice of the peace; b. 1701 or 1702 in Ireland; buried 4 April 1772 at Quebec.

Although he was born and educated in Ireland, Walter Murray was a member of the Elibank family of Great Britain and hence related to James MURRAY. Walter spent a long time in the British American colonies, as an itinerant actor according to a letter written by Guy Carleton* in 1766. When or in what capacity Murray arrived in Quebec is not known. Some authors maintain that he came as an officer in Wolfe*'s army, but it is more likely that he immigrated after the conquest; his correspondence indicates that he would never have come if friends in Maryland had not persuaded him that his family connection with the governor could be useful to him and his son Richard. In any event, he was evidently in Quebec when civil government was established in August 1764, since James Murray at that time appointed him to various important positions even though he could not speak French. Described by the governor as "a man of good Sense and Education, has lived long in the Colonies and is conversant in the nature of them," Walter Murray was sworn in as a member of the first Council of Quebec on 13 Aug. 1764. Eleven days later he was appointed a justice of the peace in the districts of Quebec and Montreal and on 14 September was made receiver general of the province. He delegated his powers as receiver general to his son. However, the right to appoint to this important office did not rest with the governor but with the lords of the Treasury Board, who chose Thomas MILLS for the post. Later Walter Murray was to be appointed commissioner of the port of Quebec.

After James Murray's departure in June 1766, Walter remained a member of the Council. On 13 October he and Paulus Æmilius IRVING, Adam MABANE, François Mounier*, and James CUTHBERT signed a remonstrance addressed to Carleton, then lieutenant governor. They objected to Carleton's summoning only part of the Council and giving precedence to councillors appointed by the king over those chosen by Murray.

Walter Murray was obviously greatly disappointed when he learned that his relative had decided not to return to Quebec. He explained his views in a letter to Murray in 1767 in which, recalling his former profession as an actor, he borrowed words from *Hamlet* to describe his own situation and that of his son. He would have liked the former governor to find him a post with a good salary in any British colony. He did not seem particularly happy to be living in Canada, "a Place destitute of every thing that can make life pass away tolerably agreeable; A Place fitt only to send Exiles to, as a punishment for their past ill spent lives." Nevertheless Walter Murray remained in Quebec until his death, attending the Council for the last time on 30 Sept. 1771. He was stricken with paralysis and died the following April.

JACQUES L'HEUREUX

PAC, MG 11, [CO 42], Q, 2, p.300; 3, p.361; 4, p.60; 8, p.155; MG 23, GII, 1, ser.1, 3, pp.203–7; RG 1, E1, 1, p.1; RG 4, A1, 11, p.4374. PRO, CO 42/1, p.397; 42/2, pp.38, 56, 80, 248; 42/3, pp.158, 163 (PAC transcripts). *Coll. of several commissions* (Maseres), 153. *Doc. relatifs à l'hist. constitutionnelle, 1759–91* (Shortt et Doughty; 1921), I, 248–52, 277. Burt, *Old prov. of Que.* (1968), I, 76, 119–20; II, 186. P.-G. Roy, *Toutes petites choses du Régime anglais* (2 sér., Québec, 1946), 1re sér., 17. F.-J. Audet, "Les législateurs de la province de Québec, 1764–1791," *BRH*, XXXI (1925), 439. É.-Z. Massicotte, "Les tribunaux de police de Montréal," *BRH*, XXVI (1920), 181. P.-G. Roy, "Josephte Murray," BRH, XLV (1939), 23–24.

MYKOK. *See* MIKAK

MYRICK, ELIZABETH. *See* OSBORN

N

NATIVITÉ, MARIE-ANNE MIGEON DE BRANSSAT, *dite* **de la.** *See* MIGEON

NAVARRE, ROBERT, notary and subdelegate of the intendant; said to have been b. 1709 at Villeroy (dept of Seine-et-Marne), France, youngest son of Antoine-Marie-François de Navarre and Jeanne Plugette (Pluiette); m. 10 Feb. 1734 Marie Lothman de Barrois at Detroit (Mich.), and six of their children grew to adulthood; d. 22 Nov. 1791 at Detroit.

A descendant of the kings of Navarre, Robert Navarre was educated in Paris. When he came to Canada is not known. He signed notarial acts at Detroit as early as 24 Nov. 1729, and in 1734, when he reached the age of majority, he received his commission as a royal notary. In 1736 he was appointed receiver of dues for the Domaine d'Occident at Detroit, a position which made him responsible for collecting the taxes levied by the intendant. He was commissioned subdelegate of the intendant in 1743 and again in 1749. The office, mainly a judicial one, empowered him to deal with personal and property matters and the selection of guardians at Detroit and "in general to execute all the instruments which permanent judges are empowered to draw up, and which require immediate attention." In 1749 Navarre was also made storekeeper at the post. His duty in this capacity was to keep records of the goods in the royal storehouses. He was replaced as subdelegate of the intendant by Jean-Marie LANDRIÈVE Des Bordes in 1752, but in 1754 he was reappointed when Landriève was recalled to Quebec. This time Navarre held the office until 1759. During his years at Detroit he acquired a familiarity with the local Indian languages and occasionally acted as an interpreter.

After British rule was established at Detroit in 1760, Navarre continued as a notary. He may have been the author of the "Journal ou dictation d'une conspiration," an account of Pontiac*'s uprising of 1763 which served as the historical basis for Francis Parkman's *The conspiracy of Pontiac*. In his later years Navarre lived west of the fort on land which had been granted to him in 1747. He was buried at Detroit on 24 Nov. 1791.

IN COLLABORATION WITH THE BURTON HISTORICAL COLLECTION STAFF

Robert Navarre is thought to be the author of *Journal of Pontiac's conspiracy, 1763*, ed. C. M. and M. A. Burton, trans. R. C. Ford (Detroit, 1912), preface.

DPL, Burton hist. coll., Journal ou dictation d'une conspiration; Registres des baptêmes, mariages et sépultures de Sainte-Anne (Detroit, Mich.), 2 Feb. 1704 – 30 Dec. 1848 (5v. in 7, MS copy), I, II; Francis Navarre papers, 23 Nov. 1791; Robert Navarre papers, 7 May 1734. *City of Detroit, Michigan, 1701–1922*, ed. C. M. Burton *et al.* (5v., Detroit, 1922), I, 165–66. *John Askin papers* (Quaife), I, 37. *Navarre, or researches after the descendants of Robert Navarre, whose ancestors are the noble Bourbons of France . . .* , comp. Christian Denissen (Detroit, 1897). PAC *Report*, 1904, app.K, 238. "Recensement de Détroit, 1779," 581–85.

Christian Denissen, *Genealogy of the French families of the Detroit River region, 1701–1911*, ed. H. F. Powell (2v., Detroit, 1976). Massicotte, "Répertoire des engagements pour l'Ouest," ANQ *Rapport*, 1929–30, 276. P.-G. Roy, *Inv. coll. pièces jud. et not.*, III, 106, 218, 226; *Inv. ord. int.*, II, 165, 197, 208–9, 277, 293; III, 9, 40, 124, 169–70, 185, 211. Francis Parkman, *The conspiracy of Pontiac and the Indian war after the conquest of Canada* (2v., Boston, 1910). M. Trudel, *L'esclavage au Canada français*, 146–47. [P.-]P.-B. Casgrain, "Landrieffe," *BRH*, II (1896), 45–46.

NEGUSHWA. *See* EGUSHWA

NEILSON, SAMUEL, printer; b. 1771 at Balmaghie (Dumfries and Galloway), Scotland, son of William Neilson and Isabel Brown; d. unmarried 12 Jan. 1793 in Quebec.

Samuel Neilson came to Quebec in 1785 to learn the compositor's craft in the printing shop of his uncle William BROWN. Brown died on 22 March 1789, and Samuel, who inherited a share of a considerable sum of money, purchased the printing shop and its newspaper the *Quebec Gazette/La Gazette de Québec*.

This paper, which had been founded on 21 June 1764, enjoyed a privileged status since the government published all its official announcements in it at a yearly contract price. But for some years the number of announcements had been increasing substantially and William Brown had had to claim for supplementary expenses each time work increased. Neilson continued to publish the official announcements, but the cost of printing was set by a list of prices that he established on 10 Oct. 1789. On 25 December his printing shop on Côte de la Montagne was damaged by fire; Neilson was nevertheless able to continue publishing his paper, thanks to William MOORE, who owned the *Quebec Herald, Miscellany and Advertiser*.

Neilson markedly improved the quality of the *Quebec Gazette*. From 1789 on he devoted more space to news and essays, and he published the opinions of both French and English speaking readers on the proposed constitutional act, which was to be passed by parliament in London in 1791. Leading articles and news from European sources, dealing in particular with the events troubling France at the time, also were given more attention. To his weekly four-page edition Neilson quite regularly added a supplement of from two to six pages.

In the early months of 1792 Neilson announced the forthcoming publication of a bilingual monthly journal, to be called the *Quebec Magazine/Le Magasin de Québec* and sold for 15 pence a copy or three dollars for a year's subscription. Neilson made Alexander Spark*, minister of the Presbyterian church in Quebec, its editor. The first issue, a 64-page number scheduled for August, came out on 13 Sept. 1792 and included a print of the city of Quebec done by J. G. Hochstetter; subsequently the magazine carried other prints and thus became the first illustrated periodical published in Quebec. The

Quebec Magazine reprinted substantial extracts from works on a wide variety of subjects: astronomy, hygiene, poetry, political institutions, history, agriculture, and meteorology. A column entitled the "Provincial Register" was devoted to news from Lower and Upper Canada. Finally, the magazine carried a register of births, marriages, and deaths, meteorological tables, and lists of consumer prices.

Samuel Neilson died of tuberculosis on 12 Jan. 1793 in Quebec. His magazine did not long outlast him for it ceased publication in May 1794. But, through dynamic management, in less than four years Neilson had expanded his printing shop more than his uncle had in 25 years. His firm went to his 16-year-old brother John*, who for some time acted under the guardianship of Alexander Spark. The latter was editor of the *Quebec Gazette* until John came of age and took over responsibility.

JOHN E. HARE

ASQ, Polygraphie, XXXV, 6[d]; Séminaire, 120, no.259. *Quebec Gazette*, 12 March 1789, 10 Jan. 1793. *Quebec Magazine*, 1792–94. Tremaine, *Bibliography of Canadian imprints*. F.-J. Audet, "John Neilson," RSC *Trans.*, 3rd ser., XXII (1928), sect.I, 81–97; "William Brown (1737–1789), premier imprimeur, journaliste et libraire de Québec; sa vie et ses œuvres," RSC *Trans.*, 3rd ser., XXVI (1932), sect.I, 97–112.

NESBITT, WILLIAM, lawyer and office-holder; m. secondly on 24 Aug. 1756 at Halifax, Nova Scotia, Rebecca Phelan, a widow; d. 23 March 1784 in Halifax, aged 77.

Nothing is known about William Nesbitt's early career. In 1749, bringing no family, he sailed with Edward CORNWALLIS' expedition to Nova Scotia as governor's clerk. In Halifax Nesbitt served for a time as clerk of the General Court and was confirmed as a notary public in April 1752. That August he was dismissed as governor's clerk upon the arrival of Governor Peregrine Thomas Hopson*; he had evidently enjoyed the office only under Cornwallis' patronage. Despite the fact that he seems to have had little formal training, Nesbitt developed an extensive legal practice, and in 1753 he succeeded Otis Little* as judge advocate of the Vice-Admiralty Court and attorney general. The latter appointment was apparently temporary; Hopson requested an impartial and proficient appointee from Great Britain, but the Board of Trade refused, stating that the salary being offered was insufficient to attract a qualified candidate.

In 1758 Nesbitt was elected to the first House of Assembly and the next year he was appointed its second speaker. In 1760 he was commissioned a justice of the peace, and in 1763 he was appointed surrogate general of the Probate Court. The same year he was nominated for a Council seat, which he declined, citing personal reasons.

Nesbitt's chief difficulty during this period was his salary as attorney general. Although it had been raised from £50 annually (established in 1755) to £100 in 1758 by Governor Charles Lawrence*, Nesbitt complained that there were no extra fees attached to the office, as was the case in other colonies. Moreover, despite Nesbitt's repeated memorials, the Board of Trade refused to place his salary on the civil list, and an additional per diem allowance granted by Lawrence ended in 1764. These difficulties doubtless induced Nesbitt to become involved in the colonial spoils system, and this activity brought him into direct conflict with Governor Francis LEGGE. In February 1774 Nesbitt was ordered by Legge to pay over £200 to the executors of an estate, a sum allegedly withheld by Nesbitt when surrogate general. Three months later Legge, attempting to purge the corrupt colonial administration, requested Nesbitt's dismissal, citing in addition to the retention of probate funds Nesbitt's laxity in collecting crown debts, his advanced age, and his legal ineptitude. Although Legge's request was refused, Nesbitt's duties were assumed for a time by his former protégé James Monk* Jr, the solicitor general.

In 1775 the provincial audit conducted by Monk, John DAY, and others revealed inaccurate accounting in Nesbitt's records, and he was sued for default by Monk over the alleged withholding of a fine collected in 1768. Charles MORRIS had noted that Nesbitt "always kept an open house for the army and Navy," and feared the attorney general would "by means of that Interest make a great party and Cabal against the present Governor," but there is no evidence to suggest that Nesbitt took such action. He allied himself with other defaulters such as Jonathan Binney* and John Newton and, exploiting the absence of the rural members, used his influential position as speaker of the assembly to direct the proceedings of the summer session to clear many of those charged, including himself. In 1776 he was accused of continuously opposing Legge from the speaker's chair; he also signed a petition to the Board of Trade which was critical of the governor. It is largely for this assiduous campaign against Legge that Nesbitt is remembered.

In 1779 Nesbitt resigned as attorney general in favour of James Brenton*, his request that he receive his salary for life having been granted. He retired from the assembly in November 1783, stating that "My firm Duty to my Sovereign, and the Prosperity and Success of this Province at all times . . . induced me to use my utmost Endeavours for the good of the same." He was rewarded for his long service with an annual pension of £100. At his death Nesbitt's personal property was worth only £168, exclusive of an extensive library; his investments in land had brought little gain. The estate was hounded by creditors, but when his family petitioned the assembly for the first instalment of his pension in order to meet them, their request was refused.

LOIS KERNAGHAN

Halifax County Court of Probate (Halifax), N17 (original estate papers of William Nesbitt). PANS, RG 1, 44, no.34. PRO, CO 217/50, ff.41–48. *Directory of N.S. MLAs*, 265. Brebner, *Neutral Yankees*. John Doull, "The first five attorney-generals of Nova Scotia," N.S. Hist. Soc., *Coll.*, XXVI (1945), 33–48.

NICK'A'THU'TIN. *See* PRIMEAU

NISSOWAQUET (Nosawaguet, Sosawaket, La Fourche, Fork), Ottawa chief; the name apparently comes from Nassauaketon, meaning forked river, the designation of one of the four Ottawa bands; b. *c.* 1715; d. 1797.

Nissowaquet was born into the Nassauaketon band, whose village was located beside Fort Michilimackinac (Mackinaw City, Mich.). In 1741, having exhausted the soil there, these Ottawas moved to L'Arbre Croche (Cross Village, Mich.), 20 miles away. Their new settlement, which numbered approximately 180 warriors, stretched for several miles along the Lake Michigan shore. Its inhabitants lived there from spring until fall, raising corn for their own needs and for trade with the French, who depended on it to provision their canoes. In the autumn they divided into family hunting bands and went southward to the valleys of the St Joseph and other rivers to hunt for furs during the winter and to make maple sugar in the spring.

Living in proximity to Fort Michilimackinac, the band developed ties with the French. Nissowaquet's bond with his sister's son, Charles-Michel MOUET de Langlade, particularly encouraged his friendship with them and his later association with the British. In 1739 the French raised a force of Ottawas to assist Pierre-Joseph Céloron* de Blainville on an expedition against the Chickasaws, who lived in the lower Mississippi valley. Nissowaquet was one of the war chiefs who participated.

There was much discontent among the Indians of the *pays d'en haut* during the 1740s, but Nissowaquet and his band maintained their alliance with the French. The band is said to have frustrated an intended uprising of western Indians in 1744 by reporting it to Paul-Joseph LE MOYNE de Longueuil. When war broke out between the French and the British in the 1750s, Nissowaquet and his warriors went east with Langlade to fight. In August 1757 a party of 70 assisted Montcalm* in the capture of Fort William Henry (also called Fort George, now Lake George, N.Y.). When the warriors returned to L'Arbre Croche they carried with them not only the spoils of war but the feared smallpox. The results were devastating. Ottawa tradition records that "Lodge after lodge was totally vacated – nothing but the dead bodies lying here and there in their lodges – entire families being swept off with the ravages of this terrible disease."

The British occupied Fort Michilimackinac in 1761, and Nissowaquet and his band accepted the new régime, as did Langlade. When in June 1763 the Ojibwas of Michilimackinac, organized by Minweweh*, captured the fort, Nissowaquet's band rescued most of the surviving soldiers and traders, whom they took to L'Arbre Croche and protected for over a month. For his services Nissowaquet obtained from the refugees a large quantity of trade goods and a personal slave. Some of the supplies he used to ransom captives from the Ojibwas, but many of the goods remained in his own lodge. A group of Ottawas escorted the refugees to Montreal and promised General GAGE, the military governor of the Montreal District, that they would be as good friends of the British as they had been of the French. The next year, when Nissowaquet attended Sir William JOHNSON's peace conference at Niagara (near Youngstown, N.Y.), he promised allegiance to the British and received in return a chief's commission and a medal.

In subsequent years Nissowaquet used these tokens of friendship to obtain presents of rum, tobacco, and clothing. Arguing that the chiefs of the Ottawas "take most of their time in serving the English, & keeping peace, among all the Nations," he obtained supplies from the commandants of Michilimackinac, particularly Robert ROGERS. He was, according to Indian agent Benjamin ROBERTS, "the richest Indian I ever Saw." All this wealth, the treasured commission, and a wampum belt received from Gage were consumed in a house fire in 1767, but Nissowaquet immediately began seeking replacement of his losses.

During the winter of 1767–68, while Nissowaquet was wintering on the Grand River (Mich.), Rogers was charged with treason and confined at Michilimackinac. Rumours circulated that Nissowaquet, the "Great Chief of the Ottawas," would help Rogers escape. When Nissowaquet returned with 40 of his warriors in the spring he was upset by Rogers' confinement, but although the Ojibwa chiefs showed their distress by throwing their British flags into the lake, he and his band returned peacefully to L'Arbre Croche. He kept tensions alive, however, by reporting the discovery of tracks of a large number of Indians with war canoes. Nissowaquet again shrewdly used the threat of attack by other Indians to bolster his own value to the British, promising at a conference in August 1768 that "as Long as you remain here you and your Garrison Shall always Sleep in Saftey, that we will watch over you, And If any bad news is hered amongst any of the Villiages you shall be informed of it Immediately as we are a check to all the Nations, whose harts are not True to the English . . . ."

When the American revolution broke out, Nissowaquet sided with the British, and his warriors took part in several expeditions. By the 1780s his active career was nearly over, although he continued to be the most important chief of L'Arbre Croche. He and his band usually made several visits to Michilimackinac in the summer to receive presents and have their hoes and guns repaired by the fort's blacksmith; he was there in 1791, 1792, and 1793. Some time in 1797 he died.

DAVID A. ARMOUR

AN, Col., C[11A], 77, ff.151, 156, 158, 160. Clements Library, Thomas Gage papers, supplementary accounts, William Lesley's deposition, 18 Feb. 1764; Henry Bostwick and Ezekiel Solomon's deposition, 25 April 1764; Frederick Spiesmacher, journal, 6 Dec. 1767 – 17 June 1768; John Askin's blacksmith accounts, 1769; George Turnbull's Indian expenses, 25 May 1770 – 25 Nov. 1772. Newberry Library (Chicago), MSS coll., George Etherington to Charles Langlade, 16, 18 June, 14 July 1763. PAC, RG 10, A2, 26, pp.14967–15076.

Bougainville, *Adventure in wilderness* (Hamilton), 126, 143, 150–51; "Journal" (A.-E. Gosselin), ANQ *Rapport*, 1923–24, 266–67, 272–73, 282, 287–88. [A. S. De Peyster], *Miscellanies, by an officer* (Dumfries, Scot., 1813), 31, 33; [2nd ed.], ed. J. W. De Peyster (2v. in 1, New York, 1888), xxxiv, xxxv. Henry, *Travels and adventures*. *Johnson papers* (Sullivan *et al.*), V, 714–15; VI, 348–49; X, 779–85; XI, 273–74; XII, 491–92. *Michigan Pioneer Coll.*, X (1886), 406; XII (1887), 261–63. *NYCD* (O'Callaghan and Fernow), IX, 1053; X, 608. [Robert Rogers], "Rogers's Michillimackinac journal," ed. W. L. Clements, American Antiquarian Soc., *Proc.* (Worcester, Mass.), new ser., 28 (1918), 247–51, 253–55. *Treason? at Michilimackinac: the proceedings of a general court martial held at Montreal in October 1768 for the trial of Major Robert Rogers*, ed. D. A. Armour (Mackinac Island, Mich., 1967), 41. Wis., State Hist. Soc., *Coll.*, I (1855), 43–48; III (1857), 198–99, 212–13; VII (1876), 125–26; XVII (1906), 372–75; XVIII (1908), 67–68, 253, 388, 390; XIX (1910), 2–3, 50–52, 153–54. A. J. Blackbird, *History of the Ottawa and Chippewa Indians of Michigan . . .* (Ypsilanti, Mich., 1887), 9–10. N. W. Caldwell, "The Chickasaw threat to French control of the Mississippi in the 1740's," *Chronicles of Oklahoma* (Oklahoma City), XVI (1938), 465–92.

NORTON, MOSES, HBC chief factor; b. *c.* 1735, son of Richard Norton* and Susannah Dupeer; d. 29 Dec. 1773 at Prince of Wales's Fort (Churchill, Man.).

Moses Norton is one of the most controversial figures in the annals of the Hudson's Bay Company. Historians of the fur trade do not agree in their assessment of him: Richard Glover denounces him as "a very sinister man" whereas Edwin Ernest Rich praises him, especially for his "uncommon energy and perception." The root of the conflict lies in the credibility of a damning character sketch of Norton written by Samuel HEARNE and first published in 1795. Hearne nursed a deep hatred for Norton and several of his allegations must be questioned.

Norton's origin remains a mystery. He was definitely not "an Indian" as Hearne claims, but owing to Hearne's statement that Norton was born at Prince of Wales's Fort it has widely been assumed that he was the mixed-blood son of his father and a native woman. Norton's will, however, suggests that both his parents were European, for he names Susannah Dupeer as his mother. Since Richard Norton had married Elizabeth McCliesh, it is possible that Moses was born of an illicit union when his father was on furlough in England in the 1730s.

The course of Moses Norton's career reinforces the improbability of his being of mixed blood. In 1744 Norton was indentured in England to one of the HBC's ship captains, George Spurrell*, for a term of seven years. His career with the company was launched in 1753 when he contracted to serve as mate of the Churchill sloop for three years at a salary of £25 per annum. In 1756 he became accountant and assistant to Ferdinand JACOBS, chief factor of Prince of Wales's Fort, assuming temporary command of the post in 1759 prior to a year's furlough in England. He was appointed chief factor in 1762 and retained command at Churchill until his death. In view of the company's official policy, which forbade intimate contact between its servants and the Indians [*see* Joseph ISBISTER], it is doubtful whether the London committee would appoint a mixed-blood to one of its most important posts. It was not until 1794 that official permission was given for mixed-blood boys to be employed in the company's service. If Norton was indeed a native of Hudson Bay, it is curious that his exceptional advancement received no mention in the company's records.

The correspondence between Norton and his superiors reveals the faith which the London committee had in his ability to carry out the arduous responsibilities connected with Prince of Wales's Fort. Three difficult tasks faced Norton: the reconstruction of poorly built sections of the stone fort, further northern exploration, and the establishment of a black whale fishery. His failure to achieve conspicuous success in any of these areas resulted from circumstances beyond his control, rather than personal incompetence as Glover maintains. Work on the fort was inevitably hampered by lack of materials and skilled artisans. From 1761 to 1764 Norton himself captained expeditions to search for the elusive northwest passage. His explorations took him as far north as Chesterfield Inlet (N.W.T.) and he was rewarded by the committee with a gratuity of £40. Norton, whose annual instructions to his sloop captains show a comprehensive grasp of affairs, improved the coastal trade with the Inuit, particularly after 1765, when he succeeded in negotiating a peace between the Inuit and their enemies, the Chipewyans. Norton's interest in the fabled northern copper mine, which had long intrigued the company's officers at Churchill, was heightened in 1767 when two Indians, Idotliazee and another (probably MATONABBEE), returned to Churchill after five years of exploration with a piece of copper ore and a draft map. During his furlough the following year, Norton was able to interest the committee in his plans for exploration which subsequently led to the dispatch of Samuel Hearne in 1769. Although Norton has been held responsible for the failure of Hearne's first two journeys, it is doubtful whether he would have deliberately tried to sabotage an undertaking in whose success he was so much interested. Norton has been unfairly castigated for the failure of the black whale fishery, which was abandoned in 1772. The project was defeated, in spite of much effort and expense, by the lack of skilled men, inadequate boats, and the short season.

In sum, the London committee had reason to consider Moses Norton a highly valuable servant, and it expressed disapproval only of the manner in which he attempted to curb private trade. Although Hearne charged that Norton was "a notorious smuggler," the problem of private trade was much worse at the posts at the bottom of the bay than at Churchill. Norton had adopted a realistic approach to curbing the abuse; he allowed his "principal Officers and Tradesmen" to trade furs with the ships' captains in return for their suppressing "illicit Trade and practices among the Inferior Class." In 1770, as part of a general attempt to deal with the problem, the London committee ordered Norton to abandon his scheme. To curb the chief factors' penchant for indulging in private trade, the committee raised their salaries to £130 per annum and allowed them a bounty of three shillings on every score of made beaver shipped to England. Norton was reprimanded for trying to curry favour by sending presents of furs to his friends on the London committee.

Within the draughty walls of Prince of Wales's Fort, Norton endeavoured to live in high style. His apartments were "not only convenient but elegant"; he imported books, pictures, and an organ from England, and even kept a pet parrot. Like his father before him, Norton showed a particular fondness for the company of Indians, who were regularly admitted to his quarters. He was a stern disciplinarian, however, and he earned the enmity of some of his men, notably Hearne, by refusing to allow them to have any dealings with Indian women [*see* George ATKINSON]. He himself had an Indian family, but there is no evidence to substantiate Hearne's claim that he lived a most debauched existence, maintaining five or six of the finest Indian girls for his pleasure and not hesitating to poison any man who refused him a wife or daughter. Norton's only known descendant was a daughter named Mary (Polly), born in the early 1760s of a Cree woman. A doting father, Norton indulged this child to such an extent that she became totally unsuited to the hardships of Indian life; although provided with a generous annuity by her father, Mary perished during the difficult winter of 1782 following Hearne's surrender of Churchill to the French under Lapérouse [GALAUP]. Like other chief factors of this period, Norton also maintained an English wife, Sarah, whom he probably married in 1753. He made regular and generous payments to her and named her the executrix of his will.

Norton died in December 1773 from a chronic disorder of the bowels. The 21-gun salute fired at his funeral would have pleased Norton, for he wanted to be remembered at his passing. To his friends and servants, he left bequests for mourning rings and apparel and "ten Gallons of English Brandy to be equally divided amongst all hands."

SYLVIA VAN KIRK

HBC Arch. A.1/39, A.1/43, A.5/1, A.6/15, A.11/14, A.16/10, A.44/1. PRO, Prob. 11/713, f.314; 11/1002, f.374. *Copy-book of letters outward &c, begins 29th May, 1680, ends 5 July, 1687*, ed. E. E. Rich and A. M. Johnson, intro. E. G. R. Taylor (Toronto, 1948). Hearne, *Journey from Prince of Wales's Fort* (Glover). *Letters from Hudson Bay, 1703–40*, ed. K. G. Davies and A. M. Johnson, intro. R. [G.] Glover (London, 1965). Rich, *History of HBC*, II.

NOSAWAGUET. *See* NISSOWAQUET

NOYAN ET DE CHAVOY, PIERRE-JACQUES PAYEN DE. *See* PAYEN

O

OAKES, FORREST, merchant and fur-trader; d. 1783 in Montreal (Que.).

Forrest Oakes was an English merchant who came to Canada during the period of military occupation. By 1761 he was a partner in the firm of MacKenzie and Oakes, and in September he hired indentured employees in Montreal to go to Michilimackinac (Mackinaw City, Mich.) under the leadership of Ignace Pinsonneau, *dit* Lafleur. Oakes accompanied the expedition and either stayed at Michilimackinac or went inland. In 1762 he was sued at Montreal for debt by Joseph Lamoureux, *dit* Saint-Germain, who had been hired as a guide in 1761. Oakes was represented at the hearing by Lawrence ERMATINGER, his partner from 1763 to 1766.

Oakes's presence at various places from Montreal to Grand Portage (near Grand Portage, Minn.) can be documented, but it is difficult to trace his activities. From 1763 to 1765 he was in the fur trade, probably in the Great Lakes region, but there is no proof that he wintered inland. In 1766 and 1768 he seems to have been in Montreal; in 1767 he appears on the list of licences issued at Michilimackinac and he was probably inland at this time.

From 1767 to 1782 Oakes received trade goods from Ermatinger, now his brother-in-law and his principal outfitter. During this period Ermatinger, in Montreal, forwarded supplies to Grand Portage on an increasing scale, from one canoe with £241 of trade goods in 1767 to canoe-loads worth from £1,300 to £1,700 in the years 1771–73, when Oakes was associated with Charles Boyer. In 1774 Oakes went into partnership with Boyer and Peter Pangman*, and Ermatinger's extensive shipments the next year were divided into four separate lots with different codes marked on each bale, suggesting that trade was being carried on in four different locations. Oakes came down to Montreal in 1776, but he spent the next two years in Grand Portage. He may have been one of the traders who pooled their stock to send Peter Pond* to the Athabasca country in 1778. In 1779, when his partnership with Pangman and Boyer ended, he became one of the partners who formed the original North West Company, capitalized at 16 shares, of which Oakes and Company held one. Ermatinger forwarded two canoes to Oakes in 1780 and 1781 but only one in 1782, a decline which may reflect the increasing competition from both other Montreal-based traders and the Hudson's Bay Company as well as the bad state of Ermatinger's finances. Oakes returned to Montreal from the Great Lakes region in the fall of 1782 and died between 17 April and 24 May 1783.

It is impossible to know how far Oakes travelled inland from Grand Portage. It seems likely that he divided his time between Michilimackinac, Sault Ste Marie (Mich.), and Grand Portage, sending down meticulously prepared indents and provision lists to Ermatinger, arranging for corn shipments from Detroit, keeping track of the wintering partners, and supervising the packaging and shipment of cargo inland and of furs to Montreal. He may have spent his winters comfortably at Michilimackinac or Sault Ste Marie with his Indian wife. He left one son, John Meticamish Oakes, a minor, who may have become John Oakes* the silversmith. The fact that Oakes left property in Handsworth (West Midlands), England, suggests that he came from there.

GEORGE E. THORMAN

ANQ-M, Chambre de milices, 5, f.16; État civil, Anglicans, Christ Church (Montréal). BL, Add. MSS 35915, f.232. PAC, MG 19, A2, ser.3, 86, 88, 89. *Docs. relating to NWC* (Wallace), 62–66, 439, 489. *John Askin papers* (Quaife), I, 51, 91, 141, 146, 149–50, 156–57. Massicotte, "Répertoire des engagements pour l'Ouest," ANQ *Rapport*, 1932–33, 268. Innis, *Fur trade in Canada* (1930), 195–219. Daniel Morison, *The doctor's secret journal* (Mackinac Island, Mich., 1960), 12–22.

A. S. Morton, "Forrest Oakes, Charles Boyer, Joseph Fulton, and Peter Pangman in the northwest, 1765–1793," RSC *Trans.*, 3rd ser., XXXI (1937), sect.II, 87–100.

OGILVIE, JOHN, Church of England clergyman; b. 1724 in New York City, son of Lieutenant William Ogilvie of the British army; m. 15 Sept. 1751 Susanna Catharine Symes of New York, and they had five children; m. secondly on 17 April 1769 Margaret Marston, widow of Philip Philipse, of New York; d. 26 Nov. 1774 in New York.

John Ogilvie enrolled in Yale College, New Haven, Connecticut, in 1745 and as an undergraduate became a candidate for holy orders; at this time he served as a lay reader in two missions. He graduated in 1748 and then sailed to England, having been recommended to the Society for the Propagation of the Gospel as "a young Gentleman of good abilities . . . of much Piety and Zeal, and of a virtuous Life." He was ordained deacon in London on 27 March 1749 and was raised to the priesthood on 2 April. On 30 June Ogilvie was licensed to officiate as an SPG missionary and was back in New York by 30 November.

On 31 March 1750 he began work at St Peter's Church in Albany (N.Y.), a mission to which was attached the care of the Indians at Fort Hunter, some 40 miles to the west. Here, during a decade of turbulence and war, he ministered in English and Dutch to his motley frontier flock. Soon he was able to read church services in Mohawk, but he used an interpreter in preaching to the Indians. In later years he maintained his interest in the Fort Hunter congregation and directed the publication of the second Mohawk prayer book. This book was a new edition of a translation which had appeared in 1715. The revision had been done under the direction of Henry Barclay, former missionary at Fort Hunter; printing was begun in 1763 but was not completed until 1769 because of Barclay's death and publishing difficulties. Christian Daniel CLAUS, who prepared a third edition in 1780, later indicated that the 1769 one was "replete with mistakes."

Before the Seven Years' War Ogilvie occasionally preached for the army, and on 1 Sept. 1756 he was appointed chaplain to the newly raised Royal American Regiment (62nd, later 60th Foot) on the recommendation of Sir William JOHNSON. In that capacity he accompanied the expedition under Johnson and Brigadier-General John Prideaux to Fort Niagara (near Youngstown, N.Y.) in the summer of 1759, and after the capture of the fort he returned to Albany for a short time. He took up chaplaincy duties again under AMHERST at Oswego, went to Montreal following its capture in 1760, and stayed there for four years. Ogilvie thus became the first minister of the Church of England to serve in Montreal. He was popular with the military and civil population, and he got along well with the Roman Catholic clergy and members of the religious orders. Since no Anglican church had been erected he conducted services in the chapel of the Hôtel-Dieu. He maintained contact with Albany and New York and he probably visited Quebec. Ogilvie performed baptisms at Sorel, Chambly, and Boucherville, near Montreal, and endeavoured to commend Anglican worship to Roman Catholic Mohawks by showing them the prayer book in their own language. In letters to the SPG in 1760 and 1763, Ogilvie observed, with some caution, that the large Sulpician and Jesuit estates might be a source for endowing missionary work among the Indians and for the establishment of the Church of England in Canada. In mentioning the Jesuit estates he anticipated an issue of major political importance in the next century [*see* Jean-Joseph CASOT; Antoine-Nicolas Braun*].

In September 1764 Ogilvie was appointed assistant minister at Trinity Church in New York, where he laboured until his death. In 1769 he was awarded an honorary degree of Doctor of Divinity by Marischal College (University of Aberdeen). Ogilvie was remembered favourably by many of his contemporaries; one commented that his "appearance was singularly prepossessing; his address and manners entirely those of a gentleman." Claus, who as an Indian department official had been closely associated with Ogilvie, wrote to the SPG in 1782 describing him as "an ornament and a blessing to the Church he belonged to."

T. R. MILLMAN

Protestant Episcopal Church in the U.S.A., Archives and Hist. Coll. – Episcopal Church (Austin, Tex.), E. L. Pennington papers, "The manuscript register and journal of the Reverend John Ogilvie, from April 22, 1750, to February 12, 1759 . . . ," ed. E. L. Pennington (typescript), in the custody of the Hist. Soc. of the Episcopal Church (Austin) (copy in Anglican Church of Canada, General Synod Archives, Toronto). *Abstracts of wills on file in the surrogate's office, city of New York* (17v., N.Y. Hist. Soc., *Coll.*, [ser.3], XXV–XLI, New York, 1892–1908), VIII: *1771–1776*, 247–48. *Archives of the general convention: the correspondence of John Henry Hobart* [1757–1811], ed. A. [E.] Lowndes (6v., New York, 1911–12), IV, 72, 123–34. [A. MacV.] Grant, *Memoirs of an American lady . . .* (New York and Philadelphia, 1846), 187. Charles Inglis, *Ser-*

mon on II Corinth. V. 6 occasioned by the death of John Ogilvie, D.D., assistant minister of Trinity Church, New-York (New York, 1774). *Johnson papers* (Sullivan *et al.*).

F. B. Dexter, *Biographical sketches of the graduates of Yale College with annals of the college history* (6v., New York and New Haven, Conn., 1885–1912), II, 174–77. *DAB*. William Berrian, *An historical sketch of Trinity Church, New York* (New York, 1847), 127–34. Joseph Hooper, *A history of Saint Peter's Church in the city of Albany*, intro. W. W. Battershal (Albany, N.Y., 1900). J. W. Lydekker, *The faithful Mohawks* (Cambridge, Eng., 1938). W. B. Sprague, *Annals of the American pulpit . . .* (9v., New York, 1857–69), V, 134–37. A. H. Young, "The Revd. John Ogilvie, D.D., an army chaplain at Fort Niagara and Montreal, 1759–60," *OH*, XXII (1925), 296–337.

OHQUANDAGEGHTE (Atquandadeghte, Kointaguettez, Kouategeté, Otkwande, Otqueandageghte), Onondaga warrior; fl. 1757–73 in the upper St Lawrence River region; m. 10 May 1760 at La Présentation (Ogdensburg, N.Y.).

In 1701 the Six Nations declared their neutrality in the conflict between the French and British in North America, but rumours of conspiracy and double-dealing among them frequently circulated among the Europeans, particularly at periods of crisis. The difficulty of assessing such reports has not lessened with the passing of time. According to Pierre Pouchot*, Ohquandageghte spied for the British and acted as an intermediary in illicit trading between them and the French commanders of Fort Frontenac (Kingston, Ont.). His supposed friendship for the British did not, however, prevent him from accepting from Governor Vaudreuil [RIGAUD] in 1757 a commission as head warrior of Oswegatchie, the village at François PICQUET's strategic mission-post of La Présentation. In April 1758 he led a raid on German Flats, a part of the Mohawk valley near the mouth of West Canada Creek. At about that time Sir William JOHNSON, the British superintendent of northern Indians, was notified that Ohquandageghte's body along with a knife inscribed "Otqueandageghte le Camera [camarade] de Jeanson" had been found. The spelling of the Onondaga name appears to be in the English style, and the story behind the report remains a mystery; the body was not Ohquandageghte's.

Pouchot believed that John BRADSTREET's capture of Fort Frontenac in August 1758 so offended Ohquandageghte that he committed himself to the French cause. The warrior's enthusiasm for fighting the British had, however, diminished by March 1760, when Pouchot arrived to command at Fort Lévis near the mission. Ohquandageghte would no longer go on war parties, claiming religious scruples arising from his recent conversion. "He understood none of our distinctions," the Frenchman remarked. Pouchot appears not to have considered that Ohquandageghte's newly found pacificism might have resulted from the British victories of the previous year. Ohquandageghte was willing to gather information for the French, however. Early in the summer of 1760 he went to Oswego to find out what the Six Nations were planning to do regarding the forthcoming British move down the St Lawrence against Montreal. He warned the Indians there that the British intended to extirpate their people; on his return he told Pouchot that he had spoken with AMHERST and he reported on the size of the assembled British force.

In 1762 he was involved in plans to make war on the British. Sir William Johnson instructed his deputy Christian Daniel CLAUS to warn him against such an action. Whether Ohquandageghte received the message is not known, but shortly after it was sent he went to the commandant of Fort William Augustus (formerly Fort Lévis), Henry GLADWIN, told him of French attempts to stir up the Indians, and gave him the names of Indians at Oswegatchie who had been implicated. He declared repentance of his own involvement and relinquished his commission from Vaudreuil. When Major-General GAGE attempted to investigate the story further, however, Ohquandageghte was reluctant to confront the people against whom he had informed.

In the fall of 1763 he was reported to be residing at Cataraqui (Kingston, Ont.) and to have planned with some Mississaugas and others to cut off the movement of troops and provisions on the St Lawrence. The next fall he was sent prisoner to Montreal for having attempted to cross the checkpoint at nearby Les Cèdres without a pass. (Pontiac*'s uprising of 1763 had aggravated British fears of conspiracy among the Indians.) He was apparently charged with further intrigues in 1766 but he denied the allegations. "Deserted by the Swegachy Indians," he was by 1769 living at St Regis. He was given a British commission as a chief and a medal but was, Claus reported, "so dashed & conscious of not deserving it [the medal] that he would not wear it."

In 1773 Ohquandageghte sided with the priest in a power struggle, the exact nature of which is not known, at St Regis. He went to see Johnson about the dispute and on returning distorted Johnson's answer to make it appear that he and his faction had the Indian superintendent's support. The Iroquois chiefs of Caughnawaga, who had some authority over St Regis, complained to Claus of Ohquandageghte's actions and pretensions. They asserted that his appointment as chief had not had their approval and that he was "an Ind^{n} that had no certain place of Abode."

IN COLLABORATION

Inv. des papiers de Léry (P.-G. Roy), III, 10. *Johnson papers* (Sullivan *et al.*). [Pierre] Pouchot, *Memoir upon the late war in North America, between the French and the English, 1755–60 . . .* , ed. and trans. F. B. Hough (2v., Roxbury, Mass., 1866). W. L. Stone, *Life of Joseph Brant – Thayendanegea . . .* (2v., New York, 1838).

OLABARATZ (De Laubara, Dolobarats), JOANNIS-GALAND D', merchant fisherman, privateer, and port captain; b. probably at Saint-Jean-de-Luz, France; d. 1778 at Bayonne, France.

The cod fishery first attracted Joannis-Galand d'Olabaratz to Louisbourg, Île Royale (Cape Breton Island). As early as 1722 he was granted a concession on the north side of the harbour for drying his catch, but he does not seem to have made the fortress his residence until the mid 1730s. He should not be confused with Jean Dolabaratz, another merchant fisherman who was also active at Louisbourg during this period.

When war came in 1744, d'Olabaratz hoped to profit by privateering. That May he accompanied in his own ship the successful expedition led by François DU PONT Duvivier against Canso (N.S.). Returning to Louisbourg in early June, he signed two agreements: one for the purchase and outfitting of the corsair *Cantabre*, which he owned in partnership with Duvivier, François BIGOT, and Jean-Baptiste-Louis Le Prévost* Duquesnel; the other with a M. Leneuf de Beaubassin, probably Philippe, captain of the corsair *Caesar*, whereby the two men agreed to share their proceeds from privateering equally for one month. The two ships sailed together in June but were separated, and the unlucky d'Olabaratz and his 93-man crew on the *Cantabre* were captured 15 leagues off Cape Cod by a Massachusetts coast guard vessel commanded by Edward Tyng*. Imprisoned in Boston for several months, d'Olabaratz returned to Louisbourg in November with information, perhaps intentionally leaked by Governor William Shirley, concerning a British amphibious assault on Louisbourg supposedly planned for the following spring. D'Olabaratz wrote a report on New England in which he noted with a privateer's eye that Boston's material wealth would permit a handsome payment to avoid pillage. He carried his report to France, where he was assigned to the fleet of Antoine-Alexis Perier de Salvert. In 1746 he was given command of a frigate in the fleet commanded by the Duc d'Anville [La Rochefoucauld*]. For these and other services, he was honoured in 1748 with the rank of fire-ship captain.

D'Olabaratz returned to Louisbourg after it was restored to France in 1748, and in 1750 he became port captain, a post previously held by Pierre Morpain*. For the next eight years he filled this position to the satisfaction of several Louisbourg administrations and in addition to his regular duties undertook soundings of the harbour and nearby coastal waters. On 6 Jan. 1758, through winter seas usually considered unnavigable, d'Olabaratz succeeded in bringing provisions to Louisbourg, which had been blockaded the previous summer by the British [*see* Augustin de Boschenry* de Drucour]. He was back in France in March 1758 when he was awarded the cross of Saint-Louis and permitted to retire with a pension of 800 *livres*. Later that year, however, he rejoined the service of the Marine as a port official at Bayonne.

D'Olabaratz's involvement with New France had not ended. Bougainville*'s request for merchant captains to command the tiny French inland fleet brought him back, lured by the hope of wartime profits. When AMHERST's army began to move down Lake Champlain on 11 Oct. 1759 to attack the French under François-Charles de Bourlamaque* at Île aux Noix, d'Olabaratz and his three poorly constructed xebecs attacked a troop-laden bateau at daybreak on 12 October near the Îles aux Quatre Vents and captured 21 Highlanders of the 42nd Foot. Sailing north, he was spotted later in the day by a British brigantine and sloop. Captain Joshua LORING chased him toward the advancing British army, but d'Olabaratz sought refuge in a bay on the western shore. Believing his escape cut off, and perhaps deliberately having run one of his vessels aground, he called a council that decided to scuttle the vessels and make for Montreal overland with the prisoners.

Had Amherst not abandoned his campaign on 18 October when he heard of the fall of Quebec, d'Olabaratz might have received a severe reprimand from his superiors, especially because the British were able to raise his vessels with nearly all of their guns intact. Governor Vaudreuil [RIGAUD] accepted his explanation after d'Olabaratz reached Montreal on 21 October, but Bourlamaque, whose position at Île aux Noix had been jeopardized by d'Olabaratz's flight, thought that he should have attacked the enemy or attempted to escape at night. A marginal note in

Montcalm*'s journal admonished that d'Olabaratz was "*a man no longer to be employed in any command.*"

Nothing is known of d'Olabaratz after 1759. As a corsair, he had served the interests of France while he served his own. During two wars his seafaring experience aided the French cause even though his personal goal was profit, the booty from privateering on the high seas or other raids. Much of the French naval effort in North America until 1760 rested on the skill and daring of men such as d'Olabaratz, Morpain, and Jean VAUQUELIN. The hasty scuttling of d'Olabaratz's vessels on Lake Champlain, however, was an illustration that the privateer lacked the discipline and judgement of the regular naval officer.

D'Olabaratz had married Catherine Despiaube, and they had at least one son, Jean, who became port ensign at Louisbourg in 1743 and eventually rose to the rank of brigadier of marine infantry.

T. A. CROWLEY

AD, Charente-Maritime (La Rochelle), B, 266, ff.24v, 59v; 268, f.156; 275, ff.67–69, 72; 279, f.3v. AMA, SHA, A[1], 3393, nos.29, 59, 60. AN, Col., B, 91, f.330; 97, f.307; 108, f.123; C[11A], 104, ff.207–7v; C[11B], 26, f.32; 28, f.126; 30, f.250; 31, f.232; 32, ff.24, 210, 316; F[3], 50, ff.302, 495, 502; Marine, C[7], 229 (dossier Olabaratz); Section Outre-mer, G[1], 466/3, f.173; G[2], 192/1, ff.22, 34v; 192/2, ff.36, 48v. ASQ, Polygraphie, V, 47. Amherst, *Journal* (Webster). *Coll. de manuscrits relatifs à la N.-F.*, III, 213–15, 477. *Coll. des manuscrits de Lévis* (Casgrain), V, 62, 65, 70, 71, 325–27, 343, 349, 350; VII, 525, 544; VIII, 125, 141; IX, 77–79. Knox, *Hist. journal* (Doughty), III, 65, 73–74. *Mémoires sur le Canada, depuis 1749 jusqu'à 1760*, 171. *NYCD* (O'Callaghan and Fernow), X, 1042, 1056. PAC *Rapport*, 1924, 1–70. McLennan, *Louisbourg*. Rawlyk, *Yankees at Louisbourg*. Stanley, *New France*.

OLD KING (Old Smoke). *See* KAIEÑ?KWAAHTOÑ

OLIVA, FRÉDÉRIC-GUILLAUME (Frederick William), physician; b. *c.* 1749, probably of German origin; m. 30 Jan. 1782 Catherine Couillard Des Islets, and they had eight children; d. 31 July 1796 in Quebeç City.

During the American revolutionary war Frédéric-Guillaume Oliva served as surgeon major in one of the regiments lent to Great Britain by the Duke of Brunswick and commanded by Friedrich Adolphus von Riedesel. Oliva's military experience, although grim, must have greatly assisted his professional development, since the German troops had their share of injuries and wounds as well as such diseases as scurvy, smallpox, and dysentery. After the war Oliva practised medicine in Saint-Thomas-de-Montmagny (Montmagny, Que.), but in 1792 he and his family moved to Quebec City, where he practised for the remainder of his life.

Oliva, like many of the German soldiers who settled in Quebec, was Roman Catholic. He was assimilated into Canadian, not English, society when he married the daughter of the co-seigneur of Rivière-du-Sud, Louis Couillard Des Islets. He joined many of his fellow citizens in signing the Loyal Declaration of 1794, which, written in response to the French revolution and against the "designing and wicked men" who would follow its example, extolled the British constitution and condemned those who were then ruling France.

Oliva seems to have been dedicated to the welfare of his patients, whatever their rank. He once requested the authorities to postpone the prison sentence given a farmer until the man had fully recovered from a severe attack of dysentery. As for his medical theories, known largely from the *Mémoires* of Philippe-Joseph Aubert* de Gaspé, they appear to have been based on a healthy scepticism about received medical opinion. Aubert de Gaspé, who was inoculated with smallpox by the doctor at the age of five, wrote that Oliva pioneered in the prescription of fresh air and daily exercise for those afflicted or inoculated with the disease, at a time when treatment usually consisted of heat and strong liquor. According to Aubert de Gaspé, Oliva once said during a smallpox epidemic, "How lucky are those unfortunates who fall ill in the country, close by a stream and under the shadow of the pine trees; ninety per cent of such will probably recover." Although many people thought him mad at the time, he used an ice bath in the cure of typhus, and it is said that he saved the life of his son, Frédéric-Godlip, in this way.

In 1788 Oliva was appointed to the first board of medical examiners for the District of Quebec, which together with a similar body at Montreal had been established by a licensing act passed that year. As an examiner he appears to have probed the more fundamental issues of medical treatment. We know, for example, that Pierre Fabre*, *dit* Laterrière, was asked by him, not to name surgical instruments, nor even to describe the circulation of the blood, but to explore the differences between the patient in the books and the patient in the bed. In 1795 Oliva, along with James Fisher*, John Mervin Nooth*, and George Longmore, was examined by the House of Assembly on the problem of contagious diseases brought into the colony by ocean-going vessels. That year the assembly passed a statute enabling the governor to quarantine ships suspected of carrying disease.

Despite his many achievements, Oliva seems to have been a modest man. The condescension and boasting characteristic of the advertisements of European-trained physicians were entirely absent in the announcement opening his Quebec City practice, and for a doctor he had an attractive humility in the face of the healing power of nature. Aubert de Gaspé wrote that his death "was an irreparable loss for Quebec, where good doctors were very rare."

F. MURRAY GREENWOOD

PAC, MG 24, L3, pp.5027–28; RG 4, B28, 47. P.[-J.] Aubert de Gaspé, *Mémoires* (Ottawa, 1866), 17–25. Bas-Canada, chambre d'Assemblée, *Journaux*, 1795. Max von Eelking, *Memoirs, and letters and journals, of Major General Riedesel, during his residence in America*, trans. W. I. Stone (2v., Albany, N.Y., 1868). Fabre, dit Laterrière, *Mémoires* (A. Garneau). *Quebec Gazette*, 10 Aug. 1786, 23 April 1789, 19 April, 14 June, 10 July 1794, 26 March 1795. Tanguay, *Dictionnaire*. Abbott, *History of medicine*, 41–49. M.-J. et G. Ahern, *Notes pour l'hist. de la médecine*, 217–23, 428–29. P.-G. Roy, "Biographies canadiennes," *BRH*, XXI (1915), 91–94.

OLIVIER DE VÉZIN (Vésin, Vézain), PIERRE-FRANÇOIS, ironmaster, director of the Saint-Maurice ironworks, and chief road officer in Louisiana; b. 28 April 1707 at Aingoulaincourt (dept of Haute-Marne), France, son of Hugues Olivier and Louise Le Roux; d. in or after 1776.

Pierre-François Olivier de Vézin was an ironmaster at Sionne (dept of Vosges), France, at the time he was hired by the king to investigate the Saint-Maurice ironworks in New France. These ironworks had virtually been abandoned after the death of their first owner, François Poulin* de Francheville, in 1733. With an annual salary of 2,400 *livres* and a special gratuity of 1,200 *livres*, Olivier de Vézin sailed on the *Héros* and reached Quebec on 3 Sept. 1735. After a five-week tour with Jean-Eustache Lanoullier* de Boisclerc to Batiscan, Champlain, and finally Saint-Maurice, he drew up a report to Maurepas, the minister of Marine, which included an assessment of the favourable and disadvantageous aspects of Poulin de Francheville's establishment, and he appended a "draft of the expenses to be incurred to set up and run the ironworks in Canada" [*see* François-Étienne Cugnet*]. He offered to oversee the undertaking himself, quite forgetting his ironworks at Sionne.

Vézin and two of Poulin de Francheville's former partners, Cugnet and Ignace GAMELIN, drew up a plan for a partnership. In the spring of 1736 they received backing from the king, who agreed to Vézin's proposal and consented to advance substantial capital. When the company was formed on 16 Oct. 1736, it also included Thomas-Jacques Taschereau*, the agent of the treasurers general of the Marine, and Jacques Simonet* d'Abergemont, an ironmaster sent from France some months earlier to help Vézin set up the ironworks. They all signed the official instrument establishing the "Société et Compagnie pour l'Exploitation des . . . mines de fer" on 11 Feb. 1737, but preparatory work had already been undertaken in 1736 under Vézin's enthusiastic direction. He enjoyed the confidence of colonial officials and had the benefit of royal bounties. However the works did not progress as quickly as he had promised and were costly. Intendant HOCQUART began to question the ironmaster's competence. Vézin had in fact been guilty of a technical error in overestimating the flow of the stream that was to run the ironworks, and he tried to conceal his error when the intendant came to visit the installations in July 1738. Not until August was the furnace first lit successfully.

Vézin went to France late in 1739 and returned the following year with his brother, the Sieur Darmeville, and several workmen. Simonet d'Abergemont had replaced him during his absence. Violent disputes now occurred between Olivier de Vézin and his partners who blamed him for spending too much money, for the workmen's bad behaviour, and for the ironworks' unprofitability. These difficulties became so serious that in 1741 bankruptcy became inevitable for the undertaking. Olivier de Vézin submitted his resignation on 13 October and immediately returned to France on the *Rubis* to plead his cause. Writing to the king on 13 March 1742, he offered to resume management of the Saint-Maurice ironworks. Instead, he was commissioned chief road officer in Louisiana the following year.

The reports drawn up by the interested parties after the bankruptcy of the ironworks all blame Olivier de Vézin. When he had been chosen to go to New France, Maurepas had stated that his qualities as an ironmaster were well known, but they were in fact frequently questioned by his partners. It is undeniable that there were other causes for the bankruptcy; the difficulty in finding really competent skilled workers and the workers' lack of discipline are two of the factors that prevent our blaming Vézin alone. Subsequent managements achieved only modest results which indicate that Olivier de Vézin's management was not the sole reason for the poor performance of the ironworks.

However that may be, in 1744 Olivier de Vézin was in Louisiana. His new duties as chief road officer did not satisfy him completely; he soon made clear his desire to undertake the exploitation of iron mines in Louisiana, but the project was stillborn. He continued to carry out the duties of chief road officer and of surveyor general for Louisiana, and in 1749 he was back in Trois-Rivières, where on 14 June he married Marie-Joseph, the daughter of Jean-Baptiste Gastineau* Duplessis. Vézin had obviously not forgotten his earlier ties with America: in his marriage certificate he indicated that he was "the first person sent by the king to this country to set up there the ironworks and furnace of Saint-Maurice, of which he was the first director." Vézin returned to Louisiana with his young wife, and on 4 July 1754 he received permission to sail for France on the *Rhinocéros* to try to persuade the king to exonerate him from responsibility in the bankruptcy of the Saint-Maurice ironworks, in which he had "lost his time, his emoluments, his youth, and his salary." He wanted the assurance of being freed of all debt.

Olivier de Vézin remained in Louisiana even after the colony was transferred to Spain in 1762. After a score of years in that colony, where he held important administrative posts, he must have acquired a certain renown as well as gratifying material rewards. He became a member of the *Cabildo*, the council of six members that replaced the Conseil Supérieur of the former French colony, when it was created in 1769, and served as *regidor perpetual* (councillor) and *alcalde mayor provincial* (chief provincial justice of the peace). In 1776 he resigned his positions in favour of one of his sons, Charles-Honoré Olivier de Saint-Maurice. This is the last piece of information we have on Pierre Olivier de Vézin. According to some sources he is supposed to have died while on a voyage in France.

His wife must have died some years before him. During the 1760s two sons, Pierre-Darmeville and Nicolas-Joseph-Godefroy, lived for a time at Trois-Rivières with their aunt, Madeleine Duplessis. On her death in 1768 she left a legacy to them and other children of Olivier de Vézin. In January 1770 Vézin was chosen guardian of those of his children who had remained in Canada. That year he went to Trois-Rivières for the last time; he was present at the marriage of his friend Michel-Eustache-Gaspard-Alain Chartier* de Lotbinière. In 1772 and 1773 Jacques PERRAULT, known as Perrault *l'aîné*, took care on his behalf of the sale of property left by Madeleine Duplessis. From that time on the Olivier family was firmly established in Louisiana. Nicolas-Joseph-Godefroy purchased a huge sugar-cane plantation at St Bernard, not far from New Orleans, and several of his descendants were prominent in the area.

M.-F. FORTIER

AD, Haute-Marne (Chaumont), État civil, Aingoulaincourt, 29 avril 1707. AN, Col., B, 62, p.56; 63/1, pp.237–39; C[11A], 63, pp.45, 58; 65, pp.154–57; 72, p.29; 76, pp.68–69; 100, pp.207–10; 110; 111; 112; C[13A], 38, pp.8–11; 42, pp.81–82; C[13C], 4, pp.238–39 (PAC transcripts). ANQ-MBF, État civil, Catholiques, Immaculée-Conception (Trois-Rivières), 14 juin 1749, 13 déc.1770; Greffe de Paul Dielle, 4, 28 nov. 1768, 3 avril 1772, 6 mars 1773; Greffe de C.-L. Maillet, 3 avril, 5 nov. 1772, 6 mars 1733; Greffe de H.-O. Pressé, 28 sept. 1737. Archives maritimes, Port de Rochefort (France), 1E, 122, f.334; S, 162, liasse 131, pièce 225. New Orleans Public Library, Dept. of Archives, Cabildo, 1769–1803, I, pp.3, 139–43, 242.

J.-N. Fauteux, *Essai sur l'industrie*, I, 55–124. Jouve, *Les franciscains et le Canada: aux Trois-Rivières*. J. S. Kendall, *History of New Orleans* (3v., New York and Chicago, 1922), III, 1069–70. E. E. Long, *Madame Olivier's mansion* (New Orleans, 1965), 11–18. Sulte, *Mélanges historiques* (Malchelosse), VI. Tessier, *Les forges Saint-Maurice*.

ONONDAMOKIN. *See* ANANDAMOAKIN

ORILLAT, JEAN, merchant-trader; b. 1733 at Barbezieux, France, son of Jean Orillat and Marie Dupuy; m. 21 Sept. 1761 Marie-Amable Filiau, *dit* Dubois, in Montreal (Que.); m. there secondly 27 Aug. 1767 Thérèse-Amable Viger; d. 1779 in Montreal.

Jean Orillat came to Canada when he was quite young and soon took an interest in business. It is not known whether he brought capital from France, but in 1757 he signed on 16 men as *engagés* to go to Michilimackinac (Mackinaw City, Mich.). The war doubtless interrupted his trade in furs, but he resumed it in 1761, investing varying but usually substantial amounts in it. From his earliest years in Canada he evidently had large sums of money since at the time of his first marriage contract he kept trade goods worth 20,000 *livres* out of the material arrangements made. Similarly, when his second marriage contract was signed, he reserved for himself the property from his first joint estate.

Orillat's business expanded in 1763 when, in partnership with Pierre Cardinal, he obtained from the merchant Benjamin Comte more than 60,000 *livres* to invest in the fur trade at La Baye (Green Bay, Wis.). The partnership probably lasted at least two years, for in 1765 numerous engagements for Michilimackinac and La Baye were signed. In the autumn of 1764 Orillat had received official permission to go to France and settle business matters.

In 1767 Orillat took on a new fur-trading partner, Jean-Gabriel Cerré*, a trader in the Illinois country. The partnership contract stipulated that Orillat would put his order for the trade goods required by Cerré to the merchants Brook Watson* and Gregory Olive, who in turn would look after selling the skins and furs on the London market. Watson and Olive was one of the largest London houses with business interests in Canada. Watson, a man of "recognized integrity," had represented British merchants at the time of the negotiations with the court of France over the liquidation of Canada paper. Furthermore he was a friend of Governor Carleton*. Nevertheless, this second company created by Orillat had only limited success; when it was dissolved in 1771, the only subject of discussion was debts.

A third partnership, this time bringing together Orillat and the merchant Pierre Foretier*, was set up in 1774. The associates carred on trade in furs as well as selling trade goods to voyageurs, secured on fur shipments to London. This latter procedure allowed them to make profits on the goods without running the risks of the fur trade itself or of fluctuations in prices on the British market, and it explains their success. When the partnership was liquidated in 1780, after Orillat's death, it declared over 160,000 *livres* owing to it in debts secured on fur shipments in England.

In addition to the company formed with Foretier, Orillat carried on trade in furs on his own account and kept a shop in Montreal where he sold trade goods and everyday articles both wholesale and retail, as was the custom of Montreal merchants. This establishment stood out because of its size (it had more than 100,000 *livres* in stock at the time of Orillat's death) and the variety of articles carried. Its clientele consisted mainly of craftsmen from Montreal and the surrounding region, and occasionally of other merchants such as Edward Chinn, Pascal Pillet, Jean-Baptiste Lemoine Despins, John Porteous, John Askin*, and Joseph Sanguinet, or furtraders such as Jean-Étienne WADDENS, Christophe Sanguinet, Pierre-Louis and Charles-Jean-Baptiste* Chaboillez, Hypolite Desrivières, Jean-Marie* and Dominique* Ducharme, Nicolas Blondeau, and Alexis Réaume, Orillat's future son-in-law.

Orillat's activity did not stop here. He also lent money on security, bought letters of credit, and acquired both urban and rural land. He even hired one of his debtors to help his farmer, and once sold for double its purchase price a piece of land he had bought that very day. He also made deals in wood and wheat. He had achieved success.

Orillat seems to have been gifted with business acumen, and his financial situation allowed him a degree of luxury. Thus his furnishings included candlesticks, silver cutlery, a mahogany table brought from England, and landscape paintings. He also owned some black slaves. At his death the strong-box "serving as a cash-box" contained 15,000 *livres* in gold and silver. All of this constituted only a small part of his estate valued at nearly 750,000 *livres*.

Like a number of other Canadian merchants, Orillat dabbled in politics, signing a few petitions to the government on matters concerning the fur trade and the value of the currency. His loyalty to the new régime was, however, complete, and it brought him an arduous experience. When the Americans invaded the province of Quebec in September 1775, some parishes in the Richelieu valley went over to the American side, and Governor Carleton tried to bring them back into line by offering amnesty. On 14 September he sent Orillat, along with a trader by the name of Léveillé, to take the amnesty proclamation to them. They reached Saint-Denis on the evening of 17 September and were offered hospitality by parish priest François Cherrier*, in whose house they spent the night. Early next morning a group of Canadian rebels besieged the house and demanded that the two visitors be handed over. Orillat and Léveillé were thus taken prisoner, conducted to the rebel camp on Île aux Noix, and then to Ticonderoga and Albany, N.Y. From there they went to Connecticut, where they were kept under house arrest, although they were not imprisoned, for fear of the impact such a gesture might have on the attitude of the Canadians towards the Americans.

The Americans had captured an important figure. Orillat wrote from Albany to the provincial Congress of New York to obtain his release. His request was forwarded to the second Continental Congress, but the New York body asked the Albany committee of safety to make his captivity as easy as possible while preventing his escape. In October 1775 Brook Watson, who had arrived in Canada in the summer, wrote to influential people in Boston trying to obtain his release.

Orillat, who had put up a stiff resistance at the time of his capture, managed to escape in late December 1775. His whereabouts between then and September 1776 are unknown. At that time the company created by Foretier and Orillat obtained from Carleton the contract to supply the Indians in 1776 and 1777. The following year

Orillat was granted a fur-trading licence for Michilimackinac; in addition he gave bond for other voyageurs, which leads us to suppose that he was taking the lead of a trading expedition. He made a second voyage in 1778 and returned to Montreal early in October. He was becoming ill and he died some time before July 1779.

Orillat was survived by his second wife and a 16-year-old daughter, Marie-Luce-Amable, who had just been married. He bequeathed his whole estate to his daughter; her husband, fur-trader Alexis Réaume, took over its management. Réaume probably had less talent than his father-in-law, for in 1786 all rights to the estate were turned over to the London firm of Rashleigh and Company. Thus vanished the largest fortune of the period.

JOSÉ E. IGARTUA

AN, Col., C[11A], 108, f.172. ANQ-M, État civil, Catholiques, Notre-Dame de Montréal, 1er juill. 1779; Greffe de P.-F. Mézière, 19 juill. 1779; Greffe de Pierre Panet, 8 mars, 30 mai, 7 juin 1757; 7 mars, 8 mai, 19 sept. 1761; 28 avril, 15, 20 sept., 13 nov. 1762; 14 janv., 11 févr., 3, 4, 26 mai 1763; 3, 15 mars, 3, 13 sept., 13, 15, 17 oct. 1764; 23 mars, 7, 16, 25 avril, 2, 8 mai, 11 juin, 13, 24, 29 août, 16 oct., 17 déc. 1767; 7 juin, 7, 30 juill., 23 sept., 31 oct. 1768; 4 févr., 25 mars, 8 mai, 20, 24 juin, 1er juill., 10 août, 13 sept., 8 nov., 5, 7 déc. 1769; 3 janv., 12, 14 févr., 10, 28 mars, 8 mai, 2, 5 juill., 25, 31 août, 18, 22 oct. 1770; 22 févr., 12 mars, 15 avril, 15, 27 mai, 4, 25 juin, 30 juill., 6, 28 août, 26, 28, 30 sept., 2, 9, 23 oct. 1771; 27 janv., 3 avril, 18 mai, 10 juin, 4, 17 sept., 12 oct., 2, 3 déc. 1772; 2 janv., 15, 30 mars, 21 avril, 1er mai, 25 août, 2 oct., 6 déc. 1773; 16 mai, 18 juin, 22 juill. 1774; 15 mars, 23 juin 1775; 24 janv. 1778; Greffe de François Simonnet, 14 août, 19 nov. 1771, 1er oct. 1773. BL, Add. MSS 21757, ff.82–84v; 45915, ff.228–33 (mfm. at PAC). McGill University Libraries, Dept. of Rare Books and Special Coll., New MS coll., Orilliat, Jean, 1733–79, Inventaire des biens de la communauté d'entre feu Mr Jean Orilliat à dame Thérèse Viger son épouse, 19 juill. 1779. PAC, MG 18, H28, 3; MG 24, L3, pp.26208–10; RG 4, B28, 115; B58, 15. PRO, CO 42/3, f.228; 42/5, ff.298–99; 42/24, ff.72–73v; 42/27, ff.140–45; 42/66, f.225 (mfm. at PAC).

American archives (Clarke and Force), 4th ser., III, 1285; IV, 917. *Invasion du Canada* (Verreau). PAC *Rapport*, 1904, app.I, 375–76. "Protêt des marchands de Montréal contre une assemblée des seigneurs, tenue en cette ville le 21 février, 1766," É.-Z. Massicotte, édit., *Canadian Antiquarian and Numismatic Journal* (Montreal), 3rd ser., XI (1914), 1–20. *Quebec Gazette*, 1 Feb., 12 April 1770, 28 Feb., 18 April, 25 July 1771, 23 July, 26 Nov. 1772, 7 Sept. 1775, 15 April, 9 Nov. 1779, 6 April 1780. Massicotte, "Répertoire des engagements pour l'Ouest," ANQ *Rapport*, 1931–32, 1932–33. Tanguay, *Dictionnaire*, IV, 25; VI, 170. A.-H. Gosselin, *L'Église du Canada après la Conquête*. J. C. Webster, *Sir Brook Watson, friend of the loyalists, first agent of New Brunswick in London* (Sackville, N.B., 1924). F.-J. Audet, "Jean Orillat," *BRH*, XL (1934), 233–34. É.-Z. Massicotte, "Le bourgeois Pierre Foretier," *BRH*, XLVII (1941), 176–79; "Orillia, Orilla et Orillat," *BRH*, XL (1934), 160–61. Gabriel Nadeau, "Jean Orillat," *BRH*, XLI (1935), 644–84.

OSBORN, ELIZABETH (Myrick; Paine; Doane), midwife; b. 1715 probably at Sandwich, Massachusetts, to Samuel Osborn and Jedidah Smith; d. 24 May 1798 at Barrington, Nova Scotia.

Elizabeth Osborn probably was educated at local schools in Eastham (Mass.) and by her father, a schoolmaster and Congregational minister there. "A young lady possessing superior ability, beauty and character," she married Captain William Myrick at Eastham on 23 Jan. 1733/34. They were residing in Boston when he was lost at sea in 1742. Elizabeth became administrator of his estate and was allowed money for house rent and maintenance of herself and the children. On 14 Jan. 1744/45 she married 50-year-old William Paine, an Eastham merchant and provincial assemblyman. He served in the 1745 expedition against Louisbourg, Île Royale (Cape Breton Island) and died there in the summer of 1746, leaving her with a son William. Elizabeth had previously been courted unsuccessfully by a childhood friend, Edmund Doane. Now a 34-year-old widow with four children, she said she believed the fates had decreed that she should marry Edmund, and she did so on 10 Nov. 1749.

After some years Doane decided to join the emigration of Cape Cod fishermen to the Cape Sable area of Nova Scotia, which was nearer to productive fishing grounds and where free land grants could be obtained because of the deportation of the Acadians [*see* Charles Lawrence*]. In 1761 Doane had his house dismantled and the frame and boards loaded on a hired vessel together with furniture, grain and vegetables, and some animals. Young William Paine was left behind to continue his education, and Elizabeth with her seven children by Doane set out for Nova Scotia. A gale blew the ship ashore; the Doanes had to salvage what they could and embark in another vessel.

An autumn storm drove their ship past Barrington to Liverpool, where they had to spend the winter in a rough storehouse. In the spring of 1762 they sailed to The Passage (Barrington Passage, N.S.), and in the frame house they built near the harbour they opened a shop, selling such goods as flour, corn, salt, molasses, rum, sugar, cloth, nails, and shoes to about 50 customers. They obtained their supplies from Elizabeth's brother-in-law, John Homer, a Boston merchant and shipowner. But the inhabitants of Barrington suffered many hardships in the early years and had little cash. Thinking of returning to Cape Cod, Edmund sold his property.

Elizabeth, however, had filled an important niche in the scattered fishing settlement. There was no physician, and being skilled in the use of roots and herbs and in nursing she was soon acting as nurse, doctor, and midwife. At the request of those relying on her services, in 1770 she took the unusual step of applying to the proprietors of Barrington for "Land to Set a house upon." Her petition was endorsed by 38 male proprietors, "She Being a . . . Expert midwife as its Said By the Woemen . . . and . . . Incomparably well Skild in fisick and Surgery." She was granted 1½ acres, and the Doanes remained in Nova Scotia. She was still practising her craft in her 70s and 80s, and when she was needed at a distance men would come to carry her over hard places in a basket.

This pioneer woman is honoured by a marker on her grave in Barrington, not for her services to medicine, but because she was the grandmother of John Howard Payne, lyricist of *Home, sweet home*.

PHYLLIS R. BLAKELEY

Barrington Municipal Clerk's Office (Barrington, N.S.), Barrington Township records, The proprietors book of records of their divisions and measurements of their lands and meadows, 1768–1803, pp.76–77; A record of births & deaths pr. Samuel O. Doane. Edwin Crowell, *A history of Barrington Township and vicinity . . . 1604–1870* (Yarmouth, N.S., [1923]; repr. Belleville, Ont., 1973). *The Doane family . . . and their descendants* . . . , comp. A. A. Doane (2nd ed., [Trenton, N.J.], 1960).

OSBORN (Osborne), HENRY, naval officer and governor of Newfoundland; baptized 27 Aug. 1694, second son of Sir John Osborn and his second wife Martha Kelynge; m. Mary Hughes, and they had two sons and three daughters; d. 4 Feb. 1771 in London, England.

Henry Osborn entered the Royal Navy as a volunteer and in July 1717 was promoted lieutenant. Before he was appointed to the command of his first ship, the *Squirrel*, on 4 Jan. 1727/28, he served on board several famous vessels. In one of these, the *Royal Oak*, he saw action at the battle of Cape Passero, Sicily, in 1718. His appointment in 1729 as the first governor of Newfoundland was to involve him in conflict of a very different kind.

During the 17th century there had been increasing competition each fishing season between the West Country, or transient, fishermen and the inhabitants of Newfoundland over the possession of the best fishing "rooms" on the island. The act 10–11 William III, c.25, passed in 1698, attempted to remedy this problem by ordering that the transients were to have first possession of rooms each year; it assigned the settlement of disputes to fishing "admirals," each of whom received this responsibility by being the first transient to enter a harbour in any year. The act had tacitly assumed that the population of Newfoundland would decrease when the transients were given more advantages in the fishery, but the War of the Spanish Succession hindered the activities of the fishing fleets and the island's population actually increased. In the years after the treaty of Utrecht in 1713 the inhabitants not only generally disregarded the act but were lawless, especially during the winter. To remedy this situation, which was unfavourable for the fishery, the government decided in April 1729 to establish a governorship over the island. But instead of appointing a "Person skill'd in the Laws," as had been recommended, it chose Osborn and thus commenced a system of naval rulers which was to last until 1841. Osborn's authority was far from extensive: he was given the power to appoint civil magistrates, but he was not to contravene the act of 1698, and he was to defer to Lord Vere Beauclerk, the commodore of the squadron which sailed to Newfoundland each year for the protection of the fisheries.

Osborn began his governorship in the fishing season of 1729 by visiting all the principal places on the island. He then divided Newfoundland into six districts and appointed for each constables and magistrates with authority to function during the winter season [*see* William Keen*]. There were no persons on the island skilled in civil government, and Osborn had to make the best choices possible from a limited number of settlers, who were not always willing to place duty before self-interest. In addition, the fishing admirals refused to accept the authority of the magistrates, whom they dubbed "winter justices." Osborn, who remained in Newfoundland as governor only during the summer fishing season, was dismayed on his return in 1730 to discover that the magistrates had been intimidated almost to inaction by the aggressive conduct of the admirals.

Among Osborn's instructions was one empowering him to select places for court houses and jails, but no money was provided for him to construct needed buildings. To raise these funds Osborn therefore imposed a tax of fish on each vessel. The legality of this action was challenged by the transient fishermen, although fortunately for Osborn not in the British courts, since he would then have faced prosecution. Osborn and Beauclerk appealed to the Board of Trade for a decision. It approved Osborn's action in the one instance only because of the necessity and because the action had not been challenged in British courts. The decision was a poor consolation for the risks taken. The obvious solution for the difficulty was a proper civil government for the island, but the probability of strong West Country parliamentary opposition to such a move made it beyond practical politics at the time.

In the autumn of 1730 the Board of Trade took up Osborn's request for a ruling on the conflicting jurisdictions of the fishing admirals and the magistrates. According to the legal advice it obtained, the admirals' authority was limited to disputes concerning property in fishing rooms and other conveniences under the act of 1698, and there was no contradiction between their powers and those of the magistrates; moreover, the establishment of magistrates was found not to contravene the act of 1698. As a result of this ruling the government became more willing to support the governor's authority against the criticisms of the West Country merchants.

Osborn did not relinquish his governorship until June 1731 because of a delay in preparing the commission of his successor, George Clinton*. He then returned to his normal duties as a naval officer, in which he experienced the most successful part of his career. Promoted admiral of the blue in February 1757, the following year he commanded the squadron which captured the Marquis DUQUESNE's ship and obliged another French force to abandon its attempt to reach Louisbourg, Île Royale (Cape Breton Island). The inability of the French to reinforce the fortress was undoubtedly a major factor in its fall to Jeffery AMHERST the same year. Osborn's active naval service ended in July 1758 when he suffered a paralysing stroke. He was nevertheless promoted vice-admiral of England in January 1763, and he represented Bedfordshire in parliament from 1758 to 1761. A contemporary opinion of his character was given by John Charnock who praised his bravery and devotion to his country but considered him to have been of "a cold, saturnine disposition, ill-habituated to the warmth of sincere friendship."

FREDERIC F. THOMPSON

National Maritime Museum, CAL/1–6. Charnock, *Biographia navalis*, IV, 199–203. *DNB*. R. H. Bonnycastle, *Newfoundland in 1842; a sequel to "The Canadas in 1841"* (2v., London, 1842), I, 88–103. R. G. Lounsbury, *The British fishery at Newfoundland, 1634–1763* (New Haven, Conn., 1934; repr. New York, 1969), 275–83. Prowse, *History of Nfld.* (1895), 286–89. John Reeves, *History of the government of the island of Newfoundland . . .* (London, 1793; repr. New York and East Ardsley, Eng., 1967), 62–101.

OTKWANDE (Otqueandageghte). *See* OHQUANDAGEGHTE

OTSINUGHYADA. *See* HOTSINOÑHYAHTAˀ

OTTROWANA (Adrawanah, Atterwana, Dyaderowane, Gatrowani), Cayuga chief; fl. 1746–74 in what is now upper New York state.

Ottrowana was known to the British as early as 1746, and he probably led one or more of the raiding parties fitted out by New York's colonel of the Six Nations, William JOHNSON, to attack Canada during the War of the Austrian Succession. He also supplied Johnson with intelligence such as the news he brought in 1747 that the Hurons had requested the Six Nations' permission to destroy the French Fort Niagara (near Youngstown, N.Y.). After hostilities between Britain and France formally closed in 1748, Ottrowana continued to provide information on French activities. In 1751 he reported that he had been at Cataraqui (Kingston, Ont.) "where they were building a large Ship, which was to have three Masts, and that some there told him when fitted was designed to come & take this Place [Oswego]. That he Saw there Six Cannon, designed for Said purpose, three Yards long with a Wide Bore. . . ." War resumed in the mid 1750s and Governor Vaudreuil [RIGAUD] invited the leaders of the Six Nations to meet with him in Montreal. At a conference with those who arrived in the summer of 1756, he denounced Iroquois diplomatic practice. "You pretend to be friends of the French and of the English, in order to obtain what you want from both sides, which makes you invent lies that an upright man would never think of," he said. The delegation privately advised the western Indians who had come to Montreal to assist the French in the war that "as they could not know yet how matters might turn out," they should go home and stay neutral. Ottrowana is not known to have attended the conference, but he reported on it to Johnson, warning him that the French had said they would attack Fort Johnson (near Amsterdam, N.Y.) in the autumn.

Early in 1758 the French appear to have made a special effort to win the friendship of the Six Nations and their dependent tribes. Daniel-Marie CHABERT de Joncaire de Clausonne set out from Montreal in the spring with a large quantity of trade goods and presents and a dozen blacksmiths who were to live in the Indian villages. It was rumoured that the French intended to win over the leaders who were most pro-British, and Ottrowana was one of those specifically invited to a meeting at the Seneca village of Chenussio (Geneseo, N.Y.). A few months later he sent Johnson word of a French army assembling at Chouaguen (Oswego). In February 1759 he and several other Cayuga chiefs went to Johnson's residence to apologize for the murder of an Englishman by one of their young men. With the close of the war, information on his activities becomes even more scant. He was present at Fort Stanwix (Rome, N.Y.) in 1768, when a treaty was signed relinquishing a large amount of land and establishing a boundary line between whites and Indians. Along with HOTSINOÑHYAHTAˀ, TEYOHAQUEANDE, and others, he attended the condolence council at Johnson Hall (Johnstown, N.Y.) following Sir William's death in 1774.

It is difficult to estimate the influence Ottrowana exercised among his people. Johnson called him "one of the leadingest men in Cajuga," but his assessment may have been coloured by optimism, since Ottrowana seems to have been genuinely pro-British. The intelligence he supplied was not always correct, but the rumours were usually based on plans under active consideration by the French. When he had first-hand knowledge, his information was exact. His political judgement, on the other hand, may be questioned. Once the French were no longer in Quebec competing for their services, the Six Nations' bargaining position was substantially weakened and their lands were more than ever coveted by the British colonists.

IN COLLABORATION

Bougainville, "Journal" (A.-E. Gosselin), ANQ *Rapport*, 1923–24, 319. *Johnson papers* (Sullivan *et al.*). *NYCD* (O'Callaghan and Fernow). [J.-G.-C. Plantavit de Margon, Chevalier de La Pause], "Relation des affaires du Canada depuis l'automne dernière 57 . . . ," ANQ *Rapport*, 1932–33, 347–50.

OUANGOTE. *See* WILLIAMS, EUNICE

OUASSON (Ousson, Owasser). *See* WASSON

OWEN, WILLIAM, naval officer and founder of a settlement on Passamaquoddy Outer Island (Campobello Island, N.B.); b. 1737 at Glam Severn (Powys), Wales, son of David Owen; d. 1778 at Madras, India.

William Owen entered the Royal Navy as a youth and by 1759 had been promoted lieutenant. During the Seven Years' War he served in support of the East India Company, and in an action against the French off Pondicherry in 1760 he suffered a wound which resulted in the loss of his right arm.

At the close of the war Owen returned to England and was placed on half pay. Not content with his "pitiful pension," in 1766 he wrote to Lord William CAMPBELL, with whom he had served in India, asking for assistance in obtaining employment. Campbell, the newly appointed governor of Nova Scotia, offered Owen the position of volunteer secretary and naval aide. Owen accompanied Campbell to Halifax in November and spent the following summer surveying and mapping nearby Shubenacadie Lake. On 30 Sept. 1767 Campbell granted Owen Passamaquoddy Outer Island in Passamaquoddy Bay; three nephews of Owen's were also included as grantees because the grant exceeded the amount normally awarded to an officer of Owen's rank. Owen left for England shortly afterwards without having visited the island.

In 1768 Owen, persuaded by "the spirit of Rambling," toured Kent and the Continent after having spent the spring ill in London. In early September he settled in Shrewsbury, where, during an election brawl, he lost the sight of one eye. It was not until August 1769, when Owen met with friends in Warrington, that arrangements were made for the settlement of the Nova Scotian island. In contrast with other parts of Nova Scotia, where settlers were given their own grants of land, Owen retained title to the land as "lord of the soil or principal proprietary." As well, he was to receive from his tenants three-sixteenths of any profits realized. His 12 partners in the project expected a fair return for their investment through the production of crops, livestock, and lumber, and the exploitation of the rich fisheries. After months of planning, in early 1770 Owen embarked at Liverpool for his American estate with 38 indentured servants of all trades who were intended to form the nucleus of the new settlement. The vessel arrived at Passamaquoddy Outer Island on 4 June. Owen almost immediately renamed the island Campobello, partly in honour of Campbell and partly because he thought the Italian meaning "fair field" suited it.

Work on building temporary shelters and the establishment of a settlement began promptly. A town was laid out and called New Warrington (Wilson's Beach) with its harbour named Port Owen. A small portion of the island had been occupied before Owen's arrival by a few New England families, and they joined with the indentured servants in building. By June 1771 considerable progress had been made; several fields had been fenced off and sown, 15 buildings, including a chapel and a grist-mill, had been constructed, and a start had even been made at a deer park. In all, 73 persons had settled on the island, and timber, potash, and shingles had been shipped for export. Owen, who had been appointed a justice of the peace shortly after his arrival, evidently believed in firm discipline, for some of the first constructions at New Warrington were a pair of stocks and a whipping post. But there was in fact little trouble.

In 1771 Britain and Spain appeared close to war over possession of the Falkland Islands, and Owen left that June for England to return to active service. Soon after his departure 27 of the indentured servants persuaded Captain Plato Denny, one of Owen's partners, to take them to England. The vessel in which they sailed, however, was lost at sea. Of the 11 original settlers left, seven eventually departed for the mainland, leaving the New England settlers practically alone. Owen never returned to Campobello, but he maintained his interest in its settlement, and in February 1772 he and his partners advertised for 10 or 12 "Industrious Farmers" to settle the island. Little more is known of Owen's career after his return to England. He was killed at Madras in 1778 while on his way from India to England with dispatches.

Owen had two sons, Edward Campbell Rich and William Fitz-William*. In 1835 William Fitz-William, who became in that year the sole proprietor of Campobello, took up residence on the island. He is known for his surveys of the Great Lakes; Owen Sound, Ontario, is named in his honour.

L. K. INGERSOLL

William Owen was the author of: "The journal of Captain William Owen . . . ," ed. W. F. Ganong, N.B. Hist. Soc., *Coll.*, I (1894–97), no.2, 193–220; II (1899–1905), no.4, 8–27; "Narrative of American voyages and travels of Captain William Owen, R.N., and the settlement of the island of Campobello in the Bay of Fundy, 1766–1771," ed. V. H. Paltsits, New York Public Library, *Bull.*, 35 (1931), 71–98, 139–62, 263–300, 659–85, 705–58.

N.B., Hist. Resources Administration (Fredericton), The Owen House, unpublished report by Louise Banville; architect's report by Ross Anderson; final departmental recommendations by David Webber, 1971. N.B. Museum (Saint John), W. F. Owen, estate papers, 1839–1907. PANB, RG 2, RS8, Attorney general, cases and opinions; RG 7, RS63. *DNB*. G.B., Adm., *Commissioned sea officers*, III. John Marshall, *Royal navy biography* . . . (4v. in 6 and 2v. supp., London, 1823–35), supp., II. B. E. Barber, *A guide book to FDR's "beloved island," Campobello Island, New Brunswick, Canada* ([Vicksburg, Miss., 1962]). Campobello Company, *Campobello* (Boston, Mass., [1882?]). Campobello Island, Board of Trade, *Campobello Island, N.B., a vacation paradise* ([Campobello Island, N.B., 1963]). W. A. R. Chapin, *The story of Campobello* (n.p., 1960). James Dugan, *The great mutiny* (New York, 1965), chaps.v–ix. M. [A.] Lewis, *The navy of Britain: a historical portrait* (London, 1948). [C. B.] G. Wells, *Campobello: an historical sketch* (Boston, Mass., 1893). L. K. Ingersoll, "A chair with naval lineage," N.B. Museum, *Museum Memo* (Saint John), 3 (1971), no.2, 4–8. D. K. Parr, "The principal proprietary of Campobello," *Atlantic Advocate* (Fredericton), 53 (1962–63), no.1, 63.

P

PAINE, ELIZABETH. *See* OSBORN

PALLISER (Pallisser), Sir HUGH, naval officer and governor of Newfoundland; b. 22 Feb. 1722/23 at Kirk Deighton (West Yorkshire), England, only son of Captain Hugh Palliser and Mary Robinson; d. 19 March 1796 at Chalfont St Giles, England.

Hugh Palliser was born into an old landed family which had estates in Yorkshire and Ireland. His parents died when he was young and he and his sisters were probably raised by his mother's relatives. Entering the Royal Navy at age 11 on board the *Aldborough*, commanded by his uncle Nicholas Robinson, he was promoted lieutenant in September 1741. Five years later he became captain of the *Captain* and during the War of the Austrian Succession commanded several ships. In one, the *Sutherland*, he was severely injured when an arms chest exploded on the quarter-deck, and he remained crippled and in pain in his left leg until his death.

Soon after the outbreak of the Seven Years' War Palliser was given command of the *Eagle*, in which he participated in the blockade of northern French ports. In 1757 he was present in Vice-Admiral Francis Holburne's fleet cruising off Louisbourg, Île Royale (Cape Breton Island), and in 1759, commanding the *Shrewsbury*, he was with SAUNDERS' fleet at the siege of Quebec. On the surrender of the town on 18 September, Palliser had the honour of landing with a party of seamen and marines to take possession of the Lower Town. In 1762, when news of the French capture of St John's [*see* Charles-Henri-Louis d'ARSAC de Ternay] reached England, he was sent to Newfoundland with a squadron. He did not, however, arrive off the coast until 19 September, the day after the French surrendered to Lieutenant-Colonel William Amherst. In April 1764 Palliser was appointed governor of Newfoundland, succeeding Thomas Graves*.

Palliser, now a commodore, arrived in St John's harbour on board the *Guernsey* on 18 April 1764. His squadron of seven ships manned by some 1,100 men testified to the Newfoundland fishery's importance to the British government. From the first, Palliser was active and energetic in visiting the different areas of his administration. In 1764 he went to the south coast and the Bay of Islands on the west coast. He was on the south coast again for over a month during the summer of 1765, and he subsequently visited the north coast, as well as the coast of Labrador, which had been placed under the jurisdiction of the governor of Newfoundland in 1763. In 1767 he once more spent the early part of the fishing season off the south coast and then paid a second visit to Labrador.

The policing of the French fishery in Newfoundland was a particularly necessary and time-consuming task during the early years of Palliser's governorship. By the treaty of Paris in February 1763, France was allowed to retain fishing rights which the treaty of Utrecht had granted her on the so-called French Shore, a stretch of coastline from Cape Bonavista to Point Riche. At the same time, she received the islands of Saint-Pierre and Miquelon as a base for her fishermen. For some time before 1763, however, British fishermen had been active on the French Shore, and they considered that they had a concurrent right to the fishery there. The French believed equally strongly that they possessed an exclusive right. The short time available for the British government to formulate detailed regulations for the 1763 fishing season meant that serious disputes broke out that year between British and French fishermen on the French Shore. In its instructions to him, the British government had ordered Palliser not to allow British subjects to interrupt the French fishery but stressed that French fishermen were to be kept strictly within their treaty limits. Palliser made it clear that although French fishermen on the treaty coast were not to be interfered with, British fishermen possessed concurrent rights there, and he early took the vitally important step of asserting that all disputes were to be settled by British officials and no French warships were to enter Newfoundland waters. Thus in July 1764, when he learned that a squadron under Commodore François-Jean-Baptiste L'Ollivier de Tronjoly had gathered at Saint-Pierre in order to visit the French Shore, he sailed to that island. After he bluntly warned Tronjoly that the proposed visitation would violate British sovereignty, it was called off. The French government protested his actions, but Palliser fully explained his policy of firmness on "national points" to his superiors, and he was supported by the Admiralty and the Board of Trade.

When Palliser himself visited the French Shore in 1765, he issued several proclamations designed to confine the French strictly to their treaty rights. Under the treaty, they were not allowed to erect buildings other than those used in the fishery, and they were forbidden to remain beyond the end of the fishing season; in addition, the British assumed that boats would not be built on the French Shore. Palliser kept the officers of his squadron busy patrolling the coasts, seizing locally built boats, and arresting Frenchmen who had stayed in Newfoundland over the winter. He sympathized with the French, however, when their huts and boats were destroyed during the winter, blaming the inhabitants of Newfoundland and lamenting his inability to curb them. The governor also dealt firmly with the problem of illegal trade and French fishing on the south coast. Early in the season of 1765 he found French boats fishing all along that shore and promptly seized those he could, simultaneously sending a stiff protest to François-Gabriel d'ANGEAC, the governor of Saint-Pierre and Miquelon. He was equally hard on British subjects guilty of wrongdoing. New England vessels found trading at Saint-Pierre were taken and sent to the vice-admiralty courts in St John's and Placentia, and south coast residents convicted of trading with the French lost their houses and fishing equipment and were themselves expelled from Newfoundland.

In his attempts to limit the French fishery to the terms of the treaty, Palliser was motivated by concern for the migratory fishermen from England who came out each year, and not for the inhabitants of Newfoundland. A naval governor, he naturally viewed the Newfoundland fishery primarily as a great "nursery" to train seamen for the British merchant marine and navy. If Newfoundland developed into a settled colony, then ships and men employed in the fishery would not return annually to Britain, the provisions and fishing gear would be only partly British, and income from fish sold abroad would not flow back to Britain. To support the annual ship fishers further, Palliser sought to limit the inhabitants' property rights in fishing places and attempted to enforce the regulations of the act of 1698. He tried continually to convert unoccupied land or land to which residents did not have clear title into ships' fishing rooms. In the fall of 1766, for example, he charged that many "idle people" had built houses and planted gardens on ships' rooms in St John's harbour. They were warned to withdraw before the next season, when everything would be cleared away to "accommodate the Ship Fishers, who must never be disappointed for want of room." Palliser also tried to enforce the clauses in the act of 1698 which required owners of fishing ships to return all their seamen to the British Isles at the end of the season. He repeatedly reprimanded Andrew Pinson*, a West Country merchant who landed his men in St John's at the end of the season without money to pay their passages home, supplying them with liquor and other goods in lieu of wages. In 1767 Palliser issued a detailed proclamation designed to rid Newfoundland of the thousands of poor fishermen left behind for the winter; masters were to ensure that their men could return home by not advancing more than half their wages during the season. Palliser was not completely successful in enforcing this measure, but during his governorship the number of persons remaining in Newfoundland over the winter decreased. His aims for the Newfoundland fishery were reflected in the Act for the Encouragement of the Ship Fishery passed by parliament in 1775. It was known as Palliser's Act because, as the Newfoundland historian Daniel Woodley Prowse* states, "Sir Hugh's hand can be traced in every line." The act gave bounties for fishing ships going to the Grand Banks, recapitulated the regulations of 1698, and incorporated the essence of Palliser's order of 1767.

One of Palliser's cherished projects was the establishment of a British ship fishery on the Labrador coast. He hoped that the fishery might flourish there as had originally been intended in Newfoundland, since the area had few settlers and it would be necessary only to establish friendly relations with the native population and exclude interlopers from the colonies and elsewhere. On his voyage to Newfoundland in 1765 Palliser was accompanied by four Moravian missionaries, including both Christian Larsen DRACHART and Jens HAVEN, who were to travel to Labrador as interpreters with instructions to stop the Inuit from trading with the French and from clashing with British fishermen. When the governor himself arrived at Chateau Bay in August, the missionaries had assembled over 500 Inuit to meet with him; friendly relations were established and a profitable trade in furs was carried on. He also made examples of persons found trading illicitly. In 1765 one of his officers raided the post of the Quebec merchants Daniel Bayne* and William Brymer at Cape Charles and found French goods. Palliser ordered the post closed and Bayne and Brymer's agent expelled from the coast. He then issued a proclamation banning inhabitants of Newfoundland and the mainland colonies from frequenting the coast. For years afterwards, however, he was harassed by law suits the irate merchants initiated to recover their damages, until he settled out of court in 1770. In the summer of 1766 a timber blockhouse was erected at Chateau Bay to protect the property of British ship fishers from Inuit and colonial crews. Palliser himself spent a good part of the summer of 1767 at Chateau Bay cultivating good relations with the Inuit and encouraging the ship fishers by giving them greater security of tenure in new posts. His efforts were marked with success; whereas no British fishing ships had been on the Labrador coast in the 1764 season, 23 fished there in the 1768 season.

Even before his appointment as governor, Palliser had worked closely with James COOK, who had been master's mate on the *Eagle* and who in 1763 had been appointed to survey Newfoundland. Although it was Thomas Graves who procured Cook his initial appointment and supplied him with the survey ship *Grenville*, Palliser secured Cook's appointment as master of the ship with his own crew. It was also due to Palliser that Cook's manuscript charts contained much information useful for the fishery; anxious to extend the range of the ship fishers, the governor ordered Cook to take every opportunity to note likely harbours and beaches for the creation of new fishing rooms. And Cook's surveys covered those coasts where the British had most to fear from French rivalry. In view of the instructions given to Palliser in 1764 he naturally first directed Cook to survey the hotly contested northern waters systematically. In 1765 he also ordered Cook to chart the coastline near Saint-Pierre and Miquelon in order to assist his squadron's patrols and to encourage British fishermen to resort there. Palliser obtained the Admiralty's permission for Cook to publish his charts, and in August 1766 he reported that the British fishery on the south coast was well established and likely to expand quickly, "to which the surveys lately taken of that coast, and published by their Lordships' orders, will greatly contribute."

As might be expected, Palliser had little use for the resident population of Newfoundland, but his administration of justice was generally humane and even-handed, and he showed himself ready on occasion to protect fishermen against highly placed merchants. In his attitudes towards the native population of Newfoundland and Labrador the governor was a person of his time. Although he saw the Labrador Inuit as barbarians who needed to be converted into good British subjects and Christians, he at least adopted a policy of conciliation rather than one of extirpation, and he was genuinely revolted at the attacks of whaling crews on the Inuit. He distrusted the Roman Catholic Micmacs who came from Nova Scotia to hunt and fish on the south coast of Newfoundland, because he believed that they were under the domination of the French at Saint-Pierre and Miquelon. He repeatedly confiscated from the Indians passports which had been issued by the Nova Scotia and Cape Breton authorities, and he admonished the offending officials to issue no more. The Newfoundland Indians, the Beothuks, were rapidly dwindling in number, and Palliser offered rewards for any brought in alive. In 1768 a little boy was captured, but he was "so young as to be of no use, not even to get a word of their language from it." Late in the same year a small expedition headed by Lieutenant John Cartwright and his brother George* was dispatched to the interior to find the Beothuks' chief settlement and establish friendly relations, but although the party travelled up the Exploits River to Red Indian Lake, the search was fruitless.

Palliser's years as governor from 1764 to 1768 brought considerable change to Newfoundland. In 1764 only 238 British ships with slightly more than 7,000 men had come out to the Newfoundland fishery, but in 1768, 389 ships carried out over 12,000 men. Conversely, the totals of resident fishermen fell from just over 10,000 to some 7,000 and the most vital statistic, the number of seamen who returned annually to the British Isles, more than doubled from 5,562 in 1764 to 11,811 in 1768. As for the rival French fishery, the number of fishermen and their total catch were well below the combined figures for the British migratory fishermen and the inhabitants of Newfoundland.

Palliser left Newfoundland for the last time in November 1768. In February 1769 John BYRON was appointed governor, and Palliser began a political career in addition to his naval one. As comptroller of the navy from 1770 to 1775 he organized and outfitted several voyages of exploration, including those of his old friend Cook. On 6 Aug. 1773 he was created a baronet and in the fall of 1774 was elected to parliament from Scarborough; the following year he was promoted rear-admiral and soon afterwards became one of the lords of the Admiralty; in addition, he was appointed lieutenant-general of marines after Saunders' death. When hostilities broke out in the American colonies, Palliser was in charge of arranging transports and victuallers for the British armies, and he organized the relief expedition which lifted the siege of Quebec in May 1776 [*see* Sir Charles DOUGLAS].

In 1778 Palliser was promoted vice-admiral and became third in command of the home fleet under Admiral Augustus Keppel. In a battle with a French fleet off Ushant on 27 July, a misunderstanding or disagreement on tactics between Palliser and Keppel contributed to the indecisive result. The incident was taken up by party politicians and the ensuing courts martial of the two admirals, who had been personal friends, bitterly divided the navy. When Keppel was exonerated in February 1779, the exultant London mob looted Palliser's house. He became so unpopular that the government was forced to dismiss him from his offices, and he resigned his seat in parliament. Even when he also was acquitted, the Earl of Sandwich, first lord of the Admiralty, dared not reinstate him but did brave the invective of opposition politicians to name him governor of Greenwich Hospital in 1780. Palliser ended his long career honourably in that comfortable sinecure. He re-entered parliament as a member for Huntingdon from 1780 to 1784 and was promoted full admiral in 1787.

Palliser died at his country house in Buckinghamshire at the age of 73. He left the bulk of his fortune to his illegitimate son George Thomas; the baronetcy and his Irish estates devolved on his grand-nephew Hugh Walters, who took the name of Palliser. In his will Palliser bequeathed £30 a year for educating and clothing 40 children at a day school he had established in his parish in 1780. Although Palliser was a tireless collector of naval papers, neither these nor the personal papers he surely must have kept have survived to the present day.

Hugh Palliser was an admirable servant of the state. As well as being a brave and aggressive sea officer, he was a methodical and industrious man of business. Prowse points out that his administration in Newfoundland lasted the unusual period of five years, owing, no doubt, to the consistent approval of his policies by the British government, and that his records are the most voluminous of the 18th-century governors. There can be little doubt that the pettiness, evasion, and idleness in the small world of St John's and the outports irritated him, and his letters and orders sometimes crackle with exasperation. But if he was stern, he was also energetic and fair. He attempted to preserve the Beothuk and Inuit, and he felt real concern for fishermen paid off in overpriced goods and left destitute on the beach after a season of dangerous toil. The friend of men like Cook, Saunders, and Joseph Banks* must have been intelligent and zealous.

At Newfoundland Palliser kept the French fishery within its treaty limits and the supervision of both fisheries firmly under his control. His attempt to retain Newfoundland and Labrador for the annual ship fishers had only limited success, however, in spite of substantial short-term gains. To try to enforce the fishing regulations of 1698 and his own rules was to attempt what was virtually impossible. Palliser is best remembered, perhaps, for his support of James Cook. Cook for his part remembered his "worthy friend" in the Palliser Isles of the South Pacific and in Cape Palliser, which guards the eastern entrance to Cook Strait in New Zealand.

WILLIAM H. WHITELEY

A portrait of Sir Hugh Palliser by Nathaniel Dance was in the possession of the last baronet in the late 19th century; a copy of this portrait hangs in the Painted Hall at Greenwich Naval College.

BL, Add. MSS 33030, 35915, 38219, 38227, 38310, 38388, 38396. PAC, MG 23, A1, ser.1, 13; A4, 17. PANL, GN2/1, 3, 4. PRO, Adm. 1/470, 1/2291–94, 1/2296, 1/2299–301, 1/4126–27, 1/5313, 2/91–93, 2/236, 2/539, 2/541–42, 3/71–76, 8/40–44, 50/19, 51/4210, 80/121; CO 194/16–18, 194/21, 194/26–28, 195/19, 324/41, 391/71–76; Prob. 11/1274, f.206; SP 41/39, 42/43, 42/65, 42/136, 44/328.

Gentleman's Magazine, 1796, 439–40. G.B., Privy Council, *Acts of P. C., col., 1766–83. The private papers of John, Earl of Sandwich, first lord of the Admiralty, 1771–1782*, ed. G. R. Barnes and J. H. Owen (4v., London, 1932–38). A. [C.] Valentine, *The British establishment, 1760–1784* . . . (2v., Norman, Okla., 1970), II, 674–75. Charnock, *Biographia navalis*, V, 483–96. *DNB*. R. M. Hunt, *The life of Sir Hugh Palliser* . . . (London, 1844). A. M. Lysaght, *Joseph Banks in Newfoundland and Labrador, 1766: his diary, manuscripts and collections* (London and Berkeley, Calif., 1971). Prowse, *History of Nfld.* (1895), 328, 344. J. H. Broomfield, "The Keppel-Palliser affair, 1778–1779," *Mariner's Mirror* (Cambridge, Eng.), 47 (1961), 195–207; "Lord Sandwich at the Admiralty Board: politics and the British navy, 1771–1778," *Mariner's Mirror*, 51 (1965), 7–17. G. O. Rothney, "The case of Bayne and Brymer; an incident in the early history of Labrador," *CHR*, XV (1934), 264–75. W. H. Whiteley, "The establishment of the Moravian mission in Labrador and British policy, 1763–83," *CHR*, XLV (1964), 29–50; "Governor Hugh Palliser and the Newfoundland and Labrador fishery, 1764–1768," *CHR*, L (1969), 141–63; "James Cook and British policy in the Newfoundland fisheries, 1763–7," *CHR*, LIV (1973), 245–72.

PANET, JEAN-CLAUDE, notary, lawyer, and judge; b., probably late in December 1719, in the parish of Saint-Germain-l'Auxerrois in Paris, France, eldest son of Jean-Nicolas Panet, a clerk with the treasurers-general of the Marine, and Marie-Madeleine-Françoise Foucher; d. 28 Feb. 1778 in Quebec.

Jean-Claude Panet had seven brothers and sisters. One of them, Nicolas-Gabriel, became clerk of the *parlement* of Paris; another, Pierre-Méru*, emigrated to New France some years after his brother, was also a notary, lawyer, and judge, and began the Montreal branch of the Panet family during the period when Jean-Claude was beginning a branch in Quebec.

Jean-Claude Panet arrived in Canada at 20 years of age as a soldier in the colonial regular troops. He had sailed from La Rochelle on 10 June 1740 aboard the *Rubis* and landed at Quebec on 12 August, having escaped the epidemic which caused the deaths of many of the crew and passengers, including Bishop François-Louis de Pourroy* de Lauberivière. Panet had certainly received a fairly advanced education, for eight months after his arrival he was working as a legal practitioner, and a little later as an attorney. He was well thought of; Intendant HOCQUART considered him "intelligent and prudent" and Governor Charles de Beauharnois* praised his "good conduct." Despite a request made by his father in Paris, he was unable to obtain the post of notary in Quebec which had been left vacant when Jean de Latour returned to France in the autumn of 1741. The appointment of Nicolas BOISSEAU as chief clerk of the Conseil Supérieur, however, created a vacancy enabling Panet to become royal notary in the provost court of Quebec on 22 Dec. 1744. His father having paid the required 150 *livres*, Jean-Claude Panet had obtained discharge from the armed forces at the beginning of the previous year. Although he held a number of other posts over the years, Panet was to practise continuously as a notary from 1745 until 1775, and his register records more than 5,860 acts.

On 8 Aug. 1759, during the siege of Quebec, a British fire-ball fell on Jean-Claude Panet's house in Lower Town, causing a fire that destroyed 166 other houses. Panet recounted the particulars in a diary entitled "Précis de ce qui s'est passé au Canada depuis la nouvelle de la flotte de M. Canon [Jacques Kanon*]," which accurately and in detail relates events of the period from 10 May to 8 September 1759. The last section of the manuscript, containing the account of the final days of the siege, has unfortunately disappeared. On 25 July 1759 Panet had been named clerk of a commission charged with suppressing looting by sailors, soldiers, and militiamen. The ordinance of 19 July creating the commission had authorized François Daine*, the lieutenant general for civil and criminal affairs of the provost court of Quebec, to sentence to death and have executed the same day looters caught in the act. Panet is supposed to have recommended this drastic measure to Daine. His diary reports that Daine had two men arrested and hanged on 31 July. After the defeat on the Plains of Abraham on 13 September, Panet, as deputy for king's attorney Jean-Baptiste-Ignace Perthuis*, was one of 25 leading citizens who signed the request for capitulation addressed to the king's lieutenant, Jean-Baptiste-Nicolas-Roch de RAMEZAY.

The military régime, from 1760 to 1763, made little change in the daily life of New France. In the interests of efficiency the British administration had to be in a position both to understand and to be understood by the Canadians, and the services of French speaking persons, such as Jacques de Lafontaine* de Belcour and François-Joseph CUGNET, were called upon. When James MURRAY, the new governor, set up a court of final appeal for the District of Quebec, which he called the "superior council," he named Jean-Claude Panet its chief clerk on 2 Nov. 1760. At the same period Panet's brother Pierre-Méru was appointed court clerk in the District of Montreal. When civil government was restored, Canadians qualified in the legal field were not affected by the theoretical obligation of important civil servants to take the oath under the Test Act, and they retained their offices. In 1765 Murray asked Jean-Claude Panet to examine the registers of the Conseil Supérieur of New France and make an inventory of the lands incorporated in the Domaine d'Occident under the French régime. The governor emphasized that only a French speaking jurist could accomplish this task and that Panet was to have free access to the documents.

In February 1765 Jean-Claude Panet, along with William Kluck, became clerk of the Court of Common Pleas, which replaced the council created by Murray. At the same time Panet and Kluck were appointed depositaries of the minutes of deceased notaries in the District of Quebec. But the following year Panet quit his post and went to France in the hope of obtaining recompense for his services under the French régime and a better post. He presented a statement to the minister of the Marine, the Duc de Choiseul, who forwarded it with a favourable recommendation to the comptroller general of finance. Panet's request apparently was rejected, for he returned to Quebec and on 6 Oct. 1767 obtained a commission as a lawyer. He had practised law for several years, had been an assessor to the Conseil Supérieur of New France in 1751 and deputy king's attorney from 1755 to 1759, and had even signed as a lawyer in 1764; so he had had a lengthy training for this profession. On his appointment, Panet withdrew into a private career as a notary and lawyer until 1775.

It was only when the Quebec Act, which was to establish a new judicial organization, came into effect that Jean-Claude Panet again held office. On 26 April 1775, Governor Guy Carleton* reappointed judges Thomas Dunn*, John Fraser, Adam MABANE, and John Marteilhe; at the same time he appointed René-Ovide HERTEL de Rouville and Panet "keepers of the peace" and commissioners, Hertel for the District of Montreal and Panet for the District of Quebec, appointments equivalent to judgeships. They thus became the first French speaking and Catholic judges under the British régime. On 13 July 1776, after the American troops had withdrawn, Dunn, Mabane, and Panet were appointed commissioners to assess damage done during the American invasion of the province. Ten days later Carleton appointed them "judges of a Court with Civil Jurisdiction within the District of Quebec." In August Panet became a justice of the peace, and on 6 March 1777 a judge of the Court of Common Pleas.

Jean-Claude Panet did not hold these various posts long. He died on 28 Feb. 1778 in the afternoon, at 58 years of age. Could his death have been due to alcoholism? An anonymous letter written in Quebec on 9 Nov. 1775 commented on "the appointment as judges of Mr. de Rouville in Montreal and Claude Panet in Quebec (who has his nip every day before noon) with salaries, it is said, of 700 *louis* a year; in short, the audacity exercised in proliferating jobs for intimate friends and sycophants by whom the governor is continually surrounded . . . has inspired universal and profound disgust."

On 23 Oct. 1747, Jean-Claude Panet had married Marie-Louise, daughter of notary Claude Barolet*, in Quebec. In 1796 Carleton, now Lord Dorchester, obtained an annual pension for Mme Panet of £80 (four-fifths of her husband's salary when he was clerk of the Court of Common Pleas), which she received until her death in 1803. Fourteen children were born between 1749 and 1764, 12 of whom were still living at the time of their father's death. Three daughters entered the Ursuline order; one left it two years later but the other two spent more than 50 years in holy orders. Two sons chose the priesthood; Bernard-Claude* became bishop of Quebec, and Jacques* was parish priest of Notre-Dame-de-Bon-Secours at L'Islet from 1779 to 1829. Jean-Baptiste became a notary and died in 1808. A notary, lawyer, and judge like his father, Jean-Antoine* was speaker of the House of Assembly and one of the outstanding political figures of his time.

ANDRÉ FRENIÈRE

AMA, SHA, A[1], 3540, ff.84–84[2], 90–90[6] (mfm. at PAC). AN, Col., B, 76/1, pp.233–35; 77, p.15; 97, p.138; 125, pp.20–21 (PAC transcripts); C[11A], 73, pp.3–7, 46–49; 76; 77, pp.312–17. ANQ-Q, AP-P-1565. ASQ, Doc. Faribault, no.149; Lettres, M, 98; Polygraphie, II, 3; XXVII, 25; Séminaire, 14/5, no.41; Université, carton 96, no.71. PAC, RG 4, A1, 12, pp.4659–60, 5726; RG 68, 89, pp.59–60; 90, pp.11–12, 22–24, 36–40, 51–52, 84–85. PAC *Rapport*, 1905, I, VIe partie. *Doc. relatifs à la monnaie sous le Régime français* (Shortt), II, 978. *Doc. relatifs à l'hist. constitutionnelle, 1759–91* (Shortt et Doughty; 1921). *Invasion du Canada* (Verreau). J.-C. Panet, "Siège de Québec en 1759," Literary and Hist. Soc. of Quebec, *Hist. Docs.*, 4th ser. (1875), 1–31. *Quebec Gazette*, 5 March 1778.

P.-G. Roy, *Les avocats de la région de Québec*; *Inv. jug. et délib., 1717–60*, IV, V, VI; *Inv. ord. int.*, III, 65; *Les juges de la prov. de Québec*. Tanguay, *Dictionnaire*. Vachon, "Inv. critique des notaires royaux," *RHAF*, IX, 551–52; XI, 405. Lanctot, *Le Canada et la Révolution américaine*. J.-E. Roy, *Hist. du notariat*, I, II. P.-G. Roy, *La famille Panet* (Lévis, Qué., 1906). Wade, *Les Canadiens français* (1966), I.

PARR, JOHN, army officer and colonial administrator; b. 20 Dec. 1725 in Dublin (Republic of Ireland), son of John Parr and Eleanor Clements; m. 1761 Sara Walmesley, and they had three sons and two daughters; d. 25 Nov. 1791 in Halifax, Nova Scotia.

Nothing is known of John Parr's early years, but in April 1745 he joined the British army as an ensign in the 20th Foot. After his baptism of fire at Fontenoy (Belgium) the same year Parr accompanied his regiment to Scotland to help suppress the Jacobite rebellion and was wounded at Culloden. When James Wolfe* became acting lieutenant-colonel of the 20th in 1749 Parr may have become his adjutant; in any event, he had an acquaintanceship with Wolfe which later secured him ministerial patronage. Promoted captain in 1756, Parr fought in several engagements during the Seven Years' War, including the bloody battle of Minden (Federal Republic of Germany) in 1759, during which he was severely wounded. After promotion to major in 1763 and six years of garrison duty at Gibraltar, Parr advanced by purchase to the rank of lieutenant-colonel of the 20th in 1770. Six years later he resigned from the army just before his regiment embarked for Quebec as part of the ill-fated BURGOYNE expedition. In 1778 he exploited his government connections to secure the comfortable sinecure of major of the Tower of London.

In July 1782, through the influence of his patron the Earl of Shelburne, secretary of state for the Home Department, Parr was appointed governor of Nova Scotia, succeeding Francis LEGGE. Instead of quiet retirement, however, he was at once confronted with the urgent and immense task of succouring and settling some 35,000 loyalists who flooded into Nova Scotia at the end of the American revolution. With the colony's population more than doubled overnight, impossible strains were placed on Nova Scotia's rudimentary administrative machinery as well as on stores and provisions. In the winter of 1782–83 ten thousand refugees arrived helpless and destitute at Halifax, and as makeshift accommodation warehouses, sheds, and churches had to be commandeered, ships detained in port, and improvised shelters erected in open places.

After the initial emergency, Parr had to locate the clamorous loyalists and disbanded soldiers on grants of land throughout the province. Aided by Surveyor General Charles Morris* Jr and an overworked team of surveyors and army engineers, Parr encouraged the newcomers to settle in unoccupied areas of Nova Scotia. These included the region of Port Roseway, which Parr renamed Shelburne in honour of his patron, the Annapolis valley, the mouth of the Saint John River, and the shores of Passamaquoddy Bay. Discontent and squabbles soon arose. The method of granting land was chaotic and inefficient, with complicated procedures, delays in surveys, a mass of previous titles, and a superabundance of barren terrain. Many ambitious applicants such as the Fifty-Five Associated Loyalists [*see* Abijah WILLARD] sought to palliate their sufferings by applying for vast tracts of land, but Parr resisted this kind of selfish importunity. The processing of some 6,220 land claims for grants up to 1,000 acres occupied the Nova Scotian authorities for several years.

Although the loyalist migration initially brought Parr unsought responsibilities, the scope of his administration was soon materially reduced. To satisfy the aspirations of settlers on the Saint John, the province of New Brunswick was carved out of Nova Scotia in 1784 and placed under the governorship of Thomas Carleton*. The same year Cape Breton was given a separate government under Joseph Frederick Wallet DesBarres*, although it remained under Parr's supervision. Two years later, Parr was reduced in rank to lieutenant governor with the appointment of Lord Dorchester [Guy Carleton*] as governor general of British North America. These changes greatly angered him, although his army acquaintance with the Carleton brothers somewhat assuaged his injured feelings. Similarly, the imperial authorities' decision to create a bishopric of Nova Scotia in 1787 obliged Parr to surrender some of the powers he had hitherto exercised over the Church of England on behalf of the crown. Nevertheless, he retained sufficient authority over appointments to church livings, the stationing of missionaries, and the issue of marriage licences to provoke occasional clashes with Bishop Charles Inglis*. Although Parr's protracted controversy with rival vestries at Shelburne over the erection of parishes and the choice of ministers was settled in 1787, he quarrelled with Inglis the next year over the presentation of a rector to St Paul's Church, Halifax. This dispute was not resolved until 1791.

Meanwhile, many of the new settlements had begun to decline in population as loyalists moved to more promising parts of North America. The most dramatic transformation occurred at Shelburne, where a township of 8,000 persons in 1784 dwindled within a few years to a mere handful. The year 1792 saw the departure from the province of 1,190 of the 3,000 black loyalists. Accorded a low priority in the settlement of land claims, enterprising blacks responded eagerly to the mission of John Clarkson, sent by the Sierra Leone Company in 1791 to recruit settlers for its colony in West Africa. Parr was uncooperative over recruitment, fearing that such an exodus would be interpreted in London as indicative of discontent with his administration. The lieutenant governor had reason to be apprehensive, since in recent years he had come under attack for his attitudes and policies towards black settlement in Nova Scotia. Thomas PETERS, one of the black leaders, had criticized Parr and his officials for discriminatory practices and long delays in establishing black loyalists in the province, and Clarkson voiced similar complaints when he arrived. The British government ordered an investigation into the charges, but Parr had died by the time the investigators submitted their report exonerating him.

Parr was particularly sensitive about his superiors' views since he had been censured in 1786 for attempting to establish a whaling industry at Dartmouth. The lieutenant governor had welcomed as settlers Nantucket Quakers, whose fortunes were threatened by the exclusion of American whale oil from the British market following the war, and prospects for a thriving fishery had seemed bright. The British government decided, however, that Parr's initiative would favour American citizens with pecuniary aid intended for loyalists, foster a colonial competitor to British producers, and facilitate the illicit entry of American oil into Britain in the guise of a colonial product. Although Parr was disappointed at the rebuff, he supported the wider imperial policy of maintaining the navigation acts in the vain hope that Nova Scotians might supplant New Englanders as carriers and suppliers of provisions to the West Indies.

Towards the end of his administration Parr became disagreeably involved in the unseemly squabbling between loyalists and established settlers which affected all aspects of Nova Scotian life. After electoral victories in 1785, the loyalists used their new majority in the assembly to attack entrenched officials and councillors, and the partisan jockeying for office and influence often acquired constitutional overtones, as in the so-called "judges' affair." In 1787 two aspiring lawyers, Jonathan Sterns and William Taylor, accused puisne judges James Brenton* and Isaac Deschamps* of incompetence and partiality in the administration of justice. The assembly demanded an investigation, but the Council dismissed the complaints as "Groundless and Scandalous" and Parr unhesitatingly repudiated the charges. Though a lonely, isolated figure rather than a willing partisan, Parr's whole training and outlook, as well as a sensitive regard for his own authority and dignity, predisposed him to support the Council and the officials when they came under attack. He viewed the two lawyers as self-seeking attorneys, "strongly tinctured with a Republican spirit," whose sole object was to replace the judges with their own loyalist cronies. In a typical outburst to Evan Nepean, under-secretary of state for the Home Department, Parr declared, "I am surrounded with a number of Fanatical, diabolical, unprincipled, expecting, disapointed, deceitful, lying Scoundrels, who exist upon Party of their own creating, eternaly finding fault with, and complaining against their Superiours in Office." While loyalist assemblymen turned their wrath against the Council for refusing to hold an investigation, the two lawyers, who had been unceremoniously struck from the roll of attorneys for their behaviour, travelled to London to plead their case. But despite a long sojourn in England they received no satisfaction and were in fact required to make abject apologies before they were readmitted to the provincial bar. After their return, the affair flared up again in 1790 as the reinvigorated assembly under the leadership of Thomas Barclay* debated whether to impeach the judges. The controversy dragged on inconclusively until Parr's death, when the appointment of loyalist John Wentworth* as lieutenant governor transformed the troubled scene.

Parr's governorship coincided with a period of profound upheaval and dislocation which would have taxed the talents and energies of any administrator: a lesser man would have been dilatory and incompetent; an abler man might have shown more dexterity and resourcefulness. Being dour, brusque, and inured to deprivation in army life, he did not display the degree of solicitous sympathy the loyalists felt they deserved, although much of their criticism of Parr reflected despondency, frustration, and anger at straitened circumstances. A short man with sharp features and a brisk, strutting gait, he was a stickler for formalities and had the tetchy stubbornness of an independent but narrow mind long accustomed to military discipline. He also lacked the accommodating manners and social graces which might have made him a more popular governor of the colony to which he found himself somewhat uncongenially exiled.

PETER BURROUGHS

PRO, CO 217/56–63, 218/9, 218/20, 218/25–27. N.S., House of Assembly, *Journal*, 1782–91. PAC *Report*, 1921, app.C, 37–40; app.E, 1–12. Le Jeune, *Dictionnaire*, II, 410–11. Judith Fingard, *The Anglican design in loyalist Nova Scotia, 1783–1816* (London, 1972), 173–80. V. T. Harlow, *The founding of the second British empire, 1763–1793* (2v., London and New York, 1964), II, 295–97. MacNutt, *Atlantic provinces*. R. W. Winks, *The blacks in Canada: a history* (London and New Haven, Conn., 1971), 67–73. Margaret Ells, "Settling the loyalists in Nova Scotia," CHA *Report*, 1934, 105–9. J. S. Macdonald, "Memoir of Governor John Parr," N.S. Hist. Soc., *Coll.*, XIV (1909), 41–78.

PASCAUD, ANTOINE, merchant; b. 18 April 1729 in Bordeaux, France, to Guillaume Pascaud, a merchant, and Marie-Anne Baulos; d. January 1786.

Through his paternal grandparents, Jean Pascaud and Anne Puyperouse, Antoine Pascaud was related to the well-known family of Antoine Pascaud* at La Rochelle. His father's elder brother, Jean Pascaud, held the royal office of lawyer in the *parlement* of Paris. Antoine's parents had brought a total of 42,000 *livres* to their marriage on 3 Dec. 1726, and during Antoine's childhood his father was the principal Bordeaux agent for their La Rochelle cousins' extensive trade with Canada. When the father suffered the reverses of fortune that were to lead him into bankruptcy in May 1753, Antoine and his brother Jean went to Canada where Jean married Élisabeth de Cournoyer of Louisbourg, Île Royale (Cape Breton Island) at Quebec on 10 April 1752. Meanwhile, another brother, Pierre, went to the West Indies and took up the slave trade.

It is not clear when Antoine Pascaud first came to Canada, but in the early 1750s he was importing food. In February 1754, when food was short, he travelled overland from Quebec to New York to obtain about 360 bushels of flour for Canada and Île Royale. By so bravely finding food at such a critical moment Pascaud won high praise from Governor DUQUESNE, Jacques PREVOST de La Croix, financial commissary at Louisbourg, and other authorities.

Pascaud's activities in Canada were at the beginning of a long career in supplying the French navy and other maritime trading. During the Seven Years' War he worked in the West Indies and immediately after the war became supply merchant to the new and short-lived colony in French Guiana which the crown hoped might take root and flourish as a substitute for the lost colonies of Île Royale and Canada. When this project failed, Pascaud was arrested by order of 18 Sept. 1767 and imprisoned in the Bastille with the Guiana officials. In a case reminiscent of the *affaire du Canada* [*see* François BIGOT] they were all charged with profiteering and defrauding the crown. Pascaud was released on 9 Aug. 1768 to go into exile on a property that he owned near Aubeterre in Angoumois (Aubeterre-sur-Dronne, dept of Charente). He then claimed to have been ruined, but in the American War of Independence was again supplying the French colonies on a large scale, sending out many ships and making secret international payments for the crown at his headquarters in Paris.

Antoine Pascaud is typical of the businessmen who worked in the French colonial field, and as a member of the Pascaud family has a special interest in that he puts the affairs of Canada in a larger perspective.

J. F. BOSHER

AD, Gironde (Bordeaux), Minutes Janeau (Bordeaux), 23 nov. 1726. AN, Col., E, 330 (dossier Pascaud). Archives municipales, Bordeaux (dép. de la Gironde, France), État civil, Saint-André, 20 avril 1729. Bibliothèque de l'Arsenal, Archives de la Bastille, 12324, ff.215ff. Jean Tarrade, *Le commerce colonial de la France à la fin de l'ancien régime: l'évolution du régime de l'Exclusif de 1763 à 1789* (2v., Paris, 1972), II.

PATTERSON (Paterson), WALTER, army officer, land proprietor, and colonial administrator; b.*c.* 1735 near Rathmelton, Co. Donegal (Republic of Ireland), eldest son of William Patterson and Elizabeth Todd; m. Hester Warren 9 March 1770 and they had at least four children; d. 6 Sept. 1798 in London, England.

The career of Walter Patterson is inextricably bound up with the land question, the foremost issue in Prince Edward Island politics prior to confederation. After St John's Island, as it was then called, passed into British hands in 1763, it was divided into 67 townships or lots of approximately 20,000 acres each. These, with the single exception of Lot 66 containing about 6,000 acres, were granted to influential individuals in Britain in the summer of 1767. The conditions attached to the grants were unrealistic and, toward the latter part of the 18th century, increasingly anachronistic: principally, each township was to be settled within ten years in the proportion of one person per 200 acres, all settlers were to be Protestants from the continent of Europe or Protestants who had lived for at least two years in North America, and quitrents of between £20 and £60 per annum were to be paid to the royal treasury. Failure by the proprietors to adhere to these stipulations carried the penalty of forfeiture to the crown. Such was the plan; in practice the proprietors did not fulfil the conditions, yet managed to retain possession. For almost a century, Island settlers, a large proportion of them tenants of absentee landlords, clamoured for the land to be confiscated and granted to them. The origins of the land question can be traced in large part to the failure of Walter Patterson, during his 17 years as governor, to cope adequately with his responsibility as public administrator of a privately owned colony.

Little is known of Patterson's early life. He entered the British army on 29 Dec. 1757 as an ensign in Thomas GAGE's 80th Foot. Gage had served in Ireland between 1744 and 1755 with the 44th Foot, and it is possible that Patterson made his acquaintance during that time. The 80th was the first British regiment to be trained from the outset in irregular tactics, and it served under ABERCROMBY in 1758 at Fort Carillon (Ticonderoga, N.Y.) and with AMHERST in 1759 on Lake Champlain, and along with Robert ROGERS' rangers it was used in skirmishing and reconnaissance and as the advance guard for the army. Patterson was promoted lieutenant on 4 Oct. 1760, and on 26 Oct. 1762 was granted leave to go to Europe. Patterson continued on leave until 24 Nov. 1764 when his name no longer appears on the list of army returns. His regiment was disbanded the following month.

With his army career behind him, Patterson seems to have turned to land speculation and colonization ventures in New York and St John's Island. In July 1764 he and Charles Lee, a former officer in the 44th, acted as intermediaries to secure Lord Holland 60,000 acres of land in New York. As a reward for their efforts Holland and the Earl of Hillsborough, president of the Board of Trade, promised to secure each of the two men 20,000 acres. On 29 November Hillsborough presided over a session of the board which recommended royal confirmation of these grants. The royal mandamus of 19 December provided for 20,000 acres "in one contiguous tract, in such part . . . of New York as he [Patterson] . . . shall choose" and was approved by the New York Council the following month. Patterson selected land on the Connecticut River, although as late as 15 Nov. 1771 a patent had not been issued. On 16 Dec. 1772 his name headed a petition for a further grant of 24,000 acres on the Connecticut River to be erected into a township. It is not known whether the petitioners were successful.

In 1764 Patterson's name was among those of 20 reduced army officers, including Allan MACLEAN, Francis MCLEAN, and Charles Lee, on a memorial of the Earl of Egmont to the Board of Trade seeking a grant of the entire island of St. John's. On 23 July 1767 17 of the officers named in the 1764 memorial, including Charles Lee, received 10,000-acre parcels of land in Lots 18 to 26 inclusive. Patterson became co-owner of Lot 19 with his brother John, the only grantee for the nine lots not on the 1764 list. The following year Patterson played an active role in the effort, supported by a majority of the proprietors, to have the Island separated from Nova Scotia, of which it was then a part, and made into a separate colony. The British government acquiesced, on condition that the proprietors agree to support the civil establishment out of the quitrent fund. Walter Patterson was appointed governor on 14 July 1769 and arrived at his capital of Charlottetown on 30 Aug. 1770.

The problems confronting Governor Patterson were daunting. The population of the entire colony was a mere 300, most of them Acadians who did not speak English. The capital city had only a few crude houses and no public buildings. The civil officers were an unpromising lot, a hungry contingent of disaffected office-seekers with little, if any, previous administrative experience, depending for a tenuous subsistence on the collection of the quitrents. The proprietors, saddled with conditions the fulfilment of which would have bankrupted all but the most wealthy, were disposed to regard their property as a windfall and their obligations an inconvenience to be avoided. In dealing with such a difficult situation the governor of a small and strategically insignificant colony could expect little attention, much less substantial assistance, from a British government preoccupied with global politics.

Patterson assumed his new duties with characteristic energy. In September 1770 he took the oath of office and appointed an executive council. During the next several years a number of ordinances were passed dealing with matters as diverse as the protection of the sea cow (walrus) industry and the prevention of masters of vessels from carrying away settlers who were in debt. It was with some trepidation that Patterson forwarded these ordinances to Hillsborough, now secretary of state for the American Colonies, asking to be excused "What ever Errors may be found in them" since they were "among the first of our productions of that nature. . . ." Patterson also obtained permission to appoint a surveyor general, Thomas Wright*, after complaining that the township boundaries were "merely imaginary, except upon the Map." Unfortunately, it was much easier to pass ordinances than to enforce them, and "imaginary boundaries" were only too appropriate for a colony where the whole scheme of settlement looked much better on paper than in reality.

Between the years 1770 and 1775 approximately 1,000 new settlers arrived in the colony, the large majority through the efforts of a few proprietors, most notably James William Montgomery [*see* William MONTGOMERY], Robert CLARK, and John MacDonald* of Glenaladale, known as Fear-a-ghlinne. Montgomery held the position of lord advocate for Scotland, one of the most important political appointments in Britain at the time. He attempted to set up a large flax farm on Lot 34 [*see* David Lawson*] and a commercial establishment at Three Rivers (the region around Georgetown) [*see* David HIGGINS]. Robert Clark, a Quaker merchant from London, with his partner Robert Campbell sent out about 200 people to the New London area of Lot 21 in 1773–74. John MacDonald purchased Lot 36 and his brother Donald accompanied a party of 210 Scottish Catholic Highlanders as settlers there in 1772. Each of these men expended, and lost, thousands of pounds; yet, according to the strict terms of the original grants, their property was liable to confiscation because none had settled his land with Protestants from outside the British Isles. Proprietor-sponsored immigration practically ceased with the outbreak of the American revolution in 1775.

Not surprisingly perhaps, Patterson took no overt action to enforce the quite unreasonable conditions of settlement; a more pressing consideration was the collection of quitrents, upon which the survival of his government depended. At first Patterson himself held the crucial position of receiver general with a deputy in London. By 1774, however, the post had been procured by William Allanby, a member of the Island Council. Allanby soon quarrelled with Patterson and departed for England, leaving behind neither a list of the proprietors nor the amount that each owed. The collection soon lapsed, frustrated by the proprietors' resistance and administrative incompetence. By 1775 roughly £3,000 had been paid, the arrears were over £6,000, and the civil officers were left to subsist under extremely adverse conditions on a fraction of their nominal salaries, a circumstance which provided both motive and justification for measures to lay hands on proprietor-owned land.

Throughout his régime, Patterson was preoccupied with the problem of enforcing the collection of quitrents through legislation. The initial effort, an ordinance passed by the Council in 1771, became an act when the first House of Assembly met in July 1773. It failed to receive royal assent and was re-enacted by the assembly in October 1774 to correct "two manifest inaccuracies." This act provided for the collection of the quitrent arrears through the seizure (distraint) of goods, or, failing that, for thc sale of sufficient land at public auction to meet the debt. No express provision was made either for advance notice to the proprietors or advertisement of the sales in Great Britain. For rather complicated reasons, largely of convenience, the legislation applied only to those proprietors who had signed the petition requesting a separate government in 1768, a document Patterson professed to regard as "a Contract between the signers of it and the Crown." Approximately 50 lots were thus exposed to the possibility of sale. Armed with this legislation, which had not yet received royal assent, Patterson wrote to Lord Dartmouth, secretary of state for the American Colonies, on 2 Sept. 1774 requesting a seven-month leave of absence, stating that he would be "of more service to the Island, by spending a little time among the Proprietors at Home, than I can possibly be of, in the same space, by remaining here." He sailed from Charlottetown on 2 Aug. 1775.

Patterson remained in England for the better part of five years. There he displayed a considerable skill in manipulating the proprietors to serve his own interests, in the guise of promoting theirs. He initiated a series of meetings, resulting in a memorial, supported by about 20 proprietors, which was forwarded to the Privy Council in February 1776. It requested that the British government make provision for the civil establishment of St John's Island, that the Quit Rent Act of 1774 be put into effect, and that some concessions be granted proprietors with regard to the payment of quitrents. On 10 April 1777 Patterson was informed that parliament had voted £3,000 to support the Island government "for the present year," an amount which became institutionalized as an annual grant. This was perhaps the outstanding achievement of his governorship, for without it reannexation to Nova Scotia would have been a virtual certainty. Early in 1776 royal assent was given to the Quit Rent Act, and on 7 August a Treasury minute was issued directing the receiver general to "take proper measures" to enforce collection of the arrears, which were to be applied to the payment of salaries still owing the civil officers for the period 1769–77. Far from receiving concessions, the proprietors had imposed on them, by order of the Treasury in 1778, the inconvenience of being obliged to pay their quitrents on the Island only, a measure apparently solicited by Patterson and opposed by Receiver General William Allanby.

Patterson returned to the Island in the summer of 1780. He now had an opportunity, perhaps unique in early Island history, to break the land monopoly of the absentee proprietors. His quitrent legislation had been ratified by the appropriate British officials, the majority of the proprietors were complacent or disinterested, and, with the outcome of the war in the colonies still uncertain, Island land was conceived to be of little value. He quickly consolidated his position by appointing his brother-in-law, William Nisbett, acting receiver general of the quitrents, and by reaching an accommodation with his attorney general, Phillips CALLBECK, who had been demanding half of Patterson's salary for officiating as governor between 1775 and 1779. On 26 Nov. 1780 he secured the agreement of the Council to put the Quit Rent Act into effect. In order to expedite proceedings, the council voted on 19 Feb. 1781 to dispense with the formality of distraint and to take action against "the land only," except where the proprietors were themselves present. This action was illegal in that it contravened the 1774 quitrent legislation. It was not to be an isolated incident.

After a series of hesitations and delays, the land sales were finally held, at the home of Charlottetown tavern-keeper John Clark, some time between 13 and 15 Nov. 1781. Secrecy, confusion, and controversy surrounded the event. The only purchasers were officers of government and no actual money was paid, the land being claimed in lieu of salary arrears. Patterson himself obtained three whole and four half townships, plus an additional 70,000 acres in the names of four of his English acquaintances. Chief Justice Peter Stewart*, who had made an appropriately tempestuous entry into Island life on board a vessel wrecked off the north shore during an autumn gale in 1775, acquired half of Lot 18, the property of William Allanby. Lieutenant Governor Thomas Desbrisay*, a man who harboured a deep resentment against the world in general and Patterson in particular, claimed Lot 33. Phillips Callbeck, now Patterson's principal officer-accomplice, outbid Chief Justice Peter Stewart for the much sought-after Lot 35.

After the land sales of 1781, Patterson spent the rest of his political life on the defensive. In orchestrating the event, he had made, or allowed, several critical errors. By claiming so much of the spoils for himself, he earned the lingering resentment of his fellow officers, particularly Stewart and Desbrisay, who were implicated but not satiated. Blunders were made, too, in the choice of which of the 50-odd available lots were to be sold. By his own admission in 1783, Patterson went out of his way, illegally, to "save" land belonging to several influential proprietors, notably George, Viscount Townshend* and James William Montgomery. His own appropriations brought him much of the most valuable land in the colony, including Lot 49, the property of Robert Clark. Lot 35, acquired by Phillips Callbeck, was known to be much coveted by John MacDonald, the owner of the adjacent Lot 36. The land of some of the inactive proprietors could probably have been seized with impunity; it was foolhardy to tamper with lots belonging to the few men who had gone to considerable expense to send out settlers.

A dispute over Lot 35 soon became the focal point of a bitter and protracted struggle. Shortly after the outbreak of the American revolution, John MacDonald had joined the Royal Highland Emigrants; he became Captain MacDonald, and spent most of the period 1775–81 at Halifax. In close contact with the officers of the Island government, he was quite aware of the impending land sales. He made an unsuccessful attempt, by emissary, to obtain an informal lien on Lot 35 by paying the quitrents. In 1782 he was in London petitioning against the sales, apparently under the impression that both lots 35 and 36 had been sold. By early 1783, with some of the other proprietors, he succeeded in having the royal assent denied a 1781 Quit Rent Act of the Island legislature, which would have included all 67 of the lots, and in having a new Quit Rent Act drawn up providing for the return of the sold lots. Governor Patterson was sent this bill by Lord North, secretary of state for the Home Department, on 24 July 1783, with explicit instructions to lay it before the assembly and recommend "in the strongest manner . . . to them the passing of the same."

Patterson later acknowledged receiving this bill in the late fall of 1783. Unwisely, he chose to do everything in his power to frustrate its intent. The bill would have provided a solid basis, sanctioned by the British government, for the future sale of land because of non-payment of quitrents. Moreover, the terms upon which the sold lots were to be returned – the former proprietors were given one month to pay the 1781 purchase price, plus interest and compensation for improvements – ensured that in only a very few instances would possession by the officers be challenged. Patterson adopted a tactic of delay. He kept the 1783 bill secret throughout the winter of 1783–84. Then, in March 1784, he called a general election in the hope of obtaining an assembly which could be trusted to reject the bill. Phillips Callbeck resigned his seat on the Council to lead the pro-governor faction. Callbeck was opposed, and defeated, by a party led by John Stewart*, an able but intemperate young man whose animosity toward the governor was intensified by the knowledge that Patterson had been intimate with his stepmother, the wife of the chief justice. Rather than entrust the bill to such an assembly, Patterson decided to implicate the Council in the effort to suppress it. On 20 March, over the strong objections of Peter Stewart and Thomas Desbrisay, the Council passed a motion stating that the bill would be withheld pending the reaction of the British government to a "humble petition and remonstrance" explaining why the overturning of the sales would be detrimental to the colony.

The already Byzantine political situation on the Island was further complicated in the summer of 1784 by the arrival of several hundred American loyalists. Patterson had been active in seeking loyalist settlers as early as the winter of 1782–83, when preparations were under way for the evacuation of New York. His brother John Patterson went to London and managed to cajole some of the proprietors into supporting yet another memorial, this one dated 29 June 1783. These proprietors agreed to give up to loyalists one-quarter of the land signed for opposite their names; in return, they requested the usual abatement of quitrents, and asked that the British government supply transportation and provisions for those loyalists wishing to go to the Island. Governor Patterson received approval in principle for this scheme late in 1783. The loyalists who came were immediately involved in the land sales controversy. Since most were given locations on the disputed lots they had a vested interest in opposing the return of this land to the original proprietors, at whose hands they quite rightly feared eviction.

In London, meanwhile, the lobbying proprietors were growing impatient. Early in 1784 John Cambridge*, Robert Clark's agent, was sent to Charlottetown, where he found the anti-Patterson faction brimming with information and ready to talk. Now in possession of a detailed account of recent proceedings on the Island, Robert Clark "and others" on 27 August petitioned the Board of Trade for redress. Their lordships expressed surprise that the governor and Council had taken it "on themselves to disobey a positive injunction of His Majesty. . . ." They observed, also, that the petition and remonstrance promised in the Council minutes of 20 March had not been forthcoming. Accordingly, a "Sloop of War" was ordered to the Island expressly to bring back "the papers and Evidence that the Governor and Council must naturally be so anxious to submit to the Lords of the Committee." When the ship returned to London in February 1785, Patterson's "Facts and Reasons" were judged inadequate. Moreover, it was now apparent that many irregularities had accompanied the sales. The former proprietors were therefore informed that they were "at liberty . . . to prosecute . . . their Remedy at Law for the Recovery of their said Lots." Emboldened by this success, the proprietors now pressed their advantage and requested that the text of the 1783 bill be revised in their favour. The delay occasioned by this procedure gave Patterson time for a few last desperate manœuvres.

In the spring of 1785 Patterson suspended the chief justice and appointed three of his own supporters to replace him, thereby effectively denying his proprietor-opponents recourse to Island law courts. He also staged another general election. This time the pro-governor faction was victorious, with strong loyalist support. On 20 April 1786 the assembly passed a bill ratifying the 1781 land sales, "any want of legal form, or other irregularity whatever in such proceedings notwithstanding. . . ." In his dispatch to Lord Sydney, secretary of state for the Home Department, justifying this legislation, Patterson remarked that since he had had no recent official communication regarding the 1783 bill, he assumed "His Majesty's Ministers in their wisdom had seen fit to let the matter drop. . . ."

It was Patterson, however, who was dropped – in three stages. The first of these had occurred two years previously: late in 1784, as a result of the rearrangement of British North America after the treaty of Paris (1783), the Island's government had been made nominally dependent on that of Nova Scotia, the salaries of the civil officers reduced, and Patterson's rank, as chief administrative officer, lowered to that of lieutenant governor. He was told, "With regard . . . to your continuance upon that Island, the matter will lay with you for your determination. . . ." As the protests of his opponents continued to mount, particularly after his bold efforts of 1785 and early 1786 to institutionalize the sales, Lieutenant Governor Patterson received a dispatch dated 30 June 1786 ordering him to repair to England "as soon as may be" to answer, in person, the charges of his accusers. Although his interim successor, Edmund Fanning*, arrived in Charlottetown on 4 November ready to assume command, Patterson contrived to remain in control throughout the winter. He made haste to call the assembly on 8 November and lay before it the 1783 Bill, which the assembly obligingly rejected. A new bill was then passed ten days later, of more local manufacture, for "setting aside and annulling" the land sales. The bill included only lots controlled directly by Patterson: there was no mention of Lot 35, nor of the land claimed by Peter Stewart and Thomas Desbrisay. The original proprietors were given twelve months to repay the purchase price, with interest and compensation for improvements. To protect loyalist settlers, all conveyances made by post-1781 proprietors were confirmed. A final communication from Whitehall was quite explicit. "His Majesty," Patterson was informed in a dispatch of 5 April 1787, "has no further occasion for your services as Lieutenant Governor of the Island of St. John."

Although now forced to give up his government to Edmund Fanning, Patterson remained on the Island for more than a year, meddling in politics, protecting his interests as a landowner, and engaging in trade. By 1789 he was back in London, making a final, and futile, attempt to regain his former influence among the proprietors. Now bankrupt and helpless before his many enemies, he was apparently imprisoned for debt, and his vast estate on the Island, for which he had risked so much, was sold to satisfy his creditors. He died in poverty at his lodgings in Castle Street, Oxford Market, London, on 6 Sept. 1798.

On 1 May 1786 Patterson had written Lord Sydney, then secretary of state for the Home Department, imploring him to abandon attempts to overturn the 1781 land sales. "What yesterday was fact, today is doctrine," Patterson had declared. The truth of this statement is evidenced by the subsequent history of the sold lots, particularly Lot 35. Although the two controversial Patterson-directed bills of 1786 and 1787 were denied the royal assent, the 1783 Bill sent out from England never was enacted into law, thus denying Captain MacDonald his long-sought remedy by legislation. After much further lobbying and expense, including a trial before a committee of the Privy Council in 1789, MacDonald succeeded in having Callbeck, Wright, and several other Patterson supporters removed from their posts and the chief justice restored. Even then, he could only acquire Lot 35 by purchase from the original proprietor, General Alexander Maitland, whose title his great exertions had merely served to protect, at the exorbitant price of £1,200. By contrast, the wily Fanning, who was rather good at converting "fact" into "doctrine," made full use of his considerable experience in colonial administration and law to acquire about 60,000 acres of Patterson's estate at a cost purported to be just slightly more than £100. Fanning's possession of this land helps to explain why, as reported by John Stewart in 1806, the majority of the sold lots tended to remain "in the quiet and peaceable possession of those claiming under the sales in 1781. . . ."

Walter Patterson has long been a favourite of Island historians. His initiative and daring have certainly distinguished him among a generally lacklustre group of colonial administrators. In recent years, some historians have tended to romanticize his career, depicting him as an Island patriot fighting for local independence against an unholy alliance of grasping absentee proprietors and an indifferent British government. Captain John MacDonald once characterized him as a man of "an amazing cleverness . . . mixed with an equal proportion of folly and madness," who "rose from nothing, & would have done extremely well, had he known where to stop. . . ." Along with a functioning, separate colonial government, under the circumstances a major achievement, he left to his successors a chaotic administration, a history of intense factional rivalry, and an entrenched system of absentee proprietorship. Patterson's failure to bring about reform during the early, malleable period when change was most possible, and the particular way in which he pursued his self-interest among the competing claims of absentee proprietors, government officials, and tenants, largely determined the issues about which the struggle over land would revolve for the following one hundred years [*see* Edmund Fanning, William Cooper*, and George Coles*].

HARRY BAGLOLE

Clements Library, Thomas Gage papers, American ser., Patterson to Gage, 16 April 1771; Gage to Patterson, 8 Aug. 1771, 7 June 1775; Germain papers, Walter Patterson, "Observations on the Island of St. John in the Gulf of St. Lawrence . . ."; Patterson to Germain, [1778], Proposal for offering America a liberal constitution and for erecting coastal forts; Shelburne papers, Patterson to Shelburne, "Mr. Paterson on the preservation of his majesty's timber in America"; Patterson to Shelburne, 22 June 1782. PAC, MG 19, E2. PRO, BT 5/2, ff.21, 28, 124; 6/102, ff.112, 118, 126; CO 226/1, ff.11–13, 21, 45–46, 95–100, 102–12; 226/2, ff.21, 27–28, 33; 226/3, ff.15–17, 58–61, 62–71; 226/4, ff.32, 65; 226/5, ff.11–12; 226/6, ff.132–34, 142; 226/7, ff.82–83; 226/8, ff.72–80, 92–93, 270; 226/9, ff.147–49; 226/10, ff.1–2, 31–32, 94; 226/17, ff.108, 115–16; 228/1, ff.40–41; 228/2, ff.69–70, 73–75; 229/2, ff.48–63, 81–82; WO 17/1490, f.3; 25/25; 25/209. Public Archives of P.E.I. (Charlottetown), MacDonald papers, John MacDonald to Nelly MacDonald, 19 July 1783; John MacDonald to Nellie and Peggy MacDonald, 27 June 1785, 27 March, 12 Sept. 1789; RG 5, "Report of Richard Jackson to the Board of Trade on acts passed in 1773," in "Proclamations and orders in Council relative to the allowance or disallowance of acts of Prince Edward Island," 1; RG 16, Conveyance registers, 1.7, ff.98–99.

Amherst, *Journal* (Webster). [J. P. Egmont], *To the king's most excellent majesty, the memorial of John, Earl of Egmont . . .* ([London, 1764?]), 31. *Gentleman's Magazine*, 1798, 815. G.B., Board of Trade, *JTP, 1764–67*, 116–17. *Johnson papers* (Sullivan *et al.*), IV, 133, 609; XIII, 328–30. *The Lee papers* (2v., N.Y. Hist. Soc., *Coll.*, [ser.3], IV, V, New York, 1871–72), I, 48–52, 92, 96, 112–16. [John MacDonald?], *The criminating complaint of the proprietors of the Island of St. John whose lands were condemned and sold in 1781* (London, 1789); *Information for the officers of the navy and army, proprietors of land in the Island of St. John's in the gulph of St. Lawrence, and for the other now remaining proprietors thereof* (n.p., n.d.), 9–10; *Remarks on the conduct of the governor and Council of the Island of St. John's, in passing an act of assembly in April of 1786 to confirm the sales of the lands in 1781 . . .* (n.p., [1789?]), 37, 81. PAC *Report*, 1905, I, pt.II, 6–10.

British officers serving in North America, 1754–1774, comp. W. C. Ford (Boston, 1894), 80. "Calendar of [New York colony] Council minutes, 1668–1783," N.Y. State Library, *Annual report* (Albany), 1902, II, 520, 526, 571. G.B., WO, *Army list*, 1759, 133; 1760, 138; 1763, 144. N.Y., Secretary of state, *Calendar of N.Y. colonial manuscripts, indorsed land papers; in the office of the secretary of state of New York, 1643–1803* (Albany, 1864), 354, 379, 547, 584. R. C. Archibald, *Carlyle's first love, Margaret Gordon, Lady Bannerman; an account of her life, ancestry, and homes, her family, and friends* (London and New York, 1910; repr. New York, 1973), 6–7, 10. Duncan Campbell, *History of Prince Edward Island* (Charlottetown, 1875; repr. Belleville, Ont., 1972), 30–31. Frank MacKinnon, *The government of Prince Edward Island* (Toronto, 1951; repr. [1974]), 11. John Stewart, *An account of Prince Edward Island, in the gulph of St. Lawrence, North America . . .* (London, 1806; repr. East Ardsley, Eng., and New York, 1967), 201. David Weale and Harry Baglole, *The Island and confederation: the end of an era* (n.p., 1973). J. M. Bumsted, "Sir James Montgomery and Prince Edward Island, 1767–1803," *Acadiensis*, VII (1977–78), no.2, 76–102.

PAULUS. *See* SAHONWAGY

PAYEN DE NOYAN ET DE CHAVOY, PIERRE-JACQUES, officer in the colonial regular troops, seigneur, and king's lieutenant at Trois-Rivières (Que.); b. 3 Nov. 1695 in Montreal (Que.), son of Pierre Payen* de Noyan and Catherine-Jeanne Le Moyne de Longueuil et de Châteauguay; d. 30 Dec. 1771 in Paris, France.

Like his father, Pierre-Jacques Payen de Noyan entered the colonial regulars; he was promoted ensign in 1712, lieutenant in 1722, and captain in 1729. In 1721 he served briefly as commandant of Fort Frontenac (Kingston, Ont.). He made several trips to the *pays d'en haut*, including one in 1729 when he led the provisioning convoy from Montreal into Michilimackinac (Mackinaw City, Mich.) as preparation for the offensive against the Foxes [*see* Kiala*]. Some time before 1724 he inherited the fief of Chavoy, near Avranches, France; in that year Maurepas, minister of Marine, arranged for him a two- or three-year delay in rendering *foi et hommage* for the property.

From 1730 to 1731 Noyan was in France, where he had been summoned to present a plan for dealing with the Foxes. His proposal was detailed and perhaps workable; along with suggestions about the conduct of military operations, he even included pattern speeches to be used before Fox leaders. The plan's most interesting feature was that the campaign should be paid for by selling fur trade permits, to relieve the crown of any expense. In the event, Noyan's scheme was not needed, for while he was in France the Foxes were defeated by Governor Beauharnois*. Nevertheless, Noyan impressed Maurepas, and from that time he was considered an authority on the west.

In 1733 Noyan was scheduled to command at Michilimackinac, but illness kept him from that post. The following year he was assigned to Pointe-à-la-Chevelure (near Crown Point, N.Y.); because of recurring sickness, however, he was there only intermittently and during the summer he was replaced. Beauharnois commented that "this officer is indeed subject to most extraordinary illness." In 1738 Noyan was appointed to command at Detroit and, following an operation on his left breast, he set out for the post the next spring.

Noyan remained at Detroit until mid 1742. There he had two serious problems, the excessive trade in brandy and an Ottawa-Huron feud. During most of his term of office he had a free hand in dealing with these problems, and he corresponded directly with Maurepas, an unusual situation on the frontier which was evidently a result of his good relations with the minister. But although he tried harder than most commandants to curtail the brandy trade, his powers were nevertheless limited and he did not succeed. To settle the Ottawa-Huron dispute, Noyan recommended that the less numerous Hurons be sent to locate near Montreal and that they be replaced by Shawnees from the Ohio valley. Opposition from the Huron missionary Armand de La Richardie* prevented the move, however. In spite of this disagreement, Noyan and the missionary remained good friends.

In 1746–47 Noyan was commandant at Fort Saint-Frédéric (near Crown Point, N.Y.), where his influence with the Iroquois (he had previously been adopted by them) proved useful during the war which had broken out in North America in 1744. One report referred to him as "a man of talent." From this period through the 1750s Noyan attended most of the conferences between the governor and the Iroquois. At a meeting in 1756 the Iroquois asked Vaudreuil [RIGAUD] to "be so good as to give us our son, Mr. de Noyan, as Commandant of Fort Frontenac."

In May 1749 Noyan became major of Montreal and in March 1756 king's lieutenant at Trois-Rivières. While still holding the latter position he was appointed to command again at Fort Frontenac. The post was a supply centre for the western garrisons, but it was in poor condition; Montcalm* referred to it as "good for nothing" and its complement of about 60 soldiers as a "feeble garrison." When a force of nearly 3,000 British and American soldiers under Lieutenant-Colonel John BRADSTREET laid siege to the fort in August 1758, it surrendered after three days. Bradstreet and Noyan worked out an arrangement in which Noyan was to be exchanged for Colonel Peter Schuyler*, and Noyan was permitted to return to Montreal because of his poor health. Vaudreuil blamed Noyan for the defeat, claiming that he was too old to fight. Stung by the governor's lack of faith, Noyan requested retirement, which was granted with a pension in January 1759. After the surrender of Canada, Noyan went to France where he was imprisoned in the Bastille from March 1762 to December 1763 in connection with the *affaire du Canada.* He seems to have been guilty of no more than negligence in checking the inventory of Joseph-Michel CADET's goods at Frontenac, and he was fined only six *livres*. He died eight years later.

On 17 Nov. 1731 at Montreal Noyan had married Louise-Catherine d'Ailleboust de Manthet, widow of Jean-Baptiste Charly* Saint-Ange, and the couple had two sons and three daughters, one of whom, Catherine-Angélique, married Pierre-Jean-Baptiste-François-Xavier LEGARDEUR de Repentigny. In 1733 Noyan had been granted a seigneury on the Rivière Richelieu which became known as Noyan, and in 1740 one on the Ottawa River near that of the Séminaire de Québec. His wife sold the former seigneury to John CAMPBELL and Gabriel CHRISTIE in 1764 and probably joined her husband in France.

Pierre-Jacques Payen de Noyan et de Chavoy was one of the better colonial officers in New France. He served with distinction and in 1741 was awarded the cross of Saint-Louis. As major of Montreal, king's lieutenant at Trois-Rivières, and commander of several western posts, he was effective, unselfish, and held in high respect by his superiors. Neither his defeat at Frontenac nor his implication in the *affaire du Canada* should affect this reputation.

DONALD CHAPUT

AN, Col., D[2C], 58, p.23ff.; 61, p.167; 222 (copies at PAC). "The French regime in Wisconsin – II," ed. R. G. Thwaites, Wis., State Hist. Soc., *Coll.*, XVII (1906), 73, 107–8, 170–72, 284–85, 326–27, 348–50. *Michigan Pioneer Coll.*, XXXIV (1905), 113–15, 186–88, 340. *NYCD* (O'Callaghan and Fernow), X, 83–88, 499–518, 825–26, 831–32, 835–55. PAC *Report*, 1904, app.K, 173–74, 198, 252; 1905, I, pt.VI, 118–19, 223. *DAB. Dictionnaire national des Canadiens français (1608–1760)* (2v., Montréal, 1958), II, 1036. Æ. Fauteux, *Les chevaliers de Saint-Louis*, 140. Le Jeune, *Dictionnaire*, II, 363–64. Tanguay, *Dictionnaire*, VI, 265. Ægidius Fauteux, *La famille d'Aillebout: étude généalogique et historique* (Montréal, 1917), 128–31. "Les seigneuries de Noyan et de Foucault," *BRH*, XXXVIII (1932), 399.

PEACHEY (Peachy, Pitchy), JAMES, surveyor, draughtsman, army officer, and artist; probably of British origin; d. 24 Nov. 1797, likely in Martinique.

Records of James Peachey begin with the first of his three visits to North America. Nothing has been discovered about his early life or training. In

1773 or 1774 he began employment in the Boston office of Samuel Jan Holland*, surveyor general of the province of Quebec and of the Northern District of North America. The Board of Trade, under whose sponsorship Holland was working, wanted the most up-to-date general maps of North America possible, especially with the approach of the American revolution. Peachey may have been hired specifically for this project. In late 1775 Holland sent him and two assistant surveyors to England. Lodged in London apartments, they were to prepare maps for a publication that never materialized. The board gave its financial support to Joseph Frederick Wallet DesBarres*'s rival proposal for the *Atlantic Neptune*, into which Holland's surveys were incorporated. Peachey not surprisingly disappeared from Holland's pay-list by 1777. Remarking on the visual similarity between the supplementary topographical views in the *Atlantic Neptune* and Peachey's works, Michael Bell has suggested that Peachey's talents were perhaps utilized in this publication.

By 1780 Peachey had again crossed the Atlantic. He spent the next few years in the Quebec region, as evidenced by the earliest known, dated examples of his artistic production. Through his portrayal of Governor HALDIMAND's entourage and of habitants in idyllic local landscape settings exquisitely executed in water-colour, Peachey captured the attention and patronage of the governor and of William Tryon, former governor of New York. In correspondence with the latter in 1784, Holland referred to Peachey as being "for Som time Draughtsman to General Haldimand" and "on the footing of a Gentleman, of which he has made himselfe deserving of, as well by his Conduct & Improvements in Drawing & Painting."

By May 1783 Peachey was employed as a deputy surveyor under Holland. His assignments were connected with surveying and laying out lots of land for disbanded troops and refugee loyalists in the future Upper Canada. Peachey and his colleagues René-Hippolyte Pepin*, *dit* Laforce, and Lewis Kotte (Koth, Cotté) were instructed to journey the north shore of Lake Ontario to Niagara (near Youngstown, N.Y.). Peachey wintered in the vicinity of Cataraqui (Kingston), where in association with Kotte until 1784 he continued the surveys of Adolphustown and Fredericksburgh (North and South Fredericksburgh) townships begun by John COLLINS the previous year. In November Peachey accompanied Haldimand to England.

Among other works Peachey then produced two distinguished series of Canadian views, frequently of identical subject. The first, represented in the collections of the Public Archives of Canada, consists of several fine small-scale water-colours, alphabetically keyed, which were probably at one time insets of a large-scale plan of the St Lawrence valley, possibly intended for publication. A second series, now dispersed, is dated 1785 and may have been commissioned by Haldimand. Peachey used the technique of pouncing to transfer the elements of his preparatory drawing in producing some of these highly finished works. He sometimes copied works after his associates Kotte, James Hunter, and Peter Couture.

Peachey capitalized on his modest success on the London scene by producing his compositions in varying formats, media, and sizes. He prepared etched outlines of topographical views related to his second visit which were then coloured by his own or another hand. He also sought professional assistance to produce aquatints, published in London in 1785 and 1786, after his Canadian views. Residing in the Mayfair district, he exhibited views of Montreal and Quebec at the Royal Academy in 1786 and three more Canadian subjects in 1787. In all likelihood his success was enhanced by his connection with Haldimand. His works may have influenced the perception that Englishmen formed of Canada.

Peachey also tried his hand at book illustration through an association with the London printer C. Buckton. He etched the frontispiece to *A primer, for the use of the Mohawk children . . .* (2nd ed., London, 1786) by Christian Daniel CLAUS and the frontispiece and 18 biblical scenes for *The Book of Common Prayer . . . translated into the Mohawk language . . . to which is added the gospel according to St. Mark, translated into the Mohawk language by Captn. Joseph Brant . . .* (4th ed., London, 1787).

On 3 Oct. 1787 Peachey obtained an ensign's commission in the 60th Foot under Haldimand's command. He arrived at Quebec in August 1788 to join the 1st battalion, then mustered at Niagara. His correspondence with Haldimand refers to a view of the Niagara Falls and a portrait of Catharine Brant [Adonwentishon*], the wife of Joseph Brant [Thayendanegea*], but no Canadian works unmistakably dated to his third visit are known to have survived. By 1790 the 60th had moved to the Montreal region, and Peachey worked under Holland as a deputy provincial surveyor. He was required to amend earlier plans and surveys and to make new ones, including a survey of the rivers St Lawrence and Ottawa above Repentigny in 1793; some of these were compiled into larger plans. On 31 Oct. 1793 he was promoted lieutenant and transferred to the 7th Foot, then stationed at Quebec. A year later the regiment moved to Halifax and in 1795 returned to England. Peachey was made captain 29 July 1795 and transferred to the 43rd Foot on 2 Feb. 1797. His death that year was likely due to an epidemic which decimated the regiment while posted in Martinique.

W. MARTHA E. COOKE and BRUCE G. WILSON

The names Wm Peachy and W. Peachy, inscribed on two aquatints after Peachey, are probably erroneous. Representative examples of Peachey's works are in ASQ, BL, the Metropolitan Toronto Library, the National Gallery of Canada (Ottawa), the New York Public Library, PAC, PAO, the Royal Ontario Museum (Toronto), and private collections.

BL, Add. MSS 21737, pp.183–84; 21784, pp.34–37; 21892, ff.13–14 (transcripts at PAC). PAC, RG 1, E15, A, 25/2–27/2; 45/1. PAO, RG 1, A-I-6, 1, Copy of instructions to Mr James Peachey . . . 15 Feb. 1793; Peachey to Holland, 28 Feb. 1793; Holland to Peachey, 17 March 1793. PRO, AO 3/140, pp.52–57, 73, 81; CO 42/16, pp.230–33; CO 323/29, pp.20–22; WO 12/5563, f.79; WO 17/1500–5. [Frederick Haldimand], "Private diary of Gen. Haldimand," PAC *Report*, 1889, 175, 243. "James Peachey (active/connu 1773–1797)," intro. and catalogue by B. G. Wilson, *Archives Canada Microfiches* (Ottawa), 2, (1975–76). Mary Allodi, *Canadian watercolours and drawings in the Royal Ontario Museum* (2v., Toronto, 1974). *Catalogue of the manuscript maps, charts, and plans, and of the topographical drawings in the British Museum* (3v., London, 1844–61; repr. Brussels, 1962), III. W. M. E. Cooke, *Catalogue of paintings, water-colours and drawings in the W. H. Coverdale collection of Canadiana* (forthcoming). Algernon Graves, *The Royal Academy of Arts: a complete dictionary of contributors and their works from its foundation in 1769 to 1904* (8v., London, 1905–6; repr. 8v. in 4, East Ardsley, Eng., 1970). G.B., WO, *Army list*, 1788–99. *Image of Canada, documentary watercolours and drawings from the permanent collection of the Public Archives of Canada*, intro. Michael Bell ([Ottawa, 1972]). *Landmarks of Canada . . . a guide to the J. Ross Robertson historical collection in the Public Reference Library, Toronto* . . . (2v., Toronto, 1917–21; [new ed.], 2v. in 1, 1967), I. [The authors wish to thank Michael Bell, Douglas Schoenherr, Mrs J. M. White, and Peter Winkworth for their assistance. W.M.E.C. and B.G.W.]

PÉAN, ANGÉLIQUE. *See* RENAUD D'AVÈNE DES MÉLOIZES

PÉAN, MICHEL-JEAN-HUGUES, officer in the colonial regular troops and adjutant at Quebec; b. in the manor-house of Contrecœur and baptized on 18 May 1723 at Saint-Ours (Que.), the son of Jacques-Hugues Péan* de Livaudière and Marie-Françoise, daughter of François-Antoine Pécaudy* de Contrecœur; d. 21 Aug. 1782 at Cangey (dept of Indre-et-Loire), France.

Michel-Jean-Hugues Péan, the eldest son of a prominent officer in the colony, progressed quite rapidly through the military ranks in New France. Joining the colonial regulars at an early age, he was appointed second ensign (1738), ensign (1742), adjutant (1745), and captain (1750), before being awarded the cross of Saint-Louis in 1756. Although Péan's military aptitudes were praised by some – for example Charles DESCHAMPS de Boishébert, his commanding officer in Acadia – his chief talent was a skill in obtaining favours from those holding the highest administrative offices in the colony. His opportunism and extraordinary gift for organization enabled him to become a favourite of governors La Jonquière [Taffanel*], DUQUESNE, and Vaudreuil [RIGAUD]. Duquesne later remarked that he was "a man of prodigious talent, ability, resourcefulness, and zeal."

Taking advantage of his privileged position as adjutant of the town and Government of Quebec from 1745 on, his marriage in 1746 to Angélique RENAUD d'Avène Des Méloizes, and family and social connections, Péan began making his fortune soon after Intendant BIGOT's arrival in 1748. He became a veritable middleman between suppliers and the intendant, participated in all the undertakings and all the contracts, and influenced the recommendations and appointments made by the intendant.

In 1749 Péan entered into partnership with Bigot, La Jonquière, and Jacques-Michel BRÉARD to operate and supply the posts of Mer de l'Ouest (the Lake Winnipeg region) and Baie-des-Puants (Green Bay, Mich.). The partners made substantial profits by having the government pay for all the trade goods as presents for the Indians. Péan managed about two per cent of the business, but his interest accrued, he said, from assignments that the partners made on their shares.

Péan also became involved in the wheat trade and in providing flour and meal for the government. In the spring of 1750 he had no difficulty in obtaining the contract for supplying flour and meal which had been cancelled by his aunt, Louise Pécaudy de Contrecœur, François Daine*'s wife; it seems, however, that this operation was carried on through a front man. In addition he received the commission to supply wheat to the king, and the Treasury advanced him the necessary funds for his purchases; in this way he bought an immense quantity of grain at a low price. Subsequently the intendant fixed the price of wheat higher, so that Péan was able to make extensive profits without spending a *sou*. Since the milling was done in his mill and the screening in his warehouses, he could collect seigneurial dues of a twelfth and of two *sous* per bushel respectively. Péan also made attractive profits from exporting flour and meal. According to the anonymous author of the "Mémoire du Canada," the huge warehouses that he had erected on his seigneury of Saint-Michel (Saint-Michel-de-Bellechasse) were the loading point for wheat being sent to the West Indies.

Numerous complaints were made to the court about Péan because of his active role in the procuring of grain and the provisioning of the troops. In reply to La Jonquière's repeated requests for promotion for this officer, Rouillé, the minister of Marine, granted him a captain's commission on 14 June 1750; he added, however, that if the accusations of corruption in the procurement of supplies involving Péan proved correct, he would have to hold up the commission. The governor rejected all the accusations. The same suspicions were expressed again in 1756, when Intendant Bigot obtained the cross of Saint-Louis for Péan from the minister of Marine, Machault. Despite this rejection of complaints, Jean-Victor VARIN de La Marre levelled the accusation against Péan during the inquiry at the Châtelet in Paris following the conquest. He declared that, at Péan's request and with Bigot's assent, he had overcharged by a quarter for the goods supplied between 1752 and 1757. Péan and Bigot had each had a 25 per cent interest in the enterprise, Bréard 20 per cent, and Varin himself 30 per cent. In 1756 Bigot and Péan are said to have formed a partnership with Varin to purchase a business belonging to Guillaume ESTÈBE and Jean-André LAMALETIE which could, as it happened, supply exactly the provisions the king's stores were lacking. The three partners then made profits of 155 per cent. At his trial Péan admitted having played a role in this business but denied having had any knowledge of its shady side.

In 1756 some entrepreneurs known as the Grande Société concentrated the economic activity of New France in their own hands. As a result the "purveyor's deal" was made, which through a contract signed at Quebec on 26 October gave them a monopoly on the sale of supplies to the king's stores and allowed them to corner trade in the colony. Although Joseph-Michel CADET was officially the director of this company, Péan was its real protector. He had no expenses; according to Cadet, he simply pocketed 50 and later 60 per cent of the profits which the director made with his protection. Through his position as adjutant and numerous trips to the *pays d'en haut*, Péan was able to give Cadet valuable advice about procurement in the forts and the composition and price of rations. Manipulating the supply inventories of the forts constituted an important commercial activity for the Grande Société. Cadet had agreed to purchase from the government the stock on hand when the contract came into effect. Louis PENNISSEAUT, who was responsible for drawing up such an inventory, was ordered by Péan to adjust the returns so as "to reduce the total by half." At the same time Péan is supposed to have given him a ration chart indicating the quantity of goods to be supplied to each establishment over and above what the garrison had actually consumed. Pennisseaut carried out this task, substantially inflating the figures for the supplies the government would have to purchase from Cadet.

Because of his association with Bigot at all levels of trade in the colony, Péan also had close commercial relations with the Gradis family of Bordeaux. In 1757 and 1758 he is supposed to have participated in providing supplies for Canada as a partner of these merchants, for whom he acted as a liaison with Bigot. It is highly probable, in fact, that Bigot had a part of the share belonging to Péan, who through this partnership accumulated a fortune which some estimates placed at nearly seven million *livres* at the time of the conquest.

Being in regular contact with the mother country, Péan was able to take advantage of the presence there of his brother, René-Pierre, who was commissary of the Marine at the port and arsenal of Brest, to promote certain commercial undertakings. Although he was Canadian by birth, Péan was closely linked to France, and this tie may explain his desire to take up residence there. It may even be conjectured that these contacts in France helped not only in his commercial undertakings but also during his trial. Péan's personal abilities and the value of his family and social connections must not be underestimated. There is no doubt, moreover, that Mme Péan's friendship with Bigot enabled her husband to occupy a privileged place in society in the colony and that his status furthered the business dealings of those close to him.

Péan invested large sums in real estate. He rounded out his seigneuries of Saint-Michel and La Livaudière through agreements with his brother, who on 16 July 1750 made over to him, for 12,000 *livres*, all his rights to them; similarly, on 1 Aug. 1757 Péan acquired all his brother's properties in Canada for the sum of 15,000 *livres*. Péan also owned several houses in the town of Quebec, including his residence, the Maison Arnoux, purchased in 1751 for 9,000 *livres*.

On the eve of the conquest Péan was one of the most prominent men in the colony. When he went to France in 1758, on the pretext of having to go to a spa for rheumatic pains, Governor Vaudreuil entrusted him with reporting Montcalm*'s latest victory, at Fort Carillon (Ticonderoga, N.Y.), to the minister. But certain people distrusted Péan; in fact, the financial commissary of wars, André Doreil*, gave Lieutenant Jacques Kanon* the task of announcing the victory at Carillon ahead of Péan and, in a letter of 12 Aug. 1758, warned Massiac, the minister of Marine, "concerning M. Péan, an officer who is M. de Vaudreuil's and M. Bigot's creature, . . . [who] has made such a quick fortune in eight years that he is held to be worth two million." In another letter, dated 31 August of the same year, he named Péan "as one of the chief causes of the bad administration and ruin of this unfortunate country." Berryer's arrival at the ministry of Marine on 1 Nov. 1758 was to bring about a sudden change in Bigot's and Péan's careers; the minister not only refused to listen to Péan, but also sent a special delegate to Canada, Charles-François PICHOT de Querdisien Trémais.

After Montreal surrendered, Bigot, Péan, and his wife sailed for France in September 1760 on the *Fanny*. In November 1761, as a result of the investigations into the administration of Canada, Bigot, Péan, and four other suspects – Varin, Pennisseaut, Boishébert, and François-Marc-Antoine LE MERCIER – were ordered to be arrested. The prisoners were taken to the Bastille where they were treated according to their rank; Bigot was entitled to 20 *livres* a day for his keep and his needs, whereas Péan had to be content with 15 *livres*. During their stay in prison they bought and had themselves sent many things, such as clothing and furniture, and every week Péan received bottles of wine from Bordeaux. After 20 Feb. 1762 the two confederates were allowed to go for a walk once or twice a week, but separately and under close guard.

On 12 Dec. 1761 a decree from the king's council had set up a court at the Châtelet to judge the officials from New France. Péan's interrogation began on 27 Jan. 1762. The proceedings went ahead, but the prisoners were still unable to have recourse to a lawyer. In the spring Mme Péan, looking after her own interests, attempted to correspond secretly with her husband by inserting letters in the lining of a coat, and she made use of her relations to keep him from being disgraced and losing his fortune.

Although Péan was one of those chiefly responsible for the scandals in the administration of Canada, he was highly successful in extricating himself from the various accusations. After having banished him for nine years, the judges reconsidered their decision and subjected him to "further inquiry for six months." On 25 June 1764 Péan's case was dismissed and he was sentenced to make restitution of 600,000 *livres* – a sum he immediately deposited in Canadian bills of exchange – but there was no hint of dishonour attached to his name.

After his release Péan retired to his domain of Orzain not far from Blois, France, where he lived as a seigneur. In 1771 he obtained permission to have his former companion, Bigot, come to visit him. Mme Péan chose to live at Blois where she supported the Canadian families who had followed them to France. Péan died at Cangey in August 1782; his wife survived him by ten years. Their daughter, Angélique-Renée-Françoise, who had been born at Quebec, had in September 1769 married Louis-Michel de Marconnay, an infantry colonel and provost marshal of Pas-de-Calais, but had died childless in March 1779.

GUY DINEL

AD, Indre-et-Loire (Tours), État civil, Cangey, 23 août 1782. ANQ-Q, AP-G-322; AP-P-1607; Greffe de Claude Barolet, 1731–61; Greffe de C.-H. Du Laurent, 1734–59; Greffe de P.-A.-F. Lanoullier Des Granges, 1749–60; Greffe de J.-C. Panet, 1745–75; Greffe de J.-A. Saillant, 1750–76; Greffe de Simon Sanguinet, 1748–71. "Les archives de la famille Gradis et le Canada," Claude de Bonnault, édit., ANQ *Rapport*, 1944–45, 267–306. Bégon, "Correspondance" (Bonnault), ANQ *Rapport*. 1934–35, 1–277. Bougainville, "Journal" (A.-E. Gosselin), ANQ *Rapport*, 1923–24, 202–393. [Charles Deschamps de Boishébert et de Raffetot], "Mémoire de M. de Boishébert au ministre sur les entreprises de guerre contre les Sauvages, novembre 1747," *BRH*, XXII (1916), 375–81. *Doc. relatifs à la monnaie sous le Régime français* (Shortt). Doreil, "Lettres" (A. Roy), ANQ *Rapport*, 1944–45, 3–171. "Mémoire du Canada," ANQ *Rapport*, 1924–25, 96–198. [L.-G. de Parscau Du Plessis], "Journal d'une campagne au Canada à bord de *la Sauvage* (mars-juillet 1756) par Louis-Guillaume de Parscau Du Plessix, enseigne de vaisseau," ANQ *Rapport*, 1928–29, 211–26.

"Archives Gradis," ANQ *Rapport*, 1957–59, 3–52. Æ. Fauteux, *Les chevaliers de Saint-Louis*. Gustave Lanctot, "L'Affaire du Canada; bibliographie du procès de Bigot," *BRH*, XXXVIII (1932), 8–17. Le Jeune, *Dictionnaire*. P.-G. Roy, *Inv. concessions; Inv. jug. et délib., 1717–60; Inv. ord. int.* Frégault, *François Bigot*. Jean de Maupassant, *Un grand armateur de Bordeaux, Abraham Gradis (1699?–1780)* (Bordeaux, 1917). P.-G.

Roy, *Bigot et sa bande; Les petites choses de notre histoire* (7 sér., Lévis, Qué., 1919–44), 3e sér., 238–39. [P.-]P.-B. Casgrain, "La maison d'Arnoux où Montcalm est mort," *BRH*, IX (1903), 1–16. Guy Frégault, "La guerre de Sept Ans et la civilisation canadienne," *RHAF*, VII (1953–54), 183–206. Juliette Rémillard, "Angélique Des Méloizes," *RHAF*, XIX (1965–66), 513–34. P.-G. Roy, "La famille Renaud d'Avène des Méloizes," *BRH*, XIII (1907), 161–81. Benjamin Sulte, "Les Saint-Michel," *BRH*, XX (1914), 292–95. Têtu, "Le chapitre de la cathédrale," *BRH*, XVI, 262.

PÉCAUDY DE CONTRECŒUR, CLAUDE-PIERRE, officer in the colonial regular troops, seigneur, and member of the Legislative Council; b. 28 Dec. 1705 at Contrecœur (Que.), son of François-Antoine Pécaudy* de Contrecœur, a seigneur and officer in the colonial regulars, and Jeanne de Saint-Ours; d. 13 Dec. 1775 in Montreal (Que.).

Claude-Pierre Pécaudy de Contrecœur's career is a good illustration of the vicissitudes in the life of a military officer who devoted himself almost entirely to the king's service. A cadet at 16, Contrecœur at 20 was given the expectancy of an ensign's commission. In 1729 he was second ensign, then in 1734 a full ensign. In 1742, as a lieutenant, he commanded a detachment at Fort Saint-Frédéric (near Crown Point, N.Y.).

On 2 March 1746 Governor Beauharnois* promised to obtain recognition for his services. In 1748 he was promoted captain. At intervals he turned his attention as best he could to his family and his seigneury of Saint-Denis. In 1749 Contrecœur served as second in command in the expedition led by Pierre-Joseph Céloron* de Blainville down the Ohio valley; his older son, Claude-François, accompanied him. Immediately after, Contrecœur was named commandant at Fort Niagara (near Youngstown, N.Y.), which was strategically situated for maintaining liaison between the settlements on the St Lawrence and the vast and still sparsely occupied regions of the west and the Ohio valley, on the route to Louisiana. In the autumn of 1752 and the following winter Governor DUQUESNE wrote several letters to Contrecœur to inform him, under the seal of secrecy, that in the spring an expedition of 2,000 men would be setting out "to establish our hold on the valley of the Belle-Rivière [Ohio River], which we are on the verge of losing." During the summer and autumn of 1753 the expedition, commanded by Paul Marin* de La Malgue, opened the route as far as the Ohio watershed and built Fort de la Rivière au Bœuf (Waterford, Pa). Marin died at the end of October and was replaced by Jacques Legardeur* de Saint-Pierre, who immediately asked to be relieved of his duties. On 25 December Duquesne gave command of the force to Contrecœur and on 27 Jan. 1754 ordered him to occupy the Ohio valley. A letter written by Contrecœur's nephew, Michel-Jean-Hugues PÉAN, reveals that, despite the privileges conceded by Duquesne and "all the other promises," the new commander, whose wife was with him at Niagara, was not enthusiastic about an order which would force him to live separate from his family.

On 16 April 1754 Contrecœur and a large force seized a fort the British were building where Pittsburgh, Pa, now stands. He called upon ensign Edward Ward and his 41 men to withdraw. After discussion, Ward agreed to leave on the 18th at noon, a decision which allowed Contrecœur to dine with him on the evening of the 17th in order to obtain more information about British manœuvres and also to negotiate the purchase of various carpenter's tools. He went on with the construction of the fort, which took Governor Duquesne's name, and held command of it until 1756. On the evening of 3 July 1754 at Fort Necessity (near Farmington, Pa) Louis Coulon* de Villiers forced George Washington to capitulate after a sharp combat that day. According to Duquesne's testimony, these events, which finally secured the French position in the Ohio region, were to be attributed to the "wise and prudent conduct of the Sieur de Contrecœur."

But despite several requests Contrecœur did not receive the reinforcements or the supplies and equipment necessary to ensure consolidation of recent gains. In the summer of 1755 Vaudreuil [RIGAUD], who had succeeded Duquesne, complained to the minister of Marine, Machault, that Fort Duquesne was actually threatened by the British, who had 3,000 men six or eight leagues away, whereas Contrecœur could count on only 1,600 "including militiamen and Indians." Nevertheless, on 9 July 1755 the French troops, who were commanded initially by Daniel-Hyacinthe-Marie Liénard* de Beaujeu, won the important battle of the Monongahela, at a place three leagues from Fort Duquesne. In a letter on 20 July Contrecœur indicated to the minister that an "unfortunate accident caused by the fatigues of the last campaign will perhaps make me unable to continue my services." He asked the minister on 28 Nov. 1755 for the cross of the order of Saint-Louis, which he received in March 1756, and for promotions for his two sons, one an ensign, the other a cadet. His military career was essentially finished, but he did not officially obtain his retirement and pension with half pay until 1 Jan. 1759.

After the conquest Contrecœur chose to remain in Canada and was finally able to attend to his affairs and his seigneury, which in 1765 counted 371 persons, 6,640 acres under cultivation, and 973 animals. Writing to Lord Hillsborough on 15 March 1769, Governor Guy Carleton* called him the third most influential Canadian. On 3 Jan. 1775 Contrecœur was appointed to the Legislative Council, and he was sworn in on 17 August. His career there was short, since he died in Montreal on 13 December, having attended only one meeting.

On 10 Jan. 1729, at Boucherville, Claude-Pierre Pécaudy de Contrecœur had married Marie-Madeleine, daughter of René Boucher* de La Perrière, and they had nine children. On 9 Sept. 1768 in Quebec, he had taken as his second wife Marguerite-Barbe Hingue de Puygibault, the widow of Étienne Rocbert de La Morandière.

FERNAND GRENIER

[The principal manuscript sources concerning Claude-Pierre Pécaudy de Contrecœur are the Contrecœur papers held at ASQ in the Fonds Viger-Verreau, cartons I to IV. This collection also contains various other papers, in particular those of Jacques Legardeur de Saint-Pierre and Paul Marin de La Malgue. A number of the Viger-Verreau documents have been published in *Papiers Contrecœur* (Grenier); its bibliography contains a description of relevant manuscript and printed sources, secondary works, and articles. Useful also are F.-J. Audet, *Contrecœur, famille, seigneurie, paroisse, village* (Montréal, 1940), and Hunter, *Forts on Pa. frontier*. F.G.]

PÉLISSIER, CHRISTOPHE (the name was sometimes written **Pellissier**), king's scrivener and director of the Saint-Maurice ironworks; b. 29 April 1728 in the parish of Saint-Pierre et Saint-Saturnin, Lyons, France, son of François-Christophe Pélissier, a merchant, and Agathe Martaud La Rigaudière; d. some time before 1800.

Christophe Pélissier seems to have come to Quebec about 1752 to work as king's scrivener there. His first contact with the Saint-Maurice ironworks probably occurred in June 1756, when as attorney for Quebec merchant Jacques Zorn he bought a house belonging to Barthélemy Sicard, *dit* Marseille, in Trois-Rivières, where they were located. Zorn left Canada before paying him, however, and Pélissier was back in Trois-Rivières in June 1758 and February 1759 because of a lawsuit over the resale of the house and the sums due him. Although on 2 April 1759 Jacques Zorn was ordered to pay him 6,242 *livres* 10 *sols*, Pélissier recovered only 2,500 *livres*.

In March 1767 Pélissier drew up an inventory of the properties and machinery of the Saint-Maurice ironworks, which he and others wanted to rent. From 1760 to 1764 the ironworks had been administered by the military government and had produced appreciable quantities of iron. They had come under civil jurisdiction in September 1764; Hector Theophilus CRAMAHÉ, Governor MURRAY's representative, had closed the enterprise down in the spring of 1765, dismissed the director, François Poulin de Courval, and the workmen, and left only a few soldiers on the premises. On 9 June 1767 Christophe Pélissier, Alexandre Dumas*, Thomas Dunn*, Benjamin Price*, Colin Drummond, Jean DUMAS Saint-Martin, George Allsopp*, James JOHNSTON, and Brook Watson* acquired a 16-year lease, signed by Guy Carleton* in the king's name, to a large tract of land on which the Saint-Maurice ironworks stood; it included the fief and seigneury of Saint-Maurice and other pieces of adjoining land. They were granted the right to cut wood, to put up any necessary building, and to exploit all mineral resources except gold and silver, in exchange for an annual payment of £25 in province of Quebec currency (£18 15*s*. in British currency). The partners undertook to repair the existing buildings, which had been abandoned two years before. On 4 April 1771 Pélissier bought the shares belonging to Dunn, Drummond, Allsopp, and Watson; he had already obtained those of Johnston, who had acquired them in the name of the partnership he had formed with John Purss*. In 1771 the company spent more than £4,500 to restore the ironworks which were in poor repair and had successfully produced iron of superior quality. That year Pierre Fabre*, *dit* Laterrière, was appointed the shareholders' agent in Quebec, with responsibility for selling their products there. Four years later he went to live at the ironworks as inspector. In his *Mémoires* he describes the spot as "a most pleasant one." According to him the ironworks were bringing in "10 to 15 thousand *louis* in every seven-month season; expenses took two thirds of [this amount]; consequently each year the parties involved had the remaining third to share." He was probably exaggerating since, according to Francis Maseres*, "the profits . . . have not answered the expectations of the undertakers, and have hardly even paid them their expences."

Laterrière's arrival at the ironworks marked, in a sense, the beginning of Pélissier's misfortunes. On 16 Oct. 1758 Pélissier had married Marthe, the daughter of surgeon Gervais Baudouin*; she died in 1763. Some years later Pélissier wanted to take as his second wife Marie-Catherine*, the daughter of his friend, silversmith Ignace-François DE-

LEZENNE. The marriage took place at Bécancour on 8 March 1775, apparently despite the opposition of the girl, who was not yet 20 and was in love with Laterrière. When the Americans invaded Canada in 1775–76 Pélissier, whom Laterrière described as a "strong supporter of John Wilkes and his system of freedom, [and] hence influenced . . . in favour of the Anglo-American rebels," collaborated with the Americans, supplying, amongst other things, ammunition, bombs, and cannon-balls for the siege of Quebec; he also wrote to the Continental Congress on 8 Jan. 1776 to point out the measures they should take for a successful siege. The luck of the American armies changed, and, learning of Carleton's displeasure with him, Pélissier thought it better to flee. On 7 June 1776 he left Trois-Rivières, taking with him "all his gold and silver, and a bill for advances made to the Congressional army amounting to 2,000 *louis*." He went to the United States, where he got his money back, and worked for a time at Ticonderoga, New York, as an engineer, with the rank of lieutenant-colonel. He then returned to Lyons, France. Meanwhile, Laterrière ran the ironworks and Marie-Catherine went to live with him. The lovers had a daughter, Dorothée, in January 1778.

In the spring of that year Pélissier sent to M. Perras in Quebec a power of attorney to sell his share in the ironworks and to arrange for his wife and the children of his first marriage to go to France. Marie-Catherine refused to leave Laterrière and her daughter. Having received permission to return to Canada, Pélissier arrived in July to go over his accounts and endeavour to secure his wife's return with him. While he and Laterrière were busy liquidating his business at the ironworks, he had Marie-Catherine abducted and shut up illegally. She succeeded in escaping and hid on the Île de Bécancour, which belonged to Laterrière, until Pélissier left in October. Before he left, the jealous husband, who was determined to separate the lovers, succeeded in revenging himself on Laterrière by getting him arrested on a charge of having collaborated with the Americans [*see* Ignace-François Delezenne]. Alexandre Dumas then took over direction of the ironworks until 1783.

Pélissier was never to return to Canada. On 18 Dec. 1799, "in view of the absence of the aforementioned Sieur Christophe Pélissier for more than 20 years," the Jesuits took back the land granted to him in the seigneury of Cap-de-la-Madeleine on 29 April 1767. Pélissier was evidently dead by then, since on 10 Oct. 1799 Pierre Fabre, *dit* Laterrière, and Marie-Catherine Delezenne had been married, Marie-Catherine "having produced adequate proof of the death of the aforementioned Sieur Pélissier, her first husband."

Despite his misadventures Pélissier did not leave only bad memories in Canada. He had often been generous to his workmen when he was director of the Saint-Maurice ironworks. On occasion he stood surety for his clerks, for example when Louis Bomer purchased a boat for 1,200 shillings; he agreed to lend 900 shillings to a "headstrong lad" who had been hired in his establishment and wanted to buy a piece of land; he gave 720 shillings as a dowry to a girl who had worked in his home "in consideration of good and faithful service"; finally, he pleaded on behalf of one of his workmen when the church refused to marry him. It also seems that for a long period he enjoyed the confidence of the colonial authorities, and of the religious and military dignitaries, whom he used to entertain with sumptuous suppers at the ironworks.

M.-F. FORTIER

ANQ-MBF, État civil, Catholiques, La Nativité de Notre-Dame (Bécancour), 8 mars 1775; Greffe de J.-B. Badeaux, 22, 23 avril, 16 oct. 1771, 16 juin, 11 nov. 1772, 2 mai, 6 juill. 1773, 11 nov. 1774, 24 sept. 1778; Greffe de C.-L. Maillet, 14 mars 1772, 20 févr. 1775, 11 nov. 1780; Greffe de Louis Pillard, 4 juin 1756, 16 juin 1758, 27 juill. 1767. ANQ-Q, Greffe de Claude Barolet, 13 oct. 1758; Greffe de J.-A. Saillant, 4 avril 1771; Greffe de Charles Voyer, 18 déc. 1799. Archives municipales, Lyon (dép. du Rhône, France), État civil, Saint-Pierre et Saint-Saturnin, 30 avril 1728.

Coll. of several commissions (Maseres), 221–33. Fabre, dit Laterrière, *Mémoires* (A. Garneau). P.-G. Roy, *Inv. jug. et délib., 1717–60*, VI, 89, 91. Jouve, *Les franciscains et le Canada: aux Trois-Rivères*. Sulte, *Mélanges historiques* (Malchelosse), VI. Tessier, *Les forges Saint-Maurice*. "Catholics and the American revolution," *American Catholic Hist. Researches* (Parkesburg, Pa.), new ser., III (1907), 144–49, 193–96.

PELLEGRIN (Pelegrin), GABRIEL, mariner and naval officer; b. 16 July 1713 in the parish of Saint-Louis at Toulon, France, son of François Pellegrin and Marie-Anne Bonnegrâce; d. 19 June 1788 at Brest, France.

Gabriel Pellegrin came to Canada in 1734 as a pilot in the French navy. On being released shortly after from duties usual to such employment he assisted the port captain of Quebec, Richard Testu* de La Richardière, in carrying out the most extensive hydrographic surveys of the French régime. In 1735 they charted the Strait of Belle Isle, at that time known chiefly to fishermen; from 1738 to 1740 they surveyed the south coast of Newfoundland, the Gulf of St Lawrence, and the shores of present-day Prince Edward Island, New Brunswick, and Nova Scotia from Baie des Chaleurs to the Strait of Canso.

On 18 Nov. 1738 Pellegrin married Madeleine Boissy at Quebec and two children were born during the next five years. Pellegrin appears to have left the colony during the War of the Austrian Succession when he may have seen active service in the navy. With the coming of peace the French attempted to improve navigation in the St Lawrence. Quebec had been without a port captain, the responsible official, for several years, but Philippe-Marie d'AILLEBOUST de Cerry took up the post in 1749 and in 1751 Pellegrin joined his staff as harbour-master. Pellegrin's chief task was to pilot naval vessels from Bic upstream to Quebec, but his broad knowledge of the St Lawrence soon led to more important duties. In 1752 he was promoted port lieutenant and the next year his annual stipend was increased by 200 *livres*.

Pellegrin caught the particular attention of the authorities in 1755 when he piloted a large squadron to France by way of the Strait of Belle Isle since the British were thought to be waiting on the usual route south of Newfoundland [*see* Emmanuel-Auguste de Cahideuc*, Comte Dubois de La Motte; Edward Boscawen*]. His success was rewarded with a bounty of 4,000 *livres*, an annual gratuity of 600 *livres*, and a promotion to deputy port captain of Quebec. While in France he constructed two charts of the full length of the St Lawrence and submitted a long critique of recently published French charts of the river. When in the spring of 1756 he travelled to Canada on the *Licorne* with Montcalm*, the new commander formed a favourable impression of him. Pellegrin's services were not in great demand, however, and in the fall he was given command of the *Abénaquise* and sent to France with dispatches. He again sailed through the northern exit from the St Lawrence and after safely reaching France was given the modest but substantive rank of fire-ship captain in the navy, a promotion which aroused the jealousy of the port captain, Cerry, who held no naval rank. In September 1757 Pellegrin returned to Quebec and was appointed royal hydrographer to replace Father Joseph-Pierre de BONNÉCAMPS. Pellegrim complained to Intendant BIGOT that there were few people studying navigation and pilotage, but more urgent matters were pressing on the colony and the post became a sinecure.

Soon after his return to Canada Pellegrin renewed his acquaintance with Montcalm and in October 1757, accompanied by the senior artillery officer, Montbeillard [POTOT], and Bougainville*, inspected the north shore from Quebec to Cap Tourmente. At the latter place the party discovered an emplacement for a defensive battery, safe from assault and so close to the navigation channel that enemy ships could be brought under fire for almost a quarter of an hour. During the winter Pellegrin continued to develop ideas for the defence of the St Lawrence distinguished by their practicality. He was probably the source of the recommendations made by Bougainville to the minister of Marine in the winter of 1758–59, which emphasized that the colony's defences should begin at Gaspé and Sept-Îles. No enemy, Bougainville wrote, could get past ten well-placed warships stationed in the St Lawrence. Several of these ships, if in danger of sinking after engaging the enemy, should be run aground to serve as batteries at locations indicated by Pellegrin. Authorities in the colony should be ordered to consult Pellegrin and René-Nicolas LEVASSEUR, the master shipbuilder, on everything relating to the riverine defences. Meanwhile Montcalm forwarded to Vaudreuil [RIGAUD] with his own endorsement a similar report signed by Pellegrin. Although in February 1759 the minister of Marine instructed the governor and intendant to employ Pellegrin, the latter's advice continued to be ignored. Whether this failure to act on his recommendations was due to neglect or to the influence of other interests, the responsibility must be laid on Governor Vaudreuil.

In May 1759, when it was learned that British ships were in the river, a proposal was made at a council of war to sink ten of the largest ships in the colony in the Traverse, the difficult passage southeast of the Île d'Orléans. Pellegrin, who was taking up marker buoys in the Traverse and substituting false aids to navigation, was not even called to the meeting; on his return he reported that it was impossible to block the passage. Six days later, on 1 June, all but a few provision ships and frigates were sent to find protection at Batiscan, 50 miles above Quebec. Soon after Pellegrin sounded the waters off the Beauport beaches to determine how close enemy warships could sail to shell the shore, but his subsequent offers of service were rejected. He took no part in the fire-ship attacks in July [*see* François-Louis Poulin* de Courval], which failed as Pellegrin had anticipated. On 15 September he was one of those who signed the articles of capitulation.

Pellegrin returned to France and resumed his naval career. In 1770 he was made a knight of the order of Saint-Louis for his long and devoted service. After several years in the East he was stationed at Brest in 1773 and remained there until his retirement. At that time he was promoted lieutenant-commander.

Gabriel Pellegrin probably had more accurate

knowledge of the St Lawrence River than anyone in New France, but he was apparently the victim of his own zeal and probity, the jealousy of his immediate superior, and perhaps also of the vested maritime interests of other influential persons. Late in June 1759 the anonymous author of the "Journal du siège de Québec" noted: "hundreds of times he has offered his services and his understanding. It appears that they absolutely do not want either. He is a perfectly upright man. If I dared, I would say that it is this quality which prevents him from having any employment." Pellegrin's Canadian career casts a small but significant sidelight on the complex internecine struggles in the last years of New France.

JAMES S. PRITCHARD

AN, Col., B, 67, f.111v; 97; 103, f.13; 109, f.66; C[11A], 68, ff.90–93; 69, ff.20–21; 94, f.40; 95, f.80; 101, f.182; 103, f.234; E, 67 (dossier Cerry); Marine, B[4], 68, f.215; C[7], 240 (dossier Pellegrin); 3JJ, 273; 4JJ, 8, no.46; 6JJ, 65, no.17; 126. Bougainville, "Journal" (A.-E. Gosselin), ANQ *Rapport*, 1923–24, 311. *Coll. des manuscrits de Lévis* (Casgrain), IV, 91–94; VI, 24, 37, 39, 41, 307, 523–26, 535. "Journal du siège de Québec" (Æ. Fauteux), ANQ *Rapport*, 1920–21, 141, 160, 208. Knox, *Hist. journal* (Doughty), III, 174–78. "La mission de M. de Bougainville en France en 1758–1759," ANQ *Rapport*, 1923–24, 21–23, 27–29, 61. *NYCD* (O'Callaghan and Fernow), X, 961–62. P.-G. Roy, *Inv. ord. int.*, II, 243–44, 291–92; III, 174, 206. Tanguay, *Dictionnaire*.

PENNISSEAUT (Pénissault, Penisseau, Pennisseault), LOUIS (baptized **Louis-André-Joachim**), merchant-trader; b. 20 March 1724 at Poitiers, France, son of Charles Pennisseaut, a lawyer at the presidial court of justice in Poitiers, and Catherine Bry; d. some time after 12 Sept. 1771.

Louis Pennisseaut arrived in Canada around 1747 and settled there, dividing his time between Quebec and Montreal. "Quick and enterprising by nature," he soon made friends with people in high office. On 2 March 1753 in Montreal, he married Marie-Marguerite, daughter of the merchant Alexis Lemoine*, *dit* Monière; the previous day Governor DUQUESNE, Intendant BIGOT, and several prominent Montreal merchants had gathered in the office of notary Louis-Claude Danré* de Blanzy for the signing of the marriage contract. If we accept Pennisseaut's own statement (according to the Sieur de Courville [AUMASSON] he was "dishonest and deceitful in all his dealings"), he went into partnership in 1754 with Brouilhet (Drouilhet), receiver general of finance in Paris, and the La Ferté brothers, who sent him merchandise from France. Their business seems to have been profiable. Pennisseaut also obtained fur-trading rights in the *pays d'en haut* from his father-in-law and thus secured a solid footing in the colony's economic system.

After Joseph-Michel CADET's appointment in 1756 as purveyor general of supplies in New France, Pennisseaut seems to have become interested in supplying the troops in the Montreal region and the *pays d'en haut*. He and François Maurin*, whom Cadet had appointed assistant purveyor general, were busy finding wheat, flour, salt pork, hay, harness, firewood, boards, kegs and barrels, oars, poles, and clubs. When at the beginning of 1757 Pennisseaut and Maurin went into partnership with Cadet, the monopoly exercised by the Grande Société [*see* Michel-Jean-Hugues PÉAN] was extended from Quebec to the entire colony. The partnership was ratified in a contract of 10 April 1758, by which Pennisseaut was to work "in his capacity," that is, as an entrepreneur, with Maurin being responsible for the bookkeeping, and each was to receive one-fifteenth of the profits. Pennisseaut by his own admission drew more than 900,000 *livres* in profits from this partnership – the figure of 1,900,000 *livres* has even been mentioned; he received 1,062,000 *livres* in bills of exchange in 1759. When Intendant Bigot was informed of these profits, he had a warning passed on to Pennisseaut and his accomplices "not to boast" of them. Such understandable prudence could conceal only the extent of the dishonesty, not its existence.

In addition to his talents as an entrepreneur, Pennisseaut could count on the charms of his wife, who was considered a beauty and who became the mistress of Péan, Montreal's assistant town major, and later of the Chevalier de LÉVIS. According to Pennisseaut, Péan ran the affairs of the Grande Société in Montreal, and Bigot played a similar role in Quebec, not only at the head of the Grande Société, but also with Mme Péan [Angélique RENAUD d'Avène Des Méloizes].

In the autumn of 1760 Pennisseaut returned to France, and on 16 Nov. 1761 he was arrested for fraud and imprisoned in the Bastille. He was tried at the Châtelet with the other defendants in the *affaire du Canada* and eagerly cooperated, all the while endeavouring to attribute his swindles to naïvety. He was nonetheless found guilty and he was sentenced on 10 Dec. 1763, as was François Maurin, to banishment from Paris, payment of a fine of 500 *livres*, and restitution of 600,000 *livres*. His wife meanwhile continued to look after his affairs and succeeded in winning the Duc de Choiseul's favour. After he received a memoir from Mme Pennisseaut describing her destitution, Choiseul suggested in July 1764 that her husband be released from the Bastille and that the bills of exchange he was offering be accepted in payment of the 600,000 *livres*. The king assented to this suggestion and Pennisseaut was released at the end of the year. No interest was imposed and at the end of 1765 Mme Pennisseaut even received a gratuity of 4,000 *livres*.

In November 1769 Louis Pennisseaut obtained letters of rehabilitation which remitted his fine and his sentence of banishment. The last record of him is a letter dated 12 Sept. 1771, in which he requested a safe-conduct and a suspension of any legal proceedings against him, circumstances having obliged him to borrow 24,000 *livres*. He probably died soon after, since his widow married first the Marquis de Fresnoy, and then a certain M. de Fontanille, before she died on 22 Dec. 1786.

JOSÉ E. IGARTUA

AN, Col., B, 115, f.168v; 118, f.58; 120, ff.253v, 310, 351; 122, ff.112, 353; 139, f.394; C[11A], 108, ff.1–90; 116, f.249; E, 92 (dossier Corpron, Maurin, Pénisseault); 332bis (dossier Pénissault). ANQ-M, État civil, Catholiques, Notre-Dame de Montréal, 2 mars 1753; Greffe de L.-C. Danré de Blanzy, 1er mars 1753; Greffe de Gervais Hodiesne, 5 avril, 17 juin 1754, 25 juin 1758; Greffe de Pierre Panet, 14 juill. 1756–13 mai 1759. ANQ-Q, NF 19, 40, pp.41–42 (copies at PAC). Archives paroissiales, Saint-Paul (Poitiers, dép. de la Vienne, France), Registre des baptêmes, mariages et sépultures, 21 mars 1724. Bibliothèque de l'Arsenal, Archives de la Bastille, 12133–68, 12501–6 (mfm. at PAC). [These documents primarily give details of the daily life of those imprisoned in the Bastille during the *affaire du Canada* and provide little information about Pennisseaut. J.E.I.] PAC, MG 18, G8, 5, pp.199–230, 232–33, 241. *Mémoires sur le Canada, depuis 1749 jusqu'à 1760*. PAC *Rapport*, 1905, I, VIe partie, 326, 344, 353, 355, 357–58, 363, 367, 396. *Quebec Gazette*, 25 July 1765. J.-E. Roy, *Rapport sur les archives de France*, 693, 860, 864, 868, 870, 873–74, 880–81. Tanguay, *Dictionnaire*. Frégault, *François Bigot*, II. P.-G. Roy, *Bigot et sa bande*, 98–105. "Les 'millionnaires' de 1759," *BRH*, L (1944), 19–20.

PÉREZ HERNÁNDEZ, JUAN JOSEF, naval officer and explorer; b. *c*. 1725 in Majorca, Spain; d. 2 Nov. 1775 at sea off the Californian coast.

Little is known of the career of Juan Josef Pérez Hernández before 1767, when he entered the department of San Blas (state of Nayarit, Mexico), the administrative headquarters of New Spain's west coast posts north of San Blas. A graduate pilot, he had previously served on the Manila galleon route and was of sufficient prominence to be included in the junta convoked at San Blas in 1768 by Visitador José de Gálvez. The junta, in response to reports of Russian expansion east from the Aleutians (Alas.), planned the colonization of Alta (present day) California. In February 1769 Pérez, in command of the packet-boat *Príncipe*, carried one of the first shiploads of colonists to San Diego and Monterey, and in subsequent years he captained vessels which supplied the new settlements. Although only a frigate ensign, Pérez was chosen in 1774 by Antonio María Bucareli y Ursúa, viceroy of New Spain, to head an expedition to ascertain the trend of the coastline north of Alta California and to scout for signs of Russian activity. Command of the expedition should have fallen to an officer of higher rank than Pérez, but at the time no one in the department, one of the most unhealthy and least desirable bases in Spanish America, outranked him.

Pérez, in the frigate *Santiago*, sailed from San Blas on 25 January and called at San Diego and Monterey. He left the latter port in June 1774 with instructions to reach at least 60°N latitude, make formal acts of possession south from that point, scout any foreign settlements, and gather information on the coastal Indians. After sailing northwest and then north, Pérez sighted land near the present Alaska-Canada border on 15 July. The next day, offshore of the northernmost of what are now called the Queen Charlotte Islands (B.C.), the expedition encountered the Haidas and established their willingness to barter furs for cloth, beads, and pieces of copper. Pérez continued north, reaching 55°30′ N on 30 July, but he was discouraged from going farther by unfavourable winds, fogs, currents, and dangerous breakers. Sailing south along what he believed to be the mainland, but which was actually Vancouver Island, Pérez discovered on 8 August an opening which he named Surgidero de San Lorenzo (Nootka Sound). The next day his crew traded with the Indians (Nootkas) and gave them presents of Californian abalone shells. The Nootkas stole from Esteban José MARTÍNEZ, the ship's second officer, several silver spoons which members of Captain James COOK's expedition four years later would cite as evidence of previous Spanish presence in the area. Prevented by contrary winds from entering the sound or sending a party ashore, Pérez continued south. He sighted the fog-shrouded coastline only occasionally thereafter. The *Santiago* sailed by the entrance to the Juan de Fuca Strait; Martínez later claimed that he had pointed the opening out to his commander, but Pérez had been reluctant to explore it. They saw a large mountain, which they named Sierra Nevada de Santa Rosalia (Mount Olympus, Wash.), and the smoke of many Indian villages. The *Santiago*, its crew sick with scurvy, sailed south to San Blas without making any further discoveries of note.

The results of the first documented European visit to the coast of present-day British Columbia were meagre. Pérez had not made the formal acts of possession necessary to secure Spain's claim to sovereignty along the northwest coast and had failed even to undertake a detailed reconnaissance of the coastline. The expedition nevertheless established the belief in the minds of Spanish officials that Spain had a right, through discovery, to Nootka Sound. Today the diaries of Pérez, Martínez, and the Franciscans Juan Crespi and Tomás de la Peña Saravia are valued for ethnographic data on the customs and life of the Nootkas at the time they met the whites.

Bucareli, disappointed by the failure of the expedition, ordered Pérez to prepare for another voyage north the following season. In the mean time, however, a contingent of competent young naval officers, sent by Madrid expressly to counter the threat of Russian encroachments on the northwest coast, arrived in San Blas. Bruno de Hezeta was placed in command of the 1775 expedition, and Pérez was relegated to second officer on the flagship *Santiago*. His name seldom appears in the account of events. The two voyages undermined his health, since on both trips the diet was so poor that most of the crew developed scurvy before their return to Alta Californian ports. Despite two months of recuperation at Monterey, Pérez died shortly after leaving for San Blas on board the *Santiago*. He was buried at sea with a mass, a salvo of muskets, and a cannonade.

WARREN L. COOK

Archivo General de la Nación (Mexico City), Sección de Historia, vol.61, exp.14, Diario de la navegación y exploración del piloto segundo don Esteban José Martínez – 17 Dec. 1774; Juan Pérez, Diario (1774). Juan Crespi, "Diario" and Tomás de la Peña Saravia, "Diario," *The California coast, a bilingual edition of documents from the Sutro collection*, ed. and trans. G. B. Griffin and D. C. Cutter (Norman, Okla., 1969), 203–78 and 135–201. Cook, *Flood tide of empire*, 52–56, 62–82, 121–22. M. E. Thurman, *The naval department of San Blas; New Spain's bastion for Alta California and Nootka, 1767 to 1798* (Glendale, Calif., 1967), 78–80, 119–22, 125–40, 145–46. J. G. Caster, "The last days of Don Juan Pérez, the Mallorcan mariner," *Journal of the West* (Los Angeles), II (1963), 15–21. D. C. Cutter, "California, training ground for Spanish naval heroes," Calif. Hist. Soc., *Quarterly* (San Francisco), XL (1961), 109–22. R. F. Heizer, "The introduction of Monterey shells to the Indians of the northwest coast," *Pacific Northwest Quarterly* (Seattle, Wash.), XXXI (1940), 399–402. F. W. Howay, "The Spanish discovery of British Columbia in 1774," CHA *Report*, 1923, 49–55. W. N. Sage, "Spanish explorers of the British Columbia coast," *CHR*, XII (1931), 390–406.

PERRAULT, JACQUES, known as **Perrault l'aîné**, merchant-trader; b. 2 June 1718 at Quebec (Que.), eldest son of François Perrault* and Suzanne Pagé, *dit* Carcy; m. 20 Oct. 1749 Charlotte, daughter of Pierre Boucher* de Boucherville at Quebec; d. there on 20 March 1775.

Almost all members of Jacques Perrault's family were involved in business. His father arrived in Quebec as a merchant around 1714, and all his brothers spent their lives in business with the exception of Joseph-François, who took holy orders. Guillaume-Michel took refuge in La Rochelle, France, in 1760 and then settled in Martinique, where he once again became prosperous. Jean-Baptiste joined an uncle in running the Saint-Maurice ironworks. Louis-François assisted Jacques in Quebec until 1760 and then was associated with Frederick HALDIMAND, who used his influence on behalf of the whole Perrault family.

Jacques Perrault was not born to high social position, but he rose in society through his work, the wealth he acquired, and the connections he established. Judging by his correspondence he evidently received a sound academic training. His father assisted by making him a partner in 1740 in the trading lease of the post on the Rivière Nontagamion (Nétagamiou) on the Labrador coast. His propitious marriage to the daughter of the co-seigneur of Boucherville linked him with important colonial officials and with families well known in the business community. Members of the upper class, including Governor La Jonquière [Taffanel*] and Intendant BIGOT, were present at the signing of his marriage contract. As a trusted middleman, with a large circle of business connections, he greatly expanded his entrepreneurial activity so that he became involved in commercial transactions with the most important French and then British figures in Canada in the period 1750–75. It was from him, for instance, that James MURRAY bought a house in 1764.

In choosing his investments Perrault seems to have been seeking security. He traded in furs and fish and ran a general store where merchandise imported from France and the West Indies was sold. He bought land and building sites, built boats, lent money, and engaged in the lucrative trade in spirits. This diversity of investments, which provided numerous opportunities for profit, allowed him to link or to separate his activities according to his assessment of the benefits or risks in prevailing economic circumstances. His principal French correspondents lived in Paris, Bordeaux, La Rochelle, Nantes, Le Havre, and the West Indies.

The war and the siege of Quebec were hard on Perrault. His business was dormant, his house was destroyed, and he and his family had to take refuge at Trois-Rivières. After the military defeat Perrault, who had been clerk of the marshalsea and churchwarden of Notre-Dame since 1758, was uncertain what to do. In the end he decided to remain in Canada, since life promised to be easier in a colony under British rule than in a defeated France burdened with repatriates. He never had reason to regret his choice. By 1760 he was able to correspond with Denis GOGUET, his most important associate in France, via New England and later via London, where he also found a reliable associate. During this period more than 20 of those in exile in France entrusted the administration of their Canadian estates to him and he managed assets worth nearly 150,000 *livres*.

With an annual turnover of between 250,000 and 300,000 *livres*, Perrault was able to leave an estate worth about 150,000 *livres* after debts and expenses were paid, including a house on Rue Saint-Pierre in Quebec which he had inherited from his father, a nearby river-lot, and a house and land in the barony of Longueuil. The dynamic businessman's widow, a lady of high social standing, was left one-half of his estate and radically altered the nature of her inheritance, letting all the commercial ventures go and keeping clothing and silverware rather than any other movable assets. The children did not benefit much from their father's estate; then 11 in number they each received slightly less than 7,000 *livres*. The strict egalitarian principles governing the division of property under the custom of Paris affected the Perrault heirs as they did all others. The dispersal of capital with each generation, which threatened to have ruinous consequences for Canadian businessmen, prompted Jacques Perrault's children to enter government or the priesthood rather than follow their father's career in business. Jacques-Nicolas*, who started out as a merchant, became a seigneur, a member of the assembly, and later a legislative councillor. Charles-François, who died in 1794, and Charles, who died in 1793, were priests. Jean-Olivier*, a lawyer and judge of the Court of King's Bench, was a member of both the Legislative and Executive Councils.

JACQUES MATHIEU

[A detailed bibliography is found in Jacques Mathieu, "Un négociant de Québec à l'époque de la Conquête: Jacques Perrault l'aîné," ANQ *Rapport*, 1970, 27–82. J.M.]

PERTHUIS (sometimes **Perthuis de La Salle**), **JOSEPH**, merchant-trader, member of the Conseil Supérieur of Quebec, commissary of royal prisons, and seigneur; b. 29 Aug. 1714 at Quebec, son of Charles Perthuis* and Marie-Madeleine Roberge; d. 19 March 1782 in Poitiers, France.

Son of a prosperous Quebec merchant, Joseph Perthuis followed in his father's steps and embarked on a career in trade. Early in the 1740s, however, business apparently left him enough time to attend Attorney General Louis-Guillaume Verrier*'s classes in law and jurisprudence on a regular basis. Thanks to assiduous attendance, he was appointed assessor to the Conseil Supérieur of Quebec on 26 Jan. 1743. He did his work so well that the following year the colonial authorities proposed his name to the minister of Marine, Maurepas, for the position left vacant by the death of councillor Louis Rouer* d'Artigny. Maurepas thought he should remain assessor for a time; he finally granted him the office of councillor on 1 Jan. 1747.

Perthuis, who was described by Intendant BIGOT as "a very good judge, the best-versed in his profession," was called upon to carry out the attorney general's duties during Verrier's stay in France in 1744–45 and 1749. Subsequently he was asked to resume these duties temporarily, following the death of the attorney general on 13 Sept. 1758; he was to hold this office until the conquest. On 18 Nov. 1754 Perthuis had been appointed by the Conseil Supérieur commissary of the king's prisons, and he held this post until 26 Jan. 1756, when he handed it over to Joseph-Étienne Nouchet*. He is also believed to have received on several occasions a commission as subdelegate of the intendant. On 25 Feb. 1747 Intendant HOCQUART had instructed him to go to start a salt-works in Kamouraska, in order to ensure the colony's supply in the event that the regular cargoes from France were captured at sea. His report was not encouraging, and no further attempt to set up salt-works there was made. He also helped to establish an observation post at Cap-des-Rosiers, and he translated some military documents that had been seized.

Perthuis never neglected his business for his judicial work, despite the potential conflict of interest, and during the 1740s and 1750s he carried on these two parallel careers. In 1755 he was one of the major suppliers in Quebec of the king's storehouses.

On 16 Sept. 1745 Perthuis had married Marie-Anne Chasle, the widow of Guillaume Gouze, a

Quebec merchant. His wife brought a dowry of 6,000 *livres*, including a house in Lower Town. At the time Perthuis was well off: he owned a house in Quebec on Rue Notre-Dame and employed a servant. He was also highly regarded in colonial society: in 1747 the Quebec merchants chose him as their representative to the colonial authorities. On several occasions his colleagues on the Conseil Supérieur appointed him to its delegation charged with welcoming governors or intendants when they arrived in the colony or when they went on a trip, or introducing them to the council. His prestige was enhanced when the king granted him a seigneury behind that of Portneuf on 1 May 1754.

After the conquest Perthuis sold to Jean Mounier for only 300 *livres* his real estate in the colony, including the still undeveloped seigneury; he then sailed for France with his family. He was in Paris in November 1767, as was his brother, Jean-Baptiste-Ignace*, who had been a merchant and king's attorney in Canada. In 1774 Joseph Perthuis became king's councillor and secretary in the chancellery in Poitiers and obtained a pension of 600 *livres* which in September 1775 was converted to an annual one of 200 *livres* for each of his sons. He died in Poitiers on 19 March 1782. Of his seven children, a daughter and two sons (Joseph, who followed a military career, and Charles-Régis) survived him.

André Lachance

AN, Col., B, 78, f.25; 81, ff.42, 60; 85, f.15; 87, f.34; 99, ff.11, 12; 109, f.6; 115, f.194; 164, f.379; C[11A], 81, ff.12, 15; 120, f.350; E, 335 (dossier Perthuis); F[3], 11, f.258. ANQ-Q, AP-P-1634; Greffe de C.-H. Du Laurent, 15 sept. 1745; NF 25, 56, nos.2108, 2118. *Doc. relatifs à la monnaie sous le Régime français* (Shortt), II, 758–59. PAC *Rapport*, 1888, 36. "Recensement de Québec, 1744," 136. Le Jeune, *Dictionnaire*. P.-G. Roy, *Fils de Québec*, I, 183–84; *Inv. concessions*, V, 83–84; *Inv. jug. et délib., 1717–60*, II, 169, 175, 177, 181; IV, 45, 117–18; V, 37, 49, 52, 71, 84, 142, 169–70, 174, 179, 193–94, 238; VI, 15, 21, 34, 56, 122, 126, 172, 180, 285–86; *Inv. ord. int.*, III, 36, 90, 203, 210. Tanguay, *Dictionnaire*, VI, 324. J.-N. Fauteux, *Essai sur l'industrie*, II, 403. Cameron Nish, *Les bourgeois-gentilshommes de la Nouvelle-France, 1729–1748* (Montréal et Paris, 1968), 135. P.-G. Roy, *Bigot et sa bande*, 281–84. J.-F. Récher, "La famille Perthuis," *BRH*, XLI (1935), 452ff.

PETER. *See* Kingminguse

PETERS, JOSEPH, soldier, schoolmaster, and postmaster; b. 11 Dec. 1729 in Dedham, Massachusetts, eldest child of William Peters and Hannah Chenery; m. Abigail Thompson and they had three children; d. 13 Feb. 1800 at Halifax, Nova Scotia.

Joseph Peters was brought up in Medfield, Massachusetts, and learned the trade of armourer in nearby Medway. Impressed into the provincial service of the colony as a foot soldier in 1752, he obtained his release in 1755 only to be "immediately kid-napped into Shirley's Regiment [50th Foot]." He was later transferred to the 1st Foot, in which he spent the Seven Years' War as a non-commissioned officer and saw service in 1758 at the capture of Louisbourg, Île Royale (Cape Breton Island). He was discharged in Nova Scotia in 1763. Between that date and his setting up as a schoolmaster in 1773 his activities are unknown, though he lived in Halifax and enjoyed a "settled livelyhood," possibly as a government clerk, and pursued in his leisure an interest in astronomy and his duties as a Freemason. In 1774, some time after leaving the Congregational Church of his forefathers to become a member of the Church of England and vestry clerk of St Paul's, Halifax, he was adopted by the Society for the Propagation of the Gospel as its teacher in the capital. As schoolmaster Peters combined the usual functions of charity teaching and private instruction, but he found the SPG stipend small compensation for his trouble during the inflationary period of the American revolutionary war. He gave up the school in 1785, a decision which marked the end of SPG support for education in Halifax. In 1782 he had become unofficial postmaster of Nova Scotia and succeeded to the office of deputy postmaster general in 1785. He held the position until his death.

A highly opinionated, vitriolic critic of the British leaders of the local establishment such as the Reverend John Breynton and Governor John Parr, Peters looked with favour in the 1770s and 1780s on the acquisition by Nova Scotia of more New Englanders, this time as loyalist refugees. He became a regular correspondent of his cousin the Reverend Samuel Andrew Peters of Hebron, Connecticut, then a refugee in London, who acted as Joseph's agent and used his influence to secure for his Nova Scotian cousin a share of the loyalist spoils. All this share really amounted to was the appointment at the post office, though Joseph never stopped dreaming of more exalted posts such as provincial secretary or naval officer for himself or his elder son. In return Joseph supported Samuel's campaign to secure the new bishopric of Nova Scotia. Joseph's acquaintance with the Church of England clergy in Nova Scotia, New Brunswick, and Cape Breton, many of whom were New Englanders, and his control of the official channels of communication, placed him in an excellent position to launch a campaign encouraging the Church of England congregations to demand a voice in the appointment of their bishop and to promote Samuel's claim to the office. Unfortunately for the cause the local response left much to be desired, and the arrival of Charles Inglis* as bishop in 1787 deprived Joseph of the prospect of an influential patron in the province.

As postmaster Peters' main innovation was to initiate a regular courier service from Halifax to Annapolis Royal, where the mail was carried by water down-river to Digby, across the Bay of Fundy, and into the jurisdiction of his New Brunswick counterpart, Christopher SOWER. By 1788 a regular service to Quebec was established to coincide with the visits of the New York-Falmouth packet at Halifax for eight months of the year [*see* Hugh Finlay*]. The irregularities, expenses, and frustrations of the postal service made Peters' life as a public servant far from enviable. Military and naval officers refused to abide by office hours, and Governor Parr ran up a bill of £70 which was only settled finally by his executors. The General Post Office in London, "that unrelenting tyrant," remained singularly unsympathetic to the pleas of the hard-pressed postmaster for a higher salary and reimbursement of the considerable expenses of his office. Although between 1785 and 1792 his stipend climbed from £50 to £250, financial anxiety constantly plagued him, as did his gout and the sluggish careers of his two sons. Failure to achieve a remunerative and comfortable niche in the civil establishment left him considerably embittered and probably confirmed his cynical opinion of 1785 that "Every dog must have his day to be sure, tho' I never had a good one yet."

JUDITH FINGARD

Halifax County Court of Probate (Halifax), Book 3, pp.208–11 (will of Joseph Peters, 22 Dec. 1798) (mfm. at PANS). PANS, MG 1, 93 (Jacob Bailey docs.), vol.3. Protestant Episcopal Church in the U.S.A., Archives and Hist. Coll. – Episcopal Church (Austin, Tex.), Samuel Peters papers, Joseph Peters letters, 1779–99, in the custody of the Hist. Soc. of the Episcopal Church (Austin) (mfm. at PANS). St Paul's Anglican Church (Halifax), Registers of baptisms, burials and marriages, 16 Feb. 1800 (mfm. at PANS). USPG, B, 25, nos.184, 211, 221, 225, 242, 255, 269, 270; Journal of SPG, 20, pp.266, 268.

Nova-Scotia Gazette and the Weekly Chronicle (Halifax), 19 Dec. 1780. *Royal Gazette and the Nova-Scotia Advertiser* (Halifax), 18 Feb. 1800. Judith Fingard, *The Anglican design in loyalist Nova Scotia, 1783–1816* (London, 1972), 13–38. C. M. Jephcott *et al.*, *The postal history of Nova Scotia and New Brunswick, 1754–1867* (Toronto, 1964), 13–43. Judith Fingard, "Attitudes towards the education of the poor in colonial Halifax," *Acadiensis*, II (1972–73), no.2, 16.

PETERS, PAULY (Paulus Petersen). *See* SAHONWAGY

PETERS (Petters), THOMAS, black soldier and leader; b. *c.* 1738; d. 25 June 1792 in Freetown, Sierra Leone.

Legend has given Thomas Peters a noble birth in West Africa, whence he was supposedly kidnapped as a young man and brought as a slave to the American colonies. The earliest documentary evidence places him in 1776 as the 38-year-old slave of William Campbell in Wilmington, North Carolina. In that year, encouraged by the proclamation issued by Governor Lord Dunmore of Virginia in 1775 promising freedom to rebel-owned slaves who joined the loyalist forces, Peters fled Campbell's plantation and enlisted in the Black Pioneers in New York. In 1779, in response to a new invitation to rebel-owned slaves to place themselves under British protection whether they wished to bear arms for the crown or not, a 26-year-old woman named Sally from Charleston, South Carolina, appeared in a British camp, and she too joined the Black Pioneers. In that service she met Peters, who by 1779 had been promoted sergeant, and they were married.

When the provisional peace agreement was signed in Paris on 30 Nov. 1782, the Peters were in New York awaiting evacuation. The ship carrying them to safety went first to Bermuda in 1783 and then to Annapolis Royal, Nova Scotia, where they disembarked in May 1784. They were among 3,500 free black loyalists taken to Nova Scotia after the revolution. Peters was placed in charge of the Annapolis County blacks, and he settled with more than 200 former Pioneers in Brindley Town, near Digby. Although loyalists were entitled to three years' worth of provisions to sustain themselves while establishing homes and farms, the Annapolis County blacks received enough to last only 80 days and, unlike the whites, were required to earn their support by working on the roads.

On 21 Aug. 1784 Peters and a fellow sergeant, Murphy Still (Steele), petitioned Governor John PARR for the land grants to which all loyalists were entitled. In response, the government surveyor, Charles Morris* Jr, ordered Thomas Millidge* to lay out one-acre town plots for 76 black families at Brindley Town. When the blacks attempted to settle on larger farming plots, however, they were twice removed because of conflicting claims to the land. Without provisions or land sufficient for farming, they sustained themselves with kitchen gardens, fishing in the Bay of Fundy, and the assistance of their white neighbours and English charities. They quickly formed Church of England and Methodist religious groups and in January 1785 the Associates of the Late Dr Bray provided financing for a school. Community life was therefore established, but the settlers lacked the means of self-support. Having again failed to obtain land in July 1785, Peters crossed to New Brunswick, where on 25 October he petitioned Governor Thomas Carleton* for farms for the Annapolis County blacks. He was told that his people would receive equal treatment with other loyalists, but his petition was unsuccessful. In fact, although slaves who joined the British cause had been promised the same rewards and considerations as white loyalists, only about one-third of those who went to Nova Scotia and New Brunswick received any land at all.

In 1790, after six years of fruitless waiting and five different petitions to colonial officials, Peters determined to appeal directly to the British government. He was given power of attorney by several hundred blacks in Nova Scotia and New Brunswick to represent their case, and by November, "at much trouble and risk," he had made his way to London. There he met the abolitionist Granville Sharp, who arranged for him to present his petition to the secretary of state for the Home Department, Henry Dundas. One of the documents Peters sent Dundas outlined the blacks' general grievances, noting that the rights of free British subjects, such as the vote, trial by jury, and access to the courts, had been denied them. The other gave a detailed account of their futile efforts to obtain land. It stated that Peters had been deputed to procure for his people "some Establishment where they may obtain a competent Settlement for themselves" and pointed out that although some blacks wished to remain in North America, others were "ready and willing to go wherever the Wisdom of Government may think proper to provide for them as free Subjects of the British Empire." This alternative was undoubtedly inspired by Peters' contact with the directors of the Sierra Leone Company, whose freed-slave colony in West Africa had been destroyed the previous year in a raid by indigenous people. Peters quickly accepted their offer to take his group into the colony, and the directors successfully negotiated with the government to pay the costs of transporting the blacks to Sierra Leone. Lieutenant John Clarkson of the Royal Navy, brother of the abolitionist Thomas Clarkson, was appointed to recruit the emigrants and organize their safe passage.

As a result of Peters' charges Governor Parr was ordered to institute an inquiry into the Annapolis area land problem. If Peters' description proved accurate the blacks were to be located immediately on good land. Those who chose not to accept grants could either enlist in a black army unit for service in the West Indies or remove to Sierra Leone. In the fall of 1791 Peters visited Annapolis and Saint John to promote the colonization scheme; Clarkson, who arrived in October, toured the black settlements in Halifax and Shelburne counties with the same intent. In New Brunswick Peters met with determined opposition from the whites, who did not wish to lose cheap labour or have his charges corroborated by mass emigration. False debts and indentures were fabricated, officials harassed Peters and his recruits by demanding proof of free status, and the story was spread that Peters would receive a fee for every black he inveigled to Africa for sale into slavery. The situation in New Brunswick was not exceptional. Agents appointed by both colonial governments to publicize the alternatives available to blacks deliberately misconstrued the Sierra Leone Company's intentions. The blacks nevertheless responded with enthusiasm to the offer of free land, racial equality, and full British rights in Sierra Leone. Some 1,200 emigrants gathered in Halifax, almost 500 of them from Peters' recruitment areas.

As the initiator of the project and natural leader of nearly half the emigrants, Peters became unofficial second in command to Clarkson. Together they inspected the ships and made arrangements for the journey. To channel complaints from individuals Clarkson appointed Peters and the preachers David George* and John Ball superintendents over the emigrants. Peters not unnaturally expected special status, and according to Clarkson he felt piqued at not having been given absolute charge of the emigration. He was less willing than the others to accept Clarkson's every word as law, and a conflict grew between the two men. No major disruptions were caused, however, and on 15 Jan. 1792 a fleet of 15 ships left Halifax for West Africa. Meanwhile Parr had appointed Alexander Howe* and Job Bennet Clarke commissioners to investigate Peters' charges. Though Dundas undoubtedly intended their investigation to include the complaints Peters made on behalf of all the blacks, the commissioners chose to interpret their task as an examination only of Peters' landless situation. Having heard evidence from Peters and the officials involved in land distribution, they upheld the facts of Peters' description but concluded that the reason he had not obtained land was his "hasty" departure for New Brunswick in 1785. The fact that blacks who had remained in Nova Scotia had received no land was ignored, and no remedial action was suggested.

Arriving in Sierra Leone early in March, the black loyalists immediately began clearing a site for their settlement, Freetown, but the promised land they expected was not to be realized. During Clarkson's recruitment mission the Sierra Leone Company had introduced a new constitution for the colony providing for a government made up of white officials appointed from London. Clarkson was made superintendent, and later governor. To add to the settlers' disappointment, rations were short, the rainy season brought fever and death, and the distribution of land was delayed by sickness, the inexperience of the administration, and the interference of the indigenous population. Instead of becoming free landed proprietors the black loyalists found themselves paid employees of the company. Their discontent was voiced at a meeting on 7 April, when Peters was chosen to represent their demands to Clarkson. Clarkson interpreted this action as an attempt to replace his government with a black one headed by Peters. A sincere humanitarian and abolitionist, he was convinced that a successful colony in Sierra Leone would benefit black people everywhere and that anarchy and disorder would destroy it. He assembled the entire population the following day and, addressing Peters as a traitor, announced that "either one or other of us would be hanged upon that tree before the palaver was settled." When he challenged the people to choose between himself and Peters, none moved to Peters' side. To extricate himself from this confrontation Clarkson chose to accept Peters' explanation that his wish had been only to act as spokesman for the settlers, but privately he feared Peters' intentions and assigned spies to watch his movements. For his part, Peters continued to remind the people at Methodist meetings of the promises made to them and the realities of their situation.

On 1 May 1792 Peters was accused of stealing from the trunk of a settler who had died of fever. His defence, that he had simply recovered property owed to him, was not accepted, and he was sentenced to return the goods and receive a public reprimand. The humiliation shattered his credibility, which was not revived before he too fell victim to fever on the night of 25 June 1792. He died in dishonour, denied the respect of the people he had led to Africa.

The end of Peters' career, like its early years, has been shrouded in legend. Posthumous stories had him travelling to England in 1793 to lay the settlers' complaints before the company's directors, becoming the first elected mayor of Freetown, and facing even Queen Victoria with the British betrayal of his people. Though untrue, these later embellishments are more faithful to Peters' legacy. His true image was not that of the sneak thief and frustrated leader. Rather he should be remembered as the courageous opponent of injustice and discrimination and as a primary inspiration for black self-expression and self-determination in both North America and West Africa. He represents a valuable tradition for Canada's racial mosaic.

James W. St G. Walker

BL, Add. MSS 41262A, 41262B, 41263, 41264. PANB, RG 10, RS108, Land petitions, bundle 16, Thomas Peters, 18 March 1789; series I, York County, no.386, Thomas Peters, 18 April [1789]; series II, Thomas Peters, in Council, 25 Oct. 1785. PANS, RG 1, 359, no.65; 376, pp.73–77. PRO, CO 217/63; CO 267/9; FO 4/1; PRO 30/55, Book of Negroes (copy at PANS). USPG, Dr Bray's Associates, minute books, 3; unbound papers, box 7. [John Clarkson], *Clarkson's mission to America, 1791–1792*, ed. and intro. C. B. Fergusson (Halifax, 1971); "Diary of Lieutenant J. Clarkson, R.N. (governor, 1792)," *Sierra Leone Studies* ([Freetown, Sierra Leone]), no.VIII (March 1927). A. M. Falconbridge, *Two voyages to Sierra Leone during the years 1791–2–3, in a series of letters* . . . (London, 1794).

F. W. Butt-Thompson, *Sierra Leone in history and tradition* (London, 1926). C. [H.] Fyfe, *A history of Sierra Leone* (London, 1962). E. G. Ingham, *Sierra Leone after a hundred years* (London, 1894). J. W. St G. Walker, *The black loyalists: the search for a promised land in Nova Scotia and Sierra Leone, 1783–1870* (London, 1976); "The establishment of a free black community in Nova Scotia, 1783–1840," *The African Diaspora: interpretive essays*, ed. M. L. Kilson and R. I. Rotberg (Cambridge, Mass., and London, 1976). R. W. Winks, *The blacks in Canada: a history* (Montreal, 1971). [A. G.] Archibald, "Story of deportation of Negroes from Nova Scotia to Sierra Leone," N.S. Hist. Soc., *Coll.*, VII (1891), 129–54. C. H. Fyfe, "Thomas Peters: history and legend," *Sierra Leone Studies* (Freetown), new ser., 1 (1953–55), 4–13. A. F. Walls, "The Nova Scotian settlers and their religion," *Sierra Leone Bull. of Religion* (Freetown), 1 (1959), 19–31.

PICARD, LOUIS-ALEXANDRE, jeweller, silversmith, and militia lieutenant; b. *c.* 1728 in the parish of Saint-Eustache, Paris, France, son of Pierre-François Picard and Marie-Jeanne Léger; d. 27 April 1799 at the Hôtel-Dieu in Montreal (Que.).

Louis-Alexandre Picard evidently learned his craft as an apprentice in Paris. Around 1750 he enlisted in the cavalry and served for two years. At the end of this period he settled in Bordeaux, where he remained for two and a half years. He arrived in Quebec in 1755, established himself on Rue de l'Escalier with silversmith Jacques TERROUX, and quickly made friends with the town's leading silversmith, Ignace-François DELEZENNE. By October, "wishing to set himself up on his own," he had suggested to Terroux that they dissolve their verbal contract of partnership and had offered to buy back his share from Terroux. Picard took a store on Rue Saint-Louis and began to work for Delezenne.

Delezenne was busy filling orders placed by BIGOT for trade silver. By the autumn of 1756, in a period when there was a dearth of specie, Bigot had deposited with Picard the impressive sum of 2,729 *livres* in gold and silver. The coins were to be used for making "articles of silver and gold and other pieces of jewellery produced by the [silversmiths'] craft." Picard developed at this time new tools which enabled him both to produce his wares more rapidly and to use less of the precious material. He engaged three apprentices in turn: Amable Maillou in 1756, Jean-François Risbé in 1757, and Charles Diverny, *dit* Saint-Germain, in 1759. Around 1758 he moved to Rue de la Montagne, where Delezenne had his workshop; his apprentice Risbé, who had been living with him the preceding year, was living with Delezenne in 1758. Documents relating to Picard's marriage in May 1759 to Françoise Maufils, who had borne him a daughter the previous January, reveal the identity of his friends. In giving evidence regarding his freedom to marry, Delezenne, "who has often been a companion of Picard in [the four years] he has been in Canada," asserted that they were the closest of friends. Delezenne was present when the marriage contract was signed a few days later, as were Christophe PÉLISSIER and the agent of the treasurers general of the Marine, Jacques Imbert*, who may have had connections with the Grande Société [*see* Michel-Jean-Hugues PÉAN].

In the summer of 1759 the hum of activity in the workshop on Rue de la Montagne was suddenly broken by the siege of Quebec. When peace was restored, Picard became heavily involved in real estate transactions which absorbed his energies for several years. He nevertheless remained in touch with Delezenne, who was still engaged in producing trade silver for numerous merchants. Eager to re-establish himself, Picard spent 1,000 *livres* to purchase "goods, wares, and polished gems . . . for his business" from his former partner Terroux. But economic conditions worsened and business apparently no longer flourished as it had. In spite of repeated attempts, Picard did not succeed in selling his house on Rue de la Montagne, even "at a very low price with very advantageous terms for the purchaser." His financial problems were compounded by difficulties with his apprentices. Philippe Bélanger cancelled his contract in 1766, and Louis Migneau ran away in 1772. Worst of all, in 1775 his son Pierre drowned and war was again imminent. In August Picard was commissioned lieutenant in the Canadian militia of Quebec. On 31 Dec. 1775 he was in the guard at the post of Près-de-Ville when Major-General Richard MONTGOMERY launched his troops against the post. In the skirmish, 13 Americans, including Montgomery, were killed and the American force was routed.

When peace came, Picard built a new house on Rue des Remparts since the one on Rue de la Montagne had been heavily damaged. But while he had stubbornly remained in Quebec, Montreal had become the centre for trade silver. Although he had enough business as a silversmith to engage Michel Létourneau as an apprentice in 1783, Picard went bankrupt. Unable to pay off 9,380 *livres* owing in instalments on his house, he was sent to prison. Released in 1785, he slowly re-established himself. He lived first on Rue Saint-Jean and later moved to Place du Marché. In 1795 he and six other Quebec silversmiths petitioned to be exempt from a law which concerned the use of forges, claiming that it would injure them in several respects [*see* Michel Forton*]. Picard made up his mind soon afterwards to move to Montreal, but it was unfortunately too late: the market was already dominated by Pierre Huguet*, *dit* Latour, Dominique Rousseau*, and Robert Cruickshank*.

Picard's work in silver is virtually unknown; only one goblet, bearing the stamp AP inside a rectangle, and held by the Musée du Québec, has been attributed to him.

ROBERT DEROME

ANQ-M, État civil, Catholiques, Notre-Dame de Montréal, 28 avril 1799. ANQ-Q, État civil, Catholiques, Notre-Dame de Québec, 7 mai 1759, 26 janv. 1762, 19 janv. 1769; Greffe de Claude Barolet, 13, 29 déc. 1756, 22 avril 1757, 6 mars, 6 mai 1759; Greffe de M.-A. Berthelot d'Artigny, 2 août 1777; Greffe de François Lemaître Lamorille, 16 déc. 1762; Greffe de Claude Louet, 2 oct. 1755, 17 janv. 1763; Greffe de J.-C. Panet, 9 juill. 1766; Greffe de J.-N. Pinguet, 13 janv. 1785, 1er mai 1786; Greffe de F.-D. Rousseau, 24 sept. 1783; Greffe de J.-A. Saillant, 15 mars 1757; QBC 26, 1, 1ère partie, 2. ASQ, S, Carton 13, no.51. IBC, Centre de documentation, Fonds Morisset, Dossier L.-A. Picard.

"Les dénombrements de Québec faits en 1792, 1795, 1798 et 1805 par le curé Joseph-Octave Plessis," ANQ *Rapport*, 1948–49, 18, 83. *Invasion du Canada* (Verreau), 121. "La milice canadienne-française à Québec en 1775," *BRH*, XI (1905), 228. "Témoignages de liberté au mariage (15 avril 1757–27 août 1763)," ANQ *Rapport*, 1951–53, 49, 83–84. *Quebec Gazette*, 27 Dec. 1764, 3 Jan. 1765, 17, 24 Nov., 15 Dec. 1766, 6 Oct. 1768, 30 July 1772, 27 July 1775, 27 Dec. 1792. Derome, *Les orfèvres de N.-F.* J. Trudel, *L'orfèvrerie en N.-F.*, 221. Robert Derome, "Delezenne, les orfèvres, l'orfèvrerie, 1740–1790" (thèse de MA, université de Montréal, 1974). Frégault, *François Bigot*. Langdon, *Canadian silversmiths*. Ouellet, *Hist. économique*. Traquair, *Old silver of Que*. Gérard Morisset, "L'orfèvre Louis-Alexandre Picard," *La Patrie* (Montréal), 30 avril 1950, 37–38.

PICHON. *See also* PICHOT

PICHON, THOMAS, known as **Thomas Tyrell (Thirel, Tirel)**, colonial official, spy, and author; b. 30 March 1700 at Vire (dept of Calvados), France, son of Jean Pichon, a minor merchant, and Marie Esnault; d. 22 Nov. 1781 at Saint Helier, Jersey.

Thomas Pichon is one of the most intriguing figures in the early history of Canada. For much of his life there is autobiographical material, though what is said about his early career is often contradictory. According to Pichon his parents wanted him to become a priest, but he left school at 14 and went to Paris to study medicine. When his father withdrew his stipend, Pichon was forced to clerk for several lawyers. Later he tutored a seigneur's children and managed his business affairs. He left this position to aid his father in a complicated law suit which took six years to resolve. His father refused to compensate him, and he resumed his work as a legal secretary. In 1741 he obtained a position, probably as a clerk, in the hospital service of the French armies in Bohemia and Bavaria. Again according to his own account, he became a forage inspector of the army in upper Alsace and in 1745 was appointed to organize hospitals on the Lower Rhine and in the Netherlands, where he met Jean-Louis de RAYMOND. In 1751 Raymond was appointed governor at Louisbourg and Pichon became his secretary, allured by promises of advancement.

Little is recorded about him during his first two years in the colony. In 1752 he accompanied Raymond on his tour of Île Royale and Île Saint-Jean (Prince Edward Island) and gained the intimate geographical knowledge of the area displayed in the book on Cape Breton he wrote eight years later. He also prepared many of the governor's reports to France, carefully retaining copies for use in his future publication. Raymond's promises proved illusory and Pichon became increasingly disenchanted with the governor's imperious conduct. Raymond recommended him to the minister of Marine for the position of king's attorney of the Admiralty Court, but was refused. Pichon drew closer to Louisbourg's financial commissary, Jacques PREVOST de La Croix, who granted favours to anyone willing to join his camp against the governor. When Raymond returned to France in 1753, Pichon remained behind. Raymond provided Pichon with a glowing recommendation and asked the minister to send him to Fort Beauséjour (near Sackville, N.B.) as commissary, noting that such an appointment would meet with the approbation of Abbé Jean-Louis LE LOUTRE. But it was Prevost who dispatched Pichon to Chignecto and requested a commission for him as scrivener and subdelegate of the intendant of New France. Pichon arrived at Beauséjour on 3 Nov. 1753. For the next two years he acted as chief clerk responsible for stores, although his commissions never arrived from France. A man of letters, well versed in the classics, Pichon served as scribe to the commandants, taking down their correspondence, editing it, and improving the grammar. Pichon also helped Le Loutre with his writing, although his suspicions about Roman Catholicism were confirmed by the missionary and he came to despise the priest.

The British commandant at nearby Fort Lawrence, Captain George Scott*, had previously met Pichon at Louisbourg. The boredom of garrison life on the Acadian frontier brought the French and British into frequent contact, and no one noticed when Scott invited Pichon to Fort Lawrence. Scott offered to advance Pichon's fortune in exchange for information about French activities. Although he later gave several explanations for accepting this overture, Pichon seems to have had little other reason than monetary gain.

For more than a year Pichon practised espionage and subterfuge against the French under the assumed name of Tyrell. He sent Scott and his successor, Captain John Hussey, detailed accounts of French activities in Quebec and Acadia, plans of forts Beauséjour and Gaspereau (near Port Elgin, N.B.), comments on the defences of Louisbourg, copies of official documents, censuses of Acadian refugees, gossip of the French court, and, most commonly, reports on French missionaries and warnings of attacks by Indians and their Acadian allies. Prior to the successful British assault on the French forts of Chignecto in the summer of 1755, Pichon supplied Scott with an outline of the steps necessary for their capture, which Lieutenant-Colonel Robert MONCKTON later used in the attack. Pichon discouraged the Acadians from joining the Indians and retarded the strengthening of Beauséjour by advising that the British would not attack that year. During the siege he further weakened the French side with his counsel to the Acadian settlers to terminate the ordeal by demanding that the commandant, Louis DU PONT Duchambon de Vergor, capitulate. Pichon also helped draft a letter sent by an Acadian settler to the commandant of Gaspereau, Benjamin Rouer* de Villeray, calling for a swift surrender. While the fighting was going on he wrote a generally accurate and dispassionate journal that was later partially reproduced in his book.

Before the fall of Beauséjour Pichon had made arrangements with the British to continue his spying. As a prisoner in Halifax, he passed on to Archibald Hinchelwood, acting secretary to Charles Lawrence*, some of the correspondence entrusted to him by a captured French naval officer, including a plan for seizing the town; the rest he carried with him to London late in 1755.

In London Pichon continued his duplicity for a short period with some Acadians and attempted to sway the allegiance of Louis-Thomas JACAU de Fiedmont, the artillery officer at Beauséjour. With a pension of £100 sterling he was able to devote much of his time to the preparation of his book, *Lettres et mémoires pour servir à l'histoire naturelle, civile et politique du Cap Breton, depuis son établissement jusqu'à la reprise de cette isle par les Anglois en 1758*, which appeared in 1760. Based on previous writings and composed in the form of letters to a friend, the book is a generally accurate but uneven description of Île Royale and Île Saint-Jean. His account of the customs and behaviour of the Micmacs and Malecites is strikingly realistic, but his discussion of the role of the missionaries is marked by a sneering contempt for the Roman Catholic Church, appropriate to an Enlightenment mind. His views on colonial government are distorted by his supposition that the bitter political factionalism of the Raymond-Prévost years characterized all adminstrations. The remainder of the book, concerned mainly with the military events he witnessed, presents little that is new or revealing. The work remains, nevertheless, one of the few reliable published sources about the French in Acadia during the 18th century.

During his early life in Paris Pichon had acquired an unsavoury reputation as a seducer of young women, and after his arrival in London, undeterred by age, he became involved in a series of amorous adventures. The most tortuous involved Marie-Barbe de Beaumont, *née* Le Prince, a novelist and the editor of a children's magazine, whose marriage had been annulled. Her infatuation with Pichon was more intense than his devotion to her; they never married, but Pichon moved into her apartment in 1757 and continued to reside there after she left England in 1760. Unable to speak English, Pichon lived in a restricted circle, but in the 1760s he took several mistresses and became a friend of John Cleland, the author of *Fanny Hill, or the memoirs of a woman of pleasure*. Some time after 1769 Pichon moved to Saint Helier. Pichon left as a legacy to his Norman birthplace all his letters, manuscripts, and a library of over 3,000 volumes, mainly works of history, science, and political economy.

Assessments of Thomas Pichon have been universally harsh. The tone of exaggerated self-importance struck in his correspondence, his ambition and avarice, his treason, and his sexual promiscuity have all led to condemnation. Pichon himself, always dissatisfied with his lot in life, was to end in mortification of spirit over his betrayal of his country. He desired to be loved, but was incapable of truly loving.

During his last years the sins and excesses of his former life overwhelmed Pichon and led to a profound spiritual crisis. Lonely and tormented, he was repulsed by the physical deterioration that accompanied his advancing years. "What a horrible thing is old age!" he wrote. "The sprightliness of my senses is worn by time, maybe by debauchery, and as they say, for having lived too much. My infirmities are constantly increasing, and my days and nights are spent in unbearable torment. My legs, once my adornment and the object of admiration at balls and gatherings, are stretched, swollen and immobile, on a chair or footstool. My cheeks, once glowing and plump, are parched and shrivelled with wrinkles; my lips are covered with tense and livid skin. I have lost, not only the power to enjoy pleasure, but the desire for enjoyment."

The thought of death confused and frightened Pichon even more. Having rejected religion, he found reason an uncomforting solace with which to meet that fate he had once ridiculed as an illusion. "I tremble in spite of myself," he wrote, "before something that threatens and which, in vain, I strive not to believe." He contemplated suicide and turned in desperation to God, dying as a Protestant. His anguish was best expressed in the epitaph he wrote for himself: "Dear God, who regards this world and the anxieties of men, take pity on my soul." But Pichon also hoped that others might learn from his example "whether or not it beseems a man of sense to live according to a system in which he does not dare to die."

T. A. CROWLEY

Thomas Pichon is the author of *Lettres et mémoires pour servir à l'histoire naturelle, civile et politique du Cap Breton, depuis son établissement jusqu'à la reprise de cette isle par les Anglois en 1758* (La Haye, Pays-Bas, 1760; réimpr. [East Ardsley, Eng.], 1966).

AD, Calvados (Cæn), F, 1894 (fonds Surlaville) (mfm. at PAC). AN, Col., C^{11B}, 31, f.51v; 33, f.70; 34, f.167v. Bibliothèque municipale de Vire (dép. du Calvados), Coll. Thomas Pichon, 1750–62 (transcripts at PAC). BL, Add. MSS 19071, pp.141–42 (transcript in PAC, MG 21). PANS, RG 1, 341–41½ (Thomas Pichon papers). *Les derniers jours de l'Acadie* (Du Boscq de Beaumont). [L.-T. Jacau de Fiedmont], *The siege of Beauséjour in 1755; a journal of the attack on Beauséjour . . .*, ed. J. C. Webster, trans. Alice Webster (Saint John, N.B., 1936). *Military affairs in North America, 1748–65* (Pargellis). Pierre Bagot, *Marie Le Prince de Beaumont, lettres à Thomas Pichon* (Vire, France, 1924). J. C. Webster, *Thomas Pichon, "the spy of Beausejour," an account of his career in Europe and America . . .* ([Sackville, N.B.], 1937). Albert David, "Le Judas de l'Acadie," *Revue de l'université d'Ottawa*, III (1933), 492–513; IV (1934), 22–35; "Thomas Pichon, le 'Judas' des Acadiens (1700–1781)," *Nova Francia* (Paris), III (1927–28), 131–38. Gustave Lanctot, "Le traître Pichon," *BRH*, XXXVI (1930), 328–40. Régis Roy, "Thomas Pichon," *BRH*, V (1899), 92–93.

PICHOT (Pichon) DE QUERDISIEN (Kerdisien de) TRÉMAIS, CHARLES-FRANÇOIS, commissary of the Marine charged with conducting the inquiry in the *affaire du Canada*; b. *c*. 1724 near Brest, France; d. 9 Aug. 1784 at L'Acul (Dominican Republic).

Charles-François Pichot de Querdisien Trémais entered the Marine in 1743 and served as commissary at Louisbourg, Île Royale (Cape Breton Island) during the 1758 siege. The following year he was principal writer at Brest. It was probably at the beginning of 1759 that it was proposed he go to Canada to investigate the financial administration, since early in February he sent the minister, Berryer, a report setting out his idea of what he would have to do in the colony. He suggested that he work in the "money office" (the office of the Marine), where Intendant BIGOT was requesting help. As a result of this report, which the minister called "well done," Querdisien Trémais received the title of commissary of the Marine and precise instructions for his mission. While aiding "M. Bigot efficiently in his duties," he was to work to uncover "all the abuses which have crept into any parts whatsoever of the service in the colony." He was therefore to inspect the supplies sent to the colony by the king, examine the profits of merchants favoured by the intendant, and above all pay close attention to purveyor general Joseph-Michel CADET's activities. He was to ensure that the hospitals' expenditures and the rent paid for warehouses and buildings were examined, that any abuse in the payment of officers and soldiers at the various posts was reported, and that the costs of the merchandise at these posts were investigated. The need for written proof of any abuses was emphasized. To facilitate his task he received a code to use for correspondence.

Bigot quickly detected Querdisien Trémais's real mission and, to prove his honesty, he obliged his partners in the Grande Société to make partial restitution. The minister's representative had to work under particularly unfavourable conditions – he had barely arrived in Quebec when the British appeared in the St Lawrence, and the intendant felt it necessary to transfer the documents of the "money office" to Trois-Rivières. Consequently Querdisien Trémais was not able to examine them and had to confine himself to collecting statements and comparing them with his own observations. Nevertheless his assessment of Bigot and the general staff of the armed forces was to result in prosecution at the Châtelet in Paris. As a reward for his services he received a pension of 1,200 *livres*. In 1761 the minister proposed that he be the person in France to settle Canadian accounts. He had to complete this task without the help of the financial commissary, Pierre-Michel MARTEL, who refused to leave the colony.

In July 1762, with the assistance of the intendant of Bordeaux, Charles-Robert Boutin, he investigated Bigot's commercial operations with the Jewish merchant Abraham Gradis; he seized documents from Gradis's offices which revealed various aspects of the Grande Société [*see* Michel-Jean-Hugues PÉAN]. Then he held an inquiry at La Rochelle into the activities of Denis GOGUET, Bigot's agent, who was responsible for the sale in Europe of furs Bigot acquired at his or the king's trading posts.

At the end of December 1762 Querdisien Trémais received 6,000 *livres*, drawn on colonial funds, and was sent to Saint-Domingue (Hispaniola) on a mission similar to the one he had carried out capably in Canada. He was appointed subdelegate general of the intendant, financial commissary of Cap-Français (Cap-Haïtien or Le Cap), and first councillor of the Conseils Supérieurs of Cap-Français and Port-au-Prince. From 23 Jan. 1769 on he served as commissary general of Saint-Domingue, and he received the appointment of commissary general of the Marine in 1771. In 1780 he was honorary councillor of the Conseil Supérieur of Cap-Français; he died four years later.

MICHEL ROBERGE

AN, Col., B, 109, ff.34, 63; 110, ff.40v, 46; 113, f.299v; 113, 2e partie, ff.11, 12, 80v; 115, f.147; C11A, 104, f.344. ANQ-M, Greffe de Pierre Panet, 10 sept. 1760. "Dossier Charles-François Pichot de Querdisien Trémais," Antoine Roy, édit., ANQ *Rapport*, 1959–60, 3–22. "Les malignités du sieur de Courville," *BRH*, L (1944), 113. Gustave Lanctot, "L'Affaire du Canada; bibliographie du procès Bigot," *BRH*, XXXVIII (1932), 8–17. [M.-L.-É.] Moreau de Saint-Méry, *Description topographique, physique, civile, politique et historique de la partie française de l'isle de Saint-Domingue*, Blanche Maurel et Étienne Taillemite, édit. (3v., Paris, 1958), 272, 1502. Frégault, *François Bigot*. P.-G. Roy, *La famille Martel de Magesse* (Lévis, Qué., 1934), 23. Pierre de Vaissière, *Saint-Domingue; la société et la vie créoles sous l'Ancien Régime (1629–1789)* (Paris, 1909), 149–50. "M. Querdisien Trémais," *BRH*, LII (1946), 349.

PICOTÉ DE BELESTRE, FRANÇOIS-MARIE, officer in the colonial regular troops, member of the Legislative Council, and chief road commissioner (*grand voyer*); b. 17 Nov. 1716 at Lachine (Que.), son of François-Marie Picoté de Belestre and Marie-Catherine Trottier Desruisseaux; d. 30 March 1793 at Montreal.

Like his father, François-Marie Picoté de Belestre chose a military career. A year after his marriage to Marie-Anne Nivard Saint-Dizier on 28 July 1738, he took part, under Charles Le Moyne* de Longueuil and Pierre-Joseph Céloron* de Blainville, in a campaign to subdue the Chickasaws. This major offensive, which had been organized over a long period, enabled the governor of Louisiana, Jean-Baptiste Le Moyne* de Bienville, to obtain a negotiated peace with that forbidding tribe. In April 1742 Governor Beauharnois* rewarded Picoté de Belestre with recommendation to a second ensigncy. From June to October 1746 Picoté de Belestre fought in Acadia with the forces under Jean-Baptiste-Nicolas-Roch de RAMEZAY; he was entrusted with the special task of recruiting through Charles GERMAIN, a missionary to the Malecites of the Saint John valley, pilots competent to guide the French ships and get them out of reach of the British fleet anchored at Port-La-Joie (Fort Amherst, P.E.I.). In 1747, along with Louis de La Corne*, known as Chevalier de La Corne, Luc de LA CORNE, and François-Josué de La Corne* Dubreuil, he was sent to invite the Indians of the *pays d'en haut* to Montreal. His popularity among the tribes had some bearing on his appointment as commandant at Fort Saint-Joseph (Niles, Mich.) the following August.

The treaty of Aix-la-Chapelle in 1748 did not prevent the pressure of Anglo-American colonization from being increasingly felt in the Ohio valley. The attraction of new trade alliances led to the migration of a considerable number of Miamis who, under the leadership of Memeskia (La Demoiselle, Old Britain), wanted to escape from the surveillance of the French Canadians at Detroit by settling farther south on the Rivière à la Roche (Great Miami River, Ohio). There they founded the village of Pickawillany (Piqua), which rapidly became "the main centre of Anglo-American trade and political intrigue in the Ohio region." In order to counter this threat to French claims to the region, Commandant General Roland-Michel Barrin* de La Galissonière dispatched a military expedition under Céloron de Blainville in 1749; the latter, because he lacked a strike force of adequate strength, decided his expedition could not attempt a punitive campaign aimed at wiping out Memeskia's Miamis. In the autumn of 1751 the new governor, La Jonquière [Taffanel*] called on Picoté de Belestre, who had become a lieutenant in April of that year, to report to the minister of the Marine on the serious deterioration of France's position in that part of the west.

Until the eve of the conquest Picoté de Belestre maintained a fairly prosperous fur-trading business concurrently with his military activity. In the period from 1749 to 1759 he signed almost 90 hiring contracts, mostly for Detroit but sometimes for Michilimackinac (Mackinaw City, Mich.) and Fort des Miamis (probably at or near Fort Wayne, Ind.).

The year 1756 saw renewal of military engagements against the British forts in Pennsylvania, Virginia, and the Carolinas. Early in the year, in compliance with the orders of Jean-Daniel DUMAS, the commandant of Fort Duquesne (Pittsburgh, Pa), Picoté de Belestre and a party of Miamis and Shawnees fell upon a Carolina village consisting of some 40 houses and a small fort; they took 300 prisoners, looted, and put everything to the torch, to the satisfaction of Governor Vaudreuil [RIGAUD]. Then in August 1757 Picoté de Belestre took part in Montcalm*'s victorious offensive against Fort George (also called Fort William Henry; now Lake George, N.Y.). In the autumn he was commissioned by Vaudreuil to go to spread terror on the north bank of the Mohawk, at German Flats (near the mouth of West Canada Creek). The governor wanted to teach a lesson to the German immigrants there who had refused to join the French. Perhaps, as historian Guy Frégault* has suggested, the crime of which they had been guilty in refusing to change their allegiance resembled that of the Acadians [*see* Charles Lawrence*]. The expedition lasted nearly two months and resulted in 40 dead and 150 prisoners. Vaudreuil had reason to be content, and the ease with which Picoté de Belestre had penetrated into enemy territory by way of the Mohawk led the governor in 1758 to conceive of a diversionary strategy in that region to draw off part of Major-General James ABERCROMBY's troops, which were concentrated on the Hudson with a view to invading Canada via Lake Champlain.

Upon Jacques-Pierre Daneau* de Muy's death in May 1758, Picoté de Belestre became commandant at Detroit, thus honouring the memory of his father, who had been there as second in command under Alphonse de Tonty*. In January 1759 he was made a knight of Saint-Louis and was named captain at the same time as his son François-Louis was recommended for an ensigncy. François-Louis assisted in rallying numerous Indian clans to the French cause. Taken prisoner by the Cherokees, he became one of their chieftains and succeeded in drawing them into taking up arms against the British in Virginia and the Carolinas, where they wreaked considerable havoc. François-Louis settled in Louisiana, and his family lived on there until the end of the 19th century.

At the time of the conquest there was still support for the French among the Indian tribes of the *pays d'en haut*. On the eve of the surrender of Detroit late in 1760, a council was held by the Hurons, Weas, Potawatomis, and Ojibwas at Picoté de Belestre's residence, during which they expressed their grief at his departure and their hope that they would not be abandoned to the British. When he visited Paris in 1762 Picoté de Belestre could thus report to the minister of Marine, the Duc de Choiseul: "These tribes are confident that the king their master will deliver them from slavery." The same Indian tribes would respond to the appeal made by Pontiac* in 1763 to incite them against the British. After turning over the fort to Robert ROGERS on 29 Nov. 1760, the last French commandant of Detroit and its garrison were taken to Fort Pitt (Pittsburgh) and then sent on to New York, where they arrived on 4 Feb. 1761. From there Picoté de Belestre was to go to Europe. In Paris on 16 June 1762 he sent a request to the Duc de Choiseul for a company in Louisiana for François-Louis.

Picoté de Belestre had had three daughters and two other sons by his first marriage. On 29 Jan. 1753, three years after his wife's death, he married Marie-Anne Magnan, *dit* L'Espérance, and they had two children. While their father was detained in Europe, the two eldest daughters gave their stepmother cause for anxiety; she tried to secure the annulment of the marriages they had contracted before a Protestant minister, and she opposed their requests for a rendering of accounts. However, captains John Wharton and William Evans, her new sons-in-law, won their case in the Montreal Chamber of Militia. Picoté de Belestre apparently did not bear a grudge against his daughters. When he drew up his will on 8 June 1791 he included them or, failing them, his grandchildren, as beneficiaries of a sum of £50 each.

Picoté de Belestre probably did not return to Canada before 1764. In Montreal he lived rather in seclusion. In 1767 he was involved in the unusual repercussions of the notorious Thomas WALKER affair. Some startling arrests had been made in November 1766 in connection with the assault on the merchant Walker; six people, amongst them such prominent figures as the judge John Fraser, Luc de La Corne, and La Corne's son-in-law John CAMPBELL, were charged. The verdict was to be reached by a grand jury, on which sat several Canadians including Picoté de Belestre, Pierre-Roch de Saint-Ours Deschaillons, Claude-Pierre PÉCAUDY de Contrecœur, and Joseph-Claude Boucher* de Niverville, all knights of Saint-Louis. Wishing to clear their compatriot Luc de La Corne of the charge, they took the occasion "cheerfully" to swear the oath of allegiance to the British crown, contrary to the commitment which the order of Saint-Louis imposed upon them "of never quitting the service of the king of France to enter that of a foreign prince without his majesty's permission and written assent." What was a breach of allegiance to their former sovereign put them on the select list that Governor Guy Carleton* presented in March 1769 to the secretary of state for the American Colonies, Lord Hillsborough, in anticipation of future appointments to the Legislative Council.

Picoté de Belestre was barely becoming familiar with his newly acquired role as a member of the Legislative Council in 1775 when the American invasion called him back to combat, this time in the Richelieu region. As Fort Saint-Jean was threatened, some one hundred Canadian volunteers, including a good number of ex-officers, rushed to its defence, under the orders of the former commandant of Detroit and of Joseph-Dominique-Emmanuel Le Moyne* de Longueuil. Picoté de Belestre stood out as a leader among those representing the Canadian nobility. The fort was under siege for 45 days. The valiant defenders had to surrender on 2 November, a fortnight after the capitulation of Fort Chambly. Picoté de Belestre was taken prisoner of war for the second time and underwent exile in Albany and New Jersey. Upon his return Carleton appointed him chief road commissioner for the province on 1 May 1776. He does not, however, seem to have undertaken active duties because of his "age" and "infirmities," as HALDIMAND, Carleton's successor, noted. One final honour crowned Picoté de Belestre's career. On 12 July 1790 he received the provincial rank of lieutenant-colonel, in recognition of his services during the American invasion.

The political scene did not afford Picoté de Belestre the opportunity to distinguish himself by feats as brilliant as those of his military career. Appointed to the Legislative Council when he was nearing 60, he served in a spirit of honest and faithful allegiance to his British king, but with a feeling of deep attachment to the social and cultural values inherited from his former mother country. This attachment explains his participation in the various steps his compatriots took to preserve their precious heritage, on both the civil and the religious planes. He made common cause with the members of the French party within the Legislative Council. He fitted so well into the new régime established by the Quebec Act that he became one of its most tenacious defenders against the reform movement which, rallying both Anglo-Scottish and Canadian bourgeois forces in the colony, was calling for a system of representative government in conformity with the rights and privileges of British subjects [*see* Pierre DU CALVET]. He must have been reassured by the constitution of 1791, since under it he was able to retain his prerogatives as a member of the Legislative Council.

On 30 March 1793 François-Marie Picoté de Belestre passed away at the age of "76 years, 4 months, 13 days." The "tremendous procession" that accompanied the funeral cortège was evidence of the high esteem in which his fellow citizens held him.

PIERRE TOUSIGNANT and
MADELEINE DIONNE-TOUSIGNANT

[François-Marie Picoté de Belestre's year of birth has been erroneously given as 1719 by all his biographers. This date is found in Æ. Fauteux, *Les chevaliers de Saint-Louis*, 170–71; Le Jeune, *Dictionnaire*, I, 154; and Turcotte, *Le Cons. législatif*, 39. However, Belestre's first wedding certificate and his burial certificate (ANQ-M, État civil, Catholiques, 28 juillet 1738, 2 avril 1793), as well as a funeral oration published in the *Montreal Gazette* on 4 April 1793, indicate that he was born on 17 Nov. 1716. P.T. and M.D.-T.]

AAQ, 1CB, V, 35. AN, Col., C[11A], 85, pp.147, 151–52; 87/1, pp.45–46, 68, 178–79, 183–84, 194; 87/2, pp.22, 35; 97, pp.217–18; 101, pp.446–48, 461–62; 102, pp.3–5; 103, pp.357–59; 105, pp.606–15; D[2C], 48, pp.69, 139, 391, 403, 424–26, 439–40; F[3], 15, pp.86–92 (PAC transcripts). ANQ-M, Chambre des milices, 6, 9 févr. 1762, 6 déc. 1763; État civil, Catholiques, La Visitation-de-la-Bienheureuse-Vierge-Marie, Sault-au-Récollet (Montréal), 11 juin 1744; Notre-Dame de Montréal, 27 mai 1714, 4 déc. 1736, 28 juillet 1738, 11 avril 1739, 18 mars 1741, 15 sept. 1742, 2 déc. 1743, 10 sept. 1746, 9 juin, 20 août 1748, 29 janv. 1753, 16 mai 1754, 17 nov. 1758, 20 juin 1791, 2 avril, 31 oct. 1793; Saint-Antoine (Longueuil), 18 mars 1743; Saints-Anges (Lachine), 26 févr. 1731; Greffe de L.-C. Danré de Blanzy, 1749–59; Greffe de Joseph Papineau, 8 juin 1791. BL, Add. MSS 21727, ff. 107, 133 (mfm. at PAC). PAC, MG 8, A1, 9, pp.220–21; 10, p.98; MG 11, [CO 42], Q, 4, pp.1, 103, 105; 5/1, p.269; 6, pp.31–33; 11, pp.11–13, 161, 258–61, 284; 27/1, pp.63–67; MG 24, L3, pp.4017–19.

American archives (Clarke and Force), 4th ser., II, 518–19. Amherst, *Journal* (Webster). Bégon, "Correspondance" (Bonnault), ANQ *Rapport*, 1934–35, 163. *Coll. de manuscrits relatifs à la N.-F.*, III, 407; IV, 82. *Coll. des manuscrits de Lévis* (Casgrain), XI, 127–42. [Charles Deschamps de Boishébert et de Raffetot], "Mémoire de M. de Boishébert au ministre sur les entreprises de guerre contre les Sauvages, novembre 1747," *BRH*, XXII (1916), 378. *Doc. relatifs à l'hist. constitutionnelle, 1759–91* (Shortt et Doughty; 1921), I, 491–94; II, 578–79. [Antoine Foucher], "Journal tenu pendant le siège du fort Saint-Jean, en 1775, par feu M. Boucher, ancien notaire de Montréal," *BRH*, XL (1934), 135–59, 197–222. *Invasion du Canada* (Verreau), 24–26, 335–36. *Journal of Pontiac's conspiracy, 1763*, ed. C. M. and M. A. Burton, trans. R. C. Ford (Detroit, 1912). [Francis Maseres], *An account of the proceedings of the British, and other Protestant inhabitants, of the province of Quebeck, in North-America, in order to obtain an house of assembly in that province* (London, 1775). "La mission de M. de Bougainville en France en 1758–1759," ANQ *Rapport*, 1923–24, 37–38. *NYCD* (O'Callaghan and Fernow), X, 49, 51, 85, 90, 115–16, 118, 145, 151, 162, 182, 423–24, 481–82, 486, 672–74, 705, 992, 1094. Robert Rogers, *Journals of Major Robert Rogers . . .* (London, 1765; repr. Ann Arbor, Mich., [1966]). "Une expédition canadienne à la Louisiane en 1739–1740," ANQ *Rapport*, 1922–23, 181, 189–90. *Quebec Gazette*, 15 July 1790.

Massicotte, "Répertoire des engagements pour l'Ouest," ANQ *Rapport*, 1930–31, 393; 1931–32, 251–59, 271–75, 279–82, 285–86, 289–93, 305–11, 363–65; 1932–33, 245–46, 250, 256. P.-G. Roy, *Inv. procès-verbaux des grands voyers*, V, 156–57. Stanley, *New France*, 20–21, 37, 176, 219, 265–66. Tousignant, "La genèse et l'avènement de la constitution de 1791." Ivanhoë Caron, "Historique de la voirie dans la province de Québec; Régime anglais: les ordonnances de

1766 et de 1777," *BRH*, XXXIX (1933), 283–84. "Références biographiques canadiennes," *BRH*, LII (1946), 227. J.-E. Roy, "La charge de grand voyer," *BRH*, II (1896), 139–40. P.-G. Roy, "Les grands voyers de 1667 à 1842," *BRH*, XXXVII (1931), 451, 455.

PICQUET, FRANÇOIS, priest, Sulpician, and missionary; b. 4 Dec. 1708 at Bourg-en-Bresse, France, son of André Picquet and Marie-Philippe Berthet; d. 15 July 1781 at Verjon (dept of Ain), France.

After studying at the Jesuit college in Bourg-en-Bresse, François Picquet then entered the Séminaire de Lyon in 1728. He took further training at the Séminaire de Saint-Sulpice in Paris, where he was ordained priest on 10 April 1734. That summer he arrived in Montreal (Que.) and served in the parish ministry there until 1739, at the same time learning Indian languages and customs. From 1739 to 1749 he lived at the Sulpician mission of Lac-des-Deux-Montagnes (Oka, Que.), which had been founded in 1721. Picquet can be credited with writing a few hymns and catechetical texts in the Iroquois language, but, despite an enthusiastic tradition to the contrary, he was not responsible for the Calvary at Oka, built by his colleague Hamon Guen* in the period 1740–42, or for other mission buildings, which had been erected well before his arrival.

His main vocation – to win over to France all Indians living to the south of the Great Lakes – seems to have taken shape about this time. In 1745 Picquet went with some Iroquois to Quebec, where Intendant Gilles HOCQUART is supposed to have conferred upon him the title of "apostle to the Iroquois"; he also met Governor Charles de Beauharnois*, who congratulated him on his work with the Iroquois. On 5 Oct. 1748 Roland-Michel Barrin* de La Galissonière, the commandant general of New France, informed Maurepas that Picquet would soon leave for Fort Frontenac (Kingston, Ont.) to find the best place to locate a village for Indians seeking Christian conversion. He chose a site downstream from Mille-Îles (Thousand Islands, Ont.) at a strategic point on a narrows in the St Lawrence.

On 1 June 1749, with 25 Frenchmen and four Indians, he founded the post of La Présentation (Oswegatchie, now Ogdensburg, N.Y.). By autumn Picquet had built a stockaded fort, with a redoubt and living quarters sheltering some 300 Iroquois, Hurons, and other Indians. But the LE LOUTRE of the *pays d'en haut* was aiming above all to wean the Six Nations from their alliance with the English. Thus in August 1752 he went to Montreal with "his" Iroquois, so that they could take an oath of allegiance to the new governor, DUQUESNE. The following summer, he sailed for France on the *Algonkin* accompanied by three Iroquois, to ask Louis XV for the additional funds that he thought necessary for his mission. Although the help given was minimal – 3,000 *livres*, some books, and a statue – the spectacle had its effect on the Iroquois. And so Picquet's 18th-century hagiographer, Joseph-Jérôme Lefrançois de Lalande, was able to write: "War had no sooner been declared in 1754 than the new children of God, of the king, and of M. Picquet thought only of proving their fidelity and valour."

Back in New France in 1754, and having vainly solicited a comfortable position as dean of the canonical chapter, the fiery Sulpician hurled himself into the final conflict between France and Britain in North America. From 1755 on he was everywhere, as military chaplain, as adviser, or even as an "army", since, according to Lalande, Governor Duquesne thought that "Abbé Picquet was worth more than ten regiments." While Abbé Pierre-Paul-François de LAGARDE worked at the mission Picquet took part in 1756 in the expeditions against Fort Bull (east of Lake Oneida, N.Y.) and Oswego (Chouaguen). Montcalm* observed that "according to Abbé Picquet, the Indians say that the English have put a price on his head." Lalande continues: "Generals, commanding officers, troops showed their esteem and gratitude in an extraordinary manner by giving him military honours . . . honours received both in the field, and at Quebec, Montreal, and Trois-Rivières, in all the forts he visited."

In March 1757 Picquet was rewarded with a pension from the king. Two months later he undertook secret negotiations with the Oneidas which resulted in a more durable alliance. But as the fighting intensified Governor Vaudreuil [RIGAUD] decided to place a military commandant, Claude-Nicolas de Lorimier* de La Rivière, at Fort de La Présentation. Insulted by this division of authority, the autocratic abbé withdrew in March 1758 to his former mission of Lac-des-Deux-Montagnes and did not emerge until 18 May. "Abbé Picquet appeared this morning from the depths of his retreat; he is like a seigneur of the royal court, who, dissatisfied, has spent two months on his estates," noted Montcalm; the latter, a good Frenchman, sided with Picquet against the governor.

"In high standing" with the Indians, Abbé Picquet led them on 8 July 1758 during the famous battle of Carillon (Ticonderoga, N.Y.); according to a song composed after the victory, he is supposed to have exhorted the army before the combat: "'My children,' he said, 'be of good spirit!/The good Lord, his Mother, all things favour you.'"

The grateful Vaudreuil appointed the affable Antoine-Gabriel-François BENOIST as commandant to replace the bad-tempered Lorimier. And when he put Pierre Pouchot* in provisional command of La Présentation in March 1759, Vaudreuil gave him strict injunctions "to show Abbé Picquet all the respect due his character and his prestige among the tribes." Yet the French resistance was crumbling. Vaudreuil, LÉVIS, Montcalm, and others might be unceasing in their praise of Picquet, who "has fought like a warrior," but he sensed after the failure of Louis de La Corne*'s expedition to Oswego in July 1759 that the end was imminent. Aware that the fortifications at La Présentation were inadequate, he decided to move his mission to a nearby island, Île Picquet. But the Indians there, "who are starving," began to flee. In the winter of 1760 Picquet went to Montreal for help. Wasted effort! All he could do was return to the island, in March 1760, rally the most desperate Indians, and in the summer take them to Montreal, now shorn of its own empire.

Unwilling, apparently, to submit to the new master, and perhaps because a price had been set on his head, Picquet secretly left Montreal just before its capitulation with 25 Frenchmen and a few Indians. In July 1761 he arrived in New Orleans, where he stayed until April 1763. He then made his last voyage back to France. His difficulties were by no means over. He was denied a pension – this man who, Lalande claims with his usual studied care, "could say that while he was in Canada there were no glorious actions for France in which he did not have a large part." The general assembly of the clergy of France, however, came to his aid and paid him 1,200 *livres* on two occasions, in 1765 and 1770.

In 1772 Picquet decided to return to his native Bresse, first exercising the parish ministry at Verjon until 1775. Finally the quick-tempered priest became chaplain to the nuns of the Visitation at Bourg-en-Bresse and held this office until 1779. In March 1777 he went to Rome, where Pius VI accorded him a private audience; "his" Visitation nuns presented him in one of their circulars as "known in the four corners of the world . . . loved by the people, respected by the Indians, esteemed by the great and particularly by Louis XV, who like the Pope had given him every sort of authority and power." That was enough to persuade him to retire and he bought a house and property near Cluny in 1779. In 1781 business brought him to Verjon, where he died of a haemorrhage and dropsy on 15 July.

ROBERT LAHAISE

[The main difficulty in writing about Abbé Picquet is in separating truth from hyperbole. The first account of his life, by his friend and compatriot, astronomer Joseph-Jérôme Lefrançois de Lalande, was published in Paris in 1783. Lalande provides no sources but tells us that Picquet did everything: he rallied all the Iroquois (and almost did the same with the "Negroes and Negresses in New England"), he made England tremble, he foresaw and directed the wars. AMHERST, advancing to Montreal, even "first informed himself as to where M. Picquet could have taken refuge."

A century after this sensational beginning, André Chagny, Catholic and royalist as only a 19th-century Frenchman could be, continued the epic. Accepting Lalande's text unconditionally, he filled in the gaps left by his predecessor's scant 60 pages with 600 pages of his own invention. We are consequently in his debt for, among other things, a defence of the Abbé's humility, as well as a final elegy worthy of his basic assumptions: "Thanks to all who defended New France at that time, and first and foremost to Abbé Picquet, we can boldly affirm that there survives on the other side of the Atlantic something of the great soul of France." Later Joseph Tassé*, Pierre Rousseau, and Auguste-Honoré Gosselin* composed minor variations on this theme. It is, however, undeniable that much contemporary praise of Picquet, bestowed by colonial authorities, is to be found, for example in the *Coll. des manuscrits de Lévis*. There is therefore evidence to visualize him as a Le Loutre of the west with accomplishments of no mean order. R.L.]

Coll. des manuscrits de Lévis (Casgrain), I, 198; II, 187; V, 254–55, 307; VII, 119, 206, 481; VIII, 97, 103; X, 189, 204. J.-J. Lefrançois de Lalande, "Mémoire sur la vie de M. Picquet, missionnaire au Canada, par M. de la Lande, de l'Académie des Sciences," *Lettres édifiantes et curieuses, écrites des missions étrangères par quelques missionnaires de la Compagnie de Jésus*, Y.-M.-M. de Querbeuf, édit. (nouv. éd., 26v., Paris, 1780–83), XXVI, 1–63. "Les malignités du sieur de Courville," *BRH*, L (1944), 69–70. [A.-J.-H. de Maurès de Malartic, comte de Malartic], *Journal des campagnes au Canada de 1755 à 1760 . . .* , Gabriel de Maurès de Malartic et Paul Gaffarel, édit. (Dijon, France, 1890). Louise Dechêne, "Inventaire des documents relatifs à l'histoire du Canada conservés dans les archives de la Compagnie de Saint-Sulpice à Paris," ANQ *Rapport*, 1969, 147–288. André Chagny, *Un défenseur de la "Nouvelle-France," François Picquet, "le Canadien" (1708–1781)* (Montréal et Paris, 1913). Frégault, *La guerre de la Conquête*. Pierre Rousseau, *Saint-Sulpice et les missions catholiques* (Montréal, 1930). M. Trudel, *L'Église canadienne*. J.-G. Forbes, "La mission d'Oka et ses missionnaires," *BRH*, VI (1900), 147. A.[-H.] Gosselin, "Le fondateur de la Présentation (Ogdensburg): l'abbé Picquet (1734–

1760)," RSC *Trans.*, 1st ser., XII (1894), sect.I, 3–28. Olivier Maurault, "Quand Saint-Sulpice allait en guerre . . . ," *Cahiers des Dix*, 5 (1940), 11–30. J. R. Porter, "Le calvaire d'Oka," *Vie des arts* (Montréal), XIX (1974–75), no.76, 88–89. P.-G. Roy, "Pierre Margane des Forêts de Lavaltrie," *BRH*, XXIII (1917), 71–77. Joseph Tassé, "L'abbé Picquet," *Revue canadienne* (Montréal), VII (1870), 5–23, 102–18. Têtu, "Le chapitre de la cathédrale," *BRH*, XV, 97–111.

PIER. *See* SAINT-AUBIN

PIERRE-BENOÎT. *See* BENOÎT

PIOT DE LANGLOISERIE (L'Angloiserie), MARIE-MARGUERITE, *dite* **Saint-Hippolyte,** sister of the Congregation of Notre-Dame and superior of the community (superior general); b. 11 Feb. 1702 at Varennes, near Montreal (Que.), daughter of Charles-Gaspard Piot* de Langloiserie and Marie-Thérèse Dugué de Boisbriand; d. 10 Feb. 1781 in Montreal.

Marie-Marguerite Piot de Langloiserie came from two families belonging to the Canadian élite. Her father was king's lieutenant at Quebec and a knight of the order of Saint-Louis; her maternal grandfather, Michel-Sidrac Dugué* de Boisbriand, had been one of the earliest seigneurs in the Montreal region. In 1721 Marie-Marguerite entered the noviciate of the Congregation of Notre-Dame in Montreal as did her sister Charlotte-Angélique, who was six years her senior. Charlotte-Angélique, named Sister Sainte-Rosalie, was a member of the community for 23 years and died on 1 March 1744, seven years before her sister's election as superior.

Sister Saint-Hippolyte's first term of office at the head of the community began in 1751 under auspicious circumstances. The sisters were in better health and no death had been recorded for nearly two years, in contrast to 19 deaths during the preceding four years. Peace and harmony reigned in the community, and both French and Canadian religious and civil authorities supported the order in many ways. Sister Saint-Hippolyte's first six years as superior were not marked by any major events, given the renewal of hostilities between France and Great Britain in America. When she resumed direction of the order in 1763 following Sister Marie-Angélique Lefebvre* Angers, *dite* Saint-Simon, the treaty of Paris had been signed. Apparently to demonstrate its determination to continue its work in spite of the permanent change in régime, the community immediately laid the foundations for a new mission, at Saint-François-de-la-Rivière-du-Sud (Saint-François-de-Montmagny). The endeavour only revealed the community's precarious financial position, but the following year the parishioners of Saint-François and their priest, Pierre-Laurent Bédard, gave the sisters a convent built for them and their boarders.

Marguerite Bourgeoys*'s work was in fact preserved. While Sister Saint-Hippolyte attended to settling the community's business in France in accordance with the agreements between the French and British crowns and resigned herself to selling some land to improve the community's financial position, the sisters continued to educate young girls in Montreal and in the nearby missions of Pointe-aux-Trembles, Lachine, Saint-Laurent, Boucherville, La Prairie, and Lac-des-Deux-Montagnes (Oka). In the Quebec region the nuns served in the missions at Champlain, Sainte-Famille, Île d'Orléans, and Pointe-aux-Trembles (Neuville). They had not yet resumed the mission in Lower Town, Quebec; the mission at Château-Richer, founded by Marguerite Bourgeoys herself in 1689, would never be restored. As for Louisbourg, Île Royale (Cape Breton Island), its mission had carried on at La Rochelle, France, after the missionaries were deported in 1758, but it came to an end with the deaths of the last two sisters, Marie-Marguerite-Daniel Arnaud*, *dite* Saint-Arsène, in 1764, and Marie Robichaud, *dite* Saint-Vincent-de-Paul, in 1766.

By 1766, when Sister Saint-Hippolyte's second term of office as superior came to an end and she was replaced by Marie-Josèphe MAUGUE-GARREAU, *dite* de l'Assomption, the community had survived the transitional period that every Canadian order went through after the conquest, a significant achievement. The Congregation of Notre-Dame no longer had reason to doubt its future.

ANDRÉE DÉSILETS

ACND, Fichier général; Personnel, III; Registre général. ANQ-M, État civil, Catholiques, Sainte-Anne (Varennes), 11 févr. 1702. Lemire-Marsolais et Lambert, *Hist. de la CND de Montréal*, IV, V. M. Trudel, *L'Église canadienne*, II, 333–49.

PITCHY. *See* PEACHEY

PORLIER, PIERRE-ANTOINE, priest; b. 19 May 1725 in Montreal (Que.), son of Claude-Cyprien-Jacques Porlier, a merchant, and Angélique Cuillerier; d. 15 Aug. 1789 at Saint-Ours (Que.).

Pierre-Antoine Porlier did his classical studies at the Petit Séminaire in Quebec and was ordained priest on 8 June 1748. Entrusted that year with the parish of Sainte-Geneviève-de-Batiscan, in 1749 he became the first resident parish priest of Sainte-Anne-de-la-Pocatière (La Pocatière), a charge he held until 1778.

When he succeeded Charles Lefebvre Duchouquet, the priest ministering to Sainte-Anne-de-la-Pocatière, Abbé Porlier seemed rather lost but enthusiastic, and above all determined to organize this parish in his own way. Noticing that certain parishioners had become somewhat casual with regard to the respect due holy places, he appealed to Intendant BIGOT, who published an ordinance on 12 April 1749 enjoining "the habitants and young men of La Pocatière not to indulge in any more quarrels outside the church . . . or to commit any irreverent acts on feast-days." Abbé Porlier was an active priest, enjoying the esteem and confidence of his colleagues and generally of Bishop BRIAND. Nevertheless his stay at Sainte-Anne-de-la-Pocatière was marked by many disputes. His correspondence reveals differences of opinion with his bishop, particularly over the amount of money the parish priest himself collected. On several occasions the bishop accused Porlier of being too demanding; in 1762 he wrote: "I have had the examples of several parish priests who [manage to] subsist and whose incomes are not as large as yours. Everyone, even the most comfortable, eats very simply at the present time. Is it fitting for priests to be unwilling to feel in any way the effects of the public distress?" In 1771 Briand made a fresh attempt and recommended that Porlier practise Christian mortification.

Abbé Porlier supported his parishioners at the time of the conquest and, as a loyalist, took a firm position against the American incursion of 1775–76 [*see* Richard MONTGOMERY]. His relations with Bishop Briand seem to have been at their best during the latter period. He kept up a copious correspondence and took pains to describe to Briand his parishioners' behaviour during the invasion in his "Mémoire d'observations sur la conduite des habitans des deux paroisses de Ste. Anne et de St. Roch au sujet de l'invasion des Bostonois rebels et de l'exécution des ordres de son excellence monsr. de Carleton pour les repousser de la pointe Levi sous les ordres de mr. de Beaujeu." Pursuing the goal of repelling the invaders he urged his parishioners to enlist in the troops recruited by the seigneur of Île aux Grues, Louis Liénard* de Beaujeu de Villemomble. But the acceptance of republican principles by a number of his parishioners [*see* Clément Gosselin*] and the massacre of Liénard's troops were painful experiences that profoundly touched him.

Abbé Porlier had to cope with many other difficulties in his 29 years as parish priest of Sainte-Anne-de-la-Pocatière. On 13 Oct. 1766 a careless workman set some wood chips alight, and the resulting fire got out of control, destroying the parish church. The walls remained standing, however, and thanks to a collection in the surrounding parishes and to some ten carpenters who volunteered their services, the church was rebuilt before the severe winter cold set in. Depressed by the disaster, Abbé Porlier is believed to have asked for a new parish charge at that time.

Drawn to the parish of Varennes, and alleging ill health, Pierre-Antoine Porlier made repeated requests for a change in the 1760s. Bishop Briand offered him a post as missionary to the Tamaroas, and then a parish in Quebec; but each time the parish priest's unreasonable demands exceeded his bishop's offers. Having at last become parish priest at Saint-Ours in 1778, replacing Abbé François Cherrier*, Porlier probably thought he would now have a more peaceful existence. But his early years at Saint-Ours were marked by many quarrels with the parish council and some of his parishioners. Everything seemed to be a source of misunderstanding: the improvement of church premises, the sale of pews, the allotment of expenses, the purchase of materials, the building of a strong-box, and so on. The smallest purchase engendered controversy, and many times the parish priest called upon Bishop Briand and the vicar general, Étienne MONTGOLFIER, to settle the dispute. Under this stress, Porlier fell ill in February 1781. His repeated requests for a curate were granted in October 1787, when Abbé Jean-Baptiste Boucher-Belleville*, who would succeed him as parish priest at his death, came to assist him.

Pierre-Antoine Porlier died at Saint-Ours on 15 Aug. 1789 and was buried two days later. Documentary sources give no indication of the cause of his death.

PIERRE MATTEAU

Archives du collège de Sainte-Anne-de-la-Pocatière (La Pocatière, Qué.), CAC 1038, nos.726.3, 726.5. Allaire, *Dictionnaire*, I, 442. Caron, "Inv. de la corr. de Mgr Briand," ANQ *Rapport*, 1929–30, 51, 87. Azarie Couillard-Després, *Histoire de la seigneurie de Saint-Ours* (2v., Montréal, 1915–17), II, 118–61. N.-E. Dionne, *Sainte-Anne de la Pocatière, 1672–1900* (Lévis, 1900). Gérard Ouellet, *Histoire de Sainte-Anne-de-la-Pocatière, 1672–1972* (La Pocatière, Qué., 1973). [P.-F.-X.-O.-M.-A.] Paradis, *Notes historiques sur la paroisse et les curés de Sainte-Anne de la Pocatière depuis les premiers établissements* (Sainte-Anne-de-la-Pocatière, 1869). N.-E. Dionne, "L'invasion de 1775–76," *BRH*, VI (1900), 132–33.

POTIER (Pottier, Pottié, or Pothier), PIERRE-PHILIPPE, Jesuit, priest, and missionary; baptized 22 April 1708 at Blandain (province of Hainaut, Belgium), son of Jacques Potier and Marie Duchatelet; d. 16 July 1781 at Notre-Dame-de-l'Assomption (Windsor, Ont.).

From 1721 to 1727 Pierre-Philippe Potier attended the Jesuit college in Tournai (Belgium) and from 1727 to 1729 the college in Douai, France. On 30 Sept. 1729 he entered the noviciate in Tournai. After studying the humanities for a year in Lille, France (1731–32), he taught for six years at the Jesuit college in Béthune. A student at the theological college in Douai from 1738 to 1742, he went to Armentières for his tertianship, and pronounced his final vows at Tournai on 2 Feb. 1743.

On 18 June 1743 Potier sailed from La Rochelle on the king's ship *Rubis* and reached Quebec on 1 October. He spent eight months at the mission of Lorette learning the Huron language. On 26 June 1744 he left Quebec for his final destination, the Huron mission at the mouth of the Detroit River, which he reached on 25 September. The superior was Father Armand de La Richardie*, who had held the position since 1728. Two years later illness forced La Richardie to leave and Potier took charge. The mission, which was located on Bois Blanc Island (Ont.), consisted of 33 Huron lodges divided into two settlements – Petit Village and Grand Village. Potier drew up a list noting the names of the heads of the lodges and the number of occupants in each. He made a record of all individuals baptized since 1728 and his numerous notebooks also include some of the mission's account-books as well as other information.

When the mission was destroyed in May 1747 by a war party from the Huron band of Nicolas [Orontony*], La Richardie came back for a short period and decided to re-establish it at La Pointe de Montréal (now part of Windsor). From 1755 until 1759 Potier was aided by Father Jean-Baptiste de Salleneuve. As was customary, one of the missionaries went with the Huron bands to their winter quarters, usually at Sandoské (Sandusky, Ohio) on the southwest shore of Lake Erie.

During the years following the conquest, Potier also took responsibility for the French settlers on the left bank of the Detroit River. In 1767 the parish of Notre-Dame-de-l'Assomption was founded, and from that year until his death in 1781 he carried on his ministry to the Hurons and French as priest of this parish, the oldest in Ontario. Despite his isolation and the circumstances in which he lived, Potier pursued intellectual interests energetically. He devoted much time to reading and recorded long passages of various works in personal notebooks, of which about half have been preserved. The 22 books in the archives of the Quebec seminary contain lecture notes; various papers in Latin or French on theology, philosophy, the sciences, the history of religion, and the church councils; devotional works, noviciate exercises, and a dictionary. The Jesuit archives in Saint-Jérôme holds various Potier manuscripts. Five pertain to the Huron language: "Radices linguae huronicae," "Elementa grammaticae huronicae," "Sermons en langue huronne," "Extraits de l'Évangile," and "De religione." Included with them are fragments on individuals, on Huron lodges and names, and some geographical information. Three manuscripts deal with other matters: one is an elaborate *précis* of *Le spectacle de la nature* by Noël-Antoine Pluche; another deals with mission affairs (the register of baptisms, marriages, and burials, and account-books); and the third groups personal notes under the title of "Gazettes" and includes travel itineraries, letters sent and received, and chronologies. Two other manuscripts are preserved in the Montreal city library: "Façons de parler proverbiales, triviales, figurées, &c des Canadiens au XVIIIe siècle" and "Vocabulaire huron-français."

The notes assembled by Potier in "Façons de parler proverbiales" constitute the only dictionary of the language spoken in New France on the eve of the conquest. From 1743 to 1758 he had recorded about a thousand words and expressions picked up in conversations; the majority relate to French speech, but there are also a fair number of Indian words and expressions. Because of its early date and its abundant information, this document has proven of inestimable value for the study of the history of language in Quebec.

ROBERT TOUPIN

[P.-P. Potier], "Façons de parler proverbiales, triviales, figurées, etc. des Canadiens au XVIIIe siècle," *Bull. du parler français au Canada* (Québec), III (1904–5), 213–20, 252–55, 291–93; IV (1905–6), 29–30, 63–65, 103–4, 146–49, 224–26, 264–67; "Huron manuscripts from Rev. Pierre Potier's collection," PAO *Report*, 1918–19; "Selections from the diary and gazette of Father Pierre Potier, S.J. (1708–1781)," ed. E. R. Ott, *Mid-America* (Chicago), 18 (1936), 199–207, 260–65.

Archives de l'État (Tournai, Belgique), État civil, Blandain, 22 avril 1708. ASJCF, MSS Potier. ASQ, MSS, 82–103. Bibliothèque de la ville de Montréal, Salle Gagnon, père Potier. *JR* (Thwaites), LXIX, 240–76; LXX, 20–70. Marcel Juneau, *Problèmes de lexicologie québécoise; prolégomènes à un trésor de la langue française au Québec* (Québec, 1977). E. J. Lajeunesse, *Outline history of Assumption parish* (n.p., n.d.). George Paré, *The Catholic Church in Detroit, 1701–1888* (Detroit, 1951). Marcel Juneau, "Un pionnier de la lexicologie québécoise: le père Pierre-Philippe Potier, S.J.," *Langue et linguistique* (Québec), 1 (1975), 51–68.

POTOT DE MONTBEILLARD, FIACRE-FRANÇOIS, artillery officer; b. 23 Dec. 1723 at Semur-en-Auxois, France, son of François-Augustin Potot de Montbeillard and Claude d'Orbigny; m. 1763 Marie-Claude Carlet de La Rozière; d. 31 Dec. 1778 at Semur-en-Auxois.

Fiacre-François Potot de Montbeillard entered the French army in 1741 and in 1756 attained the rank of second captain in the Corps Royal d'Artillerie et de Génie. In 1757 the court of Versailles approved a recommendation of the governor of New France, RIGAUD de Vaudreuil, that the artillery element in the colonial regular troops be increased from one company to two. To assist in this expansion a draft of six officers and 20 men of the regular artillery was sent to Canada on detachment. Montbeillard was the senior officer of this group, which reached Canada in the summer of 1757. He became commander of the second company of artillery. The overall commander of the artillery was Captain François-Marc-Antoine LE MERCIER, an officer of limited professional qualifications who had been in the country for many years and whom Montcalm*, commanding the regular forces in Canada, regarded as one of the colony's leading corruptionists.

Montbeillard at once became involved in the rivalries and tensions which in contemporary Canada divided Frenchman from Canadian, professional soldier from irregular, and Montcalm from Vaudreuil. He had been highly recommended to Montcalm, who moreover clearly saw in him an officer of high professional attainments and competence. Montcalm used him as an assistant and adviser in planning the defence of Quebec. Vaudreuil doubtless disliked this association. As a regular officer attached to the colonial regular troops, which were under Vaudreuil's control, Montbeillard's position was equivocal. In 1758 the governor attempted to subordinate Montbeillard to the other battery commander, Louis-Thomas JACAU de Fiedmont, who, Montbeillard claimed, was junior to him. Montcalm strongly supported Montbeillard and the difficulty seems to have been resolved without damage to Montbeillard's position. Early in 1759 he was decorated with the cross of the order of Saint-Louis. That year greatly improved his status. In August, while James Wolfe* was beleaguering Quebec, news came of the British capture of Fort Niagara (near Youngstown, N.Y.), and LÉVIS was sent west with a large detachment from Montcalm's force at Quebec to provide against attack from that direction. With him went Le Mercier, evidently in the capacity of a staff officer, to the great satisfaction of Montcalm. From this moment until the capitulation in the following year, Montbeillard is spoken of, and functions as, the artillery commander both in the Quebec area and in the colony at large.

Montbeillard commanded the French artillery (five or six guns) in the battle of the Plains of Abraham. At this time he was closely associated with Montcalm and was keeping the general's journal. To him we owe the only first-hand record of the battlefield appreciation that led Montcalm to make his fatally premature attack upon Wolfe's army: "If we give him [the enemy] time to establish himself, we shall never be able to attack him with the sort of troops we have." When the attack was delivered Montbeillard was with his artillery detachment on the French left. He moved it forward cautiously, and his prudent handling is reflected in the fact that, in spite of the total rout of the French infantry, only two of his guns were lost. In the spring of 1760 he directed the bombardment during the French siege of Quebec, and later in the season he was involved in the unsuccessful attempt to check or at least delay James MURRAY's advance up the St Lawrence against Montreal. He was a member of the council of war which on 6 Sept. 1760 advised Vaudreuil to negotiate for a capitulation. That autumn he returned to France in the same ship as Lévis.

Going back to duty with the Corps Royal d'Artillerie, Montbeillard was awarded in 1761 a pension of 400 *livres* for his command of the artillery in Canada. In 1766 he was promoted *chef de brigade* by brevet (confirmed 1767), and in 1769 he attained his final rank of lieutenant-colonel. He had evidently been appointed in 1761 (presumably as an inspector) to the *manufacture royale* at Charleville (Charleville-Mézières). How long he remained there is uncertain, but it was apparently a lady of Charleville whom he married in 1763. In 1779, shortly after his death, pensions payable from the royal treasury were awarded to her and to their two children, Jean and Louise.

C. P. STACEY

AMA, SHA, A^1, 3498–99; Y^d (dossier Montbeillard). AN, Col., B, 105, ff.50–52; 109, ff.30–33, 125; F^3, 16, ff.229–34; Marine, C^7, 216 (dossier Montbeillard).

PAC, MG 18, K10, 2. *Coll. des manuscrits de Lévis* (Casgrain), I, 192, 274; II, 386; III, 110; IV, 43, 212; VI, 44–45, 66–67, 107, 188, 227; VII, 243, 307; VIII, 115; X, 107, 172, 175; XI, 192, 240, 250. Æ. Fauteux, *Les chevaliers de Saint-Louis*, 171. Thomas Chapais, *Le marquis de Montcalm (1712–1759)* (Québec, 1911), 572–75. Kennett, *French armies in Seven Years' War*. Stacey, *Quebec, 1759*.

POULOUS (Powless). *See* SAHONWAGY

PREISSAC DE BONNEAU, LOUIS DE, officer in the French regular troops; b. 12 Dec. 1724 at Maravat (dept of Gers), France, son of Paul de Preissac, seigneur of Cadeilhan, Maravat, and Touron, and Anne de Dupré; d. some time after 1789.

Louis de Preissac de Bonneau was descended from an old family of Guyenne; like his brothers he chose a military career. In 1743 he was an ensign in the Régiment de Guyenne. He was promoted lieutenant in 1744 and captain ten years later. During the Seven Years' War four Preissac brothers came to fight in New France: Louis and his brother Paul arrived with the Régiment de Guyenne in 1755, Lambert and Jean-Gérard with the Régiment de Berry in 1757.

From 1755 to 1757 Louis de Preissac de Bonneau must have accompanied his regiment on the military campaigns under Dieskau* and later Montcalm* in the Lake Champlain region. During the winter of 1757–58 he was in Quebec, where he associated with the best society and spent his time gambling. On 6 July the following summer, two days before the battle of Carillon (Ticonderoga, N.Y.), he was taken prisoner by the British in a skirmish at the portage between Lake Champlain and Lac Saint-Sacrement (Lake George). Some days later the adjutant Michel-Jean-Hugues PÉAN wrote to LÉVIS: "I greatly miss the officers whom you have lost. My wife [Angélique RENAUD d'Avène Des Méloizes] will weep for her friend Bonneau." Captain Preissac de Bonneau, however, was permitted by Major-General James ABERCROMBY to go to Montreal to settle personal affairs, on condition that he subsequently give himself up at New York. At the end of 1759 he was exchanged, and on 28 April 1760 he fought in the battle of Sainte-Foy, in which MURRAY's army met defeat. The British artillery was captured and 22 officers, including a colonel, were taken prisoner. Bonneau noted: "We pursued them to the gates of the city; had our army not been exhausted, we should have entered the city with the English." During the combat his brother, Captain Jean-Gérard de Preissac, was seriously wounded and on 9 May died at the Hôpital Général.

Preissac de Bonneau took part in the final operations around Quebec in May 1760 and retreated with the army to Montreal. As he was known to the senior British officers, Lévis chose him to go to New York to negotiate an exchange of prisoners in the summer of 1760. His mission accomplished, he returned to France on 8 March 1761. A fortnight later he was made a knight of the order of Saint-Louis and on 13 May was reimbursed 1,898 *livres* for expenses incurred on his mission to New York. In 1763 he was taken into the Régiment du Dauphin and he transferred to the Régiment du Perche in 1775. At his retirement in 1782 he was senior captain-commandant of the Régiment du Perche and he received a pension of 1,200 *livres*. He was still living in 1789.

ÉTIENNE TAILLEMITE

AMA, SHA, X[b], 5. AN, Col., E, 39 (dossier Bonneau). BN, MSS, Fr., Chérin, 162–3299. *Coll. de manuscrits relatifs à la N.-F.*, IV, 307–8. *Coll. des manuscrits de Lévis* (Casgrain), I, 289; II, 344–45, 351; IV, 233–36, 239, 245–47, 250–54; V, 283; VI, 111; VII, 393; X, 86; XI, 164. Ægidius Fauteux, "Les quatre frères Preissac," *BRH*, XXXVIII (1932), 136–48. "Les officiers du régiment de Guyenne," *BRH*, LI (1945), 190.

PRESSART, COLOMBAN-SÉBASTIEN, priest, superior, and vicar general; b. 30 Sept. 1723 at Le Faouët (dept of Morbihan), France, son of François Pressart, a merchant, and Angélique Lorans; d. 27 Oct. 1777 in Quebec.

Colomban-Sébastien Pressart studied at the diocesan college in Quimper and received the tonsure there; on 23 Dec. 1747, minor orders and the priesthood were conferred upon him in Paris. He arrived in Canada during the summer of 1748 with Christophe de Lalane, a director of the Séminaire des Missions Étrangères who had been sent temporarily to Quebec as superior. Soon a member of the council of the seminary, Pressart was appointed a director of the Petit Séminaire (1748–50) and then of the Grand Séminaire (1750–52). He served as bursar from 1752 to 1756, assisted by Joseph-André-Mathurin JACRAU. When the superior, François SORBIER de Villars, had to return to France to attend to the seminary's affairs, the directors in Paris appointed Pressart to replace him on 26 April 1756, and this appointment was renewed in 1759. As a consequence he was in charge of the seminary during the painful years of the war and the siege of Quebec. In the summer of 1759, before the bombardment began, Abbé Pressart, Abbé Henri-François Gravé* de La Rive, and some pupils from the upper forms took refuge with the Sulpicians in Montreal. There Pressart taught theology. He returned to Quebec the following summer.

In 1762 his appointment as superior came to an end and Urbain BOIRET replaced him. Since there were few students in theology, Pressart apparently resumed the office of bursar, again with the assistance of Jacrau, who had, however, become an invalid. The work of this period of rebuilding was immense and difficult, at the seminary and the farms and mills of its seigneuries. When the Petit Séminaire reopened in 1765, it had to provide classrooms for day pupils because the Jesuits had had to give up all hope of resuming their teaching of classical studies. The institution's new orientation was approved by the seminary in Paris, which retained some authority over the activities of the seminary in Quebec, although Governor MURRAY was no longer willing to accept foreign interference. Pressart, who from 1768 till his death bore the title of "first assistant" to the superior, resigned the office of bursar on 1 June 1770 to become head of the Grand Séminaire until 1772. While he held these different offices and even afterwards, he evidently continued to teach; he was referred to as "a teacher of theology at the Séminaire de Québec" in the letters issued by Bishop BRIAND on 18 Oct. 1774, appointing him vicar general. But in this era people's health gave out early, and a man was old at 60. During the siege of Quebec by the Americans (December 1775 – May 1776), Pressart suffered "an attack of apoplexy and paralysis," which left him very weak. As soon as the siege was lifted, he obtained a room at the Hôpital Général. He stayed there several times for lengthy periods because of intermittent attacks of what was probably angina pectoris. He died on the morning of 27 Oct. 1777.

Pressart may have had some knowledge of the law. In any event he helped Jacrau write a summary of the custom of Paris, which Governor Guy Carleton* had requested of the priests of the Séminaire de Québec in 1768. It served as a basis for one of five abstracts of laws published in London in 1772 and 1773 and known collectively in Canada as the "Extrait des Messieurs." Written entirely in French, each bore a long English title. Francis Maseres*, a former attorney general of the province who supervised the publication of the abstracts, seems to have appreciated the contribution made by the priests of the seminary: in his correspondence he expressed his admiration for the "learned Mr Jacrau . . . and the very intelligent Mr Pressart. . . ."

HONORIUS PROVOST

AHGQ, Communauté, Journal, II. ASQ, Lettres, M, 160; P, 120; R, 15; MSS, 12, ff.16, 28, 36, 38; Séminaire, 3, nos.106–17. *Le séminaire de Québec* (Provost), 450. Philéas Gagnon, *Essai de bibliographie canadienne . . .* (2v., Québec et Montréal, 1895–1913), I, 2–3. A.-H. Gosselin, *L'Église du Canada après la conquête*, I. O'Reilly, *Mgr de Saint-Vallier et l'Hôpital Général*. M. Trudel, *L'Église canadienne*, II. Albert David, "Les spiritains dans l'Amérique septentrionale au XVIIIe siècle," *BRH*, XXXV (1929), 318. Leland, "François-Joseph Cugnet," *Revue de l'université Laval*, XVII, 448–56, 820–34. P.-G. Roy, "L'Extrait des Messieurs," *BRH*, III (1897), 78.

PREVOST DE LA CROIX, JACQUES, colonial administrator; b. 6 May 1715 at Brest, France; d. 9 Oct. 1791 in France.

Jacques Prevost de La Croix's grandfather, Robert Prevost, a wealthy Parisian banker, had in 1705 secured hereditary nobility for the family by purchasing the office of king's secretary. His father, Philippe, had moved to Brest and acquired the offices of director of supply and treasurer of fortifications for Brittany. In 1714 Philippe, referred to as *écuyer*, married Marie-Gabrielle-Élisabeth L'Estobec de Langristain, a nobleman's daughter. One of Jacques's uncles became bank agent and king's counsellor. His own career was marked by determined effort to advance himself and enhance his family's wealth and status.

Like three of his four brothers, Jacques entered the naval commissariat because Brest was a major seaport and he was related to an important naval family, the Le Febvre de Grivys. Beginning his Marine career in 1729, he was promoted scrivener in 1732. In 1735 he was sent to Louisbourg, Île Royale (Cape Breton Island) as principal scrivener; this post in the commissariat involved supervision of one area of the intendant's jurisdiction and was often the stepping-stone to the higher grade of commissary. Prevost did not remain in the colony long since he gained the confidence of administrators who sent him to Versailles in 1737 to report on the shortage of supplies. Falling ill after his return, he left for France again in 1738 and did not come back until François BIGOT was appointed financial commissary in 1739. Prevost was then assigned commissariat duties for the colonial regular troops and for maritime conscription.

Prevost became Bigot's protégé and the careers of the two men were closely linked in the 1740s and 1750s. Bigot trained Prevost in colonial administration, promoted his career, and defended him when necessary. During Bigot's absence from Louisbourg in 1742, Prevost replaced him, but in such a manner that he provoked Commandant Duquesnel [Le Prevost*] to complain to France about the young man's pretensions. During the 1745 siege Prevost was wounded and, after the capitulation, he returned to Rochefort where he worked on accounts with Antoine Sabatier*. When Bigot was appointed intendant of the fleet of the Duc d'Anville [La Rochefoucauld*], Prevost was promoted naval commissary in 1746 to serve under him. A series of misfortunes then befell Prevost. Two ships on which he sailed were captured by the British, and his belongings were lost in another vessel sunk off Sable Island, Nova Scotia. In 1747 he was appointed to replace the controller at Quebec, Jean-Victor VARIN de La Marre, but his ship was forced back into port by the British. After Louisbourg was returned to France by the treaty of Aix-la-Chapelle in 1748, Prevost was appointed financial commissary on 1 Jan. 1749, following Bigot's solicitation. Together with Bigot, who was now intendant of New France, Prevost re-established the civil administration at Louisbourg later that year.

Prevost became the patron of the men he placed in administrative positions at Louisbourg between 1749 and 1755, just as he himself was a client of François Bigot and of Pierre-Arnaud de Laporte, the powerful chief clerk of the Marine colonial bureau. His family was his first concern and the core of his support. By his marriage to Marguerite-Thérèse Carrerot on 14 Feb. 1745, Prevost became allied not only to her prominent merchant-administrative family, but to the Delorts as well [*see* Guillaume Delort*]. His wife's father, André Carrerot*, was promoted keeper of the seals for the Conseil Supérieur and principal scrivener shortly before his death in 1749. Two Delorts obtained seats on the Conseil Supérieur and another was employed by Prevost in the civil administration. In 1750 Prevost brought his younger brother, Pierre-François, from France to serve as scrivener and, after many years of requests, secured a promotion for him. Two of Prevost's sons and a Carrerot were enrolled in the colonial regular troops, one of them even before the age of four.

During Prevost's years at Louisbourg the civil administration was expanded, and Michel LE COURTOIS de Surlaville maintained that Prevost employed many more clerks than he could occupy. Jean LABORDE, the agent of the treasurers general of the Marine at Louisbourg, was Prevost's closest ally and benefited from the association by amassing offices and government contracts, as did his in-laws, the Morin, Daccarrette, and Milly families. Laborde's son was hired by Prevost as an assistant clerk, and in 1749 Jean-Baptiste MORIN de Fonfay, who had been Prevost's secretary, became royal notary and clerk of the Conseil Supérieur. King's Lieutenant Charles-Joseph d'Ailleboust* and Major Robert Tarride* Duhaget were identified as among several military officers who became the commissary's "creatures" in return for the special favours he dispensed.

Opposition to Prevost's empire building, and to his personal vindictiveness, formed quickly. Pierre-Jérôme Lartigue, the king's storekeeper, and Séguin, the royal controller, opposed Prevost because of irregularities they observed in his administrative practices. In 1749 Séguin's criticism led Bigot to intercede on Prevost's behalf and ask the minister to recall the controller. The lieutenant-general of the Admiralty Court, Laurent de Domingué Meyracq, also opposed Prevost, as did Antoine LE POUPET de La Boularderie. In 1750 La Boularderie requested permission to go to Versailles with Lartigue to report on the commissary's alleged misconduct; however, it was Séguin who is known to have left for France in 1751, because of ill health, and who reported to Versailles. When he returned in 1752 he carried with him instructions aimed at tightening administrative procedures to ensure financial accountability.

The arrival in 1751 of a new governor, Jean-Louis de RAYMOND, strengthened the dissident elements and caused an irrevocable split in the administration. From totally different backgrounds, Raymond and Prevost were equally headstrong and stubborn. Each came to detest the other to such a degree that personality dominated over policy for two years. Their quarrel became so intense that at one point Raymond contemplated removing Prevost from his position and replacing him with Séguin. For his part Prevost carried on a concerted campaign to remove Lartigue [*see* Jean-Baptiste Morin de Fonfay] and to discredit Meyracq by appointing judicial subdelegates for the sole purpose of reporting on the activities of the Admiralty Court in the outports. Personal animosities reached such a height that the priest Pierre Maillard* was moved later to comment to the new governor, Drucour [Boschenry*] on the "sad things [that] had passed" at Louisbourg.

Material interests were the root of this confrontation among personalities. A report prepared by Surlaville and Raymond revealed the variety of ways in which Prevost attempted to misappropriate or defraud the crown of 32,982 *livres* on the accounts for 1752. Funds were requested for unfilled administrative posts, the government was overcharged for services rendered, and supplied were purchased above the market value. Contracts were awarded to favourites such as Jean Laborde, Nicolas LARCHER, and the Rodrigue brothers, and sometimes they were rigged so that the supplier made unusually high profits. Prevost departed from standard procedure by dispensing with the controller in many financial transactions where his presence was required by regulation. He awarded two contracts for the fortifications to Claude-Audet Coeuret, an associate of the Rodrigue brothers, but the second was vetoed by France because the prices were so exorbitant.

Prevost was also at least aware of the attempt by Bigot and the Grande Société to control the supply of New France for their own profit [*see* Michel-Jean-Hugues PÉAN]. When one of the ships used by Bigot, the *Renommée* of Bordeaux, arrived at Louisbourg with supplies for the administration, Lartigue and Séguin found the cargo short. On reporting to Prevost, Lartigue discovered that the ship captain had preceded him; Prevost berated Lartigue for weighing the flour incorrectly and said he would handle the matter personally. Further, Surlaville and Raymond charged that 20,000 *livres* requested from the crown for the transport of Acadian refugees in 1752 had been diverted by Prevost to finance a ship sent to the British colonies to buy beef for Bigot.

Complaints lodged against Prevost were neutralized through the counter-offensive he waged in dispatch after dispatch and through the protection afforded him by Pierre-Arnaud de Laporte. In utter frustration Raymond resigned the governorship in 1753, thereby strengthening Prevost's grip on the administration. One more dissident voice was silenced the following year when Séguin became paralysed and was forced to return to France. Prevost removed Lartigue from his position as storekeeper and replaced him with Jean-Baptiste Morin de Fonfay, despite initial opposition from France due to soaring supply costs and criticism of Morin's integrity.

Prevost was the undisputed master of the Louisbourg administration after 1753. Not only did Laborde's government contracts grow, but his son-in-law Michel Daccarrette* and his stepson François Milly also became suppliers to the administration. Expenditures for the colony and the fortifications rose to the highest ever, although they were partially attributable to the preparations for war and to the several thousand Acadians who fled Nova Scotia and sought refuge in French territory in the early 1750s [*see* Jean-Louis LE LOUTRE].

When Governor Drucour arrived in 1754 Prevost worked assiduously to cultivate him, and the governor came to rely heavily on his advice. Within a few months Prevost had secured Drucour's agreement to the appointment to the Conseil Supérieur of four assistant councillors whom he had personally chosen. In 1755 when battalions of the French army were sent to the colonies, Prevost was appointed acting war commissary until the arrival of La Grive Des Assises, the regular quartermaster, the following year. The rapid influx of soldiers overburdened the town's facilities and led the French army officers, unaccustomed to the rigours of colonial North America, to complain about Prevost's manner of billeting and according supplies. Prevost also quarrelled with La Grive as he had with Séguin, but once again Bigot interceded, instructing the quartermaster to obey Prevost's orders as though they came from the intendant. In 1757 Prevost was promoted commissary general, the rank below intendant, with a raise in salary.

Prevost demanded absolute loyalty from his subordinates, and to his enemies he showed no quarter. One officer went so far as to accuse him in 1754 of having engineered the escape from prison of a man who had attempted to kill La Boularderie, his bitter opponent. Yet Prevost worked earnestly to resettle displaced Acadians and won praise from several quarters, notably from Abbé de L'Isle-Dieu, who lauded him to Bishop Pontbriand [Dubreil*] and felt that he would have been intendant if Bigot had been removed. Prevost had opposed Raymond's foolhardy settlement schemes and there appears to be little substance in the assertion made by James JOHNSTONE, known as the Chevalier de Johnstone, a partisan of Raymond, that Prevost retarded the economic development of Île Royale.

Little precise information is available concerning Prevost's personal affairs or any profits he may have made while in North America apart from Raymond's appraisal that Prevost's estimates for the 1753 colonial accounts were inflated by at least 33,000 *livres*. Thomas PICHON did note however that both Prevost and the engineer Louis Franquet* were "devilishly fond of money," and that while work on Louisbourg's fortifications progressed slowly in the 1750s, "some people wish the work to last a long time." Before 1745 Prevost was mentioned only as commercial agent for André Carrerot. His meagre investment of 500 *livres* in privateers in 1744 makes his later claim that he left 50,000 *livres* in France when he returned to the colony in 1749 appear unlikely, although he may have inherited money. His household staff in the 1750s numbered about ten and he acquired two houses and a piece of land on Île Royale. He rented his properties to the crown for 1,500 *livres* annually, and the costly addition to his house undertaken in 1754–55 was made at government expense. Prevost apparently loved gambling for he was admonished by the minister of Marine in 1758 for allowing games in his house where sums as large as 20,000 *livres* were lost. Jean Laborde claimed in 1763 that he had loaned the commissary 10,000 *livres* at Louisbourg, but after Prevost returned to France he considered buying land valued at 85,000 *livres*, although he said he intended to borrow for this purchase.

Prevost's role during the 1758 siege of Louisbourg was limited but critical. He consistently advocated that the French fleet remain in the harbour to defend the fortress and that the ships not be abandoned to augment the garrison. At a meeting of Drucour's war council on 26 June, he persuaded the military officers to accept Jeffery AMHERST's stringent terms of unconditional surrender because the colonists had suffered at the hands of the British long enough. Yet even in this instance Prevost's conduct was questioned. Louis-Antoine de Bougainville* maintained that Prevost, like Bigot during the 1745 siege, had advocated capitulation for pecuniary reasons. As the king's stores were situated behind one of the points of British attack, Prevost had transported the merchandise to safer locations. When the inventory of French goods was prepared, after the surrender, Bougainville claimed that Prevost failed to mention the items placed elsewhere. This booty fell to his profit and that of Louisbourg's residents.

After the capitulation Prevost returned to France to await reassignment. With the financial commissary from Rochefort, he was ordered to La Rochelle late in 1760 to investigate the large deficit owed by Laborde on his accounts from Louisbourg. The debt was still unresolved in March 1762 when Prevost officially resigned with a pension of 3,000 *livres*. The following year Laborde was imprisoned in the Bastille where he accused Prevost of having stolen the strong-box in which army funds had been stored. Already suspicious of Prevost for reasons which are not entirely clear, the Duc de Choiseul ordered his arrest on 28 April 1763.

Prevost proved his innocence and convinced the Paris lieutenant-general of police, Antoine de Sartine, who asked Choiseul to release him. Prevost was freed on 14 June but, still under suspicion, he was not permitted to leave Paris until the following April. Choiseul considered him to have been negligent at Louisbourg and ordered that he never again be employed in the Marine department. But Sartine became a new protector who in 1766 persuaded Choiseul's successor, the Duc de Praslin, to exonerate Prevost officially from any involvement in the Laborde affair.

Considering Prevost's questionable conduct in Île Royale, and his subsequent tribulations, his rise to prominence during the second half of his career was remarkable, although partially attributable to Sartine, who became minister of Marine in 1774, and to his successor, Castries. Returning to the Marine service as assistant in the Rochefort archives in 1767, the following year Prevost was sent to Corsica as financial commissary. In 1773 the *parlement* of Paris upheld his family's nobility, he became financial commissary at Lorient, and he was named knight of the order of Saint-Louis with a pension of 2,000 *livres*. Three years later he achieved his life's ambition when Sartine appointed him intendant at Toulon. After serving for five years, Prevost retired with a pension of 16,000 *livres*. The 52 years he had given to France's naval and colonial service were ultimately rewarded in 1782 when he was appointed king's councillor.

Jacques Prevost was motivated by an intense desire to give respectability to the noble status acquired by his grandfather. Despite having spent nearly two decades in Île Royale, he remained a Frenchman imbued with the values of his homeland. His colonial service was a brief interlude in a career dedicated to social ascendancy through the acquisition of wealth, a naval intendancy, land in France, and military commissions for his sons. Yet his ambition and petty vindictiveness made him abhorrent to many such as Johnstone, whose published memoirs so defamed Prevost that most historical comment about the man has been negative.

The French revolution witnessed an end to the aspirations Prevost entertained for himself and his family. His eldest son, Jacques-Marie-André, an army officer, was killed in battle in 1783. Prevost died in 1791 and his second son, naval captain Charles-Auguste, was guillotined in the following year. The youngest son, Louis-Anne, was elected by the Gironde in 1795, but his election was annulled and he died several weeks later.

T. A. CROWLEY

AD, Charente-Maritime (La Rochelle), B, 275, ff.69, 72, 92v. AMA, Inspection du Génie, Archives, art.15, pièce 5; Bibliothèque, MSS *in-4º*, 66, pp.108, 134; MSS *in-fº*, 205[b], f.49; SHA, A[1], 3457; 3498, no.174. AN, Col., B, 89, f.207; C[11A], 93, f.352; C[11B], 23, f.19; 24, f.67; 25, f.169; 34, ff.22, 253; C[11C], 13, ff.106, 149v; 14, f.105; 16, ff.31–32; D[2C], 3, ff.19–19v; 48, f.305; 60, f.23; E, 258 (dossier Lartigue); F[2C], 4, f.198; F[3], 50, f.494; Marine, C[7], 261 (dossier Prevost de La Croix); Section Outremer, G[1], 466, no.76; G[2], 192/3, pièces 7, 23; Minutier central, LII, 175. ASQ, Polygraphie, LI; LIII; LV; LVI, 15; LVII. Bibliothèque de l'Arsenal, Archives de la Bastille, 12200; 12480; 12506. BN, MSS, Fr., 29989, f.10; 31625, f.3310. PAC, MG 18, G8; J10.

Coll. de manuscrits relatifs à la N.-F., III, 469, 484. *Les derniers jours de l'Acadie* (Du Boscq de Beaumont), 126, 133. [James Johnstone], *Memoirs of the Chevalier de Johnstone*, trans. Charles Winchester (3v., Aberdeen, Scot., 1870–71). La Rue, "Lettres et mémoires," ANQ *Rapport*, 1936–37, 400, 433. [Thomas Pichon], *Lettres et mémoires pour servir à l'histoire naturelle, civile et politique du Cap Breton, depuis son établissement jusqu'à la reprise de cette isle par les Anglois en 1758* (La Haye, Pays-Bas, 1760; repr. [East Ardsley, Eng.], 1966). Crowley, "Government and interests." McLennan, *Louisbourg*. Marc Perrichet, "Plume ou épée: problèmes de carrière dans quelques familles d'officiers d'administration de la Marine au XVIIIe siècle," Congrès national des soc. savantes, Section d'hist. moderne et contemporaine, *Actes du quatre-vingt-onzième congrès, Rennes, 1966* (3v., Paris, 1969), II, 145–81.

PRIMEAU (Primault, Primo), LOUIS (Lewis) (Nick'a'thu'tin), fur-trader; b. at Quebec; fl. 1749–1800.

Nothing is known of Louis Primeau's early life, but he was probably the Louis Primot who engaged in May 1749 with Joseph Coulon* de Villiers de Jumonville and Pierre Raimbault to trade in the Nipigon region (Ont.). He was among those Canadian traders who pushed up the Saskatchewan River in the last decade of the old régime. Unlike most, he stayed in the west during the Seven Years' War. He lived with the Indians, who called him Nick'a'thu'tin, and gained much influence with them; however, the hardships of this life were such that in 1765 he made his way to the Hudson's Bay Company post of York Factory (Man.). Ferdinand JACOBS, chief at York, doubted Primeau's trustworthiness, but realizing that his knowledge of Indian languages and experience in wilderness travel would make him a valuable servant for the HBC, engaged him specifically as an inland trader. From 1765 to 1772 Primeau wintered nearly every season among the Indians. There he was supposed to promote the interests of a company whose trade was being increasingly threatened by the activities of Montreal pedlars. In 1768, however, he was forced to remain at York because he was suffering from venereal disease, an ailment common among the traders and Indians because of their promiscuous contact.

As competition with the pedlars increased, Primeau urged upon the HBC officers, Andrew Graham* in particular, the absolute necessity of their building permanent inland posts. But Primeau himself began to show signs of divided loyalty. Matthew COCKING, who travelled inland in 1772 to investigate the deteriorating trade situation, suspected that he "hath a secret kindness for his old Masters" and he did, in fact, defect the following May, going out to Quebec via the pedlars' rendezvous at Grand Portage (near Grand Portage, Minn.). The HBC formally renounced all obligations to him in 1774. Primeau's desertion made the company wary of hiring any more Canadians, even though it needed skilled inland servants.

Primeau returned to the west in the employ of "Mr. Frobisher and Partners" as their chief pilot and trader. In 1773–74 he wintered with Joseph Frobisher* on Pine Island Lake (Cumberland Lake, Sask.). In the spring he was sent by Frobisher to intercept the Athapaskan Indians on their way to Prince of Wales's Fort (Churchill, Man.) to trade. He was so successful in this undertaking at Portage de Traite (Primeau Lake, Man.) that Samuel HEARNE reported in August "few of that Valuable Tribe of Indians are gone Down to Churchill this Year." Primeau built a post at Portage de Traite, in which he wintered in 1775–76, and the next year built another, at Île-à-la-Crosse (Sask.). In the autumn of 1777 he went down to Montreal, but the next year he was back at Île-à-la-Crosse.

Primeau appears to have been a significant factor in the early Nor'Westers' success in cutting off the HBC's trade at York and Churchill. Although little is known of his subsequent career, he was probably the Primeau who was in charge of the North West Company's Cumberland House (Cumberland Lake) when David Thompson* visited it in 1798. Primeau was reported to be on the Saskatchewan as late as 1800, and a Joseph Primeau who served as an interpreter in this area in the early 1800s may have been his son.

SYLVIA VAN KIRK

HBC Arch. B.42/b/11, f.7. [Matthew Cocking], "An adventurer from Hudson Bay: journal of Matthew Cocking, from York Factory to the Blackfeet country, 1772–73," ed. and intro. L. J. Burpee, RSC *Trans.*, 3rd ser., II (1908), sect.II, 89–121. *Docs. relating to NWC* (Wallace). HBRS, XIV (Rich and Johnson); XV (Rich and Johnson). *Journals of Hearne and Turnor* (Tyrrell). Massicotte, "Répertoire des engagements pour l'Ouest," ANQ, *Rapport*, 1931–32. Morton, *History of Canadian west*. Rich, *History of HBC*, II.

PRINGLE, ROBERT, military engineer; m. 29 July 1784 a Miss Balneavis; d. 17 June 1793 at Grenada.

Nothing is known about Robert Pringle prior to his commission as an ensign in the engineers in November 1760, but he had probably been a cadet at the Royal Military Academy in Woolwich, England. He was promoted lieutenant in 1766 and six years later was sent to Newfoundland as chief engineer. Pringle supervised the construction of new defences around St John's to replace the existing decayed works and also built several roads and bridges to connect the fortifications.

Although the defences were being improved, the town's garrison remained "old, infirm" and "not capable of . . . Resistance," the result of years of neglect by the home government. The outbreak of the American revolution made this deficiency a serious problem. The appearance of numerous privateers off the coasts and their attacks upon undefended outports raised fears that St John's harbour might be raided. The supplies on which the island depended in winter were housed in the town, and their capture or destruction would have proved disastrous.

Pringle had seen the need for a more adequate garrison soon after his arrival and had recommended to the secretary of state for the American Colonies the raising of a force of local inhabitants to supplement the regulars in an emergency. He was sufficiently concerned during the winter of 1777–78 to organize 120 labourers working on the fortifications into a small auxiliary armed force, without waiting for official approval. When Governor Richard EDWARDS arrived in 1779 he approved of Pringle's measures and with his advice persuaded the inhabitants to form a militia-like force of larger size. The inhabitants of St John's who joined the Newfoundland Volunteers, as it was called, agreed to be drilled by Pringle, and also agreed to serve in case of an attack on condition that they receive an enlistment bounty and provisions. The Volunteers proved popular, and by May 1780 some 400 men had joined.

Shortly thereafter the Volunteers learned that the British government had refused to sanction the enlistment bounty, and they promptly disbanded and dispersed to the fishery. Since the labourers were due to return soon to Britain and since Edwards' squadron had captured information that suggested an imminent French attack on the island, some alternate form of defence was imperative. Again with Pringle's advice, Edwards authorized the formation of a provincial unit to be called the Newfoundland Regiment in September 1780. Pringle was promoted lieutenant-colonel in view of his past services.

Although official approval for the regiment was forthcoming, Pringle experienced several problems in forming and maintaining his unit. The British government reduced the number of companies from six of 55 men to three of 100 men, thereby halving the number of officers and burdening those who remained with double the recruiting costs. It also lowered Pringle's pay and refused the regiment certain privileges accorded other provincial units. In addition Pringle was forced to pay for regimental needs from his own funds, and he was frequently bothered by a lack of provisions and equipment. The Newfoundland Regiment was nevertheless well received in the island and probably helped deter attacks on St John's until it was disbanded in October 1783. The life of the various forces raised on the island, although brief and uneventful, was a testimony to the vision and energy of Pringle at a critical stage of the war.

Pringle apparently returned to Europe in 1783, where he resumed his regular duties. He was promoted chief engineer at Gibraltar in 1785, a position he held until at least 1788. Two years later he was promoted full lieutenant-colonel and colonel in America, and in 1792 lieutenant-colonel of engineers. The following year he was sent to Grenada, where he died of fever shortly after his arrival.

STUART R. J. SUTHERLAND

PAC, MG 23, A4, 66, pp.116–34. PRO, Adm. 1/471, ff.455–57; 1/472, f.12; 80/121, ff.75, 78, 106–7; CO 194/30, ff.114–16; 194/32, ff.76–78; 194/33, ff.5–6, 106–7, 115–16, 131–32, 138–39; 194/34, ff.3–6, 7–9, 25–28, 52, 57, 61–62, 75–76, 102–3; 194/35, ff.3–10, 36–39, 53–55, 64–72, 76–77, 82–83, 98–119, 125, 130, 133–36, 147–48, 153, 212, 222, 257, 300, 305–7, 310–11, 322–23; 195/12, ff.99, 106–8, 225–27, 228; 195/13, f.14; 195/14, ff.1–20; 195/15, ff.98, 102, 115, 155; WO 1/12, ff.207–10, 217–20; 1/13, ff.40–41; 55/1557/2–4; 55/2269, ff.2–9. *Gentleman's Magazine*, 1784, 636; 1785, 838; 1788, 267; 1793, 768. G.B., WO, *Army list*, 1761–93. *Roll of officers of the corps of Royal Engineers from 1660 to 1898 . . .*, ed. R. F. Edwards (Chatham, Eng., 1898), 8. T. W. J. Connolly, *History of the corps of Royal Sappers and Miners* (2v., London, 1855), I, 47–48. G. W. L. Nicholson, *The fighting Newfoundlander; a history of the Royal Newfoundland Regiment* (St John's, [1964?]), 13–23, 582–91. Porter, *History of Royal Engineers*, I, 215. Prowse, *History of Nfld.* (1895), 341, 652.

Q

QUADRA, JUAN FRANCISCO DE LA BODEGA Y. *See* BODEGA

QUERDISIEN TRÉMAIS, CHARLES-FRANÇOIS PICHOT DE. *See* PICHOT

QUIASUTHA. *See* KAYAHSOTA?

QUINTAL, AUGUSTIN (baptized **Joseph**), priest, Recollet, and superior; b. 18 Dec. 1683 at Boucherville (Que.), son of François Quintal and Marie Gaultier; probably d. 17 Nov. 1776.

Joseph Quintal, who was a descendant of one of the families that founded Boucherville, was ordained priest on 8 Oct. 1713 at Quebec. He had made his profession in the Recollet order, under the name of Augustin, on 20 Nov. 1707, but the absence of a bishop explains the delay in his receiving holy orders. (Bishop Laval* had died on 6 May 1708, and Bishop Saint-Vallier [La Croix*], his successor, was detained and did not reach New France until 1713.) In December 1713 Quintal was serving as a priest at Trois-Rivières. Between 1713 and 1716 he was given the additional task of ministering to three parishes then being created, Saint-Antoine-de-Padoue, Rivière-du-Loup (Louiseville), Sainte-Anne, Yamachiche, and Saint-Joseph, Maskinongé. He was entrusted from 1720 to 1723 with the office of superior of the Franciscan monastery in Montreal. Between 1724 and 1727 he again worked at Yamachiche, Rivière-du-Loup, and Maskinongé. In the years 1729–35, 1744–53, and 1755–58 he was parish priest at Trois-Rivières, while serving again as superior of the Franciscan monastery; for the interval from 1735 to 1743 he worked at setting up a parish in the mission at the Saint-Maurice ironworks. He lived in Trois-Rivières from 1759 to 1763, continuing to serve in the community.

Augustin Quintal's name is frequently mentioned in works on the history of the early art of Quebec, and certain historians and art historians have conferred upon him somewhat too readily the title of architect and wood-carver, attributing to him many 18th-century works created in the Trois-Rivières region and comparing him to another Recollet, Juconde Drué*.

Study of his movements, as well as examination of his presumed works, supports the conclusion that Augustin Quintal's reputation has been much exaggerated. Works executed when he served in the Trois-Rivières region show that Father Quintal should be credited with giving orders to wood-carvers of great talent, especially for the decoration of the church of Trois-Rivières. However his role must have been limited to making it possible for already well-trained wood-carvers to practise their art in favourable conditions. Under his authority the tabernacle of the parish church was completed in 1730; the pulpit and churchwardens' pew, which were begun in 1734, were also finished during his tenure. It was probably Noël Levasseur* who was responsible for the creation of the tabernacle, which from the stylistic point of view fits perfectly into the evolution of works that came out of his Quebec workshop. By contrast, this work has no kinship with the pieces by Gilles Bolvin* which flank it on each side of the church: the style of Bolvin, a wood-carver of French origin, is much heavier and more ornate and derives from different influences.

Augustin Quintal's activity as the so-called architect of the church at Yamachiche is even more easily explained. In this case he can be called "parish priest and builder," a term still in use. From the time of his arrival in the parish he supervised the collection of the necessary funds and organized the corvées. He also drafted plans for the church, sometimes summary ones, the master mason being responsible for all the technical aspects of construction. Quintal had apparently never spent any time in Europe; so his plans remained unvaryingly of one type.

All things considered, Augustin Quintal has enjoyed an inflated reputation as an artist, since his ministry in the developing parishes took up most of his time. He did, however, leave the mark of his good taste in sacred art upon the parishes where he served by ordering from skilful craftsmen the works his parishes needed. Augustin Quintal probably passed away on 17 Nov. 1776.

RAYMONDE GAUTHIER

ANQ-M, État civil, Catholiques, Sainte-Famille (Boucherville), 18 déc. 1683. ANQ-Q, Greffe de Romain Becquet, 16 oct. 1678. Archives de l'évêché de Trois-Rivières, Registres de la paroisse de l'Immaculée-Conception, Reddition des comptes de 1732. Archives des franciscains (Montréal), Dossier Augustin Quintal. ASN, AP-G, L.-É. Bois, Garde-notes, 1, p.218; 5, pp.368–69; 6, pp.26, 405–6, 431; 7, pp.296–97; 10, pp.243, 311; 16, p.275. ASQ, MSS, 425, f.361; Polygraphie, XVIII, 20.

Allaire, *Dictionnaire*, IV, 278. Ivanhoë Caron, "Inventaire de documents concernant l'Église du Canada sous le Régime français," ANQ *Rapport*, 1940–41, 436–38. Tanguay, *Dictionnaire*, VI, 486; *Répertoire*, 91. Napoléon Caron *et al.*, *Histoire de la paroisse d'Yamachiche (précis historique) . . .* (Trois-Rivières, 1892), 29–40. G.-R. Gareau, *Premières concessions d'habitations, 1673, Boucherville* (Montréal, 1973), 38–41. Gowans, *Church architecture in New France*. Jouve, *Les franciscains et le Canada: aux Trois-Rivières*. Raymonde [Landry] Gauthier, *Les tabernacles anciens du Québec des XVIIe, XVIIIe et XIXe siècles* (Québec, 1974); *Trois-Rivières disparue ou presque* (Montréal, 1978). Gérard Morisset, *L'architecture en Nouvelle-France* (Québec, 1949); *Coup d'œil sur les arts*, 11, 15, 27–28, 30–31, 52. Luc Noppen, *Notre-Dame de Québec, son architecture et son rayonnement*

(1647–1922) (Ottawa, 1974). M Trudel, *L'Église canadienne*, I, 99–100, 120, 350; II, 184, 186, 202, 204–5. *Les ursulines des Trois-Rivières depuis leur établissement jusqu'à nos jours* (4v., Trois-Rivières, 1888–1911), I, IV. Gérard Morisset, "Deux artistes récollets au XVIIIe siècle," *Le Droit* (Ottawa), 12 mars 1935, 2.

QUIQUINANIS. *See* WIKINANISH

R

RABY, AUGUSTIN, ship captain; b. *c.* 1706, eldest son of Mathieu Raby and Marie-Françoise Poireaux, *née* Morin; buried 19 Dec. 1782 at Quebec.

Augustin Raby was already a ship's captain on 23 April 1731 when he married Françoise Toupin, *dit* Dussault (*née* Delisle), at Quebec. The son of habitant parents, he clearly had risen in colonial society. His wife was the widow of the seigneur of Bélair, and Raby was able to present her with a dower of 1,000 *livres*. During the 1730s he was employed by François Martel* de Brouague and Pierre Trottier* Desauniers, who were exploiting concessions along the coast of Labrador, and Raby regularly sailed the St Lawrence carrying foodstuffs downstream and returning with sealskins and oil. By 1745 he was an acknowledged authority on the pilotage of the St Lawrence and resided comfortably in Quebec on the quay of the Cul-de-Sac with his wife, one child, and a domestic.

Early in the Seven Years' War, Raby was captured and taken to England. In January 1759 he was placed on the *Neptune* (90 guns), the flagship of Vice-Admiral Charles SAUNDERS, and prevailed upon to act as a pilot in the forthcoming expedition to Quebec. An old acquaintance, Théodose-Matthieu DENYS de Vitré, sailed in this ship also but was transferred to Rear-Admiral Philip Durell*'s squadron before it entered the St Lawrence. The *Neptune* was off Île aux Coudres for some time in the summer, apparently because of the difficulties of piloting so large a vessel, but she finally dropped anchor off Île Madame on 4 August. James MURRAY later referred to Raby as "the principal pilot of our fleet in 1759." In October, after the fall of the city, Raby sailed to England with Saunders, but the following year he returned to Canada as "pilot extra" in the *Kingston*. He again went back to England at the end of the season and continued to serve in naval ships until he was paid off in August 1761. Soon afterwards he returned to Quebec.

Raby's home had been burnt and pillaged during the siege, and he was reduced to indigence. The hostility of his countrymen and fear of being tried for his life should he move to France led him to petition James Murray for protection and assistance. The governor, who wanted to restore the colony's services as rapidly as possible, commissioned Raby and one Savard as river pilots in April 1762. He also forwarded Raby's petition to London with a strong recommendation that he be rewarded. "It would be a great discouragement to others," he wrote, "if his services were forgot or neglected." A similar recommendation was transmitted to the Privy Council by Admiral Saunders and early in 1764 Raby was granted a life pension of 5*s*. per diem. He spent the remainder of his days as senior pilot at Quebec.

JAMES S. PRITCHARD

AN, Col., F[2B], 11. ANQ-Q, Greffe de Claude Barolet, 21 avril 1731; Greffe de J.-É. Dubreuil, 6 mars 1714. BL, Add. MSS 11813, f.72. G. B., Privy Council, *Acts of the P.C., col., 1745–66*, IV, 665. *Inv. de pièces du Labrador* (P.-G. Roy), I, 253. "Recensement de Québec, 1744," 122. P.-G. Roy, *Inv. ord. int.*, II, 145. Tanguay, *Dictionnaire*, VI, 416, 490. Burt, *Old prov. of Que.* (1968), I, 35–36. P.-G. Roy, "Le pilote Raby," *BRH*, XIII (1907), 124–26.

RAFFETOT, CHARLES DESCHAMPS DE BOISHÉBERT ET DE. *See* DESCHAMPS

RAMEZAY (Ramesai, Ramesay, Ramsay), JEAN-BAPTISTE-NICOLAS-ROCH DE, officer in the colonial regular troops and king's lieutenant; b. 4 Sept. 1708 at Montreal (Que.), youngest son of Claude de Ramezay* and Marie-Charlotte Denys de La Ronde; brother of LOUISE and Marie-Charlotte*, *dite* de Saint-Claude de la Croix; m. 6 Dec. 1728 at Trois-Rivières Louise, daughter of René Godefroy* de Tonnancour; they had six children, five of whom died in infancy; d. 7 May 1777 at Blaye, France.

Jean-Baptiste-Nicolas-Roch de Ramezay spent his childhood at the Château de Ramezay in Montreal. On 7 May 1720, at the age of 11, he became an ensign in the colonial regulars, and after the death of his brother Charles-Hector de Ramezay de La Gesse in August 1725 his mother sought and obtained for him the deceased's lieutenancy. Promoted lieutenant on 23 April 1726, he was sent to Fort Niagara (near Youngstown, N.Y.) in a force commanded by the engineer Gaspard-Joseph CHAUSSEGROS de Léry. This force was to rebuild Niagara, which was intended to "serve as a barrier" to the expansion of the British, recently established at Oswego (N.Y.). In the spring of 1728 he took part in the expedition that Constant Le Marchand* de Lignery led against the Foxes in the Illinois country, and in 1731 Governor Beauharnois* entrusted him with the mission of pacifying the Ojibwas of Chagouamigon (near Ashland, Wis.). Three years later he was promoted captain. In 1742 he was named commandant of Fort La Tourette (also called La Maune, at the mouth of the Onaman River, Ont.).

In 1746, two years after war had been declared between France and Britain, Governor Beauharnois and Intendant HOCQUART, on the order of the minister of Marine, raised a detachment of Canadians and Indians to take part in the campaign in Acadia. They gave command of the expedition to Ramezay, who left Quebec on 5 June with 700 men on seven ships. He first landed at Baie-Verte (N.B.) on 10 July and from there sent a detachment under Joseph-Michel LEGARDEUR de Croisille et de Montesson to Port-La-Joie (Fort Amherst, P.E.I.), recently taken by the British; he then took up quarters at Beaubassin (near Amherst, N.S.).

Ramezay's mission was to meet the French squadron under the Duc d'Anville [La Rochefoucauld*], but in the absence of precise orders from the latter he was supposed to divide his forces and attack both Canso and Annapolis Royal. On 22 Sept. 1746 he learned of the arrival of the remnant of the French squadron at Chibouctou (Halifax) and the death of the Duc d'Anville, who eventually was replaced by La Jonquière [Taffanel*]. Ramezay therefore prepared to attack Annapolis Royal, which he reached on 11 October. But after waiting 23 days for La Jonquière, Ramezay, who for want of sufficient troops had established only a cordon around the fort to prevent communication between the garrison and the village, had to withdraw to Beaubassin.

In December an expeditionary force of New England troops under Lieutenant-Colonel Arthur Noble* settled in at Grand Pré with the aim of ending incursions into Nova Scotia by the Canadians and French. On learning this news Ramezay decided to attack them, and he entrusted leadership of the detachment, which left on 9 Feb. 1747, to his second in command, Captain Nicolas-Antoine Coulon* de Villiers. After being wounded in the attack Coulon was replaced by Louis de La Corne*. Following some hours of combat, Benjamin Goldthwait* surrendered and signed the act of capitulation on 12 February. Ramezay profited most from this exploit; on 15 Feb. 1748 he was decorated with the cross of Saint-Louis.

In 1749 Ramezay was appointed major of Quebec, replacing Paul-Joseph LE MOYNE de Longueuil, and thus assumed the duties of second in command to the king's lieutenant at Quebec. He held the office "with honour and distinction" for nine years, before acceding at the age of 50 to the post of king's lieutenant with a salary of 1,800 *livres*.

In the spring of 1759 Quebec was readying its defences in anticipation of an attack by the British fleet. Around the city, under the instructions of Governor Vaudreuil [RIGAUD], were gathering French sailors, French and colonial regulars, militia from the governments of Montreal, Trois-Rivières, and Quebec, and Indian allies. As the officer responsible for the defence of the Upper Town, Ramezay had under his orders 700 soldiers and sailors, a few gunners, and the townspeople who had become militiamen for the occasion. The British fleet reached the Île d'Orléans on 26 June, but apart from a destructive bombardment from Pointe-Lévy (Lauzon), the summer passed without the town being attacked. In mid August Ramezay's health forced him to enter the Hôpital Général and to delegate his powers to a subordinate. He was still there when the British forces under Wolfe* reached the Plains of Abraham on 13 September. Learning of Montcalm*'s defeat, Ramezay returned to town and resumed command of his troops. He asked Pierre-André GOHIN, Comte de Montreuil, Montcalm's assistant chief of staff, for reinforcements and received 150 French soldiers and several cannon. That evening, a council of war held at the headquarters of Governor Vaudreuil at Beauport decided on a retreat to Jacques-Cartier. Through Montcalm, who approved them on his death-bed, Ramezay received from Vaudreuil terms of surrender as well as instructions that he was "not to wait until the enemy storms the city, thus as soon as he lacks supplies he will hoist the white flag and send the most capable and most intelligent officer of the garrison to propose its capitulation." Stunned, Ramezay appealed to Montcalm, but the general was too close to death to respond.

The next day Ramezay reviewed his forces and established that he had about 2,200 men, consisting of 330 French and colonial regulars, 20 artillerymen, 500 sailors, and the rest militiamen. Rations for them and the 4,000 inhabitants would last at most for eight days. On 15 September Ramezay was again shocked when he received a "request from the burghers of Quebec" which urged him to capitulate on honourable terms [*see* François Daine*; Jean Taché*]. Ramezay called a council of war of the garrison's principal officers, to whom he reported Vaudreuil's instructions. Thirteen of the fourteen officers proposed capitulation, the sole exception being Louis-Thomas JACAU de Fiedmont. Meanwhile the town's artillery was causing damage to the British forces on the Plains of Abraham and to their ships. On the 17th LÉVIS, hastening from Montreal, met Vaudreuil at Jacques-Cartier and decided to march the army back to Quebec in the hopes of preventing the enemy from spending the winter there. Attempts were made to get food to the city and Vaudreuil sent new instructions to Ramezay to hold out until Lévis arrived. But at 3:00 P.M. on the same day Ramezay, faced not only with the request from the townspeople and the decision of the council of war but also with the imminent bombardment of Quebec from cannon being assembled on the plains and from the British fleet, hoisted the white flag. He then sent Armand de Joannès, major of Quebec, to discuss the terms for capitulation and the surrender of the town. At 11:00 P.M. Joannès returned to the British headquarters with a document signed by Ramezay. Only after his departure did Vaudreuil's second instructions arrive.

On the morning of 18 September Charles SAUNDERS and George Townshend* signed the capitulation; the next day Ramezay handed the city over to Townshend, and the soldiers of the garrison went aboard British vessels. Ramezay and the officers embarked on 22 September, but they did not sail until 19 October.

By a proxy signed before his departure Ramezay had asked his wife to sell his property in Canada and she did so on 23 Aug. 1763. In 1765 she left with her daughter Charlotte-Marguerite, her son-in-law, and their two children to join her husband in La Rochelle. Ramezay, who had been granted a meagre pension of 800 *livres*, ultimately went to live at Blaye, where he died on 7 May 1777.

The question of whether Ramezay was right to surrender still persists. After having given him precise instructions to that effect, Vaudreuil was the first to criticize him. Joannès, one of the officers who had agreed to the surrender, albeit with certain reservations, also attacked him in his memoir on the campaign. In Britain there was immediate exultation at the capture of the city, and in his report to the king Townshend emphasized the advantage there had been to signing a hasty peace, even though the conditions granted the French seemed generous to him. Ramezay's decision had been greatly influenced by the number of sick and wounded, the lack of supplies, the various pressures brought to bear by the townspeople and the officers of the garrison, and the imminent threat of renewed bombardment: these had demolished any combative spirit he had shown until then. But it was the desertion of the militia and the flight of the regular troops after the battle that played the greatest part in destroying the last hopes that a victory was still within reach. Throughout history there have been many victims of a combination of circumstances: Ramezay was simply one of them.

JEAN PARISEAU

[J.-B.-N.-R. de Ramezay], *Mémoire du sieur de Ramezay, commandant à Québec, au sujet de la reddition de cette ville, le 18 septembre 1759* [. . .] (Québec, 1861) (pt.1: "Évènements de la guerre en Canada durant les années 1759 et 1760"; "Relation du siège de Québec du 27 mai au 8 août 1759", pt.2: "Mémoire du sieur de Ramezay").

AMA, Bibliothèque du ministère de la Guerre, A[2C], 236, ff.222–24; 287; SHA, A[1], 3540, 3542–46 (mfm. at PAC). AN, Col., C[11A], 120, ff.398, 405; C[11E], 13, ff.150, 257; D[2C], 49; 57; 58; 61; 222, f.673. *Coll. des manuscrits de Lévis* (Casgrain), I, 215; II, 242–43; IV, 162–64; V, 205, 230, 232, 293, 309, 356; VI, 106, 155, 174, 186, 228; VII, 64, 551–53, 616; VIII, 68, 78, 110; X, 111–13. *Coll. doc. inédits Canada et Amérique*, II, 10–75. *Doc. relatifs à la monnaie sous le Régime français* (Shortt), II, 740–42, 744, 750, 754, 794. "Journal du siège de Québec" (Æ. Fauteux), ANQ *Rapport*, 1920–21. Knox, *Hist. journal* (Doughty), II, 108–10, 123; III, 267–95. "Mémoire du Canada," ANQ *Rapport*, 1924–25, 151–67. *Mémoires sur le Canada, depuis 1749 jusqu'à 1760*, 169–71. "Projet pour la défense du Canada pendant la campagne 1759, relativement à ses forces et aux projets que peuvent avoir les Anglois pour l'attaquer," ANQ *Rapport*, 1932–33, 368–72. [Nicolas Renaud d'Avène Des Méloizes], "Journal militaire tenu par Nicolas Renaud d'Avène Des Méloizes, ch[er], seigneur de Neuville, au Canada, du 8 mai 1759 au 21 novembre de la même année . . . ," ANQ *Rapport*, 1928–29, 76–78. *Siège de Québec en 1759* [. . .] (Québec, 1836; republished in Quebec, 1972, in *Le siège de Québec en 1759 par trois témoins*, J.-C. Hébert, édit.).

[F.-]M. Bibaud, *Le panthéon canadien; choix de biographies*, Adèle et Victoria Bibaud, édit. (2e éd., Montréal, 1891), 243–44. Æ. Fauteux, *Les chevaliers de Saint-Louis*, 145. "Historic forts and trading posts of the French regime and of the English fur trading companies," comp. Ernest Voorhis (mimeographed copy, Ottawa, 1930), 98. Le Jeune, *Dictionnaire*, II, 499–500. "Lieutenants du roi à Québec," *BRH*, XVII (1911), 381. "Les majors de Québec," *BRH*, XIX (1913), 352. J.-E. Roy. *Rapport sur les archives de France*. P.-G.

Roy, *Les officiers d'état-major des gouvernements de Québec, Montréal et Trois-Rivières sous le Régime français* (Lévis, Qué., 1919), 88–94. Tanguay, *Dictionnaire*, I, 183; III, 351. Wallace, *Macmillan dictionary*, 617–18. Antoine Champagne, *Les La Vérendrye et le poste de l'Ouest* (Québec, 1968), 138, 272. A.[G.] Doughty and G. W. Parmelee, *The siege of Quebec and the battle of the Plains of Abraham* (6v., Quebec, 1901), II, 79, 212–13; III, 104, 132, 259–60, 272–73, 292; IV, 10, 149, 154, 163–217, 219–29, 239–78; V, 1–11, 111, 225–81, 283–301, 303–26. Guy Frégault, *La civilisation de la Nouvelle-France, 1713–1744* (Montréal, 1944), 53–54; *La guerre de la Conquête*. Félix Martin, *Le marquis de Montcalm et les dernières années de la colonie française au Canada (1756–1760)* (Paris, 1898) (contains in an appendix the deliberations of the council of war presided over by Ramezay on 15 Sept. 1759). P.-G. Roy, *La famille de Ramezay* (Lévis, 1910). Stacey, *Quebec, 1759*. Stanley, *New France*. "La famille de Ramezay," *BRH*, XVII (1911), 18–22, 33–34, 44, 74, 103–10. A.[-E.] Gosselin, "Notes sur la famille Coulon de Villiers," *BRH*, XII (1906), 198–203. Victor Morin, "Les Ramezay et leur château," *Cahiers des Dix*, 3 (1938), 9–72. P.-G. Roy, "Le conseil de guerre tenu à Québec le 15 septembre 1759," *BRH*, XXII (1916), 63–64; "M. de Ramesay, lieutenant de roi à Québec, après 1759," *BRH*, XXII, 355–64; "Où fut signé la capitulation de Québec, le 18 septembre 1759?" *BRH*, XXIX (1923), 66–69.

RAMEZAY, LOUISE DE, seigneur; b. 6 July 1705 at Montreal, daughter of Claude de Ramezay*, governor of Montreal, and Marie-Charlotte Denys de La Ronde; d. 22 Oct. 1776 at Chambly (Que.).

Louise de Ramezay received her schooling at the Ursuline convent in Quebec. Having remained single like her sister Marie-Charlotte*, *dite* de Saint-Claude de la Croix, she was led when she was about 30 to take an interest in the administration of part of her family's properties. In particular she was concerned with the sawmill that her father had built early in the century on the banks of the Rivière des Hurons, in the seigneury of Chambly not far from his own seigneury of Monnoir. Shortly after his death in 1724, his widow had gone into partnership with Clément de SABREVOIS de Bleury to run the sawmill. From 1732 until 1737, however, a protracted lawsuit, which Louise de Ramezay followed closely, set the two former partners against each other. Mlle de Ramezay probably acquired at that period the knowledge necessary for running the mill, as well as the other enterprises of which she later became the owner.

For more than three decades beginning in 1739, Louise de Ramezay faithfully saw to it that the sawmill on the Rivière des Hurons was not idle, for every year the operation had to pay 112 *livres* in rent to the seigneurs of Chambly and 600 *livres* to her sisters and her brother JEAN-BAPTISTE-NICOLAS-ROCH, who were also heirs to their father's estate. The mill was well situated to saw the wood from the upper Richelieu and Lake Champlain and thus to supply timbers, planks, and sheathing to the shipyards at Quebec. Louise de Ramezay did not always run the enterprise in person. At certain periods she supervised production closely, collaborating with the foreman and going to Quebec to sell the lumber; at others, having leased the sawmill and even the right to grant land and collect the rents in the seigneury of Monnoir, she was primarily concerned with getting her share of the revenue. When she entrusted the mill to a foreman, she preferred him to know how to keep the accounts; to one who was illiterate, she gave permission in his contract "to take an hour every day to learn to read and write, and to have himself taught by one of the men hired at the mill who would take the same time to teach him." Such a clause was quite uncommon, but it gave her the hope that the foreman would eventually keep the accounts well.

Contracts for taking charge of the sawmill were made in succession at about five-year intervals until 1765, proof of success and of virtually uninterrupted operation. During her years of management, however, Louise de Ramezay had to deal with a number of problems. On the two occasions when she farmed out the sawmill she had difficulty getting the conditions of the lease carried out. First, in 1756, a lumber merchant from Chambly, François Bouthier, owed her more than 12,000 *livres* for two years of rent and goods advanced much earlier. In 1765 she again tried the experiment with Louis Boucher de Niverville de Montisambert, but at the end of a few years, as accounts were not yet settled, legal action was initiated. She no doubt was afraid at one point of finding herself dragged into a prolonged lawsuit, as her mother had been 40 years earlier. She soon agreed with Montisambert that to avoid the delays and expense of a court case it was better to have the dispute settled by the parish priest of Chambly, Médard Petrimoulx. In August 1771 the priest decided in her favour and concluded that Montisambert had to pay her 3,284 *livres*.

Louise de Ramezay was also interested in two other sawmills; these are known, however, only through documents that show her as intending to put mills into operation, in particular deeds of partnership and building transactions. In 1745 she entered into partnership with Marie-Anne Legras, the wife of Jean-Baptiste-François Hertel de Rouville, and the two entrepreneurs had a sawmill and a flour-mill built "on the seigneury of Rouville, on the stream called Notre-Dame de

Bonsecours, on a piece of land belonging to the . . . Sieur de Rouville." These two mills doubtless turned a satisfactory profit, since the partnership lasted 16 years; it was not dissolved until 1761, six years before the anticipated date. The second sawmill was to be located much farther south, in the seigneury of La Livaudière, west of Lake Champlain. This seigneury, which had initially been granted to Jacques-Hugues Péan* de Livaudière, had been withdrawn in 1741 and returned to the king's domain. When the seigneury had belonged to him, however, Péan had granted land to a habitant from Saint-Antoine-sur-Richelieu, Jean Chartier, with the authorization "to take sawn timber on the whole of the aforementioned seigneury where the lands had not been given in grants." Moreover, a stream that crossed Chartier's land and flowed into Lake Champlain by way of the Chazy River (probably the Great Chazy River, N.Y.) could supply the power needed for running a mill. It was probably this set of favourable circumstances that prompted Louise de Ramezay to go into partnership with Chartier in August 1746 and to have a sawmill built at once on his land, near the Chazy River. Moreover, in 1749 she obtained a grant from the colonial authorities of a domain on Lake Champlain, the seigneury of Ramezay-La-Gesse, which extended on both sides of the Rivière aux Sables (probably the Ausable River, N.Y.). Although a sawmill does not seem to have been built there, the interest of this property obviously lay in its abundant timber reserves.

Louise de Ramezay did not confine her activities to the lumber industry. In 1749 she bought from Charles Plessy, *dit* Bélair, the tannery that had belonged to his father Jean-Louis* and was located in Coteau-Saint-Louis on Montreal Island. In 1753 she went into partnership with a master tanner, Pierre Robereau, *dit* Duplessis, to whom she entrusted the operation of the tannery. Until she was 60, she appears to have lived mainly in Montreal, often going to Chambly and Quebec.

It is not possible with the available documentation to evaluate precisely the extent of Louise de Ramezay's economic activity. In the transactions related to the lumber or leather industries, however, she always seemed able to advance the money necessary for construction work, for fitting-out or repairs, for the foremen's and workmen's wages, for the purchase of land, equipment, and goods, or for repayment of debts contracted by a partner or employee. These are additional signs of the efficiency and success of her enterprises. She owed this success in part to her own administrative abilities, but probably even more to her social position: the descendant of a great family, the daughter of a governor, the "very noble young lady," as the documents of the period call her, enjoyed privileges that were by no means negligible. Besides an upbringing that had prepared her for the realities of her situation, her relations within the colonial aristocracy certainly on more than one occasion brought her useful advice, information, recommendations, and even a few favours in connection with the lumber industry, the exploitation of timber limits, the purchase of domains, or her own financial resources. For example, after her mother's death in 1742 she was the beneficiary of an annual and comfortable pension of 1,000 *livres*, because the authorities in France had decided to extend the pension paid to Mme de Ramezay as the widow of a former governor of Montreal. In addition, in 1746 Bishop DOSQUET gave her half of the seigneury of Bourchemin, an enclave within the seigneury of Ramezay, which she demanded in the name of her family's claims on that domain; the bishop on this occasion wrote to her: "I am delighted to have this small opportunity to give proof of my attachment to your family." Thus Louise de Ramezay owned, in her own right, half of the seigneury of Bourchemin as well as the seigneury of Ramezay-La-Gesse; in addition, in 1724, along with her brothers and sisters she had inherited from her father the seigneuries of Ramezay, Monnoir, and Sorel. When all is said and done, her economic activities could rest on the kind of substantial landed fortune of which there were but few examples in the colony in the mid 18th century.

With the conquest and the establishment of the southern border of Canada, Louise de Ramezay lost her seigneury of Ramezay-La-Gesse, and also, if indeed it still belonged to her, the mill near the Chazy River. At the same period she parted with other properties. In 1761 she sold her rights to the seigneury of Sorel to her sister Louise-Geneviève, the widow of Henri-Louis Deschamps* de Boishébert, for 3,580 *livres*. Three years later this property was sold to a Quebec merchant, John Taylor Bondfield, as was the seigneury of Ramezay on the Yamaska River, in which Louise had kept her share. In 1774, two years before her death, she also sold her half of Bourchemin. Monnoir apparently remained in the family until the end of the century; towards the end of her life she made grants of a considerable number of lots there at the request of habitants in the Richelieu valley.

Louise de Ramezay, unmarried and a member of the aristocracy, administered the properties for which she was responsible conscientiously and with remarkable constancy, at the same time drawing the greatest possible advantage from the privileges of her class.

HÉLÈNE PARÉ

[The printed sources dealing with Louise de Ramezay's economic activities have circulated certain inaccuracies, based, it seems, on a somewhat free interpretation of archival sources. Thus, following Ovide-Michel-Hengard Lapalice, *Histoire de la seigneurie Massue et de la paroisse de Saint-Aimé* (s.l., 1930), 34, various authors have wrongly located the sawmill of the Rivière des Hurons, and even that of the Ruisseau Notre-Dame de Bonsecours, placing them in the seigneury of Monnoir. Édouard-Zotique Massicotte*, "Les Sabrevois, Sabrevois de Sermonville et Sabrevois de Bleury," *BRH*, XXXI (1925), 79–80, gives Mlle de Ramezay "a couple" of tanner's shops, when the documents indicate only one; moreover, Lapalice states inaccurately that "in 1735 Lousie de Ramezay moved all the working stock of the tannery to Chambly." With regard to the debts owed to Mlle de Ramezay by various persons in 1751 and 1756, Massicotte, "Une femme d'affaires du Régime français," *BRH*, XXXVII (1931), 530, multiplies by five the sums indicated in the documents (did he intend to convert to dollars and then neglect to say so?); as a result, several authors have overvalued the importance of Louise de Ramezay's transactions. Finally, the title of "businesswoman" that Lapalice and Massicotte give Mlle de Ramezay is totally anachronistic in reference to this 18th-century noblewoman. It should be noted that the passages relating to Louise de Ramezay in the biography of her father (*DCB*, II, 548) repeat some of these inaccuracies. H.P.]

ANQ-M, État civil, Catholiques, Saint-Joseph (Chambly), 1776; Greffe d'Antoine Grisé, 6 août 1765, 8, 26 juill. 1768, 1er, 15 juill. 1769, 16 nov. 1770, 23 mai, 16, 30 août 1771, 24 oct. 1772, 25 août 1774; Greffe de Gervais Hodiesne, 14, 17 juin, 20 déc. 1745, 18 mars, 19 avril, 30 juin, 29 août 1746, 1er févr. 1749, 19 sept. 1751, 16, 30 avril 1753, 6 juill., 6 sept. 1754, 26 sept. 1756, 8 oct. 1758, 17 mars 1760, 5 mai, 1er déc. 1761; Greffe d'Antoine Loiseau, 2 sept. 1739; Greffe de François Simonnet, 26 mars 1746. Archives paroissiales, Notre-Dame (Montréal), Registre des baptêmes, mariages et sépultures, 1705. P.-G. Roy, *Inv. concessions*, II, IV, V. J.-N. Fauteux, *Essai sur l'industrie*, I, 204–10. Mathieu, *La construction navale*, 75–76, 87–90.

RAYMOND, JEAN-LOUIS DE, Comte de RAYMOND, army officer and governor of Île Royale; b.*c*. 1702; d. 12 Oct. 1771 in the parish of Saint-Antonin, Angoulême, France.

Little is known of the early life of Jean-Louis de Raymond. According to Michel LE COURTOIS de Surlaville, Raymond's family were minor provincial seigneurs, probably in Angoumois (dept of Charente). Raymond began his army career as lieutenant in the Régiment de Vexin. He was promoted captain in 1725 and lieutenant-colonel in 1743. In 1731 Raymond secured the king's lieutenancy of the town and château of Angoulême, an increasingly titular position, which brought him an annual income for life of 2,100 *livres*. He was present at the battle of Dettingen (Federal Republic of Germany) in 1743 and served with the French armies along the Rhine in 1744–45, although it seems he never engaged directly in combat. In 1747 he was accorded the non-venal general officer rank of brigadier and in 1749 was transferred to the Grenadiers de France with the rank of lieutenant-colonel. During his army career he had learned how to manipulate the mechanism of official patronage. After he had convinced the minister of War, Voyer d'Argenson, that he was a blood relation, the minister helped to obtain his promotion to major-general in 1751, and in the same year interceded with the minister of Marine, Rouillé, to secure him the governorship of Île Royale (Cape Breton Island) in succession to Charles Des Herbiers* de La Ralière.

Athough unsolicited, the governorship offered Raymond the two things he desired most: prestige and money. His lavish lifestyle had impoverished him and Rouillé offered generous terms: an initial gratuity of 10,000 *livres*; an annual salary of 9,000 *livres* plus the 1,200 *livres* annual stipend awarded both the governor and the financial commissary for travel within the colony; and permission to return to France on a year's notice. After Pierre-Arnaud de Laporte, chief clerk of the Marine colonial bureau, had flattered Raymond's ego, he readily accepted the post, although he had had no prior experience in either the Marine or the colonies.

Raymond's appointment was part of an attempt by Rouillé to upgrade the quality of personnel in the colonial service. Raymond was the last governor of a Canadian colony during the French régime to have pursued a regular army career and the only one appointed to Louisbourg who was not a Marine officer. He came to Louisbourg with superficially impressive credentials and accolades. Prior to his appointment he had purchased the tiny fief of Oyes (dept of Marne) and he was the first member of his family to be styled count, although his distant cousin, Charles de Raymond Des Rivières (who belonged to a noble branch of the family), and Surlaville doubted the legitimacy of the title.

Raymond was the most flamboyant governor of a Canadian colony between Frontenac [Buade*] and Lord Durham [Lambton*]. With Frontenac he shared an unbounded ambition and a passion for extravagant living. For both men the title of governor evoked, as Mme de Sévigné wrote, "noise, trumpets and violins." Like Durham, Raymond gloried in pomp and ceremony. The fanfare that greeted his arrival at Louisbourg on 3 Aug. 1751 was greater than that surrounding Durham's debarkation at Quebec in 1838. The celebrations he staged for the birth of the dauphin in 1752 were unsurpassed in the annals of the colony.

Raymond came to Louisbourg anxious to impress his new superiors. He was determined to allow no area to escape his attention, nor any of his activities to escape his superiors' notice. Some of his actions were preposterous. He tried to impress Rouillé by sending Canadian animals to France, and even included partridge pies that were putrid on arrival. When iron pyrites (fool's gold) was discovered, Raymond rashly announced that Île Royale was a new Peru. Because of such stories, rumours circulated in the ports of France that he was deranged. With the help of Surlaville and Thomas PICHON, he wrote a host of memoranda on many subjects. He recommended changes in the regulation of trade, the religious establishment, the administration of justice, and Louisbourg's fortifications. He maintained close surveillance on the British in Nova Scotia and in 1752 toured both Île Royale and Île Saint-Jean (Prince Edward Island), meeting with Indian allies at orchestrated parleys. Detailed but exaggerated accounts of his movements were dispatched to Versailles.

Some of Raymond's ideas were sound; all were expensive to implement. Although the financial commissary had jurisdiction over settlement, Raymond, by virtue of his responsibility for the military and public order, undertook to make Louisbourg self-sufficient in food. He paid troops to clear land for agriculture and sought to augment the island's defences by settling soldiers in agricultural communities similar to the early Roman *coloniae*. In 1752 he had 22 soldiers married and placed in a village obsequiously called Rouillé on the Rivière de Miré (Mira River). Others were located at Baie-des-Espagnols (Sydney), at Port-Toulouse (near St Peters), and on Île Saint-Jean. He also devised an ingenious plan for the coastal defence of the island and without authorization from France paid troops to build a barely passable road from Port-Toulouse to Louisbourg at a cost of 100,000 *livres*. His scheme projected a series of redoubts along the coast to aid settlement, avert smuggling, and give warning of enemy attack. The engineer Louis Franquet* opposed this plan as too costly, and it was ultimately rejected by Rouillé. To improve the colonial officer corps, Raymond instituted formal instruction in mathematics and artillery as well as reading and writing for the illiterate.

Raymond thought his role as governor was to govern in the fullest sense. Because of his inexperience, his ambition, and the flattery of Laporte, he failed to appreciate that government in New France was a diarchy in which the military and commissariat branches exercised separate and largely independent authority: the former over external relations, Indian affairs, and military discipline; the latter over justice, finances, and supply. They jointly shared the responsibility for public order. The Louisbourg financial commissary, Jacques PREVOST de La Croix, was no less vain or domineering than Raymond. Surlaville commented that "each wanted to gain control" and that both were "equally headstrong . . . vain and presumptuous." The two men clashed frequently over both petty jurisdictional and major policy matters. Prevost opposed the governor at every turn and used all means at his disposal to ensure adherents to his camp. Not only did he complain incessantly to his superiors about Raymond's high-handedness, but he distributed additional supplies to military officers who supported him. With Surlaville's aid, Raymond retaliated by preparing an extensive memorandum documenting Prevost's inflation of colonial accounts. He concluded that Prevost had defrauded the monarchy of 33,000 *livres* in one year. Unfortunately, he presented this information to the ministry in July 1754 when Rouillé had left office, and consequently no action was taken.

Unhappy with his increasingly untenable situation at Louisbourg, Raymond requested a transfer after less than a year. When DUQUESNE's appointment as governor general of New France was announced, Raymond avowed that his dignity would not permit him to serve under a man who held a rank inferior to his own. In the fall of 1753 he left the colony with a pension of 4,000 *livres*. Charles-Joseph d'Ailleboust* assumed temporary command until the arrival of Raymond's successor, Drucour [Boschenry*].

After his return to France, Raymond was reassigned to the War department. In 1755 he became commandant at Le Havre. Pathologically obsessed with his self-importance, he attempted to impress French officials with his intimate knowledge of colonial affairs. After constant pleading he gained audiences with ministers at Versailles in 1755 and 1757. In 1759 he successfully petitioned to be appointed commandant of Angoumois, but he remained king's lieutenant and received only 2,000 *livres*, one-quarter the additional salary he had requested. In the same year

Raymond was drawing 8,400 *livres* in pensions, exclusive of the pension attached to his new post: 2,100 as king's lieutenant, 800 as former lieutenant-colonel of the Vexin, 1,500 on the order of Saint-Louis, and 4,000 from the Marine. Little is known of him after the Seven Years' War.

Raymond never emerged from the debts that plagued his life, though Surlaville estimated that his income during the governorship was 86,000 *livres*. Even the major's canteen, the only officially sanctioned canteen in the fortress, which he expanded and tapped for a supplement to his income of 3,000 *livres*, went broke. Much of his money came as gratuities from Rouillé because Raymond did not degrade his status by engaging in trade. The minister cleared 20,000 *livres* of the governor's debts, but when Raymond mustered sufficient temerity to request a second gratuity of an equal amount, the minister refused. Last notice of Raymond is a 1766 petition to the minister, the Duc de Praslin, to pay a 6,000 *livres*' debt to the Bordeaux merchant David Gradis, still outstanding from the Louisbourg years. Typically Raymond attempted to improve his chances by outlining his relationship to the minister, although it was five generations removed on the distaff side. Raymond never acquired the Midas touch that alone could have supported his extravagant life.

Vain and self-centred, Raymond forced his contemporaries to be either loyal allies or bitter opponents. Numerous people, including Pichon, Franquet, Surlaville, and Joannis-Galand d'OLABARATZ, complained of his high-handed treatment. He used people with little regard, at Louisbourg getting his servant girl pregnant. Surlaville, who later annotated much of Raymond's correspondence with biting sarcasm and frequent cynicism, was perhaps most charitable when he wrote that Raymond was animated by "an intense zeal which never lets him listen at all." Yet the object of his energies was personal advancement rather than public service. Pichon observed that he knew "how to profit by the knowledge of others, and to turn it to his sole advantage." Although many of his projects had merit, they failed through his inability to concentrate his energies and his lack of discrimination, and from opposition within the colony and France. His agricultural communities withered because of his failure to appreciate the infertility of the location he chose for them; his roads project was vetoed by France on financial and security grounds; and, before his departure from Louisbourg, his schools for mathematics and artillery had begun to collapse. Raymond's two years on Île Royale had been tumultuous but ultimately his impact was negligible.

T. A. CROWLEY

[Some archival calendars and secondary sources confuse Raymond's career with that of his cousin, Charles de Raymond Des Rivières, because the Raymond dossier in AN, Marine, contains material pertaining to both men. T.A.C.]

AD, Charente (Angoulême), État civil, Saint-Antonin d'Angoulême, 13 oct. 1771. AMA, Inspection du Génie, Bibliothèque, MSS *in-f°*, 205[b], f.47; SHA, A[1], 3393, 3457, 3461, 3499, 3526, 3540, 3577, 3602, 3631; Y[3d], 2121. AN, Col., B, 100, f.109v; C[11B], 32, ff.39, 48, 61; 33, f.100; 34, f.24; C[11C], 9; F[3], 50; Marine, C[7], 270 (dossier Raymond). ASQ, Polygraphie, LV–LVII (copies at PAC). Bibliothèque municipale de Vire (dép. du Calvados), Coll. Thomas Pichon, 1750–62 (transcripts at PAC). PAC, MG 18, J10. PANS, RG 1, 341–41½ (Thomas Pichon papers). *Les derniers jours de l'Acadie* (Du Boscq de Beaumont). *Docs. relating to Canadian currency during the French period* (Shortt), II. [Thomas Pichon], *Lettres et mémoires pour servir à l'histoire naturelle, civile et politique du Cap Breton, depuis son établissement jusqu'à la reprise de cette isle par les Anglois en 1758* (La Haye, Pays-Bas, 1760; réimpr. [East Ardsley, Eng.], 1966). Groulx, *Hist. du Canada français* (1960), I, 70. McLennan, *Louisbourg*.

RENAUD, JEAN (John), merchant and chief road commissioner (*grand voyer*); b. *c.* 1734; d. 16 March 1794 at Quebec.

Nothing is known of Jean Renaud's origins or early years. The first evidence of his presence at Quebec dates from 1768, when he married Martha Sheldon on 1 October in the presence of the Anglican priest David-François De Montmollin*. That year he purchased a property in the Lower Town on Rue Saint-Pierre, where he built a quay, shed, and stable; in 1789 he sold all of these for £900. In the intervening period, in February 1775, he had bought a farm and some buildings on the Rivière Saint-Charles, in the parish of Ancienne-Lorette, and had taken up residence there. Then in 1790 the Jesuits granted him 60 acres in the seigneury of Saint-Gabriel, near Quebec.

Renaud first attracted attention during the American siege of Quebec in the winter of 1775–76, when he was a member of the British militia. Until March his house served as a meeting-place for Lower Town militiamen. On 2 December he had been promoted ensign and he was on guard duty in Rue du Sault-au-Matelot when early on the morning of 31 December the Americans attacked the barricades in the Lower Town [*see* Richard MONTGOMERY]. In recognition of his good conduct on that occasion Governor

HALDIMAND appointed him to succeed Jean-Baptiste Magnan as chief road commissioner for the District of Quebec on 10 Dec. 1782.

This office was defined by the roads ordinance of 1777. With the assistance of the militia captains and their officers the commissioner had to see that the habitants maintained the roads crossing their lands in good repair. In the winter of 1782–83 Renaud began his work by undertaking a tour of his district, which extended down river from Grondines on the north shore of the St Lawrence and Deschaillons across from it on the south shore. He was also interested in the other aspect of his duties: the laying-out of new roads. In 1784 he recommended the building, by the parishioners who would benefit from it, of a road between Baie-Saint-Paul and Quebec. In July 1792 he marked out the king's highway linking Pointe-au-Père and Trois-Pistoles.

Haldimand gave Renaud a further proof of his esteem when on 30 May 1783 he entrusted him with the task of opening up the Témiscouata portage trail from the St Lawrence to Lac Témiscouata in order to facilitate the safe dispatch of the royal mail to Fort Howe (Saint John, N.B.). The terrain was difficult, swampy, and intersected by numerous bogs. Renaud wanted to complete the work quickly and resorted to drastic measures. He obtained remuneration for the militiamen doing *corvées* and had extra rations drawn for them from the king's stores, including a supplementary one of salt pork. A group of 185 militiamen began construction on 12 June. On 30 June it was replaced by another group of 183 men, to whom Renaud added 125 more on 4 July. The road, which was "twelve leagues and sixteen *arpents* [about 30 miles]" long and which only horses could use, was completed on 20 July. The speed with which the work was carried out did not prevent criticism, from Adam MABANE in particular, of the expenses incurred.

Renaud also sought means of improving the general state of the roads. In February 1785 and December 1786 he presented reports to the colonial authorities in which he identified problems and outlined solutions. He would have liked vehicles, which were an important cause of the deterioration of the roads, to be modified, and he wanted the ordinance of 1777 and the powers of the chief road commissioner to be clarified. He objected to the fact that those most directly affected, the habitants, were often opposed to the re-siting of bad roads. In December 1793 he pointed out to the chairman of the Assembly committee studying the highways that roads in Canada could be compared to those in England, with the exception of toll-roads. Renaud had not appreciated being called before this committee, which, instead of drawing upon his expertise, wanted to know why the roads were not better maintained. The "neglect" of which the committee complained could not be said to characterize Jean Renaud's work as chief road commissioner. No one since Jean-Eustache Lanoullier* de Boisclerc had given so much attention to the roads. Renaud's reports indicate that thought was beginning to be given to the whole question of the roads.

At his death Jean Renaud left more than £930 of which £500 was in net debts due him and nearly £280 in real estate. His only heir was his wife, since his son, John Lewis, who had been born in March 1781, had lived only four months. Martha Sheldon survived her husband by many years; she died in 1810.

GRATIEN ALLAIRE

ANQ-Q, État civil, Anglicans, Cathedral of the Holy Trinity (Québec), 1 Oct. 1768; Greffe de P.-L. Descheneaux, 21, 23 févr. 1789; Greffe d'Alexandre Dumas, 28 mars, 8, 26 avril, 18 mai 1794; NF 10, 7, 8. *Journal of the principal occurences during the siege of Quebec by the American revolutionists under generals Montgomery and Arnold in 1775–76*, ed. W. T. P. Short (London, 1824); this journal is reprinted in *Blockade of Quebec in 1775–1776 by the American revolutionists (les Bastonnais)*, ed. F. C. Würtele, Literary and Hist. Soc. of Quebec, *Hist. Docs.*, 8th ser. (1906; repr., London, 1970), 55–101. "Orderly book begun by Captain Anthony Vialar of the British militia . . . ," ed. F. C. Würtele, Literary and Hist. Soc. of Quebec, *Hist. Docs.*, 7th ser. (1905), 155–265. PAC *Rapport*, 1913, app. E, 77–80; 1914, app. C, 78–83. *Quebec Gazette*, 12 Dec. 1776, 19 Dec. 1782, 6 March, 19 June 1783, 8, 29 May 1794. P.-G. Roy, *Inv. concessions*, I, 230; V, 162; *Inv. procès-verbaux des grands voyers*, I, 196–261; IV, 76–79; V, 160.

Ivanhoë Caron, *La colonisation de la province de Québec* (2v., Québec, 1923–27), I, 310, 315. G. P. de T. Glazebrook, *A history of transportation in Canada* (2v., Toronto, 1964), I, 107–9. Ivanhoë Caron, "Historique de la voirie dans la province de Québec; Régime anglais: les ordonnances de 1766 et de 1777," *BRH*, XXXIX (1933), 278–300. Léon Gérin, "La seigneurie de Sillery," RSC *Trans.*, 2nd ser., VI (1900), sect.I, 73–115. Frère Marie Victorin [Conrad Kirouac], "Le portage du Témiscouata; notes critiques et documents pour servir à l'histoire d'une vieille route coloniale," RSC *Trans.*, 3rd ser., XII (1918), sect.I, 55–93. P.-G. Roy, "Le grand voyer Jean Renaud," *BRH*, XLV (1939), 319.

RENAUD, *dit* **Cannard, PIERRE**, master mason and contractor; baptized 3 Oct. 1699 at Saint-Charles-de-Charlesbourg (Charlesbourg, Que.), son of Michel Renaud, *dit* Cannard, and Marie-Renée Réaume; buried there on 15 June 1774.

Pierre Renaud, *dit* Cannard, belonged to the second generation of masons trained in New France, a generation marked off from their predecessors by their ability to adapt their technique to the resources of the country and its climate. In the 18th century the building industry was scarcely flourishing in the city of Quebec and consequently could not support a large number of big contractors; the construction of the important secular and monastic buildings had been completed. Such were the times in which Renaud, *dit* Cannard, and his fellow masons Jean-Baptiste Boucher, *dit* Belleville, and JACQUES and Girard-Guillaume* Deguise, *dit* Flamand, were active.

Renaud, *dit* Cannard, began his career as a building contractor after his marriage with Marie Gariépy on 21 Feb. 1729 at L'Ange-Gardien. His best-known work is the second church at Cap-Santé, one of the most imposing churches of New France. An immense, twin-towered, stone structure, it was begun in 1754. Apparently the plans of the church had been drawn by Jean-Baptiste Maillou*, *dit* Desmoulins, with whom Renaud is thought to have apprenticed. Its dimensions and ostentation stemmed from a rivalry which existed at the time among the parishes. When the year 1763 began, the church was still not finished, and on 17 May Renaud agreed to let the parish priest, Joseph Fillion, continue the work as he saw fit. The construction workers had been drawn away from their building site by the Seven Years' War, which had necessitated, among other things, the building of Fort Jacques-Cartier at the mouth of the river of the same name. At the time that work resumed the price of a toise of masonry had apparently risen sharply, and Renaud was not interested in continuing construction on the terms laid down in the contract.

In the realm of domestic architecture, the principal work of Renaud, *dit* Cannard, was clearly the house that he erected in 1752 for merchant Jean-Baptiste Chevalier near the Quebec shipyards. Built of stone, it had three storeys and originally opened on the Rue du Cul-de-Sac. Today it is attached to two adjoining buildings, and the whole structure is known as the Maison Chevalier. The masonry for Renaud's building was done at the rate of "25 *livres* per running toise, with two bonuses thrown in besides."

Renaud's activities after the conquest are unknown. No notarized contract for masonry has yet been turned up, but there may have been private agreements. When he died in 1774, the contractor left his heirs three pieces of land in the city of Quebec, where he had lived for some years, in addition to property at Gros-Pin (Charlesbourg) on which there was only a wooden house of 25 feet by 18 with an extension measuring 20 by 12 feet. Under the French régime not all master masons could afford the luxury of a stone house.

RAYMONDE GAUTHIER

ANQ-Q, État civil, Catholiques, Saint-Charles-Borromée (Charlesbourg), 15 juin 1774; Greffe de Gilbert Boucault de Godefus, 20 mars 1752; Greffe d'André Genest, 18 juill. 1774; Greffe de Joseph Jacob, 15 févr. 1729. Archives paroissiales, Saint-Charles-Borromée (Charlesbourg), Registre des baptêmes, mariages et sépultures, 3 oct. 1699. IBC, Centre de documentation, Fonds Morisset, Dossier Pierre Renaud, dit Cannard. Tanguay, *Dictionnaire*, VI, 515, 542. F.-X. Gatien *et al.*, *Histoire du Cap-Santé* (Québec, 1955), 64–65. A. W. Gowans, *Church architecture in New France*, 87–88, 154; *Looking at architecture in Canada* (Toronto, 1958), 51–52. Raymonde Landry Gauthier, "L'architecture civile et conventuelle à Québec, 1680–1726" (thèse de MA, université Laval, Québec, 1976). Gérard Morisset, *Le Cap-Santé, ses églises et son trésor* (Québec, 1944), 22–23. Jean Bruchési, "De la maison Soulard à l'hôtel Chevalier," *Cahiers des Dix*, 20 (1955), 91–92.

RENAUD D'AVÈNE DES MÉLOIZES, ANGÉLIQUE (baptized **Angélique-Geneviève**) **(Péan)**, b. 11 Dec. 1722 at Quebec, daughter of Nicolas-Marie Renaud* d'Avène Des Méloizes and Angélique Chartier de Lotbinière; d. 1 Dec. 1792 at Blois, France.

Almost nothing is known about Angélique Renaud d'Avène Des Méloizes' childhood and youth. A list of pupils attending the Ursuline boarding school between 1700 and 1739 includes her name; the institution's annalist later made a note: "The famous Dame Péan, wife of the Chevalier de Livaudière [Michel-Jean-Hugues PÉAN]. She was remarkable for her beauty, her charms, and her wit." The portraits of Angélique certainly give her an expression of confidence that makes her beautiful; the rather sharp nose suggests a strong will, as do her bright, piercing eyes and equally resolute chin.

On 3 Jan. 1746 Angélique married Michel-Jean-Hugues Péan, adjutant at Quebec. All the husband's talents "lay in his wife's charms," the anonymous author of the "Mémoire du Canada" commented irreverently. Péan would soon, however, enjoy high rank in Quebec society, when he became the confidential agent of Intendant BIGOT. The couple lived in the Upper Town, where "after the intendant's house, the best one in town is M. Péan's.... All the elegant people meet at his house, and here life is carried on after the fashion of Paris." The hostess was young, engaging, witty, rather gentle and obliging; her conversation was lively and amusing. Contemporary accounts add that as mediator and protectress for her relatives and friends she was adroit, and that people unfailingly paid court to the two Péans.

Intendant Bigot's arrival in Quebec in 1748 had another consequence for the Péans. Bigot was 45 at the time, and Angélique 25. Contemporary memoirs maintain that she became "the Pompadour" of the intendant, and that her complaisant husband deliberately accepted the situation since it offered him the advantage of amassing a fortune more quickly. Sumptuous banquets and gambling were held in high regard in the intendant's circle. Mme Péan gambled with this high dignitary, and at the games fortunes changed hands. Governor Vaudreuil [RIGAUD], the prudent Vaudreuil, gave in to the prevailing fashion; he "went to the trouble of holding . . . a faro game in his home," according to Montcalm*, who in Guy Frégault*'s opinion, also belonged "to the grand Sultana's court." In one of his letters Montcalm himself mentioned "the ladies of the Péans' circle with whom I am intimate . . . to the point that people believe that I have designs on Lélie [Angélique]."

After the capitulation of Montreal, Angélique accompanied Bigot and her husband to France, sailing on the *Fanny* in September 1760. There had already been gossip in France about the scandal of their relationship. Soon accusations were levelled against the triumvirate of Bigot, Péan, and Joseph-Michel CADET, who were held responsible for the bad administration and loss of Canada. Angélique's husband was arrested in November 1761 and kept in solitary confinement in the Bastille. Mme Péan nevertheless attempted to establish a clandestine correspondence with him, and even obtained permission from the minister, Choiseul, to see him; from March to June 1764 when he was released, she visited him 58 times.

The Péans then went to live at Orzain, near Blois, on property Péan had purchased upon arrival in France in 1758, and for a time they continued their worldly existence. Mme Péan, who was to lose her husband in 1782, devoted the last 20 years of her life to the impoverished, and especially to the Canadian families who had settled in Touraine. Her only daughter, Angélique-Renée-Françoise, married Louis-Michel de Marconnay on 1 Sept. 1769; they had no children. Mme Péan died on 1 Dec. 1792, at nearly 70 years of age.

Angélique Renaud d'Avène Des Méloizes, who was extravagantly admired by the highest officials in the colony, was clearly a formidable woman. Those who liked her did not dare to say much about her. There is no argument in her defence or strong praise in the surviving documents of the period. Only Sieur de Courville [AUMASSON], the memorialist, expressed a desire that we look at the other side of the coin "and see that she had a great deal of merit, above all for her charitable temperament." This controversial figure was made the heroine of William Kirby*'s famous novel, *The golden dog* (New York, 1877), in which fiction takes over from historical truth.

JULIETTE RÉMILLARD

AD, Loir-et-Cher (Blois), État civil, Blois, 1er déc. 1792. "Les archives de la famille Gradis et le Canada," Claude de Bonnault, édit., ANQ *Rapport*, 1944–45, 273. *Coll. des manuscrits de Lévis* (Casgrain), VI, 115; VII, 219; IX, 105. Doreil, "Lettres" (A. Roy) ANQ *Rapport*, 1944–45, 158. "Mémoire du Canada," ANQ *Rapport*, 1924–25, 117–18, 188–89. Burke, *Les ursulines de Québec* (1863–66), II, 176. H.-R. Casgrain, *Guerre du Canada, 1756–1760; Montcalm et Lévis* (2v., Québec, 1891; réimpr., Tours, France, 1899). Frégault, *François Bigot*. P.-G. Roy, *La ville de Québec sous le Régime français* (2v., Québec, 1930), II, 266. Ægidius Fauteux, "Le S. . . de C. . . enfin démasqué," *Cahiers des Dix*, 5 (1940), 267–68. Juliette Rémillard, "Angélique Des Méloizes," *RHAF*, XIX (1965–66), 513–34.

REPENTIGNY, LOUIS LEGARDEUR DE. *See* LEGARDEUR

REPENTIGNY, PIERRE-JEAN-BAPTISTE-FRANÇOIS-XAVIER LEGARDEUR DE. *See* LEGARDEUR

RETOR, CLAUDE DEVAU, *dit*. *See* DEVAU

RIGAUD DE VAUDREUIL, FRANÇOIS-PIERRE DE, soldier and administrator; b. 8 Feb. 1703 in Montreal, son of Philippe de Rigaud* de Vaudreuil, governor general of New France, and Louise-Élisabeth de Joybert* de Soulanges et de Marson; d. 24 Aug. 1779 at the Château de Colliers, in the commune of Muides (dept of Loir-et-Cher), France.

François-Pierre de Rigaud de Vaudreuil, whom Canadians called "Monsieur de Rigaud," belonged to an old family from the province of Languedoc; the *Armorial de France* enumerates 11 generations prior to 1680 of the Rigauds whose descendants won fame on Canadian soil. Philippe de Rigaud de Vaudreuil, who landed at Quebec in 1687, served in the army and assumed the office of governor general of New France in 1703, retaining it until 1725. His six sons were active in the king's service, holding posts in the army, the navy, and the colonies.

The fifth son, François-Pierre, was born the year his father became governor general. Nothing is known of his childhood, or of his education, which must, however, have been rudimentary since his contemporaries, while considering him brave, also said that he was "shallow-brained" and "unintelligent." Taking advantage of the Comte de Pontchartrain's influence, his father had him appointed at the age of five to the company of gentlemen midshipmen, despite the regulation that candidates be 18. He obtained a post for him as ensign in the colonial regulars in 1712 and a lieutenancy on 2 June 1720; his mother, who lived at Versailles from 1709 to 1721, also had a hand in these appointments. The young lieutenant was initiated into military life by serving as adjutant. He first visited France in 1723, and the following year obtained command of a company, again through the influential patronage which the Vaudreuils enjoyed at court. In 1726 he returned to Canada, but went back to France to settle his father's estate two years later; he revisited it in 1730 and 1731. According to Canon Pierre HAZEUR de L'Orme, who was continually on the look-out for gossip from the colony, Rigaud de Vaudreuil went to France to see Louise, the daughter of Joseph de Fleury* de La Gorgendière and Claire Jolliet, whom he had found attractive. He came back to Quebec in 1732 on the *Rubis*, and the following year on 2 May was married in Quebec. He and his wife had five children, all of whom died in infancy.

Rigaud de Vaudreuil was not of the generation that had taken root in Canada, but rather of the one that became Canadian. A soldier, fur-trader, and seigneur, he was typical of that Canadian oligarchy which, though serving the king, endeavoured to work for Canada and for its own interests, a practice which led to frequent clashes with people who came from the mother country. From 1724, the year in which he obtained a company, until 1741, when he was appointed major, Rigaud de Vaudreuil had an inconspicuous role and concentrated mainly on his own promotion and interests. In 1732, in joint ownership with his brother Pierre de RIGAUD de Vaudreuil de Cavagnial, he obtained the seigneury of Rigaud adjoining their seigneury of Vaudreuil on the Ottawa River. In 1736 he secured the grant of the seigneury of Saint-Joseph-de-la-Nouvelle-Beauce, with a responsibility which the other local seigneurs shared of seeing to the construction of "a good carriage road." His obligations as a seigneur did not lie heavily upon him; Rigaud de Vaudreuil was no gentleman farmer.

The post of major which he obtained in 1741, and then the War of the Austrian Succession, finally gave him a chance to put his military talents to best use. Although the war occasioned massive deployments of armies in Europe, in America the Canadians stuck to skirmishing; no fewer than 27 raids spread terror in New England. Rigaud de Vaudreuil was given the responsibility of protecting Fort Saint-Frédéric (near Crown Point, N.Y.). Arriving at the fort in August 1746, and finding no British troops in the vicinity, he followed the Kaskékoué (Hoosic) River to Fort Massachusetts (Williamstown, Mass.), which he razed to the ground after a faint show of resistance by its defenders. On the way back he burned some 200 buildings along the Kaskékoué; he was in Montreal by 26 September. In June 1747 he returned with 780 men to Fort Saint-Frédéric, where he waited in vain for the British; he did not organize any offensive on his own.

In September of that year the new commandant general, Roland-Michel Barrin* de La Galissonière, brought the news of the end of hostilities in Europe. The treaty of Aix-la-Chapelle in 1748 restored peace to Europe but established only a truce in America, where the frontiers of Acadia and the Ohio region were the locations of a bitter struggle marked by constant skirmishing; La Galissonière endeavoured to fortify the strategic points on the frontiers. That year Rigaud de Vaudreuil was named king's lieutenant in the Government of Quebec, a prestigious post placing him at the centre of Quebec society. In September he obtained a seigneury on the Yamaska that would later be the site of the town of Saint-Hyacinthe (Que.).

On 1 May 1749 Rigaud de Vaudreuil succeeded Claude-Michel Bégon* de La Cour as governor of Trois-Rivières. He was thus in a good position to engage in the fur trade; he obtained a grant for two years of the post of Baie-des-Puants (Green Bay, Wis.), receiving the permanent concession in 1759. He sailed for France in 1754, and on the return voyage the following year his ship, the *Alcide*, strayed from the convoy off Cape Ray, Newfoundland, and British ships under Vice-Admiral Edward Boscawen* forced it to surrender after a broadside that raked it "from top to bottom at point-blank range." Rigaud de Vaudreuil was captured and taken to Halifax where, unsuspecting, he handed over precious documents about Louisiana to Thomas PICHON, a spy in the pay of the British. Subsequently he was interned in England; he succeeded in getting over to France and then on 4 May 1756 returned to Quebec.

By June France and Great Britain had declared

war, thus making official the state of war that existed on the frontiers of New France. Upon his arrival Rigaud de Vaudreuil was called into service. During the summer he commanded the advance guard of the forces under Montcalm*, who on 11 August invested the forts in the region of Oswego (N.Y.). Following bombardments and a three-day siege, the British capitulated. Though Montcalm took the credit for it, this splendid feat of arms nevertheless established the reputation of the Canadians and of Rigaud de Vaudreuil. In February and March 1757 he commanded an expeditionary corps of 1,500 including, it seems, 600 Canadians and 300 Indians, which went across country to ravage the region around Fort George (also called Fort William Henry; now Lake George, N.Y.), destroying the depots and the boats which were to have supported an invasion of Canada.

Since the death in January 1755 of the governor of Montreal, Charles Le Moyne* de Longueuil, a successor had been sought for his post. Traditionally the governor of Trois-Rivières replaced the governor of Montreal, and Governor General Pierre de Rigaud de Vaudreuil de Cavagnial proposed his brother. But the minister hesitated, since he did not consider François-Pierre sufficiently talented and intelligent to take the place of the governor general, should the need arise. Vaudreuil insisted, skilfully pleading his brother's cause and that of the Canadians, who had always been relegated to minor posts. On 1 May 1757 the minister assented. Rigaud de Vaudreuil assumed his duties as governor from that date. He had to quarter troops, supply them, and ensure the defence of the region. In 1758 he carried out diversionary manœuvres while Montcalm, with the main body of troops, stopped the invaders at Carillon (Ticonderoga, N.Y.). In 1759, during the Quebec campaign, the governor of Montreal was busy strengthening the line of defence along the Richelieu, which had its strong points at La Prairie and Île aux Noix, seeing that the crops were harvested and maintaining the roll of men fit for military service. After the fall of Quebec, Montreal became the capital of Canada; there, on Place Jacques-Cartier, Governor General Vaudreuil set up headquarters. There was no longer any reason for Montreal to have a governor of its own; Rigaud de Vaudreuil faded into the background at the moment New France was becoming part of history.

Then came life in exile. A British vessel carried Vaudreuil and Rigaud and their suite to France. The two brothers, who were close friends, lived in Paris and at Muides at the Château de Colliers. In March 1762 Rigaud de Vaudreuil, who was called the Marquis de Rigaud in France, obtained an annual pension of 2,000 *livres*, which he tried on several occasions to have increased. He died on 24 Aug. 1779. His wife had died in February 1775 in Saint-Domingue (Hispaniola), where she had gone with her niece.

JEAN HAMELIN and JACQUELINE ROY

[François-Pierre de Rigaud de Vaudreuil left no personal records. His correspondence and papers are dispersed throughout the major documentary series on the French régime. For his career we have used principally documents published in ANQ *Rapport*, PAC *Report*, *BRH*, *Coll. des manuscrits de Lévis* (Casgrain), and *NYCD* (O'Callaghan and Fernow).

A secondary figure, Rigaud de Vaudreuil has had little attention from historians. He has, however, been the subject of a master's thesis: Bernard Vinet, "François-Pierre Rigaud de Vaudreuil, 1703–1779" (université de Montréal, 1954). The thesis is now outdated, but its chronological framework has been useful. In addition there is material on Rigaud de Vaudreuil in various historical works: Æ. Fauteux, *Les chevaliers de Saint-Louis*; Frégault, *La guerre de la Conquête*, which has interesting pages on his role at forts Oswego and George and on the question of the appointment of Canadians to high administrative posts; Ernest Gagnon, *Le fort et le château Saint-Louis (Québec); étude archéologique et historique* (Montréal, 1925); Francis Parkman, *A half-century of conflict* (5th ed., 2v., Boston, 1893); Benjamin Sulte, "Les gouverneurs des Trois-Rivières," *BRH*, II (1896), 66–72. J.H. and J.R.]

RIGAUD DE VAUDREUIL DE CAVAGNIAL, PIERRE DE, Marquis de VAUDREUIL, officer in the colonial regulars and last governor general of New France; b. 22 Nov. 1698 at Quebec, fourth son of Philippe de Rigaud* de Vaudreuil, Marquis de Vaudreuil, and Louise-Élisabeth de Joybert* de Soulanges et de Marson; d. 4 Aug. 1778 in Paris, France.

Pierre de Rigaud de Vaudreuil de Cavagnial's father, scion of a feudal Languedoc noble family, served with the Mousquetaires before accepting the appointment of commander of the colonial regulars in Canada. He later became governor of Montreal and in 1703 succeeded Louis-Hector de Callière* as governor general of New France. He governed the colony in troubled times but won the respect and esteem of the Canadian people, and Pierre was to benefit from his father's legendary reputation to a considerable degree.

At the age of ten, Pierre was commissioned ensign in the colonial regulars; on 5 July 1711 he was promoted lieutenant and in the same year accorded the rank of midshipman on the navy list. Two years later his father sent him to the court with the year's dispatches. His mother had been there for the past four years and had received the prestigious post of under-governess of the Duc de Berry's children. She was able to influence the minister of Marine in the direction of Canadian policy and, at the same time, advance her family's interests. Pierre returned to Quebec in 1715 with the rank of captain, well grounded in the workings of the colonial administration and the methods of dealing with the officials who made the major decisions.

At Quebec, under his father's tutelage, he learned how to cope with the intrigues endemic in all the French colonies. What was more important, he acquired a thorough understanding of his father's policies for defending the interests of New France against threats posed by the British colonies to the south and the Hudson's Bay Company to the north. In 1721 he accompanied a party of senior officers on a tour of inspection of Lake Ontario. From Fort Frontenac (Kingston, Ont.) they skirted the north shore of the lake, examining possible sites for future forts. At Fort Niagara (near Youngstown, N.Y.) they held a conference with Seneca and Onondaga chiefs. This experience of Indian oratory and diplomacy was to prove useful to the young captain. On the party's return it skirted the south shore of the lake, and he thus gained a first-hand knowledge of a vital zone in Canada's extended defence system.

In 1725 Governor General Vaudreuil died. His widow crossed to France and the following year succeeded in obtaining the appointment of major of the troops in Canada for Cavagnial. Although now burdened with the management of the family's Canadian affairs he proved assiduous in the performance of his duties and introduced several long overdue administrative reforms.

In 1727 he obtained leave to go to France to assist his mother in the disposition of his father's estate, but he passed it up when word was received that the Fox nation had attacked a French detachment on the Missouri, killing an officer and seven soldiers. Governor General Charles de Beauharnois* decided that a strong counterstroke was called for. He gave Captain Constant Le Marchand* de Lignery command of a large force to crush the tribe once and for all. Cavagnial accómpanied the expedition, which accomplished little but did provide him with valuable experience in the logistic problems and difficulties attendant on warfare in the distant wilderness.

Upon his return to Quebec in 1728 Cavagnial crossed to France with his younger brother François-Pierre de RIGAUD de Vaudreuil. He made a good impression on Maurepas, the minister of Marine, and was appointed to the post of adjutant of the colonial troops. From this point on he regarded Maurepas as his protector. In 1730 he received the cross of Saint-Louis and promotion on the naval list to lieutenant-commander. When it became apparent that the governorship of Montreal would soon fall vacant – the incumbent, Jean Bouillet* de La Chassaigne, being almost moribund – Cavagnial put in a plea to the minister for the succession. In this aspiration he was disappointed, but two years later, in 1733, when the governor of Trois-Rivières, Josué Dubois* Berthelot de Beaucours, received the Montreal post, Cavagnial was appointed to the vacancy thus created. He quickly learned to dispense the modest patronage at his disposal shrewdly, building up a circle of loyal supporters. His success as a local governor can be gauged by the negative evidence: his nine years at Trois-Rivières were singularly lacking in untoward incidents.

When in 1740 his mother died in Paris, Cavagnial requested leave and the following year travelled to France. He arrived at a most propitious time. Jean-Baptiste Le Moyne* de Bienville, governor of Louisiana, worn out by four decades of incessant struggle to get the colony firmly established, had requested his recall. Just when Maurepas was casting about for a suitable replacement Cavagnial appeared at court. In April the minister made his decision. Cavagnial's official appointment was dated 1 July 1742. It represented a major advance in the imperial service, but the Marquis de Vaudreuil, as Cavagnial had begun calling himself, was already looking further ahead. He saw it as merely a steppingstone to the achievement of his great ambition, one day soon to succeed to the governor-generalship of New France.

He sailed from Rochefort on 1 Jan. 1743, accompanied by Jeanne-Charlotte de Fleury Deschambault, 15 years his senior and the impoverished widow of the king's lieutenant at Quebec, François Le Verrier* de Rousson. They must have been well acquainted before embarking on this voyage with its attendant risks, but it certainly afforded them an opportunity to come to know each other a good deal better. After a four-month voyage they landed at New Orleans on 10 May. That Vaudreuil was a cautious man who did not like to rush into things is evidenced by his waiting a further three years, until November 1746, before he married Mme Le Verrier, who was then 63. They were to remain deeply attached to each other for the ensuing 17 years.

Vaudreuil quickly discovered that his elevated post, so eagerly accepted, was not to be a tranquil one. He was responsible for the maintenance of

Rigaud de Vaudreuil

French sovereignty over the interior of the continent from the Appalachian range and Florida on the east to New Spain in the west, from the Gulf of Mexico to the Illinois River. Except for the agricultural settlements along the Mississippi from south of New Orleans to Natchez (Miss.), and in the Illinois country, the French presence was maintained among the various Indian nations, many of them hostile, only by palisaded trading posts garrisoned by a commandant with a few regular troops who deserted at the first opportunity. The total white population was less than 6,000. New Orleans, the administrative centre of this shadow empire, lay at the end of two long communication lines, both of them vulnerable. The one stretched through the dangerous Bahamas passage (Straits of Florida) and across the Atlantic to Rochefort, the other up the Mississippi and through the Great Lakes to Quebec. Months were required to reach either destination. Were a serious threat to the colony's security to arise, the governor would have to cope with the situation as best he could.

Vaudreuil was also aware that a colonial governor was merely one unit in the colonial administration, albeit an important one. Although nominally subordinate to the governor general of New France at Quebec, distance and the slowness of communications made the governor of Louisiana an independent authority, reporting to, and receiving orders directly from, the ministry of Marine. Above him were the minister and his deputy, the first clerk, who had to be courted, placated, influenced, convinced, and most of all, favourably impressed. Below were the subordinate officials and military officers who had to be kept in line, their loyalty and support gained, their hostility checked. The governor had to find ways to make them fear and respect him. He was thus under all manner of pressures and influences, many of them hidden. Intrigue and chicanery were everywhere rampant in the Byzantine government of Louis XV.

Every governor of Louisiana had to bear in mind the purpose that the colony was intended to serve in French imperial policy. Louisiana had been first established for purely political and military reasons, to block Anglo-American westward expansion. It was also hoped that eventually the colony's economy would develop to the point that it would show a profit on the imperial balance sheet. The crown, staggering from one financial crisis to the next, always sought to achieve its aims with the minimum of expenditure. The needs of the colonists rarely received much consideration. Vaudreuil found himself required to execute policies with means that were invariably inadequate. He also, being himself colonial born, felt considerable sympathy for the settlers and sought to assist them in every way he could. All too often these two objectives, furthering imperial policy and improving conditions for the Creoles, were, if not in conflict, mutually exclusive.

Bienville, Vaudreuil's predecessor, had seen the colony through its founding period. He had performed prodigies merely to avert total collapse but he had been unable to perform miracles. Being human, he wished the minister to believe that he left the colony secure, the Indian nations solidly aligned in the French interest following on his recent campaign against the redoubtable Chickasaws. Vaudreuil saw things differently. It was politically expedient for him to depict the situation that he had inherited in a bad light. He informed the minister that he would quickly restore discipline among the troops and put a stop to the civil and military abuses that were rampant. On the state of the economy he was quite optimistic, and judicious. It was the external threat that worried him most and for which he held his predecessor responsible. Perhaps he would feel more charitable a few years hence, after he had struggled to cope with the complexities that had taxed Bienville's indisputable talents. Yet he did not exaggerate when he informed the minister that French influence among the Indian nations, particularly the powerful Cherokees and Chickasaws, was minimal and that the British colonials were sowing dissension among all the tribes with their underpriced trade goods in order to win them over one by one.

Within a year of his arrival the situation was exacerbated by the outbreak of hostilities between France and Britain in the War of the Austrian Succession. Vaudreuil sought to have the Choctaws attack the Chickasaws, who were allies of the British. The Choctaws, at one time in the French allegiance, demurred. A faction in the tribe led by the chief Matahachitoux (Soulier Rouge) had been won over by the British of Carolina and Georgia by lavish gifts and cheap trade goods. The danger was great that the entire nation would go over to the British, leaving the lower colony open to devastating attacks which its feeble defences could not have withstood. The Louisiana garrison consisted of 835 officers and men, including 149 Swiss mercenaries. Four hundred militia, at most, could be raised, 200 to 300 black slaves used for non-combatant duties, and 500 to 600 Indian allies recruited from the smaller tribes. To make matters worse the supply ships from France too often failed to arrive. The supply situation at the outposts became so bad that the officers were hard pressed to feed their men, who were on the verge of mutiny. This situation was not alleviated by the policy of the commissary general, Sébastien-François-Ange Le NORMANT de Mézy, who insisted on following the ministry's budget restrictions to the letter, regardless of the political or military consequences. Vaudreuil wrote to the minister, "M. Le Normant seeks only to gain merit in your eyes by all these financial arrangements and by his retrenchment. The principle is sound, but it should not be allowed to prejudice the good of the service and the well-being of the colony."

Vaudreuil held frequent conferences with delegations from the Indian nations in his attempts to hold them fast in the French alliance and woo them away from British influence. His efforts did not go unrecognized by the minister; in 1746 he was promoted captain, a senior rank on the navy list. Vaudreuil informed the minister that the colony could flourish if the native tribes were brought to live in peace, but peace could be obtained only by eliminating the influence of the Carolina traders. An additional 100,000 *livres'* worth of trade goods was required to achieve this end, but the supply provided by the crown never seemed adequate and Le Normant's tight hold on the budget hampered his efforts at every turn. Lacking both the military force and the goods needed to counter the growing British threat, Vaudreuil was forced to use other means. The influence of Matahachitoux among the Choctaws had somehow to be countered to prevent the entire nation's being subverted. Vaudreuil put a price on his head sufficiently tempting that five months later the chief was killed by some of his own people. He also succeeded in persuading the Choctaws to attack a Carolina trading party and pillage its 60-horse pack train. The loss of their goods and horses was a serious blow to the Carolinians. They were slow to send another pack train over the mountains. This incident was not the end of the struggle but British dominance over the Louisiana tribes had been averted.

It must have been a cause for considerable satisfaction to Vaudreuil when, in March 1748, Le Normant left for Saint-Domingue (Hispaniola). This condition, however, was to be of short duration. Le Normant's successor, Honoré Michel* de Villebois de La Rouvillière, who had married into the powerful Bégon family, proved to be a far worse thorn in Vaudreuil's side than Le Normant had been. All his life a quarrelsome man, within a few months of his arrival Michel began penning savage tirades against Vaudreuil to the minister. Unfortunately for Vaudreuil his old mentor, Maurepas, was dismissed from office in April 1749. He was replaced by Antoine-Louis Rouillé, who seemed determined to make Maurepas's appointees aware that they had a new master. He accepted Michel's charges at face value, among them that the troops in the colony were insubordinate and that Vaudreuil protected his appointees who were committing all manner of crimes. Vaudreuil now found himself continually being reprimanded and forced to defend himself against a variety of charges. This he did without allowing the dispute to flare up in public. He treated Michel with polite aloofness which infuriated him all the more. Frustrated by Vaudreuil's refusal to quarrel openly, and by his own failure to find support among the local notables, Michel seethed with repressed fury which mounted until in mid December 1752 he was carried off by a fit of apoplexy. Vaudreuil sent a restrained note to Rouillé, stating that Michel's contribution to the service was well known to the minister and requesting that something be done for the deceased's son who was still at college.

This episode had been a vexing but minor one in the colony's affairs. Vaudreuil had other and far more serious problems to worry about. Several hundred miles to the north the Illinois country was a source of constant concern. Settlers were few, but the region was a keystone in France's American empire. Although officially under the jurisdiction of the governor of Louisiana the Illinois settlements were as much, if not more, under the control of the governor general at Quebec. Ironically, Vaudreuil's father had bitterly resented the detachment of the region from his jurisdiction in 1717 to strengthen John Law's Compagnie des Indes. Settled by Canadians who lived by farming, hunting, and trading with the Indians [*see* Antoine Giard*; Jean-François Mercier*], the region had economic ties with both Montreal and New Orleans. The fur trade was controlled by the Montreal merchants, but the region's surplus flour, heavy hides, and the product of the local lead mines went to New Orleans.

The Illinois settlements were also vital for the security of the communication route between Canada and Lower Louisiana. A major problem in the region was the disorders caused by renegade Canadian coureurs de bois among the Illinois tribes and those along the Missouri. They created a situation that, Vaudreuil feared, British traders would be quick to exploit were it not brought under control. Moreover, he maintained that the trade of the entire Mississippi valley belonged by rights to the Louisiana colonists; the Canadians were interlopers.

Vaudreuil had to accept the fact that the price

of trade goods was cheaper at Montreal than at New Orleans, and the Canadian fur trade efficiently organized. In his correspondence with Governor General Beauharnois at Quebec, he proposed that the Canadians be permitted to trade in Upper Louisiana for beaver and fine grade furs, but that deer skins and buffalo hides should go to New Orleans. He set about organizing a company of 20 of the leading Illinois traders and proposed to give them a monopoly of the trade on the Missouri. The company should agree to build a fort and maintain a detachment of troops to keep order in the region. This project seemed so reasonable to Vaudreuil, so well calculated to further French imperial interests in America, that he put it in motion before informing Beauharnois, fully expecting to receive both the governor general's and the minister's concurrence. Beauharnois, however, took umbrage, declaring it to be a usurpation of his authority, and the district subsequently reverted to the authority of Quebec.

Vaudreuil sought to avoid further conflicts with Quebec by obtaining a definition of the jurisdictional limits of Canada and Louisiana. When in 1746 La Jonquière [Taffanel*] was named to replace Beauharnois he was instructed to resolve the problem expeditiously. At the same time the minister began to be persuaded that it would be more economical were the Illinois country placed under the jurisdiction of Quebec since it was too remote from New Orleans for the authorities there to administer effectively. He also felt that it was a strain on Louisiana's budget, and the detachment of two companies of regular troops a thousand miles to the north weakened the lower colony's meagre defences. As for the economic factors, the furs of the region would go to Montreal, the wheat to New Orleans, regardless of jurisdictional control.

It was Roland-Michel Barrin* de La Galissonière, acting in La Jonquière's absence, who had to deal with the problem. In September 1748 he put forward a detailed plan for the defence of French sovereignty in North America against Anglo-American aggression. He concurred with Vaudreuil that the Illinois country was vital but declared that it had to depend on Canada for its defence and development. He was concerned solely with the larger picture of imperial policy; Vaudreuil, on the other hand, was loath to relinquish his authority over Upper Louisiana and the patronage it afforded him. He therefore strongly opposed the annexation of the Illinois region by Canada.

When, in 1749, a decision had to be taken Rouillé compromised. The administration of the Illinois settlements was left with Louisiana but the Ohio valley and the posts on the Ouabache (Wabash) were placed under the commandant at Detroit. Vaudreuil had long been concerned over a potential British threat to the Ohio region. In 1744 he had advocated the construction of a fort on the Ohio some 30 miles from its mouth but Maurepas had prevaricated. Meanwhile traders from Pennsylvania had begun infiltrating the valley. Without a strong French presence and an ample supply of trade goods at competitive prices Vaudreuil could do little to halt their inroads. He feared that the British would establish a fort on the Ohio, win over all the tribes, and be impossible to dislodge. The 1749 expedition of Pierre-Joseph Céloron* de Blainville to the Ohio valley revealed just how serious this threat had become. Vaudreuil then appealed to La Jonquière to employ force to drive the British out but the governor general demurred. All that Vaudreuil could do was reinforce the Illinois garrison with six additional companies, send reliable officers to try to hold the wavering allies from going over to the British, and make plans to restore the crumbling Fort de Chartres (near Prairie du Rocher, Ill.).

Just how effective the action proposed by Vaudreuil could be was demonstrated in 1752 by the daring raid of Charles-Michel MOUET de Langlade who, at the head of 200 or 250 coureurs de bois, Ottawas, and Ojibwas from Michilimackinac (Mackinaw City, Mich.), swooped down on the British trading base at Pickawillany (Piqua, Ohio) among the Miamis. They killed Memeskia (La Demoiselle), the leader of the faction serving the British interest, and 20 of his followers, took five or six British traders prisoner, and then swiftly retired. British influence in the whole region crumbled. Some of their client bands abandoned their villages, fearing like treatment. Half a dozen nations whose allegiance to the French had become doubtful now sent war parties against villages that had allied themselves with the British traders. Vaudreuil was able to report that the tribes of the Ohio valley were all making overtures to the French, hoping to be restored to grace. He warned, however, that the situation was still fluid. What was needed to maintain dominance over the region was a fort on the Ohio [*see* Claude-Pierre PÉCAUDY de Contrecœur].

Perhaps Vaudreuil's greatest achievement in Louisiana was his contribution to the establishment, for the first time in the colony's history, of relative economic prosperity. In 1744 the colonists had faced starvation; the land was neglected and a lack of both external markets and shipping had reduced the settlers to bare subsistence farming. Vaudreuil's solution to this problem was to gain access to markets in the Spanish colonies, Cuba and Mexico. The British navy was his unwitting accomplice in this endeavour. The Spanish colonial administrators, in the face of severe wartime shortages, were forced to entertain Vaudreuil's proposals to admit Louisiana produce, much of it on their contraband list. La Balise, at the mouth of the Mississippi, became an entrepôt where French goods were picked up by Spanish ships for trans-shipment to Havana, Santo Domingo (Dominican Republic), and Veracruz (Mexico). Vaudreuil estimated the value of this trade in the period 1742–44 to be 750,000 *livres*. When the war ended, the trade fell off dramatically but quickly revived. The Spanish colonies found that they could no longer do without it.

In 1743 Vaudreuil purchased a working plantation with 30 slaves on the shore of Lake Pontchartrain for 30,000 *livres*. He developed it assiduously to increase his income, his salary being a mere 12,000 *livres* a year, an amount that was quite inadequate to support his lavish mode of living. He also intended that it should encourage the other planters by example. Upon quitting the colony he sold the property for 300,000 *livres*, but likely this tenfold increase could be attributed to some degree to wartime inflation.

Vaudreuil stressed the production of indigo in Louisiana and brought about a marked improvement in its quality. Between 1743 and 1750 its price doubled and it was so much in demand that the British parliament was obliged to subsidize Carolina indigo. This subsidy resulted in a thriving contraband trade between New Orleans and Charleston (S.C.). Louisiana found itself with an additional profitable market for its indigo and the Carolina exporters collected the British subsidy; both prospered. Timber, pitch, tar, turpentine, tobacco, rice, and hides were also produced for export in increasing quantities. In 1750 a hundred ships called at La Balise from the French and Spanish West Indies, Mexico, and France. By 1751 the colony's export trade amounted to a million *livres*. By 1753 that figure had doubled. Vaudreuil could take some of the credit.

Another major contribution to the colony's prosperity for which Vaudreuil could take credit was the tripling of the budget, from 322,798 *livres* in 1742 to 930,767 in 1752. Most of this money was expended in the colony to pay the troops and officials, to build fortifications and subsidize the clergy, for "presents" to the Indians, social welfare, and a myriad of things. The greater part of it ended up in the pockets of the colonists, who now enjoyed a fair measure of economic security, and some of them were relatively affluent. Vaudreuil himself set the pace in colonial society for conspicuous consumption. He entertained lavishly, kept open table for the officers and notables, rendering it highly desirable to be granted the entrée to his circle, pernicious to earn his displeasure and be excluded.

Throughout these years Vaudreuil hoped and expected one day in the near future to be appointed governor general of New France. This had long been his main aim in life. Learning that not he but La Jonquière had been named, in 1746, to replace Beauharnois came as a terrible disappointment. La Jonquière, however, reassured him that he had accepted the post at Quebec for a three-year term and that Maurepas had stated that he would be succeeded by Vaudreuil; but then Maurepas was dismissed from office. In 1752 DUQUESNE was appointed to replace the deceased La Jonquière. Vaudreuil began to fear that he had been passed over permanently. His family was outraged. His brother François-Pierre wrote him to say that he was sure Vaudreuil would now resign from the service. He added that even though Vaudreuil would have only 4,000 *livres* a year pension he could live at his ease in Languedoc on that and be answerable to no one. It must have come as a great relief when, in a letter dated 8 June 1752, Rouillé informed Vaudreuil that he was to be replaced as governor of Louisiana by Louis Billouart de Kerlérec. He was ordered to remain at New Orleans long enough to instruct Kerlérec in the affairs of the colony and then return to France from where he would, in due course, proceed to Quebec.

Vaudreuil had won the acclaim of the Louisiana colonists. He left the colony in a far more secure and prosperous condition than he had found it. He had gained a great deal of invaluable experience in his negotiations with the Indian nations. He had also become acutely aware of the growing threat posed by the British colonies. On 24 Jan. 1753 Kerlérec's ship arrived at La Balise. On 8 May Vaudreuil and his entourage left New Orleans. He landed at Rochefort on 4 Aug. 1753 and then took up residence in Paris.

Vaudreuil's commission as governor general of New France was not issued until 1 Jan. 1755. During those 20-odd months that he spent in France there was a clash of arms in the Ohio valley between Major George Washington at the head of a party of colonial militia and a detachment from the garrison at Fort Duquesne (Pittsburgh, Pa) [*see* Louis Coulon* de Villiers]. This incident marked the beginning of hostilities between Britain and France that were to involve four continents for the ensuing nine years. Neither Vaudreuil nor the French government had any illusions about their ability to conquer the British in America. Vaudreuil's task now was to prevent them from conquering New France.

To bolster the defences of Louisbourg, Île Royale (Cape Breton Island), and Canada against anticipated British attacks, the French government in 1755 detached six of its 395 infantry battalions from the ministry of War and placed them under the ministry of Marine. Command of the army battalions in Canada was given to Baron Jean-Armand de Dieskau* with the rank of major-general. The wording of his commission, which was issued on 1 March 1755, was undertaken with the most scrupulous care. It went through several drafts to ensure that all concerned clearly understood and accepted that the commander of these battalions was under the supreme command of the governor general. The likelihood of conflicts between them was foreseen and a sincere effort was made by Pierre-Arnaud de Laporte, the first clerk of the Marine, to remove all possible causes by defining the respective spheres of authority in detail. Dieskau was required to carry out the orders of the governor general without question; the latter was expected to consult with Dieskau in formulating his strategy. Given sensible men the arrangement would have worked reasonably well.

Vaudreuil, accompanied by his wife, sailed for Quebec from Brest on 3 May 1755 with the ships that carried Dieskau and the six army battalions. The convoy eluded Vice-Admiral Edward Boscawen*'s squadron, dispatched by the British Admiralty before war had been declared to intercept and capture or sink it, and arrived at Quebec on 23 June. A week previous the British under Robert MONCKTON had taken Fort Beauséjour (near Sackville, N.B.), and an army commanded by Major-General Edward Braddock was over the Allegheny mountains, making its slow but steady way towards Fort Duquesne. Other Anglo-American forces were being massed for assaults on the French forts at Niagara and on Lake Champlain.

As governor general Vaudreuil was ultimately responsible for everything that transpired in the vast territory under his authority. Subordinate officials, principally the intendant, had charge of the civil administration, finance, and justice. The major problem of supplies for the army, and for the civilian population, was also the intendant's responsibility. BIGOT, it has to be said, discharged this task efficiently, if at staggering cost to the crown. What the armed forces required he always managed to provide. Throughout the war Vaudreuil's relations with Bigot, a man of undoubted charm, were good. After his bitter experience in Louisiana with Le Normant and Michel, who had frustrated him at every turn, it must have been a great relief to work with someone as complacent and efficient as Bigot. Vaudreuil was well aware that the intendant was amassing a fortune but he got things done, freeing Vaudreuil from worry over the logistics of the war. In any event, a governor general was not supposed to meddle in financial matters.

Military affairs and relations with the Indian nations, upon whom he had to rely heavily for military support, were the governor's responsibility. Were anything to go wrong in these spheres he would be held solely accountable. Vaudreuil's main concern, from the moment he landed at Quebec, had to be the direction of the war.

His strategy throughout was to take maximum advantage of his interior lines of communication along the St Lawrence, the Great Lakes, the Richelieu, and Lake Champlain. The Anglo-Americans could, he well knew, mass far greater forces than he had at his disposal, but there was a limit to the numbers they could usefully deploy along the invasion routes; supplies, shipping, roads, transport, these factors imposed limits. He also counted on the American colonials' disunity, their military ineptitude, and the ability of his forces to strike swiftly, summer or winter, all along their frontiers. He could move his main force by water much more swiftly than they could move theirs on forest roads; thus he could attack, inflict a defeat on one front, and then move the army to the other danger point in time to block them again. He also used the Canadian militia and Indian auxiliaries to ravage American settlements, forcing the enemy to tie down sizeable forces for defence. The ferocity of this guerrilla warfare, at which the Canadians excelled [*see* Joseph MARIN de La Malgue; Joseph-Michel LEGARDEUR de Croisille et de Montesson], terrorized the Americans and severely weakened their morale. In addition the prisoners taken provided Vaudreuil with information on the enemy's dispositions and intentions. He was thus able to mount spoiling attacks on bases and supply trains, making it difficult for an assault to be organized. Just how devastatingly effective the Canadians and Indians could be against both American militia units and British regulars was demonstrated by the destruction of Braddock's army a few miles from Fort Duquesne in July 1755 [*see* Jean-Daniel DUMAS].

During the ensuing three years Vaudreuil employed these tactics with great effectiveness. Major-General William JOHNSON's thrust towards Lake Champlain was turned back in 1755, although not with all the success that Vaudreuil had intended. The fortified American base at Oswego (Chouaguen) was destroyed the following year by Montcalm*'s forces, securing control of the Great Lakes. In 1757 Fort George (Fort William Henry; now Lake George, N.Y.) was taken after a short siege and razed to the ground, enemy assault from that quarter being thereby ruled out for another year. There was never any question of holding these captured bases. The operations were purely defensive; attack was regarded by Vaudreuil as the best defence.

This external threat, grave as it was, proved easier to cope with than the problems Vaudreuil faced with the French battalions, and more particularly with their staff officers. In the 1755 campaign against Johnson's army Dieskau had ignored Vaudreuil's orders to keep his force together and had attempted to surprise the enemy with less than half the men he had available. It was a calculated risk and he was only partially successful. The Americans were left in command of the field and Dieskau was taken prisoner. Vaudreuil informed the minister that the Canadians had lost confidence in the ability of the French staff officers to direct military operations in the field. Canadian conditions, he pointed out, were far different to those that the French troops were accustomed to and their officers were not willing to heed advice, or even orders. He therefore asked the minister not to send a general officer to replace Dieskau. This plea was rejected.

In October 1755 André Doreil*, the commissary of wars, in a dispatch to the minister of War, commented on Vaudreuil's problems and his character: "He is a general who has good, honest intentions, who is gentle, benevolent, and easily approachable, always considerate and courteous, but the circumstances and his present responsibility are a bit too much for him, he needs an adviser who is free of personal bias and who could strengthen his resolve." Doreil went on to express the hope that the commander to be sent in the spring to replace Dieskau would be responsive, good natured, and of a gentle character, for such a person would be able to govern the governor. Doreil was certainly not the best judge of character, his own leaving much to be desired, but there was some truth in what he wrote.

Had the minister of War set out to find a man possessed of the exact opposite qualities he could not have chosen better than the Marquis de Montcalm, who had never commanded more than a regiment before being appointed to command the French battalions in Canada. The minister of Marine assured Vaudreuil that "M. le Marquis de Montcalm has only the same powers as M. de Dieskau had, and he has been given the same orders and instructions. It is only under your authority that he can exercise the command that has been entrusted to him. And he will be subordinate to you in every respect." Montcalm was instructed that he had to establish and maintain good relations with Vaudreuil, but he quickly made it clear that this rapport was beyond him. He had a quick, caustic wit and an even quicker temper that he could not control. Although his personal bravery was beyond question he was a confirmed defeatist, convinced that every campaign he was engaged in would turn out badly and always anxious to ensure that the blame would fall elsewhere than on his shoulders. He resented bitterly having to take orders from an officer of the Marine, disagreed violently with Vaudreuil's strategy, and was extremely critical of the Canadian manner of waging war. He did not scruple to criticize Vaudreuil before his subordinates and servants and his words were of course promptly reported to Vaudreuil, who somehow still managed to be openly polite.

Beneath the surface, however, Vaudreuil's state of mind was far from good. He was, in fact, at the end of his tether and in danger of going to pieces. Within a few months of his arrival at Quebec he had become totally disillusioned with the situation facing him. So much so in fact that when the first ships sailed for France in the spring of 1756 he dispatched an urgent plea for his recall. He likely sent it to his elder brother Jean, Vicomte de Vaudreuil, to present to the minister. Since no such communication, nor any mention of it, appears in the official correspondence the recipient obviously chose not to act upon it. Had he done so Vaudreuil's career would no doubt have been abruptly terminated. On 26 Oct. 1756, in poor health, he wrote to his friend de Calanne at Saint-Domingue a letter, subsequently intercepted by the British, which revealed his demoralized state of mind. After mentioning the capture of Oswego he wrote: "Canada at the moment is in chaos. If I were not to return to France I should go out of my mind. I have not received one word about my return that I strongly requested at the turn of the year. Since I could expect nothing were I to be crippled in this country, and I can expect no great thanks for the vital services that I render here, I shall return to France, without permission, if the state of my health requires it. At present the war is waged in Canada as in France, with the usual panoply and baggage train. It is only the poor Canadians who are not in the like case, always being off on forays with the Indians and bearing the brunt of the enemy's fire."

Vaudreuil, in his dispatches to the minister of Marine, which Montcalm contrived to have intercepted and copied, praised the Canadians to the skies but was critical of the French battalions in general and Montcalm's leadership in particular. He was exceedingly irate over Montcalm's failure to follow his orders in 1757 and press on to destroy Fort Lydius (Fort Edward; now Fort Edward, N.Y.) after Fort George had fallen. He charged that too many French officers refused to serve with Canadian raiding parties, declaring that they had not come to Canada to wage that kind of war. All that they were willing to do was wait for the enemy to come to them, then hope to avoid a defeat. He also reported that the Canadian militia, with French solders billeted on them over the winter, resented being called out for war parties while the soldiers remained behind by the fireside. He charged that the French officers were drawing rations for grossly inflated muster rolls, disposing of the surplus, and pocketing the proceeds. Evidence from other sources supports the accusation. At the end of the war many of these officers sought to change colonial paper money into bills of exchange for amounts far in excess of what their pay and allowances had been. Vaudreuil later stated that he and Bigot had issued orders, against which Montcalm had strongly protested, to put a stop to the abuse. Their efforts in this regard enjoyed little success. It was the attitude of the French officers towards the Canadians that raised Vaudreuil's ire the most. He, and others, reported that the French troops behaved as though they were on enemy territory, pillaging and abusing the habitants with impunity. He informed the minister that nothing would benefit the colony more than the recall of these troops the moment peace was declared.

The year 1758 marked the turning point in the war and brought the long simmering conflict between Montcalm and Vaudreuil to the boil. The British government was more determined than ever to eliminate French power in North America. Heavy reinforcements of British regulars were sent across the Atlantic and assaults were mounted against Louisbourg, Carillon (Ticonderoga, N.Y.), Fort Frontenac (Kingston, Ont.), and Fort Duquesne. Louisbourg held out long enough to prevent AMHERST's besieging army from going on to attack Quebec that year. At Carillon Montcalm, despite odds of nearly four to one, won a stunning victory over Major-General ABERCROMBY. Fort Frontenac was destroyed in a surprise attack by an American force under Lieutenant-Colonel BRADSTREET. Vaudreuil had relied on the Iroquois to keep him informed of the enemy's movements in that region, but they had always resented the presence of that fort on lands they regarded as theirs; hence they gave him no warning. The garrison at Fort Duquesne, commanded by François-Marie Le Marchand* de Lignery, fought a brilliant delaying action against a vastly greater enemy force under Brigadier-General John Forbes,* inflicted heavy casualties, but was finally forced to retire to the upper Allegheny. Vaudreuil's outer defence system had begun to crumble, but the enemy was still being held well away from the central colony. He knew, however, that the assault would be renewed the following year. He informed the minister that only two things could save the colony, an early end to the war or the sending of heavy troop-reinforcements and supplies in the spring. He sent Major Michel-Jean-Hugues PÉAN to the court with his dispatches to impress on the minister the urgency of the situation. The decision was then out of his hands.

The conflict with Montcalm he had to deal with himself. Before the Carillon campaign Montcalm had disputed Vaudreuil's orders and openly ridiculed him. After his victory he levelled serious and quite wild charges against the governor general and the Canadian troops, charges that no superior officer could countenance or ignore. Montcalm also declared that he would request his recall to France. Vaudreuil was only too glad to support this request and sent a strong plea to the minister that Montcalm be promoted lieutenant-general and his undoubted talents employed in Europe. He gave permission to Bougainville* and Doreil to cross to France in the autumn of 1758 to present Montcalm's view of the situation. They arrived to find that Nicolas-René Berryer had become minister of Marine, the fourth of five to hold the post during the war, and the decrepit Maréchal de Belle-Isle, an old friend of Montcalm, was now the minister of War, the third since the beginning of hostilities. The French government could hardly have been in greater disarray.

Berryer refused to listen to Péan, but Vaudreuil's request that Montcalm be replaced by LÉVIS, and the reasons for it, were carefully considered and accepted. The decision, however, had to be referred to the king who rejected it, decreeing that, for reasons unstated, Montcalm had to remain in Canada. He was appointed lieutenant-general on 20 Oct. 1758, a promotion which created an anomalous situation. As the minister of Marine had pointed out in recommending Montcalm's recall, a lieutenant-general ranked higher than a colonial governor general. Montcalm therefore had to be given command over all the armed forces, yet Vaudreuil as governor general was still held responsible for the security of the colony. The lines of command were now hopelessly confused between two men who could not abide each other.

Meanwhile, at Quebec, Montcalm was disputing with Vaudreuil over the strategy to be employed in 1759. He demanded that the fittest men in the Canadian militia be incorporated into the ranks of the regulars, and that the forts in the west and down Lake Champlain be abandoned in order to concentrate all the available manpower for the defence of the central colony. He also made recommendations for the defence of the river below Quebec. Vaudreuil acceded to the militia's incorporation into the regulars, but he refused to abandon the outer defences. He argued that to do so would allow the enemy to advance into the central colony unopposed whereupon the fate of New France would be decided in one battle against an army vastly superior in numbers. He intended to oppose the enemy's advance every foot of the way to delay them as long as possible, hoping that the mother countries would end the war before the central colony was invaded.

In mid May 1759 Bougainville returned to Quebec accompanied by nine merchant ships with another convoy of 17 close behind [*see* Jacques Kanon*]. They relieved the grave food shortage of the preceding months and provided enough supplies for the coming campaign. All through the war the supply problem had been a vexing one. Enough ships had always reached Quebec – in 1758 over 40 – to provide for the needs of the army and civilian population. The real problem was one of distribution. A sizeable proportion of the supplies disappeared no one knew where, and the habitants were most reluctant to deliver their produce in exchange for dubious paper money.

Montcalm was overjoyed to learn of his promotion, and promised miracles. Vaudreuil could only be dejected. What also dismayed him was that his plea for strong reinforcements had, on the advice of Montcalm, been rejected. Only 336 sorry recruits landed at Quebec. Yet he was ordered to fend off the enemy and retain possession of as much of the colony as he could to strengthen France's bargaining position at a future peace settlement. The minister, having indicated that Montcalm outranked him, still addressed him as the responsible officer. Montcalm made no attempt to take over the command, and with it the responsibility for what might ensue. He was quite content to leave that to Vaudreuil. It was small solace for Vaudreuil to learn that he had been awarded the grand cross of the order of Saint-Louis with an accompanying grant of 10,000 *livres*, after having been appointed a commander of the order in 1757. He had, however, little time to feel sorry for himself since late in May 1759 it was learned that a large British fleet was moving up the river. Unaccountably, the defence measures that he and Montcalm had discussed taking had not been carried out [*see* Gabriel PELLEGRIN]. Had they been, the British fleet could have been punished severely before reaching Quebec. Vaudreuil has to be held responsible for this omission.

Vaudreuil gave provisional over-all command of the armed forces and the town to Montcalm who, ably seconded by Lévis, succeeded in holding Wolfe*'s army at bay all through the summer. By September the British had become despondent, the French and Canadians jubilant, believing that the enemy would be forced to withdraw in a matter of days and that they would end the campaign with glory. Then Wolfe switched his main force from below Quebec to above it, got it ashore on the night of 12 September, and by daylight had it drawn up within a mile of the town walls. Much ink has been spilled as to who should be held to blame, on the French side, for this turn of events. In fact, had Vaudreuil and Montcalm desired to lure Wolfe's army into a position where they could totally destroy it, they could not have hoped to find it in a more suitable place than the one that Wolfe had chosen. Montcalm, however, gave way to panic. Without stopping to take stock of the situation, to consult with Vaudreuil or his own staff, he launched an ill-conceived and worse-directed attack with a third of the forces at his disposal. Within the hour his shattered army had fled the field and he himself was mortally wounded.

Vaudreuil later stated in a dispatch to the minister that upon learning of the British disposition he sent a note to Montcalm requesting him to do nothing precipitate but to wait until they had their entire force in position to attack. When he arrived on the heights it was all over. He asserted that he tried to rally the fleeing troops without success. The Canadians alone responded. With heavy loss to themselves they checked the British on the right flank, allowing the regulars to cross the Rivière Saint-Charles unmolested. Vaudreuil then set about restoring some sort of order. He dispatched a note to Montcalm who was in the hands of the surgeons in Quebec, with only hours to live, asking for his views on what should be done. Montcalm replied that he should seek terms of capitulation for the entire colony, or launch another attack, or retire up river to join Bougainville's force of 3,000 élite troops at

Jacques-Cartier. Vaudreuil wished to launch another attack at dawn the next day. The British losses had been as great as those of the French, who still outnumbered the enemy by more than three to one and retained possession of the fortified town. He called a council of war attended by Bigot, Pierre-André GOHIN de Montreuil, Nicolas Sarrebource* Maladre de Pontleroy, Jean-Daniel Dumas, and the corps commanders. The officers had no stomach for another engagement; only Bigot was for it. The military voted unanimously to retire to Jacques-Cartier. Vaudreuil had to give way. There was little hope of a successful attack by a defeated army under such officers, and another defeat would have been fatal. Vaudreuil therefore gave the orders to retire to Jacques-Cartier under cover of darkness. The guns were spiked, the tents, equipment, and supplies abandoned. Vaudreuil sent word to Montcalm informing him of the decision and expressing a manifestly sincere hope for his recovery. To the commander of the Quebec garrison, Jean-Baptiste-Nicolas-Roch de RAMEZAY, he sent an order, previously drawn up by Montcalm, requiring him to hold out as long as he could but allowing him to surrender the city rather than sustain an assault that would have incurred, according to the rules of war, no quarter for the inhabitants. He also sent word of what had transpired to Lévis at Montreal. Lévis departed Montreal on the instant, arrived at Jacques-Cartier on the 17th, and immediately set about restoring order in the demoralized army.

Vaudreuil and Lévis agreed that the situation could still be saved if the British could be prevented from occupying Quebec. Vaudreuil sent an order to Ramezay, superseding the earlier one, this time to hold out, not to capitulate, and informing him that supplies and reinforcements would reach him in a matter of hours. Ramezay disregarded this order and surrendered Quebec on the 18th. But for that, within a matter of days the British army would have had to raise its siege and leave with the fleet that dared not risk being trapped in the river by the onset of winter. Vaudreuil sent a terse and bitter note to Ramezay informing him that he would have to account to the king himself for his action; he, Vaudreuil, could not. Nothing then remained but to get word to France with a desperate plea that strong reinforcements be sent early the next year to arrive before the British fleet brought a fresh army to Quebec. Vaudreuil arrived in Montreal on 1 October, and in November Lévis drew back with his dejected forces to rejoin him as three British armies prepared to advance on this last defenceless stronghold, all that remained of French power in America east of the Mississippi.

Vaudreuil, who had always got on well with Lévis, left the preparations for, and direction of, the ensuing campaign in his hands, giving him all the support he could. When in April 1760 he ordered the Canadian militia to join the army for the march to Quebec they responded well. Lévis won a brilliant victory over the British army under MURRAY before the walls of Quebec but the expected fleet with reinforcements from France did not appear. The French troops, even the grenadiers, as well as the Canadian regulars and militia, seeing that further resistance was futile – that it could only result in the useless loss of their lives, in rapine and the destruction of yet more farms and crops, with winter coming on to bring starvation – began to desert in droves.

When the British armies which had approached by the St Lawrence and by Lake Champlain were at the gates of Montreal, their cannon ranged on the town, Vaudreuil on the night of 6 Sept. 1760 called a council of war attended by the senior officers and Bigot. They all agreed that the situation was hopeless and discussed the terms they should ask of Amherst for the capitulation of Canada, Acadia, and the western posts as far south as the Illinois. Vaudreuil then drew up terms with great care, having two main aims in mind: first, to protect the rights of the Canadians to enjoy their religion, their property, and their laws, even in the event that Canada should not be restored to the French crown at the end of the war; second, that the troops under his command be awarded the customary honours of war and given safe passage to France. Bougainville was then deputed to go to Amherst the following morning to ask for a suspension of arms until 1 October. If by that date no word had been received of a peace settlement in Europe the French would capitulate. The whole of 7 September passed in negotiations. Amherst refused to suspend hostilities until the end of the month. He accepted most of the terms proposed by Vaudreuil, was equivocal on some, including the question of religion, but he insisted that both the French and the colonial regulars should not serve again during the war, and he churlishly refused to grant the honours of war. Bougainville passed back and forth between the lines as Vaudreuil tried repeatedly to get Amherst to grant more generous terms, but to no avail.

Late that night, when Lévis and his senior officers were informed that Amherst adamantly refused to accommodate them, they protested to Vaudreuil in the strongest terms, both orally and in writing. Lévis demanded that negotiations be broken off and that Vaudreuil grant them the right to march out with their remaining 2,400 men against the enemy or at least allow them to retire to Île Sainte-Hélène, near the town, there to defy Amherst, rather than accept terms that would deprive France of ten battalions, not to mention ruin their own careers. Vaudreuil and Montcalm had earlier received orders from the court that, no matter what, the honour of the army had to be preserved. The terms on which Governor Drucour [Boschenry*] had surrendered Louisbourg had been regarded as humiliating, and the king had made it plain that he would not countenance another such occurrence.

Vaudreuil now had to make a cruel decision. To have given way to Lévis's plea would have saved honour and pleased Louis XV, but at the cost of the slaughter of the remaining regulars, the destruction of Montreal, and incalculable suffering for the Canadian people thereby left at the mercy of an enemy who would have no need to give quarter or feel any compunction for their suffering. The British had already demonstrated in Ireland, the Scottish Highlands, and in Acadia how ruthless they could be when provoked. Displaying both common sense and strength of character, Vaudreuil rejected Lévis's demand and ordered him to submit to Amherst's conditions. In one last defiant gesture, before his troops stacked their arms on the Champ de Mars, Lévis ordered the regiments' colours burned. Later that day, 8 September, the British entered Montreal.

On 18 October Vaudreuil sailed from Quebec on a British ship and landed at Brest on 28 November. He well knew that he had caused the Canadians to be spared at the cost of his own career, which could now only end with ignominy. If he had any doubts on that score they were resolved early in December when he received, whilst still at Brest, a missive from the minister informing him that the king had been astonished to learn that his colony, Canada, had been rendered up to the enemy. The protests of Lévis and his officers were cited as evidence that, despite the heavy odds, one last attack or at least the sustaining of the enemy's assault on their position, would have obliged Amherst to grant more honourable terms to his majesty's army.

The Vicomte de Vaudreuil immediately voiced his strong resentment to the Duc de Choiseul, minister of Marine, at this treatment of his brother. Choiseul replied, courteously, as always, that he had been obliged to express the king's displeasure over the capitulation of Montreal, that the former governor general should not take it to heart, and that he would always be happy to render justice to the zeal and long service of the vicomte's brother. This response, however, was small consolation to Vaudreuil for it did not prevent his being implicated in the *affaire du Canada*.

The government had to find someone to blame for the loss of its empire in North America, and for the huge bills that had accrued for its defence. The ministries of Marine and War could not be expected to shoulder any part of the blame, Montcalm was dead, and the king would not allow the army battalions to be held culpable. Vaudreuil and Bigot were thus the obvious choice. On 17 Nov. 1761 Bigot was sent to the Bastille. Vaudreuil followed him on 30 March 1762 but was granted his provisional freedom on 18 May.

During his long drawn out trial his wife was stricken with a painful illness. Her suffering endured for months, ending only with her death in the autumn of 1763. His brother Louis-Philippe* also died during those months. Vaudreuil avowed that these afflictions, combined with all that he had had to undergo since arriving in France, had rendered life hardly worth living. Although nothing could console him for the loss of his wife, his spirits revived when, on 10 Dec. 1763, he was exonerated by the judges of the tribunal. The king then allowed him to be invested with the grand cross of the order of Saint-Louis and granted him an additional pension of 6,000 *livres* as compensation for all that he had endured while implicated in the *affaire du Canada*. In a letter dated 22 March 1764 Vaudreuil reported that the nobility, the ministers, even the princes, had demonstrated their pleasure over his justification. To cap it all, he had dined with the Duc de Choiseul who revealed that he had never given credence to the charges levelled at him by the onetime minister of Marine, Berryer, and that he was very pleased his name had finally been cleared.

Vaudreuil could now look back on his career with greater equanimity. He had reached the upper level of the imperial service and he was in receipt of a pension that allowed him to live with modest dignity. For the ensuing 14 years he resided in quiet retirement at his Paris house on the Rue des Tournelles in the Latin quarter, where he died on 4 Aug. 1778.

Pierre de Rigaud, Marquis de Vaudreuil, was obviously a highly strung, complex person who bottled up his emotions and let no one around him suspect his inner turmoil. His *crise de nerfs* of 1756 when he sought to be recalled, even though it would have terminated his career, is proof. The circumstances of his long courtship and eventual marriage, late in life, to a fortuneless woman then over 60 and 15 years his senior, also appear odd even for that age and *ambiance*.

His task as commander-in-chief in New France, bedevilled by the long-standing, bitter rivalry between the army and the Marine, was made infinitely worse by Montcalm's personal vendetta against him. He could not be blamed for the final defeat and the loss of the colony. Rather he deserves much credit for the colony's having held out as long as it did against such heavy odds. His true measure, however, was displayed when he overruled Lévis and insisted on capitulating at Montreal to spare the Canadian people further pointless death and destruction. That act required great strength of character since he must have been aware that he thereby placed his career and all that he had so long struggled for in jeopardy. Lévis summed the case up fairly and succinctly when, upon arriving at La Rochelle on 27 Nov. 1760, he wrote to the minister of Marine: "Without seeking to render misplaced eulogies I believe I can say that M. le Marquis de Vaudreuil employed, right up to the last moment, every resource of which prudence and human experience is capable."

W. J. ECCLES

[The main manuscript sources pertinent to Vaudreuil's career are AN, Col., B, C^{11A}, C^{13A}, D^2, F^3; AMA, SHA, A^1; PAC, MG 18, G2; and the Vaudreuil MSS in the Huntington Library's Loudoun papers. An excellent catalogue, virtually a calendar of these last Vaudreuil MSS, is *The Vaudreuil papers: a calendar and index of the personal and private records of Pierre de Rigaud de Vaudreuil, royal governor of the French province of Louisiana, 1743–1753*, comp. Bill Barron (New Orleans, 1975).

A sizable proportion of manuscript material has been printed, including the extensive *Coll. des manuscrits de Lévis* (Casgrain), who also edited *Extraits des archives de la Marine et de la Guerre*. Many pertinent documents have been published over the years in the ANQ *Rapport*. The *Table des matières des rapports des Archives du Québec, tomes 1 à 42 (1920–1964)* ([Québec], 1965) should be consulted under the headings Guerre, Journaux, Mémoires, Capitulations, Siège de Québec. *NYCD* (O'Callaghan and Fernow), VI, VII, IX, X, have to be used with care; neither the transcription nor the translation can be trusted.

By far the best treatment of Vaudreuil to date, but one which still leaves much to be desired, is to be found in the three works by Guy Frégault*, *François Bigot*, *Le grand marquis*, and *La guerre de la Conquête*. Particularly in the last two works Frégault felt obliged to deal at some length with the *canards* of earlier historians who had depicted Vaudreuil in a bad light. His exasperation at the way they had ignored or abused historical evidence resulted in his displaying, on occasion, an understandable acerbity. Some Anglophone historians chose to regard this as a partisan departure from the revealed conventual wisdom. Of the above-named three works only *Le grand marquis* is devoted specifically to Vaudreuil, but it addresses itself solely to his early career and his tenure as governor of Louisiana. In the other two works Vaudreuil figures prominently, but inevitably he is dwarfed by events. All three contain excellent bibliographies of the primary and secondary sources concerned with Vaudreuil and his times. The *Almanach royal* (Paris), gives terse but valuable information on Vaudreuil's service career, such as his appointments and promotions.

For brief general works dealing with the Seven Years' War in America the bibliographies appended to the biographies of Wolfe and Montcalm in vol. III of the *DCB* can be consulted. A much more extensive bibliography is to be found in Stanley, *New France*. W.J.E.]

RITCHIE, JOHN, merchant and office-holder; b. 1745 or 1746 in or near Glasgow, Scotland; d. 20 July 1790 in Annapolis Royal, Nova Scotia.

In 1770 John Ritchie, accompanied by his wife Jennet (Janet), moved from Edinburgh, Scotland, to Boston, Massachusetts. There he carried on a mercantile business aided by his uncle Andrew Ritchie, who had immigrated to Boston in 1753. Some time before 1775, perhaps in connection with his uncle's business, he moved to Annapolis Royal. In that year, an important one for Ritchie, his first son was born and his wife died. At the same time his uncle was captured by American rebels and imprisoned in Massachusetts for a year. John Ritchie's support for the mother country never wavered, although that of some of his Nova Scotian neighbours was not so certain. Fearing rebel designs on the western part of the province, he and three other Annapolis residents, the Reverend Thomas WOOD, William SHAW, and Thomas Williams, petitioned Halifax for the means to defend the area. In late July 1775 the government responded with arms, ammunition, and four six-pounders. When a company of militia was raised the following month Ritchie joined, and on 22 May 1779 he was commissioned a captain.

Fears of an American attack on Annapolis Royal were realized in 1781. In the early morning of 29 August two rebel ships entered the Annapolis Basin and seized the sleeping town. So complete was the surprise that no resistance was possible. The town was plundered and two of its prominent citizens, Ritchie and Williams, were taken hostage. They were soon released in exchange for a rebel prisoner held in Halifax. Both men were forced to swear not to bear arms against the rebels in the future; Ritchie's days in the militia were over.

The Ritchie family's long and illustrious connection with the courts began in a small way in 1779 with John Ritchie's appointment as justice of the peace for Annapolis County. In 1786 he was named one of the justices of the Inferior Court of Common Pleas. A son and four grandsons would hold judgeships; one grandson, William Johnstone Ritchie*, became chief justice of Canada in 1879.

In a 1783 by-election Ritchie offered himself as a candidate for Annapolis County and was subsequently elected; for two years he represented the area in the House of Assembly. In the general election of 1785 he was rejected by the voters of Annapolis Township in favour of a newly arrived loyalist, Stephen De Lancey*. A minor political appointment followed in 1787 when he became one of the commissioners to supervise expenditure of public money on the new Shelburne-Annapolis road.

John Ritchie's last years were troubled by worsening business affairs. His death at the age of 45 left his young family nearly destitute. In 1775 or 1776 he had married at Annapolis Alicia Maria, daughter of Francis Barclay Le Cain (Le Quesne), former ordnance master at Fort Anne. At the time of his death his four children ranged in age from five to 15. His widow survived until 1817.

Barry M. Moody

PANS, RG 1, 168, pp.551, 564; 169, p.143; 222, no.56. *Nova-Scotia Gazette and the Weekly Chronicle* (Halifax), 4 Sept. 1781. *Directory of N.S. MLAs*. Calnek, *History of Annapolis* (Savary). Savary, *Supplement to history of Annapolis*. M. C. Ritchie, "The beginnings of a Canadian family," N.S. Hist. Soc., *Coll.*, XXIV (1938), 135–54. C. St C. Stayner, "John William Ritchie," N.S. Hist. Soc., *Coll.*, XXXVI (1968), 183–277.

ROBERTS, BENJAMIN, army officer and Indian department official; fl. 1758–75.

Commissioned ensign in the 46th Foot on 23 July 1758, Benjamin Roberts served in North America during the Seven Years' War. He was present at the sieges of Fort Carillon (Ticonderoga, N.Y.), Fort Niagara (near Youngstown, N.Y.), and Havana, Cuba. In 1765 he appears to have been stationed at Fort Ontario (Oswego, N.Y.). On 12 Sept. 1762 Roberts had received his lieutenancy, but in 1766 he exchanged with a half-pay officer and was appointed an Indian department commissary by Sir William Johnson.

The post-war years were hectic for the department of northern Indians, since its responsibilities now extended into Canada. A series of Indian uprisings linked with Pontiac* occurred, and rumours of French intrigues and pan-Indian unions were rife. Wandering independent traders dealing mostly in whisky and the attendant ills of this commerce further complicated the delicate frontier situation. The British government, with Johnson's advice, reacted by imposing new regulations on the Indian trade. After 1764 white traders had to be licensed, trading was confined to designated posts, and new restrictions limited the liquor traffic. These changes expanded the role of the Indian department. The supervision of trading at the posts was its responsibility, and Johnson staffed forts along the perimeter of the Great Lakes with commissaries who were, he wrote, to have "y[e]. sole managem[t]. of the Trade & Indian affairs." The relationship of these commissaries to the commandants of the posts was not easy because the limits of their respective jurisdictions were unclear. Moreover some of the commissaries who were half-pay officers could not resist flaunting their semi-independent authority before men of superior military rank. Benjamin Roberts seems to have been prey to such official vanity.

Noted for his egocentricity, Roberts quarrelled violently in July 1766 with Captain Jonathan Rogers of Fort Ontario. Later that year he had a bitter dispute with Captain John Brown of Fort Niagara, where he had been stationed. In March 1767 Johnson appointed him commissary at Michilimackinac (Mackinaw City, Mich.), the most important trading post on the Upper Lakes. Rumours were circulating that its commandant, Robert Rogers, had been involved with the French and Spaniards in planning a Bourbon *coup d'état* in the west, and Gage, the commander-in-chief, ordered Johnson to have the Indian department interpreters and commissaries keep a close watch on him.

Roberts arrived at Michilimackinac early in the summer of 1767 and soon had a stormy scene with Rogers over control of some confiscated rum. He appears to have had justification for his actions. According to the traders Jean-Baptiste Cadot* and Alexander Henry* the elder, who wrote to Johnson in support of Roberts, Rogers was "permitting Rum to go out of this Garrison at midnight in order to carry on a Contraband trade." A clash over the provision of quarters for the Indian department's blacksmith ended with Rogers ordering Roberts to Detroit early in October, but Roberts had already been talking with Rogers' former secretary, Nathaniel Potter. Potter had left for Montreal at the end of August and there swore out an affidavit accusing Rogers of treason. Gage had Rogers arrested in December 1767 and brought to Montreal for trial the following spring; Roberts corroborated the charges, but a court martial acquitted Rogers. Bitter animosity between the two did not dissipate. In May 1769, when they encountered one another on the street in Montreal, Rogers proposed that they meet alone for a duel. Roberts, by his own account, "said I could not trust myself to such a man, who I heard had neither honor or Courage. . . . He told me he'd blow my brains out."

Roberts' position was by then unenviable. No evidence had been produced to substantiate the charges against Rogers. The post of commissary had been abolished after the new structure for the Indian department that Johnson had begun setting up was rejected by a cost-conscious British government. By the end of 1769 Roberts had decided to seek an appointment in Britain. Johnson wrote him a glowing letter of reference, and John Blackburn, one of Johnson's London correspondents, prevailed on Lord Hillsborough, the secretary of state for the American Colonies, to find him a position. Experience, however, had not improved Roberts' judgement; he lived extravagantly and from 1772 until at least 1774 he was in debtors' prison. By June 1775 he had been released and was writing to Lord Dartmouth, Hillsborough's successor. He had, observed Blackburn, "an astonishing tincture of Vanity in all He did."

DOUGLAS LEIGHTON

Clements Library, Thomas Gage papers, American series. PRO, CO 5/70, ff.39–41, 125; CO 323/30. G.B., Hist. MSS Commission, *The manuscripts of the Earl of Dartmouth* (3v., London, 1887–96). *Johnson papers* (Sullivan *et al.*). G.B., WO, *Army list*, 1758–75. J. R. Cuneo, *Robert Rogers of the rangers* (New York, 1959), 209–11, 223, 232–33, 248. R. S. Allen, "The British Indian department and the frontier in North America, 1755–1830," *Canadian Historic Sites: Occasional Papers in Archaeology and History* (Ottawa), no.14 (1975), 5–125.

ROBICHAUX (Robichau, Robeshaw), LOUIS, merchant; b. 9 Aug. 1704 at Port-Royal (Annapolis Royal, N.S.), son of Prudent Robichaux and Henriette Petitpas; m. 7 Feb. 1730 Jeanne Bourgeois at Annapolis Royal, and they had ten children; d. 20 Dec. 1780 at Quebec.

A merchant, Louis Robichaux was on good terms with the British troops at Annapolis Royal, who were by far his best customers. In addition to supplying provisions and wood for building and heating, he carried out various repair jobs for the garrison. Robichaux was one of those Acadians who in January 1729/30 took an oath to remain "completely loyal" to George II [*see* Richard Philipps*], and when war broke out between France and Britain in 1744 he and his family were employed in repairing the fortifications of Annapolis Royal. Members of his family even warned the garrison in August of the impending attack by French forces under François DU PONT Duvivier. As a result of these activities Robichaux – according to his own account – was twice plundered of his household goods and cattle and twice taken prisoner with his family by the French. Each time they managed to escape.

The Acadians suffered much during the war. Writing to Lieutenant Governor Paul Mascarene* and the Nova Scotia Council in June 1745, Robichaux and six other Acadian deputies described the distress of their people: "You know, Sirs, to what a state we are reduced by the French and the Indians in all their incursions, the latter plunder, pillage, kill us, the former overwhelm us with difficulties and labour, not giving us time to catch our breath, and from another quarter we hear that people will come from Boston to subjugate us totally, which would not be very hard since we are already much downcast in every way." The French, they pointed out, treated them "as Englishmen" and the British suspected their loyalty although they had "done nothing that might be connected with arms."

After the war Robichaux rebuilt his fortune, but his good relations with the British did not save him from the hardship of deportation in 1755. Major John Handfield* granted him only the privilege of choosing his place of exile. He opted for New England, where he hoped his loyalty to the British would be recognized and he would in consequence be treated leniently. On their arrival Robichaux and his family were ordered to Boston, where they remained until the government moved them to Cambridge in September 1756. That same month Robichaux petitioned the Massachusetts Council for permission to return to Boston, pointing out that although he had managed to support himself for the previous three months in Boston, he was unable to find work in Cambridge and promising that he and his family would "behave as peaceable good subjects & neighbours." Perhaps fearing his influence among the Acadians, the Council refused his request; he was, however, furnished with a house and occasional financial assistance in the 11 years he spent in Cambridge.

During his exile in New England Robichaux emerged as the spokesman for his compatriots there, and for their missionaries in Acadia, and became the person upon whom they all relied. In a letter dated 17 Sept. 1761 Abbé Pierre Maillard*, vicar general of the bishop of Quebec in Halifax, authorized him, in the absence of a priest, to receive the mutual consent of exiled Acadians who wished to marry; he was to obtain necessary dispensations and to report on each union solemnized. Ten years later, on 17 July 1771, Abbé Charles-François BAILLY de Messein wrote to him confirming his authority and also specifying the procedure to be followed where marriages had taken place without his authorization.

Exile was apparently less difficult for Robichaux than it was for his compatriots. His good education, his relations with Boston society, and the prestige he enjoyed with the missionaries and among his own people all helped to make his stay more agreeable. His status probably explains why his name does not appear on the lists of Acadians who applied to go to France, Canada, or Saint-Domingue (Hispaniola). Most of the Acadian families who wanted and were able to settle in Canada were there by 1766, but Robichaux did not go until 1775. He probably left the revolutionary turmoil of Boston with loyalist friends from Cambridge, such as colonels John and William Vassall and Edward Winslow*. He went to live in Quebec, where he died of smallpox on 20 Dec. 1780. His children settled in Quebec and New Brunswick; Vénérande* became the agent in Quebec for her brother Otho*, a prominent New Brunswick businessman.

DONAT ROBICHAUD

Placide Gaudet, "Généalogie des familles acadiennes avec documents," PAC *Rapport*, 1905, II, IIIe partie, 258–71. *N.S. Archives, I*, 84–85. Pierre Belliveau, *French neutrals in Massachusetts* . . . (Boston, 1972), 192–99. Calnek, *History of Annapolis* (Savary), 66, 68, 73, 75–76, 78.

ROBINSON, CHRISTOPHER, army officer, lawyer, and office-holder; b. 1763 in Virginia, probably the son of Peter Robinson and Sarah Lister; m. 1784 to Esther Sayre, and they had six children, including Peter*, John Beverley*, and William Benjamin*; d. 2 Nov. 1798 at York (Toronto).

Born into a family prominent in the public life of Virginia, Christopher Robinson was raised in the household of John Robinson, apparently his uncle. He was educated at the College of William and Mary in Williamsburg, but he may have left the college in 1780 or 1781 to go to New York to aid the loyalist cause. On 26 June 1781 he was commissioned ensign in the Queen's Rangers under the command of John Graves Simcoe*. He served with the regiment until the surrender at Yorktown, Virginia, on 19 Oct. 1781, after which the Queen's Rangers were moved north to Nova Scotia, most of the men settling in what is now the parish of Queensbury in New Brunswick. Since the regiment had been placed on the regular establishment of the British army in 1782, Robinson was able to retire on half pay.

Lack of opportunity in New Brunswick probably prompted Robinson to move in 1788 to Quebec where he and his family settled first at L'Assomption, and later at Berthier-en-Haut (Berthierville). Robinson may have begun articling to become a lawyer at this time. He seems to have remained in contact with Simcoe, who was appointed lieutenant governor of Upper Canada in 1791. Simcoe took care to find employment for disbanded officers of the Queen's Rangers, and in 1792, shortly after his arrival in Upper Canada, he appointed Robinson surveyor general of woods and forests there. The Robinsons moved to Kingston that year.

Robinson's work as surveyor general meant constant travel about the province examining reserve lands, arranging rent collection for leased reserve land, licensing the cutting of timber, and identifying potential naval timber. In 1794 he was licensed to practise law in Upper Canada and two years later he was elected member of the House of Assembly for Ontario and Addington. No record of the proceedings of the assembly survives for his period of service, except for the 1798 session. Robinson played an active role that year and sponsored a bill, which never became law, "to enable persons migrating into this province to bring their negro slaves into the same." In 1797 he had been involved in the establishment of the Law Society of Upper Canada and he became a bencher of the society.

Money problems haunted Robinson all his life. Whether because of his style of life or because of his continuing ill health, his income was never sufficient. He acquired a great deal of land, but it was not a liquid asset. At the time of his death in 1798 he was in debt to William Willcocks*, whom he had been unable to repay because of expenses incurred in moving to York earlier that year.

Of better family and education than most of the loyalists who came to Canada, Christopher Robinson was nevertheless able to obtain official preferment only because of his link with Simcoe. He seems always to have been disappointed that the more comfortable life to which he felt his birth, education, and loyalty entitled him did not materialize. One of the few Robinsons from Virginia who supported the loyalist cause, he was cut off from most of the family.

Robinson died suddenly on 2 Nov. 1798 after returning to York from a long trip on horseback. The cause of his death is uncertain, but his son John Beverley remembered it as an acute attack of gout aggravated by cold and exposure.

R. E. SAUNDERS

PAO, Robinson (Sir John Beverley) papers, "Memoranda," pp.43–46. University of Toronto Library, Thomas Fisher Rare Book Library, MS coll. 163, Robinson family papers. *Correspondence of Lieut. Governor Simcoe* (Cruikshank). PAO *Report*, 1929–31.

Julia Jarvis, *Three centuries of Robinsons: the story of a family* ([Toronto], 1967). C. W. Robinson, *Life of Sir John Beverley Robinson, bart., C.B., D.C.L., chief-justice of Upper Canada* (Toronto, 1904).

RODRIGUE, ANTOINE, ship's captain, merchant, and colonial official; b. 17 Dec. 1722 at Louisbourg, Île Royale (Cape Breton Island), son of Jean-Baptiste Rodrigue* and Anne Le Borgne de Belle-Isle; d. 2 May 1789 at Port-Louis, France.

Antoine Rodrigue, a younger brother Pierre, and an elder brother Joseph-Baptiste were declared legally adult by a court decision at the time of their mother's remarriage in 1738. By 1742, and probably before, Antoine had begun his career at sea. His business activities before the siege of Louisbourg in 1745 are little known, but during this time he was joint owner of the schooner *Salamandre* with Michel de Gannes* de Falaise, and he shared in the 5,000 *livres* paid by the financial commissary, BIGOT, for the purchase on the king's behalf of the Rodrigues' land and house on the quay in Louisbourg harbour.

In May 1749 Antoine entered a partnership with his eldest brother, Michel, and this was renewed in April 1751. Among other provisions, Antoine was supposed to be employed at 1,000 *livres* a year as the firm's agent at Louisbourg, while Michel resided at La Rochelle. In 1749, 1750, and 1751 he sailed as captain of the *Grand St Esprit* fitted out by Michel. By 1752 he had established himself in Louisbourg and had a house built there on the corner of the Rue Saint-Louis and the Rue d'Orléans. His black slave was baptized at the Louisbourg church on 9 Feb. 1754. His business activity was at first in supplying the town and garrison and chartering the company's ships to the local administrators. On the strength of a 6,000-*livre* advance from the funds of Jean LABORDE, agent of the treasurers general of the Marine, he and Beaubassin, Silvain et Compagnie got a three-year contract for meat supplies in 1752, but, unable to meet his obligations, Antoine had to withdraw. In 1753 he provided part of the hay for the cattle kept for the slaughterhouse, but a flooded meadow at Miré (Mira) prevented him from supplying enough fodder and 11 cattle died that winter.

Already relying somewhat on local credit, Antoine became further enmeshed in debt when his brother in La Rochelle failed to meet bills of exchange for over 10,000 *livres* which Antoine had drawn on him in the winter of 1752. Although Antoine made arrangements to pay, went into debt, and sold two of his shallops, he was unable to satisfy his creditors, headed by Nicolas Hamelin, Daniel Augier, Pierre Boullot, and Tanguay Merven, who formed a union to pursue the brothers in November 1753. In 1754, Antoine's affairs were in such a sorry state that his servant had to sue him for the payment of 620 *livres*' arrears in wages. Antoine and Michel shortly fell out, Antoine claiming that Michel owed him 150,925 *livres*, and the brothers took their disputes to court at La Rochelle in a series of lawsuits which ended only in 1777. While these matters were still unsettled, Antoine exploited a coal mine with Nicolas LARCHER at Louisbourg on the strength of a contract for the supply of the barracks and fortress; he also ran a fishery at Louisbourg, managed Larcher's farmland and sawmill at Miré, and owned at least one ship, the 55-ton *Deux Sœurs*, requisitioned as a fire-ship in the second siege of Louisbourg and destroyed. There is some possibility that he may have also acted as port captain at Louisbourg shortly before its fall.

After the taking of the fortress in 1758, Rodrigue was shipped back to France in the *Duke of Cumberland*, a British transport manned partly by French sailors being exchanged as prisoners of war. When the British captain refused to give his French seamen adequate rations Rodrigue bought supplies for them from his fellow-passengers out of his own pocket. This act, along with his losses in the siege, and the testimony of François-Gabriel d'ANGEAC and Jacques-François Barbel, governor and financial commissary of Saint-Pierre and Miquelon, as to his seamanship, got him the post of port captain on those islands in 1765. Rodrigue had already gone there in 1763, got a fishing concession, and set up his household; his eldest son, Antoine, also had a fishing base there. By 1767 Rodrigue and the other major entrepreneur in the islands, Jean-Baptiste DUPLEIX Silvain, claimed to have spent 80,000 *livres* between themselves and their French backers on their establishments, but the poor catches of the 1760s meant that their enterprises started slowly, and for a time they contemplated emigrating to Louisiana. By 1777, however, Rodrigue was employing 61 fishermen. Along with the other colonists he was expelled from the islands after their capture by the British in 1778, but even six years later, when they were allowed to return, he was listed as owning a brig, a schooner, seven shallops, a half-shallop, two dinghies, and two wherries. He himself probably never came back to North America, remaining instead in France. Worn out, we are told, with old age, gout, and chagrin at his business reverses, he had retired from his post of port captain in 1778.

Antoine had married Jeanne-Françoise Jacau, sister of Louis-Thomas JACAU de Fiedmont, of

Port-Dauphin on 19 May 1750; they had at least nine children. The eldest, Antoine, got the post of king's storekeeper briefly at Saint-Pierre and Miquelon in 1783 but returned to his father's business in partnership with his brother Claude, who represented him on the islands, while Michel worked at Port-Louis. Antoine Jr also soon went to Port-Louis and on 20 June 1783 married Marie-Josèphe Ramondine; they had six children. During the French revolution, the two brothers claimed to represent the inhabitants of Saint-Pierre and Miquelon and tried to persuade French authorities to give them a concession and ten-year loan of 200,000 *livres* to supply the colony with food. They were refused and went bankrupt in 1792. Antoine then made a career in the ministry of the Marine, reaching the rank of deputy commissary at Le Havre in 1796. Antoine Sr's daughter, Jeanne-Françoise, became the second wife to Charles-Gabriel-Sébastien de L'ESPÉRANCE, governor of Saint-Pierre and Miquelon, in 1775.

J. F. BOSHER and T. J. A. LE GOFF

AD, Charente-Maritime (La Rochelle), B, 1460, 1797; Minutes Chameau (La Rochelle); Minutes Fredureaux-Dumas (La Rochelle); Morbihan (Vannes), E[s], 186, État civil, Port-Louis, 3 mai 1789. AN, Col., B, 65–68; C[12], 2; 6; 12, ff.95–98v; E, 356 (dossier Rodrigue); Marine, C[2], 44, 62; C[7], 281 (dossier Rodrigue); Section Outre-mer, G[1], 408, 414, 467; G[2], 185, 201; G[3], 2041–42, 2044, 2046–47. *Calendrier des armateurs de La Rochelle*, 1748–51. J.-Y. Ribault, *Les îles Saint-Pierre et Miquelon des origines à 1814* (Saint-Pierre, 1962); "La pêche et le commerce de la morue aux îles Saint-Pierre et Miquelon de 1763 à 1793," Congrès national des soc. savantes, Section d'hist. moderne et contemporaine, *Actes du quatre-vingt-onzième congrès, Rennes, 1966* (3v., Paris, 1969), I, 251–92; "La population des îles Saint-Pierre et Miquelon de 1763 à 1793," *Revue française d'hist. d'outre-mer* (Paris), LIII (1966), 5–66.

ROGERS, ROBERT (early in his career he may have signed **Rodgers**), army officer and author; b. 8 Nov. 1731 (N.S.) at Methuen, Massachusetts, son of James and Mary Rogers; m. 30 June 1761 Elizabeth Browne at Portsmouth, New Hampshire; d. 18 May 1795 in London, England.

While Robert Rogers was quite young his family moved to the Great Meadow district of New Hampshire, near present Concord, and he grew up on a frontier of settlement where there was constant contact with Indians and which was exposed to raids in time of war. He got his education in village schools; somewhere he learned to write English which was direct and effective, if ill spelled. When still a boy he saw service, but no action, in the New Hampshire militia during the War of the Austrian Succession. He says in his *Journals* that from 1743 to 1755 his pursuits (which he does not specify) made him acquainted with both the British and the French colonies. It is interesting that he could speak French. In 1754 he became involved with a gang of counterfeiters; he was indicted but the case never came to trial.

In 1755 his military career proper began. He recruited men for the New England force being raised to serve under John WINSLOW, but when a New Hampshire regiment was authorized he took them into it, and was appointed captain and given command of a company. The regiment was sent to the upper Hudson and came under Major-General William JOHNSON. Rogers was recommended to Johnson as a good man for scouting duty, and he carried out a series of reconnaissances with small parties against the French in the area of forts Saint-Frédéric (near Crown Point, N.Y.) and Carillon (Ticonderoga). When his regiment was disbanded in the autumn he remained on duty, and through the bitter winter of 1755–56 he continued to lead scouting operations. In March 1756 William Shirley, acting commander-in-chief, instructed him to raise a company of rangers for scouting and intelligence duties in the Lake Champlain region. Rogers did not invent this type of unit (a ranger company under John Gorham* was serving in Nova Scotia as early as 1744) but he became particularly identified with the rangers of the army. Three other ranger companies were formed in 1756, one of them commanded by Rogers' brother Richard (who died the following year).

Robert Rogers won an increasing reputation for daring leadership, though it can be argued that his expeditions sometimes produced misleading information. In January 1757 he set out through the snow to reconnoitre the French forts on Lake Champlain with some 80 men. There was fierce fighting in which both sides lost heavily, Rogers himself being wounded. He was now given authority over all the ranger companies, and in this year he wrote for the army what may be called a manual of forest fighting, which is to be found in his published *Journals*. In March 1758 another expedition towards Fort Saint-Frédéric, ordered by Colonel William HAVILAND against Rogers' advice, resulted in a serious reverse to the rangers. Rogers' reputation with the British command remained high, however, and as of 6 April 1758 Major-General James ABERCROMBY, now commander-in-chief, gave him a formal commission both as captain of a ranger company and as "Major of the Rangers in his Majesty's Service." That summer Rogers with four ranger companies and two companies of Indians took part in the campaign on Lac Saint-Sacrement (Lake George) and Lake Champlain which ended with Abercromby's disastrous defeat before Fort Carillon. A month later, on 8 August, Rogers with a mixed force some 700 strong fought a fierce little battle near Fort Ann, New York, with a smaller party of Frenchmen and Indians under Joseph MARIN de La Malgue and forced it to withdraw.

British doubts of the rangers' efficiency, and their frequent indiscipline, led in this year to the formation of the 80th Foot (Gage's Light Infantry), a regular unit intended for bush-fighting. The rangers were nevertheless still considered essential at least for the moment, and Major-General Jeffery AMHERST, who became commander-in-chief late in 1758, was as convinced as his predecessors of Rogers' excellence as a leader of irregulars. Six ranger companies went to Quebec with James Wolfe* in 1759, and six more under Rogers himself formed part of Amherst's own army advancing by the Lake Champlain route. In September Amherst ordered Rogers to undertake an expedition deep into Canada, to destroy the Abenaki village of Saint-François-de-Sales (Odanak). Even though the inhabitants had been warned of his approach, Rogers surprised and burned the village; he claims to have killed "at least two hundred" Indians, but French accounts make the number much smaller. His force retreated by the Connecticut River, closely pursued and suffering from hunger. Rogers himself with great energy and resolution rafted his way down to the first British settlement to send provisions back to his starving followers. The expedition cost the lives of about 50 of his officers and men. In 1760 Rogers with 600 rangers formed the advance guard of Haviland's force invading Canada by the Lake Champlain line, and he was present at the capitulation of Montreal.

Immediately after the French surrender, Amherst ordered Rogers to move with two companies of rangers to take over the French posts in the west. He left Montreal on 13 September with his force in whaleboats. Travelling by way of the ruined posts at the sites of Kingston and Toronto (the latter "a proper place for a factory" he reported to Amherst), and visiting Fort Pitt (Pittsburgh, Pa) to obtain the instructions of Brigadier Robert MONCKTON, who was in command in the west, he reached Detroit, the only fort with a large French garrison, at the end of November. After taking it over from François-Marie PICOTÉ de Belestre he attempted to reach Michilimackinac (Mackinaw City, Mich.) and Fort Saint-Joseph (Niles), where there were small French parties, but was prevented by ice on Lake Huron. He states in his later *A concise account of North America* (but not in his report written at the time) that during the march west he met Pontiac*, who received him in a friendly manner and "attended" him to Detroit.

With the end of hostilities in North America the ranger companies were disbanded. Rogers was appointed captain of one of the independent companies of regulars that had long been stationed in South Carolina. Subsequently he exchanged this appointment for a similar one in an independent company at New York; but the New York companies were disbanded in 1763 and Rogers went on half pay. When Pontiac's uprising broke out he joined the force under Captain James Dalyell (Dalzell), Amherst's aide-de-camp, which was sent to reinforce the beleaguered garrison of Detroit [*see* Henry GLADWIN]. Rogers fought his last Indian fight, with courage and skill worthy of his reputation, in the sortie from Detroit on 31 July 1763.

By 1764 Rogers was in serious financial trouble. He had encountered at least temporary difficulty in obtaining reimbursement for the funds he had spent on his rangers, and the collapse of a trading venture with John Askin* at the time of Pontiac's uprising worsened his situation. According to Thomas GAGE he also lost money gambling. In 1764 he was arrested for debt in New York but soon escaped.

Rogers went to England in 1765 in hope of obtaining support for plans of western exploration and expansion. He petitioned for authority to mount a search for an inland northwest passage, an idea which may possibly have been implanted in his mind by Governor Arthur Dobbs of North Carolina. To enable him to pursue this project he asked for the appointment of commandant at Michilimackinac, and in October 1765 instructions were sent to Gage, now commanding in America, that he was to be given this post. He was also to be given a captain's commission in the Royal Americans; this it appears he never got.

While in London Rogers published at least two books. One was his *Journals*, an account of his campaigns which reproduces a good many of his reports and the orders he received, and is a valuable contribution to the history of the Seven Years' War in America. The other, *A concise account of North America*, is a sort of historical geography of the continent, brief and lively and profiting by Rogers' remarkably wide firsthand knowledge. Both are lucid and forceful, rather extraordinary productions from an author with his education. He doubtless got much editorial help from his secretary, Nathaniel Potter, a graduate of the College of New Jersey (Princeton University) whom he had met shortly before leaving America for England; but Sir William Johnson's description of Rogers in 1767 as "a very illiterate man" was probably malicious exaggeration at best. Both books were very well received by the London critics. A less friendly reception awaited *Ponteach; or, the savages of America: a tragedy*, a play in blank verse published a few months later. It was anonymous but seems to have been generally attributed to Rogers. John R. Cuneo has plausibly suggested that the opening scenes, depicting white traders and hunters preying on Indians, may well reflect the influence of Rogers, but that it is hard to connect him with the highflown artificial tragedy that follows. Doubtless, in Francis Parkman's phrase, he "had a share" in composing the play. The *Monthly Review: or, Literary Journal* rudely called *Ponteach* "one of the most absurd productions of the kind that we have seen," and said of the "reputed author", "in turning bard, and writing a tragedy, he makes just as good a figure as would a Grubstreet rhymester at the head of our Author's corps of North-American Rangers." No attempt seems to have been made to produce the play on the stage.

His mission to London having had, on the whole, remarkable success, Rogers returned to North America at the beginning of 1766. He and his wife arrived at Michilimackinac in August, and he lost no time in sending off two exploring parties under Jonathan Carver and James Tute, the latter being specifically instructed to search for the northwest passage. Nothing important came of these efforts.

Both Johnson, who was now superintendent of northern Indians, and Gage evidently disliked and distrusted Rogers; Gage no doubt resented his having gone to the authorities in London over his head. On hearing of Rogers' appointment Gage wrote to Johnson: "He is wild, vain, of little understanding, and of as little Principle; but withal has a share of Cunning, no Modesty or veracity and sticks at Nothing. . . . He deserved Some Notice for his Bravery and readiness on Service and if they had put him on whole Pay. to give him an Income to live upon, they would have done well. But this employment he is most unfit for, and withal speaks no Indian Language. He made a great deal of money during the War, which was squandered in Vanity and Gaming. and is some Thousands in Debt here [in New York]." Almost immediately Gage received an intercepted letter which could be read as indicating that Rogers might be intriguing with the French. Rogers was certainly ambitious and clearly desired to carve out for himself some sort of semi-independent fiefdom in the west. In 1767 he drafted a plan under which Michilimackinac and its dependencies should be erected into a "Civil Government," with a governor, lieutenant governor, and a council of 12 members chosen from the principal merchants trading in the region. The governor and council would report in all civil and Indian matters direct to the king and the Privy Council in England. This plan was sent to London and Rogers petitioned the Board of Trade for appointment as governor. Such a project was bound to excite still further the hostility of Gage and Johnson, and it got nowhere. Rogers quarrelled with his secretary Potter and the latter reported that his former chief was considering going over to the French if his plan for a separate government was not approved. On the strength of an affidavit by Potter to this effect Gage ordered Rogers arrested and charged with high treason. This was done in December 1767 and in the spring Rogers was taken east in irons. In October 1768 he was tried by court martial at Montreal on charges of "designs . . . of Deserting to the French . . . and stirring up the Indians against His Majesty and His Government"; "holding a correspondence with His Majesty's Enemies"; and disobedience of orders by spending money on "expensive schemes and projects" and among the Indians. Although these charges were supported by Benjamin ROBERTS, the former Indian department commissary at Michilimackinac, Rogers was acquitted. It seems likely that he had been guilty of no crime more serious than loose talk. The verdict was approved by the king the following year, though with the note that there had been "great reason to suspect . . . an improper and dangerous Correspondence." Rogers was not reinstated at Michilimackinac. In the summer of 1769 he went to England seeking redress and payment of various sums which he claimed as due him. He received little satisfaction and spent several periods in debtors' prison, the longest being in 1772–74. He sued Gage for false imprisonment and other injuries; the suit was later withdrawn and Rogers was granted a major's half pay. He returned to America in 1775.

The American Revolutionary War was now raging. Rogers, no politician, might have fought on either side, but for him neutrality was unlikely. His British commission made him an object of suspicion to the rebels. He was arrested in Philadelphia but released on giving his parole not to serve against the colonies. In 1776 he sought a Continental commission, but General George Washington distrusted and imprisoned him. He escaped and offered his services to the British headquarters at New York. In August he was appointed to raise and command with the rank of lieutenant-colonel commandant a battalion which seems to have been known at this stage as the Queen's American Rangers. On 21 October this raw unit was attacked by the Americans near Mamaroneck, New York. A ranger outpost was overrun but Rogers' main force stood firm and the attackers withdrew. Early in 1777 an inspector general appointed to report on the loyalist units found Rogers' in poor condition, and he was retired on half pay. The Queen's Rangers, as they came to be known, later achieved distinction under regular commanders, notably John Graves Simcoe*.

Rogers' military career was not quite over. Returning in 1779 from a visit to England, he was commissioned by General Sir Henry Clinton – who may have been encouraged from London – to raise a unit of two battalions, to be recruited in the American colonies but organized in Canada, and known as the King's Rangers. The regiment was never completed and never fought. The burden of recruiting it fell largely on Rogers' brother James, also a ranger officer of the Seven Years' War. Robert by now was drunken and inefficient, and not above lying about the number of men raised. Governor Frederick HALDIMAND wrote of him, "he at once disgraces the Service, & renders himself incapable of being Depended upon." He was in Quebec in 1779–80. At the end of 1780, while on his way to New York by sea, he was captured by an American privateer and spent a long period in prison. By 1782 he was back behind the British lines. At the end of the war he went to England, perhaps leaving New York with the British force at the final evacuation in 1783.

Rogers' last years were spent in England in debt, poverty, and drunkenness. Part of the time he was again in debtors' prison. He lived on his half pay, which was often partly assigned to creditors. He died in London "at his apartments in the Borough [Southwark]," evidently intestate; letters of administration of his estate, estimated at only £100, were granted to John Walker, said to be his landlord. His wife had divorced him by act of the New Hampshire legislature in 1778, asserting that when she last saw him a couple of years before "he was in a situation which, as her peace and safety forced her *then* to shun & fly from him so Decency *now* forbids her to say more upon so indelicate a subject." Their only child, a son named Arthur, stayed with his mother.

The extraordinary career that thus ended in sordid obscurity had reached its climax in the Seven Years' War, before Rogers was 30. American legend has somewhat exaggerated his exploits; for he often met reverses as well as successes in his combats with the French and their Indian allies in the Lake Champlain country. But he was a man of great energy and courage (and, it must be said, of considerable ruthlessness), who had something of a genius for irregular war. No other American frontiersman succeeded so well in coping with the formidable bushfighters of New France. That the frontiersman was also the author of successful books suggests a highly unusual combination of qualities. His personality remains enigmatic. Much of the evidence against him comes from those who disliked him; but it is pretty clear that his moral character was far from being on the same level as his abilities. Had it been so, he would have been one of the most remarkable Americans of a remarkable generation.

C. P. STACEY

[Robert Rogers' published works have all been reissued: *Journals of Major Robert Rogers* . . . (London, 1765) in an edition by F. B. Hough (Albany, N.Y., 1883) with an appendix of documents concerning Rogers' later career, in a reprint with an introduction by H. H. Peckham (New York, [1961]), and in a facsimile reprint (Ann Arbor, Mich., [1966]); *A concise account of North America* . . . (London, 1765) in a reprint (East Ardsley, Eng., and New York, 1966); and the play attributed to Rogers, *Ponteach; or, the savages of America: a tragedy* (London, 1766), with an introduction and biography of Rogers by Allan Nevins (Chicago, 1914) and in *Representative plays by American dramatists*, ed. M. J. Moses (3v., New York, 1918–[25]), I, 115–208. Part of the play is printed in Francis Parkman, *The conspiracy of Pontiac and the Indian war after the conquest of Canada* (2v., Boston, 1910), app.B.

Unpublished MSS or transcripts of MSS concerning Rogers are located in Clements Library, Thomas Gage papers, American series; Rogers papers; in PAC, MG 18, L4, 2, pkt.7; MG 23, K3; and in PRO, Prob. 6/171, f.160; TS 11/387, 11/1069/4957.

Printed material by or relating to Rogers can be found in *The documentary history of the state of New-York* . . . , ed. E. B. O'Callaghan (4v., Albany, 1849–51), IV; *Gentleman's Magazine*, 1765, 584–85; *Johnson papers* (Sullivan *et al.*); "Journal of Robert Rogers the ranger on his expedition for receiving the capitulation of western French posts," ed. V. H. Paltsits, New York Public Library, *Bull.*, 37 (1933), 261–76; *London Magazine, or Gentleman's Monthly Intelligencer*, XXXIV (1765), 630–32, 676–78; XXXV (1766), 22–24; *Military affairs in North America, 1748–65* (Pargellis); *Monthly Review: or, Literary Journal* (London), XXXIV (1766), pt.1, 9–22, 79–80, 242; *NYCD* (O'Callaghan and Fernow), VII, VIII, X; "Rogers's Michillimackinac journal," ed. W. L. Clements, American Antiquarian Soc., *Proc.* (Worcester, Mass.), new ser., 28 (1918), 224–73; *Times* (London), 22 May 1795; *Treason? at Michilimackinac: the proceedings of a general court martial held at Montreal in October 1768 for the trial of Major Robert Rogers*, ed. D. A. Armour (Mackinac Island, Mich., 1967).

The considerable Rogers cult that has been in evidence in the United States during the last generation probably owes a good deal to K. L. Roberts' popular historical novel, *Northwest passage* (Garden City, N.Y., 1937; new ed., 2v., 1937). Entries for Rogers are to be found in the *DAB* and *DNB*. J. R. Cuneo, *Robert Rogers of the rangers* (New York, 1959) is an excellent biography based on a wide range of sources but marred by lack of specific documentation. *See also*: Luca Codignola, *Guerra e guerriglia nell'America coloniale: Robert Rogers e la guerra dei sette anni, 1754–1760* (Venice, 1977), which contains a translation into Italian of Rogers' *Journals*; H. M. Jackson, *Rogers' rangers, a history* ([Ottawa], 1953); S. McC. Pargellis, *Lord Loudoun*, and "The four independent companies of New York," *Essays in colonial history presented to Charles McLean Andrews by his students* (New Haven, Conn., and London, 1931; repr. Freeport, N.Y., 1966), 96–123; Francis Parkman, *Montcalm and Wolfe* (2v., Boston, 1884; repr. New York, 1962); J. R. Cuneo, "The early days of the Queen's Rangers, August 1776–February 1777," *Military Affairs* (Washington), XXII (1958), 65–74; Walter Rogers, "Rogers, ranger and loyalist," RSC *Trans.*, 2nd ser., VI (1900), sect.II, 49–59. C.P.S.]

ROSS, JOHN, army officer; fl. 1762–89. He may have married the sister of John McDonell* (1750–1809).

John Ross was commissioned lieutenant in the 34th Foot on 31 July 1762. His regiment served in the attack on the Spaniards at Havana, Cuba, in 1762, in West Florida from 1764 to 1768, and in Ireland in 1769. In December 1764 Ross was sent from Louisiana to Fort de Chartres (near Prairie du Rocher) in the Illinois country, where he was received by Louis GROSTON de Saint-Ange et de Bellerive, the French commandant. The first British officer to enter the area after the peace with France, Ross was to attempt a reconciliation with the Indians there, but he found them hostile to British occupation of their lands. After a few months he returned to New Orleans. During this expedition he made a map of the route up the Mississippi River to Fort de Chartres which was later published in Thomas Jefferys, *The American atlas* (London, 1778).

Ross was promoted captain in the 34th Foot on 14 March 1772. In 1776 the regiment was part of the force sent to drive the Americans from Canada, but the exact nature of Ross's early service in Canada is not known. In July 1780 John Ross, described as a "veteran officer of high reputation," was given the temporary rank of major to raise a second battalion of the King's Royal Regiment of New York (KRRNY) at Lachine and was sent with it to work on construction at Coteau-du-Lac, west of Montreal. In September Governor HALDIMAND arranged that Ross and the 2nd battalion KRRNY would occupy Carleton Island (N.Y.) to maintain the essential link between Montreal and the upper posts. Ross arrived there on 30 Nov. 1780 with 100 men, after Haldimand had learned that the Americans were planning to seize the island as soon as winter ice made the river crossing possible. "Enterprising and resourceful," he fortified the island during the unusually mild winter. When navigation opened on 2 April 1781, provisions were sent to the upper posts.

In October 1781 Ross took a force composed of troops from his garrison and from Fort Niagara (near Youngstown, N.Y.) with a few Indians on a raid against the Mohawk valley. Advancing by way of Oswego and Oneida Lake, Ross was hampered by bad weather and inadequate support from the Indians. The troops fought a successful action at Johnstown against a larger and better armed force of American militia. However, Ross was forced to withdraw before the operation was completed. During the orderly retreat to Carleton Island Walter BUTLER, commanding the ranger detachment, was killed. That winter Ross built Fort Haldimand to protect the twin harbours of the island. In February 1782 Haldimand ordered him to occupy Oswego when navigation opened, and he arrived there on 15 April. Commanding about 500 men from Carleton Island and Fort Niagara, Ross gained Haldimand's admiration by the speed with which he fortified his new post. He was promoted major in the army on 12 June 1782.

In July 1783 Ross was sent to Cataraqui (Kingston, Ont.) to arrange for the settlement of loyalist refugees. He wintered there with an advance party of the KRRNY, constructed barracks amongst the ruins of old Fort Frontenac, and built saw and flour mills. Ross recommended the purchase of land in the area from the Mississauga Indians and the construction of a fort on nearby Point Henry, and he established a navy yard on Point Frederick.

When the main party of loyalists arrived at Cataraqui in 1784 and the KRRNY was disbanded, Ross arranged for the allocation of rations, supplies, and land and built a saw mill at present Millhaven. As an army officer responsible for the work of settlement, Ross felt he lacked legal authority to deal with civilian problems. He commented on the prevalence of disputes "between The Master & Servant" but did not feel able to prevent the severe punishments that were handed out. In response to his complaints, the government appointed Ross a magistrate in July 1784, along with Neil MCLEAN. Ross was largely responsible for the success of the loyalist settlement at Cataraqui. He, rather than Michael Grass, captain of the loyalists who settled there, should be called the "founder of Kingston."

In October 1784 Ross sought permission to return to England to attend to his aged, infirm father, and he arrived in London from Quebec on 23 April 1785. He was promoted major in the 34th Foot on 20 May. The following year, when he was back in Canada, he was arrested as a consequence of accusations by his second in command at Cataraqui, Lieutenant William Tinling, whom he had charged with a malicious attempt to injure his reputation. Ross was exonerated and given the command of the 34th Foot in Montreal in August 1786. The regiment returned to England in 1787.

Ross retired from the army on 17 Feb. 1789 and sold his commission. Details of his later life, descendants, and death are not known.

RICHARD A. PRESTON

BL, Add. MSS 21786. PRO, CO 42/18, pp.148–51 (copies at PAC). *Kingston before War of 1812* (Preston), xli–xlvii, lii–lv, 21–46, 69–71. *Orderly book of Sir John Johnson during the Oriskany campaign, 1776–1777 . . .*, ed. W. L. Stone (Albany, N.Y., 1882), 56. *Scots Magazine* (Edinburgh), 1789, 155. *The settlement of the United Empire Loyalists on the upper St Lawrence and Bay of Quinte in 1784, a documentary record*, ed. E. A. Cruikshank (Toronto, 1934; repr. 1966). G.B., WO, *Army list*, 1788, 110.

William Canniff, *The medical profession in Upper Canada, 1783–1850; an historical narrative with original documents relating to the profession, with some brief biographies* (Toronto, 1894), 457. Richard Cannon, *Historical record of the 34th or Cumberland Regiment of Foot* (London, 1844), 34–37. Graymont, *Iroquois*, 247–48. J. R. Simms, *Trappers of New York; or a biography of Nicholas Stoner and Nathaniel Foster; together with anecdotes of other celebrated hunters, and some account of Sir William Johnson, and his style of living* (Albany, N.Y., 1871), 94–95. E. A. Cruikshank, "The King's Royal Regiment of New York," *OH*, XXVII (1931), 231, 234–35, 241–42, 253, 266, 271–80, 293–318.

ROSS, MALCHOM (Malcolm, Malcholm), fur-trader; b. *c.* 1754 in the Orkney Islands (U.K.), probably in South Ronaldsay; d. autumn 1799.

Malchom Ross first contracted with the Hudson's Bay Company in 1774 to serve as a labourer at York Factory (Man.) at a wage of £6 per annum. Within two years he was serving inland under William Tomison* and Robert Longmoor* at York's outpost, Cumberland House (Sask.), and beyond. On 5 Oct. 1776 Ross joined Longmoor on a journey up the Saskatchewan River from Cumberland; they returned in February 1777 "bringing four Sledge Loads of Furrs, hauled by Dogs" after 40 days' arduous travel from "Where the Indians they left (chiefly Assinnee Poetuck) [Assiniboins] are pounding Buffelo." Other travels included summer trips with furs down to York Factory and expeditions in January and May 1778 to divert inland Indians from trading with Canadian pedlars.

By 1778 Ross was known as "an Excellent Servant and fine canoe Man equal allmost to any Indian in Shooting falls &c." The next year he was left in charge of Upper Hudson House (near Wandsworth, Sask.) by Longmoor, who wrote that "he is the fittest man that I can Trust." The company, which often had labour problems with its Orkney servants, appreciated Ross's service. Although he still ranked as a labourer, it increased his salary to £15 per annum in 1779, and beginning in 1782 granted this "most excellent Canoe Man, much beloved by the Indians" a salary of £20 per annum.

Ross was inland when the Comte de Lapérouse [GALAUP] seized York and Churchill (Man.) in 1782, and so he avoided being captured with other company servants such as Humphrey MARTEN, Samuel HEARNE, and Edward UMFREVILLE. He continued with the company and during the 1780s took on positions of increased responsibility. Besides serving as a canoe-maker, hunter, trader, and even tailor at Lower Hudson (near Wandsworth, Sask.) and Cumberland houses, he was called upon to act as temporary master at Lower Hudson in April 1780 and at Cumberland in the summer of 1783. In 1788 he was described as "occasional Master at either House" and during the 1790–91 season as temporary master, being "Every way qualified . . . cannot be a better."

Between 1790 and 1792 Ross was a valued associate of Philip TURNOR and Peter Fidler* on their journey to the Athabasca country and was listed in company books as in "Charge of Goods on the Northern Expedition" at an annual wage of £40. Ross was accompanied on these travels by "his woman and 2 children," wrote Fidler, who added that "An Indian woman at a House is particularly useful in making shoes, cutting line, netting snow shoes, cleaning and stretching Beaver skins &c., that the Europeans are not acquainted with."

The Athabascan journey revealed to the London committee the area's potential as a rich source of furs. In May 1793 Ross, who had spent "a poor, expensive Winter" above Cumberland intercepting Indian groups carrying furs to rival Canadian traders, was asked by the committee to organize an expedition to Athabasca and establish a trading post there. The plan failed to gain the support of William Tomison, by now chief inland, and the expedition, plagued by logistics problems, was postponed. During the 1794–95 season Ross elected to winter at Reed Lake (Man.), northeast of Cumberland, and spent the next season at Fairford House (near Iskwatam Lake, Sask.) to the northwest. The recurrent problem of rivalries within the company for the inland trade was highlighted by his activities, since they drew complaint from Thomas Stayner, chief at York, who had sent men to the same area. In 1796–97 Ross, although weary of frequent changes of winter quarters, was led by circumstances to build Bedford House at Reindeer Lake (Sask.), over 100 miles north of Fairford. Winter provisions got low for the "15 English men of us and two women and 3 Childering"; and the Indians proved difficult. Matters worsened in April when the Canadian Alexander Fraser* arrived to trade in the vicinity and Ross's assistant, David Thompson*, deserted into the "Canadan Service."

Ross travelled to England in 1798 and met the London committee on 28 November. It had decided after much discussion that Athabasca should be opened up from Churchill rather than York. Having ordered York not to compete in the area, the committee retained Ross "for 3 Years at £80 p. Ann" to travel from Churchill to establish trade in the Athabasca River region. In the summer of 1799 Ross joined the council at Churchill. On 6 September he made a will, the principal beneficiaries of which were a brother Charles and a natural son George, who was proposed as an apprentice at York in 1801. Shortly after making his will he departed for Athabasca. On 17 October Indians brought word to Churchill that the expedition of which so much was hoped had been halted about 150 miles upriver after Ross fell overboard and drowned in rapids.

Ross was one of the most valued and best rewarded of the company's many Orkney servants. His enterprise, ability to learn inland skills, loyalty, and modest literacy combined to raise him from labouring to officer rank and enabled him to render conspicuous service to his employers in difficult times. The premature loss of his "well known experience" was much regretted.

JENNIFER S. H. BROWN

HBC Arch. A.1/47, ff.120, 122; A.6/13, f.41; A.6/16, ff.55–56, 127, 129; A.11/116, f.43; A.30/1, ff.22, 80; A.30/2, ff.32, 52, 72; A.30/3, f.38; A.30/4, ff.14, 45, 72; A.30/5, ff.16, 42; A.32/1, f.92; B.14/a/1, ff.21, 29, 33; B.24/a/1, f.32; B.42/b/42, pp.8, 15; B.42/b/44, ff.67, 74; B.49/a/19, ff.28, 40; B.239/b/56, ff.25–25d. PRO, Prob. 11/1370, will of Malchom Ross, proved 12 Feb. 1802. St John's Anglican Cathedral (Winnipeg), Red River register of baptisms, I, no.400. HBRS, XIV (Rich and Johnson); XV (Rich and Johnson). *Journals of Hearne and Turnor* (Tyrrell). *Saskatchewan journals and correspondence: Edmonton House, 1795–1800; Chesterfield House, 1800–1802*, ed. A. M. Johnson (London, 1967).

ROUBAUD, PIERRE-JOSEPH-ANTOINE, Jesuit, priest, and missionary; b. 28 May 1724 at Avignon, France, son of Pierre-Pascal Roubaud and Marguerite Tressol; d. in Paris probably after 1789.

The eldest son of a family which was large and poor, Pierre Roubaud entered the Jesuit college in Avignon at the age of 13. His teachers noted that he was seriously lacking in prudence and judgement, but in September 1739, during his noviciate, they praised his aptitude for teaching. He taught in various Jesuit colleges for seven years before leaving for Canada in the spring of 1756.

Here Roubaud was assigned to the Abenaki mission at Saint-François-de-Sales (Odanak). Although he suffered from poor health, by the summer he was accompanying the Abenakis on their numerous military expeditions of the Seven Years' War. When the troops of Major Robert ROGERS destroyed the village of Saint-François-de-Sales on 4 Oct. 1759, Roubaud withdrew to Montreal for the winter. The following 23 March he delivered a sermon in the parish church there in which he accused the troops from France of moral laxity and blamed them for the defeat at Quebec. Stung to the quick, the officers wanted to assault him; Roubaud was obliged to hide in his order's house and later fled to Sault-Saint-Louis (Caughnawaga, Que.).

When the British forces drew near in 1760 Governor Vaudreuil [RIGAUD] requested Roubaud to bring his Abenakis to the vicinity of Montreal from Saint-Régis, where they had sought refuge after the destruction of their village; the Abenakis, fearing British reprisals, fled to the mission at Lac des Deux-Montagnes (Oka) and the Jesuit was unable to comply. By now suspect in the eyes of French officials, Roubaud took advantage of the capitulation of Montreal in September to inform AMHERST that he was prepared to give him information about Canada and to take the oath of loyalty to the British crown. One month later his superior, Father Jean-Baptiste de Saint-Pé*, ordered him to leave the Saint-François-de-Sales mission, to which he had returned, and to go immediately to one of the Jesuit residences. Roubaud complained about this to Ralph Burton*, governor of Trois-Rivières, and Burton objected to any transfer of the missionary. Several historians have asserted that the recall came about because of incidents involving morals, but it seems the real reason was that his superiors wished to put him at some distance from the Abenakis because of his change of allegiance.

In October 1762 Roubaud, in ill health, went to Quebec and spent the winter with the Jesuits, who censured his conduct and his relations with the British. Their attitude did not, however, stop him from becoming a close friend of James MURRAY or from going to live at his house in the summer. Roubaud provided information about the country to the governor and entertained him with his talents as a conversationalist and poet. But when the Jesuit wanted to make a public announcement of conversion to the Protestant faith, the governor was alarmed. In the summer of 1764 Murray sent him to England to give British officials information about the new colony. Roubaud went with the support of the Jesuits who, believing he was returning to a European house, paid his travel costs and committed themselves to send him ten guineas a month for five months. Murray subsequently required them to continue the allowance for 11 months.

Arriving in London in August 1764, Roubaud spent the first months courting ladies of the *demi-monde*. In November he entered the service of the Earl of Halifax, secretary of state for the Southern Department, who was responsible for the colonies. Roubaud drafted a number of reports for him about the Indians, the problem of French paper money, and the religious situation in Canada. Although these statements did not have any notable effect on ministerial decisions, his report on religion was the occasion of a great deal of anxiety for Canon BRIAND, who was in London trying to obtain the British government's authorization for his consecration as bishop. Roubaud claimed that the best way for Britain to gain the loyalty of the Canadians was to alienate them from their religion by depriving them of a bishop and by providing them with as few priests as possible. Satisfied with his services, Lord Halifax presented him to George III and secured him a monthly pension of 20 guineas. He was looking forward to a life free of financial cares when in July 1765 a change of government deprived him of both job and pension. He had just married a young woman of humble origins named Mitchell, and he needed more money. The Jesuits in Quebec considered that his marriage had released them from any obligation to him and refused to help him. To make ends meet Roubaud had to try his hand at numerous jobs and even became an actor of sorts.

From September 1766 Roubaud was employed by Lord Shelburne, the newly appointed secretary of state for the Southern Department. He gave Shelburne his views about the lifetime grant of land on the Baie des Puants (Green Bay, Lake Michigan) made by the king of France in the autumn of 1759 to François-Pierre de RIGAUD de Vaudreuil and his wife. As a result of the conquest, the grant had never been registered with the Conseil Supérieur and when in January 1765 the Vaudreuils sold William Grant* the territory, which carried with it exclusive fur-trading rights, certain English traders put pressure on the government to annul the sale. In his written statement Roubaud gave a verdict against the validity of the grant, and his opinion may have had some influence on the decision of the British government to refuse to acknowledge the land as the Vaudreuils' property.

Early in 1768 Shelburne left his ministerial post and Roubaud once more was unemployed. He acquired such heavy debts that he was imprisoned several times, even though at the end of 1769 he obtained a pension of £100 for service to the state. In 1769 Amherst asked the king for the grant of the Jesuit estates as a reward for his role in the conquest, and in 1770 Roubaud presented to the general a written statement designed to support this request, no doubt hoping to turn it to his own advantage. Amherst was favourably impressed, adopted Roubaud's arguments, and repeated them point by point to his agent in Canada, Colonel James Robertson. Amherst failed to obtain the estates, however, and Roubaud apparently received no reward for his services.

In November 1773 the Earl of Dartmouth, secretary of state for the American Colonies, weary of Roubaud's requests for money, procured him the post of secretary to Sir Joseph Yorke, the British ambassador to the Netherlands. Yorke was satisfied with his services and advised Dartmouth to settle his debts, with the result that Roubaud returned to the British capital early in January 1775. That summer M. de Sandray, secretary to the French ambassador in London, enlisted him to gather information about the American revolution and to report on debates in the House of Commons. In November Roubaud prepared a report recommending joint action by Great Britain and France to suppress the rebellion of the 13 colonies. He hoped that the execution of such a plan would guarantee his employment since, as he saw it, the opening moves would be given to obscure agents rather than to statesmen. But far from obtaining the result he desired, Roubaud instead brought upon himself British remonstrances and deeper French distrust.

Observing the effect of events in America upon the international scene, Roubaud conceived the idea of forging letters in which Montcalm* would predict that the British would take Canada and that the 13 colonies would revolt. The letters, entitled *Letters from the Marquis de Montcalm, governor-general of Canada; to Messrs. DeBerryer & De La Molé; in the years 1757, 1758 and 1759 . . .* , were published in London in 1777. Certain historians have gone to a great deal of trouble to demonstrate that these letters were complete forgeries, even though documents of the period prove conclusively that Roubaud's contemporaries were not fooled and that the author himself admitted the fraud.

In June 1777 the French embassy dismissed Roubaud from its service because his reports were inaccurate, and because it was clear that he was in the pay of the British government. In November 1778 the Duke of Almodóvar, the Spanish ambassador in London, employed him to report on the House of Commons debates and later to do translation. The latter task gave him access to important documents, which enabled him to inform the British ministers about certain aspects of the American revolution.

In the course of 1779 Roubaud again found himself out of work and now resorted to the lowest forms of spying in the most sordid places. He found no remunerative employment until the summer of 1783, when a large number of Canadians were in London to present plans for reform to the ministers or to settle legal actions. Gaining access to their circle, Roubaud offered to write the statements they intended to present to the ministers. Once more he took advantage of his situation to report what he learned – this time to under-secretary of state Evan Nepean – and thereby to augment his income. With Pierre DU CALVET he pursued the same line of action. Du Calvet was seeking redress from Governor HALDIMAND for imprisoning him on a charge of having collaborated with the enemy during the American invasion of Canada in 1775–76, and Roubaud was editing his material. Haldimand received daily information about his adversary's moves from Roubaud.

Du Calvet left London early in July 1785, leaving Roubaud without any livelihood. Adopting an approach he had used before when in financial difficulty, the ex-missionary tried to convince the British government that he had a right to a share of the Jesuit estates and that his colleagues had committed themselves to provide for his maintenance during his entire sojourn in London. The attempt almost succeeded this time since until he realized the absurdity of Roubaud's pretensions, Lord Sydney, secretary of state for the Home Department, supported his claims.

Roubaud, sick and unable to provide for his wife and child, left for France early in 1788. He was taken in by the Séminaire de Saint-Sulpice in Paris, where he remained until his death at an unknown date. Haldimand noted in his private diary on 17 Dec. 1789 that he was still living.

AUGUSTE VACHON

[P.-J.-A. Roubaud], "'Mr. Roubaud's deplorable case . . .,'" intro. J. G. Shea, *Hist. Magazine* (Morrisania, N.Y.), 2nd ser., VII (1870), 282–91.

AAQ, 20 A, VI, 10; 1 CB, VI, 64. AD, Vaucluse (Avignon), État civil, Saint-Pierre, 4 avril 1723, 28 mai 1724. Archives du ministère des Affaires étrangères (Paris), Corr. politique, Angleterre, 461, f.192; 515, ff.64, 66, 70, 177, 189; 525, ff.158, 312; Mémoires et doc., Angleterre, 56, ff.187–99 (mfm. at PAC). Archivo General de Simancas (Simancas, Spain), Secretaría de Estado, legajo 7021, atado 3, número 3, Roubaud à Almodóvar, 28 nov. 1778. ASQ, Fonds Viger-Verreau, Carton 13, no.35 (copy at PAC); Sér. O, 0116, pp.1–45 (copies at PAC). BL, Add. MSS 21865–66 (copies at PAC). PAC, MG 11, [CO 42], Q, 2, pp.243–45; 6, pp.111–12; 25, pp.42–43; 26, pp.89–90, 126; 55, pp.253–55; MG 23, A1, ser.1, 8, no.2991; 9, nos. 2315, 2325, 2332; 10, nos. 2373, 2383; ser.3, 5, f.22; GII, 1, ser.1, 2, p.141; 3, p.264. PRO, CO 42/15, p.225; 42/16, p.348; 42/17, p.233; 42/20, pp.52, 174–75, 184; WO 34/6, ff.12f., 47–49, 220–67; 34/39, ff.321, 325–28 (copies at PAC).

Bougainville, "Journal" (A.-E. Gosselin), ANQ *Rapport*, 1923–24, 202–393. *Coll. des manuscrits de Lévis* (Casgrain), VI, 141. *Doc. relatifs à la monnaie sous le Régime français* (Shortt). *Doc. relatifs à l'hist. constitutionnelle, 1759–91* (Shortt et Doughty; 1921). Pierre Du Calvet, *Appel à la justice de l'État . . .* (Londres, 1784); *The case of Peter Du Calvet, esq., of Montreal in the province of Quebeck* (London, 1784). *JR* (Thwaites), LXX, 90–203. PAC *Rapport*, 1885, xiv–xxii. "Pièces relatives à la mission de MM. Adhémar et Delisle en Angleterre en 1783–1784." *BRH*, XII (1906), 325–41, 353–71. *Biographie universelle* (1854–65), XXXVI, 577. T.-M. Charland, *Hist. des Abénakis*. R. C. Dalton, *The Jesuits' estates question, 1760–1888: a study of the background for the agitation of 1889* (Toronto, 1968), 8–10, 22, 28. A. [G.] Doughty and G. W. Parmelee, *The siege of Quebec and the battle of the Plains of Abraham* (6v., Quebec, 1901), VI, 122. Gustave Lanctot, *Faussaires et faussetés en histoire canadienne* (Montréal, 1948), 171–200. Rochemonteix, *Les jésuites et la N.-F. au XVIIIe siècle*, II, 143–45. M. Trudel, *L'Église canadienne*. "Les jésuites au Canada après la suppression de la Compagnie de Jésus," *BHR*, XXXVI (1930), 752–58. Gustave Lanctot, "La vie scandaleuse d'un faussaire," RSC *Trans.*, 3rd ser., L (1956), sect. I, 25–48. Arthur Maheux, "Notes sur Roubaud et sur sa responsabilité dans la nomination de M. Briand comme évêque de Québec," SCHÉC *Rapport*, 6 (1938–39), 45–60. É.-Z. Massicotte, "Pierre Ducalvet inculpé en 1775," *BRH*, XXIX (1923), 303–5.

ROUSSEAU DE VILLEJOUIN (Villejoin, Villejoint), GABRIEL, officer in the colonial regular troops; b. 24 April 1709 at Plaisance (Placentia, Nfld), son of Gabriel Rousseau de Villejouin, naval captain, and Marie-Josephte Bertrand; d. 6 Nov. 1781 at Saint-Jean-d'Angély (dept of Charente-Maritime), France.

Information on the first two decades of Gabriel Rousseau de Villejouin's career is scarce. Having entered military service as a second ensign at Île Royale (Cape Breton Island) on 9 May 1723, he was promoted ensign in March 1730 and lieutenant two months later. He evidently served at Louisbourg until 1737, when he was put in command at Port-Toulouse (St Peters, N.S.). In 1739 he returned to Louisbourg to succeed his brother-in-law, Robert Tarride* Duhaget, as assistant garrison adjutant with a captain's commission on 1 April. Two years later Villejouin received formal command of a company. This he led in defence of the King's bastion in 1745 when the fortress was successfully besieged by New England troops under the command of William Pepperrell*.

Although the record of these first 20 years is meagre, it reveals a certain ability. Villejouin was not yet 30 when made adjutant and, after leaving this position, he apparently continued to devote some time to military administration. By his own testimony, he earned the approbation of both his fellow officers and the townspeople for his success in pacifying the soldiers who mutinied at Louisbourg in 1744. Louis DU PONT Duchambon, the commandant of Île Royale, commended his valorous conduct during the siege.

In 1747 Villejouin was with the convoy commanded by La Jonquière [Taffanel*] when the British attacked and defeated it off Cape Ortegal, Spain. He may have been taken prisoner to England; in any event he was at Rochefort on 28 Feb. 1748 when he received the cross of Saint-Louis.

The treaty of Aix-la-Chapelle in 1748 restored Île Royale to France, but the attitudes of both France and Britain remained belligerent. French policy required a new and stronger fortress at Louisbourg and therefore more troops for its construction and defence; Villejouin was responsible for recruiting them in Rochefort. He then returned to Île Royale, and when Duhaget, the commandant of Port-Toulouse, was wounded in a mutiny in June 1750, Villejouin was assigned to command the post. After the death of Michel de Gannes* de Falaise in 1752, Duhaget took over the duties of town major at Louisbourg, and from 10 July 1753 to 1 April 1754 Villejouin acted as troop major, replacing Michel LE COURTOIS de Surlaville. Until 1751 the majority had been one office, and in 1754 the ministry of Marine reunited the two positions and gave them to Duhaget. Villejouin was thereupon appointed to succeed Claude-Élisabeth Denys* de Bonnaventure as major and commandant of Île Saint-Jean (Prince Edward Island).

Villejouin had been in command there for only a year when, in the late summer of 1755, the deportation of Acadians from Nova Scotia [*see* Charles Lawrence*] led to a nearly disastrous influx of refugees. Designated earlier by French policy as a farm for Île Royale, the island had yet to become even self-sufficient. Nevertheless, Villejouin actively and energetically dealt with the problems raised by the refugees and the war. He sent the sick and unfit to Quebec, supported as best he could the guerrilla activities of Charles DESCHAMPS de Boishébert, and even while establishing 1,500 new settlers invigorated the island's agriculture. "I foresaw," he wrote at Port-La-Joie (Fort Amherst) in September 1758, "being able to feed the whole island this autumn with little outside help. . . ." The fall of Louisbourg two months earlier had, however, sealed the fate of Île Saint-Jean. Andrew, Lord Rollo*, took possession of the island in August and all but 200 settlers, isolated on the western shore, were eventually deported.

On his repatriation to France in 1759 Villejouin became garrison adjutant at Rochefort. On 23 May 1760 he succeeded Bonnaventure as inspector of all colonial troops. But France's permanent loss of her North American colonies made the position redundant. Consolidation of what was left of the French empire led to Villejouin's appointment as lieutenant-colonel and governor of Désirade (in the Leeward Islands) on 1 Jan. 1763. To this small, rugged island were sent the "black sheep" of many good families. To improve its society Villejouin obtained commissions there for three of his sons and several of the old Île Royale garrison. When Désirade came under the government of Guadeloupe in 1768, he returned to France and was made a brigadier of the king's armies on 12 November. This appointment marked the end of his military career, since it seems to have carried few if any duties. He retired to Saint-Jean-d'Angély, where he died on 6 Nov. 1781.

On 11 Jan. 1733 in Louisbourg Villejouin had married Anne, daughter of Louis de Gannes* de Falaise and Marguerite Leneuf de La Vallière et de Beaubassin. The marriage was conceived of necessity; their first child was born in February. Four of their six children lived to adulthood, including Michel, who fought rearguard actions in Acadia during the Seven Years' War and who attempted a relief of Louisbourg during the 1758 siege. After Anne's death in 1751 Villejouin married, on 30 Dec. 1753 in Louisbourg, Barbe, daughter of Michel Leneuf* de La Vallière et de Beaubassin and Renée Bertrand. Only two of their four children survived infancy.

ANDREW RODGER

AMA, SHA, Y[4d]. AN, Col., A, 1, p.5; B, 72, p.420; 72/2, p.440; 88/2, pp.280, 353; 99, p.222; 107, p.274; C[11B], 10, ff.170–71v; 11, ff.61–68, 170v; 14, ff.188v, 190v; 15, f.40v; 20, f.95; 21, ff.63–64, 271; 28, ff.63–63v; 29, ff.66–71v; 32, f.242v; 33, ff.22–22v; 34, f.36v; 35, p.158; 36, pp.51, 181; 37, p.165; 38, ff.245v, 265v, p.269; C[11C], 16, pièce 26 (2e sér.); D[2C], 47; 48, ff.105, 108, 143, 168, 173, 184, 218, 240v, 369, 378, 404; 49, f.216; 60, ff.3, 11v, 12; 222; Marine, C[7], 287; Section Outre-mer, G[1], 406/2, p.301; 406/3, pp.366, 409, 489; 407, pp.133, 290; 408; 410; 411; G[2], 201, dossier 243, pièces 1, 4; 202, dossier 295, pièce 1; 207, dossier 474, f.22v (paginated references are to PAC transcripts). PAC, MG 18, H13, no.100. *Les derniers jours de l'Acadie* (Du Boscq de Beaumont). Æ. Fauteux, *Les chevaliers de Saint-Louis*. Harvey, *French régime in P.E.I.*

ROUSSON, LOUIS LE VERRIER DE. *See* LE VERRIER

ROUVILLE, RENÉ-OVIDE HERTEL DE. *See* HERTEL

ROY, LOUIS, printer; b. 24 May 1771 in Quebec, son of François Roy, a tailor, and Marie-Louise Lapérade; d. 22 Sept. 1799 in New York.

In 1786 Louis Roy became an apprentice in the printing shop of William BROWN, printer and owner of the *Quebec Gazette/La Gazette de Québec*. After Brown's death in 1789, Roy continued to work there for Samuel NEILSON, Brown's nephew, probably as a journeyman printer. It was in Montreal, however, in Fleury MESPLET's shop apparently, that the new lieutenant governor of Upper Canada, Colonel John Graves Simcoe*, found him and hired him as the first king's printer for that province. Reaching Newark (Niagara-on-the-Lake), the capital, early in the autumn of 1792, Roy on 4 November made out his first requisition for equipment needed for the printing shop. But his order apparently was made too late, given the navigation season, for him to receive the equipment before the spring of 1793. Hence he probably purchased some of it at Quebec from his former employer, Neilson, including a second-hand press with which he was able to fill some printing orders by January. Thus, one of the first printed pieces in Upper Canada was an eight-page brochure entitled *Speech of His Excellency John Graves Simcoe, esq; lieutenant governor of the province of Upper Canada, &c. &c. &c. upon opening the first session of the legislature. . . .* Then on 2 and 7 February he published official proclamations by the lieutenant governor.

On 18 April 1793 Louis Roy launched the *Upper Canada Gazette, or American Oracle*, a semi-official weekly newspaper, which was continued until 1845. The paper, which consisted of four two-column pages, appeared in English only, except for a few official documents translated into French. Advertisements and government announcements left little space for local news but, in compensation, at least one page of each issue had articles reprinted from European periodicals. This was one way in which the small population of Upper Canada could keep abreast of the events of the French revolution. Roy's paper was superior in the quality of its printing to that published by his successors. He is supposed to have printed about 45 numbers between 18 April 1793 and 31 July 1794. The last bearing his name came out, however, on 29 Aug. 1794: it was a supplement announcing a British naval victory.

Roy had assumed his post officially on 1 Oct. 1792, and in the early autumn of 1794 he left Upper Canada, never to return. On 29 October a final money order was issued in his favour; the salary being paid for the period to 31 Dec. 1794 amounted to £35 3*s*. 4½*d*., including a supplement for his keep and other needs. It seems that Roy enjoyed good salary terms, but too much work, a life of isolation, and the illiteracy of part of the population probably prompted his departure. He returned to work in Quebec, likely in the shop of John Neilson*, whose brother Samuel had died in 1793. By 8 July 1795 it was clear that he wanted to settle in Montreal. He had already bought a printing shop there, intending to publish a newspaper. He received help from his brother Joseph-Marie, who was also a printer, and on 17 August his *Montreal Gazette/Gazette de Montréal* was launched. For nearly two years Montreal was the scene of a newspaper war. Indeed, concurrently with Roy's newspaper Edward Edwards* published one with the same name. Edwards had purchased Fleury Mesplet's printing shop shortly after his death in 1794.

In his capacity as postmaster Edwards seems to have had easier access to international news. On many occasions he prevented foreign periodicals from being delivered to his competitor. Roy consequently found himself limited to local news. In addition he lacked equipment, and the clientele was too limited to support two printing shops. Consequently in 1797 he was forced to hand his newspaper over to his brother Joseph-Marie and to emigrate to New York. Roy's *Montreal Gazette* ceased publication in November that year, since Joseph-Marie and John Bennett, a former master printer in John Neilson's shop, did not succeed in their efforts.

It seems that Roy's departure for New York may also be accounted for by the prevailing political situation in Montreal. Roy, who was known for his republican principles, perhaps had not remained deaf to the approaches of the emissaries of republican France. Thus it is possible that he left Montreal to escape harassment, hoping at the same time to find an environment for work that would be more in keeping with his political ideas. In New York he worked at the *Argus, Greenleaf's New Daily Advertiser*, a newspaper founded in May 1795 whose foreman he soon became. He held this position until his death from yellow fever on 22 Sept. 1799.

The announcement of his death in this newspaper spoke of him in very flattering terms: "We condole with our Republican friends upon the loss of this Genuine Patriot and truly honest man; and we regret sincerely that we have occasion to record the death of such a worthy character." Louis Roy left in mourning his brothers Joseph-Marie and Charles and a sister, Louise-Olive de Saint-Paul, a member of the Ursulines of Quebec. Charles would become the publisher of the *Canadien* in 1806.

John E. Hare

ANQ-Q, État civil, Catholiques, Notre-Dame de Québec, 25 mai 1771; Greffe de J.-A. Saillant, 3 sept. 1768. P.-G. Roy, *Fils de Québec*, II, 154. Tremaine, *Bibliography of Canadian imprints*. Burke, *Les ursulines de Québec* (1863–66), III, 336. Gundy, *Early printers. Canadian book of printing; how printing came to Canada and the story of the graphic arts, told mainly in pictures*, ed. Marie Tremaine (Toronto, 1940). William Colgate, "Louis Roy: first printer in Upper Canada," *OH*, XLIII (1951), 123–42. P.-G. Roy, "L'imprimeur Louis Roy," *BRH*, XXIV (1918), 77. W. S. Wallace, "The periodical literature of Upper Canada," *CHR*, XII (1931), 5.

ROZINOGHYATA. *See* Hotsinoñhyahta?

S

SABREVOIS DE BLEURY, CLÉMENT DE, seigneur and merchant; baptized 16 July 1702 at Boucherville (Que.), son of Jacques-Charles de Sabrevois* and Jeanne Boucher; d. 18 April 1781 at Montreal.

Although he came from a military family, Clément de Sabrevois de Bleury did not follow his brothers Charles de Sabrevois and Christophe de Sabrevois de Sermonville into the colonial regular troops. He turned instead to commerce. Early in 1726 he formed a five-year partnership with Claude de Ramezay*'s widow, Marie-Charlotte Denys de La Ronde, to exploit a sawmill erected by her husband in the seigneury of Chambly. Because of his connections with the Bouchers and the Hertels, Bleury moved easily among the leaders of Montreal society. The list of witnesses to his marriage contract with Charlotte Guichard, signed on 19 Aug. 1728 at Montreal, reads like a directory to the military, commercial, and seigneurial élite of the town. By 1731 Bleury had entered a partnership with Louis Lepage* de Sainte-Claire to supply shipyards in the colony with planking, and as encouragement Intendant Hocquart allowed them to cut 2,000 cubic feet of oak from seigneuries that did not belong to them. In 1732 Bleury exploited the timber in the seigneuries of Chambly and Longueuil. He also ventured into intercolonial trade when the same year he joined his father-in-law, Jean Guichard, in building a 76-ton brigantine at Chambly which they sent to Martinique with a cargo of foodstuffs. Bleury made no further moves in this direction, however. He appears cautious and preferred to keep his enterprises closer to home, where greater personal supervision could be maintained.

In April 1733 he and his brother Charles obtained concessions on the Richelieu River, but they were interested only in harvesting the timber and in 1741 the two seigneuries, Bleury and Sabrevois, were retroceded to the crown for their holders' failure to encourage settlement. Bleury entered a long-term partnership in 1734 with his uncle Jean-Baptiste Boucher* de Niverville to erect and exploit a sawmill in the seigneury of Chambly. Bleury agreed to advance the required funds while his uncle supplied the land and timber. Four years later Bleury contracted with Pierre Lupien*, *dit* Baron, to supply timber to the government shipyards at Quebec. Bleury's cautious approach to trade was again revealed as he began to diversify his interests despite the flourishing state of his timber enterprises.

During the 1740s he bought lands and annuities and he also began to furnish supplies and transportation services to the government. Between 1740 and 1748 he purchased at least five pieces of land in the seigneury of Chambly near Île Sainte-Thérèse. He also loaned money and cashed annuities and bonds. In 1743 he supplied transportation to the government worth 7,654 *livres*; four years later the value of these services had grown to 48,263 *livres*. In 1747 also he supplied the government with goods worth 83,104 *livres*, over half the total value of purchases by the crown at Montreal. In brief, Bleury had become an exceedingly prosperous merchant.

He had lived at Chambly since his marriage, but in 1746 he purchased a town lot in Montreal on Rue Saint-Gabriel and soon moved with his family into a new house there to be closer to the government offices. Four years later he and his brother Charles succeeded in regaining the seigneuries retroceded nine years before and, in order to prevent a repetition of their loss, the two men went to France where they obtained royal warrants ratifying the new grants. Bleury's rise to social prominence culminated in 1754 when two of his children, Jean-Clément and Marguerite, were married in a magnificent double wedding ceremony at Montreal. The chief witnesses were Governor DUQUESNE and Intendant BIGOT, and the other guests included members of most of the important families in Canada.

With the outbreak of the Seven Years' War and the decision to fortify the Lake Champlain approaches to the colony, Bleury entered his element. He became chief of the intendant's transportation services in the region. His enormous fleet of bateaux, each built to carry three tons of cargo, moved regularly between forts Saint-Jean and Carillon (Ticonderoga, N.Y.). In 1756 Bougainville* claimed that the "admiral on Lake Champlain" was receiving 18 *sols* on every pound of freight carried for the crown. Since between 22 Sept. and 25 Oct. 1756 Bleury sent 179 bateaux to Carillon, his potential gross revenues from freight alone were immense. In addition the bateaux carried goods and supplies to be sold for his own account. To what degree Bleury earned profits from these activities cannot yet be determined. Some time in 1757 he withdrew from them but recurring illness rather than commercial difficulties may have been the reason; in 1749 he had nearly died from an infection.

After the conquest Bleury further curtailed his activities. In 1764 he sold the seigneuries of Bleury and Sabrevois to Gabriel CHRISTIE and Moses Hazen*. His private income appears to have been substantial, since thereafter he lived in quiet retirement on Rue Saint-Gabriel. Bleury was a successful merchant, but not a risk-taking entrepreneur. His ventures were of a local nature, often in association with his relatives, and his greatest success probably resulted from his connections with government officials.

JAMES S. PRITCHARD

AN, Col., C^{11A}, 60, ff.406–8; F^{2B}, 11. Bégon, "Correspondance" (Bonnault), ANQ *Rapport*, 1934–35, 1–277. Bougainville, "Journal" (A.-E. Gosselin), ANQ *Rapport*, 1923–24, 202–393. *Coll. des manuscrits de Lévis* (Casgrain), IX. P.-G. Roy, *Inv. concessions*, IV; *Inv. jug. et délib., 1717–60*, VI. Tanguay, *Dictionnaire*, VII. J.-N. Fauteux, *Essai sur l'industrie*. Mathieu, *La construction navale*. Cameron Nish, *Les bourgeois-gentilshommes de la Nouvelle-France, 1729–1748* (Montréal et Paris, 1968). É.-Z. Massicotte, "Les Sabrevois, Sabrevois de Sermonville et Sabrevois de Bleury," *BRH*, XXXI (1925), 77–84.

SAHONWAGY (Sahonwadi; the name probably means the one on his boat – Shahũwà:ke in Floyd G. Lounsbury's orthography, but he signed Sahonwagy; also known as **Paulus Petersen, Pauly Peters, Paulus, Poulous**, and **Powless)**, Mohawk sachem and schoolmaster; son of Theyanoguin*, probably b. at Fort Hunter, New York; d. after 1787, probably at the Six Nations settlement on the Grand River (Ont.).

In July 1753 the missionary John OGILVIE suggested Sahonwagy to the Society for the Propagation of the Gospel as a schoolmaster in the place of Paulus Petrus, a Mohawk who had died some time before. Sahonwagy, he added, "may at the same time officiate as Clerk, and read Prayers to the Indians in . . . [my] Absence." In December the SPG agreed to engage him at a salary of £7 per annum. Although described by Ogilvie as a Fort Hunter Mohawk, Sahonwagy established himself at Canajoharie (near Little Falls, N.Y.), where by June 1755 he was teaching upwards of 40 children every day.

Both as a sachem and as a member of an influential Mohawk family, Sahonwagy was of service to the British during the Seven Years' War. In May 1756 he attended a council between Sir William JOHNSON and the Oneida sachem Canaghquiesa (Kanaghgwasea), and that summer he drew pay as an Indian captain. He was at Fort Herkimer (Herkimer, N.Y.) in March 1758, when he promised to go on a scouting mission near Oswegatchie (Ogdensburg). Such activities cut into his work as a schoolmaster, however, and in February 1759 Ogilvie suspended his salary "because of several Complaints that he was so taken up with War-parties, that he had greatly neglected the Instruction of the Children."

Between 1761 and 1763 Sahonwagy and the other Canajoharie sachems were involved in a struggle over land claims with George Klock, a local miller who used copious quantities of rum to obtain Indian signatures to land deeds. In July 1763 Sahonwagy and Nicholas Brant wrote to Johnson complaining that Klock had threatened to kill Brant and his wife and requesting Johnson's intervention to "Provent trouble or Els there will be Mischeiff Done here on one Side or Another."

Sahonwagy was reappointed reader at Canajoharie by the missionary John Stuart* in 1775, but in 1777 the American revolution drove many of the Canajoharie and Fort Hunter Mohawks to Canada. Christian Daniel CLAUS, at the instance of these Indians, prepared a new edition of the Mohawk Book of Common Prayer in 1780, and Sahonwagy oversaw the correction of proof. The next year he was reported by Claus to be teaching the refugee Mohawks who were living near Montreal. Some time after that he moved to the Grand River settlement. He reported to Claus in August 1785 that he was well pleased with the land and that "the crops [were] all growing splendid." The lack of a teacher at the settlement disturbed him, and he offered to take up the position provided he were given supplies. He advised against the use of a white teacher, pointing out that "if he does not understand our language, he cannot restrain them [the children] from doing wrong." In February 1787 he, along with Joseph Brant [Thayendanegea*], Karonghyontye (David Hill), Kanonraron (Aaron Hill), and others, signed a deed granting land on the Grand River to some whites. The Paulus who was at Fort George (Niagara-on-the-Lake, Ont.) in August 1802 was probably his son.

GUS RICHARDSON

PAC, MG 19, F1, 3, pp.49–50; 4, p.79; 24, pp.24–25; F6, 4, pp.555–56. USPG, Journal of SPG, 12, pp.307–9; 13, pp.182–83; 14, p.186. *Johnson papers* (Sullivan *et al.*), II, 589, 624, 780; IV, 54–55, 165–66; XI, 984; XIII, 175, 274–75. *NYCD* (O'Callaghan and Fernow), VII, 112; VIII, 816. *The valley of the Six Nations . . .*, ed. and intro. C. M. Johnston (Toronto, 1964), 71. J. W. Lydekker, *The faithful Mohawks* (Cambridge, Eng., 1938).

SAILLANT (Saillant de Collégien), JEAN-ANTOINE (Antoine-Jean), royal notary, attorney to the Conseil Supérieur, and lawyer; b. 1720 in Paris, France, son of Jacques Saillant, a notary, and Anne Laurent; d. 9 Oct. 1776 at Quebec.

Jean-Antoine Saillant came from a prominent French family – his father was a lawyer, king's councillor, and controller of annuities for the city of Paris. He also had influential relatives in Canada, where, for reasons unknown, he arrived around 1745. On 27 Dec. 1749 he received a commission as royal notary to practise throughout the Government of Quebec. His clientele included such important people as Intendant BIGOT and the Péan, Duchesnay, and Duchambon families. An accomplished notary, he practised from 1750 to 1776, drawing up 2,817 deeds.

In Montreal on 12 Jan. 1750, in the presence of Governor La Jonquière [Taffanel*] and Charles Le Moyne* de Longueuil, Saillant married Véronique, the daughter of Pierre Pépin, *dit* Laforce, royal surveyor and former king's storekeeper at Fort Niagara (near Youngstown, N.Y.); he thus allied himself with a prominent family in the colony. Shortly after, probably through his relatives – he was a nephew of Nicolas BOISSEAU, chief clerk of the Conseil Supérieur, and a cousin of Nicolas-Gaspard Boisseau*, the chief clerk of the provost court of Quebec, and of Jacques PERRAULT, known as Perrault *l'aîné*, an important Quebec merchant-trader – he was appointed attorney to the Conseil Supérieur, where his services were highly esteemed.

Under the British régime Saillant continued to practise as a notary and attorney. On 29 Dec. 1760 Governor MURRAY granted him a commission as royal notary for the whole of the Government of Quebec. As attorney Saillant was the impassioned defence counsel for the Séminaire de Québec (1762), and for La Corriveau [Marie-Josephte Corriveau*] in her two trials in 1763 (both of his addresses to the court have been preserved in full). In 1765 Murray commissioned him to compile the list of recognitions of sovereignty and census of the fiefs and lands in his seigneury of Lauson. Saillant demanded such a high fee that the governor refused to pay him. After arbitration his work was deemed worth 3,600 *livres*, and he was given three months to deliver copies of the title-deeds to the habitants. On this occasion Saillant had the notarial acts drawn up on printed forms, making the first such use of printing in Canada. His good reputation was demonstrated when he became the fourth Canadian to be commissioned as a lawyer by the British authorities, on 9 July 1766, although he had already been authorized to act in this capacity before the Court of Common Pleas in 1765.

Notary, attorney, and lawyer, Saillant was never wealthy, although he inherited nearly 6,000 *livres* from his parents. When he died in Quebec on 9 Oct. 1776, his estate was so heavily burdened with debts that his second wife, Louise-Catherine Roussel, whom he had married in

Quebec in 1757, refused to act as the administrator.

ROLAND-J. AUGER

Jean-Antoine Saillant's notarial register, 1750–76, is held at ANQ-Q. ANQ-Q, NF 25, 56, no.2126; 58, no.2467. PRO, WO 71/49, pp.213–14; 71/137, p.60. *Quebec Gazette*, 21 March, 27 June, 15 Aug. 1765, 23 March 1775. "Cahier des témoignages de liberté au mariage commancé le 15 avril 1757," ANQ *Rapport*, 1951–53, 52. Labrèque, "Inv. de pièces détachées," ANQ *Rapport*, 1971, 6, 324, 360, 369, 393. P.-G. Roy, *Les avocats de la région de Québec*, 395–96; *Inv. ord. int.*, III, 137; "Les notaires au Canada sous le Régime français," ANQ *Rapport*, 1921–22, 52. J.-E. Roy, *Histoire de la seigneurie de Lauzon* (5v., Lévis, Qué., 1897–1904), III, 12–15; *Hist. du notariat*, I, 361; II, 17, 26, 29. F.-J. Audet, "Les députés du Barreau de la province de Québec," *Cahiers des Dix*, 2 (1937), 213. Luc Lacourcière, "Le triple destin de Marie-Josephte Corriveau (1733–1763)," *Cahiers des Dix*, 33 (1968), 213–42. Jacques Mathieu, "Un négociant de Québec à l'époque de la Conquête: Jacques Perrault l'aîné," ANQ *Rapport*, 1970, 31, 58, 66.

SAINT-ANGE ET DE BELLERIVE, LOUIS GROSTON DE. *See* GROSTON

SAINT-AUBIN, AMBROISE (Ambroise, Ambroise Bear, Ambroise Pier, Ambroise Var), Malecite chief; d. October 1780.

During the American revolution the governments of Nova Scotia and Massachusetts competed for control of the area that has become New Brunswick and Maine. Within this vast wilderness the Penobscot, Malecite, and Micmac Indians seemed to hold the key to victory. The colonies believed they could secure their frontier districts and damage those of their enemy by controlling these tribes. To gain such influence the governments waged campaigns combining bribery, flattery, and intimidation with restriction of Indian access to vital supplies and heavy-handed manipulation of the Roman Catholic priests serving the tribes.

Ambroise Saint-Aubin was a chief of the Malecites, who constituted a powerful force in the Saint John valley. His participation in the revolution began in September 1775 when he and Pierre TOMAH, another major Malecite chief, appeared at the Penobscot truck house (Bangor, Maine) and declared their support for Massachusetts. In July 1776 Saint-Aubin led a delegation of Malecites and Micmacs to Watertown, Mass., for a week-long conference with government leaders. The meeting resulted in a treaty under which the state promised a truck house at Machias (Maine) and the Indians agreed to provide 600 men for the Continental Army.

Although the promise of 600 fighting men was repudiated by the older Micmac chiefs, the Malecites and some Micmacs continued sympathetic to the Americans. Saint-Aubin was involved in a number of American operations, including Jonathan Eddy*'s unsuccessful attack on Fort Cumberland (near Sackville, N.B.) in the fall of 1776, and he assisted John Allan*, who became the American agent to the Malecites and Micmacs in 1777. Early in the summer of 1777 a rift in the Malecite polity became evident. An American force under Allan established itself on the Saint John at Aukpaque (near Fredericton) in June and was warmly received by the Malecites. When British ships arrived in the lower river later in the month, however, Pierre Tomah went on board HMS *Vulture* to confer. Saint-Aubin refused to go, and he and a larger part of the tribe fled to Machias, which they reached in time to help the garrison meet an assault from a British force sent by Sir George COLLIER. Saint-Aubin continued to work with Allan and spent much time travelling between Machias and Nova Scotia as a courier and spokesman among the Indians for the Americans. Although Allan noted that he was an "old man" and "very Infirm," he remained active through the summer of 1780 and his death in October was sudden. The Indians suspected that he had been poisoned, but Allan knew of no evidence for the allegation.

Although Saint-Aubin's adherence to the Americans had provided them with a useful tool in operations and reconnaissance, the Malecites played a minor role in the revolution. Impoverished by governmental neglect since 1763, they were interested only in gaining maximum benefit from the conflict, not in undertaking the large-scale hostilities to which both sides had hoped to incite them.

RICHARD I. HUNT

PAC, MG 11, [CO 217], Nova Scotia A, 72, pp.44–45; 78, pp.83–85; 83, pp.22, 303; 87, pp.123–24; 100, pp.200–1; [CO 220], Nova Scotia B, 12, pp.158–59; 13, p.126; 14, pp.50, 90–91. *Documentary history of Maine* (Willis *et al.*), XIV–XVI, XVIII, XIX, XXIV. *Military operations in eastern Maine and N.S.* (Kidder). J. H. Ahlin, *Maine Rubicon; downeast settlers during the American revolution* (Calais, Maine, 1966). R. I. Hunt, "British-American rivalry for the support of the Indians of Maine and Nova Scotia, 1775–1783" (unpublished MA thesis, University of Maine, Orono, 1973).

SAINT-AURON. *See* MAUGENEST

SAINTE-MARIE, PHILIPPE-JOSEPH D'ALLARD DE. *See* ALLARD

SAINT-FRANÇOIS, JOSEPH-HIPPOLYTE HERTEL DE. *See* Hertel

SAINT-GEORGES DUPRÉ, GEORGES-HIPPOLYTE LE COMTE DUPRÉ, known as. *See* Le Comte

SAINT-HIPPOLYTE, MARIE-MARGUERITE PIOT DE LANGLOISERIE, *dite*. *See* Piot

SAINT-HORAN (Saint-Jorand). *See* Maugenest

ST LEGER, BARRIMORE MATTHEW (Barry), army officer; the name is variously pronounced "Sill′inger" and "Saint Leg′er"; baptized 1 May 1733, probably in County Kildare (Republic of Ireland), son of Sir John St Leger and Lavina Pennefather; m. 7 April 1773 a Miss Bayly, widow of Sir Edward Mansel, and they had at least one son; d. 1789.

Educated at Eton, then at Cambridge, where he was a fellow of Peterhouse, Barrimore Matthew St Leger joined the army in April 1756 as an ensign in the 28th Foot. He served under James Abercromby in 1757 and is supposed to have gained some experience as a bush fighter. He took part in the siege of Louisbourg, Île Royale (Cape Breton Island) in 1758 and in Wolfe*'s expedition against Quebec in 1759. St Leger was named brigade-major in July 1760, serving as a staff officer in the campaign against Montreal under James Murray. He was promoted major in the 95th Foot on 16 Sept. 1762.

By the time of the American revolution St Leger was lieutenant-colonel of the 34th Foot. He took part in the operations in 1776 that drove the Americans from Quebec and up Lake Champlain to Ticonderoga (N.Y.). When Major-General John Burgoyne proposed an expedition to take Albany (N.Y.) as part of a scheme to cut the colonies in two, he suggested that St Leger command a secondary advance from Canada through the Mohawk valley.

St Leger's expedition left Montreal on 23 June 1777 and reached Oswego on 25 July. Advancing through the wilderness, the British and their Indian allies reached Fort Stanwix (Rome, N.Y.) on 2 August. Since the fort was too strong to be taken by assault, they besieged it. The chief action of the little campaign occurred when a force of militia under Brigadier-General Nicholas Herkimer attempted to relieve the fort. The Americans were ambushed and defeated in a hard-fought battle nearby at Oriskany on 6 August [*see* Kaieñ?kwaahtoñ]. During the engagement, however, the defenders of Fort Stanwix raided and looted the weakly held British positions around the fort. The Indians eventually withdrew, and St Leger, tricked into believing that a second American relief column was much closer than it actually was, raised the siege on 22 August and retreated the way he had come.

Back in Canada, he attempted once more to join Burgoyne but got no farther than Ticonderoga before Burgoyne surrendered at Saratoga (Schuylerville). For the remainder of the war St Leger commanded a force of rangers based in Montreal. He was promoted colonel in 1780, and in 1781 he led two unsuccessful enterprises. The first was an attempt to capture Philip John Schuyler, a retired American general and a leading New Yorker in the revolutionary cause. The second involved a meeting at Ticonderoga with representatives of some dissatisfied Vermonters led by Ethan Allen to discuss the possibility of Vermont's returning its allegiance to the crown. The plot was uncovered in Vermont, however, and before anything could be accomplished Lieutenant-General Charles Cornwallis surrendered at Yorktown, Virginia, effectively ending the war.

After the revolution St Leger continued to serve in Canada. Promoted brigadier-general, he was for a short time commander of the British troops after Frederick Haldimand's departure in November 1784. He suffered from ill health, however, and in spite of not receiving any orders for his relief from the home government, he gave up his command to Henry Hope late in 1785. After that year his name disappears from the *Army list*.

Authorities have generally considered St Leger a capable soldier in frontier warfare, but his record indicates that he was a better follower than a leader; G. F. G. Stanley concludes only a little too harshly that "as a commander St. Leger was neither inspiring or inspired." His chief fault in his one independent campaign was that he underestimated his opponent, but the same mistake was made by the entire British army and government.

James Stokesbury

"Colonel St. Leger's account of occurrences at Fort Stanwix" was published as app.XIII to [John Burgoyne], *A state of the expedition from Canada . . .* (London, 1780; repr. New York, 1969). Boatner, *Encyclopedia of American revolution*. D. B. Chidsey, *The war in the north; an informal history of the American revolution in and near Canada* (New York, 1967). Duncan McArthur, "Canada under the Quebec Act," *Canada and its provinces* (Shortt and Doughty), III, 107–38. J. N. McIlwraith, *Sir Frederick Haldimand* (London and Toronto, 1926), 211–12, 295–96. Hoffman

Nickerson, *The turning point of the revolution, or Burgoyne in America* (2v., Boston and New York, 1928; repr. Port Washington, N.Y., 1967). Stanley, *Canada's soldiers*. W. L. Stone, *The campaign of Lieut. Gen. John Burgoyne and the expedition of Lieut. Col. Barry St. Leger* (Albany, N.Y., 1877; repr. New York, 1970). C. [L.] Ward, *The war of the revolution*, ed. J. R. Alden (2v., New York, 1952).

SAINT-LUC, LUC DE LA CORNE, known as **LA CORNE.** *See* LA CORNE

SAINT-MARTIN, JEAN DUMAS. *See* DUMAS

SAINT-ONGE, PIERRE GARREAU, *dit*. *See* GARREAU

SAINT-SAUVEUR, ANDRÉ GRASSET DE. *See* GRASSET

SAINT-SIMON, ANTOINE-CHARLES DENIS DE. *See* DENIS

SAINT-TERONE. *See* MAUGENEST

SALTER, MALACHY (Malachi), merchant and office-holder; b. 28 Feb. 1715/16 at Boston, Massachusetts, second son of Malachy Salter and Sarah Holmes; m. there on 26 July 1744 Susanna Mulberry, and they had at least 11 children; d. 13 Jan. 1781 at Halifax, Nova Scotia.

Unlike the most successful early entrepreneurs in Halifax, Malachy Salter had been born in New England and with it, rather than England, he maintained financial and emotional ties. Before settling in Halifax, perhaps as early as 1749, he had been in turn a seaman in the American coastwise trade, an associate of his uncles Nathaniel and George Holmes in their successful Boston distillery, and the senior partner in a firm involved in the fisheries and the West Indian trade. Established tradition says that he was a frequent visitor to Chebucto Bay before the founding of Halifax in 1749.

Initially in partnership with John Kneeland, also of Boston, Salter established himself as a general merchant in Halifax, where the debtors' act protected him against the demands of the New England creditors from whom he had fled. As agent for former associates, he transacted the sale of their cargoes and sought executions in the courts for debts owed them. In his own right he engaged in shipping ventures which brought him both North American and European goods. He also extended credit, prosecuted debts, settled estates, and purchased Halifax properties, often from the over-extended poor. No doubt it was not his creditors alone who found him a "Litigious troublesome Man" "who has treated us in a Barbarous cruel manner." In 1754 Salter expanded his operations into the remunerative field of government contracts, farming the impost and retail duties on rum and importing stock from New England to supply the Germans at Lunenburg [*see* Benjamin GREEN]. He was subsequently called upon to provide certain mercantile evaluations for the government, but he was unable to establish himself in the fruitful provisions contracts as Joshua MAUGER and Thomas Saul* had done.

Having acted briefly as a constable and a clerk of the market in Boston, Salter was an early member of the grand jury in Halifax and served as a captain of militia (1761–62) and an overseer of the poor (1765–66). In 1757, in response to Governor Charles Lawrence*'s continuing refusal to call a representative assembly, he became a leader in the committee of Halifax freeholders which employed London lawyer Ferdinando John Paris to present civic complaints against the governor before the Board of Trade. When Lawrence was forced to convene an assembly in October 1758, Salter was amongst its 20 members.

In an early show of strength, the New England-dominated assembly thwarted the Council's attempt to limit its powers of patronage and nominated Salter, with John Newton, to act as collector of the impost and excise duties, a position which afforded the incumbent a ten per cent commission on revenues collected. In 1759, as another favour of government, Salter was granted land near Fort Edward (Windsor) to qualify him as an elector there. Two years later he was appointed a justice of the peace and collector of lighthouse duties, but he soon lost the first of these offices, which was held to be incompatible with his other positions. Initially a protégé of the Massachusetts-born Jonathan BELCHER, Salter fell out of favour with the lieutenant governor when he aligned himself with the New England faction of the house in opposing Belcher's calling of the assembly late in 1761 and determination to allow the debtors' act to lapse. He was removed from his offices in September 1762. Reinstated as collector of lighthouse duties and justice of the peace by Montagu Wilmot*, he appears to have held the first office only briefly.

For 15 years Salter sat in the House of Assembly, representing Halifax Township from 1759 to 1765 and Yarmouth Township from 1766 to 1772. Until 1769 he attended regularly and was active on many important committees. Later he participated in only one session, that of 1772, at the end of which his election in 1770 was declared invalid. As well as speaking for the New England community in the assembly, Salter represented their struggling Congregationalism both in Halifax and in Boston [*see also* Benjamin GERRISH].

During the Seven Years' War Salter was owner, with other Halifax entrepreneurs, of the privateer *Lawrence*. With his development of a sugar-house at Halifax in the mid 1760s he joined Mauger and John FILLIS as one of Nova Scotia's three manufacturers. His sugar-house, his friendship with Fillis, and his American trade connections enabled him to capitalize upon the embargo placed on British goods by the Thirteen Colonies in the late 1760s. Despite the promise of his diversified interests, however, and despite further government contracts during Michael FRANCKLIN's short-lived administration of St John's (Prince Edward) Island in 1768, Salter's circumstances at the end of the decade reflected the collapse of Nova Scotia's boom. His financial affairs had always been precarious and in 1768 shipping and other losses overtook him. After spending two years settling his debts in Nova Scotia and New England, he was restricted by the early 1770s to operating his sugar-house himself and in 1773 to building a vessel at Liverpool that he might go to sea, as in his youth, and thus support his family.

Salter was not a self-pitying man, but rather one who trusted in that "providence which has hitherto protected and supported me." His final years were to try his faith severely. In 1776, sailing from London, he was accused of intending English goods for Boston rather than their stated destination, Halifax. Early in 1777 he stood trial in Halifax for seditious conversation, but the jury found him innocent of any evil intent. Later the same year his brig *Rising Sun* was captured by Salem privateers and condemned as a prize. A prisoner in New England, Salter obtained a pass from the Massachusetts government to settle his family there. After his return to Halifax later in the year, he was accused of attempting to redeem Nova Scotian treasury notes for his Boston associates and charged with "secret correspondence" of "dangerous tendency" with the rebels. Finding himself harassed, he sailed for England, where he remained, settling business affairs, from early 1778 to early 1780. His absence stayed court proceedings against him, but from February 1778 until his death a recognizance on charges of misdemeanour was continued from term to term. Why the charges were not pressed after his return from England is not clear, but part of the explanation may be that James Brenton*, his lawyer at least in 1778–79, had become attorney general in October 1779.

John Bartlet Brebner* ranks Salter among the most important entrepreneurs of early Halifax, surpassed only by Mauger and Saul. Although his early Nova Scotian career points to such prominence, in the long run Salter's 75 property transactions and numberless court cases provided him with neither significant capital gains nor liquid assets. His shipping activities were minor compared with those of Mauger, Francklin, or his New England associates. Only briefly was he the official that Brebner notes, for in a town dependent upon the government in its civil and military roles he failed to establish himself securely within its profitable network. Nor did his efforts to make of Nova Scotia a new New England succeed finally in giving "the hand of Boston" any significant strength in the province.

Salter's relationship to the Mauger connection is ambiguous. There is much evidence to suggest that he was not free of its economic or political entanglements. A business associate of Mauger in the 1750s and a political ally of his forces in the 1760s, he participated with Mauger's henchmen in the establishment of government on St John's Island in 1768. Moreover, both his intimate friends, Fillis and Jonathan Prescott, and his son-in-law Thomas Bridge were Mauger's men. Yet in the 1770s Mauger's agents John BUTLER and Brook Watson* were among Salter's most pressing creditors, and Salter was the only leading Haligonian prosecuted during the American revolution who was not defended by Mauger's associates. If Salter's affairs at one time lay within Mauger's grasp, his scepticism of Mauger, his widespread American connections, and his determination to be self-sufficient appear to have ensured his independence.

S. BUGGEY

BL, Add. MSS 19069, pp.50–55 (transcripts at PAC). Halifax County Registry of Deeds (Halifax), Deeds, 1753–89 (mfm. at PANS). Harvard College Library, Harvard University (Cambridge, Mass.), fMS AM 579, Bourn papers, I, 137, 144; VI, 8, 57. Mass., Supreme Judicial Court (Boston), Records, 181, no.20931 (court files Suffolk, October 1727–December 1727); 310, no.47231 (court files Suffolk, July 1738–August 1738); 1265, no.170914 (court files Suffolk, 1751/52–1753). PAC, MG 11, [CO 217], Nova Scotia A, 84, pp.18ff; [CO 220], Nova Scotia B, 17, pp.116, 118, 121. PANS, MG 9, no.109; MS file, Malachy Salter, letters, 1766–73; Salter family docs., 1759–1802; RG 1, 163–65; 342, nos.77–85; RG 37, Halifax County, 1752–71; RG 39, C, 1–39; J, 1. PRO, CO 142/15 (mfm. at Dalhousie University Archives, Halifax); 217/16–27; 221/28–31 (mfm. at PAC). "Congregational churches in Nova Scotia," Mass. Hist. Soc., *Proc.*, 2nd ser., IV (1887–89), 67–73. Perkins, *Diary, 1766–80* (Innis). Brebner, *Neutral Yankees*; *New England's outpost*, 254–57. W. J. Stairs,

Family history, Stairs, Morrow; including letters, diaries, essays, poems, etc. (Halifax, 1906), 209–59.

SANGUINET, SIMON, merchant, notary, lawyer, and judge of the Court of Common Pleas; b. 16 March 1733 at Varennes (Que.), eldest son of Simon Sanguinet and Angélique Lefebvre, *dit* Duchouquet; d. 16 March 1790 in Montreal.

Simon Sanguinet's father, who had come from France, was royal notary at Varennes, near Montreal, from 1734 till 1748 and then settled with his family in Quebec, where he worked as a notary until 1771. What education Simon received is not known; we do know his brother Joseph attended the Séminaire de Québec, the only one of his family to do so. When Simon married Thérèse Réaume in Montreal on 15 Jan. 1759, he called himself a merchant; in April that year he was listed in a notarial act as "an employee in the king's offices in this town." He slowly learned business methods and became increasingly successful. At their marriage the couple each contributed 10,000 *livres* to their joint estate. The following year Simon bought a house on Rue Saint-Louis in Montreal from his father-in-law for 22,000 *livres*; he received 50,000 for it when he sold it in 1764. Simon Sanguinet also lent money, but he does not seem to have joined in the trade in furs that his brothers Christophe and Joseph carried on from 1763 to 1765.

In 1764 Sanguinet became a notary, and he soon acquired a substantial practice. Like a number of other notaries in the towns, he also became a lawyer, receiving his commission in July 1768. He soon had as many clients as a lawyer as he had as a notary. Sanguinet was secretary of the parish council of Notre-Dame in Montreal from 1765 and a member of a Masonic lodge from 1771; he led a busy life as a prominent member of Montreal society. The American invasion in 1775–76 was to give him the opportunity to play an important role.

A fervent royalist, Sanguinet took an active political part in the defence of Canada, using his time, his money, and his social contacts. He was one of eight Montrealers made responsible for preparing a census and military rosters, and it was on his advice that Governor Guy Carleton*, with whom he was on friendly terms, re-established the Canadian militia at the beginning of June 1775. After the Americans arrived in Montreal, the loyalism of Sanguinet and his family got them into difficulties. When Brigadier-General David Wooster decided early in January 1776 to arrest ten prominent Montrealers, Christophe, Joseph, and Simon Sanguinet were among those selected, although in the end none were arrested. In March Simon circulated a virulent letter to the "habitants of Canada," an "ungrateful people" whom he called upon to chase out the American "brigands." He also sought to inform Carleton of the situation in Montreal by sending messengers to Quebec and one of these, his young brother-in-law Charles Réaume, was taken prisoner. In mid May he went there himself with his sister-in-law Marguerite Réaume, whose husband, John Welles, meanwhile fled with the Americans, who were evacuating Montreal.

Sanguinet left a complete and detailed account of these stirring years entitled "Le témoin oculaire de la guerre des Bastonnois en Canada dans les années 1775 et 1776." The journal mainly covers the period from February 1775 to 20 June 1776, the day Carleton returned to Montreal; the three longest descriptions are of the siege of Fort Saint-Jean on the Richelieu, the occupation of Montreal, and the siege of Quebec. Sanguinet sought to present facts objectively – "I am impartial, I do not want to conceal anything" – and he comments upon them throughout his account, never failing to express his personal opinion and sparing no one: not the Americans, whose hypocrisy he denounces, or the colonial administration (he stigmatizes Carleton's wait-and-see policy and his failure to do anything about the exactions by British troops in the province), or the British merchants, or his compatriots (he accuses the population of ignorance and reproaches much of the élite for its pursuit of honours). The war, described vividly, comes out in his pages as not very bloody. Fighting went on, but with little ardour, and Sanguinet wonders if Carleton had not indeed been ordered by London to do nothing that might be considered irreparable in the hope there might yet be a reconciliation with the rebellious colonies.

Sanguinet took up his professional activities again as soon as the Americans had left Montreal and he continued his land transactions, capped in November 1782 by the acquisition of the seigneury of La Salle. Like his brother Christophe, who had become one of the seigneurs of Varennes in 1776, Sanguinet henceforth bore the title of seigneur. But his transactions were not always appreciated. In June 1779 the *Gazette littéraire, pour la ville et district de Montréal*, a publication of Fleury MESPLET and Valentin JAUTARD that had already attacked Sanguinet, described him as a contemptible man who, among other dishonest acts, had "seized an inheritance"; it did not, however, attempt to prove its accusations.

On 30 April 1785 an ordinance which forbade the simultaneous practice of the professions of lawyer and notary forced Sanguinet to make a choice. At the appointed time the following year, he decided to remain a lawyer, and he signed his final notarial act, number 2,472, on 16 July 1786. His register, written in a clear and careful hand, has been preserved intact.

Sanguinet's last years were probably painful. His wife died in March 1787 at 45 years of age. His own health deteriorated rapidly, and at the time of his marriage with Marie-Jeanne Hervieux in October 1788 his trembling signature shows that he was ill. He resigned as secretary of the parish council of Notre-Dame that year. Moreover, his brothers Christophe and Joseph were having difficulty in dealing with serious financial problems.

On 24 Dec. 1788 Sanguinet was appointed a judge of the Court of Common Pleas in the District of Montreal, perhaps in recognition of past services. One of his first tasks was to participate in the inquiry under Chief Justice William SMITH into the workings of the court itself. This occupation kept him away from the bench, and he sat only occasionally until his death.

On 14 March 1790 Simon Sanguinet, who had no children, dictated his will to notary Louis Chaboillez*, and two days later, at the age of 57, he died. The newspapers gave him obituaries worthy of a benefactor of mankind, reporting that his will provided a legacy estimated at £11,000 for the creation of a university; this legacy included his house in Montreal and the seigneury of La Salle, a significant part of a fortune of more than £15,000. Hopes were kindled in the province. On 31 October a petition bearing the signatures of 175 Canadiens and British people, including those of Charles-François BAILLY de Messein and David-François De Montmollin*, asked Carleton (now Lord Dorchester) that Sanguinet's will be carried out. In a letter about education, Dorchester told the secretary of state for the Home Department, Lord Grenville, that he too favoured the project. But a long and costly lawsuit to have the will revoked had begun in August. Throughout the proceedings the heirs, with Christophe Sanguinet in the forefront, took their stand on a report prepared by lawyer Joseph-François Perrault* emphasizing Simon's enfeebled and troubled state of mind in his last days, the incoherence of certain provisions of the will, and a claim that certain words had been stricken out after the signatures were appended. Judgement for the plaintiffs was delivered in November 1792.

It must not be thought, however, that the failure of this plan to establish a university was due to the revoking of Simon Sanguinet's will. The aftermath of the inquiry into education instituted in 1787, and Bishop HUBERT's opposition, were of greater significance than the decision in favour of Sanguinet's heirs. But the fact remains that nearly a quarter of a century before James McGill*, a prominent Canadien bequeathed part of his fortune for the creation of a university in the province of Quebec.

YVES-JEAN TREMBLAY

["Le témoin oculaire de la guerre des Bastonnois en Canada dans les années 1775 et 1776" was published by Abbé Hospice-Anthelme-Jean-Baptiste Verreau* as "Témoin oculaire de l'invasion du Canada par les Bastonnois: journal de M. Sanguinet" in *Invasion du Canada*. The validity of Sanguinet's will was discussed by Ægidius Fauteux* in "Le testament Sanguinet," *La Patrie* (Montréal), 10 May 1936, 44–45, a response to the argument developed by Joseph-François Perrault in *Mémoire en cassation du testament de Mr. Simon Sanguinet, écuyer, seigneur de la Salle, &c., précédé du testament*, published in Montreal by Fleury Mesplet early in 1791. In the same year as Fauteux, Francis-Joseph Audet* published "Simon Sanguinet et le projet d'université de 1790," RSC *Trans.*, 3rd ser., XXX (1936), sect.I, 53–70. Le Jeune, *Dictionnaire*, and Tanguay, *Dictionnaire*, are wrong in stating that Sanguinet's grandfather came to Canada. Sanguinet's register, 1764–86, is held at ANQ-M. Y.-J.T.]

ANQ-M, Doc. jud., Contrats de shérif, 1767–99, 10 sept. 1700, 31 déc. 1772, 11 mai 1773, 18 nov. 1782; Cour des plaidoyers communs, Registres, 14 août 1790, nov. 1792; État civil, Catholiques, Notre-Dame de Montréal, 15 janv. 1759, 1761, 1762, 10 mars 1787, 18 mars 1790; Sainte-Anne (Varennes), 16 mars 1733; Greffe de Louis Chaboillez, 22 oct. 1788, 3, 14 mars 1790; Greffe de L.-C. Danré de Blanzy, 14 janv. 1759, 15 sept. 1760; Greffe de J.-G. Delisle, 17 mars 1790; Greffe d'Antoine Foucher, 1er oct. 1788; Greffe de J.-P. Gauthier, 17 juin 1790, 12 mars 1792; Greffe de P.-F. Mézière, 7 sept. 1764; Greffe de Pierre Panet, 16 avril 1759; Greffe de Joseph Papineau, 23 mars, 12 avril 1790; Greffe de Simon Sanguinet, père, 1734–47; Greffe de François Simonnet, 10 sept. 1764; Insinuations, Registres des insinuations, 23 mars 1790. ANQ-Q, Greffe de Simon Sanguinet, père, 1748–71. *La Gazette littéraire pour la ville et district de Montréal*, 2 juin 1779. *Montreal Gazette*, 25 March 1790. *Quebec Gazette*, 25 March 1790. L.-P. Audet, *Le système scolaire de la province de Québec* (6v. parus, Québec, 1950–), II. J.-J. Lefebvre, "Notes sur Simon Sanguinet," *BRH*, XXXIX (1933), 83; "Les premiers notaires de Montréal sous le Régime anglais, 1760–1800," *La Revue de notariat* (Québec), 45 (1942–43), 293–321; "Les Sanguinet de LaSalle," SGCF *Mémoires*, II (1946–47), 24–49.

SAUER (Saur). *See* SOWER

SAUNDERS, Sir CHARLES, naval officer and office-holder; b. *c.* 1715, son of James Saunders;

m. 26 Sept. 1751 a Miss Buck, daughter of a London banker, James Buck; d. 7 Dec. 1775 in London, England.

Little is known about the antecedents and early life of Charles Saunders. In 1727 he entered the Royal Navy under the patronage of a relative and in 1739 was appointed first lieutenant of the *Centurion*, the flagship of Commodore George Anson in his circumnavigation of the world from 1740 to 1744. Saunders sailed a sloop around Cape Horn, captured Spanish shipping in the Pacific, and returned to England a post-captain. During the remainder of the War of the Austrian Succession he commanded several ships of the line with success; in 1746, in the *Gloucester*, he took part in the capture of a treasure ship bound for Spain and acquired about £40,000 of the booty. The following year, in the *Yarmouth*, he took two enemy warships when Admiral Edward Hawke defeated Admiral L'Étenduère off Cape Ortegal, Spain, on 19 October.

Placed on half pay in 1749 after the peace, Saunders began to combine a political career with his naval one, as did many aspiring officers. After sitting for the Admiralty borough of Plymouth in parliament from 1750 to 1754, he became a member of parliament for Hedon, Yorkshire, in 1754 and represented it until his death. The pocket borough was in the gift of Anson, now first lord of the Admiralty. When Anson died in 1761 Saunders became the borough patron and acquired considerable property in the vicinity. In 1752 he had returned to active service at sea, spending from July to October in Newfoundland as commodore of the squadron for the protection of the fisheries. In April 1754 he was appointed treasurer of Greenwich Hospital, a lucrative sinecure, and in December 1755 he became comptroller of the navy; Anson's influence was responsible for both appointments.

With the outbreak of the Seven Years' War Saunders was promoted rear-admiral of the blue in January 1756 and was hastily dispatched to Gibraltar as second in command of the Mediterranean fleet under Hawke. When Hawke returned to England early the next year Saunders assumed the command. He was unable, however, to prevent a French force under Joseph-François de Noble Du Revest from eluding his blockade and aiding Admiral Dubois de La Motte [Emmanuel-Auguste de Cahideuc*] to concentrate a large fleet in the harbour of Louisbourg, Île Royale (Cape Breton Island). In May 1757 Saunders was succeeded by Admiral Henry OSBORN and the following year was transferred to the Channel fleet off Brest, with which he served until October.

William Pitt's advent to power in 1757 brought more emphasis to the maritime and colonial aspects of the war with France. In North America this policy produced the capture of Louisbourg in 1758 [*see* Jeffery AMHERST]. The victory opened the way for an attack upon the city of Quebec via the St Lawrence River, to be coordinated with advances up the line of lakes George (Saint-Sacrement) and Champlain. Saunders had never commanded a fleet in a major action before, but on 9 Jan. 1759, recommended by Anson, he was appointed commander of the fleet bound for the St Lawrence. One month later he was promoted vice-admiral of the blue. His second in command was to be Rear-Admiral Philip Durell*, then in charge of the squadron wintering at Halifax, Nova Scotia, and his third in command was to be Rear-Admiral Charles Holmes*. Major-General James Wolfe*, the military commander, joined Saunders aboard his flagship *Neptune* on 13 February. Both men had been warned by Pitt that success depended on an "entire Good Understanding between our Land and Sea Officers." Saunders was ordered to "cover" the army against French naval intervention and keep control of the line of communication. He was left, however, to decide to what extent his fleet would directly aid Wolfe's forces.

Saunders sailed from Spithead on 17 February. His fleet was stopped by ice from making Louisbourg, the original rendezvous with the transports from America, and it sailed to Halifax, arriving there on 30 April. To the dismayed anger of Wolfe, and no doubt to Saunders' considerable surprise, Durell's squadron was still in the harbour. Although the rear-admiral had been ordered to proceed to the St Lawrence as early in the year as possible in order to cut off any French reinforcements, a severe winter had delayed his departure and he did not leave until 5 May. Saunders himself proceeded to Louisbourg ten days later and spent most of three weeks marshalling and organizing the heterogeneous armada as vessels arrived there. The main fleet finally left on 4 June, almost a month later than planned. The battle fleet was composed of 49 warships, including 22 ships of the line carrying 50 guns or more, and was manned by 13,500 seamen. About half the total fleet had been sent ahead under Durell, and Saunders now followed with 22 warships, guarding the main body of 119 transports, many of which carried flat-bottomed boats to be used in amphibious operations. He faced the task of conducting this large and unwieldy mass of ships through the difficult tides and currents of the gulf and river St Lawrence. For control purposes he divided the shipping into three divisions, each directed by a frigate and attended by sounding and buoy boats. The various types of vessels – transports, victuallers, sounding ships, anchoring and ordnance vessels, hospital ships, and tenders – were all distinguished by flags of different colours to facilitate signalling. Saunders had some fairly good charts of the river and also carried both French and English pilots, including the veteran Canadian pilot Augustin RABY and an able English pilot, John Veysey.

By 18 June Saunders was off Bic, 170 miles below Quebec. Durell had already reached Île aux Coudres, 50 miles below Quebec, and had learned that he had been preceded by French reinforcements which carried knowledge of the British campaign plan. The difficulties of the river navigation, including the dreaded twisting Traverse below the Île d'Orléans, were soon solved by ships' masters such as James COOK, and from 14 June merchantmen and warships of Durell's squadron were running continuously through the passage.

In March, while still at sea, Saunders had written to Amherst, the commanding army officer in North America, that he hoped Wolfe would be supplied with "pioneers" (labourers) by the transports, "for the situation of my squadron will render any dependence upon me, extremely precarious, as I shall be at a great distance below him in the river, and, perhaps, in constant expectation of seeing the enemy's fleet." Durell's news of the French reinforcements convinced him, however, that the possibility of French naval intervention had disappeared, and he determined to support the army closely with virtually the entire fleet under his command. On 20 June he therefore signalled the transports to proceed up river and then brought the ships of his battle fleet after them. A week later the fleet had penetrated to the Quebec Basin.

Saunders covered Wolfe's landing on the Île d'Orléans on 27 June and, after fending off an attack by French fire-ships the following night, was able to settle his fleet into a safe anchorage in the south channel between Pointe-Lévy (Lauzon and Lévis) and Pointe d'Orléans. The fleet was really a vast supply train for the army and a prearranged system of signals allowed instant communication. The troops ashore signalled for reinforcements, provisions, supplies, and boats with flags by day or sky rockets and lanterns by night. Saunders' few surviving letters to the army commanders are invariably cooperative, and his support was immediate and unstinting.

Early in the campaign Wolfe and Saunders agreed that ships and troops should be placed above Quebec to menace the French supply routes, although Saunders advised waiting until batteries were established at Pointe-Lévy to suppress the fire of the town's guns. The batteries began their bombardment on 12 July and on the night of 18–19 July a flotilla of transports and smaller warships led by the *Sutherland* (Capt. John Rous*) ran the gauntlet successfully. Wolfe's attack near the Montmorency Falls on 31 July brought about perhaps the greatest strain between the two men. The general blamed the failure partially on the lack of adequate covering fire from the navy. Saunders objected and Wolfe agreed to delete the criticism from his report to Pitt, although he plainly told the admiral that he still believed the facts were as originally stated. In spite of the criticisms of the navy which punctuated his letters, however, Wolfe referred to Saunders as a "brave zealous officer," and in his will left him his "light service of Plate."

The breakthrough which ultimately led to final victory owed much to the navy. In late August Saunders was able to reinforce the ships above Quebec in order to attack the enemy ships in the upper river. At about the same time Wolfe's brigadiers Robert MONCKTON, James MURRAY, and George Townshend*, after lengthy consultations with Saunders, proposed that military operations be shifted above the city. Saunders' opinions doubtless had an effect on the brigadiers' plan and British naval strength above Quebec now made the plan feasible.

Wolfe's landing at the Anse au Foulon in the pre-dawn blackness of 13 September involved a difficult and demanding amphibious operation. Some 1,800 troops had to be conducted in boats almost ten miles downstream from Cap Rouge in complete secrecy and landed at an exact spot, with due allowance made for currents and tides. The boats arrived at almost exactly the right place, and surprise was achieved. In Saunders' modest words, it was "a very critical Operation, and very properly & successfully conducted."

Immediately after the battle, the admiral devoted all his energy to consolidating the victory won by his dead colleague. Every night all available boats, loaded with cannon, ammunition, tents, timber, and provisions of every kind, streamed past the town to the army, now commanded by Townshend. In less than a week seamen manhandled over 100 cannon and mortars up the heights to the west of Quebec. On 17 September Saunders moved seven ships of the line to within cannonading distance of Lower Town to act in concert with a projected assault by the army. When the capitulation of the garrison followed the next morning, Saunders and Townshend signed jointly for Britain. The news of the fall of Quebec reached England on 16 October in the dispatches of Saunders and Townshend. Saunders was, as usual, succinct and modest. Holmes was duly credited for his conduct of the landing operation, and the army highly praised for its ascent of the cliff. Echoing the words of Pitt's instructions, he assured the Admiralty that there had been "a perfect good understanding between the Army & Navy."

Although Saunders was anxious to attack the enemy ships still up river, he was forced to concentrate on landing stores and provisions at Quebec before winter trapped him in the St Lawrence. He also dispatched a sloop to New York for money and collected over £3,000 from his own officers as a loan to the army, which found itself embarrassingly short of cash. On 18 October Saunders dropped down the St Lawrence in the *Somerset*, accompanied by three other ships of the line and some smaller vessels. He left two sloops and three armed schooners with the garrison and sent a powerful squadron under Lord Colvill* to Halifax, with orders to proceed to Quebec as early as possible in the spring. Saunders had a great reception when he reached London on 26 December. Pitt had already ranked him with those who had beaten armadas and he was thanked by the House of Commons when he took his seat after the Christmas recess.

Saunders' achievement at Quebec had been to organize and conduct a large expedition up a difficult river and maintain it there. The success reflected not only his professionalism, but also the advances that had been made in the navy in recent years, such as the development of reliable navigational devices, the improvements in marine surveying and charting, and the development of landing craft for amphibious operations. His contribution did not end with the capture of the fortress, for had he not supplied the garrison with cannon, ammunition, and provisions before he left, even to the extent of reducing ships' stores, Quebec might well have been recaptured by the French under LÉVIS the following spring.

In addition, a permanent contribution to the safe navigation of the St Lawrence came out of the Quebec campaign. All soundings and bearings taken had been reported to the master of the flagship in order that existing charts might be improved. In April 1760 Saunders informed the Admiralty that he had readied the materials for a new, detailed chart of the St Lawrence and he received permission to publish. The first edition appeared on 1 May under his imprint.

Saunders returned to the Mediterranean command in April 1760, remaining there for the balance of the war. He successfully blockaded the French and Spanish fleets and in the course of this duty captured many ships, the most valuable of which was the Spanish treasure ship *Hermione*. More than £500,000 in prize money was distributed, Saunders receiving £65,000 to swell his ample fortune. In October 1762 he was promoted vice-admiral of the white.

At the end of the war Sir Charles (he was knighted in 1761) retired from active service and devoted more time to politics. To some extent he was drawn into the machinations that trapped other politician-admirals of the time. He was appointed first lord of the Admiralty in September 1766 but resigned a few months later over a conflict with Pitt, now Lord Chatham. Saunders never held political office again but he retained his seat in the Commons and often spoke on matters that concerned the navy. In June 1774 he attacked the Quebec Bill for removing control of the Labrador coast from the Newfoundland governor. He was sure that the reannexation of the region to Quebec would mean that the Labrador fishery would fall into the hands of Americans and Frenchmen, warning "God knows, how much you'll find the want of seamen, whenever this country finds it necessary to equip its fleets!" Although the bill passed, Saunders' arguments were respected and the Labrador fishery continued to be supervised by the Newfoundland governor.

Sir Charles died at his London town house in December 1775 "of an access of gout in the stomach"; at the time of his death he was an admiral of the blue, having been promoted in 1770. He was eulogized in the Commons by Edmund Burke and was buried privately in Westminster Abbey. His wife apparently predeceased him and they had no children. In his will, Saunders left large bequests to Vice-Admiral Augustus Keppel, a personal friend, and to Rear-Admiral Sir Hugh PALLISER, one of his captains at Quebec, as well as a handsome annuity and his household effects to Ann Clevett (Cleverley), "a young lady that lived with him." He settled the bulk of his estate on a favourite niece, Jane Kinsey, on condition that she and her husband assume the Saunders name and coat of arms. To her also went the pictures which had hung in the dining room of the town house, a portrait of Anson and two paintings of the attacks by the fire-ships and fire-stages on the fleet before Quebec.

It is difficult to penetrate the character of a reserved man like Saunders, who left no diary and whose dispatches are terse and impersonal. He was a professional sea officer in the mould of

Anson, zealous to protect the interests of the navy and to advance those of his country. Married to a demanding profession, he had little home life and few close personal friends outside the navy. Although he never commanded in a victory at sea, he played a major role in Canada at a decisive moment in her history. Saunders spent only a single summer in Canada, besides the one in Newfoundland, but it was the high point of his career.

WILLIAM H. WHITELEY

There are portraits of Saunders by Sir Joshua Reynolds and Richard Brompton; the latter hangs in the Painted Hall at Greenwich Naval College, London.

PAC, MG 18, M, ser.1, 21. PANL, GN2/1, 1, f.353. PRO, Adm. 1/482, 1/2467, 2/524, 2/526, 2/1331; C 108, bundle 23; Prob. 11/1014; WO 34/42. *Annual Register* (London), 1775, 27. *Correspondence of William Pitt* (Kimball), II, 168. G.B., Parl., *Debates of the House of Commons in the year 1774, on the bill for making more effectual provision for the government of the province of Quebec, drawn up from the notes of Sir Henry Cavendish* ... (London, 1839; repr. [East Ardsley, Eng. and New York], 1966), 197–98. Knox, *Hist. journal* (Doughty). *The logs of the conquest of Canada*, ed. William Wood (Toronto, 1909), 84, 86–87, 97–99, 263–64, 303–4. Horace Walpole, *Memoirs of the reign of King George the Second*, ed. [H. R. V. Fox, 3rd Baron] Holland (2nd ed., 3v., London, 1847), II, 230; *Memoirs of the reign of King George the Third*, ed. Denis Le Marchant ([new ed.], ed. G. F. R. Barker, 4v., London and New York, 1894), III, 255–56, 282.

Robert Beatson, *Naval and military memoirs of Great Britain from 1727 to 1783* (2nd ed., 6v., London, 1804), II, 345. Charnock, *Biographia navalis*, V, 116–27. *DNB*. Namier and Brooke, *House of Commons*, I, 434; III, 405. W. L. Clowes, *The Royal Navy; a history from the earliest times to the present* (7v., London, 1897–1903), III, 206. J. S. Corbett, *England in the Seven Years' War: a study in combined strategy* (2v., London, 1907), I, 401, 415, 471; II, 321. A. [G.] Doughty and G. W. Parmelee, *The siege of Quebec and the battle of the Plains of Abraham* (6v., Quebec, 1901), II, 1515–54; V, 241; VI, 99–107, 137. Christopher Lloyd, *The capture of Quebec* (London, 1959). Robin Reilly, *The rest to fortune: the life of Major-General James Wolfe* (London, 1960). Stacey, *Quebec, 1759*, 103.

SAYENQUERAGHTA. *See* KAIEÑˀKWAAHTOÑ

SCHINDLER, JOSEPH (Jonas), "engineer" of mathematical instruments, silversmith, and merchant; b. in the parish of Saint-Nicolas, Glarus, Switzerland, son of Joseph Schindler and Marguerite Gaspar; d. 19 Nov. 1792 in Montreal (Que.).

Joseph Schindler sailed on the *Dauphin* from London and arrived at Quebec in 1763 with someone named Meyer. Early in November Schindler and Jeann (?) George Meyer, "both engineers of mathematical instruments," took lodgings with Jean Roy, an innkeeper and restaurateur on Rue Saint-Pierre. A few months later, in March 1764, the two tenants had debts of 864 *livres* 16 sous, which the seigneur of Beauport, Antoine Juchereau* Duchesnay, discharged. On 17 May Joseph Schindler married Geneviève Maranda at Quebec and they apparently went to live with her parents.

In November 1766, when his son Frédéric was baptized, Schindler was described as a "mathematician." But it was as a silversmith that he took on three apprentices soon afterward: Louis-Alexandre Huguet, *dit* Latour, and Joseph Lucas in December, and Jean-Nicolas Amiot in February. His abrupt switch to the silversmith's trade is easier to understand when one realizes that the training and equipment needed for making mathematical instruments are somewhat similar to those required by the silversmith. Schindler's extensive involvement in this craft must, however, have stemmed from a large order for trade silver. Jewellery and trinkets, in fact, constituted his basic stock, although as early as 1767 he was making the occasional piece of church silver. Schindler soon opened a large workshop on Rue de la Montagne and was living there in 1769.

In March 1775 he made plans with a merchant-voyageur named Monforton, who was in Montreal, to go to Michilimackinac (Mackinaw City, Mich.) towards the end of April. As Monforton's agent, Schindler hired four workers, and he took along his own apprentice, Michel Forton*. In 1776 he was brought before Philippe Dejean*, a justice of the peace in Detroit, for having produced substandard silver hollowware. In his defence he explained that having never served an apprenticeship he was a poor judge of the quality of metal, a problem compounded by his use of old silver brought in to him. Michel Forton testified in his favour. Although he was acquitted by the jury, Lieutenant Governor Henry HAMILTON and Dejean drummed him out of the settlement. Schindler was living in Montreal in 1777 and, in spite of his humiliating exit, he carried on business with the fur-traders at Detroit.

Schindler was primarily a trader who engaged apprentices to make commissioned pieces, as did Robert Cruickshank* and Pierre Huguet*, *dit* La Tour. His stamp – IS in a rectangle (which must not be confused with the one Joseph Sasseville used) – was, like theirs, more the mark of a workshop than of a single craftsman. His commercial ventures were certainly not confined to silverware. On 21 May 1784, in the presence of notary Edward William Gray*, Schindler and Christy Cramer, "Merchants of Montreal" with premises on Rue Saint-Paul, acknowledged their debt to Isaac Todd* and James McGill* "for divers Goods, Wares and Merchandises" which the latter had received from "the late Partnership of Cramer and Lymes."

On the same day, in Quebec, Schindler's mother-in-law relinquished tenure of her assets, which consisted primarily of a property there already deeded to him in 1781. She had been widowed ten days earlier and now, too old to look after herself, she came to live with her daughter in Montreal. The property, on Rue de la Montagne at the corner of L'Escalier, was put up for sale a week later through John Justus Diehl.

Schindler evidently remained active as a silversmith until his death in 1792, for in 1791 he took on Joseph Normandeau as an apprentice for five years. The suggestion has been made that his widow made silver articles herself, but this seems doubtful. She was obliged to liquidate the assets of her husband's workshop and to fulfil the contract with Normandeau. Various payments for trade silver were made to her in 1797 and 1798 by the McGill brothers, and at the time of her death on 11 Jan. 1803 she owed these traders £10 3*s*. 8*d*. for goods not yet delivered.

ROBERT DEROME

ANQ-M, État civil, Anglicans, Christ Church (Montréal), 21 Nov. 1792; Catholiques, Notre-Dame de Montréal, 21 août 1778, 13 janv. 1803; Greffe de J. G. Beek, 30 juill. 1781, 19 févr. 1783; Greffe de Louis Chaboillez, 29 sept. 1791; Greffe d'E. W. Gray, 21 mai 1784. ANQ-Q, État civil, Anglicans, Cathedral of the Holy Trinity (Québec), 5 Dec. 1774; Catholiques, Notre-Dame de Québec, 17 mai 1764, 17 nov. 1766, 3 avril, 27 mai 1769, 14 juill. 1770, 25 janv., 26 juill. 1773, 21 mai 1774; Greffe de C.-H. Du Laurent, 20 sept. 1752; Greffe de Claude Louet, 12 nov. 1763, 20 mars 1764, 20, 22 déc. 1766, 9 févr. 1767; Greffe de J.-A. Panet, 21, 23, 25 mars 1775; Greffe de F.-D. Rousseau, 17 août 1781, 21 mai 1784. AUM, P 58, Doc. divers, Q1, 3 juill. 1763. IBC, Centre de documentation, Fonds Morisset, Dossier Joseph Schindler.

Quebec Gazette, 27 May 1784. Detroit Institute of Arts, *The French in America, 1520–1880* (Detroit, 1951), 199. Tanguay, *Dictionnaire*. Robert Derome, "Delezenne, les orfèvres, l'orfèvrerie, 1740–1790" (thèse de MA, université de Montréal, 1974). Langdon, *Canadian silversmiths*, 126. Gérard Morisset, *Évolution d'une pièce d'argenterie* (Québec, 1943), 12–13, planches VI–VII. Traquair, *Old silver of Que*. F.-J. Audet, "Les habitants de la ville de Québec en 1769–1770," *BRH*, XXVII (1921), 124. F. W. Robinson, "Silversmiths of early Detroit," Detroit Hist. Soc., *Bull.*, IX (1952–53), no.2, 5–8.

SCHWARTZ, OTTO WILLIAM (Otho Wilhelm), fur-trader and local official; b. 12 May 1715 near Riga (U.S.S.R.); d. 5 Oct. 1785 in Halifax, Nova Scotia.

Otto William Schwartz, son of a portrait painter, appears to have been born into the German community which had dominated Riga and its environs for some centuries. He served a seven-year apprenticeship in the fur trade beginning in 1732 and later began travels which ended with his joining Edward CORNWALLIS' expedition to found Halifax in 1749.

When Schwartz reached Chebucto Bay on 27 June in the *Canning*, he was 34, unmarried, and had enough working capital to establish himself in the fur trade. Most of the settlers with Cornwallis were London's poor, enticed by the offer of government support. The few Swiss, Germans, and French who joined the expedition proved more industrious than their English counterparts, and Cornwallis encouraged further immigration of "foreign Protestants." Of those who arrived in the next few years, some settled in the north suburb of Halifax laid out for them, some in Lunenburg, and some in the English Halifax community.

Although Schwartz's interests lay with the English and he settled among them, he maintained a strong German identity. On 4 Dec. 1750 he married a German widow, Anna Justina Liebrich, and they had three sons and two daughters. He became the elder for life of the German religious community, which, although it formed close relations with the Church of England and began its worship at St Paul's, soon established a church of its own, the little Dutch church (St George's). He supported this church in a number of ways: in 1758 he made an interest-free loan to the congregation for completing the interior; in 1761 and 1764 he appealed to the governor and Council for funds promised by Governor Charles Lawrence* to erect a steeple; and he belonged to the Funeral Fees or Friendly Society, which paid burial expenses for the German poor.

Schwartz's ability to offer this support suggests that his business as a furrier was thriving. In 1760 he had been appointed by the provincial secretary, Richard BULKELEY, "Furrier for the Indian Commerce," an ill-defined but probably privileged and lucrative post in which he was subordinate to Bulkeley, to the commander-in-chief, and to the commissary for Indian trade, Benjamin GERRISH. Schwartz also invested in real estate. By 1782 he had 4,000 acres on the Saint John River, 1,000 on the Windsor Road, a farm in Falmouth Township, and various lots and houses in Halifax and its north suburb.

Schwartz held other offices which were not lucrative but which indicated status. He was a member of the grand jury for Halifax in 1757, rose to become captain in the militia in 1774, and was appointed one of the commissioners of sewers for Falmouth in 1776. From 1773 until his death he represented Lunenburg County in the House of Assembly. The assembly journals do not reveal his political position, but other records show that, although the success of his business depended in part on favour and influence, he had not before his election hesitated to criticize local administration. In 1753 he was associated with a deposition charging the justices of the Inferior Court of Common Pleas with partiality. Four years later he signed a petition against Governor Lawrence for his delay in establishing a representative assembly and for his arrogant attitude towards the leading inhabitants. Another petition which he signed in the same year demanded better fortifications for Halifax.

The few clues to Schwartz's character which remain suggest a shrewd, hard-working man, strongly paternal in his family and church relationships, careful of both worldly and spiritual position. He took pride in being a founder of "the Evangelical German Church," and one of his last gifts was a covering for the table and pulpit with his name "inscribed in Golden Letters." His funeral was costly, and a section of the little Dutch church floor was removed for the construction of his tomb.

Schwartz's will may reveal the vision which shaped his life. Each of his five children was generously provided for, but they were also given to hold in common a large tract of land on the Windsor Road "known by the Name of Schwartzburg." Any one who sold or gave his share to "any person or persons Who Shall not be of the Sir name of Schwartz" was to forfeit his claim. Perhaps Otto William saw himself as founder of a family dynasty in the Nova Scotian wilderness.

CATHERINE PROSS

Halifax County Court of Probate (Halifax), S19 (will of Otto William Schwartz, probated 1799) (mfm. at PANS). PANS, RG 1, 164, pp.120, 207; 166A, p.73; 168, pp.73, 383, 471; 211, 16 Feb. 1761, 24 April 1764; 411, docs.1½, 1B, 7. St Paul's Anglican Church (Halifax), Registers of baptisms, burials, and marriages, 4 Dec. 1750, 9 June 1752 (mfm. at PANS). "Letters and other papers relating to the early history of the Church of England in Nova Scotia," N.S. Hist. Soc., *Coll.*, VII (1891), 89–127. *N.S. Archives, I*, 539, 659. *Directory of N.S. MLAs*. Akins, *History of Halifax City*, 38–39, 49–50, 55, 73, 253. Bell, *Foreign Protestants*, 291n, 302, 307, 616, 625–26, 633n. Francis Partridge, "The early history of the parish of St. George, Halifax," N.S. Hist. Soc., *Coll.*, VII (1891), 73–87; "Notes on the early history of St. George's Church, Halifax," N.S. Hist. Soc., *Coll.*, VI (1888), 137–54.

SCOTT, JOSEPH, soldier, businessman, and office-holder; m. 4 Jan. 1763 Margaret Ramsey Cottnam in Halifax, Nova Scotia; d. 29 Sept. 1800 in Sackville, Nova Scotia.

Joseph Scott was a member of the interesting breed of men who combined public service with private gain so successfully in 18th-century Nova Scotia. Never an outstanding leader, he nonetheless was typical of the merchant-politician élite which dominated Halifax in the pre-loyalist era.

Although the details of his birth and early life are unknown, there is little doubt that he was a young man when he disembarked from the ship *London* as one of the original settlers of Halifax in July 1749 [*see* Edward CORNWALLIS]. He was described at that time as having been a quartermaster in Shirley's American Provincials (67th Foot). By the early 1750s he had established himself as a general merchant "at his Store near Mr. *Fairbanks*'s Wharfe," with the announced intention of selling a wide assortment of goods "Cheap for ready Money." A number of partnerships ensued. With John DAY he established the firm of Day and Scott, a partnership which apparently began in the late 1760s and which continued until Day's death in 1775. Scott also constructed a lumber mill in nearby Sackville, where he owned a tract of timber land.

His public career began in 1752, when he was appointed a justice of the peace and a judge of the Inferior Court of Common Pleas for Halifax. In 1754 he became a surveyor of lumber, undoubtedly an important post for one who was interested in the timber trade. He aligned himself with a group of influential merchants who were pressing for the establishment of an assembly and to whose demands Governor Charles Lawrence* finally acquiesced in 1758. The following year Scott was elected to the second House of Assembly as one of the first two members from Kings County. Although he sat in the assembly for only one session, he was able to use his influence to secure an additional perquisite, paymaster of the Halifax garrison for the period 1761–63.

Along with the vast majority of merchants and placemen, Scott remained loyal to the crown during the American revolution. His loyalty, however, did not extend to support for Governor Francis LEGGE. He was one of "the Principal inhabitants of Nova Scotia" who signed a petition to the Board of Trade early in 1776 praying for that hapless governor's recall. After the revolution many of the old élite were submerged by the incoming tide of loyalists. What effect this influx had on Scott personally is not known. It is certain, however, that after it he played no major role in provincial affairs, although he was commissioned *custos rotulorum* in 1784.

Little is known of Scott's family life, but it is possible that he was a brother of Colonel George Scott*. George's will leaves all of his Nova Scotian properties to a brother in Halifax named Joseph, and the fact that the Joseph of this biography acquired his Sackville property in 1767, the year of George's death, may confirm the relationship.

L. R. FISCHER

PAC, MG 23, A1, ser.1, 14, no.2516. N.S., House of Assembly, *Journal*, 4 Dec. 1759. *Halifax Gazette*, 1752–76. *Directory of N.S. MLAs*.

SECCOMBE, JOHN (while in Nova Scotia he used this spelling, although as a young man he had omitted the final "e"), Congregationalist minister; b. 25 April 1708 at Medford, Massachusetts, third son of Peter Seccomb, merchant, and Hannah Willis; m. 10 March 1736/37 Mercy Williams at Weston, Massachusetts; they had at least five children; d. 27 Oct. 1792 at Chester, Nova Scotia.

As a student at Harvard College (AB 1728, AM 1731), John Seccombe was known for his practical jokes, skirmishes with college authorities, and ready wit, rather than for his scholarship. Among the literary productions of his student years the best known is "Father Abbey's will," a 15-stanza nonsense verse celebrating the college sweeper, Matthew Abdy. First published in the *Weekly Rehearsal* (Boston) on 3 Jan. 1732, it was reprinted in London in the same year and in broadsides and periodicals as late as 1850. A reply from the sweeper at Yale, frequently printed with it, has sometimes incorrectly been attributed to Seccombe.

In 1732 Seccombe was invited to settle as the first minister of the new town of Harvard, where he was ordained on 10 Oct. 1733. His entry into the Congregationalist ministry was a movement upward socially, as was his marriage to the daughter of the well-connected Reverend William Williams of Weston. Seccombe's magnificent estate at Harvard rendered showy statement of the position he had attained by the late 1730s. His ministry, however, was not without controversy. Although he and his congregation agreed in accepting the principles of the Great Awakening, his relations with ministerial associations were sometimes strained on this account. His years at Harvard were also clouded by rumours of marital infidelity, which apparently led to his offering "Christian satisfaction for his Offence" in January 1738/39 and which may have been the cause of his requesting dismission from the church in 1757.

One of the original proprietors of Chester, Seccombe preached there in 1761 and settled his family there in 1763. His congregation of new settlers afforded him little support, but with money brought from New England he developed a family farm. His "very necessitous Circumstances" of 1769 were subsequently relieved by a family inheritance. Seccombe also preached at Mather's (St Matthew's) Church, Halifax, as early as 1761 and regularly thereafter for a quarter-century. Why he was never given an official call to Mather's is unknown. He had been warmly welcomed by the congregation, and in 1771, having preached there more often than any other dissenting minister, he found it "so natural to be with this people, that it Seemes almost as if I were their Pastor." An inclination to Presbyterianism at Mather's or his own evangelical spirit may have excluded him but, since he was an educated, clever man and a good preacher, it is more likely that his troubles at Harvard made him unacceptable to an influential segment of the congregation, which claimed pre-eminence among the dissenting churches of the province and which sought to compete for status with the Church of England establishment at St Paul's. In the 1780s schoolmaster Joseph PETERS thought that Seccombe had been imposed upon, but also blamed him for being "too easy."

In July 1770, when the first Presbyterian-Congregationalist presbytery in Nova Scotia ordained Bruin Romkes Comingo*, a Lunenburg fisherman, as pastor of a dissenting congregation in that town, Seccombe preached the ordination sermon on the theme of the necessity of sanctifying grace to the ministry. Elsewhere his highly structured, articulate sermons, for the weekly pulpit as for the bereaved, pursued the Calvinist doctrine of faith. Although he abhorred the doctrinal confusion of the followers of Henry ALLINE, in 1786 he welcomed "the awakening & concern which some among us are under." Two years later he led his congregation to accept open communion with Baptists, but he himself did not join the reorganized church.

Seccombe's summons before the Nova Scotia Council in December 1776 on charges of preaching a seditious sermon locates him clearly within the New England Congregationalist tradition, but tells more about governmental fears and Chester's proximity to the capital than about revolutionary sympathies on Seccombe's part. He was not only required to give security for his future good behaviour but forbidden to preach until he had signed a formal recantation. There is no record of his having done so, but he is known to have preached in Halifax in June 1777. Having visited New England in 1769 and having once considered returning there in case of war, Seccombe nevertheless remained in Nova Scotia during and, as one of only three Congregationalist clergymen, after the American revolution.

"A very godly man" to the Baptists, "a true Gospel minister . . . not after the *Loaves* nor the *Fishes*" to an Anglican, and "the first Character in this Province" and "the Father of all . . . [its dissenting] Churches" to a Presbyterian, Seccombe was regarded as "a great lover of good men of all ages, ranks and denominations." The contrasts and struggles of his own life bear witness to his conviction that "Christ is the thirsty Sinner's only foundation."

S. Buggey

John Seccombe is the author of *Father Abbey's will . . .* (Cambridge, Mass., 1854), first published in *Weekly Rehearsal* (Boston, Mass.), 3 Jan. 1732; "The diary of Rev. John Seccombe," ed. C. B. Fergusson, PANS *Report* (Halifax), 1959, app.B, 18–45 (the original is in PANS, MG 1, 797C); *A sermon preached at Halifax, July 3d, 1770, at the ordination of the Rev. Bruin Romcas Comingoe to the Dutch Calvanistic Presbyterian congregation at Lunenburg . . .* (Halifax, 1770); *A sermon occasioned by the death of the Honorable Abigail Belcher, late consort of Jonathan Belcher, esq . . . delivered at Halifax . . . October 20, 1771* (Boston, Mass., 1772); *A sermon, occasioned by the death of Mrs. Margaret Green; consort of the late Honourable Benjamin Green, esq; delivered at Halifax, in the province of Nova-Scotia, February 1st, 1778* (Halifax, [1778?]).

Acadia University (Wolfville, N.S.), Atlantic Baptist hist. coll., [John Seccombe], A sermon on Isaiah 55:1 preached at Halifax, April 24, 1779 . . . . [A note on the sermon wrongly attributes it to the Rev. James Munro. S.B.] Beinecke Rare Book and Manuscript Library, Yale University (New Haven, Conn.), George Gilmore to Ezra Stiles, 12 Nov. 1788. PANS, MG 1, 797C (Rev. John Seccomb(e) docs.); RG 1, 212, 23 Dec. 1776, 6 Jan. 1777. Protestant Episcopal Church in the U.S.A., Archives and Hist Coll. – Episcopal Church (Austin, Tex.), Samuel Peters papers, I, no.95; II, nos.7, 56; III, no.118, in the custody of the Hist. Soc. of the Episcopal Church (Austin) (mfm. at PANS). United Church of Canada, Maritime Conference Archives, Pine Hill Divinity Hall (Halifax), McGregor papers A, Seccombe-Comingoe letters. "Congregational churches in Nova Scotia," Mass. Hist. Soc., *Proc.*, 2nd ser., IV (1887–89), 67–73. Shipton, *Sibley's Harvard graduates*, VIII. H. S. Nourse, *History of the town of Harvard, Massachusetts, 1732–1893* (Harvard, 1894), 178–95. *Baptist Missionary Magazine of Nova-Scotia and New-Brunswick* (Saint John and Halifax), I (1827–29), 317.

SENECA KING. *See* Kaieñ?kwaahtoñ

SHANSON, GILLIOM. *See* Jeanson, Guillaume

SHAW, WILLIAM, army officer and local official; b. probably in Scotland; m. Jane, daughter of Thomas Wood, probably in 1764 at Annapolis Royal, Nova Scotia; they had "a pretty large family"; fl. 1759–89.

In 1759 William Shaw served as a volunteer with the 42nd Foot at the siege of Guadeloupe; he may also have been present at the British capture of Montreal in 1760. He purchased a commission in the 43rd Foot in October 1761 and participated in the sieges of Martinique and Havana, Cuba. Having acquitted himself well at Havana, he was promoted lieutenant in the 40th Foot. In 1763 he accompanied his regiment to Nova Scotia and two years later went with it to Ireland, where he and his wife lived for several years. Originally educated for holy orders, he applied while in Ireland to be ordained a missionary for the Society for the Propagation of the Gospel, but despite his father-in-law's support, his request was refused. Although his regiment continued to be stationed in Ireland, Shaw was granted 500 acres in Granville Township, near Annapolis Royal, in July 1767, and he is listed as head of a household in Granville Township in 1770. In 1772 he exchanged into the 47th Foot and served with it in New Jersey and Boston. While in the army he acted at various times as adjutant, paymaster, and deputy judge advocate. In 1774 he left the army "thro' necessity not choice." Family responsibilities may have weighed heavily in the face of active service, but whatever the reasons Shaw returned to Nova Scotia and engaged in "commerce."

In 1775 Shaw was elected to the House of Assembly from Annapolis County. When he was commissioned in the Loyal Nova Scotia Volunteers by Governor Francis Legge that year, he left his commercial activities, but he later lost his commission through the influence of Sir William Howe, a former commander. In 1775 the inhabitants of Annapolis County petitioned Major-General Eyre Massey, commander of the troops in Nova Scotia, to ask Shaw to raise a company of militia for the defence of the district. Commissioned a major in the militia in January 1776, Shaw raised the company by July and requested Massey that the men be furnished with pay, provisions, and equipment since they had only what Shaw had supplied. In November, now a colonel, he called out his company to face a threatened attack by American rebels and kept it on duty until the danger was past. It was charged, however, that Shaw's men had not performed the duties he had reported and that Shaw was keeping money forwarded by the government as payment for his company. Affidavits from the men cleared him of the first charge, but after a review of the second the assembly ordered him to return some money.

In January 1777 Shaw was appointed a justice of the peace and in April succeeded in being recommissioned in the Loyal Nova Scotia Volunteers. Shortly afterwards, however, he was asked to return his commission; in spite of his efforts, Shaw remained out of favour in military circles.

By 1781 Shaw had obtained the office of sheriff of Halifax County. Two years later an investigation in the assembly revealed that the sheriffs were not transmitting money collected from fines to the provincial treasury. A bill regulating their office and appointment was therefore considered; one of its stipulations was that the sheriff of Halifax County own at least a £1,000 freehold in the county. By November 1783 Shaw had lost his office. One year later, for "having refused to attend and produce vouchers to his accounts as a public accountant, having been Sheriff of Halifax County," he was pronounced in contempt of the assembly, his seat was declared vacant, and he was ordered taken into custody. He managed to avoid arrest, however, and early the following year Major-General John Campbell appointed him provost marshal of the British forces in Nova Scotia, describing him as "an Officer of long service and respectable Character." Shaw subsequently claimed that he saved the government "to the amount of £20,000" in his work of "Mustering the Loyalists &ca." How long he held the position is not clear, but by 1786 he had returned to England, where he petitioned Lord Sydney, secretary of state for the Home Department, for half pay as a provincial colonel, citing his services and complaining that he "found himself without either Appointment or Provision whatever." It is not known whether he was successful in his claim. By 1789 Shaw had once again returned to Granville, but no further record of him remains.

CATHERINE PROSS

PANS, RG 1, 168, no.492; 222, nos.56–63; 369, no.213; 443, nos.2–17. PRO, CO 217/26; 217/36; 217/37, ff.42–43. USPG, B, 25, no.80. N.S., House of Assembly, *Journal*, 23 Sept., 28 Oct. 1780; 25 Oct., 18 Nov., 2 Dec. 1783; 29 Nov. 1784. *Directory of N.S. MLAs*, 315. *Service of British regiments* (Stewart). Calnek, *History of Annapolis* (Savary), 162, 184, 207–10, 338. H. M. Chichester and George Burges-Short, *The records and badges of every regiment and corps in the British army* (2nd ed., London, 1900), 523ff., 558ff., 591ff. A. W. Savary, *French and Anglican churches at Annapolis Royal* (Annapolis Royal, N.S., 1910).

SHULDHAM, MOLYNEUX, 1st Baron SHULDHAM, naval officer and governor of Newfoundland; b. *c.* 1717, probably in Ireland, second son of the Reverend Lemuel Shuldham and Elizabeth Molyneux; m. 4 Oct. 1790 Margaret Irene Sarney; d. 30 Sept. 1798 at Lisbon, Portugal.

Molyneux Shuldham entered the Royal Navy in 1732 as a captain's servant on the *Cornwall*. He passed his examination for lieutenant on 25 Jan. 1739 and was promoted captain seven years later. In 1756 his ship, the *Warwick*, was captured by the French off Martinique and he spent two years as a prisoner in France. Following his release he was given command of the *Panther* and participated in the capture of Guadeloupe in 1759.

After holding peacetime commands in home waters, in February 1772 Shuldham succeeded John BYRON as governor of Newfoundland. Upon his arrival he investigated the fortifications at St John's and Placentia and found them greatly deteriorated. The home government subsequently ordered the construction of a new fort at St John's, and Shuldham, after consultation with the chief engineer, Lieutenant Robert PRINGLE, decided to locate it on the crest of the hill at the rear of the town. When completed in 1780, Fort Townshend became the seat of government on the island.

During the 18th century, Newfoundland's administration was characterized by an absence of any real local government, and much of Shuldham's time before his return to England in the fall each year was taken up with issuing proclamations and deciding disputes. He also did his best to uphold the sometimes shaky authority of local officials. When the St John's justices of the peace complained in 1772 that two merchants had failed to obey summonses and had threatened to crop the ears of the first constables who meddled with them, Shuldham replied soothingly that he would always support the justices to the utmost of his power but that the persons complained of should be treated with that "decency and indulgence to which they are entitled as gentlemen, merchants, and British subjects."

In August 1773 Shuldham visited the Labrador coast, which had been placed under the jurisdiction of the governor of Newfoundland in 1763. At Chateau Bay he issued a proclamation which gave British fishing firms greater security in their posts, and he dispatched "a very sensible officer," Lieutenant Roger Curtis*, to explore the northern coast and visit the Moravian missionaries at their newly established station at Nain [*see* Christian Larsen DRACHART]. Curtis' lengthy reports praised the Moravians' progress with the Inuit and extolled the potential of the northern fisheries. Shuldham himself sent much information to the British government concerning fishing posts and good harbours in southern Labrador. Although his authority over the coast ended when Labrador was reannexed to Quebec in 1774, Shuldham continued to superintend the fisheries as commander-in-chief of the squadron detailed for their protection.

In February 1775 Shuldham was succeeded as governor by Commodore Robert Duff; he was promoted rear-admiral on 31 March and the following September became commander-in-chief of the North American station. His force was not large enough to give protection to all the colonies, however, and he was unable to send Commodore Mariot ARBUTHNOT in Nova Scotia and Administrator Phillips CALLBECK in St John's (Prince Edward) Island the ships they wanted. On 17 March 1776 Shuldham evacuated the army of Lieutenant-General Sir William Howe and several thousand loyalist refugees from Boston, arriving safely at Halifax with the transports on 2 April. He now considered that Nova Scotia had become more important and urged the Admiralty to provide additional warships to guard the province. When he convoyed Howe's army to New York in June he left ships behind in the Bay of Fundy and off Cape Breton Island. The following month he was suddenly superseded by Vice-Admiral Richard, Viscount Howe but the blow was eased when he was created an Irish baron. Shuldham's active career was now effectively at an end, although he served as admiral of Plymouth dockyard from 1777 to 1782 and represented Fowey in parliament from 1774 to 1784. He became a full admiral in 1787. Married late in life, he had no children.

In Newfoundland, Shuldham was reasonably successful in a demanding post, and if he did not display any great initiative he carried out his instructions conscientiously. His interest in Labrador resulted in the first detailed information about the northern coast. On the North American station he handled the operations of his squadron competently and withdrew quietly when replaced by Howe. Although the defence of Canada was necessarily at the edge of his concern, he nevertheless recognized the importance of Halifax and took what means he could to protect Nova Scotia.

WILLIAM H. WHITELEY

[Molyneux Shuldham], *The despatches of Molyneux Shuldham, vice-admiral of the blue and commander-in-chief of his Britannic majesty's ships in North America, January–July 1776*, ed. R. W. Nesser (New York, 1913).

PANL, GN2/1, 27 July, 2, 5, 15, 16 Oct. 1772; 21 Aug., 13, 15 Oct. 1773. PRO, Adm. 1/470, 1/484, 2/550; CO 5/119, 5/205, 5/251, 194/30–32, 199/17; WO 1/2. *Gentleman's Magazine*, 1798, 909. [J.] B. Burke, *A genealogical history of the dormant, abeyant, forfeited and extinct peerages of the British empire* (3rd ed., London, 1883). Charnock, *Biographia navalis*, V, 505–8. *DNB*. A. [C.] Valentine, *The British establishment, 1760–1784* . . . (2v., Norman, Okla., 1970), II, 790.

SIERRA, ESTEBAN JOSÉ MARTÍNEZ FERNÁNDEZ Y MARTÍNEZ DE LA. *See* MARTÍNEZ

SILVAIN (Sylvain), JEAN-BAPTISTE DUPLEIX. *See* DUPLEIX

SIMONNET, FRANÇOIS, Brother Hospitaller of the Cross and of St Joseph, schoolmaster, royal notary, and king's attorney; b. 29 Dec. 1701 at Niort, France, son of Philippe Simonnet, a merchant and later comptroller of the king's tax farms, and of Marie Boismenay; d. 9 Dec. 1778 in Montreal.

Nothing is known of François Simonnet's life before his arrival in New France. It seems certain that he had been recruited by François Charon* de La Barre, and that with five other schoolmasters he had come on the *Chameau* in 1719. His presence in the colony is first indicated on 14 Sept. 1721 among the Brothers Hospitallers of the Cross and of St Joseph at the Hôpital Général in Montreal, when he signed in a register "F. Simonnet de la Croix, hospitaller and missionary," and then "schoolmaster." At that time he was teaching in the school at Longueuil. On 8 Oct. 1723 Bishop Saint-Vallier [La Croix*] approved the brothers' rules, which had been recorded in an extraordinarily beautiful hand by Simonnet. On 24 Oct. 1724, after five years of community life, in both hospital and missions, Simonnet took simple vows of poverty, chastity, obedience, and hospitality to the poor and the young. From then until 1730 he taught at Trois-Rivières, where he was in charge of the school. On 28 Sept. 1731 he was still a religious and was then teaching in Boucherville. That year the king of France discontinued the annual subsidy of 3,000 *livres* that had until then been granted to provide for schoolmasters. François Simonnet probably quit the religious life at that time, for, following the king's decision, several of the hospitallers asked to be freed from their vows.

In any case it is known that on 23 Jan. 1736 at Boucherville Simonnet married Léger Bourgy's widow, Marguerite Bougret Dufort, a 52-year-old invalid. She died on 22 April 1749 and two and a half months later, on 7 July 1749, in Montreal, he remarried. His second wife was Marguerite Neveu, daughter of Jean-Baptiste Neveu*, seigneur of Lanoraie and Dautré and colonel of the militia in the Government of Montreal, and of Françoise-Élisabeth Legras. They had one son, who died in infancy.

On 1 July 1737 François Simonnet, who had called himself a merchant at Boucherville in certain deeds signed the year before, received from Honoré Michel* de Villebois de La Rouvillière, the commissary of the Marine who was serving as intendant in HOCQUART's absence, a commission as royal notary at Boucherville and throughout the *côtes* within the Government of Montreal. On 25 Feb. 1738 Intendant Hocquart confirmed his commission but restricted it to Varennes, Cap Saint-Michel, Verchères, Contrecœur, Saint-Ours, and Chambly. This restriction was lifted on 20 Aug. 1738, however, and Simonnet obtained a new commission for the whole of the Government of Montreal. From October 1738 on, he lived in Montreal.

In 1756 Simonnet took part as a handwriting expert in the celebrated trial in Montreal of the hostage Robert Stobo*. From 1757 to 1760 he was deputy king's attorney and then regular attorney for the jurisdiction of Montreal. On 24 Nov. 1759 the members of the Conseil Supérieur at their meeting in Montreal had appointed him *ex officio* clerk in the court registry. On 20 Oct. 1760, three weeks after the surrender of Montreal, Thomas GAGE, the military governor, renewed Simonnet's commission as royal notary. Despite all his other duties, Simonnet was to draw up deeds almost without interruption until 14 Nov. 1778.

Although never an important businessman, Simonnet in the course of time became the owner of a great deal of property. In addition to inheriting the seigneuries of Lanoraie and Dautré, he purchased land in the seigneuries of Belœil, Boucherville, Cournoyer, and Prairie-de-la-Madeleine, as well as on Montreal Island. He initiated work on the seigneuries of Cournoyer and Prairie-de-la-Madeleine in 1742 and 1743 that was never finished. But in the seigneury of Boucherville and on Montreal Island he developed tracts of land and shared the proceeds equally with his farmers. In addition to owning all the buildings, equipment, and animals needed for improving his farms, he went in for sheep-raising and the cultivation of orchards.

On 14 Sept. 1768 René Cartier and his wife Angélique Sarasin Depelteau, the seigneurs of La Salle, appointed François Simonnet legal adviser in personal and general matters for their seigneury and gave him the right to manage all their property and business affairs. On the same occasion the seigneur made a grant of an arriere fief to Simonnet as an act of recognition and gratitude to him for stopping the auction of the seigneury. They were, however, really just settling in this way a legal dispute that had been entered in the Court of Common Pleas on 26 Sept. 1766 on the application of Simonnet, who complained that the seigneur Cartier was unable to honour his debts to him and to other creditors.

François Simonnet died on 9 Dec. 1778, a few weeks after his wife Marguerite Neveu. His estate was valued at more than £53,000 including £8,200 in gold and silver. He left the greater part of it to his sister Marie-Louise, and the remainder to a number of paupers.

RAYMOND DUMAIS

François Simonnet's register, 1737–78, is held at ANQ-M.

AD, Deux-Sèvres (Niort), État civil, Saint-André de Niort, 1er janv. 1702. AN, Col., C11A, 101, ff.254–91. ANQ-M, AP-M-78-8; Chambre des milices, 5, 16 août 1763; Doc. jud., Cour des plaidoyers communs, Registres, 26 sept. 1766, 5, 19, 26 juin 1772, 14 janv., 11 févr., 22 mars, 15 avril, 18 nov. 1779; Doc. jud., Pièces détachées, 30 juill. 1739; État civil, Catholiques, Notre-Dame de Montréal, 12 août 1746, 23 avril, 7 juill. 1749, 5 oct. 1751, 1er sept. 1752, 22 nov., 11 déc. 1778; Sainte-Famille (Boucherville), 23 janv. 1736; Greffe de J.-B. Adhémar, 10 août 1740, 18 févr., 26 mai 1741, 6 juin, 16 oct. 1742, 30 avril, 25 juill. 1743, 19 oct. 1744, 6 mars, 7 déc. 1745, 18 mars 1746, 9 sept. 1747, 28 mai, 1er juill. 1749, 2 mars 1753; Greffe de Louis Chaboillez, 29 mars 1793; Greffe de Jean Delisle, 24 oct. 1768, 19 janv. 1769, 28 mars, 18 oct. 1770, 19 janv., 16 févr. 1771, 14 févr. 1772, 24 sept. 1773, 8 mars, 4 avril, 10 août 1775, 30 sept., 12, 16 déc. 1778; Greffe d'Antoine Foucher, 15 févr. 1779; Greffe de Gervais Hodiesne, 1er déc. 1762, 17 janv. 1763; Greffe de J.-B. Janvrin Dufresne, 22 mars 1738, 31 déc. 1740; Greffe d'Antoine Loiseau, 21 janv., 13, 14 avril, 5 mai, 9, 15, 22 oct. 1736, 28 juill. 1739; Greffe de P.-F. Mézière, 24 mars 1763; Greffe de Pierre Panet, 6 janv. 1759, 21 oct. 1761, 18 nov. 1762, 7 févr. 1763, 30 juill., 11 août 1764, 30 juill. 1777; Greffe de C.-C.-J. Porlier, 4 mai, 18 août 1742, 11 oct., 6 déc. 1743; Greffe de J.-C. Raimbault, 28 sept. 1731; Greffe de Simon Sanguinet, 14 sept. 1768, 13 mars 1769, 26 juill. 1771, 12 mars 1774; Greffe de François Simonnet,

6 juin 1777; Greffe d'André Souste, 2 janv. 1746, 9 janv., 30 avril, 10 juin 1765, 13 juill. 1767; Recensement, Compagnie des Indes, 1741, 40. ANQ-MBF, Insinuations, 2, f.15. ANQ-Q, NF 2, 25, f.35; 26, ff.55, 177. ASGM, Frères Charon, 80; Registre des vêtures, professions, sépultures, etc., des frères Charon. ASSM, 24, Dossier 6.

"Les ordonnances et lettres de change du gouvernement de Montréal en 1759," ANQ *Rapport*, 1924–25, 248. "Procès de Robert Stobo et de Jacob Wambram pour crime de haute trahison," ANQ *Rapport*, 1922–23, 320–27. "Archives Gradis," ANQ *Rapport*, 1957–59, 38–39. Labrèque, "Inv. de pièces détachées," ANQ *Rapport*, 1971, 48–49. Hubert Létourneau, "Inventaire analytique des taxes de dépens du Conseil supérieur (1703–1759)," ANQ *Rapport*, 1973, 106. É.-Z. Massicotte, "Les frères Charon ou Frères hospitaliers de Saint-Joseph de la Croix," *BRH*, XXII (1916), 365–70; "Inventaire des documents et des imprimés concernant la communauté des frères Charon et l'Hôpital Général de Montréal sous le Régime français," ANQ *Rapport*, 1923–24, 192; "Les tribunaux et les officiers de justice de Montréal sous le Régime français," *BRH*, XXXVII (1931), 307. "Les notaires au Canada sous le Régime français," ANQ *Rapport*, 1921–22, 46. Vachon, "Inv. critique des notaires royaux," *RHAF*, XI, 99–100. Jouve, *Les franciscains et le Canada: aux Trois-Rivières*, 277–81. J.-E. Roy, *Hist. du notariat*, I, 211. P.-G. Roy, *Les mots qui restent* (Québec, 1940), 134–35. M. Trudel, *L'esclavage au Canada français*, 147. É.-Z. Massicotte, "Hospitalier, ecclésiastique, notaire et père de famille," *BRH*, XLII (1936), 305. J.-E. Roy, "Les conseillers au Conseil souverain de la Nouvelle-France," *BRH*, I (1895), 187.

SINGLETON, GEORGE, army officer and merchant; b. *c.* 1750 in Ireland; d. 21 Sept. 1789 at Fredericksburgh (North and South Fredericksburgh, Ont.).

A merchant, presumably in the province of New York, George Singleton joined the British cause early in the American revolution and may have served in the defence of Quebec during the siege of 1775–76. In June 1776 he was commissioned lieutenant in the King's Royal Regiment of New York (KRRNY), under the command of Sir John Johnson*. He served in Barrimore Matthew St Leger's Mohawk valley expedition in 1777 and was wounded and taken prisoner during the siege of Fort Stanwix (Rome, N.Y.). Local histories link Singleton with an alleged "act of shameful cruelty"; he is said to have encouraged his Indian allies to kill some prisoners. In the spring of 1778 he was allowed to go to Canada, but he remained on parole at Montreal for two years. Returning to duty in 1780 he was appointed captain in the 2nd battalion KRRNY, commanded by John Ross, and was at Carleton Island, N.Y., in October 1780, possibly his introduction to the Cataraqui (Kingston) and Bay of Quinte area. In July 1782 he joined Joseph Brant [Thayendanegea*] on a scouting expedition to the Mohawk valley. His journal of that moderately successful journey indicates that he was a man of some education and ability. He maintained good relations with the Indians and together he and Brant obtained 224 cattle for them and the garrison at Oswego, N.Y.

When hostilities ended he received land in the Cataraqui area, settling in Fredericksburgh Township. In July 1784, along with Edward Jessup* and John Stuart*, he successfully petitioned the government to delay drastic reduction of rations for the loyalists. Initially Singleton was more interested in trade than in acquiring a large landed estate. There is strong evidence to suggest that he had a trading post near the mouth of the Sagonaska (Moira) River in Thurlow Township in the summer of 1785; he was thus among the earliest settlers and was the first resident merchant at what is now Belleville, Ont. Israel Ferguson, his brother-in-law, was his trading partner. Singleton's residence-trading post on the Sagonaska was a primitive but comfortable log building. He continued to spend time also at his Fredericksburgh residence. In 1788 he was appointed justice of the peace for the Mecklenburgh District.

The "Hungry Year" of 1788, caused by drought and a poor crop and complicated by a severe winter, had disastrous consequences for Singleton. His customers were unable to make payments and he was obliged to mortgage or sell land. Since he had never claimed the full officer's allowance of 3,000 acres, he petitioned the government in August 1789 for 2,100 acres directly across from his trading post, in what is now Prince Edward County. Before the government could respond tragedy struck. Early in September Singleton set out by bateau for Kingston, where he was to obtain trading goods and to appear as a defendant in a civil court case. He was taken ill en route, and despite medical attention from the Mohawks at Tyendinaga (near Napanee) and a Kingston doctor, he died at his home in Fredericksburgh. Singleton was interred on 23 Sept. 1789, by the Reverend John Langhorn*. He was survived by his wife Nancy (Ferguson?) and his son John.

The river and location in Thurlow had been given the names Singleton's Creek and Singleton's and continued to be known in this way until the mid 1790s. Singleton's untimely death, perhaps as a result of the privations of the "Hungry Year," meant that the river and site soon took on their modern names. After 1810 his family moved to Murray Township in neighbouring Northumberland County, where his son and his grandchildren were prominent early settlers.

GERALD E. BOYCE

BL, Add. MSS 21785, 21829. Corby Public Library (Belleville, Ont.), Hastings County Hist. Soc. coll., Singleton family papers. PAC, RG 1, L5, 34. PAO, Canniff (William) papers, package 9, Notes concerning the early settlers of Belleville and Prince Edward County; Cartwright family papers, Ezra Stephens to F. M. Hill, 23 Nov. 1852; RG 1, C-IV, Fredericksburgh Township papers, abstract index; Pittsburgh Township papers, abstract index; Sidney Township papers, abstract index; Thurlow Township papers, abstract index. PRO, WO 17/1574; 28/5, ff.5, 215 (mfm. at PAC).

Orderly book of Sir John Johnson during the Oriskany campaign, 1776–1777 . . ., ed. W. L. Stone (Albany, N.Y., 1882), 13. PAO *Report*, 1917, 203–4. "Rev. John Langhorn's records, 1787–1813: burials," *OH*, I (1899), 59–63. William Canniff, *History of the settlement of Upper Canada (Ontario) with special reference to the Bay Quinte* (Toronto, 1869; repr. Belleville, Ont., 1971). Ont., Dept. of Planning and Development, *Moira valley conservation report* (Toronto, 1950). J. A. Scott, *Fort Stanwix (Fort Schuyler) and Oriskany . . .* (sesquicentennial ed., Rome, N.Y., 1927), 197. E. A. Cruikshank, "The King's Royal Regiment of New York," *OH*, XXVII (1931), 193–323. R. V. Rogers, "The first commission of the peace for the district of Mecklenburg," *OH*, VIII (1907), 49–78.

SIONGOROCHTI. *See* KAIEÑ?KWAAHTOÑ

SIRIER. *See* CIRIER

SIVERT. *See* L'ESPÉRANCE

SLADE, JOHN, sea captain, shipowner, officeholder, and merchant; b. 1719 at Poole, England, one of eight children of John Slade, a mason, and his wife Ann; m. Martha Haitor (Hayter) and they had one son; d. 17 Feb. 1792 at Poole.

John Slade's father was a man of modest means, leaving at his death in 1727 only a small plot of land with a tenement and a bequest of £10 to three sons – John, Robert, and Thomas. John, though orphaned at the age of eight, probably received some basic education in the Free School and an early apprenticeship as a mariner, for seafaring was the backbone of Poole's economic life. Indeed it was during Slade's childhood that Daniel Defoe visited Poole and in *A tour through the whole island of Great Britain* described it as the most considerable seaport in southern England. He further noted that the key to the town's growth had been "ships fitted out every year to the Newfoundland fishery." Yet in Defoe's day Poole was but approaching its main period of expansion of trade with Newfoundland. In the early eighteenth century the trade consisted largely of seasonal migratory adventures, with fishing crews drawn from members of the ship's company and divided into catching and curing crews during the summer months. Later the trade expanded rapidly and Poole merchants found it to their advantage to set up those of their servants who wished to settle in Newfoundland, and a trade based on the provisioning of these planters in return for their production of fish and other staples began to supersede the migratory fishery. It was during the years of dynamic growth and fundamental change that John Slade became involved. From the trade he amassed a respectable fortune, exerting in the process considerable economic and cultural influence upon the development of settlement in northeastern Newfoundland and Labrador.

The earliest known documentation of Slade's maritime career is for the 1740s, when he captained several Poole merchant ships on voyages to the Channel Islands, the Mediterranean, Ireland, and Newfoundland. He made his first recorded visit to Newfoundland in 1748 as master of the trader *Molly*, a vessel he commanded until 1750, sailing between Poole, Newfoundland, Cork, and Lisbon. In 1750 alone, he completed three transatlantic crossings. At this time, he was apparently in the employ of Joseph White, a Poole Quaker, then the most substantial of the Poole–Newfoundland adventurers. In 1751 Slade took command of the 100-ton *Dolphin*, owned by William Kittier, and followed the familiar routes between Newfoundland, the Mediterranean salt fish markets, and Poole for another two years.

In 1753 Slade acquired ownership of his first ship, the 90-ton *Little John*, and struck out into the Newfoundland trade on his own account. This development was undoubtedly aided by some wealth acquired from his marriage to Martha Haitor, apparently the daughter of John Hayter, a Poole–Newfoundland merchant of a slightly earlier era. It was probably also through her inheritance that Slade advanced his social position in Poole and came to reside amongst the merchants of Thames Street (Spurriers, Lesters, and Westons) in a house that for decades afterwards was identified in Poole rate books as "Mr. Hayters tenement."

Slade's early experience in Newfoundland, especially with Kittier, had given him a thorough firsthand knowledge of an expanding frontier of English exploitation: the region to the north of Bonavista Bay, especially the large and varied Notre Dame Bay district. Up to 1728 the region had formed part of the French migratory fishery, which afterwards began to shift northward of Cape St John probably because of pilfering by the Beothuks and the northward thrust of the English, who were in the habit of overwintering and usurping the best fishing places. English migratory fishermen, mainly from Poole, first occupied the area between 1728 and 1732 and it became a regular resort after 1738. The territory not only added new inshore areas prolific in codfish but also provided in the numerous estuaries and river valleys at the bottom of Notre Dame Bay some of the finer timber stands, fur-hunting areas, and salmon runs on the island. Harbours such as Fogo and Twillingate, the first to be favoured by the English, were reliable ports from which to harvest both cod in the summer and harp seals in the winter and spring, and were convenient for strikes farther northwards, even to Labrador.

In the late 1750s John Slade was developing his trade in the northern regions in competition with other small shipowners and establishing a foothold within the ranks of the Poole–Newfoundland merchant community. He was one of 30 "principal merchants and traders" of Poole who in 1758 petitioned for the exemption of fishermen from naval service and for convoy protection of shipping between Poole, Newfoundland, and the fish markets. The Poole port books show that in 1759 he exported varied provisions to Newfoundland and imported train-oil (cod oil) and furs of beaver, fox, otter, and marten, as well as seal skins. Aggressive and persistent, by the 1760s Slade had expanded his business. Between 1764 and 1770 he owned and operated three to four ships (ranging between 40 and 80 tons and averaging 60) and deployed cod fishing crews in Twillingate, Fogo, and Tilting Harbour. Occasionally he ventured north of Cape St John, despite the injunction of Governor Hugh PALLISER not to disturb the French fishery in this area. Although an intruder himself, in 1766 Slade even seized a fishing room at Fleur-de-Lys Harbour built by William Branscombe, a Devon ship's captain, whom he undoubtedly regarded as an interloper. Towards the end of the Seven Years' War other English traders had begun moving northward of Cape St John but only Slade persisted in this region beyond the period of the American revolution. Over the years he was to develop a significant and regular trade with planters there. To a far greater degree than most Poole traders, who concentrated on the cod fishery, Slade's interest in Newfoundland was diversified and directed towards furs, salmon, and seals and in this regard he was a pioneer.

During the 1760s Slade also began trading on the Labrador coast. Governor Palliser was anxious to revive the fishery as a "nursery of seamen," and in 1765 he encouraged English merchants to extend their activities to Labrador. Slade followed the other merchants including Jeremiah COGHLAN of Bristol in partnership with Nicholas DARBY of London, John Noble of Bristol and Andrew Pinson* of Dartmouth, and George Cartwright* of London, in establishing cod, seal, and salmon fisheries and a furring business there. Cartwright's journal records Slade in Labrador with a winter sealing crew in 1771 and another Slade crew bound northward from Henley Harbour in September the following year.

John Slade divided his more active working years between his home port and his Newfoundland establishments, usually in a winter-summer cycle, but he occasionally overwintered on the island. His movements are well documented in the diaries of Isaac Lester, his next-door neighbour in Poole, and of Isaac's brother Benjamin*. Their trading firm kept a keen eye on Slade's business and Benjamin, though based in Trinity, had a close association with him in Newfoundland. The diaries document Slade's migratory pattern until 1777 when he apparently gave it up in order to spend the rest of his life in Poole. He was then well enough established in Newfoundland to entrust the more vigorous aspects of business management to younger relatives.

By the outbreak of the American Revolutionary War Slade was firmly established at Twillingate, his main base, with a supply and staple collection system that served settlements and exploitation outposts throughout Notre Dame Bay and along the Labrador coast. Many of the migrant apprentices and indentured servants Slade recruited in Dorset and west Hampshire became planters once they had acquired the basic skills of fishermen, furriers, or sealers. Slade advanced supplies, food, clothing, and even servants to the planters mortgaged against their production, of cod, oil, and other staples. The planters thus became dependent on him for their continued existence, and Slade had an assured production unit when labour was scarce especially in war time, and increased his profits by acting as a retailer. Though the system was in use elsewhere, it was innovative in the area and the stability which it assured enabled Slade to resist incursions by the Lesters, whose main establishment from the 1760s was at Trinity. His shipping, though modest compared to the Lesters' fleet of 15–20 vessels, now consisted of five ships between 30 and 120 tons, with an average of 93. The larger brigs plied the Atlantic; the schooners linked Twillingate and Slade's various outports. Occasionally he sent a vessel to New York for foodstuffs.

In 1774 Slade had sought Isaac Lester's help in

securing an appointment as naval officer in Twillingate. He received the commission within five days, and was re-appointed the next year. Apparently this post was the only political office he sought or held. In Poole, apart from joining the conservative lobby of merchants led by the Lesters, Spurriers, and Westons in voicing opinions on Newfoundland affairs, he was not concerned with politics. Even in his active years, in Notre Dame Bay he was overshadowed by Jeremiah Coghlan at Fogo, the owner of eight to ten ships, who commanded significantly more economic and political influence.

The revolutionary years were difficult for Slade. American privateers plagued his ships and establishments. In August 1778 the privateer John Grimes captured one of his vessels at Charles Harbour in Labrador. Early the following spring another privateering vessel with only four guns ventured boldly into Twillingate, captured another of Slade's ships laden with fish, broke open his stores, and distributed his goods to the "poor inhabitants of the place." It next fell upon Slade's Battle Harbour premises in Labrador and captured a sloop with 22 tons of seal oil and destroyed his goods. Natural hazards added to his problems. In the fall of 1775 he lost several vessels and ten fishing boats in a storm. His wharves in Fogo were destroyed in the fall of 1782 by a gale that also washed away his stages at Twillingate with some 800 quintals of cured fish. Wartime conditions in Poole made it difficult to recruit seamen and servants because of press-gangs and at one stage Slade was desperate enough to spirit away Lester's men. In 1776 Isaac Lester noted, "John Slade our neighbour is mean enough to ship our people after they agreed with us, and conceal them. He or his son [in fact his nephew John] is at the door all day and watches to see who goes in and out of the house and nabs them and gets them into his house." For all these reasons Slade's trade suffered serious decline. In 1773 his tax rates in Poole were assessed at £3,000 annual trade; a decade later he was taxed on half that amount.

It was natural that Slade's only son, John Haitor, should have been earmarked to succeed him. When he was 15 years old he began accompanying his father on the annual trip to Newfoundland, and within a few years acted in the absence of his father as chief agent in Twillingate. In 1773, however, he died of smallpox. Slade's attention now focussed on his nephews. Several, including John, David, Robert, and Thomas, had had considerable experience with him in Newfoundland as mariners and ships' captains. According to Isaac Lester, he took John Slade, eldest son of his brother Robert, into his household in 1776 and had also contemplated adopting a boy he had fathered reputedly by a Twillingate planter's wife. From 1777 to 1792 Slade's nephew, now called John Slade Jr, was chief Newfoundland agent of John Slade and Company and in 1793 became its Poole-based principal. David Slade assisted as company factor in Twillingate, Thomas Slade commanded ships, and Robert Slade took major responsibility for Labrador operations.

This placement of his nephews proved prudent for after 1783 Slade's trade yielded the most profitable returns of his career. When Coghlan's failed in 1782 Slade opened a second major establishment in Fogo. His firm was not without competition on the northeast coast until he died, but it was the only major resident firm. In his will he divided equally among his four nephews and cousin, George Nickleson Allen, his "fishing rooms, plantations, warehouses, stages, Salmon Brooks, Sealing Ports . . . in Newfoundland and on the coast of Labrador . . . with all my boats and crafts and all my goods and property there" and "all my ships and vessels." He owned six ships between 60 and 150 tons, averaging 90 tons, and trading establishments in Fogo, Twillingate, Change Island, Conche, and Wester Head in Newfoundland and in Battle Harbour, Hawke's Port, Hawkes Bay, Lewis Bay, Matthews Cove, Caribou Tickle, and Guy's Cove in Labrador.

Slade's trading system fostered migration from Poole and Dorset and the growth of permanent settlement in Newfoundland. The surnames of many of those who live in the Twillingate-Fogo region today are those of the settlers he recruited. The most important aspect of his Newfoundland career was thus the initiation in this area of the transition from the migratory fishery to permanent residency; his heirs and their successors were to further it. As Chief Justice John Reeves* stressed in 1793: "The merchants . . . were and still are the chief encouragers of residency." In fact, only those merchants having a regular supply trade with planters survived for long in any district. The perseverance of Bideford and Barnstaple merchants in the ancient migratory mode has been given as the main reason these ports were driven out of the Newfoundland fishery. The inhabitant fishery secured for men such as Slade their major source of marketable staples during war, and if they survived they were in a better position to expand in peace-time.

The ledgers of John Slade and Company from 1783 onwards show that under the credit or truck system the firm was annually staking the ventures of some 90–100 planters in northeastern Newfoundland and employed 150–200 servants directly. In 1787–88 Slade collected from them some 2,200 seal skins, 200 tierces of salmon, 400 bundles of hoops, 32 tons of seal oil, 2,000 gallons of train-oil, 3,000 quintals of fish, 24,000 wooden staves, 15,000 feet of board, 32 sets of oars, 30 pounds of beaver skins, 25 furs (fox, otter, and marten), and sundry smaller items. Slade was also closely associated in trade with independent frontiersmen such as John Peyton*, Henry Miller, William Hooper, and William Cull*, who as salmon fishermen and furriers were drawn into contact and conflict with the dwindling remnants of the ill-fated Beothuks.

There was little that Slade did in Newfoundland for which one could not find contemporary parallels or earlier precedents. He was one of a set of adventurers, who closely copied one another's successful innovations and changing emphases in an attempt to gain a competitive advantage. Contending for the same resources, supplies, and markets, they hated one another, but they formed a closely knit community for common interests and survival. Slade's distinction lies in his persistence and his continuity of effort; his single-minded attention to business was undoubtedly the reason his firm survived when Coghlan's failed in 1782. At his death in 1792 his estate was estimated, perhaps conservatively, at £70,000, earned, as the *Western Flying Post; or, Sherborne and Yeovil Mercury* reported, from "many years extensive and lucrative trade to Newfoundland and Labrador." Through his heirs his firm continued to be a major economic and social force in northeastern Newfoundland and Labrador until the 1860s, when it was sold out of the family.

W. Gordon Handcock

Dorset Record Office (Dorchester, Eng.), D365/F2–F10; P227/OV1. Maritime History Group Archives, Memorial University of Nfld. (St John's), Hayter name file; G. N. Horvath, "Social and economic background of Fogo Island as interpreted from the Slade Fogo ledgers, 1783–1792" (typescript, 1973); John Slade name file. PANL, GN 2/1, v.4, 6 (1766, 1769, 1774–75); Slade & Sons, Fogo, Ledgers, 1782–84, 1784–86, 1787–88, 1789–92. Private archives, H. Johnstone (Poole, Eng.), Peter Thomson, Diary, 1762. PRO, Adm. 7/87; BT 6/87, pp.2, 84; CO 194/21, 30; E 190; Prob.11, 1239/618.

George Cartwright, *A journal of transactions and events, during a residence of nearly sixteen years on the coast of Labrador* . . . (3v., Newark, Eng., 1792), II, 361–62, 459–60. Daniel Defoe, *A tour through the whole island of Great Britain*, abridged and ed. Pat Rogers (Harmondsworth, Eng., and Baltimore, Md., 1971), 206. "The third report from the committee appointed to enquire into the state of the trade to Newfoundland," G.B., House of Commons, *Reports from committees of the House of Commons* (16v., London, 1803–20), X, 470. *London Chronicle*, 24 June 1782. *Western Flying Post; or, Sherborne and Yeovil Mercury* (Sherborne, Eng.), 27 Feb. 1792. *Register book of shipping* (London), 1741–75. C. G. Head, *Eighteenth century Newfoundland: a geographer's perspective* (Toronto, 1976), 57. J. P. Howley, *The Beothucks or Red Indians: the aboriginal inhabitants of Newfoundland* (Cambridge, Eng., 1915; repr. Toronto, 1974). Prowse, *History of Nfld*. B. C. Short, *Poole: the romance of its later history* (London and Aylesbury, Eng., 1932), 155.

SMITH, WILLIAM, historian, diarist, jurist, and politician; b. 18 June 1728 in New York City, eldest child of William Smith and Mary Het; m. 3 Nov. 1752 Janet Livingston, and they had 11 children; d. 6 Dec. 1793 in Quebec City.

William Smith's grandfather had been a merchant in England before immigrating to New York City in 1715. His father graduated from Yale College in 1722, became a successful lawyer, and in 1753 was appointed a member of the Council of the province of New York; his mother was from the French speaking Huguenot settlement of New Rochelle, New York. Smith graduated from Yale College in 1745 and articled in his father's law office. Licensed attorney at law in October 1750, he quickly established a lucrative practice. He became particularly skilled in the defence of what were often ill-defined landed estates, and he was prominent in efforts to raise the standards of the legal profession by adherence to British forms. In 1763 Governor Robert Monckton offered Smith, then only 35 years old, the position of chief justice of the Supreme Court. Smith hesitated, because his father had just been appointed third judge of the same court, and the opportunity was lost. In 1767, when his father retired from the colonial council, Smith was appointed to succeed him.

From an early age Smith was a prolific writer. After several literary ventures, in 1753–54 he co-authored the *Independent Reflector*, New York's first magazine. With one of his friends, William Livingston, he compiled the first collection of the *Laws of New-York from the year 1691 to 1751, inclusive*, published in 1752, and so acquired the basic material for *The history of the province of New-York*, which he published in London in 1757. This work served him well over the years, giving him a wide reputation as an authority on the colony, and he was often referred to as "the historian of New York"; 20 years later he began a second volume, published posthumously. In 1757 he was also the co-author, again with Livingston, of a pamphlet entitled *A review of the military operations in North-America*, condemning the direction of the Seven Years' War. In this polemic he took his first look at his future home: "Canada must be demolished – Delenda est Carthago – or we are undone." By now a compulsive writer, from 1763 to 1787 Smith kept a journal, intended partly as a confidant but chiefly as a historical source book, and from its publication in the mid 20th century it has served as such to historians of the British empire in North America.

Smith's talents as a writer were frequently enlisted in partisan causes. New York politics were dominated by family groupings struggling for control of patronage, and Smith espoused his father's long-standing antipathy to the De Lancey party. A Presbyterian, he opposed such Anglican enterprises as the foundation in 1754 of King's College (the future Columbia University) and the establishment of a bishop in America. William Livingston, John Morin Scott, and Smith became known as the "New York Triumvirate," whose object, one critic observed, was "to pull down Church and State." John Adams reported that Smith had "acted an intrepid, an honest and a prudent part" in the Stamp Act crisis of 1765, for which he earned the cognomen "Patriotic Billy." After his appointment to the council, however, Smith became more cautious and as his land speculations increased he turned away from some of his youthful enthusiasms. He preferred to oppose the De Lancey party and the Anglican church covertly and represented himself to successive governors as the man "above party" on whom they could rely for disinterested advice. Nevertheless, when New York began to drift into rebellion, there were those among both radical and conservative opponents of Britain who looked to him for support. In 1776 he moved to his country house in a vain attempt to sit out the crisis in rural retirement, and he refused to pledge allegiance to the new state. After two years on parole in Albany, he was finally forced to take a stand and joined the British in New York City. Although he recognized that both sides were at fault in the conflict, he believed that nothing could pardon the revolutionaries' desire to shatter the unity of the empire, and he declared his allegiance to the crown in 1778. To the British he was a prize equivalent to a repentant Samuel Adams, a sign for gentlemen "who had been lying on their oars," though there were reservations: "few Men so able, if he could be trusted." Two years later he was rewarded by appointment as chief justice of New York.

Sir Guy Carleton*'s arrival as commander-in-chief of the British forces in 1782 shaped the future course of Smith's life. The two men quickly established a rapport, conversing frequently about ideas of empire and imperial management. Smith had long been an advocate of a union of the American colonies: between 1765 and 1775 he had written several papers urging a united legislature consisting of a lord lieutenant with wide discretionary powers, a council, and an assembly chosen by indirect election. Individual colonial governments would remain as they were beneath this superstructure; the continental assembly would handle all royal requisitions for taxation. Since Carleton had initially hoped to exercise viceregal powers in New York, and was disgusted by the way his command had been shackled by the British government's determination to accept defeat, he saw great merit in the imperial structure Smith proposed, especially when Smith insinuated that the commander-in-chief was the obvious man to head it.

The British evacuated New York in 1783, and Carleton and Smith sailed for England on the same ship in December, Carleton to face a government unappreciative of his true merits, Smith to learn the numbing routine of office-seeker and claimant for compensation, although London was also a broadening experience in that he met and found himself at ease with many of the dissenting reformers of the day. Smith's fortunes were inextricably tied to those of Carleton, who had recommended his appointment as chief justice of Quebec while they were both still in New York. Put simply, if Carleton became governor of Quebec, Smith would become chief justice; if not, Smith's future was blank. It gradually became clear that even compensation for his losses as a loyalist might depend upon Carleton's success. He heard that William Pitt himself had some "Doubt of my Principles" in the recent war.

Smith viewed Quebec in the context of what he hoped was a British determination to reunite the empire in North America, and he had to encourage an often surly Carleton, determined upon a peerage before accepting any post there, with visions of what might be achieved. If the surviving colonies were put under central direction and made a shining example of the superior wisdom of British forms, then the disorganized Americans would repent of their independence and perhaps "place themselves under the same protecting Power." Carleton should be governor general of all the provinces and captain-general of the militia, with control of the navy and full authority to negotiate and conclude treaties within North America. He alone would be in contact with the imperial government, and all North American officials would correspond with him. He should approve all executive decisions, control Indian affairs and frontier defence, regulate commerce, grant crown lands and charters for towns, universities, and other public institutions, and choose all officers usually appointed by the British government. He should also have the power to confer for the levying of general taxes with a two-chamber house drawing members from all the colonies. The British government's conception of what was needed in North America, however, differed from Smith's. When Carleton was finally commissioned on 15 April 1786, it was not as governor general of a federation of colonies but as multiple governor of Quebec, Nova Scotia, and New Brunswick, with none of the overriding powers Smith had envisaged. Ennobled as Baron Dorchester, he was sent to Quebec on a fact-finding mission, to advise ministers on the constitutional problems of the province.

Dorchester and Smith arrived at Quebec on 23 Oct. 1786, and Smith took the oaths of office as councillor and chief justice on 2 November. Once again denied a full measure of power, Carleton retired from the political scene and did not attend the council. Since the next in line, Lieutenant Governor Henry HOPE, was frequently absent, Smith was left to preside over meetings, and his position was strengthened through his chairmanship of numerous council committees. The council was sharply divided along party lines drawn in the names of national groups. The majority French party saw in Smith a powerful threat of anglicization, and the hostility of its leader, Adam MABANE, was doubly assured by the fact that he himself had hoped to become chief justice. Other judges, Thomas Dunn* and Pierre-Méru Panet*, regarded him askance as a newcomer and an American, who retained large land holdings in Vermont and New York and whose reputation for equivocal conduct had preceded him. But since the English party had no leader of Mabane's calibre, men such as Hugh Finlay* and Samuel Jan Holland* at first looked to Smith to fill that role.

Smith made no secret of his wish to see massive anglophone immigration to strengthen Quebec through increased population, and one of the ways he hoped to encourage it was by anglicizing the legal system of the colony. He and Mabane soon came into conflict in a council committee called to report on the courts of justice. Among the reforms Smith proposed were new judicial districts for the loyalist settlements and the extension of optional jury trials, which since 1785 had been permitted in some civil cases, to all personal actions. Mabane, however, opposed further encroachment of English legal practice on French civil law procedures. Meanwhile, only two months after his arrival, Smith had caused a major controversy by upsetting the customary interpretation of the Quebec Act. He reversed the decision found by Mabane in the Court of Common Pleas in a case involving William Grant*, of Saint-Roch, and Alexander Gray by demonstrating that French civil law did not apply to natural-born British subjects. He argued that the Quebec Act, which had expressly granted Canadian laws to Canadians, had not expressly denied English law to British-born subjects, who were therefore entitled to their natural rights. Although he had good legal precedent for his opinion, Smith chose not to mention it, and it seemed that he was destroying singlehanded a system of laws widely regarded as holding back a flood of British immigration. His legal decision was a political challenge to the French party in the council. When he tried to embody his views in a law, Paul Roch* de Saint-Ours counter-attacked by introducing a bill to abolish optional jury trials, as well as the English law of evidence in force in commercial cases since 1777. On 22 March 1787 the council voted not to commit Smith's bill for consideration. Manœuvring to avoid defeat, Smith seized on a protest against Saint-Ours' bill, in the form of a petition from the English merchants, as a reason to shelve it. The merchants' protest was argued before the council on 14 April by the attorney general, James Monk*, who condemned the past administration of justice in such strong terms that a formal inquiry was unavoidable. Smith, the only judge not castigated by Monk, was mainly responsible for conducting the investigation and was uncomfortably prominent as one disappointed litigant after another denounced his colleagues. The accumulated evidence was sent to London with no suggestion as to what should be done; the judicial system had been discredited but continued as before; and Smith, blamed for the impasse, lost support among the English party. In April 1789 Monk was relieved of his office and replaced by Alexander Gray; feeling that he had been made the scapegoat, Monk became a bitter opponent of the chief justice.

Smith continued his efforts to clear the way for immigration when he supported, or possibly inspired, Charles-Louis Tarieu* de Lanaudière's petition in January 1788 to convert his seigneury to freehold tenure. This effort failed, but in 1790 Smith chaired a council committee that recommended voluntary conversion. Feudal tenures, he argued, had held back the expansion of the old French colony and left it weak enough to be conquered; their retention would retard the progress of Quebec now that it was an English colony. A storm of public protest greeted the committee's report, and when the legislative session opened in March 1791, the council voted unanimously to abandon a bill for voluntary conversion. Many members of the English party were themselves seigneurs.

Smith, feeling isolated, frequently demonstrated his scorn for provincial politicians, whom he found slovenly, unsophisticated, and unfit for an elective assembly. As he wrote to the London merchant Brook Watson*, "neither Protestant nor Popish Catholic, British nor Canadian, merchant nor landholder" agreed with his views. The only initiative that won nearly unanimous support was his proposal, advanced in 1789, for a provincial educational system crowned by a university with a council consisting of an equal number of French and English members. But since he opposed any denominational connection for the college, the plan was buried in London [*see also* Charles-François BAILLY de Messein; Jean-François HUBERT].

Smith had created acrimonious political controversy with himself as the focal point, a situation far different from his experience in New York, where he had been able to influence governors and yet remain in the background. And, as with the judicial investigations, to what end? Decisions were made in London, not Quebec. Dorchester's advice to the home government on the constitutional problems of the colony was mostly negative, and the chief justice fully concurred. In 1789 the initiative for reform passed to William Wyndham Grenville, the new Home secretary, who drew up a plan for dividing Quebec into two separate provinces. He sent a copy of this document, the basis of the Constitutional Act of 1791, to Dorchester for his comments; Dorchester turned it over to Smith.

Grenville's plan beat a retreat from the glorious prospect Smith cherished: a British America from Atlantic to Pacific and from the Arctic Ocean, through Louisiana, to the Gulf of Mexico. The expansion of British North America required a government that was more centralized, not further fragmented. There should, Smith argued, be a federal government uniting the existing colonies under a governor general, with a legislative council and a general assembly. The council would consist of members from each province appointed for life by the governor general; the general assembly would have members chosen by the assemblies of the various provinces. To pass in the general assembly, a bill would have to receive not only a majority vote, but also a vote representing a majority of the provinces. This double majority would not, however, be necessary in the council. The legislature would meet at the behest of the governor general at least once in two years and continue no longer than seven years between elections. There was to be no hindrance to royal appointment of the executive council or crown officers. Thus a federal system was to be superimposed on the political constitutions of the provinces. Smith's plan was included in Dorchester's reply to Grenville, but a few words from London were sufficient to dispel the dream: the plan, sniffed Grenville, was "liable to considerable objection."

The constitution of 1791 fell far short of Smith's ideas, but as chief justice, now of Lower Canada, he resolved to do his best to set the new province on a correct course. He was determined that its politics should be conducted in proper parliamentary form, and his appointment as speaker of the Legislative Council gave him the necessary authority. He drew up commissions for Black Rod and the Serjeant-at-Arms with an exact copy of the uniforms worn at Westminster. Under his direction a council committee decided that all intercourse between council and assembly should be "in strict adherence to parliamentary practice," and he saw to it that the writs issued to councillors were exact duplicates of the royal summonses to the House of Lords. He even determined the physical layout of the new legislature.

Reform of the judicial system continued to be one of Smith's main concerns. In October 1792 Grenville's successor, Henry Dundas, in an effort to make uniform the administration of justice in British North America, forwarded a plan to replace the existing Lower Canadian establishment of one chief justice and six judges of the Court of Common Pleas with two stationary courts of king's bench in Quebec and Montreal, each presided over by a chief justice. Smith opposed the change, which threatened his personal position, and set out in a draft bill a whole judicial system that, to advance the provincial autonomy of Lower Canada under the crown, would have created almost a complete duplicate of the English judicial system. (Dundas' plan went into effect, but after Smith's death.) Smith also played an important role in determining land policy in the colony as chairman of the committee charged with reporting on the land-granting clauses of the royal instructions of 1791. Although the proclamation based on his report followed ministerial intentions, much depended on interpretation, and Smith's zeal for immigration led him to interpret it in such a way that Lower Canada was opened to the worst kind of speculation. Millions of acres were petitioned for, mostly by Americans who had no intention of bringing in settlers.

Warrants of survey for large tracts of land were readily issued, and were then sold and resold in the United States, where they were accepted as proof of title. Smith's policy, in effect, defeated his aims, and the land-granting problem was not resolved during his lifetime.

Smith died on 6 Dec. 1793 after a prolonged illness. The funeral procession was led by His Royal Highness Edward Augustus*, followed by the members of the Legislative Council and the assembly, officers both civil and military, "and the most respectable and numerous concourse of Citizens ever witnessed on a similar occasion." Smith was buried – strange victory for a lifelong foe – in an Anglican cemetery. He was survived by his wife Janet and four children, including Harriet, who became the wife of Jonathan Sewell*, and William*, a future historian and member of the Executive Council.

William Smith received one of the greatest gifts any man can have, a second chance. He was one of the few loyalists able to resume a career broken by the American revolution. Consequently his life spanned not just two colonies, but two empires as well. From the perspective of the old empire he foresaw the new: a British America federated, virtually autonomous, bulwarked by British political concepts and traditions. He was able to adapt ideas formulated in the first empire while an official of the second. Yet Smith's career was one of potential rather than actual achievement. His political durability was bought at a high price. Too many men had too many reservations about him; there were too many accusations of duplicity and greed and hypocrisy. His portrait shows a man of middling stature with a high forehead and a weak chin. He was an ascetic individual, prim, self-possessed; an intellectual with a gift for crushing repartee. It was his misfortune to live in times that required clear-cut decisions or at least the appearance of straightforwardness. Smith's motto had always been *in medio tutissimus ibis*.

L. F. S. Upton

[William Smith is the author of *The history of the province of New-York, from the first discovery to the year M.DCC.XXXII.; to which is annexed, a description of the country with a short account of the inhabitants, their religious and political state, and the constitution of the courts of justice in that colony* (London, 1757), translated by M.-A. Eidous as *Histoire de la Nouvelle-York . . .* (London, 1767); *Continuation of the history of the province of New-York, to the appointment of Governor Colden, in 1762*, ed. William Smith Jr (New York, 1826); and *A review of the military operations in North-America; from the commencement of the French hostilities on the frontier of Virginia in 1753, to the surrender of Oswego, on the 14th of August, 1756 . . .* (London, 1757). With William Livingston, he compiled *Laws of New-York from the year 1691 to 1751, inclusive* (New York, 1752) and *Laws of New-York from the 11th Nov. 1752, to 22d May 1762* (New York, 1762).

W. H. W. Sabine published in New York in 1956 *Historical memoirs from 16 March 1763 to 9 July 1776 of William Smith . . .* and in 1958 *Historical memoirs from 29 July 1776 to 28 July 1778 . . .*; L. F. S. Upton has edited *The diary and selected papers of Chief Justice William Smith, 1784–1793* (2v., Toronto, 1963–65). For a more complete listing of Smith's writings, as well as a comprehensive biography, *see* L. F. S. Upton, *The loyal whig: William Smith of New York & Quebec* (Toronto, 1969). L.F.S.U.]

SOLOMONS, LUCIUS LEVY, merchant and fur-trader; b. 1730 in England; father of one child by his first marriage and 11 by his second, to Rebecca Franks on 31 May 1775; d. 18 May 1792 at Montreal (Que.).

Lucius Levy Solomons was living in the province of New York as early as 1755. During the Seven Years' War he entered a partnership with his cousin Ezekiel Solomons, Chapman Abraham, Benjamin Lyon, and Gershom Levy to supply the British army. After the fall of New France in 1760 the consortium became involved in the Canadian fur trade, and since under British rule the settlement of Jews in Quebec was legal, Solomons eventually moved his headquarters from Albany to Montreal. The partners had financial support in England and were connected with Hayman Levy of New York City, who was active in the fur trade of the Hudson valley. With such good backing they were able to do business on a larger scale than was usual in the trade at the time.

Ezekiel Solomons took a load of trade goods to Michilimackinac (Mackinaw City, Mich.) in 1761, preceding even the British troops who arrived in September to take over the post from its acting commandant Charles-Michel Mouet de Langlade. Levy Solomons was at Fort Niagara (near Youngstown, N.Y.) in 1762. During the Indian uprising of 1763 [*see* Pontiac*] four of the partners, including Levy Solomons, were captured and large quantities of goods taken from them. All eventually reached safety but they were ruined financially. Their total loss was estimated at £18,000. In 1764 a fur sale was held for their creditors, but they remained in debt. Attempts to get government compensation failed, and some of their creditors refused to agree to their declaring bankruptcy. They attempted to avail themselves of an English law that would have enabled them to go into bankruptcy nonetheless, but the British government ruled that this law did not apply in the colony [*see* George SUCKLING].

The exact outcome of their financial difficulties is not known. The partnership broke up but the members continued to be involved in the fur trade. In 1767, when the trade began to pick up, Gershom Levy provided security for two Canadian traders at Michilimackinac. In 1769 Chapman Abraham had a licence to take goods valued at £189 to the *pays d'en haut*; in 1770 Benjamin Lyon had one for £1,300. Licences granted to Ezekiel Solomons increased from £750 in 1770 to £2,050 in 1774. Levy Solomons had licences for seven canoes in 1771 with a total value of probably over £3,000; he also acted as a fur buyer, purchasing from independent traders. Although Benjamin Lyon, writing in 1770, may have exaggerated when he claimed that Levy Solomons had received the greatest part of the furs passing through Montreal that year, Solomons was undoubtedly important in the trade.

Solomons signed a petition in 1773 requesting a legislative assembly for Quebec. When the Americans captured Montreal in 1775 he cooperated with them, providing supplies to the troops and establishing three hospitals. Large quantities of his goods destined for the fur trade were appropriated by the invaders. After the Americans were driven out Solomons remained but was in great disfavour. The British turned him out of his house and threatened those who helped him. He survived, however, and remained in business until 1782. In 1784, still in Montreal, he unsuccessfully petitioned Congress to reimburse him for his losses.

In December 1768 Levy and Ezekiel Solomons were among the founders of the Shearith Israel congregation in Montreal. Levy Solomons was apparently lay leader of the congregation in 1782 and appeared as the defendant that year when the reader, Jacob Raphael Cohen*, went to the courts to collect his salary. The case was appealed and finally settled in 1784. Solomons died in Montreal eight years later.

WALTER S. DUNN JR

Pa. Hist. and Museum Commission, Division of Public Records (Harrisburg), Baynton, Wharton and Morgan coll. Wis., State Hist. Soc. (Madison), Canadian archives, Abstracts of Indian trade licenses in Canadian archives, 1767–76. *Johnson papers* (Sullivan *et al.*), III, 671.Maseres, *Maseres letters* (Wallace). Mass. Hist. Soc., *Commerce of Rhode Island, 1726–1800* (2v., Boston, 1914–15), II, 309–11. "Memorials presented to the Continental Congress," ed. Herbert Friedenwald, American Jewish Hist. Soc., *Pubs.* ([New York]), II (1894), 119–27. "A suit at law involving the first Jewish minister in Canada," ed. B. G. Sack, American Jewish Hist. Soc., *Pubs.*, XXXI (1928), 181–86. "Items relating to the Solomons family, New York," [comp. J. J. Lyons], American Jewish Hist. Soc., *Pubs.*, XVII (1920), 376–78. W. S. Dunn, "Western commerce, 1760–1774" (unpublished PHD thesis, University of Wisconsin, Madison, 1971). J. R. Marcus, *The colonial American Jew, 1492–1776* (3v., Detroit, 1970); *Early American Jewry* (2v., Philadelphia, 1951–53). Peckham, *Pontiac*. Peter Wiernik, *History of the Jews in America, from the discovery of the New World to the present time* (2nd ed., New York, 1931). I. I. Katz, "Chapman Abraham: an early Jewish settler in New York," American Jewish Hist. Soc., *Pubs.*, XL (1950–51), 81–86. Louis Rosenberg, "Some aspects of the historical development of the Canadian Jewish community," American Jewish Hist. Soc., *Pubs.*, L (1960–61), 121–42.

SORBIER DE VILLARS, FRANÇOIS, priest, superior, and vicar general; b. 8 Feb. 1720 in the former diocese of Uzès (dept of Gard), France; d. 29 Nov. 1788 in Paris.

François Sorbier de Villars, who had done part of his studies with the Sulpicians in Paris, was sent to Canada in 1744 by the Séminaire des Missions Étrangères. He arrived in Quebec at the beginning of October and was soon regarded by the members of the seminary as "an excellent acquisition." In the spring of 1746 he was appointed a director of the seminary; the following January he succeeded François-Elzéar Vallier* as bursar; then in November 1749 he became assistant to the procurator, Joseph-André-Mathurin JACRAU. The next spring the seminary in Paris recalled Christophe de Lalane, the superior of the Séminaire de Québec, and appointed Sorbier de Villars to replace him. Villars remained in office until 1756, when he too was recalled; his prestige and knowledge of the facts had led to his being chosen to present before the king's council of state the Séminaire de Québec's case against the chapter concerning the parish of Quebec [*see* René-Jean Allenou* de Lavillangevin; Jean-Félix Récher*].

Villars arrived in Paris on 6 Jan. 1757. Theoretically he was to remain only two years, but the war of the conquest changed his expectations and he never returned to Canada. Before he left, his colleagues in Quebec had entrusted him with a procuration to administer the seminary's possessions and interests in France. Until his death Villars was to remain the temporal procurator and the true moral guide of the Séminaire de Québec, sending letters and accounts punctually, even during the military régime, when Governor MURRAY had kept a close watch on correspondence to make sure that Paris was not intervening in the affairs of Quebec. A similar relationship was established between Villars and the Ursulines of Quebec; he had been their chaplain from 1747 until 1755 and helped them on numerous occasions. Bishop BRIAND, who had appointed him his vicar general in Paris on 17 Oct. 1777, said that he had "laboured hard for the diocese of Quebec with the bishops of France and other seigneurs whom he knew."

On 6 April 1757 Sorbier de Villars, whose zeal and competence were recognized, was appointed a member of the board of directors of the seminary in Paris. He became its secretary in 1761, procurator in 1763, superior in 1766 and 1769, assistant to the superior in 1772, and once more procurator from 1783 until his death. His last letter, dated 2 May 1788, discloses that he was the beneficiary of the priory of Fontmoron in the diocese of Poitiers and that he had just given up this benefice with a lifetime pension from the king in its place. He died of an attack of gout on 29 Nov. 1788. His death brought about a change in the relations between the seminary in Paris and the Séminaire de Québec; the fraternal ties they had enjoyed became simple bonds of friendship, which dissolved after the Revolution and were not renewed for a long period.

HONORIUS PROVOST

[The ASQ holds some documents in the hand of François Sorbier de Villars: a description of the capture of Fort Chouaguen (Oswego) with a summary of booty taken (Lettres, R, 16); a list of British officers taken prisoner (Polygraphie, VII, 98); a copy of a letter to the commandant of Fort Edward (Fort Edward, N.Y.) (Polygraphie, VII, 39); and two manuscripts, "Observations utiles et curieuses touchant les forts, lacs et rivières du Canada" (1756, 10 pp.) (Polygraphie, VII, 123) and "Observations sur le Canada, routes fluviales, distances, etc." (Polygraphie, IX, 30). H.P.]

ASQ, C 21, 17 oct. 1744; Évêques, 145; Lettres, P, 124; T, 156; MSS, 12, f.29; 13, 9 août 1789; Polygraphie, XVIII, 5, 6, 18, 50. Burke, *Les ursulines de Québec* (1866–78), II, 258–63; III, 188–94. A.-H. Gosselin, *L'Église du Canada après la Conquête*, I; *L'Église du Canada jusqu'à la Conquête*, III. Adrien Launay, *Mémorial de la Société des Missions étrangères* (2v., Paris, 1912–16), II, 631.

SOSAWAKET. *See* NISSOWAQUET

SOUSTE, ANDRÉ, stocking maker, merchant, and royal notary; baptized on 4 April 1692 in the parish of Saint-Léger, Chambéry, Savoy, son of Jean-Marie Souste, a merchant, and Marguerite Vulliermet; m. 28 Nov. 1720 in Montreal (Que.) Marie-Louise, daughter of Denis d'Estienne* Du Bourgué de Clérin; d. 12 Feb. 1776 in Montreal.

André Souste had been a workman and a maker of silk and woollen stockings in France before coming to Canada late in the summer of 1719, under contract to François Charon* de La Barre, founder of the Brothers Hospitallers of the Cross and of St Joseph. Souste had agreed to set up a stocking factory with François Darles, a journeyman, at the Hôpital Général in Montreal. Charon's death obliged Souste and Darles to sign another contract, dated 13 December, with Louis Turc* de Castelveyre, the newly appointed superior of the community. The partners' difficulties in meeting the terms of the contract and their increased obligations to the hospitallers caused André Souste slowly to lose interest in his work. When the two began to quarrel, Intendant Michel Bégon* was forced to intervene; on 9 July 1721 he put Darles in sole charge of the factory. Souste protested at first but he finally accepted the decision on 8 May 1722, when he ceased all relations with his partner and let it be known that he had developed an aversion for Darles.

Souste then went into business in Montreal. He apparently did well, since in July 1725 he built a stone house 50 feet by 24 on Rue Saint-Pierre, and in November he hired a servant at an annual salary of 130 *livres*, with board and lodging. He engaged in retail trade in textiles and clothing until about 1740. Through the good offices of his wife's brother-in-law Louis-Claude Danré* de Blanzy, he was then appointed notary by the Jesuits for their seigneury of Prairie-de-la-Madeleine (La Prairie). After the death of Guillaume Barette he was appointed royal notary of the seigneury of Longueuil in 1745. Commissioned by Intendant HOCQUART, he was to practise in the area "from and including the seigneury of Longueuil up to the dwellings in the southern *côtes* of the administrative district of Montreal." On 12 March 1749 Intendant BIGOT licensed Souste to practise as a notary in both the northern and the southern *côtes* of the Montreal district; his jurisdiction was extended to the town itself on 2 Aug. 1750. At the time of the conquest, GAGE renewed his commission, and Souste was permitted to practise in the city and throughout the Government of Montreal for another nine years. During his career Souste drew up nearly 1,200 instruments, more than half dating from the period 1750–59. These included the usual kinds of documents prepared by a notary of the old régime: deeds of sale, land grants, and marriage contracts.

By the end of his career, André Souste had become quite prosperous, with the house on Rue Saint-Pierre and a farm of one and a half by 20 arpents on the *côte* Saint-Laurent near Montreal.

His marriage connected him with a prominent family in the colony and probably was a factor in his being able to make a successful transition from specialized labour to the judicial circle of the colony.

André Lachance

André Souste's register, which covers 28 March 1745 to 5 Feb. 1769, is held at ANQ-M. AD, Savoie (Chambéry), État civil, Saint-Léger, 4 avril 1692. ANQ-M, Doc. jud., Pièces détachées, 21 mars 1720; Registres des audiences pour la juridiction de Montréal, 9, ff.132, 138v; État civil, Catholiques, Notre-Dame de Montréal, 28 nov. 1720, 30 oct. 1758, 13 févr. 1776, 1er mai 1780; Greffe de J.-B. Adhémar, 5 juill., 21 nov. 1725; Greffe de F.-L. Lepallieur de Laferté, 28 mars 1737; Greffe de M.-L. Lepallieur de Laferté, 27 nov. 1720, 9, 27 juin 1725; Greffe de Pierre Panet, 28 oct. 1758, 20 févr. 1761. ANQ-Q, NF 2, 7, 25 juin 1720, 9 juill. 1721; 8, 24 sept. 1722. IBC, Centre de documentation, Fonds Morisset, Dossier André Souste. PAC *Rapport*, 1918, app.B, 24–25. "Recensement de Montréal, 1741" (Massicotte), 54. É.-Z. Massicotte, "Inventaire des documents et des imprimés concernant la communauté des frères Charon et l'Hôpital Général de Montréal sous le Régime français," ANQ *Rapport*, 1923–24, 179; "Les tribunaux et les officiers de justice, à Montréal, sous le Régime français, 1648–1760," RSC *Trans.*, 3rd ser., X (1916), sect.I, 298. "Les notaires au Canada sous le Régime français," ANQ *Rapport*, 1921–22, 49. P.-G. Roy, *Inv. jug. et délib., 1717–60*, II, 3, 35; III, 82; IV, 280; *Inv. ord. int.*, I, 183, 204, 229–30; II, 99, 106, 170–71; III, 77, 121. P.-G. Roy *et al.*, *Inv. greffes not.*, XV, 71; XXIV, 1–161; XXV, 15, 65, 123, 132, 182, 191, 193. Tanguay, *Dictionnaire*, VII, 208. Vachon, "Inv. critique des notaires royaux," *RHAF*, XI, 102. J.-E. Roy, *Hist. du notariat*, I, 214. J.-J. Lefebvre, "Les premiers notaires de Montréal sous le Régime anglais, 1760–1800," *La Revue du notariat* (Québec), 45 (1942–43), 297–99.

SOWER (Sauer, Saur), CHRISTOPHER, printer and office-holder; b. 27 Jan. 1754 at Germantown (Philadelphia, Pa), eldest son of Christopher Sower and Catharine Sharpnack; m. 8 Jan. 1775 Hannah Knorr at Philadelphia, and they had five surviving children; d. 3 July 1799 at Baltimore, Md.

Christopher Sower's grandfather was a German Baptist who had established a celebrated printing business at Germantown in 1738, and Christopher joined his father as a partner in the firm in 1775. The publication in 1776 of anti-revolutionary articles brought about a partial suspension of business, and in 1778 Sower and his family were forced to flee to New York. For several years Sower worked principally as an undercover agent for Major John André. In 1781 he visited England in an ineffectual attempt to promote the peace proposals of moderate loyalists, and following the cessation of hostilities he returned there. With merchant Brook Watson*'s assistance he successfully applied for compensation for his losses and for an official post in a British North American colony. He was appointed the first king's printer and deputy postmaster general for the new province of New Brunswick.

Sower took up his new posts in 1785. He brought a press from England and began publishing his weekly newspaper, the *Royal Gazette and the New Brunswick Advertiser,* at Saint John on 11 October. His appointment was resented by William Lewis and John Ryan*, two loyalists who had been operating a post office and printing a newspaper in Saint John since 1783, and an acrimonious controversy developed. Ryan and Sower were later reconciled; Ryan operated the Sower press from 1790 until 1796 and succeeded Sower as king's printer.

From his arrival until 1798, Sower also printed the journals of the House of Assembly and the acts of the General Assembly. In 1787 and 1788, however, Ryan received the contract, perhaps as a result of quarrels between Sower and the House of Assembly. In 1792 the assembly required Sower to move his press to Fredericton; he thus undertook the first printing done in the capital. Other government contracts included such curious ephemera as a handbill forbidding members to wear creepers (spiked boot attachments useful on ice) in the parliament buildings. Sower also printed items such as a confession by two condemned criminals and a religious treatise, but the most interesting of his non-official publications were several almanacs, which continued a tradition established by his grandfather in 1739.

As deputy postmaster-general Sower was continually involved in controversy. He condemned private mail couriers, was accused of opening official mail, and conducted a fierce but unsuccessful campaign to make Saint John the overseas mail packet terminal. An excitable man, Sower interpreted the views of the radical faction in New Brunswick as a threat parallel to that posed by American rebels in 1776. But although he was a solid conservative, he was critical of the ruling faction as well. In his only entry into active politics he was defeated in his bid for a House of Assembly seat in 1795.

After living in Saint John until 1790, Sower moved to a country property on the Hammond River. He had been troubled by ill health, and reports of changed conditions in the United States so reassured him that he decided to return to the warmer climate of his birthplace. He resigned as king's printer in March 1799 and died suddenly in Baltimore while negotiating for a press.

J. RUSSELL HARPER

PRO, AO 12/38, 12/100, 13/102, 13/270. *Royal Gazette and the New Brunswick Advertiser* (Saint John), 1786–98. *Saint John Gazette and Weekly Advertiser* (Saint John, N.B.), 1786–99. *DAB*. Tremaine, *Bibliography of Canadian imprints*. James Hannay, *History of New Brunswick* (2v., Saint John, N.B., 1909). E. W. Hocker, *The Sower printing house of colonial times* (Norristown, Pa., 1948). J. R. Harper, "Christopher Sower, king's printer and loyalist," N.B. Hist. Soc., *Coll.*, no.14 (1955), 67–109. J. O. Knauss, "Christopher Saur the third," American Antiquarian Soc., *Proc.* (Worcester, Mass.), new ser., 41 (1931), 235–53.

STERLING (Stirling), JAMES, merchant and local official; b. in Ireland; m. 9 Feb. 1765 at Detroit to Angélique Cuillerier, *dit* Beaubien. Three children were born at Detroit, but they may have had seven in all. Sterling died some time after 1783.

James Sterling served as an officer in the Pennsylvania forces during the early part of the Seven Years' War. He was a commissary in the British attack on Fort Niagara (near Youngstown, N.Y.) in 1759 and in AMHERST's expedition against Montreal the following year. He subsequently became the representative in the Niagara area of the Schenectady (N.Y.) trading firm of Livingston, Rutherford, Duncan, Coventry and Syme, which in the spring of 1761 obtained from Amherst a provisional grant of 10,000 acres at the upper end of the Niagara portage. In July Sterling left for Detroit where he acted as the firm's western agent. Success came quickly to him, for he was a shrewd businessman, and his knowledge of Indian languages and French helped him gain customers. He became a householder in Detroit in 1763 and from his dwelling sold goods and dispatched merchandise to other traders as far away as Fort Miamis (probably at or near Fort Wayne, Ind.) and Michilimackinac (Mackinaw City, Mich.).

It has been suggested that Sterling's romantic involvement with Angélique Cuillerier, *dit* Beaubien, led her to tell him of Pontiac*'s plan to make a surprise attack in May 1763 on the Detroit garrison and that Sterling's warning enabled Henry GLADWIN to foil the plan. The identity of Gladwin's informant has not been established, but Angélique was in a position to know what was occurring. Shortly after their marriage Sterling wrote that she was "used to trade from her infancy, and is generally [said] to be the best interpreter of the various Indian languages at this place; her family is in great esteem amongst the Indians, so much so that her father was suspected to have been chosen by the Indians to command here in case they had succeeded."

During Pontiac's siege of the garrison in the summer of 1763 Sterling was chosen by the merchants and other volunteers to command the local militia. In 1764 he and John Duncan formed a partnership to which they later admitted John Porteous. Sterling also became a king's revenue collector and surveyor.

At the time of the American revolution, Sterling's denunciation of the administration of Lieutenant Governor Henry HAMILTON and Hamilton's appointee, Judge Philippe Dejean*, led Hamilton to accuse him of disloyalty and official misconduct and to send him to Quebec in 1777. A review of Sterling's record resulted in his release, and he returned to Detroit in December. Ill feeling between Hamilton and Sterling continued, however, and in 1778 the latter took his family first to Quebec and then to England.

Sterling's correspondence from London in 1781 indicates he continued business relations with John Porteous, then at Little Falls, N.Y. Records of accounts also document business transactions between William Park of Petite Côte (Windsor, Ont.) and Sterling until 1783. Sterling is thought to have relocated in Pennsylvania after the war, but the date and place of his death are unknown.

BURTON HISTORICAL COLLECTION STAFF

Clements Library, James Sterling, letterbook, 1761–65. DPL, Burton hist. coll., C. M. Burton, "The Beaubien or Cuillerier family of Detroit" (typescript, n.d.); John Porteous papers, Sterling to Porteous, 18 April 1781; Registres des baptêmes, mariages et sépultures de Sainte-Anne (Detroit, Mich.), 2 Feb. 1704 – 30 Dec. 1848 (5v. in 7, MS copy), II, 628, 775, 842, 852, 862; James Sterling papers, account book, 1779–83. PRO, CO 5/116, pp.291–96 (copy at PAC). *City of Detroit, Michigan, 1701–1922*, ed. C. M. Burton *et al.* (5v., Detroit, 1922), I, 202. *John Askin papers* (Quaife), I, 46–47, 108–10, 137. *Johnson papers* (Sullivan *et al.*). *Michigan Pioneer Coll.*, IX (1886), 349; XIX (1891), 310–11. *Remembrancer; or Impartial Repository of Public Events* (London), 1778, 188–91. *The revolution on the upper Ohio, 1775–1777 . . .*, ed. R. G. Thwaites and L. P. Kellogg (Madison, Wis., 1908; repr. Port Washington, N.Y., and London, 1970), 148. Christian Denissen, *Genealogy of the French families of the Detroit River region, 1701–1911*, ed. H. F. Powell (2v., Detroit, 1976). Silas Farmer, *The history of Detroit and Michigan . . .* (2nd ed., 2v., Detroit, 1889). [H. R. Howland], "The Niagara portage and its first attempted settlement under British rule," Buffalo Hist. Soc., *Pubs.* (Buffalo, N.Y.), VI (1903), 35–45.

STUDHOLME, GILFRED, army officer and office-holder; b. 1740 near Dublin (Republic of Ireland); d. unmarried 10 Oct. 1792 at Studville (Apohaqui, N.B.).

Gilfred Studholme was commissioned ensign in the 27th Foot in November 1756 and the following May was posted to Halifax, Nova Scotia. In November 1761 he received a lieutenancy in the 40th Foot and served in what he described as "the Expensive Campaigns of Martonico [Martinique] and the Havanna." When the 40th returned to Nova Scotia in 1763, Studholme was placed in command of a company stationed at Fort Frederick (Saint John, N.B.). In the summer of the same year, acting on orders from Lieutenant Governor Jonathan BELCHER of Nova Scotia, Studholme ordered a group of Acadians living in the Sainte-Anne (Fredericton) area to leave for other parts of the province. He took no measures to force their departure, however, and the Acadians remained. In 1765 Studholme left with his regiment for Ireland.

It is uncertain when he returned to Nova Scotia. In September 1771 he transferred to the 24th Foot and three years later retired from active service. With the outbreak of the American revolution his military career quickly resumed. He was commissioned in the Loyal Nova Scotia Volunteers, later served as a captain in the Royal Fencible Americans, and in December 1775 was promoted brigade-major, a rank he held until his retirement in 1783. When rebel forces under Jonathan Eddy* attempted to capture Fort Cumberland (near Sackville, N.B.) in late 1776 [*see* Joseph GOREHAM], the timely arrival of reinforcements under Major Thomas Batt and Studholme forced their retreat. American privateers and Indians incited by rebel John Allan* continued, however, to threaten settlers on the Saint John River. As a result Studholme arrived in Saint John harbour in November 1777 with orders either to repair Fort Frederick or to build a new fort.

Because of the low-lying position of Fort Frederick and the damage done to it by the rebels the previous year, Studholme decided to erect a new fortification, and his 50 men, helped by local inhabitants, began the construction of Fort Howe. In the years after its completion both the fort and its commandant Studholme made important contributions to the British cause. The "comparative security" the fort brought to the inhabitants of the Saint John area is attributed by William Odber Raymond* to "the ability and zeal" of Studholme. Fort Howe also proved useful in the complicated Indian diplomacy of Michael FRANCKLIN, superintendent of Indian affairs in Nova Scotia. Studholme himself helped in the execution of Francklin's policies and had a major role in the Indian conference of June 1780 at which the Micmacs and Malecites were neutralized. Shortly thereafter, with some satisfaction, Studholme mentioned to Lieutenant-General Frederick HALDIMAND, governor of Quebec, "The Friendship and good behaviour of the Indians in this District." Studholme conducted a correspondence with Haldimand which was necessitated by another of Fort Howe's functions, the maintenance of communications between Halifax and Quebec. He was especially attentive to this task and earned Haldimand's repeated praise for his zeal and diligence.

As the war drew to a close Studholme involved himself in a number of civilian activities. He was already leasing lands and buildings belonging to James Simonds* at the mouth of the Saint John River, and in August 1782 he received 2,000 acres as a veteran of the Seven Years' War. Shortly afterwards he acquired 5,000 acres on the Kennebecasis River, to which he gave the name Studville. The end of the war found him active in procuring land for loyalist refugees as well. In September 1783 Governor John PARR of Nova Scotia appointed him to "The care and superintending" of the loyalist settlers on the Saint John, and under his direction they were given "a hearty welcome," assigned their land, and issued materials for the construction of their homes. Surprisingly, despite the divisions among the settlers and their dislike of Parr, Studholme maintained a good relationship with both the leading loyalists and the governor. Parr turned to Studholme for advice concerning communications between Halifax and Quebec, and Studholme's acceptability to the loyalist leaders was demonstrated when he was named to the first Executive Council of the new province of New Brunswick. He remained a Council member, although never a very active one, until his death.

It might have been assumed that Studholme, a respected retired military officer with considerable property, a Council seat, and influential friends such as Ward Chipman* and Edward Winslow*, was assured a prosperous and tranquil existence. Such was not to be the case. As an agent for absentee landowners he was involved in considerable litigation; at the same time he was embroiled in disputes over his own lands and faced with a number of unpaid notes. His health, which he described as "at all times precarious and easily Shook," broke and he was a frequent invalid. He was constantly forced to beg creditors for more time in the hope that his lumber sales or hemp production would improve his financial position. By 1790 he was "very hard drove for money" and could only hope "by the sale of my Lands to get out of Debt." He retained his Kennebecasis holdings, however, and lived there until his death "with neither child nor wife to cheer his solitude." The obituary notice in the *Royal Gazette and the New Brunswick Advertiser* paid tribute to his "amiable manners, universal benevolence and liberal spirit" which "most justly endeared him to all who had the pleasure of his acquaintance." His wartime services and aid to the loyalists were deservedly remembered and appreciated by his contemporaries while his peacetime failures and difficulties were forgotten.

W. G. Godfrey

BL, Add. MSS 21723, pp.108–9; 21724, p.240; 21809, pp.57, 67, 88, 113, 139, 144–45, 160–61, 179–80, 186–89, 203, 209, 214–15, 219–22, 226–27, 230–31, 233, 235–36, 242–47, 259–60, 284, 286, 288, 293, 306–7, 309–10; 21810, pp.16, 31, 58, 76, 87, 107, 125, 134–36, 140–41, 145–46, 154–55, 171, 176, 202, 208 (PAC transcripts). PAC, MG 23, D1, 3, ff.1169–86; 6, ff.275, 296–97, 705, 727–29, 731–32, 738, 742; 18, ff.71–73, 108–9; 23, ff.76–110, 113–17; MG 23, D5, ff.14–17, 19–24, 61–67. PANB, "New Brunswick political biography," comp. J. C. and H. B. Graves (11v., typescript), IV, 40. PRO, WO 1/6, pt.2, ff.344–46. PAC *Report*, 1894, 362. "Royal commission and instructions to Governor Thomas Carleton," N.B. Hist. Soc., *Coll.*, II (1899–1905), no.6, 406. "Sunbury County documents," N.B. Hist. Soc., *Coll.*, I (1894–97), no.1, 100–18. "The James White papers," ed. W. O. Raymond, N.B. Hist. Soc., *Coll.*, II (1899–1905), no.4, 45–46, 64–65. *Winslow papers, A.D. 1776–1826*, ed. W. O. Raymond (Saint John, N.B., 1901), 119, 147, 162, 204–6, 217, 346–47, 379–80.

James Hannay, *History of New Brunswick* (2v., Saint John, 1909), I, 145–46. W. B. Kerr, *The maritime provinces of British North America and the American revolution* (Sackville, N.B., [1941?]; repr. New York, [1970]), 80–81, 91–94, 100–3. MacNutt, *New Brunswick*, 34–35, 52. L. M. B. Maxwell, *An outline of the history of central New Brunswick to the time of confederation* (Sackville, 1937), 31–33, 64, 99, 120–21. Murdoch, *History of N.S.*, III, 19–20. Raymond, *River St. John* (1943), 133, 138, 191, 216–23, 228–30, 237, 248–49, 254–55, 279. R. H. R. Smythies, *Historical records of the 40th (2nd Somersetshire) Regiment . . .* (Devonport, Eng., 1894), 553–54. E. C. Wright, *The Saint John River* (Toronto, 1949), 25, 35, 69–70. Garnet Basque, "Major Studholm's treasure," *Canadian Treasure* (Vancouver), 2, (1974), no.1, 4–9. Robert Fellows, "The loyalists and land settlement in New Brunswick, 1783–1790; a study in colonial administration," *Canadian Archivist* (Calgary), II (1971), 5–15. Neil MacKinnon, "Nova Scotia loyalists, 1783–1785," *Social History*, no.4 (1969), 17–48. W. G. Power, "Fort Howe (1777–1821)," N.B. Hist. Soc., *Coll.*, no.19 (1966), 7–16. W. O. Raymond, "Brigadier General Monckton's expedition to the River Saint John in September, 1758 . . . ," N.B. Hist. Soc., *Coll.*, III (1907–14), no.8, 113–65.

SUCKLING, GEORGE, lawyer and first attorney general of the province of Quebec; m. 8 Sept. 1759, as his second wife, Frances Duport at Halifax, Nova Scotia; fl. 1752–80.

In July 1752 George Suckling was practising law in Halifax, where he had immigrated some time before. He was also a merchant from 1753 to 1758, in partnership with William Nesbitt. Acting clerk of the General Court in 1753, he was elected to the first House of Assembly of Nova Scotia in October 1758 and soon attracted attention in Halifax and London when he violently attacked John Collier*, a judge of the Court of Vice-Admiralty, for refusing to give the house the table of the fees collected by that court. In February 1759 Suckling was accused of misappropriation of funds; although he was exonerated by the house, Governor Charles Lawrence* remained convinced of his guilt, calling him "a rascally Attorney."

When Suckling arrived in Quebec is not known. On 16 Feb. 1764 the king appointed him attorney general of the province, an office for which London merchants doing business with Canada had strongly recommended him. In this capacity his task was to give legal advice to the governor and the Council of Quebec, and to institute proceedings in the name of the crown. His commission was dated 24 Aug. 1764. A month later he was also named advocate general of the Court of Vice-Admiralty.

At the request of the Council, Suckling, with Chief Justice William Gregory, prepared the ordinance establishing civil courts. This ordinance, enacted on 17 Sept. 1764, was exceptionally important since it created a judicial organization for the province. It showed clearly, however, the juridical incompetence of the chief justice and the attorney general. The ordinance divided the province into two districts, Quebec and Montreal. It gave judicial powers to bailiffs, justices of the peace, a court of common pleas, a court of king's bench, assize courts, the governor in council, and the king in Privy Council. The jurisdiction of the bailiffs in both civil and criminal matters was limited. In court of first instance justices of the peace had authority in civil matters to judge suits dealing with property up to a value of 30 *louis* (English pounds); in appeal they could review the bailiffs' decisions. They had quite wide jurisdiction in criminal matters but it was derived more from their commissions than from the ordinance. The Court of Common Pleas, confined to civil actions, was to judge any suit involving more than 10 *louis*. The Court of King's Bench was authorized in the first instance to judge any action at law, in both civil and criminal matters; in appeal its jurisdiction extended to decisions of justices of the peace in civil matters when the object of litigation was worth more than 10 *louis*, and to those of the Court of Common Pleas when the object of litigation was worth 20 *louis* or more. The assize courts were held only rarely, although they had considerable authority in both civil and criminal matters. The ordinance gave the governor in council the right to uphold or reject appeals from judgements of the Court of King's Bench and the Court of Common Pleas in civil matters where the object of litigation exceeded £300 in value, whereas the king in his Privy Council could do the same on appeals from decisions of the governor in council when the object of litigation was worth £500 or more.

The chief justice and the attorney general erroneously believed that the Royal Proclamation of 1763 introduced British civil law into the province. Wishing to lessen the effects of this change of law and to accustom Canadians to the laws of Great Britain, they created the Court of Common Pleas to administer "equity," a vague term which the drafters of the ordinance seem to have taken in its ordinary meaning of natural justice and not in the technical sense which is given it in British law. In practice the judges of that court most often applied French laws; thus the Court of Common Pleas helped maintain those laws more than it accustomed Canadians to British laws. This judicial system was, moreover, quite illogical. When the object of litigation was worth more than 10 *louis*, the plaintiff could institute proceedings in this Court of Common Pleas or in the Court of King's Bench, which under the ordinance was supposed to apply British laws. The plaintiff thus had the choice of the laws he wanted to see applied. On appeal the situation was even worse, since there was a right of appeal from the Court of Common Pleas to the Court of King's Bench. Consequently a decision of the Court of Common Pleas based upon equity, according to the terms of the ordinance drawn up by the chief justice and the attorney general, had, by virtue of the same ordinance, to be overturned in the Court of King's Bench if British laws had not been applied. This arrangement, combined with the incompetence of most of the judges and justices of the peace, the use of English only, except in the Court of Common Pleas, and the slowness and exorbitant cost of justice, inevitably gave rise to judicial anarchy.

On the basis of Suckling's legal opinion, Governor MURRAY set up a court of chancery in the province on 1 Nov. 1764; in accordance with the generally accepted view at the time, the attorney general declared that the governor had the authority to set up such a court because, having been appointed keeper of the great seal by the king, he had in fact been appointed chancellor of the province.

Suckling did not possess the qualities required for the post of attorney general. He was a mediocre jurist, and he was acquainted neither with the French language nor with French law. He got along badly with Gregory, and even published criticisms of the chief justice in a supplement to the *Quebec Gazette* on 23 May 1765. Consequently, at Murray's request, Suckling was removed from office in 1766 and replaced by Francis Maseres*. He retained his office as advocate general, however, and practised law in the province. The ex-attorney general did not share his successor's ideas about British bankruptcy law, among other questions. Maseres advised fur-trader Lucius Levy SOLOMONS, who had been ruined and wanted to reach a final settlement with his creditors, to take advantage of the British laws on bankruptcy – laws that he claimed were in force in the province – and to have one of his creditors request a commission which, among other things, would secure the appointment of assignees charged with liquidating his assets and settling his bankruptcy. The granting of the commission by Governor Guy Carleton*, on the recommendation of Maseres and Chief Justice William HEY, upset the merchants, who protested vigorously. They alleged that the application of such laws would ruin them since they cut two ways: if they assisted merchants seeking bankruptcy, they might also put into bankruptcy merchants hoping to resolve their difficulties by other means. To defend his and Solomons' position, Maseres wrote an abstract of these laws and sent it to Carleton with a reply to the merchants' objections. William Grant* had the abstract published in the *Quebec Gazette* on 10 and 17 Dec. 1767 under the signature of "a Merchant." According to Maseres, it was Suckling and Thomas AYLWIN who defended the merchants' interests in an article published on 24 and 31 December that was signed "A Friend to Liberty, tho' not a Merchant," and that attacked the attorney general in harsh terms.

In 1768 Suckling had differences with Carleton. As advocate general he had brought an action in the Court of Vice-Admiralty, but the governor had ordered him to suspend the proceedings. Suckling protested to Hillsborough, the secretary of state for the American Colonies, and declared that this order constituted a violation of the rights and jurisdiction of both the Court of Vice-Admiralty and the advocate general.

Having disposed of his belongings, Suckling left the province in 1771, without permission and without officially resigning his office of advocate general. In October of that year, however, he was replaced by Henry KNELLER. In London, on 25 Feb. 1775, Suckling presented a petition to the king, asking for financial aid or a post; he published it in the *Quebec Gazette* on 7 September. In the petition he stated that he had already addressed himself to the "Lords Commissioners of your Majesty's Treasury," to Lord North, and to the Earl of Dartmouth, secretary of state for the American Colonies, but that he had obtained only a small sum of money. On 12 March 1776 he asked Lord George Germain for the post of secretary of Georgia or financial aid to keep him until he found employment in the legal field or else for money to enable him to settle in the West Indies with his family. His repeated demands finally met with success: in 1780 he was chief justice of the Virgin Islands. The date of his appointment is unknown, as are the date and place of his death.

JACQUES L'HEUREUX

PAC, MG 11, [CO 42], Q, 2, p.378; 3, p.3; 8, p.83; MG 23, A4, 64, p.104; C17; GII, 1, ser. 1, 2, p.189; RG 1, E1, 1, p.13; 2, pp.10, 45; RG 4, A1, 2, p.621. PRO, CO 5/114, p.57; 5/115, p.227; 5/157, p.25; 42/2, pp.44, 74 (copies at PAC). *Doc. relatifs à l'hist. constitutionnelle, 1759–91* (Shortt et Doughty; 1921), I, 180. Maseres, *Maseres letters* (Wallace). PAC *Rapport*, 1944, xxvii, xxix. *Quebec Gazette*, 23 May 1765; 10, 17, 24, 31 Dec. 1767; 7 Sept. 1775. *Directory of N.S. MLAs*, 335.

Brebner, *New England's outpost*. Burt, *Old prov. of Que.* (1968), I, 77–78, 107–9, 129, 134. A. [McK.] MacMechan, "Nova Scotia under English rule, 1713–1775," *Canada and its provinces* (Shortt and Doughty), XIII, 104–5. Neatby, *Quebec*, 35. L'Heureux, "L'organisation judiciaire," *Revue générale de droit*, 1, 266–331. W. R. Riddell, "The first court of chancery in Canada," *Boston University Law Rev.* (Boston, Mass.), II (1922), 234–36.

SURLAVILLE, MICHEL LE COURTOIS DE. *See* LE COURTOIS

SUTHERLAND, GEORGE, HBC master; b. *c.* 1755, probably in Wick (Highlands), Scotland; fl. 1774–99.

George Sutherland began his career with the Hudson's Bay Company in 1774 as the personal servant of Thomas HUTCHINS, chief at Fort Albany (Ont.), contracting for five years at £10 per annum. Although he had "received little improvement from Education" his master soon decided he was a promising employee. On 6 April 1777 Hutchins noted that he had sent Sutherland "to the Northward . . . in order to Learn him how to make Remarks in case I should send him inland." By June Sutherland had gone inland with an Indian named Caupemartissue Winnekee. Eusebius Bacchus Kitchin, chief at Moose Factory (Ont.), believed this man to be from the vicinity of Basquia (The Pas, Man.), and Hutchins in early 1778 expressed hope that, if he were, his guidance would enable Sutherland "to determine the distance of Cumberland House [Sask.] from hence," an important matter in planning inland posts and trade routes. Hutchins was pleased with Sutherland's work that year.

Listed as a labourer at £10 a year, Sutherland spent the winter of 1779–80 at Sturgeon Lake (east of Sioux Lookout, Ont.). In July 1779 he left Albany with some Canadians brought by Germain MAUGENEST into company service. Passing Gloucester House (Washi Lake, Ont.) in late August, they reached Sturgeon Lake in late September to find that Canadian traders had burned Maugenest's house there because he had absconded with furs and still owed 30,000 *livres* to Ezekiel Solomons, a Montreal merchant said to direct the local trade [*see* Lucius Levy SOLOMONS]. While building a new shelter, Sutherland learned all he could from his rivals about their trade and methods and about his remote location. Once a month he recorded in his journal detailed accounts of the pedlars and of his hardships, which included a diet of mice, boiled leather, and other "Nastyness" during late winter. Three of Maugenest's men died; the rest rejoined the Canadians. Sutherland felt that he had learned to speak the Indians' language "five times as well as any one down the bay. (my Superiors Excepted)," but his health was damaged and he was gloomy over the presence of pedlars "in Every hole and cornor."

Back at Albany in the summer of 1780, Sutherland apparently took a year's health leave. In 1781 he became steward at Albany at £20 a year. In the summer of 1785 he went to Severn House (Fort Severn, Ont.) with the packet, was briefly locum tenens there, and remained the next winter. He was transferred to York Factory (Man.) to aid Joseph Colen* during 1786–87 as "Linguist and trader" at £30, and he compiled for him "A Short Vocabulary of . . . the Northern Indian Language." In 1793 his salary reached £40.

After a year in Britain, Sutherland joined the York council at £80, taking charge of York during the 1794–95 season while Colen went home to discuss with his employers the difficulties between himself and William Tomison*, chief inland. Colen's support in London doubtless favoured Sutherland's appointment to the charge of Cumberland House in 1795–96 and the upper

Saskatchewan in 1796–97. Residing at Edmonton House (near Fort Saskatchewan, Alta), Sutherland fostered more cooperative relations with his Canadian rival, Angus Shaw*, than had Tomison. When the Fall Indians visited Edmonton House in December 1796 Sutherland and Shaw issued a joint reprimand to them for their sack of the HBC posts of Manchester House (near Pike's Peak, Sask.) and South Branch House (near Duck Lake). In mid 1797 Sutherland became the first to use large boats instead of canoes for transport on the Saskatchewan River. Two craft, each of 30 feet, were built, and they proved as useful as similar boats Sutherland had seen employed in the Albany district.

Tomison, hostile to both Colen and Sutherland and to their plans for large boats, had meanwhile visited London and regained the support of the London committee. In late 1797 he took charge once more of Edmonton and the Saskatchewan region. Sutherland was rebuked by the committee for a "rash inconsiderate Letter" to Tomison. He wintered at Buckingham House (near Lindbergh, Alta) on the North Saskatchewan River but, in the summer of 1798, refused Tomison's request that he stay inland and returned to York. Finding that Tomison had written a "most ungenerous" letter about him, he sent a public response that ended any prospect of their working together. When a letter from the London committee informed him that his brother had died in Jamaica leaving him "some considerable Property," he took the opportunity to retire.

Once in London, Sutherland convinced the committee of the benefits of using boats along the important inland route to Edmonton House. In May 1799 Tomison and the York council were told to adopt his plan to "diminish the enormous expences of the Company" and ease the scarcity of labour and the management difficulties it brought. Boats, the committee observed, "will require less than half the Number of Men employed at present in Canoes."

Sutherland had at least two children in Hudson Bay, a daughter who drowned in July 1799 at York Factory and a son, John, who served as an apprentice from 1795 until 1799, when the company granted his father's request that he join him in England. The Parklands people, a Plains Cree group of mixed origins near Duck Lake, Sask., also trace their ancestry to a George Sutherland employed by the HBC in this period.

JENNIFER S. H. BROWN

HBC Arch. A.6/16, ff.34, 55, 59, 81; A.11/116, f.178; A.11/117, ff.142, 171; A.15/15, p.467; A.30/1, ff.16, 42, 55, 72–73; A.30/2, ff.4, 40; A.30/3, ff.57, 65, 91; A.30/4, ff.23, 49; A.30/5, ff.48, 80; A.30/9, f.39; A.32/3, f.57; A.32/4, f.43; B.135/b/5, ff.24, 35; B.135/b/6, f.23; B.198/z/1, ff.129–36; B.211/a/1; B.239/a/101, ff.97, 98; B.239/f/3, f.15; B.239/f/5, f.11; B.239/f/6, ff.12, 66. *Saskatchewan journals and correspondence: Edmonton House, 1795–1800; Chesterfield House, 1800–1802*, ed. A. M. Johnson (London, 1967). D. G. Mandelbaum, "The Plains Cree," American Museum of Natural History, *Anthropological Papers* (New York), XXXVII (1941), 155–316 (especially 167).

SUTHERLAND, JAMES, HBC inland trader and master; b. *c.* 1751, probably in the Orkneys (U.K.); d. 29 April 1797 at Brandon House (Man.).

James Sutherland was recruited, probably in the Orkneys, by the Hudson's Bay Company in the summer of 1770 to serve at Prince of Wales's Fort (Churchill, Man.) for five years at £8 per annum. There he worked under Moses NORTON and probably met Samuel HEARNE. When his term of service ended in 1775 he refused to renew his contract for the same wages and so was ordered back to England by the London committee. The company, however, was firmly committed to inland expansion by the 1770s and was anxious to recruit inland traders. Sutherland, by then a resident of the London parish of St Martin's-in-the-Fields, was re-engaged on 5 Feb. 1777 for £12 per annum "to Travel from . . . [Fort Albany, Ont.] to any parts inland for the better Discovery of the Country and improving the Trade."

Sutherland's subsequent career was one of steady service and rise through company ranks. After nine months at Albany he was appointed in 1778 to serve under John Kipling, master of Gloucester House (Washi Lake, Ont.), a post which had been established the previous summer as part of the company's inland development program. In 1784 Sutherland, who was by then second at Gloucester, explored the route to Lake Nipigon and Pishocoggan Lake (Lake St Joseph). Two years later he set out from Gloucester, with John Richards and some Indians, for Lac Seul, returning on 3 Aug. 1786 after an arduous 53-day journey. In 1789 he was appointed second at Osnaburgh House and in August 1790 he continued the company's westward expansion by establishing a post on Red Lake (Ont.). In October Duncan(?) Cameron, a rival fur-trader from Montreal, arrived and built a post within 100 yards of Sutherland. The two traders spent a pleasant winter exchanging visits and celebrating various anniversaries together. Sutherland left Red Lake for Osnaburgh in the spring of 1791 with 2,400 made beaver in furs, a good return for a new post with established competition.

The endeavours of the inland traders were carefully noted by the London committee. In 1792 it informed the chief of Albany that, being particularly pleased with "the conduct and assiduity" of Sutherland, it was appointing him to the Albany council. That same year Sutherland, who was by now earning £40 with a £10 gratuity annually, built Eschabitchewan House on Lake Burdingno (Ball Lake, Ont.), and the next year he established Portage de l'Isle on the Winnipeg River near its junction with the English River (Ont.). He took charge of Osnaburgh in October 1794 at a salary of £70 per annum. Despite strong competition from the Canadian pedlars, he managed to secure a good share of the trade. In 1796 he was appointed master of Brandon House and arrived there on 13 September. By April of the next year, however, he was reported "very sick" and died the same month. He left an estate that consisted of £1,050 in consolidated Bank of England annuities.

James Sutherland was employed during a period when the company, actively competing with the Nor'Westers, had need of his dexterity with canoes, his ability to live off the land, his diplomacy with the Indians, and his willingness to undergo physical hardship. He was a religious and tolerant man, and his lack of prejudice enabled him to live in harmony with rival traders. Sutherland was eminently suited to serve the company during this highly competitive period of its history.

SHIRLEE ANNE SMITH

HBC Arch. A.1/45, ff.34d–35; A.5/4, f.27; A.6/11, f.101d; A.6/12, f.32d; A.6/15, ff.14, 16d, 17, 52d; A.11/4, f.68; A.11/14, f.136d; A.11/15, ff.6, 16; A.16/6, p.58; A.16/11, ff.76d–77; A.30/2, f.21d; A.32/3, f.14; B.3/a/74, ff.1d, 26; B.3/a/97, ff.46d–49; B.3/b/33, f.31; B.22/a/4, ff.12, 36d–37d; B.42/a/80, f.4d; B.64/a/1; B.78/a/2; B.78/a/11; B.78/a/14; B.155/a/1; B.155/a/3, f.35d; B.155/a/10, ff.14, 15, 35; B.166/a/1; B.177/a/1. *Five fur traders of the northwest . . .*, ed. C. M. Gates ([2nd ed.], St Paul, Minn., 1965). *Journals of Hearne and Turnor* (Tyrrell). Morton, *History of Canadian west*. Rich, *History of HBC*.

SYRIER. *See* CIRIER

T

TAGAWIRUNTE. *See* TEKAWIROÑTE

TARIEU DE LA NAUDIÈRE, CHARLES-FRANÇOIS (also called **Charles-François-Xavier**), officer in the colonial regular troops and seigneur; b. 4 Nov. 1710 at Sainte-Anne-de-la-Pérade (La Pérade, Que.), son of Pierre-Thomas Tarieu de La Pérade, seigneur of La Pérade, and Marie-Madeleine Jarret* de Verchères; d. 1 Feb. 1776 in Quebec.

Charles-François Tarieu de La Naudière was to serve for more than 30 years in the colonial regular troops but never acquired through the profession of arms the renown legend gave his mother, the famous Madeleine de Verchères, as a result of her youthful exploits at the Verchères fort. Yet his mother did not neglect her son's reputation, recounting that in 1722, when he was 12, he had saved her life when she was attacked by four Indian women.

Charles-François began a conventional career at an early age, and advanced through the ranks regularly like the other officers, sons of important families in the colony. In 1727 he received a commission as a second ensign. Promoted ensign in 1734 and lieutenant in 1742, in 1743 he was appointed adjutant of Quebec. On 6 Jan. 1743 he became related to a prominent family in the colony through his marriage in Quebec to Louise-Geneviève, daughter of a former captain in the colonial regular troops, Henri-Louis Deschamps* de Boishébert. Nothing is known of La Naudière's military activities during his first 20 years of service. In 1746 he apparently took part in the expedition led by Jean-Baptiste-Nicolas-Roch de RAMEZAY to blockade Annapolis Royal, Nova Scotia, but he did not participate in the attack on Grand Pré in February 1747 [*see* Arthur Noble*]. He was ordered by Governor Charles de Beauharnois* to carry out a number of missions that year. In the spring of 1748 he was sent to the Miami country, where it was important to secure the French military presence after the troubles stirred up in the west by Orontony*'s band. He seems to have carried out his mission quite well, since upon his return to Quebec in the summer of 1749 the new governor, La Jonquière [Taffanel*], requested a gratuity of 2,000 *livres* for him. The request was refused, but in May he had obtained the rank of captain.

The early 1750s marked a hiatus in La Naudière's military career. On 1 March 1750 he was granted the seigneury of Lac-Maskinongé, soon also known as Lanaudière. But he had little inclination or time to attend to his lands and instead turned to business. Having a share in a ship, in 1753 he went into partnership with commissary of the Marine Jean-Victor VARIN de La Marre to import goods from France. The following year he formed an association with his brother-in-law Jean-François Gaultier* for the exploitation of the fishing post at Chateau Bay (on the Strait of Belle Isle), of which Gaultier was the proprietor. He is also known to have had dealings with merchant-trader Jean-Baptiste Amiot* and with Pierre Révol*; in October 1756 he took part in a meeting of the creditors of Révol, who had just gone bankrupt and owed him nearly 3,000 *livres*.

But the crucial years of the Seven Years' War were beginning, and La Naudière once more was caught up in military activity. In the spring of 1756 he was in Acadia, in charge of distributing provisions to the many habitants who had had to seek refuge in the woods. He took an active part in the guerrilla operations led by his brother-in-law, Charles DESCHAMPS de Boishébert, against the English who had settled along the Saint John River. His presence the next year at the siege of Fort William Henry (also called Fort George; now Lake George, N.Y.) is not certain, but he was at Carillon (Ticonderoga, N.Y.) on 8 July 1758. Montcalm* noted his satisfactory conduct in a letter to Governor RIGAUD de Vaudreuil the day after the battle. La Naudière perhaps owed to this praise the cross of the order of Saint-Louis, bestowed on him in January 1759.

It can assuredly be said that in the following months the new knight of Saint-Louis accomplished no feats of arms. He conceived and was responsible for building *cajeux*, rafts carrying artillery, to be used to check the advance of the British fleet, then sailing up the St Lawrence. In this task he was aided by François-Louis Poulin* de Courval, who redesigned the *cajeux*. Having left for Île aux Coudres only on 22 May, La Naudière did not have time to carry out the operation. On 27 May the British landed on the island, and La Naudière beat an inglorious retreat, after ordering that the *cajeux* already built and everything of potential use to the enemy be burned. He reached Quebec on 1 June. Problems in provisioning the army were developing since relief supplies brought from France by Jacques Kanon* were insufficient. La Naudière was therefore ordered by Vaudreuil and Intendant BIGOT on 7 June to requisition all oxen and bulls in the Government of Quebec. At the end of July the ordinance was extended to the Government of Trois-Rivières. It was an unheroic but delicate and necessary task, which moved the anonymous author of a diary of the siege to observe ironically: "A bunt from a horn is not as much to be feared as a hit from a cannon." La Naudière probably took part, at the head of his soldiers, in the last two major battles of the war, on the Plains of Abraham in 1759 and at Sainte-Foy the following year.

The war years were also years of busy social activity for French and Canadian officers. In Quebec La Naudière's home was one of the centres of polite society. His company and his wife's were much appreciated during the winter months, particularly by Montcalm, who held Mme de La Naudière in high esteem and one day described M. de La Naudière to Bourlamaque* as "the best of [my] friends."

After the conquest La Naudière spent some time in France; the reasons for his trip and its duration are unknown. During his absence his wife died, in July 1762. The following summer he returned to Canada, and on 12 Jan. 1764 he married Marie-Catherine, the daughter of Charles Le Moyne* de Longueuil, second Baron de Longueuil. She was much younger than he and they had ten children. During his last years La Naudière used part of his fortune to purchase seigneuries: in 1767 he bought the fief and seigneury of Saint-Vallier from the nuns of the Hôpital Général of Quebec, and in 1769 the seigneury of Saint-Pierre-les-Becquets, which belonged to Charles Levrard. In the mean time he had transferred his rights to the seigneury of Lac-Maskinongé to Charles-Louis*, a son of his first marriage.

La Naudière's relations with the British administration were excellent. In 1766 he was one of the seigneurs in the District of Quebec who signed the address to Governor MURRAY on his departure. When Carleton* asked the British government in 1769 to admit members of the Canadian nobility to the Council of Quebec, La Naudière's was one of 12 names put forward. Indeed he did become a member of the Legislative Council created in 1775 by the Quebec Act, and the first council open to Catholics. He scarcely had time to take his seat, since he died on 1 Feb. 1776 at the Hôpital Général of Quebec.

La Naudière, who was descended from one of the great families of the colony, had an undistinguished career in the military profession to which he had devoted himself. A report written in 1761 or 1762 described him as a "very mediocre officer" but "rich." Like others, he had been able to accommodate his military career to more lucrative activities as a merchant; after the conquest he got along well with the colony's new administrators, as would his children – Charles-Louis and Xavier-Roch* in particular.

MARIE-CÉLINE BLAIS

ANQ-MBF, État civil, Catholiques, Sainte-Anne-de-la-Pérade (La Pérade), 5 nov. 1710. ANQ-Q, Greffe de

J.-C. Panet, 30 oct. 1756. "Accord entre M. de Lanaudière et M. Varin (16 octobre 1753)," *BRH*, XXXVI (1930), 395. "Charles-François-Xavier Tarieu de Lanaudière et la campagne de 1759," *BRH*, XXXII (1926), 691–95. *Coll. de manuscrits relatifs à la N.-F.*, IV, 170. *Coll. des manuscrits de Lévis* (Casgrain), III, 114, 144; IV, 104–5; V, 194, 277; VI, 94; VII, 67, 113, 422, 525, 527, 529. *Découvertes et établissements des Français dans l'ouest et dans le sud de l'Amérique septentrionale . . . mémoires et documents inédits* [1614–1754], Pierre Margry, édit. (6v., Paris, 1879–88), VI, 667–68. *Doc. relatifs à l'hist. constitutionnelle, 1759–91* (Shortt et Doughty; 1921), II, 579. *Inv. de pièces du Labrador* (P.-G. Roy), II, 100–3. "Journal du siège de Québec" (Æ. Fauteux), ANQ *Rapport*, 1920–21, 142–44, 149, 156, 163, 175, 208, 220. *NYCD* (O'Callaghan and Fernow), X, 722, 894. PAC *Rapport*, 1899, suppl., 29; 1905, I, VIe partie, 131, 279, 339.

Æ. Fauteux, *Les chevaliers de Saint-Louis*, 168. Le Jeune, *Dictionnaire*. P.-G. Roy, *Inv. concessions*, III, 237, 268–69; IV, 226; *Inv. jug. et délib., 1717–60*, VI, 43. Tanguay, *Dictionnaire*. Thomas Chapais, *Le marquis de Montcalm (1712–1759)* (Québec, 1911), 352–53, 495, 547. Frégault, *La guerre de la Conquête*, 330. P.-G. Roy, *La famille Tarieu de Lanaudière* (Lévis, Qué., 1922). Henri Têtu, "La rue Port Dauphin à Québec," *BRH*, II (1896), 78.

TEIORHÉÑHSERE? **(Tayorheasere, Teyarhasere, Tigoransera, Tiyerhasere, Tyorhansera,** called **Little Abraham** by the whites), Mohawk chief, member of the wolf clan; son of Old Abraham, a prominent chief; d. 1780 at Fort Niagara (near Youngstown, N.Y.).

Teiorhéñhsere? was a pine tree chief, an elected leader chosen for his rhetorical or military skills. He first appears in the records in 1755. In the late spring of the following year he participated in a conference between the superintendent of northern Indians, Sir William JOHNSON, and representatives of the Six Nations then gathered at Fort Johnson (near Amsterdam, N.Y.). In the Seven Years' War he led at least one war party against the French and was with AMHERST at the surrender of Montreal in 1760. He must have distinguished himself in his early career for Sir William, an accurate judge of men, called him "the Best Indian of the Mohawks."

Even in the midst of war Teiorhéñhsere? found time to use his considerable oratorical powers in a cause for which he fought most of his life – the struggle to save Mohawk lands from encroachment by whites. As one of the leaders of Fort Hunter, the lower village of the Mohawks, Teiorhéñhsere? kept up the fight for his people's lands during the 1760s. The next decade, however, was to see this struggle made much more difficult by the outbreak of revolution.

At the beginning, Teiorhéñhsere? declared that the Six Nations had "no inclination or purpose of interfering in the dispute between Old England and Boston." As he put it, the Iroquois considered the revolution "a family affair" and would "sit still and see you fight it out." Neutrality, however, proved impossible. The Mohawks were attracted to the British for many reasons: their links with the Johnson family, their regard for their missionary, John Stuart*, their resentment toward American land-grabbers, and – since the Americans could not adequately furnish the Indians with essential supplies – their reliance upon the more dependable flow of British trade goods. As a result, the Mohawks were generally regarded as friends of the crown, and after the battle of Oriskany (near Rome, N.Y.) in August 1777, many were driven from their homes to the safety of Montreal.

Teiorhéñhsere? and a few others, however, chose to remain despite considerable danger from local rebels who resented their presence. He may well have decided to stay behind because Major-General Philip John Schuyler, an American Indian commissioner, had intimated to the Mohawks that if they deserted their villages they would never be allowed to return. Quite possibly Teiorhéñhsere?, one of the few Mohawks of any stature to remain in hostile territory, did so in hopes of preventing the loss of his people's land.

While at Fort Hunter, the courageous chief tried to prevent bloodshed between rebels and loyalists, both Indian and white. Unfortunately for Teiorhéñhsere?, his neutral conduct made him a traitor in the eyes of British officials. When he went to Niagara in February 1780 to try to negotiate a prisoner exchange and to appeal for an end to Iroquois involvement in the war, he was denounced by KAIEÑ?KWAAHTOÑ and Kanonraron (Aaron Hill) and arrested by Guy JOHNSON, Sir William's successor. The ageing chief did not survive the ordeal; he died in prison. In a sense Teiorhéñhsere? was fortunate, for he was spared the pain of witnessing the irrevocable loss of his people's homeland.

RALPH T. PASTORE

National Archives (Washington), RG 360, M247, roll 172, item 153, v.1, ff.414–46, Philip Schuyler to J. Hancock, 23 Jan. 1776; roll 173, item 153, v.3, ff.286–91, Philip Schuyler to H. Laurens, 15 March 1778. New York Public Library, Manuscripts and Archives Division, Schuyler papers, Indian boxes, box 13, Conference between commissioners for Indian Affairs and the Six Nations, 26 April – 10 May 1776; box 14, Board of Commissioners for Indian Affairs in the Northern Department, minutes, 9 Jan. 1778; box 14, Jelles Fonda to the commissioners, 21 April 1778. PAC, RG 10, A2, 1822–26, 1829–32. *American archives* (Clarke and Force), 4th ser., III, 485, 487; 5th ser., I, 1040, 1045–46. *Johnson papers* (Sullivan *et al.*). *NYCD* (O'Callaghan and Fernow), VII, 115; VIII, 658–59, 725. Graymont, *Iroquois*. R. T. Pastore, "The Board of Commissioners for Indian Affairs in the Northern Department and the Iroquois Indians, 1775–1778" (unpublished PHD thesis, University of Notre Dame, Notre Dame, Ind., 1972), 125–29, 151–52, 165–77, 184, 200.

TEIYOQUANDE. *See* TEYOHAQUEANDE

TEKAWIROÑTE (Tagawirunte, William of Canajoharie, William Johnson), Mohawk warrior; the name means two infants stand out; probably born in the early 1750s at Canajoharie (near Little Falls, N.Y.), son of William JOHNSON, future superintendent of northern Indians, and an unidentified Mohawk woman; probably d. 6 Aug. 1777 at Oriskany (near Rome, N.Y.).

In 1764 his father sent Tekawiroñte to Moor's Indian Charity School in Lebanon, Connecticut. Eleazar Wheelock, the Congregationalist minister who had established the school, was at first pleased with the boy's behaviour but later complained of his pride and violent temper. The students were required to labour as well as to study, but when Tekawiroñte was ordered by Wheelock's son to saddle his horse, the boy refused because, he said, he was the son of a gentleman and Wheelock's son was not. On 10 Dec. 1766 Tekawiroñte was sent home as "too litigious."

In 1767 his father sent him to Thomas Barton, a Church of England clergyman at Lancaster, Pennsylvania, to continue his education. The youth was conducting himself well and beginning to learn surveying when some murders of Indians and other lawless actions against them by Pennsylvania frontiersmen caused him to become morose and lose interest in his work. In March 1768 he was sent home. There Tekawiroñte was often in neighbourhood trouble, and in June 1770 his father threatened to "take no farther notice of him." However in 1774, when Sir William died, he left the youth 1,000 acres of land, £100, and enough livestock to start a farm.

In May 1775, at the approach of the American revolution, Guy JOHNSON, successor to Sir William as Indian superintendent, fled to Canada, taking with him many Mohawk warriors, among them Tekawiroñte. Tekawiroñte apparently participated in the defence of Canada against the invading Americans in that summer's campaign around Lake Champlain and the upper St Lawrence. He fought at Fort Saint-Jean on 6 Sept. 1775 and was erroneously reported killed. He returned home later in the fall, boasting about his exploits and making threats. This behaviour did not please his neighbours, and brawling seems to have ensued. Late in 1775 he stabbed a man to death in a tavern fight and fled home forever.

He went first probably to the Indian country and then on to Fort Niagara (near Youngstown, N.Y.). In the spring of 1776 John BUTLER, the acting Indian agent, sent the youth to a Six Nations council at Onondaga (near Syracuse, N.Y.) in an attempt to prevent the Oneidas from breaking the Iroquois League and siding with the Americans. This embassy failed. The Oneidas were deeply attached to their rebel missionary, Samuel Kirkland, and the Americans made great efforts throughout the war to supply them with enough trade goods to live upon.

Tekawiroñte led a small party that captured two rebel soldiers near Fort Bull, east of Oneida Lake, in the fall of 1776. In the spring of 1777 he met Joseph Brant [Thayendanegea*], who was probably a relative, and about 300 other Indians and loyalists at the Indian village of Oquaga (near Binghamton, N.Y.). When Barrimore Matthew ST LEGER set out on his march to the Mohawk valley Brant's party joined him at Oswego, N.Y. It took part that summer in the siege of Fort Stanwix (Rome, N.Y.) and the ambush at Oriskany in which a William Johnson, probably Tekawiroñte, was killed.

ISABEL T. KELSAY

Hamilton College Library (Clinton, N.Y.), Kirkland MSS, Dean to Kirkland, 22 March 1776; Kirkland to Philip Schuyler, [8 June 1776]. N.Y. Hist. Soc. (New York), Tryon County committee of safety papers, 30 Dec. 1775. N.Y. State Library (Albany), Fonda papers, Jelles Fonda notebook, list of Indians killed at Oriskany. PAC, MG 19, F1, 25, p.63. *American archives* (Clarke and Force), 4th ser., III, 739, 1245; 5th ser., III, 755. *The documentary history of the state of New-York . . . ,* ed. E. B. O'Callaghan (4v., Albany, N.Y., 1849–51), IV, 351, 367. *Johnson papers* (Sullivan *et al.*). N.Y., Secretary of state, *Calendar of historical manuscripts, relating to the war of the revolution, in the office of the secretary of state, Albany, N.Y.* (2v., Albany, 1868), I, 190. *NYCD* (O'Callaghan and Fernow), VIII, 658–62, 719–21. "Proceedings of a general court martial . . . for the trial of Major General Schuyler . . . ," N.Y. Hist. Soc., *Coll.*, [ser.3], XII (1879), 103–4.

TERLAYE, FRANÇOIS-AUGUSTE MAGON DE. *See* MAGON

TERNAY, CHARLES-HENRI-LOUIS D'ARSAC DE. *See* ARSAC

TERROUX, JACQUES, silversmith and merchant; b. in Geneva (Switzerland), son of François Terroux; fl. 1725–77. [See *DCB*, III.]

ANQ-MBF, Greffe de L.-C. Maillet, 11 juill. 1777.

TESSIER (Texier), *dit* **Lavigne, PAUL** (he signed **Tesier**), master mason and contractor; b. 22 Oct.

1701 at Montreal (Que.), son of Jacques Tessier (Texier), *dit* Lavigne, and Marie Adhémar, *dit* Saint-Martin; d. 20 Oct. 1773 at Longue-Point (Montreal).

Paul Tessier, *dit* Lavigne, was the son of a Montreal Island *censitaire* and the grandson of the carpenter-sawyer who established the Tessier, *dit* Lavigne, family in Canada. In November 1719 Paul's father apprenticed him to Louis-Jean Denys, a Montreal edge-tool maker, for three years. This arrangement was short-lived, for in the following March Paul was indentured for three years to Jean Deguire to learn the stonemason's craft. Paul's cousin Dominique Janson*, *dit* Lapalme, was also a masonry contractor at this time, as had been another cousin, Pierre Couturier*, *dit* Le Bourguignon.

After his training Paul resorted, like so many others, to the fur trade in order to obtain the capital he needed to establish himself as an independent craftsman and householder. In April 1726 he and his younger brother Jacques signed on as voyageurs for Constant Le Marchand* de Lignery, Jean Lemire Marsolet, and François Augé. Jacques only made a round trip to Michilimackinac (Mackinaw City, Mich.) via "La Grande Rivière" (Grand River, Ont.), but Paul, for 300 *livres*, went into the country beyond and returned the following year. Paul's earnings allowed him to buy a town lot next to his father's property on Place d'Armes on the north side of Rue Saint-Jacques in November 1727. There he had a small, wooden, one-storey house, which he may have built for himself, since he ran up a substantial debt with Pierre COURREAUD de La Coste over the next two years. Paul's bright prospects enabled him to marry on 19 April 1728 the young widow of Jean-Baptiste Descaris, Jeanne Lefebvre, who had a daughter by her previous marriage. In his marriage contract Tessier described himself as a "master mason and stone-cutter." The Tessiers had six children of whom three daughters survived childhood. As well as bearing the responsibility of parenthood, Paul, as the eldest living son, acted on behalf of his brothers and sisters in legal matters and took care of his mother after she was widowed in 1738.

By 1737 Tessier had become a successful master builder in Montreal, employing three stonemasons and an apprentice. Private dwellings provided most of his work and the most famous of these was the Château de Ramezay, which he repaired and enlarged in 1740–41. In 1749 he embarked on construction of the king's storehouse near the Beauharnois gate. The stone structure was two and a half storeys high, with a vaulted cellar, and measured 120 by 40 *pieds*; it was Tessier's greatest undertaking. In 1756 he contracted to restore and extend the residence of the Compagnie des Indes in Montreal and to provide a cut stone entrance "like that of the intendant's palace." For each of these projects Tessier hired stonemasons and labourers and made subcontracts with wood suppliers and carriers of sand and pebbles.

Tessier's enterprise procured a comfortable existence which is revealed by the estate inventory made in 1760 after his wife's death. His home was adorned with clocks, plaster busts and parrots, and a painting of the Virgin Mary. Tessier slept on a luxurious bed worth 600 *livres* and ate at a table for which there were wineglasses, a silver service, and porcelain coffee cups and plates. Nonetheless, the builder was semi-literate and owned no books. Subtracting foodstuffs over-valued at 2,417 *livres*, Tessier had movable assets worth 5,421 *livres*, 9 *sols* against a debt of 3,300 *livres*. To his misfortune, he held paper bills of credit from the government with a face value of 18,720 *livres*. Worse still, he acquired more of this rubbish before the transfer of Canada to Great Britain and lost a considerable amount of money when the French government refused to honour the bills. To cap his misfortunes, Tessier's house was destroyed by fire in April 1768, and many of his remaining assets were sold at the suit of the merchant John Porteous, likely for debts owed. His fortune gone, Tessier appears to have moved in with the children of his uncle, Paul Tessier, *dit* Chaumine, at Longue-Pointe, and there he died.

PETER N. MOOGK

[Since there were three persons named Paul Tessier, *dit* Lavigne, in 18th-century Montreal, the researcher faces an identification problem. There were the subject of this biography, his uncle, and his cousin. P.N.M.]

AN, Col., F^3, Cartes et plans, 82, 85 (mfm. at PAC). ANQ-M, Doc. jud., Juridiction de Montréal, 11, ff.108, 218; Greffe de J.-B. Adhémar, 2 nov. 1719, 6 nov. 1724, 14 janv. 1725, 22 avril 1726, 1er févr., 7, 9 mars 1737, 6 mars 1740, 31 déc. 1743; Greffe de L.-C. Danré de Blanzy, 24 août 1756, 2 juin 1760; Greffe de Jacques David, 6 mars 1720; Greffe de N.-A. Guillet de Chaumont, 25 févr. 1729, 22 mai 1730; Greffe de J.-C. Raimbault, 9 oct. 1731; Greffe de François Simonnet, 26 sept., 7 oct. 1740, 29 mai 1741, 17 mars, 8 sept. 1749. "État général des billets d'ordonnances . . . , ANQ *Rapport*, 1924–25, 259. *L'île de Montréal en 1731: aveu et dénombrement des messieurs de Saint-Sulpice, seigneurs de Montréal*, Antoine Roy, édit. (Québec, 1943), 42–43. "Procès-verbaux sur la commodité et incommodité dressés dans chacune des paroisses de la Nouvelle-France par Mathieu-Benoît Collet, procureur général du roi au Conseil supérieur de Québec," Ivanhoë Caron, édit., ANQ *Rapport*, 1921–22, 296–97. "Recensement de Montréal, 1741" (Massicotte), 42.

Quebec Gazette, 24 Jan. 1765, 28 April, 12 May 1768, 17 Aug. 1769, 5 Dec. 1771, 6 Jan. 1774, 2 Aug. 1781, 25 Aug. 1785. Massicotte, "Répertoire des engagements pour l'Ouest," ANQ *Rapport*, 1929–30, 251. P.-G. Roy, *Inv. jug. et délib., 1717–60*, V, 85. Tanguay, *Dictionnaire*, I, 562; VII, 275. Archange Godbout, "Urbain Tessier, dit Lavigne," SGCF *Mémoires*, XI (1960), 6–21. É.-Z. Massicotte, "Maçons, entrepreneurs, architectes," BRH, XXXV (1929), 132–42. Antoine Roy, "Le coût et le goût des meubles au Canada sous le Régime français," *Cahiers des Dix*, 18 (1953), 236.

TESTARD DE MONTIGNY, JEAN-BAPTISTE-PHILIPPE, officer in the colonial regular troops; b. 15 June 1724 in Montreal (Que.), to Jacques Testard* de Montigny and Marie-Anne de La Porte de Louvigny; m. 27 Oct. 1748 in Montreal, Marie-Charlotte Trottier Desrivières, and they had nine children; d. 3 Nov. 1786 at Blois, France.

In order to learn Indian languages and customs Jean-Baptiste-Philippe Testard de Montigny probably went to Michilimackinac (Mackinaw City, Mich.) with his father, who was commandant there from 1730 to 1732. In 1736 he became a cadet in the garrison of Fort Saint-Frédéric (near Crown Point, N.Y.). His father died the following year, leaving his mother to care for five sisters, while Montigny continued to serve as a scout in the borderlands between Canada and New York. The young soldier gained a thorough knowledge of the woods, and acquired skill in leading bands of soldiers and Indians on scouting parties. Montigny's enthusiasm and ability were recognized and duly rewarded; on 1 April 1742 he was provisionally appointed second ensign and on 31 May 1743 he achieved the full rank.

In the War of the Austrian Succession, Montigny served under Paul Marin* de La Malgue during the successful attack on the fortified post of Saratoga (Schuylerville, N.Y.) in 1745. Later given an independent command, he led more than 30 raids on the New York and Connecticut frontiers. Early in 1748 he was promoted ensign in Louis Herbin's company. Montigny remained at Fort Saint-Frédéric until 1751. On 1 April 1753 he was commissioned lieutenant; Governor DUQUESNE referred to him as an active officer "who has an admirable zeal."

Tensions were increasing between France and Britain over control of the Ohio country, and Montigny was assigned to transport provisions to the western points. Between 1753 and 1755 he led a number of supply convoys to Detroit, Fort des Miamis (probably at or near Fort Wayne, Ind.), and Fort Niagara (near Youngstown, N.Y.). As hostilities flared, Montigny led a contingent of Indians to Fort Duquesne (Pittsburgh, Pa) to aid in its defence against Major-General Edward Braddock's forces, and he helped win the stunning victory of 9 July 1755. After the battle he assisted in salvaging the abandoned British artillery supplies and in retrieving the body of his commandant, Daniel-Hyacinthe-Marie Liénard* de Beaujeu, killed in the first exchanges of gunfire.

Early in 1756 Montigny was second in command to Gaspard-Joseph CHAUSSEGROS de Léry in the daring overland raid on Fort Bull (east of Oneida Lake, N.Y.), and he personally led the assault on the fort's gates. After a sharp fight the British post was overrun and destroyed, and the French retreated through the forest. Back in Montreal, Montigny organized a force of 62 men in 12 canoes to carry supplies for Montcalm*'s attack on Chouaguen (Oswego). Following the capture of that post in August, Montigny and his men went on to Detroit and Fort des Miamis, where he informed the western Indians of the declaration of war between Britain and France and urged them to fight for the French king.

Promoted captain on 1 May 1757, Montigny spent the year convoying supplies to Detroit. After another trip to Detroit in the early summer of 1758, he led 500 soldiers to reinforce Fort Niagara, which was threatened by increased British activity in the west. During the next few months he led another 600 men to Niagara, and on 1 June 1759 he was sent from that post with a force to capture Fort Pitt, which the British had built to replace Fort Duquesne, destroyed the previous year. Shortly after he left Niagara, however, it was unexpectedly besieged by the British under Brigadier-General John Prideaux and Sir William JOHNSON. Hastily recalled, Montigny joined with François-Marie Le Marchand* de Lignery, Louis LEGARDEUR de Repentigny, and Joseph MARIN de La Malgue and their men in marching to its aid. On the 24th, within sight of the fort, they ran into an ambush carefully prepared by Johnson. Their force was shot to pieces; Montigny, who suffered three wounds including a shattered hand, was captured. The Indians sold him to the British and he spent two years as a prisoner in New England before being exchanged. Early in 1762 he was apparently in Paris. That June, St John's, Newfoundland, was captured by Charles-Henri-Louis d'ARSAC de Ternay, and when reinforcements were sent to the French garrison there, Montigny was assigned to the frigate *Zéphir*, commanded by François-Louis Poulin* de Courval. The *Zéphir* was captured by British ships, however, and Montigny was briefly imprisoned in England before returning to Saint-Malo in November.

Montigny's long and distinguished military career was over. As a fitting conclusion, he had been made a knight of the order of Saint-Louis in August 1762. At the end of the Seven Years' War, lured by the Duc de Choiseul's promise of a pension, Montigny decided to remain in France rather than live under British rule in his native Canada. After returning to Canada to sell his goods and collect his family, he landed in Calais on 19 Nov. 1764 and settled into retirement at Blois, where he lived until his death.

DAVID A. ARMOUR

AN, Col., D[2C], 41, p.185; 48 (copies at PAC). PAC, MG 18, H7. Bougainville, "Journal" (A.-E. Gosselin), ANQ *Rapport*, 1923–24, 213–14, 216, 363–67. [G.-J. Chaussegros de Léry], "Journal de Joseph-Gaspard Chaussegros de Léry, lieutenant des troupes, 1754–1755," ANQ *Rapport*, 1927–28, 361–62, 371, 381; "Les journaux de campagnes de Joseph-Gaspard Chaussegros de Léry," A.[-E.] Gosselin, édit., ANQ *Rapport*, 1926–27, 350, 354–55, 358–59, 364, 374, 376, 380, 391. *NYCD* (O'Callaghan and Fernow), X. *Papiers Contrecœur* (Grenier), 49, 60, 67–69, 73, 75, 348, 390, 400, 417. [J.-G.-C. Plantavit de Margon, chevalier de La Pause], "Continuation du journal de la campagne, 1759," ANQ *Rapport*, 1933–34, 120; "Mémoire et observations sur mon voyage en Canada," ANQ *Rapport*, 1931–32, 23, 26, 29–30; "Les 'mémoires' du chevalier de La Pause," ANQ *Rapport*, 1932–33, 308–10. Æ. Fauteux, *Les chevaliers de Saint-Louis*, 191. Massicotte, "Répertoire des engagements pour l'Ouest," ANQ *Rapport*, 1931–32, 326–29, 333, 339, 342, 348–49, 351–52, 356, 358–63; 1932–33, 250. Tanguay, *Dictionnaire*, VII, 283–84. Gilbert Hagerty, *Massacre at Fort Bull, the de Léry expedition against Oneida Carry, 1756* (Providence, R.I., 1971). F. H. Severance, *An old frontier of France: the Niagara region and adjacent lakes under French control* (2v., New York, 1917).

TEYARHASERE. *See* TEIORHÉÑHSERE?

TEYOHAQUEANDE (Deiaquande, Diaquande, Teiyoquande, Tiahogwando, Tüyaguande), Onondaga warrior and sachem; fl. 1756–83.

Teyohaqueande, a chief warrior of the Onondagas, was among a delegation sent to Montreal by the Six Nations in the summer of 1756. The group conferred with Governor Vaudreuil [RIGAUD], and Teyohaqueande took the opportunity of the journey and his four weeks in Montreal to gather intelligence which he subsequently reported to Sir William JOHNSON, the British superintendent of northern Indians. He was in Canada again the following year.

In the summer of 1759, when many warriors from the Six Nations joined Johnson in attacking the French in the Niagara region, Teyohaqueande was on an expedition against the Catawbas. When he returned he met Johnson at Oswego (N.Y.), where Brigadier-General GAGE was considering an attack against La Galette (near Ogdensburg, N.Y.), the next obstacle on the route to Montreal. On 6 Sept. 1759 Teyohaqueande set off for his village, intending to return in six days with his warriors. While he was at home one of his children died but he cut short his mourning to arrive at Oswego before the end of the month. After much uncertainty the British decided to postpone the attack until the next year, and most of the Six Nations returned to their villages. When forces re-gathered at Oswego in the summer of 1760 Teyohaqueande was present and, unlike many of his people who returned home after Fort Lévis fell, he accompanied AMHERST and Johnson to Montreal.

In March 1761, bereaved by numerous deaths in his family, Teyohaqueande returned the insignia of office, a medal and a flag, which he had been awarded when Johnson recognized him as a sachem. The superintendent sent them back to him with a message of consolation and a request that Teyohaqueande retain his leadership. The sachem resumed his responsibilities and carried them through the difficult post-war years. He was present at Johnson Hall (Johnstown, N.Y.) in March 1763 for discussions concerning the murder of two members of a British trading party in Seneca country. Johnson was attempting to get the Six Nations to turn over the murderers so that British justice could be administered, but they argued "that it was better to Accomodate Matters already bad enough, than to shed further Blood thereon." At this meeting the Onondagas announced the appointment of Teyohaqueande and five others to share the responsibilities of the older sachems for the management of the confederacy. The next year they informed Johnson of the selection of Teyohaqueande and Onughranorum "to assist in their Councils." The gravity of the appointment was signified by the powerful traditional symbol of two wampum strings.

On 28 April 1765 Teyohaqueande spoke on behalf of those Six Nations warriors who had accompanied John BRADSTREET the previous summer on his expedition against Pontiac*'s supporters. Bradstreet, he claimed, had "let them Suffer greatly for want of the necessarys they expected . . . [and] a Drunken Man would have spoke & acted better than he did." The warriors wished compensation for their mistreatment. He spoke again in July at the signing of treaties between the British and the Shawnees, Delawares, and Mingos. He warned these tribes (over whom the confederacy exercised some authority) that the agreements must not be broken, for "the Supreme Being whose Worshiper & Servant our Great King & Father is can punish you, because all these promises & engagements have been entered upon before Him. . . ."

In the autumn of 1767, after more deaths in his family and the death of Karaghiagigo, an important Onondaga warrior, Teyohaqueande returned his insignia of office to Johnson. Bereavement was not his sole reason. The loss of Karaghiagigo had left the Onondagas divided, and Teyohaqueande was at the head of one faction. The lines of division are not certain, but it appears that Teyohaqueande was doubtful whether his people would ever obtain redress of their grievances against the British. Once again Johnson reassured him. In the following year he was present at the negotiation of the treaty of Fort Stanwix, which established a line demarcating the Indian domain. Early on the opening morning of a major conference at German Flats (near the mouth of West Canada Creek, N.Y.) in 1770, however, the Bunt [HOTSINOÑHYAHTAˀ] and the speaker of the Six Nations informed Johnson that Teyohaqueande had again "refused to attend to business" and had "encamped with another Nation." As he was the head warrior of the Onondagas, his behaviour would impede the proceedings, and they asked the superintendent to persuade him to return. Johnson did so after some discussion with him. In 1773 he went on behalf of Johnson to investigate the murder of some Canadian traders which had occurred in Seneca country. He returned in time to attend a conference at Johnson Hall in January 1774 called to deal with the hostilities between the whites and the Shawnees.

Teyohaqueande spoke at a gathering of September 1774 at Johnson Hall, voicing regrets at Johnson's death that summer and welcoming his successor, Guy JOHNSON. The account of the meeting describes Teyohaqueande as "a Chief who had long enjoyed Sir William's particular confidence." His alignment with the British and the Johnsons endured. He attended meetings in 1775 at which the Americans attempted to secure the neutrality of the Six Nations in the coming struggle. Replying to the American commissioners, he raised the Wyoming valley question, a land controversy long a source of grievance to the Iroquois [*see* Karaghtadie*]. In January 1777 he was among the Oneidas with a message from the British agent John BUTLER, summoning them to Fort Niagara (near Youngstown, N.Y.). The Oneidas refused to go. Most of them, like most of the Tuscaroras, favoured the Americans during the war. Majorities of other nations of the confederacy allied themselves with the British and suffered devastating raids on their settlements. Teyohaqueande spent six weeks of the summer of 1779 in Quebec as part of an attempt to get more assistance from the British. Governor HALDIMAND, who addressed the delegation on 20 August, dismissed Iroquois apprehensions of a major American attack on their villages, but as he spoke a rebel army under John Sullivan was marching into Indian country. Diplomatic missions during the rest of the war took Teyohaqueande on various journeys, but his headquarters were at Niagara with the thousands of Iroquois refugees. Haldimand was appalled at the expense of aiding the homeless families and was constantly pressing for more to be done to make them self-supporting. Groups of them were sent out to sow corn to reduce the demand for provisions; in May 1781 Teyohaqueande was listed as the chief of 277 Onondagas gone to Buffalo Creek, N.Y., to plant. In July 1783 he attended a conference at Niagara where Sir John Johnson*, superintendent general of Indian affairs, assured the Iroquois that the peace agreement between the British and Americans was not intended to deprive the Six Nations of their lands. He must have listened with a sceptical ear.

IN COLLABORATION

BL, Add. MSS 21767, ff.181, 264. PAC, MG 19, F1, 3, p.249; 25, p.169. *Johnson papers* (Sullivan *et al.*). *NYCD* (O'Callaghan and Fernow). Graymont, *Iroquois*. L. H. Morgan, *League of the Ho-dé-no-sau-nee, or Iroquois* (new ed., 2v., New York, 1901; repr. 2v. in 1, 1922). S. F. Wise, "The American revolution and Indian history," *Character and circumstance: essays in honour of Donald Grant Creighton*, ed. J. S. Moir (Toronto, 1970), 182–200.

THIREL (Tirel), THOMAS. *See* PICHON, THOMAS

TIAHOGWANDO. *See* TEYOHAQUEANDE

TIGORANSERA (Tiyerhasere). *See* TEIORHÉÑHSEREˀ

TOMAH (Tomas, Tomer, Tomma), PIERRE, Malecite chief; fl. 1775–80 in the Saint John valley (N.B.).

During the American revolution the Malecite Indians seemed important to the European conquerors of North America for the last time. The governments of rebellious Massachusetts and loyal Nova Scotia believed these inhabitants of the Saint John valley and their neighbouring tribes held the balance of power north of the Bay of Fundy. Leaders of both colonies remembered earlier struggles with the Indians and French and, anticipating similarly devastating raids, vied with each other for Indian support. The Malecites, however, were reluctant to enter combat. During the preceding century they had watched Massachusetts destroy tribe after tribe. Demoralized by these defeats and economically depressed by the decline of the fur trade, they sought to preserve what remained of their traditional way of life. The diplomatic situation was difficult for they needed to balance between Massachusetts, with its genocidal methods of warfare against Indians, and the British in Nova Scotia, with their growing presence on the Saint John. The disputes that caused the war were of no concern to the tribe, but after years of fighting colonial neglect it desperately needed the provisions that the warring colonies would furnish in return for support.

In response to a Massachusetts initiative of May 1775 the Malecites moved to establish closer relations with the Americans. Pierre Tomah and Ambroise SAINT-AUBIN arrived at the Penobscot truck house (Bangor, Maine) in September and dispatched a letter of support to the rebel government. The chiefs asked that goods be sent them and stated that they had no other place to trade. The Massachusetts government responded, and more than a year of close cooperation followed. Tomah and Saint-Aubin led a Malecite contingent which accompanied Jonathan Eddy*'s attack on Fort Cumberland (near Sackville, N.B.) in the fall of 1776. In December Tomah and others met with George Washington on the banks of the Delaware River. Massachusetts did its best to supply the tribe with provisions. Early in 1777 it even attempted to establish a truck house on the Saint John at Maugerville. The British, however, drove the Americans from the Saint John in July. This evidence that the rebels could not protect the tribe on its ancestral territory caused a rift among the Malecites. Tomah's group was willing to swear allegiance to Britain to forestall hostilities and to try to accommodate both sides. Most of the tribe, however, fled with Saint-Aubin to Machias (Maine).

From this time on, Tomah travelled freely between the British and the Americans, performing occasional services for both. He delivered letters for the American agent John Allan* and in 1778 helped him avoid a split among the Indians at Machias, some of whom, excited by France's entry into the war, wished to give her their immediate support. He also stopped a threatened assault on James White, the British deputy Indian agent for the area, who was attempting to prevent a Malecite attack on settlements near Fort Howe (Saint John). In September 1778 at a major conference at Menagouèche, near Fort Howe, Tomah signed a treaty with the British and a letter forbidding Allan to interfere with the Indians east of Machias. A year later, however, he was back in Machias, assuring Allan that he had acted out of fear and offering to renounce all connection with the British if Allan would provision the tribe. When the Americans could not meet his demands, he led the Malecites eastward to Passamaquoddy Bay. On 31 May or 1 June 1780 he told the American agent that the tribe appreciated his efforts but that poverty and religious zeal required them to meet Michael FRANCKLIN, Nova Scotia's superintendent of Indian affairs, who was waiting on the Saint John with supplies and an Acadian priest (Joseph-Mathurin BOURG). Tomah's name subsequently disappears from the records but he probably led the Malecites until after the end of the war. In any case, the policies he devised must have guided them since they "lived at the joint expense of the contending parties."

Traditional Canadian and American writers saw Tomah's activities as evidence of the manipulation of the Malecites by the government. That ethnocentric view did not admit that the Indians were capable of designing and executing a policy to meet their own purposes, and it led to castigation of the Malecites for their "weaknesses of Indian nature" and their failure to rally to the proper cause. Tomah's ability to protect his people and make the war serve their ends, however, clearly confounds such a low opinion of Indian capabilities.

RICHARD I. HUNT

PAC, MG 11, [CO 217], Nova Scotia A, 72, pp.44–45; 74, p.94; 75, pp.24–25, 41–42; 78, pp.83–85; 83, pp.19–24; 87, pp.123–24; 97, pp.209, 228; 98, pp.180–83; 101, pp.134, 268–69; 102, pp.16, 52–53; [CO 220], Nova Scotia B, 12, pp.158–59; 13, p.216; 14, pp.90–91. *Documentary history of Maine* (Willis *et al.*), XIV–XIX, XXIV. *Military operations in eastern Maine and N.S.* (Kidder). J. H. Ahlin, *Maine Rubicon; downeast settlers during the American revolution* (Calais, Maine, 1966). R. I. Hunt, "British-American rivalry for the support of the Indians of Maine and Nova Scotia, 1775–1783" (unpublished MA thesis, University of Maine, Orono, 1973). R. H. Lord *et al.*, *History of the archdiocese of Boston in the various stages of its development, 1604 to 1943* (3v., New York, 1944), I. Raymond, *River St. John.*

TONGE, WINCKWORTH, army officer, officeholder, politician, and landowner; b. 4 Feb. 1727/28 in County Wexford (Republic of Ireland); m. Martha Cottnam, and they had four sons, including William Cottnam*; d. 2 Feb. 1792 in Halifax, Nova Scotia.

Winckworth Tonge devoted his early years to a military career. He first saw service in 1743 as a volunteer in Captain Charles Knowles's expedition against the Spanish American settlements. Subsequently Tonge became an ensign in the 45th Foot and served in garrison at Louisbourg, Cape Breton Island, from 1746 to 1749, when his regiment was sent to assist in the establishment of Halifax [*see* Edward CORNWALLIS]. Commissioned lieutenant on 8 April 1755, Tonge served as assistant engineer to John BREWSE in the capture that year of Fort Beauséjour (near Sackville, N.B.) [*see* Robert MONCKTON]. He saw service under AMHERST at the siege of Louisbourg in 1758 and under Wolfe* at Quebec the following year. With the fall of Quebec his active military career came to an end, and he apparently left the army some time between 1763 and 1765.

By that time Tonge had begun to acquire large tracts of land in Nova Scotia. His first grant, about 130 acres, was received shortly after the fall of Beauséjour and was situated in what was soon to become Cumberland County. His holdings in what later became Hants County dated from 1759 and 1760 and included about 5,000 acres. Over the next 15 years he devoted considerable time and money to his property; writing in 1774, Governor Francis LEGGE observed that Tonge had spent over £3,000 in agricultural improvements. When the American revolution broke out, Tonge volunteered for military service and was made colonel in the militia on 5 Sept. 1781. Partly because his duties demanded much of his time, and partly because he suffered heavy losses at the hands of American privateers, by the end of the revolution his savings were "dissipated and a considerable debt incurr'd." He never recovered financially; by 1789 he had been forced to sell most of his property, including Winckworth, his estate in Hants County.

Although Tonge's financial affairs had taken a turn for the worse, he remained an important political figure in the colony. In 1759–60 he had sat in the House of Assembly for Cumberland County, and he represented Kings County from 1765 to 1783 and Hants County from 1785 until his death. Governor Legge wrote in 1774 that Tonge was esteemed by his constituents and "well Attached to the Interest of the Country." His involvement in provincial affairs was extensive. At various times he served as justice of the peace, *custos rotulorum* for Hants, justice of the Inferior Court of Common Pleas for Hants, and provincial surveyor or superintendent of roads, bridges, and public works.

Tonge's most important appointment came in 1773, when he was sworn in as naval officer for the colony. His chief duty was the careful regulation of shipping between Nova Scotia and Europe, Asia, Africa, and America. The position was to make him the centre of political controversy for many years. Within a few months of his appointment he managed to alienate the governor, Lord William CAMPBELL. Before 1773 the governor had appointed deputy naval officers throughout the colony, a prerogative Tonge now claimed as his own. Tonge sought to regulate the activities of these officers and claimed half their fees for himself. His behaviour created a furor in both business and political circles, especially when he increased the fees collected. Appeals were urgently sent to the Board of Trade for relief. According to Lord Dartmouth, the secretary of state for the American Colonies, Tonge was "in right of his Commission . . . to appoint Deputies" and had the power to collect fees. He made it clear, however, that the Board of Trade was opposed to the collection of fees since they felt the salary of the naval officer was sufficient for his support: "If Mr Tonge thinks fit to avail himself of the Act of Parliament, and receive Fees, their Lordships will not think him intituled to receive the Salary." Tonge opted for the salary since the fees were inconsiderable.

Tonge's political stock seems to have risen considerably in 1774, when Governor Legge recommended him, "a Gentleman of good Character & Reputation," for appointment to the Council. This political manœuvre by the governor to form an alliance with one of the leading members of a hostile assembly failed; Tonge balked at Legge's advances and the governor withdrew his recommendation.

Tonge's position as naval officer brought him into renewed conflict with the assembly and the mercantile community following the American revolution. In an attempt to limit the widespread smuggling that was taking place Tonge endeavoured to enforce the navigation laws rigidly, and to increase his income he again began to collect fees. Reaction was swift. The attorney general, Sampson Salter Blowers*, protested in 1786 that Tonge was exceeding his powers, and the assembly even debated whether the naval office should be abolished. Faced with this general assault on his position, Tonge fought back: "I do declare & can Prove, I have not in any Instance Demanded anything but what is fully authorized by Acts of Parliament . . . and that so far from being Exorbitant in my Demand of Fees, they are by no means Adequate to the Trouble and Expense of Keeping Offices Open."

The debate between Tonge, the assembly, and the mercantile community continued over the next few years. In 1790 the matter was settled and a fee table established. Although more restricted than in the past, the naval office was still intact when Tonge died, a tired but resolved man, in 1792.

RONALD H. MCDONALD

PANS, MG 1, 250A (Cunningham family docs.), 2, docs.88–92; RG 1, 31–33, 40–48; RG 5, A, 2, 1786, 3, 25 March 1790. PRO, CO 217/26, pp.161, 165ff.; 217/35, pp.236ff.; 217/50, pp.3ff., 127ff.; 217/58, pp.318ff., 324ff.; 218/5–12; 218/14; 218/17–21; 218/25–27 (mfm. at PANS). G.B., WO, *Army list*, 1756, 1763, 1765. N.S., House of Assembly, *Journal*, 1759–92. *Directory of N.S. MLAs*. Beck, *Government of N.S.* Brebner, *Neutral Yankees*. M. G. MacG. Morison, "The evolution of political parties in Nova Scotia, 1758–1848" (unpublished MA thesis, Dalhousie University, Halifax, 1949). Murdoch, *History of N.S.* Porter, *History of Royal Engineers*, I, 171. A. W. H. Eaton, "Rhode Island settlers on the French lands in Nova Scotia in 1760 and 1761," *Americana* (New York), X (1915), 1–43, 83–104, 179–97.

TONNANCOUR, CHARLES-ANTOINE GODEFROY DE. *See* GODEFROY

TONNANCOUR, LOUIS-JOSEPH GODEFROY DE. *See* GODEFROY

TOOSEY, PHILIP, Church of England clergyman and agriculturist; baptized 18 March 1744/45, son of the Reverend John Toosey, rector of Hessett (Hetheringsett), Suffolk, England; m. Sarah Denton in 1770, and they had three children; d. 14 Sept. 1797 at Quebec.

Philip Toosey attended Winchester School and St Paul's School, London, and he matriculated to Cambridge (Trinity Hall) in 1762. Ordained deacon in 1765 and priest in 1769, he became rector of Stonham, Suffolk, in the latter year and retained this living, to which another was later added, throughout his life. In 1784 the Reverend Lewis Guerry resigned as incumbent of Sorel (Que.), a parish from which he had been an absentee since 1775. The annual stipend of £200 which had been paid by the British government to Guerry was now transferred to Toosey, who immigrated to Quebec with his family in 1785. As he came without any definite ecclesiastical appointment, and as the rector of Quebec, the Reverend David-François De Montmollin*, did not require his assistance, he was able in 1786 to journey to Detroit, where he baptized Indian children. Much attracted by the land and climate of Detroit, he requested the Society for the Propagation of the Gospel to station him there as a missionary, but his request was refused.

His manners and abilities commended him to Lord Dorchester [Carleton*], as well as to the bishop of Nova Scotia, Charles Inglis*, who in 1789 licensed Toosey to assist Montmollin at English services in Quebec and appointed him ecclesiastical commissary of the eastern district of Canada. When a Church of England bishop for Quebec was being proposed, Toosey went back to England in the spring of 1792 to submit a claim for the post. Disappointed in this endeavour, he returned to Quebec in 1794, resumed clerical duties, and was appointed ecclesiastical commissary for Lower Canada by Bishop Jacob Mountain*. From July 1796 to August 1797 he was curate at Christ Church, Montreal. After his death the family returned to England. It is known that a son, James, educated under his father, had matriculated to Cambridge in 1794.

Toosey engages the interest of the historian more as a farmer than as a clergyman. His 70-acre farm in his Suffolk parish was described by the noted agriculturist Arthur Young, who found Toosey "a very accurate and ingenious cultivator." After he arrived in Quebec he obtained, in concert with Kenelm Chandler*, title to a large tract of land 18 miles from the capital. In this new township, which he named Stoneham after his English parish, Toosey set about creating an estate in the forest. His property had to be approached by water since no road had been built. In September 1791 he wrote to Young, saying that he had "erected a very complete barn, lofty enough to give shade all round it for fifty cows or oxen, stables for twelve horses, and flanked by sheephouses and hog-sties." Shortly before his death he had, according to Isaac Weld*, "a neat boarded little mansion," a farmyard "exactly in the English style," a barn, "the largest in all Canada," and he had erected several log houses for people he had brought out from England to help clear and settle the land. He was one of the founders, and director, of the Quebec Agricultural Society in 1789.

Toosey appears to have been a superior squire-parson of the 18th-century type. He apparently had private means to augment his moderate professional income and hence was able to take financial risks. His few letters in Young's *Annals of Agriculture* show him to have been an able writer with a tendency to romanticize, but also a practical, intelligent farmer and an enthusiastic promoter of settlement.

T. R. MILLMAN

BL, Add. MSS 21735/2, pp.82, 114 (PAC transcripts). PAC, MG 11, [CO 42], Q, 2, p.678; 28, p.161; 49, p.343; 59/1, p.598; 61/1, p.203; 66, pp.271–76, 281, 304–6; 69/2, pp.236–37, 402–3, 485; 72/2, pp.403–13; 77, pp.307–8; 79/2, p.343. QDA, 72 (C-1), 9, 14, 19, 23–26, 30–33, 129, 130; 84 (D-3), 20 March, 19 April, 25 June, 26 Nov. 1792. USPG, Journal of SPG, 24, p.377. Agricultural Soc. in Canada, *Papers and letters on agriculture recommended to the attention of the Canadian farmers* (Quebec, 1790). *Annals of Agriculture and Other Useful Arts* (London), ed. Arthur Young, 1784–1815. *Gentleman's Magazine*, 1791, 895, 979. [E. P. Gwillim (Simcoe)], *The diary of Mrs. John Graves Simcoe . . .*, ed. J. R. Robertson (Toronto, 1911; repr. 1973). Isaac Weld, *Travels through the states of North America, and the provinces of Upper and Lower Canada, during the years 1795, 1796, and 1797* (London, 1799). *Quebec Gazette*, 28 July 1785, 2 Nov. 1797, 21 Feb. 1799, 4 Dec. 1833. *Alumni Cantabrigienses . . .*, comp. John and J. A. Venn (2pts. in 10v., Cambridge, Eng., 1922–54), pt.II, VI. T. R. Millman, *Jacob Mountain, first lord bishop of Quebec, a study in church and state, 1793–1825* (Toronto, 1947). H. C. Stuart, *The Church of England in Canada, 1759–1793; from the conquest to the establishment of the see of Quebec* (Montreal, 1893). F.-J. Audet, "Le clergé protestant du Bas-Canada de 1760 à 1800," RSC *Trans.*, 2nd ser., VI (1900), sect.I, 140–41.

TRÉMAIS, CHARLES-FRANÇOIS PICHOT DE QUERDISIEN. *See* PICHOT

TROTTIER DUFY DESAUNIERS, THOMAS-IGNACE (he also signed **Dufy Desauniers**), merchant and militia captain; baptized 21 Dec. 1712 in Montreal, son of Pierre Trottier Desauniers, a merchant-trader, and Catherine Charest; m. in 1747, in Quebec, Marie-Thomas, daughter of Joseph de Fleury* de La Gorgendière, a merchant; d. 21 March 1777 in Montreal.

Thomas-Ignace Trottier Desauniers, who was related to several important families in Canada including the Charests, adopted from the Charests the name Dufy and subsequently was known as Dufy Desauniers. His brother, Pierre Trottier* Desauniers, and his cousin, Étienne CHAREST, seigneur of Lauson, owned thriving businesses in Quebec. It was not surprising, then, that Dufy Desauniers became a merchant. As such he was active in the deliberations of the assembly of merchant-outfitters of Montreal. In addition, in 1753 he was elected a church warden of Notre-Dame in Montreal and in 1775 the head church warden.

It is, however, Dufy Desauniers's military career that is better known. Having entered the king's service in either 1729 or 1737 (he gave both dates), he became captain of one of the companies of Montreal militia in 1745. In that capacity he took part in nearly all the campaigns of the Seven Years' War. Serving in turn under Vaudreuil [RIGAUD], Montcalm*, and LÉVIS, he earned praise as "one of those [officers] who most distinguished themselves in the Canadian militia."

In a letter of 1764 pointing out his services to the minister of the Marine, the Duc de Choiseul, Dufy Desauniers noted that he had "sacrificed his own interests for the king's service, for which, during all the time that he served, he received no allowances, emoluments, or gratuities whatever." He asked for the cross of the order of Saint-Louis, insisting he was only awaiting this favour to leave Canada for France with his family and fortune, which Vaudreuil valued at 12,000 *livres* in annual income. The decoration was denied because "His Majesty is firmly decided not to grant any to anyone for some time."

In 1772 Dufy Desauniers was somewhat surprised to receive a letter from France assuring him that the king was ready to confer the said cross when he settled in France. Now used to the new régime, and not disposed to leave his country for the pleasure of wearing a decoration, Dufy Desauniers confided his embarrassment to the lieutenant governor of Quebec, Hector-Théophilus CRAMAHÉ. Cramahé referred the problem to Lord Hillsborough, the British secretary of state for the Colonies, who informed the Duc d'Aiguillon, the French minister of foreign affairs, of the British court's surprise and hope that this offer was only an error, because Dufy Desauniers, having become a British subject, was no longer eligible for the honour. When the Duc d'Aiguillon went to the council of Marine for further information, the president explained that the Sieur Dufy was to have been decorated only if he went to live in France. Dufy Desauniers having refused to move, the incident was closed.

After the conquest Dufy Desauniers had got along well with the British authorities in Montreal. In 1775, at the time of the American invasion and the re-establishment of the Canadian militia by Governor Guy Carleton*, he was appointed colonel of the Montreal militia units. In 1777 the governor decided to call him to the Legislative Council, but Dufy Desauniers died in March.

JACQUELINE ROY

AN, Col., E, 148 (dossier Desauniers). ANQ-M, État civil, Catholiques, Notre-Dame de Montréal, 21 déc. 1712, 23 mars 1777. ANQ-Q, État civil, Catholiques, Notre-Dame de Québec, 25 mai 1747. Claude de Bonnault, "Le Canada militaire: état provisoire des officiers de milice de 1641 à 1760," ANQ *Rapport*, 1949–51, 439–41. Æ. Fauteux, *Les chevaliers de*

Saint-Louis, 81–83. P.-G. Roy, "Thomas-Ignace Trottier Dufy Desauniers," *BRH*, XXIV (1918), 379–80. "Une chambre de commerce à Montréal sous le Régime français," *BRH*, XXXII (1926), 121–22.

TÜYAGUANDE. *See* TEYOHAQUEANDE

TUGLAVINA (Tuglawina, Tukelavinia, baptized **William)**, a leader among the Labrador Inuit; b. *c.* 1738; m. *c.* 1770 to MIKAK; d. 4 Oct. 1798 at Nain, Labrador.

Tuglavina was born and raised at a time when there were no European settlements in northern Labrador and when contacts between Europeans and the Labrador Inuit were of a sporadic and often hostile nature [*see* John Christian Erhardt*]. Although little is known of his early years, the second half of his life is well documented in the diaries of the Moravian missions which were established during his lifetime at Nain (1771), Okak (1776), and Hoffenthal (Hopedale) (1782) [*see* Jens HAVEN]. When first mentioned by the Moravians, in 1770, he was an *angakok* (a native religious leader) and the husband of Mikak, who was well known to the missionaries because of her recent stay in England. With Mikak he served as a pilot on the Moravian sloop sent to select a suitable location for Nain, and once the mission was established he became a frequent visitor. In 1775 he took three of the Moravians in his own boat to seek a building site for Hoffenthal, and five years later he allowed one of the missionaries to travel with him to the caribou hunting camps in the interior.

From the early years of their marriage Tuglavina and Mikak had frequent quarrels and they eventually separated after he had taken several additional wives, one of whom was Mikak's sister. In 1782 he took a fourth wife, a mark of exceptional prestige at a time when polygyny was a common and desired form of marriage among the Labrador Inuit but when even the most successful men had only two or three spouses. Later in the same year Tuglavina made a journey to Chateau Bay (on the Strait of Belle Isle) in southern Labrador where he traded at some of the fishing and sealing posts recently established in the area. Having obtained muskets and gunpowder, which the Moravians had been unwilling to supply at their trading stores, he persuaded many of the baptized Inuit to leave the Moravian missions and follow him south on subsequent trips. He became a successful middleman, taking trade goods to the Inuit who lived north of the missions and carrying south in his large two-masted sloop valuable raw materials such as baleen. In spite of his success many of his followers left him, and he became obsessed with the fear that his enemies were plotting revenge for his part in past murders of Inuit.

Tuglavina's southern trading journeys seem to have ceased by 1790, when his sloop became unseaworthy and he had only a single dog to pull his sled. In that year he moved with his only remaining wife to the mission at Nain. He had been baptized at Chateau Bay in 1783 while suffering from a serious illness and in 1793 he was accepted into the church congregation at Nain. He seems to have become a strong advocate of Christianity in his later years. He died of pleurisy in 1798 and was buried in the mission cemetery.

J. GARTH TAYLOR

Archiv der Brueder-Unitat (Herrnhut, German Democratic Republic), Hopedale diary, 1782–84. Moravian Church Archives (London), Hopedale diary, 1784–98; Journal of the voyage of the Jersey packet to Labrador and Newfoundland taken from the papers of Jens Haven and Christian Drachard, 1770; Nain diary, 1771–98; Okak diary, 1776–98. J. G. Taylor, *Labrador Eskimo settlements of the early contact period* (Ottawa, 1974); "William Turner's journeys to the caribou country with the Labrador Eskimos in 1780," *Ethnohistory* (Tucson, Ariz.), 16 (1969), 141–64.

TURNOR, PHILIP, HBC inland surveyor; b. *c.* 1751; d. 1799 or 1800.

When first engaged by the Hudson's Bay Company on 30 April 1778, Philip Turnor was described as a resident "of Laleham Middx. 27 yrs. age not marry'd brot up in farming business." Recommended to the London committee by William WALES, who had spent the winter of 1768–69 at Prince of Wales's Fort (Churchill, Man.), Turnor signed on with the company to serve as an inland surveyor for three years at £50 per annum, and sailed for York Factory (Man.), arriving there on 24 Aug. 1778.

Although the company had previously encouraged such servants as Joseph Robson* and Anthony Henday* to survey and explore its holdings in Rupert's Land, Turnor was the first to be engaged specifically as a surveyor to map "the Lattitudes and Longitudes of all their settlements . . . also their respective distances from each regularly adjusted." After surveying the grounds of York he was ordered by Humphrey MARTEN, chief at York, to map the route to Cumberland House (Sask.) and the newly established post of Upper Hudson House (near Wandsworth, Sask.), and then, if possible, to make his way to Fort Albany and Moose Factory (Ont.) "thro the Lakes inland." He reached Cumberland on 11 Oct. 1778 and the following March he, William WALKER, and others set out with a dog-team on the 280-mile journey over ice to Upper Hudson

House, arriving there on the 19th. He was prevented from attempting to survey the Canadians' upper settlement, in the Eagle Hills (to the south of Battleford, Sask.), by the news that a band of Indians had killed two of the Canadians and plundered the post. Turnor returned to York on 15 July by canoe with the information he later incorporated into his "Chart of the rivers and lakes falling into Hudsons Bay according to a survey taken in the years 1778 & 9."

Turnor was next involved in surveying the route from Albany to its two outposts, Henley House (at the junction of the Albany and Kenogami rivers, Ont.) and Gloucester House (Washi Lake, Ont.). After spending the early winter of 1779 at Albany with Thomas HUTCHINS, Turnor set out in February 1780 to walk to Henley with five others. Eleven days later he arrived, snow-blind and exhausted. He rested until mid-March, but was prevented from continuing to Gloucester by lack of provisions, and returned to Albany. In June 1780 he set out for Gloucester once more, by canoe, and reached it on 8 July. Returning to Albany on 11 August, he sailed to Moose in September, and that December he walked back to Albany "to take a sketch of the coast as it appears in Winter." On 22 Jan. 1781 he set out to visit Rupert River (Que.) and Eastmain House (at the mouth of Rivière Eastmain, Que.). After failing in his attempt to walk to Mesagamy Lake (Kesagami Lake, Ont.) in April, Turnor travelled in May to Wapiscogamy (later Brunswick) House (near the junction of the Opasatika and Missinaibi rivers, Ont.), Moose's new outpost. He spent June surveying the route from there to Michipicoten House, a Canadian post at the mouth of the Michipicoten River on Lake Superior. He then tried to reach the Canadian post on Lake Abitibi (Ont.) but found the rivers too difficult. He was back at Moose on 13 July. A second attempt to get to Abitibi in August failed, but Turnor agreed when he renewed his contract in September 1781 to trade at Abitibi. While at Moose he drew plans in March 1782 for a new post at Henley. That May he left for Abitibi, returning on 2 August.

Although employed as a surveyor, Turnor took charge of Brunswick House on 14 Oct. 1782. During the winter he suffered so badly from rheumatism that he was unable to go down to Moose in March 1783 to consider company policy after the capture of York and Prince of Wales's Fort by the Comte de Lapérouse [GALAUP]. Turnor served as master at Brunswick until the spring of 1784, when he was ordered to establish a new post "towards Abitibi." He left Moose in June with two large and four small canoes and two new bateaux. All his craft proved defective, however, and he was forced to stop 80 miles short of Lake Abitibi. After wintering at the junction of the Abitibi and Frederick House rivers, he moved south the following spring and built a post on the shores of Frederick House Lake (Ont.). He served there as master until July 1787, when he was sent out to survey the Canadian posts in the Lake Abitibi-Lake Timiskaming region. He then returned to Moose and sailed for England in command of the *Beaver* sloop on 9 September.

In London Turnor worked on his maps and in November 1788 was paid 20 guineas by the HBC for his "Draught of several inland settlements belonging to the company." He was also probably consulted about the notion of establishing a trade route from the Saskatchewan River to Lake Athabasca (Alta) and from there to the Pacific. Peter Pond*, a Montreal-based trader, had traded at Lake Athabasca in 1778–79, making an enormous profit and producing a map which made a route to the Pacific seem feasible. The possibility of a trade route through Rupert's Land, in an age still hoping for a northwest passage to China, concerned Alexander Dalrymple, Samuel HEARNE, William Wales, and the London committee. Turnor, who had recovered his health, was engaged on 16 May 1789 primarily to establish the position of Lake Athabasca and to find a route to it from the Saskatchewan River. He reached York Factory on 27 August and left for Cumberland, arriving there on 7 October.

During the winter of 1789–90 at Cumberland Turnor taught surveying to Peter Fidler* and David Thompson*, who was recovering from a broken leg. In June 1790, while awaiting the arrival of supplies, Turnor met Alexander Mackenzie*, who told him of his trip down the Mackenzie River (N.W.T.) to the sea. Turnor wrote that Mackenzie "*thinks it the Hyperborean Sea but he does not seem acquainted with Observations which makes me think he is not well convinced where he has been.*"

The party that set out for Lake Athabasca on 13 September consisted of Malchom Ross and his Indian wife and two children, Turnor, Fidler, and four Orkney servants, all in two canoes. Badly provisioned, the party was constantly helped by Canadian traders. At Île-à-la-Crosse (Sask.) its members wintered in two houses lent to them by Patrick Small, a Canadian, who also provisioned them when they set out the following May. Turnor arrived at Fort Chipewyan (Alta), on Lake Athabasca, on 28 June 1791. From there he canoed down Slave River to Great Slave Lake (N.W.T.). Deciding it was too late to explore farther to the northwards, he returned to Lake Athabasca and spent most of August trying to find a way from the east end of the lake into

Churchill River. He then returned to a house which Ross was building near the Canadian fort. Turnor, who kept a careful record of the trade at Fort Chipewyan, considered the post to be "*the Grand Magazine of the Athapiscow Country*," and concluded that the Canadians could afford to compete at a loss elsewhere as long as they kept their monopoly of the rich Athabascan trade. Convinced that the Indians would patronize a HBC post if one were built there, he began preparations for his return journey in April, before the ice was clear from the Athabasca River, in the hope of getting to York in time to persuade the council there to send supplies and establish a post. Although he reached York on 17 July, he did not carry his point, since, as he believed, William Tomison*, chief inland, "had set his face against any undertaking to the Northward." Turnor returned to England in October 1792.

In London the apathy of the York council was overruled. In 1793 Ross was ordered to organize an expedition to the Athabasca country and to establish a post there. Though the project proved endlessly difficult it ultimately proved crucial to the company's fortunes. In the mean time Turnor worked on his maps and in 1795 was given by the London committee the watch he had used on his trips as well as £100 "in consideration of his services in having surveyed the Company's several Settlements & explored several New Tracts & laid down the same in a large and accurate Map."

In retirement Turnor lived at Rotherhithe (London), and taught navigation. Apart from his formal relations with the HBC little is known of him. Obviously a courageous and conscientious man and a competent traveller and surveyor, he left no intimate or personal records. He must have died shortly after 4 Dec. 1799, when he last wrote to the company, for on 26 March 1800 the London committee read "a Petition from Elizabeth Turnor Wife of Philip Turnor Geographer to this Company, lately deceased, praying for some pecuniary assistance."

The importance of Turnor's work lies within the general context of the surveying effort launched by the HBC in 1778. Seeking to establish the positions of its inland posts and the river routes that linked them, the company amassed a wealth of information concerning the interior of North America that was published as a map in 1795 by Aaron Arrowsmith, the London cartographer. Entitled "A map exhibiting all the new discoveries in the interior parts of North America," the Arrowsmith map was often reissued and became the basis of many subsequent maps of Canada. Indeed, as Arrowsmith wrote in 1794, the work of the company's servants, Turnor among them, "had laid the permanent Foundation for the Geography of that part of the Globe."

E. E. RICH

HBRS, XIV (Rich and Johnson), XV (Rich and Johnson). *Journals of Hearne and Turnor* (Tyrrell). [Alexander Mackenzie], *The journals and letters of Sir Alexander Mackenzie*, ed. and intro. W. K. Lamb (Cambridge, Eng., 1970). *Moose Fort journals, 1783–85*, ed. E. E. Rich and A. M. Johnson, intro. G. P. de T. Glazebrook (London, 1954). [David Thompson], *David Thompson's narrative, 1784–1812*, ed. R. [G.] Glover (new ed., Toronto, 1962). Rich, *History of HBC*, II.

TYORHANSERA. *See* TEIORHÉÑHSERE?

TYRELL, THOMAS. *See* PICHON, THOMAS

U

UMFREVILLE, EDWARD, HBC and NWC fur-trader and author; b. *c.* 1755; fl. 1771–89.

Nothing is known of Edward Umfreville's life prior to 1771, when he was engaged by the Hudson's Bay Company to serve as a writer. He shipped to York Factory (Man.) but was soon transferred to Severn House (Fort Severn, Ont.). Severn's master for the 1772–73 season, Andrew Graham*, was impressed by Umfreville, writing that he was "A very pretty Accountant and does very well at Severn." The two men worked together in drawing up a remarkably detailed loading-table of requirements for the inland posts the company proposed to establish, a project to which Graham had only recently been converted. He and Umfreville shared the conviction that success depended on the use of Canadian servants and the large birch-bark canoes developed by the Canadian pedlars. While at Severn in 1774 Umfreville met Samuel HEARNE, who had come to confer with him and Graham about the requirements of the proposed post at Pine Island Lake (Cumberland Lake, Sask.).

The next year Umfreville was transferred to York. His time there was not happy, for he was under the command of Humphrey MARTEN, who was by 1775 a sick and irritable man. Marten, for his part, described Umfreville in 1778 as diligent and sober, but of a violent temper, and early the next year he banished him from the officers' table for insolence. Umfreville was given command of the post, however, when Marten's health gave way. He subsequently served as second to Marten until 1782 when the post was captured by the Comte de Lapérouse [GALAUP], and its officers and men taken prisoner to France.

After the treaty of Paris in 1783 Umfreville made his way to London. His salary had not been credited to him while he was a prisoner, and it was almost inevitable that when he had drawn the small balance due to him "some disagreement . . . in point of salary" should have arisen between him and the company. He quit the HBC and probably wrote the letters to the *Morning Chronicle and London Advertiser* that appeared in April 1783, describing the capture of York in terms highly critical of both the company and Marten. That month Umfreville sailed for Quebec, arriving there in June. By May 1784 he had joined the North West Company and was engaged in an attempt to find an alternate way from Lake Superior to Lake Winnipeg, part of the traditional route via the Grand Portage (near Grand Portage, Minn.) having been placed within American territory by the recent treaty. Although Umfreville succeeded in finding a route via Lake Nipigon (Ont.), the Nor'Westers continued to use the old one since the American claims were not enforced.

From 1784 until 1787 Umfreville served the NWC on the North Saskatchewan, commanding at its most westerly post (near Frenchman Butte, Sask.). From that vicinity he wrote in 1785 to Edward JARVIS, master of the HBC's post at Albany (Fort Albany, Ont.), and made clear to him that the Nor'Westers' ability to compete successfully with the HBC rested on the provisions that could be got from the "Fire Country" north and northwest of Kaministikwia (Thunder Bay, Ont.). Though in the employ of the NWC he urged the HBC to push into this country from Gloucester House (Washi Lake, Ont.), its most southerly post. His suggestion was given added credibility by John Kipling, master of Gloucester, who wrote in 1786 that Umfreville was able to stay inland all year and drive a good trade.

In line with these personal contacts, Umfreville had decided by 1788 to leave the service of the NWC. He communicated his desire to re-enter the employ of the HBC to William Tomison*, chief inland. He then left his post in May to travel via Lake Superior, Montreal, and New York to London, where he proposed himself to the London committee in letters of 23 January and 22 April 1789. Tomison had recommended him the previous July as "a fitt Person for Inland service, being hardy and durable, strictly sober, and has a thurrow knowledge how business is carried on by the traders of Canada," but Umfreville and the company could not agree on terms for his re-employment. This failure marked the end of his career as a fur-trader. Even if terms had been settled, it is unlikely that he would have made a satisfactory employee, for he had presumably written *The present state of Hudson's Bay* . . . before his negotiations with the company had come to an end. The book, published in 1790, was marked by a knowledge of the country that most writers on Canada in the late 18th-century lacked. It was also characterized, however, both by extensive plagiarism from the works of other HBC officers, especially Andrew Graham, and by bitter attacks on them and the company. Umfreville's former friend, Samuel Hearne, ascribed the book's ill nature to the author's disappointment over not "succeeding to a command in the Bay, though there was no vacancy for him."

Umfreville had been "under the necessity of going abroad" even before the publication of his book, but where he went, where he lived thereafter, and where and when he died are not known.

E. E. RICH

Edward Umfreville, *The present state of Hudson's Bay* . . . (London, 1790; new ed., ed. W. S. Wallace, Toronto, 1954).

HBC Arch. A.6/10, ff.123, 126d; A.11/115, f.161. HBRS, XIV (Rich and Johnson), XXVII (Williams). Hearne, *Journey from Prince of Wales's Fort* (Tyrrell). *Nipigon to Winnipeg: a canoe voyage through western Ontario by Edward Umfreville in 1784, with extracts from the writings of other early travellers through the region*, ed. Robert Douglas (Ottawa, 1929). [David Thompson], *David Thompson's narrative, 1784–1812*, ed. R. [G.] Glover (new ed., Toronto, 1962). Morton, *History of Canadian west*. Rich, *History of HBC*.

V

VANCOUVER, GEORGE, naval officer and explorer; b. 22 June 1757 at King's Lynn, England, sixth and youngest child of John Jasper Vancouver, deputy collector of customs at King's Lynn and a descendant of the titled Van Coeverden family, one of the oldest in Holland,

and Bridget Berners, daughter of an old Essex and Norfolk family that traced its ancestry back to Sir Richard Grenville of *Revenge* fame; d. 12 May 1798 at Petersham (Greater London), England.

George Vancouver entered the Royal Navy in 1771. Some person with influence evidently brought him to the attention of James COOK, then preparing for the second of his three great voyages of discovery, for in January 1772 Cook appointed Vancouver to his ship, the *Resolution*. Though he had the nominal rank of able-bodied seaman, Vancouver was actually a midshipman-in-training. William WALES, a noted astronomer, was a supernumerary on board, and Vancouver was privileged to receive instruction under him. The voyage, in search of the legendary southern continent, lasted three years and ventured as far south as 71°10′.

In February 1776 Cook appointed Vancouver a midshipman on the *Discovery*, which was to accompany the *Resolution* on his third expedition, sent out in search of a Pacific outlet to the fabled northwest passage. The ships arrived off the northwest coast of America in March 1778. Vancouver's shipmates included Joseph Billings*, George DIXON, and Nathaniel Portlock*, all of whom later commanded trading vessels that visited this coast. When Cook happened upon King George's Sound (Nootka Sound, B.C.) on 29 March and refitted there, Vancouver and his shipmates became the first Europeans known to have landed on the coast of what is now British Columbia [*see* Juan Josef PÉREZ Hernández]. After exploring the coast well to the north, Cook sailed to the Sandwich (Hawaiian) Islands, where he was killed in a clash with the natives on 14 Feb. 1779. Vancouver had narrowly escaped a like fate the previous day. The expedition returned to England in October 1780, and on the 19th Vancouver passed the examination for lieutenant. His eight years' service with Cook had given him an incomparable opportunity to receive training in seamanship and hydrographic surveying under the greatest navigator of the age.

Vancouver's career falls into three well-defined periods: first, the years with Cook, then nine years in fighting ships, and finally, the voyage of discovery. The middle period was spent almost entirely in the Caribbean. On 9 Dec. 1780 he was appointed to the sloop *Martin*, which was sent to the West Indies early in 1782. In May he joined the much larger *Fame* (74 guns) and served in her until peace was proclaimed and she returned to England in July 1783. The end of hostilities meant that many ships were decommissioned, and Vancouver found himself on half pay for the next 15 months. In November 1784 he was appointed to the *Europa* (50 guns), flagship of Admiral Alexander Innes, the new commander-in-chief of the Jamaica station. The death rate in the West Indies from yellow fever and other diseases was appalling, but the vacancies resulting from deaths often provided opportunities for promotion. Early in 1787 Admiral Innes died and was succeeded by Commodore Alan Gardner, an energetic and progressive officer, destined to rise rapidly in the service and to become a member of the Board of Admiralty early in 1790. He also became Vancouver's friend and influential patron, and deaths enabled him to promote Vancouver second lieutenant of the *Europa* in November 1787 and first lieutenant (second in command) two months later. In 1789, after a five-year cruise, the *Europa* headed for home waters, where Vancouver was paid off in mid September.

At this time interest in the Pacific was increasing sharply. Southern whaling was attracting attention, and settlement had just begun in New Holland (Australia). But it was the northwest coast of North America that was of most immediate concern to Great Britain. Sea otter skins picked up casually by the crews of Cook's ships had brought high prices in China, and when this fact became known trading vessels began to frequent the coast [*see* James HANNA; John KENDRICK]. Britain was interested in the commercial opportunities the fur trade might offer and was not prepared to accept Spain's contention that she held exclusive title to the whole coast from San Francisco to Prince William Sound (Alas.). In addition, the Admiralty was anxious to find out once and for all whether or not a passage existed between the Pacific and the Atlantic. Cook had proved that there was none of commercial value north of 55°N. The possibility remained, however, that Alaska might be a vast island, made so by a passage farther south.

In the autumn of 1789 it was decided to send an expedition to settle the question. A suitable ship of 340 tons burthen was purchased, named *Discovery*, and commissioned on 1 Jan. 1790. The command was given to Captain Henry Roberts, who, like Vancouver, had sailed with Cook on his second and third voyages. Through Gardner's influence, Vancouver was appointed second in command.

The work of outfitting the *Discovery* was well advanced when details of the famous Nootka Sound affair reached London. The seizure of several British ships there in time of peace, by the Spanish commander Esteban José MARTÍNEZ, was denounced as an insult to the nation's honour, and Spain's claim to have the right to exclude foreign traders from the area was hotly denied. A powerful naval squadron was mobilized and Britain prepared energetically for war. Spain was in no position to fight and was forced to agree to the Nootka Sound Convention, signed on 28 Oct. 1790 in Madrid. Under its terms Spain was to make restitution to British subjects whose property had been seized, and, more important, to abandon her claim to exclusive ownership and occupation of the coast.

Mobilization had halted the outfitting of the *Discovery*; in May her officers and crew had been assigned to fighting ships. Roberts had gone to the West Indies and Vancouver had joined the *Courageux*, commanded by Gardner. When news of the signing of the convention was received early in November, preparations for the expedition to the Pacific were resumed immediately. On the 17th Vancouver was recalled to London, and on 15 December, no doubt on Gardner's recommendation, he was appointed to command the *Discovery*.

His instructions, dated 8 March 1791, dealt with two matters in addition to the survey of the coast. First, he was to receive from Spanish officers at Nootka "such lands or buildings as are to be restored to the British subjects"; secondly, he was to winter in the Sandwich Islands and while there complete a survey of them. As for the main purpose of the voyage, he was to examine the coast between 30° and 60°N and to acquire "accurate information with respect to the nature and extent of any water-communication" which might "in any considerable degree" serve as a northwest passage "for the purposes of commerce." The *Discovery*, accompanied by the small armed tender *Chatham* (131 tons), sailed from Falmouth, their last port of call in England, on 1 April 1791. The voyage to the northwest coast was to last over a year and was made by way of Tenerife (Canary Islands), the Cape of Good Hope, New Holland, New Zealand, Tahiti, and the Sandwich Islands. Vancouver had expected to meet a supply ship, the *Daedalus*, in the Sandwich Islands, but she failed to appear. He sailed on to his main objective, the coast of North America, which was sighted on 17 April 1792. The landfall was in latitude 39°27′N, about 110 miles north of San Francisco.

Sailing north, he began the survey that he was to continue through all the complexities of the coastline to a point beyond 60°. Juan de Fuca Strait, to which he had been directed to give particular attention, was reached on 29 April. Vancouver has been much criticized for his failure to enter the Columbia River, the mouth of which he passed as he sailed northward; it is evident, however, that he suspected its existence but decided to leave it for later examination. Indeed, he paid little attention to rivers, since the mountains visible in the distance made it highly unlikely that they would be navigable for any considerable distance inland. Moreover, he had been directed, in order to save time, "not to pursue any inlet or river further than it shall appear to be navigable by vessels of such burthen as might safely navigate the pacific ocean."

His plan for the survey was simple: he would trace every foot of the continental shore, so that no passage could escape him. The featureless coasts of what are now Oregon and Washington were easily surveyed, but the shore north of Juan de Fuca Strait was another matter. Vancouver first realized the difficulties of his task when he explored the maze of inlets branching off Puget Sound (Wash.). The Admiralty had sent the *Chatham* with the *Discovery* in the expectation that the smaller ship could survey narrow waters into which it would be imprudent for the *Discovery* to venture; but Vancouver quickly learned that tidal and wind conditions, and often sheer depth of water that placed the bottom beyond the reach of an anchor, created hazards even for the *Chatham*, and he was compelled after a month's experience to fall back on the ships' pinnaces, cutters, and launches, however laborious and dangerous service in open boats might be. Once the *Discovery* and *Chatham* had found a suitable anchorage the boats would set out to explore the adjacent coastline. Every inlet was traced to its head, lest it form part of the long sought northwest passage. The boats were usually provisioned for a week or ten days, but officers and men alike made every effort to extend the period if by so doing they could advance the survey. A great effort was made to treat the natives fairly and establish friendly relations with them. The boats, however, being no larger than many Indian canoes, were temptations because of their arms and provisions, and late in the survey a number of attacks had to be beaten off.

As long as his health permitted, Vancouver often took part in the boat expeditions. On 22 June 1792, when returning to the ships after exploring Howe Sound, Jervis Inlet, and what is now Vancouver harbour, he found the Spanish survey ships *Sútil* and *Mexicana*, under the command of Dionisio Alcalá-Galiano*, at anchor off Point Grey. From Alcalá-Galiano he learned that Spanish explorers had preceded him in Juan de Fuca Strait and the Strait of Georgia, though not in Puget Sound. Relations were cordial and some cooperation was decided upon, but it was limited by Vancouver's contention that his instructions prevented him from accepting any but his own survey of the continental shore.

By August Vancouver had worked his way up the full length of what is now Vancouver Island, establishing its insularity when his ships emerged in Queen Charlotte Sound on 9 August. He pushed on to Burke Channel, in 52°N, and then sailed south to Nootka Sound where he knew his supply ship and the Spanish commander, Juan Francisco de la BODEGA y Quadra, were awaiting him.

A warm friendship sprang up between Vancouver and Bodega, but they were unable to agree on the details of the property transfer provided for in the Nootka Convention. Vancouver had expected to receive an extensive area, perhaps the entire sound; inquiry had convinced Bodega that John Meares*, part owner of several of the ships seized in 1789, had occupied no more than a small plot on Friendly Cove. Both undertook to refer the matter to their respective governments and await instructions. The supply ship brought Vancouver some additional instructions dated 20 Aug. 1791, but he received no further communication from the Admiralty during the last three years of his voyage.

From Nootka Vancouver sailed south to San Francisco and Monterey, in Alta (present-day) California, and then to the Sandwich Islands where he wintered. In May 1793 he was back on the coast and by September had traced the continental shore as far north as 56°. Vancouver explored Dean Channel in June; a few weeks later he would have met Alexander Mackenzie*, who completed his overland journey to the Pacific there late in July.

At the end of the 1793 season Vancouver again visited Alta California en route to winter quarters in the Sandwich Islands. After calling at Monterey he went on to San Diego and then, fulfilling his instructions, sailed southward along the Mexican coast to extend his survey to the appointed limit of 30°. In two seasons he had thus traced the coast from 30°N to 56°N and had proved that Juan de Fuca Strait was not the entrance to a great inland sea, as Fuca* had alleged, and that the extensive waterways Bartholomew de Fonte* claimed to have entered in latitude 53° did not exist.

In the course of his third and last visit to the Sandwich Islands Vancouver completed their survey and also intervened actively in their internal affairs. With a view to ending civil strife he encouraged their political unification under King Kamehameha. He also persuaded Kamehameha to cede the island of Hawaii to Great Britain in the expectation that a small military force would be stationed there to provide protection for the islands, now that ships of many nations were frequenting them. The cession was signed on 25 Feb. 1794, but no confirming action was taken in London.

For the 1794 season Vancouver decided to sail directly to Cook Inlet (Alas.), the northern limit of his survey, and to work southward to the point reached the previous year. The last anchorage of the *Discovery* and *Chatham* was in a bay on the southeast coast of Baranof Island to which Vancouver gave the appropriate name Port Conclusion. The boats returned from the last exploring expedition on 19 August, and the completion of the survey was celebrated by "such an additional allowance of grog as was fully sufficient to answer every purpose of festivity on the occasion." Later Vancouver was to write in his *Voyage of discovery to the north Pacific ocean*: "I trust the precision with which the survey . . . has been carried into effect, will remove every doubt, and set aside every opinion of a *north-west passage*, or any water communication navigable for shipping, existing between the north pacific, and the interior of the American continent, within the limits of our researches."

The survey had been carried out with remarkable accuracy. Vancouver's latitudes vary little from modern values; the more difficult calculations for longitude show an error that varies from about one-third to one degree. It was an accomplishment worthy of comparison with the surveys of Cook, and the frequent references to Cook in the published *Voyage* show that he was ever the ideal Vancouver had in mind. John Cawte Beaglehole, the authority on Cook, remarks that of all the men who trained under him Vancouver was "the only one whose work as a marine surveyor was to put him in the class of his commander."

The long homeward voyage was made by Cape Horn, with calls at Monterey, Valparaíso (Chile), and St Helena. As Britain was at war, the *Discovery* travelled from St Helena in convoy and arrived in the estuary of the Shannon River, Ireland, on 13 Sept. 1795. Vancouver left her immediately and proceeded to London but rejoined her when she arrived in the Thames on 20 October. Thus ended the longest surveying expedition in history – over four and a half years. The distance sailed was approximately 65,000 miles, to which the boat excursions are estimated to have added 10,000 miles. The care Vancouver devoted to the health of his crews was noteworthy; only one man died of disease. Another died of poisoning and four were drowned.

Vancouver's achievement received little recognition at the time, largely because of charges that he had been overly harsh as a commander. As early as January 1793 Thomas Manby, master's mate of the *Chatham*, wrote privately that Vancouver had "grown Haughty Proud Mean and Insolent, which has kept himself and Officers in a continual state of wrangling during the whole of the Voyage." His difficulties with Archibald Menzies*, botanist and surgeon, had serious consequences because Menzies was a protégé of Sir Joseph Banks*, the influential president of the Royal Society of London. More serious was the case of Thomas Pitt, heir of Lord Camelford, one of the midshipmen-in-training in the *Discovery*. He was a difficult and unbalanced young man whose conduct so infuriated Vancouver that he discharged him in Hawaii in 1794. Pitt was closely related to the prime minister and to the first lord of the Admiralty, John Pitt, and a brother of Lady Grenville, wife of the foreign secretary, and their combined displeasure weighed heavily on Vancouver. It is evident that illness (probably some hyperthyroid condition) had made Vancouver irritable and subject to outbursts of temper, but he was not a brutal commander. He ran a taut ship, as was essential in a vessel far removed from any supporting authority, and if his officers did not like him, they respected him and admired his capability.

Vancouver retired on half pay in November 1795. He settled at Petersham, near Richmond Park, and was soon busy revising his journal for publication. He died, at the early age of 40, when the narrative, half a million words in length, was within a hundred pages of completion. His brother John finished the revision and the *Voyage* was published in 1798 in a handsome edition consisting of three quarto volumes and a folio atlas.

Almost all of the several hundred place names bestowed by Vancouver on physical features have been retained. Most notable of them is Vancouver Island, originally named Quadra and Vancouver's Island in honour of his friend the Spanish commander. Vancouver's work and memory have received more attention in recent years, and his grave in St Peter's churchyard in Petersham is the scene of an annual commemorative ceremony sponsored by the province of British Columbia.

W. Kaye Lamb

[A portrait in the National Portrait Gallery (London), long stated to be a likeness of Vancouver, is now regarded as of doubtful authenticity. No other portrait has come to light. Vancouver's original journals, including the partial copies sent to the Admiralty while his voyage of discovery was in progress, have disappeared. His logs as lieutenant in the *Martin*, *Fame*, and *Europa* are in the National Maritime Museum, ADM/L/M/16B, log of HMS *Martin*, 9 Dec. 1781–16 May 1782; ADM/L/F/115, log of HMS *Fame*, 17 May 1782–3 July 1783; ADM/L/E/155, log of HMS *Europa*, 24 Nov. 1787–23 Nov. 1788. His letters to the Admiralty are in PRO, Adm. 1/2628–30. His original dispatches are in PRO, CO 5/187. Drawings and charts relating to the voyage are in Ministry of Defence, Hydrographer of the Navy (Taunton, Eng.), 226, 228–29, 523 (surveys on the west coast of North America).

Most of the score or more officers' official logs in the PRO are concise and devoted chiefly to ships' movements and business, but two are highly informative. (1) Peter Puget, PRO, Adm. 55/17 and Adm. 55/27, January 1791–March 1794 (BL, Add. MSS 17542–45 includes rough drafts of Puget's journals and logs for January 1791–December 1793; Add. MSS 17552, papers relating to the voyage of the *Discovery* and *Chatham*, 1790–95, includes some Vancouver letters and a narrative by Puget, one page of which was wrongly described by G. S. Godwin as the only surviving fragment of Vancouver's original journal). (2) James Johnstone, PRO, Adm. 53/335, which unfortunately covers only the period January 1791–May 1792. There are three important private journals. (1) Archibald Menzies, BL, Add. MSS 32641, December 1790–February 1794; National Library of Australia (Canberra), MS 155, Archibald Menzies, Journal, 21 Feb. 1794–18 March 1795. (2) Edward Bell, National Library of New Zealand, Alexander Turnbull Library (Wellington), [Edward Bell], Journal of voyage in H.M.S. "Chatham" to the Pacific Ocean, 1 Jan. 1791–26 Feb. 1794. (3) Thomas Manby, Beinecke Rare Book and Manuscript Library, Yale University (New Haven, Conn.), Western Americana coll., Thomas Manby, Journal of the voyage of H.M.S. Discovery and Chatham, under the command of Captain George Vancouver, to the northwest coast of America, February 10, 1791, to June 30, 1793; University of B.C. Library (Vancouver), Special Coll. Division, Thomas Manby to Captain Barlow, 9 Jan. 1793 (photocopy). State Library of New South Wales, Mitchell Library (Sydney, Australia), Banks papers, Brabourne coll., v.9, includes correspondence, drafts, etc., relating to Vancouver's voyage. There are other Banks papers in California State Library, Sutro Library (San Francisco), Sir Joseph Banks coll.

[George Vancouver], *A voyage of discovery to the north Pacific Ocean, and round the world . . .*, [ed. John Vancouver] (3v. and atlas, London, 1798; repr. Amsterdam and New York, 1967; new ed., [ed. John Vancouver], 6v., London, 1801). Translations were published in French (3v. and atlas, Paris, [1799–1800]); Danish (2v., Copenhagen, 1799–1802); and Russian (6v., St Petersburg [Leningrad], 1827–38). Abridged editions appeared in German (2v., Berlin, 1799–1800) and Swedish (2v., Stockholm, 1800–1). As well, an annotated edition of the *Voyage* is in preparation for the Hakluyt Society. For a complete list of previous editions see *Navigations, traffiques & discoveries, 1774–1848: a guide to publications relating to the area now British Columbia*, comp. G. M. Strathern and M. H. Edwards (Victoria, 1970), 308–10. E. S. Meany, *Vancouver's discovery of Puget Sound: portraits and biographies of the men honored in the naming of geographic features of northwestern America* (New York and London, 1907; repr. 1915; Portland, Oreg., 1942; repr. 1949), reprints the *Voyage* for the period April to October 1792. [George Vancouver], *Vancouver in California, 1792–1794: the original account*, ed. M. [K.] E. Wilbur (3v., Los Angeles, 1953–54), reprints the portions for 1792, 1793, and 1794 that describe the visits to California.

Bern Anderson, *Surveyor of the sea: the life and voyages of Captain George Vancouver* (Seattle, Wash., 1960; repr. Toronto, 1966). G. H. Anderson, *Vancouver and his great voyage: the story of a Norfolk sailor, Captain Geo. Vancouver, R.N., 1757–1798* (King's Lynn, Eng., 1923). G. [S.] Godwin, *Vancouver; a life, 1757–1798* (London, 1930; repr. New York, 1931). J. S. and Carrie Marshall, *Vancouver's voyage* (2nd ed., Vancouver, 1967). C. F. Newcombe, *The first circumnavigation of Vancouver Island* (Victoria, 1914). H. R. Wagner, *The cartography of the northwest coast of America to the year 1800* (2v., Berkeley, Calif., 1937); *Spanish explorations in the Strait of Juan de Fuca* (Santa Ana, Calif., 1933). Glyndwr Williams, *The British search for the northwest passage in the eighteenth century* (London and Toronto, 1962). Adrien Mansvelt, "Vancouver: a lost branch of the Van Coeverden family," *British Columbia Hist. News* (Vancouver), 6 (1972–73), no.2, 20–23, and his articles "The original Vancouver in old Holland," *Vancouver Sun*, 1 Sept. 1973, 37, and "Solving the Captain Vancouver mystery," *Vancouver Sun*, 1 Sept. 1973, 36. W.K.L.]

VAR. *See* SAINT-AUBIN

VARIN, *dit* **La Pistole, JACQUES** (he signed Jacques Varin), silversmith and jeweller; baptized 3 Oct. 1736 at Notre-Dame in Montreal (Que.), son of Louis-Joseph Varin, *dit* La Pistole, and Marie-Renée Gautier; m. 27 Jan. 1777 Marie-Josette Périnault in Montreal; d. there 25 Jan. 1791.

Several authors have claimed that Jacques Varin, *dit* La Pistole, came from a family of silversmiths. In fact, his grandfather Nicolas, his uncles Jacques and Nicolas, and his father were all wet coopers. His father – to whom the silversmith's stamp LV within an ellipse has been wrongly attributed – was working as a wet cooper at the time of his marriage in 1731, and numerous documents prove that he followed this trade all his life. Jacques's sister Marie-Louise did, however, marry a silversmith; in 1755 in Montreal she became the wife of Jean Joram Chappuis, *dit* Comtois. Joram had apparently been working in Montreal for some time; in 1748 he and Jacques Gadois*, *dit* Mauger, had been present at the marriage of Ignace-François DELEZENNE. For a number of reasons it seems certain that Jacques Varin received his training as a silversmith from his brother-in-law. Gadois was dead by 1750; Delezenne had moved to Quebec in 1752; and it is unlikely that Varin trained with the silversmiths grouped about Roland Paradis*, including his apprentices Jean-Baptiste Legu, *dit* La Noue, and Jean-Baptiste Plante, or with Paradis's cousin Charles-François Delique who had come from France around 1753. Since apprenticeship was usually completed by the age of 20 or 21, it may be assumed that Varin set up his own shop about 1756–57.

In 1762, when he was living on Rue Saint-Paul, "jacque varin, merchant, silversmith," bought a site in the *faubourg* Saint-Joseph, and the following year, at a cost of 250 *livres*, he took a one-year lease on a house on Rue Capitale "for himself and his men." There are clear indications that his fortune, clientele, and reputation all grew in the ensuing years. He acquired a house in Rue Saint-Sacrement which became his permanent residence, and in March 1769 he contracted to take Eustache Larivée as an apprentice silversmith and jeweller for five years. The unusual stipulation was made that the young man's father, Charles Larivée, a Montreal merchant, had to provide 250 *livres* or "shillings in the currency of this province." When the contract expired, Eustache Larivée opened a silversmith's shop on Rue Notre-Dame and in his turn engaged an apprentice, Jean Choisser. According to his apprenticeship contract with Larivée, Varin was working as a jeweller, and it may be safely assumed that he was involved in the lucrative business of producing jewellery and trinkets for the fur trade. This concentration may explain why only a score of religious and domestic works bearing his stamp (a crown, IV, a heart [?]) have been found.

It is curious that a soup-tureen made for the Sulpicians about 1775 (and now held by the Musée de l'Église Notre-Dame in Montreal) bears the stamp of not only Varin but also Robert Cruickshank*. Cruickshank was one of the silversmiths who immigrated to Montreal after British rule was established. Yet a collaboration between the two is certainly suggested by the tureen's sober elegance of proportion and fine chasing, both characteristic of Cruickshank's work. Probably a Scot, Cruickshank may well have acquired in Great Britain and transmitted to Varin the taste for Greek and Roman antiquities manifested in the representations of human feet that form the tureen's base and in the heads, modelled after Graeco-Roman deities, that guard the handles. Such heads had protected the handles of classical pieces from being broken and prevented hot contents from being spilled on the carrier. The pagan influence the tureen displays and the technical skill of its crafting make this substantial piece one of the most magnificent and important creations of 18th-century Quebec silver-work.

Parish account books make numerous references to payments to Varin during the final period of his life. It is regrettable that we no longer have the instrument of peace – a decorated metal plaquette for the faithful to kiss – which in 1787 brought him 66 *livres* for materials and 28 *livres* for workmanship from the church of Saint-Charles-de-Lachenaie.

ROBERT DEROME

[Works by Jacques Varin, *dit* La Pistole, are held in Toronto in the Henry Birks collection; in Montreal by the Congregation of Notre-Dame, the Hôtel-Dieu, and the church of Notre-Dame; in Quebec by the Musée du Québec; and in the United States by the Detroit Institute of Arts. R.D.]

ANQ-M, État civil, Catholiques, La Nativité-de-la-Très-Sainte-Vierge (Laprairie), 31 mars 1723; Notre-Dame de Montréal, 30 avril 1731, 22 févr. 1735, 3 oct. 1736, 22 janv. 1738, 13 mars 1739, 2 oct., 11 déc. 1740, 3, 5 mars 1743, 8 janv. 1748, 30 juin 1755, 5 juin 1758, 24 avril 1760, 9 nov. 1772, 8 févr. 1773, 27 janv. 1777, 29 janv. 1791; Saint-Antoine (Longueuil), 16 juill. 1731; Greffe d'Antoine Adhémar, 20 mars 1709; Greffe de Guillaume Barette, 21 juill. 1720, 14 nov. 1722, 30 mars (not located), 26 juin 1723, 7 janv., 7 juin 1724, 25 juin 1731, 18 mai 1732, 24 mars 1733; Greffe de René Chorel de Saint-Romain, 15 juill. 1731; Greffe d'Antoine Foucher, 26 janv. 1777; Greffe de N.-A. Guillet de Chaumont, 9 juill. 1730, 29 avril 1731, 2 janv., 24 juill. 1733, 20 mars 1734; Greffe de Gervais Hodiesne, 24 juill. 1760, 31 mai 1763; Greffe de Michel Lepallieur, 28 févr. 1720; Greffe de J.-C. Raimbault, 9 avril 1731; Greffe de François Simonnet, 12 juin 1745, 31 juill. 1747, 29 janv. 1765, 2 mars 1769, 1er oct. 1774; Greffe d'André Souste, 10 sept. 1762, 27 juill. 1763. ANQ-Q, Greffe de J.-C. Panet, 4 déc. 1755.

"État général des billets d'ordonnances . . . ," ANQ *Rapport*, 1924–25, 251. "Recensement de Montréal, 1741" (Massicotte), 52–53. *Les arts au Canada français* ([Vancouver], 1959), 73. Derome, *Les orfèvres de N.-F.* Tanguay, *Dictionnaire*. J. Trudel, *L'orfèvrerie en N.-F.* Robert Derome, "Delezenne, les orfèvres, l'orfèvrerie, 1740–1790" (thèse de MA, université de Montréal, 1974). Langdon, *Canadian silversmiths*. Traquair, *Old silver of Que*. Gérard Morisset, "L'instrument de paix," RSC *Trans.*, 3rd ser., XXXIX (1945), sect.I, 145.

VARIN DE LA MARRE, JEAN-VICTOR, commissary and controller of the Marine, subdelegate of the intendant, and councillor of the Conseil Supérieur of Quebec; b. 14 Aug. 1699 at Niort, France, son of Jean Varin de La Sablonnière, an infantry officer; d. some time between 1780 and 1786, probably at Malesherbes, France.

In 1721 Jean-Victor Varin de La Marre was a scrivener in training at Rochefort, France, and the following year was a scrivener of the Marine. On 22 May 1729 he was appointed chief scrivener of the Marine in Canada, and also assumed the duties of controller, substituting for Jean-Eustache Lanoullier* de Boisclerc, whom the king had just dismissed. He sailed from La Rochelle on 28 June 1729 on the *Éléphant* with his immediate superior, financial commissary HOCQUART, and reached Quebec in mid September, after being shipwrecked near the Île aux Grues some 30 miles downstream.

As controller, and later as commissary, Varin de La Marre undertook to put the colony's finances in order. During the next ten years his work was so remarkable that Hocquart praised it virtually every year. In addition Varin took care of his own interests; he regularly asked the minister for additional remuneration and higher rank. On 18 Feb. 1733 he received letters of appointment to the office of councillor of the Conseil Supérieur of Quebec; he took his seat on 18 July, and continued to hold this office together with other posts until 1749. On 13 April 1734 he was promoted from chief scrivener to commissary and controller of the Marine in Quebec, with an annual salary of 1,800 *livres*. Meanwhile, on 19 Oct. 1733, in the presence of leading figures in Canadian society, he had married Charlotte, the daughter of Louis Liénard* de Beaujeu, a nobleman from an old family. She brought him a dowry of 6,000 *livres* to add to the 12,000 *livres* he already possessed.

In the summer of 1736 Varin de La Marre was sent to Montreal to serve as subdelegate of the intendant, an office left vacant when Honoré Michel* de Villebois de La Rouvillière came to Quebec to take over the intendant's duties during Hocquart's absence. In 1738, Varin obtained the minister's permission to go to France to settle urgent personal matters, but because he was a valued official Hocquart would not consent to his leaving until the autumn of 1740. In addition to his usual duties, he issued the playing-card money and was responsible for supervising the Saint-Maurice ironworks and the king's shipbuilding operations; his reports on these activities were well received by his superiors. He returned to Canada in April 1741, having secured a special gratuity of 1,200 *livres* from the minister, Maurepas, who two years later granted him the "haute paye" of 2,400 *livres*, the highest salary a junior official in Canada could receive. Finally, following Michel de Villebois's appointment on 1 Jan. 1747 as commissary general and *ordonnateur* in Louisiana, Maurepas, after consulting Hocquart, promoted Varin commissary of the Marine and subdelegate of the intendant in Montreal, duties he assumed in the autumn of 1747. He returned to Quebec in the summer of 1749 to replace Intendant BIGOT during the latter's visit to Île Royale (Cape Breton Island). At the beginning of September 1749 Varin set up permanent residence in Montreal, where he wielded broad powers.

For an ambitious nobleman like Varin de La Marre, who was as fond of money as of honours, Montreal provided irresistible temptations and he engaged in commercial transactions in which his private interests were clearly, and improperly, in conflict with the interests of the state. In 1748 he had formed a trading partnership with Jean-Baptiste-Grégoire Martel de Saint-Antoine, the king's storekeeper in Montreal, and Jacques-Joseph LEMOINE Despins, Martel's clerk. The company sold retail to the habitants and held interests in the trading posts in the *pays d'en haut*. In addition Varin personally sold to the king goods that he bought from merchant-traders Guillaume ESTÈBE and Jean-André LAMALETIE and Antoine PASCAUD. But since he could not at the same time buy supplies, sell them, and fix their price, he split his activities in two, and Lemoine Despins acted as a front for him. He was later to admit that from 1752 to 1757 he had increased the prices of the supplies for the king's warehouses by 25 per cent. Finally, between 1755 and 1757 he was in partnership with Jacques-Michel BRÉARD, Michel-Jean-Hugues PÉAN, and Bigot, with whom he engaged in other malpractices. Having a presentiment that the web of his dishonest operations would soon be discovered, he sought to leave the colony. On 15 Oct. 1754 he asked the minister of Marine, Machault, to post him to either Cap-Français (Cap Haïtien, Haiti) or Louisiana. Machault does not seem to have acted upon his request, since two years later, on 15 Oct. 1756, Varin de La Marre made a fresh attempt, this time asking for permission to go to France to recover his health. The minister reluctantly granted him leave on 1 April 1757, while hoping that he would avail himself of it only if his health made it indispensable. Varin de La Marre returned to France in the autumn of 1757. His health did not improve, and he retired the next spring.

During his 28 years in Canada Varin de La Marre had succeeded in accumulating capital estimated by the author of the "Mémoire du Canada" at 4,000,000 *livres*, and in an inventory prepared in France in 1763 at 1,320,000 *livres*. In December 1761 Varin was arrested in connection with the *affaire du Canada* and imprisoned in the Bastille on a charge of having "during part of the time that he served as financial commissary in Montreal, tolerated, encouraged, and committed abuses, embezzlements, acts of betrayal of office, and breaches of trust in the furnishing of goods to the king's warehouses." He was indicted at the Châtelet, and the preliminary investigation of his case took 15 months. On 10 Dec. 1763 he was found guilty of the charges against him and was sentenced to banishment for life from the kingdom of France, to a fine of 1,000 *livres*, and to the restitution of 800,000 *livres* to the king.

On 9 Sept. 1770, after about seven years in exile, Varin de La Marre received permission from Louis XV to live in Corsica through the intervention of a family friend, the Duc de Noailles. Finally, in March 1780 Louis XVI allowed him to return to France and to settle in Malesherbes, near his son Jean-Baptiste-François-Marie, a dragoon in the royal troops. He probably died there, some time before his wife, who died on 23 May 1786 in Sens.

Jean-Victor Varin de La Marre typified the ambitious official who through talent and connections was able to reach the highest posts in the king's service in Canada, but whose greed brought about his ruin.

ANDRÉ LACHANCE

AD, Deux-Sèvres (Niort), État civil, Notre-Dame de Niort, 14 août 1699. AN, Col., B, 53, ff.153, 556; 58, ff.425, 431; 61, ff.515, 536; 63, ff.471, 494; 64, f.421; 66, ff.7, 31; 68, ff.29, 51; 71, ff.35, 42; 72, f.33; 74, ff.18, 89; 76, f.61; 78, ff.56, 62; 81, f.57; 83, ff.3, 20; 85, f.25; 87, f.2; 89, ff.58, 75; 91, ff.32, 59; 95, f.10; 99, ff.27, 33; 105, f.12; 106, f.147; 107, f.7; 108, f.127; 120, ff.6, 30, 67, 84, 158; 125, f.210; 127, ff.266, 291; 137, ff.153, 165; 172, f.60; C[11A], 51, f.387; 70, f.96; 71, f.134; 73, ff.143, 417; 74, f.192; 77, f.332; 78, f.57; 80, ff.298, 304, 307, 310, 314; 81, f.398; 82, f.282; 87, f.159; 88, f.29; 89, ff.184–87; 92, ff.292–96; 93, f.299; 97, ff.219, 221; 98, f.158; 99, ff.493, 495; 100, f.143; 101, f.287; 103, ff.23, 256; E, 383 (dossier Varin de La Marre); F[3], 10, ff.268, 369; 14, ff.171, 213, 215, 223, 257; 16, ff.257–58; Marine, C[7], 337 (dossier Varin de La Marre). ANQ-Q, État civil, Catholiques, Notre-Dame de Québec, 19 oct. 1733; Greffe de Jacques Barbel, 17 oct. 1733.

Doc. relatifs à la monnaie sous le Régime français (Shortt), II, 600–1. "Mémoire du Canada," ANQ *Rapport*, 1924–25, 197. P.-G. Roy, *Inv. jug. et délib., 1717–60*, VI, 271–72. Tanguay, *Dictionnaire*, VII, 428. Frégault, *François Bigot*. Cameron Nish, *Les bour-*

geois-gentilshommes de la Nouvelle-France, 1729–1748 (Montréal et Paris, 1968), 132, 135, 138–39. P.-G. Roy, *Bigot et sa bande*, 40–41.

VASSEUR. *See* LEVASSEUR

VAUDREUIL, FRANÇOIS-PIERRE DE RIGAUD DE. *See* RIGAUD

VAUDREUIL, PIERRE DE RIGAUD DE VAUDREUIL DE CAVAGNIAL, Marquis de. *See* RIGAUD

VAUQUELIN, JEAN, naval officer; b. February 1728 at Dieppe, France; d. 10 Nov. 1772 at Rochefort, France.

Little is known of Jean Vauquelin's early career. The son of a captain in the merchant marine, he went to sea with his father at a young age and during the War of the Austrian Succession served as an officer on a privateering frigate. Becoming a captain in the merchant marine himself around 1750, he had completed 21 voyages before being recruited by the naval commandant at Le Havre at the beginning of the Seven Years' War to serve as an *officier bleu*. This term was applied to the officers of the merchant marine or naval officers who served on the king's ships as subaltern officers on a voluntary temporary basis without commissions. On 26 April 1757 Vauquelin received command of the frigate *Tourterelle* and in February 1758 he was commissioned a lieutenant in the royal navy. He was immediately given command of the *Pèlerine*, a 30-gun frigate which the king had recently bought from an outfitter at Le Havre and renamed the *Aréthuse*. Vauquelin was sent to Île Royale (Cape Breton Island) and, despite Edward Boscawen*'s blockade, succeeded in entering Louisbourg harbour on 9 June 1758. Moored broadside on, near the lagoon called the Barachois, the *Aréthuse* hindered the British landing operations significantly by keeping them under fire from the rear; Vauquelin's accurate gunfire caused substantial losses and notably delayed the construction of siegeworks. At the beginning of July Vauquelin received permission from Governor Augustin de Boschenry* de Drucour to go to France with dispatches and to inform the minister of Marine of the plight of the fortress. He set sail on the night of 14–15 July, ran the British blockade once more, and reached Europe after a rapid and uneventful crossing, casting anchor at Santander in Spain on 2 August. As a result of this brilliant manœuvre Vauquelin received a congratulatory letter from the minister, who wrote on 15 August: "The statements given me about your conduct at Louisbourg during the time that you were there are all favourable, and I cannot but be pleased with the speed of your return voyage, especially in view of the frigate's condition."

Vauquelin came to Canada in 1759 as commander of the frigate *Atalante*. Appointed a fire-ship captain for the campaign, he left Rochefort on 13 March, and on arrival in the colony he was ordered by Governor RIGAUD de Vaudreuil to inspect the batteries in the Quebec sector, as well as everything concerning the navy. Vauquelin carried out his mission with his usual dispatch, and LÉVIS expressed "the highest praise for the bravery and intelligence of this officer." It is nonetheless certain that the naval forces were badly utilized during the siege of Quebec. Although plans were made to launch fire-ships against the British fleet, the operation was not entrusted to sailors and as a result it failed lamentably. The British fleet under Charles SAUNDERS secured mastery of the St Lawrence without difficulty and so obtained freedom to manœuvre. At the end of August an attack on the British ships anchored above Quebec was envisaged, but to carry it out the sailors manning the batteries would have had to be recalled; the project was consequently abandoned.

In the spring of 1760 Vauquelin formed a small division composed of the *Atalante*, the *Pomone*, the flute *Pie*, and some light craft, which left Sorel for Quebec on 20 April to follow Lévis's army and supply it. It reached the Anse au Foulon on 28 April, the day of the French victory at Sainte-Foy. Lévis continued the siege of the city, but on 9 May a British frigate arrived before Quebec and was soon joined by another frigate and a ship of the line [*see* Robert Swanton*]. Pursued on 16 May by the *Lowestoft* and the *Diana*, Vauquelin drew them off towards Cap-Rouge to save the army's supply depots and then had to run his ship aground at Pointe-aux-Trembles (Neuville). He used up his ammunition and then, having nailed his flag to the mast under the enemy's steady fire and thrown his sword into the St Lawrence, he ordered his crew to leave the ship. He had been wounded, and he was taken prisoner with the three officers, the ship's writer, the chaplain, and the six sailors who had remained on board. The next day the British burned the *Atalante*, which had been reduced to a wreck. Vauquelin, it seems, had greatly impressed his enemies with his bravery. He was quickly released and was able to return to France.

His years of service brought Vauquelin the rank of fire-ship captain on 5 Nov. 1761 and that of lieutenant-commander on 1 Oct. 1764. After commanding the flute *Bricole* that year, he took the *Coulisse* the following year on a transport mission to Guiana, where Choiseul, the minister of Marine and the Colonies, was endeavouring to found a settlement to make up for the loss of Canada. Vauquelin was next put in command of the flute *Garonne* and in April 1767 he left Lorient for a long cruise in the Indian Ocean, where his vessel served as a station ship under the governor general of Île de France (Mauritius). In August 1768 he was ordered to transport to Madagascar Louis-Laurent de Féderbe, Comte de Maudave, who was to try to found a French colony there. Later, he took the *Garonne* on voyages between Île de France, Mozambique, and Madagascar to trade in black slaves and cattle. These voyages occasioned disputes with Pierre Poivre, the intendant of Île Bourbon (Réunion) and Île de France. Vauquelin was accused of trading illegally, and upon his return to France in December 1769 the king ordered him confined for three months in the château of Le Taureau on the Baie de Morlaix. Because his health would not withstand such imprisonment, he was transferred to Nantes and then released on 1 May 1770. The suspicions about him probably turned out to be ill founded, since on 10 Aug. 1772 he received command of the *Faune*, which had received orders to proceed to the Indian Ocean. His health, however, was seriously impaired. He fell ill and died at Rochefort three months later. It has been claimed that he was murdered, but this assertion is one of many inaccuracies to be found in accounts of Vauquelin's career.

Jean Vauquelin is a good example of an officer who, since he was born a commoner, entered the royal navy indirectly rather than through the usual route of midshipman, and who succeeded by his talents in carving out an honourable niche for himself.

ÉTIENNE TAILLEMITE

AN, Col., B, 127, f.21; C[4], 20; C[11A], 104, ff.193, 270; F[3], 50, ff.529–30; Marine, B[3], 359, f.51; 533, f.124; 543, ff.94–96; B[4], 80, f.284; 98, f.21; C[1], 174, p.1656; 180, p.228; C[7], 341 (dossier Vauquelin). *Coll. des manuscrits de Lévis* (Casgrain), I, 227; II, 305; III, 168; IV, 163, 183; VII, 540; VIII, 140, 152, 159, 171, 174, 177, 179–80, 190, 195, 198; IX, 52, 57, 89; X, 224; XI, 263–71. Knox, *Hist. journal* (Doughty). Le Jeune, *Dictionnaire*.

Jacques Aman, *Les officiers bleus dans la marine française au XVIII[e]s.* (Paris, 1976), 124–26. Gabriel Gravier, *Notice sur Vauquelain de Dieppe, lieutenant de vaisseau (1727–1764), d'après M. Faucher de Saint-Maurice* (Rouen, France, 1885). Lacour-Gayet, *La marine militaire sous Louis XV*. McLennan, *Louisbourg*, 278, 302. Stanley, *New France*, 172, 244, 250. N.-H.-É. Faucher de Saint-Maurice, "Un des oubliés de notre histoire, le capitaine de vaisseau Vauquelain," RSC *Trans.*, 1st ser., III (1885), sect.I, 35–47. Ægidius Fauteux, "Jean Vauquelin," RSC *Trans.*, 3rd ser., XXIV (1930), sect.I, 1–30.

VEAUX. *See* DEVAU

VERGOR, LOUIS DU PONT DUCHAMBON DE. *See* DU PONT

VEYSSIÈRE, LEGER-JEAN-BAPTISTE-NOËL (baptized **Leger**; named **Father Emmanuel**), Recollet priest and Church of England clergyman; b. 23 Dec. 1728 at Tulle, France, son of Étienne Veyssières and Françoise Fraysse; m. 17 April 1770 Elizabeth Lawrear (Chase; Brookes), and in 1790 the widow Christiana Gotson (Godson); d. 26 May 1800 at Trois-Rivières, Lower Canada.

Leger-Jean-Baptiste-Noël Veyssière, after completing his theology in 1750 at Cahors, France, arrived at Quebec on 15 August of that year. He took two more years of theology at the Séminaire de Québec before going in 1752 as assistant treasurer to the Séminaire de Saint-Sulpice, Montreal, where he also taught humanities for two years. After 14 months as missionary to the Iroquois of La Galette (near Ogdensburg, N.Y.), he was admitted in 1756 to the Recollet order at Quebec, taking the name Father Emmanuel. On 27 Dec. 1758 he became the last priest ordained by Bishop Pontbriand [Dubreil*]. In 1760 he was appointed by Vicar General Jean-Olivier BRIAND confessor and preacher at Quebec, where in July 1761 he received the abjuration of the Huguenot Antoine-Libéral Dumas*. The following year Briand appointed him priest of Saint-Michel de La Durantaye (Saint-Michel-de-Bellechasse), adding to his charge in February 1765 the parish of Beaumont. In January 1766 he was transferred to Saint-Nicolas.

In October 1762 Veyssière had aroused Briand's ire by complaining to Governor MURRAY that the vicar general reserved all the poorest paying parishes for the Recollets. Four years later he scandalized the Roman Catholic Church by converting to Protestantism. The *Quebec Gazette* affirmed that his conversion was apparently made "from the laudable Motive of Conscience only." Veyssière's hopes of becoming a minister at Quebec, however, were thwarted by the Reverend John BROOKE, the chaplain there, who refused to administer the oath of abjuration. Brooke acted under pressure from Lieutenant Governor Guy Carleton*, who feared further provocation of the Roman Catholic Church. Veyssière nevertheless enjoyed the support of the Huguenot attorney general, Francis Maseres*, who opposed Carleton's religious policies. Maseres hoped that if the former Recollet, whom he described as having "a little plain good sense" and "a tolerable knowledge of the points in dispute between papists and protestants," were treated well, many more priests might follow his lead, and a conversion movement begin.

Rebuffed at Quebec, Veyssière left for London in October 1767 armed with letters of recommendation from Maseres, French and British residents of Quebec, and 36 Catholics of his former parishes. Maseres expected Veyssières to give the British government a "true and exact account of the State of religion in the province," and especially to emphasize that a mistake had been made in allowing the Canadians to have a bishop in Briand. Veyssière arrived just as the Church of England was looking for French speaking ministers for Trois-Rivières and Quebec, David CHABRAND Delisle having already been placed at Montreal. Veyssière sought the Quebec position, but he was passed over in favour of David-François De Montmollin* and appointed instead to Trois-Rivières, with a salary of £200 per annum. He was back in Canada by the summer of 1768 when Carleton strongly protested his engagement in light of "his Levity and Folly both before and after his renouncing the errors of the Church of Rome." Fearing the three new appointees might cause trouble, Carleton drafted their commissions in such a manner as "to leave the Power to do all the good they can, or chuse to do, without authorizing them to do Mischief."

At Trois-Rivières Veyssière began ministering in September 1768 in the former Recollet chapel, to a congregation which until after the American revolution was largely composed of soldiers. Throughout his ministry his large parish contained a relatively constant number of Protestants – about 150 to 200; most were probably dissenters, but all decidedly indifferent.

In January 1775 Henry Caldwell*, who was named to the Legislative Council of Quebec the following year, wrote Lord Shelburne, a prominent member of the House of Lords, that the Protestant religion was "absolutely going a begging in this Country" since the Society for the Propagation of the Gospel had sent out the three French-language ministers "who Every Sunday Massacre the poor English Liturgy in the most Barbarous manner." Caldwell had particular contempt for the former Recollet who, he charged, had converted only to avoid doing penance for "his notorious debaucheries." It was not, however, the old and generally bilingual English inhabitants like Caldwell but the unilingual loyalists flooding into the colony who complained most effectively. Christian Daniel CLAUS initiated the attack supported by the Reverend John Doty*. In 1785 a report to the government warned that the Church of England could soon be extirpated in the colony "by the Cunning and perseverence of New England Emissaries [dissenting ministers], that are now creeping into the Province and poisoning the Minds of unsuspecting Inhabitants"; from their desire to get their religion in English, these people also imbibed dissenter principles. In February 1786 Evan Nepean, commissioner of the privy seal, received a memorandum describing as shameful the situation of the church at Trois-Rivières, where "the Clergyman . . . is that kind of Character, that wou'd disgrace the meanest Profession."

These complaints reached Charles Inglis*, appointed bishop of Nova Scotia in 1787 with jurisdiction over all of British North America, and himself a loyalist. In June 1789, Inglis, already determined to replace the French speaking ministers, reached Quebec to begin a pastoral visit. On 26 June he found the church at Trois-Rivières in ruins and services being held in the minister's house. "Mr. Veyssière," he noted, "is a poor little creature – he is not more than 4 feet 10 inches high," unable to speak English coherently, and capable only of degrading the church. With men like Veyssière it was no wonder, he complained, that converts to Catholicism were 20 times as numerous in the colony as those to Protestantism. In August he sought vainly to persuade Veyssière to accept an English replacement who would take half of his salary.

Veyssière clung to his post, isolated from his congregation and the church, until 1794. During a pastoral visit from the newly appointed bishop of Quebec, Jacob Mountain*, Veyssière reported that the people gave no money to the poor, the church, or the clergyman. Communion had been held three times yearly, "there being sometimes three and four persons, and often none." Catechism classes for children were advertised, but were never attended. Although ten years later John Lambert*, the author of a travel account, would consider the indifference of the Protestants at Trois-Rivières congenital, the bishop blamed it on Veyssière, who, he charged, "united to an utter incapacity of speaking so as to be understood, Mental imbecility, & notorious irregularity of conduct." Mountain appointed his brother Jehosaphat* as Veyssière's assistant, relieving the latter of all responsibilities but leaving him as nominal rector on full stipend.

Since 1777 Veyssière had lived in a wood house next to the merchant Aaron HART. He also owned a wooded lot in the seigneury of Cap-de-la-Madeleine, but it was considered almost valueless. Yet his library contained about 180 volumes, mostly religious, and all in French. When they were sold at auction shortly before his death, among the most important buyers were William Grant*; the Harts, Aaron, Ezekiel*, and Benjamin*; and several priests including François-Xavier Noiseux*, the vicar general at Trois-Rivières. The size and composition of this library would seem to refute the charges that Veyssière was imbecilic and irreligious.

Insignificant as a minister, Veyssière, by the isolation of his life, throws light on the probable fate of any Roman Catholic priest who might have converted to Protestantism after the conquest. His sufferings at the hands of Protestant and Catholic, the Church of England and the state, may have prevented similar conversions which might have seriously weakened the stature of the Roman Catholic Church at a critical period. More certainly, the Church of England's experience with Veyssière, and to a lesser degree with his colleagues Chabrand Delisle and De Montmollin, determined it to reverse its post-conquest proselytist policy. Beginning in the 1790s, it would, with a British clergy, concentrate its attentions on the colony's British Protestants.

JAMES H. LAMBERT

AAQ, 12 A, C, 109; 20 A, I, 94; 42 CD, I, 25. AD, Corrège (Tulle), État civil, Saint-Julien, 24 déc. 1728. ANQ-MBF, État civil, Anglicans, Église protestante (Trois-Rivières), 28 mai 1800; Greffe de Joseph Badeaux, 30 janv., 18 févr. 1800. Archives des franciscains (Montréal), Dossier Emmanuel Veyssière. BL, Add. MSS 21877, f.253. Lambeth Palace Library (London), Fulham papers, 1, ff.116–21, 138, 147, 163–65; 33, f.3a; 38, f.58. PAC, MG 23, A4, 14, p.27; 16, p.113; 18, p.335; C6, ser. IV, Journals, June–Aug. 1789; Letterbooks, 27 Aug. 1789; GII, 1, ser. 1, 2, pp.139–40; RG 4, A1, pp.6217–18, 7194. PRO, CO 42/28, ff.387f., 390, 398; 42/49, ff.13, 15, 57; 42/71, ff.296f.; 42/72, ff.231f. QDA, 45 (A-7), 1 July 1768; 70 (B-24), 1794; 72 (C-1), 26, 34; 73 (C-2), 136; 83 (D-2), 15 Jan. 1783, 18 Sept. 1788, 27 Aug. 1789. Trinity Cathedral Archives (Quebec), Register of marriages, 1768–95, p.6. USPG, C/CAN/Que., I, 9 Oct. 1782 (copies at PAC). Charles Inglis, *A charge delivered to the clergy of the province of Quebec, at the primary visitation holden in the city of Quebec, in the month of August 1789* (Halifax, 1790). "Inventaire des biens de feu Sr Pierre Du Calvet," J.-J. Lefebvre, édit., ANQ *Rapport*, 1945–46, 373, 381. John Lambert, *Travels through Lower Canada, and the United States of North America in the years 1806, 1807, and 1808* . . . (3v., London, 1810), I, 24–25. Maseres, *Maseres letters* (Wallace), 24–25, 57, 75, 86; *Occasional essays on various subjects chiefly political and historical* . . . (London, 1809), 364–411. *Quebec Gazette*, 27 Oct. 1766, 8 Oct. 1767, 13 Aug. 1789, 13 June 1799. Kelley, "Church and state papers," ANQ *Rapport*, 1948–49, 310, 312–15, 320, 329, 336; 1953–55, 79, 93, 95, 102–3, 106–7, 111–13. R.-P. Duclos, *Histoire du protestantisme français au Canada et aux États-Unis* (2v., Montréal, [1913]), I, 34–35. A.-H. Gosselin, *L'Église du Canada après la Conquête*, I, 17, 251. A. E. E. Legge, *The Anglican Church in Three Rivers, Quebec, 1768–1956* ([Russell, Ont.], 1956), 24–26, 28–30, 36–37. J. S. Moir, *The church in the British era, from the conquest to confederation* (Toronto, 1972), 40, 45, 59, 66. M.-A. [Roy], *Saint-Michel de la Durantaye [notes et souvenirs]: 1678–1929* (Québec, 1929), 81–82. H. S. Stuart, *The Church of England in Canada, 1759–1793; from the conquest to the establishment of the see of Quebec* (Montreal, 1893), 26. É.-Z. Massicotte, "Les mariages mixtes, à Montréal, dans les temples protestants, au 18e siècle," *BRH*, XXI (1915), 86. J.-E. Roy, "Les premiers pasteurs protestants au Canada," *BRH*, III (1897), 2. A. H. Young, "Lord Dorchester and the Church of England," CHA *Report*, 1926, 60–65.

VÉZIN (Vésin, Vézain), PIERRE-FRANÇOIS OLIVIER DE. *See* OLIVIER

VIENNE, FRANÇOIS-JOSEPH DE, writer in the office of the Marine, storekeeper, and probable author of a diary describing the 1759 siege of Quebec; b. *c.* 1711 in Paris, son of Jean de Vienne and Françoise Perdrigean; m. 20 Aug. 1748 Marie-Ursule-Antoinette Vaillant at Quebec; d. in France around 1775.

It is not known why François-Joseph de Vienne immigrated to New France. He arrived in Quebec around 1738, was enrolled in the colonial regular troops, and did not receive his discharge until 1744. By then he was already employed as a writer in the office of the Marine. In addition to his administrative work, de Vienne became involved in some commercial ventures. For example, from 1753 on he and Pierre Glemet ran a seal-hunting enterprise from land granted to François Martel* de Brouague at Baie de Phélypeaux (Brador Bay). They employed about 50 men from 20 June to 10 July each year and obtained 400 to 500 large barrels of seal oil and 4,000 to 5,000 sealskins.

De Vienne's career would have gone unnoticed had his cousin Louis-Antoine de Bougainville* not come to New France in May 1756. During his visit to Quebec Bougainville stayed with de Vienne and out of friendship resolved to secure for him the preferment he believed de Vienne deserved. A few days after the death of Pierre

Claverie* in August 1756, the intendant, Bigot, appointed de Vienne to the important and lucrative post of storekeeper at Quebec. Bougainville was pleased but wanted the appointment to emanate from the court so that the position would be a permanent one. Neither his recommendations to his brother Jean-Pierre and to his patroness Mme Héraut de Séchelles nor pressure on the intendant obtained the desired result. De Vienne held the post on a temporary basis until the conquest. The anonymous author of the "Mémoire du Canada" noted that "the Intendant has always made only interim appointments in order to have all citizens at [his] beck and call." This statement matches the experience of François-Joseph de Vienne. De Vienne may have been involved in irregularities; nearly a third of those charged in the *affaire du Canada* were storekeepers. He apparently was not troubled by the authorities, however, and his name is mentioned only three times in Attorney General Moreau's notes.

After the fall of Quebec de Vienne remained in Canada for five years to put his affairs in order. He probably sold at this time the two houses he owned on Rue des Pauvres (Côte du Palais). On 8 Sept. 1764 he sold to William Grant*, the future seigneur of Saint-Roch, an arriere fief in the seigneury of Notre-Dame-des-Anges called La Mistanguienne (also known as Grandpré and Montplaisir), a property he had bought from Guillaume Estèbe in 1757. A few days later, he transferred the house he owned on Rue de la Fabrique to a nephew. Before he left for France in the autumn of 1764, he gave a power of attorney to Colomban-Sébastien Pressart. Settling with his wife and children in Saint-Servan, a *faubourg* of Saint-Malo, de Vienne continued to correspond with the superior of the Séminaire de Québec. By 1775 his debtors had discharged their debts to him and Pressart sent him the final statement of accounts, which apparently went unacknowledged. No further trace of de Vienne has been uncovered.

Pierre-Georges Roy* and Amédée-Edmond Gosselin* attributed to de Vienne the anonymous manuscript entitled "Journal du siège de Québec du 10 mai au 18 septembre 1759." Written in lively style, the diary gives a striking account of events during these months and provides valuable information about the life of the besieged. The historians identified the storekeeper as its author on the basis of allusions to his activities and family and also through comparison of de Vienne's handwriting with the manuscript. Their hypothesis has not been universally accepted. Ægidius Fauteux* thought their proof insufficient and noted that the journal censures the storekeeper for his attitude when the city capitulated.

François Rousseau

Bougainville, "Journal" (A.-E. Gosselin), ANQ *Rapport*, 1923–24, 245. *Inv. de pièces du Labrador* (P.-G. Roy), I, 246–50. "Journal du siège de Québec" (Æ. Fauteux), ANQ *Rapport*, 1920–21, 137–241. "Mémoire du Canada," ANQ *Rapport*, 1924–25, 96–198. "Les 'papiers' La Pause," ANQ *Rapport*, 1933–34, 218. "Recensement de Québec, 1744," 30. Tanguay, *Dictionnaire*, III, 411; VII, 402. P.-G. Roy, *Inv. concessions*, I, 23–24; *Inv. jug. et délib., 1717–60*, V, 245; *Inv. ord. int.*, III, 187–88. Frégault, *François Bigot*. P.-G. Roy, *Bigot et sa bande*, 271–78, 330. "François-Joseph de Vienne," *BRH*, LIV (1948), 259–63. A.[-E.] Gosselin, "François-Joseph de Vienne et le journal du siège de Québec en 1759," ANQ *Rapport*, 1922–23, 407–16.

VILLARS, FRANÇOIS SORBIER DE. *See* Sorbier

VILLEFRANCHE, ANTOINE GRISÉ, *dit. See* Grisé

VILLEJOUIN (Villejoin, Villejoint), GABRIEL ROUSSEAU DE. *See* Rousseau

VILLIERS, FRANÇOIS COULON DE. *See* Coulon

VITRÉ, THÉODOSE-MATTHIEU DENYS DE. *See* Denys

VOX. *See* Devau

VUADENS. *See* Waddens

WABAKININE (Wabacoming, Wabicanine, Waipykanine), Mississauga Ojibwa chief and warrior; d. August 1796 near York (Toronto).

The most important event in Wabakinine's life was his death, and the story of his violent end and its consequences helps dispel the traditional belief that relations between whites and Indians in Upper Canada were generally harmonious.

Wabakinine signed several early land surrenders in present-day southern Ontario. On 9 May 1781 he was one of the Mississaugas (as the white settlers termed Ojibwas on the north shore of Lake Ontario) who confirmed the previous cession of a strip of land four miles wide along the west bank of the Niagara River. His name heads the list of ten Mississauga signatories to an agreement of 22 May 1784, which surrendered lands at the western end of Lake Ontario to the crown. It relinquished about one-half of the band's hunting grounds, reserving only the "Mississauga Tract," an area between Burlington Bay and the Credit River. Wabakinine was present at a conference of December 1792 that clarified the boundaries established by the 1784 agreement, and he signed a document of 24 Oct. 1795 conveying an additional 3,500 acres to the crown. Hundreds of American immigrants began farming in the surrendered territory and made the Mississaugas' lives a nightmare: farmers threatened to shoot the Indians for "trespassing"; vandals desecrated their graves; epidemics against which the band had no immunity reduced its population from over 500 to roughly 350 between 1787 and 1798.

Late in August 1796 Wabakinine, his wife, sister, and others went to York from the Credit River to sell some salmon. With the money they had earned, they bought liquor and began drinking. Taking advantage of the situation, a soldier named Charles McCuen approached the chief's sister. To "induce her to grant him certain favours" he offered her some rum and a dollar, and that evening, 20 August, went to the Indians' encampment. Wabakinine's wife saw him, wakened her husband, and told him the whites were going to kill his sister. The chief, half-asleep and half-drunk, stumbled towards the soldier. In the scuffle that followed, McCuen hit him soundly on the head with a rock, knocking him senseless to the ground. He later died from the blow.

Several weeks after, his wife died as well. When word reached some Mississaugas hunting around the upper Thames River that she had died of ill treatment by the whites, they called for revenge. Her brother, "said to be a considerable Chief," gathered the band and stopped Augustus Jones*, a provincial surveyor, from proceeding with his survey of the Grand River region.

The thought of a native uprising had always terrified the Upper Canadian authorities, and the deaths of Wabakinine and his wife came at a particularly tense period. A projected attack on the province by French and Spanish forces from the Mississippi valley was rumoured, and it was feared that Joseph Brant [Thayendanegea*] might lead the Indians to join them. He and the colonial authorities had been at loggerheads for a decade over his claim that the Six Nations had the right to sell and lease land on any part of their Grand River Reserve, and he was losing patience. Immediately after hearing of Wabakinine's murder, Brant sent a wampum belt to the Indians on the Upper Lakes inviting the chiefs to the Grand River the following summer. For several weeks in the late winter of 1796–97 the organization of a rebellion appeared to have begun. The fact that McCuen had been discharged for want of evidence no doubt contributed to the Indians' resentment. On 15 Feb. 1797 Ningausim, "a Principal Chief lately from Lake Huron," asked Augustus Jones, whose Indian wife was a Mississauga, to join him and several Mississaugas meeting at York. Jones later reported that Ningausim wished "to open a war against the English to get Satisfaction, for what had been done; saying that he had at the Place of his residence, a great number of young warriors, that he could bring out at his command."

No Franco-Spanish attack occurred, and the uprising never came. Peter Russell*, the administrator of Upper Canada, recognized the agreements Brant had made to sell lands to various whites. The possibility of the 400 Iroquois warriors joining the several hundred Ojibwas who would have been involved was thus removed. Too weak to act on their own, the Ojibwas abandoned the idea of avenging Wabakinine's death.

DONALD B. SMITH

Ont., Ministry of Natural Resources, Survey Records Office, surveyors letters, 28, pp.137–39, Augustus Jones to D. W. Smith, 11 March 1797. PAC, RG 10, A6, 1834, p.197. PAO, RG 22, 7, affidavits and depositions, Home District, 1796–1835. PRO, CO 42/340, f.51. *Canada, Indian treaties and surrenders . . . [1680–1906]* (3v., Ottawa, 1891–1912; repr. Toronto, 1971), I, 5–9; III, 196–97. *Correspondence of Lieut. Governor Simcoe* (Cruikshank), III, 24. *The correspondence of the Honourable Peter Russell, with allied documents relating to his administration of the government of Upper Canada . . .*, ed. E. A. Cruikshank and A. F. Hunter (3v., Toronto, 1932–36), I, 49–50, 117; II, 30, 41, 306. *Upper Canada Gazette; or, American Oracle* (West-Niagara [Niagara-on-the-Lake, Ont.]), 30 Dec. 1797, 12 May 1798. *Handbook of Indians of Canada* (Hodge), 5, 7, 9. [Kahkewaquonaby], *Life and journals of Kah-ke-wa-quo-na-by (Rev. Peter Jones), Wesleyan missionary* (Toronto, 1860).

WABUNMASHUE. *See* WAPINESIW

WADDENS (also **Vuadens, Wadins**), **JEAN-ÉTIENNE**, sometimes known as the Dutchman, northwest fur-trader; baptized 23 April 1738 at La Tour-de-Peilz, canton of Vaud, Switzerland, son of Adam Samuel Vuadens and Marie-Bernardine Ormond (Ermon); d. March 1782 at Lac La Ronge (Sask.).

Jean-Étienne Waddens lived in Switzerland until at least 1755. By 1757 he was serving in New France with the colonial regular troops, and in May of that year at Montreal he renounced "the Calvinist heresy." He remained in Montreal or the neighbourhood after the capitulation of the city in 1760, and although technically a deserter he felt so secure that he married Marie-Josephte Deguire at Saint-Laurent on 23 Nov. 1761. In 1763 he became a property holder in Montreal.

Waddens first appears in the records of the fur trade as a small independent trader. As early as 1772 he was at Grand Portage (near Grand Portage, Minn.) with a party of eight traders. The next year he had a licence for two canoes, and the value of the outfit was £750, a considerable sum in the trade. Waddens appears to have accompanied his traders, and between 1773 and 1778 he moved from Lake Winnipeg to the Saskatchewan valley; by 1779 he was on the southern edge of the Athabasca country. He had the financial backing of Richard Dobie* and John McKindlay of Montreal for part or all of this time.

In 1779, to offset "the Separate Interests . . . the Bane of that Trade," the firms trading into the far northwest joined into one association [*see* William HOLMES]. Waddens became a member of this "nine parties' agreement," a temporary combination usually regarded as the forerunner of the North West Company. At Lac La Ronge Waddens carried on a lucrative trade with "the Northward Indians" from Lake Athabasca. Late in 1781 he was joined by Peter Pond*, bound for Athabasca itself. Although both men represented the company's interests, they were on bad terms. In February 1782 they quarrelled and in March Waddens was fatally wounded in another fracas. This incident has been described as murder. In 1783 Mme Waddens petitioned Governor HALDIMAND for Pond's apprehension, submitting an affidavit of one of Waddens' men. When in 1785 Pond was in Montreal he was examined but apparently was not brought to trial, probably because Lac La Ronge lay in the territories of the Hudson's Bay Company, beyond the legal jurisdiction of the province of Quebec.

Little is known of Waddens' character, and Alexander Mackenzie*'s description of him as a man of "strict probity and known sobriety" is perhaps a formal phrase. Whatever the case, Waddens did succeed in moving up the social ladder from the private soldier of 1757 to the bourgeois of 1782. He never rose, however, to the ranks of the trader-capitalists as did James McGill*.

Few personal details survive. The children by his marriage to Marie-Josephte Deguire were all baptized at Saint-Laurent or nearby Montreal, three according to the Anglican form of the sacrament. His eldest daughter Véronique became the wife of John Bethune*, Montreal's first Presbyterian minister. Another daughter, Marguerite, whose mother was Indian, married successively Alexander McKay* and Dr John McLoughlin*.

J. I. COOPER

[I wish to acknowledge the assistance I have received from J.-J. Lefebvre and G. F. G. Stanley. J.I.C.]
Archives cantonales vaudoises (Lausanne, Suisse), Eb 129/2, p.178; 129/5, p.12. ANQ-M, État civil, Catholiques, Notre-Dame de Montréal, 1er mai 1757. Archives paroissiales, Saint-Laurent (Montréal), Registres des baptêmes, mariages et sépultures, 23 nov. 1761. *Docs. relating to NWC* (Wallace). HBRS, XIV (Rich and Johnson); XV (Rich and Johnson). PAC *Report*, 1885, note A. Tanguay, *Dictionnaire*. Davidson, *NWC*. Morton, *History of Canadian west*. H. R. Wagner, *Peter Pond, fur trader & explorer* ([New Haven, Conn.], 1955). *CHR*, XIII (1932), 205–7. T. C. Elliott, "Marguerite Wadin-McKay-McLaughlin," Oreg. Hist. Soc., *Quarterly* (Eugene), XXXVI (1935), 338–47.

WÄBER, JOHANN. *See* WEBBER, JOHN

WAIPYKANINE. *See* WABAKININE

WALES, WILLIAM, mathematician and astronomer; b. *c.* 1734 of humble parents, probably in Yorkshire, England; d. 29 Dec. 1798.

William Wales was one of a number of men of science linked through the Royal Society of London and their mutual interest in exploration who in the second half of the 18th century helped bring Hudson Bay into the public eye. His interest in the Canadian north stemmed from 1768–69, when he spent a year at the Hudson's Bay Company post of Prince of Wales's Fort (Churchill, Man.) in order to observe the transit of the planet Venus. He was the first scientist to winter in Hudson Bay, and in addition to keeping a full set of observations "on the State of the Air, Winds, Weather, &c." he presented to the Royal Society after his return a short but perceptive journal of his experiences at the bay, with information on the severity of the climate, the men's clothing and diet, and other details. Wales remained interested in the region, may well have been associated with the Royal Society's request to the HBC in 1770 for natural history specimens to be sent from the bay, and certainly advised two company servants, Andrew Graham* and Thomas HUTCHINS, on the keeping of meteorological observations at York Factory (Man.) during the 1771–72 season. His career seems to have benefited considerably from his service as astronomer on the second Pacific voyage of James COOK from 1772 to 1775, for on his return he was appointed master of the mathematical school established at Christ's Hospital, London, to train youths in navigation, and in November 1776 he was elected a fellow of the Royal Society.

Wales maintained his interest in North America, mainly through his friendship with George Samuel Wegg, vice president and treasurer of the Royal Society since 1772, and from 1774 deputy governor and then governor of the HBC. In 1778 Wales suggested Philip TURNOR to the company as the first of its proposed inland surveyors, a recommendation well worth the five guineas it paid to Wales "for his trouble." In the early 1780s Wales helped with the editing and publication of the official account of Cook's third voyage. In 1792 he intervened in a publishing matter of great import to our knowledge of the Canadian north when he negotiated the sale to Messrs Strahan and Cadell of Samuel HEARNE's journal of northern exploration, geography, and natural history. Wales had met Hearne during his stay at Prince of Wales's Fort in 1768–69. The negotiations were completed in October 1792, shortly before Hearne died, when Wales witnessed the contract that ensured the publication in 1795 of the journal under the title *A journey from Prince of Wales's Fort, in Hudson's Bay, to the northern ocean. . . .*

Wales died in 1798, active to the last at Christ's Hospital, where he was remembered as "a good man, of plain simple manners, with a large heavy person and benign countenance."

GLYNDWR WILLIAMS

[An outline of William Wales's career is given in the *DNB*, which incorrectly states that he accompanied Cook on the third as well as the second of his Pacific voyages. Other biographical details, as well as information of a more general nature about Wales, will be found in Bernard Smith, "Coleridge's *Ancient Mariner* and Cook's second voyage," Warburg and Courtauld Institutes, *Journal* (London), XIX (1956), 117–54. The observations Wales and his assistant Joseph Dymond kept at Churchill, and Wales's more personal "Journal of a voyage, made by order of the Royal Society, to Churchill River, on the north-west coast of Hudson's Bay; of thirteen months residence in that country; and the voyage back to England, in the years 1768 and 1769," are printed in Royal Soc. of London, *Philosophical Trans.*, LX (1771), 100–78. Wales's role in the publishing of Hearne's journal is outlined in the Strahan MSS 2180, in the BL; extracts from the relevant documents have been printed in Hearne, *Journey from Prince of Wales's Fort* (Glover). Some information concerning Wales's contacts with servants of the HBC will be found in *Journals of Hearne and Turnor* (Tyrrell), HBRS, XXVII (Williams), and HBC Arch. B.239/a/67, ff.1, 6d. G.W.]

WALKER, THOMAS, merchant and local official; b. in England; d. 9 July 1788 in Boston, Massachusetts.

Thomas Walker, who had emigrated to Boston in 1752, came to Montreal in 1763 and established himself as a merchant. He purchased a fine stone house on Rue Saint-Paul, near the Chateau de Ramezay, and prospered in the western trade. At this time relations between the military and civilian populations were strained, and Walker became the leading spokesman for the Montreal merchants in their quarrels with the military authorities. In September, soon after his arrival, he ignored the verdict of a military court which had found against him in a civil suit. When civilian government was established in 1764, the governor, James MURRAY, believing that the pugnacious and ambitious merchant could be useful if handled properly, appointed Walker a justice of the peace. Walker, however, used the appointment to give free rein to his animosity against the military, and he was soon quarrelling with them over the billeting of British troops. Previously, soldiers had enjoyed bedding, firewood, and the use of kitchen facilities in addition to their billets; now the magistrates, appealing to the letter of the law, forbade them these comforts. In November Walker and four other magistrates went so far as to imprison Captain Benjamin Charnock Payne, of the 28th Foot, for his refusal to vacate lodgings which a merchant claimed to have rented to another.

Relations between the merchants and the military became so acrimonious that Murray asked Walker and three other magistrates to come to Quebec on 13 December to explain their actions. But on the night of the 6th masked men broke into Walker's house, beat him severely, and cropped one of his ears. Murray wrote in his report that some 20 men had been involved in the attack and that suspicion had fallen on members of the 28th. Four men of that regiment were arrested, and the government sought to have them tried in Quebec where it would have been easy to find an impartial jury. However, Walker, who insisted on having a Protestant jury, refused to go there or to give evidence. He adopted the same position when the government sought as a compromise to hold the trial at Trois-Rivières. The trial, held on 1 July 1765, resulted in acquittal and convinced Walker that the military authorities had permitted the guilty to escape justice.

Murray's governorship had been criticized by the Montreal merchants and their allies in London, and the Walker affair was to increase their opposition. News of the affair had been used in London in April 1765 to bolster the merchants' argument that military authority was incompatible with the economic growth of the colony. Walker, who had been dismissed as a magistrate by the Council of Quebec on 22 June, carried his case to London. He returned in late May 1766 with a stiffly worded note from Henry Seymour Conway, secretary of state for the Southern Department, instructing Murray to reinstate Walker and to "support him in that unmolested Persuit of Trade, which as a British subject, he is entitled to." Shortly thereafter Murray, who had been recalled for an investigation of the affairs of the colony, sailed for England.

Walker's case was reopened in November 1766 when George McGovock, a disreputable ex-soldier who had spent four months in Walker's home, accused six respectable Montreal residents of responsibility for the attack on Walker. Unlike the previous set of defendants, who had been generally considered guilty, the accused – captains John Campbell and Daniel Disney, Lieutenant Simon Evans, John Fraser, judge of the Court of Common Pleas, the merchant Joseph Howard, and Luc de La Corne – received strong support from the public. At Walker's insistence, William Hey, chief justice of Quebec, refused to grant bail; his action brought protest on 23 November in the form of a petition signed by almost every prominent Montreal resident. The trial of Disney in March 1767 resulted in acquittal, and Walker was discouraged from proceeding against the others.

The Disney trial revealed that Montreal's mercantile community had become fragmented, with the articulate Walker now the leader of a small, radical group. In November 1773 Walker, who had petitioned Lieutenant Governor Guy Carleton* as early as 1767 on the desirability of an elected assembly, travelled to London with Zachary Macaulay* to present a similar petition to Lord Dartmouth and to solicit the support of the business community. He opposed the passage of the Quebec Act, agitated for its repeal, and became a foe of Carleton. Through his activity as a wheat buyer and speculator Walker had gained an influence in rural areas that enabled him to circulate, in Montreal and its district and in Quebec, the Continental Congress' 1774 appeal for support. By 1775 Walker was a full-fledged republican. In April he was present at a meeting of American sympathizers at the Montreal Coffee House and there urged the sending of delegates to the next Congress. He supplied military information to Benedict Arnold*, and later to Ethan Allen. In June he agitated among the habitants of Repentigny and Chambly, promising money, arms, and powder to those who would support the Americans.

When the American army invaded the colony in September [*see* Richard Montgomery], Walker, naturally regarded as an enemy and a traitor, was arrested at L'Assomption, where he owned a farm and potash plant and where he had been engaged in levying Canadians to fight the British. On 11 November, when Carleton retreated from Montreal to Quebec, Walker was placed on a ship bound for Quebec. The Americans captured the vessel, however, and Walker was released. He returned to Montreal, and there he housed Benjamin Franklin, Samuel Chase, and Charles Carroll, the three Congress delegates who arrived in the city early in 1776. When the Americans withdrew from the province later that year, Walker accompanied them and established himself in Boston. His subsequent career is obscure, but it is known that in January 1785 he petitioned Congress to recompense him for the losses he had sustained in his support of the American revolution. In that year he also visited Pierre Du Calvet in London.

Lewis H. Thomas

BL, Add. mss 21668, pp.64, 68, 80, 82, 93, 101, 141–43, 146–48, 181 (copies at PAC). Boston, Registry Division, Records of births, marriages and deaths, 9 July 1788. Library of Congress (Washington), Continental Congress papers, no.41, 10, p.665 (copy at PAC). PAC, MG 11, [CO 42], Q, 3, pp.5, 9, 29, 41, 122, 391; 4, pp.1–20, 44, 76, 79, 98, 103, 105–6, 108, 129, 133; 10, p.8; 11, pp.11, 149, 167, 192, 267, 285, 301, 307; MG 23, A1, ser.2, 1, pp.56–67; A4, 16, pp.86–88; I13, 1, pp.118–21, 169–70. Maseres, *Maseres letters* (Wallace). PAC *Rapport*, 1888, xi–xiv, 1–14. *The trial of Daniel Disney, esq. . . .* (Quebec, 1767). *Quebec Gazette*, 13 Dec. 1764, 13 June, 4 July, 12 Sept. 1765, 5 June, 29 Sept., 24 Nov., 29 Dec. 1766, 26 Jan., 9 Feb., 16, 23 March, 9 April, 15 Oct. 1767, 10 March 1768. Le Jeune, *Dictionnaire*, II, 808–9. Wallace, *Macmillan dictionary*. Burt, *Old prov. of Que.* Neatby, *Quebec*. G. F. G. Stanley, *Canada invaded, 1775–1776* (Toronto, 1973). A. L. Burt, "The mystery of Walker's ear," *CHR*, III (1922), 233–55.

WALKER, WILLIAM, HBC master; b. *c*. 1754, probably in England, son of Hannah Walker; d. 13 Oct. 1792 at South Branch House (near Duck Lake, Sask.).

Nothing is known of William Walker prior to his engagement with the Hudson's Bay Company on 17 Feb. 1768. He contracted to serve as an apprentice for seven years and sailed for York Factory (Man.) that spring. After serving his apprenticeship, Walker accompanied Samuel HEARNE to Cumberland House (Sask.) in 1775 and that October left to winter with Crees, "according to his own desire of having an Opportunity to learn the Indian Tongue." The next year he was given temporary charge of Cumberland while its master, Matthew COCKING, took the fur returns down to York. In 1778 Walker's salary was raised from £15 to £25 per annum.

Walker's career at this point highlights to some degree the hardships, tensions, and rivalries which affected HBC men inland from York. The company was dependent on poorly educated Orkney labourers, who often resented having to work with the more articulate Englishmen. Such resentment was probably a source of friction between the abrasive William Tomison*, an Orkneyman who had risen from labourer to officer rank, and Walker, who had been trained as an officer. Six months after Tomison succeeded Cocking as master of Cumberland in 1778, Walker threatened to join the pedlars, who had offered him an annual salary of £60. Two years later the York council and Humphrey MARTEN, chief at York, overruled the London committee's appointment of Walker as "Assistant to Our Chief" at York, arguing that he had not the temperament for the position. Cocking, who knew Walker from York and Cumberland, disagreed. He informed the committee that Walker was "very assiduous and Steady" and was disliked by Marten and Tomison "chiefly through prejudice." He added that Walker was entitled to consider himself worthy of promotion, but "I am sorry to say Partiality is predominent."

Walker spent six years at Cumberland House travelling into the country to meet Indians and persuade them to bring their furs down to trade. In the fall of 1781 he took command of Hudson House (near Wandsworth, Sask.); its master, Robert Longmoor*, was sent farther up the Saskatchewan to collect and stockpile food for a proposed outpost. It was a difficult year for Walker. A smallpox epidemic left the Indians "lying dead about the Barren Ground like Rotten Sheep." He looked after them in the fort as best he could and buried them when they died. Since there were fewer Indians able to hunt, Walker, who was a good shot, spent his time procuring food for the mess. In 1782 he kept the post open during the summer for the first time. This decision enabled the men to collect birch-bark and food, and furs from the Indians who had not been able to come down during the winter.

Walker spent most of the next five years at Hudson House under Tomison and Longmoor. He was frequently given the delicate task of intercepting the Indians before they reached the Nor'Westers, as well as the arduous job of hunting for meat in the winter. In 1787 he was appointed master of South Branch House. During the winter of 1788–89 he collected 6,297 made beaver, a good return for a newly established post. As a mark of the company's satisfaction with his services he was made a member of the York council in 1789.

In 1791 Walker travelled down to York intending to return to England on leave. Tomison, now chief inland, prevailed upon him to return to South Branch House by promising to recommend to the London committee that Walker should succeed him when his own contract expired in 1793. The appointment was made in May 1793, but Walker did not know of it. He had died at South Branch House on 13 Oct. 1792.

It is not known when Walker had formed a liaison with an Indian woman, but their son William was born in Rupert's Land about 1779 and entered the company's service in 1797 as an apprentice. He was killed in 1807.

Tomison was at times critical of Walker, but because the two were so different in temperament his fault finding has to be carefully considered when assessing Walker's contribution to the company. The fact that Walker had a good opinion of his own trading abilities, was more literate than Tomison or Longmoor, and was a sparing consumer of alcohol undoubtedly set him apart. He was an astute trader who understood the Indians, had their trust, and spoke their language. He could and did exercise his judgement, and had the potential to be a good chief inland. It is unfortunate that his premature death deprived him of the opportunity of utilizing his talents.

SHIRLEE ANNE SMITH

HBC Arch. A.1/45, f.19; A.1/138, p.100; A.5/3, f.110; A.6/11, f.33; A.6/12, f.133d; A.6/14, f.77d; A.6/32, f.100; A.6/116, f.19d; A.11/115, ff.142, 167d; A.11/116, ff.24d, 69, 71–72; A.11/117, ff.52–52d, 62, 134; A.16/32, f.101; A.16/33, f.37d; A.30/5, f.72; A.30/10, f.38; B.49/a/3, f.8d; B.49/a/4, f.27; B.49/a/6, ff.50d,

56d; B.49/a/7, ff.16, 26, 38, 40d, 43d; B.49/a/12; B.49/a/15, ff.29d, 49d, 51d, 52d, 55d, 61d, 62d, 63d; B.49/a/16, f.2; B.60/a/7, ff.3d–4; B.87/a/4, ff.7, 12d, 19d; B.87/a/5, f.5d; B.87/a/6–8; B.205/a/1; B.205/a/2; B.205/a/3, f.36d; B.205/a/6, f.41; B.205/a/7, ff.1, 4, 10; B.239/a/59, f.282; B.239/a/71, f.32d; B.239/a/91, f.29. HBRS, XIV (Rich and Johnson); XV (Rich and Johnson). Morton, *History of Canadian west*. Rich, *History of HBC*.

WAPINESIW (Wappenessew, Wabunmashue; the name means white bird), Cree leading Indian; fl. 1755–72.

The first documented reference to Wapinesiw comes from 1755, when Anthony Henday* of the Hudson's Bay Company met him on his expedition from York Factory (Man.) to the prairies. On 2 February Henday, camped near Devil's Pine Creek (Ghostpine Creek, Alta), noted "we are joined by a French Leader named Wappenessew." Since an Indian, before being eligible to assume the role of trading captain, or leading Indian, had to have a family and proven abilities as a hunter and trader, it is probable that Wapinesiw was at least in his early 30s when he met Henday.

Leading Indians occupied an important position in the fur trade [*see* MATONABBEE]. They served as middlemen between fur-traders and Indians who trapped the furs but were unwilling to travel to the bayside posts to trade. Henday reported that Wapinesiw "hath a great sway amongst the Indians, commands above 20 canoes and is greatly taken notice of by the French at Basquea house [The Pas, Man.], where he hath constantly frequented." He recognized that Wapinesiw, either by encouraging other Indians to come down to trade or by himself bringing down the furs, could provide a valuable service for the HBC, which had not yet committed itself to the concept of inland posts. Henday accordingly lured him away from the French with a gift of trading goods on behalf of the company. Wapinesiw travelled down to York later in 1755 and became a regular visitor at the post for roughly the next 15 years. Initially, he brought 20 canoes of prime furs with him every year, but by the 1760s this number had grown to 30. In 1762 Humphrey MARTEN, chief at York, listed him as one of the nine Cree trading captains who visited the post regularly. All of these leaders were said to bring in 30 canoes or more every year.

When the Canadian pedlars invaded York's hinterland in the late 1760s they tried to regain the allegiance of Wapinesiw. In 1770 they succeeded, and he began to use his influence to induce "the Indians to resort to the pedlars" and to protect the canoes travelling up and down from Michilimackinac (Mackinaw City, Mich.) from the interference of other tribes on the way. According to reports reaching York, he "lives in . . . [Thomas Corry's] House all the Winter, dines at Table with the Master, & his family are Cloathed . . . & no favour is refused." It is possible that he continued to visit York, if only to increase the competition for his services. Corry wrote from the Saskatchewan country on 2 June 1772 to inform Andrew Graham*, acting chief at York, both that Wapinesiw "Dwos knot go to see you this Springe But . . . will go to the Grandportge [near Grand Portage, Minn.] with me," and that "he says he will Com to see you the next Spring." That July Wapinesiw was reported accompanying Corry and seven of his canoes down to "the Grand Fort." Graham attempted to persuade him to return to the HBC by sending a present of tobacco and felt confident of success provided the Canadians' "New England Rum does not prevail." There are no further references to Wapinesiw, and it is probable that he died in the 1770s at an age of about 50 or 60.

ARTHUR J. RAY

HBC Arch. B.239/a/66, p.55; B.239/b/23, pp.14–15; E.2/4, p.53. *Docs. relating to NWC* (Wallace). HBRS, XXVII (Williams). [Anthony Henday], "York Factory to the Blackfeet country: the journal of Anthony Hendry, 1754–55," ed. and intro. L. J. Burpee, RSC *Trans.*, 3rd ser., I (1907), sect.II, 307–69.

WASSON (Ouasson, Ousson, Owasser, Warsong, Wassong), Ojibwa chief; b. probably *c.* 1730 in the Saginaw valley (Mich.); d. after 1776. At the time of Pontiac*'s uprising Wasson had several daughters of marriageable age; little else is known about his family.

On 31 May 1763 Wasson brought some 200 warriors from the Saginaw valley to join Pontiac's force in the siege of Detroit. After conferring, Wasson and Pontiac decided to end the attacks on the fort and concentrate instead on cutting off the approaches so that no supplies or reinforcements could be brought in. The plan might have succeeded had the British not been able to pass through the blockade by using the ships Charles Robertson* had built on the Niagara River in 1761 and 1762. Early in July Wasson's nephew was killed in a British sortie, and in retaliation Wasson brutally murdered a British officer, Donald Campbell*, who was a hostage in the Ottawa camp. Enraged over the loss of their prisoner, the Ottawas determined to execute John Rutherford, a prisoner of the Ojibwas. Wasson intervened, took Rutherford into his own lodge, and became so impressed with the young Englishman that he offered his daughter in marriage. In August Wasson sent a letter to the commandant, Henry GLADWIN, demanding the surrender of the fort, a demand that Gladwin ignored. As winter drew near, Wasson and the other chiefs began to have second thoughts about the campaign. In October he and others conferred with Gladwin in the fort, and soon the siege was abandoned.

Wasson was back at the fort the following summer, "begging mercy in the most submissive manner" according to Jehu HAY, and giving excuses for having missed Sir William JOHNSON's peace council at Niagara (near Youngstown, N.Y.). Several weeks later at Cedar Point (near Toledo, Ohio) he met John BRADSTREET's expedition against the unsubmissive tribes. When Bradstreet sent a party under Captain Thomas Morris* into the Illinois country, Wasson apparently agreed to accompany Morris as far as Pontiac's camp. Early in September Wasson was back in Detroit, where he was the principal Indian speaker at Bradstreet's peace conference of 7 Sept. 1764. He told the assembled officers and chiefs that this was one war not started by hotheaded young men. "Every thing that was done last Year bad," he said, "was done by the old Warriors, without Cause. . . . This day, the Young Chiefs broke all their old Chiefs." Greatly impressed, Bradstreet agreed to peace terms.

Wasson was present at another Detroit peace conference in August 1765, but it is not certain what role he played. More than a decade later, in the summer of 1776, Wasson and several Ojibwa warriors met at Fort Pitt (Pittsburgh, Pa) with commissioners appointed by the Continental Congress. On 19 May 1790 an Ojibwa chief named Wasson was with a group of Detroit chiefs including Potawatomis, Hurons, and Ottawas that negotiated the cession of land in present southwestern Ontario. This could well have been the same Wasson, aged about 60, but there is not enough evidence available to be certain.

The name of Wasson was honoured among the Saginaw Ojibwas for many years, but the various bands were never again able to achieve the unity brought about by this great chief.

HARRY KELSEY

Clements Library, Jehu Hay, diary of the siege of Detroit, p.50. National Archives (Washington), RG 75, Michigan Superintendency, Mackinac Agency, letters received, January–June 1838, 4, ff.387–88. PAC, RG 10, A2, 1825. *American archives* (Clarke and Force), 5th ser., II, 511–18. *Canada, Indian treaties and surrenders* . . . [1680–1906] (3v., Ottawa, 1891–1912; repr. Toronto, 1971), I, 1–3. [Thomas Morris], "Captain Morris' journal," ed. H. [H.] Peckham, *Old Fort News* (Fort Wayne, Ind.), VI (February 1941), 3–11; "Journal of Captain Thomas Morris, of his majesty's XVII Regiment of Infantry, Detroit, September 25, 1764," *Early western travels, 1748–1846* . . . , ed. R. G. Thwaites (32v., Cleveland, Ohio, 1904–7), I, 293–328. [Robert Navarre?], *Journal of Pontiac's conspiracy, 1763*, ed. C. M. and M. A. Burton, trans. R. C. Ford (Detroit, 1912). *The new régime, 1765–67*, ed. C. W. Alvord and C. E. Carter (Springfield, Ill., 1916), 56–57. *The revolution on the upper Ohio, 1775–1777* . . . , ed. R. G. Thwaites and L. P. Kellogg (Madison, Wis., 1908; repr. Port Washington, N.Y., and London, 1970), 201. [John Rutherford], "Rutherford's narrative – an episode in the Pontiac war, 1763 – an unpublished manuscript by Lieut. Rutherford of the 'Black Watch,'" Canadian Institute, *Trans.* (Toronto), III (1891–92), 229–52. Peckham, *Pontiac*.

WEBBER, JOHN (known in Switzerland as **Johann Wäber**, but he signed John Webber), artist on James COOK's third Pacific voyage; b. 6 Oct. 1751 in London, England; d. 29 April 1793 in London.

John Webber's father, Abraham Wäber, was a Swiss sculptor who moved to London, changed his name to Webber, and in 1744 married a Mrs Mary Quant. John, the second of six children and probably the eldest surviving, was sent to Bern in 1757 or 1758 to be raised by Rosina Wäber, a maiden aunt. Encouraged in his early aptitude for drawing, he was placed under Johann Ludwig Aberli, a landscape and portrait painter. In 1770 he was sent to Paris, where he studied under Johann Georg Wille. His French drawings show an inclination toward the rural picturesque.

Webber returned to London in 1775 and found employment decorating house interiors for a speculative builder. On the urging of his employer, he displayed his work at the 1776 exhibition of the Royal Academy of Arts. His views of Parisian environs and a portrait of his brother caught the eye of Daniel Carl Solander, assistant to the naturalist Joseph Banks*. It was probably through the agency of Banks that Webber, as Cook wrote, was "pitched upon" for the explorer's third Pacific voyage, to supply drawings of "the most memorable scenes of our transactions" that would supplement "the unavoidable imperfections" of the written account.

The expedition departed in July 1776. Webber sketched as the ships made their way across the Pacific. Two years later, while searching the northwest coast of America for a passage to the Atlantic, Cook's vessels spent four weeks refitting at Nootka Sound (B.C.). There Webber found the Indians (Nootkas) to be "wretched and wild in nature, living principally by fishing and hunting, and the country is covered with pine trees." Drawing "every thing that was curious both within and without doors," he later wrote that he had found at Yuquot, one of the villages at Nootka, "an inside which would furnish me with sufficient matter to convey a perfect Idea of the mode these people live in." He began sketching the room's two large carved and painted figures when a man, seemingly displeased, approached with a long knife and placed a mat "in such a manner as to hinder my having any further sight of them. Being certain of no further opportunity to finish my Drawing & the object too interesting for leaving unfinished, I considered a little bribery . . . and accordingly made an offer of a button from my coat, which when of metal they are much pleased with. This instantly produced the desired effect." It took all of Webber's buttons to enable him to finish.

Webber's efforts on Cook's expedition were well received and rewarded. After returning to London in August 1780, he showed his 200 sketches to George III, the Earl of Sandwich, and Fanny Burney, a noted writer. In addition to the able-bodied seaman's pay Cook had slipped him during the voyage, he received £187 for mess expenses, a back salary of 400 guineas, and a commission to supervise the engraving of 61 of his drawings for the official journals at £250 per annum. Printing was slow, and George Nicol, the king's bookseller, charged Webber with studied delay. His pay ended only in June 1785.

Webber revisited Bern in 1787, and he sketched in Derbyshire and Wales. Having been made an associate of the Royal Academy in 1785, in 1791 he was elected a full member. He printed a series of his own etchings of the voyage, and both Francesco Bartolozzi and William Byrne engraved his *Death of Cook*. Toward 1793 his health declined, and he died in his residence on Oxford Street, at the age of 41, of a kidney disease.

Although none of Webber's pictures rises to distinction, they have on the whole a consistently high quality. His depictions of Nootka Sound, of which there seem to be 29 extant, present about 17 different subjects ranging from coastal profiles to a dead sea otter. The most important drawings, those of Nootkas, the inside and outside of their houses, and their masks and rattles, are of inestimable ethnological value. Six were engraved for the published journal, which was very favourably received and ran through several printings.

DOUGLAS COLE

BL, Add. MSS 33977, ff.217–19; Egerton MSS 2180, ff.112–13. PRO, Adm. 17/7. St George's Church (London), Registers of baptisms, burials, and marriages. Staatsarchiv des Kantons Bern (Bern, Switzerland), Nachlass Sigmund Wagner. James Cook and James King, *A voyage to the Pacific Ocean . . .* (3v. and atlas, London, 1784). *Journals of Captain James Cook* (Beaglehole), III. *DNB*. Historischer Verein des Kantons Bern, Biographien-Kommission, *Sammlung Bernischer Biographien* (5v., Bern, 1887–1906), II, 295–307. *Schweizerisches Künstler-Lexikon*, ed. Carl. Brun (4v., Frauenfeld, Switzerland, 1905–17; repr. Nendeln, Liechtenstein, 1967), III, 409–10. D. I. Bushnell, *Drawings by John Webber of natives of the northwest coast of America, 1778 (with 12 plates)* (Washington, 1928). J. J. Horner and Sigmund Wagren, "Leben Johann Webers von Bern," Künstler-Gesellschaft in Zürich, *Neujahrstück*, XVII (1821), 1–13.

WENMAN (Winman), RICHARD, businessman and office-holder; b. in England; d. 28 Sept. 1781 at Halifax, Nova Scotia, in his 70th year.

In June 1749 Richard Wenman immigrated with the first settlers to Halifax in the ship *Charlton* accompanied by his wife and his son Amos. According to the list of settlers Wenman had been a quarter-gunner in HMS *Advice*. On 27 July 1751 he married a recent widow, Ann Pyke, *née* Scroope, mother of John George Pyke*. Together the Wenmans managed the orphan house in Halifax. Apart from this responsibility and his share of the civic duties required of regular inhabitants, Wenman held a number of official positions and launched a range of business ventures. He was appointed a justice of the peace in 1762, represented Halifax Township in the House of Assembly from 1765 to 1770, and was commissioned captain in the Halifax militia in 1770. His commercial activities included a brewery, a rope-walk established in 1754, contracts for supplying the jail and workhouse, and real estate dealings in town and country.

A man of considerable landed property, Wenman was assessed amongst the ten wealthiest property-owners of Halifax in 1776. His lands were obtained by grant, private treaty, auction, and mortgage. He was one of the original grantees of Lawrencetown in 1754, and ten years later he petitioned successfully for 500 acres near present Sackville known as Wenman Hall farm. His town property, much of which he leased, included some choice commercial lots such as the Market House lot, which he acquired in 1760 and for which he paid nearly £600 over 18 years. One of his houses, adjoining the orphan house property, became the temporary lodging of the Reverend Jacob Bailey* after his flight in 1779 from Pownalborough (in the vicinity of West Dresden, Maine). Bailey especially admired its English country garden stocked with hawthorns, willows, and fruit trees. Wenman was also a slave owner. Cato, a liveried house servant, ran away temporarily in 1778, but he was sufficiently esteemed by his master to be granted his freedom under the terms of Wenman's will.

In comparison with his diversified and apparently thriving entrepreneurial activities, Wenman's role as keeper of the orphan house was a minor concern. But his connection with the institution was a long one, beginning with its establishment in 1752 as a "Public Charity." Its 32-year dependence on the imperial government was unintentional on the part of its originators. In the 1750s the establishment was seen largely as a means of training a labour force in an underpopulated colony. Lieutenant Governor Charles Lawrence* also feared that the absence of such an institution would encourage destitute settlers to sell children to the Acadians, whom he described as anxious for Romish converts. It seems more likely, however, that the main function of the orphan house and, after its dissolution in the 1780s, of the facilities provided for children in the poorhouse till the mid 19th century was the care of the illegitimate offspring of the military and naval establishments in a town that catered fulsomely to the garrison presence. Criticism by the Board of Trade that the Wenmans' superintendence of the orphan house cost more than their care of the children encouraged Jonathan BELCHER to reduce the establishment of 40 children at a cost of £713 in 1760 to one of 25 children at £384 in 1762. The zealous Governor Francis LEGGE further economized by reducing the appropriation to £250 in 1774. Nonetheless, the orphan house provided a tidy sinecure for Wenman and a ready supply of labour for his rope and beer production. The day-to-day supervision devolved on Ann as matron, under the watchful eye of the Reverend John BREYNTON as guardian, and she outlived both the keeper and the asylum, dying in 1792. Meanwhile the Wenmans' daughters Susanna and Elizabeth Susanna improved their social position through marriages to Benjamin Green Jr, the provincial treasurer, and Lieutenant William Pringle of the Royal Nova Scotia Volunteers.

JUDITH FINGARD

Halifax County Court of Probate (Halifax), Book 2, pp.296–97 (will of Richard Wenman, 26 Sept. 1781); Book 3, pp.89–90 (will of Ann Wenman, 18 Feb. 1792) (mfm. at PANS). Halifax County Registry of Deeds (Halifax), 2, pp.371, 381, 391, 406; 3, p.62; 4, pp.28, 101, 119, 121, 122, 123; 5, pp.22, 140, 248; 9, pp.128, 130; 10, pp.89–91, 184; 11, p.215; 12, p.62; 15, pp.300–1; 18, pp.46–50 (mfm. at PANS). PANS, RG 1, 29, no.25; 30, no.18; 32, no.23; 164, p.195; 168, p.41; 397; 411, no.7; 417. PRO, CO 217/14, ff.186, 347; 217/16, f.237; 217/18, ff.63, 205–6, 216, 218–25; 217/19, ff.145, 151; 217/20, ff.26v–27, 30; 217/50, ff.125–26; 218/4, ff.177v–78; 218/5, f.49v; 218/6, ff.25v–26, 72v, 96v, 186. St Paul's Anglican Church (Halifax), Registers of baptisms, burials, and marriages, 27 July 1751, 30 Sept. 1781 (mfm. at PANS). N.S., House of Assembly, *Journal*, 1765–68. *N.S. Archives, I*, 507. *Halifax Gazette*, 7 July 1753, 29 June 1754. *Nova-Scotia Gazette and the Weekly Chronicle* (Halifax), 6 Oct. 1778, 2 Oct. 1781. W. S. Bartlet, *The frontier missionary: a memoir of the life of the Rev. Jacob Bailey . . .* (Boston, 1853), 168–71. Brebner, *Neutral Yankees*. Relief Williams, "Poor relief and medicine in Nova Scotia, 1749–1783," N.S. Hist. Soc., *Coll.*, XXIV (1938), 40–45.

WHEELWRIGHT, ESTHER (rebaptized **Marie-Joseph**), *dite* **de l'Enfant-Jésus**, Ursuline and superior; b. 10 April 1696 (N.S.) at Wells, Massachusetts (now Maine), daughter of Colonel John Wheelwright and Mary Snell; d. 28 Nov. 1780 at Quebec.

Esther Wheelwright's father, like her great-grandfather, the Reverend John Wheelwright, and her grandfather, Judge Samuel Wheelwright, was prominent in the town of Wells. On 14 June 1701 Esther was baptized in the local Congregationalist church.

On 21 Aug. 1703 several hundred Abenakis and some Canadians led by Alexandre Leneuf* de La Vallière et de Beaubassin ravaged Wells and nearby frontier settlements. Esther was carried off by the Abenakis to the forests between the Kennebec and Androscoggin rivers. There she was instructed in the Catholic religion by French missionaries, who rebaptized her conditionally and rechristened her Marie-Joseph. Her parents, having learned of her whereabouts, used the authority of the government of Massachusetts Bay to petition Governor Philippe de Rigaud* de Vaudreuil to obtain her release. He sent a Jesuit much revered by the Abenakis, Father Vincent Bigot*, who after some delicate negotiations persuaded the Indians to release the girl. They did so as a compliment to Vaudreuil and in exchange for a captive Indian boy sent by Esther's father from Boston to Quebec.

Late in 1708 Father Bigot brought Esther to Quebec, where she was treated by Vaudreuil with special consideration as the "daughter of the governor of a small place," a misconception arising, apparently, from the reports of Colonel Wheelwright's influence in Wells and of his position as a member of Governor Joseph Dudley's council. Wartime conditions made it difficult, however, to send Esther home immediately, and on 18 Jan. 1709 she was placed in the Ursuline boarding school.

After 18 months as a pupil, she asked to become a nun. Influenced by Father Bigot, who offered to pay the expenses of her entry with money sent from France, the Ursulines agreed to accept her. Vaudreuil objected, however, because he felt obligated to return her to her family. He withdrew her from the Ursulines in the autumn of 1710, and she spent the following winter at Château Saint-Louis, the governor's residence in Quebec. In June 1711, after receiving from Boston another demand for her release, Vaudreuil brought her to Montreal, whence he intended to send her home. Further difficulties, coupled with her own reluctance, kept him from doing so. For several months she lived at the Hôtel-Dieu, making the acquaintance of the English captives in the city, among them her cousin, Esther Sayward, and Mary Silver*. The two cousins remained friends until Esther Sayward's death in 1770. In Montreal Esther also met the zealous Sulpician, Father Henri-Antoine Meriel*, who exerted much influence on the captives. He arranged for her to stand sponsor with Nicolas Lemoyne d'Assigny at the baptism on 3 Oct.1711 of Dorothée de Noyon, whose mother was Marguerite de Noyon [Abigail Stebbins] of Deerfield, Massachusetts.

Esther was next taken to Trois-Rivières, where the Ursulines were eager to receive her into their nascent community. She preferred the Ursulines of Quebec, however, and began her postulancy with them on 2 Oct.1712. She took the habit as Esther-Marie-Joseph de l'Enfant-Jésus on 3 Jan. 1713. On this occasion Father Bigot preached a moving sermon, the manuscript of which contains what little is known of Esther's life among the Abenakis.

Esther de l'Enfant-Jésus had concluded little more than half of her noviciate when in 1714, after the signing of the treaty of Utrecht, her family again sought her return. In compliance with her earnest plea, Bishop Saint-Vallier [La Croix*] advanced the time of her profession of vows to 12 April 1714, thus ensuring that she would remain in Canada. Contact between Esther and her family was maintained through occasional visits by nephews from New England. Both her father and mother left her bequests, conditional upon her return from Canada, and gifts were exchanged.

Anxious to consolidate the good relations established with the British during 1759 and 1760, when they had acted as nurses for the British troops and Esther had been assistant superior, the Ursulines elected her superior on 15 Dec. 1760. The serene strength which made her respected in the community also made her a logical choice to govern it. She did so from 1760 to 1766, and from 1769 to 1772. She served again as assistant superior from 1772 to 1778, and as zelatrice from 1778 until her death in 1780.

Through a policy of flexibility Esther maintained good relations between the Ursulines and the British authorities. She re-established, though with difficulty, the community's affairs in France and placed it on firm ground financially by encouraging the nuns to perfect their skill in birch-bark embroidery, which became a highly profitable enterprise. The reopening of the noviciate in 1764 after a lapse of nine years had guaranteed the continuing existence of the community, which Esther de l'Enfant-Jésus had helped to restore and direct during 20 of the most difficult years of its history.

GERALD M. KELLY

AN, Col., B, 34/1, p.113 (PAC transcript); C[11A], 30, ff.422–30; 32, ff.119–23, 156–58; 33, ff.15–37, 249–53; 34, ff.333–42. ANQ-M, État civil, Catholiques, Notre-Dame de Montréal, 3 oct. 1711. AUQ, Actes d'élections des supérieures, 63, 67–69; Actes des assemblées capitulaires, 1, pp.111, 123–24, 127, 275–78, 298, 328; Actes de professions et de sépultures, 1, pp.70–71; Annales, I, pp.127–28, 216, 254, 259, 268, 277, 301, 331; Conclusions des assemblées des discrètes, 1, pp.54–55; Corr. des laïcs, Corr. de Miss C. A. Baker avec mère Sainte-Croix; Lettres, pétitions, gouverneurs anglais, juin 1761, 6 mars 1762, 2 janv. 1764, 23 avril 1767; Corr. des ursulines de Paris, 28 sept. 1747, 6 mai 1761, 31 août 1771, 20 sept. 1772, 22 août 1789; Fonds de la famille Wheelwright; Fonds dots des religieuses; Fonds sermons, Sermon du R. P. Vincent Bigot, s.j., 3 janv. 1713; Journal, 2; Livre des entrées et sorties des filles françaises et sauvages; Registre de l'examen canonique des novices, 1, pp.37–38; Registre des entrées, vêtures, professions et décès des religieuses, 1, p.11. Mass. Hist. Soc., Wheelwright family papers; A journal of the proceedings of Nathaniel Wheelwright appointed and commission'd by his Excellency William Shirley Esquire Governour and Commander in Chief in and over His Majestys Province of the Massachusetts Bay in New England from Boston to Canada in order to redeem the captives belonging to this Government in the hands of the French and Indians. Pocumtuck Valley Memorial Assoc. (Deerfield, Mass.), Papers of C. A. Baker.

Coll. de manuscrits relatifs à la N.-F., II, 506. *Maine wills, 1640–1760*, ed. W. M. Sargent (Portland, Maine, 1887), 522–26, 769–72. *Genealogical dictionary of Maine and New Hampshire*, comp. Sybil Noyes *et al.* (Portland, Maine, 1928–39). C. A. Baker, *True stories of New England captives carried to Canada during the old French and Indian wars* (Cambridge, Mass., 1897). E. E. Bourne, *The history of Wells and Kennebunk from the earliest settlement to the year 1820, at which time Kennebunk was set off, and incorporated, with biographical sketches* (Portland, Maine, 1875). Coleman, *New England captives*. M. Trudel, *L'Église canadienne*.

WHITE, JOHN, lawyer and office-holder; b. *c.* 1761, only son of John White of Hicks's Hall, parish of St Sepulchre, Middlesex, England; m. 1784 to Marrianne Lynne of Horkesley, Essex, and they had two sons and a daughter; d. 4 Jan. 1800 in York (Toronto).

John White was admitted as a student at the Inner Temple, London, on 17 Oct. 1777. In 1783 his only sister Elizabeth married his fellow student, Samuel Shepherd, who became a distinguished British jurist and throughout his life remained White's staunch friend and patron. White was called to the bar in 1785 and the following year went to Jamaica, where he practised law without success. In 1791 he was living with his family in Wales, intending to become a clergyman. Shepherd recommended him as a suitable attorney general of Upper Canada to William Osgoode*, who had been selected as chief justice of the new colony. Osgoode passed on the recommendation to Evan Nepean, a commissioner of the Privy Seal, and White was appointed on 31 Dec. 1791.

White sailed for Canada in the spring of 1792 with Osgoode and with Peter* and his sister Elizabeth Russell*, the three of whom remained his closest friends in Canada. After a brief period in Kingston, the government moved in September 1792 to Newark (Niagara-on-the-Lake); White and Osgoode lived together there until White acquired a house the following year. In 1797 he moved to York where Mrs White, from whom he had been estranged, joined him with their children. Their reconciliation was unsuccessful; in 1799 Mrs White returned to England with their daughter.

As the first attorney general of Upper Canada, White was concerned with the adaptation of the laws of Britain to the vastly different conditions of the new colony. There were many problems concerning the ownership of land, especially of land granted before the passage of the Constitutional Act of 1791 and of land transferred by the original grantee before the issuance of his deed. Prosecuting for the crown, White had difficulty getting convictions for murder, even with strong evidence. Because of the absence of jails, petty offenders were punished by fines rather than imprisonment; according to White, these fines were rarely paid.

Like other early attorneys general White carried on a private law practice to supplement his income. Irregularities occasionally resulted. In 1793 Lieutenant Governor Simcoe* was told that White, as attorney general, had prosecuted on an assault and battery charge and had then put up the bail for the defendant, lodged him in his own tent when the sheriff was looking for him, and defended him in the ensuing civil action. Simcoe ignored the complaint, possibly because the defendant was an officer in the Queen's Rangers.

White was active in the founding of the Law Society of Upper Canada in 1797; as its first treasurer he was also its first president. Alone among the lawyers attending its early meetings he supported the distinction between attorneys and barristers. His objection to combining them was overruled 12 days after his death.

During his stay in Kingston in 1792 White had been elected to the House of Assembly as the member for Leeds and Frontenac. He and the surveyor general, David William Smith*, led the support of government-sponsored legislation in the assembly, including the 1793 bill which provided for the eventual abolition of slavery in the province. White was most concerned personally with the bill establishing the Court of King's Bench and the district courts in 1794. He was not a member of the second parliament, but in 1799 he contested a by-election in Addington and Ontario. After his defeat his election expenses were paid by the government. In November 1799 he agreed to contest a seat in Lincoln, but he died before the election.

White's salary as attorney general was £300 a year, supplemented by fees for particular duties, the most important of which was drawing up land deeds. He was seriously in debt to Shepherd when he came to Canada, where he continued to live beyond his means. He constantly sought more highly paid positions and was fiercely resentful of any threatened reduction of his income. A running battle developed among White, the provincial secretary, the surveyor general, the receiver general, the clerk of the Executive Council, and the lieutenant governor, who all shared the fees from the issuance of land deeds. This quarrel deeply divided the officers of government, reduced their efficiency, and caused much bitterness.

White's first impressions of Upper Canada and Simcoe had been favourable, but he rapidly became disillusioned with the country, Simcoe, many of his colleagues, and his own prospects. As his health deteriorated he grew depressed and irascible. He had apparently had a brief affair with the wife of the clerk of the Executive Council, John Small*. Mrs Small slighted Mrs White at an assembly in York; White made a scurrilous comment about Mrs Small's virtue to D. W.

Smith. Eventually this remark reached Mrs Small, whose husband challenged White to a duel. White was shot, and died 36 hours later. Mrs Small was ostracized, Smith's appointment to the Legislative Council was postponed indefinitely, and scandal and ill-feeling permeated the insular society of York.

White died heavily in debt. His executor, Peter Russell, sent White's sons to Shepherd and tried to disentangle his estate. In response to White's requests, the Duke of Portland, secretary of state for the Home Department, had approved a land grant equivalent to that of an executive councillor; news of his decision reached York after White's death, and the land was given to his wife and children. White had attempted to make provision for his mistress in York, Mrs Susanna Page, and their two daughters, but nothing was done for them. His estate was not settled until a private bill was passed in 1837.

White was deeply involved in establishing the legal and judicial system of Upper Canada. He had difficulty, however, working with others and is now chiefly remembered for the circumstances of his death.

EDITH G. FIRTH

White's diary has been published: "The diary of John White, first attorney general of Upper Canada (1791–1800)," ed. William Colgate, *OH*, XLVII (1955), 147–70.

Metropolitan Toronto Library, John Elmsley letterbook; Elizabeth Russell papers; Peter Russell papers; John Graves Simcoe, Wolford papers; Sir David William Smith papers. PAC, MG 23, HI, 3; 5. PAO, Russell family papers; Simcoe (John Graves) papers. PRO, CO 42/21, f.234, William Osgoode to Evan Nepean, 13 Aug. 1791. "Canadian letters: description of a tour thro' the provinces of Lower and Upper Canada, in the course of the years 1792 and '93," *Canadian Antiquarian and Numismatic Journal* (Montreal), 3rd ser., IX (1912), 85–168 (offprint). *Correspondence of Lieut. Governor Simcoe* (Cruikshank). *The correspondence of the Honourable Peter Russell, with allied documents relating to his administration of the government of Upper Canada . . .* , ed. E. A. Cruikshank and A. F. Hunter (3v., Toronto, 1932–36). *Gentleman's Magazine*, 1760–1800. [E. P. Gwillim (Simcoe)], *Mrs. Simcoe's diary*, ed. M. Q. Innis (Toronto and New York, 1965). [F.-A.-F. de] La Rochefoucauld-Liancourt, *Voyage dans les États-Unis d'Amérique, fait en 1795, 1796 et 1797* (8v., Paris, [1799]), II, 64. "The probated wills of men prominent in the public affairs of early Upper Canada," ed. A. F. Hunter, *OH*, XXIII (1926), 335–36. *The town of York, 1793–1815: a collection of documents of early Toronto*, ed. E. G. Firth (Toronto, 1962). W. R. Riddell, *The bar and the courts of the province of Upper Canada, or Ontario* (Toronto, 1928); "The first attorney-general of Upper Canada – John White (1792–1800)," *OH*, XXIII (1926), 413–33.

WIKINANISH (Huiquinanichi, Quiquinanis, Wickananish, Hiyoua), Nootka chief and fur-trader; the name, spelled wikinaniš in a proper native orthography, means having no one in front of him in the canoe and suggests that, as the descendant of a long line of chiefs who had boys as their first-born, he was the direct heir to his father as chief; fl. 1788–93.

Wikinanish was the leading chief at Clayoquot Sound, on the west coast of Vancouver Island, during the period of initial European contact and of the maritime fur trade. Accounts of a Wikinanish appear in the journals of European captains visiting the area from 1788 to 1818. Probably the references are to a succession of men who held the same name. It was reported, for example, that in 1792 Wikinanish gave his name to his eldest son and took for himself the name of Hiyoua (hayuˀa, ten [whales] on the rocks).

Although not as well known as MUQUINNA, the chief at Nootka Sound, Wikinanish was probably more wealthy and therefore more powerful than his neighbour. Because Clayoquot Sound was less frequently visited by European vessels than Nootka and was not at the centre of international rivalry between Britain and Spain, Wikinanish did not receive as much attention in European accounts of the northwest coast. It also seems that relations were often less cordial with Wikinanish than they were with Muquinna. There was often tension and sometimes violence between the fur-traders and the Clayoquot Indians. In 1790 an early visitor, James Colnett*, fearing that there had been an attack on his longboat, took Wikinanish's brother hostage while he investigated the affair. The action not unnaturally incensed the Indians, who a few weeks later launched an attack on Colnett's ship. They occasionally assaulted other trading vessels and in February 1792 were subject to retaliation when one of their villages was burnt. This uneasy relationship tended to deter European visitors despite the power and influence of Wikinanish.

Like other trading leaders, Wikinanish had achieved prominence in Indian society according to traditional patterns and then, with the coming of the white man, was able to consolidate and enhance his dominion by controlling the maritime fur trade in his area. He was able to direct the trade at Clayoquot, particularly by manipulating competition between foreign vessels, in a way that raised the price of furs and therefore increased his personal wealth. He also operated as a middleman between the Europeans and other Indian groups in his vicinity. Hopeful traders arrived at other villages only to find that

Wikinanish's agents had been there already and stripped them of furs. By preventing, with force if necessary, Indian outsiders from trading directly with the ships Wikinanish was able to add his own mark-up to the furs. The captains acknowledged his power and influence. Although undoubtedly inflated, estimates of the number of men that Wikinanish could command ran as high as four to five thousand. According to John Meares*, an early visitor to the coast, "such was the power and extensive territory of Wicananish, that it was very much in our interest to conciliate his regard and cultivate his friendship."

As Meares's remark suggests, Wikinanish held sway over other Nootka groups on the west coast of Vancouver Island. When Peter John Puget*, who visited the coast with George VANCOUVER in 1792 and 1793, styled Wikinanish "the Emperor of all the coast . . . from the Streights of Fuca to the Charlottes Islands," he was probably exaggerating. But Wikinanish had defeated a number of groups in the Clayoquot area, sometimes with a considerable loss of life. Even Muquinna, to the north, considered it necessary to maintain his good will. Muquinna's daughter, Apānas, was betrothed to the eldest son of Wikinanish and, when relations with the Spaniards at Nootka Sound were strained to the point of violence in 1789, Muquinna sought the protection of Wikinanish. These actions did not, however, completely extinguish rivalry between the two great leaders.

ROBIN A. FISHER

PRO, Adm. 55/17. *The journal and letters of Captain Charles Bishop on the north-west coast of America, in the Pacific and in New South Wales, 1794–1799*, ed. and intro. Michael Roe (Cambridge, Eng., 1967). *Journals of Captain James Cook* (Beaglehole), I, II. Meares, *Voyages*. J. M. Moziño Suárez de Figueroa, *Noticias de Nutka: an account of Nootka Sound in 1792*, trans. and ed. I. H. Wilson (Seattle, Wash., 1970). Camille de Roquefeuil, *A voyage round the world between the years 1816–1819* (London, 1823), 28, 93–99. G. Vancouver, *Voyage of discovery* (J. Vancouver). *Voyages of 'Columbia'* (Howay). Cook, *Flood tide of empire*. Philip Drucker, *The northern and central Nootkan tribes* (Washington, 1951). Robin Fisher, *Contact and conflict: Indian-European relations in British Columbia, 1774–1890* (Vancouver, 1977).

WILKINS, JOHN, army officer; date and place of birth and death unknown; fl. 1748–75.

John Wilkins entered the British army about 1748. On 18 June 1753 he became adjutant in the 32nd Foot, probably as an ensign. On 29 Oct. 1754 he was promoted lieutenant, still keeping the post of adjutant, perhaps because of the additional pay. In 1755 he became a captain in the 57th Foot; the regiment (renumbered the 55th) came to America in 1757. Wilkins was made a major in the Royal Americans (60th Foot) on 9 June 1762. He commanded the garrison at Fort Niagara (near Youngstown, N.Y.) from June or July 1762 and was in command throughout Pontiac*'s uprising of 1763–64. He was severely criticized by AMHERST for his lack of aggressiveness and for his "infatuated stupidity" in failing to provide a guard for the *Huron*, sent to supply Detroit, where Henry GLADWIN was besieged by Pontiac's Indians. In September 1763, a supply convoy and two parties from the 80th Foot were ambushed by a large Indian force along the Niagara carrying place, a disaster that Wilkins might have averted with more effective patrols. In October he himself set out with a relief expedition. A storm on Lake Erie resulted in the loss of 70 or 71 men, tons of supplies, and several boats before the party was able to land at Long Beach (Ont.), whence it returned to Niagara. Despite such apparent incompetence, Wilkins was allowed to purchase the lieutenant-colonelcy of the 18th Foot at a price he later claimed was £4,000, £500 over the legal limit. He took rank from 13 June 1765 and went to Ireland to help bring the unit to America for further service.

Following his return to America, Wilkins was assigned in May 1768 to command Fort de Chartres (near Prairie du Rocher) in the Illinois country, and he reached the post on 7 September. He remained at Fort de Chartres until the summer of 1771, when he was replaced by Major Isaac Hamilton. During his three-year tenure Wilkins managed to antagonize most of the French settlers, in part because of his shady dealing with the British trading firm of Baynton, Wharton, and Morgan, but also because of his high-handed and possibly unauthorized administration of courts in the region. On Wilkins' departure Lieutenant-General GAGE advised him to begin assembling evidence to refute charges that had been made against him, and Wilkins apparently left immediately for London to do so. Nothing more is known about his career except that he left the army in 1775, perhaps selling his commission to Adam Williamson, who replaced him in the 18th Foot.

HARRY KELSEY

Huntington Library, Brock coll., BR Box 257; 80487, [G.B., WO], "All commissions in the Dragoons, and the field officers in the Foot, at ten years purchase. Captains and subalterns of Foot at nine years purchase" (broadside). PRO, WO 34/49, Amherst to Gladwin, 1 Aug. 1762, 6 Oct. 1763. Amherst, *Journal*

(Webster). *Correspondence of General Thomas Gage* (Carter), I, 4–6, 208–11, 309–12. *Johnson papers* (Sullivan *et al.*), III, 903–4; X, 815–18. *Michigan Pioneer Coll.*, XIX (1891), 27–295. *Trade and politics, 1767–1769*, ed. C. W. Alvord and C. E. Carter (Springfield, Ill., 1921). *British officers serving in North America, 1754–1774*, comp. W. C. Ford (Boston, 1894), 6, 105. G.B., WO, *Army list*, 1755, 1759, 1763, 1767–69, 1771, 1773, 1775–77. L. W. G. Butler and S. W. Hare, *The annals of the King's Royal Rifle Corps* . . . (5v., London, 1913–32), I, 20, 134–39. Peckham, *Pontiac*. Colton Storm, "The notorious Colonel Wilkins," Ill. State Hist. Soc., *Journal* (Springfield), XL (1947), 7–22.

WILLARD, ABIJAH, army officer and office-holder; b. 27 July 1724 at Lancaster, Massachusetts, second son of Samuel Willard; m. 2 Dec. 1747 Elizabeth Prescott of Groton, secondly in 1752 Anna Prentice of Lancaster, and thirdly in 1772 Mary, widow of John McKown of Boston; d. 28 May 1789 in Saint John, New Brunswick.

The Willard family of Worcester County, Massachusetts, combined land holding with a long record of provincial military service. As a result of his own military duties Abijah Willard twice became involved in Canadian history. The first period of involvement occurred between 1745 and 1760, when Massachusetts was supporting Britain's efforts to expel the French from North America. In 1745 Willard served at the siege of Louisbourg, Île Royale (Cape Breton Island), as a captain in the 4th Massachusetts Regiment, commanded by his father. Ten years later he was a captain in William Shirley's provincial regiment at the siege of Fort Beauséjour (near Sackville, N.B.). During this campaign he kept a journal which contains a vivid account of the forced dispersal of the Acadians after the French defeat. Willard was ordered by Lieutenant-Colonel Robert MONCKTON to round up the French inhabitants and to "burn all the houses that I found." He carried out his orders punctiliously but regarded the grief caused by his raids as "sumthing shoking." After the campaign he was promoted colonel, and in 1759 and 1760 he commanded a regiment under General Timothy Ruggles at Fort Edward and Lake George (Lac Saint-Sacrement), New York. In the latter year his regiment was part of the force under William HAVILAND which assisted in the capture of Montreal.

With the return of peace Willard retired from public service and for the next 14 years pursued a quiet existence as one of Lancaster's more prosperous landowners. However, the increasingly acrimonious debate within Massachusetts over British colonial policy brought him back into the public sphere. Labelled a Tory because of his long service with the British army, Willard became a natural target for public abuse by those opposed to British policies. In 1774 his position became even more difficult when Governor Thomas Hutchinson appointed him a mandamus councillor. He was seized by a mob in Connecticut and imprisoned for five days until he agreed to resign his seat. Yet crowd violence could not undermine Willard's commitment to royal government in America. After the battle of Lexington, in April 1775, he offered his services to the British army and was commissioned a captain in the first company of the Loyal American Associates. When the British evacuated Boston in March 1776, Willard accompanied the troops to Halifax and then to New York. Massachusetts formally cut her ties with this loyalist son by including him in the Banishment Act of 1778 and confiscating his property in 1779.

Willard spent the rest of the Revolutionary War as an assistant commissary on Long Island, but it was not until 1781, after a trip to England, that he obtained a regular salary. With the achievement of American independence in 1783, he prepared to immigrate to British North America, and sent his nephew Abel Willard to England to represent his interests with the loyalist claims commissioners. While still in New York that summer, Abijah Willard, along with such persons as Colin Campbell*, Ward Chipman*, Charles Inglis*, and William Wanton*, signed the controversial petition of the Fifty-Five Associated Loyalists. This petition, in which the signatories requested special grants of 5,000 acres in Nova Scotia for themselves, was bitterly resented by other loyalists, and the fact that Willard's was the first signature made him particularly vulnerable to criticism. The British government did not agree with this criticism; the claims commissioners pointedly praised Willard's scrupulous handling of his wartime accounts and granted him compensation of £2,912 as well as a yearly pension of £150. In addition, he was appointed to the Executive Council of the new province of New Brunswick, a post he held until his death.

Willard arrived at Parrtown (Saint John) in the fall of 1784. Aside from attending occasional council meetings, he did not take a conspicuous part in the public life of New Brunswick. He did acquire a good deal of property on the west side of the Saint John harbour. The parish of Lancaster was apparently named after his birthplace. Although the few personal documents remaining do not reveal Willard's particular reasons for becoming a loyalist, his position was quite typical of persons with a similar military and economic background. His decision caused him real financial hardship, and he particularly resented the failure of his former American neighbours to honour their pre-revolutionary debts. As a result, his estate was insolvent when he died. He was survived by his third wife and three children, all of whom returned to Massachusetts. No portrait of Willard is known to exist, but he is described as a "large and portly" man of "stately presence and dignified manner."

ANN GORMAN CONDON

Willard's journal has been published: "Journal of Abijah Willard of Lancaster, Mass., an officer in the expedition which captured Fort Beauséjour in 1755," ed. J. C. Webster, N.B. Hist. Soc., *Coll.*, no.13 (1930), 3–75. Huntington Library, HM 497, Abijah Willard, journal and orderly book, 1755–56. Worcester County Registry of Probate (Worcester, Mass.), Ser.A, no.65822, estate papers of Abijah Willard, 1816. G. O. Dent, "The loyalist Willards," *Acadiensis* (Saint John, N.B.), V (1905), 157–65.

WILLIAM. *See* TUGLAVINA

WILLIAM OF CANAJOHARIE. *See* TEKAWIROÑTE

WILLIAMS, EUNICE (also known as **Marie, Maria, Marguerite, Margarett, Gannenstenhawi**, meaning she brings in the corn, and **Ouangote, Aongote, Gonˀaongote**, meaning they took her and placed her as a member of the tribe); b. 17 Sept. 1696 in Deerfield, Massachusetts, daughter of John Williams* and Eunice Mather; d. 26 Nov. 1785 at Sault-Saint-Louis (Caughnawaga, Que.).

On 29 Feb. 1703/4 the town of Deerfield was destroyed by the French and their allies, the Iroquois of Sault-Saint-Louis. Approximately 50 townspeople were killed and over 100, including Eunice Williams, taken prisoner in the raid, which was under the command of Jean-Baptiste Hertel* de Rouville. Eunice was taken to Sault-Saint-Louis where she was kept by her Mohawk captor. Her father, who had been freed by Governor Philippe de Rigaud* de Vaudreuil, tried to make contact with her but was told by the Jesuit at the mission of Saint-François-Xavier at Sault-Saint-Louis that the Mohawks "would as soon part with their hearts as the child." Through Vaudreuil's intercession Williams secured an interview with his daughter, and the governor personally made several attempts to ransom her from her captors. Johannes Schuyler* of Albany, New York, who was active in negotiations for the freeing of prisoners, wrote on 18 Feb. 1706/7 that "our spies . . . saw M[r]. Williams daughter . . . she is in good health, but seemed unwilling to returne, and the Indian not very willing to part with her." Several more attempts to redeem her were made but all failed. In 1713 Schuyler came to Canada and found that she had been baptized with the name Marguerite, had married an Indian called Arosen (or François-Xavier), and had adopted the Mohawk language and style of life. Schuyler asked her to return to Deerfield to see her father; she replied through an interpreter that she would not go. Her father journeyed to Canada again and on 13 May 1714 they met, for the last time.

In later years Eunice and her husband made several trips to Massachusetts to see her relatives. In August 1740 they met two of Eunice's brothers, Warham and Stephen, in Albany, and Stephen persuaded them to go to Longmeadow, Massachusetts, where he was a minister. The news of the arrival of Eunice Williams, known as a heroine from her father's narrative, *The redeemed captive returning to Zion . . .*, filled Longmeadow with a crowd of curiosity-seekers. Joseph Kellogg* served as interpreter during the visit. The following summer she, her husband, and two of their three children returned to Longmeadow again, and they made another visit in 1761. On this last occasion Stephen Williams tried once more to persuade his sister to settle in New England, but as in the past she refused.

The descendants of Eunice Williams and Arosen retained the Williams name, in accordance with the practice of the Mohawks' matrilineal society. Thomas Williams [Tehoragwanegen*], a grandson, became a chief at Sault-Saint-Louis; later he journeyed to the western prairies as a voyageur in the fur trade and also distinguished himself as a chief of St Regis. Today the descendants of Arosen and Eunice Williams can be found among the Iroquois of both Caughnawaga and St Regis.

J. A. FRISCH

ANQ-M, État civil, Catholiques, Saint-François-Xavier (Sault-Saint-Louis, Caughnawaga). John Williams, *The redeemed captive returning to Zion: or, a faithful history of remarkable occurrences in the captivity and deliverance of Mr. John Williams . . .* (6th ed., Boston, 1795), 3, 36, 108–9. C. A. Baker, *True stories of New England captives carried to Canada during the old French and Indian wars* (Cambridge, Mass., 1897), 128–54, 380–94. Coleman, *New England captives*, I, 45; II, 54–63, 178–79. F. B. Hough, *A history of St. Lawrence and Franklin counties, New York, from the earliest period to the present time* (Albany, N.Y., 1853), 200–3. Clifton Johnson, *An unredeemed captive; being the story of Eunice Williams . . .* (Holyoke, Mass., 1897). H. H. Peckham, *Captured by Indians;*

true tales of pioneer survivors (New Brunswick, N.J., 1954), 32–49. Alexander Medlicott, "Return to this land of light: a plea to an unredeemed captive," *New England Quarterly* (Brunswick, Maine), XXXVIII (1965), 202–16.

WILLIAMS, GRIFFITH, army officer and author; m. by 1771 Ann Fothersall, and they had three daughters; d. 18 March 1790 at Woolwich (London), England. His brother John was a merchant of St John's, Newfoundland, in 1785.

Griffith Williams entered the Royal Artillery as a private in January 1743 and became a cadet at the Royal Military Academy at Woolwich the following year. His next few years are the subject of some uncertainty; according to a pamphlet he wrote later he was in Newfoundland from about 1744, but another source states that he served as an additional sub-engineer in South Carolina and Georgia from 1744 to 1749. At all events, by October 1749 Williams, now a lieutenant-fireworker of artillery, was stationed at the Newfoundland outport of Carbonear, and by 1750 he had been transferred to St John's. Rather unusually for an officer, Williams took a keen interest in the fishery and in farming; indeed, the Newfoundland historian Daniel Woodley Prowse* considers him to have been one of the pioneers of farming on the island. By the time of his departure from the island he had received and cleared a grant at Quidi Vidi.

In 1758 Williams, now a first lieutenant, was sent to Europe, and he served in the battle of Minden (Federal Republic of Germany) the following year. By 1763 he was a captain in command of a company of artillery and for two years was stationed at various London garrisons. During this time he maintained his interest in Newfoundland. He claimed to have lost over £2,000 in livestock, buildings, and crops during the French attack on the island in 1762 [*see* Charles-Henri-Louis d'ARSACde Ternay], and for several years he addressed memorials to the British government in an apparently futile attempt to obtain compensation. After his departure for the island in 1765 to become artillery commander there, a friend had Williams' observations on the fishery printed in a pamphlet, *An account of the island of Newfoundland . . .* (London, 1765). Williams served in Newfoundland for a further eight years, during which time he explored the interior of the Avalon peninsula and defended the Anglican missionary Edward LANGMAN against charges brought by his parishioners. He and his wife received more grants of land and continued their farming.

In June 1773 Williams left Newfoundland and returned to garrison duty in England. Three years later he was promoted major and sent out with the reinforcements under BURGOYNE destined for Canada. Williams served throughout the campaigns of 1776 and 1777, holding *de facto* command of the artillery in the Burgoyne expedition until he was captured at the battle of Bemis Heights (near Schuylerville, N.Y.) on 17 Oct. 1777. Released from captivity by 1780, he served as brigade-major of the New York garrison for a time. In 1782 Williams, then a lieutenant-colonel, was sent to Gibraltar to take command of the artillery during the closing stages of the siege. In December of the same year he was promoted colonel. The following year he was appointed to command the Woolwich garrison of the Royal Artillery, a post he held until 1786 and again from July 1789 until his death.

Williams' importance to Canadian history rests not on his unspectacular service as an officer, but on his pamphlet. An interesting document, it is one of the few non-official sources on Newfoundland in the 18th century. At the time of its publication the British and French governments were disputing the rights of their fishermen on the French Shore of northern Newfoundland, and Williams evidently intended his pamphlet to awaken the British public to the necessity of securing fishing rights for Britain in the region. Using some questionable and certainly unverifiable statistics, he claimed that during the years 1745 to 1752 the Newfoundland fishery had been worth £1,000,000 annually to Britain, but during the 1760s only about one-sixth of that total. This decrease Williams ascribed to the lack of adequate garrisons since 1750, which discouraged British merchants from competing with the French on the French Shore because they lacked protection in case of disputes. It is unlikely, however, that the presence of garrisons would have made much difference to the merchants, and the decline Williams noted was probably a result of the depletion of the resource following the fishery's operation at maximum capacity in the 1740s. As well, during the 1750s and 1760s the northern shore became less important to British fishermen as they began to exploit the rich Grand Banks fishery. Williams did, however, make some telling arguments against the naval governors, criticizing their negligent computation of the seasonal catch, which they often underestimated by as much as two-thirds. He also proposed interesting innovations, including the institution of a resident governor, a legal amendment that would allow fishermen to winter on the island, and a reduction in price for the equipment and food needed in the fishery. All in all, the pamphlet is a good "Account" of some aspects of 18th-century Newfoundland.

STUART R. J. SUTHERLAND

Griffith Williams is the author of *An account of the island of Newfoundland* . . . (London, 1765).

Cathedral of St John the Baptist (Anglican) (St John's), parish registers, 1752–1800, 1, ff.2, 4. PRO, Adm. 80/121, f.108; CO 194/12, ff.123–24, 196; 194/13, ff.31, 74, 137, 184, 207, 234; 194/14, ff.10, 28; 194/16, f.193; 194/20, f.19; 194/23, ff.325, 341; 194/28, ff.97, 118; 194/30, f.113; Prob. 11/1190, f.176. USPG, B, 6, nos.165, 169. *Gentleman's Magazine*, 1790, 373. *Battery records of the Royal Artillery, 1716–1859*, comp. M. E. S. Laws (Woolwich, Eng., 1952), 27–52. G.B., WO, *Army list*, 1756–90. *Officers of the Royal Regiment of Artillery*, comp. John Kane (4th ed., London, 1900), 4, 4a, 169.

J. P. Baxter, *The British invasion from the north: the campaigns of generals Carleton and Burgoyne from Canada, 1776–1777* . . . (Albany, N.Y., 1887), 286–87. John Drinkwater [Bethune], *A history of the siege of Gibraltar, 1779–1783* . . . (10th ed., London, 1861), 155. Francis Duncan, *History of the Royal Artillery, compiled from the original records* (2v., London, 1872–73), I, 315, 330, 389. C. G. Head, *Eighteenth century Newfoundland: a geographer's perspective* (Toronto, 1976). Porter, *History of Royal Engineers*, I, 166. Prowse, *History of Nfld.* (1895), 296–97, 427.

WILLIAMSON, GEORGE, army officer; b. *c.* 1704, probably in England; d. 10 Nov. 1781 at Woolwich (London), England. He had at least one son, Adam, who served as an engineer officer in North America during the Seven Years' War and later rose to the rank of lieutenant-general.

George Williamson entered the Royal Artillery as a cadet on 1 Feb. 1722 and was commissioned ensign 1 Nov. 1727, second lieutenant 1 Oct. 1731, and first lieutenant 1 Dec. 1737. On Minorca from 1731 to 1746, he was promoted captain on 1 July 1740. Williamson participated in the campaigns in Flanders from 1746 to 1748, receiving his majority on 22 June 1747. Ten years later he became a lieutenant-colonel.

Either in 1756 or early in 1757 Williamson volunteered to serve in America, and because of his reputation as "a very good & carefull officer" he was appointed to command the artillery in the force under Lord Loudoun which was being assembled for an expedition against Louisbourg, Île Royale (Cape Breton Island). Williamson reached Halifax, Nova Scotia, on 8 July 1757 with 76 pieces of artillery; with his reinforcements, the army had about 100 cannon, howitzers, and mortars, served by about 300 men. During the summer he raised a battery to guard the entrance to Halifax harbour.

After his superiors decided in August not to attack Louisbourg that year, Williamson left for New York and Albany. He spent the winter at Albany inspecting, organizing, and requisitioning weapons, ammunition, equipment, and supplies for the next campaign. Like other artillery officers of the period, he was in a rather difficult position, since he was responsible to both the commander-in-chief in North America and the Board of Ordnance in England. But as a veteran officer experienced in army politics Williamson handled both parties diplomatically, and no unusual difficulties arose. In administrating his command he favoured both maintaining strict discipline and treating his officers and men fairly and impartially. A persistent concern of his during this period was securing promotion to colonel commandant of the new battalion about to be added to the Royal Artillery. Williamson was always very sensitive about seniority, precedence, and perquisites, and he sought promotion with great avidity, probably because he appears to have been somewhat older than other officers of the same rank.

During the summer of 1758 Williamson commanded the artillery during AMHERST's siege of Louisbourg. His force consisted of about 300 men and 145 pieces of ordnance including 85 heavy guns and mortars. An expert technician thoroughly familiar with the many intricacies of his branch of the service, Williamson appears to have been responsible for preparing the main bombardment against the fortress, which opened on 22 July. When Louisbourg surrendered five days later he commanded the detail that hoisted the British flag over its walls. He then surveyed his and the French guns, equipment, and supplies with an eye to the coming campaign against Quebec and worked to make the damaged fortifications defensible again. After it was decided not to attack Quebec until 1759, the army was dispersed, and Williamson was ordered to Halifax to prepare for the next year. He arrived there early in September, but having found the storage and barrack facilities there inadequate he proceeded to Boston. He spent the winter preparing for the Quebec expedition; by February 1759 he was in New York, and he also went to Newport (R.I.), Boston, and Louisbourg in the spring. Although hard at work, he was not too busy to continue soliciting command of a battalion as well as promotion to full colonel in the army (he had been appointed local colonel late in 1758). On 4 June 1759 he left Louisbourg with Wolfe*'s army.

During the siege of Quebec that summer, Williamson commanded the artillery detachment of 330 men. In July, on Wolfe's orders, he placed three batteries consisting of seven mortars and 12 heavy cannon on the heights at Pointe-Lévy (Lauzon) opposite the city. The guns fired almost

4,500 shells and over 11,500 cannon-balls, inflicting serious damage to the Upper and Lower towns. Early in September Williamson added eight cannon to the batteries; despite continuing problems with his health, he remained on duty at Pointe-Lévy. When the army reached the Plains of Abraham on the morning of 13 September, its chief artillerist commanded a small detachment of guns that fired briskly throughout the battle; he claimed Montcalm* was mortally wounded by grape-shot from one of the cannon. Although Williamson stated that six light cannon and two small howitzers were present, most accounts mention only two light cannon, and he may well have been trying to impress the Board of Ordnance with his diligence by inflating figures. Williamson attributed the day's success to a combination of luck, planning, and perseverance, and he reported Wolfe's last words as "I thank God for [victory] & now I shall die contented." Following Quebec's surrender, Williamson again supervised the raising of the British flag, and as at Louisbourg he busied himself with assessing captured equipment and supplies and making the town defensible again. He was then ordered to Boston. Once there he wrote to the Marquess of Granby, commander of the British contingent in Germany, and Viscount Ligonier, commander-in-chief and master general of the Ordnance, both old acquaintances from Flanders, asking for help in obtaining command of a battalion. While his letters were at sea, he was promoted colonel commandant of the new third battalion (20 Nov. 1759), evidently on Amherst's recommendation. Hearing of his advancement in February 1760, the new colonel immediately began a campaign to attain brigadier's rank. He spent a busy winter in preparation for the coming year's fighting, and between January and August 1760 his duties took him to New York, Albany, and Oswego.

Given command of the artillery in Amherst's force, the able and hard-working artillerist turned his hand to naval warfare during the advance down the St Lawrence in August 1760. He placed a cannon and its crew in each of five row-galleys or cutters, and on 17 August these attacked and captured the *Outaouaise*, a French vessel of 150 tons with a crew of 100 and ten cannon. Amherst was so pleased with the success that he named the prize the "Williamson Frigate." Returning to more familiar work, the colonel commanded the batteries at the siege of Fort Lévis (east of Prescott, Ont.), where 60 hours' fire from 16 guns forced Captain Pierre Pouchot* to surrender. Williamson again directed the hoisting of the British flag.

After the capitulation of Montreal in September, Williamson proceeded to New York. His command now consisted of detachments scattered among various forts, and he spent his time on routine matters of administration, discipline, and supply. In the spring of 1761 he began the laborious task of collecting men, guns, equipment, and supplies from the forts and garrisons and forwarding them to New York, where they were being assembled for an expedition against the French West Indies. This work, conducted mainly from Albany, also involved considerable redistribution of resources among the posts. Williamson did not accompany Major-General Robert MONCKTON's expedition which sailed for Martinique in November but remained with Amherst in New York. In October 1762 he was apparently replaced as artillery commander in North America, since he was scheduled to sail for England that month.

On 20 Nov. 1762 Williamson was promoted major-general. For the remainder of his career he was stationed at the regimental headquarters and depot at Woolwich and was an active commander of his battalion. He was one of the main sources of information for John KNOX in writing his account of the war in North America, and was a supporter of William Congreve's innovative work on technical improvements in the artillery. On 25 May 1772 he was promoted lieutenant-general. A capable artillery commander whose work played an important part in the crucial engagements at Louisbourg and Quebec, George Williamson contributed significantly to the British victory in the Seven Years' War.

PETER E. RUSSELL

A portrait of George Williamson is in the PAC; it is reproduced in Knox, *Hist. journal* (Doughty), II, facing p.252. PAC, MG 18, N21. PRO, WO 34/78, 34/82–83, 34/119–21, 34/127, 34/129, 34/135–36, 34/147, 34/153–54. Knox, *Hist. journal* (Doughty), I, 7, 209; II, 541, 552–53; III, 87, 339–40. G.B., WO, *Army list. Officers of the Royal Regiment of Artillery*, comp. John Kane (4th ed., London, 1900), 2. McLennan, *Louisbourg*, 262–63.

WINMAN. *See* WENMAN

WINNINNEWAYCAPPO (Captain Jecob), leading Indian, probably Cree; d. in the autumn of 1799 in the Martin Falls (Ont.) district.

Winninnewaycappo, or Captain Jecob as he was known to Hudson's Bay Company traders, first appeared at Fort Albany (Ont.) to trade furs in the autumn of 1769. Thereafter he was one of the early arrivals at the post each May, canoeing down the Albany River from his hunting grounds in the vicinity of Eabamet and Makokibatan lakes. He seems to have attained the peak of his influence during the years 1771–84, when he came to trade with between five and 11 canoes and up to 31 people.

In his capacity as leading Indian, Jecob rendered valuable service to the HBC traders on the coast [*see also* MATONABBEE; WAPINESIW]. An important source of information on events in the Albany hinterland, he also promoted the company's interests among Indians in the interior beyond Gloucester House (Washi Lake, Ont.). In 1777 he offered to "Collect Indians to come down to Albany" and the following August paddled into Gloucester House with another leading Indian called Newaukeshickwab and 11 canoes. Supplying sturgeon, caribou, and geese to the post, which had been established only recently, Jecob was a key factor in the survival of company servants trying to exist on country provisions. In 1778 he warned John Kipling, master at Gloucester, that "Metawiss and Gang . . . is to come here in the winter and kill us." Although this attack did not materialize, Jecob's report is an indication of his informal alliance with the HBC.

Jecob was also a powerful shaman who communicated with forest spirits. In 1786 he became embroiled with another shaman, Assup, a man "looked upon as a God," when one of Assup's sons cast off a daughter of Jecob. She was found "in the woods almost naked and froze to death." Jecob promised revenge: four years later Assup was "almost torn to pieces by a Black Bear" (bears were often guided by shamans).

By 1799 Jecob was trading at Martin Falls. In May 1800 five canoes from his family reported that he had died "last fall." Jacob Corrigal, at Martin Falls, called his death "a great loss."

JAMES R. STEVENS

HBC Arch. B.3/a/62–65; B.78/a/2–4, 6–8, 13, 16–18, 21; B.123/a/5–6.

WINSLOW, JOHN, army officer and office-holder; b. 10 May 1703 at Marshfield, Massachusetts, son of Isaac Winslow and Sarah Wensley; m. in 1725 Mary Little, and they had two sons; m. secondly Bethiah Johnson, *née* Barker; d. 17 April 1774 at Hingham, Massachusetts.

John Winslow was a member of one of the most prominent families of New England; his great-grandfather and grandfather had both been governors of the Plymouth Bay colony. After holding a few minor positions in Plymouth, he was commissioned captain of a provincial company in the abortive Cuban expedition organized in 1740. Apparently through the influence of Governor William Shirley of Massachusetts, Winslow transferred soon afterwards to the British army and served as a captain in Richard Philipps*' regiment (40th Foot) at Annapolis Royal, Nova Scotia, and St John's, Newfoundland. In 1751 he exchanged with a half-pay captain of Shirley's former regiment and returned to Massachusetts, where he looked after his property and represented Marshfield in the General Court of 1752–53. In 1754 he was promoted major-general of militia by Shirley and chosen to command a force of 800 men which was sent to the Kennebec River (Maine) to consolidate British positions in the area and prevent French encroachments. There Winslow planned and built forts Western (Augusta, Maine) and Halifax (Winslow, Maine). The expedition added greatly to his popularity, and he was thus a natural choice as the lieutenant-colonel of a provincial regiment raised by Shirley in 1755 to aid Lieutenant Governor Charles Lawrence* of Nova Scotia in his attempts to sweep French influence from the province.

Winslow played a conspicuous role at the capture of Fort Beauséjour (near Sackville, N.B.) in June 1755 and in the defeat of French ambitions in the Chignecto region during the summer; his journals provide an important eye-witness account. Throughout the expedition differences of temperament had caused him to clash with the commander, Lieutenant-Colonel Robert MONCKTON, a British regular officer; problems of pay and provisioning added to the tension. Monckton appears to have used little tact in dealing with his touchy second in command, at one point ordering that Winslow's regimental colours be forcibly seized. A furious Winslow confided to his journal that "This Transaction Causd Great uneassiness to both officers & Soldiers & raisd my Temper some." He was probably equally to blame for the friction, however, since he resented not having been given command of the expedition.

After the reduction of the French forts in the Chignecto region, Winslow was ordered to proceed to Grand Pré, the largest Acadian community in the Minas area, and there carry out the removal of the population of that region. Although often believed solely responsible for carrying out the deportation, Winslow was in charge of only one segment of a much larger operation. On 5 Sept. 1755 he informed the assembled Acadian men of the Grand Pré region that they, their families, and their portable goods were to be removed from the province. Winslow termed the business "Very Disagreable to my natural make & Temper," but he carried out his orders with care, military precision, and as much compassion as circumstances allowed. The numerous delays in procuring transports caused the deportation to take far longer than had been anticipated, but by November he had shipped some 1,510 Acadians to Pennsylvania, Maryland, and other British colonies to the south. Plans had been previously made to use Winslow as an agent for the settlement of the now vacant farm lands, but they were not carried out.

Winslow instead returned to Massachusetts in November, and the following year reached the high point of his military career when he was appointed by Shirley to command the provincial troops in the expedition against Fort Saint-Frédéric (near Crown Point, N.Y.). However, he fought bitterly with Lord Loudoun, the commander-in-chief, over Loudoun's proposed integration of the provincial troops with the regulars. The provincial soldiers had enlisted to serve only under their own officers, while their officers feared that if the integration came about they would lose their rank, which they held only by colonial commission. The issue nearly developed into a mutiny of the provincial troops and a revolt of their officers, but Winslow eventually agreed to the integration under threats from Loudoun and after pleadings from Shirley. Little of military importance, however, was achieved in the campaign.

This expedition appears to have marked the end of Winslow's military career. He returned to Massachusetts in 1757 and represented Marshfield in the General Court from 1757 to 1758 and from 1761 to 1765. In 1762 he served as a member of the St Croix River boundary commission, and about 1766 moved to Hingham, where he lived the rest of his life.

Barry M. Moody

Winslow's journals have been published: "Journal of Colonel John Winslow of the provincial troops, while engaged in removing the Acadian French inhabitants from Grand Pre . . ." and "Journal of Colonel John Winslow of the provincial troops, while engaged in the siege of Fort Beausejour, in the summer and autumn of 1755 . . . ," N.S. Hist. Soc., *Coll.*, III (1883), 71–196, and IV (1885), 113–246.

Mass. Hist. Soc., Gay coll., Mascarene papers, II, p.4; III, pp.133, 135–36; Winslow papers, 61.E^1.31, 61.E^1.32, 61.E^1.33, 61.E^1.36, 61.E^1.38, 61.E^1.42, 61.E^1.60. PAC, MG 11, [CO 217], Nova Scotia A, 30, pp.55–57. PANS, RG 1, 21, f.148. *Correspondence of William Shirley* (Lincoln), II, 492–93, 495–98, 525–27. *Military affairs in North America, 1748–65* (Pargellis), 54. *N.S. Archives, I*, 396. *DAB*. *DCB*, III (biography of Charles Lawrence). Sabine, *Biographical sketches of loyalists*, II, 439–44. H. E. Dunnack, *Maine forts* (Augusta, Maine, 1924), 234. Murdoch, *History of N.S.*, II. Pargellis, *Lord Loudoun*, 88–91. G. A. Rawlyk, *Nova Scotia's Massachusetts: a study of Massachusetts-Nova Scotia relations, 1630 to 1784* (Montreal and London, 1973), 209–11. J. A. Schutz, *William Shirley, king's governor of Massachusetts* (Chapel Hill, N.C., 1961), 175–76, 178–79, 187–89, 228, 234–35. G. A. Wood, *William Shirley, governor of Massachusetts, 1741–1756; a history* (New York, 1920), 96, 98.

WOOD, THOMAS, physician, surgeon, and Church of England clergyman; b. late in 1711 in New Jersey, probably in New Brunswick, of Scottish Quaker descent; son of Thomas Wood; m. before 1752 Mary Myers, and they had one son and four daughters; d. 14 Dec. 1778, at Annapolis Royal, Nova Scotia.

Thomas Wood was "bred to Physick and Surgery" and practised medicine from New York to Philadelphia in his early years. When troops were raised in New England to relieve provincial units that had taken part in the first siege of Louisbourg, Île Royale (Cape Breton Island), Wood was appointed surgeon to Shirley's American Provincials and accompanied them to Louisbourg in May 1746. He remained there until the regiment was disbanded late in 1748. Having decided to seek ordination in the Church of England, he left for England in June 1749 and was ordained deacon by Bishop Thomas Sherlock of London on 24 September and priest five days later. The report of the Society for the Propagation of the Gospel for 1749–50 states that the citizens of New Brunswick, New Jersey, had requested that "Mr. *Wood*, a Gentleman of a very good Life and Conversation . . . might, if he should be found worthy of holy Orders, and be admitted into them, be appointed their Missionary." Wood left late in 1749 to serve the churches in New Brunswick and Elizabethtown (Elizabeth, N.J.).

Apparently Wood became dissatisfied with his mission, for in letters of 9 Nov. and 6 Dec. 1751 he petitioned the SPG for transfer to Nova Scotia. The following year, on 1 August, he asked to be allowed to exchange missions with Jean-Baptiste Moreau* of Halifax. Without receiving the Society's permission, but with the approval of Governor Edward Cornwallis of Nova Scotia, Wood left for Halifax that month. His hope of succeeding William Tutty* as missionary there was, however, disappointed by the arrival of John Breynton early in October. On Breynton's recommendation Wood was eventually made assistant at St Paul's Church, since the population of Halifax had grown to such an extent that two missionaries had become necessary.

Using Halifax as his base, Wood made many missionary journeys to the western parts of Nova Scotia and to districts as far as what is now the New Brunswick border. In 1755 he was appointed chaplain to the garrison at Fort Cumberland (near Sackville, N.B.), and in 1759 he became chaplain to the first House of Assembly in Halifax. As there appeared to be some rivalry between Wood and Breynton over who was actually in charge of the parish of St Paul, on 24 Sept. 1759 Governor Charles Lawrence* appointed Breynton rector, and Wood vicar, of St Paul's. Wood remained vicar until he went to Annapolis Royal permanently in 1764. Although little is known about his ministry at Annapolis, he seems to have continued his missionary travels. In July 1769 he advised the society of a tour he had made that summer to Maugerville (N.B.) and the Indian settlements on the Saint John River.

Wood was a good linguist and could preach in French, German, English, and Micmac. During his years in Halifax he had become friendly with Abbé Pierre Maillard*, with whom he had studied Micmac. He learned the language so well that in 1764 he began to translate the services in the Book of Common Prayer and started a Micmac grammar. On 4 Sept. 1766 he informed the SPG that he had finished the first volume of the grammar, including the creeds and the Lord's Prayer, and that he was engaged on the second and last volume. A year later he was able to read prayers to the Indians in Micmac at a service attended by the governor in St Pauls. Nothing is known of his Micmac studies after 1767.

Wood had married Mary Myers before his arrival in Halifax. She died on 17 April 1778 and Wood was buried beside her on his death eight months later. One of their daughters married William SHAW and another the surgeon John Philipps*.

C. E. THOMAS

USPG, B, 19, p.10; 20, pp.8, 97, 100; 25, nos.2, 51, 80, 85, 88, 116, 179 (mfm. at PANS). SPG, [*Annual report*] (London), 1748–49, 46. J. B. Bell, "Anglican clergy in colonial America ordained by bishops of London," American Antiquarian Soc., *Proc.* (Worcester, Mass.), 83 (1973), 159. G.B., WO, *Army list*, 1758, 159. S. A. Clark, *The episcopal church in the American colonies: the history of St. John's Church, Elizabeth Town, New Jersey, from the year 1703 to the present time . . .* (Philadelphia and New York, 1857), 62, 65. [H. M. S. Clayton], *Smith's Cove and her neighbors: the story of Smith's Cove and her neighbors in the land of the bluenoses* (2 pts., [Smith's Cove, N.S.], 1961–62), pt.1, 63. R. V. Harris, *The church of Saint Paul in Halifax, Nova Scotia: 1749–1949* (Toronto, 1949), 26. C. F. Pascoe, *Two hundred years of the S.P.G. . . .* (2v., London, 1901), 855. Savary, *Supplement to history of Annapolis.*

WOOSTER, HEZEKIAH CALVIN, Methodist minister; b. 20 May 1771, probably in Massachusetts, son of Edward Wooster; d. 6 Nov. 1798 in the United States.

Hezekiah Calvin Wooster was one of several early Methodist itinerants who emerged from obscurity in the United States and preached briefly with immense effect in Upper Canada. Nothing is known of his early years except that he was converted in 1791 and achieved sanctification or holiness in 1792. He was taken on trial in 1793 by the Methodist Episcopal Church, received into full connection in 1795, and ordained elder two years later. In 1793–94 he was on the itinerant list for the Granville, Mass., circuit and he was subsequently stationed in New Jersey and New York. In 1796 he was appointed to the Oswegatchie circuit in Upper Canada and appears to have worked there and throughout the rest of the eastern part of the province until his failing health impelled him to leave in June 1798.

In the two years he remained in Canada, Wooster became known as a man totally dedicated to his calling. To him, as to his Methodist brethren, nothing was more urgent than to awaken people to their spiritual desolation and to lead them toward conversion and sanctification. By these terms the Methodists meant that the Christian life has two phases – the initial break with one's sinful past, and the attainment of Christian perfection or holiness, in which stage one's life would be fully oriented towards the good. John Wesley believed that this entire process was the consequence of the Holy Spirit's intervention in the individual soul, but he was persuaded that holiness could be attained only in the context of devoted spiritual and moral preparation. For less sophisticated ministers such as Wooster, the new and holy life was initiated by a sequence of intense emotional experiences which they perceived to be the consequence of being smitten directly by the power of God. Hence their preaching was intended to induce their listeners to participate in a series of pentecostal experiences.

A man of fervent piety whose preaching "was not boisterous, but solemn, spiritual, powerful," Wooster was an effective evangelist. When exhausted from exertion and later from illness, he whispered or relied on an interpreter to convey his words. His exhortation "Smite them, my Lord; my Lord smite them," had a dramatic impact on his audiences. One testified: "I felt it like a tremour run through my soul, and every vein, so that it took away my limbs' power. . . ." In others his words stirred ecstasy followed by peace and changed lives. Thus to his contemporary Nathan Bangs* "he was the happy instrument of kindling up such a fire in the hearts of the people, wherever he went, particularly in Upper Canada, that all the waters of strife and opposition have not been able to quench it." Wooster's brethren recorded that "He was a man of zeal, grace, and understanding, but of a slender habit of body, and [he] could not endure all the hardships of travelling, and great exertions in preaching, which zeal, attended with a great revival of the work of God, exposed him to. . . ."

Wooster brought a measure of comfort and a new sense of direction to many who were isolated, fearful, and overwhelmed by the demands of daily life in a wilderness. Those who heeded his words may well have lived together more harmoniously and have had a greater concern for each other. More broadly, by his teaching and example Wooster contributed in a small way to the early growth of the Methodist connection in British North America and especially to the formation of a heroic myth which helped to shape and sustain its development.

G. S. French

Methodist Episcopal Church, *Minutes of the Methodist conferences, annually held in America; from 1773 to 1813 inclusive* (New York, 1813), 120, 149, 222. Nathan Bangs, *A history of the Methodist Episcopal Church* (4v., New York, 1839–41), II, 83–85. J. [S.], Carroll, *Case and his cotemporaries . . .* (5v., Toronto, 1867–77), I, 49, 50. Abel Stevens, *History of the Methodist Episcopal Church in the United States of America* (4v., New York, 1864–67).

Y

YORK, JACK, black slave; fl. 1800.

The life of Jack York is known only through a single criminal act. In 1800 he was one of several black slaves living on the farm of James Girty of Gosfield Township in the Western District of Upper Canada. Girty had served during the American revolution as a "partizan" in the Indian department with his brother Simon* and his fellow Pennsylvania loyalists and friends Matthew Elliott* and Alexander McKee. In this period all of these men became slave-holders by treating captured slaves as personal booty rather than prisoners of war. It is possible that Jack York was acquired in this manner and in 1788 was brought to the District of Hesse. Slavery had been common in that area as early as 1782. By 1807 it was becoming increasingly unpopular, but the renowned anti-slavery statute of 1793 had not changed the lot of slaves such as York; rather it had secured them as the legal property of their owners. Indeed, as late as 1798 Christopher Robinson had sponsored a bill in the House of Assembly which would have extended slavery within the province, although the efforts of Richard Cartwright* and Robert Hamilton* in the Legislative Council prevented it from passing. York's life seems to have been spent in relative ease, tending to his master's animals, possibly fathering children by a female slave Hannah, and devoting his idle hours to hunting. His relationship with his master seems to have been one neither of deference nor strict discipline.

In late August 1800 York's life changed abruptly when he was charged with burglary with intent to commit a felony. He was tried on 12 September before Justice William Dummer Powell* and an associate judge, Alexander Grant*. After a short trial a petit jury of 12 men deliberated only momentarily before finding York guilty. But the charge masked the real nature of his supposed crime, the rape of a white woman, Ruth Tufflemier. The burglary charge was sufficient to support the indictment, and spared the crown the difficulty of establishing the "usual technical Evidence of the rape being perpetrated."

The only record of the testimonies of the seven witnesses is in Powell's bench notes. Ruth Tufflemier testified that on a "star light night" about 20 August she was awakened and discovered York peering into her cabin. Being alone she took her husband's rifle and waited. Some 15 minutes later she heard a noise and noticed that the device fastening the door had been removed. Fearful of letting York know she had recognized him, she threatened to shoot if he breached the door, whereupon he burst in, hit her with a large stick, "treated her with great violence, entered her body, and did not leave untill he had completed his purpose." The removal of the door fastener was crucial to the burglary charge. Powell questioned her in order to make sure that the door had been locked in the usual manner and that she could positively identify the accused. Under cross-examination she said that "she could distinguish between a white man and a black man" and that "no private Picque or resentment" had motivated the accusation.

The sole supporting evidence was circumstantial, from a friend, Hannah Boyles, who recounted that Mrs Tufflemier had visited her home on 20 August, claiming that "she had been abused by Mr Girty's black man Jack" and had recovered from unconsciousness to find "he had ravished her," and who described injuries to Mrs Tufflemier's body suggesting that "the woman was forced" – "Her breast [was] scratched, her loins [were] bruised, and her left thigh just above the Knee was much bruised."

The testimony of Jacob Tufflemier was surprisingly ambivalent. He stated that when York was arraigned his wife had "not sworn positively to the Prisoner, but to the best of her belief." Moreover he introduced the possibility that resentment had motivated the charge by recounting a dispute he had had with York "a long time ago" over Girty's hogs which had culminated with an exchange of violent threats. Tufflemier was absent on the night of the alleged rape but he too contended it was a "Star light night."

The remaining witnesses were York's fellow slaves and master whose testimony suggested that he could not have committed the rape at the time in question. A black woman Hannah testified that she had been "in bed with him that night, untill about 10 or 11 oClock." Another slave, James, said he had seen York "strip to go to bed" and had later awakened with him to shoot an owl, after which they returned to their huts. When questioned by the prosecution, James said that he did not "know the Prisoner is attracted to white women, or that he ever expressed a desire to have connection with Stofflemire's wife." The testimony of James Girty, "a black man," who may have been Girty's illegitimate son, added to the impression that York's only activity that night had been shooting an owl. Girty's own testimony substantiated this incident; moreover he asserted that the night was overcast and that York could not have left his hut without Girty's noticing. Girty told the prosecution he evaluated York at £121 and said his only complaint about York's character was his tendency of "being free of his Tongue and that only to such as made free with him." When York himself took the stand he described a long-standing association with Ruth Tufflemier. They had met "alone in the woods and other places frequently, and [he] had never offended her." He confirmed the quarrel with Jacob Tufflemier which resulted in his own banishment from the Tufflemier abode and he proclaimed his innocence stating that he had been "in his bed at Mr Girty's all night."

During the trial Powell received personal attestations to York's "good Character from long acquaintance" from Thomas McKee*, the son of Alexander, George Ironside*, and William Hands*, all three prominent in the local community. McKee had succeeded his father as deputy superintendent of Indian affairs and was a member of the assembly for Kent. He was also the son-in-law of one of the most powerful men in the district, John Askin*. McKee tried to impugn Ruth Tufflemier's character, claiming that she "had been an Indian Prisoner, redeemed by his father, and had lived in his Kitchen, and He did not think her credit good." Ostensibly because this information was not given under oath, Powell chose to ignore it.

Powell's address to the jury was the critical juncture in the trial. Reiterating that the charge was burglary, he declared that the evidence was clear and consistent, and only the visibility possible on the night in doubt. He admonished the jury about Girty's "avowed Interest . . . in saving the Prisoner" and said "all depended upon the Credit due to the witness Ruth which was unimpeached by anything on the Trial." After the jury's speedy verdict Powell sentenced York to death.

Powell's reasoning is a matter of conjecture. In two earlier burglary cases involving black slaves prejudice does not seem to have affected his judgements, and there is no evidence it played a role in the York case. The trial of William Newberry invites comparison. Powell had sentenced him to death a month earlier after conviction on a charge of burglary, but convinced that the charge was bogus (the "real crime" was attempted rape) and the penalty of execution unjust, although he admitted the conviction was legal, he had written to Lieutenant Governor Peter Hunter* to get the sentence reduced. Newberry's father had been a loyalist spy executed "for bearing arms in the Royal Cause" and this background may have influenced Powell. In contrast, Powell's long acquaintance with Indian department frontiersmen such as Simon Girty may have had something to do with his distrust and outright dismissal of the evidence of Girty and his slaves which was in York's favour. Powell had acted on HALDIMAND's behalf against Girty, Alexander McKee, and James Duperron Baby* earlier when they were involved in 1780 in seizing slaves on a raid into Kentucky, and he had come into conflict with certain of them again on the land board of the District of Hesse between 1789 and 1791. In a note written in 1809 on the prospect of his son joining the department, Powell expressed "my personal aversion to the Indian Department . . . it holds out too many Temptations to Honesty & if persevered in has no Credit with the World."

But regardless of Powell's opinion of them,

these men, and McKee in particular, were powers to be reckoned with. McKee had financed York's defence and had made it known that he intended to apply for mercy on York's behalf. Powell had no reason or wish to defer the execution of a criminal "convicted of the most atrocious offence, without any circumstances of doubt or Alleviation." But in a move calculated to preclude political repercussions, he withheld signing the warrant for execution until Hunter could be consulted. Hunter upheld Powell's decision rejecting McKee's plea for mercy, but York was not executed. On 1 November the sheriff of the Western District, Richard Pollard*, had notified Powell of York's escape. When after several weeks York had not been recaptured, an enraged Powell informed Hunter on 24 November. Clearly Powell suspected collusion and urged Hunter to order a "serious Enquiry," but it is not known whether any action was taken.

Jack York disappeared after his escape. James Girty died in 1817 and his will of 1804 leaves a clue which may pertain to York's fate after 1800. Among his property Girty listed six slaves, aside from his "negro wench Sall," including James, Hannah, and one named Jack!

ROBERT LOCHIEL FRASER III

Metropolitan Toronto Library, William Dummer Powell papers, A27-1, Francis Gore to Powell, 13 May 1809. PAC, RG 1, L3, 204a, no.35; 496, nos.10, 18; RG 5, A1, pp.443–51, 474–75, 502–3, 506–11, 544–45; RG 8, I (C series), 1209, p.38. PAO, Hiram Walker Museum coll., 20-224; RG 1, A-I-6, 4, Jacob Tufflemear to Capt. Elliott, 2 May 1804; C-IV, Gosfield Township East, concession 1, lots 1–4; RG 8, I-3, index to land patents, 1790–1825, II, f.208; RG 22, ser.3, 164, pp.80 (6 Aug. 1800), 94 (12 Sept. 1800); ser.6-2, no.145 (James Girty). *Correspondence of Lieut. Governor Simcoe* (Cruikshank), II, 53. *John Askin papers* (Quaife), I, 476; II, 582. *Michigan Pioneer Coll.*, X (1886), 601–13. PAO *Report*, 1905, 20, 43, 60–61, 76, 78, 90, 151, 272–73; 1909, 67–72; 1910, 67, 69–70. *The Windsor border region, Canada's southernmost frontier . . .* , ed. E. J. Lajeunesse (Toronto, 1960), 54–56.

F. H. Armstrong, *Handbook of Upper Canadian chronology and territorial legislation* (London, Ont., 1967), 26, 48, 192–94, 222. C. W. Butterfield, *History of the Girtys . . .* (Cincinnati, Ohio, 1890), 65–66, 315–19, 397–99. Reginald Horsman, *Matthew Elliott, British Indian agent* (Detroit, 1964). W. D. Reid, *The loyalists in Ontario: the sons and daughters of the American loyalists of Upper Canada* (Lambertville, N.J., 1973), 125. W. R. Riddell, *The life of William Dummer Powell, first judge at Detroit and fifth chief justice of Upper Canada* (Lansing, Mich., 1924), 26–30, 60. R. W. Winks, *The blacks in Canada: a history* (Montreal, 1971), 50–51. R. S. Allen, "The British Indian department and the frontier in North America, 1755–1830," *Canadian Historic Sites: Occasional Papers in Archaeology and History* (Ottawa), no.14 (1975). John Clarke, "The role of political position and family and economic linkage in land speculation in the Western District of Upper Canada, 1788–1815," *Canadian Geographer* (Toronto), XIX (1975), 18–34. Francis Cleary, "Notes on the early history of the county of Essex," *OH*, VI (1905), 73.

YOUVILLE, CHARLES-MARIE-MADELEINE D' (he regularly signed **Ch. Youville Dufrost** or **Dufrost** to distinguish himself from his brother Joseph-François, who signed Youville), parish priest and vicar general; b. 18 July 1729 at Montreal (Que.), son of François-Madeleine d'Youville and Marie-Marguerite DUFROST de Lajemmerais; d. 7 March 1790 at Boucherville, near Montreal.

Charles-Marie-Madeleine d'Youville was barely a year old when his father died in 1730. After 1742 he studied at the Séminaire de Québec, and on 26 Aug. 1752 he was ordained priest. Two years later he was appointed parish priest at Saint-Joseph-de-la-Pointe-de-Lévy. In July 1759 Major John Dalling took him prisoner during a retaliatory raid against the Canadians, who were carrying on guerrilla warfare, and he was held until September. In November he left his parish for the Government of Montreal. He had refused to collaborate with Governor James MURRAY, and in February 1760 Bishop Pontbriand [Dubreil*] confirmed that d'Youville would not return to his parish. He took refuge with his brother Joseph-François, who was parish priest at Saint-Ours, and then succeeded Louis Lepage* de Sainte-Claire as parish priest at Sainte-Rose, Île Jésus. In October 1761 he took up his post at Saint-Joseph-de-la-Pointe-de-Lévy again, and the following spring he made his peace with Murray. In 1774 Bishop BRIAND put him in charge of the parish of Boucherville; he also served as vicar general for the District of Montreal from this date.

Throughout his ministry d'Youville enjoyed his bishop's confidence. He was very young, just 25, when Bishop Pontbriand gave him his first parish, and in 1762 he was asked to receive a wayward *confrère* into his home to assist in his rehabilitation – one of the few priests so called upon. Bishop Briand held him in high esteem, as did Bishop HUBERT, who appointed him vicar general in June 1788.

D'Youville is also remembered as the first biographer of his mother, the founder of the Sisters of Charity of the Hôpital Général of Montreal, called the Grey Nuns. He had watched the birth and growth of her life's work, and he was the natural person to describe the various stages of its development. The tone of the biography is one of admiration, but in truth Mme d'Youville was quite exceptional. The document is interesting in other respects for the details it provides about the religious practices of the period, and through it d'Youville is revealed as a simple and sincere man.

CLAUDETTE LACELLE

C.-M.-M. d'Youville is the author of "La vie de madame Youville fondatrice des Sœurs de la Charité à Montréal" and "Mémoires pour servir à la vie de M[de] Youville et tirés pour la plupart des dépositions des sœurs Despins, Lasource, Rinville et de M[de] Gamelin, et d'une autre sœur"; these manuscripts, held at the ASGM, were published as "La vie de madame Youville, fondatrice des Sœurs de la Charité à Montréal" in ANQ *Rapport*, 1924–25, 361–74.

ASGM, Maison mère, Historique, Doc., 258, 259; Mère d'Youville, Famille, c/23–23.31 (includes some copies of documents held in the AAQ or ACAM). Allaire, *Dictionnaire*, I, 543. Caron, "Inv. de la corr. de Mgr Briand," ANQ *Rapport*, 1929–30, 50, 52, 109; "Inv. de la corr. de Mgr Hubert et de Mgr Bailly de Messein," ANQ *Rapport*, 1930–31, 204, 209–10, 227. Desrosiers, "Corr. de cinq vicaires généraux," ANQ *Rapport*, 1947–48, 111–12 (ten letters from Vicar General Youville Dufrost to Bishop Hubert). A.-H. Gosselin, *L'Église du Canada après la Conquête*. J.-E. Roy, *Histoire de la seigneurie de Lauzon* (5v., Lévis, Qué., 1897–1904), II, 268, 292, 302, 340–50, 360–61, 391, 416; III, 36–37. M. Trudel, *L'Église canadienne*.

YOUVILLE, MARIE-MARGUERITE D'. *See* DUFROST DE LAJEMMERAIS

Z

ZOUBERBUHLER, SEBASTIAN, businessman and office-holder; b. 1709 or 1710, probably in Switzerland; d. 31 Jan. 1773 in Lunenburg, Nova Scotia.

Sebastian Zouberbuhler is known to have been in North America during the 1730s. As agent for Samuel Waldo*, a land speculator, he operated in South Carolina and Massachusetts. In 1743 a committee of the General Court of Massachusetts found the two men at fault for neglecting the German Protestants whom Waldo had recently settled in the eastern part of the colony, in what is now Maine. As a captain in Waldo's unit, the 2nd Massachusetts Regiment, Zouberbuhler fought in the attack on Louisbourg, Île Royale (Cape Breton Island) in 1745. During his stay at occupied Louisbourg, Zouberbuhler bought and sold lumber, cattle, and coal, apparently on his own account as well as Waldo's. He moved to Halifax, Nova Scotia, in 1749 or 1750, after Louisbourg had been returned to France. In 1750 he secured permission to import into Halifax 40 chaldrons of coal dug during the occupation; in the autumn he was in Louisbourg and sold three ships to French residents. He also represented Joshua MAUGER at Louisbourg in 1749 or 1750.

A shrewd and intelligent man, familiar with the English, French, and German languages, Zouberbuhler soon became one of the government agents dealing with the foreign Protestants in Nova Scotia. In 1753 he and John Creighton* were sent as magistrates by Governor Peregrine Thomas Hopson* to the new settlement of Germans, French, and Swiss called Lunenburg. Already suspicious of Halifax rule, the inhabitants feared that their interests were being neglected by profiteering merchants and officials. When Zouberbuhler was thwarted in his efforts to stop the widespread smuggling of rum into the town (probably by New Englanders), he advised the licensing of taverns to regulate the trade. This action was resented by some settlers.

In December 1753 Zouberbuhler became the scapegoat when smouldering discontent erupted. A rumour spread through the town that Jean Pettrequin* had a letter from London asking whether the settlers were receiving the abundant supplies which the local government had been directed to give them. Some settlers seized Pettrequin in an attempt to get the letter as evidence of corruption and neglect on the part of local officials, but he was freed by the commanding officer at Lunenburg, Patrick Sutherland*, Zouberbuhler, and others. A mob then recaptured Pettrequin and shut him in a blockhouse, demanding that he produce the document. Frightened, Pettrequin then claimed that Zouberbuhler had taken it from him. When pursued by the mob, Zouberbuhler took refuge in another blockhouse, where he was protected by some of Sutherland's soldiers.

Sutherland had sent to Halifax for reinforcements, and when the troops under Robert MONCKTON arrived an investigation was launched. Pettrequin declared that he had never had possession of the letter but that it had been read to him by John William Hoffman, who had encouraged him to spread the news of its contents. Hoffman had been justice of the peace among the foreign Protestants when they were in

Halifax but had been deprived of his commission and replaced by Zouberbuhler. He was subsequently tried in Halifax for his part in fomenting the disturbances at Lunenburg and was sentenced to a two-year prison term and a £100 fine.

Despite Zouberbuhler's apparent vindication, resentment against him may have persisted. He was defeated in the election to the first House of Assembly in 1758 but elected the following year for Lunenburg Township. Re-elected in 1761, he was appointed to the Council by Lieutenant Governor Montagu Wilmot* in 1763. His attendance at Council meetings was sporadic, especially after 1764; his duties as chief magistrate in Lunenburg and his private affairs seemed more important to him than his presence at the Halifax-dominated Council. He was active in the firewood and lumber trade in Lunenburg County. By judicious purchases he acquired several properties in Halifax city and Lunenburg town and county. With that incredible speculator Alexander McNutt* and four others he obtained during the great land-boom of 1765 a grant of 125,000 acres between Annapolis Basin and St Mary's Bay. An attempted land-grab in which Zouberbuhler and other councillors would have helped themselves to 20,000-acre grants was not allowed by the Board of Trade in England. Zouberbuhler obtained only 5,000 acres; even his title to that seems to have been questionable.

An ardent churchman, Zouberbuhler led the fight to have a German-speaking Church of England minister appointed to Lunenburg and opposed any intrusion of Lutheran and Calvinist preachers. He was also interested in education and gave a "handsome subscription" toward the erection of a school at North West Range (North West, N.S.) where many of the Montbéliardians, French Protestants who had been assimilated into the Church of England, had settled.

Zouberbuhler died, apparently of gout, at his home in Lunenburg in 1773. His two large land grants had been transferred before his death to James Boutineau Francklin, son of Michael Francklin. The rest of his property went to his daughter Catherine, Mrs Silver. A codicil ordering partial repayment of a loan received during his time in South Carolina was set aside as having originated in an unsound mind.

A. A. MacKenzie

AN, Section Outre-mer, G[3], 2041/1. Halifax County Registry of Deeds (Halifax). Mass., Office of the Secretary of the Commonwealth, Archives Division (Boston), "Mass. archives," 15A. Mass. Hist. Soc., Knox papers, 50; Waldo papers, 1743–44. PANS, MG 4, no.103 (Canon E. A. Harris' notes on Lunenburg County families); MG 7, Shipping registers, Halifax; RG 1, 164. PRO, CO 217/13, f.83. *Royal Gazette* (Halifax), 16 Feb. 1773. *Directory of N.S. MLAs*. Beck, *Government of N.S.* Bell, *Foreign Protestants*. Brebner, *Neutral Yankees*; *New England's outpost*. S. D. Clark, *Church and sect in Canada* (Toronto, 1948). M. B. DesBrisay, *History of the county of Lunenburg* (2nd ed., Toronto, 1895). R. E. Kaulbach, *Historic saga of Lehève (Lahave)* (Lower Sackville, N.S., 1971). Murdoch, *History of N.S.* H. L. Osgood, *The American colonies in the eighteenth century* (4v., New York, 1924), II.

Appendix

DU PONT DUVIVIER, JOSEPH (he signed and was known as the Chevalier Duvivier), officer in the colonial regular troops; baptized 12 Nov. 1707 at Port-Royal (Annapolis Royal, N.S.), son of François Du Pont* Duvivier and Marie Mius d'Entremont de Pobomcoup; d. 24 Nov. 1760.

Following the death of their father in 1714, Joseph Du Pont Duvivier, his elder brother FRANÇOIS, and his younger brother Michel Du Pont de Gourville all entered the military service at Île Royale (Cape Breton Island). François enrolled in 1716 and then went temporarily to France; Joseph and Michel remained in Louisbourg, where they enlisted in 1717. That year the French authorities had expressly forbidden the colonial governor to enrol officers' sons who had not reached 14, but an exception was made for Joseph and Michel. It was not until 1732, however, when Marine cadets were formally instituted, that Joseph was commissioned second ensign in the newly formed company of Michel de Gannes* de Falaise; in 1738, as first ensign, he was transferred to the company of Pierre-Paul d'Espiet de La Plagne. Although it was during these years that his brothers began to build a commercial empire based partially on official patronage, no record links Joseph to their activities. He may have had a private, non-notarial agreement with them, but it is significant that in 1738 he was not mentioned in the public petition of Louisbourg master fishermen and merchants that condemned the practices of his brothers.

In the early 1740s Joseph joined his uncle Louis DU PONT Duchambon on Île Saint-Jean (Prince Edward Island). On 6 Aug. 1744, along with two cousins (Duchambon's sons), another ensign, and 18 soldiers, he took part in his brother François's expedition against Annapolis Royal. During the siege Joseph acted as emissary to the garrison commander, Paul Mascarene*. Joseph later returned to Île Saint-Jean and was left in command of a token detachment of 20 soldiers at Saint-Pierre (St Peters). He moved this command to Port-La-Joie (Fort Amherst). In May 1745, when forces under William Pepperrell* and Peter Warren* were moving against Louisbourg, two American privateers attacked Port-La-Joie and forced its defenders to retreat up the Rivière du Nord-Est (Hillsborough River). Enlisting the support of local residents and Indians, Joseph repulsed the invaders, inflicting considerable casualties. Île Saint-Jean was included in the terms of capitulation for Louisbourg and shortly after Joseph and his men sailed for Quebec with their prisoners, arriving there on 18 Aug. 1745.

In April 1746 Governor Beauharnois* ordered Joseph to go to the lower Saint John River (N.B.) in advance of the expedition of Jean-Baptiste-Nicolas-Roch de RAMEZAY. His mission was to receive supplies from Quebec in the absence of Father Charles GERMAIN and distribute them to Indian allies. The following month he was ordered to Ramezay's headquarters at Beaubassin (near Amherst, N.S.) with any Indians he could muster. His subsequent movements are unknown, but he was promoted lieutenant in 1747. Joseph and his brother Michel returned to Louisbourg after the French reoccupation in 1749, became captains in 1750, and lived there unobtrusively. On 24 Oct. 1750 Joseph contracted an advantageous marriage with his cousin Marie-Josephe Le Borgne de Belle-Isle, widow of Jacques-Philippe-Urbain Rondeau*, the former agent of the treasurers general of the Marine. Only one of their two children survived infancy.

Duvivier served in the garrison of Île Royale until the fall of Louisbourg to AMHERST in 1758; he did not distinguish himself during the siege. Returning to France, Joseph and Michel were awarded the cross of Saint-Louis in 1760. Later that year Joseph was posted to captain the third of four companies of reinforcements sent to Canada under the command of François-Gabriel d'ANGEAC. This expedition was forced by the British navy to seek refuge at the mouth of the Restigouche River, and in the ensuing engagement Joseph served bravely until d'Angeac surrendered. On the return voyage to France, he died of smallpox on 24 Nov. 1760.

T. A. CROWLEY and BERNARD POTHIER

AN, Col., B, 39, ff.287–95v; 66, f.14½; 83, f.19; C^{11A}, 83, ff.173, 177v; C^{11B}, 20, f.304; 26, ff.70–76; D^{2C}, 47, f.483; 48, ff.24, 180, 374–77v; E, 169 (dossier Duvivier [François Du Pont Duvivier]), "Journal conténant le detail de la conduite qui a tenu Monsieur Dupont Duvivier capitaine a l'isle Royalle . . ."; Section Outre-mer, G^1, 408/1, ff.121–22; 408/2, ff.65–66; 409/2, f.42; G^2, 209, dossier 509; G^3, 2041/1, 2 nov. 1750, 4 nov. 1752; 2042, 21 juin 1754. PANS, RG 1, 26 (mfm. at PAC). Knox, *Hist. journal* (Doughty), III, 369, 375,

389–90. *NYCD* (O'Callaghan and Fernow), X, 40, 43. Ægidius Fauteux, "Les Du Pont de l'Acadie," *BRH*, XLVI (1940), 232.

KERRIVAN, PETER. In its full-blown literary form, the legend of Peter Kerrivan is as follows:

Some time around 1750 there arrived on the high barrens of the Avalon Peninsula of Newfoundland, just inland from the village of Ferryland, an Irish deserter from the Royal Navy named Peter Kerrivan, with a small band of men fleeing from the harsh life of the nearby fishing settlements. They lived as hunters on the barren land, dwelling in rude "tilts" near the coastal eminence known locally as the Butter Pot; and they were soon joined by large numbers of young men from the settlements, mostly Irish "youngsters" under bond to serve the English merchants and planters who conducted the fisheries operations. They called themselves the Society of the Masterless Men, and their fame spread until it became a dangerous and intolerable scandal to the ruling merchants and officials. The Royal Navy was ordered to proceed against the outlaws.

There were, however, delays, and the Masterless Men, led by the now expert woodsman Kerrivan, the Robin Hood of the Butter Pot, constructed cunning blind trails throughout the wilderness so that when, at last, a detachment of marines advanced over the hills, their quarry slipped quietly away. Thrice the authorities launched expeditions to rout, capture, or kill the outlaws and burn their hide-out; and thrice the nimble Masterless Men eluded them, though on one occasion four new members of the society were taken and summarily hanged from the yardarm of the nearest British frigate. So, for more than half a century (or a hundred years, in a variant literary version) the society lived outside the law, subsisting on the wild berries and caribou herds like Indians, and occasionally trading surreptitiously with friendly local fishermen of the coast, until a more settled time made it possible for them, one by one, to make their way back to the coast, marry, and live out their lives in peace. Kerrivan himself, however, never did return, but lived to a ripe old age as the patriarch of the Butter Pot, though many descendants bore his name (or its variant forms Kerwin and Caravan) among the small fishing settlements of the Southern Shore and in Trepassey and St Mary's bays.

The legend thus recounted has all the marks of "a folktale caught on the winds of tradition," though surprisingly it seems to have been transmitted by only a single family of the region to which it relates. But for the kernel of an historical basis there is support both in the general social and economic conditions of the settlements of the Southern Shore and elsewhere in the later 18th century, and in several documents concerning events in Ferryland which the legend itself wildly embroiders.

The evidence is as follows. First there is an undated petition to His Excellency John Elliot, Esq., Rear-Admiral of the Red, Governor of Newfoundland, from Robert Carter, J.P., Thomas Pyne, John Baker, Henry Sweetland and others, magistrates, merchants, and traders, representing "the inconvenience in carrying on the fishery, especially in the Harbour of Ferryland, occasioned by the riotous and unlawful assembly of people during the past winter of 1788," and requesting the construction of a jail at Ferryland and the provision of military protection during the coming winter. The governor sent a letter dated 8 Oct. 1789 to Captain Edward Pellew requesting his views on the petition and particularly information on the conditions prevailing in the Ferryland area as observed during his summer patrol. On the same date Pellew replied to Elliot affirming that, indeed, "much danger is to be apprehended" and recommending that a ship of war be stationed at Ferryland for the winter. On 9 October the governor replied to the petitioners, authorizing the building of a jail, the costs to be borne from the moneys collected as fines levied on the rioters; plans for the jail were to be approved by a committee of the Protestant inhabitants of Ferryland. On 20 October the Ferryland magistrates offered a remittance of sentence to all rioters who would give themselves up to be "sent home" to Ireland; a penalty of £50 was announced for all convicted of aiding or harbouring the rioters. A notation dated 25 October records that four men gave themselves up. On 24 March 1791, the Ferryland Surrogate Court, with Edward Pellew, Robert Carter, and Henry Sweetland presiding, convicted 137 men with Irish names of riotous and unlawful assembly in the winter of 1788, and they were penalized with fines of between £2 and £20, transportation home, or the lash. Included in the list is a Thomas Kervan, sentenced to be fined £7, given 39 lashes, and transported home. It is not clear whether all those convicted were actually present in court for the document bears the notation "sentence to be executed if they return," and opposite several names are the words "run away." On 23 June 1791 a meeting was convened at Ferryland to approve the plans for a jail and the appointment of a jailer.

The documentary evidence outlined above reflects the stresses in Newfoundland which accompanied the transition from a migratory fishery and seasonal fishermen to an immigrant shore-based enterprise and the struggle of an increasingly settled population for colonial status. By the late 18th century the traditional West Country-Newfoundland fishery, prosecuted by thousands of "youngsters" shipped over for two summers and a winter, was in decline; Irish immigration, particularly, was replacing the old pattern of seasonal migration of surplus labour [*see* John SLADE], and during the winters idleness, cold, and hunger often led to turbulence. The contemporary records are full of a sense of official anxiety; naval administrators and a rudimentary civil authority, ruling the island during a period of almost continuous foreign war, reacted sharply to perceived threats to order and this reaction is reflected in the speedy response to the Ferryland affair of 1788–91, though it is to be noted that fines, the lash, and deportation home are mild sentences for the age.

As for the still current and vigorous legend of Peter Kerrivan and the Masterless Men it is interesting as a persistent reflection of the popular version of 18th-century Newfoundland history, which traditionally casts tyrannous West Country merchants, fishing admirals, and British naval governors as the villains in a popular struggle for representative institutions and government, successfully accomplished in the opening decades of the 19th century.

G. M. STORY

[The oral tradition has been presented by Harold Horwood in "The Masterless Men of the Butter Pot barrens," *Newfoundland Quarterly* (St John's), LXV (1966–67), no.2, 4–5, and in *Newfoundland* (Toronto, 1969), 113–21, and by Farley Mowat in *The boat who wouldn't float* ([Toronto, 1969]), 32–34. Both Horwood and Mowat picked up the tale from Howard Morry, a well-known fish merchant of Ferryland whose family has long been established on the Southern Shore. Mr Morry received the tradition from his grandmother. In the printed tradition, both Charles Pedley* in *The history of Newfoundland from the earliest times to the year 1860* (London, 1863) and Daniel Woodley Prowse* in *History of Nfld.* refer briefly to a "serious riot at Ferryland" in 1788 with no elaboration. This is surprising at least in Prowse, who had a taste for the picturesque and knew the Southern Shore intimately. The petition of the Ferryland magistrates, the correspondence dealing with the petition, and the record of the meeting convened to approve plans for the Ferryland jail are in PANL, GN2/1, 12 (Documents relating to the disturbances at Ferryland). The judgement of the Ferryland Surrogate Court is in PANL, GN/5/1/C/1, 24 March 1791. Unpublished works by the historical geographer John Mannion and by the historian of the West Country-Newfoundland fishery, Keith Matthews, deal with the general background of the period to which the Kerrivan legend relates. The most accessible treatment of the Irish communities of the Southern Shore is by the anthropologist Thomas F. Nemec in "The Irish emigration to Newfoundland," *Newfoundland Quarterly* (St John's), LXIX (1972–73), no.1, 15–24; "Trepassey, 1505–1840 A.D.: the emergence of an Anglo-Irish Newfoundland outport," *ibid.*, no.4, 17–28; "Trepassey, 1840–1900: an ethnohistorical reconstruction of Anglo-Irish outport society," *ibid.*, LXX (1973–74), no.1, 15–24; and "The Irish emigration to Newfoundland: a critical review of the secondary sources" (unpublished lecture, Nfld. Hist. Soc., St John's, 1978). G.M.S.]

Supplement

CRAMAHÉ, HECTOR THEOPHILUS (baptized Théophile-Hector de Cramahé), army officer, civil secretary to governors James MURRAY, Guy Carleton*, and Frederick HALDIMAND, judge, lieutenant governor of the province of Quebec, and titular lieutenant governor of Detroit; b. 1 Oct. 1720 in Dublin (Republic of Ireland), son of Hector-François Chateigner de Cramahé et Des Rochers and Marie-Anne de Belrieux de Virazel; d. *c.* 9 June 1788 in England.

Hector Theophilus Cramahé, the tenth and last child of a Huguenot family, was baptized in the French church of St Patrick in Dublin. His father had left France towards the end of the 17th century for religious reasons. The elder Cramahé entered the service of England, for which he fought, and found shelter in Ireland, where he raised a large family. Hector Theophilus kept the patronymic Cramahé, which was linked to a fief and a château near La Rochelle owned by the Chateigners.

Following in his father's footsteps Cramahé took up a military career in 1740. Appointed ensign in January 1741, he was posted to the 15th Regiment with the rank of lieutenant three months later. He served at Cartagena (Colombia) and Cuba (1741–42), in Flanders at Ostend (Belgium) (1745), in Brittany at Lorient (1746), and then at Rochefort (1757). On 12 March 1754 he became a captain and in 1758 he went with his regiment to America, where he took part in the siege of Louisbourg, Île Royale (Cape Breton Island), and in that of Quebec the following year.

Cramahé arrived at Quebec in June 1759 and was to remain there more than 22 years, during which he ended the purely military phase of his career. On 22 September, shortly after the capital's surrender, he entered Brigadier-General Murray's service as his secretary. The fact that they had fought in the same regiment and on the same battlefields since 1741 was probably not unrelated to the solid friendship that soon linked the two men. Cramahé became indispensable to the first governor of Quebec and, since he gave up his military command in 1761 to remain with Murray, the latter had no hesitation in using his influence to obtain for him the post of civil secretary, which he held from 1764 to 1780.

At the end of 1764, even before Cramahé's future had been definitely settled, Murray sent him post-haste to London, without advising Major-General GAGE, the British commander-in-chief in North America. As the governor explained in a letter dated 27 October, "The situation of Affairs here obliges me to send him to England because I know nobody so capable of informing ye King's servants thoroughly of everything relative to this country." Cramahé would, he hoped, dispel the "doubts and misrepresentations," unmask the intrigues, and "give you every information I know," since he was "thoroughly informed of all I know." Commenting to the Board of Trade Murray observed, "There does not exist a man of more Integrity and Application" and "No man has the good of this colony more at heart." To the secretary of state for the Southern Department, Lord Halifax, he described him as "one of the best men I know."

Upon arrival in England in December 1764 Cramahé sought audiences with the principal ministers capable of expediting the study of Canadian matters and finding remedies without delay, as Murray desired. The problems fell into five categories. Firstly, the authorities in the home country had to be convinced of the necessity of giving military command to the governor of Quebec, and to that end of having Murray listed as "Extraordinary Brigadier." In this connection Murray took to task Brigadier-General Ralph Burton*, commander of the troops in the province of Quebec, who refused to recognize the military authority with which the governor believed himself vested by his commission. Feelings had been running so high that an anti-Murray clan had developed in London. Secondly, concerning civil affairs, Cramahé had to explain that it was too early to think of convoking the house of assembly demanded by the British merchants. The administration of justice was an area where the governor found himself more open to criticism; the remonstrances of the Grand Jury, to which Murray in a spirit of liberalism had allowed the new Catholic subjects to be admitted, provided the Protestant minority with sufficient ammunition to put the governor in an embarrassing situation. Revenues were a fourth subject of contention. The Treasury, which had not had the time to study this problem, complained of not having received any reports, whereas the governor maintained that he had written about it on many occasions without benefit of a reply. The delay in establishing revenues was slowing down the administration of the colony. Cramahé agreed to draw up for the chancellor of the Exchequer, George Grenville, a statement "from memory" of revenues and expenditures from the time of the conquest until his departure for England, and Murray was pleased with this financial report.

The last, but by no means the least problem that had to be discussed with the authorities was the thorny one of giving the Canadian clergy a bishop. Murray, who was convinced that a bishop was needed, favoured the vicar general of Quebec, Canon Jean-Olivier BRIAND, who, he noted, "has in all circumstances acted with a Candour, Moderation, and a Delicacy" meriting the highest praise. "None of his Gown in the Province," he wrote to Lord Shelburne, "[is] so justly deserving of the Royal Favour." It was with this recommendation by the governor that Briand, the choice of the chapter of Quebec, had set out for London in the autumn of 1764. His steps to obtain permission for his consecration were followed with interest by Cramahé, who arrived just a month later, but the governor's secretary quickly perceived that the time was unsuitable. Assertions were being made that the recent uprisings in Ireland had been fomented by priests. Moreover, the former Jesuit Pierre-Joseph-Antoine ROUBAUD, whom the governor of Quebec himself had sent to England as his protégé, impeded the appointment of a bishop for the province, particularly by the memoir he drew up on the church in Canada. Briand had to defend himself against Roubaud's allegations. Cramahé endeavoured to intervene with Roubaud, but to no avail. In February 1766 Cramahé simply recommended "all possible discretion and secrecy" to Briand, who had sought his advice. In so doing Cramahé acted as prudently as the British ministers, who according to him did not dare give official approval to Briand's proposal for fear of rousing strong opposition in parliament. In the light of this caution on Cramahé's part, it would seem unreasonable to credit the claim made after Briand's consecration by Quebec's attorney general, Francis Maseres*, that Cramahé had been "deluding people into an opinion that . . . [Briand] was not to be called bishop or to appear with all this public pomp."

Cramahé's mission to London was to last some 20 months. The change of government in July 1765 obliged him to start his canvassing all over again. In his correspondence with Murray he conscientiously noted all the steps he had taken. Although he was, as Murray stressed, timid to the point of "what at first may appear awkwardness," Cramahé's letters show that he nevertheless had sound judgement and a perceptive mind. He gave good advice, and Murray not only continued to seek his counsel but told his secretary that he took decisions only while waiting "till you can provide better." No striking results, however, crowned Cramahé's efforts. The probity, modesty, good sense, and thorough knowledge of Canadian affairs vaunted by Murray had not persuaded the British ministers to heed him. On the contrary Murray was recalled to England to give an account of his administration. Exasperated, weary, and suspecting Cramahé of having perhaps been too cautious in his reports and solicitations, the governor even reached the point of writing, not without bitterness, that he hoped "your silence has recommended you to the regards of my enemys who alone at present can do Justice to your merit." But Murray in fact needed his friend's help at such a critical moment. Carleton, who succeeded Murray, was able to recognize Cramahé's value and win him to his service.

Having returned to Canada on 12 Sept. 1766, Cramahé devoted himself to the service of the new lieutenant governor and future governor. Soon he had to undertake jointly the offices of acting receiver general, to which Carleton appointed him on 15 Aug. 1767, and judge of the Court of Common Pleas, assumed in July 1769 following François Mounier*'s death. In July 1770, however, Cramahé gave up the two offices to Thomas Dunn* to become administrator of the province during the absence of Carleton, who left on 1 August for England. The favourable opinion held of Cramahé in high places meant that Carleton had not had to plead the cause of "the eldest Counsellor"; his "Sense, Moderation, and Disinterestedness, as well as Knowledge of all public Business," the governor observed, were already known to Lord Hillsborough, secretary of state for the American Colonies. Cramahé's administration was to last four years. On 6 June 1771, ten months after Carleton's departure, he received a commission as lieutenant governor of this "very important colony," to the great satisfaction of the Council, who assured him "of an entire union and harmony in our Councils as long as you continue to preside in them." He was to hold this appointment until April 1782.

Many problems faced Cramahé as lieutenant governor, and they required thorough explanation to the authorities in London. To this task he applied himself. First and foremost Cramahé became the defender of the Canadians' rights. When on 9 Oct. 1770 he sent Carleton a petition from the Canadians asking that the laws and customs that had governed their landed property be restored, Cramahé emphasized its importance to them. Not content with the supplementary royal instructions of July 1771 confirming the maintenance of seigneurial tenure, which according to Hillsborough should "convince His Majesty's new subjects of the King's gracious intentions" towards them, Cramahé took advantage of these orders the following year to press for the application of the old property laws that were still suspended. He stressed that "the confusion and perplexity of the [present] laws," high costs, dilatory procedures, and the "disagreeable necessity" of listening to hearings in the law courts conducted in a language they did not understand, were the Canadians' main complaints. He even attributed the influence that France might still have over her former subjects to "the confusion . . . subsisting in regard to the laws." The need to set up a stable government for the province as soon as possible appears as a *leitmotiv* in nearly all Cramahé's letters to the minister. His insistence was the more understandable given Lord Hillsborough's warning that delay was unavoidable because of the delicacy and importance of the decisions to be taken.

Cramahé had another strong preoccupation: the achievement of as much religious freedom as possible for the Canadians, in order, he claimed, to gain their affection. He was sympathetic towards the Canadian-born clergy, who, he noted, were "strongly interested in preventing any change," in contrast to the French clergy and the Canadian nobility, whom he suspected of desiring a return to the former régime. On 12 July 1772, "to encourage this Disposition" of the Canadian priests, he allowed Bishop Briand to consecrate Abbé Louis-Philippe MARIAUCHAU d'Esgly as his coadjutor, to the great surprise of Lord Dartmouth, the new secretary of state for the American Colonies. To allow and indeed to desire the existence of "a clergy entirely Canadian" presupposed the acceptance of a bishop to ordain priests and a coadjutor to ensure the succession of episcopal authority; of this Cramahé did his utmost to convince the authorities in London. Dartmouth at first considered this permission granted by the lieutenant governor as "a matter of the highest importance" because no royal instruction had ever recognized episcopal authority. The creation of such a precedent required "the most serious consideration." Five months after the coadjutor had been consecrated, Dartmouth had mellowed: such toleration of the Catholic religion as had been accorded by the king could make "the admission of some episcopal authority under proper restrictions" necessary. A year later, in December 1773, he pointed out "the Justice and Expediency of giving all possible Satisfaction to the new Subjects" according to the guarantee recognized by the treaty of Paris, while assuring himself, however, that all their needs in the practice of their religion would be met within the colony itself without the necessity for recourse to a foreign jurisdiction. He was coming round to Cramahé's very ideas.

Cramahé took every occasion to reassure London about the Canadians' state of mind. His annual tour of the province brought him into contact with the people and allowed him to discover their needs and feelings. Thus he reacted vigorously against the rumour spread by the London newspapers in the spring of 1771 to the effect that the imminent prospect of war with Spain had caused the Canadians to behave "with unusual Insolence." There was "not the least reason to apprehend any stir among them," he asserted. The Canadians' relations with the Indians of the Six Nations seemed equally innocent; he had been unable to obtain any confirmation of a questionable exchange of correspondence between them. A further reason for confidence was the fact that the Canadians were against the house of assembly demanded by the Protestant minority in the province. Efforts to win them over to this cause had proved unavailing, to the great relief of Cramahé, who judiciously explained that the Canadians, suspecting the English speaking merchants of wanting their signatures only to support this request "without really intending their Participation of the Privilege," had refused to join them. Although the new subjects' docility reassured him, the agitation among the British in Montreal and Quebec, who had sent four petitions and two memoirs to London at the end of 1773, alarmed Cramahé, especially since they had conveyed certain of their projects directly to the former attorney general, Maseres, without submitting them to him beforehand. He told Dartmouth that he would try "to convince them of the irregularity of their conduct" and of the "ill example" they were setting their Canadian compatriots, from whom similar activities were to be feared given "their great superiority in point of numbers." It was preferable, he added, "to see [them] continue in [their] habits of respect and submission." In July 1774 Cramahé saw in the proposed Quebec Revenue Act, which was intended to tax spirits in order to defray the cost of the colony's administration, another reason for the British to petition for a house of assembly. The "Old Subjects," he alerted Lord Dartmouth, ". . . have in General adopted American Ideas in regard to Taxation."

Another subject on which Cramahé proved to be a valuable adviser for London was the settling of the boundaries of the province, the western hinterland having been cut off by the Royal Proclamation of 1763. The problem was important and had been getting more serious since 1768 when the mother country had relinquished control in the west, leaving the colonies free to regulate the fur trade with the Indians. Rivalry among merchants gave rise to all kinds of troubles, against which no civil government could take strong action. In 1771 an attempt to bring commissioners of the various colonies together in New York to reach a common set of regulations seemed to offer a glimmer of hope. Cramahé hastened to lend his support to this measure, corresponding with the governor of Virginia, Lord Dunmore, in order to choose the date and procedures for the meeting. It was set for 1 December but unfortunately did not take place. The project failed not only because the British government vetoed the holding of a congress but because, in Cramahé's opinion, "the interests of the two Provinces [New York and Quebec] in regard to the Indian trade differ too widely, to expect they will ever perfectly agree upon general regulations for carrying it on." There remained another solution, one envisaged on 8 April 1769 by the committee of Council that had been appointed to consider the numerous complaints of the British merchants in Montreal. Cramahé had sat on this committee, along with Chief Justice William HEY and Thomas Dunn. It had concluded that from both the geographic and the economic points of view only the extension of Quebec's jurisdiction over the west could restore order there. The legitimacy of this recommendation was confirmed by the fact that since 1770 new fur-traders had come to set up in business in Montreal, thus foreshadowing the supremacy of the St Lawrence valley. On 1 Oct. 1773 Cramahé was able to recommend to Dartmouth that before setting the boundaries of Quebec he should consider the fur trade, on which the commercial activity of the province was concentrated. If the boundaries were left as they were, he wrote, the trade would be lost to the Montreal merchants, to the advantage of those in Albany, their main rivals; this prospect the Montrealers considered all the more "unreasonable" since the southern colonies already had the West Indies trade, whereas the northern one, limited by geographical situation and climate to a scant six months of inland navigation per year, could lay claim to the western trade only. Two months later Dartmouth confirmed to Cramahé that in view of a number of considerations of which the mother country had not been aware at the time of the Royal Proclamation of 1763, it was necessary to extend the boundaries of the province of Quebec to the former limits of Canada.

The lieutenant governor's administration ended on 18 Sept. 1774, with the return of Governor Carleton to Quebec. Cramahé then limited himself to his role as civil secretary and president of the Council, where he had great influence, playing an active role within the French party. The siege of Quebec by the Americans in 1775 [*see* Richard MONTGOMERY] brought Cramahé into prominence again for some weeks. Since Carleton had set up his headquarters in Montreal at the beginning of September, the responsibility fell to Cramahé to ready as far as possible the defences of Quebec City against the approach of the American rebels. The task was hardly an easy one, as Cramahé was aware. Lacking soldiers, Carleton had been unable to post any regular troops to garrison the capital. Its defence rested on a militia re-established and trained in haste, which had been "with difficulty brought to mount guard, and [was] consequently not much to be depended on," in Cramahé's words. The British merchants in the city were just as reluctant to take up arms as were the Canadian habitants in the country. Cramahé reproached the merchants for their "damn'd Committees that had thrown the province into its present state" of indifference. For want of sufficient forces he found himself unable to take strong action against the habitants' defection. He could count upon the fidelity of the clergy, the nobility, and the Canadian bourgeoisie, but their zeal, unfortunately, had not been able to counteract the habitants' resistance. The enemy threatened the besieged as much from within as from without, to such an extent that Cramahé wished that "all of them, inclined to that cause, had done the same" and left the city. Despite the desperate situation Cramahé set to work. With the few men available he endeavoured first to repair the breaches in the walls and to place artillery along the fortifications. On 16 September, to counter pro-American espionage and propaganda, he issued a proclamation designed to enable the authorities to find out in less than two hours the intentions of every newly arrived visitor in the city. On 28 September, in order to man the armed vessels that were to keep a watch on the St Lawrence, he put an embargo on all navigation. Through this measure he was able to detain five transports that had come from Boston. He was overjoyed at the arrival of the naval sloop *Hunter* on 12 October and of the frigate *Lizard* at the beginning of November, since it meant more combatants for the defence of the city. Other developments were less encouraging: on 2 November he learned that the British army and naval commanders, General Sir William Howe and Vice-Admiral Samuel Graves, would not be able to send help from

Boston; the next day Fort Saint-Jean, on the Richelieu, was surrendered to Brigadier Richard Montgomery. At the same time an intercepted letter from Benedict Arnold* to John Dyer Mercier, a Quebec merchant, confirmed his suspicions of betrayal within the walls; it also revealed, to his great despair, the secret advance of Arnold's army along the Kennebec, and led him to predict that this force would soon be on the Chaudière and at Pointe-Lévy (Lauzon and Lévis). To prevent the enemy from crossing the St Lawrence, Cramahé quickly had all ships removed from the south shore and Île d'Orléans. On 12 November, an assembly of Quebec's leading citizens is supposed to have recommended, in view of the precarious situation, that the city surrender. The providential arrival that day of Lieutenant-Colonel Allan MACLEAN, who had come from Sorel with reinforcements, revived hopes. Despite the rebels' occupation of the city's outskirts the next day and their rash parade before the ramparts on 14 November, the besieged Quebeckers did not reply to Colonel Arnold's threatening demand for surrender. Instead the rebels' envoy was twice turned away at the city's gates. On 11 and 16 November Cramahé held a council of war with army and navy officers serving in the defence of Quebec and with two members of the Legislative Council, judges Adam MABANE and Thomas Dunn. Not only did this group vote on the 16th for the unconditional defence of the city, but it also agreed on "the absolute necessity" of maintaining the embargo and detaining the king's ships and their crews. The same day a petition to this effect was sent to the ships' captains. The wise decisions taken by Cramahé in anticipation of the siege were thus sanctioned. Thanks to Cramahé, Maclean at the head of the Royal Highland Emigrants, and Captain John Hamilton commanding the sailors, the critical first phase of the invasion, the autumn of 1775, had been weathered to the advantage of the British. On 20 November, the day after his return to Quebec, Governor Carleton was able to inform London that, considering the unfavourable circumstances, "... every thing has been done in my absence for the Defense of this Place." A captain in the British militia, Thomas Ainslie*, who was more loquacious, gave credit to Cramahé, writing in his *Journal* that "the Lieutenant Governor was indefatigable in putting the town in a proper state of defence."

In the performance of his duties Cramahé was led to take measures which did not always meet with approval. His quarrels with Chief Justice Peter LIVIUS deserve mention. In August 1777 Livius had a disagreement with the members of the Court of Appeal, over which Cramahé presided. Wishing to extend its power over the lower courts, Livius wanted to allow fresh evidence to be accepted in appeals. His colleagues refused. The following October he came into personal conflict with Cramahé, accusing him of "an usurpation and abuse of power." In Carleton's absence from the city the lieutenant governor had arrested two civilians, a tanner and his wife, on his own authority and sent them to the military prison on a charge of having used seditious language. Livius challenged Cramahé's "extraordinary proceeding," accusing him of "Acts of Illegality, Violence and Oppression." Offended in his official dignity, Livius could not tolerate the lieutenant governor's obstruction and interference in his particular responsibility, the administration of criminal justice. Claiming it was his duty to protect personal liberty, Livius maintained that the right of habeas corpus had existed in the colony since the introduction of British criminal law, whereas Cramahé claimed that the risk of rebellion justified his repressive gesture, even if the strict letter of the law did not authorize it. Like Pierre DU CALVET, whose ardent defender he would become, Livius violently opposed encroachments by the military authority upon the civil. On the strength of his office as chief justice, he denied not only that Cramahé had any legal power as long as the governor was in the province but that he had any of the authority his position was officially acknowledged to confer; he asserted that the lieutenant governor could act only as a simple justice of the peace. Livius insistently called for a trial of all the civilians imprisoned illegally by the lieutenant governor: he demanded they be brought before him so that he might deal with them "as of right," and bring the administration of justice back to its normal course. Despite his extreme statements, before taking any action Livius consulted the governor, asking for his protection and aid. Upon his return to the city Carleton temporized – but not for long: some months later, on 1 May 1778, he removed the chief justice from office.

The arrival of the new governor, Frederick Haldimand, on 27 June 1778 was to upset Cramahé's life and deprive him of the influential role he had been able to play with the two previous governors. It seems that ill feeling developed quickly between the two men, since Cramahé proposed in November 1779 to resign from his office as civil secretary. Haldimand's entreaties probably persuaded him to be patient. Their relations soon grew increasingly acrimonious, particularly over the wheat question. The governor supported two proposed ordinances which Cramahé opposed vigorously, one to fix the price of wheat, the other to make threshing of grain obligatory. Alarmed by the poor harvest of the previous year and the danger of shortages, Haldimand asked the Legislative Council in January 1780 to issue an ordinance forcing the sale of wheat at a fixed price. This proposal, supported by the French party, was defeated by one vote, Cramahé having joined the merchants in opposing it. He explained his position in two long letters to the governor on 10 and 20 February. Comparing the fixing of the price of wheat to a "tax" levied on its owners, he denied the Legislative Council had the authority to tax, since the Quebec Act did not confer it. He had no more faith in the submission and obedience of the habitants than he had had in 1775: they would either hide their wheat or go over to the enemy. The area richest in wheat, the Chambly River region (in the Richelieu valley), was in fact also the one that could least be trusted. Surely it was unnecessary to risk losing the colony for "a wretched tax," as the other 13 had been lost. Better to pay the current price for wheat and flour and profit from the good effect this liberality would have on the Canadian people. Cramahé found further justification for this expenditure in his belief that "the present emergency" should be attributed to the British Treasury, which in 1776 had counted too much on the province to supply BURGOYNE's army with flour. Haldimand retorted that his instructions did not prevent him from passing a law to set a fair price for wheat. He criticized the council for not using its authority to bring relief to the poor and end monopolies and greed. As a final argument he insisted that, given the army's extensive requirements of rations, military logistics demanded that the selling price of wheat be fixed, in order to prevent the free play of supply and demand. Haldimand had to be content, however, with an ordinance forbidding the export of supplies, which would reduce the high price of wheat and flour. This ordinance of 9 March 1780 was strangely similar to the one suggested by Cramahé in his letter of 10 February.

On 5 Jan. 1781 Cramahé again returned to the charge, tackling a proposed ordinance aimed at making it obligatory to thresh wheat. Judging the measure improper and ill advised, likely to alarm the habitants, encourage scheming, and give the government's enemies the time in which to do it harm, Cramahé suggested that the government send agents to comb the countryside buying up wheat, and then order it threshed immediately and put in the army's stores. In this way supporters of the American cause would be prevented from storing up wheat for their friends. He brandished the prospect of the habitants hiding and even destroying their wheat harvest if the unpopular obligation to thresh the grain were perceived as the forerunner of a "tax" that would set the selling price – the famous tax already debated in the council and rejected by one vote. Furthermore, in the event of another invasion he saw recourse to martial law as the only means of keeping the province in a state of submission. Not unreasonably Haldimand objected that, since the habitants never sold their wheat until March, it would be unpardonable to lose precious time trying to apply the method suggested by the lieutenant governor; in any event it would be impossible to avoid alarming the habitants with troop movements, because forces had to be shifted soon for the defence of Montreal. He wanted at all cost to avert destruction of the wheat which martial law, applied when the enemy was already among them, would make inevitable. And taking practical considerations into account, he attached greater importance to obtaining unanimous support within the council and among government officials for the adoption of vigorous measures to maintain order, experience having shown that submission and obedience were now virtually impossible in America. Perhaps he feared another rebuff from the council. Giving up the idea of an ordinance, he issued a proclamation ordering wheat to be threshed.

As he was unable to gain acceptance of his views, Cramahé resigned as civil secretary on 5 Jan. 1781, pleading ill health. Far from showing resentment, he said he was ready to give his opinion at any time if asked, and to serve in a minor capacity if the situation required it. Two months later Sir Thomas MILLS, who had advised Haldimand in September 1779 to get rid of Cramahé if he did not cooperate, urged Lord Germain to summon the lieutenant governor to England to answer before the Treasury for the province's accounts. Such an order was issued, but it seems to have been merely a pretext to get him out of the colony. As Cramahé stressed to the Home secretary, Lord Shelburne, in April 1782, three months after his arrival in London, neither Lord North nor the Treasury made any effort to have him appear before them. On 8 July 1781 Haldimand, who was only too happy with the prospect of Cramahé's departure, had suggested Henry HAMILTON to succeed him as lieutenant governor. On 27 April 1782 Shelburne confirmed the choice of Hamilton, and he justified the removal of Cramahé in the following terms: "Lt-Gov. Cramahé's character and time of life is more adapted to other situations than what he now fills." Before leaving Canada on 23 Oct. 1781 Cramahé had received the kind of stirring demonstration of gratitude, esteem, and affection which Haldimand himself was not to get when he in turn left in 1784. "The Address was signed by all the principal citizens both French and English," wrote the *Quebec Gazette*, in contrast to the custom of old and new subjects remaining separate in their public demonstrations. Reduced to the salary of judge advocate, Cramahé asked his former superior, Guy Carleton, to use his influence on his behalf. In 1786 he was appointed lieutenant governor of Detroit, but he was to hold this commission for only 16 months, as his wife Margaret indicated when asking for a pension after his death. He died on or about 9 June 1788, at his residence near Exeter in Devonshire. Cramahé was so discreet about his 22-year stay in Canada that it has been impossible to discover whom he married or whether he had children.

PIERRE TOUSIGNANT and
MADELEINE DIONNE-TOUSIGNANT

AAQ, 20 A, VI, 10; 60 CN, I, 16. ASQ, Fonds Viger-Verreau, Sér.O, 040A, pp.12, 17; 0280, p.49. BL, Add. MSS 21705, f.46; 21714, ff.151, 284, 354; 21732, f.44; 21755, ff.79–87, 89, 91, 94–101; 21890–92 (mfm. at PAC). PAC, MG 11, [CO 42], Q, 2, pp.81–88, 233–35; 6, pp.34–35, 127; 7, pp.192, 253, 266; 8, pp.18, 43–45, 47, 53–56, 74–76, 79–83, 97–98, 160–64, 168, 217–19, 221; 9, pp.34, 51–52, 91–95, 157–58; 10, pp.8, 22, 44–45, 53, 76–80; 11, pp.249–50, 256–57, 264–65, 285–89, 297–98, 319–20, 325, 328–30, 332, 339, 342, 345; 12A, pp.70, 119; 14, pp.233–36, 243, 245, 247–49, 251–52, 257–58, 260; 18, pp.22, 26–27, 216–18; 26, p.73; 26A, p.517; MG 23, GII, 1, ser. 1, 2, pp.25–28, 82–83, 109–10, 130–34, 170–78, 183–85, 188–89, 269–70, 293; 3, pp.256, 258–61, 263–64; RG 68, 89, ff.161–62, 231–33; 93, f.66. PRO, CO 42, 29, ff.70v–77; 32, f.60.

[Thomas Ainslie], *Canada preserved: the journal of Captain Thomas Ainslie*, ed. S. S. Cohen (New York, 1968). *American archives* (Clarke and Force), 4th ser., IV, 170. *Docs. relating to constitutional history, 1759–91* (Shortt and Doughty; 1918), I, 419–21, 713. *Invasion du Canada* (Verreau), 111–12, 235. [Francis Maseres], *Additional papers concerning the province of Quebeck: being an appendix to the book entitled, "An account of the proceedings of the British and other Protestant inhabitants of the province of Quebeck in North America,* [*in*] *order to obtain a house of assembly in that province"* (London, 1776), 101; *Maseres letters* (Wallace), 47, 54. PAC *Rapport*, 1914–15, app. C, 103–6. *Quebec Gazette*, September, 12, 18 Oct. 1775, 18 Oct. 1781, 25 Sept. 1788. "The Irish pensioners of William III's Huguenot regiments, 1702," ed. W. A. Shaw, Huguenot Soc. of London, *Proc.* ([Aberdeen, Scot.]), VI (1898–1901), 295–326. C. E. Lart, *Huguenot pedigrees* (2v., London, 1924–28). "Registers of the French conformed churches of St. Patrick and St. Mary, Dublin," ed. J. J. Digges La Touche, Huguenot Soc. of London, *Pub.* (Dublin), VII (1893), 40, 124, 220. Burt, *Old prov. of Que.* D.[G.] Creighton, *The empire of the St Lawrence* (Toronto, 1956). A.-H. Gosselin, *L'Église du Canada après la Conquête*. R. J. Jones, *A history of the 15th (East Yorkshire) Regiment (the Duke of York's Own), 1685 to 1914* (Beverley, Eng., 1958). Neatby, *Administration of justice under Quebec Act*; *Quebec*. P. C. Phillips, *The fur trade* (2v., Norman, Okla., 1962). G. F. G. Stanley, *Canada invaded, 1775–1776* (Toronto, 1973). M. Trudel, *L'Église canadienne*; *Le Régime militaire*. A. L. Burt, "The tragedy of Chief Justice Livius," *CHR*, V (1924), 196–212. S. S. Cohen, "Lieutenant John Starke and the defence of Quebec," *Dal. Rev.*, XLVII (1967–68), 57–64. S. M. Scott, "Civil and military authority in Canada, 1764–1766," *CHR*, IX (1928), 117–36. Têtu, "Le chapitre de la cathédrale," *BRH*, XV, 354–55; XVI, 5.

HALDIMAND, Sir FREDERICK (baptized **François-Louis-Frédéric**), army officer and colonial administrator; b. 11 Aug. 1718 at Yverdon, Switzerland, second of four sons of François-Louis Haldimand, receiver for the town, and Marie-Madeleine de Treytorrens; d. unmarried there 5 June 1791.

Frederick Haldimand apparently was attracted to a military career early in life, and in 1740 he entered the Prussian army, seemingly as an officer, and saw active service during the War of the Austrian Succession. By 1750 he had transferred to the Dutch army, where that year he became captain commandant in the regiment of Swiss Guards, with the army rank of lieutenant-colonel. Some time in 1755 he was recruited for a British infantry regiment intended for colonial campaigning and to be composed partly of Germans and Swiss. He became lieutenant-colonel of the 2nd battalion of this unit, named the Royal Americans (62nd, later 60th, Foot), in January 1756, and during the Seven Years' War he saw a considerable amount of service in North America. He participated in ABERCROMBY's assault on Fort Carillon (Ticonderoga, N.Y.) in 1758, defended Oswego (N.Y.) from Louis de La Corne* in 1759, and took part in AMHERST's campaign against Montreal in 1760.

From September 1760 until the spring of 1762 Haldimand was second in command to GAGE at Montreal, but then he temporarily replaced Ralph Burton* as military governor of Trois-Rivières. From October 1763 to September 1764 he was full governor. During his terms of office he made some changes in the administration of justice and took a keen interest in the operation of the Saint-Maurice ironworks, whose production increased substantially during the military régime. Changes instituted by the introduction of civil government in 1764 reduced Haldimand to commander of the troops in Trois-Rivières, and he went on leave in 1765. That year he was promoted from colonel (a rank awarded 19 Feb. 1762) to brigadier-general (12 Dec. 1765), and when Burton was recalled from his post as brigadier of the Northern Department Haldimand was initially considered for that position. Guy Carleton*, however, received the appointment, and Haldimand became brigadier of the Southern Department (the provinces of East and West Florida) instead. He remained in Florida from March 1767 to the spring of 1773, and during that time was promoted major-general (25 May 1772) and colonel commandant of the 2nd battalion of the 60th Foot (25 Oct. 1772). When Gage went to England on leave in 1773 Haldimand became temporary commander-in-chief, and upon his superior's return in 1774 second in command of the army at Boston. In the spring of 1775 he was replaced, and returned to England, where he received the sinecure of inspector general of the forces in the West Indies and promotion to lieutenant-general. For the next two years he remained without an active command, and then in the summer of 1777 was appointed governor of Quebec following Carleton's resignation. Adverse weather prevented his reaching the province until June 1778.

As governor, Haldimand's overriding concern until 1783 was naturally the military situation. He devoted much time and effort to strengthening the defences of the colony against a feared American invasion, and he directed the dispatching of raids of troops and pro-British Indians into the back settlements of New York and Pennsylvania, which counteracted enemy invasion preparations, diverted troops from the main theatres, and destroyed supplies [*see* John BUTLER; Walter BUTLER; KAIEÑ?KWAAHTOÑ; John ROSS]. The governor was also responsible, through the Indian department, for maintaining good relations with the Indian allies [*see* John CAMPBELL; Christian Daniel CLAUS], and for dealing with the frontier posts and the old northwest [*see* EGUSHWA; Henry HAMILTON]. A corollary to the military events was the necessity of guarding against dissident elements in the population. With the entry of France into the war in 1778, Haldimand feared that the Canadians would be much less loyal to Britain than they had been and that they would support a French invasion of the province. Thus he was particularly careful to guard against indications of disloyalty [*see* Pierre DU CALVET; Charles HAY].

In civil government, Haldimand followed the practice of Carleton. He continued the "privy council," an inner group of the Council composed of his supporters, chief among them being Adam MABANE. Haldimand agreed with Mabane and his friends in the French party such as Luc de LA CORNE that the Quebec Act represented the charter of government in Quebec, and he was consistently opposed by councillors such as Hugh Finlay*, William Grant*, and others who believed that English institutions such as commercial law and habeas corpus should be introduced into the province. Haldimand successfully resisted innovations of this sort throughout most of his governorship, although by 1784 this position was becoming increasingly difficult as opposition mounted.

The peace treaty of 1783 caused Haldimand several problems, not the least of which were the delicate tasks of reconciling the Six Nations Indians to the loss of their ancestral lands and of providing for their resettlement in British North America. No less difficult was the work necessary for the establishment of the thousands of loyalists who had flooded into Canada during the war. Rejecting the idea of mixing them with the Canadians, Haldimand determined instead to settle them on the upper St Lawrence, and provided the loyalists with a solid base for their future development.

In November 1784 Haldimand left Quebec for London on leave. While there he was consulted by the government on affairs in Quebec, but in 1786 he was replaced as governor by Carleton, now Lord Dorchester. In September 1785 he had received a knighthood. For the last five years of his life he lived quietly in retirement in London and Switzerland.

[This brief outline of Sir Frederick Haldimand's life has been included in order to give readers the main facts of his career. As the Introduction to the volume explains, a complete biography of Haldimand, with bibliographic support, will appear in volume V. DCB/DBC]

GENERAL BIBLIOGRAPHY AND LIST OF ABBREVIATIONS

List of Abbreviations

AAQ	Archives de l'archidiocèse de Québec
ACAM	Archives de la chancellerie de l'archevêché de Montréal
ACND	Archives de la Congrégation de Notre-Dame
AD	Archives départementales
AHGQ	Archives de l'Hôpital Général de Québec
AMA	Archives du ministère des Armées
AMHDQ	Archives du monastère de l'Hôtel-Dieu de Québec
AN	Archives nationales
ANQ	Archives nationales du Québec
ANQ-M	Archives nationales du Québec, dépôt de Montréal
ANQ-MBF	Archives nationales du Québec, dépôt de la Mauricie et des Bois-Francs
ANQ-Q	Archives nationales du Québec, dépôt de Québec
ASGM	Archives des sœurs Grises, Montréal
ASJCF	Archives de la Compagnie de Jésus, province du Canada français
ASN	Archives du séminaire de Nicolet
ASQ	Archives du séminaire de Québec
ASSM	Archives du séminaire de Saint-Sulpice
AUM	Archives de l'université de Montréal
AUQ	Archives du monastère des ursulines, Québec
BL	British Library
BN	Bibliothèque nationale
BRH	*Le Bulletin des recherches historiques*
CCHA	Canadian Catholic Historical Association
CÉA	Centre d'études acadiennes
CHA	Canadian Historical Association
CHR	*Canadian Historical Review*
DAB	*Dictionary of American biography*
DBF	*Dictionnaire de biographie française*
DCB	*Dictionary of Canadian biography*
DNB	*Dictionary of national biography*
DOLQ	*Dictionnaire des œuvres littéraires du Québec*
DPL	Detroit Public Library
HBC	Hudson's Bay Company
HBRS	Hudson's Bay Record Society
IBC	Inventaire des biens culturels
JR	*Jesuit relations and allied documents*
NYCD	*Documents relative to the colonial history of the state of New-York*
OH	*Ontario History*
PAC	Public Archives of Canada
PANB	Provincial Archives of New Brunswick
PANL	Provincial Archives of Newfoundland and Labrador
PANS	Public Archives of Nova Scotia
PAO	Archives of Ontario
PRO	Public Record Office
QDA	Quebec Diocesan Archives
RHAF	*Revue d'histoire de l'Amérique française*
RSC	Royal Society of Canada
SCHÉC	Société canadienne d'histoire de l'Église catholique
SGCF	Société généalogique canadienne-française
USPG	United Society for the Propagation of the Gospel

General Bibliography

The General Bibliography is based on the sources most frequently cited in the individual bibliographies in volume IV. It should not be regarded as providing a complete list of background materials for the history of Canada in the 18th century.

Section I describes the principal archival sources consulted and is arranged by country. Section II is divided into two parts: part A contains printed primary sources; part B lists contemporary newspapers. Section III includes dictionaries, nominal lists, indexes, and inventories. Section IV presents secondary works, the majority written in the 20th century; included are a number of general histories and theses. Section V describes the principal journals and the publications of various societies containing material on the 18th century.

I. ARCHIVES AND MANUSCRIPT SOURCES

CANADA

ARCHIVES CIVILES. *See* Québec, ministère de la Justice

ARCHIVES DE LA CHANCELLERIE DE L'ARCHEVÊCHÉ DE MONTRÉAL. This archives holds about 900 photographs, some 500 maps and plans, 634 registers in 17 series (mainly the correspondence of the bishops of Montreal), and some 500,000 files containing unbound items relating to dioceses, clergy, laity, institutions, missions, religious communities, etc. Pre-1896 documents are open to researchers. For further information see: *RHAF*, XIX (1965–66), 652–55; SCHÉC *Rapport*, 30 (1963), 69–70. There is a detailed inventory of a number of registers and files in *RHAF*, XIX (1965–66), 655–64; XX (1966–67), 146–66, 324–41, 669–700; XXIV (1970–71), 111–42.

The following were cited in volume IV:

Dossiers
- 350: Paroisses
  - 355.114: L'Assomption
- 901: Fonds Lartigue-Bourget
  - .001: Évêques de Québec
  - .004: Étienne Marchand, vicaire général et curé de Boucherville
  - .005: Étienne Montgolfier, vicaire général
  - .012: Gabriel-Jean Brassier, p.s.s., vicaire général
  - .115: Lettres de M. Montgolfier, p.s.s.
  - .137: Notre-Dame et Saint-Sulpice

ARCHIVES DE LA COMPAGNIE DE JÉSUS, PROVINCE DU CANADA FRANÇAIS, Saint-Jérôme. Founded in 1844 by Father Félix Martin*, first rector of the Collège Sainte-Marie in Montreal, the archives was originally known as the Archives du collège Sainte-Marie [see *DCB*, I, 686]. In 1968 it was moved to Saint-Jérôme and now forms part of the ASJCF. In the year of its founding this archives received a valuable gift from the nuns of the Hôtel-Dieu of Quebec, who had preserved a small part of the records of the old Jesuit college in Quebec (1635–1800).

In addition to thousands of photographs, miniature paintings, some 500 maps and plans (as yet unnumbered), the ASJCF contains numerous original documents (256 predating 1800) and certified copies concerning the history of the Jesuit missions in Acadia, New France, Canada, and the United States, from 1608 to about 1930 (the date at which French speaking Jesuits turned over their missions to the Indians of the Great Lakes region and Ontario to English speaking Jesuits); as well there are documents relating to the history of the Roman Catholic Church in Canada in the 19th century. All the documents from the period before 1800 have been published [see *DCB*, II, 692, *The Jesuit relations* . . .]. Finally, the ASJCF has records previously held by other archives; all organization completed by these archives has been maintained.

The following materials were cited in volume IV:

Cahier des vœux. A list of those pronouncing their vows within the boundaries of New France or Canada, 1715–72.

Fonds général. This group consists of 6,830 numbered documents, comprising, among other materials, the archives of the Collège Sainte-Marie, original documents of the 17th and 18th centuries, and materials relating to the principal religious and political conflicts of the 19th century, including the Jesuit estates question.
- 573: P. Charles Germain, s.j., Notes biographiques par le P. Arthur Jones
- 583: P.-R. Floquet, 1716–82, Notes biographiques
- 595: O. H. Marshall, "De Céloron's expedition to the Ohio in 1749"
- 596: Voyage (journal) du P. J.-P. de Bonnecamps à l'Ohio, Québec, 17 oct. 1750
- 597: P. J.-P. de Bonnecamps, s.j., Notes biographiques
- 675: Lettre de M. l'abbé Le Guerne, missionnaire de l'Acadie
- 708: Lettres des missionnaires chez les Acadiens, 1759–60
- 727: Lettre du P. L.-A. de Glapion à Hugh Finlay, 10 sept. 1788, Québec
- 740: Concession par messire P.-J.-L. Desjardins, ptre, fondé de pouvoir du P. Joseph Casot, 1798–1800
- 741: Testament (supposé) du P. Joseph Casot; notes biographiques et gravure
- 779: Correspondance d'archiviste du P. Jones, 26 oct. 1888–10 mars 1899
- 808–3: Lettre du P. Germain, s.j., adressée de la rivière Saint-Jean à un habitant de la rivière Annapolis en Nouvelle-Écosse, 19 déc. 1753
- 856–16: Extrait de la lettre de la mère Marie L. de Saint-Martin, supérieure, au P. Floquet, supérieur des jésuites à Montréal, 15 oct. 1768
- 4001–28: Papiers Rochemonteix. Includes 28 notebooks used by Camille de Rochemonteix in the preparation of *Les jésuites et la Nouvelle-France au XVIIe siècle* (3v., Paris, 1895–96) and *Les jésuites et la N.-F. au XVIIIe siècle* [*see* section IV].

Fonds Immaculée-Conception. 4,285 numbered documents, primarily miscellaneous correspondence.
- 4244.43: Note sur le soi-disant testament du P. de Glapion, 1887

Série BO. Contains papers left by Jesuits. Numbered from 1 to 154, these papers are classified by death date and by sequence of date within each file.
- 80: P. François Lemercier, Notes biographiques

Série D-7: Contains papers of Jesuit fathers leaving scant records; their classification is identical to the preceding series.
- 1: P. Félix Martin, Biographie du P. Énémond Massé, missionaire au Canada

ARCHIVES DE LA CONGRÉGATION DE NOTRE-DAME, Montréal. This archival repository, which now has completed the classification of its material, contains 300 feet of documents dating from 1658 to the present, as well as some 200 maps and plans. The documents relate to the congregation's administration, its various services, the approximately 200 houses, those operating and closed, as well as to the possessions and the sisters of the congregation.

The following series have been cited in volume IV:

Administration générale
- Documents du dépôt général, 1693–1922. 74v.
  - 13: Recettes et dépenses de la communauté; comptes des serviteurs et des fabriques, 1722–66

Documents se rapportant au personnel de la Congrégation de Notre-Dame
- Fichier général des sœurs, 1698 à nos jours
- Personnel, 1653–1900. 7v.
  - III: 1768–1807
- Registre général des sœurs, 1653 à nos jours

Maisons
- 312.640: Neuville
  - /1: Historique de la fondation, 1713–1899
  - /2: Historique suivi des Annales, 1713–1897

ARCHIVES DE L'ARCHIDIOCÈSE DE QUÉBEC. Contains some 1,200 feet of documents from 1638 to the present, about 5,000 photographs (1855 to the present), 400 maps and plans from the 18th century on, an analytical card index for all documents prior to 1930, and a six-volume general index to the official registers of the archdiocese from 1659 to the present. A guide to the archives is found in SCHÉC *Rapport*, 2 (1934–35), 65–73.

The series cited in volume IV were the following:

A: Évêques et archevêques de Québec
- 10 A: Mandements et lettres pastorales
- 12 A: Registres des insinuations ecclésiastiques
- 20 A: Lettres manuscrites des évêques de Québec
- 210 A: Registres des lettres expédiées. There is an inventory of the correspondence of a number of the bishops of Quebec in the ANQ *Rapport*. For the correspondence of Mgr BRIAND from 1741 to 1794 *see* 1929–30, 45–136; for that of

Mgr L.-P. MARIAUCHAU d'Esgly from 1740 to 1788 *see* 1930–31, 185–98; for that of Mgr HUBERT from 1768 to 1797 *see* 1930–31, 199–351 (contains as well the correspondence of Mgr C.-F. BAILLY de Messein, as coadjutor); that of Mgr Pierre Denaut* from 1794 to 1806 is in 1931–32, 129–242; and that of Mgr J.-O. Plessis*, as coadjutor of Mgr Denaut from 1797 to 1806, is in 1927–28, 213–40; 1932–33, 1–21.

22 A: Copies de lettres expédiées
30 A: Registre des actes de sépulture, oraisons funèbres, testaments, etc.

B: Chapitre de la cathédrale de Québec
10 B: Registre des délibérations
11 B: Correspondance

C: Secrétairerie et chancellerie
CB: Structures de direction
1 CB: Vicaires généraux
CD: Discipline diocésaine
42 CD: Abjurations
515 CD: Séminaire de Nicolet
516 CD: Séminaire de Québec
61 CD: Paroisses
66 CD: Registre des abjurations
81 CD: Congrégations religieuses féminines

Diocèse de Québec (now being reclassified)
CM: Église universelle
10 CM: Correspondance de Rome
7 CM: États-Unis
90 CM: Angleterre
91 CM: France
CN: Église canadienne
311 CN: Nouveau-Brunswick
60 CN: Gouvernement du Canada
CP: Église du Québec
26 CP: District de Montréal
CR: Province ecclésiastique de Québec
33 CR: Diocèse de Trois-Rivières

U: Archives des missions, paroisses et institutions
Registres des postes du Domaine du roy

W: Copies d'archives étrangères
1 W: Église du Canada

ARCHIVES DE L'HÔPITAL GÉNÉRAL DE QUÉBEC. This repository holds the archives of the community of the Augustines de la Miséricorde de Jésus (Augustinian hospital nuns) and the archives of the hospital. The former comprise 57 feet of original records from 1645 to the present, 3,000 photographs, and 85 maps and plans. The latter relate to specifically medical records.

The following series were cited in volume IV:

Communauté
Journal, 1693 à nos jours. 20v. II: 1743–93

Hôpital
Registre des décès, 1728 à nos jours
Registre des prêtres malades, 1745–1935
50: Thomas-Laurent Bédard

ARCHIVES DE L'UNIVERSITÉ DE MONTRÉAL. The Service des archives, which was created in 1966, has been responsible since 1977 for all the institutional and private archives held by the university. The institutional material includes the administrative records and printed documents of the university. The private archive groups, at present 83 in number, are organized as follows: history of the university, professors, early documents, specialized material. The archives has prepared a series of publications on the archive groups and collections that it holds.

The collection cited in volume IV was:

P 58: Collection Baby. This collection, which is part of the early documents, contains a large number of original manuscripts collected by François-Louis-Georges Baby*, who bequeathed them to the Université de Montréal. It contains more than 20,000 items covering all aspects of Canadian history from 1602 to 1905. Beginning in 1942, Camille Bertrand classified this collection and reorganized the manuscripts into two major series. Bertrand's *Catalogue de la collection François-Louis-Georges Baby* (2v., Montréal, 1971), provides useful information about the material. Manuscript copies of the greater part of the Baby collection are held by PAC.

Correspondance générale. Filed alphabetically under the names of the signatories of the letters, this series comprises about 12,000 original letters, in 120 boxes.

Documents divers. For the most part single items, these are indexed under 20 general titles, listed by the letters A to S.
B: Documents seigneuriaux
B1: Tenure seigneuriale
C: Colonisation
C2: Ventes et échanges
G: Commerce et finance
G2: Commerce, finance, affaires
Q1: Documents hors-séries

ARCHIVES DES SŒURS GRISES, Montréal. The documents which were at the Hôpital Général of Montreal when Mme d'Youville [DUFROST] became administratrix there in 1747 make up the Fonds Charon and are the source of this archival repository. Subsequently the items necessary for the general administration of the community were added. The files of this repository are classified alphabetically and the contents of each file are arranged chronologically. The archives contains 55 feet of original documents dating from 1692 to 1904, several hundred photographs, and about 100 maps and plans.

Series and documents cited in volume IV were:

Ancien journal, 1688–1877. 3v.
I: 1688–1857
II: 1857–67
III: 1867–77
Correspondance générale
Frères Charon
80: Constitutions pour les Frères hospitaliers de la Croix et de Saint-Joseph
Table des articles de la règle de Saint-Augustin
Laïcs
Maison mère
Historique
Documents
Médecins
MY/D: Mère d'Youville et ses contemporains
Mémoires de mère Élisabeth McMullen
Mère Despins
Personnel
Mère d'Youville
Correspondance
Famille
MS
Mémoire particulier, 1705–1857
Registre des baptêmes et sépultures de l'Hôpital Général de Montréal, 1725–1901. 7v.
II: 1759–76
Registre des recettes et dépenses, 1718–1854. 5v.
I: 1718–46
II: 1747–79
Registre des vêtures, professions, sépultures, etc., des frères Charon, 1701–48. 1v.

ARCHIVES DU MONASTÈRE DE L'HÔTEL-DIEU DE QUÉBEC. In addition to 2,000 photographs and 150 maps and plans, this repository contains about 200 feet of documents (from 1637 to the present) concerning the establishment, government, and administration of the Hôtel-Dieu de Québec (hospital and convent). For a description of the archives, *see* Claire Gagnon et François Rousseau, "Deux inventaires des archives de l'Hôtel-Dieu de Québec," *Archives, 73.1* (Québec), 62–82.

The following material was cited in volume IV:

Actes capitulaires, 1700–1947. 2v.
I: 1700–1922
Annales, 1636 à nos jours. 12v.
II: 1755–74
Bienfaiteurs, 1641–1964. 30 cartons.
Papiers Curot, 1784–1887
Chroniques, 1639–1930. 3v.
III: Dots et pensions
Correspondance
Anciennes mères, 1697–1769. 7 cartons.
Évêques, 1676–1947. 50 cartons.
J.-F. Hubert, 1767–91
Procureurs, 1654–1791. 14 cartons.
B.-L. Villars, 1757–88
Élections triennales et annuelles, 1683–1966. 3v.
I: 1683–1806
Notices biographiques, 1641 à nos jours
M.-L. Curot
Papier terrier, 1639 à nos jours. 115 registres.
Quartier Saint-Sauveur
Registre des comptes du monastère, 1691–1953. 29v.
Recettes (brouillons), 1691–1860. 6v.
IV: 1733–89
V: 1789–1813
Registre des malades, 1689–1907. 20v.
V: 1740–51

ARCHIVES DU MONASTÈRE DES URSULINES, Québec. This repository holds 60 feet of original documents from 1609 to the present, about 1,500 photographs, 30 daguerreotypes, and 200 maps and plans. Although the majority of the documents relate to the Ursulines, a certain number concern the laity.

The following were used in volume IV:

Actes d'élection des supérieures, 1688–1941
Actes de professions et de sépultures, 1639–1966. 2v. 1: 1639–1867.
Actes des assemblées capitulaires, 1686 à nos jours. 4v. 1: 1686–1842.
Annales, 1639 à nos jours. 8v. I: 1639–1822.
Conclusions des assemblées des discrètes, 1687 à nos jours. 4v. 1: 1687–1865.
Correspondance des laïcs (to be reclassified)
Correspondance de Miss C. A. Baker avec mère Sainte-Croix
Lettres, pétitions, gouverneurs anglais, 1760–1843
Correspondance des ursulines de Paris, 1640–1792
Fonds construction, 1642 à nos jours
Fonds de la famille Wheelwright
Fonds dots des religieuses, 1648–1865
Fonds sermons
Sermon du R.P. Vincent Bigot, s.j., le 3 janvier 1713
Journal (recettes et dépenses), 1715 à nos jours. 38v. 2: 1747–81.

Livre des entrées et sorties des filles françaises et sauvages, 1647–1720. 1v.
Livre des entrées et sorties des pensionnaires, 1720 à nos jours (being classified)
Livres de comptes, 1672 à nos jours. 6v. 1: 1672–1750.
Registre de l'examen canonique des novices, 1689–1967. 4v. 1: 1689–1807.
Registre des entrées, vêtures, professions et décès des religieuses, 1647 à nos jours. 4v. 1: 1647–1862.

ARCHIVES DU SÉMINAIRE DE NICOLET. This repository contains nearly 300 feet of documents; although the earliest predates 1638, the majority are from the 19th and 20th centuries. The ASN also has a collection of photographs and reproductions (200 albums and some 20,000 additional photographs), engravings, paintings, music notebooks, old stamps and coins, as well as plans and estimates for the college, and maps of certain seigneuries and of the province. Now being classified, the repository houses the official records of the seminary, and also important private archives such as that of the seigneury of Nicolet and the papers of Abbé Louis-Édouard Bois*. There is a catalogue index and card indexes by theme and name.

The following were cited in volume IV:
AO: Archives officielles
Polygraphie. 16v.
I: Succession Louis-Marie Brassard
Séminaire. Contains documents on the seminary predating its foundation in 1803 and up to the present. In addition to 13 volumes, numbered I to XIII, this series includes numerous volumes arranged in sections which occupy 117 linear feet; these volumes are at present being classified.
IX: Succession Paradis; université Laval; séminaire.
Titres divers et contrats de l'abbé Louis-Marie Brassard (section 3, rayon 3)
AP: Archives privées
G: Grandes collections
L.-É. Bois, 69v., 3 boîtes et 3 spicilèges de notes et de documents historiques. The Jean-Baptiste Meilleur* collection at PAC (MG 24, B26) contains copies of this series.
Garde-notes. 19v.
Succession. 20v.

ARCHIVES DU SÉMINAIRE DE QUÉBEC. One of the most important private archival repositories in North America. The records date from the seminary's founding in 1663, but Mgr Thomas-Étienne Hamel* and Mgr Amédée-Edmond Gosselin* may be considered to have founded the ASQ in the late 19th and early 20th centuries. ASQ contains some 1,172 feet of documents (seminary and private papers, the oldest dating from 1636 and the majority from 1675 to 1950), 2,800 maps and plans, and 5,000 engravings and photographs. Analytical and chronological card indexes are available.

Documents used in volume IV include:
C. Livres de comptes du séminaire. 110 manuscript notebooks, 1674–1934.
C 8: 1730–47
C 9: 1748–68
C 10: 1730–35
C 11: 1749–77
C 21: 1740–48
C 22: 1748–70
C 35: 1753–80
Chapitre. 7 cartons, 1670–1974.
Documents Faribault. 3 cartons, 1557–1943.
Évêques. 2 cartons, 1657–1920.
Fonds H.-R. Casgrain. 147 manuscript notebooks classified in Série O (0400-0547) and a number of cartons.
Série O
0423: Lettres de Duperon Baby, 1765–88
0475-0476: E.-A. Baby, Mémoires de famille par Mme C.-E. Casgrain
Fonds A.-H. Gosselin. 35 cartons (uncatalogued).
Fonds Viger-Verreau. The collections of Abbé H.-A.-J.-B. Verreau* and Jacques Viger* consist of 102 cartons and 300 manuscript notebooks. The latter are in Série O and include, among other items, the Viger collection entitled "Ma Saberdache" (095–0125; 0139–0152) (*see* Fernand Ouellet, "Inventaire de la Saberdache de Jacques Viger," ANQ *Rapport*, 1955–57, 31–176). This collection also contains a book of photos, the "Album Gaspé," and 15 registers of copies of the HALDIMAND papers, 1757–86.
Série O
035: Album Verreau, I
040A: Commissions, instructions et livre de comptes (recettes et dépenses du gouvernement civil de Québec) . . . , 1772
081: Jacques Viger, Notices sur la vie de plusieurs "Prêtres du Canada," avant 1834
0181: Les troubles de l'Église du Canada, 1728
0227: H.-A. Verreau, Histoire du Canada, I
Lettres. 36 cartons.
I: uncatalogued

M: 1685–1789
P: 1685–1887
R: 1686–1946
S: 1663–1871
T: 1731–1875
Y: 1742–1881

Missions. 2 cartons.

MSS. 870 manuscript notebooks including the journal of the seminary

2: A.-J.-M. Jacrau, prêtre, Annales du petit séminaire de Québec, 1700
12: Grand livre du séminaire de 1733–1856
13: Plumitif du Conseil du séminaire commencé en 1678. 5v.
82–103: Pierre Potier, s.j. (22 cahiers), 1739–49
146: Emmanuel Crespel, prêtre, Relations des voyages du R. P. Emmanuel Crespel, 1792
191b: Louis Crespel, Voyages et naufrage du R. P. Emmanuel Crespel, 1742
208: Pierre Hazeur, Extraits de correspondance entre Mr. Pierre Hazeur et son frère Thierry, 1730–57
424: A.-E. Gosselin, prêtre, États de service des officiers du Canada
425: A.-E. Gosselin, prêtre, Répertoire du clergé canadien, Régime français
433: A.-E. Gosselin, prêtre, Officiers et professeurs du séminaire de Québec, 1663–1860
437: A.-E. Gosselin, prêtre, Prêtres du séminaire de Québec (notices) du début à nos jours

MSS-M. 1,120 manuscript notebooks of lecture courses

67: André Couillard, Cours de philosophie par le père J.-B. de Labrosse, 1757
122: Charles Chauveau, Éclipse de soleil; Éclipse de lune; Cours de mathématiques (tous de l'abbé Thomas Bédard), 1775
199–202: Arnault Dudevant, Cours de théologie (4 cahiers), 1774
225: Bertrand, Cours de rhétorique par l'abbé François Leguerne et Urbain Boiret, 1770
228: Antoine Lapommerai, Cours de rhétorique par l'abbé Charles-François Bailly de Messein, 1774
251: T.-L. Bédard, prêtre, Cours d'Astronomie, 1792
726: Cours de théologie par l'abbé T.-L. Bédard, 1790

Paroisse de Québec. 2 cartons. 1652–1877.

Polygraphie. 324 cartons.

S. 70 cartons and 327 manuscript notebooks (identified by S-) concerning the seigneuries of the seminary.

S-184A: Aveu et dénombrement, 11 juillet 1781, par le séminaire de Québec

Séminaire. 256 cartons.

Université. 369 cartons concerning the administration and the correspondence of the university and 75 manuscript notebooks (Série U) relating to the administration and various societies.

ARCHIVES DU SÉMINAIRE DE SAINT-SULPICE, Montréal. An important archival repository for the history of the Montreal region from the beginning. The repository, divided into 67 sections, contains 500 feet of documents for the years 1586–1978, about 1,600 maps and plans, and 500 photographs.

The following sections were used in the preparation of volume IV:

Section 8: Seigneuries, fiefs, arrière-fiefs, domaines, 1658–1930
A: Seigneurie du Lac-des-Deux-Montagnes, 1660–1930
Section 11: Enseignement, 1654–1960
Section 14: Successions, 1653–1958
Section 15: Testaments, 1692–1968
Section 19: Statistiques, 1643–1886
Section 21: Correspondance générale, 1670–1920
Section 24: Histoire et géographie, biographies, divers, 1600–1920
Dossier 2: Biographies, 1642–1850
Dossier 5: Catalogue des prêtres de Saint-Sulpice, etc., 1657–1900
Dossier 6: Cahiers Faillon
Section 27: Le séminaire, les évêchés et les paroisses, 1654–1938

ARCHIVES JUDICIAIRES. *See* Québec, ministère de la Justice

ARCHIVES NATIONALES DU QUÉBEC. At the conquest, articles 43, 44, and 45 of the capitulation of Montreal – contrary to the custom of international law at that time – permitted the administrators of New France to take documents relating to the government of the colony back to France. Only records having a legal value for individuals remained in the country, and these were to suffer many misfortunes before the office of the Archives de la province de Québec – now the Archives nationales du Québec – was created in 1920. (*See* Gilles Héon, "Bref historique des Archives du Québec," ANQ *Rapport*, 1970, 13–25.) Since 1971, the ANQ, which has its head office at

Quebec, has been opening regional centres in each of the administrative regions of Quebec. In addition to the repository at Quebec there are now repositories for Mauricie/Bois-Francs (Trois-Rivières), Montréal, Outaouais (Hull), Saguenay/Lac-Saint-Jean (Chicoutimi). Those for Bas-Saint-Laurent (Rimouski) and the Eastern Townships (Sherbrooke) are in the process of organization. There are also plans to open repositories on the North Shore and in the northwest. All the repositories contain private archives and the archives of local communities, which include the records of numerous bodies including parishes, municipalities, and the school boards of each of the administrative districts. As well, they hold documents entrusted to them by the Archives civiles and the Archives judiciaires of the administrative districts. Hence the notarial *minutiers* (*greffes*), surveyors' records, registers of births, marriages, and deaths (updated lists of these documents are available at the archives), and records of various courts of justice will eventually be located at these regional centres of the ANQ [*see* section I, Québec, ministère de la Justice].

MAURICIE/BOIS-FRANCS, Trois-Rivières

The following were used in volume IV:

État civil
Insinuations, 1675–1911. 133 cahiers.
Minutiers (greffes)
Procès-verbaux des arpenteurs

MONTRÉAL

Further information on the documents held in this repository can be found in "État sommaire des Archives nationales du Québec à Montréal," ANQ *Rapport*, 1972, 1–29.

The following were cited in volume IV:

AP: Archives privées
  199: Fleury Mesplet
  M-78-8: Charles Phillips
Chambre des milices (formerly ANQ-Q, QBC 28, 1–6), 1760–64. 6v.
Documents judiciaires
  Contrats de shérif
    1767–99. 3v.
  Cour des plaidoyers communs
    Registres, 1765–1816. 48v.
    Sentences, 1765–67. 1v.
  Juridiction de Montréal (formerly ANQ-Q, NF 21), 1676–1760. 17v.
  Pièces détachées de documents judiciaires, classées par ordre chronologique, 1651–1760. 164v.
  Registres des audiences pour la juridiction de Montréal, 1665–1760. 32 registres.
État civil
Insinuations
  Registres des insinuations, 1722–1866. 49v.
Livres de comptes
Minutiers (greffes)
Procès-verbaux des arpenteurs
Recensement, Compagnie des Indes, 1741. 1 registre.
Testaments
  Testaments olographes, 1658–1875. 17v.
Tutelles et curatelles
  1658–1852. 250v.

QUÉBEC

Further information about the records housed in this repository can be found in *État général des archives publiques et privées* (Québec, 1968). It should be noted that the following material will be moved to one location on the campus of the Université Laval early in 1980: the registers of births, marriages, and deaths held by the Section de la Généalogie, 1,180 Rue Berthelot; post-1867 official documents, maps, plans, and illustrations, which are now located at 115 Côte de la Montagne; and pre-1867 official documents as well as private archives which at present are at the Parc des Champs de Bataille.

The following were cited in volume IV:

AP: Archives privées
  G: Grandes collections
  208: Port de Québec, 1779–1922
  229: Renaud d'Avène Des Méloizes, Nicolas, 1783–1811
  313: Allsopp, George, 1765–1804
  322: Affaire du Canada, 1761–63
  323: Agriculture Society, 1789–95
  398: Baillargé, François, 1784–1800
  P: Petites collections
  11: Adhémar, dit St-Martin, famille, 1689–1844
  84: Bailly, Charles, 10 mars 1651
  86: Bailly, Mlle, 5 juin 1739
  378: Lotbinière, famille, 1761–1810
  526: Delzenne, Monsieur, 1763 et 1772
  545: Deschambault, sieur, 1755–56
  659: Dupont, famille, 1580–1866
  753: Fournel, J.-Ls. et Mme Vve, 1725–65
  997: Hubert, famille, 1797
  1061: Labadie, Louis, 1796–97
  1106: Lajus, François, 1757–76
  1385: Mariaucheau d'Esgly, famille, XVIIIe siècle
  1386: Mariaucheau d'Esgly, Mgr Louis-Philippe, 1788
  1395: Martel, Michel, 1749
  1565: Panet, Monsieur, 1744–69
  1607: Péan, famille, 1575–1730
  1634: Perthuis, Joseph, 31 janv. 1743

2213: Laterrière, Pierre de Sales, 1789
État civil
Minutiers (greffes)
NF: Nouvelle-France
2: Ordonnances des intendants, 1666–1760. 46v.
4: Registres d'intendance, 1672–1759. 4v.
6: Foi et hommage, 1667–1759. 5v.
7: Aveux et dénombrements, 1723–58. 5v.
8: Déclarations des censitaires du roi, 1750–58. 4v.
10: Procès-verbaux des grands voyers, 1668–1780. 9v.
11: Registres du Conseil supérieur, 1663–1760. 69v.
12: Insinuations du Conseil supérieur, 1663–1758. 16v. (Volumes 11 to 16 are copies of the first volumes.)
13: Dossiers du Conseil supérieur, 1663–1759. 11v.
Matières criminelles, 1665–1759
19: Registres de la Prévôté de Québec, 1666–1759. 113v.
20: Documents de la Prévôté de Québec, 1668–1759. 17v.
21: *See* ANQ-M, Documents judiciaires, Juridiction de Montréal
25: Collection de pièces judiciaires et notariales, 1638–1759. 125v.
QBC: Québec et Bas-Canada
16: Seigneuries, 1766–1862. 10v.
26: Armée et milice, 1770–1871. 8v.
28: Cours de justice, 1760–1880. 61v.
Chambre des milices. *See* ANQ-M, Chambre des milices
Conseil militaire, Québec, 1760–1764

ARCHIVES OF ONTARIO, Toronto. The archives is authorized to acquire, preserve, and analyse all records of significance of the Ontario government. It also holds manuscripts, maps, photographs, pictures, and newspapers relating to the history of the province. Unpublished inventories, calendars, catalogue entries, guides, and other finding aids are available in the archives.

Materials used in volume IV include:
Baby family papers, 1759–1866
Canniff (William) papers, 1778–1900
Cartwright family papers, 1779–1913
Hiram Walker Museum collection, 1749–1971
Macaulay family papers, 1781–1921
Reive (W. G.) collection
Robinson (Sir John Beverley) papers, 1803–1905
Russell family papers, 1720–1810
Simcoe (John Graves) papers, 1665–1934
Street (Samuel) papers, 1791–1880
Upper Canada, Lieutenant governor, Letterbook, 1799–1800
RG 1: Records of the Ministry of Natural Resources
A: Offices of surveyor general and commissioner of crown lands
I: Correspondence
1: Letters received, surveyor general, 1766–1913
6: Letters received, surveyor general and commissioner
II: Reports and statements
1: Surveyor general's reports, 1788–1857
CB-1: Survey diaries, field notes, and reports
C: Lands Branch
IV: Township papers
RG 8: Records of the Department of the Provincial Secretary
I-3: Recording Office
RG 21: Municipal records
A: Records of municipalities and townships, 1790 to the present
RG 22: Court records
3: Supreme Court of Ontario
6-2: Records of the Surrogate Court of Ontario
7: Courts of General Quarter Sessions of the Peace

ARCHIVES PAROISSIALES. The parish archives in Quebec hold, in particular, the registers of baptisms, marriages, and burials, of which a copy is kept in the Archives civiles of the judicial district in which the parish is located. The Archives civiles hold the registers for one hundred years before transferring them to the ANQ. Parish archives usually contain many other records including parish account books and vestry records, and registers of the confraternities of the parish, etcetera.

CENTRE D'ÉTUDES ACADIENNES, Université de Moncton, N.-B. Established in 1969, the CÉA holds the papers formerly deposited at the Archives acadiennes; the latter had inherited the documents accumulated at the Collège Saint-Joseph since its founding in 1864. The collection includes manuscripts, books, folklore materials, maps, and newspapers. The CÉA holds copies of many series related to Acadian history; of particular interest for the 18th century are the materials copied in France in the Archives nationales and Archives départementales. For further information about the collections, *see* CÉA, *Inventaire général des sources documentaires sur les archives* (1v. to date, Moncton, N.-B., 1975–).

Materials used in volume IV include:
1: Fonds d'archives privées
A: Fonds personnels
Bourgeois, Philias (1855–1913)
Gaudet, Placide (1850–1930)
C: Généalogies acadiennes
Fonds Patrice Gallant

HUDSON'S BAY COMPANY ARCHIVES, Winnipeg. The archives as constituted at present was established in 1932, and holds records dating from 1670. Documents from the archives have been published by the Hudson's Bay Record Society since 1938 [*see* section II]. In 1974 the archives was transferred from London to Winnipeg and deposited in the Provincial Archives of Manitoba. The PRO and the PAC hold microfilm copies of the archives for the years 1670–1870. Information on PAC copies and finding aids is found in: *General inventory manuscripts, 3*.

The following were used in the preparation of volume IV:
Section A: London office records
A.1/: London minute books
A.5/: London correspondence outwards – general
A.6/: London correspondence outwards – official
A.11/: London inward correspondence from HBC posts
A.14/: Grand ledgers
A.15/: Grand journals
A.16/: Officers' and servants' ledgers and account books
A.19/: Cash books
A.30/: Lists of servants
A.32/: Servants' contracts
A.36/: Officers' and servants' wills
A.43/: Transfer book (book of assignments of stock)
A.44/: Register book of wills and administrations of proprietors, etc.
Section B: North America trading post records
B.3/a: Albany journals
B.3/b: Albany correspondence
B.14/a: Bedford House (Reindeer Lake) journals
B.22/a: Brandon House journals
B.23/a: Brunswick House journals
B.24/a: Buckingham House journals
B.42/a: Churchill journals
B.42/b: Churchill correspondence books
B.42/d: Churchill account books
B.49/a: Cumberland House journals
B.59/a: Eastmain journals
B.59/b: Eastmain correspondence books
B.60/a: Edmonton House journals
B.64/a: Escabitchewan journals
B.78/a: Gloucester House journals
B.86/a: Henley House journals
B.87/a: Hudson House (Upper) journals
B.121/a: Manchester House journals
B.123/a: Martin Fall journals
B.135/a: Moose journals
B.135/b: Moose correspondence books
B.155/a: Osnaburgh House journals
B.166/a: Portage de l'Île journals
B.177/a: Red Lake journals
B.198/a: Severn journals
B.198/d: Severn account books
B.198/z: Severn miscellaneous items
B.205/a: South Branch House journals
B.211/a: Sturgeon Lake (Albany River) journals
B.239/a: York Factory journals
B.239/b: York Factory correspondence books
B.239/d: York Factory account books
B.239/f: York Factory lists of servants
Section C: Records of ships owned or chartered by the HBC
C.1/: Ships' logs
Section E: Miscellaneous
E.2/: "Observations on Hudson's Bay." Pieces 1–3 are by James Isham, 4–13 by Andrew Graham.
Section F: Records relating to companies connected with or subsidiary to the HBC
F.3/1: North West Company correspondence
Section Z: Miscellaneous items
Z.4/1: Deeds referring to lands in Stapleford, Abbots, England

INVENTAIRE DES BIENS CULTURELS, Quebec. The documentation centre of the IBC includes a library devoted mainly to history, art history, anthropology, archaeology, and architecture, as well as a map library which has copies of both early and contemporary maps of Quebec, copies of architectural plans, a photographic collection, and a large number of manuscript files.

Materials consulted in the preparation of volume IV include the following:

Fonds Morisset. When Gérard Morisset* set up the Service de l'Inventaire des œuvres d'art in 1940, he gained official recognition for a project of recording and locating works of art which he had conducted personally for more than ten years. Aided by a staff which he himself had trained, until 1967 Morisset photographed articles of silver, works of architecture, and paintings, searched parish account books, newspapers, and notarial registers, and accumulated many thousands of documents on artisans and their work. This impressive collection (about 70,000 photographs, 40,000 biographical cards, 20,000 slides, and 5,000 old photographs) had already acquired an exceptional value as the result of the disappearance of a number of the works of art. The two principal sections of this collection comprise files dealing with the artists and artisans of Quebec (section 2) and files containing documentation on architecture and works of art by locality (section 5). As well, numerous files dealing with architecture, works of art, and the ethnography of Quebec have been added to the Morisset collection to form section 3. The photographs and slides taken by Gérard Morisset or by the staff of the IBC have been studied and classified individually in order to make the collection more accessible to the researcher.

McGill University Libraries, Department of Rare Books and Special Collections, Montreal. This repository, established in 1965, holds 350 feet of Canadian documents from 1664 to the present, about 670 engravings, and some 1,900 maps and plans. The collection includes documents relating to McGill University, and a large selection of papers of scientists and explorers, scholars and authors, businessmen, other notable figures, various families, associations, and institutions. In addition to Canadian manuscripts, the McGill University Libraries holds an important collection of European manuscripts (dating from the 9th century). For a more complete description, *see* Richard Pennington, *McGill University Library, special collections: European and American manuscripts* (Montreal, 1962); John Andreassen, *A preliminary guide to the manuscript collection, McGill University* (Montreal, 1969).

The following were cited in volume IV:

Manuscript collection
Chartier de Lotbinière family
  CH243.S221b: Miscellaneous documents, 1787–1819
Cugnet, François Joseph
  CH9.S44: Loix municipales de Quebec divisées en trois traités . . . , 1771–73
  CH191.S169: Three letters to Mr Justice Blackstone, 1773; a.l.s. to Chartier de Lotbinière via Monsieur de Longueuil . . . , 1788
Fleury Deschambault, Joseph
  CH218.S196: [Contains various memoirs by Joseph Fleury Deschambault and other documents relating to him], 1765–77
Frobisher, Joseph
  CH132.S2: Letter book of the North West Company . . . , 1787–88
Hubert, Jean François
  CH193.S171: a.l.s. to M. Dufrost, 1789
New manuscript collection
  Orillat, Jean, 1733–79, Inventaire des biens de la communauté d'entre feu Mr Jean Orillat à dame Thérèse Viger son épouse, 19 juillet 1779

Provincial Archives of New Brunswick, Fredericton. Established in 1968, the PANB contains government records from 1784 as well as private manuscript collections. Records and manuscripts formerly with the Legislative Library of New Brunswick have been transferred to the archives. For information on the manuscript holdings see *A guide to the manuscript collections in the Provincial Archives of New Brunswick*, comp. A. B. Rigby (Fredericton, 1977).

Materials used in the preparation of volume IV include:

"New Brunswick political biography." Compiled by J. C. and H. B. Graves. 11 vols., typescript.
RG 2: Records of the central executive
  RS 6: Minutes and orders-in-council of the Executive Council
  RS 7: Executive Council records, Ottawa series
  RS 8: Executive Council records, New Brunswick series
    Appointments and commissions
    Attorney General, cases and opinions
    Indians
RG 4: Records of the New Brunswick Legislative Assembly
  RS 24: Legislative Assembly sessional papers
RG 5: Records of the Superior Courts
RG 7: Records of the Probate Courts
  RS 63: Charlotte County Probate Court records
RG 10: Records of the Department of Natural Resources
  RS 107: Crown Lands and Lands Branch records
  RS 108: Land petitions
RG 18: Records of the Department of Municipal Affairs
  RS 153: Northumberland County records
    Minutes of the Inferior Court of Common Pleas and General Sessions of the Peace

Provincial Archives of Newfoundland and Labrador, St John's. Created by an act of the Newfoundland House of Assembly in 1959, the PANL took over the collection and preservation of existing public archives from Memorial University of Newfoundland, which had performed the task in the previous three years. The PANL contains both printed and unprinted government and private records. The main groups of government records are supplemented by Colonial Office correspondence from the PRO, available by means of transcript or microfilm. Private records groups contain the papers of governors, politicians, civil servants, military and naval figures, businessmen, etcetera, in addition to the records of various corporate bodies. For further information see *Preliminary inventory of the holdings . . .* and *Supplement . . .* (2 nos., St John's, 1970–74).

Materials used in the preparation of volume IV include:

Government records – Newfoundland
GN 2: Department of the Colonial Secretary
  1: Outgoing correspondence, 1749–1864, 1867–1934
  2: Incoming correspondence
GN 5: Court records
  1: Surrogate Court
  C: Southern District
  1: Minutes
P: Private records
  N. C. Crewe collection
  Slade & Sons, Fogo, records, 1782–1878

PUBLIC ARCHIVES OF CANADA, Ottawa. The following general inventories to material used in the preparation of volume IV have been published by the Manuscript Division or the Public Records Division:

General inventory manuscripts, volume 1, MG 1-MG 10 (1971).
General inventory manuscripts, volume 2, MG 11-MG 16 (1976).
General inventory manuscripts, volume 3, MG 17-MG 21 (1974).
General inventory manuscripts, volume 4, MG 22-MG 25 (1972).
General inventory manuscripts, volume 7, MG 29 (1975).
General inventory manuscripts, volume 8, MG 30 (1977).
General inventory series, no. 1, records relating to Indian affairs (RG 10) (1975).
General inventory series, no. 6, records of Statistics Canada (RG 31) (1977).

Other inventories, some of them largely superseded by unpublished inventories available at the PAC, are the following:

Record Group 1, Executive Council, Canada, 1764–1867 (1953).
Record Group 4, civil and provincial secretaries' offices, Canada East, 1760–1867; Record Group 5, civil and provincial secretaries' offices, Canada West, 1788–1867 (1953).
Record groups, no. 14: Records of parliament, 1775–1915; no. 15: Department of the Interior; no. 16: Department of National Revenue (1957).

Unpublished addenda for the above inventories and unpublished inventories of other manuscript and record groups, as well as finding aids to individual collections, are available for consultation at the PAC.

The following were found useful in the preparation of volume IV:

MG 8: Documents relatifs à la Nouvelle-France et au Québec (XVIIe–XXe siècles)
  C: District de Montréal
    10: Cour des Plaidoyers communs. Originaux, 1783–91; transcriptions, 1765–67.
  F: Documents relatifs aux seigneuries et autres lieux
    51: Longueuil. Originaux et transcriptions, 1701–1870.
    113: Soulanges. Originaux, 1739, 1756.
  G: Archives paroissiales
    10: Fort Saint-Frédéric ou fort Beauharnois (Crown Point) (église catholique). Transcriptions, 1732–60.
    14: Illinois (église catholique). Transcriptions, 1695–1834.
    17: Michilimackinac, Saint-Ignace (église catholique). Transcriptions, 1695–1799.
MG 9: Provincial, local, and territorial records
  A: New Brunswick
    5: Crown Lands Department. Transcripts, 1784–87; typescripts, 1763–1860; photocopies, 1783–1833.
  B: Nova Scotia
    1: Executive Council. Originals, 1770–75, 1841–42.
    3: Legislature. Originals, 1749–53, 1768–82; photocopies, 1749–50.
    8: Church records
    9: Local records
MG 11: Public Record Office, London, Colonial Office papers
  [CO 42]. Q series. Transcripts, 1760–1841. The Q transcripts were prepared by the PAC before the PRO reorganization of 1908–10 and include most of what is now in CO 42, material now found in CO 43, and items from other

series. Documents for the period covered by volume IV are calendared in PAC *Report*, 1890, 1891, and 1892.

[CO 217]. Nova Scotia A; Cape Breton A. Transcripts and photostats, 1603–1865. Up to 1801 these series are composites of transcripts from various sources in Great Britain, especially the PRO. By the time that the work of transcription had reached 1802 the PRO had established the CO 217 series. From 1802 on the transcripts are from CO 217 only. Documents of Nova Scotia A for the period covered by volume IV have been calendared in PAC *Report*, 1894, and of Cape Breton A in *Report*, 1895.

[CO 220]. Nova Scotia B (minutes of the Executive Council, 1720–85); Nova Scotia C (minutes of the Legislative Council, 1758–1807). Transcripts. A composite series taken principally from sources now part of PRO, CO 217 or CO 220. A calendar for Nova Scotia B has been published in PAC *Report*, 1949.

MG 17: Ecclesiastical archives
- A: Roman Catholic Church
  - 7-2: Séminaire de Saint-Sulpice, Montréal. Original, 1828; transcriptions, 1635–1899; microfilms, 1556–1945.
  - 15: Hôpital-Général de Montréal. Originals, 1908; transcriptions, 1692–1773.
- D: Moravian Brethren
  - 1: Moravian Brethren. Originals, 1827–1955; transcripts, 1752, 1770–79; microfilm, 1749–1944.

MG 18: Pre-conquest papers
- D: Hudson Bay
  - 5: Graham, Andrew. Transcripts, n.d.
- E: Religious records
  - 15: Crespel, Emmanuel. Original, 1742.
- F: Acadia and Newfoundland
  - 37: Vergor, Louis Du Pont Du Chambon de. Original, 1755.
- G: Governors and intendants of Canada
  - 2: Vaudreuil, famille. Originaux, 1718–1831; photocopie, 1786; transcriptions, 1758–59.
  - 8: Bigot, François. Originaux, 1746–52; photocopies, 1756–63; transcriptions, 1748–65.
- H: New France
  - 7: Testard de Montigny, famille. Transcriptions, vers 1659–vers 1863.
  - 13: Denys, famille. Original, 1710; photocopies, 1658, 1724; transcriptions, 1655–1787; microfilm, 1654–1870.
  - 28: Morin, Pierre-Louis. Originaux, 1836–84; transcriptions, 1504–1763.
  - 50: Lemoine Despins, famille. Originaux, 1755–1851.
- I: Detroit
  - 5: Détroit, registres de notaires de. Originaux, 1786–92; transcriptions, 1737–96.
- J: Memoirs and travel
  - 10: Johnstone, James, dit le chevalier de. Transcriptions, 1745–60.
- K: French officers
  - 3: Chartier de Lotbinière, Michel-Eustache-Gaspard, marquis de. Originaux, 1683–1832; photocopies, 1663–1792; transcriptions, 1778–88; microfilm, 1750–87.
  - 4: Benoist, Antoine-Gabriel-François, dit le chevalier. Originaux, 1706–vers 1776.
  - 10: Bougainville, Louis-Antoine de. Original, 1760; photocopies, 1756–63; transcriptions, 1756–63.
- L: British officers
  - 4: Amherst family. Photocopies, 1758–1854; transcripts, 1758–1836; microfilm, 1758–63.
- M: Northcliffe collection
- N: Military and naval documents
  - 15: Seven Years' War. Originals, 1758–60; transcripts, 1754–59.
  - 21: Williamson family. Photocopy, 1760; microfilm, 1757–76.
  - 25: Nova Scotia: British garrisons. Transcripts, 1754–56.
- O: Miscellaneous
  - 6: Couagne, famille. Originaux, vers 1761–vers 1769.

MG 19: Fur trade and Indians
- A: Fur trade, general
  - 2: Ermatinger estate. Originals, 1758–1874; photocopies, 1766–1966.
- B: Fur trade, companies and associations
  - 3: Beaver Club. Transcript, 1807–27.
- E: Red River Settlement
  - 2: Red River Settlement, 1814–30. Originals, 1822–30; transcripts, 1814–18.
- F: Indians
  - 1: Claus family. Originals, 1755–1886.
  - 2: Johnson family. Photocopies,

1763–1807; originals, 1778–1827; transcripts, 1764, 1770, 1937.
6: Brant family. Originals, 1774–1889; photocopies, 1786, 1793, 1799.
MG 23: Late eighteenth-century papers
A: British statesmen
1: Dartmouth, William Legge, 2nd Earl of. Originals, transcripts, 1688–1798.
4: Shelburne, William Fitzmaurice Petty, 2nd Earl of, 1st Marquis of Lansdowne. Typescripts, 1663–1782; transcripts, 1698–1795.
B: American revolution
3: Continental Congress. Transcripts, 1776–88.
C: Nova Scotia
17: Suckling, George. Original, 1759–60.
D: New Brunswick
1: Chipman, Ward, Sr and Jr. Originals, 1751–1844; microfilm, 1783–1839.
5: Crannell, Bartholomew. Originals, 1783–1818.
E: Prince Edward Island
6: Montgomery, Sir James William. Originals, 1792; photocopies, 1791–98.
F: Cape Breton
1: Desbarres, Joseph Frederick Wallet. Originals, 1762–1894; photocopies, 1774–1925; transcripts, 1903–17.
GI: Quebec and Lower Canada: government
5: Quebec: administration of justice. Originals, 1782, 1787.
GII: Quebec and Lower Canada: political figures
1: Murray, James. Originals, 1757–78; photocopies, 1765–93; transcripts, 1734–92.
3: Gray, Edward William. Originals, 1767–1826.
12: Hope, Henry. Originals, 1781–86; photocopies, 1779, 1789.
15: Gray, Alexander. Originals, 1784–87.
19: Monk, James and family. Originals, 1735–1888.
21: Price, Benjamin. Originals, 1767.
22: Haldimand, Sir Frederick. Originals, 1779–91.
23: Mabane, Adam. Originals, 1783–90.
GIII: Quebec and Lower Canada: merchants and settlers
5: Lindsay-Morrison papers. Photocopies, 1716–1860.
7: Porteous, John. Microfilm, 1765–1862; transcripts, 1780–1800.
8: Birnie, Samuel. Originals, 1785–94.
11: Fraser, Alexander. Originals, 1791–1810.
25: Antiquarian and Numismatic Society of Montreal. Microfilm, 1712–1930.
29: Augé, Étienne. Microfilm, 1750–80.
GIV: Quebec and Lower Canada: religious and fraternal
8: Marchand, Étienne. Original, 1765.
GV: Quebec and Lower Canada: miscellaneous
1: Boisseau, Nicolas-Gaspard. Originaux, 1784–89.
HI: Upper Canada: political figures
1: Simcoe, John Graves. Microfilm, 1765–1860; photocopies, 1768–1805; transcripts, 1724–1824.
3: Jarvis family. Originals, 1767–1901.
5: White, John. Originals, 1780–1840; photocopies, 1792–97.
8: Murray, George W. Original, 1789.
I: Colonies general
13: Sharpe, Joshua. Originals, 1760–72.
K: Military documents
3: Gage, Thomas. Photocopies, 1765, 1768.
MG 24: Nineteenth-century pre-confederation papers
A: British officials and political figures
6: Hunter, Peter. Originals, 1799, 1802; photocopy, 1800; transcript, 1799–1805.
B: North American political figures and events
1: Neilson collection. Originals, 1666–1912; transcripts, 1804–37; photocopies, 1763–68.
D: Industry, commerce and finance
3: Collection Gamelin. Originaux, 1766–1858.
4: Goring, Francis. Originals, 1776–1833.
E: Transportation
1: Merritt papers. Originals, 1775–1897; microfilm, 1780–1873.
F: Military and naval figures
3: Bell, William. Originals, 1800–36.
L: Miscellaneous
3: Collection Baby. Originaux, 1855–1879; transcriptions, 1629–1907; microfilm, 1691–1836.
MG 25: Genealogy
47: Gorham family. Transcript, 1927.
186: Collection Gérard Jalbert. Originals, n.d.

MG 28: Records of post-confederation corporate bodies
III: Business establishments
18: Robin, Jones and Whitman, Ltd. Originals, 1784–1953.
MG 29: Nineteenth-century post-confederation manuscripts
A: Economic
26: Goodwin, E. G.[?]. Original, *c.* 1946.
E: Professional and public life
74: Campbell, John Colin Armour, collection. Originals, n.d., 1903.
MG 30: Manuscripts of the first half of the twentieth century
C: Social
20: Gaudet, Placide. Originaux, vers 1900; transcriptions, vers 1900; photocopies, 1897–1914.
D: Cultural
1: Audet, Francis-Joseph. Originaux, 1888–1942.
E: Professional and public life
66: Cruikshank, Ernest Alexander. Originals, 1903–40.
MG 55/14: Miscellaneous documents
RG 1: Executive Council of Canada, 1764–1867
E: State records
1: Minute books, 1764–1867
15: Board of Audit, 1759–1867
L: Land records
3: Upper Canada and Canada, petitions, 1791–1867
3[L]: Quebec and Lower Canada, petitions, 1764–1842
4: Upper Canada, land board records, 1764–1804
5: Upper Canada, records of the Heir and Devisee Commission, 1777–1854
RG 4: Civil and provincial secretaries' offices, Quebec, Lower Canada, and Canada East
A: Civil secretary's correspondence, 1760–1841
1: Series, 1760–1841
B: Office records, 1763–1867
6: Statistical returns from public officers, 1791, 1806, 1808–40
8: Petitions for notaries' and advocates' commissions, 1760–1841
17: Suits, 1765–91, 1798–1827
28: Bonds, licences, and certificates, 1763–1867
32: Shipping returns for the port of Quebec, 1766–1819
43: Miscellaneous records relating to the St Paul's Bay disease, 1785–91
58: Customs records, 1772–1852
D: Montreal Gazette, Jan.–Dec. 1798
1: Quebec Gazette, 1764–1850, 1854–55, 1864
RG 5: Civil and provincial secretaries' offices, Canada West
A: Civil secretary's correspondence, 1791–1840
1: Upper Canada sundries
RG 8: British military and naval records
I: C series (British military records)
RG 10: Indian affairs
A: Administrative records of the imperial government, 1677–1864
1: Records of the governor general and lieutenant governors, 1787–1850
1–7: Upper Canada, civil control, 1796–1816, 1829–30, 1841–43
486–87: Lower Canada, civil control, 1801–15
2: Records of the superintendent's office, 1755–1830
8–21: Superintendent general's office, 1791–1828
26–46: Deputy superintendent general's office, correspondence, 1789–1830
1822–26, 1829–32: Minutes of Indian affairs, 1755–90
6: General office files, 1717–1864
659, 785, 1833: General administration records, Quebec and Lower Canada, 1717–1849
1834–35: General administration records, Six Nations and Niagara, 1763–1810
RG 14: Records of parliament, 1775–1972
A: Legislative Council, Quebec and Lower Canada, 1775–1841
1: Records of the clerk, 1775–91, 1807–37
RG 31: Statistics Canada
A: Census Division
1: Census records, 1825–81
RG 68: Registrar general of Canada, *c.* 1651–1978.
The PAC has recently converted the former, complex volume numbering system of RG 68 to a single continuous series from 1 to 1142. *DCB* references are to the new PAC volume numbers. However, since researchers are obliged to consult microfilm copies of RG 68 and only the old volume numbers appear on the reels, a conversion table at the PAC must be consulted to obtain the new volume numbers.

PUBLIC ARCHIVES OF NOVA SCOTIA, Halifax. Founded in 1857, the PANS holds government records, court papers, municipal records, family and business papers, collections of societies such as the Nova Scotia Historical Society, community and church records, microfilm copies of deeds and wills from county registries and courts of probate, and a collection of Nova Scotian newspapers. For further information *see* C. B. Fergusson, *The Public Archives of Nova Scotia* (PANS *Bull.*, 19, Halifax, 1963). For a description of the collections see *Inventory of manuscripts in the Public Archives of Nova Scotia* (Halifax, 1976).

Materials used in the preparation of volume IV include:

MG 1: Papers of families and individuals
MG 4: Churches and communities
MG 7: Log books, ships and shipping
  Shipping registers, Halifax
MG 9: Scrapbooks
RG 1: Bound volumes of Nova Scotia records for the period 1624–1867
  5–26: Documents relating to the governing of Nova Scotia under British rule while the governor resided at Annapolis Royal
  28–185: Documents relating to the governing of Nova Scotia, 1748–1867
    Dispatches, letterbooks, and commission books
  186–214½H: Council, minutes, 1749–1867
  215–18: Legislative Council, journals
  219–85: Miscellaneous documents, 1748–1870
  286–300: Legislative Council, selections from the files
  341–96c: Special subjects
  410–18: City of Halifax
  430–32: Indians
  443–54: Census and poll tax
  491–98: Court of Vice-Admiralty, records, 1749–94, 1813
RG 5: Records of the Legislative Assembly of Nova Scotia
  A: Assembly papers, 1758–1815
RG 20: Lands and forests
RG 37: Inferior Court of Common Pleas
RG 39: Supreme Court
  C: Civil and criminal cases
  J: Judgement books

QUÉBEC, MINISTÈRE DE LA JUSTICE. The Archives civiles and the Archives judiciaires of Quebec, which are under the jurisdiction of the Ministère de la Justice, have now been established as separate repositories, following the reclassification of the old Archives judiciaires.

ARCHIVES CIVILES. Located at the court-houses of the principal towns of the judicial districts of Quebec, these archives house documents from the last hundred years including the registers of births, deaths, and marriages, the *minutiers* or minute-books (*greffes*) of notaries, and records of surveyors who worked in the district; earlier documents are housed with ANQ.

ARCHIVES JUDICIAIRES. The new Archives judiciaires hold the records of the various courts: documents still current, roughly those of the past five years, are at the court-houses; non-current material from about the previous 25 years will be placed in one of the 13 centres now being organized by the Ministère de la Justice where some preliminary archival work will be undertaken; documents that are more than 30 years old will be placed in the regional repositories of the ANQ.

QUEBEC DIOCESAN ARCHIVES, Quebec. Early in the 20th century the Reverend H. C. Stuart began to assemble and organize the documents in this repository; the Reverend A. R. Kelley continued the work in the 1930s and 1940s. Part of this material is also held by the ANQ-Q and part by the Church Society of the Diocese of Quebec. The archives contains original records relating to the history of the Anglican diocese of Quebec from its founding in 1793; they include letters patent, registers of consecration, and bishops' papers, correspondence relating to the parishes and to various associations and institutions of the diocese, and a large number of miscellaneous items. In addition it has copies of letters and documents concerning the diocese (1759–1864) that are held in England, and two important sections of printed primary sources. For a more complete description of this archives, *see* Kelley, "Quebec Diocesan Archives," ANQ *Rapport*, 1946–47, 181–298 [section III]; A. M. Awcock, "Catalogue of the Quebec Diocesan Archives" (copy available at the archives, Shawinigan, Que., 1973).

The following documents were used in the preparation of volume IV:

Section A: Letters patent and records of consecration of bishops, 1793–1935
  45 (A-7), Copies of various letters patent, proclamations
Section B: Parishes of the Diocese of Quebec, 1793–1885
  70 (B-24), Three Rivers
Section C: Correspondence of Right Reverend Jacob Mountain, 1792–1845
  72 (C-1), 1792–96
  73 (C-2), 1796–99

Section D: Copies of letters and papers referring to Diocese of Quebec, 1759–1864
82 (D-1), 1759–80
83 (D-2), 1781–88
84 (D-3), 1789–93

FRANCE

ARCHIVES DÉPARTEMENTALES. For lists of analytical inventories *see*: France, Direction des Archives, *État des inventaires des archives nationales, départementales, communales et hospitalières au 1er janvier 1937* (Paris, 1938); *Supplément, 1937–1954* [by R.-H. Bautier] (Paris, 1955); *Catalogue des inventaires, répertoires, guides de recherche et autres instruments de travail des archives départementales, communales et hospitalières . . . à la date du 31 décembre 1961* (Paris, 1962). For copies of documents in the PAC see: *General inventory manuscripts, 1*, 87–99. There is a uniform system of classification for all departmental archives. A list of the various series may be found in *DBC*, II, 683–84.

Series cited in volume IV:
B: Cours et juridictions
C: Administrations provinciales (Intendances)
E: Titres de famille, états civils, notaires [*États civils* are often more complete in municipal archives.]
F: Fonds et collections divers
G: Clergé séculier

ARCHIVES DU MINISTÈRE DES ARMÉES, Paris.

INSPECTION DU GÉNIE. The Dépôt des fortifications was, in 1791, placed under the Direction des officiers du Génie, and later the Comité technique du Génie. The governing authority is now the Inspection du Génie. There are two repositories:

Archives du Génie. Situated at the Château de Vincennes, this archives originally included 23 articles. A certain number have been turned over to other archives, notably article 9 (Colonies françaises), which is now in AN, Section Outre-mer, Dépôt des fortifications des colonies, and article 16 (Cartes), which has passed to the BN. There remain, however, several *registres* or cartons which contain information on former French colonies.

Used in the preparation of volume IV were the following:
Article 3: Personnel
Article 8: Places françaises
Article 14: Places étrangères: Amérique septentrionale, possessions anglaises, États-Unis, Louisbourg, île Royale . . .
Article 15: Histoire militaire, campagnes et sièges

Bibliothèque du Génie, 39 Rue de Bellechasse. The manuscript items held in the library are catalogued in France, Ministère de la Guerre, *Catalogue général des manuscrits des bibliothèques publiques de France: bibliothèques de la Guerre* (Paris, 1911).

Items used in the preparation of volume IV include:
MSS *in 4°*, 66: Collection Lafitte (mémoires divers sur les sièges et campagnes)
MSS *in fol.*, 205b: "Registres des lettres écrites de rapport au service des fortifications de l'Isle Royale et du Canada." 1750–55.
MSS *in fol.*, 210d: Mémoires et dessins: Canada et île Royale

SERVICE HISTORIQUE DE L'ARMÉE. Housed at the Château de Vincennes, the archives was, before 1919, referred to as the Archives de la Guerre. The archives' organization is described in Madeleine Lenoir, "La documentation historique militaire en France," *Revue de défense nationale* (Paris), numéro hors série (déc. 1952); J.-E. Roy, *Rapport sur les archives de France* [*see* section III]. The archives consists of two collections, the historical archives and the administrative archives. A manuscript inventory is available at PAC: Louise Dechêne, "Inventaire analytique des documents relatifs à l'histoire du Canada conservés en France au Service historique de l'Armée."

The following series from the two collections were used in the preparation of volume IV:

Archives historiques
A: Archives antérieures à 1789
A1: Correspondance générale, opérations militaires. Inventoried in France, Archives de la Guerre, *Inventaire sommaire des archives historiques (archives anciennes: correspondance)* . . . , Félix Brun, compil. (Paris, 1898–1930).
M: Mémoires historiques et reconnaissances militaires. Inventoried in Louis Tuetey, *Catalogue général des manuscrits des bibliothèques publiques de France: Archives de la Guerre* (3v., Paris, 1912–20).

Archives administratives
X: Corps des troupes
Xb: Régiments d'infanterie
Y: Documents individuels
Yb: Contrôles "officiers." Classified only for the years 1715–90
Yd: Dossiers individuels. Not yet classified
Y1d: Maréchaux de France

Y^{2d}: Lieutenants-généraux
Y^{3d}: Maréchaux de camp
Y^{4d}: Brigadiers
Sub-series X^b, Y^b, and Y^d are inventoried in France, Archives de la Guerre, *Inventaire des archives conservées au Service historique de l'État-major de l'Armée, château de Vincennes (archives modernes)*, M.-A. Fabre *et al.*, édit. (2e éd., Paris, 1954).

ARCHIVES MUNICIPALES. Guides to inventories are noted above under Archives départementales. For copies of documents in the PAC see: *General inventory manuscripts, 1*, 100–2. There is a uniform system of classification for all municipal archives and a list of the pre-1790 series may be found in *DCB*, II, 684.

Series cited in volume IV:
CC: Impôts et comptabilités
DD: Biens communaux
GG: Cultes, instruction et assistance

ARCHIVES NATIONALES, Paris. The basic inventories of the Archives nationales are: France, Direction des Archives, *Inventaire sommaire et tableau méthodique des fonds conservés aux Archives nationales, 1re partie, régime antérieur à 1789* (Paris, 1871); *État sommaire par séries des documents conservés aux Archives nationales* (Paris, 1891); *Catalogue des manuscrits conservés aux Archives nationales* (Paris, 1892). Guides to finding aids are: France, Direction des Archives, *État des inventaires des archives nationales, départementales, communales et hospitalières au 1er janvier 1937* (Paris, 1938), and *Supplément, 1937–1954* [by R.-H. Bautier] (Paris, 1955); Gilles Héon, "Fonds intéressant le Canada conservés en France: quelques instruments de recherche," *Archives, 73–1* (Québec), 40–50. J.-E. Roy, *Rapport sur les archives de France* [*see* section III], and H. P. Beers, *The French in North America: a bibliographical guide to French archives, reproductions, and research missions* (Baton Rouge, La., 1957), give sketches of the history and organization of the archives. For copies in the PAC of documents in the AN see: *General inventory manuscripts, 1*, 5–48.

The basic classification of the AN is as follows:
I: Section ancienne (which includes the Fonds des Colonies and the Fonds de la Marine)
II: Service des Sceaux
III: Section moderne
IV: Section contemporaine
V: Section Outre-mer
VI: Département des activités scientifiques, culturelles, et techniques

The following material from sections I, V, and VI was used in the preparation of volume IV:

I: Section ancienne
T: Séquestre
V^1: Grande chancellerie
Y: Châtelet de Paris

Fonds des Colonies. For a description of the series and sub-series *see*: Étienne Taillemite, "Les archives des colonies françaises aux Archives nationales," *Gazette des Archives* (Paris), XLVI (1964), 93–116.
A: Actes du pouvoir souverain, 1669–1782
B: Correspondance envoyée, 1663–1815. For the 17th and 18th centuries see the following calendars: Étienne Taillemite, *Inventaire analytique de la correspondance générale avec les colonies, départ, série B (déposée aux Archives nationales), I, registres 1 à 37 (1654–1715)* (Paris, 1959), and PAC *Report*, 1899, supp., 245–548; 1904, app.K, 1–312; 1905, I, pt. VI, 3–446.
C: Correspondance générale, lettres reçues
C^4: Île de France, 1714–1810
C^{8A}: Martinique, 1663–1815. For an analysis of this series *see*: Étienne Taillemite, *Inventaire de la série Colonies C^{8A}, Martinique (correspondance à l'arrivée)* (2v., Paris, 1967–71). [Articles 1 to 121.]
C^{9A}: Saint-Domingue, 1664–1789
C^{11A}: Canada, 1458–1784. A calendar of documents is published in PAC *Report*, 1885, xxix–lxxix; 1886, xxxix–cl; 1887, cxl–ccxxxix. *See also*: Parker, *Guide*, 227ff. [*see* section III]. An unpublished index for this series exists at the PAC.
C^{11B}: Île Royale, 1712–62. Volumes 1–38 are calendared in Parker, *Guide*, 241–45, and PAC *Report*, 1887, cclxxxii–cccxciv.
C^{11C}: Amérique du Nord, 1661–1898. Papers concerning Newfoundland, Îles de la Madeleine, Île Royale, and Gaspé. Calendared in Parker, *Guide*, 246, and PAC *Report*, 1887, cccxciv–cccxcviii. An unpublished index to C^{11B} and C^{11C} is available at the Fortress of Louisbourg and on microfilm at the PAC.
C^{11D}: Acadie, 1603–1788. Calendared in Parker, *Guide*, 238–40, and PAC *Report*, 1887, ccxxxix–cclxiii. The CÉA published in 1975 an *Index des noms propres avec un choix de thèmes*, compiled by Noël Dupuis and Valéda Melanson.
C^{11E}: Canada, divers, 1651–1818. Letters etc.

dealing with boundary disputes. Calendared in Parker, *Guide*, 240–41, and PAC *Report*, 1887, cclxiii–cclxxxii.

C[12]: Saint-Pierre et Miquelon, 1763–1819
C[13A]: Louisiane, 1678–1803
C[13B]: Louisiane, 1699–1803
C[13C]: Louisiane, 1673–1782
C[14]: Guyane
D[1]: Correspondance relative aux troupes des colonies
D[2C]: Troupes des colonies, 1627–1885. Selected volumes are calendared in PAC *Report*, 1905, I, pt.VI, 508–18.
D[2D]: Personnel militaire et civil, 1685–1789
E: Personnel individuel
F[1A]: Fonds des colonies, 1670–1789. Financial documents.
F[2A]: Compagnies de commerce, 1623–1773
F[2B]: Commerce des colonies, 1663–1790
F[2C]: Colonies en général, 1704–89
F[3]: Collection Moreau de Saint-Méry, 1540–1806. Papers relating to Canada, Louisiana, Île Royale, Saint-Pierre, and Miquelon have been copied and microfilmed by the PAC. Calendared in PAC *Report*, 1899, supp., 39–191; 1905, I, pt.VI, 447–505; Parker, *Guide*, 249–53.
F[5B]: Passagers

Fonds de la Marine. The material in the Fonds extends to 1870. For descriptions of the archives *see*: Didier Neuville, *État sommaire des Archives de la Marine antérieures à la Révolution* (Paris, 1898); J.-E. Roy, *Rapport sur les archives de France*, 157–243; Étienne Taillemite, *Les archives anciennes de la Marine* (Paris, [1961]).

B: Service général. Inventoried in Didier Neuville *et al.*, *Inventaire des Archives de la Marine, série B: service général* (8v., Paris, 1885–1963).
B[2]: Correspondance, lettres envoyées, 1662–1789
B[3]: Correspondance, lettres reçues, 1660–1789. For a name and subject index to this and the preceding sub-series *see*: Étienne Taillemite *et al.*, *Tables des noms de lieux, de personnes, de matières et de navires (sous-séries B[1], B[2] et B[3])* (Paris, 1969).
B[4]: Campagnes, 1640–1789
C[1]: Officiers militaires de la Marine, 1400–1789
C[2]: Officiers civils de la Marine, 1663–1770
C[7]: Personnel individuel, 1651–1789

Service central hydrographique
3 JJ: Journaux, mémoires, correspondance, 1679–1849
4 JJ: Journaux de bord, [1594]–1789, 1815–71. For an analysis of this sub-series *see*: Georges Bourgin et Étienne Taillemite, *Inventaire des Archives de la Marine, service hydrographique, sous-série 4 JJ (journaux de bord)* . . . (Paris, 1963).
6 JJ: Cartes

V: Section Outre-mer. The Section Outre-mer came into being on 1 Jan. 1961 when the Ministère de la France d'Outre-mer ceased to exist. This section preserves post-1815 documents relating to the colonies; pre-1815 material remains in the Section ancienne as the Fonds des Colonies [*q.v.*]. Two important series dealing with the earlier period are, however, to be found in the Section Outre-mer and were of use in the preparation of volume IV.

Dépôt des fortifications des colonies. Series Amérique septentrionale and Saint-Pierre et Miquelon were used in the preparation of volume IV. A manuscript inventory of the various series is available at the AN. *See*: PAC *Report*, 1905, I, pt.III, 3–43; J.-E. Roy, *Rapport sur les archives de France*, 535–59.

G: Dépôt des papiers publics des colonies
G[1]: Registres d'état civil, recensements et documents divers
G[2]: Greffes des tribunaux
G[3]: Notariat

VI: Département des activités scientifiques, culturelles, et techniques

Minutier central des notaires de Paris et du département de la Seine

BIBLIOTHÈQUE DE L'ARSENAL, Paris. For a brief description of the Bibliothèque de l'Arsenal *see*: J.-E. Roy, *Rapport sur les archives de France* [*see* section III]; W. G. Leland *et al.*, *Guide to materials for American history in the libraries and archives of Paris* . . . (2v., Washington, 1932–43), I: *Libraries*. *See also*: H.-M.-R. Martin and Frantz Funck-Brentano, *Catalogue des manuscrits de la Bibliothèque de l'Arsenal* (9v., Paris, 1885–99). Volume IX by F. Funck-Brentano includes a history and inventory of the Archives de la Bastille. Supplements have been published in *Catalogue général des manuscrits des bibliothèques publiques de France* . . . (Paris), XLIII (1904), XLV (1915). Copies of documents in the PAC are listed in *General inventory manuscripts, 1*, and a more up-to-date inventory is available at the archives.

The following material was used in the preparation of volume IV:

5768–69: Papiers du comte d'Argenson, 1756–62

Archives de la Bastille

12110–68: Affaire du Canada, 1761–72
12200, 12480: Affaire de l'île Royale, 1758–66
12324: Affaire des colonies de la Guyane, 1767–74
12501–9: Affaire du Canada et Affaire de la Louisiane, 1760–66

BIBLIOTHÈQUE NATIONALE, Paris. The Bibliothèque nationale is divided into departments on the basis of the nature of the documents kept: Cartes et plans, Estampes, Imprimés, Manuscrits, Médailles, Musique, Périodiques. For biographical research on Canada the most important is the manuscript department, consisting of documents classified by language as well as independent collections. The French manuscripts are the most numerous and are divided among the Fonds français (Fr.), the Nouvelles acquisitions françaises (NAF), and the Clairambault, Colbert (Cinq-cents and Mélanges), Joly de Fleury, and Moreau collections. For a description of the BN *see*: J.-E. Roy, *Rapport sur les archives de France* [*see* section III]; W. G. Leland *et al.*, *Guide to materials for American history in the libraries and archives of Paris* . . . (2v., Washington, 1932–43), I: *Libraries*. *See also* the following catalogues to the French manuscripts (alphabetical indexes are available): J.-A. Taschereau *et al.*, *Catalogue des manuscrits français* (5v., Paris, 1868–1902) [Fr. 1-6170]; H.-A. Omont *et al.*, *Catalogue général des manuscrits français* (13v., Paris, 1895–1918) [Fr. 6171-33264; NAF 1-11353, 20001-2811]; BN, Dép. des MSS, *Nouvelles acquisitions françaises, 1946–1957* (Paris, 1967) [NAF 13005-4061, 24219-5100]; Auguste Molinier, *Inventaire sommaire de la collection Joly de Fleury* (Paris, 1881). For other guides and catalogues see: *Les catalogues imprimés de la Bibliothèque nationale: liste établie en 1943 suivie d'un supplément (1944–1952)* (Paris, 1953); *Catalogues et publications en vente* (Paris, 1973; nouv. éd., 1978). A revised guide to the catalogues is under way: *Les catalogues du département des Imprimés* appeared in 1970; *Les catalogues du département des Manuscrits: manuscrits occidentaux* was published in 1974.

GREAT BRITAIN

BRITISH LIBRARY, London. For a brief guide to catalogues of the manuscript collections *see*: T. C. Skeat, "The catalogues of the British Museum, 2: manuscripts," *Journal of Documentation* (London), VII (1951), 18–60; revised as *British Museum: the catalogues of the manuscript collections* (London, 1962). For copies of documents from the British Library in the PAC see: *General inventory manuscripts, 3*. Used in the preparation of volume IV were the Egerton and Additional manuscripts.

Add. MSS 9913–14: Royal Artillery muster rolls, 1721–60
Add. MSS 11813: Captain William Parry papers, 1747–61
Add. MSS 17542–51: Log-books, journals and astronomical observations of the *Discovery*, Capt. Vancouver, and the *Chatham*, Lieut. Broughton, 1791–95
Add. MSS 19069–70: Letters and papers of Paul Mascarene, commander-in-chief of Nova Scotia, 1713–57
Add. MSS 19071–73, 19075–76: Papers relating to Nova Scotia collected by Dr Andrew Brown, 1720–91
Add. MSS 21631–60: Henry Bouquet papers, 1757–65
Add. MSS 21661–892: Official correspondence and papers of Sir Frederick Haldimand, 1758–85
Add. MSS 23678: Narrative and remarks on the siege of Havana by Sir Charles Knowles in 1761 and 1762, includes journal of the siege by Patrick Mackellar
Add. MSS 24323: Letters to John Blackburn from Sir William Johnson, Sir John Johnson, and Colonel Guy Johnson, 1770–80
Add. MSS 32641: Journal of Archibald Menzies, surgeon, botanist on the *Discovery*, Dec. 1790–16 Feb. 1794
Add. MSS 32686–992: Official correspondence of Thomas Pelham Holles, Duke of Newcastle, 1697–1768
Add. MSS 33028–30: Papers relating to American and West Indian colonies which passed through the Duke of Newcastle's hands, 1701–68 (with a few of later date)
Add. MSS 33977–82: Letters addressed to Sir Joseph Banks, 1765–1821
Add. MSS 35349–36278: Hardwicke papers
Add. MSS 38190–489: Liverpool papers
Add. MSS 41262–67: Clarkson papers
Egerton MSS
2177–80: Papers relating to Captain James Cook's 2nd and 3rd voyages and the publication of his journals, 1776–84
2591: Journal of David Samwell, surgeon of *Discovery*, in Captain Cook's voyage to the Pacific, 10 Feb. 1776–29 Nov. 1779

NATIONAL MARITIME MUSEUM, London. The manuscript collection of the National Maritime Museum includes public records, business records, and private papers relating to all facets of naval and merchant shipping history and concentrating on the mid 17th to the 20th centuries. For further information see: *Guide to the manuscripts in the National Maritime Museum, volume I: the personal collections*, ed. R. J. B. Knight ([London], 1977). Volume II, describing the rest of the collection, "Public records, business records and artificial collections" is in preparation and will be published in 1980.

The following materials have been used in the preparation of volume IV:

Public records
ADM: Admiralty Board
ADM/L: Lieutenants logs, 1678–1809
HAL: Halifax Dockyard records
Personal collections
CAL: Caldwell papers
SAN: Sandwich papers
Artificial collections
HIS: History and Biography
JOD: Journals and Diaries
RUSI: Royal United Services Institution

PUBLIC RECORD OFFICE, London. For an introduction to the contents and arrangements of this archives see *Guide to the contents of the Public Record Office* (3v., London, 1963–68). For copies of PRO documents available at the PAC see *General inventory manuscripts, 2.*

Materials cited in volume IV include:

Admiralty
Accounting departments
Ship's musters
Adm. 36: Series I, 1688–1808
Admiralty and Secretariat
Adm. 1: Papers, 1660–1962
Adm. 2: Out-letters, 1656–1859
Adm. 3: Minutes, 1657–1881
Registers, returns and certificates
Adm. 6: Various, 1673–1859
Adm. 7: Miscellanea, 1563–1871
Adm. 8: List books, 1673–1893
Log books
Adm. 50: Admirals' journals, 1702–1916
Adm. 51: Captains' logs, 1669–1852
Adm. 52: Masters' logs, 1672–1840
Adm. 53: Ships' logs, 1799–1952
Adm. 55: Supplementary, series II: explorations, 1757–1861
Greenwich Hospital
Adm. 80: Various, 1639–1957
Navy Board
Adm. 106: Navy Board records, 1659–1837
Adm. 107: Passing certificates, 1691–1848
Colonial Office. [*See* R. B. Pugh, *The records of the Colonial and Dominions offices* (PRO handbooks, 3, London, 1964).]
America and West Indies
CO 5: Original correspondence, [1606]–1807
Canada
CO 42: Original correspondence, 1700–1922
CO 47: Miscellanea, 1764–1925
Jamaica
CO 142: Miscellanea, 1658–1945
Newfoundland
CO 194: Original correspondence, 1696–1922
CO 195: Entry books, 1623–1867
CO 199: Miscellanea, 1677–1903
Nova Scotia and Cape Breton
CO 217: Original correspondence, 1710–1867
CO 218: Entry books, 1710–1867
CO 221: Miscellanea, 1730–1866
Prince Edward Island
CO 226: Original correspondence, 1769–1873
CO 227: Entry books, 1769–1872
Sierra Leone
CO 267: Original correspondence, 1664–1949
Colonies General
CO 323: Original correspondence, 1689–1952
CO 324: Entry books, series I, 1662–1872
Board of Trade
CO 388: Original correspondence, 1654–1792
CO 391: Minutes, 1675–1782
Court of Bankruptcy
B 4: Commisions, docket books (registers), 1710–1849
B 6: Registers, 1733–1925
Court of Chancery
Judicial proceedings (equity side)
C 108: Masters' exhibits: Farrar, *c.* 1180–1845
Exchequer – King's Remembrancer
E 190: Port books, 1565–1798
Exchequer and Audit Department
AO 1: Declared accounts, 1536–1828
AO 3: Accounts, various, 1539–1886
Claims, American loyalists
AO 12: Series I, 1776–1831
AO 13: Series II, 1780–1835
Foreign Office. [See *Records of the Foreign Office, 1782–1939* (PRO handbooks, 13, 1969).]
FO 4: America, United States of, series I, 1782–92
High Court of Admiralty

Instance and prize courts
HCA 32: Prize papers, 1655–1855
Prerogative Court of Canterbury (formerly held at Somerset House)
Prob. 6: Act books: administrations, 1559–1858
Prob. 11: Registered copy, wills, 1384–1858
Privy Council Office
PC 2: Registers, 1540–1972
Public Record Office
Documents acquired by gift, deposit or purchase
PRO 30/8: Chatham papers, George II–George III
PRO 30/55: Carleton papers, 1747–83
State Paper Office
Domestic
SP 41: Military, 1640–1782
SP 42: Naval, 1689–1782
SP 44: Entry books, 1661–1828
Board of Trade
BT 5: Minutes, 1784–1850
BT 6: Miscellanea, 1697–1921
Treasury
T 64: Various, 1547–1905
Treasury Solicitor
TS 11: Treasury solicitor and king's proctor, papers, 1584–1856
War Office
Correspondence
WO 1: In-letters, 1732–1868
Returns
WO 12: Muster books and pay lists: general, 1732–1878
WO 17: Monthly returns, 1759–1865
WO 24: Establishments, 1661–1846
WO 25: Registers, various, 1660–1938
WO 28: Headquarters' records, 1746–1901
Private collections
WO 34: Amherst papers, 1712–86
Ordnance Office
WO 44: In-letters, 1682–1873
WO 47: Minutes, 1644–1856
WO 55: Miscellanea, 1568–1923
Judge Advocate General's Office
Courts martial
WO 71: Proceedings, 1668–1967

UNITED SOCIETY FOR THE PROPAGATION OF THE GOSPEL, London. For copies of documents from the USPG archives available in the PAC see *General inventory manuscripts, 3*.

Documents from the following groups were used in preparing volume IV:

A: Contemporary copies of letters received, 1701–38

B: Original letters received from the American colonies, the West Indies, Newfoundland, Nova Scotia, 1701–86

C/CAN: Unbound letters from Canada, 1752–1860. Letters from Newfoundland, Nova Scotia, and Quebec groupings used. Nominal card index is available at USPG. This section was subjected to reorganisation and reclassification (not completed), resulting in some confusion. Thus classifications used by Canadian authors holding microfilm of this section do not correspond to those of the archives itself.

Dr Bray's Associates, minute books and unbound papers

Journal of proceedings of the Society for the Propagation of the Gospel. Comprises bound and indexed volumes of the proceedings of the general meetings held in London from 1701, and four appendices, A, B, C, D (1701–1860).

UNITED STATES

DETROIT PUBLIC LIBRARY, Burton Historical Collection, Detroit, Mich. Founded on the private library of Clarence Monroe Burton, the collection concentrates on the history of Detroit and Michigan from the 17th century to the present. Its holdings are listed in *The national union catalog of manuscript collections* . . . (Ann Arbor and Washington, 1962–).

Materials used in volume IV include:

Munro (John) papers
Navarre (Francis) papers
Navarre (Robert) papers
Pontiac papers, Journal ou dictation d'une conspiration faite par les sauvages contre les anglais, et du siege du Fort le Detroix, 1763.
Porteous (John) papers
Registres des baptêmes, mariages et sépultures de Sainte-Anne (Detroit, Mich.), 2 Feb. 1704–30 Dec. 1848. 5 vols. in 7. Manuscript copy.
Sterling (James) papers

HUNTINGTON LIBRARY, San Marino, Calif. The collections of the Huntington Library extend from the 11th to the 20th centuries. For materials relating to 18th century Canadian history see: *Guide to American historical manuscripts at the Huntington Library* (San Marino, 1979). *See also* S. M. Pargellis, "Loudoun papers: (*a*) Colonial, 1756–58," and N. B. Cuthbert, "[Loudoun papers]: (*b*) French colonial, 1742–53," *Huntington Library Bull.* (Cambridge, Mass.), 3 (1933), 97–103, 104–7.

Collections used in volume IV include:
Abercromby papers, 1674–1787
Brock collection, 1639–1800
Loudoun papers
English colonial manuscripts (personal and official papers of John Campbell, 4th Earl of Loudoun)
French colonial manuscripts (personal and official papers of Pierre de Rigaud de Vaudreuil de Cavagnial, Marquis de Vaudreuil). These papers have been catalogued as *The Vaudreuil papers: a calendar and index of the personal and private records of Pierre de Rigaud de Vaudreuil, royal governor of the French province of Louisiana, 1743–1753*, comp. Bill Barron (New Orleans, 1975).

MASSACHUSETTS HISTORICAL SOCIETY, Boston, Mass. About half the holdings of the society are manuscripts and transcriptions. For information about the collections *see*: S. T. Riley, *The Massachusetts Historical Society, 1791–1959* (Boston, 1959); "The manuscript collections of the Massachusetts Historical Society: a brief listing," *M.H.S. Miscellany* (Boston), 5 (December 1958); *Catalog of manuscripts of the Massachusetts Historical Society* (7v., Boston, 1969).

The following collections were used in the preparation of volume IV:
Andrews-Eliot papers
Belknap papers
Gay collection
Mascarene papers
Thomas Hancock papers
Jeffries family papers
Knox papers
Louisbourg papers
Parkman collection
St John's Society collection
Waldo papers
Wheelwright family papers
Winslow papers

WILLIAM L. CLEMENTS LIBRARY, University of Michigan, Ann Arbor. The manuscript collections of the Clements Library are concentrated in the years 1740 to 1865. A large number of these collections concern Anglo-American politics in the mid 18th and early 19th centuries. The manuscripts are catalogued. Brief descriptions appear in *The national union catalog of manuscript collections . . .* (Ann Arbor and Washington, 1962–), and *Guide to the manuscript collections in the William L. Clements Library*, comp. A. P. Shy and B. A. Mitchell (3rd ed., Boston, 1978).

The following were consulted in the preparation of volume IV:
Sir Henry Clinton papers, 1750–1812
Thomas Gage papers, 1754–83
George Sackville Germain, Viscount Sackville, papers, 1683–1785
Josiah Harmar papers, 1681–1855
Jehu Hay diary, 1763–65
William Petty, Earl of Shelburne, papers, 1663–1797
Robert Rogers papers, 1759–1832
James Sterling letterbook, 1761–65
Sydney family papers, 1685–1829
Sir John Vaughan papers, 1779–81

II. PRINTED PRIMARY SOURCES

A. OFFICIAL PUBLICATIONS AND CONTEMPORARY WORKS

American archives: consisting of a collection of authentick records, state papers, debates, and letters and other notices of publick affairs, the whole forming a documentary history of the origin and progress of the North American colonies. . . . Compiled by Matthew St Clair Clarke and Peter Force. 2 ser. in 9 vols. Washington, 1837–53; reprinted [New York, 1972]. Six series covering the years 1688–1787 were projected but only the 4th and part of the 5th series appeared, covering the years 1774–76.

[AMHERST, JEFFERY.] *The journal of Jeffery Amherst, recording the military career of General Amherst in America from 1758 to 1763.* Edited by John Clarence Webster. Toronto and Chicago, [1931].

ARCHIVES DU SÉMINAIRE DE QUÉBEC, Québec
PUBLICATIONS
I: *Papiers Contrecœur* (Grenier).
II: *Le séminaire de Québec* (Provost).

ARCHIVES NATIONALES DU QUÉBEC, Québec
PUBLICATIONS [*see also* section III]
Inv. de pièces du Labrador (P.-G. Roy).
Inv. des papiers de Léry (P.-G. Roy).
Lettres de noblesse (P.-G. Roy).
Rapport. 53 vols. 1920/21–75. There is an index to the contents of the first 42 volumes: *Table des matières des rapports des Archives du Québec, tomes 1 à 42 (1920–1964)* ([Québec], 1965).

ARCHIVES OF ONTARIO, Toronto
Report. 22 vols. 1903–33.

Atlas de la Nouvelle-France/An atlas of New France. Marcel Trudel, compilateur. [Édition révisée.] [Québec], 1968.

BÉGON. *See* La Morandière

[BOUGAINVILLE, LOUIS-ANTOINE DE.] *Adventure in the wilderness: the American journals of Louis Antoine de Bougainville, 1756–1760*. Translated and edited by Edward Pierce Hamilton. Norman, Okla., [1964].

——— "Le journal de M. de Bougainville," A.[-E.] Gosselin, édit., ANQ *Rapport*, 1923–24, 202–393.

Les bourgeois de la compagnie du Nord-Ouest: récits de voyages, lettres et rapports inédits relatifs au Nord-Ouest canadien. Louis-[François-]Rodrigue Masson, éditeur. 2 vols. Québec, 1889–90; réimprimé New York, 1960.

CENSUSES. *See* Recensements

CHAMPLAIN SOCIETY, Toronto
PUBLICATIONS
50 vols. to date, exclusive of the Hudson's Bay Company series [*see* HBRS], the Ontario series [*q.v.*], and the unnumbered series. Issued only to elected members of the society, limited in number.
III: *Docs. relating to seigniorial tenure* (Munro).
VI: Hearne, *Journey from Prince of Wales's Fort* (Tyrrell).
VIII–X: Knox, *Hist. journal* (Doughty).
XVI: *Journals and letters of La Vérendrye* (Burpee).
XXI: *Journals of Hearne and Turnor* (Tyrrell).
XXII: *Docs. relating to NWC* (Wallace).
XXIX: Perkins, *Diary, 1766–80* (Innis).
XXXVI: Perkins, *Diary, 1780–89* (Harvey and Fergusson).
XXXIX: Perkins, *Diary, 1790–96* (Fergusson).
XLIII: Perkins, *Diary, 1797–1803* (Fergusson).
L: Perkins, *Diary, 1804–12* (Fergusson).
ONTARIO SERIES
10 vols. to date. Available through normal publishing channels.
II: *Royal Fort Frontenac* (Preston and Lamontagne).
III: *Kingston before War of 1812* (Preston).

Charts & views drawn by Cook and his officers.... Edited by Raleigh Ashlin Skelton. (Hakluyt Society publication.) Cambridge, Eng., 1955.

Collection de documents inédits sur le Canada et l'Amérique. [Henri-Raymond Casgrain, éditeur.] 3 vols. Québec, 1888–90. Published as a supplement to the journal *Le Canada français* (Québec), 1re sér., I–III.

Collection de manuscrits contenant lettres, mémoires, et autres documents historiques relatifs à la Nouvelle-France. . . . 4 vols. Québec, 1883–85.

Collection des manuscrits du maréchal de Lévis. Henri-Raymond Casgrain, éditeur. 12 vols. Québec, 1889–95.

A collection of several commissions, and other public instruments, proceeding from his majesty's royal authority, and other papers, relating to the state of the province in Quebec in North America, since the conquest of it by the British arms in 1760. Compiled by Francis Maseres. London, 1772; reprinted [East Ardsley, Eng., and New York], 1966.

[*Colonial records of Pennsylvania*.] Edited by Samuel Hazard. 16 vols. Harrisburg, Pa., 1838–53; vols. I–III reprinted Philadelphia, 1852. *Colonial records* is the official title, though not used in printing; vols. I–X are *Minutes of the provincial council of Pennsylvania, from the organization to the termination of the proprietary government* [1683–1775]. This collection of documents is supplemented by *Pa. archives* (Hazard *et al.*) [*q.v.*].

The correspondence of General Thomas Gage with the secretaries of state, 1763–1775. Edited by Clarence Edwin Carter. 2 vols. New Haven, Conn., and London, 1931–33; reprinted [Hamden, Conn.], 1969.

The correspondence of Lieut. Governor John Graves Simcoe, with allied documents relating to his administration of the government of Upper Canada. Edited by Ernest Alexander Cruikshank. (Ontario Historical Society publication.) 5 vols. Toronto, 1923–31.

Correspondence of William Pitt, when secretary of state, with colonial governors and military and naval commissioners in America. Edited by Gertrude Selwyn Kimball. 2 vols. New York and London, 1906.

Correspondence of William Shirley, governor of Massachusetts and military commander in America, 1731–1760. Edited by Charles Henry Lincoln. 2 vols. New York, 1912.

Les derniers jours de l'Acadie (1748–1758), correspondances et mémoires: extraits du portefeuille de M. Le Courtois de Surlaville, lieutenant-général des armées du roi, ancien major des troupes de l'île Royale. Gaston Du Boscq de Beaumont, éditeur. Paris, 1899.

DETROIT PUBLIC LIBRARY, Detroit
BURTON HISTORICAL RECORDS
I, II: *John Askin papers* (Quaife).

Documentary history of the state of Maine. Edited by William Willis *et al.* (Maine Historical Society publication.) 24 vols. Portland, Maine, and Cambridge, Mass., 1869–1916.

Documents relatifs à l'histoire constitutionnelle du Canada. . . . Adam Shortt *et al.*, éditeurs. (PAC publication.) 3 vols. Ottawa, 1907–35.

[I]: *1759–1791.* Adam Shortt et Arthur George Doughty, éditeurs. 2e édition. (PAC, Board of historical publications.) 2 vols. 1921.

[II]: *1791–1818.* Arthur George Doughty et Duncan A. McArthur, éditeurs.

Documents relating to Canadian currency, exchange and finance during the French period/Documents relatifs à la monnaie, au change et aux finances du Canada sous le Régime français. Edited by Adam Shortt. (PAC, Board of historical publications.) 2 vols. Ottawa, 1925.

Documents relating to currency, exchange and finance in Nova Scotia, with prefatory documents, 1675–1758. Edited by Adam Shortt *et al.* (PAC, Board of historical publications.) Ottawa, 1933.

Documents relating to the constitutional history of Canada. . . . Edited by Adam Shortt *et al.* (PAC publication.) 3 vols. Ottawa, 1907–35.

[I]: *1759–1791.* Edited by Adam Shortt and Arthur George Doughty. 2nd edition. (PAC, Board of historical publications.) 2 vols. 1918.

[II]: *1791–1818.* Edited by Arthur George Doughty and Duncan A. McArthur.

Documents relating to the North West Company. Edited by William Stewart Wallace. (Champlain Society publications, XXII.) Toronto, 1934.

Documents relating to the seigniorial tenure in Canada, 1598–1854. Edited by William Bennett Munro. (Champlain Society publications, III.) Toronto, 1908.

Documents relative to the colonial history of the state of New-York; procured in Holland, England and France, by John Romeyn Brodhead. . . . Edited by Edmund Bailey O'Callaghan and Berthold Fernow. 15 vols. Albany, N.Y., 1853–87.

[DOREIL, ANDRÉ.] "Lettres de Doreil," Antoine Roy, édit., ANQ *Rapport*, 1944–45, 3–171.

Édits, ordonnances royaux, déclarations et arrêts du Conseil d'état du roi concernant le Canada. [2e édition.] 3 vols. Québec, 1854–56. Title varies. [II]: *Arrêts et règlements du Conseil supérieur de Québec, et ordonnances et jugements des intendants du Canada*; [III]: *Complément des ordonnances et jugements des gouverneurs et intendants du Canada, précédé des commissions des dits gouverneurs et intendants et des différents officiers civils et de justice. . . .* A revision and expansion of a two-volume edition published in Quebec in 1803–6.

Extraits des archives des ministères de la Marine et de la Guerre à Paris; Canada, correspondance générale: MM. Duquesne et Vaudreuil, gouverneurs-généraux, 1755–1760. Henri-Raymond Casgrain, éditeur. Québec, 1890. Only correspondence for the year 1755 is included.

[FABRE, DIT LATERRIÈRE, PIERRE.] *Mémoires de Pierre de Sales Laterrière et de ses traverses.* [Alfred Garneau, éditeur.] Québec, 1873.

Gentleman's Magazine. London. 1731–1907. Monthly.

GREAT BRITAIN, BOARD OF TRADE. *Journal of the commissioners for Trade and Plantations . . .* [1704–82]. 14 vols. London, 1920–38.

——— HISTORICAL MANUSCRIPTS COMMISSION. *Report on American manuscripts in the Royal Institution of Great Britain.* [Compiled by Benjamin Franklin Stevens, edited by H. J. Brown.] 4 vols. London, etc., 1904–9.

——— PRIVY COUNCIL. *Acts of the Privy Council of England: colonial series* [1613–1783]. Edited by William Lawson Grant and James Munro. 6 vols. Hereford and London, 1908–12.

HAKLUYT SOCIETY, London

WORKS, EXTRA SERIES

XXXIV–XXXVII: *Journals of Captain James Cook* (Beaglehole *et al.*).

OTHER PUBLICATIONS

Charts & views drawn by Cook and his officers (Skelton).

HEARNE, SAMUEL. *A journey from Prince of Wales's Fort, in Hudson's Bay, to the Northern Ocean . . . in the years 1769, 1770, 1771, & 1772.* London, 1795; reprinted Edmonton, [1971]. New edition. Edited by Joseph Burr Tyrrell. (Champlain Society publications, VI.) Toronto, 1911; reprinted New York, 1968. Another edition. Edited by Richard [Gilchrist] Glover. Toronto, 1958; reprinted, [1972].

HENRY, ALEXANDER. *Travels and adventures in Canada and the Indian territories, between the years 1760 and 1776.* New York, 1809. New edition. Edited by James Bain. Toronto, 1901; reprinted Edmonton, [1969], and St Clair Shores, Mich., 1972. Part I of the original has also been published as *Attack at Michilimackinac . . .*, ed. D. A. Armour (Mackinac Island, Mich., 1971).

HUDSON'S BAY RECORD SOCIETY, Winnipeg

PUBLICATIONS

31 vols. to date. General editor for vols. I–XXII, Edwin Ernest Rich; vols. XXIII–XXV, Kenneth Gordon Davies; vols. XXVI–XXX, Glyndwr Williams; vols. XXXI– , Hartwell Bowsfield. Vols. I–XII

were issued in association with the Champlain Society [*q.v.*] and reprinted in 1968 in Nendeln, Liechtenstein.

XIV, XV: *Cumberland House journals and inland journal, 1775–82*. Edited by Edwin Ernest Rich with Alice Margaret Johnson. 2 vols. London, 1951–52.

XXI, XXII: Rich, *History of HBC* [*see* section IV].

XXVII: [Graham, Andrew.] *Andrew Graham's observations on Hudson's Bay, 1767–91*. Edited by Glyndwr Williams, introduction by Richard [Gilchrist] Glover. London, 1969.

Invasion du Canada. [Hospice-Anthelme-Jean-Baptiste] Verreau, éditeur. Montréal, 1873. A collection of five pamphlets originally issued separately between 1870 and 1872. Further volumes were projected but only one additional pamphlet appeared. See *Bibliography of Canadiana* (Staton and Tremaine) [section III].

Inventaire de pièces sur la côte de Labrador conservées aux Archives de la province de Québec. Pierre-Georges Roy, éditeur. (ANQ publication.) 2 vols. Québec, 1940–42.

Inventaire des papiers de Léry conservés aux Archives de la province de Québec. Pierre-Georges Roy, éditeur. (ANQ publication.) 3 vols. Québec, 1939–40.

The Jesuit relations and allied documents: travels and explorations of the Jesuit missionaries in New France, 1610–1791, the original French, Latin, and Italian texts, with English translations and notes.... Edited by Reuben Gold Thwaites. 73 vols. Cleveland, Ohio, 1896–1901.

The John Askin Papers. Edited by Milo Milton Quaife. (DPL, Burton historical records, I, II.) 2 vols. Detroit, 1928–31.

Johnson papers (Sullivan *et al.*). See *The papers of Sir William Johnson*.

"Journal du siège de Québec du 10 mai au 18 septembre 1759," Ægidius Fauteux, édit., ANQ *Rapport*, 1920–21, 140–241. Published separately under the same title in Quebec in 1922.

Journal and letters of Pierre Gaultier de Varennes de La Vérendrye and his sons, with correspondence between the governors of Canada and the French court, touching the search for the Western Sea. [Translated by William Dawson Le Sueur], edited by Lawrence Johnstone Burpee. (Champlain Society publications, XVI.) Toronto, 1927.

The journals of Captain James Cook on his voyages of discovery. Edited by John Cawte Beaglehole *et al.* (Hakluyt Society, Works, extra series, XXXIV–XXXVII.) 4 vols. in 5. Cambridge, Eng., and London, 1955–74. For portfolio see: *Charts & views....*

Journals of Samuel Hearne and Philip Turnor. Edited by Joseph Burr Tyrrell. (Champlain Society publications, XXI.) Toronto, 1934; reprinted New York, 1968.

Kingston before the War of 1812: a collection of documents. Edited by Richard Arthur Preston. (Champlain Society publications, Ontario series, III.) Toronto, 1959.

KNOX, JOHN. *An historical journal of the campaigns in North-America, for the years 1757, 1758, 1759, and 1760....* 2 vols. London, 1769. [New edition.] Edited by Arthur George Doughty. (Champlain Society publications, VIII–X.) 3 vols. Toronto, 1914–16; reprinted New York, 1968.

[LA RUE, PIERRE DE.] "Lettres et mémoires de l'abbé de L'Isle-Dieu," ANQ *Rapport*, 1935–36, 275–410; 1936–37, 331–459; 1937–38, 147–253.

LATERRIÈRE. *See* Fabre

Lettres de noblesse, généalogies, érections de comtés et baronnies insinuées par le Conseil souverain de la Nouvelle-France. Pierre-Georges Roy, éditeur. (ANQ publication.) 2 vols. Beauceville, Qué., 1920.

LITERARY AND HISTORICAL SOCIETY OF QUEBEC/SOCIÉTÉ LITTÉRAIRE ET HISTORIQUE DE QUÉBEC, Québec

PUBLICATIONS

Historical Documents. 9 series in 12 vols. 1838–1915. The volumes were later numbered consecutively by the society D.1, D.2, etc., irrespective of the fact that the 1st series contains 4 vols. and the remaining 8 series only 1 vol. each.

[D.1]: *Mémoires sur le Canada, depuis 1749 jusqu'à 1760*.

[D.4]: *Mémoire du sieur de Ramezay*.

Transactions. [1st series.] 5 vols. 1824/29–1861/62. New series. 30 vols. 1862/63–1924.

As a guide to contents see: *Index to the archival publications ... 1824–1924* (1923); *Index of the lectures, papers and historical documents published by the Literary and Historical Society of Quebec ... together with a list of unpublished papers read before the society* [1829–1927], comp. F. C. Würtele and J. W. Strachan (1927).

MAINE HISTORICAL SOCIETY, Portland

PUBLICATIONS

Documentary history of Maine (Willis *et al.*).

Mandements, lettres pastorales et circulaires des évêques de Québec. 18 vols. to date. Québec,

1887–19 . The first six volumes were edited by Henri Têtu and Charles-Octave Gagnon; no editors are given for later volumes. Volume numbering is peculiar: [1re série], I–IV; nouvelle [2e] série, I–V; nouvelle [3e] série, I–III; a second set of cumulative volume numbers begins with vol. V of the 2nd series and is the only volume numbering found after vol. III of the 3rd series.

[Maseres, Francis.] *The Maseres letters, 1766–1768*. Edited by William Stewart Wallace. Toronto, 1919.

Massachusetts Historical Society, Boston

PUBLICATIONS

Collections. 7 series of 10 vols. each and 11 additional vols. to date. 1792–19 .

79: *Voyages of "Columbia"* (Howay).

Proceedings. 3 series of 20 vols. each, index vols. for each series, and 29 additional vols. to date. 1859–19 .

Shipton, *Sibley's Harvard graduates* [*see* section III].

As a guide to contents and indexes see: *Handbook of the publications and photostats, 1792–1935* ([2nd ed.], 1937).

[Meares, John.] *Voyages made in the years 1788 and 1789, from China to the north west coast of America. . . .* [Compiled by William Combe.] London, 1790; reprinted Amsterdam and New York, [1967].

"Mémoire du Canada," ANQ *Rapport*, 1924–25, 96–198.

Mémoire du sieur de Ramezay, commandant à Québec, au sujet de la reddition de cette ville, le 18 septembre 1759. . . . (Literary and Historical Society of Quebec, Historical Documents, 1st series, [D.4].) Québec, 1861. The "Mémoire du sieur de Ramezay" with accompanying documents forms the second part of the compilation.

Mémoires sur le Canada, depuis 1749 jusqu'à 1760. . . . (Literary and Historical Society of Quebec, Historical Documents, 1st series, [D.1].) Québec, 1838; réimprimé, 1873.

Michigan Pioneer Collections. Lansing. 40 vols. 1874/76–1929. To avoid confusion the Michigan Historical Commission, Department of State, Lansing, has standardized the citation for these volumes, which were originally published by various historical agencies and under various titles. Volumes are traditionally cited by their spine dates. The following were particularly useful for volume IV:

IX–XI: containing "The Haldimand papers." 1886–87.

XIX: containing "Bouquet papers," "Haldimand papers." 1891.

XX: containing "Haldimand papers," "Indian affairs." 1892.

An *Index* has been published for vols. I–XV (1904) and vols. XVI–XXX (1907); an index to vols. I–XXXIX appears in vol. XXXIX.

Military affairs in North America, 1748–1765: selected documents from the Cumberland papers in Windsor Castle. Edited by Stanley [McCrory] Pargellis. New York and London, [1936]; reprinted [Hamden, Conn.], 1969.

Military operations in eastern Maine and Nova Scotia during the revolution, chiefly compiled from the journals and letters of Colonel John Allan, with notes and a memoir of Col. John Allan. Edited by Frederic Kidder. Albany, N.Y., 1867.

New Brunswick Historical Society, Saint John

PUBLICATIONS

Collections. 12 nos. in 4 vols. and 9 additional nos. to date. 1894/97–19 .

New York Historical Society, New York

PUBLICATIONS

Collections. [1st series.] 5 vols. 1809–30. 2nd series. 4 vols. 1841–59. [3rd series.] 85 vols. to date, 1868–19 .

Nova Scotia, House of Assembly, *Journal* (Halifax), 1760–19 . The journals for 1758–60 remain in manuscript form. The originals are in the Legislative Library of N.S. (Halifax); a contemporary copy is available at PANS. Title varies. *See* O. B. Bishop, *Publications of the governments of Nova Scotia, Prince Edward Island, New Brunswick, 1758–1952* (Ottawa, 1957).

[*Nova Scotia Archives, I:*] *Selections from the public documents of the province of Nova Scotia*. Edited by Thomas Beamish Akins, translations by Benjamin Curren. (PANS publication.) Halifax, 1869.

——— *II: A calendar of two letter-books and one commission-book in the possession of the government of Nova Scotia, 1713–1741*. Edited by Archibald McKellar MacMechan. (PANS publication.) Halifax, 1900.

——— *III: Original minutes of his majesty's council at Annapolis Royal, 1720–1739*. Edited by Archibald McKellar MacMechan. (PANS publication.) Halifax, 1908.

——— *IV: Minutes of his majesty's council at Annapolis Royal, 1736–1749*. Edited by Charles Bruce Fergusson. (PANS publication.) Halifax, 1967.

Ontario Historical Society, Toronto

PUBLICATIONS

Correspondence of Lieut. Governor Simcoe (Cruikshank).

The papers of Sir William Johnson. Edited by James Sullivan *et al.* 14 vols. Albany, N.Y., 1921–65.

Papiers Contrecœur et autres documents concernant le conflit anglo-français sur l'Ohio de 1745 à 1756. Fernand Grenier, éditeur. (ASQ publication, I.) Québec, 1952.

Pennsylvania archives. . . . Edited by Samuel Hazard *et al.* 9 series in 119 vols. Philadelphia and Harrisburg, Pa., 1852–1935. This collection of documents is supplemented by *Colonial records of Pa.* (Hazard) [*q.v.*]. As a guide to contents and indexes *see*: H. H. Eddy, *Guide to the published archives of Pennsylvania, covering the 138 volumes of colonial records and Pennsylvania archives, series I–IX* (Harrisburg, 1949).

[PERKINS, SIMEON.] *The diary of Simeon Perkins. . . .* Edited by Harold Adams Innis *et al.* (Champlain Society publications, XXIX, XXXVI, XXXIX, XLIII, L.) 5 vols. Toronto, 1948–78.

[I]: *1766–1780*. Edited by Harold Adams Innis.

[II]: *1780–1789*. Edited by Daniel Cobb Harvey with notes by Charles Bruce Fergusson.

[III]: *1790–1796*; [IV]: *1797–1803*; [V]: *1804–1812*. Edited by Charles Bruce Fergusson.

PUBLIC ARCHIVES OF CANADA, Ottawa

BOARD OF HISTORICAL PUBLICATIONS

Doc. relatifs à la monnaie sous le Régime français (Shortt).

Doc. relatifs à l'hist. constitutionnelle, 1759–91 (Shortt et Doughty; 1921).

Docs. relating to Canadian currency during the French period (Shortt).

Docs. relating to constitutional history, 1759–91 (Shortt and Doughty; 1918).

Docs. relating to currency in N.S., 1675–1758 (Shortt *et al.*).

NUMBERED PUBLICATIONS [*see* section III]

OTHER PUBLICATIONS [*see also* section III]

Doc. relatifs à l'hist. constitutionnelle, 1791–1818 (Doughty et McArthur).

Docs. relating to constitutional history, 1791–1818 (Doughty and McArthur).

Reports; *Rapports*. 1881–19 . Annually until 1952; irregularly thereafter.

PUBLIC ARCHIVES OF NOVA SCOTIA, Halifax

PUBLICATIONS [*see also* section III]

N.S. Archives, I (Akins).

N.S. Archives, II (MacMechan).

N.S. Archives, III (MacMechan).

N.S. Archives, IV (Fergusson).

RECENSEMENTS

NEW FRANCE

1716: *Recensement de la ville de Québec pour 1716*. Louis Beaudet, éditeur. Québec, 1887.

1741: "Un recensement inédit de Montréal, en 1741," É.-Z. Massicotte, édit., RSC *Trans.*, 3rd ser., XV (1921), sect.I, 1–61.

1744: "Le recensement de Québec, en 1744," ANQ *Rapport*, 1939–40, 3–154.

PROVINCE OF QUEBEC

1760: "Recensement des habitants de la ville et gouvernement des Trois-Rivières tel qu'il a été pris au mois de septembre mil sept cent soixante," ANQ *Rapport*, 1946–47, 5–53. Includes not only the census of 1760 but demographic information up to 1763.

1762: "Le recensement du gouvernement de Québec en 1762," A.[-E.] Gosselin, édit., ANQ *Rapport*, 1925–26, 2–143.

1765: "Le recensement des gouvernements de Montréal et des Trois-Rivières," ANQ *Rapport*, 1936–37, 2–121.

1779: "Recensement de Détroit, 1779," Lucien Brault, édit., *RHAF*, V (1951–52), 581–85.

[ROCBERT DE LA MORANDIÈRE, MARIE-ÉLISABETH.] "Correspondance de Madame Bégon, née Rocbert de La Morandière," Claude de Bonnault, édit., ANQ *Rapport*, 1934–35, 5–277.

Royal Fort Frontenac. Compiled and translated by Richard Arthur Preston, edited by Léopold Lamontagne. (Champlain Society publications, Ontario series, II.) Toronto, 1958.

Le séminaire de Québec: documents et biographies. Honorius Provost, éditeur. (ASQ publication, II.) Québec, 1964.

[VANCOUVER, GEORGE.] *A voyage of discovery to the north Pacific Ocean, and round the world. . . .* [Edited by John Vancouver.] 3 vols. London, 1798; reprinted Amsterdam and New York, [1967].

Voyages of the "Columbia" to the northwest coast, 1787–1790 and 1790–1793. Edited by Frederic William Howay. (Massachusetts Historical Society, *Collections*, 79.) [Boston], 1941; reprinted Amsterdam and New York, [1969].

WISCONSIN, STATE HISTORICAL SOCIETY, Madison

PUBLICATIONS

Collections. 31 vols. 1855–1931.

B. NEWSPAPERS

The following newspapers were particularly useful in the preparation of volume IV. For detailed information on publishers, regularity of publication, and changes in title, readers are referred to Beaulieu et Hamelin, *La presse québe-*

çoise, I, and Tremaine, *Bibliography of Canadian imprints* [*see* section III].

La Gazette littéraire pour la ville et district de Montréal. 1778–79. Weekly. Continued by the *Montreal Gazette/La Gazette de Montréal*.

Halifax Gazette. 1752–66. Weekly. Continued by the *Nova-Scotia Gazette and the Weekly Chronicle*.

Montreal Gazette/La Gazette de Montréal. 1785–1824. Weekly. A bilingual continuation of *La Gazette littéraire pour la ville et district de Montréal*. From 1824 to the present time, under differing titles, the paper has appeared only in English.

Nova-Scotia Gazette and the Weekly Chronicle. Halifax. 1770–89. Weekly. Representing a merger of the *Nova-Scotia Gazette* (Halifax, 1766–70) and the *Nova Scotia Chronicle and Weekly Advertiser* (Halifax, 1769–70). A continuation of the *Halifax Gazette* and continued by the *Royal Gazette and the Nova-Scotia Advertiser*.

Quebec Gazette/La Gazette de Québec. 1764–1832. Weekly, 1764–1817; bi-weekly, 1818–32. Bilingual. The paper remained bilingual from 1832 to 1842 but the French and English editions were published separately; from 1842 to 1874, when publication ceased, only the English edition appeared.

Quebec Herald, Miscellany and Advertiser. Quebec. 1788–93. Weekly, 1788–89, 1791–93; bi-weekly, 1789–91.

Royal Gazette and the New Brunswick Advertiser. Saint John. 1785–1815. Weekly.

Royal Gazette and the Nova-Scotia Advertiser. Halifax. 1789–1800. Weekly. A continuation of the *Nova-Scotia Gazette and the Weekly Chronicle*.

III. REFERENCE WORKS

ALLAIRE, JEAN-BAPTISTE-ARTHUR. *Dictionnaire biographique du clergé canadien-français*. 6 vols. Montréal, etc., 1908–34.
[I]: *Les anciens*. Montréal, 1910.
[II]: *Les contemporains*. Saint-Hyacinthe, Qué., 1908.
[III]: [*Suppléments*.] 6 parts in 1 vol. Montréal, etc., 1910–19.
[IV]: *Le clergé canadien-français: revue mensuelle* ([Montréal]), I (1919–20). Only one volume of this journal was published.
[V]: *Compléments*. 6 parts in 1 vol. Montréal, 1928–32.
[VI]: Untitled. Saint-Hyacinthe, 1934.

Almanach de Québec. Québec. 1780–1841. From 1792 the title varies, appearing sometimes in English, sometimes in French, and sometimes in both languages. See *DCB*, IX, 892.

ARCHIVES NATIONALES DU QUÉBEC, Québec PUBLICATIONS [*see also* section II]
P.-G. Roy, *Inv. coll. pièces jud. et not.*
——— *Inv. concessions.*
——— *Inv. contrats de mariage.*
——— *Inv. ins. Cons. souv.*
——— *Inv. ins. Prév. Québec.*
——— *Inv. jug. et délib., 1717–60.*
——— *Inv. ord. int.*
——— *Inv. procès-verbaux des grands voyers.*
——— *Inv. testaments.*
——— *Les juges de la prov. de Québec.*
——— *et al., Inv. greffes not.*

[AUBERT] DE LA CHESNAYE-DESBOIS, [FRANÇOIS-ALEXANDRE], ET ——— BADIER. *Dictionnaire de la noblesse, contenant les généalogies, l'histoire & la chronologie des familles nobles de la France*. . . . 2e édition. 15 vols. Paris, 1770–86. 3e édition. 19 vols. 1863–76; réimprimé Nendeln, Liechtenstein, 1969. First published by La Chesnaye-Desbois alone as *Dictionnaire généalogique, héraldique, chronologique et historique contenant l'origine et l'état actuel des premières maisons de France* . . . (7v., 1757–65).

BEAULIEU, ANDRÉ, ET JEAN HAMELIN. *La presse québecoise des origines à nos jours*. [2e édition.] 3 vols. to date [1764–1895]. Québec, 1973– . First published as *Les journaux du Québec de 1764 à 1964* (Université Laval, Institut d'histoire, Cahiers, 6, Québec, 1965).

BÉLISLE, LOUIS-ALEXANDRE. *Références biographiques, Canada-Québec*. [Jean-Jacques Lefebvre, éditeur.] 5 vols. Montréal, [1978].

A bibliography of Canadiana, being items in the Public Library of Toronto, Canada, relating to the early history and development of Canada. Edited by Frances Maria Staton and Marie Tremaine. Toronto, 1934; reprinted, 1965.

A bibliography of Canadiana: first supplement. . . . Edited by Gertrude Mabel Boyle with Marjorie Colbeck. Toronto, 1959; reprinted, 1969.

Biographie universelle, ancienne et moderne. . . . [Joseph-François et Louis-Gabriel Michaud, éditeurs.] 85 vols. [vols. 1–52, "A" to "Z"; vols. 53–55, *Partie mythologique*, "A" to "Z"; vols. 56–85, *Supplément*, "A" to "Vil"]. Paris, 1811–62. Nouvelle édition. [Louis-Gabriel Michaud et Eugène-Ernest Desplaces, éditeurs.] 45 vols. [1854–65]; réimprimé [Graz, Austria, 1966].

BOATNER, MARK MAYO. *Encyclopedia of the American revolution*. New York, [1966].

BURKE, JOHN. *A general and heraldic dictionary of the peerage and baronetage of the United Kingdom*. London, 1826. 105th edition. Edited by Peter Townend. 1970.

CARON, IVANHOË. "Inventaire de la correspondance de Mgr Jean-François Hubert, évêque de Québec et de Mgr Charles-François Bailly de Messein, son coadjuteur," ANQ *Rapport*, 1930–31, 199–351.

——— "Inventaire de la correspondance de Mgr Jean-Olivier Briand, évêque de Québec," ANQ *Rapport*, 1929–30, 47–136.

——— "Inventaire de la correspondance de Mgr Louis-Philippe Mariaucheau D'Esgly, évêque de Québec," ANQ *Rapport*, 1930–31, 185–98.

——— "Inventaire de la correspondance de Mgr Pierre Denaut, évêque de Québec," ANQ *Rapport*, 1931–32, 129–242.

CHARLAND, PAUL-VICTOR. "Notre-Dame de Québec: le nécrologe de la crypte ou les inhumations dans cette église depuis 1652," *BRH*, XX (1914), 137–51, 169–81, 205–17, 237–51, 269–80, 301–13, 333–47.

CHARNOCK, JOHN. *Biographia navalis; or, impartial memoirs of the lives and characters of officers of the navy of Great Britain, from the year 1660 to the present time; drawn from the most authentic sources, and disposed in a chronological arrangement*. 6 vols. London, 1794–98.

COLLEDGE, JAMES JOSEPH. *Ships of the Royal Navy: an historical index*. 2 vols. Newton Abbot, Eng., [1969–70].

DEROME, ROBERT. *Les orfèvres de Nouvelle-France: inventaire descriptif des sources*. Ottawa, 1974.

DESROSIERS, LOUIS-ADÉLARD. "Correspondance de cinq vicaires généraux avec les évêques de Québec, 1761–1816," ANQ *Rapport*, 1947–48, 73–133.

Dictionary of American biography. Edited by Allen Johnson *et al.* 20 vols., index, and 2 supplements [to 1940]. New York, 1928–58; reprinted, 22 vols. in 11 and index, [1946?–58]. 2 additional supplements to date [to 1950]. Edited by Edward James Topping *et al.* [1973]– . *Concise DAB*. [1964.]

Dictionary of national biography. Edited by Leslie Stephen and Sidney Lee. 63 vols., 3 supplements, and index and epitome [to 1900]. London, 1885–1903. 6 additional supplements to date [to 1960]. Edited by Sidney Lee *et al.* 1912– . *Concise DNB*. 2 vols. [1952]–61. *Corrections and additions to the "Dictionary of national biography"*. Boston, Mass., 1966.

Dictionnaire de biographie française. Jules Balteau *et al.*, éditeurs. 13 vols. and 3 fascicules to date ["A" to "Fouret"]. Paris, 1933– .

Dictionnaire des œuvres littéraires du Québec. Maurice Lemire *et al.*, éditeurs. 1 vol. to date [to 1900]. Montréal, [1977]– .

A directory of the members of the Legislative Assembly of Nova Scotia, 1758–1958. Introduction by Charles Bruce Fergusson. (PANS publications, Nova Scotia series, II.) Halifax, 1958.

Encyclopædia Britannica. Edited by Warren E. Preece *et al.* 23 vols. and index. Chicago and Toronto, [1966]. 15th edition. 30 vols. [1977.]

Encyclopedia Canadiana. Edited by John Everett Robbins *et al.* 10 vols. Ottawa, [1957–58]. [Revised edition.] Edited by Kenneth H. Pearson *et al.* 10 vols. Toronto, [1975].

FAUTEUX, ÆGIDIUS. *Les chevaliers de Saint-Louis en Canada*. Montréal, 1940.

GAUTHIER, HENRI. *Sulpitiana*. n.p., 1912. [2e édition.] Montréal, 1926.

GODBOUT, ARCHANGE [ALDÉRIC]. "Nos ancêtres au XVIIe siècle," ANQ *Rapport*, 1951–53, 449–544; 1953–55, 445–536; 1955–57, 379–489; 1957–59, 383–440; 1959–60, 277–354; 1965, 147–81. "A" to "Brassard" included. The last instalment has notes by R.-J. Auger.

Grand Larousse encyclopédique. 10 vols. and 2 supplements to date. Paris, [1960]– .

GREAT BRITAIN, ADMIRALTY. *The commissioned sea officers of the Royal Navy, 1660–1815*. [Editing begun by David Bonner Smith; project continued by the Royal Naval College in cooperation with the National Maritime Museum.] 3 vols. n.p., [1954?].

GREAT BRITAIN, PUBLIC RECORD OFFICE. *Calendar of Home Office papers of the reign of George III* [1760–75]. Edited by Joseph Redington and Richard Arthur Roberts. 4 vols. London, 1878–99.

——— *Calendar of state papers, colonial series, America and West Indies*. . . . Edited by William Noel Sainsbury *et al.* 44 vols. to date [1574–1738]. London, 1860–19 .

——— *Calendar of Treasury books and papers* . . . [1729–45]. Edited by William Arthur Shaw. 5 vols. London, 1897–1908.

GREAT BRITAIN, WAR OFFICE. *A list of the general and field officers as they rank in the army*.

. . . [London, 1754–1868.] The first known official army list was published in 1740 and has been reprinted as *The army list of 1740 . . . with a complete index of names and of regiments* (Soc. for Army Hist. Research, Special no., III, Sheffield, Eng., 1931).

Guide to the reports of the Public Archives of Canada, 1872–1972. Compiled by Françoise Caron-Houle. (PAC publication.) Ottawa, 1975.

Handbook of American Indians north of Mexico. Edited by Frederick Webb Hodge. 2 vols. Washington, 1907–10; reprinted New York, 1971. The Canadian material in this work has been revised and republished as an appendix to the tenth report of the Geographic Board of Canada, entitled *Handbook of Indians of Canada* (Ottawa, 1913; repr. New York, 1969). The Smithsonian Institution is currently preparing a multi-volume "Handbook of North American Indians" under the general editorship of W. C. Sturtevant; it will update and replace the original *Handbook*.

HOWAY, FREDERIC WILLIAM. *A list of trading vessels in the maritime fur trade, 1785–1825*. Edited by Richard Austin Pierce. Kingston, Ont., 1973. First published in RSC *Trans.*, 3rd ser., XXIV (1930)–XXVIII (1934) [*see* section V].

HOZIER, LOUIS-PIERRE D', *et al. Armorial général de la France. . . .* 7 vols. in 13. Paris, [1865–1908]; réimprimé [1970]. The first six volumes (or *registres*) are a reprint of the original work: L.-P. d'Hozier et A.-M. d'Hozier de Sérigny, *Armorial de la France* (6v. in 10, 1738–68). The d'Hoziers' work was continued by A.-L.-M. and A.-C. d'Hozier, who published a 7th volume: *Armorial général d'Hozier* . . . (2 pts. in 1v., 1847–48).

Index to reports of Canadian archives from 1872 to 1908. (PAC publications, 1.) Ottawa, 1909.

KELLEY, ARTHUR READING. "Church and state papers for the years 1759 to 1786, being a compendium of documents relating to the establishment of certain churches in the province of Quebec," ANQ *Rapport*, 1948–49, 293–340.

——— "The Quebec Diocesan Archives," ANQ *Rapport*, 1946–47, 181–298.

LABRÈQUE, LUCILE. "Inventaire de pièces détachées de cours de justice de la Nouvelle-France (1638–1760)," ANQ *Rapport*, 1971, 5–50.

LA CHESNAYE-DESBOIS. *See* Aubert

[LANGELIER, JEAN-CHRYSOSTOME.] *Liste des terrains concédés par la couronne dans la province de Québec de 1763 au 31 décembre 1890*. Québec, 1891. Published in English as *List of lands granted by the crown in the province of Quebec from 1763 to 31st December 1890* (1891).

LEBŒUF, JOSEPH-[AIMÉ-]ARTHUR. *Complément au dictionnaire généalogique Tanguay*. (Société généalogique canadienne-française publications, 2, 4, 6.) 3 vols. Montréal, 1957–64.

LEFEBVRE, JEAN-JACQUES. "Engagements pour l'Ouest, 1778–1788," ANQ *Rapport*, 1946–47, 303–69.

LE JEUNE, LOUIS[-MARIE]. *Dictionnaire général de biographie, histoire, littérature, agriculture, commerce, industrie et des arts, sciences, mœurs, coutumes, institutions politiques et religieuses du Canada*. 2 vols. Ottawa, [1931].

LÉTOURNEAU, HUBERT, ET LUCILE LABRÈQUE. "Inventaire de pièces détachées de la Prévôté de Québec," ANQ *Rapport*, 1971, 55–413.

MARION, MARCEL. *Dictionnaire des institutions de la France aux XVIIe et XVIIIe siècles*. Paris, 1923; réimprimé, 1968 et 1969.

MASSICOTTE, ÉDOUARD-ZOTIQUE. "Répertoire des engagements pour l'Ouest conservés dans les Archives judiciaires de Montréal . . . [1670–1821]," ANQ *Rapport*, 1929–30, 195–466; 1930–31, 353–453; 1931–32, 243–365; 1932–33, 245–304; 1942–43, 261–397; 1943–44, 335–444; 1944–45, 309–401; 1945–46, 227–340.

[MÉLANÇON, ARTHUR.] *Liste des missionnaires-jésuites: Nouvelle-France et Louisiane, 1611–1800*. Montréal, 1929.

MORICE, ADRIEN-GABRIEL. *Dictionnaire historique des Canadiens et des Métis français de l'Ouest*. Kamloops, C.-B., 1908; Québec, 1908. 2e édition. Québec, 1912.

NAMIER, LEWIS [BERNSTEIN], AND JOHN BROOKE. *The House of Commons, 1754–1790*. 3 vols. London, 1964; New York, 1964. *See also* Sedgwick, *House of Commons*.

"Les notaires au Canada sous le Régime français," ANQ *Rapport*, 1921–22, 1–58. Contains biographies of nearly 200 notaries.

PARKER, DAVID WILLSON. *A guide to the documents in the manuscript room at the Public Archives of Canada*. (PAC publications, 10.) Ottawa, 1914.

Place-names and places of Nova Scotia. (PANS publications, Nova Scotia series, III.) Halifax, 1967; reprinted Belleville, Ont., 1976.

PUBLIC ARCHIVES OF CANADA, Ottawa

NUMBERED PUBLICATIONS

1: *Index to reports of Canadian archives*.

6: J.-E. Roy, *Rapport sur les archives de France*.

10: Parker, *Guide to documents at PAC*.
OTHER PUBLICATIONS [*see also* section II]
Guide to reports of PAC (Caron-Houle).
Inventories of holdings in the manuscript division [*see* section I].
Union list of MSS (Gordon *et al.*; Maurice).
Union list of MSS, supp. (Maurice and Chabot).
PUBLIC ARCHIVES OF NOVA SCOTIA, Halifax
NOVA SCOTIA SERIES
II: *Directory of N.S. MLAs*.
III: *Place-names of N.S.*
OTHER PUBLICATIONS [*see* section II]
RAYBURN, ALAN. *Geographical names of Prince Edward Island*. Ottawa, 1973.
A register of the regiments and corps of the British army: the ancestry of the regiments and corps of the regular establishment. Edited by Arthur Swinson. London, [1972].
ROY, JOSEPH-EDMOND. *Rapport sur les archives de France relatives à l'histoire du Canada*. (PAC publications, 6.) Ottawa, 1911.
ROY, PIERRE-GEORGES. *Les avocats de la région de Québec*. Lévis, Qué., 1936.
——— *Fils de Québec*. 4 vols. Lévis, Qué., 1933.
——— *Inventaire des concessions en fief et seigneurie, fois et hommages et aveux et dénombrements, conservés au Archives de la province de Québec*. (ANQ publication.) 6 vols. Beauceville, Qué., 1927–29.
——— *Inventaire des contrats de mariage du Régime français conservés aux Archives judiciaires de Québec*. (ANQ publication.) 6 vols. Québec, 1937–38.
——— *Inventaire des insinuations de la Prévôté de Québec*. (ANQ publication.) 3 vols. Beauceville, Qué., 1936–39.
——— *Inventaire des insinuations du Conseil souverain de la Nouvelle-France*. (ANQ publication.) Beauceville, Qué., 1921.
——— *Inventaire des jugements et délibérations du Conseil supérieur de la Nouvelle-France de 1717 à 1760*. (ANQ publication.) 7 vols. Beauceville, Qué., 1932–35.
——— *Inventaire des ordonnances des intendants de la Nouvelle-France conservées aux Archives provinciales de Québec*. (ANQ publication.) 4 vols. Beauceville, Qué., 1919.
——— *Inventaire des procès-verbaux des grands voyers conservés aux Archives de la province de Québec*. (ANQ publication.) 6 vols. Beauceville, Qué., 1923–32.
——— *Inventaire des testaments, donations et inventaires du Régime français conservés aux Archives judiciaires de Québec*. (ANQ publication.) 3 vols. Québec, 1941.
——— *Inventaire d'une collection de pièces judiciaires, notariales, etc., etc., conservées aux Archives judiciaires de Québec*. (ANQ publication.) 2 vols. Beauceville, Qué., 1917.
——— *Les juges de la province de Québec*. (ANQ publication.) Québec, 1933.
——— *et al. Inventaire des greffes des notaires du Régime français*. (ANQ publication.) 23 vols. to date. Québec, [1942]– .
SABINE, LORENZO. *Biographical sketches of loyalists of the American revolution, with an historical essay*. [2nd edition.] 2 vols. Boston, Mass., 1864. First published as *The American loyalists, or biographical sketches of adherents to the British crown in the war of the revolution* ... (1847).
SEDGWICK, [RICHARD] ROMNEY. *The House of Commons, 1715–1754*. 2 vols. London, 1970; New York, 1970. *See also* Namier and Brooke, *House of Commons*.
The service of British regiments in Canada and North America.... Compiled by Charles Herbert Stewart. Ottawa, 1962. [2nd edition.] 1964.
SHIPTON, CLIFFORD KENYON. *Sibley's Harvard graduates*. . . . (Massachusetts Historical Society publication.) 17 vols. to date [1690–1771]. Cambridge and Boston, Mass., 1933– . A continuation of J. S. Sibley, *Biographical sketches of graduates of Harvard University, in Cambridge, Massachusetts* [1642–89] (3v., Cambridge, 1873–85), the volumes are numbered consecutively from it.
TANGUAY, CYPRIEN. *Dictionnaire généalogique des familles canadiennes depuis la fondation de la colonie jusqu'à nos jours*. 7 vols. [Montréal], 1871–90; réimprimé New York, 1969. *See also* Lebœuf, *Complément*.
——— *Répertoire général du clergé canadien par ordre chronologique depuis la fondation de la colonie jusqu'à nos jours*. Québec, 1868.
TREMAINE, MARIE. *A bibliography of Canadian imprints, 1751–1800*. Toronto, 1952.
TRUDEL, JEAN. *L'orfèvrerie en Nouvelle-France: une exposition organisée par la Galerie nationale du Canada*. Ottawa, 1974.
TURCOTTE, GUSTAVE. *Le Conseil législatif de Québec, 1774–1933*. Beauceville, Qué., 1933.
Union list of manuscripts in Canadian repositories/Catalogue collectif des manuscrits des archives canadiennes. Edited by Robert Stanyslaw Gordon *et al.* (PAC publication.) Ottawa, 1968. Revised edition. Edited by E. Grace Maurice. 2 vols. 1975. *Supplement/Supplément*. Edited by E. Grace Maurice and Victorin Chabot. 1976.
VACHON, ANDRÉ. "Inventaire critique des notaires royaux des gouvernements de Québec, Montréal et Trois-Rivières (1663–

1764)," *RHAF*, IX (1955–56), 423–38, 546–61; X (1956–57), 93–103, 257–62, 381–90; XI (1957–58), 93–106, 270–76, 400–6.

WALBRAN, JOHN THOMAS. *British Columbia coast names, 1592–1906, to which are added a few names in adjacent United States territory: their origin and history*. . . . Ottawa, 1909; reprinted Vancouver, 1971.

WALLACE, WILLIAM STEWART. *The Macmillan dictionary of Canadian biography*. 4th edition. Edited by William Angus McKay. Toronto, [1978]. First published as *The dictionary of Canadian biography* (1926).

WATTERS, REGINALD EYRE. *A check list of Canadian literature and background materials, 1628–1950*. . . . Toronto, [1959]. 2nd edition [. . . *1628–1960*]. Toronto and Buffalo, [1972].

IV. STUDIES (BOOKS AND THESES)

ABBOTT, MAUDE ELIZABETH [SEYMOUR]. *History of medicine in the province of Quebec*. Toronto, 1931; Montreal, 1931.

AHERN, MICHAEL-JOSEPH ET GEORGE. *Notes pour servir à l'histoire de la médecine dans le Bas-Canada depuis la fondation de Québec jusqu'au commencement du XIXe siècle*. Québec, 1923.

AKINS, THOMAS BEAMISH. *History of Halifax City*. Belleville, Ont., 1973. First published as N.S. Hist. Soc., *Coll.*, VIII (1895) [*see* section V].

ARSENAULT, BONA. *Histoire et généalogie des Acadiens*. 2 vols. Québec, [1965]. Vol. I translated in collaboration with Brian M. Upton and John G. McLaughlin as *History of the Acadians* (Quebec, [1966]).

AUDET, LOUIS-PHILIPPE. *Le système scolaire de la province de Québec* [1635–1840]. 6 vols. Québec, 1950–56.

BECK, JAMES MURRAY. *The government of Nova Scotia*. Toronto, 1957.

BELL, WINTHROP PICKARD. *The "foreign Protestants" and the settlement of Nova Scotia: the history of a piece of arrested British colonial policy in the eighteenth century*. Toronto, [1961].

BREBNER, JOHN BARTLET. *The neutral Yankees of Nova Scotia, a marginal colony during the revolutionary years*. New York, 1937; republished, introduction by William Stewart MacNutt, Toronto and Montreal, [1969]; reprint of 1937 edition, New York, [1970].

——— *New England's outpost: Acadia before the conquest of Canada*. New York and London, 1927; reprinted Hamden, Conn., 1965, and New York, [1973].

BRUNET, MICHEL. *Les Canadiens après la Conquête, 1759–1775: de la Révolution canadienne à la Révolution américaine*. Montréal, [1969].

[BURKE, CATHERINE, DITE DE SAINT-THOMAS.] *Les ursulines de Québec, depuis leur établissement jusqu'à nos jours*. 4 vols. Québec, 1863–66. [2e édition.] First two volumes only. 1878.

BURT, ALFRED LEROY. *The old province of Quebec*. Toronto and Minneapolis, Minn., 1933; republished, introduction by Hilda [Marion] Neatby, 2 vols., [Toronto, 1968]; reprint of 1933 edition, New York, [1970].

CALNEK, WILLIAM ARTHUR. *History of the county of Annapolis, including old Port Royal and Acadia, with memoirs of its representatives in the provincial parliament, and biographical and genealogical sketches of its early English settlers and their families*. Edited and completed by Alfred William Savary. Toronto, 1897; reprinted Belleville, Ont., 1972. *See also* Savary, *Supplement to history of Annapolis*.

CAMPBELL, ROBERT. *A history of the Scotch Presbyterian Church, St. Gabriel Street, Montreal*. Montreal, 1887.

Canada and its provinces: a history of the Canadian people and their institutions. Edited by Adam Shortt and Arthur George Doughty. 23 vols. Toronto, 1913–17.

Canada's smallest province: a history of P.E.I. Edited by Francis William Pius Bolger. [Charlottetown, 1973.]

CANADIAN CENTENARY SERIES. William Lewis Morton, executive editor; Donald Grant Creighton, advisory editor.
5: Stanley, *New France*.
6: Neatby, *Quebec*.
9: MacNutt, *Atlantic provinces*.

CASGRAIN, HENRI-RAYMOND. *Histoire de l'Hôtel-Dieu de Québec*. Québec, 1878.

CHARLAND, THOMAS-MARIE. *Histoire des Abénakis d'Odanak (1675–1937)*. Montréal, 1964.

CLARK, ANDREW HILL. *Acadia: the geography of early Nova Scotia to 1760*. Madison, Wis., 1968.

COLEMAN, EMMA LEWIS. *New England captives carried to Canada between 1677 and 1760 during the French and Indian wars*. 2 vols. Portland, Maine, 1925.

COOK, WARREN LAWRENCE. *Flood tide of empire: Spain and the Pacific northwest, 1543–1819*. New Haven, Conn., and London, 1973.

CROWLEY, TERENCE ALLAN. "Government and interests: French colonial administration at Louisbourg, 1713–1758." Unpublished PHD thesis, Duke University, Durham, N.C., 1975.

D'ALLAIRE, MICHELINE. *L'Hôpital-général de Québec, 1692–1764*. Montréal, [1971].

DAVIDSON, GORDON CHARLES. *The North West Company*. Berkeley, Calif., 1918; reprinted New York, [1967].

ECCLES, WILLIAM JOHN. *The Canadian frontier, 1534–1760*. New York and Toronto, [1969].

——— *France in America*. New York, [1972].

FAUTEUX, ÆGIDIUS. *The introduction of printing into Canada: a brief history*. Montreal, 1930; republished, 6 parts in 1 vol., 1957. Appeared in French as *L'introduction de l'imprimerie au Canada: une brève histoire* (6 pts. in 1v., Montréal, 1957).

[FAUTEUX, ALBINA, ET CLÉMENTINE DROUIN.] [*L'Hôpital Général de Montréal*:] *L'Hôpital Général des sœurs de la Charité (sœurs grises) depuis sa fondation jusqu'à nos jours*. 3 vols. to date [1692–1877]. Montréal, [1916]– .

FAUTEUX, JOSEPH-NOËL. *Essai sur l'industrie au Canada sous le Régime français*. 2 vols. Québec, 1927.

FRÉGAULT, GUY. *Le XVIIIe siècle canadien: études*. Montréal, 1968; réimprimé, 1970.

——— *François Bigot, administrateur français*. (Institut d'histoire de l'Amérique française, Études.) 2 vols. [Montréal], 1948.

——— *Le grand marquis: Pierre de Rigaud de Vaudreuil et la Louisiane*. (Institut d'histoire de l'Amérique française, Études.) Montréal et Paris, 1952. 2e édition. [1962.]

——— *La guerre de la Conquête*. Montréal et Paris, [1955]. Reprinted as vol. IX of *Histoire de la Nouvelle-France*, Marcel Trudel, édit. (3v. [I, II, IX], Montréal et Paris, [1963–66]). Translated by Margaret M. Cameron as *Canada: the war of the conquest* (Toronto, 1969).

GALARNEAU, CLAUDE. *La France devant l'opinion canadienne (1760–1815)*. (Université Laval, Institut d'histoire, Cahiers, 16.) Québec et Paris, 1970.

GARNEAU, FRANÇOIS-XAVIER. *Histoire du Canada depuis sa découverte jusqu'à nos jours*. 4 vols. Québec, 1845–52. 3e édition. 3 vols. 1859. 5e édition. Hector Garneau, éditeur. 2 vols. Paris, 1913–20. 8e édition. Hector Garneau, éditeur. 9 vols. Montréal, [1944–46]. Third edition translated and edited by Andrew Bell as *History of Canada, from the time of its discovery till the union year (1840–1)* (3v., Montreal, 1860; 3rd edition, 1866).

GAUMOND, MICHEL. *Les forges de Saint-Maurice*. (Société historique de Québec, Textes, 2.) Québec, 1968.

GOSSELIN, AMÉDÉE[-EDMOND]. *L'instruction au Canada sous le Régime français (1635–1760)*. Québec, 1911.

GOSSELIN, AUGUSTE[-HONORÉ]. *L'Église du Canada après la Conquête* [1760–89]. 2 vols. Québec, 1916–17.

——— *L'Église du Canada depuis Monseigneur de Laval jusqu'à la Conquête*. 3 vols. Québec, 1911–14.

GOWANS, ALAN [WILBERT]. *Church architecture in New France*. Toronto, 1955.

GRAYMONT, BARBARA. *The Iroquois in the American revolution*. Syracuse, N.Y., 1972.

GROULX, LIONEL. *Histoire du Canada français depuis la découverte*. 4 vols. [Montréal], 1950–52. 4e édition. 2 vols. Montréal et Paris, 1960; réimprimé, 1962.

GUNDY, HENRY PEARSON. *Early printers and printing in the Canadas*. Toronto, 1957. [2nd edition.] 1964.

HAMELIN, JEAN. *Économie et société en Nouvelle-France*. (Université Laval, Institut d'histoire, Cahiers, 3.) [Québec, 1960]; réimprimé, [1970].

HARRIS, RICHARD COLEBROOK. *The seigneurial system in early Canada: a geographical study*. Madison, Wis., and Quebec, 1966.

HARVEY, DANIEL COBB. *The French régime in Prince Edward Island*. New Haven, Conn., and London, 1926.

HEAGERTY, JOHN JOSEPH. *Four centuries of medical history in Canada and a sketch of the medical history of Newfoundland*. 2 vols. Toronto, 1928.

HILLER, JAMES K. "The foundation and the early years of the Moravian mission in Labrador, 1752–1805." Unpublished MA thesis, Memorial University of Newfoundland, St John's, [1968].

L'Hôpital Général de Montréal. *See* A. Fauteux et C. Drouin

HUNTER, WILLIAM ALBERT. *Forts on the Pennsylvania frontier, 1753–1758*. Harrisburg, Pa., 1960.

INNIS, HAROLD ADAMS. *The fur trade in Canada: an introduction to Canadian economic history*. New Haven, Conn., and London, 1930. Revised edition. [Edited by Mary

Quayle Innis, Samuel Delbert Clark, and William Thomas Easterbrook.] Toronto, 1956. [Abridged edition.] Based on revised edition, foreword by Robin William Winks. [1962.] Revised edition (reprint of 1956 edition with revised foreword from 1962 edition). [1970.]

INSTITUT D'HISTOIRE DE L'AMÉRIQUE FRANÇAISE, Montréal, Qué.
ÉTUDES
Frégault, *François Bigot*.
——— *Le grand marquis*.
OTHER PUBLICATIONS
M. Trudel, *L'Église canadienne*.

JOUVE, ODORIC-MARIE. *Les franciscains et le Canada: aux Trois-Rivières*. Paris, 1934.

KENNETT, LEE. *The French armies in the Seven Years' War: a study in military organization and administration*. Durham, N.C., 1967.

LACOUR-GAYET, GEORGES. *La marine militaire de la France sous le règne de Louis XV*. Paris, 1902. 2e édition. 1910.

——— *La marine militaire de la France sous le règne de Louis XVI*. Paris, 1905.

LA MORANDIÈRE, CHARLES DE. *Histoire de la pêche française de la morue dans l'Amérique septentrionale....* 3 vols. Paris, 1962–66.
I, II: *(Des origines à 1789)*.
III: *(De la Révolution à nos jours)*.

LANCTOT, GUSTAVE. *Le Canada et la Révolution américaine*. Montréal, 1965. Translated by Margaret M. Cameron as *Canada & the American revolution, 1774–1783* (Toronto and Vancouver, 1967).

——— *Histoire du Canada*. 3 vols. Montréal, 1959–64.
[I]: *Des origines au Régime royal*.
[II]: *Du Régime royal au traité d'Utrecht, 1663–1713*.
[III]: *Du traité d'Utrecht au traité de Paris, 1713–1763*.
Translated by Josephine Hambleton and Margaret M. Cameron as *A history of Canada* (3v., Toronto and Vancouver, 1963–65).

LANGDON, JOHN EMERSON. *Canadian silversmiths, 1700–1900*. Toronto, 1966.

LEMIEUX, LUCIEN. *L'établissement de la première province ecclésiastique au Canada, 1783–1844*. Montréal et Paris, [1968].

[LEMIRE-MARSOLAIS, DARIE-AURÉLIE, DITE SAINTE-HENRIETTE, ET] THÉRÈSE LAMBERT, DITE SAINTE-MARIE-MÉDIATRICE. *Histoire de la Congrégation de Notre-Dame de Montréal*. 11 vols. in 13 and an index to date. Montréal, 1941– . Before her death in 1917 Sister Sainte-Henriette had completed nine volumes of her history as well as an index; only two volumes were published, in 1910. In 1941 her complete work was published and the first two volumes reissued. The index for the first nine volumes, prepared by Sister Sainte-Henriette, was published in 1969.

MCLENNAN, JOHN STEWART. *Louisbourg from its foundation to its fall, 1713–1758*. London, 1918; reprinted without appendices, Sydney, N.S., 1957.

MACNUTT, WILLIAM STEWART. *The Atlantic provinces: the emergence of colonial society, 1712–1857*. (Canadian centenary series, 9.) [Toronto, 1965.]

——— *New Brunswick, a history: 1784–1867*. Toronto, 1963.

MATHIEU, JACQUES. *La construction navale royale à Québec, 1739–1759*. (Société historique de Québec, Cahiers d'histoire, 23.) Québec, 1971.

[MONDOUX, MARIA.] *L'Hôtel-Dieu, premier hôpital de Montréal . . . 1642–1763*. Montréal, 1942.

Monseigneur de Saint-Vallier. *See* O'Reilly

MORISSET, GÉRARD. *Coup d'œil sur les arts en Nouvelle-France*. Québec, 1941; réimprimé, 1942.

MORTON, ARTHUR SILVER. *A history of the Canadian west to 1870–71, being a history of Rupert's Land (the Hudson's Bay Company's territory) and of the North-West Territory (including the Pacific slope)*. London and Toronto, [1939]. 2nd edition. Edited by Lewis Gwynne Thomas. Toronto [and Buffalo, N.Y., 1973].

MURDOCH, BEAMISH. *A history of Nova-Scotia, or Acadie*. 3 vols. Halifax, 1865–67.

NEATBY, HILDA MARION. *The administration of justice under the Quebec Act*. London and Minneapolis, Minn., [1937].

——— *Quebec: the revolutionary age, 1760–1791*. (Canadian centenary series, 6.) [Toronto, 1966.]

[O'REILLY, HELENA, DITE SAINT-FÉLIX.] *Monseigneur de Saint-Vallier et l'Hôpital Général de Québec: histoire du monastère de Notre-Dame des Anges....* Québec, 1882.

OUELLET, FERNAND. *Histoire économique et sociale du Québec, 1760–1850: structures et conjoncture*. Montréal et Paris, [1966].

PARGELLIS, STANLEY MCCRORY. *Lord Loudoun in North America*. New Haven, Conn., and London, 1933; reprinted [Hamden, Conn.], 1968.

PECKHAM, HOWARD HENRY. *Pontiac and the Indian uprising*. Princeton, N.J., 1947; reprinted Chicago, [1961].

PORTER, WHITWORTH, AND CHARLES MOORE WATSON. *History of the corps of Royal En-*

gineers. 3 vols. London and New York, 1889–1915. Reprinted as first three vols. of Whitworth Porter *et al.*, *History of the corps of Royal Engineers* (9v., Chatham, Eng., 1951–58).

PROWSE, DANIEL WOODLEY. *A history of Newfoundland from the English, colonial, and foreign records*. London and New York, 1895. 2nd edition. London, 1896. 3rd edition. Edited by James Raymond Thoms and Frank Burnham Gill. St John's, 1971. Reprint of 1895 edition. Belleville, Ont., 1972.

RAWLYK, GEORGE ALEXANDER. *Yankees at Louisbourg*. Orono, Maine, 1967.

RAYMOND, WILLIAM ODBER. *The River St. John, its physical features, legends and history from 1604 to 1784*. Saint John, N.B., 1910. [2nd edition.] Edited by John Clarence Webster. Sackville, N.B., 1943; reprinted, 1950.

RICH, EDWIN ERNEST. *The history of the Hudson's Bay Company, 1670–1870*. (HBRS publications, XXI, XXII.) 2 vols. London, 1958–59. Another edition. 3 vols. Toronto, 1960. A copy of this work available at PAC contains notes and bibliographical material omitted from the printed version.

ROCHEMONTEIX, CAMILLE DE. *Les jésuites et la Nouvelle-France au XVIIIe siècle*. . . . 2 vols. Paris, 1906.

ROY, JOSEPH-EDMOND. *Histoire du notariat au Canada depuis la fondation de la colonie jusqu'à nos jours*. 4 vols. Lévis, Qué., 1899–1902.

ROY, PIERRE-GEORGES. *Bigot et sa bande et l'affaire du Canada*. Lévis, Qué., 1950.

SAVARY, ALFRED WILLIAM. *Supplement to the history of the county of Annapolis*. . . . Toronto, 1913; reprinted Belleville, Ont., 1973. *See also* Calnek, *History of Annapolis* (Savary).

SHY, JOHN [WILLARD]. *Toward Lexington: the role of the British army in the coming of the American revolution*. Princeton, N.J., 1965.

SOCIÉTÉ HISTORIQUE DE QUÉBEC, Québec.
CAHIERS D'HISTOIRE
23: Mathieu, *La construction navale*.
TEXTES
2: Gaumond, *Les forges de Saint-Maurice*.

SOCIÉTÉ HISTORIQUE DU SAGUENAY, Chicoutimi, Qué.
PUBLICATIONS
3: Tremblay et Angers, *L'hist. du Saguenay*.
21: Tremblay, *Hist. du Saguenay*.

STACEY, CHARLES PERRY. *Quebec, 1759: the siege and the battle*. Toronto, 1959.

STANLEY, GEORGE FRANCIS GILMAN. *New France: the last phase, 1744–1760*. (Canadian centenary series, 5.) [Toronto, 1968.]

——— WITH HAROLD MCGILL JACKSON. *Canada's soldiers, 1604–1954: the military history of an unmilitary people*. Toronto, 1954. [Revised edition.] 1960. 3rd edition. [1974.]

SULTE, BENJAMIN. *Histoire des Canadiens-français, 1608–1880*. . . . 8 vols. Montréal, 1882–84.

——— *Mélanges historiques*. . . . Gérard Malchelosse, éditeur. 21 vols. Montréal, 1918–34. This series is a mixture of volumes of articles and monographs.

TESSIER, ALBERT. *Les forges Saint-Maurice, 1729–1883*. Trois-Rivières, 1952; réimprimé, [Montréal, 1974].

TOUSIGNANT, PIERRE. "La genèse et l'avènement de la constitution de 1791." Thèse de PHD, université de Montréal, 1971.

TRAQUAIR, RAMSAY. *The old silver of Quebec*. Toronto, 1940.

TREMBLAY, VICTOR. *Histoire du Saguenay depuis les origines jusqu'à 1870*. Nouvelle édition. (Société historique du Saguenay publications, 21.) [Chicoutimi, Qué.], 1968. First published as [Victor Tremblay et Lorenzo Angers], *L'histoire du Saguenay depuis l'origine jusqu'à 1870* (Société historique du Saguenay publications, 3, Chicoutimi, Qué., 1938).

TRUDEL, MARCEL. *L'Église canadienne sous le Régime militaire, 1759–1764*. (Institut d'histoire de l'Amérique française publication.) 2 vols. [Montréal et] Québec, 1956–57.

——— *L'esclavage au Canada français: histoire et conditions de l'esclavage*. Québec, 1960.

——— *Le Régime militaire dans le gouvernement des Trois-Rivières, 1760–1764*. Trois-Rivières, 1952.

UNIVERSITÉ LAVAL, INSTITUT D'HISTOIRE, Québec.
CAHIERS
3: Hamelin, *Économie et société*.
6: Beaulieu et Hamelin, *Les journaux du Québec* [*see* section III].
16: Galarneau, *La France devant l'opinion canadienne*.

Les ursulines de Québec. *See* Burke

VACHON, ANDRÉ. *Histoire du notariat canadien, 1621–1960*. Québec, 1962.

WADE, MASON. *The French Canadians, 1760–1945*. Toronto, 1955; reprinted, 1956. Revised edition [. . . *1760–1967*]. 2 vols. Toronto, 1968. A French edition covering the years 1760–1963 and translated by Adrien Venne and Francis Dufau-Labeyrie has been published as *Les Canadiens français de 1760 à nos jours* (2v., [Ottawa, 1963]).

V. JOURNALS AND STUDIES (ARTICLES)

Acadiensis: Journal of the History of the Atlantic Region/Revue de l'histoire de la région atlantique. Fredericton. Published by the Department of History of the University of New Brunswick. I (1971–72)– .

Beaver: a Magazine of the North. Winnipeg. Published by the HBC. I (1920–21)– . *Index*: I (1920–21)–outfit 284 (June 1952–March 1954).

Le Bulletin des recherches historiques. Published usually in Lévis, Qué. Originally the organ of the Société des études historiques, it became in March 1923 the journal of the Archives de la province de Québec (now the ANQ). I (1895)–LXX (1968). *Index*: I (1895)–XXXI (1925) (4v., Beauceville, Qué., 1925–26). For subsequent years there is a manuscript index at the ANQ-Q.

Les Cahiers des Dix. Montréal et Québec. Published by "Les Dix." I (1936)– .

CANADIAN CATHOLIC HISTORICAL ASSOCIATION/SOCIÉTÉ CANADIENNE D'HISTOIRE DE L'ÉGLISE CATHOLIQUE, Ottawa. Publishes simultaneously a *Report* in English and a *Rapport* in French, of which the contents are entirely different. 1 (1933–34)– . *Index*: 1 (1933–34)–25 (1958). Title varies: *Study Sessions/Sessions d'étude* from 1966.

CANADIAN HISTORICAL ASSOCIATION/SOCIÉTÉ HISTORIQUE DU CANADA, Ottawa. *Annual Report*. 1922– . *Index*: 1922–51; 1952–68. Title varies: *Historical Papers/Communications historiques* from 1966.

Canadian Historical Review. Toronto. I (1920)– . *Index*: I (1920)–X (1929); XI (1930)–XX (1939); XXI (1940)–XXX (1949); XXXI (1950)–LI (1970). Université Laval has also published an index: *Canadian Historical Review, 1950–1964: index des articles et des comptes rendus de volumes*, René Hardy, comp. (Québec, 1969). A continuation of the *Review of Historical Publications relating to Canada*: I (1895–96)–XXII (1917–18); *Index*: I (1895–96)–X (1905); XI (1906)–XX (1915).

Dalhousie Review. Halifax. Published by Dalhousie University. I (1921–22)– .

GANONG, WILLIAM FRANCIS. "A monograph of historic sites in the province of New Brunswick," RSC *Trans.*, 2nd ser., V (1899), sect. II, 213–357.

LELAND, MARINE. "François-Joseph Cugnet, 1720–1789," *La Revue de l'université Laval* (Québec), XVI (1961–62), 3–13, 129–39, 205–14, 411–20, 618–29, 929–36; XVII (1962–63), 64–73, 145–55, 445–56, 820–41; XVIII (1963–64), 337–60, 717–33; XIX (1964–65), 144–57, 254–65, 658–71; XX (1965–66), 143–50, 267–74, 359–65, 832–44, 923–33; XXI (1966), 178–91, 378–96.

L'HEUREUX, JACQUES. "L'organisation judiciaire au Québec de 1764 à 1774," *Revue générale de droit* (Ottawa), 1 (1970), 266–331.

New England Historical and Genealogical Register. Published usually in Boston, Mass., by the New England Historic Genealogical Society. I (1847)– . *Index*: I (1847)–L (1896) (5v., Boston, 1907–11; repr., 4v., Baltimore, Md., 1972).

NOVA SCOTIA HISTORICAL SOCIETY, Halifax. *Collections*. I (1878)– . Index: I (1878)–XXXII (1959).

Ontario History. Toronto. Published by the Ontario Historical Society. I (1899)– . An index to volumes I (1899) to LXIV (1972) appears in *Index to the publications of the Ontario Historical Society, 1899–1972* (1974). Title varies: *Papers and Records* to 1946.

Revue d'histoire de l'Amérique française. Montréal. Published by the Institut d'histoire de l'Amérique française. I (1947–48)– . Index: I (1947–48)–X (1956–57); XI (1957–58)–XX (1966–67); XXI (1967–68)–XXX (1976–77).

ROYAL SOCIETY OF CANADA/SOCIÉTÉ ROYALE DU CANADA, Ottawa. *Proceedings and Transactions/Mémoires et comptes rendus*. 1st series: I (1882–83)–XII (1894). 2nd series: I (1895)–XII (1906). 3rd series: I (1907)–LVI (1962). 4th series: I (1963)– . *General index*: 1st series–2nd series; *Subject index*: 3rd series, I (1907)–XXXI (1937); *Author index*: 3rd series, I (1907)–XXXV (1941).

Social History, a Canadian Review/Histoire sociale, revue canadienne. Ottawa. Published under the direction of an interdisciplinary committee from various Canadian universities. 1 (April 1968)– .

SOCIÉTÉ GÉNÉALOGIQUE CANADIENNE-FRANÇAISE, Montréal. *Mémoires*. I (1944–45)– . The society's numbered publications include 2, 4, 6: Lebœuf, *Complément* [*see* section III].

TÊTU, HENRI. "Le chapitre de la cathédrale de Québec et ses délégués en France: lettres des chanoines Pierre Hazeur de L'Orme et Jean-Marie de la Corne, 1723–1773," *BRH*, XIII (1907), 225–43, 257–83, 289–308, 321–38, 353–61; XIV (1908), 3–22, 33–40, 65–79,

97–109, 129–46, 161–75, 193–208, 225–39, 257–70, 289–98, 321–37, 353–64; XV (1909), 3–16, 33–48, 65–79, 97–111, 129–42, 161–76, 193–211, 225–41, 257–74, 289–301, 321–28, 353–60; XVI (1910), 3–10, 33–44, 65–75, 97–109, 129–41, 161–75, 193–206, 225–40, 257–74, 289–302, 321–30, 353–64.

Contributors

ABLER, THOMAS S. Associate professor of anthropology, University of Waterloo, Ontario.
Kaieñ?kwaahtoñ. Kayahsota?.

ALLAIRE, GRATIEN. Edmonton, Alberta.
Jean Renaud.

ANGUS, MARGARET SHARP. Writer, Kingston, Ontario.
Robert Macaulay.

ARCHER, CHRISTON I. Professor of history, University of Calgary, Alberta.
Esteban José Martínez Fernández y Martínez de la Sierra.

ARMOUR, DAVID ARTHUR. Assistant superintendent, Mackinac Island State Park Commission, Michigan, U.S.A.
René Bourassa, dit *La Ronde*. *Laurent Ducharme. Pierre Du Jaunay. Nissowaquet. Jean-Baptiste-Philippe Testard de Montigny.*

ARMSTRONG, FREDERICK H. Professor of history, University of Western Ontario, London, Ontario.
Alexander Aitken.

ARTHUR, M. ELIZABETH. Professor of history, Lakehead University, Thunder Bay, Ontario.
Henry Hamilton. Paulus Æmilius Irving. Adam Mabane.

AUGER, ROLAND-J. Responsable des publications de généalogie, Archives nationales du Québec, Québec.
Étienne Charest. Jean-Antoine Saillant.

BAGLOLE, HARRY. Writer, Belfast, Prince Edward Island; editor, *The Island Magazine*.
Walter Patterson.

BAILLARGEON, NOËL, PTRE. Historien, Séminaire de Québec, Québec.
Thomas-Laurent Bédard.

BARRY, FRANCINE. Québec.
Guillaume Estèbe.

BECK, J. MURRAY. Professor of political science, Dalhousie University, Halifax, Nova Scotia.
Edward Cornwallis. Philip Augustus Knaut.

BÉLANGER, JULES. Professeur de littérature, Collège de la Gaspésie, Gaspé, Québec.
Bertrand de Latour.

BÉRUBÉ, ANDRÉ. Région du Québec, Parcs Canada, Québec, Québec.
James Johnston.

BISHOP, CHARLES A. Professor of anthropology, State University of New York, Oswego, New York, U.S.A.
John Long.

BLAIS, MARIE-CÉLINE. Pigiste dans le domaine de l'édition, Québec, Québec.
Michel Blais [in collaboration with J. Morin]. *Charles-François Tarieu de La Naudière.*

BLAKELEY, PHYLLIS R. Associate provincial archivist, Public Archives of Nova Scotia, Halifax, Nova Scotia.
Richard Bulkeley. Benoni Danks. Shubael Dimock. Charles Morris. Elizabeth Osborn (Myrick; Paine; Doane).

BOSHER, J. F. Professor of history, York University, Downsview, Ontario.
François Bigot [in collaboration with J.-C. Dubé]. *Jacques-Michel Bréard. Joseph-Michel Cadet. Philippe-Antoine de Cuny Dauterive. Alexandre-Robert Hillaire de La Rochette. Jean Laborde. Jean-Mathieu Mounier. Antoine Pascaud. Antoine Rodrigue* [with T. Le Goff].

BOUCHARD, RENÉ. Centre d'études sur la langue, les arts et les traditions populaires des francophones en amérique du Nord, Université Laval, Québec, Québec.
André Corbin.

BOWLER, R. ARTHUR. Associate professor of history, State University of New York at Buffalo, New York, U.S.A.
John Butler [in collaboration with B. Wilson]. *John Montresor.*

BOWSFIELD, HARTWELL. Associate professor of history, York University, Downsview, Ontario.
Cuthbert Grant.

BOYCE, GERALD E. Writer; teacher of history, Moira Secondary School, Belleville, Ontario.
George Singleton.

BROWN, JENNIFER S.H. Publications editor, Middle American Research Institute, Tulane University, New Orleans, Louisiana, U.S.A.
George Atkinson. Isaac Batt. Malchom Ross. George Sutherland.

BROWN, WALLACE. Professor of history, University of New Brunswick, Fredericton, New Brunswick.
Benjamin Marston.

BROWNE, G. PETER. Professor of history, Carleton University, Ottawa, Ontario.
James Murray.

BUGGEY, SUSAN. Head, Construction history, Research Division, Parks Canada, Ottawa, Ontario.
Jonathan Belcher. Malachy Salter. John Seccombe.

BUMSTED, J. M. Professor of history, Simon Fraser University, Burnaby, British Columbia.
Henry Alline. Henry Denny Denson. David Higgins. Francis Legge. James MacDonald. John Mackay. William Montgomery.

BURROUGHS, PETER. Professor of history, Dalhousie University, Halifax, Nova Scotia.
John Parr.

BURTON HISTORICAL COLLECTION STAFF. Detroit Public Library, Detroit, Michigan, U.S.A.
Robert Navarre. James Sterling.

CAISSIE, FRANCES. Historienne, Québec, Québec.

Louis-Joseph Godefroy de Tonnancour [in collaboration with P. Lahoud].

CASTONGUAY, JACQUES. Doyen de la faculté des arts, Collège militaire royal de Saint-Jean, Québec.
Ignace-Philippe Aubert de Gaspé.

CERBELAUD SALAGNAC, GEORGES. Directeur littéraire des Éditions Tequi, Paris, France.
Charles-Henri-Louis d'Arsac de Ternay. Jean-Gabriel Berbudeau.

CHAMPAGNE, ANTOINE. Professeur à la retraite, Winnipeg, Manitoba.
François Gaultier Du Tremblay.

CHAPUT, DONALD. Senior curator of history, National History Museum, Los Angeles, California, U.S.A.
Alexandre Dagneau Douville. Daniel-Maurice Godefroy de Linctot. Louis Groston de Saint-Ange et de Bellerive. Louis Le Verrier de Rousson. Joseph Marin de La Malgue. Pierre-Jacques Payen de Noyan et de Chavoy.

CHARD, DONALD F. Historic park planner, Atlantic Region, Parks Canada, Halifax, Nova Scotia.
Mariot Arbuthnot. Benjamin Green. Joshua Mauger.

†CHARLAND, THOMAS-M., O.P. Bibliothécaire et archiviste, Couvent des Dominicains, Montréal, Québec.
Joseph-Louis Gill. Joseph-Hippolyte Hertel de Saint-François.

CHARTERS, DAVID. Formerly manuscript editor, *Dictionary of Canadian biography/Dictionnaire biographique du Canada*, University of Toronto Press, Ontario.
Walter Butler. Joseph Goreham [in collaboration with S. Sutherland].

CHAUSSÉ, GILLES, S.J. Chargé de cours, Département d'histoire, Université de Montréal, Québec.
Jean-François Hubert. Étienne Marchand.

COGHLAN, FRANCIS A. Chairman, Department of history, University of New Brunswick, Fredericton, New Brunswick.
Lord William Campbell.

COLE, DOUGLAS. Historian, Simon Fraser University, Burnaby, British Columbia.
John Webber.

COLTHART, JAMES M. Academic relations officer, Canadian Embassy, Washington, District of Columbia, U.S.A.
Robert Ellice.

CONDON, ANN GORMAN. Assistant professor of history, University of New Brunswick, Saint John, New Brunswick.
Elias Hardy. Abijah Willard.

COOK, WARREN L. Professor of history and anthropology, Castleton State College, Castleton, Vermont, U.S.A.
Juan Francisco de la Bodega y Quadra. Juan Joseph Pérez Hernández.

COOKE, W. MARTHA E. Ottawa, Ontario.
James Peachey [in collaboration with B. Wilson].

COOPER, JOHN IRWIN. Professor emeritus of history, McGill University, Montreal, Quebec.
Jean-Étienne Waddens.

COSSETTE, JOSEPH, S.J. Archiviste, Archives de la Compagnie de Jésus, Saint-Jérôme, Québec.
Joseph-Pierre de Bonnécamps. Jean-Joseph Casot. Pierre-René Floquet. Joseph Huguet.

CÔTÉ, PIERRE-L. Saint-Félicien, Québec.
Ange Duquesne de Menneville.

CROWLEY, TERENCE ALLAN. Assistant professor of history, University of Guelph, Ontario.
François-Gabriel d'Angeac. Louis Du Pont Duchambon [in collaboration with B. Pothier]. *François Du Pont Duvivier* [with B. Pothier]. *Joseph Du Pont Duvivier* [with B. Pothier]. *James Johnstone. Michel Le Courtois de Surlaville. Charles-Gabriel-Sébastien de L'Espérance. Joannis-Galand d'Olabaratz. Thomas Pichon. Jacques Prevost de La Croix. Jean-Louis de Raymond.*

CYR, CÉLINE. Assistante, *Dictionnaire biographique du Canada/Dictionary of Canadian biography*, Les Presses de l'université Laval, Québec, Québec.
Pierre-Jean-Baptiste-François-Xavier Legardeur de Repentigny.

DAY, GORDON M. Eastern Canada ethnologist, Canadian Ethnology Service, National Museum of Man, National Museums of Canada, Ottawa, Ontario.
Glossary of Native Peoples.

DEGRÂCE, ÉLOI. Archiviste-historien, Shippagan, Nouveau-Brunswick.
Joseph-Mathurin Bourg.

DEROME, ROBERT. Conservateur intérimaire de l'art canadien ancien, Galerie nationale du Canada, Ottawa, Ontario.
Ignace-François Delezenne. Louis-Alexandre Picard. Joseph Schindler. Jacques Varin, dit *La Pistole.*

DÉSILETS, ANDRÉE. Professeur titulaire d'histoire, Université de Sherbrooke, Québec.
Marie-Josèphe Maugue-Garreau, dite *de l'Assomption. Marie-Marguerite Piot de Langloiserie*, dite *Saint-Hippolyte.*

DESJARDINS, ÉDOUARD, M.D. Rédacteur en chef, *l'Union médicale du Canada*, Montréal, Québec.
James Bowman.

DESROSIERS, RENÉ, F.C. Conseiller pédagogique en documentation, Commission scolaire régionale Saint-François, Drummondville, Québec.
Joseph Deguire, dit *Desrosiers.*

DEVEAU, J.-ALPHONSE. Directeur du Centre acadien, Université Sainte-Anne, Church Point, Nouvelle-Écosse.
Pierre Doucet. Guillaume Jeanson. Pierre Le Blanc.

DINEL, GUY. Division des archives, Bibliothèque, Université Laval, Québec, Québec.
Charles Hay. Michel-Jean-Hugues Péan.

DIONNE-TOUSIGNANT, MADELEINE. Recherchiste, Montréal, Québec.
Hector Theophilus Cramahé. François-Joseph Cugnet. Pierre Du Calvet. René-Ovide Hertel de Rouville. Luc de La Corne. François-Marie Picoté de Belestre. [All biographies done in collaboration with P. Tousignant.]

DOUGLAS, W. A. B. Director, Directorate of history, National Defence Headquarters, Ottawa, Ontario.
John Byron. Sir Charles Douglas. Joshua Loring.

DOUVILLE, RAYMOND. Ex-sous-secrétaire et ex-archiviste du gouvernement du Québec, Québec.
Jean-Baptiste Badeaux [in collaboration]. *John Bruyères* [in collaboration]. *Pierre Garreau*, dit *Saint-Onge*. *Conrad Gugy* [in collaboration]. *Marie-Françoise Guillimin*, dite *de Saint-Antoine*. *François Guillot*, dit *Larose*.

DUBÉ, JEAN-CLAUDE. Professeur titulaire d'histoire, Université d'Ottawa, Ontario.
François Bigot [in collaboration with J. Bosher].

†DUFF, WILSON. Professor of anthropology, University of British Columbia, Vancouver, British Columbia.
Koyah.

DUMAIS, RAYMOND. Archiviste, Archives nationales du Québec, Centre régional de Montréal, Québec.
Ignace Gamelin. *Pierre-Joseph Gamelin*. *François Simonnet*.

DUNLOP, ALLAN C. Research assistant, Provincial Archives of Nova Scotia, Halifax, Nova Scotia.
John Butler.

DUNN, WALTER S., JR. Director, Buffalo & Erie County Historical Society, Buffalo, New York, U.S.A.
Daniel-Marie Chabert de Joncaire de Clausonne [in collaboration]. *Lucius Levy Solomons*.

ECCLES, W. J. Professor of history, University of Toronto, Ontario.
François Coulon de Villiers. *François de Lévis*. *Pierre de Rigaud de Vaudreuil de Cavagnial*.

EDMUNDS, R. DAVID. Professor of history, Texas Christian University, Fort Worth, Texas, U.S.A.
Glikhikan.

EINHORN, ARTHUR. Associate professor of anthropology, Jefferson Community College, Watertown, New York, U.S.A.
Hotsinoñhyahta? [in collaboration].

ELLIOTT, SHIRLEY B. Legislative librarian, Nova Scotia Legislative Library, Halifax, Nova Scotia.
Robert Fletcher.

FELLOWS, JO-ANN. Graduate student in public administration, Carleton University, Ottawa, Ontario.
Abraham De Peyster.

†FERGUSSON, CHARLES BRUCE. Archivist emeritus of Nova Scotia, Public Archives of Nova Scotia, Halifax, Nova Scotia; associate professor of history, Dalhousie University, Halifax, Nova Scotia.
John Doggett.

FINGARD, JUDITH. Associate professor of history, Dalhousie University, Halifax, Nova Scotia.
Joseph Peters. *Richard Wenman*.

FINN, GÉRARD. Chef, Recherches historiques, Région de l'ouest, Parcs Canada, Calgary, Alberta.
François Le Guerne. *Jean-Louis Le Loutre*.

FIRTH, EDITH G. Head, Canadian history department, Metropolitan Toronto Library, Ontario.
John White.

FISCHER, L.R. Assistant professor of history, Memorial University of Newfoundland, St John's, Newfoundland.
Michael Francklin. *Joseph Scott*.

FISHER, ROBIN A. Associate professor of history, Simon Fraser University, Burnaby, British Columbia.
Glossary of Native Peoples. *Muquinna*. *Wikinanish*.

FORTIER, MARIE-FRANCE. Trois-Rivières, Québec.
Pierre-François Olivier de Vézin. *Christophe Pélissier*.

FRASER, ROBERT L. Hamilton, Ontario.
Jack York.

FRENCH, GOLDWIN SYLVESTER. President, Victoria University, Toronto, Ontario.
Hezekiah Calvin Wooster.

FRENIÈRE, ANDRÉ. Chef du service de la Gestion des Documents, Ministère des Travaux Publics et de l'Approvisionnement, Québec, Québec.
Jean-Claude Panet.

FRISCH, JACK A. Executive director, Clearfield Co. Area Agency on Aging, Clearfield, Pennsylvania, U.S.A.
Eunice Williams.

GAGNON, CLAIRE, A.M.J. Archiviste, Archives des Augustines, Monastère de l'Hôtel-Dieu de Québec, Québec.
Marie-Louise Curot, dite *de Saint-Martin*.

GALARNEAU, CLAUDE. Professeur titulaire d'histoire, Université Laval, Québec, Québec.
Charles-François Bailly de Messein. *Arnauld-Germain Dudevant*. *Valentin Jautard*. *David McLane*. *Fleury Mesplet*.

GAUMOND, MICHEL. Direction de l'archéologie, Ministère des Affaires culturelles, Québec, Québec.
François Jacquet [in collaboration].

GAUTHIER, RAYMONDE. Professeur d'histoire de l'art, Université du Québec à Montréal, Québec.
Jacques Deguise, dit *Flamand* [in collaboration with M. Lacombe]. *François-Noël Levasseur*. *Jean-Baptiste-Antoine Levasseur*, dit *Delor*. *Augustin Quintal*. *Pierre Renaud*, dit *Cannard*.

GÉRIN-LAJOIE, MARIE. Ottawa, Ontario.
Jean-Louis Besnard, dit *Carignant* [in collaboration with J. Igartua].

GERVAIS, JEAN-FRANCIS. Maître de Conférences, Université du Maroc, Maroc.
William Brown [in collaboration]. *Thomas Gilmore*. *François Lévesque*.

GIGUÈRE, GEORGES-ÉMILE, S.J. Historien, Montréal, Québec.
Augustin-Louis de Glapion.

GILLESPIE, BERYL C. Research assistant, University of Iowa City, Iowa, U.S.A.
Matonabbee.

GODFREY, WILLIAM G. Associate professor of history, Mount Allison University, Sackville, New Brunswick.
John Bradstreet. *Alexander Fraser*. *Gilfred Studholme*.

GOUGH, BARRY MORTON. Associate professor of history, Wilfrid Laurier University, Waterloo, Ontario.
George Dixon. *Charles Duncan*.

GRAHAM, JANE E. Associate editor, *Dictionary of Canadian biography/Dictionnaire biographique du Canada*, University of Toronto Press, Ontario.
Jean-Baptiste de Couagne.

GRAYMONT, BARBARA. Professor of history, Nyack College, Nyack, New York, U.S.A.
Glossary of Native Peoples. *Koñwatsi?tsiaiéñni*.

GREENWOOD, FRANK MURRAY. Assistant professor of history, University of British Columbia, Vancouver, British Columbia.
Sir Thomas Mills. Frédéric-Guillaume Oliva.

GREER, ALLAN R. Graduate student in history, York University, Downsview, Ontario.
George Davison.

GRENIER, FERNAND. Directeur général, Teléuniversité, Université du Québec, Québec.
Claude-Pierre Pécaudy de Contrecœur.

GRIFFITHS, N.E.S. Dean of arts, Carleton University, Ottawa, Ontario.
Introductory essay: *The Acadians.*

GWYN, JULIAN. Professor of history, University of Ottawa, Ontario.
Sir George Collier. Sir Charles Hardy. Sir William Johnson.

HAMELIN, JEAN. Directeur général adjoint, *Dictionnaire biographique du Canada/Dictionary of Canadian biography*, Les Presses de l'université Laval; professeur d'histoire, Université Laval, Québec, Québec.
François-Pierre de Rigaud de Vaudreuil [in collaboration with J. Roy].

HANDCOCK, GORDON. Assistant professor of geography, Memorial University of Newfoundland, St John's, Newfoundland.
John Slade.

HARE, JOHN E. Professeur agrégé d'histoire, Université d'Ottawa, Ontario.
Samuel Neilson. Louis Roy.

HAREL, J.-BRUNO, P.S.S. Archiviste, Séminaire de Saint-Sulpice de Montréal, Québec.
Jean-Baptiste Curatteau. Jacques Degeay. Vincent-Fleuri Guichart. Pierre-Paul-François de Lagarde. François-Auguste Magon de Terlaye. Jean-Claude Mathevet.

HARPER, JOHN RUSSELL. Professor of fine arts, Concordia University, Montreal, Quebec.
Christopher Sower.

HAY, DOUGLAS. Associate professor of history, Memorial University of Newfoundland, St John's, Newfoundland.
Glossary of Native Peoples.

HAYWARD, ROBERT J. Archives branch, Public Archives of Canada, Ottawa, Ontario.
John Collins.

HÉBERT, LÉO-PAUL. Professeur d'histoire, Collège d'enseignement général et professionnel de Joliette, Québec.
Jean-Baptiste de La Brosse.

HENDERSON, SUSAN W. Claims representative, Social Security Administration, Portland, Maine, U.S.A.
Jean-Baptiste d'Aleyrac. François-Prosper Douglas. Pierre-André Gohin.

HICKERSON, HAROLD. Associate professor of anthropology, Simon Fraser University, Burnaby, British Columbia.
Glossary of Native Peoples.

HICKS, FRANKLYN H., M.D. Ottawa, Ontario.
John Hicks.

HILLER, JAMES K. Associate professor of history, Memorial University of Newfoundland, St John's, Newfoundland.
Christian Larsen Drachart. Jens Haven. Kingminguse.

HOLMAN, HARRY TINSON. Assistant archivist, Public Archives of Prince Edward Island, Charlottetown, Prince Edward Island.
Phillips Callbeck. Robert Clark.

HORSMAN, REGINALD. UWM Distinguished professor of history, University of Wisconsin-Milwaukee, Wisconsin, U.S.A.
Egushwa. Alexander McKee. Normand MacLeod.

HORTON, DONALD J. Assistant professor of history, University of Waterloo, Ontario.
Guillaume Guillimin. Gilles Hocquart.

HUNT, RICHARD I. Staff associate, Canadian-American Center, University of Maine at Orono, Maine, U.S.A.
Ambroise Saint-Aubin. Pierre Tomah.

HUNTER, WILLIAM A. Formerly chief, Division of history, Pennsylvania Historical and Museum Commission, Harrisburg, Pennsylvania, U.S.A.
Glossary of Native Peoples. *Anandamoakin.*

IGARTUA, JOSÉ E. Assistant professor of history, University of Western Ontario, London, Ontario.
Étienne Augé. Jean-Louis Besnard, dit *Carignant* [in collaboration with M. Gérin-Lajoie]. *Pierre Courreaud de La Coste. Jean Dumas Saint-Martin. Jacques-Joseph Lemoine Despins. Jean Orillat. Louis Pennisseaut.*

INGERSOLL, L.K. Director, Museums Branch, Historical Resources Administration, Fredericton, New Brunswick.
William Owen.

JANSON, GILLES. Archiviste, Université du Québec à Montréal, Québec.
Charles-Elemy-Joseph-Alexandre-Ferdinand Feltz. Louis-Nicolas Landriaux.

JARRELL, RICHARD. Associate professor of natural science, Joseph E. Atkinson College, York University, Downsview, Ontario.
Pehr Kalm.

JARVIS, RUTH RICHEY. Formerly high school science teacher; history researcher and writer, Findlay, Ohio, U.S.A.
Gabriel Cotté.

JOHNSON, J.K. Professor of history, Carleton University, Ottawa, Ontario.
John Munro.

JOHNSON, MICHELINE D. Professeur adjoint d'histoire, Université de Sherbrooke, Québec.
Charles Germain. Jacques Girard. Jean-Pierre de Miniac.

JOHNSTON, BASIL H. Lecturer in American Indian history, Royal Ontario Museum, Toronto, Ontario.
Glossary of Native Peoples.

JONES, FREDERICK. Senior lecturer in history, Dorset Institute of Higher Education, England.
Edward Langman.

KELLY, GERALD M. Port Chester, New York, U.S.A.
Esther Wheelwright, dite *de l'Enfant-Jésus.*

KELSAY, ISABEL T. Freelance historian, Media, Pennsylvania, U.S.A.
Tekawiroñte.

KELSEY, HARRY. Chief curator of history, Los Angeles County Museum of Natural History, Los Angeles, California, U.S.A.
Wasson. John Wilkins.

KERNAGHAN, LOIS KATHLEEN. Historical researcher, Boutilier's Point, Nova Scotia.
William Nesbitt.

KRUGLER, JOHN DAVID. Associate professor of history, Marquette University, Milwaukee, Wisconsin, U.S.A.
William Haviland.

LACELLE, CLAUDETTE. Division des recherches, Parcs Canada, Ottawa, Ontario.
Marie-Marguerite Dufrost de Lajemmerais (Youville). Marguerite-Thérèse Lemoine Despins. Charles-Marie-Madeleine d'Youville.

LACHANCE, ANDRÉ. Directeur, Département d'histoire, Université de Sherbrooke, Québec.
Nicolas Boisseau. Jean-Baptiste Decoste. Claude Devau, dit *Retor. André Grasset de Saint-Sauveur. Jean-Marie Landriève Des Bordes. Joseph Perthuis. André Souste. Jean-Victor Varin de La Marre.*

LACOMBE, MARTHE. Direction de l'archéologie, Ministère des Affaires culturelles, Québec, Québec.
Jacques Deguise, dit *Flamand* [in collaboration with R. Gauthier].

LAFLEUR, JEAN. Professeur d'histoire, École secondaire M.S.C., Beauport, Québec.
Thomas Aylwin.

LAHAISE, ROBERT. Professeur d'histoire, Université du Québec à Montréal, Québec.
François Picquet.

LAHOUD, PIERRE. Historien, Québec, Québec.
Louis-Joseph Godefroy de Tonnancour [in collaboration with F. Caissie].

LAMB, J. WILLIAM. United Church minister, Islington, Ontario.
Charles Justin McCarty.

LAMB, WILLIAM KAYE. Formerly dominion archivist and national librarian, Vancouver, British Columbia.
George Vancouver.

LAMBERT, JAMES. Assistant, *Dictionnaire biographique du Canada/Dictionary of Canadian biography*, Les Presses de l'université Laval, Québec, Québec.
John Brooke. David Chabrand Delisle. Leger-Jean-Baptiste-Noël Veyssière.

LANDRY, ALBERT, O.F.M. CAP. Fraternité des Capucins, Bathurst, Nouveau-Brunswick.
Alexis Landry.

LAPOINTE, GABRIELLE, O.S.U. Monastère des Ursulines, Québec, Québec.
Marie-Anne Migeon de Branssat, dite *de la Nativité.*

LEBLANC, PHYLLIS E. Recherchiste, Centre d'études acadiennes, Université de Moncton, Nouveau-Brunswick.
Charles Deschamps de Boishébert et de Raffetot.

LEE, DAVID. Historian, Research Division, Parks Canada, Ottawa, Ontario.
Nicholas Cox. François Lefebvre de Bellefeuille.

LEFEBVRE, JEAN-JACQUES. Ex-archiviste en chef, Cour supérieure, Montréal, Québec.
Antoine Grisé. Claude Hantraye.

LE GOFF, T.J.A. Associate professor of history, York University, Downsview, Ontario.
Jean-Baptiste Dupleix Silvain. Bertrand Imbert. Jean-Baptiste Morin de Fonfay. Antoine Rodrigue [in collaboration with J. Bosher].

LEIGHTON, DOUGLAS. Assistant professor of history, Huron College, University of Western Ontario, London, Ontario.
John Campbell. Joseph Chew. Christian Daniel Claus. Benjamin Roberts.

LEMAY, THÉRÈSE P. Assistante, *Dictionnaire biographique du Canada/Dictionary of Canadian biography*, Les Presses de l'université Laval, Québec, Québec.
Joseph Brassard Deschenaux. Joe. François Lajus.

LEMIEUX, LUCIEN. Professeur agrégé, Faculté de théologie, Université de Montréal, Québec.
Gabriel-Jean Brassier. Étienne Montgolfier.

LESSARD, CLAUDE. Professeur et directeur des archives, Université du Québec à Trois-Rivières, Québec.
Louis-Marie Brassard.

LEWIS, G. MALCOLM. Senior lecturer in geography, University of Sheffield, England.
Richard McCarty.

L'HEUREUX, JACQUES. Professeur de droit, Université d'Ottawa, Ontario.
Henry Kneller. Walter Murray. George Suckling.

LOCHHEAD, DOUGLAS. Director of Canadian studies, Mount Allison University, Sackville, New Brunswick.
Anthony Henry.

MACBEATH, GEORGE. Historical resources administrator, Province of New Brunswick, Fredericton, New Brunswick.
Joseph Godin, dit *Bellefontaine*, dit *Beauséjour.*

MCDONALD, RONALD H. Historian, Atlantic Region, Parks Canada, Halifax, Nova Scotia.
Winckworth Tonge.

MCGEE, TIMOTHY J. Professor of music, University of Toronto, Ontario.
James Lyon.

MACKENZIE, A. ANTHONY. Assistant professor of history, St Francis Xavier University, Antigonish, Nova Scotia.
John Fillis. Sebastian Zouberbuhler.

MACKINNON, CLARENCE STUART. Assistant professor of history, University of Alberta, Edmonton, Alberta.
Samuel Hearne.

MACLEAN, TERRENCE D. Senior historian, Fortress of Louisbourg National Historic Park, Nova Scotia.
Philippe-Joseph d'Allard de Sainte-Marie.

MACLEOD, MALCOLM. Associate professor of history, Nova Scotia Teachers College, Truro, Nova Scotia.

Joseph-Michel Legardeur de Croisille et de Montesson.

McMullen, Lorraine. Associate professor of English, University of Ottawa, Ontario.
Frances Moore (Brooke).

†MacNutt, William Stewart. Professor emeritus of history, University of New Brunswick, Fredericton, New Brunswick.
Charles Newland Godfrey Jadis [in collaboration].

Major-Frégeau, M. Agent de recherche historique, Section des tableaux, dessins et estampes. Archives publiques du Canada, Ottawa, Ontario.
François Malepart de Beaucourt.

Marcil, Eileen. Historian, Orsainville, Québec.
Patrick Beatson.

Marshall, Peter. Professor of American history and institutions, University of Manchester, England.
William Hey.

Mathieu, Jacques. Professeur d'histoire, Université Laval, Québec, Québec.
René-Nicolas Levasseur. Jacques Perrault.

Matteau, Pierre. Professeur d'histoire, Collège de Sainte-Anne-de-La-Pocatière, La Pocatière, Québec.
Pierre-Antoine Porlier.

Middleton, Richard. Lecturer in history, Queen's University, Belfast, Northern Ireland.
James Abercromby.

Miller, Virginia P. Assistant professor of anthropology, Dalhousie University, Halifax, Nova Scotia.
Glossary of Native Peoples. *Nicholas Akomápis. Jean-Baptiste Arimph. Philip Bernard.*

Millman, Thomas R. Formerly archivist, Anglican Church of Canada, Toronto, Ontario.
John Ogilvie. Philip Toosey.

Mimeault, Mario. Professeur d'histoire, École Camille-Pouliot, Gaspé, Québec.
Raymond Bourdages.

Miquelon, Dale. Professor of history, University of Saskatchewan, Saskatoon, Saskatchewan.
Jacques Baby, dit *Dupéront. Marie-Anne Barbel (Fornel). Denis Goguet. Jean-André Lamaletie. Antoine Le Poupet de La Boularderie.*

Mitchell, Elaine Allan. Toronto, Ontario.
James Grant.

Momryk, Myron. Ottawa, Ontario.
Lawrence Ermatinger.

Moody, Barry M. Assistant professor of history, Acadia University, Wolfville, Nova Scotia.
John Ritchie. John Winslow.

Moogk, Peter N. Associate professor of history, University of British Columbia. Vancouver, British Columbia.
John Burch. Barthélemy Cotton. Joseph Huppé, dit *Lagroix. John Hendricks Lÿdius. Paul Tessier*, dit *Lavigne.*

Moore, Christopher. Formerly staff historian, Fortress of Louisbourg National Historic Park, Nova Scotia.
Pierre-Antoine Castaing. Nicolas Larcher.

Morgan, Robert J. Director, Beaton Institute, College of Cape Breton, Sydney, Nova Scotia.
Richard Gibbons. David Mathews.

Morin, Jacques. Rimouski, Québec.
Michel Blais [in collaboration with M.-C. Blais].

Nicolini-Maschino, Sylvette. Historienne, New York, New York, U.S.A.
Michel Chartier de Lotbinière [in collaboration with F. Thorpe].

O'Flaherty, Patrick. Professor of English, Memorial University of Newfoundland, St John's, Newfoundland.
Laurence Coughlan.

Ouellet, Fernand. Professeur titulaire d'histoire, Université d'Ottawa, Ontario.
Gabriel Christie. Benjamin Frobisher.

Pannekoek, Frits. Chief, Historical research, Prairie Region, Parks Canada, Winnipeg, Manitoba.
Edward Jarvis. Humphrey Marten.

Paquette, Normand. CÉGEP, Trois-Rivières, Québec.
Charles-Antoine Godefroy de Tonnancour.

Paré, Hélène. Chercheur en histoire, Montréal, Québec.
François-Jean-Daniel d'Ailleboust de La Madeleine. Louise de Ramezay.

Pariseau, Jean. Historien en chef, Service historique, Défense nationale, Ottawa, Ontario.
François-Marc-Antoine Le Mercier. Jean-Baptiste-Nicolas-Roch de Ramezay.

Pastore, Ralph T. Associate professor of history, Memorial University of Newfoundland, St John's, Newfoundland.
Teiorhéñhsere?.

Patterson, Stephen E. Professor of history, University of New Brunswick, Fredericton, New Brunswick.
Benjamin Gerrish. Joseph Gerrish.

Pelletier, Jean-Guy. Ministère des affaires intergouvernementales, Québec, Québec.
Jean-Baptiste-Amable Adhémar. Emmanuel Crespel. Pierre-Herman Dosquet. Joseph-Marie de La Corne de Chaptes. Louis-Philippe Mariauchau d'Esgly.

Pierce, Richard A. Professor of history, Queen's University, Kingston, Ontario.
James Hanna. John Kendrick.

Poirier, Jean. Archiviste, Archives nationales du Québec à Montréal, Québec.
James Cuthbert.

Porter, John R. Conservateur adjoint de l'art canadien ancien, Galerie nationale du Canada, Ottawa, Ontario; chargé de cours, Université Laval, Québec, Québec.
Jean-Antoine Aide-Créquy. Antoine Cirier. Louis Foureur, dit *Champagne.*

Pothier, Bernard. Historian, Canadian War Museum, National Museums of Canada, Ottawa, Ontario.
Joseph Dugas. Louis Du Pont Duchambon [in collaboration with T. Crowley]. *Louis Du Pont Duchambon de Vergor. François Du Pont Duvivier* [with T. Crowley]. *Joseph Du Pont Duvivier* [with T. Crowley].

PRESTON, RICHARD ARTHUR. Director, Canadian Studies Center, Duke University, Durham, North Carolina, U.S.A.
Neil McLean. John Ross.

PRITCHARD, JAMES S. Associate professor of history, Queen's University, Kingston, Ontario.
Philippe-Marie d'Ailleboust de Cerry. Théodose-Matthieu Denys de Vitré. Sébastien-François-Ange Le Normant de Mézy. Gabriel Pellegrin. Augustin Raby. Clément de Sabrevois de Bleury.

PROSS, CATHERINE A. Lunenburg County, Nova Scotia.
Otto William Schwartz. William Shaw.

PROVOST, HONORIUS, PTRE. Archiviste, Séminaire de Québec, Québec.
Urbain Boiret. Eustache Chartier de Lotbinière. Joseph-André-Mathurin Jacrau. Colomban-Sébastien Pressart. François Sorbier de Villars.

RAY, ARTHUR J. Professor of geography, York University, Downsview, Ontario.
William Holmes. Wapinesiw.

REMILLARD, JULIETTE. Directeur du secrétariat, Institut d'histoire de l'Amérique française; secrétaire de la Fondation Lionel-Groulx, Outremont, Québec.
Angélique Renaud d'Avène Des Méloizes (Péan).

RICH, EDWIN ERNEST. Emeritus Vere Harmsworth professor of imperial and naval history, University of Cambridge, England.
John Cole. Philip Turnor. Edward Umfreville.

RICHARDSON, A. J. H. Formerly chief of research, Parks Canada, Ottawa, Ontario; formerly chief, National Map Collection, Public Archives of Canada, Ottawa, Ontario.
Thomas Busby. Edward Harrison. Henry Hope. Joseph Howard. Alexander Johnston. Jacob Jordan. Georges-Hippolyte Le Comte Dupré.

RICHARDSON, GUS. Formerly manuscript editor, *Dictionary of Canadian biography/Dictionnaire biographique du Canada*, University of Toronto Press, Ontario.
Sahonwagy.

ROBERGE, MICHEL. Analyste, Archives nationales du Québec, Direction, Québec, Québec.
Michel Fortier. Pierre-Michel Martel. Charles-François Pichot de Querdisien Trémais.

ROBICHAUD, DONAT, PTRE. Beresford, Nouveau-Brunswick.
Louis Robichaux.

RODGER, ANDREW. Archivist, National Photography Collection, Public Archives of Canada, Ottawa, Ontario.
Jean-François Bourdon de Dombourg. Joseph Fleury Deschambault. Paul-Joseph Le Moyne de Longueuil. Gabriel Rousseau de Villejouin.

ROSSIE, JONATHAN G. Professor of history, St Lawrence University, Canton, New York, U.S.A.
Guy Johnson.

ROUSSEAU, FRANÇOIS. Étudiant gradué en histoire, Université Laval, Québec, Québec.
Louis-Léonard Aumasson de Courville. François-Joseph de Vienne.

ROY, JACQUELINE. Assistante, *Dictionnaire biographique du Canada/Dictionary of Canadian biography*, Les Presses de l'université Laval, Québec, Québec.
François-Pierre de Rigaud de Vaudreuil [in collaboration with J. Hamelin]. *Thomas-Ignace Trottier Dufy Desauniers.*

RUSSELL, PETER E. Graduate student in history, University of Michigan, U.S.A.
James Abercrombie. Henry Gladwin. Jehu Hay. George Williamson.

RYDER, DOROTHY E. Reference collection development specialist, National Library of Canada, Ottawa, Ontario.
William Moore.

SAUNDERS, ROBERT E. Education officer, Ontario Ministry of Education, Toronto, Ontario.
Christopher Robinson.

SMALE, RUTH GARIÉPY. Archiviste, Archives nationales du Québec, Centre régional de Montréal, Québec.
Maurice Desdevens de Glandons.

SMITH, DONALD B. Associate professor of history, University of Calgary, Alberta.
Glossary of Native Peoples. *Wabakinine.*

SMITH, SHIRLEE ANNE. Archivist, Hudson's Bay Company Archives, Winnipeg, Manitoba.
Ferdinand Jacobs. James Sutherland. William Walker.

SPRAY, WILLIAM ARTHUR. Professor of history, St Thomas University, Fredericton, New Brunswick.
William Davidson.

SPRY, IRENE M. Professor emeritus of economics, University of Ottawa, Ontario.
Matthew Cocking.

SPURR, JOHN WHEELOCK, Chief librarian emeritus, Royal Military College of Canada, Kingston, Ontario.
Patrick Mackellar.

STACEY, CHARLES P. Emeritus professor of history, University of Toronto, Ontario.
Jeffery Amherst. John Knox. Fiacre-François Potot de Montbeillard. Robert Rogers.

STANLEY, DELLA M. M. Graduate student in history, University of New Brunswick, Fredericton, New Brunswick.
Jean-Baptiste-Marie Castanet. Jean-Antoine Ledru. Thomas-François Le Roux.

STANLEY, GEORGE F. G. Professor emeritus of Canadian studies, Mount Allison University, Sackville, New Brunswick; formerly Dean of arts, Royal Military College of Canada, Kingston, Ontario.
Allan Maclean.

STEELE, IAN K. Professor of history, University of Western Ontario, London, Ontario.
Robert Monckton.

STEVENS, JAMES R. Writer; folklorist, Confederation College, Thunder Bay, Ontario.
Winninnewaycappo.

STEWART, GORDON. Associate professor of history, Michigan State University, East Lansing, Michigan, U.S.A.

Ebenezer Moulton.

STOKESBURY, JAMES. Professor of history, Acadia University, Wolfville, Nova Scotia.

John Burgoyne. Barrimore Matthew St Leger.

STORY, G. M. Professor of English, Memorial University of Newfoundland, St John's, Newfoundland.

Peter Kerrivan.

SUTHERLAND, MAXWELL. Chief historian, Research Division, Parks Canada, Ottawa, Ontario.

John Brewse. Robert George Bruce.

SUTHERLAND, STUART R. J. Manuscript editor, *Dictionary of Canadian biography/Dictionnaire biographique du Canada*, University of Toronto Press, Ontario.

Joseph Goreham [in collaboration with D. Charters]. *Richard Gridley. Richard Montgomery. Robert Pringle. Griffith Williams.*

TAILLEMITE, ÉTIENNE. Inspecteur général des Archives de France, Direction des Archives de France, Paris, France.

Antoine-Gabriel-François Benoist. Antoine-Charles Denis de Saint-Simon. Jean-Daniel Dumas. Jean-François de Galaup. Louis-Thomas Jacau de Fiedmont. Louis Legardeur de Repentigny. Anne-Joseph-Hippolyte de Maurès de Malartic. Louis de Preissac de Bonneau. Jean Vauquelin.

TAYLOR, J. GARTH. Head, Urgent Ethnology Programme, Canadian Ethnology Service, National Museum of Man, Ottawa, Ontario.

Glossary of Native Peoples. *Tuglavina.*

THÉRIAULT, FIDÈLE. Historien, Caraquet, Nouveau-Brunswick.

Bonaventure Carpentier.

THOMAS, CHRISTMAS EDWARD. Research assistant, Public Archives of Nova Scotia, Halifax, Nova Scotia.

John Breynton. Thomas Wood.

THOMAS, LEWIS HERBERT. Professor of history, University of Alberta, Edmonton, Alberta.

Thomas Walker.

THOMPSON, FREDERIC FRASER. Professor and head, Department of history, Royal Military College of Canada, Kingston, Ontario.

Francis William Drake. Richard Edwards. John Jones. Henry Osborn.

THORMAN, GEORGE E. Formerly principal, Parkside Collegiate, St Thomas, Ontario.

Germain Maugenest. Forrest Oakes.

THORPE, FREDERICK J. Chief, History division, National Museum of Man, National Museums of Canada, Ottawa, Ontario.

Michel Chartier de Lotbinière [in collaboration with S. Nicolini-Maschino]. *Gaspard-Joseph Chaussegros de Léry. Michel de Couagne. Jean-Nicolas Desandrouins. Pierre-Jacques Druillon de Macé.*

THORPE, WENDY L. Research assistant, Public Archives of Nova Scotia, Halifax, Nova Scotia.

John Day.

TOUPIN, ROBERT, S.J. Professeur d'histoire, Université Laurentienne, Sudbury, Ontario.

Pierre-Philippe Potier.

TOUSIGNANT, PIERRE. Professeur agrégé d'histoire, Université de Montréal, Québec.

Hector Theophilus Cramahé. François-Joseph Cugnet. Pierre Du Calvet. René-Ovide Hertel de Rouville. Luc de La Corne. François-Marie Picoté de Belestre. [All biographies done in collaboration with M. Dionne-Tousignant.] Introductory essay: *The integration of the province of Quebec into the British empire, 1763–91.* Part I: *From the Royal Proclamation to the Quebec Act.*

TRAP, PAUL. Teacher, Grand Haven Public Schools, Grand Haven, Michigan, U.S.A.

Charles-Michel Mouet de Langlade.

TRATT, GERTRUDE E. N. Teacher, Halifax, Nova Scotia.

John Eagleson.

TREMBLAY, YVES-JEAN. Archiviste, Archives nationales du Québec, Centre régional de Montréal, Québec.

Jean-Baptiste Barsalou. François-Pierre Cherrier. Simon Sanguinet.

TRIGGER, BRUCE G. Professor of anthropology, McGill University, Montreal, Quebec.

Glossary of Native Peoples.

TURNBULL, JAMES R. Historian, Peterborough, Ontario.

Benoît-François Bernier.

UPTON, L. F. S. Professor of history, University of British Columbia, Vancouver, British Columbia.

Pierre Benoît. Joseph Claude. Peter Livius. William Smith.

VACHON, ANDRÉ. Historien, Québec, Québec.

Jean-Olivier Briand.

VACHON, AUGUSTE. Chef, Section des médailles de l'héraldique et du costume, Archives publiques du Canada, Ottawa, Ontario.

Pierre-Joseph-Antoine Roubaud.

VAN KIRK, SYLVIA. Assistant professor of history, University of Toronto, Ontario.

Joseph Isbister. Moses Norton. Louis Primeau.

VAUGEOIS, DENIS. Historien; éditeur, Trois-Rivières, Québec.

Aaron Hart. Samuel Jacobs.

VOISINE, NIVE. Professeur agrégé d'histoire, Université Laval, Québec, Québec.

Pierre Hazeur de L'Orme.

WALKER, JAMES. Associate professor of history, University of Waterloo, Ontario.

John Marrant. Thomas Peters.

WALLACE, CARL MURRAY. Associate professor of history, Laurentian University, Sudbury, Ontario.

William Lewis.

WHITELEY, WILLIAM HENRY. Professor of history, Memorial University of Newfoundland, St John's, Newfoundland.

Jeremiah Coghlan. Nicholas Darby. Mikak. Sir Hugh Palliser. Sir Charles Saunders. Molyneux Shuldham.

WICKWIRE, FRANKLIN. Professor of history, University of Massachusetts, Amherst, Massachusetts, U.S.A.

Francis McLean.

WILLIAMS, GLYNDWR. Professor of history, Queen Mary College, University of London, England.

CONTRIBUTORS

Charles Clerke. James Cook. Thomas Hutchins. James King. William Wales.

WILSON, BRUCE G. Archivist, Public Archives of Canada, Ottawa, Ontario.
John Butler [in collaboration with R. A. Bowler]. *James Peachey* [with W. M. E. Cooke].

WISE, SYDNEY FRANCIS. Director, Institute of Canadian Studies, Carleton University, Ottawa, Ontario.
Thomas Gage.

YOUNG, D. MURRAY. Professor and former chairman, Department of history, University of New Brunswick, Fredericton, New Brunswick.
Beamsley Perkins Glasier.

Index of Identifications

Like the network of cross-references within biographies, this index is designed to assist readers in following their interests through the volume. Most of the groupings are by occupations within Canada, and some of the categories require explanation. Under "agriculture" is to be found a variety of people known to have been actively engaged in the development of land; those who operated outside the area of seigneurial tenure we have called "improvers" and under that sub-classification have included land agents, gentlemen farmers, and colonizers. The distinction between "fine arts" and "artisans" was difficult to make; in the end, silversmiths were placed under fine arts and potters were considered artisans. "Mariners" includes civilian captains, pilots, navigators, and privateers; naval officers appear as a sub-group of the armed forces. The category entitled "colonial administrators" contains high ranking officials: governors, lieutenant governors, administrators, and intendants. Fur-traders, although they might have appeared under "business," are given a separate listing since they are so numerous. Some divisions have been established to help readers who approach the past from other perspectives, such as the study of a particular ethnic group. Women form a category of their own, a reflection of the recent interest in their history, but they may also be found under the occupations in which they engaged. Where it has seemed most useful, groups have been sub-divided geographically.

Although the DCB/DBC attempts by its assignments to encourage research in new areas as well as familiar ones, its selection of individuals to receive biographies reflects the survival of documentation and the areas historians have chosen to investigate. This index should not, therefore, be used for quantitative judgements about the 18th century; it is merely a guide to what is contained in volume IV.

BLACKS

BUSINESS

FRENCH RÉGIME

ACADIA AND ÎLE ROYALE

CANADA

BRITISH RÉGIME

ATLANTIC COLONIES

INDEX OF IDENTIFICATIONS

FUR-TRADERS

ATLANTIC COLONIES

Knaut, Philip Augustus
Schwartz, Otto William

GREAT LAKES REGION

Ailleboust de La Madeleine, François-Jean-Daniel d'
Baby, *dit* Dupéront, Jacques
Bourassa, *dit* La Ronde, René
Campion, Étienne-Charles
Cotté, Gabriel
Couagne, Jean-Baptiste de
Dagneau Douville, Alexandre
Ducharme, Laurent
Grant, James
Howard, Joseph
McCarty, Richard
McKee, Alexander
MacLeod, Normand
Mouet de Langlade, Charles-Michel
Oakes, Forrest
Primeau, Louis

HUDSON BAY – PRAIRIES REGION

Atkinson, George
Batt, Isaac
Cocking, Matthew
Cole, John
Grant, Cuthbert
Hearne, Samuel
Holmes, William
Hutchins, Thomas
Isbister, Joseph
Jacobs, Ferdinand
Jarvis, Edward
Long, John
Marten, Humphrey
Maugenest, Germain
Norton, Moses
Ross, Malchom
Sutherland, George
Sutherland, James
Turnor, Philip
Umfreville, Edward
Waddens, Jean-Étienne
Walker, William

PACIFIC COAST

Dixon, George
Duncan, Charles
Hanna, James
Kendrick, John

INDIAN AFFAIRS

Baby, *dit* Dupéront, Jacques
Butler, John (d. 1796)
Campbell, John
Chabert de Joncaire de Clausonne, Daniel-Marie
Chew, Joseph
Claus, Christian Daniel
Couagne, Jean-Baptiste de
Dagneau Douville, Alexandre
Francklin, Michael
Godefroy de Linctot, Daniel-Maurice
Godin, *dit* Bellefontaine, *dit* Beauséjour, Joseph
Goreham, Joseph
Hay, Jehu
Hertel de Saint-François, Joseph-Hippolyte
Johnson, Guy
Johnson, Sir William
La Corne, Luc de
Lÿdius, John Hendricks
McKee, Alexander
MacLeod, Normand
Mouet de Langlade, Charles-Michel
Roberts, Benjamin

JOURNALISTS

Brown, William
Gilmore, Thomas
Henry, Anthony
Jautard, Valentin
Mesplet, Fleury
Moore, William

LEGAL AND JUDICIAL

Judges

Belcher, Jonathan
Butler, John (d. 1791)
Butler, John (d. 1796)
Cramahé, Hector Theophilus
Cugnet, François-Joseph
Denson, Henry Denny
Doggett, John
Gamelin, Ignace
Gerrish, Joseph
Gibbons, Richard
Green, Benjamin
Guillimin, Guillaume
Hertel de Rouville, René-Ovide
Hey, William
Johnston, Alexander
Langman, Edward
Livius, Peter
Mabane, Adam
McKee, Alexander
McLean, Neil
Morris, Charles
Munro, John
Nesbitt, William
Panet, Jean-Claude
Ritchie, John
Sanguinet, Simon
Smith, William
Tonge, Winckworth

Justices of the peace

Adhémar, Jean-Baptiste-Amable
Aylwin, Thomas
Baby, *dit* Dupéront, Jacques
Badeaux, Jean-Baptiste

Index

Included in the index are the names of persons mentioned in volume IV. They are listed by their family names, with titles and first names following. Wives are entered under their maiden names with their married names in parentheses. Persons who appear in incomplete citations in the text are fully identified when possible. An asterisk indicates that the person has received a biography in a volume already published, or will probably receive one in a subsequent volume. A death date or last floruit date refers the reader to the volume in which the biography will be found. Numerals in bold face indicate the pages on which a biography appears. Titles, nicknames, variant spellings, married and religious names are fully cross-referenced.